Contents

Contents

SURVIVAL GUIDE

PETR KOVALENKOV/SHUTTERSTOCK ©

Right: Parisian
cafe (p391)

WELCOME TO
Europe

As with many young travellers, Europe is where my life on the road began – in the late 1980s with a £140 InterRail ticket. Not having travelled outside Britain as a child, I'll never forget the excitement of arriving at Paris' Gare du Nord late at night and becoming instantly infatuated by the 'City of Light'. Since then, I've travelled around Europe multiple times returning regularly to my favourite haunts and revelling in the diversity, intensity and complexity of this multilayered continent that I'll need at least 10 lifetimes to explore properly.

By Brendan Sainsbury, Writer
🐦 @sainsburyb
For more about our writers, see p1248

Europe

GREENLAND

Greenland Sea

Fjords, Norway
Sublime Scandinavian scenery (p849)

Faxaflói **ICELAND**
Reykjavík

Norwegian Sea

ATLANTIC OCEAN

Faroe Islands (Denmark)

Amsterdam, the Netherlands
Ply boat-filled canals under ornamental bridges (p799)

Shetland

NORWAY

Oslo

Orkney

Outer Hebrides **SCOTLAND**

London, Britain
Enjoy nightlife in pubs, clubs and concert halls (p164)

NORTHERN IRELAND

Edinburgh

North Sea

Skagerrak

Copenhagen

DENMARK

Belfast

Irish Sea **BRITAIN**

Elbe

Berlin

IRELAND
Dublin

ENGLAND

WALES

NETHERLANDS

Amsterdam

GERMANY

Paris, France
Ascend the Eiffel Tower (p378)

St George's Channel

Cardiff

London

Brussels

Rhine

Channel Islands

English Channel

BELGIUM

Luxembourg City

LUXEMBOURG

Seine

Paris

Barcelona, Spain
Be humbled by La Sagrada Família (p1055)

FRANCE

Loire

LIECHTENSTEIN

Bern Vaduz

SWITZERLAND

Bay of Biscay

Mt Blanc (4807m) **ALPS**

Venice

San Marino

Po

Lisbon, Portugal
Lose yourself in the Alfama's alleyways (p895)

PYRENEES

Golfe du Lion

Monaco

MONACO

Corsica (France)

ITALY

Rome

Andorra la Vella **ANDORRA**

Barcelona

Lisbon

Madrid

SPAIN

Sardinia (Italy)

Tyrrhenian Sea

PORTUGAL

Balearic Islands (Spain)

Mediterranean Sea

Modeira (Portugal)

Strait of Gibraltar

ALGERIA

TUNISIA

Rabat

The Matterhorn, Switzerland
Most iconic Swiss Alps (p1135)

Venice, Italy
Drift along the winding canals (p686)

MOROCCO

Marrakesh

Canary Islands (Spain)

Berlin, Germany
Historic encounters at the
Berlin Wall (p458)

St Petersburg, Russia
Imperial palaces
packed with art (p966)

Tallinn, Estonia
Soak up the city's
vibrant vibe (p337)

Prague, Czech Republic
Iconic castle, diverse
neighbourhoods and art (p283)

Budapest, Hungary
Museums, thermal baths
and nightlife (p574)

Transylvania, Romania
Explore the mountains and
spooky castles (p932)

İstanbul, Turkey
Marvel at the
stunning mosques (p1156)

Ohrid, North Macedonia
Wander the seductive
Old Town (p833)

Dubrovnik, Croatia
Walk the old city walls
at dusk (p272)

Europe's Top Experiences

1 CASTLES & PALACES

Europe is full of muscular fortifications and showy palaces constructed to cement the legacy of whoever held the reins of power when they were built. It's not difficult to track the evolution of these noble citadels from the Palatine Hill in Rome to the UK's Tower of London, to St Petersburg's Winter Palace. Ostentatious but built to last, they reflect the tumultuous history of the continent.

The Illustrious Alhambra

Granada's 1,000-year-old fort and palace complex was built by the Moors and rises like a heavenly apparition at the foot of the Sierra Nevada. After admiring the ornate residences and manicured gardens of its foppish Nasrid rulers, everything else threatens to be anticlimactic. p1091

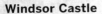

Windsor Castle

Home to British royalty for nearly 1000 years, Windsor is a historical heavyweight even by European standards. Surrounded by a humongous park and host to a soaring gothic chapel, it's a castle fit for a queen – which is probably why she still lives there. p187

Château of Versailles

Conceived by France's imperial Sun King in the 1600s, Versailles has been the measuring stick for every palace built since. Not surprisingly, the baroque beauty gets more annual visitors than many small countries. p398

2 COOL CAFÉ CULTURE

Snap a street scene in Paris, Vienna, Trieste or Barcelona and, chances are, it'll include a café. Picture striped awnings jutting over shaded pavements, tight crowds squeezed around marble tables, and fashionable patrons sipping cappuccinos from porcelain cups. Cafes are as important to European culture as churches and battlefields. Revolutions have been plotted in them, books written, and love affairs ignited. Order a drink and soak up the atmosphere.

Parisian Style

You haven't been to Paris until you've decamped outside a Latin Quarter café with a croissant and *chocolat* and eavesdropped on a 21st century reincarnation of Simone de Beauvoir and Jean-Paul Sartre. p378

Below: Parisian cafe, Latin Quarter

Viennese People-Watching

When the Turks dumped their coffee outside the gates of Vienna in 1683, they did the continent a huge favour. Unchanged in decades, the cosmopolitan cafes of the Austrian capital are heavy with the air of refinement. Observe human behaviour, play cards, admire the drapes, and imbibe the fin-de-siècle atmosphere with your coffee. p73

Above left: Viennese café

Espresso in Turin

The home of Lavazza and chocolate makes a good place to perch among the chandeliers, starched tablecloths and waistcoated wait staff while taking a well-earned '*pausa*'. Discuss the latest corruption scandal with the barista before necking your piping hot espresso and going on your merry way. p677

Above right: Turin café

3 CAPTIVATING CITIES

Stuffed with culture, history, and a healthy dose of *je ne sais quoi*, European cities have deep roots and complex personalities. There's ancient Athens and spa-centric Budapest, up-all-hours Madrid and bike-friendly Amsterdam. Life in the urban entrails of the 'old' continent is often a little less futuristic and more haphazard than elsewhere. Sometimes you have to stay longer and dig a bit deeper. The joy is in the details.

Cosmopolitan London

Historic, constantly evolving, and hugely diverse, London is a truly global city. The British capital has an electric atmosphere that gets under your skin. Stay for a week and you'll feel like you've put your finger on the planet's pulse. p164

Above: Houses of Parliament (p164)

Eternal Rome

Other cities rise and fall, but Rome remains constant, revered as much for its trademark thin-crust pizza as it is for its ancient ruins. You can peel off the past in layers, admire multiple historical eras and even visit another country within the city limits. p651

Top: Spanish Steps (p656)

Gothic Prague

Welcome to Europe's biggest museum, a love letter to gothic architecture, bohemian art and Kaftaesque literature, where drinking beer is a spiritual experience, and the last revolution was more velvet than violent. It's not quite urban perfection, but it's dangerously close. p283

Bottom: Charles Bridge (p288)

4 EURO-SOUNDS

Spewing forth from the bars, garages and backstreet balconies of Europe are multiple seams of individual sounds. Some have gone global; others have barely left the region that spawned them. From the soaring harmonies of The Beatles to Pavarotti belting 'Nessun dorma'. From Krautrock to the Eurovision Song Contest. From South London Grime to Czech polkas. Hit the Scala, Glastonbury, Roskilde or a decrepit old tavern in Seville and partake in a bit of live entertainment.

Seville's Flamenco Scene

Roma rhythms, Spanish folk songs, Jewish chants and Moorish laments, flamenco is a raw and powerful art best witnessed in its western Andalucian heartland. p1084

Below: Flamenco dancers, Plaza de España (p1085), Seville

All You Need is Liverpool

The Beatles kicked the door open. A veritable conveyor belt of talented bands has been milking it ever since. Take a bus down Penny Lane in Liverpool and see where it all started. p206

Above left: The Beatles Story museum, Liverpool

A Night at the Scala

Opera is the kind of rousing melodramatic music that only the Italians could have invented – and where better to see it than in Milan's Scala. p683

Above right: Teatro alla Scala, Milan

5 TRACKING THE COAST

Europe's jagged coastline takes in a huge sweep of show-stopping scenery. There's rugged Norway where deep, narrow fjords penetrate icy mountain ranges, plucky Ireland whose giant emerald-topped cliffs collide with the raging Atlantic, and Spain's Costa de la Luz where epic sandy beaches provide launch sites for kite-surfers. Choose your water and select your terrain. The Mediterranean or the Baltic; Dutch dykes or Scottish Mountains.

CANADASTOCK/SHUTTERSTOCK ©

K. SAMURKAS/SHUTTERSTOCK ©

KIEVVICTOR/SHUTTERSTOCK ©

Bay of Kotor

There's a sense of secrecy and mystery to the Bay of Kotor. Grey mountain walls rise steeply from steely blue waters, getting higher and higher as you progress through their folds to the hidden reaches of the inner bay. p785

Above: Bay of Kotor

The Precipitous Amalfi

Blessed with a lattice of steep walking paths that link a network of medieval towns and villages, the precipitous Italian coastline south of Naples is a dazzling array of terraced fields, steeply stacked houses, and aromatic lemon groves. p714

Left: Positano (p716), Amalfi Coast

Below left: Positano (p716), Amalfi Coast

Swanky Côte d'Azur

First colonized by aristocrats, then artists and later rock royalty, the Côte d'Azur is a synonym for posh, glossy and rich. Elegant resorts front ritzy beaches. p438

Opposite page, bottom: Côte d'Azur

IGORZH/SHUTTERSTOCK ©

6 ISLAND-HOPPING ARCHIPELAGOS

From the Britain Isles to diminutive Malta, Europe is dotted with archipelagos. Sweden has more islands than any other country in the world, while Greece is famed for its idyllic clusters of holiday isles. Irrespective of national identities, archipelagos have their own nuances and flavours, adding extra complexity to Europe's already complicated cultural patchwork. Whether you like them chilly and bleak (Skye), or sandy and fertile (Hvar), the continent's got it covered.

Above: Oia (p550), Santorini

Cyclade Beaches

Start with Mykonos, Santorini and Naxos, and work your way down the list. Greece is famous for its individualistic islands that juxtapose perfect golden beaches with idiosyncratic classical legends. p546

Left: Mykonos (p546), Cyclades

Deluxe Dalmatia

There are over 70 islands off Croatia's Dalmatian coast, including halcyon Adriatic retreats like Hvar which mixes swank with elegance and deluxe beaches with abandoned ancient hamlets. p262

Below left: Hvar (p270), Dalmatia
Below right: Dalmation coastline (p262)

7 A LESSON IN ART HISTORY

The birthplace of Da Vinci, Rembrandt, Picasso, and Velázquez. Need we say more. Europe was the continent that nurtured the 'Old Masters', first committed oil to canvas, and effortlessly evolved baroque, Dada, cubism, and pointillism. Art galleries are legion here, stuffed full of priceless works, as are many churches, stately homes and palaces. Choose a muse and follow the story from Giotto to Miró.

ANIBAL TREJO/SHUTTERSTOCK ©

Left: Museo del Prado, Madrid
Below: Museo del Prado, Madrid

Museo del Prado

The best of Titian, Ve-
lázquez's greatest hits,
a top ten of Flemish
masters; the Prado is the
premier gallery in a country not short on great artists – and you'll find them
all inside these hallowed
walls. p1038

Musée du Louvre

The world's largest art
museum is also one of its
oldest and most visited.
The masses arrive to see
hordes of priceless treasure, including some of the
finest paintings put on
canvas. p382

Top left: Musée du Louvre, Paris

Bottom left: Musée du Louvre, Paris

State Hermitage Museum

Only slightly smaller and
younger than the Louvre,
the Hermitage is a lesson
in art history with paintings amassed by succes-
sive Tsars and communist
leaders. p967

Above: State Hermitage Museum, St
Petersburg

8 LIMITLESS LANDSCAPES

Despite being settled, farmed, and modified for millennia, Europe's landscapes can still shock and awe. The Alps have epic scale, England's patchwork of fields and hedgerows are loaded with pastoral charm, while Northern Norway exhibits a natural rawness that wouldn't be out of place in Alaska. Visitors sometimes bypass Europe's rural idylls for art and culture, but there are few finer experiences than watching Tuscany's hillcrests poke through the morning mist.

Iceland

Europe's Nordic island outpost is a land of ice and fire where geothermal springs bubble and volatile volcanos can lead to flight cancelations. All the more reason to stay longer. p596

Below: Strokkur geyser (p606), the Golden Circle

JAKL LUBOS/SHUTTERSTOCK ©

The Matterhorn

The most famous and dramatically shaped mountain in the world stabs the sky above the timber-chalet-filled village of Zermatt looking, at once, magnificent and terrifying. p1135

Above: Matterhorn

Norway's Fjords

Mind-boggling in more ways than one, Norway's spectacularly twisted coastline indented with fjords would encircle the world two and a half times if it was stretched out fully. p849

Right: Sognefjorden (p854)

9 FABULOUS FOOD SCENE

ALEXANDRE ROTENBERG/SHUTTERSTOCK ©

PURIPAT LERTPUNYAROJ/SHUTTERSTOCK ©

NATALIA KABLIUK/SHUTTERSTOCK ©

Home to some the world's best-loved and widely copied food, European cuisine oscillates between posh French escargot and salt of the earth British fish n chips. Somewhere along the way, you'll also want to dip your fingers into Ukrainian borscht, Neapolitan pizza, Greek baklava, Spanish tapas and Wiener schnitzel. And that just the hors d'oeuvres. You could fill a library with the nuances of European food. Bring a good appetite and get ready to experiment.

Gourmet Copenhagen

The Danish capital is a gourmet destination in its own right: people come here just for the food, a true smorgasbord of Nordic cuisine. p320

No Fuss Naples

Forget celebrity food boffins and molecular gastronomy; eating doesn't get any better than the simple, passed-down-through-the-generations pizzas and pastas of Italy's gloriously decrepit southern capital. p710

Michelin-Starred San Sebastián

While most cities are happy with one Michelin star, this Spanish Basque powerhouse has created a constellation with nouvelle cuisine restaurants competing with old-style taverns plying *pintxos*. p1072

Above: *Pintxos*, San Sebastián

Need to Know

For more information, see Survival Guide (p1195)

Currency

Euro (€) Austria, Belgium, Estonia, France, Germany, Greece, Republic of Ireland, Italy, Kosovo, Latvia, Lithuania, Luxembourg, the Netherlands, Montenegro, Portugal, Slovakia, Slovenia, Spain

Pound (£; also called 'pound sterling') Britain, Northern Ireland

Local currency elsewhere.

Visas

EU citizens don't need visas for other EU countries. Australians, Canadians, New Zealanders and Americans don't need visas for visits of less than 90 days.

Money

ATMs are common; credit and debit cards are widely accepted.

Time

Britain, Ireland and Portugal: GMT. Central Europe: GMT plus one hour. Greece, Turkey & Eastern Europe: GMT plus two hours. Russia: GMT/UTC plus three hours.

When to Go

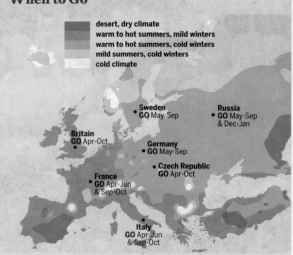

desert, dry climate
warm to hot summers, mild winters
warm to hot summers, cold winters
mild summers, cold winters
cold climate

Sweden GO May-Sep

Russia GO May-Sep & Dec-Jan

Britain GO Apr-Oct

Germany GO May-Sep

Czech Republic GO Apr-Oct

France GO Apr-Jun & Sep-Oct

Italy GO Apr-Jun & Sep-Oct

High Season (Jun–Aug)

➡ Everybody comes to Europe and all of Europe hits the road.

➡ Hotel prices and temperatures are at their highest.

➡ Expect all the major attractions to be nightmarishly busy.

Shoulder (Apr– May & Sep–Oct)

➡ Crowds and prices drop, except in Italy, where it's still busy.

➡ Temperatures are comfortable but it can be hot in southern Europe.

➡ Overall these are the best months to travel in Europe.

Low Season (Nov–Mar)

➡ Outside ski resorts, hotels drop their prices or close down.

➡ The weather can be cold and days short, especially in northern Europe.

➡ Some places, such as resort towns, are like ghost towns.

Useful Websites

The Man in Seat Sixty-One (www.seat61.com) Encyclopedic site dedicated to train travel plus plenty of other tips.

Hidden Europe (www.hidden europe.co.uk) Fascinating magazine and online dispatches from all the continent's corners.

Couchsurfing (www.couch surfing.org) Find a free bed and make friends in any European country.

VisitEurope (www.visiteurope.com) With information about travel in 33 member countries.

Spotted by Locals (www.spot tedbylocals.com) Insider tips for cities across Europe.

Lonely Planet (www.lonely planet.com/europe) Destination information, hotel bookings, traveller forum and more.

Important Numbers

The number 112 can be dialled free for emergencies in all EU states. See individual countries for country-specific emergency numbers.

France country code	☏33
Germany country code	☏49
Italy country code	☏39
Spain country code	☏34
UK country code	☏44

Exchange Rates

Australia	A$1	€0.62
Canada	C$1	€0.66
Japan	¥100	€0.80
New Zealand	NZ$1	€0.59
UK	£1	€1.11
USA	US$1	€0.87

For current exchange rates, see www.xe.com.

Daily Costs

**Budget:
Less than €70**

➡ Dorm beds: €15–30

➡ Museum admission: €5–15

➡ Pizza or pasta: €8–12

**Midrange:
€70–200**

➡ Double room in a small hotel: €70–120

➡ Short taxi trip: €10–20

➡ Meals in good restaurants: per person €20–40

**Top end:
More than €200**

➡ Stay at iconic hotels: from €150

➡ Car hire: per day from around €35

➡ Theatre tickets: €15–150

Accommodation

Europe offers the fullest possible range of accommodation for all budgets. Book up to two months in advance for a July visit or for ski resorts over Christmas and New Year.

Hotels Range from the local pub to restored castles.

B&Bs Small, family-run houses generally provide good value.

Hostels Enormous variety from backpacker palaces to real dumps.

Homestays and farmstays A great way to really find out how locals live.

Arriving in Europe

Schiphol Airport (Amsterdam) Trains to the centre (20 minutes).

Heathrow Airport (London) Trains (15 minutes) and tube (one hour) to the centre.

Aéroport de Charles de Gaulle (Paris) Many buses (one hour) and trains (30 minutes) to the centre.

Frankfurt Airport Trains (15 minutes) to the centre.

Leonardo da Vinci Airport (Rome) Buses (one hour) and trains (30 minutes) to the centre.

Barajas Airport (Madrid) Buses (40 minutes) and metro (15 minutes) to the centre.

Getting Around Europe

Train Europe's train network is fast and efficient but rarely a bargain unless you book well in advance or use a rail pass wisely.

Bus Usually taken for short trips in remoter areas, though long-distance intercity buses can be cheap.

Car You can hire a car or drive your own through Europe. Roads are excellent but petrol is expensive.

Ferry Boats connect Britain and Ireland with mainland Europe; Scandinavia to the Baltic countries and Germany; and Italy to the Balkans and Greece.

Air Speed things up by flying from one end of the continent to the other.

Bicycle Slow things down on a two-wheeler; a great way to get around just about anywhere.

For much more on **getting around**, see p1208

Month by Month

PLAN YOUR TRIP

TOP EVENTS

Carnevale, Venice
February

Hellenic Festival, Athens June

White Nights, St Petersburg June

Edinburgh International Festival August

Oktoberfest, Munich September

January

It's cold but most towns are relatively tourist-free and hotel prices are rock bottom. Head to Eastern Europe's ski slopes for wallet-friendly prices, with Bosnia and Bulgaria your best bets.

📷 Orthodox Christmas, Eastern Europe

Christmas is celebrated in different ways in Eastern Europe: many countries celebrate on Christmas Eve (24 December), with an evening meal and midnight Mass. In Russia, Ukraine, Belarus, Moldova, Serbia, Montenegro and North Macedonia, Christmas falls in January, as per the Julian calendar.

✯✯ Küstendorf Film & Music Festival, Serbia

Created and curated by Serbian director Emir Kusturica, this international indie-fest (http://kustendorf-filmandmusicfestival.org) in the town of Drvengrad, near Zlatibor in Serbia, eschews traditional red-carpet glitz for oddball inclusions vying for the 'Golden Egg' prize.

✯✯ Kiruna Snöfestivalen, Sweden

In the last weekend of January this Lapland snow festival (www.snofestivalen.com), based around a snow-sculpting competition, draws artists from all over Europe. There's also a husky-dog competition and a handicrafts fair.

February

Carnival in all its manic glory sweeps the Catholic regions. Cold temperatures are forgotten amid masquerades, street festivals and general bacchanalia. Expect to be kissed by a stranger.

✯✯ Carnevale, Italy

In the period before Ash Wednesday, Venice goes mad for masks (www. venice-carnival-italy.com). Costume balls, many with traditions centuries old, enliven the social calendar in this storied old city. Even those without a coveted invite are swept up in the pageantry.

✯✯ Karneval, Croatia

For colourful costumes and nonstop revelry head to Rijeka (www.rijecki-karneval.hr), where Karneval (Carnival) is the pinnacle of the year's calendar. Zadar and Samobor host Karneval celebrations too, with street dancing, concerts and masked balls.

✯✯ Carnaval, Netherlands

Pre-Lent is celebrated with greater vigour in Maastricht than anywhere else in northern Europe. While the rest of the Netherlands hopes the canals will freeze for ice skating, this Dutch corner cuts loose with a celebration that would have done its former Roman residents proud.

✯✯ Fasching, Germany

Germany doesn't leave the pre-Lent season solely to its neighbours. Fasching (or Karneval) is celebrated with abandon in the traditional Catholic regions including Bavaria, along the Rhine and particularly vibrantly in Cologne.

March

Spring arrives in southern Europe. Further north the rest of the continent continues to freeze, though days are often bright.

✯✯ St Patrick's Day, Ireland

Parades and celebrations are held on 17 March in Irish towns big and small to honour the beloved patron saint of Ireland. While elsewhere the day is a commercialised romp of green beer, in his home country it's time for a parade and celebrations with friends and family.

✯ Ski-Jumping World Cup, Slovenia

This exciting international competition (www.planica. si) takes place on the world's largest ski-jumping hill, in the Planica Valley at Rateče near Kranjska Gora. Held the third weekend in March, it's a must for adrenaline junkies.

April

Spring arrives with a burst of colour, from the glorious bulb fields of Holland to the blooming orchards of Spain. On the most southern beaches it's time to shake the sand out of the umbrellas.

📅 Semana Santa, Spain

There are parades of penitents and holy icons in Spain, notably in Seville, during Easter week (www. semana-santa.org). Thousands of members of religious brotherhoods parade in traditional garb before thousands more spectators. Look for the pointed *capirotes* (hoods).

📅 Settimana Santa, Italy

Italy celebrates Holy Week with processions and passion plays. By Holy Thursday, Rome is thronged with the faithful and even nonbelievers are swept up in the emotion and piety of hundreds of thousands thronging the Vatican and St Peter's Basilica.

✯ Budapest Spring Festival, Hungary

This two-week festival in early April is one of Europe's top classical-music events (www.springfestival. hu). Concerts are held in a number of beautiful venues, including stunning churches, the opera house and the national theatre.

✯✯ Orthodox Easter, Greece

The most important festival in the Greek Orthodox calendar has an emphasis on the Resurrection, meaning it's a celebratory event. The most significant part is midnight on Easter Saturday, when candles are lit and fireworks and a procession hit the streets.

✯✯ Feria de Abril, Spain

Hoods off! A weeklong party (http://feriadesevilla. andalunet.com) in Seville in late April counterbalances the religious peak of Easter. The beautiful old squares of this gorgeous city come alive during the long, warm nights for which the nation is known.

✯✯ Koninginnedag (Queen's Day), The Netherlands

The nationwide celebration of Queen's Day on 27 April is especially fervent in Amsterdam, awash with orange costumes and fake Afros, beer, dope, leather bags, temporary roller coasters, clogs and general craziness.

May

May is usually sunny and warm and full of things to do – an excellent time to visit. It's not too hot or too crowded, though you can still expect the big destinations to feel busy.

✯ Queima das Fitas, Portugal

Coimbra's annual highlight is this boozy week of fado music and revelry that begins on the first Thursday in May (www.facebook. com/queimadasfitas coimbra), when students celebrate the end of the academic year.

✯✯ Beer Festival, Czech Republic

An event dear to many travellers' hearts, this Prague beer festival (www.ceskypiv nifestival.cz) offers lots of food, music and – most importantly – around 70 beers from around the country from mid- to late May.

✯ Brussels Jazz Weekend, Belgium

Around-the-clock jazz performances hit Brussels

during the second-last weekend in May (www.brusselsjazzweekend.be). The saxophone is the instrument of choice for this international-flavoured city's most joyous celebration.

June

The huge summer travel season hasn't started yet, but the sun has broken through the clouds and the weather is generally gorgeous across the continent.

Festa de Santo António, Portugal

Feasting, drinking and dancing in Lisbon's Alfama in honour of St Anthony (12–13 June) top the even grander three-week Festas de Lisboa (www.festasde lisboa.com), which features processions and dozens of street parties.

White Nights, Russia

By mid-June the Baltic sun just sinks behind the horizon at night, leaving the sky a grey-white colour and encouraging locals to forget routines and party hard. The best place to join the fun is St Petersburg, where balls, classical-music concerts and other summer events keep spirits high.

Karneval der Kulturen, Germany

This joyous street carnival (www.karneval-berlin.de) celebrates Berlin's multicultural tapestry with parties, global nosh and a fun parade of flamboyantly costumed dancers, DJs, artists and musicians.

Festa de São João, Portugal

Elaborate processions, live music on Porto's plazas and merrymaking all across Portugal's second city. Squeaky plastic hammers (for sale everywhere) come out for the unusual custom of whacking one another. Everyone is fair game – expect no mercy.

Glastonbury Festival, Britain

The town's youthful summer vibe peaks for this long weekend of music, theatre and New Age shenanigans (www.glastonburyfestivals.co.uk). It's one of England's favourite outdoor events and more than 100,000 turn up to writhe around in the grassy fields (or deep mud) at Pilton's (Worthy) Farm.

Roskilde Festival, Denmark

Northern Europe's largest music festival (www.roskilde-festival.dk) rocks Roskilde each summer. It takes place in late June to early July but advance ticket sales are on offer in December and the festival usually sells out.

Hellenic Festival, Greece

The ancient theatre at Epidavros and the Odeon of Herodes Atticus are the headline venues of Athens' annual cultural shindig (www.greekfestival.gr). The festival, which runs from mid-June to August, features music, dance, theatre and much more.

July

One of the busiest months for travel across the continent with outdoor cafes, beer gardens and beach clubs all hopping. Expect beautiful – even steamy – weather anywhere you go.

Il Palio, Italy

Siena's great annual event is the Palio (2 July and 16 August; www.thepalio.com), a pageant culminating in a bareback horse race around Il Campo. The city is divided into 17 *contrade* (districts), of which 10 compete for the *palio* (silk banner), with emotions exploding.

EXIT Festival, Serbia

Eastern Europe's most talked-about music festival (www.exitfest.org) takes place within the walls of the Petrovaradin Citadel in Serbia's second city, Novi Sad. Book early as it attracts music lovers from all over the continent with big international acts headlining.

Východná, Slovakia

Slovakia's standout folk festival, Východná (www.festivalvychodna.sk) is held in a village nestled just below the High Tatras.

Bažant Pohoda, Slovakia

Slovakia's largest music festival (www.pohodafestival.sk) represents all genres of music from folk and rock to orchestral over eight different stages. It's firmly established as one of Europe's biggest and best summer music festivals.

⭐ Ultra Europe, Croatia

Held over three days in Split's Poljud Stadium, this electronic music fest (www. ultraeurope.com) includes a huge beach party.

⭐ Bastille Day, France

Fireworks, balls, processions, and – of course – good food and wine, for France's national day on 14 July, celebrated in every French town and city. Go to the heart of town and get caught up in this patriotic festival.

⭐ Gentse Feesten, Belgium

Ghent is transformed into a 10-day party of music and theatre (www.gentse feesten.be), a highlight of which is a vast techno celebration called 10 Days Off.

⭐ Medieval Festival of the Arts, Romania

The beautiful Romanian city of Sighişoara hosts open-air concerts, parades and ceremonies, all glorifying medieval Transylvania and taking the town back to its fascinating 12th-century origins.

⭐ Paléo Festival Nyon, Switzerland

More than 250 shows and concerts are staged for this premier music festival (http://yeah.paleo.ch) held above the town of Nyon.

August

Everybody's going someplace as half of Europe shuts down to enjoy the traditional month of holiday with the other half.

If it's near the beach, from Germany's Baltic to Spain's Balearics, it's mobbed and the temperatures are hot, hot, hot!

⭐ Salzburg Festival, Austria

Austria's most renowned classical-music festival (www.salzburgfestival.at) attracts international stars from late July to the end of August. That urbane person sitting by you having a glass of wine who looks like a famous cellist, probably is.

⭐ Edinburgh International Festival, Britain

Three weeks of innovative drama, comedy, dance, music and more (www.eif. co.uk). Two weeks overlap with the celebrated Fringe Festival (www.edfringe. com), which draws acts from around the globe. Expect cutting-edge productions that often defy description.

⭐ Amsterdam Gay Pride, The Netherlands

Held at the beginning of August, this is one of Europe's best GLBT events (www.amsterdamgaypride. nl). It's more about freedom and diversity than protest.

⭐ Sziget Music Festival, Hungary

A weeklong, great-value world-music festival (www. sziget.hu) held all over Budapest. Sziget features bands from around the world playing at more than 60 venues.

⭐ Guča Trumpet Festival, Serbia

Guča's Dragačevo Trumpet Assembly (www.guca.rs)

is one of the most exciting and bizarre events in all of Eastern Europe. Hundreds of thousands of revellers descend on the small Serbian town to damage their eardrums, livers and sanity in four cacophonous days of celebration.

⭐ Zürich Street Parade, Switzerland

Zürich lets its hair down with an enormous techno parade (www.streetparade. com). All thoughts of numbered accounts are forgotten as bankers, and everybody else in this otherwise staid burg, party to orgasmic, deep-base thump, thump, thump.

⭐ Notting Hill Carnival, Britain

This is Europe's largest – and London's most vibrant – outdoor carnival (www. thelondonnottinghillcarni val.com), where London's Caribbean community shows the city how to party. Food, frolic and fun are just a part of this vast multicultural two-day celebration.

September

It's cooling off in every sense, from the northern countries to the romance started on a dance floor in Ibiza. Maybe the best time to visit: the weather's still good but the crowds have thinned.

⭐ Venice International Film Festival, Italy

The Mostra del Cinema di Venezia (www.labiennale. org) is Italy's top film fest and the longest running in the world (since 1932). The judging here is seen as an early indication of what to look for at the next year's Oscars.

🍺 Oktoberfest, Germany

Despite its name, Germany's legendary beer-swilling party (www.oktoberfest. de) starts mid-September in Munich and finishes a week into October. Millions descend for litres of beer and carousing that has no equal. If you didn't plan ahead, you'll have to sleep in Austria.

🎆 Festes de la Mercè, Spain

Barcelona knows how to party until dawn and it outdoes itself for the Festes de la Mercè (around 24 September). The city's biggest celebration has four days of concerts, dancing, *castellers* (human-castle builders), fireworks and *correfocs* – a parade of fireworks-spitting dragons and devils.

October

Another good month to visit – almost everything is still open, while prices and visitor numbers are way down. Weather can be unpredictable, though, and even cold in northern Europe.

🍷 Wine Festival, Moldova

Wine-enriched folkloric performances in Moldova draw oenophiles and innocent bystanders for

CHRISTMAS MARKETS

In December, Christmas markets (www.christmas markets.com) are held across Europe, with particularly good ones in Germany, Austria, Slovakia and Czech Republic. The most famous are in Nuremberg (the Christkindlmarkt) and Vienna. Warm your hands through your mittens holding a hot mug of mulled wine and find that special (or kitsch) present. Slovak Christmas markets are regarded as some of Europe's best and a great opportunity to taste *medovina* (mead) and *lokše* (potato pancakes).

National Wine Day in early October when over 60 producers hold court in Chişinău's main square.

☆ Belfast International Arts Festival

Held at several venues throughout the city, this huge arts festival (www. belfastinternationalartsfes tival.com) has been around since 1962. Over two and a half weeks, the city sheds its gritty legacy and celebrates the intellectual and the creative without excessive hype.

November

Leaves have fallen and snow is about to in much of Europe. Even in the temperate zones around the Med it can get chilly, rainy and blustery. Most seasonal attractions have closed for the year.

☆ Guy Fawkes Night, Britain

Bonfires and fireworks erupt across Britain on 5 November, recalling the foiling of a plot to blow up

the Houses of Parliament in the 1600s. Go to high ground in London to see glowing explosions erupt everywhere.

☆ Iceland Airwaves, Iceland

Roll on up to Reykjavík for Iceland Airwaves (www. icelandairwaves.is), a great music festival featuring both Icelandic and international acts.

December

Despite freezing temperatures this is a magical time to visit Europe, with Christmas decorations brightening the dark streets. Prices remain surprisingly low provided you avoid Christmas and New Year's Eve.

🎄 Natale, Italy

Italian churches set up an intricate crib or a *presepe* (nativity scene) in the lead-up to Christmas. Some are quite famous, most are works of art, and many date back hundreds of years and are venerated for their spiritual ties.

Itineraries

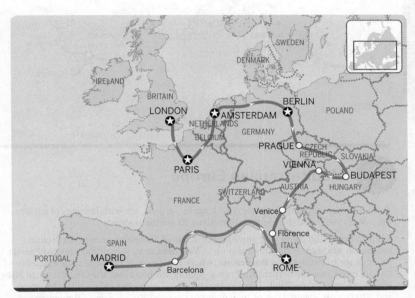

 First-Time Europe

If this is your first visit to Europe you'll want to experience as many of its famous cultural cities as possible – this is where your dreams become reality.

London is calling. The former capital of a huge empire is a city of massive museums, regal parks and electrifying nightlife.

Take the Eurostar to **Paris** and prepare to be seduced by the Eiffel Tower, Versailles and the Louvre. The art theme continues in **Amsterdam**, where you can admire works by Van Gogh and Rembrandt. Next travel to cosmopolitan, hedonistic **Berlin** in Germany where you can see the remains of the wall.

Prague in the Czech Republic is a city of intangible medieval magic. **Budapest** could be Prague's twin, offering refined music and a youthful nocturnal scene. **Vienna** is known for its gilded coffee bars.

Time to hit southern Europe. Start in glorious **Venice** with its canals and gondoliers, jump on a train to the Renaissance time capsule of **Florence**, and then proceed to **Rome**. Leapfrog southern France to Spain, stopping in **Barcelona** where Gaudí meets Gothic, before having a grand finale in **Madrid**.

5 WEEKS Mediterranean Europe

Think Europe doesn't do beaches? Think again – it does, but with lashings of culture on the side, as you'll find during this romp along its southern shores.

Fly to Spain and claim your sun-lounger at one of Europe's warmest year-round beaches in **Málaga**. Follow the coast up to **Valencia** next, the culinary home of paella. Pay homage to Catalonia in **Barcelona**, where you can soak up the seaside ambience of Gaudí's city. Cross the border into France, then beach-hop along the Côte d'Azur to **Nice** with its palm-lined seafront. Take the twisty coastal corniches to beguiling **Monaco** and, afterwards, spend a day or two inland in the beautiful villages of **Provence**.

Return to Nice and take the train southeast to historic **Rome**. Continue south to energetic **Naples**, walk through ill-fated **Pompeii** and explore the narrow footpaths and ancient staircases of the precipitous Amalfi Coast. Cross Italy to understated **Bari**, from where you head across the Adriatic by ferry to the Croatian pearl of **Dubrovnik** with its spectacular city walls.

Bus it south through Montenegro and Albania. Pause at the walled town of **Kotor** in the former and the white crescent-shaped beaches of **Drymades** in the latter.

Greece's Ionian Islands are next and the best is **Corfu**. Take a ferry to **Patra**, from where you can get a bus on to venerable **Athens**, capital of the ancient world. Move on to the port of Piraeus for an island-hopping expedition of the Cyclades, dreamy islands that include sophisticated **Mykonos**, laid-back **Paros** and volcanic **Santorini**. When you've had enough of Greek salads, set sail for Turkish port Kuşadası from lush, mountainous Samos.

Visit ancient **Ephesus**, one of the greatest surviving Graeco-Roman cities. Travel by bus north along the Aegean coast to the ruins of Troy and **Çanakkale**, the base for visiting Gallipoli Peninsula. Finish in beautiful, chaotic **İstanbul**.

Top: Whirling dervishes, İstanbul (p1156), Turkey

Bottom: Roman Baths (p191), Bath, Britain

ANTB/SHUTTERSTOCK ©

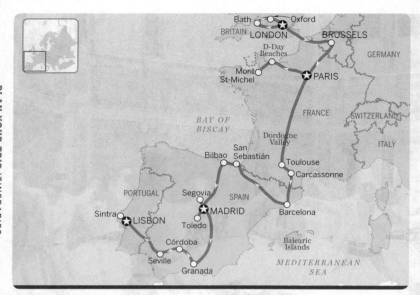

3 WEEKS From London to the Sun

Combining the best of both worlds, this itinerary begins with the urban powerhouse of London and ends with soaking up the sun in Spain and Portugal.

Enjoy several days in **London** for museums, galleries and clubbing, then take a train to **Bath** to appreciate Roman and Georgian architecture. Save time on the way back for **Oxford**, the fabled university town.

Back in London, take the Eurostar from grand St Pancras station to **Brussels**, the ethnically diverse headquarters of the EU.

The Eurostar will whisk you southwest to romantic **Paris**. Having dipped into the City of Light's cultural sights and gourmet delights, make side trips to the **D-Day beaches** north of Bayeux and the iconic abbey of **Mont St-Michel**, which reaches for the sky from its rocky island perch.

Head south by rail, stopping at lively **Toulouse**. Detour to the fairy-tale fortified city of **Carcassonne**. Cross into Spain, pausing at supercool **Barcelona**, where you can indulge in avant-garde Spanish cuisine.

Zip north to Basque seaside resort **San Sebastián**, with its envelope-pushing food scene, and then to the curvaceous Museo Guggenheim in happening **Bilbao**. Turn south, making a beeline for energetic **Madrid**, for some of Europe's best bars. From here plan day trips to **Toledo**, the so-called 'city of three cultures', and enchanting **Segovia** with its Roman aqueduct.

Continue south to **Granada** to explore the exquisite Islamic fortress complex of the Alhambra. Continue your Andalucian adventures with the one-of-a-kind Mezquita of **Córdoba**, before dancing flamenco in **Seville**. Get the bus to Portugal's captivating hillside capital **Lisbon**, where you can eat custard tarts by the sea. Finish in the wooded hills of **Sintra**, home to fairy-tale-like palaces and gardens.

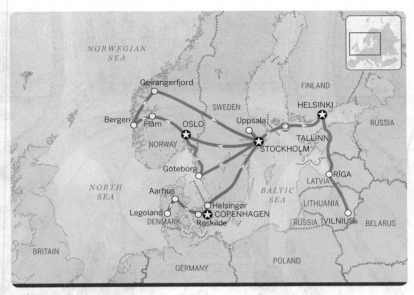

Scandinavian & Baltic Highlights

4 WEEKS

Three weeks is sufficient for the classic sights of northern Europe, though you can easily spend longer. Extra time allows detailed exploration and side trips to quieter places.

Start in Danish capital **Copenhagen**, the hipster of the Nordic block. Make day trips to the cathedral and Viking-boat museum at **Roskilde**; 'Hamlet's' castle Kronborg Slot at **Helsingør**; Denmark's second but no-less-trendy city **Aarhus** with its incredible art at ARoS Aarhus Kunstmuseum; and the country's top tourist attraction, **Legoland**.

Take the train to charming **Stockholm**. Sweden's capital spills across 14 islands with Gamla Stan the oldest and most beautiful. Side-trip to university town **Uppsala**, Sweden's spiritual heart, and spend the night. Creative and happening **Gothenburg**, the country's second city, has interesting galleries and museums, including a great one for kids.

It's a 3½-hour bus ride to **Oslo**, where you can check out Munch's work in a stunning setting. Norway's capital has plenty of museums and galleries, plus the iconic Oslo Opera House.

From Oslo, take the long but scenic 'Norway in a Nutshell' rail day trip to **Flåm** and ride the world's steepest railway that runs without cable or rack wheels. Continue by boat and bus along the stunning Sognefjord – Norway's deepest fjord – to **Bergen**. Admire this pretty town from a cable car and explore the quayside Bryggen district of historic buildings. From Bergen take a side trip to the mighty 20km-long emerald-green **Geirangerfjord**.

Return to Stockholm for a cruise circuit of the Baltic. First stop in quirky, design-diva **Helsinki**, a great base for exploring the natural wonders of Finland.

Wind up proceedings in the Baltic States starting in **Tallinn**, the charming Estonian capital where the Old Town is a jumble of turrets, spires and winding streets. Next is Latvia's gorgeous art nouveau **Rīga** followed by Lithuania's capital **Vilnius**, the baroque bombshell of the Baltics.

Top: Great Synagogue (p577), Budapest, Hungary

Bottom: Acueducto (p1051), Segovia, Spain

 4 WEEKS

The Alps to the Balkans

If you fancy visiting gorgeous towns on the shores of brilliant-blue lakes surrounded by turreted Alpine peaks, followed by a sojourn through the capitals of Eastern Europe, then head to Switzerland and jump on this itinerary.

Start with a few days in the spectacular **Swiss Alps**, ideal for hiking in summer and skiing in winter. Visit the oft-overlooked Swiss capital of **Bern**, and sophisticated, lake-side **Zürich**. Take the train to the top of Jungfrau (it's Europe's highest station) before heading down to visit lovely **Lucerne** where candy-coloured houses are reflected in a cobalt lake.

Turn east into Austria next, where, on the banks of the Danube, you'll find elegant **Vienna**. Track south into Slovenia, pausing by emerald-green **Lake Bled** and nearby but much less-developed **Lake Bohinj** with the picturesque Julian Alps as the backdrop.

Time to decamp to Croatia's **Dalmatian coast**, a holiday paradise of sun-dappled islands, limestone cliffs, ancient towns and Mediterranean cuisine. Aptly named **Split** on the Adriatic displays an interesting split between tradition and modernity, and guards Diocletian's Palace, one of Europe's most incredible Roman ruins. Further south, the walled marble town of **Dubrovnik** is heavy with history and tourists. Inland and across the border in Bosnia and Hercegovina lies **Sarajevo**. Forget its grisly recent past, this is a city on the rebound and a good place for winter activities, especially skiing.

Travel east through Serbia, stopping off in gritty but lively **Belgrade** to experience its famous nightlife and explore historic Kalemegdan Citadel. Then take a train to the relaxed Bulgarian capital of **Sofia** with its cityscape of onion-domed churches and Cold War–era monuments.

A train zips you through the mountains to Bulgaria's loveliest town, **Veliko Târnovo**, laced with cobbled lanes and surrounded by forested hills. Finish off in seaside **Varna**, your base for Black Sea beaches, archaeology museums and enormous parks.

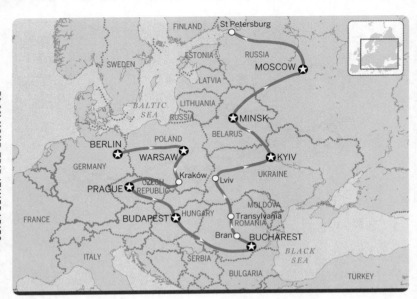

4 WEEKS Eastern Europe Today

Forget the stereotypes of the grim and grey 'Eastern Bloc' of the early 1990s – this half of Europe is one of the most dynamic and fast-changing places in the world.

The natural starting point is **Berlin**, once a city divided but now a veritable music, art and nightlife mecca.

Cross the now nonexistent iron curtain to Poland's capital **Warsaw**, a vibrant city that's survived all that history could throw at it and was meticulously restored after WWII. Further south is beautiful **Kraków**, the preserved royal capital which miraculously was spared destruction in WWII.

Cut across Slovakia into the Czech Republic and another remarkably intact medieval city: **Prague**, which has one of Eastern Europe's most romantic historical centres.

Moving back east, you'll encounter the Hungarian capital, **Budapest**, where you can freshen up at the thermal baths.

Romania had to wait a long time for its place in the sun, but it has come, especially in dynamic capital **Bucharest** with the world's largest parliament building.

For another side of Romania, make a beeline for **Transylvania** where you can sharpen your fangs at 'Dracula's' castle in **Bran** and enjoy the gorgeous old towns nearby.

Head north into western Ukraine where epiphanies are rife in charming **Lviv**, whose cityscape, like Kraków's, miraculously survived WWII. Continue on to bustling Ukrainian capital **Kyiv**, one of the former Soviet Union's more pleasant metropolises, before journeying into the past on a train to **Minsk** in Belarus to see how things were under communism.

Take another train to modern-day supercity **Moscow**, where the imposing Kremlin and adjacent Red Square are guaranteed to strike you with awe. Finally, head north to the old imperial capital of **St Petersburg**.

On the Road

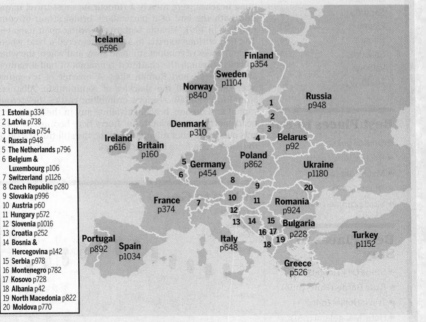

Albania

POP 2.93 MILLION

Best Places to Eat

➜ Onufri (p51)

➜ Pasta e Vino (p55)

➜ Met Kodra (p46)

➜ Otium (p48)

➜ Mrizi i Zanave (p48)

Best Places to Stay

➜ Stone City Hostel (p52)

➜ Rose Garden Hotel (p55)

➜ Trip'n'Hostel (p46)

➜ Hotel Mangalemi (p51)

➜ Hotel Rilindja (p57)

➜ B&B Tirana Smile (p46)

Why Go?

Closed to outsiders for much of the 20th century, Albania has long been Mediterranean Europe's enigma. Until fairly recently its rumpled mountains, fortress towns and sparkling beaches were merely a rumour on most travel maps. But, with the end of a particularly brutal strain of communism in 1991, Albania tentatively swung open its gates. The first curious tourists to arrive discovered a land where ancient codes of conduct still held sway and where the wind whistled through the shattered remnants of half-forgotten ancient Greek and Roman sites. A quarter of a century after throwing off the shackles of communism, Albania's stunning mountain scenery, crumbling castles, boisterous capital and dreamy beaches rivalling any in the Mediterranean continue to enchant. But hurry here because as word gets out about what Albania is hiding, the still-tiny trickle of tourists threatens to become a flood.

When to Go
Tirana

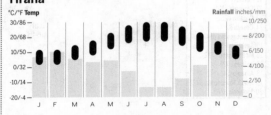

Jun Enjoy the perfect Mediterranean climate and deserted beaches.

Jul–Aug Albania's beaches may be packed, but this is a great time to explore the mountains.

Dec See features and shorts at the Tirana Film Festival, while the intrepid can snowshoe to Theth.

Entering the Country

Albania has good connections in all directions: daily buses go to Kosovo, Montenegro, North Macedonia and Greece. There are no international train routes to/from Albania. The southern seaport of Saranda is a short boat trip from Greece's Corfu, while in summer ferries also connect Himara and Vlora to Corfu. Durrës has regular ferries to Italy.

ITINERARIES

One Week

Spend a day in busy Tirana (p45), checking out the various excellent museums as well as the Blloku bars and cafes. On day two, make the three-hour trip to the Ottoman-era town of Berat (p49). Overnight there before continuing down the coast for a couple of days on the beach in Himara (p54) or Ksamil (p53). Make sure you leave time for Butrint (p54) before spending your last night in charming Gjirokastra (p51) and returning to Tirana.

Two Weeks

Follow the first week itinerary and then head north into Albania's incredible Accursed Mountains (p56). Start in Italian-flavoured Shkodra (p54), from where you can get transport to Koman (p56) for the stunning morning ferry ride to Fierzë. Continue the same day to the charming mountain village of Valbona (p56) for the night, before trekking to Theth (p57) and spending your last couple of nights in the beautiful Theth National Park before heading back to Tirana.

Essential Food & Drink

Byrek Pastry with cheese or meat.

Fergesë Baked peppers, egg and cheese, and occasionally meat.

Midhje Wild or farmed mussels, often served fried.

Paçë koke Sheep's head soup, usually served for breakfast.

Qofta Flat or cylindrical minced-meat rissoles.

Sufllaqë Doner kebab.

Tavë Meat baked with cheese and egg.

Konjak Local brandy.

Raki Popular spirit made from grapes.

Raki mani Spirit made from mulberries.

AT A GLANCE

Area 28,748 sq km

Capital Tirana

Country Code ☑ 355

Currency Lek (plural lekë); the euro (€) is widely accepted.

Emergency Ambulance ☑127; Fire ☑128; Police ☑129

Language Albanian

Time Central European Time (GMT/UTC plus one hour)

Visas Nearly all visitors can travel visa-free to Albania for a period of up to 90 days

Sleeping Price Ranges

The following price categories are based on the cost of a double room in high season.

€ less than €40

€€ €40–80

€€€ more than €80

Eating Price Ranges

The following price categories are based on the cost of a main course.

€ less than 500 lekë

€€ 500–1200 lekë

€€€ more than 1200 lekë

Albania Highlights

1 Accursed Mountains (p56)
Doing the wonderful day trek between the isolated mountain villages of Valbona and Theth and experiencing some of Albania's best scenery.

2 Berat (p49)
Exploring this Unesco World Heritage–listed museum town, known as the 'city of a thousand windows'.

3 Albanian Riviera (p52) Catching some sun at just one of the many gorgeous beaches on the Albanian Riviera.

4 Tirana (p45)
Feasting your eyes on the wild colour schemes and experiencing Blloku cafe culture in the plucky Albanian capital.

5 Gjirokastra (p51) Taking a trip to this traditional Albanian mountain town, with its spectacular Ottoman-era mansions and impressive hilltop fortress.

6 Butrint (p54)
Searching for the ghosts of Ancient Greece and Rome among the forest-dappled ruins of one of Europe's finest archaeological sites.

TIRANA

📍 04 / POP 557,000

Lively, colourful Tirana is where this tiny nation's hopes and dreams coalesce into a vibrant whirl of traffic, brash consumerism and unfettered fun. Having undergone a transformation of extraordinary proportions since awaking from its communist slumber in the early 1990s, Tirana's centre is now unrecognisable from those grey days, with buildings painted in primary colours, and public squares and pedestrianised streets that are a pleasure to wander.

Trendy Blloku buzzes with the well-heeled hanging out in bars and cafes, while the city's grand boulevards are lined with fascinating relics of its Ottoman, Italian and communist past – from delicate minarets to loud socialist murals. Add to this some excellent museums and you have a compelling list of reasons to visit.

⦿ Sights

The centre of Tirana is Sheshi Skënderbej (Skanderbeg Sq), a large traffic island with an equestrian statue of the eponymous Albanian national hero at its centre. Most of the city's sights are within walking distance of the square.

★ Bunk'Art   MUSEUM
(📞 067 207 2905; www.bunkart.al; Rr Fadil Deliu; 500 lekë; ⊙ 9am-4pm Wed-Sun) This fantastic conversion – from a massive Cold War bunker on the outskirts of Tirana into a history and contemporary art museum – is Albania's most exciting new sight and easily a Tirana highlight. With almost 3000 sq metres of space underground spread over several floors, the bunker was built for Albania's political elite in the 1970s and remained a secret for much of its existence. Now it hosts exhibits that combine the modern history of Albania with pieces of contemporary art.

★ National History Museum   MUSEUM
(Muzeu Historik Kombëtar; www.mhk.gov.al; Sheshi Skënderbej; 200 lekë; ⊙ 9am-7pm) The largest museum in Albania holds many of the country's archaeological treasures and a replica of Skanderbeg's massive sword (how he held it, rode his horse and fought at the same time is a mystery). The lighting might be poor but fortunately the excellent collection is almost entirely signed in English and takes you chronologically from ancient Illyria to the postcommunist era. The collection of statues, mosaics and columns from Greek and Roman times is breathtaking.

National Gallery of Arts   GALLERY
(Galeria Kombëtare e Arteve; 📞 04 223 3975; www.galeriakombetare.gov.al/en/home/index.shtml; Blvd Dëshmorët e Kombit; adult/student 200/60 lekë; ⊙ 9am-7pm) Tracing the relatively brief history of Albanian painting from the early 19th century to the present day, this beautiful space also has temporary exhibitions. The interesting collection includes 19th-century paintings depicting scenes from daily Albanian life and others with a far more political dimension including some truly fabulous examples of Albanian socialist realism.

The ground-floor part of the gallery is given over to temporary exhibitions of a far more modern and challenging kind.

Bunk'Art 2   MUSEUM
(📞 067 207 2905; www.bunkart.al; Rr Sermedin Toptani; 500 lekë; ⊙ 9am-9pm) The little cousin to the main Bunk'Art, this museum, which is within a communist-era bunker and underground tunnel system below the Ministry of Internal Affairs, focuses on the role of the police and security services in Albania through the turbulent 20th century. While this might not sound especially interesting, the whole thing has been very well put together and makes for a fascinating journey behind police lines.

House of Leaves   MUSEUM
(📞 04 222 2612; www.muzeugjethi.gov.al; Rr Ibrahim Rugova; 700 lekë; ⊙ 9am-7pm May–mid-Oct, 10am-5pm Tue-Sat, 9am-2pm Sun mid-Oct–Apr) This grand old 1930s building started life as Albania's first maternity hospital, but within a few years the focus turned from creating new life to ending lives as the hospital was converted to an interrogation and surveillance centre (read: torture house). It remained as such until the fall of the communist regime. Today, the House of Leaves is a museum dedicated to surveillance and interrogation in Albania.

Mt Dajti National Park   NATIONAL PARK
Just 25km east of Tirana is Mt Dajti National Park. It is the most accessible mountain in the country, and many locals go there to escape the city rush and have a spit-roast lamb lunch. A sky-high, Austrian-made cable car, **Dajti Express** (📞 067 208 4471; www.dajtiekspres.com; Rr Dibrës; one-way/return 500/800 lekë; ⊙ 9am-10pm Jul-Aug, to 9pm May-Jun & Sep-Oct, to 7pm Nov-Apr), takes 15 minutes to make the scenic trip (almost) to the top (1611m).

National Archaeological Museum MUSEUM

(Muzeu Arkeologjik Nacional; Sheshi Nënë Tereza; 300 lekë; ⊙10am-2.30pm Mon-Fri) The collection here is comprehensive and impressive in parts, but there's only minimal labelling in Albanian and none at all in English (nor are tours in English offered), so you may find yourself a little at a loss unless this is your field. A total renovation is on the cards, but as one staff member pointed out to us, they've been waiting for that since 1985 – so don't hold your breath.

🍂 Tours

Tirana Free Tour TOURS

(☑069 631 5858; www.tiranafreetour.com) This enterprising tour agency has made its name by offering a free daily tour of Tirana that leaves at 10am year-round. In July, August and September a second tour is offered at 3pm. Tours meet outside the Opera House on Sheshi Skënderbej (look on the website for a photo indicating the exact meeting spot).

🛏 Sleeping

⭐Trip'n'Hostel HOSTEL €

(☑068 304 8905; www.tripnhostel.com; Rr Musa Maci 1; dm/d from €10/30; 🛜) Tirana's coolest hostel is on a small side street, housed in a design-conscious self-contained house with a leafy garden out the back, a bar lined with old records, a kitchen and a cellar-like chill-out lounge downstairs. Dorms have handmade fixtures, curtains between beds for privacy and private lockable drawers, while there's also a roof terrace strewn with hammocks.

Tirana Backpacker Hostel HOSTEL €

(☑068 313 3451, 068 468 2353; www.tiranahostel. com; Rr Bogdani 3; dm from €8, d €27; 🅱@🛜) Albania's first-ever hostel continues to go from strength to strength. Housed in a charmingly decorated house, which has something of the air of the hazy hippy backpacker days of the 1970s to it, this super-friendly place has a funky design and an excellent location. There's always a big crew of globally wandering backpackers staying.

⭐B&B Tirana Smile HOTEL €€

(☑068 406 1507, 068 406 1561; www.bbtirana smile.com; Rr Bogdani; d incl breakfast €42; 🅱🛜) The owners could not have picked a better name for this inspirational hotel. The eight rooms are bright, modern, colourful and all have light summery touches. Each has a big workspace and good beds (though bathrooms are small). The best part is the communal lounge with sofas, books and a large table where a breakfast of homemade products is served.

Green House BOUTIQUE HOTEL €€

(☑069 205 7599; www.greenhouse.al; Rr Jul Variboba 6; d incl breakfast €60; 🅿🌸🛜) You've got a fantastic location at this 10-room hotel with downlit, stylish rooms that might be some of the city's coolest. Some have balconies, all have low-slung beds, shag-pile carpets, minibars and sleek furnishings. Downstairs is a large terrace restaurant where guests take breakfast each morning, and the whole place looks up at one of Tirana's more quirkily decorated buildings.

🍴 Eating

Most of Tirana's best eating is in and around Blloku, a square of some 10 blocks of shops, restaurants, cafes and hotels situated west of Blvd Dëshmorët e Kombit, but there are other options elsewhere. Particularly good kebabs can be found on Rr e Kavajës. The area known as the new market (Pazari i ri), where Rr Luigj Gurakuqi runs into Sheshi Avni Rustemi, has a growing number of good traditional restaurants.

⭐Met Kodra ALBANIAN €

(Sheshi Avni Rustemi; qofte 100 lekë; ⊙6am-9.30pm Sun-Thu, to midnight Fri & Sat) One of the great classics of Tirana dining. This tiny place which consists of nothing but a small smoky grill, does one thing and one thing only – *qoftas* (rissoles) – and the same lady and her family have been making them to exactly the same recipe since 1957.

King House ALBANIAN €

(☑067 223 3335; www.king-house.net; Rr Ibrahim Rugova 12; mains 300-800 lekë; ⊙8am-11pm) Enough Albanian traditional artefacts to shame an ethnographic museum bedeck the walls of this charming Blloku place. There's an excellent selection of traditional Albanian cooking – try the delicious Korça meatballs – as well as Italian pasta and pizza, and prices are low. There's a good terrace dining area if the interior is a little too much for you.

Era ALBANIAN, ITALIAN €€

(☑04 224 3845; www.era.al; Rr Ismail Qemali; mains 400-900 lekë; ⊙11am-midnight; 🍴) This local institution serves traditional Albanian and Italian fare in the heart of Blloku. The inventive menu includes oven-baked veal

Tirana

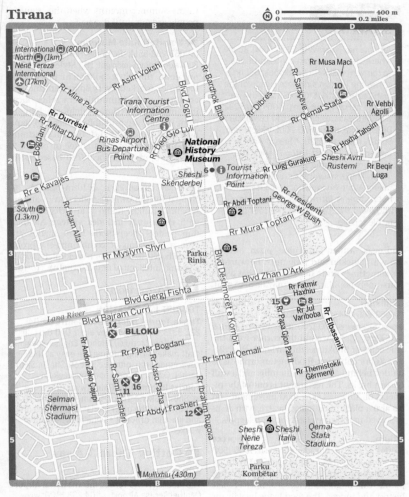

ALBANIA TIRANA

Tirana

◎ Top Sights
1 National History Museum.....................B2

◎ Sights
2 Bunk'Art 2..C3
3 House of Leaves...B3
4 National Archaeological Museum........C5
5 National Gallery of Arts..........................C3

✪ Activities, Courses & Tours
6 Tirana Free Tour...C2

⬢ Sleeping
7 B&B Tirana Smile.......................................A2

8 Green House..C4
9 Tirana Backpacker Hostel.....................A2
10 Trip'n'Hostel... D1

✗ Eating
11 Era...B4
12 King House...B5
13 Met Kodra... D2
14 Otium...B4

⬡ Drinking & Nightlife
15 Komiteti Kafe Muzeum...........................C4
16 Radio...B4

DON'T MISS

SLOW FOOD

Albania has a growing 'Slow Food' scene where chefs use organic local produce to reinvent classic local dishes. Set on a sprawling farm in a remote village of the lush Lezhë District, 65km north of Tirana, the **Mrizi i Zanave** (☎ 069 210 8032; www.mrizizanave.com/mrizi; Rr Lezhë-Vau i Dejës, Fishtë; mains 600-2000 lekë; ☺ from 8pm by reservation; ☎ ☑) restaurant is owned by Altin and Anton Prenga, the pioneers of Albania's slow-food movement. The restaurant is credited with taking Albanian food back to basics: fresh, organic farm-to-table produce and meat that celebrates the country's fertile terrain.

and eggs, stuffed aubergine, pizza, and pilau with chicken and pine nuts. Be warned: it's sometimes quite hard to get a seat as it's fearsomely popular, so you may have to wait.

Mullixhiu ALBANIAN €€
(☎ 069 666 0444; www.mullixhiu.al; Lazgush Poradeci St; mains 800-1200 lekë; ☺ noon-4pm & 6-10.30pm; ☎ ☑) Around the corner from the chic cafes of Blloku neighbourhood, chef Bledar Kola's Albanian food metamorphosis is hidden behind a row of grain mills and a wall of corn husks. The restaurant is one of the pioneers of Albania's slow-food movement and it's also a place of culinary theatre, with dishes served in treasure chests or atop teapots.

Otium FRENCH €€€
(☎ 04 222 3570; Rr Brigada e VIII; mains 1000-1500 lekë; ☺ noon-11pm Mon-Sat, to 6pm Sun) With its lace window curtains and tubs of flowering plants, this might look like a simple French bistrot and indeed, the food leans heavily on Gallic cuisine. But a meal here reveals a refined operation as attentive waiters talk you through the daily menu of artfully executed seasonal dishes, typically including seafood options and some fabulous starters.

🍷 Drinking & Nightlife

Tirana runs on caffeine during the day then switches over to alcohol after nightfall. Popular places to get both are concentrated in the Blloku neighbourhood, and indeed several streets are almost nothing but bars and cafes, and become jam-packed at night. Nightlife in Tirana goes late, particularly

in the summer months when the beautiful people are out until dawn.

⭐**Komiteti Kafe Muzeum** BAR
(☎ 069 262 5514; Rr Fatmir Haxhiu; raki around 200 lekë; ☺ 8am-midnight; ☎) Styled as a cafe-museum, this little bohemian place looks like a flea market. Every spare centimetre is crammed with communist-era relics, farming implements (those pitchforks hanging from the bar are probably a warning), Japanese fans, old clocks and so on. It's certainly a memorable spot for a coffee or one of 25 varieties of *raki*, the local fruit-based spirit.

Radio BAR
(Rr Ismail Qemali 29/1; ☺ 10am-midnight; ☎) Named for the owner's collection of antique Albanian radios, Radio is an eclectic dream with decor that includes vintage Albanian film posters, deep-1950s lamp shades and even a collection of communist-era propaganda books to read over a cocktail. It attracts a young, intellectual and alternative crowd.

ℹ Information

TOURIST INFORMATION

Tirana Tourist Information Centre (☎ 04 222 3313; www.tirana.gov.al; Rr Ded Gjo Luli; ☺ 8am-4pm Mon-Fri) Friendly English-speaking staff make getting information easy at this government-run initiative just off Sheshi Skënderbej. Oddly, it's only open on weekdays.

Tourist Information Point (www.tirana.gov.al; Sheshi Skënderbej; ☺ 8am-4pm Mon-Fri) A sub-office of the main tourist information office and like that office, it's unhelpfully closed at weekends.

ℹ Getting There & Away

AIR

The modern **Nënë Tereza International Airport** (Mother Teresa Airport; ☎ 04 238 1800; www.tirana-airport.com; Rinas) is at Rinas, 17km northwest of Tirana. The Rinas Express airport bus operates an on-the-hour (6am to 6pm) service, with **departures** from the corner of Rr Mine Peza and Rr e Durrësit (a few blocks from the National History Museum) for 250 lekë one way. The going taxi rate is 2000 to 2500 lekë. The airport is about 20 minutes' drive away, but plan for possible traffic jams and give yourself plenty of time to get there if you're catching a flight.

BUS

There is no one official bus station in Tirana. Instead, there are numerous bus stations around the city from which buses to specific destinations leave.

International services depart from the aptly named **International Bus Station** (off Rr Durresit) just off Rr Durresit. There are multiple services to Skopje (€13 to €20, eight hours) and Ohrid (€17.50, four hours) in North Macedonia, to Pristina (via Prizren) in Kosovo (€10, four hours), and services to Budva, Kotor and Podgorica in Montenegro (€20 to €25, four hours). At present there is no direct bus to Ulcinj from Tirana, and your best bet is to change buses in Shkodra. Other international destinations include Istanbul, Dubrovnik, Sofia, Thessaloniki and Athens. It's best to double-check all international services locally, as routes and timings change with great frequency.

Furgons (shared minibuses) to Bajram Curri (1000 lekë, 5½ hours, hourly 5am to 2pm), the jumping-off point for Valbona or the far side of Lake Koman, leave from **North Station** on Rr Dritan Hoxha, a short distance from the Zogu i Zi roundabout. Note that this service passes through Kosovo. Services to Shkodra (300 lekë, two hours, hourly until 5pm) also leave from here.

Departures to the south leave from – yes, you guessed it – **South Station** (Rr Muhedin Llagani) on Rr Muhedin Llagani. These include services to Berat (400 lekë, 2½ to three hours, every 30 minutes until 6pm), Himara (1000 lekë, five hours, 1pm and 6pm), Saranda (1300 lekë, seven hours, roughly hourly 5am to midday) and Gjirokastra (1000 lekë, five to six hours, regular departures until midday, also at 2.30pm and 6.30pm). Services to Himara and Saranda will drop you off at any of the coastal villages along the way.

ⓘ Getting Around

There's now a good network of city buses running around Tirana costing 40 lekë per journey (payable to the conductor), although most of the sights can be covered easily on foot.

TAXI

Taxi stands dot the city, and taxis charge from 300 to 400 lekë for a ride within Tirana, and from 500 to 600 lekë at night and to destinations outside the city centre. Reach an agreement on the fare with the driver before setting off; while drivers are supposed to use meters, they almost never do. **Speed Taxi** (☏ 04 222 2555; www.speedtaxi.al), with 24-hour service, is reliable.

CENTRAL ALBANIA

Berat

☏ 032 / POP 35,000

Berat weaves its own very special magic, and is easily a highlight of visiting Albania. Its most striking feature is the collection of white Ottoman houses climbing up the hill to its castle, earning it the title of 'town of a thousand windows' and helping it join Gjirokastra on the list of Unesco World Heritage sites in 2008. Its rugged mountain setting is particularly evocative when the clouds swirl around the tops of the minarets, or break up to show the icy peak of Mt Tomorri. Despite now being a big centre for tourism in Albania, Berat has managed to retain its easy-going charm and friendly atmosphere.

⊙ Sights

★**Kalaja** FORTRESS

(100 lekë; ⊙24hr, ticket booth 9am-6pm) Hidden behind the crumbling walls of the fortress that crowns the hill above Berat is the whitewashed, village-like neighbourhood of Kala; if you walk around the quiet cobbled streets of this ancient neighbourhood for long enough you'll invariably stumble into someone's courtyard thinking it's a church or ruin (no one seems to mind, though).

★**Onufri Museum** GALLERY

(Kalaja; 200 lekë; ⊙9am-6pm May–mid-Oct, to 4pm Tue-Sat, to 2pm Sun mid-Oct–Apr) The Onufri Museum is situated in the Kala quarter's biggest church, the **Church of the Dormition of St Mary** (Kisha Fjetja e Shën Mërisë). The church itself dates from 1797 and was built on the foundations of an earlier 10th-century chapel. Today Onufri's spectacular 16th-century religious paintings are displayed along with the church's beautifully gilded 19th-century iconostasis. Don't miss the chapel behind the iconostasis, or

---

WORTH A TRIP

APOLLONIA

The evocative ruins of the ancient Illyrian city of **Apollonia** (Pojan; 400 lekë; ⊙8am-6pm Apr-Oct, to 5pm Nov-Mar) sit on a windswept hilltop some 12km west of the city of Fier. While a large part of the ruins remains buried under the ground, what has been excavated within the 4km of city walls is pure poetry. The highlights include the theatre and the elegant pillars of the restored facade of the city's 2nd-century-CE administrative centre.

Few foreigners visit, but Apollonia is popular with locals for afternoon picnics.

Berat

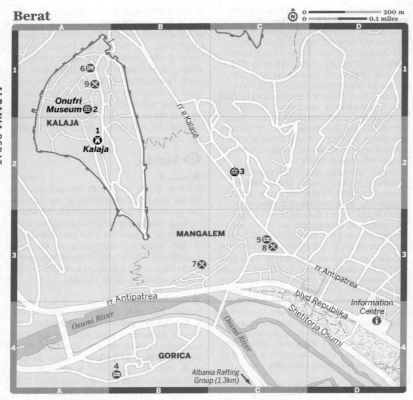

N 0 ———————————— 200 m
0 ———————————— 0.1 miles

Berat

◎ Top Sights
1 Kalaja	A2
2 Onufri Museum	A1

◎ Sights
3 Ethnographic Museum	C2

🛏 Sleeping
4 Berat Backpackers	B4

| | |
|---|---|
| 5 Hotel Mangalemi | C3 |
| 6 Hotel Restaurant Klea | A1 |

⊗ Eating
7 Lili Homemade Food	B3
8 Mangalemi Restaurant	C3
9 Onufri	A1

its painted cupola, whose frescoes are now faded almost to invisibility.

Ethnographic Museum MUSEUM
(☏ 032 232 224; www.muzeumet-berat.al; 200 lekë; ◎ 9am-7.30pm May-Sep, to 4pm Mon-Sat & to 2pm Sun Oct-Apr) Just off the steep hillside that leads up to Berat's castle is this excellent museum, which is housed in a beautiful 18th-century Ottoman house that's as much of an attraction as the exhibits within. The ground floor has displays of traditional clothes and the tools used by silversmiths and weavers, while the upper storey has kitchens, bedrooms and guest rooms decked out in traditional style.

🏃 Activities

Albania Rafting Group RAFTING
(☏ 067 200 6623; www.albrafting.com; Hotel Castle Park, Rr Berat–Përmet) 🏵 This pioneering group runs rafting tours for all levels to some stunning gorges around Berat and

Përmet. Everyone from children to pensioners is welcome. Rafting starts at €50 per person and hiking tours start from €20 per person per day.

🛏 Sleeping

★ Berat Backpackers
HOSTEL €

(☑ 069 785 4219; www.beratbackpackers.com; 295 Gorica; tents/dm/r without bathroom €7/10/25; ☉ Apr–Oct; @ 🛜) This transformed traditional house in the Gorica quarter houses one of Albania's friendliest hostels. The vine-clad establishment contains a basement bar and restaurant, an alfresco drinking area and a relaxed atmosphere that money can't buy. There are two airy dorms with original ceilings, and four gorgeous, excellent-value double rooms with antique furnishings. Shaded camping area and cheap laundry also available.

Hotel Restaurant Klea
GUESTHOUSE €

(☑ 032 234 970; Rr Shën Triadha, Kala; tw/d/tr incl breakfast €31/33/35) From the castle gates, go straight ahead and you'll find this gorgeous hilltop hideaway, run by a friendly English-speaking family. There are just five compact wood-panelled rooms, each with its own clean and modern bathroom. The downstairs restaurant adjoins a wonderful garden and has a daily changing specials menu featuring tasty Albanian fare (200 lekë to 450 lekë).

★ Hotel Mangalemi
HISTORIC HOTEL €

(☑ 068 232 3238; www.mangalemihotel.com; Rr Mihail Komneno; s/d/tr from €25/35/50; P ❄ @ 🛜) A true highlight of Berat is this gorgeous place inside two sprawling Ottoman houses where all the rooms are beautifully furnished in traditional Berati style and balconies (superior rooms only) give memorable views. Its terrace **restaurant** (mains 300-800 lekë; ☉ noon-11pm; 🛜) is the best place to eat in town with great Albanian food with bonus views of Mt Tomorri.

🍴 Eating

★ Onufri
ALBANIAN €

(Rr Shën Triadha, Kalaja; mains 200-300 lekë, mixed plates from 1500 lekë; ☉ noon-4pm) In the pretty village-like cobbled streets of the kalaja (castle; p49), Onufri is the closest you'll get to a homestyle Albanian feast without actually gatecrashing a family lunch. Expect to be brought a heaving plate of stuffed peppers, *byrek* (stuffed savoury pastries), *qofta* (rissoles), stuffed aubergines and grilled chicken. Finish up with a slice of homemade honey cake and you've got a meal to remember.

Lili Homemade Food
ALBANIAN €€

(☑ 069 234 9362; Mangalem; mains 500-700 lekë; ☉ noon-3pm & 6.30-10pm) This charming family home deep in the Mangalem Quarter below the castle is the setting for one of Berat's best restaurants. Lili speaks English and will invite you to take a table in his backyard where you can order a meal of traditional Berati cooking. We heartily recommend the *gjize ferges,* a delicious mash of tomato, garlic and cheese.

ℹ Information

TOURIST INFORMATION

Information Centre (Rr Antipatrea; ☉ 9am-noon & 2-6pm Mon-Fri) This tourist information centre can be found on Berat's main square, and has lots of local information and English-speaking staff.

ℹ Getting There & Away

Berat now has a bus terminal, around 3km from the town centre on the main road to Tirana. Bus services run to Tirana (400 lekë, three hours, half-hourly until 3pm). There are also buses to Vlora (300 lekë, two hours, hourly until 2pm), Durrës (300 lekë, two hours, six per day) and Saranda (1600 lekë, six hours, two daily at 8am and 2pm), one of which goes via Gjirokastra (1000 lekë, four hours, 8am). To get to the bus station from the centre, ask locals to put you on a bus to 'Terminali Autobusave'.

Gjirokastra
☑ 084 / POP 43,000

Defined by its castle, roads paved with chunky limestone and shale, imposing slate-roofed houses and views out to the Drina Valley, Gjirokastra is a magical hillside town described beautifully by Albania's most famous author, Ismail Kadare (b 1936), in *Chronicle in Stone.* There has been a settlement here for 2500 years, though these days it's the 600 'monumental' Ottoman-era houses in town that attract visitors.

◉ Sights

★ Gjirokastra Castle
CASTLE

(200 lekë; ☉ 9am-6pm mid-Apr–mid-Oct, 8am-4pm mid-Oct–mid-Apr) Gjirokastra's eerie hilltop castle is one of the biggest in the Balkans. There's been a fortress here since the 12th century, although much of what can be seen today dates to the early 19th century.

The castle remains somewhat infamous due to its use as a prison under the communists. Inside there's a collection of armoury, two good museums, plenty of crumbling ruins to scramble around and superb views over the valley.

Cold War Tunnel
TUNNEL

(Sheshi Çerçiz Topulli; 200 lekë; ⊘8am-4pm Mon-Fri, 10am-2pm Sat, 9am-3pm Sun) Gjirokastra's most interesting sight in no way relates to its traditional architecture, but instead to its far more modern kind: this is a giant bunker built deep under the castle for use by the local authorities during the full-scale invasion that communist leader Enver Hoxha was so paranoid about. Built in secret during the 1960s, it has 80 rooms and its existence remained unknown to locals until the 1990s. Personal guided tours run from the tourist information booth on the main square all day.

🛏 Sleeping & Eating

★ Stone City Hostel
HOSTEL €

(☑069 348 4271; www.stonecityhostel.com; Rr Alqi Kond; dm/d without bathroom incl breakfast €11/27; ⊘Apr-Oct; ❋🤝) This hostel is a fantastic conversion of an Old Town house, created and run by Dutchman Walter. The attention to detail and respect for traditional craftsmanship is extremely heartening, with beautiful carved wooden panels in all the rooms. Choose between the dorm rooms with custom-made bunks or a double room, all of which share spotless communal facilities.

Gjirokastra Hotel
HISTORIC HOTEL €

(☑068 409 9669, 084 265 982; hhotelgjirokastra@yahoo.com; Rr Sheazi Çomo; tw/d incl breakfast €35/40; ❋🤝) Combining modern facilities with traditional touches, this lovely family-run hotel inside a 300-year-old house has rooms that boast huge balconies and gorgeously carved wooden ceilings. If you can afford the extra then the suite (which sleeps four), with its long Ottoman-style sofa, original wooden doors and ceiling, and magnificent stone walls, is like sleeping inside a museum.

Odaja Restaurant
ALBANIAN €

(☑069 580 8687; Rr Gjin Bue Shpata; mains 250-600 lekë; ⊘10am-11pm) Cooking up a storm since 1937, Odaja is a small and cute 1st-floor restaurant serving good, honest home-cooked Albanian mountain dishes. Tuck into the oh-so-succulent meatballs with cheese, devour some stuffed peppers and relish the superb moussaka and you'll quickly come to understand just how good Albanian food can be.

ℹ Information

TOURIST INFORMATION

Information Centre (☑084 269 044; www.gjirokastra.org; Sheshi Çerçiz Topulli; ⊘9am-5pm Mar-Nov, to 3pm Dec-Feb) In a kiosk on the main square at the entrance to the Old Town, the staff here are suitably clued up on things to do and places to stay in and around the town. Tickets for the Cold War Tunnel are also on sale here. In low season it might be briefly closed when staff are conducting a tour.

ℹ Getting There & Away

Buses stop at the ad hoc bus station just after the Eida petrol station on the new town's main road. Services include Tirana (1000 lekë, seven hours, every one to two hours until 5pm), Saranda (300 lekë, one hour, hourly) and Berat (1000 lekë, four hours, 9.15am). A taxi between the Old Town and the bus station is 300 lekë.

THE ALBANIAN RIVIERA & THE EAST

The Albanian Riviera was a revelation a decade or so ago, when backpackers discovered the last virgin stretch of the Mediterranean coast in Europe, flocking here in droves, setting up ad hoc campsites and exploring scores of little-known beaches. Since then, things have become significantly less pristine, with overdevelopment blighting many of the once-charming coastal villages. But worry not: while some beaches may be well and truly swarming in summer, with a little persistence you can still find spots to kick back and enjoy the empty beaches the region was once so famous for.

ℹ Getting There & Away

The best way to explore this part of Albania is with your own wheels. Buses do connect the towns along the coast, but they're irregular and sometimes full – give yourself plenty of time and be patient when things don't go to plan.

From Tirana, buses to Saranda (1300 lekë, five hours) leave at 6am, 9am and midday and take the coastal road via the riviera villages. From Saranda, a daily bus travels up the riviera to Vlora (1300 lekë, three hours, 7am) and can drop you anywhere along the way, while there are also Vlora buses (900 lekë; also three hours) at 7.30am and 1pm that go via the coast. An 11.30am bus from Saranda heads to Himara (500 lekë, two hours) via the coast.

Saranda

📞 0852 / POP 38,000

Saranda is the unofficial capital of the Albanian Riviera, and come the summer months it seems like half of Tirana relocates here to enjoy the busy beach and busier nightlife along its crowd-filled seaside promenade. What was once a sleepy fishing village is now a thriving city, and while Saranda has lost much of its quaintness in the past two decades, it has retained much of its charisma. The town's beaches are nothing special, but Saranda is a great base for exploring the beaches of the riviera if you have your own transport.

🛏 Sleeping & Eating

SR Backpackers HOSTEL €
(📱 069 434 5426; www.backpackerssr.hostel.com; Rr Mitat Hoxha 10; dm from €11; @ 🛜) Your host at Saranda's most central hostel is the gregarious, English-speaking Tomi and he does much to give this place its party atmosphere. The 14 beds here are spread over three dorms, each with its own balcony, but sharing one bathroom and a communal kitchen. In Tomi's own words, 'It's not really suitable for couples after privacy'. You've been warned!

Hairy Lemon HOSTEL €
(📱 069 889 9196; cnr Mitat Hoxha & E Arberit, 8th fl; dm incl breakfast from €9; 🛜) With a prime 8th-floor location, a clean beach at its base and a friendly, helpful atmosphere, this Irish-run backpacker hostel is a good place to chill. There's an open-plan kitchen and lounge, and two cramped and often quite hot dorm rooms, although the fans and sea breezes help temper things a bit. The unlimited breakfast pancakes are always a hit.

Follow the port road for around 10 minutes and continue when it becomes dirt; it's the orange-and-yellow apartment block on your right.

⭐ Mare Nostrum INTERNATIONAL €€
(📱 0852 24 342; Rr Jonianët; mains 700-1200 lekë; ⊙ 8am-2pm & 6.30pm-midnight Apr-Oct) This sleek restaurant immediately feels different to the others along the seafront: here there's elegant decor that wouldn't look out of place in a major European capital, the buzz of a smart, in-the-know crowd and an imaginative menu that combines the seafood and fish you'll find everywhere else with dishes such as Indonesian chicken curry and burgers.

ℹ Information

ZIT Information Centre (📞 0852 24 124; Rr Skënderbeu; ⊙ 8am-midnight May-Sep, to 4pm Mar-Apr & Oct-Nov, 9am-5pm Dec-Feb) Saranda's tiny but excellent ZIT information centre provides information about transport and local sights and is staffed by friendly and helpful English-speaking staff. It's in a UFO-shaped building right on the waterfront.

ℹ Getting There & Away

BUS

The ZIT Information Centre has up-to-date bus timetables. Most buses leave just uphill from the ruins on Rr Vangjel Pando, right in the centre of town. Buses to Tirana (1300 lekë, eight hours) go inland via Gjirokastra (300 lekë, two hours) and leave regularly between 5am and 10.30am. There are later buses at 2pm and 10pm. The 7am Tirana bus takes the coastal route (1300 lekë, eight hours). There is also one bus a day to Himara at 11.30am (500 lekë, two hours), which can stop at any point along the way to let you off at riviera villages.

Ksamil

📞 0852 / POP 3000

Delightful Ksamil, 17km south of Saranda, sits on a narrow arm of land bordering a sparkling lagoon famed for its mussels and a cobalt-coloured sea. The entire area surrounding the small town is a protected zone and the dusty tracks and pathways leading over olive-studded hills and along ancient water canals are a joy to explore. The coastline around Ksamil is also unusually attractive. Blessed with three small, dreamy islands (sadly, one of which is being quarried for construction material) within swimming distance of shore and dozens of pretty cove beaches, Ksamil is the kind of place where you can happily while away many sun-drenched days. However, do try and avoid high season when the place is overrun with other Nirvana seekers. Late September is idyllic.

Ksamil is an ideal base for the stunning ruins of nearby Butrint (p54).

🛏 Sleeping & Eating

Hotel Joni HOTEL €€
(📱 069 543 1378, 069 209 1554; Sheshi Miqesia; d incl breakfast from €70; ❄ 🛜) This popular hotel in the middle of Ksamil is not on the

BUTRINT

Early in the morning, before the tourist crowds arrive and when the rocks are still tinged in the yellow dawn light, you might just imagine that the ancient walls of **Butrint** (www.butrint.al; Butrint National Park; adult 700 lekë, children under 8yrs free, family ticket per person 300 lekë; ☺ 8am-sunset, museum 8am-4pm) are whispering secrets to you of long-past lives. Easily the most romantic and beautiful – not to mention the largest – of Albania's ancient sites, Butrint, 18km south of Saranda, is worth travelling a long way to see.

Although the site was inhabited long before, Greeks from Corfu settled on the hill in Butrint (Buthrotum) in the 6th century BCE. Within a century Butrint had become a fortified trading city with an acropolis. The lower town began to develop in the 3rd century BCE, and many large stone buildings had already been built by the time the Romans took over in 167 BCE. Butrint's prosperity continued throughout the Roman period, and the Byzantines made it an ecclesiastical centre. The city then went into a long decline and was abandoned until 1927, when Italian archaeologists arrived.

Buses from Saranda (100 lekë, 20 minutes, hourly from 8.30am to 5.30pm) leave from outside the ZIT Information Centre (p53), returning from Butrint hourly on the hour.

beach, but its smart brick-and-timber-lined rooms are some of the best value around. It's within easy walking distance of several good places to swim, not to mention dozens of good eating and drinking spots.

Mussel House   SEAFOOD €€
(Km 10, Rr Sarande-Butrint; mains 500-1000 lekë; ☺ noon-midnight) With a winning view out over the vast Butrint lagoon and fronting the famed mussel beds, this laid-back, beach-shack-like restaurant a kilometre or so back along the road to Saranda dishes up mussels in any style you might care to think of. It also serves excellent grilled fish and other seafood.

❶ Getting There & Away

Any bus running between Saranda and Butrint will drop you off in Ksamil. The cost is 100 lekë.

Himara

☎ 0393 / POP 5700

The busy resort of Himara is the biggest town on the riviera north of Saranda. Despite this, the beaches here – book-ended by forested cliffs – are fairly attractive and the whole place has a more well-kept feel than some quieter beaches elsewhere on the coast. For those with their own wheels, there are heaps of other attractive beaches within a short drive.

⛺ Sleeping & Eating

The seafront promenade along the main town beach is lined with restaurants, all of which sell a fairly similar, but decent, range of seafood and Italian dishes.

Himara Downtown Hostel   HOSTEL €
(☎ 067 201 7574; https://himaradowntownhostel.business.site; dm/d €10/30) This small hostel has helpful staff and just three dorms each with six beds, plus there's one double room for couples who want some privacy. The hostel walls are covered in squiggly bright wall art. When full it can feel a bit claustrophobic. It's just one block back from the town's main beach and is in the thick of the action.

Kamping Himare   CAMPGROUND €
(☎ 068 529 8940; www.himaracamping.com; Potami Beach; camping per person/car/electricity 700/420/240 lekë; ☺ May-Oct; ☎) Set up a tent under the olive trees at this chilled-out camping ground across the main road from the beach. Facilities are basic but nice touches include midnight movies in an open-air cinema and a lamp-lit bar-restaurant that serves as a natural social centre for guests. It's on the second (southern) beach in Himara if you're coming from Tirana.

❶ Getting There & Away

There are four buses a day (most in the morning) to Tirana (1000 lekë, five to six hours) and five a day to Saranda with the last one leaving at 1pm (500 lekë, two hours).

Shkodra

☎ 022 / POP 135,000

Shkodra, the traditional centre of the Gheg cultural region, is one of the oldest cities in Europe and arguably the most attractive urban centre in Albania. The ancient Rozafa Fortress has stunning views over Lake

Shkodra, while the pastel-painted buildings in the Old Town have a distinct Italian ambience. Many travellers rush through here while travelling between Tirana and Montenegro, or en route to the Lake Koman Ferry and the villages of Theth and Valbona, but it's worth spending a night or two to soak up this pleasant and welcoming place and to check out the interesting museums before moving on to the mountains, the coast or the capital.

◎ Sights

★ Rozafa Fortress CASTLE
(200 lekë; ⊗9am-8pm Apr-Oct, to 4pm Nov-Mar) With spectacular views over the city and Lake Shkodra, the Rozafa Fortress is the most impressive sight in town. Founded by the Illyrians in antiquity and rebuilt much later by the Venetians and then the Turks, the fortress takes its name from a woman who was allegedly walled into the ramparts as an offering to the gods so that the construction would stand.

★ Marubi National Photography Museum GALLERY
(Muzeu Kombëtari i Fotografise Marubi; ☑022 400 500; Rr Kolë Idromeno 32; adult/student 700/200 lekë; ⊗9am-7pm Apr-Oct, to 5pm Nov-Mar) The Marubi Museum is a one-of-a-kind Albanian photographic museum. The core of the collection is the impressive work of the Marubi 'dynasty', Albania's first and foremost family of photographers. The collection includes the first-ever photograph taken in Albania, by Pjetër Marubi in 1858, as well as fascinating portraits, street scenes and early photojournalism, all giving a fascinating glimpse into old Albania and the rise and fall of communism.

Site of Witness & Memory Museum MUSEUM
(Vendi i Dëshmisë dhe Kujtesës; Blvd Skënderbeu; 150 lekë; ⊗9am-2.30pm Mon-Fri, 9.30am-12.30pm Sat) During the communist period this building, which started life as a Franciscan seminary, was officially used as the Shkodra headquarters of the Ministry of Internal Affairs. What that actually means is that it was an interrogation centre and prison for political detainees. Over the years, thousands of people spent time here – some never to re-emerge. The museum does a reasonable job of illustrating the horrors that took place here although much of the signage is in Albanian.

▭ Sleeping

Wanderers Hostel HOSTEL €
(☑069 212 1062; www.thewandershostel.com; Rr Gjuhadol; dm/d incl breakfast €8/25; ❄☎) Very popular with a young Anglophone crowd, this central and convivial hostel is a great place to hang out by the garden bar and make fast travel buddies. Dorms are frills-free and the bathrooms basic, but everyone seems to be having too much of a good time to care. Bikes are available for hire.

Mi Casa Es Tu Casa HOSTEL €
(☑069 381 2054; www.micasaestucasa.it; Blvd Skenderbeu 22; dm €10-13, d €35, apt €40, campsites per person with/without own tent €5/7; @☎) Shkodra's original hostel is a gorgeous arty space, and with a peaceful garden and open-air bar (selling local craft beers) you'd hardly guess that you were almost right in the heart of the city. There are attractive communal spaces littered with musical instruments and artwork and a bunch of friendly dogs. Dorms have between six and 10 beds.

★ Rose Garden Hotel BOUTIQUE HOTEL €
(☑022 245 296, 069 311 7127; www.rosegarden hotel.al; Rr Justin Godard 18; d incl breakfast from €36; ❄☎) A wonderfully restored old townhouse, the Rose Garden is all clean modern lines dusted with touches of old-fashioned class. Rooms are exceptionally inviting and include filigree door frames. The real highlight of a stay, though, is the hidden courtyard garden (which extends its botanical knowledge to more than just roses); sitting here with a good book is just perfect.

✗ Eating

★ Pasta e Vino ITALIAN €€
(☑069 724 3751; www.facebook.com/pastaevino shkoder; Rr Gjergj Fishta; mains 400-600 lekë; ⊗noon-11pm) Casually dressed waiters with tattoos, dried tree branches dressed with herbs, and artworks made from wine corks all help to make this one of the more visually memorable places to eat in Shkodra. But what about the food? Well, it's classic Italian, it's authentic and it's very well prepared and presented. What's not to like?!

Restaurant Elita ALBANIAN €€
(☑069 206 2193; Rr Gjergj Fishta; mains 600-800 lekë; ⊗8am-4pm & 6.30-11pm) Respected and smart restaurant with an emphasis on imaginative recreations of classic Albanian and Italian dishes. The slow-cooked pork served

in an inverted wine glass is just one such example. Very good value considering the quality of the food. Earlier in the evening it seems to be mainly other foreigners eating here, so for a more Albanian clientele, come later.

ℹ️ Information

Tourist Information (Rr Teuta; ⊙9am-7pm Mon-Sat) The small tourist information office has a few token leaflets to hand out but not much else of use. As it's a new office, there was no telephone number available at the time of research.

ℹ️ Getting There & Away

BUS

There is no bus station in Shkodra, but most services leave from around Sheshi Demokracia in the centre of town. There are hourly *furgons* (minibuses; 400 lekë) and buses (300 lekë) to Tirana (two hours, 6am to 5pm), which depart from outside Radio Shkodra near Hotel Rozafa. There are also several daily buses to Kotor, Ulcinj and Podgorica in Montenegro (€5 to €8, two to three hours) from outside the Ebu Bekr Mosque.

To get up into the mountains, catch the 6.30am bus to Lake Koman (600 lekë, two hours) in time for the wonderful Lake Koman Ferry to Fierzë. Several *furgons* also depart daily for Theth between 6am and 7am (1200 lekë, four hours). In both cases hotels can call ahead to get the *furgon* to pick you up on its way out of town.

THE ACCURSED MOUNTAINS & THE NORTH

Names don't come much more evocative than the 'Accursed Mountains' (Bjeshkët e Namuna; also known as the Albanian Alps), but the dramatic peaks of northern Albania truly live up to the wonder in their name. Offering some of the country's most impressive scenery, and easily its finest hiking, the mountains spread over the borders of Albania, Kosovo and Montenegro, and in Albania they reach a respectable height of 2694m. But as we all know, size isn't everything and what these mountains lack in Himalayan greatness, they more than make up for with lyrical beauty. There are deep green valleys, thick forests where wolves prowl, icy-grey rock pinnacles and quaint stone villages where old traditions hold strong. Indeed, this is where shepherds still take their flocks to high summer pastures and blood feuds continue to hold sway, and it feels as if you're far, far away from 21st-century Europe.

Valbona

📞 0213 / POP 200

Valbona has a gorgeous setting on a wide plain surrounded by towering mountain peaks, and its summer tourism industry is increasingly well organised. The village itself consists virtually only of guesthouses and

---

WORTH A TRIP

THE LAKE KOMAN FERRY

One of Albania's undisputed highlights is the superb three-hour **ferry ride** (www.komanilakeferry.com/en/ferry-lines-in-the-komani-lake) across vast Lake Koman, connecting the towns of Koman and Fierzë.

The best way to experience the journey is to make a three-day, two-night loop beginning and ending in Shkodra, and taking in Koman, Fierzë, Valbona and Theth. Every hotel in Shkodra and Valbona organises packages for the route for 2000 lekë. This includes a 6.30am *furgon* (shared minibus) pick-up from your hotel in Shkodra which will get you to the ferry departure point at Koman by 8.30am. There are normally two ferries daily and both leave from Koman at 9am. One of the two, the Berisha, carries up to ten cars, which cost 700 lekë per square metre of space they occupy. There's also a big car ferry that leaves at 1pm, but it only runs when demand is high enough – call ahead to make a reservation.

On arrival in Fierzë, the boats are met by furgons that will take you to either Bajram Curri or to Valbon. Hikers will want to head straight for Valbona, where you can stay for a night or two before doing the stunning day hike to Theth. After the hike you can stay for another night or two in glorious Theth before taking a furgon back to Shkodra (not included in the standard packages). It's also possible to do the whole thing independently, though you won't save any money or time by doing so.

HIKING

Most people come here to do the popular hike between Valbona and Theth, which takes between five and seven hours depending on your fitness and where in either village you start or end. It's not a particularly hard walk and it is attempted by many first-time mountain walkers. Even so, it's quite long and steep and can get very hot, and if you don't have much mountain walking experience you should allow extra time.

You can walk it either way, though the majority of people seem to go from Valbona to Theth as this allows for a neat circle going from Shkodra via the Lake Koman ferry. The trail begins a couple of kilometres beyond Valbona, and many people get a lift to the trailhead; it's a tiring and monotonous walk over a dry – and often very hot – stone riverbed otherwise. On the whole the trail itself is decently marked with red and white way markings and there are a number of tea houses where you can get refreshments (and even a bed). Eventually you will arrive at the Valbona Pass (1800m) for memorable views over an ocean of jagged mountains.

camping grounds, nearly all of which have their own restaurants attached. Most travellers just spend a night here before trekking to Theth, which is a shame as there are a wealth of other excellent hikes to do in the area.

🛏 Sleeping

★ Hotel Rilindja
GUESTHOUSE €

(☑ 067 301 4637; www.journeytovalbona.com; Quku i Valbonës; tent/dm/d incl breakfast €4/12/35; 🛜) Pioneering tourism in Valbona since 2005, the Albanian–American–run Rilindja is a fairy-tale wooden house in the forest 3km downhill from Valbona village centre. It's hugely popular with travellers, who love the comfortable accommodation, easy attitude and excellent food. The simple rooms in the atmospheric farmhouse share a bathroom, except for one with private facilities.

Jezerca
GUESTHOUSE €

(☑ 067 309 3202; r from €30; 🛜) Named after one of the soaring mountain peaks nearby, this guesthouse on Valbona's main (well, only) street has freestanding pine huts in a pleasant field, which sleep two, three or five people. The best huts have attached bathrooms and little terraces with hanging flower baskets. There's a small restaurant which tries hard to use only locally sourced products.

❶ Getting There & Away

Valbona can be reached from Shkodra via the Lake Koman Ferry and a connecting *furgon* (minibus) from Fierzë (400 lekë, one hour). Alternatively it can be reached by *furgon* from Bajram Curri (200 lekë, 45 minutes). In general most people just organise the entire trip as one package from Shkodra (2000 lekë).

Theth

☑ 022 / POP 400

This unique mountain village easily has the most dramatic setting in Albania. Just the journey here is quite incredible, whether you approach over the mountains on foot from Valbona or by vehicle over the high passes from Shkodra. Both a sprawling village along the valley floor amid an amphitheatre of slate-grey mountains and a national park containing stunning landscapes and excellent hiking routes, Theth is now well on its way to being Albania's next big thing. An improved – though still incomplete – asphalt road from Shkodra has made access to this once virtually unknown village far easier in recent years, bringing with it the familiar problem of overdevelopment. Come quickly while Theth retains its incomparable romance and unique charm.

◉ Sights

Blue Eye
NATURAL POOL

A superb half-day hike from Theth is to the Blue Eye, a natural pool of turquoise waters fed by a small waterfall, up in the mountains to the southwest of Theth. The walk will take you through forests and steeply up into the mountains and in summer it can get very hot, so you'll probably be keen for a swim when you get to the pool. But, be warned: the water is glacier cold. Are you brave enough?

🛏 Sleeping

Vila Pisha
GUESTHOUSE €€

(☑ 069 325 6415, 068 278 5057; r per person incl breakfast €34; 🛜) Next to the church, right in the centre of the village, this place has been totally rebuilt from the ground upwards. It is one of the best guesthouses in the village, with friendly, English-speaking owners, smart en-suite rooms with radiators for those cold mountain nights, large beds and wooden floors.

Vila Zorgji   GUESTHOUSE €
(☑ 068 231 9610, 068 361 7309; pellumbkola@ gmail.com; r per person incl full board €35; ☺ Apr-Oct; 🛜) Zorgji is a gorgeous stone farmhouse with big, bright en-suite rooms and a dining room full of drying corn and old farming implements. The garden is equally attractive and is lined with grape vines and tomato plants. It's a little to the north of the village centre and up on the hillside near the turquoise-painted school.

❶ Getting There & Away

A daily *furgon* (1200 lekë, two hours) leaves from Shkodra at 7am and will pick you up from your hotel if your hotel owner calls ahead for you. The return trip leaves between 1pm and 2pm, arriving late afternoon in Shkodra. During the summer months it's also easy to arrange a shared *furgon* (around €50) transfer to Shkodra with other hikers from Valbona.

SURVIVAL GUIDE

❶ Directory A–Z

ACCESSIBLE TRAVEL

High footpaths and unannounced potholes make life difficult for mobility-impaired travellers. Tirana's top hotels do cater to people with disabilities, and some smaller hotels are making an effort to be more accessible. The roads and castle entrances in Gjirokastra, Shkodra, Berat and Kruja are cobblestone, although taxis can get reasonably close.

ACCOMMODATION

Hotels and guesthouses, including an expanding number of boutique and heritage properties, are easily found throughout Albania as tourism continues to grow. You will rarely have trouble finding a room for the night, though seaside towns are often booked out in late July and August.

Homestays abound in Theth and Valbona, while the number of camping grounds is increasing; you'll find them at Himara, Livadhi, Dhërmi and Drymades. Most have hot showers and on-site restaurants.

LGBTIQ+ TRAVELLERS

Extensive antidiscrimination legislation became law in 2010, but did not extend to legalising same-sex marriage. Gay and lesbian life in Albania is alive and well but is not yet organised into clubs or organisations. The alternative music and party scene in Tirana is queer-friendly, but most contacts are made on the internet. As with elsewhere in the Balkans, discretion is generally the way to go for LGBTIQ+ travellers.

MONEY

ATMs are widely available in most towns. Acceptance of credit cards is normally confined to upper-end hotels, restaurants and shops, although every year their usage becomes more widespread.

OPENING HOURS

Banks 9am to 3.30pm Monday to Friday
Cafes & Bars 8am to midnight
Offices 8am to 5pm Monday to Friday
Restaurants 8am to midnight
Shops 8am to 7pm; siesta time can be any time between noon and 4pm

PUBLIC HOLIDAYS

New Year's Day 1 January
Summer Day 16 March
Nevruz 23 March
Catholic Easter March or April
Orthodox Easter March or April
May Day 1 May
Mother Teresa Day 19 October
Independence Day 28 November
Liberation Day 29 November
Christmas Day 25 December

TELEPHONE

Albania's country phone code is 355. Mobile coverage is excellent, though it's limited in very remote areas (though most places have some form of connection including Theth).

TOURIST INFORMATION

The country's main tourist board website is www.albaniantourist.com.

WOMEN TRAVELLERS

Albania is a safe country for women travellers, but outside Tirana it is mainly men who go out and sit in bars and cafes in the evenings. You may tire of being asked why you're travelling alone, but you'll rarely feel the target of more than curiosity.

❶ Getting There & Away

ENTERING THE COUNTRY

All citizens of European and North American countries may enter Albania visa-free for up to 90 days. This is also true for Australians, New Zealanders, Japanese and South Korean citizens. Citizens of most other countries must apply for a visa.

AIR

Nënë Tereza International Airport (p48) is a modern, well-run terminal 17km northwest of Tirana. There are no domestic flights within Albania. Airlines flying to and from Tirana include **Adria Airways** (www.adria.si), **Alitalia** (www.alitalia.com), **Austrian Airlines** (www.austrian.com), **Lufthansa** (www.lufthansa.com), **Olympic Air** (www.olympicair.com), **Pegasus Airlines** (www.flypgs.com) and **Turkish Airlines** (www.turkishairlines.com).

LAND
Border Crossings

There are no passenger trains into Albania, so your border-crossing options are buses, *furgons* (minibuses), taxis or walking to a border and picking up transport on the other side.

Montenegro The main crossings link Shkodra to Ulcinj (via Muriqan, Albania, and Sukobin, Montenegro) and to Podgorica (via Hani i Hotit).

Kosovo The closest border crossing to the Lake Koman Ferry terminal is Morina, and further south is Qafë Prush. Near Kukës, use Morinë for the highway to Tirana.

North Macedonia Use Blato to get to Debar, and Qafë e Thanës or Tushemisht, each to one side of Pogradec, for accessing Ohrid.

Greece The main border crossing to and from Greece is Kakavija on the road from Athens to Tirana. It's about half an hour from Gjirokastra and 250km southeast of Tirana, and can take up to three hours to pass through in summer. Kapshtica (near Korça) to Krystallopigi also gets long lines in summer. Konispoli (near Butrint in Albania's south) and Leskovik (between Gjirokastra and Korça) are both far less busy.

Bus

From Tirana, regular buses head to Pristina, Kosovo; to Skopje in North Macedonia; to Ulcinj in Montenegro; and to Athens and Thessaloniki in Greece. *Furgons* (minibuses) and buses leave Shkodra for Montenegro, and buses head to Kosovo from Durrës. Buses travel to Greece from Albanian towns on the southern coast as well as from Tirana.

Car & Motorcycle

Travellers heading south from Croatia can pass through Montenegro to Shkodra (via Ulcinj), and loop through Albania before heading into North Macedonia via Pogradec or into Kosovo via the Lake Koman Ferry or the excellent Albania–Kosovo highway.

To enter Albania with you own vehicle you'll need a Green Card (proof of third-party insurance, issued by your insurer); check that your insurance covers Albania.

Taxi

Heading to North Macedonia, taxis from Pogradec will drop you off just before the border at Tushemisht/Sveti Naum. Alternatively, it's an easy 4km walk to the border from Pogradec. It's possible to organise a taxi (or, more usually, a person with a car) from where the Lake Koman Ferry stops in Fierzë to Gjakova in Kosovo. Taxis commonly charge €50 from Shkodra to Ulcinj in Montenegro.

SEA

Two or three boats per day ply the route between Saranda and Corfu, in Greece, and there are plenty of ferry companies making the journey to Italy from Vlora and Durrës. There are additional ferries from Vlora and Himara to Corfu in the summer.

ⓘ Getting Around

BUS

Bus and *furgon* (privately run minibuses) are the main forms of public transport in Albania. Fares are low, and you either pay the conductor on board or when you hop off, which can be anywhere along the route.

Municipal buses operate in Tirana, Durrës, Shkodra, Berat, Korça and Vlora, and trips usually cost 40 lekë.

CAR & MOTORCYCLE

Despite severe neglect under the communists, nowadays the road infrastructure is improving; there's an excellent highway from Tirana to Kosovo, and the coastal route from the Montenegro border to Butrint, near Saranda, is in good condition.

Tourists are driving cars, motorbikes and mobile homes into the country in greater numbers, and, apart from heavy traffic and bad drivers, it's generally hassle free. One issue is the huge number of traffic cops running speed traps. If they stop you for speeding, you'll have to pay a 'fine' in cash (around €20).

Off the main routes a 4WD isn't a bad idea. Driving at night is particularly hazardous; following another car on the road is a good idea as there are rarely any road markings or street lighting. A valid foreign driving licence is all that's required to drive a car in Albania.

Austria

POP 8.8 MILLION

Includes →

Best Places to Eat

→ Vollpension (p71)

→ Der Steirer (p78)

→ Esszimmer (p83)

→ Restaurant zum Salzbaron (p85)

→ Die Wilderin (p87)

Best Places to Stay

→ Hotel am Domplatz (p76)

→ Haus Ballwein (p82)

→ Magdas (p70)

→ Hotel Weisses Kreuz (p87)

→ Hotel Wiesler (p78)

Why Go?

For such a small country, Austria is ridiculously large on inspiration. This is the land where Mozart was born, Strauss taught the world to waltz and Julie Andrews grabbed the spotlight with her twirling entrance in *The Sound of Music*. It's where the Habsburgs ruled over their spectacular, sprawling 600-year empire.

These past glories still shine in the resplendent baroque palaces and chandelier-lit coffee houses of Vienna, Innsbruck and Salzburg, but beyond its storybook cities, Austria's allure is one of natural beauty and outdoor adventure. Whether you're schussing down the legendary slopes of Kitzbühel, climbing high in the Alps of Tyrol or cycling the banks of the mighty Danube, you'll find the kind of landscapes to which no well-orchestrated symphony or singing nun could ever quite do justice.

When to Go

Vienna

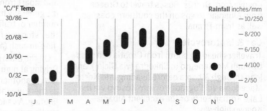

Jul–Aug Alpine hiking in Tyrol, lake swimming in Salzkammergut and lots of summer festivals.

Sep–Oct New wine in vineyards near Vienna, golden forest strolls and few crowds.

Dec–Jan Christmas markets, skiing in the Alps and Vienna waltzing into the New Year.

Entering the Country

Austria is well connected to the rest of the world. Vienna and several regional capitals are served by no-frills airlines (plus regular airline services). Europe's extensive bus and train networks criss-cross the country and there are major highways from Germany and Italy. It's also possible to enter Austria by boat from Hungary, Slovakia and Germany. Trains from Vienna run to many Eastern European destinations, including Bratislava, Budapest, Prague and Warsaw; there are also connections south to Italy via Klagenfurt and north to Berlin. Salzburg is within sight of the Bavarian border, with many Munich-bound trains. Innsbruck is on the main rail line from Vienna to Switzerland, and two routes also lead to Munich. Look out for the fast, comfortable RailJet services to Germany and Switzerland.

ITINERARIES

Two Days

Make the most of Vienna (p64), spending your first day visiting the Habsburg palaces and Stephansdom before cosying up in a *Kaffeehäus* (coffee house). At night, check out the pumping bar scene.

One Week

Plan for two long and lovely days in Vienna, plus another day exploring the Wachau (Danube Valley; p75) wine region, a day each in Salzburg (p79) and Innsbruck (p86), a day in Kitzbühel (p88) hiking or skiing, and then a final day exploring the Salzkammergut (p84) lakes.

Essential Food & Drink

Make it meaty Go for a classic Wiener schnitzel, *Tafelspitz* (boiled beef with horseradish sauce) or *Schweinebraten* (pork roast). The humble *Wurst* (sausage) comes in various guises.

On the side Lashings of potatoes, either fried (*Pommes*), roasted (*Bratkartoffeln*), in a salad (*Erdapfelsalat*) or boiled in their skins (*Quellmänner*); or try *Knödel* (dumplings) and *Nudeln* (flat egg noodles).

Kaffee und Kuchen Coffee and cake is Austria's sweetest tradition. Must-tries: flaky apple strudel, rich, chocolatey *Sacher Torte* and *Kaiserschmarrn* (sweet 'scrambled' pancakes with raisins).

Wine at the source Jovial locals gather in rustic *Heurigen* (wine taverns) in the wine-producing east, identified by an evergreen branch above the door. Sip crisp Grüner Veltliner whites and spicy Blaufränkisch wines.

Cheese fest Dig into gooey *Käsnudeln* (cheese noodles) in Carinthia, *Kaspressknodel* (fried cheese dumplings) in Tyrol and *Käsekrainer* (cheesy sausages) in Vienna. The hilly Bregenzerwald is studded with dairies.

AT A GLANCE

Area 83,871 sq km

Capital Vienna

Country Code 43

Currency euro (€)

Emergency 112

Language German

Time Central European Time (GMT/UTC plus one hour)

Visas Schengen rules apply

Sleeping Price Ranges

The following price ranges refer to a double room with a bathroom for two people, including breakfast.

€ less than €80

€€ €80–200

€€€ more than €200

Eating Price Ranges

The following price ranges refer to the cost of a two-course meal, excluding drinks.

€ less than €15

€€ €15–30

€€€ more than €30

Resources

Embassy of Austria (www.austria.org)

Lonely Planet (www.lonelyplanet.com/austria)

Österreich Werbung (www.austria.info)

Tiscover (www.tiscover.com)

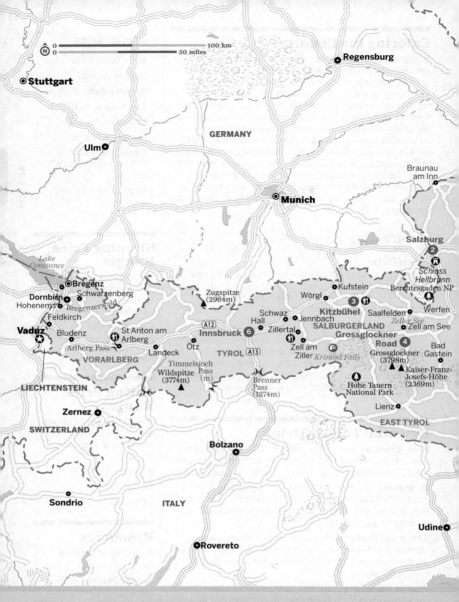

Austria Highlights

① Vienna (p64) Discovering opulent Habsburg palaces, coffee houses and cutting-edge galleries.

② Salzburg (p79) Surveying the baroque cityscape from the giddy heights of 900-year-old Festung Hohensalzburg.

③ Kitzbühel (p88) Sending your spirits soaring from peak to peak hiking and skiing.

④ Grossglockner Road (p89) Buckling up for a rollercoaster ride of Alps and glaciers on one of Austria's greatest drives.

5 Salzkammergut (p84)
Diving into the crystal-clear lakes of Austria's summer playground.

6 Innsbruck (p86) Whizzing up to the Tyrolean Alps in Zaha Hadid's space-age funicular.

7 Danube Valley (p75) Exploring the romantic Wachau and technology trailblazer Linz.

VIENNA

📷 01 / POP 1.9 MILLION

Few cities in the world waltz so effortlessly between the present and the past like Vienna. Its splendid historical face is easily recognised: grand imperial palaces and bombastic baroque interiors, revered opera houses and magnificent squares. But Vienna is also one of Europe's most dynamic urban spaces. A stone's throw from Hofburg (the Imperial Palace), the MuseumsQuartier houses provocative and high-profile contemporary art behind a striking basalt facade. In the Innere Stadt (Inner City), up-to-the-minute design stores sidle up to old-world confectioners, and Austro-Asian fusion restaurants stand alongside traditional *Beisl* (small taverns).

◉ Sights

Vienna's magnificent series of boulevards, the Ringstrasse, encircles the Innere Stadt, with many of the city's most famous sights situated on or within it, including the monumental Hofburg palace complex. Just outside the Ringstrasse are exceptional museums including the Kunsthistorisches Museum and the ensemble making up the MuseumsQuartier, while attractions further afield include the sumptuous palaces Schloss Schönbrunn and Schloss Belvedere.

★ Hofburg
PALACE

(Imperial Palace; www.hofburg-wien.at; 01, Michaelerkuppel; adult/child €13.90/8.20; ⊘9am-5.30pm; 🚌 1A, 2A Michaelerplatz, 🚋 D, 1, 2, 46, 49, 71 Burgring, Ⓤ Herrengasse) Nothing symbolises Austria's resplendent cultural heritage more than its Hofburg, home base of the Habsburgs from 1273 to 1918. The oldest section is the 13th-century Schweizerhof (Swiss Courtyard), named after the Swiss guards who used to protect its precincts. The Renaissance Swiss gate dates from 1553. The courtyard adjoins a larger courtyard, In der Burg, with a monument to Emperor Franz II adorning its centre. The palace now houses the Austrian president's offices and a raft of museums.

★ Kaiserappartements
PALACE

(Imperial Apartments; 📞01-533 75 70; www.hofburg-wien.at; 01, Michaelerplatz; adult/child €13.90/8.20, incl guided tour €16.90/9.70; ⊘9am-6pm Jul & Aug, to 5.30pm Sep-Jun; Ⓤ Herrengasse) The Kaiserappartements, once the official living quarters of Franz Josef I and Empress Elisabeth, are dazzling in their chandelier-lit opulence. The highlight is the Sisi Museum, devoted to Austria's most beloved empress, which has a strong focus on the clothing and jewellery of Austria's monarch. Multilingual audio guides are included in the admission price. Guided tours take in the Kaiserappartements, the Sisi Museum and the Silberkammer (Silver Depot), whose largest silver service caters for 140 dinner guests.

★ Kaiserliche Schatzkammer
MUSEUM

(Imperial Treasury; www.kaiserliche-schatzkammer.at; 01, Schweizerhof; adult/child €12/free; ⊘9am-5.30pm Wed-Mon; Ⓤ Herrengasse) The Hofburg's Kaiserliche Schatzkammer contains secular and ecclesiastical treasures (including devotional images and altars, particularly from the baroque era) of priceless value and splendour – the sheer wealth of this collection of crown jewels is staggering. As you walk through the rooms you'll see magnificent treasures such as a golden rose, diamond-studded Turkish sabres, a 2680-carat Colombian emerald and, the highlight of the treasury, the imperial crown.

★ Stephansdom
CATHEDRAL

(St Stephen's Cathedral; www.stephanskirche.at; 01, Stephansplatz; tours adult/child €6/2.50; ⊘6am-10pm Mon-Sat, 7am-10pm Sun, tours 10.30am Mon-Sat; Ⓤ Stephansplatz) Vienna's Gothic masterpiece Stephansdom – or Steffl (Little Stephan), as it's ironically nicknamed – is Vienna's pride and joy. A church has stood here since the 12th century, and reminders of this are the Romanesque Riesentor (Giant Gate) and Heidentürme (Towers of the Heathens). From the exterior, the first thing that will strike you is the glorious tiled roof, with its dazzling row of chevrons and Austrian eagle. Inside, the magnificent Gothic stone pulpit presides over the main nave, fashioned in 1515 by Anton Pilgrim.

★ Kunsthistorisches Museum Vienna
MUSEUM

(KHM, Museum of Art History; www.khm.at; 01, Maria-Theresien-Platz; adult/child incl Neue Burg museums €15/free; ⊘10am-6pm Fri-Wed, to 9pm Thu; Ⓤ Museumsquartier, Volkstheater) One of the unforgettable experiences of any trip to Vienna is a visit to the Kunsthistorisches Museum Vienna, brimming with works by Europe's finest painters, sculptors and artisans. Occupying a neoclassical building as sumptuous as the art it contains, the museum takes you on a time-travel treasure hunt from Classical Rome to Egypt and the Renaissance. If your time's limited, skip straight to the Picture

Gallery, where you'll want to dedicate at least an hour or two to the Old Masters.

★ **Neue Burg Museums** MUSEUM
(☑ 01-525 240; www.khm.at; 01, Heldenplatz, Hofburg; adult/child €12/free; ⊙ 10am-6pm Wed-Sun; 🚊 D, 1, 2, 71 Burgring, Ⓤ Herrengasse, Museumsquartier) The Neue Burg is home to the three Neue Burg Museums. The **Sammlung Alter Musik Instrumente** (Collection of Ancient Musical Instruments) contains a wonderfully diverse array of instruments. The **Ephesos Museum** features artefacts unearthed during Austrian archaeologists' excavations at Ephesus in Turkey between 1895 and 1906. The **Hofjägd und Rüstkammer** (Arms and Armour) museum contains armour dating mainly from the 15th and 16th centuries. Admission includes the Kunsthistorisches Museum Vienna and all three Neue Burg museums. Audio guides cost €4.

★ **Staatsoper** NOTABLE BUILDING
(www.wiener-staatsoper.at; 01, Opernring 2; tour adult/child €9/4; Ⓤ Karlsplatz) Few concert halls can hold a candle to the neo-Renaissance Staatsoper, Vienna's foremost opera and ballet venue. Even if you can't snag tickets to see a tenor hitting the high notes, you can get a taste of the architectural brilliance and musical genius that have shaped this cultural bastion by taking a 40-minute guided tour. Tours (in English and German) generally depart on the hour between 10am and 4pm.

★ **MuseumsQuartier** MUSEUM
(Museum Quarter; MQ; www.mqw.at; 07, Museumsplatz; ⊙ information & ticket centre 10am-7pm; Ⓤ Museumsquartier, Volkstheater) The MuseumsQuartier is a remarkable ensemble of museums, cafes, restaurants and bars inside former imperial stables designed by Fischer von Erlach. This breeding ground of Viennese cultural life is the perfect place to hang out and watch or meet people on warm evenings. With over 90,000 sq metres of exhibition space – including the Leopold Museum, MUMOK, **Kunsthalle** (Arts Hall; ☑ 01-521 890; www.kunsthallewien.at; adult/child €8/free; ⊙ 11am-7pm Tue, Wed & Fri-Sun, to 9pm Thu), **Architekturzentrum** (Vienna Architecture Centre; ☑ 01-522 31 15; www.azw.at; adult/child €9/2.50; ⊙ architecture centre 10am-7pm, library 10am-5.30pm Mon, Wed & Fri, to 7pm Sat & Sun) and **Zoom** (☑ 01-524 79 08; www.kindermuseum.at; exhibition adult/child €6/free, activities child €5-7, accompanying adult free; ⊙ 12.45-5pm Tue-Sun Jul & Aug, 8.30am-4pm Tue-Fri, 9.45am-4pm Sat & Sun

Sep-Jun, activity times vary; 👣) – the complex is one of the world's most ambitious cultural hubs.

★ **MUMOK** GALLERY
(Museum Moderner Kunst; Museum of Modern Art; www.mumok.at; 07, Museumsplatz 1; adult/child €12/free; ⊙ 2-7pm Mon, 10am-7pm Tue, Wed & Fri-Sun, 10am-9pm Thu; 🚊 49 Volkstheater, Ⓤ Volkstheater, Museumsquartier) The dark basalt edifice and sharp corners of the Museum Moderner Kunst are a complete contrast to the MuseumsQuartier's historical sleeve. Inside, MUMOK contains Vienna's finest collection of 20th-century art, centred on fluxus, nouveau realism, pop art and photo-realism. The best of expressionism, cubism, minimal art and Viennese Actionism is also represented in a collection of 9000 works that are rotated and exhibited by theme – but note that sometimes all this Actionism is packed away to make room for temporary exhibitions.

★ **Leopold Museum** MUSEUM
(www.leopoldmuseum.org; 07, Museumsplatz 1; adult/child €13/8; ⊙ 10am-6pm Fri-Wed, to 9pm Thu; Ⓤ Volkstheater, Museumsquartier) Part of the MuseumsQuartier, the Leopold Museum is named after ophthalmologist Rudolf Leopold, who, after buying his first Egon Schiele for a song as a young student in 1950, amassed a huge private collection of mainly 19th-century and modernist Austrian artworks. In 1994 he sold the lot – 5266 paintings – to the Austrian government for €160 million (individually, the paintings

---

SPIN OF THE RING

One of the best deals in Vienna is a self-guided tour on tram 1 or 2 of the monumental **Ringstrasse** boulevard encircling much of the Innere Stadt, which turns 150 in 2015. For the price of a single ticket you'll take in the neo-Gothic **Rathaus** (City Hall; ☑ 01-502 55; www.wien.gv.at; 01, Rathausplatz 1; ⊙ tours 1pm Mon, Wed & Fri Sep-Jun, 1pm Mon-Fri Jul & Aug; 🚊 D, 1, 2 Rathaus, Ⓤ Rathaus) **FREE**, the Greek Revival–style parliament, the 19th-century **Burgtheater** (National Theatre; ☑ 01-514 44 4440; www.burgtheater.at; 01, Universitätsring 2; seats €10-61, standing room €3.50; ⊙ box office 9am-5pm Mon-Fri; 🚊 D, 1, 2 Rathaus, Ⓤ Rathaus) and the baroque Karlskirche (p69), among other sights.

AUSTRIA VIENNA

Central Vienna

AUSTRIA VIENNA

A

Bauernmarkt
Yppenplatz
(1.3km)

Ostarichi
Park

Rooseveltplatz

Währinger Str

29

Sigmund Freud
Museum (500m)

Börsegasse/
Wipplingerstrasse

Alser Str

Universitätsstr

Schottentor
Votivpark

Schottentor

Börseplatz

1

Schlösselgasse

Wickenburggasse

Landesgerichtsstr

Liebiggasse

Ebendorferstr

Reichsratstr

Mölker Bastei

Helfertorferstr

Börsegasse

Wipplingerstr

Hohenstaufengasse

Buchfeldgasse

Tulpengasse

Friedrich-
Schmidt-Platz

Felderstr

Rathauspark

Renngasse

Tiefer Graben

Färbergasse

Am Hof

42

Freyunggasse

Herrengasse

30

Am Hof

Bognergasse

Naglergasse

Rathaus

11

Rathaus

Rathausplatz

44

37

Rathausplatz/
Burgtheater

Bankgasse

**INNERE
STADT 1**

Fähnengasse

Kohlmarkt

Josefstädter Str

Weinstube
Josefstadt
(150m)

Friedrich-Schmidt

Stadiongasse

Minoritenplatz

Herrengasse

Schauflergasse

3

Kaiserappartements

In der Burg

Michaelerplatz

40

Hofburg 2

2

3

Lange Gasse

Josefsgasse

Trautsongasse

Doblhoffgasse

Auerspergstr

Hansenstr

Stadiongasse/
Parlament

Ballhausplatz

Volksgarten

Dr Karl-
Renner-
Ring

Heldenplatz

36

Josefsplatz

**Kaiserliche
Schatzkammer**

In der Burg

Dirndlherz
(250m)

Lerchenfelder Str

Museumstr

Volksgartenstr

Bellariastr

Burgring (Ringstrasse)

Neue
Burg

Neue Burg
Museums

10

Reitschulstr

Augustinerstr

4

Neustiftgasse

Volkstheater

Maria-
Theresien-
Platz

Burggarten

23

5

Burggasse

my MOjO
vie (800m)

Hotel am
Brillantengrund
(550m)

Breite Gasse

Stiftgasse

16

MUMOK

8

9
MuseumsQuartier

Kunsthalle Wien

7 **Leopold
Museum**

21

**Kunsthistorisches
Museum Vienna**

6

Babenbergerstr

Burgring

Goethegasse

Helmut-
Zilk-Platz
(Albertinaplatz)

Opernring

6

Siebensterngasse

Karl-Schweighofer-Gasse

Mariahilfer Str

Rahlgasse

Elisabethstr

Museumsquartier

Schillerplatz

Opernring
(Ringstrasse)

NEUBAU 7

Shades Tours (500m)

Mariahilfer Str

Theobaldgasse

Gumpendorfer Str

Getreidemarkt

13

Secession

Friedrichstr

Karlsplatz

Treitlstr

Hotel Riede (3.1km);
Schloss Schönbrunn
(3.2km)

Windmühlgasse

Fillgradergasse

32

Lehárgasse

Girardigasse

41

26

7

28

Barnabitengasse

Gumpendorfer Str

Laimgrubengasse

**MARIAHILF
6**

Rechte Wienzeile

27

Schadekgasse

Esterházy
Park

Fritz-
Grünbaum-
Platz

Linke Wienzeile

Kettenbrückengasse

Schleifmühlgasse

Schikanedergasse

Opernring

Wiedner Hauptstr

Kaffeefabrik
(260m)

A **B** **C** **D**

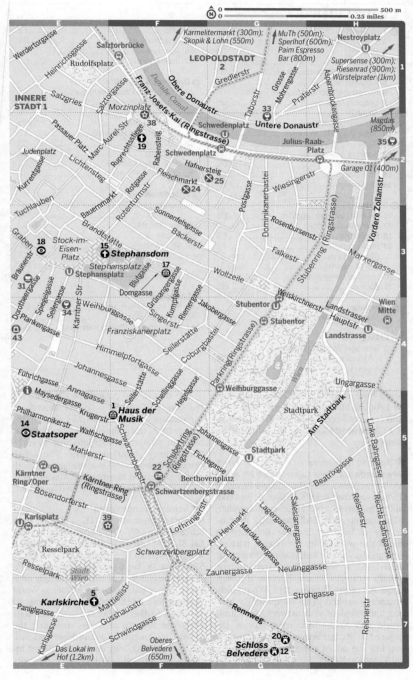

Central Vienna

would have made him €574 million), and the Leopold Museum was born. **Café Leopold** (www.cafeleopold.wien; ⊙9.30am-1am Mon-Fri, 9.30am-midnight Sat & Sun; 🛜) is located on the top floor.

★ **Schloss Belvedere** PALACE
(www.belvedere.at; Prinz-Eugen-Strasse 27; adult/child Oberes Belvedere €15/free, Unteres Belvedere €13/free, combined ticket €22/free; ⊙9am-6pm Sat-Thu, to 9pm Fri; 🚊D, 71 Schwarzenbergplatz, Ⓤ Taubstummengasse, Südtiroler Platz) A masterpiece of total art, Schloss Belvedere is one of the world's finest baroque palaces. Designed by Johann Lukas von Hildebrandt (1668–1745), it was built for the brilliant military strategist Prince Eugene of Savoy, conqueror of the Turks in 1718. What giddy romance is evoked in its sumptuously frescoed halls, replete with artworks by Klimt, Schiele and Kokoschka; what stories are conjured in its landscaped gardens, which drop like the fall of a theatre curtain to reveal Vienna's skyline.

The first of the palace's two buildings is the **Oberes Belvedere** (Upper Belvedere), showcasing Gustav Klimt's *The Kiss* (1908), the perfect embodiment of Viennese art nouveau, alongside other late-19th- to early-20th-century Austrian works. The lavish **Unteres Belvedere** (Lower Belvedere), with its richly frescoed Marmorsaal (Marble Hall), sits at the end of sculpture-dotted gardens.

★ **Schloss Schönbrunn** PALACE
(www.schoenbrunn.at; 13, Schönbrunner Schlossstrasse 47; adult/child Imperial Tour €14.20/10.50, Grand Tour €17.50/11.50, Grand Tour with guide €20.50/13; ⊙8am-6.30pm Jul & Aug, to 5.30pm Apr-Jun, Sep & Oct, to 5pm Nov-Mar; ⓊHietzing) The Habsburgs' overwhelmingly opulent summer palace is now a Unesco World Heritage Site. Of the palace's 1441 rooms, 40 are open to the public; the Imperial Tour takes you into 26 of these, including the private apartments of Franz Josef and Sisi, while the Grand Tour covers all 40 and includes the precious 18th-century interiors

from the time of Maria Theresia. These mandatory tours are done with an audio guide or, for an additional charge, a tour guide.

★ Haus der Musik · MUSEUM

(www.hausdermusik.com; 01, Seilerstätte 30; adult/child €13/6, incl Mozarthaus Vienna €18/8; ⏲10am-10pm; 🖼; 🚌2, 71 Schwarzenbergplatz, ⓊKarlsplatz) The Haus der Musik explains the world of sound and music to adults and children alike in an amusing and interactive way (in English and German). Exhibits are spread over four floors and cover everything about how sound is created, from Vienna's Philharmonic Orchestra to street noises. The staircase between floors acts as a piano; its glassed-in ground-floor courtyard hosts musical events. Admission is discounted after 8pm.

Mozarthaus Vienna · MUSEUM

(⏰01-512 17 91; www.mozarthausvienna.at; 01, Domgasse 5; adult/child €11/4.50, incl Haus der Musik €18/8; ⏲10am-7pm; ⓊStephansplatz) The great composer spent 2½ happy and productive years at this residence between 1784 and 1787. Exhibits include copies of music scores and paintings, while free audio guides recreate the story of his time here. Mozart spent a total of 11 years in Vienna, changing residences frequently and sometimes setting up his home outside the Ringstrasse in the cheaper *Vorstädte* (inner suburbs) when his finances were tight. Of these the Mozarthaus Vienna is the only one that survives.

★ Prater · PARK

(www.wiener-prater.at; 🖼; ⓊPraterstern) Spread across 60 sq km, central Vienna's biggest park comprises woodlands of poplar and chestnut, meadows and tree-lined boulevards, as well as children's playgrounds, a swimming pool, a golf course and a race track. Fringed by statuesque chestnut trees that are ablaze with russet and gold in autumn and frilly with white blossom in spring, the central Hauptallee avenue is the main vein, running straight as a die from the Praterstern to the Lusthaus (⏰01-728 95 65; 02, Freudenau 254; mains €13-20; ⏲noon-11pm Mon-Fri, to 6pm Sat & Sun, shorter hours winter; 🛜; 🚌77A).

Twirling above the **Würstelprater** (Prater 7; rides €1.50-5; ⏲10am-midnight; 🖼; ⓊPraterstern) amusement park is one of the city's most visible icons, the **Riesenrad** (www.wienerriesenrad.com; 02, Prater 90; adult/child €12/5; ⏲9am-11.45pm, shorter hours winter; 🖼; ⓊPraterstern). Built in 1897, this 65m-high Ferris wheel of *The Third Man* fame affords far-reaching views of Vienna.

Sigmund Freud Museum · MUSEUM, HOUSE

(www.freud-museum.at; 09, Berggasse 19; adult/child €12/4; ⏲10am-6pm; 🚌1, D Schlickgasse, ⓊSchottentor, Schottenring) Sigmund Freud is a bit like the telephone – once he happened, there was no going back. This is where Freud spent his most prolific years and developed the most significant of his groundbreaking theories; he moved here with his family in 1891 and stayed until forced into exile by the Nazis in 1938.

★ Secession · MUSEUM

(www.secession.at; 01, Friedrichstrasse 12; adult/child €9/6; ⏲10am-6pm Tue-Sun; ⓊKarlsplatz) In 1897, 19 progressive artists swam away from the mainstream Künstlerhaus artistic establishment to form the *Wiener Secession* (Vienna Secession). Among their number were Gustav Klimt, Josef Hoffman, Kolo Moser and Joseph M Olbrich. Olbrich designed the new exhibition centre of the Secessionists, which combined sparse functionality with stylistic motifs. Its biggest draw is Klimt's exquisitely gilded *Beethoven Frieze*. Guided tours in English (€3) lasting one hour take place at 11am Saturday. An audio guide costs €3.

★ Karlskirche · CHURCH

(St Charles Church; www.karlskirche.at; 04, Karlsplatz; adult/child €8/4; ⏲9am-6pm Mon-Sat, noon-7pm Sun; ⓊKarlsplatz) Built between 1716 and 1739, after a vow by Karl VI at the end of the 1713 plague, Vienna's finest baroque church rises at the southeast corner of Resselpark. It was designed and commenced by Johann Bernhard Fischer von Erlach and completed by his son Joseph. The huge elliptical copper dome reaches 72m; the highlight is the lift to the cupola (included in admission) for a close-up view of the intricate frescoes by Johann Michael Rottmayr.

Pestsäule · MEMORIAL

(Plague Column; 01, Graben; ⓊStephansplatz) Graben is dominated by the twisting outline of this gold-topped baroque memorial, designed by Fischer von Erlach in 1693 at the behest of Emperor Leopold I to commemorate the 75,000 Viennese victims of the Black Death, the bubonic plague epidemic that swept through Vienna in 1679.

🏃 Activities & Tours

Vienna steps effortlessly between urban and outdoors. The Wienerwald to the west is criss-crossed with hiking and cycling trails, while the Danube, Alte Donau, Donauinsel and Lobau to the east offer boating, swimming, cycling and inline skating. There are over 1200km of cycle paths, and the city is dotted with parks, some big (Prater), some small (Stadtpark).

★ **Space & Place** WALKING
(📱 0680 125 43 54; http://spaceandplace.at; walking tours €10, Coffeehouse Conversations €11) For the inside scoop on Vienna, join Eugene on one of his fun, quirky tours. The alternative line-up keeps growing: from Vienna Ugly tours, homing in on the capital's ugly side, to Smells Like Wien Spirit, a playful exploration of the city through smell, and the sociable Coffeehouse Conversations. See the website for dates, further details and meeting points.

Shades Tours WALKING
(📱 01-997 19 83; www.shades-tours.com; Impact Hub Vienna, Lindengasse 56; walking tours €18) A world apart from the bog-standard city tour, Shades reveals central Vienna from a unique perspective, with two-hour walks guided by formerly homeless residents. Offered in English and German, the tours are a real eye-opener. It also provides integration-aimed tours led by refugees. See the website for dates, bookings and meeting points.

★ **Festivals & Events**

★ **Christkindlmärkte** CHRISTMAS MARKET
(www.wien.info/en/shopping-wining-dining/markets/christmas-markets; ⊘ mid-Nov–24 Dec) Vienna's much-loved Christmas market season runs from around mid-November to Christmas Eve. Magical *Christkindlmärkte* set up in streets and squares, with stalls selling wooden toys, holiday decorations and traditional food such as *Wurst* (sausages) and *Glühwein* (mulled wine). The centrepiece is the **Rathausplatz Christkindlmarkt** (www.christkindlmarkt.at; 🚋 D, 1, 2 Rathaus, Ⓤ Rathaus).

Donauinselfest MUSIC
(https://donauinselfest.at; ⊘ late Jun) FREE Held over three days on a weekend in late June, the Donauinselfest features a feast of rock, pop, folk and country performers, and attracts almost three million onlookers. Best of all, it's free!

Wiener Festwochen ART
(Vienna Festival; www.festwochen.at; ⊘ mid-May–mid-Jun) A wide-ranging program of theatrical productions, concerts, dance performances and visual arts from around the world, the month-long Wiener Festwochen takes place from mid-May to mid-June at various venues city-wide.

Opernball CULTURAL
(www.wiener-staatsoper.at; ⊘ Feb; Ⓤ Karlsplatz) Of the 300 or so balls held in January and February, the Opernball (Opera Ball) is number one. Held in the Staatsoper (p73) on the Thursday preceding Ash Wednesday, it's a supremely lavish affair, with the men in tails and women in shining white gowns.

🛏 **Sleeping**

my MOjO vie HOSTEL $
(📱 0676 551 11 55; www.mymojovie.at; 07, Kaiserstrasse 77; dm/d/tr/q €25/80/100/120, s/d/tr/q with shared bathroom €44/60/80/100; 🛜; Ⓤ Burggasse-Stadthalle) An old-fashioned cage lift rattles up to these design-focused backpacker digs. Everything you could wish for is here – well-equipped dorms with two power points per bed, a self-catering kitchen, tablets for surfing, guidebooks for browsing and musical instruments for your own jam session. There's no air-con but fans are available in summer.

Hotel am Brillantengrund HOTEL $
(📱 01-523 36 62; www.brillantengrund.com; 07, Bandgasse 4; s/d/tr/q from €59/69/89/109; @🛜; 🚌 49 Westbahnstrasse/Zieglergasse, Ⓤ Zieglergasse) In a lemon-yellow building set around a sociable courtyard strewn with potted palms, this community linchpin works with local artists and hosts regular exhibitions, along with DJs, live music and other events such as pop-up markets and shops. Parquet-floored rooms are simple but decorated with vintage furniture, and variously incorporate local artworks, funky wallpapers and retro light fittings. Breakfast included.

Hotel Riede B&B $$
(📱 01-813 85 76; www.hotelriede.at; Niederhofstrasse 18; s €65-76, d €70-100; 🅿🛜; Ⓤ Niederhofstrasse) Around a 15-minute stroll east of Schönbrunn, this family-run hotel in a gorgeous art nouveau building has a spiral staircase curling up to parquet-floored rooms that are simple but spacious, comfortable and well kept. Tots can stay free in their parents' room. Bring cash as credit cards aren't accepted.

★ **Magdas** BOUTIQUE HOTEL $$
(📱 01-720 02 88; www.magdas-hotel.at; 02, Laufbergergasse 2; d €70-150; Ⓤ Praterstern) How

clever: the Magdas is a hotel making a difference as the staff who welcome guests are refugees. The former retirement home turned boutique hotel opened its doors in 2016 and hit the ground running. The rooms are retro cool, with one-of-a-kind murals, knitted cushions and upcycling. The pick of them have balconies overlooking the Prater, just around the corner.

Grand Ferdinand Hotel   DESIGN HOTEL $$
(☑01-918 80; www.grandferdinand.com; 01, Schubertring 10-12; dm/d/ste from €30/180/600; ✳ 🛜 🅿; 🚊2, 71 Schwarzenbergplatz) An enormous taxidermied horse stands in the reception area of this ultrahip hotel, which is shaking up Vienna's accommodation scene by offering parquet-floored dorms with mahogany bunks alongside richly coloured designer rooms with chaise longues and chandeliered suites with private champagne bars. Breakfast (€29) is served on the panoramic rooftop terrace, adjacent to the heated, open-air infinity pool.

🍴 Eating

Würstelstande (sausage stands) are great for a cheap bite on the run, and the city also has a booming international restaurant scene and many multi-ethnic markets. Self-caterers can stock up at central Hofer, Billa and Spar supermarkets. Some have delis that make sandwiches to order.

★ Vollpension   CAFE $
(www.vollpension.wien; 04, Schleifmühlgasse 16; dishes €4.60-8.90; ⊙9am-10pm Tue-Sat, to 8pm Sun; 🖉; Ⓤ Karlsplatz) This white-painted brick space with mismatched vintage furniture, tasselled lampshades and portraits on the walls is run by 15 *omas* (grandmas) and *opas* (grandpas) along with their families, with more than 200 cakes in their collective repertoire. Breakfast, such as avocado and feta on pumpernickel bread, is served until 4pm; lunch dishes include a vegan goulash with potato and tofu.

Das Lokal in Hof   INTERNATIONAL $
(☑01-971 91 41; https://daslokal.at; Viktorgasse 22; mains €11.90-19.90, lunch special €6.90-7.90; ⊙11am-11pm Mon-Fri; Ⓤ Hauptbahnhof) Snuggled away in the courtyard of an old dairy is this cracking cafe-restaurant, with a stripped-back interior and open kitchen. Robert and Barbara run the place with love and an imaginative eye, serving food that is honest, generous and delicious – be it pumpkin gnocchi with lingonberries and cashews or black pudding spring roll with apple mousse and chive sauce.

Bitzinger Würstelstand am Albertinaplatz   STREET FOOD $
(www.bitzinger-wien.at; 01, Albertinaplatz; sausages €3.50-4.70; ⊙8am-4am; 🚊D, 1, 2, 71 Kärntner Ring/Oper, Ⓤ Karlsplatz, Stephansplatz) Behind the Staatsoper, Vienna's best sausage stand has cult status. Bitzinger offers the contrasting spectacle of ladies and gents dressed to the nines, sipping beer, wine or Joseph Perrier Champagne (€19.90 for 0.2L) while tucking into sausages at outdoor tables or the heated counter after performances. Mustard comes in *süss* (sweet, ie mild) or *scharf* (fiercely hot).

ef16   AUSTRIAN $$
(☑01-513 23 18; www.ef16.net; Fleischmarkt 16; mains €16.50-32.50; ⊙5.30-11.30pm; 🚊1, 2, 31 Schwedenplatz, Ⓤ Schwedenplatz) What a joy it is to step into this quirkily named restaurant and wine bar, where you'll dine by candlelight in a vaulted, red-walled space. In summer, the vine-rimmed *Schanigarten* (courtyard-garden) is among Vienna's prettiest. The beautifully presented food reveals profound flavours in such dishes as venison carpaccio with black nuts and cranberry mayonnaise, and guinea fowl with olive polenta.

Skopik & Lohn   EUROPEAN $$
(☑01-219 89 77; www.skopikundlohn.at; 02, Leopoldsgasse 17; mains €13-28; ⊙6pm-1am Tue-Sat; Ⓤ Taborstrasse) The spidery web of scrawl that creeps across the ceiling at Skopik & Lohn gives an avant-garde edge to an otherwise French-style brasserie – all wainscoting, globe lights, cheek-by-jowl tables and white-jacketed waiters. The menu is modern European with a Mediterranean slant, delivering spot-on dishes like slow-braised lamb with mint-pea purée, almonds and polenta, and pasta with summer truffle and monkfish.

Griechenbeisl   BISTRO $$
(☑01-533 19 77; www.griechenbeisl.at; 01, Fleischmarkt 11; mains €15-28; ⊙11.30am-11.30pm; 🖉;

DON'T MISS

FOOD MARKET FINDS

The sprawling **Naschmarkt** (06, Linke & Rechte Wienzeile; ☉6am-7.30pm Mon-Fri, to 6pm Sat; Ⓤ Karlsplatz, Kettenbrückengasse) is the place to *nasch* (snack) in Vienna. Stalls are piled high with meats, fruits, vegetables, cheeses, olives, spices and wine. There are also plenty of cafes dishing up good-value lunches, along with delis and takeaway stands.

Bio-Markt Freyung (www.biobauernmarkt-freyung.at; 01, Freyungasse; ☉9am-6pm Fri & Sat; Ⓤ Herrengasse, Schottentor) 🏵 sells farm-fresh produce, as does the bustling **Karmelitermarkt** (02, Karmelitermarkt; ☉6am-7.30pm Mon-Fri, to 5pm Sat; 🚃2 Karmeliterplatz, Ⓤ Taborstrasse). Head to the Saturday farmers market at the latter for brunch at one of the excellent deli-cafes or, if you like your markets with a little more edge, head to **Bauernmarkt Yppenplatz** (16, Yppenplatz; ☉9am-1pm Sat; 🚃44 Yppengasse, Ⓤ Josefstädter Strasse).

🚃1, 2, 31 Schwedenplatz, Ⓤ Schwedenplatz) Dating from 1447 and frequented by Beethoven, Brahms, Schubert and Strauss among other luminaries, Vienna's oldest restaurant has vaulted rooms, wood panelling and a figure of Augustin trapped at the bottom of a well inside the front door. Every classic Viennese dish is on the menu, along with three daily vegetarian options. In summer, head to the plant-fringed front garden.

🍷 Drinking & Nightlife

★ Das Loft   BAR
(www.dasloftwien.at; 02, Praterstrasse 1; ☉noon-2am; 🚃2 Gredlerstrasse, Ⓤ Schwedenplatz) Wow, what a view! Take the lift to Das Loft on the Sofitel's 18th floor to reduce Vienna to toytown scale. From this slinky, glass-walled lounge, you can pick out landmarks such as the Stephansdom and the Hofburg over a tonka bean sour or mojito. By night, the backlit ceiling swirls with an impressionist painter's palette of colours.

Botanical Gardens   COCKTAIL BAR
(www.botanicalgarden.at; 09, Kolingasse 1; ☉6pm-2am Tue-Thu, to 3am Fri & Sat; Ⓤ Schottentor) A subterranean mirror of Cafe Stein's sunny spaces above, Botanical Gardens makes for a cosy, magical retreat once Vienna's weather turns chilly. A dark nautical theme ticks all the cocktail-revival-scene boxes, but with enough local eccentricity to keep things interesting.

Weinstube Josefstadt   WINE BAR
(08, Piaristengasse 27; ☉4pm-midnight Apr-Dec; Ⓤ Rathaus) Weinstube Josefstadt is one of the loveliest *Stadtheurigen* (city wine taverns) in Vienna. A leafy green oasis nestled between towering residential blocks, its tables of friendly, well-liquored locals are squeezed in between the trees and shrubs looking onto a pretty, painted *Salettl* (wooden summerhouse). Wine is local and cheap, and food is typical, with a buffet-style meat and fritter selection.

Strandbar Herrmann   BAR
(www.strandbarherrmann.at; 03, Herrmannpark; ☉10am-2am Apr-early Oct; 🎵; 🚃O Hintere Zollamtstrasse, Ⓤ Schwedenplatz) You'd swear you're by the sea at this hopping canalside beach bar, with beach chairs, sand, DJ beats and hordes of Viennese livin' it up on summer evenings. Cocktail happy hour is from 5pm to 6pm. Cool trivia: it's located on Herrmannpark, named after picture-postcard inventor Emanuel Herrmann (1839–1902).

Loos American Bar   COCKTAIL BAR
(www.loosbar.at; 01, Kärntner Durchgang 10; ☉noon-4am; Ⓤ Stephansplatz) Loos is *the* spot in the Innere Stadt for a classic cocktail such as its signature dry martini, expertly whipped up by talented mixologists. Designed by Adolf Loos in 1908, this tiny 27-sq-metre box (seating just 20 or so patrons) is bedecked with onyx and polished brass, with mirrored walls that make it appear far larger.

Ammutson Craft Beer Dive   BAR
(📞0664 479 91 30; www.facebook.com/Ammutson; 06, Barnabitengasse 10; ☉4pm-1am Mon, to 2am Tue & Wed, to 4am Thu-Sat, 2pm-midnight Sun; 🚃U3 Neubaugasse) Tucked into a cobbled alley, Ammutson is a welcoming bar with simple wooden communal bench seating and quirky art on its white brick walls. Twelve taps pour 'proudly independent' brews from Austrian and European craft beer makers. Come for the chatty, laid-back atmosphere fostered by owner Misho and his passionate team.

☆ Entertainment

Vienna is, was and will always be the European capital of opera and classical music. The line-up of music events is never-ending and even the city's buskers are often classically trained musicians. Box offices generally open from Monday to Saturday and sell cheap (€3 to €6) standing-room tickets around an hour before performances. For weekly listings, visit Falter (www.falter.at), while Tourist Info Wien (http://events.wien.info/en) lists concerts up to 18 months in advance.

⭐ **Staatsoper** OPERA

(📞01-514 44 7880; www.wiener-staatsoper.at; 01, Opernring 2; tickets €13-239, standing room €3-4; U Karlsplatz) The glorious Staatsoper is Vienna's premier opera and classical-music venue. Productions are lavish, formal affairs, where people dress up accordingly. In the interval, wander the foyer and refreshment rooms to fully appreciate the gold-and-crystal interior. Opera is not performed here in July and August (but tours still take place). Tickets can be purchased up to two months in advance.

Musikverein CONCERT VENUE

(📞01-505 81 90; www.musikverein.at; 01, Musikvereinsplatz 1; tickets €25-105, standing room €7-15; ⊙ box office 9am-8pm Mon-Fri, to 1pm Sat Sep-Jun, 9am-noon Mon-Fri Jul & Aug; U Karlsplatz) The opulent Musikverein holds the proud title of the best acoustics of any concert hall in Austria, which the Vienna Philharmonic Orchestra embraces. The lavish interior can be visited by 45-minute guided tour (in English; adult/child €8.50/5) at 1pm Tuesday to Saturday.

Smaller-scale performances are held in the Brahms Saal. There are no student tickets.

Theater an der Wien THEATRE

(📞01-588 85; www.theater-wien.at; 06, Linke Wienzeile 6; tickets €5-148; ⊙ box office 10am-6pm Mon-Sat, 2-6pm Sun; U Karlsplatz) The Theater an der Wien has hosted some monumental premiere performances, including Beethoven's *Fidelio*, Mozart's *Die Zauberflöte* and Strauss Jnr's *Die Fledermaus*. These days, besides staging musicals, dance and concerts, it's re-established its reputation for high-quality opera. Student tickets go on sale 30 minutes before shows; standing-room tickets are available one hour prior to performances.

Jazzland LIVE MUSIC

(📞01-533 25 75; www.jazzland.at; 01, Franz-Josefs-Kai 29; cover €11-20; ⊙ 7pm-2am Mon-Sat mid-Aug–mid-Jul, live music from 9pm; 🚌1, 2, 31 Schwedenplatz, U Schwedenplatz) Buried in a former wine cellar beneath **Ruprechtskirche** (St Rupert's Church; 📞01-535 60 03; www.ruprechtskirche.at; 01, Ruprechtsplatz 1; ⊙ 10am-noon Mon & Tue, 10am-noon & 3-5pm Wed, 10am-5pm Thu & Fri, 11.30am-3.30pm Sat), Jazzland is Vienna's oldest jazz club, dating back nearly 50 years. The music covers the whole jazz spectrum, and features both local and international acts. Past performers have included Ray Brown, Teddy Wilson, Big Joe Williams and Max Kaminsky.

DON'T MISS

COFFEE HOUSE CULTURE

Vienna's legendary *Kaffeehäuser* (coffee houses) houses rank on the Unesco list of Intangible Cultural Heritage, which defines them as 'places where time and space are consumed, but only the coffee is found on the bill'. Grand or humble, poster-plastered or chandelier-lit, this is where you can join the locals for coffee, cake and a slice of living history.

Café Central (www.cafecentral.wien; 01, Herrengasse 14; ⊙ 7.30am-10pm Mon-Sat, 10am-10pm Sun; 🛜; U Herrengasse)

Café Leopold Hawelka (www.hawelka.at; 01, Dorotheergasse 6; ⊙ 8am-midnight Mon-Thu, to 1am Fri & Sat, 10am-midnight Sun; U Stephansplatz)

Café Sperl (www.cafesperl.at; 06, Gumpendorfer Strasse 11; ⊙ 7am-10pm Mon-Sat, 10am-8pm Sun; 🛜; U Museumsquartier, Kettenbrückengasse)

Sperlhof (02, Grosse Sperlgasse 41; ⊙ 4pm-1.30am; 🛜; U Taborstrasse)

Supersense (02, Praterstrasse 70; 2-course lunch €10, breakfast €3.80-9.20; ⊙ 9.30am-7pm Tue-Fri, 10am-5pm Sat; U Praterstern)

IMPERIAL ENTERTAINMENT

The world-famous Vienna Boys' Choir performs on Sunday at 9.15am (late September to June) in the **Burgkapelle** (Royal Chapel) in the Hofburg (p64). **Tickets** (☏ 01-533 99 27; www.hofmusikkapelle.gv.at; 01, Schweizerhof; tickets €11-37; Ⓤ Herrengasse) should be booked around six weeks in advance. The group also performs on Friday afternoons at the **MuTh** (☏ 01-347 80 80; www.muth.at; 02, Obere Augartenstrasse 1e; Vienna Boys' Choir Fri tickets €39-89; ⊙ 4-6pm Mon-Fri & 1 hour before performances; Ⓤ Taborstrasse).

Another Habsburg legacy is the **Spanish Riding School** (Spanische Hofreitschule; ☏ 01-533 90 31-0; www.srs.at; 01, Michaelerplatz 1; tickets €25-217; ⊙ hours vary; ▤ 1A, 2A Michaelerplatz, Ⓤ Herrengasse), where Lipizzaner stallions gracefully perform equine ballet to classical music. For morning training sessions, same-day tickets are available at the nearby visitor centre.

Shopping

With a long-standing history of craftsmanship, in recent years this elegant city has spread its creative wings in the fashion and design world. Whether you're browsing for hand-painted porcelain in the Innere Stadt, new-wave streetwear in Neubau or epicurean treats in the Freihausviertel, you'll find inspiration, a passion for quality and an attentive eye for detail.

Dorotheum ANTIQUES
(www.dorotheum.com; 01, Dorotheergasse 17; ⊙ 10am-6pm Mon-Fri, 9am-5pm Sat; Ⓤ Stephansplatz) The Dorotheum is among the largest auction houses in Europe, and for the casual visitor it's more like a museum, housing everything from antique toys and tableware to autographs, antique guns and, above all, lots of quality paintings. You can bid at the regular auctions held here; otherwise just drop by (it's free) and enjoy browsing.

Information

Most hostels and hotels in Vienna offer free wi-fi, called WLAN (pronounced vee-lan) in German. As well as 400 city hotspots that can be found at www.wien.gv.at/stadtplan, cafes, coffee houses and bars also offer free wi-fi; check locations at www.freewave.at/en/hotspots.

Tourist Info Wien (☏ 01-245 55; www.wien. info; 01, Albertinaplatz; ⊙ 9am-7pm; 🛱; 🚋 D, 1, 2, 71 Kärntner Ring/Oper, Ⓤ Stephansplatz) Vienna's main tourist office has free maps and racks of brochures.

Getting There & Away

AIR
Located 19km southwest of the city centre, **Vienna International Airport** (VIE; ☏ 01-700 722 233; www.viennaairport.com; 🛱) operates services worldwide. The fastest transport into the centre is **City Airport Train** (CAT; www. cityairporttrain.com; single/return €12/21), which runs every 30 minutes and takes 16 minutes between the airport and Wien Mitte; book online for a discount. The cheaper but slower S7 suburban train (€4.20, 37 minutes) does the same journey.

BUS
Eurolines (☏ 01-798 29 00; www.eurolines.at; 03, Erdbergstrasse 200; ⊙ office 6.30am-9pm; Ⓤ Erdberg) has basically tied up the bus routes connecting Austria with the rest of Europe. Its main terminal is at the U3 U-Bahn station Erdberg, but some buses stop at the U6 and U1 U-Bahn and train station Praterstern, and at Südtiroler Platz by Vienna's *Hauptbahnhof*.

CAR & MOTORCYCLE
The Gürtel is an outer ring road that joins up with the A22 on the north bank of the Danube and the A23 southeast of town. All the main road routes intersect with this system, including the A1 from Linz and Salzburg, and the A2 from Graz.

TRAIN
Austria's train network is a dense web reaching the country's far-flung corners. The system is fast, efficient, frequent and well used. **Österreiche Bundesbahn** (ÖBB; www.oebb.at) is the main operator, and has information offices at all of Vienna's main train stations. Tickets can be purchased online, at ticket offices or from train-station ticket machines. Long-distance train tickets can be purchased on board but incur a €3 service charge. Tickets for local, regional and intercity trains must be purchased before boarding.

Getting Around

BICYCLE
Citybike Wien (Vienna City Bike; www.city bikewien.at; 1st/2nd/3rd hour free/€1/2, per hour thereafter €4) has more than 120 bicycle

stands across the city. A credit card and €1 registration fee is required to hire bikes; swipe your card in the machine and follow the multilingual instructions.

PUBLIC TRANSPORT

Vienna's unified public transport network encompasses trains, trams, buses, and underground (U-Bahn) and suburban (S-Bahn) trains. Free maps and information pamphlets are available from **Wiener Linien** (🖉 01-7909-100; www.wienerlinien.at). All tickets must be validated at the entrance to U-Bahn stations and on buses and trams (except for weekly and monthly tickets).

THE DANUBE VALLEY

The stretch of Danube between Krems and Melk, known locally as the Wachau, is arguably the loveliest along the entire length of this long, long river. Both banks are dotted with ruined castles and medieval towns, and lined with terraced vineyards. Further upstream is the industrial city of Linz, Austria's avantgarde art and new technology trailblazer.

Krems an der Donau

🖉 02732 / POP 24,610

Sitting on the northern bank of the Danube against a backdrop of terraced vineyards, Krems marks the beginning of the Wachau. It has an attractive cobbled centre, some good restaurants and the gallery-dotted Kunstmeile.

◉ Sights & Activities

Kunsthalle Krems GALLERY
(www.kunsthalle.at; Franz-Zeller-Platz 3; €10; ⊙10am-6pm Tue-Sun) The flagship of Krems' Kunstmeile, an eclectic collection of galleries and museums, the Kunsthalle has a program of changing exhibitions. These might be mid-19th-century landscapes or hard-core conceptual works, but are always well curated. Guided tours (€3) run on Sundays at 2pm.

Weingut der Stadt Krems WINE
(www.weingutstadtkrems.at; Stadtgraben 11; ⊙9am-noon & 1-5pm Mon-Fri, 9am-noon Sat) This city-owned vineyard yielding 200,000 bottles per year, with almost all Grüner Veltliner and riesling, offers a variety of wine for tasting and purchase.

🛌 Sleeping

Arte Hotel Krems DESIGN HOTEL **$$**
(🖉 02732-711 23; www.arte-hotel.at; Dr-Karl-Dorrek-Strasse 23; s/d €109/161; P🐕🖥️) The art of the title might be a stretch, but what you do get here are large, well-designed rooms with open-plan bathrooms, all scattered with '60s-tilting furniture and big, bright patterns.

ℹ️ Information

Krems Tourismus (🖉 02732-826 76; www.krems.info; Utzstrasse 1; ⊙9am-6pm Mon-Fri, 11am-6pm Sat, 11am-4pm Sun, shorter hours winter) Helpful office well stocked with info and maps.

ℹ️ Getting There & Away

For boats, the **river station** is near Donaustrasse, about 1.5km west of the train station.

Frequent daily trains connect Krems with Vienna (€18.40, 70 minutes).

Melk

🖉 02752 / POP 5529

With its blockbuster abbey-fortress set high above the valley, Melk is a high point of any visit to the Danube Valley. Separated from the river by a stretch of woodland, this pretty town makes for an easy and rewarding day trip from Krems or even Vienna. Post abbey visit, you'll find plenty of restaurants and cafes with alfresco seating line the Rathausplatz. **Melk Tourist Office** (🖉 02752-511 60; www.stadt-melk.at; Kremser Strasse 5; ⊙9.30am-6pm Mon-Sat, 9.30am-3.30pm Sun May-Sep, shorter hours rest of year) should be your first port of call.

★ Stift Melk ABBEY

(Benedictine Abbey of Melk; www.stiftmelk.at; Abt Berthold Dietmayr Strasse 1; adult/child €12.50/6.50, with guided tour €14.50/8.50; ⊙9am-5.30pm, tours 10am-4pm Apr-Oct, tours only 11am & 2pm Nov-Mar) Of the many abbeys in Austria, Stift Melk is the most famous. Possibly Lower Austria's finest, the monastery church dominates the complex with its twin spires and high octagonal dome. The interior is baroque gone barmy, with regiments of smirking cherubs, gilt twirls and polished faux marble. The theatrical high-altar scene, depicting St Peter and St Paul (the church's two patron saints), is by Peter Widerin. Johann Michael Rottmayr created most of the ceiling paintings, including those in the dome.

ℹ Getting There & Away

Boats leave from the canal by Pionierstrasse, 400m north of the abbey. There are regular train services to Melk from Vienna (€18.40, 50 minutes, twice hourly).

UPPER AUSTRIA

Linz

☎ 0732 / POP 204,846

'It begins in Linz' goes the Austrian saying, and it's true. The technology trailblazer and European Capital of Culture 2009 is blessed with a leading-edge cyber centre and world-class contemporary-art gallery.

Sitting astride the Danube, Linz also harbours a charming Altstadt filled with historic baroque architecture.

◉ Sights

★ **Lentos**　　　　　　　　　　GALLERY
(www.lentos.at; Ernst-Koref-Promenade 1; adult/child €8/4.50, guided tours €3; ◷ 10am-6pm Tue, Wed & Fri-Sun, 10am-9pm Thu) Overlooking the Danube, the rectangular glass-and-steel Lentos is strikingly illuminated by night. The gallery guards one of Austria's finest modern-art collections, including works by Warhol, Schiele, Klimt, Kokoschka and Lovis Corinth, which sometimes feature in the large-scale exhibitions. There are regular guided tours in German and 30-minute tours in English at 4pm on the first Saturday of the month. Alternatively, download Lentos' app from the website.

★ **Ars Electronica Center**　　　MUSEUM
(www.aec.at; Ars-Electronica-Strasse 1; adult/child €9.50/7.50; ◷ 9am-5pm Tue, Wed & Fri, 9am-7pm Thu, 10am-6pm Sat & Sun; 🚼) The technology, science and digital media of the future are in the spotlight at Linz' biggest crowd-puller. In the labs you can interact with robots, animate digital objects, print 3D structures, turn your body into musical instruments, and (virtual-ly) travel to outer space. Kids love it. Designed by Vienna-based architectural firm Treusch, the centre resembles a futuristic ship by the Danube after dark, when its LED glass skin kaleidoscopically changes colour.

Mural Harbour　　　　　　　PUBLIC ART
(www.muralharbor.at; Industriezeile 40; guided tours €15-25) Street art comes into its own on the graffiti-blasted industrial facades in Linz' harbourside Hafenviertel. You'll find eye-catching, larger-than-life, Instagramm-able works from the likes of Roa (Belgium), Lords (USA), Aryz (Spain) and a host of ball-sy Austrian artists. For more insider info, join one of the regular walks, workshops or cruises. Visit the website for times and dates.

🍴 Sleeping & Eating

★ **Hotel am Domplatz**　　　DESIGN HOTEL $$
(☎ 0732-77 30 00; www.hotelamdomplatz.at; Stifterstrasse 4; d €114-178, ste €310-350; 🅿❄🛜) ❁ Adjacent to the neo-Gothic **Mariendom** (Neuer Dom; Herrenstrasse 26; ◷ 7.30am-7pm Mon-Sat, 8am-7.15pm Sun) (ask for a room overlooking the cathedral), this glass-and-concrete cube filled with striking metal sculptures has streamlined, Nordic-style pristine-white and blond-wood rooms with semi-open bathrooms. Wind down with a view in the rooftop spa. In fine weather the cathedral-facing terrace is a prime spot for breakfast (€19), which includes a glass of bubbly.

★ **Cafe Jindrak**　　　　　　　CAFE $
(www.jindrak.at; Herrenstrasse 22; dishes €3-8.80; ◷ 8am-6pm Mon-Sat, 8.30am-6pm Sun; 🚼) Join the cake-loving locals at this celebrated cafe – the original shop (1929) of a now nine-strong chain that produces over 100,000 of its famous *Linzer Torte* each year made to its family recipe. You'd need a huge fork (and appetite) to tackle the torte that set a Guinness World Record in 1999, measuring 4m high and weighing 650kg.

ℹ Information

Tourist Information Linz (☎ 0732-7070 2009; www.linztourismus.at; Hauptplatz 1; ◷ 9am-7pm Mon-Sat, 10am-7pm Sun May-Sep, 9am-5pm Mon-Sat, 10am-5pm Sun Oct-Apr) Upper Austria information as well as brochures and accommodation listings.

LINZ CARD

The **Linz Card** (one day adult/child €18/15, three days €30/25) grants unlimited use of public transport, entry to major museums, plus discounts on other sights, city tours and river cruises.

Getting There & Away

Ryanair flies to the **Blue Danube Airport** (LNZ; 07221-60 00; www.linz-airport.com; Flughafenstrasse 1, Hörsching), 13km southwest of Linz. An hourly shuttle bus (€3.20, 22 minutes) links the airport to the main train station.

Linz is on the main rail route between Vienna (€36.20, 1½ hours) and Salzburg (€27.50, 1¼ hours); express trains run twice hourly in both directions.

THE SOUTH

Austria's southern states often feel worlds apart from the rest of the country, both in climate and attitude. Styria (Steiermark) is a blissful amalgamation of genteel architecture, rolling green hills, vine-covered slopes and soaring mountains. Its capital, Graz, is one of Austria's most attractive cities. A glamorous crowd heads to sun-drenched Carinthia (Kärnten) in summer. Sidling up to Italy, its sparkling lakes and pretty lidos are as close to Mediterranean as this landlocked country gets.

Graz

0316 / POP 286,292

Austria's second-largest city is relaxed and good-looking, with ample green spaces, red rooftops and a narrow, fast-flowing river gushing through its centre. Architecturally, Graz hints at nearby Italy with its Renaissance courtyards and baroque palaces. But there's a youthful, almost Eastern European energy too, with a handful of edgily modern buildings, a vibrant arts scene and great nightlife (thanks in part to its large student population).

Sights

Graz' most compelling sights can easily be seen in a day or two and are easily accessible by foot or a quick tram ride.

★ Kunsthaus Graz   GALLERY

(0316-8017 92 00; www.museum-joanneum.at; Lendkai 1; adult/child €9.50/3.50; 10am-5pm Tue-Sun; 1, 3, 6, 7 Südtiroler Platz) Designed by British architects Peter Cook and Colin Fournier, this world-class contemporary-art space is known as the 'friendly alien' by locals. The building is signature Cook, a photovoltaic-skinned sexy biomorphic blob that is at once completely at odds with its pristine historic surroundings but sitting rather lyrically within it as well. Exhibitions change every three to four months.

Schlossberg   VIEWPOINT

(one way €2.40; 4, 5 Schlossbergplatz) **FREE** Rising to 473m, Schlossberg is the site of the original fortress where Graz was founded and is marked by the city's most visible icon – the **Uhrturm** (Clock Tower; 4, 5 Schlossplatz/Murinsel) **FREE**. Its wooded slopes can be reached by a number of bucolic and strenuous paths, but also by lift or Schlossbergbahn funicular. It's a brief walk or take tram 4 or 5 to Schlossplatz/Murinsel for the lift.

★ Schloss Eggenberg   PALACE

(0316-8017 95 32; www.museum-joanneum.at; Eggenberger Allee 90; adult/child €15/6; tours hourly 10am-4pm, except 1pm Tue-Sun Apr-Oct, exhibitions 10am-5pm Tue-Sun Apr-Oct; 1 Schloss Eggenberg) Graz' elegant palace was created for the Eggenberg dynasty in 1625 by Giovanni Pietro de Pomis (1565–1633) at the request of Johann Ulrich (1568–1634). Admission is via a highly worthwhile guided tour during which you learn about the idiosyncrasies of each room, the stories told by the frescoes and about the Eggenberg family itself.

★ Neue Galerie Graz   GALLERY

(0316-8017 91 00; www.museum-joanneum. at; Joanneumsviertel; adult/child €9.50/3.50; 10am-5pm Tue-Sun; 1, 3, 4, 5, 6, 7 Hauptplatz) The Neue Galerie is the crowning glory of the three museums inside the Joanneumsviertel complex. The collection of works on level 0 is the highlight, which is regularly curated from visual arts works since 1800. It also has changing exhibitions on level 1, and a section about Styrian artists; finally, the Bruseum (a separate museum) on level 0 is dedicated to the Styrian artist Günter Brus and his followers.

🛏 Sleeping & Eating

Graz does fine dining with aplomb, but you'll also find plenty of cheap eats near Universität Graz, particularly on Halbärthgasse, Zinzendorfgasse and Harrachgasse.

Stock up for a picnic at the farmers markets on Kaiser-Josef-Platz and Lendplatz. For fast-food stands, head for Hauptplatz and Jakominiplatz.

Hotel Daniel   HOTEL $
(☑ 0316-71 10 80; www.hoteldaniel.com; Europaplatz 1; d €75-350; 🅿 ❄ @ 🛜; 🚊 1, 3, 6, 7 Hauptbahnhof) The Daniel's rooms are well designed and super-simple, and while its small 'smart' rooms scrape into budget territory, it also offers the super-exclusive loft cube on the roof if you're looking for something out of the ordinary. The lobby area is a lot of fun – a great space in which to work or just hang out.

★ Hotel Wiesler   HOTEL $$
(☑ 0316-70 66-0; www.hotelwiesler.com; Grieskai 4; d €141-246; 🅿 ❄ @ 🛜; 🚊 1, 3, 6, 7 Südtiroler Platz) The riverside Wiesler, a *Jugenstil* (art nouveau) gem from 1901, has been transformed into Graz' most glamorous hotel, complete with oriental-style spa. Hotelier Florian Weltzer has shaken up everything, including the notion of room categories, and ensured that this is a luxury experience that is far from stuffy.

Kunsthauscafé   INTERNATIONAL $
(☑ 0316-71 49 57; www.kunsthauscafe.co.at; Südtirolerplatz 2; mains €7-16.50; ⊙ 9am-midnight

STYRIAN TUSCANY

Head south of Graz to what's known as *Steirische Toskana* (Styrian Tuscany), for lush wine country that's reminiscent of Chianti: gentle rolling hills cultivated with vineyards or patchwork farmland, dotted with small forests where deer roam. Apart from its stellar whites, it's also famous for Kürbiskernöl, the rich pumpkin-seed oil generously used in Styrian cooking. The picturesque 'capital' of **Ehrenhausen**, on the road to the Slovenian border, makes a fine base for wine tasting and exploring.

Mon-Thu, to 2am Fri & Sat, to 8pm Sun; 🚊 1, 3, 6, 7 Südtiroler Platz) A happy, young crowd fills the long tables here for a menu that incorporates burgers (from big beef to chickpea), creative salads and international flavours from noodle bowls to steak tartare with skinny fries. It's very very loud – but fun if you're in the mood. The lunch special goes for just €6.80.

★ Der Steirer   AUSTRIAN, TAPAS $$
(☑ 0316-70 36 54; www.der-steirer.at; Belgiergasse 1; weekday lunch menu €8.90, mains €11.50-24; ⊙ 11am-midnight; 🌱; 🚊 1, 3, 6, 7 Südtiroler Platz) This neo-*Beisl* (bistro pub) and wine bar has a beautiful selection of Styrian dishes, including great goulash, crispy *Backhendl* (fried breaded chicken) and seasonal game dishes, all done in a simple, contemporary style. Its Styrian tapas concept is a nice way to sample local flavours.

Aiola Upstairs   INTERNATIONAL $$
(☑ 0316-81 87 97; http://upstairs.aiola.at; Schlossberg 2; pasta €16-17.50, mains €19.90-34; ⊙ 9am-midnight; 🛜 🌱; 🚊 4, 5 Schlossbergplatz/Murinsel (for lift)) This cracking restaurant atop Schlossberg (p77) has fabulous views from both its glass box interior and summer terrace. Even better, the cooking up here is some of the city's best, with chefs putting a novel spin on regional, seasonal and global ingredients, along the lines of blueberry and chanterelle risotto or wild brook trout with aubergines, fresh cheese and tomato salsa.

🍷 Drinking & Nightlife

The bar scene in Graz is split between three main areas: around the university; east of the Kunsthaus in hipster Lend; and on Mehlplatz and Prokopigasse (dubbed the 'Bermuda Triangle').

Blendend   COFFEE
(☑ 0660 4714 753; www.blendend.at; Mariahilferstrasse 24; ⊙ 6pm-2am Mon-Fri, 9am-2am Sat, 9am-midnight Sun; 🛜; 🚊 1, 3, 6, 7 Südtiroler Platz) A rambling, warm and endearingly boho addition to Lend's usual line-up of grungy bars, Blendend is a great drinking and snacking spot during the week and then turns all-day cafe on weekends with beautiful homemade cakes and desserts competing with the spritzs and excellent local beers. In warmer weather all the action happens at the courtyard tables.

Freiblick Tagescafe ROOFTOP BAR

(☑ 0316-83 53 02; http://freiblick.co.at; Kastner & Öhler, Sackstrasse 7-11; ⊙ 9.30am-7pm Mon-Fri, to 6pm Sat; 🛜; 🚃 1, 3, 4, 5, 6, 7 Hauptplatz) This huge terrace cafe-bar tops the Kastner & Öhler department store and has the best view in the city. Enjoy the clouds and rooftops over a breakfast platter and coffee or a lunchtime soup or salad. Or stop by in the afternoon for something from the Prosecco spritz menu or a Hugo Royal – Moët Chandon splashed with elderflower (€15).

ℹ Information

Graz Tourismus (☑ 0316-807 50; www. graztourismus.at; Herrengasse 16; ⊙ 10am-5pm Jan-Mar & Nov, to 6pm Apr-Oct & Dec; 🛜; 🚃 1, 3, 4, 5, 6, 7 Hauptplatz) Graz' main tourist office, with loads of free information on the city and helpful and knowledgeable staff.

ℹ Getting There & Away

Graz airport (GRZ; ☑ 0316-290 21 72; www. flughafen-graz.at) is 10km south of the centre and is served by carriers including easy-Jet, Austrian Airlines, KLM, Eurowings and Lufthansa.

Trains to Vienna depart hourly (€39, 2½ hours), and five daily go to Salzburg (€58 to €69, four to 5½ hours). International train connections from Graz include Ljubljana (€31.90, 3½ hours) and Budapest (€56.40 to €79, 5½ hours).

Klagenfurt

☑ 0463 / POP 100,369

With its captivating location on Wörthersee and its beauty more Renaissance than baroque, Klagenfurt has a distinct Mediterranean feel and is surprisingly lively. Carinthia's capital makes a handy base for exploring Wörthersee's lakeside villages and elegant medieval towns to the north.

⊙ Sights & Activities

Boating and swimming are usually possible from May to September.

Europapark PARK

(🛝) The green expanse and its *Strandbad* (beach) on the shores of the Wörthersee are centres for aquatic fun and especially great for kids. The park's biggest draw is **Minimundus** (www.minimundus.at; Villacher Strasse 241; adult/child €19/10; ⊙ 9am-6pm Mar, Apr, Oct & Nov, to 7pm May-Sep; 🛝), a 'miniature world' with 140 replicas of the world's architectural icons, downsized to a scale of 1:25. To get here, take bus 10, 11, 12 or 22 from Heiligengeistplatz.

🛏 Sleeping & Eating

Das Domizil APARTMENT $$

(☑ 0664 843 30 50; www.das-domizil.at; Bahnhofstrasse 51; apt €92; 🅿🛜) This large, light and sweetly decorated apartment is in a grand 19th-century building just beyond the historic centre's ring. It's extremely well equipped with a full kitchen, laundry facilities and lots of space. Owner Ingo Dietrich is a friendly and fashionable young local who is generous with his insider tips and time. Courtyard parking is €12 per day extra.

ℹ Information

Tourist Office (☑ 0463-287 46 30; www. visitklagenfurt.at; Neuer Platz 5; ⊙ 9am-5pm Mon-Fri, 10am-3pm Sat) Sells Kärnten Cards and books accommodation.

ℹ Getting There & Away

Klagenfurt's **airport** (KLU; www.klagenfurt-airport.com; Flughafenstrasse 60-66) is 3km north of town. Eurowings flies from here to a number of destinations including London Heathrow and Cologne-Bonn in Germany.

Two-hourly direct trains run from Klagenfurt to Vienna (€54.40, four hours) and Salzburg (€41.20, three hours). Trains to Graz depart every two to three hours (€42, 2¾ hours). Trains to western Austria, Italy, Slovenia and Germany go via Villach (€8.10, 25 to 40 minutes, two to four per hour).

SALZBURG

☑ 0662 / POP 150,887

The joke 'If it's baroque, don't fix it' is a perfect maxim for Salzburg: the tranquil Old Town nested between steep hills looks much as it did when Mozart lived here 250 years ago.

A Unesco World Heritage Site, Salzburg's overwhelmingly 17th-century Altstadt (old town) is entrancing both at ground level and from Hohensalzburg fortress high above. Across the fast-flowing Salzach River rests

Salzburg

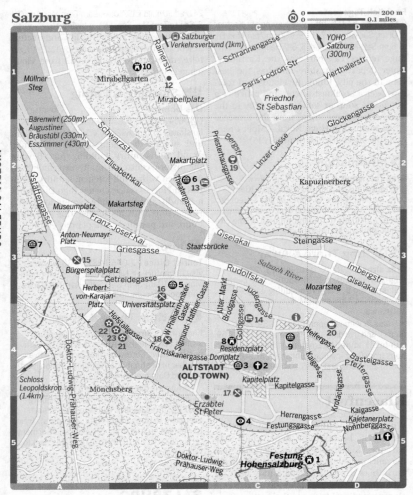

Schloss Mirabell, surrounded by gorgeous manicured gardens. You can of course, bypass the baroque grandeur and head straight for kitsch-country via a tour of *The Sound of Music* film locations.

◉ Sights

★ Festung Hohensalzburg
FORT

(www.salzburg-burgen.at; Mönchsberg 34; adult/child/family €9.40/5.40/20.90, incl funicular €12.20/7/27.10; ⊙ 9.30am-5pm Oct-Apr, 9am-7pm May-Sep) Salzburg's most visible icon is this mighty, 900-year-old clifftop fortress, one of the biggest and best preserved in Europe.

It's easy to spend half a day up here, roaming the ramparts for far-reaching views over the city's spires, the Salzach River and the mountains. The fortress is a steep 15-minute walk from the centre or a speedy ride up in the glass **Festungsbahn** (Festungsgasse 4; one way/return adult €6.90/8.60, child €3.70/4.70; ⊙ 9am-8pm May-Sep, to 5pm Oct-Apr) funicular.

Residenz
PALACE

(www.domquartier.at; Residenzplatz 1; DomQuartier ticket adult/child €13/8; ⊙ 10am-5pm Wed-Mon Sep-Jun, 10am-5pm Thu-Tue, to 8pm Wed Jul & Aug) The crowning glory of Salzburg's DomQuartier, the Residenz is where the

Salzburg

AUSTRIA SALZBURG

prince-archbishops held court until Salzburg became part of the Habsburg Empire in the 19th century. An audio-guide tour takes in the exuberant **state rooms**, lavishly adorned with tapestries, stucco and frescoes by Johann Michael Rottmayr. The 3rd floor is given over to the **Residenzgalerie**, where the focus is on Flemish and Dutch masters. Must-sees include Rubens' *Allegory on Emperor Charles V* and Rembrandt's chiaroscuro *Old Woman Praying*.

Museum der Moderne GALLERY
(www.museumdermoderne.at; Mönchsberg 32; adult/child €8/6; ⊙10am-6pm Tue-Sun, to 8pm Wed; ⌖) Straddling Mönchsberg's cliffs, this contemporary glass-and-marble oblong of a gallery stands in stark contrast to the fortress, and shows first-rate temporary exhibitions of 20th- and 21st-century art. The works of Alberto Giacometti, Dieter Roth, Emil Nolde and John Cage have previously been featured. There's a free guided tour of the gallery at 6.30pm every Wednesday. The **Mönchsberg Lift** (Gstättengasse 13; one way/return €2.40/3.70, incl gallery entry €9.10/9.70; ⊙8am-11pm Jul & Aug, 8am-7pm Mon, to 9pm Tue-Sun Sep-Jun) whizzes up to the gallery year-round.

Salzburg Museum MUSEUM
(www.salzburgmuseum.at; Mozartplatz 1; adult/child €8.50/3; ⊙9am-5pm Tue-Sun; ⌖) Housed in the baroque Neue Residenz palace, this flagship museum takes you on a fascinating romp through Salzburg past and present. Ornate rooms showcase everything from Roman excavations to royal portraits. There are free guided tours at 6pm every Thursday.

Stift Nonnberg CONVENT
(Nonnberg Convent; Nonnberggasse 2; ⊙7am-dusk) FREE A short climb up the Nonnbergstiege staircase from Kaigasse or along Festungsgasse brings you to this Benedictine convent, founded 1300 years ago and made famous as the nunnery in *The Sound of Music*. You can visit the beautiful rib-vaulted **church**, but the rest of the convent is off limits. Take €0.50 to switch on the light that illuminates the beautiful **Romanesque frescoes**.

Dom CATHEDRAL
(Cathedral; ☎0662-804 77 950; www.salzburgerdom.at; Domplatz; ⊙8am-7pm Mon-Sat, from 1pm Sun May-Sep, shorter hours Oct-Apr) Gracefully crowned by a bulbous copper dome and twin spires, the Dom stands out as a masterpiece of baroque art. Bronze portals symbolising faith, hope and charity lead into the cathedral. In the nave, both the intricate stucco and Arsenio Mascagni's ceiling frescoes recounting the Passion of Christ guide the eye to the polychrome dome.

Mozart's Geburtshaus MUSEUM
(Mozart's Birthplace; www.mozarteum.at; Getreidegasse 9; adult/child €11/3.50; ⊙8.30am-7pm Jul & Aug, 9am-5.30pm Sep-Jun) Wolfgang Amadeus Mozart, Salzburg's most famous son, was born in this bright yellow townhouse in 1756, and spent the first 17 years of his life here. Today's museum harbours a collection of instruments, documents and portraits. Highlights include the mini-violin he played as a toddler, plus a lock of his hair and buttons from his jacket.

Mozart-Wohnhaus
MUSEUM

(Mozart's Residence; www.mozarteum.at; Makartplatz 8; adult/child €11/3.50; ⏰ 8.30am-7pm Jul & Aug, 9am-5.30pm Sep-Jun) Tired of the cramped living conditions on Getreidegasse, the Mozart family moved in 1773 to this roomier abode, where the prolific Wolfgang composed works such as the *Shepherd King* (K208) and *Idomeneo* (K366). Emanuel Schikaneder, a close friend of Mozart and the librettist of *The Magic Flute,* was a regular guest here. An audio guide accompanies your visit, serenading you with opera excerpts. Alongside family portraits and documents, you'll find Mozart's original fortepiano.

☞ Tours

Fräulein Maria's Bicycle Tours
CYCLING

(www.mariasbicycletours.com; Mirabellplatz 4; adult/child €30/18; ⏰ 9.30am Apr-Oct, plus 4.30pm Jun-Aug; 🏃) Belt out *The Sound of Music* faves as you pedal on one of these jolly 3½-hour bike tours, taking in locations from the film including the **Mirabellgarten** (Mirabellplatz 4; ⏰ Marble Hall 8am-4pm Mon, Wed & Thu, from 1pm Tue & Fri, gardens 6am-dusk) **FREE**, Stift Nonnberg (p81), **Schloss Leopoldskron** (www.schloss-leopoldskron.com; Leopoldskronstrasse 56-58) and Hellbrunn. No advance booking is necessary; just turn up at the meeting point on Mirabellplatz.

✨ Festivals & Events

Salzburg Festival
CULTURAL

(Salzburger Festspiele; www.salzburgerfestspiele. at; ⏰ Jul & Aug) The absolute highlight of the city's events calendar is the Salzburg Festival. It's a grand affair, with some 200 productions – including theatre, classical music and opera – staged in the impressive surrounds of the **Grosses Festspielhaus**

> ### ⓘ SALZBURG CARD
>
> If you're planning on doing lots of sightseeing, save by buying the **Salzburg Card** (1-/2-/3-day card €29/38/44). The card gets you entry to all of the major sights and attractions, unlimited use of public transport (including cable cars) and numerous discounts on tours and events. The card is half-price for children and €3 cheaper in the low season.
>
> The card can be purchased at the airport, tourist office, most hotels and online at www.salzburg.info.

(☎ 0662-804 50; Hofstallgasse 1), **Haus für Mozart** (House for Mozart; ☎ 0662-804 55 00; www.salzburgerfestspiele.at; Hofstallgasse 1) and the baroque **Felsenreitschule** (Summer Riding School; Hofstallgasse 1). Tickets vary in price between €11 and €430; book well ahead.

🛏 Sleeping

⭐ Haus Ballwein
GUESTHOUSE $

(☎ 0662-82 40 29; www.haus-ballwein.at; Moosstrasse 69a; s €55-65, d €72-85, tr €85-90, q €90-100; 🅿 🐾) With its bright, pine-filled rooms, mountain views, free bike hire and garden, this place is big on charm. The largest, quietest rooms face the back and have balconies and kitchenettes. It's a 10-minute trundle from the Altstadt; take bus 21 to Gsengerweg. Breakfast is a wholesome spread of fresh rolls, eggs, fruit, muesli and cold cuts.

Yoho Salzburg
HOSTEL $

(☎ 0662-87 96 49; www.yoho.at; Paracelsusstrasse 9; dm €20-26, d €70-88; @ 🐾) Free wi-fi, secure lockers, comfy bunks, plenty of cheap beer and good-value schnitzels – what more could a backpacker ask for? Except, perhaps, a merry singalong with *The Sound of Music* screened daily (yes, *every* day). The friendly crew can arrange tours, adventure sports such as rafting and canyoning, and bike hire.

Arte Vida
GUESTHOUSE $$

(☎ 0662-87 31 85; www.artevida.at; Dreifaltigkeitsgasse 9; d €110-145, apt €170-220; 🐾) Arte Vida has the boho-chic feel of a Marrakech *riad,* with its lantern-lit salon, communal kitchen and serene garden. Asia and Africa have provided the inspiration for the rich colours and fabrics that dress the individually designed rooms. Affable hosts Herbert and Karoline happily give tips on Salzburg and its surrounds, and can arrange massages and private yoga sessions.

Hotel am Dom
BOUTIQUE HOTEL $$

(☎ 0662-84 27 65; www.hotelamdom.at; Goldgasse 17; s €109-219, d €149-349; ❄ 🐾) Antique meets boutique at this Altstadt hotel, where the original vaults and beams of the 800-year-old building contrast with razor-sharp design features. Artworks inspired by the musical legends of the Salzburg Festival grace the rooms, which sport caramel-champagne colour schemes, funky lighting, velvet throws and ultra-glam bathrooms.

⭐ Villa Trapp
HOTEL $$$

(☎ 0662-63 08 60; www.villa-trapp.com; Traunstrasse 34; s €65-130, d €114-280, ste €290-580;

P 🛜) Marianne and Christopher have transformed the original von Trapp family home into a beautiful guesthouse (for guests only, we might add). The 19th-century villa is elegant, if not *quite* as palatial as in the movie, with tasteful wood-floored rooms and a balustrade for sweeping down à la Baroness Schräder.

✖ Eating

Self-caterers can find picnic fixings at the **Grünmarkt** (Green Market; Universitätsplatz; ⏰7am-7pm Mon-Fri, to 3pm Sat).

Stiftsbäckerei St Peter　　　　　BAKERY $
(Kapitelplatz 8; ⏰8am-5.30pm Mon & Tue, 7am-5.30pm Thu & Fri, 7am-1pm Sat) Next to the monastery, where the watermill turns, this 700-year-old bakery turns out Salzburg's best sourdough loaves from a wood-fired oven.

Bärenwirt　　　　　AUSTRIAN $$
(📞0662-42 24 04; www.baerenwirt-salzburg.at; Müllner Hauptstrasse 8; mains €12-20; ⏰11am-11pm) Sizzling and stirring since 1663, Bärenwirt is Austrian through and through. Go for hearty *Bierbraten* (beer roast) with dumplings, locally caught trout or organic wild-boar bratwurst. A tiled oven warms the woody, hunting-lodge-style interior in winter, while the river-facing terrace is a summer crowd-puller. The restaurant is 500m north of Museumplatz.

Triangel　　　　　AUSTRIAN $$
(📞0662-84 22 29; Wiener-Philharmoniker-Gasse 7; mains €12-38; ⏰11.30am-10pm Tue-Sat) The menu is market-fresh at this arty bistro, where the picture-clad walls pay tribute to Salzburg Festival luminaries. It does gourmet salads, a mean Hungarian goulash with organic beef, and delicious house-made ice cream. Lunch specials go for just €7.90.

Afro Café　　　　　INTERNATIONAL $$
(www.afrocafe.at; Bürgerspitalplatz 5; lunch €8.90, mains €14-19; ⏰9am-11pm Mon-Thu, to midnight Fri & Sat) Hot-pink walls, butterfly chairs and artworks made from beach junk...this Afro-chic cafe is totally groovy. Staff keep the good vibes and food coming – from breakfasts to ostrich burgers, and from samosas to steaks sizzling hot from the grill. It also does a good line in coffee, rooibos teas, juices and cakes.

★ Esszimmer　　　　　FRENCH $$$
(📞0662-87 08 99; www.esszimmer.com; Müllner Hauptstrasse 33; 3-course lunch €45, tasting menus €79-128; ⏰noon-2pm & 6.30-9.30pm Tue-Sat)

ℹ DOMQUARTIER

Salzburg's DomQuartier (www.dom quartier.at) showcases the most fabulous baroque monuments and museums in the historic centre. A single ticket (adult/child €13/8) gives you access to the Residenz (p80) state rooms and gallery, the upper galleries of the Dom (p81), the **Dommuseum** (www.dom quartier.at; Domplatz; DomQuartier ticket adult/child €13/8; ⏰10am-5pm Wed-Mon) and **Erzabtei St Peter** (St Peter's Abbey; www.stift-stpeter.at; Sankt-Peter-Bezirk 1-2; catacombs adult/child €2/1.50; ⏰church 8am-noon & 2.30-6.30pm, cemetery 6.30am-7pm, catacombs 10am-6pm). The free multilingual audio guide whisks you through the quarter in 90 minutes, though you could easily spend half a day absorbing all of its sights. For an insight into the DomQuartier's history and architecture, you can download the audioguide to your phone, tablet or PC from the website before you visit.

Andreas Kaiblinger puts an innovative spin on market-driven French cuisine at Michelin-starred Esszimmer. Eye-catching art, playful backlighting and a glass floor revealing the Almkanal stream keep diners captivated, as do gastronomic show-stoppers such as Arctic char with calf's head and asparagus. Buses 7, 21 and 28 to Landeskrankenhaus stop close by.

🍷 Drinking & Nightlife

★ Augustiner Bräustübl　　　　　BREWERY
(www.augustinerbier.at; Augustinergasse 4-6; ⏰3-11pm Mon-Fri, from 2.30pm Sat & Sun) Who says monks can't enjoy themselves? Since 1621, this cheery, monastery-run brewery has served potent homebrews in beer steins, in the vaulted hall and beneath the chestnut trees of the 1000-seat beer garden. Get your tankard filled at the foyer pump and visit the snack stands for hearty, beer-swigging grub including *Stelzen* (ham hock), pork belly and giant pretzels.

Kaffee Alchemie　　　　　CAFE
(www.kaffee-alchemie.at; Rudolfskai 38; ⏰7.30am-6pm Mon-Fri, from 10am Sat & Sun) Making coffee really is rocket science at this vintage-cool cafe by the river, which spotlights high-quality, fair-trade, single-origin beans. Talented baristas make spot-on espressos

(on a Marzocco GB5, in case you wondered), cappuccinos and speciality coffees, which go nicely with the selection of cakes and brownies. Not a coffee fan? Try the super-smooth coffee-leaf tea.

Enoteca Settemila   WINE BAR
(www.facebook.com/enotecasettemila; Bergstrasse 9; ⊙5-11pm Wed-Sat) This bijou wine shop and bar brims with the enthusiasm and passion of Rafael Peil and Nina Corti. Go to sample their well-curated selection of wines, including Austrian, organic and biodynamic ones, with *taglieri* – sharing plates of cheese and *salumi* (salami, ham, prosciutto and the like) – from small Italian producers.

❶ Information

Most hotels and bars offer free wi-fi, and there are several cheap internet cafes near the train station. *Bankomaten* (ATMs) are all over the place.

Tourist Office (📞 0662-88 98 73 30; www. salzburg.info; Mozartplatz 5; ⊙9am-8pm Apr-Sep, 9am-6pm Mon-Sat Oct-Mar) Helpful tourist office with a ticket-booking service (www.salzburgticket.com) in the same building.

❶ Getting There & Away

Flights from the UK and the rest of Europe, including low-cost airlines **Ryanair** (www. ryanair.com) and **easyJet** (www.easyjet.com) service **Salzburg airport** (SZG; 📞 0662-858 00;

SCHLOSS HELLBRUNN

A prince-archbishop with a wicked sense of humour, Markus Sittikus built Italianate **Schloss Hellbrunn** (www. hellbrunn.at; Fürstenweg 37; adult/child/family €12.50/5.50/26.50, gardens free; ⊙9am-9pm Jul & Aug, to 5.30pm Apr-Jun, Sep & Oct; 🚸) as a 17th-century summer palace and an escape from his Residenz functions. While the whimsical palace interior is worth a peek, the eccentric **Wasserspiele** (trick fountains) are the big draw in summer. Be prepared to get soaked in the mock Roman theatre, the shell-clad Neptune Grotto and the twittering Bird Grotto. In the palace gardens, look out for *The Sound of Music* pavilion of 'Sixteen Going on Seventeen' fame. Bus 25 (€2, every 20 minutes) runs to Hellbrunn, 4.5km south of Salzburg, from Mozartsteg/Rudolfskai in the Altstadt.

www.salzburg-airport.com; Innsbrucker Bundesstrasse 95; 📞), a 20-minute bus ride from the centre.

Salzburger Verkehrsverbund (📞24hr hotline 0662-63 29 00; www.svv-info.at) buses depart from just outside the Hauptbahnhof on Südtiroler Platz.

Trains leave frequently for Vienna (€54.10, 2½ to three hours) and Linz (€27.50, 1¼ hours). There is a two-hourly express service to Klagenfurt (€41.20, three hours).

❶ Getting Around

A Velo (📞0676-435 59 50; Mozartplatz; bicycle rental half-day/full day/week €12/18/55, e-bike €18/25/120; ⊙9.30am-5pm Apr-Jun & Sep, to 7pm Jul & Aug) is just across the way from the tourist office.

Bus routes are shown at bus stops and on some city maps; buses 1 and 4 start from the Hauptbahnhof and skirt the pedestrian-only Altstadt. Bus drivers sell single (€2.60), 24-hour (€5.70) and weekly tickets (€16). Single tickets bought in advance from machines are slightly cheaper.

THE SALZKAMMERGUT

A wonderland of deep blue lakes and tall craggy peaks, the Lake District has long been a favourite holiday destination for Austrians, luring a throng of summertime visitors to sail, fish, swim, hike or just laze on the shore. Bad Ischl is the region's hub, but Hallstatt is its true jewel.

❶ Information

For info visit **Salzkammergut Tourismus** (📞06132-2400 051; www.salzkammergut.co.at; Götzstrasse 12, Bad Ischl; ⊙9am-6pm Mon-Fri, 9am-2pm Sat & Sun, closed Sun Sep-Jun). The Salzkammergut Card (€4.90, available May to October) provides up to 30% discounts on sights, ferries, cable cars and some buses.

Hallstatt
📞 06134 / 📞778

With pastel-coloured houses that cast shimmering reflections onto the glassy waters of the lake and with towering mountains on all sides, Hallstatt is a beauty with a great backstory. Now a Unesco World Heritage Site, Hallstatt was settled 4500 years ago and over 2000 Iron Age graves have been discovered in the area, most of them dating from 1000 to 500 BCE.

⊙ Sights & Activities

Salzwelten
MINE

(☎ 06132-200 24 00; www.salzwelten.at; Salzberg-strasse 21; funicular return & tour adult/child/family €34/17/71; ☻ 9.30am-2.30pm early Mar–late Mar & late Sep–mid-Dec, to 4.30pm late-Mar–late Sept) The fascinating *Salzbergwerk* (salt mine) is situated high above Hallstatt on Salzberg (Salt Mountain) and is the lake's major cultural attraction. The bilingual German-English tour details how salt is formed and the history of mining, and takes visitors down into the depths on miners' slides – the largest is 60m (on which you can get your photo taken).

Beinhaus
CHURCH

(Bone House; Kirchenweg 40; adult/child €1.50/0.50; ☻ 10am-5pm May-Oct, 11.30am-3.30pm Wed-Sun Nov-Apr) This small ossuary contains rows of neatly stacked skulls, painted with decorative designs and the names of their former owners. Bones have been exhumed from the overcrowded graveyard since 1600, and although the practice waned in the 20th century, the last joined the collection in 1995. It stands in the grounds of the 15th-century Catholic **Pfarrkirche** (parish church), which has some attractive Gothic frescoes and three winged altars inside.

🛏 Sleeping & Eating

Pension Sarstein
GUESTHOUSE $$

(☎ 06134-82 17; Gosaumühlstrasse 83; d €110, apt for 2/3/4 people €140/180/210, breakfast €8 per person; ☻ 🤶) The affable Fischer family takes pride in its little guesthouse, a few minutes' walk along the lakefront from central Hallstatt. The old-fashioned rooms are not flash, but they are neat, cosy and have balconies with dreamy lake and mountain views. Family-sized apartments come with kitchenettes. Doubles can be rented for a night, but apartments only for three or more (five in summer). Wi-fi is not in the rooms themselves.

★ Halstätt Hideaway
BOUTIQUE HOTEL $$$

(☎ 0677 617 105 18; www.hallstatt-hideaway.com; Dr. Friedrich-Morton-Weg 24; ste €270-480; ☻ 🤶) Six splendidly modern, beautifully textured private suites make up what is the region's most stylish accommodation choice. While prices reflect the varying sizes and facilities of each of the suites, they all have their own particular appeal – be that alpine charm, a stuccoed ceiling or contemporary design pieces and killer terraces with hot tub in the penthouse.

WORTH A TRIP

OBERTRAUN

Across the lake from the Hallstatt throngs, down-to-earth Obertraun is the gateway for some geological fun. The many 1000-year-old caves of the **Dachstein Rieseneishöhle** (www.dachstein-salzkammergut.com; All cable car sections plus caves adult/child €48.20/26.60, one section plus caves €42.60/23.40; ☻ 9.20am-3.30pm late Apr–mid-Jun & mid-Sep–Oct, to 4pm mid-late Jun, to 5pm late Jun–mid-Sep) extend into the mountain for almost 80km in places.

From Obertraun it's also possible to catch a cable car to **Krippenstein** (www.dachstein-salzkammergut.com; cable car return adult/child €32/17.60; ☻ mid-Jun–Oct), where you'll find the freaky but fabulous **5 Fingers viewing platform**, which protrudes over a sheer cliff face – not for sufferers of vertigo.

Restaurant zum Salzbaron
EUROPEAN $$

(☎ 06134-82 63-0; www.gruenerbaum.cc; Marktplatz 104; mains €21.90-32.90; ☻ noon-10pm; 🤶🍴) One of the best gourmet acts in town, the Salzbaron is perched alongside the lake inside the **Seehotel Grüner Baum** (s €150, d €250-380, ste €450; ☻🤶) and serves a seasonal pan-European menu – the wonderful local trout features strongly in summer.

ⓘ Getting There & Away

Ferry excursions (☎ 06134-82 28; www.hallstattschifffahrt.at) do the circuit of Hallstatt Lahn via Hallstatt Markt, Obersee, Untersee and Steeg return (€10, 90 minutes) three times daily from July to early September.

Trains connect Hallstatt and Bad Ischl (€5.20, 20 minutes, hourly). Hallstatt Bahnhof (train station) is across the lake from the village, and boat services (€2.50, 10 minutes, last ferry to Hallstatt Markt 6.50pm) coincide with train arrivals.

TYROL

Tyrol is as pure Alpine as Austria gets, with mountains that make you want to yodel out loud and patchwork pastures chiming with cowbells. After the first proper dump of snow in winter, it's a Christmas-card scene, with snow-frosted forests and skiers whizzing down some of the finest slopes in

Europe. Summer is lower key: hiking trails thread high to peaks and mountain huts, while folk music gets steins swinging down in the valleys.

Innsbruck

📞 0512 / POP 132,493 / ELEV 574M

Tyrol's capital is a sight to behold. Jagged rock spires are so close that within 25 minutes it's possible to travel from the heart of the city to over 2000m above sea level. Summer and winter outdoor activities abound, and it's understandable why some visitors only take a peek at Innsbruck proper before heading for the hills. But to do so is a shame, for Innsbruck is in many ways Austria in microcosm, with an authentic late-medieval Altstadt (Old Town), inventive architecture and a vibrant student-driven nightlife.

⊙ Sights

★ Hofkirche   CHURCH
(www.tiroler-landesmuseum.at; Universitätsstrasse 2; adult/child €7/free; ⊙ 9am-5pm Mon-Sat, 12.30-5pm Sun) Innsbruck's pride and joy is the Gothic Hofkirche, one of Europe's finest royal court churches. It was commissioned in 1553 by Ferdinand I, who enlisted top artists of the age such as Albrecht Dürer, Alexander Colin and Peter Vischer the Elder. Top billing goes to the empty **sarcophagus of Emperor Maximilian I** (1459–1519), a masterpiece of German Renaissance sculpture, elaborately carved from black marble.

Schloss Ambras   PALACE
(www.schlossambras-innsbruck.at; Schlosstrasse 20; palace adult/child €10/free, gardens free; ⊙ palace 10am-5pm, gardens 6am-dusk, closed Nov; 🖭) Picturesquely perched on a hill and set among beautiful gardens, this Renaissance pile was acquired in 1564 by Archduke Ferdinand II, then ruler of Tyrol, who transformed it from a fortress into a palace.

FREE GUIDED HIKES

From late May to October, Innsbruck Information arranges daily guided hikes from Monday to Friday, including sunrise walks, lantern-lit strolls and half-day mountain jaunts, which are, incredibly, free to anyone with an Innsbruck guest card. Pop into the tourist office to register and browse the program.

Don't miss the centrepiece **Spanische Saal** (Spanish Hall), the dazzling **Armour Collection** and the gallery's Velázquez and Van Dyck originals.

Hofburg   PALACE
(Imperial Palace; www.hofburg-innsbruck.at; Rennweg 1; adult/child €9/free; ⊙ 9am-5pm) Grabbing attention with its pearly white facade and cupolas, the Hofburg was built as a castle for Archduke Sigmund the Rich in the 15th century, expanded by Emperor Maximilian I in the 16th century and given a baroque makeover by Empress Maria Theresia in the 18th century. The centrepiece of the lavish rococo state apartments is the 31m-long **Riesensaal** (Giant's Hall).

Goldenes Dachl   MUSEUM
(Golden Roof; Herzog-Friedrich-Strasse 15; museum adult/child €4.80/2.40; ⊙ 10am-5pm May-Sep, 10am-5pm Tue-Sun Oct & Dec-Apr) Innsbruck's golden wonder and most distinctive landmark is this Gothic oriel, built for Holy Roman Emperor Maximilian I (1459–1519), lavishly decorated with murals and glittering with 2657 fire-gilt copper tiles. It is most impressive from the exterior, but the museum is worth a look – especially if you have the Innsbruck Card – with an audio guide whisking you through the history. Keep an eye out for the grotesque tournament helmets designed to resemble the Turks of the rival Ottoman Empire.

Bergisel   VIEWPOINT
(www.bergisel.info; adult/child €9.50/4.50; ⊙ 9am-6pm Jun-Oct, 10am-5pm Wed-Mon Nov-May) Rising above Innsbruck like a celestial staircase, this glass-and-steel ski jump was designed by much-lauded Iraqi architect Zaha Hadid. It's 455 steps or a two-minute funicular ride to the 50m-high **viewing platform**, with a breathtaking panorama of the Nordkette range, Inntal and Innsbruck. Tram 1 trundles here from central Innsbruck.

🏃 Activities

Nordkettenbahnen   CABLE CAR
(www.nordkette.com; single/return to Hungerburg €5.40/9, to Seegrube €18.60/31.10, to Hafelekar €20.70/34.50; ⊙ Hungerburg 7.15am-7.15pm Mon-Fri, 8am-7.15pm Sat & Sun, Seegrube 8.30am-5.30pm daily, Hafelekar 9am-5pm daily) Zaha Hadid's space-age funicular runs every 15 minutes, whizzing you from the Congress Centre to the slopes in no time. Walking trails head off in all directions from **Hungerburg** and

Seegrube. For more of a challenge, there is a downhill track for mountain bikers and two fixed-rope routes (*Klettersteige*) for climbers.

Inntour ADVENTURE SPORTS
(www.inntour.com; Leopoldstrasse 4; ⊘9am-6pm Mon-Sat) Inntour arranges guided cycling and mountain biking trips, including routes along the Inn River.

🍴 Sleeping & Eating

Nepomuk's HOSTEL $
(☑0512-58 41 18; www.nepomuks.at; Kiebachgasse 16; dm/d from €24/58; 🛜) Could this be backpacker heaven? Nepomuk's sure comes close, with its Altstadt location, well-stocked kitchen and high-ceilinged dorms with nice touches like CD players. The delicious breakfast in attached Cafe Munding, with homemade pastries, jam and fresh-roasted coffee, gets your day off to a grand start.

★ Hotel Weisses Kreuz HISTORIC HOTEL $$
(☑0512-594 79; www.weisseskreuz.at; Herzog-Friedrich-Strasse 31; s €66-105, d €100-180; 🅿@🛜) Beneath the arcades, this atmospheric Altstadt hotel has played host to guests for 500 years, including a 13-year-old Mozart. With its wood-panelled parlours, antiques and twisting staircase, the hotel oozes history with every creaking beam. Rooms are supremely comfortable, staff are charming and breakfast is a lavish spread.

Breakfast Club BREAKFAST $
(www.breakfast-club.at; Maria-Theresien-Strasse 49; breakfast €5-13; ⊘8am-4pm; 🛜🍽) Hip, wholesome and nicely chilled, the Breakfast Club does what it says on the tin: all-day breakfast and brunch. And boy are you in for a treat: free-range eggs, Tyrolean mountain cheese, organic breads, homemade spreads, cinnamon-dusted waffles with cranberries and cream, French toast, Greek omelettes – take your pick. It also does fresh-pressed juices and proper Italian coffee.

Die Wilderin AUSTRIAN $$
(☑0512-56 27 28; www.diewilderin.at; Seilergasse 5; mains €12.50-20; ⊘5pm-midnight Tue-Sun) 🌿 Take a gastronomic walk on the wild side at this modern-day hunter-gatherer of a restaurant, where chefs take pride in local sourcing and using top-notch farm-fresh and foraged ingredients. The menu sings of the seasons, be it asparagus, game, strawberries or winter veg. The vibe is urbane and relaxed.

Il Convento ITALIAN $$
(☑0512-58 13 54; www.ilconvento.at; Burggraben 29; mains €13.50-25, 2-course lunch €17.50-18.50; ⊘10am-3pm & 5pm-midnight Mon-Sat) Neatly tucked into the old city walls, this Italian job is run with passion by Peppino and Angelika. It's a winner, with its refined look (white tablecloths, wood beams, Franciscan monastery views from the terrace) and menu. Dishes such as clam linguine, braised veal and salt-crusted cod are cooked to a T and served with wines drawn from the well-stocked cellar.

🍷 Drinking & Nightlife

Moustache BAR
(www.cafe-moustache.at; Herzog-Otto-Strasse 8; ⊘11am-2am Tue-Sat, 10am-1am Sun; 🛜) Playing Spot-the-Moustache (Einstein, Charlie Chaplin and co) is the preferred pastime at this retro bolthole, with table football and a terrace overlooking pretty Domplatz. The bartenders knock up a mean pisco sour.

Tribaun CRAFT BEER
(www.tribaun.com; Museumstrasse 5; ⊘6pm-1am Mon-Thu, to 3am Fri & Sat) This cracking bar taps into craft-beer culture, with a wide variety of brews – from stouts and porters to IPA, sour, amber, honey and red ales. The easygoing vibe and fun-loving crew add to its appeal.

360° BAR
(Rathaus Galerien; ⊘10am-1am Mon-Sat) Grab a cushion and drink in 360-degree views of the city and Alps from the balcony that skirts this spherical, glass-walled bar. It's a nicely chilled spot for a coffee or sundowner.

ⓘ Information

Innsbruck Information (☑0512-598 50, 0512-535 60; www.innsbruck.info; Burggraben 3; ⊘9am-6pm Mon-Sat, 10am-4.30pm Sun) Main tourist office with truckloads of info on the city and surrounds, including skiing and walking.

❶ Getting There & Away

EasyJet flies to **Innsbruck Airport** (INN; ☑ 0512-22 52 50; www.innsbruck-airport.com; Fürstenweg 180), 4km west of the city centre. Buses depart every 15 or 20 minutes from Maria-Theresien-Strasse (16 minutes).

The A12 and the parallel Hwy 171 are the main roads heading west and east. The B177, to the west of Innsbruck, continues north to Germany and Munich while the A13 toll road (€9.50) runs south through the Brenner Pass to Italy.

Fast trains depart daily every two hours for Bregenz (€38.90, 2½ hours) and Salzburg (€47.20, 11¾ hours). From Innsbruck to the Arlberg, the best views are on the right-hand side of the train. Two-hourly express trains serve Munich (€42.60, 1¾ hours) and Verona (€43, 3½ hours). Direct services to Kitzbühel also run every two hours (€15.80, 1¼ hours).

❶ Getting Around

Single tickets on buses and trams cost €3 from the driver or €2.40 if purchased in advance. If you plan to use the city's public transport frequently you're better off buying a 24-hour ticket (€5.60).

Kitzbühel

☑ 05356 / POP 8272 / ELEV 762M

Ever since Franz Reisch slipped on skis and whizzed down the slopes of Kitzbüheler Horn way back in 1893, so christening the first alpine ski run in Austria, Kitzbühel has carved out its reputation as one of Europe's foremost ski resorts. It's renowned for the white-knuckled Hahnenkamm downhill ski race in January and the reliable excellence of its slopes.

🏃 Activities

Downhill skiers flock here for the 185km of slopes that are mostly intermediate and focused on Hahnenkamm-Pengelstein. Kitzbüheler Horn is much loved by beginners. If you're an intermediate skiier, pick a good day to cruise the unforgettable 35km **Ski Safari**. Anyone wanting to up the fear ante should brave the heart-stopping World Cup **Streif**. Kitzbühel makes a terrific base for walking in summer, with scores of well-marked trails, including the 15km **Kaiser Trail** with superlative views of the jagged Kaisergebirge massif. All cable cars are covered by ski passes in winter and by the **Summer Card** (adult three/seven days €52.50/73.50) in summer. The card is sold at cable-car base stations.

🛏 Sleeping & Eating

Rates leap by up to 50% in the winter season.

Snowbunny's Hostel   HOSTEL $
(☑ 0676 794 02 33; www.snowbunnys.com; Bichlstrasse 30; dm €24-48, d €66-146; 🛜) This friendly, laid-back hostel is a bunny-hop from the slopes. Dorms are fine, if a tad dark; breakfast is DIY-style in the kitchen. There's a TV lounge, a ski storage room and cats to stroke.

⭐ Villa Licht   HOTEL $$
(☑ 05356-622 93; www.villa-licht.at; Franz-Reisch-Strasse 8; d apt €130-580; 🅿️@🛜🛏) Pretty gardens, spruce modern apartments with pine trappings, living rooms with kitchenettes, balconies with mountain views, peace – this charming Tyrolean chalet has the lot, and owner Renate goes out of her way to please. Kids love the outdoor pool in summer.

Huberbräu Stüberl   AUSTRIAN $$
(☑ 05356-656 77; Vorderstadt 18; mains €9-19; ⊙8am-11.30pm Mon-Sat, 9am-11.30pm Sun; 🪑) An old-world Tyrolean haunt with vaults and pine benches, this tavern favours substantial portions of Austrian classics, such as schnitzel, goulash and dumplings, cooked to perfection.

Bring cash as cards are not accepted.

❶ Getting There & Away

Trains run frequently from Kitzbühel to Innsbruck (€15.80, 1¼ hours) and Salzburg (€31.50 to €43.80, two to 2½ hours). For Kufstein (€10.20, 51 minutes), change at Wörgl.

Lienz

☑ 04852 / POP 11,844 / ELEV 673M

The Dolomites rise like an amphitheatre around Lienz, which straddles the Isel and Drau Rivers just 40km north of Italy. The capital of East Tyrol is a scenic staging point for travels through the Hohe Tauern National Park.

◉ Sights & Activities

Lienz is renowned for its 64km of cross-country skiing trails; the town fills up for the annual Dolomitenlauf cross-country race in mid-January. A €47.50 day pass covers the downhill slopes on nearby Zettersfeld and Hochstein peaks.

KRIMML FALLS

The thunderous, three-tier **Krimmler Wasserfälle** (Krimml Falls; ☑06564-72 12; www.wasserfaelle-krimml.at; adult/child €4/1; ⊙9am-5pm mid-Apr–Oct) is Europe's highest waterfall at 380m, and one of Austria's most unforgettable sights. The **Wasserfallweg** (Waterfall Trail), which starts at the ticket office and weaves gently uphill through mixed forest, has numerous viewpoints with photogenic close-ups of the falls. It's about a two-hour return-trip walk.

The pretty Alpine village of Krimml has a handful of places to sleep and eat – contact the **tourist office** (☑06564-72 39; www.krimml.at; Oberkrimml 37; ⊙8am-noon & 2-5pm Mon-Fri, 8.30-11.30am Sat) for more information.

Buses run year-round from Krimml to Zell am See (€10.20, 1¼ hours, every two hours), with frequent onward train connections to Salzburg (€19.60, 1½ hours). The village is about 500m north of the waterfall, on a side turning from the B165. There are parking spaces near the falls.

🛏 Sleeping & Eating

Gasthof Schlossberghof
HOTEL **$$**

(☑04852-632 33; https://schlossberghof.at; Iseltaler Strasse 21; s/d €65/100; P) With rooms revamped in a contemporary style, this rustic, chalet-style guesthouse is a 10-minute stroll from the centre and is watched over by the Dolomites.

Garage
EUROPEAN **$$**

(☑04852-645 54; www.garage-lienz.at; Südtiroler Platz 2; mains €10-26, lunch special €8.50; ⊙11am-3pm & 6-11pm Tue-Sat) At this garage-style restaurant in the heart of Lienz, the decor is an atmospheric new-old combination of dark beams, monochrome tones, marble-topped tables and vintage picture frames. Alongside faves like organic *Wiener Schnitzel,* you'll find bright flavours in dishes like basil felafel with rocket, five-spice sirloin with rosemary dumplings, and coconut-lemongrass chicken curry.

❶ Information

The **tourist office** (Lienzer Dolimiten; ☑050 212 212; www.osttirol.com; Mühlgasse 11; ⊙8am-6pm Mon-Fri, 9am-noon & 4-6pm Sat) sells walking (€4) and via ferrate (€1) maps, can advise on the high-altitude trails that thread through the Dolomites' peaks and has brochures on all the adventure sports operators.

❶ Getting There & Away

Most trains to the rest of Austria, including Salzburg (€40.70, 3½ hours to 4½ hours, hourly), go east via Spittal-Millstättersee, where you usually have to change. Buses to Kitzbühel (€15.80, 1¾ hours) are quicker and more direct than the train, but less frequent.

Hohe Tauern National Park

Straddling Tyrol, Salzburg and Carinthia, this national park is the largest in the Alps; a 1786-sq-km wilderness of 3000m peaks, alpine meadows and waterfalls. At its heart lies Grossglockner (3798m), Austria's highest mountain, which towers over the 8km-long Pasterze Glacier, best seen from the outlook at Kaiser-Franz-Josefs-Höhe (2369m).

The 48km **Grossglockner Road** (www.grossglockner.at; day ticket car/motorbike €36/26; ⊙6am-8pm May, 5am-9.30pm Jun-Aug, 6am-7.30pm Sep & Oct) from Bruck in Salzburgerland to Heiligenblut in Carinthia is one of Europe's greatest Alpine drives. A feat of 1930s engineering, the road swings giddily around 36 switchbacks, passing jewel-coloured lakes, forested slopes and wondrous glaciers.

The major village on the Grossglockner Road is **Heiligenblut**, famous for its 15th-century pilgrimage church. Here the **tourist office** (☑04824-27 00 20; www.heiligenblut.at; Hof 4; ⊙9am-6pm Mon-Fri, 2-6pm Sat & Sun) can advise on guided ranger hikes, mountain hiking and skiing. The village also has a spick-and-span **Jugendherberge** (☑04824-22 59; www.oejhv.or.at; Hof 36; dm/s/d €23.50/31.50/58; P🛜).

Bus 5002 runs frequently between Lienz and Heiligenblut on weekdays (€8.70, one hour), and less frequently at weekends. From late June to late September, four buses run from Monday to Friday, and three at weekends between Heiligenblut and Kaiser-Franz-Josefs-Höhe (€5.90, 32 minutes).

SURVIVAL GUIDE

❶ Directory A–Z

ACCOMMODATION

Tourist offices invariably keep lists and details of accommodation; some arrange bookings (free, or for a small fee).

Hotels From budget picks to five-star luxury in palatial surrounds.

B&Bs Also called pensions and *Gasthöfe*; range from simple city digs to rustic mountain chalets.

Private rooms *Privat Zimmer* usually represent great value (doubles go for as little as €50).

Farmstays Well geared towards families. Some only operate during the summer months.

Alpine huts These go with the snow, opening from roughly late June to mid-September. Advance bookings are essential.

Camping Most resorts and cities have campgrounds, usually in pretty, natural settings.

Booking Services

Local city and regional tourist office websites often have excellent accommodation booking functions.

Austrian Hotelreservation (www.austrian-hotelreservation.at) Find hotels Austria-wide by theme and/or destination.

Austrian National Tourist Office (www.austria.info) The Austrian National Tourist Office has a number of overseas offices. There is a comprehensive listing on the ANTO website.

Bergfex (www.bergfex.at) Hotels, guesthouses, hostels, B&Bs, farms and huts searchable by region.

Best Alpine Wellness Hotels (www.wellnesshotel.com) The pick of Austria's top family-run spa hotels.

Camping in Österreich (https://www.camping.info/österreich) Search for campgrounds by location, facilities or reviews.

Lonely Planet (lonelyplanet.com/austria/hotels) Recommendations and bookings.

MONEY

➡ Austria's currency is the euro. An approximate 10% tip is expected in restaurants. Pay it directly to the server; don't leave it on the table.

➡ ATMs are widely available. Maestro direct debit and Visa and MasterCard credit cards accepted in most hotels and midrange restaurants. Expect to pay cash elsewhere.

OPENING HOURS

Banks 8am or 9am–3pm Monday to Friday (to 5.30pm Thursday)

Cafes 7am or 8am–11pm or midnight; traditional cafes close at 7pm or 8pm

Offices and government departments 8am–3.30pm, 4pm or 5pm Monday to Friday

Post offices 8am–noon and 2–6pm Monday to Friday; some open Saturday morning

Pubs and Bars Close between midnight and 4am

Restaurants Generally 11am–2.30pm or 3pm and 6–11pm or midnight

Shops 9am–6.30pm Monday to Friday (often to 9pm Thursday or Friday in cities), 9am–5pm Saturday

PUBLIC HOLIDAYS

New Year's Day (Neujahr) 1 January

Epiphany (Heilige Drei Könige) 6 January

Easter Monday (Ostermontag) March/April

Labour Day (Tag der Arbeit) 1 May

Whit Monday (Pfingstmontag) 6th Monday after Easter

Ascension Day (Christi Himmelfahrt) 6th Thursday after Easter

Corpus Christi (Fronleichnam) 2nd Thursday after Whitsunday

Assumption (Maria Himmelfahrt) 15 August

National Day (Nationalfeiertag) 26 October

All Saints' Day (Allerheiligen) 1 November

Immaculate Conception (Mariä Empfängnis) 8 December

Christmas Day (Christfest) 25 December

St Stephen's Day (Stephanitag) 26 December

SAFE TRAVEL

Theft Take usual common-sense precautions: keep valuables out of sight (on your person and in parked cars). Pickpockets occasionally operate on public transport and at major tourist sights.

Natural dangers Every year people die from landslides and avalanches in the Alps. Always check weather conditions before heading out; consider hiring a guide when skiing off-piste. Before going on challenging hikes, ensure you have the proper equipment and fitness. Inform someone at your hotel/guesthouse where you're going and when you intend to return.

TELEPHONE

➡ Austrian telephone numbers consist of an area code followed by the local number.

➡ Austria's international access code is 00; its country code is 43.

➡ Phone shops sell prepaid SIM cards from around €15.

➡ Phone cards in different denominations are sold at post offices and *Tabak* (tobacconist) shops. Call centres are widespread in cities, and many internet cafes are geared for Skype calls.

TOURIST INFORMATION

Austria Info (www.austria.info) is the official tourism website for the low-down on Austria, including hotels, itineraries, activities and excellent information on walking in Austria, from themed day hikes to long-distance treks. Also has details on national parks and nature reserves, hiking villages and special walking packages. Region-specific brochures are available for downloading.

Getting There & Away

AIR

Vienna is the main transport hub for Austria, but Graz, Linz, Klagenfurt, Salzburg and Innsbruck all receive international flights. Flights to these cities are often a cheaper option than those to the capital, as are flights to Airport Letisko (Bratislava Airport), which is only 60km east of Vienna, in Slovakia. Bregenz has no airport; there are limited flights to nearby Friedrichshafen in Germany and much better connections at Zürich in Switzerland.

BUS

Buses depart from Austria for as far afield as England, the Baltic countries, the Netherlands, Germany and Switzerland. Most significantly, they provide access to Eastern European cities small and large – from the likes of Sofia and Warsaw to Banja Luka, Mostar and Sarajevo.

Services operated by **Eurolines** (www.euro lines.at) leave from Vienna and from several regional cities.

CAR & MOTORCYCLE

There are numerous entry points into Austria by road from Germany, the Czech Republic, Slovakia, Hungary, Slovenia, Italy and Switzerland. All border-crossing points are open 24 hours.

Standard European insurance and paperwork rules apply.

TRAIN

The main services in and out of the country from the west normally pass through Bregenz, Innsbruck or Salzburg en route to Vienna. Trains to Eastern Europe leave from Vienna. Express services to Italy go via Innsbruck or Villach; trains to Slovenia are routed through Graz.

For online timetables and tickets, visit the **ÖBB** (www.oebb.at) website. SparSchiene (discounted tickets) are often available when you book online in advance. **Deutsche Bahn** (www.bahn. com) is also useful.

RIVER

Hydrofoils run to Bratislava and Budapest from Vienna; slower boats cruise the Danube between the capital and Passau.

ⓘ Getting Around

AIR

Flying within a country the size of Austria is rarely necessary. The main exception is to/from Innsbruck (in the far west of Austria).

The national carrier **Austrian Airlines** (www. austrian.com) offers several flights daily between Vienna and Graz, Innsbruck, Klagenfurt, Linz and Salzburg.

BICYCLE

➜ Most regional tourist boards have brochures on cycling facilities and routes within their region.

➜ Separate bike tracks are common in cities, and long-distance tracks and routes also run along many of the major valleys such as the Danube, Enns and Mur.

➜ The **Danube cycling trail** is like a Holy Grail for cyclists, following the entire length of the river in Austria between the borders with Germany and Slovakia.

BOAT

The Danube serves as a thoroughfare between Vienna and Lower and Upper Austria. Services are generally slow, scenic excursions rather than functional means of transport.

BUS

Rail routes are often complemented by **Postbus** (www.postbus.at) services, which really come into their own in the more inaccessible mountainous regions. Buses are fairly reliable, and usually depart from outside train stations

CAR & MOTORCYCLE

➜ A *Vignette* (toll sticker) is imposed on all motorways. *Vignette* can be purchased at border crossings, petrol stations and *Tabak* shops.

➜ Winter or all-weather tyres are compulsory from 1 November to 15 April. Carrying snow chains in winter is highly recommended.

➜ Speed limits are 50km/h in built-up areas, 130km/h on autobahn and 100km/h on other roads.

TRAIN

ÖBB (www.oebb.at) is the main operator, supplemented by a handful of private lines. Tickets and timetables are available online.

➜ Reservations cost €3.50 for most 2nd-class express services within Austria.

➜ Fares quoted are for 2nd-class tickets.

➜ Passengers with disabilities can use the 24-hour 05-17 17 customer number for special travel assistance; do this at least 24 hours ahead of travel (48 hours ahead for international services).

Belarus

POP 9.55 MILLION

Best Places to Eat

➡ Bistro de Luxe (p98)

➡ Jules Verne (p101)

➡ Kukhmystr (p98)

➡ Enzo (p98)

Best Places to Stay

➡ Hotel Manastyrski (p97)

➡ Hermitage Hotel (p101)

➡ Willing Hotel (p98)

➡ Kamyanyuki Hotel Complex (p103)

Why Go?

Long regarded by travellers as little more than a curiosity, Belarus has suddenly emerged as one of Europe's 'it' destinations. Fuelling that rise are relaxed visa requirements, a sneaky-good art and cafe scene, and hospitable locals. Political dissent had been muted until the disputed results of the August 2020 election – officially a landslide victory for the incumbent – sparked mass street protests, which were curbed by a huge police crackdown.

The capital has a pulsing nightlife, excellent museums and an impressive ensemble of Stalin-era architecture. Minsk has also become a hub for global summits and sporting events. Elsewhere, the western cities of Brest and Hrodna are Europeanised nooks, while around the Belarusian heartland you'll turn up ancient castles and national parks where rare *zubr* (European bison) roam.

When to Go

Minsk

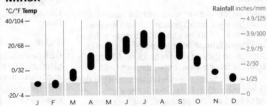

Jun–Aug Come to Belarus to escape the crowds elsewhere in Eastern Europe.

Jul Catch two superb festivals, countrywide Kupalle and Slavyansky Bazaar in Vitsebsk.

Oct Pleasantly cool temps, fall foliage and a good time to spot wildlife in national parks.

Entering the Country

You must arrive and depart by air in Minsk to take advantage of the 30-day visa-free regime. You'll generally need a visa if you arrive overland – visa-free zones (p103) in Brest and Hrodna are the exceptions.

ITINERARIES

Five Days

Five days gives you enough time to explore Minsk (p95) and get a taste of rural Belarus. Spend day one exploring the capital's Soviet past. Walk along massive pr Nezalezhnastsi (p95), take in the the Great Patriotic War Museum (p95), and pop in for a vodka at Tsentralny (p98). Day two is for culture. Check out an art museum, pop into a gallery on vul Kastrychnitskaya (p95), and go bar-hopping in the lively Old Town. Next, explore castle towns Mir (p100) and Nyasvizh (p100), with a potential overnight in either. Spend your last day cycling around Minsk's outskirts, or do another day trip.

Ten Days

After a few days in and around Minsk, hop a train or drive to the appealing western city of Brest (p100), which mixes European cafe culture with a slew of Soviet historical attractions. On day seven, head north along the Polish border to Belavezhskaya Pushcha National Park (p103), where lovely cycling trails and rare European bison await. Next, keep driving north to pleasant Hrodna (p103) with its preserved pre-WWII architecture. Alternatively, take a night train from Brest (or drive) east to Chagall's hometown, Vitsebsk (p101), before heading back to Minsk.

Essential Food & Drink

Belavezhskaya A bitter herbal alcoholic drink.

Draniki Potato pancakes, usually served with sour cream (*smetana*).

Khaladnik A local variation on cold *borshch,* a soup made from beetroot and garnished with sour cream, chopped-up hard-boiled eggs and potatoes.

Kindziuk A pig-stomach sausage filled with minced pork, herbs and spices.

Kletsky Dumplings stuffed with mushrooms, cheese or potato.

Kolduni Potato dumplings stuffed with meat.

Kvas A mildly alcoholic drink made from black or rye bread and commonly sold on the streets.

Machanka Pork stew served over pancakes.

AT A GLANCE

Area 207,600 sq km

Capital Minsk

Country Code ☑375

Currency Belarusian rouble (BYN)

Emergency Ambulance ☑03, Fire ☑01, Police ☑02

Language Belarusian, Russian

Time Eastern European time (GMT/UTC plus three hours)

Visas Not required for stays of 30 days or less for citizens of 74 countries, but must fly in/out of Minsk.

BELARUS

Sleeping Price Ranges

The following price ranges refer to a double room with bathroom during high season.

€ less than US$40

€€ US$40–100

€€€ more than US$100

Eating Price Ranges

The following price ranges refer to a main course.

€ less than BYN10

€€ BYN10–20

€€€ more than BYN20

Useful Websites

Belarus Feed (www.belarusfeed.com)

Belarus Tourism (www.belarus.by/en)

Minsk Tourism (http://minsktourism.by/en)

Gulf of Riga	

LATVIA

⊛ **RĪGA**

● **Jelgava**

● **Rēzekne**

P18

● **Šiauliai**

● **Daugavpils** ⊛

P46

P133

Daugava (Zapadnaya Dvina)

RUSSIA

● **Panevėžys**

LITHUANIA

Novopolatsk ● ● **Polatsk**

● **Hlybokoye**

Vitsebsk ❼

P46

Byarezinski Biosphere Reserve

M3

M8

A141

● **Smolensk**

Kaunas

P45

● **Lepel**

Neris (Vilija)

M3

P28

● **Khatyn**

● **Orsha**

VILNIUS ⊛

E28

● **Maladzechna**

● **Barysau**

M1

Mahileu (Mogilev) ●

A101

● **Krichev**

● **Druskininkai**

● **Lida**

Minsk ❶

M6

Mir ❸

P11

● **Dudutki**

Dnyapro (Dnieper)

P43

❻ **Hrodna**

● **Bruzgi**

Navahrudak (Novogrudok)

P68

E28

Nyasvizh ❹

● **Babrujsk**

● **Slonim**

● **Baranavichy**

● **Slutsk**

● **Zhlobin**

M8

● **Homel**

M10

Białystok

POLAND

❺ Belavezhskaya Pushcha National Park

P43

● **Svetlahorsk**

P31

● **Rechitsa**

Kamyanyuki ●

P136

● **Zhytkavichy**

● **Kobryn**

M1

Bug

❷ **Brest**

Terespol

P17

● **Pinsk**

M10

● **Turau**

Lyaskavichy ● ● **Mazyr**

Pripyatsky National Park

Polesye State Radioecological Reserve

Chornobyl Exclusion Zone

● **Chornobyl**

● **Chernihiv**

Desna

● **Chełm**

UKRAINE

● **Zamość**

● **Lutsk**

KYIV ⊛

Kyivske Reservoir

● **Zhytomyr**

Belarus Highlights

❶ **Minsk** (p95) Taking in the architecture, the rowdy nightlife and the burgeoning arts scene of Belarus' capital.

❷ **Brest** (p100) Strolling through the streets of this cosmopolitan city and gaping at its epic WWII memorials.

❸ **Mir Castle** (p100) Training your lens on this fairy-tale

16th-century castle – and its equally famous reflection.

❹ **Nyasvizh** (p100) Exploring this tranquil provincial town's parks and impeccably restored castle.

❺ **Belavezhskaya Pushcha National Park** (p103) Cycling around Europe's oldest

wildlife refuge in search of rare European bison.

❻ **Hrodna** (p103) Checking out its ruined Old Castle, museums and pre-WWII architecture.

❼ **Vitsebsk** (p101) Discovering the childhood home of painter Marc Chagall and excellent art museums.

MINSK МIНСК

📄 17 / POP 2.01 MILLION

Minsk will almost certainly surprise you. The capital of Belarus is, contrary to its dreary reputation, a progressive, modern and clean place. Fashionable cafes, impressive restaurants and crowded nightclubs vie for your attention, while sushi bars and art galleries have taken up residence in a city centre once totally remodelled to the tastes of Stalin. Despite the strong police presence and obedient citizenry, Minsk is a thoroughly pleasant place that's easy to become fond of.

◉ Sights

If you're short on time, have a wander around the attractive Old Town, or Verkhni Horad (Upper City). This was once the city's thriving Jewish quarter, and while most of it was destroyed in the war, a smattering of pre-war buildings along vul Internatsyanalnaya and a rebuilt **ratusha** (Town Hall; pl Svabody) on **pl Svabody** emit a whiff of history.

Many of the most bombastic buildings from the Soviet and Lukashenko eras lie well outside the centre. The most jaw-dropping specimens are northeast of the centre along pr Nezalezhnastsi and out toward **Minsk Arena** (📄 17 3634 598; http://minskarena.

by; pr Peramozhtsaŭ) on pr Peramozhtsaŭ (take the no 1 bus from pl Svabody). A good way to see a bunch of these is to take a **City Tour** (📄 17 3996 969; http://citytour.by; pl Privakzalnaya; adult/child BYN30/15; ☉ tours 11am, 1.30pm, 4pm & 6.30pm) bus tour.

★ Museum of the Great Patriotic War   MUSEUM

(📄 17 2030 792; www.warmuseum.by; pr Peramozhtsaŭ 8; adult/student BYN9/7, audioguide BYN4, guided tours BYN35; ☉ 10am-6pm Tue-Sun) Housed in a garish new building, Minsk's best museum houses an excellent display detailing Belarus' suffering and heroism during the Nazi occupation. With English explanations throughout, atmospheric dioramas and a range of real tanks, airplanes and artillery from WWII, it's one of the capital's few must-see attractions.

★ Vul Kastrychnitskaya   STREET

Vul Kastrychnitskaya – still known by its Soviet name, ulitsa Oktyabrskaya – has blossomed into Minsk's unofficial arts district. Brazilian street artists have spray-painted brilliant murals on the giant facades of the street's apartment blocks, warehouses and factories, many of which now house event spaces, galleries and hipster cafes. President

MINSK'S MAIN DRAG

Inconspicuous **pr Nezalezhnastsi (Independence Ave)** is a good way to take Minsk's pulse while also taking in a few sights. It runs the length of the modern city, from stubbornly austere and expansive **pl Nezalezhnastsi (Independence Sq)** to the pinnacle of Lukashenko-approved hubris, the rhombicuboctahedron-shaped **National Library of Belarus** (📄 17 2932 966; www.nlb.by; pr Nezalezhnastsi 116; library BYN1.50, viewing platform BYN3.50; ☉ library 10am-8pm, closed Sun & last Mon of the month; viewing platform noon-11pm; Ⓜ Uschod). The avenue is the world's premier embodiment of the post-WWII Stalinist Empire style, marked by expansive squares, utopian parks and palatial architectural gems like the **Central Post Office** (pr Nezalezhnastsi 10).

At pl Nezalezhnastsi you can't miss the imposing Belarusian Government Building, fronted by a Lenin Statue. It is one of several fine examples of pre-WWII constructivist architecture in Minsk. Heading northeast you'll pass the post office, the ominous **KGB headquarters** (pr Nezalezhnastsi 17) and daunting **Kastrychnitskaya pl** (Oktyabrskaya Pl) before crossing the Svislach River, straddled by the city's two main parks.

Just across the bridge is the **former residence of Lee Harvey Oswald** (vul Kamyunistychnaya 4). The alleged assassin of former US president John F Kennedy lived here for a couple of years in his early 20s. He arrived in Minsk in January 1960 after leaving the US Marines and defecting to the USSR. Once here, he truly went native: he got a job in a radio factory, married a Minsk woman, had a child – and even changed his name to Alek. But soon he returned to the United States and...you know the rest. His apartment is thought to be at the far left (northwest) side of the building on the 3rd floor.

Just 100m northeast of here, **pl Peramohi (Victory Sq)** is marked by a giant Victory Obelisk and its eternal flame, which is directly beneath the obelisk underground. From here you can hop on the Metro to go out to the National Library 5km away.

BELARUS MINSK

Minsk

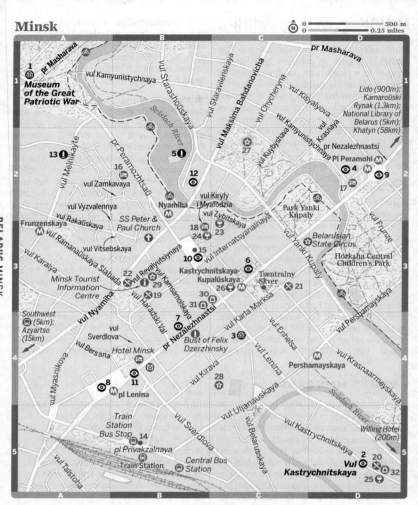

0 500 m
0 0.25 miles

BELARUS MINSK

Lukashenko has allowed creative expression to flourish here with the expectation that it not spread to other parts of the capital, which remain sanitised and generally free of street art.

The district exudes a refreshing counter-culture spirit and is one of the few places where you'll hear locals speaking Belarusian and/or talking about politics.

Belarusian State Art Museum MUSEUM
(☑17 3277 163; vul Lenina 20; adult/student BYN8/4, audioguide BYN3, excursion BYN20; ☺11am-7pm Wed-Mon) This excellent museum

in one of Minsk's iconic buildings (built in 1939) includes definitive works by Soviet social realists and Russian masters, including Valentin Volkov's social realist *Minsk on July 3, 1944* (1944–5), depicting the Red Army's arrival in the ruined city. Several works by Yudel Pen, Chagall's teacher, are here, including his 1914 portrait of Chagall, and Chagall exhibitions often rotate through here.

Trinity Hill HISTORIC SITE
(Traetskae Pradmestse) Trinity Hill is a pleasant – if tiny – recreation of Minsk's pre-war buildings on a pretty bend of the river just

Minsk

⊙ **Top Sights**
1 Museum of the Great Patriotic War.......A1
2 Vul Kastrychnitskaya.............................D5

⊙ **Sights**
3 Belarusian State Art Museum...............C4
4 Former Residence of Lee Harvey
    Oswald...D2
5 Island of Courage & Sorrow..................B2
6 Kastrychnitskaya Pl..............................C3
7 KGB Headquarters................................B4
8 Pl Nezalezhnastsi.................................A4
9 Pl Peramohi..D2
10 Pl Svabody...B3
11 Pr Nezalezhnastsi................................B4
    Ratusha..(see 10)
12 Trinity Hill...B2
13 Zaslavsky Jewish Monument A2

⊕ **Activities, Courses & Tours**
14 City Tour..B5
15 Free Walking Tour Minsk......................B3

⊟ **Sleeping**
16 DoubleTree by Hilton............................B2

17 Hostel Tower 31/18 ....D2
18 Hotel Manastyrski.................................B3

✕ **Eating**
19 Bistro de Luxe B3
20 Enzo...D5
21 Kukhmystr...C3
22 Lido..B3

⊙ **Drinking & Nightlife**
23 Beercap Barshop...................................C3
24 Bessonitsa...B3
25 Hooligan..D5
26 Tsentralny...C3

⊕ **Entertainment**
27 Bolshoi Theatre of Belarus...................C2
28 Dinamo Stadium....................................C4
29 TNT..B3

⊟ **Shopping**
30 GUM...C3
31 Kirmash...B3
32 Vialiki Dziakuj D5

BELARUS MINSK

a little north of the centre. It has a few little cafes, restaurants and shops, and a walking bridge leads over to the **Island of Courage & Sorrow** (Island of Tears), an evocative Afghan war memorial known locally as the Island of Tears.

Kamaroůski Rynak   MARKET
(Komarovskiy Market; vul Very Kharuzhay; ⊙9am–7pm; Ⓜ Ploshcha Jakuba Kolasa) Market buffs should not miss Minsk's air-hangar-like main market, one of Minsk's collectivist masterpieces. It's a colourful smorgasbord of seasonal (and unseasonal) fruits and vegetables, breads and all manner of meat.

☞ Tours

Minsk Guide   TOURS
(☑29 3846 689; www.minsktours.by) Andrei is a professional guide who speaks excellent English and leads tours around the country. He specialises in Jewish heritage tours but is well versed on all things Belarus. He also has a lovely, log-cabin-like farmstay southwest of Minsk out towards Mir.

Free Walking Tour Minsk   WALKING
(☑44 5398 306; http://freewalkingtour.by) In addition to the two-hour free walking tour, which kicks off daily at 11am in front of the

ratusha on pl Svabody, this group leads Soviet tours, Jewish tours and more.

⊟ Sleeping

Hostel Tower 31/18   HOSTEL €
(☑33 6250 305; pr Nezalezhnastsi 31; dm/r BYN20/55; @🛜) JFK assassin Lee Harvey Oswald lived under the same roof (in a different apartment) in the 1960s. If that doesn't interest you, then the welcoming vibe, clean dorms and pleasant kitchen/hangout area at this quiet hostel will. It's five storeys up (no lift), in apartment 18; the door access code is 18C.

★**Hotel Manastyrski**   HISTORIC HOTEL €€
(☑17 3290 300; http://monastyrski.by/en; vul Kiryly i Myafodzia 6; s/d incl breakfast from US$65/$75; ❈🛜) Housed in the converted remains of a Benedictine Monastery in the heart of Minsk's bustling Old Town, this 48-room gem cannot be beaten for location and atmosphere. Rooms are smart and comfortably furnished with dark-wood fittings, while the impressive corridors are decorated with frescoes (found during the renovation) and wrought-iron chandeliers. Booking directly on the website nets a 10% discount.

Willing Hotel
BOUTIQUE HOTEL €€

(☑17 3369 000; vul Lenina 50; r US$70-100, ste US$150; ❄@🖥; Ⓜ Praletarskaya) This new hotel announces its presence with a giant mural facing artsy vul Kastrychnitskaya. The creativity continues inside, where a circular atrium awaits and colourful carpeting with a squiggly motif covers all floor space. The suitably snazzy rooms feature contemporary art and bathtubs, and the deluxe rooms have kitchenettes with bar seating. The in-house Simple Cafe is wonderful.

DoubleTree by Hilton
HOTEL €€€

(☑17 3098 000; www.doubletree.com; pr Peramozhtsaŭ 9; s/d incl breakfast from US$160/170; ❄@🖥) A short walk from the Old Town, this 21-storey high-rise is the capital's best all-around hotel. The ship-shape, well-appointed rooms are what you'd expect from a four-star hotel. It's the extras that make it stand out: the excellent gym, the ground-level coffee shop and adjacent patio bar, the bike-rental service, and the sumptuous breakfast complete with a unique 'honey bar'.

🍴 Eating

Lido
CAFETERIA €

(pr Nezalezhnasti 49/1; mains BYN3-7; ⊙8am-11pm Mon-Fri, from 11am Sat & Sun; 🖥🅿; Ⓜ Ploshcha Jakuba Kolasa) This large, upscale *stolovaya* (cafeteria) with Latvian roots has a huge array of food on display, so it's easy for non-Russian speakers: just point at what you want. Classic Russian soups and salads, grilled trout and cheesy meat dishes are highlights.

Another branch is on **vul Nyamiha** (vul Nyamiha 5; dishes BYN3-7; ⊙10am-10pm; 🖥).

★Enzo
BISTRO €€

(☑29 1770 088; vul Kastrychnitskaya 23; mains BYN10-20, steaks BYN30-60; ⊙11am-midnight Sun-Thu, to 3am Fri & Sat; ❄🖥) A hip and happening bistro worthy of the hip and happening street that it's on, Enzo is justifiably popular, mainly for its burgers and succulent steaks served on bread boards, but also for its towering salads and inventive desserts. Outside is prime people-watching, while inside classic-rock and alternative music videos are projected onto a brick wall behind the bar.

★Kukhmystr
BELARUSIAN €€

(☑17 3274 848; vul Karla Marksa 40; mains BYN15-30; ⊙noon-11pm, closed last Sat of month; ❄🖥) A stone's throw from the president's office, this charming Belarusian place boasts wooden beams, a tiled fireplace, wrought-iron light fittings and antique knick-knacks. Staff are equally pleasant, and the menu is among the most authentically Belarusian in town.

★Bistro de Luxe
BISTRO €€€

(☑44 7891 111; vul Haradski Val 10; mains BYN15-45; ⊙8am-midnight Mon-Fri, from 11am Sat & Sun; ❄🖥) Housed in a gorgeous space with chandeliers, sleek brasserie-style furnishings, a chessboard floor and luxury toilets, Bistro de Luxe has charm and atmosphere in spades. The food is excellent – it leans towards French – and service is impeccable. Breakfast is served until noon. Reservations recommended, especially if you want to sit outside.

🍷 Drinking & Nightlife

★Hooligan
BAR

(vul Kastrychnitskaya 16; ⊙5pm-midnight, from 8am Sat & Sun, to 4am Fri & Sat; 🖥) The haphazard look is very much by design at this brick-walled hipster hangout on vul Kastrychnitskaya. Belly up to the recycled-wood bar, play table football under exposed pipes or kick back in old leather couches. It offers 'twisted and classic' cocktails (BYN10 to BYN12), beer, and a few single malts and other high-end spirits.

Bessonitsa
COCKTAIL BAR

(Insomnia; vul Hertsena 1; ⊙noon-late) *The* place in the Old Town for professional cocktails (try the bourbon sour or a gimlet) and late-night eats. It has Minsk's longest bar, a lively interior and a bustling patio tailor-made for people-watching.

Tsentralny
BAR

(pr Nezalezhnastsi 23; ⊙8am-11pm) It's known as a place where you can drown your sorrows with BYN1.80 vodka shots – and therein lies its beauty. While models and hipsters crash the Old Town, real people with real problems hit the ground floor of this department store on Minsk's main drag. Order from the cashier and take a window seat.

Beercap Barshop
CRAFT BEER

(vul Hertsena 10; ⊙5-11pm, to 1am Fri & Sat; 🖥) This is a generously stocked craft-beer place at the very centre of the Old Town action. Choose from about a dozen draught beers inside, with about half a dozen additional varieties on tap outside. Tunes roar and the whole place gets jumping at weekends.

⭐ Entertainment

TNT
LIVE MUSIC

(☑ 29 6555 555; www.tntrock.by; vul Revalyut-siynaya 9a; cover Fri & Sat BYN10; ☺ noon-2am Sun-Thu, to 4am Fri & Sat) An early pioneer of Minsk's rock-music renaissance, this multi-room venue in the centre of town draws top local and regional talent and is a good bet for those who want to rock out midweek. The cocktails are strong, and on some nights it gets several bands.

Bolshoi Theatre of Belarus
PERFORMING ARTS

(☑ 17 2895 493; http://bolshoibelarus.by; pl Parizh-skoy Kamunni 1; tickets BYN5-120; ☺ performances 7pm, closed Jul & Aug) In an iconic pre-WWII collectivist building, the national opera has an excellent reputation and stages a range of classical ballets and operas.

🔒 Shopping

Kirmash
CLOTHING

(www.kirmash.by; pr Nezalezhnastsi 19; ☺ 10am-9pm Mon-Fri, to 6pm Sat & Sun) This is *the* place buy embroidered shirts and dresses, table-cloths and other national-flavoured textiles. Much of the clothing blends traditional and modern motifs, with several contemporary designers represented.

Vialiki Dziakuj
GIFTS & SOUVENIRS

(vul Kastrychnitskaya 23; ☺ noon-10pm) Personable, Belarusian-speaking Valentin is a printer and brander by trade, and it shows in his wonderful collection of original mugs and T-shirts. You'll also find cool wallets, handbags, pins and other knick-knacks, plus bottled craft beer that can be enjoyed in the courtyard outside.

ℹ️ Information

MEDICAL SERVICES

24-Hour Pharmacy (vul Karla Marksa 20; ☺ 24hr) Well stocked.

Apteka #4 (vul Kirava 3; ☺ 24hr) A 24-hour pharmacy.

Ecomedservice (☑ 160, 17 2077 474; www.ems.by; vul Talstoha 4; ☺ 8am-9pm; 🛜) Reliable, Western-style clinic. Bring a translator.

TOURIST INFORMATION

Minsk Tourist Information Centre (☑ 17 2033 995; www.minsktourism.by/en; vul Revaly-utsiynaya 13-119; ☺ 8.45am-1pm & 2-6pm Mon-Fri) The main tourist office is central but well hidden in the courtyard behind vul Revalyutsiynaya 13.

BelarusTourService (☑ 33 3332 666; www.visa.by; vul Rozy Lyuksemburg 89) An excellent source for visa support, hotel bookings and transfers, plus tours.

ℹ️ Getting There & Away

AIR

Minsk National Airport (☑ 17 2791 300; www.airport.by) All flights in and out of Belarus are through this airport about 40km east of the centre. There are no domestic flights in Belarus.

BUS

The vast majority of intercity domestic and international services leave from the **Central Bus Station** (Tsentralny Aŭtavakzal; ☑ 114; vul Babruyskaya 6).

TRAIN

The busy and modern **Minsk train station** (☑ 105, 17 2257 000; pl Privakzalnaya; ☺ 24hr) is pretty easy to deal with. You can buy tickets here, or opposite the station at the less crowded **International Train Ticket Office** (vul Kirava 2; ☺ 8am-noon & 1-5pm). Downstairs is a well-signed **left luggage office** (per 24hr BYN1.25-1.50; ☺ 24hr).

ℹ️ Getting Around

TO/FROM THE AIRPORT

Minsk National Airport Handy Bus A300Э goes to/from the Central Bus Station (platform 2), passing by the train station (BYN4.40, 55 minutes). It runs roughly hourly around the clock. Head left when you exit the terminal and look for the dedicated **bus stop** (Minsk National Airport).

The 35-minute taxi ride into town costs a flat BYN30 provided you book it at one of several dedicated taxi booths in the arrivals area.

BICYCLE

Renting a bicycle is an ideal way to explore Minsk and its vast boulevards. Riding on the sidewalk is encouraged – indeed many sidewalks have designated bike lanes – and a beautiful 26km two-way bike route cuts right through the centre of Minsk. **City Bike** (vul Kastrychnitskaya 16; per day BYN15-20; ☺ 7am-10pm) and **Speedy Go** (☑ 29 1445 030; http://speedygo.by; pr Nezalezhnastsi 37a; bicycles per day BYN15; ☺ 10am-10pm) rent bikes.

CAR

Rental cars are widely available and work great for day trips out of town. **Avis** (☑ 17 2099 489; www.avis.by; Hotel Minsk, pr Nezalezhnastsi 11) and **Europcar** (☑ 29 1336 553; www.europcar.by; Hotel Minsk, pr Nezalezhnastsi 11; ☺ 9am-6pm) both have outlets at Hotel Minsk and at the airport; for a cheaper local option try **AvtoGurman**

(☑ 29 6887 070; http://auto-rent.by; vul Chycheryna 4; per day from €25).

PUBLIC TRANSPORT

Minsk's metro isn't hugely useful to travellers unless you're exploring the vast suburbs. It's open daily from dawn until just after midnight. One ride costs 65 kopeks.

Buses, trams and trolleybuses cost 60 kopeks per ride, and you can buy tickets on board. The most useful services for travellers are bus 1 and bus 69, which depart from the **train station bus stop** (vul Kirava), pass by pl Svabody in the Old Town, then continue along pr Peramozhtsaŭ.

TAXI

Ordering a taxi via a ride-hailing app or by phone is the way forward. Trips within the centre cost just BYN3 to BYN5 – much cheaper and less hassle than negotiating with street taxis. Yandex Taxi and NextApp are apps that work well in Minsk (Uber also works, via Yandex). Otherwise dial 152 or 7788 for a taxi (find a translator, though, in case the operators don't speak English).

AROUND MINSK

Worthwhile trips from the capital include **Dudutki** (☑ 29 6025 250; www.dudutki.by; adult/child BYN10/6; ☉10am-5pm Tue-Wed, to 6pm Thu-Sun), an open-air folk museum 40km south of Minsk (take bus 323 from Minsk's Central Bus Station; p99); and **Khatyn** (☑ 1774 55 787; www.khatyn.by; photo exhibit BYN1; ☉complex 24hr, photo exhibit 10.30am-4pm Tue-Sun) FREE, a sobering memorial to a village wiped out by the Nazis 60km north of Minsk (accessible only by private transport). The latter can be combined with the **Stalin Line Museum** (http://stalin-line.by; Rt 28, Lashany; adult/student BYN14/7; ☉10am-6pm), 25km northwest of Minsk in Lashany – a must for military buffs with all manner of Soviet war paraphernalia on display in an open field.

Nyasvizh   Нясвіж

This green and attractive town 120km southwest of Minsk is home to the splendid **Nyasvizh Castle** (☑ 1770 20 602; www.niasvizh.by/en; adult/student BYN16/8, audioguide BYN3, excursion BYN39; ☉10am-7pm May-Sep, to 6pm Oct-Apr, closed last Wed of month). It was erected by the Radziwill family in 1583 but was rebuilt and restored often over the centuries and encompasses many styles. With more than 30 fully refurbished state rooms,

a very impressive inner courtyard and clearly labelled displays, you can easily spend a couple of hours looking around. Access to the castle is via a causeway leading away from the parking lot, with lovely lakes on either side.

From Minsk's Central Bus Station, there are five daily buses to and from Nyasvizh (BYN8, two hours). The last trip back to Minsk is around 6pm. There's a 2.30pm bus to Hrodna (BYN16, six hours) via Mir (BYN2, 45 minutes).

Mir   Mip

The charming small town of Mir, 85km southwest of Minsk, is dominated by the impossibly romantic 16th-century **Mir Castle** (☑ 1596 28 270; www.mirzamak.by; adult/student BYN14/7, audioguide BYN3; ☉museum 10am-6pm, 9am-7pm Fri-Sun Jun-Aug; courtyard 24hr), reflected magnificently in an adjoining pond. A recent renovation has the place looking simply lovely, with gorgeous grounds and impressively restored interiors that have been converted into a museum with beautifully done displays on the life and times of the Radziwills. Definitely splash out for the audioguide, which offers fascinating descriptions of more than 120 items.

From Minsk's Central Bus Station, buses to Mir's small **bus station** (pl 17 Sentyabrya), on the town square, depart roughly hourly (BYN7, 1½ hours). The last trip back to Minsk is around 4.15pm; buy a return ticket when you arrive to avoid getting stuck. There's also a daily bus to Nyasvizh around 5pm (BYN2, 45 minutes) and a daily bus to Hrodna around 3pm (BYN14, five hours).

BREST   БРЕСТ

☑ 162 / POP 300,000

This prosperous and cosmopolitan border town looks far more to the neighbouring EU than to Minsk. Brest and the city of Hrodna to the north can now be visited visa-free for 10 days if you are arriving overland from Poland, provided you secure the proper paperwork.

⊙ Sights

Most sights are in and around Brest Fortress (p102), which flanks the Bug and Mukhavets rivers just a whisper from the Polish border. It's about a 4km walk from central **vul**

VITSEBSK

The historic city of Vitsebsk (known universally outside Belarus by its Russian name, Vitebsk) lies a short distance from the Russian border and almost 300km from Minsk. It was an important centre of Jewish culture when it was one of the major cities of the 'Pale of Settlement', where Jews were allowed to live in the Russian Empire. The city was immortalised in the early work of Marc Chagall, the city's most famous son.

Today Vitsebsk is an agreeable regional centre with pedestrianised vul Suvorova at its heart, along with several fine churches and museums, including two dedicated to Chagall. First and foremost among these is the **Marc Chagall Art Center** (www.chagall. vitebsk.by; vul Putna 2; adult/student BYN2.50/1.50, tours in Russian BYN9; ⊙11am-7pm Tue-Sun Apr-Sep, Wed-Sun Oct-Mar), which has about 300 of Chagall's graphic works, less than one-quarter of which is on display at any given time. Across the town's river is the **Marc Chagall House Museum** (☑212 663 468; vul Pokrovskaya 11; adult/student BYN2.50/1.50; ⊙11am-7pm Tue-Sun Apr-Sep, Wed-Sun Oct-Mar), where the artist lived as a child from 1897 to 1910 – a period beautifully evoked in his autobiography, *My Life*.

The dining and drinking scene in Vitsebsk is concentrated in the Old Town on vul Talstoha near the base of pedestrianised vul Suvorova – just follow the music. It's worth trying to time your visit for **Slavyansky Bazaar** (Slavic Bazaar; www.festival.vitebsk.by; ⊙mid-Jul), a popular festival that takes place over 10 days in July and brings in dozens of singers and performers from Slavic countries for a week-long series of concerts.

One or two daily express trains (BYN8, 3¾ hours) and a handful of slower trains (from BYN8.60, four to nine hours) head to Minsk. The **train station** (vul Kasmanaŭtaŭ) is just over the main bridge on the west side of the Dvina River.

BELARUS MIR

Savetskaya, a pleasant walking street lined with bars and restaurants.

★ Museum of Railway Technology
MUSEUM

(pr Masherava 2; adult/student BYN2.50/2; ⊙10am-6pm Tue-Sun) The outdoor Museum of Railway Technology has a superb collection of locomotives and carriages dating from 1903 (eg the Moscow–Brest Express, with shower rooms and a very comfy main bedroom) to 1988 (far more proletarian Soviet passenger carriages).

St Nicholas Brotherly Church
CHURCH

(cnr vul Savetskaya & vul Mitskevicha) With its gold cupolas and yellow-and-blue facades shining gaily in the sunshine, this finely detailed 200-year-old Orthodox church is one of several lovely churches in Brest.

🛏 Sleeping

Hotel Bug
HOTEL €€

(☑162 278 800; www.hotelbug.by; vul Lenina 2; s/d from BYN64/90; 🛜) An unfortunate name, but this 1950s hotel near the train station is great value. The functional rooms have hot water, desks, and working wi-fi. The vintage Soviet foyer, with utopian murals and white-marble statues of Lenin and others, is

definitely a highlight. The staff do not speak English but are friendly.

Hermitage Hotel
HOTEL €€€

(☑162 276 000; www.hermitagehotel.by; vul Chkalova 7; s/d incl breakfast from BYN215/260; 🅿❄❅🛜) This 55-room hotel is heads above the local competition and is priced accordingly. Housed in a sensitively designed modern building, it has more than a little old-world style, with spacious, grand and well-appointed rooms, as well as impressive public areas and a top-notch restaurant.

🍴 Eating & Drinking

★ Jules Verne
INTERNATIONAL €€

(vul Hoholya 29; mains BYN10-25; ⊙5pm-1am Mon-Fri, from noon Sat & Sun; 🛜🍴) Decked out like a traditional gentlemen's club and with a travel theme, this dark, atmospheric joint manages to be refined without being stuffy. It serves up cracking dishes, from mouthwatering Indian curries and French specialities to sumptuous desserts and the best coffee in town. Don't miss it.

Fania Braverman's House
EASTERN EUROPEAN €€

(vul Savetskaya 53; mains BYN10-25; ❄🛜) Who was Fania Braverman? We have no idea.

BREST FORTRESS

The city's main sight is the **Brest Fortress** (Brestskaya krepost; www.brest-fortress.by; pr Masherava) `FREE`, a moving WWII memorial where Soviet troops held out far longer than expected against the Nazi onslaught in the early days of Operation Barbarossa.

The fortress was built between 1833 and 1842, but by WWII it was being used mainly as a barracks. The two regiments bunking here when German troops launched a surprise attack in 1941 defended the fort for an astounding month and became venerated as national legends thanks to Stalin's propaganda machine.

Enter the Brest Fortress complex through a tunnel in the shape of a huge socialist star, then walk straight ahead several hundred metres to the fortress's most iconic site: **Courage**, a chiselled soldier's head projecting from a massive rock, flanked by a sky-scraping memorial obelisk.

There are several museums in and around the sprawling grounds, the most interesting of which are a pair museums that commemorate the siege and related events in WWII: the comprehensive **Defence of Brest Fortress Museum** (adult/student BYN5/2.50, audioguide BYN3; ⊙9am-6pm, closed Mon & last Tue of month) inside the fortresses' northern bastion; and the newer, more visual **Museum of War, Territory of Peace** (adult/student BYN5/2.50, audioguide BYN3; ⊙10am-7pm, closed Tue & last Wed of month) in the southern bastion.

But we know there is possibly no more pleasant place in Brest to spend an evening people-watching. Top-quality acoustic musicians play out on the terrace most evenings in the warm months. Order from the meat-heavy menu or just have a drink.

★ **Korova** COCKTAIL BAR
(vul Savetskaya 73; ⊙noon-2am Sun-Thu, to 5am Fri & Sat) Just an average grill and bar along vul Savetskaya by day, Korova morphs at night into a superb lounge-club, with slick bartenders serving expertly made cocktails and craft beer, while an all-types, somewhat older crowd gets their groove on to talented DJs and live bands at weekends.

Paragraph Cafe CAFE
(vul Savetskaya 30; ⊙8am-11pm Mon-Fri, from 10am Sat & Sun) This little space on Brest's main drag caters to writers and artists with strong coffee and a paint-splattered interior. Besides coffee it also has smoothies, shakes, lemonade and a few light bites, such as muesli for breakfast.

Coyote Club LIVE MUSIC
(vul Dzyarzhynskaha 14; BYN10 after 11pm Fri & Sat; ⊙4pm-midnight Sun-Thu, to 3am Fri & Sat) Bartenders dancing on the bar and loud live music are the calling cards of this raucous bar. Terrific fun any night of the week, it really gets going on weekends, when the best bands play and shots flow.

🛍 Shopping

Knyaz Vitaŭt CLOTHING
(vul Savetskaya 55; ⊙10am-9pm) Absolutely original clothing including wonderful T-shirts and embroidered traditional shirts and dresses. Also has handbags, leather goods and even socks and playing cards with national motifs.

ℹ Information

MEDICAL SERVICES

Vita Fari (vul Hoholya 32; ⊙24hr) Pharmacy open 24 hours.

City Emergency Hospital (☑103; vul Lenina 15)

TRAVEL AGENCIES

Contact travel agencies in advance to arrange paperwork for visa-free entry. They charge €10 to €15.

Brest City Tour (☑333 444 223; www.brest citytour.by; vul Zubachova 25/1) This useful agency at Brest Fortress has English-speaking guides for BYN40 per hour and leads two-hour city tours in a brightly painted van (BYN10 to BYN12 per person, minimum five people).

ℹ Getting There & Away

From the **train station** (☑105), express business-class trains serve Minsk (from BYN12, 3¼ hours, three to four daily), while slower *pasazhirsky* (passenger) trains trundle to Minsk (from BYN7, 4½ hours to nine hours, frequent), Homel (from BYN 13, 9½ hours, two daily) and Vitsebsk (from BYN15, nine to 17 hours, three daily).

From the **bus station** (📍114; vul Mitskevicha), there are *marshrutky* (fixed-route minivans) to Hrodna (BYN13 to BYN17, 3½ to four hours, six daily), plus a slower bus or two.

Daily train 127 serves Warsaw (BYN35 to BYN55, two hours). Other trains to Warsaw are possible but are less regular and cost triple or quadruple (www.ecolines.net) buses to Warsaw (€18, 3½ hours, three daily), which originate in Minsk, are another option.

You'll need a proper Belarusian visa for international bus travel to Ukrainian destinations such as Lviv (BYN23, 7½ hours, two daily).

ⓘ Getting Around

For a taxi, try the 7220 ride-sharing app, or call 7220 or 5656.

Bike N' Roll (📍29 5051 286; vul Hoholya 32; bicycles per day BYN15; ⊙10am-7pm Mon-Fri, to 5pm Sat & Sun) Nice selection of mountain and city bikes available for hourly or daily rental.

Koleso (📍162 566 699; https://prokatkoles. by/en; pr Masherava 22) The best place to rent cars in town, with a good website and prices starting at €20 per day.

AROUND BREST

Belavezhskaya Pushcha National Park
Белавежская Пушча

Unesco World Heritage Site **Belavezhskaya Pushcha National Park** (📍1631 56 398; www.npbp.by; cost varies per activity; ⊙ticket office 9am-6pm) is the oldest wildlife refuge in Europe and the pride of Belarus. At least 55 mammal species call this park home, but the area is most celebrated for its 300 or so European bison, the continent's largest land mammal. You have a chance to spot these beasts in the wild on a tour of the park, although you have to be a bit lucky.

At the National Park headquarters in Kamyanyuki, 55km north of Brest, you can arrange to tour the park by bus tour (adult/child BYN10/6, three hours, 11am and 2pm, in Russian only) or by bicycle (BYN9 to BYN15), which can be hired at the park entrance. There are several sealed bike trails to choose from; the 27km 'big journey' and the 16km 'animal crossing' offer the best chance of spotting wildlife.

You can spend the night at one of several comfortable hotels in the **Kamyanyuki Hotel Complex** (📍1631 56 200; https://npbp.by/eng; s/d incl breakfast from BYN74/148; ❄️ 🐾 🌐) near the park entrance. To get to the park from Brest, take a bus or *marshrutka* from the bus station (BYN5, 1¼ hours, seven daily).

HRODNA   ГРОДНА

📍152 / POP 320,000

Hrodna is a laid-back, friendly city with plenty of intact pre-WW2 architecture and a host of good bars and cafes. You can visit the city overland from Poland or Lithuania without a visa – just play by the rules and do not wander outside the fairly limited confines of Hrodna district (*rayon*).

⊙ Sights

Hrodna's two main sights are right next to each other on the banks of the Neman River. While mostly in ruins, the **Old Castle** (vul Zamkavaya 20; grounds free, museum adult/student BYN6.20/4.90; ⊙10am-6pm Tue-Sun) does have one restored wing that houses the Hrodna History and Archaeology Museum, a comprehensive walk through the history of the Hrodna region. The rococo **New Castle** (vul Zamkavaya 20; admission BYN7, or per exhibit BYN3, audioguide BYN3; ⊙10am-6pm Tue-Sun), built in the 18th century by Polish-Lithuanian rulers to replace the Old Castle, is an eclectic art museum that features

ⓘ VISA-FREE TRAVEL TO BREST & HRODNA

You can travel to Brest and Hrodna visa-free for up to 10 days provided you have the proper paperwork (€8 to €15) secured in advance through a travel agency like Nemnovo Tour (p104) in Hrodna. The regimes for Brest and Hrodna are separate – you cannot travel between the two, and there are strict limits on which borders you can cross and where you can travel once over the border (ask your supporting travel agency). The law requires you to purchase a minimum of two travel services in advance from your supporting travel agency, but these can be as minor as a taxi reservation or museum entry.

attractive 19th-century oils and the brilliant *Man with a Shovel*, thought to be by Russian avant-garde master Kazimir Malevich.

🛏 Sleeping

⭐ Hostel Sarmatiya   HOSTEL €

(📞152 723 027; www.hostelgrodno.by; vul Karla Marksa 11; dm BYN25) This mid-sized hostel is a real find, with a perfect central location, an airy and attractive common room, and the best dorm beds in town complete with personal lights and charging stations. Features include lockers, laundry, six-bed female dorm, small kitchen, and bike rental (BYN3 per hour).

🍴 Eating & Drinking

⭐ Nesterka   VEGAN €

(vul Davyda Haradzenskaha; dishes BYN4-8; ⏰2pm-midnight, to 2am Fri & Sat; 🌱) 🍴 Hrodna's alternative kids head here for falafel sandwiches, craft beer and poetry slams – you get the idea. The dirt-cheap food satisfies the impoverished artists among the crowd. DJs or live bands occasionally play inside or in a separate space downstairs.

Nasha Kava   COFFEE

(vul Zamkavaya 11; ⏰9am-11pm Mon-Thu, to 1am Fri & Sat; 🌐) The cool crowd gravitates to this cosy and contemporary coffee shop with huge mirrors, pendant lighting, lovely wood tables, a small patio out front and great specialty coffee. There are sweets to nibble on plus mulled wine and hot grog.

Faradey   COCKTAIL BAR

(vul Satsiyalistychnaya 32; ⏰6pm-4am Sun-Thu, to 6am Fri & Sat) Marked by an eccentric design and strong cocktails, this self-described 'emotion lab' is the best all-around bar in town. You'll see plenty of good-looking faces here on weekends when the DJs fire it up and it morphs into an intimate club.

❶ Information

Nemnovo Tour (📞152 742 943; www.nemnovotour.by; vul Elizy Azheshka 38; ⏰9am-6pm Mon-Fri; 🌐) This super-friendly agency near the train station arranges visa-free travel to both Hrodna and Brest, and has useful hardcopy and online maps highlighting Hrodna's main attractions.

❶ Getting There & Away

Trains to Minsk (from BYN10, 4¾ to eight hours, six daily) leave from the **train station** (vul Budzyonnaha 37). *Marshrutky* (fixed-route mini-

vans) from Hrodna's **central bus station** (📞152 752 292; vul Chyrvonarmeyskaya 7) do the trip faster (BYN7, three hours, hourly).

For Brest, you're best off with a *marshrutka* (BYN13 to BYN17, 3½ to four hours, six daily). There is an 11.35am bus to Nyasvizh (BR16, six hours) via Mir (BR14, five hours).

For Białystok in Poland via the Bruzgi–Kuźnica border (4½ hours) there are frequent minibuses (BYN15) and a daily Ecolines (www.ecolines.net) bus (€15, 1.40pm); the latter continues to Warsaw (€20, 7½ hours). There's also a daily late-afternoon train to Kraków (BYN52, seven hours) via Białystok (BYN18, two hours) and Warsaw (BYN38, 3½ hours).

About four buses per day serve Druskininkai in Lithuania via the Pryvalki border (BYN10, three hours).

❶ Getting Around

Buses 14 and 3 link the train station and central pl Savetskaya, with the latter also passing by the bus station. To hail a taxi, download the 'Taxi 7220' app.

SURVIVAL GUIDE

❶ Directory A–Z

INTERNET ACCESS

Wi-fi is ubiquitous at restaurants and hotels and is almost always free. Local SIM cards with data (4G) are easy to purchase. Data is cheap and fast and coverage is excellent, including on major highways.

LEGAL MATTERS

Police take quality-of-life infractions such as jaywalking or public alcohol consumption seriously. Should you be cited, police will issue a ticket for about BYN25 that you can pay in most banks.

MONEY

ATMs are the best way to obtain Belarusian roubles (BYN). Credit cards are widely used for payment in Minsk and other cities, but are unlikely to be accepted in rural areas.

OPENING HOURS

Banks 9am to 5pm Monday to Friday

Office hours 9am to 6pm Monday to Friday

Restaurants and bars 10am or noon to 10pm or midnight

Shops 9am or 10am to 9pm Monday to Saturday, to 6pm Sunday (if at all)

PUBLIC HOLIDAYS

New Year's Day 1 January

Orthodox Christmas 7 January

International Women's Day 8 March
Constitution Day 15 March
Catholic & Orthodox Easter March/April
Unity of Peoples of Russia and Belarus Day 2 April
International Labour Day (May Day) 1 May
Victory Day 9 May
Independence Day 3 July
Dzyady (Day of the Dead) 2 November
Catholic Christmas 25 December

TELEPHONE

There are four mobile-phone companies that can sell you a SIM-card package with oodles of data for next to nothing. Bring your passport, a Belarusian address and your unlocked phone. To place a call or send a text from a local mobile phone, dial either +375 or 80, plus the nine-digit number.

VISAS

Citizens of 74 countries can enter Belarus visa-free for up to 30 days as long as they arrive and depart from Minsk National Airport (p99). If arriving or departing by land, everybody needs a visa – unless going to either Brest or Hrodna, the two special visa-free zones. If arriving visa-free, you must purchase a Belarusian health insurance policy upon landing in Minsk to cover the length of your stay (about €1 per day). Your home policy may work if you can prove to authorities that it covers Belarus.

Registration

If you are staying in Belarus for more than five working days, you must register with the local authorities. Most hotels do this automatically, and it's included in the room price. If you are staying with an individual or with a hostel that does not handle registration, you or your host will have to register your visa at the main **AGIM** (Citizenship & Migration Department; ☑17 284 5923, 17 284 5960; vul Very Kharuzhay 3; ☉8am-5pm Tue & Fri, 11am-8pm Wed, 8am-1pm Thu & Sat; Ⓜ Ploshcha Jakuba Kolasa) office in Minsk, or at any regional AGIM office. The cost is BYN24. Do not lose your white registration slips – border officers may demand to see these when you leave the country.

ℹ Getting There & Away

Minsk is the main hub for all domestic travel and is also surprisingly well connected by both air

---

ℹ WARNING: TRANSITING THROUGH RUSSIA

Via Air Flying via Moscow when departing or arriving in Minsk will require a Russian transit visa; you will not be allowed to board your flight without one.

Via Land It is illegal for foreigners to enter or leave Belarus overland via Russia – even if you have valid Russian and Belarusian visas.

---

and land to Eastern and Western Europe, as well as, of course, most former Soviet countries.

AIR

All international flights to Belarus fly in and out of Minsk National Airport (p99). Belarus' national airline, **Belavia** (☑17 2202 555; www.belavia. by; vul Nyamiha 14, Minsk; ☉9am-8pm Mon-Sat, to 6pm Sun), has lots of flights to Moscow and former Soviet states, and it also serves a few Western European cities.

LAND

Car & Motorcycle

➡ You can drive your own car or motorcycle into Belarus via legal border crossings (see http://gpk.gov.by/en/maps for the list). Make sure your vehicle insurance and other documents are in order.

➡ Foreign-registered cars (not motorcycles) are subject to stiff tolls on major Belarusian highways. Study up on the system and pre-purchase your electronic payment device at http://beltoll.by/index.php/en.

ℹ Getting Around

Trains are extremely cheap and plenty comfortable; buses are cheap but less comfortable. For train schedules and prices, see www.rw.by.

Air There are no domestic flights within Belarus.

Bus A bit cheaper than trains, but can be slower. Zippy *marshrutky* (public minivans), on the other hand, are less comfortable but generally faster than buses or trains.

Car Hiring a car is recommended for exploring around Minsk, with car-hire widely available.

Train Efficient and usually on time. Try the business-class express trains for quick hops between cities.

Belgium & Luxembourg

POP 11.4 MILLION/576,000

Best Places to Eat

➜ The Jane (p132)

➜ Comme Chez Soi (p115)

➜ Le Sud (p137)

➜ Arcadi (p115)

➜ De Stove (p122)

Best Places to Stay

➜ 1898 The Post (p127)

➜ Guesthouse Nuit Blanche (p121)

➜ Chambres d'Hôtes du Vaudeville (p114)

➜ Villa Botanique Guesthouse (p114)

➜ La Pipistrelle (p136)

Why Go?

Stereotypes of comic books, chips and sublime chocolates are just the start in eccentric little Belgium. Its self-deprecating people have quietly spent centuries producing some of Europe's finest art and architecture. Bilingual Brussels is the dynamic yet personable EU capital, also sporting what's arguably the world's most beautiful city square. Flat, Dutch-speaking Flanders has many other alluring medieval cities, all easily linked by regular train hops. Much of hilly, French-speaking Wallonia is contrastingly rural – its castles and extensive cave systems easier to reach by car – though fascinating Mons is well connected by public transport. Independent Luxembourg, the EU's richest country, is compact and attractive with its own wealth of castle villages, while its capital city is famed both for banking and for its fairy-tale Unesco-listed Old Town. Meanwhile the brilliant beers of Belgium and the sparkling wines of Luxembourg's Moselle Valley lubricate some of Europe's best dining.

When to Go
Brussels

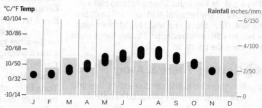

Pre-Easter weekends Belgium hosts many of Europe's weirdest carnivals, not just at Mardi Gras.

Feb–Mar Both countries symbolically burn the spirit of winter on the first weekend after Carnival.

Jul–Aug Countless festivals; hotels are packed in Bruges but cheaper in Brussels and Luxembourg City.

Entering the Country

As part of the Schengen area, there are usually no controls at land borders. The main airport is at Brussels but those at Charleroi, and to a lesser extent Luxembourg, have a good range of budget flights.

ITINERARIES

Four Days

Belgium's four finest 'art cities' all make easy stops or short excursions while you're train-hopping between Paris and Amsterdam. Bruges (p119) is the fairy-tale 'Venice of the north', Ghent (p125) has similar canalside charms without the tourist hordes, Brussels' (p110) incomparable Grand Place is worth jumping off any train for, and cosmopolitan Antwerp (p129) goes one further, adding in fashion and diamonds to its rich artistic and architectural heritage.

Ten Days

Stay longer in each of the above, then return south from Antwerp dropping into lively Leuven (p133), charming Lier (p133) and spiritual Mechelen (p134). From Brussels, visit the world-famous battle site at Waterloo (p118) then take the train across the rolling Ardennes to wealthy little Luxembourg (p136) with its compact Unesco-listed capital and quaint, accessible castle villages.

Essential Food & Drink

Belgium's famous lagers (eg Stella Artois) and white beers (Hoegaarden) are global brands, but what has connoisseurs really drooling are the robust, rich abbey-brewed 'Trappist beers'. Chimay, Rochefort, Westmalle and Orval are widely known, but the one that really counts is ultra-rare Westvleteren XII. Luxembourg's Moselle region produces creditable white wines and excellent *crémants* (bubbles). While top restaurants often have a French-fusion focus, home-style local dishes are making a resurgence. Classics include the following:

Boulettes Meatballs

Chicons au gratin Endives rolled in ham and cooked in cheese/béchamel sauce.

Filet Américain A blob of raw minced beef, typically topped with equally raw egg yolk.

Judd mat gaardebounen Luxembourg's national dish: smoked pork neck in a cream-based sauce with chunks of potato and broad beans.

Mosselen/moules Cauldrons of in-the-shell mussels, typically steamed in white wine with celery and onions and served with a mountain of *frites* (chips).

Paling in 't groen Eel in a sorrel or spinach sauce.

Stoemp Mashed veg-and-potato dish.

Waterzooi A cream-based chicken or fish stew.

AT A GLANCE (BELGIUM/ LUXEMBOURG)

Area 30,528/2586 sq km

Capital Brussels/ Luxembourg City

Country Code +32/+352

Currency euro (€)

Emergency 112

Languages Dutch (Flanders), French (Wallonia), both (Brussels); Letzeburgisch, French and German (Luxembourg)

Time Central European Time (GMT/UTC plus one hour)

Visas Schengen rules apply

Sleeping Price Ranges

The following ranges refer to the cost of a double room in high season.

€ less than €60

€€ €60–140

€€€ more than €140

Eating Price Ranges

The following price ranges refer to the cost of a typical main course.

€ less than €15

€€ €15–25

€€€ more than €25

Resources

Visit Brussels https://visit.brussels/en

Visit Flanders www.visitflanders.com

Visit Luxembourg www.visitluxembourg.com

BELGIUM & LUXEMBOURG

Belgium & Luxembourg Highlights

❶ Bruges (p119) Visiting on weekdays off-season to appreciate the picture-perfect canal scenes of this medieval city.

❷ Ghent (p125) Being wooed by one of Europe's greatest underappreciated all-round discoveries.

❸ Brussels (p110) Savouring the 'world's most beautiful square', then seeking out remarkable *cafés* (pubs or bars) and chocolate shops.

❹ Antwerp (p129) Following fashion and Rubens to this hip yet historic port city.

❺ Luxembourg City (p136) Spending the weekend in the UNESCO-listed Old Town then heading out to the grand duchy's evocative castle villages.

❻ Waterloo (p118) Tramping across the world-famous battlefield where Napoleon met his Abba song.

❼ Ypres (p123) Pondering the heartbreaking futility of WWI in Flanders' fields.

❽ Lier (p133) Discovering the quaintest Flemish canal city that nobody's heard of.

❾ Moselle Valley (p140) Tasting your way through a range of Luxembourg white wines and sparking *crémants* while watching the Moselle River glide by.

BRUSSELS

POP 1.2 MILLION / 📞02

Belgium's capital, and the EU's administrative heart, Brussels is historic yet hip, bureaucratic yet bizarre, self-confident yet unshowy, and multicultural to its roots. All this plays out in a cityscape that swings from majestic to quirky to rundown and back again. Organic art nouveau facades face off against 1960s concrete developments, and regal 19th-century mansions contrast with a Gotham City of brutal glass that forms the EU district. This whole maelstrom swirls out from Brussels' medieval core, where the Grand Place is surely one of the world's most beautiful squares.

⊙ Sights

To see a bunch of top sites, consider the **BrusselsCard** (www.brusselscard.be; 24/48/72hr €26/34/42) which includes free city transport. However, avoid buying one for Mondays when much is closed or on the first Wednesday afternoon of each month when many major museums are free.

◈ Central Brussels

★ Grand Place   SQUARE
(Ⓜ Gare Centrale) Brussels' magnificent Grand Place is one of the world's most unforgettable urban ensembles. Oddly hidden, the enclosed cobblestone square is only revealed as you enter on foot from one of six narrow side alleys: Rue des Harengs is the best first approach. The focal point is the spired 15th-century city hall, but each of the antique guildhalls (mostly 1697–1705) has a charm of its own. Most are unashamed exhibitionists, with fine baroque gables, gilded statues and elaborate guild symbols.

Musées Royaux des Beaux-Arts   GALLERY
(Royal Museums of Fine Arts; 📞 02-508 32 11; www. fine-arts-museum.be; Rue de la Régence 3; adult/6-25yr/BrusselsCard €10/3/free, incl Magritte Museum €15; ⊙10am-5pm Tue-Fri, 11am-6pm Sat & Sun; Ⓜ Gare Centrale, Parc) This prestigious museum incorporates the **Musée d'Art Ancien** (ancient art); the **Musée d'Art Moderne** (modern art), with works by surrealist Paul Delvaux and fauvist Rik Wouters; and the purpose-built Musée Magritte. The 15th-century Flemish Primitives are wonderfully represented in the Musée d'Art Ancien: there's Rogier Van der Weyden's *Pietà* with its hallucinatory sky, Hans Memling's refined portraits, and the richly textured *Madonna*

with Saints by the anonymous artist known as Master of the Legend of St Lucy.

Musée Magritte   GALLERY
(📞 02-508 32 11; www.musee-magritte-museum. be; Place Royale 1; adult/under 26yr/BrusselsCard €10/3/free; ⊙10am-5pm Tue-Fri, 11am-6pm Sat & Sun; Ⓜ Gare Centrale, Parc) The beautifully presented Magritte Museum holds the world's largest collection of the surrealist pioneer's paintings and drawings. Watch his style develop from colourful Braque-style cubism in 1920 through a Dali-esque phase and a late-1940s period of Kandinsky-like brushwork to his trademark bowler hats of the 1960s. Regular screenings of a 50-minute documentary provide insights into the artist's unconventionally conventional life.

MIM   MUSEUM
(Musée des Instruments de Musique; 📞 02-545 01 30; www.mim.be; Rue Montagne de la Cour 2; adult/concession €10/8; ⊙9.30am-5pm Tue-Fri, from 10am Sat & Sun; Ⓜ Gare Centrale, Parc) Strap on a pair of headphones, then step on the automated floor panels in front of the precious instruments (including world instruments and Adolphe Sax' inventions) to hear them being played. As much of a highlight as the museum itself are the premises – the art nouveau Old England Building. This former department store was built in 1899 by Paul Saintenoy and has a panoramic rooftop *café* (pub/bar) and outdoor terrace.

Galeries St-Hubert   ARCHITECTURE
(📞 02-545 09 90; www.grsh.be; Rue du Marché aux Herbes; Ⓜ Gare Centrale) When opened in 1847 by King Léopold I, the glorious Galeries St-Hubert formed Europe's very first shopping arcade. Many enticing shops lie behind its neoclassical glassed-in arches flanked by marble pilasters. Several eclectic *cafés* spill tables onto the gallery terrace, safe from rain beneath the glass roof. The arcade is off Rue du Marché aux Herbes.

Musée Mode & Dentelle   MUSEUM
(Fashion & Lace Museum; 📞 02-213 44 50; www. costumeandlacemuseum.brussels; Rue de la Violette 12; adult/child/BrusselsCard €8/free/free; ⊙10am-5pm Tue-Sun; Ⓜ Gare Centrale) Lace making has been one of Flanders' finest crafts since the 16th century. While *kloskant* (bobbin lace) originated in Bruges, *naaldkant* (needlepoint lace) was developed in Italy but was predominantly made in Brussels. This excellent museum reveals lace's applications for underwear and outerwear over the

CINQUANTENAIRE & THE EU AREA

While far less famous than the Paris equivalent, Brussels has its very own triumphal arch. It's the centrepiece of the **Parc du Cinquantenaire** (Rue de la Loi & Rue Belliard; Ⓜ Mérode), built to celebrate 50 years of Belgian independence but only finished in 1905, 25 years late. A surrounding cluster of museums includes the **Musée Art & Histoire** (☑ 02-741 73 01; www.artandhistory.museum; Parc du Cinquantenaire 10; adult/child/Brussels-Card €10/4/free; ⊙ 9.30am-5pm Tue-Fri, from 10am Sat & Sun; Ⓜ Mérode), chock-a-block with priceless antiquities, and **Autoworld** (www.autoworld.be; Parc du Cinquantenaire; adult/concession/BrusselsCard €10/€7/free; ⊙ 10am-6pm Apr-Sep, to 5pm Oct-Mar; Ⓜ Mérode) with its huge collection of vintage cars. Around a kilometre west, the thought-provoking **Musée des Sciences Naturelles** (☑ 02-627 42 11; www.naturalsciences.be; Rue Vautier 29; adult/concession/child/BrusselsCard €7/6/4.50/free; ⊙ 9.30am-5pm Tue-Fri, 10am-6pm Sat & Sun; 🚌 38) is a highly interactive science museum featuring a unique 'family' of iguanodons – 10m-high dinosaurs found in a Hainaut coal mine in 1878. The museum is directly south of the **EU Parliament** (☑ 02-284 34 57; www.europarl.europa.eu; Rue Wiertz 43; ⊙ tours 10am & 3pm Mon-Thu, 10am Fri; 🚌 38, Ⓜ Trône) FREE.

centuries, as well as displaying other luxury textiles in beautifully presented exhibitions. There's a new focus here on Belgium's ahead-of-the-curve fashion industry, with changing exhibitions of contemporary textiles.

Manneken Pis
MONUMENT

(cnr Rue de l'Étuve & Rue du Chêne; Ⓜ Gare Centrale) Rue Charles Buls – Brussels' most unashamedly touristy shopping street, lined with chocolate and trinket shops – leads the hordes three blocks from the Grand Place to the Manneken Pis. This fountain-statue of a little boy taking a leak is comically tiny and a perversely perfect national symbol for surreal Belgium. Most of the time the statue's nakedness is hidden beneath a costume relevant to an anniversary, national day or local event: his ever-growing wardrobe is displayed at the **Maison du Roi** (Musée de la Ville de Bruxelles; Grand Place; Ⓜ Gare Centrale).

◉ Beyond the Centre

Atomium
MONUMENT

(☑ 02-475 47 75; www.atomium.be; Av de l'Atomium; adult/teen/child €15/8/free; ⊙ 10am-6pm; Ⓜ Heysel, 🚌 51) The space-age Atomium looms 102m over north Brussels' suburbia, resembling a steel alien from a '60s Hollywood movie. It consists of nine house-sized metallic balls linked by steel tube-columns containing escalators and lifts. The balls are arranged like a school chemistry set to represent iron atoms in their crystal lattice...except these are 165 billion times bigger. It was built as a symbol of postwar progress for the 1958 World's Fair and became an architectural icon, receiving a makeover in 2006.

Cantillon Brewery
BREWERY

(Musée Bruxellois de la Gueuze; ☑ 02-520 28 91; www.cantillon.be; Rue Gheude 56; €9.50; ⊙ 10am-5pm Mon, Tue & Thu-Sat; Ⓜ Clemenceau) Beer lovers shouldn't miss this unique living brewery-museum. Atmospheric and family run, it's Brussels' last operating lambic brewery and still uses much of the original 19th-century equipment. After hearing a brief explanation, visitors take a self-guided tour, including the barrel rooms where the beers mature for up to three years in chestnut wine casks. The entry fee includes two taster glasses of Cantillon's startlingly acidic brews.

Africa Museum
MUSEUM

(☑ 02-769 52 11; www.africamuseum.be/en/home; Leuvensesteenweg 13, Tervuren; adult €12, concessions free-€8; 🚌 44) The revived Africa Museum is a big draw, and a world away from its earlier dusty colonial incarnation. The exhibits are predominantly from former Belgian colony the Congo, and include some beautiful musical instruments, masquerade masks and artfully carved pot lids. Resident artists and a digital project give the space a contemporary focus.

Train World
MUSEUM

(☑ 02-224 74 98; www.trainworld.be; Place Princesse Elisabeth 5; adult/concession/BrusselsCard €12/9/free; ⊙ 10am-5pm Tue-Sun; 🚌 58, 59, 🚊 7, 92, 🚆 Schaerbeek) Wonderful old engines gleam in the low light of this imaginative and beautiful museum, located in the renovated 1887 Schaerbeek station: exhibits include *Le Belge*, the country's first locomotive. You can climb on board the engines, wander into a historic station cottage and

Central Brussels

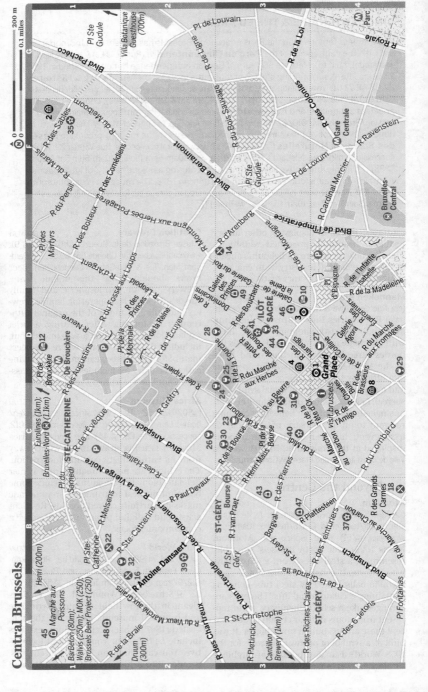

200 m
0.1 miles

Pl Ste Gudule

Villa Botanique Guesthouse (700m)

Pl de Louvain

Blvd Pachéco

R de la Loi

R de la Ligne

R du Bois Sauvage

R des Colonies

Parc

R Royale

Blvd de Berlaimont

R du Meiboom

R des Comédiens

R Montagne aux Herbes Potagères

Pl Ste Gudule

R de Loxum

Gare Centrale

R Ravenstein

R des Sables

2

35

R du Marais

R du Persil

R des Boiteux

R d'Arenberg

Blvd de l'Impératrice

R Cardinal Mercier

Bruxelles-Central

Pl des Martyrs

R d'Argent

R du Fossé-aux-Loups

R Léopold

R Neuve

R des Princes

Pl de la Monnaie

R de la Reine

R de l'Écuyer

R de la Madeleine

R de la Montagne

Pl d'Espagne

R de l'Infante Isabelle

R de la Madeleine

R de la Montagne

R Montagne du Roi

Galerie du Roi

Galerie des Princes

14

R des Dominicains

49

ÎLOT SACRÉ

Galerie de la Reine

R des Bouchers

46

10

3

Galerie des Éperonniers

Galerie Agora

R du Marché aux Fromages

28

41

33

44

Petite R des Bouchers

25

R de la Fourche

24

R des Harengs

27

R de la Colline

R du Marché aux Herbes

4

1

Grand Place

8

R des Brasseurs

29

Pl de Brouckère

De Brouckère

12

R des Augustins

Pl de la Monnaie

Pl de Brouckère

R Grétry

R des Fripiers

Blvd Anspach

R de l'Évêque

STE-CATHERINE

Eurolines (1km);
Bruxelles-Nord (1.1km)

R du Marché au Charbon

au Charbon

R de l'Étuve

17

31

R au Beurre

R du Midi

40

R Henri Maus

Pl de la Bourse

43

47

R des Pierres

R Plattesteen

Borgval

R St-Géry

R-J van Praet

R des Teinturiers

R des Riches-Claires

R de la Grande Île

ST-GÉRY

Blvd Anspach

R du Marché au Charbon

R des Grands Carmes

18

37

R du Lombard

visit.brussels
au Charbon

de l'Amigo

26

30

23

R de la Bourse

R Paul Devaux

Bourse

R Melsens

R des Halles

R de la Vierge Noire

R Ste-Catherine

Pl du Samedi

Pl Ste-Catherine

22

32

16

39

R Antoine Dansaert

R des Poissonniers

R Van Arteveld

Pl St-Géry

ST-GÉRY

R de la Grande Île

R St-Christophe

R des Chartreux

R des 6 Jetons

Pl Fontainas

Henri (200m)

Marché aux Poissons

45

BarBëton (80m);
Walvis (250m); MOK (250);
Brussels Beer Project (250)

48

R de la Braie

Druum (300m)

R du Vieux Marché aux Grains

Cantillon Brewery (1km)

R Pletinckx

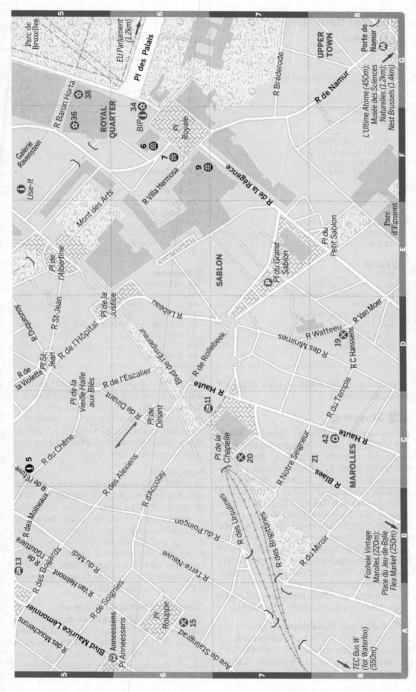

Central Brussels

walk over a railway bridge. A train simulator is an added bonus.

🛏 Sleeping

Hostel-wise, HI-affiliated **Hostel Bruegel** (📞02-511 04 36; www.jeugdherbergen.be/en/brussels; Rue du St-Esprit 2; dm/tw adult €23.90/64, youth €21.60/60; ⊗lockout 10am-2pm, curfew 1am-7am; ⊜@🛜; ⓂLouise) is helpfully central if rather institutional, while **Centre van Gogh** (📞02-217 01 58; www.chab.be; Rue Traversière 8; dm €22-26, s/tw/tr €35/60/90; @🛜; ⓂBotanique) has a hip lobby bar but less glamrous rooms (plus a 35-year-old upper age limit). A good network of B&Bs and guesthouses offer fine mid-budget alternatives. With much of Brussels' upper-market accommodation scene aimed squarely at business travellers, many top-end hotels drop their rates dramatically at weekends.

Villa Botanique Guesthouse   GUESTHOUSE €
(📞0496 59 93 79; http://villabotaniqueguesthouse.be; Chaussée de Haecht 31; dm/d €30/€60; 🛜; ⓂBotanique) This idiosyncratic, warmly friendly venture is housed in an impressive 1830s mansion near the botanical gardens and has a mix of dorms and private rooms. Guests connect with each other over a simple breakfast (included in the price) at a long table in the dining room. A kitchen in which guests can self-cater overlooks a spacious communal garden.

Train Hostel   HOSTEL €
(📞02-808 61 76; www.trainhostel.be/en; Ave Georges Rodenbach 6; dm/d/ste €18/45/129; 🛜; 🚌58, 58, 🚋7, 92, 🚉Schaerbeek) Anyone hankering for the days of interrailing should check in to the family-friendly Train Hostel, where you sleep in real old sleeper carriages, albeit restored and cosy ones. The dorms have bunk beds, and there is a spacious suite, as well as train-themed apartments nearby. Breakfast is €8, sleeping bag rental €15.

Chambres d'Hôtes du Vaudeville   B&B €€
(📞0484 59 46 69; www.theatreduvaudeville.be; Galerie de la Reine 11; d from €120; 🛜; 🚉Bruxelles Central) 🍃 This classy B&B has an incredible location right within the gorgeous (if reverberant) Galeries St-Hubert (p110). Delecta-

ble decor styles include African, modernist and 'Madame Loulou' (with 1920s nude sketches). Larger front rooms have claw-foot bathtubs and *galerie* views, but can be noisy with clatter that continues all night. Get keys via the art deco–influenced Café du Vaudeville, where breakfast is included.

Druum
B&B €€

(☎ 0472 05 42 40; www.druum.be; Rue du Houblon 63; s/d €105/115; ☎; ⬛51) Brussels' most stylish B&B appeared after the owners gave artists carte blanche to rework the six bedrooms. Now this former pipe factory is a quirky homage to apartment-style living with incredible one-offs like a gigantic concrete bed for four and the cassette tapes of former studio recordings found in the stripped-back HS63 room.

La Casa-BXL
B&B €€

(☎ 0475 29 07 21; www.downtownbxl.com; Rue du Marché au Charbon 16; d €109-119; ⬛Anneessens) Three B&B rooms are decked out in Moroccan-Asian style in a quiet but central location.

Nest Brussels
B&B €€

(☎ 0488 38 80 29; http://bb-the-nest.hotelsbrussels.net/en; Rue Wayenberg 24; d €80-110; ☎; ⬛38, ⬛Porte de Namur) This beautifully tasteful B&B has subtly coloured Turkish carpets, ikat cushions and Moroccan tiles. Run by a young family, it offers great value in the EU district, and a personal atmosphere. Three rooms; a simple breakfast is provided.

Hôtel Métropole
HOTEL €€€

(☎ 02-217 23 00, reservations 02-214 24 24; www.metropolehotel.com; Place de Brouckère 31; d €170-350, weekend rates from €130; ⬛🌀☎; ⬛De Brouckère) This 1895 showpiece has a jaw-droppingly sumptuous French Renaissance–style foyer with marble walls, coffered ceiling and beautifully etched stained-glass back windows. The *café* is indulgent and the bar (with frequent live music) features recently 'rediscovered' murals by a student of Horta. One of the lifts is an 1895 original.

✕ Eating

The central area is ideal for classic bar-cafés and good Asian places, while in Ste-Catherine you'll find classy seafood restaurants along with ever-popular fishmonger takeaway-window **Mer du Nord** (Noordzee; www.vishandel noordzee.be; Rue Ste-Catherine 45; items from €7; ☺8am-6pm Tue-Fri, to 5pm Sat; ⬛Ste-Catherine) and enticing 1902 cheese shop **Cremerie de Linkebeek** (☎ 02-512 35 10; Rue du Vieux Marché aux Grains 4; items from €5; ☺9am-3pm Mon, to 6pm Tue-Sat; ⬛Ste-Catherine). There are delightful chocolate-shop cafes around the Sablon and some quirky dining choices in the Marolles. Excellent neighbourhood restaurants like **L'Ultime Atome** (☎ 02-513 13 67; www.ultimeatome.be; Rue St-Boniface 14; mains €11-19; ☺8.30am-1am Mon-Fri, 10am-1am Sat & Sun; ⬛Porte de Namur) abound in Ixelles, though that's a little off the main tourist circuit. For the very finest restaurants like **Comme Chez Soi** (www.commechezsoi.be; Place Rouppe 23; mains from €49; ☺7-9pm Tue & Wed, noon-1.30pm & 7-9pm Thu-Sat; ⬛Anneessens), you'll generally need to book months in advance.

Arcadi
BRASSERIE €

(☎ 02-511 33 43; www.arcadicafe.be; Rue d'Arenberg 1b; mains €10-15; ☺8am-11.45pm Tue-Fri, from 7.30am Sat, from 9am Sun; ⬛Gare Centrale) The jars of preserves, beautiful cakes and fruit tarts at this classic and charming bistro entice plenty of Brussels residents, as do well-priced meals such as lasagne and steak, all served nonstop by courteous staff. With a nice location on the edge of the Galeries St-Hubert, this is a great spot for an indulgent, creamy hot chocolate.

Le Perroquet
CAFE €

(☎ 02-512 99 22; Rue Watteeu 31; light meals €9-15; ☺noon-11.30pm; ⬛Porte de Namur) Perfect for a drink, but also good for a simple bite (think salads and variations on croque-monsieurs), this art nouveau cafe with its stained glass, marble tables and timber panelling is an atmospheric, inexpensive stop in an area that's light on such places. Popular with expats.

MOK
VEGETARIAN €

(☎ 02-513 57 87; www.mokcoffee.be; Rue Antoine Dansaert 196; mains €10-20; ☺8.30am-6pm Mon-Fri, from 10am Sat & Sun; ✎; ⬛Comte de Flandre) MOK serves some of the capital's best coffee and offers a wide range of vegan-inspired recipes prepared by Josefien Smets – think crispy tofu and pickled cucumber sandwiches or the legendary avocado toast. A big picture window looks out onto Rue Dansaert.

Dandoy
BAKERY €

(☎ 02-511 03 26; www.maisondandoy.com; Rue au Beurre 31; snacks from €6; ☺9.30am-7pm Mon-Sat, from 10.30am Sun; ⬛Bourse) Established in 1829, Brussels' best-known *biscuiterie* has five local branches, this one with an attached tearoom. The chocolate for Dandoy's choc-dipped biscuits is handmade by Laurent Gerbaud.

BOURSE CAFE CLASSICS

Many of Brussels' most historic drinking holes are within stumbling distance of the Bourse, Brussels' classically columned stock exchange building. Don't miss **Le Cirio** (☑ 02-512 13 95; Rue de la Bourse 18; ☺ 10am-midnight; 🚇 Bourse), a sumptuous yet affordable 1866 marvel full of polished brasswork serving great-value pub meals. Three more classics are hidden up shoulder-wide alleys: the medieval yet unpretentious **A l'Imaige de Nostre-Dame** (Rue du Marché aux Herbes 8; ☺ noon-midnight Mon-Fri, 3pm-1am Sat, 4-10.30pm Sun; 🚇 Bourse); the 1695 Rubenseque **Au Bon Vieux Temps** (☑ 02-217 26 26; Impasse St-Nicolas; ☺ 11am-midnight; 🚇 Bourse), which sometimes stocks ultra-rare Westvleteren beers; and lambic specialist **À la Bécasse** (☑ 02-511 00 06; www.alabecasse.com; Rue de Tabora 11; ☺ 11am-midnight, to 1am Fri & Sat; Ⓜ Gare Centrale) with its vaguely Puritanical rows of wooden tables.

Henri
FUSION €€

(☑ 02-218 00 08; www.restohenri.be; Rue de Flandre 113; mains €17-24; ☺ noon-2pm Tue-Fri & 6-10pm Tue-Sat; Ⓜ Ste-Catherine) In an airy white space on this street to watch, Henri concocts tangy fusion dishes such as tuna with ginger, soy and lime, artichokes with scampi, lime and olive tapenade, or Argentine fillet steak in parsley. It has an astutely curated wine list and staff who know their stuff.

Les Brigittines
FRENCH, BELGIAN €€

(☑ 02-512 68 91; www.lesbrigittines.com; Place de la Chapelle 5; mains €16-24; ☺ noon-2.30pm & 7-10.30pm Mon-Fri, to 11pm Sat; 🖥; Ⓜ Louise) Offering grown-up eating in a muted belle époque dining room, Les Brigittines dishes up traditional French and Belgian food. Its classic (and very meaty) dishes include veal cheek, pigs' trotters and steak tartare. Staff are knowledgeable about local beer and artisanal wines, and can advise on pairing these with your food.

Drinking & Nightlife

In most cities, tourists stop in at cafes in between visiting the sights. Here the cafés are the sights; visiting a museum just gives your liver necessary respite. Beer in multitudinous variety is the main draw.

On the Grand Place itself, 300-year-old gems like **Le Roy d'Espagne** (☑ 02-513 08 07; www.roydespagne.be; Grand Place 1; ☺ 9.30am-1am; Ⓜ Gare Centrale) and **Chaloupe d'Or** (☑ 02-511 41 61; https://chaloupedor.be/en; Grand Place 24; ☺ 11am-1am; Ⓜ Gare Centrale) are magnificent if predictably pricey. It's just a short stumble to the 'Bourse Classics', to **Délirium** (www.deliriumcafe.be; Impasse de la Fidélité 4a; ☺ 10am-4am Mon-Sat, to 2am Sun; Ⓜ Gare Centrale) for an astonishing brew variety with a party atmosphere, to **Cercle des Voyageurs** (☑ 02-514 39 49; www.lecercledesvoyageurs.com; Rue des Grands Carmes 18; mains €15-21; ☺ 11am-midnight; 🖥; 🚇 Bourse, Anneessens) to sit in settees reading travel books, or to **Celtica** (www.celticpubs.com/celtica; Rue de Marché aux Poulets 55; 🚇 Bourse) if you just want cheep booze (and maybe a dance). In Ste-Catherine, meet the locals at **Monk** (☑ 02-511 75 11; www.monk.be; Rue Ste-Catherine 42; ☺ 11am-2am Mon-Sat, from 2pm Sun; Ⓜ Ste-Catherine), hit **BarBeton** (☑ 02-513 83 63; www.barbeton.be; Rue Antoine Dansaert 114; ☺ 10am-midnight; 🖥; Ⓜ Ste-Catherine) or **Walvis** (☑ 02-219 95 32; www.cafewalvis.be; Rue Antoine Dansaert; ☺ 11am-2am Mon-Thu & Sun, to 4am Fri & Sat; 🖥; Ⓜ Ste-Catherine) for DJ-led hipster minimalism, and **Brussels Beer Project** (☑ 02-502 28 56; www.beerproject.be; Rue Antoine Dansaert 188; ☺ 2-10pm Thu-Sat; 🚇 51) for inventive new microbrewed beers.

Toone
BAR

(Rue du Marche des Herbes 66; beer from €2.50; ☺ noon-midnight Tue-Sun; Ⓜ Gare Centrale) At the home to Brussels' classic **puppet theatre** (☑ 02-511 71 37; www.toone.be; adult/child €10/7; ☺ typically 8.30pm Thu & 4pm Sat), this irresistibly quaint and cosy timber-framed bar serves beers and basic snacks.

Goupil le Fol
BAR

(☑ 02-511 13 96; www.goupillefol.com; Rue de la Violette 22; ☺ 4pm-2am; Ⓜ Gare Centrale) Overwhelming weirdness hits you as you acid-trip your way through this sensory overload of rambling passageways, ragged old sofas and inexplicable beverages mostly based on madly fruit-flavoured wines (no beer is served). Unmissable.

☆ Entertainment

Home to the National Orchestra, **BOZAR** (www.bozar.be; Palais des Beaux-Arts, Rue Ravenstein 23; Ⓜ Gare Centrale) is a Horta-designed mega-venue with splendid acoustics incorporating **Cinematek** (☏02-507 83 70; www.cinematheque.be) where silent movies are screened with live piano accompaniment. Intimate jazz venues include **Sounds** (☏02-512 92 50; www.soundsjazzclub.be; Rue de la Tulipe 28; ☉8pm-4am Mon-Sat; Ⓜ Porte de Namur), **Music Village** (☏02-513 13 45; www.themusicvillage.com; Rue des Pierres 50; cover €7.50-20; ☉from 7.30pm Wed-Sat; ⓂBourse) and **L'Archiduc** (☏02-512 0652; www.archiduc.net; Rue Antoine Dansaert 6; ☉4pm-5am; ⓂBourse) which is free at 5pm on Saturdays...if you can get in. **Art Base** (☏02-217 29 20; www.art-base.be; Rue des Sables 29; ☉Fri & Sat; Ⓜ Rogier) hosts salon-style gigs, from classical to Greek *rebetiko* to Indian classical while brassy **Cabaret Mademoiselle** (☏0474 58 57 61; www.cabaretmademoiselle.be; Rue du Marché au Charbon 53; ☉7pm-late Wed-Sat; ⓂBourse) 𝗙𝗥𝗘𝗘 is a burlesque cabaret combining drag, circus, comedy and good beer. For extensive listings check www.agenda.be, www.thebulletin.be and http://thewordmagazine.com/neighbourhood-life. Discounted tickets for arts, music and cinema are sold by **Arsène50** (www.arsene50.be; Rue Royale 2; ☉12.30-5pm; Ⓜ Parc).

Shopping

Supermarkets stock many of the 'standard' Belgian beers, but for rare brews try well-stocked **de Biertempel** (☏02-502 19 06; http://biertempel.wixsite.com/debiertempel; Rue du Marché aux Herbes 56b; ☉9.30am-7pm; ⓂBourse). Gorgeous chocolate boutiques are dotted around the Sablon and in the magical Galleries-St Hubert (p110) shopping passage, though for non conoisseurs, pralines from the ubiquitous Leonidas chain can taste almost as good for around a third of the price. Brussels is also great for fashion, from funky vintage shops like **Foxhole Vintage Marolles** (☏0477 20 53 36; https://foxholevintage.com; Rue des Renards 6; ☉10am-6.30pm Thu-Sun; ⓂLouise) to chic boutiques on Ave Louise and alternative designer outlets around Rue Antoine Dansaert, notably **Stijl** (☏02-512 03 13; www.stijl.be; Rue Antoine Dansaert 74; ☉10.30am-6.30pm Mon-Sat; ⓂSte-Catherine) and **ICON** (☏02-502 71 51; www.icon-shop.be; Place du Nouveau Marché aux Grains 5; ☉10.30am-6.30pm Mon-Sat; ⓂDansaert).

For unique if downmarket shopping experiences, visit the **Jeu-de-Balle Flea Market** (www.marcheauxpuces.be; Place du Jeu-de-Balle; ☉6am-2pm Mon-Fri, to 3pm Sat & Sun; Ⓜ Porte de Hal, ⓂLemonnier) and the vast, multicultural Sunday morning market around the **Gare du Midi**.

Manufacture
Belge de Dentelles ARTS & CRAFTS
(☏02-511 44 77; www.mbd.be; Galerie de la Reine 6-8; ☉9.30am-6pm Mon-Sat, 10am-4pm Sun; Ⓜ Gare Centrale) Excellent stock of antique lace, and staff who love the stuff.

Tropismes BOOKS
(☏02-512 88 52; http://tropismes.com; Galerie des Princes 11; ☉11am-6.30pm Mon, 10am-6.30pm Tue-Thu, 10am-7.30pm Fri, 10.30am-7pm Sat,

BELGIUM & LUXEMBOURG BRUSSELS

COMIC-STRIP CULTURE

In Belgium, comic strips *(bandes dessinées)* are revered as the 'ninth art'. Dozens of cartoon murals enliven Brussels buildings and serious comic fans might enjoy Brussels' comprehensive **Centre Belge de la Bande Dessinée** (Belgian Comic Strip Centre; ☏02-219 19 80; www.comicscenter.net; Rue des Sables 20; adult/concession €10/7; ☉10am-6pm; Ⓜ Rogier) in a distinctive Horta-designed art nouveau building.

For an immersive Tintin experience, **Musée Hergé** (☏010-48 84 21; www.museeherge.com; Rue du Labrador 26; adult/child €9.50/5; ☉10.30am-5.30pm Tue-Fri, 10am-6pm Sat & Sun) is highly recommended, but it's in Louvain-la-Neuve, a €5.50 train ride from Brussels taking around 50 minutes including a quick change at Ottignies.

Comic-book shops include **Brüsel** (www.brusel.com; Blvd Anspach 100; ☉10.30am-6.30pm Mon-Sat, from noon Sun; ⓂBourse) and **Multi-BD** (☏02-513 72 35; http://bulledor.blogspot.com; Blvd Anspach 122-124; ☉10.30am-7pm Mon-Sat, 12.30-6.30pm Sun; ⓂBourse).

WORTH A TRIP

WATERLOO

Tourists have been swarming to Waterloo ever since Napoleon's 1815 defeat, a pivotal event in European history. Inaugurated for the 2015 bicentenary, **Memorial 1815** (☑ 02-385 19 12; www.waterloo1815.be; Rte du Lion, Hameau du Lion; adult/child €16/13, with Wellington & Napoleon HQ museums €20/16; ☉ 9.30am-6.30pm Apr-Sep, to 5.30pm Oct-Mar) is a showpiece underground museum and visitor centre at the main battlefield area (known as Hameau du Lion). There's a detailed audio guide and some enjoyable technological effects. The climax is an impressive 3D film that sticks you right into the middle of the cavalry charges. It includes admission to various other battlefield attractions, including the **Butte du Lion**, a lion-topped memorial hill from which you can survey the terrain, and the restored **Hougoumont farmhouse** that played a key part in the battle.

Hameau du Lion is 5km south of Waterloo town. Rather than the train, use twice-hourly TEC bus W from Ave Fonsny outside Bruxelles-Midi station (€3.50, one hour).

1.30-6.30pm Sun; Ⓜ Gare Centrale) With its gold-wreath-encircled columns and ornate gilded ceiling, this is about the prettiest bookshop you could imagine. The literary connections are hot too: this is where the exiled Victor Hugo visited his lover/assistant Juliette Drouet. Some titles are in English.

Belge une fois ARTS & CRAFTS
(☑ 02-503 85 41; www.belgeunefois.com; Rue Haute 89; ☉ 11am-6pm Wed-Sat, 1-6pm Sun; 🚌 92, 93) Belge une fois is a concept store selling creations by the eponymous designers' collective. It also sells artefacts, accessories and light fixtures by other Belgian designers. Expect everything from simple postcards and concrete cactus holders to large photographic prints.

ℹ Information

Use-It (☑ 02-218 39 06; www.brussels.use-it. travel; Galerie Ravenstein 17; ☉ 10am-6pm Mon-Sat; 🛜; Ⓜ Gare Central) Youth-oriented office with a list of nightly events, great guide-maps and a free city tour.

Visit.Brussels (☑ 02-513 89 40; www.visit. brussels; Hôtel de Ville, Grand Place; ☉ 9am-6pm; 🚇 Bourse) High-quality information on the main square, a booth at Gare du Midi and an office on Rue Royale, where you'll also find **BIP** (☑ 02-563 63 99; http://bip.brussels/en; Rue Royale 2-4; ☉ 9.30am-5.30pm Mon-Fri, 10am-6pm Sat & Sun; Ⓜ Parc) and the **Arsène50** desk for discounted events tickets.

ℹ Getting There & Away

BUS

Eurolines (☑ 02-274 13 50; www.eurolines.be; Rue du Progrès 80; 🚇 Gare du Nord) and **Flix-Bus** (www.flixbus.co.uk) operate international services to London, Amsterdam, Paris and

beyond, mostly starting from Bruxelles-Nord. Pre-book online.

TEC Bus W for Waterloo starts from Ave Fosny outside Buxelles-Midi station.

TRAIN

Bruxelles-Midi (Gare du Midi; luggage office per day per article €4, luggage lockers per 24hr small/large €3/4; ☉ luggage office 6am-9pm; Ⓜ Gare du Midi, 🚊 Bruxelles-Midi) is the only stop for Eurostar, TGV and Thalys high-speed international trains (prebooking compulsory). Other mainline trains also stop at more convenient **Bruxelles-Central** (Gare Centrale). For enquiries consult www.belgiantrain.be/en.

ℹ Getting Around

TO/FROM BRUSSELS AIRPORT

Brussels Airport (https://www.brussels airport.be/en) is 14km northeast of Brussels.

Airport City Express (tickets €9; ☉ 5.30am-12.20am) trains (€10) run four times hourly to the city's three main train stations, Bruxelles-Nord (15 minutes), Bruxelles-Central (20 minutes) and Bruxelles-Midi (25 minutes). Taxis are a very bad idea in rush-hour traffic.

TO/FROM CHARLEROI AIRPORT

Misleadingly known as 'Brussels South', **Charleroi Airport** (www.brussels-charleroi-airport.com) is 46km southeast of the city. It's mainly used by budget airlines, including Ryanair and WizzAir.

Buses to Brussels Gare du Midi leave around half an hour after flight arrivals (€14.20/28.40 one way/return, 1½ hours). Bus-train combination tickets via Charleroi station are also worth considering.

BICYCLE

Villo! (☑ 078-05 11 10; http://en.villo.be; subscription day/week €1.60/8.20) is a system of 180 automated stations for short-term bicycle rental (under 30/30/60/90/120 minutes free/€0.50/1/1.50/2) with a subscription (€1.60/8.20/32.60 day/week/year), credit or debit-card essential. Read instructions carefully.

For longer bike hires, try **FietsPunt/PointVelo** (☑ 02-513 04 09; www.cyclo.org; Carrefour de l'Europe 2; per day/week €15/45; ☺7am-7pm Mon-Fri; ⓡ Bruxelles-Central), on the left as you leave Bruxelles-Central station via the day-time-only Madeleine exit. **Maison des Cyclistes** (☑ 02-502 73 55; www.provelo.be; Rue de Londres 15; ☺noon-6pm Mon-Fri, 10am-6pm Sat & Sun Apr-Oct; Ⓜ Trone) also offers bike tours.

PUBLIC TRANSPORT
STIB/MIVB (☑ 02-515 20 00; www.stib.be; ☺10am-6pm Mon-Sat) tickets are sold at metro stations, kiosks, newsagents and on buses and trams. Single-/five-/10-journey tickets cost €2.10/8/14 including transfers, valid for an hour from mandatory validation. Unlimited one-day passes cost €6. Airport buses are excluded. Slightly higher 'jump' fares apply if you want to connect to city routes operated by De Lijn (Flanders bus), TEC (Wallonia bus) or SNCB/NMBS (rail). Children under six travel free.

FLANDERS

Bruges
☑ 050 / POP 118,284

If you set out to design a fairy-tale medieval town, it would be hard to improve on central Bruges (Brugge in Dutch). Picturesque cobbled lanes and dreamy canals link photogenic squares lined with soaring towers, historical churches and photogenic old whitewashed almshouses. Of course the secret is already out and during the busy summer months you'll be sharing Bruges' with constant streams of tourists. If you can stand the cold, come midweek in the depths of winter (except Christmas time) to avoid the crowds. And do stay overnight to enjoy the city's stunning nocturnal floodlighting.

☉ Sights

Old-town Bruges is an ambler's dream. At its heart, **Markt** is the old market square, lined with pavement cafes beneath step-gabled facades. The buildings aren't always quite as medieval as they look, but together they create a fabulous scene, and soaring above is the **Belfort** (Belfry; ☑ 050-44 87 43; www.visit bruges.be/nl/belfort; Markt 7; adult/child €12/10;

☺9.30am-6pm), Belgium's most famous belfry. Its iconic octagonal tower is arguably better appreciated from afar than by climbing the 366 claustrophobic steps to the top. Immediately east, **Burg** is a less theatrical but still enchanting square that's been Bruges' administrative centre for centuries and retains several unmissable buildings. To escape the crowds, explore east of pretty Jan van Eykplein and seek out city gateways and windmills around the oval-shaped moat.

Groeningemuseum GALLERY
(☑ 050-44 87 11; www.visitbruges.be/en/groeninge museum-groeninge-museum; Dijver 12; adult/concession/under 18yr €12/10/free; ☺9.30am-5pm Tue-Sun) Bruges' most celebrated art gallery boasts an astonishingly rich collection that's strong in superb Flemish Primitive and Renaissance works, depicting the conspicuous wealth of the city with glittering realistic artistry. Meditative works include Jan Van Eyck's radiant masterpiece *Madonna with Canon Van der Paele* (1436) and the *Madonna Crowned by Angels* (1482) by the Master of the Embroidered Foliage, where the rich fabric of the Madonna's robe meets the 'real' foliage at her feet with exquisite detail.

Museum Sint-Janshospitaal MUSEUM
(Memlingmuseum; ☑ 050-44 87 43; www.visit bruges.be/en/sint-janshospitaal-saint-johns-hospi tal; Mariastraat 38; adult/concession/under 18yr €12/10/free; ☺9.30am-5pm Tue-Sun) In the restored chapel of a 12th-century hospital building with superb timber beamwork, this museum shows various torturous-looking medical implements, hospital sedan chairs and a gruesome 1679 painting of an anatomy class. But it's much better known for

LOCAL KNOWLEDGE
WHAT'S A BEGIJNHOF?
Usually enclosed around a central garden, a *begijnhof* (*béguinage* in French) is a pretty cluster of historic houses originally built to house lay sisters. The idea originated in the 12th century when many such women were left widowed by their crusader-knight husbands. Today 14 of Flanders' historic *begijnhoven* have been declared Unesco World Heritage Sites with great examples at Diest, Lier, Turnhout, Kortrijk and Bruges, which also has dozens of smaller *godshuizen* (almshouses).

Bruges

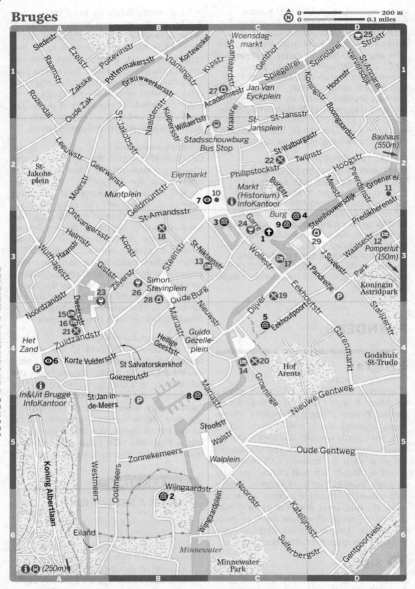

its six masterpieces by 15th-century artist Hans Memling, including the enchanting reliquary of St Ursula. This gilded oak reliquary looks like a miniature Gothic cathedral, painted with scenes from the life of St Ursula, including highly realistic Cologne cityscapes.

Begijnhof HISTORIC BUILDING

(Wijngaardstraat; ⏰ 6.30am-6.30pm) **FREE** Bruges' delightful *begijnhof* dates from the 13th century. Despite the hordes of summer tourists, it remains a remarkably tranquil haven. Outside the 1776 gateway bridge lies a tempting (if predictably tourist-priced) array of

Bruges

◉ Sights
1 Basiliek van het Heilig Bloed............... C3
2 Begijnhof B6
3 Belfort C3
4 Brugse Vrije... C3
5 Groeningemuseum C4
6 Het Zand Square A4
7 Markt.. B2
8 Museum Sint-Janshospitaal............... B5
9 Stadhuis C3

☺ Activities, Courses & Tours
10 Legends Walking Tours...................... C2
11 Quasimundo D2

⬚ Sleeping
12 B&B Dieltiens.................................... D3
13 B&B SintNik B3
14 Guesthouse Nuit Blanche C4
15 Hotel Bla Bla A4
16 Passage Bruges.................................. A4
17 Relais Bourgondisch Cruyce C3

✖ Eating
18 De Stove B3
19 Den Dyver C3
20 Den Gouden Harynck C4
21 Gran Kaffee De Passage..................... A4
22 Lieven... C2

◉ Drinking & Nightlife
23 Cafédraal A3
24 De Garre C3
25 Herberg Vlissinghe............................. D1
26 't Brugs Beertje.................................. B3

⬚ Shopping
27 Bacchus Cornelius C1
28 Chocolate Line................................... B3
29 Vismarkt D3

terraced restaurants, lace shops and waffle peddlers.

The classic way to arrive here from Markt is by horse-carriage, but walking allows you to seek out lesser-known almshouses en route. Don't miss a romantic stroll in the **Minnewater Park** around the 'Lake of Love'.

☞ Tours

The city's must-do activity is a 30-minute **canal-boat tour** (adult/child €8/4; ☺10am–6pm Mar–mid-Nov). Boats depart roughly every 20 minutes from various jetties south of the Burg. Each operator does essentially the same loop for the same price, so just pick the shortest queue. **Legends** (☏0472 26 87 15; www.legendstours.be/walking-tours-bruges; Markt) **FREE** conducts wildly popular 'free'

(ie tips-based) walking tours – book your slot online. **Quasimundo** (☏050-33 07 75; www.quasimundo.eu; Predikherenstraat 28; adult/student €28/26; ☺Mar-Oct) leads cycle tours into the countryside around Bruges, with bike rental included.

⬚ Sleeping

Bauhaus HOSTEL €
(St Christopher's Hostel; ☏050-34 10 93; www.bauhaus.be; Langestraat 133-137; dm/d from €21/39; @☎) One of Belgium's most popular hangouts for young travellers, this backpacker village incorporates a hostel, apartments, a nightclub, internet cafe and a little chill-out room that's well hidden behind the reception and laundrette section at Langestraat 145. Simple and slightly cramped dorms are operated with key cards; hotel-section double rooms have private shower cubicles. Bike hire is also available.

B&B Dieltiens B&B €€
(☏050-33 42 94; www.bedandbreakfastbruges.be; Waalsestraat 40; s/d/tr from €70/80/90; ☎) Old and new art fills this lovingly restored classical mansion, which remains an appealing real home run by charming musician hosts. Superbly central yet quiet. It also operates a holiday flat (from €75 per night) nearby in a 17th-century house.

Hotel Bla Bla HOTEL €€
(☏050-33 90 14; www.hotelblabla.com; Dweersstraat 24; s/d incl breakfast from €85/95; ☎) A shuttered and step-gabled building given an elegant makeover, with parquet floors, modern artworks and soothingly pale rooms. Excellent buffet breakfast.

B&B SintNik B&B €€
(☏050-61 03 08; www.sintnik.be; St-Niklaasstraat 18; s/d from €125/135; ☎) Room 1 has a clawfoot bath and antique glass panel, but it's the other two rooms' remarkable Pisa-like belfry views that make this welcoming B&B so special and popular.

★ Guesthouse Nuit Blanche B&B €€€
(☏0494 40 04 47; www.bb-nuitblanche.com; Groeninge 2; d from €185; P❋☎) Pay what you like, nowhere else in Bruges can get you a more romantic location than this fabulous B&B, which started life as a 15th-century tannery. It oozes history, retaining original Gothic fireplaces, stained-glass roundels and some historical furniture, while bathrooms and beds are luxury-hotel standard.

Relais Bourgondisch Cruyce
BOUTIQUE HOTEL €€€

(☑ 050-33 79 26; www.relaisbourgondischcruyce. be; Wollestraat 41-47; d from €245; P ❄ 🛜) This luxurious little boutique hotel occupies a part-timbered medieval house that's been tastefully updated and graced with art, antiques, Persian carpets and fresh orchids. A special delight is relaxing in the canal-side lounge while envious tourists cruise past on their barge tours.

✖ Eating

De Stove
INTERNATIONAL €€

(☑ 050-33 78 35; www.restaurantdestove.be; Kleine St-Amandsstraat 4; mains €19-36, menu with/without wine €69/51; ⊙ 7-9pm Fri-Tue, noon-1.30pm Sun) Having just 20 seats keeps this gem intimate. Fish caught daily is the house speciality, but the monthly changing menu also includes the likes of wild boar fillet on oyster mushrooms. Everything, from the bread to the ice cream, is homemade. Despite perennially rave reviews, this calm one-room family restaurant remains friendly, reliable and inventive, without a hint of tourist-tweeness.

Lieven
BELGIAN €€

(☑ 050-68 09 75; www.etenbijlieven.be; Philipstockstraat 45; mains €22-34; ⊙ noon-10pm Tue-Sun) You'll need to book ahead for a table at this extremely popular, excellent-value Belgian bistro. It works wonders with local ingredients, and is recognised by its peers from around the country. Simple food done well in a trendy but relaxed environment.

Gran Kaffee De Passage
BISTRO €€

(☑ 050-34 02 32; www.passagebruges.com; Dweersstraat 26-28; mains €10-18; ⊙ 5-11pm Tue-Thu & Sun, noon-11pm Fri & Sat) A mix of regulars and travellers staying at the adjoining hostel (d/tr from €64/98; 🛜) give this candlelit, alternative art deco–style bistro one of the best atmospheres in town. Its menu of hearty traditional dishes, such as *stoverij* (local meat in beer sauce), as well as filling tofu creations, is a bargain.

Den Dyver
BELGIAN €€€

(☑ 050-33 60 69; www.dyver.be; Dijver 5; mains €23-47, tasting menu €45; ⊙ noon-2pm & 6.30-9.30pm Fri-Mon) Den Dyver is a pioneer of fine beer dining where you match the brew you drink with the one the chef used to create the sauce on your plate. This is no pub: beers come in wine glasses served on starched tablecloths in an atmosphere of Burgundian grandeur. The lunch menu includes an *amuse-bouche*, nibbles and coffee.

Den Gouden Harynck
INTERNATIONAL €€€

(☑ 050-33 76 37; www.goudenharynck.be; Groeninge 25; set lunch menu €45, midweek dinner €65, surprise menu €95; ⊙ noon-1.30pm & 7-8.30pm Tue-Fri, 7-8.30pm Sat) Behind an ivy-clad facade, this uncluttered Michelin-starred restaurant garners consistent praise and won't hurt the purse quite as severely as some better-known

BRUGES' BURG

The centrepiece of this tree-shaded central square is Bruges' beautiful 1420 city hall, the **Stadhuis** (City Hall; ☑ 050-44 87 43; www.visitbruges.be/en/stadhuis-city-hall; Burg 12; adult/concession/under 18yr €6/5/free; ⊙ 9.30am-5pm). Its exterior is fancifully smothered with statues of the counts and countesses of Flanders – convincing replicas of originals that were torn down in 1792 by French soldiers. Inside, the highlight is the dazzling **Gotische Zaal** (Gothic Hall) with its polychrome ceiling, hanging vaults and romantic murals. Entrance also includes admission to parts of the adjacent **Brugse Vrije** (Liberty of Bruges; ☑ 050-44 87 11; Burg 11a; €6; ⊙ 9.30am-noon & 1.30-5pm) where the Renaissancezaal has a remarkable 1531 carved chimneypiece.

The western end of the stadhuis morphs into the **Basiliek van het Heilig Bloed** (Basilica of the Holy Blood; ☑ 050-33 67 92; www.holyblood.com; Burg 13; €2; ⊙ 9.30am-noon & 2-5pm, closed Wed afternoons mid-Nov–Mar), a small basilica that takes its name from a phial supposedly containing a few drops of Christ's blood, brought here after the 12th-century Crusades. The right-hand door leads upstairs to a colourfully adorned chapel where the relic is hidden behind a flamboyant silver tabernacle and is brought out for pious veneration at 2pm daily.

BELGIUM & LUXEMBOURG BRUGES

competitors. Its lovely location is both central and secluded. Exquisite dishes might include noisettes of venison topped with lardo and quince purée, or seed-crusted fillet of bream.

🍷 Drinking & Nightlife

Beer-specialist *cafés* include **'t Brugs Beertje** (☑ 050-33 96 16; www.brugsbeertje.be; Kemelstraat 5; ⊙ 4pm-midnight Mon, Thu & Sun, to 1am Fri & Sat) and alley-hidden **De Garre** (☑ 050-34 10 29; www.degarre.be; De Garre 1; ⊙ noon-midnight Sun-Thu, to 12.30am Fri, 11am-12.30am Sat) serving its own fabulous 11% Garre house brew. Old-world classic **Herberg Vlissinghe** (☑ 050-34 37 37; www.cafevlissinghe.be; Blekersstraat 2; ⊙ 11am-10pm Wed-Sat, to 7pm Sun) dates from 1515; local legend has it that Rubens once painted an imitation coin on the table here and then did a runner. Eiermarkt, just north of Markt, has many plain but lively bars, with DJs and seemingly endless happy hours. For cocktails try suavely classy **Cafédraal** (☑ 050-34 08 45; www.cafedraal.be; Zilverstraat 38; ⊙ 6pm-1am Tue-Thu, to 3am Fri & Sat).

🛍 Shopping

There are morning markets at **Markt** (Wednesday) and **Het Zand** (Saturday), plus a fish market at colonnaded **Vismarkt** (Fish Market; Vismarkt; ⊙ 7am-1pm Tue-Fri). Supermarkets stock standard beers (Leffe, Chimay etc), but for rare brews try **Bacchus Cornelius** (☑ 050-34 53 38; www.bacchuscornelius.com; Academiestraat 17; ⊙ 1-6.30pm). Of some 50 chocolate shops, **Chocolate Line** (☑ 050-82 01 26; www.thechocolateline.be; Simon Stevinplein 19; per kg €50; ⊙ 10am-6pm) is among the most experimental, though for great value, ubiquitous Leonidas can save you a packet.

ℹ Information

There are three main info locations in Bruges.

Tourist Information Counter (☑ 050-44 46 46; www.visitbruges.be; Stationsplein; ⊙ 10am-5pm Mon-Fri, to 2pm Sat & Sun)

Tourist Office (In&Uit Brugge) (☑ 050-44 46 46; www.visitbruges.be; Concertgebouw, 't Zand 34; ⊙ 10am-5pm Mon-Sat, 10am-2pm Sun)

Markt (Historium) InfoKantoor (☑ 050-44 46 46; Markt 1; ⊙ 10am-5pm)

They, and hostels, generally stock the excellent free *Use-it* map/guide (www.use-it.be), also available online.

WORTH A TRIP

DAMME

Charming Damme village is little more than a single street plus a historic main square sporting a fine Gothic stadhuis. It's 5km from Bruges via a perfectly straight canal, with a cycleway on one side and a road on the other. A classic (if somewhat over-rated) way to arrive is using paddle-steamer **Lamme Goedzak** (☑ 050-28 86 10; www.bootdamme-brugge.be; Noorweegse Kaai 31; adult/child one way €8.50/6, return €10.50/9.50; ⊙ 10am-5pm Easter–mid-Oct), taking a dawdling 35 minutes from Bruges' Noorweegse Kaai (every two hours). Cycling is arguably more enjoyable and in summer it's worth continuing beyond Damme to much quieter areas of very beautiful tree-lined canals.

ℹ Getting There & Around

Intercity trains and international bus services use Bruges central station, 1.5km south of the Markt – a lovely walk via Minnewater. Both **Eurolines** (www.eurolines.eu) and **Flixbus** (www.flixbus.co.uk) have overnight buses to London. Book online.

Trains run twice-hourly to Brussels (€14.50, one hour) via Ghent (€7, 23 minutes) and hourly to Antwerp (€15.40, 80 minutes). For Ypres (Ieper), take the train to Roeselare then bus 95 via Langemark or 94 via Passendale, Tyne Cot and Zonnebeke, all WWI-related sights that you're likely to want to see anyway.

City buses operate 5.30am to 11pm (€3/8 per one-hour ride/day pass). Services marked 'Centrum' run to Markt. For the station, the most central stop is **Stadsschouwburg** (Vlamingstraat 58).

Ypres

☑ 057 / POP 34,964

Only the hardest of hearts are unmoved by historic Ypres (Ieper in Dutch). In the Middle Ages it was an important cloth town ranking alongside Bruges and Ghent. In WWI some 300,000 Allied soldiers plus countless more civilians and German troops died in Flanders Fields, aka the 'Salient', a bow-shaped bulge that formed the front line around the town. Ypres remained unoccupied by German forces, but was utterly flattened by bombardment. After the war, the city's beautiful medieval core was convincingly rebuilt and the restored **Lakenhalle** is today one of the most spectacular buildings in Belgium.

Sights

Central Ypres

In Flanders Fields Museum MUSEUM
(☑ 057-23 92 20; www.inflandersfields.be; Grote Markt 34; adult/under 26yr/child €9/5/4; ⊘ 10am-6pm Apr–mid-Nov, to 5pm Tue-Sun mid-Nov–Mar) No museum gives a more balanced yet moving and user-friendly introduction to WWI history. It's a multisensory experience combining soundscapes, videos, well-chosen exhibits and interactive learning stations at which you 'become' a character and follow his or her progress through the wartime period. An electronic 'identity' bracelet activates certain displays.

Ramparts CWGC Cemetery CEMETERY
(Lille Gate Cemetery; Lille Gate) One of Ypres' most attractive military graveyards, this Commonwealth War Graves Commission site is found 1km south of the Grote Markt.

Ypres Salient

Flanders' WWI battlefields are famed for red poppies, both real and metaphorical. From 1914 the area suffered four years of brutal fighting in a muddy, bloody quagmire where the world first saw poison-gas attacks and as thousands of diggers valiantly tunnelled underground to dynamite enemy trenches.

Tourism here still revolves around widely spaced WWI cemeteries, memorials, bunkers

> **DON'T MISS**
>
> ### LAST POST
>
> A block east of Ypres central square lies a huge stone gateway called the **Menin Gate** (Menenpoort; Menenstraat). It's inscribed with 54,896 names: British and Commonwealth casualties of WWI whose bodies were never found. At 8pm daily, traffic through the gateway is halted while buglers sound the **Last Post** (www.lastpost.be; ⊘ 8pm) FREE in remembrance of the dead, a moving tradition that started in 1928. Every evening the scene is somewhat different, possibly accompanied by pipers, troops of cadets or maybe a military band.

and museums. The following are relatively accessible between Bruges and Ypres, all within 600m of Ypres–Roeselare bus routes 94 and 95, which run once or twice hourly on weekdays, and five times daily on weekends.

Having your own wheels makes visits much easier, or join the various half-day guided bus tours organised by **British Grenadier** (☑ 057-21 46 57; www.salienttours.be; Menenstraat 5; tours from €40; ⊘ 10am-1.30pm). The office is between the Grote Markt and Menin Gate in central Ypres.

**Memorial Museum
Passchendaele 1917** MUSEUM
(☑ 051-77 04 41; www.passchendaele.be; Berten Pilstraat 5A, Zonnebeke; €10.50; ⊘ 9am-6pm Feb–mid-Dec; ☐ 94) Within the grounds of Kasteelpark Zonnebeke you'll find this polished WWI museum charting local battle progressions with plenty of multilingual commentaries. The big attraction here is descending into its multiroom 'trench experience', with low-lit, wooden-clad subterranean bunk rooms and a soundtrack. Explanations are much more helpful here than in 'real' trenches elsewhere.

Tyne Cot CWGC Cemetary CEMETERY
(Vijfwegestraat, Zonnebeke; ⊘ 24hr, visitor centre 10am-6pm Feb-Nov; ☐ 94) Probably the most-visited Salient site, this is the world's biggest British Commonwealth war cemetery, with 11,956 graves. A huge semicircular wall commemorates another 34,857 lost-in-action soldiers whose names wouldn't fit on Ypres' Menin Gate. The name Tyne Cot was coined by the Northumberland Fusiliers who fancied that German bunkers on the hillside here looked like Tyneside cottages. Two such dumpy concrete bunkers sit amid the graves, with a third visible through the metal wreath beneath the white Cross of Sacrifice.

**Langemark Deutscher
Soldatenfriedhof** CEMETERY
(Klerkenstraat, Langemark) The Salient's largest German WWI cemetery is smaller than Tyne Cot but arguably more memorable, sited amid oak trees and trios of squat, mossy crosses. Some 44,000 corpses were grouped together here, up to 10 per granite grave slab; four eerie silhouette statues survey the site. Entering takes you through a black concrete tunnel that clanks and hisses with distant war sounds, while four short video montages commemorate the tragedy of war.

🛏 Sleeping & Eating

Ariane Hotel
HOTEL €€

(📞057-21 82 18; www.ariane.be; Slachthuisstraat 58; d from €129; P🛜) This peaceful, professionally managed large hotel has a designer feel to its rooms and popular restaurant. Wartime memorabilia dots the spacious common areas.

Main Street Hotel
GUESTHOUSE €€€

(📞057-46 96 33; www.mainstreet-hotel.be; Rijselstraat 136; d incl breakfast from €180; 🛜) Jumbling eccentricity with historical twists and luxurious comfort, this is a one-off that oozes character. The smallest room is designed like a mad professor's experiment. The breakfast room has a Tiffany glass ceiling.

De Ruyffelaer
FLEMISH €€

(📞057-36 60 06; www.deruyffelaer.be; Gustave de Stuersstraat 9; mains €15-26; ⏱11.30am-3.30pm Sun, 5.30-9.30pm Fri-Sun) Traditional local dishes are served in an adorable wood-panelled interior with old chequerboard floors and *brocante* (vintage) decor including dried flowers, old radios and antique biscuit tins.

ℹ Information

Tourist Office (📞057-23 92 20; www.toerismeieper.be; Grote Markt 34, Lakenhalle; ⏱9am-6pm Mon-Fri, 10am-6pm Sat & Sun Apr–mid-Nov, to 5pm mid-Nov–Mar) Has an extensive bookshop.

ℹ Getting There & Around

Buses depart from Ypres Station, 500m southwest of centre, and also pick up at the Grote Markt bus stop (check the direction carefully).

Trains run hourly to Brussels (€18.40, 1¾ hours) via Ghent and Kortrijk (30 minutes), where you could change for Bruges or Antwerp.

Bike hire is available from **Hotel Ambrosia** (📞057-36 63 66; www.ambrosiahotel.be; D'Hondtstraat 54; bike per day €15; ⏱7.30am-7.30pm).

Ghent
📞09 / POP 248,358

One of Europe's greatest hidden gems, Ghent (Gent in Dutch) is small enough to feel cosy but big enough to stay vibrant. There's a wealth of medieval and classical architecture here, contrasted by large post-industrial areas undergoing urban development, and with a lively student population to inject life. Magical canalside views from Korenmarkt and Graslei give Bruges a run for its money, there's an abundance of quirky bars, and Ghent has some of Belgium's most fascinating museums; altogether this is a city you really won't want to miss.

⊙ Sights

The Adoration of the Mystic Lamb GALLERY
(Het Lam Gods; 📞09-269 20 45; www.sintbaafskathedraal.be; St-Baafskathedraal, Sint-Baafsplein; adult/child/audioguide €4/1.50/1; ⏱9.30am-5pm Mon-Sat, 1-5pm Sun Apr-Oct, 10.30am-4pm Mon-Sat, 1-4pm Sun Nov-Mar) Art enthusiasts swarm the **Sint-Baafskathedraal** (⏱8.30am-6pm Mon-Sat, 10am-6pm Sun Apr-Oct, to 5pm Nov-Mar) **FREE** to glimpse *The Adoration of the Mystic Lamb* (De Aanbidding van het Lams God), a lavish representation of medieval religious thinking that is one of the earliest-known oil paintings. Completed in 1432, it was painted as an altarpiece by Flemish Primitive artists the Van Eyck brothers, and has 20 panels.

Gravensteen CASTLE
(📞09-225 93 06; https://gravensteen.stad.gent/en; St-Veerleplein 11; adult/concession/child €10/6/free; ⏱10am-6pm Apr-Oct, 9am-5pm Nov-Mar) Flanders' quintessential 12th-century stone castle comes complete with moat, turrets and arrow slits. It's all the more remarkable considering that during the 19th century the site was converted into a cotton mill. Meticulously restored since, the interior sports the odd suit of armour, a guillotine and torture devices. The relative lack of furnishings is compensated for by a handheld 45-minute movie guide, which sets a tongue-in-cheek historical costumed drama in the rooms, prison pit and battlements.

Belfort HISTORIC BUILDING
(📞09-375 31 61; www.belfortgent.be; Sint-Baafsplein; adult/concession €8/3; ⏱10am-6pm) Ghent's Unesco-listed 14th-century belfry (91m) is topped by a large dragon weathervane: he's become something of a city mascot. You'll meet two previous dragon incarnations on the 350-stair climb to the top; there are lifts to help some of the way. Enter through the **Lakenhalle**, Ghent's cloth hall that was left half-built in 1445 and only completed in 1903. Hear the carillon at 11.30am Fridays and 11am on summer Sundays.

MSK GALLERY
(Museum voor Schone Kunsten, Museum of Fine Arts Ghent; 📞09-323 67 00; www.mskgent.be; Fernand Scribedreef 1; adult/youth/child €8/2/free; ⏱9.30am-5.30pm Tue-Fri, 10am-6pm Sat &

Ghent Centre

Sun) Styled like a Greek temple, this superb 1903 fine-art gallery introduces a veritable A–Z of great Belgian and other Low Countries' painters from the 14th to mid-20th centuries. Highlights include a happy family of coffins by Magritte, luminist canvases by Emile Claus, and Pieter Brueghel the Younger's 1621 *Dorpsadvocaat* – a brilliant portrait of a village lawyer oozing with arrogance. English-language explanation cards are available in each room.

Museum Dr Guislain MUSEUM
(☏ 09-398 69 50; www.museumdrguislain.be; Jozef Guislainstraat 43; adult/concession €8/3; ⊙ 9am-

5pm Tue-Fri, 1-5pm Sat & Sun; 🚌 1) Hidden away in an 1857 neo-Gothic psychiatric hospital, this enthralling mental-health museum takes visitors on a trilingual, multicultural journey through the history of psychiatry, from gruesome Neolithic trepanning to contemporary brain scans via cage beds, straightjackets, shackles and phrenology. Dr D'Arsonval's extraordinary 1909 radiographic apparatus looks like a Dr Frankenstein creation.

S.M.A.K. GALLERY
(Museum of Contemporary Art; ☏ 09-240 76 01; www.smak.be; Jan Hoetplein 1; adult/concession/

Ghent Centre

◉ Sights
1	Belfort	D4
2	Gravensteen	B2
3	Sint-Baafskathedraal	E5
4	The Adoration of the Mystic Lamb	E5

⬛ Sleeping
5	1898 The Post	B4
6	Hostel 47	F1
7	Hotel Erasmus	A4

⊗ Eating
8	Balls & Glory	B5
9	't Oud Clooster	B5

◉ Drinking & Nightlife
10	Café Labath	A4
11	Dulle Griet	D3
12	Het Waterhuis aan de Bierkant	C3
13	Rococo	C2
14	't Dreupelkot	C3

✪ Entertainment
15	Hot Club Gent	C3

(☑ 0486 67 80 33; www.ecohostel.be; Bargiekaai 35; dm/d incl breakfast from €23/68; ⊙ reception 2-8pm; P 🖅; ☐ 1) and indoor camping at **Treck Hostel** (☑ 09-310 76 20; www.treck hostel.be; Groendreef 51; dm/van from €19/35; 🖅). Numerous B&Bs can be found through www. gent-accommodations.be and www.bed andbreakfast-gent.be.

Hostel 47   HOSTEL €
(☑ 0478 71 28 27; www.hostel47.com; Blekerijstraat 47-51; dm/d incl breakfast from €27/72; 🖅) Unusually calm yet pretty central, this inviting hostel is in a revamped a high-ceilinged historical house with virginal white walls, spacious bunk rooms and designer fittings. Free lockers and cursory breakfast with Nespresso coffee; no bar.

Hotel Erasmus   HERITAGE HOTEL €€
(☑ 09-224 21 95; www.erasmushotel.be; Poel 25; s/d incl breakfast from €79/99; ⊙ reception 7am-10.30pm; 🖅) A suit of armour guards the breakfast in this creaky 16th-century building. Its 12 guest rooms have a mixture of old and antique furniture, giving it an atmospheric feeling of times gone by.

★ 1898 The Post   LUXURY HOTEL €€€
(☑ 09-277 09 60; www.zannierhotels.com/1898 thepost/en; Graslei 16; d/ste €175/315; ❄🖅) This beautiful boutique offering is housed

child €8/2/free; ⊙ 9.30am-5.30pm Tue-Sun; ☐ 5) Ghent's highly regarded Museum of Contemporary Art is one of Belgium's largest. Works from its 3000-strong permanent collection (dating from 1939 to the present) are regularly curated to complement visiting temporary exhibitions of provocative, cutting-edge installations, which sometimes spill out right across the city.

⬛ Sleeping

Ghent offers innovative accommodation in all price ranges. There's plenty for budget travellers including a big, central HI Hostel, the recycled barge 'Eco'-hostel **Andromeda**

PARTY TIME IN GHENT

Mid-July's raucous **Gentse Feesten** (http://gentsefeesten.stad.gent) is a vast, city-wide festival during which many squares become venues for a variety of street-theatre performances, and there are big associated techno and jazz festivals. Those wanting a merrily boozy party atmosphere will love it. But consider avoiding Ghent at this time if you don't.

in Ghent's spectacular twin-turreted former post office. The property's common areas, guestrooms and suites are dark and moody in a wonderful way, with elements of great design at every turn (though note the standard rooms are compact for the price). The hotel also offers fine dining and an ultra-atmospheric bar.

Eating

Cosy, upmarket restaurants in the delightful cobbled alleyways of Patershol cover most cuisines. Several eateries jostle for summer terrace space on Graslei's gorgeous canal-side terrace; there's fast food around Korenmarkt, great-value Turkish food on Sleepstraat and numerous vegetarian choices city-wide.

Balls & Glory BELGIAN €
(☑0486 67 87 76; www.ballsnglory.be; Jakobijnenstraat 6; balls €4.40-6; ☺10am-9pm Mon-Sat; ☑) This easy-going eatery is popular with students and hipsters for its classy interiors and good value. It serves big meaty or vegetarian balls (a bit like a hybrid of a traditional meatball and an arancini) that you can take away in a box or devour on-site.

't Oud Clooster CAFE €€
(☑09-233 78 02; www.toudclooster.be; Zwartezusterstraat 5; mains €16-22; ☺11.45am-2.30pm & 6-10.30pm Mon-Fri, 11.45am-2.30pm & 5.30-10.30pm Sat, 5.30-9.30pm Sun) Mostly candle-lit at night, this atmospheric double-level cafe is built into sections of what was long ago a nunnery, hence the sprinkling of religious statues and cherub lamp-holders. Well-priced light meals are presented with unexpected style.

Drinking & Entertainment

Try the snug **Hot Club** (☑09-256 71 99; www.hotclub.gent; Schuddevisstraatje 2; ☺3pm-late) for live jazz, gyspy or blues music; **Hotsy Totsy** (☑09-224 20 12; www.facebook.com/Hotsy.Totsy.Gent; Hoogstraat 1; ☺6pm-1am Mon-Fri, 8pm-2am Sat & Sun, from 8pm daily Jul & Aug) for free Thursday jazz; and beautifully panelled **Rococo** (☑09-224 30 35; Corduwaniersstraat 5; ☺9pm-late Tue-Sun) for candlelit late-night conversation. **Café Labath** (☑09-225 28 25; www.cafelabath.be; Oude Houtlei 1; ☺8am-7pm Mon-Fri, 9am-7pm Sat, 10am-6pm Sun) is ideal for a coffee fix, **Dulle Griet** (☑09-224 24 55; www.dullegriet.be; Vrijdagmarkt 50; ☺noon-1am Tue-Sat, to 7pm Sun, 4.30pm-1am Mon) and **Het Waterhuis aan de Bierkant** (☑09-225 06 80; Groentenmarkt 9; ☺11am-1am) are traditional brown-bar gems, with brick-thick beer menus while next door to the latter, **'t Dreupelkot** (☑09-224 21 20; www.dreupelkot.be; Groentenmarkt 12; ☺11am-1.30am Mon-Thu, to 2am Fri-Sun) is a timeless jenever bar with a hundred variants on Flemish and Dutch 'gin'.

As a wide-ranging events venue, it's hard to beat **Vooruit** (☑09-267 28 20; www.vooruit.be; St-Pietersnieuwstraat 23; ☺10am-1am; ☑5) whose 1912 building is a visionary architectural premonition of art deco.

Information

CityCard Gent (48-/72-hour €30/35) gives free entrance to all of Ghent's top museums and monuments, and allows unlimited travel on trams and city buses, plus a boat trip. It's excellent value. Buy one at participating museums, major bus offices or the **tourist office** (☑09-266 56 60; https://visit.gent.be; St-Veerleplein 5; ☺10am-6pm).

Getting There & Around

Gent-Dampoort Station, 1km west of the old city, is handy for trains to Antwerp (€9.90, fast/slow 42/64 minutes, three per hour) and Bruges (€7, 36 minutes, hourly), and is a pick-up point for international buses. Bigger **Gent-Sint-Pieters Station**, 2.5km south of the centre by tram 1, has many more Bruges-bound trains and twice hourly services to Brussels (€9.40, 36 minutes).

Biker (☑09-224 29 03; www.bikerfietsen.be; Steendam 16; per day from €9; ☺9am-12.30pm & 1.30-6pm Tue-Sat) and **De Fiets**

Ambassade (The Bike Embassy; ☑ 09-242 80 40; https://fietsambassade.gent.be/en; Voskenslaan 27; per half-day/day/week €7/10/30; ⊙7am-7pm Mon-Fri) rent out bicycles.

Antwerp

☑ 03 / POP 521,700

Known as Antwerpen in Dutch and Anvers in French, the port city of Antwerp is Belgium's capital of cool. In the mid-16th century it was one of Europe's most important cities and home to baroque superstar painter Pieter Paul Rubens, and today it remains a powerful magnet for everyone from fashion moguls and club queens to art lovers and diamond dealers.

⊙ Sights

⊙ City Centre

★**Onze-Lieve-Vrouwekathedraal** CATHEDRAL
(☑ 03-213 99 51; www.dekathedraal.be; Handschoenmarkt; adult/reduced/under 12yr €6/4/free; ⊙10am-5pm Mon-Fri, to 3pm Sat, 1-5pm Sun) Belgium's finest Gothic cathedral was 169 years in the making (1352–1521). Wherever you wander in Antwerp, its gracious, 123m-high spire has a habit of popping unexpectedly into view and it rarely fails to prompt a gasp of awe. The sight is particularly well framed when looking up Pelgrimstraat in the afternoon light.

Grote Markt SQUARE
As is the case with every great Flemish city, Antwerp's medieval heart is a classic Grote Markt (market square). Here the triangular, pedestrianised space features the voluptuous, baroque **Brabo Fountain** depicting the hero of Antwerp's giant-killing, hand-throwing foundation legend. Flanked on two sides by very photogenic guildhalls, the square is dominated by an impressive Italo-Flemish Renaissance-style **stadhuis** (Town Hall; Grote Markt) completed in 1565.

★**Museum Plantin-Moretus** MUSEUM, HISTORIC BUILDING
(☑ 03-221 14 50; www.museumplantinmoretus. be; Vrijdagmarkt 22; adult/reduced/child €8/6/free; ⊙10am-5pm Tue-Sun, last entry 4.30pm) The medieval building and 1622 courtyard garden alone would be worth a visit, but it's the world's oldest printing press, priceless manuscripts and original type sets that justify this museum's Unesco World Heritage status. It's been a museum since 1876 and its other great highlights include a 1640 library, a bookshop dating from 1700 and rooms lined with gilt leather.

Rubenshuis MUSEUM
(☑ 03-201 15 55; www.rubenshuis.be; Wapper 9-11; adult/reduced €8/6; ⊙10am-5pm Tue-Sun) This delightfully indulgent 1611 mansion was built as a home and studio for celebrated painter Pieter Paul Rubens. It was rescued from ruins in 1937 and has been very sensitively restored with furniture that dates from Rubens' era plus a priceless collection of 17th-century art. There are around a dozen Rubens canvases, most memorably his world-famous hatted self-portrait and a large-scale canvas of Eve glancing lustfully at Adam's fig leaf.

Museum Mayer van den Bergh MUSEUM
(☑ 03-232 42 37; www.museummayervandenbergh. be; Lange Gasthuisstraat 19; adult/reduced €8/6, with Rubenshuis €10/8; ⊙10am-5pm Tue-Sun) Styled as a 16th-century town house, this superb place was actually constructed in 1904 as one of the first museums in the world built around a single collection. Fritz Mayer van den Bergh's collection is indeed as rich as that of many a national gallery with its notable paintings, sculptures, tapestries, drawings, jewellery and stained-glass windows. The undoubted highlight is the Brueghel Room, whose centrepiece is Pieter Brueghel the Elder's brilliantly grotesque *Dulle Griet* (Mad Meg), painted in 1561 and restored in 2018.

Snijder-Rockoxhuis MUSEUM
(☑ 03-201 92 50; www.snijdersrockoxhuis.be; Keizerstraat 10-12; adult/reduced €8/6; ⊙10am-5pm Tue-Sun) Combining the impressive 17th-century houses of artist Frans Snijders and of Antwerp lawyer, mayor and Rubens-patron Nicolaas Rockox, this recently revamped museum does a superb job of making accessible a fine collection of 16th- and 17th-century masterpieces with a very helpful tablet tour, headphones and two six-minute films.

St-Carolus-Borromeuskerk CHURCH
(www.mkaweb.be/site/english/062.mv; Hendrik Conscienceplein 6; ⊙10am-12.30pm & 2-5pm Mon-Sat) **FREE** Rubens turned interior designer as part of the team that created this superb 1621 baroque church, designed to give worshippers a very visceral foretaste of heaven's delights. A wonder of its era, the remarkable altarpiece allowed vast canvases to be changed using a series of wire pulleys.

Antwerp

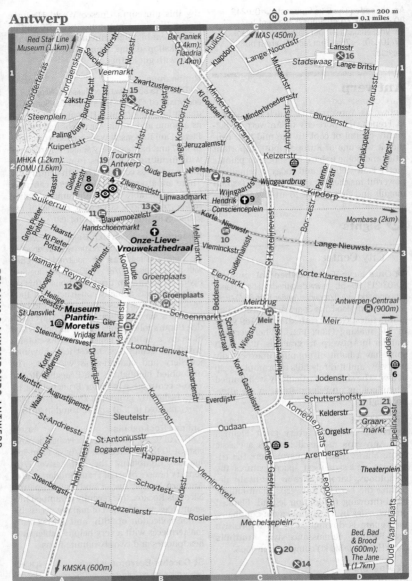

👁 't Zuid & Zurenborg

Heading south from the centre, the Fashion District morphs into 't Zuid, a dining, drinking and museum zone interspersed by some areas of relatively grand urban residences. The highlight here is the world-class gallery,

KMSKA (www.kmska.be; Leopold de Waelplaats), housed in a monumental neoclassical building topped with winged charioteer statues. There is also an important modern art gallery, **MHKA** (☏ 03-260 99 99; www.muhka.be; Leuvenstraat 32; some floors free, exhibitions adult/student/under 26yr/child €10/5/1/free; ⊙ 11am-

Antwerp

◉ Top Sights

6pm Tue-Sun, to 9pm Thu), and photography museum **FoMu** (Fotomuseum; ☑03-242 93 00; www.fotomuseum.be; Waalsekaai 47; adult/pensioner/under 26yr/child €10/5/3/free; ◷10am-6pm Tue-Sun, last tickets 5.30pm). Further southeast, Zurenborg has a wealth of art nouveau and belle-époch residential architecture, notably around Waterloostraat.

◉ 't Eilandje

Starting around 800m north of Grote Markt, 't Eilandje is a regenerated dockland area with a scattering of in-vogue bars, a marina and a parked lightship. From here, the **Flandria** (☑03-472 21 40 56; www.flandria.nu; Kattendijkdok; adult/child €19/3; ◷noon Thu, Sat & Sun Apr-Nov) makes three-hour cruises of the greater Antwerp harbour area, passing Zaha Hadid's 2016 architectural flight of fancy, the Port House.

MAS   MUSEUM
(Museum aan de Stroom; ☑03-338 44 00; www.mas.be; Hanzestedenplaats; viewpoint free, mus-

eum adult/reduced €10/8, btwn exhibitions €5/3; ◷viewpoint 9.30am-11.30pm Tue-Sun, museum 10am-4.45pm Tue-Sun) Opened in 2011, MAS is a 10-storey complex that redefines the idea of a museum-gallery. Floors are designed around big-idea themes using a barrage of media, from old master paintings and tribal artefacts to video installations. But many people come just for the views over the city (no ticket required), which transform as you climb somewhat laboriously by a series of escalators and three flights of stairs (no public lifts).

Red Star Line Museum   MUSEUM
(☑03-298 27 70; www.redstarline.be; Montevideostraat 3; adult/reduced €8/6; ◷10am-5pm Tue-Sun, reservations required on weekends) Over two million passengers sailed from Antwerp on Red Star Line ships between 1873 and 1934, the great majority of them immigrants bound for America. This museum, housed in the very building where those many embarkations took place, is beautifully designed and extremely engaging, telling the story of individual journeys through photographs, recreations and objects, including some gorgeous period model ships.

🛏 Sleeping

ABhostel   HOSTEL €
(☑0473-57 01 66; www.abhostel.com; Kattenberg 110; dm/tw €25/55; ◷reception noon-3pm & 6-8pm; 🖥; 🚊10, 24 to Drink) ❂ This adorable, family-run hostel in Borgerhout is a great place to get to know fellow travellers while fixing breakfast from provided ingredients

---

BOLLEKE

To sound like a local, ask for a *bolleke*. No, that's not an insult, but the nickname for 'little bowl' (ie glass) of De Koninck, Antwerp's favourite brown ale. Timeless old-world places to try one include the following:

Oud Arsenaal (Pijpelincxstraat 4; ◷10am-10pm Wed-Fri, 7.30am-7.30pm Sat & Sun),

De Kat (☑03-233 08 92; www.facebook. com/cafeDeKat; Wolstraat 22; ◷noon-2am Mon-Sat, 5pm-2am Sun),

Den Engel (www.cafedenengel.be; Grote Markt 3; ◷9am-2am)

De Duifkens (Graanmarkt 5; ◷10am-late Mon-Thu, from noon Fri-Sun)

THE FASHION DISTRICT

Antwerp may seem far more sartorially laid-back than fashion heavyweights Paris or Milan, but it punches above its weight. Few places in the world have such a covetable concentration of designer boutiques, end-of-line discounters, upmarket vintage stores and designer consignment shops. Most lie within a couple of blocks from Dries Van Noten's iconic flagship store **Het Modepaleis** (www.driesvannoten. be; Nationalestraat 16; ⊙10am-6.30pm Mon-Sat). Browse Nationalestraat, Lombardenvest, Huidevettersstraat and Schuttershofstraat, not missing Kammenstraat for streetwear and up-and-coming designers.

in the kitchen-bar, or relaxing in hammocks in the small yard-garden. Helpful traveller staff are a mine of information to help you make the most of the odd-ball location's opportunities and hot spots.

Bed, Bad & Brood   B&B €€
(☑03-248 15 39; www.bbantwerp.com; Justitiestraat 43; s/d/q from €62/76/135; ⊜@) In a 1910, belle époque–era town house near the vast Gerechtshof (former courthouse), this B&B impresses with authentic wooden floors, high ceilings and beautifully eclectic furniture. The three rooms are remarkably spacious and comfortable for the price and rates include a bountiful breakfast.

Hotel O   BOUTIQUE HOTEL €€
(☑03-500 89 50; www.hotelokathedral.com; Handschoenmarkt 3; rear s/d from €79/89, d with view €99-154; ☀️🛜) The immediate selling point of this excellent-value 39-room hotel is its unbeatable location, with oblique views across the square to the cathedral frontage. Expect moody decor with baths or showers in black-framed glass boxes and – in most rooms – giant 17th-century paintings reproduced as either headboards or covering whole walls.

Hotel Julien   BOUTIQUE HOTEL €€€
(☑03-229 06 00; www.hotel-julien.com; Korte Nieuwstraat 24; d €184-284, ste €334; ☀️@🛜) In a grand old mansion with lots of designer detail, this discreet 21-room boutique hotel has a suave, understated elegance, impressive lounge and bar spaces, and a staff attitude that hits the sweet spot between

friendly and professional. Every room is different. Choose pricier versions for high ceilings, exposed beams, coffee maker etc. The breathtaking rooftop terrace view is a well-kept secret.

✖️ Eating

Locals often head south of centre to dine in 't Zuid, where there are great mid-range choices around Leopold de Waelplaats, Vlaamsekaai and Marnixplaats. Troonplaats is an up-and-coming place to eat, while just one block away, contrastingly ungentrified Brederodestraat has excellent-value Turkish bakeries, kebab shops and Eastern European groceries. More centrally, **Little Ethiopia** (☑03-336 22 93; www.little-ethiopia.be; Zirkstraat 8; mains €9-19.50; ⊙noon-10pm Wed-Mon) serves Ethiopian cuisine in a veritable museum of African artefacts, while **Nimmanhaemin** (☑03-345 35 38; www.nimmanhaemin.be; Stadswaag 9; starters €6-10, mains €13-20; ⊙6-10pm) offers richly flavoured Thai food by a pretty, tree-shaded square.

Elfde Gebod   BELGIAN €€
(www.11gebod.com; Torfbrug 10; mains €14-24.50, sandwiches €8.50; ⊙noon-11pm) In the heart of the tourist zone, this ivy-clad medieval masterpiece has an astounding interior decked with angels, saints, pulpits and several deliciously sacrilegious visual jokes.

Life Is Art   INTERNATIONAL €€
(www.rebeccavanherck.wixsite.com/lifeisart; St-Jorisoord 21-23; lunch salads €15, starters/ mains €13/22; ⊙11am-3pm & 7-10pm Thu & Fri, 10am-10pm Sat & Sun) Loose cushions on bench seats, *brocante* mirrors, an old piano and a dangling canoe-skeleton all conspire to create a casually quirky venue for super-fresh food that changes so regularly that you'll have to ask the waitstaff for details.

De Groote Witte Arend   BELGIAN €€
(☑03-233 50 33; www.degrootewittearend.be; Reyndersstraat 18; lunches €8-15, mains €16-26; ⊙noon-9pm Sun-Thu, to 10pm Fri & Sat; 🛜) Retaining the Tuscan stone arcade of a 15th-to-17th-century convent building, as well as a little family chapel, this place combines the joys of a good beer bar with the satisfaction of well-cooked, sensibly priced Flemish home cuisine.

★ The Jane   INTERNATIONAL €€€
(☑03-808 44 65; www.thejaneantwerp.com; Paradeplein 1; 12/14 courses €110/130, Upper Room lunch plates €7-22; ⊙7pm, 7.30pm or 8pm Tue-Sat,

bar noon-2am; 9 to Zurenborg) In a stunningly repurposed old military-hospital chapel, the Jane's sublime two-Michelin-star dining is such an overwhelmingly fabulous experience that you'll need to book online exactly three months ahead...on the dot of 8am.

Drinking & Nightlife

Around Mechelseplein, stylishly unkempt drinking holes like **Korsåkov** (☑0485 46 45 06; www.facebook.com/vokasrov; Mechelseplein 21; ☺noon-4am Mon-Thu, 2pm-5am Fri & Sat, noon-midnight Sun) open super-late. Less centrally, **Bar Paniek** (Kattendijkdok-Oostkai 21B; ☺11am-11pm) is an artists' collective bar in old harbour warehouses. The pre-gentrified inner-suburb of Borgerhout has several absolute gems, most notably **Mombasa** (☑0498 52 11 94; Moorkensplein 37; ☺3pm-2am Tue-Sun).

❶ Information

Tourism Antwerp (☑03-232 01 03; www. visitantwerpen.be; Grote Markt 13; ☺10am-5pm) sells tram/bus passes and books tickets here. They have a booth at Antwerpen-Centraal station (open 9am to 5pm). Ask for the excellent, free *Use It guide maps* (www.antwerp. use-it.travel). For events and offbeat visitor ideas consult www.thisisantwerp.be.

❶ Getting There & Away

An attraction in itself, the gorgeous main station **Antwerpen-Centraal** (Koningin Astridplein 27; ☺ticket office 5.45am-10pm) has regular IC trains to Amsterdam (from €37.40 booked online, two hours), Bruges (€15.50, 90 minutes), Brussels (€7.70, 46 minutes), Leuven (€7.70, 46 minutes), Lier (€3, 25 minutes) and Mechelen (€4.10, 20 minutes).

❶ Getting Around

Velo-Antwerpen (☑03-206 50 30; www. velo-antwerpen.be; Kievitplein 7; day/week membership €4/10; ☺11am-5pm Mon-Thu, 9am-3pm Fri) is a super-handy short-hop bike rental service with around 100 docking stations. Sign up online and get the phone app for an interactive map showing availability and spaces.

Cyclant (☑03-232 01 09; www.cyclant. com; Pelikaanstraat 3/1050; per 4/12/24hr €9/12/15; ☺10am-6pm Sun, Mon, Wed & Thu, to 7pm Fri & Sat) has longer-term bike rental. The shop is tucked into the outer west side of Antwerpen-Centraal.

De Lijn (www.delijn.be) runs an integrated bus and tram service. One ride costs €3 and a day-pass €8 (or €6 if pre-purchased).

Lier

☑03 / POP 35.700

Delightful Lier is one of Flanders' overlooked historical gems. The centre retains a satisfying architectural integrity and is ringed by a circular waterway followed by a walkable green rampart where the city walls once stood. Founded in 1258, the Unesco-listed **Begijnhof** (Sint-Margaretastraat) is one of Belgium's prettiest, a picture-perfect grid of cobbled lanes lined with archetypal houses around the baroque-fronted 1671 St-Margaretakerk. Two blocks away is the intriguing **Zimmertoren** (☑03-800 03 95; www. zimmertoren.be; Zimmerplein; museum adult/child €4.50/2; ☺10am-noon & 1-5pm Tue-Sun), a partly 14th-century tower incorporating a fanciful 1930 timepiece that's eccentrically overendowed with dials and zodiac signs. On the fine central square, it's worth visiting the **tourist office** (☑03-800 05 55; www.visit lier.be; Grote Markt 58; ☺9am-4.30pm Mon-Fri, to 4pm Sat & Sun Apr-Oct, 9am-4.30pm Mon-Fri & closed weekends & lunchtimes Nov-Mar) if only to admire the splendid chandeliers, ceiling mural and portrait of Leopold I.

Bed Muzet (☑03-488 60 36; www.vjh.be; Volmolenstraat 65; dm/d €27/62; ☺check-in 4.30-7pm), Lier's swish modern hostel, occupies a repurposed former monastery, while the atmospheric, riverside **Hof van Aragon** (☑03-491 08 00; www.hofvanaragon.be; Mosdijk 6; small s/d €79/94, extra-large s/d/tr €109/124/157; ☎) has a minor maze linking its 20 comfortable rooms in a series of knocked-together historic riverside houses.

Grote Markt, Eikelstraat and Zimmerplein are lined with inviting places to eat and drink, with other characterful restaurants scattered in lanes near Lier's huge Gothic church, **St-Gummaruskerk** (www. topalier.be/bezoeken; Kardinaal Mercierplein; treasury €3; ☺2-4.30pm daily & 10am-noon Tue-Fri, closed Nov-Easter),

Frequent Lier–Antwerp trains (€3) take under 20 minutes.

Leuven

☑016 / POP 101.200

Lively, self-confident Leuven (Louvain in French; www.leuven.be) is Flanders' oldest university town and home to the vast **Stella Artois brewery** (www.breweryvisits.com; Aarschotsesteenweg 22; adult/concession €8.50/7.50; ☺1pm & 3pm Sat & Sun). Its greatest attraction is the flamboyant 15th-century city hall, the **Stadhuis** (Grote Markt 9; tours €4; ☺tours 3pm), lavished with intricate exterior statuary. Other architectural attractions are patchy due to heavy damage sustained in 20th-century wars, but the iconic **university library** (www.bib.kuleuven.be; Monseigneur Ladeuzeplein 21; library/library plus tower €2/7; ☺library 9am-8pm Mon-Thu, to 7pm Fri, 10am-5pm Sat & Sun, tower 10am-7pm Mon-Fri, to 5pm Sat & Sun) has been rebuilt. Twice.

Mirroring the ornate Gothic look of the nearby Stadhuis, **The Fourth** (☑016-22 75 54; www.th4th.com; Grote Markt 5; r from €107, peak times €245-295) is a highly automated, luxury hotel within a 1479 guildhouse. Peaceful **Martin's Klooster Hotel** (☑016-21 31 41; www.martinshotels.com; Onze-Lieve-Vrouwstraat 18; d €115-230, ste €299; @ 🕾) also successfully recycles a medieval building, while for backpackers there's an HI hostel and the homey **Leuven City Hostel** (☑016 84 30 33; www.leuvencityhostel.com; Bogaardenstraat 27; s/d/tr/q with bathroom €70/80/95/120, dm/d/tr without bathroom €22/52/53; ☺reception 4-8pm; @ 🕾).

Casually stylish restaurants fill flag-decked **Muntstraat**, while low prices and quirky character make **De Werf** (www.dewerf-leuven.be; Hogeschoolplein 5; snacks €5-7, pasta & salads €8-15; ☺9am-midnight Mon-Fri, kitchen to 9pm) a student dining classic. For the full-on Leuven pub experience, be blown away by the cacophanous overload of **Oude Markt** (Oude Markt; ☺8am-7am), a whole square packed with drinking revelry that's collectively nicknamed 'Europe's Longest Bar'.

Trains are frequent to Brussels (€5.50, 30 minutes), Lier (€7.20, 45 minutes) and Mechelen (€4.70, 30 minutes).

Mechelen

☑015 / POP 86,140

Belgium's religious capital, Mechelen (Malines in French) is centred on the **St-Romboutskathedraal cathedral** (www.sintromboutstoren.mechelen.be; Grote Markt; church free, tower adult/under 26yr €8/3; ☺church 9am-5.30pm, tower 1-4.40pm Sun-Fri, 10am-4.40pm Sat) featuring a 97m, 15th-century tower. It soars above a particularly memorable central market square from which IJzerenleen, a street of fine baroque facades, leads south. There are several other splendid churches around town, and along Keizerstraat the courthouse and theatre buildings were once royal palaces in the days when the Low

Countries were effectively run from Mechelen. Other top sights include the brilliantly wide-ranging **Speelgoedmuseum** (☑015-55 70 75; www.speelgoedmuseum.be; Nekkerstraat 21; adult/child €9.80/7.30; ☺10am-5pm Tue-Sun; 🖐) toy museum, the harrowing **Kazerne Dossin** (☑015-29 06 60; www.kazernedossin.eu; Goswin de Stassartstraat 153; memorial free, museum adult/reduced/under 21yr €10/8/4; ☺museum 9.30am-5pm Thu-Tue, memorial from 10am) remembering WWII Nazi deportations, and the contrastingly uplifting **Hof van Busleyden** (☑015-29 40 30; www.hofvanbusleyden.be; Sint-Janstraat 2A; adult/under 26yr/child €11/5/free), a state-of-the-art history museum in a gracious medieval mansion.

The HI **Hostel De Zandpoort** (☑015-27 85 39; www.mechelen-hostel.com; Zandpoortvest 70; dm €23-26, tw €55-58; ☺check-in 5-10pm; 🅿🕾) is handy for budget visitors. For more classy accommodation try stylish **Martins Patershof** (☑015-46 46 46; www.facebook.com/MartinsPatershof; Karmelietenstraat 4; d €100-399; 🅿❄🕾) 🍴, set in a 1867 Franciscan monastery.

There's a compact bar-cafe zone on Vismarkt beside the canal, but don't miss **Het Anker** (www.hetanker.be; Guido Gezellelaan 49; ☺tours 11am Tue-Sun & 1pm Fri-Sun, brasserie 10am-11pm, kitchen 11.30am-9pm), a classic brewery whose brasserie is great for Belgian meals as well as for tasting their own top-rated Gouden Carolus beers.

Trains from Brussels (€4.70, 30 minutes) and Antwerp (€4.10, 20 minutes) run to Mechelen station. Some slower services also call at conveniently central Mechelen-Nekerspoel.

WALLONIA

Wallonia (La Wallonie) is Belgium's mostly French-speaking southern half. It includes many a pretty rustic village in rolling green countryside, interspersed by a scattering of post-industrial cities. The heavily wooded Ardennes is a major area for outdoors activities, but for those without wheels, the regions's most accessible historic cities are Mons and Tournai.

Mons

☑065 / POP 95,300

Historic Mons (Bergen in Dutch; www.visitmons.be) has a characterful medieval centre

BOULLON

Wallonia and Luxembourg have many magnificent castles in widely scattered rural towns and villages. If you're only going to visit one, a great choice is the **Château de Bouillon** (☏ 061-46 62 57; www.bouillon-initiative.be; Rue du Château; adult/senior/student & child €7/6.50/5; ⏱10am-6.30pm Jul & Aug, 10am-5pm or 6pm Mar-Jun & Sep-Nov, see website for winter hours; P☑), the hefty ruins of Belgium's finest feudal castle dominating a tight loop of the Semois River. Accessed by two stone bridges between crags, the fortress harks back to 988, but is especially associated with the knight Godefroid (Godefroy) de Bouillon who sold it to help fund the 1096 First Crusade. The super-atmospheric castle has many an eerie nook and cranny to explore with dank dripping passageways, musty half-lit cell rooms and rough-hewn stairwells. From March to October, entertaining falconry shows at 11.30am, 2pm and 3.30pm are included in the ticket price.

To reach Bouillon, take a train to Libramont, then bus 8 (€3.50, 45 minutes, roughly hourly weekdays, two-hourly weekends).

---

with a fine **Grand Place** (main square), a Unesco-listed **belfry** (www.beffroi.mons.be; Parc du Château; adult/child €9/6; ⏱10am-6pm Tue-Sun) and a large, 15th-century Gothic church, the **Collégiale Ste-Waudru** (www.waudru.be; Place du Chapitre; ⏱9am-6pm). The latter's small treasury displays a sword-slashed skull relic, supposedly that of sainted Merovingian king Dagobert II whose murder in 675 CE was, according to some conspiracy theorists, an attempt to put an end to the 'Jesus bloodline'. Mons received a substantial facelift in 2015 when it was a European Capital of Culture and the legacy includes a handful of modern museums, most notably the superb **Memorial Museum** (☏ 065-40 53 20; www.monsmemorialmuseum.mons.be; Blvd Dolez 51; adult/child €9/2; ⏱10am-6pm Tue-Sun) covering the city's experience of two world wars.

Accommodation-wise there's a central **HI hostel** (☏065-87 55 70; www.lesaubergesdejeunesse.be; Rampe du Château 2; dm/d/q incl breakfast €26/56/104; P@☎) and several midrange hotels set in historic buildings, including **Dream Hôtel** (☏065-32 97 20; www.dream-mons.be; Rue de la Grand Triperie 17; s €94, d €113-130, ste €180-350; P✲@☎) that brings Belgian eccentricity to a revamped 19th-century convent.

Dining is a treat with great bistros like **L'Envers** (☏ 065-35 45 10; www.lenvers-mons.be; Rue de la Coupe 20; mains €15-29; ⏱noon-2.15pm & 6.15-10.15pm, closed Wed & Sun; ☎✍) and creative brasserie **Oscar** (☏065-95 96 12; www.brasserie-oscar.be; Rue de Nimy 14; mains €18-22; ⏱noon-2pm & 6-9.30pm Tue-Fri, 6-10pm Sat, noon-2pm Sun; ✍).

Regular trains connect Mons to Brussels (€9.90, 52 minutes), Charleroi (€6.80, 35 minutes) and Tournai (€7.70, 30 to 50 minutes). Free city shuttle buses link the station and the Grand Place.

Tournai

☏ 069 / POP 69,600

If you want to go by train between France and Belgium without paying for high-speed services, a good tactic is to transit via Tournai to/from Lille. While you're passing through, don't miss Tournai's particularly splendid five-towered **cathedral** (www.cathedrale-tournai.be; Place de l'Évêché; ⏱9am-6pm Mon-Fri, to noon & 1-6pm Sat & Sun Apr-Oct, to 5pm Nov-Mar) **FREE**, whose interior shows a fascinating evolution of architectural styles combining an Romanesque nave with an early-Gothic choir whose soaring pillars bend disconcertingly. Tournai's gorgeous triangular main square, the **Grand Place**, is ringed with cafes in fine gable-fronted guildhouses and features Belgium's oldest belfry-tower. Art lovers shouldn't miss the **Musée des Beaux-Arts** (☏069-33 24 31; www.tournai.be; Enclos St-Martin 3; adult/child €2.60/2.10; ⏱9.30am-12.30pm & 1.30-5pm Wed-Mon Apr-Oct, 9.30am-noon & 2-5pm Mon & Wed-Sat, 2-5pm Sun Nov-Mar), a Horta-designed gallery whose rich collection features work by Monet, Rubens and most notably Rogier Van de Weyden.

Tournai's train station is around 1km northeast of the Grand Place. Regular trains serve **Brussels** (€13.40, 70 minutes), Lille, France (€6.60, 30 minutes) and Mons (€7.70, 30 to 55 minutes).

BELGIUM & LUXEMBOURG TOURNAI

LUXEMBOURG

Stretching just 82km and 57km at its longest and widest points respectively, diminutive Luxembourg (www.visitluxembourg.com) is a charming slice of northern Europe ruled by its own monarchy. It consistently ranks among the world's top three nations in both wealth and wine consumption. Getting around is easy: wherever you go by public transport within the country the fare is just €2 for up to two hours' journey, €4 for the whole day. Luxembourg has its own language, Lëtzebuergesch, but most Luxembourgers also speak French and German.

Luxembourg City

POP 116,323

The scenic capital has a Unesco-listed old core that's majestically set across the deep gorges of the Alzette and Pétrusse rivers. Some outstanding museums add to a lively drinking and dining scene. Since city accommodation is primarily geared to bankers and Eurocrats, hotel prices drop dramatically at weekends when those folks head home. Sundays can be deathly quiet, but summer Saturday nights see many a festival.

⊙ Sights

Chemin de la Corniche   STREET

Hailed as 'Europe's most beautiful balcony', this pedestrian promenade winds along the course of the 17th-century city ramparts with views across the river canyon towards the hefty fortifications of the Wenzelsmauer (Wenceslas Wall). The rampart-top walk continues along Blvd Victor Thorn to the **Dräi Tier** (Triple Gate) tower, stretching 600m in total.

Bock Casemates   FORTRESS

(www.luxembourg-city.com; Montée de Clausen; adult/child €6/3; ⊙10am-5.30pm mid-Feb–Mar & Oct-early Nov, 10am-8.30pm Apr-Sep) Beneath the Montée de Clausen, the clifftop site of Count Sigefroi's once-mighty fort, the Bock Casemates are an atmospheric honeycomb of rock galleries and passages initially carved by the Spaniards from 1644 onwards. They were extended by French engineer Vauban in the 1680s, and again by the Austrians in the mid-18th century. Over the years the casemates have housed everything from garrisons to bakeries and slaughterhouses; during WWI and WWII they sheltered 35,000 locals. Kids will adore exploring the passageways.

Mudam   GALLERY

(Musée d'Art Moderne; ☑45 37 85 1; www.mudam.lu; 3 Parc Dräi Eechelen; adult/child €8/free; ⊙10am-6pm Thu-Mon, to 9pm Wed) Ground-breaking exhibitions of modern, installation and experiential art take place in this airy architectural icon designed by Pritzker-winning architect IM Pei (best known for his glass pyramid entrance to Paris' Louvre museum). The collection includes everything from photography to fashion, design and multimedia. Regional products are used in local specialities at its glass-roofed cafe, which hosts free concerts on Wednesday evenings.

Musée d'Histoire de la Ville de Luxembourg   MUSEUM

(Luxembourg City History Museum; ☑47 96 45 00; www.citymuseum.lu; 14 Rue du St-Esprit; adult/child €5/free, after 6pm Thu free; ⊙10am-6pm Tue, Wed & Fri-Sun, to 8pm Thu) Hidden within a series of 17th- to 19th-century houses, including a former 'holiday home' of the Bishop of Orval, the city's history museum is engrossing. Permanent collections on its lower levels cover the city's industrial, handicraft and commercial heritage, with models, plans and engravings, textiles, ceramics, posters, photographs and household items. Upper floors host temporary exhibitions. Its enormous glass lift provides views of the rock foundations, the Grund valley and Rham plateau; there's also a lovely garden and panoramic terrace.

⌂ Sleeping

Midweek, accommodation can seem dauntingly overpriced. Prices are marginally cheaper around the train station, a slightly sleazy area by Luxembourg's high standards, where the **Hotel Bristol** (☑48 58 30; www.hotel-bristol.lu; 11 Rue de Strasbourg; s/d/studio incl breakfast from €75/120/130, d without bathroom incl breakfast from €85; ☎) is a decent bet. For budget travellers there's a handily central **HI hostel** (☑26 27 66 65 0; www.youthhostels.lu; 5 Rue du Fort Olisy; dm €25.15-26.15; P✲@☎), plus another at attractively rural **Larochette** (☑26 27 66 550; www.youthhostels.lu; 45 Rue Osterbour; dm/s/d €24.70/39.70/60.40; P☎), 25km away by Luxembourg–Diekirch bus route 100.

La Pipistrelle   B&B €€€

(☑621 300 351; www.lapipistrelle.lu; 26 Montée de Grund; s/d from €185/220; ☎) Just four sumptuous suites and a charming location mean you'll have to book early to enjoy this intimate B&B-style hotel. Carved into the rock face, the 18th-century property retains period features but the spacious rooms are stylishly rendered with designer fabrics and open bathrooms. Breakfast is an extra €16; bars and restaurants abound close by. A nearby public lift zips you up to the Old Town

Hôtel Le Place d'Armes BOUTIQUE HOTEL €€€
(☑27 47 37; www.hotel-leplacedarmes.com; 18 Place d'Armes; d incl breakfast from €295; ✻ ⑨) On the city's busiest central square, seven 18th-century buildings have been combined into an enchanting labyrinth incorporating part-cave meeting rooms with stone walls, light-touch modern lounges and inner courtyards. Each of the 28 luxurious rooms is different, with details including fireplaces, beams or timber ceilings.

Hotel Les Jardins d'Anaïs BOUTIQUE HOTEL €€€
(☑27 04 83 71; https://jardinsdanais.lu; 2 Place Ste-Cunégonde; s/d from €150/180; ⑫✻⑨) Behind an ivy-clad facade, Hotel Les Jardins d'Anaïs's seven rooms spread over two floors, served by a lift. Each has an individual theme, such as sunflower-yellow Provence, Bibliothéque ('library') with a wooden bookcase framing the tartan-quilted bed, and pink-accented Roses with wrought-iron furniture. Its glass-paned, Michelin-starred restaurant opens to a magical garden with a pond and a gazebo.

✗ Eating & Drinking

Cafe and restaurants spill summer tables on to city squares such as leafy Place d'Armes. For atmospheric options, explore the alleys and passages directly behind the Royal Palace, collectively nicknamed 'Îlot Gourmand'. For inexpensive, if mostly characterless, Asian eateries, search towards the train station. Grund has many great drinking spots, with **Scott's** (www.scotts-pub.com; 4 Bisserweg; ⊙noon-1am Mon-Fri, from 11am Sat & Sun; ⑨) perfectly perched overlooking the river. Nightlife is centred on the Rives de Clausen, with numerous bar-resto-clubs and a handy night bus running back to the centre.

Am Tiirmschen BISTRO €€
(☑26 27 07 33; www.amtiirmschen.lu; 32 Rue de l'Eau; mains €19-29; ⊙noon-2pm Tue-Fri, 7-10.30pm Mon-Sat) At this cosy restaurant with exposed-stone walls and heavy bowed beams, Luxembourg specialities include *Judd mat Gaardebounen* (smoked pork with broad beans), *Gromperekichelcher* (a

spiced potato pancake), *Rieslingspaschtéit* (a loaf-shaped meat pie made with Riesling) and *Kniddelen mam Speck* (flour-based dumplings topped with bacon and served with apple sauce). Wines are predominantly from Luxembourg's Moselle Valley.

★Le Sud FRENCH €€€
(☑26 47 87 50; www.le-sud.lu; 8 Rives de Clausen; mains €37-42, 2-/3-course lunch menu €28/32, 5-course dinner menu €78; ⊙kitchen noon-3pm & 7.30-10pm Tue-Fri, 7.30-10pm Sat, noon-3pm Sun, bar 6pm-1am Tue-Thu, 6pm-3am Fri & Sat, 2-6pm Sun; ⑨) *Crémant*-poached lobster, brioche-crumbed garlic snails, line-caught John Dory with artichoke mousseline and Grand Marnier soufflé are among the refined French dishes at this stone-walled restaurant in the historic Rives de Clausen neighbourhood. Stupendous views extend over the area's rooftops and wooded hillsides from the bar's panoramic rooftop terrace.

Dipso WINE BAR
(☑26 20 14 14; 4 Rue de la Loge; ⊙5pm-1am Tue-Thu, 5pm-3am Fri, 3pm-1am Sat; ⑨) Dating from 1453, this stone building with leaded glass windows incorporates part of the old city walls. Its wines, including 20-plus available by the glass, are accompanied by cheese and charcuterie platters. DJs hit the decks on Friday nights year-round; umbrella-shaded tables set up on its tiny, fight-for-a-seat cobbled terrace in summer.

Brauerei BREWERY
(www.bigbeercompany.lu; 12 Rives de Clausen; ⊙4.30pm-1am Mon-Thu, to 3am Fri & Sat; ⑨) Dating from 1511, this vast brick brewery complex retains its copper boilers and steam engines. Beers now brewed at its latest incarnation include blonde, amber and bruin

Luxembourg City

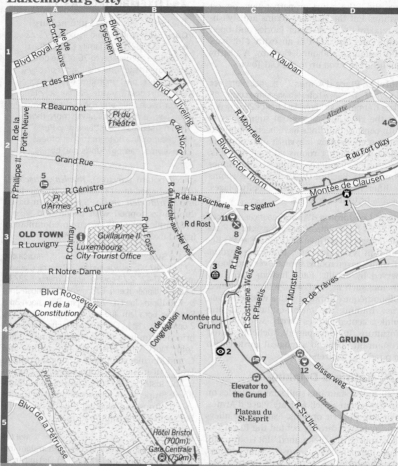

varieties. Soak them up with Bavarian specialities such as sausages, pretzels, *Spätzle* (hand-rolled noodles) and sauerkraut. The huge main brewhall reverberates when DJs spin tunes on weekends.

ℹ Information

Luxembourg City Tourist Office (LCTO; ☎22 28 09; www.luxembourg-city.com; 30 Place Guillaume II; ⊗8.30am-7pm Mon-Sat, to 6pm Sun mid-Jul–Aug, 9am-7pm Mon-Sat Apr–mid-Jul & Sep, 9am-6pm Mon-Sat Oct-Mar) Has maps, walking-tour leaflets and event guides.

ℹ Getting There & Away

Luxembourg Airport (LUX; www.lux-airport.lu; Rue de Treves), 8km northwest of centre, is well connected to other European cities by national carrier **Luxair** (www.luxair.lu) and other airlines including budget operator EasyJet.

For most overland connections, www.mobiliteit. lu has the timetables including bus 401 from Luxembourg-Kirchberg to Bitburg, Germany (€2, 1¼ hours, up to two per hour) via Echternach (45 minutes).

Pre-bookable **Flibco** (www.flibco.com) buses shuttle from Luxembourg City to German and Belgian airports at Frankfurt, Frankfurt Hahn

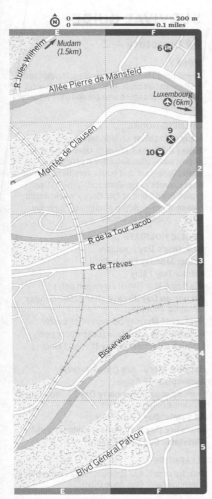

Luxembourg City

⊙ Sights
1	Bock Casemates	D2
2	Chemin de la Corniche	C4
3	Musée d'Histoire de la Ville de Luxembourg	C3

🛏 Sleeping
4	Auberge de Jeunesse	D2
5	Hôtel Le Place d'Armes	A2
6	Hotel Les Jardins d'Anaïs	F1
7	La Pipistrelle	C4

🍴 Eating
8	Am Tiirmschen	C3
9	Le Sud	F2

🍷 Drinking & Nightlife
10	Brauerei	F2
11	Dipso	C3
12	Scott's	D4

1am), and between **Montée du Pfaffenthal and Pfaffenthal** (⊙ 6am-1am).

BICYCLE

Velóh (☏ 800 611 00; www.en.veloh.lu; subscription per week €1, 1st 30min free/subsequent hour €1; ⊙ 24hr) Short-hop shared bike-hire scheme with 683 bikes across 75 docking stations. The initial subscription is payable by credit card at one of 25 special stands; locations are listed online.

Vélo en Ville (☏ 47 96 42 71; www.vdl.lu; 8 Bisserweg; per day/week bike hire from €20/75, helmet €3.50/10; ⊙ 8am-noon & 1-8pm Mon-Fri, 10am-noon & 1-8pm Sat & Sun Apr-Sep, 7am-3pm Mon-Fri Oct-Mar) Hires out city bikes and tandems.

BUS & TRAM

➜ Tickets (€2/4 per two hours/day) are sold at vending machines, at the train station or from bus drivers. They are valid for trams, buses and domestic trains.

➜ Route maps are available at www.vdl.lu.

➜ Buses run from 5.30am to 10pm; trams run till midnight (all night on Saturday evenings).

and Charleroi. They leave from the main train station, Gare Centrale, 1km south of the Old City.

Train services (www.cfl.lu) include Brussels (€43.60 to €50.40, 3¾ hours, hourly), Diekirch (€2, 45 minutes, every 30 minutes) via Ettelbrück (35 minutes), and Paris (€92 to €110, 2¼ hours, six daily) via Metz (€18.40, 40 minutes). Trains run hourly to Trier (€19.90 to €24.60, one hour, hourly) but on weekdays it's much cheaper to use commuter bus routes 118/117 from Kirchberg (one hour)/the station (45 minutes).

🛈 Getting Around

Handy lifts link the valleys with the city centre, between **Plateau St-Esprit and Grund** (⊙ 6am-

Northern Luxembourg

Understandably popular as a weekend getaway, magical little **Vianden** (www.vianden-info.lu) is dominated by a vast slate-roofed **castle** (☏ 83 41 08; www.castle-vianden.lu; Montée du Château; adult/child €7/2; ⊙ 10am-4pm Nov-Feb, to 5pm Mar & Oct, to 6pm Apr-Sep) and its impregnable stone walls glow golden in the evening's floodlights. Cobbled Grand Rue descends 700m from there to the riverside tourist office, passing the **HI hostel** (☑26 27 66 80 0; www.youthhostels.lu; 3 Montée du Château; dm/s/d €24.70/39.70/60.40; 🛜) and several appealing family hotels, notably **Auberge Aal Veinen** (☑83 43 68; http://vianden. beimhunn.lu; 114 Grand-Rue; s/d €60/90; ⊘ closed mid-Dec–mid-Jan; 🛜) and **Hôtel Heintz** (☑83 41 55; www.hotel-heintz.lu; 55 Grand-Rue; d/tr/f from €75/110/145; ⊘ Easter-Sep; 🅿🛜).

Bus 570 (18 minutes) connects at least hourly to **Diekirch**, which is home to **Musée National d'Histoire Militaire** (☑80 89 08; www.mnhm.net; 10 Rue Bamertal; adult/child €5/3; ⊘10am-6pm Tue-Sun), the most comprehensive and visual of many museums commemorating 1944's devastating midwinter Battle of the Ardennes. Diekirch has twice-hourly trains to Luxembourg City (40 minutes) via Ettelbrück (10 minutes). From the latter, bus 545 gets you within 2km of isolated **Château de Bourscheid** (☑99 05 70; http:// chateau.bourscheid.lu; Rue du Château; adult/child €5/3; ⊘9.30am-6pm Apr–mid-Oct, 11am-4pm mid-Oct–Mar), Luxembourg's most evocative medieval ruined castle.

Moselle Valley

Smothering the Moselle River's steeply rising banks are the neatly clipped vineyards that produce Luxembourg's balanced Rieslings, fruity rivaners and excellent *crémants* (sparkling *méthode traditionelle* wines). Many wineries offer tastings, but if you choose just one, make it the grand **Caves Bernard-Massard** (☑75 05 45 1; www.bernard -massard.lu; 8 Rue du Pont, Grevenmacher; tour incl 1 glass of wine €6; ⊘tours 9.30am-6pm Tue-Sun Apr-Oct, by reservation Nov-Mar, shop 10am-noon & 1.30-6pm Mon-Fri, 10am-1pm Sat) in central **Grevenmacher** where frequent 20-minute winery tours are multilingual and spiced with humour. Further south at Remerschen near Schengen (where the EU's agreement ensuring free movement of people was signed), don't miss the **Valentiny Foundation** (www.valentiny-foundation.com; 34 Rte du Vin, Remerschen; ⊘2-6pm Tue-Sun) **FREE**, a 2016 Arctic-white exhibition space featuring displays about modern architecture.

A good way of visiting the area is renting a bicycle from **Rentabike Miselerland** (www. entente-moselle.lu/en/rentabike/presentation; standard/mountain/electric bike hire per day €12/15/20). Pick up at one of 11 points and drop off at another: just make sure that you check closing times and take ID.

SURVIVAL GUIDE

ℹ Directory A-Z

MONEY

Credit cards are widely accepted, though some B&Bs insist on cash. ATMs are very prevalent but money changers are rare and offer generally poor rates.

OPENING HOURS

Many sights close on Mondays.

Banks 8.30am–3.30pm or later Monday to Friday, some also Saturday morning

Bars 10am–1am, but hours very flexible

Restaurants noon–2pm and 7pm–9.30pm, typically with one or two days a week closed

Shops 10am–6.30pm Monday to Saturday; Sunday opening is limited

PUBLIC HOLIDAYS

New Year's Day 1 January

Easter Monday March/April

Labour Day 1 May

Iris Day 8 May (Brussels region only)

Ascension Day 39 days after Easter Sunday (always a Thursday)

Pentecost Monday 50 days after Easter

National Day 23rd June (Luxembourg only)

Flemish Community Day 11 July (Flanders only)

National Day 21 July (Belgium only)

Assumption 15 August

Francophone Community Day 27 September (Wallonia only)

All Saints' Day 1 November

Armistice Day 11 November (Belgium only)

Christmas Day 25 December

TELEPHONE

Country codes: +32 Belgium, +352 Luxembourg. International access code 0015.

ℹ Getting There & Away

AIR

Brussels Airport (BRU, www.brusselsairport. be) is Belgium's most globally connected airport.

Charleroi Airport (CRL, www.brussels -charleroi-airport.com), sometimes misleadingly called Brussels-South, is a major hub for budget airline RyanAir.

Luxembourg Airport (LUX, www.lux-airport.lu) has a wide range of European connections.

For long-haul flights it can be worth comparing costs with flying into neighbouring countries via Frankfurt, Amsterdam or Paris, then continuing to Belgium overland.

LAND
Bus

Long-distance international bus fares can be remarkable bargains if prebooked well in advance.

Eurolines (www.eurolines.eu) and **Flixbus** (www.flixbus.be) both have very extensive European networks.

Ecolines (www.ecolines.net) specialises in mostly Baltic and Eastern European destinations.

Flibco (www.flibco.com) runs long-distance shuttles between major airports in Belgium, Luxembourg and Germany.

Car & Motorcycle

➔ Northern Europe is one vast web of motorways, so Belgium is easily accessed from anywhere.

➔ If driving from the southeast, fill your tank in Luxembourg for Western Europe's lowest petrol prices.

➔ As in France, the *priorité à droite* rule gives right of way to vehicles emerging from the right even from a small side lane, unless otherwise indicated.

➔ Motorway speed limits are 120km/h in Belgium and 130km/h in Luxembourg.

➔ The centres of most larger Flemish cities (especially Bruges and Ghent) are highly pedestrianised making access very awkward for motorists. Use park-and-ride facilities outside town and shuttle in.

➔ Driving into Antwerp is complicated by its Low Emission Zone (https://lez.antwerpen. be). Read the website carefully and, assuming your car is neither Belgian nor Dutch, allow at 10 days' application time to get the necessary permit (apply online with scans of the vehicle's original registration documents).

➔ While Belgium's motorway system is extensive and toll-free, traffic often grinds to a halt, especially on the ring roads around Brussels and Antwerp (during rush hour, September to June), on the Brussels–Ghent–Ostend highway (sunny weekends) and on the Ardennes-bound E411 (holidays and snowy weekends).

Train

High-speed trains offer easy connections between Brussels and London, and from Belgium to the broader French, Dutch and German networks. Such trains require reservations and can prove expensive, especially if demand is high. Although advance-purchase discounts can be massive, you'll usually forfeit the right to make changes.

Less-publicised ordinary trains run on several international sectors, including Antwerp–Breda–Amsterdam, Antwerp–Roosendaal, Tournai–Lille Flandres, Liège–Maastricht and Luxembourg–Trier–Koblenz. Using these routes combined with domestic tickets is slower but can prove far cheaper than high-speed services for last-minute journeys. There are no assigned seats, but booking online (self-printing or use the e-ticket service) saves a cheeky €6 in-station international ticketing fee for fares ex-Belgium. See www.b-europe.com, Belgian Railways' international site, for details.

SEA

P&O (www.poferries.com) operates a Zeebrugge–Hull service (14 hours, overnight). The quickest way across the channel is via the French port of Calais, around an hour's drive west of Ostend.

ⓘ Getting Around

BICYCLE

Bicycle on train Free in Luxembourg, ticket required in Belgium (€5/8 for one journey/whole day).

Bike helmets Rarely worn and not a legal requirement.

Cycle paths Very extensive in Belgium, especially Flanders. Most tourist offices sell regional cycling maps, while www.fietsroute.org, http://ravel.wallonie.be and www.randovelo.org are very helpful online resources.

Bike rental Available near most major train stations. Short-hop hire schemes operate in many cities: you'll need a credit card to sign up, then be sure to return the bike to any other automated stand within 30 minutes to avoid extra charges.

BUS

Where bus and train options link the same two cities, the bus is usually cheaper but far slower. Single tickets are valid for transfers for up to an hour after the ticket's validation (or 90 minutes for TEC Horizon) plus however long the final leg of your ride takes.

TRAIN

In Belgium, trains are run by **NMBS/SNCB** (www.belgianrail.be). Tickets should be pre-purchased; buying once aboard incurs a €7 surcharge. Fares a calculated by distance, with return tickets costing twice the price except for over-65-year-olds and for anyone on weekends, when there's a discounted return for travel after 7pm Friday, returning by Sunday night.

For under-26s, a Go-Pass 1 (€6.40) allows any one-way trip within Belgium or, for €8.20, an added border crossing to Roosendaal or Maastricht in the Netherlands.

In Luxembourg, trains (www.cfl.lu) are included in the nationwide flat-fare ticketing system (two hours/all day €2/4).

Bosnia & Hercegovina

POP 3.51 MILLION

Best Places to Eat

➡ Tima-Irma (p153)

➡ Avlija (p148)

➡ Rajska Vrata (p149)

➡ Željo (p148)

➡ Park Prinčeva (p148)

Best Places to Stay

➡ Isa-begov Hamam Hotel (p148)

➡ Pansion Čardak (p153)

➡ Halvat Guest House (p148)

➡ Hotel Aziza (p148)

➡ Hostel Polako (p156)

Why Go?

Craggily beautiful Bosnia and Hercegovina is most intriguing for its East-meets-West atmosphere born of blended Ottoman and Austro-Hungarian histories filtered through a Southern Slavic lens. Many still associate the country with the heartbreaking civil war of the 1990s, and the scars from that time are all too visible. But today's visitors are likely to remember the country for its deep, unassuming human warmth, its beautiful mountains, numerous medieval castle ruins, raftable rivers, impressive waterfalls and bargain-value skiing.

Major drawcards include the reincarnated historical centres of Sarajevo and Mostar, counterpointing splendid Turkish-era stone architecture with quirky bars, inviting street-terrace cafes, traditional barbecue restaurants and vibrant arts scenes. There's plenty of interest to discover in the largely rural hinterland too, all at prices that make the country one of Europe's best-value destinations.

When to Go
Sarajevo

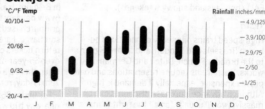

Apr–Jun Beat the heat in Hercegovina; flowers blooming in Bosnia; rivers at peak flows.

Jul & Aug Gets sweaty and accommodation fills up, but festivals keep things lively.

Mid-Jan–mid-Mar Skiing gets cheaper after the New Year holidays.

Entering the Country

Bosnia has four main international airports, although only Sarajevo has an extensive range of flights. Depending on where in the country you're heading to, it's often worth comparing prices on flights to Dubrovnik, Split or Zagreb in Croatia, then connecting to Bosnia by land. Belgrade (Serbia) and Podgorica (Montenegro) are also options.

Bosnia has multiple border crossings with Croatia, Serbia and Montenegro.

ITINERARIES

Four Days

Devote your first two days to exploring Sarajevo (p145). On day three, stop to admire the rebuilt Ottoman bridge in Konjic (p151) on your way to the even more famous rebuilt Ottoman bridge in Mostar (p150). The next day, stop in Blagaj (p154), the Kravica Waterfall (p154) and Počitelj (p155) en route to Trebinje (p155).

Seven Days

Spend your first day soaking up the sights of the Una River Valley (p156) and your second exploring the lakes, waterfall and historical old centre of Jajce (p157). The next day, take a leisurely trip to Sarajevo then continue with the four-day itinerary above.

Essential Food & Drink

Bosanska Kava Traditional Bosnian coffee, made and served in a *džezva* (small long-handled brass pot).

Burek Bosnian *burek* are cylindrical or spiral lengths of filo pastry usually filled with minced meat. *Sirnica* is filled with cheese, *krompiruša* with potato and *zeljanica* with spinach. Collectively these pies are called *pita*.

Ćevapi (Ćevapčići) Minced meat formed into cylindrical pellets and served in fresh bread with melting *kajmak*.

Hurmašice Syrup-soaked sponge fingers.

Kajmak Thick semi-soured cream.

Lokum Turkish delight.

Pljeskavica Patty-shaped *ćevapi*.

Rakija Grappa or fruit brandy.

Sarma Steamed dolma-parcels of rice and minced meat wrapped in cabbage or other green leaves.

Tufahija Whole stewed apple with walnut filling.

AT A GLANCE

Area 51,129 sq km

Capital Sarajevo

Country Code ☑ 387

Currency Convertible mark (KM, BAM)

Emergency Ambulance ☑ 124, Fire ☑ 123, Police ☑ 122

Languages Bosnian, Serbian and Croatian (all variants of the same language)

Money ATMs accepting Visa and MasterCard are ubiquitous

Time Central European Time (GMT/UTC plus one hour)

Visas Not required for most visitors (see www. mvp.gov.ba)

Sleeping Price Ranges

The following price ranges refer to a double room with bathroom during high season.

€ less than 80KM

€€ 80KM–190KM

€€€ more than 190KM

Eating Price Ranges

The following price ranges refer to a main course.

€ less than 10KM

€€ 10KM–20KM

€€€ more than 20KM

BOSNIA & HERCEGOVINA

Bosnia & Hercegovina Highlights

1 Sarajevo (p145)
Padding around Baščaršija's fascinating Turkic-era alleyways and downing heart-stopping Bosnian coffee and the nation's best *burek* and *ćevapi*.

2 Mostar (p150) Gawping as young men throw themselves off the magnificently rebuilt

stone bridge at the centre of the city's old Ottoman quarter.

3 Jajce (p157) Watching the waterfall tumble photogenically past castle-crowned Old Town.

4 Trebinje (p155) Enjoying this fetching regional centre's low-key pace, with its walled

riverside Old Town and leafy squares and parks.

5 Kravica Waterfall (p154) Cooling off in the turquoise waters beneath the fantastical falls.

6 Počitelj (p155) Soaking up the atmosphere of a tiny, picture-perfect Ottoman hillside town.

SARAJEVO

📱 033 / POP 395,000

Ringed by mountains, Sarajevo is a singular city with a enticing East-meets-West vibe all of its own. It was once renowned as a religious melting pot, earning it the epithet 'the Jerusalem of Europe'. Within a few blocks you can still find large Catholic and Orthodox cathedrals, Ashkenazi and Sephardic synagogues, and numerous mosques. However, the Jewish population was decimated during WWII and Sarajevo is now a divided city, with most of the Orthodox Christians living in Istočno Sarajevo (East Sarajevo) on the Republika Srpska side.

During the 20th century, two violent events thrust Sarajevo into the world's consciousness: the assassination which sparked WWI, and the brutal almost-four-year siege of the city in the 1990s. The scars of the longest siege in modern European history are still painfully visible, yet Sarajevo is once again a wonderful place to visit – for its intriguing architectural medley, vibrant street life and irrepressible spirit.

⦿ Sights

⦿ Baščaršija

Centred on what foreigners call Pigeon Square, Baščaršija (pronounced barsh-*char*-shi-ya) is the very heart of old Sarajevo. The name is derived from the Turkish for 'main market' and it's still lined with stalls, a lively (if tourist-centric) coppersmiths' alley, grand Ottoman mosques, *caravanserai* (inn) restaurants and lots of inviting little cafes. The east-west lane, Sarači, broadens out into the wide pedestrian boulevard Ferhadija, where Austro-Hungarian–era buildings take over. Some particularly grand examples line the waterfront.

★ Sarajevo City Hall   ARCHITECTURE
(Gradska vijećnica Sarajevo; Obala Kulina bana bb, Baščaršija; adult/child 10/5KM; ⊘9am-6pm) A storybook neo-Moorish striped facade makes the triangular Vijećnica (1896) Sarajevo's most beautiful Austro-Hungarian–era building. Seriously damaged during the 1990s siege, it finally reopened in 2014 after laborious reconstruction. Its colourfully restored interior and stained-glass ceiling are superb. Your ticket also allows you to peruse the excellent *Sarajevo 1914–2014* exhibition in the octagonal basement. This gives well-explained potted histories of the city's various 20th-century periods, insights into fashion and music subcultures, and revelations about Franz Ferdinand's love life.

★ Galerija 11/07/95   MUSEUM
(📱033-953 170; www.galerija110795.ba; 3rd fl, Trg Fra Grge Martića 2, Baščaršija; admission/audioguide/tour 12/3/4KM; ⊘9am-10pm, guided tours 10.15am & 7.15pm) This gallery uses stirring photography, video footage and audio testimonies of survivors and family members to create a powerful memorial to the 8372 victims of the Srebrenica massacre, one of the most infamous events of the Bosnian civil war. You'll need well over an hour to make the most of a visit, and it's worth paying the extra for the audioguide to get more insight.

Gazi Husrev-beg Mosque   MOSQUE
(Gazi Husrev-begova džamija; 📱033-573 151; www.begovadzamija.ba; Sarači 18, Baščaršija; mosque 3KM, incl museum 5KM; ⊘9am-noon, 2.30-4pm & 5.30-7pm May-Sep, 9am-11am Oct-Apr) Bosnia's second Ottoman governor, Gazi Husrev-beg, funded a series of splendid 16th-century buildings of which this 1531 mosque, with its 45m minaret, is the greatest. The domed interior is beautifully proportioned and even if you can't look inside, it's worth walking through the courtyard with its lovely fountain, chestnut trees and the *turbe* (tomb) of its founder.

⦿ Other Areas

★ Sarajevo Cable Car   CABLE CAR
(Sarajevska žičara; 📱033-292 800; www.zicara.ba; off Franjevačka, Babića bašča; single/return 15/20KM; ⊘10am-8pm) Reopened in 2018 after being destroyed during the war, Sarajevo's cable car shuttles people on a nine-minute ride, climbing 500m to a viewpoint 1164m up on Mt Trebević. From here it's a short walk to the wreck of the Olympic bobsled track, seemingly held together by layers of graffiti.

★ War Childhood Museum   MUSEUM
(Muzej ratnog djetinjstva; 📱033-535 558; www.warchildhood.org; Logavina 32, Logavina; adult/child 10/5KM; ⊘11am-7pm) This affecting museum had its genesis in a 2013 book edited

Central Sarajevo

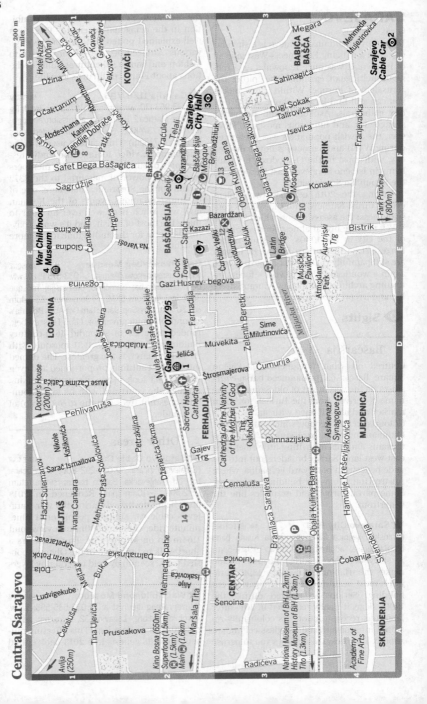

Central Sarajevo

by Jasminko Halilović, in which he asked a simple question of survivors of the Sarajevo siege: 'What was a war childhood for you?' Of the hundreds of replies received, 50 short written testimonies are presented here, each illustrated by personal effects donated by the writer, such as diaries, drawings, toys and ballet slippers. It's a lighter, less gore-filled approach to the conflict than you'll find elsewhere, but equally devastating.

National Museum of BiH   MUSEUM
(Zemaljski muzej BiH; www.zemaljskimuzej.ba; Zmaja od Bosne 3, Marijin dvor; adult/child 6/3KM; ☺10am-7pm Tue-Fri, to 2pm Sat & Sun) Bosnia's biggest and best-endowed museum of ancient and natural history is housed in an impressive, purpose-built quadrangle of neoclassical 1913 buildings. It's best known for housing the priceless Sarajevo Haggadah illuminated manuscript, but there's much more to see. Along with the Haggadah, the main building houses extraordinary Greek pottery and Roman mosaics. Behind this, the central courtyard has a pretty little botanical garden and an exceptional collection of medieval *stećci* (stone funerary monuments).

History Museum of BiH   MUSEUM
(☑033-226 098; www.muzej.ba; Zmaja od Bosne 5, Novo Sarajevo; adult/child 5/2KM; ☺9am-7pm) Somewhat misleadingly named, this small yet engrossing museum occupies a striking, still partly war-damaged 1960s social-ist-modernist building originally dubbed the Museum of the Revolution. It regularly hosts high-profile international exhibitions but the main attraction is the permanent *Surrounded Sarajevo* display, which charts local people's life-and-death battles for survival between 1992 and 1995. Alongside some heartbreaking photographs are personal effects such as self-made lamps, examples of food aid, stacks of Monopoly-style 1990s dinars and a makeshift siege-time 'home'.

Also interesting is the collection of 1996–2011 before-and-after Sarajevo images in the hallway. Directly behind the building, the tongue-in-cheek Tito (Zmaja od Bosne 5, Novo Sarajevo; ☺7am-11pm) bar is a museum in its own right.

Tunnel of Hope   MUSEUM
(Tunel Spasa; ☑033-778 672; www.tunelspasa.ba; Tuneli 1, Ilidža; adult/child 10/5KM; ☺9am-4pm) During the 1992–95 siege, when Sarajevo was surrounded by Bosnian Serb forces, the only link to the outside world was an 800m-long, 1m-wide, 1.6m-high tunnel between two houses on opposite sides of the airport runway. Walking through a 25m section is the moving culmination of a visit to the shell-pounded house which hid the western tunnel entrance. The story of the siege and the tunnel's construction is told via video, information boards and an audioguide accessible via free wi-fi.

🛏 Sleeping

Doctor's House   HOSTEL €
(☑061 222 914; www.thedoctorshousehostel.com; Pehlivanuša 67, Bjelave; dm/d from 24/70KM; 🛜) The Doctor's House is a healthy choice, if only for the workout you'll get walking up the hill from the centre of town. It's a nice neighbourhood; the French ambassador lives next door. The dorms all have privacy curtains, reading lights, power points and lockers, and there are also a couple of tidy private rooms.

★Halvat Guest House   GUESTHOUSE €€
(☑033-237 715; www.halvat.com.ba; Kasima Efendije Dobrače 13, Kovači; s/d/tr 80/113/132KM;

P ✳ 🛜) The six rooms at this friendly, family-run guesthouse are clean and spacious, and surprisingly quiet for such a central location. Breakfast is available at an additional charge – but with Baščaršija (p145) just down the road, you might choose to skip it. Only the narrowest of vehicles and drivers should brave the secure garage (charged separately).

Hotel VIP
HOTEL €€

(📞033-535 533; www.hotelvip.info; Jaroslava Černija 3, Baščaršija; s/d 138/177KM; P ✳ 🛜) Tucked away on a quiet lane in the centre of town, this smart modern block only has a dozen rooms but the ambience, professional service, valet parking and well-provisioned breakfast buffet might have you think you're staying somewhere far ritzier. The bathrooms are excellent, and some rooms have balconies.

★ Isa-begov Hamam Hotel
HERITAGE HOTEL €€€

(📞033-570 050; www.isabegovhotel.com; Bistrik 1, Bistrik; s/d from €80/100; ✳) After many years of restoration this ornate 19th-century *hammam* (Turkish bath), founded in 1462, reopened with a hotel attached in 2015. The 15 rooms are designed to evoke the spirit of the age, with lashings of handcrafted darkwood furniture, ornately carved bedsteads and tube-glass chandeliers. Guests get free use of the *hammam*, which is also open to the general public.

Hotel Aziza
HOTEL €€€

(📞033-257 940; www.hotelaziza.ba; Saburina 2, Vratnik; r/ste 196/235KM; P ✳ 🛜) Not just an extremely comfortable and friendly family-run hotel, this place invites you to enter into the love story of its owners, Mehmed and Aziza Poričanin. The 17 spacious, light-filled rooms are numbered according to significant years in the couple's life, such as the births of children and grandchildren. A daily sauna is included in the rates.

✖ Eating

★ Željo
BALKAN €

(📞033-447 000; Kundurdžiluk 19 & 20, Baščaršija; mains 3.5-7KM; ⊙8am-10pm; 🛜) Locals are willing to brave the tourist throngs at Željo as it's quite possibly the best place for *ćevapi* (spicy beef or pork meatballs) in Sarajevo. There are two branches diagonally across from each other. Both have street seating; neither serves alcohol.

★ Avlija
EUROPEAN €€

(📞033-444 483; www.avlija.ba; Sumbula Avde 2, Višnjik; mains 7-15KM; ⊙8am-11pm Mon-Sat; 🛜) Locals and a few in-the-know expats cosy up at painted wooden benches in this colourful, buzzing covered yard, dangling with trailing pot plants, strings of peppers and the odd birdcage. Local specialities are served, along with pasta, risotto and schnitzel. Wash them down with inexpensive local draught beers and wines.

Superfood
INTERNATIONAL €€

(www.facebook.com/SuperfoodStrEatArt; Husrefa Redžića 14, Ciglane; mains 5-27KM; ⊙11am-11pm Tue-Sat, noon-8pm Sun; 🛜) Tucked away among a set of much-graffitied apartment blocks, this hip café/restaurant wouldn't be out of place on the back streets of Auckland or Melbourne. It's a great place for brunch or a lunchtime sandwich, and they're particularly proud of their gourmet hamburgers here. Most of the ingredients are local, organic and free range.

Cakum Pakum
EUROPEAN €€

(📞061 955 310; Kaptol 10, Centar; mains 7-26KM; ⊙11am-11pm) A collection of antique suitcases, fringed lamps, gingham curtains and bright tartan tablecloths set the scene at this hip, wee restaurant with only half a dozen small tables. The food is simple but delicious – think savoury pancakes, salads, a large range of pasta and a small selection of grills.

Park Prinčeva
BALKAN €€€

(📞061 222 708; www.parkprinceva.ba; Iza Hrida 7, Hrid; mains 14-30KM; ⊙9am-11pm; P ✳) Gaze out over a superb city panorama from this hillside perch, like Bono and Bill Clinton before you. From the open-sided terrace, the City Hall (p145) is beautifully framed between rooftops, mosques and twinkling lights. Charming waiters in bow ties and red waistcoats deliver traditional dishes such as dumplings with cheese, veal *ispod sača* (roasted under a metal dome) and skewers.

🍷 Drinking & Entertainment

★ Zlatna Ribica
BAR

(📞033-836 348; Kaptol 5, Centar; ⊙8am-late) Sedate and outwardly grand, the tiny and eccentric 'Golden Fish' adds understated humour to a cosy treasure trove of antiques and kitsch, reflected in big art nouveau mirrors. Drink menus are hidden in old books that dangle by phone cords and the toilet is

OLYMPIC SKIING

Bjelašnica

The modest ski resort of **Bjelašnica** (www.bjelasnica.org; Babin Do bb; ski pass day/night 35/25KM, lift from 10KM in summer; ☉8am-4pm & 6.30-9pm ski season, 10am-5pm May-Oct), around 25km south of Sarajevo, hosted the men's alpine events during the 1984 Winter Olympics. There's usually enough snow to ski from around Christmas, and New Year is the busiest time, though February is more reliable for good piste conditions. Floodlit night skiing is offered and the main lift also operates May to October, allowing walkers easy access to high-altitude paths. In summer, there are magical mountain villages to explore.

Jahorina

Of Sarajevo's two Olympic skiing resorts, multi-piste **Jahorina** (☑057-270 020; www.oc-jahorina.com; Olimpijska bb, Jahorina; ski pass per day 44-50KM, night 30-38KM, day & night 61-73KM; ☉Nov-Mar) (26km southeast of the city, on the Republika Srpska side) has the widest range of hotels, each within 300m of one of seven main ski lifts. There are still lots of bombed-out buildings to be seen, but reconstruction is continuing apace. The ski season usually starts in mid-November and continues through to late March. The resort is at its busiest during the New Year holidays.

Beside the longest slope, **Rajska Vrata** (☑057-272 020; www.jahorina-rajskavrata.com; Olimpijska 41, Jahorina; mains 8-20KM; ☉9am-10pm Dec-Mar, to 5pm Apr-Nov; ℗☎) is a charming ski-in alpine chalet restaurant that sets diners beside a central fire with a giant metallic chimney or on the piste-side terrace. Upstairs, six Goldilocks-esque pine-walled guest bedrooms have handmade beds fashioned from gnarled old branches.

---

an experience in itself. Music swerves unpredictably between jazz, Parisian crooners, opera, reggae and the Muppets.

Art Kuća Sevdaha
CAFE

(Halači 5, Baščaršija; ☉10am-6pm Tue-Sun; ☎) Sit in the intimate fountain courtyard of an Ottoman-era building sipping Bosnian coffee, juniper or rose sherbet, or herb-tea infusions while nibbling local sweets. The experience is accompanied by the lilting wails of *sevdah* (traditional Bosnian music) – usually recorded, but sometimes live. Within the building is a museum celebrating great 20th-century *sevdah* performers (5KM) along with a store selling CDs.

Kino Bosna
ARTS CENTRE

(Kinoteka BiH; www.facebook.com/kinobosna; Alipašina 19, Koševo; ☉hours vary) This historical cinema overflows on Mondays during smoky singalongs to the house band playing Bosnian *sevdah* songs. Yugo-nostalgics pack in for New Wave nights and other themed parties. The building, originally industrial, was adapted into a workers' club, then a theatre from the 1940s. It houses the national film archive.

National Theatre Sarajevo PERFORMING ARTS
(Narodno pozorište Sarajevo; ☑033-221 682; www.nps.ba; Obala Kulina bana 9, Centar) Classically adorned with fiddly gilt mouldings, this proscenium-arch theatre hosts a ballet, opera, play or classical concert most nights from mid-September to mid-June. The grand, column-fronted, Renaissance-style building dates from 1921, adapted from its 1899 original form.

❶ Information

Sarajevo University Clinical Centre (Klinički centar univerziteta u Sarajevu; ☑033-445 522, 033-297 000; www.kcus.ba; Bolnička 25) Within the vast Koševo Hospital complex there's an English-speaking VIP outpatient clinic for people with foreign health insurance. The hospital also offers emergency care, including an emergency paediatrics department.

Tourist Information Centre (Turistički informativni centar; ☑033-580 999; www.sarajevo-tourism.com; Sarači 58, Baščaršija; ☉9am-9pm May-Oct, to 5pm Nov-Apr) Helpful official information centre. Beware of commercial imitations.

ℹ Getting There & Away

AIR

The centrally located **Sarajevo International Airport** (SJJ; www.sarajevo-airport.ba; Kurta Schorka 36; ◷5am-11pm) is about 10km south-west of Baščaršija (p145).

BUS

→ Sarajevo's main **bus station** (☑033-213 100; Put života 8, Novo Sarajevo; ◷24hr) has daily services to all neighbouring countries and to as far afield as Amsterdam and Istanbul. There are good links to Bosnian destinations including Mostar (20KM, 2½ hours, 10 daily) and Bihać (42KM, 6½ hours, four daily).

→ Further services to Republika Srpska (RS) and Serbia leave from the **Istočno Sarajevo Bus Station** (☑057-317 377; www.centrotrans-ad.com; Srpskih vladara 2, Lukavica; ◷6am-11.15pm), although this isn't convenient for most travellers.

TRAIN

Trains departing Sarajevo's **railway station** (Željeznička stanica; ☑033-655 330; www.zfbh.ba; Trg žrtava genocida u Srebrenici, Novo Sarajevo; ◷ticket office 6.30am-8pm), adjacent to the bus station, head to destinations including Konjic (7.90KM, one hour, three daily), Mostar (18KM, two hours, two daily) and Bihać (37KM, 6¼ hours, daily).

ℹ Getting Around

TO/FROM THE AIRPORT

→ On the meter, airport-bound taxis charge around 7KM from Ilidža or 16KM from Baščaršija, plus 2KM per bag for luggage in some cabs. However, at the terminal it's not always easy to find a taxi prepared to use the meter.

→ A Centrotrans bus marked Aero-drom-Baščaršija (5KM, pay on-board) departs from outside the terminal and takes around 30 minutes to central Sarajevo. However, departures are (at most) once an hour. Buses follow the main tram route, heading east along the river via Obala Kulina bana and then looping back to the airport along Mula Mustafe Bašeskije, stopping on demand at all the main stops along the way.

PUBLIC TRANSPORT

Sarajevo has an extensive network of trams, buses, trolleybuses and minibuses, all operated by **GRAS** (☑033-293 333; www.gras.ba). Except for the airport bus, all single-ride tickets cost 1.60KM if pre-purchased from kiosks, or 1.80KM if bought from the driver; they must be stamped once aboard. Two-ride (3KM), five-ride (7.10KM) and day tickets (*dnevna karta*, 5.30KM) are also available, but these are sold at official GRAS kiosks, which are few and far between.

HERCEGOVINA

Hercegovina ('hair-tse-go-*vi*-na') is the sun-scorched southern part of the country, shadowing Croatia's Dalmatian coast. It takes its name from 15th-century duke (*herceg* in the local lingo) Stjepan Vukčić Kosača, under whose rule it became a semi-independent duchy of the Kingdom of Bosnia.

Its arid Mediterranean landscape has a distinctive beauty punctuated by barren mountain ridges and photogenic river valleys. Famed for its fine wines and sun-packed fruits, Hercegovina is sparsely populated but has some intriguing historical towns and even has one little toehold on the Adriatic coast.

These days Western Hercegovina is dominated by Bosnian Croats while Eastern Hercegovina is part of the Republika Srpska. Bosniak Muslims maintain an uneasy position between the two, especially in the divided but fascinating city of Mostar. Not counting the Catholic pilgrims who flood Međugorje, Mostar is far and away Hercegovina's biggest tourist drawcard. Trebinje is lesser known but has an appealing old core.

Mostar

☑036 / POP 105,800

Mostar is the largest city in Hercegovina, with a small but thoroughly enchanting old town centre. At dusk, the lights of numerous millhouse restaurants twinkle across gushing streams, narrow **Kujundžiluk** bustles joyously with trinket sellers and, in between, the Balkans' most celebrated bridge forms a majestic stone arc between medieval towers.

Stay into the evening to see it without the summer hordes of day trippers. Stay even longer to enjoy memorable attractions in the surrounding area and to ponder the city's darker side – beyond the cobbled lanes of the attractively restored Ottoman quarter are whole blocks of bombed-out buildings, a poignant legacy of the 1990s conflict.

Between November and April most tourist facilities go into hibernation, while summer here is scorchingly hot. Spring and autumn are ideal times to visit.

KONJIC

Resting alongside the icy green Neretva River, the small town of Konjic was battered in both WWII and the 1990s war, but has revived its compact historical core centred on a beautiful six-span **Old Stone Bridge** (Stara kamena ćuprija; Konjic). Originally built in 1682, it was dynamited at the end of WWII by retreating Nazi forces but accurately reconstructed in 2009 on its original footings.

The area is also home to **D-O ARK** (Tito's Bunker; ☑036-734 811; www.titosbunker.ba; per person 20KM; ☉tours 10am, noon & 2pm), one of the most extraordinary remnants of the Cold War, designed to keep Yugoslav president Tito and his high command safe from a 25-megaton blast. Built in secret between 1953 and 1979, this extensive subterranean command centre is reputed to have cost the equivalent of US$4 billion. It's located 4km southeast of Konjic; follow the signs.

There's also good hiking in the surrounding mountains and rafting downstream on the Neretva. **RaftKor** (☑061 474 507; www.raft-kor.com; Varda 40/1; per person €35) is a reliable outfit that starts its tours with a visit to Boračko Lake. Rafting and canyoning trips can also be booked through **Visit Konjic** (☑061 072 027; www.visitkonjic.com; Donje polje bb; ☉8am-8pm).

Numerous buses, including all Sarajevo–Mostar services, pass through Konjic. Three trains a day head north to Sarajevo (7.90KM, one hour) and south to Mostar (11KM, 50 minutes).

◎ Sights

★ Stari Most   BRIDGE
The world-famous Stari Most (meaning simply 'Old Bridge') is Mostar's indisputable visual focus. Its pale stone magnificently reflects the golden glow of sunset or the tasteful night-time floodlighting. The bridge's swooping arch was originally built between 1557 and 1566 on the orders of Suleiman the Magnificent. The current structure is a very convincing 21st-century rebuild following the bridge's 1990s bombardment during the civil war. Numerous well-positioned cafes and restaurants tempt you to sit and savour the splendidly restored scene.

Partisan Memorial Cemetery   MEMORIAL
(Partizansko spomen-groblje; Kralja Petra Krešimira IV bb) Although sadly neglected and badly vandalised, fans of 20th-century socialist architecture should seek out this magnificent memorial complex, designed by leading Yugoslav-era architect Bogdan Bogdanović and completed in 1965. Paths wind up past a broken bridge, a no-longer-functioning water feature and cosmological symbols to an almost Gaudi-esque upper section made of curved and fluted concrete, which contains the graves of 810 Mostar Partisans who died fighting fascism during WWII.

Kajtaz House   MUSEUM
(Kajtazova kuća; ☑061 339 897; www.facebook.com/KajtazsHouse; Gaše Ilića 21; adult/child 4KM/free; ☉9am-6pm Apr-Oct) Hidden behind tall walls, Mostar's most interesting old house was once the harem (women's) section of a larger homestead built for a 16th-century Turkish judge. Full of original artefacts, it still belongs to descendants of the original family but is now under Unesco protection. A visit includes a very extensive personal tour.

Hamam Museum   MUSEUM
(☑036-580 200; www.facebook.com/thehamam museum; Rade Bitange bb; adult/child 4/3KM; ☉10am-6pm) This late 16th-century bathhouse has been attractively restored with whitewashed interiors, bilingual panels explaining *hammam* (Turkish bath) culture and glass cabinets displaying associated traditional accoutrements. A wordless five-minute video gives a slickly sensual evocation of an imagined latter-day bathhouse experience.

War Photo Exhibition   GALLERY
(Stari Most; admission 6KM; ☉9am-9pm Jul-Sep, 10am-6pm Mar-Jun & Oct) This collection of around 50 powerful wartime photos by New Zealand photojournalist Wade Goddard is displayed in the western tower guarding Stari Most, above the Bridge Divers' Club.

Bridge Divers' Club   ADVENTURE SPORTS
(☑061 388 552; Stari Most; training/membership €10/25; ☉10am-dusk) In summer, young men leap from the parapet of Stari Most in a

Mostar

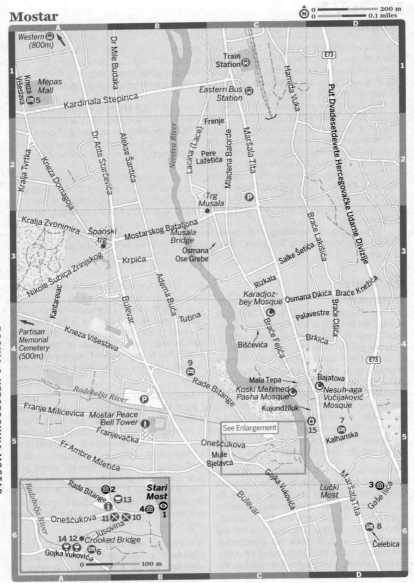

BOSNIA & HERCEGOVINA MOSTAR

tradition dating back centuries, plummeting more than 20m into the freezing cold Neretva. It's a hilarious spectacle, involving much stretching, preening and posing in speedos and cajoling the crowd for donations. Divers won't leap until 50KM has been collected (in winter it's double).

If you want to experience one of Bosnia's ultimate adrenaline rushes for yourself, you'll first need to pay for training dives from a much lower perch at the riverside downstream. If you prove capable you can then join the club and test your mettle with the real thing. You'll get a certificate to prove

Mostar

your achievement. Don't underestimate the dangers – diving badly can prove fatal. But if you love it, your life membership means you can subsequently dive as often as you like.

🛏 Sleeping

Taso's House HOSTEL €
(📞061 523 149; www.guesthousetaso.com; Maršala Tita 187; dm/r from €8/20; ❋🛜) There's nothing flash about this cramped little hostel, but backpackers love it for its chilled-out vibe and the friendliness of the family who runs it. There's only one private twin room and three dorms, one of which is in an annex nearby.

★Pansion Čardak GUESTHOUSE €€
(📞036-578 249; www.pansion-cardak.com; Jusovina 3; r from €60; P❋🛜) This old stone house on a central lane has been thoroughly modernised and now offers seven spacious ensuite rooms with feature walls emblazoned with forest scenes. There's also a small guest kitchen.

Villa Fortuna HOTEL €€
(📞036-580 625; www.villafortuna.ba; Rade Bitange 34; s/d 68/95KM; P❋🛜) Set back from a street leading to the old bridge, this eight-room family-run hotel offers welcome drinks in a sweet little private courtyard area at the rear. Fresh if compact rooms lead off a hallway decorated with a museum-like collection of local tools and metalwork.

Shangri La GUESTHOUSE €€
(📞061 169 362; www.shangrila.com.ba; Kalhanska 10; r €53-69; P❋🛜) Behind an imposing 1887 facade, eight individually themed rooms are presented to hotel standards, and there's a fine roof terrace with comfy parasol-shaded seating, dwarf citrus trees and panoramic city views. The English-speaking hosts are faultlessly welcoming without being intrusive. Breakfast costs €6 extra. The location is wonderfully peaceful, just three minutes' walk from Stari Most (p151) up a narrow lane.

Hotel Mepas HOTEL €€€
(📞036-382 000; www.mepas-hotel.ba; Kneza Višeslava bb; s/d from 167/203KM; P❋🛜🏊) Mostar's first five-star hotel inhabits a corner of the large Mepas Mall complex. The bright, glitzy reception is on the ground floor, but rooms, pool and spa centre are all on the 8th and 9th floors.

🍴 Eating

★Tima-Irma BALKAN €
(📞066 905 070; www.cevabdzinica-tima.com; Onešćukova bb; mains 5-11KM; ⊙8am-11pm; 🛜) Despite the constant queues at this insanely popular little grill joint, the staff maintain an impressive equanimity while delivering groaning platters of *ćevapi* (skinless sausage), *pljeskavica* (burger meat) and shish kebabs. Unusually for this kind of eatery, most dishes are served with salad. Sandwiches and burgers are also on offer.

Šadrvan BALKAN €€
(📞061 891 189; www.facebook.com/SadrvanMostar; Jusovina 11; mains 3.60-20KM; ⊙9am-midnight; 🛜) On a vine- and tree-shaded corner where the pedestrian lane from Stari Most (p151) divides, this tourist favourite has tables set around a trickling fountain made of old Turkish-style metalwork. Obliging, costumed waiters can help explain a menu that covers many bases and takes a stab at some vegetarian options.

🍷 Drinking & Nightlife

Black Dog Pub PUB
(www.facebook.com/Blackdogpubmostar; Jusovina 5; ⊙4pm-midnight) This Black Dog really starts to howl on summer nights, when

musicians set up on the cobbles facing the Crooked Bridge and everyone lounges around on cushions. Inside, the historical millhouse is decked out with flags and car number plates. Grab a seat on the riverside terrace and sip on some local craft beer.

Ima i Može Craft Beer Garden CRAFT BEER
(☑061 799 398; www.facebook.com/oldbridz; Južni logor bb; ⊙9am-11pm) You're liable to hear old-school punk or Bowie blasting out of this open-sided wooden pavilion above the Radobolja River, given the predilections of the owner-manager, who's also behind the OldbridZ Brewery. Take a tasting flight of their excellent range, then start sampling the guest craft brews from elsewhere in Bosnia, Croatia and Serbia, accompanied by Mexican food or Bosnian cheese.

Café de Alma CAFE
(☑063 315 572; www.facebook.com/cafedealma; Rade Bitange bb; ⊙9.30am-6pm Apr-Dec) Step back to Ottoman times at this excellent coffee roastery, with a shady front terrace and cool interior. The only things served are homemade juices and Bosnian-style coffee, and on your first visit you'll be taken through the whole traditional coffee-drinking ritual. Enquire about Alma's Tales personalised city tours (€30).

❶ Information

Grad Mostar (www.turizam.mostar.ba)

Tourist Info Centre (☑036-580 275; www.hercegovina.ba; Rade Bitange 5; ⊙9am-noon May-Oct)

Visit Mostar (www.visitmostar.org)

❶ Getting There & Away

AIR
Mostar Airport (OMO; ☑036-352 770; www.mostar-airport.ba) is 7km south of town off the

Čapljina road. The only year-round flights are to Zagreb on Croatia Airlines, with additional airlines running seasonal services.

BUS
Mostar has two bus stations, only 1.5km apart – one for each half of its ethnic divide. The main one is the **eastern bus station** (Autobusni stanica; ☑036-552 025; Trg Ivana Krndelja), located right beside the train station; it's more convenient for travellers than the **western bus station** (Autobusni kolodvor; ☑036-348 680; Vukovarska bb; ⊙5.30am-10pm). Domestic destinations include Trebinje (21KM, 3½ hours, four daily), Sarajevo (20KM, 2½ hours, 10 daily) and Jajce (26KM, 4¼ hours, three daily); most services stop at both stations.

TRAIN
Trains from Mostar's **railway station** (Željeznička stanica; ☑036-550 608; www.zfbh.ba; Trg Ivana Krndelja 1), adjacent to the eastern bus station, depart every morning and evening for Konjic (11KM, 50 minutes) and Sarajevo (18KM, two hours).

❶ Getting Around

Local bus services, which extend as far as peripheral towns such as Blagaj, are operated by **Mostar Bus** (☑036-552 250; www.mostarbus.ba).

Blagaj
036 / POPULATION 2530
An easy day trip from Mostar, pretty Blagaj hugs the turquoise Buna River as it gushes out of a cave past a historical tekke (Sufi dervish spiritual house), several enticing restaurants and Ottoman-era homesteads.

Blagaj Tekke ISLAMIC SITE
(Blagajska tekija; ☑061 371 005; www.tekijablagaj.ba/en; Blagaj bb; admission 5KM; ⊙8am-10pm May-Oct, to 6pm Nov-Apr) Forming Blagaj's signature attraction, the centrepiece of this

DON'T MISS

KRAVICA WATERFALL

There's a slightly unreal Disney-esque quality to this outstanding **waterfall** (Slap Kravica; www.kravica.ba; adult/child 10/5KM; ⊙7am-10pm Jun-Sep, to 6pm Oct-Apr, to 8pm May), where the Trebižat River plummets in a broad 25m-high arc into an emerald pool. In spring, this gorgeous mini-Niagara pounds itself into a dramatic, steamy fury. In summer it's a more gentle cascade, but the basin offers an idyllic respite from the sweltering heat for hundreds of locals and tourists.

The falls are a 15-minute walk from a car park that's 4km down a dead-end road that is well signposted from the M6 (Čapljina–Ljubuški Rd). There's no public transport, but many Mostar group tours combine a stop at the falls with visits to Blagaj and Počitelj.

POČITELJ

The stepped medieval fortress village of Počitelj is one of the most picture-perfect architectural ensembles in the country. Cupped in a steep rocky amphitheatre, it's a warren of steps climbing between ramshackle stone-roofed houses and pomegranate bushes.

The village was badly damaged by Bosnian Croat forces in 1993, including the beautiful **Hajji Alija Mosque** (Hadži Alijina džamija; adult/child 3KM/free; ⊘ 9am-6pm Apr-Oct), which was deliberately targeted. This 1563 structure has now been restored, although photos displayed within show how much of the decorative paintwork has been lost.

Nearby is a 16m Ottoman **clock tower**, while further up the hill is a partly ruined fortress, capped by the octagonal **Gavrakapetan Tower**. You can climb up the tower or save your energy for even better panoramas from the uppermost rampart bastions.

Počitelj is 28km south of Mostar. Buses from Mostar to Čapljina or Metković (Croatia) take this route.

complex of traditional stone-roofed buildings is a very pretty half-timbered dervish house with wobbly rug-covered floors, carved doorways, curious niches and a bathroom with star-shaped coloured glass set into the ceiling. The dervishes follow a mystical strand of Islam in which the peaceful contemplation of nature plays a part, hence the *tekke*'s idyllic positioning above the cave mouth from which the Buna River's surreally blue-green waters flow forth.

🛏 Sleeping & Eating

Hotel Blagaj HOTEL €€
(☎ 036-573 805; www.hotel-blagaj.com; Blagaj bb; s/d/apt €34/49/70; ⊘ reception 7am-midnight; 🅿 ❄ 🛜) Built in 2015, this professional 27-room hotel contrasts white and lavender-wash walls with sepia scenes of old Mostar. It's just beyond the main town car park en route to Blagaj Tekke.

Restoran Vrelo INTERNATIONAL €€
(☎ 036-572 556; www.restoranvrelo.com; Blagaj bb; mains 9-30KM; ⊘ 10am-10.30pm; 🛜) Across the river from the tekke, this restaurant serves reliably good food on terraces overlooking a horseshoe of rapids. Local trout is served in a variety of styles, including *'probaj ova'* (literally 'try this') which comes in lemon sauce with pumpkin seeds. There are also schnitzels, steaks, seafood or meat platters, and delicious squid stuffed with three cheeses.

ℹ Information

The small **tourist information booth** (⊘ 8am-8pm May-Sep) is in the main car park, 650m short of the tekke.

ℹ Getting There & Away

City bus routes 10 and 11 from Mostar run to Blagaj (2.10KM, 30 minutes), with a total of 10 services on weekdays (fewer on weekends).

Trebinje

☑ 059 / POP 31,500

By far the prettiest city in Republika Srpska, Trebinje has a compact centre with a tiny walled Old Town flanked by a leafy market square. The Trebišnjica River is slow and shallow as it passes through, its banks lined with swimming spots and replicas of waterwheels, which were once used for irrigation. Mountains provide a sun-baked backdrop, while hills topped with Orthodox churches punctuate the suburbs.

It's barely 30km from Dubrovnik, but in tourist terms it's a world away – not to mention vastly cheaper. Some canny travellers base themselves here and 'commute'.

Trebinje's always been a Serb-majority town but more so since the war, with the proportion rising from 70% to 94%.

◉ Sights

Hercegovačka Gračanica CHURCH
(Херцеговачка Грачаница; Miloša Šarabe bb) Offering phenomenal views, this hilltop complex comprises a bell tower, gallery, cafe-bar and bishop's palace, but most notably the compact but eye-catching Presvete Bogorodice (Annunciation) Church. The latter's design is based very symbolically on the 1321 Gračanica monastery in Kosovo, a historically significant building that's considered sacred by many Serbs. The Trebinje version

was erected in 2000 to rehouse the bones of local poet-hero Jovan Dučić.

Arslanagić Bridge BRIDGE
(Perovića Most, Перовића мост) This unique double-backed structure was built in 1574 under the direction of Grand Vizier Mehmed Pasha Sokolović, who was also behind the Višegrad **bridge** (Most Mehmed-paše Sokolovića; P), though this one was named for the toll collector. It was originally 10km further upstream from its present location but in 1965 it disappeared beneath the rising waters of the Gorica reservoir. Rescued stone by stone, it took six years to be finally reassembled.

Sleeping

★**Hostel Polako** HOSTEL €
(066 380 722; www.hostelpolakotrebinje.com; Vožda Karađorđa 7; dm/r from €11/28; Jan-Nov;) Run by a friendly American/Polish couple, this much-loved hostel offers dorms and two private doubles; bathrooms are shared. It's a ten-minute walk from both the bus station and the Old Town. Rates include pancakes for breakfast.

Hotel Platani HOTEL €€
(059-274 050; www.hotel-platani-trebinje.com; Riste i Bete Vukanović 1; s/d/apt 72/105/164KM; P) Taking pride of place on Trebinje's pretty, central **square** (Трг слободе), this landmark hotel evokes the elegance of the Austro-Hungarian era. Downstairs is one of Trebinje's best restaurants (mains 10KM to 34KM), while upstairs are spacious, well-presented rooms. One huge corner room is after named *Matrix* actress Monica Bellucci who stayed here while filming locally. There's also an annex across the square.

Sesto Senso HOTEL €€
(059-261 160; www.facebook.com/sestosenso trebinje; Obala Mića Ljubibratića 3; s/d from €42/52; P) Wrapped up in an attractive white-stone-and-glass package, this modern four-storey block is big on 21st-century style. The cheapest rooms only have tiny, high windows; it's worth paying extra for a balcony and river view. Downstairs on the terrace is one of Trebinje's best international restaurants (7am to 11pm; mains 8KM to 29KM), serving everything from local grills to chicken curries.

Information

The extremely helpful **tourist office** (059-273 410; www.gotrebinje.com; Jovan Dučića bb; 8am-4pm Mon-Fri, 9am-2pm Sat) is next to the Catholic cathedral, across the park from the Old Town's western gate.

Getting There & Away

Trebinje's **bus station** (Autobuska stanica; 059-220 466; Vojvode Stepe Stepanovića bb) is 600m southwest of the Old Town. Destinations include Mostar (21KM, 3½ hours, four daily), Konjic (26KM, two daily), Istočno Sarajevo (27KM, 4¾ hours, three daily) and Dubrovnik (8KM, one hour, one or two daily).

WESTERN BOSNIA

Travelling through this region of green wooded hills, river canyons, rocky crags and mildly interesting historical towns you'll find yourself constantly passing in and out of Bosniak-Croat Federation territory and the Republika Srpska. You'll always know when you're in the latter by the red-blue-and-white Serbian flags which sprout in profusion whenever you enter it. Prominent towns include the old Ottoman administrative capital Travnik, the gorgeous hilltop settlement of Jajce, and Republika Srpska's quasi capital Banja Luka. In the west, the Una River gushes flamboyantly over a series of waterfalls before joining the Sava on its rush to the Danube and, ultimately, the Black Sea.

Una River Valley

The adorable Una River goes through widely varying moods. In the lush green gorges to the northeast, some sections are as calm as mirrored opal, while others gush over widely fanned rafting rapids. The river broadens and gurgles over a series of shallow falls as it passes through the unassuming town of Bihać (population 39,700). Occasionally it leaps over impressive falls, notably at Štrbački Buk (p157), which forms the centrepiece of the 198-sq-km **Una National Park** (www.nationalpark-una.ba).

Sights & Activities

Rafting is a draw here; in addition, there's kayaking, fly-fishing (day's licence 40KM; two-fish maximum) and 'speed river diving', a sport invented here involving scuba diving in fast-flowing waters. Each activity centre has its own campsite and provides transfers from Bihać.

JAJCE & THE VRBAS RIVER

Jajce is a historical gem, with a highly evocative walled Old Town and **fortress** (Tvrđava u Jajcu; adult/child 2/1KM; ☉8am-8pm May-Oct, to 4pm Nov-Apr) clinging to a steep rocky knoll with rivers on two sides. The Pliva River tumbles into the Vrbas River by way of an impressive urban **waterfall** (Vodopad) right at the very foot of the town walls. Immediately to the west, the Pliva is dammed to form two pretty **lakes** (Plivsko Jezero) which are popular with swimmers, strollers, bikers and boaters.

Further up the Vrbas towards Banja Luka, **Kanjon Rafting Centre** (☑066 714 169; www.raftingnavrbasu.com; Karanovac bb; ☉9am-8pm Apr-Oct) is a reliable extreme-sports outfit specialising in rafting (35-70KM) but also offering guided hiking and canyoning trips (40KM, six person minimum). Rafting requires at least four people but joining with others is sometimes possible in summer; phone to enquire.

Jajce's centrally located bus station has services to Bihać (25KM, 3½ hours, five daily), Sarajevo (27KM, 3½ hours, five daily) and Mostar (26KM, 4¼ hours, three daily).

Ostrožac Fortress
FORTRESS

(☑061 236 641; www.ostrozac.com; Ostrožac; admission 2KM; ☉9am-dusk) Ostrožac is one of Bosnia's most photogenic castles, a spooky Gothic place high above the Una Valley, up 3km of hairpins towards Cazin. There's plenty to explore from various epochs, ramparts to walk, towers to climb and a manor house on the verge of collapse that all add to the thrill (and danger) of poking about. Off-season you might have to call the caretaker to get in, but it's only officially closed if it's snowing.

Štrbački Buk
WATERFALL

(Una National Park Entry Gate 3; adult/child 6/4KM; ☉dawn-dusk) A strong contender for the title of the nation's most impressive waterfall, Štrbački Buk is a seriously dramatic 40m-wide cascade, pounding 23.5m down three travertine sections, including over a superbly photogenic 18m drop-off, overlooked by a network of viewing platforms. The easiest access is 8km along a graded but potholed unpaved road from Orašac on the Kulen Vakuf road. There are swimming spots to stop at along the way.

Milančev Buk
WATERFALL

(Una National Park Entry Gate 5, Martin Brod; adult/child 2/1.50KM; ☉dawn-dusk) Collectively, this group of cascades tumbles down a vertical height of more than 50m, with a wide arc of rivulets pouring into a series of pools surrounded by lush, green foliage. The main viewpoint is a minute's walk from the ticket gate, 1.3km off the Bihać–Dravar Rd in Martin Brod village. Make sure you check out the view from the red footbridge near the car park, too.

ⓘ Getting There & Away

➠ Bihać's **bus station** (Autobuska stanica Bihać; ☑037-311 939; www.unatransport.ba; Put Armije Republike BiH bb) is 1km west of the centre. Destinations include Jajce (25KM, 3½ hours, five daily) and Sarajevo (42KM, 6½ hours, four daily).

➠ A daily train heads to **Bihać Railway Station** (☑037-312 282; www.zfbh.ba; Bihaćkih Branilaca 20) from Sarajevo (37KM, 6¼ hours).

SURVIVAL GUIDE

ⓘ Directory A–Z

ACCOMMODATION

Accommodation is remarkably fair value by European standards. There's a good supply of guesthouses, rental apartments, motels and hostels (many homestay-style), plus some boutique and character hotels. Business and five-star hotels are rarer. Ski areas have some upmarket resorts. Most hotels in Bosnia include some type of breakfast in the rates.

LGBTIQ+ TRAVELLERS

Although Bosnia decriminalised homosexuality in 1998 (2000 in the Republika Srpska), attitudes remain very conservative and attacks have occurred at queer festivals in the past. LGBTIQ+ advocacy organisation Sarajevo Open Centre (www.soc.ba) is active in fighting sexuality-based discrimination. In Sarajevo, the highlight of the queer year is the Merlinka Film Festival (www.merlinka.com) held in January or February. Sarajevo has a weekend-only gay bar but you won't find any elsewhere.

MONEY

ATMs accepting Visa and MasterCard are ubiquitous.

OPENING HOURS

Closing times for many eateries and bars depends on custom. In tourist areas such as Mostar, hotels and restaurants may close in the off season.

Banks 8am to 6pm Monday to Friday, 8.30am to 1.30pm Saturday.

Bars and clubs Most bars are cafes by day, opening at 8am and closing at 11pm or later. Pubs and clubs open later and, at weekends, might close at 3am.

Office hours Typically 8am to 4pm Monday to Friday.

Restaurants 7am to 10.30pm or until the last customer.

Shops 8am to 6pm daily, many stay open later.

PUBLIC HOLIDAYS

Nationwide holidays:

New Year's Day 1 and 2 January

May Day 1 and 2 May

Additional holidays in the Federation:

Independence Day 1 March

Catholic Easter Sunday March or April (in majority-Croat areas)

Catholic Easter Monday March or April (in majority-Croat areas)

Ramadan Bajram June (in majority-Bosniak areas)

Kurban Bajram August or September (in majority-Bosniak areas)

All Saints Day 1 November (in majority-Croat areas)

Statehood Day 25 November

Catholic Christmas 25 December (in majority-Croat areas)

Additional holidays in the Republika Srpska:

Orthodox Christmas 7 January

Republika Day 9 January

Orthodox New Year 14 January

Orthodox Good Friday March or April

Orthodox Easter Saturday March or April

Orthodox Easter Sunday March or April

Victory Day 9 May

Dayton Agreement Day 21 November

SAFE TRAVEL

Landmines and unexploded ordnance still affect 2% of Bosnia and Hercegovina's land area. **BHMAC** (www.bhmac.org) removes more every year. Progress was slowed by floods in 2014 which added to the complexity of locating the last mines. For your safety, stick to asphalt/ concrete surfaces or well-worn paths in affected areas, and avoid exploring war-damaged buildings.

TELEPHONE

Country code 387

International access code 00

Local directory information 1182 (Federation), 1185 (Republika Srpska), 1188 (Hrvatska pošta Mostar)

VISAS

It's wise to double-check the latest visa requirements by entering your nationality on the Ministry of Foreign Affairs website (www.mvp. gov.ba). Currently stays of less than 90 days require no visa for citizens of most European and American nations, plus Australia, New Zealand, Israel and several Arab and East Asian countries. If none of the visa-free conditions apply then check carefully at which specified embassies you are expected to apply (eg that means London or Tripoli for South Africans). Visitors without access to 150KM per day could be refused entry.

Note that you do not need a Bosnia and Hercegovina visa to transit (without stopping) through Neum between Split and Dubrovnik, as long as you have the right to reenter Croatia.

🚉 Getting There & Away

AIR

Bosnia doesn't have a national carrier.

Sarajevo International Airport (p150) Bosnia's busiest, with flights all over Europe and the Middle East.

Banja Luka International Airport (BNX, Међународни аеродром Бања Лука; ☑ 051-535 210; www.banjaluka-airport.com; Mahovljani bb, Laktaši) Only used by Air Serbia (to Belgrade) and Ryanair (Charleroi, Memmingen and Stockholm-Skavsta).

Mostar Airport (p154) Year-round Croatia Airlines flights to Zagreb plus seasonal services.

Tuzla International Airport (www.tuzla-airport.ba) Tiny but a hub for budget airline WizzAir, with flights to Austria, Switzerland, Germany, The Netherlands and Sweden.

LAND

Bus

Direct bus connections link Bosnia to all of its neighbours and to as far afield as Sweden. In most cases, passports are collected on the bus and handed over at the border; you usually won't leave the bus unless there's an issue that needs resolving. Useful websites include www.bustick et4.me, www.eurolines.com, www.getbybus. com and www.vollo.net.

Car & Motorcycle

Drivers need Green Card insurance and an EU or International Driving Permit. Transiting Neum in a Croatian hire car is usually not problematic.

Note that while most cars rented in Bosnia are covered for visits to neighbouring countries, Kosovo tends to be an exception, with insurance voided if you drive there. Since Croatia joined the EU in July 2013, many previously open minor border crossings with Bosnia and Hercegovina have been closed to international traffic, and border queues can be annoyingly long at busy times.

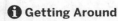 Getting Around

BUS

Bus services are excellent and relatively inexpensive. There are often different companies handling each route, so prices can vary substantially. Luggage stowed in the baggage compartment under the bus costs extra (around 2KM a piece).

Bus stations pre-sell tickets. Between towns it's normally easy enough to wave down any bus en route. Advance reservations are sometimes necessary for overnight routes or at peak holiday times. The biggest companies include Auto-prevoz (www.autoprevoz.ba), Centrotrans (www.centrotrans.com) and Globtour (www.globtour.com). Useful websites offering schedules and bookings include www.busticket4.me, www.vollo.net and www.getbybus.com.

Frequency on some routes drops drastically at weekends. Some shorter routes stop on Sundays.

CAR & MOTORCYCLE

Bosnia and Hercegovina's winding roads are lightly trafficked and a delight for driving if you aren't in a hurry. Driving makes sense to reach the country's more remote areas. There are a few toll motorways in the centre of the country; collect your ticket from the machine at the set of booths where you enter, then pay at the booths where you leave the motorway.

TRAIN

Trains are slower and far less frequent than buses but generally slightly cheaper. ŽFBH (www.zfbh.ba) has an online rail timetable search. The main routes are Sarajevo–Bihać and Sarajevo–Konjic–Mostar.

Britain

POP 66 MILLION

Best Traditional British Pubs

➜ Ye Olde Mitre (p182)

➜ Turf Tavern (p195)

➜ Old Thatch Tavern (p198)

➜ Blue Bell (p203)

Best Museums

➜ Natural History Museum (p169)

➜ Victoria & Albert Museum (p172)

➜ Ashmolean Museum (p194)

➜ National Railway Museum (p201)

Why Go?

Few places cram so much history, heritage and scenery into such a compact space as Britain. Twelve hours is all you'll need to travel from one end to the other, but you could spend a lifetime exploring – from the ancient relics of Stonehenge and Avebury, to the great medieval cathedrals of Westminster and Canterbury, and the magnificent mountain landscapes of Snowdonia and Skye.

In fact, Britain isn't really one country at all, but three. While they haven't always been easy bedfellows, the contrasts between England, Wales and Scotland make this a rewarding place to visit. With a wealth of rolling countryside, stately cities, world-class museums and national parks to explore, Britain really is one of Europe's most unmissable destinations. And despite what you may have heard, it doesn't rain all the time – but even so, a brolly and a raincoat will certainly come in handy.

When to Go
London

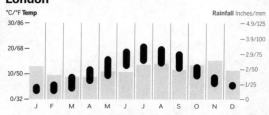

Easter–May Fewer crowds, especially in popular spots like Bath, York and Edinburgh.

Jun–Aug The weather is at its best but the coast and national parks are busy.

Mid-Sep–Oct Prices drop and the weather is often surprisingly good.

Entering the Country

Most visitors reach Britain by air. As London is a global transport hub, it's easy to fly to Britain from just about anywhere.

The other main option for travel between Britain and mainland Europe (and Ireland) is ferry, either port-to-port or combined with a long-distance bus trip, although journeys can be long and financial savings not huge compared with budget airfares.

International trains are much more comfortable and a 'green' option; the Channel Tunnel allows direct rail services between Britain, France and Belgium, with onward connections to many other European destinations.

ITINERARIES

One Week

With just seven days, you're pretty much limited to sights in England. Spend three days seeing the sights in London (p164), then head to Oxford (p193) for a day, followed by a day each at Stonehenge (p190) and historic Bath (p190), before returning for a final day in London.

Two Weeks

Follow the one-week itinerary, but instead of returning to London on day seven, head north to Stratford-upon-Avon (p196) for everything Shakespeare. Continue north with a day in the Lake District (p205), followed by two days in Scotland's capital, Edinburgh (p210). After a day trip to Loch Ness (p221), recross the border for two days to see York (p201) and Castle Howard (p203). Then, stop off in Cambridge (p199) on the way back to London.

Essential Food & Drink

Britain once had a reputation for bad food, but the nation has enjoyed something of a culinary revolution and you can now easily find fine dining based on fresh local produce.

Fish and chips Long-standing favourite, best sampled in coastal towns.

Haggis Scottish icon, mainly offal and oatmeal, traditionally served with mashed 'tatties and neeps' (potatoes and turnips).

Laverbread Laver is a type of seaweed, mixed with oatmeal and fried to create this traditional Welsh speciality.

Roast beef and Yorkshire pudding Traditional lunch on Sunday for the English.

Cornish pasty Savoury pastry; a southwest speciality, now available countrywide.

Real ale Traditionally brewed beer served at room temperature.

Scotch whisky Spirit distilled from malted and fermented barley, then aged in oak barrels for at least three years.

AT A GLANCE

Area 88,500 sq miles

Capitals London (England and the United Kingdom), Cardiff (Wales), Edinburgh (Scotland)

Country Code 44

Currency pound sterling (£)

Emergency 999 or 112

Languages English, Welsh, Scottish Gaelic

Time Greenwich Mean Time (GMT/UTC)

Visas Schengen rules do not apply

Sleeping Price Ranges

The following price ranges refer to a double room with private bathroom in high season (London/elsewhere). Hotels in London are more expensive than the rest of the country, so have different price ranges.

£ less than £100/£65

££ £100–200/£65–130

£££ more than £200/£130

Eating Price Ranges

The following price ranges refer to a main dish (London/elsewhere).

£ less than £12/£10

££ £12–25/£10–20

£££ more than £25/£20

Britain Highlights

1 London (p164)
Exploring the streets of one of the world's greatest capital cities.

2 Bath (p190)
Visiting Roman baths and admiring grand Georgian architecture.

3 Stratford-upon-Avon (p196) Enjoying a Shakepeare play in the town where he was born.

4 Snowdonia National Park
(p209) Marvelling at the mountainous landscape of Wales' first national park.

5 York (p201)
Delving into the city's history – Roman, Viking and medieval.

6 Oxford (p193)
Getting lost among the dreaming spires.

7 Stonehenge
(p190) Stepping back in time while

ATLANTIC OCEAN

SHETLAND ISLANDS

Mainland

ORKNEY ISLANDS

Mainland

NORTH SEA

St Kilda

OUTER HEBRIDES

Lewis

Harris

North Uist

South Uist

The Minch

Durness

Sutherland

Ullapool

Thurso
John O'Groats
Wick

Strathfarrar

Inverness

Moray Firth

Elgin

Findhorn

Aberdeen

Sea of the Hebrides

Isle of Skye

Rhum

Kyle of Lochalsh

Loch Ness

Aviemore

Cairngorms National Park

SCOTLAND

Don

Coll

Tiree

INNER HEBRIDES

Tobermory

Mull

Fort William

Ben Nevis

Oban

Loch Awe

Loch Lomond

Loch Lomond & The Trossachs National Park

Perth

Dundee

St Andrews

Stirling

Jura

Islay

Arran

North Channel

Glasgow

Alloway

Galloway

Edinburgh

Melrose

Hadrian's Wall

Northumberland National Park

Newcastle-

200 km
100 miles

wandering around the great trilithons of this ancient site.

8 Edinburgh (p210) Joining the party in Scotland's festival city.

9 Skye (p222) Heading north through the Scottish Highlands to experience the epic scenery of this rugged island.

10 Lake District National Park (p205) Following in the footsteps of Romantic poet William Wordsworth.

ENGLAND

POP 53 MILLION

By far the biggest of the three nations that comprise Great Britain, England offers a tempting spread of classic travel experiences, from London's vibrant theatre scene and the historic colleges of Oxford to the grand cathedrals of Canterbury and York and the mountain landscapes of the Lake District.

London

POP 8.8 MILLION

Everyone comes to London with preconceptions shaped by a multitude of books, movies, TV shows and pop songs. Whatever yours are, prepare to have them exploded by this endlessly intriguing city. Its streets are steeped in fascinating history, magnificent art, imposing architecture and popular culture. When you add a bottomless reserve of cool to this mix, it's hard not to conclude that London is one of the world's great cities, if not the greatest.

The only downside is cost: London is Europe's most expensive city for visitors, whatever their budget. But with some careful planning and a bit of common sense, you can find excellent bargains and freebies among the popular attractions. And many of London's finest assets – its wonderful parks, bridges, squares and boulevards, not to mention many of its landmark museums – come completely free.

◉ Sights

◉ The West End

★ **Westminster Abbey**   CHURCH

(Map p174; ☎020-7222 5152; www.westminster-abbey.org; 20 Dean's Yard, SW1; adult/child £22/9; ⊗9.30am-3.30pm Mon, Tue, Thu & Fri, to 6pm Wed, to 3pm Sat May-Aug, to 1pm Sat Sep-Apr; ⓤWestminster) A splendid mixture of architectural

---

BIG BEN

The Houses of Parliament's most famous feature is the clock tower known as **Big Ben** (Map p174; www.parliament.uk/visiting-and-tours/tours-of-parliament/bigben; Bridge St; ⓤWestminster). Strictly speaking, however, Big Ben is the tower's 13-ton bell, named after Benjamin Hall, commissioner of works when the tower was completed in 1858.

---

styles, Westminster Abbey is considered the finest example of Early English Gothic. It's not merely a beautiful place of worship – the Abbey is still a working church and the stage on which history unfolds. For centuries, the country's greatest have been interred here, including 17 monarchs from King Henry III (died 1272) to King George II (1760). Much of the Abbey's architecture is from the 13th century, but it was founded much earlier, in 960 CE.

Houses of Parliament   HISTORIC BUILDING

(Map p174; ☎tours 020-7219 4114; www.parliament.uk; Parliament Sq, SW1; guided tour adult/child/under 5yr £28/12/free, audio guide tour £20.50/8.50/free; ⓤWestminster) A visit here is a journey to the heart of UK democracy. The Houses of Parliament are officially called the Palace of Westminster, and its oldest part is 11th-century **Westminster Hall**, one of only a few sections that survived a catastrophic 1834 fire. The rest is mostly a neo-Gothic confection built over 36 years from 1840. The palace's most famous feature is its clock tower, Elizabeth Tower – but better known as Big Ben – covered in scaffolding until restoration works are finished in 2022.

Tate Britain   GALLERY

(☎020-7887 8888; www.tate.org.uk/visit/tate-britain; Millbank, SW1; ⊗10am-6pm; ⓤPimlico) **FREE** On the site of the former Millbank Penitentiary, the older and more venerable of the two Tate siblings opened in 1892 and celebrates British art from 1500 to the present, including pieces from William Blake, William Hogarth, Thomas Gainsborough and John Constable, as well as vibrant modern and contemporary pieces from Lucian Freud, Barbara Hepworth, Francis Bacon and Henry Moore. The stars of the show are, undoubtedly, the light-infused visions of JMW Turner in the Clore Gallery.

Trafalgar Square   SQUARE

(Map p174; ⓤCharing Cross or Embankment) Opened to the public in 1844, Trafalgar Sq is the true centre of London, where rallies and marches take place, tens of thousands of revellers usher in the New Year and locals congregate for anything from communal open-air cinema and Christmas celebrations to political protests. It is dominated by the 52m-high **Nelson's Column**, guarded by four **bronze lion statues**, and ringed by many splendid buildings, including the National Gallery (p165) and the church of **St Martin-in-the-Fields** (Map p174; ☎020-7766

London

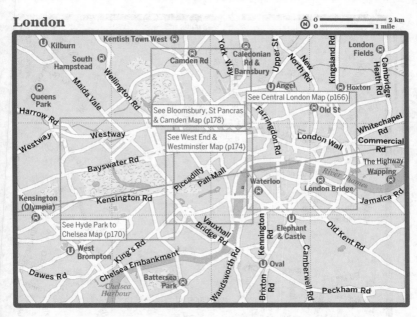

1100; www.stmartin-in-the-fields.org; ⊙8.30am-6pm Mon-Fri, 9am-6pm Sat & Sun).

★**National Gallery**   GALLERY
(Map p174; ☑020-7747 2885; www.nationalgallery.org.uk; Trafalgar Sq, WC2; ⊙10am-6pm Sat-Thu, to 9pm Fri; Ⓤ Charing Cross) **FREE** With more than 2300 European masterpieces in its collection, this is one of the world's great galleries, with seminal works from the 13th to the mid-20th century, including masterpieces by Leonardo da Vinci, Michelangelo, Titian, Vincent van Gogh and Auguste Renoir. Many visitors flock to the eastern rooms on the main floor (1700–1930), where works by British artists such as Thomas Gainsborough, John Constable and JMW Turner, and Impressionist and post-Impressionist masterpieces by Van Gogh, Renoir and Claude Monet await.

Madame Tussauds   MUSEUM
(Map p178; ☑0870 400 3000; www.madame-tussauds.com/london; Marylebone Rd, NW1; adult/child 4-15yr £35/30; ⊙10am-6pm; Ⓤ Baker St) It may be kitschy and pricey, but Madame Tussauds makes for a fun-filled day. There are photo ops with your dream celebrity (be it Daniel Craig, Lady Gaga, Benedict Cumberbatch, Audrey Hepburn or the Beckhams), the Bollywood gathering (sparring studs Hrithik Roshan and Salman Khan) and the

Royal Appointment (the Queen, Harry and Meghan, William and Kate). Book online for much cheaper rates and check the website for seasonal opening hours.

Piccadilly Circus   SQUARE
(Map p174; Ⓤ Piccadilly Circus) Architect John Nash had originally designed Regent St and Piccadilly in the 1820s to be the two most elegant streets in London but, restrained by city planners, he couldn't fully realise his dream. He may be disappointed, but suitably astonished, by Piccadilly Circus today: a traffic maelstrom, deluged by visitors and flanked by flashing advertisement panels.

Buckingham Palace   PALACE
(Map p174; ☑0303 123 7300; www.rct.uk/visit/the-state-rooms-buckingham-palace; Buckingham Palace Rd, SW1; adult/child/under 5yr £25/14/free, incl Royal Mews & Queen's Gallery £45/24.50/free; ⊙9.30am-7pm mid-Jul–Aug, to 6pm Sep; Ⓤ Green Park or St James's Park) Built in 1703 for the Duke of Buckingham, Buckingham Palace replaced St James's Palace as the monarch's official London residence in 1837. Queen Elizabeth II divides her time between here, Windsor Castle and, in summer, Balmoral Castle in Scotland. If she's in residence, the square yellow, red and blue Royal Standard is flown; if not, it's the Union Flag. The 19 lavishly furnished **State Rooms** are open

BRITAIN LONDON

Central London

Mansell St

Prescot St

Royal Mint St

East Smithfield

St Katharine Dock

Draw Bridge

9

South Mall Bridge

Mill St

Jamaica Rd

Royal Observatory (6km)

Neckinger St

Enid St

G

Minories

Tower Hill

Tower of London

3

Crutched Friars

Queen Elizabeth St

Tooley St

13

Tower Bridge Rd

BERMONDSEY

Abbey St

Fenchurch St

Crutched Friars

Mark La

Great Tower St

Lower Thames St

River Thames

William Curtis Park

Druid St

Tanner St

14

Abbey St

Bermondsey Market

F

Lime St

Fenchurch St

Eastcheap

Monument

Tooley St

Bermondsey St

Decima St

Gracechurch St

Cannon St

London Bridge

Thames Path

London Bridge

St Thomas St

8

Weston St

Snowfields

Long La

Law St

E

Bank

King William St

Walbrook

Cannon St

Upper Thames St

Montague Cl

Stoney St

London Bridge

4

Borough High St

Newcomen St

Mermaid Ct

D

Queen Victoria St

Watling St

Queen St

Mansion House

Southwark Bridge

Bankside

Clink St

Park St

Redcross Way

Lant St

Great Dover St

Trinity St

Falmouth Rd

Borough Rd

Harper Rd

Newington Causeway

St Paul's Churchyard

THE CITY

Millennium Bridge

Shakespeare's Globe

1

Park St

Southwark Bridge Rd

Sumner St

SOUTHWARK

Southwark St

Lavington St

10

Union St

Sawyer St

Great Suffolk St

Lancaster St

Borough Rd

London Rd

C

Carter La

White Lion

5

Hill

Blackfriars

Blackfriars Bridge

Hopton St

SOUTHWARK

Southwark St

Meymott St

Blackfriars Rd

Webber St

BOROUGH

Waterloo Rd

B

Tudor St

Bouverie St

Victoria Embankment

Rennie St

Hatfields St

Roupell St

6

Cornwall Rd

Waterloo East

12

21

The Cut

18

Ufford St

St George's Rd

Bayls Rd

LAMBETH

Aldwych

Strand

Temple

Arundel St

Waterloo Bridge

Upper Ground

Stamford St

York Rd

SOUTH BANK

Waterloo Rd

Jubilee Gardens

Belvedere Rd

19

Waterloo

Lower Marsh

Westminster Bridge Rd

Carlisle La

Lambeth Palace Rd

Waterloo Rd

A

5   **6**   **7**   **8**

BRITAIN LONDON

Central London

to visitors when Her Majesty is on holiday from mid-July to September.

Changing the Guard CEREMONY
(Map p174; www.royal.uk/changing-guard; Buckingham Palace, Buckingham Palace Rd, SW1; ⏰11am Sun, Mon, Wed, Fri Aug-May, 11am daily Jun & Jul; Ⓤ St James's Park or Green Park) FREE The full-on pageantry of soldiers in bright-red uniforms and bearskin hats parading down the Mall and into Buckingham Palace (p165) is madly popular with tourists. The event lasts about 45 minutes and ends with a full military band playing music from traditional marches, musicals and pop songs. The pomp and circumstance can feel far away indeed when you're in a row 15 deep, trying to watch the ceremony through a forest of selfie sticks. Get here at least 45 minutes before the main event.

◎ The City

⭐**St Paul's Cathedral** CATHEDRAL
(Map p166; ☎020-7246 8357; www.stpauls.co.uk; St Paul's Churchyard, EC4; adult/child £18/8; ⏰8.30am-4.30pm Mon-Sat; Ⓤ St Paul's) Towering over diminutive Ludgate Hill in a superb position that's been a place of Christian worship for over 1400 years (and pagan before that), St Paul's is one of London's most magnificent buildings. For Londoners, the vast dome is a symbol of resilience and pride, standing tall for more than 300 years. Viewing Sir Christopher Wren's masterpiece from the inside and climbing to the top for sweeping views of the capital is a celestial experience.

⭐**Tower of London** CASTLE
(Map p166; ☎020-3166 6000; www.hrp.org.uk/tower-of-london; Petty Wales, EC3; adult/child £26.80/12.70, audio guide £4; ⏰9am-4.30pm Tue-Sat, from 10am Sun & Mon; Ⓤ Tower Hill) The unmissable Tower of London (actually a castle of 22 towers) offers a window into a gruesome and compelling history. A former royal residence, treasury, mint, armoury and zoo, it's perhaps now most remembered as the prison where a king, three queens and many nobles met their deaths. Come here to see the colourful Yeoman Warders (or Beefeaters), the spectacular Crown Jewels, the soothsaying ravens and armour fit for a *very* large king.

Tower Bridge BRIDGE
(Map p166; ☎020-7403 3761; www.towerbridge.org.uk; Tower Bridge, SE1; ⏰24hr; Ⓤ Tower Hill) One of London's most recognisable sights, familiar from dozens of movies, Tower Bridge doesn't disappoint in real life. Its neo-Gothic towers and sky-blue suspension struts add extraordinary elegance to what is a supremely functional structure. London was a thriving port in 1894 when it was built as a much-needed crossing point in the east, equipped with a then-revolutionary steam-driven bascule (counterbalance) mechanism that could raise the roadway to make way for oncoming ships in just three minutes.

◎ The South Bank

⭐**Shakespeare's Globe** HISTORIC BUILDING
(Map p166; ☎020-7902 1500; www.shakespearesglobe.com; 21 New Globe Walk, SE1; tours adult/

child £17/10; ⊙9am-5pm; ⚡; Ⓤ Blackfriars or London Bridge) The new Globe was designed to resemble the original as closely as possible, which means having the arena open to the fickle London skies, leaving the 700 'groundlings' (standing spectators) to weather London's spectacular downpours. Visits to the Globe include tours of the theatre (half-hourly) as well as access to the exhibition space, which has fascinating exhibits on Shakespeare, life in Bankside and theatre in the 17th century.

Tate Modern
GALLERY

(Map p166; ☑020-7887 8888; www.tate.org.uk; Bankside, SE1; ⊙10am-6pm Sun-Thu, to 10pm Fri & Sat; ⚡; Ⓤ Blackfriars, Southwark or London Bridge) FREE One of London's most amazing attractions, this outstanding modern- and contemporary-art gallery is housed in the creatively revamped Bankside Power Station south of the Millennium Bridge (Map p166; Ⓤ St Paul's or Blackfriars). A spellbinding synthesis of modern art and capacious industrial brick design, Tate Modern has been extraordinarily successful in bringing challenging work to the masses, through both its free permanent collection and fee-paying big-name temporary exhibitions. The stunning Blavatnik Building opened in 2016, increasing the available exhibition space by 60%.

London Eye
VIEWPOINT

(Map p174; www.londoneye.com; near County Hall; adult/child £28/23; ⊙11am-6pm Sep-May, 10am-8.30pm Jun-Aug; Ⓤ Waterloo or Westminster) Standing 135m high in a fairly flat city, the London Eye affords views 25 miles in every direction, weather permitting. Interactive tablets provide great information (in six languages) about landmarks as they appear in the skyline. Each rotation – or 'flight' – takes a gracefully slow 30 minutes. At peak times (July, August and school holidays) it can feel like you'll spend more time in the queue than in the capsule; book premium fast-track tickets (adult/child £37/32) to jump the line.

◉ Kensington & Hyde Park

★ Natural History Museum
MUSEUM

(Map p170; www.nhm.ac.uk; Cromwell Rd, SW7; ⊙10am-5.50pm; ⚡; Ⓤ South Kensington) FREE This colossal and magnificent-looking building is infused with the irrepressible Victorian spirit of collecting, cataloguing and interpreting the natural world. The Dinosaurs Gallery (Blue Zone) is a must for children, who gawp at the animatronic T-rex, fossils

BRITISH MUSEUM

The country's largest museum and one of the oldest and finest in the world, the British Museum (Map p174; ☑020-7323 8000; www.britishmuseum.org; Great Russell St, WC1; ⊙10am-5.30pm Sat-Thu, to 8.30pm Fri; Ⓤ Tottenham Court Rd or Russell Sq) is a famous museum opened in 1759 and boasts vast Egyptian, Etruscan, Greek, Roman, European and Middle Eastern galleries, among others. It's London's most visited attraction, drawing 5.9 million people annually. Don't miss the Rosetta Stone, the key to deciphering Egyptian hieroglyphics; the controversial Parthenon sculptures, taken from Athens' Acropolis by Lord Elgin (British ambassador to the Ottoman Empire at the time); and the large collection of Egyptian mummies.

and excellent displays. Adults will love the intriguing Treasures exhibition in the Cadogan Gallery (Green Zone), which houses a host of unrelated objects, each telling its own unique story, from a chunk of moon rock to a dodo skeleton.

Science Museum
MUSEUM

(Map p170; ☑020-7942 4000; www.sciencemuseum.org.uk; Exhibition Rd, SW7; ⊙10am-6pm; ⚡; Ⓤ South Kensington) FREE This scientifically spellbinding museum will mesmerise adults and children alike with its interactive and educational exhibits covering everything from early technology to space travel. On the ground floor, a perennial favourite is Exploring Space, a gallery featuring genuine rockets and satellites and a full-size replica of the Eagle, the lander that took Neil Armstrong and Buzz Aldrin to the surface of the moon in 1969. The Making the Modern World Gallery next door is a visual feast of locomotives, planes, cars and other revolutionary inventions.

The 2nd-floor displays cover a host of subjects. The fantastic Information Age Gallery showcases how information and communication technologies – from the telegraph to smartphones – have transformed our lives since the 19th century. Standout displays include wireless messages sent by a sinking Titanic, the first BBC radio broadcast and a Soviet BESM 1965 supercomputer. The Clockmaker's Museum is a fascinating collection of timepieces, while Mathematics:

BRITAIN LONDON

Hyde Park to Chelsea

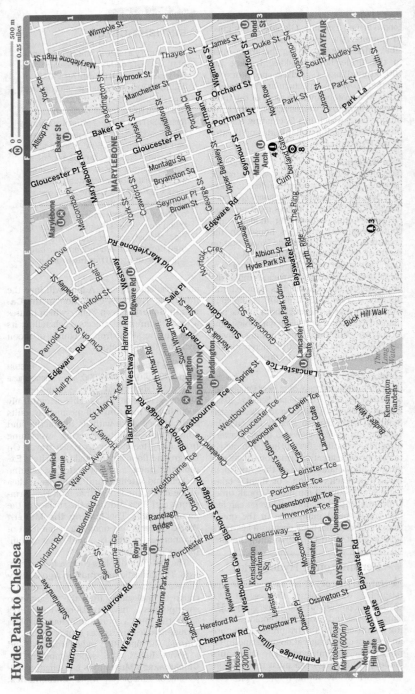

500 m
0.25 miles

WESTBOURNE GROVE

MARYLEBONE

MAYFAIR

PADDINGTON

BAYSWATER

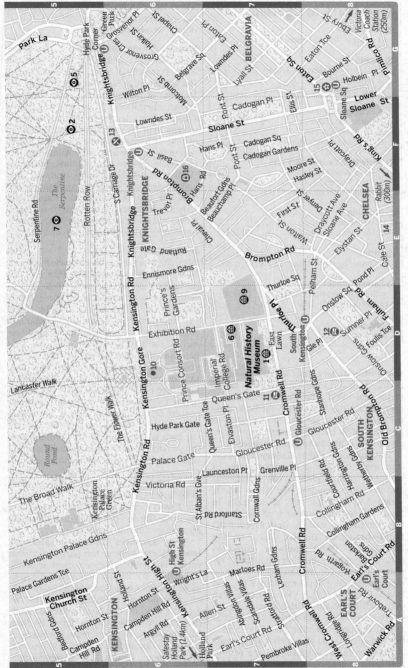

Hyde Park to Chelsea

the **Winton Gallery**, designed by Zaha Hadid Architects, is a riveting exploration of maths in the real world. The **Medicine Galleries**, opened in 2019, look at the medical world using objects from the museum's collections and those of Sir Henry Wellcome, pharmacist, entrepreneur, philanthropist and collector.

The 3rd floor's **Flight Gallery** (free tours 1pm most days) is a favourite place for children, with its gliders, hot-air balloons and aircraft, including the Gipsy Moth, which Amy Johnson flew to Australia in 1930. The rest of the floor is all about getting interactive, with a **Red Arrows 3D flight-simulation theatre** (£5), the **Fly 360-degree flight-simulator capsules** (£12 per capsule), another simulator, **Typhoon Force** (£5), replicating a low-level mission aboard a Typhoon fighter jet, and **Space Descent** (£7), a VR experience with (a digital) Tim Peake, British astronaut. Also on the 3rd floor, **Wonderlab** (adult/child £10/8) explores scientific phenomena in a fun and educational way, with daily shows.

If you've got kids under the age of five, pop down to the basement and the **Garden**, where there's a fun-filled play zone, including a water-play area, besieged by tots in orange waterproof smocks.

Victoria & Albert Museum MUSEUM
(V&A; Map p170; ☑ 020-7942 2000; www.vam. ac.uk; Cromwell Rd, SW7; ☉10am-5.45pm Sat-Thu, to 10pm Fri; ⓊSouth Kensington) FREE The Museum of Manufactures, as the V&A was known when it opened in 1852, was part of Prince Albert's legacy to the nation in the aftermath of the successful Great Exhibition of 1851. It houses the world's largest collection of decorative arts, from Asian ceramics to Middle Eastern rugs, Chinese paintings, Western furniture, fashion from all ages and modern-day domestic appliances. The (ticketed) temporary exhibitions are another highlight, covering anything from David Bowie and designer Alexander McQueen retrospectives to special materials and trends.

Hyde Park PARK
(Map p170; www.royalparks.org.uk/parks/hyde-park; ☉5am-midnight; ⓊMarble Arch, Hyde Park Corner, Knightsbridge or Queensway) Hyde Park is central London's largest green space, expropriated from the church in 1536 by Henry VIII and turned into a hunting ground and later a venue for duels, executions and horse racing. The 1851 Great Exhibition was held here, and during WWII the park became an enormous potato field. These days it's a place to stroll and picnic, boat on the **Serpentine lake** (Map p170; ☑ 020-7262 1330; ⓊLancaster Gate or Knightsbridge), or to catch a summer concert or outdoor film during the warmer months. In winter, the southeast area of the park is the site of **Winter Wonderland** (https://hydeparkwinterwonderland.com), with fairground rides, ice skating and other seasonal attractions. Year-round look out for the **Holocaust Memorial Garden** (Map p170), a simple but evocative memorial to the Jewish victims of the Nazi regime, and the **Rose Garden** (Map p170), a wonderfully scented spot during the summer.

While **Speakers' Corner** (Map p170; Park Lane; ⓊMarble Arch) in the park's northeast corner is intended for oratorical acrobats, these days it's largely eccentrics and religious fanatics who address bemused onlookers, maintaining a tradition begun in 1872 as a response to rioting. Nearby **Marble Arch** (Map p170; ⓊMarble Arch), designed by John Nash in 1828 as the entrance to Buckingham Palace, was moved here in 1851. It replaced the infamous Tyburn Tree, a three-legged gallows that was the place of execution for up to 50,000 people between 1196 and 1783.

⊙ North London

ZSL London Zoo   ZOO

(Map p178; www.zsl.org/zsl-london-zoo; Outer Circle, Regent's Park, NW1; adult/child £25/22, discounts if booked in advance online; ⊙10am-6pm Apr-Sep, to 5.30pm Mar & Oct, to 4pm Nov-Feb; 🚹; 🚇274) Opened in 1828, London Zoo is among the oldest in the world. The emphasis nowadays is firmly on conservation, breeding and education, with fewer animals and bigger enclosures. Highlights include **Land of the Lions**, **Gorilla Kingdom**, **Tiger Territory**, the walk-through **In with the Lemurs** and **Penguin Beach**. There are regular feeding sessions and talks, various experiences are available, such as Keeper for a Day, and you can even spend the night in the Gir Lion Lodge.

Regent's Park   PARK

(Map p178; www.royalparks.org.uk; ⊙5am-dusk; 🚇Regent's Park, Baker St) The most elaborate and formal of London's many parks, Regent's Park is one of the capital's loveliest green spaces. Among its many attractions are London Zoo, **Regent's Canal** (Map p178), an ornamental lake, and sports pitches where locals meet to play football, rugby and volleyball. **Queen Mary's Gardens**, towards the south of the park, are particularly pretty, especially in June when the roses are in bloom. Performances take place here in an **open-air theatre** (Map p178; 📞0844 826 4242; www.openairtheatre.org; ⊙May-Sep; 🚹; 🚇Baker St) during summer.

⊙ Greenwich

An extraordinary cluster of buildings has earned 'Maritime Greenwich' its place on Unesco's World Heritage list. It's also famous for straddling the hemispheres; this is the degree zero of longitude, home of the Greenwich Meridian and Greenwich Mean Time. Greenwich is easily reached on the DLR train (to Cutty Sark station), or by boat – Thames Clippers (p187) depart from the London Eye every 20 minutes.

Royal Observatory   HISTORIC BUILDING

(📞020-8312 6565; www.rmg.co.uk/royal-observatory; Greenwich Park, Blackheath Ave, SE10; adult/child £10/6.50, incl Cutty Sark £20/11.50; ⊙10am-5pm Sep-Jun, to 6pm Jul & Aug; 🚇Greenwich or Cutty Sark) Rising like a beacon of time atop **Green-**

wich Park (www.royalparks.org.uk; King George St, SE10; ⊙6am-around sunset; 🚇Greenwich, Maze Hill or Cutty Sark), the Royal Observatory is home to the **prime meridian** (longitude 0° 0' 0''). Tickets include access to the Christopher Wren–designed **Flamsteed House** (named for the first Royal Astronomer) and the **Meridian Courtyard**, where you can stand with your feet straddling the eastern and western hemispheres. You can also see the Great Equatorial Telescope (1893) inside the onion-domed observatory and explore space and time in the **Weller Astronomy Galleries**.

Cutty Sark   MUSEUM

(📞020-8312 6608; www.rmg.co.uk/cuttysark; King William Walk, SE10; adult/child £13.50/7; ⊙10am-5pm; 🚇Cutty Sark) The last of the great clipper ships to sail between China and England in the 19th century, the *Cutty Sark* endured massive fire damage in 2007 during a £25 million restoration. The exhibition in the hold of the fully restored ship tells its story as a tea clipper. Launched in 1869 in Scotland, it made eight voyages to China in the 1870s, sailing out with a mixed cargo and coming back with tea.

Old Royal Naval College   HISTORIC BUILDING

(www.ornc.org; 2 Cutty Sark Gardens, SE10; ⊙10am-5pm, grounds 8am-11pm; 🚇Cutty Sark) **FREE** Sir Christopher Wren's baroque masterpiece in Greenwich, and indeed Britain's largest ensemble of baroque architecture, the Old Royal Naval College contains the neoclassical **Chapel of St Peter and St Paul** (www.ornc.org/chapel; SE10; ⊙10am-5pm) and the extraordinary **Painted Hall** (📞020-8269 4799; www.ornc.org; adult/child £12/free; ⊙10am-5pm) **FREE**. The entire Old Royal Naval College, including the chapel, the **visitor centre** (www.ornc.org/visitor-centre; Pepys Bldg, King William Walk, SE10; ⊙10am-5pm) **FREE**, and the grounds, can be visited for free. Volunteers lead free 45-minute tours throughout the day from the visitor centre.

National Maritime Museum   MUSEUM

(📞020-8312 6565; www.rmg.co.uk/national-maritime-museum; Romney Rd, SE10; ⊙10am-5pm; 🚇Cutty Sark) **FREE** Narrating the long, briny and eventful history of seafaring Britain, this excellent museum's exhibits are arranged thematically, with highlights including *Miss Britain III* (the first boat to top 100mph on open water) from 1933, the 19m-long golden state barge built in 1732 for Frederick, Prince of Wales, the huge ship's propeller and the colourful figureheads installed on the

BRITAIN LONDON

West End & Westminster

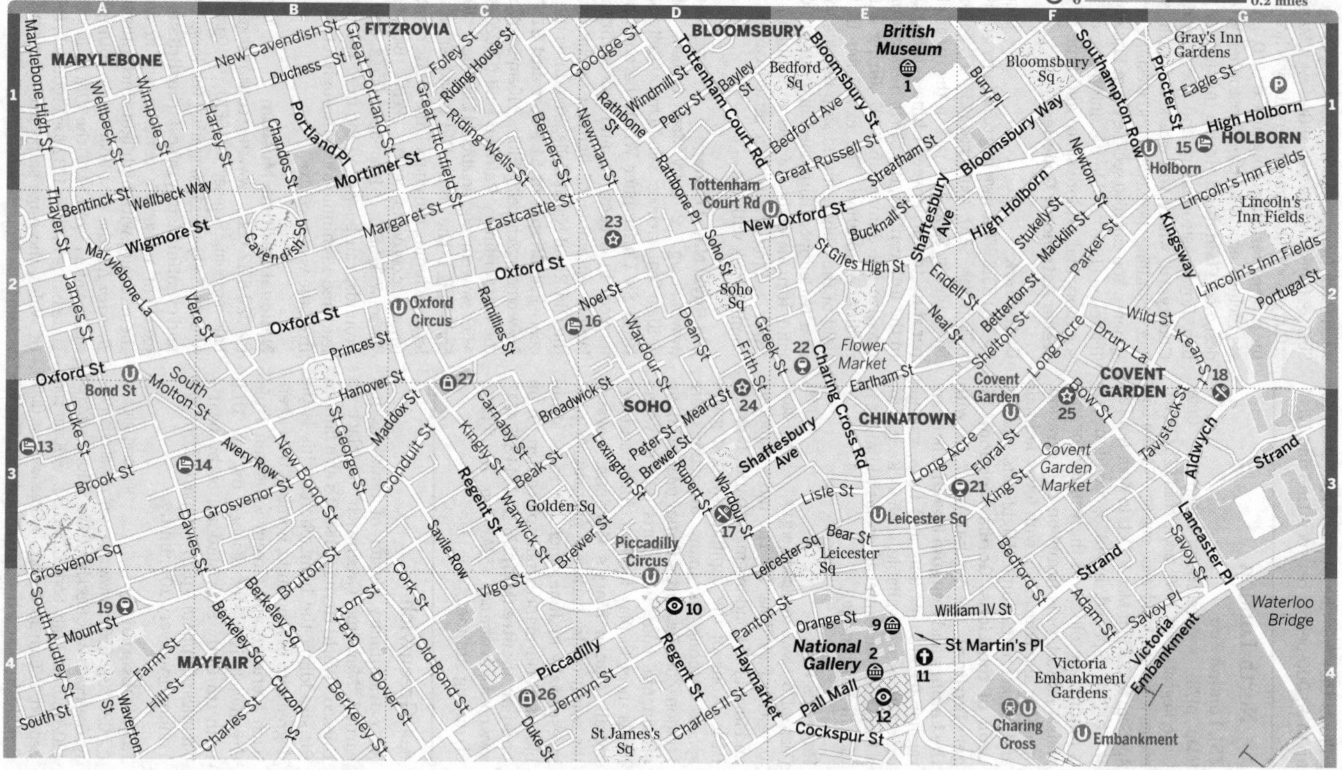

400 m
0.2 miles

MARYLEBONE

FITZROVIA

BLOOMSBURY

HOLBORN

COVENT GARDEN

SOHO

CHINATOWN

MAYFAIR

British Museum 1

National Gallery 2

Charing Cross Rd

Tottenham Court Rd

Oxford Circus

Piccadilly Circus

Leicester Sq

Covent Garden

Holborn

Bond St

Charing Cross

Embankment

Waterloo Bridge

Lincoln's Inn Fields

Gray's Inn Gardens

Victoria Embankment Gardens

Covent Garden Market

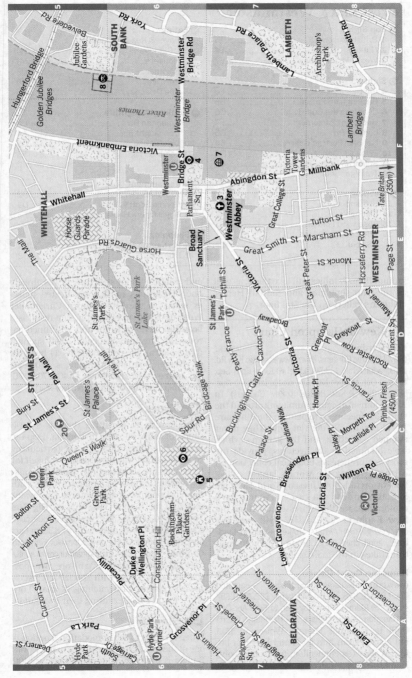

SOUTH BANK

York Rd

Belvedere Rd

Jubilee Gardens

Hungerford Bridge

Golden Jubilee Bridges

River Thames

Westminster Bridge

Westminster Bridge Rd

LAMBETH

Lambeth Palace Rd

Archbishop's Park

Lambeth Rd

Lambeth Bridge

Victoria Embankment

Westminster

Bridge St

4

7

Abingdon St

Millbank

Victoria Tower Gardens

Tate Britain (350m)

Parliament Sq

3

Westminster Abbey

Great College St

Tufton St

WESTMINSTER

WHITEHALL

Whitehall

Horse Guards Parade

Horse Guards Rd

Broad Sanctuary

Great Smith St

Marsham St

Monck St

Great Peter St

Horseferry Rd

Page St

Vincent Sq

The Mall

St James's Park

St James's Park Lake

Tothill St

Victoria St

St James's Park

Petty France

Caxton St

Broadway

Greycoat Pl

Greycoat St

Rochester Row

ST JAMES'S

St James's Palace

The Mall

Birdcage Walk

Buckingham Gate

Palace St

Cardinal Walk

Howick Pl

Francis St

Ashley Pl

Morpeth Tce

Carlisle Pl

Pimlico Fresh (450m)

Bury St

St James's St

20

Queen's Walk

Spur Rd

6

K

5

Buckingham Palace Gardens

Victoria St

Bressenden Pl

Wilton Rd

Victoria

Bridge Pl

Green Park

Bolton St

Half Moon St

Curzon St

Piccadilly

Duke of Wellington Pl

Constitution Hill

Green Park

Hyde Park Corner

Deanery St

Park La

Park St

South Carriage Dr

Hyde Park

Grosvenor Pl

Chapel St

Chester St

Wilton St

Halkin St

Belgrave Sq

BELGRAVIA

Lower Grosvenor Pl

Ebury St

Wilton St

Eccleston St

Eaton Sq

Belgrave Sq

Eaton Sq

West End & Westminster

ground floor. Families will love these, as well as the ship simulator and the 'All Hands' children's gallery on the 2nd floor.

◉ Kew & Hampton Court

Kew Gardens   GARDENS
(Royal Botanic Gardens, Kew; www.kew.org; Kew Rd, TW9; adult/child £13.50/4.50; ⊙10am-6pm Sep, to 5pm Oct, to 3pm Nov-Jan, closes later Feb-Aug; ⛴Kew Pier, 🚆Kew Bridge, ⓊKew Gardens) In 1759 botanists began rummaging around the world for specimens to plant in the 3-hectare Royal Botanic Gardens at Kew. They never stopped collecting, and the gardens, which have bloomed to 121 hectares, provide the most comprehensive botanical collection on earth (including the world's largest collection of orchids). A Unesco World Heritage Site, the gardens can easily devour a day's exploration; for those pressed for time, the **Kew Explorer** (☑020-8332 5648; www.kew. org/kew-gardens/whats-on/kew-explorer-land-train; adult/child £5/2) hop-on/hop-off road train takes in the main sights.

Hampton Court Palace   PALACE
(www.hrp.org.uk/hamptoncourtpalace; Hampton Court Palace, KT8; adult/child/family £22.70/11.35/40.40; ⊙10am-4.30pm Nov-Mar, to 6pm Apr-Oct; ⛴Hampton Court Palace, 🚆Hampton Court) Built by Cardinal Thomas Wolsey in 1515 but coaxed from him by Henry VIII just before Wolsey (as chancellor) fell from favour, Hampton Court Palace is England's largest and grandest Tudor structure. It was already one of Europe's most sophisticated palaces when, in the 17th century, Christopher Wren designed an extension. The result is a beautiful blend of Tudor and 'restrained baroque' architecture. You could easily spend a day exploring the palace and its 24 hectares of riverside gardens, including a 300-year-old **maze** (adult/child/family £4.40/2.70/12.80; ⊙10am-5.15pm Apr-Oct, to 3.45pm Nov-Mar).

⛢ Tours

From erudite to eccentric, there is a multitude of tours on offer in London. Hop-on, hop-off bus tours, although not particularly cool, are a great way for orienting yourself for those who are short on time. Specialist walking and bus tours cover a range of topics, with the most popular being the three Rs: royalty, rock and the Ripper (Jack, that is). **Big Bus Tours** (☑020-7808 6753; www.bigbustours.com; adult/child £37/19; ⊙every 5-20min 8.30am-6pm Apr-Sep, to 5pm Oct & Mar, to 4.30pm Nov-Feb) and **Original Tour** (www.theoriginaltour.com; adult/child £32/15; ⊙8.30am-8.30pm) are two possible options. Those with special interests – Jewish London, birdwatching, Roman London – might consider hiring their own guide.

🛌 Sleeping

When it comes to accommodation, London is one of the most expensive places in the world. Budget is pretty much anything below £100 per night for a double; double rooms ranging between £100 and £200 per night are considered midrange; more expensive options fall into the top-end category. Public transport is good, so you don't need to sleep at Buckingham Palace to be at the heart of things.

The West End

The city's major theatres, as well some of its best attractions, dining and drinking, are right on your doorstep here. Though moderately priced hotels are scarce, Bloomsbury is a haven of B&Bs and guesthouses, and Cartwright Gardens, north of Russell Square (within easy walking distance of the West End), has some of central London's best-value small hotels.

Generator London HOSTEL £
(Map p178; ☑ 020-7388 7666; www.generatorhotels.com/london; 37 Tavistock Pl, WC1; dm/r from £9/44; ❋ 🛜; ⓤ Russell Sq) With its industrial lines and funky decor, the huge Generator (it has more than 870 beds) is one of central London's grooviest budget spots. The bar, complete with pool tables, stays open until 3am and there are frequent themed parties. Dorm rooms have between four and 12 beds; backing it up are twins and triples.

YHA London Oxford Street HOSTEL £
(Map p174; ☑ 020-7734 1618; www.yha.org.uk/hostel/yha-london-oxford-street; 14 Noel St, W1; dm £18-36, tw £50-85; @ 🛜; ⓤ Oxford Circus) The most central of London's seven YHA hostels is also one of the most intimate with just 104 beds. The excellent shared facilities include a fuchsia-coloured kitchen and a bright, funky lounge. Dormitories have three or four beds, and there are doubles and twins. The in-house shop sells coffee and beer. Free wi-fi in common areas.

Arosfa Hotel B&B ££
(Map p178; ☑ 020-7636 2115; www.arosfalondon.com; 83 Gower St, WC1; s/tw/tr/f from £90/135/155/210, d £140-175; @ 🛜; ⓤ Goodge St) The Philippe Starck furniture and modern look in the lounge are more lavish than the decor in the guest rooms, with cabin-like bathrooms in many of them. Fully refurbished, the 16 rooms are small but remain good value. There are a couple of family rooms; room 4 looks on to a small but charming garden in the back.

★ Rosewood London HOTEL £££
(Map p174; ☑ 020-7781 8888; www.rosewoodhotels.com/en/london; 252 High Holborn, WC1; d/ste

from £390/702; 🅿 ❋ @ 🛜 🐾; ⓤ Holborn) What was once the grand Pearl Assurance building (dating from 1914) now houses the stunning Rosewood hotel, where an artful marriage of period and modern styles thanks to designer Tony Chi can be found in its 262 rooms and 44 suites. British heritage is carefully woven throughout the bar, restaurant, deli, lobby and even the housekeepers' uniforms.

The South Bank

Immediately south of the river is good if you want to immerse yourself in workaday London and still be central.

★ citizenM BOUTIQUE HOTEL ££
(Map p166; ☑ 020-3519 1680; www.citizenm.com/london-bankside; 20 Lavington St, SE1; r £89-329; ❋ @ 🛜; ⓤ Southwark) If citizenM had a motto, it would be 'Less fuss, more comfort'. The hotel has done away with things it considers superfluous (room service, reception, heaps of space) and instead has gone all out on mattresses and bedding (heavenly super-king-sized beds), state-of-the-art technology (everything from mood lighting to TV is controlled through a tablet computer) and superb decor.

Kensington & Hyde Park

This classy area offers easy access to the museums and big-name fashion shops, but at a price that reflects the upmarket surroundings.

Meininger HOSTEL £
(Map p170; ☑ 020-3318 1407; www.meininger-hotels.com; Baden Powell House, 65-67 Queen's Gate, SW7; dm £16-50, s/tw from £60/70; ❋ @ 🛜; ⓤ Gloucester Rd, South Kensington) Housed in the late-1950s Baden Powell House opposite the Natural History Museum, this 48-room German-run 'city hostel and hotel' has spick-and-span rooms – most are dorms of between four and 12 beds, with podlike showers. There is also a handful of private rooms. It has good security and nice communal facilities, including a bar and a big roof terrace, plus a fantastic location.

Lime Tree Hotel BOUTIQUE HOTEL ££
(☑ 020-7730 8191; www.limetreehotel.co.uk; 135-137 Ebury St, SW1; s incl breakfast £125-165, d & tw £185-215, tr £240; @ 🛜; ⓤ Victoria) Family run for over three decades, this beautiful 25-bedroom Georgian town-house hotel is all comfort, British design and understated elegance. Rooms are individually decorated,

BRITAIN LONDON

Bloomsbury, St Pancras & Camden

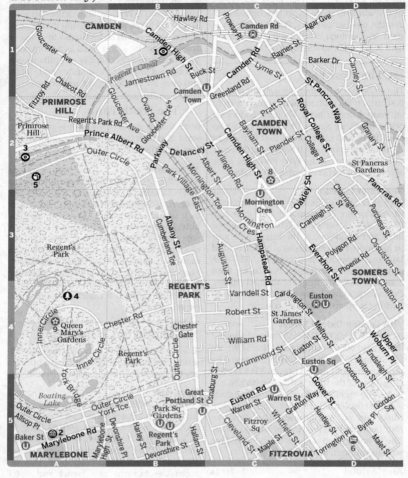

Bloomsbury, St Pancras & Camden

many with open fireplaces and sash windows, but some are smaller than others, so enquire. There is a lovely back garden for late-afternoon rays (picnics encouraged on summer evenings). Rates include a hearty full English breakfast. No lift. If you don't like climbing stairs, try to secure a room on a lower floor.

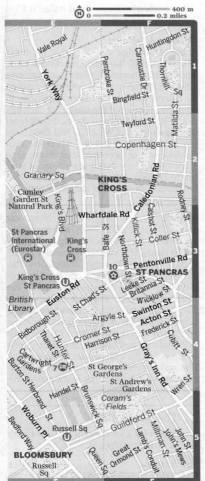

North London

Sleeping options in North London are concentrated around the King's Cross area, where you'll find the best in both budget and top-end accommodation.

★ Clink78
HOSTEL **£**

(Map p166; ☑020-7183 9400; www.clinkhostels.com/london/clink78; 78 King's Cross Rd, WC1; dm/r incl breakfast from £16/65; @ 🛜; Ⓤ King's Cross St Pancras) This fantastic 630-bed hostel is housed in a 19th-century magistrates' courthouse where Charles Dickens once worked as a scribe and members of the Clash stood trial in 1978. It features pod beds (including overhead storage space) in four- to 16-bed dormitories. There's a top kitchen with a huge dining area and a busy bar – Clash – in the basement.

West London

West London is well supplied with accommodation choices, from excellent hostels in leafy parks to boutique hotels, family-run B&Bs and apartments. It's so popular with travelling Antipodeans that it's been nicknamed Kangaroo Valley.

Safestay Holland Park
HOSTEL **£**

(☑020-3326 8471; www.safestay.co.uk; Holland Walk, W8; dm £20, r from £60; 🛜; Ⓤ High St Kensington, Holland Park) This fresh place replaced the long-serving YHA hostel that ran here since 1958. With a bright and bold colour design, the hostel has four- to eight-bunk dorm rooms, twin-bunk and single-bunk rooms, free wi-fi in the lobby and a fabulous location in the Jacobean east wing of Holland House in **Holland Park** (Ilchester Pl; ⏰7.30am–dusk), the only part that survived a Luftwaffe onslaught.

★ Number Sixteen
HOTEL **£££**

(Map p170; ☑020-7589 5232; www.firmdalehotels.com/hotels/london/number-sixteen; 16 Sumner Pl, SW7; s from £192, d £240-396; ❋ @ 🛜 ❖; Ⓤ South Kensington) With uplifting splashes of colour, choice art and a sophisticated-but-fun design ethos, Number Sixteen is simply ravishing. There are 41 individually designed rooms, a cosy drawing room and a fully stocked library. And wait till you see the idyllic, long back garden set around a fountain, or sit down for breakfast in the light-filled conservatory. Great amenities for families.

★ Main House
HOTEL **££**

(☑020-7221 9691; www.themainhouse.co.uk; 6 Colville Rd, W11; ste £130-150; 🛜; Ⓤ Ladbroke Grove, Notting Hill Gate, Westbourne Park) The four adorable suites at this peach of a Victorian midterrace house on Colville Rd make this a superb choice. Bright and spacious rooms are excellent value and come with vast bathrooms and endless tea and coffee. Cream of the crop is the uppermost suite, occupying the entire top floor. There's no sign, but look for the huge letters 'SIX'. Minimum three-night stay.

✕ Eating

Once the butt of many a culinary joke, London has transformed itself over the last few decades and today is a global dining destination. World-famous chefs can be found at the helm of several top-tier restaurants, but it is the sheer diversity on offer that is head-spinning: from Afghan to Zambian, London delivers an A to Z of world cuisine.

✕ The West End

Hoppers
SRI LANKAN **£**
(Map p174; www.hopperslondon.com; 49 Frith St, W1; dishes £5-21; ⊘noon-2.30pm & 5.30-10.30pm Mon-Thu, noon-10.30pm Fri & Sat; Ⓤ Tottenham Court Rd or Leicester Sq) This pint-sized, enormously popular place specialises in the Sri Lankan national dish of hoppers: thin pancakes of rice flour and coconut milk with spices. Eat them (or dosas) with various types of *kari* (curry) or *kothu*, a dish of chopped flatbread with spices and meat, fish, crab or vegetables.

The decor here is Old Ceylon, and the service swift but personable.

★ Palomar
MIDDLE EASTERN **££**
(Map p174; ☑020-7439 8777; www.thepalomar. co.uk; 34 Rupert St, W1; dishes £7.50-26; ⊘noon-2.30pm & 5.30-11pm Mon-Sat, 12.30-3.30pm & 6-9pm Sun; 🛜; Ⓤ Piccadilly Circus) With a stack of 'restaurant of the year' awards, Palomar is a firm favourite, and the wait for one of the 16 bar stools or 40 seats is testament to that. It celebrates modern Jerusalem cuisine, with flavours stretching from the Levant to the Maghreb. *Kubaneh* (bread dipped in tomato and tahini), 'octo-hummus' and balsamic-glazed chicken livers are a few of the must-orders.

The Delaunay
EUROPEAN **££**
(Map p174; ☑020-7499 8558; www.thedelaunay. com; 55 Aldwych, WC2; mains £14.50-35; ⊘7am-11pm Mon-Fri, from 8am Sat, 9am-10pm Sun; 🛜🍴; Ⓤ Temple or Covent Garden) This smart spot channels the majesty of the grand cafes of *Mitteleuropa* (Central Europe). Schnitzels and wieners take pride of place on the menu, which is rounded out with Alsatian *tarte flambée* (thin crust pizzas usually topped with *crème fraiche*, onions and bacon lardons) and a rotating *Tagesteller* (dish of the day).

Its location in Theatreland makes it ideal for pre- or post-show eats.

★ Foyer & Reading Room at Claridge's
BRITISH **£££**
(Map p174; ☑020-7107 8886; www.claridges.co.uk; Brook St, W1; afternoon tea £65, with champagne £75-85; ⊘afternoon tea 2.45-5.30pm; 🛜; Ⓤ Bond St) Extend that pinkie finger to partake in afternoon tea within the classic art deco foyer and Reading Room of the landmark hotel **Claridge's** (Map p174; ☑020-7629 8860; r/ste from £450/780; 🅿🅿✳@🛜🐾), where the gentle clink of fine porcelain and champagne glasses could be a defining memory of your trip to London. The setting is gorgeous and the dress code is smart casual to befit the surroundings.

Portrait
MODERN EUROPEAN **£££**
(Map p174; ☑020-7312 2490; www.npg.org.uk/visit/shop-eat-drink/restaurant; 3rd fl, National Portrait Gallery, St Martin's Pl, WC2; mains £19.50-29.50; ⊘10am-4.30pm daily, 5.30-8.30pm Thu-Sat; 🛜; Ⓤ Charing Cross or Leicester Sq) This stunningly located restaurant above the excellent **National Portrait Gallery** (Map p174; ☑020-7306 0055; ⊘10am-6pm Sat-Thu, to 9pm Fri) `FREE` comes with dramatic views over Trafalgar Sq and down to the Houses of Parliament and London Eye. Prices are a bit steep, but it's a fine choice for tantalising food and the chance to luxuriously relax after hours of picture-gazing at the gallery. It's best to book in advance.

✕ The South Bank

For a feed with a local feel, head to Borough Market or Bermondsey St.

Watch House
CAFE **£**
(Map p166; ☑020-7407 6431; www.thewatch house.com; 199 Bermondsey St, SE1; mains from £4.95; ⊘7am-6pm Mon-Fri, 8am-6pm Sat & Sun; 🍴; Ⓤ Borough or London Bridge) Saying that the Watch House nails the sandwich wouldn't really do justice to this tip-top cafe: the sandwiches really are delicious. There is also great coffee, and treats for the sweet-toothed. The small but lovely setting is a renovated 19th-century watch-house from where guards kept an eye on the next-door cemetery. No bathroom.

Padella
ITALIAN **£**
(Map p166; www.padella.co; 6 Southwark St, SE1; dishes £4-11.50; ⊘noon-3.45pm & 5-10pm Mon-

Sat, noon-3.45pm & 5-9pm Sun; ⏲; Ⓤ London Bridge) A fantastic part of the foodie enclave of **Borough Market** (Map p166; www.borough market.org.uk; ☺ full market 10am-5pm Wed & Thu, 10am-6pm Fri, 8am-5pm Sat), Padella is a small, energetic bistro specialising in handmade pasta dishes, inspired by the owners' extensive culinary adventures in Italy. The portions are small, which means that, joy of joys, you can (and should!) have more than one dish. Outstanding, but be prepared to queue (no reservations taken).

Anchor & Hope GASTROPUB ££
(Map p166; ✆ 020-7928 9898; www.anchorandhope pub.co.uk; 36 The Cut, SE1; mains £12-20; ☺ 5-11pm Mon, 11am-11pm Tue-Sat, 12.30-3.15pm Sun; Ⓤ Southwark) The Anchor & Hope is a quintessential gastropub: elegant but not formal, serving utterly delicious European fare with a British twist. The menu changes daily, but could include grilled sole served with spinach, or roast rabbit with green beans in a mustard and bacon sauce. Bookings taken for Sunday lunch only.

Skylon MODERN EUROPEAN £££
(Map p166; ✆ 020-7654 7800; www.skylon-restau rant.co.uk; 3rd fl, Royal Festival Hall, Southbank Centre, Belvedere Rd, SE1; 3-course menu grill/restaurant £25/30; ☺ grill noon-11pm Mon-Sat, to 10pm Sun, restaurant 12.30-2.30pm & 5-10.30pm Mon-Sat; ☎⛭; Ⓤ Waterloo) This excellent restaurant inside the Royal Festival Hall (p184) is divided into grill and fine-dining sections by a large bar. The decor is cutting-edge 1950s, with muted colours and period chairs (trendy then, trendier now), while floor-to-ceiling windows bathe you in magnificent views of the Thames and the city. Booking is advised.

✖ Kensington & Hyde Park

Pimlico Fresh CAFE £
(✆ 020-7932 0030; 86 Wilton Rd, SW1; mains from £4.50; ☺ 7.30am-6pm Mon-Fri, 8.30am-6pm Sat & Sun; Ⓤ Victoria) This friendly two-room cafe will see you right, whether you need breakfast (French toast, bowls of porridge laced with honey or maple syrup), lunch (homemade quiches and soups, 'things' on toast) or just a good old latte and cake.

★ Rabbit MODERN BRITISH ££
(✆ 020-3750 0172; www.rabbit-restaurant.com; 172 King's Rd, SW3; small plates £6-13, set lunch of 2/3 courses £14.50/19.50; ☺ noon-midnight Tue-Sat,

noon-6pm Sun, 6-11pm Mon; ⏲; Ⓤ Sloane Sq) Three brothers grew up on a farm. One became a farmer, another a butcher, while the third worked in hospitality. So they pooled their skills and came up with Rabbit, a breath of fresh air in upmarket Chelsea. The restaurant rocks the agri-chic look, and the creative, seasonal Modern British cuisine is fabulous.

**★ Dinner
by Heston Blumenthal** MODERN BRITISH £££
(Map p170; ✆ 020-7201 3833; www.dinnerby heston.com; Mandarin Oriental Hyde Park, 66 Knightsbridge, SW1; 3-course set lunch £45, mains £33-52; ☺ noon-2pm & 6-10.15pm Mon-Fri, noon-2.30pm & 6.30-10.30pm Sat & Sun; ☎; Ⓤ Knightsbridge) Sumptuously presented Dinner is a gastronomic tour de force, taking diners on a journey through British culinary history (with inventive modern inflections). Dishes carry historical dates to convey context, while the restaurant interior is a design triumph, from the glass-walled kitchen and its overhead clock mechanism to the large windows looking onto the park. Book ahead.

⚑ Drinking & Nightlife

You need only glance at William Hogarth's *Gin Lane* prints from 1751 to realise that Londoners and alcohol have had more than a passing acquaintance. The metropolis offers a huge variety of venues to wet your whistle in – from cosy neighbourhood pubs to glitzy all-night clubs, and everything in between.

⚑ The West End

★ Dukes London COCKTAIL BAR
(Map p174; ✆ 020-7491 4840; www.dukeshotel. com/dukes-bar; Dukes Hotel, 35 St James's Pl, SW1; ☺ 2-11pm Mon-Sat, 4-10.30pm Sun; ☎; Ⓤ Green Park) Sip to-die-for martinis in a gentlemen's-club-like ambience at this classic bar where white-jacketed masters mix up perfect preparations. James Bond fans in particular should make a pilgrimage here: author Ian Fleming used to frequent the place, where he undoubtedly ordered his drinks 'shaken, not stirred'. Smokers can ease into the secluded Cognac and Cigar Garden to light up cigars purchased here.

American Bar BAR
(Map p174; ✆ 020-7499 1001; www.thebeaumont. com/dining/american-bar; Beaumont, Brown Hart

Gardens, W1; ⊙11.30am-midnight Mon-Sat, to 11pm Sun; ☎; Ⓤ Bond St) Sip a bourbon or a classic cocktail in the 1920s art deco ambience of this stylish bar at the hallmark **Beaumont hotel** (Map p174; d/studio/ste from £550/865/1475; ❋☎). It's central, glam and like a private members' club, but far from stuffy. Only a few years old, the American Bar feels like it's been pouring drinks since the days of the flapper and the jazz age.

★ Lamb & Flag
PUB

(Map p174; ☑020-7497 9504; www.lambandflag coventgarden.co.uk; 33 Rose St, WC2; ⊙11am-11pm Mon-Sat, noon-10.30pm Sun; Ⓤ Covent Garden) Perpetually busy pint-sized Lamb & Flag is full of charm and history, and has been a public house since at least 1772. Rain or shine, you'll have to elbow your way through the merry crowd drinking outside to get to the bar.

The main entrance is at the top of tiny, cobbled Rose St.

Connaught Bar
COCKTAIL BAR

(Map p174; ☑020-7314 3419; www.the-connaught. co.uk/mayfair-bars/connaught-bar; Connaught Hotel, Carlos Pl, W1; ⊙11am-1am Mon-Sat, to midnight Sun; Ⓤ Bond St) Drinkers who know their stuff single out the travelling martini trolley for particular praise, but almost everything at this sumptuous bar at the exclusive and very British Connaught Hotel gets the nod: lavish art deco–inspired lines, faultless and cheerful service, and some of the best drinks in town.

Cocktails – classic and those given a thoroughly contemporary twist – start at £18.

Swift
COCKTAIL BAR

(Map p174; ☑020-7437 7820; www.barswift.com; 12 Old Compton St, W1; ⊙3pm-midnight Mon-Sat, 3-10.30pm Sun; Ⓤ Leicester Sq or Tottenham Court Rd) One of our favourite spots for a tipple, Swift has a sleek, candlelit Upstairs Bar designed for those who want a quick drink before dinner or the theatre, while the Downstairs Bar is a whisky-lover's dream, with 250 bottles and counting, plus art deco–inspired sofas that invite lounging, especially when live blues and jazz are played on Friday and Saturday nights.

🍴 The South Bank

★ King's Arms
PUB

(Map p166; ☑020-7207 0784; www.thekingsarms london.co.uk; 25 Roupell St, SE1; ⊙11am-11pm

Mon-Sat, noon-10.30pm Sun; Ⓤ Waterloo) Relaxed and charming, this neighbourhood boozer is found at the corner of Roupell St, a terraced Waterloo backstreet. The large traditional bar area, complete with open fire in winter, serves up a changing selection of ales and bottled beers. It gets packed with after-work crowds between 6pm and 8pm.

★ Oblix
BAR

(Map p166; www.oblixrestaurant.com; 32nd fl, Shard, 31 St Thomas St, SE1; ⊙noon-11pm; Ⓤ London Bridge) The views from Oblix on the 32nd floor of **the Shard** (Map p166; www.the viewfromtheshard.com; 32 London Bridge St, SE1; adult/child £30.95/24.95; ⊙10am-10pm) aren't quite as impressive as the panoramas from the 69th-floor viewing platform, but you'll still be wowed. Relax with a cocktail (from £13.50) in the stylish bar and enjoy views towards the City, East and South London. Live music or DJ most nights from 7pm. Smart dress recommended.

Little Bird
COCKTAIL BAR

(Map p166; www.littlebirdgin.com; Maltby St, SE1; ⊙5-10pm Thu & Fri, 10am-10pm Sat, 11am-4pm Sun; Ⓤ London Bridge or Bermondsey) This South London–based gin distillery has a bar in the arches at **Maltby Street Market** (Map p166; www.maltby.st; dishes £5-10; ⊙10am-5pm Sat, 11am-4pm Sun), ready to ply merry punters with devilishly good cocktails served in jam jars.

🍷 Clerkenwell, Shoreditch & Spitalfields

Ye Olde Mitre
PUB

(Map p166; www.yeoldemitreholborn.co.uk; 1 Ely Ct, EC1; ⊙11am-11pm Mon-Fri; ☎; Ⓤ Farringdon) A delightfully cosy historic pub with an extensive beer selection, tucked away in a backstreet off Hatton Garden, Ye Olde Mitre was originally built in 1546 for the servants of Ely Palace. There's no music, so rooms echo only with amiable chit-chat. Queen Elizabeth I danced around the cherry tree by the bar, or so they say.

★ Zetter Townhouse Cocktail Lounge
COCKTAIL BAR

(Map p166; ☑020-7324 4545; www.thezettertown house.com/clerkenwell/bar; 49-50 St John's Sq, EC1; ⊙7am-midnight Sun-Wed, to 1am Thu-Sat; ☎; Ⓤ Farringdon) Behind an unassuming door on St John's Sq, this ground-floor bar is decorated with plush armchairs, stuffed animal heads and a legion of lamps. The cocktail list takes its theme from the area's distilling history – recipes of yesteryear plus homemade tinctures and cordials are used to create interesting and unusual tipples.

Cargo
CLUB

(Map p166; www.cargo-london.com; 83 Rivington St, EC2; ⊘noon-1am Sun-Wed, to 3am Thu & Fri, to midnight Sat; [U]Shoreditch High St) Cargo has seen better days but still packs in a crowd several nights weekly. Under its brick railway arches, you'll find a dance floor and bar, and there's also an outside terrace with two stencil works by Banksy. Drinks can be insanely overpriced, and the cover charge at peak times is steep – know what you're getting into or be too drunk to care.

☆ Entertainment

Whatever it is that sets your spirits soaring or your booty shaking, you'll find it in London. The city's been a world leader in theatre ever since a young bard from Stratford-upon-Avon set up shop here in the 16th century. And if London started swinging in the 1960s, its live rock and pop scene has barely let up since.

Theatre

A night out at the theatre is as much a must-do London experience as a trip on the top deck of a double-decker bus. London's Theatreland in the dazzling West End – from Aldwych in the east, past Shaftesbury Ave to Regent St in the west – has a concentration of theatres only rivalled by New York's Broadway. It's a thrillingly diverse scene, encompassing Shakespeare's classics performed with old-school precision, edgy new works, raise-the-roof musicals and some of the world's longest-running shows.

Old Vic
THEATRE

(Map p166; ✆0844 871 7628; www.oldvictheatre. com; The Cut, SE1; [U]Waterloo) Artistic director Matthew Warchus (who directed *Matilda the Musical* and the film *Pride*) aims to bring eclectic programming to the Old Vic theatre: expect new writing, as well as dynamic revivals of old works and musicals.

Young Vic
THEATRE

(Map p166; ✆020-7922 2922; www.youngvic.org; 66 The Cut, SE1; [U]Southwark or Waterloo) This groundbreaking theatre is as much about showcasing and discovering new talent as it is about people discovering theatre. The Young Vic features actors, directors and plays from across the world, many tackling

contemporary political and cultural issues, such as the death penalty, racism or corruption, and often blending dance and music with acting. Discounts are available for children, students and over-60s.

Royal Court Theatre
THEATRE

(Map p170; ✆020-7565 5000; www.royalcourtthe atre.com; Sloane Sq, SW1; tickets £12-38; [U]Sloane Sq) Equally renowned for staging innovative new plays and old classics, the Royal Court is among London's most progressive theatres and has continued to foster major writing talent across the UK for over 60 years. There are two auditoriums: the main Jerwood Theatre Downstairs, and the much smaller studio Jerwood Theatre Upstairs. Tickets for Monday performances are £12.

Live Music

★ KOKO
LIVE MUSIC

(Map p178; www.koko.uk.com; 1a Camden High St, NW1; [U]Mornington Cres) Once the legendary Camden Palace, where Charlie Chaplin, the Goons and the Sex Pistols performed, and where Prince played surprise gigs, KOKO is maintaining its reputation as one of London's better gig venues. The theatre has a dance floor and decadent balconies, and attracts an indie crowd. There are live bands most nights and hugely popular club nights on Saturdays. Check the website to find out what's on, and when to show up.

100 Club
LIVE MUSIC

(Map p174; ✆020-7636 0933; www.the100club. co.uk; 100 Oxford St, W1; tickets £8-20; ⊘check website for gig times; [U]Oxford Circus or Tottenham Court Rd) This heritage London venue at the same address since 1942 started off as a jazz club but now leans towards rock. Back in the day it showcased Chris Barber, BB King and the Rolling Stones, and it was at the centre of the punk revolution and the '90s indie scene. It hosts dancing gigs, the occasional big name, where-are-they-now bands and top-league tributes.

Ronnie Scott's
JAZZ

(Map p174; ✆020-7439 0747; www.ronniescotts. co.uk; 47 Frith St, W1; ⊘6pm-3am Mon-Sat, noon-4pm & 6.30pm-midnight Sun; [U]Leicester Sq or Tottenham Court Rd) Ronnie Scott's jazz club opened in 1959 and became widely known as Britain's best, hosting such luminaries as Miles Davis, Charlie Parker, Ella Fitzgerald, Count Basie and Sarah Vaughan. The club continues to build upon its formidable

LBGTIQ+ LONDON

London is a world gay capital on par with New York and San Francisco, with visible gay, lesbian and transgender communities and enlightened laws to protect them. It's rare to encounter any problem with sharing rooms or holding hands in the inner city, although it would pay to keep your wits about you at night and be conscious of your surroundings. The West End, particularly Soho, is the visible centre of gay and lesbian London, with numerous venues clustered around Old Compton St – but many other areas have their own miniscenes. The easiest way to find out what's going on is to pick up the free press from a venue; the gay section of *Time Out* (www.timeout.com/london/lgbt) is also useful.

reputation by presenting a range of big names and new talent. Book in advance, or come for a more informal gig at Upstairs @ Ronnie's.

Scala
LIVE MUSIC

(Map p178; ☏020-7833 2022; www.scala.co.uk; 275 Pentonville Rd, N1; Ⓤ King's Cross St Pancras) Opened in 1920 as a salubrious golden-age cinema, Scala slipped into porn-movie hell in the 1970s, only to be reborn as a club and live-music venue in the early 2000s. It's one of the top places in London to catch an intimate gig and is a great dance space too, hosting a diverse range of club nights.

Classical Music, Opera & Dance

★ **Royal Albert Hall**
CONCERT VENUE

(Map p170; ☏0845 401 5034; 020-7589 8212; www.royalalberthall.com; Kensington Gore, SW7; Ⓤ South Kensington) This splendid Victorian concert hall hosts classical music, rock and other performances, but is famously the venue for the BBC-sponsored Proms. Booking is possible, but from mid-July to mid-September Promenaders queue for £5 standing tickets that go on sale one hour before curtain-up. Otherwise, the box office and prepaid-ticket collection counter are through door 12 (south side of the hall).

A variety of tours of the Albert Hall are also available, ranging from a **Grand Tour** (Map p170; adult/child £14/7; ⊙ hourly 9.30am-4.30pm), giving a general overview of the building, to a **Behind the Scenes Tour** (Map p170; ☏0845 401 5045; www.royalalberthall.com; adult/children £16/8.75). These can be followed by afternoon tea in the bright, chic Verdi restaurant (£30).

Royal Opera House
OPERA

(Map p174; ☏020-7304 4000; www.roh.org.uk; Bow St, WC2; ⊙ gift shop & cafe from 10am; Ⓤ Covent Garden) Opera and ballet have a fantastic setting on Covent Garden Piazza, and a night here is a sumptuous affair. Although the program has modern influences, the main attractions are still the classic productions, which feature world-class performers. A three-year, £50-million revamp finished in October 2018, with new areas open to the non-ticketed public for the first time, including a swish cafe.

Sadler's Wells
DANCE

(Map p166; ☏020-7863 8000; www.sadlerswells.com; Rosebery Ave, EC1; Ⓤ Angel) A glittering modern venue that was first established in 1683, Sadler's Wells is the most eclectic modern-dance and ballet venue in town, with experimental dance shows of all genres and from all corners of the globe. The Lilian Baylis Studio stages smaller productions.

Royal Festival Hall
CONCERT VENUE

(Map p166; ☏020-3879 9555; www.southbankcentre.co.uk; Southbank Centre, Belvedere Rd, SE1; ☎; Ⓤ Waterloo) The Royal Festival Hall is Europe's largest centre for performing and visual arts. The amphitheatre seats 2500 and is one of the best places for catching world- and classical-music artists. The sound is fantastic, the programming impeccable and there are frequent free gigs in the wonderfully expansive foyer.

🔒 Shopping

Department Stores

London's famous department stores are an attraction in themselves, even if you're not interested in buying.

★ Fortnum & Mason
DEPARTMENT STORE

(Map p174; ☏020-7734 8040; www.fortnumandmason.com; 181 Piccadilly, W1; ⊙ 10am-9pm Mon-Sat, 11.30am-6pm Sun; Ⓤ Green Park or Piccadilly Circus) With its classic eau-de-Nil (pale green) colour scheme, the 'Queen's grocery store' established in 1707 refuses to yield to modern times. Its staff – men and women – still wear old-fashioned tailcoats, and its glamorous food hall is supplied with hampers, marmalade and speciality teas. Stop for a spot of afternoon tea at the Diamond Jubilee Tea Salon, visited by Queen Elizabeth II in 2012.

Harrods
DEPARTMENT STORE

(Map p170; ☎020-7730 1234; www.harrods.com; 87-135 Brompton Rd, SW1; ⊙10am-9pm Mon-Sat, 11.30am-6pm Sun; Ⓤ Knightsbridge) Garish and stylish in equal measure, perennially crowded Harrods is an obligatory stop for visitors, from the cash-strapped to the big spenders. The stock is astonishing, as are many of the price tags. High on kitsch, the 'Egyptian Elevator' resembles something out of an Indiana Jones epic, while the memorial fountain to Dodi and Di (lower ground floor) merely adds surrealism.

★ Liberty
DEPARTMENT STORE

(Map p174; ☎020-7734 1234; www.libertylondon. com; Regent St, entrance on Great Marlborough St, W1; ⊙10am-8pm Mon-Sat, 11.30am-6pm Sun; ☎; Ⓤ Oxford Circus) One of London's most recognisable shops, Liberty department store has a white-and-wood-beam Tudor Revival facade that lures shoppers in to browse luxury contemporary fashion, homewares, cosmetics and accessories, all at sky-high prices. Liberty is known for its fabrics and has a full haberdashery department; a classic London gift or souvenir is a Liberty fabric print, especially in the form of a scarf.

Markets

Perhaps the biggest draw for visitors is the capital's famed markets. A treasure trove of small designers, unique jewellery pieces, original framed photographs and posters, colourful vintage pieces and bric-a-brac, they are the antidote to impersonal, carbon-copy shopping centres.

★ Portobello Road Market
MARKET

(www.portobellomarket.org; Portobello Rd, W10; ⊙8am-6.30pm Mon-Wed, Fri & Sat, to 1pm Thu; Ⓤ Notting Hill Gate or Ladbroke Grove) Lovely on a warm summer's day, Portobello Road Market is an iconic London attraction with an eclectic mix of street food, fruit and veg, antiques, curios, collectables, fashion and trinkets. The shops along Portobello Rd open daily and the fruit and veg stalls (from Elgin Cres to Talbot Rd) only close on Sunday. But while some an-

tique stalls operate on Friday, the busiest day by far is Saturday, when antique dealers set up shop (from Chepstow Villas to Elgin Cres).

Camden Market
MARKET

(Map p178; www.camdenmarket.com; Camden High St, NW1; ⊙10am-late; Ⓤ Camden Town or Chalk Farm) Although – or perhaps because – it stopped being cutting-edge several thousand cheap leather jackets ago, Camden Market attracts millions of visitors each year and is one of London's most popular attractions. What started out as a collection of attractive craft stalls beside Camden Lock on the Regent's Canal now extends most of the way from Camden Town tube station to Chalk Farm tube station.

Broadway Market
MARKET

(www.broadwaymarket.co.uk; Broadway Market, E8; ⊙9am-5pm Sat; ☐394) There's been a market down here since the late 19th century, but the focus these days is artisanal food, handmade gifts and unique clothing. Cafes along both sides of the street do a roaring trade with coffee-drinking shoppers. Stock up on edible treats then head to **London Fields** (Richmond Rd, E8; Ⓤ London Fields) for a picnic.

❶ Information

Visit London (www.visitlondon.com) can fill you in on everything from tourist attractions and events (Changing the Guard, Chinese New Year parade etc) to river trips and tours, accommodation, eating, theatre, shopping, children's activities and LGBT+ venues. Kiosks are dotted about the city and can provide maps and brochures; some branches book theatre tickets.

❶ Getting There & Away

BUS

Long-distance and international buses arrive and depart from **Victoria Coach Station** (164

❶ MAPS

There was a time when no Londoner would be without a pocket-sized *London A–Z* map-book. It's a great resource if you don't have a smartphone. You can buy them at news stands and shops everywhere. For getting around the London Underground system (the tube), maps are free at underground stations.

Buckingham Palace Rd, SW1; Victoria), close to the Victoria tube and rail stations.

TRAIN

Most of London's main-line rail terminals are linked by the Circle line on the tube. The terminals listed here serve the following destinations:

Charing Cross Canterbury

Euston Manchester, Liverpool, Carlisle, Glasgow

King's Cross Gatwick airport, Cambridge, Hull, York, Newcastle, Edinburgh, Aberdeen

Liverpool Street Stansted airport (Express), Cambridge

London Bridge Gatwick airport, Brighton

Marylebone Birmingham

Paddington Heathrow airport (Express), Oxford, Bath, Bristol, Exeter, Plymouth, Cardiff

St Pancras Gatwick and Luton airports, Brighton, Nottingham, Sheffield, Leicester, Leeds, Paris Eurostar

Victoria Gatwick airport (Express), Brighton, Canterbury

Waterloo Windsor, Winchester, Exeter, Plymouth

ⓘ Getting Around

TO/FROM THE AIRPORTS
Gatwick

National Rail (www.nationalrail.co.uk) Regular train services to/from London Bridge (30 minutes, every 15 to 30 minutes), London King's Cross (55 minutes, every 15 to 30 minutes) and London Victoria (30 minutes, every 10 to 15 minutes). Fares vary, but allow £10 to £20 for a single.

EasyBus (www.easybus.co.uk) Runs 13-seater minibuses to Gatwick every 15 to 20 minutes from Victoria Coach Station (one way from £1.95). The service runs round the clock. Journey time averages 75 minutes.

Heathrow

The Underground (known as 'the tube') is the cheapest way of getting to Heathrow (£6, one hour,

every three to nine minutes from around 5am to midnight, all night Friday and Saturday, with reduced frequency). Buy tickets at the station.

Heathrow Express (www.heathrowexpress. com; one way/return £27/42;) and **Heathrow Connect** (☏ 0343 222 1234; www.tfl.gov. uk; adult single/open return £10.20/12.50), trains run every 30 minutes, to Paddington train station from around 5am and between 11pm and midnight. Heathrow Express trains take a mere 15 minutes to reach Paddington.

London City

Docklands Light Railway (DLR; www.tfl.gov. uk/dlr) stops at the London City Airport station (one way £2.80 to £3.30). Trains depart every eight to 10 minutes from just after 5.30am to 12.15am Monday to Saturday, and 7am to 11.15pm Sunday. The journey to Bank takes just over 20 minutes.

A metered black-cab trip to the City/Oxford St/Earl's Court costs about £25/35/50.

Luton

National Rail (www.nationalrail.co.uk) has 24-hour services (one way from £14, 26 to 50 minutes, departures every six minutes to one hour) from London St Pancras International to Luton Airport Parkway station, where an airport shuttle bus (one way/return £2.20/3.50) will take you to the airport in 10 minutes.

Airbus A1 (www.nationalexpress.com; one way from £11) runs over 60 times daily to London Victoria Coach Station (one way from £5), via Portman Sq, Baker St, St John's Wood, Finchley Rd and Golders Green. It takes around 1½ hours.

Stansted

Stansted Express (☏ 0345 600 7245; www.stanstedexpress.com; one way/return £17/29) rail service (45 minutes, every 15 to 30 minutes) links the airport and Liverpool St station. From the airport, the first train leaves at 5.30am, the last at 12.30am. Trains depart

---

ⓘ OYSTER CARD

The Oyster Card is a smart card on which you can store credit towards 'prepay' fares, as well as Travelcards valid for periods from a day to a year. Oyster Cards are valid across the entire public transport network in London. When entering a station, touch your card on a reader (which has a yellow circle with the image of an Oyster Card on it) and then touch again on your way out. The system will then deduct the appropriate amount of credit from your card. For bus journeys, you only need to touch once upon boarding. The benefit is that fares for Oyster Card users are lower than standard ones. If you are making many journeys during the day, you will never pay more than the appropriate Travelcard (peak or off-peak) once the daily 'price cap' has been reached. Oyster Cards can be bought (£5 refundable deposit required) and topped up at any Underground station, travel information centre or shop displaying the Oyster logo. To get your deposit back along with any remaining credit, simply return your Oyster Card at a ticket booth.

Liverpool St station from 4.40am (on some days at 3.40am) to 11.25pm.

Airbus A6 (☑ 0871 781 8181; www.national express.com; one way from £10) runs to Victoria Coach Station (around one hour to 1½ hours, every 20 minutes) via Marble Arch, Paddington, Baker St and Golders Green

EasyBus (www.easybus.co.uk) runs services to Baker St and Old St tube stations every 15 minutes. The journey (one way from £4.95) takes one hour from Old St or 1¼ hour from Baker St.

BICYCLE

Tens of thousands of Londoners cycle to work every day, and it is generally a good way to get around the city, although traffic can be intimidating for less-confident cyclists and it's important to keep your wits about you. The city has tried hard to improve the cycling infrastructure, by opening new 'cycle superhighways' for commuters, while the public bike hire scheme **Santander Cycles** (☑ 0343 222 6666; www.tfl.gov.uk/modes/cycling/santander-cycles) is particularly useful for visitors.

Transport for London (www.tfl.gov.uk) publishes 14 free maps of London's cycle routes.

CAR

Don't. As a visitor, it's very unlikely you'll need to drive in London. If you do, you'll incur an £11.50 per day congestion charge (7am to 6pm weekdays) simply to take a car into central London. If you're hiring a car to continue your trip around Britain, take the tube or train to a major airport and pick it up from there.

PUBLIC TRANSPORT
Boat

Thames Clipper (www.thamesclippers.com; all zones adult/child £9.90/4.95) boats run regular services between Embankment, Waterloo (London Eye), Blackfriars, Bankside (Shakespeare's Globe), London Bridge, Tower Bridge, Canary Wharf, Greenwich, North Greenwich and Woolwich piers from 6.55am to around midnight (from 9.29am weekends).

Bus

London's ubiquitous red double-decker buses operate from 5am to 11.30pm and afford great views of the city, but be aware that the going can be slow, thanks to traffic jams and dozens of commuters getting on and off at every stop.

Cash cannot be used on London's buses. Instead you must pay with an Oyster Card, Travelcard or a contactless payment card. Bus fares are a flat £1.50, no matter the distance travelled.

Underground & DLR

The London Underground ('the tube'; 11 colour-coded lines) is part of an integrated-transport system that also includes the **Docklands Light Railway** (DLR; www.tfl.gov.uk/dlr). It's the quickest and easiest way of getting around the city, if not the cheapest.

The first trains operate from around 5.30am Monday to Saturday and 6.45am Sunday. The last trains leave around 12.30am Monday to Saturday and 11.30pm Sunday.

Additionally, selected lines (the Victoria and Jubilee lines, plus most of the Piccadilly, Central and Northern lines) run all night on Friday and Saturday to get revellers home (on what is called the 'Night Tube'), with trains every 10 minutes or so.

Single fares cost from £2.40/4.90 with/without an Oyster Card.

TAXI

London's famous black cabs are available for hire when the yellow sign above the windscreen is lit; just stick your arm out to signal one. Fares are metered, with the flagfall charge of £2.60 (covering the first 235m during a weekday), rising by increments of 20p for each subsequent 117m.

Minicabs, which are licensed, are (usually) cheaper competitors. Unlike black cabs, minicabs cannot be hailed on the street; they must be hired by phone or directly from one of the minicab offices.

Windsor & Eton

POP 32,184

Facing each other across the Thames, with the massive bulk of Windsor Castle looming above, the twin riverside towns of Windsor and Eton have a rather surreal atmosphere. Windsor on the south bank sees the daily pomp and ritual of the changing of the guards, while schoolboys dressed in formal tailcoats wander the streets of tiny Eton to the north. **Eton College** (www.etoncollege.com) is England's most famous 'public' – as in private and fee-paying – boys' school, and arguably the most enduring symbol of the British class system. High-profile alumni include 19 British prime ministers, countless princes, kings and maharajas, Princes William and Harry, George Orwell, John Maynard Keynes, Bear Grylls and Eddie Redmayne. It can only be visited on guided tours, on summer Fridays, which take in the chapel and the Museum of Eton Life. Book online.

THE MAKING OF HARRY POTTER

Whether you're a fairweather fan or a full-on Potterhead, this studio **tour** (☑ 0345 084 0900; www.wbstudiotour. co.uk; Studio Tour Dr, Leavesden, WD25; adult/child £41/33; ⏰ 8.30am-10pm Jun-Sep, hours vary Oct-May; P ♿) is well worth the admittedly hefty admission price. You'll need to pre-book your visit for an allocated timeslot and then allow two- to three hours to do the complex justice. It starts with a short film before you're ushered through giant doors into the actual set of Hogwarts' Great Hall – the first of many 'wow' moments. It's near Watford, northwest of London.

★ Windsor Castle
CASTLE

(☑ 03031-237304; www.royalcollection.org.uk; Castle Hill; adult/child £21.20/12.30; ⏰ 9.30am-5.15pm Mar-Oct, 9.45am-4.15pm Nov-Feb, last admission 1¼hr before closing, all or part of castle subject to occasional closures; ♿; 🚌 702 from London Victoria, 🚆 London Waterloo to Windsor & Eton Riverside, 🚆 London Paddington to Windsor & Eton Central via Slough) The world's largest and oldest continuously occupied fortress, Windsor Castle is a majestic vision of battlements and towers. Used for state occasions, it's one of the Queen's principal residences; when she's at home, the Royal Standard flies from the Round Tower.

Frequent, free guided tours introduce visitors to the castle precincts, divided into the Lower, Middle and Upper Wards. Free audio tours guide everyone through its lavish State Apartments and beautiful chapels; certain areas may be off limits if in use.

ℹ Information

Tourist Office (☑ 01753-743900; www. windsor.gov.uk; Old Booking Hall, Windsor Royal Shopping Arcade, Thames St, Windsor; ⏰ 10am-5pm Apr-Sep, to 4pm Oct-Mar) Tickets for attractions and events, plus guidebooks and walking maps.

ℹ Getting There & Away

The quickest rail route from London connects London Paddington with Windsor & Eton Central, opposite the castle, but you have to change at Slough (£10.50, 30 to 45 minutes). London Waterloo has slower but direct services to Windsor & Eton Riverside, on Dachet Rd (£10.50, 45 minutes to one hour).

Canterbury

☑ 01227 / POP 55,240

Canterbury tops the charts for English cathedral cities. Many consider the World Heritage–listed cathedral that dominates its centre to be one of Europe's finest, and the town's narrow medieval alleyways, riverside gardens and ancient city walls are a joy to explore.

◉ Sights

★ Canterbury Cathedral
CATHEDRAL

(www.canterbury-cathedral.org; adult/concession/child £12.50/10.50/8.50, tours adult/child £5/4, audio guide £4/3; ⏰ 9am-5.30pm Mon-Sat, 12.30-2.30pm Sun) A rich repository of more than 1400 years of Christian history, the Church of England's mother ship is a truly extraordinary place with an absorbing history. This Gothic cathedral, the highlight of the city's World Heritage Sites, is southeast England's top tourist attraction as well as a place of worship. It's also the site of English history's most famous murder: Archbishop Thomas Becket was done in here in 1170. Allow at least two hours to do the cathedral justice.

🛏 Sleeping & Eating

Kipp's Independent Hostel
HOSTEL £

(☑ 01227-786121; www.kipps-hostel.com; 40 Nunnery Fields; dm £12.50-24.50, s £22.50-40, d £40-68; @ 🛜) Occupying a century-old red-brick town house in a quietish residential area less than a mile from the city centre, these superb backpacker digs enjoy a homey atmosphere, clean (though cramped) dorms, a good kitchen for self-caterers and a large TV lounge.

★ ABode Canterbury
BOUTIQUE HOTEL ££

(☑ 01227-766266; www.abodecanterbury.co.uk; 30-33 High St; r from £64; 🛜) The 72 rooms at this super-central hotel, the only boutique hotel in town, are graded from 'comfortable' to 'fabulous' (via 'enviable'), and for the most part live up to their names. They come with features such as handmade beds, chesterfield sofas, tweed cushions and beautiful modern bathrooms. There's a splendid champagne bar, restaurant and tavern too.

Tiny Tim's Tearoom
CAFE £

(www.tinytimstearoom.com; 34 St Margaret's St; mains £6-10; ⏰ 9.30am-5pm Mon-Sat, 10.30am-5pm Sun) It's no mean feat to be declared 'Kent Tearoom of the Year', but this swish 1930s cafe was awarded the accolade in 2015. It offers hungry shoppers big breakfasts packed with Kentish ingredients, and tiers of cakes, crumpets, cucumber sandwiches and scones plastered in clotted cream. On busy shopping days you are guaranteed to queue for a table.

★ **Goods Shed** MARKET ££
(☑ 01227-459153; www.thegoodsshed.co.uk; Station Rd West; mains £17.50-20; ⊙ market 9am-7pm Tue-Sat, to 4pm Sun, restaurant noon-2.30pm & 6pm-last customer) Aromatic farmers market, food hall and fabulous restaurant rolled into one, this converted warehouse by the Canterbury West train station is a hit with everyone from self-caterers to sit-down gourmets. The chunky wooden tables sit slightly above the market hubbub but in full view of its appetite-whetting stalls. Daily specials exploit the freshest farm goodies the Garden of England offers.

ⓘ Information

Tourist Office (☑ 01227-862162; www.canterbury.co.uk; 18 High St; ⊙ 9am-6pm Mon-Wed & Fri, to 8pm Thu, to 5pm Sat, 10am-5pm Sun; 🛜) Located in the Beaney House of Art & Knowledge. Staff can help book accommodation, excursions and theatre tickets.

ⓘ Getting There & Away

There are two train stations: Canterbury East for London Victoria and Canterbury West for London's Charing Cross/St Pancras stations. Canterbury connections:

London St Pancras (£38.70, one hour, hourly) High-speed service.

London Victoria/Charing Cross (£32.60, 1¾ hours, two hourly)

Salisbury

☑ 01722 / POP 40,300

Centred on a majestic cathedral that's topped by the tallest spire in England, Salisbury makes an appealing Wiltshire base. It's been an important provincial city for more than a thousand years.

⊙ Sights

★ **Salisbury Cathedral** CATHEDRAL
(☑ 01722-555120; www.salisburycathedral.org.uk; The Close; requested donation adult/child £7.50/3; ⊙ 9am-5pm Mon-Sat, noon-4pm Sun) England is endowed with countless stunning churches, but few can hold a candle to the grandeur and sheer spectacle of 13th-century Salisbury Cathedral. This early English Gothic-style structure has an elaborate exterior decorated with pointed arches and flying buttresses, and a sombre, austere interior designed to keep its congregation suitably pious. Its statuary and tombs are outstanding; don't miss the daily **tower tours** (adult/child £13.50/8.50; ⊙ 2-5 tours daily, May-Sep) and the cathedral's original, 13th-century copy of the **Magna Carta** (⊙ 9.30am-5pm Mon-Sat, noon-4pm Sun Apr-Oct, 9.30am-4.30pm Mon-Sat, noon-3.45pm Sun Nov-Mar).

Salisbury Museum MUSEUM
(☑ 01722-332151; www.salisburymuseum.org.uk; 65 The Close; adult/child £8/4; ⊙ 10am-5pm Mon-Sat year-round, plus noon-5pm Sun Jun-Sep) The hugely important archaeological finds here include the Stonehenge Archer, the bones of a man found in the ditch near the stone circle – one of the arrows found alongside probably killed him. With gold coins dating from 100 BCE and a Bronze Age gold necklace, it's a powerful introduction to Wiltshire's prehistory.

🛏 Sleeping & Eating

Cathedral View B&B ££
(☑ 01722-502254; www.cathedral-viewbandb.co.uk; 83 Exeter St; s £85-95, d £99-140; 🅿🛜) Admirable attention to detail defines this Georgian town house, where miniature flower displays and home-baked biscuits sit in quietly elegant rooms. Breakfasts include prime Wiltshire sausages and the B&B's own bread

AVEBURY

While the tour buses usually head straight to Stonehenge, prehistoric purists make for **Avebury Stone Circle** (NT; ☑ 01672-539250; www.nationaltrust.org.uk; ⊙ 24hr; 🅿) FREE. Though it lacks the dramatic trilithons ('gateways') of its sister site across the plain, Avebury is the largest stone circle in the world and a more rewarding place to visit simply because you can get closer to the giant boulders.

A large section of Avebury village is actually inside the circle, meaning you can sleep, or at least have lunch and a pint, inside the mystic ring.

Take bus 2 from Salisbury to Devizes (£6, one hour, hourly Monday to Saturday), where bus 49 runs hourly to Avebury (£3, 15 minutes).

and jam, while homemade lemon drizzle cake will be waiting for your afternoon tea.

★ **Chapter House** INN **£££**
(☑ 01722-341277; www.thechapterhouseuk.com; 9 St Johns St; s £115-145, d £135-155; 🛜) In this 800-year-old boutique beauty, wood panels and wildly wonky stairs sit beside duck-your-head beams. The cheaper bedrooms are swish but the posher ones are stunning, starring slipper baths and the odd heraldic crest. The pick is room 6, where King Charles is reputed to have stayed. Lucky him.

King's House CAFE **£**
(☑ 01722-332151; www.salisburymuseum.org.uk; 65 The Close; snacks from £4; ⊙ 11am-3pm Tue-Sat) A cafe just made for sightseeing: attached to Salisbury Museum, with fine views of the soaring spire of neighbouring Salisbury Cathedral from the flower-framed garden. A perfect spot to refuel on well-filled sandwiches and decadent cakes.

ⓘ Information

Tourist Office (☑ 01722-342860; www. visitsalisbury.co.uk; Fish Row; ⊙ 9am-5pm Mon-Fri, 10am-4pm Sat, 10am-2pm Sun; 🛜)

ⓘ Getting There & Away

BUS

National Express (www.nationalexpress.com) services stop at Millstream Approach, near the train station. Direct services include the following:
Bath (£11, 1¼ hours, one daily)
Bristol (£6, 2¼ hours, one daily)
London Victoria via Heathrow (£10, three hours, three daily Monday to Saturday)

TRAIN

Salisbury's train station is half a mile northwest of the cathedral. Half-hourly connections include the following:
Bath (£10, one hour)
Bristol (£16, 1¼ hours)
London Waterloo (£42, 1½ hours)

Stonehenge

This compelling ring of monolithic stones has been attracting a steady stream of pilgrims, poets and philosophers for the last 5000 years and is easily Britain's most iconic archaeological site.

An ultramodern makeover at ancient Stonehenge (EH; ☑ 0370 333 1181; www.english -heritage.org.uk; near Amesbury; adult/child same-

> ### ⓘ STONE CIRCLE ACCESS VISITS
>
> Visitors to Stonehenge normally have to stay outside the stone circle. But on **Stone Circle Access Visits** (☑ 0370 333 0605; www.english-heritage.org.uk; adult/child £38.50/23.10) you get to wander round the core of the site, getting up-close views of the bluestones and trilithons. The walks take place in the evening or early morning, so the quieter atmosphere and the slanting sunlight add to the effect. Each visit only takes 26 people; to secure a place book at least two months in advance.

day tickets £19.50/11.70, advance booking £17.50/ 10.50; ⊙ 9am-8pm Jun-Aug, 9.30am-7pm Apr, May & Sep, 9.30am-5pm Oct-Mar; 🅿) has brought an impressive visitor centre and the closure of an intrusive road (now restored to grassland). The result is a far stronger sense of historical context, with dignity and mystery returned to an archaeological gem.

Stonehenge is one of Britain's great archaeological mysteries: despite countless theories about the site's purpose, ranging from a sacrificial centre to a celestial timepiece, in truth, no one knows for sure what drove prehistoric Britons to expend so much time and effort on its construction. Admission is through timed tickets – secure a place well in advance.

ⓘ Getting There & Away

There is no public transport to the site. The **Stonehenge Tour** (☑ 01202-338420; www. thestonehengetour.info; adult/child/family £30/20/90) leaves Salisbury's train station half-hourly from June to August, and hourly from September to May.

Bath

☑ 01225 / POP 88,850

Britain is littered with beautiful cities, but precious few compare to Bath, founded on top of natural hot springs that led the Romans to build a magnificent bathhouse here. Bath's heyday was during the 18th century, when local entrepreneur Ralph Allen and the father-and-son architects John Wood the Elder and Younger turned this sleepy backwater into the toast of Georgian society, and constructed fabulous landmarks such as the Circus and Royal Crescent.

⊙ Sights

★ Roman Baths
HISTORIC BUILDING

(☑ 01225-477785; www.romanbaths.co.uk; Abbey Churchyard; adult/child/family £17.50/10.25/48; ⊙ 9.30am-5pm Nov-Feb, 9am-5pm Mar–mid-Jun, Sep & Oct, 9am-9pm mid-Jun–Aug) In typically ostentatious style, the Romans built a bathhouse complex above Bath's 46°C (115°F) hot springs. Set alongside a temple dedicated to the healing goddess Sulis-Minerva, the baths now form one of the world's best-preserved ancient Roman baths, and are encircled by 18th- and 19th-century buildings. To dodge the worst of the crowds avoid weekends, and July and August; buy fast-track tickets online to by-pass the queues. Saver tickets covering the Roman Baths and the Fashion Museum cost adult/child/family £22.50/12.25/58.

Royal Crescent
ARCHITECTURE

Bath is famous for its glorious Georgian architecture, and it doesn't get any grander than this semicircular terrace of majestic town houses overlooking the green sweep of Royal Victoria Park. Designed by John Wood the Younger (1728–82) and built between 1767 and 1775, the houses appear perfectly symmetrical from the outside, but the owners were allowed to tweak the interiors, so no two houses are quite the same. No 1 Royal Crescent (☑ 01225-428126; www.no1royal crescent.org.uk; 1 Royal Cres; adult/child/family £10.30/5.10/25.40; ⊙ 10am-5pm) offers you an intriguing insight into life inside.

Jane Austen Centre
MUSEUM

(☑ 01225-443000; www.janeausten.co.uk; 40 Gay St; adult/child £12/6.20; ⊙ 9.45am-5.30pm Apr-Oct, 10am-4pm Sun-Fri, 9.45am-5.30pm Sat Nov-Mar) Bath is known to many as a location in Jane Austen's novels, including *Persuasion* and *Northanger Abbey*. Although Austen lived in Bath for only five years, from 1801 to 1806, she remained a regular visitor and a keen student of the city's social scene. Here, guides in Regency costumes regale you with Austen-esque tales as you tour memorabilia relating to the writer's life in Bath.

🛏 Sleeping

Bath YHA
HOSTEL £

(☑ 0345 371 9303; www.yha.org.uk; Bathwick Hill; dm £23, d/q from £49/69; ⊙ check-in 3-11pm; P @ 🛜) Split across an Italianate mansion and modern annexes, this impressive hostel is a steep climb (or a short hop on bus U1) from the city. The listed building means the

rooms are huge, and some have period features such as cornicing and bay windows.

★ Three Abbey Green
B&B ££

(☑ 01225-428558; www.threeabbeygreen.com; 3 Abbey Green; s £108-144, d £120-200, q £240; 🛜) Rarely in Bath do you get somewhere as central as this Georgian town house with such spacious rooms. Elegant, 18th-century-style furnishings are teamed with swish wet-room bathrooms, while the opulent Lord Nelson suite features a vast four-poster bed. There's a fabulous vibe here – friendly, family-run and proud of it.

Hill House Bath
B&B ££

(☑ 01225-920520; www.hillhousebath.co.uk; 25 Belvedere; r £115-135; P 🛜) When you walk through the door here it almost feels like you're staying with friends. The decor is quietly quirky: moustache-themed cushions, retro pictures and objets d'art abound.

Breakfasts are a cut above – how many other B&Bs add dollops of dill crème fraiche to homemade potato cakes, smoked salmon and poached egg?

★ Grays Bath
B&B £££

(☑ 01225-403020; www.graysbath.co.uk; 9 Upper Oldfield Park; r £115-245; P 🛜) Boutique treat Grays is a beautiful blend of modern, pared-down design and family treasures, many picked up from the owners' travels. All the rooms are individual: choose from floral, polka dot or maritime stripes. Perhaps the pick is the curving, six-sided room 12 in the attic, with partial city views.

✗ Eating & Drinking

Sally Lunn's
CAFE £

(☑ 01225-461634; www.sallylunns.co.uk; 4 North Pde Passage; mains £6-17, afternoon tea £8-40;

DON'T MISS

THE THERMAE BATH SPA

Taking a dip in the Roman Baths might be off limits, but you can still sample the city's curative waters at this fantastic modern **spa complex** (☑ 01225-331234; www.thermaebathspa.com; Hot Bath St; spa £36-40, treatments from £65; ⊙ 9am-9.30pm, last entry 7pm), housed in a shell of local stone and plate glass. The showpiece attraction is the open-air rooftop pool, where you can bathe with a backdrop of Bath's cityscape – a don't-miss experience best enjoyed at dusk.

Bath

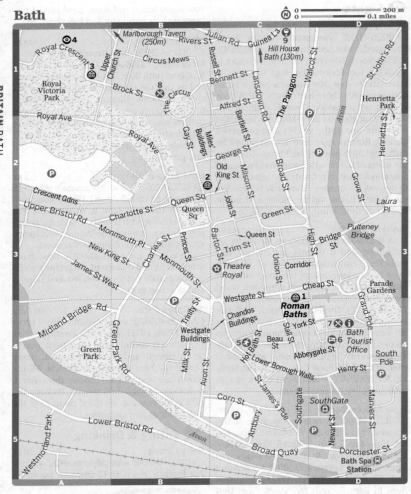

en has turned this bistro into one of Bath's destination addresses. Her taste is for British dishes with a Continental twist, à la British food writer Elizabeth David: rabbit, Wiltshire lamb and West Country fish are all infused with herby flavours and rich sauces. It occupies an elegant town house near the Circus. Reservations recommended.

10am-9pm) Eating a bun at Sally Lunn's is a Bath tradition. It's all about proper English tea here, brewed in bone-china teapots, with finger sandwiches and dainty cakes served by waitresses in frilly aprons.

The trademark Sally Lunn's bun is the house speciality – but there are heartier plates too, such as Welsh rarebit and 'Trencher' dishes (with the 'bun' acting as plate).

★**The Circus** MODERN BRITISH **££**
(☐ 01225-466020; www.thecircusrestaurant.co.uk; 34 Brock St; mains lunch £12-15, dinner £16-23; ⏰10am-midnight Mon-Sat; ☐) Chef Ali Gold-

Marlborough Tavern GASTROPUB **££**
(☐ 01225-423731; www.marlborough-tavern.com; 35 Marlborough Bldgs; mains £13-25; ⏰ bar noon-11pm, food noon-2pm & 6-9.30pm) The queen of Bath's gastropubs has food that's closer to that of a fine-dining restaurant – smoked

Bath

◎ Top Sights

◎ Sights

✦ Activities, Courses & Tours

⊜ Sleeping

✕ Eating

◎ Drinking & Nightlife

white-bean purée, and crab and ginger salad rather than bog-standard meat-and-two-veg. Chunky wooden tables and racks of wine behind the bar give it an exclusive, classy feel.

Canny diners head here in the early evening to get 25% off the food bill.

★ Menu Gordon Jones   MODERN BRITISH £££
(☑ 01225-480871; www.menugordonjones.co.uk; 2 Wellsway; 5-course lunch £50, 6-course dinner £55; ⊘ 12.30-2pm & 7-9pm Tue-Sat) If you enjoy dining with an element of surprise, then Gordon Jones' restaurant will be right up your culinary boulevard. Menus are dreamt up daily and showcase the chef's taste for experimental ingredients (expect mushroom mousse and Weetabix ice cream) and eye-catching presentation (test tubes and paper bags). It's superb value given the skill on show. Reservations essential.

★ Star   PUB
(☑ 01225-425072; www.abbeyales.co.uk; 23 The Vineyards, off the Paragon; ⊘ noon-2.30pm & 5.30-11pm Mon-Fri, noon-midnight Sat, to 10.30pm Sun) Few pubs are registered relics, but the Star is just that, and it still has many of its 19th-century bar fittings. It's the brewery tap for Bath-based Abbey Ales; some ales are served in traditional jugs, and you can even ask for a pinch of snuff in the 'smaller bar'.

❶ Information

Bath Tourist Office (☑ 01225-614420; www.visitbath.co.uk; 2 Terrace Walk; ⊘ 9.30am-5.30pm Mon-Sat, 10am-4pm Sun, closed Sun Nov-Jan) Offers advice and information. Also runs an accommodation booking service and sells a wide range of local books and maps.

❶ Getting There & Away

Inter-city bus links through National Express (www.nationalexpress.com) are cheaper than the train – sample connections include those to London (£20, 2½ hours, hourly) and Bristol (£5, 45 minutes, two daily)

Train services are regular and reliable, although some intercity ones require a change at Bristol. Direct connections include those to London Paddington (from £35, 90 minutes, half-hourly), Cardiff Central (£21, one hour, hourly) and Bristol (£8, 15 minutes, half-hourly).

Oxford

☑ 01865 / POP 161,300
One of the world's most famous university cities, Oxford is both beautiful and privileged. It's a wonderful place to wander: the elegant honey-toned buildings of the university's 38 colleges wrap around tranquil courtyards and narrow cobbled lanes where a studious calm reigns. But along with the rich history, tradition and energetic academic life, there is a busy, lively town beyond the college walls.

◎ Sights

Not all of Oxford's colleges are open to the public, and visiting hours vary seasonally; check www.ox.ac.uk for details.

★ Bodleian Library   LIBRARY
(☑ 01865-287400; www.bodleian.ox.ac.uk/bodley; Catte St; Divinity School £2, with audio tour £4, guided tours £6-14; ⊘ 9am-5pm Mon-Sat, from 11am Sun) At least five kings, dozens of prime ministers and Nobel laureates, and luminaries such as Oscar Wilde, CS Lewis and JRR Tolkien have studied in Oxford's Bodleian Library, a magnificent survivor from the Middle Ages. Wander into its central 17th-century quad, and you can admire its ancient buildings for free, while it costs just £1 to enter the most impressive of these, the 15th-century Divinity School. To see the rest of the complex, though, you'll have to join a guided tour.

★ Christ Church   COLLEGE
(☑ 01865-276492; www.chch.ox.ac.uk; St Aldate's; adult/child Jul & Aug £10/9, Sep-Jun £8/7; ⊘ 10am-5pm Mon-Sat, from 2pm Sun, last admission 4.15pm) With its compelling combination of majestic architecture, literary heritage and double

identity as (parts of) Harry Potter's Hogwarts, Christ Church attracts tourists galore. Among Oxford's largest colleges – *the* largest, if you include its bucolic meadow – and proud possessor of its most impressive quad, plus a superb art gallery and even a cathedral, it was founded in 1525 by Cardinal Wolsey. It later became home to Lewis Carroll, whose picnic excursions with the then-dean's daughter gave us *Alice's Adventures in Wonderland*.

Ashmolean Museum
MUSEUM

(☑ 01865-278000; www.ashmolean.org; Beaumont St; ◷ 10am-5pm Tue-Sun, to 8pm last Fri of month) **FREE** Britain's oldest public museum, Oxford's wonderful Ashmolean Museum is surpassed only by the British Museum in London. It was established in 1683, when Elias Ashmole presented Oxford University with a collection of 'rarities' amassed by the well-travelled John Tradescant, gardener to Charles I. A new exhibition celebrates Ashmole's 400th birthday by displaying original treasures including the hat worn by the judge who presided over the trial of Charles I, and a mantle belonging to 'Chief Powhatan', the father of Pocahontas.

Magdalen College
COLLEGE

(☑ 01865-276000; www.magd.ox.ac.uk; High St; adult/child £6/5; ◷ 10am-7pm late Jun-late Sep, 1pm-dusk or 6pm late Sep-late Jun) Guarding access to a breathtaking expanse of private lawns, woodlands, river walks and even its own deer park, Magdalen ('mawd-lin'), founded in 1458, is one of Oxford's wealthiest and most beautiful colleges. Beyond its elegant Victorian

---

MESSING ABOUT ON THE RIVER

An unmissable Oxford experience, punting is all about sitting back and quaffing Pimms (the quintessential English summer drink) as you watch the city's glorious architecture float by. Which, of course, requires someone else to do the hard work – punting is far more difficult than it appears. If you decide to go it alone, a deposit is usually charged. Most punts hold five people including the punter. Hire them from **Magdalen Bridge Boathouse** (☑ 01865-202643; www.oxfordpunting.co.uk; High St; chauffeured 4-person punts per 30min £32, punt rental per hour £22; ◷ 9.30am-dusk Feb-Nov) or **Cherwell Boat House** (☑ 01865-515978; www.cherwellboathouse.co.uk; 50 Bardwell Rd; punt rental per hour Mon-Fri £17, Sat & Sun £19; ◷ 10am-dusk mid-Mar–mid-Oct).

---

gateway, you come to its medieval chapel and glorious 15th-century tower. From here, move on to the remarkable 15th-century **cloisters**, where the fantastic grotesques (carved figures) may have inspired CS Lewis' stone statues in *The Chronicles of Narnia*.

🛏 Sleeping

Oxford YHA
HOSTEL £

(☑ 01865-727275; www.yha.org.uk; 2a Botley Rd; dm/r £26/110; ☎) Set in a purpose-built modern building behind the station, Oxford's large YHA is a cut above other local hostels, with the feel of a chain hotel – and the prices too, for a private twin or double. The simple, comfortable four- and six-bed en suite dorms are better value. Abundant facilities include a restaurant, a library, a garden, a laundry, lounges and private lockers.

Tower House
GUESTHOUSE ££

(☑ 01865-246828; www.towerhouseoxford.co.uk; 15 Ship St; s/d £100/125, d without bathroom £110; ☎) In a peaceful central location, this listed 17th-century town house holds eight good-value double rooms, simple but tastefully decorated. Some share bathrooms (not always on the same floor), while larger en suites also have attractive tongue-and-groove panelling. Run in conjunction with the excellent Turl Street Kitchen (p195) next door – slightly higher room rates include breakfast there – it donates profits to a community charity.

Acorn Guest House
B&B ££

(☑ 01865-247998; www.oxford-acorn.co.uk; 260 Iffley Rd; s/d £50/75; ℗ ☎ 🐾) Spread through two adjoining houses, the friendly Acorn offers eight comfortable rooms at very reasonable prices, close to great pubs and restaurants and a short bus ride from the centre. Single rooms and 'budget' doubles share bathrooms; en suite facilities cost just £5 more. Everything has the feel of a family home, complete with resident labradoodle Annie (visiting dogs welcome).

Head of the River
HOTEL £££

(☑ 01865-721600; www.headoftheriveroxford.co.uk; Folly Bridge, St Aldates; r incl breakfast £189; ☎) A genuine jewel among Oxford hotels, this large and characterful place, at Folly Bridge immediately south of Christ Church, was originally a Thames-side warehouse. Each of its 20 good-sized rooms is individually decorated with contemporary flair, featuring exposed brickwork and/or tongue-and-groove panelling plus modern fittings, while rates include breakfast cooked to order in

DON'T MISS

BLENHEIM PALACE

One of the country's greatest stately homes, **Blenheim Palace** (📞01993-810530; www. blenheimpalace.com; Woodstock; adult/child £26/14.50, park & gardens only £16/7.40; ⊙ palace 10.30am-5.30pm, park & gardens 9am-6.30pm or dusk; 🅿) is a monumental baroque fantasy designed by Sir John Vanbrugh and Nicholas Hawksmoor between 1705 and 1722. Now a Unesco World Heritage Site, it's home to the 12th Duke of Marlborough. Highlights include the **Great Hall**, a vast space topped by 20m-high ceilings adorned with images of the first duke in battle; the various grand **state rooms** with their plush decor and priceless china cabinets; and the magnificent 55m **Long Library**. You can also visit the **Churchill Exhibition**, dedicated to the life, work and writings of Sir Winston, who was born at Blenheim in 1874. Blenheim Palace is near the town of Woodstock, a few miles northwest of Oxford. Take Stagecoach bus S3 (£3.20, 30 minutes) from Oxford, which stops outside Blenheim Palace.

the (excellent) **pub** (⊙ 8am-10.30pm Sun-Thu, to 11.30pm Fri & Sat) downstairs.

✖ Eating

★ Edamamé
JAPANESE £

(📞01865-246916; www.edamame.co.uk; 15 Holywell St; mains £7-10.50; ⊙ 11.30am-2.30pm Wed, 11.30am-2.30pm & 5-8.30pm Thu-Sat, noon-3.30pm Sun; 🍴) No wonder a constant stream of students squeeze in and out of this tiny diner – it's Oxford's top spot for delicious, gracefully simple Japanese cuisine. Changing noodle and curry specials include fragrant chicken miso ramen, tofu stir-fries, or mackerel with soba noodles; it only serves sushi or sashimi on Thursday evenings. No bookings; arrive early and be prepared to wait.

Covered Market
MARKET £

(www.oxford-coveredmarket.co.uk; Market St; ⊙ hours vary, some close Sun; 📶🍴) A haven for impecunious students, this indoor marketplace holds 20 restaurants, cafes and takeaways. Let anyone loose here, and something's sure to catch their fancy. Brown's no-frills cafe, famous for its apple pies, is the longest-standing veteran. Look out too for Georgina's, serving quiches and burgers upstairs; Burt's superlative cookies; two excellent pie shops; and good Thai and Chinese options.

★ Turl Street Kitchen
MODERN BRITISH ££

(📞01865-264171; www.turlstreetkitchen.co.uk; 16-17 Turl St; mains £10-16; ⊙ 8-10am, noon-2.30pm & 6.30-10pm; 🍴) 🌿 Whatever time you drop into this laid-back, not-quite-scruffy, seductively charming all-day bistro, with its fairy lights and faded-wood tables, you can expect to eat well. Fresh local produce is thrown into creative combinations, with the changing menu featuring the likes of roasted beetroot, braised lamb or, on Sunday, roast beef and Yorkshire pudding. It also serves good cakes and coffee.

Magdalen Arms
BRITISH ££

(📞01865-243159; www.magdalenarms.co.uk; 243 Iffley Rd; mains £14-42; ⊙ 5-11pm Mon, from 10am Tue-Sat, 10am-10.30pm Sun; 🍴🍴) A mile beyond Magdalen Bridge, this extra-special neighbourhood gastropub has won plaudits from the national press. A friendly, informal spot, it offers indoor and outdoor space for drinkers, and dining tables further back. From vegetarian specials such as broadbean tagliatelle to the fabulous sharing-size steak-and-ale pie – well, it's a stew with a suet-crust lid, really – everything is delicious, with gutsy flavours.

Oxford Kitchen
MODERN BRITISH £££

(📞01865-511149; www.theoxfordkitchen.co.uk; 215 Banbury Rd; set menus £22.50-65; ⊙ noon-2.30pm & 6-9.30pm Tue-Sat) Oxford's not renowned for high-end, cutting-edge cuisine, so if you're crying out for a few foams, mousses, funny-shaped plates and bumpy slates, make haste to Summertown's contemporary Oxford Kitchen.

We jest; its modern British food, served as set menus ranging from £22.50 for a weekday lunch up to the £65 weekend tasting menu, is superb.

🍸 Drinking & Nightlife

Turf Tavern
PUB

(📞01865-243235; www.turftavern-oxford.co.uk; 4-5 Bath Pl; ⊙ 11am-11pm; 📶) Squeezed down an alleyway and subdivided into endless nooks and crannies, this medieval rabbit warren dates from around 1381. The definitive Oxford pub, this is where Bill Clinton famously 'did not inhale'; other patrons have included Oscar Wilde, Stephen Hawking and Margaret Thatcher.

Home to a fabulous array of real ales and ciders, it's always pretty crowded, but there's outdoor seating too.

The Perch
PUB

(☑ 01865-728891; www.the-perch.co.uk; Binsey Lane, Binsey; ⏱ 10.30am-11pm Mon-Sat, to 10.30pm Sun; 🅿 🐕) This thatched and wonderfully rural 800-year-old inn can be reached by road, but it's more enjoyable to walk half an hour upstream along the Thames Path, then follow an enchanting footpath punctuated by floral pergolas. Its huge willow-draped garden is an idyllic spot for a pint or two of Fullers, but summer crowds can mean a long wait for food.

Lamb & Flag
PUB

(12 St Giles; ⏱ noon-11pm Mon-Sat, to 10.30pm Sun; 🛜) This relaxed 17th-century tavern remains one of Oxford's nicest pubs for a sturdy pint or glass of wine. Thomas Hardy wrote (and set) parts of *Jude the Obscure* at these very tables, while CS Lewis and JRR Tolkien shifted their custom here in later years. The food's nothing special, but buying a pint helps fund scholarships at St John's College.

❶ Information

Tourist Office (☑ 01865-686430; www.experienceoxfordshire.org; 15-16 Broad St; ⏱ 9am-5.30pm Mon-Sat, 10am-4pm Sun Jul & Aug, 9.30am-5pm Mon-Sat, 10am-4pm Sun Sep-Jun) Covers the whole of Oxfordshire and sells Oxford guidebooks, makes reservations for local accommodation and walking tours, and sells tickets for events and attractions.

❶ Getting There & Away

Oxford's chaotic outdoor **bus station** (Gloucester Green) is in the centre near the corner of Worcester and George Sts. Destinations:
Bath (£11.30, two hours)
Cambridge (X5; £13.50, 3¾ hours)
London Victoria (Oxford Tube/X90; £15, 1¾ hours)

Oxford's main train station is just west of the city centre, roughly 10 minutes' walk from Broad St. Destinations include the following:
London Marylebone (£7 to £29, 1¼ hours)
London Paddington (£9.50 to £26.50, 1¼ hours)

The Cotswolds

Undulating gracefully across six counties, the Cotswolds region is a delightful tangle of golden villages, thatched cottages, evocative churches and honey-coloured mansions. In 1966 it was designated an Area of Outstanding Natural Beauty, surpassed for size in England only by the Lake District.

Travel by public transport requires careful planning and patience; for the greatest flexibility, and the potential to get off the beaten track, having your own car is unbeatable. Alternatively, the **Cotswolds Discoverer One-Day Pass** (www.cotswoldsaonb.org.uk/visiting-and-exploring; adult/child £10/5) gives you unlimited travel on participating bus or train routes.

Stratford-upon-Avon

☑ 01789 / POP 27,455

The author of some of the most quoted lines ever written in the English language, William Shakespeare was born in Stratford in 1564 and died here in 1616. Experiences linked to his life in this unmistakably Tudor town range from the touristy (medieval recreations and Bard-themed tearooms) to the humbling (Shakespeare's modest grave in Holy Trinity Church) and the sublime (taking in a play by the world-famous Royal Shakespeare Company).

◉ Sights

★ Shakespeare's Birthplace
HISTORIC BUILDING

(☑ 01789-204016; www.shakespeare.org.uk; Henley St; adult/child £17.50/11.50; ⏱ 9am-5pm Apr-Aug, to 4.30pm Sep & Oct, 10am-3.30pm Nov-Mar) Start your Shakespeare quest at the house where the renowned playwright was born in 1564 and spent his childhood days. John Shakespeare owned the house for a period of 50 years. William, as the eldest surviving son, inherited it upon his father's death in 1601 and spent his first five years of marriage here. Behind a modern facade, the house has restored Tudor rooms, live presentations from famous Shakespearean characters and an engaging exhibition on Stratford's favourite son.

★ Shakespeare's New Place
HISTORIC SITE

(☑ 01789-338536; www.shakespeare.org.uk; cnr Chapel St & Chapel Lane; adult/child £12.50/8; ⏱ 10am-5pm Apr-Aug, to 4.30pm Sep & Oct, to 3.30pm Nov-Feb) When Shakespeare retired, he swapped the bright lights of London for a comfortable town house at New Place, where he died of unknown causes in April 1616. The house was demolished in 1759, but an attractive Elizabethan knot garden occupies part of the grounds. A major restoration project has uncovered Shakespeare's kitchen and incorporated new exhibits in a reimagining of the house as it would have been. You can also

WORTH A TRIP

GLASTONBURY

To many people, Glastonbury is synonymous with the **Glastonbury Festival of Contemporary Performing Arts** (www.glastonburyfestivals.co.uk; tickets from £238; ⊙ Jun or Jul), a majestic (and frequently mud-soaked) extravaganza of music, theatre, dance, cabaret, carnival, spirituality and general all-round weirdness that's been held on farmland in Pilton, just outside Glastonbury, since 1970 (bar the occasional off-year to let the farm recover).

The town owes much of its spiritual fame to nearby **Glastonbury Tor** (NT; ⊙ 24hr) **FREE**, a grassy hump about a mile from town, topped by the ruins of St Michael's Church. According to local legend, the tor is said to be the mythical Isle of Avalon, King Arthur's last resting place. It's also allegedly one of the world's great spiritual nodes, marking the meeting point of many mystical lines of power known as ley lines.

There is no train station in Glastonbury, but buses run from Wells (£3.70, 15 minutes, several times per hour) and Taunton (£5.70, 1½ hours, four to seven daily Monday to Saturday).

explore the adjacent Nash's House, where Shakespeare's granddaughter Elizabeth lived.

Shakespeare's School Room HISTORIC SITE
(☑ 01789-203170; www.shakespearesschoolroom.org; King Edward VI School, Church St; adult/child £8/5; ⊙ 11am-5pm) Shakespeare's alma mater, King Edward VI School (still a prestigious grammar school today), incorporates a vast black-and-white timbered building, dating from 1420, that was once the town's guildhall, where Shakespeare's father John served as bailiff (mayor). In the Bard's former classroom, you can sit in on mock-Tudor lessons, watch a short film and test yourself on Tudor-style homework.

It's adjacent to the 1269-built **Guild Chapel** (www.guildchapel.org.uk; cnr Chapel Lane & Church St; by donation; ⊙ 10am-4pm).

Anne Hathaway's Cottage HISTORIC BUILDING
(☑ 01789-338532; www.shakespeare.org.uk; Cottage Lane, Shottery; adult/child £12.50/8; ⊙ 9am-5pm Apr-Aug, to 4.30pm Sep & Oct, 10am-3.30pm Nov-Mar) Before tying the knot with Shakespeare, Anne Hathaway lived in Shottery, 1 mile west of the centre of Stratford, in this delightful thatched farmhouse. As well as period furniture, it has gorgeous gardens and an orchard and arboretum, with examples of all the trees mentioned in Shakespeare's plays. A footpath (no bikes allowed) leads to Shottery from Evesham Pl. The **City Sightseeing** (☑ 01789-299123; www.city-sightseeing.com; adult/child 24hr £16.82/8.41, 48hr £25.52/13; ⊙ 9.30am-5pm Apr-Sep, to 4pm Oct-Mar) bus stops here.

Holy Trinity Church CHURCH
(☑ 01789-266316; www.stratford-upon-avon.org; Old Town; Shakespeare's grave adult/child £3/2; ⊙ 9am-6pm Mon-Sat, 12.30-5pm Sun Apr-Sep, re-

duced hours rest of year) The final resting place of the Bard, where he was also baptised and where he worshipped, is said to be the most visited parish church in England. Inside are handsome 16th- and 17th-century tombs (particularly in the Clopton Chapel), some fabulous carvings on the choir stalls and, of course, the grave of William Shakespeare, with its ominous epitaph: 'cvrst be he yt moves my bones'.

🛏 Sleeping

Stratford-upon-Avon YHA HOSTEL £
(☑ 0345 371 9661; www.yha.org.uk; Wellesbourne Rd, Alveston; dm/d/glamping from £13/58/49; ℗ 🛜) Set in a large 200-year-old mansion 1.5 miles east of the town centre, this superior 134-bed hostel attracts travellers of all ages. Of its 32 rooms and dorms, 16 are en suite. There's a canteen, bar and kitchen. Buses 6 and X17 (£3.50, 12 minutes, up to two per hour) run here from Bridge St. Wi-fi is in common areas only. Tepee-style glamping tents and hutlike camping pods with kitchenettes are available from April to September.

Stag at Red Hill INN ££
(☑ 01789-764634; www.stagredhill.co.uk; Alcester Rd, Alcester; d/f incl breakfast from £99/109; ℗ 🛜) Stratford's formidable one-time courthouse and prison, dating back over 500 years, is now an idyllic country inn 4 miles west of the town centre. Its nine rooms (including a family room with a pull-out sofa) are individually decorated; deluxe rooms have chesterfield sofas. Standout pub fare includes Red Hill sausages with spring onion mash. Countryside views unfold from its beer garden.

Townhouse BOUTIQUE HOTEL £££
(☑ 01789-262222; www.stratfordtownhouse.co.uk; 16 Church St; d incl breakfast from £130; 🛜) Some

of the dozen rooms at this exquisite hotel have free-standing claw-foot bathtubs, and all have luxurious bedding and Temple Spa toiletries. The building is a centrally located 400-year-old gem with a first-rate **restaurant** (mains £9.50-24; ⊗ kitchen noon-3pm & 5-10pm Mon-Fri, noon-10pm Sat, to 8pm Sun, bar 8am-midnight Mon-Sat, to 10.30pm Sun; 🛜). Light sleepers should avoid room 1, nearest the bar. There's a minimum two-night stay on weekends.

🍴 Eating & Drinking

Sheep St is rammed with upmarket eating options, mostly aimed at theatre goers (look out for good-value pre-theatre menus). Picnickers will find some delightful spots in the surrounding countryside, including the grounds of Mary Arden's Farm.

Fourteas   CAFE £
(📞 01789-293908; www.thefourteas.co.uk; 24 Sheep St; dishes £4.60-7.55, afternoon tea with/without Prosecco £20/15; ⊗ 9.30am-5pm Mon-Sat, 11am-4.30pm Sun) Breaking with Stratford's Shakespearean theme, this tearoom takes the 1940s as its inspiration with beautiful old teapots, framed posters and staff in period costume. As well as premium loose-leaf teas and homemade cakes, there are all-day breakfasts, soups, sandwiches (including a

> ### ℹ️ SHAKESPEARE HISTORIC HOMES
>
> Five of the most important buildings associated with Shakespeare – Shakespeare's Birthplace (p196), Shakespeare's New Place (p196), **Hall's Croft** (📞 01789-338533; www.shakespeare.org.uk; Old Town; adult/child £8.50/5.50; ⊗ 10am-5pm Apr-Aug, to 4.30pm Sep & Oct, 11am-3.30pm Nov-Feb), Anne Hathaway's Cottage (p197) and **Mary Arden's Farm** (📞 01789-338535; www.shakespeare.org.uk; Station Rd, Wilmcote; adult/child £15/10; ⊗ 10am-5pm Apr-Aug, to 4.30pm Sep & Oct; 🐾) – contain museums that form the core of the visitor experience at Stratford. All are run by the Shakespeare Birthplace Trust (www.shakespeare.org.uk). A Full Story ticket (adult/child £22/14.50) covering all five properties is available online or at the sites and provides up to a 60% discount off individual admission prices.

chicken and bacon 'Churchill club') and lavish afternoon teas.

Edward Moon's   BRITISH ££
(📞 01789-267069; www.edwardmoon.com; 9 Chapel St; mains £12.25-17; ⊗ noon-2.30pm & 5-9.30pm Mon-Fri, noon-3pm & 5-10pm Sat, noon-3pm & 5-9pm Sun; 🐾) Named after a famous travelling chef who cooked up the flavours of home for the British colonial service, this snug independent restaurant serves hearty English dishes, such as steak-and-ale pie and meltingly tender lamb shank with redcurrant gravy. Kids get a two-course menu for £6.95.

⭐ Salt   BRITISH £££
(📞 01789-263566; www.salt-restaurant.co.uk; 8 Church St; 2-/3-course menus lunch £33.50/37, dinner £37/45; ⊗ noon-2pm & 6.30-10pm Wed-Sat, noon-2pm Sun) Stratford's gastronomic star is this intimate, beam-ceilinged bistro. In the semi-open kitchen, owner-chef Paul Foster produces stunning creations influenced by the seasons: spring might see glazed parsley root with chicory and black-truffle shavings, onglet of beef with malted artichoke, cured halibut with oyster and apple emulsion, and sea-buckthorn mille-feuille with fig and goat's-milk ice cream.

⭐ Old Thatch Tavern   PUB
(www.oldthatchtavernstratford.co.uk; Greenhill St; ⊗ 11.30am-11pm Mon-Sat, from noon Sun; 🛜) To truly appreciate Stratford's olde-worlde atmosphere, join the locals for a pint at the town's oldest pub. Built in 1470, this thatch-roofed treasure has great real ales and a gorgeous summertime courtyard.

☆ Entertainment

⭐ Royal Shakespeare Company   THEATRE
(RSC; 📞 box office 01789-403493; www.rsc.org.uk; Waterside; tours adult £7-9, child £4.50-5, tower adult/child £2.50/1.25; ⊗ tour times vary, tower 10am-5pm Sun-Fri, 10am-12.15pm & 2-5pm Sat mid-Mar–mid-Oct, 10am-4.30pm Sun-Fri, to 12.15pm Sat mid-Oct–mid-Mar) Stratford has two grand stages run by the world-renowned Royal Shakespeare Company – the **Royal Shakespeare Theatre** and the **Swan Theatre** on Waterside – as well as the smaller **Other Place** (22 Southern Lane). The theatres have witnessed performances by such legends as Lawrence Olivier, Richard Burton, Judi Dench, Helen Mirren, Ian McKellan and Patrick Stewart. Various one-hour guided tours take you behind the scenes.

WARWICK

Regularly namechecked by Shakespeare, the town of Warwick is a treasure-house of medieval architecture. It is dominated by the soaring turrets of **Warwick Castle** (☑01926-495421; www.warwick-castle.com; Castle Lane; castle adult/child £27/24, castle & dungeon £32/28; ☺10am-5pm Apr-Sep, to 4pm Oct-Mar; P), founded in 1068 by William the Conqueror, and later the ancestral home of the Earls of Warwick. It's now been transformed into a major tourist attraction by the owners of Madame Tussauds, with family-friendly activities and waxworks populating the private apartments.

Stagecoach bus 18A goes to Stratford-upon-Avon (£4.30, 45 minutes, half-hourly). Trains run to Birmingham (£6.80, 40 minutes, half-hourly), Stratford-upon-Avon (£6.60, 30 minutes, hourly) and London Marylebone (£31.80, 1½ hours, every 20 minutes). Stagecoach bus X18 runs to Stratford-upon-Avon (£5.40, 40 minutes, two per hour Monday to Saturday, hourly Sunday).

Trains run to Stratford-upon-Avon (£6.90, 30 minutes, every two hours) and London Marylebone (£34, 1½ hours, every 30 minutes; some require a change in Leamington Spa).

ℹ Information

The **tourist office** (☑01789-264293; www.shakespeares-england.co.uk; Bridge Foot; ☺9am-5.30pm Mon-Sat, 10am-4pm Sun) is just west of Clopton Bridge.

ℹ Getting There & Away

BUS

National Express coaches and other bus companies run from Stratford's Riverside bus station (behind the Stratford Leisure Centre on Bridgeway). National Express services include the following:

London Victoria (£13.10, three hours, two direct services per day)

Oxford (£10.10, 1¼ hours, one per day)

TRAIN

From Stratford-upon-Avon train station, London Midland runs to Birmingham (£8, 50 minutes, two per hour), Chiltern Railways serves London Marylebone (£30.40, 2¾ hours, up to two per hour) with a change in Leamington Spa, and East Midlands runs to Warwick (£6.90, 30 minutes, every two hours).

Cambridge

☑01223 / POP 123,900

Abounding with exquisite architecture, oozing history and tradition, and renowned for its quirky rituals, Cambridge is a university town extraordinaire. The tightly packed core of ancient colleges, the picturesque 'Backs' (college gardens) leading on to the river and the leafy green meadows that surround the city give it a far more tranquil appeal than its historic rival Oxford.

☉ Sights

Cambridge University comprises 31 colleges, though not all are open to the public. Opening hours are only a rough guide, so contact the colleges or the tourist office (p201) for more information.

★ **King's College Chapel** CHURCH
(☑01223-331212; www.kings.cam.ac.uk; King's Pde; adult/child £9/6; ☺9.30am-3.15pm Mon-Sat, 1.15-2.30pm Sun term time, 9.30am-4.30pm daily university holidays) In a city crammed with showstopping buildings, this is a scene-stealer. Grandiose 16th-century King's College Chapel is one of England's most extraordinary examples of Gothic architecture. Its inspirational, intricate 80m-long fan-vaulted ceiling is the world's largest and soars upwards before exploding into a series of stone fireworks. This hugely atmospheric space is a fitting stage for the chapel's world-famous choir; hear it sing during the free and magnificent **evensong** in term time (5.30pm Monday to Saturday; 10.30am and 3.30pm Sunday).

★ **Trinity College** COLLEGE
(☑01223-338400; www.trin.cam.ac.uk; Trinity St; adult/child £3/1; ☺10am-4.30pm Jul-Oct, to 3.30pm Nov-Jun) The largest of Cambridge's colleges, Trinity offers an extraordinary Tudor gateway, an air of supreme elegance and a sweeping Great Court – the largest of its kind in the world. It also boasts the renowned and suitably musty **Wren Library** (☺noon-2pm Mon-Fri year-round, plus 10.30am-12.30pm Sat term time) FREE, containing 55,000 books published before 1820 and more than 2500 manuscripts. Works include those by Shakespeare, St

PUNTING ON THE BACKS

Gliding a self-propelled punt along the Backs is a blissful experience – once you've got the hang of it. It can also be a manic challenge for beginners. If you wimp out, you can always opt for a relaxing chauffeured punt.

Punt hire costs around £24 to £30 per hour; 45-minute chauffeured trips of the Backs cost about £14 to £20 per person. One-way trips to Grantchester (1½ hours) start at around £28 per person.

Jerome, Newton and Swift – and AA Milne's original *Winnie the Pooh;* both Milne and his son, Christopher Robin, were graduates.

Fitzwilliam Museum   MUSEUM
(www.fitzmuseum.cam.ac.uk; Trumpington St; by donation; ⏱ 10am-5pm Tue-Sat, from noon Sun) FREE
Fondly dubbed 'the Fitz' by locals, this colossal neoclassical pile was one of the first public art museums in Britain, built to house the fabulous treasures that the seventh Viscount Fitzwilliam bequeathed to his old university. Expect Roman and Egyptian grave goods, artworks by many of the great masters and some quirkier collections: banknotes, literary autographs, watches and armour.

The Backs   PARK
Behind the Cambridge colleges' grandiose facades and stately courts, a series of gardens and parks line up beside the river. Collectively known as the Backs, the tranquil green spaces and shimmering waters offer unparalleled views of the colleges and are often the most enduring image of Cambridge for visitors. The picture-postcard snapshots of student life and graceful bridges can be seen from the riverside pathways and pedestrian bridges – or from the comfort of a chauffeured punt.

🛏 Sleeping

Cambridge YHA   HOSTEL £
(☎ 0345-371 9728; www.yha.org.uk; 97 Tenison Rd; dm/d £25/60; @ 🛜) A smart, friendly and deservedly popular hostel with compact dorms and good facilities. Handily, it's very near the train station. The choice of rooms for families is particularly good.

★ Varsity   BOUTIQUE HOTEL £££
(☎ 01223-306030; www.thevarsityhotel.co.uk; Thompson's Lane; d £195-360; ❄ @ 🛜) In the 44 individually styled rooms of riverside Varsity, wondrous fixtures and furnishings (such as roll-top baths and travellers' trunks) sit beside floor-to-ceiling glass windows, espresso machines and smartphone docks. The views out over the colleges from the roof terrace are utterly sublime. Valet parking costs £20 a night.

🍴 Eating & Drinking

Pint Shop   MODERN BRITISH ££
(☎ 01223-352293; www.pintshop.co.uk; 10 Peas Hill; snacks from £5, mains £12-22; ⏱ noon-10pm Mon-Fri, 11am-10.30pm Sat, 11am-10pm Sun) Popular Pint Shop's vision is to embrace eating and drinking equally. To this end, it's both a busy bar specialising in draught craft beer and a stylish dining room serving classy versions of traditional grub (dry-aged steaks, gin-cured sea trout, coal-baked fish and meat kebabs). All in all, hard to resist.

Kingston Arms   PUB FOOD ££
(☎ 01223-319414; www.facebook.com/pg/Kingston Arms; 33 Kingston St; from £8; ⏱ 5-11pm Mon-Thu, noon-midnight Fri & Sat, to 11pm Sun; 🛜) A hike from the centre, but worth the trek for its real ales, relaxed crowd of locals and students, and gastropub grub – from roasts to homemade risotto and gourmet sausages. There's also an outdoor courtyard. It's 1 mile southeast of the centre, off Mill Rd.

★ Midsummer House   MODERN BRITISH £££
(☎ 01223-369299; www.midsummerhouse.co.uk; Midsummer Common; 5/8 courses £69/145; ⏱ noon-1.30pm Wed-Sat, 7-9pm Tue-Sat; 🍴) At the region's top table, chef Daniel Clifford's double-Michelin-starred creations are distinguished by depth of flavour and immense technical skill. Savour transformations of pumpkin (into velouté), mackerel (with Jack Daniels), quail, sea scallops and grouse, before a coriander white-chocolate dome, served with coconut, mango and jasmine rice.

Eagle   PUB
(☎ 01223-505020; www.eagle-cambridge.co.uk; Bene't St; ⏱ 11am-11pm Sun-Thu, to midnight Fri & Sat; 🛜 ♿) Cambridge's most famous pub has loosened the tongues and pickled the

grey cells of many an illustrious academic, among them Nobel Prize–winning scientists Crick and Watson, who discussed their research into DNA here (note the blue plaque by the door). Fifteenth-century, wood-panelled and rambling, the Eagle's cosy rooms include one with WWII airmen's signatures on the ceiling. The food (mains £10 to 15), served all day, is good too; it includes some thoughtful options for children.

❶ Information

As well as running escorted tours, the **tourist office** (📞 01223-791500; www.visitcambridge. org; The Guildhall, Peas Hill; ⏱ 9.30am-5pm Mon-Sat Nov-Mar, plus 11am-3pm Sun Apr-Oct) has information about self-guided walks.

❶ Getting There & Away

Buses run by **National Express** (📞 0871 781 8181; www.nationalexpress.com; Parkside; 📶) leave from Parkside. Direct services include the following:

Heathrow (£31, 2¾ hours, hourly)

London Victoria (£11, 2½ hours, every two hours)

Oxford (£14, 3½ hours, hourly)

The train station is 1.5 miles southeast of the centre. Direct services include the following:

London King's Cross (£25, one hour, two to four per hour)

Stansted Airport (£11, 35 minutes, every 30 minutes)

York

📞 01904 / POP 152,841

No other city in northern England says 'medieval' quite like York, a city of extraordinary cultural and historical wealth that has lost little of its pre-industrial lustre. A magnificent circuit of 13th-century walls encloses a medieval spider's web of narrow streets. At its heart lies the immense, awe-inspiring York Minster; York's long history and rich heritage is woven into virtually every brick and beam.

❍ Sights

Don't miss the chance to walk York's **City Walls** (www.yorkwalls.org.uk), which follow the line of the original Roman walls and give a whole new perspective on the city. Allow 1½ to two hours for the full circuit of 4.5 miles or, if you're pushed for time, the short

stretch from Bootham Bar to Monk Bar is worth doing for the views of the minster.

★ York Minster   CATHEDRAL

(📞 01904-557200; www.yorkminster.org; Deangate; adult/child £10/free, incl tower £15/5; ⏱ 9am-6pm Mon-Sat, 12.30-6pm Sun, last admission 4.30pm Mon-Sat, 3pm Sun) York Minster is the largest medieval cathedral in northern Europe, and one of the world's most beautiful Gothic buildings. Seat of the archbishop of York, primate of England, it is second in importance only to Canterbury, seat of the primate of *all* England – the separate titles were created to settle a debate over the true centre of the English Church. Note that the quire, east end and undercroft close in preparation for evening service around the time of last admission.

★ Jorvik Viking Centre   MUSEUM

(📞 ticket reservations 01904-615505; www.jorvik -viking-centre.co.uk; Coppergate; adult/child £11/8; ⏱ 10am-5pm Apr-Oct, to 4pm Nov-Mar) Interactive multimedia exhibits aimed at bringing history to life often achieve exactly the opposite, but the much-hyped Jorvik manages to pull it off with aplomb. It's a smells-and-all reconstruction of the Viking settlement unearthed here during excavations in the late 1970s, experienced via a 'time-car' monorail that transports you through 9th-century Jorvik (the Viking name for York). You can reduce time waiting in line by booking timed-entry tickets online; there is almost always a queue to get in.

★ National Railway Museum   MUSEUM

(www.nrm.org.uk; Leeman Rd; ⏱ 10am-6pm Apr-Oct, to 5pm Nov-Mar; 🅿🚻) **FREE** York's National Railway Museum – the biggest in the world, with more than 100 locomotives – is well presented and crammed with fascinating stuff. It is laid out on a vast scale and is housed in a series of giant railway sheds – allow at least two hours to do it justice. The museum also now includes a high-tech simulator experience of riding on the **Mallard** (£4), which set the world speed record for a steam locomotive in 1938 (126mph).

The Shambles   STREET

The Shambles takes its name from the Saxon word *shamel,* meaning 'slaughterhouse' – in 1862 there were 26 butcher shops on this street. Today the butchers are long gone, but this narrow cobbled lane, lined with

15th-century Tudor buildings that overhang so much they seem to meet above your head, is the most picturesque in Britain, and one of the most visited in Europe, often filled with visitors wielding cameras.

Yorkshire Museum　　　　　　MUSEUM
(www.yorkshiremuseum.org.uk; Museum St; adult/child £7.50/free; ☉10am-5pm) Most of York's Roman archaeology is hidden beneath the medieval city, so the superb displays in the Yorkshire Museum are invaluable if you want to get an idea of what Eboracum Roman York was like. There are maps and models, funerary monuments, mosaic floors and wall paintings, and a 4th-century bust of Emperor Constantine. Kids will enjoy the dinosaur exhibit, centred on giant ichthyosaur fossils from Yorkshire's Jurassic coast.

There are excellent galleries dedicated to Viking and medieval York as well, including priceless artefacts such as the beautifully decorated 9th-century York helmet.

☞ Tours

★ Brewtown　　　　　　　BEER TOUR
(☑01904-636666; www.brewtowntours.co.uk; £60; ☉11.30am-5pm) These craft-brewery minivan tours are a fuss-free way to get behind the scenes at Yorkshire's smaller breweries, some of which only open to the public for these tours. Owner Mark runs different routes (around York, Malton or Leeds) depending on the day of the week; each tour visits three breweries with tastings along the way, and sometimes even beer-pairing nibbles.

Ghost Hunt of York　　　　　WALKING
(☑01904-608700; www.ghosthunt.co.uk; adult/child £6/4; ☉tours 7.30pm) The kids will just love this award-winning and highly entertaining 75-minute tour laced with authentic ghost stories. It begins at the top end of the Shambles, whatever the weather (it's never cancelled), and there's no need to book – just turn up and wait till you hear the handbell ringing...

🛏 Sleeping

Beds can be hard to find in midsummer, even with high-season rates. The tourist office offers an accommodation booking service, which costs £4.

Safestay York　　　　　　HOSTEL £
(☑01904-627720; www.safestay.com; 88-90 Micklegate; dm/tw/f from £15/60/75; @🛜) Housed in a Grade I Georgian townhouse, this is a large boutique hostel with colourful decor and good facilities including a bar with pool table. Rooms are mostly en suite and have a bit more character than you'd usually find in hostels, with the added intrigue of plaques outside doors describing the history of different rooms in the house.

Fort　　　　　　　　　　HOSTEL £
(☑01904-620222; www.thefortyork.co.uk; 1 Little Stonegate; dm/d from £22/85; 🛜) This boutique hostel showcases the interior design of young British talents, creating affordable accommodation with a dash of character and flair. There are six- and eight-bed dorms, along with five doubles, but don't expect a peaceful retreat – it's central and there's a lively club downstairs (earplugs are provided!). Towels are included, as well as free tea, coffee and laundry.

★ The Lawrance　　　　APARTMENT ££
(☑01904-239988; www.thelawrance.com/york/; 74 Micklegate; 1-/2-bed apt from £75/160; ✳🛜) Set back from the road in a huddle of old red-brick buildings that once formed a factory, the Lawrance is an excellent find: super-swish serviced apartments with all mod cons on the inside and heritage character on the outside. Some apartments are split-level and all are comfy and spacious, with leather sofas, flatscreen TVs and luxurious fixtures and fittings.

Dairy Guesthouse　　　　　B&B ££
(☑01904-639367; www.dairyguesthouse.co.uk; 3 Scarcroft Rd; s/d/f from £130/160/200; P🛜) This Victorian home offers tasteful rooms that mesh fresh decor and five-star bathrooms with original features like cast-iron fireplaces. The flower- and plant-filled courtyard is a lovely place to pause for a rest after a day of sightseeing. It leads to a pair of private cottage-style rooms. Two-night minimum stay required.

St Raphael　　　　　　　B&B ££
(☑01904-645028; www.straphaelguesthouse.co.uk; 44 Queen Anne's Rd; d/tr/q £99/139/169; P🛜) Set in a historic house with that distinctively English half-timbered look, this B&B has a great central location, seven

bright, airy and simple bedrooms, and the smell of home-baked bread wafting up from the breakfast room.

★ Grays Court
HISTORIC HOTEL £££

(☑ 01904-612613; www.grayscourtyork.com; Chapter House St; d £190-235, ste £270-290; P 🛜) This medieval mansion with just 11 rooms feels like a country-house hotel. It's set in lovely gardens with direct access to the city walls, and bedrooms combine antique furniture with modern comfort and design. The oldest part of the building was built in the 11th century, and King James I once dined in the Long Gallery.

✗ Eating & Drinking

★ Mannion & Co
CAFE, BISTRO £

(☑ 01904-631030; www.mannionandco.co.uk; 1 Blake St; mains £7-12; ⊙ 9am-5pm Mon-Sat, 10am-4.30pm Sun) Expect to queue for a table at this busy bistro (no reservations), with its convivial atmosphere and selection of delicious daily specials. Regulars on the menu include eggs Benedict for breakfast, a chunky Yorkshire rarebit (cheese on toast) made with home-baked bread, and lunch platters of cheese and charcuterie. Oh, and pavlova for pudding.

Hairy Fig
CAFE £

(☑ 01904-677074; www.thehairyfig.co.uk; 39 Fossgate; mains £5-12; ⊙ 9am-4.30pm Mon-Sat) This cafe-deli is a standout in York. On the one side you've got the best of Yorkshire tripping over the best of Europe, with Italian white anchovies and truffle-infused olive oil stacked alongside York honey mead and baked pies; on the other you've got a Dickensian-style sweet shop and backroom cafe serving dishes crafted from the deli.

No 8 Bistro
BISTRO ££

(☑ 01904-653074; www.no8york.co.uk/bistro; 8 Gillygate; dinner mains £17-19; ⊙ noon-10pm Mon-Fri, 9am-10pm Sat & Sun; 🛜🍴) 🍴 A cool little place with modern artwork mimicking the Edwardian stained glass at the front, No 8 offers a day-long menu of top-notch bistro dishes using fresh local produce, such as Jerusalem artichoke risotto with fresh herbs, and Yorkshire lamb slow-cooked in hay and lavender. It also does breakfast (mains £6 to £9) and Sunday lunch. Booking recommended.

★ Cochon Aveugle
FRENCH £££

(☑ 01904-640222; www.lecochonaveugle.uk; 37 Walmgate; 4-course lunch £40, 8-course tasting menu £60; ⊙ 6-9pm Wed-Sat, noon-1.30pm Sat) 🍴 Black-pudding macaroon? Strawberry and elderflower sandwich? Blowtorched mackerel with melon gazpacho? Fussy eaters beware – this small restaurant with huge ambition serves an ever-changing tasting menu (no à la carte) of infinite imagination and invention. You never know what will come next, except that it will be delicious. Bookings are essential.

★ Blue Bell
PUB

(☑ 01904-654904; 53 Fossgate; ⊙ 11am-11pm Mon-Thu, to midnight Fri & Sat, noon-10.30pm Sun; 🛜) This is what a proper English pub looks like – a tiny, 200-year-old wood-panelled room with a smouldering fireplace, decor untouched since 1903, a pile of ancient board games in the corner, friendly and efficient bar staff, and weekly cask-ale specials chalked on a board. Bliss, with froth on top – if you can get in (it's often full). Cash only.

🛈 Information

York Tourist Office (☑ 01904-550099; www.visityork.org; 1 Museum St; ⊙ 9am-5pm Mon-Sat, 10am-4pm Sun) Visitor and transport info for all of Yorkshire, plus accommodation bookings (for a small fee) and ticket sales.

🛈 Getting There & Away

York does not have a bus station; intercity buses stop outside the train station, while local and regional buses stop here and also on Rougier St, about 200m northeast of the train station. Services include the following:

Edinburgh (£40, 5½ hours, two daily)

London from (£36, 5½ hours, three daily)

York is a major train hub, with frequent direct services to many British cities, including **Edinburgh** (£70, 2½ hours, two to three per hour) and **London King's Cross** (£80, two hours, every 30 minutes)

Castle Howard

Stately homes may be two a penny in England, but you'll have to try pretty damn hard to find one as breathtakingly stately as **Castle Howard** (☑ 01653-648333; www.castlehoward.co.uk; adult/child house & grounds £18.95/9.95, grounds only £11.95/7.95; ⊗ house 10am-4pm, grounds 10am-5pm, last admission 4pm; P)), a work of theatrical grandeur and audacity set in the rolling Howardian Hills. This is one of the world's most beautiful buildings, instantly recognisable from its starring role in the 1980s TV series *Brideshead Revisited* and in the 2008 film of the same name (both based on Evelyn Waugh's 1945 novel of nostalgia for the English age of aristocracy).

Castle Howard is 15 miles northeast of York, off the A64. Bus 181 from York goes to Malton via Castle Howard (£10 return, one hour, four times daily Monday to Saturday year-round).

Chester

☑ 01244 / POP 118,200

With a red-sandstone Roman wall wrapped around a tidy collection of Tudor and Victorian buildings, Chester is one of English history's greatest gifts to the contemporary visitor. The walls were built when this was Castra Devana, the largest Roman fortress in Britain.

◉ Sights

★ City Walls
LANDMARK

A good way to get a sense of Chester's unique character is to walk the 2-mile circuit along the walls that surround the historic centre. Originally built by the Romans around 70 CE, the walls were altered substantially over the following centuries, but have retained their current position since around 1200. The tourist office's *Walk Around Chester Walls* leaflet is an excellent guide and you can also take a 90-minute guided walk.

★ Rows
ARCHITECTURE

Besides the City Walls, Chester's other great draw is the Rows, a series of two-level galleried arcades along the four streets that fan out in each direction from the **Central Cross**. The architecture is a handsome mix of Victorian and Tudor (original and mock) buildings that house a fantastic collection of independently owned shops.

Chester Cathedral
CATHEDRAL

(☑ 01244-324756; www.chestercathedral.com; 12 Abbey Sq; ⊗ 9am-6pm Mon-Sat, 1-4pm Sun) FREE Chester Cathedral was originally a Benedictine abbey built on the remains of an earlier Saxon church dedicated to St Werburgh (the city's patron saint); it was shut down in 1540 as part of Henry VIII's Dissolution frenzy, but reconsecrated as a cathedral the following year. Despite a substantial Victorian facelift, the cathedral retains much of its original 12th-century structure. You can amble about freely, but the **tours** (adult/child full tour £8/6, short tour £6; ⊗ full tour 11am & 3pm daily, short tour 12.30pm & 1.15pm Mon-Tue, also 2pm & 4pm Wed-Sat) are excellent, as they take you up to the top of the panoramic bell tower.

🛏 Sleeping & Eating

★ Edgar House
BOUTIQUE HOTEL ££

(☑ 01244-347007; www.edgarhouse.co.uk; 22 City Walls; ⊗ r from £105) These award-winning digs are the ultimate in boutique luxury. This Georgian house has seven rooms, each decorated in its own individual style – some have free-standing claw-foot tubs and French doors that lead onto an elegant terrace. There's beautiful art on the walls and fabulous touches of the owners' gorgeous aesthetic throughout. The superb **Twenty2** (www.restauranttwenty2.co.uk; tasting menu £59; ⊗ 6-9pm Wed-Sat, afternoon tea noon-4pm Fri-Sun) restaurant is open to nonguests.

Joseph Benjamin
MODERN BRITISH ££

(☑ 01244-344295; www.josephbenjamin.co.uk; 134-140 Northgate St; mains £11-18; ⊗ noon-3pm Tue-Sat, also 6-9.30pm Thu-Sat & noon-4pm Sun) A bright star in Chester's culinary firmament is this combo restaurant, bar and deli that delivers carefully prepared local produce to take away or eat in. Excellent sandwiches and gorgeous salads are the mainstay of the takeaway menu, while the more formal dinner menu features fine examples of Modern British cuisine.

★ Simon Radley at the Grosvenor
MODERN BRITISH £££

(☑ 01244-324024; www.chestergrosvenor.com; 58 Eastgate St, Chester Grosvenor Hotel; tasting menu/à la carte menu £99/75; ⊗ 6.30-9pm Tue-Sat) Simon Radley's formal restaurant (you're instructed to arrive 30 minutes early for drinks and canapés) has served near-perfect Modern British cuisine since 1990, when it was first awarded the Michelin star that it has kept ever since. The food is divine and the wine list extensive. It's one of Britain's best, but why no second star? Note that attire must be smart and no children under 12 are permitted.

Information

Tourist Office (☎01244-402111; www.visitchester.com; Town Hall, Northgate St; ⊙9am-5.30pm Mon-Sat, 10am-5pm Sun Mar-Oct, 9am-5pm Mon-Sat, 10am-4pm Sun Nov-Feb)

Getting There & Away

National Express (☎08717 81 81 81; www.nationalexpress.com) coaches stop on Vicar's Lane, just opposite the tourist office by the Roman amphitheatre. Destinations include London (£33, 5½ hours, three daily).

The train station is about a mile from the city centre. Destinations include London Euston (£85.90, 2½ hours, hourly).

Lake District National Park

A dramatic landscape of ridges, lakes and peaks, including England's highest mountain, Scafell Pike (978m), the Lake District is one of Britain's most scenic corners. Among the many writers who found inspiration here were William Wordsworth, Samuel Taylor Coleridge, Arthur Ransome and Beatrix Potter. Often called simply the Lakes, the national park and surrounding area attract around 15 million visitors annually. But if you avoid summer weekends it's easy enough to miss the crush, especially if you do a bit of hiking. There's a host of B&Bs and country-house hotels in the Lakes, plus more than 20 YHA hostels, many of which can be linked by foot if you wish to hike.

Information

The national park's main visitor centre is at **Brockhole** (☎015394-46601; www.brockhole.co.uk; ⊙10am-5pm), just outside Windermere, and there are tourist offices in Windermere, Bowness, Ambleside, Keswick, Coniston and Carlisle.

Getting There & Around

To get to the Lake District via the main West Coast train line, you need to change at Oxenholme for Kendal and Windermere.

There's one daily National Express coach from London to Windermere (£46, eight hours) via Lancaster and Kendal.

Bus 555/556 Lakeslink (£4.70 to £9.80) runs at least hourly every day from Windermere train station to Brockhole Visitor Centre (seven minutes), Ambleside (£4.70, 15 minutes), Grasmere (£7.20, 30 minutes) and Keswick (£9.80, one hour).

> **DON'T MISS**
>
> **HILL TOP**
>
> The cute-as-a-button farmhouse of **Hill Top** (NT; ☎015394-36269; www.nationaltrust.org.uk/hill-top; adult/child £10.90/5.45, admission to garden & shop free; ⊙10am-5.30pm Jun-Aug, to 4.30pm Sat-Thu Apr, May, Sep & Oct, weekends only Nov-Mar) is a must for Beatrix Potter fans: it was her first house in the Lake District, and is also where she wrote and illustrated several of her famous tales.
>
> The cottage is in Near Sawrey, 2 miles from Hawkshead. The **Cross Lakes Experience** (☎015394-43360; www.mountain-goat.co.uk/Cross-Lakes-Experience; adult/child return Bowness to Hawkshead £12.75/7.10; ⊙Apr-Oct) provides boat and minibus transport from Bowness, 1.5 miles southwest of Windermere.

Windermere

POP 5423

Stretching for 10.5 miles between Ambleside and Newby Bridge, Windermere isn't just the queen of Lake District lakes – it's also the largest body of water anywhere in England, closer in stature to a Scottish loch. It's been a centre for tourism since the first trains chugged into town in 1847 and it's still one of the national park's busiest spots.

★Windermere & the Islands LAKE

Windermere gets its name from the old Norse, *Vinandr mere* (Vinandr's lake; so 'Lake Windermere' is actually tautologous). Encompassing 5.7 sq miles between Ambleside and Newby Bridge, the lake is a mile wide at its broadest point, with a maximum depth of about 220m. It's a nice place to hire a boat for the afternoon, but it is far and away the busiest of the lakes. **Windermere Lake Cruises** (☎015394-43360; www.windermere-lakecruises.co.uk; tickets from £2.70) offers sightseeing cruises, departing from Bowness Pier.

★Rum Doodle B&B ££

(☎015394-45967; www.rumdoodlewindermere.com; Sunny Bank Rd, Windermere Town; d £95-139; P 📶) Named after a classic travel novel

OTHER BRITISH PLACES WORTH A VISIT

Some other places in Britain we recommend for day trips or longer visits:

Cornwall The southwestern tip of Britain is ringed with rugged granite seacliffs, sparkling bays, picturesque fishing villages and white sandy beaches.

Liverpool The city's waterfront is a World Heritage Site crammed with top museums, including the International Slavery Museum and the Beatles Story.

Hadrian's Wall One of the country's most dramatic Roman ruins, this 2000-year-old procession of abandoned forts and towers marches across the lonely landscape of northern England.

Glen Coe Scotland's most famous glen combines those two essential qualities of Highlands landscape: dramatic scenery and deep history.

Pembrokeshire Wales' western extremity is famous for its beaches and coastal walks, as well as being home to one of Britain's finest Norman castles.

---

about a fictional mountain in the Himalayas, this B&B zings with imagination. Its rooms are themed after places and characters in the book, with details such as book-effect wallpaper, vintage maps and old suitcases. Top of the heap is the Summit, snug under the eaves with a separate sitting room. Two-night minimum in summer.

The Hideaway B&B ££
(☑ 015394-43070; www.thehideawayatwindermere. co.uk; Phoenix Way; d £90-170; P🗑) There's a fine range of rooms available at this much-recommended B&B in a former schoolmaster's house. There's a choice for all budgets, from Standard Comfy (simple decor, not much space) all the way to Ultimate Comfy (claw-foot tub, split-level mezzanine, space galore). Regardless which you choose, you'll be treated to spoils such as homemade cakes and afternoon tea every day.

★ **Mason's Arms** PUB FOOD ££
(☑ 015395-68486; www.masonsarmsstrawberry bank.co.uk; Winster; mains £12.95-18.95) Three miles east of Crosthwaite, near Bowlands Bridge, the marvellous Mason's Arms is a local secret. The rafters, flagstones and cast-iron range haven't changed in centuries, and the patio has to-die-for views across fields and fells. The food is hearty – Cumbrian stewpot, slow-roasted Cartmel lamb – and there are lovely rooms and cottages for rent (£175 to £350). In short, a cracker.

Grasmere

POP 1458

Grasmere is a gorgeous little Lakeland village, all the more famous because of its links with Britain's leading Romantic poet, William Wordsworth.

★ **Dove Cottage & The Wordsworth Museum** HISTORIC BUILDING
(☑ 015394-35544; www.wordsworth.org.uk; adult/child £8.95/free; ⊙ 9.30am-5.30pm Mar-Oct, 10am-4.30pm Nov, Dec & Feb) On the edge of Grasmere, this tiny, creeper-clad cottage (formerly a pub called the Dove & Olive Bough) was famously inhabited by William Wordsworth between 1799 and 1808. The cottage's cramped rooms are full of artefacts – try to spot the poet's passport, a pair of his spectacles and a portrait (given to him by Sir Walter Scott) of his favourite dog, Pepper. Entry is by timed ticket to avoid overcrowding and includes an informative guided tour.

The Wordsworth family graves are tucked into a quiet corner of the churchyard at nearby **St Oswald's Church.**

★ **Forest Side** BOUTIQUE HOTEL £££
(☑ 015394-35250; www.theforestside.com; Keswick Rd; r incl full board £230-400; P🗑) For out-and-out-luxury, plump for this boutique beauty. Run by renowned hotelier Andrew Wildsmith, it's a design palace: chic interiors decorated with crushed-velvet sofas, bird-of-paradise wallpaper, stag heads and 20 swish rooms from 'Cosy' to 'Jolly Good', 'Superb', 'Grand' and 'Master'. Chef Kevin Tickle previously worked at **L'Enclume** (☑ 015395-36362; www.lenclume.co.uk; Cavendish St; set lunch £59, lunch & dinner menu £155; ⊙ noon-1.30pm & 6.30-8.30pm Tue-Sun), and now runs the stellar restaurant here using produce from its kitchen garden.

Keswick

POP 4821

The main town of the north Lakes, Keswick sits beside lovely Derwent Water, a silvery curve studded by wooded islands and criss-crossed by puttering cruise boats, operated by the **Keswick Launch** (☑017687-72263; www.keswick-launch.co.uk; round-the-lake pass adult/child/family £10.75/5.65/25.50).

Keswick YHA HOSTEL £
(☑0845 371 9746; www.yha.org.uk; Station Rd; dm £15-35; ☺reception 7am-11pm; ☞) Refurbished after flooding in 2015, Keswick's handsome YHA looks as good as new. Its premium facilities include an open-plan ground-floor cafe, a seriously smart kitchen and cracking views over Fitz Park and the rushing River Greta. The dorm decor is standard YHA, but some rooms have private riverside balconies. What a treat!

★**Howe Keld** B&B ££
(☑017687-72417; www.howekeld.co.uk; 5-7 The Heads; s £65-90, d £110-140; ℙ☞) This gold-standard B&B pulls out all the stops: goose-down duvets, slate-floored bathrooms, chic colours and locally made furniture. The best rooms have views across Crow Park and the golf course, and the breakfast is a pick-and-mix delight. Free parking is available on The Heads if there's space.

★**Cottage in the Wood** HOTEL £££
(☑017687-78409; www.thecottageinthewood. co.uk; Braithwaite; d £130-220; ☺restaurant 6.30-9pm Tue-Sat; ℙ☞) For a secluded indulgence, head for this out-of-the-way bolthole, on the road to Whinlatter Forest, in a completely modernised coaching inn. Elegant rooms survey woods and countryside: the Mountain View rooms overlook the Skiddaw Range, but we liked the super-private Attic Suite and the Garden Room, with its wood floors and wet-room. The restaurant's fantastic too (set dinner menu £45).

WALES

☑029 / POP 3.1M

Lying to the west of England, Wales is a nation with Celtic roots, its own language and a rich historical legacy. While some areas in the south are undeniably scarred by coal mining and heavy industry, Wales boasts a scenic landscape of wild mountains, rolling hills and rich farmland, and the bustling capital city of Cardiff.

Cardiff

POP 349,941

The capital of Wales since just 1955, Cardiff has embraced the role with vigour, emerging in the new millennium as one of Britain's leading urban centres. Spread between an ancient fort and an ultramodern waterfront, compact Cardiff seems to have surprised even itself with how interesting it has become.

◉ Sights

★**Cardiff Castle** CASTLE
(☑029-2087 8100; www.cardiffcastle.com; Castle St; adult/child £13/9.25, incl guided tour £16/12; ☺9am-6pm Mar-Oct, to 5pm Nov-Feb) There's a medieval keep at its heart, but it's the later additions to Cardiff Castle that really capture the imagination. In Victorian times, extravagant mock-Gothic features were grafted onto this relic, including a clock tower and a lavish banqueting hall. Some but not all of this flamboyant fantasy world can be accessed with regular castle entry; the rest can be visited as part of a (recommended) guided tour. Look for the *trebuchet* (medieval siege engine) and falcons on the grounds.

★**National Museum Cardiff** MUSEUM
(☑0300 111 2 333; www.museumwales.ac.uk; Cathays Park; ☺10am-5pm Tue-Sun; ℙ) FREE Devoted mainly to natural history and art, this grand neoclassical building is the centrepiece of the seven institutions dotted around the country that together form the Welsh National Museum. It's one of Britain's best museums; you'll need at least three hours to do it justice, but it could easily consume the best part of a rainy day. On-site parking, behind the museum, is £6.50.

Wales Millennium Centre ARTS CENTRE
(☑029-2063 6464; www.wmc.org.uk; Bute Pl, Cardiff Bay; ☺9am-7pm, later on show nights) The centrepiece and symbol of Cardiff Bay's regeneration is the £106 million Wales Millennium Centre, an architectural masterpiece of stacked Welsh slate in shades of purple, green and grey topped with an overarching bronzed steel shell. Designed by Welsh architect Jonathan Adams, it opened in 2004 as Wales' premier arts complex, housing ma-

jor cultural organisations such as the Welsh National Opera, National Dance Company, BBC National Orchestra of Wales, Literature Wales, HiJinx Theatre and Tŷ Cerdd (Music Centre Wales).

Castell Coch
CASTLE

(Cadw; www.cadw.gov.wales; Castle Rd, Tongwynlais; adult/child £6.90/4.10; ⏱ 9.30am-5pm Mar-Jun, Sep & Oct, to 6pm Jul & Aug, 10am-4pm Mon-Sat, from 11am Sun Nov-Feb; 🅿) Cardiff Castle's fanciful little brother sits perched atop a thickly wooded crag on the northern fringes of Cardiff. It was the summer retreat of the third marquess of Bute and, like Cardiff Castle, was designed by oddball architect William Burges in gaudy Gothic-revival style. Raised on the ruins of Gilbert de Clare's 13th-century Castell Coch (Red Castle), the Butes' Disneyesque holiday home is a monument to high camp. An excellent audio guide is included in the admission price.

🛏 Sleeping

⭐ River House
HOSTEL £

(☑ 029-2039 9810; www.riverhousebackpackers.com; 59 Fitzhamon Embankment, Riverside; dm/s/d incl breakfast from £16/33/38; @ 🛜) Professionally run by a helpful young brother-and-sister team, River House has a well-equipped kitchen, a laundry, a small garden and a cosy TV lounge, and it's right across the Taff from Millennium Stadium. There's a mix of small dorms and private rooms with double beds, all sharing bathrooms, and a free breakfast of cereal, toast, pastries and fruit is provided.

⭐ Lincoln House
HOTEL ££

(☑ 029-2039 5558; www.lincolnhotel.co.uk; 118-120 Cathedral Rd, Pontcanna; d/penthouses from £125/250; 🅿🛜) Walking a middle line between a large B&B and a small hotel, Lincoln House is a generously proportioned Victorian property with heraldic emblems in the stained-glass windows of its book-lined sitting room, and a separate bar. There are 21 rooms and a loft penthouse sleeping up to four; for added romance, book a four-poster room.

Number 62
GUESTHOUSE ££

(☑ 029-2041 2765; www.number62.com; 62 Cathedral Rd, Pontcanna; s/d from £74/83; 🛜) The only thing preventing Number 62 from being a B&B is that breakfast is only offered as an add-on (served at the Beverley Hotel across the road). The cosy rooms come with thoughtful extras such as body lotion, make-up wipes and cotton buds, and the front gar-

den is one of the most immaculate of all the houses on this strip.

Park Plaza
HOTEL £££

(☑ 029-2011 1111; www.parkplazacardiff.com; Greyfriars Rd; s/d £125/175; ❄🛜🐾) Luxurious without being stuffy, the Plaza has all the five-star facilities you'd expect from an upmarket business-oriented hotel, including a gym for guests, a spa, a restaurant and bar (open to all) and Egyptian cotton on the beds. The slick reception has a gas fire blazing along one wall and rear rooms have leafy views over the Civic Centre.

🍴 Eating & Drinking

Coffee Barker
CAFE £

(☑ 029-2022 4575; Castle Arcade; mains £6-7; ⏱ 8.30am-5.30pm Mon-Wed, to 11pm Thu-Sat, 9.30am-4.30pm Sun; 🛜🐾) This cool cafe, a series of rooms at the entrance to one of Cardiff's Victorian arcades, is good for coffee, indulgent pancake stacks, daily soups and thick milkshakes served in glass milk bottles. Despite its size, soft chairs and quirky decor give it a cosy vibe. Usually busy, it also includes a cruisy bar, open until 11pm Thursday to Saturday.

Purple Poppadom
INDIAN ££

(☑ 029-2022 0026; www.purplepoppadom.com; 185a Cowbridge Rd E, Canton; mains £15-17, 2-course lunch £15; ⏱ noon-2pm & 5.30-11pm Tue-Sat, 1-9pm Sun) Trailblazing a path for 'nouvelle Indian' cuisine, chef and author Anand George adds his own twist to dishes from all over the subcontinent – from Kashmir to Kerala. Thankfully, the emphasis is on the perfection of tried-and-tested regional delights rather than anything unnecessarily wacky.

Porter's
BAR

(☑ 029-2125 0666; www.porterscardiff.com; Bute Tce; ⏱ 5pm-12.30am Sun-Wed, 4pm-3am Thu & Fri, noon-3am Sat) Owned by a self-confessed 'failed actor', this friendly, attitude-free bar has something on most nights, whether it's a quiz, live music, comedy, theatre or a movie screening (there's a little cinema attached). Local drama is showcased in the 'Other Room', the adjoining 44-seat theatre, while under the shadow of the train tracks out the back is a wonderful beer garden.

ℹ Information

Tourist Office (☑ 029-2087 3573; www.visitcardiff.com; Yr Hen Lyfrgell, The Hayes; ⏱ 10am-3pm Sun-Thu, to 5pm Fri & Sat)

ⓘ Getting There & Away

BUS

Cardiff's old central bus station was demolished in 2008; its replacement is due to open near the train station in 2023. In the meantime, buses call at temporary stops scattered around the city. See www.traveline.cymru for details.

Megabus (http://uk.megabus.com) offers one-way coach journeys from London to Cardiff (via Newport) from as little as £8.30.

National Express (www.nationalexpress.com) coaches depart from **Cardiff Coach Station** (Sophia Gardens) to destinations including Bristol (£8.70, 1¼ hours, six daily) and London (from £15, 3¾ hours, frequent).

TRAIN

Trains from major British cities arrive at Cardiff Central station, on the southern edge of the city centre. Direct services to/from Cardiff include London Paddington (from £62, 2¼ hours, two per hour) and Holyhead (£47, five hours, seven daily). For the latest timetables and bookings, see www.thetrainline.com.

Snowdonia National Park (Parc Cenedlaethol Eryri)

Wales' best-known slice of nature became the country's first national park (www.eryri-npa.gov.uk) in 1951. Every year more than 400,000 people walk, climb or take the train to the 1085m summit of Snowdon, Wales' highest mountain. Yet the park offers much more – its 823 sq miles embrace stunning coastline, forests, valleys, rivers, bird-filled estuaries and Wales' biggest natural lake. The Welsh for Snowdonia is Eryri (*eh*-ruh-ree) – 'highlands'.

Snowdon (Yr Wyddfa)

No Snowdonia experience is complete without coming face-to-face with Snowdon (1085m) – 'Yr Wyddfa' in Welsh (pronounced uhr-with-vuh, meaning 'the Tomb'). On a clear day the views stretch to Ireland and the Isle of Man. Even on a gloomy day you could find yourself above the clouds. At the top is the striking **Hafod Eryri** (https://snowdonrailway.co.uk; ⊙10am-20min before last train departure Easter-Oct; 🛜) visitor centre.

Six paths of varying length and difficulty lead to the summit, all taking around six hours return, or you can cheat and catch the **Snowdon Mountain Railway** (☑01286-870223; www.snowdonrailway.co.uk; adult/child return diesel £29/20, steam £37/27; ⊙9am-5pm

CONWY CASTLE

On the north coast of Wales, the historic town of Conwy is dominated by the Unesco-designated cultural treasure of **Conwy Castle** (Cadw; ☑01492-592358; www.cadw.wales.gov.uk; Castle Sq; adult/child £9.50/5.70; ⊙9.30am-5pm Mar-Jun, Sep & Oct, to 6pm Jul & Aug, 10am-4pm Mon-Sat, from 11am Sun Nov-Feb; ℗), the most stunning of all Edward I's Welsh fortresses. Built between 1277 and 1307 on a rocky outcrop, it has commanding views across the estuary and Snowdonia National Park.

mid-Mar–Oct), which opened in 1896 and is still the UK's only public rack-and-pinion railway.

However you get to the summit, take warm, waterproof clothing, wear sturdy footwear and check the weather forecast before setting out.

YHA Snowdon Ranger   HOSTEL £
(☑0845 3719 659; www.yha.org.uk; Rhyd Ddu; dm/tw from £23/50; ℗🛜) On the A4085, 5 miles north of Beddgelert at the trailhead for the Snowdon Ranger Path, this former inn has its own adjoining beach on the shore of Llyn Cwellyn, and is close to the hiking and climbing centres of Llanberis and Beddgelert. It's basic, dependable accommodation within sight of Snowdon.

Pen-y-Gwryd   HOTEL ££
(☑01286-870211; www.pyg.co.uk; Nant Gwynant; s/d £58/115; ℗🛜🐕) Eccentric but full of atmosphere, this Georgian coaching inn was used as a training base by the 1953 Everest team, and memorabilia from their stay includes signatures on the restaurant ceiling. TV, wi-fi and mobile-phone signals don't penetrate here; instead, there's a comfy games room, a sauna, and a lake for those hardy enough to swim. Meals and packed lunches are available.

You'll find the hotel below Pen-y-Pass, at the junction of the A498 and A4086.

ⓘ Getting There & Away

The Welsh Highland Railway (www.festrail.co.uk) and Snowdon Sherpa buses (single/day ticket £2/5) link various places in Snowdonia with the town of Caernarfon, which can be reached by train from London Euston.

SCOTLAND

POP 5.45 MILLION

Despite its small size, Scotland has many treasures crammed into its compact territory – big skies, lonely landscapes, spectacular wildlife, superb seafood and hospitable, down-to-earth people. From the cultural attractions of Edinburgh to the heather-clad hills of the Highlands, there's something for everyone.

Edinburgh

☑ 0131 / POP 513,210

Edinburgh is a city that just begs to be explored. From the imposing castle to the Palace of Holyroodhouse to the Royal Yacht *Britannia*, every corner turned reveals sudden views and unexpected vistas – green sunlit hills, a glimpse of rust-red crags, a blue flash of distant sea. But there's more to Edinburgh than sightseeing – there are top shops, world-class restaurants and a bacchanalia of bars to enjoy.

⊙ Sights

★ Edinburgh Castle   CASTLE

(☑ 0131-225 9846; www.edinburghcastle.gov.uk; Castle Esplanade; adult/child £18.50/11.50, audio guide £3.50/1.50; ⊙ 9.30am-6pm Apr-Sep, to 5pm Oct-Mar, last entry 1hr before closing; ☐ 23, 27, 41, 42, 67) Edinburgh Castle has played a pivotal role in Scottish history, both as a royal residence – King Malcolm Canmore (r 1058–93) and Queen Margaret first made their home here in the 11th century – and as a military stronghold. The castle last saw military action in 1745; from then until the 1920s it served as the British army's main base in Scotland. Today is one of Scotland's most atmospheric and popular tourist attractions.

★ National Museum of Scotland   MUSEUM

(☑ 0300 123 6789; www.nms.ac.uk/national -museum-of-scotland; Chambers St; ⊙ 10am-5pm; 👬; ☐ 45, 300) 【FREE】 Elegant Chambers St is dominated by the long facade of the National Museum of Scotland. Its extensive collections are spread between two buildings: one modern, one Victorian – the golden stone and striking architecture of the new building (1998) make it one of the city's most distinctive landmarks. The museum's five floors trace the history of Scotland from geological beginnings to the 1990s, with many imaginative and stimulating exhibits. Audio guides are available in several languages. Fees apply for special exhibitions.

Real Mary King's Close   HISTORIC BUILDING

(☑ 0131-225 0672; www.realmarykingsclose.com; 2 Warriston's Close; adult/child £15.50/9.50; ⊙ 10am-9pm Apr-Oct, reduced hours rest of year; ☐ 23, 27, 41, 42) Edinburgh's 18th-century City Chambers were built over the sealed-off remains of Mary King's Close, and the lower levels of this medieval Old Town alley have survived almost unchanged amid the foundations for 250 years. Now open to the public, this spooky, subterranean labyrinth gives a fascinating insight into the everyday life of 17th-century Edinburgh. Costumed characters lead tours through a 16th-century town house and the plague-stricken home of a 17th-century gravedigger. Advance booking recommended.

Palace of Holyroodhouse   PALACE

(☑ 03031237306; www.royalcollection.org.uk/visit/ palace-of-holyroodhouse; Canongate, Royal Mile; adult/child incl audio guide £14/8.10; ⊙ 9.30am-6pm, last entry 4.30pm Apr-Oct, to 4.30pm, last entry 3.15pm Nov-Mar; ☐ 6, 300) This palace is the royal family's official residence in Scotland, but is more famous as the 16th-century home of the ill-fated Mary, Queen of Scots. The highlight of the tour is **Mary's Bedchamber**, home to the unfortunate queen from 1561 to 1567. It was here that her jealous second husband, Lord Darnley, restrained the pregnant queen while his henchmen murdered her secretary – and favourite – David Rizzio. A plaque in the neighbouring room marks the spot where Rizzio bled to death.

Scottish Parliament Building   NOTABLE BUILDING

(☑ 0131-348 5200; www.parliament.scot; Horse Wynd; ⊙ 9am-6.30pm Tue-Thu, 10am-5pm Mon, Fri & Sat in session, 10am-5pm Tue-Thu in recess; 👬; ☐ 6, 300) 【FREE】 The Scottish Parliament Building, on the site of a former brewery and designed by Catalan architect Enric Miralles (1955–2000), was opened by the Queen in October 2004. The ground plan of the complex is said to represent a 'flower of democracy rooted in Scottish soil' (best seen looking down from Salisbury Crags). Free, one-hour tours (advance bookings recommended) include visits to the Debating Chamber, a committee room, the Garden Lobby and the office of a member of parliament (MSP).

Royal Yacht Britannia   SHIP

(www.royalyachtbritannia.co.uk; Ocean Terminal; adult/child incl audio guide £16/8.50; ⊙ 9.30am-6pm Apr-Sep, to 5.30pm Oct, 10am-5pm Nov-Mar, last entry 1½hr before closing; 🅿; ☐ 11, 22, 34,

36, 200, 300) Built on Clydeside, the former Royal Yacht *Britannia* was the British Royal Family's floating holiday home during their foreign travels from the time of its launch in 1953 until its decommissioning in 1997, and is now permanently moored in front of **Ocean Terminal** (☑ 0131-555 8888; www.oceanterminal.com; Ocean Dr; ⊙ 10am-8pm Mon-Fri, to 7pm Sat, 11am-6pm Sun; ⬤). The tour, which you take at your own pace with an audio guide (available in 30 languages), lifts the curtain on the everyday lives of the royals, and gives an intriguing insight into the Queen's private tastes.

🛏 Sleeping

Edinburgh offers a wide range of accommodation options, from moderately priced guesthouses set in lovely Victorian villas and Georgian town houses to expensive and stylish boutique hotels. There are also plenty of chain hotels, and a few truly exceptional hotels housed in magnificent historic buildings. At the budget end of the range, there is no shortage of youth hostels and independent backpacker hostels, which often have inexpensive double and twin rooms.

Code - The Loft   HOSTEL £
(☑ 0131-659 9883; www.codehostel.com; 50 Rose St N Lane; dm from £25, d £99; ⬤; 🚌 Princes St) This upmarket hostel, bang in the middle of the New Town, combines cute designer decor with innovative sleeping pods that offer more privacy than bunks (four to six people per dorm, each with en suite shower room). There's also a luxurious double apartment called the Penthouse, complete with kitchenette and roof terrace.

Safestay Edinburgh   HOSTEL £
(☑ 0131-524 1989; www.safestay.com; 50 Blackfriars St; dm £34-40, tw £139; @⬤; 🚌 300) A big, modern hostel, with a convivial cafe where you can buy breakfast, and mod cons such as keycard access and charging stations for mobile phones, MP3 players and laptops. Lockers in every room, a huge bar and a central location just off the Royal Mile make this a favourite among the young, party-mad crowd – don't expect a quiet night!

★ **Two Hillside Crescent**   B&B ££
(☑ 0131-556 4871; www.twohillsidecrescent.com; 2 Hillside Cres; r from £115; @⬤; 🚌 19, 26, 44) Five spacious and individually decorated bedrooms grace this gorgeous Georgian town house – it's worth splashing out for the 'superior' room with twin floor-to-ceiling windows overlooking the gardens. Guests take breakfast around a large communal table in a stylishly modern dining room – smoked salmon and scrambled eggs is on the menu – and your hosts could not be more helpful.

14 Hart Street   B&B ££
(☑ 07795 203414; http://14hartstreet.co.uk; 14 Hart St; s/d £115/125; ⬤; 🚌 8) Centrally located and child friendly, 14 Hart Street is steeped in Georgian elegance and old Edinburgh charm. Run by a retired couple, the B&B has three generous bedrooms, all en suite, and a sumptuous dining room where guests can enjoy breakfast at a time of their choosing. Indulgent extras include whisky decanters and shortbread in every room.

★ **Principal**   BOUTIQUE HOTEL £££
(☑ 0131-341 4932; www.phcompany.com/principal/edinburgh-charlotte-square; 38 Charlotte Sq; r from £245; P⬤; 🚌 all Princes St buses) Arriving in this modern makeover of a classic Georgian New Town establishment (formerly the Roxburghe Hotel) feels like being welcomed into a country-house party. Service is friendly and attentive without being intrusive, and the atmosphere is informal; in the bedrooms, designer decor meets traditional tweed, and breakfast is served in a lovely glass-roofed garden courtyard.

🍴 Eating

Scott's Kitchen   SCOTTISH, CAFE £
(☑ 0131-322 6868; https://scottskitchen.co.uk; 4-6 Victoria Tce; mains £8-10; ⊙ 9am-6pm; P⬤; 🚌 23, 27, 41, 42, 67) Green tile, brown leather and arched Georgian windows lend an elegant feel to this modern cafe, which combines fine Scottish produce with great value. Fill up on a breakfast (served till 11.45am) of eggs Benedict, bacon baps or porridge with honey, banana and almonds, or linger over

---

FESTIVAL CITY

Edinburgh boasts a frenzy of festivals throughout the year, including the world-famous **Edinburgh Festival Fringe** (☑ 0131-226 0026; www.edfringe.com), held over 3½ weeks in August. The last two weeks overlap with the first two weeks of the **Edinburgh International Festival** (☑ 0131-473 2000; www.eif.co.uk). See www.edinburghfestivalcity.com for more.

Central Edinburgh

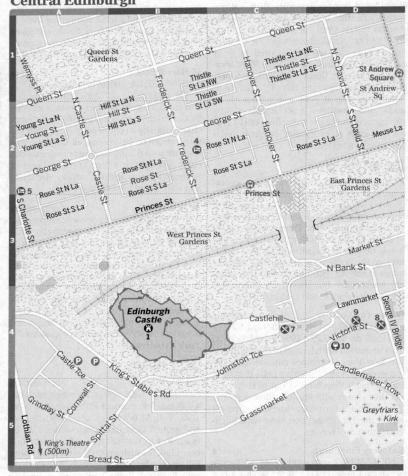

a lunch of Cullen skink (smoked haddock soup), venison casserole or haggis.

★ **Gardener's Cottage**　SCOTTISH ££
(☏ 0131-558 1221; www.thegardenerscottage.co; 1 Royal Terrace Gardens, London Rd; 4-course lunch £21, 7-course dinner £50; ⏰ noon-2pm & 5-10pm Mon-Fri, 10am-2pm & 5-10pm Sat & Sun; ➔ all London Rd buses) 🌿 This country cottage in the heart of the city, bedecked with flowers and fairy lights, offers one of Edinburgh's most interesting dining experiences – two tiny rooms with communal tables made of salvaged timber, and a set menu based on fresh local produce (most of the vegetables and

fruit are from its own organic garden). Bookings essential; brunch served at weekends.

Cannonball Restaurant　SCOTTISH ££
(☏ 0131-225 1550; www.contini.com/cannonball; 356 Castlehill; mains £15-25; ⏰ noon-3pm & 5.30-10pm Tue-Sat; 🛜 🚼; ➔ 23, 27, 41, 42) The historic Cannonball House next to Edinburgh Castle's esplanade has been transformed into a sophisticated restaurant (and whisky bar) where the Contini family work their Italian magic on Scottish classics to produce dishes such as haggis balls with spiced pickled turnip and whisky marmalade, and lobster with wild garlic and lemon butter.

12.30-10.30pm Sun; 🛜🐾♿; 🚌16, 22, 36, 300)
This cosy little restaurant, tucked beneath a
17th-century signal tower, is one of the city's
best seafood places. The menu ranges widely
in price, from cheaper dishes such as classic fish cakes with lemon-and-chive mayonnaise to more expensive delights such as Fife
lobster and chips (£40).

★ **Ondine** SEAFOOD **£££**
(📞0131-226 1888; www.ondinerestaurant.co.uk; 2
George IV Bridge; mains £18-38, 2-/3-course lunch
£19/24; ☉noon-3pm & 5.30-10pm Mon-Sat; 🛜;
🚌23, 27, 41, 42) Ondine is one of Edinburgh's
finest seafood restaurants, with a menu
based on sustainably sourced fish. Take a
seat at the curved Oyster Bar and tuck into
oysters Kilpatrick, smoked-haddock chowder, lobster thermidor, a roast-shellfish platter or just good old haddock and chips (with
minted pea purée, just to keep things posh).

🍷 Drinking & Nightlife

★ **Bennet's Bar** PUB
(📞0131-229 5143; www.bennetsbaredinburgh.co.uk;
8 Leven St; ☉11am-1am; 🚌all Tollcross buses) Situated beside the **King's Theatre** (📞0131-529
6000; www.capitaltheatres.com/kings; 2 Leven St;
☉box office 10am-6pm), Bennet's (established
in 1839) has managed to hang on to almost
all of its beautiful Victorian fittings, from
the stained-glass windows and the ornate
mirrors to the wooden gantry and the brass

Aizle SCOTTISH **££**
(📞0131-662 9349; http://aizle.co.uk; 107-109 St
Leonard's St; 5-course dinner £55; ☉5-9pm Wed-
Sat; 🛜; 🚌14) If you tend to have trouble
deciding what to eat, Aizle (the name is an
old Scots word for 'spark' or 'ember') will do
the job for you. There's no menu here, just a
five-course dinner conjured from a monthly
'harvest' of the finest and freshest local produce (listed on a blackboard), and presented
beautifully – art on a plate.

Fishers Bistro SEAFOOD **££**
(📞0131-554 5666; www.fishersbistros.co.uk; 1 The
Shore; mains £14-25; ☉noon-10.30pm Mon-Sat,

THE QUEENSFERRY CROSSING

The famous Forth Bridge (1890) and Forth Road Bridge (1964), which soar across the Firth of Forth to the west of Edinburgh, have been joined by the impressive Queensferry Crossing, a road bridge that opened in 2017.

water taps on the bar (for your whisky – there are over 100 from which to choose).

★ **Bow Bar**　　　　　　　　　　PUB
(www.thebowbar.co.uk; 80 West Bow; ⊙noon-midnight Mon-Sat, to 11.30pm Sun; ▣2, 23, 27, 41, 42) One of the city's best traditional-style pubs (it's not as old as it looks), serving a range of excellent real ales, Scottish craft gins and a vast selection of malt whiskies, the Bow Bar often has standing-room only on Friday and Saturday evenings.

Café Royal Circle Bar　　　　　PUB
(☑0131-556 1884; www.caferoyaledinburgh.co.uk; 17 W Register St; ⊙11am-11pm Mon-Wed, to midnight Thu, to 1am Fri & Sat, to 10pm Sun; ☎; ▣Princes St) Perhaps *the* classic Edinburgh pub, the Café Royal's main claims to fame are its magnificent oval bar and its Doulton tile portraits of famous Victorian inventors. Sit at the bar or claim one of the cosy leather booths beneath the stained-glass windows, and choose from the seven real ales on tap.

Roseleaf　　　　　　　　　　BAR
(☑0131-476 5268; www.roseleaf.co.uk; 23-24 Sandport Pl; ⊙10am-1am; ☎▣; ▣16, 22, 36, 300) Cute, quaint and decked out in flowered wallpaper, old furniture and rose-patterned china (cocktails are served in teapots), the Roseleaf could hardly be further from the average Leith bar. The real ales and bottled beers are complemented by a range of speciality teas, coffees and fruit drinks (including rose lemonade), and well-above-average pub grub (served from 10am to 10pm).

★ **Cabaret Voltaire**　　　　　　CLUB
(www.thecabaretvoltaire.com; 36-38 Blair St; ⊙5pm-3am Tue-Sat, 8pm-1am Sun; ☎; ▣all South Bridge buses) An atmospheric warren of stone-lined vaults houses this self-consciously 'alternative' club, which eschews huge dance floors and egotistical DJ worship in favour of a 'creative crucible' hosting an eclectic mix

of DJs, live acts, comedy, theatre, visual arts and the spoken word. Well worth a look.

☆ Entertainment

The comprehensive source for what's on is The List (www.list.co.uk).

★ **Sandy Bell's**　　　　TRADITIONAL MUSIC
(www.sandybellsedinburgh.co.uk; 25 Forrest Rd; ⊙noon-1am Mon-Sat, 12.30pm-midnight Sun; ▣2, 23, 27, 41, 42, 45) This unassuming pub has been a stalwart of the traditional-music scene since the 1960s (the founder's wife sang with the Corries). There's music every weekday evening at 9pm, and from 2pm Saturday and 4pm Sunday, plus lots of impromptu sessions.

ⓘ Information

Edinburgh Tourist Office (Edinburgh iCentre; ☑0131-473 3868; www.visitscotland.com/info/services/edinburgh-icentre-p234441; Waverley Mall, 3 Princes St; ⊙9am-7pm Mon-Sat, 10am-7pm Sun Jul & Aug, to 6pm Jun, to 5pm Sep-May; ☎; ▣St Andrew Sq) Accommodation booking service, currency exchange, gift shop and bookshop, internet access, and counters selling tickets for Edinburgh city tours and Scottish Citylink bus services.

ⓘ Getting There & Away

AIR

Edinburgh Airport (EDI; ☑0844 448 8833; www.edinburghairport.com), 8 miles west of the city, has numerous flights to other parts of Scotland and the UK, Ireland and mainland Europe.

BUS

Edinburgh Bus Station (left-luggage lockers per 24hr £5-10; ⊙4.30am-midnight Sun-Thu, to 12.30am Fri & Sat; ▣St Andrew Sq) is at the northeastern corner of St Andrew Sq, with pedestrian entrances from the square and from Elder St. For timetable information, contact **Traveline** (☑0871 200 22 33; www.travelinescotland.com).

　Scottish Citylink (☑0871 266 3333; www.citylink.co.uk) buses connect Edinburgh with all of Scotland's cities and major towns including Glasgow (£7.90, 1¼ hours, every 15 minutes), Stirling (£8.70, one hour, hourly) and Inverness (£32.20, 3½ hours to 4½ hours, hourly).

　It's also worth checking with **Megabus** (☑0141-352 4444; www.megabus.com) for cheap intercity bus fares (from as little as £5) from Edinburgh to London, Glasgow and Inverness.

TRAIN

The main rail terminus in Edinburgh is Waverley train station, in the heart of the city. Trains arriving from, and departing for, the west also stop at Haymarket station, which is more convenient for the West End.

ScotRail (☏ 0344 811 0141; www.scotrail. co.uk) operates regular train services to Glasgow (£14.40, 50 minutes, every 15 minutes) and Inverness (£40, 3½ hours).

Glasgow

☏ 0141 / POP 596,500

With a population around 1½ times that of Edinburgh, and a radically different history rooted in industry and trade rather than politics and law, Glasgow stands in complete contrast to the capital. The city offers a unique blend of friendliness, energy, dry humour and urban chaos, and also boasts excellent art galleries and museums – including the famous Burrell Collection (due to reopen in 2022) – as well as numerous good-value restaurants, countless pubs, bars and clubs, and a lively performing-arts scene. Just 50 miles to the west of Edinburgh, Glasgow makes an easy day trip by train or bus.

⊙ Sights

Glasgow's main square in the city centre is grand **George Square**, built in the Victori-

an era to show off the city's wealth, and dignified by statues of notable Scots, including Robert Burns, James Watt, John Moore and Sir Walter Scott.

★**Kelvingrove Art Gallery & Museum**   GALLERY, MUSEUM
(☏ 0141-276 9599; www.glasgowmuseums.com; Argyle St; ⊙ 10am-5pm Mon-Thu & Sat, from 11am Fri & Sun) **FREE** A magnificent sandstone building, this grand Victorian cathedral of culture is a fascinating and unusual museum, with a bewildering variety of exhibits. You'll find fine art alongside stuffed animals, and Micronesian shark-tooth swords alongside a Spitfire plane, but it's not mix 'n' match: rooms are carefully and thoughtfully themed, and the collection is of a manageable size. It has an excellent room of Scottish art, a room of fine French impressionist works, and quality Renaissance paintings from Italy and Flanders.

★**Riverside Museum**   MUSEUM
(☏ 0141-287 2720; www.glasgowmuseums.com; 100 Pointhouse Pl; ⊙ 10am-5pm Mon-Thu & Sat, from 11am Fri & Sun; ⊕) **FREE** This visually impressive modern museum at Glasgow Harbour owes its striking curved forms to late British-Iraqi architect Zaha Hadid. A transport museum forms the main part of the collection, featuring a fascinating series of cars made in Scotland, plus assorted railway locos, trams, bikes (including the world's first

---

THE GENIUS OF CHARLES RENNIE MACKINTOSH

Charles Rennie Mackintosh (1868–1928) is to Glasgow what Gaudí is to Barcelona. A designer, architect and master of the art nouveau style, his quirky, linear and geometric designs are seen all over Glasgow.

Many of his buildings are open to the public, though his masterpiece, the **Glasgow School of Art**, was extensively damaged by fires in 2014 and 2018. If you're a fan, be sure to visit the following:

Mackintosh at the Willow (☏ 0141-204 1903; www.mackintoshatthewillow.com; 217 Sauchiehall St; exhibition admission adult/child £5.50/3.50; ⊙ tearoom 9am-5pm, exhibition 9am-5.30pm Mon-Sat, 10am-5pm Sun, last entry 1hr before closing)

Mackintosh House (☏ 0141-330 4221; www.hunterian.gla.ac.uk; 82 Hillhead St; adult/child £6/3; ⊙ 10am-5pm Tue-Sat, 11am-4pm Sun)

House for an Art Lover (☏ 0141-353 4770; www.houseforanartlover.co.uk; Bellahouston Park, Dumbreck Rd; adult/child £6/4.50; ⊙ check online, roughly 10am-4pm Mon-Fri, to noon Sat, to 2pm Sun)

Hill House (☏ 01436-673900; www.nts.org.uk; Upper Colquhoun St, Helensburgh; adult/child £10.50/7.50; ⊙ 11.30am-5pm Mar-Oct)

Glasgow

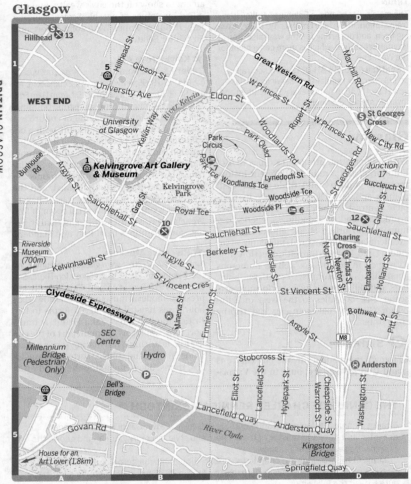

pedal-powered bicycle from 1847) and model Clyde-built ships. An atmospheric recreation of a Glasgow shopping street from the early 20th century puts the vintage vehicles into a social context. There's also a cafe.

Glasgow Cathedral CATHEDRAL
(HES; ☑0141-552 6891; www.historicenvironment.scot; Cathedral Sq; ⊙9.30am-5.30pm Mon-Sat, 1-5pm Sun Apr-Sep, 10am-4pm Mon-Sat, from 1pm Sun Oct-Mar) Glasgow Cathedral has a rare timelessness. The dark, imposing interior conjures up medieval might and can send a shiver down the spine. It's a shining example of Gothic architecture, and unlike nearly all

of Scotland's cathedrals, it survived the turmoil of the Reformation mobs almost intact. Most of the current building dates from the 15th century.

Glasgow Science Centre MUSEUM
(☑0141-420 5000; www.glasgowsciencecentre.org; 50 Pacific Quay; adult/child £11.50/9.50, IMAX, Glasgow Tower or Planetarium extra £2.50-3.50; ⊙10am-5pm daily Apr-Oct, to 3pm Wed-Fri, to 5pm Sat & Sun Nov-Mar; ﴾﴿) This brilliant science museum will keep the kids entertained for hours (that's middle-aged kids too!). It brings science and technology alive through hundreds of interactive exhibits on four

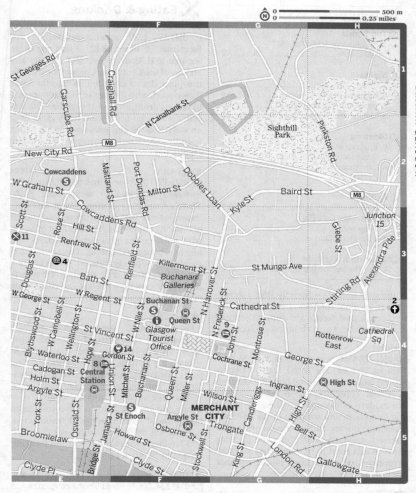

floors: a bounty of discovery for inquisitive minds. There's also an **IMAX theatre** (see www.cineworld.com for current screenings), a rotating 127m-high **observation tower**, a **planetarium** and a **Science Theatre**, with live science demonstrations. To get here, take bus 89 or 90 from Union St.

🛏 Sleeping

Glasgow SYHA   HOSTEL **£**
(📞0141-332 3004; www.hostellingscotland.org.uk; 8 Park Tce; dm/s/tw £29/52/69; @🛜) Perched on a hill overlooking Kelvingrove Park in a charming townhouse, this place is one of Scotland's best official hostels. Dorms are mostly four to six beds with padlocked lockers, and all have their own en suite. The common rooms are spacious, plush and good for lounging about in. There's no curfew, it has a good kitchen, and meals are available.

★Grasshoppers   HOTEL **££**
(📞0141-222 2666; www.grasshoppersglasgow. com; 87 Union St; r £90-138; ❄🛜❄) Discreetly hidden atop a time-worn railway administration building alongside Central station, this small, well-priced hotel is a modern, upbeat surprise. Rooms are compact (a few are larger) but well appointed, with unusual views over the station roof's glass sea.

Glasgow

Top Sights
1 Kelvingrove Art Gallery & Museum ... A2

Sights
2 Glasgow Cathedral ... H4
3 Glasgow Science Centre ... A5
4 Mackintosh at the Willow ... E3
5 Mackintosh House ... A1

Sleeping
6 15Glasgow ... C3
7 Glasgow SYHA ... C2
8 Grasshoppers ... E4
9 Z Hotel ... G4

Eating
10 Ox & Finch ... B3
11 Saramago Café Bar ... E3
12 Singl-end ... D3
13 Ubiquitous Chip ... A1

Drinking & Nightlife
14 The Horseshoe Bar ... F4

Numerous touches – friendly staff, interesting art, in-room cafetière, free cupcakes and ice cream, and weeknight suppers – make this one of the centre's homiest choices.

Z Hotel HOTEL ££
(0141-212 4550; www.thezhotels.com; 36 North Frederick St; r £90-165;) Just off George Sq, the facade of a historic building conceals a stylish contemporary hotel. Chambers are modern but compact – the idea is that you sleep here and socialise in the bar area, especially during the afternoon wine-and-cheese session. Big flatscreens and pleasing showers add comfort to rooms that are often overpriced but can be great value if advance booked.

★15Glasgow B&B £££
(0141-332 1263; www.15glasgow.com; 15 Woodside Pl; d/ste £130/160;) Glasgow's 19th-century merchants certainly knew how to build a beautiful house, and this 1840s terrace is a sumptuous example. Huge rooms with lofty ceilings have exquisite period detail complemented by attractive modern greys, striking bathrooms and well-chosen quality furniture.

Your welcoming host makes everything easy for you: the in-room breakfast, overlooking the park, is a real treat. They prefer no under-five-year-olds.

Eating & Drinking

Saramago Café Bar CAFE, VEGAN £
(0141-352 4920; www.cca-glasgow.com; 350 Sauchiehall St; mains £8-12; food noon-10pm Sun-Wed, to 11.30pm Thu-Sat;) In the airy atrium of the Centre for Contemporary Arts, this place does a great line in eclectic vegan fusion food, with a range of top flavour combinations from around the globe. The upstairs bar (open from 4pm) has a great deck on steep Scott St and packs out inside with a friendly arty crowd enjoying the DJ sets and quality tap beers.

Singl-end CAFE ££
(0141-353 1277; www.thesingl-end.co.uk; 265 Renfrew St; dishes £7-13; 9am-5pm;) There's something glorious about this long basement cafe with its cheery service and air of brunchy bonhomie. It covers a lot of bases, with good coffee, generous breakfasts and lunches, booze and baking. Dietary requirements are superbly catered for, with fine vegan choices and clear labelling. On a diet? Avert your eyes from the 'eat-me' cornucopia of meringues and pastries by the door.

★Ox & Finch FUSION ££
(0141-339 8627; www.oxandfinch.com; 920 Sauchiehall St; small plates £4-10; noon-10pm;) This fashionable place could almost sum up the thriving modern Glasgow eating scene, with a faux-pub name, sleek but comfortable contemporary decor, tapas-sized dishes and an open kitchen. Grab a cosy booth and be prepared to have your taste buds wowed by innovative, delicious creations aimed at sharing, drawing on French and Mediterreanean influences but focusing on quality Scottish produce.

★Ubiquitous Chip SCOTTISH £££
(0141-334 5007; www.ubiquitouschip.co.uk; 12 Ashton Lane; 2-/3-course lunch £20/24, mains £20-30, brasserie mains £13-16; restaurant noon-2.30pm & 5-11pm Mon-Sat, 12.30-3pm & 5-10pm Sun;) The original champion of Scottish produce, Ubiquitous Chip is legendary for its still-unparalleled cuisine and lengthy wine list. Named to poke fun at Scotland's culinary reputation, it offers a French touch but resolutely Scottish ingredients, carefully selected and following sustainable principles. The elegant courtyard space offers some of Glasgow's best dining, while, above, the cheaper brasserie (open longer hours) offers exceptional value for money.

The Horseshoe Bar PUB
(☑ 0141-248 6368; www.thehorseshoebarglasgow. co.uk; 17 Drury St; ⊙ 10am-midnight Sun-Fri, from 9am Sat) This legendary city pub and popular meeting place dates from the late 19th century and is largely unchanged. It's a picturesque spot, with the longest continuous bar in the UK, but its main attraction is what's served over it – real ale and good cheer. Upstairs in the lounge is some of the best-value pub food (dishes £4 to £10) in town.

ℹ️ Information

Glasgow Tourist Office (www.visitscotland. com; 158 Buchanan St; ⊙ 9am-5pm Mon-Sat, 10am-4pm Sun Nov-Apr, 9am-6pm Mon-Sat, 10am-4pm Sun May, Jun, Sep & Oct, 9am-7pm Mon-Sat, 10am-5pm Sun Jul & Aug; 🛜) The city's tourist office is in the centre of town. It opens at 9.30am on Thursday mornings.

ℹ️ Getting There & Away

Glasgow is easily reached from Edinburgh by bus (£7.90, 1¼ hours, every 15 minutes) or train (£14.40, 50 minutes, every 15 minutes).

Loch Lomond & the Trossachs

The 'bonnie banks' and 'bonnie braes' of Loch Lomond have long been Glasgow's rural retreat. The main tourist focus is on the loch's western shore, along the A82. The eastern shore, followed by the **West Highland Way** long-distance footpath, is quieter. The region's importance was recognised when it became the heart of **Loch Lomond & the Trossachs National Park** (☑ 01389-722600; www.lochlomond-trossachs.org) – Scotland's first national park, created in 2002.

The nearby Trossachs is a region famous for its thickly forested hills and scenic lochs. It first gained popularity in the early 19th century when curious visitors came from across Britain, drawn by the romantic language of Walter Scott's poem *Lady of the Lake,* inspired by Loch Katrine, and his novel *Rob Roy,* about the derring-do of the region's most famous son.

The main centre for Loch Lomond boat trips is Balloch, where **Sweeney's Cruises** (☑ 01389-752376; www.sweeneyscruiseco.com; Balloch Rd) offers a range of outings, including a one-hour cruise to Inchmurrin and back (adult/child £10.20/7, five times daily April to October, twice daily November to March).

Loch Katrine Cruises (☑ 01877-376315; www.lochkatrine.com; Trossachs Pier, Loch Katrine; 1hr cruise adult £12-14, child £6.50-7.50) runs boat trips from Trossachs Pier at the eastern end of Loch Katrine; some are aboard the fabulous centenarian steamship *Sir Walter Scott.* One-hour scenic cruises run one to four times daily; there are also departures to Stronachlachar at the other end of the loch (two hours return).

🛏️ Sleeping & Eating

★ **Callander Hostel** HOSTEL £
(☑ 01877-331465; www.callanderhostel.co.uk; 6 Bridgend; dm/d £19.50/60; P @ 🛜) ✔ This hostel in a mock-Tudor building has been a

---

DON'T MISS

STIRLING CASTLE

Hold Stirling and you control Scotland. This maxim has ensured that a fortress of some kind has existed here since prehistoric times. You cannot help drawing parallels with Edinburgh Castle, but many find **Stirling Castle** (HES; www.stirlingcastle.gov.uk; Castle Wynd; adult/child £15/9; ⊙ 9.30am-6pm Apr-Sep, to 5pm Oct-Mar, last entry 45min before closing; P) more atmospheric – the location, architecture, historical significance and commanding views combine to make it a grand and memorable sight.

The current castle dates from the late 14th to the 16th century, when it was a residence of the Stuart monarchs. The undisputed highlight of a visit is the fabulous **Royal Palace** – during restoration the idea was that it should look brand new, just as when it was constructed by French masons under the orders of James V in the mid-16th century, with the aim of impressing his new (also French) bride and other crowned heads of Europe.

The suite of six rooms – three for the king, three for the queen – is a sumptuous riot of colour. Particularly notable are the fine fireplaces, the **Stirling Heads** – modern reproductions of painted oak discs in the ceiling of the king's audience chamber – and the fabulous series of **tapestries** that have been painstakingly woven over many years. Stirling is 35 miles northwest of Edinburgh, and easily reached by train (£9.10, one hour, half-hourly).

major labour of love by a local youth project and is now a top-class facility. Well-furnished dorms offer bunks with individual lights and USB charge ports, while en suite doubles have super views. Staff are lovely, and it has a spacious common area and share kitchen as well as a cafe and garden.

Oak Tree Inn
INN ££

(☑ 01360-870357; www.theoaktreeinn.co.uk; Balmaha; s/d £80/100; ℗ 🛜) An attractive traditional inn built in slate and timber, this place offers bright, modern bedrooms for pampered hikers, plus super-spacious superior chambers, self-catering cottages and glamping pods with their own deck. The rustic restaurant brings locals, tourists and walkers together and dishes up hearty meals that cover lots of bases (mains £10 to £13; open noon to 9pm). There's plenty of outdoor seating. But it doesn't end there; the Oak Tree is an impressive set-up that brews its own beers, makes its own ice cream (and sells it in an adjacent cafe), and smokes its own fish. In fact, Balmaha basically is the Oak Tree these days.

★Callander Meadows
SCOTTISH ££

(☑ 01877-330181; www.callandermeadows.co.uk; 24 Main St; dinner mains £13-19; ⊙ 10am-2.30pm & 6-8.30pm Thu-Sun year-round, plus Mon May-Sep; 🛜) Informal and cosy, this well-loved restaurant in the centre of Callander occupies the front rooms of a Main St house. It's truly excellent; there's a contemporary flair for presentation and unusual flavour combinations, but a solidly British base underpins the cuisine. There's a great beer/coffee garden out the back, where you can also eat. Lighter lunches such as sandwiches are also available.

Drover's Inn
PUB FOOD ££

(☑ 01301-704234; www.thedroversinn.co.uk; Inverarnan; bar meals £9-14; ⊙ 11.30am-10pm Mon-Sat, to 9.30pm or 10pm Sun; ℗ 🛜) Don't miss this low-ceilinged howff (drinking den), just north of Ardlui, with its smoke-blackened stone, kilted bartenders, and walls adorned with moth-eaten stags' heads and stuffed birds. The convivial bar, where Rob Roy allegedly dropped by for pints, serves hearty hill-walking fuel and hosts live folk music on weekends.

❶ Getting There & Away

Balloch, at the southern end of Loch Lomond, can be easily reached from Glasgow by bus (£5.30, 1½ hours, at least two per hour) or train (£5.60, 45 minutes, every 30 minutes).

For exploring the Trossachs, your own transport is recommended.

Inverness

☑ 01463 / POP 61,235

Inverness, the primary city and shopping centre of the Highlands, has a great location astride the River Ness at the northern end of the Great Glen. It's a jumping-off point for exploring Loch Ness and northern Scotland, with the railway line from Edinburgh branching east to Elgin and Aberdeen, north to Thurso and Wick, and west to Kyle of Lochalsh (the nearest train station to the Isle of Skye). The latter route is one of Britain's great scenic rail journeys.

✖ Eating & Sleeping

Black Isle Bar & Rooms
HOSTEL £

(☑ 01463-229920; www.blackislebar.com; 68 Church St; dm/s/d £25/55/100; 🛜) It's a beer drinker's dream come true – top-quality hostel accommodation in a central location, upstairs from a bar that serves real ales from the local Black Isle Brewery.

Ardconnel House
B&B ££

(☑ 01463-240455; www.ardconnel-inverness.co.uk; 21 Ardconnel St; r per person £45-50; 🛜) The six-room Ardconnel is one of our favourites (advance booking is essential, especially in July and August) – a terraced Victorian house with comfortable en suite rooms, a dining room with crisp white table linen, and a breakfast menu that includes Vegemite for homesick Antipodeans. Kids under 10 years not allowed.

Ach Aluinn
B&B ££

(☑ 01463-230127; www.achaluinn.com; 27 Fairfield Rd; r per person £40-45; ℗ 🛜) This large, detached Victorian house is bright and homey, and offers all you might want from a B&B – a private bathroom, TV, reading lights, comfy beds with two pillows each, and an excellent breakfast. Less than 10 minutes' walk west from the city centre.

★Trafford Bank
B&B £££

(☑ 01463-241414; www.traffordbankguesthouse.co.uk; 96 Fairfield Rd; d £130-150; ℗ 🛜) Lots of rave reviews for this elegant Victorian villa, which was once home to a bishop, just a mitre's-toss from the Caledonian Canal and 10 minutes' walk west from the city centre. The luxurious rooms include fresh flowers and fruit, bathrobes and fluffy towels – ask for the Tartan Room, which has a wrought-iron king-size bed and Victorian roll-top bath.

★ **Café 1** BISTRO ££

(☑ 01463-226200; www.cafe1.net; 75 Castle St; mains £12-28; ☺ noon-2.30pm & 5-9.30pm Mon-Fri, 12.30-3pm & 6-9.30pm Sat; 🅿🚼) 🌐 Café 1 is a friendly, appealing bistro with candlelit tables amid elegant blond-wood and wrought-iron decor. There is an international menu based on quality Scottish produce, from Aberdeen Angus steaks to crisp pan-fried sea bass and meltingly tender pork belly. There's a separate vegan menu.

Kitchen Brasserie MODERN SCOTTISH ££

(☑ 01463-259119; www.kitchenrestaurant.co.uk; 15 Huntly St; mains £11-22; ☺ noon-3pm & 5-10pm; 🛜🚼) This spectacular glass-fronted restaurant offers a great menu of top Scottish produce with a Mediterranean or Asian touch, and a view over the River Ness – try to get a table upstairs. Offers a great value two-course lunch (£10; noon to 3pm) and early-bird menu (£14; 5pm to 7pm).

ℹ Information

Inverness Tourist Office (☑ 01463-252401; www.visithighlands.com; 36 High St; ☺ 9am-5pm Mon & Wed-Sat, from 10am Tue, 10am-3pm Sun, longer hours Mar-Oct; 🛜) Accommodation booking service; also sells tickets for tours and cruises.

ℹ Getting There & Away

BUS

Services depart from **Inverness bus station** (Margaret St). Most intercity routes are served by **Scottish Citylink** (☑ 0871 266 3333; www.citylink.co.uk) and **Stagecoach** (☑ 01463-233371; www.stagecoachbus.com). **National Express** (☑ 08717 818181; www.nationalexpress.com) has services to London (from £30, 13½ hours, one daily – more frequent services require changing at Glasgow).

Edinburgh (£32.20, 3½ to 4½ hours, seven daily)

Glasgow (£32.20, 3½ to 4½ hours, hourly)

Portree (£26.40, 3¼ hours, two daily)

If you book far enough in advance, **Megabus** (☑ 0141-352 4444; www.megabus.com) offers fares from as little as £1 for buses from Inverness to Glasgow and Edinburgh, and £10 to London.

TRAIN

Edinburgh (£40, 3½ hours, eight daily)

Kyle of Lochalsh (£20, 2½ hours, four daily Monday to Saturday, two Sunday) One of Britain's great scenic train journeys.

London (£180, eight to nine hours, one daily direct; others require a change at Edinburgh)

Loch Ness

Deep, dark and narrow, Loch Ness stretches for 23 miles between Inverness and Fort Augustus. Its bitterly cold waters have been extensively explored in search of the elusive Loch Ness monster, but most visitors see her only in cardboard cut-out form at the monster exhibitions. The village of **Drumnadrochit** is a hotbed of beastie fever, with two monster exhibitions battling it out for the tourist dollar.

Urquhart Castle CASTLE

(HES; ☑ 01456-450551; adult/child £9/5.40; ☺ 9.30am-8pm Jun-Aug, to 6pm Apr, May & Sep, to 5pm Oct, to 4.30pm Nov-Mar; 🅿) Commanding a superb location 1.5 miles east of Drumnadrochit, with outstanding views (on a clear day), Urquhart Castle is a popular Nessie-hunting hot spot. A huge visitor centre (most of which is beneath ground level) includes a video theatre (with a dramatic 'reveal' of the castle at the end of the film) and displays of medieval items discovered in the castle. The site includes a huge gift shop and a restaurant, and is often very crowded in summer.

Loch Ness Centre & Exhibition MUSEUM

(☑ 01456-450573; www.lochness.com; adult/child £7.95/4.95; ☺ 9.30am-6pm Jul & Aug, to 5pm Easter-Jun, Sep & Oct, 10am-4pm Nov-Easter; 🅿🚼) This Nessie-themed attraction adopts a scientific approach that allows you to weigh the evidence for yourself. Exhibits include original equipment – sonar survey vessels, miniature submarines, cameras and sediment coring tools – used in various monster hunts, plus original photographs and film footage of sightings.

You'll find out about hoaxes and optical illusions, as well as learning a lot about the ecology of Loch Ness – is there enough food in the loch to support even one 'monster', let alone a breeding population?

Nessie Hunter BOATING

(☑ 01456-450395; www.lochness-cruises.com; adult/child £16/10; ☺ Easter-Oct) One-hour monster-hunting cruises, complete with sonar and underwater cameras. Cruises depart from Drumnadrochit hourly (except 1pm) from 10am to 6pm daily.

★ Loch Ness Inn INN ££

(☑ 01456-450991; www.staylochness.co.uk; Lewiston; s/d/f £99/120/140; 🅿🛜) Loch Ness Inn

THE NORTH COAST 500

This 500-mile circuit of northern Scotland's stunning coastline (www.northcoast500.com) has become hugely popular, with thousands of people completing the route by car, campervan, motorbike or bicycle.

ticks all the weary traveller's boxes, with comfortable bedrooms (the family suite sleeps two adults and two children), a cosy bar pouring real ales from the Cairngorm and Isle of Skye breweries, and a rustic restaurant (mains £10 to £20) serving wholesome fare. It's conveniently located in the quiet hamlet of Lewiston, between Drumnadrochit and Urquhart Castle.

ⓘ Getting There & Away

Stagecoach (p221) buses run from Inverness to Drumnadrochit (£3.70, 30 minutes, six to eight daily, five on Sunday) and Urquhart Castle car park (£4, 35 minutes).

Skye

POP 10,000

The Isle of Skye is the biggest of Scotland's islands (linked to the mainland by a bridge at Kyle of Lochalsh), a 50-mile-long smorgasbord of velvet moors, jagged mountains, sparkling lochs and towering sea cliffs. It takes its name from the old Norse *sky-a*, meaning 'cloud island', a Viking reference to the often mist-enshrouded Cuillin Hills, Britain's most spectacular mountain range. The stunning scenery is the main attraction, including the cliffs and pinnacles of the Old Man of Storr, Kilt Rock and the Quiraing, but there are plenty of cosy pubs to retire to when the rainclouds close in.

Portree is the main town, with Broadford a close second; both have banks, ATMs, supermarkets and petrol stations.

⊙ Sights & Activities

Dunvegan Castle CASTLE
(☎ 01470-521206; www.dunvegancastle.com; adult/child £14/9; ⊙ 10am-5.30pm Easter–mid-Oct; P) Skye's most famous historic building, and one of its most popular tourist attractions, Dunvegan Castle is the seat of the chief of Clan MacLeod. In addition to the usual castle stuff – swords, silver and family portraits – there are some interesting artefacts, including the Fairy Flag, a diaphanous silk banner that dates from some time between the 4th and 7th centuries, and Bonnie Prince Charlie's waistcoat and a lock of his hair, donated by Flora MacDonald's granddaughter.

Skye Tours BUS
(☎ 01471-822716; www.skye-tours.co.uk; adult/child £40/30; ⊙ Mon-Sat) Five-hour sightseeing tours of Skye in a minibus, taking in the Old Man of Storr, Kilt Rock and Dunvegan Castle. Tours depart from Kyle of Lochalsh train station at 11.30am, connecting with the 8.55am train from Inverness, and returning to Kyle by 4.45pm in time to catch the return train at 5.13pm.

�Sleeping

Portree, the island's capital, has the largest selection of accommodation, eating places and other services.

★ **Cowshed Boutique Bunkhouse** HOSTEL £
(☎ 07917 536820; www.skyecowshed.co.uk; Uig; dm/tw/pod £20/80/70; P 🛜 🐾) This hostel enjoys a glorious setting overlooking Uig Bay, with superb views from its ultra-stylish lounge. The dorms have custom-built wooden bunks that offer comfort and privacy, while the camping pods (sleeping up to four, but more comfortable with two) have heating and en suite shower rooms; there are even mini 'dog pods' for your canine companions.

Portree Youth Hostel HOSTEL £
(SYHA; ☎ 01478-612231; www.syha.org.uk; Bayfield Rd; dm/tw £26/78; P 🛜) This SYHA hostel (formerly Bayfield Backpackers) was completely renovated in 2015 and offers brightly decorated dorms and private rooms, a stylish lounge with views over the bay, and outdoor seating areas. Its location in the town centre just 100m from the bus stop is ideal.

Ben Tianavaig B&B B&B ££
(☎ 01478-612152; www.ben-tianavaig.co.uk; 5 Bosville Tce; r £80-98; P 🛜) 🚭 A warm welcome awaits from the Irish-Welsh couple who run this appealing B&B bang in the centre of town. All four bedrooms have a view across the harbour to the hill that gives the house its name, and breakfasts include free-range eggs and vegetables grown in the garden. Two-night minimum stay April to October; no credit cards.

Eating

★ Cafe Sia
CAFE, PIZZERIA ££

(☑ 01471-822616; www.cafesia.co.uk; Rathad na h-Atha; mains £7-17; ⊙ 10am-9pm; 🕏 🖶) 🖋 Serving everything from eggs Benedict and cappuccino to cocktails and seafood specials, this appealing cafe specialises in wood-fired pizzas (also available to take away) and superb artisanal coffee. There's also an outdoor deck with great views of the Red Cuillin. Takeaway coffee from 8am.

Scorrybreac
MODERN SCOTTISH ££

(☑ 01478-612069; www.scorrybreac.com; 7 Bosville Tce; 3-course dinner £42; ⊙ 5-9pm Wed-Sun year-round, noon-2pm mid-May–mid-Sep) 🖋 Set in the front rooms of what was once a private house, and with just eight tables, Scorrybreac is snug and intimate, offering fine dining without the faff. Chef Calum Munro (son of Donnie Munro, of Gaelic rock band Runrig fame) sources as much produce as possible from Skye, including foraged herbs and mushrooms, and creates the most exquisite concoctions.

★ Loch Bay
SEAFOOD £££

(☑ 01470-592251; www.lochbay-restaurant.co.uk; Stein, Waternish; 3-course dinner £43.50; ⊙ 12.15-1.45pm Wed-Sun, 6.15-9pm Tue-Sat Apr-early Oct; Ⓟ) 🖋 This cosy farmhouse kitchen of a place, with terracotta tiles and a wood-burning stove, is one of Skye's most romantic restaurants and was awarded a Michelin star in 2018. The menu includes most things that swim in the sea or live in a shell, but there are non-seafood choices too. Best to book ahead.

Three Chimneys
MODERN SCOTTISH £££

(☑ 01470-511258; www.threechimneys.co.uk; Colbost; 3-course lunch/dinner £40/68; ⊙ 12.15-1.45pm Mon-Sat mid-Mar–Oct, plus Sun Easter-Sep, 6.30-9.15pm daily year-round; Ⓟ🕏) 🖋 Halfway between Dunvegan and Waterstein, the Three Chimneys is a superb romantic retreat combining a gourmet restaurant in a candlelit crofter's cottage with sumptuous five-star rooms (double £345) in the modern house next door. Book well in advance, and note that children are not welcome in the restaurant in the evenings.

ℹ Information

Portree Tourist Office (☑ 01478-612992; www.visitscotland.com; Bayfield Rd; ⊙ 9am-6pm Mon-Sat, 10am-4pm Sun Jun-Aug, shorter hours Sep-May; 🕏) The only tourist office on the island, it provides internet access and an accommodation booking service. Ask for the free *Art Skye – Gallery & Studio Trails* booklet.

ℹ Getting There & Away

BOAT

Despite the bridge, there are still a couple of ferry links between Skye and the mainland. Ferries also operate from Uig on Skye to the Outer Hebrides.

The **CalMac** (☑ 0800 066 5000; www.calmac.co.uk) ferry between Mallaig and Armadale (passenger/car £2.90/9.70, 30 minutes, eight daily Monday to Saturday, five to seven on Sunday) is very popular on weekends and in July and August. Book ahead if you're travelling by car.

The **Glenelg-Skye Ferry** (☑ 07881 634726; www.skyeferry.co.uk; car with up to 4 passengers £15; ⊙ Easter–mid-Oct) runs a tiny vessel (six cars only) on the short Kylerhea to Glenelg crossing (five minutes, every 20 minutes). The ferry operates from 10am to 6pm daily (till 7pm June to August).

BUS

There are buses from Glasgow to Portree (£44, seven hours, three daily), and Uig (£44, 7½ hours, two daily) via Crianlarich, Fort William and Kyle of Lochalsh, plus a service from Inverness to Portree (£26.40, 3¼ hours, three daily).

SURVIVAL GUIDE

ℹ Directory A-Z

ACCOMMODATION

Booking your accommodation in advance is recommended, especially in popular holiday areas and on islands (where options are often limited). Summer and school holidays (including half-terms) are particularly busy. Book at least two months ahead for July and August.

B&Bs These small, family-run houses generally provide good value. More luxurious versions are more like boutique hotels.

Hotels British hotels range from half a dozen rooms above a pub to restored country houses and castles, with a commensurate range in rates.

Hostels There's a good choice of both institutional and independent hostels, many housed in rustic and/or historic buildings.

ACTIVITIES

Walking is the most popular outdoor activity in Britain, for locals and visitors alike: firstly, because it opens up some beautiful corners of the country, and secondly, because it can be done virtually on a whim. In fact, compared to hiking and trekking in some other parts of the world, it doesn't take much planning at all.

Good maps and websites include the following:

Ordnance Survey UK's national mapping agency; Explorer series 1:25,000 scale.

Harvey Maps Specially designed for walkers; Superwalker series 1:25,000 scale.

www.walkhighlands.co.uk Superb database for walks of all lengths in Scotland.

www.walkingenglishman.com Short walks in England and Wales.

www.nationaltrail.co.uk Great for specifics on long-distance trails in England and Wales.

www.scotlandsgreattrails.com Long-distance trails in Scotland.

LGBT+ TRAVELLERS

Britain is a generally tolerant place for gays and lesbians. London, Manchester and Brighton have flourishing gay scenes, and in other sizeable cities (even some small towns), you'll find communities not entirely in the closet. That said, you'll still find pockets of homophobic hostility in some areas. Resources include the following:

Diva (www.divamag.co.uk)

Gay Times (www.gaytimes.co.uk)

Switchboard LGBT+ Helpline (0300 330 0630; www.switchboard.lgbt)

MONEY

➜ The currency of Britain is the pound sterling (£). Banknotes come in £5, £10, £20 and £50 denominations, although some shops don't accept £50 notes.

➜ ATMs, often called cash machines, are easy to find in towns and cities.

➜ Most banks and some post offices offer currency exchange.

➜ Visa and MasterCard credit and debit cards are widely accepted in Britain. Nearly everywhere uses a 'Chip and PIN' system (instead of signing).

➜ Smaller businesses may charge a fee for credit-card use, and some take cash or cheque only.

➜ Tipping is not obligatory. A 10% to 15% tip is fine for restaurants, cafes, taxi drivers and pub meals; if you order drinks and food at the bar, there's no need to tip.

OPENING HOURS

Opening hours may vary throughout the year, especially in rural areas where many places have shorter hours or close completely from October or November to March or April.

Banks 9.30am–4pm or 5pm Monday to Friday; some open 9.30am–1pm Saturday

Pubs and bars Noon–11pm Monday to Saturday (many till midnight or 1am Friday and Saturday, especially in Scotland) and 12.30–11pm Sunday

Restaurants Lunch noon–3pm, dinner 6–9pm or 10pm (or later in cities)

Shops 9am–5.30pm (or to 6pm in cities) Monday to Saturday, and often 11am–5pm Sunday; big-city convenience stores open 24/7

PUBLIC HOLIDAYS

Holidays for the whole of Britain:

New Year's Day 1 January (plus 2 January in Scotland)

Easter March/April (Good Friday to Easter Monday inclusive)

May Day First Monday in May

Spring Bank Holiday Last Monday in May

Summer Bank Holiday Last Monday in August

Christmas Day 25 December

Boxing Day 26 December

If a public holiday falls on a weekend, the nearest Monday is usually taken instead. In England and Wales most businesses and banks close on official public holidays (hence the quaint term 'bank holiday'). In Scotland, bank holidays are just for the banks, and many businesses stay open. Many Scottish towns normally have a spring and autumn holiday, but the dates vary.

On public holidays, some small museums and places of interest close, but larger attractions have their busiest times. If a place closes on Sunday, it'll probably be shut on bank holidays as well.

Virtually everything – attractions, shops, banks, offices – closes on Christmas Day, although pubs open at lunchtime. There's usually no public transport on Christmas Day, and a very minimal service on Boxing Day.

SCHOOL HOLIDAYS

Roads get busy and hotel prices go up during school holidays.

Easter holiday Week before and week after Easter.

Summer holiday Third week of July to first week of September.

Christmas holiday Mid-December to first week of January.

There are also three week-long 'half-term' school holidays – usually late February (or early March), late May and late October. These vary between Scotland, England and Wales.

SAFE TRAVEL

Britain is a remarkably safe country, but crime is not unknown – especially in London and other cities.

➜ Watch out for pickpockets and hustlers in crowded areas popular with tourists, such as around Westminster Bridge in London.

➜ When travelling by tube, tram or urban train services at night, choose a carriage containing other people.

➜ Many town centres can be rowdy on Friday and Saturday nights when the pubs and clubs are emptying.

➜ Unlicensed minicabs – a driver with a car earning money on the side – operate in large cities, and are worth avoiding unless you know what you're doing.

TELEPHONE

The UK uses the GSM 900/1800 network, which covers the rest of Europe, Australia and New Zealand, but isn't compatible with the North American GSM 1900. Most modern mobiles can function on both networks, but check before you leave home just in case.

VISAS

Generally not needed for stays of up to six months. You will need to show your passport when arriving and leaving from a UK border point. Visa regulations are always subject to change so it's essential to check with your local British embassy, high commission or consulate before leaving home.

ⓘ Getting There & Away

AIR

Visitors to the UK arriving by air generally do so at one of London's two largest airports, Heathrow and Gatwick, which have a huge range of international flights to pretty much all corners of the globe. International flights also serve the capital's three other airports (Stansted, Luton and London City) and regional hubs such as Manchester, Bristol and Edinburgh.

London Airports

The national carrier is **British Airways** (www.britishairways.com).

The main airports are as follows:

Heathrow (www.heathrowairport.com) Britain's main airport for international flights; often chaotic and crowded. About 15 miles west of central London.

Gatwick (www.gatwickairport.com) Britain's number-two airport, mainly for international flights, 30 miles south of central London.

Stansted (www.stanstedairport.com) About 35 miles northeast of central London, mainly handling charter and budget European flights.

TRAVELINE

Traveline (www.traveline.info) is a very useful information service covering bus, coach, taxi and train services nationwide.

Luton (www.london-luton.co.uk) Some 35 miles north of central London, well known as a holiday-flight airport.

London City (www.londoncityairport.com) A few miles east of central London, specialising in flights to/from European and other UK airports.

LAND
Bus

You can easily get between Britain and other European countries via long-distance bus or coach. The international network **Eurolines** (www.eurolines.com) connects a huge number of destinations; you can buy tickets online via one of the national operators.

Services to/from Britain are operated by **National Express** (www.nationalexpress.com). Sample journeys and times to/from London include Amsterdam (12 hours), Barcelona (24 hours), Dublin (12 hours), and Paris (eight hours).

If you book early, and can be flexible with timings (ie travel when few other people want to), you can get some very good deals, eg between London to Paris or Amsterdam from about £25 one way (although paying £35 to £45 is more usual).

Train

High-speed **Eurostar** (www.eurostar.com) passenger services shuttle at least 10 times daily between London and Paris (2½ hours) or Brussels (two hours). Buy tickets from travel agencies, major train stations or the Eurostar website.

The normal one-way fare between London and Paris/Brussels costs around £154; advance booking and off-peak travel gets cheaper fares, as low as £29 one way.

Drivers use **Eurotunnel** (www.eurotunnel.com). At Folkestone in England or Calais in France, you drive onto a train, get carried through the tunnel and drive off at the other end.

Trains run about four times an hour from 6am to 10pm, then hourly through the night. Loading and unloading takes an hour; the journey lasts 35 minutes.

Book in advance online or pay on the spot. The standard one-way fare for a car and up to nine passengers is between £75 and £100 depending on the time of day; promotional fares often bring it down to £59 or less.

SEA

The main ferry routes between Great Britain and other European countries are as follows:

➜ Dover–Calais (France)

- Dover–Boulogne (France)
- Newhaven–Dieppe (France)
- Liverpool–Dublin (Ireland)
- Holyhead–Dublin (Ireland)
- Fishguard–Rosslare (Ireland)
- Pembroke Dock–Rosslare (Ireland)
- Newcastle–Amsterdam (Netherlands)
- Harwich–Hook of Holland (Netherlands)
- Hull–Rotterdam (Netherlands)
- Hull–Zeebrugge (Belgium)
- Cairnryan–Larne (Northern Ireland)
- Portsmouth–Santander (Spain)
- Portsmouth–Bilbao (Spain)

Book direct with one of the operators listed below, or use the very handy www.directferries. co.uk – a single site covering all sea-ferry routes, plus Eurotunnel.

Brittany Ferries (www.brittany-ferries.com)
DFDS Seaways (www.dfdsseaways.co.uk)
Irish Ferries (www.irishferries.com)
P&O Ferries (www.poferries.com)
Stena Line (www.stenaline.com)

ⓘ Getting Around

Having your own car makes the best use of time and helps reach remote places, but rental, fuel costs and parking can be expensive – so public transport is often the better way to go.

Cheapest but slowest are long-distance buses (called coaches in Britain). Trains are faster but much more expensive.

AIR

If you're really pushed for time, flights on longer routes across Britain (eg London to Inverness) are handy. On some shorter routes (eg London to Edinburgh) trains compare favourably with planes on time, once airport downtime is factored in. On costs, you might get a bargain airfare, but trains can be cheaper if you buy tickets in advance. Some of Britain's domestic airline companies are as follows:

British Airways (www.britishairways.com)
EasyJet (www.easyjet.com)

CONNECTIONS

The quickest way to Europe from Britain is via the Channel Tunnel, which has direct Eurostar rail services from London to Paris and Brussels. Ferries sail from southern England to French ports in a couple of hours; other routes connect eastern England to the Netherlands, Germany and northern Spain, and Ireland from southwest Scotland and Wales.

FlyBe (www.flybe.com)
Loganair (www.loganair.co.uk)
Ryanair (www.ryanair.com)

BUS

If you're on a tight budget, long-distance buses are nearly always the cheapest way to get around, although they're also the slowest – sometimes by a considerable margin. Many towns have separate stations for local buses and long-distance coaches; make sure you go to the right one!

National Express (www.nationalexpress. com) is the main coach operator, with a wide network and frequent services between main centres. North of the border, services tie in with those of **Scottish Citylink** (www.citylink.co.uk), Scotland's leading coach company. Fares vary: they're cheaper if you book in advance and travel at quieter times, and more expensive if you buy your ticket on the spot and it's Friday afternoon. As a guide, a 200-mile trip (eg London to York) will cost £15 to £25 if you book a few days in advance.

Megabus (www.megabus.com) operates a budget coach service between about 30 destinations around the country. Go at a quiet time, book early and your ticket will be very cheap. Book later, for a busy time and... You get the picture.

CAR & MOTORCYCLE

Traffic drives on the left; steering wheels are on the right side of the car. Most rental cars have manual gears (stick shift).

Rental

Compared with many countries (especially the USA), hire rates are expensive in Britain: the smallest cars start at about £130 per week, and it's around £190 upwards per week for a medium car. All rates include insurance and unlimited mileage, and can rise at busy times (or drop at quiet times).

Main players are as follows:

Avis (www.avis.co.uk)
Budget (www.budget.co.uk)
Europcar (www.europcar.co.uk)
Sixt (www.sixt.co.uk)
Thrifty (www.thrifty.co.uk)

Another option is to look online for small local car-hire companies in Britain that can undercut the international franchises. Generally those in cities are cheaper than in rural areas. Using a rental-broker or comparison site such as **UK Car Hire** (www.ukcarhire.net) or **Kayak** (www.kayak. com) can also help find bargains.

Road Rules

A foreign driving licence is valid in Britain for up to 12 months.

Drink-driving is taken very seriously; you're allowed a maximum blood-alcohol level of 80mg/100mL (0.08%) in England and Wales, and 50mg/100mL (0.05%) in Scotland.

Some other important rules:
➡ Drive on the left.
➡ Wear fitted seatbelts in cars.
➡ Wear helmets on motorcycles.
➡ Give way to your right at junctions and round-abouts.
➡ Always use the left lane on motorways and dual carriageways unless overtaking (although so many people ignore this rule, you'd think it didn't exist).
➡ Don't use a mobile phone while driving unless it's fully hands-free (another rule frequently flouted).

TRAIN

About 20 different companies operate train services in Britain, while Network Rail operates track and stations. For some passengers this system can be confusing at first, but information and ticket-buying services are mostly centralised. If you have to change trains, or use two or more train operators, you still buy one ticket – valid for the whole journey. The main railcards and passes are also accepted by all train operators.

Where more than one train operator services the same route, eg York to Edinburgh, a ticket purchased from one company may not be valid on trains run by another. So if you miss the train you originally booked, it's worth checking which later services your ticket will be valid for.

Classes

There are two classes of rail travel: first and standard. First class costs around 50% more than standard fare (up to double at busy periods) and gets you bigger seats, more leg-room and usually a more peaceful business-like atmosphere, plus extras such as complimentary drinks and newspapers. At weekends some train operators offer 'upgrades' to first class for an extra £5 to £25 on top of your standard class fare, payable on the spot.

Your first stop should be **National Rail Enquiries** (www.nationalrail.co.uk), the nationwide time-table and fare information service. Its website advertises special offers and has real-time links to station departure boards and downloadable maps of the rail network.

Tickets & Reservations

For longer journeys, on-the-spot fares are always available, but tickets are much cheaper if bought in advance. The earlier you book, the cheaper it gets. You can also save if you travel off-peak. Advance purchase usually gets a reserved seat too.

SCOTTISH BANKNOTES

Scottish banks issue their own sterling banknotes. They are interchangeable with Bank of England notes, but you'll sometimes run into problems outside Scotland – shops in the south of England may refuse to accept them. They are also harder to exchange once you get outside the UK, though British banks will always exchange them.

Whichever operator you travel with and wherever you buy tickets, these are the three main fare types:

Anytime Buy anytime, travel anytime – usually the most expensive option.

Off-peak Buy ticket any time and travel off-peak (what is off-peak depends on the journey).

Advance Buy ticket in advance and travel only on specific trains – usually the cheapest option.

For an idea of the (substantial) price differences, an Anytime single ticket from London to York will cost £127 or more, an Off-peak around £109, with an Advance around £44 to £55. The cheapest fares are usually nonrefundable, so if you miss your train you'll have to buy a new ticket.

Mobile train tickets are gradually becoming more common across the network, but it's a slow process – for now printed tickets are still the norm.

Train Passes

If you're staying in Britain for a while, passes known as **Railcards** (www.railcard.co.uk) are worth considering:

16-25 Railcard For those aged 16 to 25, or full-time UK students.

Two Together Railcard For two specified people travelling together.

Senior Railcard For anyone over 60.

Family & Friends Railcard Covers up to four adults and four children travelling together.

Railcards cost £30 (valid for one year; available from major stations or online) and give a 33% discount on most train fares, except those already heavily discounted. With the Family card, adults get 33% and children get 60% discounts, so the fee is easily recouped in a couple of journeys.

For country-wide travel, **BritRail** (www.britrail.net) passes are available for visitors from overseas. They must be bought in your country of origin (not in Britain) from a specialist travel agency. They're available in seven different versions (eg England only; Scotland only; all of Britain; UK and Ireland) for periods from four to 30 days.

Bulgaria

POP 7.19 MILLION

Includes →

Why Go?

Soul-stirring mountains, golden beaches and cities that hum with music and art. There's a lot to love about Bulgaria: no wonder the Greeks, Romans, Byzantines and Turks all fought to claim it as their own. Billed as the oldest nation on the continent, Bulgaria is rich with ancient treasure. The mysterious Thracians left behind dazzling hauls of gold and silver, and tombs that can be explored to this day. The Romans built cities of breathtaking scale, the bathhouses, walls and amphitheatres of which sit nonchalantly in the midst of modern cities. Centuries later, Bulgaria still beguiles with its come-hither coastline and fertile valleys laden with vines and roses. Sofia has cool cred to rival any major metropolis, and lively Black Sea resorts teem with modern-day pleasure pilgrims.

Best Places to Eat

→ Rosé (p248)

→ Ethno (p248)

→ Niko'las (p234)

→ Pavaj (p240)

→ Tam's House (p241)

Best Places to Stay

→ Hotel Doro (p248)

→ Canapé Connection (p233)

→ Hostel Old Plovdiv (p239)

→ At Renaissance Square (p239)

→ Hotel Astra (p242)

When to Go
Sofia

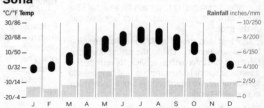

Feb It's still winter and cold, but you can pop your cork at Melnik's Golden Grape Festival.

June Warm weather is ideal for celebrating the harvest at Kazanlâk's Rose Festival.

July–Sep Spend lazy days on the Black Sea beaches and warm nights at Bulgaria's best clubs.

Entering the Country

Travel to Bulgaria does not pose any unusual problems. Sofia has air connections with many European cities, and train and long-haul bus services are frequent. At the time of research, Bulgaria was not a member of the EU's common customs and border area, the Schengen area, so even if you're entering from an EU member state (including Romania), you'll still have to show a passport or valid EU identity card. Note that border and ferry crossings can get crowded, so be sure to allow yourself plenty of time.

ITINERARIES

One Week

Take a full day to hit Sofia (p231) and its main attractions, then take the bus to Veliko Târnovo (p243) for a few days of sightseeing and hiking. For the rest of the week, head to Varna (p245) for some sea and sand, or veer south to the ancient beach towns of Nesebâr (p247) and Sozopol (p249).

Two Weeks

Spend a few extra days in Sofia (p231), adding in a day trip to Rila Monastery (p237), then catch a bus to Plovdiv (p239) to wander the cobbled lanes of the Old Town. From there, take the mountain air in majestic Veliko Târnovo (p243). Make for the coast, with a few nights in Varna (p245) and lively Sozopol (p249).

Essential Food & Drink

Fresh fruit, vegetables, dairy produce and grilled meat form the basis of Bulgarian cuisine, which has been heavily influenced by Greek and Turkish cookery. Tripe features heavily on traditional menus.

Banitsa Flaky cheese pastry, often served fresh and hot.

Beer Zagorka, Kamenitza and Shumensko are the most popular nationwide brands.

Kavarma This 'claypot meal', or meat stew, is normally made with either chicken or pork.

Kebabche Thin, grilled pork sausage, a staple of every *mehana* (tavern) in the country.

Mish-Mash Summer favourite made from tomatoes, capsicum, eggs, feta and spices.

Shishcheta Shish-kebab consisting of chicken or pork on wooden skewers with mushrooms and peppers.

Shkembe chorba Traditional stomach soup is one of the more adventurous highlights of Bulgarian cuisine.

Tarator Delicious chilled cucumber and yoghurt soup, served with garlic, dill and crushed walnuts.

Wine They've been producing wine here since Thracian times and there are some excellent varieties to try.

AT A GLANCE

Area 110,879 sq km

Capital Sofia

Country Code ☑ 359

Currency Lev (lv)

Emergency ☑ 112

Language Bulgarian

Money ATMs are everywhere.

Visas Not required for citizens of the EU, USA, Canada, Australia and New Zealand for stays of less than 90 days.

BULGARIA

Sleeping Price Ranges

The following price ranges refer to a double room with bathroom in high season. Unless otherwise stated, breakfast is included in the price.

€ less than 60 lv

€€ 60–120 lv (to 200 lv in Sofia)

€€€ more than 120 lv (more than 200 lv in Sofia)

Eating Price Ranges

The following price ranges refer to a standard main course. Unless otherwise stated, service charge is included in the price.

€ less than 10 lv

€€ 10–20 lv

€€€ more than 20 lv

Bulgaria Highlights

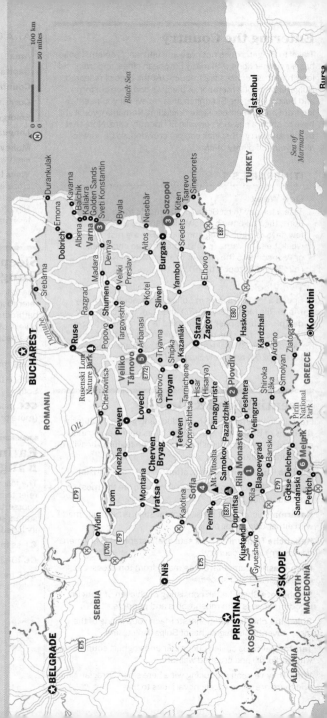

1 Rila Monastery (p237)
Exploring artistic and religious treasures.

2 Plovdiv (p239) Soaking up the city's ancient ambience and revitalised artistic quarter.

3 Sozopol (p249) and Varna (p245) Sun-worshipping or clubbing all night long at Black Sea resorts.

4 Aleksander Nevski Cathedral (p231) Experiencing the majesty of Sofia's neo-Byzantine Orthodox church.

5 Veliko Tărnovo (p243) Visiting the Tsars' medieval stronghold in this monumental, riverside town.

6 Melnik (p238) Sipping a glass or three of Bulgarian vino in this photogenic wine town.

SOFIA СОФИЯ

02 / POP 1.2 MILLION

Bulgaria's pleasingly laid-back capital is often overlooked by visitors heading to the coast or the ski resorts, but they're missing something special. Sofia is no grand metropolis, but it's a modern, youthful city, with a scattering of onion-domed churches, Ottoman mosques and stubborn Red Army monuments that lend an eclectic, exotic feel. Excavation work carried out during construction of the metro unveiled a treasure trove of Roman ruins from nearly 2000 years ago, when the city was called 'Serdica'. Away from the buildings and boulevards, vast parks and manicured gardens offer a welcome respite, and the ski slopes and hiking trails of mighty Mt Vitosha are just a short bus ride from the centre. Home to many of Bulgaria's finest museums, galleries, restaurants and clubs, Sofia may persuade you to stick around and explore further.

Sights

Ploshtad Aleksander Nevski

★ Aleksander Nevski Cathedral CHURCH
(pl Aleksander Nevski; 7am-7pm; Sofiyski Universitet) One of *the* symbols not just of Sofia but of Bulgaria itself, this massive, awe-inspiring church was built between 1882 and 1912 in memory of the 200,000 Russian soldiers who died fighting for Bulgaria's independence during the Russo-Turkish War (1877–78). It is named in honour of a 13th-century Russian warrior-prince.

★ Sveta Sofia Church CHURCH
(02-987 0971; ul Parizh 2; museum adult/child 6/2 lv; church 7am-7pm Mar-Sep, to 5pm Oct-Feb, museum 9am-5pm Tue-Sun; Sofiyski Universitet) Sveta Sofia is one of the capital's oldest churches, and gave the city its name. A subterranean **museum** houses an ancient necropolis, with 56 tombs and the remains of four other churches. Outside are the Tomb of the Unknown Soldier and an eternal flame, and the grave of Ivan Vazov, Bulgaria's most revered writer.

Aleksander Nevski Crypt GALLERY
(Museum of Icons; pl Aleksander Nevski; adult/child 6/3 lv; 10am-5.30pm Tue-Sun; Sofiyski Universitet) Originally built as a final resting place for Bulgarian kings, this crypt now houses Bulgaria's biggest and best collection of icons, stretching back to the 5th century. Enter to the left of the eponymous church's main entrance.

Sofia City Garden & Around

Archaeological Museum MUSEUM
(02-988 2406; www.naim.bg; ul Saborna 2; adult/child 10/2 lv; 10am-6pm daily May-Oct, to 5pm Tue-Sun Nov-Apr; Serdika) Housed in a former mosque built in 1496, this museum displays a wealth of Thracian, Roman and medieval artefacts. Highlights include a mosaic floor from the Church of Sveta Sofia, a 4th-century BCE Thracian gold burial mask, and a magnificent bronze head, thought to represent a Thracian king.

Ancient Serdica Complex RUINS
(pl Nezavisimost; 6am-11pm; Serdika) FREE This remarkable, partly covered excavation site, situated just above the Serdika metro station, displays the remains of the Roman city, Serdica, that once occupied this area. The remains were unearthed from 2010 to 2012 during construction of the metro. There are fragments of eight streets, an early Christian basilica, baths and houses dating from the 4th to 6th centuries. Plenty of signage in English.

Sveti Georgi Rotunda CHURCH
(Church of St George; 02-980 9216; www.svgeorgi-rotonda.com; bul Dondukov 2; services daily 8am, 9am & 5pm; Serdika) Built in the 4th century CE, this tiny red-brick church is Sofia's oldest preserved building. The murals inside were painted between the 10th and 14th centuries. It's a busy, working church, but visitors are welcome. To find the church, enter through an opening on ul Sâborna.

Sveta Petka Samardzhiiska Church CHURCH
(bul Maria Luisa 2; 9am-5pm; Serdika) This tiny church, located in the centre of the Serdika metro complex, was built during the early years of Ottoman rule (late 14th century), which explains its sunken profile and inconspicuous exterior. Inside are some 16th-century murals. It's rumoured that the Bulgarian national hero Vasil Levski is buried here.

Museum of Socialist Art MUSEUM
(02-902 1862; www.nationalgallery.bg; ul Lachezar Stanchev 7, Iztok; 6 lv; 10am-5.30pm Tue-Sun; GM Dimitrov) If you wondered where all those unwanted statues of Lenin ended up, you'll find some here, along with the red star from atop Sofia's Party House. There's a gallery of paintings, with catchy titles such as *Youth Meeting at Kilifarevo Village to Send Worker-Peasant Delegation to the USSR,* and stirring old propaganda films are shown.

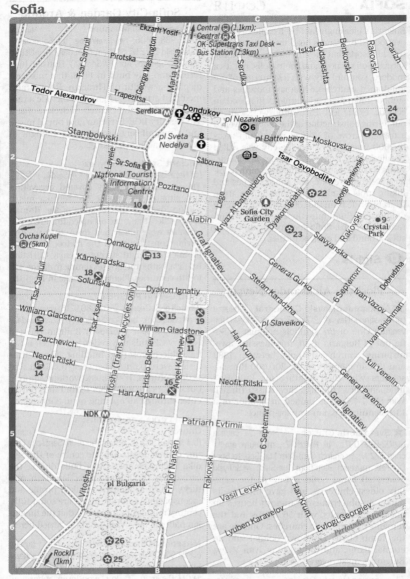

BULGARIA SOFIA

Sofia City Garden PARK

(M Serdika) This small, central park, bounded on its northern end by ul Tsar Osvoboditel, is favoured by Sofia's chess-playing pensioners. It's home to the National Theatre (p235), and until 1999 held the mausoleum of Bulgaria's first communist ruler, Georgi Dimitrov.

Tours

Free Sofia Tour WALKING

(☎ 0988920461; www.freesofiatour.com; cnr ul Alabin & bul Vitosha; ⊗ 10am, 11am & 6pm Apr-Oct, 11am, 2pm & 6pm Nov-Mar; M Serdika) FREE Explore Sofia's sights in the company of friendly and enthusiastic English-speaking

BULGARIA SOFIA

Balkan Bites   FOOD & DRINK
(☏0877613992; www.balkanbites.bg; by donation; ☉tours 2pm; Ⓜ Sofiyski Universitet, ☐9) This two-hour guided walking tour focuses on food and includes tastings and drinks at restaurants around town. The basic tour is free but a donation is expected. Walks depart at 2pm from the statue of Stefan Stambolov in Crystal Park.

⊨ Sleeping

★**Canapé Connection**   GUESTHOUSE **€€**
(☏0896893278; www.canapeconnection.com; ul William Gladstone 12a; s/d from 60/80 lv; ☎; ☐1, 6, 7) Formerly a hostel, Canapé reinvented itself as a guesthouse in 2016, retaining its same attention to cleanliness and a refreshingly simple, rustic design. The six rooms are divided into singles and doubles, with a larger

young locals on this two-hour guided walk. No reservation is needed; just show up outside the Palace of Justice on the corner of ul Alabin and bul Vitosha a few minutes before the tour. Check the website for other themed, paid tours, including on culture, communism and alternative Sofia.

room upstairs to accommodate families. There's a quiet garden outside to relax in.

Art Hostel
HOSTEL €€

(☑02-987 0545; www.art-hostel.com; ul Angel Kânchev 21a; dm/s/d from 22/50/64 lv; @🛜; 🖵12) This bohemian hostel stands out from the crowd with its summertime art exhibitions, live music, dance performances and more. Dorms are appropriately arty and bright; private rooms are airy and very welcoming. There's a great basement bar and a peaceful little garden at the back.

Hotel Niky
HOTEL €€

(☑02-952 3058; www.hotel-niky.com; ul Neofit Rilski 16; r/ste from 150/200 lv; P🌀❄🛜; MNDK, 🖵1) The hotel's popularity has allowed the owners to hike prices in recent years, though the excellent city-centre location, comfortable rooms and gleaming bathrooms make the place still a decent value. The smart suites come with kitchenettes. Frequently full; be sure to book ahead.

Hotel Les Fleurs
BOUTIQUE HOTEL €€€

(☑02-810 0800; www.lesfleurshotel.com; bul Vitosha 21; r from 250 lv; P🌀❄🛜; MSerdika, 🖵10) You can hardly miss this very central hotel with gigantic blooms on its facade. The flowery motif is continued in the large, carefully styled rooms, and there's a very good restaurant on site. The location, right at the start of the pedestrian-only stretch of bul Vitosha, is ideal.

✖ Eating

Made In Home
INTERNATIONAL €€

(☑0876884014; ul Angel Kânchev 30a; mains 14-23 lv; ⊙noon-9pm Sun, to 10pm Mon, to 10.30pm Tue-Thur, to 11pm Fri & Sat; 🛜✦; MNDK) Sofia's popular entrant into the worldwide, locally sourced, slow-food trend (the name refers to the fact that all items are made in-house). The cooking is eclectic, with dollops of Middle Eastern (eg hummus) and Turkish items, as well as ample vegetarian and vegan offerings. The playfully rustic interior feels straight out of a Winnie-the-Pooh book. Reservations essential.

Boho
INTERNATIONAL €€

(☑0896451458; www.facebook.com/boho.sofia; ul Hristo Belchev 29; mains 9-16 lv; ⊙noon-11pm; 🛜) Contemporary eclectic favorites like burgers and sweet-potato fries, hummus, pulled pork, avocado toast, and pancakes -- all reasonably priced and served in a bright, stylish locale. There's a huge garden out back for nice

weather. A top in-town choice for brunch, but it's worth reserving at least a day in advance.

Manastirska Magernitsa
BULGARIAN €€

(☑02-980 3883; www.magernitsa.com; ul Han Asparuh 67; mains 10-18 lv; ⊙11-2am; MNDK) This traditional *mehana* (tavern) is among the best places in Sofia to sample authentic Bulgarian cuisine. The enormous menu features recipes collected from monasteries across the country, with dishes such as 'drunken rabbit' stewed in wine, as well as salads, fish, pork and game options. Portions are generous and the service attentive. Dine in the garden in nice weather.

MoMa Bulgarian Food & Wine
BULGARIAN €€

(☑0885622 20; www.moma-restaurant.com; ul Solunska 28; mains 10-24 lv; ⊙11am-10pm; 🛜✦; MSerdika) An update on the traditional *mehana* (taverna), serving typical Bulgarian foods such as grilled meats and meatballs, but in a more modern and understated interior. The result is one of the best nights out in town. Start off with a shot of *rakia* (Bulgarian brandy) and a salad, and move on to the ample main courses. Book ahead.

★Niko'las
BULGARIAN €€€

(☑0876888471; www.nikolas.bg; pl Rayko Daskalov 3; mains 21-28 lv, 5-/7-course tasting menu 60/80 lv; ⊙noon-11pm Mon-Sat; 🛜; MSerdika) The menu boasts a 'taste of the Balkans with an Asian twist', which undersells the amazing food on offer here. Expect the likes of smoked trout topped with beetroot, goat cheese and poached pear, or grilled seabass with Bulgarian caviar. The open kitchen allows direct interaction with the chefs. The wood-clad walls are warm without being folksy. Reservations recommended.

🍷 Drinking & Nightlife

There's a seemingly inexhaustible supply of watering holes all over Sofia. The cheapest places to grab a beer are the kiosks in the city's parks; if you're looking for a more sophisticated ambience, the city centre has plenty of swish bars.

One More Bar
BAR

(☑0882539592; www.facebook.com/OneMoreBar; ul Shishman 12; ⊙8.30am-2am; 🛜; MSofiyski Universitet) Inside a gorgeous old house, this shabby-chic hot spot wouldn't be out of place in Melbourne or Manhattan; an extensive cocktail list, a delightful summer garden and jazzy background music add to its cosmopolitan appeal.

Raketa Rakia Bar
BAR

(📞 02-444 6111; www.facebook.com/RaketaRakia Bar; ul Yanko Sakazov 17; ⏱11am-midnight; 📶; 🚇11, Ⓜ Sofiyski Universitet) Unsurprisingly, this rakish communist-era retro bar has a huge selection of *rakia* on hand; before you start working your way down the list, line your stomach with meat-and-cream-heavy snacks and meals. Reservations essential.

DaDa Cultural Bar
BAR

(📞 0877062455; www.dadaculturalbar.com; ul Georgi Benkovski 10; ⏱5pm-midnight Mon-Thu, to 2am Fri & Sat, to 10pm Sun; 📶; Ⓜ Serdika, 🚌20, 22) A local institution, DaDa bar is far more than a place to drink. The mission here is culture, and expect to find live music, art installations, readings or happenings. The website usually has an up-to-date program. Friendly staff and a welcoming vibe.

☆ Entertainment

If you read Bulgarian, or at least can decipher some Cyrillic, the magazine *Programata* is the most comprehensive source of entertainment listings; otherwise check out its excellent English-language website, www.programata.bg.

You can search for events and book tickets online at www.eventim.bg or www.ticketpro.bg.

Live Music

Sofia Live Club
LIVE MUSIC

(📞 0886661045; www.sofialiveclub.com; pl Bulgaria 1; ⏱8pm-7am; Ⓜ NDK) This slick venue, located in the National Palace of Culture (NDK), is the city's largest live-music club. All swished up in cabaret style, it hosts local and international jazz, alternative, world-music and rock acts.

Bulgaria Hall
CLASSICAL MUSIC

(📞 02-988 3195; www.sofiaphilharmonic.com; ul Aksakov 1; ⏱box office 9.30am-2.30pm & 3pm-7.30pm Mon-Fri, from 11am Sat & Sun; Ⓜ Serdika) Home of the excellent Sofia Philharmonic Orchestra.

RockIT
LIVE MUSIC

(📞 0888666991; www.facebook.com/bar.RockIT; bul Petko Karavelov 5; ⏱8pm-7am; 🚌1, 6) If you're into rock and metal, get your horns up here. Dance parties are best on Friday and Saturday nights, while the scene is mellower during the week. In addition to metal music and beers, the kitchen pushes out decent burgers and bar food.

Performing Arts

National Palace of Culture
CONCERT VENUE

(NDK; 📞 02-916 6300; www.ndk.bg; pl Bulgaria; ⏱ticket office 10am-8pm; 📶; Ⓜ NDK) The 'NDK' (as it's usually called) has 15 halls and is the country's largest cultural complex. It maintains a regular program of events throughout the year, including film screenings, trade shows and big-name international music acts.

National Opera House
OPERA

(📞 tickets 02-987 7011; www.operasofia.bg; bul Dondukov 30; ⏱box office 9am-2pm & 2.30-7pm Mon-Fri, 11am-7pm Sat, 11am-4pm Sun; 🚌20, 22) Opened in 1953, this monumental edifice is the venue for classical opera and ballet performances, as well as special concerts for children. Enter from ul Vrabcha.

Ivan Vazov National Theatre
THEATRE

(📞 02-811 9219; www.nationaltheatre.bg; ul Dyakon Ignatiy 5; ⏱ticket office 9.30am-7.30pm Mon-Fri, from 11.30am Sat & Sun; Ⓜ Serdika) One of Sofia's most elegant buildings, the Viennese-style National Theatre opened in 1907 and is the city's main stage for Bulgarian drama.

ℹ Information

National Tourist Information Centre (📞 02-933 5826; www.tourism.government.bg; pl Sveta Nedelya 1; ⏱9am-5.30pm Mon-Fri; Ⓜ Serdika) Helpful, English-speaking staff and glossy brochures for destinations around Bulgaria. The office is a little hard to find, hidden near a small side street, a few steps southwest of pl Sveta Nedelya.

Sofia Tourist Information Centre (📞 02-491 8344; www.visitsofia.bg; Sofiyski Universitet metro underpass; ⏱9.30am-6pm Mon-Fri; Ⓜ Sofiyski Universitet) Lots of free leaflets and maps, and helpful English-speaking staff.

Pirogov Hospital (📞 emergency 02-915 4411; www.pirogov.eu; bul General Totleben 21; 🚌4, 5) Sofia's main public hospital for emergencies.

ℹ Getting There & Away

AIR

Sofia Airport (📞 info 24hr 02-937 2211; www.sofia-airport.bg; off bul Brussels; 📶; 🚌84, Ⓜ Sofia Airport), the city's and country's main air gateway, is located 10km east of the centre. The airport has two terminals (1 and 2). Most flights use the more modern Terminal 2, but a few budget carriers fly in and out of Terminal 1. Both terminals have basic services, ATMs and OK-Supertrans Taxi (p236) desks.

The only domestic flights within Bulgaria are between Sofia and the Black Sea coast. **Bulgaria Air** (📞 02-402 0400; www.air.bg; ul Ivan Vazov

MT VITOSHA & BOYANA

The Mt Vitosha range, 23km long and 13km wide, lies just south of Sofia; it's sometimes referred to as the 'lungs of Sofia' for the refreshing breezes it deflects onto the capital. The mountain is part of the 227-sq-km **Vitosha Nature Park** (www.park-vitosha. org), the oldest of its kind in Bulgaria (created in 1934). The main activities are hiking in summer and skiing in winter (mid-December to April). All of the park's areas have good hiking; Aleko, the country's highest ski resort, is best for skiing.

On weekends chairlifts, starting around 4km from the village of **Dragalevtsi**, run all year up to Goli Vrâh (1837m); take bus 66 or 93. Another option is the six-person gondola at Simeonovo, reachable by buses 122 or 123 (also weekends only).

A trip out here could be combined with a visit to **Boyana**, home to the fabulous, Unesco-listed **Boyana Church** (☑02-959 0939; www.boyanachurch.org; ul Boyansko Ezero 3, Boyana; adult/child 10/2 lv, combined ticket with National Historical Museum 12 lv, guide 10 lv; ⊙9.30am-5.30pm Apr-Oct, 9am-5pm Nov-Mar; ⬜64, 107), located en route between central Sofia and the mountains. This tiny church is adorned with 90 colourful murals dating to the 13th century, considered among the most important examples of medieval Bulgarian art. A combined ticket includes entry to both the church and the **National Museum of History** (☑02-955 4280; www.historymuseum.org/en; ul Vitoshko Lale 16, Boyana; adult/child 10/1 lv, combined ticket with Boyana Church 12 lv, guided tours in English 30 lv; ⊙9.30am-6pm Apr-Oct, 9am-5.30pm Nov-Mar; ⬜63, 111, ⬜2), 2km away. Take bus 64 or 107 to reach Boyana.

2; ⊙9.30am-noon & 12.30-5.30pm Mon-Fri; Ⓜ Serdika) flies daily to Varna, with two or three daily flights running between July and September. Bulgaria Air also flies between the capital and Burgas.

BUS

Sofia's **Central Bus Station** (Tsentralna Avtogara; ☑info 090063099; www.bgrazpisanie. com; bul Maria Luisa 100; ⊙24hr; 🖥; Ⓜ Central Railway Station) is located beside the train station and accessed via the same metro stop. It handles services to most big towns in Bulgaria as well as international destinations. There are dozens of counters for individual private companies, as well as an information desk and an **OK-Supertrans taxi desk** (☑02-973 2121; www.oktaxi.net; Centrailt Bus Station; ⊙6am-10pm; Ⓜ Central Railway Station).

Departures are less frequent between November and April. Sample destinations and fares include Burgas (32 lv, eight hours, eight daily), Kazanlâk (16 lv, 3½ hours, five daily), Nesebâr (37 lv, seven hours, five daily), Plovdiv (14 lv, 2½ hours, hourly), Sozopol (32 lv, seven hours, seven daily), Varna (33 lv, eight hours, every 45 minutes) and Veliko Târnovo (22 lv, four hours, hourly).

TRAIN

Sofia's **Central Train Station** (☑info 0700 10 200, international services 02-931 0972, tickets 0884 193 758; www.bdz.bg; bul Maria Luisa 102a; ⊙ticket office 7.30am-7pm; Ⓜ Central Railway Station) is the city's and country's main rail gateway. The station itself is a massive, cheerless modern structure that's been extensively renovated, but which feels empty

and lacks many basic services. It's located in an isolated part of town about 1km north of the centre, though it's the terminus of a metro line and easy to reach. It's 100m (a five-minute walk) from the Central Bus Station.

Same-day tickets are sold at counters on the ground floor, while advance tickets are sold in the gloomy basement, accessed via an unsigned flight of stairs near some snack bars. Counters are open 24 hours, but normally only a few are staffed and queues are long, so don't turn up at the last moment to purchase your ticket, and allow some extra time to work out the confusing system of platforms (indicated with Roman numerals) and tracks.

Sample destinations and fares include Burgas (26 lv, seven hours, six daily), Plovdiv (10 lv, three hours, several daily) and Varna (39 lv, eight hours, six daily).

❶ Getting Around

TO/FROM THE AIRPORT

Sofia's metro connects Terminal 2 to the centre (Serdika station) in around 30 minutes. Buy tickets in the station, which is located just outside the terminal exit. Bus 84 also shuttles between the centre and both terminals. Buy tickets (1.60 lv, plus an extra fare for large luggage) from the driver.

A taxi to the centre will cost anywhere from 12 lv to 16 lv. Prebook your taxi at the **OK-Supertrans Taxi** (☑02-973 2121; www.oktaxi.net; 0.79/0.90 lv per km day/night) counter. They will give you a slip of paper with the three-digit code of your cab. The driver will be waiting outside.

CAR & MOTORCYCLE

Sofia's public transport is excellent and traffic can be heavy, so there's no need to drive a private or rented car in Sofia. If you wish to explore further afield, however, a car might come in handy. The **Union of Bulgarian Motorists** (02-935 7935, road assistance 02-91 146; www.uab.org) provides emergency roadside service.

PUBLIC TRANSPORT

Sofia has a comprehensive public transport system based on trams, buses, trolleybuses and underground metro. Public transport generally runs from 5.30am to around 11pm every day. The **Sofia Urban Mobility Centre** (info 070013233; www.sofiatraffic.bg) maintains a helpful website with fares and an updated transport map. Attractions in the centre are normally located within easy walking distance, and you're not likely to need the tram or trolley in most instances.

Sofia's shiny metro links the city centre to both Sofia Airport and the central train and bus stations. It's divided into two lines, with the lines crossing at central Serdika station. Other helpful stations include NDK, at the southern end of bul Vitosha, and Sofiyski Universitet, close to Sofia University. Tickets cost 1.60 lv, but cannot be used on other forms of public transport. Buy tickets at windows and ticket machines located in the stations.

Tickets for trams, buses and trolleybuses cost 1.60 lv each and can be purchased at kiosks near stops or from on-board ticket machines. Consider buying a day pass (4 lv) to save the hassle of buying individual tickets.

TAXI

Taxis are an affordable alternative to public transport. By law, taxis must use meters, but those that wait around the airport, luxury hotels and within 100m of pl Sveta Nedelya may try to negotiate an unmetered fare – which, of course, will be considerably more than the metered fare. All official taxis are yellow, have fares per kilometre displayed in the window, and have obvious taxi signs (in English or Bulgarian) on top. The standard fare is 0.79 lv per minute during the day, 0.90 lv per minute at night. Never accept a lift in a private, unlicensed vehicle.

SOUTHERN BULGARIA

Some of Bulgaria's most precious treasures are scattered in the towns, villages and forests of the stunning south. The must-visit medieval Rila Monastery is nestled in the deep forest but easily reached by bus; tiny Melnik is awash in ancient wine; and the cobbled streets of Plovdiv, Bulgaria's second city, are lined with timeless reminders of civilisations come and gone.

The region is a scenic and craggy one; the **Rila Mountains** (www.rilanationalpark.bg) are just south of Sofia, the **Pirin Mountains** (www.pirin-np.com) rise towards the Greek border, and the **Rodopi Mountains** loom to the east and south of Plovdiv. There's great hiking to be had, and the south is also home to three of Bulgaria's most popular ski resorts: Borovets, Bansko and Pamporovo; see www.bulgariaski.com for information.

Rila Monastery
Рилски Манастир

Rising out of a forested valley in the Rila Mountains, 120km south of Sofia, Bulgaria's most famous monastery has been a spiritual centre for more than 1000 years. Rila Monastery's fortress-like complex engulfs 8800 sq m, and within its stone walls you'll find remarkably colourful architecture and religious art. Visitors can't fail to be struck by its elegant colonnades, archways striped in black, red and white, and the bright yellow domes of its main church, beneath which dance apocalyptic frescoes. Most travellers visit Rila Monastery on a day trip, but you can stay at or near the monastery to experience its tranquillity after the tour buses leave, or explore the hiking trails that begin here.

The monastery was founded in 927 CE and, inspired by the powerful spiritual influence of hermit monk Ivan Rilski, the monastery complex was heavily restored in 1469 after raids. It became a stronghold of Bulgarian culture and language during Ottoman rule. Set in a magnificent forested valley, the monastery is famous for its mural-plastered **Church of Rozhdestvo Bogorodichno** (Church of the Nativity; Rila Monastery; 7am-8pm) dating from the 1830s. The attached **museum** (5 lv; 8.30am-4.30pm) is home to the astonishing **Rafail's Cross**, an early-19th-century double-sided crucifix, with biblical scenes painstakingly carved in miniature. The monastery compound is open from 6am to 10pm. Visitors should dress modestly.

You can stay in simple **rooms** (0896872010; www.rilamonastery.pmg-blg.com; r 30-60 lv) at the monastery or, for something slightly more upmarket, try **Gorski Kut** (0888710348, 07054-2170; www.gorski-kut.eu; d/tr/ste 55/65/80 lv;), 5km west. Tour buses such as **Rila Monastery Bus**

(☎02-489 0885; www.rilamonasterybus.com; adult/child 60/50 lv) are a popular option for a day trip from Sofia. By public transport, one daily morning bus (11 lv, 2½ hours) goes from Sofia's Ovcha Kupel (Zapad) bus station, returning in the afternoon.

Melnik Мелник

☎07437 / POP 390

Steep sandstone pyramids form a magnificent backdrop in tiny Melnik, 20km north of the Bulgaria–Greece border. These natural rock formations, some 100m in height, resemble wizard hats and mushrooms, and they gave the village its name (the Old Slavonic word *mel* means 'sandy chalk').

But it's a 600-year-old wine culture that has made Melnik famous, and the village's wonderfully restored National Revival architecture looks all the better after a glass or two of the town's signature 'Melnik 55' red. Seeing the village only requires a day, even with an earnest ramble around its many ruins, though an overnight stop is best to soak up its peaceful charms after the tour buses leave.

The major sights here, unsurprisingly, are wineries. Melnik's wines, celebrated for more than 600 years, include the signature dark red, Shiroka Melnishka Loza; it was a favourite tipple of Winston Churchill. Shops and stands dot Melnik's cobblestone paths; better yet, learn the history and tools of Melnik's winemaking trade at the **Museum of Wine** (☎0878661930; www.facebook.com/Muzeinavinoto; Melnik 91; 5 lv; ⏲10am-7pm).

Kordopulov House MUSEUM

(☎0877576120; www.kordopulova-house.com; 3.50 lv; ⏲9.30am-6.30pm Apr-Sep, to 4pm Oct-Mar) Bulgaria's largest Revival-era building, this whitewashed and wooden mansion beams down from a cliff face at the eastern end of Melnik's main road. Dating to 1754, the four-storey mansion was formerly the home of a prestigious wine merchant family. Its naturally cool rooms steep visitors in luxurious period flavour, from floral stained-glass windows to Oriental-style fireplaces and a sauna. It's located at the top of a hill at the far eastern end of the town.

Golden Grapes Festival WINE

(Zlaten Grozd; ⏲2nd weekend Feb) It's hardly Bacchanalian – this is small-town Bulgaria, after all – but this annual knees-up gathers local wine producers to showcase their wares and tempt tourists with wine tastings, all set to a backdrop of singing competitions and other folkish entertainment. It's usually on the second weekend of February; ask at the tourist office for details.

★**Hotel Bolyarka** HOTEL €€

(☎07437-2383; www.melnikhotels.com; Melnik 34; s/d/apt 50/60/130 lv; P ❄ @ ᯤ) The right blend of old-world nostalgia and modern comfort has made this one of Melnik's favourite hotels. The Bolyarka has elegant rooms, a snug lobby bar, a Finnish-style sauna and one of Melnik's best restaurants. For a touch of added charm, reserve a deluxe apartment (130 lv) with fireplace.

Hotel Melnik HOTEL €€

(☎0879131459, 07437-2272; www.hotelmelnik.com; ul Vardar 2; s/d/apt 40/60/120 lv; P ❄ ᯤ) This pleasant hotel is shaded by fig and cherry trees, and peeps down over Melnik's main road. White-walled rooms with simple furnishings don't quite match the old-world reception and the *mehana* (tavern) with a bird's-eye view. But it's great value and the location – up a cobbled lane, just on the right as you enter the village – is very convenient.

★**Mehana Chavkova Kâshta** BULGARIAN €€

(☎0893505090; www.themelnikhouse.com; 8-15 lv) Sit beneath 500-year-old trees and watch Melnik meander past at this superb spot. Like many places in town, grilled meats and Bulgarian dishes are specialities (try the *satch*, a sizzling flat pan of meat and vegetables); the atmosphere and friendly service give it an extra nudge above the rest. It's 200m from the bus stop, on the left side along the main road.

Information

Melnik Tourist Information Centre (www.sandanskicrossborder.com; Obshtina Building; ⏲9am-5pm) Located behind the bus stop, on the *obshtina* (municipality) building's upper floor, this centre advises on accommodation and local activities, though opening times can be spotty (especially outside summer). Bus and train timetables are posted outside.

Getting There & Away

Direct buses connect Melnik with Sofia (18 lv, 4½ hours, one daily) and Blagoevgrad (8 lv, two hours, two daily). Two daily minibuses go from Sandanski to Melnik, continuing to Rozhen, though there may be insufficient seats if local shoppers are out in force.

By train, the closest station is Damyanitsa, 12km west.

Plovdiv   Пловдив

☑ 032 / POP 343,420

With an easy grace, Plovdiv mingles invigorating nightlife among millennia-old ruins. Like Rome, Plovdiv straddles seven hills; but as Europe's oldest continuously inhabited city, it's far more ancient. It is best loved for its romantic old town, packed with colourful and creaky 19th-century mansions that are now house-museums, galleries and guesthouses.

But cobblestoned lanes and National Revival–era nostalgia are only part of the story. Bulgaria's cosmopolitan second city has always been hot on the heels of Sofia and renovations in the Kapana creative quarter and Tsar Simeon Gardens have given the city new confidence. Music and art festivals draw increasing crowds, giving Plovdiv an edge. Once an amiable waystation between Bulgaria and Greece or Turkey, the city has flowered into a destination in its own right – and one that should be on any itinerary through central Bulgaria.

◉ Sights

Most of Plovdiv's main sights are in and around the Old Town. Its meandering cobblestone streets, overflowing with atmospheric house museums, art galleries, antique stores, are also home to welcoming nooks for eating, drinking and people-watching.

★ Roman Amphitheatre   HISTORIC SITE

(Ancient Theatre of Philippopolis; ☑ 032-622 209; www.oldplovdiv.com; ul Hemus; adult/student 5/2 lv; ☺ 9am-6pm) Plovdiv's magnificent 2nd-century CE amphitheatre, built during the reign of Emperor Trajan, was uncovered during a freak landslide in 1972. It once held about 7000 spectators. Now largely restored, it's one of Bulgaria's most magical venues, once again hosting large-scale special events and concerts. Visitors can admire the amphitheatre for free from several look-outs along ul Hemus, or pay admission for a scarper around.

Balabanov House   MUSEUM

(☑ 032-622 209; www.oldplovdiv.com; ul K Stoilov 57; adult/child 5/2 lv; ☺ 9am-6pm Apr-Oct, to 5.30pm Nov-Mar) One of Plovdiv's most beautiful Bulgarian National Revival–era mansions, Balabanov House is an enjoyable way to experience old town nostalgia as well as contemporary art. The house was faithfully reconstructed in 19th-century style during the 1970s. The lower floor has an impressive collection of paintings by local artists, while upper rooms are decorated with antiques and elaborately carved ceilings.

Ethnographical Museum   MUSEUM

(☑ 032-625 654; www.ethnograph.info; ul Dr Chomakov 2; adult/student 6/2 lv; ☺ 9am-6pm Tue-Sun May-Oct, to 5pm Nov-Apr) Even if you don't have time to step inside, it would be criminal to leave Plovdiv's old town without glancing into the courtyard of this stunning National Revival–era building. Well-manicured flower gardens surround a navy-blue mansion ornamented with golden filigree and topped with a distinctive peaked roof. There is more to admire inside, especially the upper floor's sunshine-yellow walls and carved wooden ceiling hovering above displays of regional costumes.

⛏ Sleeping

Hikers Hostel   HOSTEL €

(☑ 0896764854; www.hikers-hostel.org; ul Săborna 53; 14-/8-bed dm 18/20 lv; @ 🛜) In a mellow Old Town location, Hikers has wood-floored dorms and standard hostel perks such as a laundry and a shared kitchen. Bonuses such as a garden lounge, hammocks and mega-friendly staff make it a worthy option. Staff can help organise excursions to Bachkovo Monastery (southern mountains), Buzludzha Monument (central mountains) and more. Off-site private rooms (from 50 lv) are available in the Kapana area.

★ Hostel Old Plovdiv   HOSTEL €€

(☑ 032-260 925; www.hosteloldplovdiv.com; ul Chetvarti Yanuari 3; dm/s/d/tr/q 22/58/78/98/118 lv; 🅿 🛜) This marvellous old building (1868) is more akin to a boutique hotel than a hostel. Remarkably restored by charismatic owner Hristo Giulev and his wife, this genial place in the middle of the Old Town is all about old-world charm. Every room features hand-picked antiques (from the decor to the beds themselves), and the courtyard is desperately romantic.

At Renaissance Square   BOUTIQUE HOTEL €€€

(☑ 032-266 966; www.atrenaissancesq.com; pl Vâzhrazhdane 1; s/d from 135/155 lv; 🅿 ❄ @ 🛜) Recreating National Revival–era grandeur is a labour of love at this charming little hotel, between the old town and Plovdiv's shopping streets. Its five rooms are individually decorated with handsome wood floors, billowy drapes, and floral wall and ceiling

Old Plovdiv

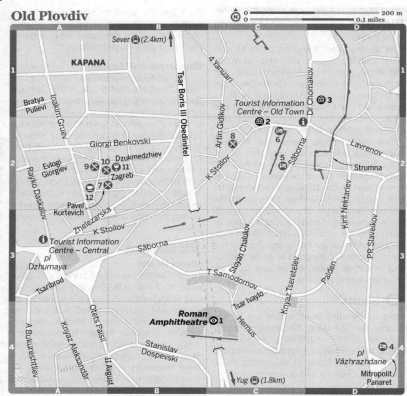

Old Plovdiv

◎ Top Sights
1 Roman Amphitheatre	C4

◎ Sights
2 Balabanov House	C2
3 Ethnographical Museum	D1

🛏 Sleeping
4 At Renaissance Square	D4
5 Hikers Hostel	C2
6 Hostel Old Plovdiv	C2

✕ Eating
7 Green Library	A2
8 Hebros Restaurant	C2
9 Pavaj	A2
10 Tam's House	A2

🍸 Drinking & Nightlife
11 Kotka i Mishka	B2
12 Monkey House	A2

paintings. The friendly, English-speaking owner is a font of local knowledge and extends the warmest of welcomes.

✕ Eating & Drinking

Green Library   VEGAN €
(☎ 0894796657; www.facebook.com/GoGreen.Enjoy Life; ul Pavel Kurtevich 1; mains 5-8 lv; ⊙ 9am-7pm Mon-Sat, 10am-6pm Sun; 🤝🍴) You can't miss the screaming bright green facade of Kapana's 'Green Library', not a repository of books but rather of healthy foods, smoothies, sandwiches, cakes and breads. Eat in, take away, or simply enjoy a vegan chocolate-cherry cake and coffee on the pavement terrace.

★ Pavaj   BULGARIAN €€
(☎ 0878111876; www.facebook.com/pavaj.plovdiv; ul Zlatarska 7; mains 10-15 lv; ⊙ noon-11pm Tue-

MYSTERIES OF THRACE

Plovdiv makes an excellent base for half-day trips to the windblown ruins and spiritual sights of Bulgarian Thrace. Magnificent **Bachkovo Monastery** (☑ 03327-2277; www. bachkovskimanastir.com; Bachkovo; monastery free, refectory 6 lv, museum 2 lv, ossuary 6 lv; ⊙ 7am-8pm Jun-Sep, to 7pm Oct-May), founded in 1083, is about 30km south of Plovdiv. Its church is decorated with 1850s frescoes by renowned artist Zahari Zograf and houses a much-cherished icon of the Virgin Mary. Take any bus to Smolyan from Plovdiv's Rodopi bus station, disembark at the turn-off about 1.2km south of Bachkovo village and walk about 500m uphill.

Asen's Fortress (Assenovgrad; adult/student 4/2 lv; ⊙ 9am-6pm Wed-Sun Apr-Oct, to 5pm Nov-Mar), 19km southeast of Plovdiv, squats precariously on the edge of a cliff. Over the centuries, Roman, Byzantine and Ottoman rulers admired its impenetrable position so much that they continued to build and rebuild, adding chapels and thickening its walls to a battering-ram-proof 3m. Taxis from Plovdiv will charge about 40 lv for a return trip to the fortress; better yet, negotiate for a driver to take you to both the fortress and Bachkovo Monastery.

Sun) This tiny hole-in-the-wall is one of Kapana's most happening restaurants. The formula for success follows can't-miss international trends like seasonal, farm-fresh ingredients and local favorites like sausages, meatballs and baked lamb given a lighter, more modern gloss. The wine list is superb. The space is cramped and you'll have to book in advance or turn up at odd hours.

Tam's House INTERNATIONAL €€
(☑ 0887242727; www.facebook.com/TamssHouse; ul Zagreb 4; mains 12-15 lv; ⊙ 11am-11pm) This labour of love fuses Bulgarian and South American cuisines by way of California. Expect a little of everything: steaks, burgers, tapas, and pilafs, prepared with care and given appealing, minimalist platings. Finish off with Tam's star attraction: a cheesecake 'egg' (mango cheesecake encased in white chocolate). Reserve in advance.

★ **Hebros Restaurant** BULGARIAN €€€
(☑ 032-625 929; www.hebros-hotel.com; ul K Stoilov 51; mains 16-28 lv; 🐾) Genteel service and a tranquil setting is exactly what you would expect from the restaurant of the boutique Hebros Hotel. Classic Bulgarian flavours are gently muddled with Western European influences, creating mouthwatering morsels such as Smilyan beans with parmesan, rabbit with prunes, and grilled sea bream.

Kotka i Mishka BAR
(☑ 0878407578; www.facebook.com/Cat.and. Mouse.Craft.Beer.Bar; ul Hristo Dyukmedjiev 14; ⊙ 10am-midnight) The crowd at this hole-in-the-wall craft-beer hangout spills onto the street – such is the bar's deserved popularity, even against stiff competition in buzzing Kapana. The industrial-feel decorations – such as hamster cages hanging from the ceiling – are a nod to its name: 'cat and mouse'. Decent stop for afternoon tea or coffee and a perfect choice to start a late-night crawl.

Monkey House CAFE
(☑ 0889678333; www.facebook.com/monkeyhouse cafe; ul Zlatarska 3; ⊙ 10am-midnight) Coffee lovers can rest easy in the stripped-bare decor of Monkey House, purveyors of Plovdiv's best flat white. The interior is ornamented with bicycles and moustachioed pillows; seats range from tree stumps and wheelbarrows to comfy chairs; and light bulbs dangle on ropes from the beamed ceiling. It's good fun, and the coffee's even better. Cocktails emerge after sundown.

❶ Information

Tourist Information Centre – Central (☑ 032-620 229; www.visitplovdiv.com; ul Rayko Daskalov 1; ⊙ 9am-5.30pm) Multilingual, friendly information centre near the main post office.

Tourist Information Centre – Old Town (☑ 032-620 453; www.visitplovdiv.com; ul Sâborna 22; ⊙ 9am-5.30pm) Helpful tourist information office in Plovdiv's Old Town.

❶ Getting There & Away

BUS

Plovdiv has several bus stations; find more info on www.avtogara-plovdiv.info. Schedules can be found on www.bgrazpisanie.com. Most destinations of interest to travellers are served from the **Yug bus station** (South Bus Station; ☑ 032-626 937; www.bgrazpisanie.com; bul Hristo Botev 47), diagonally opposite the train station and a

15-minute walk from the centre. Both public and private buses operate from here, and there's often no way of predicting whether you'll get a big, modern bus or a cramped minibus – though the latter is likely for rural destinations. The following services typically leave from Yug: Sofia (14 lv, 2½ hours, many daily) and Varna (24-26 lv, seven hours, three daily).

Sever bus station (North Bus Station; ☎ 032-953 705; www.bgrazpisanie.com; ul Dimitar Stambolov 2; ☐ 99), 3.5km from the old town in the northern suburbs, also serves several useful destinations, including Burgas (14 lv, 2½ hours, many daily), Kazanlâk (9 lv, two hours, three daily), Nesebâr (22 lv, five hours, one daily) and Veliko Târnovo (18 lv, 4½ hours, three daily).

TRAIN

Plovdiv **train station** (www.bdz.bg; bul Hristo Botev) is well organised. Computer screens at the entrance and in the underpass leading to the platforms list recent arrivals and upcoming departures. International bus and train tickets can be booked along with domestic tickets at the **Yug bus station** and the train station. The following direct services leave from the train station: Burgas (15 lv, six hours, two daily), Sofia (10 lv, three hours, 15 daily) and Varna (18-22 lv, six hours, four daily).

CENTRAL BULGARIA

Bulgaria's mountainous centre is arguably the country's historic heart. Dramatic past events played out on both sides of the Stara Planina range: to the west is museum village Koprivshtitsa, while the lowlands town of Kazanlâk accesses Thracian tombs and the famously fragrant Valley of the Roses. The hub is magnificent Veliko Târnovo, former capital of the Bulgarian tsars, crowned with one of Europe's most spectacular citadels.

Koprivshtitsa Копривщица

☎ 07184 / POP 2500

Behind colourful house fronts and babbling streams broods Koprivshtitsa's revolutionary spirit. This museum-village immediately pleases the eye with its numerous restored National Revival–period mansions. It's a peaceful, touristy place, but Koprivshtitsa was once the heart of Bulgaria's revolution against the Ottomans. Todor Kableshkov declared an uprising against the Turks on 20 April 1876 from Kalachev Bridge (also called 'First Shot Bridge'). Today, Koprivshtitsa's few streets are dotted with historic homes interspersed with rambling, overgrown

lanes, making it a romantic getaway and a good place for families.

⊙ Sights

Oslekov House   MUSEUM

(☑ 0878175613; www.koprivshtitza.com; ul Gerenilo-to 4; 2 lv; ⊙ 9.30am-6.30pm Apr-Oct, 9am-5pm Nov-Mar, closed Mon) With its triple-arched entrance and interior restored in shades from scarlet to sapphire blue, Oslekov House is arguably the most beautifully restored example of Bulgarian National Revival–period architecture in Koprivshtitsa. It was built between 1853 and 1856 by a rich merchant who was executed after his arrest during the 1876 April Uprising. Now a house-museum, it features informative, multilingual displays (in Bulgarian, English and French) about 19th-century Bulgaria.

Kableshkov House   MUSEUM

(www.koprivshtitza.com; ul Todor Kableshkov 8; adult/student 4/2 lv; ⊙ 9.30am-5.30pm Tue-Sun Apr-Oct, 9am-5pm Tue-Sun Nov-Mar) Todor Kableshkov is revered as having (probably) been the person who fired the first shot in the 1876 uprising against the Turks. After his arrest, he committed suicide rather than allowing his captors to decide his fate. This, his glorious former home (built in 1845), contains exhibits about the April Uprising.

🛏 Sleeping

Hotel Astra   GUESTHOUSE €€

(☑ 07184-2033; bul Hadzhi Nencho Palaveev 11; d/apt incl breakfast 80/90 lv; ℗) Beautifully set in a garden at the northern end of Koprivshtitsa, the hospitable Astra has large, well-kept rooms and serves an epic homemade breakfast spread of pancakes, thick yoghurt and more. Book well in advance.

✗ Eating

Chuchura   BULGARIAN €€

(☑ 0888347770; www.mehana.eu; bul Hadzhi Nencho Palaveev 66; mains 8-15 lv; ⊙ 11am-11pm) This family-run tavern is the place to visit for authentic Bulgarian cooking. Nothing fancy, just well-done classics like pork *kavarma* (cooked in a clay pot), meatballs or roast lamb, all served in suitably rustic surrounds.

Dyado Liben   BULGARIAN €€

(☑ 0887532096; bul Hadzhi Nencho Palaveev 47; mains 8-15 lv; ⊙ 11am-midnight; 🛜) Traditional fare is served at this atmospheric 1852 mansion with tables set in a warren of halls, graced with ornate painted walls and worn wood floors. Find it just across the bridge leading from the main square, inside the facing courtyard.

ℹ️ Information

Tourist Information Centre (☎07184-2191; www.koprivshtitza.com; pl 20 April 6; ⊙9.30am-5.30pm Tue, Wed & Fri-Sun Apr-Oct, to 5pm Nov-Mar) Information centre in a small building on the main square.

ℹ️ Getting There & Away

Without private transport, getting to Koprivshtitsa can be inconvenient: the train station is 9km north of the village, requiring a taxi or shuttle bus (4 lv, 15 minutes), which isn't always dependably timed to meet incoming and outgoing trains. Find timetables for the shuttle bus posted at the train station or bus station.

Trains come from Sofia (6 lv to 9 lv, two hours, four daily) and Karlovo (3 lv to 4 lv, one to 1½ hours, two to four daily). Alternatively, Koprivshtitsa's **bus stop** (☎07184-3044; bul Palaveev 76) is central and has decent connections to Sofia (13 lv, two hours) and sporadic service to Plovdiv (12 lv, two hours).

Veliko Târnovo
Велико Търново

☑062 / POP 72,938

Medieval history emanates from Veliko Târnovo's fortified walls and cobbled lanes. One of Bulgaria's oldest towns, Veliko Târnovo has as its centrepiece the magnificent restored Tsarevets Fortress, citadel of the Second Bulgarian Empire. Historic Târnovo is tucked into the dramatic bends of the Yantra River, clasped by an amphitheatre of forested hills. Bulgaria's 19th-century National Revival splendour is easy to relive along historic lanes such as ul Gurko; similarly evocative is the handicraft market, Samovodska Charshiya, which retains the same atmosphere it must have had two centuries ago. The modern town has burst these tidy seams, splaying west from busy bul Bulgaria. Today's Târnovo has Bulgaria's second-largest university and is home to a multicultural expat scene.

⊙ Sights

★Tsarevets Fortress   FORTRESS
(☎0885105282; adult/student 6/2 lv, scenic elevator 2 lv; ⊙8am-7pm Apr-Oct, 9am-5pm Nov-Mar) The inescapable symbol of Veliko Târnovo, this reconstructed fortress dominates the skyline and is one of Bulgaria's most beloved

monuments. The former seat of the medieval tsars, it hosts the remains of more than 400 houses, 18 churches, the royal palace, an execution rock and more. Watch your step: there are lots of potholes, broken steps and unfenced drops. The fortress morphs into a psychedelic spectacle with a magnificent night-time Sound & Light Show (p244).

Ulitsa General Gurko   STREET
(ul General Gurko) The oldest street in Veliko Târnovo, ul Gurko is a must-stroll with arresting views towards the Yantra River and Asen Monument. Its charmingly crumbling period houses – which appear to be haphazardly piled on one another – provide a million photo opportunities and conversations that start with 'Imagine living here...' Sturdy shoes are a must.

Sarafkina Kâshta   MUSEUM
(☎0885105282; ul General Gurko 88; adult/student 6/2 lv; ⊙9am-5.30pm Tue-Sat) Built for a wealthy banker in 1861, this National Revival–style house-museum spans five storeys. Within, 19th-century earrings, bracelets and other delicate silverware are on display, alongside antique ceramics, woodcarvings and traditional costumes and jewellery.

🛏️ Sleeping

Hotel Anhea   HOTEL €
(☎062-577 713; www.anheabg.com; ul Nezavisimost 32; s/d/tr from 32/50/60 lv; ﹡🐾) This superb budget hotel in an early-1900s building has a restful air, despite its central location. Crisp beige and cream rooms are arranged across two buildings, between which lies a peaceful courtyard and breakfast area – this secret garden is decorated with pretty iron railings and fountains, and is overseen by resident rabbit Emma.

Hostel Mostel   HOSTEL €
(☎0897859359; www.hostelmostel.com; ul Iordan Indjeto 10; campsites/dm/s/d incl breakfast 18/20/46/60 lv; @🐾) The famous Sofia-based Hostel Mostel has a welcoming branch in Târnovo, with clean, modern dorm rooms and doubles with sparkling bathrooms. It's just 150m from Tsarevets Fortress – good for exploring there, but a long walk from the city centre. Service is cheerful and multilingual, and there's barbecue equipment out back.

★Hotel-Mehana Gurko   HISTORIC HOTEL €€
(☎0887858965; www.hotel-gurko.com; ul General Gurko 33; d/apt incl breakfast from 110/150 lv;

WORTH A TRIP

TOMBS & BLOOMS: KAZANLÂK

For centuries Kazanlâk has been the sweet-smelling centre of European rose-oil production. This nondescript town is also the gateway to the Valley of the Thracian Kings, meaning you can combine fragrant flowers with awe-inspiring tombs in a single visit.

Roses (the aromatic *Rosa damascena*, to be precise) bloom around mid-May to mid-June. Their delicate oils are used in everything from moisturising balms, liqueurs, jams and candies. Kazanlâk's **Rose Festival** (⊙1st weekend Jun) is the highlight of the season. You can explore the history of rose-oil production year-round at the **Museum of Roses** (☑0431-64 057; www.muzei-kazanlak.org; bul Osvobozhdenie 10; adult/student 6/2 lv; ⊙9am-5.30pm), or on a visit to **Enio Bonchev Rose Distillery** (☑0885640999; www.eniobonchev.com; Tarnichene; with/without rose picking 10/7 lv), 27km west of Kazanlâk (call or email in advance to fix a time).

Long before a single seed was sown, the Thracians – a fierce Indo-European tribe – ruled the roost. Archaeologists believe there are at least 1500 Thracian burial mounds and tombs in the vicinity. Most visitors to Kazanlâk head to a nearby replica of the **Thracian Tomb of Kazanlâk** (www.muzei-kazanlak.org; Tyulbe Park; adult/child 6/2 lv; ⊙9am-5pm). More (and better) tombs can be reached via tour bus or your own vehicle: between Kazanlâk and the village of Shipka you can step inside 4th-century BCE **Shushmanets Tomb** (☑0431-99 031; www.muzei-kazanlak.org; adult/student 6/2 lv; ⊙9am-5pm) and the mysterious **Ostrusha Tomb** (☑0431-99 050; www.muzei-kazanlak.org; adult/student 6/2 lv; ⊙9am-5pm), whose sarcophagus was carved from a single slab of stone.

Day trips taking in both regions can be arranged at the Kazanlâk **tourist information centre** (☑0431-99 553; ul Iskra 4; ⊙8am-5pm Mon-Fri). The **Roza Hotel** (☑0431-50 005; www.hotelrozabg.com; ul Rozova Dolina 2; r 60-120 lv; P❋@⸗) in town makes a comfortable and good-value base. Buses run from Kazanlâk to Sofia (17 lv, three hours, five daily) and Plovdiv (10 lv, two hours, three daily). See www.bdz.bg/en for train schedules.

P❋@⸗) Sitting pretty on Veliko Tãrnovo's oldest street, with blooms spilling over its wooden balconies and agricultural curios littering the exterior, the Gurko is one of the best places to sleep (and eat) in town. Its 21 rooms are spacious and soothing, each individually decorated and offering great views.

✕ Eating & Drinking

Shtastliveca
BULGARIAN €€

(☑062-600 656; www.shtastliveca.com; ul Stefan Stambolov 79; mains 10-20 lv; ⊙11am-midnight; ⸗☝) Inventive dishes and amiable service have solidified the 'Lucky Man' as a favourite among locals and expats. Sauces pairing chocolate and cheese are drizzled over chicken, while strawberry and balsamic vinegar lend piquancy to meaty dishes. There is a pleasing range for vegetarians.

★ Han Hadji Nikoli
INTERNATIONAL €€€

(☑062-651 291; www.hanhadjinikoli.com; ul Rakovski 19; mains 17-30 lv; ⊙10am-11pm; ⸗) Countless Veliko Tãrnovo inns were ransacked under Ottoman rule, as they were popular meeting places for revolution-minded locals. Fortunately Han Hadji Nikoli survived, and today the town's finest restaurant occupies

this beautifully restored 1858 building with an upstairs gallery. Well-executed dishes include Trakia chicken marinated in herbs and yoghurt, mussels sautéed in white wine, and exquisitely prepared pork neck.

Tam
BAR

(☑0889879693; www.facebook.com/TAMVELIKO TARNOVO; ul Marno Pole 2A; ⊙4pm-3am Mon-Sat) Open the nondescript door, and up the stairs you'll find the city's friendliest, most-open-minded hang-out. Tam is the place to feel the pulse of VT's arty crowd. You might stumble on art installations, movie screenings, or language nights in English, French or Spanish. Punters and staff extend a genuine welcome and drinks flow late.

☆ Entertainment

Sound & Light Show
LIVE PERFORMANCE

(☑0885080865; www.soundandlight.bg; ul N Pikolo 6; 20-25 lv) Marvel as Veliko Tãrnovo's Tsarevets Fortress (p243) skyline is bathed in multicoloured light and lasers during the Sound & Light Show. This 40-minute audiovisual display uses choral music and flashes of light in homage to the rise and fall of the Second Bulgarian Empire. Check the website for a current schedule and to buy tickets for paid performances.

Shopping

⭐ **Samovodska Charshiya** ARTS & CRAFTS
(ul Rakovski) Veliko Tārnovo's historic quarter is a true centre of craftsmanship, with genuine blacksmiths, potters and cutlers, among other artisans, still practising their trades here. Wander the cobblestone streets to discover bookshops and purveyors of antiques, jewellery and art, housed in appealing National Revival houses.

ℹ Information

Tourist Information Centre (☑ 062-622 148; www.velikoturnovo.info; ul Hristo Botev 5; ⊙ 9am-6pm Mon-Fri, 10am-5pm Sat & Sun) Helpful English-speaking staff offering local info and advice.

ℹ Getting There & Away

BUS

Most services arrive at and depart from the city's two main bus stations; always double-check the timetable to get the right station. **Zapad Bus Station** (West Bus Station; ☑ 062-640 908; ul Nikola Gabrovski 74), about 3km south of the tourist information centre, is the main intercity one (it's sometimes labelled simply as 'Bus Station' on timetables). Local buses 10, 12, 14, 70 and 110 go there, along ul Vasil Levski. There's also a left-luggage office. Closer to the centre is **Yug bus station** (South Bus Station; ☑ 062-620 014; ul Hristo Botev 74), 700m south of the tourist information centre.

Sample destinations and fares from Zapad include Burgas (18 lv to 25 lv, four hours, four daily), Kazanlāk (9 lv, three hours, five daily) and Plovdiv (20 lv, four hours, four daily). Destinations served from Yug include Sofia (22 lv, four hours, several daily) and Varna (21 lv, four hours, several daily).

TRAIN

Check train schedules with the tourist information centre, or on www.bdz.bg, as Veliko Tārnovo's two main train stations are located 10km apart. Irregular trains link the two stations (1.50 lv, 20 minutes, seven daily).

The more walkable of the two is **Veliko Tārnovo train station** (☑ 0885397701; www.bdz.bg), 1.5km west of town. Direct connections from this station are limited, and services to cities like Plovdiv, Sofia and the coastal resorts require a change of trains in Gorna Oryakhovitsa, Stara Zagora or Dabovo. **Gorna Oryakhovitsa train station** (☑ 061-826 118; www.bdz.bg; ul Tsar Osvoboditel), 8.5km northeast of town, is along

the main line between Sofia and Varna. There are daily services to/from Sofia (18 lv, four to five hours, eight daily). Direct trains also reach Varna (13 lv, 3½ to four hours, five daily).

BLACK SEA COAST

Bulgaria's long Black Sea coastline is the country's summertime playground, attracting not just Bulgarians but tourists from across Europe and beyond. The big, purpose-built resorts here have become serious rivals to those of Spain and Greece, while independent travellers will find plenty to explore away from the parasols and jet skis. Sparsely populated sandy beaches to the far south and north, the bird-filled lakes around Burgas, and picturesque ancient towns such as Nesebâr and Sozopol are rewarding destinations. The 'maritime capital' of Varna and its seaside rival, Burgas, are two of Bulgaria's most vibrant cities. Both are famous for summer festivals and nightlife as well as their many museums and galleries.

Varna Варна
☑ 052 / POP 335,170

Bulgaria's third city and maritime capital, Varna is the most interesting and cosmopolitan town on the Black Sea coast. A combination of port city, naval base and seaside resort, it's an appealing place to while away a few days, packed with history yet thoroughly modern, with an enormous park to amble round and a lengthy beach to lounge on. In the city centre you'll find Bulgaria's largest Roman baths complex and its finest archaeological museum, as well as a lively cultural and restaurant scene.

⊙ Sights & Activities

⭐ **Archaeological Museum** MUSEUM
(☑ 052-681 030; www.archaeo.museumvarna.com; ul Maria Luisa 41; adult/child 10/2 lv; ⊙10am-5pm Apr-Sep, Tue-Sat Oct-Mar; ➌8, 9, 109, 409) Exhibits at this vast museum, the best of its kind in Bulgaria, include 6000-year-old bangles, necklaces and earrings said to be the oldest worked gold found in the world. You'll also find Roman surgical implements, Hellenistic tombstones and touching oddments including a marble plaque listing, in Greek, the names of the city's school graduates for 221 CE. All of the exhibits are helpfully signposted in English, with excellent

explanatory text. There's a large collection of icons on the 2nd floor.

Beach BEACH

(⏲9am-6pm) Varna has a long stretch of public beach, starting near the port and stretching north some 4km. Generally, the quality of the sand and water improve and the crowds thin as you stroll north. The easiest way to access the beach is to walk south on bul Slivnitsa to Primorski Park and follow the stairs to the beach.

Baracuda Dive Center DIVING

(☎0898706604; www.baracudadive.com; ul General Gurko 43; half-day beginning instruction from 110 lv) Offers diving instruction for beginners and advanced divers, as well as guided diving excursions along the Black Sea coast. Rates include equipment.

Sleeping

Varna has no shortage of accommodation, although the better (or at least more central) places get very busy during the summer months.

★Yo Ho Hostel HOSTEL €

(☎0884729144; www.yohohostel.com; ul Ruse 23; dm/s/d from 15/38/55 lv; @📶; 🚌8, 9, 109) Shiver your timbers at this cheerful, pirate-themed place, with four- and 11-bed dorm rooms, an all-female dorm and private options. Staff offer free pick-ups and can organise camping and rafting trips. The location is an easy walk to the main sights.

Hotel Odessos HOTEL €€

(☎052-640 300; www.odessos-bg.com; bul Slivnitsa 1; s/d from 85/105 lv; P❄📶) Enjoying a great location opposite the main entrance to Primorski Park, this is an older establishment with smallish and pretty average rooms, but it's convenient for the beach. Only the pricier 'sea view' rooms have balconies.

Eating & Drinking

Varna has some of the best eating on the Black Sea coast, with everything from beachside shacks to fine dining.

Morsko Konche PIZZA €

(☎052-600 418; www.morskokonche.bg; pl Nezavisimost, cnr ul Zamenhof; pizzas 5-10 lv; ⏲8.30am-10pm; 📶🖉; 🚌8, 9, 109) The 'Seahorse' is a cheap and cheerful pizza place with a big menu featuring all the standard varieties, plus some inventive creations of its own: the 'exotic' pizza comes with bananas and blueberries.

★Stariya Chinar BULGARIAN €€

(☎052-949 400; www.stariachinar.com; ul Preslav 11; mains 12-20 lv; ⏲8am-midnight) This is upmarket Balkan soul food at its best. Try the baked lamb, made to an old Bulgarian recipe, or the barbecued pork ribs; it also boasts some rather ornate salads. Outdoor seating is lovely in summer; park yourself in the traditional interior when the cooler weather strikes.

Mr Baba SEAFOOD €€€

(☎0896505050; www.mrbaba.net; bul Primorski; mains 15-30 lv; ⏲8am-midnight; 📶; 🚌20) The coast-long trend for novelty ship restaurants has come to Varna, with this handsome, wooden-hulled venture stranded at the far southern end of the beach off bul Primorski, near the port. It features a pricey but tasty menu of steak and fish dishes, including sea bass, trout and bluefish. Indoor and outdoor seating. Reserve in advance.

The Black Sheep Beer House PUB

(☎0878623426; www.theblacksheep.bg; bul Knyaz Boris I 62; ⏲9am-2am) This centrally located pub and microbrewery is always hopping. Stop by to try out the house brew, Zlatna Varna, or nibble on some very decent pub grub like salads, burgers and grilled pork ribs. Tables can normally be had on off nights, like Mondays or Tuesdays, but book in advance over the weekend.

Entertainment

Varna Opera Theatre OPERA

(☎box office 052-665 022; www.tmpcvarna.com; pl Nezavisimost 1; ⏲ticket office 10am-1pm & 2-7pm; 🚌8, 9, 109, 409) Varna's grand opera house hosts performances by the Varna Opera and Philharmonic Orchestra all year, except July and August, when some performances are staged at the Open-Air Theatre in Primorski Park.

Information

Tourist Information Centre (☎052-820 690; www.visit.varna.bg; pl Kiril & Metodii; ⏲9am-7pm May-Sep, 8.30am-5.30pm Mon-Fri Oct-Apr; 🚌8, 9, 109, 409) Plenty of free brochures and maps, and helpful multilingual staff. The Tourist Information Centre also operates free three-hour walking tours of the city on select days from June to September.

Getting There & Away

AIR

Varna's international **airport** (VAR; ☎052-573 323; www.varna-airport.bg; Aksakovo; 🚌409) has scheduled and charter flights from all over Europe, as well as regular flights to and from Sofia. Bus 409 goes to the airport from the centre.

BUS

Varna's **central bus station** (Avtoexpress; ☑ information 052-757 044, tickets 052-748 349; www.autogaravn.com; bul Vladislav Varenchik 158; ☺24hr; ☐148, 409) is about 2km northwest of the city centre. Most intercity coaches depart from here. There are regular buses to Sofia (33 lv, seven hours, 10 daily), Burgas (14 lv, 2½ hours, several daily) and other major destinations in Bulgaria: see www.bgrazpisanie.com/en for fares and schedules.

TRAIN

Facilities at Varna's **train station** (☑052-630 444; www.bdz.bg; pl Slaveikov; ☐8, 9, 109) include a **left luggage office** (pl Slaveikov; per day 2 lv; ☺7am-7pm) and cafe. Rail destinations from Varna include Ruse (15 lv, four hours, two daily), Sofia (30 lv, seven to eight hours, seven daily), Plovdiv (25 lv, seven hours, three daily) and Shumen (7 lv, 1½ hours, 10 daily).

Nesebâr   Несебър

☑ 0554 / POP 13,340

On a small rocky outcrop 37km northeast of Burgas and connected to the mainland by a narrow, artificial isthmus, pretty-as-a-postcard Nesebâr is famous for its surprisingly numerous, albeit mostly ruined, medieval churches. It has become heavily commercialised and transforms into one huge, open-air souvenir market during the high season; outside summer, it's a ghost town. Designated by Unesco as a World Heritage site, Nesebâr has its charms, but in summer these can be overpowered by the crowds and the relentless parade of tacky shops. With Sunny Beach (Slânchev Bryag) just across the bay, meanwhile, you have every conceivable water sport on hand. The 'new town' on the other side of the isthmus has the newest and biggest hotels and the main beach, but the sights are all in the old town.

⊙ Sights & Activities

Archaeological Museum   MUSEUM
(☑0554-46 019; www.ancient-nessebar.com; ul Mesembria 2; adult/child 6/3 lv; ☺9am-7pm Jun & Sep, to 8pm Jul & Aug, to 5pm Oct-May) Explore the rich history of Nesebâr – formerly Mesembria – at this fine museum. Greek and Roman pottery, statues and tombstones, as well as Thracian gold jewellery and ancient anchors, are displayed here. There's also a collection of icons from Nesebâr's numerous churches.

Sveti Stefan Church   CHURCH
(☑0554-46 019; www.ancient-nessebar.com; ul Ribarska; adult/child 6/3 lv; ☺9am-7pm Mon-Fri, 10.30am-2pm & 2.30-7pm Sat & Sun May-Sep, 9am-5pm Mon-Fri, from 10am Sat & Sun Oct-Apr) Built in the 11th century and reconstructed 500 years later, this is the best-preserved church in town. If you only visit one, this is the church to choose. Its beautiful 16th- to 18th-century murals cover virtually the entire interior. Come early, as it's popular with tour groups.

Aqua Paradise   WATER PARK
(☑0885208055; www.aquaparadise-bg.com; Hwy E87, Ravda; adult/child 42/21 lv, after 3pm 30/15 lv; ☺10am-6.30pm Jun-Sep; ⊕) Organised watery fun is on hand at Aqua Paradise, a huge water park just off the main highway on the western outskirts of Nesebâr, with a variety of pools, slides and chutes. A free minibus, running every 15 minutes, makes pick-ups at signed stops around Nesebâr and Sunny Beach.

🛏 Sleeping & Eating

★Boutique
Hotel St Stefan   BOUTIQUE HOTEL €€
(☑0554-43 603; www.hotelsaintstefan.com; ul Ribarska 11; r/ste 95/160 lv; P❋☞) One of the nicest hotels in Nesebâr, the St Stefan offers rooms with views out over the harbour and Black Sea. There's a small sauna on the premises as well as a terrace for drinks and light meals. Rooms feature original artwork by Bulgarian artists. Breakfast costs 8 lv. Book well in advance for summer dates.

★**Gloria Mar**   BULGARIAN €€€
(☑0893550055; www.gloriamar-bg.com; ul Kraybrezhna 9; mains 12-30 lv; ☺11am-11pm) For our money, this is the best dining option in touristy Nesebâr. Fresh seafood, wood-fired pizzas and grilled meats are on offer, as well as harder-to-find risottos and paellas. There's an extensive wine list and dining on three levels, including a rooftop terrace. It's on the southern side of old Nesebâr, facing the marina and passenger ferry terminal.

ℹ Getting There & Away

Nesebâr is well connected to coastal destinations by public transport, and the town's **bus station** (☑0554-42 721; www.bgrazpisanie.com; ul Andzhelo Ronkali) is on the small square just outside the city walls. The stop before this on the mainland is for the new town. Buses run in season every few minutes to Sunny Beach (1 lv, 10 minutes). Longer-haul destinations include Burgas (7 lv, one hour, hourly), Varna (14 lv, two hours, four daily) and Sofia (37 lv, seven hours, three daily). In season, high-speed **Fast Ferry** (📞0885808001; www.fastferry.bg; Passenger Ferry Port; ⏱8.30am-8.30pm Jun-Sep) hydrofoils and catamarans run daily from Nesebâr's passenger ferry port (on the southern side of Nesebâr) to Sozopol.

Burgas   Бургас

📄056 / POP 202,766

For most visitors, the port city of Burgas (sometimes written as 'Bourgas') is no more than a transit point for the more appealing resorts and historic towns further up and down the coast. If you do decide to stop over, you'll find a lively, well-kept city with a neat, pedestrianised centre, a long, uncrowded beach, a gorgeous seafront **Maritime Park**, and some interesting museums. A clutch of reasonably priced hotels, as well as some of the best restaurants in this part of the country, makes it a practical base for exploring the southern coast, too.

⊙ Sights

St Anastasia Island   ISLAND

(📞0882004124; www.anastasia-island.com; return boat trip adult/child 12/10 lv; ⏱departures 10.30am & 1.30pm May-Oct) This small volcanic island makes for a fun day of exploring. The island, which has served as a religious retreat, a prison and pirate bait (according to legend, a golden treasure is buried in its sands), is today dominated by a lighthouse and a monastery, where visitors can sample various healing herb potions. At least two (and usually more) ships leave daily from May to October from the **passenger ferry terminal** (📄information 882004124; Magazia 1, Southeast of ul Knyaz Al Battenberg 1) south of the bus and train stations.

🛏 Sleeping

Old House Hostel   HOSTEL **€**

(📞056-841 558; www.burgashostel.com; ul Sofroniy 3; dm/d 18/41 lv; ❄🗫) This charming hostel makes itself at home in a lovely 1895 house. Dorms are airy and bright (and bunk-free!), while doubles have access to a sweet little courtyard. The location is central and about 400m from the beach.

Hotel Doro   HOTEL **€€**

(📞056-820 808; www.hoteldoro.com; ul Sredna Gora 28; s/d 70/80 lv; 🅿❄🗫) The location is better than it looks at first glance: ignore the slightly depressed neighbourhood setting by keeping in mind that the central restaurants

and Maritime Park are both just a short walk away. Once inside the hotel, things brighten considerably. Enjoy spotlessly clean rooms (some with balconies) and what might very well be Bulgaria's best breakfast buffet.

🍴 Eating

⭐**Rosé**   INTERNATIONAL **€€**

(📞0885855099; www.facebook.com/roseburgas; bul Aleko Bogoridi 19; mains 8-20 lv; ⏱11am-11pm; 🗫) Choose from a wide menu of grilled meats and fish, including a superlative lamb-shank offering, or fresh pasta at this superb restaurant in the city centre. Finish off with a cake or homemade ice cream. There's a small terrace for nice weather; otherwise, eat in the main dining room, which is just formal enough for a special night out.

Ethno   SEAFOOD **€€**

(📞0887877966; www.facebook.com/EthnoRest aurant; ul Aleksandrovska 49; mains 7-20 lv; ⏱11am-11pm; 🗫) This downtown restaurant does splendid things with seafood: the Black Sea mussels alone are worth a trip to Burgas. With inviting blue-and-white surrounds that recall the city's Greek heritage, superb (English-speaking) service and a summery vibe, Ethno is classy without being uptight.

HashtagSTUDIO   CAFE

(📞0883376370; www.facebook.com/HashtagStu dioBurgas; ul Aboba 1; ⏱7am-11pm) As hip as it gets in Burgas: artisanal coffees, craft beers, a stylish interior of exposed concrete walls and hanging lightbulbs, attentive service, and an all-round cool vibe. Check the Facebook page for occasional parties and live events.

❶ Getting There & Away

AIR

Bulgaria Air (www.air.bg) links **Burgas Airport** (BOJ; 📄information 056-870 248; www.burgas-airport.bg; Hwy E87, Sarafovo; 🗫; 🚌15), 10km northeast of town, with Sofia daily (April to October). **Wizz Air** (www.wizzair.com) connects Burgas with London Luton. Other carriers service cities throughout Europe and select destinations in the Middle East, including Tel Aviv and Beirut. The airport is linked to the centre via public bus 15.

BUS

Outside the train station at the southern end of ul Aleksandrovska, **Yug bus station** (📄0884981220; www.bgrazpisanie.com; pl Tsaritsa Yoanna) is where most travellers will arrive or leave. There are regular buses to coastal destinations. Departures are less frequent outside summer. A **left-luggage office** (☉ 6am-10pm) is located inside the station. There are regular buses to coastal destinations, including Nesebâr (5 lv, 40 minutes, half-hourly), Varna (12 lv, two hours, half-hourly) and Sozopol (5 lv, 40 minutes, every 45 minutes). Several daily buses also go to and from Sofia (30 lv, seven to eight hours) and Plovdiv (20 lv, four hours). Departures are less frequent outside summer.

The Burgas Bus website (www.burgasbus.info) is in Bulgarian only, but has a handy timetable for both major bus stations (on the upper left side of the opening page).

TRAIN
The historic and well-maintained **train station** (☑ information 056-845 022; www.bdz.bg; ul Ivan Vazov; ☉ information office 6am-10pm) was built in 1902. There are clearly marked ticket windows for buying both domestic and international tickets. There's also an ATM and a cafe. Trains run to Plovdiv (16 lv, five to six hours, five daily) and Sofia (22 lv, seven to eight hours, five daily).

Sozopol   Созопол
☑ 0550 / POP 5700

Ancient Sozopol, with its charming old town of meandering cobbled streets and pretty wooden houses, huddled together on a narrow peninsula, is one of the coast's highlights. With two superb beaches, a genial atmosphere, plentiful accommodation and good transport links, it has long been a popular seaside resort and makes an excellent base for exploring the area. Although not quite as crowded as Nesebâr, it is becoming ever more popular with international visitors. There's a lively cultural scene, too, with plenty of free concerts and other events in summer.

The new town, known as 'Harmanite', lies south of the tiny bus station. The best beach is in this part of town, but otherwise, it's mainly modern hotels and residential areas.

☉ Sights

Sozopol has two great beaches: **Harmanite Beach** has all the good-time gear (waterslide, paddle boats, beach bar), while to the north, the smaller **Town Beach** packs in the serious sun-worshippers.

Archaeological Museum   MUSEUM
(☑ 0550-22 226; ul Han Krum 2; adult/child 7/2 lv; ☉ 8.30am-6pm Jun-Sep, 8.30am-noon & 1.30pm-5.30pm Mon-Fri Oct-May) Housed in a drab concrete box near the port, this museum has a small but fascinating collection of local finds from its Apollonian glory days and beyond.

In addition to a wealth of Hellenic treasures, the museum occasionally exhibits the skeleton of a local 'vampire', found with a stake driven through its chest.

Sveti Ivan   ISLAND
The largest Bulgarian island in the Black Sea (0.7 sq km), Sveti Ivan lies 3km north of Sozopol's old town. The island's history stretches back to Thracian and Roman times, and includes a monastery from the 4th century CE. Sveti Ivan made international headlines in 2010 with the purported discovery of the remains of St John the Baptist. There are no scheduled excursions to the island, but private trips (from around 60 lv) can be arranged along the **Fishing Harbour** (ul Kraybrezhna).

✾✿ Festivals & Events

Apollonia Arts Festival   ART, MUSIC
(www.apollonia.bg; ☉ late Aug–mid-Sep) This is the highlight of Sozopol's cultural calendar, with concerts, theatrical performances, art exhibitions, film screenings and more held across town.

🛏 Sleeping & Eating

★ **Just a Hostel**   HOSTEL €
(☑ 0550-22 175; ul Apolonia 20; dm 20 lv; 🛜) This clean, cosy, centrally located hostel sits in the centre of the Old Town, a few minutes' walk from the beach. Dorm-bed accommodation with shared bath and shower. The price includes traditional breakfast (pancakes) and coffee.

Art Hotel   HOTEL €€
(☑ 0550-24 081, 0878650160; www.arthotel-sbh.com; ul Kiril & Metodii 72; d/studios 85/105 lv; ❊🛜) This peaceful old house, belonging to the Union of Bulgarian Artists, is within a walled courtyard towards the tip of the peninsula, away from the crowds. It has a small selection of bright, comfortable rooms with balconies, most with sea views; breakfast is served on the terraces overlooking the sea.

Panorama Sv. Ivan   SEAFOOD €€
(☑ 0888260820; ul Morski Skali 21; mains 10-22 lv; ☉ 10am-11pm) This lively place has an open terrace with a fantastic view towards Sveti Ivan island. Fresh, locally caught fish is the mainstay of the menu. It's one of the best of many seafood spots on this street.

❶ Getting There & Away
The small public **bus station** (☑ 0550-23 460; www.bgrazpisanie.com; ul Han Krum) is just

south of the old town walls. Buses leave for Burgas (6 lv, 40 minutes) about every 30 minutes between 6am and 9pm in summer, and about once an hour in the low season. Public buses leave two to three times a day for Sofia (30 lv, seven hours). **Fast Ferry** (📞 0889182914, booking 0885808001; www.fastferry.bg) operates from a kiosk at the harbour and runs three daily high-speed catamarans or hydrofoils to Nesebâr (one way/return from 27/54 lv, 40 minutes) from June to September.

SURVIVAL GUIDE

ⓘ Directory A–Z

ACCESSIBLE TRAVEL

Bulgaria is not an easy destination for travellers with disabilities. Uneven and broken footpaths pose challenges, and ramps and toilets designed for disabled people are few and far between, other than in a handful of top-end hotels in Sofia and other big cities. Public transport is not generally geared toward the needs of travellers with disabilities. One organisation worth contacting is the Center for Independent Living (www.cil.bg) in Sofia.

ACCOMMODATION

Accommodation is most expensive in Sofia and other big cities, notably Plovdiv and Varna. Elsewhere, prices are relatively cheap by Western European standards. Demand and prices are highest in coastal resorts between July and August, and in the skiing resorts between December and February. Outside the holiday seasons, these hotels often close down, or operate on a reduced basis.

Guesthouses Usually small, family-run places and great value, with cosy rooms and home-cooked breakfasts.

Hizhas The mountain huts in Bulgaria's hiking terrain are convenient, though basic, places to sleep.

Hotels Bulgaria has a good range of hotels from budget to luxury.

INTERNET ACCESS

Most hotels and hostels offer free internet access to guests, and wi-fi hotspots can be found in many restaurants, cafes and other businesses. With the increasing availability of wi-fi, internet cafes have become something of a rarity in Bulgaria.

LGBTIQ+ TRAVELLERS

Homosexuality is legal in Bulgaria, but gay culture remains discreet. Same-sex relationships have no legal recognition. Attitudes are changing, and there are several gay clubs and bars in Sofia and small scenes in Varna and Plovdiv. There is an annual Gay Pride march in Sofia (www.sofiapride.org). For more information see www.gay.bg.

MONEY

ATMs are widely available. Credit cards are accepted in most hotels and restaurants; smaller guesthouses or rural businesses may only accept cash.

Currency

The local currency is the lev (plural: leva), comprised of 100 stotinki. It is almost always abbreviated as lv (лв). The lev is a stable currency and linked to the euro at a rate of around 2 leva per 1 euro. For major purchases, such as organised tours, airfares, car rental and midrange and top-end hotels, prices are sometimes quoted in euros, although payment is carried out in leva.

Money Changers

Foreign-exchange offices can be found in all large towns, and rates are always displayed prominently. They are no longer allowed to charge commission, but that doesn't always stop them trying; always check the final amount that you will be offered before handing over your cash. Avoid exchange offices at train stations, airports or in tourist resorts, as rates are often poor.

OPENING HOURS

Standard opening hours are as follows:

Banks 9am to 4pm Monday to Friday

Bars 11am to midnight

Government offices 9am to 5pm Monday to Friday

Post offices 8.30am to 5pm Monday to Friday

Restaurants 11am to 11pm

Shops 9am to 6pm

PUBLIC HOLIDAYS

New Year's Day 1 January

Liberation Day 3 March

Orthodox Easter March/April/May

May Day 1 May

St George's Day/Bulgarian Army Day 6 May

Cyrillic Alphabet/Culture and Literacy Day 24 May

Unification Day 6 September

Bulgarian Independence Day 22 September

Christmas 25 and 26 December

TELEPHONE

➡ To call Bulgaria from abroad, dial the international access code (which varies from country to country), add 359 (the country code for Bulgaria), the area code (minus the first zero) and then the number.

➡ To make an international call from Bulgaria, dial 00 followed by the code of the country you are calling, then the local area code, minus the initial 0.

➡ To make domestic calls within Bulgaria, dial the area code, which will be between 2 and 5 digits long, followed by the number you wish to call. If you are making a domestic call from your mobile phone, you will also have to insert the country code (+359) first, unless you are using a Bulgarian SIM card.

➡ To call a Bulgarian mobile phone from within Bulgaria, dial the full number, including the initial 0.

Mobile Phones

Visitors from elsewhere in Europe will be able to use their mobile phones in Bulgaria. Local SIM cards are easy to buy in mobile phone stores (bring your passport) and can be used in most phones.

TOURIST INFORMATION

Bigger cities, and smaller towns popular with tourists, have dedicated tourist information centres, which provide free maps, leaflets and brochures. National parks often have information centres offering advice.

ℹ Getting There & Away

Most international visitors enter and leave Bulgaria via Sofia Airport (p235), and there are frequent flights to the capital from other European cities. Bulgaria is also easily accessible by road and rail from neighbouring countries, and its railway is part of the InterRail system and so can be included in a longer European rail journey. Long-distance coaches reach Bulgarian cities from Turkey, Greece, Romania, Serbia and North Macedonia. There are regular ferry crossings that carry both vehicles and foot passengers across the Danube from Romania.

If you prefer something more structured, several companies offer organised tours and package holidays to Bulgaria.

Flights, cars and tours can be booked online at www.lonelyplanet.com/bookings.

AIR

Bulgaria has good air links with numerous European cities, as well as some cities in the Middle East. There are currently no direct flights to Bulgaria from further afield, so visitors from, for example, North America or Australia will need to pick up a connecting flight elsewhere in Europe.

LAND
Bus

Buses travel to Bulgarian cities from destinations all over Europe, most arriving at Sofia, with some direct to Plovdiv. You will either get off the bus at the border and walk through customs to present your passport, or be visited on the bus

by officials. Long delays can be expected. A good timetable for international connections can be found at www.bgrazpisanie.com.

Car & Motorcycle

In order to drive on Bulgarian roads, you will need to display a vignette (15/30 lv for one week/month) sold at all border crossings into Bulgaria, petrol stations and post offices. Rental cars hired within Bulgaria should already have a vignette. Petrol stations and car-repair shops are common around border crossing areas and along main roads.

Train

Trains run to/from destinations in Romania, Serbia and Turkey, though at present, no trains travel directly between Bulgaria and North Macedonia. Bulgarian international train services are operated by Bulgarian State Railways (BDZ; www.bdz.bg).

ℹ Getting Around

AIR

The only scheduled domestic flights within Bulgaria are between Sofia and Varna and Sofia and Burgas. Both routes are operated by Bulgaria Air (www.air.bg).

BUS

Buses link all cities and major towns and connect villages with the nearest transport hub. Several private companies operate frequent modern, comfortable buses between larger towns, while older, often cramped minibuses run on routes between smaller towns. Buses provide the most comfortable and quickest mode of public transport in Bulgaria, though the type of bus you get can be a lottery.

Though it isn't exhaustive, many bus and train schedules can be accessed at www.bgrazpisanie.com.

CAR & MOTORCYCLE

The best way to travel around Bulgaria – especially when visiting remote villages, monasteries and national parks – is to hire a car or motorbike. The Union of Bulgarian Motorists (p237) is the main national organisation for motorists, though little information is available in English.

TRAIN

The Bulgarian State Railways (БДЖ; www.bdz.bg) links most towns and cities, although some are on a spur track and only connected to a major railway line by infrequent services. Most trains tend to be antiquated, shabby and not especially comfortable, and journey times are usually longer than for buses. On the plus side, the scenery is likely to be more rewarding.

Croatia

POP 4.3 MILLION

Best Places to Eat

➡ Pelegrini (p264)

➡ Restaurant 360° (p276)

➡ Konoba Marjan (p268)

➡ Bistro Apetit (p257)

Best Places to Stay

➡ Art Hotel Kalelarga (p263)

➡ Meneghetti (p261)

➡ Studio Kairos (p257)

➡ Karmen Apartments (p275)

➡ Korta (p268)

Why Go?

If your Mediterranean fantasies feature balmy days by sapphire waters in the shade of ancient walled towns, Croatia is the place to turn them into reality.

The extraordinary Adriatic coastline, speckled with 1244 islands and strewn with historic towns, is Croatia's main attraction. The standout is Dubrovnik, its remarkable Old Town ringed by mighty defensive walls. Split showcases Diocletian's Palace, one of the world's most impressive Roman monuments, where bars, restaurants and shops thrive amid the ancient walls. In the heart-shaped peninsula of Istria, Rovinj is a charm-packed fishing port with narrow cobbled streets.

Away from the coast, Zagreb, Croatia's lovely capital, has a booming cafe culture and art scene, while Plitvice Lakes National Park offers a verdant maze of turquoise lakes and cascading waterfalls.

When to Go
Zagreb

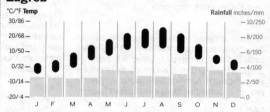

May, Jun, Sep & Oct Best time to visit: good weather, fewer people, lower prices, festival season.

Jul & Aug Lots of sunshine, warm sea and summer festivals; many tourists and highest prices.

Dec & Jan Christmas vibes in Zagreb and skiing on Mt Medvednica.

Entering the Country

Getting to Croatia is becoming easier year-on-year, with both budget and full-service airlines flying to various airports in summer. On top of this, buses, trains and ferries also shepherd holidaymakers into the country. Flights, cars and tours can be booked online at lonelyplanet.com/bookings.

ITINERARIES

Three Days
Base yourself in Dubrovnik (p272) and explore the compact old town; start early and take a walk along the city walls (p273) before it gets too hot. Catch the cable car up Srđ (p273) and explore the surrounding beaches. Once you've seen the sights and had a swim, consider boat trips to Cavtat (p277) and Lokrum (p276).

One Week
Base yourself in Croatia's exuberant second city Split (p265) for two days of sightseeing and nightlife, including a trip to the nearby postcard-perfect walled town of Trogir (p264). Spend the next few days island hopping by fast catamaran to Hvar Town (p270), the vibrant capital of the island of the same name, and photogenic walled Korčula Town (p272). Continue by catamaran to Dubrovnik (p272) and follow the itinerary above.

Essential Food & Drink

Croatian food echoes the varied cultures that have influenced the country over its history. There's a sharp divide between the Italian-style cuisine along the coast and the flavours of Hungary, Austria and Turkey in the continental parts. From grilled sea bass smothered in olive oil in Dalmatia to robust, paprika-heavy meat stews in Slavonia, each region proudly touts its own speciality, but regardless of the region you'll find tasty food made from fresh, seasonal ingredients. Here are a few essential food and drink items to look out for while in Croatia:

Beer Two popular brands of Croatian *pivo* (beer) are Zagreb's Ožujsko and Karlovačko from Karlovac.

Brodet/Brodetto/Brudet/Brujet Slightly spicy seafood stew served with polenta.

Paški sir Pungent sheep's cheese from the island of Pag, soaked in olive oil.

Pašticada Beef stewed in wine, prunes and spices and served with gnocchi.

Rakija Strong Croatian grappa comes in different flavours, from plum to honey.

Ražnjići Small chunks of pork grilled on a skewer.

AT A GLANCE

Area 56,538 sq km

Capital Zagreb

Country Code ☑385

Currency Kuna (KN)

Emergency Ambulance ☑94, Police ☑92

Language Croatian

Time Central European Time (GMT/UTC plus one hour)

Visas Not required for most nationalities for stays of up to 90 days.

CROATIA

Sleeping Price Ranges

The following price ranges refer to a double room with a bathroom in July and August.

€ less than 450KN

€€ 450KN–900KN

€€€ more than 900KN

Eating Price Ranges

The following price ranges refer to a main course.

€ less than 70KN

€€ 70KN–120KN

€€€ more than 120KN

Resources

Chasing the Donkey (www.chasingthedonkey.com)

Croatian Tourism (www.croatia.hr)

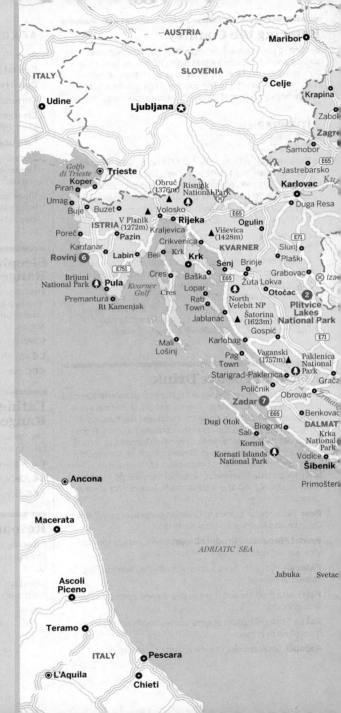

Croatia Highlights

1 Dubrovnik (p272) Circling the historic city's mighty walls and then catching the cable car up Mt Srđ for breathtaking views from above.

2 Plitvice Lakes National Park (p261) Marvelling at the otherworldly turquoise lakes and dramatic waterfalls of Croatia's top natural attraction.

3 Hvar Town (p270) Capping off endless beach days with sunset cocktails and back-lane boogie sessions.

4 Split (p265) Discovering the city's ancient heart in Diocletian's Palace, a quarter that buzzes day and night.

5 Zagreb (p256) Exploring the quirky museums and cafes of Croatia's cute little capital.

6 Rovinj (p260) Roam the steep cobbled streets and piazzas of Istria's showpiece coastal town.

7 Zadar (p262) Exploring Roman ruins, intriguing museums, local eateries and hip bars within the marbled streets of the old town.

ZAGREB

♪ 01 / POP 803,700

Zagreb is made for strolling. Wander through the Upper Town's red-roof and cobblestone glory, peppered with church spires. Crane your neck to see the domes and ornate upper-floor frippery of the Lower Town's mash-up of secessionist, neobaroque and art deco buildings. Search out the grittier pockets of town where ugly-bland concrete walls have been transformed into colourful murals by local street artists. This city rewards those on foot.

Afterwards, do as the locals do and head to a cafe. The cafe culture here is just one facet of this city's vibrant street life, egged on by a year-round swag of events that bring music, pop-up markets and food stalls to the plazas and parks. Even when there's nothing on, the centre thrums with youthful energy, so it's no surprise that Croatia's capital is now bringing in the city-break crowd. Zagreb is the little city that could.

◉ Sights

As the oldest part of Zagreb, the Upper Town (Gornji Grad), which includes the neighbourhoods of Gradec and Kaptol, has landmark buildings and churches from the earlier centuries of Zagreb's history. The Lower Town (Donji Grad), which runs between the Upper Town and the train station, has the city's most interesting art museums and fine examples of 19th- and 20th-century architecture.

★ Mirogoj   CEMETERY
(Aleja Hermanna Bollea 27; ⊙ 6am-8pm Apr-Oct, 7.30am-6pm Nov-Mar) A 10-minute ride north of the city centre (or a 30-minute walk through leafy streets) takes you to one of the most beautiful cemeteries in Europe, sited at the base of Mt Medvednica. It was designed in 1876 by Austrian-born architect Herman Bollé, who created numerous buildings around Zagreb. The majestic arcade, topped by a string of cupolas, looks like a fortress from the outside, but feels calm and graceful on the inside.

Museum of Broken Relationships   MUSEUM
(www.brokenships.com; Ćirilometodska 2; adult/ student 40/30KN; ⊙ 9am-10.30pm Jun-Sep, to 9pm Oct-May) From romances that withered to broken family connections, this wonderfully quirky museum explores the mementos left over after a relationship ends. Displayed amid a string of all-white rooms are donations from around the globe, each with a story attached. Exhibits range from the hilarious (the toaster someone nicked so their ex could never make toast again) to the heartbreaking (the suicide note from somebody's mother). In turns funny, poignant and moving, it's a perfect summing-up of the human condition.

Croatian Museum of Naïve Art   MUSEUM
(Hrvatski Muzej Naivne Umjetnosti; ♪ 01-48 51 911; www.hmnu.hr; Ćirilometodska 3; adult/concession 25/15KN; ⊙ 10am-6pm Mon-Sat, to 1pm Sun) A feast for fans of Croatia's naive art (a form that was highly fashionable locally and worldwide during the 1960s and '70s and has declined somewhat since), this small museum displays 80 artworks (a smidgen of the museum's total 1900 holdings) that illustrate the full range of colourful, and often dreamlike, styles within the genre. The discipline's most important artists, such as Generalić, Mraz, Rabuzin and Smajić, are all displayed here.

Dolac Market   MARKET
(off Trg Bana Jelačića; ⊙ open-air market 6.30am-3pm Mon-Sat, to 1pm Sun, covered market 7am-2pm Mon-Fri, to 3pm Sat, to 1pm Sun) Right in the heart of the city, Zagreb's bustling fruit and vegetable market has been trader-central since the 1930s when the city authorities set up a market space on the 'border' between the Upper and Lower Towns. Sellers from all over Croatia descend here daily to hawk fresh produce.

Katarinin Trg   VIEWPOINT
(Katarinin trg) One of the best views in town – across red-tile roofs towards the cathedral – is from this square behind the Jesuit Church of St Catherine (Crkva Svete Katarine; Katarinin trg bb; ⊙ Mass 6pm Mon-Fri, 11am Sun). It's the perfect spot to begin or end an Upper Town wander. The square is also home to Zagreb's most famous street art; the Whale, gracing the facade of the abandoned Galerija Gradec building, is a 3D work by French artist Etien.

Cathedral of the Assumption
of the Blessed Virgin Mary   CHURCH
(Katedrala Marijina Uznešenja; Kaptol 31; ⊙ 10am-5pm Mon-Sat, 1-5pm Sun) This cathedral's twin spires – seemingly permanently under repair – soar over the city. Formerly known as St Stephen's, the cathedral's original Gothic structure has been transformed many times over, but the sacristy still contains a cycle of frescos dating from the 13th century. An earthquake in 1880 badly damaged the building and reconstruction in a neo-Gothic style began around the turn of the 20th century.

Archaeological Museum
MUSEUM

(Arheološki Muzej; ☑ 01-48 73 101; www.amz.hr; Trg Nikole Šubića Zrinskog 19; adult/child/family 30/15/50KN; ⊙10am-6pm Tue, Wed, Fri & Sat, to 8pm Thu, to 1pm Sun) Spread over three floors, the artefacts housed here stretch from the prehistoric era to the medieval age. The 2nd floor holds the most interesting – and well-curated – exhibits. Here, displays of intricate Roman minor arts, such as decorative combs and oil lamps, and metal curse tablets are given as much prominence as the more usual show-stopping marble statuary. An exhibit devoted to Croatia's early-medieval Bijelo Brdo culture displays a wealth of grave finds unearthed in the 1920s.

Zrinjevac
SQUARE

(Trg Nikole Šubića Zrinskog) Officially called Trg Nikole Šubića Zrinskog but lovingly known as Zrinjevac, this verdant square is a major hang-out during sunny weekends and hosts pop-up cafe stalls during the summer months. It's also a venue for many festivals and events, most centred on the ornate music pavilion that dates from 1891.

🛏 Sleeping

Swanky Mint Hostel
HOSTEL €

(☑01-40 04 248; www.swanky-hostel.com/mint; Ilica 50; dm 170-200KN; s/d 400/600KN; ❄@🛜❄) This backpacker vortex, converted from a 19th-century textile-dye factory, has a very happening bar at its heart. Dorms are small but thoughtfully kitted out with lockers, privacy curtains and reading lamps, while private rooms are bright and large. The hostel's popularity, however, lies in its supersocial, friendly vibe, with welcome shots of *rakija* (grappa), organised pub crawls and an on-site travel agency.

Studio Kairos
B&B €

(☑01-46 40 690; Vlaška 92; s/d/tr/q from €36/50/65/70; ❄🛜) This adorable B&B in a street-level apartment has four well-appointed rooms decked out by theme – Writers, Crafts, Music and Granny's. The cosy common space, where a delicious breakfast is served, and the enthusiastic hosts, who are a fount of knowledge on all things Zagreb, add to this place's intimate and homely appeal. Bikes are also available for rent.

★ Hotel Jägerhorn
HISTORIC HOTEL €€€

(☑01-48 33 877; www.hotel-jagerhorn.hr; Ilica 14; s/d/ste 950/1050/1500KN; 🅿❄@🛜) The oldest hotel in Zagreb (around since 1827) is a peaceful oasis, brimming with character.

The 18 rooms are elegantly outfitted, with soft neutral decor offset by blue accents, king-sized beds, kettles, and swish, contemporary bathrooms. Top-floor rooms have views over leafy Gradec. Staff are charming and the downstairs terrace cafe is the perfect hang-out after your sightseeing is done.

🍴 Eating

Heritage
CROATIAN €

(Petrinjska 14; mains 18-39KN; ⊙11am-8pm Mon-Sat; ❄) Tapas dishes, Croatian-style. This teensy place, with just one counter and a few bar stools, serves cheese and meat platters using all locally sourced ingredients. Try the flatbreads with prosciutto from Zagora, black-truffle spread and cheese from Ika, or the *kulen* (spicy paprika-flavoured sausage) with grilled peppers and cream cheese. Service is warm and friendly.

★ Mali Bar
TAPAS €€

(☑01-55 31 014; www.facebook.com/MaliBarZagreb; Vlaška 63; dishes 45-150KN; ⊙12.30pm-midnight Mon-Sat; ❄) This earthy-toned spot by star chef Ana Ugarković is all about small plates, with influences cherry-picked from across the Mediterranean, the Middle East and Asia. Dig into *labneh* (strained yoghurt cheese) balls on a bed of chard and roasted beetroot, smoked tuna dressed in saffron and Chinese pork dumplings all in the same sitting.

★ Bistro Apetit
EUROPEAN €€€

(☑01-46 77 335; www.bistroapetit.com; Jurjevska 65a; mains 132-202KN; ⊙10am-midnight Tue-Sun; ❄) High up on villa-lined Jurjevska steet, this restaurant run by chef Marin Rendić, who previously worked at Copenhagen's Noma, serves up Zagreb's suavest contemporary dishes. Start with tuna tartare with pear and sesame seeds then move on to beef cheeks on bean spread, laced by carrot and pistachio. Opt for a degustation menu (five/seven courses 420/620KN) for flavour-packed feasting.

Zinfandel's
INTERNATIONAL €€€

(☑01-45 66 644; www.zinfandels.hr; Mihanovićeva 1; mains 165-230KN; ⊙6am-11pm Mon-Sat, 6.30am-11pm Sun; ❄) One of the top tables in town, Zinfandel's is headed by chef Ana Grgić, whose menu of creative flair is served in the grand dining room of the **Esplanade Zagreb Hotel** (☑01-45 66 666; www.esplanade.hr; r from €130; 🅿❄@🛜). Don't miss the confit pigeon with beetroot and cherries with a rhubarb sauce. After dinner move onto the Oleander Terrace for a drink and prime people-watching across Starčevićev Trg.

Zagreb

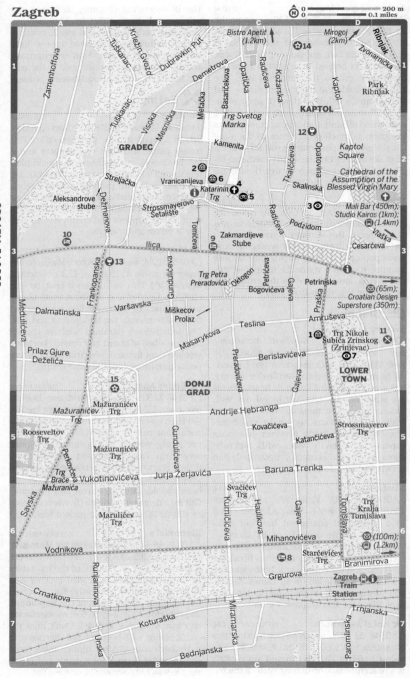

N 0 ——————— 200 m
0 ——————— 0.1 miles

Krležin Gvozd
Zamenhoffova
Tuškanac
Dubravkin Put

Bistro Apetit
(1.2km)

Mirogoj
(2km)

Ribnjak
Zvonarnička

14

Demetrova
Opatička
Radićeva
Kozarska
Kaptol

KAPTOL

Park
Ribnjak

Visoka
Mesnička
Mletačka
Basaričekova
Kožarska

Trg Svetog
Marka

12

GRADEC

Kamenita

Opatovina

Kaptol
Square

Streljačka

Dežmanova

2

Vranicanijeva

6
4

Katarinin
Trg

5

Thalčićeva

Skalinska

Cathedral of the
Assumption of the
Blessed Virgin Mary

Aleksandrove
stube

Strossmayerovo
Šetalište

Tomićeva

3

Radićeva

Podzidom

Mali Bar (450m);
Studio Kairos (1km);
(1.4km)

Vlaška

10

Ilica

9

Zakmardijeve
Stube

Cesarčeva

Frankopanska
Gundulićeva

13

Trg Petra
Preradovića

Oktogon
Petrićeva
Bogovićeva

Gajeva

Petrinjska

(65m);
Croatian Design
Superstore (350m)

Medulićeva
Dalmatinska

Varšavska

Miškecov
Prolaz

Masarykova

Teslina

Preradovićeva

Berislavićeva

Amruševa

1

Trg Nikole
Subića Zrinskog
(Zrinjevac)

11

Prilaz Gjure
Deželića

7

LOWER
TOWN

Rooseveltov
Trg

15

Mažuranićev
Trg

DONJI
GRAD

Andrije Hebranga

Kovačićeva

Strossmayerov
Trg

Perkovčeva
Trg
Braće
Mažuranića

Mažuranićev
Trg

Vukotinovićeva

Gundulićeva

Jurja Žerjavića

Katančićeva

Baruna Trenka

Gajeva

Savska

Marulićev
Trg

Kumičićeva

Haulikova

Svačićev
Trg

Mihanovićeva

Trg
Kralja
Tomislava

Tomislava

Vodnikova

8

Starčevićev
Trg

(100m);
(1.2km)

Runjaninova

Grgurova

Zagreb
Train
Station

Branimirova

Crnatkova

Unska

Koturaška

Miramarska

Bednjanska

Paromlinska

Trnjanska

Zagreb

🍷 Drinking & Entertainment

In the Upper Town, Tkalčićeva is throbbing with bars and cafes. With half a dozen bars and sidewalk cafes between Trg Petra Preradovića (known locally as Cvjetni trg) and Bogovićeva in the Lower Town, the scene on summer nights resembles a vast outdoor party. Things wind down by midnight, though, and get quieter from mid-July through late August.

Pupitres   WINE BAR
(☎ 098 16 58 073; http://pupitres.hr; Frankopanska 1; ⊙ 9am-11pm Mon-Thu, to 1am Fri & Sat; 🛜) When a wine bar is run by a top sommelier, you know you're in good hands. Jelene Šimić Valentić's casual-chic place is the best spot in town to get acquainted with Croatia's plethora of wines. Service is charming and genuinely helpful and the wine list is (unsurprisingly) a roll-call of the country's best cellars.

Craft Room   CRAFT BEER
(www.facebook.com/craftroombeer; Opatovina 35; ⊙ 10am-2am; 🛜) In the city centre, this is the number-one stop for anyone interested in Croatia's craft-beer scene. Plenty of local beers are on tap and there's a huge menu of bottled international brands.

Booze & Blues   LIVE MUSIC
(www.booze-and-blues.com; Tkalčićeva 84; ⊙ 8am-midnight Sun-Tue, to 2am Wed-Sat; 🛜) It does what it says on the tin. Perched at the top of the buzzy Tkalča strip, this haven of jazz, blues and soul rhythms stands out with its weekend live-music line-up. The interior is designed in the tradition of American blues and jazz clubs, with music-history memorabilia, and Heineken on tap flowing from a functioning saxophone.

ℹ️ Information

Emergency Health Clinic (☎ 01-63 02 911; Heinzelova 87; ⊙ 24hr)

KBC Rebro Hospital (☎ 8am-4pm 01-23 88 029; www.kbc-zagreb.hr; Kišpatićeva 12; ⊙ 24hr) Good public hospital with an emergency department. It's the teaching hospital of the University of Zagreb.

Main Tourist Office (☎ information 0800 53 53, office 01-48 14 051; www.infozagreb.hr; Trg Bana Jelačića 11; ⊙ 8.30am-8pm Mon-Fri, 9am-6pm Sat, 10am-4pm Sun) Distributes free city maps and leaflets. Has branches throughout the city.

ℹ️ Getting There & Away

AIR

Located 17km southeast of the city, **Zagreb Airport** (☎ 01-45 62 170; www.zagreb-airport. hr; Rudolfa Fizira 21, Velika Gorica), with its supermodern terminal, is Croatia's major airport, offering a range of international and domestic services.

BUS

The **Zagreb bus station** (☎ 060 313 333; www. akz.hr; Avenija M Držića 4) is located 1km east of the train station. If you need to store bags, there's a *garderoba* (per hour 5KN). Major destinations include Zadar (from 89KN, 4½ hours, 30 daily), Split (from 120KN, five to 8½ hours, 32 daily) and Dubrovnik (from 188KN, 10 hours, 12 daily).

TRAIN

The **train station** (www.hzpp.hr; Trg Kralja Tomislava 12) is in the southern part of the city centre. The station has a *garderoba* (locker per 24 hours 15KN) if you need to store bags. Destinations include Split (208KN, seven hours, three daily).

ℹ️ Getting Around

TO/FROM THE AIRPORT

The **Croatia Airlines bus** (www.plesoprijevoz. hr) runs from the airport to Zagreb bus station every half-hour or hour (depending on flight schedules) from 7am to 10.30pm (30KN, 40 minutes). Returning to the airport, bus services run from 4am to 8.30pm.

Bus line 290 (8KN, 1¼ hour) runs between Kvaternik Trg, just east of the city centre, and the airport every 35 minutes between 4.20am and midnight.

Taxis cost between 150KN and 200KN from the airport to the city centre.

PUBLIC TRANSPORT

Zagreb's public transport (www.zet.hr) is based on an efficient network of trams and buses. Tram maps are posted at most stations, making the system easy to navigate. Buy single-use tickets at newspaper kiosks or from the driver for 4KN (for 30 minutes) or 10KN (90 minutes). You can use the same ticket when transferring trams or buses but only in one direction. Night tram single-use tickets are 15KN. Make sure you validate your ticket when you get on the tram or bus by getting it time-stamped in the yellow ticket-validation box at the front of the vehicle – the other boxes only work for multi-use transport cards.

ISTRA

☑ 052

Continental Croatia meets the Adriatic in Istria (Istra to Croats), the heart-shaped, 3600-sq-km peninsula in the country's northwest. The bucolic interior of rolling hills and fertile plains attracts food- and culture-focused visitors to Istria's hilltop villages, rural hotels and farmhouse restaurants, while the indented coastline is enormously popular with the sun-and-sea set. Though vast hotel complexes line much of the coast and the rocky beaches are not Croatia's best, facilities are wide-ranging, the sea is clean and secluded spots are still plentiful.

Istria's madly popular coast gets flooded with central European tourists in summer, but you can still feel alone and undisturbed in the peninsula's interior, even in mid-August. Add acclaimed gastronomy (starring fresh seafood, prime white truffles, wild asparagus, top-rated olive oils and award-winning wines), sprinkle it with historical charm and you have a little slice of heaven.

Rovinj

POP 14,300

Rovinj (Rovigno in Italian) is coastal Istria's star attraction. While it can get overrun with tourists in summer and there aren't a lot of actual sights, it remains an intensely charming place. The old town is contained within an egg-shaped peninsula, webbed with steep cobbled streets and small squares, and punctuated by a tall church tower rising from the highest point. Originally an island, it was only connected to the mainland in 1763 when the narrow channel separating it was filled.

The main residential part of Rovinj spreads back from the old town and up the low hills that surround it, while resort-style hotels hug the coast to the north and south. When the crowds get too much, the 14 islands of the Rovinj archipelago make for a pleasant afternoon away.

◎ Sights

★ St Euphemia's Church   CHURCH

(Crkva Sv Eufemije; Trg Sv Eufemije bb; tower 20KN; ⊙10am-6pm Jun-Sep, to 4pm May, to 2pm Apr) FREE Built from 1725 to 1736, this imposing structure – the largest baroque church in Istria – dominates Rovinj from its hilltop location in the middle of the old town. Its 61m-high bell tower is older than the present church; construction commenced in 1654 and lasted 26 years. It's modelled on the campanile of St Mark's in Venice, and is topped by a 4m copper statue of St Euphemia, who shows the direction of the wind by turning on a spindle.

Rovinj City Museum   MUSEUM

(Muzej grada Rovinj; ☑052-816 720; www.muzej-rovinj.hr; Trg Maršala Tita 11; adult/child Jun-Aug 65/40KN, Sep-May 15/10KN; ⊙10am-10pm Jun-Aug, to 1pm Tue-Sat Sep-May) Housed in a 17th-century baroque palace, this museum displays temporary exhibitions on the ground floor, 20th-century and contemporary art on the 1st floor, and 16th- to 19th-century works on the top floor. Croatian artists are well represented, along with Venetian luminaries such as Jacopo Bassano.

⌂ Sleeping

Roundabout Hostel   HOSTEL €

(☑052-817 387; www.roundabouthostel.com; Trg na križu 6; dm 140-187KN; ▣❋🖙) This simple budget option has bunks with individual reading lights, lockers and a small shared kitchen. It's located on the big roundabout as you come into Rovinj, about a kilometre from the old town.

Villa Dobravac   HOTEL €€

(☑052-813 006; www.villa-dobravac.com; Karmelo 1; r €100-128; ▣❋🖙) As well as making wine and olive oil, the Dobravac family rents a set of 10 spacious, modern rooms in this lovely old peach-coloured villa in the residential part of Rovinj. Most have a terrace and a sea view.

★ Casa Alice
HOTEL €€€

(📞052-821104; www.casaalice.com; Paola Deperisa 1; r €200-220; 🅿❄🌐📶🍴) Escape the masses in this lovely 10-room hotel in Rovinj's suburban fringes, a 20-minute walk from the centre but only five minutes from the sea. If walking sounds too hard you can always laze around the blue-tiled pool and help yourself to coffee and cake. Some of the rooms have terraces and most have a spa bath.

✕ Eating & Drinking

Pizzeria Da Sergio
PIZZA €

(📞052-816 949; www.facebook.com/DaSergioRv; Grisia 11; pizzas 35-82KN; ⏰11am-3pm & 6-11pm; 📶🍴) It's worth waiting in line to get a table at this old-fashioned, two-floor pizzeria. It dishes out Rovinj's best thin-crust pizza, with a huge range of toppings to choose from. It also serves decent house wine.

Monte
ISTRIAN €€€

(📞052-830 203; www.monte.hr; Montalbano 75; 3-/4-/6-course menu 619/719/849KN; ⏰6.30-11pm May-Sep; 🍴) The first restaurant in Croatia to be awarded a Michelin star, Monte offers a choice of three differently themed six-course Modern Istrian menus (one focused on local ingredients, one exclusively vegetarian and the last emphasising modern techniques). Or you can build your own three- or four-course meal, mixing and matching from all three.

Mediterraneo
COCKTAIL BAR

(www.facebook.com/mediterraneo.rovinj; Sv Križa 24; ⏰9am-2am Apr-Sep; 📶) Clinging to the old-town sea cliffs, this gorgeous little bar feels like a secret. It's not, of course – Rovinj's fashionable set are already here, holding court on the pastel-coloured stools right by the water. It's a very relaxed Adriatic scene, with friendly waitstaff and good cocktails, too.

ℹ Information

Medical Centre (📞052-840 702; Istarska bb; ⏰24hr)

Tourist Office (📞052-811 566; www.rovinj-tourism.com; Pina Budicina 12; ⏰8am-10pm Jul & Aug, to 8pm mid-May–Jun & Sep)

ℹ Getting There & Away

The **bus station** (📞060 333 111; Trg na lokvi 6) is just to the southeast of the old town, with services to/from Zagreb (150KN, 4½ hours, 10 daily).

WORTH A TRIP

RURAL LUXURY

The focus is firmly on quality at **Meneghetti** (📞052-528 800; www.meneghetti.hr; Stancija Meneghetti 1; r from €279, mains 190-290KN; ⏰Apr-Dec; 🅿❄🌐📶🍴) – whether that be the estate's top-notch wine and olive oil, the architecture of the guest blocks, which sympathetically embrace the historic house at its core, or the exquisite modern Istrian cuisine served at the **restaurant**. Plus there's a private beach, accessed by a 25-minute walk through the vineyard. Sheer bliss.

PLITVICE LAKES NATIONAL PARK
📋053

By far Croatia's top natural attraction and the absolute highlight of Croatia's Adriatic hinterland, this glorious expanse of forested hills and turquoise lakes is exquisitely scenic – so much so that in 1979 Unesco proclaimed it a World Heritage Site. The name is slightly misleading though, as it's not so much the lakes that are the attraction here but the hundreds of waterfalls that link them. It's as though Croatia decided to gather all its waterfalls in one place and charge admission to view them.

The extraordinary natural beauty of the **park** (📞053-751 015; www.np-plitvicka-jezera.hr; adult/child Jul & Aug 250/110KN, Apr-Jun, Sep & Oct 150/80KN, Nov-Mar 55/35KN; ⏰7am-8pm) merits a full day's exploration, but you can still experience a lot on a half-day trip from Zadar or Zagreb. You must be able to walk a fair distance to get the most out of the place.

🛏 Sleeping & Eating

★ House Župan
GUESTHOUSE €

(📞047-784 057; www.sobe-zupan.com; Rakovica 35, Rakovica; s/d 250/370KN; 🅿❄📶) With an exceptionally welcoming hostess and clean, contemporary and reasonably priced rooms, this is a superb choice. There's even a guest kitchen and plenty of other diversions when you want to relax after a hike. It's set back from the highway in the small town of Rakovica, 11km north of Plitvice Lakes National Park.

Lička Kuća
CROATIAN €€

(📞053-751 024; Rastovača; mains 70-195KN; ⏰11am-10pm Mar-Nov) Built in 1972 and fully rebuilt in traditional stone-walled style in 2015 after burning to the ground three years earlier, Lička Kuća is touristy and extremely busy in high season, but the food is excellent. Specialities include slow-cooked lamb, dry-cured local prosciutto, and mountain trout, making it one of the best places for tradition-al dishes in the Northern Dalmatian interior.

ℹ Information

Both of the park's two main entrances have parking (7/70KN per hour/day) and an infor-mation office stocking brochures and maps. The main park **office** (☑ 053-751 014; www.np-plitvicka-jezera.hr; Josipa Jovića 19, Plitvička Jezera) is in Plitvička Jezera.

ℹ Getting There & Away

Buses stop at both park entrances; there's a small ticket office at the stop near Entrance 2. Destinations include Šibenik (118KN, four hours, three daily), Split (174KN, 4½ hours, six daily), Zadar (95KN, 2½ hours, seven daily) and Zagreb (89KN, two hours, frequent).

DALMATIA

Serving the classic cocktail of historic towns, jewel-like waters, rugged limestone moun-tains, sun-kissed islands, gorgeous climate and Mediterranean cuisine, Dalmatia is a holidaymaker's dream.

Hot spots include the buzzing Mediter-ranean-flavoured cities of Zadar and Split, and gorgeous little Hvar Town, where the cashed meet the trashed on the Adriatic's most glamorous party island. Yet one lo-cation understandably eclipses any discus-sion of Dalmatia: the remarkable old town of Dubrovnik. Ringed by mighty defensive walls that dip their feet in the cerulean sea, the city encapsulates the very essence of a medieval fantasy.

If it's relaxation you're after, there are se-ductive sandy beaches and pebbly coves scat-tered about islands near and far. Yachties can still sail between unpopulated islands with-out a shred of development, lost in dreams of the Mediterranean of old, while hikers can wander lonely trails in the mountainous hin-terland, where bears and wolves still dwell.

Zadar

☑ 023 / POP 75,437

Boasting a historic old town of Roman ru-ins, medieval churches, cosmopolitan cafes and quality museums set on a small penin-sula, Zadar is an intriguing city. It's not too crowded and its two unique attractions – the sound-and-light spectacle of the Sea Organ and the Sun Salutation – need to be seen and heard to be believed.

While it's not a picture-postcard kind of place from every angle, the mix of ancient relics, Habsburg elegance and its coastal setting all offset the unsightly tower blocks climbing up the hilly hinterland. It's no Dubrovnik, but it's not a museum town ei-ther – this is a living, vibrant city, enjoyed by residents and visitors alike.

Zadar is also a key transport hub, with superb ferry connections to the surrounding islands.

◉ Sights

★ **Sea Organ** MONUMENT
(Morske orgulje; Istarska Obala) **FREE** Zadar's incredible *Sea Organ,* designed by local ar-chitect Nikola Bašić, is unique. Set within the perforated stone stairs that descend into the sea is a system of pipes and whistles that exudes wistful sighs when the movement of the sea pushes air through it. The effect is hypnotic, the mellifluous tones increasing in volume when a boat or ferry passes by. You can swim from the steps off the promenade while listening to the sounds.

★ **Sun Salutation** MONUMENT
(Pozdrav Suncu; Istarska Obala) Another wacky and wonderful creation by Nikola Bašić, this 22m-wide circle set into the pavement is filled with 300 multilayered glass plates that collect the sun's energy during the day. Together with the wave energy that makes the *Sea Organ's* sound, it produces a trip-py light show from sunset to sunrise that's meant to simulate the solar system. It also collects enough energy to power the entire harbour-front lighting system.

Roman Forum RUINS
(Zeleni trg) One of the most intriguing things about Zadar is the way Roman ruins seem to sprout randomly from the city's streets. No-where is this more evident than at the site of the ancient Forum, constructed between the 1st century BCE and the 3rd century CE. As in Roman times, it's the centre of civic and religious life, with St Donatus' Church dominating one side of it.

St Donatus' Church CHURCH
(Crkva Sv Donata; Šimuna Kožičića Benje bb; 20KN; ⊙9am-9pm May-Sep, to 4pm Oct-Apr) Dating

from the beginning of the 9th century, this unusual circular Byzantine-style church was named after the bishop who commissioned it. As one of only a handful of buildings from the early Croatian kingdom to have survived the Mongol invasion of the 13th century, it's a particularly important cultural relic. The simple and unadorned interior includes two complete Roman columns, recycled from the Forum. Also from the Forum are the paving slabs that were revealed after the original floor was removed.

St Anastasia's Cathedral CATHEDRAL
(Katedrala Sv Stošije; Trg Sv Stošije; ☉6.30-7pm Mon-Fri, 8-9am Sat, 8-9am & 6-7pm Sun) FREE Built in the 12th and 13th centuries, Zadar's cathedral has a richly decorated facade and an impressive three-nave interior with the remains of frescoes in the side apses. The cathedral was badly bombed during WWII and has since been reconstructed. On the altar in the left apse is a marble sarcophagus containing the relics of St Anastasia, while the choir contains lavishly carved stalls. A glass vestibule allows you to peer inside when the cathedral's closed, which is often.

Archaeological Museum MUSEUM
(Arheološki Muzej; ☎023-250 516; www.amzd.hr; Trg Opatice Čike 1; adult/child 30/15KN; ☉9am-9pm Jun & Sep, to 10pm Jul & Aug, to 3pm Apr, May & Oct, 9am-2pm Mon-Fri, to 1pm Sat Nov-Mar) A wealth of prehistoric, ancient and medieval relics, mainly from Zadar and its surrounds, awaits at this fascinating museum. Highlights include a 2.5m-high marble statue of Augustus from the 1st century CE, and a model of the Forum as it once looked.

🛏 Sleeping

Windward Hostel HOSTEL €
(☎091 62 19 197; www.facebook.com/windward. hostel.zadar; Gazica 12; dm/d 112/450KN; ✳🛜) Just 1.5km from the old town, this 20-bed, yachting-themed hostel is run by a passionate sailor. Rooms are immaculate, with big lockers, electric window blinds and private reading lights. There's a supermarket and bakery nearby, and staff can organise sailing tours and lessons.

Boutique Hostel Forum HOSTEL €€
(☎023-253 031; www.hostelforumzadar.com; Široka 20; dm/d/ste from 155/665/725KN) Wonderfully colourful dorm rooms and stylish, white-and-black doubles and suites, some with top skyline and partial water views, make this easily

the best hostel and midrange hotel in the old centre. The location couldn't be better and the rooms are terrific for the price.

★ Art Hotel Kalelarga HOTEL €€€
(☎023-233 000; www.arthotel-kalelarga.com; Majke Margarite 3; s/d incl breakfast 1515/1810KN; ✳🛜) Built and designed under strict conservation rules due to its old-town location, this 10-room boutique hotel is understated and luxurious beauty. Exposed stonework and mushroom hues imbue the spacious rooms with plenty of style and character. The gourmet breakfast is served in the hotel's own stylish cafe, **Gourmet Kalelarga** (www.arthotel-kalelarga.com/gourmet; Široka 23; breakfast 28-60KN; mains 59-155KN; ☉7am-10pm).

🍴 Eating

★ Kaštel MEDITERRANEAN €€
(☎023-494 950; www.hotel-bastion.hr; Bedemi Zadarskih Pobuna 13; mains 70-190KN; ☉7am-11pm) Hotel Bastion's fine-dining restaurant offers contemporary takes on classic Croatian cuisine (octopus stew, stuffed squid, Pag cheese). France and Italy also make their presence felt, particularly in the delectable dessert list. Opt for the white-linen experience inside or dine on the battlements overlooking the harbour for a memorable evening.

Pet Bunara DALMATIAN €€
(☎023-224 010; www.petbunara.com; Stratico 1; mains 65-160KN; ☉noon-11pm) With exposed stone walls inside and a pretty terrace lined with olive trees, this is an atmospheric place to tuck into Dalmatian soups and stews, homemade pasta and local faves such as octopus and turkey. Save room for a traditional Zadar fig cake or cherry torte.

Corte Vino & More INTERNATIONAL €€€
(☎023-335 357; www.facebook.com/cortevinomore; Braće Bersa 2; mains 80-180KN; ☉noon-2.30pm & 7-10.30pm) One of the classiest dining experiences in Zadar, Corte Vino & More in the Al Mayer Heritage Hotel has a gorgeous setting, wonderfully attentive service and high-quality food that changes with the seasons, taking Croatian traditional dishes and riffing in subtle, new and creative directions. Fabulous wine list and knowledgeable waiters, too.

🍷 Drinking & Nightlife

Podroom CLUB
(☎099 74 98 451; www.podroom.club; Marka Marulića bb; ☉midnight-6am Fri, 1-6.30am Sat)

WORTH A TRIP

ŠIBENIK

The coastal city of Šibenik has a magnificent medieval heart, gleaming white against the placid waters of the bay, something that may not be immediately apparent as you drive through the somewhat-shabby outskirts. The stone labyrinth of steep backstreets and alleys is a joy to explore.

It's well worth a detour here to see **St James' Cathedral** (Katedrala Svetog Jakova; Trg Republike Hrvatske; adult/child 20KN/free; ☺9.30am-6.30pm), the crowning architectural glory of the Dalmatian coast and a World Heritage Site. It was constructed entirely of stone quarried from the islands of Brač, Korčula, Rab and Krk, and is reputed to be the world's largest church built completely of stone without brick or wooden supports. The structure is also unique in that the interior shape corresponds exactly to the exterior.

Other lures include **Pelegrini** (☎022-213 701; www.pelegrini.hr; Jurja Dalmatinca 1; mains 79-185KN, 3-/4-/5-course set menu 440/570/700KN; ☺noon-midnight), one of Croatia's top restaurants, and the character-filled **Medulić Palace Rooms & Apartments** (☎095 53 01 868; www.medulicpalace.com; Ivana Pribislavića 4; r 310-630KN, apt 365-815KN; ❋ ⊚).

Šibenik's **bus station** (☎060 368 368; Draga 14) has services to Dubrovnik (148KN, 6½ hours, at least two daily), Split (48KN, 1½ hours, 12 daily), Zadar (43KN, 1½ hours, at least hourly) and Zagreb (from 132KN, five to seven hours, at least hourly).

One of Zadar's biggest clubs, Podroom draws a regular cast of Croatian and international DJs, especially in summer. It's within staggering distance of the old town and really only kicks off around 2am. Live acts also take to the stage to get things going. Admission prices vary depending on who's on the bill.

❶ Information

Tourist Office (☎023-316 166; www.zadar. travel; Jurja Barakovića 5; ☺8am-11pm May-Jul & Sep, to midnight Aug, 8am-8pm Mon-Fri, 9am-2pm Sat & Sun Oct-Apr; ⊚) Publishes a good colour map and rents audioguides (40KN) for a self-guided tour around the town.

Zadar General Hospital (Opća Bolnica Zadar; ☎023-505 505; www.bolnica-zadar.hr; Bože Peričića 5)

❶ Getting There & Away

AIR

Recently upgraded **Zadar Airport** (☎023-205 800; www.zadar-airport.hr) is 12km east of the town centre. Croatia Airlines flies to Zadar from Zagreb.

BUS

The **bus station** (☎060 305 305; www. liburnija-zadar.hr; Ante Starčevića 1) is about 1km southeast of the old town. Domestic destinations include Dubrovnik (182KN, eight hours, up to six daily), Šibenik (43KN, 1½ hours, at least hourly), Split (86KN, three hours, hourly) and Zagreb (110KN, 3½ hours, hourly).

❶ Getting Around

TO/FROM THE AIRPORT

Timed around all Croatia Airlines flights, buses (25KN one way) depart from outside the main terminal, and from the old town (Liburnska Obala) and the bus station one hour prior to flights.

A taxi will cost around 150KN to the old town and 180KN to Borik.

BUS & BIKE

Liburnija (www.liburnija-zadar.hr) runs buses on 10 routes, which all loop through the bus station. Tickets cost 10KN on board – or 16KN for two from a *tisak* (news-stand). Buses 5 and 8 (usually marked 'Puntamika') head to/from Borik regularly.

Calimero (☎023-311 010; www.rent-a-bike-zadar.com; Zasjedanja Zavnoh 1; per hour/day from 40/120KN; ☺8am-8pm Mon-Fri, to 1pm Sat) is Zadar's best place to rent a bicycle. It's an easy walk from the old town.

Trogir

☎021 / POP 13,200

Gorgeous Trogir (called Trau by the Venetians) is set within medieval walls on a tiny island, linked by bridges to both the mainland and to the far larger Čiovo Island. On summer nights everyone gravitates to the wide seaside promenade lined with bars, cafes and yachts, leaving the knotted, mazelike marble streets gleaming mysteriously under old-fashioned streetlights.

The old town has retained many intact and beautiful buildings from its age of glory between the 13th and 15th centuries. In 1997 its profuse collection of Romanesque and Renaissance buildings earned it World Heritage status.

While it's easily reached on a day trip from Split, Trogir also makes a good alternative base to the big city and a relaxing place to spend a few days.

◎ Sights

★ St Lawrence's Cathedral   CATHEDRAL
(Katedrala svetog Lovre; ☑ 021-881 426; Trg Ivana Pavla II; 25KN; ⊙ 8am-8pm Mon-Sat, noon-6pm Sun Jun-Aug, to 6pm Sep-May) Trogir's show-stopping attraction is its three-naved Venetian cathedral, one of the finest architectural works in Croatia, built between the 13th and 15th centuries. Master Radovan carved the grand Romanesque **portal** in 1240, flanked by a nude Adam and Eve standing on the backs of lions. At the end of the portico is another fine piece of sculpture: the 1464 cherub-filled **baptistery** sculpted by Andrija Aleši.

Sacred Art Museum   MUSEUM
(Muzej sakralne umjetnosti; ☑ 021-881426; Trg Ivana Pavla II 6; 10KN; ⊙ 8am-8pm Mon-Sat, 11.30am-7pm Sun Jun-Sep) Highlights of this small museum include illuminated manuscripts; a large painting of St Jerome and St John the Baptist by Bellini; an almost-life-size, brightly painted *Crucifix with Triumphant Christ;* and the darkly lit fragments of a 13th-century icon that once adorned the cathedral's altar.

🛏 Sleeping & Eating

Hostel Marina Trogir   HOSTEL €
(☑ 021-883 075; www.hostelmarina-trogir.com; Cumbrijana 16; dm 175KN; ⊙ May-Oct; ❄ 🛜) Run by an expat German couple, this excellent hostel has only four dorms, each sleeping seven or eight people. The custom-built wooden bunks have suitcase-sized lockers underneath, reading lights and privacy curtains for the lower bunk (but not the top one). Plus there's a communal kitchen and separate men's and women's bathrooms.

Villa Moretti   HISTORIC HOTEL €€
(☑ 021-885 326; www.villamoretti.com; Lučica 1; r €90-120; 🅿 ❄ 🛜) Owned by the same family since 1792, this 17th-century palazzo has five spacious, antique-filled rooms accessed by a grand marble and wrought-iron stairway. Two rooms open onto a large rear terrace, but all have million-dollar views over the old town. The bathrooms are large but a tad dated.

Konoba Trs   DALMATIAN €€€
(☑ 021-796 956; www.konoba-trs.com; Matije Gupca 14; mains 105-230KN; ⊙ 11am-midnight Mon-Sat, 5pm-midnight Sun) As traditional-looking as they come, this rustic little tavern has wooden benches and old stone walls inside, and an inviting courtyard shaded by grapevines. Yet the menu adds clever, contemporary twists to Dalmatian classics, featuring the likes of panko-crumbed octopus tentacles, and the signature dis:, nutmeg-spiced lamb *pašticada* (stew), served with savoury pancakes.

❶ Information

Tourist Office (☑ 021-885 628; www.tztrogir. hr; Trg Ivana Pavla II 1; ⊙ 8am-8pm May-Sep, 9am-5pm Mon-Fri Oct-Apr) Inside the town hall; distributes town maps.

❶ Getting There & Away

BOAT
Bura Line (☑ 095 83 74 320; www.buraline. com; Obala kralja Zvonimira bb; adult/child 35/18KN) has a small boat heading to and from Split that runs four to six times a day from May to September.

BUS
Intercity buses stop at the **bus station** (☑ 021-882 947; Kneza Tripimira bb) on the mainland near the bridge to Trogir. Destinations include Zagreb (148KN, 6½ hours, 10 daily), Zadar (73KN, 2½ hours, 11 daily), Split (20KN, 30 minutes, frequent) and Dubrovnik (137KN, 5½ hours, five daily). Split city bus 37 (17KN) takes the slower coastal road through Kaštela every 20 minutes, also stopping at the airport.

❶ Getting Around

In summer, small passenger **boats** depart from Obala Bana Berislavića, right in front of Hotel Concordia, heading to the beaches of Okrug Gornji (25KN) and Medena (20KN). The journey takes about 45 minutes.

Split
☑ 021 / POP 178,000

Croatia's second-largest city, Split (Spalato in Italian) is a great place to see Dalmatian life as it's really lived. Always buzzing, this exuberant city has just the right balance between tradition and modernity. Step inside

Central Split

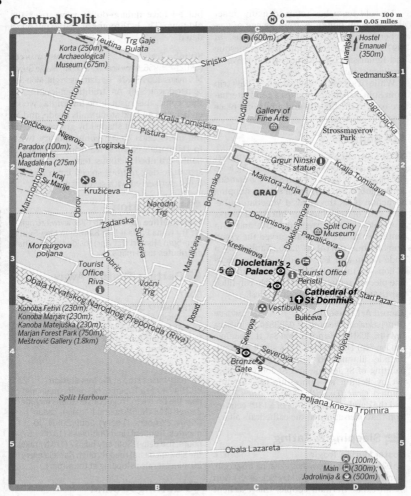

CROATIA SPLIT

Diocletian's Palace (a Unesco World Heritage Site and one of the world's most impressive Roman monuments) and you'll see dozens of bars, restaurants and shops thriving amid the atmospheric old walls where Split has been humming along for thousands of years.

To top it off, Split has a unique setting. Its dramatic coastal mountains act as the perfect backdrop to the turquoise waters of the Adriatic and help divert attention from the dozens of shabby high-rise apartment blocks that fill its suburbs. It's this thoroughly lived-in aspect of Split that means it will never be a fantasy land like Dubrovnik, but perhaps it's all the better for that.

⊙ Sights

The ever-frenetic waterfront promenade – officially called Obala hrvatskog narodnog preporoda (Croatian National Revival Waterfront) but more commonly known as the Riva – is your best central reference point in Split. East of here, past the wharf, are the buzzy beaches of Bačvice, Firule, Zenta and Trstenik bays. The wooded Marjan Hill dominates the western tip of the city and has even better beaches at its base.

★ Diocletian's Palace   HISTORIC SITE
Taking up a prime harbourside position, this extraordinary complex is one of the most

Central Split

imposing ancient Roman structures in existence today, and it's where you'll spend most of your time while in Split. Don't expect a palace, though, nor a museum – this is the city's living heart, its labyrinthine streets packed with people, bars, shops and restaurants. Built as a military fortress, imperial residence and fortified town, the palace measures 215m from north to south and 180m east to west.

➡ **Cathedral of St Domnius**

(Katedrala sv Duje; Peristil bb; cathedral/belfry 35/20KN; ⊙8am-8pm Jun-Sep, 7am-noon & 5-7pm May & Oct, 7am-noon Nov-Feb, 8am-5pm Mar & Apr) Split's octagonal cathedral is one of the best-preserved ancient Roman buildings still standing. It was built as a mausoleum for Diocletian, the last famous persecutor of the Christians, who was interred here in 311 CE. In the 5th century the Christians got the last laugh, destroying the emperor's sarcophagus and converting his tomb into a church dedicated to one of his victims. Note that a ticket for the cathedral includes admission to its crypt, treasury and baptistery (Temple of Jupiter).

➡ **Temple of Jupiter**

(Jupiterov hram; 10KN; free with cathedral ticket; ⊙8am-7pm Mon-Sat, 12.30-6.30pm Sun May-Oct, to 5pm Nov-Apr) Although it's now the cathedral's baptistery, this wonderfully intact building was originally an ancient Roman temple dedicated to the king of the gods. It still has its original barrel-vaulted ceiling and decorative frieze, although a striking bronze statue of St John the Baptist by Ivan Meštrović now fills the spot where Jupiter once stood. The font is

made from 13th-century carved stones recycled from the cathedral's rood screen.

➡ **Split City Museum**

(Muzej grada Splita; ☎021-360 171; www.mgst.net; Papalićeva 1; adult/child 22/12KN; ⊙8.30am-9pm Apr-Sep, 9am-5pm Tue-Sat, to 2pm Sun Oct-Mar) Built by Juraj Dalmatinac in the 15th century for one of the many noblemen who lived within the old town, the Large Papalić Palace is considered a fine example of late-Gothic style, with an elaborately carved entrance gate that proclaimed the importance of its original inhabitants. The interior has been thoroughly restored to house this museum, which has interesting displays on Diocletian's Palace and on the development of the city.

➡ **Diocletian's Palace Substructure**

(Supstrukcije Dioklecijanove palače; www.mgst. net; Obala hrvatskog narodnog preporoda bb; adult/child 42/22KN; ⊙8.30am-9pm Apr-Sep, to 5pm Oct, 9am-5pm Mon-Sat, to 2pm Sun Nov-Apr) The Bronze Gate of Diocletian's Palace once opened straight from the water into the palace basements, enabling goods to be unloaded and stored here. Now this former tradesman's entrance is the main way into the palace from the Riva. While the central part of the substructure is now a major thoroughfare lined with souvenir stalls, entry to the chambers on either side is ticketed.

Archaeological Museum   MUSEUM

(Arheološki muzej; ☎021-329 340; www.armus. hr; Zrinsko-Frankopanska 25; adult/child 20/10KN; ⊙9am-2pm & 4-8pm Mon-Sat Jun-Sep, closed Sat afternoon & Sun Oct-May) A treasure trove of classical sculpture and mosaics is displayed at this excellent museum, a short walk north of the town centre. Most of the vast collection originated from the ancient Roman settlements of Split and neighbouring **Salona** (☎021-213 358; Don Frane Bulića bb, Solin; adult/child 30/15KN; ⊙9am-7pm Mon-Sat, to 2pm Sun) (Solin), and there's also some Greek pottery from the island of Vis. There are displays of jewellery and coins, and a room filled with artefacts dating from the Palaeolithic to the Iron Age.

Meštrović Gallery   GALLERY

(Galerija Meštrović; ☎021-340 800; www.mestro vic.hr; Šetalište Ivana Meštrovića 46; adult/child 40/20KN; ⊙9am-7pm Tue-Sun May-Sep, to 4pm Tue-Sun Oct-Apr) At this stellar art museum you'll see a comprehensive, well-arranged collection of works by Ivan Meštrović, Croatia's premier modern sculptor, who built the grand mansion as a personal residence in the 1930s. Although Meštrović intended to retire here, he emigrated to the USA soon after WWII. Admission includes entry to the nearby **Kaštilac** (Šetalište Ivana Meštrovića 39; ⊘9am-7pm Tue-Sun May-Sep), a fortress housing other Meštrović works.

Marjan Forest Park PARK
(Park-šuma Marjan; www.marjan-parksuma.hr) Looming up to 178m over Split's western fringes, this nature reserve occupies a big space in Split's psyche. The views over the city and surrounding islands are extraordinary, and the shady paths provide a welcome reprieve from both the heat and the summertime tourist throngs. Trails pass through fragrant pine forests to scenic lookouts, a 16th-century Jewish cemetery, medieval chapels and cave dwellings once inhabited by Christian hermits. Climbers take to the cliffs near the end of the peninsula.

For an afternoon away from the city buzz, consider taking a long walk through the park and descending to **Kašjuni beach** (Šetalište Ivana Meštrovića bb) to cool off before catching the bus back.

🛏 Sleeping

⭐**Korta** APARTMENT €€
(☑021-571 226; www.kortasplit.com; Plinarska 31; apt from €94; ﷽🖧) Set around a courtyard in the historic Veli Varoš neighbourhood, these simple but elegant apartments have stone-tiled bathrooms and white walls hung with huge TVs and photos of rustic Croatian scenes. Many have balconies.

Apartments Magdalena APARTMENT €€
(☑098 423 087; www.magdalena-apartments.com; Milićeva 18; apt 465-611KN; ﷽🖧) You may never want to leave Magdalena's top-floor apartment once you see the old-town view from the dormer window. The three apartments are comfortable and fully furnished, and the hospitality offered by the off-site owners is exceptional: beer and juice in the fridge, a back-up toothbrush in the cupboard and even a mobile phone with credit on it.

⭐**Heritage Hotel Antique Split** HERITAGE HOTEL €€€
(☑021-785 208; www.antique-split.com; Poljana Grgura Ninskog 1; r from €267; ﷽🖧) Palace living at its most palatial, this boutique complex has eight chic rooms with stone walls and impressive bathrooms. In some you'll wake up to incredible views over the cathedral.

Villa Split B&B €€€
(☑091 40 34 403; www.villasplitluxury.com; Bajamontijeva 5; r from €215; 🅿﷽🖧) Built into the Roman-built wall of Diocletian's Palace, this wonderful boutique B&B has only three rooms, the best of which is the slightly larger one in the attic. If you're happy to swap the ancient for the merely medieval, there are six larger rooms in a 10th-century building on the main square.

🍴 Eating

Kruščić BAKERY €
(☑099 26 12 345; www.facebook.com/Kruscic. Split; Obrov 6; items 6-15KN; ⊘8am-2pm) Spit's best bakery serves delicious bread, pastries and pizza slices. The focus is more savoury than sweet, although you'll find sweet things, too.

Konoba Fetivi DALMATIAN, SEAFOOD €€
(☑021-355 152; www.facebook.com/KonobaFetivi; Tomića stine 4; mains 70-95KN; ⊘noon-11pm Tue-Sun) Informal and family-run, with a TV screening sports in the corner, Fetivi feels more like a tavern than most that bear the *konoba* name. However, that doesn't detract from the food, which is first rate. Seafood is the focus here. The cuttlefish stew with polenta is highly recommended, but the whole fish is wonderfully fresh, too.

Konoba Matejuška DALMATIAN, SEAFOOD €€
(☑021-814 099; www.konobamatejuska.hr; Tomića Stine 3; mains 75-140KN; ⊘noon-11pm Apr-Oct, to 9pm Wed-Mon Nov-Mar) This cosy, rustic tavern, in an alleyway minutes from the seafront, specialises in well-prepared seafood – as epitomised in its perfectly cooked fish platter for two. The grilled squid is also excellent, served with the archetypal Dalmatian side dish, *blitva* (Swiss chard with slightly mushy potato, drenched in olive oil). Book ahead.

⭐**Konoba Marjan** DALMATIAN, SEAFOOD €€€
(☑098 93 46 848; www.facebook.com/konobamarjan; Senjska 1; mains 84-160KN; ⊘noon-11pm Mon-Sat; 🖧) Offering great-quality Dalmatian fare, this friendly little Veli Varoš tavern features daily specials such as cuttlefish *brujet* (a flavour-packed seafood stew – highly recommended), *gregada* (fish stew with potato) and prawn pasta. The wine list is excellent, showcasing some local boutique wineries, and there are a few seats outside on the street leading up to Marjan Hill.

KLIS FORTRESS

Controlling the valley leading into Split, this imposing **fortress** (Tvrđava Klis; ☑021-240 578; www.tvrdavaklis.com; Klis bb; adult/child 40/15KN; ☺9.30am-4pm) spreads along a limestone bluff, reaching 385m at its highest point. Its long and narrow form (304m by 53m) derives from constant extensions over the course of millennia. Inside, you can clamber all over the fortifications and visit the small museum, which has displays of swords and costumes and detailed information on the castle's brutal past.

Game of Thrones fans will recognise the fortress as Meereen, where Daenerys Targaryen had all those nasty slave-masters crucified in season four.

Klis is located 12km northeast of the city centre, and can be reached by city bus 22 (13KN) from Trg Gaje Bulata or Split's local bus station.

Zoi   MEDITERRANEAN €€€
(☑021-637 491; www.zoi.hr; Obala hrvatskog narodnog preporoda 23; mains 120-180KN; ☺6.30pm-midnight) Accessed by a discreet door on the waterfront promenade, this upstairs restaurant serves sophisticated modern Mediterranean dishes that look as divine as they taste. The decor is simultaneously elegant and extremely hip, with the exposed walls of Diocletian's Palace offset with bright bursts of magenta. Head up to the roof terrace for one of Split's most memorable dining spaces.

🍷 Drinking & Nightlife

⭐**Marcvs Marvlvs Spalatensis**   WINE BAR
(www.facebook.com/marvlvs; Papalićeva 4; ☺11am-midnight Jun-Aug, to 11pm Mon-Sat Sep-May; 🛜) Fittingly, the 15th-century Gothic home of the 'Dante of Croatia', Marko Marulić, now houses this wonderful little 'library jazz bar' made up of small rooms crammed with books and frequented by ageless bohemians, tortured poets and wistful academics. Cheese, chess, cards and cigars are all on offer, and there's often live music.

⭐**Paradox**   WINE BAR
(☑021-787 778; www.paradox.hr; Bana Josipa Jelačića 3; ☺8am-midnight; 🛜) This stylish wine and cheese bar has a fantastic rooftop terrace, a massive selection of Croatian wines (more than 120, including 40 by the glass) and an array of local cheeses to go with them. The clued-up staff members really know their stuff, and there's live music most weekends.

ⓘ Information

KBC Split (Klinički bolnički centar Split; ☑021-556 111; www.kbsplit.hr; Spinčićeva 1)

Tourist Office Riva (☑021-360 066; www.visit split.com; Obala hrvatskog narodnog preporoda 9; ☺8am-9pm Jun-Sep, 8am-8pm Mon-Sat, to 5pm Sun Apr, May & Oct, 9am-4pm Mon-Fri, to 2pm Sat Nov-Mar) Stocks the free 72-hour Split Card, which offers free or discounted access to attractions, car rental, restaurants, shops and theatres. You're eligible for the card if you're staying in Split more than four nights from April to September, or staying in designated hotels for more than two nights at other times.

ⓘ Getting There & Away

The bus, train and ferry terminals are clustered on the eastern side of the harbour, a short walk from the old town.

AIR

Split Airport (SPU, Zračna luka Split; ☑021-203 555; www.split-airport.hr; Dr Franje Tuđmana 1270, Kaštel Štafilić) is in Kaštela, 24km northwest of central Split. In summer, dozens of airlines fly here from all over Europe but only Croatia Airlines, Eurowings and Trade Air fly year-round.

BOAT

Split's ferry harbour is extremely busy and can be hard to negotiate, so you're best to arrive early. Most domestic ferries depart from Gat Sv Petra, the first of the three major piers, which has **ticket booths** for both Jadrolinija and Kapetan Luka. The giant international ferries depart from Gat Sv Duje, the second of the piers, where there's a large **ferry terminal** with ticketing offices for the major lines. In July and August, and at weekends, it's often necessary to appear hours before departure for a car ferry, and put your car in the line for boarding. There is rarely a problem or a long wait obtaining a space in the low season.

Jadrolinija (☑021-338 333; www.jadrolinija. hr; Gat Sv Duje bb) operates most of the ferries between Split and the islands. Car ferry services include Stari Grad on Hvar (per person/car 47/310KN, two hours, up to seven daily) and Vela Luka on Korčula (60/470KN, 2¾ hours, two daily). Summertime catamaran destinations include Dubrovnik (210KN, six hours, daily), Hvar Town (55KN to 110KN, one to two hours, up to eight daily) and Korčula Town (160KN, 3¾ hours, daily).

Kapetan Luka (Krilo; ☑ 021-645 476; www.krilo.hr) has daily high-speed catamaran services to Hvar (90KN, one hour) and Korčula (130KN, 2½ hours). From May to mid-October, they also head to Dubrovnik (210KN, 4¼ hours)

BUS

Most intercity buses arrive at the **main bus station** (Autobusni Kolodvor Split; ☑ 060 327 777; www.ak-split.hr; Obala kneza Domagoja bb) beside the harbour. In summer it's best to purchase bus tickets with seat reservations in advance. If you need to store bags, there's a **garderoba** (left-luggage office; Obala kneza Domagoja 12; 1st hour 5KN, additional hours 1.50KN; ⊘ 6am-10pm May-Sep) nearby. Domestic destinations include Zagreb (157KN, five hours, at least hourly), Zadar (90KN, three hours, at least hourly) and Dubrovnik (127KN, 4½ hours, at least 11 daily).

TRAIN

Trains head to **Split Train Station** (Željeznica stanica Split; ☑ 021-338 525; www.hzpp.hr; Obala kneza Domagoja 9; ⊘ 6am-10pm) from Zagreb (194KN, 6½ hours, four daily). The station has lockers (15KN per day) that will fit suitcases, but you can't leave bags overnight. There's another **garderoba** (☑ 098 446 780; Obala kneza Domagoja 5; per day 15KN; ⊘ 6am-10pm Jul & Aug, 7.30am-9pm Sep-Jun) nearby, out on the street.

❶ Getting Around

TO/FROM THE AIRPORT

Airport Shuttle Bus (☑ 021-203 119; www.plesoprijevoz.hr; 1 way 30KN) Makes the 30-minute journey between the airport and Split's main bus station (platform 1) at least 14 times a day.

City buses 37 & 38 The regular Split–Trogir bus stops near the airport every 20 minutes. The journey takes 50 minutes from the local bus station on Domovinskog Rata, making it a slower option than the shuttle but also cheaper (17KN from Split, 13KN from Trogir).

Taxi A cab to central Split costs between 250KN and 300KN.

BUS

Promet Split (☑ 021-407 888; www.promet-split.hr) operates local buses on an extensive network throughout Split (per journey 11KN) and as far afield as Klis (13KN) and Trogir (17KN). You can buy tickets on the bus, but if you buy from the **local bus station** or from a kiosk, a two-journey (ie return, known as a 'duplo') central-zone ticket costs only 17KN. Buses run about every 15 minutes from 5.30am to 11.30pm.

Hvar Island

☑ 021 / POP 11,080

Long, lean Hvar is vaguely shaped like the profile of a holidaymaker reclining on a sun-lounger, which is altogether appropriate for the sunniest spot in the country (2724 sunny hours each year) and its most luxurious beach destination.

Hvar Town offers swanky hotels, elegant restaurants and a general sense that, if you care about seeing and being seen, this is the place to be. Rubbing shoulders with the posh yachties are hundreds of young partygoers, dancing on tables at the town's legendary beach bars. The northern coastal towns of Stari Grad and Jelsa are far more subdued.

Hvar's interior hides abandoned ancient hamlets, craggy peaks, vineyards and the lavender fields that the island is famous for. This region is worth exploring on a day trip, as is the island's southern coast, which has some of Hvar's most beautiful and isolated coves.

Hvar Town

POP 4260

The island's hub and busiest destination, Hvar Town is estimated to draw around 20,000 people a day in the high season. It's amazing that they can all fit in the small bay town, where 13th-century walls surround beautifully ornamented Gothic palaces and traffic-free marble streets, but fit they do.

Visitors wander along the main square, explore the sights on the winding stone streets, swim at the numerous beaches or pop off to the Pakleni Islands to get into their birthday suits – but most of all they come to party. Hvar's reputation as Croatia's premier party town is well deserved.

There are several good restaurants, bars and hotels here, but thanks to the island's appeal to well-heeled guests, the prices can be seriously inflated. Don't be put off if you're on a more limited budget, though, as private accommodation and multiple hostels cater to a younger, more diverse crowd.

◉ Sights

Trg Sv Stjepana SQUARE
(St Stephen's Sq) Stretching from the harbour to the cathedral, this impressive rectangular

square was formed by filling in an inlet that once reached out from the bay. At 4500 sq metres, it's one of the largest old squares in Dalmatia. Hvar Town's walled core, established in the 13th century, covers the slopes to the north. The town didn't spread south until the 15th century.

Fortica
FORTRESS

(Tvrđava Španjola; ☑ 021-742 608; Biskupa Jurja Dubokovica bb; adult/child 40/20KN; ⊘ 8am-9pm Apr-Oct) Looming high above the town and lit with a golden glow at night, this medieval castle occupies the site of an ancient Illyrian settlement dating from before 500 BCE. The views looking down over Hvar and the Pakleni Islands are magnificent, and well worth the trudge up through the old-town streets. Once you clear the town walls it's a gently sloping meander up the tree-shaded hillside to the fortress – or you can drive to the very top (100KN in a taxi).

🏃 Activities

Most of the swimming spots on the promenade heading west from the centre are tiny, rocky bays, some of which have been augmented with concrete sunbathing platforms. If you don't mind a hike, there are larger pebbly beaches in the opposite direction. A 30-minute walk will bring you to the largest of them, **Pokonji Dol**. From here, a further 25 minutes via a scenic but rocky path will bring you to secluded **Mekićevica**.

Otherwise, grab a taxi boat to the Pakleni Islands or to one of the beaches further east along the coast such as **Milna** or **Zaraće**. **Dubovica** is particularly recommended; if you have your own wheels you can park on the highway, not far from where it turns inland towards the tunnel, and reach it via a rough stony path.

🛏 Sleeping

Kapa
HOSTEL **€**

(☑ 091 92 41 068; karmentomasovic@gmail.com; Martina Vučetića 11; dm/r from €28/60; ⊘ May-Oct; [P][❄][🖙]) The advantages of Kapa's south-end-of-town location are the spacious surrounds and the brilliant sunset views. It's run by a young brother-and-sister team, operating out of a large family house. Dorms sleep four to six people, and there are private doubles with their own bathrooms.

Apartments Ana Dujmović
APARTMENT **€€**

(☑ 098 838 434; www.visit-hvar.com/apartments-ana-dujmovic; Biskupa Jurja Dubokovića 36; apt from €65; [P][❄][🖙]) This brace of comfortable holiday apartments is set behind an olive grove, only a 10-minute walk from the centre of town and, crucially, five minutes from the beach and the Hula-Hula bar. Call ahead and the delightful owner will pick you up from the town centre.

Apartments Komazin
APARTMENT **€€**

(☑ 091 60 19 712; www.croatia-hvar-apartments.com; Nikice Kolumbića 2; r/apt from €80/110; [❄][🖙]) With six bright apartments and two private rooms sharing a kitchen, bougainvillea-draped Komazin is an attractive option near the top of the private-apartment heap. What the apartments may lack in style they more than compensate for in size. And the host couldn't be more welcoming.

🍴 Eating & Drinking

Dalmatino
DALMATIAN **€€€**

(☑ 091 52 93 121; www.dalmatino-hvar.com; Sv Marak 1; mains 80-265KN; ⊘ 11am-midnight Mon-Sat Apr-Nov; [🖙]) Calling itself a 'steak and fish house', this place is always popular – due, in part, to the handsome waiters and the free-flowing *rakija* (grappa). Thankfully, the food is also excellent; try the *gregada* (fish fillet served on potatoes with a thick, broth-like sauce).

Hula-Hula Hvar
BAR

(☑ 095 91 11 871; www.hulahulahvar.com; Šetalište Antuna Tomislava Petrića 10; ⊘ 9am-11pm Apr-Oct) *The* spot to catch the sunset to the sound of techno and house music, Hula-Hula is known for its après-beach party (4pm to 9pm), where all of young, trendy Hvar seems to descend for sundowner cocktails. Dancing on tables is pretty much compulsory.

Kiva Bar
BAR

(☑ 091 51 22 343; www.facebook.com/kivabar.hvar; Obala Fabrika 10; ⊘ 9pm-2am Apr-Dec) A happening place in an alleyway just off the waterfront, Kiva is packed to the rafters most nights, with patrons spilling out and filling up the lane. DJs spin a popular mix of old-school dance, pop and hip-hop classics to an up-for-it crowd.

ⓘ Information

Emergency Clinic (Dom Zdravlja; ☑ 021-717 099; Biskupa Jurja Dubokovića 3) About 400m west of the town centre.

Tourist Office (☑ 021-741 059; www.tzhvar.hr; Trg Sv Stjepana 42; ⊘ 8am-10pm Jul & Aug, 8am-8pm Mon-Sat, 8am-1pm & 4-8pm Sun Jun & Sep, 8am-2pm Mon-Fri, to noon Sat Oct-May) In the Arsenal building, right on Trg Sv Stjepana.

WORTH A TRIP

KORČULA ISLAND

Rich in vineyards, olive groves and small villages, the island of Korčula is the sixth-largest Adriatic island, stretching nearly 47km in length. Quiet coves and small sandy beaches dot the steep southern coast while the northern shore is flatter and more pebbly. Tradition is alive and kicking on Korčula, with age-old religious ceremonies, folk music and dances still being performed to the delight of an ever-growing influx of tourists. Arguably the best of all Croatian whites is produced from the indigenous grape *pošip*, particularly from the areas around the villages of **Čara** and **Smokvica**. The *grk* grape, cultivated around Lumbarda, also produces quality dry white wine.

Korčula Town is a stunner. Ringed by imposing defences, this coastal citadel is dripping with history, with marble streets rich in Renaissance and Gothic architecture. Its fascinating fishbone layout was cleverly designed for the comfort and safety of its inhabitants: western streets were built straight in order to open the city to the refreshing summer *maestral* (strong, steady westerly wind), while the eastern streets were curved to minimise the force of the winter *bura* (cold northeasterly wind). The town cradles a harbour, overlooked by round defensive towers and a compact cluster of red-roofed houses. There are rustling palms all around and several beaches an easy walk away.

Dominating the little square at Korčula Town's heart is the magnificent 15th-century **St Mark's Cathedral** (Katedrala svetog Marka; Trg Sv Marka; church 10KN; bell tower adult/child 20/15KN; ⏰9am-9pm Jul & Aug, hours vary Sep-Jun), built from Korčula limestone in a Gothic-Renaissance style by Italian and local artisans. The sculptural detail of the facade is intriguing, particularly the naked squatting figures of Adam and Eve on the door pillars, and the two-tailed mermaid and elephant on the triangular gable cornice at the very top.

Some of Korčula's best eating experiences can be found at local taverns in its small villages. If you've got your own transport, it's well worth seeking out **Konoba Mate** (☑020-717 109; www.konobamate.hr; Pupnat 28; mains 60-118KN; ⏰11am-2pm & 7pm-midnight Mon-Sat, 7pm-midnight Sun May-Sep; 🐾) in the sleepy farming village of **Pupnat**. The turnoff to the island's best beach, **Pupnatska Luka**, is nearby.

The island has three major ferry ports: Korčula Town's West Harbour, Dominče (3km east of Korčula Town) and Vela Luka. **Jadrolinija** (☑020-715 410; www.jadrolinija.hr; Plokata 19 travnja 1921 br 19) has car ferries between Orebić and Dominče (passenger/car 16/76KN, 15 minutes), departing roughly every hour. From June to September, a daily catamaran heads from West Harbour to Dubrovnik (130KN, two hours), Hvar (120KN, 1½ hours) and Split (160KN, 3¾ hours). **Kapetan Luka** (☑021-645 476; www.krilo.hr) sails daily catamarans to Hvar (110KN, 1¼ hours) and Split (130KN, 2½ hours), adding Dubrovnik (130KN, 1¾ hours) from May to mid-October. In July and August, G&V Line (p278) has four catamarans per week to West Harbour from Dubrovnik (90KN, 2½ hours).

Tourist Office Information Point (☑021-718 109; Trg Marka Miličića 9; ⏰8am-9pm Mon-Sat, 9am-1pm Sun Jun-Sep) In the bus station; a summertime annexe of the main tourist office.

ⓘ Getting There & Away

Jadrolinija (☑021-741 132; www.jadrolinija.hr; Obala Riva bb) operates the following high-speed catamarans:

➡ Daily from Split (55KN, one hour).

➡ From May to September, up to five times a day between Hvar Town and Split (110KN, one hour).

➡ From June to September, daily from Split (110KN, two hours), Korčula (120KN, 1½ hours) and Dubrovnik (210KN, 3½ hours).

Kapetan Luka (p270) tickets can be purchased from **Pelegrini Tours** (☑021-742 743; www.

pelegrini-hvar.hr; Obala Riva 20) for the daily catamaran to Split (90KN, one hour) and Korčula (110KN, 1¼ hours). From May to mid-October, it also heads to Dubrovnik (210KN, three hours).

Hvar Town's **bus station** (Trg Marka Miličića 9) is east of the main square. Buses head to/from the Stari Grad car-ferry port (27KN, 20 minutes, six daily).

In summer taxi boats line Hvar's harbour, offering rides to the Pakleni Islands and isolated beaches further along the coast.

Dubrovnik

☑020 / POP 28,500

Regardless of whether you are visiting Dubrovnik for the first time or the hundredth, the sense of awe never fails to descend when you set eyes on the beauty of the old town. Indeed it's hard to imagine anyone becoming jaded by the city's limestone streets, baroque buildings and the endless shimmer of the Adriatic, or failing to be inspired by a walk along the ancient city walls that protected the capital of a sophisticated republic for centuries.

Although the shelling of Dubrovnik in 1991 horrified the world, the city has bounced back with vigour to enchant visitors again. Marvel at the interplay of light on the old stone buildings; trace the peaks and troughs of Dubrovnik's past in museums replete with art and artefacts; take the cable car up to Mt Srđ; exhaust yourself climbing up and down narrow lanes – then plunge into the azure sea.

⊙ Sights

★ City Walls & Forts   FORT
(Gradske zidine; ☑ 020-638 800; www.wallsof dubrovnik.com; adult/child 150/50KN; ⊙ 8am-6.30pm Apr-Oct, 9am-3pm Nov-Mar) No visit to Dubrovnik would be complete without a walk around the spectacular city walls, the finest in the world and the city's main claim to fame. From the top, the view over the old town and the shimmering Adriatic is sublime. You can get a good handle on the extent of the shelling damage in the 1990s by gazing over the rooftops: those sporting bright new terracotta suffered damage and had to be replaced.

Srđ   VIEWPOINT
(Srđ bb) From the top of this 412m-high hill, Dubrovnik's old town looks even more surreal than usual – like a scale model of itself or an illustration on a page. The views take in all of Dubrovnik and Lokrum, with the Elafiti Islands filling the horizon. It's this extraordinary vantage point that made Srđ a key battleground during the 1990s war. That story is told in **Dubrovnik During the Homeland War** (Dubrovnik u Domovinskom ratu; ☑ 020-324 856; adult/child 30/15KN; ⊙ 8am-10pm; Ⓟ), an exhibition housed in Fort Imperial at the summit.

The easiest and quickest way to get to the top is by **cable car** (Žičara; ☑ 020-414 355; www.dubrovnikcablecar.com; Petra Krešimira IV bb, Ploče; adult/child return 140/60KN, one way 85/40KN; ⊙ 9am-midnight Jun-Aug, to 10pm Sep, to 8pm Apr, May & Oct, to 4pm Nov-Mar), or you can drive (follow the signs to Bosanka), walk via the **Way of the Cross** (Križni put; Jadranska cesta, Srđ), or catch bus 17 from the Pile stop to Bosanka and then walk the final 1.5km.

War Photo Limited   GALLERY
(☑ 020-322 166; www.warphotoltd.com; Antuninska 6; adult/child 50/40KN; ⊙ 10am-10pm May-Sep, to 4pm Wed-Mon Apr & Oct) An immensely powerful experience, this gallery features compelling exhibitions curated by New Zealand photojournalist Wade Goddard, who worked in the Balkans in the 1990s. Its intention is to expose the everyday, horrific and unjust realities of war. There's a permanent exhibition on the upper floor devoted to the wars in Yugoslavia; the changing exhibitions cover a multitude of conflicts.

Rector's Palace   PALACE
(Knežev dvor; ☑ 020-321 497; www.dumus.hr; Pred Dvorom 3; adult/child 80/25KN, incl in multi-museum pass adult/child 120/25KN; ⊙ 9am-6pm Apr-Oct, to 4pm Nov-Mar) Built in the late 15th century for the elected rector who governed Dubrovnik, this Gothic-Renaissance palace contains the rector's office and private chambers, public halls, administrative offices and a dungeon. During his one-month term the rector was unable to leave the building without the permission of the senate. Today the palace has been turned into the **Cultural History Museum**, with artfully restored rooms, portraits, coats of arms and coins, evoking the glorious history of Ragusa.

Cathedral of the Assumption   CATHEDRAL
(Katedrala Marijina Uznesenja; Držićeva poljana; treasury 20KN; ⊙ 8am-5pm Mon-Sat, 11am-5pm Sun Easter-Oct, 9am-noon & 4-5pm Mon-Sat Nov-Easter) Built on the site of a 7th-century basilica, Dubrovnik's original cathedral was enlarged in the 12th century, supposedly funded by a gift from England's King Richard I, the

> ### ⓘ MUSEUMS OF DUBROVNIK PASS
>
> Perhaps a cunning plan to get you through the doors of some of the town's more marginal museums, a multi-museum pass (adult/child 120/25KN) allows access to nine of Dubrovnik's institutions. The only must-see among them though is the Rector's Palace, which is also the only one ticketed separately. If you're interested in visiting the excellent **Museum of Modern Art** (Umjetnička galerija; ☑ 020-426 590; www.ugdubrovnik.hr; Frana Supila 23, Ploče; ⊙ 9am-8pm Tue-Sun), then it's worth buying the pass. The other museums could easily be skipped.

CROATIA DUBROVNIK

Dubrovnik

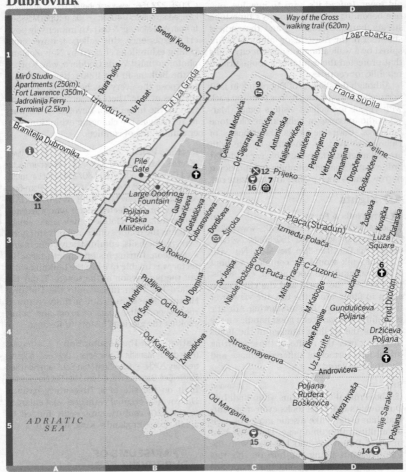

Lionheart, who was saved from a shipwreck on the nearby island of Lokrum. Soon after the first cathedral was destroyed in the 1667 earthquake, work began on this, its baroque replacement, which was finished in 1713.

St Blaise's Church
CHURCH

(Crkva Sv Vlahe; Luža Sq; ☺8am-noon & 4-5pm Mon-Sat, 7am-1pm Sun) Dedicated to the city's patron saint, this exceptionally beautiful church was built in 1715 in the ornate baroque style. The interior is notable for its marble altars and a 15th-century silver gilt statue of St Blaise (within the high altar), who is holding a scale model of pre-earthquake Dubrovnik.

Note also the stained-glass windows designed by local artist Ivo Dulčić in 1971.

Dominican Monastery
& Museum
CHRISTIAN MONASTERY

(Dominikanski samostan i muzej; ☑020-321 423; www.dominicanmuseum.hr; Sv Dominika 4; adult/child 30/20KN; ☺9am-5pm) This imposing structure is an architectural highlight, built in a transitional Gothic-Renaissance style and containing an impressive art collection. Constructed around the same time as the city walls in the 14th century, the stark exterior resembles a fortress more than a religious complex. The interior contains a

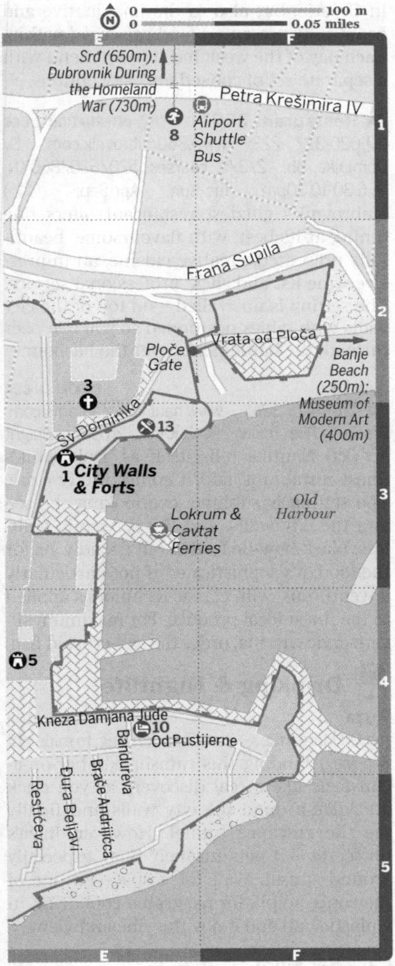

Dubrovnik

Top Sights
1 City Walls & Forts E3

Sights
2 Cathedral of the Assumption D4
3 Dominican Monastery & Museum E2
4 Franciscan Monastery & Museum B2
5 Rector's Palace E4
6 St Blaise's Church D3
7 War Photo Limited C2

Activities, Courses & Tours
8 Cable Car E1

Sleeping
9 Hostel Angelina C1
10 Karmen Apartments E4

Eating
11 Nautika A3
12 Nishta C2
13 Restaurant 360° E3

Drinking & Nightlife
14 Bard Mala Buža D5
15 Buža C5
16 D'vino C2

graceful 15th-century **cloister** constructed by local artisans after the designs of the Florentine architect Maso di Bartolomeo.

Franciscan Monastery & Museum CHRISTIAN MONASTERY
(Franjevački samostan i muzej; ☎020-321 410; Placa 2; 30KN; ⏱9am-6pm Apr-Oct, to 2pm Nov-Mar) Within this monastery's solid stone walls are a gorgeous mid-14th-century **cloister**, a historic **pharmacy** and a small **museum** with a collection of relics and liturgical objects, including chalices, paintings and gold jewellery, and pharmacy items such as laboratory gear and medical books.

Fort Lawrence FORTRESS
(Tvrđava Lovrjenac; www.citywallsdubrovnik.hr; Pile; 50KN, free with city walls ticket; ⏱8am-6.30pm Apr-Oct, 9am-3pm Nov-Mar) St Blaise gazes down from the walls of this large free-standing fortress, constructed atop a 37m-high promontory adjacent to the old town. Built to guard the city's western approach from invasion by land or sea, its walls range from 4m to 12m thick. There's not a lot inside, but the battlements offer wonderful views over the old town and its large courtyard is often used as a venue for summer theatre and concerts.

Sleeping

Hostel Angelina HOSTEL €
(☎091 89 39 089; www.hostelangelinaoldtowndubrovnik.com; Plovani skalini 17a; dm from €49; ❄📶) Hidden away in a quiet nook of the old town, this cute little hostel offers bunk rooms, a small guest kitchen and a bougainvillea-shaded terrace with memorable views over the rooftops. Plus you'll get a great glute workout every time you walk up the lane. It also has private rooms in three old-town annexes (from €110).

★**Karmen Apartments** APARTMENT €€
(☎020-323 433; www.karmendu.com; Bandureva 1; apt from €95; ❄📶) These four inviting

WORTH A TRIP

LOKRUM

Lush **Lokrum** (☑ 020-311 738; www. lokrum.hr; adult/child incl boat 150/25KN; ⊙ Apr-Nov) is a beautiful, forested island full of holm oaks, black ash, pines and olive trees, only a 10-minute ferry ride from Dubrovnik's Old Harbour. It's a popular swimming spot, although the beaches are rocky. Boats leave roughly hourly in summer (half-hourly in July and August). The public boat ticket price includes the entrance fee, but if you arrive with another boat, you're required to pay 120KN at the information centre on the island.

apartments enjoy a great location a stone's throw from Ploče harbour. All have plenty of character with art, splashes of colour, tasteful furnishings and books to browse. Apartment 2 has a little balcony while apartment 1 enjoys sublime port views. Book well ahead.

★ **Miró Studio**
Apartments   APARTMENT €€€
(☑ 099 42 42 442; www.mirostudioapartments dubrovnik.com; Sv Đurđa 16, Pile; apt €145-200; ❄ 🞉) Located in a quiet residential nook only metres from the sea, hidden between the old-town walls and Fort Lawrence, this schmick complex is an absolute gem. The decor marries ancient stone walls and whitewashed ceiling beams with design features such as uplighting, contemporary bathrooms and sliding glass partitions.

✕ Eating

Shizuku   JAPANESE €€
(☑ 020-311 493; www.facebook.com/ShizukuDub rovnik; Kneza Domagoja 1f, Batala; mains 70-85KN; ⊙ 5pm-midnight Tue-Sun; 🞉) Attentive local wait staff usher you to your table in the clean-lined, modern dining room of this popular restaurant, tucked away in a residential area between Gruž Harbour and Lapad Bay. The Japanese owners will be in the kitchen, preparing authentic sushi, sashimi, udon, crispy *karaage* chicken and gyoza dumplings. Wash it all down with Japanese beer or sake.

Nishta   VEGAN €€
(☑ 020-322 088; www.nishtarestaurant.com; Prijeko bb; mains 98-108KN; ⊙ 11.30am-11.30pm Mon-Sat; 🖉) The popularity of this tiny old-town restaurant is testament not just to the paucity of options for vegetarians and vegans

in Croatia, but also to the imaginative and beautifully presented food produced within. Each day of the week has its own menu with a separate set of cooked and raw options.

★ **Restaurant 360°**   INTERNATIONAL €€€
(☑ 020-322 222; www.360dubrovnik.com; Sv Dominika bb; 2/3/5 courses 520/620/860KN; ⊙ 6.30-10.30pm Tue-Sun Apr-Sep;   🞉) Dubrovnik's glitziest restaurant offers fine dining at its best, with flavoursome, beautifully presented, creative cuisine, an impressive wine list and slick, professional service. The setting is unrivalled – on top of the city walls with tables positioned so you can peer through the battlements over the harbour.

Nautika   EUROPEAN €€€
(☑ 020-442 526; www.nautikarestaurants.com; Brsalje 3, Pile; mains 290-360KN; ⊙ 6pm-midnight Apr-Oct) Nautika bills itself as 'Dubrovnik's finest restaurant' and it comes pretty close. The setting is sublime, overlooking the sea and the city walls, and the service is faultless: black-bow-tie formal but friendly. As for the food, it's sophisticated if not particularly adventurous, with classic techniques applied to the finest local produce. For maximum silver-service drama, order the salt-crusted fish.

🍷 Drinking & Nightlife

Buža   BAR
(off Od Margarite; ⊙ 8am-2am Jun-Aug, to midnight Sep-May) Finding this ramshackle bar-on-a-cliff feels like a real discovery as you duck and dive around the city walls and finally see the entrance tunnel. However, Buža's no secret – it gets insanely busy, especially around sunset. Wait for a space on one of the concrete platforms, grab a cool drink in a plastic cup and enjoy the vibe and views.

Cave Bar More   BAR
(www.hotel-more.hr; Šetalište Nika i Meda Pucića bb, Babin Kuk; ⊙ 10am-midnight Jun-Aug, to 10pm Sep-May) This little beach bar serves coffee, snacks and cocktails to bathers reclining by the dazzlingly clear waters of Lapad Bay, but that's not the half of it – the main bar is set in an actual cave. Cool off beneath the stalactites in the side chamber, where a glass floor exposes a water-filled cavern.

D'vino   WINE BAR
(☑ 020-321 130; www.dvino.net; Palmotićeva 4a; ⊙ 9am-midnight Mar-Nov; 🞉) If you're interested in sampling top-notch Croatian wine, this convivial bar is the place to go. As well as

a large and varied wine list, it offers tasting flights presented by cool and knowledgeable staff (three wines from 55KN) plus savoury breakfasts, snacks and platters. Sit outside for the authentic old-town-alley ambience, but check out the whimsical wall inscriptions inside.

❶ Information

Dubrovnik's tourist board has offices in **Pile** (☑ 020-312 011; www.tzdubrovnik.hr; Brsalje 5; ☺8am-8pm), **Gruž** (☑ 020-417 983; Obala Pape Ivana Pavla II 1; ☺8am-8pm Jun-Oct, 8am-3pm Mon-Fri, to 1pm Sat Nov-Mar, 8am-8pm Mon-Fri, to 2pm Sat & Sun Apr & May) and **Lapad** (☑ 020-437 460; Dvori Lapad, Masarykov put 2; ☺8am-8pm Jul & Aug, 8am-noon & 5-8pm Mon-Fri, 9am-2pm Sat Apr-Jun, Sep & Oct) that dispense maps, information and advice.

Dubrovnik General Hospital (Opća bolnica Dubrovnik; ☑ 020-431 777, emergency 194; www.bolnica-du.hr; Dr Roka Mišetića 2, Lapad)

Public hospital with a 24-hour emergency department.

Marin Med Clinic (☑ 020-400 500; www.marin-med.com; Dr Ante Starčevića 45, Montovjerna; ☺8am-8pm Mon-Fri, to 1pm Sat) Large private health centre with English-speaking doctors.

Travel Corner (Avansa Travel; ☑ 020-492 313; www.dubrovnik-travelcorner.com; Obala Stjepana Radića 40, Gruž; internet per hr 25KN, left luggage per 2hr/day 10/40KN) This handy one-stop shop has a left-luggage service and internet terminals, dispenses tourist information, books excursions and sells Kapetan Luka ferry tickets.

❶ Getting There & Away

AIR

Dubrovnik Airport (DBV, Zračna luka Dubrovnik; ☑ 020-773 100; www.airport-dubrovnik.hr; Čilipi) is in Čilipi, 19km southeast of Dubrovnik. Croatia Airlines, British Airways, Iberica, Trade Air, Turkish Airlines and Vueling

---

WORTH A TRIP

CAVTAT

Set on a petite peninsula embraced by two harbours, the ancient town of Cavtat (pronounced *tsav*-tat) has a pretty waterfront promenade peppered with restaurants, pebbly beaches and an interesting assortment of artsy attractions. These include the glorious **Račić Family Mausoleum** (Mauzolej obitelji Račić; www.migk.hr; Groblje sv Roka, Kvaternikova bb; 20KN; ☺10am-5pm Mon-Sat Apr-Oct), created in the 1920s by preeminent Croatian sculptor Ivan Meštrović. Cavtat's most revered artist is painter Vlaho Bukovac (1855–1922), whose work can be seen in **St Nicholas' Church** (Crkva svetog Nikole; Obala Ante Starčevića bb; ☺hours vary), the **Our-Lady-of-the-Snow Monastery** (Samostan Gospe od snijega; ☑020-678 064; www.franjevacki-samostan-cavtat.com; Šetalište Rat 2; ☺7am-9pm), the **Baltazar Bogišić Collection** (Obala Ante Starčevića 18; adult/child 25/10KN; ☺9.30am-1.30pm Mon-Sat Apr-Oct, 9am-1pm Mon-Fri Nov-Mar) and displayed in his childhood home, **Bukovac House** (Kuća Bukovac; ☑020-478 646; www.kuca-bukovac.hr; Bukovčeva 5; 30KN; ☺9am-6pm Mon-Sat, to 2pm Sun Apr-Oct, 10am-6pm Tue-Sat, 9am-1pm Sun Nov-Mar).

Not just the best restaurant on Cavtat's seafront strip, **Bugenvila** (☑020-479 949; www.bugenvila.eu; Obala Ante Starčevića 9; mains 90-275KN; ☺noon-4pm & 6.30-10pm; 🐾📶) is one of the culinary trendsetters of the Dalmatian coast. Local ingredients are showcased in adventurous dishes served with artistic flourishes. Visit at lunchtime to take advantage of the three-course special menu (180KN).

Without Cavtat there would be no Dubrovnik, as it was refugees from Epidaurum (the Roman incarnation of Cavtat) who established the city in 614. The walls of its famous offshoot are visible in the distance and the two are well connected by both boat and bus, making Cavtat either an easy day-trip destination from Dubrovnik or a quieter (not to mention cheaper) alternative base.

During the tourist season at least three different operators offer boats to Cavtat from Dubrovnik's Old Harbour (one-way/return 100/60KN, 45 minutes), with departures at least every half hour. In winter this reduces to three to five a day, weather dependent. Bus 10 runs roughly half-hourly to Cavtat (25KN, 30 minutes) from Dubrovnik.

fly to Dubrovnik year-round. In summer they're joined by dozens of other airlines.

BOAT

The **ferry terminal** (Obala Pape Ivana Pavla II 1, Gruž) is in Gruž, 3km northwest of the old town. Ferries for **Lokrum and Cavtat** depart from the Old Harbour.

→ **Jadrolinija** (☑ 020-418 000; www.jadrolinija. hr; Obala Stjepana Radića 40, Gruž) has daily ferries to the Elafiti Islands. From June to September, there's also a daily catamaran to Korčula (130KN, two hours), Hvar (210KN, 3½ hours) and Split (210KN, six hours).

→ **G&V Line** (☑ 020-313 119; www.gv-line.hr; Obala Ivana Pavla II 1, Gruž) has a catamaran to Korčula (90KN, 2½ hours) four times a week in July and August.

→ **Kapetan Luka** (Krilo; ☑ 021-645 476; www. krilo.hr) has a daily fast boat from May to mid-October to/from Korčula (130KN, 1¾ hours), Hvar (210KN, three hours) and Split (210KN, 4¼ hours).

BUS

Buses from **Dubrovnik Bus Station** (Autobusni kolodvor; ☑ 060 305 070; www.libertasdub rovnik.hr; Obala Pape Ivana Pavla II 44a, Gruž; ⊘ 4.30am-10pm; 🛜) can be crowded, so purchase tickets online or book in advance in summer. Domestic destinations include Split (127KN, 4½ hours, 11 daily), Zadar (182KN, eight hours, five daily) and Zagreb (259KN, 11¾ hours, 10 daily).

⊙ Getting Around

TO/FROM THE AIRPORT

Atlas runs the **airport shuttle bus** (☑ 020-642 286; www.atlas-croatia.com; one-way/return 40/70KN), timed around flight schedules. Buses to Dubrovnik stop at the Pile Gate and the bus station; buses to the airport pick up from the bus station and from the bus stop near the cable car.

City buses 11, 27 and 38 also stop at the airport but are less frequent and take longer (28KN, seven daily, no Sunday service).

Allow up to 280KN for a taxi to Dubrovnik. Dubrovnik Transfer Services (www. dubrovnik-transfer-services.com) offers a set-price taxi transfer service to the city (€30) and Cavtat (€16), and to as far away as Zagreb, Sarajevo, Podgorica and Tirana.

BUS

Dubrovnik has a superb bus service. The fare is 15KN if you buy from the driver and 12KN if you buy a ticket at a *tisak* (news-stand). Timetables are available at www.libertasdubrovnik.hr.

SURVIVAL GUIDE

ⓘ Directory A–Z

ACCOMMODATION

Croatia is extremely popular in summer and good places book out well in advance in July and August. It's also very busy in June and September.

Hotels These range from massive beach resorts to boutique establishments.

Apartments Privately owned holiday units are a staple of the local accommodation scene; they're especially good for families.

Guesthouses Usually family-run establishments where spare rooms are rented at a bargain price – sometimes with their own bathrooms, sometimes not.

Hostels Mainly in the bigger cities and more popular beach destinations, with dorms and sometimes private rooms too.

Campgrounds Tent and caravan sites, often fairly basic.

MONEY

ATMs are widely available. Credit cards are accepted in most hotels and restaurants. Smaller restaurants, shops and private-accommodation owners only take cash.

OPENING HOURS

Opening hours vary throughout the year. We've provided high-season opening hours; hours generally decrease in the shoulder and low seasons.

Banks 8am or 9am to 8pm weekdays and 7am to 1pm or 8am to 2pm Saturday.

Cafes and bars 8am or 9am to midnight.

Offices 8am to 4pm or 8.30am to 4.30pm weekdays.

Post offices 7am to 8pm weekdays and 7am to 1pm Saturday; longer hours in coastal towns in summer.

Restaurants Noon to 11pm or midnight; often closed Sundays outside peak season.

Shops 8am to 8pm weekdays, to 2pm or 3pm Saturday; some take a break from 2pm to 5pm. Shopping malls have longer hours.

PUBLIC HOLIDAYS

Croats take their holidays very seriously. Shops and museums are shut and boat services are reduced. On religious holidays, the churches are full; it can be a good time to check out the artwork in a church that is usually closed.

New Year's Day 1 January

Epiphany 6 January

Easter Sunday & Monday March/April

Labour Day 1 May

Corpus Christi 60 days after Easter
Day of Antifascist Resistance 22 June
Statehood Day 25 June
Homeland Thanksgiving Day 5 August
Feast of the Assumption 15 August
Independence Day 8 October
All Saints' Day 1 November
Christmas 25 & 26 December

TELEPHONE

➡ To call Croatia from abroad, dial your international access code, then 385 (the country code for Croatia), then the area code (without the initial 0) and the local number.

➡ To call from region to region within Croatia, start with the full area code (drop it when dialling within the same code).

Getting There & Away

ENTERING THE COUNTRY/REGION

With an economy that depends heavily on tourism, Croatia has wisely kept red tape to a minimum for foreign visitors.

Passport

Your passport must be valid for at least another three months after the planned departure from Croatia, as well as issued within the previous 10 years.

Citizens of EU countries can enter Croatia with only their ID card.

Croatian authorities require all foreigners to register with the local police when they arrive in a new area of the country, but this is a routine matter normally handled by the hotel, hostel, campground or agency securing your private accommodation. If you're staying elsewhere (eg with relatives or friends), your host should take care of it for you.

AIR

There are direct flights to Croatia from a variety of European and Middle Eastern cities year-round, with dozens of seasonal routes and charters added in summer. **Croatia Airlines** (OU; ☎ 01-66 76 555; www.croatiaairlines.hr) is the national carrier; it's part of the Star Alliance. Croatia has an astonishing eight airports welcoming international flights, although some of them are highly seasonal. The main ones are Dubrovnik Airport (p277), Split Airport (p269), Zadar Airport (p264) and Zagreb Airport (p259).

LAND

Croatia has border crossings with Slovenia, Hungary, Serbia, Bosnia and Hercegovina, and Montenegro.

Bus

Direct bus connections link Croatia to all of its neighbours and to as far afield as Norway. In most cases, passports are collected on the bus and handed over at the border; you usually won't leave the bus unless there's an issue that needs resolving. Useful websites include www.euro lines.com, www.buscroatia.com, www.getbybus. com and www.vollo.net.

Train

Zagreb is Croatia's main train hub. In most cases, passports are checked on the train.

SEA

Regular ferries connect Croatia with Italy; Split is the main year-round hub.

Jadrolinija (www.jadrolinija.hr) Overnight services between Split and Ancona year-round, between Zadar and Ancona from June to September, and between Dubrovnik and Bari from April to November.

SNAV (www.snav.com) Overnight services on the Split–Ancona route from April to October.

Venezia Lines (www.venezialines.com) Ferries ply the Venice–Rovinj route from May to September.

Getting Around

AIR

Croatia Airlines flies from Zagreb to Dubrovnik, Split and Zadar. **Trade Air** (TDR; ☎ 091 62 65 111; www.trade-air.com) flies between Split and Dubrovnik.

BOAT

Numerous ferries connect the main coastal centres and their surrounding islands year-round, with services extended in the tourist season. Split is the main hub.

BUS

Bus services are excellent and relatively inexpensive. There are often a number of different companies handling each route, so prices can vary substantially. Luggage stowed in the baggage compartment under the bus costs extra (around 10KN a piece). Note that buses between Split and Dubrovnik pass through Bosnian territory so you'll need to keep your passport handy.

TRAIN

Croatia's train network is limited and trains are less frequent than buses. For information about schedules, prices and services, contact **HŽPP** (☎ 01-37 82 583; www.hzpp.hr).

Czech Republic

POP 10.65 MILLION

Best Places to Eat

➔ Field (p292)

➔ Krčma v Šatlavské (p300)

➔ Entree (p306)

➔ Levitate Restaurant (p291)

➔ Buffalo Burger Bar (p297)

Best Places to Stay

➔ Hostel Mitte (p303)

➔ Dominican Hotel (p291)

➔ Long Story Short (p306)

➔ Hotel Myší Díra (p300)

➔ Hotel Romance Puškin (p301)

Why Go?

Since the fall of communism in 1989 and the opening up of Central and Eastern Europe, Prague has evolved into one of Europe's most popular travel destinations. The city offers an intact medieval core that transports you back – especially when strolling the hidden streets of the Old Town – some 600 years. The 14th-century Charles Bridge, traversing two historic neighbourhoods across a slow-moving river, is one of the continent's most beautiful sights.

Prague is not just about history. It's a vital urban centre with a rich array of cultural offerings. Outside the capital, in the provinces of Bohemia and Moravia, castles and palaces abound – including the audacious hilltop chateau at Český Krumlov – which illuminate the stories of powerful dynasties whose influence was felt throughout Europe. Olomouc, the historic capital of Moravia to the east, boasts much of the beauty of Prague without the crowds.

When to Go
Prague

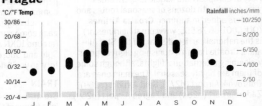

May Prague Spring Festival makes this the capital's most popular month.

Sep Lovely strolling weather in West Bohemia's spa towns.

Dec Svařák (mulled wine) and music at Christmas markets in town squares across the country.

Entering the Country

The Czech Republic lies at the centre of Europe and has good rail and road connections to surrounding countries. Prague's international airport is a major air hub for Central Europe.

Flights, cars and tours can be booked online at lonely planet.com/bookings.

ITINERARIES

One Week

Experience the exciting combination of a tumultuous past and energetic present in Prague (p283). Top experiences include the grandeur of Prague Castle (p283), Josefov's Prague Jewish Museum (p285), and getting lost amid the bewildering labyrinth of the Old Town. Take an essential day trip to Karlštejn (p295), and then head south to Český Krumlov (p298) for a few days of riverside R&R.

Two Weeks

Begin in Prague (p283) before heading west for the spa scene at Karlovy Vary (p301). Balance the virtue and vice ledger with a few Bohemian brews in Plzeň (p296) before heading south for relaxation and rigour around Český Krumlov (p298). Head east to the Renaissance grandeur of Telč (p302) and the cosmopolitan galleries and museums of Brno (p302). From Moravia's largest city, it's just a skip to stately Olomouc (p305).

Essential Food & Drink

Beer Modern pils (light, amber-coloured lager) was invented in the city of Plzeň in the 19th century, giving Czechs bragging rights to having the best beer (*pivo*) in the world.

Becherovka A shot of this sweetish herbal liqueur from Karlovy Vary is a popular way to start (or end) a big meal.

Braised beef Look out for *svíčková na smetaně* on menus. This is a satisfying slice of roast beef, served in a cream sauce, with a side of bread dumplings and a dollop of cranberry sauce.

Carp This lowly fish (*kapr* in Czech) is given pride of place every Christmas at the centre of the family meal. *Kapr na kmíní* is fried or baked carp with caraway seeds.

Dumplings Every culture has its favourite starchy side dish; for Czechs it's *knedlíky* – big bread dumplings that are perfect for mopping up gravy.

Roast pork Move over beef, pork (*vepřové maso*) is king here. The classic Bohemian dish, seen on menus around the country, is *vepřo-knedlo-zelo,* local slang for roast pork, bread dumplings and sauerkraut.

AT A GLANCE

Area 78,866 sq km

Capital Prague

Country Code ☑ 420

Currency Crown (Kč)

Emergency ☑ 112

Language Czech

Time Central European Time (GMT/UTC plus one hour)

Visas Schengen rules apply; visas not required for most nationalities for stays of up to 90 days

Sleeping Price Ranges

The following price ranges refer to the cost of a standard double room per night in high season.

€ less than 1600Kč

€€ 1600–3700Kč

€€€ more than 3700Kč

Eating Price Ranges

The following price ranges refer to the price of a main course at dinner.

€ less than 200Kč

€€ 200–500Kč

€€€ more than 500Kč

Resources

CzechTourism (www.czechtourism.com)

Lonely Planet (www.lonelyplanet.com/czech-republic)

Prague City Tourism (www.prague.eu)

CZECH REPUBLIC

Czech Republic Highlights

1 Charles Bridge (p288) Strolling across in the early morning or late evening when the crowds thin out.

2 U Kroka (p292) Enjoying an evening in an old-school Czech pub.

3 Astronomical Clock (p285) Joining the appreciative throngs at the top of the hour.

4 Český Krumlov (p298) Walking the streets of one of the prettiest towns in Central Europe.

5 Pilsner Urquell Brewery (p296) Touring this brewery in Plzeň to see where it all started.

6 Olomouc (p305) Ambling through this stately town, the most amazing place you've never heard of.

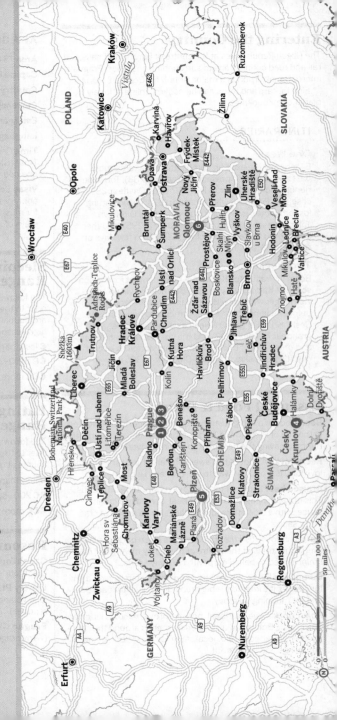

PRAGUE

POP 1.3 MILLION

It's the perfect irony of Prague: you're lured here by the past, but compelled to linger by the present and the future. Fill your days with its illustrious artistic and architectural heritage – from Gothic and Renaissance to art nouveau and cubist. If Prague's seasonal legions of tourists wear you down, that's OK. Just drink a glass of the country's legendary lager, relax and rest reassured that quiet moments still exist: a private dawn on Charles Bridge, the glorious cityscape of Staré Město or getting lost in the intimate lanes of Malá Strana.

◉ Sights

As seen on the map, the Vltava River winds through the middle of Prague like a giant question mark, with the city centre straddling its lower half. There is little method in Prague's haphazard sprawl – it's a city that has grown organically from its medieval roots, snagging villages and swallowing suburbs as it spread out into the wooded hills of Central Bohemia.

The oldest parts of the city cluster tightly just south of the river bend – **Hradčany**, the medieval castle district, and **Malá Strana** (Little Quarter) on the western bank; **Stáre Město** (Old Town), **Nové Město** (New Town) and the ancient citadel of **Vyšehrad** on the eastern bank.

◉ Hradčany

★**Prague Castle**   CASTLE
(Pražský hrad; Map p284; ☏224 372 423; www.hrad.cz; Hradčanské náměstí 1; adult/concession from 250/125Kč; ⊙grounds 6am-10pm, gardens 10am-6pm Apr-Oct, historic buildings 9am-5pm Apr-Oct, to 4pm Nov-Mar; Ⓜ Malostranská, ☒22, 23) Prague's most popular attraction. Looming above the Vltava's left bank, its serried ranks of spires, towers and palaces dominate the city centre like a fairy-tale fortress. Within its walls lies a varied and fascinating collection of historic buildings, museums and galleries that are home to some of the Czech Republic's greatest artistic and cultural treasures. Note that visitors must pass through a security check before entering the grounds, so bring your passport or EU identification card.

★**St Vitus Cathedral**   CHURCH
(Katedrála sv Víta; Map p284; ☏257 531 622; www.katedralasvatehovita.cz; Prague Castle; ⊙9am-5pm, from noon Sun, to 4pm Nov-Mar; ☒22, 23) Built over a time span of almost 600 years, St Vitus is one of the most richly endowed cathedrals in central Europe. It is pivotal to the religious and cultural life of the Czech Republic, housing treasures that range from the 14th-century mosaic of the Last Judgement and the tombs of St Wenceslas and Charles IV, to the baroque silver tomb of St John of Nepomuk, the ornate Chapel of St Wenceslas and art nouveau stained glass by Alfons Mucha.

Old Royal Palace   PALACE
(Starý královský palác; Map p284; Prague Castle; ⊙9am-5pm, to 4pm Nov-Mar; ☒22, 23) The Old Royal Palace is one of the oldest parts of Prague Castle, dating from 1135. It was originally used only by Czech princesses, but from the 13th to the 16th centuries it was the king's own palace. At its heart is the grand Vladislav Hall and the Bohemian Chancellery, scene of the famous Defenestration of Prague in 1618.

Golden Lane   STREET
(Zlatá ulička; Map p284; Prague Castle; ⊙9am-5pm, to 4pm Nov-Mar; ☒22, 23) This picturesque alley runs along the northern wall of the castle. Its tiny, colourful cottages were built in the 16th century for the sharpshooters of the castle guard, but were later used by goldsmiths. In the 19th and early 20th centuries they were occupied by artists, including the writer Franz Kafka (who stayed at his sister's house at No 22 from 1916 to 1917).

Story of Prague Castle   MUSEUM
(Map p284; www.hrad.cz; Prague Castle; adult/child 140/70Kč; ⊙9am-5pm, to 4pm Nov-Mar; ☒22, 23) Housed in the Gothic vaults beneath the Old Royal Palace, this huge and impressive collection of artefacts ranks alongside the Lobkowicz Palace as one of the most interesting exhibits in the castle. It traces 1000 years of the castle's history, from the building of the first wooden palisade to the present day, illustrated by models of the site at various stages in its development.

Lobkowicz Palace   MUSEUM
(Lobkovický palác; Map p284; ☏233 312 925; www.lobkowicz.com; Jiřská 3; adult/concession 295/220Kč; ⊙10am-6pm; ☒22, 23) This 16th-century palace houses a private museum known as the Princely Collections, which includes priceless paintings, furniture and musical memorabilia. Your tour includes an audio guide dictated by owner

Prague Castle

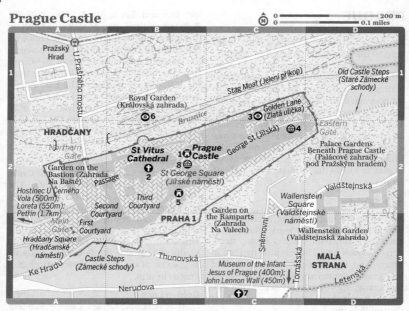

Prague Castle

◎ Top Sights

◎ Sights

William Lobkowicz and his family – this personal connection really brings the displays to life, and makes the palace one of the castle's most interesting attractions.

Strahov Library   HISTORIC BUILDING
(Strahovská knihovna; ☎ 233 107 718; www.strahovskyklaster.cz; Strahovské nádvoří 1; adult/child 120/60Kč; ☺ 9am-noon & 1-5pm; ☒ 22, 23) Strahov Library is the largest monastic library in the country, with two magnificent baroque halls dating from the 17th and 18th centuries. You can peek through the doors but, sadly, you can't go into the halls themselves – it was found that fluctuations in humidity caused by visitors' breath was endangering the frescoes. There's also a display of historical curiosities.

Loreta   CHURCH
(☎ 220 516 740; www.loreta.cz; Loretánské náměstí 7; adult/child 150/80Kč, photography permit 100Kč; ☺ 9am-5pm Apr-Oct, 9.30am-4pm Nov-Mar; ☒ 22, 23) The Loreta is a baroque place of pilgrimage founded by Benigna Kateřina Lobkowicz in 1626, designed as a replica of the supposed Santa Casa (Sacred House; the home of the Virgin Mary) in the Holy Land. Legend says that the original Santa Casa was carried by angels to the Italian town of Loreto as the Turks were advancing on Nazareth.

Royal Garden   GARDENS
(Královská zahrada; Map p284; ☺ 10am-6pm Apr-Oct; ☒ 22, 23) **FREE** A gate on the northern side of Prague Castle leads to the **Powder Bridge** (Prašný most; 1540), which spans the Stag Moat and leads to the Royal Garden, which started life as a Renaissance garden built by Ferdinand I in 1534. It is graced by several gorgeous Renaissance structures.

◎ Staré Město

★ **Old Town Square**   SQUARE
(Staroměstské náměstí; Map p286; Ⓜ Staroměstská) **FREE** One of Europe's biggest and most beautiful urban spaces, Old Town Square (Staroměstské náměstí, or Staromák for short) has been Prague's principal public square since the 10th century, and was its

main marketplace until the beginning of the 20th century.

Astronomical Clock
HISTORIC SITE

(Map p286; Staroměstské náměstí; ☺ chimes on the hour 9am-9pm; Ⓜ Staroměstská) Every hour, on the hour, crowds gather beneath the Old Town Hall Tower (p285) to watch the Astronomical Clock in action. Despite a slightly underwhelming performance that takes only 45 seconds, the clock is one of Europe's best-known tourist attractions, and a 'must-see' for visitors to Prague. After all, it's historic, photogenic and – if you take time to study it – rich in intriguing symbolism.

Old Town Hall
HISTORIC BUILDING

(Staroměstská radnice; Map p286; ☑ 236 002 629; www.staromestskaradnicepraha.cz; Staroměstské náměstí 1; adult/child 250/150Kč; ☺ 11am-6pm Mon, 9am-6pm Tue-Sun; Ⓜ Staroměstská) Prague's Old Town Hall, founded in 1338, is a hotchpotch of medieval buildings acquired piecemeal over the centuries, presided over by a tall Gothic tower with a splendid Astronomical Clock. As well as housing the Old Town's main tourist information office, the town hall has several historic attractions, and hosts art exhibitions on the ground floor and the 2nd floor.

Old Town Hall Tower
TOWER

(Věž radnice; Map p286; ☑ 236 002 629; www.staromestskaradnicepraha.cz; Staroměstské náměstí 1; adult/child 250/150Kč; ☺ 11am-10pm Mon, 9am-10pm Tue-Sun; Ⓜ Staroměstská) The Old Town Hall's best feature is the view across the Old Town Square from its 60m-tall clock tower. It's well worth the climb up the modern, beautifully designed steel spiral staircase; there's also a lift.

Church of Our Lady Before Týn
CHURCH

(Kostel Panny Marie před Týnem; Map p286; ☑ 222 318 186; www.tyn.cz; Staroměstské náměstí; suggested donation 50Kč; ☺ 10am-1pm & 3-5pm, to noon Sun Mar-Dec; Ⓜ Staroměstská) Its distinctive twin Gothic spires make the Týn Church an unmistakable Old Town landmark. Like something out of a 15th-century – and probably slightly cruel – fairy tale, they loom over Old Town Square, decorated with a golden image of the Virgin Mary made in the 1620s from the melted-down Hussite chalice that previously adorned the church.

Church of St James
CHURCH

(Kostel sv Jakuba; Map p286; ☑ 224 828 814; http://praha.minorite.cz; Malá Štupartská 6; ☺ 9.30am-noon & 2-4pm Tue-Sat, 2-4pm Sun; Ⓜ Náměstí Republiky) FREE The great Gothic mass of the Church of St James began in the 14th century as a Minorite monastery church, and was given a beautiful baroque facelift in the early 18th century. But in the midst of the gilt and stucco is a grisly memento: on the inside of the western wall (look up to the right as you enter) hangs a shrivelled human arm.

CZECH REPUBLIC PRAGUE

DON'T MISS

PRAGUE'S JEWISH MUSEUM

The **Prague Jewish Museum** (Židovské muzeum Praha; Map p286; ☑ 222 749 211; www.jewishmuseum.cz; Reservation Centre, Maiselova 15; combined-entry ticket adult/child 350/250Kč; ☺ 9am-6pm Sun-Fri, to 4.30pm Nov-Mar; Ⓜ Staroměstská) – a collection of four synagogues (the **Maisel**, **Pinkas**, **Spanish** and **Klaus**), the former **Ceremonial Hall** and the **Old Jewish Cemetery** – is one of the city's treasures. The monuments are clustered together in **Josefov** (Jewish Quarter), a small corner of the Old Town that was home to Prague's Jews for some 800 years before an urban renewal project at the start of the 20th century and the Nazi occupation during WWII brought this all to an end.

The monuments cannot be visited separately but require a combined-entry ticket that is good for all of the sights and available at ticket windows throughout Josefov. A fifth synagogue, the **Old-New Synagogue** (Staronová synagóga; Map p286; ☑ 222 749 211; www.jewishmuseum.cz; Červená 2; adult/child 220/150Kč; ☺ 9am-6pm Sun-Fri, to 4.30pm Nov-Mar; 🖾 17), is still used for religious services, and requires a separate ticket or additional fee.

The museum was first established in 1906 to preserve objects from synagogues that were demolished during the slum clearance at the turn of the 20th century. The collection grew richer as a result of one of the most grotesquely ironic acts of WWII. During the Nazi occupation, the Germans took over management of the museum in order to create a 'museum of an extinct race'. To that end, they brought in objects from destroyed Jewish communities throughout Bohemia and Moravia.

Central Prague

Vltava River

Prague Boats (70m)

JOSEFOV

19

Kozí

U obecního dvora

Dvořákovo nábřeží

Bílkova

Dušní

Elišky Krásnohorské

Vězeňská

Alšovo nábřeží

17. listopadu

Josefov

U starého hřbitova

14
Červená

V Kolkovně

Kozí

Masná

Mánes Bridge
(Mánesův
most)

15

Prague
Jewish
Museum 3

Pařížská

Dušní

Týnská

22

Týnská ulička

Jan Palach Square
(Náměstí
Jana Palacha)

Široká

Maiselova

Týn Courtyard
(Týnský dvůr)

John Lennon
Wall (650m);
St Nicholas
Church (700m);
Museum of the Infant
Jesus of Prague (850m);
Prague Castle (1.3km);
Loreta (1.7km);
Hostinec U Černého
Vola (1.7km);
Strahov Library (2km)

Staroměstská

23

Valentinská

Žatecká

Kaprova

Veleslavínova

Křižovnická

Platnéřská

Uradnice

Old Town
Square

2

6

7

Celetná

13

12

STARÉ MĚSTO

Mariánské
náměstí

Linhartská

1
Charles
Bridge

Křížovnické
náměstí

Karlova

Little Square
(Malé náměstí)

Železná

Former Fruit
Market
(Ovocný trh)

Anenská

Lilová

Řetězová

Husova

Jilská

Michalská

Melantrichova

Havlíská

Rytířská

Provaznická

Open-Air
Market

Anenské
náměstí

Zlatá

Havelská

Náprstkova

V Kotcích

Můstek

Betlémská

Bethlehem Square
(Betlémské
náměstí)

Skořepka

Uhelný
trh

Perlová

28. října

Karoliny Světlé

Konviktská

Na Perštýně

16

Martinská

Jungmannovo
náměstí

25

Můstek

Bartolomějská

Národní
Třída

Franciscan Garden
(Františkánská
zahrada)

Legion
Bridge
(Legií
most)

Jazz Dock
(750m)

Národní třída

24

K (David
Černý
Sculpture)

Smetanovo nábřeží

Divadelní

Voršilská

Mikulandská

Národní Třída

Purkyňova

Jungmannova

Palackého

Masarykovo nábřeží

P

27

Ostrovní

Spálená

Vladislavova

Vodičkova

Slav Island
(Slovanský
ostrov)

V Jirchářích

Křemencova

U Kroka (1.5km);
Biko Adventures
Prague (1.5km);
Vyšehrad
Citadel (2km)

Nastruze

Pštrossova

National Memorial
to the Heroes of the
Heydrich Terror (300m)

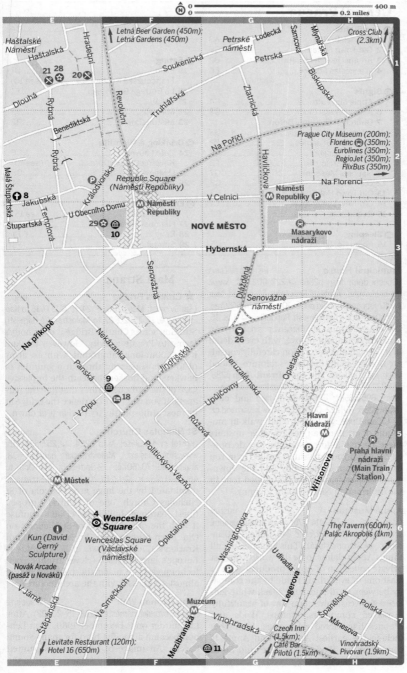

N 0 — 400 m
0 — 0.2 miles

Letná Beer Garden (450m);
Letná Gardens (450m)

Haštalské
Náměstí

Haštalská
Hradební

Petrské
náměstí

Lodecká
Šamcova
Mlynářská

Cross Club
(2.3km)

21 28
20

Soukenická
Petrská
Biskupská

Dlouhá
Rybná

Truhlářská
Revoluční

Zlatnická

Benediktská

Na Poříčí

Prague City Museum (200m);
Florenc (350m);
Eurolines (350m);
RegioJet (350m);
FlixBus (350m)

Rybná

Havlíčkova

Na Florenci

Malá Štupartská

Jakubská
Templová

8

Králodvorská

Republic Square
(Náměstí Republiky)

V Celnici

Náměstí
Republiky

Náměstí
Republiky

Štupartská

U Obecního Domu

29
10

NOVÉ MĚSTO

Masarykovo
nádraží

Hybernská

Senovážná

Dlážděná

Senovážné
náměstí

Na příkopě

Nekázanka

Jindřišská

Jeruzalémská

26

Opletalova

Panská

9
18

Růžová

V Cípu

Up-účovny

Hlavní
Nádraží

Wilsonova

Praha hlavní
nádraží
(Main Train
Station)

Politických Vězňů

Můstek

4
Wenceslas
Square

Wenceslas Square
(Václavské
náměstí)

Opletalova

Washingtonova

The Tavern (600m);
Palác Akropolis (1km)

Kun (David
Černý
Sculpture)

Novák Arcade
(pasáž u Nováků)

U divadla

Legerova

V Jámě
Štěpánská

Ve Smečkách

Mezibranská

Muzeum

Vinohradská

Španělská

Mánesova

Polská

Levitate Restaurant (120m);
Hotel 16 (650m)

11

Czech Inn
(1.5km);
Café Bar
Pilotů (1.5km)

Vinohradský
Pivovar (1.9km)

CZECH REPUBLIC PRAGUE

Central Prague

Municipal House   HISTORIC BUILDING
(Obecní dům; Map p286; ☑ 222 002 101; www.
obecnidum.cz; náměstí Republiky 5; guided tour
adult/concession/child under 10yr 290/240Kč/free;
⊙7.30am-11pm; Ⓜ Náměstí Republiky, ☐ 6, 8, 15,
26) Prague's most exuberantly art nouveau
building is a labour of love, with every detail
of its design and decoration carefully considered, every painting and sculpture loaded
with symbolism. The **restaurant** (Map p286;
☑ 602 433 524; www.francouzskarestaurace.cz;
mains 695-855Kč; ⊙noon-11pm; ☎) and **cafe**
(Map p286; ☑ 222 002 763; www.kavarnaod.cz;
⊙7.30am-11pm; ☎) here are like walk-in museums of art nouveau design, while upstairs
there are half a dozen sumptuously decorated halls that you can visit by guided tour. You
can look around the lobby and the downstairs bar for free, or book a guided tour in
the information centre (10am to 8pm).

Apple Museum   MUSEUM
(Map p286; ☑ 774 414 775; www.applemuseum.
com; Husova 21; adult/child 240/110Kč; ⊙10am-
10pm; Ⓜ Staroměstská) This shrine to all
things Apple claims to be the world's biggest
private collection of Apple products, with at
least one of everything made by the company between 1976 and 2012. Sleek white galleries showcase row upon row of beautifully
displayed computers, laptops, iPods and
iPhones like sacred reliquaries; highlights
include the earliest Apple I and Apple II
computers, an iPod 'family tree' and Steve
Jobs' business cards.

◎ Malá Strana

⭐ **Charles Bridge**   BRIDGE
(Karlův most; Map p286; ⊙24hr; ☐ 2, 17, 18 to Karlovy lázně, 12, 15, 20, 22 to Malostranské náměstí)
Strolling across Charles Bridge is everybody's
favourite Prague activity. However, by 9am
it's a 500m-long fairground, with an army
of tourists squeezing through a gauntlet of
hawkers and buskers beneath the impassive
gaze of the baroque statues that line the parapets. If you want to experience the bridge at
its most atmospheric, try to visit it at dawn.

St Nicholas Church   CHURCH
(Kostel sv Mikuláše; Map p284; ☑ 257 534 215;
www.stnicholas.cz; Malostranské náměstí 38;
adult/child 70/50Kč; ⊙9am-5pm Mar-Oct, to
4pm rest of year; ☐ 12, 15, 20, 22) Malá Strana is
dominated by the huge green cupola of St
Nicholas Church, one of Central Europe's
finest baroque buildings. (Don't confuse
it with the other Church of St Nicholas on
Old Town Square.) On the ceiling, Johann
Kracker's 1770 *Apotheosis of St Nicholas* is
Europe's largest fresco (clever trompe l'oeil
techniques have made the painting merge
almost seamlessly with the architecture).

John Lennon Wall   HISTORIC SITE
(Velkopřevorské náměstí; ☐ 12, 15, 20, 22) After
his murder on 8 December 1980, John Lennon became a pacifist hero for many young
Czechs. An image of Lennon was painted
on a wall in a secluded square opposite the

CZECH REPUBLIC PRAGUE

French embassy (there is a niche on the wall that looks like a tombstone), along with political graffiti and occasionally Beatles lyrics.

Museum of the Infant Jesus of Prague
CHURCH

(Muzeum Pražského Jezulátka; ☑ 257 533 646; www.pragjesu.cz; Karmelitská 9; ☺ 8.30am-7pm, to 8pm Sun; ⬛ 12, 15, 20, 22) FREE The Church of Our Lady Victorious (kostel Panny Marie Vítězné), built in 1613, has on its central altar a 47cm-tall waxwork figure of the baby Jesus, brought from Spain in 1628 and known as the Infant Jesus of Prague (Pražské Jezulátko). At the back of the church is a museum (open from 9.30am to 5.30pm, from 1pm Sunday), displaying a selection of the frocks used to dress the Infant.

Petřín
GARDENS

(☺ 24h; ⬛ Nebozízek, Petřín) This 318m-high hill is one of Prague's largest green spaces. It's great for quiet, tree-shaded walks and fine views over the 'City of a Hundred Spires'. Most of the attractions atop the hill, including a lookout tower and mirror maze, were built in the late 19th to early 20th century, lending the place an old-fashioned, fun-fair atmosphere.

◉ Nové Město

★ Wenceslas Square
SQUARE

(Václavské náměstí; Map p286; Ⓜ Můstek, Muzeum) More a broad boulevard than a typical city square, Wenceslas Square has witnessed a great deal of Czech history – a giant Mass was held here during the revolutionary upheavals of 1848; in 1918 the creation of the new Czechoslovak Republic was celebrated here; and it was here in 1989 where many anticommunist protests took place. Originally a medieval horse market, the square was named after Bohemia's patron saint during the nationalist revival of the mid-19th century.

National Museum
MUSEUM

(Národní muzeum; Map p286; ☑ 224 497 111; www.nm.cz; Václavské náměstí 68; adult/child 250/170Kč; ☺ 10am-6pm; Ⓜ Muzeum) Looming above Wenceslas Square is the neo-Renaissance bulk of the National Museum, designed in the 1880s by Josef Schulz as an architectural symbol of the Czech National Revival. Its magnificent interior is a shrine to the cultural, intellectual and scientific history of the Czech Republic.

Mucha Museum
GALLERY

(Muchovo muzeum; Map p286; ☑ 224 216 415; www.mucha.cz; Panská 7; adult/child 240/160Kč; ☺ 10am-6pm; ⬛ 3, 5, 6, 9, 14, 24) This fascinating (and busy) museum features the sensuous art nouveau posters, paintings and decorative panels of Alfons Mucha (1860–1939), as well as many sketches, photographs and other memorabilia. The exhibits include countless artworks showing Mucha's trademark Slavic maidens with flowing hair and piercing blue eyes, bearing symbolic garlands and linden boughs.

National Memorial to the Heroes of the Heydrich Terror
MUSEUM

(Národní památník hrdinů Heydrichiády; ☑ 224 916 100; www.vhu.cz/muzea/ostatni-expozice/krypta; Resslova 9a; ☺ 9am-5pm Tue-Sun; Ⓜ Karlovo Náměstí) FREE The Church of Sts Cyril & Methodius houses a moving memorial to the seven Czech paratroopers who were involved in the assassination of Reichsprotektor Reinhard Heydrich in 1942, with an exhibit and video about Nazi persecution of the Czechs. The church appeared in the 2016 movie based on the assassination, *Anthropoid*.

Prague City Museum
MUSEUM

(Muzeum hlavního města Prahy; ☑ 221 709 674; www.muzeumprahy.cz; Na Poříčí 52; adult/child 150/60Kč; ☺ 9am-6pm Tue-Sun; Ⓜ Florenc) This excellent museum, opened in 1898, is devoted to the history of Prague from prehistoric times to the 20th century (labels are in English as well as Czech). Among the many intriguing exhibits are an astonishing scale model of Prague, and the Astronomical Clock's original 1866 calendar wheel with Josef Mánes' beautiful painted panels representing the months – that's January at the top, toasting his toes by the fire, and August near the bottom, sickle in hand, harvesting the corn.

Kun (David Černý Sculpture)
PUBLIC ART

(Horse; Map p286; Lucerna Palace, Vodičkova 36; ⬛ 3, 5, 6, 9, 14, 24) David Černý's wryly amusing counterpart to the equestrian statue of St Wenceslas in Wenceslas Square hangs in the middle of the Lucerna Palace shopping arcade. Here, St Wenceslas sits astride a horse that is decidedly dead; Černý never comments on the meaning of his works, but it's safe to assume that this Wenceslas (Václav in Czech) is a reference to Václav Klaus, president of the Czech Republic from 2003 to 2013.

K (David Černý Sculpture)   PUBLIC ART

(Statue of Kafka; Map p286; Quadrio, Spálená 22; M Národní Třída) FREE Located in the courtyard of the Quadrio shopping centre above Národní třída metro station, David Černý's giant rotating bust of Franz Kafka is formed from some 39 tonnes of mirrored stainless steel. It's a mesmerising show as Kafka's face rhythmically dissolves and re-emerges, possibly playing on notions of the author's ever-changing personality and sense of self-doubt.

👁 Holešovice

Letná Gardens   PARK

(Letenské sady; ⏱24hr; 🚻; 🚊1, 8, 12, 25, 26 to Letenské náměstí) Lovely Letná Gardens occupies a bluff over the Vltava River, north of the Old Town, and has postcard-perfect views out over the city, river and bridges. It's ideal for walking, jogging and beer-drinking at a popular **beer garden** (📞233 378 200; www.letenskyzamecek.cz; Letenské sady 341; ⏱11am-11pm May-Sep; 🚊1) at the eastern end of the park. From the Old Town, find the entrance up a steep staircase at the northern end of Pařížská ulice (across the bridge). Alternatively, take the tram to Letenské náměstí and walk south for about 10 minutes.

👁 Smíchov & Vyšehrad

★ Vyšehrad Citadel   FORTRESS

(📞261 225 304; www.praha-vysehrad.cz; ⏱24hr; M Vyšehrad) FREE The Vyšehrad Citadel refers to the complex of buildings and structures atop Vyšehrad Hill that have played an important role in Czech history for over 1000 years – as a royal residence, religious centre and military fortress. While most of the surviving structures date from the 18th century, the citadel is still viewed as the city's spiritual home. The sights are spread out over a wide area, with commanding views out over the Vltava and surrounding city.

🧭 Tours

★ Biko Adventures Prague   CYCLING

(📞733 750 990; www.bikoadventures.com; Vratislavova 3, Vyšehrad; bike hire per day 490Kč, tours per person from 1300Kč; ⏱9am-6pm Apr-Oct; 🚊2, 3, 7, 17, 21) Italian owner Fillippo Mari loves to cycle, ski and hike and has created this small outfit dedicated to outdoor pursuits of all kinds. From April to October Biko rents bikes as well as offering day-long guided cycling trips for riders of all levels. Rental

bikes include standard mountain bikes and high-end hardtails from Giant.

Prague Boats   CRUISE

(Evropská Vodní Doprava; 📞724 202 505; www.prague-boats.cz; Čechův most, Pier 5; adult/child from 300/200Kč; ⏱9am-10pm; 🚊17) Offers a one-hour cruise to Charles Bridge and back, with views of the castle (half-hourly from 10am April to October, and hourly 11am to 7pm November to March); and a two-hour cruise to Vyšehrad and back (at 3pm year-round, plus 4.30pm April to October).

🎉 Festivals & Events

Prague Spring   MUSIC

(Pražské jaro; 📞box office 227 059 234, program 257 310 414; www.festival.cz; ⏱May) Prague Spring is the Czech Republic's biggest annual cultural event and one of Europe's most important festivals of classical music. Concerts are held in theatres, churches and historic buildings across the city. Tickets go on sale from mid-December the preceding year. Buy tickets online or at the festival box office at the Rudolfinum (p293).

Prague Fringe Festival   ART

(www.praguefringe.com; ⏱late May/early Jun) A wild week of happenings, theatre pieces, concerts and comedy shows. Much of it is in English. Buy tickets online or at venue box offices before shows.

🛏 Sleeping

Gone are the days when Prague was a cheap destination. The Czech capital now ranks alongside most Western European cities when it comes to the quality, range and price of hotels. Accommodation ranges from cosy, romantic hotels set in historic townhouses to the new generation of modish design hotels and hostels. Book as far in advance as possible (especially during festival season in May, and at Easter and Christmas/New Year).

Czech Inn   HOSTEL, HOTEL €

(📞210 011 100; www.czech-inn.com; Francouzská 76, Vršovice; dm 280-500Kč, s/d 1400/1800Kč, apt from 2600Kč; P❄@🖥; 🚊4, 22) The Czech Inn calls itself a hostel, but a boutique label wouldn't be out of place. Everything seems sculpted by an industrial designer, from the iron beds to the brushed-steel flooring and minimalist square sinks. It offers a variety of accommodation, from standard hostel dorm rooms to good-value doubles (with or without private bathroom) and apartments.

Ahoy! Hostel
HOSTEL €

(Map p286; ☑ 773 004 003; www.ahoyhostel.com; Na Perštýně 10; dm/r from 460/1800Kč; @ ☎; M Národní Třída, ☷ 2, 9, 18, 22) No big signs or branding here, just an inconspicuous card by the blue door at No 10. But inside is a very pleasant, welcoming and peaceful hostel (definitely not for the party crowd), with eager-to-please staff, some self-consciously 'arty' decoration, clean and comfortable six- or eight-bed dorms, and a couple of private twin rooms. Ideal location too.

Hotel 16
HOTEL €€

(☑ 224 920 636; www.hotel16.cz; Kateřinská 16; s/d from 2400/3500Kč; ❀ ❄ @ ☎; ☷ 4, 6, 10, 16, 22) Hotel 16 is a friendly, family-run little place with just 14 rooms, tucked away in a very quiet corner of town where you're more likely to hear birdsong than traffic. The rooms vary in size and are simply but smartly furnished; the best, at the back, have views onto the peaceful terraced garden. Staff are superb, and can't do enough to help.

NYX Hotel
BOUTIQUE HOTEL €€

(Map p286; ☑ 226 222 800; www.leonardo-hotels.com/nyx-prague; Panská 9; r from 2800Kč; @ ☎; ☷ 3, 5, 6, 9, 14, 24) NYX is a centrally located boutique for travellers looking for bold contemporary style and high-end amenities who are willing to splash out for it. Many of the rooms are quite spacious – the 'Heaven Suite' is a whopping 80 sq metres – and can be excellent value if sleeping four. The location, just near to Wenceslas Square, is convenient for sights and transport.

★ Dominican Hotel
HOTEL €€€

(Map p286; ☑ 224 248 555; www.dominicanhotel.cz; Jilská 7; r from 4900Kč; ❄ @ ☎; M Můstek) From the complimentary glass of wine when you arrive to the comfy king-size beds, the Dominican certainly knows how to make you feel pampered. Housed in the former monastery of St Giles, the hotel is bursting with character and is full of delightful period details including old stone fireplaces, beautiful painted timber ceilings and fragments of frescoes.

✖ Eating

In the last decade the number, quality and variety of Prague's restaurants has expanded beyond all recognition. You can now enjoy a wide range of international cuisine, from Afghan to Argentinian, Korean to Vietnamese, and even expect service with a smile in the majority of eating places. However, don't let this kaleidoscope of cuisines blind you to the pleasures of good old-fashioned Czech grub.

Mistral Café
BISTRO €

(Map p286; ☑ 222 317 737; www.mistralcafe.cz; Valentinská 11; mains 150-260Kč; ⊙ 8am-11pm, from 9am Sat & Sun; ☎ ⬛; M Staroměstská) Is this the coolest bistro in the Old Town? Pale stone, bleached birchwood and potted shrubs make for a clean, crisp, modern look, and the clientele of local students and office workers clearly appreciate the competitively priced, well-prepared food. Fish and chips in crumpled brown paper with lemon and black-pepper mayo – yum!

Lokál
CZECH €

(Map p286; ☑ 734 283 874; www.lokal-dlouha.ambi.cz; Dlouhá 33; mains 155-265Kč; ⊙ 11am-1am, to midnight Sun; ☎; ☷ 6, 8, 15, 26) Who'd have thought it possible? A classic Czech beer hall (albeit with slick modern styling); excellent *tankové pivo* (tanked Pilsner Urquell); a daily-changing menu of traditional Bohemian dishes; and smiling, efficient, friendly service! Top restaurant chain Ambiente has turned its hand to Czech cuisine, and the result has been so successful that the place is always busy.

The Tavern
BURGERS €

(www.thetavern.cz; Chopinova 26, Vinohrady; burgers 190-230Kč; ⊙ 11.30am-10pm; ☎; M Jiřího z Poděbrad, ☷ 11, 13) This cosy sit-down burger joint is the dream of a husband-and-wife team of American expats who wanted to create the perfect burger using organic products and free-range, grass-fed beef. Great pulled-pork sandwiches, fries and bourbon-based cocktails too. Reservations are taken via the website.

★ Levitate Restaurant
GASTRONOMY €€

(☑ 724 516 996; www.levitaterestaurant.cz; Štěpánská 611/14; mains 250-590Kč; ⊙ noon-3pm Thu-Sun, 6pm-midnight Tue-Sun; ❄; ☷ Štěpánská) One of Prague's hidden treats, this gastronomy restaurant combines Asian traditions with Nordic flavours, using local ingredients. You simply can't come here 'just to eat'. A calm oasis near the bustling heart of Prague, this restaurant is aiming for the stars. Make sure to reserve your table.

Maitrea
VEGETARIAN €€

(Map p286; ☑ 221 711 631; www.restaurace-maitrea.cz; Týnská ulička 6; weekday lunch 145Kč; mains 200-250Kč; ⊙ 11.30am-11.30pm, from noon Sat & Sun; ☑ ⬛; M Staroměstská) Maitrea (a Buddhist term meaning 'the future Buddha') is a beautifully designed space full of flowing curves and organic shapes, from the sensuous polished-oak furniture and fittings to the blossom-like lampshades. The menu is inventive and wholly vegetarian, with dishes such as Tex-Mex quesadillas, spicy goulash with wholemeal dumplings, and spaghetti with spinach, crispy shredded tofu and rosemary pesto.

U Kroka CZECH €€

(☑ 775 905 022; www.ukroka.cz; Vratislavova 12, Vyšehrad; mains 170-295Kč; ☉ 11am-11pm; ☏; 🚋 2, 3, 7, 17, 21) Cap a visit to historic Vyšehrad Citadel with a hearty meal at this traditional pub that delivers not just excellent beer but very good food as well. Classic dishes like goulash, boiled beef, rabbit and duck confit are served in a festive setting. Daily lunch specials (around 140Kč) are available from 11am to 3pm. Reservations (advisable) are only possible after 3pm.

La Bottega Bistroteka ITALIAN €€

(Map p286; ☑ 222 311 372; www.bistroteka.cz; Dlouhá 39; mains 265-465Kč; ☉ 9am-10.30pm, to 9pm Sun; ☏; 🚋 6, 8, 15, 26) You'll find smart and snappy service at this stylish deli-cum-bistro, where the menu makes the most of all that delicious Italian produce artfully arranged on the counter; the beef-cheek cannelloni with parmesan sauce and fava beans, for example, is just exquisite. It's best to book, but you can often get a walk-in table at lunchtime.

Field CZECH €€€

(Map p286; ☑ 222 316 999; www.fieldrestaurant.cz; U Milosrdných 12; mains 590-620Kč, 6-course tasting menu 2800Kč; ☉ 11am-2.30pm & 6-10.30pm Mon-Fri, noon-3pm & 6-10pm Sat & Sun; ☏; 🚋 17) 🍴 This Michelin-starred restaurant is unfussy and fun. The decor is an amusing art-meets-agriculture blend of farmyard implements and minimalist chic, while the chef creates painterly presentations from the finest of local produce along with freshly foraged herbs and edible flowers. You'll have to book at least a couple of weeks in advance to have a chance of a table.

🍷 Drinking & Nightlife

Bars in Prague go in and out of fashion with alarming speed, and trend spotters are forever flocking to the latest 'in' place only to desert it as soon as it becomes mainstream. The best areas to go looking for good drinking dens include Vinohrady, Žižkov, Karlín, Holešovice, the area south of Národní třída,

in Nové Město and the lanes around Old Town Square in Staré Město.

★ Vinograf WINE BAR

(Map p286; ☑ 214 214 681; www.vinograf.cz; Senovážné náměstí 23; ☉ 11.30am-midnight, from 5pm Sat & Sun; ☏; 🚋 3, 5, 6, 9, 14, 24) With knowledgeable staff, a relaxed atmosphere and an off-the-beaten-track feel, this appealingly modern wine bar is a great place to discover Moravian wines. There's good finger food, mostly cheese and charcuterie, to accompany your wine, with food and wine menus (in Czech and English) on big blackboards behind the bar. Very busy at weekends, when it's worth booking a table.

Cross Club CLUB

(☑ 775 541 430; www.crossclub.cz; Plynární 23; live shows 100-200Kč; ☉ 6pm-5am Sun-Thu, to 7am Fri & Sat; ☏; Ⓜ Nádraží Holešovice) An industrial club in every sense of the word: the setting in an industrial zone; the thumping music (both DJs and live acts); and the interior, an absolute must-see jumble of gadgets, shafts, cranks and pipes, many of which move and pulsate with light to the music. The program includes occasional live music, theatre performances and art happenings.

Café Bar Pilotů COCKTAIL BAR

(☑ 739 765 694; www.facebook.com/cafebarpilotu; Dónská 19, Vršovice; drinks 160-180Kč; ☉ 7pm-1am Mon-Thu, to 2am Fri & Sat; ☏; 🚋 4, 13, 22) This old-fashioned cocktail bar, with a big wooden serving bar and walls of books behind, features inventive cocktails based on favourite locales around the neighbourhood. There are plenty of tables or you can hang out on the street until 10pm. Friendly and professional service.

Vinohradský Pivovar PUB

(☑ 222 760 080; www.vinohradskypivovar.cz; Korunní 106, Vinohrady; ☉ 11am-midnight; ☏; 🚋 10, 16) This popular and highly recommended neighbourhood pub and restaurant offers its own home-brewed lagers as well as a well-regarded IPA. There's seating on two levels and a large events room at the back for concerts and happenings. The restaurant features classic Czech pub dishes at reasonable prices (180Kč to 230Kč). Book in advance for an evening meal.

Cafe Louvre CAFE

(Map p286; ☑ 724 054 055; www.cafelouvre.cz; 1st fl, Národní třída 22; ☉ 8am-11.30pm, from 9am Sat & Sun; 🚋 2, 9, 18, 22) The French-style Cafe Louvre is arguably the most amenable of

Prague's grand cafes, as popular today as it was in the early 1900s when it was frequented by the likes of Franz Kafka and Albert Einstein. The atmosphere is wonderfully olde worlde, and it serves good Czech food as well as coffee. Check out the billiard hall and the ground-floor art gallery.

Hostinec U Černého Vola
PUB

(☑ 220 513 481; Loretánské náměstí 1; ⊙ 10am-10pm; ⬚ 22, 23) Many religious people make a pilgrimage to the Loreta, but just across the road, the 'Black Ox' is a shrine that pulls in pilgrims of a different kind. This surprisingly inexpensive beer hall is visited by real-ale aficionados for its authentic atmosphere and lip-smackingly delicious draught beer, Velkopopovický Kozel (31Kč for 0.5L), brewed in a small town southeast of Prague.

U Medvídků
BEER HALL

(At the Little Bear; Map p286; ☑ 224 211 916; www.umedvidku.cz; Na Perštýně 7; ⊙ 11.30am-11pm; ☎; ⓂNárodní Třída, ⬚ 2, 9, 18, 22) The most micro of Prague's microbreweries, with a capacity of only 250L, U Medvídků started producing its own beer in 2005, though its trad-style beer hall has been around for many years. There's also Budvar on tap (45Kč for 0.5L). The in-house restaurant serves very good Czech food. Reservations recommended.

☆ Entertainment

Across the spectrum, from ballet to blues, jazz to rock and theatre to film, there's a bewildering range of entertainment on offer in this eclectic city. Prague is now as much a European centre for jazz, rock and hip-hop as it is for classical music. The biggest draw, however, is still the Prague Spring festival of classical music and opera.

Performing Arts

Smetana Hall
CLASSICAL MUSIC

(Smetanova síň; Map p286; ☑ 770 621 580; www.obecnidum.cz; Municipal House, náměstí Republiky 5; tickets 600-1300Kč; ⊙ box office 10am-8pm; ⓂNáměstí Republiky) The Smetana Hall, centrepiece of the stunning Municipal House (p288), is the city's largest concert hall, seating 1200 beneath an art nouveau glass dome. The stage is framed by sculptures representing the Vyšehrad legend (to the right) and Slavonic dances (to the left). It's the home venue of the Prague Symphony Orchestra (Symfonický orchestr hlavního města Prahy; www.fok.cz), and stages performances of folk dance and music.

Dvořák Hall
CONCERT VENUE

(Dvořákova síň; Map p286; ☑ 227 059 227; www.ceskafilharmonie.cz; náměstí Jana Palacha 1, Rudolfinum; tickets 200-1400Kč; ⊙ box office 10am-6pm Mon-Fri, to 3pm Jul & Aug; ⓂStaroměstská) The Dvořák Hall in the neo-Renaissance **Rudolfinum** (Map p286) is home to the world-renowned Czech Philharmonic Orchestra (Česká filharmonie). Sit back and be impressed by some of the best classical musicians in Prague.

National Theatre
OPERA, BALLET

(Národní divadlo; Map p286; ☑ 224 901 448; www.narodni-divadlo.cz; Národní třída 2; tickets 100-1290Kč; ⊙ box office 9am-6pm, from 10am Sat & Sun; ⬚ 2, 9, 18, 22) The much-loved National Theatre provides a stage for traditional opera, drama and ballet by the likes of Smetana, Shakespeare and Tchaikovsky, sharing the program alongside more modern works by composers and playwrights such as Philip Glass and John Osborne. The box offices are in the Nový síň building next door, in the Kolowrat Palace (opposite the Estates Theatre) and at the State Opera.

Live Music

★ Palác Akropolis
LIVE MUSIC

(☑ 296 330 913; www.palacakropolis.cz; Kubelíkova 27, Žižkov; ticket prices vary; ⊙ 7pm-5am; ☎; ⬚ 5, 9, 15, 26) The Akropolis is a Prague institution, a labyrinthine, sticky-floored shrine to alternative music and drama. Its various performance spaces host a smorgasbord of musical and cultural events, from DJs and string quartets to Macedonian Roma bands, local rock gods and visiting talent – Marianne Faithfull, the Flaming Lips and the Strokes have all played here.

Jazz Dock
JAZZ

(☑ 774 058 838; www.jazzdock.cz; Janáčkovo nábřeží 2, Smíchov; tickets 170-400Kč; ⊙ 3pm-4am Mon-Thu, from 1pm Fri-Sun Apr-Sep, 5pm-4am Mon-Thu, from 3pm Fri-Sun Oct-Mar; ☎; ⓂAnděl, ⬚ 9, 12, 15, 20) Most of Prague's jazz clubs are cellar affairs, but this riverside club is a definite step up, with clean, modern decor and a decidedly romantic view out over the Vltava. It draws some of the best local talent and occasional international acts. Go early or book to get a good table. Shows normally begin at 7pm and 10pm.

Roxy
LIVE MUSIC

(Map p286; ☑ 608 060 745; www.roxy.cz; Dlouhá 33; tickets 100-700Kč; ⊙ 7pm-5am; ⬚ 6, 8, 15, 26) Set in the ramshackle shell of an art deco cinema, the legendary Roxy has nurtured the more independent end of Prague's club spectrum for more than two decades. This is the place to see the Czech Republic's top DJs. On the 1st floor is NoD, an 'experimental space' that stages drama, dance, cinema and live music.

ℹ Information

The easiest and cheapest way to obtain Czech currency is through a bank ATM, drawn on your home credit or debit card. For exchanging cash, the big banks are preferable to private exchange booths (*směnárna*) and normally charge a lower commission (around 2% with a 50Kč minimum fee).

Na Homolce Hospital (☑ 257 271 111; www. homolka.cz; 5th fl, Foreign Pavilion, Roentgenova 2, Motol; 🚌 167, 168 to Nemocnice Na Homolce) Widely considered to be the best hospital in Prague, equipped and staffed to Western standards.

Prague City Tourism (Prague Welcome; Map p286; ☑ 221 714 714; www.prague.eu; Staroměstské náměstí 1, Old Town Hall; ⊙ 9am-7pm, to 6pm Jan & Feb; Ⓜ Staroměstská) The busiest of the Prague City Tourism branches occupies the ground floor of the Old Town Hall.

Globe Bookstore & Café (☑ 224 934 203; www.globebookstore.cz; Pštrossova 6, Nové Město; per min 1Kč; ⊙ 10am-midnight Mon-Thu, 9.30am-1am Fri-Sun; 🛜; Ⓜ Karlovo Náměstí) Offers a bank of computers for customer use; handy for visitors arriving without a laptop or web-enabled smartphone.

ℹ Getting There & Away

AIR

Václav Havel Airport Prague (Prague Ruzyně International Airport; ☑ 220 111 888; www.prg. aero; K letišti 6, Ruzyně; 🛜; 🚌 100, 119), 17km west of the city centre, is the main international gateway to the Czech Republic and hub for the national carrier Czech Airlines, which operates direct flights to Prague from many European cities. There are also direct flights from North America (from April to October) as well as to select cities in the Middle East and Asia.

The airport has two terminals: Terminal 1 for flights to/from non–Schengen Zone countries (including the UK, Ireland and countries outside Europe); Terminal 2 for flights to/from Schengen Zone countries (most EU nations plus Switzerland, Iceland and Norway).

The arrivals halls in both terminals have exchange counters, ATMs, accommodation agencies, public-transport information desks (in Terminal 2 and in the connecting corridor to Terminal 1), tourist information offices, taxi services and 24-hour left-luggage counters (Terminal 2 only; per piece per day 120Kč). Car-hire agencies

are in the 'Parking C' multistorey car park opposite Terminal 1.

BUS

Several bus companies offer long-distance coach services connecting Prague to cities around Europe. Nearly all international buses (and most domestic services) use the renovated and user-friendly **Florenc bus station** (ÚAN Praha Florenc; ☑ 900 144 444; www.florenc.cz; Pod výtopnou 13/10, Karlín; ⊙ 5am-midnight; 🛜; Ⓜ Florenc).

Important international bus operators with extensive networks and ticket offices at Florenc bus station include the following:

Flixbus (https://global.flixbus.com; Křižíkova 2b, ÚAN Florenc; ⊙ 7am-8pm)

RegioJet (Student Agency; ☑ 222 222 221; www.regiojet.cz; Křižíkova 2b, ÚAN Praha Florenc; ⊙ 5am-11.30pm)

Eurolines (☑ 731 222 111; www.elines.cz; Křižíkova 2b, ÚAN Praha Florenc; ⊙ 7am-6.30pm, to 4pm Sat; 🛜; Ⓜ Florenc)

CAR & MOTORCYCLE

Prague lies at the nexus of several European four-lane highways and is a relatively easy drive from major regional cities, including Munich (four hours), Berlin (four hours), Nuremberg (three hours), Vienna (four hours) and Budapest (five hours).

TRAIN

Prague is well integrated into European rail networks. Train travel makes the most sense if travelling to/from Berlin and Dresden to the north or Vienna, Kraków, Bratislava and Budapest to the east and south. Most domestic and all international trains arrive at **Praha hlavní nádraží** (Prague Main Train Station; ☑ information 221 111 122; www.cd.cz; Wilsonova 8, Nové Město; ⊙ 3.30am-12.30am; Ⓜ Hlavní nádraží), Prague's main station.

Most services are operated by the Czech state rail operator, České dráhy (p309), though two private rail companies, **Leo Express** (www. le.cz; Wilsonova 8, Praha hlavní nádraží; ⊙ ticket office 7.10am-8.10pm; Ⓜ Hlavní Nádraží) and **RegioJet** (Student Agency; www.regiojet.cz; Wilsonova 8, Praha Hlavní Nádraží; ⊙ 8am-8pm; Ⓜ Hlavní nádraží), compete with České dráhy on some popular lines, including travel to/from the Moravian cities Olomouc and Ostrava and points east. These companies can sometimes be cheaper and faster. Leo Express trains are identified as 'LEO' on timetables; RegioJet trains are 'RJ'.

ℹ Getting Around

TO/FROM THE AIRPORT

The cheapest way to get into Prague from the airport is by public transport. Bus 119 stops outside both arrivals terminals every 10 minutes from 4am to midnight, taking passengers to metro stop Nádraží Veleslavín (metro line A), from where you can catch a continuing metro into the centre. The entire journey (bus plus metro) requires one full-price public-transport ticket (32Kč) plus a half-fare (16Kč) ticket for every suitcase larger than 25cm x 45cm x 70cm. Buy tickets from Prague Public Transport Authority desks (located in each arrivals hall).

For connecting directly to Praha hlavní nádraží (the main train station), the **Airport Express bus** (AE; ☑ 296 191 817; www.dpp.cz; ticket 60Kč, luggage free; ☉ 5.30am-10.30pm) stops outside both arrivals terminals and runs every half-hour. The trip takes 35 minutes. Buy tickets from the driver.

Official airport taxis line up outside the arrivals area of both terminals and can take you into the centre for 500Kč to 700Kč, depending on the destination. The drive takes about 30 minutes.

PUBLIC TRANSPORT

Prague's excellent public-transport system combines tram, metro and bus services. It's operated by the **Prague Public Transport Authority** (DPP; ☑ 296 191 817; www.dpp.cz; ☉7am-9pm), which has information desks in both terminals of Prague's Václav Havel Airport and in several metro stations, including the Můstek, Anděl, Hradčanská and Nádraží Veleslavín stations. The metro operates from 5am to midnight.

Tickets valid on all metros, trams and buses are sold from machines at metro stations, as well as at DPP information offices and many newsstands and kiosks. Tickets can be purchased individually or as discounted day passes valid for one or three days. A full-price individual ticket costs 32/16Kč per adult/senior aged 65 to 70, and is valid for 90 minutes of unlimited travel. For shorter journeys, buy short-term tickets that are valid for 30 minutes of unlimited travel.

TAXI

Taxis are frequent and relatively inexpensive. The official rate for licensed cabs is 40Kč flagfall plus 28Kč per kilometre and 6Kč per minute while waiting. On this basis, any trip within the city centre – say, from Wenceslas Sq to Malá Strana – should cost no more than 200Kč. The following taxi companies offer 24-hour service and English-speaking operators:

AAA Radio Taxi (☑14014, 222 333 222; www.aaataxi.cz)

City Taxi (☑257 257 257; www.citytaxi.cz)

ProfiTaxi (☑14015; www.profitaxi.cz)

Liftago (www.liftago.com) is a locally owned ride-share service, similar to Uber, where you download an app to your phone for ordering and paying for rides.

AROUND PRAGUE

Karlštejn

Rising above the village of Karlštejn, 30km southwest of Prague, medieval **Karlštejn Castle** (Hrad Karlštejn; ☑ tour bookings 311 681 617; www.hradkarlstejn.cz; adult/child from 260/190Kč; ☉9am-6.30pm Jul & Aug, 9.30am-5.30pm Tue-Sun May, Jun & Sep, shorter hours rest of year) is in such good shape it wouldn't look out of place at Disneyworld. The crowds come in theme-park proportions as well, but the peaceful surrounding countryside offers views of Karlštejn's stunning exterior that rival anything you'll see on the inside.

The castle was born of a grand pedigree, originally conceived by Emperor Charles IV in the 14th century as a bastion for hiding the crown jewels. Run by an appointed burgrave, the castle was surrounded by a network of landowning knight-vassals, who came to the castle's aid whenever enemies moved against it. Karlštejn again sheltered the Bohemian and the Holy Roman Empire crown jewels during the Hussite Wars of the 15th century, but fell into disrepair as its defences became outmoded. Considerable restoration work in the late-19th century returned the castle to its former glory.

Entry is by guided tour only (three main tours available), and best booked in advance by phone or email.

Tour 1 (50 minutes) passes through the Knight's Hall, still daubed with the coats-of-arms and names of the knight-vassals, Charles IV's Bedchamber, the Audience Hall and the Jewel House, which includes treasures from the Chapel of the Holy Cross and a replica of the St Wenceslas Crown.

Tour 2 (100 minutes, May to October only) takes in the Marian Tower, with the Church of the Virgin Mary and the Chapel of St Catherine, then moves to the Great Tower for the castle's star attraction, the exquisite Chapel of the Holy Cross, its walls and vaulted ceiling adorned with thousands of polished semiprecious stones set in gilt stucco in the form of crosses, and with religious and heraldic paintings.

Tour 3 (40 minutes, May to October only) visits the upper levels of the Great Tower, which provide stunning views over the surrounding countryside.

From Prague, there are frequent train departures daily from Prague's main station.

The journey takes 45 minutes and costs 56Kč each way.

Kutná Hora

In the 14th century, Kutná Hora, 60km southeast of Prague, rivalled the capital in importance because of the rich deposits of silver ore below the ground. The ore ran out in 1726, leaving the medieval townscape largely unaltered. Now with several fascinating and unusual historical attractions, the Unesco World Heritage–listed town is a popular day trip from Prague.

Interestingly, most visitors come not for the silver splendour but rather to see an eerie monastery, dating from the 19th century, with an interior crafted solely from human bones. Indeed, the remarkable **Sedlec Ossuary** (Kostnice; ☑ information centre 326 551 049; www.ossuary.eu; Zámecká 127; adult/concession 90/60Kč; ⊙ 8am-6pm Mon-Sat, 9am-6pm Sun Apr-Sep, shorter hours rest of year), or 'bone church', features the remains of no fewer than 40,000 people who died over the years from wars and pestilence.

Closer to the centre of Kutná Hora is the town's greatest monument: the Gothic **Cathedral of St Barbara** (Chrám sv Barbora; ☑ 327 515 796; www.khfarnost.cz; Barborská; adult/concession 120/50Kč; ⊙ 9am-6pm Apr-Oct, shorter hours rest of year). Rivalling Prague's St Vitus in size and magnificence, its soaring nave culminates in elegant, six-petalled ribbed vaulting, and the ambulatory chapels preserve original 15th-century frescoes. Other leading attractions include the **Hrádek** (České muzeum stříbra; ☑ 327 512 159; www.cms-kh.cz; Barborská 28; adult/concession from 70/40Kč; ⊙ 10am-6pm Tue-Sun Jul & Aug, from 9am May, Jun & Sep, shorter hours rest of year) from the 15th century, which now houses the Czech Silver Museum.

Both buses and trains make the trip to Kutná Hora from Prague, though the train is usually a better bet. Direct trains depart from Prague's main train station to Kutná Hora hlavní nádraží every two hours (220Kč return, 55 minutes). It's a 10-minute walk from here to Sedlec Ossuary, and a further 2.5km (30 minutes) to the Old Town. Buses (136Kč return, 1¾ hours) depart from Prague's Háje bus station on the far southern end of the city. On weekdays, buses run hourly, with reduced services on weekdays.

BOHEMIA

Beyond the serried apartment blocks of Prague's outer suburbs, the city gives way to the surprisingly green hinterland of Bohemia, a land of rolling hills, rich farmland and thick forests dotted with castles, chateaux and picturesque towns. Rural and rustic, yet mostly within two to three hours' drive of the capital, the Czech Republic's western province has for centuries provided an escape for city-dwellers.

It's a region of surprising variety. Český Krumlov, with its riverside setting and Renaissance castle, is in a class by itself, but lesser-known towns in the south and west exude an unexpected charm. Big cities like Plzeň offer great museums and restaurants, while the famed 19th-century spa towns of western Bohemia retain an old-world lustre.

Plzeň

POP 164,180

Plzeň (Pilsen in German) is famed among beer-heads worldwide as the mother lode of all lagers, the fountain of eternal froth. Pilsner lager was invented here in 1842. It's the home of Pilsner Urquell *(Plzeňský prazdroj)*, the world's first and arguably best lager beer – 'Urquell' (in German; *prazdroj* in Czech) means 'original source' – and beer drinkers from around the world flock to worship at the Pilsner Urquell brewery.

The second-biggest city in Bohemia after Prague, Plzeň's other attractions include a pretty town square and historic underground tunnels, while the Techmania Science Centre joins the zoo and puppet museum to make this a kid-friendly destination. The city is close enough to Prague to see the sights in a long day trip, but you'll enjoy the outing much more if you plan to spend the night.

⊙ Sights

★ **Pilsner Urquell Brewery**   BREWERY
(Prazdroj; ☑ 377 062 888; www.prazdrojvisit.cz; U Prazdroje 7; guided tour adult/child 250/150Kč; ⊙ 8.30am-6pm, to 5pm Oct-Mar) Plzeň's most popular attraction is the tour of the Pilsner Urquell Brewery, in operation since 1842 and arguably home to the world's best beer. Entry is by guided tour only, with at least four tours daily in English (10.45am, 1pm, 2.45pm and 4.30pm). Tour highlights include a trip to the old cellars (dress warmly) and a glass of unpasteurised nectar at the

end. The brewery is located about 300m east of the centre (about 10 minutes on foot).

Underground Plzeň TUNNEL

(Plzeňské historické podzemí; ☑ 377 235 574; www.plzenskepodzemi.cz; Veleslavínova 6; adult/child 120/80Kč; ☉ 10am-7pm Apr-Sep, to 5pm Oct-Dec & Feb-Mar) This extraordinary 60-minute guided tour explores the passageways below the old city. The earliest were probably dug in the 14th century, perhaps for beer production or defence; the latest date from the 19th century. Of an estimated 11km that have been excavated, some 500m of the tunnels are open to the public. Bring extra clothing – it's a chilly 10°C underground. Tours are given in English at 2.20pm daily from April to October; English-language audio guides are available at other times.

Brewery Museum MUSEUM

(☑ 377 224 955; www.prazdrojvisit.cz; Veleslavínova 6; adult/child 90/60Kč; ☉ 10am-6pm, to 5pm Oct-Mar) The Brewery Museum offers an insight into how beer was made (and drunk) in the days before Pilsner Urquell was founded. Highlights include a mock-up of a 19th-century pub, a huge wooden beer tankard from Siberia and a collection of beer mats. All have English captions and there's a good printed English text available.

Techmania Science Centre MUSEUM

(☑ 737 247 585; www.techmania.cz; U Planetária 1; 190Kč; ☉ 10am-6pm; ℙ 🚗; 🚌 15, 17) Kids will have a ball at this high-tech, interactive science centre where they can play with infrared cameras, magnets and many other instructive and fun exhibits. There's a 3D planetarium (included with admission fee) and a few full-sized historic trams and trains manufactured at the Škoda engineering works. Take the trolleybus; it's a 2km hike southwest from the city centre.

🛏 Sleeping

The city has a decent range of pensions, budget and midrange hotels, many aimed at business and student visitors. The City Information Centre (p298) can find and book accommodation for a small fee.

Hotel Roudna HOTEL €€

(☑ 377 259 926; www.hotelroudna.cz; Na Roudné 13; s/d 1400/1700Kč; ℙ 🅿 🛜) Perhaps the city's best-value lodging, across the river to the north of the old town, the Roudna's exterior isn't much to look at, but inside the rooms are well proportioned with high-end

amenities such as flat-screen TVs, minibars and desks. Breakfasts are fresh and ample, and reception is friendly. Note there's no lift.

Hotel Rous BOUTIQUE HOTEL €€

(☑ 377 320 260; www.hotelrous.cz; Zbrojnická 7; s/d from 1800/2400Kč; ℙ @ 🛜) This 600-year-old building combines the historic character of the original stone walls with modern furnishings. Bathrooms are art deco cool in black and white. Breakfast is taken in a garden cafe concealed amid remnants of Plzeň's defensive walls. Downstairs, the Caffe Emily serves very good coffee.

🍴 Eating & Drinking

Plzeň is a good place to try traditional Czech pub grub, washed down with excellent local Pilsner Urquell beer.

Everest Restaurant INDIAN €

(☑ 774 048 597; www.indickaplzen.cz; Lochotínská 11; mains 140-180Kč; ☉ 11am-10pm Mon-Thu, to 11pm Fri & Sat; 🛜 🚗) The region's best Indian restaurant offers a spicy alternative to pork and dumplings. All of the standard chicken and lamb dishes, plus many vegetarian options, cooked to a high standard. The location, on a busy road outside the centre, and plain appearance are not encouraging, but push through the doors to find a comfy, crowded restaurant inside. Reservations recommended.

Na Parkánu CZECH €

(☑ 377 324 485; www.naparkanu.com; Veleslavínova 4; mains 169-299Kč; ☉ 11am-11pm, to 1am Fri & Sat, to 10pm Sun; 🛜) Don't overlook this pleasant pub-restaurant, attached to the Brewery Museum. It may look a bit touristy, but the traditional Czech food is top-rate, and the beer, naturally, could hardly be better. Try to snag a spot in the summer garden. Don't leave without trying the *nefiltrované pivo* (unfiltered beer). Reservations are an absolute must.

★ Buffalo Burger Bar AMERICAN €€

(☑ 733 124 514; www.facebook.com/barBuffalo Burger; Dominikánská 3; mains 165-385Kč; ☉ 11am-11pm, to 1am Fri & Sat; 🛜) Tuck into some of the best burgers in the Czech Republic at this American-style diner, with cool timber decor the colour of a well-done steak. Everything is freshly made, from the hand-cooked tortilla chips, zingy salsa and guacamole, to the perfect French fries, coleslaw and the juicy burgers themselves.

Aberdeen Angus Steakhouse STEAK €€
(☑ 725 555 631; www.angussteakhouse.cz; Pražská 23; mains 215-600Kč; ⊙ 11am-11pm, to midnight Fri & Sat; ☏) One of the best steakhouses in the Czech Republic. The meats hail from a nearby farm, where the livestock is raised organically. There are several cuts and sizes on offer; lunch options include a tantalising cheeseburger. The downstairs dining room is cosy; there's also a creek-side terrace. Book in advance.

★ **Měšťanská Beseda** PUB
(☑ reservations 378 035 415; http://web.mestanska-beseda.cz; Kopeckého sady 13; ⊙ 9am-10pm, from 11am Sat & Sun; ☏) Cool heritage cafe, pub, expansive exhibition space and occasional art-house cinema – the elegant art nouveau Měšťanská Beseda is hands-down Plzeň's most versatile venue. The beautifully restored 19th-century pub is perfect for a leisurely beer or coffee. Check out who's performing at the attached theatre.

ℹ Information

City Information Centre (Informační centrum města Plzně; ☑ 378 035 330; www.pilsen.eu/tourist; náměstí Republiky 41; ⊙ 9am-7pm, to 6pm Oct-Mar; ☏) Plzeň's well-stocked tourist information office is a first port of call for visitors. Staff here can advise on sleeping and eating options, and there are free city maps and a stock of brochures on what to see and do.

ℹ Getting There & Away

BUS

Plzeň's **bus station** (Centrální autobusové nádraží, CAN; ☑ 377 237 237; www.csadplzen. cz; Husova 60; ◲ 11, 28), marked on maps and street signs as 'CAN', is 1km west of the centre. The city is well-connected by bus to regional towns and cities. **RegioJet** (Student Agency; ☑ 377 333 222; www.regiojet.cz; náměstí Republiky 9; ⊙ 9am-6pm Mon-Fri) runs half-hourly buses during the day between Plzeň and Prague (99Kč, one hour). Note most Plzeň-bound buses depart Prague from Zličín station, the last stop on metro line B (yellow).

TRAIN

Plzeň's **train station** (Plzeň hlavní nádraží; www.cd.cz; Nádražní 102) is 1km east of the historic centre. Train connections are frequent between Plzeň and Prague's main train station (120Kč, 1½ hours). There's also regular direct train service to České Budějovice (179Kč, 2 hours) and Mariánské Lázně (114Kč, 1 hour), among other regional cities.

Český Krumlov

POP 13,141

Český Krumlov, in Bohemia's deep south, is one of the most picturesque towns in Europe. It's a little like Prague in miniature – a Unesco World Heritage Site with a stunning castle above the Vltava River, an old town square, Renaissance and baroque architecture, and hordes of tourists milling through the streets – but all on a smaller scale; you can walk from one side of town to the other in 20 minutes. There are plenty of lively bars and riverside picnic spots – in summer it's a popular hangout for backpackers. It can be a magical place in winter, though, when the crowds are gone and the castle is blanketed in snow.

Český Krumlov is best approached as an overnight destination; it's too far for a comfortable day trip from Prague. Consider staying at least two nights, and spend one of the days hiking or biking in the surrounding woods and fields.

⊙ Sights

★ **Český Krumlov State Castle** CASTLE
(☑ 380 704 721; www.zamek-ceskykrumlov.eu; Zámek 59; adult/concession from 240/170Kč; ⊙ 9am-5pm Tue-Sun Jun-Aug, to 4pm Apr, May, Sep & Oct) Český Krumlov's striking Renaissance castle, occupying a promontory high above the town, began life in the 13th century. It acquired its present appearance in the 16th to 18th centuries under the stewardship of the noble Rožmberk and Schwarzenberg families. The interiors are accessible by guided tour only, though you can stroll the grounds on your own. Book tours at castle ticket windows, over the website or through the Infocentrum (p300).

Castle Museum & Tower MUSEUM, TOWER
(☑ 380 704 721; www.zamek-ceskykrumlov.eu; Zámek 59; museum adult/child 100/70Kč, tower 100/70Kč; ⊙ 9am-5pm Jun-Aug, to 4pm Apr, May, Sep & Oct, to 3pm Tue-Sun Nov-Mar) Located within the castle complex, this small museum and adjoining tower is an ideal option if you don't have the time or energy for a full castle tour. Through a series of rooms, the museum traces the castle's history from its origins to the present day. Climb the tower for the perfect photo ops of the town below.

Museum Fotoateliér Seidel MUSEUM
(☑ 736 503 871; www.seidel.cz; Linecká 272; adult/child 100/40Kč; ⊙ 9am-noon & 1-6pm May-Sep, 9am-noon & 1-5pm Tue-Sun Oct-Apr) This photography museum presents a moving retrospective of

Český Krumlov

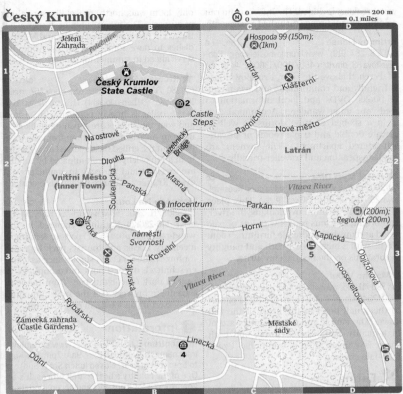

the work of local photographers Josef Seidel and his son František. Especially poignant are the images recording early-20th-century life in nearby villages. In the high season you should be able to join an English-language tour; if not, let the pictures tell the story.

Egon Schiele Art Centrum MUSEUM
(☑ 380 704 011; www.schieleartcentrum.cz; Široká 71; adult/child under 6yr 180Kč/free; ⊙ 10am-6pm) This excellent private gallery houses a small retrospective of the controversial Viennese painter Egon Schiele (1890–1918), who lived in Krumlov in 1911 and raised the ire of the townsfolk by hiring young girls as nude models. For this and other sins he was eventually driven out. The centre also houses interesting temporary exhibitions.

🛏 Sleeping

There are thousands of beds in Český Krumlov, but accommodation is still tight in summer. Winter rates drop by up to 30%. Ac-

Český Krumlov

◎ Top Sights
1 Český Krumlov State Castle B1

◎ Sights
2 Castle Museum & Tower B1
3 Egon Schiele Art Centrum................. A3
4 Museum Fotoateliér Seidel B4

🛏 Sleeping
5 Hotel Myší Díra D3
6 Krumlov House D4
7 U Malého Vítka................................ B2

✕ Eating
8 Hospoda Na Louži B3
9 Krčma v Šatlavské.......................... B3
10 Nonna Gina................................... C1

commodation can be noisy in the Old Town, and parking expensive. Consider alternative accommodation a short walk out of town. For budget accommodation, expect to pay from 500Kč per person for a private room, often with breakfast included. The Infocentrum can recommend mid-range furnished apartments.

Krumlov House
HOSTEL €

(📞728 287 919; www.krumlovhostel.com; Rooseveltova 68; dm/d/tr 450/1100/1300Kč; 😊@🛜)
🏊 Perched above the river, Krumlov House is friendly and comfortable, and has plenty of books, DVDs and local information to feed your inner wanderer. Accommodation is in a six-bed en-suite dorms as well as private double and triple rooms or private, self-catered apartments. The owners are English-speaking and traveller-friendly.

★ Hotel Myší Díra
HOTEL €€

(📞380 712 853; www.hotelmysidira.com; Rooseveltova 28; d/tr 2500/3100Kč; 🅿🛜) This place has a superb location overlooking the river, and bright, spacious rooms with lots of pale wood and quirky handmade furniture; room No 12, with a huge corner bath and naughty decorations on the bed, is a favourite.

U Malého Vítka
HOTEL €€

(📞380 711 925; www.vitekhotel.cz; Radniční 27; s/d 1700/2040Kč; 🅿😊🛜) There is a lot of charm to this small hotel in the heart of the Old Town. The simple room furnishings are of high-quality, hand-crafted wood, and each room is named after a traditional Czech fairy-tale character.

✗ Eating

Although there are dozens of places to eat in town, the large number of visitors means that booking ahead for dinner is recommended from April to October and on weekends year-round.

Nonna Gina
ITALIAN €

(📞380 717 187; www.facebook.com/pages/Pizzeria-Nonna-Gina/228366473858301; Klášterní 52; mains 130-200Kč; ⏰11am-11pm) Authentic Italian flavours from the Massaro family feature at this long-established pizzeria, where the quality of food and service knocks the socks off more expensive restaurants. Superb antipasti, great pizza and Italian wines at surprisingly low prices make for a memorable meal. Grab an outdoor table and pretend you're in Naples, or retreat to the snug and intimate upstairs dining room.

Hospoda 99
BURGERS €

(📞380 713 813; www.hostel99.cz/hospoda-99; Věžní 99; mains 120-300Kč; ⏰10am-11pm, to 10pm Oct-May; 🛜) This pub with a big summer terrace is far enough away from the busy centre (though

only 150m walk north) to feel like something of an oasis. The menu is big on burgers, but throws in nicely prepared steaks and Mexican dishes to have something for everyone. Reserve ahead in summer for dinner.

★ Krčma v Šatlavské
CZECH €€

(📞380 713 344; www.satlava.cz; Horní 157; mains 180-355Kč; ⏰11am-midnight) This medieval barbecue cellar is hugely popular with visitors and your tablemates are much more likely to be from Austria or China than from the town itself, but the grilled meats served up with gusto in a funky labyrinth illuminated by candles are excellent and perfectly in character with Český Krumlov. Advance booking is essential.

Hospoda Na Louži
CZECH €€

(📞380 711 280; www.nalouzi.cz; Kájovská 66; mains 140-280Kč) Nothing's changed in this wood-panelled *pivo* (beer) parlour for almost a century. Locals and tourists pack Na Louži for huge plates of Czech staples such as chicken schnitzels or roast pork and dumplings, as well as dark (and light) beer from the local Eggenberg brewery. Get the fruit dumplings for dessert if you see them on the menu.

ℹ Information

Infocentrum (📞380 704 622; www.ckrumlov. info; náměstí Svornosti 2; ⏰9am-7pm Jun-Aug, to 5pm rest of year; closed lunch Sat & Sun) One of the country's best tourist offices. It's a good source for transport and accommodation info, maps, internet access (per five minutes 5Kč) and audio guides (per hour 100Kč). You can purchase bus tickets and the **Český Krumlov Card** (www.ckrumlov.cz/card; adult/child 300/150Kč) here. A guide for visitors with disabilities is available.

ℹ Getting There & Away

BUS

RegioJet (Student Agency; 📞841 101 101; www. regiojet.cz; Nemocniční 586) coaches (170Kč, three hours, hourly) leave from Prague's Na Knížecí bus station at Anděl metro station (Line B). Book in advance for weekends or in July and August. Český Krumlov **bus station** (Autobusové nádraží; Nemocniční 586) is about a 10-minute walk east of the historic centre.

TRAIN

The train from Prague (210Kč, 3½ hours, four to six daily) requires a change in České Budějovice. There's regular train service between České Budějovice and Český Krumlov (40Kč, 45 minutes). It is quicker and cheaper to take the bus. Český Krumlov **train station** (Vlakové nádraží; www.cd.cz;

Třída Míru 1) is located 2km north of the historic centre. A **taxi** (☑ 380 712 712; www.green-taxi.cz) from the station costs around 100Kč.

Karlovy Vary

POP 51,800

Karlovy Vary (Carlsbad), or simply 'Vary' to Czechs, has stepped up its game in recent years, thanks largely to a property boom spurred by wealthy Russian investors. Indeed, the first thing you'll notice is the high number of Russian visitors, all following in the footsteps of Tsar Peter the Great, who stayed here for treatments in the early 18th century. Day trippers come to admire the grand 19th-century spa architecture and to stroll the impressive colonnades, sipping on the supposedly health-restoring sulphurous waters from spouted ceramic drinking cups.

Despite its exalted spa reputation, Karlovy Vary is not entirely welcoming to walk-ins looking for high-end treatments such as exotic massages and peelings; these services are available but should be booked in advance.

◉ Sights & Activities

★ Mill Colonnade
SPRING

(Mlýnská kolonáda; www.karlovyvary.cz/en/colon nades-and-springs; ⊘ 24hr) FREE The most impressive piece of architecture in Karlovy Vary is the neo-Renaissance Mill Colonnade (built 1871–81), with five different springs, rooftop statues depicting the months of the year, and a little bandstand. The Petra Restaurant, opposite, is the spot (but not the original building) where Peter the Great allegedly stayed in 1711.

Hot Spring Colonnade
SPRING

(Vřídelní kolonáda; www.karlovyvary.cz/en/colon nades-and-springs; ⊘ 9am-5pm, from 10am Sat & Sun) FREE The Hot Spring Colonnade is in an incongruous concrete-and-glass functionalist structure built in 1975 and once dedicated to Soviet cosmonaut Yuri Gagarin. It houses the most impressive of the town's geysers, Pramen Vřídlo, which spurts some 12m into the air; people lounge about inhaling the vapours or sampling the waters from a line of taps in the main hall.

Market Colonnade
SPRING

(Tržní kolonáda; www.karlovyvary.cz/en/colonnades-and-springs; Lázeňská; ⊘ 24hr) FREE The only one of the town's colonnades to be crafted from wood, this beautiful neoclassical structure dates from the 1880s and was the work of the fabled Viennese architectural firm of Fellner & Helmer. The bronze panel above the Charles IV Spring (pramen Karla IV) depicts the discovery of the hot springs by Emperor Charles in the 14th century.

Park Colonnade
SPRING

(Sadová kolonáda; www.karlovyvary.cz/en/colonn ades-and-springs; ⊘ 24hr) FREE Also known as the Garden Colonnade, this elegant wrought-iron structure dates from 1880 and is the first of the main colonnades that you reach as you enter the spa zone from the north. It was designed by the Viennese architectural firm of Fellner & Helmer, the same company that designed the Market Colonnade.

Castle Spa
SPA

(Zámecké Lázně; ☑ 353 225 502; www.castle-spa. com; Zámecký vrch 1; 30min massage from 676Kč; ⊘ 7.30am-7.30pm) Most Karlovy Vary accommodation offers some kind of spa treatment for a fee, but if you're just a casual visitor or day tripper, consider this modernised spa centre complete with a subterranean thermal pool. Visit the website for a full menu of treatments and massages.

✦✦ Festivals & Events

Karlovy Vary International Film Festival
FILM

(www.kviff.com; ⊘ early Jul) This film festival always features the year's top films as well as attracting plenty of (B-list) stars. It's rather behind the pace of the likes of Cannes, Venice and Berlin but is well worth the trip.

⎸⎦ Sleeping & Eating

Accommodation prices in Karlovy Vary have risen in recent years to be similar to those in Prague, especially in July during the annual Karlovy Vary International Film Festival. Indeed, if you're planning a July arrival, make sure to book well in advance. Infocentrum (p302) can help with hostel, pension and hotel bookings.

★ Hotel Romance Puškin
HOTEL €€

(☑ 353 222 646; www.hotelromance.cz; Tržiště 37; s/d 2800/3800Kč; ❀☎☞) In a great location just across from the Hot Spring Colonnade, the Puškin has renovated rooms with fully updated baths and very comfortable beds. These are just some of the charms at one of the nicest mid-range hotels in the spa area. The breakfast is a treat; the usual sausage and eggs is supplemented by inventive salads and smoked fish.

WORTH A TRIP

UNESCO HERITAGE ARCHITECTURE IN TELČ

The Unesco-protected town of Telč, perched on the border between Bohemia and Moravia, possesses one of the country's prettiest and best-preserved historic town squares. The main attraction is the beauty of the square, **náměstí Zachariáše z Hradce**, itself, which is lined with Renaissance burghers' houses. Most of the structures were built in the 16th century after a fire levelled the town in 1530. Famous houses include No 15, which shows the characteristic Renaissance sgraffito. The house at No 48 was given a baroque facade in the 18th century. **Telč Chateau** (Zámek; 567 243 943; www.zamek-telc.cz; náměstí Zachariáše z Hradce 1; adult/concession from 100/80Kč; 10am-4pm Tue-Sun May-Sep, to 3pm Apr & Oct), another Renaissance masterpiece, guards the northern end of the square.

If you decide to spend the night, the **Hotel Celerin** (567 243 477; www.hotelcelerin.cz; náměstí Zachariáše z Hradce 43; s/d 1300/1850Kč;) offers 12 comfortable rooms, with decor ranging from cosy wood to white-wedding chintz (take a look first).

There are a handful of daily buses that run from Prague's Florenc bus station (168Kč, 3 hours), though many connections require a change in Jihlava. The situation is similarly poor for bus travel to/from Brno (106Kč, two hours). Check the online timetable at http://jizdnirady.idnes.cz for times.

Bagel Lounge
BAGELS €

(720 022 123; www.bagellounge.cz; TG Masaryka 45; sandwiches 99-140Kč; 8am-8pm;) Ideal spot for a quick breakfast, a lunch of soup and bagel sandwich, or simply a coffee or cold drink. The terrace is great for people-watching, and the 1950s diner–inspired retro interior is fun. The 'Bacon-Bagel' sandwich (99Kč) makes for a filling breakfast.

Tusculum
CZECH €€

(739 541 008; www.tusculumkv.cz; Sadová 31; mains 180-400Kč; 11am-10pm;) One of the better dinner options. Tusculum features organic, locally sourced ingredients on a small menu of traditional favourites like duck and pork, spiced up with surprise starters like Thai soup and hummus. There are lots of vegetarian options on the menu, and (big plus) allergy and food-sensitivity information is clearly marked on the menu. Attractive terrace for alfresco dining.

ℹ Information

Infocentrum Spa (Infocentrum Lázeňská; 355 321 176; www.karlovyvary.cz; Lázeňská 14; 8am-6pm;) The main tourist information office within the main spa area. Can provide maps and advice on accommodation, events, transport info and spa treatments.

Infocentrum TG Masaryka (Infocentrum TGM; 355 321 171; www.karlovyvary.cz; TG Masaryka 53; 8am-6pm Mon-Fri, 9am-1pm & 1.30-5pm Sat & Sun) This branch of the main tourist information office is within easy walk of the bus and train stations.

ℹ Getting There & Away

BUS
Buses from Prague (150Kč, 2¼ hours, hourly) arrive at Karlovy Vary's terminal **bus station** (Autobusové Nádraží Terminal; 353 504 518; Západní 2a; 3, 6, 18, 23). Both Flixbus (www.flixbus.cz) and **RegioJet** (841 101 101; www.regiojet.cz; Západní 2a; 7am-7pm Mon-Fri, 8.30am-6.30pm Sat & Sun; 3, 6, 18, 23) operate regular service to and from Karlovy Vary. Check www.vlak-bus.cz for timetables.

TRAIN
Trains from Prague (330Kč, 3¼ hours, every two hours) take a circuitous route that is much slower and more expensive than the bus. Unless you have nothing else to do, it's not recommended.

MORAVIA

The Czech Republic's eastern province, Moravia is yin to Bohemia's yang. If Bohemians love beer, Moravians love wine. If Bohemia is about towns and cities, Moravia is all rolling hills and pretty landscapes. The Moravian capital, Brno, has the museums, but the northern city of Olomouc has the captivating architecture.

Brno

POP 377,440

Moravia's capital city just keeps getting better and better. The thousands of university students here have always ensured a lively club and entertainment scene, but a wave of next-gen cafes, restaurants and cocktail bars in the past few years has put the city on the map and even invited positive comparisons with Prague. The churches and museums are great too. If you add in some daring modern architecture from the early 20th century, such as the Unesco-protected Vila Tugendhat, there's plenty to reward more than a transit stop.

◎ Sights

★ Vila Tugendhat — ARCHITECTURE
(Villa Tugendhat; ☑ 515 511 015; www.tugendhat.eu; Černopolni 45; adult/concession from 300/180Kč; ☺10am-6pm Tue-Sun Mar-Dec, 9am-5pm Wed-Sun Jan & Feb; ☒ 3, 5, 9) Brno had a reputation in the 1920s as a centre for modern architecture in the Bauhaus style. Arguably the finest example is this family villa, designed by modern master Mies van der Rohe for Greta and Fritz Tugendhat in 1930. The house was the inspiration for British author Simon Mawer in his 2009 bestseller *The Glass Room*. Entry is by guided tour booked in advance by phone or email. Two tours are available: basic (one hour) and extended (1½ hours).

Labyrinth under the Cabbage Market — TUNNELS
(Brněnské podzemí; ☑ 542 212 892; www.ticbrno.cz; Zelný trh 21; adult/concession 160/80Kč; ☺9am-6pm Tue-Sun; ☒ 4, 8, 9) In recent years, the city has opened several sections of extensive underground tunnels to the general public. This tour takes around 40 minutes to explore several cellars situated 6m to 8m below the Cabbage Market, which has served as a food market for centuries. The cellars were built for two purposes: to store goods and to hide in during wars.

Old Town Hall — HISTORIC BUILDING
(Stará radnice; ☑ 542 427 150; www.ticbrno.cz; Radnická 8; tower adult/concession 70/40Kč; ☺10am-10pm May-Aug, to 6pm Sep & Oct, 10am-6pm Fri-Sun Nov; ☒ 4, 8, 9) No visit to Brno would be complete without a peek inside the city's medieval Old Town Hall, parts of which date back to the 13th century. The tourist office (p305) is here, plus oddities including a crocodile hanging from the ceiling (known affectionately as the Brno 'dragon') and a wooden wagon wheel with a unique story. You can also climb the tower.

Capuchin Monastery — CEMETERY
(Kapucínský klášter; ☑ 511 145 796; www.kapucini.cz; Kapucínské náměstí; adult/concession 70/35Kč; ☺9am-noon & 1-6pm Mon-Sat, 11am-5pm Sun, reduced hours Nov-Mar; ☒ 4, 8, 9) One of the city's leading attractions is this ghoulish cellar crypt that holds the mummified remains of several city noblemen from the 18th century. Apparently, the dry, well-ventilated crypt has the natural ability to turn dead bodies into mummies. Up to 150 cadavers were deposited here prior to 1784, the desiccated corpses including monks, abbots and local notables.

Špilberk Castle — CASTLE
(Hrad Špilberk; ☑ 542 123 677; www.spilberk.cz; Špilberk 210/1; adult/concession 280/170Kč; ☺10am-6pm Apr-Sep, 9am-5pm Tue-Sun Oct-Mar) Brno's spooky hilltop castle is considered the city's most important landmark. Its history stretches back to the 13th century, when it was home to Moravian margraves and later a fortress. Under the Habsburgs in the 18th and 19th centuries, it served as a prison. Today it's home to the Brno City Museum, with several temporary and permanent exhibitions.

⌒ Sleeping

Brno is a popular venue for international trade fairs, and hotels routinely jack up rates by 40% or more during large events (in February, April, August, September and October especially). Check www.bvv.cz for event dates and try to plan your visit for an off week. Always book ahead if possible.

★ Hostel Mitte — HOSTEL €
(☑ 734 622 340; www.hostelmitte.com; Panská 22; incl breakfast dm 455Kč; s/d 900/1400Kč; ☒ @ ☎ ; ☒ 4, 8, 9) Set in the heart of the Old Town, this clean and stylish hostel smells and looks brand new. The rooms are named after famous Moravians (eg Milan Kundera) or famous events (Austerlitz) and decorated accordingly. There are six-bed dorms and private singles, doubles and quads. Cute cafe on the ground floor.

Hotel Europa — HOTEL €
(☑ 515 143 100; www.hotel-europa-brno.cz; třída kpt Jaroše 27; s/d 1250/1400Kč; ⓟ ☎ ☎ ; ☒ 3, 5) Set in a quiet neighbourhood a 10-minute walk from the city centre, this self-proclaimed 'art' hotel (presumably for the futuristic lobby furniture) offers clean and tastefully furnished modern rooms in a historic 19th-century building. Rooms come in 'standard' and more expensive 'superior', with the chief difference being size. There is free parking out the front and in the courtyard.

Hostel Fléda

HOSTEL €

(☑731 651 005; www.hostelfleda.com; Štefánikova 24; dm/d from 270/800Kč; ❂☎; 🖫1, 6) One of Brno's best music clubs offers funky and colourful rooms, and a cafe and good bar reinforce the social vibe. It's a quick tram ride from the centre to the Hrnčirská stop.

Barceló Brno Palace

LUXURY HOTEL €€€

(☑532 156 777; www.barcelo.com; Šilingrovo nám 2; r from 3600Kč; P❂❋@☎; 🖫4, 6, 12) Five-star heritage luxury comes to Brno at the Barceló Brno Palace. The lobby blends glorious 19th-century architecture with thoroughly modern touches, and the spacious rooms are both contemporary and romantic. The location on the edge of Brno's Old Town is excellent.

✕ Eating

As the second-biggest city in the Czech Republic, Brno also has some of the country's best restaurants – at prices to match. For travellers on a budget, there are plenty of cafes and pubs where you can grab cheaper – but still very good – grub.

Spolek

CZECH €

(☑774 814 230; www.spolek.net; Orli 22; mains 90-180Kč; ❂9am-10pm, from 10am Sat & Sun; ☎🖉🕭; 🖫2, 4, 11) You'll get friendly, unpretentious starts at this coolly 'bohemian' (yes, we're in Moravia) haven with interesting salads and soups, and a concise but diverse wine list. Photojournalism on the walls is complemented by a funky mezzanine bookshop. It has excellent coffee too.

Bistro Franz

CZECH €

(☑720 113 502; www.bistrofranz.cz; Veveří 14; mains 165-195Kč; ❂8am-3.30pm Mon, to 9pm Tue-Fri, 9am-8.30pm Sat & Sun; ☎🖉; 🖫6, 12) Colourfully retro Bistro Franz is one of a new generation of restaurants that focuses on locally sourced, organic ingredients. The philosophy extends to the relatively simple menu of soups, baked chicken drumsticks, curried lentils and other student-friendly food. The wine is carefully chosen and the coffee is sustainably grown. Excellent choice for morning coffee and breakfast.

★ Pavillon

INTERNATIONAL €€

(☑541 213 497; www.restaurant-pavillon.cz; Jezuitská 6; mains 300-550Kč; ❂11am-11pm Mon-Sat, noon-10pm Sun; ☎🖉; 🖫1) High-end dining in an elegant, airy space that recalls the city's heritage in functionalist architecture. The menu changes with the season, but usually features one vegetarian entrée as well as mains with locally sourced ingredients, such as wild boar or lamb raised in the Vysočina highlands. Daily lunch specials (295Kč) including soup, main and dessert, are good value.

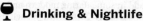

Drinking & Nightlife

Whether your beverage of choice is coffee, beer or cocktails, Brno has you covered. Thousands of students mean dozens of watering holes, and the cafes are every bit as cool as Prague's, while the cocktail bars are even better. Central Dvořákova street, particularly the area behind the Church of St James, is a popular area for clubs and bars.

★ Cafe Podnebi

CAFE

(☑542 211 372; www.podnebi.cz; Údolní 5; ❂8am-midnight, from 9am Sat & Sun; ☎🕭; 🖫4) This homey, student-oriented cafe is famous citywide for its excellent hot chocolate, but it also serves very good espresso drinks. There are plenty of baked goods and sweets to snack on. In summer the garden terrace is a hidden oasis, and there's a small play area for kids.

Super Panda Circus

COCKTAIL BAR

(☑734 878 603; www.superpandacircus.cz; Šilingrovo náměstí 3, enter from Husova; ❂6pm-2am Mon-Sat; ☎; 🖫4, 6, 12) From the moment the doorman ushers you through an unmarked door into this bar, you feel you've entered a secret world like out of the movie *Eyes Wide Shut*. The dark interior, lit only in crazy colours emanating from the bar, and inventive drinks add to the allure. Hope for an empty table since it's not possible to book.

Bar, Který Neexistuje

COCKTAIL BAR

(☑734 878 602; www.barkteryneexistuje.cz; Dvořákova 1; ❂5pm-2am, to 3am Wed & Thu, to 4am Fri & Sat; ☎; 🖫4, 8, 9) 'The bar that doesn't exist' boasts a long, beautiful bar backed by every bottle of booze imaginable. It anchors a row of popular, student-oriented bars along trendy Dvořákova. For a bar that 'doesn't exist', it gets quite crowded, so it's best to book ahead.

SKØG Urban Hub

CAFE

(☑607 098 557; www.skog.cz; Dominikánské nám 5; ❂8am-1am, to 2am Fri, 10am-2am Sat, noon-10pm Sun; ☎) Exposed brick walls, unadorned light bulbs hanging from the ceiling, loads of effortless attitude and, naturally, some of the best coffee and cakes in the centre of town. SKØG Urban Hub also moonlights as a gallery and performance space, and has pretty good salads and hummus as well.

☆ Entertainment

Fléda   LIVE MUSIC
(☑ 533 433 559; www.fleda.cz; Štefánikova 24; tickets 200-500Kč; ⊙ 7pm-2am; �🚊 1, 6) Brno's best up-and-coming bands, occasional touring performers and DJs all rock the stage at Brno's top music club. Buy tickets at the venue. Shows start around 9pm. Take the tram to the Hrnčirská stop.

**Brno Philharmonic
Orchestra**   CLASSICAL MUSIC
(Besední dům; ☑ 539 092 811; www.filharmonie-brno.cz; Komenského náměstí 8; tickets 300-450Kč; ⊙ box office 9am-2pm Mon & Wed, 1-6pm Tue, Thu & Fri, plus 45 mins before performances; 🚊 5, 6, 12, 13) The Brno Philharmonic is the city's leading orchestra for classical music. It conducts some 40 concerts each year, plus tours around the Czech Republic and Europe. It's particularly strong on Moravian-born, early-20th-century composer Leoš Janáček. Most performances are held at Besední dům concert house. Buy tickets at the box office, located around the corner from the main entrance on Besední.

ℹ Information

Tourist Information Centre (TIC Brno; ☑ 542 427 150; www.gotobrno.cz; Radnická 8, Old Town Hall; ⊙ 8.30am-6pm, from 9am Sat & Sun) Brno's main tourist office is located within the Old Town Hall complex. The office has loads of great information on the city in English, including events calendars and walking maps. Lots of material on the city's rich architectural heritage is also available, as well as self-guided tours. There's a free computer to check email.

Information Centre for South Moravia (Informační centrum – Jižní Morava; ☑ 542 211 123; www.ccrjm.cz; Radnická 2; ⊙ 9am-noon & 12.45-5pm Mon-Fri) Just next to the main city tourist information centre, this office focuses on South Moravia, outside of the city. It's a good place to stock up on ideas and information if your travels will take you to Olomouc, Mikulov, Znojmo, Valtice-Lednice and other attractions in the region.

ℹ Getting There & Away

BUS

Hourly buses connect Brno to Prague as well as cities and towns throughout the region. Buses use one of two stations, so be sure to look at the ticket or booking closely to be sure of the station you need. Most services use Brno's central bus station, **Zvonařka** (ÚAN Zvonařka; ☑ 543 217 733; www.vlak-bus.cz; Zvonařka; ⊙ information 6am-8pm, to 4pm Sat & Sun), which is located behind the main train station. Access is through a tunnel that begins below the train station and runs through a shopping centre.

Several popular services, however, including handy Prague-bound services with **RegioJet** (Student Agency; ☑ 539 000 860; www.regiojet.cz; náměstí Svobody 17; ⊙ 9am-6pm Mon-Fri) as well as Flixbus (https://global.flixbus.com) and some others, arrive at and depart from the small **Grand Hotel Bus Stop** in front of the main train station.

There are regular coach services throughout the day to Prague (210Kč, 2½ hours), Bratislava (180Kč, two hours), Olomouc (96Kč, one hour) and Vienna (200Kč, two hours).

TRAIN

Brno's hulking **train station** (Brno hlavní nádraží; www.cd.cz; Nádražní 1) is a major domestic and international train hub, with regular services to Prague, as well as Vienna, Bratislava and Budapest. There are domestic and international ticket offices, train information, a left-luggage office and lockers, as well as several places to stock up on train provisions.

Express trains to Brno depart Prague's Hlavní nádraží (main train station; 219Kč, three hours) every couple of hours during the day. Brno is a handy junction for onward train travel to Vienna (220Kč, two hours) and Bratislava (210Kč, 1½ hours).

Olomouc

POP 100,160

Olomouc is a sleeper. Practically unknown outside the Czech Republic and underappreciated at home, the city is surprisingly majestic. The main square is among the country's nicest, surrounded by historic buildings and blessed with a Unesco-protected trinity column. The evocative central streets are dotted with beautiful churches, testament to the city's long history as a bastion of the Catholic church. Explore the foundations of ancient Olomouc Castle at the must-see Archdiocesan Museum, then head for one of the city's many pubs or microbreweries, fuelled by the thousands of students who attend university here. Don't forget to try the cheese, *Olomoucký sýr* or *tvarůžky*, reputedly the smelliest in the Czech Republic.

⊙ Sights

Holy Trinity Column   MONUMENT
(Sloup Nejsvětější Trojice; Horní náměstí) The town's pride and joy is this 35m-high baroque sculpture that dominates Horní náměstí and is a popular meeting spot for

CZECH REPUBLIC OLOMOUC

local residents. The trinity column was built between 1716 and 1754 and is allegedly the biggest single baroque sculpture in Central Europe. In 2000 the column was added to Unesco's World Heritage Site list.

Archdiocesan Museum   MUSEUM
(Arcidiecézní muzeum; ☑ 585 514 111; www.olmuart.cz; Václavské náměstí 3; adult/concession 70/35Kč; ☉ 10am-6pm Tue-Sun; ☐ 2, 3, 4, 6) The impressive holdings of the Archdiocesan Museum trace the history of Olomouc back 1000 years. The thoughtful layout, with helpful English signage, takes you through the original Romanesque foundations of Olomouc Castle, and highlights the cultural and artistic development of the city during the Gothic and baroque periods. Don't miss the magnificent Troyer Coach, definitely the stretch limo of the 18th century. Entry is free on Sundays.

St Moritz Cathedral   CHURCH
(Chrám sv Mořice; ☑ 585 223 179; www.moric-olomouc.cz; Opletalova 10; ☉ tower 9am-5pm, from noon Sun; ☐ 2, 3, 4, 6) FREE This vast Gothic cathedral is Olomouc's original parish church, built between 1412 and 1540. The western tower is a remnant of its 13th-century predecessor. The cathedral's amazing sense of peace is shattered every September with an International Organ Festival; the cathedral's organ is Moravia's mightiest. The tower (more than 200 steps) provides the best view in town.

Civil Defence Shelter   HISTORIC SITE
(Kryt Civilní Obrany; www.tourism.olomouc.eu; Bezručovy sady; 30Kč; ☉ tours 10am, 1pm & 4pm Sat mid-Jun–Sep) Olomouc is all about centuries-old history, but this more-recent relic of the Cold War is also worth exploring on a guided tour. The shelter was built between 1953 and 1956 and was designed to keep a lucky few protected from the ravages of a chemical or nuclear strike. Book tours at the Olomouc Information Centre, which is also where they start.

🛏 Sleeping

The old centre has plenty of reasonably priced pensions, guesthouses and a couple of very good hostels.

Long Story Short   HOSTEL €
(☑ 606 090 469; www.longstoryshort.cz; Koželužská 31; dm 340-400, r 1100-2000Kč; ☉ 🛜) Clean, sleek, modern hostel has won international design awards for its creative fusion of old and new. Sleeping is in six- to 10-bed dorms, and private single and double rooms.

Facilities include an in-house bar, co-working space and garden terrace. Breakfast costs an additional 130Kč; laundry costs 200Kč.

Poets' Corner Hostel   HOSTEL €
(☑ 777 570 730; www.poetscornerhostel.com; 4th fl, Sokolská 1; dm 300-400, s/d 750/850Kč; ☉ 🛜; ☐ 2, 3, 4, 6) The couple who mind this friendly and exceptionally well-run hostel are a wealth of local information. There are eight-bed dorms, as well as private singles and doubles. Bicycles can be hired for 100Kč per day. In summer there's sometimes a two-night minimum stay, but Olomouc is worth it, and there's plenty of day-trip information on offer.

★ Penzión Na Hradě   PENSION €€
(☑ 585 203 231; www.penzionnahrade.cz; Michalská 4; s/d 1490/1890Kč; ☉ ✳ 🛜) In terms of price:quality ratio, this may be Olomouc's best deal, and worth the minor splurge if you can swing it. The location, tucked away in the shadow of St Michael's Church, is ideally central and the sleek, cool rooms have a professional design touch. There's also a small garden terrace for relaxing out the back. Book ahead in summer.

🍴 Eating & Drinking

With its large population of students, Olomouc's food options tend towards the simple and affordable. Most restaurants offer a good lunch deal of soup and main course for not much more than 100Kč. Nearly every restaurant will offer some version of the local cheese (Olomoucký sýr or tvarůžky), a stringy, fragrant dairy product that makes for either a filling starter or an accompaniment to beer.

Entree Restaurant   CZECH €€
(☑ 585 312 440; www.entree-restaurant.cz; Ostravská 1; mains 285-445Kč, 5-course tasting menu from 950Kč; ☉ 11am-2pm & 5pm-midnight; ✳ 🛜 🅿) The highest-rated restaurant in Olomouc and among the top 10 in the country, Entree emphasises locally sourced ingredients and natural materials. Award-winning Czech chef Přemek Forejt deconstructs and rearranges traditional Czech dishes in ways that make them unrecognisable yet memorable. The out-of-centre location is a 15-minute walk east of the train station or a short taxi ride. Reserve online.

Svatováclavský Pivovar   CZECH €€
(☑ 585 207 517; www.svatovaclavsky-pivovar.cz; Mariánská 4; mains 180-290Kč; ☉ 10am-11pm Mon & Tue, to midnight Wed-Fri, 11am-midnight Sat, 11am-

10pm Sun; 🔊; 🚌 2, 3, 4, 6) This warm and inviting pub makes its own beer and serves plateloads of Czech specialities such as duck confit and beer-infused *guláš* (goulash). Stop by for lunch mid-week for an excellent-value soup and main course for around 150Kč. Speciality beers include unpasteurised wheat and cherry-flavoured varieties.

The Black Stuff PUB
(📞 774 697 909; www.blackstuff.cz; 1 máje 19; ⏱ 5pm-2am, to 3am Sat, to midnight Sun; 🔊; 🚌 2, 3, 4, 6) Cosy, old-fashioned Irish bar with several beers on tap and a large and growing collection of single malts and other choice tipples. Attracts a mixed crowd of students, locals and visitors.

☆ Entertainment

Jazz Tibet Club LIVE MUSIC
(📞 777 746 887; https://jazztibet.cz/en; Sokolská 48; tickets 100-300Kč; ⏱ 11am-midnight Mon-Sat; 🔊) Blues, jazz and world music, including occasional international acts, feature at this popular spot, which also incorporates a good restaurant and wine bar. See the website for the program during your visit. Buy tickets at the venue on the day of the show or in advance at the Olomouc Information Centre.

Moravian Philharmonic Olomouc CLASSICAL MUSIC
(Moravská Filharmonie Olomouc; 📞 585 206 514; www.mfo.cz; Horní náměstí 23; tickets 90-270Kč) The local orchestra presents regular concerts and hosts Olomouc's International Organ Festival. Buy tickets one week in advance at the Olomouc Information Centre or at the venue one hour before the performance starts.

ℹ Information

Olomouc Information Centre (Olomoucká Informační Služba; 📞 585 513 385; www. tourism.olomouc.eu; Horní náměstí; ⏱ 9am-7pm) Located in the historic town hall and very helpful when it comes to securing maps, brochures and tickets for events around town. It also offers one-hour sightseeing tours of the city centre (70Kč) several times daily from mid-June to September.

ℹ Getting There & Away

BUS

Olomouc is connected by around 15 buses daily to/from Brno (96Kč, 1¼ hours). Regional bus services are excellent. The best way of getting to Prague, however, is by train. The **bus station** (Autobusové nádraží Olomouc; 📞 585 313 848; www.vlak-bus.cz; Sladkovského 142/37; 🚌 1, 2, 3, 4, 5, 6, 7) is located just behind the train station, about 2km east of the centre.

TRAIN

Olomouc is on a main international rail line, with regular services from both Prague (250Kč, two to three hours) and Brno (110Kč, 1½ hours). From Prague, you can take normal trains or faster, high-end private trains run by **RegioJet** (Student Agency; 📞 539 000 931; www.regiojet.cz; Jeremenkova 23; ⏱ 5.15am-8.30pm, from 6.15am Sat & Sun; 🚌 1, 2, 3, 4, 5, 6, 7) or **LEO Express** (📞 220 311 700; www.le.cz; Jeremenkova 23, Main Train Station; ⏱ 8am-7.50pm; 🚌 1, 2, 3, 4, 5, 6, 7). Buy tickets online or at ticket counters in either train station. Olomouc's **train station** (Olomouc hlavní nádraží; www.cd.cz; Jeremenkova; 🚌 1, 2, 3, 4, 5, 6, 7) is around 2km east of the centre and accessible via several tram lines.

SURVIVAL GUIDE

ℹ Directory A–Z

ACCOMMODATION

Accommodation in the Czech Republic runs the gamut from summer campsites to family pensions to hotels at all price levels. Places that pull in international tourists – Prague, Karlovy Vary and Český Krumlov – are the most expensive and beds can be hard to find during peak periods, but there's rarely any problem finding a place to stay in smaller towns.

LEGAL MATTERS

Foreigners in the Czech Republic are subject to the laws of the host country. Most visitors aren't likely to have any issues. Handy things to know:
➜ The legal blood-alcohol level for drivers is zero.
➜ Cannabis occupies a grey area; it's been decriminalised but is not technically legal. Police will rarely hassle someone for smoking a joint, but always exercise discretion and do not smoke indoors. Buying and selling drugs of any kind, including cannabis, is illegal.

LGBTIQ+ TRAVELLERS

The Czech Republic is a relatively tolerant destination for gay and lesbian travellers. Homosexuality is legal, and since 2006, same-sex couples have been able to form registered partnerships.

Prague has a lively gay scene and is home to Eastern Europe's biggest gay pride march (www.praguepride.cz), normally held in August.

Attitudes are less accepting outside the capital, but even here homosexual couples are not likely to suffer overt discrimination.

Useful websites include Prague Saints (www.praguesaints.cz) and Travel Gay Europe (www.travelgayeurope.com).

MONEY

ATMs are widely available. Credit and debit cards are accepted in most hotels and restaurants.

OPENING HOURS

Most places adhere roughly to the following hours.

Banks 9am to 4pm Monday to Friday; some 9am to 1pm Saturday

Bars 11am to 1am Tuesday to Saturday; shorter hours Sunday and Monday

Museums 9am to 6pm Tuesday to Sunday; some close or have shorter hours October to April

Restaurants 11am to 11pm; kitchens close 10pm

Shops 9am to 6pm Monday to Friday, some 9am to 1pm Saturday; tourist shops and malls have longer hours and are normally open daily.

PUBLIC HOLIDAYS

Banks, offices, department stores and some shops are closed on public holidays. Restaurants, museums and tourist attractions tend to stay open, though many may close on the first working day after a holiday.

New Year's Day 1 January

Easter Monday March/April

Labour Day 1 May

Liberation Day 8 May

Sts Cyril & Methodius Day 5 July

Jan Hus Day 6 July

Czech Statehood Day 28 September

Republic Day 28 October

Struggle for Freedom & Democracy Day 17 November

Christmas Eve (Generous Day) 24 December

Christmas Day 25 December

St Stephen's Day 26 December

TELEPHONE

Most Czech telephone numbers, both landline and mobile (cell), have nine digits. There are no city or area codes. To call any Czech number, simply dial the unique nine-digit number.

➨ To call abroad from the Czech Republic, dial the international access code (00), then the country code, then the area code (minus any initial zero) and the number.

➨ To dial the Czech Republic from abroad, dial your country's international access code, then 420 (the Czech Republic country code) and then the unique nine-digit local number.

TOURIST INFORMATION

Czech Tourism (www.czechtourism.com) maintains a wonderful website, with a trove of useful information. There's a large English-language section on festivals and events, accommodation and tips on what to see and do all around the country. **Prague City Tourism** (www.prague.eu) and **GoToBrno** (www.gotobrno.cz) are also useful.

Nearly all cities have decent tourist offices. If you turn up in a city that doesn't have a tourist office, you're pretty much on your own. Local bookshops or newsagents can sometimes sell a local map.

🕄 Getting There & Away

AIR

Prague's Václav Havel Airport (p294) is one of Central Europe's busiest airports, and daily flights connect the Czech capital with major cities throughout Europe, the UK, the Middle East and Asia. From April to October, direct flights link Prague to a handful of cities in North America.

LAND

The country is integrated into the European road and rail network. Trains and buses to neighbouring countries are frequent, and road travel poses no unusual problems.

Bus

Several bus companies offer long-distance coach services connecting cities in the Czech Republic to cities around Europe. For travel to and from Prague, nearly all international buses (and most domestic services) use the city's renovated and user-friendly Florenc bus station (p294).

Important international bus operators with extensive networks and ticket offices at the Florenc bus station include Flixbus (p294), RegioJet (p294) and Eurolines (p294).

The Florenc bus station website has a good timetable of buses, both foreign and domestic, arriving in and departing from the capital.

Car & Motorcycle

The Czech Republic has generally good roads, with some limited stretches of four-lane highway.

➨ All drivers, if stopped by the police, must be prepared to show the vehicle's registration, proof of insurance (a 'green' card) and a valid driving licence.

➨ In lieu of paying highway tolls, all motorists are required to display a special prepaid sticker (dálniční známka) on car windscreens. Buy these at large petrol stations near the border or immediately after crossing the border. A sticker valid for 10 days costs 310Kč, for 30 days 440Kč, and for a year 1500Kč.

Train

The Czech national railway, České dráhy (ČD; www.cd.cz) forms part of the European rail grid, and there are decent connections to neighbouring countries. Frequent international trains connect German cities like Berlin and Dresden with Prague. From here, fast trains head southeast to Brno, with excellent onward service to points in Austria, Slovakia and Hungary. The German Rail (www.bahn.de) website has a handy international train timetable.

In addition to ČD, two private railways operate in the Czech Republic and service international destinations.

➡ RegioJet (p294) Train service to select destinations in the Czech Republic, with onward service to Slovakia. Identified as 'RJ' on timetables.

➡ LEO Express (p294) Train service to select destinations in the Czech Republic, with onward coach service to destinations in Poland, Slovakia and Ukraine. Identified as 'LEO' on timetables.

ℹ Getting Around

AIR

At the time of writing there were no domestic flights in operation. The size of the country makes air travel impractical.

BICYCLE

Cycling is a popular weekend activity in nice weather, though its full potential has yet to be realised. Southern Moravia, especially along a marked wine trail that runs between vineyards, is ideal for cycling.

➡ A handful of large cities, including Prague, do have dedicated cycling lanes, but these are often half-hearted efforts and leave cyclists at the mercy of often-aggressive drivers.

➡ It's possible to hire or buy bicycles in many major towns, though not all. Rates average from 400Kč to 600Kč per day.

➡ A helpful website for getting started and planning a cyclist route in the Czech Republic is Cyclists Welcome (Cyklisté vítáni; www.cykliste vitani.cz).

BUS

Long-haul and regional bus services are an important part of the transport system in the Czech Republic. Buses are often faster, cheaper and more convenient than trains, and are especially handy for accessing areas where train services are poor, such as Karlovy Vary and Český Krumlov.

➡ Bus stations are usually (but not always) located near train stations to allow for easy transfer between the two. In Prague, the Florenc bus station (p294) is the main departure and arrival point, though some buses arrive at and depart from smaller stations along outlying metro lines.

➡ Check the online timetable at IDOS (http://jizdnirady.idnes.cz) to make sure you have the right station.

➡ RegioJet (p294) and Flixbus (p294) are popular private carriers with extensive networks to key destinations, including Prague, Brno, Karlovy Vary, Plzeň and Český Krumlov. Buy tickets online or at station ticket windows.

CAR & MOTORCYCLE

Driving has compelling advantages. With your own wheels, you're free to explore off-the-beaten-track destinations and small towns. That said, driving in the Czech Republic is not ideal, and if you have the chance to use alternatives like the train and bus, these can be more relaxing options.

➡ Roads, including the most important highways, are in the midst of a long-term rebuilding process, and delays and detours are more the norm than the exception.

➡ Most highways are two lanes, and can be choked with cars and trucks. When calculating arrival times, figure on covering about 60km to 70km per hour.

TRAIN

The Czech rail network is operated by **České dráhy** (ČD, Czech Rail; ☎ national hotline 221 111 122; www.cd.cz). Train travel is generally comfortable, reasonably priced and efficient. Trains are particularly useful for covering relatively long distances between major cities, such as between Prague and Brno, or Prague and Olomouc.

Two smaller private operators, RegioJet (p294) and LEO Express (p294), operate daily high-speed trains from Prague to the Moravian cities of Olomouc and Ostrava, with the possibility to connect to onward coach services to Slovakia and Poland. Timetable information for all trains is available online at IDOS (http://jizdnirady.idnes.cz).

Denmark

POP 5.8 MILLION

Best Places to Eat

→ Kadeau (p320)

→ Admiralgade 26 (p320)

→ Høst (p321)

→ Restaurant No 61 (p326)

→ Aarhus Street Food (p328)

Best Places to Stay

→ Hotel Nimb (p319)

→ Urban House (p319)

→ Hotel Guldsmeden (p327)

→ Babette Guldsmeden (p319)

Why Go?

It's heart-warming to know there's still a country where the term 'fairy tale' can be used freely – from its most enduring literary legacy to its textbook castles. In a nutshell, Denmark gets it right: old-fashioned charm embraces the most avowedly forward-looking design and social developments. The country wins a regular place on lists of both the most liveable and the happiest nations on earth, and you won't have to search hard to find much-prized hygge, a uniquely Danish trait best described as a merger of cosiness, camaraderie and contentment. From art and architecture, to sustainable living and dining, Denmark's capital, Copenhagen, is a global leader, punching well above its weight. Supporting cities such as Odense and Aarhus harbour their own urbane drawcards, with no shortage of photogenic hamlets, country trails and sweeping coastline in between.

When to Go
Copenhagen

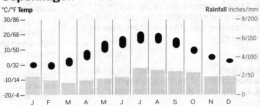

Jun & Jul Long days, buzzing beachside towns, Copenhagen Jazz and A-list rock fest Roskilde.

Sep & Oct Fewer crowds, golden landscapes and snug nights by crackling open fires.

Dec Twinkling Christmas lights, ice-skating rinks and gallons of warming *gløgg* (mulled wine).

Entering the Country

Getting to Denmark is simple. The capital, Copenhagen, has worldwide air links, and some carriers fly into regional airports around the small nation. Train, road and bridge links exist to Germany and Sweden, and there are ferry connections to/from several countries.

ITINERARIES

One Week

You could comfortably spend four days in Copenhagen (p313) exploring the museums, hunting down Danish design and taste-testing its lauded restaurants and bars. A trip north along the coast to the magnificent modern-art museum Louisiana (p315), and then further north still to Kronborg Slot (p324), before returning south via Roskilde (p324), is a top option for the remaining three days.

Two Weeks

After time in and around Copenhagen (p313), head west, stopping off to see Hans Christian Andersen's birthplace in Odense (p325). Continue further west to the Jutland peninsula (p327) for the understated cool of Aarhus (p327), home to one of Denmark's top modern-art museums. Indulge your inner child with a visit to Legoland (p331), then head north to luminous Skagen (p330) for art, local seafood and duelling seas.

Essential Food & Drink

Beer Beyond Carlsberg is an armada of top-notch craft brews from microbreweries like Mikkeller.

Akvavit An alcoholic spirit commonly made with potatoes and spiced with caraway.

Kanelsnegle The sticky, ubiquitous 'cinnamon snail' is sometimes laced with chocolate.

Koldskål A cold, sweet buttermilk soup made with vanilla and traditionally served with crunchy biscuits such as *kammerjunkere*.

New Nordic Contemporary Danish cooking merges locavore ingredients, Nordic traditions and bold creativity into one spectacular whole.

Sild Smoked, cured, pickled or fried, herring is a local staple.

Smørrebrød Denmark's famous 'open sandwich' sees rye or white bread topped with anything from beef tartare to egg and shrimp.

Flæskesteg Danish-style roast pork is famed for its crackling, cooked with bay leaves and often served with both boiled and caramelised potatoes.

Fiskefrikadeller Succulent, pan-fried Danish fish cakes are made with codfish, onion, dill, parsley and lemon, and commonly served with tartare-like *remoulade*.

AT A GLANCE

Area 43,094 sq km

Capital Copenhagen

Currency Danish krone (DKK or kr)

Country Code ☑ 45

Emergency ☑ 112

Language Danish

Time Central European Time (GMT/UTC plus one hour)

Visas Generally not required for stays of up to 90 days. Not required for members of EU or Schengen countries.

Sleeping Price Ranges

The following price ranges refer to a double room without breakfast in high season. Unless otherwise noted, rooms have private bathrooms.

€ less than 700kr

€€ 700kr–1500kr

€€€ more than 1500kr

Eating Price Ranges

The following price ranges refer to a standard main course.

€ less than 125kr

€€ 125kr–250kr

€€€ more than 250kr

Resources

Visit Denmark (www.visitdenmark.com)

Visit Copenhagen (www.visitcopenhagen.com)

Rejseplanen (www.rejseplanen.dk)

Lonely Planet (www.lonelyplanet.com/denmark)

DENMARK

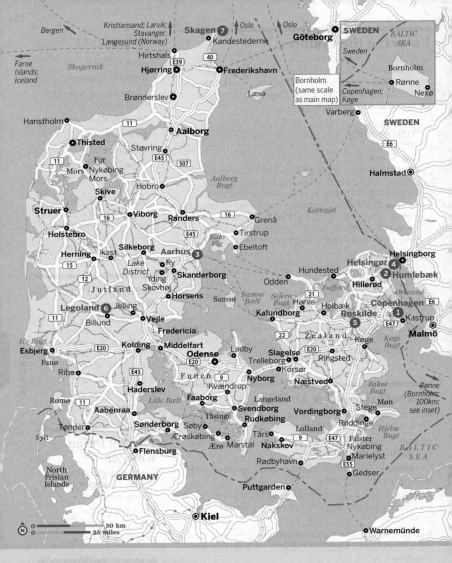

Denmark Highlights

❶ Copenhagen (p313) Lapping up the good looks, flavours and style of Europe's capital of cool.

❷ Louisiana (p315) Finding inspiration in art, architecture and nature at a world-famous modern-art museum.

❸ Aarhus (p327) Exploring bars, eateries and artist

Olafur Eliasson's spectacular installation in Denmark's burgeoning second city.

❹ Kronborg Slot (p324) Snooping around Hamlet's gargantuan home in seaside Helsingør.

❺ Roskilde Festival (p324) Finding your groove

at Scandinavia's biggest summertime music festival.

❻ Legoland (p331) Imagining the world as a giant Lego set, then jumping on a few rides.

❼ Skagen (p330) Winding down in one of Denmark's most evocative, artistically inspiring coastal towns.

COPENHAGEN

POP 602,480

Copenhagen is the epitome of Scandi cool. Modernist lamps light New Nordic tables, lateral-thinking drives contemporary architecture, and locals wear edgy, alt-chic threads like runway naturals. When cities seek enlightenment, it's here they often turn. The hometown of architect Jan Gehl – one of the world's leading authorities on sustainable urban planning – the Danish capital regularly tops world liveability lists. After all, this is one of the globe's greenest, cleanest, most sustainable urban centres, a place where cycling is serious transport, where transport runs around the clock, and where the harbour is squeaky clean enough for a bracing dip. Innovation fuels Scandinavia's hottest restaurant scene, not to mention a plethora of museums and galleries that celebrate everything from Viking culture and Islamic arts to impressionist brushstrokes and industrial Danish design. Best of all, it all comes in a compact, inclusive, user-friendly package that makes for one seamless, deeply rewarding city break.

◉ Sights

One of the great things about Copenhagen is its size. Virtually all of Copenhagen's major sightseeing attractions are in or close to the medieval city centre. Only the perennially disappointing *Little Mermaid* statue lies outside of the city proper, on the harbourfront.

◉ Rådhuspladsen & Tivoli

★ **Tivoli Gardens** AMUSEMENT PARK

(☑ 33 15 10 01; www.tivoligardens.com; Vesterbrogade 3; adult/child 3-7yr 120/50kr, Fri after 7pm 175/100kr; ◷ 11am-11pm Sun-Thu, to midnight Fri & Sat early Apr–late Sep, reduced hours rest of year; ⊞; ◻ 2A, 5C, 9A, 12, 14, 26, 33, 250S, Ⓜ København H, Ⓢ København H) Dating from 1843, tasteful Tivoli wins fans with its dreamy whirl of amusement rides, twinkling pavilions, carnival games and open-air stage shows. Visitors can ride the renovated, century-old **roller coaster**, enjoy the famous Saturday evening **fireworks display** or just soak up the story-book atmosphere. A good tip is to go on Friday during summer when the open-air Plænen stage hosts free rock concerts by Danish bands (and the occasional international superstar) from 10pm – go early if it's a big-name act.

Nationalmuseet MUSEUM

(National Museum; ☑ 33 13 44 11; https://en.natmus.dk; Ny Vestergade 10; adult/child 95kr/free; ◷ 10am-5pm Tue-Sun; ⊞; ◻ 1A, 2A, 9A, 12, 14, 26, 37, Ⓜ Rådhuspladsen) For a crash course in Danish history and culture, spend an afternoon at Denmark's National Museum. It has first claim on virtually every antiquity uncovered on Danish soil, including Stone Age tools, Viking weaponry, rune stones and medieval jewellery. Among the many highlights is a finely crafted 3500-year-old Sun Chariot, as well as bronze *lurs* (horns), some of which date back 3000 years and are still capable of blowing a tune.

Ny Carlsberg Glyptotek MUSEUM

(☑ 33 41 81 41; www.glyptoteket.com; Dantes Plads 7, HC Andersens Blvd; adult/child 115kr/free, Tue free; ◷ 11am-6pm Tue, Wed & Fri-Sun, until 10pm Thu; ◻ 1A, 2A, 9A, 37, Ⓜ Rådhuspladsen, Ⓢ København H) Fin de siècle architecture meets with an eclectic mix of art at Ny Carlsberg Glyptotek. The collection is divided into two parts: Northern Europe's largest booty of antiquities, and an elegant collection of 19th-century Danish and French art. The latter includes the largest collection of Rodin sculptures outside of France and no less than 47 Gauguin paintings. These are displayed along with works by greats like Cézanne, Van Gogh, Pissarro, Monet and Renoir.

◉ Slotsholmen

Slotsholmen is a compact island and all of its attractions are within walking distance of each other. Many of these are located at Christiansborg Slot, including the Royal Reception Rooms, Royal Stables, Royal Kitchen and medieval castle ruins. Both single-attraction and combined tickets are available. The palace complex is also home

---

ⓘ COPENHAGEN CARD

The **Copenhagen Card** (www.copenhagencard.com; adult/child 10-15yr 24hr 399/199kr, 48hr 569/289kr, 72hr 689/349kr, 120hr 899/449kr), available at the Copenhagen Visitor Service and online, gives you access to almost 90 museums and attractions in the city and surrounding area, as well as free public transport. Note, though, that several of the city's attractions are either free or at least free one day of the week.

to the Theatre Museum and the neighbouring Royal Danish Arsenal Museum. Directly north of the palace is Thorvaldsens Museum, while directly south are the Danish Jewish Museum and the Royal Library. A short walk to the west is the Kongernes Lapidarium.

★ De Kongelige Repræsentationslokaler   HISTORIC BUILDING
(Royal Reception Rooms at Christiansborg Slot; www.christiansborg.dk; Slotsholmen; adult/child 90kr/free; ⊘9am-5pm, closed Mon Oct-Apr; ☐1A, 2A, 9A, 26, 37, 66, ⊞Det Kongelige Bibliotek, Ⓜ Gammel Strand) The grandest part of Christiansborg, this series of palace rooms and halls was used by the queen to hold royal banquets and entertain heads of state. The Queen's Library is especially memorable, a gilded wonderland adorned with dripping chandeliers, ornate stucco, ceiling storks and a small part of the royal family's centuries-old book collection. Top billing goes to the Great Hall, home to riotously colourful wall tapestries depicting 1000 years of Danish history. Guided tours in English at 3pm.

Thorvaldsens Museum   MUSEUM
(☑33 32 15 32; www.thorvaldsensmuseum.dk; Bertel Thorvaldsens Plads 2; adult/child 70kr/free, Wed free; ⊘10am-5pm Tue-Sun; ☐1A, 2A, 26, 37, 66, Ⓜ Gammel Strand) What looks like a colourful Greco-Roman mausoleum is in fact a museum dedicated to the works of illustrious Danish sculptor Bertel Thorvaldsen (1770–1844). Heavily influenced by mythology after four decades in Rome, Thorvaldsen returned to Copenhagen and donated his private collection to the Danish public. In return the royal family provided this site for the construction of what is a remarkable complex housing Thorvaldsen's drawings,

plaster moulds and statues. The museum also contains Thorvaldsen's own collection of Mediterranean antiquities.

Ruinerne under Christiansborg   RUINS
(Ruins under Christiansborg; ☑33 92 64 92; www.christiansborg.dk; adult/child 50kr/free; ⊘10am-5pm, closed Mon Oct-Apr; ☐1A, 2A, 9A, 26, 37, 66, ⊞Det Kongelige Bibliotek, Ⓜ Gammel Strand) A walk through the crypt-like bowels of Slotsholmen, known as Ruinerne under Christiansborg, offers a unique perspective on Copenhagen's well-seasoned history. In the basement of the current palace are the ruins of Slotsholmen's original fortress – built by Bishop Absalon in 1167 – and its successor, Copenhagen Castle. Among these remnants are each building's ring walls, as well as a well, baking oven, sewerage drains and stonework from the castle's Blue Tower.

◉ Christianshavn

★ Christiania   AREA
(www.christiania.org; Prinsessegade; ☐9A, Ⓜ Christianshavn) Escape the capitalist crunch and head to Freetown Christiania, a hash-scented commune straddling the eastern side of Christianshavn. Since its establishment by squatters in 1971, the area has drawn non-conformists from across the globe, attracted by the concept of collective business, workshops and communal living. Explore beyond the settlement's infamous 'Pusher St' – lined with shady hash and marijuana dealers who do not appreciate photographs – and you'll stumble upon a semi-bucolic wonderland of whimsical DIY homes, cosy garden plots, eateries, beer gardens and music venues.

◉ Nyhavn & the Royal Quarter

★ Nyhavn   CANAL
(Nyhavn; ☐1A, 26, 66, 350S, Ⓜ Kongens Nytorv) There are few nicer places to be on a sunny day than sitting at an outdoor table at a cafe on the quayside of the Nyhavn canal. The canal was built to connect Kongens Nytorv to the harbour and was long a haunt for sailors and writers, including Hans Christian Andersen. He wrote *The Tinderbox, Little Claus and Big Claus* and *The Princess and the Pea* while living at No 20, and also spent time living at Nos 18 and 67.

★ Designmuseum Danmark   MUSEUM
(☑33 18 56 56; www.designmuseum.dk; Bredgade 68; adult/child 115kr/free; ⊘10am-6pm Tue & Thu-Sun, to 9pm Wed; ♿; ☐1A, Ⓜ Kongens Nytorv)

SUPERKILEN

Copenhagen's gritty, indie-hearted Nørrebro neighbourhood is home to **Superkilen** (Nørrebrogade 210; ☐5C, Ⓜ Nørrebro, Ⓢ Nørrebro), an out-of-the-box, 1km-long park pimped with objects sourced from around the globe. With the purpose of celebrating diversity, its items include a tile fountain from Morocco, bollards from Ghana, swing chairs from Baghdad, and neon signs from Russia and China. Even the benches, manhole covers and rubbish bins hail from foreign lands.

THE OTHER LOUISIANA

Even if you don't have a consuming passion for modern art, Denmark's outstanding **Louisiana Museum of Modern Art** (☑49 19 07 19; www.louisiana.dk; Gammel Strandvej 13, Humlebæk; adult/student/child 125/110kr/free; ☺11am-10pm Tue-Fri, to 6pm Sat & Sun; ☒388, ☒Humlebæk) should be high on your 'to do' list. Along with its important, ever-changing exhibitions, much of the thrill here is the glorious presentation. A maze-like web of halls and glass corridors weaves through rolling gardens in which magnificent trees, lawns, a lake and a beach view set off monumental abstract sculptures by greats including Henry Moore, Jean Arp, Max Ernst and Barbara Hepworth.

Louisiana is in the pretty coastal town of Humlebæk, 30km north of Copenhagen. From Humlebæk train station, the museum is a 1.5km signposted walk northeast. Trains to Humlebæk run at least twice hourly from Copenhagen (92kr, 35 minutes) but if you're day-tripping, the 24-hour Copenhagen ticket (adult/child 150/75kr) is much better value.

The 18th-century Frederiks Hospital is now the outstanding Denmark Design Museum. A must for fans of the applied arts and industrial design, its fairly extensive collection includes Danish textiles and fashion, as well as the iconic design pieces of modern innovators like Kaare Klint, Poul Henningsen and Arne Jacobsen. The museum gift shop is one of the city's best.

Little Mermaid   MONUMENT
(Den Lille Havfrue; Langelinie, Østerport; ☒1A, 26, ☒Nordre Toldbod) New York has its Lady Liberty and Sydney its (Danish-designed) Opera House. When the world thinks of Copenhagen, the chances are they're thinking of the *Little Mermaid*. Love her or loathe her (watch Copenhageners cringe at the very mention of her), this small, underwhelming statue is arguably the most photographed sight in the country, as well as the cause of countless 'Is that it?' shrugs from tourists who have trudged the kilometre or so along an often windswept harbourfront to see her.

◉ Nørreport

★Rosenborg Slot   CASTLE
(☑33 15 32 86; www.kongernessamling.dk/en/rosenborg; Øster Voldgade 4A; adult/child 110kr/free; ☺9am-6pm mid-Jun–mid-Sep, reduced hours rest of year; ☒6A, 42, 184, 185, 350S, ☒Nørreport, ☒Nørreport) A 'once upon a time' combo of turrets, gables and moat, the early-17th-century Rosenborg Slot was built in Dutch Renaissance style between 1606 and 1633 by King Christian IV to serve as his summer home. Today the castle's 24 upper rooms are chronologically arranged, housing the furnishings and portraits of each monarch from Christian IV to Frederik VII. The pièce de résistance is the basement Treasury, home to the dazzling crown jewels, among them Christian IV's glorious crown and Christian III's jewel-studded sword.

★Statens Museum for Kunst   MUSEUM
(☑33 74 84 94; www.smk.dk; Sølvgade 48-50; adult/child 120kr/free; ☺11am-5pm Tue & Thu-Sun, to 8pm Wed; ☒6A, 26, 42, 184, 185) Denmark's National Gallery straddles two contrasting, interconnected buildings: a late-19th-century 'palazzo' and a sharply minimalist extension. The museum houses medieval and Renaissance works and impressive collections of Dutch and Flemish artists, including Rubens, Breughel and Rembrandt. It claims the world's finest collection of 19th-century Danish 'Golden Age' artists, among them Eckersberg and Hammershøi, foreign greats like Matisse and Picasso, and modern Danish heavyweights including Per Kirkeby.

Kongens Have   PARK
(King's Gardens; http://parkmuseerne.dk/kongens-have; Øster Voldgade; ☺7am-10pm mid-Jun–mid-Aug, reduced hours rest of year; ☒; ☒26, ☒Nørreport, ☒Nørreport) FREE The oldest park in Copenhagen was laid out in the early 17th century by Christian IV, who used it as his vegetable patch. These days it has a little more to offer, including wonderfully romantic paths, a fragrant rose garden, some of the longest mixed borders in northern Europe and a marionette theatre with free performances from mid-July to mid-August (2pm and 3pm Tuesday to Sunday).

☂ Activities

Islands Brygge Havnebadet   SWIMMING
(☑30 89 04 69; https://svoemkbh.kk.dk/indhold/havnebade; Islands Brygge; ☺24hr Jun-Sep,

Central Copenhagen (København)

Superkilen (1km)

Coffee Collective Nørrebro (400m)

Assistens Kirkegård

27 33
41

Blegdamsvej

Guldbergsgade
Møllegade
Sankt Hans Torv

Lassøesgade
Ryesgade

Fredensbro

Skt Hans Gade

37

Elmegade

Sølvgade

Nørrebrogade

Fælledvej

Sortedam Dossering

Sortedams Sø

Øster Søgade

NØRREBRO

Ravnsborggade

Stengade
Baggesensgade

Rantzausgade
Kapelvej
Griffenfeldsgade
Korsgade

Dronning Louises Bro

Blågårds Plads

Øster Farimagsgade

Åblvd

Frederiksborggade

Gothersgade
Rømersgade
Linnésgade

Nørreport

Coffee Collective Frederiksberg (1km)

Åblvd

Peblinge Dossering

Peblinge Sø

Nørre Søgade

Vendersgade

Nørreport

30
36

Nørreport

Israels Plads

Rosengården

Nansensgade

Nørre Farimagsgade

Gyldenløvesgade

H.C. Ørsteds Vej
Rosenørns Allé

Forum

Turesensgade

Nørre Voldgade

Nørregade

Fiolstræde

Sankt Marcus Allé

VESTERBRO

Ørsteds Parken

Larslejsstræde

Krystalgade

Kannikestræde

Danasvej

H C Andersens Blvd

Vor Frue Plads

Nørre Voldgade

Vester-Søgade

Niels Ebbesens Vej

Nyropsgade

14

Studiestræde

Gammeltorv

Sankt Jørgens Sø

Kampmannsgade

Vester Farimagsgade

Hammerichsgade

Vester Voldgade

Vestergade
Frederiksberggade (Strøget)

STRØGET

23

Rådhusstræde

Fornåbningsholms Allé
Vodroffsvej

Vesterport

Rådhuspladsen

Rådhuspladsen
16

Farvergade

Bag Rådhuset

Copenhagen Visitor Service

Axeltorv

Lavendelstræde

Regnbuepladsen

Stormgade

Gammel Kongevej Amend

Tivoli Gardens
7

TIVOLI

Vester

Vesterbrogade

24

Banegårdspladsen

Dantes Plads

18 25

Bernstorffsgade

Tietgensgade

11

Bertrams Guldsmeden (250m)

39

Viktoriagade
Gasværksvej

Istedgade

København Hovedbanegården (Central Station)

Otto Mønstedsgade

Mitchellsgade

Hambrosgade

20

Dannebrogsgade
Eskildsgade
Absalonsgade
Halmtorvet

Kødbyen (Meatpacking District)

Ingerslevsgade

Carsten Niebuhrs Gade

Kalvebod Brygge

Vega Live (350m)

Sønder Blvd

VESTERBRO

Kalvebod Bølge

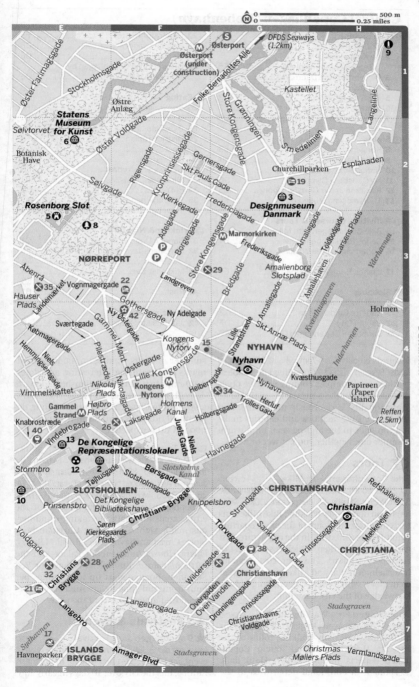

△ 0 ──────── 500 m
Ⓝ ⊙ 0 ──────── 0.25 miles

DFDS Seaways
(1.2km)

❶ 9

Østerport Ⓢ
Ⓜ Østerport
Østerport
(under
construction)
Folke Bernadottes Allé

Kastellet

Østre Farimagsgade

Stockholmsgade

Østre
Anlæg
Øster Voldgade

Store Kongensgade

Grønningen

Smedelinen

Langelinie

**Statens
Museum
for Kunst**
6 🏛

Sølvtorvet

Botanisk
Have

Sølvgade

Gernersgade

Skt Pauls Gade

Churchillparken

🏛 19

Esplanaden

🏛 3
**Designmuseum
Danmark**

Rosenborg Slot
5 🏰

❹ 8

Rigensgade

Kronprinsessegade

Kr Klerkegade

Fredericiagade

Adelgade

Borgergade

Store Kongensgade

Amaliegade

Toldbodgade

Larsens Plads

Viderhavnen

Ⓜ Marmorkirken

Frederiksgade

NØRREPORT

Ⓟ
Ⓟ

Landgreven

✖ 29

Bredgade

Amalienborg
Slotsplad

Amaliehavn

Kvæsthusgraven

Holmen

Abenrå

✖ 35

Vognmagergade

22 🏛

Landemærket

Hauser
Plads

Gothersgade

🏛 42

Ny Østergade

Ny Adelgade

Amaliegade

Kvæsthusgraven

Inderhavnen

Sværtegade

Gammel Mønt

Ny Østergade

Pilestræde

Købmagergade

Niels

Hemmingsensgade

Østergade

Lille Kongensgade

Kongens
Nytorv
15 ●

Lille Strandstræde

Skt Annæ Plads

NYHAVN

Nyhavn
4 ◉

Kvæsthusgade

Papirøen
(Paper
Island)

Reffen
(2.5km)

Vimmelskaftet

Nikolaj
Plads

Nikolajgade

Kongens
Nytorv Ⓜ

Heibergsgade

✖ 34

Nyhavn

Trolles Gade

Herluf

Inderhavnen

**Gammel
Strand** Ⓜ
Højbro
Plads

Holmens
Kanal

Holbergsgade

Knabrostræde

❚ 40
⊗

Yindelbrogade

26 ✖

Laksegade

Juels Gade

Niels

Havnegade

13 🏛
**De Kongelige
Repræsentationslokaler**

Ⓢ
12 ✖ 2 🏛

Tøjhusgade

Børsgade

Slotsholms
Kanal

CHRISTIANSHAVN

Refshalevej

Stormbro

Slotsholmsgade

SLOTSHOLMEN

Det Kongelige
Bibilliotekshave

Christians Brygge

Knippelsbro

Strandgade

Christiania
1 ◉

🏛
10

Prinsensbro

Søren
Kierkegaards
Plads

Inderhavnen

Torvegade

⊖ 38

Sankt Annæ Gade

Prinsessegade

Mælkevejen

CHRISTIANIA

Voldgade

✖ 32

Christians
Brygge

✖ 28

Wildersgade

31

Ⓜ
Christianshavn

Overgaden
Oven Vandet

Dronningensgade

Prinsessegade

Stadsgraven

21 🏛

Langebro

Langebrogade

Langebrogade

Christianshavns
Voldgade

Søndhavnen

17
⊗

**ISLANDS
BRYGGE**

Havneparken

Amager Blvd

Stadsgraven

Christmas
Møllers Plads

Vermlandsgade

DENMARK COPENHAGEN

Central Copenhagen (København)

lifeguards on duty 11am-7pm; 🚻; 🚎5C, 12, Ⓜ Islands Brygge) **FREE** Copenhagen's coolest outdoor pool complex comprises three pools and sits right in the central city's main canal. Water quality is rigorously monitored, and the lawns, BBQ facilities and eateries make it a top spot to see and be seen on a warm summer day, whether you get wet or not.

🕝 Tours

Bike Copenhagen with Mike   CYCLING
(📞 26 39 56 88; www.bikecopenhagenwithmike.dk; Sankt Peders Stræde 47; per person 300kr; 🚎5C, 6A) If you don't fancy walking, Bike Mike runs three-hour cycling tours of the city, departing Sankt Peders Stræde 47 in the city centre, just east of Ørstedsparken (which is southwest of Nørreport Station). The tour cost includes bike, helmet rental and Mike himself, a great character with deep, attention-grabbing knowledge of the city. Cash only.

Copenhagen Free Walking Tours   WALKING
(www.copenhagenfreewalkingtours.dk) **FREE** This outfit runs free daily walking tours of the city. The three-hour Grand Tour of Copenhagen departs Rådhus (Town Hall) daily at 11am, with additional departures in the summer months, taking in famous landmarks and featuring interesting anecdotes. A 90-minute tour of Christianshavn departs daily at 3pm from Højbro Plads. There's also a 90-minute Classical Copenhagen Tour, departing Fridays, Saturdays and Sundays at noon. A tip is expected.

Canal Tours Copenhagen   BOATING
(📞 32 96 30 00; www.stromma.dk; Nyhavn; 1hr tour adult/child 85/43kr; ⊙9.30am-9pm late Jun–mid-Aug, reduced hours rest of year; 🚻; 🚎1A, 26, 66, 350S, Ⓜ Kongens Nytorv) Canal Tours Copenhagen runs one-hour cruises of the city's canals and harbour, taking in numerous major sights, including Christiansborg Slot, Christianshavn, the Royal Library, Opera House, Amalienborg Palace and the *Little Mermaid*. Embark at Nyhavn or Ved Stranden. Boats depart up to six times per hour from mid-June to late August, with reduced frequency the rest of the year.

🎊 Festivals & Events

★**Copenhagen Jazz Festival**   MUSIC
(www.jazz.dk; ⊙Jul) Copenhagen's single largest event, and the biggest jazz festival in northern Europe, hits the city over 10 days in early July.

The program covers jazz in all its forms, with an impressive line-up of local and international talent. A nationwide winter edition, called Vinterjazz, takes place in February.

Distortion MUSIC
(www.cphdistortion.dk; ⊘ May/Jun) Taking place over five heady days in late May and early June, Copenhagen Distortion celebrates the city's street life and club culture. Expect raucous block parties and top-name DJs spinning dance tracks in bars and clubs across town.

Copenhagen Cooking & Food Festival FOOD & DRINK
(www.copenhagencooking.dk; ⊘ Aug) Scandinavia's largest food festival serves up a gut-rumbling program spanning cooking demonstrations from A-list chefs to tastings and foodie tours of the city. Events are held in venues and restaurants across town, usually over 10 days in August.

🛌 Sleeping

🛌 Vesterbro & Frederiksberg

⭐ **Urban House Copenhagen by MEININGER** HOSTEL, HOTEL €
(✍ 89 88 32 69; www.urbanhouse.me; Colbjørnsensgade 5-11, Vesterbro; dm/d from 160/595kr; @ 🛜; 🚌6A, 10, 14, 26, Ⓜ København H, Ⓢ København H) This huge hostel spans a trio of historic buildings close to Central Station and Vesterbro's on-trend venues. Slumber options range from modern single rooms to dorms with bunks for up to 10 people; all have private bathrooms. Bed linen and towels are included in the price, while in-house facilities include a communal kitchen, laundry, games room and even a small cinema. Breakfast costs 65kr.

Axel Guldsmeden BOUTIQUE HOTEL €€€
(✍ 33 31 32 66; www.guldsmedenhotels.com; Helgolandsgade 7-11, Vesterbro; d from 1145kr; @ 🛜; 🚌6A, 10, 14, 26, Ⓜ København H, Ⓢ København H) 🏊 Part of the reputable eco-hotel chain, Axel Guldsmeden puts a Nordic spin on Balinese chic. Rooms are spacious and plushly decorated, oriental carpets contrasting against parquet flooring and pale paintwork. There's a luxe spa on site with sauna, cold tub, steam bath and hot tub, plus lushly planted garden and fireplace for warming your toes on chilly evenings.

Bertrams Guldsmeden BOUTIQUE HOTEL €€€
(✍ 70 20 81 07; www.guldsmedenhotels.com; Vesterbrogade 107, Vesterbro; d from 1525kr; @ 🛜;

🚌3A, 6A) 🏊 Like the rest of the gorgeous Guldsmeden hotels (there are several in town), Bertrams features raw stone, bare wood, crisp white linen, spectacular bath tubs and exotic Bali-style decor. The hotel is eminently comfortable, with underfloor heating and plenty of squishy sofas and comfortable seating spaces; the breakfast is also a slice above the norm.

🛌 Nyhavn & the Royal Quarter

⭐ **Babette Guldsmeden** BOUTIQUE HOTEL €€
(✍ 33 14 15 00; www.guldsmedenhotels.com; Bredgade 78; d from 995kr; @ 🛜 🐾; 🚌1A) 🏊 The 98-room Babette is part of the superb Guldsmeden hotel chain, with the same (unexpectedly) harmonious blend of Nordic and Indonesian design aesthetics. Though on the smaller side, the rooms are inviting and tactile, with four-poster beds, sheepskin throws and vibrant artworks. There's a rooftop spa and sauna, tranquil leafy courtyard, buzzing bar popular with locals, as well as decent organic breakfasts (225kr).

🛌 Rådhuspladsen & Tivoli

Cabinn City HOTEL €
(✍ 33 46 16 16; www.cabinn.com; Mitchellsgade 14; s/d 495/645kr; @ 🛜; 🚌5C, 250S, Ⓜ København H, Ⓢ København H) If you're not intent on surrounding yourself with fancy Danish design, but just want somewhere clean and relatively comfortable to lie your head, Cabinn may be your hotel in shining armour. Rooms are small but functional, making clever use of the limited space. And it's close to the action.

Danhostel Copenhagen City HOSTEL €
(✍ 33 11 85 85; www.danhostel.dk; HC Andersens Blvd 50; dm/d from 250/800kr; @ 🛜; 🚌5C, 250S, Ⓜ København H, Ⓢ København H) Step into the lobby here with its cafe-bar and it looks more like a hotel than a hostel. Set in a tower block overlooking the harbour just south of Tivoli Gardens (did we mention the views?), the dorms and private rooms are all bright, light and modern, each with bathroom. Laundry facilities available on-site. Book ahead.

⭐ **Hotel Nimb** BOUTIQUE HOTEL €€€
(✍ 88 70 00 00; www.nimb.dk; Bernstorffsgade 5; r from 3000kr; P @ 🛜 🐾; 🚌2A, 5C, 9A, 66, 250S, Ⓜ København H, Ⓢ København H) Part of historic Tivoli Gardens, this boutique belle offers 38 individually styled rooms and suites that fuse clean lines, handpicked art and antiques,

and luxury fabrics. All but one room enjoy views over the amusement park, while in-house perks include a rooftop terrace with pool, savvy cocktail lounge and herbivore-focused hotspot restaurant Gemyse.

🏠 Nørreport

★ Generator Hostel
HOSTEL €

(📞 78 77 54 00; www.generatorhostel.com; Adelgade 5-7; dm/d from 135/695kr; @ 🛜; 🚌 350S, 1A, 26, Ⓜ Kongens Nytorv) A solid choice for 'cheap chic', upbeat, design-literate Generator sits on the edge of the city's medieval core. It's kitted out with designer furniture, slick communal areas (including a bar and outdoor terrace) and friendly, young staff. While the rooms can be a little small, all are bright and modern, with bathrooms in private rooms and dorms.

🍴 Eating

🍴 Rådhuspladsen & Tivoli

Blox Eats
CAFE €

(📞 28 93 65 55; www.meyersfb.dk/restauranter/BLOXEATS; Bryghuspladsen 14, Blox; pastries from 25kr; ⏰ 8am-10pm; 🛜; 🚌 66, 🚢 Det Kongelige Bibliotek) Spilt into a ground-floor cafe and upstairs restaurant space, spacious, light-filled Blox Eats is owned by New Nordic food pioneer Claus Meyer. The cafe – speckled with the odd banana tree and designer woollen sofa – is the better option, its simple, quality bites including organic pastries, overnight oats, housemade sourdough toast served with marmalade and Danish cheeses, as well as panini. Organic coffee to boot.

Lillian's Smørrebrød
DANISH €

(📞 33 14 20 66; http://lillians-smorrebrod.dk; Vester Voldgade 108; smørrebrød from 17kr; ⏰ 6am-2pm Mon-Fri; 🚌 66) Tiny 1970s throwback Lillian's is one of the best and least costly smørrebrød places in town. Decked out in white deli-style tiles, with kitsch artwork and just a handful of tables, its generous, open-faced sandwiches are classic: think marinated herring, chicken salad and roast beef with remoulade. However, while the coffee here is also a bargain, you'll get a much better cup elsewhere.

🍴 Strøget & the Latin Quarter

★ Schønnemann
DANISH €€

(📞 33 12 07 85; www.restaurantschonnemann.dk; Hauser Plads 16; smørrebrød 75-185kr; ⏰ 11.30am-

5pm Mon-Sat; 🛜; 🚌 6A, 42, 150S, 184, 185, Ⓜ Nørreport, Ⓢ Nørreport) A veritable institution, Schønnemann has been lining bellies with smørrebrød and *snaps* since 1877. Originally a hit with farmers in town selling their produce, the restaurant's current fan base includes revered chefs like René Redzepi; try the smørrebrød named after him: smoked halibut with creamed cucumber, radishes and chives on caraway bread.

★ Admiralgade 26
INTERNATIONAL €€

(📞 33 33 79 73; www.admiralgade26.dk; Admiralgade 26; dishes 95-195kr, tasting menu 550kr; ⏰ 11.30am-midnight Mon-Sat; 🛜; Ⓜ Gammel Strand) There are some restaurants you could return to time and time again. Admiralgade 26 is one of them. An artful balance of vintage Danish furniture and contemporary artworks, its menu is modern, sophisticated and genuinely intriguing. Here, silky carpaccio might find its match in dehydrated watermelon, while smoked duck heart is taken to new heights with a pairing of black rice vinegar and peach.

🍴 Christianshavn

★ Reffen
STREET FOOD €

(https://reffen.dk; Refshalevej 167a; meals from 80kr; ⏰ noon-8pm Mon-Sun Apr-Sep, hours vary Oct-Mar; 🚲 ♿ 🛜; 🚌 9A, 🚢 Refshaløen) 🌿 This harbourside street-food market is a veritable village of converted shipping containers, peddling sustainable bites from across the globe. Multiculti options include organic polenta and pasta, dosas, burgers, sushi, satay skewers and Filipino BBQ. You'll also find a number of bars (open until 10pm or later Friday and Saturday). These include an outpost of Copenhagen's cult-status microbrewery Mikkeller.

★ Kadeau
NEW NORDIC €€€

(📞 33 25 22 23; www.kadeau.dk; Wildersgade 10B; tasting menu 2150kr, wine/juice pairings 1350/800kr; ⏰ 6.30pm-midnight Tue-Sat, also noon-4pm Sat; 🚌 2A, 9A, 37, 350S, Ⓜ Christianshavn) The big-city spin-off of the Bornholm original, this Michelin-two-starred standout has firmly established itself as one of Scandinavia's gastronomic powerhouses. Whether it's salted and burnt scallops drizzled with clam bouillon, or an unexpected combination of lardo, thyme, cherry blossom and Korean pine, each dish manages to evoke moods and landscapes with extraordinary creativity and skill.

Nyhavn & the Royal Quarter

★ District Tonkin   VIETNAMESE €

(📞 60 88 86 98; http://district-tonkin.com; Dronningens Tværgade 12; baguettes 58-62kr, soups & salads 70-120kr; ⏰ 11am-9.30pm Sun-Wed, to 10pm Thu-Sat; 🚌 1A, 26, Ⓜ Kongens Nytorv) With a playful interior channelling the streets of Vietnam, casual, convivial District Tonkin peddles fresh, gut-filling *bánh mì* (Vietnamese baguettes), stuffed with coriander, fresh chilli and combos like Vietnamese sausage with marinated pork, homemade pâté and BBQ sauce. The menu also includes gorgeous, less-common Vietnamese soups, among them tomato-based *xíu mai* (with pork and mushroom meatballs).

PMY   LATIN AMERICAN €€

(Papa-Maiz-Yuca; 📞 50 81 00 02; www.restaurant-pmy.com; Tordenskjoldsgade 11; 4 servings 395kr, 6 servings 495kr, à la carte 85-195kr; ⏰ 5.30pm-11pm Tues-Thurs, 5pm-midnight Fri-Sat; 📷; 🚌 1A, 26, Ⓜ Kongens Nytorv) PMY stands for Papa, Maiz, Yuca: the three main ingredients from the trio of chefs' home countries, with the bold and flavourful Latin American menu boasting dishes and cocktails from Mexico, Venezuela and Peru. For the full experience at the best price, indulge in the six-serving menu showcasing two dishes from each of the featured cuisines.

Nørreport

★ Torvehallerne KBH   MARKET €

(www.torvehallernekbh.dk; Israels Plads; dishes from around 55kr; ⏰ 10am-7pm, to 10pm Fri, to 6pm Sat, 11am-5pm Sun; Ⓜ Nørreport, Ⓢ Nørreport) Food market Torvehallerne KBH is an essential stop on the Copenhagen foodie trail. A delicious ode to the fresh, the tasty and the artisanal, the market's beautiful stalls peddle everything from seasonal herbs and berries to smoked meats, seafood and cheeses, smørrebrød, fresh pasta and hand-brewed coffee. You could easily spend an hour or more exploring its twin halls.

★ Høst   NEW NORDIC €€€

(📞 89 93 84 09; https://cofoco.dk/en/restaurants/hoest; Nørre Farimagsgade 41; 3-/5-course menu 350/450kr; ⏰ 5.30pm-midnight, last order 9.30pm; Ⓜ Nørreport, Ⓢ Nørreport) Høst's phenomenal popularity is easy to understand: award-winning interiors and New Nordic food that's equally fabulous and filling. The set menu is superb, with smaller 'surprise dishes' thrown

in and evocative creations like birch-smoked scallops with horseradish and green beans, or a joyful blueberry sorbet paired with Norwegian brown cheese and crispy caramel.

Nørrebro & Østerbro

★ Bæst   ITALIAN €€

(📞 35 35 04 63; www.baest.dk; Guldbergsgade 29; pizzas 85-145kr; ⏰ 5-10.30pm, plus noon-3pm Thu-Sun; 🍴; 🚌 3A, 5C) Owned by powerhouse Italo-Scandi chef Christian Puglisi, Bæst remains hot years after its 2014 launch. Charcuterie, cheese and competent woodfired pizzas are the drawcards here. The produce is sustainable and organic, and both the commendable charcuterie and hand-stretched mozzarella are made upstairs (the latter made using jersey milk from Bæst's own farm). To fully appreciate its repertoire, opt for the sharing menu (lunch/dinner 225/375kr).

Bæst also has an adjoining bakery and cafe called **Mirabelle** (📞 35 35 47 24; http://mirabelle-bakery.dk; pastries from 28kr, sandwiches 65kr, lunch & dinner dishes 115-175kr; ⏰ 7am-10pm; 🍴).

🍷 Drinking & Nightlife

Strøget & the Latin Quarter

★ Ruby   COCKTAIL BAR

(📞 33 93 12 03; www.rby.dk; Nybrogade 10; ⏰ 4pm-2am, from 6pm Sun; 🍴; 🚌 1A, 2A, 14, 26, 37, Ⓜ Gammel Strand) Cocktail connoisseurs raise their glasses to high-achieving Ruby, hidden away in an unmarked 18th-century townhouse. Inside, suave mixologists whip up near-flawless, seasonal libations created with craft spirits and homemade syrups, while a lively crowd spills into a labyrinth of cosy, decadent rooms. For a gentlemen's club vibe, head downstairs among chesterfields, oil paintings and wooden cabinets lined with spirits.

Christianshavn

Christianshavns Bådudlejning & Café BAR
(📞 32 96 53 53; www.baadudlejningen.dk; Overgaden Neden Vandet 29; ⏰ 10am-midnight Jun-Aug, reduced hours rest of year; 🍴; 🚌 2A, 9A, 37, 350S, Ⓜ Christianshavn) Right on Christianshavn's main canal, this festive, wood-decked cafe-bar is a wonderful spot for drinks by the water. It's a cosy, affable hang-out, with jovial crowds and strung lights. There's grub for the peckish and gas heaters and tarpaulins to ward off any northern chill.

🍷 Nørrebro & Østerbro

★ Coffee Collective
COFFEE

(www.coffeecollective.dk; Jægersborggade 57, Nørrebro; ⊙7am-7pm, from 8am Sat & Sun; 🚌8A, Ⓜ Nørrebros Runddel) Copenhagen's most prolific microroastery, Coffee Collective has helped revolutionise the city's coffee culture. Head in for rich, complex cups of caffeinated magic. The baristas are passionate about their single-origin beans and the venue itself sits at one end of creative Jægersborggade in Nørrebro. There are several other outlets, including at gourmet food market Torvehallerne KBH (p321) and in **Frederiksberg** (🚌60 15 15 25; Godthåbsvej 34B; ⊙7.30am-6pm, from 9am Sat, from 10am Sun; 🚌2A, 8A, Ⓜ Aksel Møllers Have).

Rust
CLUB

(🖉35 24 52 00; www.rust.dk; Guldbergsgade 8, Nørrebro; ⊙hours vary; 🛜; 🚌3A, 5C, 350S) A smashing, multilevel place attracting one of the largest, coolest, most relaxed crowds in Copenhagen. Live acts focus on alternative or upcoming indie rock, hip-hop or electronica. At 11pm, the venue transforms into a club, with local and international DJs pumping out anything from classic hip-hop to electro, house and more.

Barking Dog
COCKTAIL BAR

(🖉35 36 16 00; http://thebarkingdog.dk; Sankt Hans Gade 19, Nørrebro; ⊙6pm-midnight, to 2am Fri & Sat; 🚌3A, 5C, 350S) Far from hostile, this Barking Dog is affable, unpretentious and not too loud. Not surprisingly, it draws a somewhat older crowd, who head in to chat over well-mixed, fairly priced cocktails. Signature libations include the Tree Hugger, a concoction of Danish gin, Piedmontese vermouth and organic agave reputedly created when the moon was aligned with Sankt Hans Gade.

🍷 Vesterbro & Frederiksberg

★ Mikkeller Bar
BAR

(🖉33 31 04 15; http://mikkeller.dk; Viktoriagade 8B-C, Vesterbro; ⊙1pm-1am, to 2am Thu & Fri, noon-2am Sat; 🛜; 🚌6A, 26, Ⓜ København H, Ⓢ København H) Low-slung lights, green floors and 20 brews on tap: cool, cult-status Mikkeller flies the flag for craft beer, its rotating cast of suds including Mikkeller's own acclaimed creations and guest drops from microbreweries from around the globe. Expect anything from tequila-barrel-aged stouts to yuzu-infused fruit beers. The bottled offerings are equally inspired, with cheese and snacks to soak up the foamy goodness.

☆ Entertainment

Most events can be booked through **Ticketmaster** (🖉70 15 65 65; www.ticketmaster.dk), which has outlets at Tivoli and city-centre department stores Magasin du Nord and Illum. You can also try **Billetlugen** (🖉70 26 32 67; www.billetlugen.dk).

★ Jazzhus Montmartre
JAZZ

(🖉tickets 70 20 20 96, venue 91 19 19 19; www.jazzhusmontmartre.dk; Store Regnegade 19A; ⊙varies, see website; 🚌1A, 26, Ⓜ Kongens Nytorv) Saxing things up since the late 1950s, this is one of Scandinavia's great jazz venues, with past performers including Dexter Gordon, Ben Webster and Kenny Drew. Today, it continues to host local and international talent. On concert nights, you can also tuck into a decent, three-course set menu (325kr) at the **cafe-restaurant** from 6pm.

Vega Live
LIVE MUSIC

(🖉33 25 70 11; www.vega.dk; Enghavevej 40, Vesterbro; ⊙varies; 🛜; 🚌3A, 10, 14, Ⓜ Enghave Plads) The daddy of Copenhagen's live-music venues, Vega hosts everyone from big-name rock, pop, blues and jazz acts to underground indie, hip-hop and electro up-and-comers. Gigs take place on either the main stage (Store Vega), small stage (Lille Vega) or the ground-floor Ideal Bar. Performance times vary; check the website.

ℹ Information

Copenhagen Visitor Service (🖉70 22 24 42; www.visitcopenhagen.com; Vesterbrogade 4A; ⊙9am-8pm Mon-Fri, to 6pm Sat & Sun Jul & Aug, reduced hours rest of year; 🛜; 🚌2A, 5C, 6A, 12, 14, 26, Ⓜ København H, Ⓢ København H) Copenhagen's excellent and informative information centre has a cafe with free wi-fi; it also sells the money-saving Copenhagen Card.

ℹ Getting There & Away

AIR

Copenhagen Airport (🖉32 31 32 31; www.cph.dk; Lufthavnsboulevarden, Kastrup; Ⓜ Lufthavnen, Ⓢ Københavns Lufthavn) is Scandinavia's busiest air hub, with direct flights to cities in Europe, North America and Asia, as well as a handful of Danish cities. Located in Kastrup, 9km southeast of central Copenhagen, it's connected to the city by both metro and regional train services.

BOAT

DFDS Seaways (📞 33 42 30 00; www.dfds-seaways.com; Dampfærgevej 30; ⑤ Nordhavn) operates one nightly service to/from Oslo (one way from 600kr, 17 hours). Ferries depart from Søndre Frihavn, just north of Kastellet.

BUS

Flixbus (www.flixbus.dk) connects Copenhagen to various European destinations, including cities in Sweden and Norway. Pricing is dynamic, so book ahead for the best deals.

TRAIN

Regional, national and international trains arrive and depart from Central Station, known officially as Københavns Hovedbanegård. A *billetautomat* (ticket machine) is the quickest way to purchase a ticket. Located inside the station, **DSB Billetsalg** (DSB Ticket Office; 📞 70 13 14 15; www.dsb.dk; Central Station, Bernstorffsgade 16-22; ⏰ 7am-8.30pm Mon-Fri, 8am-6pm Sat & Sun; ⑤ København H) is best for reservations and for purchasing international train tickets. Alternatively, you can make reservations on its website.

ℹ Getting Around

TO/FROM THE AIRPORT

➡ The 24-hour metro (www.m.dk) runs every four to 20 minutes between the airport terminal station (Lufthavnen) and the city centre. Journey time from the airport to Kongens Nytorv is 14 minutes (36kr).

➡ DSB trains (www.dsb.dk) connect the airport terminal to Copenhagen Central Station (Københavns Hovedbanegård, commonly known as København H) around every 10 minutes. Journey time is 14 minutes (36kr). Check schedules at www.rejseplanen.dk.

BICYCLE

Copenhagen vies with Amsterdam as the world's most bike-friendly city. The city's superb, citywide **Bycyklen** (City Bikes; www.bycyklen.dk; per hr 30kr) bike-share system features high-tech 'Smart Bikes' with touchscreen tablets, GPS, multispeed electric motors, puncture-resistant tyres and locks. The bikes must be paid for by credit card via the website or the bike's touchscreen.

BOAT

Movia (📞 36 13 14 00; www.moviatrafik.dk) operates the city's yellow commuter ferries, known as Harbour Buses. Routes 991 and 992 are virtually the same: 991 ferries run south, 992 ferries run north. There are nine stops each way, including Det Kongelige Bibliotek (Royal Library), Nyhavn and Operaen (Opera House).

BUS

City buses are frequent, convenient and also run by Movia. Single tickets can be purchased

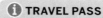

ℹ TRAVEL PASS

Rejsekort (www.rejsekort.dk) is a touch-on, touch-off smart card valid for all zones and all public transport across Denmark. Available from the Rejsekort machines at metro stations, Central Station or the airport, the card costs 180kr (80kr for the card and 100kr in credit). To use, tap the Rejsekort against the dedicated sensors at train and metro stations or when boarding buses and commuter ferries, then tap off when exiting. Only tap off at the very end of your journey – if your journey involves a metro ride followed immediately by a bus ride, tap on at the metro station and again on the bus, but only tap off once you exit the bus.

on board, though it usually makes more sense to purchase a rechargeable Rejsekort (available at train and metro stations).

METRO

The efficient, 24-hour metro system consists of four lines : M1, M2, M3 and M4. The M2 line runs to the airport, while M3 is known as the 'City Circle' line. Passengers can change between all routes at Kongens Nytorv. See www.m.dk for more information.

TRAIN

Copenhagen's 'S-tog' suburban train network runs seven lines through Central Station (København H) and is useful for reaching both the airport and the Louisiana Museum of Modern Art. Regional DSB trains connect Copenhagen to Helsingør.

ZEALAND

Though Copenhagen is the centre of gravity for most visitors to Denmark's eastern island, there is no shortage of drawcards beyond the city limits, especially Kronborg Slot and the remarkable Viking ships of Roskilde.

Helsingør

POP 47,270

Fascinating Helsingør commands the narrowest point of the Øresund, the sound that separates Denmark from today's Sweden. While its most famous attraction is the gigantic Kronborg Slot (p324), it's also home to an outstanding, modern maritime museum.

⊙ Sights

★ Kronborg Slot
CASTLE

(☑ 49 21 30 78; www.kronborg.dk; Kronborgvej; interior adult/child 140kr/free; ⊙ 10am-5.30pm Jun-Sep, 11am-4pm Apr, May & Oct, 11am-4pm Tue-Sun Nov-Mar) Best known as the Elsinore Castle of Shakespeare's *Hamlet*, this Unesco World Heritage Site is a vast Renaissance masterpiece topped by baroque green-copper spires. It's ringed by moats, fortifications and powerful Vaubanesque star bastions that you can discover without a ticket. But it's well worth the entry fee to explore the inner palace's rooms, tapestries, ceiling paintings and viewpoints and, best of all, to delve into the spooky maze of casemates – subterranean dungeon passages barely lit by flickering paraffin lamps.

★ M/S Museet for Søfart
MUSEUM

(Maritime Museum of Denmark; www.mfs.dk; Ny Kronborgvej 1; adult/child 120kr/free; ⊙ 10am-6pm Jul & Aug, 11am-5pm Tue-Sun Sep-Jun) Ingeniously built into a dry dock beside Kronborg Slot, this subterranean museum merits a visit as much for its design as for its informative multimedia galleries. These explore Denmark's maritime history and culture in dynamic, contemporary ways. Alongside nautical instruments, sea charts and wartime objects, exhibitions explore themes including the representation of sailors in popular culture, trade and exploitation in Denmark's overseas colonies, and the globe-crossing journeys of modern shipping containers.

🛏 Sleeping

Danhostel Helsingør
HOSTEL €

(☑ 49 28 49 49; www.danhostelhelsingor.dk; Nordre Strandvej 24; dm/s/d/tr 225/495/550/650kr; P 🛜; 🚌 842) Right on its own little sandy beach with fireplace, lawns and kayak hire, this remarkable hostel is based around a count's 1907 summer mansion. Only five of the 40 rooms are within that building, but the restaurant section remains very grand with sea views. Dorm beds are available only in peak summer season. Sheet hire (59kr) obligatory.

🍴 Eating

Café Hyacint
DANISH €

(☑ 49 21 69 70; Bjergegade 4; salads 99kr, mains 109-169kr; ⊙ noon-5pm Mon-Thu, 11am-6pm Fri & Sat; 🛜🚼) Celebrating Hyacinth Bucket, the Patricia Routledge character from a classic British TV sitcom, this terraced cafe sprawls

its summer seats onto the joyously buzzing Axeltorv Sq. One particularly good-value lunch option comprises three classic smørrebrød, a beer and a shot of *snaps* (119kr).

ℹ Information

Kulturværftet (Cultureyard; https://kuto.dk; Allegade 2; ⊙ 10am-9pm, to 4pm Sat & Sun) Pick up tourist brochures in the foyer of this waterfront cultural centre.

ℹ Getting There & Away

DSB trains to Copenhagen (108kr, 46 minutes) run about three times hourly from before 5am to around midnight.

Roskilde
POP 50,780

Most foreigners who have heard of Roskilde know it either as the home of one of northern Europe's best music festivals, or the site of several remarkable Viking ship finds. To the Danes, however, it is a city of great royal and religious significance, as it was the capital city long before Copenhagen.

The **Roskilde Festival** (www.roskilde-festival.dk; Darupvej; tickets from 2100kr; ⊙ late Jun/early Jul) takes place over a long weekend in early July, in fields just outside the city centre. It attracts the biggest international rock and pop names, along with 75,000 music fans, and is renowned for its relaxed, friendly atmosphere. Most visitors camp on-site.

⊙ Sights

★ Viking Ship Museum
MUSEUM

(Vikingeskibsmuseet; ☑ 46 30 02 00; www.viking eskibsmuseet.dk; Vindeboder 12; adult/child 130kr/free; ⊙ 10am-5pm late Jun–mid-Aug, to 4pm rest of year; P 🚼) Five original Viking ships, discovered at the bottom of Roskilde Fjord, are displayed in the main hall of this must-see museum. A short walk away, the same ticket gives access to the workshops of **Museumsø**, where archaeological and reconstruction work takes place, and **Nordic longboats** (per person 100kr; ⊙ May-Sep) depart. There are free daily guided tours (45 minutes) in English in the summer; see the website for times.

★ Roskilde Domkirke
CATHEDRAL

(☑ 46 35 16 24; www.roskildedomkirke.dk; Domkirkestræde 10; adult/pensioner/child 60/40kr/free; ⊙ 10am-6pm Mon-Sat, 1-4pm Sun Jun-Aug, reduced hours rest of year) The crème de la crème of Danish cathedrals, this twin-spired giant was started by Bishop Absalon in 1170, but has been rebuilt and tweaked so many times that it's now a superb showcase of 850 years' worth of Danish architecture. As the royal mausoleum, it contains the crypts of 37 Danish kings and queens and is now a Unesco World Heritage Site. The entry fee includes a comprehensive, full-colour 48-page guidebook.

Ragnarock   MUSEUM
(📱 46 31 68 54; www.museumragnarock.dk; Rabalderstræde 16; adult/child 95kr/free; ⏰ 10am-5pm Tue & Thu-Sun, to 10pm Wed; 🅿; 🚌 202A) Within a startling architectural statement of a building, this spirit-lifting, highly interactive museum delivers a multisensory, experiential and often humorous journey through the evolution of rock music and youth culture from the 1950s to the present. Walls of headphones let you listen to music time capsules, and spin-to-hear turntables explain about gramophones. Play with interactive musical lights, learn why toilets were integral to Danish music production and practise various dance steps on the hot-spot stage beside the 'world's biggest mirror ball'.

🛏 Sleeping

Danhostel Roskilde   HOSTEL **€**
(📱 46 35 21 84; www.danhostelroskilde.dk; Vindeboder 7; dm/s/d 250/575/700kr; 🅿🛜; 🚌 203) Roskilde's swish, five-star hostel has a superb position on the waterfront right next door to the Viking Ship Museum. Decorated with funky black-and-white murals, each of the 40 large rooms has its own shower and toilet, and beds are proper doubles.

🍴 Eating & Drinking

Bryggergården   PUB
(📱 46 35 01 03; www.restaurantbryggergaarden. dk; Algade 15; ⏰ 10.30am-11pm Mon-Thu, 10.30am-midnight Fri & Sat, noon-9pm Sun) This quietly classy wood-panelled bar-restaurant has a sunny street terrace and offers a wide range of Danish pub meals along with several beers, supplementing Jacobsen IPA with various local Herslev brews.

Café Vivaldi   CAFE
(📱 46 37 40 05; http://cafevivaldi.dk/cafe/Roskilde-staendertorvet; Stændertorvet 8; lunch dishes 79-159kr, dinner mains 139-249kr; ⏰ 10am-10pm,

to 11pm Fri & Sat; 🛜📶) Slap bang on the main square, cathedral views included, this chain-bistro is a good place to sit back and people-watch over drinks or abundant servings of tasty, if stock-standard, cafe grub.

Kloster Kælderen   CRAFT BEER
(📱 31 17 11 14; www.klosterkaelderen.beer; Store Gråbrødrestræde 23; ⏰ 2pm-midnight Mon-Thu, noon-2am Fri, 10am-2am Sat) Cosy, candlelit yet unpretentious, this beer cellar, with walls made of giant boulders, has 15 regularly changing craft beers on tap, sometimes including Hornbeer Strong Porter, a remarkably smoky stout. There's also an astounding selection of bottled beers, including almost 30 Trappist brews – including the very rarest.

❶ Getting There & Away

Trains between Copenhagen and Roskilde run around the clock, up to six times an hour (84kr, 23 to 28 minutes), with reduced services at night. Holders of the Copenhagen Card get free train travel to Roskilde.

Other useful train services include Odense (232kr, 73 minutes). For northeastern Zealand change in Copenhagen.

FUNEN

Funen is Denmark's proverbial middle child. Lacking Zealand's capital-city pull or Jutland's geographic dominance, it's often overlooked by visitors, who perhaps make a whistle-stop visit to Hans Christian Andersen's birthplace in Odense.

Odense

POP 202,350

Pronounced *o*-thn-se (or *ohn*-se if you're local), Funen's millennium-old hub is Denmark's third-biggest city, a buzzing place undergoing a very major revamp. The birthplace of fairy-tale writer extraordinaire Hans Christian Andersen, there's a profusion of Andersen-related attractions, including museums, a children's centre and sculptures interpreting his most famous stories.

◉ Sights

★ HC Andersens Hus   MUSEUM
(www.museum.odense.dk; Hans Jensens Stræde 45; adult/child 125kr/free; ⏰ 10am-5pm Jul & Aug,

reduced hours rest of year; 🚼) Lying amid the seemingly miniaturised streets of the former poor quarter is the sparse little cottage where Hans Christian Andersen was born. Visiting it is a small part of a much bigger, modern museum experience that gives a thorough, lively account of Andersen's extraordinary life. His achievements are put into interesting historical context and leavened by some engaging audiovisual material and quirky exhibits.

There's also a reconstruction of his Copenhagen study, displays of his pen-and-ink sketches and paper cuttings, and a voluminous selection of his books, which have been translated into some 140 languages. The ticket gets you same-day entry to **HC Andersens Barndomshjem** (Munkemøllestræde 3-5; adult/child 75kr/free; ⊙10am-5pm Jul & Aug, reduced hours rest of year), **HC Andersen Museum** (☑65 51 46 01; Claus Bergs Gade 11; adult/child 125kr/free; ⊙10am-5pm Jul & Aug, reduced hours rest of year), Møntergården and **Børnekulturhuset Fyrtøjet** (Tinderbox Children's Culturehouse; Møntestræde 1; adult/child 125kr/free; ⊙10am-5pm Jul & Aug, reduced hours rest of year; 🚼).

Møntergården
MUSEUM

(www.museum.odense.dk; Møntstræde 1; adult/child 75kr/free; ⊙10am-5pm Jul & Aug, reduced hours rest of year) The new, stylishly designed main section of this city-history museum takes visitors on a thematic walk through humorously named 'Funen – Centre of the Universe', looking at world events and cultural currents through a Funen lens. Different areas cover pre-Viking gods, the Industrial Revolution's effect on villages, WWII occupation, the Cold War and how Funen came to be known as 'Denmark's garden' (the gigantic apple dominating the entry-level hall is a bit of a hint).

Brandts
MUSEUM

(☑65 20 70 00; www.brandts.dk; Brandts Torv 1; adult/child 90kr/free, after 5pm Thu free; ⊙10am-5pm Tue, Sat & Sun, to 9pm Wed-Fri) This sprawling arts centre occupies a beautifully converted 1887 textile mill. Most of the gallery space is used for well-curated, frequently changing modern-art exhibitions, but at least two rooms display highlights of the Brandts Samling permanent collection, tracing 250 years of Danish art.

🛏 Sleeping

Billesgade
B&B €

(☑20 76 42 63; www.billesgade.dk; Billesgade 9; d/apt from 585/900kr; 🅿🛜) This spotless B&B has six hotel-standard rooms, each trio sharing a bathroom. There's a communal kitchenette with free coffee and tea, or you can opt for an agreeable breakfast (75kr) made with eggs laid by the hosts' own chickens.

🍴 Eating & Drinking

Cafe Skt Gertrud
FRENCH €€

(☑65 91 33 02; www.gertruds.dk; Jernbanegade 8; mains 148-288kr; ⊙9am-1am Mon-Wed, to 2am Thu, to 3am Fri & Sat, 10am-midnight Sun, kitchen closes 10pm; 🛜) Affecting the attitude of a Parisian brasserie complete with Bar-Tabac sign, this very inviting street cafe serves French favourites like mussels in white wine or *confit de canard* (duck confit), as well as steak, salads, fish and a house burger.

★ Restaurant No 61
EUROPEAN €€€

(☑61 69 10 35; www.no61.dk; Kongensgade 61; 1-/2-/3- course menu 195/275/325kr; ⊙5-10pm Mon-Sat; 🛜🚼) Family-friendly yet gastronomically oriented, this farmhouse-chic bistro has a short, simple, monthly changing menu of seasonal dishes using produce plucked straight from the Funen fields: white asparagus with truffle-infused hollandaise sauce perhaps, or a confection of strawberry, rhubarb, white chocolate and crème anglaise. Reservations recommended.

Nelle's Coffee & Wine
COFFEE

(☑88 97 77 00; www.nellesbar.dk; Pantheonsgade; ⊙8am-10pm Mon-Thu, to 11pm Fri, 9am-11pm Sat, 10am-6pm Sun; 🛜) Many locals rate Nelle's fair trade Ugandan coffee as the best in town. There are three locations to choose from, all airy, bright places in which you might want to linger.

ℹ Information

The **tourist office** (☑63 75 75 20; www.visit odense.com; Vestergade 2; ⊙9.30am-6pm Mon-Fri, 10am-3pm Sat, 11am-2pm Sun Jul & Aug, 10am-4.30pm Mon-Fri, to 1pm Sat Sep-Jun; 🛜), located in the townhall, and its excellent website are very useful resources.

ℹ Getting There & Away

Odense is on the main railway line between Copenhagen (278kr, 1¼ to 1¾ hours, at least hourly) and Aarhus (246kr, 1½ hours, at least hourly).

JUTLAND

Denmark doesn't have a north–south divide; culturally, spiritually and to a great extent politically, it is divided into Jutland...and all the rest. Its boat-filled harbours, glittering lakes and thatch-roofed villages have inspired centuries of great Danish art, while its largest city, Aarhus, buzzes with art, gastronomy and understated cool.

Aarhus

POP 269,020

Aarhus (*oar*-hus) has long laboured in the shadow of consummate capital Copenhagen, but transformation is afoot. Denmark's second-largest city is busy staking a claim for visitor attention and building a reputation as an emerging European destination for savvy city-breakers, festival-goers, art and food fans, and those looking beyond the capital-city conga.

⊙ Sights

★ **ARoS Aarhus Kunstmuseum**   MUSEUM
(☑ 87 30 66 00; www.aros.dk; Aros Allé 2; adult/child 130kr/free; ⊙10am-5pm Tue & Thu-Sun, to 10pm Wed; ⊛) Inside the cubist, red-brick walls of Aarhus' showpiece art museum are nine floors of sweeping curves, soaring spaces and white walls showcasing a wonderful selection of Golden Age works, Danish modernism and an abundance of arresting and vivid contemporary art. The museum's cherry-on-top is the spectacular Your Rainbow Panorama, a 360-degree rooftop walkway offering views of the city through its glass panes in all shades of the rainbow.

★ **Den Gamle By**   MUSEUM
(The Old Town; ☑ 86 12 31 88; www.dengamleby.dk; Viborgvej 2; adult/child 135kr/free; ⊙10am-6pm Jul–early Sep, reduced hours rest of year; ⊛) The Danes' seemingly limitless enthusiasm for dressing up and re-creating history reaches its zenith at Den Gamle By. It's an engaging, picturesque open-air museum of over 70 half-timbered houses brought here from all corners of Denmark and reconstructed as a provincial market town from the era of Hans Christian Andersen. It also includes a recreated neighbourhood from 1974.

Moesgaard Museum   MUSEUM
(☑ 87 39 40 00; www.moesgaardmuseum.dk; Moesgård Allé; adult/child 140kr/free; ⊙10am-5pm

Tue & Thu-Sun, to 9pm Wed; ⊛) Don't miss the reinvented Moesgaard Museum, 10km south of the city, housed in a spectacularly designed, award-winning modern space. The star attraction is the 2000-year-old **Grauballe Man**, whose astonishingly well-preserved body was found in 1952 in the village of Grauballe, 35km west of Aarhus. Aside from the Grauballe Man, the museum brings various eras (from the Stone Age to the Viking era) to life with cutting-edge archaeological and ethnographic displays.

Aarhus Domkirke   CHURCH
(www.aarhus-domkirke.dk; Store Torv; ⊙9.30am-4pm Mon-Sat May-Sep, 10am-3pm Mon-Sat Oct-Apr) With a lofty nave spanning nearly 100m in length, Aarhus Domkirke is Denmark's longest church. The original Romanesque chapel at the eastern end dates from the 12th century, while most of the rest of the church is 15th-century Gothic.

☞ Tours

★ **Cycling Aarhus**   CYCLING
(☑ 27 29 06 90; www.cycling-aarhus.dk; Frederiksgade 78; 2½/3hr tour 299/349kr; ⊙bike rental 9am-1pm May-Oct, other times by arrangement) Helping you join the cycling locals, this company offers two-wheeled tours of the city. The Must See Tour takes in Aarhus' highlights over 12km and three hours, departing at 10.30am daily from the company's central base (where bike rental is also available). Schedules and bookings are online.

🛏 Sleeping

Cabinn Aarhus Hotel   HOTEL €
(☑ 86 75 70 00; www.cabinn.com; Kannikegade 14; s/d from 495/625kr; P@⊛) 'Best location, best price' is the Cabinn chain's motto and, given that this huge branch overlooks the river and is in the centre of town, it's pretty spot on. The 400 functional rooms are based on ships' cabins (hence the name) – the cheapest is *tiny,* but all come with bathroom, kettle and TV.

★ **Hotel Guldsmeden**   BOUTIQUE HOTEL €€
(☑ 86 13 45 50; http://guldsmedenhotels.com/aarhus; Guldsmedgade 40; d with/without bathroom from 1075/895kr; ⊛) 🌿 A top pick for its excellent location, warm staff, French Colonial-style rooms with Persian rugs, pretty garden oasis and relaxed, stylish ambience. Bumper breakfasts (mainly organic) are included,

Aarhus

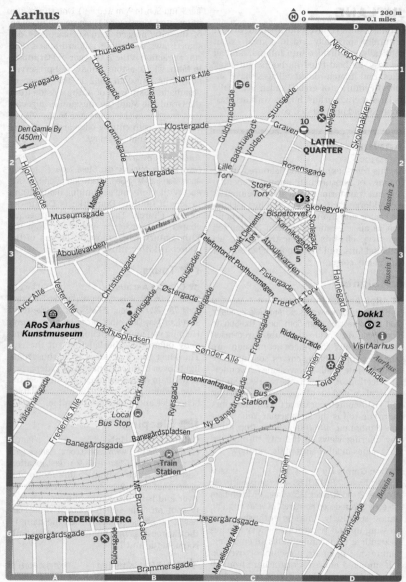

as is Guldsmeden's own organic toiletries range. *Guldsmed* means both goldsmith and dragonfly in Danish – look for sweet use of the dragonfly motif in the decor.

🍴 Eating & Drinking

⭐ **Aarhus Street Food**   FOOD HALL €
(www.aarhusstreetfood.com; Ny Banegårdsgade 46; mains 50-150kr; ⏱ 11.30am-9pm Sun-Thu, to 10pm

Aarhus

Fri & Sat; 🛜🥤) 🍴 A former garage at the back of the bus station (p330) now houses a buzzing street-food venue serving everything from pizza slices to bumper burgers, by way of Thai curries, Chinese dumplings and Vietnamese baguettes. The place is one of *the* places to meet, greet and graze in town – on-site bars stay open until midnight Friday – and Saturday.

★ OliNico INTERNATIONAL €
(📞86 25 05 70; www.olinico.dk; Mejlgade 35; mains 65-165kr; ⊙11.30am-2pm & 5.30-9pm, eve only Sun) You may need to fight for one of the sought-after tables at OliNico, a small, understatedly cool deli-restaurant with a menu of classic dishes at excellent prices. The daily-changing, three-course dinner menu (for a bargain 140kr) may be Aarhus' best-kept food secret.

★ La Cabra CAFE
(www.lacabra.dk; Graven 20; ⊙8am-6pm Mon-Sat, 9am-5pm Sun) First-rate bean sourcing and roasting combine with fine barista skills to make La Cabra the city's best coffee spot, and the queue for a takeaway brew attests to that. An airy interior, alfresco seats and delectable housemade pastries and sandwiches help to round out its justified appeal.

St Pauls Apothek DANISH €€€
(📞86 12 08 33; www.stpaulsapothek.dk; Jægergårdsgade 76; 2-/3-course menu 265/345kr;

⊙5.30pm-midnight Tue-Thu, to 2am Fri & Sat) What was once a pharmacy is now one of Aarhus' hottest dining destinations: a Brooklyn-esque combo of hipster mixologists, vintage architectural detailing and slinky mood lighting. The menu is small on choice but big on Nordic produce and confident food pairings – and for 595kr, you can enjoy three courses matched with inspired cocktails. Book ahead.

☆ Entertainment

Train LIVE MUSIC
(📞86 13 47 22; www.train.dk; Toldbodgade 6) Aarhus' premier club, Train is first and foremost a concert venue, with shows a couple of nights a week and some big international acts on the program. Train opens as a late-night club as well on Friday and Saturday nights, with room for up to 1300 party-people and top-notch DJ talent. The complex also incorporates Kupé, a cool lounge club.

ℹ Information

VisitAarhus (📞87 31 50 10; www.visitaarhus. com; Hack Kampmanns Plads 2; ⊙10am-4pm Mon-Sat, 11am-2pm Sun) has a good website, touchscreens around town and a free app. Its social media pages are useful for up-to-date info. The main staffed information desk is a small one inside **Dokk1** (📞89 40 92 00; www. dokk1.dk; Hack Kampmanns Plads 2; ⊙8am-10pm Mon-Fri, 10am-4pm Sat & Sun; 🚻).

ℹ Getting There & Away

Aarhus is well connected by train. Services to Copenhagen (388kr, three to 3½ hours), via Odense (246kr, 1½ hours) leave roughly half-hourly.

ℹ Getting Around

Aarhus' city centre is compact and best explored on foot or bike. The bus network is good for getting to sights and natural attractions on the city outskirts.

BICYCLE

Donkey Republic (www.donkey.bike/cities/ bike-rental-aarhus) is the city's official bike-share provider, its bright-orange bikes available for rent (one day 100kr) from locations around the city. To unlock the bikes, you will need to download the Donkey Republic app. See the website for details.

Cycling Aarhus (p327) offers bike rental (one day 110kr) as well as city cycling tours from a central location. See its website for details of its free city app with suggestions for cycling destinations.

BUS

Aarhus has an extensive, efficient local bus network. Most in-town (yellow) buses **stop** (Park Allé) close to the train station on Park Allé. You can buy your ticket on-board (single ticket 20kr) or using the **Midttrafik** (☑ 70 21 02 30; www.midttrafik.dk) app.

Information on tickets, passes, routes and schedules is available from the **bus station** (Rutebilstation; Fredensgade 45) on Fredensgade or through Midttrafik, which has good info in English on its website.

LIGHT RAIL

The first phase of Aarhus' light-rail line (known as the Aarhus Letbane) runs north from Aarhus train station via the harbour (stopping at Dokk1; p329) to Skolebakken, where the line divides into two tracks, including one that runs via Nørreport, the university and main hospital. In early 2019, the Letbane was expanded to Grenaa in Djursland. From Aarhus train station, the line runs south to Odder via Mølleparken.

Skagen

POP 8090

Located at Jutland's northern tip where the Baltic meets the North Sea, Skagen (pronounced 'skain') lures with its rich art heritage, fresh seafood, photogenic neighbourhoods and salubrious summer crowds.

◎ Sights

★ Gammel Skagen
VILLAGE, BEACH

There's a touch of Cape Cod in refined Gammel Skagen ('Old Skagen', also known as Højen), renowned for its gorgeous sunsets, upmarket hotels and well-heeled summer residents.

It was a fishing hamlet before sandstorms ravaged this windswept area and forced many of its inhabitants to move to Skagen on the more protected east coast. It's a pleasant bike ride 4km west of Skagen: head towards Frederikshavn and turn right at Højensvej, which takes you to the waterfront.

★ Skagens Museum
MUSEUM

(☑ 98 44 64 44; www.skagensmuseum.dk; Brøndumsvej 4; adult/child 110kr/free; ☺ 10am-5pm, to 9pm Wed Jun-Aug, reduced hours rest of year; ④) This wonderful gallery showcases the outstanding art that was produced in Skagen between 1870 and 1930. Artists discovered Skagen's luminous light and its wind-blasted heath-and-dune landscape in the mid-19th century and fixed eagerly on the romantic imagery of the area's fishing life that had earned the people of Skagen a hard living for centuries. Their work established a vivid figurative style of painting that became known internationally as the 'Skagen School'.

★ Grenen
BEACH

Appropriately enough for such a neat and ordered country, Denmark doesn't end untidily at its most northerly point, but on a neat finger of sand just a few metres wide. You can actually paddle at its tip, where the waters of the Kattegat (an arm of the Baltic Sea) and Skagerrak (part of the North Sea) clash, and you can put one foot in each sea – but not too far. Bathing here is forbidden because of the ferocious tidal currents.

Anchers Hus
MUSEUM

(☑ 98 44 64 44; www.skagenkunstmuseer.dk; Markvej 2; adult/child 80kr/free; ☺ 10am-5pm Jun-Aug, reduced hours Apr, May, Sep & Oct, closed rest of year) Time stands still at the atmospheric former home of renowned Skagen painters Anna and Michael Ancher, its interiors unchanged since Anna Ancher's passing in 1935. You can inspect the family's personal possessions and around 250 works of art from Scandinavian, German, Dutch and British artists. The venue also includes a cafe, small shop and separate gallery for temporary exhibitions.

⑤ Tours

Sandormen
BUS

(☑ 40 30 50 42; www.sandormen.dk; Grenen; adult/child return 30/15kr; ☺ mid-Apr–late Oct; ④) Sandormen is a tractor-pulled bus that can take you out to the point at Grenen (otherwise it's about a 20-minute walk along the sand from the car park). It leaves from the car park from 10am daily and runs regularly all day, according to demand. Cash payment only.

⨌ Sleeping

Danhostel Skagen
HOSTEL €

(☑ 98 44 22 00; www.danhostelskagen.dk; Rolighedsvej 2; dm/s/d 199/555/666kr; ☺ Mar-Dec; ℗ 圇) Always a hive of activity, this hostel is modern, functional and spick and span. It's decent value, particularly for families or groups. Low-season prices drop sharply. It's 1km towards Frederikshavn from the Skagen train station (if you're coming by train, get off at Frederikshavnsvej). Breakfast/linen costs 60/60kr.

DON'T MISS

LEGOLAND

Revisit your tender years at Denmark's most visited tourist attraction (beyond Copenhagen), **Legoland** (☑ 75 33 13 33; www.legoland.dk; Nordmarksvej; one-day ticket adult/child 379/359kr; ☺ 10am-8pm early Jul–mid-Aug, shorter hours Apr–early Jul & mid-Aug–early Nov, closed rest of year; 🅿 ⛟). Located 1km north of the Lego company town of Billund, the sprawling theme park is a gobsmacking ode to those little plastic building blocks, with everything from giant Lego models of famous cities, landmarks and wild beasts to re-created scenes from the *Star Wars* film series. Admission is slightly cheaper if you buy your tickets in advance online.

In the heart of Billund, **Lego House** (☑ 82 82 04 00; www.legohouse.com; Ole Kirks Plads 1; Experience Zones ticket 229kr; ☺ 9.30am-8.30pm) offers a stellar year-round reason to visit Billund (even in winter, when Legoland is closed). Designed by Danish starchitect Bjarke Ingels and resembling a stack of 21 gigantic Lego bricks, the hands-on 'experience centre' incorporates top-quality museum displays of the company's history, plus exhibition areas and rooftop terraces. The ground level (home to eateries and a Lego shop) has free public access; access to the Experience Zones requires a prebooked ticket (with allocated entry time).

Billund lies in central Jutland. By train, the most common route is to disembark at either Vejle or Kolding and catch a bus from there. Buses 43 and 143 run from Vejle (62kr, 35 minutes), while bus 166 runs from Kolding (72kr, 60 minutes). To plan your travel, use www.rejseplanen.dk.

✕ Eating & Drinking

Jorgens Spisehus   DANISH €
(☑ 98 44 26 24; www.joergensspisehus.dk; Sardinvej 7; mains 70-209kr; ☺ 10am-7.30pm, from 11am Sat & Sun) While you probably won't remember the decor and ambience, down-to-earth Jorgens is dependable for no-fuss traditional dishes and cheerful service. Tuck into old-school Danish specialities like *stjerneskud* (one pan-fried and one steamed fish fillet, plus shrimp and asparagus on bread) and smørrebrød, or hit the spot with a burger or Wiener schnitzel. The kitchen closes 7pm; takeaway available too.

Skagen Bryghus   MICROBREWERY
(☑ 98 45 00 50; www.skagenbryghus.dk; Kirkevej 10; ☺ 10.30am-6pm Mon-Thu, to 7pm Fri & Sat, to 4pm Sun) Lots of summertime live music, a snack-worthy menu and a big beer garden make this microbrewery an ideal spot for a lazy afternoon. Sample your way through the beer varieties, starting with the award-winning Drachmann pilsner.

ⓘ Information

Tourist Office (☑ 98 44 13 77; www.skagen-tourist.dk; Vestre Strandvej 10; ☺ 9am-4pm Mon-Sat, 10am-2pm Sun late Jun–mid-Aug, reduced hours rest of year) In front of the harbour, with loads of info on regional sights, attractions and activities.

ⓘ Getting There & Away

Trains run to Frederikshavn roughly every 30 to 60 minutes (60kr, 40 minutes), where you can change for destinations further south.

In July and August the handy Nordjyllands Trafikselskab's summer buses are in operation. Bus 99 (also known as Skagerakkeren) runs along the west coast connecting Skagen to Gammel Skagen, Tversted, Hirtshals, Løkken, Fårup Sommerland and Blokhus. See www.nordjyllandstrafikselskab.dk for details.

SURVIVAL GUIDE

ⓘ Directory A–Z

ACCOMMODATION

High standards are the norm. It's good to book ahead; in peak summer (late June to mid-August), bookings are essential in popular holiday areas.

LGBT+ TRAVELLERS

Denmark's liberal attitude makes the country a popular destination for LGBT+ travellers. Copenhagen in particular has an active gay community with numerous venues. Landsforeningen for Bøsser, Lesbiske, Biseksuelle og Transpersoner (www.lgbt.dk) is the Danish national association for the LGBT+ community.

MONEY

ATMs are widely available. Credit cards are accepted in most hotels, restaurants and shops.

OPENING HOURS

Opening hours vary throughout the year, especially for sights and activities. Use the following hours as a guideline only.

Banks 10am–4pm Monday to Friday

Bars & Clubs 4pm–midnight, to 2am or later Friday and Saturday (on weekends clubs may open until 5am)

Cafes 8am–5pm or midnight

Restaurants noon–10pm (maybe earlier on weekends for brunch)

Shops 10am–6pm Monday to Friday, to 4pm Saturday, some larger stores may open Sunday

Supermarkets 8am–9pm (many with in-store bakeries opening around 7am)

PUBLIC HOLIDAYS

Many Danes take their main work holiday during the first three weeks of July, but there are numerous other holidays as well.

New Year's Day (Nytårsdag) 1 January

Maundy Thursday (Skærtorsdag) Thursday before Easter

Good Friday (Langfredag) Friday before Easter

Easter Day (Påskedag) Sunday in March or April

Easter Monday (2. påskedag) Day after Easter

Great Prayer Day (Store Bededag) Fourth Friday after Easter

Ascension Day (Kristi Himmelfartsdag) Sixth Thursday after Easter

Whitsunday (Pinsedag) Seventh Sunday after Easter

Whitmonday (2. pinsedag) Seventh Monday after Easter

Constitution Day (Grundlovsdag) 5 June

Christmas Eve (Juleaften) 24 December (from noon)

Christmas Day (Juledag) 25 December

Boxing Day (2. juledag) 26 December

New Year's Eve (Nytårsaften) 31 December (from noon)

TELEPHONE

➡ All telephone numbers in Denmark have eight digits; there are no area codes.

➡ Prepaid local SIM cards are available at supermarkets, kiosks and petrol stations. Look for prepaid SIM-card packages from Lycamobile (www.lycamobile.dk) and Lebara (www.lebara.dk). Lycamobile is best – SIM cards can be obtained for free (see the website) and topped up online.

TIME

Time in Denmark is one hour ahead of GMT/UTC, the same as in neighbouring European countries. Clocks are moved forward one hour for daylight saving time from the last Sunday in March to the last Sunday in October.

TOILETS

In towns and cities, public toilets are generally easy to find. There may be a small fee to use the facilities at shopping centres or large train stations.

ⓘ Getting There & Away

AIR

The majority of overseas flights into Denmark land at Copenhagen Airport (p322) in Kastrup, about 9km southeast of central Copenhagen.

LAND

➡ Technically, Denmark's only land crossing is with Germany, although the bridge over the Øresund from Sweden functions in the same way.

➡ FlixBus (www.flixbus.dk) runs frequent long-distance buses between Denmark and other European destinations.

➡ Reliable, regular train services link Denmark to Sweden, Germany and Norway. Tickets booked online in advance can be cheaper. See www.dsb.dk for details.

SEA

Ferry connections are possible between Denmark and Norway, Sweden, Germany, Poland (via Sweden), Iceland and the Faroe Islands.

Fares on these routes vary wildly, by season and by day of the week. The highest prices tend to occur on summer weekends and the lowest on winter weekdays. Discounts are often available.

If travelling in peak times, in particular if you are transporting a car, you should always make reservations well in advance.

Major operators and their routes are listed here.

Faroe Islands & Iceland

Smyril Line (www.smyrilline.com) Sails from the Northern Jutland port of Hirtshals to Tórshavn, the capital of the Faroe Islands (36 hours, once weekly year-round, twice weekly in summer peak), and from Hirtshals to Seyðisfjörður (Iceland) via Tórshavn (48 hours, once weekly).

Germany

Bornholmslinjen (www.bornholmslinjen.com) Sails from Rønne (on Bornholm) to Sassnitz (3½ hours) four to five times weekly from April to October (daily in July and August). Departures are reduced significantly at other times of the year.

Scandlines (www.scandlines.dk) Sails from Rødbyhavn (on Lolland) to Puttgarden (45

minutes, every half-hour) and from Gedser (on Falster) to Rostock (1¾ to two hours, up to 10 daily).

Sylt Ferry (www.syltferry.com) Sails from Havneby (on west-coast Rømø) to the German island of Sylt (45 minutes, up to nine daily).

Norway

Color Line (www.colorline.com) Sails from Hirtshals to Kristiansand (3¼ hours, once or twice daily) and Larvik (3¾ hours, once or twice daily).

DFDS Seaways (www.dfdsseaways.com) Copenhagen to Oslo (17 hours, daily).

Fjordline (www.fjordline.com) Offers a fast catamaran service from Hirtshals to Kristiansand (2¼ hours, two or three services daily mid-April to mid-September). Also sails year-round from Hirtshals to Bergen via Stavanger (Stavanger 10½ hours, Bergen 16½ hours, once daily), and to Langesund (4½ hours, once daily).

Stena Line (www.stenaline.dk) Frederikshavn to Oslo (9¼ hours, six to seven weekly).

Poland

Polferries (www.polferries.com) connects Świnoujście with Ystad in southern Sweden (6½ to eight hours, two to three daily). From Ystad there is a free connecting shuttle-bus service to Copenhagen via the Øresund Bridge for foot passengers; those in cars receive a pass for passage across the bridge. From Ystad there are frequent ferries to Bornholm.

TT-Line (www.ttline.com) has a direct weekly ferry service in summer connecting Rønne (on Bornholm) and Świnoujście.

Sweden

Bornholmslinjen (www.bornholmslinjen.dk) Rønne (Bornholm) to Ystad (80 minutes, up to eight times daily).

Scandlines (www.scandlines.dk) Helsingør to Helsingborg (20 minutes, up to four sailings an hour).

Stena Line (www.stenaline.dk) Sails from Frederikshavn to Gothenburg (3½ hours, up to six times daily) and from Grenaa to Varberg (4¼ to five hours, once or twice daily).

ⓘ Getting Around

AIR

Denmark's small size and efficient train network mean that domestic air traffic is limited, usually

ⓘ THE ESSENTIAL TRANSPORT WEBSITE

For getting around in Denmark, the essential website is www.rejseplanen.dk. It allows you to enter your start and end point, date and preferred time of travel, and will then give you the best travel option, which may involve walking or taking a bus or train. Bus routes are linked, travel times are given, and fares listed. Download the app for easy access.

to business travellers and people connecting from international flights through Copenhagen, from where there are frequent services to a few of the more distant corners of the country.

BICYCLE

Denmark offers excellent cycling routes. Bicycles can be taken on ferries and trains for a modest fee.

BUS

Long-distance buses run a distant second to trains. Still, some cross-country bus routes work out to about 25% cheaper than trains. Check out FlixBus (www.flixbus.dk) and Thinggaard Express (www.expressbus.dk), and search online at www.rejseplanen.dk for regional and long-distance options.

CAR & MOTORCYCLE

➡ Roads are well maintained and usually well signposted. Except during rush hour, traffic is quite light.

➡ Cyclists often have the right of way; check cycle lanes before turning.

➡ Denmark's extensive ferry network carries vehicles at reasonable rates. It's wise to make ferry reservations in advance, even if it's only a couple of hours ahead of time.

TRAIN

DSB runs virtually all trains in Denmark and services are reliable, frequent and reasonably priced. The network extends to most corners of the country, with the exception of the southern islands and a pocket of northwestern Jutland. In these areas, a network of local buses connects towns (and there are frequent services to the nearest train station).

Estonia

POP 1.3 MILLION

Best Places to Eat

➡ Mr Jakob (p346)

➡ Manna La Roosa (p343)

➡ Ö (p343)

➡ Rataskaevu 16 (p342)

➡ Retro (p351)

Best Places to Stay

➡ Pädaste Manor (p350)

➡ Antonius Hotel (p348)

➡ Georg Ots Spa Hotel (p351)

➡ Hektor Design Hostel (p347)

➡ Tabinoya (p342)

Why Go?

Estonia doesn't have to struggle to find a point of difference; it's completely unique. It shares a similar geography and history with Latvia and Lithuania, but culturally it's distinct. Its closest ethnic and linguistic buddy is Finland, though 50 years of Soviet rule in Estonia have separated the two. For the last 300 years Estonia has been linked to Russia, but the two states have as much in common as a barn swallow and a bear (their respective national symbols).

With a newfound confidence, singular Estonia has crept from under the Soviet blanket and leapt into the arms of Europe. The love affair is mutual. Europe has fallen head over heels for the charms of Tallinn and its Unesco-protected Old Town. Put simply, Tallinn is now one of the continent's most captivating cities. And in overcrowded Europe, Estonia's sparsely populated countryside and extensive swathes of forest provide spiritual sustenance for nature-lovers.

When to Go

Tallinn

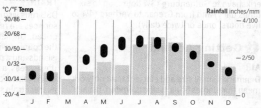

May–Sep Clement weather and summer festivals make this the best time to visit.

Nov–Jan Yuletide markets and the raising of a Christmas tree on Tallinn's main square.

Dec–Mar Fans of cross-country skiing should make for Otepää, the unofficial winter capital.

Entering the Country

Seventeen European airlines have scheduled services to Tallinn year-round, with additional routes and airlines added in summer. There are reliable bus services between Estonia and the other Baltic states.

Estonia is easily accessed by boat from major port cities around the Baltic Sea. Ferries run from Tallinn to Helsinki, St Petersburg, Mariehamn and Stockholm.

There are no border checks when driving between Estonia and Latvia thanks to the Schengen agreement.

Trains between Estonia and Latvia route through Valga, but services aren't linked. Estonian trains operated by Elron (www.elron.ee) head to Elva, Tartu and Tallinn from Valga. There is direct service to Tallinn from St Petersburg and Moscow.

ITINERARIES

Three Days

Base yourself in Tallinn (p337) and spend your first day exploring Old Town. The following day, venture to the other side of the tracks to Telliskivi Creative City (p340) before heading out of town to the wonderful Estonian Open-Air Museum (p340). On your last day, hire a car or take a day tour to Lahemaa National Park (p345).

One Week

Spend your first three days in Tallinn (p337), then allow a full day to explore Lahemaa (p345) before bedding down within the national park. The following day, continue on to Tartu (p347) for a night or two and then finish up in Pärnu (p348).

Essential Food & Drink

Estonian gastronomy mixes Nordic, Russian and German influences, and prizes local and seasonal produce.

Desserts On the sweet side, you'll find delicious chocolates, marzipan and cakes.

Favourite drinks Õlu (beer) is the favourite alcoholic drink. Popular brands include Saku and A Le Coq, and aficionados should seek out the product of the local microbreweries such as Tallinn's Põhjala. Other tipples include vodka (Viru Valge and Saremaa are the best-known local brands) and Vana Tallinn, a syrupy sweet liqueur, also available in a cream version.

Other favourites Black bread, sauerkraut, black pudding, smoked meat and fish, creamy salted butter and sour cream, which is served with almost everything.

Pork and potatoes The traditional stodgy standbys, prepared a hundred different ways.

Seasonal Summer menus feature berries in sweet and savoury dishes; forest mushrooms are the craze in autumn.

ESTONIA

AT A GLANCE

Area 45,339 sq km

Capital Tallinn

Country Code ☑ 372

Currency euro (€)

Emergency Police ☑ 110; ambulance & fire ☑ 112

Language Estonian

Time Eastern European Time (GMT/UTC plus two hours)

Visas Not required for citizens of the EU, USA, Canada, Japan, New Zealand and Australia.

Sleeping Price Ranges

The following price ranges refer to a double room in high (but not necessarily peak) season.

€ less than €35

€€ €35–100

€€€ more than €100

Eating Price Ranges

The following Estonian price ranges refer to a standard main course.

€ less than €10

€€ €10–15

€€€ more than €15

Estonia Highlights

1 **Tallinn** (p337) Embarking on a medieval quest for atmospheric restaurants and hidden bars in the history-saturated lanes.

2 **Lahemaa National Park** (p345) Wandering the forest paths, bog boardwalks and abandoned beaches.

3 **Tartu** (p347) Furthering your education among the museums and student bars of Estonia's second city.

4 **Saaremaa** (p350) Unwinding among the windmills and exploring the island's castles, churches, cliffs, coast and crater.

5 **Muhu** (p349) Hopping over to Koguva village and the gastronomic delights of Padaste Manor.

6 **Pärnu** (p348) Strolling the sands and streets of Estonia's summer capital.

7 **Otepää** (p346) Getting back to nature at the winter capital.

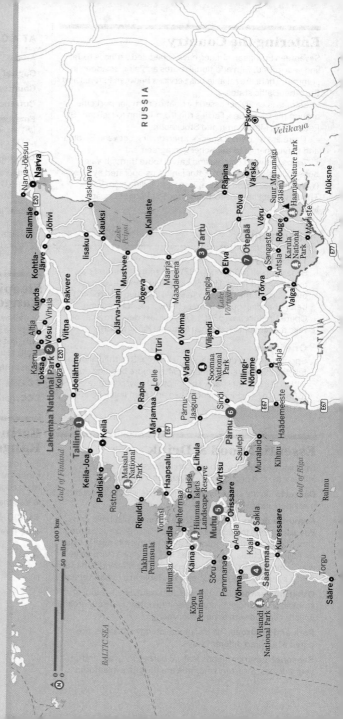

TALLINN

POP 426,540

No longer the plaything of greater powers – Danish, Swedish, Polish, German and Soviet – Tallinn is now a proud European capital with an allure all of its own. It's lively yet peaceful, absurdly photogenic and bursting with wonderful sights – ancient churches, medieval streetscapes and noble merchants' houses. Throw in delightful food and vibrant modern culture and it's no wonder Tallinn seems in danger of being loved to death, especially after a few cruise ships dock. But it's one of those blessed places that seems to cope with all the attention.

Despite the boom of 21st-century development, Tallinn safeguards the fairy-tale charms of its Unesco-listed Old Town – one of Europe's most complete walled cities. Some examples of exuberant post-Soviet development aside, the city clearly realises it's better to be classy than brassy. Hence the blossoming of first-rate restaurants, atmospheric hotels and a well-oiled tourist machine that makes visiting a breeze.

Sights

Old Town

Tallinn's medieval Old Town (Vanalinn) is without doubt the country's most fascinating locality. It's divided into Toompea (the upper town) and the lower town, which is still surrounded by much of its 2.5km defensive wall.

Toompea

Lording it over the Lower Town is the ancient hilltop citadel of Toompea. In German times this was the preserve of the feudal nobility, literally looking down on the traders and lesser beings below. It's now almost completely given over to government buildings, churches, embassies and shops selling amber knick-knacks and fridge magnets.

Alexander Nevsky Orthodox Cathedral   CATHEDRAL

(☑644 3484; http://tallinnanevskikatedraal.eu; Lossi plats 10; ⊙8am-7pm, to 4pm winter) The positioning of this magnificent, onion-domed Russian Orthodox cathedral (completed in 1900) at the heart of the country's main administrative hub was no accident: the church was one of many built in the last part of the 19th century as part of a general wave of Russification in the empire's Baltic provinces. Orthodox believers come here in droves, alongside tourists ogling the interior's striking icons and frescoes. Quiet, respectful, demurely dressed visitors are welcome, but cameras aren't.

St Mary's Lutheran Cathedral   CHURCH

(Tallinna Püha Neitsi Maarja Piiskoplik toomkirik; ☑644 4140; www.toomkirik.ee; Toom-Kooli 6; church/tower €2/5; ⊙9am-5pm May & Sep, to 6pm Jun-Aug, shorter hrs/days rest of year) Tallinn's cathedral (now Lutheran, originally Catholic) had been initially built by the Danes by at least 1233, although the exterior dates mainly from the 15th century, with the tower completed in 1779. This impressive building was a burial ground for the rich and titled, and the whitewashed walls are decorated with the elaborate coats of arms of Estonia's noble families. Fit view-seekers can climb the tower.

Lower Town

Picking your way along the lower town's narrow, cobbled streets is like strolling into the 15th century – not least due to the tendency of local businesses to dress their staff up in medieval garb. The most interesting street is Pikk (Long St), which starts at the Great Coast Gate and includes Tallinn's historic guild buildings.

Tallinn Town Hall   HISTORIC BUILDING

(Tallinna raekoda; ☑645 7900; www.raekoda.tal linn.ee; Raekoja plats; adult/student €5/3; ⊙10am-4pm Mon-Sat Jul & Aug, shorter hrs rest of year; 🔄) Completed in 1404, this is the only surviving Gothic town hall in northern Europe. Inside, you can visit the Trade Hall (whose visitor book drips with royal signatures), the Council Chamber (featuring Estonia's oldest woodcarvings, dating from 1374), the vaulted Citizens' Hall, a yellow-and-black-tiled councillor's office and a small kitchen. The steeply sloped attic has displays on the building and its restoration. Details such as brightly painted columns and intricately carved wooden friezes give some sense of the original splendour.

★Town Hall Square   SQUARE

(Raekoja plats) In Tallinn all roads lead to Raekoja plats, the city's pulsing heart since markets began setting up here in the 11th century. One side is dominated by the Gothic town hall, while the rest is ringed by pretty pastel-coloured buildings dating from the 15th to 17th centuries. Whether bathed in sunlight or sprinkled with snow, it's always a photogenic spot.

Tallinn

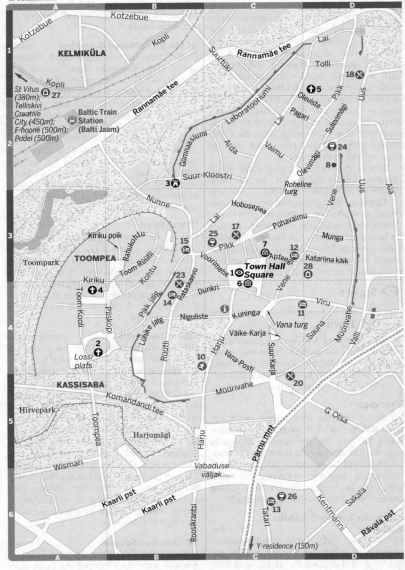

Town Council Pharmacy HISTORIC BUILDING
(Raeapteek; ☎631 4860; www.raeapteek.ee; Raekoja plats 11; ⊙10am-6pm Mon-Sat) Nobody's
too sure on the exact date it opened but by
1422 this pharmacy was already on to its
third owner, making it the oldest continually operating pharmacy in Europe. In 1583
Johann Burchardt took the helm, and a de-
scendant with the same name ran the shop
right up until 1913 – 10 generations in all!
Inside there are painted beams and a small
historical display, or you can just drop in to
stock up on painkillers and prophylactics.

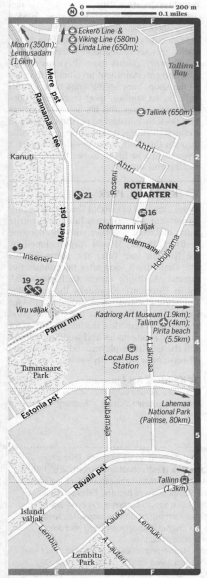

reaches a still-respectable 124m and you can take a tight, confined, 258-step staircase up the tower (adult/child €3/1) for wonderful views of Toompea and over the lower town's rooftops.

Lower Town Wall   FORTRESS
(Linnamüür; ☎ 644 9867; Väike-Kloostri 1; adult/child €2/1; ◷ 11am-7pm Jun-Aug, shorter hrs/days rest of year) The most photogenic stretch of Tallinn's remaining walls connects nine towers lining the western edge of Old Town. Visitors can explore the barren nooks and crannies of three of them (there are modest displays on weaponry and castle-craft

St Olaf's Church   CHURCH
(Oleviste kirik; ☎ 641 2241; www.oleviste.ee; Lai 50; ◷ 10am-6pm Apr-Jun & Sep-Oct, to 8pm Jul & Aug) From 1549 to 1625, when its 159m steeple was struck by lightning and burnt down, this (now Baptist) church was one of the tallest buildings in the world. The current spire

inside) with cameras at the ready for the red-rooftop views. The gardens outside the wall are pretty and relaxing.

👁 Kalamaja

Immediately northwest of the Old Town, this enclave of tumbledown wooden houses and crumbling factories swiftly transitioned into one of Tallinn's most interesting neighbourhoods thanks to local hipsters opening cafes and bars in abandoned warehouses and rickety storefronts. The intimidating hulk of Patarei Prison had seemed to cast a malevolent shadow over this part of town, so its transformation over the last several years has been nothing short of extraordinary.

★ Lennusadam   MUSEUM
(Seaplane Harbour; ☑ 620 0550; www.meremuuseum.ee; Vesilennuki 6; adult/child €14/7; ⊙ 10am-7pm daily May-Sep, to 6pm Tue-Sun Oct-Apr; 🅿) Surrounded on two sides by island-dotted waters, Estonia has a rich maritime history, explored in this fascinating museum filled with interactive displays. When the building, with its triple-domed hangar, was completed in 1917, its reinforced-concrete shell frame construction was unique in the world. Resembling a classic Bond-villain lair, the vast space was completely restored and opened to the public in 2012. Highlights include exploring the cramped corridors of a 1930s naval submarine, and the ice-breaker and minehunter ships moored outside.

Telliskivi Creative City   AREA
(Telliskivi Loomelinnak; www.telliskivi.eu; Telliskivi 60a; ⊙ shops 10am-6pm Mon-Sat, 11am-5pm Sun; 🖳) Once literally on the wrong side of the tracks, this set of abandoned factory buildings is now Tallinn's most alternative shopping and entertainment precinct, with cafes, a bike shop, bars selling craft beer, graffiti walls, artist studios, food trucks and pop-up concept stores. But it's not only hipsters who flock to Telliskivi to peruse the fashion and design stores, drink espressos and riffle through the stalls at the weekly flea market – you're just as likely to see families rummaging and sipping.

👁 Kadriorg Park

About 2km east of the Old Town, this beautiful park's ample acreage is Tallinn's favourite patch of green. Together with the baroque Kadriorg Palace, it was commissioned by the Russian tsar Peter the Great for his wife Catherine I soon after his conquest of Estonia (Kadriorg means Catherine's Valley in Estonian). Nowadays the oak, lilac and horse chestnut trees provide shade for strollers and picnickers, the formal pond and gardens provide a genteel backdrop for romantic promenades and wedding photos, and the children's playground is a favourite off-leash area for the city's youngsters.

★ Kadriorg Art Museum   MUSEUM
(Kadrioru kunstimuuseum; ☑ 606 6400; www.kadriorumuuseum.ekm.ee; Kadriorg Palace, A

ESTONIAN OPEN-AIR MUSEUM

If tourists won't go to the countryside, let's bring the countryside to them. That's the modus operandi of this excellent sprawling **complex** (Eesti vabaõhumuuseum; ☑ 654 9101; www.evm.ee; Vabaõhumuuseumi tee 12, Rocca Al Mare; adult/child high season €10/7, low season €8/6; ⊙ 10am-8pm 23 Apr–28 Sep, to 5pm 29 Sep–22 Apr), where historic Estonian buildings have been plucked and transplanted among the tall trees. In summer the time-warping effect is highlighted by staff in period costume performing traditional activities among the wooden farmhouses and windmills. There's a chapel dating from 1699 and an old wooden tavern, Kolu Kõrts, serving traditional Estonian cuisine.

Activities such as weaving, blacksmithing, and traditional cooking are put on, kids love the horse-and-carriage rides (adult/child €9/6) and bikes can be hired (per hour €3). If you find yourself in Tallinn on Midsummer's Eve (23 June), come here to witness the traditional celebrations, bonfire and all.

To get here from the centre, take Paldiski mnt. When the road nears the water, veer right onto Vabaõhumuuseumi tee. Bus 21, which departs from the railway station (p345) at least hourly, stops right out front. Combined family tickets are available that include **Tallinn Zoo** (Tallinna loomaaed; ☑ 694 3300; www.tallinnzoo.ee; Paldiski mnt 145, Veskimetsa; adult/child €8/5; ⊙ 9am-8pm May-Aug, to 7pm Mar, Apr, Sep & Oct, to 5pm Nov-Feb), which is a 20-minute walk away.

Weizenbergi 37; adult/child €6.50/4.50; ☺10am-6pm Tue & Thu-Sun, to 8pm Wed May-Sep, 10am-8pm Wed, to 5pm Thu-Sun Oct-Apr) Kadriorg Palace, a baroque beauty built by Peter the Great between 1718 and 1736, houses a branch of the Estonian Art Museum devoted to Dutch, German and Italian paintings from the 16th to the 18th centuries, and Russian works from the 18th to early 20th centuries (check out the decorative porcelain with communist imagery upstairs). The pink building is exactly as frilly and fabulous as a palace ought to be, and there's a handsome French-style formal garden at the rear.

★ **Kumu**   GALLERY
(☑602 6000; www.kumu.ekm.ee; A Weizenbergi 34; adult/student €8/6; ☺10am-6pm Wed & Fri-Sun, to 8pm Thu year-round, plus 10am-6pm Tue Apr-Sep) This futuristic, Finnish-designed, seven-storey building is a spectacular structure of limestone, glass and copper that's nicely integrated into the landscape. Kumu (the name is short for *kunstimuuseum,* or art museum) contains the country's largest repository of Estonian art as well as constantly changing contemporary exhibits. There's everything from venerable painted altarpieces to the work of contemporary Estonian artists such as Adamson-Eric.

◉ **Pirita**

Pirita's main claim to fame is that it was the base for the sailing events of the 1980 Moscow Olympics; international regattas are still held here. It's also home to Tallinn's largest and most popular beach.

Tallinn TV Tower   VIEWPOINT
(Tallinna teletorn; ☑686 3005; www.teletorn.ee; Kloostrimetsa tee 58a; adult/child €13/7; ☺10am-6pm) Opened in time for the 1980 Olympics, this futuristic 314m tower offers brilliant views from its 22nd floor (175m). Press a button and frosted glass discs set in the floor suddenly clear, giving a view straight down. Once you're done gawping, check out the interactive displays in the space-age pods. Daredevils can try the exterior, 175m-high 'edge walk' (€30, 10am to 6pm).

🏃 **Activities**

Harju Ice Rink   ICE SKATING
(Harju tänava uisuplats; ☑56246739; www.ui-suplats.ee; Harju; per hr adult/child €7/5; ☺10am-10pm Dec-Mar; 👟) Wrap up warmly to join the locals at Old Town's outdoor ice rink –

very popular in the winter months. You'll have earned a *hõõgvein* (mulled or 'glowing' wine) in the warm indoor cafe by the end of your skating session. Skate rental costs €3.

Sage Traveling   TOUR
(www.sagetraveling.com) This worldwide outfit bills itself as a European travel expert for disabled travellers. Its three-hour 'Essential Tallinn Accessible Walking Tour' thoughtfully traces a step-free route without missing out on the major sights.

🧭 **Tours**

Tallinn Traveller Tours   TOURS
(☑58374800; www.traveller.ee) This outfit runs entertaining tours, including a two-hour Old Town walk departing from outside the tourist office (p344; private groups of one to 15 people from €80), or there's a larger free tour (which also starts at the tourist office – you should tip the engaging guides). There are also ghost tours (€15), bike tours (from €19), pub crawls (€20) and day trips as far afield as Rīga (€55).

City Bike   CYCLING
(☑5111819; www.citybike.ee; Vene 33; ☺10am-7pm, to 6pm Oct-Apr) This friendly den of cycle-monkeys offers 'Welcome to Tallinn' tours (€19, two hours) from 11am year-round that include Kadriorg and Pirita. 'Other Side' tours take in Kalamaja and **Stroomi Beach** (from €19, 2½ hours), while 'Countryside Cycling & Old Town Walking' tours head as far as the Open-Air Museum (€47, four hours). It also hires out bikes from €7/15 per hour/day.

Epic Bar Crawl   TOURS
(☑56243088; www.freetour.com; €15; ☺10pm Thu-Sat) Billing itself as 'the most fun and disorderly pub crawl in Tallinn' (although somehow also the best organised), this five-hour tour includes a welcome beer or cider, a shot in each of three bars and entry to a nightclub. Epic Bar Crawl also offers particularly ignominious packages designed for stags. The meeting point is Red Emperor bar on Aia 10.

🛏 **Sleeping**

📷 **Old Town**

★ **Welcome Hostel**   HOSTEL €€
(☑650 4100; www.welcomehostel.ee; Rotermanni 12; dm/d from €18/60; 🛜) Plush beds, exposed brick walls, high ceilings and mid-century modern furnishings put this Rotermann

Quarter hostel at the top of the heap for cheaper picks in Tallinn. The 26 rooms sleep between two and 11 people and each floor has a fully-stocked kitchen. Snacks and drinks are available for purchase, and there are plenty of food options nearby.

Tabinoya HOSTEL €€
(✆632 0062; www.tabinoya.com; Nunne 1; dm/d from €17/50; @ 🛜) The Baltic's first Japanese-run hostel occupies the two top floors of a charming old building, with dorms (the four-person one is for females only) and a communal lounge at the top, and spacious private rooms, a kitchen and a sauna below. Bathroom facilities are shared. The vibe's a bit more comfortable and quiet than most of Tallinn's hostels. Book ahead.

Old House Apartments APARTMENT €€€
(✆641 1464; www.oldhouseapartments.ee; Rataskaevu 16; apt from €109; P 🛜) The name 'Old House' does poor justice to this wonderfully refurbished 14th-century merchant's house. It's been split into beautifully furnished apartments (including a spacious two-bedroom unit with traces of a medieval painted ceiling), and there are a further 20-odd units scattered around Old Town. All are in similar buildings, but the quality and facilities vary.

★Hotel Cru HOTEL €€€
(✆611 7600; www.cruhotel.eu; Viru 8; s/d/ste €170/285/585; 🛜) Behind the pretty powder-blue facade of this boutique hotel you'll find 15 richly furnished rooms scattered along a rabbit warren of corridors. All make sensitive use of original 14th-century features such as timber beams and limestone walls, but the cheapest are a little snug. The attached restaurant prides itself as one of Tallinn's best.

🛏 City Centre

Monk's Bunk HOSTEL €
(✆636 3924; www.themonksbunk.com; Tatari 1; dm/r from €15/50; @ 🛜) The only monk we can imagine fitting in here, at Tallinn's self-described 'Number One Party Hostel', is Friar Tuck. There are organised activities every night, including legendary pub crawls aimed at maximum intoxication (Wednesday to Sunday nights, €15, with shots at each bar). The facilities are good, with high ceilings, free lockers and underfloor heating in the bathrooms.

Y-residence APARTMENT €€
(✆5021477; www.facebook.com/YResidence; Pärnu mnt 32; apt from €65; 🛜) The 'Y' stands for 'yoga', which seems a strange name for a collection of clean-lined new apartments in several locations around Tallinn, until you realise the operators also run yoga, tai chi and meditation sessions. You can expect friendly staff, a basic kitchenette and, joy of joys, a washing machine!

Hotel Telegraaf HOTEL €€€
(✆600 0600; www.telegraafhotel.com; Vene 9; r €225-255; P ✴ 🛜 ≋) This upmarket hotel in a converted 19th-century former telegraph station delivers style in spades. It boasts a spa, a pretty courtyard, an acclaimed restaurant, swanky modern-art decor, and smart, efficient service. 'Superior' rooms, in the older part of the building, have more historical detail but we prefer the marginally cheaper 'executive' rooms for their bigger proportions and sharp decor.

🍴 Eating

🍴 Old Town

Vegan Restoran V VEGAN €
(✆626 9087; www.veganrestoran.ee; Rataskaevu 12; mains €8-13; ⊘noon-11pm Sun-Thu, to 11.30pm Fri-Sat; 🍴) Visiting vegans are spoiled for choice in this wonderful restaurant. In summer everyone wants one of the four tables on the street, but the atmospheric interior is just as appealing. The food is excellent – expect the likes of quinoa and turnip cutlet with roasted garlic purée and spicy oven-baked seitan tacos.

Clayhills Gastropub PUB FOOD €€
(✆641 9312; www.clayhills.ee; Pikk 13; mains €10-20; ⊘10am-midnight Sun-Wed, to 2am Thu-Sat; 🛜) With live bands, comfy couches, a stone-walled upstairs room and sunny summer terrace, Clayhills is a very pleasant place to take a break from a day's wandering of Old Town. It serves up quality grub too: try the miso/sesame-glazed duck breast, the wild mushroom risotto or the ribeye with chimichurri.

Rataskaevu 16 ESTONIAN €€
(✆642 4025; www.rataskaevu16.ee; Rataskaevu 16; mains €9-20; ⊘noon-11pm Sun-Thu, to midnight Fri & Sat; 🍴) If you've ever had a hankering for braised elk roast, this warm, stone-walled

place, named simply for its Old Town address, can sate it. Although it's hardly traditional, plenty of Estonian faves fill the menu – fried Baltic herring, grilled pork tenderloin and Estonian cheeses among them. Finish, if you can, with a serve of the legendary warm chocolate cake.

Must Puudel CAFE €€
(☑ 5056258; www.facebook.com/mustpuudel; Müürivahe 20; mains €7-16; ☺ 9am-11pm Sun-Tue, to 2am Wed-Sat; ☎) With eclectic retro furniture matched by an equally wide-roaming soundtrack, courtyard seating, excellent coffee, long opening hours and select nights of live music and DJs, the 'Black Poodle' must be Old Town's hippest cafe. It's also charming, welcoming and capable of slinging seriously good cocktails and casual meals.

★ Manna La Roosa GASTRONOMY €€€
(☑ 620 0249; www.mannalaroosa.com; Vana-Viru 15; mains €15-23; ☺ noon-11pm Sun-Tue, to 1am Wed-Thu, to 3am Fri-Sat) This restaurant-bar is truly a multi-sensory adventure. Housed in an old apothecary, the interior is a curated kaleidoscope of wacky sculptures, nonsensical paintings and plush furnishings, all sourced from around the world by revered Estonian designer Soho Fond. It's a lot to take in – thankfully the top-notch gastronomy, deliciously inventive cocktails and super-cool staff make it easy to linger.

★ Tchaikovsky RUSSIAN, FRENCH €€€
(☑ 600 0600; www.telegraafhotel.com; Vene 9; mains €20-30; ☺ 6-11pm; ☎) Located in a glassed-in pavilion within the Hotel Telegraaf (p342), Tchaikovsky offers a dazzling tableau of blinged-up chandeliers, gilt frames and greenery. Service is formal and faultless (as is the carefully contemporaried menu of Franco-Russian classics) and the experience is capped by live chamber music. The €25 three-course weekday lunch is excellent value and there's terrace seating in summer.

★ Tai Boh ASIAN €€€
(☑ 629 9218; www.taiboh.com; Vana-Viru 15; mains €11-24; ☺ 5-11pm Mon-Thu, 5pm-1am Fri-Sat, 2-11pm Sun) Located above Manna La Roosa, this superb pan-Asian eatery feels like a Brutalist-meets-Baroque fever dream. It's hard to pick a focal point among the opulent kitsch...until your eye catches the chandelier adorned with mannequin arms and dove

feathers. Images of historical icons span the ceiling – diners savour quality sashimi, curry or satay under the watchful eye of Barack Obama in the Dalai Lama's garb.

★ Leib ESTONIAN €€€
(☑ 611 9026; www.leibresto.ee; Uus 31; mains €15-24; ☺ noon-11pm Mon-Sat) *Leib* (Estonian black bread) is a thing of great beauty and quiet national pride, and you'll find a peerless rendition here: dense, moist, almost fruity in its Christmas-cake complexity. Thick-sliced and served with salt-flaked butter, it's the ideal accompaniment to the delightful new-Nordic ('new Estonian'?) food at this garden restaurant in the Old Town headquarters of Tallinn's Scottish club (really!).

✖ City Centre

★ Ö NEW NORDIC €€€
(☑ 661 6150; www.restoran-o.ee; Mere pst 6e; degustation menus €59-76; ☺ 6-11pm Mon-Sat, closed Jul) Award-winning Ö (pronounced 'er' and named for Estonia's biggest island, Saaremaa) has carved a unique space in Tallinn's culinary world, delivering inventive degustation menus showcasing seasonal Estonian produce. There's a distinct 'New Nordic' influence at play, deploying unusual ingredients such as fermented birch sap and spruce shoots, and the understated dining room nicely complements the theatrical but always delicious cuisine.

✖ Kalamaja

F-hoone PUB FOOD €
(☑ 53226855; www.fhoone.ee; Telliskivi 60a; mains €5-11; ☺ kitchen 9am-11pm Mon-Sat, to 9pm Sun; ☎☑) The trailblazing watering hole of the uberhip Telliskivi complex (p340), the industrial-chic 'Building F' offers a quality menu of pasta, burgers, soups, salads and desserts in an always-lively atmosphere. Wash down your food with a craft beer from the extensive selection and remember to book a table on buzzing weekend evenings.

★ Moon RUSSIAN €€€
(☑ 631 4575; www.restoranmoon.ee; Võrgu 3; mains €15-19; ☺ noon-11pm Mon-Sat, 1-9pm Sun, closed some of Jul) Quietly but consistently the best restaurant in increasingly hip Kalamaja, Moon ('poppy') is a Tallinn gem, combining Russian and broader European influences to delicious effect. The staff are delightfully

friendly and switched-on, the decor is cheerily whimsical, and dishes such as *piroshki* (little stuffed pies) and reputation-transforming chicken Kiev showcase a kitchen as dedicated to pleasure as to technical excellence.

Pirita

★ NOA
INTERNATIONAL €€€

(☑ 5080589; www.noaresto.ee; Ranna tee 3; mains €14-28; ☉ noon-11pm Mon-Thu, to midnight Fri & Sat, to 10pm Sun; ☑) It's worth the trek out to the far side of Pirita to reach this top-notch waterside restaurant, which consistently backs up its elevated reputation. Housed in a stylish low-slung pavilion with superb views over Tallinn Bay to Old Town, it plays knowledgeably with Asian influences while keeping a focus on the best Estonian and European ingredients and techniques.

Drinking & Nightlife

★ No Ku Klubi
BAR

(☑ 631 3929; Pikk 5; ☉ noon-1am Mon-Thu, to 3am Fri, 2pm-3am Sat, 6pm-1am Sun) A nondescript red-and-blue door, a key-code to enter, a clubbable atmosphere of regulars lounging in mismatched armchairs – could this be Tallinn's ultimate 'secret' bar? Once the surreptitious haunt of artists in Soviet times, it's now free for all to enter – just ask one of the smokers outside for the code. Occasional evenings of low-key music and film are arranged.

★ Levist Väljas
BAR

(☑ 504 6048; www.facebook.com/levistvaljas; Olevimägi 12; ☉ 5pm-3am Sun-Thu, to 6am Fri & Sat) Inside this much-loved Tallinn cellar bar (usually the last pit stop of the night) you'll find broken furniture, cheap booze and a refreshingly motley crew of friendly punks, grunge kids and anyone else who strays from the well-trodden tourist path. The discreet entrance is down a flight of stairs.

St Vitus
CRAFT BEER

(☑ 655 5354; www.vitus.ee; Telliskivi 61b; beers from €3.50, mains €7-11; ☉ noon-11pm Tue-Thu, to 2am Fri-Sat, to 9pm Sun & Mon) Friendly staff and tasty drinking food are agreeable supplements to the great range of craft beers at this Telliskivi pub. You'll find a vast selection of Estonian brews, plus several from around Europe, and a handful from the US and Asia. Cider- and wine-lovers are looked after, too, with enough variety to please a range of tastes.

Pudel
BAR

(☑ 58664496; www.pudel.ee; Telliskivi 60a; ☉ 4pm-midnight Sun, Tue & Wed, 4pm-2am Thu & Fri, noon-2am Sat) Laid-back and intimate, this friendly spot in the Telliskivi Creative City (p340) complex offers plenty of craft beers on tap, plus great booze-soaking snacks to go with them.

X-Baar
LGBTIQ+

(☑ 641 9478; www.facebook.com/xbaar; Tatari 1; ☉ 4pm-1am Sun-Thu, to 4am Fri & Sat) Tucked behind a sex shop and a hostel, this stalwart of Tallinn's tiny gay scene hosts a mixed and welcoming crowd.

Shopping

★ Masters' Courtyard
ARTS & CRAFTS

(Meistrite Hoov; www.hoov.ee; Vene 6; ☉ 10am-6pm) Archetypal of Tallinn's amber-suspended medieval beauty, this cobbled 13th-century courtyard offers rich pickings – a cosy chocolaterie/cafe, a guesthouse and artisans' stores and workshops selling quality ceramics, glass, jewellery, knitwear, woodwork and candles.

Balti Jaama Turg
MARKET

(Baltic Station Market; https://astri.ee/bjt; Kopli 1; ☉ 9am-7pm Mon-Sat, to 5pm Sun) The gentrification of the train station precinct is manifest in this sleek market complex, where niche food vendors trade from tidy huts on the former site of a famed but slightly seedy outdoor market. There's also a supermarket, meat, dairy and seafood halls, green grocers, fashion retailers, a gym and underground parking.

Information

Tallinn Tourist Information Centre (☑ 645 7777; www.visittallinn.ee; Niguliste 2; ☉ 9am-7pm Mon-Sat, to 6pm Sun Jun-Aug, shorter hrs rest of year) Has a full range of brochures, maps, event schedules and other info for Tallinn and for Estonia generally.

Getting There & Away

BUS

Regional and international buses depart from Tallinn's **Central Bus Station** (Tallinna bussijaam; ☑ 12550; www.bussijaam.ee; Lastekodu 46; ☉ ticket office 7am-9pm Mon-Sat, 8am-8pm Sun), about 2km southeast of Old Town and linked by two tram lines and eight buses. Services depart from here for Latvia, Lithuania, Poland and other European destinations.

The national bus network is extensive, linking Tallinn to pretty much everywhere you might care to go. All services are summarised on the extremely handy Tpilet site (www.tpilet.ee). The following are some of the main routes:

Tartu (€7 to €14, 2½ hours, at least every half-hour)

Pärnu (€6.50 to €11, two hours, at least hourly)

Kuressaare (€15 to €17, four hours, 11 daily)

TRAIN

The **Baltic Train Station** (Balti Jaam; Toompuiestee 35) is on the northwestern edge of Old Town; despite the name, it has no direct services to other Baltic states. **GoRail** (www.gorail.ee) runs a daily service stopping in Narva (€8.10, 2½ hours) en route to St Petersburg and Moscow.

Domestic routes are operated by **Elron** (www.elron.ee) and include the following destinations:

Narva (€11.50, 2¾ hours, three daily)

Tartu (€10.60, two to 2½ hours, eight daily)

Pärnu (€7.90, 2¼ hours, three daily)

❶ Getting Around

Tallinn has an excellent network of buses, trams and trolleybuses running from around 6am to 11pm or midnight. The major **local bus station** is beneath the Viru Keskus shopping centre, although some buses terminate their routes on the surrounding streets. All local public transport timetables are online at www.tallinn.ee.

Public transport is free for Tallinn residents, children under seven and adults with children under three. Others need to pay, either buying a paper ticket from the driver (€2 for a single journey, exact change required) or by using the e-ticketing system. Buy a Ühiskaart (a smart card, requiring a €2 deposit that can't be recouped within six months of validation) at an R-Kiosk, post office or the Tallinn City Government customer service desk, add credit, then validate the card at the start of each journey using the orange card-readers. E-ticket fares are €1.10/3/6 for an hour/day/five days.

The Tallinn Card (www.tallinncard.ee) includes free public transport on all services for the duration of its validity.

NORTHERN ESTONIA

Lahemaa National Park

Estonia's largest *rahvuspark* (national park), the 'Land of Bays' is 725 sq km of rural landscape and the perfect retreat from the nearby capital. A microcosm of Estonia's natural charms, the park takes in a stretch of deeply indented coast with several peninsulas and bays, plus 475 sq km of pine-fresh hinterland encompassing forest, lakes, rivers and peat bogs, and areas of historical and cultural interest.

There is an extensive network of forest trails for walkers, cyclists and even neo-knights on horseback. In winter, the park is transformed into a magical wonderland of snowy shores, frozen seas and sparkling black trees.

Loksa, the main town within the park, has a popular sandy beach but is otherwise rather down-at-heel. Võsu, the next largest settlement, is much nicer, with its long sandy beach and summertime bars. It fills up with young revellers in peak season, despite being just a somewhat overgrown village.

Palmse Manor HISTORIC BUILDING
(☑ 55599977; www.palmse.ee; adult/child €9/7; ⊙ 10am-6pm) Fully restored Palmse Manor is the showpiece of Lahemaa National Park, housing the visitor centre in its former stables. The pretty manor house (1720, rebuilt in the 1780s) is now a museum containing period furniture and clothing. Other estate buildings have also been restored and put to new use: the distillery is a hotel, the steward's residence is a guesthouse, the lakeside bathhouse is a summertime restaurant and the farm labourers' quarters became a tavern.

★ Merekalda APARTMENT €€
(☑ 323 8451; www.merekalda.ee; Neeme tee 2, Käsmu; r €49, apt €69-99; ⊙ May-Sep; 🅿 🛜) At the entrance to Käsmu, this peaceful retreat is set around a lovely large garden right on the bay. Ideally you'll plump for an apartment with a sea view and terrace, but you'll need to book ahead. Boat and bike hire are available.

Altja Kõrts ESTONIAN €€
(☑ 324 0070; www.palmse.ee; Altja; mains €10-16; ⊙ noon-8pm Apr-Sep) Set in a thatched, wooden building with a large terrace, this uber-rustic place is run by the same folks behind Palmse Manor. Operating in spring and summer, it serves delicious plates of traditional fare (baked pork with sauerkraut, for instance) at candlelit wooden tables. It's extremely atmospheric and a lot of fun.

❶ Information

Lahemaa National Park Visitor Centre
(☑ 329 5555; www.loodusegakoos.ee; ⊙ 9am-5pm daily mid-May–mid-Sep, 9am-5pm Mon-Fri mid-Sep–mid-May) This excellent centre stocks the essential map of Lahemaa (€1.90), as well as information on hiking trails, accommodation and guiding services. It's worth starting your

park visit with the free 17-minute film titled *Lahemaa – Nature and Man.*

ℹ Getting There & Away

If you have your own wheels, Lahemaa National Park is an easy 45-minute drive from Tallinn or Rakvere. Note that most roads within the park are narrow and unmarked. There is next to nothing in terms of street lighting, so plan accordingly if arriving later in the day.

Direct buses can get you from Rakvere to Palmse, Altja, Võsu and Käsmu – but you'll still have to hike a considerable amount to get deep into nature.

ℹ Getting Around

Lahemaa is best explored by car or bicycle as there are only limited bus connections within the park. The main bus routes through the park include Rakvere to Sagadi (€1.55 to €2.55, 45 minutes, one to four daily), Palmse (€1.75 to €2, 50 minutes, one daily), Altja (€1.90 to €2.25, one hour, most days), Võsu (€1.95 to €2.30, one hour, six daily) and Käsmu (€2.20 to €2.55, one hour, four daily).

SOUTHERN ESTONIA

Otepää

POP 1900

The small hilltop town of Otepää, 44km south of Tartu, is the centre of a picturesque area of forests, lakes and rivers. The district is beloved by Estonians for its natural beauty and its many possibilities for hiking, biking and swimming in summer, and cross-country skiing in winter. It's often referred to as Estonia's winter capital, and winter weekends here are busy and loads of fun. Some have even dubbed the area (tongue firmly in cheek) the 'Estonian Alps' – a reference not to its peaks but to its excellent ski trails. The 63km Tartu Ski Marathon kicks off here every February but even in summer you'll see professional athletes and enthusiasts hurtling around on roller skis.

The main part of Otepää is centred on the intersection of the Tartu, Võru and Valga highways, where you'll find the main square, shops and some patchy residential streets.

◉ Sights

Pühajärv
LAKE

According to legend, 3.5km-long, 8.5m-deep Pühajärv (Holy Lake) was formed from the tears of the mothers who lost their sons in a battle of the *Kalevipoeg* epic. Its five islands are said to be their burial mounds. Pagan associations linger, with major midsummer festivities held here every year. The popular sandy **beach** (Ranna tee) on the northeastern shore has waterslides, a swimming pontoon, a cafe and lifeguards in summer.

⌯ Sleeping

Murakas
HOTEL €€

(☑ 731 1410; www.murakas.ee; Valga mnt 23a; s/d €50/60; P ⅏ ⧈) With only 10 bedrooms, Murakas is more like a large, friendly guesthouse than a hotel. Stripey carpets, blonde wood and balconies give the rooms a fresh feel and there's a similarly breezy breakfast room downstairs (breakfast €7 per person).

GMP Clubhotel
APARTMENT €€€

(☑ 799 7000; www.clubhotel.ee; Tennisevälja 1; apt from €105; P ⧈) This super-slick lakeside block is decked out with kitchenettes, funky furniture, comfy beds and oversized photos. The icing on the cake is the luxurious pair of single-sex saunas on the top level, open in the evenings for those who fancy a sunset sweat.

✗ Eating

Pühajärve Restaurant
MODERN EUROPEAN €€

(☑ 799 7000; www.clubhotel.ee; Tennisevälja 1; mains €13-27; ⊙ noon-10pm) From the 1960s to 1980s this was Otepää's most famous restaurant, but when the Soviet Union went down the gurgler it followed in its wake. The opening of the attached Clubhotel gave Pühajärve a new lease of life and it now offers a tasty menu on a terrace above its namesake.

★ Mr Jakob
MODERN ESTONIAN €€€

(☑ 53753307; www.otepaagolf.ee; Mäha küla; mains €14-18; ⊙ noon-9pm daily, closed Mon-Thu Nov-Mar; ⧈) Otepää's best restaurant is hidden away at the golf club, 4km west of Pühajärv. The menu is as contemporary and playful as the decor, taking Estonian classics such as pork ribs and marinated herring fillets and producing something quite extraordinary. Add to that charming service and blissful views over the course and surrounding fields.

ℹ Information

Otepää Tourist Information Centre (☑ 766 1200; www.otepaa.eu; Tartu mnt 1; ⊙ 10am-5pm Mon-Fri, to 3pm Sat & Sun mid-May–mid-Sep, 10am-5pm Mon-Fri, to 2pm Sat rest of year) Well-informed staff distribute maps and brochures, and make recommendations for activities, guide services and lodging in the area.

ℹ️ Getting There & Away

The **bus station** (Tartu mnt 1) is next to the tourist office. Destinations include Tallinn (€13, 3½ hours, daily), Narva (€12, 4¼ hours, twice weekly), Tartu (€4.20, one hour, 10 daily), Sangaste (€1.70, 30 minutes, six daily) and Valga (€3.30, one hour, four daily).

Tartu

POP 98,000

Tartu lays claim to being Estonia's spiritual capital, with locals talking about a special Tartu *vaim* (spirit), created by the time-stands-still feel of its wooden houses and stately buildings, and the beauty of its parks and riverfront. Tartu was the cradle of Estonia's 19th-century national revival, and escaped Soviet town planning to a greater degree than Tallinn. Its handsome centre is lined with classically designed 18th-century buildings, many of which have been put to innovative uses.

Small and provincial, with the tranquil Emajõgi River flowing through it, Tartu is Estonia's premier university town; students comprise nearly a seventh of the population. This injects a boisterous vitality into the leafy, historic setting and grants it a vibrant nightlife for a city of its size. On long summer nights, those students who haven't abandoned the city for the beach can be found on the hill behind the Town Hall, flirting and drinking.

⊙ Sights

★ Estonian Print & Paper Museum   MUSEUM

(Eesti Trüki- ja Paberimuuseum; ☑ 5682 8117; www.trykimuuseum.ee; Kastani 48f; adult/student €8/4; ⊙ noon-6pm Wed-Sun) A treat for word nerds, design hounds and print junkies alike, this interactive museum focuses on the history of printing and paper-making. Machinery from across the ages is on permanent display, most of it kept in working order, and there's a gallery with rotating exhibitions plus a small selection of handmade notebooks for sale. Tickets include an hour-long tour in English, complete with demonstrations and the opportunity to make your own paper or prints on one of the antique presses.

University of Tartu Museum   MUSEUM

(Tartu Ülikool muuseum; ☑ 737 5674; www.muuseum.ut.ee; Lossi 25; adult/child €5/4; ⊙ 10am-6pm Tue-Sun May-Sep, 11am-5pm Wed-Sun Oct-Apr) Atop Toomemägi are the ruins of a Gothic cathedral, originally built by German knights in the 13th century. It was substantially rebuilt in the 15th century, despoiled during the Reformation in 1525, used as a barn, and partly rebuilt between 1804 and 1809 to house the university library, and is now a museum. Inside there are a range of interesting exhibits chronicling student life.

★ Estonian National Museum   MUSEUM

(Eesti rahva muuseum; ☑ 736 3051; www.erm.ee; Muuseumi tee 2; adult/child €14/10; ⊙ 10am-6pm Tue & Thu-Sun, 10am-8pm Wed) This immense, low-slung, architectural showcase is a striking sight and had both Estonian patriots and architecture-lovers purring when it opened in late 2016. The permanent exhibition covers national prehistory and history in some detail. Fittingly, for a museum built over a former Soviet airstrip, the Russian occupation is given in-depth treatment, while the 'Echo of the Urals' exhibition gives an overview of the various peoples that speak tongues in the Estonian language family. There's also a restaurant and cafe.

Town Hall Square   SQUARE

(Raekoja plats) Tartu's main square is lined with grand buildings and echoes with the chink of glasses and plates in summer. The centrepiece is the Town Hall itself, fronted by a statue of students kissing under a spouting umbrella. On the south side of the square, look out for the communist hammer-and-sickle relief that still remains on the facade of No 5.

Aparaaditehas   AREA

(☑ 56674704; www.aparaaditehas.ee; Kastani 42) Aparaaditehas (the Widget Factory) is an old 14,000-sq-metre industrial complex that once functioned as a factory for refrigeration equipment and secret submarine parts during the Soviet era. It underwent development in 2014 and has since been resurrected as Tartu's hippest dining, drinking, shopping and cultural hub, akin to the extremely popular Telliskivi Creative City in Tallinn.

🛏️ Sleeping

★ Hektor Design Hostel   HOSTEL €

(☑ 740 5100; www.hektorhostels.com; Riia mnt 26; dm/s/d from €15/31/35) A 1950s warehouse coated charcoal-grey and enlivened with splashes of vivid colour, Hektor raises the bar for hostels. Modern, functional design and super-cosy beds are just the start – there's also a gym, a yoga room and sauna, plus a movie projector and laundry room. Little more expensive than dorms, private rooms have fridges and microwaves, and some their own bathrooms.

Villa Margaretha   BOUTIQUE HOTEL **€€**
(✆731 1820; www.margaretha.ee; Tähe 11/13; s €55-85, d €65-95, ste €175; P🌐) Like something out of a fairy tale, this wooden art-nouveau house has a sweet little turret and romantic rooms decked out with sleigh beds and artfully draped fabrics. The cheaper rooms in the modern extension at the rear are bland in comparison. It's a little away from the action but still within walking distance of Old Town.

Tampere Maja   GUESTHOUSE **€€**
(✆738 6300; www.tamperemaja.ee; Jaani 4; s/d/tr/q from €54/84/110/132; P🅿@🌐) With strong links to the Finnish city of Tampere (Tartu's sister city), this cosy guesthouse features seven warm, light-filled guest rooms in a range of sizes. Breakfast is included and each room has access to cooking facilities. And it wouldn't be Finnish if it didn't offer an authentic sauna (one to four people €15; open to nonguests).

Antonius Hotel   HOTEL **€€€**
(✆737 0377; www.hotelantonius.ee; Ülikooli 15; s/d/ste from €95/120/220; ✳🌐) Sitting plumb opposite the main university building, this first-rate 18-room boutique hotel is loaded with antiques and period features. Breakfast is served in the 18th-century vaulted cellar, which in the evening morphs into a top-notch restaurant.

✖ Eating

Aparaat   INTERNATIONAL **€**
(✆730 3090; www.aparaadiresto.ee; Aparaaditehas, Kastani 42; mains €5-14; hnoon-11pm Mon-Thu, to 1am Fri-Sat, to 6pm Sun) Set in the courtyard of Aparaaditehas (p347), Tartu's hipster enclave, Aparaat serves simple and well-executed food to share, socialise over, and drink wine with. The interior makes little attempt to hide its industrial ancestry, with stripped-brick walls and big, functional windows, but no-one seems to mind – lounging at bare wooden tables sipping negronis and nibbling at burgers and sharing plates.

Meat Market   STEAK **€€€**
(✆653 3455; www.meatmarket.ee; Küütri 3; mains €9-19; ⊙noon-11pm Mon-Thu, to 1am Fri & Sat, to 10pm Sun) The name says it all, with dishes ranging from standards like sirloin with truffle butter or black-garlic lamb chops, to bull testicles or wild goose with duck heart sauce. The veggie accompaniments (think buckthorn-potato purée and mushroom pâté) are excellent too. It's open late for cocktails.

ℹ Information

Tartu Tourist Information Centre (✆744 2111; www.visittartu.com; Town Hall, Raekoja plats; ⊙9am-6pm Mon, 9am-5pm tue-Fri, 10am-2pm Sat mid-Sep–mid-May, shorter hours rest of year) Stocks local maps and brochures, books accommodation and tour guides, and has free internet access.

ℹ Getting There & Away

Tartu's beautifully restored wooden **train station** (✆673 7400; www.elron.ee; Vaksali 6), built in 1877, is 1.5km southwest of the Old Town at the end of Kuperjanovi street. Six express (two-hour) and four regular (2½-hour) services head to Tallinn daily (both €12), and there are also three trains a day to Sangaste (€4.20, one hour) and Valga (€4.90, 70 minutes).

ℹ Getting Around

Tartu is easily explored on foot but there is also a local bus service. You can buy a single-use ticket from any kiosk (€0.83) or from the bus driver (€1.50); be sure to validate the ticket once on board or risk a fine. Kiosks also sell day passes (€2.50).

WESTERN ESTONIA & THE ISLANDS

Pärnu

POP 52,000

Local families, hormone-sozzled youths and German, Swedish and Finnish holidaymakers join together in a collective prayer for sunny weather while strolling the beaches, sprawling parks and picturesque historic centre of Pärnu (*pair*-nu), Estonia's premier seaside resort. In these parts, the name Pärnu is synonymous with fun in the sun; one hyperbolic local described it to us as 'Estonia's Miami', but it's usually called by its slightly more prosaic moniker, the nation's 'summer capital'.

In truth, most of Pärnu is quite docile, with leafy streets and expansive parks intermingling with turn-of-the-20th-century villas that reflect the town's fashionable, more decorous past. Older visitors from Finland and the former Soviet Union still visit, seeking rest, rejuvenation and Pärnu's vaunted mud treatments.

Sights

★ Pärnu Beach
BEACH

Pärnu's long, wide, sandy beach – sprinkled with volleyball courts, cafes and changing cubicles – is easily the city's main draw. A curving path stretches along the sand, lined with fountains, park benches and an excellent playground. Early-20th-century buildings are strung along Ranna pst, the avenue that runs parallel to the beach. Across the road, the formal gardens of **Rannapark** are ideal for a summertime picnic.

★ Museum of New Art
GALLERY

(Uue kunstimuuseum; ☑443 0772; www.mona. ee; Esplanaadi 10; adult/child €4/2; ⊙9am-9pm Jun-Aug, 9am-7pm Sep-May) Pärnu's former Communist Party headquarters now houses one of Estonia's edgiest galleries. As part of its commitment to pushing the cultural envelope, it stages an international nude art exhibition every summer. The gallery also hosts the annual **Pärnu Film Festival**, founded by film-maker Mark Soosaar.

Sleeping

Inge Villa
GUESTHOUSE €€

(☑443 8510; www.ingevilla.fi; Kaarli 20; s/d/ ste €56/70/82; ❀☺) Describing itself as a 'Swedish-Estonian villa hotel', low-key and lovely Inge Villa occupies a prime patch of real estate near the beach. Its 11 rooms are simply decorated in muted tones with Nordic minimalism to the fore. The garden, lounge and sauna seal the deal.

Villa Ammende
HOTEL €€€

(☑447 3888; www.ammende.ee; Mere pst 7; s/d/ ste €225/275/475; ℗❀☺) Luxury abounds in this refurbished 1904 art-nouveau mansion, which lords it over handsomely manicured grounds. The gorgeous exterior – looking like a Paris metro stop writ large – is matched by an elegant lobby and individually antique-furnished rooms. Rooms in the gardener's house are more affordable but lack a little of the wow factor. It's a lot cheaper outside of July.

ⓘ Information

Pärnu Tourist Information Centre (☑447 3000; www.visitparnu.com; Uus 4; ⊙9am-6pm mid-May–mid-Sep, 9am-5pm Mon-Fri, 10am-2pm Sat & Sun mid-Sep–mid-May) A very helpful centre stocking maps and brochures, booking accommodation and rental cars (for a small fee), and providing a left-luggage service (per day €2). There's a small gallery attached as well as a toilet and showers.

ⓘ Getting There & Away

Three daily trains run between Tallinn and Pärnu (€7.90, 2¼ hours), but this isn't a great option given that **Pärnu station** (Liivi tee) is an inconvenient 5km east of the town centre in a spot that's difficult to find and to access, on a major road. There's no station office; buy tickets on the train. Note, if you're coming from Tallinn, make sure you get in the right carriages, as part of the train unhooks at Lelle and continues on a different track to Viljandi.

ⓘ Getting Around

There are local buses but given that all the sights are within walking distance of each other, you probably won't need to bother with them. Tickets for local journeys are €0.64 if pre-purchased or €1 from the driver.

Muhu
POP 1560

Connected to Saaremaa by a 2.5km causeway, the island of Muhu has the undeserved reputation as the 'doormat' for the bigger island – lots of people passing through on their way from the ferry, but few stopping. In fact, Estonia's third-biggest island offers plenty of excuses to hang around, including one of the country's best restaurants and some excellent accommodation options.

Sights

Muhu Museum
MUSEUM

(☑454 8872; www.muhumuuseum.ee; Koguva; adult/concession €4/3; ⊙9am-6pm mid-May– mid-Sep, 10am-5pm Tue-Sat rest of year) Koguva, 6km off the main road on the western tip of Muhu, is an exceptionally well-preserved, old-fashioned island village, now protected as an open-air museum. One ticket allows you to wander through an old schoolhouse, a house displaying beautiful traditional textiles from the area (including painstakingly detailed folk costumes) and a farm that was the ancestral home of author Juhan Smuul

(1922–71). You can poke around various farm buildings, one of which contains a collection of Singer sewing machines.

⊨ Sleeping

★ Pädaste Manor HOTEL €€€
(☑ 454 8800; www.padaste.ee; Pädaste; r €254-481, ste €416-875; ☺ Mar-Oct; 🅿🛜) If money's no object, here's where to part with it. This manicured bayside estate encompasses the restored manor house (14 rooms and a fine-dining restaurant), a stone carriage house (nine rooms and a spa centre) and a separate stone 'sea house' brasserie. The attention to detail is second-to-none, from the pop-up TVs to the antique furnishings and Muhu embroidery.

ℹ Getting There & Away

Buses take the ferry from the mainland and continue through to Saaremaa via the causeway, stopping along the main road. Some Kuressaare–Kuivastu services also divert to Koguva and Pädaste on weekdays. Major destinations include Tallinn (€12 to €14, three hours, 15 daily), Tartu (€17, five hours, two daily), Viljandi (€15, four hours, two daily), Pärnu (€8.80, 2½ hours, two daily) and Kuressaare (€5 to €5.60, one hour, 27 daily).

Saaremaa

POP 33,950

To Estonians, Saaremaa (literally 'island land') is synonymous with space, spruce and fresh air – and bottled water, vodka and killer beer. Estonia's largest island (roughly the size of Luxembourg) is still substantially covered in forests of pine, spruce and juniper, while its windmills, lighthouses and tiny villages seem largely unbothered by the passage of time.

Kuressaare, the capital of Saaremaa, is on the south coast (75km from the Muhu ferry terminal) and is a natural base for visitors. It's here among the upmarket hotels that you'll understand where the island got its nickname, 'Spa-remaa'. When the long days arrive, so too do the Finns and Swedes, jostling for beach and sauna space with Estonian urban-escapees.

ℹ Getting There & Away

Most travellers reach Saaremaa by taking the ferry from Virtsu to Muhu and then driving in a personal vehicle or by bus across the 2.5km causeway connecting the islands.

ℹ Getting Around

There are more than 400km of paved roads on Saaremaa and many more dirt roads. Hitching is not uncommon on the main routes but you'll need time on your hands; there's not much traffic on minor roads.

Local buses putter around the island, but not very frequently. The main terminus is **Kuressaare bus station** (Kuressaare Bussijaam; ☑ 453 1661; www.bussipilet.ee; Pihtla tee 2) and there's a route planner online at www.bussipilet.ee.

Kuressaare

POP 13,540

What passes for the big smoke in these parts, Kuressaare has a picturesque town centre with leafy streets and a magnificent castle rising up in its midst, surrounded by the usual scrappy sprawl of housing and light industry. The town built a reputation as a health centre as early as the 19th century, when the ameliorative properties of its coastal mud were discovered and the first spas opened. Now they're a dime a dozen, ranging from Eastern-bloc sanatoriums to sleek and stylish resorts.

Apart from the castle, the best of Kuressaare's historic buildings are grouped around the central square, Keskväljak. The tourist office is housed in the town hall (1670), a baroque building guarded by a fine pair of stone lions. Directly across the square the Vaekoja pub inhabits a former weigh-house, also from the 17th century.

◉ Sights

★ Kuressaare Castle CASTLE
(www.saaremaamuuseum.ee) Majestic Kuressaare Castle stands facing the sea at the southern end of the town, on an artificial island ringed by a moat. It's the best-preserved castle in the Baltic and the region's only medieval stone castle that has remained intact. The castle grounds are open to the public at all times but to visit the keep you'll need to buy a ticket to Saaremaa Museum.

Saaremaa Museum MUSEUM
(☑ 455 4463; www.saaremaamuuseum.ee; adult/concession €6/3; ☺ 10am-7pm May-Aug, 11am-6pm Wed-Sun Sep-Apr) Occupying the keep of Kuressaare Castle, this museum is devoted to the island's nature and history. A large part of the fun is exploring the warren of chambers, halls, passages and stairways, apt to fuel anyone's *Game of Thrones* fantasies.

One room near the bishop's chamber looks down to a dungeon where, according to legend, condemned prisoners were dispatched to be devoured by hungry lions (recorded growls reinforce the mental image).

🛌 Sleeping

★ Ekesparre
BOUTIQUE HOTEL €€€

(☑ 453 8778; www.ekesparre.ee; Lossi 27; r €175-215; ☺ Apr-Oct; 🅿🛜) Holding pole position on the castle grounds, this elegant 10-room hotel has been returned to its art-nouveau glory. Period wallpaper and carpet, Tiffany lamps and a smattering of orchids add to the refined, clubby atmosphere, while the 3rd-floor guests' library is a gem. As you'd expect from the price, it's a polished operator.

★ Georg Ots Spa Hotel
HOTEL €€€

(Gospa; ☑ 455 0000; www.gospa.ee; Tori 2; r €185-225, ste €295; 🅿✳🛜♨) Named after a renowned Estonian opera singer, Gospa has modern rooms with wildly striped carpet, enormous king-sized beds and a warm but minimalist design. Most rooms have balconies, and there's a fitness centre and excellent spa centre, including a pool and multiple saunas. Separate freestanding 'residences' are also available, and families are very well catered to. Prices vary widely.

🍴 Eating

★ Retro
CAFE €€

(☑ 5683 8400; www.kohvikretro.ee; Lossi 5; mains €9-14; ☺ noon-9pm Mon-Thu, to midnight Fri & Sat; 🛜🍴) The menu at this hip little cafe-bar is deceptively simple (pasta, burgers, wraps, grilled fish), but Retro takes things to the next level, making its own pasta and burger buns, and using the best fresh, local produce. Desserts are delicious, too. There's also a great selection of Estonian craft beer, perfect for supping on the large rear terrace.

Ku Kuu
MODERN EUROPEAN €€

(☑ 453 9749; www.kuressaarekuursaal.ee; Lossipark 1; mains €8-15; ☺ 11am-midnight May–mid-Sep; 🛜) Occupying the elegant Spa Hall from which it takes its name (Ku Kuu is short for Kuressaare Kuursaal), this is Saaremaa's loveliest dining room. The wood panelling and panes of coloured glass provide an atmospheric backdrop for a tasty menu of seafood and island produce, prepared with a strong French accent.

ℹ Information

Kuressaare Tourist Office (☑ 453 3120; www.kuressaare.ee; Tallinna 2; ☺ 9am-6pm Mon-Fri, 10am-4pm Sat & Sun mid-May–mid-Sep, 9am-5pm Mon-Fri rest of year) Inside the old town hall, it sells maps and guides, arranges accommodation and has information on boat trips and island tours.

SURVIVAL GUIDE

ℹ Directory A–Z

ACCOMMODATION
During July and August, the best accommodation books up quickly in Tallinn, which is especially busy on most weekends. Book a month ahead anytime from May to September.

High season in Estonia means summer. Prices drop substantially at other times. The exception is Otepää, when there's also a corresponding peak in winter.

LEGAL MATTERS
After dark, pedestrians are required to wear reflectors in order to remain visible to passing drivers. This is regularly enforced by police and violators may face a fine up to €40.

LGBTIQ+ TRAVELLERS
Estonia is a fairly tolerant and safe home to its gay and lesbian citizens – certainly much more so than its neighbours. Unfortunately, that general acceptance hasn't translated into a wildly exciting scene (only Tallinn has gay venues).

OPENING HOURS
Opening hours vary considerably throughout the year, due to the stark contrast between summer and winter – some places close entirely from October to March. The hours indicated here are during high summer season (June to August) when most places are open, and working hours are longest.

Banks 9am or 10am to 5pm or 6pm Monday to Friday

Restaurants noon to midnight

Cafes 8am to 4pm

Bars noon to midnight

Museums 10am to 6pm

Shops 10am to 6pm Monday to Friday, 11am to 5pm Saturday and Sunday

Shopping Centres 9am to 9pm

Supermarkets 8am to 11pm

PUBLIC HOLIDAYS

New Year's Day (Uusaasta) 1 January

Independence Day (Iseseisvuspäev; Anniversary of 1918 declaration) 24 February

Good Friday (Suur reede) March/April

Easter Sunday (Lihavõtted) March/April

Spring Day (Kevadpüha) 1 May

Pentecost (Nelipühade) Seventh Sunday after Easter (May/June)

Victory Day (Võidupüha; commemorating the anniversary of the Battle of Võnnu, 1919); 23 June

St John's Day (Jaanipäev, Midsummer's Day) 24 June

Day of Restoration of Independence (Taasiseseisvumispäev; marking the country's return to Independence in 1991); 20 August

Christmas Eve (Jõululaupäev) 24 December

Christmas Day (Jõulupüha) 25 December

Boxing Day (Teine jõulupüha) 26 December

Taken together, Victory Day and St John's Day are the excuse for a week-long midsummer break for many people.

TELEPHONE

There are no area codes in Estonia; if you're calling anywhere within the country, just dial the number as it's listed. All landline phone numbers have seven digits; mobile (cell) numbers have seven or eight digits and begin with 5. Estonia's country code is 372. To make a collect call dial 16116, followed by the desired number. To make an international call, dial 00 before the country code.

Public telephones accept chip cards, available at post offices, hotels and most kiosks. For placing calls outside Estonia, an international telephone card with a pin, available at many kiosks and supermarkets, is better value. Note that these cards can only be used from landlines, not mobile phones.

🛈 Getting There & Away

ENTERING THE COUNTRY

Entering Estonia from other parts of the EU is usually a breeze – no border checkpoints and no customs – thanks to the Schengen Agreement. If arriving from outside the Schengen area, old-fashioned travel document and customs checks are required. For more information, check the Estonian Foreign Ministry's website at www.vm.ee

AIR

The following airlines operate services to Tallinn year-round, with additional routes and airlines added in summer:

airBaltic (www.airbaltic.com) Multiple daily flights between Tallinn and Rīga.

Finnair (www.finnair.ee) Up to seven flights a day between Helsinki and Tallinn, and daily flights between Helsinki and Tartu.

LAND

Bus

The following bus companies all have services between Estonia and the other Baltic states:

Ecolines (www.ecolines.net) Major routes: Tallinn–Pärnu–Rīga (seven daily), six of which continue on to Vilnius; Tallinn–St Petersburg (six daily); Tartu–Valga–Rīga (two daily); Vilnius–Rīga–Tartu–Narva–St Petersburg (four daily).

Lux Express & Simple Express (www.luxexpress.eu) Major routes: Tallinn–Pärnu–Rīga (up to 13 daily), eight of which continue on to Panevėžys and Vilnius; Tallinn–Rakvere–Sillamäe–Narva–St Petersburg (four daily); Tallinn–Tartu–Võru–Moscow (daily); Rīga–Valmiera–Tartu–Sillamäe–Narva–St Petersburg (nine to 10 daily).

Eurolines (www.eurolines.lt) Two daily Tallinn–Pärnu–Rīga–Panevėžys–Vilnius–Kaunas–Warsaw buses.

Car & Motorcycle

With the Schengen agreement, there are no border checks when driving between Estonia and Latvia. There's usually no problem taking hire cars across the border but you'll need to let the rental company know at the time of hire if you intend to do so; some companies will charge an additional fee.

Train

Valga is the terminus for both the Estonian and Latvian rail systems, but the train services don't connect up. From Valga, Estonian trains operated by **Elron** (www.elron.ee) head to Elva, Tartu and Tallinn, while Latvian trains operated by **Pasažieru vilciens** (www.pv.lv) head to Valmiera, Cēsis, Sigulda and Rīga. There are also direct trains to Tallinn from St Petersburg and Moscow.

SEA

Eckerö Line (📞 6000 4300; www.eckeroline.fi; Passenger Terminal A, Vanasadam; adult/child/car from €15/10/19; 🕐 ticket office 8.30am-7pm Mon-Fri, to 3pm Sat & Sun) Twice-daily car ferry from Helsinki to Tallinn (2½ hours).

Linda Line (📞 699 9331; www.lindaliini.ee; Patarei Sadam, Linnahall Terminal) Smaller and faster vessels operate from late March to late December.

Tallink (📞 631 8320; www.tallink.com; Terminal D, Lootsi 13) Daily services between Tallinn and Helsinki plus an overnight ferry to Stockholm and Tallinn, via the Åland islands.

Viking Line (666 3966; www.vikingline.com; Terminal A, Vanasadam; passenger & vehicle from €42) At least four daily car ferries between Helsinki and Tallinn (2½ hours).

❶ Getting Around

AIR

There is very little in the way of domestic flights in Estonia. Direct flights run from Tallinn to Kuressaare and Tallinn to Kärdla, operated by **Saartelennuliinid** (www.saartelennuliinid.ee) twice daily on weekdays and once on Saturdays and Sundays. Other flights from Tallinn to the rest of the country require a connection outside of Estonia.

In winter, when sea travel is impossible, **Luftverkehr Friesland-Harle** (LFH, www.lendame. ee) operates flights between Pärnu and Kuressaare to the island of Ruhnu on Thursdays, Fridays and Sundays.

BOAT

There are ferries between mainland Estonia and its many islands, Saaremaa, Hiiumaa, Kihnu, Ruhnu and Vormsi being the most frequented by visitors. **Praamid** (www.praamid.ee) and **Kihnu**

Veeteed (www.veeteed.com) are the major operators – check websites for exact routes and prices.

BUS

The national bus network is extensive, linking all the major cities to each other and the smaller towns to their regional hubs. All services are summarised on the extremely handy **T pilet** (www.tpilet.ee) site.

CAR & MOTORCYCLE

Estonian roads are generally very good and driving is easy. In rural areas, particularly on the islands, some roads are unsealed and without lines indicating lanes, but they're usually kept in good condition.

TRAIN

Train services have been steadily improving in recent years. Domestic routes are run by **Elron** (www.elron.ee) but it's also possible to travel between Tallinn and Narva on the Russian-bound services run by **GoRail** (www.gorail.ee).

The major domestic routes are Tallinn–Rakvere (five daily, with four continuing to Narva), Tallinn–Tartu (11 daily), Tallinn–Viljandi (five daily) and Tartu–Sangaste–Valga (four daily).

ESTONIA SURVIVAL GUIDE

Finland

POP 5.52 MILLION

Best Places to Eat

➜ Rakas (p368)

➜ Smor (p363)

➜ Kuu (p360)

➜ Vanha Kauppahalli (p359)

➜ Aanaar (p370)

Best Places to Stay

➜ Arctic Treehouse Hotel (p368)

➜ Clarion Hotel Helsinki (p358)

➜ Hotel F6 (p359)

➜ Wilderness Hotel Inari (p370)

➜ Lossiranta Lodge (p366)

➜ Dream Hostel (p364)

Why Go?

Inspired design, technology and epicurean scenes meet epic stretches of wilderness here in Europe's deep north, where summer's endless light balances winter's eerie frozen magic.

Whatever the season, there's something pure in the Finnish air and spirit that's vital and exciting. With towering forests, speckled by picture-perfect lakes, Suomi (Finnish for Finland) offers some of Europe's best hiking, kayaking and canoeing. After the snowfall, pursuits include skiing, sledding with dogs or reindeer, snowmobiling or trekking across snowy solitudes, lit by a beautiful, pale winter sun. And of course, there's catching the majestic aurora borealis (Northern Lights).

Vibrant cities stock the south, headlined by the capital, Helsinki, a cutting-edge urban space with world-renowned design and music scenes where 'new Suomi' cuisine is flourishing, bringing locally foraged flavours to the fore. Beyond Helsinki, Tampere and Turku are especially engaging, with spirited university-student populations.

When to Go
Helsinki

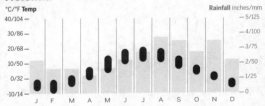

Mar–Apr There's still plenty of snow, but enough daylight to enjoy winter sports.

Jul Everlasting daylight, countless festivals and summer budget accommodation.

Sep The stunning *ruska* (autumn colours) season make this prime hiking time up north.

Entering the Country

Entering Finland is a breeze and you'll experience no problems if your papers are in order. Most Western nationals don't need a tourist visa for stays of less than three months.

Finland is easily accessed from the rest of Europe and beyond. There are direct flights from numerous destinations, while Baltic ferries are another good option.

Flights, cars and tours can be booked online at www.lonelyplanet.com/bookings.

ITINERARIES

One Week

Helsinki (p357) demands at least a couple of days and is a good base for a day trip to Tallinn (Estonia; p337) or Porvoo (p361). In summer head to the Lakeland and explore Savonlinna (p366). In winter take an overnight train or flight to Lapland (p367), visiting Santa, exploring Sámi culture and mushing with huskies. A Helsinki–Savonlinna–Rovaniemi–Helsinki route is a good option.

Two Weeks

Spend a few days in Helsinki (p357) and Porvoo (p361), visit the harbour town of Turku (p362) and lively Tampere (p364). Next stop is Savonlinna (p366) in the beautiful Lakeland. Head up to Rovaniemi (p367), and perhaps as far north as the Sámi capital Inari (p369). You could also fit in a summer festival, some hiking, or a quick cycling trip to Åland (p363).

Essential Food & Drink

Coffee Eight or nine cups a day is about right, best accompanied with a *pulla* (cardamom-flavoured pastry).

Offbeat meats Unusual meats appear on menus: reindeer is a staple up north; elk and bear are available during autumn's hunting season.

Fresh food The kauppahalli (market hall) offers a stunning array of produce. In summer, stalls at the kauppatori (market square) sell delicious fresh vegetables and fruit.

Gastronomy Helsinki is the best venue for fabulous New Suomi cuisine, with sumptuous, inventive degustation menus presenting traditional Finnish ingredients in crest-of-the-wave ways.

Alcoholic drinks Beer is a staple, and great microbreweries are on the increase. Finns also love dissolving things in vodka – try a shot of *salmiakkikossu* (which has a salty-liquorice flavour) or *fisu* (Fisherman's Friend flavour).

Fish Salmon is ubiquitous, and tasty lake fish include Arctic char, lavaret, pike-perch and scrumptious fried *muikku* (vendace).

Brunssi Weekend *brunssi* (brunch) is increasingly popular in Helsinki and other cities. Book ahead for these sumptuous all-you-can-eat spreads.

AT A GLANCE

Area 338,145 sq km

Capital Helsinki

Country Code ☑ 358

Currency euro (€)

Emergency ☑ 112

Languages Finnish, Swedish, Sámi languages

Time Eastern European Time (EET; UTC/GMT plus two hours)

Visas Generally not required for stays of up to 90 days; some nationalities will need a Schengen visa.

FINLAND

Sleeping Price Ranges

The following price ranges refer to a double room in high season.

€ less than €70

€€ €70–€160

€€€ more than €160

Eating Price Ranges

The following price ranges refer to a standard main course.

€ less than €17

€€ €17–€27

€€€ more than €27

Finland Highlights

1 Helsinki (p357) Exploring Finland's harbourside capital, a creative melting pot for the latest in Finnish food, drink, design and nightlife.

2 Savonlinna (p366) Marvelling at the shimmering lakescapes of this picturesque town and catching top-quality opera in its medieval castle.

3 Turku (p362) Combining history with contemporary culture in one of Finland's most dynamic and engaging cities.

4 Rovaniemi (p367) Crossing the Arctic Circle, hitting the awesome Arktikum museum, and visiting Santa in his grotto.

5 Inari (p369) Learning about Sámi culture, husky-sledding and meeting reindeer in this northern Lapland village.

HELSINKI

☑ 09 / POP 643,272

It's fitting that harbourside Helsinki, capital of a country with such watery geography, entwines so spectacularly with the Baltic's bays, inlets and islands.

While Helsinki can seem a younger sibling to the Scandinavian capitals, it's the one that went to art school, scorns pop music and works in a cutting-edge studio. The design scene here is one of the most electrifying in the world today, with boutiques, workshops and galleries proliferating in the Design District, Helsinki's thoroughfares and intriguing backstreets. The city's foodie scene is also flourishing, with hip eateries offering locally sourced tasting menus, and craft-beer bars, coffee roasteries and microdistilleries popping up at dizzying speed.

◎ Sights

Tuomiokirkko
CHURCH

(Lutheran Cathedral; www.helsinginseurakunnat.fi; Unioninkatu 29; ⊘ 9am-midnight Jun-Aug, to 6pm Sep-May) FREE One of CL Engel's finest creations, the chalk-white neoclassical Lutheran cathedral presides over Senaatintori. Created to serve as a reminder of God's supremacy, its high flight of stairs is now a popular meeting place. Zinc statues of the 12 Apostles guard the city from the roof of the church. The spartan, almost mausoleum-like interior has little ornamentation under the lofty dome apart from an altar painting and three stern statues of Reformation heroes Luther, Melanchthon and Mikael Agricola.

★ Ateneum
GALLERY

(☑ 029-450-0401; www.ateneum.fi; Kaivokatu 2; adult/child €15/free; ⊘ 10am-6pm Tue & Fri, to 8pm Wed & Thu, to 5pm Sat & Sun) Occupying a palatial 1887 neo-Rennaisance building, Finland's premier art gallery offers a crash course in the nation's art. It houses Finnish paintings and sculptures from the 'golden age' of the late 19th century through to the 1950s, including works by Albert Edelfelt, Hugo Simberg, Helene Schjerfbeck, the von Wright brothers and Pekka Halonen. Pride of place goes to the prolific Akseli Gallen-Kallela's triptych from the Finnish national epic, the *Kalevala,* depicting Väinämöinen's pursuit of the maiden Aino.

Helsinki Art Museum
MUSEUM

(HAM; ☑ 09-3108-7001; www.hamhelsinki.fi; Eteläinen Rautatiekatu 8; adult/child €12/free; ⊘ 11am-7pm Tue-Sun) Inside the **Tennispalatsi** (Tennis Palace; Eteläinen Rautatiekatu), Helsinki's contemporary-art museum oversees 9000 works, including 3500 citywide public artworks. The overwhelming majority of its 20th- and 21st-century works are by Finnish artists; it also presents rotating exhibitions by emerging artists. Exhibits change every seven weeks. There's always at least one free exhibition that doesn't require a ticket to the museum's main section.

Kamppi Chapel
CHAPEL

(www.helsinginseurakunnat.fi; Simonkatu 7; ⊘ 8am-8pm Mon-Fri, 10am-6pm Sat & Sun) Built in 2012 by Helsinki architectural firm K2S, this exquisite, ultracontemporary curvilinear chapel is constructed from wood (wax-treated spruce outside, oiled alder planks inside, with pews crafted from ash) and offers quiet contemplation in cocoon-like surrounds. Its altar cross is the work of blacksmith Antti Nieminen. Known as the Chapel of Silence, the Lutheran chapel is ecumenical and welcomes people of all (or no) faiths. True to its name, inside is the purest silence you'll find in Helsinki.

★ Suomenlinna
FORTRESS

(Sveaborg; www.suomenlinna.fi) Suomenlinna, the 'fortress of Finland', straddles a cluster of car-free islands connected by bridges. The Unesco World Heritage Site was originally built by the Swedes as Sveaborg in the mid-18th century. Several museums, former bunkers and fortress walls, as well as Finland's only remaining WWII submarine, are fascinating to explore. Cafes and picnic spots are plentiful.

Ferries (www.hsl.fi; day ticket €5, 15 minutes, four hourly, fewer in winter) depart from the passenger quay at Helsinki's **kauppatori**.

✦ Activities

★ Allas Sea Pool
SWIMMING

(www.allasseapool.fi; Katajanokanlaituri 2; day ticket adult/child €14/7, towel rental €5; ⊘ 6.30am-9pm Mon-Fri, 9am-9pm Sat, 9am-8pm Sun) Constructed from Finnish fir, this 2016-built swimming complex sits right on the harbour against a spectacular city backdrop. It incorporates a bracing Baltic seawater pool, two freshwater pools – one for adults, one for kids; both heated to 27°C (80.6°F) – and three saunas (male, female and mixed). Regular events include DJs or full-moon all-night nude swimming. Its restaurant serves Nordic cuisine.

★ Kotiharjun Sauna
SAUNA

(☑ 09-753-1535; www.kotiharjunsauna.fi; Harjutorinkatu 1; adult/child €13/7; ⊘ 2-9.30pm Tue-Sun)

Helsinki

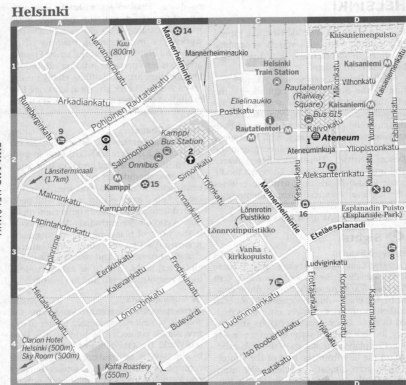

Helsinki's only original traditional public wood-fired sauna dates back to 1928. It's a classic experience, where you can also get a scrub down and massage (from €30). There are separate saunas for men and women; bring your own towel or rent one (€3). It's a 150m stroll southwest of the Sörnäinen metro station.

🛏 Sleeping

From mid-May to mid-August bookings are strongly advisable, although July is a quieter time for business and high-end hotels.

Hostel Diana Park   HOSTEL €

(☎ 09-642-169; www.dianapark.fi; Uudenmaankatu 9; dm €28-33, s/d from €58/68; 🛜) More like a guesthouse, Helsinki's most characterful and laid-back hostel occupies the 3rd (top) floor of a walk-up building in a lively street of bars and restaurants. Its 50 beds are spread across 15 rooms; all share bathrooms but have in-room sinks. Private rooms offer

more peace and there's a great lounge for socialising. Breakfast costs €7.

★ Clarion Hotel Helsinki   HOTEL €€

(☎ 010-850-3820; www.nordicchoicehotels.com/hotels/finland/helsinki/clarion-hotel-helsinki; Tyynenmerenkatu 2; d/ste from €118/350; 🛜🏊; 🚇 Jätkäsaari) Arguably Helsinki's trendiest place to stay, this architectural showpiece has pleasing rooms with supermodern everything. All have views, but the higher floors (more expensive) are best. Our only complaint – it's a pity the windows aren't a bit bigger. The rooftop swimming pool is almost as cool as the rooftop bar, **Sky Room** (⊘ 4pm-midnight Mon-Thu, 3pm-2am Fri & Sat, 3-9pm Sun).

Hotelli Helka   HOTEL €€

(☎ 09-613-580; www.hotelhelka.com; Pohjoinen Rautatiekatu 23; s/d/ste from €138/158/228; 🅿🛜) One of Helsinki's best midrange hotels, the Helka has friendly staff and excellent facilities, including parking if you can bag one of the 28 spots. Best are the rooms, with Alvar

Helsinki

◎ Top Sights

◎ Sights

◎ Activities, Courses & Tours

◎ Sleeping

◎ Eating

◎ Drinking & Nightlife

◎ Entertainment

◎ Shopping

Aalto–designed furniture, ice-block bedside lights and a backlit print of a rural Suomi scene over the bed. Saunas are situated on the top floor, adjoining the rooftop terrace.

★ Hotel F6 — BOUTIQUE HOTEL €€€
(☎ 09-6899-9666; www.hotelf6.fi; Fabianinkatu 6; r €129-325; ✴ 🕸) 🖉 Stunningly designed, this 2016 hotel ranges around an internal courtyard (some rooms have direct access and patios); superior rooms come with French balconies. All 66 rooms are spacious (even the smallest are 27 sq metres) and stylishly furnished with cushion-strewn sofas. The courtyard's herb garden supplies the bar (serving great cocktails). Breakfast is organic, and wind and water power all electricity.

✕ Eating

Good budget options are in short supply but lunch specials are available in most places and there are plenty of self-catering opportunities.

Karl Fazer Café — CAFE €
(☎ 020-729-6702; www.fazer.fi; Kluuvikatu 3; dishes €5-14; 🕖 7.30am-10pm Mon-Fri, 9am-10pm Sat, 10am-6pm Sun; 🕸🖉🖫) Founded in 1891 and fronted by a striking art deco facade, this cavernous cafe is the flagship for Fazer's chocolate empire. The glass cupola reflects sound, so locals say it's a bad place to gossip. It's ideal, however, for buying dazzling confectionery, fresh bread, salmon or shrimp sandwiches, or digging into towering sundaes or spectacular cakes. Gluten-free dishes are available.

★ Vanha Kauppahalli — MARKET €
(www.vanhakauppahalli.fi; Eteläranta 1; 🕗 8am-6pm Mon-Sat, 10am-5pm Sun; 🖉) 🖉 Alongside the harbour, this is Helsinki's iconic market hall. Built in 1888, it's still a traditional Finnish market, with wooden stalls selling local flavours such as liquorice, Finnish cheeses, smoked salmon and herring, berries, forest mushrooms and herbs. Its centrepiece is its

superb cafe, **Story** (☑0190-666-8458; www. restaurantstory.fi; snacks from €4, mains €12.50-19; ⊙kitchen 8am-3pm Mon-Fri, to 5pm Sat, bar to 6pm Mon-Sat; 🖉) 🍷.

★ Suomenlinnan Panimo FINNISH €€
(☑020-742-5307; www.panimoravintola.fi; Suomenlinna C1; mains €19.50-30, set menu €49; ⊙noon-10pm Mon-Sat, to 6pm Sun Jun-Aug, shorter hours Sep-May) By the main quay, this microbrewery is the best place to drink or dine on Suomenlinna. It brews three ciders and seven different beers, including a hefty porter, plus several seasonal varieties, and offers good food to accompany it, such as smoked roast reindeer calf or spiced lamb sausages with the house mustard.

★ Kuu FINNISH €€
(☑09-2709-0973; www.ravintolakuu.fi; Töölönkatu 27; mains €20-33, 2-/3-course lunch menus €25/29; ⊙11.30am-midnight Mon-Fri, 2pm-midnight Sat, 4-11pm Sun) Traditional Finnish fare is given a sharp, contemporary twist at Kuu, which creates seasonal dishes from local ingredients that could include smoked reindeer heart with pickled forest mushrooms or pan-friend liver with lingonberries and bacon sauce. Wines aren't cheap, but there are some interesting choices. Its casual bistro sibling, KuuKuu, is located 800m south.

Ravintola Aino FINNISH €€€
(☑09-624-327; www.ravintolaaino.fi; Pohjoisesplanadi 21; mains €17.50-38.50, 3-course set menus €48-56.50; ⊙11.30am-11pm Mon-Fri, 4-11pm Sat) In a minimalist dining space in the heart of town, Aino is a popular choice for assured Finnish cooking that is faithful to local traditions, but with the occasional twist; the creamy salmon soup for starters is superb, while the reindeer fillet and shank with porcini potato cake is also rather tasty. The wine list is similarly well chosen.

🍷 Drinking & Nightlife

The city centre is full of bars and clubs. For the cheapest beer in Helsinki (€3 to €4 a pint), hit working-class Kallio (near Sörnäinen metro station), north of the centre.

★ Holiday BAR
(http://holiday-bar.fi; Kanavaranta 7; ⊙4-11pm Tue-Thu, to 2am Fri, noon-2am Sat; 🖲) Even on the greyest Helsinki day, this colourful waterfront bar transports you to more tropical climes with vibrant rainforest wallpapers and plants, tropical-themed cocktails such as frozen margaritas and mojitos (plus two dozen different gins) and a seafood menu that includes softshell crab. A small market is often set up out the front in summer, along with ping-pong tables.

★ Kaffa Roastery COFFEE
(☑010-422-6702; www.kaffaroastery.fi; Pursimiehenkatu 29A; ⊙7.45am-6pm Mon-Wed, to 9pm Thu & Fri, 10am-9pm Sat; 🖲) Processing up to 4000kg of beans every week, this vast coffee roastery supplies cafes throughout Helsinki, Finland and beyond. You can watch the roasting in progress through the glass viewing windows while sipping Aeropress, syphon or V60 brews in its polished-concrete surrounds. It also stocks a range of coffee grinders, espresso machines and gadgets.

☆ Entertainment

★ Musiikkitalo CONCERT VENUE
(Helsinki Music Centre; ☑020-707-0400; www. musiikkitalo.fi; Mannerheimintie 13; tickets free-€30) Home to the Helsinki Philharmonic Orchestra, Finnish Radio Symphony Orchestra and Sibelius Academy, the glass- and copper-fronted Helsinki Music Centre, opened in 2011, hosts a diverse program of classical, jazz, folk, pop and rock. The 1704-capacity main auditorium, visible from the foyer, has stunning acoustics. Five smaller halls seat 140 to 400. Buy tickets at the door or from www.ticketmaster.fi.

Tavastia LIVE MUSIC
(☑09-7746-7420; www.tavastiaklubi.fi; Urho Kekkosenkatu 4; ⊙7pm-1am Sun-Thu, 9pm-4am Fri, 8pm-4.30am Sat) One of Helsinki's legendary rock venues and going strong since 1970, Tavastia attracts both up-and-coming local acts and bigger international groups, with a band virtually every night of the week. Most gigs start at 9pm; doors open two hours beforehand. Also check out what's on at its adjoining venue, **Semifinal** (Urho Kekkosenkatu 6; ⊙8pm-1am Sun-Thu, 9pm-2am Fri, 8pm-4am Sat), where new talent and young local bands take the stage.

🛍 Shopping

★ World of Tre DESIGN
(☑029-170-0430; www.worldoftre.com; Mikonkatu 6; ⊙10am-7pm Mon-Fri, 10am-6pm Sat, noon-5pm Sun) If you only have time to visit one design store in Helsinki, this 2016 emporium is a brilliant bet. Showcasing the works of

Finnish designers in fashion, jewellery and accessories, including umbrellas, furniture, ceramics, textiles, stationery and art, it also stocks a range of architecture and design books to fuel inspiration.

★ **Artek** DESIGN
(☑ 010-617-3480; www.artek.fi; Keskuskatu 1B; ⊙ 10am-7pm Mon-Fri, to 6pm Sat) Originally founded by architects and designers Alvar Aalto and his wife Aino Aalto in 1935, this iconic Finnish company maintains the simple design principle of its founders. Textiles, lighting and furniture are among its homewares. Many items are only available at this 700-sq-metre, two-storey space.

ℹ Information

Helsinki City Tourist Office (☑ 09-3101-3300; www.myhelsinki.fi; Kaivokatu 1, Central Railway Station; ⊙ 9am-7pm Mon-Fri, 10am-5pm Sat & Sun Jun-Sep, 9.30am-5.30pm Mon-Fri, 10am-4pm Sat & Sun Oct-May) Busy multilingual office with a great quantity of information on the city. Also has an office at the **airport** (Terminal 2, Helsinki-Vantaa Airport; ⊙ 10am-8pm May-Sep, 10am-6pm Mon-Sat, noon-6pm Sun Oct-Apr).

ℹ Getting There & Away

AIR
Helsinki-Vantaa Airport (www.helsinki-vantaa.fi), 19km north of the city, is Finland's main air terminus. Direct flights serve many major European cities and several intercontinental destinations.
Finnair (☑ 09-818-0800; www.finnair.fi) covers 18 Finnish cities, usually at least once per day.

BOAT
International ferries sail to Stockholm (Sweden), Tallinn (Estonia), St Petersburg (Russia) and German destinations. There is also regular fastboat service to Tallinn. There are five main ferry terminals.

BUS
Kamppi bus station (☑ 0200-4000; www.matkahuolto.fi; Salomonkatu) has a terminal for local buses to Espoo in one wing, while longer-distance buses also depart from here to destinations throughout Finland. **Onnibus** (www.onnibus.com; Kamppi bus station, Salomonkatu) runs budget routes to several Finnish cities.

Destinations with several daily departures include the following:

WORTH A TRIP

PORVOO
Finland's second-oldest town is an ever-popular day trip or weekender destination from Helsinki. Porvoo (Swedish: Borgå) officially became a town in 1380, but even before that it was an important trading post. The town's fabulous historic centre includes the famous brick-red former warehouses along the river that once stored goods bound for destinations across Europe. During the day, old-town craft shops bustle with visitors, but staying on a weeknight will mean you could have the place more or less to yourself. The old painted buildings are spectacular in the setting sun. Frequent buses depart for Porvoo from Helsinki's Kamppi bus station.

Jyväskylä From €8.70, 4½ hours, up to three hourly
Kuopio From €11.40, six hours, hourly
Lappeenranta From €7.70, 3½ hours, up to three hourly
Oulu From €19.70, 9½ hours, up to 13 per day
Savonlinna From €8.70, 5½ hours, nine daily
Tampere From €4.70, 2½ hours, up to four hourly
Turku From €5.70, 2½ hours, up to four hourly

TRAIN
Helsinki's central **train station** (Rautatieasema; www.vr.fi; Kaivokatu 1) is linked to the metro (Rautatientori stop) and situated 500m east of Kamppi bus station.

The train is the fastest and cheapest way to get from Helsinki to major centres.

Destinations include the following:
Joensuu From €22.30, 4½ hours, three daily
Kuopio From €22.20, 4¼ hours, one to four daily
Lappeenranta €28, two hours, one to six daily
Oulu From €56, 7¼ hours, four daily
Rovaniemi €80, eight hours, four daily
Tampere From €8.90, 1½ hours, two hourly
Turku From €8.90, two hours, hourly

There are also daily trains (buy tickets from the international counter) to the Russian cities of Vyborg, St Petersburg and Moscow; you'll need a Russian visa.

ⓘ Getting Around

TO/FROM THE AIRPORT
Bus

Bus 615 (€3.50, 50 minutes, every 30 minutes, 24 hours) shuttles between Helsinki-Vantaa airport and the Rautatientori (Railway Sq), next to Helsinki's train station.

Taxi

Door-to-door **Yellow Line Airport Taxis** (📞 0600-555-555; www.airporttaxi.fi) need to be booked the previous day before 6pm if you're leaving Helsinki (per two/four passengers €19.50/50).

A regular **Taksi Helsinki** (📞 010-00700; www.taksihelsinki.fi) cab should cost around €40.

Train

The airport–city rail link (www.hsl.fi, €5, 30 minutes, 5.05am to 12.05am) serves Helsinki's train station. It's quick and easy and not subject to traffic complications.

BICYCLE

With a flat inner city and well-marked cycling paths, Helsinki is ideal for cycling. Pick up the free *Ulkoilukartta* Helsinki cycling map at the tourist office, or view it online at www.ulkoilukartta.fi.

Launched in 2016, Helsinki's shared-bike scheme, City Bikes (www.hsl.fi/citybikes), has some 1500 bikes at 150 stations citywide. Bikes are €5/10 for a day/week pass; the first 30 minutes are free, then it's €1 for each additional 30 minutes per ride. Register online.

LOCAL TRANSPORT

HSL (www.hsl.fi) operates buses, metro, local trains, trams and the Suomenlinna ferry. A single-trip ticket for any HSL transport costs €3.20 when purchased on board or €2.90 when purchased in advance. Day or multiday tickets (per 24/48/72 hours €9/13.50/18, tickets up to seven days available) are worthwhile. Buy tickets at the Rautatientori and Hakaniemi metro stations, R-kioskis and the tourist office.

TURKU

📞 02 / POP 188,435

Turku (Swedish: Åbo) is Finland's second city – or first, by some accounts, as it was the capital until 1812. The majestic Turun Linna (Turku Castle) and ancient Turun Tuomiokirkko (Turku Cathedral) – both dating from the 13th century – are testament to the city's long and storied past.

Contemporary Turku is even more enticing, a hotbed of experimental art and vibrant music festivals, designer boutiques and innovative restaurants. University students populate the cafes and clubs, keeping the place buzzing.

Through the age-old network of bustling streets and squares, the Aurajoki meanders picturesquely, heading out to sea. For nature lovers, Turku is the gateway to the glorious Turku Archipelago. As one of the country's main ports of entry (many visitors arrive by ferry from Sweden and Åland), it's a fabulous introduction to mainland Finland.

⊙ Sights

★ Turun Linna   CASTLE

(Turku Castle; 📞 02-262-0300; www.turku.fi/turun linna; Linnankatu 80; adult/child €11/5; ⊘ 10am-6pm daily Jun-Aug, to 6pm Tue-Sun Sep-May) Founded in 1280 at the mouth of the Aurajoki, mammoth Turku Castle is easily Finland's largest fortress. Highlights include two dungeons and sumptuous banqueting halls, as well as a fascinating **historical museum** of medieval Turku in the castle's Old Bailey. Models depict the castle's growth from a simple island fortress to a Renaissance palace. Guided tours in English run four to six times daily from June to August.

★ Aboa Vetus & Ars Nova   MUSEUM, GALLERY

(📞 020-718-1640; www.aboavetusarsnova.fi; Itäinen Rantakatu 4-6; adult/child €10/5.50; ⊘ 11am-7pm) Art and archaeology unite here under one roof. Aboa Vetus (Old Turku) draws you underground to Turku's medieval streets, showcasing some of the 37,000 artefacts unearthed from the site (digs still continue). Back in the present, Ars Nova has contemporary-art exhibitions upstairs. English-language tours lasting 45 minutes (included in admission) take place daily from 11.30am in July and August.

★ Turun Tuomiokirkko   CATHEDRAL

(Turku Cathedral; 📞 040-341-7100; www.turun seurakunnat.fi; Tuomiokirkonkatu 1; cathedral free, museum adult/child €2/1; ⊘ cathedral & museum 9am-6pm) The 'mother church' of Finland's Lutheran faith, Turku Cathedral towers over Turku. Consecrated in 1300, the colossal brick Gothic building was rebuilt many times over the centuries after damaging fires, but it still looks majestic and historic. Upstairs, a small **museum** traces the stages of the cathedral's construction, and contains medieval sculptures and religious paraphernalia. Free summer organ concerts (www.turkuorgan.fi) take place at 8pm Tuesday.

English-language services are held at 4pm every Sunday year-round except December.

✦ Festivals & Events

★ Ruisrock
MUSIC

(☏ 044-966-1384; www.ruisrock.fi; 1-/2-/3-day ticket €90/135/155; ☉ Jul) Finland's oldest and largest annual rock festival – held since 1969 and attracting 100,000-strong crowds – takes over Ruissalo island for three days.

🛏 Sleeping

Laivahostel Borea
HOSTEL €

(☏ 040-843-6611; www.msborea.fi; Linnankatu 72; dm/s/tw/d from €32/55/88/98; 🅿 🛜) Built in Sweden in 1960, the enormous passenger ship SS *Bore* is docked outside the Forum Marinum museum, just 500m northeast of the ferry terminal. It now contains an award-winning HI-affiliated hostel with 120 vintage en suite cabins. Most are squishy, but if you want room to spread out, higher-priced doubles have a lounge area. Rates include a morning sauna.

★ Park Hotel
BOUTIQUE HOTEL €€

(☏ 02-273-2555; www.parkhotelturku.fi; Rauhankatu 1; r/f/ste from €102/189/237; 🅿 🛜) Overlooking a hilly park, this art nouveau building was the home of a shipyard magnate. Nowadays it's a truly atmospheric place to stay, with classical music playing in the lift and a resident parrot in the lobby. Its 20 rooms are decorated in a lovably chintzy style. This is the antithesis of a chain hotel, thanks to the owners' wonderful hospitality.

🍴 Eating

Tårget
MODERN EUROPEAN €€

(☏ 040-052-2707; http://matbar.fi; Linnankatu 3A; pizzas €14-17, mains €20-29, 5-course set menu €55; ☉ 11am-10pm Mon-Thu, 11am-11pm Fri, noon-11pm Sat, 1-7pm Sun, bar to 2am Fri & Sat) There's fancier fare on the menu, but the reason to come to Tårget is to try the exceptional pizzas with unusual topping combinations (goat cheese and strawberries, barbecue pork, crayfish and lemon crème fraiche etc). Among the mains is deep-fried feta cheese... Great food, jovial atmosphere.

★ Smor
GASTRONOMY €€€

(☏ 02-536-9444; www.smor.fi; Läntinen Rantakatu 3; 3-/5-/7-course set menu €55/65/75; ☉ 4-11pm Mon-Thu, 4pm-midnight Fri & Sat) A vaulted cellar lit by flickering candles makes a roman-

tic backdrop for appetising, organic, locally sourced food, such as roast lamb with organic currant sauce or the catch of the day with roasted hay sauce. Desserts are truly inspired: try quark mousse with wild blueberries and oat ice cream or caramelised yoghurt with thyme cookies and honey.

🍷 Drinking & Nightlife

Boat bars such as **Donna** (☏ 02-251-5940; www.donna.fi; Itäinen Rantakatu; ☉ 11am-3am Apr-Sep) open along the river from around April to September.

★ Tiirikkala
COCKTAIL BAR

(☏ 020-741-7337; www.tiirikkala.fi; Linnankatu 3; ☉ 11am-10pm Tue-Thu, 11am-2am Fri & Sat, noon-10pm Sun) This cool, contemporary Nordic-style space inhabits a gorgeous old wooden house that opens to a street-level terrace and fabulous roof terrace. Unique cocktails and tasty tapas soothe the soul, as does the jazz and blues heading up the weekend live-music program. Weekend brunch is also a highlight.

ℹ Information

Tourist Office (☏ 02-262-7444; www.visitturku.fi; Aurakatu 2; ☉ 8.30am-6pm Mon-Fri year-round, plus 9am-4pm Sat & Sun Apr-Sep, 10am-3pm Sat & Sun Oct-Mar; 🛜) Busy but helpful office with information on the entire region.

WORTH A TRIP

THE ÅLAND ARCHIPELAGO

The glorious Åland archipelago is a geo-political anomaly: the islands belong to Finland, the spoken language is Swedish, but they have their own parliament, flag and stamps. Åland is the sunniest spot in northern Europe and its sweeping white-sand beaches and flat, scenic cycling routes have great appeal. Outside the lively capital, Mariehamn, a sleepy haze hangs over the islands' tiny villages and finding your own remote beach among the 6500 skerries and islets is surprisingly easy. A lattice of bridges and free cable ferries connect the central islands, while larger car ferries run to the archipelago's outer reaches. Several car ferries head to Åland, including those that connect Turku and Helsinki with Stockholm. Bikes are the best way to explore and are easily rented.

❶ Getting There & Away

BOAT

The harbour, southwest of the city centre, has terminals for Tallink/Silja and Viking Line services to Stockholm (10½ hours) via the Åland islands. Prices vary according to season and class.

BUS

Long-distance buses use the **bus station** (www.matkahuolto.fi; Aninkaistenkatu 20), while regional buses (including for Naantali) depart from the **kauppatori** (www.foli.fi; s ride before/after 11pm €3/4, day pass €7.50).

Major intercity services:

Helsinki From €5.70, 2½ hours, up to four hourly

Pori From €12, 2¼ hours, hourly

Tampere From €7.90, 2½ hours, hourly

TRAIN

Turku's train station is 400m northwest of the city centre; trains also stop at the ferry harbour.

Direct trains include the following:

Helsinki €20, two hours, hourly

Oulu €59 to €77, six to 10 hours, one to two daily

Tampere From €19, 1¾ hours, six daily

TAMPERE

📞 03 / POP 229,475

Set between two vast lakes, scenic Tampere has a down-to-earth vitality and pronounced cultural focus that make it a favourite for many visitors. The Tammerkoski rapids churn through the centre, flanked by grassy banks that stand in contrast with the red brick of the imposing fabric mills that once drove the city's economy. Regenerated industrial buildings now house quirky museums, enticing shops, pubs, cinemas and cafes.

◉ Sights

★**Tuomiokirkko** CHURCH

(📞040-804-8765; www.tampereenseurakunnat.fi; Tuomiokirkonkatu 3; ⊙10am-5pm May-Aug, 11am-3pm Sep-Apr) FREE An iconic example of National Romantic art nouveau architecture, Tampere's cathedral dates from 1907. Hugo Simberg created the frescoes and stained glass; you'll appreciate that they were controversial. A procession of naked childlike apostles holds the 'garland of life', graves and plants are tended by skeletal figures, and in the upstairs gallery a wounded angel

is stretchered off by two children. Magnus Enckell's dreamlike Resurrection altarpiece is designed in a similar style. The serpent on the dome adds to the strange ambience.

★**Amurin Työläismuseokortteli** MUSEUM

(Amuri Museum of Workers' Housing; 📞03-5656-6690; www.museokortteli.fi; Satakunnankatu 49; adult/child €7/3, 3-6pm Fri free; ⊙10am-6pm Tue-Sun mid-May–early Sep) An entire block of wooden houses – including 32 apartments in five residential buildings, a bakery, a shoemaker, a public sauna, two general shops and a cafe – is preserved at the Amuri Museum of Workers' Housing, evoking life from 1882 to 1973. Interpretative panels (English translation available) outlining the fictional lives of residents give plenty of historical information and make for a visit that is as entertaining as it is educational. There's a good on-site cafe (soup lunch €7).

🛏 Sleeping

★**Dream Hostel** HOSTEL €

(📞045-236-0517; www.dreamhostel.fi; Åkerlundinkatu 2; dm/s from €23/65, d & tw from €69; ❄@🅿) 🍃 With its contemporary Nordic design, switched-on staff and good facilities, this hostel is consistently ranked Finland's best. Narrow dorms (mixed and female-only) have small underbed lockers; bathrooms are barracks-like but clean. Facilities include a laundry and fully kitted-out self-catering kitchen (free tea and coffee). It's a 200m walk southeast of the train station in a quiet area. Breakfast costs €6.50.

★**Lapland Hotel Tampere** DESIGN HOTEL €€

(📞03-383-000; www.laplandhotels.com; Yliopistonkatu 44; s/d from €131/144; 🅿❄@🅿) Part of the excellent portfolio of contemporary hotels operated by the Lapland hotel group, this place has a chic ground-floor lounge bar, a sauna, well-equipped and extremely comfortable rooms (soothing colours, plus reindeer antlers above the bed) and a restaurant where a generous and delicious buffet breakfast is served. Staff members are young and very helpful; on-site parking costs €18.

Solo Sokos Hotel Torni Tampere HOTEL €€€

(📞020-123-4634; www.sokoshotels.fi/en/tampere/solo-sokos-hotel-torni-tampere; Ratapihankatu 43; s/d €314/334) Opened in 2014, this architectural showpiece has rooms up to the 16th floor – upper-floor rooms cost more, but have superlative Tampere views. Rooms have a contemporary slant with Tampere wall maps and bold colours. The styling won't be to everyone's taste, but if you spend most of your time looking out the window at the view you should be fine.

✕ Eating

The city's speciality, *mustamakkara*, is a mild, tasty sausage made with cow's blood, normally eaten with lingonberry jam. Try it at the kauppahalli (covered market).

Bull   BURGERS €

(☑ 050-345-5422;   www.gastropub.net/bull; Hatanpään valtatie 4; burgers €8.50-15.50; ⊙ 4-10pm Mon, Wed & Thu, 11am-11pm Fri, 1-11pm Sat, 1-6pm Sun; ☑) Patties made from 100% Black Angus beef are the centrepiece of many of Bull's towering burgers, including Dirty Harry (with blue cheese and red onion) and the Porn Master (with Thai spices). It also has a horsemeat version, as well as veggie and vegan options cooked on a separate grill.

Heinätori   FINNISH €€

(☑ 032-121-205; www.heinatori.com; Pyynikintori 5; mains €18-28, 3-course set menu €45; ⊙ noon-10pm Tue-Fri, 1-10pm Sat, 1-5pm Sun) Inhabiting the old weighing room in the central town square, Heinätori has local specialities like wild-mushroom soup, reindeer and fried vendace (a local lake whitefish), plus a few rarities such as roasted guinea fowl.

Hella & Huone   GASTRONOMY €€€

(☑ 010-322-3898; http://hellajahuone.fi; Salhojanka-tu 48; 6-/12-course menu €68/90, wine pairing €55/78; ⊙ 4-10pm Tue-Thu, to midnight Fri, 2pm-midnight Sat) Acclaimed chef Arto Rastas serves cutting-edge contemporary Nordic cuisine in this minimalist space where black high-backed chairs provide a sharp contrast to the stark-white tablecloths. Menus change with the season (usually every two months). Organic European drops dominate the wine list.

🍷 Drinking & Nightlife

★ Mokka Mestarit   COFFEE

(☑ 03-253-0145; www.mokkamestarit.fi; Verkeh-taankatu 9; ⊙ 10am-6pm Mon-Fri, to 4pm Sat; 🛜) 🍴 Despite being the most caffeine-addicted nation on earth, Finland doesn't generally do coffee well. Fortunately this stylish cafe and roastery bucks the trend. Espresso, cold-drip and Aeropress variations are on offer, along with hippie variations such as chai lattes and matcha bowls. It also has a huge range of tea and an array of panini and cakes to snack on – we love it.

Moro Sky Bar   BAR

(☑ 010-786-0121;   www.raflaamo.fi/en/tampere/moro-sky-bar; Ratapihankatu 43; ⊙ 11am-midnight Sun-Tue, to 2am Wed-Sat) Finland's highest bar sits on the 25th floor of the Solo Sokos Hotel Torni, Finland's tallest hotel, at 88m. Floor-to-ceiling glass windows offer a dizzying panorama of the city, as does Finland's highest terrace. Local Olympians and other champion athletes are commemorated on its 'wall of heroes'. Craft beers are a speciality. Children are welcome until 9pm.

🛍 Shopping

Taito Pirkanmaa   DESIGN

(☑ 03-225-1415; www.taitopirkanmaa.fi; Hatanpään valtatie 4A; ⊙ 10am-6pm Mon-Fri, to 3pm Sat) 🍴 Handcrafted Finnish products – including clothing (woolly jumpers, cardigans, socks, caps, scarves, babywear), textiles (blankets, towels, tea towels, traditional woven rugs), confectionery (chocolates, liquorices, boiled sweets), toys and jewellery – are beautifully displayed at this corner boutique and make ideal gifts to take back home. It also has an extensive selection of hand-printed cards.

ℹ Information

Visit Tampere (☑ 03-5656-6800; www.visit tampere.fi; 🛜) Online tourist information. Can book activities and events.

ℹ Getting There & Away

AIR

Tampere-Pirkkala Airport (TMP; ☑ 020-708-5521; www.finavia.fi; Tornikaari 50) is situated 17km southwest of the city. Airlines flying to/from Tampere:

AirBaltic Flies to Rīga, Latvia.

Finnair Flies to Helsinki (though the train is more convenient), with connections to other Finnish cities.

Ryanair Flies to Budapest, Hungary, twice weekly.

SAS Flies to Stockholm, Sweden, and Málaga, Spain.

BUS

From the **bus station** (Hatanpään valtatie 7), express buses serve Helsinki (€4.70 to €27, 2¾ hours, up to four hourly) and Turku (€2 to €12, two hours, hourly). There are services to most other major towns in Finland.

TRAIN

Trains link Tampere's central **train station** (www.vr.fi; Rautatienkatu 25) with Helsinki (from €8.90, 1½ to 1¾ hours, up to three hourly), Turku

DON'T MISS

SAUNAS

For centuries the sauna has been a place to meditate, warm up and even give birth, and most Finns still use it at least once a week. Saunas are usually taken in the nude (public saunas are nearly always sex-segregated) and Finns are quite strict about its nonsexual – even sacred – nature.

Shower first. Once inside (with a temperature of 80°C to 100°C), water is thrown onto the stove using a *kauhu* (ladle), producing *löyly* (steam). A *vihta* (whisk of birch twigs and leaves, known as a *vasta* in eastern Finland) is sometimes used to lightly strike the skin, improving circulation. Cool off with a cold shower or preferably by jumping into a lake. Repeat. The sauna beer afterwards is also traditional.

(from €9.70, 1¾ hours, up to six daily) and other cities.

THE FINNISH LAKELAND

Savonlinna

📞 015 / POP 35,800

The historic frontier settlement of Savonlinna is one of Finland's prettiest towns and most compelling tourist destinations. Scattered across a garland of small islands strung between Haukivesi and Pihlajavesi lakes, its major attraction is the visually dramatic Olavinlinna Castle, constructed in the 15th century and now the spectacular venue of July's world-famous Savonlinna Opera Festival. In summer, when the lakes shimmer in the sun and operatic arias waft through the forest-scented air, the place is quite magical. In winter it's often blanketed in fairy-tale-like snow. If you find yourself in the newer part of town, you may wonder what all of the fuss is about. But fear not: magic lies just around the corner.

🎯 Sights

★ Olavinlinna   CASTLE

(St Olaf's Castle; 📞 029-533-6932; www.kansallis museo.fi/en/olavinlinna/frontpage; adult/child/family €10/5/22; ⏰ 10am-5pm Jun–mid-Aug, 10am-4pm Mon-Fri, 11am-4pm Sat & Sun May,

10am-4pm Tue-Fri, 11am-4pm Sat & Sun mid-Aug–Dec & Feb-Apr, closed Jan) Built directly on rock in the middle of the lake (now accessed via bridges), this heavily restored 15th-century fortification was constructed as a military base on the Swedes' restless eastern border. The currents in the surrounding water ensure that it remains unfrozen in winter, which prevented enemy attacks over ice. To visit the castle's upper levels, including the towers and chapel, you must join an hour-long guided tour. Guides bring the castle to life with vivid accounts of its history.

🛏️ Sleeping

★ Lossiranta Lodge   BOUTIQUE HOTEL €€

(📞 044-511-2323; www.lossiranta.net; Aino Acktén Puistotie; s €100-175, d €110-315, extra person €65; 🅿️ 🛜) The dress-circle views of Olavinlinna Castle are one of many good reasons to stay at this boutique hotel on the lakeshore. There are five rooms sleeping between two and four on offer year-round, the best of which has its own wood sauna and outdoor spa. All are attractively decorated and most have kitchenettes. Staff are both friendly and helpful.

Hotel Saima   BOUTIQUE HOTEL €€

(📞 015-515-340; www.kahvilasaima.fi; Linnankatu 11; r €110-225) The six stunning rooms here have a winning combination of wood, wrought iron and white linen, with plenty of space and the occasional period touch. Each room is different (check the website for photos) and the on-site cafe and **design shop** (📞 015-515-320; www.facebook.com/saimatalonkauppa; ⏰ 10am-5pm Mon-Fri, to 3pm Sat) mean that you can indulge many needs without even leaving the property.

🍴 Eating

Kahvila Saima   CAFE €

(📞 015-515-340; www.kahvilasaima.net; Linnankatu 11; mains €8-17; ⏰ 9.30am-5pm Jun-Aug, 10.30am-4.30pm Wed-Sun Sep-May) Set inside a wooden villa with stained-glass windows, and opening to a wide terrace out the back, this charmingly old-fashioned cafe is adorned with striped wallpaper and serves home-style Finnish food, including good cakes and baked items.

Perlina di Castello   ITALIAN €€

(📞 010-764-2440; Kauppatori 4-6; mains €16-31; ⏰ noon-10pm Mon-Thu, to midnight Fri & Sat, to 6pm Sun) This elegant place effortlessly combines the casual with the sophisticated. The menu includes thin-crust, wood-fired Italian pizzas, grilled meats and pasta such as deep-fried ravioli.

Drinking & Nightlife

★Huvila
MICROBREWERY

(☑015-555-0555; www.panimoravintolahuvila.fi; Puistokatu 4; mains €23-35, 3-course menu €45-52; ☉noon-10pm Jun-Aug, shorter hours Sep-May; ☜) Sitting across the harbour, Huvila is operated by the Waahto brewery and is a delightful destination in warm weather, when its lakeside deck is full of patrons relaxing over a pint or two of the house brew (try the Golden Ale). There's also an attractive dining area in the old timber house. Sadly the menu promises more than it delivers.

❶ Information

Savonlinna has no official tourist office, but the ticket desk in the **Riihisaari** (Lake Saimaa Nature & Culture Centre; ☑044-417-4466; www.savonlinna.fi/museo; adult/child €7/3, incl Olavinlinna €10/4.50; ☉10am-5pm Tue-Sun Sep-Apr, 9am-5pm Mon-Fri & 10am-5pm Sat & Sun May, 10am-5pm daily Jun-Aug) stocks maps and brochures about the city and region. Limited information can be accessed via www.savonlinna.fi/en/tourist.

❶ Getting There & Away

AIR

Savonlinna Airport (SVL; ☑020-708-8101; www.finavia.fi; Lentoasemantie 50) is 14km north of town, and is predominantly used by charter flights. Finnair flies here during the opera season.

BOAT

Boats connect Savonlinna's **passenger harbour** (Satamapuistonkatu) with many lakeside towns; check www.oravivillage.com for seasonal schedules. The M/S *Puijo*, operated by **Saimaan Laivamatkat Oy** (☑015-250-250; www.mspuijo.fi; Satamapuistonkatu; one way €95, return by car same day €130, return with/without overnight cabin €180/150; ☉mid-Jun–mid-Aug), cruises between Savonlinna and both Kuopio and Lappeenranta in summer.

BUS

Savonlinna is not on major bus routes, but buses link the **bus station** (Tulliportinkatu 1) with Helsinki (€32, 4¾ to 6½ hours, up to nine daily), Mikkeli (from €22, 1½ hours, up to 14 daily) and Jyväskylä (from €32, 3½ hours, up to eight daily).

TRAIN

Punkaharju (€2.70, 30 minutes, at least four daily) is one of the few destinations that can be accessed via a direct service from Savonlinna. To get to

Helsinki (from €41, 4¼ hours, up to four daily) and Joensuu (€25, 2¼ hours, up to four daily), you'll need to change in Parikkala. The train station is in the town centre near the kauppatori. Buy your ticket at the machines – there's no ticket office.

LAPLAND

Lapland casts a powerful spell: there's something lonely and intangible here that fills it with Arctic magic. The midnight sun, the Sámi peoples, the aurora borealis (Northern Lights) and roaming reindeer are all components of this – as is Santa Claus himself, who 'officially' resides here – along with the awesome latitudes: at Nuorgam, the northernmost point, you have passed Iceland and nearly all of Canada and Alaska.

Spanning 30% of Finland's land area, Lapland is home to just 3% of its population. Its vast wilderness is ripe for exploring on foot, skis or sled. The sense of space, pure air and big skies are what's most memorable here, more so than the towns.

Lapland's far north is known as Sápmi, home of the Sámi, whose main communities are around Inari, Utsjoki and Hetta. Rovaniemi, on the Arctic Circle, is the most popular gateway to the north.

Rovaniemi

☑016 / POP 61,816

Right by the Arctic Circle, the 'official' terrestrial residence of Santa Claus is the capital of Finnish Lapland and a tourism boom town. Its wonderful Arktikum museum is the perfect introduction to these latitudes, and Rovaniemi is a fine base from which to organise activities, visit Santa and generally get a taste for the Arctic.

Thoroughly destroyed by the retreating Wehrmacht in 1944, the town was rebuilt to a plan by Alvar Aalto, with the major streets in the shape of a reindeer's head and antlers (the stadium near the bus station is the eye). Its utilitarian buildings are compensated for by its marvellous riverside location.

❍ Sights

★Arktikum
MUSEUM

(☑016-322-3260; www.arktikum.fi; Pohjoisranta 4; adult/child €13/6; ☉9am-6pm Jun-Aug, 10am-6pm Tue-Sun mid-Jan–May & Sep-Nov, 10am-6pm Dec–mid-Jan) With its beautifully designed glass tunnel stretching out to the Ounasjoki, this is one of Finland's finest museums. One half deals with Lapland, with information on Sámi culture and the history of Rovaniemi; the other offers a wide-ranging display on the Arctic, with superb static and interactive displays focusing on flora and fauna, as well as on the peoples of Arctic Europe, Asia and North America. Downstairs an audiovisual – basically a pretty slide show – plays on a constant loop.

🏃 Activities

Rovaniemi is Finnish Lapland's most popular base for winter and summer activities, offering the convenience of frequent departures and professional trips with multilingual guides. Check the tourist-office website (www.visitrovaniemi.fi) for activities including river cruises, reindeer- and husky-sledding, rafting, snowmobiling, skiing and mountain biking.

🛏 Sleeping

Guesthouse Borealis   GUESTHOUSE €
(☑ 044-313-1771; www.guesthouseborealis.com; Asemieskatu 1; s/d/tr/apt from €60/72/105/190; 🅿🛜) Friendly owners and proximity to trains make this family-run spot a winner. Rooms are simple, bright and clean, and guests can use a kitchen. Breakfast, served in an airy dining room, features Finnish porridge. The two apartments each have their own entrance and full kitchen; one has a private balcony and private sauna.

★ Arctic Treehouse Hotel   DESIGN HOTEL €€€
(☑ 050-517-6909; https://arctictreehousehotel.com; Tarvantie 3; r €300-567; 🅿🛜) Forget the theme-park ambience of the nearby Santa quarter, because this place, opened in 2016, is something special. Designer rooms are swathed in local wood and reindeer rugs, with massive windows looking out from amid the trees, and combine a oneness with nature and supreme levels of comfort and cosiness no matter what the weather's like outside.

🍴 Eating

Nili   FINNISH €€
(☑ 040-036-9669; www.nili.fi; Valtakatu 20; mains €18-35, 4-course menu €62, with paired wines €110; ⊙ 5-11pm Sun-Fri, noon-11pm Sat) A timber-lined interior with framed black-and-white photos of Lapland, kerosene lamps, traditional fishing nets, taxidermied bear and reindeer heads, and antler chandeliers gives this hunting-lodge-style spot a cosy, rustic charm. Local ingredients are used in dishes such as zandar lake fish with tar-and-mustard foam and reindeer with pickled cucumber and lingonberry jam, accompanied by Finnish beers, ciders and berry liqueurs.

★ Rakas   FINNISH €€€
(☑ 050-517-6952; https://rakasrestaurant.com; Tarvantie 3, Arctic Treehouse Hotel; mains €20-36; ⊙ noon-10pm Sun-Thu, to 11pm Fri & Sat) The home kitchen of UK chef Jonathan Guppy, Rakas is one of Lapland's most exciting places to eat. The seasonal menu could include reindeer served with wild mushrooms, lingonberry and red wine sauce or king crab salad. It's the simple things that make this place different – local ingredients and the use of juniper or spruce oil instead of olive oil.

ℹ Information

Metsähallitus (☑ 020-564-7820; www.metsa.fi; Pilke Tiedekeskus, Ounasjoentie 6; ⊙ 9am-6pm Mon-Fri, 10am-4pm Sat & Sun mid-Jun–Aug, shorter hours rest of year) Information centre for the national parks; sells maps and fishing permits.
Tourist Office (☑ 016-346-270; www.visitrovaniemi.fi; Maakuntakatu 29; ⊙ 9am-5pm Mon-Fri; 🛜) On the square in the middle of town.

ℹ Getting There & Around

AIR
Rovaniemi's **airport** (RVN; ☑ 020-708-6506; www.finavia.fi; Lentokentäntie), 8km northeast of the city, is the 'official airport of Santa Claus' (he must hangar his sleigh here) and a major winter destination for charter flights. Finnair and Norwegian have several flights daily to/from Helsinki. There are car-hire desks, cafes, ATMs,

---

LAPLAND SEASONS

It's important to time your trip in Lapland carefully. In the far north there's no sun for 50 days of the year, and no night for 70-odd days. In June it's very muddy, and in July insects can be hard to deal with. If you're here to walk, August is great and September brings the spectacle of the *ruska* (autumn leaves). There's usually thick snow cover from mid-October to May; December draws charter flights looking for Santa, real reindeer and a white Christmas, but the best time for skiing and husky/reindeer/snowmobile safaris is March and April, when you get a decent amount of daylight and less-extreme temperatures. October, November and March seem to be particularly good for the aurora borealis.

SEEING SANTA

The southernmost line at which the sun doesn't set on at least one day a year, the Arctic Circle (Napapiiri in Finnish) crosses the Sodankylä road 7.5km north of Rovaniemi (although the Arctic Circle can actually shift several metres daily). There's an **Arctic Circle marker** here; surrounding it is the 'official' **Santa Claus Village** (www.santaclausvillage. info; Tarvantie 2; ☺9am-6pm Jun-Aug, 10am-5pm mid-Jan–May, Sep & Nov, 9am-7pm Dec–mid-Jan) `FREE`, a touristy complex of shops, activities and accommodation including the **Santa Claus Holiday Village** (☏040-159-3811; www.santaclausholidayvillage.fi; Tähtikuja 2; d from €109; P🖥) cabins, and the new **Snowman World** (http://snowmanworld.fi), with glass-sided apartments and a winter-only ice hotel complete with restaurant and bar.

The **Santa Claus Post Office** (www.santaclausvillage.info; Sodankyläntie; ☺9am-6pm Jun-Aug, 10am-5pm mid-Jan–May, Sep & Nov, 9am-7pm Dec–mid-Jan) `FREE` receives over half a million letters yearly from children all over the world. Your postcard sent from here will bear an official Santa stamp, and you can arrange to have it delivered at Christmas. For €4.45, Santa will send you a Christmas letter.

At the tourist-information desk you can get your Arctic Circle certificate (€4.50).

But the top attraction for most is, of course, Santa himself, who sees visitors year-round in a rather impressive **grotto** (www.santaclausvillage.info; Sodankyläntie; visit free, photographs from €25; ☺9am-6pm Jun-Aug, 10am-5pm mid-Jan–May, Sep & Nov, 9am-7pm Dec–mid-Jan) `FREE`, with a huge clock mechanism (it slows the earth's rotation so that Santa can visit the whole world's children on Christmas Eve). A private chat (around two minutes) is absolutely free, but you'll need to pay for official photographs (no other photography is allowed). You can also get a certificate of 'niceness' or of meeting Santa (each €10).

Other attractions include a **husky park** (☏040-824-7503; www.huskypark.fi; Joulumaantie 3, Napapiiri; adult/child €10/5; ☺11am-4pm Jun-Aug, 10am-4pm Sep-May); reindeer-pulled **sleigh rides** (on wheels in summer, traditional runners in snow; from €18/14 per adult/child for 400m); ice sculpting; and varying Christmassy exhibitions.

Bus 8 (Rovakatu P; Poromiehentie) heads here from Rovaniemi's train station, via the city and airport (€4.25, 25 minutes, up to three hourly 6.30am to 6.30pm).

Closer to Rovaniemi town centre, the separate Christmas theme park **Santapark** (https://santaparkarcticworld.com/santapark; Tarvantie 1; adult/child winter €34/28.50, summer €18.50/16; ☺10am-6pm late Nov–mid-Jan, to 5pm Mon-Sat mid-Jun–mid-Aug) is also linked by bus 8.

money changers, a children's playground and a Santa Claus Post Office outpost.

Airport minibuses (☏016-362-222; http://airportbus.fi; per person €7) meet arriving flights, dropping off at hotels in the town centre (€7, 15 minutes). They pick up along the same route about an hour before departures.

A taxi to the city centre costs €20 to €30 depending on the time of day and number of passengers.

BUS

Express buses go south from the **bus station** (Matkahuolto Rovaniemi; ☏020-710-5435; www.matkahuolto.fi; Lapinkävijäntie 2) to Kemi (€20, 1½ hours, up to six daily) and Oulu (€9 to €24, 3½ hours, up to eight daily). Night buses serve Helsinki (from €45, 13 hours, up to four daily). Daily connections serve just about everywhere else in Lapland. Some buses continue north into Norway.

TRAIN

One direct train per day runs from Rovaniemi to Helsinki (from €34.80, 8½ hours), with two more requiring a change in Oulu (from €12.60, 2½ hours).

There's one train daily northeast to Kemijärvi (€11, 1¼ hours).

Inari

☏016 / POP 617

The tiny village of Inari (Sámi: Anár) is Finland's Sámi capital and the ideal starting point to immerse yourself in Sámi culture. Home to the wonderful Siida museum and Sajos (cultural centre and seat of the Finnish Sámi parliament), it also has a string of superb handicrafts shops and it's a great base for forays into Lemmenjoki National Park and the Kevo Strict Nature Reserve.

The village sits on Lapland's largest lake, Inarijärvi, a spectacular body of water with more than 3000 islands in its 1084-sq-km area.

⦿ Sights

★ Siida
MUSEUM

(☑ 040-0089-8212; www.siida.fi; Inarintie 46; adult/child €10/5; ⊙ 9am-7pm daily Jun-Aug, 9am-6pm Sep, 10am-5pm Tue-Sun Oct-May) One of Finland's most absorbing museums, state-of-the-art Siida offers a comprehensive overview of the Sámi and their environment. The main exhibition hall consists of a fabulous nature exhibition around the edge, detailing northern Lapland's ecology by season, with wonderful photos and information panels. The centre of the room has detailed information on the Sámi, from their former semi-nomadic existence to modern times.

★ Sajos
CULTURAL CENTRE

(☑ 010-839-3100; www.samediggi.fi; Siljotie 4; ⊙ 9am-5pm Mon-Fri) **FREE** The spectacular wood-and-glass Sámi cultural centre stands proud in the middle of town. It holds the Sámi parliament as well as a library and music archive, a restaurant, exhibitions and a craft shop. Guided tours start at noon.

🛏 Sleeping & Eating

Uruniemi Camping
CAMPGROUND €

(☑ 050-371-8826; www.uruniemi.fi; Uruniementie 7; tent sites €18, d with shared bathroom from €25, cabins €30-125; ⊙ Jun–mid-Sep; P 🛇) The most pleasant place to pitch a tent hereabouts is this well-equipped lakeside campground 2km south of town. Along with campsites, there are basic rooms and cottages; facilities include a cafe and a sauna, and kayaks, boats and bikes for hire. Heated cottages are available year-round.

★ Wilderness Hotel Inari
HOTEL €€

(☑ 050-430-7600; https://nellim.fi/destinations/wilderness-hotel-inari; Inarintie 2; s €99-150, d €129-180, cabins €170-440) Just outside town, this terrific lakeside place has a cosy feel in its tastefully decorated rooms and cabins, with some igloos as well. The decor features dark wood and reindeer skins and some rooms have glass ceilings for watching the aurora. The public areas have a similarly warm and welcoming feel.

★ Aanaar
FINNISH €€

(☑ 016-511-7100; www.hotelkultahovi.fi; Saarikoskentie 2; mains €19.40-28.50, 3-/5-course menu €43.50/62.50, with paired wines €61/86; ⊙ 11am-2.30pm & 5-10.30pm) 🍴 A panoramic glassed-in dining room overlooks the Juutuanjoki's Jäniskoski rapids at Inari's best restaurant, situated in the **Tradition Hotel Kultahovi** (d with/without sauna from €140/110; P 🛇). Seasonal local produce is used in dishes such as morel and angelica-root soup, smoked reindeer heart with pine-needle vinaigrette, grilled Inarijärvi lake trout with white wine and dill sauce and a cauliflower puree, or Arctic king crab with nettle butter.

🛍 Shopping

Inarin Hopea
JEWELLERY

(☑ 016-671-333; www.inarinhopea.fi; Inarintie 61; ⊙ 9am-8pm mid-Jun–Aug, 9am-5pm Sep, 10am-5pm Mon-Fri Oct–mid-Jun) You can watch gold- and silversmith Matti Qvick at work in his studio, which is filled with his traditional handmade jewellery (rings, bracelets, pendants, earrings and more, at all price points) based on Sámi designs and local wildlife such as Arctic foxes and Scandinavian lynx. He's been crafting here since 1982. Pieces can be custom fitted while you wait.

ⓘ Information

Inari's **tourist office** (☑ 040-168-9668; www.inarisaariselka.fi; Inarintie 46; ⊙ 9am-7pm daily Jun-Aug, 9am-6pm Sep, 10am-5pm Tue-Sun Oct-May; 🛜) is in the Siida museum and is open the same hours. There's also a nature information point here.

ⓘ Getting There & Away

Inari is 38km northwest of Ivalo on the E75. Up to four daily buses run here from Ivalo (€8.20, 30 minutes). Shuttle buses (€30, 45 minutes) serving **Ivalo Airport** (IVL; ☑ 020-708-8610; www.finavia.fi; Lentokentäntie 290) can be booked through Inari's tourist-office website (www.inarisaariselka.fi).

Two direct daily buses serve Inari from Rovaniemi (€60.10, 5½ hours). Both continue to Norway: one to Karasjok (€23.70, three hours) and, in summer, on to Nordkapp (€77.90, 5½ hours); and another to Tana bru (€37.60, three hours, up to four per week).

SURVIVAL GUIDE

ⓘ Directory A-Z

ACCOMMODATION

Many rural accommodation options open only in summer, and ski areas book out in winter – reserve well ahead. Most properties don't have 24-hour reception.

Hotels Chains such as Sokos and Scandic dominate, but boutique and/or designer hotels are emerging. Most rooms have twin beds that can be pushed together rather than double beds.

Camping Campgrounds open throughout the countryside in the warmer months.

Cottages In Finnish tradition, lakeside and coastal cabins are popular in the warmer months.

Hostels Typically basic, even in larger cities.

Student residences During the summer break, student residences often rent rooms to travellers. Facilities vary widely.

ACTIVITIES

Water sports Every waterside town has a place (frequently the campground) where you can rent a canoe, kayak or rowboat. Rental cottages often have rowboats that you can use free of charge to investigate the local lake. Rafting options abound.

Fishing Several permits are required for foreigners but they are very easy to arrange. See www. mmm.fi for details.

Hiking Finland has some of Europe's greatest hiking, best done from June to September, although in July mosquitoes and other biting insects can be a big problem in Lapland. Wilderness huts line the northern trails. Numerous national parks (www.nationalparks.fi) provide a well-maintained network of marked trails across the nation.

Skiing The ski season runs from late November to early May and slightly longer in the north.

Dog-sledding Expeditions can range from one-hour tasters to multiday trips with overnight stays in remote forest huts.

Snowmobiling If you want to drive one, a driving licence is required.

Saunas Many hotels, hostels and campgrounds have saunas that are free with a night's stay. Large towns have public saunas.

INTERNET ACCESS

Wireless internet access is widespread. Several cities have extensive free networks and nearly all hotels, as well as many restaurants, cafes and bars, offer free access to customers and guests.

Data is very cheap. If you have an unlocked smartphone, you can pick up a local SIM card for a few euros and charge it with a month's worth of data at a decent speed for under €20. Ask at R-kioski shops for the latest deals.

LGBT+ TRAVELLERS

Finland's cities are open, tolerant places. Helsinki has a small but welcoming gay scene and the country's largest pride festival. Tampere and Turku also host pride festivals. Same-sex marriage became legal in Finland on 1 March 2017.

The tourist-board website, www.visitfinland. com, is a good starting point for information.

MONEY

ATMs Using ATMs with a credit or debit card is by far the easiest way of getting cash.

Credit cards Widely accepted.

Money changers Travellers cheques and cash can be exchanged at banks; in cities, independent exchange facilities such as Forex (www. forex.fi) usually offer better rates.

Tipping Service is considered to be included in bills, so there's no need to tip unless you want to reward exceptional service.

OPENING HOURS

Many attractions in Finland only open for a short summer season, typically mid-June to late August. Opening hours tend to be shorter in winter in general.

Alko (state alcohol store) 9am–8pm Monday to Friday, to 6pm Saturday

Banks 9am–4.15pm Monday to Friday

Businesses and shops 9am–6pm Monday to Friday, to 3pm Saturday

Nightclubs 10pm–4am Wednesday to Saturday

Pubs 11am–1am (often later on Friday and Saturday)

Restaurants 11am–10pm, lunch 11am–3pm; last orders are generally an hour before closing

TELEPHONE

➔ Public telephones basically no longer exist in Finland.

➔ If you have an unlocked phone, the cheapest and most practical solution is to purchase a Finnish SIM card.

➔ You can buy a prepaid SIM card at any R-kioski shop. Top the credit up at the same outlets, online or at ATMs.

➔ The country code for Finland is 358.

➔ To dial abroad, the international access code is 00.

TOURIST INFORMATION

The main website of the Finnish Tourist Board is www.visitfinland.com. Cities, large towns and major tourist destinations have tourist offices.

VISAS

Most Western nationals don't need a tourist visa for stays of less than three months. South Africans, Indians and Chinese, however, are among those who need a Schengen visa. For more information, contact the nearest Finnish embassy or consulate, or check the website https://um.fi/entering-finland.

❶ Getting There & Away

AIR

Finland is easily reached by air, with direct flights to Helsinki from many European, North American and Asian destinations. It's also served by budget carriers from several European countries. Most other flights are with Finnair, Norwegian or Scandinavian Airlines (SAS).

Most flights land at Helsinki-Vantaa airport (p361), 19km north of the capital. Winter charters serve Rovaniemi (p368), Lapland's main airport, and other smaller regional airports. Other international airports include Tampere-Pirkkala Airport (p365), **Turku** (TKU; www.finavia.fi; Lentoasemantie 150) and **Oulu** (OUL; www.finavia.fi; Lentokentäntie 720; ☎). The website www.finavia.fi includes information for Finnish airports.

LAND

There are several border crossings from northern Sweden and Norway to northern Finland, with no passport or customs formalities. Buses link northern Finland and Norway, while the shared bus station at Tornio (Finland) and Haparanda (Sweden) links the public-transport systems of those countries.

Between Finland and Russia, there are nine main border crossings, including several in the southeast and two in Lapland. Buses and trains run from Helsinki and other cities to Russia. You must already have a Russian visa.

SEA

Baltic ferries connect Finland with Estonia, Russia, Germany and Sweden. Book ahead in summer, at weekends and if travelling with a vehicle.

Ferry companies have detailed timetables and fares on their websites. Fares vary according to season. Main operators include the following:

Eckerö Line (☑ 0600-04300; www.eckeroline.fi) Finland–Estonia

Finnlines (☑ 010-343-4810; www.finnlines.com) Finland–Sweden, Finland–Germany

St Peter Line (☑ 09-6187-2000; https://stpeterline.com) Finland–Russia

Tallink/Silja Line (☑ 0600-15700; www.tallinksilja.com) Finland–Sweden, Finland–Estonia

Viking Line (☑ 0600-41577; www.vikingline.fi) Finland–Sweden, Finland–Estonia

Wasaline (☑ 020-771-6810; www.wasaline.com; Laivanvarustajankatu 4, Helsinki) Finland–Sweden

❶ Getting Around

AIR

Finnair (www.finnair.com) runs a fairly comprehensive domestic service out of Helsinki. Standard prices are expensive, but check the website for offers. Multitrip journeys can be significantly cheaper than one-way flights. Some Lapland destinations are winter only.

BICYCLE

Finland is as bicycle friendly as any country you'll find, with plenty of paths and few hills. Bikes can be taken on most trains, buses and ferries. Åland is particularly good for cycling.

Helmets are recommended but no longer required by law.

BOAT

Lake boats were once important summer transport providers. These services are now largely kept on as cruises, and make a great, leisurely way to journey between towns. The most popular routes are Tampere–Hämeenlinna, Tampere–Virrat, Savonlinna–Kuopio and Lahti–Jyväskylä.

Coastal routes include Turku–Naantali, Helsinki–Porvoo and ferries to the Åland Archipelago.

The website http://lautta.net is handy for domestic lake-boat and ferry services.

BUS

Bus is the main form of long-distance transport in Finland, with a far more comprehensive network than the train system. Buses run on time and are rarely full.

Ticketing is handled by Matkahuolto (www.matkahuolto.fi), which has an excellent website with all the timetables. Matkahuolto offices work normal business hours, but you can always just buy the ticket from the driver.

Towns have a *linja-autoasema* (bus terminal), with local timetables displayed (*lähtevät* is departures, *saapuvat* arrivals).

Separate from the normal system (though its timetables appear on the Matkahuolto website), Onnibus (www.onnibus.com) runs a variety of budget intercity routes in comfortable double-decker buses. Most of these radiate from Helsinki and can be much cheaper than normal fares if booked in advance.

CAR & MOTORCYCLE

Finland's road network is excellent, although there are few motorways. When approaching a town or city, *keskusta* on signs indicates the town centre. There are no road tolls but *lots* of speed cameras.

Petrol is expensive in Finland; check current prices at www.fuel-prices-europe.info. Many petrol stations are unstaffed, but machines take cash and most (but not all) chip- and PIN-enabled credit and debit cards. Change for cash is not given.

Hire

Car rental is expensive, but rates can work out to be reasonable with advance booking or with a group. A small car costs from €55/200 per day/week with 300km free per day, including basic insurance. One-way rentals attract a surcharge and are not always possible. Book ahead at peak times to ensure a car is available. As ever, the cheapest deals are online.

In larger towns, look out for weekend rates. These can cost little more than the rate for a single day, and you can pick up the car early afternoon on Friday and return it late Sunday or early Monday.

Car-hire franchises with offices in many Finnish cities include the following:

→ Avis (www.avis.com)
→ Budget (www.budget.com)
→ Europcar (www.europcar.com)
→ Hertz (www.hertz.com)
→ Sixt (www.sixt.com)

Road Conditions & Hazards

Conditions Snow and ice on the roads, potentially from September to April, and as late as June in Lapland, make driving a serious undertaking. Snow chains are illegal: people use either snow tyres, which have studs, or special all-weather tyres. The website http://liikennetilanne.liikennevirasto.fi has road webcams around Finland that are good for checking conditions. Select 'Kelikamerat' on the map.

Wildlife Beware of elk and reindeer, which don't respect vehicles and can dash onto the road unexpectedly. This sounds comical, but elk especially constitute a deadly danger. Notify the police if there is an accident involving these animals. Reindeer are very common in Lapland; slow right down if you see one, as there will be more nearby.

Road Rules

→ Finns drive on the right.
→ The speed limit is 50km/h in built-up areas, from 80km/h to 100km/h on highways, and 120km/h on some motorways.
→ Use headlights at all times.
→ Seat belts are compulsory for all.
→ Blood alcohol limit is 0.05%.

An important feature of Finland is that there are fewer give-way signs than most countries. Traffic entering an intersection from the right has right of way. While this doesn't apply to highways or main roads, in towns cars will often nip out from the right without looking: you must give way, so be careful at smaller intersections in towns.

TRAIN

State-owned Valtion Rautatiet (VR; www.vr.fi) runs Finnish trains. It's a fast, efficient service, with prices roughly equivalent to buses on the same route.

VR's website has comprehensive timetable information. Major stations have a VR office and ticket machines. Tickets can also be purchased online, where you'll also find discounted advance fares. You can board and pay the conductor, but if the station where you boarded had ticket-purchasing facilities, you'll be charged a small penalty fee (€2 to €5).

Costs

Fares vary slightly according to the type of train, with Pendolino the priciest. A one-way ticket for a 100km Express train journey costs approximately €25 in 2nd ('eco') class. First-class ('extra') tickets cost around 35% more than a 2nd-class ticket. A return fare gives a 10% discount. Online discounts are considerable.

Children under 17 pay half fare; those under six years travel free (but without a seat). A child travels free with every adult on long-distance trips, and there are also discounts for seniors, local students and any group of three or more adults travelling together.

Train Passes

Various passes are available for rail travel within Finland, or in European countries including Finland. There are cheaper passes for students, people aged under 26 and seniors. Supplements (eg for high-speed services) and reservation costs are not covered, and terms and conditions change – check carefully before buying. Always carry your passport when using the pass.

Eurail

Eurail (www.eurail.com) offers a good selection of passes available to residents of non-European countries, which should be purchased before arriving in Europe. Most of the passes offer discounts of around 25% for under-26s, or 15% for two people travelling together.

The Eurail Country Pass, valid for a single country, costs €182/245 for five/eight days' 2nd-class travel in a one-month period within Finland.

Eurail Global Passes offer a variety of options for travel in 28 European countries, from €468 for five days' travel within a one-month period to €942 for one month's continuous travel. The Global Passes are much better value for under-26s, as those older have to buy a 1st-class pass.

On most Eurail passes, children aged between four and 11 get a 50% discount on the full adult fare.

Eurail passes give a 30% to 50% discount on several ferry lines in the region; check the website for details.

InterRail

If you've lived in Europe for more than six months, you're eligible for an InterRail pass (www.interrail.eu). The InterRail Finland pass offers travel only in Finland for three/four/six/eight days in a one-month period, costing €105/126/164/198 in 2nd class. The Global Pass offers travel in 30 European countries and costs from €208 for five days' travel in any 15-day period, to €510 for a month's unlimited train travel. On both passes, there's a 33% discount for under-26s.

InterRail passes give a 30% to 50% discount on several ferry lines in the region; check the website for details.

France

POP 67 MILLION

Why Go?

France seduces travellers with its iconic landmarks and unfalteringly familiar culture woven around cafe terraces, markets and lace-curtained bistros with their *plat du jour* (dish of the day) chalked on the board. Nowhere else does the simple rhythm of daily life transform everyday rituals into exquisite moments quite like *la belle France:* a coffee and croissant in the Parisian cafe where Jean-Paul Sartre and Simone de Beauvoir met, a stroll through the lily-clad gardens Monet painted, a walk on a beach in Brittany scented with the subtle infusion of language, music and mythology brought by 5th-century Celtic invaders.

France is the world's top tourism destination, attracting some 89 million visitors each year with its exceptional wealth of museums and galleries, world-class art and architecture, tempting cuisine, and incredible bounty of outdoor experiences. Go slowly and enjoy.

Best Places to Eat

➡ L'Assiette Champenoise (p409)

➡ Restaurant AT (p391)

➡ 1741 (p412)

➡ Le Musée (p420)

Best Places to Stay

➡ Hôtel Ritz Paris (p390)

➡ Hôtel Particulier Montmartre (p390)

➡ Château Les Crayères (p409)

➡ Cour du Corbeau (p411)

When to Go

Paris

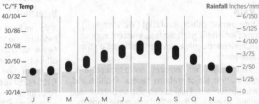

Dec–Mar Christmas markets in Alsace, snow in the Alps and decadent black truffles in the south.

Apr–Jun France is at its springtime best, with good weather and far smaller crowds.

Sep–Oct Cooling temperatures, abundant local produce and the *vendange* (grape harvest).

Entering the Country

Air France (www.airfrance.com) is the national carrier, with plenty of both domestic and international flights in and out of major French airports. Rail services link France with virtually every country in Europe. Eurolines (www.eurolines.eu), a grouping of 32 long-haul coach operators (including the UK's National Express), links France with cities all across Europe, Morocco and Russia.

FRANCE

ITINERARIES

One Week

Start with a couple of days exploring Paris (p378), taking in the Louvre, the Eiffel Tower, Montmartre and a boat trip along the Seine. Day-trip to magnificent Versailles (p398) and then spend the rest of the week in Normandy (p404) to visit WWII's D-Day beaches and glorious Mont St-Michel. Or head east to Champagne (p408) to sample the famous bubbly and visit Reims' (p408) magnificent cathedral.

Two Weeks

With Paris and surrounds having taken up much of the first week, hop on a high-speed TGV to Avignon (p436) or Marseille (p432) and take in the delights of Provence's Roman heritage, its beautiful hilltop villages and its famous artistic legacy. Finish your stay with a few days in Nice (p438), enjoying its glittering Mediterranean landscapes and sunny cuisine. Alternatively, head southwest to elegant Bordeaux (p425) and its world-famous vineyards before pushing inland to the Dordogne (p424) with its hearty gastronomy and unique prehistoric-art heritage.

Essential Food & Drink

Bordeaux and Burgundy wines You'll find France's signature reds in every restaurant; now find out more by touring the vineyards.

Bouillabaisse Marseille's signature hearty fish stew, eaten with croutons and rouille (garlic-and-chilli mayonnaise).

Champagne Tasting in century-old cellars is an essential part of Champagne's bubbly experience.

Foie gras and truffles The Dordogne features goose and 'black diamonds' from December to March. Provence is also good for indulging in the aphrodisiacal fungi.

Fondue and raclette Warming cheese dishes in the French Alps.

Oysters and white wine Everywhere on the Atlantic coast, but especially in Cancale and Bordeaux.

Piggy-part cuisine Lyon is famous for its juicy *andouillette* (pig-intestine sausage), a perfect marriage with a local Côtes du Rhône red.

Sleeping Price Ranges

The following price ranges refer to a double room in high season, with private bathroom, excluding breakfast unless noted.

€ less than €90 (€130 in Paris)

€€ €90–190 (€130–250 in Paris)

€€€ more than €190 (€250 in Paris)

Eating Price Ranges

The following price ranges refer to the average cost of a two-course à la carte meal (starter and main, or main and dessert), or a two- or three-course *menu* (set meal at a fixed price).

€ less than €20

€€ €20–40

€€€ more than €40

Resources

France.fr (www.france.fr)

France 24 (www.france24.com/en/france)

France Highlights

❶ Paris (p378)
Gorging on the iconic sights and sophistication of Europe's most impossibly romantic city.

❷ Loire Valley (p412) Reliving the French Renaissance with extraordinary châteaux built by kings and queens.

❸ Chamonix (p422) Doing a Bond and swooshing down slopes in the shadow of Mont Blanc.

❹ Mont St-Michel (p406) Dodging tides, strolling moonlit sand and immersing yourself in legend at this island abbey.

❺ Provence (p432) Savouring ancient ruins, modern art, markets, lavender and hilltop villages.

❻ Dune du Pilat (p429) Romping up and down Europe's largest sand dune.

❼ Épernay (p410) Tasting bubbly in ancient *caves* (cellars) in the heart of Champagne.

❽ Lyon (p417) Tucking into France's piggy-driven cuisine in a traditional *bouchon* (Lyonnais bistro).

❾ Casino de Monte Carlo (p445) Hitting the big time in Monaco's sumptuous gaming house.

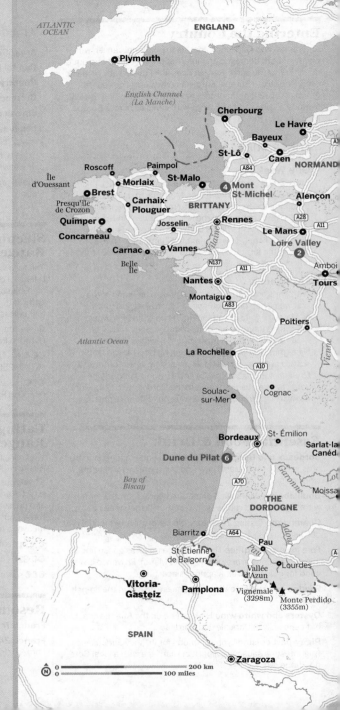

PARIS

POP 2.2 MILLION

What can be said about the timelessly sexy, sophisticated City of Lights that hasn't already been said myriad times before? Quite simply, this is one of the world's great metropolises – a trendsetter, market leader and cultural capital for over a thousand years and still going strong.

As you might expect, Paris is strewn with historic architecture, glorious galleries and cultural treasures galore. But the modern-day city is much more than just a museum piece: a new wave of multimedia galleries, creative wine bars, design shops and tech start-ups ensure it stays right up-to-the-minute and a delightful place to simply be: stroll the boulevards, shop until you drop, flop riverside or simply do as the Parisians do and watch the city's unique world buzz by from a cafe pavement terrace.

Sights

Most sights offer discounted tickets (*tarif réduit*) for students and seniors (over 60) provided they have valid ID. Children are often free; the cut-off age for 'child' is between six and 18 years. EU citizens under 26 years get in for free at national monuments and museums. The **Paris Museum Pass** (http://en.parismuseumpass.com; two/four/six days €48/62/74) covers admission to 50-plus venues – often via a different entrance to bypass ridiculously long ticket queues. The **Paris Passlib'** (www.parisinfo.com; two/three/five days €109/129/155) pass includes the above plus unlimited public transport in zones 1 to 3, a boat cruise and a one-day hop-on, hop-off open-top bus sightseeing tour around central Paris.

Left Bank

★ Eiffel Tower
TOWER

(☑ 08 92 70 12 39; www.toureiffel.paris; Champ de Mars, 5 av Anatole France, 7e; adult/child lift to top €25/12.50, lift to 2nd fl €16/8, stairs to 2nd fl €10/5; ⏱ lifts & stairs 9am-12.45am mid-Jun–Aug, lifts 9.30am-11.45pm, stairs 9.30am-6.30pm Sep–mid-Jun; Ⓜ Bir Hakeim or RER Champ de Mars–Tour Eiffel) No one could imagine Paris today without it. But Gustave Eiffel only constructed this elegant, 324m-tall signature spire as a temporary exhibit for the 1889 World's Fair. Luckily, the art nouveau tower's popularity assured its survival. Prebook online to avoid painfully long ticket queues. Lifts ascend to the tower's three floors; change lifts on the 2nd floor for the final ascent to the top. Energetic visitors can climb as far as the 2nd floor via the south pillar's 720 stairs (no prebooking).

★ Musée du Quai Branly – Jacques Chirac
MUSEUM

(☑ 01 56 61 70 00; www.quaibranly.fr; 37 quai Branly, 7e; adult/child €10/free; ⏱ 11am-7pm Tue, Wed & Sun, 11am-9pm Thu-Sat, plus 11am-7pm Mon during school holidays; Ⓜ Alma Marceau or RER Pont de l'Alma) A tribute to the diversity of human culture, Musée du Quai Branly's highly inspiring overview of indigenous and folk art spans four main sections – Oceania, Asia, Africa and the Americas. An impressive array of masks, carvings, weapons, jewellery and more make up the body of the rich collection, displayed in a refreshingly unorthodox interior without rooms or high walls. Look out for excellent temporary exhibitions and performances.

★ Hôtel des Invalides
MONUMENT, MUSEUM

(www.musee-armee.fr; 129 rue de Grenelle, 7e; adult/child €12/free; ⏱ 10am-6pm Apr-Oct, to 5pm Nov-Mar; Ⓜ Varenne or La Tour Maubourg) Flanked by the 500m-long Esplanade des Invalides lawns, Hôtel des Invalides was built in the 1670s by Louis XIV to house 4000 *invalides* (disabled war veterans). On 14 July 1789, a mob broke into the building and seized 32,000 rifles before heading on to the prison at Bastille and the start of the French Revolution. Admission includes entry to all Hôtel des Invalides sights (temporary exhibitions cost extra). Hours for individual sites can vary – check the website for updates.

★ Musée Rodin
MUSEUM, GARDEN

(☑ 01 44 18 61 10; www.musee-rodin.fr; 79 rue de Varenne, 7e; adult/child €10/free, garden only €4/free; ⏱ 10am-5.45pm Tue-Sun; Ⓜ Varenne or Invalides) Sculptor, painter, sketcher, engraver and collector Auguste Rodin donated his entire collection to the French state in 1908 on the proviso that it dedicate his former workshop and showroom, the beautiful 1730 Hôtel Biron, to displaying his works. They're now installed not only in the mansion itself, but also in its rose-filled garden – one of the most peaceful places in central Paris and a wonderful spot to contemplate his famous work *The Thinker*. Prepurchase tickets online to avoid queuing.

★ Musée d'Orsay
MUSEUM

(☑ 01 40 49 48 14; www.musee-orsay.fr; 1 rue de la Légion d'Honneur, 7e; adult/child €14/free;

9.30am-6pm Tue, Wed & Fri-Sun, to 9.45pm Thu; M Assemblée Nationale or RER Musée d'Orsay) The home of France's national collection from the impressionist, post-impressionist and art nouveau movements spanning from 1848 to 1914 is the glorious former Gare d'Orsay train station – itself an art nouveau showpiece – where a roll-call of masters and their world-famous works are on display. Top of every visitor's must-see list is the painting collection, centred on the world's largest collection of impressionist and post-impressionist art. Allow ample time to swoon over masterpieces by Manet, Monet, Cézanne, Renoir, Degas, Pissarro and Van Gogh.

★ **Église St-Germain des Prés**   CHURCH
(Map p380; 0155428118; www.eglise-saintgermain despres.fr; 3 place St-Germain des Prés, 6e; ⊙9am-8pm; M St-Germain des Prés) Paris' oldest standing church, the Romanesque St Germanus of the Fields, was built in the 11th century on the site of a 6th-century abbey and was the main place of worship in Paris until the arrival of Notre Dame. It's since been altered many times. The oldest part, **Chapelle de St-Symphorien**, is to the right as you enter; St Germanus (496–576), the first bishop of Paris, is believed to be buried there.

★ **Jardin du Luxembourg**   PARK
(Map p380; www.senat.fr/visite/jardin; 6e; ⊙hours vary; M Mabillon, St-Sulpice, Rennes, Notre Dame des Champs or RER Luxembourg) This inner-city oasis of formal terraces, chestnut groves and lush lawns has a special place in Parisians' hearts. Napoléon dedicated the 23 gracefully laid-out hectares of the Luxembourg Gardens to the children of Paris, and many residents spent their childhood prodding 1920s wooden **sailboats** (sailboat rental per 30min €4; ⊙11am-6pm Apr-Oct) with long sticks on the octagonal **Grand Bassin** pond, watching puppets perform puppet shows at the **Théâtre du Luxembourg** (01 43 29 50 97; www.marionnettesduluxembourg.fr; tickets €6.40; ⊙Wed, Sat & Sun, daily during school holidays) and riding the *carrousel* (merry-go-round) or **ponies** (Map p380; 06 07 32 53 95; www.animaponey.com; 600m/900m pony ride €6/8.50; ⊙3-6pm Wed, Sat, Sun & school holidays).

★ **Panthéon**   MAUSOLEUM
(Map p380; 01 44 32 18 00; www.paris-pantheon. fr; place du Panthéon, 5e; adult/child €9/free; ⊙10am-6.30pm Apr-Sep, to 6pm Oct-Mar; M Maubert-Mutualité or RER Luxembourg) The Panthéon's stately neoclassical dome is an icon of the Parisian skyline. Its vast interior is an architectural masterpiece: originally an abbey church dedicated to Ste Geneviève and now a mausoleum, it has served since 1791 as the resting place of some of France's greatest thinkers, including Voltaire, Rousseau, Braille and Hugo. A copy of Foucault's pendulum, first hung from the dome in 1851 to demonstrate the rotation of the earth, takes pride of place.

★ **Les Catacombes**   CEMETERY
(01 43 22 47 63; www.catacombes.paris.fr; place Denfert-Rochereau, 14e; adult/child €13/free, online booking incl audio guide €29/5; ⊙10am-8.30pm Tue-Sun; M Denfert-Rochereau) Paris' most macabre sight are these skull- and bone-lined underground tunnels. In 1785 it was decided to rectify the hygiene problems of Paris' overflowing cemeteries by exhuming the bones and storing them in disused quarry tunnels, and the Catacombes were created in 1810. After descending 20m (via 131 narrow, dizzying spiral steps), you follow dark, subterranean passages to the ossuary (1.5km in all). Exit up 112 steps via a 'transition space' with gift shop onto 21bis av René Coty, 14e.

⊙ The Islands

★ **Cathédrale Notre Dame de Paris**   CATHEDRAL
(Map p380; www.notredamedeparis.fr; 6 Parvis Notre Dame – place Jean-Paul-II, 4e; ⊙closed indefinitely; M Cité) While its interior is closed off to visitors following the devastating fire of April 2019, this masterpiece of French Gothic architecture remains the city's geographic and spiritual heart. It's grand exterior, with its two enduring towers and flying buttresses, is rightly still an alluring attraction to countless visitors.

★ **Sainte-Chapelle**   CHAPEL
(Map p380; 01 53 40 60 80, concerts 01 42 77 65 65; www.sainte-chapelle.fr; 8 bd du Palais, 1er; adult/child €10/free, joint ticket with Conciergerie €15/free; ⊙9am-7pm Apr-Sep, to 5pm Oct-Mar; M Cité) Try to save Sainte-Chapelle for a sunny day, when Paris' oldest, finest stained glass is at its dazzling best. Enshrined within the Palais de Justice (Law Courts), this gem-like Holy Chapel is Paris' most exquisite Gothic monument. It was completed in 1248, just six years after the first stone was laid, and was conceived by Louis IX to house his personal collection of holy relics, including the famous Holy Crown.

Central Paris

FRANCE PARIS

Central Paris

◉ Right Bank

★ Musée du Louvre — MUSEUM
(Map p380; ☑ 01 40 20 53 17; www.louvre.fr; rue de Rivoli & quai des Tuileries, 1er; adult/child €15/free, 6-9.45pm 1st Sat of month free; ☉9am-6pm Mon, Thu, Sat & Sun, to 9.45pm Wed, Fri & 1st Sat of month; Ⓜ Palais Royal–Musée du Louvre) It isn't until you're standing in the vast courtyard of the Louvre, with sunlight shimmering through the glass pyramid and crowds milling about beneath the museum's ornate facade, that you can truly say you've been to Paris. Holding tens of thousands of works of art – from Mesopotamian, Egyptian and Greek antiquities to masterpieces by artists such as da Vinci (including his incomparable *Mona Lisa*), Michelangelo and Rembrandt – it's no surprise that this is one of the world's most visited museums.

★ Jardin des Tuileries — PARK
(rue de Rivoli, 1er; ☉7am-9pm Apr-late Sep, 7.30am-7.30pm late Sep-Mar; Ⓜ Tuileries or Concorde) Filled with fountains, ponds and sculptures, the formal 28-hectare Tuileries Garden, which begins just west of the Jardin du Carrousel, was laid out in its present form in 1664 by André Le Nôtre, architect of the gardens at Versailles. The Tuileries soon became the most fashionable spot in Paris for parading about in one's finery. It now forms part of the Banks of the Seine Unesco World Heritage Site.

★ Arc de Triomphe — LANDMARK
(www.paris-arc-de-triomphe.fr; place Charles de Gaulle, 8e; viewing platform adult/child €12/free; ☉10am-11pm Apr-Sep, to 10.30pm Oct-Mar; Ⓜ Charles de Gaulle–Étoile) If anything rivals the Eiffel Tower (p378) as the symbol of Paris, it's this magnificent 1836 monument to Napoléon's victory at Austerlitz (1805), which he commissioned the following year. The intricately sculpted triumphal arch stands sentinel in the centre of the Étoile (Star) roundabout. From the viewing platform on top of the arch (50m up via 284 steps and well worth the climb) you can see the dozen avenues.

★ Église St-Eustache — CHURCH
(Map p380; www.st-eustache.org; 2 impasse St-Eustache, 1er; ☉9.30am-7pm Mon-Fri, 10am-7.15pm Sat, 9am-7.15pm Sun; Ⓜ Les Halles or RER Châtelet–Les Halles) Just north of the gardens adjoining the city's old marketplace, now the **Forum**

des Halles (Map p380; www.forumdeshalles.com; 1 rue Pierre Lescot, 1er; ⏱shops 10am-8pm Mon-Sat, 11am-7pm Sun), is one of the most beautiful churches in Paris. Majestic, architecturally magnificent and musically outstanding, St-Eustache was constructed between 1532 and 1632 and is primarily Gothic. Artistic highlights include a work by Rubens, Raymond Mason's colourful bas-relief of market vendors (1969) and Keith Haring's bronze triptych (1990) in the side chapels.

★ **Centre Pompidou** MUSEUM
(Map p380; ☎01 44 78 12 33; www.centrepompidou.fr; place Georges Pompidou, 4e; museum, exhibitions & panorama adult/child €14/free, panorama only ticket €5/free; ⏱11am-9pm Wed-Mon, temporary exhibits to 11pm Thu; Ⓜ Rambuteau) Renowned for its radical architectural statement, the 1977-opened Centre Pompidou brings together galleries and cutting-edge exhibitions, hands-on workshops, dance performances, cinemas and other entertainment venues, with street performers and fanciful fountains outside. The **Musée National d'Art Moderne**, France's national collection of art dating from 1905 onwards, is the main draw; a fraction of its 100,000-plus pieces – including Fauvist, cubist, surrealist, pop art and contemporary works – is on display. Don't miss the spectacular Parisian panorama from the rooftop.

★ **Musée National Picasso** MUSEUM
(Map p380; ☎01 85 56 00 36; www.museepicassoparis.fr; 5 rue de Thorigny, 3e; adult/child €12.50/free; ⏱10.30am-6pm Tue-Fri, from 9.30am Sat & Sun; Ⓜ Chemin Vert or St-Paul) One of Paris' most treasured art collections is showcased inside the mid-17th-century Hôtel Salé, an exquisite private mansion owned by the city since 1964. The Musée National Picasso is a staggering art museum devoted to Spanish artist Pablo Picasso (1881–1973), who spent much of his life living and working in Paris. The collection includes more than 5000 drawings, engravings, paintings, ceramic works and sculptures by the *grand maître* (great master), although they're not all displayed at the same time.

★ **Cimetière du Père Lachaise** CEMETERY
(☎01 55 25 82 10; www.pere-lachaise.com; 16 rue du Repos & 8 bd de Ménilmontant, 20e; ⏱8am-6pm Mon-Fri, from 8.30am Sat, from 9am Sun mid-Mar–Oct, shorter hours Nov–mid-Mar; Ⓜ Père Lachaise or Gambetta) Opened in 1804, Père Lachaise is today the world's most visited cemetery. Its 70,000 ornate tombs of the rich and famous form a verdant, 44-hectare sculpture

'I LOVE YOU' PARIS-STYLE

Few visitors can resist a selfie in front of Montmartre's 'I Love You' wall, **Le Mur des je t'aime** (www.lesjetaime.com; Sq Jehan Rictus, place des Abbesses ,18e; ⏱8am-9.30pm Mon-Fri, from 9am Sat & Sun mid-May–Aug, shorter hours Sep–mid-May; Ⓜ Abbesses), a public artwork created in a small park by artists Frédéric Baron and Claire Kito in the year 2000. Made from 511 dark-blue enamel tiles, the striking mural features the immortal phrase 'I love you' 311 times in nearly 250 different languages (the red fragments, if joined together, would form a heart). Find a bench beneath a maple tree and brush up your language skills romantic-Paris-style.

garden. The most visited are those of 1960s rock star Jim Morrison (division 6) and Oscar Wilde (division 89). Pick up cemetery maps at the **conservation office** (Bureaux de la Conservation; 16 rue du Repos, 20e; ⏱8.30am-12.30pm & 2-5pm Mon-Fri; Ⓜ Philippe Auguste, Père Lachaise) near the main bd de Ménilmontant entrance. Other notables buried here include composer Chopin, playwright Molière, poet Apollinaire, and writers Balzac, Proust, Stein and Colette.

★ **Basilique du Sacré-Cœur** BASILICA
(☎01 53 41 89 00; www.sacre-coeur-montmartre.com; Parvis du Sacré-Cœur, 18e; basilica free, dome adult/child €6/4, cash only; ⏱basilica 6am-10.30pm, dome 8.30am-8pm May-Sep, 9am-5pm Oct-Apr; Ⓜ Anvers or Abbesses) Begun in 1875 in the wake of the Franco-Prussian War and the chaos of the Paris Commune, Sacré-Cœur is a symbol of the former struggle between the conservative Catholic old guard and the secular, republican radicals. It was finally consecrated in 1919, standing in contrast to the bohemian lifestyle that surrounded it. The view over Paris from its parvis is breathtaking. Avoid walking up the steep hill by using a regular metro ticket aboard the **funicular** (www.ratp.fr; place St-Pierre, 18e; ⏱6am-12.45am; Ⓜ Anvers or Abbesses) to the **upper station** (www.ratp.fr; rue du Cardinal Dubois, 18e; ⏱6am-12.45am; Ⓜ Abbesses).

☞ Tours

A boat cruise down the Seine is the most relaxing way to acquaint or reacquaint yourself with the city's main monuments as you watch

Montmartre

N 0 ————— 400 m
0 ————— 0.2 miles

Montmartre

⊙ Top Sights
1 Basilique du Sacré-Cœur C1
2 Le Mur des je t'aime C2

🛏 Sleeping
3 Hôtel Particulier Montmartre B1
4 Hoxton D5

✖ Eating
5 Le Grenier à Pain C2
6 Le Potager de Charlotte D3

7 L'Office D4
8 Richer D4

🍷 Drinking & Nightlife
Le Très Particulier ....(see 3)

✪ Entertainment
9 Kiosque Théâtre Madeleine A5
10 Moulin Rouge B2
11 Palais Garnier B5

Paris glide by. **Bateaux-Mouches** (☑ 01 42 25 96 10; www.bateaux-mouches.fr; Port de la Conférence, 8e; adult/child €14/6; ⏲ 10am-10.30pm Mon-Fri, 10.15am-9.20pm Sat & Sun Apr-Sep, every 40min 11am-9.20pm Oct-Mar; Ⓜ Alma Marceau) is Paris' largest river-cruise company; boats depart from just east of the Pont de l'Alma on the Right Bank. An alternative to a regular tour is the hop-on, hop-off Batobus (p397).

⭐ **Parisien d'un Jour – Paris Greeters** WALKING
(www.greeters.paris; by donation) See Paris through local eyes with these two- to three-hour city tours. Volunteers – mainly knowledgeable Parisians passionate about their city – lead groups (maximum six people) to their favourite spots. Minimum two weeks' notice is needed.

Meeting the French CULTURAL, TOURS
(☑ 01 42 51 19 80; www.meetingthefrench.com; tours & courses from €12) Cosmetics workshops, backstage cabaret tours, fashion-designer showroom visits, French table decoration, art embroidery classes, market tours, baking with a Parisian baker – the repertoire of cultural and gourmet tours and behind-the-scenes experiences offered by Meeting the French is truly outstanding. All courses and tours are in English.

Street Art Paris WALKING
(☑ 09 50 75 19 92; www.streetartparis.fr; tours €20; ⏲ by reservation) Learn about the history of graffiti on fascinating tours taking in Paris' vibrant street art. Tours take place in Belleville and Montmartre and on the Left Bank. If you're inspired to try it yourself, book into a 2½-hour mural workshop (€35).

🛏 Sleeping

🛏 Left Bank

⭐ **Hôtel Diana** HOTEL $
(Map p380; ☑ 01 43 54 92 55; http://hotel-diana-paris.com; 73 rue St-Jacques, 5e; s €78-98, d €105-145, tr €160-195; 🛜; Ⓜ Maubert-Mutualité) Footsteps from the Sorbonne, two-star Diana is budget-traveller gold. Owner extraordinaire, Thérèse Cheval, has been at the helm here since the 1970s and the pride and joy she invests in the hotel is boundless. Spacious rooms sport a stylish contemporary decor with geometric-patterned fabrics, the odd retro furniture piece, and courtesy tray with kettle and white-mug twinset. Breakfast €10.

⭐ **Hôtel Henriette** DESIGN HOTEL $$
(☑ 01 47 07 26 90; www.hotelhenriette.com; 9 rue des Gobelins, 13e; s €69-209, d €79-309, tr €89-339, q €129-499; 🌬🛜; Ⓜ Les Gobelins) Interior designer Vanessa Scoffier scoured Paris' flea markets to source Platner chairs, 1950s lighting and other unique vintage pieces for the 32 rooms at bohemian Henriette – one of the Left Bank's most stunning boutique addresses. Guests can mingle in the light-flooded glass atrium and adjoining plant-filled patio with wrought-iron furniture.

Off Paris Seine HOTEL $$
(Map p380; ☑ 01 44 06 62 66; www.offparisseine.com; 85 quai d'Austerlitz, 13e; d from €169; 🛜🖂; Ⓜ Gare d'Austerlitz) Should the idea of being gently rocked to sleep take your fancy, check in to Paris' first floating hotel by the highly recommended Parisian Elegancia hotel group. The sleek, 80m-long catamaran-design structure moored by Pont Charles de Gaulle sports sun terraces overlooking the Seine, a chic bar with silver beanbags by a 15m-long dipping pool, a lounge and 58 stunningly appointed rooms and suites.

🛏 Right Bank

⭐ **Generator Hostel** HOSTEL $
(☑ 01 70 98 84 00; www.generatorhostels.com; 9-11 place du Colonel Fabien, 10e; dm/d from €33/92; 🌬@🛜; Ⓜ Colonel Fabien) From the 9th-floor rooftop bar overlooking Sacré-Cœur and the stylish ground-floor cafe-restaurant to the vaulted basement bar-club styled like a Paris metro station, and supercool bathrooms with 'I love you' tiling, this ultra-contemporary hostel near Canal St-Martin is sharp. Dorms have USB sockets and free lockers, and the best doubles have fabulous terraces with views. Women-only dorms are available.

⭐ **Hôtel du Dragon** HOTEL $
(☑ 01 45 48 51 05; www.hoteldudragon.com; 36 rue du Dragon, 6e; d €95-150, tr €130-180; 🛜; Ⓜ St-Sulpice) It's hard to believe that such a gem of a budget hotel still exists in this ultrachic part of St-Germain. A family affair for the last five generations, today the ever-charming Roy runs the 28-room Dragon with his children, Sébastien and Marie-Hélène. Spotlessly clean rooms are decidedly large by Paris standards, often with exposed wooden beams and lovely vintage furnishings.

⭐ **Hôtel Georgette** DESIGN HOTEL $$
(Map p380; ☑ 01 44 61 10 10; www.hotelgeorgette.com; 36 rue du Grenier St-Lazare, 3e; d from €240;

The Louvre

A HALF-DAY TOUR

Successfully visiting the Louvre is a fine art. Its complex labyrinth of galleries and staircases spiralling across three wings and four floors renders discovery a snakes-and-ladders experience. Initiate yourself with this three-hour itinerary – a playful mix of *Mona Lisa*–obvious and up-to-the-minute unexpected.

Arriving in the newly renovated ❶ **Cour Napoléon** beneath IM Pei's glass pyramid, pick up colour-coded floor plans at an information stand, then ride the escalator up to the Sully Wing and swap passport or credit card for a multimedia guide (there are limited descriptions in the galleries) at the wing entrance.

The Louvre is as much about spectacular architecture as masterful art. To appreciate this, zip up and down Sully's Escalier Henri II to admire ❷ **Venus de Milo**, then up parallel Escalier Henri IV to the palatial displays in ❸ **Cour Khorsabad**. Cross Room 236 to find the escalator up to the 1st floor and the opulent ❹ **Napoléon III apartments**. Next traverse 25 consecutive galleries (thank you, floor plan!) to flip conventional contemplation on its head with Cy Twombly's ❺ **The Ceiling**, and the hypnotic ❻ **Winged Victory of Samothrace**, which brazenly insists on being admired from all angles. End with the impossibly famous ❼ **Raft of the Medusa**, ❽ **Mona Lisa** and ❾ **Virgin & Child**.

TOP TIPS

➡ Don't even consider entering the Louvre's maze of galleries without a floor plan, free from the information desk in the Hall Napoléon.

➡ The Denon Wing is always packed; visit on late nights (Wednesday or Friday) or trade Denon in for the notably quieter Richelieu Wing.

➡ Tickets to the Louvre are valid for the whole day, meaning that you can nip out for lunch.

BRIAN KINNEY /SHUTTERSTOCK ©

Napoléon III Apartments
1st Floor, Richelieu
Napoléon III's gorgeous gilt apartments were built from 1854 to 1861, featuring an over-the-top decor of gold leaf, stucco and crystal chandeliers that reaches a dizzying climax in the Grand Salon and State Dining Room.

Jardin du Carrousel

Galerie du Carrousel Entrances

Porte des Lions

LOUVRE AUDITORIUM

Classical-music concerts are staged several times a week at the Louvre Auditorium (off the main entrance hall). Don't miss the Thursday lunchtime concerts featuring emerging composers and musicians. The season runs from September to April or May, depending on the concert series.

Mona Lisa
Room 711, 1st Floor, Denon
No smile is as enigmatic or bewitching as hers. Da Vinci's diminutive *La Joconde* hangs opposite the largest painting in the Louvre – sumptuous, fellow Italian Renaissance artwork *The Wedding at Cana*.

The Raft of the Medusa
Room 700, 1st Floor, Denon
Decipher the politics behind French romanticism in Théodore Géricault's *Raft of the Medusa*.

Cour Khorsabad
Ground Floor, Richelieu
Time travel with a pair of winged human-headed bulls to view some of the world's oldest Mesopotamian art. **DETOUR»** Night-lit statues in Cour Puget.

PRZMAT / SHUTTERSTOCK ©

The Ceiling
Room 663, 1st Floor, Sully
Admire the blue shock of Cy Twombly's 400-sq-metre contemporary ceiling fresco – the Louvre's latest, daring commission. **DETOUR»** *The Braque Ceiling*, Room 662.

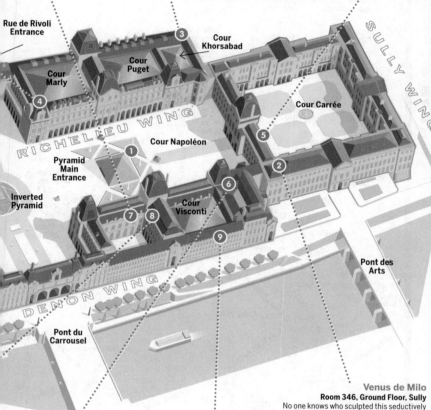

Rue de Rivoli Entrance

Cour Khorsabad

Cour Puget

Cour Marly

SULLY WING

Cour Carrée

RICHELIEU WING

Cour Napoléon

Pyramid Main Entrance

Cour Visconti

Inverted Pyramid

Pont des Arts

DENON WING

Pont du Carrousel

③ ④ ⑤ ① ② ⑥ ⑦ ⑧ ⑨

Venus de Milo
Room 346, Ground Floor, Sully
No one knows who sculpted this seductively realistic goddess from Greek antiquity. Naked to the hips, she is a Hellenistic masterpiece.

Winged Victory of Samothrace
Room 703, 1st Floor, Sully
Draw breath at the aggressive dynamism of this headless, handless Hellenistic goddess. **DETOUR»** The razzle-dazzle of the Apollo Gallery's crown jewels.

Virgin & Child
Grande Galerie, 1st Floor, Denon
In the spirit of artistic devotion save the Louvre's most famous gallery for last: a feast of Virgin-and-child paintings by Da Vinci, Raphael, Domenico Ghirlandaio, Giovanni Bellini and Francesco Botticini.

TUTTI FRUTTI / SHUTTERSTOCK ©

Greater Paris

COURBEVOIE

Seine

Île de la Grande Jatte

LEVALLOIS-PERRET

CLICHY

Porte de St-Ouen

Bd Bessières

Porte de Clichy

R Cardinet

R Guy Môquet

17E

R de Rome

La Fourche

Bd Bineau

Bd Victor Hugo

Porte de Villiers

R Anatole France

Péreire-Lavallois

Av de Villiers

Av Niel

Av de Wagram

Bd Malesherbes

Place de Clichy

NEUILLY-SUR-SEINE

Av Charles de Gaulle

Av du Roule

Parking Pershing

Av des Ternes

Bd de Courcelles

Gare St-Lazare

Bd Maurice Barrès

Jardin d'Acclimatation

Av Mac Mahon

Av Hoche

Bd Haussmann

St-Augustin

Auber

Mare St-James

Neuilly-Porte Maillot

Air France Buses

8E

Lac Pour le Patinage

Allée de Longchamp

Pl du Maillot de Lattre de Tassigny

Av Foch

1 Charles de Gaulle Étoile

Arc de Triomphe

Bois de Boulogne

Avenue Foch

Av Victor Hugo

Av Kléber

Av Marceau

Av des Champs-Élysées

TRIANGLE D'OR

15

Lac Inférieur

Avenue Henri Martin

Trocadéro

Le Bus Direct

Cours la Reine

10

Jardin des Tuileries

17

5

16E

Jardins du Trocadéro

Av de New York

8

Q d'Orsay

Q Anatole France

Av Paul Doumer

Batobus Stop

Q Branly

Musée du Quai Branly

Esplanade des Invalides

Musée d'Orsay

7

Musée d'Orsay

Boulainvilliers

R du Ranelagh

3 Eiffel Tower

Champ de Mars-Tour Eiffel

Hôtel des Invalides

4

Musée Rodin

9

7E

Lac Supérieur

Av Mozart

Avenue du Président Kennedy

Av de Suffren

14

LEFT BANK

Bd Raspail

12

Porte d'Auteuil

R Jean de la Fontaine

Batobus Stop

Bir Hakeim

21

École Militaire

Bd des Invalides

29

30

24

R de Sèvres

R de Rennes

Ste-Périne

Q André Citroën

Javel

Av de Versailles

Av Émile Zola

R de la Convention

Av de la Motte-Picquet

Av de Saxe

Gare Montparnasse

R du Départ

6E

Bd Exelmans

R Balard

R de la Croix Nivert

R Lecourbe

R de Vaugirard

Bd Pasteur

Bd Raspail

Porte d'Auteuil

Boulevard Victor

Bd Victor

20

15E

R de Vouillé

R d'Alésia

R Froidevaux

Av du Maine

Bd Périphérique

Bd Lefebvre

Porte de Vanves

14E

Av du Général Leclerc

Issy-Val de Seine

Île St-Germain

Jacques Henri Lartigue

Bd Périphérique

Bd Lefebvre

VANVES

Issy Ville

MONTROUGE

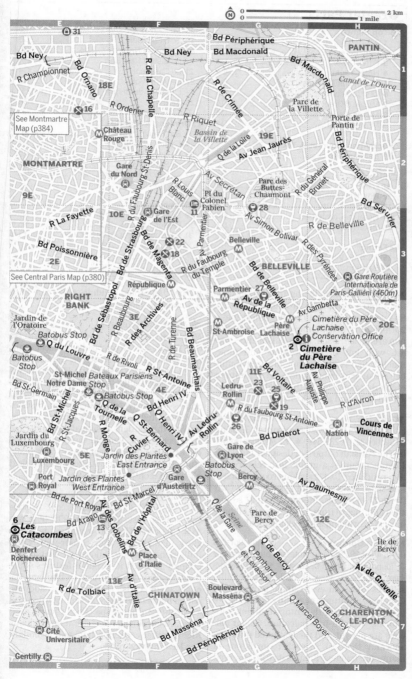

FRANCE PARIS

Greater Paris

✳ 🛜; Ⓜ Rambuteau) Taking inspiration from the Centre Pompidou around the corner, this vivacious hotel's 19 rooms reflect major 20th-century artistic movements, including pop art, op art, Dada, new realism and street art, with lots of bold colours and funky touches like Andy Warhol–inspired Campbell's-soup-can lampshades. Art exhibitions regularly take place in the bright lobby. It's gay-friendly and all-welcoming.

★ **Hoxton** DESIGN HOTEL **$$**
(☑ 01 85 65 75 00; www.thehoxton.com; 30-32 rue du Sentier, 2e; d €239-549; ✳ 🛜; Ⓜ Bonne Nouvelle) The Parisian outpost of designer hotel The Hoxton occupies a grand 18th-century former residence. Its 172 striking rooms come in four sizes: Shoebox (from 13 sq metres), Cosy (from 17 sq metres), Roomy (from 21 sq metres) and Biggy (from 32 sq metres). All have intricate cornicing and reclaimed oak floors.

Hôtel Le Comtesse BOUTIQUE HOTEL **$$**
(☑ 01 45 51 29 29; www.comtesse-hotel.com; 29 av de Tourville, 7e; d from €229; ✳ @ 🛜; Ⓜ École Militaire) A five-star view of Mademoiselle Eiffel seduces guests in every single room at The Countess, an utterly charming boutique hotel at home in a 19th-century building with alluring wrought-iron balconies. Colour palettes are playful, and the feathered quill pen adorning the desk in each room is one of many cute touches. Breakfast (€19) is served in the glamorous, boudoir-styled cafe with pavement terrace.

★ **Hôtel Particulier Montmartre** BOUTIQUE HOTEL **$$$**
(☑ 0153418140; www.hotel-particulier-montmartre. com; Pavillon D, 23 av Junot, 18e; ste €390-590; ✳ 🛜; Ⓜ Lamarck–Caulaincourt) Hidden down a stone-paved alley behind a high wall, this mansion is one of the city's most magical addresses. Its five sweeping designer suites are decorated with retro flea-market finds, but it's the garden, designed by landscape architect Louis Benech, and fashionable **cocktail bar** (⊙ 6pm-2am Tue-Sat) that really stun. Ring the buzzer outside the unmarked black-gated entrance at No 23.

★ **Hôtel Ritz Paris** HISTORIC HOTEL **$$$**
(☑ 01 43 16 30 30; www.ritzparis.com; 15 place Vendôme, 1er; d/ste from €1000/1900; ⓟ ✳ @ 🛜 ♿; Ⓜ Opéra) The Ritz reopened in all its glory in mid-2016 after a four-year, €400 million head-to-toe renovation that painstakingly restored its original features while incorporating 21st-century technology. It's once again Paris' most rarefied address, with a manicured French formal garden and a world-first Chanel spa (Coco Chanel lived here). Also reinvigorated are its prestigious Ritz Escoffier cookery school and legendary Bar Hemingway (p394).

Eating

Left Bank

Café de la Nouvelle Mairie
CAFE **$**

(Map p380; ☑ 01 44 07 04 41; 19 rue des Fossés St-Jacques, 5e; mains €11-17; ☺ 8am-12.30am Mon-Fri, kitchen noon-2.30pm & 8-10.30pm Mon-Thu, 8-10pm Fri; Ⓜ Cardinal Lemoine) Shhhh…just around the corner from the Panthéon (p379) but hidden away on a small, fountained square, this hybrid cafe-restaurant and wine bar is a tip-top neighbourhood secret, serving natural wines and delicious seasonal bistro fare from oysters and ribs *(à la française)* to grilled lamb sausage over lentils. It takes reservations for dinner but not lunch – arrive early.

★ Bouillon Racine
BRASSERIE **$$**

(Map p380; ☑ 01 44 32 15 60; www.bouillonracine.fr; 3 rue Racine, 6e; 2-course weekday lunch menu €17.50, 3-course menu €35, mains €17-24.50; ☺ noon-11pm; ☝; Ⓜ Cluny–La Sorbonne) Inconspicuously situated in a quiet street, this heritage-listed art nouveau 'soup kitchen', with mirrored walls, floral motifs and ceramic tiling, was built in 1906 to feed market workers. Despite the magnificent interior, the food – inspired by age-old recipes – is no afterthought and superbly executed (stuffed, spit-roasted suckling pig, pork shank in Rodenbach red beer, scallops and shrimps with lobster coulis).

Le Beurre Noisette
BISTRO **$$**

(☑ 01 48 56 82 49; www.restaurantbeurrenoisette. com; 68 rue Vasco de Gama, 15e; 2-/3-course lunch menu €25/34, 3-/5-course dinner menu €38/46, mains €19; ☺ noon-2pm & 7-10.30pm Tue-Sat; Ⓜ Lourmel) *Beurre noisette* (brown butter sauce, named for its hazelnut colour) features in dishes such as tender veal loin with homemade fries and caramelised pork belly

tender with braised red cabbage and apple, at pedigreed chef Thierry Blanqui's neighbourhood neobistro. Filled with locals, the chocolate-toned dining room is wonderfully convivial – be sure to book. Fantastic value.

Le Cassenoix
MODERN FRENCH **$$**

(☑ 01 45 66 09 01; www.le-cassenoix.fr; 56 rue de la Fédération, 15e; 3-course menu €34; ☺ noon-2pm & 7-10.30pm Mon-Fri; Ⓜ Bir Hakeim) The Nutcracker is everything a self-respecting neighbourhood bistro should be. *'Tradition et terroir'* (tradition and provenance) dictate the menu that inspires owner-chef Pierre Olivier Lenormand to deliver feisty dishes such as braised veal chuck with mashed potato and caramelised onions or grilled hake with parsnips and hazelnut-parmesan crumble. Vintage ceiling fans add to the wonderful retro vibe. Book ahead.

★ Restaurant AT
GASTRONOMY **$$$**

(Map p380; ☑ 01 56 81 94 08; www.atsushitanaka. com; 4 rue du Cardinal Lemoine, 5e; 6-course lunch menu €55, 12-course dinner tasting menu €95, with paired wines €170; ☺ 12.15-2pm & 8-9.30pm Mon-Sat; Ⓜ Cardinal Lemoine) Trained by some of the biggest names in gastronomy (Pierre Gagnaire included), chef Atsushi Tanaka showcases abstract artlike masterpieces incorporating rare ingredients (charred bamboo, kohlrabi turnip cabbage, juniper berry powder, wild purple fennel, Nepalese Timut pepper) in a blank-canvas-style dining space on stunning outsized plates. Reservations essential.

Right Bank

Marché Bastille
MARKET **$**

(Map p380; bd Richard Lenoir, 11e; ☺ 7am-2.30pm Thu, to 3pm Sun; Ⓜ Bastille or Bréguet–Sabin) If you only get to one open-air street market

FRANCE PARIS

TOP THREE PICNIC STOPS

When a light bite for lunch or between sights beckons – be it a pastry, well-filled baguette sandwich or sweet bite – head to one of these favourite *boulangeries* and patisseries.

Ladurée (Map p380; ☑ 01 44 07 64 87; www.laduree.fr; 34 rue Bonaparte, 6e; ☺ 8.30am-7.30pm Mon-Fri, 8.30am-8.30pm Sat, 10am-7.30pm Sun; Ⓜ St-Germain des Prés) One of Paris' oldest patisseries (1862), baking its iconic ganache-filled macarons since the 1930s.

Du Pain et des Idées (www.dupainetdesidees.com; 34 rue Yves Toudic, 10e; breads €1.20-7, pastries €2.50-6.50; ☺ 6.45am-8pm Mon-Fri, closed Aug; Ⓜ Jacques Bonsergent) Traditional bakery near Canal St-Martin with an exquisite 1889 interior.

Le Grenier à Pain (www.legrenierapain.com; 38 rue des Abbesses, 18e; pastries €1.10-4.50; ☺ 7.30am-8pm Thu-Mon; Ⓜ Abbesses) Perfect Montmartre picnic stop.

in Paris, this one – stretching between the Bastille and Richard Lenoir metro stations – is among the very best. Its 150-plus stalls are piled high with fruit and vegetables, meats, fish, shellfish, cheeses and seasonal specialities such as truffles. You'll also find clothing, leather handbags and wallets, and a smattering of antiques.

★ **Jacques Genin**   PASTRIES $
(Map p380; ☑ 01 45 77 29 01; www.jacquesgenin. fr; 133 rue de Turenne, 3e; pastries €9; ⊙ 11am-7pm Tue-Fri & Sun, to 7.30pm Sat; M Oberkampf or Filles du Calvaire) Wildly creative *chocolatier* Jacques Genin is famed for his flavoured caramels, *pâtes de fruits* (fruit jellies) and exquisitely embossed *bonbons de chocolat* (chocolate sweets). But what completely steals the show at his elegant chocolate showroom is the *salon de dégustation* (aka tearoom), where you can order a pot of outrageously thick hot chocolate and legendary Genin *millefeuille,* assembled to order.

★ **Breizh Café**   CRÊPES $
(Map p380; ☑ 01 42 72 13 77; www.breizhcafe.com; 109 rue Vieille du Temple, 3e; crêpes & galettes €6.80-18.80; ⊙ 10am-11pm; M St-Sébastien–Froissart) Everything at the Breizh ('Breton' in Breton) is 100% authentic, including its organic-flour crêpes and *galettes* (savoury buckwheat crêpes) that top many Parisians' lists for the best in the city. Other specialities include Cancale oysters and 20 types of cider. Tables are limited and there's often a wait; book ahead or try its deli, **L'Épicerie** (Map p380; ☑ 01 42 71 39 44; 111 rue Vieille du Temple, 3e; crêpes & galettes €6.80-18.80; ⊙ 10am-10pm), next door.

Le Verre Volé   BISTRO $
(☑ 01 48 03 17 34; www.leverrevole.fr; 67 rue de Lancry, 10e; mains €11-22, sandwiches €7.90; ⊙ bistro 12.30-2.30pm & 7.30-11.30pm, wine bar 10am-2am; ☎; M Jacques Bonsergent) The tiny 'Stolen

Glass' – a wine shop with a few tables – is one of Paris' most popular wine bar–restaurants, with outstanding natural and unfiltered wines and expert advice. Unpretentious, hearty *plats du jour* are excellent. Reserve in advance for meals, or stop by to pick up a gourmet sandwich (such as mustard-smoked burrata with garlic-pork sausage) and a bottle.

Richer   BISTRO $
(www.lericher.com; 2 rue Richer, 9e; mains €17-28; ⊙ noon-2.30pm & 7.30-10.30pm; M Poissonnière or Bonne Nouvelle) Run by the same team as across-the-street neighbour **L'Office** (☑ 01 47 70 67 31; www.office-resto.com; 3 rue Richer, 9e; 2-/3-course lunch menus €22/27, mains €22-29; ⊙ noon-2pm & 7.30-10.30pm Mon-Fri), Richer's pared-back, exposed-brick decor is a smart setting for genius creations including smoked-duck-breast ravioli in miso broth, and quince-and-lime cheesecake for dessert. It doesn't take reservations, but it serves snacks and Chinese tea, and has a full bar (open until midnight). Fantastic value.

L'Avant Comptoir de la Mer   SEAFOOD $
(Map p380; ☑ 01 42 38 47 55; www.hotel-paris -relais-saint-germain.com; 3 Carrefour de l'Odéon, 6e; tapas €5-25, oysters per 6 €17; ⊙ noon-11pm; M Odéon) One of Yves Camdeborde's stunning line-up of St-Germain hors d'oeuvre bars – alongside **Le Comptoir** (Map p380; ☑ 01 44 27 07 97; 9 Carrefour de l'Odéon, 6e; lunch mains €15-30, dinner menu €60; ⊙ noon-6pm & 8.30-11.30pm Mon-Fri, noon-11pm Sat & Sun), **L'Avant Comptoir de la Terre** (Map p380; 3 Carrefour de l'Odéon, 6e; tapas €5.50-13.50; ⊙ noon-11pm) and **L'Avant Comptoir du Marché** (Map p380; 15 rue Lobineau, 6e; tapas €5.50-21; ⊙ noon-11pm; M Mabillon) – serves succulent Cap Ferret oysters (straight, Bloody Mary–style or with chipolata sausages), herring tartine, cauliflower and trout roe, blood-orange razor clams, roasted scallops and salmon cro-

---

TOP THREE VEGETARIAN & VEGAN

Abattoir Végétal (www.abattoirvegetal.fr; 61 rue Ramey, 18e; 2-/3-course lunch menu €16.50/19, mains €10-16.50; ⊙ 9am-6pm Tue, 9am-10.30pm Wed-Fri, 10am-10.30pm Sat, 11am-4.30pm Sun; ☎☑; M Jules Joffrin) Plant-filled vegan cafe in Montmartre.

Le Potager de Charlotte (☑ 01 44 65 09 63; www.lepotagerdecharlotte.fr; 12 rue de la Tour d'Auvergne, 9e; mains €14.50-16, Sunday brunch €29; ⊙ 7-10.30pm Wed & Thu, noon-2.30pm & 7-10.30pm Fri & Sat, 11am-3pm Sun; ☑; M Cadet) Gourmet vegan restaurant.

Gentle Gourmet Café (Map p380; ☑ 01 43 43 48 49; https://gentlegourmet.fr; 24 bd de la Bastille, 12e; 2-/3-course lunch menu €23/30, mains €21-25; ⊙ noon-2.30pm & 6.30-10pm Tue-Sun; ☎☑✦; M Quai de la Rapée or Bastille) ✿ All of the dishes are vegan and most are organic at this light-filled cafe.

TOP THREE FOOD TRUCKS

Street food continues to take the city by storm as food trucks roll out across Paris. Find the day's location online.

Le Camion Qui Fume (https://lecamionquifume.com; burger & fries €13-15) This 'smoking truck' serving gourmet burgers started the local food-truck craze.

KimPop (www.facebook.com/kimpopfoodtruck; dishes €5.50-12.50) Korean food truck KimPop serves soup, pork, beef or tofu *bibimbap* ('mixed rice') salad bowls, *kimbap* (sushi-style rolls) and more.

La Cabane de Cape Cod (www.facebook.com/cabanecapecod; dishes €11-16) Choose from classic fish and chips, salmon gravlax, tuna tataki and other seafood dishes.

---

quettes, complemented by fantastic artisanal bread, hand-churned flavoured butters, sea salt and Kalamata olives.

★ Au Passage
BISTRO **$$**

(Map p380; ☎ 01 43 55 07 52; www.restaurant-aupassage.fr; 1bis passage St-Sébastien, 11e; small plates €8-18, meats to share €25-70; ☺ 7-11pm Tue-Sat, bar to 1.30am Tue-Sat; Ⓜ St-Sébastien–Froissart) Rising-star chefs continue to make their name at this *petit bar de quartier* (little neighbourhood bar). Choose from a good-value, uncomplicated selection *of petites assiettes* (small tapas-style plates) of cold meats, raw or cooked fish, vegetables and so on, and larger meat dishes such as slow-roasted lamb shoulder or *côte de bœuf* (rib-eye steak) to share. Reservations are essential.

Le Bistrot Paul Bert
BISTRO **$$**

(☎ 01 43 72 24 01; 18 rue Paul Bert, 11e; 3-course menu €41, mains €29; ☺ noon-2pm & 7.30-11pm Tue-Thu, 7.30-11pm Fri, noon-2.30pm Sat, closed Aug; Ⓜ Faidherbe-Chaligny) When food writers list Paris' best bistros, Paul Bert's name consistently pops up. The timeless decor and classic dishes such as *steak-frites* (steak and chips) and hazelnut-cream Paris-Brest pastry reward those booking ahead. Siblings in the same street: **L'Écailler du Bistrot** (☎ 01 43 72 76 77; 22 rue Paul Bert, 11e; oysters per half-dozen €9-22, mains €32-48, seafood platters per person from €40; ☺ noon-2.30pm & 7.30-11pm Tue-Sat) for seafood; **La Cave Paul Bert** (☎ 01 58 53 50 92; 16 rue Paul Bert, 11e; ☺ noon-midnight, kitchen noon-2pm & 7.30-11.30pm), a wine bar with small plates; and **Le 6 Paul Bert** (☎ 01 43 79 14 32; www.le6paulbert.com; 6 rue Paul Bert, 12e; mains €24-34; ☺ noon-2pm & 7.30-11pm Tue-Fri, 7.30-11pm Sat) for modern cuisine.

Maison Maison
MEDITERRANEAN **$$**

(Map p380; ☎ 09 67 82 07 32; www.restaurant-maisonmaison.com; 63 Parc Rives de Seine, 1er; 2-/3-course lunch menu €20/25, small plates €7-

16; ☺ kitchen 7-10pm Mon, noon-3pm & 7-10pm Tue-Sun, bar to 2am; Ⓜ Pont Neuf) Halfway down the stairs by Pont Neuf is this wonderfully secret space beneath the *bouquinistes* (used-book sellers), where you can watch the *bateaux-mouches* (river-cruise boats) float by as you dine on creations such as beetroot and pink-grapefruit-cured bonito or gnocchi with white asparagus and broccoli pesto. In nice weather, cocktails at the glorious riverside terrace are not to be missed.

Balagan
ISRAELI **$$**

(☎ 01 40 20 72 14; www.balagan-paris.com; 9 rue d'Alger, 1er; mains €24-34; ☺ 7-10.30pm; Ⓜ Tuileries) Cool navy blues and creamy diamond tiling contrast with the chic vibe at this Israeli hot spot. Come here to sample delectable starters – deconstructed kebabs, crispy halloumi cheese with dates, onion confit Ashkenazi chicken liver or a spicy, succulent tuna tartare with fennel, coriander, capers and pistachios – followed by praiseworthy mains such as the sea bream black pasta.

★ Septime
GASTRONOMY **$$$**

(☎ 01 43 67 38 29; www.septime-charonne.fr; 80 rue de Charonne, 11e; 4-course lunch menu with/without wine €80/42, 7-course dinner menu €135/80; ☺ 7.30-10pm Mon, 12.15-2pm & 7.30-10pm Tue-Fri; Ⓜ Charonne) The alchemists in Bertrand Grébaut's Michelin-starred kitchen produce truly beautiful creations, served by blue-aproned waitstaff. The menu reads like an obscure shopping list: each dish is a mere listing of three ingredients, while the mystery *carte blanche* dinner *menu* puts you in the hands of the innovative chef. Reservations require planning and perseverance – book at least three weeks in advance.

🍷 Drinking & Nightlife

The line between bars, cafes and bistros is blurred at best. It costs more to sit at a table

BAR-HOPPING STREETS

Prime Parisian streets for a soirée:

Rue Vieille du Temple, 4e Marais cocktail of gay bars and chic cafes.

Rue Oberkampf, 11e Edgy urban hang-outs.

Rue de Lappe, 11e Boisterous Bastille bars and clubs.

Rue de la Butte aux Cailles, 13e Village atmosphere and fun local haunts.

Rue Princesse, 6e Student and sports bars.

than to stand at the counter, more on a fancy square than a backstreet, and more in the 8e than in the 18e. After 10pm many cafes charge a pricier *tarif de nuit* (night rate).

Left Bank

★ Coutume Café
COFFEE

(☑ 01 45 51 50 47; www.coutumecafe.com; 47 rue de Babylone, 7e; ☺ 8.30am-5.30pm Mon-Fri, 9am-6pm Sat & Sun; 🚊; Ⓜ St-François Xavier) 🍴 The Parisian coffee revolution is thanks in no small part to Coutume, artisanal roaster of premium beans for scores of establishments around town. Its flagship cafe – a light-filled, post-industrial space – is ground zero for innovative preparation methods including cold extraction and siphon brews. Couple some of Paris' finest coffee with tasty, seasonal cuisine and the place is always packed out.

Les Deux Magots
CAFE

(Map p380; ☑ 01 45 48 55 25; www.lesdeuxmagots.fr; 6 place St-Germain des Prés, 6e; ☺ 7.30am-1am; Ⓜ St-Germain des Prés) If ever there was a cafe that summed up St-Germain des Prés' early-20th-century literary scene, it's this former hang-out of anyone who was anyone. You'll spend substantially more here to sip *un café* (€4.80) in a wicker chair on the pavement terrace shaded by dark-green awnings and geraniums spilling from window boxes, but it's an undeniable piece of Parisian history.

Right Bank

★ Bar Hemingway
COCKTAIL BAR

(www.ritzparis.com; Hôtel Ritz Paris, 15 place Vendôme, 1er; ☺ 6pm-2am; 🚊; Ⓜ Opéra) Black-and-white photos and memorabilia (hunting trophies, old typewriters and framed hand-written letters by the great writer) fill this snug bar inside the Ritz (p390). Head bartender Colin Peter Field mixes monumental cocktails, including three different Bloody Marys made with juice from freshly squeezed seasonal tomatoes. Legend has it that Hemingway himself, wielding a machine gun, helped liberate the bar during WWII.

★ Le Baron Rouge
WINE BAR

(www.lebaronrouge.net; 1 rue Théophile Roussel, 12e; ☺ 5-10pm Mon, 10am-2pm & 5-10pm Tue-Fri, 10am-10pm Sat, 10am-4pm Sun; Ⓜ Ledru-Rollin) Just about the ultimate Parisian wine-bar experience, this wonderfully unpretentious local meeting place, where everyone is welcome, has barrels stacked against the bottle-lined walls and serves cheese, charcuterie, and oysters in season. It's especially busy on Sunday after the Marché d'Aligre wraps up. For a small deposit, you can fill up 1L bottles straight from the barrel for less than €5.

★ Le Perchoir
ROOFTOP BAR

(☑ 01 48 06 18 48; www.leperchoir.tv; 14 rue Crespin du Gast, 11e; ☺ 6pm-2am Tue-Sat; 🚊; Ⓜ Ménilmontant) Sunset is the best time to head up to this 7th-floor bar for a drink overlooking Paris' rooftops, where DJs spin on Saturday nights. Greenery provides shade in summer; in winter it's covered by a sail-like canopy and warmed by fires burning in metal drums. It's accessed off an inner courtyard via a lift (or a spiralling staircase).

Candelaria
COCKTAIL BAR

(Map p380; www.quixotic-projects.com; 52 rue de Saintonge, 3e; ☺ bar 6pm-2am, taqueria noon-10.30pm Sun-Wed, to 11.30pm Thu-Sat; Ⓜ Filles du Calvaire) A lime-green *taqueria* serving homemade tacos, quesadillas and tostadas conceals one of Paris' coolest cocktail bars through an unmarked internal door. Phenomenal cocktails made from agave spirits, including mezcal, are inspired by Central and South America, such as a Guatemalan El Sombrerón (tequila, vermouth, bitters, hibiscus syrup, pink-pepper-infused tonic and lime). Weekend evenings kick off with DJ sets.

Pavillon Puebla
BEER GARDEN

(www.leperchoir.tv; Parc des Buttes Chaumont, 39 av Simon Bolivar, 19e; ☺ 6pm-2am Wed-Fri, from noon Sat, noon-10pm Sun; 🚊; Ⓜ Buttes Chaumont) Strung with fairy lights, this rustic ivy-draped cottage's two rambling terraces in the Parc des Buttes Chaumont evoke a *guinguette* (old-fashioned outdoor tavern/dance venue), with a 21st-century vibe provided by its Moroccan decor, contemporary furniture, and DJ beats from Thursdays to Saturdays. Alongside mostly French wines and craft beers, cocktails include its signature Spritz du Pavillon (Aperol, Prosecco and soda).

☆ Entertainment

France's Opéra National de Paris and Ballet de l'Opéra National de Paris perform at Paris' two opera houses: the **Palais Garnier** (www.operadeparis.fr; place de l'Opéra, 9e; Ⓜ Opéra) and **Opéra Bastille** (Map p380; ☑ international calls 01 71 25 24 23, within France 08 92 89 90 90; www.operadeparis.fr; 2-6 place de la Bastille, 12e; ⊙ box office 11.30am-6.30pm Mon-Sat, 1hr prior to performances Sun; Ⓜ Bastille). The season runs between September and July.

On the day of performance, theatre, opera and ballet tickets are sold for half price (plus €3.50 commission) at the central **Kiosque Théâtre Madeleine** (www.kiosqueculture.com; opposite 15 place de la Madeleine, 8e; ⊙ 12.30-2.30pm & 3-7.30pm Tue-Sat, 12.30-3.45pm Sun Sep-Jun, closed Sun Jul & Aug; Ⓜ Madeleine). Paris' top listings guide, *L'Officiel des Spectacles* (www.offi.fr; €1), is published in French but is easy to navigate. It's available from news stands on Wednesday, and is crammed with everything that's on in the capital.

★ **La Seine Musicale** CONCERT VENUE
(☑ 01 74 34 54 00; www.laseinemusicale.com; Île Seguin, Boulogne-Billancourt; Ⓜ Pont de Sèvres) A landmark addition to Paris' cultural offerings, La Seine Musicale opened on the Seine island of Île Seguin in 2017. Constructed of steel and glass, the egg-shaped auditorium has a capacity of 1150, while the larger, modular concrete hall accommodates 6000. Ballets, musicals and concerts from classical to rock are all staged here, alongside exhibitions.

★ **Café Universel** JAZZ, BLUES
(Map p380; ☑ 01 43 25 74 20; www.facebook.com/cafeuniversel.paris05; 267 rue St-Jacques, 5e; ⊙ concerts from 8.30pm Tue-Sat, cafe 8.30am-3pm Mon, 8.30am-1am Tue-Fri, 4.30pm-1am Sat, 1.30pm-1am Sun; 🛜; Ⓜ Censier Daubenton or RER Port Royal) Café Universel hosts a brilliant array of live concerts with everything from be-bop and Latin sounds to vocal jazz sessions. Plenty of freedom is given to young producers and artists, and its convivial, relaxed at-mosphere attracts a mix of students and jazz lovers. Concerts are free, but you should tip the artists when they pass the hat around.

Moulin Rouge CABARET
(☑ 01 53 09 82 82; www.moulinrouge.fr; 82 bd de Clichy, 18e; show only from €87, lunch & show from €165, dinner & show from €190; ⊙ show only 2.45pm, 9pm & 11pm, lunch & show 1.45pm, dinner & show 7pm; Ⓜ Blanche) Immortalised in Toulouse-Lautrec's posters and later in Baz Luhrmann's film, Paris' legendary cabaret twinkles beneath a 1925 replica of its original red windmill. Yes, it's packed with bus-tour crowds, but from the opening bars of music to the last high cancan kick, it's a whirl of fantastical costumes, sets, choreography and Champagne. Book in advance and dress smartly (no trainers or sneakers).

🛍 Shopping

Paris has it all: broad boulevards lined with international chains, luxury avenues studded with designer fashion houses, famous *grands magasins* (department stores) and fabulous markets. But the real charm lies in strolling the city's backstreets, where tiny speciality shops and quirky boutiques selling everything from strawberry-scented wellington boots to heavenly fragranced candles are wedged between cafes, galleries and churches.

Paris' twice-yearly *soldes* (sales) generally last five to six weeks, starting around mid-January and again around mid-June.

★ **Merci** CONCEPT STORE
(Map p380; ☑ 01 42 77 00 33; www.merci-merci.com; 111 bd Beaumarchais, 3e; ⊙ 10am-7.30pm

> ### LGBT+ PARIS
>
> Le Marais (4e), especially the areas around the intersection of rue Ste-Croix de la Bretonnerie and rue des Archives, and eastwards to rue Vieille du Temple, has been Paris' centre of gay nightlife for some three decades. The single best source of info is the **Centre Gai et Lesbien de Paris** (Map p380; ☑ 01 43 57 21 47; www.centrelgbtparis.org; 63 rue Beaubourg, 3e; ⊙ centre & bar 3.30-8pm Mon-Fri, 1-7pm Sat, library 6-8pm Mon-Wed, 5-7pm Fri & Sat; Ⓜ Rambuteau), with a large library and happening bar.

FRANCE PARIS

DON'T MISS

MARKET SHOPPING

Spanning 9 hectares, **Marché aux Puces de St-Ouen** (www.marcheauxpuces-saintouen.com; rue des Rosiers, St-Ouen; ⏰ Sat-Mon; Ⓜ Porte de Clignancourt) is a vast flea market that was founded in 1870 and is said to be Europe's largest. Over 2000 stalls are grouped into 15 *marchés* (markets) selling everything from 17th-century furniture to 21st-century clothing. Each market has different opening hours – check the website for details. There are miles upon miles of 'freelance' stalls; come prepared to spend some time.

Mon-Sat, noon-7pm Sun; Ⓜ St-Sébastien–Froissart) 🏷 A Fiat Cinquecento marks the entrance to this unique concept store, which donates all its profits to a children's charity in Madagascar. Shop for fashion, accessories, linens, lamps and nifty designs for the home. Complete the experience with a coffee in its hybrid used-bookshop-cafe, a juice at its **Cinéma Café** (⏰ 11am-7pm Mon-Sat) or lunch in its stylish **La Cantine de Merci** (mains €16-21; ⏰ noon-5pm Mon-Fri, to 6pm Sat).

★**Shakespeare & Company**   BOOKS
(Map p380; 📞 01 43 25 40 93; www.shakespeareandcompany.com; 37 rue de la Bûcherie, 5e; ⏰ 10am-10pm; Ⓜ St-Michel) Enchanting nooks and crannies overflow with new and secondhand English-language books. The original shop (12 rue l'Odéon, 6e; closed by the Nazis in 1941) was run by Sylvia Beach and became the meeting point for Hemingway's 'Lost Generation'. Readings by emerging and illustrious authors regularly take place and there's a wonderful **cafe** (2 rue St-Julien le Pauvre, 5e; ⏰ 9.30am-7pm Mon-Fri, to 8pm Sat & Sun; 🖥) 🏷 next door.

★**Le Bonbon au Palais**   FOOD
(Map p380; 📞 01 78 56 15 72; www.lebonbonaupalais.com; 19 rue Monge, 5e; ⏰ 10.30am-7.30pm Tue-Sat; Ⓜ Cardinal Lemoine) Kids and kids-at-heart will adore this sugar-fuelled *tour de France*. The school-geography-themed boutique stocks rainbows of artisanal sweets from around the country. Old-fashioned glass jars brim with treats like *calissons* (diamond-shaped, icing-sugar-topped ground fruit and almonds from Aix-en-Provence), *rigolettes* (fruit-filled pillows from Nantes), *berlingots* (striped, triangular boiled sweets from Carpentras and elsewhere) and *papalines*

(herbal liqueur-filled pink-chocolate balls from Avignon).

★**La Grande Épicerie de Paris**   FOOD & DRINKS
(www.lagrandeepicerie.com; 38 rue de Sèvres, 7e; ⏰ 8.30am-9pm Mon-Sat, 10am-8pm Sun; Ⓜ Sèvres-Babylone) The magnificent food hall of department store **Le Bon Marché** (📞 01 44 39 80 00; www.24sevres.com; 24 rue de Sèvres, 7e; ⏰ 10am-8pm Mon-Wed, Fri & Sat, 10am-8.45pm Thu, 11am-7.45pm Sun; Ⓜ Sèvres-Babylone) sells 30,000 rare and/or luxury gourmet products, including 60 different types of bread baked on-site and delicacies such as caviar ravioli. Its fantastical displays of chocolates, pastries, biscuits, cheeses, fresh fruit and vegetables and deli goods are a sight in themselves. Wine tastings regularly take place in the basement.

ℹ Information

Paris Convention & Visitors Bureau (Paris Office de Tourisme; Map p380; 📞 01 49 52 42 63; www.parisinfo.com; 29 rue de Rivoli, 4e; ⏰ 9am-7pm May-Oct, 10am-7pm Nov-Apr; 🖥; Ⓜ Hôtel de Ville) Paris' main tourist office is at the Hôtel de Ville. It sells tickets for tours and several attractions, plus museum and transport passes.

ℹ Getting There & Away

AIR

Aéroport de Charles de Gaulle (CDG; 📞 01 70 36 39 50; www.parisaeroport.fr) Most international airlines fly to Aéroport de Charles de Gaulle (also known as Roissy), 28km northeast of central Paris.

Aéroport d'Orly (ORY; 📞 01 70 36 39 50; www.parisaeroport.fr) Located 19km south of central Paris.

BUS

Eurolines (Map p380; 📞 08 92 89 90 91; www.eurolines.fr; 55 rue St-Jacques, 5e; ⏰ 10am-1pm & 2-6pm Mon-Fri; Ⓜ Cluny–La Sorbonne) connects all major European capitals to Paris' international bus terminal, **Gare Routière Internationale de Paris-Galliéni** (28 av du Général de Gaulle, Bagnolet; Ⓜ Galliéni). The terminal is in the eastern suburb of Bagnolet; it's about a 15-minute metro ride to the more central République station.

Major European bus company FlixBus (www.flixbus.com) uses western **Parking Pershing** (16-24 bd Pershing, 17e; Ⓜ Porte Maillot).

TRAIN

Paris has six major train stations serving both national and international destinations. For mainline train information, check **SNCF** (www.sncf-voyages.com).

Gare du Nord (www.gares-sncf.com; rue de Dunkerque, 10e; Ⓜ Gare du Nord) Trains to/from the UK, Belgium, Germany and northern France.

Gare de l'Est (www.gares-sncf.com; place du 11 Novembre 1918, 10e; Ⓜ Gare de l'Est) Trains to/from Luxembourg, southern Germany and points further east; TGV Est trains to areas of France east of Paris (Champagne, Alsace and Lorraine).

Gare de Lyon (bd Diderot, 12e; Ⓜ Gare de Lyon) Trains to/from Provence, the Riviera, the Alps and Italy. Also serves Geneva.

Gare d'Austerlitz (bd de l'Hôpital, 13e; Ⓜ Gare d'Austerlitz) Terminus for a handful of trains from the south, including services to/from Toulouse. High-speed trains to/from Barcelona and Madrid also use Austerlitz.

Gare Montparnasse (av du Maine & bd de Vaugirard, 15e; Ⓜ Montparnasse Bienvenüe) Trains to/from the southwest and west (Brittany, the Loire and Bordeaux), Spain and Portugal. Some services will eventually move to Gare d'Austerlitz.

Gare St-Lazare (www.gares-sncf.com; rue Intérieure, 8e; Ⓜ St-Lazare) Trains to Normandy.

ⓘ Getting Around

TO/FROM THE AIRPORTS

Getting into town is straightforward and inexpensive thanks to a raft of public-transport options. Bus drivers sell tickets. Children aged four to 11 years pay half-price on most services.

Aéroport de Charles de Gaulle

RER B line (€11.40, 50 minutes, every 10 to 20 minutes) Stops at Gare du Nord, Châtelet–Les Halles and St-Michel–Notre Dame stations. Trains run from 4.50am to 11.50pm; fewer trains on weekends.

Le Bus Direct line 2 (€17, one hour, every 30 minutes, 5.45am to 11pm) Links the airport with the Arc de Triomphe via the Eiffel Tower and Trocadéro.

Le Bus Direct line 4 (€17, 50 to 80 minutes, every 30 minutes, 6am to 10.30pm from the airport, 5.30am to 10.30pm from Montparnasse) Links the airport with Gare Montparnasse (80 minutes) in southern Paris via Gare de Lyon (50 minutes) in eastern Paris.

RATP bus 350 (€6 or three metro tickets, 70 minutes, every 30 minutes, 5.30am to 11pm) Links the airport with Gare de l'Est.

Taxi (€50 to Right Bank and €55 to Left Bank, plus 15% surcharge between 7pm and 7am and on Sundays) It takes 40 minutes to city centre.

Aéroport d'Orly

RER B and Orlyval (€13.25, 35 minutes, every four to 12 minutes, 6am to 11.35pm) The nearest RER station to the airport is Antony, where you connect on the dedicated Orlyval automatic train.

Le Bus Direct line 1 (€12, one hour, every 20 minutes, 5.50am to 11.30pm from Orly, 4.50am to 10.30pm from the Arc de Triomphe) Runs to/from the Arc de Triomphe (one hour) via Gare Montparnasse (40 minutes), La Motte-Picquet and Trocadéro.

Orlybus (€8.70, 30 minutes, every 15 to 20 minutes, 6am to 12.30am from Orly, 5.35am to midnight from Paris) Runs to/from place Denfert-Rochereau in southern Paris.

Taxi (€30 to the Left Bank and €35 to the Right Bank, plus 15% between 7pm and 7am and on Sundays) It takes 30 minutes to city centre.

BICYCLE

Paris is increasingly bike-friendly, with more cycling lanes and efforts from the City of Paris to reduce the number of cars on the roads.

BOAT

Batobus (www.batobus.com; adult/child 1-day pass €17/8, 2-day pass €19/10; ⊙10am-9.30pm late Apr-Aug, shorter hours Sep-late Apr) runs glassed-in trimarans that dock every 20 to 25 minutes at nine small piers along the Seine: Beaugrenelle, Eiffel Tower, Musée d'Orsay, St-Germain des Prés, Jardin des Plantes/Cité de la Mode et du Design, Hôtel de Ville, Musée du Louvre and Champs-Élysées. (At time of printing, the Notre Dame pier was closed.) Buy tickets online, at ferry stops or at tourist offices.

PUBLIC TRANSPORT

Paris' public transit system is operated by the **RATP** (www.ratp.fr).

➡ The same RATP tickets are valid on the 14-line metro, the RER (for travel on five main lines within the city limits), buses, trams and the Montmartre funicular.

➡ A ticket – white in colour and called *Le Ticket t+* – costs €1.90 (half price for children aged four to nine years) if bought individually; a *carnet* (book) of 10 costs €14.90 for adults.

➡ One ticket lets you travel between any two metro stations (no return journeys) for a period of 1½ hours, no matter how many transfers are required. You can also use it on the RER for travel within zone 1, which encompasses all of central Paris.

➡ Keep your ticket until you exit from your station or risk a fine.

Bus

➡ Buses run runs from approximately 5am to 1am Monday to Saturday; services are drastically reduced on Sunday and public holidays.

➡ Normal bus rides embracing one or two bus zones cost one metro ticket; longer rides require two or even three tickets.

➡ Validate your ticket in the ticket machine near the driver. If you don't have a ticket, the driver can sell you one for €2 (correct change required).

Metro & RER

➡ Trains usually start at around 5.30am, with the last train beginning its run between 12.35am and 1.15am (2.15am on Friday and Saturday).

➡ The RER is faster than the metro, but the stops are much further apart. Some attractions, particularly those on the Left Bank (eg the Musée d'Orsay, Eiffel Tower and Panthéon), can be reached far more conveniently by the RER than by the metro.

➡ If you're going out to the suburbs (eg Versailles or Disneyland), ask for help on the platform – finding the right train can be confusing. Also make sure your ticket is for the correct zone.

Tourist Passes

Mobilis Allows unlimited travel for one day and costs from €7.50 (for two zones) to €17.80 (five zones). Buy it at any metro, RER or SNCF station in the Paris region. Depending on how many times you plan to hop on/off the metro in a day, a *carnet* (book of 10 tickets) might work out cheaper.

Paris Visite Allows unlimited travel as well as discounted entry to certain museums, and other discounts and bonuses. The 'Paris+Suburbs+Airports' pass includes transport to/from the airports and costs €25.25/38.35/53.75/65.80 for one/two/three/five days. The cheaper 'Paris Centre' pass, valid for zones 1 to 3, costs €12/19.50/26.65/38.35 for one/two/three/five days. Children aged four to 11 years pay half price.

Navigo If you're staying in Paris more than three or four days, the cheapest and easiest way to use public transport is to get a rechargeable Navigo (www. navigo.fr) pass. A weekly pass costs €22.80 and is valid Monday to Sunday. You'll also need to pay €5 for the Navigo card and provide a passport photo.

TAXI

➡ Flagging down a taxi in Paris can be difficult; it's best to find an official taxi stand.

➡ To order a taxi, call or reserve online with **Taxis G7** (☑ 01 41 27 66 99, 3607; www.g7.fr) or **Alpha Taxis** (☑ 01 45 85 85 85; www. alphataxis.fr).

➡ The minimum taxi fare for a short trip is €7.10. The *prise en charge* (flagfall) is €4. Within the city limits, it costs €1.07 per kilometre for travel between 10am and 5pm Monday to Saturday. At night (5pm to 10am), on Sunday from 7am to midnight and in the inner suburbs, the rate is €1.29 per kilometre.

AROUND PARIS

Splendid architecture, including some of the most magnificent châteaux and gardens in the country, are within easy striking distance of the French capital.

Versailles

POP 87,550

Louis XIV transformed his father's hunting lodge into the monumental Château de Versailles in the mid-17th century, and it remains France's most famous and grand palace. Situated in the leafy, bourgeois suburb of Versailles, 22km southwest of central Paris, the baroque château was the kingdom's political capital and the seat of the royal court from 1682 up until the fateful events of 1789 when revolutionaries massacred the palace guard. Louis XVI and Marie Antoinette were ultimately dragged back to Paris, where they were ingloriously guillotined.

◉ Sights

★ **Château de Versailles** PALACE
(☑ 01 30 83 78 00; www.chateauversailles.fr; place d'Armes; adult/child passport ticket incl estate-wide access €20/free, with musical events €27/free, palace €18/free except during musical events; ⊙ 9am-6.30pm Tue-Sun Apr-Oct, to 5.30pm Tue-Sun Nov-Mar; ⓜ RER Versailles-Château–Rive Gauche) Amid magnificently landscaped formal **gardens** (free except during musical events; ⊙ gardens 8am-8.30pm Apr-Oct, to 6pm Nov-Mar, park 7am-8.30pm Apr-Oct, 8am-6pm Nov-Mar), this splendid and enormous palace was built in the mid-17th century during the reign of Louis XIV – the Roi Soleil (Sun King) – to project the absolute power of the French monarchy, which was then at the height of its glory. The château has undergone relatively few alterations since its construction, though almost all the interior furnishings disappeared during the Revolution and many of the rooms were rebuilt by Louis-Philippe (r 1830–48).

✖ Eating

Rue de Satory is lined with restaurants and cafes. More local options can be found on and around rue de la Paroisse, where you'll also find Versailles' **markets** (rue de la Paroisse; ⊙ food market 7am-2pm Tue, Fri & Sun, covered market 7am-7.30pm Tue-Sat, to 2pm Sun, flea market 11am-7pm Wed, Thu & Sat).

ⓘ TOP VERSAILLES TIPS
....

➡ Monday is out for obvious reasons (it's closed).

➡ Arrive early morning and avoid Tuesday, Saturday and Sunday, its busiest days.

➡ Pre-purchase tickets on the château's website or at **Fnac** (☎ 08 92 68 36 22; www. fnactickets.com) branches and head straight to **Entrance A** (Château de Versailles).

➡ Versailles is free on the first Sunday of every month from November to March.

➡ Prebook a **guided tour** (☎ 01 30 83 77 88; www.chateauversailles.fr; Château de Versailles; tours €10, plus palace entry; ⊙ English-language tours 11am, 1.30pm & 3pm Tue-Sun) to access areas otherwise off limits.

➡ Try to time your visit for summertime's **Grandes Eaux Musicales** (www.chateauversailles -spectacles.fr; adult/child €9.50/8; ⊙ 9am-7pm Tue, Sat & Sun mid-May–late Jun, 9am-7pm Sat & Sun Apr–mid-May & late Jun-Oct) or the after-dark **Grandes Eaux Nocturnes** (adult/child €24/20; ⊙ 8.30-11.30pm Sat mid-Jun–mid-Sep), magical 'dancing water' displays – set to music composed by baroque- and classical-era composers – in the grounds.

★ **Ore** FRENCH $$
(☎ 01 30 84 12 96; www.ducasse-chateauversailles. com; 1st fl, Pavillon Dufour, Château de Versailles; breakfast menus €12-20, mains €20-36, afternoon-tea platters €35; ⊙ 9am-6.30pm Tue-Sun Apr-Oct, to 5.30pm Nov-Mar; 🛜🚹) Full-length windows frame the Cour d'Honneur and Cour Royale at this resplendent light-flooded restaurant inside the Château de Versailles. Created by superstar chef Alain Ducasse, it offers breakfast (mini pastries, organic eggs), small lunchtime plates (like citrus-marinated mackerel with horseradish crème) and afternoon tea (such as chocolate soufflé with Ducasse's Paris-made bean-to-bar chocolate, or laden platters with tea or coffee).

ⓘ Information

Tourist Office (☎ 01 39 24 88 88; www. versailles-tourisme.com; 2bis av de Paris; ⊙ 9.30am-6pm Mon, 8.30am-7pm Tue-Sun Apr-Oct, 11am-5pm Mon, 8.30am-6pm Tue-Sun Nov-Mar)

ⓘ Getting There & Away

Take RER C5 (return €7.10, 40 minutes, frequent) from Paris' Left Bank RER stations to Versailles-Château–Rive Gauche station.

Chartres

POP 41,588

The magnificent 13th-century **Cathédrale Notre Dame** (www.cathedrale-chartres.org; place de la Cathédrale; ⊙ 8.30am-7.30pm daily year-round, also to 10pm Tue, Fri & Sun Jun-Aug) of Chartres, crowned by two very different spires – one Gothic, the other Romanesque – rises from rich farmland 88km southwest of Paris and dominates the medieval town. The cathedral's west, north and south entrances have superbly ornamented triple portals and its 105m-high **Clocher Vieux** (Old Bell Tower) is the tallest Romanesque steeple still standing. Superb views of three-tiered flying buttresses and the 19th-century copper roof, turned green by verdigris, reward the 350-step hike up the 112m-high **Clocher Neuf** (New Bell Tower; adult/child €7.50/free; ⊙ 9.30am-12.30pm & 2-4.30pm Mon-Sat, 2-4.30pm Sun).

Inside, 172 extraordinary stained-glass windows, mainly from the 13th century, form one of the most important ensembles of medieval stained glass in the world. The three most exquisite – renowned for the depth and intensity of their tones, famously known as 'Chartres blue' – are above the west entrance and below the rose window.

ⓘ Information

Tourist Office (☎ 02 37 18 26 26; www.chartres -tourisme.com; 8-10 rue de la Poissonnerie; ⊙ 10am-6pm Mon-Sat, to 5.30pm Sun) Rents 1½-hour English-language audio-guide tours (€5.50/8.50 per one/two) of the medieval city, as well as binoculars (€2), which are fabulous for seeing details of the cathedral close up.

ⓘ Getting There & Away

Frequent SNCF trains link Paris' Gare Montparnasse (€16, 55 to 70 minutes) with Chartres' **train station** (place Pierre Semard).

Giverny

POP 518

The tiny village of Giverny, 74km northwest of Paris, was the **home of impressionist**

Versailles

A DAY IN COURT

Visiting Versailles – even just the State Apartments – may seem overwhelming at first, but think of it as a house where people ate, drank, worked, slept and conspired and you'll be on the right path.

Some two decades into his long reign, Louis XIV began turning his father's hunting lodge into a palace large enough to house his entire court (to keep closer tabs on the 6000-strong army of courtiers). Sparing no expense, the Sun King employed the greatest artists and craftspeople of the day and by 1682 he'd created the most extravagant dormitory in history.

The royal schedule was as accurate and predictable as a Swiss watch. By following this itinerary of rooms you can recreate the king's day, starting with the ❶ **King's Bedchamber** and the ❷ **Queen's Bedchamber**, where the royal couple was roused at about the same time. The royal procession then leads through the ❸ **Hall of Mirrors** to the ❹ **Royal Chapel** for morning Mass and returns to the ❺ **Council Chamber** for late-morning meetings with ministers. After lunch the king might ride or hunt or visit the ❻ **King's Library**. Later he could join courtesans for an 'apartment evening' starting from the ❼ **Hercules Drawing Room** or play billiards in the ❽ **Diana Drawing Room** before supping at 10pm.

VERSAILLES BY NUMBERS

Rooms 700 (11 hectares of roof)

Windows 2153

Staircases 67

Gardens and parks 800 hectares

Trees 200,000

Fountains 50 (with 620 nozzles)

Paintings 6300 (measuring 11km laid end to end)

Statues and sculptures 2100

Objets d'art and furnishings 5000

Visitors 5.3 million per year

Queen's Bedchamber
Chambre de la Reine
The queen's life was on constant public display and even the births of her children were watched by crowds of spectators in her own bedchamber. **DETOUR »** The Guardroom, with a dozen armed men at the ready.

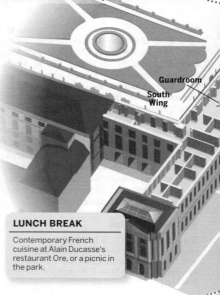

Guardroom

South Wing

LUNCH BREAK

Contemporary French cuisine at Alain Ducasse's restaurant Ore, or a picnic in the park.

Hercules Drawing Room
Salon d'Hercule
This salon, with its stunning ceiling fresco of the strong man, gave way to the State Apartments, which were open to courtiers three nights a week. **DETOUR»** Apollo Drawing Room, used for formal audiences and as a throne room.

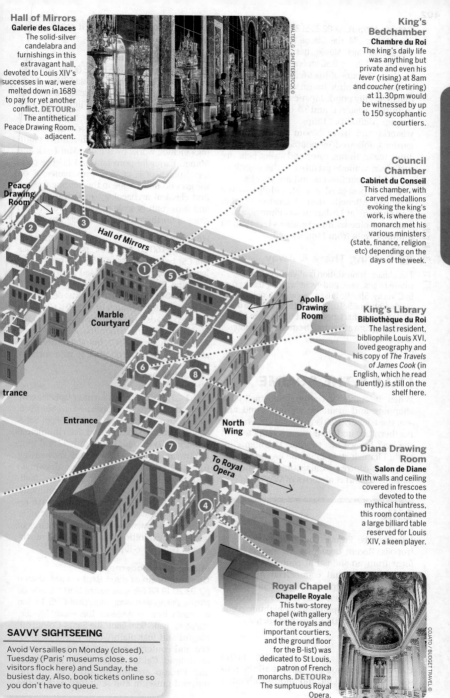

Hall of Mirrors
Galerie des Glaces
The solid-silver candelabra and furnishings in this extravagant hall, devoted to Louis XIV's successes in war, were melted down in 1689 to pay for yet another conflict. **DETOUR»** The antithetical Peace Drawing Room, adjacent.

WALTER_G / SHUTTERSTOCK ©

King's Bedchamber
Chambre du Roi
The king's daily life was anything but private and even his *lever* (rising) at 8am and *coucher* (retiring) at 11.30pm would be witnessed by up to 150 sycophantic courtiers.

Council Chamber
Cabinet du Conseil
This chamber, with carved medallions evoking the king's work, is where the monarch met his various ministers (state, finance, religion etc) depending on the days of the week.

Peace Drawing Room

Hall of Mirrors

Marble Courtyard

Apollo Drawing Room

trance

Entrance

North Wing

To Royal Opera

King's Library
Bibliothèque du Roi
The last resident, bibliophile Louis XVI, loved geography and his copy of *The Travels of James Cook* (in English, which he read fluently) is still on the shelf here.

Diana Drawing Room
Salon de Diane
With walls and ceiling covered in frescoes devoted to the mythical huntress, this room contained a large billiard table reserved for Louis XIV, a keen player.

Royal Chapel
Chapelle Royale
This two-storey chapel (with gallery for the royals and important courtiers, and the ground floor for the B-list) was dedicated to St Louis, patron of French monarchs. **DETOUR»** The sumptuous Royal Opera.

COJATO / BUDGET TRAVEL ©

SAVVY SIGHTSEEING

Avoid Versailles on Monday (closed), Tuesday (Paris' museums close, so visitors flock here) and Sunday, the busiest day. Also, book tickets online so you don't have to queue.

Claude Monet (☎02 32 51 28 21; www.fondation -monet.com; 84 rue Claude Monet; adult/child €9.50/5.50, incl Musée des Impressionnismes Giverny €17/9; ⏰9.30am-6pm Easter-Oct) for the last 43 years of his life. You can visit the artist's pastel-pink house and famous gardens with lily pond, Japanese bridge draped in purple wisteria, and so on. Early to late spring, daffodils, tulips, rhododendrons, wisteria and irises bloom in the flowery gardens, followed by poppies and lilies. By June, nasturtiums, roses and sweet peas are in flower, while September is the month to see dahlias, sunflowers and hollyhocks.

Pre- or post-garden visit, indulge in the inventive Michelin-starred cuisine of chef Eric Guerin's at Le Jardin des Plumes, a gorgeous sky-blue-trimmed address less than 10 minutes' walk from Monet's pad.

ⓘ Getting There & Away

The closest train station is at Vernon, from where buses, taxis and cycle/walking tracks run to Giverny. Shuttle buses (www.sngo-giverny.fr; single/return €5/10, 20 minutes, up to five daily Easter to October) meet most trains from Paris' Gare St-Lazare at Vernon (from €9, 45 minutes to one hour).

LILLE & THE SOMME

When it comes to culture, cuisine, beer, shopping and dramatic views of land and sea, the friendly Ch'tis (residents of France's northern tip) and their region compete with the best France has to offer. Highlights include Flemish-style Lille, the cross-Channel shopping centre of Calais, and the moving battlefields and cemeteries of WWI.

Lille

POP 233,900

Lille may be France's most underrated metropolis. Recent decades have seen it transform from an industrial centre into a glittering cultural and commercial hub, with enchanting old town, magnificent French and Flemish architecture, renowned art museums, stylish shopping and a nightlife scene bolstered by 67,000 university students.

⊙ Sights

The **Lille City Pass** (24/48/72 hours €25/35/45) gets you into almost all the museums in greater Lille and affords unlimited use of public transport; buy it at the tourist office or online.

★ Palais des Beaux Arts   MUSEUM
(Fine Arts Museum; ☎03 20 06 78 00; www.pba-lille. fr; place de la République; adult/child €7/4; ⏰2-6pm Mon, 10am-6pm Wed-Sun; Ⓜ République-Beaux-Arts) Inaugurated in 1892, Lille's illustrious Fine Arts Museum claims France's second-largest collection after Paris' Musée du Louvre. Its cache of sublime 15th- to 20th-century paintings include works by Rubens, Van Dyck and Manet. Exquisite porcelain and faience (pottery), much of it of local provenance, is on the ground floor, while in the basement you'll find classical archaeology, medieval statuary and 18th-century scale models of the fortified cities of northern France and Belgium.

Hôtel de Ville   HISTORIC BUILDING
(☎03 20 49 50 00; www.lille.fr; place Augustin Laurent CS; belfry adult/child €7/5.50; ⏰belfry 10am-1pm & 2-5.30pm; Ⓜ Mairie de Lille) Built between 1924 and 1932, Lille's city hall is topped by a slender, 104m-high belfry that was designated a Unesco-listed monument in 2004. Climbing 100 steps leads to a lift that whisks you to the top for a stunning panorama over the town. An audio guide costs €2; binoculars are available for €1. Ring the doorbell to gain entry.

★ La Piscine Musée d'Art et d'Industrie   GALLERY
(☎03 20 69 23 60; www.roubaix-lapiscine.com; 23 rue de l'Espérance, Roubaix; adult/child €9/6; ⏰11am-6pm Tue-Thu, 11am-8pm Fri, 1-6pm Sat & Sun; Ⓜ Gare Jean Lebas) An art deco municipal swimming pool built between 1927 and 1932 is now an innovative museum showcasing fine arts (paintings, sculptures, drawings) and applied arts (furniture, textiles, fashion) in a delightfully watery environment: the pool is still filled and sculptures are reflected in the water. It reopened in October 2018 with a new wing and 2000 sq metres of additional exhibition space. It's 12km northeast of Gare Lille-Europe in Roubaix.

Musée d'Art Moderne, d'Art Contemporain et d'Art Brut – LaM   MUSEUM
(☎03 20 19 68 68; www.musee-lam.fr; 1 allée du Musée, Villeneuve-d'Ascq; adult/child €7/5, 1st Sun of month free; ⏰museum 10am-6pm Tue-Sun, sculpture park 9am-6pm Tue-Sun) Colourful, playful and just plain weird works of modern and contemporary art by masters such as Braque, Calder, Léger, Miró, Modigliani and Picasso are the big draw at this renowned museum and sculpture park in the

Lille suburb of Villeneuve-d'Ascq, 9km east of Gare Lille-Europe. Take metro line 1 to Pont de Bois, then bus L4 six stops to 'LaM'.

🛏 Sleeping & Eating

Dining hot spots in Vieux Lille include rue de Gand, rue de la Monnaie and its side streets, alleys and courtyards. Keep an eye out for *estaminets* (traditional Flemish eateries).

★**Hôtel L'Arbre Voyageur** DESIGN HOTEL **$$**
(✉ 03 20 20 62 62; http://hotelarbrevoyageur.com; 45 bd Carnot; d/f/ste from €119/214/219; 🌐🖥; Ⓜ Gare Lille-Flandres) 🌿 Behind a fretted glass-and-steel facade in the former Polish Consulate's post-Soviet building, the 2016-opened Hôtel L'Arbre Voyageur has 48 stylised rooms (including four suites) with custom-made furniture and minibars stocked with free soft drinks, and a bamboo- and palm-filled courtyard. Green initiatives span solar panels to a free drink for guests who don't want their linen changed every day.

Papà Raffaele PIZZA **$**
(www.facebook.com/paparaffaelepizzeria; 5 rue St-Jacques; pizza €7.50-14; ⊘ noon-2pm & 7-10pm Mon-Thu, noon-2pm & 6.30-11pm Fri, noon-3pm & 6.30-11pm Sat & Sun; 🖥🖥; Ⓜ Gare Lille-Flandres) The queues at Papà Raffaele are as legendary as its pizzas (it doesn't take reservations), so come early or late to this post-industrial space with recycled timber tables, vintage chairs and cured meats hanging from the ceiling. Wood-fired pizzas (like Cheesus Christ, with six cheeses) are made with Naples-sourced ingredients; coffee, craft beers and wine are all Italian. Takeaway is available.

★**L'Assiette du Marché** FRENCH **$$**
(✉ 03 20 06 83 61; www.assiettedumarche.com; 61 rue de la Monnaie; 2-/3-course menus €19.50/25, mains €16-25; ⊘ noon-2.30pm & 7-10.30pm Mon-Fri, to 11pm Sat & Sun; Ⓜ Rihour) Entered via a grand archway, a 12th-century aristocratic mansion – a mint under Louis XIV, hence the street's name, and a listed historical monument – is the romantic setting for contemporary cuisine (tuna carpaccio with Champagne vinaigrette, roast duckling with glazed turnips and smoked garlic). Dine under its glass roof, in its intimate dining rooms, or on its cobbled courtyard in summer.

🍷 Drinking & Nightlife

Small, stylish bars line rue Royale and rue de la Barre, while university students descend on the bars along rue Masséna and

DON'T MISS
WONDERFUL WAFFLES

Famed for its *gaufres* (waffles) made with Madagascar vanilla, **Meert** (✉ 03 20 57 07 44; www.meert.fr; 27 rue Esquermoise; waffles & pastries €3-7.60, tearoom dishes €4.50-11.50, restaurant mains €26-32; ⊘ shop 2-7.30pm Mon, 9.30am-7.30pm Tue-Fri, 9am-7.30pm Sat, 9am-7pm Sun, tearoom 2-7pm Mon, 9.30am-10pm Tue-Fri, 9am-10pm Sat, 9am-6.30pm Sun, restaurant noon-2.30pm & 7.30-10pm Tue-Sat, 11am-2pm Sun; 🖥; Ⓜ Rihour) has served kings, viceroys and generals since 1761. The sumptuous chocolate shop's coffered ceiling, painted wooden panels, wrought-iron balcony and mosaic floor date from 1839. Its *salon de thé* (tearoom) is a delightful spot for a morning arabica or a mid-afternoon tea. Also here is a French gourmet restaurant.

rue Solférino. In warm weather, cafes on place du Général de Gaulle and place du Théâtre spill onto table-filled terraces.

★**La Capsule** CRAFT BEER
(✉ 03 20 42 14 75; www.bar-la-capsule.fr; 25 rue des Trois Mollettes; ⊘ 5.30pm-1am Mon-Wed, 5.30pm-3am Thu & Fri, 4pm-3am Sat, 5.30pm-midnight Sun; 🖥; Ⓜ Rihour) Spread across three levels – a vaulted stone cellar, a beamed-ceilinged ground floor and an upper level reached by a spiral staircase – Lille's best craft beer bar has 28 varieties on tap and over 100 by the bottle. Most are French (such as Lille's Lydéric and Paris' BapBap) and Belgian (eg Cantillon), but small-scale brewers from around the world are also represented.

ℹ Information

Tourist Office (✉ 03 59 57 94 00; www.lilletourism.com; 3 rue du Palais Rihour; ⊘ 9.30am-1pm & 2-6pm Mon-Sat, 10am-12.30pm & 1.15-4.30pm Sun; Ⓜ Rihour)

ℹ Getting There & Around
AIR
Aéroport de Lille (LIL; www.lille.aeroport.fr; rte de L'Aéroport, Lesquin), 11km southeast of the centre, is linked to destinations around France and southern Europe by a variety of low-cost carriers. To get to/from the city centre (Gare Lille-Europe), take a shuttle bus (return €8, 20 minutes, hourly).

THE SOMME BATTLEFIELDS

The First Battle of the Somme, a WWI Allied offensive waged in the villages and wood-lands northeast of Amiens, was designed to relieve pressure on the beleaguered French troops at Verdun. On 1 July 1916, British, Commonwealth and French troops 'went over the top' in a massive assault along a 34km front. But German positions proved virtually unbreachable, and on the first day of the battle an astounding 21,392 British troops were killed and another 35,492 were wounded. By the time the offensive was called off in mid-November, a total of 1.2 million lives had been lost on both sides. The British had advanced 12km, the French 8km.

The battlefields and memorials are numerous and scattered – joining a tour can therefore be a good option, especially if you don't have your own transport. Tourist offices in **Péronne** (☑03 22 84 42 38; www.hautesomme-tourisme.com; 16 place André Audinot; ◷9.30am-12.30pm & 1.30-6.30pm Mon-Sat, 10am-noon & 2-5pm Sun Jul & Aug, 9am-12.30pm & 2-6pm Mon-Fri, 9am-noon & 2-6pm Sat Apr-Jun, Sep & Oct, shorter hour Nov-Mar) and **Albert** (☑03 22 75 16 42; www.tourisme-paysducoquelicot.com; 9 rue Gambetta; ◷9am-12.30pm & 1.30-6.30pm Mon-Fri, 9am-12.30pm & 2-6.30pm Sat, 9am-1pm Sun May-Aug, 9am-12.30pm & 1.30-5pm Mon-Fri, 9am-noon & 2-5pm Sat Sep-Apr) can help with booking tours and accommodation.

TRAIN

Lille has two main train stations: **Gare Lille-Flandres** for trains to Paris Gare du Nord (€47 to €63, one hour, at least hourly) and intra-regional TER services; and ultramodern **Gare Lille-Europe** for Eurostar trains to London, TGV/Thalys/Eurostar trains to Brussels-Midi, half of the TGVs to Paris Gare du Nord and most province-to-province TGVs. The two stations, 400m apart, are linked by metro line 2 (one stop).

NORMANDY

Famous for cows, cider and Camembert, this largely rural region (www.normandie-tourisme.fr) is one of France's most traditional, and most visited, thanks to world-renowned sights such as the Bayeux Tapestry, the historic D-Day beaches and spectacular Mont St-Michel.

Bayeux

POP 13,900

Bayeux has become famous throughout the English-speaking world thanks to a 68.3m-long piece of painstakingly embroidered cloth: the 11th-century Bayeux Tapestry, with its 58 scenes that vividly tell the story of the Norman invasion of England in 1066.

The town is also one of the few in Normandy to have survived WWII practically unscathed, with a centre crammed with 13th- to 18th-century buildings, timber-framed Norman-style houses, and a spectacular Norman Gothic **cathedral** (rue du Bienvenu;

◷8.30am-7pm). It makes a great base for exploring D-Day beaches.

◉ Sights

A 'triple ticket' good for all three of Bayeux' outstanding municipal museums costs €15/13.50 for an adult/child (€12/10 for two museums).

★**Bayeux Tapestry** MUSEUM
(☑02 31 51 25 50; www.bayeuxmuseum.com; 13bis rue de Nesmond; adult/child incl audio guide €9.50/5; ◷9.30am-12.30pm & 2-5.30pm Mon-Sat, 10am-1pm & 2-5.30pm Sun Feb, Mar, Nov & Dec, to 6pm Apr-Jun, Sep & Oct, 9am-7pm Mon-Sat, 9am-1pm & 2-6pm Sun Jul & Aug, closed Jan) The world's most celebrated embroidery depicts the conquest of England by William the Conqueror in 1066 from an unashamedly Norman perspective. Commissioned by Bishop Odo of Bayeux, William's half-brother, for the opening of Bayeux' cathedral in 1077, the well-preserved cartoon strip tells the dramatic, bloody tale with verve and vividness as well as some astonishing artistry. Particularly incredible are its length – nearly 70m long – and fine attention to detail.

★**Musée d'Art et d'Histoire Baron Gérard** MUSEUM
(MAHB; ☑02 31 92 14 21; www.bayeuxmuseum.com; 37 rue du Bienvenu; adult/child €7.50/5; ◷9.30am-6.30pm May-Sep, 10am-12.30pm & 2-6pm Oct-Apr, closed 3 weeks in Jan) Make sure you drop by this museum – one of France's most gorgeously presented provincial museums – where exhibitions cover everything

from Gallo-Roman archaeology through medieval art to paintings from the Renaissance and on to the 20th century, including a fine work by Gustave Caillebotte. Other highlights include impossibly fine local lace and Bayeux-made porcelain. The museum is housed in the former bishop's palace.

🛏 Sleeping & Eating

Local specialities to keep an eye out for include products made from *cochon de Bayeux* (a local heritage pig breed). Near the tourist office, along rue St-Jean and rue St-Martin, there is a variety food shops and cheap eateries.

Hôtel Reine Mathilde   HOTEL $
(📞 02 31 92 08 13; www.hotel-bayeux-reinemathilde. fr; 23 rue Larcher; d/ste/studio from €50/90/95; 🛜) Occupying a superbly central location, this friendly hotel has comfortable accommodation, with an assortment of sleek and spacious rooms in the annexe, a converted barn by the Aure River. Rooms, named after historic figures, are attractively designed with beamed ceilings, and elegant lines, excellent lighting and modern bathrooms; studios come with a small kitchenette. A decent restaurant is also on-site.

Au Ptit Bistrot   MODERN FRENCH $$
(📞 02 31 92 30 08; 31 rue Larcher; lunch menus €17-20, dinner menus €29-35, mains €18-22; ⊙ noon-2pm & 7-9pm Tue-Sat) Near the cathedral, this friendly, welcoming eatery whips up creative, beautifully prepared dishes that highlight the Norman bounty without pre-tension. The kids' menu is €11. Reservations essential.

ℹ Information

Tourist Office (📞 02 31 51 28 28; www. bayeux-bessin-tourisme.com; Pont St-Jean; ⊙ 9am-7pm Mon-Sat, 10am-1pm & 2-6pm Sun Jul & Aug, shorter hours rest of year)

ℹ Getting There & Away

Direct trains link Bayeux with Caen (€6, 15 to 20 minutes, hourly), from where there are connections to Paris' Gare St-Lazare and Rouen.

D-Day Beaches

Early on 6 June 1944, Allied troops stormed 80km of beaches north of Bayeux, codenamed (from west to east) Utah, Omaha, Gold, Juno and Sword. The landings on D-Day – called *Jour J* in French – ultimately led to the liberation of Europe from Nazi occupation. For context, see www.normandie memoire.com and www.6juin1944.com.

The most brutal fighting on D-Day took place 15km northwest of Bayeux along the stretch of coastline now known as **Omaha Beach**, today a glorious stretch of fine golden sand partly lined with sand dunes and summer homes. **Circuit de la Plage d'Omaha**, a trail marked with a yellow stripe, is a self-guided tour along the beach, surveyed from a bluff above by the huge **Normandy American Cemetery & Memorial** (📞 02 31 51 62 00; www.abmc.gov; Colleville-sur-Mer; ⊙ 9am-6pm mid-Apr–mid-Sep, to 5pm mid-Sep–

WORTH A TRIP

MODERN ART MUSEUMS

Two of Paris' foremost art institutions, the Louvre and the Centre Pompidou, have satellite outposts in northern France that art lovers won't want to miss.

Centre Pompidou-Metz (www.centrepompidou-metz.fr; 1 parvis des Droits de l'Homme; adult/child €7/free; ⊙ 10am-6pm Mon & Wed-Thu, to 7pm Fri-Sun) concentrates mainly on abstract and experimental art. The building itself is worth the trip, designed by Japanese architect Shigeru Ban, with a curved roof resembling a space-age Chinese hat. Trains run direct from Paris (€77 to €82, 1½ hours) and Strasbourg (€27.80, 1½ hours).

Louvre-Lens (📞 03 21 18 62 62; www.louvrelens.fr; 99 rue Paul Bert, Lens; temporary exhibitions adult/child €10/5; ⊙ 10am-6pm Wed-Mon) **FREE** showcases hundreds of the Louvre's treasures in a purpose-built, state-of-the-art exhibition space in Lens, 35km southwest of Lille. A second building, the glass-walled **Pavillon de Verre**, displays temporary themed exhibits. Free half-hourly shuttle buses link the museum with Lens' train station, linked by regular trains to/from Paris' Gare du Nord (€33, 1¼ hours) and Lille-Flandres (from €8.30, 45 minutes).

mid-Apr) FREE. Featured in the opening scenes of Steven Spielberg's *Saving Private Ryan*, this is the largest American cemetery in Europe.

Caen's high-tech, hugely impressive **Mémorial – Un Musée pour la Paix** (Memorial – A Museum for Peace; ☑ 02 31 06 06 44; www.memorial-caen.fr; esplanade Général Eisenhower; adult/child/family pass €19.80/17.50/51; ⊙ 9am-7pm Apr-Sep, 9.30am-6pm Oct-Dec, 9am-6pm Feb-Mar, closed 3 weeks in Jan, shut most Mon in Nov & Dec) uses sound, lighting, film, animation and lots of exhibits to graphically explore and evoke the events of WWII, the D-Day landings and the ensuing Cold War.

Lots of local companies offer guided minibus tours of the D-Day beaches; reserve at Bayeux tourist office (p405).

ⓘ Getting There & Away

Bus Verts (☑ 09 70 83 00 14; www.busverts. fr) links Bayeux' train station and place St-Patrice with many of the villages along the D-Day beaches.

Mont St-Michel

POP 44

It's one of France's most iconic images: the slender spires, stout ramparts and rocky outcrops of Mont St-Michel rising dramatically from the sea – or towering over slick, shimmering sands laid bare by the receding tide. The surrounding bay is famed for having Europe's highest tidal variations; the difference between low and high tides – only about six hours apart – can reach an astonishing 15m.

The Mont's one main street, the **Grande Rue**, leads up the slope – past souvenir shops, touristy eateries and a forest of elbows – to the abbey. Be prepared for hundreds of steps.

The Mont's star attraction is the stunning ensemble crowning its top: the **abbey** (☑ 02 33 89 80 00; www.abbaye-mont-saint-michel.fr/en; adult/child incl guided tour €10/free; ⊙ 9am-7pm May-Aug, 9.30am-6pm Sep-Apr, last entry 1hr before closing). Most areas can be visited without a guide, but it's worth taking the 1¼-hour tour included in the ticket. Admission is free the first Sunday of the month from November to March. For spectacular views of the bay and people trudging through the mud at low tide, walk along the top of the entire eastern section of the Mont's **ramparts**, from Tour du Nord (North Tower) to the Porte du Roy.

ⓘ Information

La Caserne Tourist Office (☑ 02 14 13 20 15; www.bienvenueaumontsaintmichel.com; La Caserne car park; ⊙ 10am-6pm)

Mont St-Michel Tourist Office (☑ 02 33 60 14 30; www.ot-montsaintmichel.com; bd Avancée, Corps de Garde des Bourgeois; ⊙ 9.30am-7pm Jul & Aug, to 6.30pm Mon-Sat, 9.30am-12.30pm & 1.30-6pm Sun Apr, May, Jun & Sep, shorter hours rest of year; ☎)

ⓘ Getting There & Away

For all manner of details on getting to the Mont, see www.bienvenueaumontsaintmichel.com.

Bus 1 (every hour or two, more frequently in July and August), operated by **Transdev** (☑ 02 14 13 20 15), links La Caserne with the train station in Pontorson (€3.20, 18 minutes); times are coordinated with some trains to/from Caen and Rennes.

BRITTANY

Brittany is for explorers. Its wild, dramatic coastline, medieval towns and thick forests make an excursion here well worth the detour off the beaten track. This is a land of prehistoric mysticism, proud tradition and culinary wealth, where fiercely independent locals celebrate Breton culture, and Paris feels a long way away indeed.

Quimper

POP 66,926

Small enough to feel like a village, with its slanted half-timbered houses and narrow cobbled streets, and large enough to buzz as the troubadour of Breton culture and arts, Quimper (kam-pair) is Finistère's thriving capital. With some excellent museums, standout crêperies, a history of faience (pottery) production, one of Brittany's loveliest old quarters and a delightful setting along the Odet River, Quimper deserves serious exploration. Beside the **Cathédrale St-Corentin**, recessed behind a magnificent stone courtyard, Quimper's superb **Musée Départemental Breton** showcases Breton history, furniture, crafts and archaeology in a former bishop's palace.

Quimper has a bewildering choice of exceptional crêperies centred on place au Beurre and rue du Sallé. The covered market **Halles St-François** (www.halles-cornouaille. com; 16 quai du Stéir; ⊙ 7am-7.30pm Mon-Sat, to 1pm Sun) has a slew of salad and sandwich options, or dine brasserie-style at one of Quimper's oldest addresses, **L'Épée** (☑ 02 98 95 28 97; http://cafedelepee.fr; 14 rue du Parc; mains €12-32, menus €15.50-39; ⊙ brasserie noon-2.30pm & 7-10.30pm Mon-Sat, cafe 10.30am-midnight Mon-Sat, noon-2.30pm Sun).

ⓘ Information

Tourist Office (☑ 02 98 53 04 05; www. quimper-tourisme.bzh; 8 rue Élie Fréron; ⊙ 9am-7pm Mon-Sat, 10am-12.45pm & 3-5.45pm Sun Jul & Aug, shorter hours rest of year; ☎) Sells the Pass Quimper (€12), which gives admission to four museums, sights or tours from a list of participating organisations.

ⓘ Getting There & Away

Frequent trains serve Paris' Gare Montparnasse (€67 to €108, 4¾ hours).

St-Malo

POP 46,589

The enthralling mast-filled port of fortified St-Malo is inextricably tied up with the deep briny blue: the town became a key harbour during the 17th and 18th centuries, functioning as a base for merchant ships and government-sanctioned privateers. These days it's a busy cross-Channel ferry port and summertime getaway.

◉ Sights

Walking on top of the sturdy 17th-century ramparts (1.8km) affords fine views of the old walled city known as **Intra-Muros** (Within the Walls), or Ville Close; access the ramparts from any of the city gates.

★ Château de St-Malo   CASTLE

(place Chateaubriand; ⊙ 10am-12.30pm & 2-6pm Apr-Sep, 10am-noon & 2-6pm Tue-Sun Oct-Mar) Château de St-Malo was built by the dukes of Brittany in the 15th and 16th centuries, and is now the home of the **Musée d'Histoire de St-Malo** (☑ 02 99 40 71 57; www.ville-saint-malo.fr/culture/les-musees; adult/child €6/3; ⊙ 10am-12.30pm & 2-6pm Apr-Sep, 10am-noon & 2-6pm Tue-Sun Oct-Mar), which examines the life and history of the city, while the lookout tower offers eye-popping views of the old city.

Ramparts   WALLS

Constructed at the end of the 17th century under military architect Vauban, and measuring 1.8km, the ramparts of St-Malo can be accessed from several points, including all the main city gates.

Île du Grand Bé & Fort du Petit Bé   ISLAND, CASTLE

(☑ 06 08 27 51 20; fort guided tours adult/child €6/4; ⊙ fort by reservation, depending on tides & weather) At low tide, cross the beach to walk out via Porte des Bés to Île du Grand Bé, the rocky islet where the great St-Malo-born, 18th-century writer Chateaubriand is buried. About 100m beyond Grand Bé is the privately owned, Vauban-built, 17th-century Fort du Petit Bé. Once the tide rushes in, the causeway remains impassable for about six hours; check tide times with the tourist office (p408) so you don't get trapped on the island.

🛏 Sleeping & Eating

★ Le Valmarin   HISTORIC HOTEL $$

(☑ 02 99 81 94 76; www.levalmarin.com; 7 rue Jean XXIII, St-Servan; s €80-125, d €85-165, f €149-230; ☎) If you're yearning for an aristocratic overlay to your St-Malo experience then this peaceful 18th-century mansion should do the job nicely. It has 12 high-ceilinged rooms dressed in late-19th-century style, and glorious gardens full of flowers and shade trees. Minus: some bathrooms feel a bit dated. It's a soothing escape from the St-Malo hubbub, on the edge of the village-like St-Servan quarter.

Breizh Café   CRÊPES $

(☑ 02 99 56 96 08; www.breizhcafe.com; 6 rue de l'Orme; crêpes €10-15, menu €15.80; ⊙ noon-2pm & 7-10pm Wed-Sun) This will be one of your most memorable meals in Brittany, from the delicious menu at this international name to the excellent service. The creative chef combines traditional Breton ingredients and *galette* and crêpe styles with Japanese flavours, textures and presentation, where seaweed and delightful seasonal pickles meet local ham, organic eggs and roast duck.

★ Bistro Autour du Beurre   BISTRO $$

(☑ 02 23 18 25 81; www.lebeurrebordier.com; 7 rue de l'Orme; 3-course weekday lunch menu €22, mains €19-26; ⊙ noon-2pm & 7-10pm Tue-Sat Jul & Aug, noon-2pm Tue & Wed, plus 7-10pm Thu-Sat Sep-Oct, Apr & Jun, noon-2pm Tue-Thu, plus 7-10pm Fri & Sat Nov-Mar) This casual bistro showcases the cheeses and butters handmade by the world-famous Jean-Yves Bordier; you'll find his **shop** (☑ 02 99 40 88 79; 9 rue de l'Orme; ⊙ 9am-1pm & 3.30-7.30pm Mon-Sat, 9am-1pm Sun Jul & Aug, closed Mon Sep-Jun) next door. At the bistro, the butter sampler and bottomless bread basket are just the start to creative, local meals that change with the seasons.

ⓘ Information

Tourist Office (☎ 08 25 13 52 00; www.
saint-malo-tourisme.com; esplanade St-
Vincent; ⊙ 9am-7.30pm Mon-Sat, 10am-7pm
Sun Jul & Aug, shorter hours rest of year; 🛜)

ⓘ Getting There & Away

Brittany Ferries (www.brittany-ferries.com)
sails between St-Malo and Portsmouth; Condor
Ferries (www.condorferries.co.uk) runs to/from
Poole via Jersey or Guernsey.

TGV train services go to Paris' Gare Montparnasse (€74, 2¾ hours, three direct TGVs daily).

CHAMPAGNE

POP 1.3 MILLION

Known in Roman times as Campania,
meaning 'plain', the agricultural region
of Champagne is synonymous these days
with its world-famous bubbly. This multimillion-dollar industry is strictly protected
under French law, ensuring that only grapes
grown in designated Champagne vineyards
can truly lay claim to the hallowed title.
The town of Épernay, 30km south of the
regional capital of Reims, is the best place
to head for *dégustation* (tasting); self-drive
Champagne Routes (www.tourisme-en
-champagne.com) wend their way through
the region's most celebrated vineyards.

Reims

POP 186,971

Rising golden and imperious above the
city, Reims' gargantuan Gothic cathedral
is where, over the course of a millennium
(816 to 1825), some 34 sovereigns – among
them two dozen kings – began their reigns.
Meticulously restored after WWI and again
following WWII, Reims is endowed with
handsome pedestrian boulevards, Roman
remains, art deco cafes and a flourishing
fine-dining scene that counts among it four
Michelin-starred restaurants.

⊙ Sights & Activities

The musty *caves* (cellars) and dusty bottles
of the 10 Reims-based Champagne producers
(known as *maisons* – literally, 'houses') can be
visited on guided tours. Major *maisons* such
as **Veuve Clicquot Ponsardin** (☎ 03 26 89 53
90; www.veuveclicquot.com; 1 place des Droits de
l'Homme; public tours & tastings €26-53, private tour
& tasting €250; ⊙ tours 9.30am, 10.30am, 12.30pm,

1.30pm, 2pm, 3.30pm & 4.30pm Tue-Sat Mar-Dec),
Mumm (☎ 03 26 49 59 70; www.mumm.com; 34
rue du Champ de Mars; tours incl tasting €20-39;
⊙ tours 9.30am-1pm & 2-6pm daily, shorter hours
& closed Sun Oct-Mar) and **Taittinger** (☎ 03 26
85 45 35; https://cellars-booking.taittinger.fr; 9 place
St-Nicaise; tours €19-55; ⊙ tours 10am-4.30pm) all
have fancy websites, cellar temperatures of
10°C to 12°C (bring warm clothes!) and frequent English-language tours that end, *na-
turellement*, with a tasting session.

★**Cathédrale Notre Dame**   CATHEDRAL
(☎ 03 26 47 81 79; www.cathedrale-reims.fr; 2 place
du Cardinal Luçon; tower adult/child €8/free, incl
Palais du Tau €11/free; ⊙ 7.30am-7.30pm, tower tours
10am, 11am & 2-5pm Tue-Sat, 2-5pm Sun May-Aug,
10am, 11am & 2-4pm Sat, 2-4pm Sun Sep, Oct & mid-
Mar–Apr) Imagine the extravagance of a French
royal coronation. The focal point of such
pomposity was Reims' resplendent Gothic cathedral, begun in 1211 on a site occupied by
churches since the 5th century. The interior is
a rainbow of stained-glass windows; the finest
are the western facade's great rose window,
the north transept's rose window and the vivid Marc Chagall creations (1974) in the central
axial chapel. The tourist office (p409) rents
out audio guides for self-paced tours.

★**Palais du Tau**   MUSEUM
(www.palais-du-tau.fr; 2 place du Cardinal Luçon;
adult/child €8/free, incl cathedral tower €11/free;
⊙ 9.30am-6.30pm Tue-Sun May–mid-Sep, 9.30am-
12.30pm & 2-5.30pm Tue-Sun mid-Sep–Apr) A
Unesco World Heritage Site, this lavish former archbishop's residence, redesigned in
neoclassical style between 1671 and 1710, was
where French princes stayed before their
coronations – and where they threw sumptuous banquets afterwards. Now a museum,
it displays truly exceptional statuary, liturgical objects and tapestries from the cathedral,
some in the impressive, Gothic-style **Salle de
Tau** (Great Hall). Treasures worth seeking out
include the 9th-century talisman of Charlemagne and St Rémi's golden, gem-encrusted
chalice, which dates from the 12th century.

Basilique St-Rémi   BASILICA
(place du Chanoine Ladame; ⊙ 9am-7pm) This
121m-long former Benedictine abbey church,
a Unesco World Heritage Site, mixes Romanesque elements from the mid-11th century
(the worn but stunning nave and transept)
with early Gothic features from the latter
half of the 12th century (the choir, with a
large triforium gallery and, way up top,

tiny clerestory windows). Next door is the **Musée St-Rémi** (http://musees-reims.fr; 53 rue Simon; adult/child €5/free; ⊙10am-noon & 2-6pm Tue-Sun).

🛏 Sleeping

Les Telliers
B&B $$

(☑09 53 79 80 74; https://telliers.fr; 18 rue des Telliers; s €68-85, d €80-121, tr €117-142, q €133-163; [P] [奈]) Enticingly positioned down a quiet alley near the cathedral, this bijou B&B extends one of Reims' warmest *bienvenues* (welcomes). The high-ceilinged rooms are big on art deco character, and handsomely decorated with ornamental fireplaces, polished oak floors and the odd antique. Breakfast costs an extra €9 and is a generous spread of pastries, fruit, fresh-pressed juice and coffee.

⭐Château Les Crayères
LUXURY HOTEL $$$

(☑03 26 24 90 00; www.lescrayeres.com; 64 bd Henry-Vasnier; d €395-755; [P] [✲] [@] [奈]) Such class! If you've ever wanted to stay in a palace, this romantic château on the fringes of Reims is the real McCoy. Manicured lawns sweep to the graceful turn-of-the-century estate, where you can play golf or tennis, dine in two-Michelin-starred finery, and stay in the lap of luxury in exuberantly furnished, chandelier-lit interiors – all at a price, naturally.

🍴 Eating & Drinking

A tempting array of delis, patisseries and chocolatiers lines rue de Mars, near **Halles du Boulingrin**. Place du Forum is a great place to watch the world drift languidly by at bistros, cafes and bars with pavement seating.

Le Wine Bar by Le Vintage
WINE BAR

(http://winebar-reims.com; 16 place du Forum; ⊙6pm-12.30am Tue-Thu, to 1.30am Fri & Sat) This bijou wine bar is a convivial spot to chill over a glass of wine or Champagne (some 500 are offered) with a tasting plate of charcuterie and cheese. The friendly brothers who own the place are happy to give recommendations.

Chez Jérôme
BISTRO $

(☑03 26 24 36 73; 23 rue de Tambour; menus €15-20; ⊙11am-6pm Tue-Fri, to 10.30pm Sat) So cosy it's like stepping into a friend's eccentric dining room, this bistro is run with passion by the inimitable one-man-band that is Jérôme – cook, waiter and chief bottle-washer. Made

according to the chef's whim and what's available, the tasty, unfussy *menus* are prepared with seasonal, market-fresh ingredients. Everything, from the vintage lights to ceramics and furnishings, is for sale.

l'Alambic
FRENCH $$

(☑03 26 35 64 93; www.restaurant-lalambic.fr; 63 bis rue de Chativesle; mains €14-25; ⊙noon-2pm & 7-9.30pm Tue-Fri, 7-9.30pm Sat & Mon; [♿]) 🍴 Ideal for an intimate dinner, this vaulted cellar dishes up well-prepared French classics – along the lines of home-smoked trout with horseradish, cod fillet with Champagne-laced *choucroute* (sauerkraut), and pigeon served two ways with Reims mustard sauce. Save room for terrific desserts such as crème brûlée with chicory ice cream. The *plat du jour* (dish of the day) is a snip at €11.

⭐L'Assiette Champenoise
GASTRONOMY $$$

(☑03 26 84 64 64; www.assiettechampenoise.com; 40 av Paul-Vaillant-Couturier, Tinqueux; menus €95-315; ⊙noon-2pm & 7.30-10pm Thu-Mon) Heralded far and wide as one of Champagne's finest tables and crowned with the holy grail of three Michelin stars, L'Assiette Champenoise is headed up by chef Arnaud Lallemen. Listed by ingredients, his intricate, creative dishes rely on outstanding produce and play up integral flavours – be they Breton scallops or milk-fed lamb with preserved vegetables. One for special occasions.

ⓘ Information

Tourist Office (☑03 26 77 45 00; www.reims-tourisme.com; 6 rue Rockefeller; ⊙10am-5pm Mon-Sat, 10am-12.30pm & 1.30-5pm Sun; [奈])

ⓘ Getting There & Away

from Reims train station, 1km northwest of the cathedral, frequent services include Paris Gare de l'Est (€28 to €61, 46 minutes to one hour) and Épernay (€7.20, 30 minutes).

Épernay

POP 24,456

Prosperous Épernay, the self-proclaimed *capitale du Champagne* and home to many of the world's most celebrated Champagne houses, is the best place for touring subterranean cellars and sampling bubbly. The town also makes an excellent base for exploring the Champagne Routes.

◉ Sights & Activities

★ Avenue de Champagne   STREET

Épernay's handsome av de Champagne fizzes with *maisons de champagne* (Champagne houses). The boulevard is lined with mansions and neoclassical villas, rebuilt after WWI. Peek through wrought-iron gates at Moët's private **Hôtel Chandon**, an early-19th-century pavilion-style residence set in landscaped gardens, which counts Wagner among its famous past guests. The haunted-looking **Château Perrier**, a red-brick mansion built in 1854 in neo–Louis XIII style, is aptly placed at number 13!

Atelier 1834: Champagne Boizel   WINE

(☑ 03 26 55 91 49; www.boizel.com; 46 av de Champagne; tours incl 2 Champagne tastings €22-40; ⊙10am-1pm & 2.30-5.30pm Mon-Fri, 10am-1pm & 2.30-6pm Sat) This wonderfully intimate Champagne house is still run with passion and prowess by the Boizel family, with a winemaking tradition dating from 1834. Unlike many of the *maisons* that open their doors to the public, these are still very much working cellars. Hidden away here are the real treasures – several bottles (still drinkable, apparently) hail from 1834.

Moët & Chandon   WINE

(☑ 03 26 51 20 20; www.moet.com; 20 av de Champagne; 1½hr tour with tasting €25-40, 10-17yr €10; ⊙tours 9.30-11.30am & 2-4.30pm) Flying the Moët, French, European and Russian flags, this prestigious *maison* is the world's biggest producer of Champagne. It has frequent 90-minute tours that are among the region's most impressive, offering a peek at part of its 28km labyrinth of *caves* (cellars).

⊨ Sleeping & Eating

Épernay's main eat street is rue Gambetta and adjacent place de la République. For picnic fixings, head to rue St-Thibault.

Hôtel Jean Moët   HISTORIC HOTEL $$

(☑ 03 26 32 19 22; www.hoteljeanmoet.com; 7 rue Jean Moët; d €168-212, ste €235-265; ❋ ⊚ ⊛) Housed in a beautifully converted 18th-century mansion, this old-town hotel is big on atmosphere, with its skylit tearoom and revamped antique-meets-boutique-chic rooms. Exposed beams add a dash of romance and there are modern comforts like Nespresso makers.

★ La Grillade Gourmande   FRENCH $$

(☑ 03 26 55 44 22; www.lagrilladegourmande.com; 16 rue de Reims; lunch menus €21, dinner menus €33-59, mains €20-26; ⊙noon-1.45pm & 7.30-9.30pm Tue-Sat) This chic, red-walled, art-slung bistro is an inviting spot to try chargrilled meats and dishes rich in texture and flavour, such as crayfish pan-fried in Champagne and lamb cooked in rosemary and honey until meltingly tender. Diners spill out onto the covered terrace in the warm months. Both the presentation and service are flawless.

ⓘ Information

Tourist Office (☑ 03 26 53 33 00; www.ot-epernay.fr; 7 av de Champagne; ⊙9am-12.30pm & 1.30-7pm Mon-Sat, 10.30am-1pm & 2-4.30pm Sun mid-Apr–mid-Oct, 9.30am-12.30pm & 1.30-5.30pm Mon-Sat mid-Oct–mid-Apr; ⊚)

ⓘ Getting There & Away

The **train station** (place Mendès-France) has direct services to Reims (€7.20, 27 minutes, 14 daily) and Paris Gare de l'Est (€24 to €69, 1¼ to 2¾ hours, seven daily).

LOCAL KNOWLEDGE

TASTE LIKE A PRO

You can taste Champagne anywhere, but you might get more out of the two-hour workshop at **Villa Bissinger** (☑ 03 26 55 78 78; www.villabissinger.com; 15 rue Jeanson, Ay), home to the International Institute for the Wines of Champagne. Besides covering the basics like names, producers, grape varieties and characteristics, the workshop includes a tasting of four different Champagnes. The institute is in Ay, 3.5km northeast of Épernay. Call ahead to secure your place.

ALSACE & LORRAINE

Teetering on the tempestuous frontier between France and Germany, the neighbouring regions of Alsace and Lorraine are where the worlds of Gallic and Germanic culture collide. Half-timbered houses, lush vineyards and forest-clad mountains hint at Alsace's Teutonic leanings, while Lorraine is indisputably Francophile.

Strasbourg

POP 276.170

Strasbourg is the perfect overture to all that is idiosyncratic about Alsace – walking a fine tightrope between France and Germany and between a medieval past and a progressive future, it pulls off its act in inimitable Alsatian style. Roam the old town's twisting alleys lined with fairy-tale half-timbered houses, feast in snug *winstubs* (Alsatian taverns) by the canals in Petite France, and marvel at how a city that does Christmas markets and gingerbread so well can also be home to the glittering EU Quarter and France's second-largest student population.

☉ Sights

★ **Cathédrale Notre-Dame** CATHEDRAL
(www.cathedrale-strasbourg.fr; place de la Cathédrale; adult/child astronomical clock €3/2, platform €5/3; ◷ 9.30-11.15am & 2-5.45pm, astronomical clock noon-12.45pm, platform 9am-7.15pm; 🚇 Grand'Rue) Nothing prepares you for your first glimpse of Strasbourg's Cathédrale Notre-Dame, completed in all its Gothic grandeur in 1439. The lace-fine facade lifts the gaze little by little to flying buttresses, leering gargoyles and a 142m spire. The interior is exquisitely lit by 12th- to 14th-century **stained-glass windows**, including the western portal's jewel-like rose window. The Gothic-meets-Renaissance **astronomical clock** strikes solar noon at 12.30pm with a parade of figures portraying the different stages of life and Jesus with his apostles.

★ **Grande Île** HISTORIC SITE
(🚇 Grand'Rue) History seeps through the twisting lanes and cafe-rimmed plazas of Grande Île, Strasbourg's Unesco World Heritage–listed island bordered by the River Ill. These streets – with their photogenic line-up of wonky, timber-framed houses in sherbet colours – are made for aimless ambling. They cower beneath the soaring magnificence of the cathedral and its sidekick, the ginger-bready 15th-century **Maison Kammerzell** (rue des Hallebardes), with its ornate carvings and leaded windows. The alleys are at their most atmospheric when lantern-lit at night.

Petite France AREA
(🚇 Grand'Rue) Criss-crossed by narrow lanes, canals and locks, Petite France is where artisans plied their trades in the Middle Ages. The half-timbered houses, sprouting veritable thickets of scarlet geraniums in summer, and the riverside parks attract the masses, but the area still manages to retain its Alsatian charm, especially in the early morning and late evening. Drink in views of the River Ill and the Barrage Vauban from the much-photographed **Ponts Couverts** (Covered Bridges; 🚇 Musée d'Art Moderne) and their trio of 13th-century towers.

★ **Palais Rohan** HISTORIC BUILDING
(2 place du Château; adult/child per museum €6.50/free, all 3 museums €12/free; ◷ 10am-6pm Wed-Mon; 🚇 Grand'Rue) Hailed as a 'Versailles in miniature', this opulent 18th-century residence is loaded with treasures. The basement **Musée Archéologique** takes you from the Palaeolithic period to 800 CE. On the ground floor is the **Musée des Arts Décoratifs**, where rooms adorned with Hannong ceramics and gleaming silverware evoke the lavish lifestyle of the nobility in the 18th century. On the 1st floor, the **Musée des Beaux-Arts'** collection of 14th- to 19th-century art includes El Greco, Botticelli and Flemish Primitive works.

Barrage Vauban VIEWPOINT
(Vauban Dam; ◷ viewing terrace 7.15am-9pm, shorter hours winter; 🚇 Faubourg National) FREE
A triumph of 17th-century engineering, the Barrage Vauban bears the architectural imprint of the leading French military engineer of the age – Sébastien Le Prestre de Vauban. The dam has been restored to its former glory and is now free to visit. Ascend to the terrace for a tremendously photogenic view that reaches across the canal-woven Petite France district to the Ponts Couverts and cathedral spire beyond.

🛏 Sleeping

It can be tricky to find last-minute accommodation from Monday to Thursday when the European Parliament is in plenary session (see www.europarl.europa.eu for dates).

★ **Cour du Corbeau** BOUTIQUE HOTEL $$
(📞 03 90 00 26 26; www.cour-corbeau.com; 6-8 rue des Couples; r €157-275, ste €220-260; ✹ 🛜;

FRANCE STRASBOURG

Porte de l'Hôpital) A 16th-century inn lovingly converted into a boutique hotel, Cour du Corbeau wins you over with its half-timbered charm and its location, just steps from the river. Gathered around a courtyard, rooms blend original touches such as oak parquet and Louis XV furnishings with mod cons including flat-screen TVs.

Hôtel du Dragon HOTEL $$
(📋 03 88 35 79 80; www.dragon.fr; 12 rue du Dragon; r €80-154; @ 🛜 🗶; 🚇 Porte de l'Hôpital) Step through a tree-shaded courtyard and into the, ahhh...blissful calm of this bijou hotel. The Dragon receives glowing reviews for its crisp interiors, attentive service and prime location near Petite France (p411).

🍴 Eating

Try canalside Petite France for Alsatian fare and half-timbered romance; Grand'Rue for curb-side kebabs and *tarte flambée* (thin Alsatian-style pizza topped with crème fraiche, onions and lardons); and rue des Veaux or rue des Pucelles for hole-in-the-wall eateries serving the world on a plate.

Winstub S'Kaechele FRENCH $
(📋 03 88 22 62 36; www.skaechele.fr; 8 rue de l'Argile; mains €12.50-18.50; ⏰ 7-9.30pm Mon, 11.45am-1.30pm & 7-9.30pm Tue-Fri; 🚇 Grand'Rue) Traditional French and Alsatian grub doesn't come more authentic than at this snug, amiable *winstub* (wine tavern), run with love by couple Karine and Daniel. Cue wonderfully cosy evenings spent in stone-walled, lamp-lit, wood-beamed surrounds, huddled over dishes such as escargots oozing Roquefort, fat pork knuckles braised in pinot noir, and *choucroute garnie* (sauerkraut garnished with meats).

★1741 GASTRONOMY $$$
(📋 03 88 35 50 50; www.1741.fr; 22 quai des Bateliers; 3-course lunch menus €42, 3-/5-course dinner menus €95/129; ⏰ noon-2pm & 7-10pm Thu-Mon; 🚇 Porte de l'Hôpital) A team of profoundly passionate chefs runs the show at this Michelin-starred number facing the River Ill. Murals, playful fabrics and splashes of colour add warmth to the dining room, where waiters bring well-executed, unfussy dishes, such as sea bass with Jerusalem artichoke and Alsatian venison with root vegetables, to the table. Service is excellent, as is the wine list.

ℹ️ Information

Tourist Office (📋 03 88 52 28 28; www.otstrasbourg.fr; 17 place de la Cathédrale; ⏰ 9am-7pm; 🚇 Grand'Rue) Buy a money-saving **Strasbourg Pass** (adult/child €21.50/15) here, valid for three consecutive days and covering one museum visit, access to the cathedral platform and astronomical clock, half a day's bicycle rental and a boat tour.

ℹ️ Getting There & Around

AIR

Strasbourg's **airport** (SXB; www.strasbourg.aeroport.fr), 17km southwest of town, is served by major carriers and budget airline Ryanair (London Stansted). A shuttle train links it to Strasbourg train station (€4.30, nine minutes, four hourly).

TRAIN

Train services include the following:
Lille (€128 to €151, four hours, 17 daily)
Lyon (€54 to €194, 4½ hours, 14 daily)
Paris (€90 to €113, 1¾ hours, 19 daily)

THE LOIRE VALLEY

One step removed from the French capital, this valley was historically the place where princes, dukes and notable nobles established their country getaways, and the countryside is littered with some of the most extravagant architecture outside Versailles.

Blois

POP 46,350

Towering above the northern bank of the Loire, Blois' royal château, one-time feudal seat of the powerful counts of Blois, offers a gripping introduction to some key periods in French history and architecture. Parts of the city still have a medieval vibe, and Blois makes an excellent base for visits to the châteaux, villages and towns of the central Loire Valley.

⊙ Sights

Billets combinés (combo tickets; €15.50 to €26.50), sold at the château, Maison de la Magie and Fondation du Doute, can save you some cash.

★ Château Royal de Blois CHATEAU
(📋 02 54 90 33 33; www.chateaudeblois.fr; place du Château; adult/child €12/6.50, audio guide €4; ⏰ 9am-6.30pm or 7pm Apr-Oct, 10am-5pm Nov-Mar) Seven French kings lived in Blois' royal château, whose four grand wings were built during four distinct periods in French architecture: Gothic (13th century), Flamboyant

Gothic (1498–1501), early Renaissance (1515–20) and classical (1630s). You can easily spend a half-day immersing yourself in the château's dramatic and bloody history and its extraordinary architecture. In July and August there are free tours in English (at 10.30am, 1.15pm and 3pm).

Maison de la Magie   MUSEUM
(☑ 02 54 90 33 33; www.maisondelamagie.fr; 1 place du Château; adult/child €10/6.50; ⊙ 10am-12.30pm & 2-6.30pm Apr-Aug & mid-Oct–early Nov, 2-6.30pm daily plus 10am-12.30pm Sat & Sun 1st 2 weeks Sep; ⏸) This museum of magic occupies the one-time home of watchmaker, inventor and conjurer Jean Eugène Robert-Houdin (1805–71), after whom the American magician Harry Houdini named himself. Dragons emerge roaring from the windows every half-hour, while inside the museum has exhibits on Robert-Houdin and the history of magic, displays of optical trickery, and several daily magic shows.

🛏 Sleeping & Eating

Hôtel Anne de Bretagne   HOTEL $
(☑ 02 54 78 05 38; www.hotelannedebretagne.com; 31 av du Dr Jean Laigret; s/d/tr/q €60/69/76/95, winter s/d €45/55; ⊙ reception 7am-11pm; P 🛜) This ivy-covered hotel, in a great location midway between the train station and the château, has friendly staff, a cosy piano-equipped *salon* and 29 brightly coloured rooms with bold bedspreads. A packed three-course picnic lunch costs €11.50. Also rents out bicycles (€16) and has free enclosed bike parking.

L'Orangerie du Château   GASTRONOMY $$$
(☑ 02 54 78 05 36; www.orangerie-du-chateau.fr; 1 av du Dr Jean Laigret; menus €40-86; ⊙ noon-1.45pm & 7-9.15pm Tue-Sat; P) This Michelin-starred restaurant serves *cuisine gastronomique inventive* inspired by both French tradition and culinary ideas brought from faraway lands. The excellent wine list comes on a tablet computer. For dessert try the house speciality, *soufflé chaud* (hot soufflé).

ℹ Information

Tourist Office (☑ 02 54 90 41 41; www.blois chambord.co.uk; 6 rue de la Voûte du Château; ⊙ 9am-7pm Apr-Sep, 10am-12.30pm & 2-5pm Mon-Sat, plus Sun school holidays, Oct-Mar)

ℹ Getting There & Away

BUS

The tourist office has a brochure detailing public-transport options to nearby châteaux. A

DON'T MISS

A ROOM WITH A VIEW

At home in the Château de Chambord's former kennels in front of the castle, **Relais de Chambord** (☑ 02 54 81 01 01; www.relaisdechambord.com; place St-Louis, Chambord; d from €165; P ❄ @ 🛜) is a four-star hotel that offers larger-than-life views of the château from some rooms and a sensational bar and restaurant terrace. Contemporary rooms are country-chic, dining is modern French and the hotel has a spa. Guests can borrow electric bicycles to cruise around the vast private estate. Rates include breakfast.

navette (shuttle bus; €6) run by **Rémi** (☑ 02 54 58 55 44; www.remi-centrevaldeloire.fr) makes it possible to do a Blois–Chambord–Cheverny–Beauregard–Blois circuit on Wednesday, Saturday and Sunday from early April to 5 November. From early April to August, this line runs daily during school-holiday periods and on public holidays.

TRAIN

Blois-Chambord train station (av Dr Jean Laigret) is 600m west (up the hill) from Blois' château.

Amboise (€7.20, 20 minutes, 15 to 20 daily)
Paris Gare d'Austerlitz (€18 to €32.40, 1½ hours, five direct daily)
Tours (€11.20, 30 to 46 minutes, 16 to 22 daily)

Around Blois

The peaceful, verdant countryside around the former royal seat of Blois is home to some of France's finest châteaux.

◎ Sights

★ **Château de Chambord**   CHATEAU
(☑ info 02 54 50 40 00, tour & show reservations 02 54 50 50 40; www.chambord.org; adult/child €13/free, parking distant/near €4/6; ⊙ 9am-6pm Apr-Oct, to 5pm Nov-Mar; ⏸) One of the crowning achievements of French Renaissance architecture, the Château de Chambord – with 426 rooms, 282 fireplaces and 77 staircases – is the largest, grandest and most visited château in the Loire Valley. Begun in 1519 by François I (r 1515–47) as a weekend hunting retreat, it quickly grew into one of the most ambitious – and expensive – building projects ever undertaken by a French monarch. A French-style **formal garden** opened in 2017.

Château de Chaumont-sur-Loire   CHATEAU
(☑02 54 20 99 22; www.domaine-chaumont.fr;
adult/child Apr-Oct €18/12, Jan-Mar, Nov & Dec
€12/7; ⏱9.30am or 10am-5pm or 6pm Nov-Mar,
to 8pm Apr-Oct) Set on a strategic bluff with
sweeping views along the Loire, Chaumont-
sur-Loire is known for three things: the
château itself, which has a medieval exteri-
or (cylindrical towers, a sturdy drawbridge)
and an interior courtyard that is very much
of the Renaissance; world-class exhibitions
of striking **contemporary art**; and the
Festival International des Jardins (⏱late
Apr-early Nov), for which 30 magnificent gardens are created each year by jury-selected
teams led by visual artists, architects, set designers and landscape gardeners.

Amboise

POP 13,370

Elegant Amboise, childhood home of
Charles VIII and final resting place of the
incomparable Leonardo da Vinci, is gorgeously situated on the southern bank of the
Loire, guarded by a soaring château. With
some seriously posh hotels, outstanding dining and one of France's most vivacious weekly markets (on Sunday morning), Amboise
is a convivial base for exploring the Loire
countryside and nearby châteaux by car or
bicycle.

◉ Sights

★ **Château Royal d'Amboise**   CHATEAU
(☑02 47 57 00 98; www.chateau-amboise.com;
place Michel Debré; adult/child €11.70/7.80, incl
audio guide €15.70/10.80; ⏱9am-5.45pm Dec-
Feb, to btwn 6.30pm & 8pm Mar-Nov, last entry 1hr
before closing) Perched atop a rocky escarp-
ment above town, Amboise's castle was a
favoured retreat for all of France's Valois and
Bourbon kings. Only a few of the château's
original structures survive, but you can still
visit the furnished **Logis** (Lodge) – Gothic
except for the top half of one wing, which
is Renaissance – and the Flamboyant Gothic
Chapelle St-Hubert (1493), where Leonardo da Vinci's presumed remains have been
buried since 1863. The ramparts afford
thrilling views of the town and river.

Le Clos Lucé   HISTORIC BUILDING
(☑02 47 57 00 73; www.vinci-closluce.com; 2 rue
du Clos Lucé; adult/child €15.50/11, mid-Nov–Feb
€13.50/10.50; ⏱9am-7pm or 8pm Feb-Oct, 9am

or 10am-6pm Nov-Jan, last entry 1hr before closing; ⊞) It was at the invitation of François
I that Leonardo da Vinci (1452–1519), aged
64, took up residence in this grand manor
house, built in 1471. An admirer of the
Italian Renaissance, the French monarch
named Da Vinci 'first painter, engineer and
king's architect', and the Italian spent his
time here sketching, tinkering and dreaming up ingenious contraptions.

Château Gaillard   CHATEAU
(☑02 47 30 33 29; www.chateau-gaillard-amboise.
fr; 95-97 av Léonard de Vinci & 29 allée du Pont
Moulin; adult/child €12/8; ⏱1-7pm Apr-early Nov)
The most exciting Loire château to open
to visitors in years, Gaillard is the earliest
expression of the Italian Renaissance in
France. Begun in 1496, the château was inspired by the refined living that Charles VIII
fell in love with during his Italian campaign.
The harmonious, Renaissance-style **gardens** were laid out by master gardener Dom
Pacello (1453–1534), an Italian Benedictine
monk who brought the first orange trees to
France.

🛏 Sleeping & Eating

L'Écluse   FRENCH $$
(☑02 47 79 94 91; www.ecluse-amboise.fr; rue
Racine; lunch menu €19, other menus €25-39;
⏱noon-1.30pm & 7-9pm Tue-Sat) On the banks
of the bubbling L'Amasse (or La Masse) Riv-
er next to an *écluse* (river lock), L'Écluse has
generated enthusiasm and glowing reviews.
The sharply focused menu is made up of just
three starters, three mains and three des-
serts, expertly prepared with fresh seasonal
products from a dozen Loire-area producers.

ⓘ Information

Tourist Office (☑02 47 57 09 28; www.amboise
-valdeloire.co.uk; quai du Général de Gaulle;
⏱9am or 10am-6pm or 7pm Mon-Sat, 10am-
1pm & 2-5pm Sun Apr-Oct, 10am-12.30pm &
2-5pm Mon-Sat Nov-Mar; 🛜)

ⓘ Getting There & Away

Amboise's **train station** (bd Gambetta) is 1.5km
north of the château, on the opposite side of
the Loire.

Blois (€7.20, 20 minutes, 15 to 20 daily)
Paris (€18.50 to €60.50, two hours) A handful
of direct trains go to Gare d'Austerlitz, other
trains serve Gare Montparnasse.

Around Amboise

A trio of world-class châteaux lies within easy day-trip reach of Amboise. Your own wheels – two or four – is the easiest means of getting around, although the towns of Chenonceaux (€7, 25 minutes, nine to 11 trains daily) and Azay-le-Rideau (€5.90, 26/41 minutes by train/bus, six to eight daily) are both served by public transport to/from the town of Tours.

◉ Sights

★Château de Chenonceau   CHATEAU
(☑02 47 23 90 07; www.chenonceau.com; adult/child €14/11, with audio guide €18/14.50; ☺9am-6.30pm or later Apr-Oct, to 5pm or 6pm Nov-Mar) Spanning the languid Cher River atop a graceful arched bridge, Chenonceau is one of France's most elegant châteaux. It's hard not to be moved and exhilarated by the glorious setting, the formal gardens, the magic of the architecture and the château's fascinating history, shaped by a series of powerful women. The interior is decorated with rare furnishings and an **art collection** that includes works by Tintoretto, Correggio, Rubens, Murillo, Van Dyck and Ribera (look for an extraordinary portrait of Louis XIV).

★Château de Villandry   CHATEAU
(☑02 47 50 02 09; www.chateauvillandry.com; 3 rue Principale; château & gardens adult/child €11/7, gardens only €7/5, cheaper Dec-Feb, audio guide €4; ☺9am-5pm or 6.30pm year-round, château interior closed mid-Nov–late Dec & early Jan-early Feb) Villandry's six glorious landscaped gardens *à la française* are some of France's finest, with more than 6 hectares of kitchen gardens, cascading flowers, ornamental vines, manicured lime trees, razor-sharp box hedges and tinkling fountains. Try to visit when the gardens – all of them organic – are blooming, between April and October. Tickets are valid all day (get your hand stamped). The website has details on special events.

Château d'Azay-le-Rideau   CHATEAU
(☑02 47 45 42 04; www.azay-le-rideau.fr; adult/child €10.50/free, audio guide €3; ☺9.30am-11pm Jul & Aug, to 6pm Apr-Jun & Sep, 10am-5.15pm Oct-Mar) Romantic, moat-ringed Azay-le-Rideau is celebrated for its elegant turrets, perfectly proportioned windows, delicate stonework and steep slate roofs. Built in the early 1500s on a natural island in the middle of the Indre River, it is one of the Loire's loveliest castles: Honoré

de Balzac called it a 'multifaceted diamond set in the River Indre'. The famous, Italian-style **loggia staircase** overlooking the central courtyard is decorated with the salamanders and ermines of François I and Queen Claude.

BURGUNDY

Burgundy (Bourgogne in French) offers some of France's most gorgeous countryside: rolling green hills dotted with mustard fields and medieval villages. Its handsome capital, Dijon, is heir to a glorious architectural heritage and peerless food and wine culture: Burgundy's tantalising vineyards are a treasured Unesco World Heritage Site.

Dijon

POP 159,168

Filled with elegant medieval and Renaissance buildings, dashing Dijon is Burgundy's capital, and the spiritual home of French mustard. Its lively old town is wonderful for strolling and shopping, interspersed with some snappy drinking and dining.

◉ Sights & Activities

English-language minibus tours operated by **Authentica Tours** (☑06 87 01 43 78; www.authentica-tours.com; group tours per person €65-130) and **Wine & Voyages** (☑03 80 61 15 15; www.wineandvoyages.com; tours €63-120) introduce the Côte d'Or vineyards. Reserve by phone, internet or via the tourist office.

**Palais des Ducs et des
États de Bourgogne**   PALACE
(Palace of the Dukes & States of Burgundy; place de la Libération) Once home to Burgundy's powerful dukes, this monumental palace with a neoclassical facade overlooks place de la Libération, old Dijon's magnificent central square dating from 1686. The palace's eastern wing houses the outstanding Musée des Beaux-Arts (p415), whose entrance is next to the **Tour de Bar**, a squat 14th-century tower that once served as a prison. The remainder of the palace houses municipal offices that are off limits to the public.

★Musée des Beaux-Arts   MUSEUM
(☑03 80 74 52 09; http://beaux-arts.dijon.fr; 1 rue Rameau; audio guide €4, guided tour €6; ☺10am-6.30pm Jun-Sep, 9.30am-6pm Oct-May, closed Tue

year-round) **FREE** Nearing the end of a nine-year renovation, these sprawling galleries in Dijon's monumental Palais des Ducs are works of art in themselves and constitute one of France's most outstanding museums. The star attraction is the wood-panelled **Salle des Gardes**, which houses the ornate, carved late-medieval sepulchres of dukes John the Fearless and Philip the Bold. Other sections focus on Egyptian art, the Middle Ages in Burgundy and Europe, and six centuries of European painting, from the Renaissance to modern times.

Tour Philippe le Bon   TOWER
(place de la Libération; adult/child €3/1.50; ⊙ guided tours every 45min 10.30am-noon & 1.45-5.30pm Tue-Sun Apr-mid-Nov, hourly 2-4pm Tue, 11am-4pm Sat & Sun mid-Nov-Mar) Adjacent to the ducal palace, this 46m-high, mid-15th-century tower affords fantastic views over the city. On a clear day you can see all the way to Mont Blanc. Dijon's tourist office handles reservations.

🛏 Sleeping & Eating

Find loads of restaurants on buzzy rue Berbisey, around place Émile Zola, on rue Amiral Roussin and around the perimeter of the covered market. In warm months, outdoor cafes and brasseries (restaurants) fill place de la Libération.

Hôtel Le Chambellan   HOTEL $
(☑ 03 80 67 12 67; www.hotel-chambellan.com; 92 rue Vannerie; s €44-59, d €59-66, q from €79, s/d with shared bathroom €37/39; ⊛) This budget favourite in the heart of medieval Dijon has a whole new look, mixing modern flair (remodelled bathrooms, bold colours, phone-charging ports, spiffy new reading lamps) with the three Ps – *poutres, pierre, parquet* (exposed beams, stone and wood floors) – that epitomise owner Christophe Comte's long-standing fondness for the rustic.

★**L'Age de Raisin**   WINE BAR
(☑ 03 80 23 24 82; 67 rue Berbisey; ⊙6pm-2am Tue-Sat) Stone walls, red-and-white-checked tablecloths and gracious service set the mood at this cosiest of Dijon wine bars. With late hours and a wealth of local vintages hand-selected by affable owners Jeff and Nadine, it doubles as a bistro, serving fabulous

home-cooked *plats du jour* built from locally sourced organic produce. Reserve ahead at dinner time; it fills up fast!

ℹ Information

Tourist Office (☑ 08 92 70 05 58; www.destinationdijon.com; 11 rue des Forges; ⊙9.30am-6.30pm Mon-Sat, 10am-6pm Sun Apr-Sep, 9.30am-1pm & 2-6pm Mon-Sat, 10am-4pm Sun Oct-Mar; ⊛)

ℹ Getting There & Away

Transco (☑ 03 80 11 29 29; www.mobigo-bourgogne.com; single ticket/day pass €1.50/6.60) Buses stop in front of the train station. Bus 44 goes to Nuits-St-Georges (45 minutes) and Beaune (1¼ hours).

Frequent rail services from Dijon's train station include the following:
Lyon-Part Dieu (€32 to 37, 1½ to two hours)
Marseille (€81, 3¾ hours)
Paris Gare de Lyon (€35 to €61, 1½ to three hours)

Beaune
POP 22,418

Beaune (pronounced similarly to 'bone'), 44km south of Dijon, is the unofficial capital of the Côte d'Or and wine is its raison d'être. The jewel of its old city hides a subterranean labyrinth of centuries-old wine cellars where some of the world's most prestigious wines repose. The amoeba-shaped old city is enclosed by thick stone ramparts and a stream, which is in turn encircled by a one-way boulevard with seven names. The ramparts, which shelter wine cellars, are lined with overgrown gardens and ringed by a pathway that makes for a lovely stroll. Beaune's flagship sight is the magnificent Gothic **Hôtel-Dieu des Hospices de Beaune** (☑ 03 80 24 45 00; www.hospices-de-beaune.com; 2 rue de l'Hôtel-Dieu; adult/child €7.50/3; ⊙9am-6.30pm mid-Mar–mid-Nov, 9-11.30am & 2-5.30pm rest of year), built as a hospital in 1443 and famously topped by stunning turrets and pitched rooftops covered in multicoloured tiles.

The **tourist office** (☑ 03 80 26 21 30; www.beaune-tourisme.fr; 6 bd Perpreuil; ⊙9am-6.30pm Mon-Sat, to 6pm Sun Apr-Oct, shorter hours Nov-Mar) has information on wine tasting and visiting nearby vineyards. An annexe opposite the Hôtel-Dieu keeps shorter hours.

A TRIP BETWEEN VINES

Burgundy's most renowned vintages come from the **Côte d'Or** (Golden Hillside), a range of hills made of limestone, flint and clay that runs south from Dijon for about 60km. The northern section, the **Côte de Nuits**, stretches from Marsannay-la-Côte south to Corgoloin and produces reds known for their robust, full-bodied character. The southern section, the **Côte de Beaune**, lies between Ladoix-Serrigny and Santenay and produces great reds and whites.

Tourist offices provide brochures. The signposted **Route des Grands Crus** (www.road-of-the-fine-burgundy-wines.com) visits some of the most celebrated Côte de Nuits vineyards; mandatory tasting stops for oenophiles seeking nirvana include 16th-century **Château du Clos de Vougeot** (📞03 80 62 86 09; www.closdevougeot.fr; rue de la Montagne, Vougeot; adult/child €7.50/2.50; ☺9am-6.30pm Sun-Fri, to 5pm Sat Apr-Oct, 10am-5pm Nov-Mar), which offers excellent guided tours, and **L'Imaginarium** (📞03 80 62 61 40; www.imaginarium-bourgogne.com; av du Jura, Nuits-St-Georges; adult incl basic/grand cru tasting €10/21, child €7; ☺2-7pm Mon, 10am-7pm Tue-Sun, last admission 5pm), an entertaining wine museum in **Nuits-St-Georges**.

❶ Getting There & Away

Bus 44, operated by **Transco** (📞03 80 11 29 29; www.mobigo-bourgogne.com), links Beaune with Dijon (€1.50, 1¼ hours), stopping at Côte d'Or villages.

LYON

POP 514,000

Commanding a strategic spot at the confluence of the Rhône and the Saône Rivers, Lyon has been luring people ever since the Romans named it Lugdunum in 43 BCE. As France's third-largest city, it cooks up outstanding museums, a dynamic cultural life, busy clubbing and drinking scenes, fantastic shopping and stupendous gastronomy. Don't leave without sampling Lyonnais specialities in a *bouchon* (Lyonnais bistro) – the quintessential Lyon experience.

◉ Sights

The excellent-value **Lyon City Card** (www.lyoncitycard.com; 1/2/3 days adult €25/35/45, child €17/24/31) offers free admission to every Lyon museum, the roof of Basilique Notre Dame de Fourvière, guided city tours, Guignol puppet shows and river excursions (April to October), along with numerous other discounts. The card also includes unlimited public transport.

◉ Vieux Lyon

Lyon's Unesco-listed old town is a rabbit warren of narrow streets lined with medi-

eval and Renaissance houses, especially on rue du Bœuf, rue St-Jean and rue des Trois Maries. Crane your neck upwards to see gargoyles and other cheeky stone characters carved on window ledges along rue Juiverie, home to Lyonnais Jews in the Middle Ages.

Cathédrale St-Jean-Baptiste CATHEDRAL (www.cathedrale-lyon.fr; place St-Jean, 5e; ☺cathedral 8.15am-7.45pm Mon-Fri, 8am-7pm Sat & Sun, treasury 9.30am-noon & 2-6pm Tue-Sat; Ⓜ Vieux Lyon) Lyon's partly Romanesque cathedral was built between the late 11th and early 16th centuries. The portals of its Flamboyant Gothic facade, completed in 1480 (and recently renovated), are decorated with 280 square stone medallions. Inside, the highlight is the astronomical clock in the north transept.

◉ Fourvière

More than two millennia ago, the Romans built the city of Lugdunum on the slopes of Fourvière – an **amphitheatre** is all that remains. Footpaths wind uphill from Vieux Lyon, but the funicular is less taxing.

Basilique Notre Dame de Fourvière CHURCH (📞04 78 25 13 01; www.fourviere.org; place de Fourvière, 5e; rooftop tour adult/child €10/5; ☺basilica 7am-7pm, tours 9am-12.30pm & 2-6pm Mon-Fri, 9am-12.30pm & 2-4.45pm Sat, 2-4.45pm Sun Apr-Nov; Ⓕ Fourvière) Crowning the hill, with stunning city panoramas from its terrace, this superb example of late-19th-century French ecclesiastical architecture is lined with magnificent mosaics. From April to November,

Lyon

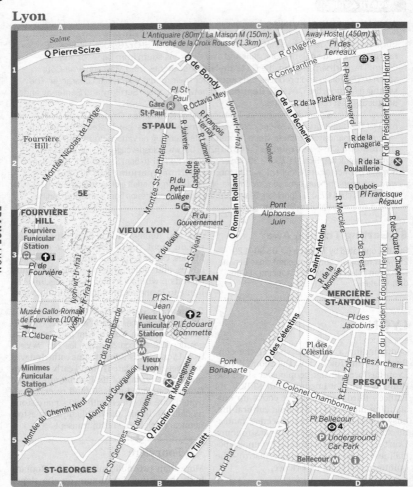

free 30-minute discovery visits take in the main features of the basilica and crypt; otherwise, 90-minute rooftop tours ('Visite Insolite') climax on the stone-sculpted roof. Reserve tickets in advance online for the latter.

Musée Gallo-Romain de Fourvière MUSEUM (📞 04 73 38 49 30; www.museegalloromain.grandlyon.com; 17 rue Cléberg, 5e; adult/child €4/free; ⏰ 11am-6pm Tue-Fri, from 10am Sat & Sun; 🚋 Fourvière) For an enlightening historical perspective on the city's past, start your visit at this archaeological museum on the hillside of Fourvière. It hosts a wide-ranging collection of ancient artefacts found in the Rhône Valley as well as superb mosaics.

◉ Presqu'île & Confluence

Lyon's city centre lies on this peninsula, 500m to 800m wide, bounded by the rivers Rhône and Saône, and pierced by **place Bellecour** (Ⓜ Bellecour), one of Europe's largest public squares. Past Gare de Perrache lies **Lyon Confluence** (www.lyon-confluence.fr) the city's newest neighbourhood.

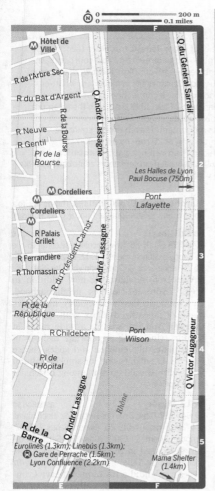

Lyon

ⓞ Sights
1 Basilique Notre Dame de
   Fourvière A3
2 Cathédrale St-Jean-Baptiste............. B4
3 Musée des Beaux-Arts D1
4 Place Bellecour...................................... D5

🛏 Sleeping
5 Cour des Loges.................................. B2

⊗ Eating
6 Cinq Mains B4
7 La Cuisinerie B5
8 Le Musée D2

★ **Musée des Confluences**   MUSEUM
(☎ 04 28 38 12 12; www.museedesconfluences.fr; 86
quai Perrache, 6e; adult/child €9/free; ⊙ 11am-7pm
Tue, Wed & Fri, to 10pm Thu, 10am-7pm Sat & Sun;
🚊 T1) This eye-catching building, designed
by the Viennese firm Coop Himmelb(l)au,
is the crowning glory of the Confluence, at
Presqu'île's southern tip. Lying at the confluence of the Rhône and Saône rivers, this
ambitious science-and-humanities museum
is housed in a futuristic steel-and-glass transparent crystal. Its distorted structure is one
of the city's iconic landmarks.

🛏 Sleeping

Lyon's **tourist office** (☎ 04 72 77 69 69; www.
lyon-france.com; place Bellecour, 2e; ⊙ 9am-6pm;
🛜; Ⓜ Bellecour) runs a free reservation service
(http://book.lyon-france.com/en/accommoda
tion) and occasionally offers deals like free
breakfasts or discounts on multinight stays.

★ **Away Hostel**   HOSTEL $
(☎ 04 78 98 53 20; www.awayhostel.com; 21 rue
Alsace Lorraine, 1er; dm €25-30, d €95; @ 🛜;
Ⓜ Croix-Paquet) One of Lyon's best new
budget sleeps, Away Hostel has attractive,
sunny rooms with tall ceilings, wood floors
and oversized windows. The cafe is a good
place to meet other travellers, and there are
loads of events going on (walking tours, yoga
brunches, communal dinners).

★ **Mob Hotel**   BOUTIQUE HOTEL $$
(☎ 04 58 55 55 88; www.mobhotel.com; 55 quai
Rambaud, 2e; d/ste from €120/170; Ⓟ 🛜; 🚊 T1) A
stellar new addition to Lyon, the Mob Hotel
is a magnet for designers and the creative
set. Metal lacework encases the avant-garde
building overlooking the Saône, while the

★ **Musée des Beaux-Arts**   MUSEUM
(☎ 04 72 10 17 40; www.mba-lyon.fr; 20 place des
Terreaux, 1er; adult/child €8/free; ⊙ 10am-6pm
Wed, Thu & Sat-Mon, 10.30am-6pm Fri; Ⓜ Hôtel de
Ville) This stunning and eminently manage-
able museum showcases France's finest col-
lection of sculptures and paintings outside
of Paris, from antiquity onwards. Highlights
include works by Rodin, Monet and Picas-
so. Pick up a free audio guide and be sure
to stop for a drink or meal on the delightful
stone terrace off its cafe-restaurant or take
time out in its tranquil cloister garden.

DON'T MISS

LYON'S HIDDEN LABYRINTH

Deep within Vieux Lyon and the hilltop quartier of Croix-Rousse, *traboules* (secret passages) wind their way through apartment blocks, under streets and into courtyards. In all, 315 passages link 230 streets, with a combined length of 50km. Most were constructed by *canuts* (silk weavers) in the 19th century to transport silk in inclement weather.

Vieux Lyon's most celebrated *traboules* include those connecting 27 rue St-Jean with 6 rue des Trois Maries and 54 rue St-Jean with 27 rue du Bœuf (push the intercom button to buzz open the door). Step into Croix-Rousse's underworld at 9 place Colbert, crossing cour des Voraces – renowned for its monumental seven-storey staircase – to 14bis montée St-Sébastien, and eventually emerging at 29 rue Imbert Colomès.

For detailed descriptions and maps, download the free iPhone app **Traboules de Lyon**. Guided walking **tours** (☎04 72 77 69 69; www.visiterlyon.com; tours adult/child €13/8; ⊙by reservation) by Lyon's tourist office also visit *traboules*.

inside is a playful mixture of polished concrete, pale blond woods, artful lighting and subtle pastels. Book a Master Mob room for a balcony and ample space.

Mama Shelter HOTEL **$$**
(☎04 78 02 58 00; www.mamashelter.com/en/lyon; 13 rue Domer, 7e; r €79-323; P❄@; M Jean Macé) Lyon's branch of this trendy hotel chain has sleek decor, carpets splashed with calli-graffiti, firm beds, plush pillows, modernist lighting and big-screen Macs offering free in-room movies. A youthful crowd fills the long bar in the low-lit restaurant. The residential location 2km outside the centre may feel remote, but it's only three metro stops from Gare de la Part-Dieu and place Bellecour.

★**Cour des Loges** HOTEL **$$$**
(☎04 72 77 44 44; www.courdesloges.com; 2-8 rue du Bœuf, 5e; d €250-450, ste €430-580; ❄@; M Vieux Lyon) Four 14th- to 17th-century houses wrapped around a *traboule* (secret passage) with preserved features such as Italianate loggias make this an exquisite place to stay. Individually decorated rooms draw guests with designer bathroom fittings and bountiful antiques, while decadent facilities include a spa, a Michelin-starred restaurant (*menus* €105 to €145), a swish cafe and a cross-vaulted bar.

Eating

Lyon's famed indoor food market **Les Halles de Lyon Paul Bocuse** (☎04 78 62 39 33; www.hallespaulbocuse.lyon.fr; 102 cours Lafayette, 3e; ⊙7am-10.30pm Tue-Sat, to 4.30pm Sun; M Part-Dieu) has more than 60 stalls selling their renowned wares and ample spots to squat and quaff freshly shucked oysters. Lyon's premier outdoor food market is the bustling **Marché de la Croix Rousse** (bd de la Croix Rousse, 1er; ⊙6am-1pm Tue-Sun; M Croix Rousse).

La Cuisinerie FUSION **$**
(☎04 78 60 91 86; www.lacuisinerie.com; 16 rue St-Georges; lunch menu €11-17, small plates €6-13; ⊙noon-2pm & 7pm-midnight Mon-Sat; ✎; M Vieux Lyon) A charming new addition to Vieux Lyon's St-Georges neighbourhood, La Cuisinerie has a deliciously innovative menu of tapas-sized plates with global influences. You can sample a wide range of flavours (including vegetarian dishes) in small plates like chicken and goat's cheese *churros*, crayfish ravioli, or smoked salmon blinis with wasabi cream, among dozens of other options.

★**Le Musée** BOUCHON **$$**
(☎04 78 37 71 54; 2 rue des Forces, 2e; lunch mains €14, lunch menus €19-26, dinner menus €23-32; ⊙noon-1.30pm & 7.30-9.30pm Tue-Sat; M Cordeliers) Housed in the stables of Lyon's former Hôtel de Ville, this delightful *bouchon* serves a splendid array of meat-heavy Lyonnais classics, including a divine *poulet au vinaigre* (chicken cooked in vinegar). The daily changing *menu* features 10 appetisers and 10 main dishes, plus five scrumptious desserts, all served on cute china plates at long family-style tables.

Cinq Mains NEOBISTRO **$$**
(☎04 37 57 30 52; www.facebook.com/cinqmains; 12 rue Monseigneur Lavarenne, 5e; menu lunch/dinner €19/33; ⊙noon-1.30pm & 7.30-9.30pm; M Vieux Lyon) When young Lyonnais Grégory Cuilleron and his two friends opened this neobistro in early 2016, it was an instant hit. They're working wonders at this cool loft-like space with a mezzanine, serving up tantalising creations based on what they find at

the market. A new generation of chefs, and a new spin for Lyonnais cuisine.

★ Restaurant Paul Bocuse GASTRONOMY $$$

(☑ 04 72 42 90 90; www.bocuse.com; 40 quai de la Plage, Collonges au Mont d'Or; menus €175-275; ⊘ noon-1.30pm & 8-9pm) Some 7km north of Lyon, this triple-Michelin-starred restaurant was the flagship of the city's most decorated chef, Paul Bocuse. Although Bocuse is no longer around, his recipes continue to dazzle foodies, with the likes of escargots with parsley butter, thyme-roasted rack of lamb and Bocuse's signature *soupe aux truffes noires VGE* (truffle soup created for French president Valéry Giscard d'Estaing in 1975).

🍷 Drinking & Nightlife

Vieux Lyon and rue Ste-Catherine behind place des Terreaux sport extraordinary concentrations of British and Irish pubs. Along quai Victor Augagneur on the Rhône's left bank, a string of *péniches* (barges with onboard bars) serve drinks from midafternoon onwards; many rock until the wee hours with DJs and/or live bands.

L'Antiquaire COCKTAIL BAR

(☑ 06 34 21 54 65; 20 rue Hippolyte Flandrin, 1er; ⊘ 5pm-1am Tue & Wed, to 3am Thu-Sat, 6.30pm-1am Sun & Mon; Ⓜ Hôtel de Ville) Old-time jazz, flickering candles and friendly suspenders-wearing barkeeps set the mood in this atmospheric speakeasy-style bar. The painstakingly prepared cocktails are first-rate (try a Penicillin made from scotch, ginger, honey, lemon and peat whisky) and are best sipped slowly at one of the dark wood and leather booths.

La Maison M CLUB

(☑ 04 72 00 87 67; http://mmlyon.com; 21 place Gabriel Rambaud, 1er; ⊘ 7.30pm-4am Wed-Sat; Ⓜ Hôtel de Ville) A fantastic addition to Lyon's nightlife scene, La Maison M has three separate spaces: a tropical-style bar near the entrance, a dance floor to the left and a cosy lounge off to the right. DJ parties feature nights of samba (with Brazilian cocktails to match), cumbia, hip-hop and new-wave disco.

★ Le Sucre LIVE MUSIC

(www.le-sucre.eu; 50 quai Rambaud, 2e; ⊘ 8.30pm-midnight Wed & Thu, 6.30pm-1am Fri, to 5am Sat, 4-11pm Sun; ⓐ T1) Down in the Confluence neighbourhood, Lyon's most innovative club hosts DJs, live shows and eclectic arts events on its super-cool roof terrace atop a 1930s sugar factory, La Sucrière.

ℹ Information

Tourist Office (p419) offers excellent guided tours, many themed.

ℹ Getting There & Away

AIR

Lyon-St-Exupéry Airport (LYS; www.lyonaeroports.com) Located 25km east of the city, with 40 airlines (including many budget carriers) serving more than 120 direct destinations across Europe and beyond.

BUS

International bus companies **Eurolines** (☑ 08 92 89 90 91; www.eurolines.fr; Gare de Perrache, 2e; ⊘ 6.30am-9.15pm Mon-Sat, noon-4pm & 8.15-10pm Sun; Ⓜ Perrache) and **Linebús** (☑ 04 72 41 72 27; www.linebus.es; Gare de Perrache; ⊘ 7am-9pm Mon-Sat, noon-4pm Sun; Ⓜ Perrache) offer services to Spain, Portugal, Italy and Germany from the Centre d'Échange building at the north end of the Perrache train complex. Follow signs for 'Cars Grandes Lignes' and 'Galerie A: Gare Routière Internationale'.

TRAIN

Lyon has two main-line train stations: **Gare de la Part-Dieu** (place Charles Béraudier, 3e; Ⓜ Part-Dieu), 1.5km east of the Rhône, and **Gare de Perrache** (cours de Verdun Rambaud, 2e; Ⓜ Perrache). Destinations by direct TGV include the following:

Marseille (€52, 1¾ hours, every 30 to 60 minutes)

Paris Charles de Gaulle Airport (€88, two hours, at least 11 daily)

Paris Gare de Lyon (€75, two hours, every 30 to 60 minutes)

ℹ Getting Around

Buses, trams, a four-line metro and two funiculars linking Vieux Lyon to Fourvière and St-Just are operated by TCL (www.tcl.fr) and run from around 5am to midnight.

> **DON'T MISS**
>
> ### FESTIVAL OF LIGHTS
>
> **Fête des Lumières** (Festival of Lights; www.fetedeslumieres.lyon.fr; ⊘ Dec) Over four days around the Feast of the Immaculate Conception (8 December), magnificent sound-and-light shows are projected onto key buildings, while locals illuminate window sills with candles. This is Lyon's premier festival, and it's so colourful that it's worth timing your trip around it. Note that every hotel will be fully booked.

FRANCE LYON

Tickets cost €1.90 (€16.90 for a *carnet* of 10) and are available from bus and tram drivers as well as machines at metro entrances. Tickets allow two consecutive hours of travel after 9am or unlimited travel after 7pm cost €3, and an all-day ticket costs €5.80. Time-stamp tickets on all forms of public transport or risk a fine.

THE FRENCH ALPS

Hiking, skiing, soul-soaring panoramas – the French Alps have it all when it comes to the great outdoors. But you'll also find excellent gastronomy, good nightlife and plenty of history.

Chamonix

POP 8906 / ELEV 1035M

Mountains loom large almost everywhere you look in Chamonix – France's original winter-sports hub rediscovered as a tourist destination by Brits William Windham and Richard Pococke in 1741. In 1924 Chamonix hosted the first ever Winter Olympics.

Downtown Chamonix hums with life. Streets are lined with Michelin-starred restaurants, sports gear shops and some of the French Alps' fanciest hotels. And if you do the nightlife justice, it'll exhaust you as much as the mountains.

⊙ Sights & Activities

The ski season runs from mid-December to mid-April. Summer activities – hiking, biking, canyoning, mountaineering etc – generally start in June and end in September. The **Compagnie des Guides de Chamonix** (📋04 50 53 00 88; www.chamonix-guides. com; 190 place de l'Église, Maison de la Montagne; ⊙8.30am-noon & 2.30-7.30pm mid-Dec–late Apr & mid-June–mid-Sep, closed Sun & Mon rest of year) is the most famous of all the guide companies and has guides for virtually every activity, whatever the season.

★ Aiguille du Midi   VIEWPOINT

The great rocky fang of the Aiguille du Midi (3842m), rising from the Mont Blanc massif, is one of Chamonix' most distinctive features. The 360-degree views of the French, Swiss and Italian Alps from the summit are (quite literally) breathtaking. Year-round, you can float via cable car from Chamonix to the Aiguille du Midi on the vertiginous **Téléphérique de l'Aiguille du Midi** (www.compagniedu montblanc.co.uk; place de l'Aiguille du Midi; adult/

child return to Aiguille du Midi €61.50/52.30, to Plan de l'Aiguille €32.50/27.60; ⊙1st ascent btwn 6.30am & 8.10am, last btwn 4pm & 5.30pm, mid-Dec–early Nov). Dress warmly: even in summer, temperatures at the top rarely rise above -10°C (in winter prepare for -25°C).

SkyWay Monte Bianco   CABLE CAR

(www.montebianco.com; Pointe Helbronner; single/return €37/49; ⊙6.30am-4.30pm Jul & Aug, 8.30am-4pm Sep–mid-Nov & Dec-May, 7.30am-4.20pm Jun) This spectacular, international cable car links France with Italy, from Pointe Helbronner to Courmayeur in the Val d'Aosta. The cars rotate a full 360 degrees, affording peerless views of Mont Blanc, the Matterhorn and Gran Paradiso. To get there, take the Aiguille du Midi and **Télécabine Panoramique Mont Blanc** (📋04 50 53 22 75; www.montblancnaturalresort.com; Aiguille du Midi; adult/child return from Chamonix €89/75.70; ⊙7.30am-4.30pm Jul & Aug, 8am-4pm Jun, 9am-3.30pm Sep) cable cars.

★ Mer de Glace   GLACIER

France's largest glacier, the 200m-deep 'Sea of Ice', flows 7km down the northern side of Mont Blanc, scarred with crevasses formed by the immense pressure of its 90m-per-year movement. The **Train du Montenvers** (📋04 50 53 22 75; www.montblancnaturalresort. com; 35 place de la Mer de Glace; adult/child return €32.50/27.60; ⊙10am-4.30pm late Dec–mid-Mar, to 5pm mid-Mar–Apr), a picturesque, 5km-long cog railway opened in 1909, links Gare du Montenvers with Montenvers (1913m), from where a cable car descends to the glacier and, 420 stairs later, the **Grotte de Glace** FREE. Also worth a visit is the **Glaciorium**, an exhibition on the formation (and future) of glaciers.

🛌 Sleeping

Le Vert Hôtel   HOTEL $

(📋04 50 53 13 58; www.verthotel.com; 964 rte des Gaillands; d €55-120, q €85-190; 🅿 🛜) This lively hotel has 21 compact rooms – all with new bathrooms and some with fantastic Aiguille du Midi views. There's also a more-than-decent restaurant (dinner *menu* €22.50) and in-house ski rental. In winter, the bar regularly hosts international DJs (Gilles Peterson and Krafty Kuts, to name two). *Navettes* (shuttle buses) to central Chamonix, 2km to the northeast, stop right outside.

Terminal Neige   HOTEL $$

(Refuge du Montenvers; 📋04 50 53 87 70; http://montenvers.terminal-neige.com; Le Montenvers; half-board dm €80-100, d €190-270, tr €275-395, q €360-

500; ☺Nov-Sep; @ ☎) There's just one way to access this iconic mountain address, overlooking the shimmering ice of Mer de Glace – by the Train du Montenvers cog railway. Its 20 designer-chic, wood-panelled rooms have glacier views, and hikers and families are well catered for with an insanely stylish 10-bed dorm, cosy duplex rooms for five or seven, and five-person bunk-bed rooms. Rates include dinner and breakfast.

★ **Grand Hôtel des Alpes** HISTORIC HOTEL $$$
(☑ 04 50 55 37 80; www.grandhoteldesalpes.com; 75 rue du Docteur Paccard; d/ste from €175/294; ☺ mid-Dec–mid-Apr & mid-June–late Sep; P ☎ ☀) Exuding belle époque charm, this buttercup and powder-blue hotel is one of the prettiest buildings in Chamonix. Established in 1840, the hotel's 30 rooms have a classic style: flowing drapes, wood-panelled ceilings and glossy marble bathrooms. There's a glamorous-feeling wellness centre, and in winter a scrumptious teatime cake buffet (4pm to 6pm) greets skiers back from the slopes.

✗ Eating

Pizzeria des Moulins PIZZA $
(☑ 06 68 70 99 82, 06 47 07 75 10; www.facebook.com/pizzeriadesmoulins; 107 rue des Moulins; pizzas from €15; ☺ noon-2.30pm & 6.30-11pm) Cham's best pizzas, piled with buffalo mozzarella, forest mushrooms and Savoyard ham, puff up in the oven of this little gourmet joint. Reservations are essential for dining in, but you can always get takeaway if (or rather, when) they're packed with ravenous diners.

Munchie FUSION $$
(☑ 04 50 53 45 41; www.streamcreek.com/munchie; 87 rue des Moulins; mains €23-29; ☺ 7pm-2am winter & summer) Franco-Japanese-Scandinavian fusion may not be the most obvious recipe for success, but this casual, Swedish-skippered restaurant has been making diners happy since 1997. There's a sharing plate concept with sushi plates resembling little works of art, and the excellent seafood and passion-fruit ceviche, teriyaki duck and alcoholic Oreo milkshakes have brought local acclaim. Reservations recommended.

★ **Le Cap Horn** FRENCH, SEAFOOD $$$
(☑ 04 50 21 80 80; www.caphorn-chamonix.com; 74 rue des Moulins; lunch/dinner menus from €23/42; ☺ noon-3pm & 7-10.30pm; ☑) Housed in a candelit, two-storey chalet decorated with model sailing boats – joint homage to the Alps and Cape Horn – this highly praised

restaurant, which opened in 2012, serves French and Asian dishes such as pan-seared duck breast with honey and soy sauce, an ample sushi menu, and a marvellous range of seafood like red tuna *taquitos* and fish stew. Reserve for dinner Friday and Saturday in winter and summer.

🍷 Drinking & Nightlife

For a bar crawl, head to central rue des Moulins, where wall-to-wall watering holes keep buzzing until about 1am.

★ **Chambre Neuf** BAR
(☑ 04 50 53 00 31; www.facebook.com/chambre.neuf; 272 av Michel Croz; ☺ 7am-1am; ☎) A favourite among seasonal workers letting off steam, 'Room 9' boasts the most spirited (rather, loudest) après-ski party in Cham (from 3pm or 4pm). There's live rock music (from Sunday to Friday), dancing on the tables, and themed events (if DJ sets or circus-themed parties sound like your jam). Action spills out of the front door, and the terrace opens in spring.

Jekyll & Hyde PUB
(☑ 04 50 55 99 70; www.facebook.com/jekyllchamonix; 71 rte des Pélerins, Chamonix Sud; ☺ 4pm-2am Mon-Fri, opens earlier Sat & Sun; ☎) This British-owned après-ski mainstay has a split personality: upstairs the 'Jekyll' has really good pub food (from seafood tapas and sweet and sour duck to plenty of veggie options), live music, DJs and comedy; check their Facebook page for events. Downstairs, the 'Hyde' is cosier and more relaxed. Both have good Irish beer and a friendly vibe.

MBC MICROBREWERY
(Micro Brasserie de Chamonix; ☑ 04 50 53 61 59; www.mbchx.com; 350 rte du Bouchet; ☺ 4pm-2am Mon-Fri, 10am-2am Sat & Sun) This Canadian-run microbrewery is one of Chamonix' most unpretentious and gregarious watering holes, pouring its own locally made blonde, stout, pale ale, German-style wheat beer and mystery beer of the month. Soaking it up is a menu of huge burgers, poutine (chips with cottage cheese and gravy) and vegetarian choices. Eclectic live music (usually from 9pm) could mean anything from soul to hard rock. Enormously satisfying.

❶ Information

Tourist Office (☑ 04 50 53 00 24; www.chamonix.com; 85 place du Triangle de l'Amitié; ☺ 9am-7pm mid-Jun–mid-Sep & mid-Dec-Apr, 9am-12.30pm & 2-6pm rest of year, closed Sun Oct & Nov; ☎)

FRANCE CHAMONIX

ⓘ Getting There & Away

BUS

Drop by the **bus station** (☑ 04 50 53 01 15; 234 av Courmayeur, Chamonix Sud; ⊙ ticket 8am-noon & 1.15-6.30pm in winter, shorter hours rest of year) for timetables and reservations (highly recommended) or book online with **Ouibus** (www.ouibus.com). Direct daily buses serve Lyon Perrache (from €26, 3½ to 4½ hours) and Geneva in Switzerland (€19, 1½ to two hours). **Savda** (www.savda.it) operates four daily buses to Courmayeur in Italy (€15, 45 minutes), with onward connections to Aosta and Milan.

TRAIN

The scenic, narrow-gauge **Mont Blanc Express** (www.mont-blanc-express.com) glides from the Swiss town of Martigny to Chamonix, taking in Argentière and Vallorcine en route.

For destinations around France, including Lyon, Annecy and Paris, you'll need to change trains at St-Gervais-Le-Fayet first (€11.40, 45 minutes, hourly).

THE DORDOGNE

Tucked into the green southwestern corner of *la belle France,* the Dordogne fuses history, culture and culinary sophistication in one unforgettably scenic package. The region is best known for its sturdy *bastides* (fortified towns), earthy cuisine, clifftop châteaux teetering above the mighty Dordogne River and spectacular prehistoric cave paintings.

Sarlat-la-Canéda

POP 9030

A picturesque tangle of honey-coloured buildings, alleyways and secret squares make up the beautiful town of Sarlat-la-Canéda. Boasting some of the region's best-preserved medieval architecture, it's a popular base for exploring the Vézère Valley, and a favourite location for film directors.

⊙ Sights & Activities

Part of the fun of wandering around Sarlat is losing yourself in its twisting alleyways and backstreets. Rue Landry, rue de la Liberté and rue Jean-Jacques Rousseau are good starting points.

★**Weekly Markets** MARKET
(place de la Liberté; ⊙ 8.30am-1pm Wed & Sat) For an introductory French market experience, visit Sarlat's heavily touristed Saturday market, which takes over the streets around

---

DON'T MISS

PREHISTORIC CAVE ART

The Vézère Valley is littered with some of Europe's most impressive prehistoric cave art. The most famous is **Grotte de Lascaux**, 2km southeast of Montignac, which features the largest collection of paintings ever discovered. The original cave has been closed since 1963 to prevent damage, but a perfect replica can be viewed at **Lascaux IV** (International Centre for Cave Art; ☑ 05 53 50 99 10; www.lascaux.fr; Montignac; adult/child €16/10.40; ⊙ 8.30am-10pm Jul & Aug, shorter hours rest of year). Using laser technology and 3D printing to re-create the rock paintings in what feels like a real cave – complete with muffled sounds, semi-darkness, damp smells and prehistoric fauna – the whole experience is legitimately spine-tingling. Advance reservations (up to two days in advance online) are highly recommended. Several other caves in the valley remain open to the public; reserve well ahead.

Grotte de Font de Gaume (☑ 05 53 06 86 00; www.sites-les-eyzies.fr; 4 av des Grottes; adult/child €10/free; ⊙ guided tours 9.30am-5.30pm Sun-Fri mid-May–mid-Sep, 9.30am-12.30pm & 2-5.30pm Sun-Fri mid-Sep–mid-May) About 14,000 years ago, prehistoric artists created the gallery of over 230 figures, including bison, reindeer, horses, mammoths, bears and wolves, of which 25 are on permanent display; 1km northeast of Les Eyzies.

Abri du Cap Blanc (☑ 05 53 59 60 30; www.sites-les-eyzies.fr; adult/child €8/free; ⊙ guided tours 10am-6pm Sun-Fri mid-May–mid-Sep, 10am-12.30pm & 2-5.30pm Sun-Fri mid-Sep–mid-May) Showcases an unusual sculpture gallery of horses, bison and deer; 7km east of Les Eyzies.

Grotte de Rouffignac (☑ 05 53 05 41 71; www.grotractderouffignac.fr; Rouffignac-St-Cernin-de-Reilhac; adult/child €7.80/5.10; ⊙ 9-11.30am & 2-6pm Jul & Aug, 10-11.30am & 2-5pm Apr-Jun, Sep & Oct, closed Nov-Mar) Sometimes known as the 'Cave of 100 Mammoths' because of its painted mammoths. Access to the caves, hidden in woodland 15km north of Les Eyzies, is aboard a trundling electric train.

PÉRIGUEUX

Founded by Gallic tribes, and later developed by the Romans into the important city of Vesunna, Périgueux, 85km northwest of Sarlat, is the Dordogne's biggest and busiest town. Medieval buildings and Renaissance mansions dot a charming old town, radiating out from the Gothic **Cathédrale St-Front** (place de la Clautre; ⊙ 8.30am-7pm). In the old Roman quarter of La Cité, the **Gallo-Roman museum** (☑ 05 53 53 00 92; www.perigueux -vesunna.fr; 20 rue du 26e Régiment d'Infanterie, Parc de Vésone; adult/child €6/4, audioguide €1; ⊙ 10am-7pm Jul & Aug, shorter hours rest of year), designed by French architect Jean Nouvel around a 1st-century Roman domus (townhouse), is a Dordogne highlight.

Périgueux' wonderful street markets – a prime spot for seasonal black truffles, wild mushrooms and foie gras – explode into action on Wednesday and Saturday. Michelin-starred **L'Essentiel** (☑ 05 53 35 15 15; www.restaurant-perigueux.com; 8 rue de la Clarté; lunch menus €29-47, dinner menus €45-81; ⊙ noon-1.30pm & 7.30-9.30pm Tue-Sat) or down-to-earth, utterly delicious **Café de la Place** (☑ 05 53 08 21 11; www.cafedelaplace24.com; 7 place du Marché au Bois; mains €9.50-20; ⊙ restaurant noon-2.30pm & 7-10.30pm, bar 8am-2am) are memorable lunch spots.

Cathédrale St-Sacerdos. Depending on the season, delicacies include local mushrooms and duck- and goose-based products such as foie gras. The Wednesday version is a smaller affair. An atmospheric, largely organic **night market** (place du 14 Juillet; ⊙ 6-10pm Thu) operates on Thursdays.

Église Ste-Marie MARKET
(place de la Liberté; elevator adult/child €4/1) Église Ste-Marie was ingeniously converted by acclaimed architect Jean Nouvel, whose parents still live in Sarlat, into the town's touristy **Marché Couvert** (Covered Market; place de la Liberté; ⊙ 8.30am-2pm daily mid-Apr–mid-Nov, closed Mon, Thu & Sun rest of year). Its **panoramic elevator** (buy tickets at tourist office) offers 360-degree views across Sarlat's countryside.

🛏 Sleeping & Eating

⭐ **Le Grand Bleu** GASTRONOMY $$$
(☑ 05 53 31 08 48; www.legrandbleu.eu; 43 av de la Gare; lunch menus €25, dinner menus €54-125; ⊙ 12.30-2pm Thu-Sun, 7.30-9.30pm Tue-Sat) This eminent Michelin-starred restaurant run by chef Maxime Lebrun is renowned for its creative cuisine, with elaborate *menus* making maximum use of luxury produce: truffles, lobster, turbot and scallops, with a wine list to match. Cooking courses are also available. Located 1.5km south of the centre.

ℹ Information

Tourist Office (☑ 05 53 31 45 45; www.sarlat -tourisme.com; 3 rue Tourny; ⊙ 9am-7.30pm

Mon-Sat, 10am-1pm & 2-6pm Sun Jul & Aug, shorter hours rest of year; 📶)

ℹ Getting There & Away

The **train station** (av de la Gare) is 1.3km south of the old city. Services include Bordeaux (€28.20, 2½ hours, three daily) and Périgueux (€16.30, 1½ to three hours, five daily).

ATLANTIC COAST

With quiet country roads winding through vine-striped hills and wild stretches of coastal sands interspersed with misty islands, the Atlantic coast is where France returns to nature. If you're a surf nut or beach bum, the sandy bays around Biarritz will be right up your alley, while oenophiles can sample the fruits of the vine in the high temple of French winemaking, Bordeaux.

Bordeaux

POP 250,776

An intoxicating cocktail of 18th-century savoir-faire, millennial hi-tech and urban street life, France's sixth largest city is among Europe's most exciting players. Its art and architecture are utterly sublime (half the city is Unesco-listed), the dining scene is exceptional, and the majestic River Garonne fuels bags of riverside fun and action on its leggy route north past traditional wine-producing châteaux to the Atlantic Ocean. Bordeaux' flagship wine museum and surrounding vineyards make the city a key stop for wine lovers.

◉ Sights & Activities

Consider buying a **Bordeaux Métropole City Pass** (www.bordeauxcitypass.com; 24/48/72hr €29/39/46) online before arrival. The pass covers admission to major museums as well as a free guided tour and unlimited use of public transport

★ La Cité du Vin   MUSEUM

(☑05 56 16 20 20; www.laciteduvin.com; 134-150 Quai de Bacalan, 1 Esplanade de Pontac; adult/child €20/free; ☺10am-7pm Apr-Aug, shorter hours rest of year) The complex world of wine is explored in depth at ground-breaking La Cité du Vin, a stunning piece of contemporary architecture resembling a wine decanter on the banks of the River Garonne. The curvaceous gold building glitters in the sun and its 3000 sq metres of exhibits are equally sensory and sensational. Digital guides lead visitors around 20 themed sections covering everything from vine cultivation, grape varieties and wine production to ancient wine trade, 21st-century wine trends and celebrated personalities.

★ Cathédrale St-André   CATHEDRAL

(☑05 56 44 67 29; www.cathedrale-bordeaux.fr; place Jean Moulin; ☺2-7pm Mon, 10am-noon & 2-6pm Tue-Sun) FREE The Cathédrale St-André, a Unesco World Heritage Site prior to the city's classification, lords it over the city. The cathedral's oldest section dates from 1096; most of what you see today was built

in the 13th and 14th centuries. Enjoy exceptional masonry carvings in the north portal.

Musée d'Aquitaine   MUSEUM

(☑05 56 01 51 00; www.musee-aquitaine-bordeaux. fr; 20 cours Pasteur; adult/child €5/free; ☺11am-6pm Tue-Sun) Gallo-Roman statues and relics dating back 25,000 years are among the highlights at this bright and spacious, well-curated history and civilisations museum. Grab a bilingual floor plan at the entrance and borrow an English-language catalogue to better appreciate the exhibits that span prehistory through to 18th-century Atlantic trade and slavery, world cultures and the emergence of Bordeaux as a world port in the 19th century. Temporary exhibitions cost extra.

★ Miroir d'Eau   FOUNTAIN

(Water Mirror; place de la Bourse; ☺10am-10pm summer) FREE A fountain of sorts, the Miroir d'Eau is the world's largest reflecting pool. Covering an area of 3450 sq metres of black granite on the quayside opposite the imposing Palais de la Bourse, the 'water mirror' provides hours of entertainment on warm sunny days when the reflections in its thin slick of water – drained and refilled every half-hour – are stunning. Every 23 minutes a dense fog-like vapour is ejected for three minutes to add to the fun (and photo opportunities).

École du Vin de Bordeaux   WINE

(Bordeaux Wine School; ☑05 56 00 22 85; www. bordeaux.com; 3 cours du 30 juillet; introductory workshops €32) Serious students of the grape

---

DON'T MISS

WINE-TASTING IN SITU

Diminutive neighbour to nearby Château Haut-Briond, which is rated among the top 'first growths' in the 1855 classification, **Château Les Carmes Haut Briond** (☑07 77 38 10 64; www.les-carmes-haut-brion.com; 20 rue des Carmes; 1½hr guided visit incl tasting €30; ☺9.30am-12.30pm & 2-6pm Mon-Sat) is named after Carmelite monks – Les Carmes – who tended vines here from 1584 until the French Revolution. The 16th-century château is very much intact and contrasts beautifully with its millennial cellars and tasting room designed by French designer Philippe Starck. Resembling a majestic ship, the striking building 'floats' in a pool of water and is accessed by footbridges.

Guided visits include a tour of the 19th-century château gardens and cellar, and end with wine tasting. Advance reservations online or by telephone are essential. The château is 4km southwest of the cathedral, in Pessac. Take tram line A from Hôtel de Ville to the François Mitterrand stop, a 10-minute walk from the château.

can enrol at this highly regarded wine school inside the Maison du Vin de Bordeaux (Bordeaux House of Wine). It hosts introductory two-hour workshops the last Saturday of each month and daily from July to September (€32), plus more complex two- to three-day courses from May to October.

🛏 Sleeping

Central Hostel HOSTEL $
(http://centralhostel.fr; 2 place Projet; d €19-30, d €90-150) Urban-chic dorms and swish doubles with USB plugs aplenty and en suite bathrooms are spread across four floors at this dead-central, designer hostel in Saint-Pierre. Glam to the core, the 97-bed hostel promises a bespoke guest experience, with a bar, sun-drenched terrace designed for summertime chilling and a locally sourced restaurant, open 24 hours.

★ Hôtel La Cour Carrée BOUTIQUE HOTEL $$
(📞 05 57 35 00 00; www.lacourcarree.com; 5 rue de Lurbe; d €125-250; P ❄ @ 🛜) Tucked in an 18th-century house on a quiet side street with little passing traffic, this design-driven boutique hotel oozes natural style and peace. Soft, muted colours and contemporary Scandinavian furnishings complement ancient gold-stone walls in its 16 elegant rooms, and the pièce de résistance is the interior courtyard – a much-appreciated alfresco lounge in summer. Breakfast/parking €12/13.

Mama Shelter DESIGN HOTEL $$
(📞 05 57 30 45 45; www.mamashelter.com/en/bordeaux; 19 rue Poquelin Molière; d/tr from €80/130; ❄ @ 🛜) With personalised iMacs, video booths and free movies in every room, Mama Shelter is up-to-the-minute. White rooms are small, medium or large; XL doubles have a sofa bed. The ground-floor restaurant (mains €13 to €29) sports the same signature rubber rings strung above the bar as other Philippe Starck–designed hotels. Summertime drinks and dinner are served on the sensational rooftop terrace.

🍴 Eating

Timeless dining icons mingle with new openings and cheaper eats in the tasty tangle of pedestrian streets in Saint-Pierre and Saint-Paul. North along the river, quai des Chartons is laced with waterfront restaurants and bars – particularly enchanting at sunset.

Chez Jean-Mi SEAFOOD $
(place des Capucins, Maré des Capucins; breakfast €1-7.50, seafood €6-25; ⏰ 7am-2.30pm Tue-Fri, to 3.30pm Sat & Sun) If there's one stall at the city's iconic food market that sums up the contagious *joie de vivre* of Les Capus (as locals call the market), it is this *bistrot à huitres* (oyster bar). Jean-Mi greets regulars and first-timers with the same huge smile, and his freshly shucked oysters, fish soup and copious seafood platters are of the finest quality money can buy.

★ Magasin Général INTERNATIONAL $
(📞 05 56 77 88 35; www.magasingeneral.camp; 87 quai des Queyries; mains €10-20; ⏰ 8am-6pm Mon, to 7pm Tue & Wed, to midnight Thu & Fri, 8.30am-midnight Sat, 8.30am-6pm Sun; 🛜) Follow the hip crowd across the river to this huge industrial hangar on the right bank, France's biggest and best organic restaurant with a gargantuan terrace complete with vintage sofa seating, ping-pong table and table football. Everything here – from vegan burgers and superfood salads to smoothies, pizzas, wine and French bistro fare – is *bio* (organic) and sourced locally. Sunday brunch is a bottomless feast.

Au Bistrot FRENCH $$
(📞 06 63 54 21 14; www.facebook.com/aubistrot bordeaux; 61 place des Capucins; mains €18-24; ⏰ noon-2.30pm & 7-11pm Wed-Sun) There's nothing flashy or fancy about this hardcore French bistro, an ode to traditional market cuisine with charismatic François front of house and talented French-Thai chef Jacques In'On in the kitchen. Marinated herrings, lentil salad topped with a poached egg, half a roast pigeon or a feisty *andouillette* (tripe sausage) roasted in the oven – 80% of produce is local or from the surrounding Aquitaine region.

★ Le Bordeaux CAFE $$
(📞 05 57 30 43 46; https://bordeaux.intercontinen tal.com; 2-5 place de la Comédie; 2-/3-course lunch menu from €29/39, mains €27; ⏰ 7am-10.30pm) A homage to the rich fruits of Bordeaux's extraordinary terroir (land), the brasserie of double Michelin-starred chef Gordon Ramsay cooks up a different *plat du jour* daily in addition to a memorable Sunday brunch (€68) and French classics like Cap Ferret oysters, slow-cooked lamb, duck, the fishy catch of the day or pasta laced with aromatic palourdes (clams), garlic and parsley.

LOCAL KNOWLEDGE

BREAKFAST & BRUNCH

Whatever the time of day, **Horace** (☑ 05 56 90 01 93; 40 rue Poquelin Molière; mains €8-14; ⊗ 8.30am-6.30pm Mon, to 9.30pm Tue-Fri, 9.30am-9.30pm Sat, 9.30am-6.30pm Sun) can do no wrong. Outstanding speciality coffee roasts (including Oven Heaven beans roasted locally), sophisticated fruit- and veg-packed breakfasts, homemade brioches and breads, and lunch/dinner menus bursting with creativity are the quality hallmarks of this coffee shop, owned by the same talented barista as Bordeaux' **Black List** (☑ 06 89 91 82 65; www. facebook.com/blacklistcafe; 27 place Pey Berland; ⊗ 8am-6pm Mon-Fri, 9.30am-6pm Sat). Sunday brunch (€21) is a sell-out every week.

La Tupina FRENCH $$$
(☑ 05 56 91 56 37; www.latupina.com; 6 rue Porte de la Monnaie; lunch menu €18, dinner menus €44-52, mains €20-32; ⊗ noon-2pm & 7-11pm Tue-Sun) Filled with the aroma of soup simmering inside a *tupina* ('kettle' in Basque) over an open fire, this iconic bistro is feted for its seasonal southwestern French fare: calf kidneys with fries cooked in goose fat, milk-fed lamb, tripe and goose wings. Dining is farmhouse-style, in a maze of small elegant rooms decorated with vintage photographs, antique furniture and silver tableware.

🍷 Drinking & Nightlife

Medieval Saint-Pierre teems with atmospheric cafe pavement terraces, as do Chartron's riverside quays. Mainstream nightclubs congregate on busy quai du Paladate near the train station.

⭐ **Symbiose** COCKTAIL BAR
(Old-Fashioned Stories; ☑ 05 56 23 67 15; www. facebook.com/symbiosebordeaux; 4 quai des Chartrons; ⊗ noon-2.30pm Mon, noon-2.30pm & 6.30pm-2am Tue-Fri, 6.30pm-2am Sat) There is something inviting about this clandestine address with a soft green facade across from the river on the fringe of the Chartrons district. This is the secret speakeasy that introduced good cocktails with gastronomic food pairings to Bordeaux. The chef uses locally sourced artisanal products, and cocktails rekindle old-fashioned recipes packed with homemade syrups and 'forgotten', exotic or unusual ingredients.

⭐ **Bar à Vin** WINE BAR
(☑ 05 56 00 43 47; http://baravin.bordeaux.com; 3 cours du 30 Juillet; ⊗ 11am-10pm Mon-Sat) The decor – herringbone parquet, grandiose stained glass depicting the godly Bacchus, and sky-high ceiling – matches the reverent air that fills this wine bar inside the hallowed halls of the Maison du Vin de Bordeaux. Dozens of Bordeaux wines are served by the glass (€3.50 to €8) which, paired with a cheese or charcuterie platter, transport foodies straight to heaven. Gracious sommeliers know their *vin*.

⭐ **Night Beach** BAR
(https://bordeaux.intercontinental.com; 2-5 place de la Comédie, 7th fl, Grand Hôtel de Bordeaux; ⊗ 7pm-1am late May-late Sep) There is no finer, more elegant or more romantic rooftop bar in Bordeaux than this achingly hip drinking-and-hobnobbing joint on the 7th floor of the historic Grand Hôtel de Bordeaux. Views of the city, River Garonne and the vineyards beyond are a panoramic 360 degrees. French-chic seating is sofa-style beneath parasols, and DJ sets play at weekends.

I.Boat CLUB
(☑ 05 56 10 48 37; www.iboat.eu; quai Armand Lalande, Bassins à Flot 1; ⊗ 7.30pm-6am) Hip-hop, rock, indie pop, psyche blues rock, punk and hardcore are among the varied sounds that blast out of this fun nightclub and concert venue, on a decommissioned ferry moored in the increasingly trendy, industrial Bassins à Flot district in the north of the city. Live music starts at 7pm, with DJ sets kicking in on the club dance floor from 11.30pm.

ℹ️ Information

Tourist Office (☑ 05 56 00 66 00; www. bordeaux-tourisme.com; 12 cours du 30 Juillet; ⊗ 9am-6.30pm Mon-Sat, to 5pm Sun)

ℹ️ Getting There & Away

Aéroport de Bordeaux (Bordeaux Airport; BOD; ☑ Information 05 56 34 50 50; www. bordeaux.aeroport.fr) is 10km west of the city centre in the suburb of Mérignac.

Major train services to/from from Bordeaux train station **Gare St-Jean** (Cours de la Marne) include Paris Gare Montparnasse (€69, 3¼ hours, at least 16 daily) and Toulouse (€39, 2¼ hours, hourly).

Biarritz

POP 25,500

Edge your way south along the coast towards Spain and you arrive in stylish Biarritz, which is just as ritzy as its name suggests. The resort took off in the mid-19th century and it still shimmers with architectural treasures from the belle époque and art deco eras. Big waves – some of Europe's best – and a beachy lifestyle are a magnet for Europe's hip surfing set.

Biarritz' raison d'être is its fashionable beaches, particularly central **Grande Plage** and **Plage Miramar**. North of Pointe St-Martin, the adrenaline-pumping surfing beaches of **Anglet** continue northwards for more than 4km. Take bus 10 or 13 from the bottom of av Verdun (just near av Édouard VII).

🛏 Sleeping & Eating

Biarritz is a pricey place to sleep, with a massive premium during July and August – although off-season discounts are often available, especially in winter when the town is largely deserted.

Shop for beach-perfect picnic supplies at the covered **Les Halles** (www.halles-biarritz.fr; rue des Halles; ⊙7am-2pm) market.

Auberge de Jeunesse de Biarritz   HOSTEL **$**
(☑ 05 59 41 76 00; www.hihostels.com; 8 rue Chiquito de Cambo; dm/s incl sheets & breakfast €26/44; ⊙ reception 9am-noon & 6-10pm, closed mid-Dec–early Jan; @🛜) This popular, well-run place has a lot going for it: clean dorms, a lively cafe-bar and a sunny terrace for summer barbecues. From the train station, follow the railway line westwards for 800m.

★ Hôtel de Silhouette   BOUTIQUE HOTEL **$$$**
(☑ 05 59 24 93 82; www.hotel-silhouette-biarritz. com; 30 rue Gambetta; d from €175; ❄🛜) Come here if you want to splash out. It's just steps from the covered market, but is surprisingly secluded thanks to being set back from the street. It's full of fun, from the weird faces on the wallpaper to the odd bear and sheep sculptures, and there's a gorgeous garden. The building dates from 1610, but it's metropolitan modern in style.

Haragia   STEAK **$$$**
(☑ 05 35 46 68 92; www.facebook.com/haragia64; 26 rue Gambetta; mains €30-50; ⊙8pm-1am Thu-Sun, to 5pm Sun) Tucked back in a tiny alley near the central market, this convivial steakhouse has a few small tables and an open kitchen with the grill on show as the friendly brothers cook up your evening meal. The meat menu is simple – steak, veal and pork – but the wine menu is vast!

ⓘ Information

Tourist Office (☑ 05 59 22 37 10; www.tour isme.biarritz.fr; Square d'Ixelles; ⊙9am-7pm Jul–mid-Sep, shorter hours rest of year)

ⓘ Getting There & Around

AIR

Domestic and international flights leave from **Aéroport Biarritz Pays Basque** (BIQ; ☑05 59 43 83 83; www.biarritz.aeroport.fr). Chronoplus (www.chronoplus.eu) Line C buses run from the train station in Biarritz, while Line 14 leaves from near the Biarritz tourist office. Both run every half-hour or so and take about 10 minutes. A single fare costs €1.

TRAIN

Trains to Biarritz stop at the **train station** (☑ 08 92 35 35 35; allée du Moura) 3.5km southeast of the town centre. Chronoplus bus 10 runs regularly into the city centre. Services include Paris Gare Montparnasse (€50 to €109, 4¼ hours, five daily) and Bordeaux (€35 to €50, 2¼ hours, 10 daily).

LANGUEDOC-ROUSSILLON

POP 2.7 MILLION

Languedoc-Roussillon comes in three distinct flavours: Bas-Languedoc (Lower

---

DON'T MISS

DUNE DU PILAT

This colossal **sand dune** (sometimes referred to as the Dune de Pyla because of its location in the resort town of Pyla-sur-Mer), an easy day trip from Bordeaux 65km west, stretches from the mouth of the Bassin d'Arcachon southwards for almost 3km. Already the largest in Europe, it's spreading eastwards at 4.5m a year – it has swallowed trees, a road junction and even a hotel. Take care swimming in this area: powerful currents swirl out to sea from the deceptively tranquil *baïnes* (little bays).

WORTH A TRIP

TOULOUSE

Elegantly set at the confluence of the Canal du Midi and the Garonne River , this vibrant southern city – nicknamed *la ville rose* (the pink city) after the distinctive hot-pink stone used in many buildings – is one of France's liveliest metropolises. Busy, buzzy and bustling with students, this riverside dame has a history stretching back over 2000 years and has been a hub for the aerospace industry since the 1930s.

Lavish **place du Capitole** is the classic starting point to explore Toulouse, before wandering south into the pedestrianised **Vieux Quartier** (Old Quarter). Most of the city's major galleries, museums and **Couvent des Jacobins** (☑05 61 22 23 82; www. jacobins.toulouse.fr; rue Lakanal; cloister adult/child €4/free; ☉10am-6pm Tue-Sun) are easily accessed from metro stops Esquirol, Jean Jaurès and Jeanne d'Arc, all on the red A line.

The fantastic **Cité de l'Espace** (☑05 67 22 23 24; www.cite-espace.com; av Jean Gonord; adult €21-26, child €15.50-19; ☉10am-7pm daily Jul & Aug, to 5pm or 6pm Sep-Dec & Feb-Jun, closed Mon in Feb, Mar & Sep-Dec, closed Jan; ⊞), on the city's eastern outskirts, brings Toulouse's illustrious aeronautical history to life through hands-on exhibits. Plane-spotters can arrange a guided tour of Toulouse's massive JL Lagardère **Airbus factory** (☑05 34 39 42 00; www.manatour.fr; allée André Turcat, Blagnac; tours adult/child €15.50/13; ☉Mon-Sat by reservation), near the airport in Blagnac, 10km northwest of the city centre.

When France's sacrosanct aperitif hour beckons, head to **N°5 Wine Bar** (☑05 61 38 44 51; www.n5winebar.com; 5 rue de la Bourse; ☉6pm-1am Mon-Sat), followed by dinner at always-packed **La Pente Douce** (☑05 61 46 16 91; www.lapentedouce.fr; 6 rue de la Concorde; menus €23-28, mains €18-24; ☉noon-1.30pm Tue & Wed, noon-1.30pm & 8-9.30pm Thu-Sat).

Toulouse is served by frequent fast TGVs, which run west to Bordeaux (from €17, two hours, 13 daily) and east to Carcassonne (from €16.50, 45 minutes to one hour, up to 23 daily) and beyond.

Languedoc), home to the biggest beaches, rugby and robust red wines; Haut Languedoc (Upper Languedoc), a mountainous, sparsely populated terrain made for lovers of the great outdoors; and Roussillon, to the south, snug against the rugged Pyrenees and frontier to Spanish Catalonia.

Nîmes

This lively city boasts some of France's best-preserved classical buildings, including a famous Roman amphitheatre, although the city is most famous for its sartorial export, *serge de Nîmes* – better known to cowboys, clubbers and couturiers as denim.

☉ Sights

Save money by purchasing a **Pass Nîmes Romaine** (adult/child €13/11), covering admission to a trio of Roman sights (including Les Arènes) and valid for three days.

★**Les Arènes**   ROMAN SITE
(☑04 66 21 82 56; www.arenes-nimes.com; place des Arènes; adult/child incl audio guide €10/8; ☉9am-8pm Jul & Aug, 9am-6.30pm Apr-Jun & Sep, 9am-6pm Mar & Oct, 9.30am-5pm Jan, Feb, Nov & Dec) Nîmes' twin-tiered amphitheatre is the best preserved in France. Built around 100 BCE, the arena once seated 24,000 spectators and staged gladiatorial contests and public executions; it's still an impressive venue for gigs and events. An audio guide provides context as you explore the arena, seating areas, stairwells and corridors (known to Romans as *vomitoria*), and afterwards you can view replicas of gladiatorial armour and original bullfighters' costumes in the museum.

Musée de la Romanité   MUSEUM
(☑04 48 21 02 10; 16 bd des Arènes; adult/child €8/3; ☉10am-8pm Jul & Aug, 10am-7pm Sep-Nov & Apr-Jun, 10am-6pm Wed-Mon Dec-Mar) Opened in mid-2018, this futuristic steel-and-glass structure faces Les Arènes right in the heart of the city. Within, the ambitious archaeological museum's permanent exhibitions are devoted to regional archaeology, with more than 5000 artefacts including well-preserved mosaics and ceramics.

🛏 Sleeping & Eating

Place aux Herbes, place de l'Horloge and place du Marché are great places to watch the world drift languidly by at bistros, cafes and bars with pavement seating.

Hôtel des Tuileries   HOTEL **$**
(☑ 04 66 21 31 15; www.hoteldestuileries.com; 22 rue Roussy; d €60-81, tr €70-93, ste €85-118; P ❄ 🌐) Run by an English couple, this well-priced 11-room hotel within strolling distance from Les Arènes (p430) features simple yet satisfyingly equipped rooms, some with covered balconies. Breakfast costs €9. Its private parking garage (€10 to €15) is just down the street, but there are only five car spaces, so reserve ahead.

Les Halles   MARKET **$**
(www.leshallesdenimes.com; rues Guizot, Général Perrier & des Halles; ⊙ 7am-1pm Mon-Sat, to 1.30pm Sun) With over 100 stalls in 3500 sq metres, Nîmes' covered market is the best place for supplies. Look out for local specialities including *picholines* – a local green olive with its own AOP (Appellation d'Origine Protégée) – and *brandade* (salt cod). You'll also find a couple of great eateries.

ℹ Getting There & Around

AIR
Aéroport de Nîmes Alès Camargue Cévennes (FNI; ☑ 04 66 70 49 49; www.aeroport-nimes. fr; St-Gilles) Nîmes' airport, 10km southeast of the city on the A54, is served only by Ryanair. An airport bus (€6.80, 30 minutes) to/from the **train station** (bd Sergent Triaire) connects with all flights.

BUS
From the **bus station** (☑ 08 10 33 42 73; rue Ste-Félicité), local buses run by Edgard (www.edgard-transport.fr) serve Pont du Gard (Line B21, €1.50, 40 minutes, two or three daily Monday to Saturday).

TRAIN
TGVs run hourly to/from Paris' Gare de Lyon (from €45, three hours) from the train station.

Pont du Gard

Southern France has no shortage of superb Roman sites, but nothing can top the Unesco World Heritage-listed **Pont du Gard** (☑ 04 66 37 50 99; www.pontdugard.fr; adult/child €8.50/6, Pass Aqueduc incl guided visit of topmost tier €11.50/6; ⊙ 9am-11pm Jul & Aug, to 10pm Jun & Sep, to 9pm May, to 8pm Apr & Oct, to 6pm Nov-Mar), 21km northeast of Nîmes. One of the most impressive surviving Roman ruins in Europe, this extraordinary three-tiered aqueduct is a definite highlight in any trip to France. It was once part of a 50km-long system of channels built around 19 BCE to transport water from Uzès to Nîmes. The scale is huge: the bridge is 48.8m high, 275m long and graced with 52 precision-built arches. It

FRANCE PONT DU GARD

DON'T MISS

CARCASSONNE

Perched on a rocky hilltop and bristling with zigzag battlements, stout walls and spiky turrets, the fortified city of Carcassonne (population 49,400) looks like something out of a children's storybook from afar. A Unesco World Heritage Site since 1997, it's most people's idea of the perfect medieval castle.

Built on a steep spur of rock, Carcassonne's rampart-ringed fortress dates back more than two millennia. The fortified town is encircled by two sets of battlements and 52 stone towers, topped by distinctive 'witch's hat' roofs (added by architect Viollet-le-Duc during 19th-century restorations). Inside the gates, cobbled lanes and courtyards in the **Cité Médiévale** (enter via Porte Narbonnaise or Porte d'Aude; ⊙ 24hr) **FREE** lead to a bounty of touristy shops and restaurants.

To walk the ramparts and visit the keep built for the viscounts of Carcassonne in the 12th century, buy a **Château et Remparts** (www.remparts-carcassonne.fr; 1 rue Viollet le Duc, Cité Médiévale; adult/child €9/free; ⊙ 10am-6.30pm Apr-Sep, 9.30am-5pm Oct-Mar) ticket.

The **tourist office** (☑ 04 68 10 24 30; www.tourisme-carcassonne.fr; impasse Agnès de Montpellier, Cité Médiévale; ⊙ 9.30am-7pm Jul & Aug, 9am-6pm Apr-Jun, Sep & Oct, 9.30am-1pm & 1.30-5.30pm Nov-Mar) in the Cité Médiévale runs regular 1¼-hour guided walking tours (adult/child €8/6) of the old city in English (Saturdays and Sundays at 1.30pm), French and Spanish (daily).

was the highest in the Roman Empire. At the visitors centre on the northern bank, there's an impressive, high-tech **museum** featuring the bridge, the aqueduct and the role of water in Roman society.

For a unique perspective on the Pont du Gard (p431), view it from the water afloat the Gard River. Rent kayaks from **Canoë Le Tourbillon** (☏ 04 66 22 85 54; www.canoeletour billon.com; 3 chemin du Gardon, Collias; adult/child from €23/17; ☺ 9am-7pm Apr-Sep) in Collias, 8km and a two-hour paddle from the Pont du Gard.

PROVENCE

Provence conjures up images of rolling lavender fields, blue skies, gorgeous villages, wonderful food and superb wine. It certainly delivers on all those fronts, but it's not just worth visiting for its good looks – dig a little deeper and you'll also discover the multicultural metropolis of Marseille, the artistic haven of Aix-en-Provence and Roman Arles.

Marseille

POP 861,635

Grit and grandeur coexist seamlessly in Marseille, an exuberantly multicultural port city with a pedigree stretching back to classical Greece and a fair claim to the mantle of France's second city. Track down its vibrant heart and soul in the Vieux Port (old port), mast-to-mast with yachts and pleasure boats; uphill in the ancient Le Panier neighbourhood; and looking out to sea on the contemporary rooftop of its flagship museum, MuCEM.

◉ Sights

The **Marseille City Pass** (www.resamarseille. com; 24/48/72hr €26/33/41) covers admission to city museums and public transport, and includes a guided city tour and a Château d'If boat trip, plus other discounts. It's not necessary for children under 12, as many attractions are greatly reduced or free. Buy it online or at the tourist office.

★ Vieux Port   PORT
(Old Port; Ⓜ Vieux Port) Ships have docked for millennia at Marseille's birthplace, the vibrant Vieux Port. The main commercial docks were transferred to the Joliette area in the 1840s, but the old port remains a

thriving harbour for fishing boats, pleasure yachts and tourist boats. Guarded by the forts **St-Jean** (Ⓜ Vieux Port) and **St-Nicolas** (1 bd Charles Livon; ☐ 83), both sides of the port are dotted with bars, brasseries and cafes, with more to be found around place Thiars and cours Honoré d'Estienne d'Orves, where the action continues until late.

★ Musée des Civilisations de l'Europe et de la Méditerranée   MUSEUM
(MuCEM, Museum of European & Mediterranean Civilisations; ☏ 04 84 35 13 13; www.mucem.org; 7 promenade Robert Laffont; adult/child incl exhibitions €9.50/free; ☺ 10am-8pm Wed-Mon Jul & Aug, 11am-7pm Wed-Mon May-Jun & Sep-Oct, 11am-6pm Wed-Mon Nov-Apr; ♿; Ⓜ Vieux Port, Joliette) The icon of modern Marseille, this stunning museum explores the history, culture and civilisation of the Mediterranean region through anthropological exhibits, rotating art exhibitions and film. The collection sits in a bold, contemporary building designed by Algerian-born, Marseille-educated architect Rudy Ricciotti, and Roland Carta. It is linked by a vertigo-inducing footbridge to the 13th-century Fort St-Jean, from which there are stupendous views of the Vieux Port and the surrounding sea. The fort grounds and gardens are free to explore.

Le Panier   AREA
(Ⓜ Vieux Port) 'The Basket' is Marseille's oldest quarter – site of the original Greek settlement and nicknamed for its steep streets and buildings. Its close, village-like feel, artsy ambience, cool hidden squares and sun-baked cafes make it a delight to explore. Rebuilt after destruction in WWII, its mishmash of lanes hide artisan shops, *ateliers* (workshops) and terraced houses strung with drying washing. Its centrepiece is **La Vieille Charité** (☏ 04 91 14 58 80; www. vieille-charite-marseille.com; 2 rue de la Charité; museums adult/child €6/free; ☺ 10am-6pm Tue-Sun mid-Sep–mid-May, longer hours in summer; Ⓜ Joliette), which houses several museums.

Basilique Notre Dame de la Garde   BASILICA
(Montée de la Bonne Mère; ☏ 04 91 13 40 80; www. notredamedelagarde.com; rue Fort du Sanctuaire; ☺ 7am-8pm Apr-Sep, to 7pm Oct-Mar; ☐ 60) Occupying Marseille's highest point, La Garde (154m), this opulent 19th-century Romano-Byzantine basilica is Marseille's most-visited icon. Built on the foundations of a 16th-century fort, which was itself an enlarge-

ment of a 13th-century chapel, the basilica is ornamented with coloured marble, superb Byzantine-style mosaics, and murals depicting ships sailing under the protection of La Bonne Mère (The Good Mother). The campanile supports a 9.7m-tall gilded statue of said Mother on a 12m-high pedestal, and the hilltop gives 360-degree panoramas of the city.

Château d'If CASTLE
([☎] 06 03 06 25 26; www.if.monuments-nationaux. fr; Île d'If; adult/child €6/free; ⊙10am-6pm Apr-Sep, to 5pm Tue-Sun Oct-Mar) Commanding access to Marseille's Vieux Port, this photogenic island-fortress was immortalised in Alexandre Dumas' 1844 classic *The Count of Monte Cristo*. Many political prisoners were incarcerated here, including the Revolutionary hero Mirabeau and the Communards of 1871. Other than the island itself there's not a great deal to see, but it's worth visiting just for the views of the Vieux Port. **Frioul If Express** ([☎] 04 96 11 03 50; www.frioul-if-express. com; 1 quai de la Fraternité) runs boats (return €11, 20 minutes, up to 10 daily) from Quai de la Fraternité.

🛏 Sleeping

★Vertigo Vieux-Port HOSTEL $
([☎] 04 91 54 42 95; www.hotelvertigo.fr; 38 rue Fort Notre Dame; dm/tw €26/76; ⊙; Ⓜ Vieux Port) This award-winning hostel shows a swanky sleep is possible on a shoestring budget – for your euro you can expect breakfast, murals by local artists, vintage furniture, stripped wooden floors and original architectural details such as exposed wooden beams and stone arches. All rooms have their own mod-

ern bathrooms, and there are lockers, a good kitchen and a TV lounge.

★Hôtel Edmond Rostand DESIGN HOTEL $$
([☎] 04 91 37 74 95; www.hoteledmondrostand.com; 31 rue Dragon; s/d/tr €100/110/135; ✱@⊙; Ⓜ Estrangin-Préfecture) Push past the unassuming facade of this great-value hotel in the Quartier des Antiquaires to find a stylish interior in olive-grey and citrus, with a communal lounge area, a cafe and 15 rooms dressed in crisp white and soothing natural hues. Some rooms overlook a tiny private garden and others the Basilique Notre Dame de la Garde.

Mama Shelter DESIGN HOTEL $$
([☎] 04 84 35 20 00; www.mamashelter.com; 64 rue de la Loubière; d from €113; Ⓟ✱⊙; Ⓜ Notre Dame du Mont-Cours Julien) Part of a funky mini-chain of design-forward hotels, Marseille's Mama Shelter offers 125 Philippe Starck–imagined rooms over five floors. It's all about keeping the cool kids happy here – with sleek white-and-chrome colour schemes, a live stage and bar, and a giant *babi foot* (foosball) table. Smaller rooms are oddly shaped, however, and it's a walk from the Vieux Port.

🍴 Eating

The Vieux Port and surrounding pedestrian streets teem with cafe terraces, but choose carefully (some rely on tourists to pay too much for average food). For world cuisine, try cours Julien and nearby rue des Trois Mages. For pizza, roast chicken, and Middle Eastern food under €10, nose around the streets surrounding **Marché des Capucins**

WORTH A TRIP

LES CALANQUES

Marseille abuts the wild and spectacular **Parc National des Calanques** (www.calanques-parcnational.fr), a 20km stretch of high, rocky promontories rising from brilliant-turquoise Mediterranean waters.

The sheer cliffs are occasionally interrupted by small idyllic beaches, some impossible to reach without a kayak. Among the most famous are the calanques of Sormiou, Port-Miou, Port-Pin and En-Vau.

From October to June, the best way to see the Calanques is to hike, and the best access is from the small town of Cassis. Its **tourist office** ([☎] 08 92 39 01 03; www.ot-cassis. com; quai des Moulins; ⊙9am-6.30pm Mon-Sat, 9.30am-12.30pm & 3-6pm Sun May-Aug, shorter hours rest of year; ⊙) has maps. In July and August, trails close because of fire danger: take a boat tour from Marseille or Cassis; sea kayak with **Raskas Kayak** ([☎] 04 91 73 27 16; www.raskas-kayak.com; impasse du Dr Bonfils, Auberge de Jeunesse Marseille; half/full day €40/70); drive; or take a bus.

(Marché de Noailles; place des Capucins; ⊘8am-7pm Mon-Sat; Ⓜ Noailles, 🚊 Canebière Garibaldi).

⭐**L'Arôme**　　　　　　　　　　　　FRENCH **$$**
(🖉 04 91 42 88 80; 9 rue de Trois Rois; menus €23-28; ⊘7.30-11pm Mon-Sat; Ⓜ Notre Dame du Mont) Reserve ahead to snag a table at this fabulous little restaurant just off cours Julien. From the service – relaxed, competent and friendly without over familiarity – to the street art on the walls and the memorable food, it's a complete winner. Well-credentialled chef-owner Romain achieves sophisticated simplicity in dishes such as roast duckling served with polenta and a pecorino *beignet* (doughnut).

🍸 **Drinking & Nightlife**

Near the Vieux Port, head to place Thiars and cours Honoré d'Estienne d'Orves for cafes that bask in the sun by day and buzz into the night. Cours Julien is a fine place on a sunny day to watch people come and go. Le Panier, place de Lenche and rue des Pistoles are ideal places to while away an afternoon soaking up the area's boho charms.

⭐**Waaw**　　　　　　　　　　　　　　　　　BAR
(🖉 04 91 42 16 33; www.waaw.fr; 17 rue Pastoret; ⊘4pm-midnight Wed & Sat, from 6pm Tue, Thu & Fri; Ⓜ Notre Dame du Mont) Marseille's creative chameleon and the heart of the cours Julien scene, Waaw ('What an Amazing World') has everything you could possibly want for a night out, whether that's a cold cocktail, a late-night dancehall DJ set or an innovative dinner made from local market produce. The city's unofficial cultural headquarters also offers music, film, festivals and much more.

⭐**La Friche La Belle de Mai**　　ARTS CENTRE
(🖉 04 95 04 95 04; www.lafriche.org; 41 rue Jobin; ⊘ticket kiosk 11am-6pm Mon, to 7pm Tue-Sat, from 12.30pm Sun; 🚊49, 52) This 45,000-sq-metre former tobacco factory is now a vibrant arts centre with a theatre, cinema, bar, bookshop, artists' workshops, multimedia displays, skateboard ramps, electro- and world-music parties and much more. Check the program online. The on-site restaurant, **Les Grandes Tables** (🖉 04 95 04 95 85; www.lesgrandestables. com; mains €16; ⊘noon-2pm Sun-Wed, noon-2pm

& 8-10pm Thu-Sat), is a great bet for interesting, locally sourced food.

ℹ️ **Information**

Tourist Office (🖉 08 26 50 05 00, box office 04 91 13 89 16; www.marseille-tourisme.com; 11 La Canebière; ⊘9am-6pm; Ⓜ Vieux Port)

ℹ️ **Getting There & Around**

For local transport information in and around Marseille, see www.lepilote.com.

AIR

Aéroport Marseille-Provence (Aéroport Marseille-Marignane; MRS; 🖉 08 20 81 14 14; www.marseille.aeroport.fr) is 25km northwest of Marseille in Marignane. There are regular year-round flights to nearly all major French cities, plus major hubs in the UK, Germany, Belgium, Italy and Spain.

Navette Marseille (www.lepilote.com; one way/return €8.30/14; ⊘4.30am-11.30pm) buses link the airport and Gare St-Charles (30 minutes) every 15 to 20 minutes.

The airport's train station has direct services to several cities including Arles and Avignon – a free shuttle bus runs to/from the airport terminal.

BOAT

Gare Maritime de la Major (Marseille Fos; www.marseille-port.fr; Quai de la Joliette; Ⓜ Joliette), the passenger ferry terminal, is just south of place de la Joliette.

Corsica Linea (🖉 08 25 88 80 88; www.corsicalinea.com; quai du Maroc; ⊘8.30am-8pm) has regular ferries from Marseille to Corsica and Sardinia, plus long-distance routes to Algeria and Tunisia.

TRAIN

Eurostar (www.eurostar.com) offers two to 10 weekly services between Marseille and London (from €213, seven hours) via Lille or Paris. As always, the earlier you book, the cheaper the fare.

Regular and TGV trains serve **Gare St-Charles** (🖉 04 91 08 16 40; www.rtm.fr; rue Jacques Bory; Ⓜ Gare St-Charles SNCF), which is a junction for both metro lines. The **left-luggage office** (Consignes Automatiques; ⊘8.15am-9pm) is next to platform A. Sample fares:

Avignon (€22, 1¼ hours, hourly)

Nice (€38, 2½ hours, up to six per day)

Paris Gare de Lyon (from €76, 3½ hours, at least hourly)

Aix-en-Provence

POP 142,668

Aix-en-Provence is to Provence what the Left Bank is to Paris: a pocket of bohemian chic crawling with students. It's hard to believe that 'Aix' (pronounced ex) is just 25km from chaotic, exotic Marseille. The city has been a cultural centre since the Middle Ages (two of the town's most famous sons are painter Paul Cézanne and novelist Émile Zola), but for all its polish, it's still a laid-back Provençal town at heart.

◉ Sights

A stroller's paradise, Aix' highlight is the mostly pedestrian old city, **Vieil Aix**. South of cours Mirabeau, the **Quartier Mazarin** was laid out in the 17th century, and is home to some of Aix' finest buildings.

The **Aix City Pass** (http://booking.aixen provencetourism.com; adult 24/48/72hr €25/34/43, child €17/21/26) covers entry to all the major museums and Cézanne sights, plus public transport and a guided walking tour.

★**Musée Granet**   MUSEUM
(☑04 42 52 88 32; www.museegranet-aixenprovence.fr; place St-Jean de Malte; adult/child €5.50/free;

◷10am-7pm Tue-Sun mid-Jun–Sep, noon-6pm Tue-Sun Oct–mid-Jun) Aix established one of France's first public museums here, on the site of a former Hospitallers' priory, in 1838. Nearly 200 years of acquisitions (including bequests by the eponymous François Marius Granet, himself a painter of note) have resulted in a collection of more than 12,000 works, including pieces by Picasso, Léger, Matisse, Monet, Klee, Van Gogh and, crucially, nine pieces by local boy Cézanne. This fabulous art museum sits right near the top of France's artistic must-sees.

★**Caumont Centre d'Art**   HISTORIC BUILDING
(☑04 42 20 70 01; www.caumont-centredart.com; 3 rue Joseph Cabassol; adult/child €6.50/free; ◷10am-7pm May-Sep, to 6pm Oct-Apr) The Caumont is a stellar art space housed inside the Mazarin quarter's grandest 18th-century *hôtel particulier* (mansion). While there are three quality exhibitions each year, plus concerts and other events, it's the building itself that's the star of the show. Built from local honey-coloured stone, its palatial rooms are stuffed with antiques and objets d'art attesting to the opulence of the house's aristocratic past.

WORTH A TRIP

VAN GOGH'S ARLES

If the winding streets and colourful houses of Arles seem familiar, it's hardly surprising – Vincent van Gogh lived here for much of his life in a yellow house on place Lamartine, and the town regularly featured in his canvases. His original house was destroyed during WWII, but you can still follow in Vincent's footsteps on the evocative **Van Gogh walking circuit** – the **tourist office** (☑04 90 18 41 20; www.arlestourisme.com; 9 blvd des Lices; ◷9am-6.45pm Apr-Sep, 9am-4.45pm Mon-Sat, 10am-1pm Sun Oct-Mar; ☏) sells maps (€1). You won't see many of the artist's masterpieces in Arles, however, although the modern art gallery **Fondation Vincent Van Gogh** (☑04 90 93 08 08; www.fondation-vincentvan gogh-arles.org; 35ter rue du Docteur Fanton; adult/child €9/free; ◷10am-7pm Jul & Aug, from 11am Sep-Jun) always has one on show, as well as contemporary exhibitions inspired by the Impressionist.

Two millennia ago, Arles was a major Roman settlement. The town's 20,000-seat amphitheatre, known as **Les Arènes** (Amphithéâtre; ☑08 91 70 03 70; www.arenes-arles.com; Rond-Point des Arènes; adult/child €6/free, incl Théâtre Antique €9/free; ◷9am-8pm Jul & Aug, to 7pm May, Jun & Sep, shorter hours Oct-Apr), nowadays hosts outdoor spectacles, concerts, races and the *corrida* – bullfighting that is banned in most parts of France and which has come under intense scrutiny for its cruelty.

There are buses to/from Aix-en-Provence (€11, 1¼ hours) and regular trains to/from Nîmes (€7.50, 30 minutes to one hour), Marseille (€13, one hour) and Avignon (€6, 20 minutes).

Atelier Cézanne
MUSEUM

(☑ 04 42 21 06 53; www.atelier-cezanne.com; 9 av Paul Cézanne; adult/child €6.50/free, audio guide €3; ☺ 10am-6pm Jun-Sep, 10am-12.30pm & 2-6pm Apr & May, 10.30am-12.30pm & 2-5pm Oct-Mar, closed Sun Dec-Feb; 🚌 5, 12) Cézanne's last studio, where he worked from 1902 until his death four years later, has been painstakingly preserved. Some elements have been recreated: not all the tools and still-life models strewn around the room were his. Though the studio is inspiring, and home to periodic exhibitions, none of Cezanne's works actually hang there. It's a leisurely walk to the studio at Lauves hill, 1.5km north of central Aix, or you can take the bus.

🛌 Sleeping

★ Hôtel les Quatre Dauphins
BOUTIQUE HOTEL **$$**

(☑ 04 42 38 16 39; www.lesquatredauphins.fr; 54 rue Roux Alphéran; s/d €101/123; ❄🌐) This sweet 13-room hotel slumbers in a former 19th-century mansion in one of the loveliest parts of town. Rooms are fresh and clean, decorated with a great eye and equipped with excellent modern bathrooms. Those with sloping, beamed ceilings in the attic are quaint but are not for those who don't pack light – the terracotta-tiled staircase is not suitcase friendly.

🍴 Eating

No spot revs up taste buds more than the city's daily **food market** on place Richelme. Restaurant terraces spill out across dozens of charm-heavy old-town squares: place des Trois Ormeaux, place des Augustins, place Ramus and vast Forum des Cardeurs are particular favourites.

★ Farinoman Fou
BAKERY **$**

(www.farinomanfou.fr; 3 rue Mignet; bread €1.40-3; ☺ 7am-7pm Tue-Sat) To appeal to bread connoisseurs, in Aix as in any part of France, you need to know your dough. Judging by the lines typically spilling out of this shop onto place des Prêcheurs, artisanal *boulanger* Benoît Fradette clearly does. The bakery has no need to invest in a fancy shopfront – customers jostle for space with bread ovens and dough-mixing tubs.

Jardin Mazarin
FRENCH **$$**

(☑ 04 28 31 08 36; www.jardinmazarin.com; 15 rue du 4 Septembre; lunch/dinner menus €23/29; ☺ 9am-3pm & 7-10.30pm Mon-Sat) This elegant restaurant is set perfectly on the ground floor of a handsome 18th-century *hôtel particulier* in the Quartier Mazarin. Two salons sit beneath splendid beamed ceilings, but the real gem is the verdant fountain-centred garden, which comes into its own in summer. Expect knowledgeable treatment of local, seasonal produce (such as truffles and asparagus) from the kitchen.

❶ Information

Tourist Office (☑ 04 42 16 11 61; www.aixen provencetourism.com; 300 av Giuseppe Verdi, Les Allées; ☺ 8.30am-7pm Mon-Sat, 10am-1pm & 2-6pm Sun Apr-Sep, 8.30am-6pm Mon-Sat Oct-Mar; 🌐)

❶ Getting There & Around

Consult www.lepilote.com for timetables, fares and itineraries for public transport journeys to/from Aix and www.navetteaixmarseille.com for shuttle buses to/from Marseille.

BUS

Aix' **bus station** (Gare routière; ☑ 04 42 91 26 80, 08 91 02 40 25; 6 bd Coq) is a 10-minute walk southwest from La Rotonde. Services include Avignon (€18, 1¼ hours, six daily), Marseille (€9, 40 minutes, every 10 minutes Monday to Saturday, fewer on Sunday) and Nice (€30, 2¼ hours, three to five daily).

TRAIN

The **city centre train station** (☑ 08 00 11 40 23; www.ter.sncf.com/paca; av Maurice Blondel; ☺ 5am-1am Mon-Sat, from 6am Sun), at the southern end of av Victor Hugo, serves Marseille (€8.30, 45 minutes).

Aix' **TGV station** (☑ 0892 35 35 35; www. gares-sncf.com; rte Départementale 9; ☺ 5.30am-1am), 15km from the centre, is a stop on the high-speed Paris–Marseille line. Destinations include Avignon (from €13, 25 minutes, one or two per hour) and Lyon (from €33, 1½ hours, around hourly).

Bus 40 runs from the TGV station to Aix' bus station (€4.30, 15 minutes, every 15 minutes).

Avignon

POP 91,250

Hooped by 4.3km of superbly preserved stone ramparts, this graceful city is the belle of Provence's ball. Its turn as the papal seat of power has bestowed Avignon with a treasury of magnificent art and architecture, none grander than the massive World Heritage–listed fortress-cum-palace known as the Palais des Papes. Famed for its annual performing arts festival, these days Avignon is a lively student city and an ideal spot to step out into the surrounding region.

◉ Sights

With the free **Avignon Passion** card, available at the tourist office and museums, pay full price at the first museum or monument you visit, then get a discount at every subsequent site visited.

★ Palais des Papes   PALACE
(Papal Palace; ☑ tickets 04 32 74 32 74; www.palais -des-papes.com; place du Palais; adult/child €12/10, with Pont St-Bénézet €14.50/11.50; ☺9am-8pm Jul, to 8.30pm Aug, shorter hours Sep-Jun) The largest Gothic palace ever built, the Palais des Papes was erected by Pope Clement V, who abandoned Rome in 1309 in the wake of violent disorder after his election. Its immense scale illustrates the medieval might of the Roman Catholic church.

Ringed by 3m-thick walls, its cavernous halls, chapels and antechambers are largely bare today – but tickets now include tablet 'Histopads' revealing virtual-reality representations of how the building would have looked in all its papal pomp.

Musée du Petit Palais   MUSEUM
(☑04 90 86 44 58; www.petit-palais.org; place du Palais; adult/child €6/free; ☺10am-1pm & 2-6pm Wed-Mon) The archbishops' palace during the 14th and 15th centuries now houses outstanding collections of primitive, pre-Rennaissance, 13th- to 16th-century Italian religious paintings by artists including Botticelli, Carpaccio and Giovanni di Paolo – the most famous is Botticelli's *La Vierge et l'Enfant* (1470).

★ Pont St-Bénézet   BRIDGE
(☑ tickets 04 32 74 32 74; bd de la Ligne; adult/child 24hr ticket €5/4, with Palais des Papes €14.50/11.50; ☺9am-8pm Jul, to 8.30pm Aug, shorter hours Sep-Jun) Legend says Pastor Bénézet (a former shepherd) had three visions urging him to build a bridge across the Rhône. Completed in 1185, the 900m-long bridge linked Avignon with Villeneuve-lès-Avignon. It was rebuilt several times before all but four of its 22 spans were washed away in the 1600s,

leaving the far side marooned in the middle of the Rhône. There are fine (and free) views from Rocher des Doms park, Pont Édouard Daladier and Île de la Barthelasse's chemin des Berges.

★彡 Festivals & Events

★ Festival d'Avignon   PERFORMING ARTS
(☑ box office 04 90 14 14 14; www.festival-avignon. com; ☺Jul) The three-week annual Festival d'Avignon is one of the world's great performing-arts festivals. Over 40 international works of dance and drama play to 100,000-plus spectators at venues around town. Tickets don't go on sale until springtime, but hotels sell out by February.

🛏 Sleeping

★ Les Jardins de Baracane   B&B $$
(☑06 11 14 88 54; www.lesjardinsdebaracane.fr; 12 rue Baracane; r €125-310; 🅿❄🌐📶) This 18th-century house near place des Corps Saints is owned by an architect, so it's been sensitively and tastefully renovated. Wood beams, stone walls and period detailing feature in all rooms, but the best are the two suites, which are posh enough for a pope. There's a great pool, and breakfast is served in the garden under a huge wisteria tree.

★ Hôtel La Mirande   HOTEL $$$
(☑04 90 14 20 20; www.la-mirande.fr; 4 place de la Mirande; d from €450; ❄@📶) The address to sleep in Avignon *en luxe*. It's located literally in the shadow of the palace, and stepping inside feels more like entering an aristocrat's château than a hotel, with oriental rugs, gold-threaded tapestries, marble statues and oil paintings everywhere you look. Rooms are equally opulent, and the best overlook the interior garden where afternoon tea is served.

🍽 Eating

Place de l'Horloge is crammed with touristy restaurants that don't offer the best cuisine or value in town. Delve instead into the pedestrian old city where ample pretty squares like place des Châtaignes or place de la Principle tempt.

★ Maison Violette   BAKERY $
(☑06 59 44 62 94; place des Corps Saints; ☺7am-7.30pm Mon-Sat) We simply defy you to

walk into this bakery and not instantly be tempted by the stacks of baguettes, *ficelles* and *pains de campagnes* loaded up on the counter, not to mention the orderly ranks of éclairs, *millefeuilles,* fruit tarts and cookies lined up irresistibly behind the glass. Go on, a little bit of what you fancy does you good, *non*?

Hygge CAFE **$**
(☑04 65 81 06 87; 25 place des Carmes; 2-/3-course lunch €13.90/15.90; ☺8am-3pm Mon-Wed, 8am-3pm & 6-10pm Thu-Sat) 🍴 Having worked at a smorgasbord of high-flying restaurants (including Copenhagen's Noma and Avignon's La Mirande), Jacques Pampiri opened his own place in Avignon, and it's a big hit with the locals. Hearty, wholesome organic food is dished up canteen-style to keep costs down, and the mix-and-match thrift-shop decor is great fun. Arrive early for a prime table on the square.

★ **Restaurant L'Essentiel** FRENCH **$$**
(☑04 90 85 87 12; www.restaurantlessentiel.com; 2 rue Petite Fusterie; menus €32-46; ☺noon-2pm & 7-9.45pm Tue-Sat) In the top tier of Avignon's restaurants for many a year, this elegant restaurant remains (as its name suggests) as essential as ever. First there's the setting: a lovely, honey-stoned *hôtel particulier* (mansion) with a sweet courtyard garden. Then there's the food: rich, sophisticated French dining of the first order, replete with the requisite foams, veloutés and reductions.

ℹ Information

Tourist Office (☑04 32 74 32 74; www.avignon-tourisme.com; 41 cours Jean Jaurès; ☺9am-6pm Mon-Sat, 10am-5pm Sun Apr-Oct, shorter hours Nov-Mar) Guided walking tours, information on boat trips along the River Rhône and wine-tasting trips to nearby vineyards.

ℹ Getting There & Around

AIR

Aéroport Avignon-Provence (AVN; ☑04 90 81 51 51; www.avignon.aeroport.fr) is in Caumont, 8km southeast of Avignon, and has direct flights to London, Birmingham and Southampton in the UK.

From the airport, LER bus 22 (www.info-ler.fr; €1.50) goes to the Avignon bus station and TGV station.

BUS

Avignon's **bus station** (bd St-Roch; ☺information window 8am-7pm Mon-Fri, to 1pm Sat) is a major bus hub for the Vaucluse *département*. Services include Aix-en-Provence (€18, 1¼ hours, two to six daily) and Arles (€7.80, 50 minutes, five daily).

TRAIN

Avignon has two train stations: **Gare Avignon Centre** (42 bd St-Roch), on the southern edge of the walled town, and **Gare Avignon TGV**, 4km southwest in Courtine. Shuttle trains link the two every 15 to 20 minutes (€1.60, six minutes, 6am to 11pm).

Eurostar (www.eurostar.com) services operate one to five times weekly between Avignon TGV and London St Pancras (from €78, 5¾ hours) en route to/from Marseille.

Frequent TGV services include Aix-en-Provence (€12.50 to €21, 25 minutes), Marseille (€12.50 to €19, 40 minutes), Nice (€36 to €62, 3¼ hours) and Paris (€45 to €90, 3½ hours).

THE FRENCH RIVIERA & MONACO

With its glistening seas, idyllic beaches and fabulous weather, the French Riviera (Côte d'Azur in French) screams exclusivity, extravagance and glitz. It has been a favourite getaway for the European jet set since Victorian times and there is nowhere more chichi or glam in France than St-Tropez, Cannes and super-rich, sovereign Monaco.

Nice

POP 342,522
With its mix of real-city grit, old-world opulence, year-round sunshine, vibrant street life and shimmering seaside shores, no place in France compares with Nice. But then this is the queen of the Riviera who truly understand what good living is all about: the very best of Mediterranean food, free museums, exceptional art, and alpine wilderness within an hour's drive.

◉ Sights & Activities

The **French Riviera Pass** (www.frenchriviera pass.com; 1/2/3 days €26/38/56) includes access to a number of sights in Nice and along the Riviera. Buy it online or at the Nice **tourist office** (☑04 92 14 46 14; www.nicetourisme.com; 5 Promenade des Anglais; ☺9am-7pm daily Jun-Sep, to 6pm Mon-Sat Oct-May; 🛜; 🚎8, 52, 62 to Massenet).

★ **Promenade des Anglais**   ARCHITECTURE
(🚍8, 52, 62) The most famous stretch of sea-front in Nice – if not France – is this vast paved promenade, which gets its name from the English expat patrons who paid for it in 1822. It runs for the whole 4km sweep of the Baie des Anges with a dedicated lane for cyclists and skaters; if you fancy joining them, you can rent skates, scooters and bikes from **Roller Station** (☑04 93 62 99 05; www.roller -station.fr; 49 quai des États-Unis; skates, boards & scooters per hour/day €5/15, bicycles €5/18; ☻9am-8pm Jul & Aug, 10am-7pm May, Jun, Sep & Oct, to 6pm Nov-Apr).

★ **Vieux Nice**   HISTORIC SITE
(🚍1 to Opéra-Vieille Ville/Cathédrale-Vieille Ville) Getting lost among the dark, narrow, winding alleyways of Nice's old town is a highlight. The layout has barely changed since the 1700s, and it's now packed with delis, restaurants, boutiques and bars, but the centrepiece remains **cours Saleya**: a massive market square that's permanently thronging in summer. The **food market** (☻6am-1.30pm Tue-Sun) is perfect for fresh produce and foodie souvenirs, while the **flower market** (☻6am-5.30pm Tue-Sat, 6.30am-1.30pm Sun) is worth visiting just for the colours and fragrances. A **flea market** (Marché à la Brocante; ☻7am-6pm Mon) is held on Monday.

Colline du Château   PARK
(Castle Hill; ☻8.30am-8pm Apr-Sep, to 6pm Oct-Mar) **FREE** For the best views over Nice's red-tiled rooftops, climb the winding staircases up to this wooded outcrop on the eastern edge of the old town. It's been occupied since ancient times; archaeological digs have revealed Celtic and Roman remains, and the site was later occupied by a medieval castle that was razed by Louis XIV in 1706 (only the 16th-century **Tour Bellanda** remains). There are various entrances, including one beside the tower, or you can cheat and ride the free **lift** (Ascenseur du Château; rue des Ponchettes; ☻9am-8pm Jun-Aug, to 7pm Apr, May & Sep, 10am-6pm Oct-Mar).

Musée Masséna   MUSEUM
(☑04 93 91 19 10; 65 rue de France; museum pass 24hr/7 days €10/20; ☻10am-6pm Wed-Mon late Jun–mid-Oct, from 11am rest of year; 🚍8, 52, 62 to Congrès/Promenade) Originally built as a holiday home for Prince Victor d'Essling (the grandson of one of Napoléon's favourite generals, Maréchal Massena), this lavish belle époque building is another of the city's iconic architectural landmarks. Built between 1898 and 1901 in grand neoclassical style with an Italianate twist, it's now a fascinating museum dedicated to the history of the Riviera – taking in everything from holidaying monarchs to expat Americans, the boom of tourism and the enduring importance of Carnaval.

Musée d'Art Moderne et d'Art Contemporain   GALLERY
(MAMAC; ☑04 97 13 42 01; www.mamac-nice.org; place Yves Klein; museum pass 24hr/7 days €10/20; ☻10am-6pm Tue-Sun late Jun–mid-Oct, from 11am rest of year; 🚍1 to Garibaldi) European and American avant-garde works from the 1950s to the present are the focus of this sprawling multilevel museum. Highlights include many works by Christo and Nice's neorealists: Niki de Saint Phalle, César, Arman and Yves Klein. The building's rooftop also works as an exhibition space (with knockout panoramas of Nice to boot).

★ **Musée Matisse**   GALLERY
(☑04 93 81 08 08; www.musee-matisse-nice.org; 164 av des Arènes de Cimiez; museum pass 24hr/7 days €10/20; ☻10am-6pm Wed-Mon late Jun–mid-Oct, from 11am rest of year; 🚍15, 17, 20, 22 to Arènes/Musée Matisse) This museum, 2km north of the city centre in the leafy Cimiez quarter, houses a fascinating assortment of works by Matisse, including oil paintings, drawings, sculptures, tapestries and Matisse's famous paper cut-outs. The permanent collection is displayed in a red-ochre 17th-century Genoese villa in an olive grove. Temporary exhibitions are in the futuristic basement building. Matisse is buried in the **Monastère Notre Dame de Cimiez** (place du Monastère; ☻8.30am-12.30pm & 2.30-6.30pm) cemetery, across the park from the museum.

🎊 Festivals & Events

★ **Carnaval de Nice**   CARNIVAL
(www.nicecarnaval.com; ☻Feb-Mar) Held over a two-week period in late February and early March since 1294. Highlights include the *batailles de fleurs* (battles of flowers) and the ceremonial burning of the carnival king on Promenade des Anglais, followed by a fireworks display.

FRANCE NICE

Nice

FRANCE NICE

Nice

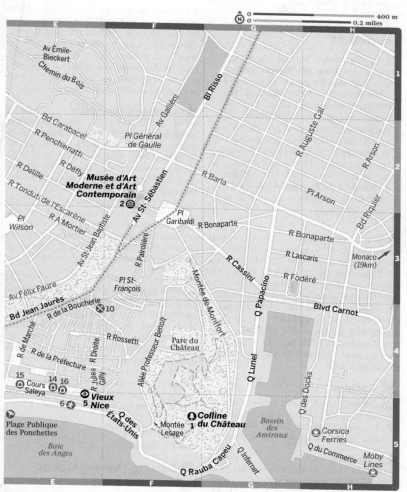

🛏 Sleeping

⭐**Hostel Meyerbeer Beach** HOSTEL **$**
(☎04 93 88 95 65; www.hostelmeyerbeer.com; 15
rue Meyerbeer; dm €25-50, s €80-90, d €90-100;
🚌7, 9, 22, 27, 59, 70 to Rivoli) A welcoming mood
prevails throughout this cosy little hostel,
thanks to the congenial, international staff
of four, a kitchen small enough to make
you feel like you're cooking at home, and a
cheerful, immaculate mix of private rooms
and four- to eight-bed dorms, each with its
own en suite bathroom.

⭐**Hôtel Windsor** BOUTIQUE HOTEL **$$**
(☎04 93 88 59 35; www.hotelwindsornice.com; 11
rue Dalpozzo; d €92-290; ❄@🛜🚭; 🚌7, 9, 22, 27,
59, 70 to Grimaldi or Rivoli) Don't be fooled by
the staid stone exterior: inside, owner Odile
Redolfi has enlisted the collective creativity
of several well-known artists to make each
of the 57 rooms uniquely appealing. Some
are frescoed and others are adorned with
experimental chandeliers or photographic
murals. The garden and pool out the back
are delightful, as are the small bar and at-
tached restaurant.

DAY TRIP INTO RURAL PROVENCE

Chugging between the mountains and the sea, the **Train des Pignes** (Pine Cone Train; www.trainprovence.com; single/return Nice to Digne €24.10/48.20; 🚊1 to Libération) is one of Provence's most picturesque train rides. The 151km track between Nice and Digne-les-Bains rises to 1000m for breathtaking views as it passes through Haute-Provence's scarcely populated backcountry. The service runs four times daily from **Gare de Nice-CF de Provence** (rue Alfred Binet; 🚊1 to Libération) and is ideal for a day trip inland.

★**Nice Garden Hôtel**   BOUTIQUE HOTEL **$$**
(🔇04 93 87 35 62; www.nicegardenhotel.com; 11 rue du Congrès; s €75-85, d €110-140; ⏱reception 8.30am-9pm; ❄🛜; 🚌7, 9, 22, 27, 59, 70 to Grimaldi) Behind heavy iron gates hides this gem: the nine beautifully appointed rooms – the work of the exquisite Marion – are a subtle blend of old and new and overlook a delightful garden with a glorious orange tree. Amazingly, all this charm and peacefulness is just two blocks from the promenade. Breakfast costs €9.

✖ Eating

To lunch with locals, grab a pew in the midday sun on one of the many place Garibaldi cafe terraces. There are lots of restaurants on cours Saleya, but quality can be variable.

★**Mama Baker**   BAKERY **$**
(🔇06 23 91 33 86; www.facebook.com/Mamabakernice; 13 rue de Lépante; items from €2; ⏱7am-2pm & 3-7pm Mon-Fri, 7am-6pm Sat; 🚌4 to Toselli) Great bakeries abound in France, but even here, truly creative artisanal ones stand out. Witness Mama Baker, where organic grains and speciality ingredients go into a host of unique goodies. Don't miss the delectable *bouchées aux olives,* soft and crispy bitesized bits of olive-studded cheesy dough, or *pompe à l'huile,* a semisweet roll flavoured with olive oil and orange blossoms.

★**Chez Palmyre**   FRENCH **$**
(🔇04 93 85 72 32; 5 rue Droite; 3-course menu €18; ⏱noon-1.30pm & 7-9.30pm Mon, Tue, Thu & Fri) Look no further for authentic Niçois cooking than this packed, cramped, convivial little space in the heart of the old town. The menu is very meat-heavy, with plenty of tripe, veal, pot-cooked chicken and the like, true to the traditional tastes of Provençal cuisine. It's a bargain, and understandably popular. Book well ahead, even for lunch.

★**La Femme du Boulanger**   BISTRO **$$**
(🔇04 89 03 43 03; www.facebook.com/femmeduboulanger; 3 rue Raffali; mains €20-25, tartines €16-22; ⏱9am-3pm & 7-11pm; 🚌8, 52, 62 to Massenet) This back-alley gem with pavement seating is a vision of French bistro bliss. Mains like duck *à l'orange,* honeybalsamic glazed lamb shank, or perfect *steak au poivre* (pepper steak) with *gratin dauphinois* (cheesy potatoes) and perfectly tender veggies are followed up with raspberry clafoutis, tiramisu and other scrumptious desserts. Tartines on wood-fired homemade bread are the other house speciality.

★**Peixes**   SEAFOOD **$$**
(🔇04 93 85 96 15; 4 rue de l'Opéra; small plates €12-19, mains €17-35; ⏱noon-10pm Tue-Sat) This chic modern seafood eatery is the latest jewel in the crown of Niçois master restaurateur Armand Crespo. All done up in white-and-turquoise nautical decor, with dangling fish eyeball light fixtures and murals of a tentacle-haired mermaid ensnaring a fishing boat, it specialises in fresh local fish turned into delicious ceviches, tartares and Japanese-style tatakis by chefs in the open kitchen.

ℹ Information

Tourist Office (p438)

ℹ Getting There & Around

AIR

Nice-Côte d'Azur Airport (NCE; 🔇08 20 42 33 33; www.nice.aeroport.fr; 🛜; 🚌98, 99, 🚊2) is France's second-largest airport and has international flights to Europe, North Africa and the USA, with regular and low-cost airlines.

Buses 98 and 99 link the airport's terminal with Promenade des Anglais and Nice train station respectively (€6, 35 minutes, every 20 minutes).

BOAT

Corsica Ferries (🔇04 92 00 42 76; www.corsicaferries.com; quai du Commerce; 🚌2 to Port Lympia) and **Moby Lines** (🔇08 00 90 11 44;

www.mobylines.fr; Quai du Commerce; 🚌 2 to Port Lympia) offer regular ferry services from Nice to Corsica. Corsica Ferries also serves Golfo Aranci in Sardinia.

TRAIN
From Nice's train station, 1.2km north of the beach, there are frequent services to Cannes (€7.20, 40 minutes), Marseille (€36 to €42, 2¾ hours), Monaco (€4.10, 25 minutes) and other Riviera destinations.

Cannes
POP 74,285

Most have heard of Cannes and its celebrity film festival. The latter only lasts for two weeks in May, but the buzz and glitz linger all year thanks to regular visits from celebrities who come here to indulge in designer shopping, beaches and the palace hotels of the Riviera's most glam seafront strip, bd de la Croisette.

◉ Sights & Activities

★ La Croisette
ARCHITECTURE

The multi-starred hotels and couture shops lining the iconic bd de la Croisette (aka La Croisette) may be the preserve of the rich and famous, but anyone can enjoy strolling the palm-shaded promenade – a favourite pastime among Cannois at night, when it twinkles with bright lights. Views of the Baie de Cannes and nearby Estérel mountains are beautiful, and seafront hotel palaces dazzle in all their stunning art deco glory.

Le Suquet
HISTORIC SITE

Follow rue St-Antoine and snake your way up through the narrow streets of Le Suquet, Cannes' oldest district. Up top you'll find the site of Cannes' medieval castle, place de la Castre, flanked by the 17th-century Église Notre-Dame de l'Esperance. Climb the adjacent ramparts for great views of the bay.

Îles de Lérins
ISLAND

Although just 20 minutes away by boat, Cannes' tranquil islands feel far from the madding crowd. Île Ste-Marguerite, where the mysterious Man in the Iron Mask was incarcerated during the late 17th century, is known for its bone-white beaches, eucalyptus groves and small marine museum. Tiny Île St-Honorat has been a monastery since the 5th century; you can visit the church and small chapels and stroll through the monks' vineyards.

Boats leave Cannes from quai des Îles on the western side of the harbour. Trans Côte d'Azur (📞04 92 98 71 30; www.trans-cote-azur.com; quai Max Laubeuf), Riviera Lines (📞04 92 98 71 31; www.riviera-lines.com; quai Max Laubeuf) and Horizon (📞04 92 98 71 36; www.horizon-lerins.com; quai Laubeuf) all run ferries to Île Ste-Marguerite, while Planaria (📞04 92 98 71 38; www.cannes-ilesdelerins.com; quai Max Laubeuf) covers Île St-Honorat.

🛏 Sleeping & Eating

Most private beaches have restaurants: expect to pay around €25 to €30 for a main of grilled fish or meat, or gourmet salad. Several

DON'T MISS

THE CORNICHES

Some of the Riviera's most spectacular scenery stretches east between Nice and Monaco. A trio of *corniches* (coastal roads) hugs the cliffs between the two seaside cities, each higher up the hill than the last. The middle *corniche* ends in Monaco; the upper and lower continue to Menton near the France–Italy border.

Corniche Inférieure (lower) Skimming the glittering, villa-studded shoreline, this road is all about belle époque glamour, the height of which can be seen at the extravagant **Villa Ephrussi de Rothschild** (📞04 93 01 33 09; www.villa-ephrussi.com/en; adult/child €14/11; ⊙10am-6pm Feb-Jun, Sep & Oct, to 7pm Jul & Aug, 2-6pm Mon-Fri, 10am-6pm Sat & Sun Nov-Jan) in St-Jean-Cap Ferrat.

Moyenne (middle) Corniche The jewel in the Riviera crown undoubtedly goes to Èze, a medieval village spectacularly located on a rocky outcrop with dazzling views of the Med.

Grande (upper) Corniche The epitome of 'scenic drive', with sublime panoramas unfolding at every bend. Stop in **La Turbie** for dramatic views of Monaco.

streets just inland, such as rue Hoche, are filled with restaurants and bistros. Cheaper eats can be found in and around Cannes' atmospheric food market, **Marché Forville** (11 rue du Marché Forville; ⊙ 7.30am-1pm Tue-Fri, to 2pm Sat & Sun).

★**Hôtel de Provence**   HOTEL **$$**
(☑ 04 93 38 44 35; www.hotel-de-provence.com; 9 rue Molière; s €93-140, d €110-247, ste €246-340; ⊙ closed mid-Jan–early Mar; ❋ 🐾) This traditional Provençal townhouse with buttermilk walls, lavender-blue shutters and a palm-lined entryway disguises a minimalist-chic interior. Almost every room sports a balcony, climaxing with a 7th-floor suite with stunning rooftop terrace. The Provence also has self-catering studios in the neighbourhood for three to six people. Breakfast costs €10.80.

★**Bobo Bistro**   MEDITERRANEAN **$$**
(☑ 04 93 99 97 33; www.facebook.com/BoboBistro Cannes; 21 rue du Commandant André; pizzas €14-20, mains €18-31; ⊙ noon-11pm) Predictably, it's a 'bobo' (bourgeois bohemian) crowd that gathers at this achingly cool bistro in Cannes' fashionable Carré d'Or. Decor is stylishly retro, with attention-grabbing objets d'art including a tableau of dozens of spindles of coloured yarn. Cuisine is local, seasonal and invariably organic: artichoke salad, tuna carpaccio with passion fruit, or roasted cod with mash *fait masion* (homemade).

★**Table 22**   MODERN EUROPEAN **$$$**
(Mantel; ☑ 04 93 39 13 10; www.restaurantmantel. com; 22 rue St-Antoine; menus €39-65, mains €35-46; ⊙ noon-2pm Wed-Sun, 7.30-10pm daily) Discover why Noël Mantel is the hotshot of the Cannois gastronomic scene at his refined old-town restaurant. Service is stellar and the seasonally inspired cuisine divine – Mantel's food maximises local ingredients but isn't afraid to experiment with unusual flavours and cooking techniques. Spot the classic film stars on the walls, from Cary Grant to Alfred Hitchcock.

❶ Information

Tourist Office (☑ 04 92 99 84 22; www. cannes-destination.fr; 1 bd de la Croisette; ⊙ 9am-7pm Mar-Oct, to 8pm Jul & Aug, 10am-6pm Nov-Feb; 🐾)

❶ Getting There & Away

Cannes' gleaming white train station is well connected with other towns along the coast.
Marseille (€33, 2¼ hours, half-hourly)
Monaco (€10, one hour, at least twice hourly)
Nice (€7.20, 40 minutes, every 15 minutes)

St-Tropez

POP 4305

In the soft autumn or winter light, it's hard to believe the pretty terracotta fishing village of St-Tropez is a stop on the Riviera celebrity circuit. It seems far removed from its glitzy siblings further up the coast, but come spring or summer, it's a different world: the population increases tenfold, prices triple and fun-seekers pile in to party till dawn, strut around the luxury-yacht-packed **Vieux Port** and enjoy the creature comforts of exclusive A-listers' beaches in the **Baie de Pampelonne**.

◉ Sights & Activities

About 4km southeast of town is the start of magnificently sandy (and nudist) **Plage de Tahiti** and its continuation, celebrity **Plage de Pampelonne**, studded with legendary drinking and dining haunts.

★**Musée de l'Annonciade**   GALLERY
(☑ 04 94 17 84 10; www.saint-tropez.fr/fr/culture/ musee-de-lannonciade; place Grammont; adult/ child €6/free; ⊙ 10am-6pm daily mid-Jun–Sep, Tue-Sun Oct–mid-Jun) In a gracefully converted 16th-century chapel, this small but famous museum showcases an impressive collection of modern art infused with that legendary Côte d'Azur light. Pointillist Paul Signac bought a house in St-Tropez in 1892 and introduced other artists to the area. The museum's collection includes his *St-Tropez, Le Quai* (1899) and *St-Tropez, Coucher de Soleil au Bois de Pins* (1896). Vuillard, Bonnard and Maurice Denis (the self-named 'Nabis' group) have a room to themselves.

★**La Ponche**   HISTORIC SITE
Shrug off the hustle of the port in St-Tropez' historic fishing quarter, La Ponche, northeast of the Vieux Port. From the southern end of quai Frédéric Mistral, place Garrezio sprawls east from 10th-century **Tour**

Suffren to place de l'Hôtel de Ville. From here, rue Guichard leads southeast to iconic **Église de St-Tropez** (Eglise Notre Dame de l'Assomption; rue Commandant Guichard). Follow rue du Portail Neuf south to **Chapelle de la Miséricorde** (1-5 rue de la Miséricorde; ☺10am-6pm).

★**Citadelle de St-Tropez**   MUSEUM
(☑04 94 97 59 43; www.saint-tropez.fr/fr/culture/citadelle; 1 montée de la Citadelle; adult/child €3/free; ☺10am-6.30pm Apr-Sep, to 5.30pm Oct-Mar; 🖱) Built in 1602 to defend the coast against Spain, the citadel dominates the hillside overlooking St-Tropez to the east. The views are fantastic, as are the exotic peacocks wandering the grounds. Its dungeons are home to the excellent **Musée de l'Histoire Maritime**, an interactive museum that traces the history of humans at sea through fishing, trading, exploration, travel and the navy. The particular focus, of course, is Tropezienne and Provençal seafarers.

🛏 Sleeping & Eating

Celebrity-studded St-Trop is no shoestring destination, although campgrounds do sit southeast along Plage de Pampelonne.

Tuesday and Saturday mornings mean market day on place des Lices. Don't leave town without sampling *tarte Tropézienne*, an orange-blossom-flavoured double sponge cake filled with thick cream, created by Polish baker A Mickla in 1955.

★**Le Café**   CAFE **$$**
(☑04 94 97 44 69; www.lecafe.fr; Traverse des Lices; 2-course lunch menu €18, mains €22-29; ☺8am-11pm) Wetting whistles since 1789, this historic cafe is where artists and painters preferred to hang out back in the days when St-Trop was still a sleepy port. Happily, it has clung on to its no-nonsense roots – you'll find solid dishes such as pot-roasted chicken, mussels and grilled fish on the menu.

❶ Information

Tourist Office (☑08 92 68 48 28; www.sainttropeztourisme.com; quai Jean Jaurès; ☺9.30am-1.30pm & 3-7.30pm Jul & Aug, 9.30am-12.30pm & 2-7pm Apr-Jun, Sep & Oct, to 6pm Mon-Sat Nov-Mar) Runs occasional walking tours April to October, and also has a

kiosk (☺9am-6pm Jul & Aug) in Parking du Port in July and August.

❶ Getting There & Away

VarLib (☑09 70 83 03 80; www.varlib.fr) tickets cost €3 from the **bus station** (Gare Routière; ☑04 94 56 25 74; av du Général de Gaulle) for anywhere within the Var département (except Toulon-Hyères airport). Destinations include Ramatuelle (35 minutes, up to six daily) and St-Raphaël (1¼ to three hours, depending on traffic, hourly) via Grimaud and Port Grimaud, and Fréjus.

Buses serve Toulon-Hyères airport (€15, 1½ hours), but some require a transfer.

Monaco

POP 37,550 / TEL +377

Squeezed into just 200 hectares, this confetti principality might be the world's second-smallest country (the Vatican is smaller), but what it lacks in size it makes up for in attitude. Glitzy, glam and screaming hedonism to the core, Monaco is truly beguiling.

It is a sovereign state but has no border control. It has its own flag (red and white) and national holiday (19 November), and it uses the euro even though it's not part of the EU. Renowned as one of the world's most notorious tax havens and home to the annual Formula One Grand Prix, it can easily be visited as a day trip from Nice.

◉ Sights

★**Casino de Monte Carlo**   CASINO
(☑98 06 21 21; www.casinomontecarlo.com; place du Casino; morning visit incl audio guide adult/child Oct-Apr €14/10, May-Sep €17/12, salons ordinaires gaming Oct-Apr €14, May-Sep €17; ☺visits 9am-1pm, gaming 2pm-late) Peeping inside Monte Carlo's legendary marble-and-gold casino is a Monaco essential. The building, open to visitors every morning, including the exclusive *salons privés*, is Europe's most lavish example of belle époque architecture. Prince Charles III spearheaded the casino's development and in 1866, three years after its inauguration, the name 'Monte Carlo' – Ligurian for 'Mount Charles' in honour of the prince – was coined. To gamble here, visit after 2pm (when a strict over-18s-only admission rule kicks in).

★**Musée**
Océanographique de Monaco AQUARIUM
(📞93 15 36 00; www.oceano.mc; av St-Martin; adult/child high season €16/12, low season €11/7; ☺9.30am-8pm Jul & Aug, 10am-7pm Apr-Jun & Sep, to 6pm Oct-Mar) Stuck dramatically to the edge of a cliff since 1910, the world-renowned Musée Océanographique de Monaco, founded by Prince Albert I (1848–1922), is a stunner. Its centrepiece is its aquarium with a 6m-deep lagoon where sharks and marine predators are separated from colourful tropical fish by a coral reef. Upstairs, two huge colonnaded rooms retrace the history of oceanography and marine biology (and Prince Albert's contribution to the field) through photographs, old equipment, numerous specimens and interactive displays.

Le Rocher HISTORIC SITE
Monaco Ville, also called Le Rocher, is the only part of Monaco to have retained its original old town, complete with small, windy medieval lanes. The old town thrusts skywards on a pistol-shaped rock, its strategic location overlooking the sea that became the stronghold of the Grimaldi dynasty. There are various staircases up to Le Rocher; the best route up is via Rampe Major, which starts from place d'Armes near the port.

✗ Eating

French and Italian cuisine prevail, though you'll find a full line-up of international fare. Don't miss the quintessential Monégasque speciality, *barbajuans* (deep-fried ravioli). Key restaurant zones include bd des Moulins near the Casino, the Les Condamines port and market, and the narrow streets behind the cathedral in Le Rocher.

★**Marché de la Condamine** MARKET $
(www.facebook.com/marche.condamine; 15 place d'Armes; ☺7am-3pm Mon-Sat, to 2pm Sun) For tasty, excellent-value fare around shared tables, hit Monaco's fabulous food court, tucked beneath the arches behind the open-air place d'Armes market. Rock-bottom budget faves include fresh pasta from **Maison des Pâtes** (📞93 50 95 77; pasta €6.40-12; ☺7am-3.30pm) and traditional Niçois *socca* from **Chez Roger** (📞93 50 80 20; socca €3; ☺10am-3pm); there's also pizza and seafood from **Le Comptoir**, truffle cuisine from **Truffle Bistrot**, a deli, a cafe, a cheesemonger and more.

★**La Montgolfière** FUSION $$$
(📞97 98 61 59; www.lamontgolfiere.mc; 16 rue Basse; 3-/4-course menu €47/54; ☺noon-2pm & 7.30-9.30pm Mon, Tue & Thu-Sat) Monégasque chef Henri Geraci has worked in some of the Riviera's top restaurants, but he's now happily settled at his own establishment down a shady alleyway near the palace. Escoffier-trained, he's faithful to the French classics, but his travels have inspired a fondness for Asian flavours, so expect some exotic twists. The restaurant's small and sought after, so reserve ahead.

ⓘ Information

Tourist Office (📞92 16 61 16; www.visitmonaco.com; 2a bd des Moulins; ☺9am-7pm Mon-Sat, 11am-1pm Sun)

ⓘ Getting There & Away

Trains run about every 20 minutes to Nice (€4.10, 25 minutes). Access to the **station** (av Prince Pierre) is through pedestrian tunnels, lifts and escalators from allée Lazare Sauvaigo, pont Ste-Dévote, place Ste-Dévote and bd de Belgique/bd du Jardin Exotique.

CORSICA

The rugged island of Corsica (Corse in French) is officially a part of France but remains fiercely proud of its own culture, history and language. It's one of the Mediterranean's most dramatic islands, with a bevy of beautiful beaches, glitzy ports and a mountainous, maquis-covered interior to explore, as well as a wild, independent spirit all of its own.

Ajaccio

POP 68,490

Commanding a lovely sweep of bay, the handsome city of Ajaccio has the self-confidence that comes with a starring role in world history. Looming over this elegant port city is the spectre of Corsica's great general: Napoléon Bonaparte was born here in 1769 and the city is dotted with statues and museums relating to him.

◎ Sights & Activities

Kiosks on the quayside at the foot of place du Maréchal Foch sell tickets for seasonal boat trips around the Golfe d'Ajaccio and Îles Sanguinaires (adult/child €27/15), and excursions to the Réserve Naturelle de Scandola (adult/child €58/38).

Maison Bonaparte   MUSEUM

(📞 04 95 21 43 89; www.musees-nationaux-napo leoniens.org; rue St-Charles; adult/child €7/free; ⏰ 10am-12.30pm & 1.15-5.30pm Tue-Sun Apr-Sep, 10.30am-12.30pm & 1.15-4.30pm Tue-Sun Oct-Mar) Unremarkable from the outside, the old-town house where Napoléon was born and spent his first nine years was ransacked by Corsican nationalists in 1793, requisitioned by English troops from 1794 to 1796, and eventually rebuilt by his mother. It's now preserved as a museum, filled with interesting displays and memorabilia despite the loss of its original furnishings and decor. Highlights include a glass medallion containing a lock of Napoléon's hair.

Palais Fesch –
Musée des Beaux-Arts   GALLERY

(📞 04 95 26 26 26; www.musee-fesch.com; 50-52 rue du Cardinal Fesch; adult/child €8/5; ⏰ 9.15am-6pm May-Sep, 9am-5pm Oct-Apr) Established by Napoléon's uncle, cardinal Joseph Fesch (1763–1839), Ajaccio's superb art museum holds the largest French collection of Italian paintings outside the Louvre. Masterpieces by Titian, Fra Bartolomeo, Veronese, Bellini and Botticelli – look out for his *Vierge à l'Enfant Soutenu par un Ange* (Mother and Child Supported by an Angel) – are complemented by temporary exhibitions. Several rooms are devoted to Napoléon and his family, with one unlikely painting showing Napoléon atop a dromedary.

🛏 Sleeping & Eating

Key spots to linger over a lazy lunch include waterfront quai Napoléon at the old port, the main commercial street cours Napoléon, the car-free place de Gaulle, and the citadel end of beach-bound bd Pascal Rossini.

Hôtel Napoléon   HOTEL **$$**

(📞 04 95 51 54 00; www.hotel-napoleon-ajaccio. fr; 4 rue Lorenzo Vero; d €130-150; ❄ 🛜) The warmth of a family-run hotel, coupled with a prime location on a side street in the heart of town, make the Napoléon an excellent midrange choice. Rooms are clean, bright and comfortable, despite their rather uninspiring decor; some of the nicest are on the 7th floor, with high ceilings and tall shuttered windows looking out on a leafy backyard.

⭐**Hôtel Demeure**
Les Mouettes   BOUTIQUE HOTEL **$$$**

(📞 04 95 50 40 40; www.hotellesmouettes.fr; 9 cours Lucien Bonaparte; d €170-520; ⏰ Apr-Oct; ❄ 🛜 ⛱) Nestled right at the water's edge, 1.5km west of the old town, this colonnaded, peach-coloured 19th-century mansion is a dream. Views of the bay from its terraces – some rooms have their own private ones – and (heated) pool are exquisite; you may spot dolphins at dawn or dusk. Inside, the decor is elegantly understated and the service superb.

⭐**Le 20123**   CORSICAN **$$**

(📞 04 95 21 50 05; www.20123.fr; 2 rue du Roi de Rome; menu €36.50; ⏰ 7-11pm Apr-Oct, closed Mon Nov-Mar) This fabulous, one-of-a-kind restaurant originated in the village of Pila Canale (postcode 20123). When the owner moved to Ajaccio, the village came too – water fountain, life-sized dolls, central square and all. That might sound tacky, but it works; lively year-round, it's a charming, characterful night out, where everyone feasts on a seasonal four-course menu that's rich in meaty traditional cuisine.

⭐**L'Altru Versu**   BISTRO **$$**

(📞 04 95 50 05 22; www.facebook.com/mezzac quiresto; rte des Sanguinaires; mains €18-38, menus €29-54; ⏰ 12.30-2pm & 7.30-10.30pm Thu-Mon, plus 7.30-10.30pm Tue & Wed mid-May–mid-Oct, closed Jan & Feb) At this perennial favourite on Ajaccio's waterfront, 2.5km west of the old town, magnificent sea views complement the exquisite gastronomic creations of the Mezzacqui brothers (Jean-Pierre front of house, David powering the kitchen), from crispy minted prawns with pistachio cream to pork with honey and clementine zest.

ℹ Information

Tourist Office (📞 04 95 51 53 03; www. ajaccio-tourisme.com; 3 bd du Roi Jérôme; ⏰ 8am-8pm Mon-Sat, 9am-1pm Sun Jul-Aug, shorter hours Sep-June, closed Sun Nov-Mar; 🛜)

ℹ Getting There & Around

AIR
The **Aéroport d'Ajaccio Napoléon Bonaparte** (📞 04 95 23 56 56; www.2a.cci.fr/Aeroport

-Napoleon-Bonaparte-Ajaccio), 6km east of the town centre around the bay, is connected with the French mainland, and in summer with London Stansted, by Air Corsica. It's linked by the hourly bus 8 (€5, 30 minutes) to Ajaccio's train station (bus stop Marconajo). A taxi into town will cost around €25.

BOAT

Corsica Linea (☑ 04 95 57 69 10, 08 25 88 80 88; www.corsicalinea.com), **Corsica Ferries** (☑ 08 25 09 50 95; www.corsica-ferries.fr) and **La Méridionale** (☑ 04 91 99 45 09, 09 70 83 13 20; www.lameridionale.com) sail to the French mainland ports of Toulon (seven to 11 hours), Nice (6¼ to 10 hours) and Marseille (12 hours) from Ajaccio's **Gare Maritime** (☑ 04 95 51 55 45; quai L'Herminier). Buy tickets before sailings inside the combined bus and ferry terminal.

BUS

Local bus companies have ticket kiosks inside the ferry terminal building, the arrival/departure point for buses. Daily services include Bonifacio (€20, three hours), Porto (€12, two hours) and Porto-Vecchio (€20, 3¼ hours).

TRAIN

Services from the **train station** (☑ 04 95 23 11 03; www.cf-corse.corsica; place de la Gare), 1km north of the old town and 500m north of the ferry terminal, include the following:

Bastia (€21.60, 3¾ hours, five daily)

Calvi (€25.10, 4¾ hours, two daily; change at Ponte Leccia)

Bastia

POP 43,675

The bustling old port of Bastia has an alluring magnetism. Allow yourself at least a day to drink in the narrow old-town alleyways of Terra Vecchia, the seething Vieux Port, the dramatic 16th-century citadel perched up high, and the compelling history museum.

◉ Sights & Activities

★ Terra Vecchia   OLD TOWN

Criss-crossed by narrow lanes, Terra Vecchia is Bastia's heart and soul. Shady place de l'Hôtel de Ville hosts a lively morning market on Saturday and Sunday. One block west, baroque **Chapelle de l'Immaculée Conception** (rue des Terrasses; ◷ 8am-7pm), with its elaborately painted barrel-vaulted ceiling, served as the seat of the short-lived Anglo-Corsican parliament in 1795. Further north, **Chapelle St-Roch** (rue Napoléon; ◷ 8am-7pm) holds an 18th-century organ and trompe l'œil roof.

★ Terra Nova   OLD TOWN

Looming above the harbour, Bastia's stern-walled citadel was built between the 15th and 17th centuries for the city's Genoese masters. Known as the Terra Nova, despite looking much older than the lower town, it's largely residential and uncommercialised. The amber-hued Palais des Gouverneurs now houses the Musée de Bastia, while the majestic **Cathédrale Ste-Marie** (rue de l'Évêché; ◷ 8am-noon & 2-6.30pm Mon-Sat, to 5.30pm Oct-Mar, 8am-noon Sun) and the rococo **Église Ste-Croix** (rue de l'Évêché; ◷ 9am-noon & 2-6pm Mon-Sat, to 5pm Oct-Mar), home to a mysterious black-oak crucifix found in the sea in 1428, stand side by side a few streets south.

★ Vieux Port   HARBOUR

Bastia's Vieux Port is ringed by precariously tall, pastel-coloured tenements and buzzy brasseries, and overlooked by the twin-towered **Église St-Jean Baptiste** (4 rue du Cardinal Viale Préla; ◷ 8am-noon & 3-7pm Mon-Sat). The best views of the harbour are from the citadel or the hillside park of Jardin Romieu, reached via a stately old staircase that twists up from the waterfront.

Musée de Bastia   MUSEUM

(☑ 04 95 31 09 12; www.musee-bastia.com; place du Donjon; adult/child €5/2.50, Oct-Apr free; ◷ 10am-6.30pm daily Jul & Aug, Tue-Sun May-Jun & Sep, 9am-noon & 2-5pm Tue-Sat Oct-Apr) Occupying the former palace of Bastia's Genoese governors, set into the formidable walls of the citadel, this museum retraces the city's history from its early days as a Roman trading port. Expect plenty of busts and portraits of local dignitaries such as Louis-Napoleon Mattei, inventor of the Cap Corse aperitif. Admission also gives access to the palace's lovely upper gardens, with views over the port.

⌂ Sleeping & Eating

Market stalls packed with local produce spill across place de l'Hôtel de Ville every Saturday and Sunday morning.

★ Hôtel-Restaurant La Corniche   HOTEL $$

(☑ 04 95 31 40 98; www.hotel-lacorniche.com; D31, San Martino di Lota; d €88-130; ◷ mid-Feb–Dec;

✴ 🛜 📶) Perched high in the hills, 8km along a tortuous road northwest of Bastia, this veteran family-run hotel makes a brilliant halfway house between city and wilderness. Summertime ushers in dreamy lounging in the bijou back garden, by the pool or on the panoramic terrace – the sea views will leave you smitten.

A Scudella
CORSICAN $$

(✆ 09 51 70 79 46, 06 25 27 26 25; 10 rue Pino; mains €13-18, menu €25; ⏱ 6-11.30pm Tue-Sat) Tucked down a back alley near the Vieux Port, this is a superb spot to sample traditional mountain cuisine, from appetisers of fine Corsican charcuterie and *beignets de brocciu* (sweet, lemon-scented fritters filled with ricotta-like Brocciu cheese) to *veau aux olives* (stewed veal with olives) and *flan à la châtaigne* (chestnut flan).

ℹ Information

Tourist Office (✆ 04 95 54 20 40; www. bastia-tourisme.com; place St-Nicolas; ⏱ 8am-8pm Mon-Sat, 8am-1pm & 3-7pm Sun Jul & Aug, 8am-6pm Mon-Sat, to noon Sun May, Jun, Sep & Oct, 8.30am-noon & 2-6pm Mon-Fri Nov-Apr; 🛜)

ℹ Getting There & Away

BOAT

Ferry companies including **Corsica Ferries** (✆ 08 25 09 50 95; www.corsica-ferries.fr), **Corsica Linea** (✆ 08 25 88 80 88; www.corsica linea.com), **La Méridionale** (✆ 04 91 99 45 09, 09 70 83 13 20; www.lameridionale.com) and **Moby** (✆ 09 74 56 20 75, 04 95 34 84 94; www. mobycorse.fr) have information offices at **Bastia Port** (www.bastia.port.fr); they usually open for same-day ticket sales a couple of hours before sailings. Ferries sail to/from Marseille, Toulon and Nice (mainland France), and Livorno, Savona and Genoa (Italy).

TRAIN

Services from the **train station** (www.cf-corse. corsica; av Maréchal Sébastiani) run to Ajaccio (€21.60, 3¾ hours, five daily) via Corte (€10.10, 1¾ hours), and Calvi (€16.40, 3¼ hours, two daily) via Île Rousse (€13.50, 2¾ hours).

Bonifacio

POP 3015

With its glittering harbour, dramatic perch atop creamy white cliffs, and a stout citadel teetering above the cornflower-blue waters of the Bouches de Bonifacio, this dazzling port is an essential stop. Just a short hop from Sardinia, Bonifacio has a distinctly Italianate feel: sun-bleached townhouses, dangling washing lines and murky chapels cram the web of alleyways of the old citadel, while, down below on the harbourside, brasseries and boat kiosks tout their wares to the droves of day trippers.

◉ Sights

★ Citadel
HISTORIC SITE

(Haute Ville) The great joy of visiting Bonifacio lies in strolling the tangled medieval lanes of the citadel. The paved steps of montée du Rastello and montée St-Roch lead up from the marina to its old gateway, the **Porte de Gênes**, complete with an original 16th-century drawbridge. Immediately inside, the **Bastion de l'Étendard** (adult/child €2.50/free, incl Escalier du Roi d'Aragon €3.50/free; ⏱ 9am-8pm mid-Apr–Sep, 10am-5pm rest of year) was the main stronghold of the fortified town. Built to hold heavy artillery, it now houses a small museum, and provides access to the ramparts, which offer jaw-dropping views.

Îles Lavezzi
ISLAND

(day trips from Bonifacio adult/child €35/17.50) Paradise! If you love to splash in tranquil lapis-lazuli waters, this protected clutch of uninhabited islets was made for you. The largest, the 65-hectare Île Lavezzi itself, is the most accessible. In summer, operators based at Bonifacio's marina (and also in Porto-Vecchio) offer boat trips; bring a picnic lunch.

Escalier du Roi d'Aragon
HISTORIC SITE

(adult/child €2.50/free, incl Bastion de l'Étendard €3.50/free; ⏱ 9am-sunset Apr-Oct) Only accessible from the top, this impressive staircase cuts down Bonifacio's southern cliff-face. Legend says that during the siege of 1420, Aragonese troops carved its 187 steep steps from the bottom up in a single night, only to be rebuffed by Bonifacio's defenders at the top. In reality the steps gave access to an underground freshwater well.

🛏 Sleeping & Eating

Hôtel Le Colomba
HOTEL $$

(✆ 04 95 73 73 44; www.hotel-bonifacio-corse.fr; 4-6 rue Simon Varsi; d €167; 🅿 ✴ 🛜) Occupying a tastefully renovated 14th-century building, this hotel enjoys a prime location on a picturesque (steep) street, bang in the heart of the old town. Rooms are simple and smallish, but fresh and decorated with amenities including wrought-iron bedsteads, country fabrics, carved bedheads and/or chequerboard tiles. Other pluses include friendly staff and breakfast served in a medieval vaulted cellar.

★ **Kissing Pigs**   CORSICAN **$**
(☑ 04 95 73 56 09; 15 quai Banda del Ferro; mains €9-23, menus €21-23; ☺11.30am-2.30pm & 6.30-11pm Tue-Sun) At water's edge beneath the citadel, and festooned with swinging sausages, this seductively cosy and friendly restaurant-cum-wine bar serves wonderfully rich and predominantly meaty Corsican dishes. Hearty casseroles include pork stewed with muscat and chestnuts, while the cheese and charcuterie platters are great for sharing. The Corsican wine list is another hit.

❶ Information

Tourist Office (☑ 04 95 73 11 88; www.boni facio.fr; 2 rue Fred Scamaroni; ☺9am-8pm Jul & Aug, shorter hours rest of year, closed Sat & Sun Nov-Mar; ☎)

❶ Getting There & Around

AIR
Aéroport de Figari-Sud-Corse (☑ 04 95 71 10 10; www.2a.cci.fr/Aeroport-Figari-Sud-Corse), 20km north of Bonifacio, welcomes domestic flights from France, plus seasonal services from London Stansted on Air Corsica, and London Gatwick on EasyJet. There's no shuttle-bus service to Bonifacio, though **Transports Rossi** (☑ 04 95 73 11 88; www.corsicabus.org) runs shuttles to Porto-Vecchio. Car rental is available, while a taxi into Bonifacio costs about €45.

BOAT
Italian ferry operators **Moby** (☑ 04 95 34 84 94, 09 74 56 20 75; www.mobycorse.fr) and **Blu Navy** (☑ 05 65 26 97 10; www.blunavytraghetti. com) run seasonal boats between Bonifacio and Santa Teresa Gallura (Sardinia); sailing time is 50 minutes.

BUS
Eurocorse Voyages (☑ 04 95 21 06 30; www. eurocorse.com) runs daily buses to Porto-Vecchio (€8, 30 minutes) and Ajaccio (€20, three hours).

SURVIVAL GUIDE

❶ Directory A–Z

ACCESSIBLE TRAVEL
While France presents evident challenges for *visiteurs handicapés* (disabled visitors), particularly those with mobility issues – think cobblestones, cafe-lined streets that are a nightmare to navigate in a wheelchair *(fauteuil roulant)*, a lack of kerb ramps, older public facilities and many budget hotels without lifts – efforts are being made to improve the situation.
➡ Paris' tourist office runs the excellent 'Tourisme & Handicap' initiative whereby museums, cultural attractions, hotels and restaurants that provide access or special assistance or facilities for those with physical, mental, visual and/or hearing disabilities display a special logo at their entrances. For a list of qualifying places, go to www.parisinfo.com and click on 'Practical Paris'.

Accès Plus (☑ 03 69 32 26 26, 08 90 64 06 50; www.accessibilite.sncf.com) is a SNCF assistance service for rail travellers with disabilities.

Tourisme et Handicaps (☑ 01 44 11 10 41; www.tourisme-handicaps.org; 43 rue Marx Dormoy, 18e) issues the 'Tourisme et Handicap' label to tourist sites, restaurants and hotels that comply with strict accessibility and usability standards.

ACCOMMODATION
Be it a fairy-tale château, a boutique hideaway or floating pod on a lake, France has accommodation to suit every taste and pocket.

B&Bs Enchanting properties with maximum five rooms.

Camping Sites range from wild and remote to brash resorts with pools, slides etc.

Hostels New-wave hostels are design-driven, lifestyle spaces with single and double rooms as well as dorms.

Hotels Hotels embrace every budget and taste. Breakfast is rarely included in rates.

Refuges and Gîtes d'Étape Huts for hikers on trails in mountainous areas.

INTERNET ACCESS
➡ Wi-fi (pronounced 'wee-fee' in French) is available at major airports, in most hotels, and at many cafes, restaurants, museums and tourist offices.

➡ In cities free wi-fi is available in hundreds of public places, including parks, libraries and municipal buildings. In Paris look for a purple 'Zone Wi-Fi' sign. To connect, select the 'PARIS_WI-FI_' network. Sessions are limited to two hours (renewable). For complete details and a map of hot spots, see www.paris.fr/wifi.

→ Tourist offices is some larger cities, including Lyon and Bordeaux, rent out pocket-sized mobile wi-fi devices that you carry around with you, ensuring a fast wi-fi connection while roaming the city.

LEGAL MATTERS

→ French police have wide powers of search and seizure and can ask you to prove your identity at any time – whether or not there is 'probable cause'.

→ Foreigners must be able to prove their legal status in France (eg with a passport, visa or residency permit) without delay.

→ French law does not distinguish between 'hard' and 'soft' drugs; penalties can be severe.

LGBT+ TRAVELLERS

Laissez-faire perfectly sums up France's liberal attitude towards homosexuality and people's private lives in general.

→ Paris has been a thriving gay and lesbian centre since the late 1970s, and most major organisations are based there today. Bordeaux, Lille and Lyon are among other LGBT-active towns.

→ Attitudes towards homosexuality tend to be more conservative in the countryside and villages.

→ France's lesbian scene is less public than its gay male counterpart and is centred mainly on women's cafes and bars.

→ Same-sex marriage has been legal in France since May 2013.

→ Gay Pride marches are held in major French cities mid-May to early July.

OPENING HOURS

Banks 9am–noon and 2pm–5pm Monday to Friday or Tuesday to Saturday

Bars 7pm–1am

Cafes 7am–11pm

Clubs 10pm–3am, 4am or 5am Thursday to Saturday

Restaurants Noon–2.30pm and 7pm–11pm six days a week

Shops 10am–noon and 2pm–7pm Monday to Saturday; longer, and including Sunday, for shops in defined ZTIs (international tourist zones)

PUBLIC HOLIDAYS

New Year's Day (Jour de l'An) 1 January

Easter Sunday & Monday (Pâques & Lundi de Pâques) Late March/April

May Day (Fête du Travail) 1 May

Victoire 1945 8 May

Ascension Thursday (Ascension) May; on the 40th day after Easter

Pentecost/Whit Sunday & Whit Monday (Pentecôte & Lundi de Pentecôte) Mid-May to mid-June; on the seventh Sunday after Easter

Bastille Day/National Day (Fête Nationale) 14 July

Assumption Day (Assomption) 15 August

All Saints' Day (Toussaint) 1 November

Remembrance Day (L'onze Novembre) 11 November

Christmas (Noël) 25 December

SAFE TRAVEL

France is generally a safe place, despite a rise in crime and terrorism in recent years.

→ Never leave baggage unattended, especially at airports or train stations.

→ At museums and monuments, bags are routinely checked on entry.

→ Sporadic train strikes and striking taxi drivers can disrupt travel.

→ France's hunting season is September to February: if you see signs reading *'chasseurs'* or *'chasse gardée'* tacked to trees, don't enter the area.

→ In the Alps, check the day's avalanche report and stick to groomed pistes. Summer thunderstorms can be sudden and violent.

→ On the Atlantic Coast watch for powerful tides and undertows; only swim on beaches with lifeguards.

TELEPHONE

→ French mobile phone numbers begin with 06 or 07.

→ France uses GSM 900/1800, which is compatible with the rest of Europe and Australia but not with the North American GSM 1900 or the totally different system in Japan (though some North Americans have tri-band phones that work here).

→ It is usually cheaper to buy a local SIM card from a French provider such as Orange, SFR, Bouygues or Free Mobile, which gives you a local phone number. To do this, ensure your phone is unlocked.

→ Recharge cards are sold at most *tabacs* (tobacconist-newsagents), supermarkets and online through websites such as Topengo (www.topengo.fr) or Sim-OK (https://recharge. sim-ok.com).

→ To call France from abroad dial your country's international access code, then 33 (France's country code), then the 10-digit local number without the initial zero.

→ To call internationally from France dial 00, the country code, the area code (without the initial zero if there is one) and the local number.

ℹ Getting There & Away

AIR

International airports include the following; there are many smaller ones serving European destinations only.

Aéroport de Charles de Gaulle, Paris (p397)

Aéroport d'Orly, Paris (p397)

Aéroport Lyon-St Exupéry (p421)

Aéroport Marseille-Provence (p434)

Aéroport Nice-Côte d'Azur (p442)

LAND

Bus

Eurolines (☏ 08 92 89 90 91; www.eurolines. eu), a grouping of 32 long-haul coach operators (including the UK's National Express), links France with cities all across Europe, Morocco and Russia.

Flixbus (www.flixbus.com) offers low-cost, intercity bus travel between 27 countries in Europe aboard comfy buses equipped with a toilet, snacks, plug sockets to keep devices charged and free wi-fi, and runs night services too.

Car & Motorcycle

A right-hand-drive vehicle brought to France from the UK or Ireland must have deflectors affixed to the headlights to avoid dazzling oncoming traffic.

A foreign motor vehicle entering France must display a sticker or licence plate identifying its country of registration.

High-speed **Eurotunnel Le Shuttle** (☏ France 08 10 63 03 04; UK 08443 35 35 35; www.euro tunnel.com) trains whisk bicycles, motorcycles, cars and coaches in 35 minutes from Folkestone through the Channel Tunnel to Coquelles, 5km southwest of Calais. Shuttles run 24 hours a day, with up to three departures an hour during peak periods. Fares for a car, including up to nine passengers, start at £30 (€37).

Train

Rail services – including a dwindling number of overnight services to/from Spain, Italy and Germany, and Eurostar services to/from the UK – link France with virtually every country in Europe.
➜ Book tickets and get train information from Rail Europe (www.raileurope.com). In the UK contact Railteam (www.railteam.co.uk).

SEA

Regular ferries travel to France from the UK, Ireland and Italy. To get the best fares, check Ferry Savers (www.ferrysavers.com). Several ferry companies ply the waters between Corsica and Italy.

Brittany Ferries (www.brittany-ferries.co.uk) Links between England/Ireland and Brittany and Normandy.

Condor Ferries (www.condorferries.co.uk) Ferries between England/Channel Islands and Normandy and Brittany.

Corsica Linea (www.corsicalinea.com) Sailings to/from France and Sardinia, Tunisia and Algeria.

P&O Ferries (www.poferries.com) Ferries between England and northern France.

ℹ Getting Around

AIR

France's high-speed train network renders rail travel between some cities (eg from Paris to Lyon, Marseille and Bordeaux) faster and easier than flying.

Air France (www.airfrance.com) and its subsidiaries Hop! (www.hop.com) and Transavia (www.transavia.com) control the lion's share of France's domestic airline industry.

Budget carriers offering flights within France include EasyJet (www.easyjet.com), Twin Jet (www.twinjet.net) and Air Corsica (www.air corsica.com).

BICYCLE

The SNCF does its best to make travelling with a bicycle easy; see www.velo.sncf.com for full details.

Most French cities and towns have at least one bike shop that rents out *vélos tout terrains* (mountain bikes; around €15 a day), known as VTTs, as well as more road-oriented *vélos tout chemin* (VTCs) or cheaper city bikes. You usually have to leave ID and/or a deposit (often a credit-card slip of €250) that you forfeit if the bike is damaged or stolen.

A growing number of cities have automatic bike-rental systems, intended to encourage cycling as a form of urban transport, with computerised pick-up and drop-off sites all over town.

BUS

Buses are widely used for short-distance travel within *départements,* especially in rural areas with relatively few train lines (eg Brittany and Normandy). Unfortunately, services in some regions are infrequent and slow, in part because they were designed to get children to their schools in the towns rather than transport visitors around the countryside.

Some less-busy train lines have been replaced by SNCF buses, which, unlike regional buses, are free if you've got a rail pass.

CAR & MOTORCYCLE

A car gives you exceptional freedom and allows you to visit more remote parts of France.
➜ All drivers must carry a national ID card or passport; a valid driving licence, car-ownership papers, known as a *carte grise* (grey card), and proof of third-party (liability) insurance.

SNCF TRAIN FARES & DISCOUNTS

The Basics

➧ 1st-class travel, where available, costs 20% to 30% extra.

➧ Ticket prices for some trains, including most TGVs, are pricier during peak periods.

➧ The further in advance you reserve, the lower the fares.

➧ Children under four travel for free, or for €9 with a *forfait bambin* to any destination if they need a seat.

➧ Children aged four to 11 travel for half-price.

Discount Tickets

Prem's The SNCF's most heavily discounted, use-or-lose tickets are sold online, by phone and at ticket windows/machines. Prem's are available from Thursday evening to Monday night, for last-minute travel that weekend; Saturday-return Prem's are valid for return travel on a Saturday; and three-month Prem's can be booked a maximum of 90 days in advance.

Intercités 100% Éco can be booked from three months to the day of departure, and offer cheap tickets between any stops, in any direction, on four main lines: Paris–Toulouse, Paris–Bordeaux, Paris–Nantes and Paris–Strasbourg. A single fare costs €15 to €35.

Ouigo (www.ouigo.com) is a low-cost TGV service whereby you can travel on high-speed TGVs for a snip of the usual price. Purchase tickets online from three weeks until four hours before departure.

Discount Cards

Reductions of 25% to 60% are available with several discount cards (valid for one year):

Carte Jeune (€50) Available to travellers aged 12 to 27.

Carte Enfant+ (€75) For one to four adults travelling with a child aged four to 11.

Carte Weekend (€75) For people aged 26 to 59. Discounts on return journeys of at least 200km that either include a Saturday night away or only involve travel on a Saturday or Sunday.

Carte Sénior+ (€60) For travellers over 60.

➧ Many French motorways (*autoroutes*) are fitted with toll (*péage*) stations that charge a fee based on the distance you've travelled; factor in these costs when driving. See www.autoroutes.fr.

➧ In the cities, traffic and finding a place to park can be a major headache. During holiday periods and bank-holiday weekends, roads throughout France also get backed up with traffic jams (*bouchons*).

➧ **Bison Futé** (www.bison-fute.gouv.fr) is also a good source of information about traffic conditions.

➧ Theft from cars can be a major problem in France, especially in the south.

TRAIN

➧ France's superb rail network is run by the **SNCF** (Société Nationale des Chemins de fer Français, French National Railway Company; ☑ France 36 35, abroad +33 8 92 35 35 35; http://en.voyages-sncf.com); many rural towns not on the rail network are served by SNCF buses instead.

➧ Few train stations have *consignes automatiques* (left-luggage lockers). In larger stations you can leave your bags in a *consigne manuelle* (staffed left-luggage facility) where items are handed over in person and X-rayed before being stowed. Charges are around €7 for up to 10 hours and €12 for 24 hours; payment must be made in cash.

➧ Before boarding the train, paper tickets must be validated (*composter*) by time-stamping them in a *composteur,* a yellow post located on the way to the platform.

Germany

POP 83.2 MILLION

Best Places to Eat

➡ Schwein (p470)

➡ Stadtpfeiffer (p477)

➡ Fraunhofer (p486)

➡ Bürgerspital Weinstube (p492)

➡ Zu den 12 Aposteln (p504)

Best Places to Stay

➡ 25hours Hotel Bikini (p469)

➡ Hotel Schloss Eckberg (p475)

➡ Flushing Meadows (p485)

➡ Hotel Reikartz Vier Jahreszeiten (p489)

Why Go?

Few countries have had as much impact on the world as Germany. It has given us the printing press, the automobile, aspirin and historical heavyweights from Luther to Bach to Hitler. You'll encounter history in towns where streets were laid out long before Columbus set sail, and in castles that loom above prim, half-timbered villages where flower boxes billow with crimson geraniums. The great cities – Berlin, Munich and Hamburg among them – come in more flavours than a jar of jelly beans, but will all wow you with a cultural kaleidoscope that spans the arc from art museums and high-brow opera to naughty cabaret and underground clubs. Germany's storybook landscapes will also likely leave an even bigger imprint on your memories. There's something undeniably artistic in the way Germany's scenery unfolds from the dune-fringed northern coasts via romantic river valleys to the off-the-charts Alpine splendour.

When to Go
Berlin

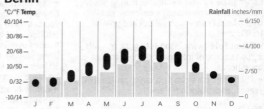

Jun–Aug Warm summers cause Germans to shed their clothes; night never seems to come.

Sep Radiant foliage and often-sunny skies invite outdoor pursuits; festivals galore (Oktoberfest anyone?).

Dec It's icy, it's cold but lines are short and Alpine slopes and twinkly Christmas markets beckon.

Entering the Country

Entering Germany is usually a very straightforward procedure. If you're arriving from any of the 25 other Schengen
countries, such as the Netherlands, Poland, Austria or the
Czech Republic, you no longer have to show your passport or
go through customs in Germany, no matter which nationality
you are. If you're coming in from non-Schengen countries, full
border procedures apply.

ITINERARIES

Three Days

Come on, is that all you got? If the answer really is yes,
drive down the Romantic Road (p490), stopping in Rothenburg ob der Tauber (p491) and Füssen (p489), then
spend the rest of your time in Munich (p481).

Five Days

Spend a couple of days in Berlin (p458), head south to
Dresden (p474) and Nuremberg (p493) or Bamberg
(p494) for half a day each and wrap up your trip in Munich (p481) and surrounds.

One Week

This gives you a little bit of time to tailor a tour beyond
the highlights mentioned above. Art fans might want
to build Cologne (p508) or Düsseldorf (p511) into
their itinerary; romantics could consider Heidelberg
(p498), a Rhine cruise or a trip down the Romantic Road
(p490); while outdoorsy types are likely to be lured by
Garmisch-Partenkirchen (p488), Berchtesgaden (p488)
or the Black Forest (p499).

Essential Food & Drink

As in Britain, Germany has redeemed itself gastronomically
over the past decade. These days culinary offerings are often
slimmed down and healthier as many chefs let seasonal,
regional and organic ingredients steer their menus. Of course,
if you crave traditional comfort food, you'll still find plenty of
pork, potatoes and cabbage on the menus. Here are our top-
five classic German culinary treats:

Sausage (Wurst) A favourite snack food, links come in
1500 varieties, including finger-sized Nürnbergers, crunchy
Thüringers and tomato-sauce-drowned Currywurst.

Schweinshaxe The mother of all pork dishes, this one presents itself as entire knuckle roasted to crispy perfection.

Königsberger Klopse A simple but elegant plate of golf-ball-
sized veal meatballs in a caper-laced white sauce and served
with a side of boiled potatoes and beetroot.

Bread Get Germans talking about bread and often their
eyes will water as they describe their favourite type – usually
hearty and wholegrained in infinite variations.

AT A GLANCE

Area 356,866 sq km

Capital Berlin

Country Code ☑ 49

Currency euro (€)

Emergency ☑ 112

Language German

Time Central European
Time (GMT/UTC plus
one hour)

Visas Schengen rules
apply

Sleeping Price Ranges

The following price ranges
refer to the cost of a double
room with private bathroom,
including 7% VAT.

€ less than €80

€€ €80– 160

€€€ more than €160

Eating Price Ranges

The following price ranges
refer to a standard main
course. Unless otherwise
stated, 19% tax is included
in the price.

€ less than €12

€€ €12–22

€€€ more than €22

Resources

**German National Tourist
Office**
(www.germany.travel)

Deutsche Welle
(www.dw.com)

Facts About Germany
(www.tatsachen-ueber-
deutschland.de/en)

GERMANY

Germany Highlights

① Berlin (p458)
Discovering your inner party animal in the capital; save sleep for somewhere else as there's no time here with all the clubs, museums and bars.

② Munich (p481)
Experiencing Oktoberfest, a bacchanale of suds, or just soaking up the vibe in a beer garden.

③ Bamberg
(p494) Going slow in Germany's alluring small towns like this gem, with winding lanes, smoked beer and a lack of cliché.

④ Cologne (p508)
Comparing the soaring spires of the Dom with the slinky glasses of this city's famous beer.

⑤ Black Forest
(p499) Going cuckoo in the Black Forest, discovering its chilly

Label *Labe*

PRAGUE ✪

CZECH
REPUBLIC

Plzeň ●

● Passau

AUSTRIA

Klagenfurt ●

Bavarian Forest

Zwickau ●

Plauen ●

Hof ●

Marktredwitz ●

Regensburg ●

● Landshut

● Rosenheim

Chiemsee

Berchtesgaden ●

Salz

Salzburg ●

Hohe Tauern
National Park

Bressanone ●

Kitzbüheler Alpen

Kufstein ●

Innsbruck ●

Bavarian Alps

Mittenwald ●

Lech

Zugspitze
(2962m) ▲

Garmisch-
Partenkirchen

ITALY

Weimar ●
Erfurt ●

Thuringian Forest

Coburg ●

Bayreuth ●

Erlangen ●

Nuremberg ● ⑩

Schweinfurt ●

Bamberg ● ③

Suhl ●

Fulda ●

Würzburg ●

Rothenburg
ob der
Tauber ●

Nördlingen ●

Ingolstadt ●

Dachau ●

Munich ● ②

Augsburg ●

BAVARIA

Danube

Memmingen ●

Kempten ●

Füssen ● Schloss, ⑨
Neuschwanstein

Oberammergau ●

Wieskirche ✝

Oberstdorf ●

Lechtaler Alpen

*Lake
Starnberg*

Aachen ●
Cologne ④

Bonn ●

Siegen ●

Marburg ●

Giessen ●

HESSE

Frankfurt-
am-Main ●

Offenbach ●
Wiesbaden ●
Mainz ●

Darmstadt ●

Aschaffenburg ●

Main

Heilbronn ●

Stuttgart ●

Ulm ●

Tübingen ●

BADEN-
WÜRTTEMBERG

Konstanz ●

*Lake
Constance*

Meersburg ●

Lindau ●

Friedrichshafen ●

Zürich ●

SWITZERLAND

VADUZ ✪

Rhein

Koblenz ●

Braubach ●

Burg
Eltz ●

Cochem ●

St Goar ●

Bacharach ●

Bingen ●

Bernkastel-
Kues ●

Trier ● ⑧

RHINELAND-
PALATINATE

LUXEMBOURG

LUXEMBOURG
CITY ✪

BELGIUM

Kaiserslautern ●

Saarbrücken ●

Worms ●

Mannheim ●

Heidelberg ●

Speyer ●

Karlsruhe ●

Baden-
Baden ●

Pforzheim ●

Offenburg ●

Black Forest ⑤

Triberg ●

Höllental

Freiburg im
Breisgau ●

Strasbourg ●

FRANCE

Vallée de la Meurthe

Épinal ●

Nancy ●

Rhine

Rhein

Basel ●

Besançon ●

*Lac de
Neuchâtel*

crags, misty peaks and
endless trails.

⑥ Dresden (p474)
Getting into the
swing of this city,
with a creative
culture beyond the
restorations.

⑦ Hamburg (p514)
Cruising around
one of the world's
great harbours, then
following the trail of
the Beatles.

⑧ Trier (p507)
Discovering the best-
preserved Roman ruins
north of the Alps in this
delightful wine town on
the Moselle.

**⑨ Schloss
Neuschwanstein**
(p490) Diving into
the mind of a loopy
Bavarian monarch at
this dreamy palace
cradled by the Alps.

⑩ Nuremberg
(p493) Tapping into
this city's medieval
roots, enjoying the
famous local sausages,
and pondering its Nazi
past.

BERLIN

📖 030 / POP 3.71 MILLION

Berlin is a bon vivant, passionately feasting on the smorgasbord of life and never taking things – or itself – too seriously. Its unique blend of glamour and grit is bound to mesmerise anyone keen to connect with its vibrant culture, superb museums, fabulous food, intense nightlife and tangible history.

When it comes to creativity, the sky's the limit in Berlin, Europe's newest start-up capital. In the last 20 years, the city has become a giant lab of cultural experimentation thanks to an abundance of space, cheap rent and a free-wheeling spirit that nurtures and encourages new ideas.

All this trendiness is a triumph for a city that staged a revolution, was headquartered by the Nazis, bombed to bits, divided in two and finally reunited – and that was just in the 20th century! Must-sees and aimless explorations – Berlin delivers it all in one exciting and memorable package.

👁 Sights

Key sights such as the Reichstag, Brandenburger Tor and Museumsinsel cluster in the walkable historic city centre – Mitte – which also cradles the Scheunenviertel, a maze-like hipster quarter around Hackescher Markt. Further north, residential Prenzlauer Berg has a lively cafe and restaurant scene, while to the south loom the contemporary high-rises of Potsdamer Platz. Further south, gritty but cool Kreuzberg and Neukölln are party central, as is student-flavoured Friedrichshain east across the Spree River. Western Berlin's hub is Charlottenburg, with great shopping and a swish royal palace.

👁 Stasi Prison

Victims of Stasi persecution often ended up in this grim remand prison, now a memorial site officially called **Gedenkstätte Berlin-Hohenschönhausen** (Gedenkstätte Berlin-Hohenschönhausen; 📞 030-9860 8230; www.stiftung-hsh.de; Genslerstrasse 66; tours adult/concession €6/3, exhibit free; ⏰ tours in English 10.30am, 12.30pm & 2.30pm Mar-Oct, 11.30am & 2.30pm Nov-Feb, exhibit 9am-6pm, German tours more frequent; 🅿; 🚋M5). Tours – often conducted by former inmates – reveal the full extent of the terror and cruelty perpetrated upon thousands of suspected regime opponents, many utterly innocent. A permanent exhibit uses photographs, objects and a free audioguide to document daily life behind bars and also opens up the offices of the prison administration.

👁 City West & Charlottenburg

⭐ **Schloss Charlottenburg** PALACE (Charlottenburg Palace; 📞 030-320 910; www.spsg. de; Spandauer Damm 10-22; day pass to all 4 bldgs adult/concession €17/13; ⏰ hours vary by bldg; 🚌M45, 109, 309, Ⓤ Richard-Wagner-Platz, Sophie-Charlotte-Platz) Charlottenburg Palace is one of Berlin's few sites that still reflect the one-time grandeur of the Hohenzollern clan, which ruled the region from 1415 to 1918. Originally a petite summer retreat, it grew into an exquisite baroque pile with opulent private apartments, richly decorated festival halls, collections of precious porcelain and paintings by French 18th-century masters. It's lovely in fine weather, when you can fold a stroll in the palace park into a day of peeking at royal treasures.

BERLIN IN...

One Day

Book ahead for an early lift ride to the **Reichstag dome** (p461), then snap a picture of the **Brandenburger Tor** (p461) before walking quietly through the **Holocaust Memorial** (p461) and admiring the contemporary architecture of **Potsdamer Platz** (p466). Ponder Cold War madness at **Checkpoint Charlie**, then head to **Museumsinsel** (p462) for an audience with Queen Nefertiti and the Ishtar Gate. Finish up with a night of mirth and gaiety around **Hackescher Markt**.

Two Days

Kick off day two coming to grips with what life was like in divided Berlin at the **Gedenkstätte Berliner Mauer** (p467). Intensify the experience at the **DDR Museum** (p463) or on a walk along the **East Side Gallery**. Spend the afternoon soaking up the urban spirit of **Kreuzberg** (p462) with its sassy shops and street art, grab dinner along the canal, drinks around Kottbusser Tor and finish up with a night of clubbing.

Berlin

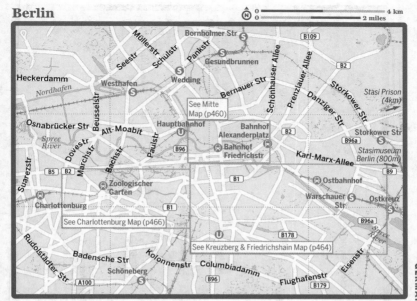

Schlossgarten Charlottenburg PARK
(Charlottenburg Palace Park; ☎030-320 910;
www.spsg.de; Spandauer Damm 20-24; ☺8am-
dusk; ☒M45, 109, 309, ⓤSophie-Charlotte-Platz,
Richard-Wagner-Platz) FREE The expansive
park behind Schloss Charlottenburg is part
formal French, part unruly English and all
picturesque playground. Hidden among
the shady paths, flower beds, lawns, mature
trees and carp pond are two smaller royal
buildings, the sombre **Mausoleum** (Spandauer Damm 10-22; €3; ☺10am-5.30pm Tue-Sun Apr-
Oct) and the dainty **Belvedere** (Spandauer
Damm 20-24; adult/concession €4/3; ☺10am-
5.30pm Tue-Sun Apr-Oct). It's a lovely place for
strolling, jogging or lazing on a sunny day.

Museum Berggruen MUSEUM
(☎030-266 424 242; www.smb.museum/mb;
Schlossstrasse 1; adult/concession incl Sammlung
Scharf-Gerstenberg €10/5; ☺10am-6pm Tue-
Fri, from 11am Sat & Sun; ℗; ☒M45, 109, 309,
ⓤRichard-Wagner-Platz, Sophie-Charlotte-Platz,
Ⓢ Westend) Classic modern art is the ammo
of this delightful museum where Picasso is
especially well represented, with paintings,
drawings and sculptures from all his major
creative phases. Elsewhere it's off to Paul
Klee's emotional world, Henri Matisse's paper cut-outs, Alberto Giacometti's elongated

sculptures and a sprinkling of African art
that inspired both Klee and Picasso.

**Schloss Charlottenburg –
Altes Schloss** PALACE
(Old Palace; ☎030-320 910; www.spsg.de;
Spandauer Damm 10-22; adult/concession
€10/7; ☺10am-5.30pm Tue-Sun Apr-Oct, to
5pm Tue-Sun Nov & Dec, to 4.30pm Tue-Sun Jan-
Mar; ☒M45, 109, 309, ⓤRichard-Wagner-Platz,
Sophie-Charlotte-Platz) Fronted by Andreas
Schlüter's equestrian statue of the *Great
Elector* (1699), the baroque living quarters
of Friedrich I and Sophie-Charlotte are an
extravaganza in stucco, brocade and overall
opulence. Highlights include the Oak Gallery, a wood-panelled festival hall draped
in family portraits; the charming Oval Hall
overlooking the park; Friedrich I's bedchamber, with the first-ever bathroom in
a baroque palace; the fabulous Porcelain
Chamber, smothered in Chinese and Japanese blue ware; and the Eosander Chapel,
with its trompe l'oeil arches.

◉ Friedrichshain

★East Side Gallery LANDMARK
(Map p464; www.eastsidegallery-berlin.de; Mühlenstrasse btwn Oberbaumbrücke & Ostbahnhof;

GERMANY BERLIN

Mitte

5 Hamburger Bahnhof –
Museum für Gegenwart

Invalidenstr Hannoversche
Str

Chausseestr

Gedenkstätte Berliner
Mauer (1km)
Museum für
Naturkunde (150m)

Berlin Tourist
Info – Hauptbahnhof
(500m)

Prater Garten (1.5km);
Mrs Robinson's (2.2km)

EastSeven Berlin
Hostel (660m)

Linienstr

Mulackstr

Steinstr

Gormannstr

Rosa-
Luxemburg-
Platz

Rosa-
Luxemburg-
Platz

Max-Beer-Str

Alte Schönhauser Str

Weinmeisterstr

Rosenthaler Str

SCHEUNENVIERTEL

Gipsstr

Sophienstr

Grosse Hamburger Str

14

19

Koppenplatz

Augustsstr

Krausnickstr

15

Tucholskystr

Linienstr

Torstr

Oranienburger Str

Oranienburger
Tor

Friedrichstr

Oranienburger Str

Johannisstr

Ziegelstr

Kalkscheunenstr

20

13

Monbijou
Park

Monbijouplatz

Hackescher
Markt

Hackescher
Markt

Burgstr

Weinmeisterstr

Münzstr

Dircksenstr

Rochstr

Rosenstr

Spandauer Str

Berlin Tourist Office –
Alexanderplatz (150m);
Zeiss Grossplanetarium (2.4km)

Gontardstr

Alexanderplatz

17 18

4

Fernsehturm

Karl-Liebknecht-Str

Rathausstr

Grunerstr

Judenstr

Molkenmarkt

Poststr

Rathausstr

Spree River

Liebknechtbrücke

DDR
Museum

2

12

Lustgarten

11

Am Zeughaus

Schlossbrücke

Oberwallstr

Spreekanal

Deutsches
Historisches
Museum

3

Bebelplatz

21

Unter den Linden

Charlottenstr

Mittelstr

Dorotheenstr

Friedrichstr

Friedrichstr

Georgenstr

Planckstr

Am Kupfergraben

Geschwister-Scholl-Str

Hegelplatz

Bahnhof
Friedrichstr

Am Zirkus

Bertolt-
Brecht-Platz

Reichstagufer

Schiffbauerdamm

Reinhardtstr

Marienstr

Albrechtstr

16

Schumannstr

Karlplatz

Charité-
Platz

Luisenstr

Hannoversche
Str

Museumsinsel

Pergamonmuseum

Neues
Museum

6 10

8

7

Friedrichsbrücke

Friedrichstr

Spree River

Reichstag

9

Bundestag

Platz der
Republik

Paul-Löbe-Allee

Otto-von-
Bismarck-Allee

Spreebogenpark

Alexanderufer

Kapelleufer

Scheidemannstr

Brandenburger
Tor

Brandenburger
Tor

Pariser
Platz

1

Platz des
18 März

Berlin Tourist Info – Brandenburg Gate

Brandenburger Gate

Mitte

⊙ 24hr; Ⓤ Warschauer Strasse, Ⓢ Ostbahnhof, Warschauer Strasse) 𝙁𝙍𝙀𝙀 In 1989, after 28 years, the Berlin Wall, that grim and grey divider of humanity, was finally torn down. Most of it was quickly dismantled, but along Mühlenstrasse, paralleling the Spree, a 1.3km stretch became the East Side Gallery, the world's largest open-air mural collection. In more than 100 paintings, dozens of international artists translated the era's global euphoria and optimism into a mix of political statements, drug-induced musings and truly artistic visions.

⊙ Historic Mitte

★ Brandenburger Tor   LANDMARK
(Brandenburg Gate; Map p460; Pariser Platz; Ⓢ Brandenburger Tor, Ⓤ Brandenburger Tor) A symbol of division during the Cold War, the landmark Brandenburg Gate now epitomises German reunification. Carl Gotthard Langhans found inspiration in Athens' Acropolis for the elegant triumphal arch, completed in 1791 as the royal city gate.

★ Reichstag   HISTORIC BUILDING
(Map p460; www.bundestag.de; Platz der Republik 1, Visitors Centre, Scheidemannstrasse; ⊙ lift 8am-midnight, last entry 9.45pm, Visitors Centre 8am-8pm Apr-Oct, to 6pm Nov-Mar; ♠; ▣ 100, Ⓢ Brandenburger Tor, Hauptbahnhof, Ⓤ Brandenburger Tor, Bundestag) 𝙁𝙍𝙀𝙀 It's been burned, bombed, rebuilt, buttressed by the Wall, wrapped in fabric and finally turned into the modern home of the German parliament by Norman Foster: the 1894 Reichstag is indeed one of Berlin's most iconic buildings. Its most distinctive feature, the glittering glass dome, is served by a lift and affords fabulous 360° city views.

For guaranteed access, make free reservations online; otherwise try scoring tickets at the **Reichstag Visitors' Centre** (⊙ 8am-8pm Apr-Oct, to 6pm Nov-Mar) for the same or next day. Bring ID.

★ Holocaust Memorial   MEMORIAL
(Memorial to the Murdered Jews of Europe; Map p464; ☑ 030-2639 4336; www.stiftung-denkmal. de; Cora-Berliner-Strasse 1; audioguide €3; ⊙ 24hr; Ⓢ Brandenburger Tor, Ⓤ Brandenburger Tor) 𝙁𝙍𝙀𝙀 Inaugurated in 2005, this football-field-sized memorial by American architect Peter Eisenman consists of 2711 sarcophagi-like concrete columns rising in sombre silence from the undulating ground. You're free to access this maze at any point and make your individual journey through it. For context visit the subterranean **Ort der Information** (Information Centre; Map p464; ☑ 030-7407 2929; www.holocaust-mahnmal.de; audio guide €3; ⊙ 10am-8pm Tue-Sun Apr-Sep, to 7pm Oct-Mar, last admission 45min before closing) 𝙁𝙍𝙀𝙀, whose exhibits will leave no one untouched. Audioguides and audio translations of exhibit panels are available.

★ Topographie des Terrors   MUSEUM
(Topography of Terror; Map p464; ☑ 030-2545 0950; www.topographie.de; Niederkirchner Strasse 8; ⊙ 10am-8pm, grounds close at dusk or 8pm at the latest; ▣ M41, Ⓢ Potsdamer Platz, Ⓤ Potsdamer Platz) 𝙁𝙍𝙀𝙀 In the spot where the most feared institutions of Nazi Germany (including the Gestapo headquarters and the SS central command) once stood, this compelling exhibit chronicles the stages of terror and persecution, puts a face on the perpetrators and details the impact these brutal institutions had on all of Europe. A second exhibit outside zeroes in on how life changed for Berlin and its people after the Nazis made it their capital.

GERMANY BERLIN

DON'T MISS

MORE MUSEUM ISLAND TREASURES

While the Pergamonmuseum and the Neues Museum are the highlights of Museum Island, the other three museums are no slouches in the treasure department either. Fronting the Lustgarten park the Altes Museum (p463) presents Greek, Etruscan and Roman antiquities. At the northern tip of the island, the Bode-Museum (p465) has a prized collection of European sculpture from the Middle Ages to the 18th century. Finally, there's the Alte Nationalgalerie (p465), whose thematic focus is on 19th-century European painting. A combined day pass for all five museums costs €18 (concession €9).

★ **Deutsches Historisches Museum** MUSEUM
(German Historical Museum; Map p460; ☑ 030-203 040; www.dhm.de; Unter den Linden 2; adult/concession/child under 18 incl IM Pei Bau €8/4/free; ◷ 10am-6pm; 🚋 100, 200, Ⓤ Hausvogteiplatz, Ⓢ Hackescher Markt) If you're wondering what the Germans have been up to for the past 1500 years, take a spin around the baroque Zeughaus, formerly the Prussian arsenal and now home of the German Historical Museum. Upstairs, displays concentrate on the period from the 6th century CE to the end of WWI in 1918, while the ground floor tracks the 20th century all the way through to the early years after German reunification.

★ **Gendarmenmarkt** SQUARE
(Map p464; Ⓤ Französische Strasse, Stadtmitte) This graceful square is bookended by the domed German and French cathedrals and punctuated by a grandly porticoed concert hall, the **Konzerthaus** (Map p464; ☑ 030-203 092 333; www.konzerthaus.de). It was named for the Gens d'Armes, an 18th-century Prussian regiment consisting of French Huguenot refugees.

⊙ Kreuzberg & Neukölln

★ **Jüdisches Museum** MUSEUM
(Jewish Museum; Map p464; ☑ 030-2599 3300; www.jmberlin.de; Lindenstrasse 9-14; adult/concession €8/3, audioguide €3; ◷ 10am-8pm; Ⓤ Hallesches Tor, Kochstrasse) In a landmark building by American-Polish architect Daniel Libeskind, Berlin's Jewish Museum offers a chronicle of the trials and triumphs in 2000 years of Jewish life in Germany. The exhibit smoothly navigates all major periods, from the Middle Ages via the Enlightenment to the community's post-1990 renaissance. Find out about Jewish cultural contributions, holiday traditions, the difficult road to emancipation, outstanding individuals (eg Moses Mendelssohn and Levi Strauss) and the fates of ordinary people.

König Galerie @ St Agnes Kirche GALLERY
(Map p464; ☑ 030-2610 3080; www.koeniggalerie.com; Alexandrinenstrasse 118-121; ◷ 11am-7pm Tue-Sat, from noon Sun; Ⓤ Prinzenstrasse) **FREE** If art is your religion, a pilgrimage to this church-turned-gallery is a must. Tucked into a nondescript part of Kreuzberg, this decommissioned Catholic church, designed in the mid-1960s by architect and city planner Werner Düttmann, is a prime example of Brutalist architecture in Berlin. In 2012, it was leased by the gallerist Johann König and converted into a spectacular space that presents interdisciplinary, concept-oriented and space-based art.

Deutsches Technikmuseum MUSEUM
(German Museum of Technology; Map p464; ☑ 030-902 540; http://sdtb.de/technikmuseum; Trebbiner Strasse 9; adult/concession/child under 18 €8/4/after 3pm free; ◷ 9am-5.30pm Tue-Fri, 10am-6pm Sat & Sun; Ⓟ 🏍; Ⓤ Gleisdreieck, Möckernbrücke) A roof-mounted 'candy bomber' (the plane used in the 1948 Berlin Airlift) is merely the overture to this enormous and hugely engaging shrine to technology. Fantastic for kids, the giant museum includes the world's first computer, an entire hall of vintage locomotives and exhibits on aerospace and navigation in a modern annexe. At the adjacent **Science Center Spectrum** (Map p464; ☑ 030-9025 4284; www.sdtb.de; Möckernstrasse 26; ◷ 9am-5.30pm Tue-Fri, 10am-6pm Sat & Sun; Ⓟ; Ⓤ Möckernbrücke, Gleisdreieck), entered on the same ticket, kids can participate in hands-on experiments.

⊙ Museumsinsel & Alexanderplatz

★ **Museumsinsel** MUSEUM
(Map p460; ☑ 030-266 424 242; www.smb.museum; day tickets for all 5 museums adult/concession/under 18 €18/9/free; ◷ varies by museum; 🚋 100, 200, TXL, Ⓢ Hackescher Markt, Friedrichstrasse, Ⓤ Friedrichstrasse) Walk through ancient Babylon, meet an Egyptian queen, clamber up a Greek

altar or be mesmerised by Monet's ethereal landscapes. Welcome to Museumsinsel (Museum Island), Berlin's most important treasure trove, spanning 6000 years' worth of art, artefacts, sculpture and architecture from Europe and beyond. Spread across five grand museums built between 1830 and 1930, the complex takes up the entire northern half of the little Spree Island where Berlin's settlement began in the 13th century.

★ **Pergamonmuseum**　　MUSEUM
(Map p460; ☑ 030-266 424 242; www.smb.museum; Bodestrasse 1-3; adult/concession/under 18yr €12/6/free; ☺ 10am-6pm Fri-Wed, to 8pm Thu; ☑ 100, 200, TXL, Ⓢ Hackescher Markt, Friedrichstrasse, Ⓤ Friedrichstrasse) Opening a fascinating window on to the ancient world, this palatial three-wing complex unites a rich feast of classical sculpture and monumental architecture from Greece, Rome, Babylon and the Middle East, including the radiant-blue Ishtar Gate from Babylon, the Roman Market Gate of Miletus and the Caliph's Palace of Mshatta. Note that extensive renovations put the namesake Pergamon Altar and several rooms off-limits until 2023. Budget at least two hours for this amazing place and be sure to use the free and excellent audio guide.

★ **Neues Museum**　　MUSEUM
(New Museum; Map p460; ☑ 030-266 424 242; www.smb.museum; Bodestrasse 1-3; adult/concession/under 18yr €12/6/free; ☺ 10am-6pm Fri-Wed, to 8pm Thu; ☑ 100, 200, TXL, Ⓢ Hackescher Markt, Friedrichstrasse, Ⓤ Friedrichstrasse) David Chipperfield's reconstruction of the bombed-out Neues Museum is now the residence of Queen Nefertiti, the showstopper of the Egyptian Museum, which also features mummies, sculptures and sarcophagi. Pride of place at the Museum of Pre- and Early History (in the same building) goes to Trojan antiquities, a Neanderthal skull and the 3000-year-old 'Berliner Goldhut', a golden conical hat. Skip the queue by buying your timed ticket online.

★ **Fernsehturm**　　LANDMARK
(TV Tower; Map p460; ☑ 030-247 575 875; www.tv-turm.de; Panoramastrasse 1a; adult/child €15.50/9.50, fast track online ticket €19.50/12; ☺ 9am-midnight Mar-Oct, 10am-midnight Nov-Feb, last ascent 11.30pm; ☑ 100, 200, TXL, Ⓤ Alexanderplatz, Ⓢ Alexanderplatz) Germany's tallest structure, the TV Tower has been soaring 368m high since 1969 and is as iconic to Berlin as the Eiffel Tower is to Paris.

On clear days, views are stunning from the observation deck (with bar) at 203m or from the upstairs **Sphere restaurant** (Map p460; ☑ 030-247 575 875; www.tv-turm.de/en/bar-restaurant; mains lunch €10.50-18, dinner €12.50-28; ☺ 10am-11pm; ☎), which makes one revolution per hour.

★ **DDR Museum**　　MUSEUM
(GDR (East Germany) Museum; Map p460; ☑ 030-847 123 731; www.ddr-museum.de; Karl-Liebknecht-Strasse 1; adult/concession €9.80/6; ☺ 10am-8pm Sun-Fri, to 10pm Sat; ☑ 100, 200, TXL, Ⓢ Hackescher Markt) This touchy-feely museum does an insightful and entertaining job of pulling back the iron curtain on daily life in socialist East Germany. You'll learn how kids were put through collective potty training, engineers earned little more than farmers, and everyone, it seems, went on nudist holidays. A perennial crowd-pleaser among the historic objects on display is a Trabi, the tinny East German standard car – sit in it to take a virtual spin around an East Berlin neighbourhood.

Altes Museum　　MUSEUM
(Old Museum; Map p460; ☑ 030-266 424 242; www.smb.museum; Am Lustgarten; adult/concession/under 18 €10/5/free; ☺ 10am-6pm Tue, Wed & Fri-Sun, to 8pm Thu; ☑ 100, 200, TXL, Ⓢ Friedrichstrasse, Hackescher Markt, Ⓤ Friedrichstrasse) A curtain of fluted columns gives way to the Pantheon-inspired rotunda of the grand neoclassical Old Museum, which harbours a prized antiquities collection. In the downstairs galleries, sculptures, vases, tomb reliefs and jewellery shed light on various facets of life in ancient Greece, while upstairs the focus is on the Etruscans and Romans. Top draws include the *Praying Boy* bronze sculpture, Roman silver vessels, an 'erotic cabinet' (over 18s only!) and portraits of Caesar and Cleopatra.

Berliner Dom　　CHURCH
(Berlin Cathedral; Map p460; ☑ ticket office 030-2026 9136; www.berlinerdom.de; Am Lustgarten; adult/concession €7/5; ☺ 9am-8pm Apr-Sep, to 7pm Oct-Mar; ☑ 100, 200, TXL, Ⓢ Hackescher Markt) Pompous yet majestic, the Italian Renaissance–style former royal court church (1905) does triple duty as house of worship, museum and concert hall. Inside it's gilt to the hilt and outfitted with a lavish marble-and-onyx altar, a 7269-pipe Sauer organ and elaborate royal sarcophagi. Climb up the 267 steps to the gallery for glorious city views.

GERMANY BERLIN

Kreuzberg & Friedrichshain

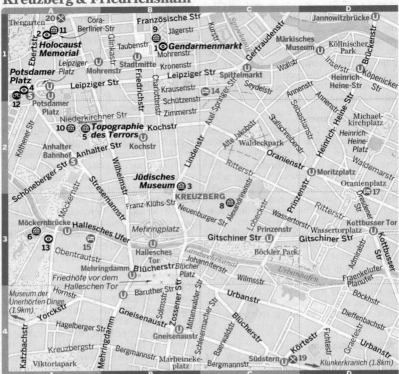

GERMANY BERLIN

Kreuzberg & Friedrichshain

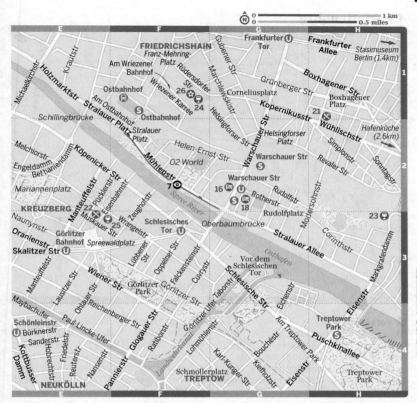

Bode-Museum
MUSEUM

(Map p460; ☏ 030-266 424 242; www.smb.museum; cnr Am Kupfergraben & Monbijoubrücke; adult/concession/under 18 €12/6/free; ⏰10am-6pm Tue, Wed & Fri-Sun, to 8pm Thu; Ⓢ Hackescher Markt, Friedrichstrasse) On the northern tip of Museumsinsel, this palatial edifice houses a comprehensive collection of European sculpture from the early Middle Ages to the 18th century, including priceless masterpieces by Tilman Riemenschneider, Donatello and Giovanni Pisano. Other rooms harbour a precious coin collection and a smattering of Byzantine art, including sarcophagi and ivory carvings.

Alte Nationalgalerie
MUSEUM

(Old National Gallery; Map p460; ☏ 030-266 424 242; www.smb.museum; Bodestrasse 1-3; adult/concession €10/5; ⏰10am-6pm Tue, Wed & Fri-Sun, to 8pm Thu; ☐100, 200, TXL, Ⓢ Hackescher Markt) The Greek temple–style Old National Gallery is a three-storey showcase of 19th-century European art. To get a sense of the period's virtuosity, pay special attention to the moody landscapes by Romantic heart-throb Caspar David Friedrich, the epic canvases by Franz Krüger and Adolf Menzel glorifying Prussia, the Gothic fantasies of Karl Friedrich Schinkel, and the sprinkling of French and German impressionists.

◉ Potsdamer Platz & Tiergarten

★ Tiergarten
PARK

(Map p466; Strasse des 17 Juni; ☐100, 200, Ⓢ Potsdamer Platz, Brandenburger Tor, Ⓤ Brandenburger Tor) Berlin's rulers used to hunt boar and pheasants in the rambling Tiergarten until garden architect Peter Lenné landscaped the grounds in the 19th century. Today it's one of the world's largest urban parks, popular for strolling, jogging, picnicking, frisbee tossing and, yes, nude sunbathing and gay cruising (especially around the Löwenbrücke).

Charlottenburg

★ **Potsdamer Platz** AREA

(Map p464; Alte Potsdamer Strasse; ☐ 200, ⑤ Potsdamer Platz, Ⓤ Potsdamer Platz) The rebirth of the historic Potsdamer Platz was Europe's biggest building project of the 1990s, a showcase of urban renewal masterminded by such top international architects as Renzo Piano and Helmut Jahn. An entire city quarter sprouted on terrain once bifurcated by the Berlin Wall and today houses offices, theatres and cinemas, hotels, apartments and museums. Highlights include the glass-tented Sony Center and the Panoramapunkt observation deck.

★ **Sony Center** NOTABLE BUILDING

(Map p466; www.potsdamer-platz.net; Potsdamer Strasse; ☐ 200, Ⓤ Potsdamer Platz, ⑤ Potsdamer Platz) Designed by Helmut Jahn, the visually dramatic Sony Center is fronted by a 26-floor, glass-and-steel tower and integrates rare relics from the prewar era of Potsdamer Platz, such as the opulent Kaisersaal. The heart of the Sony Center, though, is a central plaza canopied by a tentlike glass roof with supporting beams radiating like bicycle spokes. The plaza and its many cafes are popular places to hang out and people-watch.

★ **Gemäldegalerie** GALLERY

(Gallery of Old Masters; Map p466; ☎ 030-266 424 242; www.smb.museum/gg; Matthäikirchplatz;

adult/concession/under 18 €10/5/free; ☉ 10am-6pm Tue, Wed & Fri, to 8pm Thu, 11am-6pm Sat & Sun; ⦿; ☐ M29, M48, M85, 200, ⑤ Potsdamer Platz, Ⓤ Potsdamer Platz) This museum ranks among the world's finest and most comprehensive collections of European art with about 1500 paintings spanning the arc of artistic vision from the 13th to the 18th century. Wear comfy shoes when exploring the 72 galleries: a walk past masterpieces by Titian, Dürer, Hals, Vermeer, Gainsborough and many more Old Masters covers almost 2km. Don't miss the Rembrandt Room (Room X).

Panoramapunkt VIEWPOINT

(Map p464; ☎ 030-2593 7080; www.panoramapunkt.de; Potsdamer Platz 1; adult/concession €7.50/6, without wait €11.50/9; ☉ 10am-8pm Apr-Oct, to 6pm Nov-Mar; ☐ M41, 200, ⑤ Potsdamer Platz, Ⓤ Potsdamer Platz) Europe's fastest lift, Panoramapunkt yo-yos up and down the red-brick postmodern Kollhoff Tower in 20 seconds. From the bilevel viewing platform at a lofty 100m, you can pinpoint the sights, make a java stop in the 1930s-style cafe, enjoy sunset from the terrace and check out the exhibit that peels back the layers of the square's history.

Martin-Gropius-Bau GALLERY

(Map p464; ☎ 030-254 860; www.gropiusbau.de; Niederkirchner Strasse 7; cost varies, usually €10-12, under 16 free; ☉ 10am-7pm Wed-Mon; ☐ M41,

Charlottenburg

people on both sides of it. There's a great outlook from the centre's viewing platform.

★ **Zeiss Grossplanetarium** PLANETARIUM
(☑ 030-4218 4510; www.planetarium.berlin; Prenzlauer Allee 80; adult €8-9.50, concession €6-7.50; ▣ M2, ⓢ Prenzlauer Allee) It was the most advanced planetarium in East Germany at its opening in 1987 and after the recent renovation it has upped the scientific, technology and comfort factor ante once again to become one of the most modern in Europe. It's a beautiful space to delve into the mysteries not only of the cosmos but of science in general. Many programs are in English, some are set to music, others are geared to children. Tickets are available online.

(ⓢ Potsdamer Platz, Ⓤ Potsdamer Platz) With its mosaics, terracotta reliefs and airy atrium, this Italian Renaissance–style exhibit space named for its architect (Bauhaus founder Walter Gropius' great-uncle) is a celebrated venue for high-calibre art and cultural exhibits. Whether it's a David Bowie retrospective, the latest works of Ai Weiwei or an ethnological exhibit on the mysteries of Angkor Wat, it's bound to be well curated and utterly fascinating.

◉ Prenzlauer Berg

★ **Gedenkstätte Berliner Mauer** MEMORIAL
(Berlin Wall Memorial; ☑ 030-467 986 666; www.berliner-mauer-gedenkstaette.de; Bernauer Strasse btwn Schwedter Strasse & Gartenstrasse; ◔ visitor & documentation centre 10am-6pm Tue-Sun, open-air exhibit 8am-10pm daily; ⓢ Nordbahnhof, Bernauer Strasse, Eberswalder Strasse) 𝐅𝐑𝐄𝐄 For an insightful primer on the Berlin Wall, visit this outdoor memorial, which extends for 1.4km along Bernauer Strasse and integrates an original section of Wall, vestiges of the border installations and escape tunnels, a chapel and a monument. Multimedia stations, panels, excavations and a Documentation Centre provide context and explain what the border fortifications looked like and how they shaped the everyday lives of

◉ Scheunenviertel

★ **Hamburger Bahnhof – Museum für Gegenwart** MUSEUM
(Contemporary Art Museum; Map p460; ☑ 030-266 424 242; www.smb.museum; Invalidenstrasse 50-51; adult/concession €10/5, free 4-8pm 1st Thu of the month; ◔ 10am-6pm Tue, Wed & Fri, to 8pm Thu, 11am-6pm Sat & Sun; ▣ M5, M8, M10, ⓢ Hauptbahnhof, Ⓤ Hauptbahnhof) Berlin's contemporary art showcase opened in 1996 in an old railway station, whose grandeur is a great backdrop for this Aladdin's cave of paintings, installations, sculptures and video art. Changing exhibits span the arc of post-1950 artistic movements – from conceptual

WORTH A TRIP

SCHLOSS & PARK SANSSOUCI

Easily reached in half an hour from central Berlin, the former royal Prussian seat of Potsdam lures visitors to its splendid Unesco-recognised palaces and parks dreamed up by 18th-century King Friedrich II (Frederick the Great).

Headlining the roll call of royal pads is **Schloss Sanssouci** (☎0331-969 4200; www.spsg.de; Maulbeerallee; adult/concession incl tour or audioguide €12/8; ⏰10am-5.30pm Tue-Sun Apr-Oct, to 5pm Nov & Dec, to 4.30pm Jan-Mar; 🚌614, 650, 695), a celebrated rococo palace and the king's favourite summer retreat. Standouts on the audio-guided tour include the whimsically decorated concert hall, the intimate library and the domed Marble Hall. Admission is limited and by timed ticket only; book online (http://tickets.spsg.de) to avoid wait times and/or disappointment. Tickets must be printed out. Tours run by the Potsdam **tourist office** (☎0331-2755 8899; www.potsdam-tourism.com; Potsdam Hauptbahnhof; ⏰9.30am-6pm Mon-Sat; ⓈPotsdam Hauptbahnhof) guarantee entry.

Schloss Sanssouci is surrounded by a sprawling park dotted with numerous other palaces, buildings, fountains, statues and romantic corners. The one building not to be missed is the **Chinesisches Haus** (Chinese House; ☎0331-969 4200; www.spsg.de; Am Grünen Gitter; adult/concession €4/3; ⏰10am-5.30pm Tue-Sun May-Oct; 🚌605, 606, 🚋91), an adorable clover-leaf-shaped pavilion whose exterior is decorated with exotically dressed gilded figures shown sipping tea, dancing and playing musical instruments.

Another park highlight is the **Neues Palais** (New Palace; ☎0331-969 4200; www.spsg.de; Am Neuen Palais; adult/concession incl tour or audioguide €8/6; ⏰10am-5.30pm Mon & Wed-Sun Apr-Oct, to 5pm Nov-Dec, to 4.30pm Jan-Mar; 🚌605, 606, 695, Ⓢ Potsdam Charlottenhof) at the far western end. It has built-to-impress dimensions and is filled with opulent private and representative rooms.

Each building charges separate admission; a day pass to all costs €19 (concession €14).

On a nice day, it's worth exploring Potsdam's watery landscape and numerous other palaces on a **boat cruise** (☎0331-275 9210; www.schiffahrt-in-potsdam.de; Lange Brücke 6; ⏰Apr-Oct; 🚌605, 610, 631, 694, 🚋91, 92, 93, 98). The most popular one is the 90-minute Schlösserundfahrt (palace cruise; €16). Boats leave from docks near the Hauptbahnhof.

Regional trains leaving from Berlin-Hauptbahnhof and Zoologischer Garten need only 25 minutes to reach Potsdam Hauptbahnhof. The S-Bahn S7 from central Berlin makes the trip in about 40 minutes. You need an ABC ticket (€3.40) for either service.

art and pop art to minimal art and Fluxus – and include seminal works by such major players as Andy Warhol, Cy Twombly, Joseph Beuys and Robert Rauschenberg.

Sammlung Boros   GALLERY
(Boros Collection; Map p460; ☎030-2759 4065; www.sammlung-boros.de; Reinhardtstrasse 20; adult/concession €12/6; ⏰tours 3-6.30pm Thu, 10.30am-6.30pm Fri, 10am-6.30pm Sat & Sun; 🚋M1, Ⓢ Friedrichstrasse, Ⓤ Oranienburger Tor, Friedrichstrasse) This Nazi-era bunker presents one of Berlin's finest private contemporary art collections, amassed by advertising guru Christian Boros who acquired the behemoth in 2003. A third selection of works includes installations by Katja Novitskova, digital paintings by Avery Singer and photo series by Peter Piller. Book online (weeks, if not months, ahead) to join a guided tour (also in

English) and to pick up fascinating nuggets about the building's surprising other peacetime incarnations.

Hackesche Höfe   HISTORIC SITE
(Hackesche Courtyards; Map p460; ☎030-2809 8010; www.hackesche-hoefe.com; enter from Rosenthaler Strasse 40/41 or Sophienstrasse 6; 🚋M1, Ⓢ Hackescher Markt, Ⓤ Weinmeisterstrasse) The Hackesche Höfe is the largest and most famous of the courtyard ensembles peppered throughout the Scheunenviertel. Built in 1907, the eight interlinked *Höfe* reopened in 1996 with a congenial mix of cafes, galleries, shops and entertainment venues. The main entrance on Rosenthaler Strasse leads to **Court I**, prettily festooned with art nouveau tiles, while Court VII segues to the romantic **Rosenhöfe** with a sunken rose garden and tendril-like balustrades.

Museum für Naturkunde MUSEUM

(Museum of Natural History; ☏030-2093 8591; www.naturkundemuseum.berlin; Invalidenstrasse 43; adult/concession incl audioguide €8/5; ⊙9.30am-6pm Tue-Fri, 10am-6pm Sat & Sun; ⛟; ☐M5, M8, M10, 12, ⓤNaturkundemuseum) Fossils and minerals don't quicken your pulse? Well, how about Tristan, the T-Rex? His skeleton is among the best-preserved in the world and, along with the 12m-high *Brachiosaurus branchai*, part of the Jurassic superstar lineup at this highly engaging museum. Elsewhere you can wave at Knut, the world's most famous dead polar bear; marvel at the fragile bones of an ultrarare *Archaeopteryx* protobird, and find out why zebras are striped.

Neue Synagoge SYNAGOGUE

(Map p460; ☏030-8802 8300; www.centrumjudaicum.de; Oranienburger Strasse 28-30; adult/concession €5/4, audioguide €3; ⊙10am-6pm Mon-Fri, to 7pm Sun, closes 3pm Fri & 6pm Sun Oct-Mar; ☐M1, ⓤOranienburger Tor, ⓢOranienburger Strasse) The gleaming gold dome of the Neue Synagoge is the most visible symbol of Berlin's revitalised Jewish community. The 1866 original was Germany's largest synagogue but its modern incarnation is not so much a house of worship (although prayer services do take place), as a museum and place of remembrance called **Centrum Judaicum**. The dome can be climbed from April to September (adult/concession €3/2.50).

👁 Schöneberg

Museum der Unerhörten Dinge MUSEUM

(Museum of Unheard of Things; ☏030-781 4932, 0175 410 9120; www.museumderunerhoertendinge.de; Crellestrasse 5-6; ⊙3-7pm Wed-Fri; ⓤKleistpark, ⓢJulius-Leber-Brücke) **FREE** 'Every object tells a story' could be the motto of this kooky collection of curiosities. Find madness nibbling at your psyche as you try to find the meaning in displays about Swiss cowpat-worshippers or Goethe's stone rose. It may all be a mind-bending spoof or a complete exercise in irony by founder Roland Albrecht. But one thing's certain: it will challenge the way you look at museums.

👉 Tours

Berliner Unterwelten TOURS

(☏030-4991 0517; www.berliner-unterwelten.de; Brunnenstrasse 105; adult/concession €12/10; ⊙Dark Worlds tours in English 11am Wed-Sun, 11am & 1pm Mon year-round, 3pm Mon, Wed-Sun, 1pm & 3pm Wed-Sun Apr-Oct; ⓢGesundbrunnen, ⓤGesundbrunnen) After you've checked off the Brandenburg Gate and the TV Tower, why not explore Berlin's dark and dank underbelly? Join Berliner Unterwelten on its 1½-hour 'Dark Worlds' tour of a WWII underground bunker and pick your way through a warren of claustrophobic rooms, past heavy steel doors, hospital beds, helmets, guns, boots and lots of other wartime artefacts.

Fat Tire Tours Berlin CYCLING

(Map p460; ☏030-2404 7991; www.fattiretours.com/berlin; Panoramastrasse 1a; adult/concession/under 12yr incl bicycle from €28/26/14; ⓢAlexanderplatz, ⓤAlexanderplatz) This top-rated outfit runs English-language tours by bike, e-bike and Segway. Options include a classic city spin; tours with a focus on Nazi Germany, the Cold War or 'Modern Berlin'; a trip to Potsdam; and an evening food tour. Tours leave from the Fernsehturm (TV Tower) main entrance. Reservations advised.

🛏 Sleeping

🛏 City West & Charlottenburg

★ 25hours Hotel
Bikini Berlin DESIGN HOTEL €€

(Map p466; ☏030-120 2210; www.25hours-hotels.com; Budapester Strasse 40; r €110-250; ⓟ🐕❄️ @ 🛜; ☐100, 200, ⓢZoologischer Garten, ⓤZoologischer Garten) The 'urban jungle' theme of this lifestyle outpost in the iconic 1950s Bikini Haus plays on its location between the zoo and main shopping district. Rooms are thoughtfully cool, and drip with clever design touches; the best face the animal park. Quirks include an on-site bakery, hammocks in the public areas and the 'jungle-sauna' with zoo view.

Sir Savigny BOUTIQUE HOTEL €€

(Map p466; ☏030-323 015 600; www.hotel-sir-savigny.de; Kantstrasse 144; r from €130; 🐕❄️🛜; ⓢSavignyplatz) Global nomads with a hankering for style would be well advised to point their compass to this cosmopolitan crash pad. Each of the 44 rooms exudes delightfully risqué glamour and teems with mod cons and clever design touches. And yes, the beds are fab. If you're feeling social, report to the book-filled 'kitchen' lounge or the cool bar and burger joint.

🛏 Friedrichshain

⭐ Plus Berlin
HOSTEL €

(Map p464; ☑ 030-311 698 820; www.plushostels. com/plusberlin; Warschauer Platz 6; dm/d from €18/90; P✱@🛜🏊; Ⓤ Warschauer Strasse, Ⓢ Warschauer Strasse) A hostel with a pool, steam room and yoga classes? Yep. Close to Berlin's best nightlife, this flashpacker favourite is like a hostel resort. There's a bar for easing into the night and a tranquil courtyard to soothe that hangover. Spacious dorms have four or six bunks, desks and lockers, while private rooms have TV and air-con. All have en suites.

🛏 Historic Mitte

⭐ Adina Apartment Hotel Berlin Checkpoint Charlie
APARTMENT €€

(Map p464; ☑ 030-200 7670; www.adinahotels. com; Krausenstrasse 35-36; studio/1-bedroom apt from €120/145; P✱@🛜🏊♨; Ⓤ Stadtmitte, Spittelmarkt) Adina's contemporary one- and two-bedroom, stylishly functional apartments with full kitchens are tailor-made for cost-conscious families, anyone in need of elbow room, and self-caterers (a supermarket is a minute away). Roomy studios with kitchenette are also available. The spa area with its 17m-long indoor pool and sauna helps combat post-flight fatigue. Optional breakfast is €19.

🛏 Kreuzberg & Neukölln

⭐ Grand Hostel Berlin Classic
HOSTEL €

(Map p464; ☑ 030-2009 5450; www.grandhostel -berlin.de; Tempelhofer Ufer 14; dm €10-44, tw €75-150, tw without bathroom €50-110; ♨@🛜; Ⓤ Möckernbrücke) Cocktails in the library bar? Check. Free German lessons? Got 'em. Canal views? Yep. Ensconced in a fully renovated 1870s building, the 'five-star' Grand Hostel is one of Berlin's most supremely comfortable, convivial and atmospheric hostels. Breakfast is €7.50.

Orania.Berlin
HOTEL €€

(Map p464; ☑ 030-6953 9680; www.orania.berlin; Oranienstrasse 40; d from €150; ♨✱🛜🏊♨; Ⓤ Moritzplatz) This gorgeous hotel in a sensitively restored 1913 building wraps everything that makes Berlin special – culture, class and culinary acumen, infused with a freewheeling cosmopolitan spirit – into one tidy package. Great warmth radiates from the open lobby bar, whose stylish furniture, sultry lighting and open fireplace exude living-room flair. Catch shuteye in 41 comfy rooms that mix retro and modern touches.

🛏 Prenzlauer Berg

⭐ EastSeven Berlin Hostel
HOSTEL €

(☑ 030-9362 2240; www.eastseven.de; Schwedter Strasse 7; dm/d from €25/65; ♨@🛜; Ⓤ Senefelderplatz) An excellent choice for solo travellers, this small indie hostel has personable staff who go out of their way to make all feel welcome. Make new friends while chilling in the lounge or garden (hammocks!), firing up the barbecue or hanging out in the 24-hour kitchen. Brightly painted dorms feature comfy pine beds and lockers. Linen is free, breakfast €3.

🍴 Eating

🍴 City West & Charlottenburg

Kuchenladen
CAFE €

(Map p466; ☑ 030-3101 8424; www.derkuchenladen.de; Kantstrasse 138; cakes €2.50-4.50; ⏲ 10am-8pm; Ⓢ Savignyplatz) Even size-0 locals can't resist the siren call of this classic cafe whose homemade cakes are like works of art wrought from flour, sugar and cream. From cheesecake to carrot cake to the ridiculously rich *Sacher Torte*, it's all delicious down to the last crumb.

⭐ Schwein
INTERNATIONAL €€€

(Map p466; ☑ 030-2435 6282; www.schwein.online; Mommsenstrasse 63; dishes €13-37, 4-/5-course menu €65/75; ⏲ 6pm-midnight Mon-Fri, to 2am Sat; 🛜🍴; Ⓢ Savignyplatz) This casual fine-dining lair delivers the perfect trifecta – fabulous food, wine and long drinks. Order the multicourse menu to truly experience the genius of kitchen champion Christopher Kümper, who creates globally inspired and regionally sourced symphonies of taste and textures. Or keep it 'casual' with just a bite and a gin and tonic.

🍴 Friedrichshain

Silo Coffee
CAFE €

(Map p464; www.facebook.com/silocoffee; Gabriel-Max-Strasse 4; dishes €6-12; ⏲ 8.30am-5pm Mon-Fri, 9.30am-6pm Sat & Sun; 🛜🍴; 🚊 M10, M13, Ⓤ Warschauer Strasse, Ⓢ Warschauer Strasse) If you've greeted the day with bloodshot eyes, get back in gear at this Aussie-run coffee and breakfast joint favoured by Friedrichshain's hip and expat crowds. Beans from Fjord coffee roasters ensure possibly the best flat white in town, while bread from Sironi (Markthalle Neun) adds scrumptiousness to the poached-egg avo toast.

Michelberger INTERNATIONAL €€
(Map p464; 030-2977 8590; www.michelberger hotel.com; Warschauer Strasse 39; 3-course lunch €12, dinner dishes €8-15; ⊙7-11am, noon-2.30pm & 6.30-11pm; ⊛⊘; ⒮Warschauer Strasse, ⓊWarschauer Strasse) ✈ Ensconced in one of Berlin's coolest **hotels** (Map p464; Warschauer Strasse 39; d €95-190; Ⓟ⊝⊛), Michelberger makes creative dishes that often combine unusual organic ingredients (eg wild boar with miso, scallops, cabbage and gooseberry). Sit inside the lofty, white-tiled restaurant or in the breezy courtyard.

Hafenküche INTERNATIONAL €€
(030-4221 9926; www.hafenkueche.de; Zur Alten Flussbadeanstalt 5; lunch €5.50-6.50, dinner mains €12-19; ⊙10am-11pm Mon-Fri, 9pm-11.30 Sat & Sun; ⊛; ☐21) The erstwhile staff restaurant of the adjacent bus operator is now a top address for seasonal and regional cuisine in a dreamy location right on the Spree River. It's a great lunch destination while on riverside bike rides. Dinners are more elaborate and best enjoyed on the romantically lit terrace. In good weather, the waterfront beer garden has cold drinks and grilled meats.

✕ Historic Mitte

India Club NORTH INDIAN €€
(Map p464; 030-2062 8610; www.india-club -berlin.com; Behrenstrasse 72; mains €16-27; ⊙6-10.30pm; ⊘; ⒮Brandenburger Tor) No need to book a flight to Mumbai or London: authentic Indian cuisine has finally landed in Berlin. Thanks to top toque Manish Bahukhandi, these curries are like culinary poetry, the chicken tikka perfectly succulent and the stuffed cauliflower an inspiration. The dark mahogany furniture is enlivened by splashes of colour in the plates, the chandeliers and the servers' uniforms.

✕ Kreuzberg & Neukölln

Sironi BAKERY €
(Map p464; www.facebook.com/sironi.de; Eisenbahnstrasse 42, Markthalle Neun; snacks from €2.50; ⊙8am-8pm Mon-Wed, Fri & Sat, to 10pm Thu; ⓊGörlitzer Bahnhof) The focaccia and ciabatta

are as good as they get without taking a flight to Italy, thanks to Alfredo Sironi, who hails from the Boot and now treats Berlin bread lovers to his habit-forming carb creations. Watch the flour magicians whip up the next batch in his glass bakery right in the iconic **Markthalle Neun** (Map p464; 030-6107 3473; www.markthalleneun.de; Eisenbahnstrasse 42-43; ⊙noon-6pm Mon-Wed & Fri, noon-10pm Thu, 10am-6pm Sat), then order a piece to take away.

Fes Turkish Barbecue TURKISH €€
(Map p464; 030-2391 7778; http://fes-turkish bbq.de; Hasenheide 58; meze €4-10, meat from €15; ⊙5-10pm Tue-Sun; ⓊSüdstern) If you like a DIY approach to dining, give this innovative Turkish restaurant a try. Perhaps borrowing a page from the Koreans, it requires you to cook your own slabs of marinated chicken, beef fillet and tender lamb on a grill sunk right into your table.

✕ Prenzlauer Berg

Mrs Robinson's INTERNATIONAL €€
(030-5462 2839, 01520 518 8946; www.mrs robinsons.de; Pappelallee 29; mains €16-20; ⊙6-11pm Thu-Mon; ⊛⊘; ☐12, ⓊSchönhauser Allee, ⒮Schönhauser Allee) When Israel transplant Ben Zviel and his partner Samina Raza launched their minimalist parlour (white-brick walls, polished wooden tables) in 2016, they added another rung to Berlin's food ladder. The menu is constantly in flux, but by turning carefully edited ingredients into shareable small and big plates, Ben fearlessly captures the city's adventurous and uninhibited spirit. Casual fine dining at its best.

✕ Schöneberg

BRLO Brwhouse INTERNATIONAL €€
(Map p466; 0151 7437 4235; www.brlo-brwhouse. de; Schöneberger Strasse 16; mains from €18;

GERMANY BERLIN

ℹ BUS TOUR ON THE CHEAP

Get a crash course in 'Berlinology' by hopping on bus 100 or 200 at Zoologischer Garten or Alexanderplatz and letting the landmarks whoosh by for the price of a standard bus ticket. Bus 100 goes via the Tiergarten and bus 200 via Potsdamer Platz. Without traffic and getting off, trips take about 30 minutes.

⊘ restaurant 5pm-midnight Tue-Fri, noon-midnight Sat & Sun, beer garden noon-midnight Apr-Sep; 🔊 📶; Ⓤ Gleisdreieck) The house-crafted suds flow freely at this shooting star among Berlin's craft breweries. Production, taproom and restaurant are all housed in 38 shipping containers fronted by a big beer garden with a sand box and views of Gleisdreieckpark. Shareable dishes are mostly vegetable-centric, although missing out on the meat prepared to succulent perfection in a smoker would be a shame.

🍷 Drinking & Nightlife

⭐ Prater Garten   BEER GARDEN

(📞 030-448 5688; www.pratergarten.de; Kastanienallee 7-9; snacks €2.50-7.50; ⊘ noon-late Apr-Sep, weather permitting; 📶; 🚋 M1, 12, Ⓤ Eberswalder Strasse) Berlin's oldest beer garden has seen beer-soaked days and nights since 1837 and is still a charismatic spot for guzzling a custom-brewed Prater pilsner (self-service) beneath the ancient chestnut trees. Kids can romp around the small play area.

Bar am Steinplatz   COCKTAIL BAR

(Map p466; 📞 030-554 4440; www.hotelsteinplatz.com; Steinplatz 4; ⊘ 4pm-late; Ⓤ Ernst-Reuter-Platz) This liquid playground at the art-deco **Hotel am Steinplatz** (Map p466; r €100-290; 🅿 ⊛ ❄ @ 🔊 🐾) has made history several times, most recently as Germany's first alcohol-free hotel-based cocktail bar. Mix-meister Willi Bittorf combines nonalco-

holic distillates with kombucha, rose water, syrups, herbs and juices to create guilt- and hangover-free libations. Handy and hygienic: the menu is printed on the tables.

Berghain/Panorama Bar   CLUB

(Map p464; www.berghain.de; Am Wriezener Bahnhof; ⊘ Fri-Mon; Ⓢ Ostbahnhof) Only world-class spin-masters heat up this hedonistic bass-junkie hellhole inside a labyrinthine ex-powerplant. Hard-edged minimal techno dominates the ex-turbine hall (Berghain), while house dominates at Panorama Bar, one floor up. Long lines, strict door, no cameras. Check the website for midweek concerts and record-release parties at the main venue and the adjacent **Kantine am Berghain** (Map p464; admission varies; ⊘ hours vary).

Clärchens Ballhaus   CLUB

(Map p460; 📞 030-282 9295; www.ballhaus.de; Auguststrasse 24; Sun-Thu free, Fri & Sat €5; ⊘ 11am-late; 🚋 M1, Ⓢ Oranienburger Strasse) Yesteryear is now at this early-20th-century dance hall where groovers and grannies hoof it across the parquet without even a touch of irony. There are different sounds nightly – salsa to swing, tango to disco – and a live band on Saturday. Dancing kicks off from 9pm or 9.30pm. Ask about dance lessons. Tables can only be reserved if you plan on eating.

Schwarze Traube   COCKTAIL BAR

(Map p464; 📞 030-2313 5569; www.schwarzetraube.de; Wrangelstrasse 24; ⊘ 7pm-2am Sun-Thu, to 5am Fri & Sat; Ⓤ Görlitzer Bahnhof) Mixologist Atalay Aktas was Germany's Best Bartender of 2013 and hasn't missed a step since. He and his staff still create their magic potions in this pint-sized drinking parlour with living-room looks. There's no menu, meaning each drink is calibrated to the taste and mood of each patron using premium spirits, expertise and a dash of psychology.

://about blank   CLUB

(Map p464; www.aboutparty.net; Markgrafendamm 24c; ⊘ hours vary, always Fri & Sat; Ⓢ Ostkreuz) At this gritty multifloor party pen with lots of nooks and crannies, a steady line-up of top DJs feeds a diverse bunch of revellers with dance-worthy electronic gruel. Intense club nights usually segue into the morning and beyond. Run by a collective, the venue also hosts cultural, political and gender events.

ℹ DISCOUNT CARDS

Berlin Welcome Card (www.berlin-welcomecard.de; travel in AB zones 48/72 hours €19.90/28.90, AB zones 72 hours plus admission to Museumsinsel €45) Valid for unlimited public transport for one adult and up to three children under 14 plus up to 50% discount to 200 sights, attractions and tours. Sold online, at the tourist offices, from U-Bahn and S-Bahn station ticket vending machines and on buses.

Museumspass Berlin (adult/concession €29/14.50) Buys admission to the permanent exhibits of about 30 museums for three consecutive days, including big draws like the Pergamonmuseum. Sold at tourist offices and participating museums.

☆ Entertainment

Staatsoper Berlin   OPERA

(Map p460; ☑ 030-2035 4554; www.staatsoper
-berlin.de; Unter den Linden 7; tickets €12-250;
🚆 100, 200, TXL, Ⓤ Französische Strasse) Berlin's
most famous opera company performs at the
venerable neoclassical Staatsoper Unter den
Linden. Its repertory includes works from
four centuries along with concerts and classical and modern ballet, all under the musical leadership of Daniel Barenboim. Some
performances are shortened to appeal to
families.

Berliner Philharmoniker   CLASSICAL MUSIC

(Map p466; ☑ tickets 030-2548 8999; www.berliner
-philharmoniker.de; Herbert-von-Karajan-Strasse 1;
tickets €21-290; 🚆 M29, M48, M85, 200, Ⓢ Potsdamer Platz, Ⓤ Potsdamer Platz) One of the
world's most famous orchestras, the Berliner
Philharmoniker, is based at the tent-like **Phil-
harmonie** (Map p466; ☑ 030-2548 8156; tours
adult/concession €5/3; ☉ tours 1.30pm Sep-Jun),
designed by Hans Scharoun in the 1950s and
built in the 1960s. In 2018, Sir Simon Rattle,
who had been chief conductor since 2002,
passed on the baton to the Russia-born Kirill
Petrenko. Tickets can be booked online.

ℹ Information

Alexanderplatz (☑ 030-250 025; www.visit
berlin.de; lobby Park Inn, Alexanderplatz 7;
☉ 7am-9pm Mon-Sat, 8am-6pm Sun)

Brandenburg Gate (Map p460; ☑ 030-250
023; Pariser Platz, Brandenburger Tor, south
wing; ☉ 9.30am-7pm Apr-Oct, to 6pm Nov-Mar)

Central Bus Station (ZOB) (Masurenallee 4-6;
☉ 8am-8pm Mon, Fri & Sat, to 4pm Tue-Thu &
Sun; Ⓢ Messe Nord/ICC)

Europa-Center (Map p466; ☑ 030-2500 2333;
Tauentzienstrasse 9, ground fl; ☉ 10am-8pm
Mon-Sat; 🚆 100, 200, Ⓤ Kurfürstendamm,
Zoologischer Garten, Ⓢ Zoologischer Garten)

Hauptbahnhof (☑ 030-250 025; www.visit
berlin.de; Hauptbahnhof, Europaplatz entrance,
ground fl; ☉ 8am-10pm)

ℹ Getting There & Away

AIR

Most visitors arrive in Berlin by air. Berlin's new
central airport, about 24km southeast of the
city centre, next to Schönefeld Airport, opened
in 2020.

BUS

Most long-haul buses arrive at the **Zentraler
Omnibusbahnhof** (ZOB, Central Bus Station;
☑ 030-3010 0175; www.zob-berlin.de; Messe-
damm 8; Ⓢ Messe/ICC Nord, Ⓤ Kaiserdamm)
near the trade fair grounds in far western Berlin.
The U2 U-Bahn line links to the city centre. Some
bus operators also stop at Alexanderplatz and
other points around town.

TRAIN

Berlin has several train stations, but most trains
converge at the **Hauptbahnhof** (Main Train Station; Europaplatz, Washingtonplatz; Ⓢ Hauptbahnhof, Ⓤ Hauptbahnhof) in the heart of the city.

ℹ Getting Around

TO/FROM THE AIRPORT

Schönefeld Airport Airport-Express trains
(RB14 or RE7) to central Berlin twice hourly (30
minutes), and S9 trains every 20 minutes for
Friedrichshain and Prenzlauer Berg, €3.40; taxi
to city centre €45 to €50.

PUBLIC TRANSPORT

➡ One ticket is valid on all forms of public transport, including the U-Bahn, buses, trams and
ferries. Most rides require a Tariff AB ticket,
which is valid for two hours (interruptions and
transfers allowed, but not return trips).

➡ Tickets are available from bus drivers, vending machines at U- and S-Bahn stations and
on trams and at station offices. Expect to pay
cash (change given) and be sure to validate
(stamp) your ticket or risk a €60 fine during
spot-checks.

➡ Services operate from 4am to 12.30am and all night Friday, Saturday and public holidays.

➡ For trip planning, check the **BVG** (🛈 hotline 030-194 49; www.bvg.de) website or call the 24-hour hotline.

SAXONY

POP 4 MILLION

Placed where northern plains abut mountain ranges and German efficiency meets Slavic flamboyance, and packed with elegant hilltop castles and lavish baroque palaces, Saxony is the definition of Central Europe. It was also at the centre of events during the most decisive points in European history, such as the Reformation, the Napoleonic Wars, and the velvet revolutions that dismantled Communist regimes in the late 1980s.

Dresden

🛈 0351 / POP 563,000

Proof that there is life after death, Dresden has become one of Germany's most visited cities, and for good reason. Restorations have returned its historical core to its 18th-century heyday when it was famous throughout Europe as 'Florence on the Elbe'. Scores of Italian artists, musicians, actors and master craftsmen flocked to the court of Augustus the Strong, bestowing countless masterpieces upon the city. The devastating bombing raids in 1945 levelled most of these treasures. But Dresden is a survivor and many of the most important landmarks have since been rebuilt, including the elegant Frauenkirche. Today there's a constantly evolving arts and cultural scene and zinging pub and nightlife quarters, especially in the Outer Neustadt.

☉ Sights

Dresden straddles the Elbe River, with the attraction-studded Altstadt (old town) in the south and the Neustadt (new town) pub and student quarter to the north.

★ Zwinger　　　　　　　　PALACE

(🛈 0351-4914 2000; www.der-dresdner-zwinger. de; Theaterplatz 1; ticket for all museums adult/concession €12/9, courtyard free; ☉ 6am-10pm Apr-Oct, to 8pm Nov-Mar) A collaboration between the architect Matthäus Pöppelmann

and the sculptor Balthasar Permoser, the Zwinger was built between 1710 and 1728 on the orders of Augustus the Strong, who, having returned from seeing Louis XIV's palace at Versailles, wanted something similar for himself. Primarily a party palace for royals, the Zwinger has ornate portals that lead into the vast fountain-studded courtyard, which is framed by buildings lavishly adorned with evocative sculpture. Today it houses three superb museums within its baroque walls.

★ Gemäldegalerie Alte Meister　　MUSEUM

(Old Masters Gallery; www.skd.museum; Zwinger, Theaterplatz 1; adult/concession €12/9, audioguide €3; ☉ 10am-6pm Tue-Sun) This astounding collection of European art from the 16th to 18th centuries houses an incredible number of masterpieces, including Raphael's famous *Sistine Madonna* (1513), which dominates the enormous main hall on the ground floor, as well as works by Titian, Tintoretto, Holbein, Dürer, and Cranach, whose *Paradise* (1530) is particularly arresting. Upstairs you'll find an exquisite display of Rembrandt, Botticelli, Veronese, Van Dyck, Vermeer, Brueghel and Poussin. Finally, don't miss Canaletto's sumptuous portrayals of 18th-century Dresden on the top floor.

★ Albertinum　　　　　　　GALLERY

(Galerie Neue Meister; 🛈 0351-4914 2000; www.skd.museum; enter from Brühlsche Terrasse or Georg-Treu-Platz 2; adult/concession/child under 17yr €10/7.50/free; ☉ 10am-6pm Tue-Sun) The Renaissance-era former arsenal is the stunning home of the **Galerie Neue Meister** (New Masters Gallery), which displays an array of paintings by some of the great names in art from the 18th century onwards. Caspar David Friedrich and Claude Monet's landscapes compete with the abstract visions of Marc Chagall and Gerhard Richter, all in gorgeous rooms orbiting a light-filled courtyard. There's also a superb sculpture collection spread over the lower floors.

★ Historisches Grünes Gewölbe　MUSEUM

(Historic Green Vault; 🛈 0351-4914 2000; www.skd.museum; Residenzschloss; €12; ☉ 10am-6pm Wed-Mon) The Historic Green Vault displays some 3000 precious items in the same fashion as during the time of August der Starke, namely on shelves and tables without glass

SACHSENHAUSEN CONCENTRATION CAMP

A mere 35km north of Berlin, Sachsenhausen was built by prisoners and opened in 1936 as a prototype for other concentration camps. By 1945 some 200,000 people had passed through its sinister gates, most of them political opponents, Jews, Roma people and, after 1939, POWs. Tens of thousands died from hunger, exhaustion, illness, exposure, medical experiments and executions. The camp became a **memorial site** (Memorial & Museum Sachsenhausen; ☑ 03301-200 200; www.stiftung-bg.de; Strasse der Nationen 22, Oranienburg; ◷ 8.30am-6pm mid-Mar–mid-Oct, to 4.30pm mid-Oct–mid-Mar, museums closed Mon mid-Oct–mid-Mar; P; S Oranienburg) FREE in 1961. A tour of the grounds, remaining buildings and exhibits will leave no one untouched. Unless you're on a guided tour, pick up a leaflet (€0.50) or, better yet, an audioguide (€3, including leaflet) at the visitor centre to get a better grasp of this huge site. Between mid-October and mid-March avoid visiting on a Monday when all indoor exhibits are closed. The S-Bahn S1 makes the trip to Oranienburg train station thrice hourly (ABC ticket €3.40, 45 minutes), from where it's a 2km signposted walk or a ride on hourly bus 804 to the site.

protection in a series of increasingly lavish rooms. Admission is by timed ticket only, and only a limited number of visitors per hour may pass through the 'dust lock'. Get advance tickets online or by phone, since only 40% are sold at the palace box office for same-day admission.

Frauenkirche CHURCH
(☑ 0351-6560 6100; www.frauenkirche-dresden.de; Neumarkt; audioguide €2.50, cupola adult/student €8/5; ◷ 10am-noon & 1-6pm Mon-Fri, weekend hours vary) The domed Frauenkirche – Dresden's most beloved symbol – has literally risen from the city's ashes. The original church graced the skyline for two centuries before collapsing after the February 1945 bombing, and was rebuilt from a pile of rubble between 1994 and 2005. A spitting image of the original, today's structure may not bear the gravitas of age but that only slightly detracts from its beauty, inside and out. The altar, reassembled from nearly 2000 fragments, is especially striking.

Neues Grünes Gewölbe MUSEUM
(New Green Vault; ☑ 0351-4914 2000; www.skd. museum; Residenzschloss; adult/child under 17yr incl audioguide €12/free; ◷ 10am-6pm Wed-Mon) The New Green Vault presents some 1000 objects in 10 modern rooms. Key sights include a frigate fashioned from ivory with wafer-thin sails, a cherry pit with 185 faces carved into it, and an exotic ensemble of 132 gem-studded figurines representing a royal court in India. The artistry of each item is

dazzling. To avoid the worst crush of people, visit during lunchtime.

★☆ Festivals & Events

Striezelmarkt CHRISTMAS MARKET
(Altmarkt; ◷ Dec) During December, sample the famous Dresdner Stollen (fruit cake) at one of Germany's oldest and best Christmas markets.

🛏 Sleeping & Eating

The Neustadt has oodles of cafes and restaurants, especially along Königstrasse and the streets north of Albertplatz. The latter is also the centre of Dresden's nightlife. Altstadt restaurants are more tourist-geared and pricier.

★ Hotel Schloss Eckberg HOTEL €€
(☑ 0351-809 90; www.schloss-eckberg.de; Bautzner Strasse 134; d Kavaliershaus/Schloss from €99/134; P ✳ ⟨⟩) This romantic castle set in its own riverside park east of the Neustadt is a breathtaking place to stay. Rooms in the Schloss itself are pricier and have oodles of historic flair, but staying in the modern Kavaliershaus lets you enjoy almost as many amenities and the same dreamy setting.

Gewandhaus Hotel BOUTIQUE HOTEL €€€
(☑ 0351-494 90; www.gewandhaus-hotel.de; Ringstrasse 1; d from €157; P ✳ @ ⟨⟩ ✱) Revamped as a boutique hotel a few years ago, the stunning Gewandhaus, an 18th-century trading house of tailors and fabric merchants that burned down in 1945, boasts sleek public

WORTH A TRIP

MEISSEN

Straddling the Elbe around 25km upstream from Dresden, Meissen is the cradle of European porcelain, which was first cooked up in 1710 in its imposing castle, the **Albrechtsburg** (☑03521-470 70; www.albrechtsburg-meissen.de; Domplatz 1; adult/concession incl audioguide €8/6.50, with Dom €11/8; ☺10am-6pm Mar-Oct, to 5pm Nov-Feb). An exhibit on the 2nd floor chronicles how it all began. Highlights of the adjacent **cathedral** (☑03521-452 490; www.dom-zu-meissen.de; Domplatz 7; adult/concession €4.50/3, with Albrechtsburg €11/8; ☺9am-6pm Apr-Oct, 10am-4pm Nov-Mar) include medieval stained-glass windows and an altarpiece by Lucas Cranach the Elder. Both squat atop a ridge overlooking Meissen's handsome Altstadt (old town).

Since 1863, porcelain production has taken place in a custom-built factory, about 1km south of the Altstadt. Next to it is the **Erlebniswelt Haus Meissen** (☑03521-468 208; www.meissen.com; Talstrasse 9; adult/concession €10/6; ☺9am-6pm May-Oct, to 5pm Nov-Apr), a vastly popular porcelain museum where you can witness the astonishing artistry and craftsmanship that makes Meissen porcelain unique. Note that entry is timed and only in groups, so you may have to wait a while during high season.

For details and further information about the town, stop by the **tourist office** (☑03521-419 40; www.touristinfo-meissen.de; Markt 3; ☺10am-6pm Mon-Fri, to 4pm Sat & Sun Apr-Oct, to 5pm Mon-Fri, to 3pm Sat Nov, Dec, Feb & Mar).

Half-hourly S1 trains run to Meissen from Dresden's Hauptbahnhof and Neustadt train stations (€6, 20 minutes). For the Erlebniswelt, get off at Meissen-Triebischtal. Boats operated by **Sächsische Dampfschiffahrt** (☑03521-866 090; www.saechsische-dampfschiffahrt.de; one way/return €16.50/21.50; ☺May-Sep) make the trip to Meissen from the Terrassenufer in Dresden in two hours. Consider going one way by boat and the other by train.

areas, beautiful and bright rooms, and a breakfast that sets a high bar for the city.

Little India
INDIAN €€

(☑0351-3232 6400; www.littleindia-dresden.de; Louisenstrasse 48; mains €10-15; ☺11am-2.30pm & 5-11pm Tue-Sat, to 10pm Sun; ☑) Bright, minimalist and informal, this fantastic Indian restaurant is a world away from most in Dresden, and its popularity is obvious (be prepared to wait for a table when it's busy). The large menu (available in English) includes superb tandoori dishes and an entire vegetarian section, as well as standard chicken, lamb and pork mains. The naan is heavenly.

★ Restaurant Genuss-Atelier
GERMAN €€€

(☑0351-2502 8337; www.genuss-atelier.net; Bautzner Strasse 149; mains €15-27; ☺5-11pm Wed-Fri, noon-3.30pm & 5-11pm Sat & Sun; ☑11 to Waldschlösschen) Lighting up Dresden's culinary scene is this fantastic place that's well worth the trip on the 11 tram. The creative menu is streets ahead of most offerings elsewhere, although the best way to experience the 'Pleasure-Atelier' is to book a surprise menu (three/four/five courses €39/49/59) and let the chefs show off their craft. Reservations essential.

☆ Entertainment

Semperoper Dresden
OPERA

(☑0351-491 1705; www.semperoper.de; Theaterplatz 2; ☺ticket office 10am-6pm Mon-Fri, to 5pm Sat & Sun) Dresden's famous opera house is the home of the Sächsische Staatsoper Dresden, which puts on brilliant performances that usually sell out.

ⓘ Information

There are tourist office branches inside the **Hauptbahnhof** (☑0351-501 501; www.dresden. de; Wiener Platz; ☺8am-8pm) and near the **Frauenkirche** (☑0351-501 501; www.dresden. de; QF Passage, Neumarkt 2; ☺10am-7pm Mon-Fri, to 6pm Sat, to 3pm Sun). Both book rooms and tours and rent out audioguides.

ⓘ Getting There & Away

Dresden International Airport (DRS; ☑0351-881 3360; www.dresden-airport.de; Flughafenstrasse) is about 9km north of the city centre and linked by the S2 train several times hourly (€2.30, 20 minutes).

Fast trains make the trip to Dresden from Berlin-Hauptbahnhof in two hours (€40) and Leipzig in 1¼ hours (€19.90). The S1 local train runs half-hourly to Meissen (€6.20, 40 minutes) and Bad Schandau in Saxon Switzerland (€6.20, 45 minutes).

Leipzig & Western Saxony

The more industrialised western part of Saxony centres on Leipzig, a green, hip and vibrant city with many stories to tell and places to enjoy. Hugely important in the history of music, it was home to Johann Sebastian Bach and Richard Wagner.

Leipzig

📱 0341 / POP 590,300

Hypezig! cry the papers. The New Berlin, says just about everybody. Yes, Leipzig is Saxony's coolest city, a playground for nomadic young creatives who have been displaced even by the fast-gentrifying German capital. But Leipzig is also a city of enormous history and is known as the *Stadt der Helden* (City of Heroes) for its leading role in the 1989 'Peaceful Revolution' that helped bring the Cold War to an end. The city is solidly in the sights of classical music lovers due to its intrinsic connection to the lives and work of Bach, Mendelssohn and Wagner.

◉ Sights

★ Museum der Bildenden Künste   MUSEUM
(📱 0341-216 990; www.mdbk.de; Katharinenstrasse 10; adult/concession €10/7, audio guide €2; ⊙ 10am-6pm Tue & Thu-Sun, noon-8pm Wed) This imposing modernist glass cube is the home of Leipzig's fine art museum and its world-class collection of paintings from the 15th century to today, including works by Caspar David Friedrich, Cranach, Munch and Monet. Highlights include rooms dedicated to native sons Max Beckmann, Max Klinger and Neo Rauch. Exhibits are playfully juxtaposed and include sculpture, installation and religious art. The collection is enormous, so set aside at least two hours to do it justice.

★ Nikolaikirche   CHURCH
(Church of St Nicholas; www.nikolaikirche.de; Nikolaikirchhof 3; ⊙ 10am-6pm Mon-Sat, to 4pm Sun) This church has Romanesque and Gothic roots, but since 1797 has sported a striking neoclassical interior with palm-like pillars and cream-coloured pews. While the design is certainly gorgeous, the church is most famous for playing a key role in the nonviolent movement that led to the downfall of the

East German government. As early as 1982 it hosted 'peace prayers' every Monday at 5pm (still held today), which over time inspired and empowered local citizens to confront the injustices plaguing their country.

Asisi Panometer   GALLERY
(📱 0341-355 5340; www.asisi.de; Richard-Lehmann-Strasse 114; adult/concession €11.50/10; ⊙ 10am-5pm Mon-Fri, to 6pm Sat & Sun; 🚌 16 to Richard-Lehmann/Zwickauer Strasse) The happy marriage of a *pano*rama (a giant 360-degree painting) and a gas*ometer* (a giant gas tank) is a panometer. The unusual concept is the brainchild of Berlin-based artist Yadegar Asisi, who uses paper and pencil and computer technology to create bafflingly detailed monumental scenes drawn from nature or history. Each work is about 100m long and 30m high.

🛏 Sleeping & Eating

★ Steigenberger Grandhotel Handelshof   HOTEL €€€
(📱 0341-350 5810; www.steigenberger.com; Salzgässchen 6; r from €182; ❈ ❄ @ 🛜) Behind the imposing historic facade of a 1909 municipal trading hall, this exclusive boutique luxury joint outclasses most of Leipzig's hotels with its super-central location, charmingly efficient team and modern rooms with crisp white-silver-purple colours, high ceilings and marble bathrooms. The stylish bi-level spa is the perfect bliss-out station.

★ Stadtpfeiffer   INTERNATIONAL €€€
(📱 0341-217 8920; www.stadtpfeiffer.de; Augustusplatz 8; 4-/6-course menu €108/128; ⊙ 6-11pm Tue-Sat) Petra and Detlef Schlegel give deceptively simple-sounding dishes the star treatment, and were deservedly the first in Leipzig to get the Michelin nod. Pairing punctilious artisanship with bottomless imagination, they create such exquisitely calibrated dishes as smoked Arctic char with foie gras or warm chocolate cake with lavender ice cream. It's a relaxed spot inside the Gewandhaus concert hall.

Auerbachs Keller   GERMAN €€€
(📱 0341-216 100; www.auerbachs-keller-leipzig.de; Mädlerpassage, Grimmaische Strasse 2-4; mains Keller €16-28, Weinstuben €33-35; ⊙ Keller noon-11pm daily, Weinstuben 6-11pm Mon-Sat) Founded in 1525, Auerbachs Keller is one of Germany's best-known restaurants. It's cosy and touristy, but the food's actually quite good and the

setting memorable. There are two sections: the vaulted Grosser Keller for hearty Saxonian dishes and the four historic rooms of the Historische Weinstuben for upmarket German fare. Reservations are highly advised.

☆ Entertainment

Gewandhausorchester CLASSICAL MUSIC
(☑ 0341-127 0280; www.gewandhausorchester.de; Augustusplatz 8) Led by Latvian conductor Andris Nelsons, the Gewandhaus is one of Europe's finest and oldest civic orchestras. With a history harking back to 1743, it became an orchestra of European renown a century later under music director Felix Mendelssohn-Bartholdy.

❶ Information

Tourist Office (☑ 0341-710 4260; www.leipzig.travel; Katharinenstrasse 8; ☉10am-6pm Mon-Fri, to 4pm Sat, to 3pm Sun) Room referral, ticket sales, maps and general information. Also sells the **Leipzig Card** (one/three days €11.90/23.50), which is good for free or discounted admission to attractions, plus free travel on public transport.

❶ Getting There & Away

Leipzig-Halle Airport (LEJ; ☑ 0341-2240; www.leipzig-halle-airport.de) is about 21km west of Leipzig.

High-speed trains frequently serve Frankfurt (€88, 3¾ hours), Dresden (€26.50, 1¼ hours) and Berlin (€49, 1¼ hours), among other cities.

CENTRAL GERMANY

Crucial to its culture, science, industry and history, Mitteldeutschland is Germany's beating heart. It is studded with cities whose historical importance matches their modern vitality (Weimar, Erfurt and Kassel are just the first names on this list). Ridged by low, forested mountains that loom large in German mythology, it's also edified by museums, cathedrals and castles without number.

Weimar

☑ 03643 / POP 64,426

Historical epicentre of the German Enlightenment, Weimar is an essential stop for anyone with a passion for German history and culture. A pantheon of intellectual and creative giants lived and worked here: Goethe, Schiller, Bach, Cranach, Liszt, Nietzsche, Gro-

pius, Herder, Feininger, Kandinsky...the list goes on. In summer, Weimar's many parks and gardens lend themselves to quiet contemplation of the town's intellectual and cultural onslaught, or to taking a break from it.

◉ Sights

★ Gedenkstätte Buchenwald MEMORIAL
(☑ 03463-4300; www.buchenwald.de; Buchenwald; ☉9am-6pm Apr-Oct, to 4pm Nov-Mar; ℗) Between 1937 and 1945, hidden from Weimarers and surrounding villagers, 250,000 men, women and children were incarcerated here, some 56,500 of whom were murdered. Buchenwald ('Beech Forest') has been preserved almost untouched as a memorial, with visitors encouraged to wander quietly and freely around the numerous structures, including the crematorium. Tours, pamphlets and books in English are available, as are excellent multilanguage audio guides (€3, or €5 with images). Last admission is 30 minutes before closing.

★ Goethe-Nationalmuseum MUSEUM
(☑ 03643-545 400; www.klassik-stiftung.de; Frauenplan 1; adult/concession €12.50/9; ☉9.30am-6pm Tue-Sun Apr-Oct, to 4pm Nov-Mar) This is the world's leading museum on Johann Wolfgang von Goethe, Germany's literary colossus. It incorporates his home of 50 years, gifted by Duke Carl August to keep him in Weimar, and left largely as it was upon his death in 1832. This is where Goethe worked, studied, researched, and penned *Faust* and other immortal works. In a modern annexe, documents and objects shed light on the man and his achievements in literature, art, science and politics.

★ Herzogin Anna Amalia Bibliothek LIBRARY
(☑ 03643-545 400; www.klassik-stiftung.de; Platz der Demokratie 1; adult/concession €8/6.50; ☉9.30am-2.30pm Tue-Sun) Assembled by Duchess Anna Amalia (1739–1807), the power (and purse) behind Weimar's classical florescence, this Unesco-listed library has been beautifully reconstructed after a fire in 2004 destroyed much of the building and its priceless contents. Some of the most precious tomes are housed in the magnificent Rokokosaal (Rococo Hall), and were once used by Goethe, Schiller, Christoph Wieland, Johann Herder and other Weimar hot shots, whose various busts and paintings still keep watch over the collection.

🛏 Sleeping & Eating

Labyrinth Hostel HOSTEL €

(📞 03643-811 822; www.weimar-hostel.com; Goetheplatz 6; dm/d €18/48, linen €2; @ 🛜) This super-friendly, professionally run hostel offers imaginative, artist-designed rooms. In one double the bed perches on stacks of books, while the 'purple room' features a wooden platform bed. There are en suites and shared bathrooms, plus a communal kitchen and lovely rooftop terrace. Breakfast costs €4, and the hostel will buy ingredients for guests to cook shared meals from their home countries.

★ Design

Apartments Weimar APARTMENT €€

(📞 017 2356 2210; www.hier-war-goethe-nie.de; Fuldaer Strasse 85; 1-/2-/3-bedroom apt from €60/95/95; 🛜) Get in quick to snap up one of these enormous, self-contained, fully renovated heritage apartments run by charming and generous hosts. The three apartments (with one, two or three bedrooms) are designed by Bauhaus University graduates: if you like their choice in fittings, they're available from the online shop. The ideal base from which to explore the delights of Weimar.

Gretchen's Cafe & Restaurant CAFE €€

(📞 03643-457 9877; http://gretchens-weimar.de; Seifengasse 8; mains €19-20; ⏱ 9am-11pm; 👶) 🍃 Located on the ground floor of the Familienhotel, and thus family-friendly, this passionately locavore cafe offers great alternatives to the Thuringian standards available across Weimar. For those intent only on snacking and chatting, it serves great cakes, tea and coffee, but the meals (including great-value €7.50 midday specials such as salmon en papillote, with abundant salad) are wholesome and delightful.

ℹ Information

Tourist Office (📞 03643-7450; www.weimar. de; Markt 10; ⏱ 9.30am-6pm Mon-Sat, to 2pm Sun Apr-Oct, 9.30am-5pm Mon-Fri, to 2pm Sat & Sun Nov-Mar) Pick up a great-value **Weimar Card** (€30 for two days) for free admission to most museums, free iGuides, free travel on city buses and discounted tours.

ℹ Getting There & Away

Frequent regional trains go from Weimar Hauptbahnhof, 1km north of Goetheplatz, to Erfurt (€5.80, 15 minutes), Jena (€5.80, 15 minutes), Gotha (€10, 40 minutes) and Eisenach (€16, one hour).

Erfurt

📞 0361 / POP 212,988

A little river courses through this Instagram-pretty medieval pastiche of sweeping squares, time-worn alleyways, a house-lined bridge (Krämerbrücke) and lofty church spires. Erfurt also boasts one of Germany's oldest universities, founded by rich merchants in 1392, where Martin Luther studied philosophy before becoming a monk at the local monastery. It's a refreshingly untouristed spot and well worth exploring

👁 Sights

Erfurt's main sights cluster in the old town, about a 10-minute walk from the train station (or quick ride on tram 3, 4 or 6).

★ Erfurter Dom CATHEDRAL

(Mariendom; 📞 0361-646 1265; www.dom-erfurt. de; Domplatz; ⏱ 9.30am-6pm Mon-Sat, 1-6pm Sun May-Oct, to 5pm Nov-Apr) FREE Erfurt's cathedral, where Martin Luther was ordained a priest, grew over the centuries from a simple 8th-century chapel into the stately Gothic pile of today. Standouts in its treasure-filled interior include the stained-glass windows; the 'Wolfram' (an 850-year-old bronze candelabrum in the shape of a man); the 'Gloriosa' (the world's largest free-swinging medieval bell); a Romanesque stucco Madonna; Cranach's *The Mystic Marriage of St Catherine*; and the intricately carved choir stalls. Group tours start at €4.50 per person.

★ Zitadelle Petersberg FORTRESS

(📞 0361-664 00; Petersberg 3; tour adult/concession €8/4; ⏱ 7pm Fri & Sat May-Oct) Situated on the Petersberg hill northwest of Domplatz, this 36-hectare citadel ranks among Europe's largest and best-preserved baroque fortresses. While most interior buildings are closed to the public (and daubed with stencils by guerrilla artists), it sits above a honeycomb of tunnels that can be explored on two-hour guided tours (in German), run by the tourist office. Otherwise, it's free to roam the external grounds, and to enjoy fabulous views over Erfurt.

🛏 Sleeping & Eating

Opera Hostel HOSTEL €

(📞 0361-6013 1360; www.opera-hostel.de; Walkmühlstrasse 13; dm €15-22, s/d/tr €50/60/80, linen €2.50; @ 🛜) This upmarket hostel in an 18th-century hotel scores big with

WARTBURG CASTLE

On the edge of the Thuringian forest, Eisenach is the birthplace of Johann Sebastian Bach, but even the town's **museum** (☎03691-793 40; www.bachhaus.de; Frauenplan 21; adult/concession €9.50/5; ☺10am-6pm) dedicated to the great composer plays second fiddle to its main attraction: the awe-inspiring 11th-century **Wartburg** (☎03691-2500; www.wartburg-eisenach.de; Auf der Wartburg 1; tour adult/concession €9/5, museum & Luther study only €5/3; ☺tours 8.30am-5pm Apr-Oct, 9am-3.30pm Nov-Mar, English tour 1.30pm) castle.

Perched high above the town (views!), the humungous pile hosted medieval minstrel song contests and was the home of Elisabeth, a Hungarian princess later canonised for her charitable deeds. Its most famous resident, however, was Martin Luther, who went into hiding here in 1521 after being excommunicated and placed under papal ban. During this 10-month stay, he translated the New Testament from Greek into German, contributing enormously to the development of the written German language. His modest study is part of the guided tour. Back in town, there's an exhibit about the man and his historical impact in the **Lutherhaus** (☎03691-298 30; www.lutherhaus-eisenach.com; Lutherplatz 8; permanent & special collections adult/concession €8/6; ☺10am-5pm, closed Mon Nov-Mar), where he lived as a schoolboy.

In summer, arrive before 11am to avoid the worst of the crowds. From April to October, bus 10 runs hourly from 9am to 5pm from the Hauptbahnhof to the Eselstation stop, from where it's a steep 10-minute walk up to the castle.

Regional trains run frequently to Erfurt (€14, 45 minutes) and Weimar (€15, one hour). The tourist office can help with finding accommodation.

wallet-watching global nomads, especially as reception's open round the clock and there's no lockout or curfew. Rooms are bright and spacious, many with sofas. Make friends in the communal kitchen and on-site lounge-bar, or pedal around the city on one of the hostel's bikes (€10 per day).

★**Hotel Brühlerhöhe**   BOUTIQUE HOTEL €€
(☎0361-241 4990; www.hotel-bruehlerhoehe-erfurt.de; Rudolfstrasse 48; s/d from €80/95; P🖸) This Prussian officers' casino turned chic city hotel gets high marks for its opulent breakfast spread (€12.50) and smiling, quick-on-its-feet staff. Rooms are cosy and modern with chocolate-brown furniture, solid timberwork, thick carpets and sparkling baths. It's a short ride on tram 4 (from the Justizzentrum stop) into central Erfurt.

Faustfood   BARBECUE €
(☎0361-6443 6300; www.faustfood.de; Waagegasse 1; mains €10; ☺11am-11pm Wed-Sat, to 7pm Sun) Despite its casual, student-y vibe, this rambunctious grill house is a great place for traditional Thuringian grills (*Rostbrätel* and bratwurst), plus more international meaty treats such as spare ribs, steak and cheeseburgers. Dine in (under the canopy of grill-smoke that hangs below the rafters of what was a medieval barn) or take away, but head elsewhere if you're vegetarian!

★**Zum Wenigemarkt 13**   GERMAN €€
(☎0361-642 2379; www.wenigemarkt-13.de; Wenigemarkt 13; mains €13-18; ☺11.30am-11pm) This upbeat restaurant in a delightful spot (an 18th-century house on the small marketplace at the eastern end of the Krämerbrücke) serves traditional and updated takes on Thuringian cuisine, starring regionally hunted and gathered ingredients where possible. Tender neck fillets of pork with sauerkraut and Thuringian dumplings and roasted char with potato-coconut purée are both menu stars.

ⓘ Information

Tourist Office Erfurt (☎0361-664 00; www.erfurt-tourismus.de; Benediktsplatz 1; ☺10am-6pm Mon-Sat, to 3pm Sun) Sells the 48-hour **ErfurtCard**, available in two configurations: the Classic (€13) provides a free tour (in German) entry to the Alte Synagoge and discounts to all major attractions, while the Mobil (€18) also includes free use of the city's transport.

ⓘ Getting There & Away

Direct IC/ICE trains connect Erfurt with Berlin (from €40, two hours), Dresden (from €25, two hours) and Frankfurt (from €30, 2½ hours). Direct regional trains also run regularly to Weimar (€5.80, 15 minutes) and Eisenach (€14, 45 minutes).

BAVARIA

POP 13.1 MILLION

From the cloud-shredding Alps to the fertile Danube plain, Bavaria (Bayern) is a place that keeps its clichéd promises. Storybook castles bequeathed by an oddball king poke through dark forest, cowbells tinkle in flower-filled meadows, the thwack of palm on Lederhosen accompanies the clump of frothy stein on timber, and medieval walled towns go about their time-warped business.

But there's so much more than the chocolate-box idyll. Learn about Bavaria's state-of-the-art motor industry in Munich, discover its Nazi past in Nuremberg and Berchtesgaden, sip world-class wines in Würzburg or take a mindboggling train ride up Germany's highest mountains.

Munich

089 / POP 1.46 MILLION / ELEV 520M

If you're looking for Alpine clichés, they're all here, but Munich also has plenty of unexpected cards down its Dirndl. Munich's walkable centre retains a small-town air but holds some world-class sights, especially art galleries and museums. Throw in royal Bavarian heritage, an entire suburb of Olympic legacy and a kitbag of dark tourism, and it's clear why southern Germany's metropolis is such a favourite among those who seek out the past but like to hit the town once they're done.

◉ Sights

Munich's major sights cluster around the Altstadt, with the main museum district just north of the Residenz. However, it will take another day or two to explore bohemian Schwabing, the sprawling Englischer Garten and trendy Haidhausen to the east. Northwest of the Altstadt you'll find cosmopolitan Neuhausen, the Olympiapark and Schloss Nymphenburg.

◉ Altstadt

Munich Residenz PALACE

(089-290 671; www.residenz-muenchen.de; Max-Joseph-Platz 3; Museum & Schatzkammer each adult/concession/under 18yr €7/6/free, combination ticket €11/9/free; ⊘9am-6pm Apr–mid-Oct, 10am-5pm mid-Oct–Mar, last entry 1hr before closing; UOdeonsplatz) Generations of Bavarian rulers expanded a medieval fortress into this vast and palatial compound that served as their primary residence and seat of government from 1508 to 1918. Today it's an Aladdin's cave of fanciful rooms and collections through the ages, which can be seen on an audio-guided tour of what is called the **Residenzmuseum** (Residenzstrasse 1). Allow at least two hours to see everything at a gallop.

GERMANY MUNICH

LOCAL KNOWLEDGE

BEER HALLS & BEER GARDENS

Beer drinking is not just an integral part of Munich's entertainment scene– it's a reason to visit. A few enduring faves:

Augustiner Bräustuben (089-507 047; www.braeustuben.de; Landsberger Strasse 19; ⊘10am-midnight; Holzapfelstrasse) Depending on the wind, an aroma of hops envelops you as you approach this traditional beer hall inside the Augustiner brewery. The Bavarian fare is superb, especially the *Schweinshaxe* (pork knuckle). Due to the location the atmosphere in the evenings is slightly more authentic than that of its city-centre cousins, with fewer tourists at the long tables.

Chinesischer Turm (089-383 8730; www.chinaturm.de; Englischer Garten 3; ⊘10am-11pm late Apr-Oct; Chinesischer Turm, Tivolistrasse) This one's hard to ignore because of its English Garden location and pedigree as Munich's oldest beer garden (open since 1791). Camera-toting tourists and laid-back locals, picnicking families and businessmen sneaking a sly brew clomp around the wooden pagoda, showered by the strained sounds of possibly the world's drunkest oompah band.

Hofbräuhaus (089-290 136 100; www.hofbraeuhaus.de; Am Platzl 9; ⊘9am-midnight; Kammerspiele, SMarienplatz, UMarienplatz) Every visitor to Munich should make a pilgrimage to this mothership of all beer halls, if only once. Within this major tourist attraction you'll discover a range of spaces in which to do your mass lifting: the horse chestnut–shaded garden, the main hall next to the oompah band, tables opposite the industrial-scale kitchen and quieter corners.

Central Munich

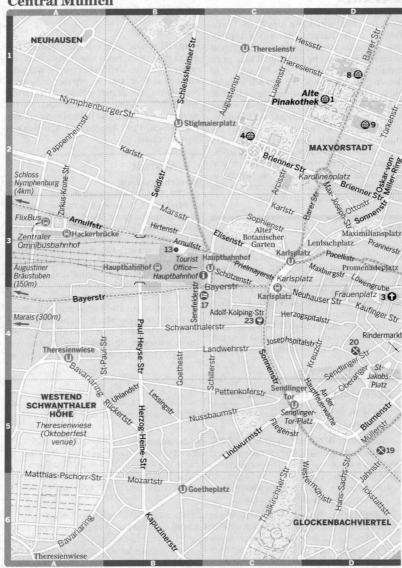

Highlights include the fresco-smothered **Antiquarium** banqueting hall and the exuberantly rococo **Reiche Zimmer** (Ornate Rooms). The **Schatzkammer** (Treasure Chamber) displays a veritable banker's bonus worth of jewel-encrusted bling of yesteryear, from golden toothpicks to finely crafted swords, from miniatures in ivory to gold-entombed cosmetics trunks.

Marienplatz   SQUARE
(**S** Marienplatz, **U** Marienplatz) The epicentral heart and soul of the Altstadt, Marienplatz is a popular gathering spot and packs a lot

till late at night. Many walking tours leave from here.

Frauenkirche CHURCH
(Church of Our Lady; www.muenchner-dom.de; Frauenplatz 1; ⊘7.30am-8.30pm; ⑤Marienplatz) The landmark Frauenkirche, built between 1468 and 1488, is Munich's spiritual heart and the Mt Everest among its churches. No other building in the central city may stand taller than its onion-domed twin towers, which reach a skyscraping 99m. The south tower can be climbed, but has been under urgent renovation for several years.

St Peterskirche CHURCH
(Church of St Peter; Rindermarkt 1; church free, tower adult/child €3/2; ⊘tower 9am-6pm Mon-Fri, from 10am Sat & Sun; ⑪Marienplatz, ⑤Marienplatz) Some 306 steps divide you from the best view of central Munich via the 92m tower of St Peterskirche, central Munich's oldest church

of personality into a compact frame. It's anchored by the **Mariensäule** (St Mary's Column), built in 1638 to celebrate victory over Swedish forces during the Thirty Years' War. This is the busiest spot in all Munich, with throngs of tourists swarming across its expanse from early morning

OKTOBERFEST

Hordes come to Munich for **Oktoberfest** (www.oktoberfest.de; ☉ mid-Sep–early Oct), running the 15 days before the first Sunday in October. Reserve accommodation well ahead and go early in the day so you can grab a seat in one of the hangar-sized beer tents spread across the Theresienwiese grounds, about 1km southwest of the Hauptbahnhof. While there is no entrance fee, those €11 1L steins of beer (called *Mass*) add up fast. Although its origins are in the marriage celebrations of Crown Prince Ludwig in 1810, there's nothing regal about this beery bacchanalia now: expect mobs, expect to meet new and drunken friends, expect decorum to vanish as night sets in and you'll have a blast.

(1150). Inside awaits a virtual textbook of art through the centuries. Worth a closer peek are the Gothic St-Martin-Altar, the baroque ceiling fresco by Johann Baptist Zimmermann and rococo sculptures by Ignaz Günther.

Viktualienmarkt MARKET
(☉ Mon-Fri & morning Sat; ⓤ Marienplatz, ⓢ Marienplatz) Fresh fruit and vegetables, piles of artisanal cheeses, tubs of exotic olives, hams and jams, chanterelles and truffles – Viktualienmarkt is a feast of flavours and one of central Europe's finest gourmet markets.

◉ Maxvorstadt, Schwabing & Englischer Garten

North of the Altstadt, Maxvorstadt is home to Munich's main university and top-drawer art museums. It segues into equally cafe-filled Schwabing, which rubs up against the vast Englischer Garten. Note that many major museums, including all the Pinakothek galleries, charge just €1 admission on Sundays.

★ Alte Pinakothek MUSEUM
(☑ 089-238 0516; www.pinakothek.de; Barer Strasse 27; adult/concession/child €7/5/free, Sun €1, audio guide €4.50; ☉ 10am-8pm Tue, to 6pm Wed-Sun; ☐ Pinakotheken, ☐ Pinakotheken) Munich's main repository of Old European Masters is crammed with all the major players who decorated canvases between the 14th and 18th centuries. This neoclassical temple was masterminded by Leo von Klenze and is a delica-

cy even if you can't tell your Rembrandt from your Rubens. The collection is world famous for its exceptional quality and depth, especially when it comes to German masters.

Neue Pinakothek MUSEUM
(☑ 089-2380 5195; www.pinakothek.de; Barer Strasse 29; adult/child €7/free, Sun €1; ☉ 10am-6pm Thu-Mon, to 8pm Wed; ☐ Pinakotheken, ☐ Pinakotheken) The Neue Pinakothek harbours a well-respected collection of 19th- and early-20th-century paintings and sculpture, from rococo to *Jugendstil* (art nouveau). All the world-famous household names get wall space here, including crowd-pleasing French impressionists such as Monet, Cézanne and Degas as well as Van Gogh, whose boldly pigmented *Sunflowers* (1888) radiates cheer.

Pinakothek der Moderne MUSEUM
(☑ 089-2380 5360; www.pinakothek.de; Barer Strasse 40; adult/child €10/free, Sun €1; ☉ 10am-6pm Tue, Wed & Fri-Sun, to 8pm Thu; ☐ Pinakotheken, ☐ Pinakotheken) Germany's largest modern-art museum unites four significant collections under a single roof: 20th-century art, applied design from the 19th century to today, a graphics collection and an architecture museum. It's housed in a spectacular building by Stephan Braunfels, whose four-storey interior centres on a vast eye-like dome through which soft natural light filters throughout the blanched-white galleries.

Englischer Garten PARK
(English Garden; ⓤ Universität) The sprawling English Garden is among Europe's biggest city parks – it even rivals London's Hyde Park and New York's Central Park for size – and is a popular playground for locals and visitors alike. Stretching north from Prinzregentenstrasse for about 5km, it was commissioned by Elector Karl Theodor in 1789 and designed by Benjamin Thompson, an American-born scientist working as an adviser to the Bavarian government.

Lenbachhaus MUSEUM
(Municipal Gallery; ☑ 089-2333 2000; www.lenbachhaus.de; Luisenstrasse 33; adult/child incl audioguide €10/5; ☉ 10am-8pm Tue, to 6pm Wed-Sun; ☐ Königsplatz, ⓤ Königsplatz) With its fabulous wing added by noted architect Norman Foster, this glorious gallery is the go-to place to admire the vibrant canvases of Wassily Kandinsky, Franz Marc, Paul Klee and other members of ground-breaking modernist group Der Blaue Reiter (The Blue Rider), founded in Munich in 1911.

⊙ Further Afield

★ Schloss Nymphenburg — PALACE

(www.schloss-nymphenburg.de; castle adult/child €6/free, all sites €11.50/free; ☉ 9am-6pm Apr–mid-Oct, 10am-4pm mid-Oct–Mar; ⛴ Schloss Nymphenburg) This commanding palace and its lavish gardens sprawl around 5km northwest of the Altstadt. Begun in 1664 as a villa for Electress Adelaide of Savoy, the stately pile was extended over the next century to create the royal family's summer residence. Franz Duke of Bavaria, head of the once-royal Wittelsbach family, still occupies an apartment here.

BMW Museum — MUSEUM

(www.bmw-welt.de; Am Olympiapark 2; adult/child €10/7; ☉ 10am-6pm Tue-Sun; Ⓤ Olympiazentrum) This silver, bowl-shaped museum comprises seven themed 'houses' that examine the development of BMW's product line and include sections on motorcycles and motor racing. Even if you can't tell a head gasket from a crankshaft, the interior design – with its curvy retro feel, futuristic bridges, squares and huge backlit wall screens – is reason enough to visit.

🖝 Tours

★ Radius Tours & Bike Rental — TOURS

(☏ 089-543 487 7740; www.radiustours.com; Arnulfstrasse 3, Hauptbahnhof; ☉ 8.30am-8pm; ⛴ Hauptbahnhof, Ⓤ Hauptbahnhof, Ⓢ Hauptbahnhof) Entertaining and informative English-language tours include the two-hour Discover Munich walk (€15), the fascinating 2½-hour Third Reich tour (€17.50) and the three-hour Bavarian Beer tour (€36). The company also runs popular excursions to Neuschwanstein, Salzburg and Dachau, and has hundreds of bikes for hire (€14.50 per day).

New Europe Munich — WALKING

(www.neweuropetours.eu; ☉ tours 10am, 10.45am & 2pm; Ⓢ Marienplatz, Ⓤ Marienplatz) Departing from Marienplatz, these English-language walking tours tick off all Munich's central landmarks in three hours. Guides are well informed and fun, though they are under pressure at the end of the tour to get as much as they can in tips. The company also runs (paid) tours to Dachau (€24) and Neuschwanstein (€40).

🛏 Sleeping

Room rates in Munich tend to be high, and they skyrocket during the Oktoberfest. Book well ahead.

Wombats City Hostel Munich — HOSTEL €

(☏ 089-5998 9180; www.wombats-hostels.com; Senefelderstrasse 1; dm/d from €25/95; 🅿 @ 🛜; ⛴ Hauptbahnhof, Ⓤ Hauptbahnhof) Munich's top hostel is a professionally run affair with a whopping 300 dorm beds plus private rooms. Dorms are painted in cheerful pastels and outfitted with wooden floors, en suite facilities, sturdy lockers and comfy pine bunks, all in a central location near the train station.

★ Flushing Meadows — DESIGN HOTEL €€

(☏ 089-5527 9170; www.flushingmeadowshotel.com; Fraunhoferstrasse 32; studios around €150; 🅿 ✳ 🛜; Ⓢ Fraunhoferstrasse) Urban explorers keen on up-to-the-minute design cherish this new contender on the top two floors of a former postal office in hip Glockenbachviertel. Each of the 11 concrete-ceilinged lofts reflects the vision of a locally known personality, while three of the five penthouse studios have a private terrace. Breakfast costs €10.50.

Hotel Laimer Hof — HOTEL €€

(☏ 089-178 0380; www.laimerhof.de; Laimer Strasse 40; s/d from €65/85; 🅿 🛜; ⛴ Romanplatz) A mere a five-minute aristocratic amble from Schloss Nymphenburg, this commendably tranquil refuge is run by a friendly team who take time to get to know their guests. No two of the 23 rooms are alike, but all boast antique touches, oriental carpets and golden beds. Free bike rental, and coffee and tea in the lobby. Breakfast costs €12.

La Maison — DESIGN HOTEL €€

(☏ 089-3303 5550; www.hotel-la-maison.com; Occamstrasse 24; r from €109; 🅿 ✳ 🛜; Ⓤ Münchner Freiheit) Situated in the cool area of Schwabing, this discerningly retro hotel comes immaculately presented in shades of imperial purple and ubercool grey. Rooms at this sassy number wow with heated oak floors, jet-black washbasins and starkly

GERMANY MUNICH

NO WAVE GOODBYE

Possibly the last sport you might expect to see being practised in Munich is surfing, but go to the southern tip of the English Garden at Prinzregentenstrasse and you'll see scores of people leaning over a bridge to cheer on wetsuit-clad daredevils as they hang on an artificially created wave in the **Eisbach** (www.eisbachwelle.de; Prinzregentenstrasse; ⛴ Nationalmuseum/Haus der Kunst). It's only a single wave, but it's a damn fine one!

contrasting design throughout – though the operators can't resist putting a pack of gummy bears on the expertly ruffed pillows! Cool bar on ground level.

Louis Hotel
HOTEL €€€

(☎089-411 9080; www.louis-hotel.com; Viktualienmarkt 6/Rindermarkt 2; r €179-320; ☎; Ⓢ Marienplatz) An air of relaxed sophistication pervades the scene-savvy Louis, where 72 good-sized rooms are furnished in nut and oak, natural stone and elegant tiles. Rooms come equipped with the latest technology. All have small balconies facing either the courtyard or the Viktualienmarkt. Views are also terrific from the rooftop bar and restaurant.

✕ Eating

Marais
CAFE €

(www.cafe-marais.de; Parkstrasse 2; dishes €5-13; ⊙8am-8pm Tue-Sat, 10am-6pm Sun; ⏃; 🚊 Holzapfelstrasse) Is it a junk shop, a cafe or a sewing shop? Well, Westend's oddest coffee house is in fact all three, and everything you see in this converted haberdashery – the knick-knacks, the cakes and the antique chair you're sitting on – is for sale.

Weisses Brauhaus
BAVARIAN €€

(☎089-290 1380; www.weisses-brauhaus.de; Tal 7; mains €7-20; ⊙8am-12.30am; Ⓢ Marienplatz, Ⓤ Marienplatz) One of Munich's classic beer halls, this place is charged in the evenings with red-faced, ale-infused hilarity, with Alpine whoops accompanying the rabble-rousing oompah band. The *Weisswurst* (veal sausage) here sets the standard for the rest to aspire to; sluice down a pair with the unsurpassed Schneider *Weissbier,* but only before noon. Understandably very popular and reservations are recommended after 7pm.

★ Fraunhofer
BAVARIAN €€

(☎089-266 460; www.fraunhofertheater.de; Fraunhoferstrasse 9; mains €5-20; ⊙4.30pm-1am; ⏃; 🚊 Müllerstrasse) With its screechy parquet

floors, stuccoed ceilings, wood panelling and virtually no trace that the last century even happened, this wonderfully characterful inn is perfect for exploring the region with a fork. The menu is a seasonally adapted checklist of southern German favourites, but also features at least a dozen vegetarian dishes and the odd exotic ingredient. Cash only.

Prinz Myshkin
VEGETARIAN €€

(☎089-265 596; www.prinzmyshkin.com; Hackenstrasse 2; mains €9-20; ⊙11am-12.30am; ⏃; Ⓢ Marienplatz, Ⓤ Marienplatz) This place is proof, if any were needed, that the vegetarian experience has well and truly left the sandals, beards and lentils era. Ensconced in a former brewery, Munich's premier meat-free dining spot occupies a gleamingly whitewashed, vaulted space where health-conscious eaters come to savour imaginative dishes such as curry-orange-carrot soup, unexpectedly good curries and 'wellness desserts'.

Alois Dallmayr
DELI €€

(☎089-213 50; www.dallmayr.de; Dienerstrasse 14; ⊙9.30am-7pm Mon-Sat; Ⓢ Marienplatz, Ⓤ Marienplatz) A pricey gourmet delicatessen right in the thick of the Altstadt action, Alois Dallmayr is best known for its coffee but has so much more, including cheeses, ham, truffles, wine, caviar and exotic foods from every corner of the globe.

Tantris
INTERNATIONAL €€€

(☎089-361 9590; www.tantris.de; Johann-Fichte-Strasse 7; menu from €100; ⊙noon-3pm & 6.30pm-1am Tue-Sat Oct-Dec, closed Tue Jan-Sep; ☎; Ⓤ Dietlindenstrasse) Tantris means 'the search for perfection' and here, at one of Germany's most famous restaurants, it's not far off it. The interior design is full-bodied '70s – all postbox reds, truffle blacks and illuminated yellows. The food is sublime and the service is sometimes as unobtrusive as it is efficient. The wine cellar is probably Germany's best. Reservations essential.

🍷 Drinking & Nightlife

Generally speaking, student-flavoured places abound in Maxvorstadt and Schwabing, while traditional beer halls and taverns cluster in the Altstadt. Haidhausen attracts trendy types, and the Gärtnerplatzviertel and Glockenbachviertel are alive with gay bars and hipster haunts.

★ Schumann's Bar
BAR

(☎089-229 060; www.schumanns.de; Odeonsplatz 6-7; ⊙8am-3am Mon-Fri, 6pm-3am Sat & Sun;

DACHAU CONCENTRATION CAMP

Officially called the **KZ-Gedenkstätte Dachau** (Dachau Concentration Camp Memorial Site; ☑ 08131-669 970; www.kz-gedenkstaette-dachau.de; Peter-Roth-Strasse 2a, Dachau; ⊗ 9am-5pm) **FREE**, the first Nazi concentration camp opened in 1933 in a bucolic village about 16km northwest of central Munich. All in all, it 'processed' more than 200,000 inmates, killing at least 43,000, and is now a haunting memorial. Expect to spend two to three hours exploring the grounds and exhibits. For deeper understanding, pick up an audioguide (€4), join a 2½-hour tour (€3.50) or watch the 22-minute English-language documentary at the main museum. From the Hauptbahnhof take the S2 to Dachau station (two-zone ticket; €5.80, 22 minutes), then catch frequent bus 726 (direction: Saubachsiedlung) to the camp.

Odeonsplatz) Urbane and sophisticated, Schumann's shakes up Munich's nightlife with libational flights of fancy and an impressive range of concoctions. It's also good for weekday breakfasts. Cash only.

★ Alter Simpl   PUB
(☑ 089-272 3083; www.altersimpl.com; Türkenstrasse 57; ⊗ 11am-3am Mon-Fri, to 4am Sat & Sun; Schellingstrasse) Thomas Mann and Hermann Hesse used to knock 'em back at this well-scuffed and wood-panelled thirst parlour. A bookish ambience still pervades, making this an apt spot at which to curl up with a weighty tome over a few Irish ales. The curious name is an abbreviation of the satirical magazine *Simplicissimus*.

Harry Klein   CLUB
(☑ 089-4028 7400; www.harrykleinclub.de; Sonnenstrasse 8; ⊗ from 11pm; Karlsplatz, Karlsplatz, Karlsplatz) Follow the gold-lined passageway off Sonnenstrasse to what some regard as one of the best *Elektro-clubs* in the world. Nights here are an amazing alchemy of electro sound and visuals, with live video art projected onto the walls Kraftwerk-style and blending to awe-inspiring effect with the music.

☆ Entertainment

★ FC Bayern München   FOOTBALL
(☑ 089-6993 1333; www.fcbayern.de; Allianz Arena, Werner-Heisenberg-Allee 25, Fröttmaning; Fröttmaning) Germany's most successful team both domestically and on a European level plays home games at the impressive Allianz Arena, built for the 2006 World Cup. Tickets can be ordered online.

❶ Information

Tourist office branches include **Hauptbahnhof** (☑ 089-21 800; www.muenchen.de; Bahnhofplatz 2; ⊗ 9am-8pm Mon-Sat, 10am-6pm Sun; Hauptbahnhof, Hauptbahnhof, Hauptbahnhof) and **Marienplatz** (☑ 089-2339 6500; www.muenchen.de; Marienplatz 2; ⊗ 9am-7pm Mon-Fri, to 4pm Sat, 10am-2pm Sun; Marienplatz, Marienplatz).

❶ Getting There & Away

AIR
Munich Airport (MUC; ☑ 089-975 00; www.munich-airport.de) is about 30km northeast of town and linked to the Hauptbahnhof every 10 minutes by S-Bahn (S1 and S8; €10.80, 40 minutes) and every 20 minutes by the **Lufthansa Airport Bus** (€10.50, 45 minutes, between 5.15am and 7.55pm).

Allgäu Airport (FMM; ☑ 08331-984 2000; www.allgaeu-airport.de; Am Flughafen 35, Memmingen) The Allgäu Airport Express also leaves from Arnulfstrasse at the Hauptbahnhof, making the trip up to seven times a day. The journey takes one hour 40 minutes and the fare is €13 (return €19.50).

BUS
The **Zentraler Omnibusbahnhof** (Central Bus Station, ZOB; www.muenchen-zob.de; Arnulfstrasse 21; Hackerbrücke), next to the Hackerbrücke S-Bahn station, handles the vast majority of international and domestic coach services. The main operator is the low-cost coach company **Flixbus** (☑ 030 300 137 300; www.flixbus.com; Zentraler Omnibusbahnhof, Arnulfstrasse 21), which links Munich to countless destinations across Germany and beyond.

TRAIN
All services leave from the **Hauptbahnhof** (Central Station). Staffed by native English speakers, **Euraide** (www.euraide.de; Desk 1, Reisezentrum, Hauptbahnhof; ⊗ 10am-7pm Mon-Fri Mar-Apr & Aug-Dec, 9.30am-8pm May-Jul; Hauptbahnhof, Hauptbahnhof, Hauptbahnhof) is a friendly agency.

Frequent fast and direct services include trains to Nuremberg (€40 to €60, one hour), Frankfurt (€105, 3¼ hours), Berlin (€150, 5¼ hours) and Vienna (€99, four hours), and thrice daily services to Zürich (€84, 4¾ hours).

ⓘ Getting Around

Central Munich is compact enough to explore on foot. The outlying suburbs are easily reachable by public transport, which is extensive and efficient, if showing its age slightly.

S-Bahn Reaches out into the suburbs and beyond. All *S-Bahn* trains follow the Stammstrecke (central line) through central Munich.

U-Bahn Serves the centre and the inner suburbs.

Tram These link the centre with the suburbs.

For public transport information, consult MVV (www.mvv-muenchen.de).

Bavarian Alps

Stretching west from Germany's remote southeastern corner to the Allgäu region near Lake Constance, the Bavarian Alps (Bayerische Alpen) form a stunningly beautiful natural divide along the Austrian border. Ranges further south may be higher, but these mountains shoot up from the foothills so abruptly that the impact is all the more dramatic.

Garmisch-Partenkirchen

📞 08821 / POP 27.024

A paradise for skiers and hikers, Garmisch-Partenkirchen is blessed with a fabled setting a snowball's throw from Germany's highest peak, the 2962m-high Zugspitze. Garmisch has a more cosmopolitan feel, while Partenkirchen retains an old-world Alpine village vibe. The towns were merged for the 1936 Winter Olympics.

◎ Sights

★**Zugspitze**   MOUNTAIN

(www.zugspitze.de; return adult/child €56/32; ⊙train 8.15am-2.15pm) On good days, views from Germany's rooftop extend into four countries. The return trip starts in Garmisch aboard a cogwheel train (Zahnradbahn) that chugs along the mountain base to the Eibsee, an idyllic forest lake. From here, the Eibsee-Seilbahn, a super-steep cable car, swings to the top at 2962m. When you're done admiring the views, the Gletscherbahn cable car takes you to the Zugspitze glacier at 2600m, from where the cogwheel train heads back to Garmisch.

Partnachklamm   CANYON

(www.partnachklamm.eu; adult/child €5/2; ⊙8am-6pm May & Oct, 6am-10pm Jun-Sep, 9am-6pm Nov-Apr) A top attraction around Garmisch is this narrow and dramatically beautiful 700m-long gorge with walls rising up to 80m. The trail hewn into the rock is especially spectacular in winter when you can walk beneath curtains of icicles and frozen waterfalls.

🛏 Sleeping & Eating

Reindl's Partenkirchner Hof   HOTEL €€

(📞 08821-943 870; www.reindls.de; Bahnhofstrasse 15; s/d €100/150; P 🏡) Reindl's may not look worthy of its five stars from street level, but this elegant, tri-winged luxury hotel is stacked with perks, a wine bar and a top-notch gourmet restaurant. Renovated to perfection on a rolling basis, the rooms are studies in folkthemed elegance and some enjoy gobsmacking Alpine views to get you in the mood.

Gasthof Fraundorfer   BAVARIAN €€

(📞 08821-9270; www.gasthof-fraundorfer.de; Ludwigstrasse 24; mains €5-23; ⊙7am-midnight Thu-Mon, from 5pm Wed) If you've travelled to the Alps to experience yodelling, knee slapping and beetroot-faced locals squeezed into Lederhosen, you just arrived at the right address. Steins of frothing ale fuel the increasingly raucous atmosphere as the evening progresses and monster portions of plattered pig meat push belt buckles to the limit. Decor ranges from baroque cherubs to hunting trophies and the 'Sports Corner'. Unmissable.

ⓘ Information

Tourist Office (📞 08821-180 700; www.gapa.de; Richard-Strauss-Platz 2; ⊙9am-5pm Mon-Fri, to 3pm Sat) Friendly staff hand out maps, brochures and advice.

ⓘ Getting There & Away

Numerous tour operators run day trips to Garmisch-Partenkirchen from Munich, but there's also at least hourly direct train services (€22, 80 minutes).

Berchtesgaden

📞 08652 / POP 7791

Plunging deep into Austria and framed by six high-rise mountain ranges, the Berchtesgadener Land is a drop-dead-gorgeous corner of Bavaria steeped in myths and legends. Framed by Germany's second-highest mountain, the Watzmann (2713m), its dreamy, fir-lined valleys are filled with gurgling streams and peaceful Alpine villages. Much of the area is protected within the 210-sq-km Berchtesgaden National Park, a Unesco Biosphere Reserve. The village of Berchtesgaden is the obvious base for hiking circuits into the park.

◉ Sights & Activities

Berchtesgaden's main sights are all a car or bus ride away from town. Seeing everything in a day without your own transport is virtually impossible.

★ Eagle's Nest
HISTORIC SITE

(Kehlsteinhaus; ☑08652-29 69; www.kehlstein haus.de; Obersalzberg; tour €30.50; ⊗ buses 8.30am-4.50pm mid-May–Oct) At 1834m above sea level, the Eagle's Nest was built as a mountaintop retreat for Hitler, and gifted to him on his 50th birthday. It took around 3000 workers a mere two years to carve the precipitous 6km-long mountain road, cut a 124m-long tunnel and a brass-panelled lift through the rock, and build the lodge itself (now a restaurant). It can only be reached by special shuttle bus from the Kehlsteinhaus bus station.

★ Königssee
LAKE

(Schönau am Königsee) Gliding serenely across the wonderfully picturesque, emerald-green Königssee makes for some unforgettable memories and photo opportunities. Cradled by steep mountain walls some 5km south of Berchtesgaden, the Königssee is Germany's highest lake (603m), with drinkably pure waters shimmering into fjordlike depths. Bus 841/843 makes the trip out here from the Berchtesgaden train station roughly every hour. **Boat tours** (☑08652-963 60; www.seenschifffahrt.de; Schönau; return boat €15; ⊗ boats 8am-5.15pm mid-Jun–mid-Sep, shorter hours rest of the year) run up to every 30 minutes in both directions.

Dokumentation Obersalzberg
MUSEUM

(☑08652-947 960; www.obersalzberg.de; Salzbergstrasse 41, Obersalzberg; adult/child €3/free, audioguide €2; ⊗ 9am-5pm daily Apr-Oct, 10am-3pm Tue-Sun Nov-Mar, last entry 1hr before closing) In 1933 the tranquil Alpine settlement of Obersalzberg (3km from Berchtesgaden) in essence became the second seat of Nazi power after Berlin, a dark period that's given the full historical treatment at this superb exhibition. Various rooms document the forced takeover of the area, the construction of the compound and the daily life of the Nazi elite. All facets of Nazi terror are dealt with, including Hitler's near-mythical appeal, his racial politics, the resistance movement, foreign policy and the death camps.

🍽 Sleeping & Eating

★ Hotel Reikartz Vier Jahreszeiten
HOTEL €€

(☑08652-9520; www.hotel-vierjahreszeiten-ber chtesgaden.de; Maximilianstrasse 20; r from €70; ⊗ reception 7am-11pm; P🐾🛜❄) For a taste of Berchtesgaden's storied past, stay at this traditional lodge where Bavarian royalty once crumpled the sheets. Rooms are very well kept and the south-facing (more-expensive) quarters offer dramatic views of the peaks. After a day's sightseeing, dinner in the hunting lodge–style Hubertusstuben restaurant is a real treat.

Bräustübl
BAVARIAN €€

(☑08652-976 724; www.braeustueberl-bercht esgaden.de; Bräuhausstrasse 13; mains €7-17; ⊗ 10am-midnight) Past the vaulted entrance painted in Bavaria's white and blue diamonds, this lively but cosy beer hall–beer garden is run by the local brewery. Expect a carnivorous feast with favourites such as pork roast and the house speciality: breaded calf's head (tastes better than it sounds). On Friday and Saturday, an oompah band launches into knee-slapping action.

ℹ Information

Tourist Office (☑08652-896 70; www. berchtesgaden.com; Königseer Strasse 2; ⊗ 8.30am-6pm Mon-Fri, 9am-5pm Sat, shorter hours mid-Oct–Mar) Near the train station, this very helpful office has detailed information on the entire Berchtesgaden region.

ℹ Getting There & Away

Travelling from Munich by train involves a change from Meridian to BLB (Berchtesgadener Land Bahn) trains at Freilassing (€36.40, 2½ hours, at least hourly connections). The best option between Berchtesgaden and Salzburg is RVO bus 840 (45 minutes).

Füssen

☑08362 / POP 15,558

In the foothills of the Alps, Füssen itself is a charming town, although most visitors skip it and head straight for Schloss Neuschwanstein and Hohenschwangau, the two most famous castles associated with King Ludwig II. You can see both on a long day trip from Munich, although only when spending the night, after all the day-trippers have gone, will you sense a certain Alpine serenity.

◉ Sights

★ Schloss Neuschwanstein   CASTLE
(☑ tickets 08362-930 830; www.neuschwanstein.de; Neuschwansteinstrasse 20; adult/child €13/free, incl Hohenschwangau €25/free; ⊙ 9am-6pm Apr–mid-Oct, 10am-4pm mid-Oct–Mar) Appearing through the mountaintops like a mirage, Schloss Neuschwanstein was the model for Disney's *Sleeping Beauty* castle. King Ludwig II planned this fairy-tale pile himself, with the help of a stage designer rather than an architect. He envisioned it as a giant stage on which to recreate the world of Germanic mythology, inspired by the operatic works of his friend Richard Wagner. The most impressive room is the **Sängersaal** (Minstrels' Hall), whose frescos depict scenes from the opera *Tannhäuser*.

Schloss Hohenschwangau   CASTLE
(☑ 08362-930 830; www.hohenschwangau.de; Alpseestrasse 30; adult/child €13/free, incl Neuschwanstein €25/free; ⊙ 8am-5pm Apr–mid-Oct, 9am-3pm mid-Oct–Mar) King Ludwig II grew up at the sun-yellow Schloss Hohenschwangau and later enjoyed summers here until his death in 1886. His father, Maximilian II, built this palace in a neo-Gothic style atop 12th-century ruins left by Schwangau knights. Far less showy than Neuschwanstein, Hohenschwangau has a distinctly lived-in feel where every piece of furniture is a used original. After his father died, Ludwig's main alteration was having stars, illuminated with hidden oil lamps, painted on the ceiling of his bedroom.

---

❶ CASTLE TICKETS & TOURS

Schloss Neuschwanstein and Schloss Hohenschwangau can only be visited on guided tours (in German or English), which last about 35 minutes each (Hohenschwangau is first). Strictly timed tickets are available from the **Ticket Centre** (☑ 08362-930 830; www.hohenschwangau.de; Alpseestrasse 12; ⊙ 7.30am-5pm Apr–mid-Oct, 8.30am-3pm mid-Oct–Mar) at the foot of the castles. In summer, come as early as 8am to ensure you get in that day.

Enough time is left between tours for the steep 30- to 40-minute walk between the castles. Alternatively, you can take a horse-drawn carriage, which is only marginally quicker.

▦ Sleeping & Eating

Hotel Sonne   DESIGN HOTEL €€
(☑ 08362-9080; www.hotel-fuessen.de; Prinzregentenplatz 1; s/d from €90/110; [P] 🛜) Although traditional looking from outside, this Altstadt favourite offers an unexpected design-hotel experience within. Themed rooms feature everything from swooping bed canopies to big-print wallpaper, and huge pieces of wall art to sumptuous fabrics. The public spaces are littered with pieces of art, period costumes and design features – the overall effect is impressive and slightly unusual for this part of Germany.

Zum Hechten   BAVARIAN €€
(Ritterstrasse 6; mains €8-19; ⊙ 10am-10pm) Füssen's best hotel restaurant has six different spaces to enjoy and keeps things regional with a menu of Allgäu staples like schnitzel and noodles, Bavarian pork-themed favourites, and local specialities such as venison goulash from the Ammertal.

❶ Information

Tourist Office (☑ 08362-938 50; www.fuessen.de; Kaiser-Maximilian-Platz; ⊙ 9am-5pm Mon-Fri, 9.30am-3.30pm Sat) Can help find rooms.

❶ Getting There & Away

Füssen is the southern terminus of the Romantic Road Coach.

If you want to do the castles in a single day from Munich, you'll need to start very early. The first train leaves Munich at 4.48am (€28.40, change in Kaufbeuren), reaching Füssen at 6.49am. Otherwise, direct trains leave Munich once every two hours throughout the day.

RVO buses 78 and 73 (www.rvo-bus.de) serve the castles from Füssen Bahnhof (€4.40 return, eight minutes, at least hourly).

The Romantic Road

Stretching 400km from the vineyards of Würzburg to the foot of the Alps, the Romantic Road (Romantische Strasse) is by far the most popular of Germany's holiday routes. This well-trodden trail cuts through a cultural and historical cross-section of southern Germany as it traverses Franconia and clips Baden-Württemberg in the north before plunging into Bavaria proper to end at Ludwig II's crazy castles.

❶ Getting There & Away

Frankfurt and Munich are the most popular gateways for exploring the Romantic Road. The ideal way to travel is by car, though many prefer to take the **Romantic Road Coach** (www. romanticroadcoach.de), which can get incredibly crowded in summer. From April to October this special coach runs daily in each direction between Frankfurt and Füssen (for Neuschwanstein); the entire journey takes around 12 hours. There's no charge for breaking the journey and continuing the next day.

Tickets are available for the entire route or for short segments, and reservations are only necessary during peak-season weekends.

Rothenburg ob der Tauber

📞 09861 / POP 11,106

With its jumble of half-timbered houses enclosed by Germany's best-preserved ramparts, Rothenburg ob der Tauber lays on the medieval cuteness with a trowel. It's an essential stop on the Romantic Road but, alas, overcrowding can detract from its charm. Visit early or late in the day (or, ideally, stay overnight) to experience this historic wonderland sans crowds.

❍ Sights

Jakobskirche   CHURCH
(Church of St Jacob; Klingengasse 1; adult/child €2.50/1.50; ⊙9am-5pm Apr-Oct, shorter hours Nov-Mar) One of the few places of worship in Bavaria to charge admission, Rothenburg's Lutheran parish church was begun in the 14th century and finished in the 15th. The building sports some wonderfully aged stained-glass windows, but the top attraction is Tilman Riemenschneider's **Heilig Blut Altar** (Altar of the Holy Blood). The gilded cross above the main scene depicting the Last Supper incorporates Rothenburg's most treasured reliquary – a rock crystal capsule said to contain three drops of Christ's blood.

Rathausturm   HISTORIC BUILDING
(Town Hall Tower; Marktplatz; adult/child €2/0.50; ⊙9.30am-12.30pm & 1-5pm Apr-Oct, 10.30am-2pm & 2.30-6pm Sun-Thu, to 7pm Fri & Sat Dec, noon-3pm Sat & Sun Jan-Mar & Nov) The Rathaus on Marktplatz was begun in Gothic style in the 14th century and was completed during the Renaissance. Climb the 220 steps of the medieval town hall to the viewing platform of the Rathausturm to be rewarded with widescreen views of the Tauber.

✦ Festivals & Events

Christmas Market   CHRISTMAS MARKET
(www.rothenburg.de; ⊙Advent) The Rothenburger Reiterlesmarkt, as it's officially known, is the town's Christmas market and one of the most romantic in Germany. It's set out around the central Marktplatz during Advent.

🛏 Sleeping & Eating

Altfränkische Weinstube   HOTEL €€
(📞09861-6404; www.altfraenkische.de; Klosterhof 7; d €80-130; 🛜) This very distinctive, 650-year-old inn has eight wonderfully romantic, realistically priced rural-style rooms with exposed half-timber, bath-tubs and four-poster or canopied beds in most rooms. From 6pm onwards, the tavern serves up sound regional fare with a dollop of medieval cheer.

Burg-Hotel   HOTEL €€€
(📞09861-948 90; www.burghotel.eu; Klostergasse 1-3; s €100-135, d €125-195; 🅿🌣🛜) Each of the 17 elegantly furnished guest rooms at this boutique hotel built into the town walls has its own private sitting area. The lower floors shelter a decadent spa with tanning beds, saunas and rainforest showers, and a cellar with a Steinway piano; while phenomenal valley views unfurl from the breakfast room and stone terrace.

Zur Höll   FRANCONIAN €€
(📞09861-4229; www.hoell.rothenburg.de; Burggasse 8; mains €7-20; ⊙5-11pm Mon-Sat) This medieval wine tavern is in the town's oldest original building, with sections dating back to 900 CE. The menu of regional specialities is limited but refined, though it's the superb selection of Franconian wines that people really come for.

❶ Information

Tourist Office (📞09861-404 800; www.tourismus.rothenburg.de; Marktplatz 2; ⊙9am-6pm Mon-Fri, 10am-5pm Sat & Sun May-Oct, 9am-5pm Mon-Fri, 10am-1pm Sat Nov-Apr) Helpful office offering free internet access.

❶ Getting There & Away

The Romantic Road Coach pauses in town for 45 minutes.

You can go anywhere by train from Rothenburg as long as it's Steinach. Change there for services to Würzburg (€15.70 – 70 minutes). Travel to and from Munich (from €29, three to four hours) can involve up to three different trains.

Würzburg

📞 0931 / POP 126,635

Straddling the Main River, scenic Würzburg is renowned for its art, architecture and delicate wines. The definite highlight is the Residenz, one of Germany's finest baroque buildings and a Unesco World Heritage Site, though there's plenty more to see besides.

◉ Sights

★ Würzburg Residenz   PALACE

(www.residenz-wuerzburg.de; Balthasar-Neumann-Promenade; adult/child €7.50/free; ⊙9am-6pm Apr-Oct, 10am-4.30pm Nov-Mar, 45min English tours 11am & 3pm, plus 1.30pm & 4.30pm Apr-Oct) The vast Unesco-listed Residenz, built by 18th-century architect Balthasar Neumann as the home of the local prince-bishops, is one of Germany's most important and beautiful baroque palaces. Top billing goes to the brilliant zigzagging **Treppenhaus** (staircase) lidded by what still is the world's largest fresco, a masterpiece by Giovanni Battista Tiepolo depicting allegories of the four then-known continents (Europe, Africa, America and Asia).

Dom St Kilian   CHURCH

(www.dom-wuerzburg.de; Domstrasse 40; ⊙8am-7pm Mon-Sat, to 8pm Sun) `FREE` Würzburg's highly unusual cathedral has a Romanesque core that has been altered many times over the centuries. The elaborate stucco work of the chancel contrasts starkly with the bare whitewash of the austere Romanesque nave that is capped with a ceiling that wouldn't look out of place in a 1960s bus station. The whole mishmash creates quite an impression and is possibly Germany's oddest cathedral interior. The Schönbornkapelle by Balthasar Neumann returns a little baroque order to things.

Festung Marienberg   FORTRESS

(tour adult/child €3.50/free; ⊙tours 11am, 2pm, 3pm & 4pm Tue-Sun, plus 10am & 1pm Sat & Sun mid-Mar–Oct, 11am, 2pm & 3pm Sat & Sun Nov–mid-Mar) Enjoy panoramic city and vineyard views from this hulking fortress whose construction was initiated around 1200 by the local prince-bishops who governed here until 1719. Dramatically illuminated at night, the structure was only penetrated once, by Swedish troops during the Thirty Years' War, in 1631. Inside, the **Fürstenbaumuseum** (closed November to mid-March) sheds light on its former residents' opulent lifestyle, while the Mainfränkisches Museum presents city history and works by local late-Gothic master carver Tilman Riemenschneider and other famous artists.

🛏 Sleeping & Eating

Babelfish   HOSTEL €

(📞 0931-304 0430; www.babelfish-hostel.de; Haugerring 2; dm/s/d €25/65/80; ⊙reception 8am-midnight; 🛜) With a name inspired by a creature in Douglas Adams' novel *The Hitchhiker's Guide to the Galaxy*, this uncluttered and spotlessly clean hostel has 74 beds spread over two floors and a sunny rooftop terrace. The communal areas are inviting places to down a few beers in the evening and there's a well-equipped guest kitchen. Breakfast costs €5.90.

Hotel Zum Winzermännle   HOTEL €€

(📞 0931-541 56; www.winzermaennle.de; Domstrasse 32; s €60-80, d €90-110; 🅿🛜) This family-run converted winery is a feel-good retreat in the city's pedestrianised heart. Rooms are well furnished, if a little on the old-fashioned side; some among those facing the quiet courtyard have balconies. Communal areas are bright and often seasonally decorated. Breakfast costs €7.

★ Bürgerspital Weinstube   FRANCONIAN €€

(📞 0931-352 880; www.buergerspital-weinstuben.de; Theaterstrasse 19; mains €7-25; ⊙10am-midnight) If you are going to eat out just once in Würzburg, the aromatic and cosy nooks of this labyrinthine medieval place probably provide the top local experience. Choose from a broad selection of Franconian wines (some of Germany's best) and wonderful regional dishes and snacks, including *Mostsuppe* (a tasty wine soup). Buy local whites in the adjoining wine shop.

❶ Information

Tourist Office (📞 0931-372 398; www.wuerzburg.de; Marktplatz 9; ⊙10am-6pm Mon-Fri, to 3pm Sat, to 2pm Sun May-Oct, closed Sun & slightly shorter hours Nov-Apr) Within the attractive Falkenhaus, this efficient office can help you with room reservations and tour booking.

❶ Getting There & Away

Frequent trains run to Bamberg (€22, one hour), Frankfurt (€20 to €36, one hour), Nuremberg (€20, one hour) and Rothenburg ob der Tauber (via Steinach; €15.70, one hour).

Nuremberg & Franconia

Nuremberg

📍 0911 / POP 511,600

Nuremberg (Nürnberg) woos visitors with its wonderfully restored medieval Altstadt, its grand castle and, in December, its magical *Christkindlmarkt* (Christmas market). The town played a key role during the Nazi years. It was here that the fanatical party rallies were held, the boycott of Jewish businesses began and the anti-Semitic Nuremberg Laws were enacted. After WWII the city was chosen as the site of the Nuremberg Trials of Nazi war criminals.

🔘 Sights

Nuremberg's city centre is best explored on foot, but the Nazi-related sights are a tram ride away.

★ Kaiserburg   CASTLE

(Imperial Castle; 📍 0911-244 6590; www.kaiserburg -nuernberg.de; Auf der Burg; adult/child incl Sinwell Tower €7/free, Palas & Museum €5.50/free; ⊙9am-6pm Apr-Sep, 10am-4pm Oct-Mar) This enormous castle complex above the Altstadt poignantly reflects Nuremberg's medieval might. The main attraction is a tour of the renovated residential wing (Palas) to see the lavish Knights' and Imperial Hall, a Romanesque double chapel and an exhibit on the inner workings of the Holy Roman Empire. This segues to the Kaiserburg Museum, which focuses on the castle's military and building history. Elsewhere, enjoy panoramic views from the Sinwell Tower or peer 48m down into the Deep Well.

Deutsche Bahn Museum   MUSEUM

(📍 0800-3268 7386; www.dbmuseum.de; Lessingstrasse 6; adult/child €6/3; ⊙9am-5pm Tue-Fri, 10am-6pm Sat & Sun) Forget Dürer and wartime rallies: Nuremberg is a railway town at heart. Germany's first passenger trains ran between here and Fürth, a fact reflected in the unmissable German Railways Museum, which explores the history of Germany's legendary rail system. The huge exhibition that continues across the road is one of Nuremberg's top sights, especially if you have a soft spot for things that run on rails.

Memorium Nuremberg Trials   MEMORIAL

(📍 0911-3217 9372; www.memorium-nuremberg. de; Bärenschanzstrasse 72; adult/child incl audioguide €6/1.50; ⊙9am-6pm Mon & Wed-Fri, 10am-6pm Sat & Sun Apr-Oct, slightly shorter hours Nov-Mar) Göring, Hess, Speer and 21 other Nazi leaders were tried for crimes against peace and humanity by the Allies in Schwurgerichtssaal 600 (Court Room 600) of this still-working courthouse. Today the room forms part of an engaging exhibit detailing the background, progression and impact of the trials using film, photographs, audiotape and even the original defendants' dock. To get here, take the U1 towards Bärenschanze and get off at Sielstrasse.

Reichsparteitagsgelände   HISTORIC SITE

(Luitpoldhain; 📍 0911-231 7538; www.museen. nuernberg.de/dokuzentrum; Bayernstrasse 110; grounds free, Documentation Centre adult/child incl audio guide €6/1.50; ⊙grounds 24hr, Documentation Centre 9am-6pm Mon-Fri, 10am-6pm Sat & Sun) If you've ever wondered where the infamous B&W images of ecstatic Nazi supporters hailing their Führer were taken, it was here in Nuremberg. Much of the grounds were destroyed during Allied bombing raids, but enough remain to get a sense of the megalomania behind it, especially after visiting the excellent **Dokumentationszentrum** (Documentation Centre). It's served by tram 8 from the Hauptbahnhof.

🛏 Sleeping

Five Reasons   HOSTEL €

(📍 0911-9928 6625; www.five-reasons.de; Frauentormauer 42; dm/d from €18/50; @🛜) This crisp, 21st-century 90-bed hotel-hostel boasts spotless dorms, the trendiest hostel bathrooms you are ever likely to encounter, premade beds, card keys, fully equipped kitchen, a small bar and very nice staff. Breakfast is around €5 extra depending on what option you choose. Overall a great place to lay your head in a very central location.

★ Hotel Deutscher Kaiser   HOTEL €€

(📍 0911-242 660; www.deutscher-kaiser-hotel.de; Königstrasse 55; s/d from €90/110; 🛜) Aristocratic in its design and service, this centrally located treat of a historic hotel has been in the same family since the turn of the 20th century. Climb the castle-like granite stairs to find rooms of understated simplicity, flaunting oversize beds, Italian porcelain, silk lampshades and real period furniture (*Biedermeier* and *Jugendstil*).

🍴 Eating & Drinking

Don't leave Nuremberg without trying its famous finger-sized *Nürnberger Bratwürste*. You'll find them everywhere around town.

★ **Albrecht Dürer Stube** FRANCONIAN €€
([☎] 0911-227 209; www.albrecht-duerer-stube.de;
cnr Albrecht-Dürer-Strasse & Agnesgasse; mains
€6-15.50; ⊘ 6pm-midnight Mon-Sat plus 11.30am-
2.30pm Fri & Sun) This unpretentious and
intimate dining room has a Dürer-inspired
dining room, prettily laid tables, a ceramic
stove keeping things toasty and a menu of
Nuremberg sausages, steaks, sea fish, seasonal specials, Franconian wine and *Landbier*
(regional beer). There aren't many tables so
booking ahead at weekends is recommended.

Kloster PUB
(Obere Wörthstrasse 19; ⊘ 5pm-1am) One of
Nuremberg's best drinking dens is all dressed
up as a monastery replete with ecclesiastic
knick-knacks, including coffins emerging
from the walls. The monks here pray to the
god of *Landbier* (regional beer) and won't be
up at 5am for matins, that's for sure.

ℹ Information

Tourist Office Hauptmarkt ([☎] 0911-233 60;
www.tourismus.nuernberg.de; Hauptmarkt 18;
⊘ 9am-6pm Mon-Sat, 10am-4pm Sun)
Tourist Office Künstlerhaus ([☎] 0911-233 60;
www.tourismus.nuernberg.de; Königstrasse 93;
⊘ 9am-7pm Mon-Sat, 10am-4pm Sun)

ℹ Getting There & Away

Nuremberg is connected by train to Berlin (from
€80, three to 3½ hours, hourly), Frankfurt (€30
to €60, 2¼ hours, at least hourly), Hamburg
(from €80, 4½ hours, hourly) and Munich (€40
and €60, one hour, twice hourly).

Bamberg

[☎] 0951 / POP 75,743
Off the major tourist routes, Bamberg is one
of Germany's most delightful and authentic
towns. It has a bevy of beautifully preserved
historic buildings, palaces and churches in
its Unesco-recognised Altstadt, plus a lively
student population and its own style of beer.

◉ Sights

★ **Bamberger Dom** CATHEDRAL
(www.erzbistum-bamberg.de; Domplatz; ⊘ 9.30am-
6pm Apr-Oct, to 5pm Nov-Mar) Beneath the
quartet of spires, Bamberg's cathedral is
packed with artistic treasures, most famously the slender equestrian statue of the **Bamberger Reiter** (Bamberg Horseman), whose
true identity remains a mystery. It overlooks
the tomb of cathedral founders, Emperor
Heinrich II and his wife Kunigunde, splen-

didly carved by Tilmann Riemenschneider.
The marble tomb of Clemens II in the west
choir is the only papal burial site north of
the Alps. Nearby, the Virgin Mary altar by
Veit Stoss also warrants closer inspection.

Altes Rathaus HISTORIC BUILDING
(Old Town Hall; Obere Brücke; adult/child €6/5;
⊘ 10am-4.30pm Tue-Sun) Like a ship in dry
dock, Bamberg's 1462 Old Town Hall was
built on an artifical island in the Regnitz
River, allegedly because the local bishop had
refused to give the town's citizens any land
for its construction. Inside you'll find the
Sammlung Ludwig, a collection of precious
porcelain, but even more enchanting are the
richly detailed frescos adorning its facades
– note the cherub's leg cheekily protruding
from the eastern facade.

Neue Residenz PALACE
(New Residence; [☎] 0951-519 390; Domplatz 8;
adult/child €4.50/free; ⊘ 9am-6pm Apr-Sep, 10am-
4pm Oct-Mar) This splendid episcopal palace
gives you an eyeful of the lavish lifestyle of
Bamberg's prince-bishops who, between
1703 and 1802, occupied its 40-odd rooms
that can only be seen on guided 45-minute
tours (in German). Tickets are also good for
the **Bavarian State Gallery**, with works
by Lucas Cranach the Elder and other Old
Masters. The baroque Rose Garden delivers
fabulous views over the town.

☞ Tours

BierSchmecker Tour WALKING
(www.bier.bamberg.info; adult €22.50) Possibly the
most tempting tour of the amazingly varied
offerings at the tourist office is the self-guided
BierSchmecker Tour. The price includes entry to the Fränkisches Brauereimuseum (depending on the route taken), plus five beer
vouchers valid in five pubs and breweries,
an English information booklet, a route map
and a souvenir stein. Not surprisingly, it can
take all day to complete the route.

🛏 Sleeping & Eating

Obere Sandstrasse near the cathedral and
Austrasse near the university are both good
eat and drink streets. Try Bamberg's unique
style of beer called *Rauchbier* (smoked beer).

★ **Hotel Sankt Nepomuk** HOTEL €€
([☎] 0951-984 20; www.hotel-nepomuk.de; Obere
Mühlbrücke 9; s/d from €90/130; [P][☎]) Aptly
named after the patron saint of bridges, this
is a classy establishment in a half-timbered

former mill right on the Regnitz. It has a superb restaurant (mains €15 to €30) with a terrace, and 24 new-fangled rooms of recent vintage. Breakfast is an extra €5.

Hotel Residenzschloss HOTEL €€
(☑ 0951-609 10; www.residenzschloss.com; Untere Sandstrasse 32; r from €100; P ☎) Bamberg's grandest digs occupy a palatial building formerly used as a hospital. But have no fear, as the swanky furnishings – from the Roman-style steam bath to the flashy piano bar – have little in common with institutional care. High-ceilinged rooms are business standard though display little historical charm. Take bus 916 from the ZOB.

Klosterbräu PUB FOOD €
(Obere Mühlbrücke 1-3; mains €7-13; ☺ 11.30am-10pm Mon-Sat, to 2pm Sun) This beautiful half-timbered brewery is Bamberg's oldest. It draws *Stammgäste* (regulars) and tourists alike who wash down filling slabs of meat and dumplings with its excellent range of ales in the unpretentious dining room.

★ **Schlenkerla** GERMAN €
(☑ 0951-560 60; www.schlenkerla.de; Dominikanerstrasse 6; mains €7-13; ☺ 9.30am-11.30pm) Beneath wooden beams as dark as the superb *Rauchbier* poured straight from oak barrels, locals and visitors gather around a large ceramic stove to dig into scrumptious Franconian fare at this legendary flower-festooned tavern. Staff will pass beers through a tiny window in the entrance for those who just want to taste a beer but not sit.

ⓘ Information

Tourist Office (☑ 0951-297 6200; www.bamberg.info; Geyerswörthstrasse 5; ☺ 9.30am-6pm Mon-Fri, to 4pm Sat, to 2.30pm Sun) Staff sell the **Bambergcard** (€14.90), valid for three days of free bus rides and free museum entry.

ⓘ Getting There & Away

Getting to and from Bamberg by train usually involves a change in Würzburg.

Regensburg & the Danube

Regensburg

☑ 0941 / POP 150,894
In a scene-stealing locale on the wide Danube River, Regensburg has relics of historical periods reaching back to the Romans, yet doesn't get the tourist mobs you'll find in other

CHRISTMAS MARKETS

Beginning in late November every year, central squares across Germany are transformed into Christmas markets or *Christkindlmarkt* (also known as *Weihnachtsmärkte*). Folks stamp about between the wooden stalls, perusing seasonal trinkets (from hand-carved ornaments to plastic angels) while warming themselves with *Glühwein* (mulled, spiced red wine) and grilled sausages. Locals love 'em and, not surprisingly, the markets are popular with tourists, so bundle up and carouse for hours. Markets in Nuremberg, Dresden, Cologne and Munich are especially famous.

equally attractive German cities. Though big on the historical wow factor, today's Regensburg is a laid-back and unpretentious student town with a distinct Italianate flair.

ⓞ Sights

★ **Dom St Peter** CHURCH
(www.bistum-regensburg.de; Domplatz; ☺ 6.30am-7pm Jun-Sep, to 6pm Apr, May & Oct, to 5pm Nov-Mar) It takes a few seconds for your eyes to adjust to the dim interior of Regensburg's soaring landmark, the Dom St Peter, one of Bavaria's grandest Gothic cathedrals with its stunning kaleidoscopic stained-glass windows and an opulent, silver-sheathed main altar. The cathedral is home of the Domspatzen, a 1000-year-old boys' choir that accompanies the 10am Sunday service (only during the school year). The Domschatzmuseum (Cathedral Treasury) brims with monstrances, tapestries and other church treasures.

Altes Rathaus HISTORIC BUILDING
(Old Town Hall; Rathausplatz; adult/child €7.50/4; ☺ tours in English 3pm Easter-Oct, 2pm Nov & Dec, in German every 30min) From 1663 to 1806, the Reichstag (imperial assembly) held its gatherings at Regensburg's old town, an important role commemorated by an exhibit in today's Reichstagsmuseum. Tours take in the lavish assembly hall and the original torture chambers in the cellar. Buy tickets at the tourist office in the same building. Note that access is by tour only. Audioguides are available for English speakers in January and February.

Steinerne Brücke BRIDGE
(Stone Bridge) An incredible feat of engineering for its day, Regensburg's 900-year-old

Stone Bridge was at one time the only fortified crossing of the Danube. Damaged and neglected for centuries (especially by the buses that once used it) the entire expanse has undergone renovation in recent years.

🛏 Sleeping & Eating

★ Elements Hotel
HOTEL €€

(🗷941-2007 2275; www.hotel-elements.de; Alter Kornmarkt 3; d from €105; 🗟) Four elements, four rooms, and what rooms they are! 'Fire' blazes in plush crimson; while 'Water' is a wellness suite with a hot tub; 'Air' is playful and light and natural wood; and stone and leather reign in colonial-inspired 'Earth'. Breakfast in bed costs an extra €10.

Hotel Orphée
HOTEL €€

(🗷0941-596 020; www.hotel-orphee.de; Untere Bachgasse 8; s €40-120, d €80-155; 🗟) Behind a humble door lies a world of genuine charm, unexpected extras and ample attention to detail. The striped floors, wrought-iron beds, original sinks and common rooms with soft cushions and well-read books give the feel of a lovingly attended home. Check-in and breakfast is nearby in the Cafe Orphée at Untere Bachgasse 8. Additional rooms are available above the cafe.

Historische Wurstkuchl
GERMAN €

(🗷0941-466 210; www.wurstkuchl.de; Thundorferstrasse 3; 6 sausages €9.60; ⊙9am-7pm) Completely submerged several times by the Danube's fickle floods, this titchy eatery has been serving the city's traditional finger-size sausages, grilled over beech wood and dished up with its own sauerkraut and sweet grainy mustard, since 1135 and lays claim to being the world's oldest sausage kitchen.

★ Dicker Mann
BAVARIAN €€

(🗷0941-573 70; www.dicker-mann.de; Krebsgasse 6; mains €9-21; ⊙9am-1am; 🗟) The 'Chubby Chappy', a stylish, tranquil and very traditional inn, is one of the oldest restaurants in town, allegedly dating back to the 14th century. All the staples of Bavarian sustenance are plated up, plus a few other dishes for good measure. On a balmy eve, be sure to bag a table in the lovely beer garden out the back.

❶ Information

Tourist Office (🗷0941-507 4410; https://tourismus.regensburg.de; Rathausplatz 4; ⊙9am-6pm Mon-Fri, to 4pm Sat, 9.30am-4pm Sun Apr-Oct, to 2.30pm Sun Nov-Mar; 🗟) In the historic Altes Rathaus. Sells tickets, tours, rooms and an audioguide for self-guided tours.

❶ Getting There & Away

Frequent trains leave for Munich (€29.70, 1½ hours) and Nuremberg (€23.20, one to two hours), among other cities.

STUTTGART & THE BLACK FOREST

POP 12.6 MILLION

The high-tech urbanite pleasures of Stuttgart, one of the engines of the German economy, form an appealing contrast to the historical charms of Heidelberg, home to the country's oldest university and a romantic ruined castle. Beyond lies the myth-shrouded Black Forest (Schwarzwald in German), a pretty land of misty hills, thick forest and cute villages with youthful and vibrant Freiburg as its only major town.

Stuttgart

🗷0711 / POP 628.032

Stuttgart residents enjoy an enviable quality of life that's to no small degree rooted in its fabled car companies – Porsche and Mercedes – which show off their pedigree in two excellent museums. Hemmed in by vine-covered hills the city also has plenty in store for fans of European art.

❍ Sights

Königsstrasse, a long, pedestrianised shopping strip, links the Hauptbahnhof to the city centre with the Schloss and the art museums. The Mercedes-Benz Museum is about 5km northeast and the Porsche Museum 7km north of here.

★ Staatsgalerie Stuttgart
GALLERY

(🗷0711-470 400; www.staatsgalerie.de; Konrad-Adenauer-Strasse 30-32; adult/concession €7/5; ⊙10am-6pm Tue, Wed & Fri-Sun, to 8pm Thu; 🆄 Staatsgalerie) The neoclassical-meets-contemporary Staatsgalerie bears British architect James Stirling's curvy, colourful imprint. Alongside big-name exhibitions, the gallery harbours a stellar collection of European art from the 14th to the 21st centuries, and American post-WWII avant-gardists. Highlights include works by Miró, Picasso, Matisse, Kandinsky and Klee. Special billing goes to masterpieces such as Dalí's

The Sublime Moment (1938), Rembrandt's pensive, chiaroscuro *Saint Paul in Prison* (1627), Max Beckmann's utterly compelling, large-scale *Resurrection* (1916) and Monet's diffuse *Fields in the Spring* (1887).

Schlossgarten
GARDENS

(U Neckartor) A terrific park for a wander right in the heart of the city, Stuttgart's sprawling Schlossgarten threads together the **Mittlerer Schlossgarten** (Middle Palace Garden; U Neckartor), with its fine beer garden for summer imbibing, the sculpture-dotted **Unterer Schlossgarten** (Lower Palace Garden; U Stöckach), and the **Oberer Schlossgarten** (Upper Palace Garden; U Charlottenplatz), home to stately landmarks such as the **Staatstheater** (☎ 0711-202 090; www.staatstheater-stuttgart.de; Oberer Schlossgarten 6; U Schlossplatz) and the glass-fronted **Landtag** (State Parliament; U Charlottenplatz).

Mercedes-Benz Museum
MUSEUM

(☎ 0711-173 0000; www.mercedes-benz.com; Mercedesstrasse 100; adult/concession €10/5; ⏰ 9am-6pm Tue-Sun, last admission 5pm; S Neckarpark) A futuristic swirl on the cityscape, the Mercedes-Benz Museum takes a chronological spin through the Mercedes empire. Look out for legends such as the 1885 Daimler Riding Car (the world's first petrol-powered vehicle) and the record-breaking Lightning Benz that hit 228km/h at Daytona Beach in 1909.

Porsche Museum
MUSEUM

(☎ 0711-9112 0911; www.porsche.com/museum; Porscheplatz 1; adult/concession €8/4; ⏰ 9am-6pm Tue-Sun; S Neuwirtshaus) Like a pearly white spaceship preparing for lift-off, the barrier-free Porsche Museum is a car-lover's dream. Audioguides race you through the history of Porsche from its 1948 beginnings. Stop to glimpse the 911 GT1 that won Le Mans in 1998. Call ahead for details of the factory tours that can be combined with a museum visit.

🛌 Sleeping

Hostel Alex 30
HOSTEL €

(☎ 0711-838 8950; www.alex30-hostel.de; Alexanderstrasse 30; dm €25-29, s/d €43/64; P 🛜; U Olgaeck) Fun-seekers on a budget should thrive at this popular hostel within walking distance of the city centre. Rooms are kept spick and span, and the bar, sun deck and communal kitchen are ideal for swapping stories with fellow travellers. Light sleepers might want to pack earplugs for the thin walls and street noise. Breakfast costs €8.

BOHEMIAN BEANS

To really slip under Stuttgart's skin, mosey through the **Bohnenviertel** (Bean District), one of the city's lesser-known neighbourhoods. Walk south to Hans-im-Glück Platz, centred on a fountain depicting the caged Grimm's fairy-tale character Lucky Hans, and you'll soon reach the boho-flavoured Bohnenviertel, named after beans introduced in the 16th century. Back then they were grown everywhere as the staple food of the poor tanners, dyers and craftsmen who lived here.

Aloft
DESIGN HOTEL €€

(☎ 0711-8787 5000; www.aloftstuttgarthotel.com; Milaneo Shopping Mall, Heilbronner Strasse 70; d €95-293; 🛜; U Stadtbibliothek) It looks pretty nondescript from outside but don't be fooled – this newcomer to Stuttgart's hotel scene is a slick, open-plan design number, with lots of retro-cool touches, pops of bright colour and terrific views. Rooms ramp up the modern-living factor with creature comforts from Bliss Spa toiletries to coffee-making facilities.

🍴 Eating & Drinking

Reiskorn
INTERNATIONAL €€

(☎ 0711-664 7633; www.das-reiskorn.de; Torstrasse 27; mains €11-15.50; ⏰ 5-10pm Tue-Sat; 🍴; U Rathaus) With an easygoing vibe and bamboo-green retro interior, this imaginative culinary globetrotter serves everything from celery schnitzel with mango-gorgonzola cream to meltingly tender beef braised in chocolate-clove sauce, and banana and yam curry. There are plenty of vegetarian and vegan choices. It's always busy.

★ Weinstube am Stadtgraben
GERMAN €€€

(☎ 0711-567 006; www.weinstube-stadtgraben.de; Am Stadtgraben 6, Stuttgart-Bad Cannstatt; 4-course menu €45; ⏰ 6-10pm; U Daimlerplatz) The Swabian food served at this warm, rustic, wood-beamed wine tavern in Bad Cannstatt is the real deal, albeit with a refined touch. Expect dishes that go with the seasons – be it spot-on suckling pig in dark beer sauce, fresh fish with pumpkin purée or duck breast with red cabbage and spinach dumplings. The wines hail from local vines.

Kraftpaule
MICROBREWERY

(www.kraftpaule.de; Nikolausstrasse 2; ⏰ 4-10pm Tue-Fri, 11am-10pm Sat; U Stöckach) Competition is stiff but for our money this might just be Stuttgart's coolest new-wave craft microbrewery and bar. The bartenders really know their stuff, the selection of beers – from IPAs to stouts, single hop brews and wheat beers – is *wunderbar*, and the vibe easygoing in the bare-wood-tabled and terracotta-tiled interior. Check the website for details on tastings.

ⓘ Information

Tourist Office (☑ 0711-222 80; www.stuttgart -tourist.de; Königstrasse 1a; ⊙ 9am-8pm Mon-Fri, to 6pm Sat, 10am-5pm Sun) Can help with room bookings (for a €3 fee). There's also a branch at the **airport** (☑ 0711-222 8100; Stuttgart Airport; ⊙ 8am-7pm Mon-Fri, 9am-1pm & 1.45-4.30pm Sat, 10am-1pm & 1.45-5.30pm Sun).

ⓘ Getting There & Around

Stuttgart Airport (SGT; ☑ 0711-9480; www. stuttgart-airport.com), a major hub for Eurowings, is 13km south of the city and linked to the Hauptbahnhof by S2 and S3 trains (€4.20, 30 minutes).

There are train services to all major German cities, including Frankfurt (€50 to €66, 1¼ hours) and Munich (€54, 2¼ hours).

Heidelberg

☑ 06221 / POP 159,914

Germany's oldest and most famous university town is renowned for its lovely Altstadt, its plethora of pubs and its evocative half-ruined castle. Millions of visitors are drawn each year to this photogenic assemblage, thereby following in the footsteps of Mark Twain who kicked off his European travels in 1878 in Heidelberg, later recounting his bemused observations in *A Tramp Abroad*.

⊙ Sights

★ **Schloss Heidelberg**   CASTLE
(☑ 06221-658 880; www.schloss-heidelberg.de; Schlosshof 1; adult/child incl Bergbahn €7/4, tours €5/2.50, audioguide €5; ⊙ grounds 24hr, castle 8am-6pm, English tours hourly 11.15am-4.15pm Mon-Fri, from 10.15am Sat & Sun Apr-Oct, fewer tours Nov-Mar) Towering over the Altstadt, Heidelberg's ruined Renaissance castle cuts a romantic figure, especially across the Neckar River when illuminated at night. Along with fabulous views, attractions include the **Deutsches Apotheken-Museum** (German Pharmacy Museum; incl in Schloss Heidelberg ticket; ⊙ 10am-6pm Apr-Oct, to 5.30pm Nov-Mar). The castle is reached either via a steep,

cobbled trail in about 10 minutes or by taking the **Bergbahn** (cogwheel train) from Kornmarkt station. The only way to see the less-than-scintillating interior is by tour. After 6pm you can stroll the grounds for free.

Alte Brücke   BRIDGE
(Karl-Theodor-Brücke) Heidelberg's 200m-long 'old bridge', built in 1786, connects the Altstadt with the river's right bank and the Schlangenweg (Snake Path), whose switchbacks lead to the **Philosophenweg** (Philosophers' Walk; Neckar River north bank). Next to the tower gate on the Altstadt side of the bridge, look for the brass sculpture of a monkey holding a mirror. It's the 1979 replacement of the original 17th-century sculpture.

Studentenkarzer   HISTORIC SITE
(Student Jail; ☑ 06221-541 2813; www.uni-heidel berg.de; Auginergasse 2; adult/child incl Universitätsmuseum €3/2.50; ⊙ 10am-6pm Tue-Sun Apr-Oct, to 4pm Mon-Sat Nov-Mar) From 1823 to 1914, students convicted of misdeeds such as public inebriation, loud nocturnal singing, freeing the local pigs or duelling were sent to this student jail for at least 24 hours. Judging by the inventive wall graffiti, some found their stay highly amusing. Delinquents were let out to attend lectures or take exams. In certain circles, a stint in the Karzer was considered a rite of passage.

🛏 Sleeping

★ **Hotel Villa Marstall**   HISTORIC HOTEL €€
(☑ 06221-655 570; www.villamarstall.de; Lauerstrasse 1; s/d/ste from €115/135/165; ⊙ reception 7am-10pm Mon-Sat, 8am-6pm Sun; ❀ ☞) A 19th-century neoclassical mansion directly overlooking the Neckar River, Villa Marstall is a jewel with cherrywood floors, solid-timber furniture and amenities including a lift. Its 18 exquisite rooms are decorated in whites, creams and bronzes, and come with in-room fridges (perfect for chilling a bottle of regional wine). A sumptuous breakfast buffet (€12) is served in the red-sandstone vaulted cellar.

Arthotel Heidelberg   BOUTIQUE HOTEL €€
(☑ 06221-650 060; www.arthotel.de; Grabengasse 7; s €109-172, d €125-198; ᴾ ❀ ☞) This charmer is a winning blend of historic setting and sleek contemporary design. Equipped with huge bathrooms (tubs!), the 24 rooms are spacious and modern – except for three that sport painted ceilings from 1790. There's a courtyard as well as a roof garden (but avoid

rooms below it in summer, when you can hear people walking above). Breakfast costs €13.50.

✖ Eating & Drinking

Schnitzelbank GERMAN €€
(📞06221-211 89; www.schnitzelbank-heidelberg.de; Bauamtsgasse 7; mains €15-22; ⏰5pm-11.30pm Mon-Fri, from 11.30am Sat & Sun, bar to 1am) Small and often jam-packed, this cosy wine tavern has you sampling the local tipples (all wines are regional) and cuisine while crouched on wooden workbenches from the time when this was still a cooperage. It's these benches that give the place its name, incidentally, not the veal and pork schnitzel on the menu.

Zum Roten Ochsen PUB
(Red Ox Inn; www.roterochsen.de; Hauptstrasse 217; ⏰5pm-midnight Mon-Wed, from 11.30am Thu-Sat) Fronted by a red-painted, blue-grey-shuttered facade, Heidelberg's most historic student pub has black-and-white frat photos on the dark wooden walls and names carved into the tables. Along with German luminaries, visitors who've raised a glass here include Mark Twain, John Wayne and Marilyn Monroe. Live piano plays from 7.30pm, with plenty of patrons singing along.

ℹ Information

Tourist Office – Hauptbahnhof (📞06221-5844 444; www.heidelberg-marketing.de; Willy-Brandt-Platz 1; ⏰9am-7pm Mon-Sat, 10am-6pm Sun Apr-Oct, 9am-6pm Mon-Sat Nov-Mar) Right outside the main train station.
Tourist Office – Marktplatz (www.heidelberg-marketing.de; Marktplatz 10; ⏰8am-5pm Mon-Fri) In the old town.

ℹ Getting There & Away

From the **Hauptbahnhof** (Willy-Brandt-Platz), 3km west of the Schloss, there are up to three services per hour to/from Frankfurt (€19.90 to €29.90, one to 1½ hours) and Stuttgart (€23.90 to €39.90, 40 minutes to one hour).

The Black Forest

As deep, dark and delicious as its famous cherry gateau, the Black Forest gets its name from its canopy of evergreens. With deeply carved valleys, thick woodlands, luscious meadows, stout timber farmhouses and wispy waterfalls, it looks freshly minted for a kids' bedtime story. Many of the Black Forest's most impressive sights are in the triangle delimited by the lively university city of Freiburg, 15km east of the Rhine in the southwest; Triberg, cuckoo-clock capital in the north; and the river-valley city of St Blasien in the southeast.

Baden-Baden

📞07221 / POP 54,160
The northern gateway to the Black Forest, Baden-Baden is one of Europe's most famous spa towns and its mineral-rich waters have reputedly cured the ills of celebs from Queen Victoria to Victoria Beckham. An air of old-world luxury hangs over this beautiful town that's also home to a palatial casino.

🏃 Activities

★Friedrichsbad SPA
(📞07221-275 920; www.carasana.de; Römerplatz 1; 3hr ticket €25, incl soap-&-brush massage €37; ⏰9am-10pm, last admission 7pm) If it's the body of Venus and the complexion of Cleopatra you desire, abandon modesty to wallow in thermal waters at this palatial 19th-century marble-and-mosaic-adorned spa. As Mark Twain said, 'after 10 minutes you forget time; after 20 minutes, the world', as you slip into the regime of steaming, scrubbing, hot-cold bathing and dunking in the Roman-Irish bath.

Caracalla Spa SPA
(📞07221-275 940; www.carasana.de; Römerplatz 11; 2/3hr €16/19, day ticket €23; ⏰8am-10pm, last admission 8pm) This modern, glass-fronted spa has a cluster of indoor and outdoor pools, grottoes and surge channels, making the most of the mineral-rich spring water. For those who dare to bare, saunas range from the rustic 'forest' to the roasting 95°C 'fire' variety.

🛏 Sleeping & Eating

Hotel am Markt HISTORIC HOTEL €€
(📞07221-270 40; www.hotel-am-markt-baden.de; Marktplatz 18; s €65-88, d €105-128, apt €110-138; 🅿🛜) Sitting pretty in front of the **Stiftskirche** (Marktplatz; ⏰8am-6pm), this hotel, which is almost three centuries old, has 23 homey, well-kept rooms. It's quiet up here apart from your wake-up call of church bells, but then you wouldn't want to miss out on the great breakfast.

Weinstube im Baldreit GERMAN €€
(📞07221-231 36; Küferstrasse 3; mains €12.50-19; ⏰5-10pm Tue-Sat) Well hidden down cobbled lanes, this wine-cellar restaurant is tricky to find, but worth looking for. Baden-Alsatian

fare such as *Flammkuchen* (Alsatian pizza) topped with Black Forest ham, Roquefort and pears is expertly matched with local wines. Eat in the ivy-swathed courtyard in summer, and the vaulted interior in winter.

ⓘ Information

Main Tourist Office (☎ 07221-275 200; www. baden-baden.com; Schwarzwaldstrasse 52, B500; ⏰ 9am-6pm Mon-Sat, to 1pm Sun) Situated 2km northwest of the centre.

Branch Tourist Office (Kaiserallee 3; ⏰ 10am-5pm Mon-Sat, 2-5pm Sun; ☎) In the Trinkhalle. Sells events tickets.

ⓘ Getting There & Away

Karlsruhe-Baden-Baden Airport (Baden Airpark; ☎ 07229-662 000; www.badenairpark.de), 15km west of Baden-Baden, is served by Ryanair.

Twice-hourly trains run to destinations including Freiburg (€23.70 to €40, 45 to 90 minutes) and Karlsruhe (€11 to €16, 15 to 30 minutes).

Triberg

☎ 07722 / POP 4771

Cuckoo-clock capital, Black Forest–cake pilgrimage site and Germany's highest waterfall – Triberg is a torrent of Schwarzwald superlatives and attracts gushes of guests.

◉ Sights

★ **Triberger Wasserfälle**   WATERFALL
(adult/concession €5/4.50) Niagara they ain't but Germany's highest waterfalls do exude their own wild romanticism. The Gutach River feeds the seven-tiered falls, which drop a total of 163m and are illuminated until 10pm. A paved trail accesses the cascades. Pick up a bag of peanuts at the ticket counter to feed the tribes of inquisitive red squirrels. Entry is cheaper in winter. The falls are in central Triberg.

⌂ Sleeping

Gasthaus Staude   GUESTHOUSE €€
(☎ 07722-4802; http://gasthaus-staude.com; Obertal 20, Triberg-Gremmelsbach; s €55, d €86-104; P ☎) A beautiful example of a 17th-century Black Forest farmhouse, with its hip roof, snug timber-clad interior and wonderfully rural setting in the forest, Gasthaus Staude is worth going the extra mile for. The rooms are silent and countrified, with chunky wood furnishings – the most romantic one

has a four-poster bed. It's a 15-minute drive east of town on the B500.

ⓘ Information

Tourist Office (☎ 07722-866 490; www. triberg.de; Wallfahrtstrasse 4; ⏰ 9am-5pm Mon-Fri, 10am-5pm Sat & Sun) Inside the Schwarzwald-Museum.

ⓘ Getting There & Away

From the Bahnhof (train station), 1.5km north of the centre, trains loop southeast to Konstanz (€27.50, 1½ hours, hourly), and northwest to Offenburg (€13.50, 46 minutes, hourly).

Freiburg

☎ 0761 / POP 229,636

Sitting plump at the foot of the Black Forest's wooded slopes and vineyards, Freiburg is a sunny, cheerful university town whose Altstadt is a storybook tableau of gabled town houses, cobblestone lanes and cafe-rimmed plazas. Party-loving students spice up the local nightlife and give Freiburg its relaxed air.

◉ Sights

★ **Freiburger Münster**   CATHEDRAL
(Freiburg Minster; www.freiburgermuenster.info; Münsterplatz; tower adult/concession €2/1.50; ⏰ 10am-5pm Mon-Sat, 1-7pm Sun, tower 9.30am-5pm Mon-Sat, 1-5pm Sun) With its lacy spires, cheeky gargoyles and intricate entrance portal, Freiburg's 11th-century minster cuts an impressive figure above the central market square. It has dazzling kaleidoscopic stained-glass windows that were mostly financed by medieval guilds and a high altar with a masterful triptych by Dürer protégé Hans Baldung Grien. Square at the base, the tower becomes an octagon higher up and is crowned by a filigree 116m-high spire. On clear days you can spy the Vosges Mountains in France.

Augustinermuseum   MUSEUM
(☎ 0761-201 2501; www.freiburg.de; Augustinerplatz 1; adult/concession/child €7/5/free; ⏰ 10am-5pm Tue-Thu, Sat & Sun, to 7pm Fri) Dip into the past as represented by artists working from the Middle Ages to the 19th century at this superb museum in a sensitively modernised monastery. The Sculpture Hall on the ground floor is especially impressive for its fine medieval sculptures and masterpieces by Renaissance artists Hans Baldung Grien

and Lucas Cranach the Elder. Head upstairs for eye-level views of mounted gargoyles.

🛌 Sleeping

Green City Hotel Vauban   HOTEL €€
(📞0761-888 5740; http://hotel-vauban.de; Paula-Modersohn-Platz 5; d €96-116, apt €150; 🛜) 🖋 This ecofriendly hotel fits in neatly to Freiburg's Vauban neighbourhood, a shining model of sustainability with its PlusEnergy housing and car-free streets. The light, bright rooms are furnished with local woods and plump white bedding. The pick of the doubles have balconies. To reach it, take tram 3 from Freiburg Hauptbahnhof to Freiburg Paula-Modersohn-Platz.

The Alex   BOUTIQUE HOTEL €€
(📞0761-296 970; www.the-alex-hotel.de; Rheinstrasse 29; d €94-148; 🅿✳🛜) The Alex stands head and shoulders above most hotels in town. Its clean, contemporary aesthetic includes lots of plate glass, blond wood, natural materials and a muted palette of colours. Besides modern rooms with rain showers, there's a bar, Winery29, where you can try locally produced wines.

🍴 Eating & Drinking

Markthalle   MARKET €
(www.markthalle-freiburg.de; Martinsgasse 235; light meals €4-8; ⏰8am-8pm Mon-Thu, to midnight Fri & Sat) Eat your way around the world – from curry to sushi, oysters to antipasti – at the food counters in this historical market hall, nicknamed 'Fressgässle'.

Gasthaus zum Kranz   GERMAN €€
(📞0761-217 1967; www.gasthauszumkranz.de; Herrenstrasse 40; mains €15-26; ⏰11.30am-3pm Mon, 11.30am-3pm & 5.30pm-midnight Tue-Sat, noon-3pm & 5.30pm-midnight Sun) There's always a good buzz at this rustic, quintessentially Badisch tavern. Pull up a hefty chair at one of the even heftier timber tables for well-prepared regional favourites such as roast suckling pig, *Maultaschen* (pork and spinach ravioli) and *Sauerbraten* (beef pot roast with vinegar, onions and peppercorns).

⭐ Kreuzblume   INTERNATIONAL €€€
(📞0761-311 94; www.hotel-kreuzblume.de; Konviktstrasse 31; mains €18-32, 3-course menu €42.50; ⏰6-11pm Wed-Sun; 🖋) On a flower-festooned lane, this pocket-sized restaurant with clever backlighting, slick monochrome decor and a menu fizzing with bright, sunny flavours

SOARING ABOVE THE FOREST
Freiburg seems tiny as you drift up above the city and over a tapestry of meadows and forest on the **Schauinslandbahn** (www.schauinslandbahn.de; Schauinslandstrasse, Oberried; return adult/child €12.50/8, one way €9/6; ⏰9am-5pm Oct-Jun, to 6pm Jul-Sep) to the 1284m **Schauinsland** (www.bergwelt-schauinsland.de) peak, great for hiking, downhill scooter racing or simply surveying the view, which reaches all the way to the Rhine Valley and Alps on clear days. The lift provides a speedy link between Freiburg and the Black Forest highlands.

attracts a rather food-literate clientele. Each dish combines just a few hand-picked ingredients in bold and tasty ways: apple, celery and chestnut soup, say, or roast duck breast with wild herb salad. Service is tops.

Hausbrauerei Feierling   MICROBREWERY
(www.feierling.de; Gerberau 46; ⏰11am-midnight Sun-Thu, to 1am Fri & Sat) This stream-side microbrewery and beer garden is a relaxed spot to quaff a cold one under the chestnut trees in summer or next to the copper vats in winter. Pretzels and sausages (€3 to €9.50) soak up the malty, organic brews.

ℹ Information
Tourist Office (📞0761-388 1880; www.visit.freiburg.de; Rathausplatz 2-4; ⏰8am-8pm Mon-Fri, 9.30am-5pm Sat, 10.30am-3.30pm Sun Jun-Sep, 8am-6pm Mon-Fri, 9.30am-2.30pm Sat, 10am-noon Sun Oct-May) Pick up the three-day **WelcomeKarte** (€26) at Freiburg's central tourist office.

ℹ Getting There & Away
There are frequent departures from the Hauptbahnhof for destinations such as Basel (€19.10 to €26.60, 45 minutes) and Baden-Baden (€23.70 to €40, 45 minutes to 1½ hours).

SOUTHERN RHINELAND
Defined by the mighty Rhine, fine wines, medieval castles and romantic villages, Germany's heartland speaks to the imagination. Even Frankfurt, which may seem all buttoned-up business, reveals itself as a

Frankfurt-am-Main

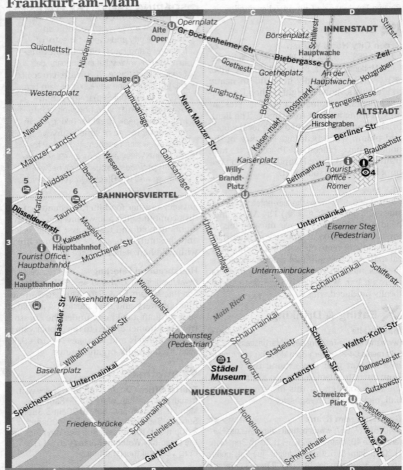

laid-back metropolis with fabulous museums and pulsating nightlife.

Frankfurt am Main

☏ 069 / POP 732.688

Unashamedly high-rise, Frankfurt-on-the-Main (pronounced 'mine') is a true capital of finance and business and hosts some of Europe's key trade fairs. But despite its business demeanour, Frankfurt consistently ranks highly among Germany's most liveable cities thanks to its rich collection of museums, expansive parks and greenery, a lively student scene and excellent public transport.

◉ Sights

★ **Städel Museum**   MUSEUM

(☏ 069-605 098; www.staedelmuseum.de; Schaumainkai 63; adult/child €16/14; ⊙ 10am-7pm Tue, Wed, Sat & Sun, to 9pm Thu & Fri; ☒ 15|16 Otto-Hahn-Platz) Founded in 1815, this world-renowned art gallery has an outstanding collection of European art from masters including Dürer, Rembrandt, Rubens, Renoir, Picasso and Cézanne, dating from the Middle Ages to today. More contemporary works by artists including Francis Bacon and Gerhard Richter are showcased in a subterranean extension lit by circular skylights. Admis-

after 1562, consecrated and crowned) in the *Wahlkapelle* at the end of the right aisle (look for the 'skull' altar). The cathedral was rebuilt both after an 1867 fire and after the bombings of 1944, which left it a burnt-out shell.

Römerberg SQUARE
(ⓤDom|Römer) The Römerberg is Frankfurt's old central square. Ornately gabled half-timbered buildings, reconstructed after WWII, give an idea of how beautiful the city's medieval core once was. In the square's centre is the **Gerechtigkeitsbrunnen** (Fountain of Justice; Römerberg).

🛌 Sleeping

If a big trade show is in town (and it often is) prices can triple. In general, rates drop on weekends.

Five Elements HOSTEL €
(☎069-2400 5885; www.5elementshostel.de; Moselstrasse 40; dm/s/d/apt from €22.50/34.50/82.90/134.50; 🛜; ℞Hauptbahnhof) The location mightn't be Frankfurt's most salubrious, but once you're inside the turn-of-the-20th-century gabled building it's a sanctuary of parquet floors, boldly coloured walls and designer furniture. Facilities include a laundry and 24-hour bar with a billiard table; breakfast costs €6.50. The apartment, sleeping up to four people, has a private bathroom and kitchen.

25hours Hotel by Levi's DESIGN HOTEL €€
(☎069-256 6770; www.25hours-hotels.com; Niddastrasse 58; d from €112; 🅿🅰🛜; ℞Hauptbahnhof)

sion prices can vary according to temporary exhibitions. Queues can be lengthy, so save time by pre-booking tickets online.

Kaiserdom CATHEDRAL
(Imperial Frankfurt Cathedral; www.dom-frankfurt.de; Domplatz 1; tower adult/child €3/1.50; ☯church 9am-8pm Sun-Thu, from 1pm Fri, tower 9am-6pm Apr-Oct, 10am-5pm Nov-Apr; ⓤDom|Römer) Frankfurt's red-sandstone cathedral is dominated by a 95m-high Gothic tower, which can be climbed via 328 steps. Construction began in the 13th century; from 1356 to 1792, the Holy Roman Emperors were elected (and,

APPLE-WINE TAVERNS

Apple-wine taverns are Frankfurt's great local tradition. They serve *Ebbelwei* (Frankfurt dialect for *Apfelwein*), an alcoholic apple cider, along with local specialities like Handkäse mit Musik (literally, 'hand-cheese with music'). This is a round cheese soaked in oil and vinegar and topped with onions; your bowel supplies the music. Anything with *Grüne Sosse*, a herb sauce, is also a winner. **Fichtekränzi** (www.fichtekraenzi. de; Wallstrasse 5; ⊙5pm-1am Mon-Sat, from 4pm Sun; ⊟14|18 Frankensteiner Platz) and **Adolf Wagner** (⊘069-612 565; www. apfelwein-wagner.com; Schweizer Strasse 71; mains €10-19.50; ⊙11am-midnight; Ⓤ Schweizer Platz) in Alt-Sachsenhausen are recommended traditional taverns.

Inspired by Levi's (yes, the jeans brand), this hip hotel has a rooftop terrace, free bike hire and a Gibson Music Room for jamming on drums and guitars. Its 76 rooms are themed by decade, from the 1930s (calm colours) to the 1980s (tiger-print walls, optical-illusion carpets). Be aware that its denim-blue bathrooms have no doors. Breakfast costs €18.

★ Villa Orange
BOUTIQUE HOTEL €€

(⊘069-405 840; www.villa-orange.de; Hebelstrasse 1; s/d from €140/170; P❈@☎; ⊟12|18 Friedberger Platz) ⊘ Offering a winning combination of tranquillity, modern German design and small-hotel comforts (such as a quiet corner library), this century-old, tangerine-coloured villa has 38 spacious rooms, some with free-standing baths and four-poster beds. Everything is organic – the sheets, the soap and the bountiful buffet breakfast (included in the rate) – with bikes also available to hire.

✗ Eating & Drinking

The pedestrian strip west of Hauptwache square is nicknamed Fressgass (literally 'Grazing Street') thanks to its many (average) eateries. Cosy apple-wine taverns cluster in Alt-Sachsenhausen south of the Main.

Kleinmarkthalle
MARKET €

(www.kleinmarkthalle.de; Hasengasse 5-7; ⊙8am-6pm Mon-Fri, to 4pm Sat; Ⓤ Dom|Römer) ⊘ Aromatic stalls inside this bustling traditional market hall sell artisanal smoked sausages, cheeses, roasted nuts, breads, pretzels, loose-leaf teas, pastries, cakes and chocolates, along with fruit, vegetables, spices, fresh pasta, olives, meat, poultry and, downstairs, fish. It's unmissable for picnickers or self-caterers, or anyone wanting to experience Frankfurt life. The upper-level wine bar opens onto a terrace.

★ Zu den 12 Aposteln
GERMAN €€

(⊘069-288 668; www.12aposteln-frankfurt.de; Rosenbergerstrasse 1; mains €9-24; ⊙11.30am-1am; Ⓤ Konstablerwache) Glowing with sepia-toned lamplight, the 12 Apostles has ground-floor and cellar dining rooms serving traditional German dishes: *Matjes* (herring) with sour cream, apple and fried onion; roast pork knuckle with pickled cabbage; Frankfurter schnitzel with *Grüne Sosse* (green sauce); and *Käsespätzle* (handmade cheese noodles with onions). It brews its own light and dark beers on the premises.

Dauth-Schneider
GERMAN €€

(⊘069-613 533; www.dauth-schneider.de; Neuer Wall 5; mains €8-13.50; ⊙11.30am-midnight; Ⓡ Lokalbahnhof) With a history stretching back to 1849 (the basement housed an apple winery), this convivial tavern is a wonderful place to sample both the local drop and classic regional specialities such as *Sulz Fleisch* (cold meat and jelly terrine), *Gekochte Haspel* (pickled pork knuckle) with sauerkraut, and various tasting platters. Tables fill the tree-shaded terrace in summer.

ⓘ Information

Tourist office locations include: **Hauptbahnhof** (⊘069-2123 8800; www.frankfurt-tourismus. de; Main Hall, Hauptbahnhof; ⊙8am-9pm Mon-Fri, 9am-6pm Sat & Sun; Ⓡ Hauptbahnhof) and **Römer** (⊘069-2123 8800; www. frankfurt-tourismus.de; Römerberg 27; ⊙9.30am-5.30pm Mon-Fri, to 4pm Sat & Sun; Ⓤ Dom|Römer), a smallish office in the central square.

ⓘ Getting There & Around

AIR

Frankfurt Airport (FRA; www.frankfurt-airport. com; Hugo-Eckener-Ring; ☎; Ⓡ Flughafen Regionalbahnhof), 12km southwest of the city centre, is Germany's busiest. S-Bahn lines S8 and S9 shuttle between the airport and city centre (one way €4.90, 11 minutes, every 15 minutes).

BUS

Eurolines (www.eurolines.de) and Flixbus (www. flixbus.com) can take you inexpensively to cities across Germany and Europe. Both operate from the main **bus station** (Mannheimer Strasse 15; 🚉 Hauptbahnhof).

TRAIN

There are direct trains to pretty much everywhere, including Berlin (€90, four hours), Cologne (€39, 1¼ hours) and Munich (€60, 3¼ hours, hourly).

Romantic Rhine Valley

Between Rüdesheim and Koblenz, the Rhine cuts deeply through the Rhenish slate mountains, meandering between hillside castles and steep fields of wine-producing grapes. This is Germany's landscape at its most dramatic – forested hillsides alternate with craggy cliffs and near-vertical terraced vineyards. Idyllic villages appear around each bend, their half-timbered houses and Gothic church steeples seemingly plucked from the world of fairy tales.

Bacharach

✔ 06743 / POP 1880

One of the prettiest of the Rhine villages, tiny Bacharach – 24km downriver from Bingen – conceals its considerable charms behind a 14th-century wall. From the B9, pass through one of the thick arched gateways under the train tracks to reach its medieval old town filled with half-timbered buildings.

For gorgeous views of village, vineyards and river, take a stroll atop the **medieval ramparts**, which are punctuated by guard towers. An especially scenic panorama unfolds from the **Postenturm** at the north end of town, from where you can also spy the filigreed ruins of the **Wernerkapelle**, a medieval chapel, and the turrets of the 12th-

century hilltop **Burg Stahleck** (✔ 06743-1266; www.jugendherberge.de; Stahleckstrasse; dm/s/d from €22.50/34.50/69; 🅿 @), a castle turned youth hostel.

Dating from 1421, the olde-worlde tavern **Zum Grünen Baum** (www.weingut-bastian-bacharach.de; Oberstrasse 63; ⊙ noon-10pm Apr-Oct, shorter hours Nov-Mar) serves some of Bacharach's best whites; the Weinkarussel (€22.50) lets you sample 15 of them.

Trains link Bacharach with Koblenz (€11.60, 35 minutes) and Mainz (€13.70, 40 minutes).

Loreley & St Goar Region

POP 4457

The most fabled spot along the Romantic Rhine, **Loreley** is an enormous, almost vertical slab of slate that owes its fame to a mythical maiden whose siren songs are said to have lured sailors to their death in the river's treacherous currents. Heinrich Heine told the tale in his 1824 poem *Die Lorelei*.

The nearby village of **St Goarshausen**, 2.5km north, is lorded over by the sprawling ruins of **Burg Rheinfels** (✔ 06741-7753; www.st-goar.de; Schlossberg 47; adult/child €5/2.50, guided mine tour €7/free; ⊙ 9am-6pm Apr-Oct, to 5pm Mar & Nov, guided mine tours by reservation), once the mightiest fortress on the Rhine. It's linked by car ferry with its twin across the river, St Goar.

A classy spot to spend the night is **Romantik Hotel Schloss Rheinfels** (✔ 06741-8020; www.schloss-rheinfels.de; Schlossberg 47; s/d/ste from €110/140/270; 🅿 🛜 🏊), right by the castle. Its three restaurants enjoy a fine reputation, but there are plenty more down in the village.

Koblenz is linked by train with St Goarshausen (€8.10, 30 minutes hourly).

ⓘ EXPLORING THE ROMANTIC RHINE

Each mode of transport on the Rhine has its own advantages and all are equally enjoyable. Try combining several.

Boat From about Easter to October (winter services are very limited), passenger ships run by **Köln-Düsseldorfer** (KD; ✔ 0221-208 8318; www.k-d.com) link villages on a set timetable. You're free to get on and off as you like.

Car No bridges span the Rhine between Koblenz and Bingen, but you can easily change banks by using a car ferry *(Autofähre)*. There are five routes: Bingen–Rüdesheim, Niederheimbach–Lorch, Boppard–Filsen, Oberwesel–Kaub and St Goar–Goarshausen.

Train Villages on the Rhine's left bank (eg Bacharach and Boppard) are served regularly by local trains on the Koblenz–Mainz run. Right-bank villages such as Rüdesheim, St Goarshausen and Braubach are linked hourly to Koblenz' Hauptbahnhof and Frankfurt by the RheingauLinie train.

Koblenz

📞 0261 / POP 112,586

Founded by the Romans, Koblenz sits at the confluence of the Rhine and Moselle Rivers, a point known as **Deutsches Eck** (German Corner) and dominated by a bombastic 19th-century statue of Kaiser Wilhelm I on horseback. On the right Rhine bank high above the Deutsches Eck – and reached by an 850m-long **Seilbahn** (cable car; 📞 0261-2016 5850; www.seilbahn-koblenz.de; Rheinstrasse 6; adult/child return €9.90/4.40, incl Festung Ehrenbreitstein €13.80/6.20; ⊙ 9.30am-7pm Jul-Sep, to 6pm Easter-Jun & Oct, 10am-5pm Nov-Easter) – is the **Festung Ehrenbreitstein** (📞 0261-6675 4000; www.tor-zum-welterbe.de; adult/child €7/3.50, incl cable car €13.80/6.20, audioguide €2; ⊙ 10am-6pm Apr-Oct, to 5pm Nov-Mar), one of Europe's mightiest citadels. Views are great and there's a restaurant and a regional museum inside.

Moselle Valley

Like a vine right before harvest, the Moselle hangs heavy with visitor fruit. Castles and towns with half-timbered buildings are built along the sinuous river below steep, rocky cliffs planted with vineyards. It's one of Germany's most evocative regions, with stunning views revealed at every river bend. Unlike the Romantic Rhine, it's spanned by plenty of bridges. The most scenic section unravels between Bernkastel-Kues and Cochem, 50km apart and linked by the B421. At the head of the valley is whimsically turreted **Burg Eltz** (📞 02672-950 500; www.burg-eltz.de; Burg-Eltz-Strasse 1, Wierschem; tour adult/child €9/6.50; ⊙ 9.30am-5.30pm Apr-Oct), one of Germany's most romantic medieval castles.

Cochem

📞 02671 / POP 5332

Cochem is one of the most popular destinations on the Moselle thanks to its fairytale-like **Reichsburg** (📞 02671-255; www.reichsburg-cochem.de; Schlossstrasse 36; tours adult/child €6/3; ⊙ tours 9am-5pm mid-Mar–Oct, shorter hours Nov–mid-Mar). The 40-minute tours (some in English; leaflet/audioguide otherwise available) take in decorative rooms reflecting 1000 years' worth of tastes and styles.

To taste and buy exceptional wines made from grapes grown on the hillside behind, stop by **VinoForum** (📞 02671-917 1777; www.vinoforum-ernst.de; Moselstrasse 12-13, Ernst; ⊙ 10am-6pm Apr-Oct, 1-5pm Nov-Mar).

The **tourist office** (📞 02671-600 40; www.ferienland-cochem.de; Endertplatz 1; ⊙ 9am-5pm Mon-Sat, 10am-3pm Sun mid-Jun–Sep, shorter hours Oct–mid-Jun) can suggest local wineries and hikes, and provide transport advice.

Cochem is 55km from Koblenz via the scenic B327 and B49. By train, destinations include Koblenz (€11.80, 40 minutes) and Trier (€14.90, 55 minutes).

Beilstein

📞 02673 / POP 140

Picture-perfect Beilstein is little more than a cluster of higgledy-piggledy houses surrounded by steep vineyards. Its historic highlights include the **Marktplatz** and the ruined hilltop castle **Burg Metternich** (📞 02673-936 39; www.burg-metternich.de; adult/child €2.50/1; ⊙ 9am-6pm Apr-Nov). The **Zehnthauskeller** (📞 02673-900 907; www.zehnthauskeller.de; Marktplatz 1; ⊙ 11am-10pm Tue-Sat, from noon Sun; 🔊) houses a romantically dark, vaulted wine tavern owned by the same family that also runs two local hotels.

Buses link Beilstein with Cochem (€3.80, 20 minutes, every two hours).

Bernkastel-Kues

📞 06531 / POP 6987

These charming twin towns are the hub of the *Mittelmosel* (Middle Moselle) region. Bernkastel, on the right (eastern) bank, is a symphony in half-timber, stone and slate, and teems with wine taverns.

Get your heart pumping by hoofing it up to **Burg Landshut** (☑ 06531-972 770; www.bur glandshut.de; Bernkastel; ☺ noon-9pm Thu-Tue), a ruined 13th-century castle on a bluff above town. Allow 30 minutes to be rewarded with glorious valley views. Since 2018, it has harboured a **restaurant** (☑ 06531-972 770; www. burglandshut.de; Burg Landshut, Bernkastel; mains €14-25; ☺ noon-2pm & 6-9pm Thu-Tue Easter-Nov) dishing up modern German cuisine.

Christiana's Wein & Art Hotel (☑ 06531-6627; www.wein-arthotel.de; Lindenweg 18, Kues; s/d/ste from €69/89/111; P ※ ☎) is a charming boutique base, with each of the 17 rooms named after a Moselle vineyard.

The **tourist office** (☑ 06531-500 190; www. bernkastel.de; Gestade 6; audioguides 3 hrs/1 day €6/8; ☺ 9am-5pm Mon-Fri, from 10am Sat, to 1pm Sun May-Oct, 9.30am-4pm Mon-Fri Nov-Apr) is in Bernkastel. Coming from Trier, drivers should follow the B53. Buses run to Bullay (€12.60, 1¼ hours) and Trier (€11.55, 2¼ hours).

Trier

☑ 0651 / POP 114, 914

With an astounding nine Unesco World Heritage Sites, Germany's oldest city shelters the country's finest ensemble of Roman monuments, among them a mighty gate, amphitheatre, elaborate thermal baths, an imperial throne room and the country's oldest bishop's church, which retains Roman sections. Architectural treasures from later ages include Germany's oldest Gothic church, and Karl Marx' baroque birthplace.

⊙ Sights

★**Porta Nigra** ROMAN SITE

(adult/child €4/2.50; ☺ 9am-6pm Apr-Sep, to 5pm Mar & Oct, to 4pm Nov-Feb) Trier's most famous landmark, this brooding 2nd-century Roman city gate – blackened by time, hence the name, which is Latin for 'black gate' – is a marvel of engineering, since it's held together by nothing but gravity and iron clamps. In the 11th century, the structure was turned into a church to honour Simeon, a Greek hermit who spent six years walled up in its east tower. After his death in 1134, he was buried inside the gate and later became a saint.

Konstantin Basilika ROMAN SITE

(Constantine's Throne Room; ☑ 0651-9949 1200; www.konstantin-basilika.de; Konstantinplatz 10; ☺ 10am-6pm Mon-Sat, 1-6pm Sun Apr-Oct, shorter hours rest of year) **FREE** Constructed around 310 CE as Constantine's throne room, this brick-built basilica is now an austere Protestant church. With built-to-impress dimensions (some 67m long, 27m wide and 33m high), it's the largest single-room Roman structure still in existence. Its organ, with 87 registers and 6500 pipes, generates a seven-fold echo.

Liebfrauenbasilika CHURCH

(Church of Our Lady; www.trierer-dom.de; Liebfrauenstrasse; ☺ 10am-6pm Mon-Fri, to 4.30pm Sat, 12.30-6pm Sun Apr-Oct, shorter hours rest of year) Germany's oldest Gothic church was built in the 13th century. It has a cruciform structure supported by a dozen pillars symbolising the 12 Apostles (look for the black stone from where all 12 articles of the Apostle's Creed painted on the columns are visible) and some colourful post-war stained glass.

★**Trierer Dom** CATHEDRAL

(☑ 0651-979 0790; www.trierer-dom.de; Liebfrauenstrasse 12; ☺ 6.30am-6pm Apr-Oct, to 5.30pm Nov-Mar) Looming above the Roman palace of Helena (Emperor Constantine's mother), this cathedral is Germany's oldest bishop's church and still retains Roman sections. Today's edifice is a study in nearly 1700 years of church architecture with Romanesque, Gothic and baroque elements. Intriguingly, its floorplan is of a 12-petalled flower, symbolising the Virgin Mary.

To see some dazzling ecclesiastical equipment and peer into early Christian history, head upstairs to the **Domschatz** (Cathedral Treasury; ☑ 0651-710 5378; www.trierer-dom. de/bauwerk/domschatz; adult/child €1.50/0.50; ☺ 10am-5pm Mon-Sat, from 12.30pm Sun Apr-Oct & Dec, 11am-4pm Tue-Sat, from 12.30pm Sun Nov & Jan-Mar) or around the corner to the **Museum am Dom Trier** (☑ 0651-710 5255; www.bistum-trier.de/museum; Bischof-Stein-Platz 1; adult/child €3.50/2; ☺ 9am-5pm Tue-Sat, from 1pm Sun).

Kaiserthermen ROMAN SITE

(Imperial Baths; Weberbachstrasse 41; adult/child €4/2.50; ☺ 9am-6pm Apr-Sep, to 5pm Mar & Oct, to 4pm Nov-Feb) Get a sense of the layout of this vast Roman thermal bathing complex with its striped brick-and-stone arches from the corner lookout tower, then descend into an underground labyrinth consisting of cavernous hot and cold water baths, boiler rooms and heating channels.

Amphitheatre ROMAN SITE

(Olewiger Strasse; adult/child €4/2.50; ☺ 9am-6pm Apr-Sep, to 5pm Mar & Oct, to 4pm Nov-Feb)

Trier's mighty Roman amphitheatre could accommodate 20,000 spectators for gladiator tournaments and animal fights. Beneath the arena are dungeons where prisoners sentenced to death waited next to starving beasts for the final showdown.

🛏 Sleeping

⭐ Hotel Villa Hügel   BOUTIQUE HOTEL €€
(☑0651-937 100; www.hotel-villa-huegel.de; Bernhardstrasse 14; s/d from €118/163; P@🛜🌊) You can begin the day with sparkling wine over breakfast at this chic 1914-built hillside villa, and end it luxuriating in the indoor or rooftop pools and Finnish sauna. The 45 rooms are decorated with honey-toned woods; higher-category 'relax' rooms have balconies. Panoramic views extend from its glass-walled gourmet restaurant and flower-filled summer terrace.

Becker's   DESIGN HOTEL €€
(☑0651-938 080; www.beckers-trier.de; Olewiger Strasse 206; hotel s €95-125, d €140-190, ste €210-240, Weinhaus s/d €85/110; P🌸@🛜) In the peaceful wine district of Olewig, across the creek from the old monastery church, 3km southeast of the centre, classy Becker's pairs supremely tasteful rooms – ultramodern in its hotel; rustically traditional in its Weinhaus – with stellar **dining** (1-/3-course lunch menu €18/28, 3-/4-course dinner menu €45/58, mains €21-34; ⊙noon-2pm & 6-10pm Tue-Sun).

🍴 Eating & Drinking

⭐ Weinwirtschaft Friedrich-Wilhelm   GERMAN €€
(☑0651-994 7480; www.weinwirtschaft-fw.de; Weberbach 75; mains €12.50-27.50; ⊙11.30am-2.30pm & 5.30-10pm Mon-Fri, 11.30am-10pm Sat & Sun) A historical former wine warehouse with exposed brick and joists now houses this superb restaurant. Creative dishes incorporate local wines, such as trout poached in sparkling white wine with mustard sauce and white asparagus, or local sausage with Riesling sauerkraut and fried potatoes. Vines trail over the trellis-covered garden; the attached wine shop is a great place to stock up.

Alt Zalawen   GERMAN €€
(☑0651-286 45; www.altzalawen.de; Zurlaubener Ufer 79; mains €6-18; ⊙kitchen 11am-10pm, closed Sun Nov-Mar; 🛜) The pick of the cluster of bar-restaurants right on the riverfront, with terraces extending to the path running along the grassy bank, timber-panelled Alt Zalawen is a picturesque spot for traditional German specialities (schnitzels, sausages, *Spätzle*) and local Trierer Viez cider.

ℹ Information

Tourist Office (☑0651-978 080; www.trier-info.de; An der Porta Nigra; ⊙9am-6pm Mon-Sat, 10am-5pm Sun Mar-Dec, 10am-5pm Mon-Sat Jan & Feb)

ℹ Getting There & Away

Trier has frequent train connections to Saarbrücken (€20.90, one to 1½ hours) and Koblenz (€24, 1½ to two hours). There are also regular trains to Luxembourg City (€19.40, 50 minutes).

COLOGNE & NORTHERN RHINELAND

POP 17.9 MILLION (NORTH RHINE–WESTPHALIA)

Cologne's iconic Dom has twin towers that might as well be exclamation marks after the word 'welcome'. Flowing behind the cathedral, the Rhine provides a vital link for some of the region's highlights – Düsseldorf, with its great nightlife, architecture and shopping; and Bonn, the former capital, which hums to Beethoven. Away from the river, Aachen still echoes to the beat of the Holy Roman Empire and Charlemagne.

Cologne

☑0221 / POP 1.07 MILLION

Cologne (Köln) offers lots of attractions, led by its famous cathedral whose filigree twin spires dominate the skyline. The city's museum landscape is especially strong when it comes to art, but also has something in store for fans of chocolate, sports and Roman history. Its people are well known for their joie de vivre and it's easy to have a good time right along with them year-round in the beer halls of the Altstadt.

👁 Sights

⭐ Kölner Dom   CATHEDRAL
(Cologne Cathedral; ☑0221-9258 4720; www.koelner-dom.de; Domkloster 4; tower adult/concession €4/2; ⊙6am-9pm May-Oct, to 7.30pm Nov-Apr, tower 9am-6pm May-Sep, to 5pm Mar, Apr & Oct, to 4pm Nov-Feb; 🚊5, 16, 18 Dom/Hauptbahnhof) Cologne's geographical and spiritual heart – and its single-biggest tourist draw – is the magnificent Kölner Dom. With its soaring twin spires, this is the Mt Everest of cathedrals, jam-packed with art and treasures. For an exercise fix, climb the 533 steps up the Dom's

south tower to the base of the steeple that dwarfed all buildings in Europe until Gustave Eiffel built a certain tower in Paris. The Domforum visitor centre is a good source of info and tickets.

Römisch-Germanisches Museum   MUSEUM
(Roman Germanic Museum; ☑0221-2212 4438; www.roemisch-germanisches-museum.de; Roncalliplatz 4; adult/concession/under 18yr €6.50/3.50/free; ☺10am-5pm Tue-Sun; ☐5, 16, 18 Dom/Hauptbahnhof) Sculptures and ruins displayed outside the entrance are merely the overture to a full symphony of Roman artefacts found along the Rhine. Highlights include the giant Poblicius tomb (30–40 CE), the magnificent 3rd-century Dionysus mosaic, and astonishingly well-preserved glass items. Insight into daily Roman life is gained from toys, tweezers, lamps and jewellery, the designs of which have changed surprisingly little since Roman times.

Museum Ludwig   MUSEUM
(☑0221-2212 6165; www.museum-ludwig.de; Heinrich-Böll-Platz; adult/concession €12/8, more during special exhibits; ☺10am-6pm Tue-Sun; ☐5, 16, 18 Dom/Hauptbahnhof) A mecca of modern art, Museum Ludwig presents a tantalising mix of works from all major genres. Fans of German expressionism (Beckmann, Dix, Kirchner) will get their fill here as much as those with a penchant for Picasso, American pop art (Warhol, Lichtenstein) and Russian avant-garde painter Alexander Rodchenko. Rothko and Pollock are highlights of the abstract collection, while Gursky and Tillmanns are among the reasons the photography section is a must-see.

Wallraf-Richartz-Museum & Fondation Corboud   MUSEUM
(☑0221-2212 1119; www.wallraf.museum; Obenmarspforten; adult/concession €9/5.50; ☺10am-6pm Tue-Sun; ☐1, 7, 9 Heumarkt, ☐5 Rathaus) One of Germany's finest art museums, the Wallraf-Richartz presents a primo collection of European art from the 13th to the 19th centuries in a minimalist cube designed by the late OM Ungers. All the marquee names are here – Rubens and Rembrandt to Manet and Monet – along with a prized sampling of medieval art, most famously Stefan Lochner's *Madonna in Rose Bower,* nicknamed the 'Mona Lisa of Cologne'.

Schokoladenmuseum   MUSEUM
(Chocolate Museum; ☑0221-931 8880; www. schokoladenmuseum.de; Am Schokoladenmuseum 1a; adult/student/child €11.50/9/7.50; ☺10am-6pm Tue-Fri, 11am-7pm Sat & Sun, last entry 1hr before closing; ☐133 Schokoladenmuseum) This boat-shaped, high-tech temple to the art of chocolate making has plenty of engaging exhibits on the 5000-year cultural history of the 'elixir of the gods' (as the Aztecs called it) as well as on the cocoa-growing process. The walk-through tropical forest is a highlight, although most visitors are more enthralled by the glass-walled miniature production facility and a sample at the chocolate fountain.

🛏 Sleeping & Eating

There are plenty of beer halls and restaurants in the tourist-adored Altstadt, but for a more local vibe head to student-flavoured Zülpicher Viertel or the Belgisches Viertel, both in the city centre. Local breweries turn out a variety called *Kölsch,* which is relatively light and served in skinny 200mL glasses.

★ 25hours Hotel The Circle   HOTEL €€
(☑0221-162 530; www.25hours-hotels.com; Im Klapperhof 22-24; d €120-220; ☐🕸❄📶; ☐Friesenplatz) The Cologne edition of this mod lifestyle hotel chain occupies a listed circular building (a former insurance company headquarters) and is bathed in a retro-futuristic design theme. Past the vast lobby with bike rental and DJ corner are good-sized rooms that bulge with quirks, character and zeitgeist-capturing amenities such as Bluetooth speakers.

CARNIVAL IN COLOGNE

Carnival in Cologne is one of the best parties in Europe and a thumb in the eye of the German work ethic. It all starts with *Weiberfastnacht,* the Thursday before Ash Wednesday, when women rule the day (and do things like chop off the ties of their male colleagues and bosses). The party continues through the weekend, with more than 50 parades of ingenious floats and wildly dressed lunatics dancing in the streets. By the time it all comes to a head with the big parade on *Rosenmontag* (Rose Monday), the entire city has become unglued. Those still capable of swaying and singing will live it up one last time on Shrove Tuesday before the curtain comes down on Ash Wednesday.

Cologne

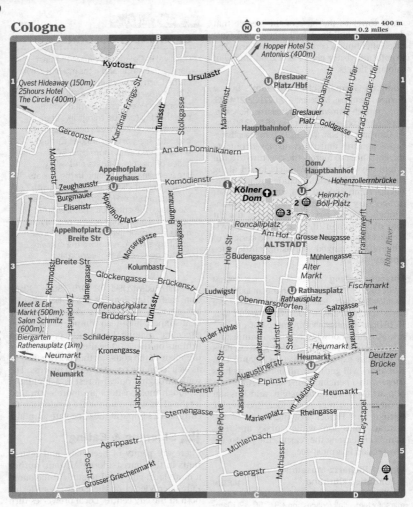

Cologne

◎ Top Sights

◎ Sights

Hopper Hotel St Antonius   HOTEL €€
(☑0221-166 00; www.hopper.de; Dagobertstrasse 32; d €95-100; ᴾ➔@🛜🐾; ⓊEbertplatz) His-

tory and high-tech mix nicely at this 54-room retreat in a historical journeyman's hostel with plenty of eye candy for the style-conscious. The romantic courtyard garden and small spa in the brick-vaulted cellar are great bliss-out spots, while the mounted photographs add artsy splashes.

Qvest Hideaway   DESIGN HOTEL €€€
(☑0221-278 5780; www.qvest-hotel.com; Gereonskloster 12; d from €150; ➔🛜; ⓇChristophstrasse/Mediapark) This dazzling alchemy of historical setting and up-to-the-minute design touches is hidden within the neo-Gothic ribbed vaults and stone pillars of the former

city archives. The carefully chosen art, design classics, midcentury furniture and amenities are likely to inspire loads of decorating ideas (hint: there's a shop that sells some of the objects). Optional breakfast is €20.

Meet & Eat Markt MARKET €
(www.meet-and-eat.koeln; Rudolfplatz; ⊙4-9pm Thu; Ⓤ Rudolfplatz) A combination of farmers market and street-food fair, Meet & Eat draws locals of all ages to Rudolfplatz on Thursday evenings. Aside from fresh produce, you can pick up homemade pesto, chutney, organic cheeses and other artisanal products or sit down at a covered table for a vegan sausage or succulent burger.

★**Salon Schmitz** EUROPEAN €€
(☑0221-139 5577; www.salonschmitz.com; Aachener Strasse 28-34; mains from €10; ⊙9am-1am Sun-Thu, open end Fri & Sat; 🚋1, 7, 12, 15 Rudolfplatz) Spread over three historical row houses, the Schmitz empire is your one-stop shop for excellent food and drink. Greet the day with a lavish breakfast in the retro-hip 1950s and '60s setting of the Salon; order cake, quiche or a hot dish in the Metzgerei, a historical butcher's shop turned deli; or indulge in a fine brasserie-style dinner in the art nouveau–styled Bar.

★**Biergarten Rathenauplatz** BEER GARDEN
(☑0221-801 7349; www.rathenauplatz.de/biergarten; Rathenauplatz 30; ⊙noon-11.30pm Apr-Sep; 🚋9, 12, 15 Zülpicher Platz) A large, leafy park has one of Cologne's best places for a drink: a community-run beer garden. Tables sprawl under huge old trees, while simple snacks such as salads and very good *Frikadelle* (spiced hamburger) issue forth from a cute little hut.

ⓘ Information

Tourist Office (☑0221-346 430; www.cologne-tourism.com; Kardinal-Höffner-Platz 1; ⊙9am-8pm Mon-Sat, 10am-5pm Sun; Ⓤ Köln Dom/Hauptbahnhof) Excellent; near the cathedral. The app is well done.

ⓘ Getting There & Around

AIR
Köln Bonn Airport (CGN; Cologne Bonn Airport; ☑02203-404 001; www.koeln-bonn-airport.de; Kennedystrasse; 🚉Köln/Bonn Flughafen) is about 18km southeast of the city centre and connected to the Hauptbahnhof by the S-Bahn S13 train every 20 minutes (€2.80, 15 minutes).

TRAIN
From Cologne's **Hauptbahnhof** (www.bahnhof.de/bahnhof-de/Köln_Hbf-1032796; Trankgasse 11; 🚋16, 18 Breslauer Platz/Hauptbahnhof, 🚉5 Dom/Hauptbahnhof), services are fast and frequent in all directions and include fast Thalys and ICE trains to Brussels (€59, two hours) where you can connect to the Eurostar for London and Paris.

Northern Rhineland

North of Koblenz, the scenery bordering the Rhine is not quite as romantic as along the Middle Rhine further south. Instead the river takes on the mightiness of an urban stream as it courses through such cities as Bonn and Düsseldorf. Many towns in the region started out as Roman settlements some 2000 years ago, and it was also the Romans who gave the Rhine its name (*rhenus* in Latin).

Düsseldorf
☑0211 / POP 628,000
Düsseldorf dazzles with boundary-pushing architecture, zinging nightlife and an art scene to rival many a metropolis. It's a posh and modern city whose economy is dominated by banking, advertising, fashion and telecommunications. However, a couple of hours of partying in the boisterous pubs of the Altstadt, the historical quarter along the Rhine, is all you need to realise that locals have no problem letting their hair down once they slip out of those Boss jackets.

⊙ Sights

★**K20 Grabbeplatz** MUSEUM
(☑0211-838 1204; www.kunstsammlung.de; Grabbeplatz 5; adult/concession/child €12/10/2.50; ⊙10am-6pm Tue-Fri, 11am-6pm Sat & Sun; Ⓤ Schadowstrasse) A collection that spans the arc of 20th-century artistic vision gives the K20 an enviable edge in the art world. It encompasses major works by Picasso, Matisse and Mondrian and more than 100 paintings and drawings by Paul Klee. Americans represented include Jackson Pollock, Andy Warhol and Jasper Johns. Düsseldorf's own Joseph Beuys has a major presence as well.

K21 Ständehaus MUSEUM
(☑0211-838 1204; www.kunstsammlung.de; Ständehausstrasse 1; adult/concession/child €12/10/2.50; ⊙10am-6pm Tue-Fri, 11am-6pm Sat & Sun; Ⓤ Graf-Adolf-Platz) A stately 19th-century parliament building forms a fabulously

dichotomous setting for the cutting-edge art of the K21 – a collection only showcasing works created after the 1980s. Large-scale film and video installations and groups of works share space with site-specific rooms by an international cast of artists including Andreas Gursky, Candida Höfer, Bill Viola and Nam June Paik.

Medienhafen ARCHITECTURE
(Am Handelshafen; 726, 732 Erftstrasse/Grand Bateau) Where sweat once dripped off dockland workers' foreheads, creative minds now forge ad campaigns and newspaper headlines. The Medienhafen (Media Harbour) is Düsseldorf's most spectacular urban revitalisation project, an old commercial harbour transformed by such architectural heavyweights as Richard Meier, Helmut Jahn and Claude Vasconi into a tableau of avant-garde buildings. Top billing goes to Frank Gehry's Neuer Zollhof, a trio of sculptural high-rises sheathed in stainless steel, red brick and white plaster, respectively.

🛏 Sleeping

Backpackers Düsseldorf HOSTEL €
(📞 0211-302 0848; www.backpackers-duesseldorf. de; Fürstenwall 180; dm €18.50-25, s/d €32/50; ⏲ reception 8am-10pm; 🅿 @ 🛜; Ⓤ Kirchplatz) Düsseldorf's adorable indie hostel sleeps 60 in clean four- to 10-bed dorms outfitted with individual backpack-sized lockers. Bathrooms are shared. It's a low-key place with a kitchen and a relaxed lounge where cultural and language barriers melt quickly. The vending machine is filled with beer. Rates include a small breakfast; linen costs €3.

Hotel Orangerie HOTEL €€
(📞 0211-866 800; www.hotel-orangerie-mcs.de; Bäckergasse 1; r €130-250; 🅿 😊 🛜; Ⓤ Benrather Strasse) Ensconced in a neoclassical mansion in a quiet corner of the Altstadt, this place puts you within staggering distance of pubs, the river and museums, yet offers a serene and stylish refuge to retire to. Some of the 27 minimalist rooms skimp somewhat on size, but all are as bright, modern and uncluttered as the lobby and breakfast room.

✕ Eating & Drinking

★**Brauerei im Füchschen** GERMAN €€
(📞 0211-137 4716; www.fuechschen.de; Ratinger Strasse 28; mains €9-17; ⏲ 9am-1am Mon-Thu, to 2am Fri & Sat, to midnight Sun; Ⓤ Tonhalle/Ehrenhof) Boisterous, packed and drenched with local colour, the 'Little Fox' in the Altstadt is

all you expect a Rhenish beer hall to be. The kitchen is especially famous for its mean *Schweinshaxe* (roast pork leg) served in a high-ceilinged interior that echoes with the mirthful roar of people enjoying their meals.

Zum Uerige BEER HALL
(📞 0211-866 990; www.uerige.de; Berger Strasse 1; ⏲ 10am-midnight; Ⓤ Heinrich-Heine-Allee) Local colour by the bucketful (despite the high tourist contingent) is what awaits at this cavernous *Altbier* brewpub. The suds flow so quickly from giant copper vats that the waiters – called *Köbes* – simply carry huge trays of brew and plonk down a glass whenever they spy an empty. Even on a cold day, the outside tables are alive with merriment.

ℹ Information

Tourist Office – Altstadt (📞 0211-1720 2840; www.duesseldorf-tourismus.de; cnr Marktstrasse & Rheinstrasse; ⏲ 10am-6pm; Ⓤ Heinrich-Heine-Allee) Right in the heart of the old centre.

Tourist Office – Hauptbahnhof (📞 0211-1720 2844; www.duesseldorf-tourismus.de; Immermannstrasse 65b; ⏲ 9.30am-7pm Mon-Fri, to 5pm Sat; Ⓤ Hauptbahnhof) The main tourist office, across from the train station; has a currency exchange window.

ℹ Getting There & Around

Düsseldorf International Airport (DUS; 📞 0211-4210; www.dus.com; 🚆 Düsseldorf Flughafen), 10km north of the **Hauptbahnhof** (www.bahnhof.de/bahnhof-de/Düsseldorf_Hbf-1021118; Konrad-Adenauer-Platz 14; Ⓤ Hauptbahnhof), is linked to the city centre by S-Bahn.

ICE/IC trains departing from the Hauptbahnhof head to Berlin (€116, 4¼ hours), Hamburg (€86, 3½ hours), Frankfurt (€86, 1¾ hours) and many other destinations.

Aachen

📞 0241 / POP 254,000

Aachen makes for an excellent day trip from Cologne or Düsseldorf as well as a worthy overnight stop. The Romans nursed their war wounds and stiff joints in the steaming waters of Aachen's mineral springs, but it was Charlemagne who put the city firmly on the European map. His legacy lives on in the stunning Dom, which in 1978 became Germany's first Unesco World Heritage Site, as well as the **Centre Charlemagne** (📞 0241-432 4956; www.centre-charlemagne.eu; Katschhof 1; adult/concession €6/3; ⏲ 10am-5pm Tue-Sun).

◎ Sights

★ Aachener Dom   CATHEDRAL
(☑ 0241-4770 9110; www.aachendom.de; Münsterplatz; tours adult/concession €4/3; ☉ 7am-7pm Apr-Dec, to 6pm Jan-Mar) It's impossible to overestimate the significance of Aachen's magnificent cathedral. The burial place of Charlemagne, it's where more than 30 German kings were crowned and where pilgrims have flocked since the 12th century. Before entering the church, stop by **Dom Information** (☑ 0241-4770 9145; Johannes-Paul-II-Strasse 1; ☉ 10am-5pm Jan-Mar, to 6pm Apr-Dec) for info and tickets for tours and the cathedral **treasury** (Cathedral Treasury; ☑ 0241-4770 9127; Johannes-Paul-II-Strasse 2; adult/concession €5/4; ☉ 10am-2pm Mon, to 5pm Tue-Sun Jan-Mar, 10am-2pm Mon, to 6pm Tue-Sun Apr-Dec). English tours run daily at 2pm.

Rathaus   HISTORIC BUILDING
(Town Hall; ☑ 0241-432 7310; http://rathaus-aachen.de; Markt; adult/concession/under 22yr incl audioguide €6/3/free; ☉ 10am-6pm) Fifty life-sized statues of German rulers, including 30 kings crowned in Aachen between 936 and 1531 CE, adorn the facade of Aachen's splendid Gothic town hall. Inside, the undisputed highlight is the vaulted coronation hall where the post-ceremony banquets were held. Note the epic 19th-century frescoes and replicas of the imperial insignia: a crown, orb and sword (the originals are in Vienna).

🛏 Sleeping & Eating

Aachen's students have their own 'Latin Quarter' along Pontstrasse northeast of the Markt.

Hotel Drei Könige   HOTEL €€
(☑ 0241-483 93; www.h3k-aachen.de; Büchel 5; d €129-169; ❄ 🤍 🐾) The sunny Mediterranean design and quirky touches are an instant mood-lifter at this family-run favourite with its super-central location. Some of the 10 rooms are a tad wee. Breakfast, on the 4th floor, comes with dreamy views over the rooftops and the cathedral.

★ Am Knipp   GERMAN €€
(☑ 0241-331 68; www.amknipp.de; Bergdriesch 3; mains €9-24; ☉ 5-10.30pm Mon & Wed-Fri, 6-10.30pm Sat & Sun; 🤍) Hungry grazers have stopped by this traditional inn since 1698, and you too will have a fine time enjoying hearty German cuisine served amid a flea market's worth of knick-knacks or, if weather permits, in the big beer garden.

★ Café zum Mohren   CAFE €
(☑ 0241-352 00; www.cafezummohren.de; Hof 4; mains €4.50-10; ☉ 10am-7pm) This darling cafe just off the tourist trail is famous for its cakes, especially a wicked chocolate one called *Krippekratz* (local slang for 'devil') and sumptuous ice-cream cakes. Also a good spot for breakfast or light meals. Outside tables overlook a courtyard flanked by Roman columns.

ⓘ Information

Tourist Office (☑ 0241-180 2950; www.aachen-tourist.de; Friedrich-Wilhelm-Platz; ☉ 10am-6pm Mon-Fri, to 2pm Sat & Sun Apr-Dec, shorter hours Jan-Mar)

ⓘ Getting There & Away

Regional trains to Cologne (€17.50, one hour) run twice hourly from the Hauptbahnhof, with some proceeding beyond. Aachen is a stop for high-speed trains to/from Brussels (€40, 1¼ hours) and Paris.

Bonn

☑ 0228 / POP 322,000

South of Cologne on the Rhine River, Bonn served as West Germany's capital from 1949 until 1990. For visitors, the birthplace of Ludwig van Beethoven has plenty in store, not least the great composer's birth house, a string of top-rated museums and the lovely riverside setting.

◎ Sights

★ Beethoven-Haus Bonn   MUSEUM
(Beethoven House; ☑ 0228-981 7525; www.beethoven-haus-bonn.de; Bonngasse 20; adult/concession €6/4.50; ☉ 10am-6pm Apr-Oct, 10am-5pm Mon-Sat, 11am-5pm Sun Nov-Mar) Star composer Ludwig van Beethoven was born in 1770 in this rather humble townhouse, where today original scores, letters, paintings and instruments, including his last grand piano, offer insight into his work, routines and feelings. Of special note are the huge ear trumpets he used to combat his growing deafness. Tickets are also good for the new media exhibit in the adjacent building, where you can experience the composer's genius during a spacey, interactive 3D multimedia tour.

Haus der Geschichte   MUSEUM
(Museum of History; ☑ 0228-916 5400; www.hdg.de; Willy-Brandt-Allee 14; ☉ 9am-7pm Tue-Fri, 10am-6pm Sat & Sun; 🅿; 🚊 16, 63, 66 Heussallee/Museumsmeile) **FREE** The Haus der Geschichte der Bundesrepublik Deutschland presents

a smart, fun romp through recent German history, starting from the end of WWII. Walk through the fuselage of a Berlin airlift *Rosinenbomber* plane, watch classic clips in a 1950s cinema, imagine free love in a VW microbus, examine Erich Honecker's arrest warrant, stand in front of a piece of the Berlin Wall or watch John F Kennedy's famous *'Ich bin ein Berliner'* speech.

✖ Eating

Brauhaus Bönnsch GERMAN €€
(☑ 0228-650 610; www.boennsch.de; Sterntorbrücke 4; mains €10-22; ⊙ 11am-1am Mon-Thu, to 3am Fri & Sat; 🖩) The unfiltered ale is a must at this congenial brewpub adorned with photographs of famous politicians great and failed, from Willy Brandt to, yes, Arnold Schwarzenegger. Schnitzel, Rhenish specialities and fry-ups dominate the menu, but the *Flammkuchen* (tarte flambée) is always a crowd-pleaser.

ℹ Information

Bonn Tourist Office (☑ 0228-775 000; www.bonn-region.de; Windeckstrasse 1; ⊙ 10am-6pm Mon-Fri, to 4pm Sat, to 2pm Sun) Lots of free information and combined bus-and-walking tours in English (adult/concession €16/8).

ℹ Getting There & Away

Bonn is linked to Cologne many times hourly by U-Bahn lines U16 and U18 (€7.90, 54 minutes).

NORTHERN GERMANY

POP 6.5 MILLION

Germany's windswept and maritime-flavoured north is dominated by Hamburg, a metropolis shaped by water and commerce since the Middle Ages. Bremen is a fabulous stop with fairy-tale character, and not only because of the famous Brothers' Grimm fairy tale starring a certain donkey, dog, cat and rooster. Those with a sweet tooth should not miss a side trip to Lübeck, renowned for its superb marzipan.

Hamburg

☑ 040 / POP 1.8 MILLION

Hamburg's historic label, 'The gateway to the world', might be a bold claim, but Germany's second-largest city and biggest port has never been shy. Hamburg has engaged in business with the world ever since it joined the Hanseatic League back in the Middle Ages. Its maritime spirit infuses the entire city; from architecture to menus to the cry of gulls, you always know you're near the water. The city has given rise to vibrant neighbourhoods awash with multicultural eateries, as well as the gloriously seedy Reeperbahn red-light district. Hamburg nurtured the early promise of the Beatles, and today its distinctive live- and electronic-music scene thrives in unique harbourside venues.

⊙ Sights

The seven-storey red-brick warehouses lining the **Speicherstadt** archipelago are a famous Hamburg symbol and they're increasingly filled with fine museums. **HafenCity,** crowned by the superlative Elbphilharmonie, is Hamburg's most architecturally dynamic corner, with a world seemingly being created before your eyes.

★ **Elbphilharmonie** ARTS CENTRE
(Elbe Philharmonic Hall; ☑ 040-3576 6666; www.elbphilharmonie.de; Platz der Deutschen Einheit 4; ⊙ 9am-11.30pm; Ⓢ Baumwall) 𝗙𝗥𝗘𝗘 Welcome to one of the most Europe's most exciting recent architectural creations. A squat brown-brick former warehouse at the far west of HafenCity was the base for the architecturally bold Elbphilharmonie, a major concert hall and performance space, not to mention architectural icon. Pritzker Prize–winning Swiss architects Herzog & de Meuron were responsible for the design, which captivates with details like 1096 individually curved glass panes.

Hamburger Kunsthalle MUSEUM
(☑ 040-428 131 200; www.hamburger-kunsthalle.de; Glockengiesserwall; adult/child €14/free, Thu evening €8/free; ⊙ 10am-6pm Tue, Wed & Fri-Sun, to 9pm Thu; Ⓤ Hauptbahnhof-Nord) A treasure trove of art from the Renaissance to the present day, the Kunsthalle spans two buildings linked by an underground passage. The main building houses works ranging from medieval portraiture to 20th-century classics, such as Klee and Kokoschka. There's also a memorable room of 19th-century landscapes by Caspar David Friedrich. Its stark white modern cube, the Galerie der Gegenwart, showcases contemporary German artists.

Rathaus HISTORIC BUILDING
(☑ 040-428 3124; Rathausmarkt 1; tours adult/under 14yr €5/free; ⊙ tours half-hourly 11am-4pm Mon-Fri, 10am-5pm Sat, to 4pm Sun, English tours

ST PAULI & THE REEPERBAHN

No discussion of Hamburg is complete without mentioning St Pauli, home to one of Europe's most (in)famous red-light districts. Sex shops, table-dance bars and strip clubs still line its main drag, the Reeperbahn, and side streets, but the popularity of prostitution has declined dramatically in the internet age. Today St Pauli is Hamburg's main nightlife district, drawing people of all ages and walks of life to live music and dance clubs, chic bars and theatres. In fact, street walkers are not even allowed to hit the pavement before 8pm and then are confined to certain areas, the most notorious being the gated Herbertstrasse (no women and men under 18 years allowed). Nearby, the cops of the Davidwache police station keep an eye on the lurid surrounds. A short walk west is the side street called Grosse Freiheit, where the Beatles cut their teeth at the Indra Club (No 64) and the Kaiserkeller (No 36). Both are vastly different venues today, but there's a small monument to the Fab Four in a courtyard behind No 35.

depend on demand; U Rathausmarkt, Jungfernstieg, S Jungfernstieg) With its spectacular coffered ceiling, Hamburg's baroque Rathaus is one of Europe's most opulent, and is renowned for its Emperor's Hall and Great Hall. The 40-minute tours take in only a fraction of this beehive of 647 rooms. A good secret to know about is the inner courtyard, where you can take a break from exploring the Rathaus on comfy chairs with tables.

St Michaelis Kirche
CHURCH

(Church of St Michael; ☑ 040-376 780; www.st-michaelis.de; Englische Planke 1; tower adult/child €5/3.50, crypt €4/2.50, combo ticket €7/4, church only €2; ☉ 9am-7.30pm May-Oct, 10am-5.30pm Nov-Apr, last entry 30min before closing; U Rödingsmarkt) 'Der Michel', as it is affectionately called, is one of Hamburg's most recognisable landmarks and northern Germany's largest Protestant baroque church. Ascending the tower (by steps or lift) rewards visitors with great panoramas across the city and canals. The crypt has an engaging multimedia exhibit on the city's history.

Mahnmal St-Nikolai
MEMORIAL

(Memorial St Nicholas; ☑ 040-371 125; www.mahnmal-st-nikolai.de; Willy-Brandt-Strasse 60; adult/child €5/3; ☉ 10am-6pm May-Sep, to 5pm Oct-Apr; U Rödingsmarkt) St Nikolai church was the world's tallest building from 1874 to 1876, and it remains Hamburg's second-tallest structure (after the TV tower). Mostly destroyed in WWII, it is now called Mahnmal St-Nikolai. You can take a glass lift up to a 76.3m-high viewing platform inside the surviving spire for views of Hamburg's centre, put into context of the wartime destruction.

The crypt houses an unflinching underground exhibit on the horrors of war.

★ Fischmarkt
MARKET

(Grosse Elbstrasse 9; ☉ 5am-9.30am Sun Apr-Oct, from 7am Nov-Mar; ☐ 112 to Fischmarkt, S Reeperbahn) Here's the perfect excuse to stay up all Saturday night. Every Sunday in the wee hours, some 70,000 locals and visitors descend upon the famous Fischmarkt in St Pauli. The market has been running since 1703, and its undisputed stars are the boisterous *Marktschreier* (market criers) who hawk their wares at full volume. Live bands also entertainingly crank out cover versions of ancient German pop songs in the adjoining **Fischauktionshalle** (Fish Auction Hall).

Auswanderermuseum BallinStadt
MUSEUM

(Emigration Museum; ☑ 040-3197 9160; www.ballinstadt.de; Veddeler Bogen 2; adult/child €13/7; ☉ 10am-6pm Apr-Oct, to 4.30pm Nov-Mar; ☐ Veddel) Sort of a bookend for New York's Ellis Island, Hamburg's excellent emigration museum looks at the conditions that drove about five million people to leave Germany for the USA and South America in search of better lives from 1850 until the 1930s. Multilingual displays address the hardships endured before and during the voyage and upon arrival in the New World. About 4km southeast of the city centre, BallinStadt is easily reached by S-Bahn.

Chilehaus
HISTORIC BUILDING

(☑ 040-349 194 247; www.chilehaus.de; Fischertwiete 2; S Messberg) One of Hamburg's most beautiful buildings is the crowning gem of the new Unesco-anointed Kontorhaus

Hamburg

Map labels:

Schröderstiftstr · Bundesstr · Sternschanzenpark · Sternschanze · Altonaer-Str · Max-Brauer-Allee · Bartelstr · 20 · 17 · 16 · Lagerstr · Rentzelstr · St-Petersburger-Str · SCHANZENVIERTEL · Susannenstr · Schulterblatt · Schanzenstr · Kampstr · Grabenstr · Karolinenstr · Lippmannstr · 14 · Stresemannstr · Wöhlers Allee · Bernstorffstr · Neuer Pferdemarkt · SCHANZENVIERTEL · Sternstr · Marktstr · Holstenglacis · Messehallen · Kleine Wallanlagen · Otzenstr · Thadenstr · Neuer Kamp · Feldstrasse · 9 · Feldstr · Johannes Brahms Platz · Kaiser-Wilhelm-Str · GaumenGanoven (1.9km) · HEILIGENGEISTFELD · Pilatuspool · Gilbertstr · Budapester-Str · Glacischaussee · Holstenwall · Paul-Roosen-Str · Armenstr · Clemens-Schultz-Str · Grosse Wallanlagen · Peterstr · Paul-Roosen-Str · 19 · Simon-von-Utrecht-Str · Hein-Hoyer-Str · Sts-Pauli-Str · 12 · ST PAULI · St Pauli · Hütten · Grossneumarkt · Holstenstr · Grosse Freiheit · Talstr · Seilerstr · Millerntorplatz · Reeperbahn · Reeperbahn · Hans-Albers-Platz · Reeperbahn · Zirkusweg · Ludwig-Erhard-Str · 21 · Davidstr · Baldurstr · Friedrichstr · Kastanienallee · Hopfenstr · Elbpark · 8 · Böhmkenstr · Venusberg · Silbersacktwiete · Bernhard-Nocht-Str · St-Pauli-Hafenstr · Seewartenstr · Tourist Information am Hafen · Landungsbrücken · Ditmar-Koel-Str · Wolfgangsweg · Stubbenhuk · Herrengraben · 2 · St-Pauli-Fischmarkt · 18 · Baumwall · Fischmarkt · Elbe River · St Pauli Elbtunnel · St Pauli Harbour · Johannisbollwerk · Vorsetzen

---

District. The brown-brick 1924 Chilehaus is shaped like an ocean liner, with remarkable curved walls meeting in the shape of a ship's bow and staggered balconies that look like decks. It was designed by architect Fritz Höger for a merchant who derived his wealth from trading with Chile. Casual visitors are not really welcome inside, but it's the exterior that you come here to see.

Miniatur Wunderland   MUSEUM
(📞 040-300 6800; www.miniatur-wunderland. de; Kehrwieder 2; adult/child €15/7.50; ⊙ hours vary; Ⓤ Baumwall) Even the worst cynics are

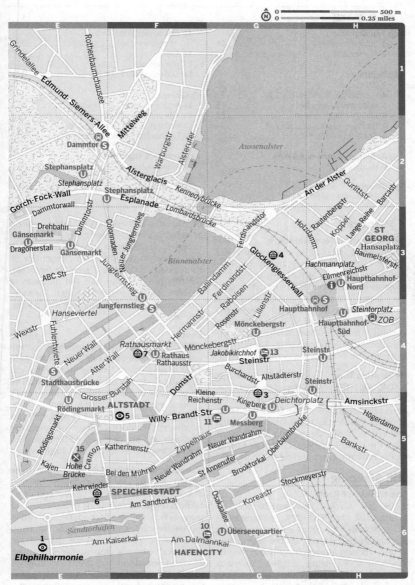

quickly transformed into fans of this vast miniature world that goes on and on. The model trains wending their way through the Alps are impressive, if slightly predictable, but when you see a model A380 swoop out of the sky and land at the fully functional model of Hamburg's airport, you can't help

but gasp! On weekends and in summer holidays, pre-purchase your ticket online to skip the queues.

The current display is a mind-numbing 1300 sq metres; tiny details abound as days change to night.

Hamburg

☞ Tours

★ Sandemans New Hamburg   TOURS
(www.neweuropetours.eu; by donation up to €12; ⊙11am & 2pm daily) These highly regarded free city tours begin at Rathausplatz and explore most of central Hamburg's attractions over three hours. These guides work hard and if you enjoy the tour, a tip is expected. They also run tours of St Pauli (€12, 7pm) that leave from the Clock Tower, and a popular Hamburg Pub Crawl (€12, 9.30pm) that starts in Beatles Platz, Reeperbahn.

★ Beatles Tour   WALKING
(☑040-3003 3790; www.hempels-musictour.com; tour €28; ⊙6pm Sat Apr-Nov; ⓤFeldstrasse) For an entertaining look at the Beatles in Hamburg, try this Beatles tour offered by the fun and engaging Stephanie Hempel. It starts from the U-Bahn station Feldstrasse and includes museum entry and a small concert.

🛏 Sleeping

Superbude St Pauli   HOTEL €
(☑040-807 915 820; www.superbude.de; Juliusstrasse 1-7; r from €65; @🛜; ⓤSternschanze, Ⓢ Sternschanze) The young and forever-young mix and mingle without a shred of prejudice at this rocking design hotel-hostel combo that's all about living, laughing, partying and, yes, even sleeping well. All rooms have comfy beds and sleek private bathrooms, breakfast is served until noon and there's even a 'rock star suite' with an Astra beer as a pillow treat.

★ Henri Hotel   HOTEL €€
(☑040-554 357 557; www.henri-hotel.com; Bugenhagenstrasse 21; s/d from €98/118; 🛜; Ⓢ Möncke-

bergstrasse) Kidney-shaped tables, plush armchairs, vintage typewriters – the Henri channels the 1950s so successfully that you half expect to run into Don Draper. Its 65 rooms and studios are a good fit for urban lifestyle junkies who like the alchemy of modern comforts and retro design. For more elbow room get an L-sized room with a king-size bed.

East   HOTEL €€
(☑040-309 933; www.east-hamburg.de; Simon-von-Utrecht-Strasse 31; r €100-225; ❄🛜; ⓤSt Pauli) In an old iron foundry, East's bold and dramatic design never fails to impress. The walls, lamps and huge pillars of this hotel's public areas emulate organic forms – droplets, flowers, trees – giving it a warm, rich and enveloping feel. Rooms come with handmade furniture and are accented with tactile fabrics and leather. It's on a cool St Pauli street.

25hours Hotel HafenCity   HOTEL €€
(☑040-257 7770; www.25hours-hotel.de; Übersee-allee 5; r €100-225; P❄🛜; ⓤÜberseequartier) Offbeat decor, an infectious irreverence and postmodern vintage flair make this pad a top choice among global nomads. Sporting maritime flourishes, the decor channels an old-timey seaman's club in the lobby, the excellent restaurant and the 170 cabin-style rooms. Enjoy views of the emerging Hafen-City neighbourhood from the rooftop sauna.

★ Adina Apartment Hotel
Speicherstadt   APARTMENT €€
(☑040-334 6080; www.adinahotels.com/hotel/hamburg-speicherstadt; Willy-Brandt-Strasse 25; r from €144; P❄🛜☒; ⓤMessberg) An excellent addition to the Adina portfolio, this sophisti-

cated place ticks all the boxes when it comes to location (within easy walking distance to most attractions), price (much more reasonable than many Hamburg apartment hotels) and comfort (the studio rooms are large, stylish and exceptionally soundproof). The swimming pool, gym and sauna are all nice touches. Multinight stays attract discounts.

✗ Eating

Fischbrötchenbude Brücke 10　SEAFOOD €
(☎040-3339 9339; www.bruecke-10.de; Landungsbrücken, Pier 10; sandwiches €3-9.50; ⊙10am-10pm; ⑤Landungsbrücken, ⑪Landungsbrücken) There are a gazillion fish sandwich vendors in Hamburg, but we're going to stick our neck out and say that this vibrant, clean and contemporary outpost makes the best. Try a classic *Bismarck* (pickled herring) or *Matjes* (brined herring), or treat yourself to a bulging shrimp sandwich. Lovely tables outside.

Altes Mädchen　EUROPEAN €€
(☎040-800 077 750; www.altes-maedchen. com; Lagerstrasse 28b; mains €6-29; ⊙noon-late Mon-Sat, 10am-late Sun; ⑤Sternschanze, ⑪Sternschanze) The lofty red-brick halls of a 19th-century animal market have been up-cycled into a hip culinary destination that includes a coffee roastery, a celebrity chef restaurant, and this beguiling brewpub with a central bar, in-house bakery and garden.

Bullerei　INTERNATIONAL €€
(☎040-3344 2110; www.bullerei.com; Lagerstrasse 34b; mains €10-25; ⊙11am-11pm; ⑤Sternschanze) One of the coolest dining spaces in the city, Bullerei inhabits a converted former slaughterhouse with lovely high ceilings and a real buzz that bounces off the walls – don't come here for a quiet romantic dinner. Service is cool and attentive, and the menu revolves around steak dishes and Italian-inflected choices.

★Alt Hamburger Aalspeicher　GERMAN €€€
(☎040-362 990; www.aalspeicher.de; Deichstrasse 43; mains €13-27; ⊙noon-11pm Wed-Sun; ⑪Rödingsmarkt) Despite its tourist-friendly location, the knick-knack-filled dining room and warm service at this restaurant, in a 400-year-old canalside building, make you feel like you're dining in your *Oma's* (grandma's) house – it's a real slice of old Hamburg where you'd least expect it. Smoked eel from its own smokehouse is a speciality.

🍷 Drinking & Nightlife

Partying in Hamburg concentrates on the Schanzenviertel and St Pauli, a few streets further south.

★Strandperle　BAR
(☎040-8809 9508; www.strandperle-hamburg.de; Oevelgönne 60; ⊙10am-11pm Mon-Fri, from 9am Sat & Sun May-Sep, shorter hours & Fri-Sun only Oct-Apr; 🚌112) Hamburg's original beach bar is a must for primo beer, burgers and people-watching. All ages and classes gather, mingle and wriggle their toes in the sand, especially at sunset, right on the Elbe, as huge freighters glide past. Get here by taking ferry 62 from Landungsbrücken or bus 112 from Altona station to Neumühlen/Oevelgönne.

★Katze　COCKTAIL BAR
(☎040-5577 5910; Schulterblatt 88; ⊙1pm-3am Mon-Sat, to midnight Sun; ⑤Sternschanze) Small and sleek, this 'kitty' (*Katze* = cat) gets the crowd purring for well-priced cocktails (the best caipirinhas in town) and great music (there's dancing on weekends). It's one of the most popular among the watering holes on this main Schanzenviertel booze strip.

★Zum Silbersack　PUB
(☎040-314 589; www.facebook.com/zumsilber sack1949; Silbersackstrasse 9; ⊙5pm-1am Sun, to 3am Mon-Wed, to 4am Thu, 3pm-5pm Fri & Sat; ⑤Reeperbahn) A real St Pauli icon, Zum Silbersack is one of our favourites in the area. It's the sort of place where you'll find students, junkies, executives, greenies, millionaires and sex workers. Anything seems possible and it can be a little rough around the edges, but it's *very* St Pauli.

Indra Club　CLUB
(www.indramusikclub.com; 64 Grosse Freiheit; ⊙9pm-late Wed-Sun; ⑤Reeperbahn) The Beatles' small first venue is open again and has live acts some nights. The interior is vastly different from the 1960s and there is a fine beer garden.

ℹ Information

Tourist Information am Hafen (☎040-3005 1701; www.hamburg-travel.com; btwn piers 4 & 5, St Pauli Landungsbrücken; ⊙9am-6pm Sun-Wed, to 7pm Thu-Sat; ⑤Landungsbrücken) No hotel bookings, but plenty of information.

Tourist Information Hauptbahnhof (☎040-3005 1701; www.hamburg-travel.com;

Hauptbahnhof, near Kirchenallee exit; ◷ 9am-7pm Mon-Sat, 10am-6pm Sun; ⓡ Hauptbahnhof, ⓤ Hauptbahnhof) Busy all the time.

❶ Getting There & Away

AIR

Hamburg Airport (Flughafen Hamburg Helmut Schmidt; HAM; ☑ 040-507 50; www.hamburg-airport.de; Flughafenstrasse; ⓡ Hamburg Airport) is linked to the city centre every 10 minutes by the S-Bahn line S1 (€3.30, 25 minutes). A taxi takes about a half-hour and cost around €30.

BUS

The **ZOB** (Zentraler Omnibusbahnhof, Central Bus Station; ☑ 040-247 576; www.zob-hamburg.de; Adenauerallee 78; ⓡ Hauptbahnhof, ⓤ Hauptbahnhof-Süd), southeast of the Hauptbahnhof, has many domestic and international departures by Eurolines, Flixbus and many other operators.

TRAIN

Frequent trains serve regional and long-distance destinations from Hamburg. There are two mainline stations worth noting: **Hamburg Hauptbahnhof** (Main Train Station; www.hamburger-hbf.de; ⓡ Hauptbahnhof) and **Hamburg Altona** (ⓢ Altona).

Frequent trains serve Lübeck (from €14.50, 45 minutes), Bremen (from €20, one hour), Berlin-Hauptbahnhof (from €30, 1¾ hours), Cologne (from €36, four hours) and many other cities.

❶ Getting Around

For public transport information, go to **HVV** (☑ 040-194 49; www.hvv.de). The city is divided into zones. Fare zone A covers the city centre, inner suburbs and airport.

Schleswig-Holstein

Sandy beaches, jaunty red-and-white striped lighthouses, deep fjords carved by glaciers, and wildlife like sandpipers and seals have made this sweeping peninsula between the North and Baltic Seas Germany's most elite summer retreat. Don't miss Lübeck, the magnificently preserved medieval headquarters of the Hanseatic League. Flensburg, too, is a lively harbour town.

Lübeck

☑ 0451 / POP 218,523

Compact and charming Lübeck makes for a great day trip from Hamburg. Looking like a pair of witches' hats, the pointed towers of its landmark Holstentor (Holsten Gate)

form the gateway to its historic centre that sits on an island embraced by the arms of the Trave River. The Unesco-recognised web of cobbled lanes flanked by gabled merchants' homes and spired churches is an enduring reminder of Lübeck's role as the one-time capital of the medieval Hanseatic League trading power. Today it enjoys fame as Germany's marzipan capital, best sampled at **Niederegger** (☑ 0451-530 1126; www.niederegger.de; Breite Strasse 89; ◷ 9am-7pm Mon-Fri, 9am-6pm Sat, 10am-6pm Sun).

◉ Sights

★ Holstentor   LANDMARK

(Holsten Gate) Built in 1464 and looking so settled-in that it appears to sag, Lübeck's charming red-brick city gate is a national icon. Its twin pointed cylindrical towers, leaning together across the stepped gable that joins them, captivated Andy Warhol (his print is in the St Annen Museum), and have graced postcards, paintings, posters and marzipan souvenirs. Discover this and more inside the **Museum Holstentor** (☑ 0451-122 4129; www.museum-holstentor.de; Holstentor; adult/child €7/2.50; ◷ 10am-6pm Apr-Dec, 11am-5pm Tue-Sun Jan-Mar), which sheds light on the history of the gate and on Lübeck's medieval mercantile glory days.

★ Museumsquartier St Annen   MUSEUM

(Museum Quarter St Annen; ☑ 0451-122 4137; www.museumsquartier-st-annen.de; St-Annen-Strasse; adult/child €12/6; ◷ 10am-5pm Tue-Sun Apr-Dec, from 11am Jan-Mar) This museum quarter includes an old synagogue, church and medieval buildings along its uneven streets. The namesake **St Annen Museum** details the diverse history of the neighbourhood as it traces 700 years of art and culture. The adjoining **St Annen Kunsthalle** has ecclesiastical art (including Hans Memling's 1491 *Passion Altar*) and contemporary art, including Andy Warhol's print of Lübeck's Holstentor. There's a chic little cafe in the courtyard.

★ Europäisches Hansemuseum   MUSEUM

(European Hanseatic Museum; ☑ 0451-809 0990; www.hansemuseum.eu; An der Untertrave 1; adult/child €12.50/7.50; ◷ 10am-6pm) Opened in 2015, this brilliant museum tells the remarkable story of the Hanseatic League, Lübeck and the region. For 600 years, city states in northern Europe and along the Baltic discovered that shared interests in trade made everybody's life better than war. Transfixing

ANNE FRANK & BERGEN-BELSEN

Nazi-built **Bergen-Belsen** (Bergen-Belsen Memorial Site; ☑ 05051-475 90; www.bergen -belsen.de; Anne-Frank-Platz, Lohheide; ☉ Documentation Centre 10am-6pm Apr-Sep, to 5pm Oct-Mar, grounds until dusk) FREE began its existence in 1940 as a POW camp, but became a concentration camp after being taken over by the SS in 1943, initially to imprison Jews as hostages in exchange for German POWs held abroad. In all, 70,000 prisoners perished here, most famously Anne Frank. A modern Documentation Centre chronicles the fates of the people who passed through here. A small section deals with Anne Frank, and there's also a memorial grave stone for her and her sister, Margot, near the cemetery's Jewish Monument. The memorial site is in the countryside about 60km northeast of Hanover and a bit complicated to reach if you don't have your own wheels. See the website for detailed driving and public transport directions.

exhibits use every modern technology to tell a story as dramatic as anything on *Game of Thrones*. The complex includes the beautifully restored medieval **Castle Friary**.

Rathaus   HISTORIC BUILDING
(Town Hall; ☑ 0451-122 1005; Breite Strasse 62; adult/concession €4/2; ☉ tours 11am, noon & 3pm Mon-Fri, 1.30pm Sat & Sun) Sometimes described as a 'fairy tale in stone', Lübeck's 13th- to 15th-century Rathaus is widely regarded as one of the most beautiful in Germany. Inside, a highlight is the *Audienzsaal* (audience hall), a light-flooded hall decked out in festive rococo.

🛏 Sleeping & Eating

★ Hotel Haase   BOUTIQUE HOTEL €€
(☑ 0451-7074 90 1; www.hotel-haase-luebeck.de; Glockengießerstrasse 24; s/d from €100/116; 🖥) Gorgeous rooms with exposed brick walls and polished hardwood floors inhabit this beautifully restored 14th-century home in the heart of town. The public areas in particular sparkle with character, and service never misses a beat.

Klassik Altstadt Hotel   BOUTIQUE HOTEL €€
(☑ 0451-702 980; www.klassik-altstadt-hotel.de; Fischergrube 52; s/d from €55/120; 🖥) Each of the 29 rooms at this elegantly furnished boutique hotel are dedicated to a different, mostly German, writer or artist, such as Thomas Mann or Johann Sebastian Bach. Single rooms (some share baths and are great value) feature travelogues by famous authors.

Grenadine   BISTRO €€
(☑ 0451-307 2950; www.grenadine-hl.de; Wahmstrasse 40; mains €10-23; ☉ 9am-4pm Mon, to 10pm Tue-Thu, to midnight Fri & Sat, to 3pm Sun; 🖥) This narrow, elongated bar leads through to a gar-

den out the back. Enjoy bistro fare amid chic, retro-minimalist style. The long drinks menu goes well with tapas choices. Sandwiches, salads and pasta, plus a gorgeous breakfast buffet (€14.50 to €17.50), are served.

★ Im Alten Zolln   PUB
(☑ 0451-723 95; www.alter-zolln.de; Mühlenstrasse 93-95; ☉ 11am-late; 🖥) This classic pub inhabits a 16th-century customs post. There's an excellent beer selection. Patrons people-watch from terrace and pavement tables in summer and watch bands (rock and jazz) inside in winter. Fortify yourself with schnitzel and Lübeck's best roast potatoes.

ℹ️ Information

Tourist Office (☑ 0451-889 9700; www. luebeck-tourismus.de; Holstentorplatz 1; ☉ 9am-7pm Mon-Fri, 10am-4pm Sat, 10am-3pm Sun Jun-Aug, shorter hours Sep-Apr) One of Schleswig-Holstein's better tourist offices, with a cafe and internet terminals.

ℹ️ Getting There & Away

Lübeck is reached via the A1 from Hamburg. Lübeck has connections every hour to Hamburg (€14.50, 45 minutes) and Kiel (from €18.70, 1¼ hours).

LOWER SAXONY & BREMEN

POP 7.9 MILLION (LOWER SAXONY), 671,489 (BREMEN)
Lower Saxony (Niedersachsen) is the largest German state after Bavaria. West to east, it stretches from the World Heritage-listed Wattenmeer tidal flats and the East Frisian Islands to Wolfsburg. Bremen, the smallest of the German states, packs a punch for its

size. At the mouth of the Weser, its port city of Bremerhaven upholds a rich seafaring tradition.

Bremen City

☑ 0421 / POP 568,006

It's a shame the donkey, dog, cat and rooster in Grimm's *Town Musicians of Bremen* never actually made it here – they would have fallen in love with the place. This little city is big on charm, from the fairy-tale character statue to a jaw-dropping expressionist laneway and impressive town hall. On top of that, the Weser riverside promenade is a relaxing, bistro- and beer garden–lined refuge and the lively student district ('Das Viertel') along Ostertorsteinweg is filled with indie boutiques, cafes, art-house cinemas and alt-flavoured cultural venues.

◉ Sights & Activities

Bremen's Unesco World Heritage–protected **Marktplatz** is striking, especially for its ornate, gabled and sculpture-adorned **Rathaus**. On the town hall's western side is a sculpture of the animal quartet of lore, the **Town Musicians of Bremen** (Stadtmusikanten).

★**Kunsthalle**　　　　　　GALLERY

(☑0421-329 080; www.kunsthalle-bremen. de; Am Wall 207; adult/child €9/free; ⊙10am-5pm Wed-Sun, to 9pm Tue; 🚊2, 3 to Theater am Goetheplatz) For art lovers, the highlight of Bremen's *Kulturmeile* (Cultural Mile) is the Kunsthalle, which presents a large permanent collection of paintings, sculpture and copperplate engravings from the Middle Ages into the modern era – some of the masterpieces here are more than 600 years old. The collection includes work by van Dyck, Rubens, Monet, Van Gogh and Picasso, as well as 10 sculptures by Rodin. Rotating exhibitions display both classical and contemporary art.

Böttcherstrasse　　　　　　STREET

(www.boettcherstrasse.de) The charming medieval coopers lane was transformed into a prime example of mostly expressionist architecture in the 1920s at the instigation of coffee merchant Ludwig Roselius. Its red-brick houses sport unique facades, whimsical fountains, statues and a carillon; many house artisanal shops and art museums. Its most striking feature is Bernhard Hoetger's golden **Lichtbringer** (Bringer of Light) relief, which keeps an eye on the north entrance.

Dom St Petri　　　　　　CHURCH

(St Petri Cathedral; ☑0421-334 7142; www.stpetri dom.de; Sandstrasse 10-12; tower adult/child €2/1, museum free; ⊙10am-5pm Mon-Fri, to 2pm Sat, 2-5pm Sun Oct-May, Mon-Fri & Sun to 6pm Jun-Sep) Bremen's Protestant main church has origins in the 8th century, though its ribbed vaulting, chapels and two high towers date from the 13th century. Aside from the imposing architecture, the intricately carved pulpit and the baptismal font in the western crypt deserve a closer look. For panoramic views, climb the 265 steps to the top of the south **tower** (April to October). The Dom museum displays religious artefacts and

WORTH A TRIP

BACK TO THE ROOTS IN BREMERHAVEN

Standing on the spot where more than 7.2 million emigrants set sail for the USA, South America and Australia between 1830 and 1942, the spectacular **Deutsches Auswandererhaus** (German Emigration Centre; ☑0471-902 200; www.dah-bremerhaven.de; Columbusstrasse 65; adult/child €14.80/8.80; ⊙10am-6pm Mar-Oct, to 5pm Nov-Feb) museum does a superb job commemorating some of their stories. The visitor relives stages of their journey, which begins at the wharf where passengers huddle together before boarding 'the ship', clutching the biographical details of one particular traveller and heading towards their new life. A second exhibit, opened in 2012, reverses the theme and tells of immigration to Germany since the 17th century. Everything is available in both German and English. Bremerhaven is some 70km north of Bremen and is served by regional train (€12.95, 40 minutes). From the station, take bus 502, 505, 506, 508 or 509 to 'Havenwelten' to get to the museum and the harbour with its many old vessels (including a WWII sub) and striking contemporary architecture.

treasures found here in a 1970s archaeological dig.

Beck's Brewery Factory Tour
BREWERY

(☎ 0421-5094 5555; www.becks.de/besucherzentrum; Am Deich 18/19; tours €12.90; ⏰ tours 1pm, 3pm & 4.30pm Mon-Wed, 10am, 11.30am, 1pm, 3pm, 4.30pm & 6pm Thu-Sat; 🚃 1, 2, 3 to Am Brill) Two-hour tours of one of Germany's most internationally famous breweries must be booked online through either the Beck's or tourist office websites. Expect a tasting at the end. The 3pm tour is also in English. Minimum age 16. Meet at the brewery's visitor centre; take the tram to Am Brill, cross the river, then turn right onto Am Deich.

🛏 Sleeping & Eating

Tourist-oriented places to eat cluster around Markt, which is pretty dead after dark. Das Viertel has an alternative, student-flavoured feel, while the waterfront promenade, Schlachte, is pricier and more mainstream.

Atlantic Grand
HOTEL €€

(☎ 0421-620 620; www.atlantic-hotels.de; Bredenstrasse 2; r from €119) The simple but effortlessly stylish, dark-wood rooms pitched around a central courtyard and the top-notch service from attentive staff make this classy hotel an excellent choice. It's moments from Bremen's quirky Böttcherstrasse and steps from the riverside Schlachte.

Hotel Überfluss
DESIGN HOTEL €€

(☎ 0421-322 860; www.designhotel-ueberfluss.de; Langenstrasse 72; s/d from €111/116; ❄ 🚻 🏊; 🚃 1, 2, 3 to Am Brill) Just metres above river level, this cutting-edge-cool hotel is a good choice for design-minded urban nomads. Black, white and chrome create a sleek, postmodern vibe that extends to the rooms (those with views are €15 more). There's one suite (from €328) with a river view and a private sauna and hot tub – perfect for a honeymoon. Breakfast costs €14.50.

Engel Weincafe
CAFE €

(☎ 0421-6964 2390; www.engelweincafe-bremen.de; Ostertorsteinweg 31; dishes €4.50-15.60; ⏰ 9am-1am Mon-Fri, from 10am Sat & Sun; 🚻 🐾; 🚃 2, 6 to Wulwesstrasse) Situated on a sunny corner in Das Viertel, this popular hang-out exudes the nostalgic vibe of the old-fashioned pharmacy it once was. The menu features breakfast, a hot lunch special, crispy *Flammkuchen* (like a French pizza, with crème fraiche), carpaccio, or just some cheese and a glass of wine from the international list.

★ Bremer Ratskeller
GERMAN €€

(☎ 0421-321 676; www.ratskeller-bremen.de; Am Markt 11; mains €9-30; ⏰ 11am-midnight; 🚻) Ratskellers were traditionally built underneath the Rathaus (town hall) in every German town to keep the citizens and civil servants fed. Bremen's – in business since 1405! – is quite the experience, with high vaulted ceilings, private booths in little cubbies (the better to discuss town business), and good, heavy, no-fuss German food and beer. Service is attentive and friendly.

ℹ Information

Tourist office branches include **Böttcherstrasse** (☎ 0421-308 0010; www.bremen-tourism.de; Böttcherstrasse 4; ⏰ 9.30am-6.30pm Mon-Fri, to 5pm Sat, 10am-4pm Sun; 🚻) a full-service tourist office with friendly staff near Marktplatz, and **Hauptbahnhof** (☎ 0421-308 0010; www.bremen-tourism.de; Hauptbahnhof; ⏰ 9am-6.30pm Mon-Fri, 9.30am-5pm Sat & Sun; 🚻), handily located at the main train station. These offices can help book tours and offer free wi-fi.

ℹ Getting There & Around

Bremen Airport (BRE; ☎ 0421-559 50; www.airport-bremen.de) is about 3.5km south of the city and well connected to the city by the line 6 tram (€2.80, 15 minutes).

Frequent IC trains go to Hamburg (€30, one hour), Hanover (€31, one hour) and Cologne (€69, three hours). Less frequent IC trains go to Berlin (€93, three hours).

SURVIVAL GUIDE

ℹ Directory A-Z

ACCOMMODATION

Outside of high season, around holidays and during major trade shows it's generally not necessary to book accommodation in advance.

DISCOUNT CARDS

Many towns offer free guest cards (*Gästekarte*), available from your hotel at the time of check-in, which entitle visitors to discounts on museums, sights and tours, plus sometimes the use of local public transport.

INTERNET ACCESS

➡ Some cafes and bars have wi-fi hot spots that let customers hook up for free, although you usually need to ask for a password.

➡ Wi-fi is available for a fee on select ICE train routes, including Berlin to Cologne and Frankfurt to Munich and in DB Lounges (free in 1st class).

• Locate wi-fi hot spots at www.hotspot-loca
tions.com.

LGBT+ TRAVELLERS

Germany is a magnet for *schwule* (gay) and *les-bische* (lesbian) travellers, with the rainbow flag flying especially proudly in Berlin and Cologne.

→ Same-sex marriage is legal.

→ Gay pride marches are held throughout Germany in springtime, the largest are in Cologne and Berlin.

→ Attitudes tend to be more conservative in the countryside, among older people and in the eastern states.

MONEY

→ ATMs (*Geldautomat*) are widely available in cities and towns, but rarely in villages. Most are linked to international networks such as Cirrus, Plus, Star and Maestro.

→ Cash is king in Germany. Always carry some with you and plan to pay cash almost everywhere.

→ Credit cards are becoming more widely accepted, but it's best not to assume you'll be able to use one – ask first.

OPENING HOURS

The following are typical opening hours; these may vary seasonally and between cities and villages. We've provided those applicable in high season. For specifics, see individual listings.

Banks 9am–4pm Monday to Friday, extended hours usually Tuesday and Thursday, some open Saturday

Bars 6pm–1am

Cafes 8am–8pm

Clubs 11pm to early morning

Post offices 9am–6pm Monday to Friday, 9am–1pm Saturday

Restaurants 11am–11pm (food service often stops at 9pm in rural areas)

Major stores and supermarkets 9.30am–8pm Monday to Saturday (shorter hours outside city centres)

PUBLIC HOLIDAYS

The following are *gesetzliche Feiertage* (public holidays):

Neujahrstag (New Year's Day) 1 January

Ostern (Easter) March/April; Good Friday, Easter Sunday and Easter Monday

Christi Himmelfahrt (Ascension Day) Forty days after Easter

Maifeiertag/Tag der Arbeit (Labour Day) 1 May

Pfingsten (Whit/Pentecost Sunday & Monday) Fifty days after Easter

Tag der Deutschen Einheit (Day of German Unity) 3 October

Weihnachtstag (Christmas Day) 25 December

Zweiter Weihnachtstag (Boxing Day) 26 December

TELEPHONE

German phone numbers consist of an area code (three to six digits), starting with 0, and the local number (three to nine digits). If dialling from a landline within the same city, you don't need to dial the area code. You must dial it if using a mobile.

Country code 49

International access code 00

TOURIST INFORMATION

→ German National Tourist Office (www.germany. travel) Should be your first port of call for travel in Germany.

ⓘ Getting There & Away

AIR

Huge Frankfurt Airport (p504) is Germany's busiest, with Munich (p487) a close second and Düsseldorf (p512) getting a good share of flights as well. Airports in Berlin (p473), Hamburg (p520) and Cologne are comparatively small.

BUS

Long-distance coach travel to Germany from such cities as Milan, Vienna, Amsterdam and Copenhagen has become a viable option thanks to a new crop of companies offering good-value connections aboard comfortable buses with snack bars and free wi-fi. Major operators include **MeinFernbus** (☑ 030-300 137 300; www.meinfernbus. de), **Flixbus** (☑ 030-300 137 300; https://global. flixbus.com), **Megabus** (☑ UK 0900 1600 900; www.megabus.com) and **Eurolines** (☑ in the UK 08717-818177; www.eurolines.com). For routes, times and prices, check www.busliniensuche.de (also in English).

CAR & MOTORCYCLE

When bringing your own vehicle to Germany, you need a valid driving licence, car registration and proof of third-party insurance. Foreign cars must display a nationality sticker unless they have official European plates. You also need to carry a warning (hazard) triangle and a first-aid kit.

TRAIN

→ Germany has an efficient railway network with excellent links to other European destinations. Ticketing is handled by **Deutsche Bahn** (Germany Railways; ☑ 0180-699 66 33; www.bahn.de).

→ Seat reservations are a good idea for Friday and Sunday travel on long-distance trains and highly recommended during the peak summer season and around major holidays.

→ Eurail and Interrail passes are valid on all German national trains.

SEA

Germany's main ferry ports are Kiel and Trave-münde (near Lübeck) in Schleswig-Holstein, and Rostock and Sassnitz (on Rügen Island) in Mecklenburg–Western Pomerania. All have services to Scandinavia. For details and tickets, go to www.ferrysavers.com.

ℹ Getting Around

Germans are whizzes at moving people around, and the public transport network is one of the best in Europe. The best ways of getting around the country are by car and by train.

AIR

Unless you're flying from one end of the country to the other, say from Berlin or Hamburg to Munich, planes are only marginally quicker than trains once you factor in the check-in and transit times.

BICYCLE

→ Cycling is allowed on all roads and highways but not on the autobahns (motorways).

→ Bicycles may be taken on most trains but require a separate ticket (Fahrradkarte) and a reservation if travelling on an IC/EC train. They are not allowed on ICE trains.

→ **Call a Bike** (www.callabike-interaktiv.de) is an automated cycle-hire scheme operated by Deutsche Bahn (German Rail) in some 50 German towns and cities.

BOAT

From April to October, boats operate on set timetables along sections of the Rhine, the Elbe and the Danube.

BUS

→ Buses are cheaper and slower than trains and have a growing long-haul network. Regional bus services fill the gaps in areas not served by rail. **Flixbus** (www.flixbus.com) is the dominant operator.

→ In some rural areas buses may be your only option for getting around without your own vehicle. Commuter-geared routes offer limited or no service in the evenings and on weekends.

→ In cities, buses generally converge at the Busbahnhof or Zentraler Omnibus Bahnhof (ZOB; central bus station), which is often near the Hauptbahnhof (central train station).

CAR & MOTORCYCLE

→ Driving is on the right side of the road.

→ Unless posted otherwise, speed limits are 50km/h in cities, 100km/h on country roads and no limit on the autobahn.

→ With few exceptions, no tolls are charged on public roads.

TIPPING

Hotels €1 per bag is standard. It's also nice to leave a little cash for the room cleaners, say €1 or €2 per day.

Restaurants Restaurant bills always include Bedienung (service charge), but most people add 5% or 10%.

Bars About 5%, rounded to the nearest euro. For drinks brought to your table, tip as for restaurants.

Taxis Tip about 10%, rounded to the nearest euro.

Toilet attendants Loose change.

→ Cars are impractical in urban areas. Leaving your car in a central Parkhaus (car park) can cost €20 per day or more.

→ Visitors from most countries do not need an International Driving Permit to drive in Germany. Automatic transmissions are rare and must be booked well in advance.

LOCAL TRANSPORT

→ Bigger cities, such as Berlin and Munich, integrate buses, trams, U-Bahn (underground, subway) trains and S-Bahn (suburban) trains into a single network.

→ Fares are determined by zones or time travelled, sometimes by both. A multi-ticket strip (Streifenkarte or 4-Fahrtenkarte) or day pass (Tageskarte) generally offers better value than a single-ride ticket.

→ Normally, tickets must be stamped upon boarding in order to be valid. Fines are levied if you're caught without a valid ticket.

TRAIN

→ Of the several train types, ICE trains are the fastest and most comfortable. IC trains (EC if they cross borders) are almost as fast but older and less snazzy. RE and RB trains are regional. S-Bahn are suburban trains operating in large cities and conurbations.

→ At larger stations, you can store your luggage in a locker (Schliessfach) or a left-luggage office (Gepäckaufbewahrung).

→ Seat reservations for long-distance travel are highly recommended, especially if you're travelling on a Friday or Sunday afternoon, during holiday periods or in summer. Reservations can be made online and at ticket counters as late as 10 minutes before departure.

→ Buy tickets online (www.bahn.de) or at stations from vending machines or ticket offices (Reisezentrum). Only conductors on ICE and IC/EC trains sell tickets on board at a surcharge.

Greece Ελλάδα

POP 10.7 MILLION

Best Places to Eat

➡ Koukoumavlos (p552)

➡ Klimataria (p568)

➡ Seychelles (p534)

➡ Bougatsa Iordanis (p558)

➡ Marco Polo Cafe (p561)

Best Places to Stay

➡ Athens Was (p533)

➡ Bella Venezia (p567)

➡ Caravan (p544)

➡ Aroma Suites (p552)

➡ Casa Leone (p558)

Why Go?

It's easy to understand how so many myths of gods and giants originated in the vast and varied wonderland of Greece, with its wide skies, island-speckled ocean and stunning terrain. Meander along Byzantine footpaths and shores, through villages, lush forests and olive groves. Swim in gorgeous clear waters. Lose yourself in sun-bleached ancient ruins – Acropolis, Delphi, Delos and Knossos. Greece is a treasure chest where socially spirited families and friends gather in cafes and play late into the summer evenings in plazas. Passionate about politics and art, the population embraces culture, and dances and festivals abound. Its celebrated cuisine highlights regional produce from local gardens, herbs and mountain greens, and the world's best olives and tomatoes; prepared as they have been for generations, or adapted into fabulous modern dishes. Ultimately, however, the locals themselves are the highlight. Think *filoxenia* (hospitality) personified. Greece is a legendary destination indeed.

When to Go
Athens

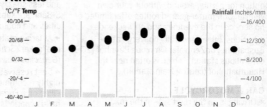

May–Aug Sights, tours and transport are running full tilt. Accommodation prices can double.

Apr, Sep & Oct Crowds thin, temperatures are more mild, and island ferries have reduced schedules.

Nov–Mar Many hotels, sights and restaurants shut down, especially on the islands.

Entering the Country

Greece is easy to reach by aeroplane or ferry – particularly in summer when it opens its arms (and schedules) wide. Getting to or from Greece overland takes more planning, but isn't impossible. Most visitors to Greece arrive by air, which tends to be the fastest and cheapest option, if not the most environmentally friendly.

ITINERARIES

Two Weeks

Begin in Athens (p528), visiting the grand sites plus cool bars, markets and cutting-edge eateries. Fly to Hania (p556), a vibrant Cretan town, then explore the Minoan ruins of Knossos (p556).

It's island hopping and ferry time. Take a ferry to Rhodes Town (p560) and get lost in the medieval old town. Then head to Kos (p561) and spend a couple days on the lovely sandy Kefalos Bay (p562), or Kos Town (p562). Next stop? Samos (p563), to spend a night or two bar-hopping in the small but active capital, Vathy (p563). The final island is Lesvos (p564). Chill out here for a few days, exploring the island's olive groves, the delightful village of Molyvos (p565) and the petrified forests of the island's barren eastern half.

Three Weeks

Fly direct to Thessaloniki (p542) and immerse yourself in the city's vibrant arts scene, fabulous local cuisine and funky accommodation. Head inland to Meteora (p542), to marvel at the extraordinary pinnacles and monasteries. Head next to Ancient Delphi (p541) and (pretend to) consult the oracle at this magical, ancient site. Go west via Patras to the Peloponnese Peninsula to take in the ancient site of Olympia (p541), where the first Olympic games played out. Wander east to your last stop, Nafplio (p539). This was Greece's former capital, a gorgeous town on the water featuring extraordinary Ottoman and Venetian architecture and three fortresses.

Essential Food & Drink

Tzatziki Yoghurt, cucumber and garlic.

Gyros Pork or chicken shaved from a revolving stack of sizzling meat and wrapped in pitta bread with tomato, onion, fried potatoes and lashings of *tzatziki*.

Mousakas Layers of aubergine and mince, topped with béchamel sauce and baked.

Baklava Thin layers of pastry filled with honey and nuts.

Pastitsio Baked dish of macaroni with minced meat and béchamel sauce.

Yemista Either tomatoes or green peppers stuffed with minced meat and rice.

AT A GLANCE

Area 131,944 sq km

Capital Athens

Country Code 30

Currency euro (€)

Emergency 112

Language Greek

Time Eastern European Time (GMT/UTC plus two hours) and three hours on daylight-saving time.

Visas Generally not required for stays up to 90 days. Schengen rules apply.

Sleeping Price Ranges

The following price ranges refer to a double room in high season (May to August). For the Cyclades, the price ranges are based on the rates in July and August. Unless otherwise stated, all rooms have private bathroom facilities.

€ less than €60 (less than €90 in Athens; less than €110 in Mykonos and Santorini)

€€ €60–150 (€90–180 in Athens; €110–250 in Mykonos and Santorini)

€€€ more than €150 (more than €185 in Athens; more than €250 in Mykonos and Santorini)

Eating Price Ranges

The following price ranges refer to the average cost of a main course (not including service charges):

€ less than €10

€€ €10–20

€€€ more than €20

GREECE

Greece Highlights

① Nafplio (p539) Basing yourself in this quaint town and exploring fabulous Peloponnesian sites nearby.

② Corfu Town (p566) Getting lost in the back alleys of the Venetian-style old town.

③ Naxos (p548) Choosing between swimming, visiting ruins or enjoying the local delights of this diverse island.

④ Thessaloniki (p542) Getting your taste buds to go 'high-end Greek' in this thriving city.

⑤ Ancient Olympia (p541) Rubbing shoulders with ghosts of great athletes at this atmospheric site.

⑥ Delphi (p541) Imagining yourself as a pilgrim and consulting the oracle at this historic place.

⑦ Lesvos (p564; Mytilini)

Sipping ouzo while munching grilled octopus on this olive-tree-covered island.

⑧ Rhodes Town (p560) Meandering through the old town and imagining yourself as a player in its medieval past.

⑨ Meteora (p542) Heading out on foot for an alternative perspective of the lofty, monastery-strewn rock pinnacles.

ATHENS

ΑΘΗΝΑ

POP 3.1 MILLION

With equal measures of grunge and grace, Athens is a heady mix of history and edginess. Iconic monuments mingle with first-

rate museums, bustling shops and stylish, alfresco dining. Even in the face of financial struggles, Athens is more cosmopolitan than ever with hip hotels, artsy-industrial neighbourhoods and entertainment quarters showing its modern face.

⊙ Sights

★ Acropolis　　　　HISTORIC SITE

(📞 210 321 4172; http://odysseus.culture.gr; adult/concession/child €20/10/free; ⊙ 8am-8pm May-Sep, reduced hours in winter, last entry 30min before closing; Ⓜ Akropoli) The Acropolis is the most important ancient site in the Western world. Crowned by the Parthenon, it stands sentinel over Athens, visible from almost everywhere within the city. Its monuments and sanctuaries of white Pentelic marble gleam in the midday sun and gradually take on a honey hue as the sun sinks, while at night they stand brilliantly illuminated above the city. A glimpse of this magnificent sight cannot fail to exalt your spirit.

★ Acropolis Museum　　　　MUSEUM

(📞 210 900 0900; www.theacropolismuseum.gr; Dionysiou Areopagitou 15, Makrygianni; adult/child €10/free; ⊙ 8am-4pm Mon, to 8pm Tue-Sun, to 10pm Fri Apr-Oct, reduced hours rest of year; Ⓜ Akropoli) This dazzling museum at the foot of the Acropolis' southern slope showcases its surviving treasures. The collection covers the Archaic period to the Roman one, but the emphasis is on the Acropolis of the 5th century BCE, considered the apotheosis of Greece's artistic achievement. The museum reveals layers of history: ruins are visible in its floor, and, through floor-to-ceiling windows, the Acropolis is always visible above. The surprisingly good-value restaurant has superb views; there's also a fine museum shop.

Benaki Museum of Greek Culture　　MUSEUM

(📞 210 367 1000; www.benaki.gr; Koumbari 1, cnr Leoforos Vasilissis Sofias, Kolonaki; adult/student/child €9/7/free, 6pm-midnight Thu free; ⊙ 9am-5pm Wed & Fri, to midnight Thu & Sat, to 4pm Sun; Ⓜ Syntagma, Evangelismos) Antonis Benakis, a politician's son born in Alexandria, Egypt, in the late 19th century, endowed what is perhaps the finest museum in Greece. Its three floors showcase impeccable treasures from the Bronze Age up to WWII. Especially gorgeous are the Byzantine icons and the extensive collection of Greek regional costumes, as well as complete sitting rooms from Macedonian mansions, intricately carved and painted. Benakis had such a good eye that even the agricultural tools are beautiful.

Museum of Islamic Art　　　　MUSEUM

(📞 210 325 1311; www.benaki.gr; Agion Asomaton 22, Keramikos; adult/student/child €9/7/free; ⊙ 10am-6pm Thu-Sun; Ⓜ Thissio) While not particularly large, this museum houses one of the world's most significant collections of Islamic art. Four floors of a mansion display, in ascending chronological order, exceptionally beautiful weaving, jewellery, porcelain and even a marble-floored reception room from a 17th-century Cairo mansion. It's all arranged for maximum dazzle, with informative signage. In the basement, part of Athens' ancient Themistoklean wall is exposed, and the top floor has a small cafe with a view of Kerameikos.

★ National Archaeological Museum　　MUSEUM

(📞 213 214 4800; www.namuseum.gr; Patision 44, Exarhia; adult/child €10/free mid Apr-Oct; €5/free Nov-mid Apr; ⊙ 8am-8pm Wed-Mon, 12.30am-8pm Tue mid Apr-Oct, reduced hours Nov-mid Apr; 🚌 2, 3, 4, 5 or 11 to Polytechnio, Ⓜ Viktoria) This is one of the world's most important museums, housing the world's finest collection of Greek antiquities in an enormous neoclassical building. Treasures offering a view of Greek art and history – dating from the Neolithic era to Classical periods, including the Ptolemaic era in Egypt – include exquisite sculptures, pottery, jewellery, frescoes and artefacts found throughout Greece. The beautifully presented exhibits are displayed mainly thematically.

Temple of Olympian Zeus　　TEMPLE

(Olympieio; 📞 210 922 6330; http://odysseus.culture.gr; Leoforos Vasilissis Olgas; adult/student/child €6/3/free; ⊙ 8am-3pm Oct-Apr, to 8pm May-Sep; Ⓜ Akropoli, Syntagma) A can't-miss on two counts: it's a marvellous temple, the largest in Greece, and it's smack in the centre of Athens. The temple is impressive for the sheer size of its 104 Corinthian columns (17m high with a base diameter of 1.7m), of which 15 remain – the fallen column was blown down in a gale in 1852.

Roman Agora　　　　HISTORIC SITE

(📞 210 324 5220; http://odysseus.culture.gr; Dioskouron, Monastiraki; adult/student/child €6/3/free; ⊙ 8am-3pm Mon-Fri, to 5pm Sat & Sun, mosque from 10am; Ⓜ Monastiraki) This was the city's market area under Roman rule, and it occupied a much larger area than the current site borders. You can see a lot from outside the fence, but it's worth going in for a closer look at the well-preserved **Gate of Athena Archegetis**, the propylaeum (entrance gate) to the market, as well as an Ottoman mosque and the ingenious and

Central Athens

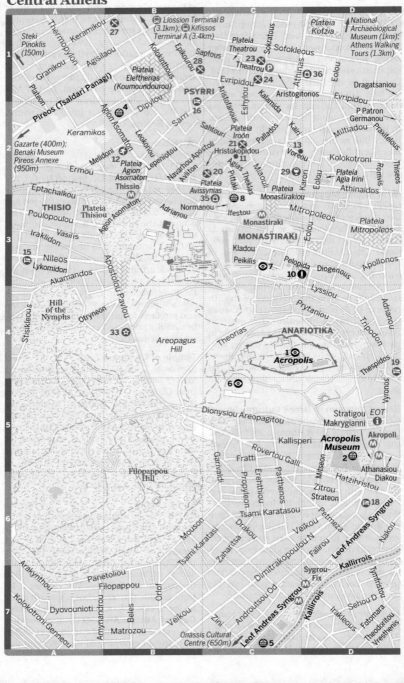

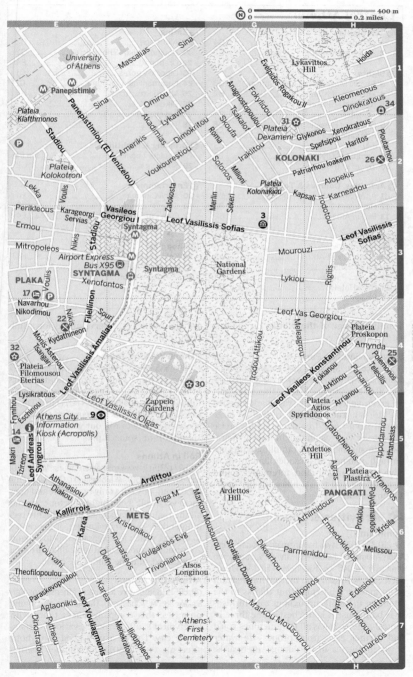

Central Athens

beautiful **Tower of the Winds**, on the east side of the site.

Stavros Niarchos Park
PARK

(www.snfcc.org; Synggrou 364, Kallithea; ⊙6am-midnight Apr-Oct, to 8pm Nov-Mar; 🚌 550 to Onasseio, 10 to Epaminonda) **FREE** Athens is short on green spaces, so this vast park, opened in 2016, is a true breath of fresh air. A large central lawn hosts free dance and exercise classes, as well as midnight movie marathons in summer, while rambling paths cut through patches of lavender and rows of olive trees. A playground, interactive sound installations and rental bikes (€1 per hour) add to the fun.

🏃 Activities & Tours

Hammam
SPA

(☎ 210 323 1073; www.hammam.gr; Melidoni 1, cnr Agion Asomaton, Keramikos; 1hr €25, bath-scrub combos from €45; ⊙11-10pm Mon-Fri, 10am-10pm Sat & Sun; Ⓜ Thissio) The marble-lined steam room may be a bit small, but thanks to the attention to detail throughout this Turkish-style bathhouse it is the best of the three in central Athens. It has all the amenities you'd find further east, from proper-size water bowls to hot tea in the lounge afterwards.

For the full effect, reserve ahead for a full-body scrub.

Athens Walking Tours
TOURS

(☎ 694 585 9662, 210 884 7269; www.athenswalkingtours.gr) Runs a full range of guided tours around and outside the city, but is especially notable for its cooking class (€77) in a Thisio taverna, which cuts no corners and even shows you how to roll out your own filo for *spanakopita* (spinach pie).

Roll in Athens
CYCLING

(☎ 6974231611; www.rollinathens.tours; Voreou 10; half-day tours €30; Ⓜ Monastiraki, Omonia) This small company does only two tours, and does them both very well: a city highlights tour, around all the main central sights, and – highly recommended – an excursion out of the centre to the sea, which is a pleasant way to expand your understanding of Athens. Bikes are well maintained, and the guides are great.

Alternative Athens
TOURS

(☎ 6951518589; www.alternativeathens.com; Karaïskaki 28; Ⓜ Monastiraki, Thissio) As the name promises, this company offers tours with less-typical slants, covering various corners of the city. There's a very good three-hour street-art tour (€40), and another visiting

Athenian designers (€50), as well as an LGBT+ bar crawl, food tours and even day trips out of town.

✨✨ Festivals & Events

Athens &

Epidaurus Festival   PERFORMING ARTS

(Hellenic Festival; ☎ 210 928 2900; www.greekfestival.gr; ☉ Jun-Aug) The ancient **Theatre of Epidavros** (adult/concession €12/6; ☉ 8am-8pm Apr-Aug, reduced hours rest or year) and Athens' **Odeon of Herodes Atticus** (Herodeon; ☎ 210 324 1807; Ⓜ Akropoli) are the headline venues for Greece's annual cultural festival, running since 1955 and featuring a top line-up of local and international music, dance and theatre.

🛏 Sleeping

Book well ahead for July and August.

City Circus   HOSTEL €

(☎ 213 023 7244; www.citycircus.gr; Sarri 16, Psyrri; dm incl breakfast €27-31.50, s/d incl breakfast from €36/72; ❄✳@🤖; Ⓜ Thissio, Monastiraki) It's not the cheapest hostel going, but with its jaunty style and helpful staff, City Circus does lift the spirit more than most ultra-budget lodgings. Its bright, well-designed rooms have modern bathrooms; some have kitchens. Book on its website for free breakfast at the chic bistro downstairs.

Phaedra   HOTEL €

(☎ 210 323 8461; www.hotelphaedra.com; Herefontos 16, Plaka; s/d/tr from €60/80/90; ✳@🤖; Ⓜ Akropoli) Almost all the rooms at this small, family-run hotel have balconies overlooking a church or the Acropolis. The rooms are basic and range from small to snug; a few have private bathrooms across the hall. Given the rooftop terrace, the friendly staff and the unbeatable location, it's one of the best deals in Plaka.

Hera Hotel   BOUTIQUE HOTEL €€

(☎ 210 923 6682; www.herahotel.gr; Falirou 9, Makrygianni; d/ste incl breakfast from €145/280; ✳@🤖; Ⓜ Akropoli) Behind its elegant neoclassical facade, this boutique hotel has been totally rebuilt. But the formal interior design stays true to exterior style, with lots of brass and dark wood. It's a short walk to the Acropolis and Plaka, and the rooftop Peacock restaurant and bar have fine views and good service. Northside rooms, away from an adjacent music bar, are preferable.

Be My Guest Athens   HOTEL €€

(☎ 213 044 9929; www.bemyguestathens.gr; Nileos 33, Thisio; d/tr/ste with breakfast €102/126/150; ✳🤖; Ⓜ Thissio) Opened in 2017, this 14-room hotel is for those seeking calm: the minimalist black-white-and-grey colour scheme is soothing, and its residential location (about 15 minutes' walk to the Acropolis) is quiet. The cheapest double rooms don't have balconies, but it's not much to upgrade. The suites have kitchens (handy grocery store downstairs).

★ Athens Was   BOUTIQUE HOTEL €€€

(☎ 210 924 9954; www.athenswas.gr; Dionysiou Areopagitou 5, Makrygianni; d/ste incl breakfast from €390/465; ✳@🤖; Ⓜ Akropoli) The location, a three-minute walk to the Acropolis east gate, couldn't be better. Staff are friendly, adding a warm touch to the minimalist decor, and standard rooms have big balconies overlooking the pedestrianised street. Korres amenities are another plus. Breakfast is excellent and the terrace has a magnificent view. Suites on the 5th and 6th floors also have Acropolis views.

Electra Palace   LUXURY HOTEL €€€

(☎ 210 337 0000; www.electrahotels.gr; Navarhou Nikodimou 18, Plaka; d/ste incl breakfast from €255/440; ℗✳@🤖; Ⓜ Syntagma) This classically elegant place is for the romantics: have breakfast under the Acropolis on your balcony (in higher-end rooms) and dinner in the chic rooftop restaurant. The well-appointed rooms are buffered from the

> ## ⓘ CHEAPER BY THE HALF-DOZEN
>
> A €30 unified ticket from the Acropolis (valid for five days) includes entry to the other significant ancient sites: Ancient Agora, Roman Agora, Keramikos, Temple of Olympian Zeus and the Theatre of Dionysos. For museums, a €15 ticket covers the National Archaeological Museum, the Byzantine & Christian Museum, the Epigraphic Museum and the Numismatic Museum. It's valid for three days.
>
> Enter the sites free on the first Sunday of the month from November to March, and on certain holidays. Anyone aged under 18 years or with an EU student card gets in free.

GREECE ATHENS

sounds of the city streets. There's a gym and an indoor swimming pool, as well as a rooftop pool with Acropolis views.

✕ Eating

Diporto Agoras
TAVERNA €

(☑210 321 1463; Sokratous 9 & Theatrou; plates €5-7; ☻7am-7pm Mon-Sat, closed 1-25 Aug; ⓜOmonia, Monastiraki) This quirky old taverna is an Athens dining gem. There's no signage – two doors lead to a rustic cellar where there's no menu, just a few dishes that haven't changed in years. The house speciality is *revythia* (chickpeas), usually followed by grilled fish and paired with wine from one of the giant barrels lining the wall.

Bougatsadiko I Thessaloniki
PIES €

(☑210 322 2088; Plateia Iroön 1, Psyrri; pita €2; ☻24hr; ⓜMonastiraki) Unexpected for its location on a key nightlife square in Psyrri, this place makes excellent *pitta* (pies), with filo crust that's 'opened' (rolled out by hand) every day. *Bougatsa* (filo with custard) is great for breakfast, the meat pies are a treat after drinks and *spanakopita* (spinach pie) hits the spot anytime.

Cremino
ICE CREAM €

(Nikis 50a, Plaka; scoops €2.20; ☻11.30am-6.30pm, later in spring & summer; ⓜSyntagma, Akropoli) The lovely proprietress at Cremino makes gelato and sorbet that's both intensely flavoured and incredibly light, using cow and buffalo milk. Flavours change daily, but

CONTEMPORARY ART

Athens is not all about ancient art. For a taste of the contemporary, visit the following:

TAF (The Art Foundation; ☑210 323 8757; www.theartfoundation.gr; Normanou 5, Monastiraki; ☻noon-9pm Mon-Sat, to 7pm Sun, cafe-bar open late; ⓜMonastiraki) Eclectic art and music gallery.

Onassis Cultural Centre (p536) Multimillion-euro visual and performing-arts centre.

National Museum of Contemporary Art (EMST; ☑211 101 9000; www. emst.gr; Kallirrois & Frantzi, Koukaki-Syngrou; ⓜSygrou-Fix) In spectacularly renovated quarters, with top-notch rotating exhibits.

look for creamy-chewy kaïmaki, a classic recipe with Chios mastic resin and orchid root.

Oikeio
MEDITERRANEAN €

(☑210 725 9216; www.facebook.com/oikeio/?rf= 170935649625545; Ploutarhou 15, Kolonaki; mains €10-12; ☻12.30pm-midnight Mon-Thu, to 1am Fri & Sat, to 6pm Sun; ⓜEvangelismos) With excellent home-style cooking, this modern taverna lives up to its name (meaning 'homey'). It's decorated like a cosy bistro, and tables on the footpath allow people-watching without the usual Kolonaki bill. Pastas, salads and international fare are tasty, but try the daily *mayirefta* (ready-cooked meals), such as the excellent stuffed zucchini. Book ahead on weekends.

Mavro Provato
MEZEDHES €

(Black Sheep; ☑210 722 3466; www.tomauroprovato.gr; Arrianou 31-33, Pangrati; dishes €6-17.50; ☻1pm-1am Mon-Sat, until 7pm Sun; ⓜEvangelismos) Book ahead for this wildly popular modern *mezedhopoleio* (mezedhes restaurant) in Pangrati, where tables line the footpath and delicious small (well, small for Greece) plates are paired with regional Greek wines.

★Seychelles
GREEK €€

(☑210 118 3478; www.seycheles.gr; Kerameikou 49, Metaxourgio; mains €8.50-14.50; ☻2pm-12.30am Sun-Thu, until 1am Fri & Sat; ⓜMetaxourgio) Gutsy, fresh food, an open kitchen, earnest service, a handwritten daily menu and David Bowie on the soundtrack: Seychelles may be the Platonic ideal of a restaurant. Dishes can look simple – meaty pan-fried mushrooms with just a sliver of sheep's cheese, say, or greens with fish roe – but the flavour is incomparable. Go early or book ahead; it's deservedly popular.

Athiri
GREEK €€

(☑210 346 2983; www.athirirestaurant.gr; Plateon 15, Keramikos; mains €17-20; ☻7pm-11.30pm Tue-Sat, plus 1-5pm Sun Oct-May; ⓜThissio) Athiri's lovely garden courtyard is a verdant surprise in this pocket of Keramikos. The small but innovative menu plays on Greek regional classics, with seasonal specialities. This might include Santorini fava and hearty beef stew with *myzithra* (sheep's-milk cheese) and handmade pasta from Karpathos.

Telis
TAVERNA €€

(☑210 324 9582; Evripidou 86, Psyrri; meal with salad €13; ☻noon-midnight Mon-Sat; ⓜThissio)

A fluorescent-lit beacon of good food and kind service on a grimy block, Telis has been serving up simplicity since 1978. There's no menu, just a set meal: a small mountain of charcoal-grilled pork chops atop chips, plus a side vegetable. Greek salad is optional, as is beer or rough house wine.

Akordeon MEZEDHES €€

(📞 210 325 3703; Hristokopidou 7, Psyrri; dishes €6-16; ⊙ 7pm-1am Thu, to 2am Fri & Sat, 1-8pm Sun Sep-May; Ⓜ Monastiraki, Thissio) Slide into this charming butter-yellow house across from a church in a quiet Psyrri side street for a warm welcome by musician-chefs Pepi and Achilleas (and their spouses), who run this excellent venue for local music and mezedhes. They'll help you order authentic Greek fare, then surround you with their soulful songs.

Karamanlidika tou Fani GREEK €€

(📞 210 325 4184; www.karamanlidika.gr; Sokratous 1, Psyrri; dishes €7-18; ⊙ 11am-midnight; Ⓜ Monastiraki) At this modern-day *pastomageireio* (combo tavern-deli) tables are set alongside the deli cases, and staff offer tasty morsels while you're looking at the menu. Beyond the Greek cheeses and cured meats, there's good seafood, such as marinated anchovies, as well as rarer wines and craft beers. Service is excellent, as is the warm welcome from Fani herself.

Drinking & Nightlife

One local favoured pastime is going for coffee. Athens' ubiquitous, packed cafes have some of Europe's most expensive coffee – you're essentially hiring the chair and can linger for hours. Many daytime cafes and restaurants turn into bars and clubs at night.

The city's hottest scene masses around Kolokotroni north of Plateia Syntagmatos, and around Plateia Agia Irini in Monastiraki. A cafe-thick area in Monastiraki is Adrianou, along the Ancient Agora, where people fill shady tables. Psyrri has seen a recent resurgence, while Kolonaki steadfastly attracts the trendier set, and Gazi remains tried and true. For the best dancing in summer, cab it to beach clubs along the coast near Glyfada – city locations close earlier.

English-language entertainment information appears daily in the 'Kathimerini' supplement in the *International Herald Tribune*. For comprehensive events listings, with links

TO MARKET, TO MARKET...

Most Athens neighbourhoods have a weekly *laïki agora*, a street market for fruit, veg and household miscellany, and **Kolonaki's** (www.laikesagores.gr; Xenokratous; ⊙ 7am-2pm Fri; Ⓜ Evangelismos) is a good one. Local regulars come to buy fresh fruit, vegetables, fish, olives, honey, handmade products and flowers.

Varvakios Agora (Athens Central Market; Athinas, btwn Sofokleous & Evripidou, Omonia; ⊙ 7am-6pm Mon-Sat; Ⓜ Panepistimio, Omonia) is a huge old wrought-iron market hall dedicated to fish and meat, with row upon row of lamb carcasses, hanging in just-barely-EU-compliant glass cases. In the surrounding streets are olives, cheeses and spices. For Monastiraki Flea Market (p536), head to Plateia Avyssinias where dusty *palaiopoleia* ('old-stuff sellers') rule. For the best rummaging, come on Sunday mornings, when the bric-a-brac explodes out onto the pavements, including on Astingos and even across Ermou in Psyrri.

to online ticket sales points, try the following: www.elculture.gr, www.tickethour.com, www.tickethouse.gr and www.ticketservices.gr.

★ Gazarte LIVE MUSIC

(📞 210 346 0347; www.gazarte.gr; Voutadon 32-34, Gazi; tickets from €10; Ⓜ Kerameikos) At this varied arts complex, you'll find a cinema-sized screen playing videos, amazing city views taking in the Acropolis, mainstream music and a trendy 30-something crowd. A ground-level theatre hosts music and comedy. There's occasional live music and a restaurant to boot.

★ Couleur Locale BAR

(📞 216 700 4917; www.couleurlocaleathens.com; Normanou 3, Monastiraki; ⊙ 10am-2am Sun-Thu, to 3am Fri & Sat; Ⓜ Monastiraki) Look for the entrance to this rooftop bar down a narrow pedestrian lane, then inside the arcade. From there, a lift goes to the 3rd floor and its lively all-day bar-restaurant. It's a go-to spot for Athenians who love a chill coffee or a louder evening, all in view of their beloved Acropolis.

★ Six d.o.g.s.
BAR

(☏ 210 321 0510; www.sixdogs.gr; Avramiotou 6-8, Monastiraki; ⏰ 10am-late; Ⓜ Monastiraki) The core of this supercreative events space is a rustic, multilevel back garden, a great place for quiet daytime chats over coffee or a relaxed drink. From there, you can head in to one of several adjoining buildings to see a band, art show or other generally cool happening.

☆ Entertainment

★ Stavros Niarchos Foundation Cultural Center
CULTURAL CENTRE

(☏ 216 809 1001; www.snfcc.org; Leoforos Syngrou 364, Kallithea; 🚍 550 to Onasseio, 10 to Epaminonda) FREE Spreading its winged roof on a hill above Faliron Bay, this Renzo Piano building, surrounded by a vast park (p532), made a big splash on the Athens cultural scene when it opened in 2017. Architecture buffs will love seeing the structure. Otherwise, check the schedule for arts events by the grand pool or at the National Opera of Greece, inside the complex.

Theatro Skion Tasou Konsta
PUPPET THEATRE

(☏ 210 322 7507; www.fkt.gr; Flisvos Park, Palaio Faliro; €3.50; ⏰ 8.30pm Fri-Sun Jun-Sep; ☻; 🚊 Park Flisvou) Greece's wise fool, Karagiozis, gave his name to the art of shadow puppetry (*karagiozi*), and they're on beautiful display in this tiny outdoor theatre every summer. Sure it's all in Greek, but the humour is slapstick and there's plenty of music in the various shows. After the 45-minute performance, kids can file backstage to see how the magic happens.

Onassis Cultural Centre
CULTURAL CENTRE

(☏ info & tickets 210 900 5800; www.sgt.gr; Leoforos Syngrou 107-109, Neos Kosmos; 🚍 10 or 550 to Panteio, Ⓜ Sygrou-Fix, 🚊 Kassomouli) This eye-catching visual- and performing-arts centre livens up the dull urbanity of Leoforos Syngrou. Cloaked in a net of white marble, it glows at night when it hosts big-name productions, installations and lectures. Check the schedule for free events. It's 1.5km southwest of the Sygrou-Fix metro station.

Steki Pinoklis
TRADITIONAL MUSIC

(☏ 210 577 7355; www.facebook.com/pinoklis; Megalou Alexandrou 102, Kerameikos; ⏰ 5pm-3am Mon-Sat, 2-1am Sun; Ⓜ Kerameikos) Although this taverna opened in 2017, its musical taste and style skews much older. This is an excellent place to hear *rembetika* (blues) songs from Smyrna and other traditional Greek music, with a band playing most nights (starting at 9.30pm or 10pm) and Sunday afternoons (usually from 4pm). Food is average, but not expensive.

🛍 Shopping

Central Athens is the city's original commercial district, and is still one big shopping hub, with an eclectic mix of shops. The area is still organised roughly by category – lace and buttons on one block, light bulbs on the next.

Find boutiques around Syntagma, from the Attica department store past Voukourestiou and on Ermou; designer brands and cool shops in Kolonaki; and souvenirs, folk art and leather in Plaka and Monastiraki with its fun **Monastiraki Flea Market** (Plateia Avyssinias; ⏰ daily May-Oct, Sun-Wed & Fri Nov-Apr; Ⓜ Monastiraki).

ℹ Information

SAFE TRAVEL
Since the financial crisis, crime has risen in Athens. But this is a rise from almost zero, and violent street crime remains relatively rare. Nonetheless, travellers should be alert. Stay aware of your surroundings at night, especially in streets southwest of Omonia, where sex workers and junkies gather, as well as by the Mavromateon bus terminal, as the adjacent park is a rather grim homeless encampment.

➡ Pickpockets favour the metro, particularly the Piraeus–Kifisia line, and crowded streets around Omonia, Athinas and the Monastiraki Flea Market.

➡ Athens taxi drivers have a reputation for mistreating foreigners with the usual tricks: failing to turn on the meter; setting the night rate (tariff set to '2' rather than '1') by day; claiming you gave them a smaller bill than you did; taking the longer route etc.

REMBETIKA

Athens has some of the best *rembetika* (Greek blues) in intimate, evocative venues. Performances usually include both *rembetika* and *laïka* (urban popular music), start at around 11.30pm and do not have a cover charge, though drinks can be expensive. Most close May to September, so in summer try live-music tavernas around Plaka, Psyrri and Exarhia.

→ Bar scams are commonplace, particularly in Plaka and Syntagma. Beware the over-friendly!

TOURIST INFORMATION

EOT (Greek National Tourism Organisation; ☑ 210 331 0347, 210 331 0716; www.visit greece.gr; Dionysiou Areopagitou 18-20, Makrygianni; ⊗ 8am-8pm Mon-Fri, 10am-4pm Sat & Sun May-Sep, 9am-7pm Mon-Fri Oct-Apr; Ⓜ Akropoli) Free Athens map, current site hours, and bus and train information.

Athens City Information Kiosks Airport (☑ 210 353 0390; www.athensconvention bureau.gr/en/content/info-kiosk-athens -international-airport; Eleftherios Venizelos International Airport; ⊗ 8am-8pm; Ⓜ Airport), Acropolis (www.thisisathens.org; Syntagma; Ⓜ Syntagma) Maps, transport information and all Athens info.

❶ Getting There & Away

AIR

Athens' modern **Eleftherios Venizelos International Airport** (ATH; ☑ 210 353 0000; www.aia. gr) is 27km east of Athens.

BOAT

Most ferry, hydrofoil and high-speed catamaran services to the islands leave from the massive port at **Piraeus** (☑ 210 455 0000, €0.89 per 1min 14541; www.olp.gr), southwest of Athens. Purchase tickets online at **Greek Ferries** (☑ 2810 529000; www.greekferries.gr), over the phone or at booths on the quay next to each ferry. Travel agencies selling tickets also surround each port; there is no surcharge.

Some services for Evia and the Cyclades arrive at/depart from the small port of Rafina, due east of Athens and the airport. To reach Athens from Rafina, take a KTEL bus (€2.60, one hour, approx half-hourly 6am to 10.45pm), which arrives at the Mavromateon Terminal, north of Athens centre.

BUS

Athens has two main intercity bus stations, 5km and 7km north and west of Omonia, plus a small bay for buses bound for south and east Attica. Pick up timetables at the tourist office, or see the relevant KTEL operator's website. Find a master list of KTEL companies at www.ktelbus. com; **KTEL Attikis** (☑ 210 880 8000; www. ktelattikis.gr) covers the Attica peninsula. **KTEL Argolida** (☑ 210 513 4588; www.ktelargolida.gr; one way €13) serves Epidavros, with dedicated buses during the summer festival season. Advance tickets for most buses can be purchased at the **ticket office** (☑ 210 523 3810; Sokratous 59, Omonia; ⊗ 7am-5.15pm Mon-Fri; Ⓜ Omonia) near Omonia.

SUMMER CINEMA

One of the delights of Athens is the enduring tradition of open-air cinema, where you can watch the latest Hollywood or art-house flick in the warm summer air. The settings are old-fashioned gardens and rooftops, with modern sound and projection. Cinemas start up in early May and usually close in September. Try **Thission** (☑ 210 342 0864; www.cine-thisio.gr; Apostolou Pavlou 7, Thisio; tickets €6-8; ⊗ May-Oct; Ⓜ Thissio), **Cine Dexameni** (☑ 210 362 3942; www.cinedexameni.gr; Plateia Dexameni, Kolonaki; adult/child €8/5,; Ⓜ Evangelismos), **Cine Paris** (☑ 210 322 0721; www. cineparis.gr; Kydathineon 22, Plaka; ⊗ May-Oct; Ⓜ Syntagma) or **Aegli Cinema** (☑ 210 336 9300; www.aeglizappiou.gr; Zappeio Gardens; adult/child €8.50/6.50; ⊗ screenings at 9pm & 11pm May-Oct; Ⓜ Syntagma).

For international buses (from Bulgaria, Turkey etc), there is no single station; some come to Kifissos, while others stop between Plateia Karaïskaki and Plateia Omonias. **Tourist Service** (www.tourist-service.com) is one operator from Piraeus and Athens to Bulgaria.

CAR & MOTORCYCLE

The airport has all major car-hire companies, and the north end of Leoforos Syngrou, near the Temple of Olympian Zeus, is dotted with firms. Expect to pay €45 per day, less for three or more days.

TRAIN

Intercity (IC) trains to central and northern Greece depart from the central Larisis train station, about 1km northwest of Plateia Omonias.

For the Peloponnese, take the suburban rail to Kiato and change for a bus there. The Patra train line is chronically closed for repairs, so OSE buses, via Kiato, replace its services. Because of this, it's easier to just take a bus from Athens' Kifissos Bus Terminal A to your ultimate destination.

❶ Getting Around

TO/FROM THE AIRPORT
Bus

Express buses operate 24 hours between the airport and key points in the city. At the airport, buy tickets (€6; not valid for other forms of public transport) at the booth near the stop.

GREECE ATHENS

Plateia Syntagmatos Bus **X95** (tickets €6; ⊙24hr), one to 1½ hours, every 20 to 30 minutes. The Syntagma stop is on Othonos St.

Kifissos Terminal A and Liossion Terminal B bus stations Bus X93, one hour (terminal B) to 1½ hours (terminal A), every 20 to 30 minutes (60 minutes at night).

Piraeus Bus X96, 1½ hours, every 20 minutes. To Plateia Karaïskaki.

Metro

Metro line 3 goes from the airport to the city centre. Trains run every 30 minutes, leaving the airport between 6.30am and 11.30pm, on the hour and half-hour. Coming from the centre, trains leave Monastiraki between 5.40am and 11pm; some terminate early at Doukissis Plakentias, so disembark and wait for the airport train (displayed on the train and platform screen).

Tickets from the airport are priced separately from the rest of the metro. The cost is €10 per adult or €18 return (return valid seven days). A €22 pass, good for three days, includes a return-trip airport service and all other transit in the centre.

Taxi

From the airport to the centre, fares are flat day/night €38/54 rates; tolls are included. The ride takes 30 to 45 minutes. For Piraeus (one hour), expect day/night €50/60.

To the airport, drivers will usually propose a flat fare of €40 from the centre. You can insist on the meter, but with all the legitimate add-ons – tolls, airport fee, luggage fees – it usually works out the same.

To prebook a taxi, contact **Welcome Pickups** (www.welcomepickups.com), at the same flat rate as regular taxis.

PUBLIC TRANPORT

The transit system uses the unified Ath.ena Ticket, a reloadable paper card available from ticket offices and machines in the metro. You can load it with a set amount of money or buy a number of rides (€1.40 each; discounted when you buy five or 10) or a 24-hour/five-day travel pass for €4.50/9.

Children under six travel free; people under 18 or over 65 are technically eligible for half-fare, but you must buy the Ath.ena Ticket from a person at a ticket office.

Swipe the card at metro turnstiles or, on buses and trams, validate the ticket in the machine as you board, and keep it with you in case of spot-checks. One swipe is good for 90 minutes, including any transfers or return trips.

Bus & Trolleybus

Local express buses, regular buses and electric trolleybuses operate every 15 minutes from 5am to midnight. In lieu of maps, use Google Maps for directions or the trip planner at the website of the bus company, **OASA** (Athens Urban Transport Organisation; ☏11185; www.oasa. gr; ⊙6.30am-11.30pm Mon-Fri, from 7.30am Sat & Sun) (click 'Telematics'). The most useful lines for tourists are trolleybuses 2, 5, 11 and 15, which run north from Syntagma past the National Archaeological Museum. For all buses, board at any door; swipe your ticket on validation machines.

Metro

The metro works well and posted maps have clear icons and English labels. Trains operate from 5.30am to 12.30am, every four minutes during peak periods and every 10 minutes off-peak. On Friday and Saturday, lines 2 and 3 run till 2.30am. Get information at www.stasy.gr. All stations have wheelchair access.

Taxi

Athens' taxis are excellent value and can be the key for efficient travel on some routes. But it can be tricky getting one, especially during rush

---

WORTH A TRIP

ISLANDS IN A DAY: AEGINA & HYDRA

For islands within easy reach of Athens, head to the Saronic Gulf. **Aegina** (*eh-yee-nah*; www.aeginagreece.com), just a half-hour from Piraeus, is home to the impressive **Temple of Aphaia**, said to have served as a model for the construction of the Parthenon. The catwalk queen of the Saronics, **Hydra** (*ee-drah*; www.hydra.gr, www.hydraislandgreece.com) is a delight, an hour and a half from Piraeus. Its picturesque horseshoe-shaped harbour town with gracious stone mansions stacked up the rocky hillsides is known as a retreat for artists, writers and celebrities. There are no motorised vehicles – apart from sanitation trucks – leading to unspoilt trails along the coast and into the mountains.

From Hydra, you can return to Piraeus, or carry on to Spetses and the Peloponnese (Metohi, Ermione and Porto Heli). Check Hellenic Seaways (www.hsw.gr) and Aegina Flying Dolphins (www.aegeanflyingdolphins.gr).

hour, so it can be much easier to use the mobile app **Beat** (www.thebeat.co/gr) or **Taxiplon** (✆18222; www.taxiplon.gr) – you can pay in cash. Or call a taxi from dispatchers such as **Athina 1** (✆210 921 0417, 210 921 2800; www.athens1.gr), **Enotita** (✆6980666720, 18388, 210 649 5099; www.athensradiotaxienotita.gr) or **Parthenon** (✆210 532 3300; www.radiotaxi-parthenon.gr). Short trips around central Athens cost about €5; there are surcharges for luggage and pick-ups at transport hubs. At night and during holidays, the fare is about 60% higher.

Train
Suburban rail (Proastiakos; ✆14511; www.trainose.gr) is fast, but not commonly used by visitors – though it goes to the airport and as far as Piraeus and the northern Peloponnese. The airport–Kiato line (€14, 1½ hours) connects to the metro at Doukissis Plakentias and Neratziotissa. Two other lines cross the metro at Larisis station.

PELOPONNESE
ΠΕΛΟΠΟΝΝΗΣΟΣ

The Peloponnese offers lofty, snowcapped mountains, vast gorges, sandy beaches and azure waters. *Filoxenia* (hospitality) is strong here; the food is among Greece's best; and the region's vineyards are contributing to Greece's wine renaissance.

Nafplio   Ναύπλιο
POP 33,000

Nafplio is one of Greece's prettiest and most romantic towns. It occupies a knockout location, on a small port beneath the towering Palamidi fortress, and is graced with attractive narrow streets, elegant Venetian houses, neoclassical mansions and interesting museums. The town is an ideal base from which to explore many nearby ancient sites.

◎ Sights

★Palamidi Fortress   FORTRESS
(✆27520 28036; adult/concession €8/4; ◷8am-8pm May-Aug, reduced hours Sep-Apr) This vast, spectacular citadel, reachable either by steep ascent on foot or a short drive, stands on a 216m-high outcrop of rock that gives all-encompassing views of Nafplio and the Argolic Gulf. It was built by the Venetians between 1711 and 1714, and is regarded as a masterpiece of military architecture in spite of being successfully stormed in one night by Greek troops in 1822, causing the Turkish garrison within to surrender without a fight.

★Archaeological Museum   MUSEUM
(✆27520 27502; Plateia Syntagmatos; adult/child €6/3; ◷8am-3pm Tue-Sun) Inside a splendid Venetian building, this museum traces the social development of Argolis, from the hunter-gatherers of the Fracthi cave to the sophisticated Mycenaean-era civilisations, through beautifully presented archaeological finds from the surrounding area. Exhibits include Paleolithic fire middens (32,000 BCE), elaborately painted amphorae (c 520 BCE) plus – a real highlight – the only existing bronze armour from near Mycenae (3500 years old, with helmet and boar tusk). Excellent audio guides are available in several languages (leave a government-issued ID).

Peloponnesian Folklore Foundation Museum   MUSEUM
(✆27520 28379; www.pli.gr; Vasileos Alexandrou 1; adult/concession €5/3; ◷9am-2.30pm Mon-Sat, 9.30am-3pm Sun) Established by its philanthropic owner, Nafplio's award-winning museum is a beautifully arranged collection of folk costumes and household items from Nafplio's 19th- and early-20th-century history. Be wowed by the intricate embroidery of traditional costumes and the heavy silver adornments, admire the turn-of-the-20th-century couture and look out for the

cute horse-tricycle. The gift shop sells high-quality local crafts.

🛏 Sleeping & Eating

★ Pension Marianna
HOTEL €€

(📱27520 24256; www.hotelmarianna.gr; Potamianou 9; s/d/tr/q incl breakfast €55/80/90/105; 🅿✳🛜) Vibrant Pension Marianna is one of Nafplio's long-standing and outstanding favourites; you can't do better for value, Greek authenticity, and setting (all fabulous). Many of the bright and airy, squeaky-clean rooms provide superb vistas from the hilltop position. The welcoming Zotos family epitomises Greek *filoxenia* (hospitality), and serves up conviviality, travel advice and delicious breakfasts (using their own farm produce).

Pidalio
GREEK €

(📱27520 22603; 25 Martiou 5; mains €7-9; ⊙12.30pm-midnight Wed-Mon) One of several excellent new spots in the 'new town' frequented mainly by locals who might steer clear of those in the more touristy 'old town', this lovely taverna serves excellent Greek fare at fair prices. It's warm and lively, and you'll smell the aromas before you spot it.

To Omorfo Tavernaki
GREEK €€

(📱27520 25944; Olgas 1; mains €7-15; ⊙1pm-late Fri-Wed; 🖋) Ample servings of homemade delights are served in a convivial restaurant adorned with antique oddments. The mezedhes (starters) – zucchini balls, feta with honey, tzatziki etc – are particularly good, as are the meat dishes, including the slow-cooked pork belly. If meat isn't your thing, it has some fabulous contemporary-style salads as well.

ⓘ Information

Staikos Tours (📱27520 27950; www.rentacar nafplio.gr; Bouboulinas 50; ⊙8.30am-2.30pm & 5.30-9pm) Run by the personable, English-speaking Christos. Offers full travel services, including ferry tickets, plus Sixt rental cars.

ⓘ Getting There & Away

The **KTEL Argolis bus station** (📱27520 27323; www.ktelargolida.gr; Syngrou) has buses to Athens (€14.40, 2½ hours, 11 to 13 daily). Other services include the following:

Argos (€1.80, 30 minutes, hourly)

Epidavros (€4.20, 45 minutes, six Monday to Friday, four Saturday, one Sunday)

Mycenae (€3.20, one hour, three Monday to Friday, two Saturday)

DON'T MISS

MYSTRAS　　　ΜΥΣΤΡΑΣ

The captivating ruins of churches, libraries, strongholds and palaces in the fortress town of Mystras, a World Heritage–listed site, spill from a spur of the Taÿgetos Mountains 7km west of Sparta. It's among the most important historical sites in the Peloponnese. This is where the Byzantine Empire's richly artistic and intellectual culture made its last stand before an invading Ottoman army, almost 1000 years after its foundation.

Traveller facilities are split between Mystras village, 1km or so below the main gate of ancient Mystras, and Pikoulianika village, 1.3km from Mystras' fortress gate.

Mycenae　　　Μυκήνες

In the barren foothills of Mt Agios Ilias (750m) and Mt Zara (600m) stand the sombre and mighty ruins of **Ancient Mycenae** (📱27510 76585; http://odysseus.culture.gr; adult/concession €12/6; ⊙8am-8pm May-Aug, reduced hours Sep-Apr), home of the mythical Agamemnon. For 400 years (1600–1200 BCE) this kingdom was the most powerful in Greece, holding sway over the Argolid and influencing other Mycenaean kingdoms.

Two to three daily buses (excluding Sundays) head to Mycenae from Nafplio (€3.20, one hour) and Argos (€1.80, 30 minutes). Buses stop both in the village and at the ancient site.

Epidavros　　　Επίδαυρος

In its day **Epidavros** (📱27530 22009; http://odysseus.culture.gr; adult/concession €12/6; ⊙8am-8pm May-Aug, reduced hours Sep-Apr; 🅿), 30km east of Nafplio, was famed and revered as far away as Rome as a place of miraculous healing. Visitors came great distances to the tranquil **Sanctuary of Asclepius** (adult/concession €12/6; ⊙8am-8pm Apr-Aug, reduced hours rest of year), the god of medicine, to seek a cure for their ailments. Today the World Heritage Site's amazingly well-preserved theatre (p533) remains a venue during the **Athens & Epidavros Festival** (📱21092 82900; www.greekfestival.gr/en; ⊙Jul & Aug) for Classical Greek plays, which were first performed here up to 2000 years ago.

There are buses from Nafplio to Epidavros (€4.20, 45 minutes, six Monday to Friday, three Saturday, one Sunday).

Olympia   Ολυμπία

The compact village of Olympia, lined with souvenir shops and eateries, caters to the coach-loads of tourists who pass through on their way to the most famous sight in the Peloponnese: Ancient Olympia. This is where myth and fact merge. According to one (of many different) legends, Zeus held the first Olympic Games to celebrate beating his father Cronos at wrestling. This is the birthplace of the ideal that still brings states together, differences aside, for the sake of friendly athletic competition, just as it did more than 4000 years ago.

Just 500m south of the village, across the Kladeos River, are the remains of **Ancient Olympia** (☑ 26240 22517; adult/concession €12/6; ☺ 8am-8pm Apr-Sep, to 6pm Oct, to 3pm Nov-Mar). As you walk around, or stand at the starting line of the ancient stadium, contemplate the influence of this site through millennia.

The Olympic Games took place here every four years for at least 1000 years, until their abolition by Emperor Theodosius I in 393 CE. The Olympic flame is still lit here for the modern Games. Thanks to the destruction ordered by Theodosius II and various subsequent earthquakes, little remains of the magnificent temples and athletic facilities, but enough exists to give you a hint of this World Heritage-listed sanctuary's former glory. Ticket includes entry to the remarkable **archaeological museum** (adult/concession incl site €12/6; ☺ 8am-8pm, to 3pm Nov-Apr).

Buses depart from the train station in the middle of town, one block east of the main street. There are services to Pyrgos (€2.30, 30 minutes, eight to 13 daily), with three handy Athens connections (€30.10, four hours).

CENTRAL GREECE
ΚΕΝΤΡΙΚΗ ΕΛΛΑΔΑ

Central Greece's dramatic landscape of deep gorges, rugged mountains and fertile valleys is home to the magical stone pinnacle-topping monasteries of Meteora and the iconic ruins of ancient Delphi, where Alexander the Great sought advice from the Delphic oracle. Established in 1938, **Parnassos National Park** (☑ 22340 23529; http://en.par nassosnp.gr), to the north of Delphi, attracts naturalists, hikers (it's part of the E4 European long-distance path) and skiers.

Delphi   Δελφοί
POP 2370

Modern Delphi and its adjoining ruins hang stunningly on the slopes of Mt Parnassos overlooking the shimmering Gulf of Corinth.

According to mythology, Zeus released two eagles at opposite ends of the world and they met here, thus making Delphi the centre of the world. By the 6th century BCE, **Ancient Delphi** (☑ 22650 82312; http://ancient-greece.org/history/delphi.html; combined ticket for site & museum adult/student/child, €12/6/free; ☺ 8am-8pm Apr-Sep, to 6pm Oct, to 3pm Nov-Mar) had become the Sanctuary of Apollo. Thousands of pilgrims flocked here to consult the female oracle who sat at the mouth of a fume-emitting chasm. After sacrificing a sheep or goat, pilgrims would ask a question, and a priest would translate the oracle's response into verse. Wars, voyages and business transactions were undertaken on the strength of these prophecies.

In the town centre, **Rooms Pitho** (☑ 22650 82850; www.pithohotel.gr; Vasileon Pavlou & Friderikis 40a; s/d/tr incl breakfast from €45/55/70; ☀ ✳ ☎) and **Fedriades Hotel** (☑ 22650 82370; www.fedriades.com; Vasileon Pavlou & Friderikis 46; s/d/tr/ste incl breakfast €45/55/65/130; ✳ ☎ ⊛) are both friendly,

GREECE OLYMPIA

MT OLYMPUS

Just as it did for the ancients, Greece's highest mountain, **Olympus** (Όρος Όλυμπος), the cloud-covered lair of the Greek pantheon, fires the visitor's imagination today. The highest of Olympus' eight peaks is **Mytikas** (2917m), which is popular with trekkers, who use **Litohoro** (305m), 5km inland from the Athens–Thessaloniki highway, as their base. The main route up takes two days, with a stay overnight at one of the refuges. Good protective clothing is essential, even in summer. **EOS Litohoro** (Greek Alpine Club; ☑ 23520 84544, 23520 82444; http://eoslitohorou.blogspot.com; ☺ 9.30am-12.30pm & 6-8pm Mon-Sat Jun-Sep) has information.

tidy bets, the latter offering breakfast and bikes. Fill up on traditional dishes at the excellent, family-run **Taverna Vakhos** (☑ 22650 83186; www.vakhos.com; Apollonos 31; mains €8-16; ☺ noon-10:30pm; 🛜 🐾).

⊙ Getting There & Away

Buses depart from the eastern end of Vasileon Pavlou and Friderikis, next to the In Delphi restaurant, where tickets can be purchased between 9am and 8pm (the bus system's closing time). If you're taking an early bus, plan ahead and buy tickets the day before. This especially applies in high season when buses fill up quickly. Travellers to Kalambaka/Meteora will find better connections via Lamia and Trikala, rather than Larissa.

Meteora Μετέωρα

The World Heritage–listed Meteora (meh-teh-o-rah) is an extraordinary place and one of the most visited in all of Greece. The massive pinnacles of smooth rock are the perfect setting for a science-fiction or fantasy tale. The monasteries atop them add to the strange and beautiful landscape.

⊙ Sights & Activities

While there were once monasteries on all 24 pinnacles, only six are still occupied: **Megalou Meteoro** (Grand Meteoron; €3; ☺ 9am-4pm Wed-Mon Apr-Oct, to 3pm Thu-Mon Nov-Mar), **Varlaam** (€3; ☺ 9am-4pm Sat-Thu Apr-Oct, to 3pm Sat-Wed Nov-Mar), **Agiou Stefanou** (St Stephen's; €3; ☺ 9am-1.30pm & 3.30-5.30pm Tue-Sun Apr-Oct, 9am-1pm & 3-5pm Tue-Sun Nov-Mar), **Agias Triados** (Holy Trinity; €3; ☺ 9am-5pm Fri-Wed Apr-Oct, to 4pm Fri-Tue Nov-Mar), **Agiou Nikolaou** (Monastery of St Nikolaou Anapafsa; €3; ☺ 9am-4pm Sat-Thu) and **Agias Varvaras Rousanou** (€3; ☺ 9am-5pm Thu-Tue Apr-Oct, to 2pm Thu-Tue Nov-Mar).

Strict dress codes apply (no bare shoulders or knees and women must wear skirts; you can borrow a long skirt at the door). Walk the footpaths between monasteries, drive the asphalt road, or take the bus that departs from Kalambaka and Kastraki at 9am and returns at 1pm (12.40pm on weekends).

Meteora's stunning rocks are also a climbing paradise. **Visit Meteora** (☑ 24320 23820; www.visitmeteora.travel; Patriarchou Dimitriou 2; ☺ 9am-9pm) offers some excellent opportunities with professional guides, including hiking and walking tours.

🛏 Sleeping

Much of the best lodging around the Meteora is in the village of **Kastraki**, often with amazing close-up views. It's just 2km from Kalambaka.

Pyrgos Adrachti   BOUTIQUE HOTEL €€
(☑ 24320 22275; www.hotel-adrachti.gr; d/tr incl breakfast from €90/108; 🅿 🌀 ❄ 🛜 🐾) Slick and cool sums up this place – think subtle designer-style touches throughout the 14 rooms, bar and common areas, and an up-close-and-personal rock experience. Plus there's a tidy garden to relax in post-activities. It feels remote, but in fact it's a short stroll to the village square. A boutique hotel for real. Follow the signs.

⊙ Getting There & Away

Kalambaka's **KTEL bus station** (☑ 24320 22432; www.ktel-trikala.gr; Ikonomou) is 50m down from Plateia Dimarhiou (the town-hall square) and the large fountain, and is the arrival/departure point for regular Trikala bus connections. For Delphi, travellers should go via Trikala (not Larissa). The trip requires three straightforward bus changes: Kalambaka to Trikala, Trikala to Lamia, Lamia to Amfissa, and finally Amfissa to Delphi. It sounds fiddly, but the buses all connect; enquire at the station.

Trains depart from the Kalambaka **train station** (☑ 24320 22451; www.trainose.gr). For trains to Athens and Thessaloniki you may need to change at Paleofarsalos. For Volos you must change at Larissa.

NORTHERN GREECE
ΒΟΡΕΙΑ ΕΛΛΑΔΑ

Diversity should be northern Greece's second name – the region stretches across more cultures and terrains than any other in the country. Mighty civilisations, including Macedonians, Thracians, Romans, Byzantines, Slavs and Turks, have left traces here and this is nowhere more apparent than in Greece's second city, Thessaloniki.

Thessaloniki Θεσσαλονίκη

POP 788,952

Thessaloniki is easy to fall in love with – it has beauty, chaos, history and culture, a remarkable cuisine and wonderful, vast sea views. When you climb up to the Byzantine walls and take in the whole of Thessaloniki

Thessaloniki

Thessaloniki

◎ Top Sights
1 Archaeological Museum D4

◎ Sights
2 Museum of Byzantine Culture..............D4
3 Rotunda of Galerius D2
4 Thessaloniki Museum of
   Photography A2

🛏 Sleeping
5 Caravan...B1
6 Rent Rooms Thessaloniki.....................D2

🍽 Eating
7 Chatzis B2
8 I Nea Follia C1
9 Mourgá C2

at sunset, you see what a sprawling, organic city it is. Old and new cohabit wonderfully while Thessaloniki's most famous sight, the White Tower, anchors a waterfront packed with cocktail bars.

◉ Sights

★ **Archaeological Museum**   MUSEUM
(☎2310 830 538; www.amth.gr; Manoli Andronikou 6; adult/concession €8/4; ⏰8am-8pm Apr-Oct,

9am-4pm Nov-Mar) Macedonia's major pre-historic and ancient Macedonian and Hellenistic finds are housed in this museum (except for Vergina's gold tomb finds, which are exhibited in Vergina). Highlights include the **Derveni Crater** (330–320 BCE), a huge, ornate Hellenistic bronze-and-tin vase. Used for mixing wine and water, and later as a funerary urn, it's marked by intricate relief carvings of Dionysos, along with mythical figures, animals and ivy vines. The **Derveni**

ZAGOROHORIA & VIKOS GORGE
ΤΑ ΖΑΓΟΡΟΧΩΡΙΑ & ΧΑΡΑΔΡΑ ΤΟΥ ΒΙΚΟΥ

Try not to miss the spectacular **Zagori region**, with its deep gorges, abundant wildlife, dense forests and snowcapped mountains. Some 46 charming villages, famous for their grey-slate architecture, and known collectively as the Zagorohoria, are sprinkled across a large expanse of the Pindos Mountains north of Ioannina. These beautifully restored gems were once only connected by stone paths and arching footbridges, but paved roads now wind between them. Get information on walks from Ioannina's **EOS** (Greek Alpine Club; ☑ 26510 22138; www.orivatikos.gr; Smyrnis 15; ☉ hours vary) office.

Monodendri is a popular departure point for treks through dramatic 12km-long, 900m-deep **Vikos Gorge**, with its sheer limestone walls. Exquisite inns with attached tavernas abound in remote (but popular) twin villages **Megalo Papingo** and **Mikro Papingo**. It's best to explore by rental car from Ioannina.

Treasure contains Greece's oldest surviving papyrus piece (320–250 BCE).

Museum of Byzantine Culture   MUSEUM
(☑ 2313 306 400; www.mbp.gr; Leoforos Stratou 2; adult/student Apr-Oct €8/4, Nov-Mar €4; ☉ 8am-8pm Apr-Oct, 9am-4pm Nov-Mar) This fascinating museum has plenty of treasures to please Byzantine buffs, plus simple explanations to introduce the empire to total beginners. More than 3000 Byzantine objects, including mosaics, intriguing tomb paintings, jewellery and glassware, are showcased with characterful asides about daily life. You'll be confidently discerning early-Christian from late-Byzantine icons in no time.

Rotunda of Galerius   HISTORIC BUILDING
(☑ 2310 204 868; Plateia Agiou Georgiou; €2; ☉ 9am-5pm Nov-Mar, 8am-7pm Apr-Oct) FREE In 306 CE Roman emperor Galerius built this stocky 30m-high brick structure as his future mausoleum. But instead of being laid to rest within the 6m-thick walls of the Rotunda, he was buried in today's Serbia after succumbing to an unpleasant disease that still puzzles historians. Later, Constantine the Great made the Rotunda Thessaloniki's first church (Agios Georgios; observe drag-on-slaying St George above the door). The Ottomans made it a mosque (note the restored minaret).

Thessaloniki Museum of Photography   MUSEUM
(☑ 2310 566 716; www.thmphoto.gr; Warehouse A, Port; adult/concession €2/1; ☉ 11am-7pm Tue-Thu, Sat & Sun, to 10pm Fri) This 1910 port warehouse is home to thought-provoking exhibitions of historic and contemporary photography. These temporary displays change every four months or so.

🛏 Sleeping & Eating

⭐ Caravan   HOTEL €€
(☑ 2313 062 780; www.thecaravan.gr; cnr Rebelou & Vamvaka; d/ste incl breakfast €70/150; 🛜) This beautiful hotel is a mix between a travellers' haven and contemporary design hotel – with luxury thrown in. Opened by three friends from Thessaloniki who love travel, the aim here is to make guests feel at home. Therefore, you get smart rooms in cool colours, a friendly common area and plenty of advice on where to go from fabulous reception staff.

Rent Rooms Thessaloniki   HOSTEL €€
(☑ 2310 204 080; www.rentrooms-thessaloniki. com; Konstantinou Melenikou 9; dm/s/d/tr/q incl breakfast €25/69/79/90/100; 🌐🛜) What it lacks in contemporary style, it makes up for with services: a charming back-garden cafe, where you can tuck into a choice of filling breakfasts with views of the Rotunda of Galerius; super-friendly and helpful staff; and a can-do attitude. It's handily located near the university. Dorms and adequate private rooms are available plus security lockers and luggage storage.

⭐ Mourgá   GREEK €
(☑ 2310 268 826; Christopoulou 12; mains €5-14; ☉ 1pm-late) This has to be the place that will linger in your sensory memory for decades – elegant and relaxed, Mourgá will make you fall in love with Greek food, Thessaloniki style. Taste the buttery pan-fried shrimp, fava bean purée with preserved caper leaves

that melt on your tongue, incredible Cretan seaweed, a fantastic cheese selection and local wine.

Chatzis
SWEETS €

(☏ 2310 221 655; http://chatzis.gr; Mitropoleos 24; sweets €1.40-4; ◷ 8am-midnight) Glistening syrup-soaked treats have been luring dessert fans into Chatzis since 1908, back when Thessaloniki was still an Ottoman city. Try the moist, sugar-rush-inducing *revani* (syrupy semolina cake), chickpea and raisin halva, or *rizogalo* (rice pudding) scented with cinnamon.

★ I Nea Follia
GREEK €€

(☏ 2310 960 383; cnr Aristomenous & Haritos; mains €7.50-12; ◷ 2pm-late Sep-Jun; ☏) I Nea Follia is nothing special to look at, but once you sit down to a table and get served a beetroot and pistachio salad, an excellent veal steak or a juicy set of shrimp, you'll be coming back over and over again. The chef-owner, Girogos Hlazas, specialises in classic Greek fare with a contemporary twist.

ⓘ Information

Tourism Office (☏ 2310 229 070; www.thessaloniki.travel; Plateia Aristotelous; ◷ 10am-5pm) A very helpful tourism office on Plateia Aristotelous with maps, brochures and local information. Can also provide lists of hotels and assist with tours and excursions beyond Thessaloniki.

ⓘ Getting There & Away

Thessaloniki is northern Greece's transport hub and gateway to the Balkans. Major European airlines and budget airlines fly to Thessaloniki and within Greece.

AIR

Besides Greece's **Aegean Airlines** (https://en.aegeanair.com), many foreign carriers use Thessaloniki for domestic and international flights. Prices and routes are fluid, so ascertain which companies are currently flying from the **Makedonia International Airport** (SKG; ☏ 2310 985 000; www.thessalonikiairport.com) website. Then visit a travel agent or book online.

If you're visiting Thessaloniki briefly, you can store luggage with Sky Bag at the airport.

BOAT

Ferries from Thessaloniki port are limited and change annually. To access the Sporades, you must depart from Volos (all year) or Agios Konstantinos further south during the summer

period only. With private yacht charters you can sail to Italy, Turkey and Albania.

See www.ferries.gr for details and booking options for ferries from Thessaloniki.

BUS

Thessaloniki's main bus station, **KTEL Makedonia** (☏ 2310 595 444; www.ktelmacedonia.gr; Giannitson 244), is 3km west of the city centre. Each destination has its own specific ticket counter, signposted in Greek and English.

For Athens *only*, avoid the trip by going instead to **Monastiriou bus station** (☏ 2310 500 111; http://ktelthes.gr; Monastiriou 67) – next to the train station – where Athens-bound buses start before calling in at KTEL Makedonia.

Buses leave for Halkidiki from the eastern Thessaloniki **Halkidiki bus terminal** (☏ 2310 316 555; www.ktel-chalkidikis.gr; Km 9 Thessaloniki-Halkidiki road). The terminal is out towards the airport, reached via city buses 45A or 45B.

TRAIN

Direct ICE trains serve Athens (€55.40, 5¼ hours, seven daily), Paleofasala (for Meteora; €24.50, one hour, 10 daily) and Larissa (€14 to €22, two hours, 15 daily). Regular trains also serve Veria, Edessa and Florina (mostly via Platy). Only two daily trains currently serve Xanthi, Komotini and Alexandroupoli in Thrace.

Thessaloniki's **train station** (☏ 2310 121 530; www.trainose.gr; Monastiriou) has ATMs, card phones and small modern eateries, plus an Orthodox chapel. Self-serve luggage storage lockers start from €3.

ⓘ Getting Around

TO/FROM THE AIRPORT

Buses X1 (during the day) and N1 (at night) run half-hourly from the airport (17km southeast of town), heading west through the city to the main bus station (KTEL Makedonia) via the train station. Tickets cost €2 from the airport to the bus station; €1 for short journeys.

Taxis to the airport cost around €20 – it is a set rate, even if the meter reads a lower fee (this allows for airport charges and the differences in central locations). Call in advance if you need them to pick you up from town; the operator speaks English.

BUS

Bus 1 connects the main bus station (KTEL Makedonia) and the train station. From the train station, major points on Egnatia are constantly served by buses such as 10 and 14.

Buy tickets at *periptera* (street kiosks) for €1, or from on-board blue ticket machines (€1.10).

Validate the former in the orange machines. Machines neither give change nor accept bills; when boarding, be sure you have the right change and buy your ticket immediately. Thessaloniki's ticket police pounce at any sign of confusion. If they nab you, you'll pay €60.

TAXI
Thessaloniki's blue-and-white taxis carry multiple passengers, and only take you if you're going the same way. The minimum fare is €3.40. A more expensive 'night rate' takes effect from midnight until 5am. To book a cab for an airport transfer, try **Taxi Way** (☑ 2310 214 900, 2310 866 866; www.taxiway.gr).

CYCLADES ΚΥΚΛΑΔΕΣ

On a quest to find the Greek island of your dreams? Start, here, in the Cyclades, with rugged, sun-drenched outcrops of rock, anchored in azure seas and liberally peppered with snow-white villages and blue-domed churches, this is Greece straight from central casting, with stellar archaeological sites and dozens of postcard-worthy beaches. Throw in a blossoming food scene, some renowned party destinations and a good dose of sophistication, and you really do have the best of Greece's ample charms.

Mykonos Μύκονος

POP 10,134

Mykonos is the great glamour island of Greece and flaunts its sizzling St-Tropez-meets-Ibiza style and party-hard reputation. The high-season mix of hedonistic holidaymakers, cruise-ship crowds and posturing fashionistas throngs Mykonos Town (aka Hora), a traditional whitewashed Cycladic maze, delighting in its cubist charms and its chichi cafe-bar-boutique scene.

There are a few provisos about visiting here. Come only if you are prepared to pay top dollar, jostle with street crowds and sit bum cheek to cheek with oiled-up loungers at the packed main beaches.

◉ Sights

The island's most popular beaches, thronged in summer, are on the southern coast. About 5km southwest of Hora are family-oriented **Agios Ioannis** (where *Shirley Valentine* was filmed) and **Kapari**. The nearby packed and noisy **Ornos** and the package-holiday resort of **Platys Gialos** have boats for the glitzier beaches to the east. In between these two is **Psarou**, a magnet for the Greek cognoscenti.

Approximately 1km south of Platys Gialos you'll find **Paraga Beach**, which has a small gay section. Party people should head about 1km east to famous **Paradise**. **Elia** is a long, lovely stretch of sand. A few minutes' walk west from here is the secluded **Agrari**. Further east, **Kalafatis** is a hub for water sports (including diving and windsurfing), and **Lia** has a remote, end-of-the-road feel.

Hora (also known as Mykonos), the island's well-preserved port and capital, is a warren of narrow alleyways and whitewashed buildings overlooked by the town's famous windmills. In the heart of the waterfront Little Venice quarter, tiny flower-bedecked churches jostle with glossy boutiques, and there's a cascade of bougainvillea around every corner.

🛏 Sleeping & Eating

It's best not to arrive in July or August without a reservation, as there will be few vacancies. Some places insist on a minimum stay during the peak period. Noise levels in Hora and popular resorts are high in summer.

Pension Kalogera PENSION €
(☑ 6972483263, 22890 24709; www.pensionkalogeramykonos.webs.com; Mavrogenous; s/d/tr/q €100/140/180/200; ❄ 🛜) For a town with so few options for the budget traveller, this comes as welcome relief and a delightful surprise. The ultra-kind and hospitable owner, Aggeliki, runs a simple, clean and super-central place and is a wealth of information. She also restores faith that the town is not out to squeeze every last dollar of your beer money.

Fresh Hotel BOUTIQUE HOTEL €€
(☑ 22890 24670; www.hotelfreshmykonos.com; Kalogera 31; d incl breakfast from €200; ❄ 🛜) In the heart of town, with a lush and leafy garden and highly regarded on-site restaurant, Fresh comes with a bit of attitude; it is indeed fresh, but with compact and stylishly minimalist rooms. Rates fall to around €90 in the low season.

Kadena CAFE €€
(☑ 22890 29290; mains €10-23; ◷ 7am-late; 🛜) Less pretentious than many other eateries, this place has a small menu of Mediterra-

DELOS

Southwest of Mykonos, the island of **Delos** (☑22890 22259; museum & site adult/concession €12/6; ⊙8am-8pm Apr-Oct, to 2pm Nov-Mar), a Unesco World Heritage Site, is the Cyclades' archaeological jewel. The mythical birthplace of twins Apollo and Artemis, splendid Ancient Delos was a shrine-turned-sacred treasury and commercial centre. It was inhabited from the 3rd millennium BCE and reached its apex of power around the 5th century BCE.

Overnight stays are forbidden (as is swimming) and boat schedules allow a maximum of four hours at Delos. A simple cafe is located by the museum, but it pays to bring water and food. Weat a hat, sunscreen and walking shoes.

Boats from Mykonos to Delos (€20 return, 30 minutes) go between 9am and 5pm in summer, and return between 12.15pm and 8pm. Departure/return times are posted at the **Delos Boat Ticket Kiosk** (☑22890 28603; www.delostours.gr; adult/child return ticket €20/10), at the foot of the jetty at the southern end of the old harbour, as well as online. Buy tickets online or from the kiosk or various travel and transport agencies. When buying tickets, establish which boat you can return on.

nean dishes, good breakfasts, friendly staff, and protection from the north wind.

★**M-Eating** MEDITERRANEAN €€€
(☑22890 78550; www.m-eating.gr; Kalogera 10; mains €24-64; ⊙7pm-1am; 🛜) A classy act, run by a chef-husband and wife team. Attentive service, soft lighting and relaxed luxury are the hallmarks of this creative restaurant specialising in fresh Greek produce prepared with flair. Sample anything from sea bass tartare to rib-eye veal with honey truffle. Don't miss the dessert of Mykonian honey pie.

🍷 Drinking & Nightlife

Night action in Hora starts around 11pm and warms up by 1am. From posh cocktail spots to the colourful bars of Hora's Little Venice (where there are also some hip clubs), Hora has the lot. Another prime spot is the Tria Pigadia (Three Wells) area on Enoplon Dynameon. Outside of town, each major beach has at least one beach bar that gets going during the day. Bring a bankroll – the high life doesn't come cheap. Beach clubs are generally open June to September, but July and August is when the scene is most intense. See websites for events and ticket info.

Cavo Paradiso CLUB
(☑22890 26124; www.cavoparadiso.gr; Paradise Beach; ⊙11.30pm-7am) When dawn gleams just over the horizon, hard-core bar-hoppers move from Hora to Cavo Paradiso at Paradise Beach, the open-air clifftop mega-club that has featured top international DJs since 1994.

ⓘ Getting There & Away

AIR

Mykonos Airport (☑22890 79000; www.mykonos-airport.com), 3km southeast of the town centre, has flights year-round to Athens with Sky Express (www.skyexpress.gr) and Aegean Airlines (https://en.aegeanair.com), among others, and to Thessaloniki with Aegean Airlines.

BOAT

Year-round ferries serve mainland ports Piraeus and Rafina (the latter is usually quicker if you are coming directly from Athens airport). In the high season, Mykonos is well connected with all neighbouring islands, including Paros and Santorini. Hora is loaded with ticket agents.

Mykonos has two ferry quays: the **Old Port**, 400m north of town, where a couple of fast ferries dock, and the **New Port**, 2km north of town, where the bigger fast ferries and all conventional ferries dock. When buying outgoing tickets, double-check which quay your ferry leaves from.

Excursion boats for Delos depart from the quay just off the waterfront of Mykonos Town.

ⓘ Getting Around

TO/FROM THE AIRPORT

Buses from the southern bus station serve Mykonos' airport (€2). Some hotels and guesthouses offer free airport and port transfers. Otherwise, arrange airport transfer with your accommodation (around €10) or take a taxi to town (€10 or €15 depending on which side of town you are on).

BOAT

Mykonos Cruises (☑22890 23995; www.mykonos-cruises.gr; ⊙8am-7pm Apr-Oct) is an association of sea-taxi operators offering services to the island's best beaches. See the timetables online. The main departure point is **Platys Gialos**, with drop-offs and pick-ups at Ornos, Paraga, Paradise, Super Paradise, Agrari and Elia beaches (return trips cost between €5 and €7). Cruises and personalised itineraries can also be arranged.

The **Sea Bus** (☑ 6978830355; www. mykonos-seabus.gr; one way €2) water-taxi service connects the New Port with Hora, running hourly from 9am to 10pm (more frequently when a cruise ship is in port).

BUS

The **KTEL Mykonos** (☑ 22890 26797, 22890 23360; www.mykonosbus.com) bus network has two main terminals plus pick-up points at the Old and New Ports.

Low-season services are much reduced, but buses in high season run frequently; the fare is €1 to €2 depending on the distance travelled. Timetables are on the website. In July and August, some bus services run until 2am or later from the beaches.

Terminal A, the **southern bus station** (www. mykonosbus.com; Fabrika Sq), known as Fabrika, serves Ornos and Agios Ioannis Beach, Platys Gialos, Paraga and Super Paradise beaches.

Terminal B, the **northern bus station** (www. mykonosbus.com), sometimes called Remezzo, is behind the OTE office and has services to Agios Stefanos via Tourlos, Ano Mera, and Kalo Livadi, Kalafatis and Elia beaches.

CAR & MOTORCYCLE

Hire cars start at €45 per day in high season and €30 in low season. Scooters/quads are around €20/40 in high season and €15/30 in low season.

Avis and Sixt are among the agencies at the airport, and there are dozens of hire places all over the island, particularly near the ports and bus stations (which is where the large public car parks are found – you can't drive into Hora proper).

TAXI

Taxis (☑ 22890 23700, 22890 22400) queue at Hora's Plateia Manto Mavrogenous (Taxi Sq), bus stations and ports, but waits can be long in high season. All have meters, and the minimum fare is €3.50 (plus €0.50 per bag and €3.30 for phone booking).

Approximate fares from Hora include New Port (€6), Ornos (€10), Platys Gialos (€10), Paradise (€11), Kalafatis (€18) and Elia (€18).

Naxos   ΝΑΞΟΣ

POP 18,900

The largest of the Cyclades, Naxos packs a lot of bang for its buck. Its main city of Hora (known also as Naxos) has a gorgeous waterfront and a web of steep cobbled alleys below its hilltop *kastro*, all filled with the hubbub of tourism and shopping. You needn't travel far, though, to find isolated beaches, atmospheric mountain villages and ancient sites.

◉ Sights

★ Kastro   AREA

The most alluring part of Hora is the 13th-century residential neighbourhood of Kastro, which Marco Sanudo made the capital of his duchy in 1207. Behind the waterfront, get lost in the narrow alleyways scrambling up to its spectacular hilltop location. Venetian mansions survive in the centre of Kastro, and you can see the remnants of the castle, the **Tower of Sanoudos**. To see the Bourgos area of the old town, head into the winding backstreets behind the northern end of Paralia.

★ Temple of Apollo   ARCHAEOLOGICAL SITE

(The Portara; ◷ 24hr) **FREE** From Naxos Town harbour, a causeway leads to the Palatia islet and the striking, unfinished Temple of Apollo, Naxos' most famous landmark (also known as the Portara, or 'Doorway'). Simply two marble columns with a crowning lintel, it makes an arresting sight, and people gather at sunset for splendid views.

Panagia Drosiani   CHURCH

(donations appreciated; ◷ 10am-7pm May–mid-Oct) Located 2.5km north of Halki, just below Moni, the small, peaceful Panagia Drosiani is among the oldest and most revered churches in Greece. Inside is a series of cavelike chapels. In the darkest chapels, monks and nuns secretly taught Greek language and religion to local children during the Turkish occupation. Several frescoes still grace the walls, and date from the 7th century.

Look for the depiction of Mary in the eastern chapter; the clarity and expression is incredible.

◉ Beaches

The popular beach of **Agios Georgios** is just a 10-minute walk south from the main waterfront.

Beaches south of here include beautiful **Agios Prokopios**, which is sandy and shallow and lies in a sheltered bay to the south of the headland of Cape Mougkri. It merges with **Agia Anna**, a stretch of shining white sand that's quite narrow but long enough to feel uncrowded towards its southern end.

Sandy beaches continue as far as Pyrgaki, passing the beautiful turquoise waters of the long, dreamy **Plaka Beach** and gorgeous sandy bays punctuated with rocky outcrops. You'll find plenty of restaurants, accommodation and bus stops along this stretch.

At **Mikri Vigla**, golden granite slabs and boulders divide the beach into two. This beach is becoming an increasingly big deal on the kitesurfing scene, with reliable wind conditions.

◉ Villages

Heading north from the mountains inland, the roads wind and twist like spaghetti, eventually taking you to the somewhat scrappy seaside village of **Apollonas**. Tavernas line the waterfront and serve the freshest of fish. In an ancient quarry on the hillside above the village is a colossal 7th-century BCE **kouros** (youth) statues. Follow the small signs to get here.

Apiranthos seems to grow out of the stony flanks of rugged Mt Fanari (883m), about 25km east of Hora. The village's unadorned stone houses and marble-paved streets reflect a rugged individualism that is matched by the villagers themselves. Many of them are descendants of refugees who migrated from Crete. Apiranthos people have always been noted for their spirited politics and populism, and the village is peppered with quirky shops, galleries and cafes.

Halki is a vivid reflection of historic Naxos, with the handsome facades of old villas and tower houses a legacy of its wealthy past as the island's long-ago capital. Today it's home to a small but fascinating collection of shops and galleries, drawing artists and culinary wizards. Halki lies at the heart of the Tragaea mountainous region, about 20 minutes' drive (15km) from Hora.

🛌 Sleeping

Hotel Galini   HOTEL €€
(☑ 22850 22114; www.hotelgalini.com; d incl breakfast from €100; ❄ ☎) A nautical theme lends this super-friendly, family-run place loads of character. Updated, spacious rooms have small balconies, plus some rooms have creative decor fashioned from seashells and driftwood. The location is first-rate – close to the old town and the beach – and the breakfast is hearty. Prices drop significantly outside high season.

KITRON-TASTING IN HALKI

The historic village of **Halki** is a top spot to try *kitron*, a liqueur unique to Naxos. While the exact recipe is top secret, visitors can taste it and stock up on supplies at **Vallindras Distillery** (☑ 22850 31220; ☉ 10am-10pm Jul & Aug, to 6pm May-Jun & Sep-Oct) in Halki's main square. There are free tours of the old distillery's atmospheric rooms, which contain ancient jars and copper stills. *Kitron* tastings round out the trip.

Xenia Hotel   HOTEL €€
(☑ 22850 25068; www.hotel-xenia.gr; Plateia Pigadakia; d/tr incl breakfast from €95/120/130; ❄ ☎) Sleek and minimalist, this hotel is in the heart of the action in the old-town, close to everything, and the staff are attentive. Balconies overlook the bustle of the streets, but thick glass keeps the noise out when you decide to call it a night. Restaurants and cafes are right outside the front door.

🍴 Eating & Drinking

★ Doukato   GREEK €
(☑ 22850 27013; www.facebook.com/doukatonaxos; Old Town; mains €8-16; ☉ 6pm-late May-Oct; dinner Fri & Sat, lunch Sun Nov-Apr) One of the Cyclades' best eating experiences, in a magical setting that has been a monastery, church and a school, Doukato is rightly capturing attention. Owner Dimitris grows much of the produce, or sources it locally. The result? Top Naxian specialities such as *gouna* (sundried mackerel), *kalogeras* (beef, eggplant and cheese) and their unbelievably delicious Doukato 'Special' souvlaki.

Naxos Cafe   BAR
(☑ 22850 26343; Old Market St; ☉ 8pm-2am) If you want to drink but don't fancy the club scene, here's your answer. This atmospheric, traditional bar is small and candlelit and spills into the cobbled Bourgos street. Drink Naxian wine with the locals.

ℹ Getting There & Around

AIR

The **airport** (JNX; www.naxos.net/airport) is 3km south of Hora. There's no shuttle bus, but buses to Agios Prokopios Beach and Agia Anna pass close by. A taxi costs around €15; luggage costs extra. There are daily flights to/from Athens (around €95, 40 minutes) with Olympic Air

GREECE NAXOS

(www.olympicair.com), Aegean Airlines (https://en.aegeanair.com/) and Sky Express (www.skyexpress.gr).

BOAT

Like Paros, Naxos is something of a ferry hub in the Cyclades, with a similar number of conventional and fast ferries making regular calls to/from Piraeus, plus the mainland port of Rafina via the northern Cyclades.

PUBLIC TRANSPORT

Frequent buses run to Agios Prokopios Beach and Agia Anna from Hora. Several buses daily serve Filoti via Halki, Apiranthos and Apollonas (€6.20), Pyrgaki (€2.30) and Melanes.

Buses leave from the end of the ferry quay in Hora; timetables are posted outside the **bus information office** (☑ 22850 22291; www.naxosdestinations.com; Harbour), diagonally left and across the road from the bus stop. You have to buy tickets from the office or from the machine outside (not from the bus driver).

Santorini ΣΑΝΤΟΡΙΝΗ

POP 15,550

You'll either love or hate Santorini. Its magnet, the multicoloured cliffs that soar above the sea-drowned caldera, are amazing indeed. The main towns of Fira and Oia – a snow-drift of white Cycladic houses that line the cliff tops and spill like icy cornices down the terraced rock – will take your breath away. And then there's the island's fascinating history, best revealed at the Minoan site of Akrotiri.

Santorini's main town of Fira is a vibrant place, if bursting at its seams. Its caldera edge is layered with swish hotels, cave apartments, infinity pools, all backed by a warren of narrow streets packed with shops, more bars and restaurants. And people.

DON'T MISS

ANCIENT AKROTIRI

In 1967, excavations in the southwest of Santorini uncovered **Ancient Akrotiri** (☑ 22860 81366; http://odysseus.culture.gr; adult/concession €12/6; ⊙ 8am-8pm May-Sep, to 3pm Oct-Apr), an ancient Minoan city buried deep beneath volcanic ash from the catastrophic eruption of 1613 BCE. Housed within a cool, protective structure, wooden walkways allow you to pass through the city. Peek inside three-storey buildings that survived, and see roads, drainage systems and stashes of pottery.

☉ Sights

★**Museum of Prehistoric Thera**   MUSEUM
(☑ 22860 22217; www.santorini.com/museums; Mitropoleos; adult/child €3/free; ⊙ 8.30am-3pm Wed-Mon) Opposite the bus station, this well-presented museum houses extraordinary finds excavated from Akrotiri and is all the more impressive when you realise just how old they are. Most remarkable is the glowing gold ibex figurine, dating from the 17th century BCE and in mint condition. Also look for fossilised olive tree leaves from within the caldera, which date back to 60,000 BCE.

★**Art Space**   GALLERY
(☑ 22860 32774; www.artspace-santorini.com; Exo Gonia; ⊙ 11am-sunset Apr-Oct) FREE This atmospheric gallery is on the way to Kamari, in Argyros Canava, one of the oldest wineries on the island. The atmospheric old wine caverns are hung with some superb artworks, while sculptures transform lost corners and niches. The collection features around 32 Greek and international modern artists. Winemaking is still in the owner's blood, and part of the complex produces some stellar vintages under the Art Space Wines label. Tastings (from €10) enhance the experience.

Ancient Thira   ARCHAEOLOGICAL SITE
(☑ 22860 25405; http://odysseus.culture.gr; adult/child €4/free; ⊙ 8am-3pm Tue-Sun) First settled by the Dorians in the 9th century BCE, Ancient Thira consists of Hellenistic, Roman and Byzantine ruins and is an atmospheric and rewarding site to visit. The ruins include temples, houses with mosaics, an *agora* (market), a theatre and a gymnasium. Views are splendid. If you're driving, take the narrow, switchbacked road from Kamari for 3km. From Perissa, a hike up a dusty path takes a bit over an hour to reach the site.

☉ Oia

Perched on the northern tip of the island, the village of Oia reflects the renaissance of Santorini after the devastating earthquake of 1956. Restoration work has whipped up beauty. You will struggle to find a more stunning spot in the Cyclades. Built on a steep slope of the caldera, many of its dwellings nestle in niches hewn into the volcanic rock.

Not surprisingly, Oia draws enormous numbers of tourists, and overcrowding is

Santorini

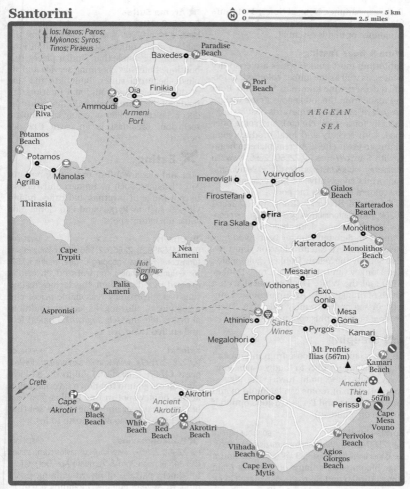

the price it pays for its good looks. Try to visit in the morning or spend the night here; afternoons and evenings often bring busloads from the cruise ships moored in the bay.

🏃 Activities

Beaches

Santorini's best beaches are on the east and south coasts. Sunbeds, beach bars and water-sports operators are here to serve.

The long stretch of black sand, pebbles and pumice stones at **Perissa**, **Perivolos** and **Agios Georgios** is backed by bars, tavernas, hotels and shops, and remains fairly relaxed.

Red (Kokkini) Beach, near Ancient Akrotiri in the south, has impressive red cliffs. Caïques from **Akrotiri Beach** can take you there and on to **White (Aspri)** and **Black (Mesa Pigadia) Beaches** for about €5 return.

Vlihada, also on the south coast, has a beach backed by weirdly eroded cliffs as well as tavernas; it also has a photogenic fishing harbour.

Kamari is Santorini's best-developed resort, with a long beach of black sand. The beachfront road is dense with restaurants and bars, and things get extremely busy in high season. Boats connect Kamari with

Perissa in summer. Note: at times, Santorini's black-sand beaches become so hot that a sunlounge or mat is essential.

Wine & Beer Tasting

Santorini's most lauded wines are crisp dry whites, as well as the amber-coloured, unfortified dessert wine known as Vinsanto. Both are made from the indigenous grape variety, *assyrtiko.* Most local vineyards host tastings (usually for a small charge), and some offer food, with scenery and local produce combining to great effect. A great place to begin is with **SantoWines** (☑ 22860 22596; www.san towines.gr; tours & tastings from €11; ⏰ 9am-10pm), Santorini's cooperative of grape-growers on the caldera edge near the port.

Santorini Brewery Company (☑ 22860 30268; www.santorinibrewingcompany.gr; ⏰ noon-5pm Mon-Sat summer, shorter hours rest of year) is home to in-demand Donkey beers (you may have seen the eye-catching logo on your travels). Sample the Yellow Donkey (golden ale), Red Donkey (amber ale), the Crazy Donkey (IPA) and the White Donkey (wheat with a touch of orange peel). All are unfiltered, unpasteurised and extremely palatable. There are free tastings, plus cool merchandise.

🛏 Sleeping

There's so much to choose from in Fira and Oia, from luxury digs to 'budget' pensions. Away from these main towns, the biggest concentration of rooms can be found in and around Kamari and Perissa (a good option if you are on a budget).

Zorzis Hotel   BOUTIQUE HOTEL €
(☑ 22860 81104; www.santorinizorzis.com; Perissa; d incl breakfast from €99; ❋ 🛜 🏊) Behind a huge bloom of geraniums on Perissa's main street, Hiroko and Spiros (a Japanese-Greek couple) run an immaculate 10-room hotel. It's a pastel-coloured sea of calm (no kids), with delightful garden, pool and eye-catching mountain backdrop.

Karterados Caveland Hostel   HOSTEL €
(☑ 22860 22122; www.cave-land.com; Karterados; dm from €26, d incl breakfast €100, apt €200; ⏰ Mar-Oct; 🅿 ❋ 🛜 🏊) This fabulous, chilled-out hostel is based in an old winery complex in Karterados about 2km from central Fira (see website for directions). Dorms (four-, six- and 10-bed) are in the big old wine caves, all of them with creative, colourful decor and good facilities. (Warning: claustrophobes might find the tiny windows problematic.) The garden swimming pool tops it off.

★**Aroma Suites**   BOUTIQUE HOTEL €€
(☑ 22860 24112; www.aromasuites.com; Agiou Mina; d from €230; ❋ @ 🛜) Overlooking the caldera at the quieter southern end of Fira, and more accessible than similar places, this boutique hotel has charming service and six plush, beautiful suites. Built into the side of the caldera, the traditional interiors are made all the more lovely with monochrome decor. Balconies offer a feeling of complete seclusion. Breakfast is an extra €12 per person.

🍴 Eating

Fira and Oia are full of top eating options. Most beaches, such as Kamari and Perissa, have a range of tavernas and cafes. Inland villages such as Pyrgos and Exo Gonia hide some top eating spots.

To Ouzeri   TAVERNA €
(☑ 6945849921, 22860 21566; http://ouzeri-san torini.com; Fabrika Shopping Centre; mains €7.50-15; ⏰ lunch & dinner) Central and cheerfully dressed in red gingham, this terrace restaurant has surprisingly reasonable prices and a good local following. Expect top traditional dishes like mussels *saganaki,* baked feta and stuffed calamari.

Krinaki   TAVERNA €€
(☑ 22860 71993; www.krinaki-santorini.gr; Finikia; mains €17-27; ⏰ noon-late) All-fresh, all-local ingredients go into top-notch taverna dishes at this homey spot in tiny Finikia, just east of Oia. Local beer and wine, plus a sea (but not caldera) view looking north to Ios.

★**Koukoumavlos**   GREEK €€€
(☑ 22860 23807; www.koukoumavlos.com; mains €15-34; ⏰ noon-3pm & 7pm-late Apr–Oct) Gleeful diners partake of award-winning fresh, modern Aegean cuisine (including a worthwhile degustation at €78). Creativity reigns here, at one of Greece's top eateries, and the menu is poetic, elevating dishes to new heights. The likes of 'slow-cooked shoulder of lamb with potato mousseline flavoured with jasmine, fig and Greek coffee sauce'. It's 30m north of the cathedral.

ℹ Information

Dakoutros Travel (☑ 22860 22958; www.dak outrostravel.gr; Fira; ⏰ 8.30am-midnight Jul & Aug, 9am-9pm Sep-Jun) Helpful travel agency and de facto tourist office on the main street, just before Plateia Theotokopoulou. Ferry and air tickets sold; assistance with excursions, accommodation and transfers.

❶ Getting There & Away

AIR

Santorini Airport (JTR; ☑ 22860 28400; www.santoriniairport.com) has flights year-round to/from Athens (from €65, 45 minutes) with Olympic Air (www.olympicair.com) and Aegean Airlines (https://en.aegeanair.com). Seasonal European connections from London, Rome, Geneva and Milan are plentiful with some budget carriers.

Give yourself plenty of time when flying back out as tourism infrastructure hasn't kept up with the island's growing popularity and it can be mayhem at the small airport terminal.

BOAT

There are plenty of ferries each day to and from Piraeus and many Cyclades islands.

Santorini's main port, Athinios, stands on a cramped shelf of land at the base of sphinx-like cliffs. It's a scene of marvellous chaos (that works itself out), except when ferries have been cancelled and arrivals and departures merge. Advice? Be patient. It clears, if eventually. Buses (and taxis) meet all ferries and then cart passengers up the towering cliffs through an ever-rising series of S-bends to Fira. Accommodation providers can usually arrange transfers (to Fira per person is around €10 to €15).

❶ Getting Around

TO/FROM THE AIRPORT

There are frequent bus connections between Fira's bus station and the airport, 5km east of Fira (€1.80, 20 minutes, 7am to 9pm). Most accommodation providers will arrange paid transfers.

BUS

KTEL Santorini Buses (☑ 22860 25404; http://ktel-santorini.gr) has a good website with schedules and prices. Tickets are purchased on the bus.

In summer buses leave Fira regularly for Oia, with more services pre-sunset (€1.80). There are also numerous daily departures for Akrotiri (€1.80), Kamari (€1.80), Perissa and Perivolos Beach (€2.40), and a few to Monolithos (€1.80).

Buses leave Fira for the port of Athinios (€2.30, 30 minutes) a half-dozen times per day, but it's wise to check times in advance. Buses for Fira meet all ferries, even late at night.

CAR & MOTORCYCLE

A car is the best way to explore the island during high season, when buses are intolerably overcrowded and you'll be lucky to get on one at all. Be very patient and cautious when driving – the narrow roads and heavy traffic, especially in and around Fira, can be a nightmare.

There are representatives of all the major international car-hire outfits, plus dozens of local operators in all tourist areas. You'll pay from around €65 per day for a car and €35/50 for a scooter/four-wheeler in high season, but it pays to shop around.

CRETE ΚΡΗΤΗ

POP 623,000

There's something undeniably artistic in the way the Cretan landscape unfolds, from the sun-drenched beaches in the north to the rugged canyons spilling out at the cove-carved and cliff-lined southern coast. Trek through Europe's longest gorge, hike to the cave where Zeus was born or cycle among orchards on the Lasithi Plateau. Leave time to plant your footprints on a sandy beach, and boat, kayak or snorkel in the crystalline waters.

Crete's natural beauty is equalled only by the richness of its history. The island is the birthplace of the Minoans, the first advanced society on European soil, and you'll find evocative vestiges like the famous Palace of Knossos. History imbues Hania and Rethymno, where labyrinthine lanes are lorded over by mighty fortresses, restored Renaissance mansions, mosques and Turkish bathhouses.

Iraklio ΗΡΑΚΛΕΙΟ

POP 140,730

Crete's capital city, Iraklio (also called Heraklion), is Greece's fifth-largest city and the island's economic and administrative hub. It's also home to Crete's blockbuster sights. Take the time to explore its layers and wander its backstreets. You'll discover a low-key urban sophistication with a thriving restaurant scene. A revitalised waterfront invites strolling and the newly pedestrianised historical centre is punctuated by bustling

DON'T MISS

IRAKLIO MARKET

An Iraklio institution, just south of the Lion Fountain, narrow **Odos 1866** (1866 St) is part market, part bazaar and, despite being increasingly tourist-oriented, a fun place to browse and stock up on picnic supplies from fruit and vegetables, creamy cheeses and honey to succulent olives and fresh breads. Other stalls sell pungent herbs, leather goods, hats, jewellery and some souvenirs.

Crete

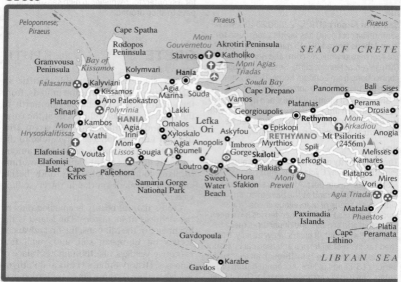

squares flanked by buildings from the time when Christopher Columbus first set sail.

<0> Sights & Activities

★ Heraklion

Archaeological Museum MUSEUM
(www.heraklionmuseum.gr; Xanthoudidou 2; adult/reduced/child €10/5/free, with Palace of Knossos adult/reduced €16/8; ⊙ 8am-8pm Mon & Wed-Sun, 10am-8pm Tue mid-Apr-Oct, 8am-4pm Nov-mid-Apr) This state-of-the-art museum is one of the largest and most important in Greece. The two-storey revamped 1930s Bauhaus building makes a gleaming showcase for artefacts spanning 5500 years from Neolithic to Roman times, including a Minoan collection of unparalleled richness. The rooms are colour coded and displays are arranged both chronologically and thematically, and presented with descriptions in English.

A visit here will greatly enhance your understanding of Crete's rich history. Don't skip it.

Cretan Adventures OUTDOORS
(☑ 6944790771; www.cretanadventures.gr) ⬤ This well-regarded local company run by friendly and knowledgeable English-speaking Fondas organises hiking tours, mountain biking and extreme outdoor excursions. It also coordinates fabulous week-long self-guided hiking tours including detailed hiking instructions, accommodation with breakfast and luggage transfer (from around €800). Fondas' office is up on the 3rd floor and easy to miss.

⌓ Sleeping & Eating

Hotel Mirabello HOTEL €
(☑ 28102 85052; www.mirabello-hotel.gr; Theotokopoulou 20; s/d from €40/50; ❋@⬤) Despite its dated Plain-Jane looks, this friendly and low-key hotel offers excellent value for money. Assets include squeaky-clean rooms with modern bathrooms, beds with individual reading lamps, a fridge and kettle plus a location close to, well, everything. The nicest units have a balcony.

Olive Green Hotel HOTEL €€
(☑ 28103 02900; www.olivegreenhotel.com; cnr Idomeneos & Meramvellou; d incl breakfast €109-126; ❋⬤) ⬤ This 'contemporary chic' and uber-smart place is one of Iraklio's newcomers to the hotel scene. Its clean rooms feature minimalistic white and olive-green decor, with separate shower and toilet (as opposed to the usual Greek-style all-in-one bathroom). It promotes itself as 'eco-friendly' but this seems to be limited to solar panels and low-impact building materials. Helpful reception staff.

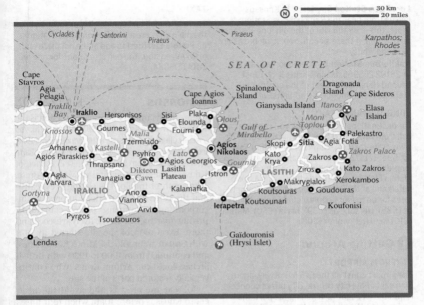

Phyllo Sofies
CAFE €

(www.phyllosophies.gr; Plateia Venizelou 33; mains €3.50-12.50; ⊘ 6am-midnight; 🛜) With tables sprawling out towards the Morosini Fountain, this is a great place to sample *bougatsa* (creamy semolina pudding wrapped in a pastry envelope and sprinkled with cinnamon and sugar). The less-sweet version is made with *myzithra* (sheep's-milk cheese).

★ Merastri
CRETAN €€

(🗗 28102 21910; www.facebook.com/merastri; Chrisostomou 17; mains €7-13; ⊘ 7pm-late) If there's a reason to come to Iraklio, it's to enjoy one of the most authentic Cretan meals, served in this stunning home, a former music building. The family of owners is passionate about their products (they use whatever they produce – oil and wine), and will conjure up everything from slow-cooked lamb to porterhouse steak with sage and wine.

Ippokambos
SEAFOOD €€

(🗗 28102 80240; Sofokli Venizelou 3; mains €7-17; ⊘ 12.30am-midnight Mon-Sat; 🛜) This long-running *ouzerie* (place that serves ouzo and light snacks) specialises in fish – freshly caught (if not, they state if it's frozen), simply but expertly prepared and sold at fair prices. In summer, park yourself on the covered waterfront terrace.

🛈 Getting There & Away

AIR

About 5km east of Iraklio city centre, the **Nikos Kazantzakis International Airport** (HER; 🗗 28103 97800; www.ypa.gr/en/our-airports/kratikos-aerolimenas-hrakleioy-n-kazantzakhs) has an ATM, a duty-free shop and a cafe-bar.

BOAT

The **ferry port** (🗗 28103 38000; www.portheraklion.gr) is 500m to the east of the Koules Fortress and old harbour. The Regional Bus Station is about 500m south, while the local bus terminal is outside the port entrance. Iraklio is a major port for access to many of the islands, though services are spotty outside high season. Tickets can be purchased online or through local travel agencies, including central **Paleologos** (🗗 28103 46185; www.paleologos.gr; 25 Avgoustou 5; ⊘ 9am-8pm Mon-Fri, to 3pm Sat). Daily ferries from Iraklio's port include services to Piraeus and faster catamarans to Santorini and other Cycladic islands. Ferries sail east to Rhodes via Sitia, Kasos, Karpathos and Halki.

BUS

Regional Bus Station (🗗 28102 46530; www.ktelherlas.gr; Leoforos Ikarou 9; 🛜) East of Koules Fortress on Ikarou, this depot serves major destinations in eastern and western Crete, including Hania, Rethymno, Agios Nikolaos, Sitia and the Lassithi Plateau.

Local Bus Station City bus 2 to Knossos leaves from near the Regional Bus Station (note: this is on the site of the old long-distance bus station; if there's confusion, local buses are blue and white).

Iraklio Bus Station B (Chanioporta Station; 📳 28102 255965; Machis Kritis 3; 🛜) Just beyond Hania Gate, west of the centre, this station serves Anogia, a traditional village.

LONG-DISTANCE TAXI

For destinations around Crete, you can order a cab from **Crete Taxi Services** (📳 6970021970; www.crete-taxi.gr; ⊘24hr) or **Heraklion Taxi** (📳 6955171473; www.crete.cab). There are also long-distance cabs waiting at the airport, at Plateia Eleftherias (outside the Capsis Astoria hotel) and at the Regional Bus Station. Sample fares for up to four people include Agios Nikolaos (€85), Hersonisos (€39), Malia (€50), Matala (€101) and Rethymno (€108).

🛈 Getting Around

TO/FROM AIRPORT

The airport is just off the E75 motorway, about 5km east of the city centre. City buses connects it with the city centre, including the port, the regional (and local) bus stations and Plateia Eleftherias, every few minutes. These include bus numbers 6, 8, 10, 11, 12 and 31. The bus stop is to the left as you exit the terminal. Taxis wait outside the departures terminal with official fares posted. The fare into town is about €20.

CAR

Iraklio's streets are narrow and chaotic so it's best to drop your vehicle in a car park (about €6 per day) and explore on foot. All the international car-hire companies have branches at the airport. Local outlets line the northern end of 25 Avgoustou.

PHAESTOS ΦΑΙΣΤΟΣ

Phaestos (📳 28920 42315; http://odysseus.culture.gr; Iraklio-Phaestos Rd; adult/concession/under 18yr €8/4/free; ⊘8am-8pm Apr-Oct, 8am-3pm Nov-Mar; 🅿), 63km southwest of Iraklio, is Crete's second-most important Minoan palatial site. More unreconstructed and moody than Knossos, Phaestos (fes-*tos*) is also worth a visit for its stunning views of the surrounding Mesara plain and Mt Psiloritis (2456m; also known as Mt Ida). The smaller site of **Agia Triada** (📳 28920 91564; www.interkriti.org; off Phaestos-Matala Rd; adult/concession/under 18yr €4/2/free; ⊘9am-4pm; 🅿) is 3km west.

TAXI

There are small taxi stands all over town, but the main ones are at the Regional Bus Station, on **Plateia Eleftherias** and at the northern end of 25 Avgoustou. You can also phone for one on 2814 003084.

Knossos ΚΝΩΣΣΟΣ

Crete's most famous historical attraction is the **Palace of Knossos** (📳 2810 231940; http://odysseus.culture.gr; Knossos; adult/concession €15/8, incl Heraklion Archaeological Museum €16/8; ⊘8am-8pm Apr-Aug, to 5pm Sep-Mar; 🅿; 🚌2) Palace of Knossos, the grand capital of Minoan Crete, 5km south of Iraklio. The setting is evocative and the ruins and recreations impressive, incorporating an immense palace, courtyards, private apartments, baths, lively frescoes and more. Excavation of the site started in 1878 with Cretan archaeologist Minos Kalokerinos, and continued from 1900 to 1930 with British archaeologist Sir Arthur Evans, who controversially restored parts of the site.

To beat the crowds and avoid the heat, get to Knossos before 10am when tour buses start arriving, or later in the afternoon when it's cooler and the light is good for photographs. Budget a couple of hours to do the place justice.

Optional guided tours last about 1½ hours and leave from the little kiosk past the ticket booth. Most tours are in English, though other languages are available too. Prices vary according to group numbers (€10 per person in a group with an eight-person minimum). Private tours cost €80 with a maximum of six people.

🛈 Getting There & Away

Getting to Knossos is easy. City bus 2 runs from Iraklio's city centre – from the Regional Bus Station or from outside Hotel Capsis Astoria – every 15 minutes. Tickets cost €1.70 if purchased from a kiosk or vending machine and €2.50 from the bus driver. If driving, from Iraklio or the coastal road there are signs directing you to Knossos. There is free parking across from the souvenir shops, but the spaces fill quickly.

Hania ΧΑΝΙΑ

POP 54,000

Hania (also spelled Chania) is Crete's most evocative city, with its pretty Venetian quarter, criss-crossed by narrow lanes, culminating at a magnificent harbour. Remnants of

SOUTHWEST COAST VILLAGES

Crete's southern coastline at its western end is dotted with remote, attractive little villages that are brilliant spots to take it easy for a few days.

Paleohora Isolated on a peninsula with a sandy beach to the west and a pebbly beach to the east. On summer evenings the main street is closed to traffic and the tavernas move onto the road.

Sougia At the mouth of the **Agia Irini gorge**, Sougia (soo-yah) is a laid-back and refreshingly undeveloped spot with a wide curve of sand-and-pebble beach. The 14.5km (six hours) walk from Paleohora is popular, as is the Agia Irini gorge walk that ends (or starts) in Sougia.

Loutro This tiny village is a particularly picturesque spot, curled around the only natural harbour on the southern coast of Crete. With no vehicle access, the only way in is by boat or on foot. The village beach, great walks, rental kayaks, and boat transfers to excellent Sweetwater Beach fill peaceful days.

Hora Sfakion Renowned in Cretan history for its people's rebellious streak, this is the place where thousands of Allied troops were evacuated by sea after the Battle of Crete. Hora Sfakion's seafront tavernas serve fresh seafood and *Sfakianes pites*, which look like crêpes filled with sweet or savoury local cheese.

Venetian and Turkish architecture abound, with old townhouses now transformed into atmospheric restaurants and boutique hotels. Although all this beauty means the old town is deluged with tourists in summer, it's still a great place to unwind. The Venetian Harbour is super for a stroll, indie boutiques provide good shopping and, with a multitude of creative restaurants, you'll eat very well here. It's an excellent base for exploring nearby idyllic beaches and a spectacular mountainous interior.

◎ Sights

★**Venetian Harbour** HISTORIC SITE
(◎24hr) **FREE** There are few places where Hania's historic charm and grandeur is more palpable than in the old Venetian Harbour. It's lined by pastel-coloured buildings that punctuate a maze of narrow lanes lined with shops and tavernas. The eastern side is dominated by the domed **Mosque of Kioutsouk Hasan** (Mosque of the Janissaries), now an exhibition hall, while a few steps further east, the impressively restored Grand Arsenal houses the **Centre for Mediterranean Architecture**.

★**Hania Archaeological Museum** MUSEUM
(☑28210 90334; http://chaniamuseum.culture.gr; Halidon 28; adult/concession/child €4/2/free; ◎8.30am-8pm Wed-Mon Apr-Oct, to 4pm Wed-Mon Nov-Mar) The setting alone in the beautifully restored 16th-century Venetian Church of San Francisco is reason to visit this fine col-

lection of artefacts from Neolithic to Roman times. Late-Minoan sarcophagi catch the eye as much as a large glass case with an entire herd of clay bulls (used to worship Poseidon). Other standouts include Roman floor mosaics out the back, Hellenistic gold jewellery, clay tablets with Linear A and Linear B script, and a marble sculpture of Roman emperor Hadrian.

★**Maritime Museum of Crete** MUSEUM
(☑28210 91875; www.mar-mus-crete.gr; Akti Koundourioti; adult/concession €3/2; ◎9am-5pm Mon-Sat, 10am-6pm Sun May-Oct, 9am-3.45pm Mon-Sat Nov-Apr) Part of the hulking Venetian-built **Firkas Fortress** (◎8am-2pm Mon-Fri) at the western port entrance, this museum celebrates Crete's nautical tradition with model ships, naval instruments, paintings, photographs, maps and memorabilia. One room is dedicated to historical sea battles, while upstairs there's thorough documentation on the WWII-era Battle of Crete.

☐ Sleeping & Eating

Hania's Venetian quarter brims with chic boutique hotels and family-run atmospheric pensions in restored Venetian buildings. Most hotels have no lift. They tend to be open year-round, but it's a good idea to book ahead for weekends and in summer.

Pension Theresa PENSION **€**
(☑28210 92798; www.pensiontheresa.gr; Angelou 8; d €50-80; ❋⬤) This creaky old Venetian

house with a long and steep winding staircase and antique furniture delivers eight snug rooms with character aplenty. The location is excellent, the ambience rustic and convivial, and the views lovely from the rooftop terrace, plus there's a communal kitchen stocked with basic breakfast items. It's close to plenty of bars and restaurants.

★ **Casa Leone** BOUTIQUE HOTEL €€€
(☎ 28210 76762; www.casa-leone.com; Parodos Theotokopoulou 18; d/ste incl breakfast from €135/190; ❄ ☎) This Venetian residence has been converted into a lovely romantic family-run boutique hotel. The rooms are spacious and well appointed, with drape-canopy beds and sumptuous curtains, though some show ever-so-slight signs of wear and bathrooms are small. Some have balconies overlooking the harbour. The central salon is delightful; it sits above the harbour.

★ **Bougatsa Iordanis** CRETAN €
(☎ 28210 88855; www.iordanis.gr; Apokoronou 24; bougatsa €3; ☉ 6am-2.30pm Mon-Sat, to 1.30pm Sun; ⚱) Locals start salivating at the mere mention of this little bakery-cafe dedicated to making the finest *bougatsa* since 1924. The flaky treat, filled with sweet or savoury cheese, is cooked fresh in enormous slabs and carved up in front of your eyes. Pair it with a coffee and you're set for the morning. There's nothing else on the menu!

Kouzina EPE CRETAN €
(☎ 28210 42391; www.facebook.com/kouzinaepe; Daskalogianni 25; mezhedes €4-9.50; ☉ noon-7.30pm Mon-Sat) This cheery lunch spot gets contemporary designer flair from the concrete floor, country-white tables and groovy lighting. It hands-down wins the area's 'local favourite' by serving great-value, delicious blackboard-listed *mayirefta* (ready-cooked meals) prepared by the owner; you can inspect what you're about to eat in the open kitchen.

To Maridaki SEAFOOD €€
(☎ 28210 08880; www.tomaridaki.gr; Daskalogianni 33; mezhedes €4-14; ☉ noon-midnight Mon-Sat) This modern seafood *mezedhopoleio* (restaurant specialising in mezedhes) is often packed to the gills with chatty locals. Dishes straddle the line between tradition and innovation with to-die-for mussels *saganaki* and crisp and delicious house white wine. The complimentary panna cotta is a worthy finish.

🍷 Drinking & Entertainment

The cafe-bars around the Venetian Harbour are nice places to sit, but charge top euro. For a more local vibe, head to Plateia 1821 in the Splantzia quarter, to the interior streets near Potie, or to alt-flavoured Sarpidona on the eastern end of the harbour.

★ **Fagotto Jazz Bar** LIVE MUSIC
(☎ 28210 71877; Angelou 16; ☉ 8.30am-noon & 9pm-late) Established in 1978, this Hania institution in a Venetian building offers smooth (mostly recorded but occasionally live) jazz, soft rock and blues in a setting brimming with jazz paraphernalia, including a saxophone beer tap. The action picks up after 10pm. It morphs into a cafe too, and serves breakfasts.

ⓘ Getting There & Away

AIR

Hania's **airport** (☎ 28210 83800; www.chania-airport.com) is 14km east of town on the Akrotiri Peninsula, and is served year-round from Athens and Thessaloniki and seasonally from throughout Europe. Carriers include Aegean Airlines and Ryanair.

BOAT

Hania's port is at Souda, 7km southeast of town (and the site of a NATO base). The port is linked to town by bus (€2, or €2.50 if bought aboard) and taxi (around €12). Hania buses meet each boat, as do buses to Rethymno.

Anek Lines (☎ 28210 24000; www.anek.gr; Leoforos Karamanlis 70; ☉ 7.30am-3.30pm Mon-Fri) runs a nightly overnight ferry between Piraeus and Hania (from €38, nine hours). Buy tickets online or at the port; reserve ahead for cars.

BUS

Hania's **KTEL bus station** (☎ info 28210 93052, tickets 28210 93306; http://e-ktel.com; Kelaidi 73-77; ☎) has an information kiosk with helpful staff and timetables, plus a cafeteria, mini-market and left-luggage service. Check the excellent website for the current schedule.

ⓘ Getting Around

Hania town is best navigated on foot, since most of it is pedestrianised.

TO/FROM THE AIRPORT

KTEL (www.e-ktel.com) buses link the airport with central Hania roughly every 30 minutes, with the last departure at around 11pm (€2.50, 25 minutes). Taxis between any place in the city and the airport cost €25.

PREVELI

Head south from the coastal city of **Rethymno** (reth-im-no), itself an architectural treasure, through the **Kourtaliotiko Gorge** towards Crete's southern coast. Here, a smooth ribbon of road soars up to the historic **Moni Preveli** (Μονή Πρεβέλης; ☑28320 31246; www.preveli.org; Koxaron-Moni Preveli Rd; €2.50; ⊙9am-6pm Apr & May, 9am-1pm & 3.30-7pm Jun-Oct; ℗), which cuts an imposing silhouette high above the Libyan sea. Like most Cretan monasteries, it was a centre of resistance during the Turkish occupation and also played a key role in WWII when hiding trapped Allied soldiers from the Nazis until they could escape to Egypt by submarine.

Below stretches **Preveli Beach** (Παραλία Πρέβελη), one of Crete's most celebrated strands. At the mouth of the gorge, where the river Megalopotamos empties into the Libyan Sea, the palm-lined river banks have freshwater pools good for a dip. The beach is backed by rugged cliffs and punctuated by a heart-shaped boulder at the water's edge. A steep path leads down to the beach (10 minutes) from a car park (€2), 1km before Moni Preveli.

BUS

Local buses are operated by **Chania Urban Buses** (☑28210 98115; http://chaniabus.gr). Zone A/B tickets cost €1.20/1.70 if bought from a kiosk or vending machine and €2/2.50 from the driver.

A handily central stop for Souda port, Halepa, Nea Hora and other local destinations is on Giannari, near the *agora* market hall.

CAR & MOTORCYCLE

Major car-hire outlets are at the airport or on Halidon. There's free parking just west of Firkas Fortress and along the waterfront towards Nea Hora beach, or by the eastern edge of the harbour off Kyprou; but avoid areas marked residents-only.

Samaria Gorge
ΦΑΡΑΓΓΙ ΤΗΣ ΣΑΜΑΡΙΑΣ

Hiking the 16km-long **Samaria Gorge** (☑28210 45570; www.samaria.gr; Omalos; adult/child €5/free; ⊙6am-4pm May–mid-Oct) is considered one of Crete's must-do experiences, which is why you'll rarely be without company. Nevertheless, there's an undeniable raw beauty to Samaria, where vertical walls soar up to 500m and are just 3m apart at the narrowest point (150m at the broadest). The hike begins at 1230m at Xyloskalo just south of Omalos and ends in the coastal village of Agia Roumeli. It's especially scenic in April and May when wildflowers brighten the trail.

In peak season, up to 3000 people a day tackle the stony trail, and even in spring and autumn, there's rarely fewer than 1000 hikers. The vast majority arrive on organised coach excursions from the big northern re-sorts. You'll encounter a mix of serious trekkers and less-experienced types attempting the trail in flip-flops.

Samaria is home to the *kri-kri,* a rarely seen endangered wild goat. The gorge was made a national park in 1962 to save the *kri-kri* from extinction. You are unlikely to see these shy animals, which show a marked aversion to hikers, but you might spot golden eagles overhead.

ⓘ Getting There & Away

Most people hike Samaria one way going north–south on an organised day trip from every sizeable town and resort in Crete. Confirm that tour prices include the €5 admission to the gorge or the boat ride from Agia Roumeli to Sougia or Hora Sfakion.

With some planning, it's possible to do the trek on your own. There are early-morning public buses to Omalos from Hania. Check www.e-ktel.com for the seasonally changing schedule. Taxis are another option. At the end of the trail, in Agia Roumeli, ferries go to Sougia or Hora Sfakion; some are met by public buses to Hania.

DODECANESE
ΔΩΔΕΚΑΝΗΣΑ

Strung out along the coast of western Turkey, the 12 main islands of the Dodecanese (*dodeca* means 12) have suffered a turbulent past of invasions and occupations that have endowed them with a fascinating diversity. Conquered successively by the Romans, the Arabs, the Knights of St John, the Turks and the Italians, then liberated from the Germans by British and Greek commandos in

GREECE SAMARIA GORGE

1944, the Dodecanese became part of Greece in 1947. These days, tourists rule.

Rhodes ΡΟΔΟΣ

POP 115,500

By far the largest and historically the most important of the Dodecanese islands, Rhodes (*ro*-dos) abounds in beaches, wooded valleys and ancient history. Whether you arrive in search of buzzing nightlife, languid sun worshipping, diving in crystal-clear waters, or to embark on a culture-vulture journey through past civilisations, it's all here.

Rhodes Town

POP 90,000

Rhodes Town is really two distinct and very different towns. The **Old Town** lies within but utterly apart from the New Town, sealed like a medieval time capsule behind a double ring of high walls and a deep moat. Nowhere else in the Dodecanese can boast so many layers of architectural history, with ruins and relics of the Classical, medieval, Ottoman and Italian eras entangled in a mind-boggling maze of twisting alleys. Strolling its hauntingly pretty cobbled lanes, especially at night, is an experience no traveller should miss. Half the fun is letting yourself get lost. The **New Town**, to the north, boasts upmarket shops and waterfront bars servicing the package crowd, along with the city's best beach, while bistros and bars lurk in the backstreets.

◉ Sights

A wander around Rhodes' Unesco World Heritage-listed Old Town is a must. It is reputedly the world's finest surviving example of medieval fortification, with 12m-thick walls. A mesh of Byzantine, Turkish and Latin architecture, the Old Town is divided into the Kollakio (the Knights' Quarter, where the Knights of St John lived during medieval times), the Hora and the Jewish Quarter. The Knights' Quarter contains most of the medieval historical sights while the Hora, often referred to as the Turkish Quarter, is primarily Rhodes Town's commercial sector with shops and restaurants, thronged by tourists.

The Knights of St John lived in the **Knights' Quarter** in the northern end of the Old Town. The cobbled Avenue of the Knights (Ippoton) is lined with magnificent medieval buildings, the most imposing of which is the **Palace of the Grand Master** (☑ 22410 23359, 22413 65270; €6; ⊘ 8am-8pm Apr-Oct, to 3pm Nov-Mar), which was restored, but never used, as a holiday home for Mussolini. From the palace, explore the **D'Amboise Gate**, the most atmospheric of the fortification gates that takes you across the moat.

The beautiful 15th-century Knights' Hospital, closer to the seafront, now houses the excellent **Archaeological Museum** (☑ 22413 65200; Plateia Mousiou; adult/child €8/free; ⊘ 8am-8pm daily Apr-Oct, to 3pm Tue-Sun Nov-Mar). The splendid building was restored by the Italians and has an impressive collection that includes the ethereal marble statue *Aphrodite of Rhodes*.

The pink-domed **Mosque of Süleyman**, at the top of Sokratous, was built in 1522 to commemorate the Ottoman victory against the knights, then rebuilt in 1808.

🛏 Sleeping & Eating

The most magical sleeping options are all in the Old Town. In summer it's essential to reserve ahead. In winter most budget options close altogether. Be warned, too, that most Old Town hotels are not accessible by taxi, so you'll have to haul your luggage along the narrow, cobbled lanes.

★ **Marco Polo Mansion** BOUTIQUE HOTEL €€
(☑ 22410 25562; www.marcopolomansion.gr; Agiou Fanouriou 40; d incl breakfast €80-160, apt €130-180; ⊘ Apr-Oct; ❄ 🕸 🛜) With its stained-glass windows, dark-wood furniture, wood floors and raised beds, Marco Polo lovingly recreates an Ottoman ambience with verve and style, and is unlike anything else in the Old Town. This former 15th-century pasha's house is like a journey back in time. There are two apartments (with kitchenettes) too. Breakfast is served in the stunning flowering courtyard.

★ **Spirit of the Knights** BOUTIQUE HOTEL €€€
(☑ 22410 39765; www.rhodesluxuryhotel.com; Alexandridou 14; s/d incl breakfast from €160/200; ❄❄ 🛜) This gorgeously finished boutique hotel has six stunning suites dripping with medieval atmosphere. Imagine thick rugs, dark woods, stained-glass windows and a sense of tranquillity. Perfectly isolated down a side street close to the Old Town walls, this fine hotel is a work of passion and vision. There's a library and a fragrant garden courtyard to read in and take breakfast.

★ **Marco Polo Cafe**   MEDITERRANEAN €€

(☑ 22410 25562; www.marcopolomansion.gr; Agiou Fanouriou 40-42; mains €15-25; ⊙ 7-11pm Apr-Oct) 🖉 Don't be surprised if you are asked to taste a wine or culinary creation, a possible new addition to the menu that includes gourmet treats like skewered lamb with rosemary and pistachio, pork loin with figs, or octopus in sea-urchin sauce. It's served up with sincerity and style in a lemon-fragrant garden courtyard. Reserve ahead to ensure you don't miss out.

Nireas   SEAFOOD €€

(☑ 22410 21703; Sofokleous 45-47; mains €10-17; ⊙ noon-late Mar-Oct; ❄) Nireas' status as one of Rhodes' better seafood restaurants owes much to the sheer verve of enthusiastic owner Theo, from Symi – that and the well-prepared food served beneath a vine-shaded canopy outside, in the Jewish Quarter. Be sure to sample the Symi shrimp, salted mackerel and, if you're in the mood, the 'Viagra' salad of small shellfish.

❶ Getting There & Away

AIR

Diagoras Airport (RHO; ☑ 22410 88700; www. rhodes-airport.org) is 16km southwest of Rhodes Town. Taxis cost €25; the local bus €2.50.

Olympic Air (☑ 22410 24571; www.olympicair. com; Ierou Lohou 9) connects the island with Athens and destinations throughout Greece, including several Dodecanese islands.

Sky Express (☑ 28102 23800; www.sky express.gr) flies up to six days a week to Heraklion on Crete (€90, one hour) and once weekly to Samos (€73, 45 minutes).

BOAT

Inter-island ferries use the **Commercial Harbour** (aka Akandia), while catamarans use **Kolana Harbour**. Excursion boats and private yachts are based at Mandraki Harbour.

Two inter-island companies operate from Rhodes Old Town. **Dodekanisos Seaways** (☑ 22410 70590; www.12ne.gr/en; Afstralias 3, Rhodes Town) sails from Kolona Harbour immediately beyond the walls, with daily high-speed catamarans running north up the chain of the Dodecanese. **Blue Star Ferries** (☑ 22410 22461; www. bluestarferries.com; Amerikis 111, Rhodes Town; ⊙ 9am-8pm), operating from the Commercial Harbour, a five-minute taxi from the Old Town, provides slower and less frequent services to several of the same islands, continuing west to Astypalea and Piraeus. It also heads southwest to Karpathos and east to Kastellorizo. Anek

DON'T MISS

LINDOS

Your first glimpse of the ancient and unbelievably pretty town of Lindos is guaranteed to steal your breath away: the towering Acropolis radiant on the cypress-silvered hill, and the sugar-cube houses of the whitewashed town tumbling below it towards the aquamarine bay. Entering the town itself, you'll find yourself in a magical warren of hidden alleys, packed with the ornate houses of long-vanished sea captains that now hold appetising tavernas, effervescent bars and cool cafes. Pick your way past donkeys as you coax your calves up to the Acropolis and one of the finest views in Greece.

Lines (www.anek.gr) runs to Kasos and Crete. Tickets are available at the dock and from travel agents in Rhodes Town.

In addition, daily excursion boats head to Symi from Mandraki Harbour in summer (around €20).

❶ Getting Around

Two bus terminals, a block apart in Rhodes Town, serve half the island each. There is regular transport across the island all week, with fewer services on Saturday and only a few on Sunday. Pick up schedules from the kiosks at either terminal, or from the EOT (Greek National Tourist Organisation; www.visitgreece.gr) office.

Rhodes Town's main **taxi** rank is east of Plateia Rimini, on the northern edge of the Old Town. There are two zones on the island for taxi meters: zone one is Rhodes Town and zone two (for which rates are slightly higher) is everywhere else. Rates double between midnight and 5am. Set taxi fares are posted at the rank.

GREECE KOS

Kos   ΚΩΣ

POP 33,400

Fringed by the finest beaches in the Dodecanese, dwarfed beneath mighty crags, and blessed with lush valleys, Kos is an island of endless treasures. Visitors soon become blasé at sidestepping the millennia-old Corinthian columns that poke through the rampant wildflowers – even in Kos Town, the lively capital, ancient Greek ruins are scattered everywhere you turn, and a mighty medieval castle still watches over the harbour.

◉ Sights & Activities

★ Asklepieion
ARCHAEOLOGICAL SITE

(☑ 22420 28763; adult/child €8/free; ⊙ 8am-7.30pm Apr-Oct, 8am-2.30pm Tue-Sun Nov-Mar) The island's most important ancient site stands on a pine-covered hill 3km southwest of Kos Town, commanding lovely views across towards Turkey. A religious sanctuary devoted to Asclepius, the god of healing, it was also a healing centre and a school of medicine. It was founded in the 3rd century BCE, according to legend by Hippocrates himself, the Kos-born 'father' of modern medicine. He was already dead by then, though, and the training here simply followed his teachings.

◉ Kefalos Bay

Enormous Kefalos Bay, a 12km stretch of high-quality sand, lines the southwest shoreline of Kos. For most of its length the beach itself is continuous, but the main road runs along a crest around 500m inland, so each separate section served by signposted tracks has its own name. Backed by scrubby green hills and lapped by warm water, these are the finest and emptiest beaches on the island. Kamari, at the western extremity of this black-pebbled beach, is a low-key resort with plenty of cafes, tavernas and accommodation, as well as decent water sports.

The most popular stretch of sand is **Paradise Beach**, while the least developed is **Exotic Beach**. **Langada Beach** (which you may also see referred to as Banana Beach) makes a good compromise, but the best of the lot is **Agios Stefanos Beach**, at the far western end. A small beachfront promontory here is topped by a ruined 5th-century basilica, while the absurdly photogenic islet of **Kastri** stands within swimming distance immediately offshore.

Buses to and from Kos Town (€4.40, three to four daily) stop nearby at Kamari Beach.

◉ Kos Town

A handsome harbour community, fronted by a superb medieval castle and somehow squeezed amid a mind-blowing array of ancient ruins from the Greek, Roman and Byzantine eras, Kos Town is the island's capital, main ferry port and only sizeable town. In the lovely cobblestoned Plateia Platanou, you can pay your respects to the **Hippocrates' plane tree**, under which Hippocrates is said to have taught his pupils.

Long, sandy **Kritika Beach**, in easy walking distance of the town centre, is lined with hotels and restaurants. Southeast of the harbour the thin strip of sand known as **Kos Town Beach** is dotted with parasols in summer and offers deep water for swimming.

⌟ Sleeping & Eating

Nowhere else on the island has the culinary diversity of Kos Town: *ouzeries* (places that serve ouzo and light snacks), seafood restaurants, *kafeneia* (coffee houses) and upmarket dining.

★ Hotel Afendoulis
HOTEL €

(☑ 22420 25321; www.afendoulishotel.com; Evripilou 1; s/d/tr from €35/50/60; ⊙ Mar-Nov; ❄ @ 🤏) This family-run hotel has sparkling rooms with TVs, balconies, hairdryers and comfy beds. Downstairs, the open breakfast room and breezy terrace have wrought-iron tables and chairs for reading or enjoying the memorable breakfast that features homemade jams and much more. There may be plusher hotels in Kos, but none with the soul of the Afendoulis, where nothing is too much trouble.

Hotel Sonia
HOTEL €€

(☑ 22420 28798; www.hotelsonia.gr; Irodotou 9; d/tr/f incl breakfast €80/95/140; ❄ 🤏) A block from the waterfront on a peaceful backstreet, this pension offers 14 sparkling rooms with tiled floors, fridges and smart bathrooms. Rooms 4 and 5 have the best sea views; around five rooms have balconies. If you want to, you can have breakfast outside in the rear garden. There's a decent book exchange. Prices are significantly reduced outside high season.

★ Pote Tin Kyriaki
TAVERNA €

(☑ 6930352099; Pisandrou 9; mezhedes 2.50-8; ⊙ 7pm-2am Mon-Sat) Named 'Never on a Sunday' to reflect its opening hours (yes, that's its day of rest), this traditional rough-and-ready *ouzerie* serves delicious specialities such as stuffed zucchini flowers, dolmadhes and steamed mussels. Come late, and you'll be cheek by jowl with the locals.

★ Elia
GREEK €€

(☑ 22420 22133; Appelou Ifestou 27; mains €9-16; ⊙ 12.30pm-late; ❄ 🤏 ✎ 🖶) 🖉 With its traditional wood-beamed ceiling and partly exposed stone walls covered in murals of the gods of the pantheon, Elia is earthy and friendly, while its small menu is fit for a hard-to-please local deity. At the time of research, there were plans to introduce a more Greek fusion and Mediterranean-focused menu. Whatever the plans, they should be good.

ℹ Getting There & Away

AIR

Kos' **airport** (KGS; ☑ 22420 56000; www. kosairportguide.com) is in the middle of the island, 24km southwest of Kos Town. Agean Airlines (https://en.aegeanair.com) and Olympic Air (www.olympicair.com) offer up to four daily flights to Athens (from €100, 55 minutes) and regular flights to Rhodes (€80, 30 minutes) and Leros (€100, 55 minutes). Flights to some other islands, such as Naxos, go via Athens.

BOAT

From the island's main ferry port, in front of the castle in Kos Town, Dodekanisos Seaways (p561) runs catamarans up and down the archipelago, southeast to Rhodes via Nisyros, Tilos, Halki and Symi, and north to Samos, with stops including Kalymnos, Leros and Patmos. Blue Star Ferries (p561) also sails to Rhodes, as well as west to Astypalea and Piraeus.

The **Panagia Spiliani** (Diakomihalis Travel & Shipping Agency; ☑ 22420 31015; www. visitnisyros.gr/en; Mandraki), which also runs day trips from Nisyros to Kos in summer, carries passengers and cars to Nisyros on sailings that leave from Kos Town three to four days a week, and from Kardamena on the other three days.

Eight daily ferries also connect Mastihari with Kalymnos (€4.50, 50 minutes); see www.12ne.gr, www.anekalymnou.gr and www.anemferries.gr.

ℹ Getting Around

TO/FROM THE AIRPORT

The airport is served by several daily buses to and from Kos Town's bus station (€3.20). A taxi to Kos Town costs around €37. Note that Kefalos-bound buses stop at the big roundabout near the airport entrance.

The airport is so far from Kos Town that if you're planning to rent a car anyway, it's worth doing so when you first arrive. All the international chains have airport offices.

BICYCLE

Cycling is very popular, so you'll be tripping over bicycles for hire. Prices range from as little as €5 per day for a boneshaker, up to €20 for a decent mountain bike.

BUS

The island's main **bus station** (☑ 22420 22292; www.ktel-kos.gr; Kleopatras 7; ⊙ Information office 8am-9pm Mon-Sat Apr-Oct, to 3pm Mon-Fri Nov-Mar) is well back from the waterfront in Kos Town. It is the base for KTEL, which has services

to all parts of the island, including the airport and south-coast beaches.

NORTHEASTERN AEGEAN ISLANDS
ΤΑ ΝΗΣΙΑ ΤΟΥ ΒΟΡΕΙΟ ΑΝΑΤΟΛΙΚΟ ΑΙΓΑΙΟΥ

One of Greece's best-kept secrets, these far-flung islands are strewn across the north-eastern corner of the Aegean, closer to Turkey than mainland Greece. They harbour unspoilt scenery, welcoming locals and fascinating independent cultures, and remain relatively calm even when other Greek islands are bulging with tourists at the height of summer.

Samos   ΣΑΜΟΣ
POP 33,000

A lush mountainous island only 3km from Turkey, Samos has a glorious history as the legendary birthplace of Hera, wife and sister of god-of-all-gods Zeus. Samos was an important centre of Hellenic culture, and the mathematician Pythagoras and storyteller Aesop are among its sons. The island has beaches that bake in summer, and a hinterland that is superb for hiking. Spring brings with it pink flamingos, wildflowers, and orchids that the island grows for export, while summer brings throngs of package tourists.

Vathy   Βαθύ Σάμου
POP 1900

The island's capital, Vathy (also called Samos) enjoys a striking setting within the fold of a deep bay, where its curving waterfront is lined with bars, cafes and restaurants. The historical quarter of Ano Vathy, filled with steep, narrow streets and red-tiled, 19th-century, hillside houses, brims with atmosphere.

The first-rate **Archaeological Museum** (☑ 22730 27469; adult/concession €4/2, 1st Sun of month Nov-Mar free; ⊙ 8am-3pm Tue-Sun) is one of the best in the islands and the **Museum of Samos Wines** (☑ 22730 87510, ext 548; www.samoswine.gr; €2; ⊙ 10am-5pm May-Oct; 🅿) **FREE** offers tours and taste-testing with one of the island's best vinters. On the hilltop, the bright rooms at **Pension Dreams** (☑ 22730 24350, 6976425195; Areos 9; d €35-40, tr €45-50; 🅿 ❄ 🛜) have large terraces over a lush garden. Elegant **Ino Village Hotel**

(✆22730 23241; www.inovillagehotel.com; Kalami; d incl breakfast €60-125; P❄🛜🅿) in the hills north of the ferry quay has **Elea Restaurant** with terrace views over town and the harbour.

ITSA Travel, opposite the quay, is helpful with travel enquiries, excursions, accommodation and luggage storage.

ℹ️ Getting Around

The **bus station** (✆22730 27262; www.samospublicbusses.gr; Themistokleous Sofouli) and nearby **taxi rank** (✆22730 28404) serve as a departure point to destinations all around the island.

Pythagorio   Πυθαγόρειο

POP 1330

Little Pythagorio, 11km south of Vathy, is where you'll disembark if you've come by boat from Patmos. It is a small, enticing town with a yacht-lined harbour and a busy, holiday atmosphere, which is overwhelming to some.

The 1034m-long **Evpalinos Tunnel** (✆22730 61400; www.eupalinos-tunnel.gr; adult/child €8/4; ⏱8.40am-2.40pm Tue-Sun Mar-Dec), built in the 6th century BCE, was dug by political prisoners and used as an aqueduct to bring water from Mt Ampelos (1140m).

Heraion (adult/child €6/3; ⏱8am-3pm Tue-Sun), the legendary birthplace of the goddess Hera, is 8km west of Pythagorio. The temple at this World Heritage Site was enormous – four times the size of the Parthenon – though only one column remains.

The impeccable **Pension Despina** (✆22730 61677, 6936930381; A Nikolaou; studio/apt €35/40; ❄🛜) is a relaxing spot with a garden, while **Polyxeni Hotel** (✆22730 61590; www.polyxenihotel.com; s/d incl breakfast from €65/72; ❄🛜) is in the heart of the waterfront action. Tavernas and bars line the waterfront.

ℹ️ Getting There & Away

There are five buses daily to Vathy (25 minutes) and five buses daily to Ireon (15 minutes) for Heraion. A taxi to the airport costs €10 to/from Pythagorio and €25 to/from Vathy. Taxis also ply the route between Pythagorio and Vathy (useful for ferry arrivals and departures) for around €20.

Northern Samos

Northern Samos is a wonderful mix of stunning sea and mountain scenery, marble gravel beaches and quirky villages favoured as a base by local and foreign artisans. The relatively remote, hence uncrowded **Potami Beach** is the area's crown jewel, especially as it is a short trek away from waterfalls and pools of cool crystal water beneath the thick canopy of a broadleaf forest.

ℹ️ Getting There & Around

AIR

Samos' airport is 4km west of Pythagorio. Aegean Airlines (https://en.aegeanair.com), Olympic Air (www.olympicair.com) and Sky Express (www.skyexpress.gr) all serve Samos and have offices at the airport.

Buses run to/from the airport three to four times daily (€2.30). Taxis from the airport cost €25 to Vathy, or €10 to Pythagorio, from where there are local buses to Vathy.

Boat

Samos is home to three ports – Vathy (aka Samos), Pythagorio and Karlovasi.

By Ship Travel (✆22730 62285; www.byshiptravel.gr) has an office in Pythagorio; check ferry and catamaran schedules with them. Alternatively, ask the **port police** (✆22730 61225).

In Karlovasi, **By Ship Travel** (✆22730 35252) will help you with travel tickets, including to Turkey.

Lesvos   ΛΕΣΒΟΣ

POP 86,436

Lesvos, or Mytilini as it is often called, tends to do things in a big way. The third-largest of the Greek islands after Crete and Evia, Lesvos produces half the world's ouzo and is home to over 11 million olive trees. Mountainous yet fertile, the island has world-class local cuisine, and presents excellent hiking and birdwatching opportunities, but remains refreshingly untouched in terms of tourism.

Mytilini Town   Μυτιλήνη

POP 29,650

The capital and main port, Mytilini, is a lively student town with great eating and drinking options, plus eclectic churches and grand 19th-century mansions and museums. It is built between two harbours (north and south) with an imposing fortress on the promontory to the east. All ferries dock at the southern harbour, and most of the town's action is around this waterfront.

SAPPHO, LESBIANS & LESVOS

Sappho, one of Greece's great ancient poets, was born on Lesvos during the 7th century BCE. Most of her work was devoted to love and desire, and the objects of her affection were often female. Because of this, Sappho's name and birthplace have come to be associated with female homosexuality.

These days, Lesvos is visited by many lesbians paying homage to Sappho. The whole island is very gay-friendly, in particular the southwestern beach resort of **Skala Eresou**, which is built over ancient Eresos, where Sappho was born. The village is well set up to cater to lesbian needs and has a **Women Together** festival held annually in September. See www.womensfestival.eu and www.sapphotravel.com for details.

⊙ Sights

★ Teriade Museum   MUSEUM
(☑ 22510 23372; http://museumteriade.gr; Varia; €3; ⊙ 9am-2pm Tue-Sun) Extraordinary. It's worth coming to Lesvos just for this museum and its astonishing collection of paintings by artists including Picasso, Chagall, Miró, Le Corbusier and Matisse. The museum honours the Lesvos-born artist and critic Stratis Eleftheriadis, who brought the work of primitive painter and Lesvos native Theophilos to international attention. Located in Varia, 4km south of Mytilini.

Fortress   FORTRESS
(Kastro; €2; ⊙ 8am-3pm Tue-Sun) Mytilini's imposing early-Byzantine fortress was renovated in the 14th century by Genoese overlord Francisco Gatelouzo, and then the Turks enlarged it again. Flanked by pine trees, it's popular for a stroll, with some good views included.

🛌 Sleeping & Eating

Theofilos Paradise
Boutique Hotel   BOUTIQUE HOTEL €€
(☑ 22510 43300; www.theofilosparadise.gr; Skra 7; d incl breakfast €114, ste €140-160, f €160; P 🕸 ❄ ☎ 🕸) This smartly restored 100-year-old mansion is elegant and good value, with modern amenities and a traditional *hammam*. The 22 swanky rooms (plus two luxe suites) are spread among three adjacent buildings surrounding an inviting courtyard.

Cafe P   CAFE €
(☑ 22510 55594; Samou 2; mains €3-7; ⊙ 11am-3am) This hip back-alley bistro draws a crowd mostly from the university for its unusual and well-priced small plates, eclectic music mix and all-round chilled atmosphere. Sautéed shrimps, served with a draught beer, costs around €8. Cheap daily

special too. It's about 50m in from Plateia Sapphou (Sappho Sq). Look for a sign with a single Greek letter, 'Π'.

ⓘ Getting There & Around

The **airport** (Mitiline Airport; ☑ 22510 38700, 22510 61212; www.mjt-airport.gr/en) is 8km south along the coast.

Mytilini Town is the island's main port, with connections to other northeastern Aegean Islands and Piraeus (Athens).

The **long-distance bus station** (KTEL; ☑ 22510 28873; www.ktel-lesvou.gr; El Venizelou) is beside Irinis Park, near the domed church. Travelling between smaller places often requires changing in Kalloni, which receives one to three buses daily (except Sunday) from Mytilini (€4.90, 45 minutes). Two to three daily buses also go north from Mytilini Town to Mantamados (for Moni Taxiarhon; €4.50, one hour).

Mytilini's **local bus station** (KTEL; ☑ 22510 46436; Pavlou Kountourioti), near Plateia Sapphou, serves in-town destinations and nearby Loutra, Skala Loutron and Tahiarhis.

Molyvos   Μόλυβος
POP 1500

Molyvos, also known as Mithymna, is a well-preserved Ottoman-era town of narrow cobbled lanes and stone houses, with jutting wooden balconies wreathed in flowers, overlooking a sparkling pebble beach below. Its grand 14th-century Byzantine castle, some good nearby beaches and its north-central island location make it a great launch pad from which to explore Lesvos.

⊙ Sights

Byzantine-Genoese Castle   CASTLE
(☑ 22530 71803; €2; ⊙ 8am-3pm Tue-Sun) This handsome 14th-century castle stands guard above Molyvos. A steep climb is repaid by sweeping views over the town and sea – even

across to Turkey, shimmering on the horizon. In summer the castle hosts several festivals.

🛏 Sleeping

Nadia Apartments & Studios　　PENSION €
(📱 22530 71345; www.apartments-molivos.com; studio/apt €43/60; ※ 🐾) On the road to Sikamenea and a short walk from the Old Town, these large motel-style rooms surrounding an expansive shady courtyard are owned by the organised Nadia. Her trademark cakes are complimentary; it's open all year.

ℹ Getting There & Away

At least one to two buses daily connect Molyvos with Mytilini Town (€7.50, 1½ hours).

Around Lesvos

Hire a car and tour the incredible countryside. Southern Lesvos is dominated by **Mt Olympus** (968m), and grove-covered valleys. Visit wonderful mountain village **Agiasos**, with its artisan workshops making everything from handcrafted furniture to pottery. **Plomari** in the far south is the land of ouzo distilleries; tour fascinating **Varvagianni Ouzo Museum** (📱 22520 32741; www.barbayanni-ouzo. com; ⊙ 9am-4pm Mon-Fri Apr-Oct, 10am-2pm Mon-Fri Nov-Mar, by appointment Sat & Sun) **FREE**.

Western Lesvos is known for its **petrified forest** (📱 22510 47033; www.petrifiedforest.gr; entry fee varies; ⊙ park 9am-5pm Jul-Sep, 8.30am-4.30pm Oct-Jun), with petrified wood at least 500,000 years old, and for the gay-friendly town of **Skala Eresou**, the birthplace of Sappho. You can stay over in peaceful **Sigri**, with its broad beaches, to the southwest.

IONIAN ISLANDS
ΤΑ ΕΠΤΑΝΗΣΑ

With their cooler climate, abundant olive and cypress trees, and forested mountains, the Ionians are a lighter, greener variation on the Greek template. Venetian, French and British occupiers have all helped to shape the islands' architecture, culture and (excellent) cuisine, and contributed to the unique feel of Ionian life. The Ionians hold something new for adventure seekers, food lovers, culture vultures and beach bums alike.

Corfu　　　　　ΚΕΡΚΥΡΑ

POP 102,070

Still recognisable as the idyllic refuge where the shipwrecked Odysseus was soothed and sent on his way home, Corfu continues to welcome weary travellers with its lush scenery, bountiful produce and pristine beaches. While certain regions of the island have succumbed to overdevelopment, particularly those close to Corfu Town, Corfu is large enough to make it possible to escape the crowds.

Corfu Town　　　Κέρκυρα

POP 30,000

Imbued with Venetian grace and elegance, historic Corfu Town (also known as Kerkyra) stands halfway down the island's east coast. The name Corfu, meaning 'peaks', refers to its twin hills, each topped by a massive fortress built to withstand Ottoman sieges. Sitting between the two, the Old Town is a tight-packed warren of winding lanes, majestic architecture, high-class museums and no fewer than 39 churches.

⊙ Sights

★ Palaio Frourio　　　　FORTRESS
(Old Fort; 📱 26610 48310; adult/concession €6/3; ⊙ 8am-8pm Apr-Oct, 8.30am-3pm Nov-Mar) The rocky headland that juts east from Corfu Town is topped by the Venetian-built 14th-century Palaio Frourio. Before that, already enclosed within massive stone walls, it cradled the entire Byzantine city. A solitary bridge crosses its seawater moat.

Only parts of this huge site, which also holds later structures from the British era, are accessible to visitors; wander up to the **lighthouse** on the larger of the two hills for superb views.

Palace of St Michael & St George　　PALACE
(adult/concession €6/3; ⊙ 8am-8pm Apr-Oct, 9am-4pm Tue-Sun Nov-Mar) Beyond the northern end of the Spianada, the smart Regency-style Palace of St Michael & St George was built by the British from 1819 onwards, to house the High Commissioner and the Ionian Parliament. It's now home to the prestigious **Corfu Museum of Asian Art** (📱 26610 30443; www.matk.gr; adult/child incl palace entry

€6/3). Two municipal art galleries I (☑26610 48690; www.artcorfu.com; Palace of St Michael & St George; €3; ☉10am-4pm Tue-Sun) and II (free entry) are housed in one annex, and its small formal **gardens** make a pleasant refuge.

Mon Repos Estate
PARK

(Kanoni Peninsula; ☉8am-3pm Tue-Sun) **FREE** This park-like wooded estate 2km around the bay south of the Old Town was the site of Corfu's most important ancient settlement, Palaeopolis. More recently, in 1921, the secluded neoclassical villa that now holds the **Museum of Palaeopolis** (☑26610 41369; Mon Repos, Kanoni Peninsula; adult/concession €4/2; ☉8am-3pm Tue-Sun) was the birthplace of Prince Philip of Greece, who went on to marry Britain's Queen Elizabeth II. Footpaths lead through the woods to ancient ruins, including those of a Doric temple atop a small coastal cliff.

Antivouniotissa Museum
MUSEUM

(Byzantine Museum; ☑26610 38313; www.antiv ouniotissamuseum.gr; off Arseniou; adult/concession €4/2; ☉8am-3pm Tue-Sun) Home to an outstanding collection of Byzantine and post-Byzantine icons and artefacts, the exquisite, timber-roofed **Church of Our Lady of Antivouniotissa** doubles as both church and museum. It stands atop a short, broad stairway that climbs from shore-front Arseniou, and frames views out towards the wooded Vidos island.

🛏 Sleeping & Eating

★Bella Venezia
BOUTIQUE HOTEL €€

(☑26610 46500; www.bellaveneziahotel.com; N Zambeli 4; d incl breakfast from €130; ❋🕸) Enter this neoclassical, historic villa, set in a peaceful central street, and you'll be seduced by its charms. It features an elegant lobby with candelabras, velvet chairs and a piano. The plush, high-ceilinged rooms (some with balconies) have fine city or garden views, while the garden breakfast area is delightful. The cheaper loft rooms have horizontal windows but no outlook.

Siorra Vittoria
BOUTIQUE HOTEL €€€

(☑26610 36300; www.siorravittoria.com; Stefanou Padova 36; d incl breakfast from €205; 🅿❋🕸) Expect luxury and style at this quiet 19th-century Old Town mansion, where restored traditional architecture meets modern amenities; marble bathrooms, crisp linens and genteel service make for a relaxed stay. Breakfast is served either in your room or beneath an ancient magnolia in the peaceful garden.

Pane & Souvlaki
GRILL €

(☑26610 20100; www.panesouvlaki.com; Guilford 77; mains €6-13.50; ☉noon-1am) Arguably the Old Town's best-value budget option (the locals rave), with outdoor tables on the Town Hall square, this quick-fire restaurant does exactly what its name suggests, serving up three skewers of chicken or pork with chunky chips, dipping sauce and warm pitta in individual metal trays. The salads and burgers are good too.

Starenio
BAKERY €

(☑26610 47370; www.facebook.com/stareniobak ery; Guilford 59; sweets & pastries from €2; ☉8am-8pm Mon-Sat) This magical little bakery, dripping with bougainvillea, is where in-the-know locals linger at little tables on the sloping pedestrian street to savour cakes, coffee, pastries, and delicious fresh pies with vegetarian fillings such as mushrooms or nettles.

To Tavernaki tis Marinas
TAVERNA €€

(☑26611 00792; Velissariou 35; mains €8-15; ☉noon-11.30pm) The stone walls, hardwood floors and cheerful staff lift the ambience of this taverna. As locals will tell you, check the daily specials or choose anything from *mousakas* (baked layers of eggplant or zucchini, minced meat and potatoes topped with cheese sauce) or sardines-in-the-oven to steak. Accompany it all with a dram of ouzo or *tsipouro* (distilled spirit similar to raki).

❶ Getting There & Around

Corfu Town is at the centre of an efficient network of local buses, and you can get pretty much anywhere on the island from the **long-distance bus station** (☑26610 28900; https://green buses.gr; Lefkimmis 13) in the New Town.

Most Corfu Town car-rental companies are based along the northern waterfront.

Local blue buses depart from the **local bus station** (☑26610 31595; www.astikok telkerkyras.gr; Plateia G Theotoki) in Corfu Old Town. Journeys cost €1.20 or €1.70. Buy tickets at the booth on Plateia G Theotiki, or on the bus

IONIAN PLEASURES

Paxi (Πάξοι) Paxi lives up to its reputation as one of the Ionians' most idyllic and picturesque islands. At only 10km by 4km it's the smallest of the main holiday islands and makes a fine escape from Corfu's quicker-paced pleasures.

Kefallonia (Κεφαλλονιά) Tranquil cypress- and fir-covered Kefallonia, the largest Ionian island, is breathtakingly beautiful with rugged mountain ranges, rich vineyards, soaring coastal cliffs and golden beaches. Not yet overrun with package tourism, it remains low-key outside resort areas and is a perfect spot for kayaking.

Ithaki (Ιθάκη) Odysseus' long-lost home in Homer's *Odyssey*, Ithaki (ancient Ithaca) remains a verdant, pristine island blessed with cypress-covered hills and beautiful turquoise coves. It's a walkers' paradise, best reached from Kefallonia.

Lefkada (Λευκάδα) Lefkada has some of the best beaches in Greece, if not the world, and an easygoing way of life.

itself. All trips are less than 30 minutes. Service is reduced on weekends.

Around Corfu

To explore the island fully your own transport is best. Much of the coast just north of Corfu Town is overwhelmed with beach resorts, while the south is quieter and the west has a beautiful, if popular, coastline. **The Corfu Trail** (ww.thecorfutrail.com) traverses the island north to south.

North of CorfuTown, in **Kassiopi**, picturesque **Manessis Apartments** (☑ 6973918416; www.manessiskassiopi.com; Kassiopi; 4-person apt €110; ❄️ 🛜) offers water-view apartments. South of Corfu Town, **Achillion Palace** (☑ 26610 56245; www.achillion-corfu.gr; Gastouri; adult/concession €8/6; ⊙8am-8pm Apr-Nov, to 4pm Dec-Mar) pulls 'em in for over-the-top royal bling. Don't miss a dinner at one of the island's best tavernas, **Klimataria** (☑ 26610 71201; www.klimataria-restaurant.gr; Benitses; mains €8-15; ⊙ dinner Mon-Sat, lunch Sun Jun-Sep, lunch Sun mid-Feb–May & Oct-Nov), in nearby **Benitses**.

To gain an aerial view of the gorgeous cypress-backed bays around **Paleokastritsa**, the west coast's main resort, go to the quiet village of **Lakones**. For beautiful rooms just 20m from the pretty beach, check in to **Hotel Zefiros** (☑ 26630 41244; www.zefiroscorfu hotel.gr; Paleokastritsa; d/tr/q from €95/130/155; ❄️ 🛜). Further south good beaches surround tiny **Agios Gordios**.

ⓘ Getting There & Around

AIR

Corfu's **airport** (CFU; ☑ 26610 89600; www. corfu-airport.com) is on the southwestern fringes of Corfu Town, just over 2km southwest of the Old Town.

Aegean Airlines (https://en.aegeanair. com) has direct flights to Athens and European destinations.

Sky Express (www.skyexpress.gr) operates a thrice-weekly island-hopping route to Preveza, Kefallonia and Zakynthos. It flies twice weekly to Thessaloniki.

Taxis between the airport and Corfu Town cost around €12, while local bus 15 runs to both Plateia G Theotoki (Plateia San Rocco) in town and the Neo Limani (New Port) beyond.

BOAT

Ferries depart from **Neo Limani** (New Port), northwest of Corfu Town's Old Town.

Ticket agencies line Ethnikis Antistaseos in Corfu Town, facing the Neo Limani.

SURVIVAL GUIDE

ⓘ Directory A-Z

ACCESSIBLE TRAVEL

Travel Guide to Greece (www.greecetravel. com/handicapped) Links to local articles, resorts and tour groups catering for tourists with physical disabilities.

Sailing Holidays (www.charterayachtingreece. com/dryachting/index.html) Two-day to two-week sailing trips around the Greek islands in fully accessible yachts.

Sirens Resort (☑ 27410 91161; www.disableds -resort.gr; Skalouma) Family-friendly resort with accessible apartments, tours and ramps into the sea.

LEGAL MATTERS

Greek citizens are presumed always to have identification on them and the police presume foreign visitors do too. If you are arrested by police insist on an interpreter (*dierminéas;* say '*the*-lo dhi-ermi-*nea*') and/or a lawyer (*dikigóros;* say '*the*-lo dhi-ki-*go*-ro').

Greek drug laws are among the strictest in Europe. Greek courts make no distinction between possession and pushing. Possession of even a small amount of marijuana is likely to land you in jail.

LGBT+ TRAVELLERS

In a country where the Church still plays a prominent role in shaping society's views on issues such as sexuality, it comes as no surprise that homosexuality is generally frowned upon by many locals – especially outside major cities. While there is no legislation against homosexual activity, it pays to be discreet.

Some areas of Greece are, however, extremely popular destinations for LGBT+ travellers, including Athens, Mykonos and Lesvos (Mytilini).

MONEY

➡ The main credit cards are MasterCard and Visa, both of which are widely accepted.

➡ ATMs are found in most towns and almost all the tourist areas.

➡ Be aware that ATMs on the islands can lose their connection for a day or two at a time, making it impossible to withdraw money. It's useful to have a backup source of money.

➡ Automated foreign-exchange machines are common in major tourist areas.

OPENING HOURS

Opening hours vary throughout the year. High-season opening hours are provided below; hours decrease significantly in the shoulder and low seasons, when many places shut completely. Shops in tourist locations tend to have a licence for longer or alternative operating hours to those listed.

Banks 8.30am–2.30pm Monday to Thursday, 8am–2pm Friday

Restaurants 11am–3pm and 7pm–1am

Cafes 10am–midnight

Bars 8pm–late

Clubs 10pm–4am

Post offices 7.30am–2pm Monday to Friday (rural); 7.30am–8pm Monday to Friday, 7.30am–2pm Saturday (urban)

Shops 8am–2pm Monday, Wednesday and Saturday; 8am–2pm and 5pm–9pm Tuesday, Thursday and Friday

PUBLIC HOLIDAYS

New Year's Day 1 January

Epiphany 6 January

First Sunday in Lent February

Greek Independence Day 25 March

Good Friday 22 April 2022, 14 April 2023

Orthodox Easter Sunday 24 April 2022, 16 April 2023

May Day (Protomagia) 1 May

Whit Monday (Agiou Pnevmatos) 13 June 2022, 5 June 2023

Feast of the Assumption 15 August

Ohi Day 28 October

Christmas Day 25 December

St Stephen's Day 26 December

TELEPHONE

Mobile Phones

There are several mobile service providers in Greece, among which Cosmote, Vodafone and Wind are the best known. Of these three, Cosmote tends to have the best coverage in remote areas. All offer 2G connectivity and pay-as-you-talk services for which you can buy a rechargeable SIM card and have your own Greek mobile number.

TOILETS

➡ Public toilets at transport terminals (bus and train) sometimes have Ottoman/Turkish squat-style toilets.

➡ The Greek plumbing system can't handle toilet paper; the pipes are often too narrow and anything larger than a postage stamp seems to cause a problem. Toilet paper etc must be placed in the small bin provided next to every toilet.

TOURIST INFORMATION

The Greek National Tourist Organisation (www. visitgreece.gr) is known as GNTO abroad and EOT within Greece. The quality of service from office to office varies dramatically; in some you'll get information aplenty and in others you'll be hard-pressed to find anyone behind the desk. EOT offices can be found in major tourist locations. In some regions, such as the Peloponnese, tourist offices are run by the local government/ municipality.

❶ Getting There & Away

AIR

Aegean Airlines (A3; ☑ 801 112 0000; https:// en.aegeanair.com) and its subsidiary, **Olympic Air** (☑ 801 801 0101; www.olympicair.com), have flights between Athens and destinations throughout Europe, as well as to Cairo, İstanbul, Tel Aviv and Toronto.

LAND

Make sure you have all of your visas sorted out before attempting to cross land borders into or out of Greece. Before travelling, also check the status of borders with the relevant embassies.

Border Crossings

Albania Kakavia (60km northwest of Ioannina); Krystallopigi (14km west of Kotas); Mertziani (17km west of Konitsa); Sagiada/Mavromati (28km north of Igoumenitsa)

Bulgaria Exohi (50km north of Drama); Ormenio (41km from Serres); Promahonas (109km northeast of Thessaloniki)

North Macedonia Doïrani (31km north of Kilkis); Evzoni (68km north of Thessaloniki); Niki (16km north of Florina)

Turkey Kastanies (139km northeast of Alexandroupoli); Kipi (43km east of Alexandroupoli)

Train

The railways organisation **OSE** (Organismos Sidirodromon Ellados; ☑ 14511; www.trainose.gr) runs daily trains from Thessaloniki to Sofia, Skopje and Belgrade (with connection services to European cities from Belgrade).

SEA

Check ferry routes and schedules at www.greekferries.gr and www.openseas.gr. If you are travelling on a rail pass, check to see if ferry travel between Italy and Greece is included. Some ferries are free; others give a discount. On some routes you will need to make reservations.

Albania

For Saranda, **Petrakis Lines** (☑ 26610 38690; www.ionian-cruises.com) has daily hydrofoils to Corfu (25 minutes).

Italy

Routes vary so check online.

Ancona Patra (20 hours, three daily, summer)

Bari Patra (15 hours, daily) via Corfu (10 hours) and Keffalonia (14 hours); also to Igoumenitsa (11½ hours, daily)

Brindisi Patra (15 hours, April to early October) via Igoumenitsa (11 hours)

Venice Patra (30 hours, up to 12 weekly, summer) via Corfu (25 hours)

Turkey

Boat services operate between Turkey's Aegean coast and the Greek islands.

🛈 Getting Around

AIR

The vast majority of domestic mainland flights are handled by the country's national carrier Aegean Airlines and its subsidiary, Olympic Air. You'll find offices wherever there are flights, as well as in other major towns. There are also a number of smaller Greek carriers, including Thessaloniki-based airline **Sky Express** (☑ 28102 23800; www.skyexpress.gr).

BICYCLE

Cycling is not popular among Greeks – but it's gaining popularity, plus kudos with tourists. You'll need strong leg muscles to tackle the mountains; or you can stick to some of the flatter coastal routes. Bike lanes are rare to non-existent; helmets are not compulsory. The island of Kos is about the most bicycle-friendly place in Greece.

➡ You can hire bicycles in most tourist places. Prices range from €10 to €15 per day, depending on the type and age of the bike.

➡ Bicycles are carried free on ferries but cannot be taken on the fast ferries (catamarans and the like).

BOAT

Greece has an extensive network of ferries – the only means of reaching many of the islands. Schedules are often subject to delays due to poor weather (note: this is a safety precaution) plus the occasional industrial action, and prices fluctuate regularly. Timetables are not announced until just prior to the season due to competition for route licences. In summer, ferries run regular services between all but the most out-of-the-way destinations; however, services seriously slow down in winter (and in some cases stop completely).

Be flexible. Boats seldom arrive early, but often arrive late. And some don't come at all. You may have the option of 'deck class', which is the cheapest ticket, or 'cabin class' with air-con assigned seats. On larger ferries there are lounges and restaurants for everyone serving fast food or snacks. Tickets can be bought at the dock, but in high season, boats are often full – plan ahead. Check www.openseas.gr or www.gtp.gr for schedules, costs and links to individual boat company websites. The Greek Ships app for smartphones tracks ferries in real time.

BUS

The bus network is comprehensive. All long-distance buses, on the mainland and the islands, are operated by regional collectives known as **KTEL** (www.ktelbus.com). Within towns and cities, different companies run inter-urban services. The fares are fixed by the government; bus travel is reasonably priced. All have good safety records.

CAR & MOTORCYCLE

No one who has travelled on Greece's roads will be surprised to hear that the road-fatality rate is still a lot higher than the EU average. Overtaking is listed as the greatest cause, along with speed. Heart-stopping moments aside, your own car is a great way to explore off the beaten track. The road network has improved enormously in recent

ⓘ SAFE TRAVEL

If you take the usual precautions, Greece is a safe place to travel and you're more likely to suffer from heat exhaustion or sunburn than from any kind of crime.

➡ An unhealthy economy has led to an increase in pickpocketing; always be vigilant in busy bus stations, markets or on crowded streets.

➡ Watch out for adulterated drinks made from cheap illegal imports, and drink spiking, especially at party resorts.

➡ If you have an issue, go first to the *touristikíastynomía* (tourist police) in cities and popular tourist destinations; at least one staff member will speak English.

years. There are regular (if costly) car-ferry services to almost all islands.

Car Hire

➡ All the big multinational companies are represented in Athens; most have branches in major towns and the majority of islands have at least one outlet.

➡ High-season weekly rates with unlimited mileage start at about €280 for the smallest models (eg a Fiat Seicento), dropping to about €150 per week in winter.

➡ On the islands, you can rent a car for the day for around €35 to €60, including all insurance and taxes.

➡ The minimum driving age in Greece is 18 years, but most car-hire firms require you to be at least 21 (or 23 for larger vehicles).

The major car-hire companies in Greece:

Avis (www.avis.gr)

Budget (www.budget.gr)

Europcar (www.europcar.gr)

Moped & Motorcycle Hire

➡ These are available for hire wherever there are tourists to rent them.

➡ You must produce a licence that shows proficiency to ride the category of bike you wish to rent.

➡ Rates start from about €20 per day for a moped or 50cc motorcycle, ranging to €35 per day for a 250cc motorcycle.

Road Rules

➡ Outside built-up areas, unless signed otherwise, traffic on a main road has right of way at intersections. In towns, vehicles coming from the right have right of way. This includes roundabouts – even if you're in the roundabout, you must give way to drivers coming on to the roundabout to your right.

➡ Seatbelts must be worn in front seats, and in back seats if the car is fitted with them.

➡ Children under 12 years of age are not allowed in the front seat.

➡ A blood-alcohol content of 0.05% can incur a fine, while over 0.08% is a criminal offence.

LOCAL TRANSPORT

All the major towns have local buses.

Athens has a good underground system, and Thessaloniki is in the process of constructing one too (expected to open in 2023).

TAXI

Taxis are widely available in Greece, except on very small or remote islands. They are reasonably priced by European standards. City cabs are metered, with rates doubling between midnight and 5am. Additional costs are charged for trips from an airport or a bus, port or train station, as well as for each piece of luggage over 10kg.

TRAIN

Trains are operated by the railways organisation OSE (p570; now an Italian-run company). The railway network is extremely limited with lines closed in recent years in areas such as the Peloponnese. OSE's northern line is the most substantial. Standard-gauge services run from Athens to Dikea in the northeast via Thessaloniki and Alexandroupoli. There are also connections to Florina and the Pelion Peninsula. The Peloponnese network runs only as far as Kiato, with bus services to Plata for ferry connections.

Due to financial instability, prices and schedules are very changeable. When you can, double-check on the OSE website. Information on departures from Athens or Thessaloniki are also available by calling 1440.

Hungary

POP 9.78 MILLION

Best Places to Eat

➔ Borkonyha (p581)

➔ Tiszavirág Restaurant (p591)

➔ Macok Bistro & Wine Bar (p592)

➔ Kispiac (p580)

Best Places to Stay

➔ Aria Hotel Budapest (p580)

➔ Sopronbánfalva Monastery Hotel (p585)

➔ Shantee House (p579)

➔ Hotel Senator Ház (p592)

➔ Club Hotel Füred (p586)

Why Go?

Stunning architecture, vital folk art, thermal spas and Europe's most exciting capital after dark: Hungary is just the place to kick off a European adventure. Lying virtually in the centre of the continent, this land of Franz Liszt and Béla Bartók, paprika-lashed dishes, superb wines and the romantic Danube River continues to enchant visitors. The allure of Budapest, once an imperial city, is immediate at first sight, and it also boasts the region's liveliest nightlife.

Pécs, the warm heart of the south, and Eger, wine capital of the north, also have much to offer travellers, as does the Great Plain, where cowboys ride and cattle roam. And how about lazing in an open-air thermal spa while snow patches glisten around you? That's at Hévíz, at the western edge of Lake Balaton, continental Europe's largest lake and Hungary's 'inland sea', which offers innumerable opportunities for rest and recreation.

When to Go
Budapest

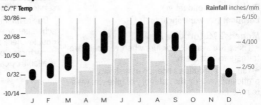

May Spring is in full swing, meaning reliable weather, cool temperatures and flowers.

Jul–Aug Sunny but often hot; decamp to the hills or Lake Balaton (book ahead).

Sep–Oct Blue skies, mild temperatures and grape-harvest festivals.

Entering the Country

Hungary is well connected with frequent air, bus and train services to its seven neighbouring countries and beyond.

ITINERARIES

One Week

Spend at least three days in Budapest (p574), checking out the sights, museums, cafes and 'ruin pubs'. On your fourth day take a day trip to a Danube Bend town such as Szentendre (p584) or Esztergom (p585). Day five can be spent getting a morning train to Pécs (p588) to see Turkish remains, museums and galleries. If you've still got the travel bug, on day six head for Eger (p591), a baroque town set in red-wine country. On your last day recuperate back in one of Budapest's wonderful thermal baths.

Two Weeks

After a week in Budapest and the Danube Bend towns, spend two days exploring the towns and grassy beaches around Lake Balaton (p586). Tihany (p589) is a rambling hillside village set on a protected peninsula, Keszthely (p587) is an old town with a great palace in addition to beaches, and Hévíz (p588) has a thermal lake. On day 10, head to the Great Plain (p589) – Szeged (p590) is a splendid university town on the Tisza River, and Kecskemét (p590) a centre of art nouveau architecture. Finish your trip in Tokaj (p592), home of Hungary's famous sweet wine.

Essential Food & Drink

Traditional Hungarian food is heavy and rich. Meat, sour cream and fat abound, and the omnipresent seasoning is paprika. Things are lightening up, though, with vegetarian, 'New Hungarian' and world cuisines increasingly available.

Gulyás (goulash) Hungary's signature dish, though here it's more like a soup than a stew and made with beef, onions and tomatoes.

Halászlé Highly recommended freshwater fish soup.

Lángos Street food; fried dough topped with cheese and/or *tejföl* (sour cream).

Palacsinta Thin crêpes eaten as a savoury main course or filled with jam, sweet cheese or chocolate sauce for dessert.

Pálinka A strong brandy distilled from all kinds of fruit but especially plums and apricots.

Paprika The omnipresent seasoning in Hungarian cooking, which comes in two varieties: strong (*erős*) and sweet (*édes*).

Pörkölt Paprika-infused stew; closer to what non-Hungarians would call goulash.

Wine Best known are the sweet dessert wine Tokaji Aszú and Egri Bikavér (Eger Bull's Blood), a full-bodied red.

AT A GLANCE

Area 93,030 sq km

Capital Budapest

Country Code ☑ 36

Currency Forint (Ft)

Emergency Ambulance ☑ 104, emergency assistance ☑ 112, fire ☑ 105, police ☑ 107

Language Hungarian

Time Central European Time (GMT/UTC plus one hour)

Visas Not required for citizens of the EU, USA, Canada, Israel, Japan, Australia and New Zealand

Sleeping Price Ranges

The following price ranges refer to a double room with bathroom in high season.

Budapest

€ less than 15,000Ft

€€ 15,000–33,500Ft

€€€ more than 33,500Ft

Provinces

€ less than 9000Ft

€€ 9000–16,500Ft

€€€ more than 16,500Ft

Eating Price Ranges

The following price ranges refer to a main course in the provinces and the cost of a two-course meal with a drink in Budapest.

Budapest

€ less than 3500Ft

€€ 3500–7500Ft

€€€ more than 7500Ft

Provinces

€ less than 2000Ft

€€ 2000–3500Ft

€€€ more than 3500Ft

Hungary Highlights

1 **Budapest** (p574) Losing yourself in the 'ruin pubs', wine bars and nightclubs of Hungary's capital.

2 **Eger** (p591) Understanding the sobering history of Turkish attacks, and sampling the region's famed Bull's Blood wine.

3 **Pécs** (p588) Absorbing the mild climate and historic architecture.

4 **Lake Balaton** (p586) Taking a pleasure cruise across Central Europe's largest body of fresh water.

5 **Hévíz** (p588) Easing your aching muscles year-round in the warm waters of this thermal lake.

6 **Hortobágy National Park** (p591) Watching Hungarian cowboys' shows in the Great Plain.

7 **Szentendre** (p584) Mill about with artists and day trippers at cute town.

BUDAPEST

♪ 1 / POP 1.75 MILLION

The beauty of Hungary's capital is both natural and built. Straddling a gentle curve in the Danube, the city is flanked by the Buda Hills on the west bank and the beginnings of the Great Plain to the east. Architecturally, the city is a treasure trove of baroque, neoclassical, Eclectic and art nouveau buildings. The city is also blessed with an abundance of hot springs, and in recent years Budapest has taken on the role of the region's party town.

◉ Sights & Activities

◉ Buda

Castle Hill (Várhegy) is Buda's biggest tourist draw and a first port of call for any visit to the city. Here, you'll find most of Budapest's remaining medieval buildings, the Royal Palace and sweeping views of Pest across the river. You can walk to Castle Hill up the Király lépcső, the 'Royal Steps' that lead northwest off Clark Ádám tér, or take the **Sikló** (www.bkv.hu; I Szent György tér & Clark Ádám tér; one-way/return adult 1200/1800Ft, child 3-14yr 700/1100Ft; ⊙7.30am-10pm, closed 1st & 3rd Mon of month; ◻16, 105, ◻19, 41), a funicular railway built in 1870 that ascends from Clark Ádám tér to Szent György tér near the Royal Palace.

★ **Royal Palace**   PALACE

(Királyi Palota; Map p576; I Szent György tér; ◻16, 16A, 116) The former Royal Palace has been razed and rebuilt at least half a dozen times over the past seven centuries. Béla IV established a royal residence here in the mid-13th century, and subsequent kings added to the complex. The palace was levelled in the battle to drive out the Turks in 1686; the Habsburgs rebuilt it but spent very little time here. The Royal Palace now contains the **Hungarian National Gallery** (Magyar Nemzeti Galéria; Map p576; ☑1-201 9082; www.mng.hu; Bldgs A-D; adult/concession 1800/900Ft, audio guide 800Ft; ⊙10am-6pm Tue-Sun), the **Castle Museum** (Vármúzeum; Map p576; ☑1-487 8800; www.btm.hu; Bldg E; adult/concession 2400/1200Ft; ⊙10am-6pm Tue-Sun Mar-Oct, to 4pm Tue-Sun Nov-Feb; ◻19, 41), and the **National Széchenyi Library** (Országos Széchenyi Könyvtár, OSZK; Map p576; ☑1-224 3700; www.oszk.hu; Bldg F; ⊙9am-8pm Tue-Sat, stacks to 7pm Tue-Fri, to 5pm Sat).

Matthias Church   CHURCH

(Mátyás templom; Map p576; ☑1-489 0716; www.matyas-templom.hu; I Szentháromság tér 2; adult/concession 1500/1000Ft; ⊙9am-5pm Mon-Fri, 9am-noon Sat, 1-5pm Sun; ◻16, 16A, 116) Parts of Matthias Church date back 500 years, notably the carvings above the southern entrance, but essentially the church (named after King Matthias Corvinus who married Queen Beatrix here in 1474) is a neo-Gothic confection designed by the architect Frigyes Schulek in 1896.

★ **Gellért Baths**   BATHHOUSE

(Gellért Gyógyfürdő; ☑06 30 849 9514, 1-466 6166; www.gellertbath.hu; XI Kelenhegyi út 4, Danubius Hotel Gellért; incl locker/cabin Mon-Fri 5600/6000Ft, Sat & Sun 5800/6200Ft; ⊙6am-8pm; ◻7, 86, ⓂM4 Szent Gellért tér; ◻18, 19, 47, 49) Soaking in the art nouveau Gellért Baths, open to both men and women in mixed sections (bring a swimsuit), has been likened to taking a bath

in a cathedral. The six thermal pools (one outdoors and one a swimming pool) range in temperature from 35°C to 40°C.

Memento Park   HISTORIC SITE

(☑1-424 7500; www.mementopark.hu; XXII Balatoni út & Szabadkai utca; adult/student 1500/1200Ft; ⊙10am-dusk; ◻101B, 101E, 150) Home to more than 40 statues, busts and plaques of Lenin, Marx, Béla Kun and others whose likenesses have ended up on trash heaps elsewhere, Memento Park, 10km southwest of the city centre, is truly a mind-blowing place to visit. Ogle the socialist realism and try to imagine that some of these relics were erected as recently as the late 1980s.

⊙ Margaret Island

Leafy Margaret Island is neither Buda nor Pest, but its shaded walkways, gardens, thermal spa and large swimming complexes offer refuge to the denizens of both sides of the river. The largest and best series of indoor and outdoor pools in the capital is the now year-round **Palatinus Strand** (☑1-340 4500; www.palatinusstrand.hu; XIII Margit-sziget; adult/child May-Sep Mon-Fri 3100/2400Ft, Sat & Sun 3500/2600Ft, Oct-Apr Mon-Fri 2400/2000Ft, Sat & Sun 2800/2300Ft; ⊙8am-8pm; ◻26), with 10 pools (two with thermal water), wave machines, water slides and kids' pools.

⊙ Pest

Andrássy út   ARCHITECTURE

(Map p578; ⓂM1 Opera) Andrássy út starts a short distance northeast of Deák Ferenc tér and stretches for 2.5km, ending at **Heroes' Sq** (Hősök tere; ◻105, ⓂM1 Hősök tere) and the sprawling **City Park** (Városliget; ◻20E, 30, ⓂM1 Hősök tere, Széchenyi fürdő, ◻trolleybus 70, 72, 75, 79). Listed by Unesco as a World Heritage Site in 2002, it is a tree-lined parade of knock-out architecture and is best enjoyed as a long stroll from the **Hungarian State Opera House** (Magyar Állami Operaház; Map p578; ☑06 30 279 5677, 1-332 8197; www.operavisit.hu; VI Andrássy út 22; adult/concession 2490/2200Ft; ⊙tours in English 2pm, 3pm & 4pm; ⓂM1 Opera) out to the park.

★ **Parliament**   HISTORIC BUILDING

(Országház; Map p578; ☑1-441 4904, 1-441 4415; http://latogatokozpont.parlament.hu/en; V Kossuth Lajos tér 1-3; adult/student EU citizen 2400/1200Ft, non-EU citizen 6000/3100Ft; ⊙8am-6pm Apr-Oct, to 4pm Nov-Mar; ⓂM2 Kossuth Lajos tér, ◻2) The Eclectic-style Parliament, designed by Imre

Buda

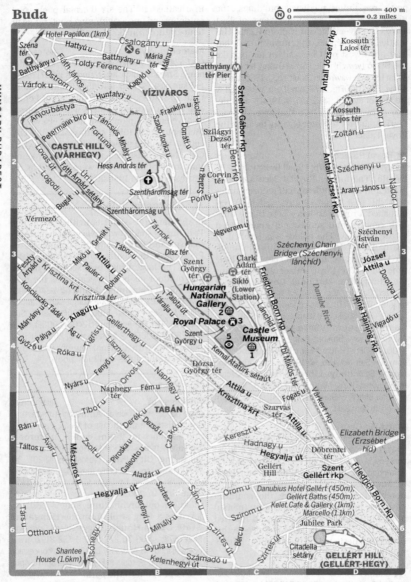

Steindl and completed in 1902, has 691 sumptuously decorated rooms. You'll get to see several of these and other features on a guided tour of the North Wing: the Golden Staircase; the Dome Hall, where the **Crown of St Stephen**, the nation's most important national icon, is on display; the **Grand Staircase** and its wonderful landing; **Loge Hall**; and **Congress Hall**, where the House of Lords of the one-time bicameral assembly sat until 1944.

Basilica of St Stephen   CATHEDRAL
(Szent István Bazilika; Map p578; ☑ 1-338 2151, 06 30 703 6599; www.basilica.hu; V Szent István tér;

Buda

requested donation 200Ft; ⊙9am-7pm Mon-Sat, 7.45am-7pm Sun; ⓂM3 Arany János utca) **FREE** Budapest's neoclassical cathedral is the most sacred Catholic church in all of Hungary and contains its most revered relic: the mummified right hand of the church's patron, King St Stephen. It was built over half a century to 1905. Much of the interruption during construction had to do with a fiasco in 1868 when the dome collapsed during a storm, and the structure had to be demolished and then rebuilt from the ground up. The view from the **dome** (Panoráma kilátó; Map p578; ☑1-269 1849; adult/child 600/400Ft; ⊙10am-6pm Jun-Sep, to 5.30pm Apr, May & Oct, to 4.30pm Nov-Mar) is phenomenal.

House of Terror

MUSEUM

(Terror Háza; Map p578; ☑1-374 2600; www.terror haza.hu; VI Andrássy út 60; adult/concession 3000/1500Ft, audio guide 1500Ft; ⊙10am-6pm Tue-Sun; ⓂM1 Vörösmarty utca, ☒4, 6) The headquarters of the dreaded ÁVH secret police houses the disturbing House of Terror, focusing on the crimes and atrocities of Hungary's fascist and Stalinist regimes in a permanent exhibition called Double Occupation. The years after WWII leading up to the 1956 Uprising get the lion's share of the exhibition space (almost three-dozen spaces on three levels). The reconstructed prison cells in the basement and the Perpetrators' Gallery on the staircase, featuring photographs of the turncoats, spies and torturers, are chilling.

Hungarian National Museum

MUSEUM

(Magyar Nemzeti Múzeum; Map p578; ☑1-327 7773, 1-338 2122; www.hnm.hu; VIII Múzeum körút 14-16; adult/concession/family 1600/800/3600Ft; ⊙10am-6pm Tue-Sun; ⓂM3/4 Kálvin tér, ☒47, 49) The Hungarian National Museum houses the nation's most important collection of historical relics in an impressive neoclassical building, purpose built in 1847. Exhibits on the 1st floor trace the history of the Carpathian Basin from earliest times to the arrival of the Magyars in the 9th century; the ongoing story of the Magyar people resumes on the 2nd floor, from the conquest of the basin to the end of communism.

★ Great Synagogue

SYNAGOGUE

(Nagy Zsinagóga; Map p578; ☑1-413 5584, 1-413 1515; www.greatsynagogue.hu/gallery_syn.html; VII Dohány utca 2; adult/concession/family incl museum 4000/3000/9000Ft; ⊙10am-7.30pm Sun-Thu, to 3.30pm Fri May-Sep, 10am-5.30pm Sun-Thu, to 3.30pm Fri Mar, Apr & Oct, 10am-3.30pm Sun-Thu, to 1.30pm Fri Nov-Feb; ⓂM2 Astoria, ☒47, 49) Budapest's stunning Great Synagogue is the world's largest Jewish house of worship outside New York City. Built in 1859, the synagogue has both Romantic and Moorish architectural elements. Inside, the **Hungarian Jewish Museum & Archives** (Magyar Zsidó Múzeum és Levéltár; Map p578; ☑1-413 5500; www.milev.hu) contains objects relating to both religious and everyday life. On the synagogue's north side, the **Holocaust Tree of Life Memorial** (Map p578; Raoul Wallenberg Memorial Park, opp VII Wesselényi utca 6; ⓂM2 Astoria, ☒47, 49) presides over the mass graves of those murdered by the Nazis.

Széchenyi Baths

BATHHOUSE

(Széchenyi Gyógyfürdő; ☑1-363 3210, 06 30 462 8236; www.szechenyibath.hu; XIV Állatkerti körút 9-11; tickets incl locker/cabin Mon-Fri 5200/5700Ft, Sat & Sun 5400/5900Ft; ⊙6am-10pm; ⓂM1 Széchenyi fürdő) These thermal baths are particularly popular with visitors and have helpful, English-speaking attendants. There are 15 indoor thermal pools (water temperatures up to 40°C) and three outdoor pools, including an activity pool with whirlpool. The baths are open year-round, and it's quite a sight to watch men and women playing chess on floating boards when it's snowing.

György Ráth Museum

MUSEUM

(Ráth György Múzeum; ☑1-416 9601; www.imm. hu/en/contents/262; VI Városligeti fasor 12; adult/ concession 2000/1000Ft; ⊙10am-6pm Tue-Sun; ☒trolleybus 70,78, ⓂM1 Bajza utca) The onetime home of the eponymous first director (1828–1905) of the Museum of Applied Arts has recently opened and is a shrine to art nouveau/Secessionist art, showing items from the museum (now under renovation). Rooms on the first floor include Ráth's fully furnished study and dining and sitting rooms; other galleries on the same floor and

Central Pest

Palatinus
Strand (2.1km);
Földes Józsi Konyhája
(2.4km)

Szent István krt

Váci út

Nyugati
Train Station

TERÉZVÁROS

Heroes' Square (950m);
City Park (1km);
Budapest Info (1.1km);
Széchenyi Baths (1.8km)

Nyugati pu

Balaton u

Stollár Béla u

Falk Miksa u

Honvéd u

Markó u

Vörösmarty u

Szobi u

Szondi u

Eötvös u

Csengery u

Izabella u

Szív u

Bajnok u

Balassi Bálint u

Nagy
Ignác u

Bihari János út

Jókai u

Teréz krt

Aradi u

Vörösmarty u

Association of
Hungarian Rural &
Agrotourism (150m);
György Ráth
Museum (630m)

Parliament
3

Kossuth
Lajos tér

Alkotmány u

Kálmán Imre u

Weiner Leó u

Lovag u

Dessewffy u

Zichy Jenő u

Jókai u

Mozsár u

Andrássy út

7

Vörösmarty u

Garibaldi u

Zoltán u

Steindl Imre u

Széchenyi u

Vécsey u

Perczel M u

Nagysándor J u

LIPÓTVÁROS

Szabadság
tér

Bank u

Podmaniczky
Frigyes tér

Arany
János u

Hajós u

Ó u

16

Oktogon

Jókai tér

Nagymező u

Hegedű u

24

Király u

Erzsébet krt

Kürt u

Vigyázó
Ferenc u

Nádor u

Október 6 u

Sas u

Szent
István tér

5

Révay u

Paulay Ede u

Vasvári
Pál u

Kis Diófa u

Dob u

20

18

Kertész u

Hungarian
State Opera
House
2
4

Opera

ERZSÉBETVÁROS

Zrínyi u

Mérleg u

17

14

10

Bajcsy-
Zsilinszky út

12

Király u

Kazinczy u

Klauzál
tér

Márkus Emília u

19

Akácfa u

13

Centre of Rural
Tourism (400m)

Keleti
(1.2km)

Great
Synagogue

8

6

1

Rákóczi út

21

JÓZSEFVÁROS

11

9

Astoria

Kálvin tér

22

Liberty Bridge
(Szabadság-híd)

Central Pest

◉ **Top Sights**
1 Great Synagogue C5
2 Hungarian State Opera House C3
3 Parliament... A2

◎ **Sights**
4 Andrássy út... C3
5 Basilica of St Stephen B3
  Basilica of St Stephen Dome.........(see 5)
6 Holocaust Tree of Life Memorial........... C5
7 House of Terror D2
8 Hungarian Jewish Museum &
  Archives... C5
9 Hungarian National Museum................. C6

🛏 **Sleeping**
10 Aria Hotel Budapest............................... B4
11 Brody House C6
12 Wombat's C4

🍴 **Eating**
13 Barack & Szilva D4
14 Borkonyha B4
15 Kispiac.. B2
16 Pizzica C3

🍷 **Drinking & Nightlife**
17 DiVino Borbár B4
18 Fogas D4
19 Füge Udvar D4
20 Instant D4
21 Neked Csak Dezső! D5

🎭 **Entertainment**
22 Budapest Music Center C7
23 Gödör Klub... B4
24 Liszt Music Academy D3

🛍 **Shopping**
25 Nagycsarnok C7

---

the one above walk you through the history of the style in France, Austria and Britain as well as Hungary. An absolute gem.

★☆ Festivals & Events

Sziget Festival   MUSIC
(www.szigetfestival.com; ⊘ mid-Aug) One of Europe's biggest and most popular music festivals is held in mid-August on Budapest's Hajógyár (Óbuda) Island, with a plethora of Hungarian and international bands and as many as 500,000 revellers.

Budapest Spring Festival   PERFORMING ARTS
(www.springfestival.hu; ⊘ mid-Apr) The capital's largest and most important cultural festival, with 200 events, takes place over 18 days in mid-April at dozens of venues across the city.

🛏 Sleeping

🛏 Buda

★ Shantee House   HOSTEL €
(☑ 06 30 402 0328, 1-385 8946; www.shantee house.com; XI Takács Menyhért utca 33; beds in yurt €10-13, large/small dm from €11/14, d €32-55; P @ 🛜; 🚃 7, 153, 🚊 19, 49) Budapest's first hostel (then known as the Back-Pack Guesthouse), the Shantee has added two floors to its colourful suburban 'villa' in south Buda. It's all good and the fun (and sleeping bodies in high season) spills out into a lovely back garden, with hammocks, a yurt and a gazebo. Two of the five doubles are en suite.

Hotel Papillon   HOTEL €€
(☑ 1-212 4750; www.hotelpapillon.hu; II Rózsahegy utca 3/b; s/d/tr €49/69/75, apt €84-99; P ✳ 🛜 🌊; 🚃 4, 6) This cosy hotel in Rózsadomb (Rose Hill) has a delightful back garden with a small swimming pool, and some of the 20 rooms have balconies. There are also four apartments available in the same building, one boasting a lovely roof terrace, as well as more apartments (studio to three-bedroom ones) next door. The staff are on the ball and helpful.

Danubius Hotel Gellért   HOTEL €€€
(☑ 1-889 5500; www.danubiushotels.com/our-hotels-budapest/danubius-hotel-gellert; XI Szent Gellért tér 1; s/d/ste from €84/170/268; P ✳ @ 🛜 🌊; M M4 Szent Gellért tér, 🚃 18, 19, 47, 49) Buda's grande dame is a 234-room four-star hotel with loads of character. Completed in 1918, the hotel contains examples of art nouveau, notably the thermal spa's entrance hall and Zsolnay ceramic fountains. Prices depend on which way your room faces and what sort of bathroom it has. Hotel guests get a 30% discount for the thermal bath.

The Gellért was the inspiration (but not the actual film location) for the hotel in Wes Anderson's *The Grand Budapest Hotel* (2014).

🛏 Pest

Brody House   BOUTIQUE HOTEL €€
(Map p578; ☑ 06 70 774 9621, 1-550 7363; www.brody.land; VIII Bródy Sándor utca 10; r €80-120;

✳ @ 🛈; Ⓜ M3 Kálvin tér, 🚌 47, 49) Offering retro chic at its hippest, this one-time residence of the prime minister when parliament sat at No 8 (today's Italian Cultural Centre) has been refurbished but not altered substantially. It features antique furnishings and modern art blending seamlessly in its eight unique guestrooms and three suites dedicated to local and international artists. A minor drawback is the lack of a lift.

Wombat's
HOSTEL €€

(Map p578; 📞 1-883 5065; http://wombats.rocks/; Király utca 20; dm €13-21, d €50-65; 🛈; Ⓜ M1/2/3 Deák Ferenc tér) Directly opposite the Király utca entrance to buzzing Gozsdu udvar, this slick and well-equipped hostel can accommodate a whopping 465 guests in its 120 rooms. Choose from four- to eight-bed dorms or doubles, all of which are en suite. There's a clean, cool design throughout and a large common area set in a colourful glass-roofed atrium.

★ Aria Hotel Budapest
HOTEL €€€

(Map p578; 📞 1-445 4055; www.ariahotelbudapest. com; V Hercegprímás utca 5; d/ste from €220/640; P ✳ 🛈; 🚌 15,115, Ⓜ M1 Bajcsy-Zsilinszky út) Our favourite new hotel in Budapest, the Aria is a music-themed affair built around an old townhouse, with Jazz, Opera, Classical and Pop Wings. Each of the 49 rooms has a balcony and bears the name of a musician or composer – they are also filled with portraits of, books about and CDs by the same. There's a fabulous wellness centre in the basement.

Eating

✕ Buda

Marcello
ITALIAN €

(📞 1-466 6231, 06 30 243 5229; www.marcelloetter em.hu/en; XI Bartók Béla út 40; mains 1600-3600Ft; ⊘ noon-10pm Sun-Wed, to 11pm Thu-Sat; 🚌 19, 47, 49) A long-time favourite with students from the nearby university since it opened almost three decades ago, this family-owned operation just down the road from XI Szent Gellért tér offers reliable Italian fare at affordable prices. The pizzas (1350Ft to 1900Ft) and the salad bar are good value, as is the lasagne (1800Ft), which is legendary in these parts.

★ Csalogány 26
INTERNATIONAL €€

(Map p576; 📞 1-201 7892; www.csalogany26.hu; I Csalogány utca 26; mains 4500-6500Ft; ⊘ noon-

3pm & 7-10pm Tue-Sat; 🚌 11, 39, 111) The decor is spartan at this intimate restaurant, which turns out creative and superb food. Try the roasted lamb with butter squash *lecsó* (a kind of ratatouille, 5000Ft) or other meat-heavy dishes that make the most of local ingredients. An eight-course tasting menu costs 6000Ft (23,000Ft with paired wines) though there is a budget-pleasing three-course set lunch on weekdays for just 3100Ft.

Földes Józsi Konyhája
HUNGARIAN €€

(📞 06 70 500 0222; www.foldesjozsikonyhaja.hu; II Bécsi út 31; mains 2100-4400Ft; ⊘ 11.30am-3.30pm Mon, 11.30am-4pm & 6-10pm Tue-Sun; 🚌 4, 6, 17) In a lovely old townhouse, this rustic place established by former hotel chef Joe Earthy – hey, that's what his name means! – some years back still serves excellent Hungarian homestyle dishes, including veal stew with dumplings (2750Ft) and a good range of *főzelék* (vegetables in a roux, 850Ft). Lovely garden seating in the warmer months too

✕ Pest

Pizzica
PIZZA €

(Map p578; 📞 06 30 993 5481; www.facebook.com/ pizzicapizza; VI Nagymező utca 21; pizza slices 290-490Ft; ⊘ 11am-midnight Mon-Thu, to 3am Fri & Sat; Ⓜ M1 Oktogon) If there is better pizza in Budapest, we don't know where to find it. Owned and operated by Italians Paolo and Enrico, Pizzica serves the real McCoy, with such toppings as potato and sage and mortadella. It's a tiny place but there's more seating in the small art gallery upstairs.

Barack & Szilva
HUNGARIAN €€

(Peach & Plum; Map p578; 📞 1-798 8285, 06 30 258 0965; www.barackesszilva.hu; VII Klauzál utca 13; mains 3300-6200Ft; ⊘ 6pm-midnight Mon-Sat; 🚌 trolleybus 74, Ⓜ M2 Blaha Lujza tér) This is the kind of perfectly formed restaurant that every neighbourhood wishes it could claim. Run by a friendly husband-and-wife team, the 'Peach & Plum' serves high-quality and exceptionally well-prepared Hungarian provincial food in a bistro setting. Try the duck pâté with dried plums (2970Ft) and the red-wine beef *pörkölt* (goulash, 4200Ft). Lovely terrace in summer and live music, too.

Kispiac
HUNGARIAN €€

(Map p578; 📞 1-269 4231, 06 30 430 0142; www. kispiac.eu; V Hold utca 13; mains 2450-4450Ft; ⊘ noon-10pm Mon-Sat; Ⓜ M3 Arany János utca)

This small retro-style restaurant – an absolute favourite – serves seriously Hungarian things like stuffed *csülök* (pig's trotter – and way better than it sounds, 2950Ft), roast *malac* (piglet, 3250Ft) and the ever-popular wild boar spare ribs (3950Ft), as well as an infinite variety of *savanyúság* (pickled vegetables). Perfectly selected wine list and a warm welcome.

★ Borkonyha HUNGARIAN €€€

(Wine Kitchen; Map p578; ☑1-266 0835; www.borkonyha.hu; V Sas utca 3; mains 3450-7950Ft; ⊙noon-4pm & 6pm-midnight Mon-Sat; ⛢15, 115, Ⓜ︎M1 Bajcsy-Zsilinszky út) Chef Ákos Sárközi's approach to Hungarian cuisine at this Michelin-starred restaurant is contemporary, and the menu changes every week or two. Go for the signature foie gras appetiser with apple and celeriac and a glass of sweet Tokaji Aszú wine. If *mangalica* (a special type of Hungarian pork) is on the menu, try it with a glass of dry Furmint.

Drinking & Nightlife

Buda

Kelet Cafe & Gallery CAFE

(Kelet Kávézó és Galéria; ☑06 20 456 5507; www.facebook.com/keletkavezo; XI Bartók Béla út 29; ⊙7.30am-11pm Mon-Fri, 9am-11pm Sat & Sun; Ⓜ︎M4 Móricz Zsigmond körtér, ⛢18, 19, 47, 49) This super-cool cafe moonlights as a used-book exchange on the ground floor and boasts a large, bright gallery with additional seating upstairs. There are foreign newspapers to read and soups (890Ft to 1100Ft), sandwiches (from 1200Ft) and fried rice or curry (1890Ft), should you feel peckish. Try the super hot chocolate.

Oscar American Bar BAR

(Map p576; ☑06 70 700 0222; http://oscarbarbudapest.hu; I Ostrom utca 14; ⊙5pm-midnight Wed, to 4am Thu-Sat; Ⓜ︎M2 Széll Kálmán tér) The decor is cinema-inspired (Hollywood memorabilia on the wood-panelled walls, leather director's chairs) and the beautiful crowd often act like they're on camera. Not to worry: the potent cocktails (950Ft to 2250Ft) – from daiquiris and cosmopolitans to champagne cocktails and mojitos – go down a treat. There's music most nights.

Pest

★ Neked Csak Dezső! CRAFT BEER

(You're only Dezső!; Map p578; ☑06 20 316 0931, 06 30 177 7424; www.nekedcsak.hu; VIII Rákóczi út 29; ⊙9am-midnight Sun-Tue, to 1am Wed, to 2am Thu-Sat) This temple to craft beer, which takes its odd name from the slaughtered pig (note the wooden portrait on the wall) in the iconic Hungarian 1969 film *A Tanú* (The Witness), has 32 taps a-flowing, with such essential local IPAs and lagers as Horizont, Mad Scientist and four of their own brewed in house. Great place to start (or end) an evening.

★ Instant CLUB

(Map p578; ☑06 70 638 5040; www.instant.co.hu; VII Akácfa utca 51; ⊙4pm-6am; ⛢trolleybus 70, 74, 78, ⛢4, 6) Many still love this 'ruin bar' even in its new location as part of the **Fogas** (Map p578; ☑06 70 638 5040; www.fogashaz.hu; VII Akácfa utca 49; ⊙4pm-6am; ☏; ⛢trolleybus 70, 74, 78, ⛢4, 6) stable and so do all our friends. It has a couple of dozen rooms to get lost in, seven bars, seven stages and two gardens with underground DJs and dance parties. It's always heaving.

BUDAPEST'S RUIN PUBS

Ruin pubs (*romkocsmák*) began to appear in the city from the early 2000s, when entrepreneurial freethinkers took over abandoned buildings and turned them into pop-up bars. At first very much a word-of-mouth scene, the ruin bars' popularity grew exponentially, and many have transformed from ramshackle, temporary sites full of flea-market furniture to more slick, year-round fixtures with covered areas to protect patrons from the winter elements. Start with **Füge Udvar** (Map p578; ☑06 20 200 1000; http://legjobbkocsma.hu; VII Klauzál utca 19; ⊙4pm-4am; Ⓜ︎M2 Blaha Lujza tér, ⛢4, 6), an enormous ruin pub with a large covered courtyard (all are on the Pest side).

DiVino Borbár
WINE BAR

(Map p578; ☑ 06 70 935 3980; www.divinoborbar. hu; V Szent István tér 3; ☺ 4pm-midnight Sun-Wed, to 2am Thu-Sat; Ⓜ M1 Bajcsy-Zsilinszky út) Central and always heaving, DiVino is Budapest's most popular wine bar, as the crowds spilling out onto the square in front of the Basilica of St Stephen in the warm weather will attest. Choose from more than 120 wines produced by some three-dozen winemakers, but be careful: those 150mL glasses (from 850Ft) go down quickly. Wine glass deposit is 500Ft.

☆ Entertainment

Handy websites for booking theatre and concert tickets include www.jegymester.hu and www.kulturinfo.hu.

★ Liszt Music Academy
CLASSICAL MUSIC

(Liszt Zeneakadémia; Map p578; ☑ 1-462 4600, box office 1-321 0690; www.zeneakademia.hu; VI Liszt Ferenc tér 8; 1400-19,800Ft; ☺ box office 10am-6pm; Ⓜ M1 Oktogon, ⓠ 4, 6) Performances at Budapest's most important concert hall are usually booked up at least a week in advance, but more expensive (though still affordable) last-minute ones can sometimes be available. It's always worth checking.

Budapest Music Center
CONCERT VENUE

(BMC; Map p578; ☑ 1-216 7894; www.bmc.hu; IX Mátyás utca 8; tickets 1500-3000Ft; ☺ library 9am-4.30pm Mon-Fri; Ⓜ M4 Fővám tér) Hosting a fantastic line-up of mainly Hungarian jazz and classical performances, the Budapest Music Center comprises a classy 350-capacity concert hall (tickets 1500Ft to 3000Ft), the Opus Jazz Club (and restaurant) with concerts at 8pm Tuesday to Saturday, a library and recording studios.

Gödör Klub
LIVE MUSIC

(Map p578; ☑ 06 20 201 3868; www.godorklub.hu; VI Király utca 8-10, Central Passage; ☺ 6pm-2am Mon-Wed, to 4am Thu-Sat; ☏; Ⓜ M1/2/3 Deák Ferenc tér) In the bowels of the Central Passage shopping centre on Király utca, Gödör has maintained its reputation for scheduling an excellent variety of indie, rock, jazz, electronic and experimental music, as well as hosting quality club nights in its spare, industrial space. Exhibitions and movies in summer too.

🛍 Shopping

★ Nagycsarnok
MARKET

(Great Market Hall; Map p578; ☑ 1-366 3300; www. piaconline.hu; IX Vámház körút 1-3; ☺ 6am-5pm Mon, to 6pm Tue-Fri, to 3pm Sat; Ⓜ M4 Fővám tér, ⓠ 47, 49) Completed in 1897, this is Budapest's biggest market, though it has become a tourist magnet since its renovation for the millecentenary celebrations in 1996. Still, plenty of locals come here for fruit, vegetables, deli items, fish and meat. Head up to the 1st floor for Hungarian folk costumes, dolls, painted eggs, embroidered tablecloths, carved hunting knives and other souvenirs.

ℹ Information

ATMs are everywhere in Budapest, including in train and bus stations and at airport terminals. Avoid moneychangers (especially those on V Váci utca) in favour of banks if possible. Arrive about an hour before closing time to ensure the bureau de change desk is still open.

INTERNET ACCESS

Wireless (wi-fi) access is available at all hostels and hotels and very few hotels charge for the service. Many restaurants and bars and most cafes offer wi-fi, usually free to paying customers.

Electric Cafe (☑ 1-781 0098; www.electric cafe.hu; VII Dohány utca 37; per hr 300Ft; ☺ 9am-midnight; ☏; Ⓜ M2 Blaha Lujza tér) Large place with attached laundrette.

Vist@netcafe (☑ 06 70 585 3924; www.vist anetcafe.com; XIII Váci út 6; per hour 500Ft; ☺ 7am-midnight; Ⓜ M3 Nyugati pályaudvar) Another of the very few internet cafes open late.

MEDICAL SERVICES

Foreigners are entitled to first-aid and ambulance services only when they have suffered an accident; follow-up treatment and medicine must be paid for.

FirstMed Centers (☑ 1-224 9090; www. firstmedcenters.com; I Hattyú utca 14, 5th fl; ☺ 8am-8pm Mon-Fri, 9am-3pm Sat, urgent care 24hr; Ⓜ M2 Széll Kálmán tér) Modern private medical clinic with very expensive round-the-clock emergency treatment.

Király Dent (☑ 06 30 971 4812, 1-411 1511; https://kiralydent.hu/en; VI Király utca 14; ☺ 24hr Mon-Sat, 8am-9pm Sun; Ⓜ M1/2/3 Deák Ferenc tér) Reputable dental clinic with three branches in Budapest.

TOURIST INFORMATION

Budapest Info (Map p578; ☑1-576 1401; www.budapestinfo.hu; V Sütő utca 2; ⊙8am-8pm; Ⓜ M1/2/3 Deák Ferenc tér, ☒47, 49) This office near Deák Ferenc tér is about the best single source of information about Budapest; stocks information about attractions, purchasable maps; can be crowded in summer.

❶ Getting There & Away

AIR

Budapest's **Ferenc Liszt International Airport** (BUD; ☑1-296 7000; www.bud.hu/en) has two modern terminals side by side 24km southeast of the city centre.

BUS

All international buses and domestic ones to/from western Hungary and some destinations in the southeast of the country arrive at and depart from **Népliget bus station** (☑1-219 8086, international ticket office 1-219-8040; IX Üllői út 131; ⊙ticket office 6am-6pm Mon-Fri, to 5pm Sat & Sun; Ⓜ M3 Népliget) in Pest. The international ticket office is upstairs. The German line FlixBus (p594) is represented here, as is the Hungarian Volánbusz (p594). There are left-luggage lockers in the basement costing 600/880Ft for a small/large backpack or suitcase for 24 hours. Népliget bus station is on the blue metro M3 (station: Népliget).

Stadion bus station (☑1-220-6227; XIV Hungária körút 48-52; ⊙ticket office 6am-6pm Mon-Fri, to 4pm Sat & Sun; Ⓜ M2 Puskás Ferenc Stadion, ☒1) Generally serves cities and towns in eastern and northeastern Hungary.

Árpád-híd bus station (☑1-412 2597; XIII Árbóc utca 1; Ⓜ M3 Árpád Híd) Located on the Pest side of Árpád Bridge, this is the place to catch buses for the Danube Bend and towns to the northwest of Budapest.

CAR & MOTORCYCLE

All the international car-hire firms, including **Avis** (☑1-318 4240; www.avis.hu; V Arany János utca 26-28; ⊙7am-6pm Mon-Fri, 8am-2pm Sat & Sun; Ⓜ M3 Arany János utca) and **Europcar** (☑1-505 4400; www.europcar.hu; V Erzsébet tér 7-8; ⊙8am-6pm Mon & Fri, to 4.30pm Tue-Thu, to noon Sat; Ⓜ M1/2/3 Deák Ferenc tér), have offices in Budapest, and online rates, particularly if you choose the 'pay now' option, are very reasonable.

TRAIN

MÁV (p595) links up with the European rail network in all directions. Most international trains (and domestic traffic to/from the north and northeast) arrive at **Keleti train station**

(Keleti pályaudvar; ☑06 40 494 949; www.mavcsoport.hu; VIII Kerepesi út 2-6; Ⓜ M2/M4 Keleti pályaudvar).

Trains from some international destinations (eg Romania) and from the Danube Bend and Great Plain generally arrive at **Nyugati train station** (Western Train Station; ☑1-349 4949; VI Nyugati tér). Trains from some destinations in the south, eg Osijek in Croatia and Sarajevo in Bosnia, as well as some trains from Vienna, arrive at **Déli train station** (Déli pályaudvar; ☑1-349 4949; I Krisztina körút 37; Ⓜ M2 Déli pályaudvar).

All three stations are on metro lines.

❶ Getting Around

TO/FROM THE AIRPORT

Minibuses, buses and trains to central Budapest from Ferenc Liszt International Airport run from 4.30am to 11.50pm (700Ft to 2000Ft). Taxis cost from 6000Ft to Pest and 7000Ft to Buda.

PUBLIC TRANSPORT

Public transport operates from 4.30am to between 9am and 11.50pm, depending on the line. After hours some 40 bus lines run along main roads. Tram 6 on the Big Ring Rd operates round the clock.

A single ticket for all forms of transport is 350Ft (60 minutes of uninterrupted travel on the same metro, bus, trolleybus or tram line without transferring/changing); a book of 10 tickets is 3000Ft. A 'transfer ticket' allowing unlimited stations with one change within one hour costs 530Ft. The three-day travel card (4150Ft) or the seven-day pass (4950Ft) make things easier, allowing unlimited travel inside the city limits. The fine for riding without a ticket is 8000Ft on the spot, or 16,000Ft if you pay within 30 days at the **BKK penalty office** (☑1-258 4636; www.bkk.hu; VII Akácfa utca 22; ⊙9am-8pm Mon-Fri; Ⓜ M2 Blaha Lujza tér).

TAXI

Taxis in Budapest are cheap by European standards, and are – at long last – highly regulated, with uniform flagfall (700Ft) and per-kilometre charges (300Ft). Never get into a taxi that does not have a yellow licence plate and an identification badge displayed on the dashboard (as required by law), plus the logo of one of the reputable taxi firms on the outside of the side doors and a table of fares clearly visible on the right-side back door. Reputable taxi firms include **Budapest Taxi** (☑1-777 7777; www.budapesttaxi.hu), **City Taxi** (☑1-211 1111; www.citytaxi.hu), **Fő Taxi** (☑1-222 2222; www.fotaxi.hu) and **Taxi 4** (☑1-444 4444; www.taxi4.hu)

DANUBE BEND & WESTERN TRANSDANUBIA

The Danube Bend is a region of peaks and picturesque river towns to the north of Budapest. The name is quite literal: this is where hills on both banks force the river to turn sharply and flow southward. It is the most beautiful stretch of the Danube along its entire course, and several historical towns vie for visitors' attention. Szentendre has its roots in Serbian culture and became an important centre for art early in the 20th century. Around the bend is tiny Visegrád, Hungary's 'Camelot' in the 15th century and home to Renaissance-era palace ruins and an enchanting hilltop fortress. Esztergom, once the pope's 'eyes and ears' in Hungary, is now a sleepy town with the nation's biggest cathedral. The Danube meanders towards Western Transdanubia where you'll find Sopron, a historic city that's been around since the Roman Empire.

ⓘ Getting There & Away

BUS & TRAIN

Regular buses serve towns on the west bank of the Danube, but trains only go as far as Szentendre and (on a separate line) Esztergom. For Visegrád, you can take one of the regular trains from Budapest to the opposite bank of the river and then take a ferry across (sailings are linked to train arrivals).

BOAT

Regular **Mahart PassNave** (Map p578; ☑1-484 4013, 1-484 4013; www.mahartpassnave.hu; V Belgrád rakpart; ☺8am-5pm Mon-Fri) boats run to and from Budapest in season. From May to August, a boat departs Pest's Vigadó tér at 9am (from Batthyány tér in Buda 10 minutes later) from Tuesday to Sunday bound for Szentendre (one way/return 2310/3470Ft, 1½ hours) and Visegrád (2890/4330Ft, 3½ hours) before carrying on to Esztergom (3470/5200Ft, 5½ hours). It returns from Esztergom at 4pm, Visegrád at 5.40pm and Szentendre at 7pm, reaching Budapest at 8pm. The service is reduced to Saturday-only in April and September.

In addition, there is a boat to Szentendre (only) at 10.30am daily in July and August, from Tuesday to Sunday in May, June, September and October, and on Saturday in April. It returns from Szentendre at 5pm. A 2pm sailing to Szentendre departs Tuesday to Sunday in July and August, returning from Szentendre at 7pm

Hydrofoils travel from Budapest to Visegrád (one way/return 4300/6500Ft, one hour) and Esztergom (5300/8000Ft, 1½ hours) Tuesday to Sunday from May to September; boats leave at 10am and return at 5.30pm from Esztergom and 6pm from Visegrád.

Szentendre

☑26 / POP 26,450

Szentendre ('St Andrew' in Hungarian) is the southern gateway to the Danube Bend but has none of the imperial history or drama of Visegrád or Esztergom. As an art colony turned lucrative tourist centre, Szentendre strikes many travellers as a little too 'cute', and it is rammed with visitors most of the year. Still, it's an easy train trip from the capital 19km away, and the town's dozens of art museums, galleries and churches are well worth the trip. Just try to avoid visiting on weekends in summer.

The charming old centre around **Fő tér** (Main Square) (Main Square) has plentiful cafes and galleries, as well as beautiful baroque Serbian Orthodox churches. Meanwhile the **Art Mill** (Művészet Malom; ☑06 20 779 6657; www.muzeumicentrum.hu/en/artmill; Bogdányi utca 32; adult/6-26yr 1400/700Ft; ☺10am-6pm) exhibits cutting-edge art installations across three floors.

ⓘ Information

Tourinform (☑26-317 965; https://iranyszen tendre.hu/en; Dumtsa Jenő utca 22; ☺10am-6pm), on the way to/from the train station, has lots of information about Szentendre and the Danube Bend.

ⓘ Getting There & Away

The easiest way to reach Szentendre from Budapest is to catch the H5 HÉV suburban train from Batthyány tér in Buda (660Ft, 40 minutes, every 10 to 20 minutes). In addition, there are efficient ferry services to Szentendre from Budapest between April and October

---

Visegrád

☑26 / POP 1840

Soporific, leafy Visegrád (from the Slavic words for 'high castle') has the most history of the main towns on the Danube Bend. While much of it has crumbled to dust over the centuries, reminders of its grand past can still be seen in its mighty 13th-century **Citadel** (Fellegvár; ☑26-398 101; https://park-erdo.hu/turizmus/latnivalok/visegradi-fellegvar; Várhegy; adult/concession 1700/850Ft; ☺9am-5pm mid-Mar–Apr & Oct, to 6pm May-Sep, to 4pm

Nov–mid-Mar), which offers spectacular views from high above a curve in the river, and its partially Renaissance **Royal Palace** (Mátyás Király Múzeum, Királyi Palota; ☑ 26-597 010; http://visegradmuzeum.hu/en/palota2; Fő utca 23; adult/concession 1100/550Ft; ☉ 9am-5pm Tue-Sun Mar-Oct, 10am-4pm Tue-Sun Nov-Feb), seat of power during Visegrád's golden age in the 15th century under the reign of King Matthias Corvinus and to whom the museum there is dedicated.

ⓘ Information

Visegrád Info (☑ 26-397 188; www.visitvisegrad.hu; Dunaparti út 1; ☉ 10am-6pm daily Apr-Oct, to 4pm Tue-Sun Nov-Mar) is a good source of local information.

ⓘ Getting There & Away

Visegrád buses are very frequent to/from Budapest's Újpest-Városkapu train station (745Ft, 1¼ hours, 39km). You can also reach Szentendre (465Ft, 45 minutes, 24km, hourly) and Esztergom (465Ft, 45 minutes, 25km). Regular ferry services link Visegrád with Budapest between April and September.

Esztergom

☑ 33 / POP 27,850

Esztergom's massive basilica, sitting high above the town and Danube River, is an incredible sight, rising out of what seems like nowhere in a rural stretch of country. But Esztergom's attraction goes deeper than that domed structure: the nation's first king, St Stephen, was born here in 975. It was a royal seat from the late 10th to the mid-13th centuries and has been the seat of Roman Catholicism in Hungary for more than a thousand years. In fact, **Esztergom Basilica** (Esztergomi Bazilika; ☑ 33-402 354; www.bazilika-esztergom.hu; Szent István tér 1; basilica free, crypt 300Ft, dome adult/concession 700/500Ft, treasury adult/concession 900/450Ft, combination ticket 1500/1000Ft; ☉ 8am-6pm, crypt & treasury 9am-5pm, dome 9am-6pm) is Hungary's largest church. At the southern end of the hill is the extensive **Castle Museum** (Vármúzeum; ☑ 33-415 986; www.mnmvarmuzeuma.hu; Szent István tér 1; adult/concession 1600/800Ft; ☉ 10am-6pm Tue-Sun Apr-Oct, to 4pm Tue-Sun Nov-Mar), housed in the former Royal Palace built during Esztergom's golden age. Below Castle Hill in the former Bishop's Palace, the **Christian Museum** (Keresztény Múzeum; ☑ 33-413 880; www.christianmuseum.hu; Mindszenty hercegprímás

tere 2; adult/concession 900/450Ft; ☉ 10am-5pm Wed-Sun Mar-Dec) contains the finest collection of medieval religious art in Hungary. A picturesque town, packed with historic attractions, Esztergom makes a great day trip from Budapest and amply rewards those who linger longer.

ⓘ Information

A private travel agency in the centre called **Cathedralis Tours** (☑ 33-520 260; Bajcsy-Zsilinszky utca 26; ☉ 9am-5pm Mon-Fri, to noon Sat) is the only place in town for information.

ⓘ Getting There & Away

Frequent buses run to/from Budapest (1120Ft, 1¼ hours), Visegrád (465Ft, 45 minutes) and Szentendre (930Ft, 1½ hours). Trains depart from Budapest's Nyugati train station (1120Ft, one hour) half-hourly. Ferries travel regularly from Budapest to Esztergom between April and September.

Sopron

☑ 99 / POP 62,450

Sopron is the most beautiful town in western Hungary. Its medieval Inner Town (Belváros) is intact and its cobbled streets are a pleasure to wander. And if that weren't enough, it's also famous for its wine, surrounded as it is by flourishing vineyards.

◎ Sights

★ **Storno House & Collection** MUSEUM
(Storno-ház és Gyűjtemény; ☑ 99-311 327; www.muzeum.sopron.hu; Fő tér 8; adult/concession Storno House 1000/500Ft, Boundless Story 700/350Ft; ☉ 10am-6pm Tue-Sun) Built in 1417, Storno House has an illustrious history: King Matthias stayed here in 1482–83, and Franz Liszt played a number of concerts here in the mid-19th century. Later it was taken over by the Swiss-Italian family of Ferenc Storno, chimney sweep turned art restorer, whose re-carving of Romanesque and Gothic monuments throughout Transdanubia remains controversial. Don't miss the **Storno Collection**, the family's treasure trove. The **Boundless Story** exhibition of local history is also worth a peek.

🛏 Sleeping

★ **Sopronbánfalva Monastery Hotel** MONASTERY €€€
(Sopronbánfalvi Kolostor Hotel; ☑ 06 70 684 9117, 99-505 895; www.banfalvakolostor.hu;

Kolostorhegy utca 1; s/d/ste €84/128/174; P 🤶) Having worn many hats over the centuries – Carmelite convent, home for coal miners, mental hospital – this 15th-century monastery has now been sensitively restored as a beautiful 20-room hotel/retreat. The vaulted singles and light-filled doubles look out on to the forest. Upstairs there's an art gallery and a tranquil common space, the library. The **Refektórium** (📞 99-505 895; www.banfalvakolostor.hu; Kolostorhegy utca 2, Sopronbánfalva Monastery Hotel; mains 3800-7600Ft; ⏱ 6-9pm daily, noon-3pm Sat & Sun; 📋) restaurant serves among the best meals in Sopron.

Erhardt Pension　　　GUESTHOUSE €€€
(📞 99-506 711; www.erhardts.hu; Balfi út 10; s/d from €68/83; P ✳ 🤶) This great central spot comprises nine compact and homey rooms decked out in soothing creams and browns, complete with super-comfy mattresses, and one of the best **restaurants** (📞 99-506 711; www.erhardts.hu; Balfi út 10; mains 2990-4990Ft; ⏱ 11.30am-10pm Sun-Thu, to 11pm Fri & Sat; 📋) in town. Three newer and more up-to-date rooms are in a separate building on nearby Halász utca.

🍷 Drinking

TasteVino Borbár & Vinotéka　　WINE BAR
(📞 06 30 519 8285; www.tastevino.hu; Várkerület 5; ⏱ noon-midnight Tue-Sat) This is a vaulted bar and wine shop all in one, where you can sample the best that Sopron's wineries have to offer and also purchase your tipples of choice.

ℹ Information

Tourinform (📞 99-951 975; http://turizmus. sopron.hu; Szent György utca 2; ⏱ 10am-6pm) in the Inner Town has information on Sopron and surrounds, including local vintners.

ℹ Getting There & Away

BUS

There are direct buses to Esztergom (3410Ft, four hours, four daily), Keszthely (2520Ft, 3¼ hours, two daily) and Balatonfüred (3130Ft, four hours, two daily).

TRAIN

Direct services from the **train station** (Állomás utca), a 10-minute walk from the heart of Sopron, run to Budapest's Keleti train station (4735Ft, 2½ hours, six daily) and Vienna's Hauptbahnhof and Meidling (5000Ft, 1½ hours, three daily).

LAKE BALATON & SOUTHERN TRANSDANUBIA

Extending roughly 80km like a skinny, lopsided paprika, at first glance Lake Balaton seems to simply be a happy, sunny expanse of opaque tourmaline-coloured water in which to play. But step beyond the beaches of Europe's biggest and shallowest body of water and you'll encounter vine-filled forested hills, historic towns and a wild peninsula jutting out 4km, nearly cutting the lake in half.

Then there's Southern Transdanubia, where whitewashed farmhouses with thatched roofs dominate a countryside that hasn't changed in centuries. Anchoring its centre is one of Hungary's most alluring cities, Pécs, where a Mediterranean feel permeates streets filled with relics of Hungary's Ottoman past and a head-spinning number of exceptional museums.

Balatonfüred
📞 87 / POP 13,140

Balatonfüred is not only the oldest resort on Lake Balaton's northern shore, it's also the most fashionable. In days gone by the wealthy and famous built large villas on its tree-lined streets, and their architectural legacy can still be seen today. Yes, it's highly touristy, but it's an excellent place to base yourself on the lake, with its endless lodging and dining options, and a superb tree-lined promenade along the shore where everyone goes for their pre- or postprandial dinner strolls. The town also has the most stylish marina on the lake and is known for the thermal waters of its world-famous heart hospital.

🛏 Sleeping

Aqua Haz　　　　　　　PENSION €€
(Aqua House; 📞 87-342 813; www.aquahaz.hu; Garay utca 2; s/d/tr 9500/11,500/15,000Ft; P 🤶) This family-run pension, in a pale-yellow three-storey house, is conveniently located between the lake and the train and bus stations. Most of the 21 rooms feature bright balconies, and free bikes are available for tooling around town. Excellent breakfast (1100Ft).

⭐ **Club Hotel Füred**　　　　RESORT €€€
(📞 06 70 458 1242, 87-482 411; www.clubhotel fured.hu; Anna sétány 1-3; r/ste from €70/185; P ✳ 🤶) This stunner of a resort hotel, right on the lake, about 1.5km from the town

centre, has 43 rooms and suites in several buildings spread over 2.5 hectares of parkland and lush gardens. There's an excellent spa centre with sauna, steam room and pool, but the real delight is the private beach at the end of the garden. Stellar service.

✗ Eating & Drinking

★ **Bistro Sparhelt**   BISTRO €€€
(✆87-950 406, 06 70 639 9944; http://bistro sparhelt.hu; Szent István tér 7; mains 3190-6990Ft; ⊙11.30am-10pm Wed-Sun; ✐) Head inland from the lake to the town hall for a rare gastronomic treat. Chef Balázs Elek presides over a sleek, minimalist restaurant with a succinct menu that changes monthly, its dishes dictated by whatever is market-fresh. Expect to be treated to the likes of duck liver with crab and wakame or leg of lamb with plum and sweet potatoes. Superb stuff.

Baricska Csárda   HUNGARIAN €€€
(✆87-950 738; www.baricska.hu; Baricska dűlő; mains 3100-5500Ft; ⊙noon-10pm Thu-Mon, 5-10pm Wed) If you are going to eat typical Hungarian fare, let it be here, under the trellises covered in creeping vines and among the vineyards. The setting is particularly magical in the evenings, and the dishes – paprika catfish with cottage cheese noodles, smoked duck breast with red cabbage and other Hungarian classics – are beautifully presented. There's an extensive list of Balaton wines.

Kredenc Borbisztró   WINE BAR
(✆06 20 518 9960, 87-343 229; www.kredencbor bisztro.hu; Blaha Lujza utca 7; ⊙9am-midnight) This family-run retro-style wine bar and bistro is a peaceful retreat near the lakefront. The menu is stacked with local wines, and the owner is often on hand to recommend the best tipple according to your tastes. The wine bar sells bottles of everything they serve plus an extensive selection of regional wines. Weekend DJ sets and live music.

❶ Information

Tourinform (✆87-580 480; www.balaton fured.info.hu; Blaha Lujza utca 5; ⊙9am-7pm Mon-Fri, to 5pm Sat, 10am-4pm Sun Jun-Aug, 9am-5pm Mon-Fri, 9am-3pm Sat Sep-May) In the centre has scads of information on Balatonfüred and other towns along the lake.

❶ Getting There & Away

BOAT
In July and August up to seven daily **Balaton Shipping Company** (Balatoni Hajózási Rt;

84-310 050; www.balatonihajozas.hu; Krúdy sétány 2, Siófok) ferries link Balatonfüred with Siófok and Tihany (adult/child 1400/700Ft). From April to June and September to late October, at least four daily ferries depart for those same ports.

BUS & TRAIN
Buses reach Tihany (310Ft, 30 minutes, 14 daily) and Keszthely (1300Ft, 1½ hours, eight daily). For Budapest buses (2520, three hours) and trains (2725Ft, two hours) are much of a muchness but bus departures are more frequent (up to nine daily) against the three trains.

Keszthely

✆83 / POP 19,390

Keszthely is a town of gently crumbling grand town houses perched at the western edge of Lake Balaton. It's hands down one of the loveliest spots to stay in the area, and far removed from the tourist hot spots on the lake. You can take a dip in small, shallow beaches by day, absorb the lively yet relaxed ambience by night, and get a dose of culture by popping into the town's handful of museums and admiring its historical buildings. Whatever you do, don't miss the Festetics Palace, a lavish baroque home fit for royalty.

◉ Sights

★ **Festetics Palace**   PALACE
(Festetics Kastély; ✆06 30 556 7719, 83-314 194; www.helikonkastely.hu; Kastély utca 1; Palace & Coach Museum adult/6-26yr 2500/1250Ft; ⊙9am-6pm Jul & Aug, to 5pm May, Jun & Sep, to 5pm Tue-Sun Oct-Apr) The glimmering white, 100-room Festetics Palace was begun in 1745, and the two wings were extended out from the original building 150 years later. Some 18 splendid rooms in the baroque south wing are now part of the **Helikon Palace Museum**, as is the palace's greatest treasure, the **Helikon Library**, with its 90,000 volumes and splendid carved furniture.

Helikon Beach   BEACH
(Helikon Strand; adult/concession 500/350Ft; ⊙8am-7pm May–mid-Sep) Reedy Helikon Beach, north of City Beach, is good for swimming and sunbathing. It has a unique view of both the north and south shores of the lake.

🛏 Sleeping & Eating

★ **Ilona Kis Kastély Panzió**   PENSION €€
(Ilona Little Castle Pansion; ✆83-312 514; www. balaton-airport.com; Móra Ferenc utca 22; s/d/apt incl breakfast 9500/12,500/17,500Ft; 🅿❄🕿)

HOT SPRINGS OF HÉVÍZ

Hévíz (population 4630), just 8km northwest of Keszthely, is the most famous of Hungary's spa towns because of the **Gyógy-tó** (Hévíz Thermal Lake; 📞 83-342 830, 06 30 959 1002; www.spaheviz.hu; Dr Schulhof Vilmos sétány 1; per 3hr/4hr/day 3000/3700/5200Ft; ⏰ 8am-7pm Jun-Aug, 9am-6pm May & Sep, to 5.30pm Apr & Oct, to 5pm Nov-Mar) – Europe's largest 'thermal lake'. A dip into this water-lily-filled lake is essential for anyone visiting the Lake Balaton region.

Fed by 80 million litres of thermal water daily, the lake is an astonishing sight. The temperature averages 33°C and never drops below 22°C in winter, allowing bathing even when there's ice on the fir trees of the surrounding Park Wood.

Buses link Hévíz with Keszthely (250Ft, 20 minutes) every half-hour.

With its pointed turrets, this delightful pension resembles a miniature castle. The five rooms might be on the compact side, but some have balconies, while the apartments are positively spacious. A generous, varied breakfast is included.

★ **Pura Vida Port**   MEDITERRANEAN €€€
(📞 06 30 860 4629; www.facebook.com/puravida portkeszthely; Vitorlás-kikötő; mains 3690-5690Ft; ⏰ 11am-10pm) On a breezy terrace by the marina, this new Mediterranean restaurant serves up mains such as osso bucco and confit leg of lamb but keeps holidaymakers happy with less complicated fare such as pizzas (1700Ft to 3200Ft) and burgers (2990Ft to 3490Ft). The dishes are well executed, and the staff is amiable and prompt.

ℹ Information

Tourinform (📞 83-314 144; www.keszthely.hu; Kossuth Lajos utca 30; ⏰ 9am-7pm mid-Jun–Aug, 9am-5pm Mon-Fri, to 1pm Sat Sep–mid-Jun) on the main street is an excellent source of information on Keszthely and the west Balaton area. Lots of brochures, plus bicycles for rent (2200Ft per day).

ℹ Getting There & Away

BUS

Buses link Keszthely with Hévíz (250Ft, 20 minutes, half-hourly), Budapest (3410Ft, three to four hours, up to 12 daily) and Pécs (3130Ft, 3¼ hours, up to six daily).

TRAIN

Keszthely has train links to Balatonfüred (1490Ft, two hours, 10 daily) with a change at Tapolca, and to Budapest (3705Ft, 3¼ hours, nine daily). Budapest trains mostly arrive at Déli station, but occasionally go to Budapest Keleti.

Pécs

📞 72 / POP 144,190

Blessed with a mild climate, an illustrious past and a number of fine museums and monuments, Pécs is one of the most pleasant and interesting cities to visit in Hungary. With its handful of universities, the nearby Mecsek Hills and the lively nightlife, it's second only to Budapest on many travellers' Hungarian bucket lists.

◉ Sights

★ **Zsolnay**
Cultural Quarter   NOTABLE BUILDING
(Zsollnay Kulturális Negyed; 📞 72-500 350; www.zskn.hu; 48hr combination ticket adult/concession/family 4990/3000/10,000Ft; ⏰ 9am-6pm daily Apr-Oct, to 5pm Tue-Sun Nov-Mar) The sprawling Zsolnay Cultural Quarter, built on the grounds of the original Zsolnay porcelain factory, is divided into four sections (craftspeople, family and children, creative, and university) and is a lovely place to stroll around. Highlights include the **Gyugi Collection** of 700 Zsolnay pieces, the street of artisans' shops, the exhibition tracing the history of the Zsolnay factory and its founding family, and the still-functioning **Hamerli Glove Manufactury** dating from 1861.

Mosque Church   CHURCH
(Mecset templom; 📞 06 30 373 8900; https://pecsi egyhazmegye.hu/en/attractions/mosque-of-pasha-gazi-kassim; Hunyadi János út 4; adult/concession 1800/900Ft; ⏰ 9am-5pm Mon-Sat, 1-5pm Sun) The largest building extant from the time of the Turkish occupation, the former Pasha Gazi Kassim Mosque (now the Inner Town Parish Church) dominates the main square in Pécs. The Ottomans built the square-based mosque in the mid-16th century with the stones of the ruined Gothic Church of St Bertalan. The Catholics moved back in the early 18th century. The Islamic elements include windows with distinctive Turkish ogee arches, a *mihrab* (prayer niche), faded verses from the Koran and lovely geometric frescoes.

🛏 Sleeping

Nap Hostel
HOSTEL **€**

(☑ 06 30 252 2972; www.naphostel.com; Király utca 23-25; dm 3000-3500Ft, d 9000Ft, apt 10,000Ft; @ 🛜) This welcoming hostel has three dorm rooms (each with between six and eight beds), a double with washbasin and a three-person apartment on the 1st floor of a former bank (dating from 1885). One of the six-bed dorm rooms has a corner balcony, and there's a communal kitchen. Enter through the main entrance of the hostel bar.

★ Hotel Arkadia
BOUTIQUE HOTEL **€€€**

(☑ 72-512 550; www.hotelarkadiapecs.hu; Hunyadi János út 1; s/d/tr €53/65/90; P 🗶 🛜) This Bauhaus-style hostelry, spread across two buildings, has plenty of polished steel, exposed brick and Corbusier-style furniture in its public areas. The 32 guestrooms follow in the same vein with lots of straight lines and solid colours, but thick throws and ample doses of natural light lend them a cosy vibe. Avoid the mansard rooms at the top.

🍴 Eating & Drinking

★ Blöff Bisztró
BALKAN **€€**

(☑ 72-497 469; Jókai tér 5; mains 1800-4500Ft; ☉ 11am-midnight) This (mostly) Balkan bad boy has quickly acquired a solid following in town. It may be to do with its supercentral location, but really the main draw is the quality of the simple, satisfying dishes – fried *papalina* (sprats) with garlic and parsley, carp crackling, *csevap* (Balkan-style grilled meat) and not-often-seen *lepények* (pies stuffed with meat or cheese) – and the friendly service.

Nappali Bar
BAR

(☑ 72-585 705; www.facebook.com/nappali.bar; Király utca 23-25; ☉ 9am-2am Sun-Thu, to 3am Fri & Sat) Nappali is one of the hippest gathering spots in town for a coffee or a glass of wine. Its outdoor seating fills up on warm, lazy evenings, and there's live music some nights. For breakfast (from 1500Ft) or lunch, head next door to sister-establishment Reggeli Bar, open from 8am to 3pm daily.

ℹ Information

Tourinform (☑ 06 30 681 7195, 72-213 315; www.iranypecs.hu; Széchenyi tér 1; ☉ 8am-6pm Mon-Fri, 10am-6pm Sat & Sun) has both knowledgeable staff and copious information on Pécs and surrounds.

ℹ Getting There & Away

BUS

Buses connect Pécs with Budapest (3690Ft, 4¼ hours, 10 daily), Szeged (3410Ft, 3¼ hours, eight daily) and Kecskemét (3410Ft, 3¼ hours, two daily).

TRAIN

Up to nine direct trains connect Pécs with Budapest's Keleti station (4305Ft, three hours, daily). Most destinations in Southern Transdanubia are best reached by bus.

GREAT PLAIN

Like the outback for Australians or the Wild West for Americans, the Nagyalföld (Great Plain) – also known as the *puszta* – holds a romantic appeal for Hungarians. Many

---

WORTH A TRIP

HISTORIC TIHANY

While in Balatonfüred, don't miss the chance to visit Tihany (population 1480), a peninsula jutting 5km into the lake and the place with the greatest historical significance on Lake Balaton. Tihany is home to the celebrated **Benedictine Abbey Church** (Bencés Apátság Templom; ☑ 87-538 200; www.tihanyiapatsag.hu; András tér 1; adult/concession/family incl abbey museum 1200/700/3200Ft; ☉ 9am-6pm Mon-Sat, 11.15am-6pm Sun May-Sep, 10am-5pm Mon-Sat, 11.15am-5pm Sun Apr & Oct, 10am-4pm Mon-Sat, 11.15am-4pm Sun Nov-Mar), filled with fantastic altars, pulpits and screens carved in the mid-18th century by an Austrian lay brother; all are baroque-rococo masterpieces. The church attracts a lot of tourists, but the peninsula itself has an isolated, almost wild feel. Hiking is one of Tihany's main attractions; a good map outlining the trails is available from the **Tourinform** (☑ 87-448 804; www.tihany.hu; Kossuth Lajos utca 20; ☉ 9am-6pm Mon-Fri, 10am-6pm Sat & Sun mid-Jun–Aug, 9am-5pm Mon-Fri, 10am-4pm Sat & Sun Sep–mid-Jun) office just down from the church. Buses bound for Tihany depart from Balatonfüred's bus/train station (310Ft, 30 minutes, 15 daily). The bus stops at both ferry landings before climbing to Tihany village.

of these notions come as much from the collective imagination as they do from history, but there's no arguing the spellbinding potential of big-sky country. The Hortobágy region is where the myth of the lonely *pásztor* (shepherd), the wayside *csárda* (inn) and Gypsy violinists – kept alive in literature and art – was born. The horse and herding show at Hortobágy National Park recreates this pastoral tradition. The Great Plain is also home to cities of graceful architecture and history. Szeged is a centre of art and culture, Kecskemét is full of art nouveau gems and Debrecen is the 'Calvinist Rome'.

Szeged

📞 62 / POP 161,120

Szeged is a bustling border town with a handful of historic sights that line the embankment along the Tisza River and a clutch of sumptuous art nouveau town palaces. Importantly, it's also a big university town, which means lots of culture, lots of partying and an active festival scene that lasts throughout the year.

⊙ Sights

Reök Palace   ARCHITECTURE
(Reök Palota; 📞 62-471 411; www.reok.hu; Magyar Ede tér 2; ⊙ 10am-6pm Tue-Sun) The Reök Palace

---

> **WORTH A TRIP**
>
> ## TREASURES OF KECSKEMÉT
>
> Ringed with vineyards and orchards, the lovely city of Kecskemét (population 110,640) lies halfway between the Danube and the Tisza Rivers in the heart of the southern Great Plain. It's a green, pedestrian-friendly place with beautiful art nouveau architecture, including the masterful **Ornamental Palace** (Cifrapalota; Rákóczi út 1), the sandy-pink, stepped-roof **City Hall** (Városház; 📞 76-513 513; Kossuth tér 1; ⊙ by arrangement) and the restored **Otthon Cinema** (Széchenyi tér 4).
>
> **Tourinform** (📞 76-481 065; www.irany kecskemet.hu/en; Kossuth tér 1; ⊙ 8.30am-5.30pm Mon-Fri, 9am-1pm Sat mid-May–Sep, 8am-4pm Mon-Fri Oct–mid-May) is centrally located in City Hall on the main square. Kecskemét is served by hourly buses to/from Budapest (1680Ft, 1½ hours) and Szeged (1680Ft, two hours).

---

is a mind-blowing green-and-lilac art nouveau structure, built in 1907, that looks like a decoration at the bottom of an aquarium. It's been polished up to regain its original lustre in recent years and now hosts regular photography and visual-arts exhibitions. There's also a lovely retro-style **cafe** (Reök Craft Cakeshop; 📞 06 30 668 8059; www.facebook.com/reokcukraszda; cakes 300-750Ft; ⊙ 8am-9pm) here.

Anna Baths   SPA
(Anna Fürdő; 📞 62-553 330; www.szegedsport. hu/intezmenyek/anna-furdo; Tisza Lajos körút 24; adult/child 1900/1600Ft, after 9pm 1200Ft; ⊙ 6am-8pm & 9pm-midnight Mon-Fri, 6am-8pm Sat & Sun) The lovely, cream-coloured Anna Baths were built in 1896 to imitate the tilework and soaring dome of a Turkish bath. Rich architectural detail surrounds all the modern saunas and bubbly pools you'd expect. There's a fountain spouting free thermal drinking water in front of the building.

⚹ Festivals & Events

★ **Szeged Open-Air Festival**   CULTURAL
(Szegedi Szabadtéri Játékok; 📞 62-541 205; www. szegediszabadteri.hu; ⊙ Jun-Aug) The Szeged Open-Air Festival held in Dom tér from June to August is the largest cultural festival in Hungary outside of Budapest. The outdoor theatre in front of the Votive Church seats up to 6000 people. Main events include an opera, an operetta, a play, folk dancing, classical music, ballet and a rock opera.

🛌 Sleeping

Familia Vendégház   GUESTHOUSE €€
(Family Guesthouse; 📞 62-441 122; www.familia panzio.hu; Szentháromság utca 71; s/d/tr 7500/12,000/14,000Ft; P ❋ 🗟) Families and international travellers love this family-run guesthouse with contemporary, if nondescript, furnishings in a great Old Town building close to the train station. The 24 rooms have high ceilings, lots of wood and brick walls, and loads of light from tall windows. Air-conditioning costs an extra 500Ft.

Art Hotel Szeged   BUSINESS HOTEL €€€
(📞 62-592 888, 06 30 697 4681; www.arthotel szeged.hu; Somogyi utca 16; s/d/ste from €90/106/120; ❋ 🗟) Business travellers love this upbeat 71-room hotel for its ubercentral location just off Somogyi utca and its large underground garage (parking costs €11 extra). Other travellers will love the primary colours, the neon and the interesting artwork. Rooms are generously proportioned,

DEBRECEN: CULTURE & COWBOY COUNTRY

Debrecen (population 202,210) is Hungary's second-largest city, and its array of museums and thermal baths will keep you busy for a day or two. Start with the colourful **Calvinist College** (Református Kollégium; ☎52-614 370; www.reformatuskollegium.ttre. hu; Kálvin tér 16; adult/concession/family 900/500/2000Ft; ☉10am-4pm Mon-Sat Mar-Oct, 10am-4pm Mon-Fri Nov-Feb), before splashing around the slides and waterfalls within **Aquaticum Debrecen Spa** (☎52-514 1174; www.aquaticum.hu/en; Nagyerdei Park 1; adult/ concession thermal baths 2050/1650Ft, with saunas 2900/2600Ft; ☉7am-9pm); you can sleep here, too.

Next take a trip to **Hortobágy National Park**, 40km west, once celebrated for its sturdy *csikósok* (cowboys), inns and Gypsy bands. You can see a staged historical recreation at the **Máta Stud Farm** (Mátai Ménes; ☎06 70 492 7655, 52-589 368; www.hortobagy. eu/hu/matai-menes; Hortobágy-Máta; adult/child 3000/1500Ft; ☉10am, noon & 2pm mid-Mar–Oct, plus 4pm Apr–mid-Oct).

Buses reach Debrecen from Eger (2520Ft, 2½ hours, six daily) and Szeged (3950Ft, five hours, four daily), while trains go direct from Budapest (3950Ft, 3½ hours, hourly). Six buses stop daily at Hortobágy village on runs between Debrecen (745Ft, 40 minutes) and Eger (1680Ft, 1¾ hours).

and some bathrooms have tubs. The centrepiece of the 3rd-floor fitness centre is a hot tub facing the Votive Church.

✗ Eating

Malata BURGERS €€
(☎06 30 190 2500; www.facebook.com/malata kezmuves; Somogyi utca 13; mains 1590-3590Ft; ☉noon-11pm Sun-Thu, to 1am Fri & Sat; 🍴) This great new hipster hang-out is part ruin garden, part pub/cafe and counts upwards of a dozen craft beers on tap. The food is mostly gourmet burgers but not exclusively so, with good choices for vegetarians. Order and pay at the bar. In winter and rain, sit in the colourful cafe, where books and frying pans dangle from the ceiling.

★ Tiszavirág Restaurant HUNGARIAN €€€
(☎62-554 888; http://tiszaviragszeged.hu; Hajnóczy utca 1/b; mains 3250-4900Ft; ☉noon-3pm & 6-10pm Tue-Sat) The restaurant at the **Tiszavirág Hotel** (d/ste €110/160; ❄🐾) serves beautifully presented international and modernised Hungarian dishes, such as guinea fowl with Jerusalem artichokes, and pigeon with couscous and beetroot. The selection of Hungarian wines by the glass is excellent and the service both warm and efficient. Simple but elegant decor, with great lighting.

ℹ Information

The exceptionally helpful **Tourinform** (☎62-488 699; www.szegedtourism.hu; Széchenyi tér 12; ☉9am-6pm Mon-Fri , to 1pm Sat Jun-Aug, 9am-5pm Mon-Fri, to 1pm Sat Apr, May, Sep & Oct,

9am-5pm Mon-Fri Nov-Mar) office is in swanky new premises facing leafy Széchenyi tér.

ℹ Getting There & Away

BUS
Buses run to Pécs (3410Ft, 3¼ hours, eight daily) and Debrecen (3950Ft, five hours, four daily). You can also get to the Serbian cities of to Novi Sad (2520Ft, 3½ hours, once daily) and to Subotica (1300Ft, 1½ hours, three to four times daily).

TRAIN
Szeged is on the main rail line to Budapest's Nyugati train station (3705Ft, 2½ hours, hourly); many trains also stop halfway along in Kecskemét (1830Ft, one hour).

NORTHERN HUNGARY

Northern Hungary is the home of Hungary's two most famous wines – honey-sweet Tokaj and Eger's famed Bull's Blood – and a region of microclimates conducive to wine production. The chain of wooded hills in the northeast constitutes the foothills of the Carpathian Mountains, which stretch along the Hungarian border with Slovakia.

Eger

☎36 / POP 53,440
Filled with beautifully preserved baroque buildings, Eger is a jewellery box of a town with loads to see and do. Explore the bloody

WORTH A TRIP

TOKAJ WINE COUNTRY

Since the 15th century, the world-renowned sweet wines of Tokaj (population 4150) have been produced in this picturesque little town of old buildings, nesting storks and cellars. **Tourinform** (☑47-352 125, 06 70 388 8870; www.visit-tokaj.com; Serház utca 1; ☺9am-6pm Mon-Fri, 10am-6pm Sat, 10am-2pm Sun Jun-Aug, 9am-4pm Mon-Fri, 10am-2pm Sat & Sun Sep-May) can help with winery tours and accommodation. Up to 16 trains a day head west for Budapest (4485Ft, 3¼ hours) through Miskolc, and south to Debrecen (1680Ft, two hours).

history of Turkish occupation and defeat at the hilltop castle; climb an original Ottoman minaret; listen to an organ performance at the colossal basilica; or relax in a renovated Turkish bath. Then spend time traipsing from cellar to cellar in the Valley of Beautiful Women, tasting the celebrated Eger Bull's Blood (Egri Bikavér) and other local wines from the cask. Flanked by northern Hungary's most inviting range of hills, the Bükk, Eger also provides nearby opportunities for hiking and other outdoor excursions.

◉ Sights

★**Eger Castle**   FORTRESS
(Egri Vár; ☑36-312 744; www.egrivar.hu; Vár köz 1; castle grounds adult/child 850/425Ft, incl museum 1700/850Ft; ☺exhibits 10am-6pm daily Apr-Oct, to 4pm Tue-Sun Nov-Mar, castle grounds 8am-10pm Apr-Oct, to 6pm Nov-Mar) Climb up cobbled Vár köz from Tinódi Sebestyén tér to reach the castle, erected in the 13th century after the Mongol invasion. Models, drawings and artefacts such as armour and Turkish uniforms in the **Castle History Exhibition**, on the 1st floor of the former Bishop's Palace (1470), painlessly explain the castle's story. On the eastern side of the complex are foundations of the Gothic 12th-century **St John's Cathedral**. Enter the **castle casemates** (Kazamata), hewn from solid rock, via the nearby **Dark Gate**.

Lyceum Library   LIBRARY
(Liceumi Könyvtar; ☑06 30 328 3030, 36-325 211; Eszterházy tér 1, Lyceum, Room 223; adult/child 1000/500Ft; ☺9.30am-3.30pm Tue-Sun May-Sep, 9.30am-1.30pm Tue-Sun Oct, Nov, Mar &

Apr) This 160,000-volume, all-wood library on the 1st floor of the Lyceum's south wing contains hundreds of priceless manuscripts, medical codices and incunabula. The trompe l'oeil ceiling fresco painted by Bohemian artist Johann Lukas Kracker in 1778 depicts the Counter-Reformation's Council of Trent (1545–63), with a lightning bolt setting heretical manuscripts ablaze. It was Eger's – and its archbishop's – response to the Enlightenment and the Reformation.

Valley of the Beautiful Women   WINE
(Szépasszony-völgy; www.ieger.com/valley-beautiful-woman.html) More than 24 wine cellars are carved into rock at the evocatively named Valley of the Beautiful Women. The choice can be daunting, so walk around first and have a look. Try ruby-red Bull's Blood or any of the whites – *leányka, olaszrizling* and *hárslevelű* – from nearby Debrő. The valley is a little more than 1km southwest across Rte 25 and off Király utca. Walk, or hop on a **Dottika** (☑06 30 928 8161; www.facebook.com/KisvonatEger; Kisvölgy 21; 1000Ft; ☺10.30am-6.30pm Apr-Oct) mini-train.

⌕ Sleeping

Agria Retur Vendégház   GUESTHOUSE €
(☑06 20 259 7291; www.returvendeghaz.hu; Knézich Károly utca 18; s/d/tr 4400/7800/10,800Ft; @☏) You couldn't receive a more inviting welcome than the one you'll get at this guesthouse near the minaret. Walking up three flights of stairs, you enter a cheery, communal, fully equipped kitchen/eating area that's central to four mansard rooms. Out the back is a huge garden with tables and a barbecue at your disposal. Just read the fan mail on the wall.

★**Hotel Senator Ház**   BOUTIQUE HOTEL €€€
(Senator House Hotel; ☑06 30 489 8744, 36-411 711; www.senatorhaz.hu; Dobó István tér 11; s/d €55/76; ❄@☏) Eleven cosy rooms with traditional furnishings fill the upper floors of this delightful 18th-century inn – a home away from home – on the main square. The ground floor is shared between a quality restaurant and a reception area stuffed with antiques and curios. Expect the warmest of welcomes.

✖ Eating & Drinking

★**Macok Bistro & Wine Bar**   HUNGARIAN €€€
(Macok Bisztró és Borbár; ☑36-516 180; www.imolaudvarhaz.hu/en/the-macok-bisztro-wine-bar.html; Tinódi Sebestyén tér 4; mains 3190-5290Ft;

🕑 noon-10pm Sun-Thu, to 11pm Fri & Sat) With its inventive menu and excellent wine cellar, this stylish eatery at the foot of the castle has been named among the top dozen restaurants in Hungary, and who are we to disagree? We'll come back in particular for the duck liver *brûlée* (2590Ft) and the roasted rabbit with liver 'crisps' (3250Ft). There's a lovely dining-room courtyard with a water feature.

Bíboros   CLUB
(☑ 06 70 199 2733; www.facebook.com/biboros eger; Bajcsy-Zsilinszky utca 6; 🕑 11am-3am Mon-Fri, 1pm-3am Sat, 3pm-midnight Sun) A subdued ruin bar by day, the 'Cardinal' transforms into a raucous dance club late in the evening; the cops at the door most weekend nights are a dead giveaway. Enjoy.

❶ Information

Meant to promote both the town and areas surrounding Eger, **Tourinform** (☑ 06 20 378 0514, 36-517 715; www.eger.hu; Bajcsy-Zsilinszky utca 9; 🕑 8am-6pm Mon-Fri, 9am-1pm Sat & Sun Jul & Aug, 8am-5pm Mon-Fri, 9am-1pm Sat Apr-Jun, Sep & Oct, 8am-5pm Mon-Fri Nov-Mar) here is surprisingly unhelpful.

❶ Getting There & Away

BUS
From Eger, buses serve Debrecen (2520Ft, 2½ hours, six daily), Kecskemét (3130Ft, four hours, two daily) and Szeged (3950Ft, five hours, two daily).

TRAIN
Up to seven direct trains a day head for Budapest's Keleti train station (2520Ft, two hours).

SURVIVAL GUIDE

❶ Directory A–Z

ACCESSIBLE TRAVEL
Hungary has made great strides in recent years in making public areas and facilities more accessible to the disabled. Wheelchair ramps, toilets fitted for the disabled and inward-opening doors, though not as common as they are in Western Europe, do exist, and audible traffic signals for the blind are becoming commonplace in the cities.

For more information, contact the **Hungarian Federation of Disabled Persons' Associations** (MEOSZ; ☑ 1-388 2387; www.meosz.hu; III San Marco utca 76).

ACCOMMODATION
Hungary has a wide range of accommodation. Book a couple of months in advance for Budapest, Lake Balaton and the Danube Bend in high season.

Camping Options range from private sites with few facilities to enormous caravan campgrounds with swimming pools.

Hostels Inexpensive, prevalent in Budapest, and with lots of backpacker facilities.

Hotels Anything from socialist-era brutalist architecture to elegant five-star places, quirky boutique hotels and converted manor houses.

Pensions, inns and B&Bs Often cosy, family-run places with all the facilities of a small hotel.

Private homes and apartments Book a room or an entire place (usually) with English-speaking hosts.

Booking Services
Camping One of the best resources for finding a campsite in a particular part of the country is http://en.camping.info; another good website is www.camping.hu.

Farmhouses For information, contact the **Association of Hungarian Rural & Agrotourism** (FATOSZ; ☑ 1-352 9804; www.fatosz. eu; VII Király utca 93; 🚋 trolleybus 70, 78) or the **Centre of Rural Tourism** (☑ 1-788-9932; www.falutur.hu; VII Dohány utca 86; 🚋 4, 6) in Budapest.

Hostels The Hungarian Youth Hostel Association (www.miszsz.hu) lists a number of places across the country associated with Hostelling International (HI), but not all HI-associated hostels provide discounts to HI card-holders.

Pensions, Inns & B&Bs A useful website is www.hoteltelnet.hu/en/pensions.

LEGAL MATTERS
There is a 100% ban on alcohol when driving and it is taken very seriously. Police conduct routine roadside checks with breathalysers and if you are found to have even 0.005% of alcohol in your blood, you could be fined up to 300,000Ft on the spot; police have been known to fine for less than that level of alcohol, so it's best not to drink at all. In the event of an accident, the drinking party is automatically regarded as guilty.

LGBTIQ+ TRAVELLERS
Budapest offers a reasonable gay scene for its size but there's not much going on publicly elsewhere in Hungary.

Háttér Society (Háttér Társaság; ☑ info & counselling hotline 1-329 3380, office 1-329 2670; www.hatter.hu) Operates an information and counselling hotline from 6pm to 11pm.

Labrisz Lesbian Association (☑ 06 30 295 5415; www.labrisz.hu) Has info on Hungary's lesbian scene.

MONEY

ATMs are widely available. Credit and debit cards are accepted in most hotels and restaurants.

OPENING HOURS

With rare exceptions, opening hours (*nyitvatartás*) are posted on the front doors of businesses; *nyitva* means 'open' and *zárva* 'closed'.

Banks 7.45am or 8am to 5pm Monday to Thursday, to 2pm or 4pm Friday

Bars 11am to midnight Sunday to Thursday, to 2am Friday and Saturday

Businesses 9am or 10am to 6pm Monday to Friday, to 1pm or 2pm Saturday

Clubs 4pm to 2am Sunday to Thursday, to 4am Friday and Saturday; some only open on weekends

Grocery stores and supermarkets 7am to 7pm Monday to Friday, to 3pm Saturday; some also 7am to noon Sunday

Restaurants 11am to 11pm; breakfast venues open by 8am

Shops 10am to 6pm Monday to Friday, to 1pm Saturday

PUBLIC HOLIDAYS

Hungary celebrates 10 *ünnep* (public holidays) each year.

New Year's Day 1 January

1848 Revolution/National Day 15 March

Easter Monday March/April

International Labour Day 1 May

Whit Monday May/June

St Stephen's/Constitution Day 20 August

1956 Remembrance Day/Republic Day 23 October

All Saints' Day 1 November

Christmas holidays 25 and 26 December

TELEPHONE

Hungary has extensive mobile (cell) phone network coverage. You can make domestic and international calls from public telephones, though these are all but obsolete with the advent of cheap mobile phone calls and WhatsApp, Skype and other VOIP services.

🛈 Getting There & Away

ENTERING THE COUNTRY/REGION

Hungary maintains 65 or so border road crossings with its neighbours. Border formalities with Austria, Slovenia and Slovakia are virtually nonexistent. However, you may only enter or leave Hungary via designated border-crossing points during opening hours when travelling to/from the non-Schengen nations of Croatia, Romania, Ukraine and Serbia. In the wake of the Syrian refugee crisis, a controversial border wall now stretches along Hungary's border with Serbia and Croatia. For the latest on border formalities, check www.police.hu.

AIR

International flights land at Ferenc Liszt International Airport (p583), 24km southeast of Budapest. In general, flights to/from Schengen countries use Terminal 2A, while Terminal 2B serves non-Schengen countries.

Hungary's only other year-round commercial international airport is **Debrecen International Airport** (DEB; ☑ 06 20 467 9899; www.debrecenairport.com; Mikepércsi út), 5km south of Debrecen, with Wizz Air and Lufthansa flights to half a dozen cities, including London, Munich, Paris and Tel Aviv.

LAND

Hungary is well connected to neighbouring countries by road and rail, though most transport begins or ends its journey in Budapest.

Timetables for both domestic and international trains and buses use the 24-hour system. Be aware that Hungarian names are sometimes used for cities and towns in neighbouring countries on bus and train schedules.

Bus

Crossing the continent by bus is the cheapest option. Most international buses are run by the German company **FlixBus** (www.flixbus.hu) and link with its Hungarian associate **Volánbusz** (☑ 1-382 0888; www.volanbusz.hu). Buses depart Budapest's Népliget station to many cities across Western Europe. From the same station there are good bus connections with destinations in Croatia, Romania, the Czech Republic and Poland, among others.

Car & Motorcycle

Drivers and motorbike riders will need the vehicle's registration papers, liability insurance and an international driver's permit in addition to their domestic licence.

Hungary's motorways may only be accessed with a motorway pass (*matrica*), to be purchased beforehand from petrol stations and post offices (see www.autopalya.hu for more details).

Train

MÁV links up with international rail networks in all directions, and its schedule is available online. Some direct train connections from Budapest include Austria, Slovakia, Romania, Ukraine, Croatia, Serbia, Germany, Slovenia, Czech Republic, Poland, Switzerland, Italy and Bulgaria.

Seat reservations are required for international destinations and are included in the price of the ticket.

RIVER

Mahart PassNave (p584), which runs hydrofoils and other passenger boats to and from the towns of the Danube Bend, no longer offers a regularly scheduled hydrofoil service between Budapest and Vienna. It does, however, offer two-day excursions (adult/child under 12 years 53,990/43,990Ft) to the Austrian capital and back over selected weekends in June, July and August.

🛈 Getting Around

AIR

There are no scheduled flights within Hungary. Hungary is small enough to get everywhere by train or bus within the span of a day.

BOAT

From April to late October Budapest-based **Mahart PassNave** (1-484 4010, 1-484 4013; www.mahartpassnave.hu; V Belgrád rakpart; ⊗9am-5pm Mon-Fri; 🚋2) runs excursion boats on the Danube from Budapest to Szentendre, Visegrád and Esztergom, and, between May and September, hydrofoils from Budapest to Vác, Visegrád and Esztergom.

From spring to autumn, some 20 ports around Lake Balaton are well served by Balaton Shipping Company (p587) passenger ferries.

BUS

Hungary's Volánbusz network comprehensively covers the whole country.

Some larger bus stations have luggage lockers or left-luggage rooms that generally close early (around 6pm). The left-luggage offices at nearby train stations keep much longer hours.

Tickets can be purchased directly from the driver. There are sometimes queues for intercity buses, so arrive around 30 minutes before departure time. Buses are reasonably comfortable and have adequate leg room. On long journeys there are rest stops every couple of hours.

CAR & MOTORCYCLE

Driving in Hungary is useful for exploring the remotest rural corners of the country; trains and buses take care of the rest.

LOCAL TRANSPORT

Public transport is efficient and extensive in Hungarian cities, with bus and, in some case, trolleybus services. Budapest, Szeged and Debrecen also have trams, and there's an extensive metro and a suburban commuter railway in Budapest. Purchase tickets (around 300Ft to 350Ft) at news stands before travelling and validate them once aboard. Inspectors frequently check tickets.

TRAIN

MÁV (Magyar Államvasutak, Hungarian State Railways; ☑1-349 4949; www.mavcsoport.hu) operates clean, punctual and relatively comfortable (if not ultramodern) train services with free wi-fi. Budapest is the hub for main railway lines, though many secondary lines link provincial cities and towns. There are three mainline stations in Budapest, each serving largely (but not exclusively) destinations from the following regions:

Keleti (Eastern Railway) station Northern Uplands and the Northeast

Nyugati (Western Railway) station Great Plain and Danube Bend

Déli (Southern Railway) station Transdanubia and Lake Balaton

Departures and arrivals are always shown on a printed timetable: yellow is for *indul* (departures) and white for *érkezik* (arrivals); fast trains are marked in red and local trains in black. The number (or sometimes letter) next to the word *vágány* indicates the platform from which the train departs or arrives.

All train stations have left-luggage offices, some of which stay open 24 hours.

Iceland

POP 350,000

Includes →

Best Places to Eat
- → Dill (p604)
- → Slippurinn (p604)
- → Bjargarsteinn Mathús (p612)
- → Siglunes Guesthouse Restaurant (p613)
- → Lindin (p607)

Best Places to Stay
- → Héraðsskólinn (p607)
- → Árból (p613)
- → Hótel Egilsen (p611)
- → Loft Hostel (p603)
- → Icelandair Hotel Reykjavík Marina (p603)

Why Go?
The energy is palpable on this magical island, where astonishing natural phenomena inspire the welcoming, creative locals and draw an increasing number of visitors in search of its untrammelled splendour. A vast volcanic laboratory, here the earth itself is restless and alive. Admire thundering waterfalls, glittering glaciers carving their way to black-sand beaches, explosive geysers, rumbling volcanoes and contorted lava fields.

In summer, permanent daylight illuminates Iceland's lively capital, Reykjavík, with its wonderful cafe and bar scene. Fashion, design and music are woven into the city's fabric, and the museums are tops. In winter, with luck, you may see the Northern Lights shimmering across the sky. Year-round, though, adventure tours abound, getting you up close and personal with sights and sounds that will stay with you for life.

When to Go
Reykjavík

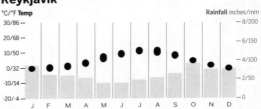

May–Jun Prime birdwatching season happily coincides with the two driest months and fewer crowds.

Aug It's full throttle in Reykjavík, the country teems with visitors and it's almost always light.

Nov–Apr The best months for Northern Lights and bare minimalism.

Entering the Country

Iceland is part of the Schengen Agreement.

ITINERARIES

Three Days

Arrive in Reykjavík (p598) on a weekend to catch the decadent all-night *djammið* (partying pub crawl). Sober up over brunch at Bergsson Mathús (p604) or in Laugardalur's geothermal pool (p602), admire the views from Hallgrímskirkja (p599), cruise the cafes and shops near Laugavegur (p603), then absorb Viking history at the National Museum (p599) or the Settlement Exhibition (p599). On day three, visit Gullfoss (p606), Geysir (p606) and Þingvellir National Park (p606) in the Golden Circle (p606), and soak in the Blue Lagoon (p608) on the way home.

Seven Days

With four more days, head to West Iceland for the excellent Settlement Centre (p611) in Borgarnes (p611) and Snæfellsnes Peninsula (p611) with its ravishing Snæfellsjökull National Park (p611), or head inland to Langjökull with its ice cave (p611), and nearby Viðgelmir lava tube (p611). In South Iceland explore: Hekla volcano (p608), Skógar (p608) with its waterfalls and hikes, Vík (p608) with gorgeous ocean-front landscapes, or take a super-Jeep or amphibious bus to Þórsmörk (p608). Vatnajökull National Park (p611) and Skaftafell (p611) are worth a trip for amazing scenery and outdoor adventures. Or hop a flight to Akureyri (p612) and check out the North, or Ísafjörður (p612) and explore the Westfjords.

Essential Food & Drink

Traditional Icelandic dishes *Harðfiskur* (dried strips of haddock with butter), *plokkfiskur* (a hearty fish-and-potato gratin) and delicious, yoghurt-like *skyr*. Brave souls try *svið* (singed sheep's head), *súrsaðir hrútspungar* (pickled ram's testicles) and *hárkarl* (fermented shark meat). Icelandic lamb is among the tastiest on the planet, fish graces most menus, reindeer meat from the eastern highlands is a high-end treat.

Whale-meat controversy Many restaurants serve whale meat, but 75% of Icelanders never buy whale meat. Tourists are responsible for most of the consumption of these protected species, as well as puffins and the Greenland shark used in *hárkarl*. Find whale-free spots at www.icewhale.is/whale-friendly-restaurants.

Favourite drinks Traditional *brennivín*, fondly known as 'black death', is schnapps made from potatoes and caraway seeds. Craft beers include Kaldi, Borg Brugghús and Einstök. Coffee is a national institution.

AT A GLANCE

Area 103,000 sq km

Capital Reykjavík

Country Code ☏ 354

Currency Icelandic króna (kr)

Emergency ☏ 112

Languages Icelandic, English widely spoken

Money Credit cards (PIN often required at petrol pumps) and ATMs everywhere

Time Western European Time Zone (equal to GMT)

Visas Generally not required for stays up to 90 days. Member of Schengen Convention. Check Icelandic Directorate of Immigration (www.utl.is) for details.

ICELAND

Sleeping Price Ranges

The following price categories are based on the high-season price for a double room:

€ less than 15,000kr (€120)

€€ 15,000–30,000kr (€120–240)

€€€ more than 30,000kr (€240)

Eating Price Ranges

The following price ranges refer to a main course.

€ less than 2000kr (€16)

€€ 2000–5000kr (€16–40)

€€€ more than 5000kr (€40)

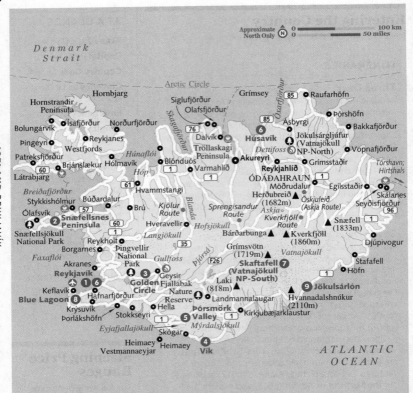

Iceland Highlights

❶ **Reykjavík** (p598)
Partying till dawn on the weekend pub crawl *djammið*, then hitting excellent museums, shops and cafes.

❷ **Snæfellsnes Peninsula** (p611) Riding horses, climbing glaciers, trekking lava fields or soaking in hot-pots.

❸ **Golden Circle** (p606)
Joining the droves exploring the scintillating Gullfoss waterfall, exploding geysers and rift valley Þingvellir.

❹ **Vík** (p608) Exploring black-sand beaches and off-shore rock formations.

❺ **Þórsmörk** (p608) Taking a wilderness hike in this dramatic valley.

❻ **Húsavík** (p612) Going whale watching in Húsavík or Reykjavík.

❼ **Skaftafell** (p611)
Exhausting your camera's memory card at Skaftafell in Vatnajökull National Park and nearby Jökulsárlón glacial lagoon.

❽ **Blue Lagoon** (p608)
Swimming through steam clouds at this world-famous milky-blue geothermal pool.

REYKJAVÍK

POP 217,711

The world's most northerly capital combines colourful buildings, quirky, creative people, eye-popping design, wild nightlife and a capricious soul. You'll find Viking history, captivating museums, cool music, and off-beat cafes and bars. And it's a superb base for touring Iceland's natural wonders.

Reykjavík's heart lies between Tjörnin (the Pond) and the harbour, and along Laugavegur, with nearly everything for visitors within walking distance.

◉ Sights

★ Old Reykjavík
AREA

With a series of sights and interesting historic buildings, the area dubbed Old Reykjavík is the heart of the capital, and the focal point of many historic walking tours. The area is anchored by Tjörnin, the city-centre lake, and sitting between it and Austurvöllur park to the north are the Ráðhús (city hall) and Alþingi (parliament).

★ National Museum
MUSEUM

(Þjóðminjasafn Íslands; ☑ 530 2200; www.national museum.is; Suðurgata 41; adult/child 2000kr/free; ⊙ 10am-5pm May–mid-Sep, closed Mon mid-Sep–Apr; ☑ 1, 3, 6, 12, 14) Artefacts from settlement to the modern age fill the creative display spaces of Iceland's superb National Museum. Exhibits give an excellent overview of Iceland's history and culture, and the free smartphone audio guide adds a wealth of detail. The strongest section describes the Settlement Era – including the rule of the chieftans and the introduction of Christianity – and features swords, drinking horns, silver hoards and a powerful bronze figure of Thor. The priceless 13th-century Valþjófsstaðir church door is carved with the story of a knight, his faithful lion and a passel of dragons.

★ Settlement Exhibition
MUSEUM

(Landnámssýningin; ☑ 411 6370; www.reykjavik museum.is; Aðalstræti 16; adult/child 1650kr/free; ⊙ 9am-6pm) This fascinating archaeological ruin-museum is based around a 10th-century Viking longhouse unearthed here from 2001 to 2002 and other Settlement-Era finds from central Reykjavík. It imaginatively combines technological wizardry and archaeology to give a glimpse into early Icelandic life. Don't miss the fragment of **boundary wall** at the back of the museum that is older still (and the oldest human-made structure in Reykjavík). Among the captivating high-tech displays, a wraparound panorama shows how things would have looked at the time of the longhouse.

★ Hallgrímskirkja
CHURCH

(☑ 510 1000; www.hallgrimskirkja.is; Skólavörðustígur; tower adult/child 1000/100kr; ⊙ 9am-9pm May-Sep, to 5pm Oct-Apr) Reykjavík's immense white-concrete church (1945–86), star of a thousand postcards, dominates the skyline and is visible from up to 20km away. An elevator trip up the 74.5m-high tower reveals an unmissable view of the city. In contrast to the high drama outside, the Lutheran church's interior is quite plain. The most eye-catching feature is the vast 5275-pipe organ installed in 1992. The church's size and radical design caused controversy, and its architect, Guðjón Samúelsson (1887–1950), never saw its completion.

★ Reykjavík Art Museum
GALLERY

(Listasafn Reykjavíkur; www.artmuseum.is; adult/child 1650kr/free) The excellent Reykjavík Art Museum is split over three superbly curated sites: the large, modern **Hafnarhús** (☑ 411 6400; Tryggvagata 17; adult/child 1650kr/free; ⊙ 10am-5pm, to 10pm Thu; ☑ 1, 3, 6, 11, 12, 13, 14), focusing on contemporary art; **Kjarvalsstaðir** (☑ 411 6420; Flókagata 24, Miklatún Park; adult/child 1650kr/free; ⊙ 10am-5pm), in a park just east of Snorrabraut, which displays rotating exhibits of modern art; and **Ásmundarsafn** (Ásmundur Sveinsson Museum; ☑ 411 6430; Sigtún; adult/child 1650kr/free; ⊙ 10am-5pm May-Sep, 1-5pm Oct-Apr; ☑ 2, 4, 14, 15, 17, 19), a peaceful haven near Laugardalur for viewing sculptures by Ásmundur Sveinsson. One ticket (valid for 24 hours) gains entry to all three sites.

Old Harbour
AREA

(Geirsgata; ☑ 1, 3, 6, 11, 12, 13, 14) Largely a service harbour until recently, the Old Harbour and the neighbouring Grandi area have blossomed into tourist hot spots, with key art galleries, several museums, volcano and Northern Lights films, and excellent restaurants. Whale-watching and puffin-viewing trips depart from the pier. Photo ops abound with views of fishing boats, the Harpa concert hall and snowcapped mountains beyond.

On the western edge of the harbour, the Grandi area, named after the fish factory there, is burgeoning with eateries and shops.

Culture House
GALLERY

(Þjóðmenningarhúsið; ☑ 530 2210; www.culture house.is; Hverfisgata 15; adult/child incl National Museum 2000kr/free; ⊙ 10am-5pm May–mid-Sep, closed Mon mid-Sep–Apr) This fantastic collaboration between the National Museum, National Gallery and four other organisations creates a superbly curated exhibition covering the artistic and cultural heritage of Iceland from settlement to today. Priceless artefacts are arranged by theme, and highlights include 14th-century manuscripts, contemporary art and the skeleton of a great auk (now extinct). Check the website for free guided tours.

National Gallery of Iceland
MUSEUM

(Listasafn Íslands; ☑ 515 9600; www.listasafn. is; Fríkirkjuvegur 7; adult/child 1800kr/free;

Central Reykjavík

12

11

15

Mýrargata

27

9

Matur og Drykkur (350m);
Grandi Mathöll (800m);
Dive.is (1.3km)

Small
cruise
ship dock

Harpa
2

Sterna

Vesturgata

10

Geirsgata

Egilsgata

Ránargata

18

**Reykjavík Art
Museum –
Hafnarhús**
4

Tryggvagata

Nauotin

Bárugata

Öldugata

Gardastræti

Mjóstræti

Fisch

34

30

Sæbraut

Tryggvagata

P

Landakotskirkja
(100m)

Túngata

Grjótag

Ingólfstorg

Veltus

Hafnarstræti

20

Airport
Express

Árnarhóll

Ingólfsstræti

**Settlement
Exhibition** 5

Adalstræti

Austurstræti

13

25

Hverfisgata

6

Samtökin
'78

Kirkjustræti

Austurvöllur

Posthist

Bankastræti

16

23

Gardastræti

P

**Old
Reykjavík** 3

Albingi

Dómkirkja

Lækjargata

26

Skólastræti

Suourgata

P

Vonarstræti

Templarasund

22

Amtmannsst

Ráðhús

Main
Tourist
Office

Bókhlöoust

Tjarnargata

Laufásvegur

Miost

Pingholtsstræti

Ingólfsstræti

Hallveigastigur

35

Gardastræti

Frikirkjuvegur

Skálholtsst

**Fríkirkjan
í Reykjavík**

8

Bjargarst

Spítalast

Bergstaðastræti

Skólavörðustigur

National Museum (200m);
Bike Cave (1.8km)

Hallargaðurinn

Pingholtsstræti

Hellus

Grundarst

Oðinsgata

Freyjugata

Bjarkargata

Skothúsvegur

Tjörnin

Sóleyjargata

Flókagata

Baldursgata

Laufásvegur

Nönnugata

28

Urðarst

Baldursgata

Hringbraut

Tjörnin

7

Bragagata

Njarðargata

Reykjavík Excursions (650m);
SBA-Norðurleið (650m);
Reykjavík Domestic (1.3km)

ICELAND REYKJAVÍK

Central Reykjavík

◎ Top Sights

◎ Sights

✪ Activities, Courses & Tours

🛏 Sleeping

✗ Eating

⦿ Drinking & Nightlife

✪ Entertainment

10am-5pm daily mid-May–mid-Sep, 11am-5pm Tue-Sun mid-Sep–mid-May) This pretty stack of marble atriums and spacious galleries overlooking Tjörnin offers ever-changing exhibits drawn from a 10,000-piece collection. The museum can only exhibit a small sample at any one time; shows range from 19th- and 20th-century paintings by Iceland's favourite artists (including Jóhannes Kjarval and Nína Sæmundsson) to sculptures by Sigurjón Ólafsson and others.

Volcano House   MUSEUM
(555 1900; www.volcanohouse.is; Tryggvagata 11; adult/child 1990/1000kr; 9am-10pm) This modern theatre with a hands-on lava exhibit in the foyer screens a 55-minute pair of films in English (hourly) about the Vestmannaeyjar volcanoes and Eyjafjallajökull. They show in German, French, Icelandic or Swedish once daily in summer.

Laugardalur   AREA, PARK
(2, 5, 14, 15, 17) Laugardalur encompasses a verdant stretch of land 4km east of the city centre. It was once the main source of Reykjavík's hot-water supply: it translates as 'Hot-Springs Valley', and in the park's centre you'll find relics from the old wash house. The park is a favourite with locals for its huge **swimming complex** (411 5100; www.reykjavik.is/stadir/laugardalslaug; Sundlaugavegur 30a; adult/child 950/150kr; suit/towel rental 850/570kr; 6.30am-10pm Mon-Fri, 8am-10pm Sat & Sun;), fed by the geothermal spring, alongside a spa, **cafe** (Flóran; 553 8872; www.floran.is; Botanic Gardens; cakes from 950kr, mains 1550-3150kr; 8am-10pm May-Sep;) , skating rink, botanical gardens, sporting and concert arenas, and a zoo/entertainment park for kids.

Tours

Walking, bike and bus tours are the main way to take in the city. Whale-watching, puffin-spotting and sea-angling trips allow a jaunt offshore. Reykjavík is also the main hub for tours to amazing landscapes and activities around Iceland. Those without wheels, time or the desire to travel the countryside independently can take tours ranging from super-Jeeps and buses to horse riding, snowmobiling and heli-tours. Regional operators like Midgard Adventure (p608) and Southcoast Adventure (p608) also pick up in Reykjavík (often with an extra charge).

Elding Adventures at Sea   WILDLIFE
(519 5000; www.whalewatching.is; Ægisgarður 5; adult/child 11,000/5500kr; harbour kiosk 8am-9pm; 14) The city's most established and ecofriendly whale-watching tours feature a whale exhibition set in a converted fishing vessel; refreshments are sold on board. Elding also offers angling (adult/child 14,900/7450kr) and puffin-watching trips (adult/child from 6500/3250kr) and combo tours. It also runs the ferry to Viðey (533 5055; www.videy.com; Skarfabakki; return adult/child 1500/750kr; from Skarfabakki hourly 10.15am-5.15pm mid-May–Sep, 1.15-4.30pm Sat & Sun Oct–mid-May). Pick-up available.

Reykjavík Excursions   BUS
(Kynnisferðir; 580 5400; www.re.is; BSÍ Bus Terminal, Vatnsmýrarvegur 10; tours 8000-47,300kr) The largest and most popular bus-tour operator (with large groups) has an enormous booklet full of summer and winter programs. Extras include horse riding, snowmobiling and themed tours tying in with festivals. It also offers 'Iceland on Your Own' bus tickets and passports for transport, and operates the Flybus (p614) to Keflavík International Airport.

Arctic Adventures   ADVENTURE
(562 7000; www.adventures.is) With young and enthusiastic staff, this company specialises in action-filled tours including kayaking (from 13,000kr), rafting (from 14,000kr), horse riding, quad-biking and glacier walking (16,000kr).

Icelandic Mountain Guides   ADVENTURE
(Iceland Rovers; 587 9999; www.mountainguides.is; Stórhöfði 33) Highly respected, full-action outfit specialising in mountaineering, trekking, ice climbing (from 24,900kr) and the like. It also markets itself as 'Iceland Rovers' for its super-Jeep tours (Essential Iceland tour 35,000kr).

Festivals & Events

Reykjavikers turn out in force for a day and night of art, music, dance and fireworks in mid-August on **Culture Night** (www.menningarnott.is). In November, the fab **Iceland Airwaves** international music festival (www.icelandairwaves.is) is one of the world's premier showcases for new music (Icelandic and otherwise). The **Secret Solstice** music festival (www.secretsolstice.is) lights up in June.

Sleeping

Book well ahead for summer high season.

★ Reykjavík Downtown Hostel   HOSTEL €
(553 8120; www.hostel.is; Vesturgata 17; 4-/10-bed dm 9200/5700kr, d with/without bathroom

20,800/18,400kr; @ 🤖; 🖵14) The reviews are so good for this squeaky clean, charming and well-run hostel that it regularly lures large groups and the nonbackpacker set. Enjoy friendly service, a guest kitchen and excellent rooms. Discount 800kr for HI members.

★**Nest Apartments**　　　APARTMENT €€
(☑ 893 0280; www.nestapartments.is; Bergthorugata 15; apt from 20,000kr; 🤖) Four thoroughly modern apartments with neat antique touches make a superb home away from home on this central, peaceful street. Ranged over a tall townhouse, the apartments sleep two to four people – the one in the loft steals the show with water and mountain views. There's a two-night minimum.

**Forsæla
Apartmenthouse**　　　GUESTHOUSE, APARTMENT €€
(☑ 551 6046; www.apartmenthouse.is; Grettisgata 33b; d/tr without bathroom incl breakfast 25,700/34,500kr, apt/house from 45,150/90,300kr; 🤖) A 100-year-old wood-and-tin house is the star of the show here. It sleeps four to eight people and comes with old beams and tasteful mod cons. Smaller apartments have cosy bedrooms and sitting rooms, kitchens and washing machines. Or opt for the B&B lodging alongside. There's a minimum three-night stay.

Loft Hostel　　　HOSTEL €€
(☑ 553 8140; www.lofthostel.is; Bankastræti 7; dm 8500-9900kr, d/q 26,200/36,700kr; @ 🤖) Perched high above the action on bustling Bankastræti, this modern hostel attracts a decidedly young crowd, including locals who come for its trendy bar and cafe terrace. This sociable spot comes with neat dorms with linen included and en suite bathrooms.

★**Reykjavík Residence**　　　APARTMENT €€€
(☑ 561 1200; www.rrhotel.is; Hverfisgata 45; 2-/3-/8-person apt 33,500/37,300/87,000kr; @ 🤖) Plush city-centre living feels just right in this array of apartments set in six historic mansions. Linens are crisp, service attentive and the light a glowing gold. The pick of the lot are the Royal Suites in the former home of an Icelandic Prime Minister – named after onetime visitors, the king and queen of Denmark.

Apotek　　　BOUTIQUE HOTEL €€€
(☑ 512 9000; www.keahotels.is; Austurstræti 16; d incl breakfast from 42,200kr; 🤖) Apotek is set in one of the city's most iconic buildings – a well-renovated, former pharmacy smack in the centre of Old Reykjavík, which dates

from 1917 and was designed by Guðjón Samúelsson. It offers slick contemporary rooms in muted tones and a popular ground-floor tapas-style **restaurant-bar** (☑ 551 0011; www.apotekrestaurant.is; mains 2800-6000kr; ☉noon-11pm Sun-Thu, to midnight Fri & Sat).

**Icelandair Hotel
Reykjavík Marina**　　　BOUTIQUE HOTEL €€€
(☑ booking 444 4000, hotel 560 8000; www.icelandairhotels.is; Mýrargata 2; d 34,850-42,500kr, ste from 47,600kr; @ 🤖; 🖵14) Captivating art, cool nautical-chic decor and up-to-the-second mod cons ensure this harbourside design hotel is a gorgeous retreat. Clever ways to conserve space make the small rooms winners. The attic bedrooms facing the harbour have excellent sea views. The lobby is home to the happening **Slippbarinn** (☑ 560 8080; www.slippbarinn.is; ☉noon-midnight Sun-Thu, to 1am Fri & Sat; 🤖) cocktail bar.

✕ Eating

★**Gló**　　　ORGANIC, VEGETARIAN €
(☑ 553 1111; www.glo.is; Laugavegur 20b; mains 1000-2400kr; ☉11.30am-10pm; 🤖 🖊) Join the cool cats in this airy upstairs restaurant serving fresh daily specials loaded with Asian-influenced herbs and spices. Though not exclusively vegetarian, it's a wonderland of raw and organic foods, with a broad bar of elaborate salads, from root veggies to Greek.

★**Grandi Mathöll**　　　STREET FOOD €
(☑ 577 6200; www.grandimatholl.is; Grandagarður 16; mains from 1200kr; ☉11am-9pm Mon-Thu, to 10pm Fri-Sun) There's no neater encapsulation of Grandi's rejuvenation than the transformation of this old fish factory into a pioneering street-food hall. Long trestle tables sit beside stalls selling a diverse range of lamb, fish and veggie delights; look out for the Gastro Truck, its succulent signature chicken burger has quite a jalapeño kick.

Sægreifinn　　　SEAFOOD €
(Seabaron; ☑ 553 1500; www.saegreifinn.is; Geirsgata 8; mains from 1500kr; ☉11.30am-10pm) Sidle into this green harbourside shack for the most famous lobster soup in the capital, or choose from a fridge full of fresh fish skewers to be grilled on the spot. Though the original sea baron sold the restaurant some years ago, the place retains its unfussy, down-to-earth charm.

Bakarí Sandholt　　　BAKERY €
(☑ 551 3524; www.sandholt.is; Laugavegur 36; snacks 700-2700kr; ☉7am-7pm Sun-Thu, 6.30am-

9pm Fri & Sat; 🛜) Reykjavík's favourite bakery is usually crammed with folks hoovering up the generous assortment of fresh baguettes, croissants, pastries and sandwiches. The soup of the day (1850kr) comes with delicious sourdough bread.

★ Hlemmur Mathöll
FOOD HALL €

(www.hlemmurmatholl.is; Laugavegur 107; mains from 800kr; ⊗ 8am-11pm) If only all bus terminals had a food court like this. Some 10 vendors rustle up multicultural foods including Danish smørrebrød (open sandwiches), Mexican tacos and Vietnamese street food. The pick is innovative SKÁL! (🖉 775 2299; www.skalrvk.com; mains 1000-2500kr; ⊗ noon-10pm Sun-Wed, to 11pm Thu-Sat; 🖉). Most stalls kick into action by lunchtime.

Bæjarins Beztu
HOT DOGS €

(www.bbp.is; Tryggvagata; hot dogs 450kr; ⊗ 10am-1am Sun-Thu, to 4.30am Fri & Sat) Icelanders swear the city's best hot dogs are found at this truck near the harbour (patronised by Bill Clinton and late-night bar-hoppers). Use the vital phrase 'eina með öllu' (one with everything) to get the quintessential favourite with sweet mustard, ketchup and crunchy onions.

★ Messinn
SEAFOOD €€

(🖉 546 0095; www.messinn.com; Lækjargata 6b; lunch mains 1850-2200kr, dinner mains 2700-4200kr; ⊗ 11.30am-3pm & 5-10pm; 🛜) Make a beeline to Messinn for the best seafood that Reykjavík has to offer. The speciality here is the amazing pan-fried dishes: your pick of fish is served up in a sizzling cast-iron skillet, accompanied by buttery potatoes and salad. The mood is upbeat and comfortable and the staff friendly.

★ Matur og Drykkur
ICELANDIC €€

(🖉 5718877; www.maturogdrykkur.is; Grandagarður 2; lunch/dinner mains from 1900/3400kr, tasting menu 10,000kr; ⊗ 11.30am-3pm & 6-10pm, closed Sun lunch; 🖉; 🚌14) One of Reykjavík's top high-concept restaurants, Matur og Drykkur means 'Food and Drink', and you'll surely be plied with the best of both. The brainchild of brilliant chef Gísli Matthías Auðunsson, who also owns the excellent Slippurinn (🖉 481 1515; www.slippurinn.com; Strandvegur 76; lunch 2400-7200kr, dinner mains 3700-4900kr, set menu 6400-9900kr; ⊗ noon-2.30pm & 5-10pm early May–mid-Sep; 🛜), it creates inventive versions of traditional Icelandic fare. Book ahead in high season and for dinner.

Bergsson Mathús
CAFE €€

(🖉 571 1822; www.bergsson.is; Templarasund 3; mains 2200-2800kr; ⊗ 7am-7pm Mon-Fri, to 5pm Sat & Sun; 🖉) There's nothing fancy here, but the homemade breads and fresh produce mean you'll be eating among locals as they flip through magazines, gossip and devour tasty brunch plates.

★ Dill
ICELANDIC €€€

(🖉 552 1522; www.dillrestaurant.is; Hverfisgata 12; 5/7 courses 11,900/13,900kr; ⊗ 6-10pm Wed-Sat) Exquisite New Nordic cuisine is the major drawcard at Reykjavík's elegant Michelin-starred bistro. Skilled chefs use a small number of ingredients to create highly complex dishes in a parade of courses. The owners are friends with Copenhagen's famous Noma clan and take Icelandic cuisine to similarly heady heights. It's hugely popular; book well in advance.

★ Grillmarkaðurinn
FUSION €€€

(Grill Market; 🖉 571 7777; www.grillmarkadurinn.is; Lækjargata 2a; mains 3500-9500kr; ⊗ 11.30am-2pm & 6-10.30pm, closed Sat & Sun lunch) Top-notch dining is the order of the day here, from the moment you enter the glass atrium with its golden-globe lights to your first snazzy cocktail, and on throughout the meal. Service is impeccable, and locals and visitors alike rave about the food, which uses Icelandic ingredients prepared with culinary imagination by master chefs.

Þrír Frakkar
ICELANDIC, SEAFOOD €€€

(🖉 552 3939; www.facebook.com/3frakkar.is; Baldursgata 14; mains 4200-6250kr; ⊗ 11.30am-2.30pm & 6-10pm Mon-Fri, 6-11pm Sat & Sun) Owner-chef Úlfar Eysteinsson has built up a consistently excellent reputation at this snug little restaurant. Specialities range throughout the aquatic world from salt cod and halibut to plokkfiskur (fish stew) with black bread. Non-fish items run towards guillemot, horse, and whale.

🍷 Drinking & Nightlife

Reykjavík is renowned for its weekend djammið, when folks buy booze from Vín-búðin (state alcohol shop), have a pre-party at home, then hit the town at midnight. Many of the cool-cat cafes around town morph into bars at night. The Reykjavík Appy Hour smartphone app lists local happy hours. Minimum drinking age is 20.

★ Kaffibarinn
BAR

(🖉 551 1588; www.kaffibarinn.is; Bergstaðastræti 1; ⊗ 3pm-1am Sun-Thu, to 4.30am Fri & Sat; 🛜) This old house with the London Underground symbol over the door contains one of Reykjavík's coolest bars; it even had a starring role in the cult movie *101 Reykjavík* (2000). At weekends you'll feel like you need either a famous face or a battering ram to get in. At other times it's a place for artistic types to chill with their Macs.

★ Kaldi
BAR

(☏ 581 2200; www.kaldibar.is; Laugavegur 20b; ⊙ noon-1am Sun-Thu, to 3am Fri & Sat) Effortlessly cool with mismatched seats and teal banquettes, plus a popular smoking courtyard, Kaldi is awesome for its range of five Kaldi microbrews, not available elsewhere. Happy hour (4pm to 7pm) gets you a beer for 750kr. Anyone can play the in-house piano.

★ Kaffi Vínyl
CAFE

(☏ 537 1332; www.facebook.com/kaffivinyl; Hverfisgata 76; ⊙ 8am-11pm Sun-Thu, to 1am Fri & Sat; ☏) 'Vegan is the new black' reads the neon sign, vinyl discs spin on the decks and a cool crowd tucks into meat-free noodles, burgers and pasta (mains from 1400kr). Happy hour lasts from 4pm to 7pm here – an ideal time to try an Icelandic beer or a vegan whiskey sour.

Port 9
WINE BAR

(☏ 832 2929; www.facebook.com/portniu; Veghúsastígur 7; ⊙ 4-11pm Tue-Sat, to 9pm Sun & Mon) Port 9 sauntered onto Reykjavík's drinking scene supremely confident in the quality of its wines and the knowledge of its staff – offerings here range from affordable tipples by the glass to vintages to break the bank. Low lighting, an arty clientele and a secret hang-out vibe (it's tucked down a tiny street) make it worth tracking down.

Reykjavík Roasters
CAFE

(☏ 517 5535; www.reykjavikroasters.is; Kárastígur 1; ⊙ 7am-6pm Mon-Fri, 8am-5pm Sat & Sun) These folks take their caffeine seriously. The tiny hipster joint is easily spotted on warm days thanks to its smattering of wooden tables on a small square. Swig a perfect latte and savour a flaky croissant and the scent of roasting coffee beans.

Paloma
CLUB

(http://palomaclub.is; Naustin 1; ⊙ 8pm-1am Thu & Sun, to 4.30am Fri & Sat) At one of Reykjavík's best late-night dance clubs DJs lay down reggae, electronica and pop upstairs and a dark deep house dance scene in the basement. Find it in the same building as the Dubliner.

ICELANDIC POP

Iceland produces a disproportionate number of world-class musicians. Björk (and the Sugarcubes) and Sigur Rós are Iceland's most famous musical exports. Sigur Rós' concert movie *Heima* (2007) is a must-see. New sounds surface all the time, ranging from indie-folk Of Monsters and Men, bluesy Kaleo, soulful Júníus Meyvant, quirky troubadour Ásgeir Trausti and indie band Seabear (which produced hit acts Sin Fang and Sóley), to electronica (FM Belfast, GusGus and múm). Visit www.icelandmusic.is for more info.

☆ Entertainment

The ever-changing vibrant Reykjavík performing-arts scene features shows at bars and cafes, local theatres and the Harpa concert hall. There are often performances at late-night bars and cafes, and venues such as **Húrra** (www.facebook.com/hurra.is; Tryggvagata 22; ⊙ 6pm-1am Mon-Thu, to 4.30am Fri & Sat, to 11.30pm Sun; ☏) and **Mengi** (☏ 588 3644; www.mengi.net; Óðinsgata 2; ⊙ noon-5pm Tue-Sat & for performances). Local theatres and **Harpa concert hall** (☏ box office 528 5050; www.harpa.is; Austurbakki 2; ⊙ 8am-midnight, box office noon-6pm) bring in all of the performing arts.

Reykjavík's **National Theatre** (Þjóðleikhúsið; ☏ 551 1200; www.leikhusid.is; Hverfisgata 19; ⊙ closed Jul) stages plays, musicals and operas. Cool, central cinema **Bíó Paradís** (☏ 412 7711; www.bioparadis.is; Hverfisgata 54; adult 1600-1800kr; ☏) screens films with English subtitles. To see what's on, consult Grapevine (www.grapevine.is), Visit Reykjavík (www.visitreykjavik.is), What's On in Reykjavík (www.whatson.is/magazine), Musik.is (www.musik.is) or city music shops.

🛍 Shopping

Reykjavík's vibrant design culture makes for great shopping: from sleek fish-skin purses and knitted *lopapeysur* (Icelandic woollen sweaters) to unique music or Icelandic schnapps *brennivín*. Laugavegur is the most dense shopping street. You'll find interesting shops all over town, but fashion concentrates near the Frakkastígur and Vitastígur end of Laugavegur. Skólavörðustígur is strong for arts and jewellery, while Bankastræti and Austurstræti have touristy shops.

❶ Information

DISCOUNT CARDS

Reykjavík City Card (www.citycard.is; 24/48/72hr 3800/5400/6500kr) offers admission to 10 of Reykjavík's municipal swimming/thermal pools and to most of the main galleries and museums, plus discounts on some tours, shops and entertainment. It also gives free travel on the city's Strætó buses and on the ferry to Viðey. Get cards at the Main Tourist Office, some travel agencies, 10-11 supermarkets, HI hostels and some hotels.

MEDICAL SERVICES

Health Centre (Heilsugæslan Miðbæ; ☑ 513-5950; Vesturgata 7; ⊕ by appointment) Book in advance.

Læknavaktin (☑ doctor on duty 1770; ⊕ 5-11.30pm Mon-Fri, 8am-11.30pm Sat & Sun) Nonemergency after-hours medical advice.

Landspítali University Hospital (☑ 543 1000, doctor on duty 1770; www.landspitali.is; Fossvogur) Hospital and emergency centre.

TOURIST INFORMATION

Main Tourist Office (Upplýsingamiðstöð Ferðamanna; ☑ 411 6040; www.visitreykjavik.is; Ráðhús, Tjarnargata 11; ⊕ 8am-8pm; 🛜) Friendly staff and mountains of free brochures, plus maps, Reykjavík City Card and Strætó city bus tickets. Books accommodation, tours and activities.

❶ Getting Around

BICYCLE

Reykjavík has a steadily improving network of cycle lanes; ask the Main Tourist Office for a map. You are allowed to cycle on pavements as long as you don't cause pedestrians problems.

You can rent from **Reykjavík Bike Tours** (☑ 694 8956; www.icelandbike.com; Ægisgarður 7; bike rental per 4hr from 3500kr, tours from 7500kr; ⊕ 9am-5pm Jun-Aug, shorter hours Sep-May; 🚌14) in the Old Harbour, or **Örninn** (☑ 588 9890; www.orninn.is; Faxafen 8; ⊕ 10am-6pm Mon-Fri, 11am-3pm Sat) in southeast Reykjavík. The **Bike Cave** (☑ 770 3113; www.facebook.com/bikecavereykjavik; Einarsnes 36; ⊕ 9am-10pm, shorter hours in winter; 🚌12), near Reykjavík Domestic Airport, can help with repairs.

BUS

Strætó (☑ 540 2700; www.straeto.is) operates regular buses around Reykjavík and its suburbs (Seltjarnarnes, Kópavogur, Garðabær, Hafnarfjörður and Mosfellsbær); it also operates long-distance buses. It has online schedules, a smartphone app and a printed map. Many free maps like *Welcome to Reykjavík City Map* also include bus-route maps.

Buses run from 7am until 11pm or midnight daily (from 11am on Sunday). Services depart at 15-minute or 30-minute intervals. A limited night-bus service runs until 4.30am on Friday and Saturday. Buses only stop at designated bus stops, marked with a yellow letter 'S'.

TAXI

Taxi prices are high. Flagfall starts at around 700kr. Tipping is not required. Taxis wait outside bus stations, airports and bars on weekend nights (huge queues for the latter), plus on Bankastræti near Lækjargata.

AROUND REYKJAVÍK

The Golden Circle

The Golden Circle takes in three popular attractions all within 100km of the capital: Þingvellir, Geysir and Gullfoss. It is a 300km artificial tourist circuit (there is no valley; natural topography marks its extent) that is loved (and marketed) by thousands and easy to see on one day-long circular drive or tour. Dozens of tour buses stop here, but visiting during off-hours allows a more subdued experience.

Þingvellir National Park (www.thingvellir.is; Rte 36/Þingvallavegur; parking 300-500kr) is inside an immense rift valley, caused by the separating North American and Eurasian tectonic plates. It's Iceland's most important historical location and a Unesco World Heritage Site: early Icelanders established the world's first democratic parliament, the Alþingi (pronounced ál-thingk-ee), here in 930 CE.

Geysir (Biskupstungnabraut) FREE, after which all spouting hot springs are named, only erupts rarely. Luckily, alongside it is the ever-reliable Strokkur, which spouts up to 30m approximately every five minutes.

Ten kilometres east, **Gullfoss** (Golden Falls; www.gullfoss.is; Rte 35/Kjalvegur) FREE is a spectacular rainbow-tinged double waterfall, which drops 32m before thundering away down a vast canyon.

Laugarvatn makes a good base for overnights and has the swanky lakeside **Fontana** (☑ 486 1400; www.fontana.is; Hverabraut 1; adult/

child 3800/2000kr; ⊘10am-11pm early Jun-late Aug, 11am-10pm late Aug-early Jun) geothermal spa.

🛏 Sleeping & Eating

Gljasteinn Skálinn   CABIN, GUESTHOUSE €
(☑486 8757; www.gljasteinn.is; Myrkholt; dm adult/child 6500/4000kr, d without bathroom 11,000kr; 🛜) This beautiful farm in the widening sweep of the valley between Geysir and Gullfoss has a clutch of tidy houses, one of which has sleeping-bag accommodation dorms (four beds each) and doubles with shared bathrooms, plus a kitchen and living room. It also has cabins with dorm beds in the highlands on the Kjölur route (F35).

Laugarvatn HI Hostel   HOSTEL €
(☑486 1215; www.laugarvatnhostel.is; Laugarvatnsvegur; dm/d without bathroom 5100/9900kr, d/tr/q 14,200/16,100/20,300kr; ⊘Feb-Nov; 🅿@🛜🏊) This large, clean and friendly hostel is housed in a renovated two-storey building with plenty of kitchen space (great lake views while washing up or from the dining room). There's also a pool table, bar and breakfast buffet (for an additional 1500kr), plus a room discount for HI members.

Þingvellir Campsite   CAMPGROUND €
(www.thingvellir.is; Rte 361; sites per adult/tent/child 1300/300kr/free; ⊘Jun-Sep) A primitive campground opposite the **information centre** (Leirar Þjónustumiðstöð; www.thingvellir.is; Rte 36; ⊘9am-10pm May-Aug, to 6pm Sep-Apr), where there are bathrooms and camping supplies.

★Efstidalur II   GUESTHOUSE €€
(☑486 1186; www.efstidalur.is; Efstidalur 2, Bláskógabyggð; s/d/tr incl breakfast from 19,800/24,200/34,200kr; 🅿🛜) Located 12km northeast of Laugarvatn on a working dairy farm, Efstidalur offers wonderfully welcoming digs, tasty meals and amazing ice cream. Adorable semi-detached cottages have brilliant views of hulking Hekla, and the **restaurant** (ice cream per scoop 500kr, mains 2250-5800kr; ⊘ice-cream bar 10am-10pm, restaurant 11.30am-10pm; 🅿🛜) serves beef from the farm and trout from the lake. The ice-cream bar scoops farm ice cream and has windows looking into the dairy barn.

★Héraðsskólinn   HOSTEL, GUESTHOUSE €€
(☑537 8060; www.heradsskolinn.is; 840 Laugarvatn; dm/d/q without bathroom from 4700/

11,100/23,000kr, d with bathroom 18,500kr; 🅿🛜) A beautifully unique lakeside boutique (originally built in 1928 by Guðjón Samúelsson) identifiable by its distinctive peaked green roofs. The interiors are sleek retro, with subtle nods to its old schoolhouse days. Design features include wooden desks, vintage maps and '50s-style chairs. It offers both private rooms with shared bathrooms (some sleep up to six) and dorms.

Hótel Geysir   HOTEL €€
(☑480 6800; www.hotelgeysir.is; Biskupstungnabraut; s/d incl breakfast from 18,000/22,900kr; 🅿@🛜) This four-star, 77-room hotel is minimalist cool. The facade has an entirely wooden front with only a small single doorway, which opens into a grand lobby, and the relics of the walls from the original building – once a training facility for glíma (Scandinavian martial art used by the Vikings). B&W photography of historic athletes decorates the walls.

Mengi   GUESTHOUSE €€
(☑780 1414; www.mengi-kjarnholt.com; Kjarnholt; d without bathroom from 17,500kr; 🅿🛜) This freshly renovated farmhouse in the countryside 10km south of Geysir has 10 rooms with sweeping pastoral views. Each is stylish with colourful artwork, wooden floors and crisp white sheets and walls. The on-site bar and hang-out space can be used by guests and there's a shared geothermal hot tub.

Ion Adventure Hotel   BOUTIQUE HOTEL €€€
(☑482 3415; www.ioniceland.is; Nesjavellir 801; d from 44,000kr; 🅿@🛜🏊) 🌿 Ion is hip, ultra modern and remote. Using sustainable practices throughout, it has a geothermal pool, organic spa and a **restaurant** (mains lunch 2600-4500kr, dinner 4000-12,000kr, 3-course dinner from 9900kr; ⊘11.30am-10pm) with slow-food local ingredients. The ubercool bar has designer cardboard lampshades and floor-to-ceiling windows for Northern Lights watching. Rooms are a tad small, but kitted out impeccably.

★Lindin   ICELANDIC €€
(☑486 1262; www.laugarvatn.is; Lindarbraut 2; mains 2200-5600kr; ⊘noon-10pm May-Sep, shorter hours Oct-Apr; 🅿🛜) Owned by Baldur, an affable, celebrated chef, Lindin could be the best restaurant for miles. In a sweet little silver house, with simple decor and wooden tables, the restaurant faces the lake and is purely

gourmet, with high-concept Icelandic fare featuring local or wild-caught ingredients. Order everything from soup to an amazing reindeer burger. Book ahead for dinner in high season.

Blue Lagoon

Arguably Iceland's most famous attraction is the **Blue Lagoon** (Bláa Lónið; ☑420 8800; www.bluelagoon.com; Norðurljosavegur 9; adult/child from 7000kr/free, premium entry from 9600kr/free; ⊙7am-midnight Jul–mid-Aug, to 11pm late May-Jun, 8am-10pm Jan-late May & mid-Aug–Sep, to 9pm Oct-Dec), a milky-blue geothermal pool set in a massive black lava field, 50km southwest of Reykjavík on the Reykjanes Peninsula. The futuristic Svartsengi geothermal plant provides an other-worldly backdrop, as well as the spa's water – 70% sea water, 30% fresh water, at a perfect 38°C. Daub yourself in silica mud and loll in the hot-pots with an iceblue cocktail. The mineral-rich waters dry hair to straw – use plenty of the provided hair conditioner.

You must book in advance, and to beat enormous crowds, go early or very late in the day. Reykjavík Excursions (p602) buses serve the BSÍ bus terminal (or hotels and the airport on request), and there are two swanky hotels on-site.

THE SOUTH

As you work your way east from Reykjavík, Rte 1 (the Ring Road) emerges into austere volcanic foothills punctuated by surreal steam vents and hot springs around **Hveragerði**, then swoops through the no-frills town of **Selfoss** and a flat, wide coastal plain, full of verdant horse farms and greenhouses, before the landscape suddenly begins to grow wonderfully jagged, after **Hella** and **Hvolsvöllur**. Hvolsvöllur's **LAVA Centre** (Iceland Volcano & Earthquake Centre; ☑415 5200; www.lavacentre.is; Austurvegur 14; adult/child 2400kr/free, cinema only 1200kr/free, exhibition & cinema 3200kr; ⊙exhibition 9am-7pm, lava house to 9pm) showcases the volcanic terrain with multimedia exhibits. Mountains thrust upwards on the inland side of the Ring Road, some of them volcanoes wreathed by mist (such as **Eyjafjallajökull**, site of the 2010 eruption), and the first of the awesome glaciers appears, as enormous rivers like the **Þjórsá** cut their way to the black-sand beaches rimming the Atlantic.

Throughout, roads pierce deep inland, to realms of lush waterfall-doused valleys like **Þjórsádalur** and **Fljótshlíð**, and awe-inspiring volcanoes such as **Hekla** (F255, off Rte 26). Two of the most renowned inland spots are **Landmannalaugar**, where vibrantly coloured rhyolite peaks meet bubbling hot springs; and **Þórsmörk**, a gorgeous, forested valley tucked away from the brutal northern elements under a series of ice caps. They are linked by the rightly famous 55km **Laugavegurinn hike**, Iceland's most popular trek (for more information, check Ferðafélag Íslands' website, www.fi.is). Since these areas lie inland on roads impassable by standard vehicles, most visitors access them on tours or amphibious buses from the southern Ring Road. Þórsmörk, one of Iceland's most popular hiking destinations, can be done as a day trip.

Skógar is the leaping-off point for Þórsmörk and boasts **Skógar Folk Museum** (Skógasafn; ☑487 8845; www.skogasafn.is; Skógavegur, near Rte 1; adult/child 2000kr/free; ⊙9am-6pm Jun-Aug, 10am-5pm Sep-May), plus nearby waterfalls **Seljalandsfoss & Gljúfurárbui** (off Rte 249, near Rte 1; parking 700kr) and **Skógafoss** (Skogafossvegur, off Rte 1). One of the easiest glacial tongues to reach is **Sólheimajökull** (Rte 221), just east of Skógar, but only climb onto the glacier accompanied by a local guide – conditions are often, and invisibly, shifting. **Vík** is surrounded by glaciers, vertiginous cliffs and black beaches such as **Reynisfjara** (Rte 215) with the offshore rock formation **Dyrhólaey** (Rte 218). South of the Ring Road, the tiny fishing villages of **Stokkseyri** and **Eyrarbakki** are refreshingly local-feeling.

Churning seas lead to the **Vestmannaeyjar** archipelago offshore (sometimes called the Westman Islands), with its zippy puffins and small town **Heimaey** tucked between lava flows, explained at the excellent volcano museum **Eldheimar** (Pompeii of the North; ☑488 2700; www.eldheimar.is; Gerðisbraut 10; adult/child 2300/1200kr; ⊙11am-6pm).

Public transport (and traffic) is solid along the Ring Road. **Midgard Adventure** (☑578 3370; www.midgardadventure.is; Dufbaksbraut 14; tours 14,000-34,000kr) and **Southcoast Adventure** (☑867 3535; www.southadventure.is; Hamragarðar Campground, Rte 249; 3-/5hr tours from 22,900/32,900kr, price based on 2 people) run excellent hiking, adventure and super-Jeep tours in the region.

The popular southwest area (www.south.is) is developing quickly and infrastructure keeps improving, with family farms offering lovely guesthouses. Nevertheless, it gets very busy in high seasons (eg summer, Christmas), so advanced accommodation booking is essential.

🛏 Sleeping & Eating

🛏 Hveragerði to Hvolsvöllur

★**River Hotel** HOTEL €€
(📞 487 5004; www.riverhotel.is; Þykkvabæjarvegur, Rte 25, Hella; d/f from 20,000/26,000kr; 🅿🛜) Relax and watch the river glide by through giant plate-glass windows in the lounge areas of this immaculate hotel on the banks of the Ytri-Rangá river. Contemporary rooms and a separate cottage are super-comfortable and there's an on-site restaurant for dinner. It's ideal for Northern Lights watching as well, and the owners are avid anglers. It gets booked up quickly.

Midgard Base Camp HOSTEL €€
(📞 578 3180; www.midgard.is; Dufþaksbraut 14, Hvolsvöllur; dm/d from 5300/23,300kr; 🅿🛜) Smart bunk beds, crafted by local iron smiths, in dorms of four to six. Private rooms have fabulous views, also enjoyed from the communal rooftop with hot tub and sauna. Downstairs there's foosball and a comfy lounge area, plus a restaurant offering hearty meals that hit the spot after a day of outdoor adventures. The highland tours (p608) run from here get glowing reviews.

Guesthouse Nonni GUESTHOUSE €€
(📞 894 9953; Arnarsandur 3, Hella; s/d without bathroom incl breakfast 14,700/18,000kr; 🛜) Run by friendly Nonni, who loves cooking a large breakfast (fresh bread and flower-shaped waffles) for his guests, this small guesthouse on a residential street has four wooden-walled rooms tucked up a cork stairwell.

★**Hótel Rangá** HOTEL €€€
(📞 487 5700; www.hotelranga.is; Hjarðarbrekka, Hella; d/ste incl breakfast from 54,000/119,000kr; @🛜) Just south of the Ring Road, 8km east of Hella, Hótel Rangá, with its stuffed polar bear in the lobby, looks like a log cabin but caters to Iceland's high-end travellers. Service is top-notch, and the wood-panelled rooms and luxurious common areas are cosy. The restaurant (mains 2600kr to 10,500kr) has broad windows looking across open pastures.

★**Kaffi Krús** INTERNATIONAL €€
(📞 482 1266; www.kaffikrus.is; Austurvegur 7, Selfoss; mains 1200-4900kr; ☺10am-10pm Jun-Aug,

shorter hours Sep-May) The 'Coffee Jar' is a popular cafe and restaurant in a charming, cosy old orange house along the main road. There's great outdoor space and a large selection of Icelandic and international dishes, from salads and pastas to fish and farmers-market dishes. The pizza (try the duck or langoustine) and burgers are excellent too.

Skyrgerðin CAFE €€
(📞 481 1010; www.skyrgerdin.is; Breiðamörk 25, Hveragerði; mains 2000-2500kr; ☺11am-10pm Mon-Thu, to 11pm Fri-Sun; 🛜) This chilled-out cafe-cum-restaurant incorporates rough wood furniture, antiques and vintage photos. Creative meals are crafted from fresh Icelandic ingredients and include fresh *skyr* (Icelandic yoghurt) smoothies and drinks, sliders, lasagne and fish, plus grand cakes that are just too tempting to resist. The building also contains the oldest *skyr* factory, hence its name.

🛏 Skógar & Around

★**Skógar Guesthouse** GUESTHOUSE €€
(📞 894 5464; www.skogarguesthouse.is; Ytri Skógar, off Skógaveur; d/tr without bathroom incl breakfast 23,800/35,700kr; 🛜) This charming white farmhouse is tucked in a strand of trees, beyond the Hótel Edda, almost to the cliff face. A friendly family offers quaint, impeccably maintained rooms with crisp linens and cosy quilts, and a large immaculate kitchen. A hot tub on a wood deck sits beneath the maples. It feels out of the tourist fray, despite being just a 10-minute walk from Skógafoss.

Hótel Skógafoss HOTEL €€
(📞 487 8780; www.hotelskogafoss.is; Skógafossvegur, off Rte 1; d incl breakfast 27,200-29,500kr; 🛜) Nineteen well-put-together, modern rooms (half of which have views of Skógafoss) and good bathrooms. There's a well-located **bistro-bar** (mains 1900-3300kr; ☺11am-9pm), with plate-glass windows looking onto the falls, and local beer on tap.

🛏 Vík & Around

★**Vík HI Hostel** HOSTEL €
(Norður-Vík Hostel; 📞 487 1106; www.hostel.is; Suður-víkurvegur 5; dm/s/d incl breakfast without bathroom 6500/10,200/18,000kr, cottages from 40,000kr; @🛜) 🚲 Vík's small, cosy, year-round hostel is in the beige house on the hill behind the village centre. Good facilities include a guest kitchen, and several standalone cottages sleep up to eight people. Staff can arrange local tours such as zip-lining and paragliding (May

to September, 14,900kr and 35,000kr). There's a discount for HI members. Green-certified.

★ Grand Guesthouse Garðakot
B&B €€

(☑894 2877; www.ggg.is; Garðakotsvegur, Garðakot farm; entire house 60,000kr; 🛜) Set on a pastoral sheep farm, this small, tidy house is rented out as a whole. It holds four beautiful rooms, two with private bathrooms and two that share. Heated hardwood floors downstairs, sweeping views of volcanoes and sea upstairs, and friendly proprietors, pretty decor, serenity and flat-screen TVs. It's 14km west of Vík, south of the Ring Road on Rte 218. Two-night minimum stay.

★ Garðar
GUESTHOUSE €€

(☑487 1260; www.reynisfjara-guesthouses.com; Reynisfjara, Rte 215; cottages 16,000-29,000kr) At the end of Rte 215, to the west of Vík, Garðar

is a magical, view-blessed place. Friendly farmer Ragnar rents out five self-contained beachside huts: one stone cottage sleeps four, while other timber cottages sleep two to four. Four of them have kitchen facilities, toilets and showers.

Guesthouse Carina
B&B €€

(☑699 0961; www.guesthousecarina.is; Mýrarbraut 13, off Rte 1; s/d/tr without bathroom from 16,900/21,900/25,900kr; 🅿🛜) Friendly Carina and her husband Ingvar run one of the best lodging options in Vík. Neat-as-a-pin, spacious rooms with good light and clean shared bathrooms fill a large converted house near the centre of town.

Icelandair Hotel Vík
HOTEL €€€

(☑487 1480, bookings 444 4000; www.icelandair hotels.com; Klettsvegur 1-5; d economy/regular

---

ICELANDIC SETTLEMENT & SAGAS

Rumour, myth and fantastic tales of fierce storms and barbaric dog-headed people kept most early explorers away from the great northern ocean, *oceanus innavigabilis*. Irish monks who regularly sailed to the Faroe Islands looking for seclusion were probably the first to stumble upon Iceland. It's thought that they settled around the year 700 but fled when Norsemen began to arrive in the early 9th century.

The Age of Settlement

The Age of Settlement is traditionally defined as between 870 and 930, when political strife on the Scandinavian mainland caused many to flee. Most North Atlantic Norse settlers were ordinary citizens: farmers and merchants who settled across Western Europe, marrying Britons, Westmen (Irish) and Scots.

Among Iceland's first Norse visitors was Norwegian Flóki Vilgerðarson, who uprooted his farm and headed for Snæland (the archaic Viking name for Iceland) around 860. He navigated with ravens, which, after some trial and error, led him to his destination and provided his nickname, Hrafna-Flóki (Raven-Flóki). Hrafna-Flóki sailed to Vatnsfjörður on the west coast but became disenchanted with the conditions. On seeing the icebergs in the fjord he dubbed the country Ísland (Iceland) and returned to Norway. He did eventually settle in Iceland's Skagafjörður district.

According to the 12th-century *Íslendingabók* (a historical narrative of the Settlement Era), Ingólfur Arnarson fled Norway with his blood brother Hjörleifur, landing at Ingólfshöfði (southeast Iceland) in 871. He was then led to Reykjavík by a pagan ritual: he tossed his high-seat pillars (a symbol of authority) into the sea as they approached land. Wherever the gods brought the pillars ashore would be the settlers' new home. Ingólfur named Reykjavík (Smoky Bay) after the steam from its thermal springs. Hjörleifur settled near the present town of Vík, but was murdered by his slaves shortly thereafter.

Descendants of the first settlers established the world's first democratic parliament, the Alþingi, in 930 at Þingvellir (Parliament Plains).

The Saga Age

The late 12th century kicked off the Saga Age, when the epic tales of the earlier 9th-to-10th-century settlement were recorded by historians and writers. These sweeping prose epics or sagas detail the family struggles, romance, vendettas and colourful characters of the Settlement Era. They are the backbone of medieval Icelandic literature and a rich source for historical understanding. Try *Egil's Saga*, the colourful adventures of a poet-warrior and grandson of a shape-shifter.

from 22,000/45,000kr; P🛜) This sleek black-window-fronted hotel has merged with the former next-door Hótel Edda. It sits on the eastern edge of town with 88 rooms, some suitably swanky, while the former Hótel Edda rooms are still modern but an economical option. Choose from views to the rear cliffs or the sea. The light, natural decor is inspired by the local environment. Breakfast costs 3000kr.

★ **Suður-Vík**   ICELANDIC, ASIAN €€
(🗹487 1515; www.facebook.com/Sudurvik; Suður-víkurvegur 1; mains 1300-5350kr; ⊙noon-10pm, shorter hours in winter) The friendly ambience, in a warmly lit building with hardwood floors, exposed beams and interesting artwork, helps to elevate this restaurant beyond its competition. Food is Icelandic hearty, ranging from farm plates and quinoa salad with chicken to pizzas and Asian dishes (think spicy Panang curry with rice). Book ahead in summer. For a nightcap head to the **Man Cave** (beers from 1000kr; ⊙6pm-late) downstairs.

Smiðjan Brugghús   MICROBREWERY
(http://smidjanbrugghus.is; Sunnubraut 15; ⊙11.30am-midnight Sun-Thu, to 1am Fri & Sat) Vík's hippest hang-out is warehouse-style with grey walls, windows looking onto the brewing room and blackboards displaying 10 craft beers on tap. Hop aficionados can try Icelandic India Pale Ales, pale ale, porter and farmhouse ale with a handful of different burgers (including a vegan patty).

WEST ICELAND

Geographically close to Reykjavík yet far, far away in sentiment, West Iceland (known as Vesturland; www.west.is) is a splendid microcosm of what Iceland has to offer. The long arm of **Snæfellsnes Peninsula** is a favourite thanks to its glacier, Snæfellsjökull. The area around **Snæfellsjökull National Park** (🗹436 6860; www.snaefellsjokull.is) is tops for birding, whale watching, lava field hikes and horse riding.

Inland beyond **Reykholt** you'll encounter waterfalls like **Hraunfossar** (Rte 518), lava tubes such as **Viðgelmir** (🗹783 3600; www.thecave.is; off Rte 518; tour per adult/child from 6500kr/free) and remote highland glaciers, including enormous **Langjökull** with its **Into the Glacier** (Langjökull Ice Cave; 🗹578 2550; www.intotheglacier.is) ice cave. **Hótel Húsafell** (🗹435 1551; www.hotelhusafell.com; Rte 518; d incl breakfast from 34,200kr; P🛜) with

SKAFTAFELL & VATNAJÖKULL NATIONAL PARK

Skaftafell, the jewel in the crown of **Vatnajökull National Park** (www.vjp.is), encompasses a breathtaking collection of peaks and glaciers. It's the country's favourite wilderness: 300,000 visitors per year come to marvel at thundering waterfalls, twisted birch woods, the tangled web of rivers threading across the *sandar* (sand deltas) and brilliant blue-white Vatnajökull with its myriad ice tongues.

Icelandic Mountain Guides (IMG; 🗹Reykjavík 587 9999, Skaftafell 894 2959; www.mountainguides.is) and **Glacier Guides** (Arctic Adventures; 🗹562 7000; www.glacierguides.is) lead glacier walks and adventure tours.

ICELAND WEST ICELAND

its top-notch rooms and gourmet restaurant offers high-end digs and camping, too.

Icelanders honour West Iceland for its local sagas: two of the best known, *Laxdæla Saga* and *Egil's Saga,* took place along the region's brooding waters, marked today by haunting cairns and an exceptional **Settlement Centre** (Landnámssetur Íslands; 🗹437 1600; www.settlementcentre.is; Brákarbraut 13-15; adult/child 2500kr/free; ⊙10am-9pm) in lively **Borgarnes**, which also has good lodging, such as **Bjarg** (🗹437 1925; www.facebook.com/bjargborgarnes; Bjarg farm; d with/without bathroom incl breakfast 20,700/17,300kr; 🛜) and **Egils Guesthouse & Apartments** (🗹860 6655; www.egilsguesthouse.is; Brákarbraut 11; d with/without bathroom incl breakfast 22,000/18,000kr, studios from 19,125kr; P🛜), and fine eats.

West Iceland offers everything from windswept beaches to historic villages and awe-inspiring terrain in one neat, little package. **Stykkishólmur** makes a great base, with its fine hotels and guesthouses such as **Hótel Egilsen** (🗹554 7700; www.egilsen.is; Aðalgata 2; s/d from 26,320/31,900kr; @🛜), excellent eateries like **Narfeyrarstofa** (🗹533 1119; www.narfeyrarstofa.is; Aðalgata 3; mains 2000-5000kr; ⊙11.30am-10pm May-Sep, reduced hours Oct-Apr; 🗹) and **Sjávarpakkhúsið** (🗹438 1800; www.sjavarpakkhusid.is; Hafnargata 2; mains 2800-3500kr; ⊙noon-10pm; 🛜), interesting museums such as **Norska Húsið** (Norwegian House; 🗹433 8114; www.norskahusid.is; Hafnargata 5; adult/child 1000kr/free; ⊙11am-6pm May-Aug, 2-5pm Tue-Thu Sep-Apr) and boats around **Breiðafjörður**

WILD WESTFJORDS

Some of Iceland's least touristed but wildest scenery lies in the far north-west of the country, in the craggy rainbow-prone Westfjords (www.west-fjords.is). **Ísafjörður** is the largest city and base, with tiny fjord-side hamlets dotting the rest of the far-flung fjord fingers. Highlights include the remote **Hornstrandir Nature Reserve** (☑ 591 2000; www.ust.is/hornstrandir), thunder-ing **Dynjandi waterfall** and the gor-geous **Rauðasandur** pink-sand beach with its nearby **Látrabjarg bird cliffs**.

operated by **Seatours** (Sæferðir; ☑ 433 2254; www.seatours.is; Smiðjustígur 3; ☺ 8am-8pm mid-May–mid-Sep, 9am-5pm rest of year). Find the re-gion's top cuisine at **Bjargarsteinn Mathús** (☑ 438 6770; www.facebook.com/Bjargarsteinnres-taurant; Sólvellir 15; mains 2800-4900kr; ☺ 4-10pm Jun-Aug, 5-9pm Sep–mid-Dec & mid-Jan–May; 🖱) in nearby **Grundarfjörður**, across from icon-ic mountain, **Kirkjufell**.

NORTH ICELAND

Iceland's mammoth and magnificent north is a wonderland of moonlike lava fields, belching mudpots, epic waterfalls, snow-capped peaks and whale-filled bays.

Little **Akureyri**, with its surprising mo-ments of big-city living, is the best base in the north. From here you can explore by car or bus, and tour the region's highlights.

Húsavík is Iceland's premier whale-watching destination, with up to 11 species coming to feed in summer. Go out whale and puffin spotting with **North Sailing** (☑ 464 7272; www.northsailing.is; Garðarsbraut; 3hr tours adult/child 10,500/3500kr), **Gentle Gi-ants** (☑ 464 1500; www.gentlegiants.is; Garðars-braut; 3hr tours adult/child 10,400/4400kr) or **Salka** (☑ 464 3999; www.salkawhalewatching.is; Garðarsbraut 7; 3hr tours adult/child 9950/4200kr; ☺ May-Sep). **Siglufjörður** on the **Tröllaska-gi Peninsula** offers vast vistas and rugged mountainscapes.

Visit otherworldy lake **Mývatn** for its lava castles and hidden fissures. Thunderously roaring **Dettifoss** is one of Iceland's grand-est waterfalls. Nearby **Goðafoss** (Waterfall of the Gods; Rte 1) rips straight through the Bárðardalur lava field along Rte 1.

On the east side of the lake, the giant jagged lava field at **Dimmuborgir** (Rte 884) (literally 'Dark Castles') is one of the most fascinating flows in the country. Dominat-ing the lava fields on the eastern edge of Mývatn is the classic tephra ring **Hverfjall** (off Rte 848) (also called Hverfell). This near-symmetrical crater appeared 2700 years ago in a cataclysmic eruption. The dramatic lava cave at **Lofthellir** is a stunning destination, with magnificent natural ice sculptures (ice trolls?) dominating the interior. Book with **Geo Travel** (☑ 464 4442; www.geotravel.is) to get there.

The magical, ochre-toned world of **Hverir** (Rte 1) (also called Hverarönd) is a lunar-like landscape of mud cauldrons, steaming vents, radiant mineral deposits and piping fumaroles.

For birdwatching background, swing by **Sigurgeir's Bird Museum** (Fuglasafn Sigur-geirs; ☑ 464 4477; www.fuglasafn.is; off Rte 1, Ytri-Neslönd farm; adult/child 1500/800kr; ☺ noon-5pm mid-May–Oct, reduced hours rest of year), housed in a beautiful lakeside building that fuses modern design with a traditional turf house.

☞ Tours

Saga Travel (☑ 558 8888; www.sagatravel.is; Fjölnisgata 6a; ☺ booking office 8am-4pm Mon-Fri, to 2pm Sat & Sun) offers diverse year-round excursions and activities throughout the north.

🛏 Sleeping & Eating

🛏 Akureyri & Around

Stay at **Sæluhús** (☑ 412 0800; www.saeluhus.is; Sunnutröð; studios/houses from 26,750/32,250kr; 🖱) with its well-equipped modern studi-os and houses, or **Skjaldarvík** (☑ 552 5200; www.skjaldarvik.is; Rte 816; s/d without bathroom incl breakfast 20,900/22,600kr; @ 🖱), a slice of guesthouse nirvana, in a farm setting 6km north of town. There's an unexpected touch of the Mediterranean at outstanding **Hall-landsnes** (☑ 895 6029; www.halllandsnes.is; Rte 1; apt from 18,900kr; 🖱), 6km east of Akureyri along Rte 1.

Akureyri Backpackers (☑ 571 9050; www.akureyribackpackers.com; Hafnarstræti 98; dm from 4900kr; d without bathroom 14,300kr; 🖱) offers great budget digs, and **Icelandair Ho-tel Akureyri** (☑ 518 1000; www.icelandairhotels.com; Þingvallastræti 23; d from 22,100kr; @ 🖱) hits the top-end mark.

🛏 Around the North

On Tröllaskagi Peninsula, Dalvík's excellent **HI Hostel** (☑ 699 6616, 865 8391; www.dalvikhostel.com; Hafnarbraut 4; dm/d/tr without bathroom 5700/15,200/18,900kr; 🛜) and wonderful cafe **Gísli, Eiríkur, Helgi** (Kaffihús Bakkabræðra; ☑ 666 3399; www.facebook.com/bakkabraedur kaffi; Grundargata 1; soup & salad buffet 1990kr; ☺ 10am-10pm, to 1am Fri & Sat, to 7pm Sun) make the sleepy village a good option. The wow factor delights at **Apartment Hótel Hjalteyri** (☑ 897 7070, 462 2770; www.hotelhjalteyri.is; Hjalteyri; d/apt incl breakfast from 21,400/26,000kr; 🛜), a renovated schoolhouse en route to Hjalteyri's harbour. In Siglufjörður, stay over at charming **Herring Guesthouse** (☑ 868 4200; www.theherringhouse.com; Hávegur 5; s/d without bathroom 14,700/19,200kr, 4-person apt 48,200kr; 🛜) or **Siglunes Guesthouse** (☑ 467 1222; www.hotelsiglunes.is; Lækjargata 10; d with/without bathroom from 23,000/19,1000kr, q 30,100kr; ☺ restaurant 6-9pm Tue-Thu, to 10pm Fri-Sun; 🛜), which has an excellent Moroccan **restaurant** (mains 3000-4000kr; ☺ 6-9pm Tue-Thu, to 10pm Fri-Sun).

Near Mývatn, **Vogafjós** (☑ 464 3800; www.vogafjos.net; Rte 848; dishes 2000-5900kr; ☺ 10am-11pm Jun-Aug, shorter hours rest of year; 🛜☑🚼) in Reykjahlíð serves up top local vittles and offers a nearby guesthouse.

In Húsavík, try cosy guesthouse **Árból** (☑ 464 2220; www.arbol.is; Ásgarðsvegur 2; s/d/q without bathroom incl breakfast 12,400/21,100/36,500kr; 🛜) or spectacularly peaceful seafront **Tungulending** (☑ 896 6948; www.tungulending.is; off Rte 85; d/tr without bathroom incl breakfast from 17,000/23,900kr; 🛜), 11km north of town.

SURVIVAL GUIDE

ℹ Directory A–Z

ACCESSIBLE TRAVEL
Iceland can be trickier than many places in northern Europe when it comes to access for travellers with disabilities. For details on accessible facilities, contact the information centre for people with disabilities, **Þekkingarmiðstöð Sjálfsbjargar** (Sjálfsbjörg Knowledge Centre; ☑ 550 0118; www.thekkingarmidstod.is; Hátún 12, Reykjavík).

Particularly good for tailor-made accessible trips around the country are **All Iceland Tours** (http://alliceland.is) and **Iceland Unlimited** (www.icelandunlimited.is).

Reykjavík's city buses are accessible courtesy of ramps; elsewhere, public buses don't have ramps or lifts.

ACCOMMODATION
Iceland has a broad range of accommodation, but demand often outstrips supply. If you're visiting in the shoulder and high seasons (from May to September), book early. Generally, accommodation prices are very high compared to mainland European lodging. All hostels and some guesthouses and hotels offer cheaper rates if guests use their own sleeping bags. Booking.com is widely used across Iceland.

Campgrounds Camping allows spontaneity. Campervans are very popular. Most towns have designated camping areas – generally open mid-May to mid-September. The Camping Card (www.campingcard.is) can be a good deal for longer stays.

Hostels Hostelling International Iceland (www.hostel.is) administers 34 of Iceland's superb youth hostels; Akureyri and Reykjavík have private ones, too.

Guesthouses (*gistiheimilð*) Run the gamut from homestyle B&Bs to large hotel-like properties, and often have shared bathrooms. Many only open mid-May to mid-September. Check Hey Iceland (www.heyiceland.is) for great countryside accommodation.

Hotels From small, bland and business-like to designer dens with all the trimmings (and prices to match).

Mountain huts Walking clubs and Ferðafélag Íslands (www.fi.is) maintain basic huts on many popular hiking tracks – reservations essential.

ACTIVITIES
➡ Hiking and mountaineering is stunning all over the country, especially in national parks and nature reserves. July, August and September are the best months for walking. For details check Ferðafélag Íslands (www.fi.is).

➡ A vast menu of adventure tours combine ice climbing, snowmobiling, caving etc with super-Jeeps or bus tours. Most pick up from Reykjavík – see Tours (p602).

➡ Stables offer everything from 90-minute horse rides to multiday tours, and can combine riding with other activities, such as visiting the Golden Circle or Blue Lagoon. Some offer guesthouse accommodation.

➡ Hvítá river, located along the Golden Circle, is a top spot for white-water rafting near Reykjavík. Trips run from Reykholt, but offer Reykjavík pick-ups. Contact **Arctic Rafting** (☑ 562 7000; www.arcticrafting.com; Drumboddsstaðir; rafting/rafting & horse riding/rafting & ATV tours per person from 19,000/30,000/34,000kr; ☺ mid-May–mid-Sep).

➡ Scuba-diving tours with **Dive.is** (☑ 578 6200; www.dive.is; Hólmaslóð 2; 2 dives at Þingvellir

SMARTPHONE APPS

There's an incredible range of smartphone apps. Useful ones include **112 Iceland** app for safe travel, **Veður** (weather), and apps for bus companies such as Strætó and Reykjavík Excursions. The **Reykjavík Appy Hour** app gets special mention for listing happy hours and their prices!

34,000kr) go to Þingvellir's rift waters, which have astonishing 100m visibility.

➡ Every town has a geothermal public pool, and natural hot-pots abound.

➡ Whale watching is best from mid-May to September. Boats depart from Reykjavík and Akureyri, although northern Húsavík is renowned for whale watching.

➡ Northern Lights tours feature in winter, and flight tours cover the whole country.

INTERNET ACCESS

Wi-fi is common at most sleeping and eating venues and N1 service stations. Find computers for public internet access at libraries and tourist offices.

LGBT+ TRAVELLERS

Icelanders have a very open attitude towards homosexuality, though the gay scene is low-key, even in Reykjavík. LGBT+ organisation **Samtökin '78** (⌨ 552 7878; www.samtokin78.is; Suður-gata 3; ☉ office 1-4pm Mon-Fri, Queer Centre 8-11pm Thu, closed Jul) provides information. **Pink Iceland** (⌨ 562 1919; www.pinkiceland. is; Hverfisgata 39; ☉ 9am-5pm Mon-Fri) is Iceland's first gay-and-lesbian-owned-and-focused travel agency.

MONEY

Credit cards are ubiquitous, but many transactions (such as purchasing petrol) require a PIN – get one before leaving home. ATMs take MasterCard, Visa, Cirrus, Maestro and Electron cards. VAT and service are included in marked prices. Tipping is not required. Spend over 6000kr in a single shop and claim a tax refund (see www.tollur.is).

POST

The Icelandic postal service (www.postur.is) is reliable and efficient, and rates are comparable to those in other Western European countries.

PUBLIC HOLIDAYS

New Year's Day 1 January

Easter March or April; Maundy Thursday and Good Friday to Easter Monday (changes annually)

First Day of Summer First Thursday after 18 April

Labour Day 1 May

Ascension Day May or June (changes annually)

Whit Sunday and Whit Monday May or June (changes annually)

National Day 17 June

Commerce Day First Monday in August

Christmas 24 to 26 December

New Year's Eve 31 December

SAFE TRAVEL

Safetravel (www.safetravel.is) provides information on ICE-SAR's 112 Iceland app for smartphones (useful in emergencies) and explains procedures for leaving a travel plan with ICE-SAR or a friend/contact.

TELEPHONE

Iceland's international access code is ⌨ 00 and its country code is ⌨ 354; there are no area codes. For international directory assistance and reverse-charge (collect) calls, dial ⌨ 1811. Mobile coverage is widespread. Visitors with GSM 900/1800 phones can make roaming calls. Local SIM cards are sold at grocery stores and petrol stations (for unlocked mobiles).

TOILETS

Tourists doing their business in public or in inappropriate places (eg car parks and cemeteries) are guaranteed to madden the locals. Stick to real facilities.

Getting There & Away

AIR

Iceland is connected by year-round flights (including budget carriers) from Keflavík International Airport (KEF; www.kefairport.is), 48km southwest of Reykjavík, to a multitude of European destinations, as well as to the United States and Canada. Icelandair (www.icelandair. com) offers stopovers between the continents, and flights to Akureyri in the North. Internal flights and those to Greenland and the Faroe Islands use the small Reykjavík Domestic Airport (REK; Reykjavíkurflugvöllur; www.reykjavikair port.is) in central Reykjavík.

SEA

Smyril Line (www.smyrilline.com) operates a weekly car ferry, the *Norröna*, from Hirtshals (Denmark) through Tórshavn (Faroe Islands) to Seyðisfjörður in East Iceland. See website for more.

Getting Around

TO/FROM THE AIRPORT

Flybus (⌨ 580 5400; www.re.is; one-way ticket 2950kr; ☎) and **Airport Express** (⌨ 540 1313; www.airportexpress.is; ☎) have buses connecting the airport with Reykjavík (50 minutes), and Flybus also goes to the Blue Lagoon (4990kr). They offer pick-up/drop-off at many city accommodations (to bus station/hotel from 2700/3300kr). **Airport Direct** (☑497 5000; www.reykjaviksightseeing.is/airport-direct; one way/return from 5500/10,000kr; 🛜) minibuses link accommodation and the airport. Strætó (p606) bus 55 also connects the BSÍ bus terminal and the airport (1840kr, 1¼ hours, nine daily Monday to Friday).

Taxis from Keflavík airport to Reykjavík cost around 16,100kr.

AIR

Iceland has an extensive network of domestic flights, which locals use almost like buses. In winter a flight can be the only way to get between destinations, but weather at this time of year can play havoc with schedules. Domestic flights depart from the small **Reykjavík Domestic Airport** (Reykjavíkurflugvöllur; www.isavia.is; Innanlandsflug), *not* from the major international airport at Keflavík.

Check **Air Iceland Connect** (☑570 3030; www.airicelandconnect.is; Reykjavík Domestic Airport) and **Eagle Air** (☑562 2640; www.eagleair.is; Reykjavík Domestic Airport), who also offer tours.

BICYCLE

Cycling is an increasingly popular way to see the country's landscapes, but be prepared for harsh conditions. Most buses carry bikes (some charge fees). Icelandic Mountain Bike Club (http://fjallahjolaklubburinn.is) has info and links to the annually updated *Cycling Iceland* map.

BOAT

Several year-round ferries operate in Iceland.
Landeyjahöfn to Vestmannaeyjar islands (www.seatours.is)
Árskógssandur, north of Akureyri, to Hrísey (www.hrisey.is)
Stykkishólmur in West Iceland to Brjánslækur in the Westfjords, via the island of Flatey (www.seatours.is)
Dalvík in North Iceland to Grímsey (www.saefari.is)

From June to August, boat services run from Bolungarvík and Ísafjörður to Hornstrandir (Westfjords).

BUS

Iceland has a shrinking network of long-distance bus routes, with services provided by a handful of main companies. The free *Public Transport in Iceland* map has an overview of routes; pick it up at tourist offices or view it online at www.publictransport.is.

➡ From roughly June to August, regular scheduled buses run to most places on the Ring Road, into the popular hiking areas of the Southwest, and to larger towns in the Westfjords and Eastfjords, and on the Reykjanes and Snæfellsnes Peninsulas. The rest of the year, services range from daily, to a few weekly, to nonexistent.

➡ In summer, 4WD buses run along some F roads (mountain roads), including the highland Kjölur, Sprengisandur and Askja routes (inaccessible to 2WD cars).

➡ Many buses can be used as day tours: buses spend a few hours at the final destination before returning to the departure point, and may stop for a half-hour at various tourist destinations en route.

➡ Bus companies may operate from different terminals or pick-up points. Reykjavík has several bus terminals; in small towns, buses usually stop at the main petrol station or camping ground, but it pays to double-check.

➡ Many buses are equipped with free wi-fi.

Main bus companies:
Reykjavík Excursions (☑580 5400; www.ioyo.is)
SBA-Norðurleið (☑550 0700; www.sba.is)
Sterna (☑551 1166; www.icelandbybus.is)
Strætó (☑540 2700; www.bus.is)
Trex (☑587 6000; www.trex.is)

CAR & CAMPERVAN

Driving in Iceland gives you unparalleled freedom to discover the country. Booking ahead is usually cheapest. The Ring Road is almost entirely paved, but many backcountry areas are served by dirt tracks. Most rental cars are not allowed on highland (F) roads. Driving off-road is strictly prohibited. To hire a car you must be at least 20 years old (23 to 25 years for a 4WD) and hold a valid licence. Campervans offer even more independence – Camper Iceland (www.camper iceland.is) is just one of many outfits.

HITCHING

Hitching is never entirely safe, and it's not recommended. Travellers who hitch should understand that they are taking a small but potentially serious risk. Check out Carpooling in Iceland (www.samferda.is) for rides – note there is an expectation that passengers will contribute to fuel costs.

Ireland

POP REPUBLIC OF IRELAND 4.76 MILLION; NORTHERN IRELAND 1.87 MILLION

Best Traditional Pubs

➜ Kyteler's Inn (p627)

➜ O'Connor's (p631)

➜ Peadar O'Donnell's (p643)

➜ Crane Bar (p636)

Best Places to Eat

➜ Fade Street Social (p623)

➜ Market Lane (p629)

➜ Oscar's (p635)

Why Go?

Few countries have an image so plagued by cliché. From shamrocks and *shillelaghs* (Irish fighting sticks) to leprechauns and lovable rogues, there's a plethora of platitudes to wade through before you reach the real Ireland.

The Emerald Isle is one of Europe's gems, a scenic extravaganza of lakes, mountains, sea and sky. From picture-postcard County Kerry to the rugged coastline of Northern Ireland (part of the UK, distinct from the Republic of Ireland), there are countless opportunities to get outdoors and explore, whether cycling the Causeway Coast or hiking the hills of Killarney and Connemara.

There are cultural pleasures too in the land of James Joyce and William Butler Yeats, U2 and the Undertones. Dublin, Cork and Belfast all have world-class art galleries and museums, and you can enjoy foot-stomping traditional music in the bars of Galway and Killarney. So push aside the shamrocks, and experience the real Ireland.

When to Go
Dublin

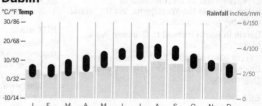

Late Mar Spring flowers are everywhere and St Patrick's Day festivities beckon.

Jun Best chance of dry weather, with long summer evenings. Bloomsday celebrates Joyce's *Ulysses* in Dublin.

Sep–Oct Summer crowds thin. Autumn colours reign and surf's up on the west coast.

Entering the Country

Dublin Airport Private coaches run every 10 to 15 minutes to the city centre (€7). Taxis take 30 to 45 minutes and cost €20 to €25.

Dun Laoghaire Ferry Port Public bus takes around 45 minutes to the centre of Dublin; DART (suburban rail) takes about 25 minutes. Both cost €3.25.

Dublin Port Terminal Buses are timed to coincide with arrivals and departures; they cost €3 to the city centre.

Belfast International Airport Airport Express 300 bus runs hourly from Belfast International Airport (one way/return £7.50/10.50, 30 to 55 minutes). A taxi costs around £30.

George Best Belfast City Airport Airport Express 600 bus runs every 20 minutes from George Best Belfast City Airport (one way/return £2.50/3.80, 15 minutes). A taxi costs around £10.

ITINERARIES

One Week

Spend a couple of days in Dublin (p619) ambling through the excellent national museums, and gorging yourself on Guinness and good company in Temple Bar. Get medieval in Kilkenny (p626) before heading on to Cork (p627) and discovering why they call it 'The Real Capital'. Head west for a day or two exploring the scenic Ring of Kerry (p632) and enchanting Killarney (p631).

Two Weeks

Follow the one-week itinerary, then make your way north from Killarney to bohemian Galway (p633). Using Galway as your base, explore the alluring Aran Islands (p636) and the hills of Connemara (p637). Finally head north to see the Giant's Causeway (p641) and experience the optimistic vibe in fast-changing Belfast (p637).

Essential Food & Drink

Potatoes Still a staple of most traditional meals and presented in a variety of forms.

Meat and seafood Beef, lamb and pork are common options. Seafood is widely available in restaurants and is often excellent, especially in the west. Oysters, trout and salmon are delicious, particularly if they're direct from the sea or a river rather than a fish farm.

Soda bread The most famous Irish bread is made with bicarbonate of soda to make up for soft Irish flour that traditionally didn't take well to yeast.

The fry Who can say no to a plate of fried bacon, sausages, black pudding, white pudding, eggs and tomatoes? For the famous Ulster fry, common throughout the North, simply add fadge (potato bread).

AT A GLANCE

Area 84,421 sq km

Capitals Dublin (Republic of Ireland), Belfast (Northern Ireland)

Country Code Republic of Ireland ☏ 353, Northern Ireland 44

Currency euro (€) in Republic of Ireland; pound sterling (£) in Northern Ireland

Emergency ☏ 112

Languages English, Irish Gaelic

Time Winter: Greenwich Mean Time (UTC/GMT+00:00); Summer (UTC/GMT+01:00)

Visas Schengen rules do not apply

Sleeping Price Ranges

The following price ranges are based on a double room with private bathroom in high season (Republic/Dublin/Northern Ireland).

€/£ less than €80/€150/£50

€€/££ €80–180/€150–250/£50–120

€€€/£££ more than €180/€250/£12

Eating Price Ranges

The following price ranges refer to the cost of a main course at dinner (Republic/Dublin/Northern Ireland).

€/£ less than €12/€15/£12

€€/££ €12–25/€15–28/£12–20

€€€/£££ more than €25/€28/£20

Ireland Highlights

1 Dublin (p619) Meandering through museums, pubs and literary haunts.

2 Galway (p633) Hanging out in bohemian Galway, with its hip cafes and live-music venues.

3 Giant's Causeway (p641) Hiking along the Causeway Coast.

4 Skellig Michael (p632) Taking a boat trip to the 6th-century monastery perched atop this wild rocky islet.

5 Irish pubs (p623) Supping a pint of Guinness while tapping your toes to a live-music session.

6 Gap of Dunloe (p631) Cycling through the

spectacular lake and mountain scenery of the Gap of Dunloe.

7 Titanic Belfast (p639) Discovering the industrial history of the city that built the famous ocean liner.

8 Aran Islands (p636) Wandering the wild, limestone shores of the remote and craggy Aran Islands.

DUBLIN

POP 1.3 MILLION

Sultry rather than sexy, Dublin exudes the personality of a city that has managed to turn careworn into carefree. The halcyon days of the Celtic Tiger (the Irish economic boom of the late 1990s), when cash cascaded like a free-flowing waterfall, have long since disappeared, and the city has once again been forced to grind out a living. But Dubliners know how to enjoy life. They do so through their music, art and literature – cultural riches that Dubs often take for granted but generate immense pride. Dublin has world-class museums, superb restaurants and the best range of entertainment available anywhere in Ireland – and that's not including its pubs, the ubiquitous centre of the city's social life and an absolute must for any visitor. And should you wish to get away from it all, the city has a handful of seaside towns at its edges that make for wonderful day trips.

◉ Sights

Dublin's relatively compact size means that the vast majority of sights – including most of the big hitters – are within walking distance of each other, on either side of the Liffey in the city centre. The exceptions are the Guinness Storehouse, the Irish Museum of Modern Art and Kilmainham Gaol, which are clustered together on the western edge of the city south of the river; they're easily reached by tram or bus, and conveniently they're also on all the the hop-on, hop-off bus itineraries, so you can take your time with each attraction. On the north side of the river, also west of the centre, the decorative arts branch of the National Museum is just a handful of stops away on the tram line.

★ Trinity College   HISTORIC BUILDING
(☑ 01-896 1000; www.tcd.ie; College Green; ⊗ 8am-10pm; ☐ all city centre, ☐ Westmoreland or Trinity) **FREE** Ireland's most prestigious university is a 16th-century bucolic retreat in the heart of the city. Ambling about its cobbled squares, it's easy to imagine it in those far-off days when all good gentlemen (for they were only men until 1904) came equipped with a passion for philosophy and a love of empire. The student body is a lot more diverse these days, even if the look remains the same.

★ National Museum of Ireland – Archaeology   MUSEUM
(www.museum.ie; Kildare St; ⊗ 10am-5pm Tue-Sat, 1-5pm Sun; ☐ all city centre) **FREE** Ireland's most important cultural institution was established in 1877 as the primary repository of the nation's archaeological treasures. These include the most famous of Ireland's crafted artefacts, the Ardagh Chalice and the Tara Brooch, dating from the 12th and 8th centuries respectively. They are part of the Treasury, itself part of Europe's finest collection of Bronze and Iron Age gold artefacts, and the most complete assemblage of medieval Celtic metalwork in the world.

★ Guinness Storehouse   BREWERY, MUSEUM
(www.guinness-storehouse.com; St James's Gate, South Market St; adult/child from €18.50/16, Connoisseur Experience €55; ⊗ 9.30am-7pm Sep-Jun, 9am to 8pm Jul & Aug; ☎; ☐ 13, 21A, 40, 51B, 78, 78A, 123 from Fleet St, ☐ James's) The most popular visit in town is this multimedia homage to Guinness in a converted grain storehouse that is part of the 26-hectare brewery. Across its seven floors you'll discover everything about Guinness before getting to taste the brew in the top-floor Gravity Bar, with panoramic views. The floor directly below has a very good restaurant. Pre-booking your tickets online will save you time and money.

★ Chester Beatty Library   MUSEUM
(☑ 01-407 0750; www.cbl.ie; ⊗ 10am-5pm Mon-Fri, 11am-5pm Sat & Sun Mar-Oct, 10am-5pm Tue-Fri, 11am-5pm Sat & Sun Nov-Feb; ☐ all city centre) **FREE** This world-famous library, in the grounds of **Dublin Castle** (☑ 01-645 8813; www.dublincastle. ie; Dame St; guided tours adult/child €12/6, self-guided tours €8/4; ⊗ 9.45am-5.45pm, last admission 5.15pm; ☐ all city centre), houses the collection of mining engineer Sir Alfred Chester Beatty (1875–1968), bequeathed to the Irish State on his death. Spread over two floors, the breathtaking collection includes more than 20,000 manuscripts, rare books, miniature paintings, clay tablets, costumes and other objects of artistic, historical and aesthetic importance. Free tours run at 1pm Wednesdays, 2pm Saturdays and 3pm Sundays.

★ Kilmainham Gaol   MUSEUM
(☑ 01-453 5984; www.kilmainhamgaolmuseum.ie; Inchicore Rd; adult/child €9/5; ⊗ 9am-7pm Jun-Aug, 9.30am-5.30pm Oct-Mar, 9am-6pm Apr, May & Sep; ☐ 69, 79 from Aston Quay, ☐ 13, 40 from O'Connell St) If you have *any* desire to understand Irish history – especially the long-running resistance to British rule – then a visit to this former prison is an absolute must. A threatening grey building, built in 1796, it's played a role in virtually every act of Ireland's painful path to independence, and even today,

Dublin

A | **B** | **C** | **D**

Upper Dominick St
Mountjoy St
St Mary's Tce
Granby Row
12
N Parnell Sq
W Rutland Pl
N Great George's St
Parnell St

Henrietta
Garden of
Remembrance
E Parnell Sq
W Parnell Sq

Henrietta St
Dominick Pl
Parnell Sq
Parnell
Britain Pl
Cathal Brugha St

Henrietta Pl
Lower Dominick St
Granby Row
Parnell Sq
21

Bolton St
King's Inns St
Granby Pl
Parnell St
O'Connell-
Upper
Thomas La
Marlborough St
Cathedral St

Capel St
Loftus La
Dominick
Moore St
Moore La
Dublin Bus
Upper O'Connell St
N Earl St
11

N King St
Halston St
Green St
Parnell St
Wolfe Tone St
Upper Jervis La
Sampson's La
Henry Pl
Henry St
N Prince's St
O'Connell-GPO
Marlborough
Sackville Pl
Marlborough St

Little Britain St
Jervis St
Mary St
Upper Liffey St
Lower O'Connell St
Abbey St
20

Little Green St
17
Little Mary St
Lower Jervis La
Wolfe Tone Sq
Middle Abbey St
Harbour Ct
Eden Quay

Mary's Abbey
Capel St
Jervis St
Jervis
Great Strand St
Lower Liffey St
Lotts Row
Litton La
O'Connell Bridge
Burgh Quay
Hawkins St

Quartier Bloom
Bachelor's Walk
Aston Quay
D'Olier St

10
Lower Ormond Quay
Boardwalk
Crampton Quay
Westmoreland
Westmoreland St
College St
Trinity

Upper Ormond Quay
River Liffey
Wellington Quay
Temple Bar
Fleet St
Trinity College

Wood Quay
Essex Quay
Parliament St
Meeting House Sq
Temple Bar Sq
Anglesea St
Front Sq
5
Old Library & Book of Kells
4

Winetavern St
Lower Exchange St
22
Essex Gate
Essex St E
Eustace St
Cecilia St
Crow St
Dame St
Trinity St
College Green
Grafton St
Nassau St

Christchurch Pl
Lord Edward St
Sycamore St
Dame St
Dame La
Dame Ct
College Green
Suffolk St
St Andrew's St
Visit Dublin Centre
13
Wicklow St
Dawson

Guinness Storehouse (1.2km);
Kilmainham Gaol (2.7km)
Castle St
Werburgh St
Cork Hill
2
Dublin Castle
Lower Yard
Palace St
Exchequer St
George's St
Castle Market
GRAFTON STREET
Grafton Arc

Ross Rd
Great Ship St
Palace St
Upper Yard
Dublinn Garden
1
Chester Beatty Library
Fade St
Drury St
18
Coppinger Row
Royal Hibernian Way
S Anne St
Dawson St

Bride Rd
Chancery La
Upper Stephen St
16
19 14
8
S William St
Westbury Mall
Clarendon St

Nicholas St
Patrick St
Bull Alley St
St Patrick's Park
Golden La
Whitefriar St
Aungier St
Lower Stephen St
Johnston Pl
Lower Mercer St
S King St
Grafton St
15

7
Whitefriar St
Peter Row
Peter St
Whelan's (250m);
Anseo (400m)
Sophie's @ the Dean (350m)
St Stephen's Green W
St Stephen's Green N

A | **B** | **C** | **D**

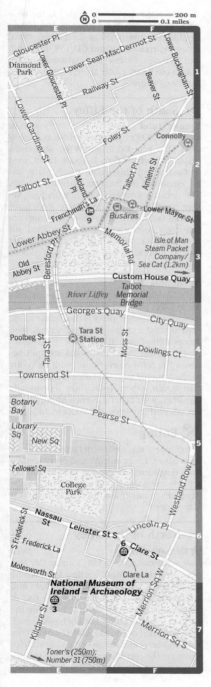

Dublin

⊙ Top Sights
1	Chester Beatty Library	B6
2	Dublin Castle	B5
3	National Museum of Ireland – Archaeology	E7
4	Old Library & Book of Kells	D5
5	Trinity College	D5

⊙ Sights
6	National Gallery	F6
7	St Patrick's Cathedral	A7

🛏 Sleeping
8	Brooks Hotel	C6
9	Isaacs Hostel	E3
10	Morrison Hotel	B4

🍴 Eating
11	101 Talbot	D2
12	Chapter One	C1
13	Cornucopia	C6
14	Fade Street Social	C6
15	Greenhouse	D7
16	L'Gueuleton	C6
17	Oxmantown	A3

🍷 Drinking & Nightlife
18	Grogan's Castle Lounge	C6
19	No Name Bar	C6

🎭 Entertainment
20	Abbey Theatre	D3
21	Gate Theatre	C1
22	Smock Alley Theatre	A5

despite closing in 1924, it still has the power to chill. Book online as far in advance as possible to get your preferred visiting time.

National Gallery   MUSEUM
(www.nationalgallery.ie; W Merrion Sq; ⊙9.15am-5.30pm Tue-Wed, Fri & Sat, to 8.30pm Thu, 11am-5.30pm Sun-Mon; ⃞4, 7, 8, 39A, 46A from city centre) FREE A magnificent Caravaggio and a breathtaking collection of works by Jack B Yeats – William Butler's younger brother – are the main reasons to visit the National Gallery, but not the only ones. Its excellent collection is strong in Irish art, and there are also high-quality collections of every major European school of painting.

St Patrick's Cathedral   CATHEDRAL
(☑01-453 9472; www.stpatrickscathedral.ie; St Patrick's Close; adult/student €8/7; ⊙9.30am-5pm Mon-Fri, 9am-6pm Sat, 9-10.30am, 12.30-2.30pm & 4.30-6pm Sun Mar-Oct, shorter hours rest of year; ⃞50, 50A, 56A from Aston Quay, 54, 54A from Burgh Quay) Ireland's largest church, St Patrick's Cathedral was built between 1191

and 1270 on the site of an earlier church that had stood since the 5th century. It was here that St Patrick himself reputedly baptised the local Celtic chieftains, making this bit of ground some fairly sacred turf: the well in question is in the adjacent St Patrick's Park, which was once a slum but is now a lovely spot to sit and take a load off.

Sleeping

A surge in tourist numbers and a relative lack of beds means hotel prices are higher than they were during the Celtic Tiger years. There are good midrange options north of the Liffey, but the biggest spread of accommodation is south of the river, from midrange Georgian townhouses to the city's top hotels.

North of the Liffey

★Isaacs Hostel   HOSTEL €
(☎01-855 6215; www.isaacs.ie; 2-5 Frenchman's Lane; dm/tw from €22/99; @ 🛜; 🚌 all city centre, 🚇 Connolly) The northside's best hostel – actually for atmosphere alone it's the best in town – is in a 200-year-old wine vault just around the corner from the main bus station. With summer barbecues, live music in the lounge, internet access, colourful dorms and even a sauna, this terrific place generates consistently good reviews from backpackers and other travellers.

Morrison Hotel   HOTEL €€€
(☎01-887 2400; www.morrisonhotel.ie; Lower Ormond Quay; r €350; P@🛜; 🚌 all city centre,

---

BOOK OF KELLS
....
The world-famous **Book of Kells** (www.tcd.ie; Library Sq; adult/student/family €11/11/28, fast-track €14/11/28; ⊗8.30am-5pm Mon-Sat, 9.30am-5pm Sun May-Sep, 9.30am-5pm Mon-Sat, noon-4.30pm Sun Oct-Apr; 🚌 all city centre, 🚇 Westmoreland or Trinity) contains the four gospels of the New Testament, written in Latin, as well as prefaces, summaries and other text. If it were merely words, the *Book of Kells* would simply be a very old book – it's the extensive and amazingly complex illustrations (the illuminations) that make it so wonderful. The superbly decorated opening initials are only part of the story, for the book has smaller illustrations between the lines.

🚇 Jervis) Space-age funky design is the template at this hip hotel, part of the Hilton Doubletree group. King-sized beds (with fancy mattresses), 40in LCD TVs, free wi-fi and deluxe toiletries are just some of the hotel's offerings. Easily the northside's most luxurious address.

South of the Liffey

Brooks Hotel   HOTEL €€
(☎01-670 4000; www.brookshotel.ie; 59-62 Drury St; r from €210; P✳@🛜; 🚌 all cross-city, 🚇 St Stephen's Green) About 120m west of Grafton St, this small, plush place has an emphasis on familial, friendly service. The decor is nouveau classic with high veneer-panelled walls, decorative bookcases and old-fashioned sofas, while bedrooms are extremely comfortable and come fitted out in subtly coloured furnishings. The clincher though is the king- and superking-sized beds in all rooms, complete with pillow menu.

★Number 31   GUESTHOUSE €€
(☎01-676 5011; www.number31.ie; 31 Leeson Close; r from €220; P🛜; 🚌 all city centre) The city's most distinctive property is the former home of modernist architect Sam Stephenson, who successfully fused 1960s style with 18th-century grace. Its 21 bedrooms are split between the retro coach house, with its coolly modern rooms, and the more elegant Georgian house, where rooms are individually furnished with tasteful French antiques and big, comfortable beds. Breakfast included.

Eating

The choice of restaurants in Dublin has never been better. Every cuisine and every trend – from doughnuts on the run to kale with absolutely everything – is catered for, as the city seeks to satisfy the discerning taste buds of its diners.

North of the Liffey

★Oxmantown   CAFE €
(www.oxmantown.com; 16 Mary's Abbey, City Markets; sandwiches €6.50; ⊗8am-4pm Mon-Fri; 🚇 Four Courts, Jervis) Delicious breakfasts and excellent sandwiches make this cafe one of the standout places for daytime eating on the north side of the Liffey. Locally baked bread, coffee supplied by Cloud Picker (Dublin's only microroastery) and meats sourced from Irish farms are the ingredients, but it's the way it's all put together that makes it so worthwhile.

101 Talbot
MODERN IRISH €€

(www.101talbot.ie; 100-102 Talbot St; mains €17-24; ⊘noon-3pm & 5-10pm Tue-Thu, to 11pm Fri-Sat; 🖳all city centre) This Dublin classic has expertly resisted every trendy wave and has been a stalwart of good Irish cooking since opening more than two decades ago. Its speciality is traditional meat-and-two-veg dinners but with Mediterranean influences: pan-fried sea bass with garlic new potatoes; squid and chorizo salad; and confit duck with peach and goat's cheese salad. Superb.

★Chapter One
MODERN IRISH €€€

(☑01-873 2266; www.chapteronerestaurant.com; 18 N Parnell Sq; 2-course lunch €36.50, 4-course dinner €80; ⊘12.30-2pm Fri, 5-10.30pm Tue-Sat; 🖳3, 10, 11, 13, 16, 19, 22 from city centre) Flawless haute cuisine and a relaxed, welcoming atmosphere make this Michelin-starred restaurant in the basement of the Dublin Writers Museum our choice for the best dinner experience in town. The food is French-inspired contemporary Irish; the menus change regularly; and the service is top-notch. The three-course pre-theatre menu (€42) is great if you're going to the **Gate** (☑01-874 4045; www.gatetheatre.ie; 1 Cavendish Row; ⊘performances 7.30pm Tue-Fri, 2.30pm & 7.30pm Sat; 🖳all city centre) around the corner.

✖ South of the Liffey

Cornucopia
VEGETARIAN €

(www.cornucopia.ie; 19-20 Wicklow St; salads €6-10, mains €13-15; ⊘8.30am-9pm Mon, to 10pm Tue-Sat, noon-9pm Sun; 🖉; 🖳all city centre) Dublin's best-known vegetarian restaurant is a terrific eatery that serves three sizes of wholesome salads, sandwiches, and a selection of hot main courses from a daily changing menu. There's live musical accompaniment on Thursday and Friday evenings. The 2nd-floor dining-room windows to the street below are good spots for people-watching.

Fade Street Social
MODERN IRISH €€

(☑01-604 0066; www.fadestreetsocial.com; 4-6 Fade St; mains €20-36, tapas €6-17; ⊘5-10.30pm Mon-Wed, 12.30-3pm & 5-10.30pm Thu, to 11pm Fri-Sat, to 10.30pm Sun; 🖘; 🖳all city centre) 🍃 Two eateries in one, courtesy of renowned chef Dylan McGrath: at the front, the buzzy tapas bar, which serves up gourmet bites from a beautiful open kitchen. At the back, the more muted restaurant specialises in Irish cuts of meat – from veal to rabbit – served with home-grown, organic vegetables. There's a bar upstairs too. Reservations recommended.

Sophie's @ the Dean
ITALIAN €€

(☑01-607 8100; www.sophies.ie; 33 Harcourt St; mains €14-34; ⊘7am-10.30pm Mon-Wed, to 1.30am Thu-Fri, 8am-1.30am Sat, 8am-10.30pm Sun; 🖳10, 11, 13, 14, 15A, 🖳Harcourt) There's perhaps no better setting in all of Dublin – a top-floor glasshouse restaurant with superb views of the city – in which to enjoy this quirky take on Italian cuisine. Delicious pizzas come with nontraditional toppings (pulled pork with barbecue sauce?) and the fillet steak is done to perfection. A good spot for breakfast too.

★Greenhouse
SCANDINAVIAN €€€

(☑01-676 7015; www.thegreenhouserestaurant. ie; Dawson St; 2-/3-course lunch menu €45/55, 4-/6-course dinner menu €110/129; ⊘noon-2pm & 6-9.30pm Tue-Sat; 🖳all city centre, 🖳St Stephen's Green) Chef Mickael Viljanen might just be the most exciting chef working in Ireland today thanks to his Scandi-influenced tasting menus, which have made this arguably Dublin's best restaurant. Wine selections are in the capable hands of Julie Dupouy, who in 2017 was voted third-best sommelier in the world, just weeks before the restaurant was awarded a Michelin star. Reservations necessary.

🍷 Drinking & Nightlife

If there's one constant about life in Dublin, it's that Dubliners will always take a drink. Come hell or high water, the city's pubs will never be short of customers, and we suspect that exploring a variety of Dublin's legendary pubs and bars ranks pretty high on the list of reasons you're here.

★Toner's
PUB

(☑01-676 3090; www.tonerspub.ie; 139 Lower Baggot St; ⊘10.30am-11.30pm Mon-Thu, to 12.30am Fri & Sat, 11.30am-11.30pm Sun; 🖳7, 46 from city centre) Toner's, with its stone floors and antique snugs, has changed little over the years and is the closest thing you'll get to a country pub in the heart of the city. Next door, Toner's Yard is a comfortable outside space. The shelves and drawers are reminders that it once doubled as a grocery shop.

★Grogan's Castle Lounge
PUB

(www.facebook.com/groganscastlelounge; 15 S William St; ⊘10.30am-11.30pm Mon-Thu, to 12.30am Fri & Sat, 12.30-11pm Sun; 🖳all city centre) Known simply as Grogan's (after the original owner), this is a city-centre institution. It has long been a favourite haunt of Dublin's writers and painters, as well as others from the alternative bohemian set, who enjoy a fine Guinness while they wait for that inevitable moment when they're discovered.

No Name Bar   BAR
(www.nonamebardublin.com; 3 Fade St; ⊗1.30-11.30pm Mon-Wed, to 1am Thu, 12.30-2.30am Fri & Sat, noon-11pm Sun; ◙all city centre) A low-key entrance just next to the trendy French restaurant **L'Gueuleton** (✎01-675 3708; www.lgueuleton.com; 1 Fade St; mains €20-31; ⊗12.30-4pm & 5.30-10pm Mon-Wed, to 10.30pm Thu-Sat, noon-4pm & 5.30-9pm Sun) leads upstairs to one of the nicest bar spaces in town, consisting of three huge rooms in a restored Victorian townhouse plus a sizeable heated patio area for smokers. There's no sign or a name – folks just refer to it as the No Name Bar.

Anseo   BAR
(18 Lower Camden St; ⊗4-11.30pm Mon-Thu, to 12.30am Fri & Sat, to 11pm Sun; ◙14, 15, 65, 83) Unpretentious, unaffected and incredibly popular, this cosy alternative bar – which is pronounced 'an-*shuh*', the Irish for 'here' – is a favourite with those who live by the credo that to try too hard is far worse than not trying at all. The pub's soundtrack is an eclectic mix; you're as likely to hear Peggy Lee as Lee Perry.

☆ Entertainment

Believe it or not, there is life beyond the pub. There are comedy clubs and classical concerts, recitals and readings, marionettes and music – lots of music. The other great Dublin treat is the theatre, where you can enjoy a light-hearted musical alongside the more serious stuff by Beckett, Yeats and O'Casey – not to mention a host of new talent.

Smock Alley Theatre   THEATRE
(✎01-677 0014; www.smockalley.com; 6-7 Exchange St; ◙all city centre) One of the city's most diverse theatres is hidden in this beautifully restored 17th-century building. It boasts a diverse program of events (expect anything from opera to murder mystery nights, puppet shows and Shakespeare) and many events also come with a dinner option.

Whelan's   LIVE MUSIC
(✎01-478 0766; www.whelanslive.com; 25 Wexford St; ◙16, 122 from city centre) Perhaps the city's most beloved live-music venue is this midsized room attached to a traditional bar. This is the singer-songwriter's spiritual home: when they're done pouring out the contents of their hearts on stage, you can find them filling up in the bar along with their fans.

Abbey Theatre   THEATRE
(✎01-878 7222; www.abbeytheatre.ie; Lower Abbey St; ◙all city centre, ◙Abbey) Ireland's national theatre was founded by WB Yeats in 1904 and was a central player in the development of a consciously native cultural identity. Expect to see a mix of homegrown theatre from Irish playwrights, as well as touring performances from around the world.

❶ Information

A handful of official-looking tourism offices on Grafton and O'Connell Sts are actually privately run enterprises where members pay to be included.

Visit Dublin Centre (www.visitdublin.com; 25 Suffolk St; ⊗9am-5.30pm Mon-Sat, 10.30am-3pm Sun; ◙all city centre) The main tourist information centre, with free maps, guides and itinerary planning, plus booking services for accommodation, attractions and events.

Grafton Medical Centre (✎01-671 2122; www.graftonmedical.ie; 34 Grafton St; ⊗8.30am-6pm Mon-Thu, to 5pm Fri; ◙all city centre) One-stop shop with male and female doctors as well as physiotherapists. You'll usually need to give a day's advance notice, but same-day appointments are often available.

Hickey's Pharmacy (✎01-679 0467; 21 Grafton St; ⊗8am-8pm Mon-Wed & Fri, to 8.30pm Thu, 9am-8pm Sat, 10am-7pm Sun; ◙all city centre) Well-stocked pharmacy on Grafton St.

St James's Hospital (✎01-410 3000; www.stjames.ie; James's St; ◙James's) Dublin's main 24-hour accident and emergency department.

❶ Getting There & Away

AIR
Dublin Airport (p644), about 13km north of the city centre, is Ireland's major international gateway, with direct flights from Europe, North America and Asia. Most international flights (including most US flights) use Terminal 2; Ryanair and select others use Terminal 1.

BOAT
The **Dublin Port Terminal** (✎01-855 2222; Alexandra Rd; ◙53 from Talbot St) is 3km northeast of the city centre.

Irish Ferries (✎0818 300 400; www.irishferries.com; Ferryport, Terminal Rd South) Holyhead in Wales (€200 return, three hours)

Isle of Man Steam Packet Company/Sea Cat (www.steam-packet.com; Terminal 1, Dublin Port; ⊗4.30am-10pm; ◙53 from city centre) Isle of Man (€110 return, 1½ hours)

P&O Irish Sea (☑ 01-686 9467; www.poferries.com; Terminal 3) Liverpool (€180 return, 8½ hours or four hours on fast boat)

BUS

Dublin's central bus station, **Busáras** (☑ 01-836 6111; www.buseireann.ie; Store St; 🚊 Connolly) is just north of the river behind the Custom House. It has different-sized luggage lockers costing from €6 to €10 per day.

It's possible to combine bus and ferry tickets from major UK centres to Dublin on the bus network. The journey between London and Dublin takes about 12 hours and costs from €29 return (but note it's €42 for one way). For details in London, contact **Eurolines** (☑ 01-836 6111; https://eurolines.buseireann.ie).

From Dublin, Bus Éireann (p645) buses serve the whole national network, including buses to towns and cities in Northern Ireland.

TRAIN

All trains in the Republic are run by Irish Rail (p645). Dublin has two main train stations: **Heuston Station** (☑ 01-836 6222; 🚊 Heuston), on the western side of town near the Liffey; and **Connolly Station** (☑ 01-703 2359; 🚊 Connolly, 🚊 Connolly Station), a short walk northeast of Busáras, behind the Custom House.

Connolly Station is a stop on the DART line into town; the Luas Red Line serves both Connolly and Heuston stations.

ⓘ Getting Around

TO/FROM THE AIRPORT

Aircoach (www.aircoach.ie) Buses every 10 to 15 minutes between 6am and midnight, then hourly from midnight until 6am (one way/return €7/12).

Airlink Express (☑ 01-873 4222; www.dublinbus.ie; one way/return €7/12) Bus 747 runs every 10 to 20 minutes from 5.45am to 12.30am between the airport, central bus station (Busáras) and the Dublin Bus Office on Upper O'Connell St. Bus 757 runs every 15 to 30 minutes from 5am to 12.25am between the airport and various stops in the city, including Grand Canal Dock, Merrion Sq and Camden St.

Taxi There is a taxi rank directly outside the arrivals concourse of both terminals. It should take about 45 minutes to get into the city centre and cost about €25, including an initial charge of €3.60 (€4 between 10pm and 8am and on Sundays and bank holidays). Make sure the meter is switched on.

BICYCLE

Typical rental for a hybrid or touring bike is around €25 a day or €140 a week.

Dublinbikes (www.dublinbikes.ie) A public bicycle-rental scheme with more than 100 stations spread across the city centre. Purchase

a €10 smart card (as well as pay a credit-card deposit of €150) or a three-day card online or at any station before 'freeing' a bike for use, which is then free of charge to use for the first 30 minutes and €0.50 for each half-hour thereafter.

Cycleways (www.cycleways.com; 31 Ormond Quay Lwr; ⊙ 8.30am-6pm Mon-Fri, 10am-6pm Sat; 🚊 all city centre) An excellent bike shop that rents out hybrids and touring bikes during the summer months (May to September).

PUBLIC TRANSPORT
Bus

The **Dublin Bus Office** (☑ 01-873 4222; www.dublinbus.ie; 59 Upper O'Connell St; ⊙ 9am-5.30pm Tue-Fri, to 2pm Sat, 8.30am-5.30pm Mon; 🚊 all city centre) has free single-route time-tables for all its services. Buses run from around 6am (some start at 5.30am) to about 11.30pm.

Fares are calculated according to stages (stops):

Stages	Cash Fare (€)	Leap Card Fare (€)
1-3	2.10	1.50
4-13	2.85	2.15
more than 13	3.30	2.60

A **Leap Card** (www.leapcard.ie), available from most newsagents, is not just cheaper but also more convenient as you don't have to worry about tendering exact fares. Register the card online and top it up with whatever amount you need. When you board a bus, DART, Luas (light rail) or suburban train, just swipe your card and the fare is automatically deducted. If paying with cash, you will need to tender the exact fare; otherwise, you will get a receipt for reimbursement, which is only possible at the Dublin Bus main office.

If you're travelling within the College Green Bus Corridor (roughly between Parnell Sq to the north and St Stephen's Green to the south) you can use the €0.50 special City Centre fare.

Train

Dublin Area Rapid Transport (DART; ☑ 01-836 6222; www.irishrail.ie) provides quick rail access to the coast as far north as Howth (about 30 minutes) and as far south as Greystones in County Wicklow. Pearse and Tara St stations are convenient for central Dublin south of the Liffey, and Connolly Station for north of the Liffey. Single fares cost €2.50 to €6; a one-day pass costs €12.

Tram

The **Luas** (www.luas.ie) light-rail system has two lines: the green line (running every five to 15 minutes) connects St Stephen's Green with Sandyford in south Dublin via Ranelagh and Dundrum; and the red line (every 20 minutes) runs from the Point Village to Tallaght via the north quays and Heuston Station. The new cross-city line connects the green and red lines with a route from

St Stephen's Green through Dawson St, around Trinity College and over the river. A typical short-hop fare (around four stops) is €2.50.

Taxi

All taxi fares begin with a flagfall of €3.60 (€4 from 10pm to 8am), followed by €1.10 per km thereafter (€1.40 from 10pm to 8am). For taxi service, call **National Radio Cabs** (☑ 01-677 2222; www.nrc.ie).

THE SOUTHEAST

Kilkenny

POP 26,500

Kilkenny is the Ireland of many visitors' imaginations. Built from dark-grey limestone flecked with fossil seashells, Kilkenny (from the Gaelic 'Cill Chainnigh', meaning the Church of St Canice) is also known as 'the marble city'. Its picturesque 'Medieval Mile' of narrow lanes and historical buildings strung between castle and cathedral along the bank of the River Nore is one of the southeast's biggest tourist draws. It's worth braving the crowds to soak up the atmosphere of one of Ireland's creative crucibles – Kilkenny is a centre for arts and crafts, and home to a host of fine restaurants, cafes, pubs and shops.

☉ Sights

★ **Kilkenny Castle** CASTLE
(☑ 056-770 4100; www.kilkennycastle.ie; The Parade; adult/child €8/4; ☉ 9am-5.30pm Jun-Aug, 9.30am-5.30pm Apr, May & Sep, 9.30am-5pm Mar, 9.30am-4.30pm Oct-Feb) Rising above the River Nore, Kilkenny Castle is one of Ireland's most visited heritage sites. Stronghold of the powerful Butler family, it has a history dating back to the 12th century, though much of its present look dates from Victorian times.

During the winter months (November to January) visits are by 40-minute guided tours only, which shift to self-guided tours from February to October. Highlights include the Long Gallery with its painted roof and carved marble fireplace. There's an excellent tearoom in the former castle kitchens.

★ **St Canice's Cathedral** CATHEDRAL
(☑ 056-776 4971; www.stcanicescathedral.ie; Coach Rd; cathedral/round tower/combined adult €4.50/4/7, child €3.50/4/6.50; ☉ 9am-6pm Mon-Sat, 1-6pm Sun Jun-Aug, shorter hours Sep-May) Ireland's second-largest medieval cathedral

(after St Patrick's in Dublin) has a long and fascinating history. The first monastery was built here in the 6th century by St Canice, Kilkenny's patron saint. The present structure dates from the 13th to 16th centuries, with extensive 19th-century reconstruction, its interior housing ancient grave slabs and the tombs of Kilkenny Castle's Butler dynasty. Outside stands a 30m-high round tower, one of only two in Ireland that you can climb.

National Design & Craft Gallery GALLERY
(☑ 056-779 6147; www.ndcg.ie; Castle Yard; ☉ 10am-5.30pm Tue-Sat, from 11am Sun) FREE
Contemporary Irish crafts are showcased at these imaginative galleries, set in former stables across the road from Kilkenny Castle, next to the shops of the **Kilkenny Design Centre** (☑ 056-772 2118; www.kilkennydesign. com; ☉ 9am-6pm). Ceramics dominate, but exhibits often feature furniture, jewellery and weaving from the members of the Crafts Council of Ireland. Family days are held the third Saturday of every month, with a tour of the gallery and free hands-on workshops for children. For additional workshops and events, check the website.

✦ Festivals & Events

Kilkenny hosts several world-class events throughout the year, attracting thousands of revellers.

Kilkenny Rhythm & Roots MUSIC
(www.kilkennyroots.com; ☉ Apr-May) More than 30 pubs and other venues participate in hosting this major music festival in late April/ early May, with an emphasis on country and 'old-time' American roots music.

Kilkenny Arts Festival ART
(www.kilkennyarts.ie; ☉ Aug) In August the city comes alive with theatre, cinema, music, literature, visual arts, children's events and street spectacles for 10 action-packed days.

⮸ Sleeping

Kilkenny Tourist Hostel HOSTEL €
(☑ 056-776 3541; www.kilkennyhostel.ie; 35 Parliament St; dm/tw/q from €18/48/88; @ ☎) Inside an ivy-covered 1770s Georgian townhouse, this fairly standard 60-bed IHH hostel has a sitting room warmed by an open fireplace, and a timber- and leadlight-panelled dining room adjoining the self-catering kitchen. Excellent location, but a place for relaxing rather than partying.

Celtic House
B&B €

(☑ 056-776 2249; www.celtic-house-bandb.com; 18 Michael St; d from €85; 🤏) Artist and author Angela Byrne extends one of Ireland's warmest welcomes at this homey and comfortable B&B. Some of the brightly decorated bedrooms have sky-lit bathrooms, others have views of the castle, and Angela's landscapes adorn many of the walls. Book ahead.

★ Rosquil House
GUESTHOUSE €€

(☑ 056-772 1419; www.rosquilhouse.com; Castlecomer Rd; d/tr/f from €95/120/130, 2-person apt from €80; P 🤏) Rooms at this immaculately maintained guesthouse are decorated with dark-wood furniture and pretty paisley fabrics, while the guest lounge is similarly tasteful with sink-into sofas, brass-framed mirrors and leafy plants. The breakfast is above average, with homemade granola and fluffy omelettes. There's also a well-equipped and comfortable self-catering apartment (minimum three-night stay).

✕ Eating & Drinking

Gourmet Store
SANDWICHES €

(☑ 056-777 1727; www.facebook.com/gourmet storekk; 56 High St; sandwiches €4.50; ☺ 8am-5.30pm Mon-Sat) In this crowded little deli, takeaway sandwiches are assembled from choice imported meats and cheeses (plus a few top-notch local varieties).

★ Foodworks
BISTRO, CAFE €€

(☑ 056-777 7696; www.foodworks.ie; 7 Parliament St; mains €17.50-26.50, 3-course dinner menus €26-29; ☺ noon-9pm Wed & Thu, to 9.30pm Fri & Sat, to 5pm Sun; 🤏🚼) 🍴 The owners of this cool and casual bistro keep their own pigs and grow their own salad leaves, so it would be churlish not to try their pork belly stuffed with black pudding, or confit pig's trotter – and you'll be glad you did. Delicious food, excellent coffee and friendly service make this a justifiably popular venue; it's best to book a table.

★ Kyteler's Inn
PUB

(☑ 056-772 1064; www.kytelersinn.com; 27 St Kieran's St; ☺ 11am-11.30pm Mon-Fri, to 2am Fri & Sat, 12.15pm-midnight Sun) Dame Alice Kyteler's old house was built back in 1224 and has seen its share of history: she was charged with witchcraft in 1323. Today the rambling bar includes the original building, complete with vaulted ceiling and arches. There is a beer garden, a courtyard and a large upstairs room for live bands (nightly from March to October), ranging from trad to blues.

☆ Entertainment

Watergate Theatre
THEATRE

(☑ box office 056-776 1674; www.watergatetheatre.com; Parliament St) Kilkenny's top theatre venue hosts drama, comedy and musical performances. If you're wondering why intermission lasts 18 minutes, it's so patrons can nip across to **John Cleere's pub** (☑ 056-776 2573; www.cleeres.com; 28 Parliament St; ☺ noon-12.30am) for a pint.

❶ Information

Kilkenny Tourist Office (☑ 056-775 1500; www.visitkilkenny.ie; Rose Inn St; ☺ 9am-5pm Mon-Sat, 10am-4pm Sun) Stocks guides and walking maps. Located in Shee Alms House, dating from 1582 and built in local stone by benefactor Sir Richard Shee to help the poor.

❶ Getting There & Away

BUS

Bus Éireann (p645) and DublinCoach (www.dublincoach.ie) services stop (Dublin Rd) at the train station and on Ormonde Rd (nearer the town centre); JJ Kavanagh (www.jjkavanagh.ie) buses to Dublin airport stop on Ormonde Rd only.

Cork (€15, 2½ hours, every two hours)
Dublin (€19, 3½ hours, four daily) Bus Éireann X4.

TRAIN

Kilkenny's **MacDonagh train station** (Dublin Rd) is a 10-minute walk northeast of the town centre. Trains run to Dublin Heuston (€13, 1½ hours, six daily) and Waterford (€7.50, 40 minutes, seven daily).

THE SOUTHWEST

Cork

POP 208,670

Ireland's second city is first in every important respect – at least according to the locals, who cheerfully refer to it as the 'real capital of Ireland'. The compact city centre is surrounded by interesting waterways and is chock-full of great restaurants fed by arguably the best foodie scene in the country.

◎ Sights

★ English Market
MARKET

(www.englishmarket.ie; main entrance Princes St; ☺ 8am-6pm Mon-Sat) It could just as easily be called the Victorian Market for its ornate vaulted ceilings and columns, but the English Market is a true gem, no matter what

Cork

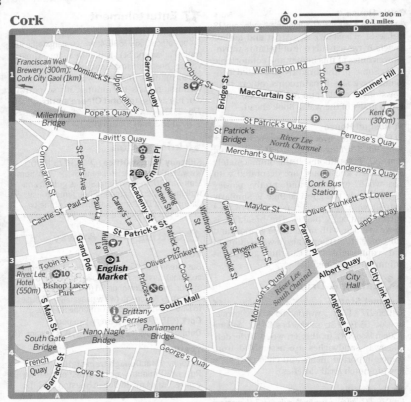

Cork

◎ Top Sights
1 English Market B3

◎ Sights
2 Crawford Art Gallery B2

🛏 Sleeping
3 Auburn House D1
4 Brú Bar & Hostel D1

🍴 Eating
Farmgate Cafe ....(see 1)
5 Market Lane...C3
6 Nash 19...B3

🍷 Drinking & Nightlife
7 Mutton Lane Inn...................................B3
8 Sin É... B1

🎭 Entertainment
9 Cork Opera House B2
Half Moon Theatre.......................(see 9)
10 Triskel Arts Centre A3

you name it. Scores of vendors set up colourful and photogenic displays of the region's very best local produce, including meat, fish, fruit, cheeses and takeaway food. On a sunny day, take your lunch to nearby Bishop Lucey Park, a popular alfresco eating spot.

★ **Cork City Gaol**   MUSEUM
(☏ 021-430 5022; www.corkcitygaol.com; Convent Ave; adult/child €10/6; ◎ 9.30am-5pm Apr-Sep, 10am-4pm Oct-Mar) This imposing former prison is well worth a visit, if only to get a sense of how awful life was for prisoners a century ago. An audio tour (€2 extra) guides you around the restored cells, which feature models of suffering prisoners and sadistic-looking guards. Take a bus to UCC, and from there walk north along Mardyke Walk, cross the river and follow the signs uphill (10 minutes).

Crawford Art Gallery   GALLERY
(☏ 021-480 5042; www.crawfordartgallery.ie; Emmet Pl; ◎ 10am-5pm Mon-Wed, Fri & Sat, to 8pm Thu, 11am-4pm Sun) **FREE** Cork's public gallery

houses a small but excellent permanent collection covering the 17th century through to the modern day. Highlights include works by Sir John Lavery, Jack B Yeats and Nathaniel Hone, and a room devoted to Irish women artists from 1886 to 1978 – don't miss the pieces by Mainie Jellet and Evie Hone.

🛏 Sleeping & Eating

Brú Bar & Hostel
HOSTEL €

(☎ 021-455 9667; www.bruhostel.com; 57 MacCurtain St; dm/tw from €20/57; @ 🛜) This buzzing hostel has its own internet cafe, with free access for guests, and a fantastic bar, popular with backpackers and locals alike. The dorms (each with a bathroom) have four to six beds and are clean and stylish – ask for one on the upper floors to avoid bar noise. Breakfast is included.

⭐ Auburn House
B&B €€

(☎ 021-450 8555; www.auburnguesthouse.com; 3 Garfield Tce, Wellington Rd; s/d/tr €58/90/135; P 🛜) There's a warm family welcome at this neat B&B, which has smallish but well-kept rooms brightened by window boxes. Try to bag one of the back rooms, which are quieter and have sweeping views over the city. Breakfast includes vegetarian choices, and the location near the fun of MacCurtain St is a plus.

⭐ River Lee Hotel
HOTEL €€€

(☎ 021-425 2700; www.doylecollection.com; Western Rd; r from €185; P 🛜 🏊) This modern riverside hotel brings a touch of luxury to the city centre. It has gorgeous public areas with huge sofas, a designer fireplace, a stunning five-storey glass-walled atrium and superb service. There are well-equipped bedrooms (nice and quiet at the back, but request a corner room for extra space) and possibly the best breakfast buffet in Ireland.

⭐ Farmgate Cafe
CAFE, BISTRO €

(☎ 021-427 8134; www.farmgate.ie; Princes St, English Market; mains €8-14; ⊙ 8.30am-5pm Mon-Sat) 🍴 An unmissable experience at the heart of the English Market (p627), the Farmgate is perched on a balcony overlooking the food stalls below, the source of all that fresh local produce on your plate – everything from crab and oysters to the lamb in your Irish stew. Go up the stairs and turn left for table service, or right for counter service.

⭐ Market Lane
IRISH, INTERNATIONAL €€

(☎ 021-427 4710; www.marketlane.ie; 5 Oliver Plunkett St; mains €12-28; ⊙ noon-9.30pm Mon-Wed, to 10pm Thu, to 10.30pm Fri & Sat, 1-9.30pm Sun;

🛜 🖶) 🍴 It's always hopping at this bright corner bistro. The menu is broad and hearty, changing to reflect what's fresh at the English Market: perhaps roast cod with seaweed butter sauce, or pea and barley risotto with goat's cheese. No reservations for fewer than six diners; sip a drink at the bar till a table is free. Lots of wines by the glass.

⭐ Nash 19
INTERNATIONAL €€

(☎ 021-427 0880; www.nash19.com; Princes St; mains €10-17; ⊙ 7.30am-4pm Mon-Fri, from 8.30am Sat) 🍴 A superb bistro and deli where locally sourced food is honoured at breakfast and lunch, either sit-in or takeaway. Fresh scones draw crowds early; daily lunch specials (soups, salads, desserts etc), free-range chicken pie and platters of smoked fish from **Frank Hederman** (☎ 021-481 1089; www.frankhederman. com; Belvelly; free for individuals, charge for groups; ⊙ by reservation 10am-5pm Mon-Fri) 🍴 keep them coming for lunch – the Producers Plate, a sampler of local produce, is sensational.

🍷 Drinking & Nightlife

In Cork pubs, locally brewed Murphy's and Beamish stouts, not Guinness, are the preferred pints.

Given the city's big student population, the small selection of nightclubs does a roaring trade. Entry ranges from free to €15; most are open until 2am on Fridays and Saturdays.

⭐ Sin É
PUB

(☎ 021-450 2266; www.facebook.com/sinecork; 8 Coburg St; ⊙ noon-11.30pm Mon-Thu, to 12.30am Fri & Sat, to 11pm Sun) You could easily spend an entire day at this place, which is everything a craic-filled pub should be – long on atmosphere and short on pretension (Sin É means 'that's it!'). There's music every night from 6.30pm May to September, and regular sessions Tuesday, Friday and Sunday during the rest of the year, many of them traditional but with the odd surprise.

⭐ Mutton Lane Inn
PUB

(☎ 021-427 3471; www.facebook.com/mutton.lane; Mutton Lane; ⊙ 10.30am-11.30pm Mon-Thu, to 12.30am Fri & Sat, 12.30-11pm Sun) Tucked down the tiniest of alleys off St Patrick's St, this inviting pub, lit by candles and fairy lights, is one of Cork's most intimate drinking holes. It's minuscule, so try to get in early to bag the snug, or perch on the beer kegs outside.

⭐ Franciscan Well Brewery
PUB

(☎ 021-439 3434; www.franciscanwellbrewery.com; 14 North Mall; ⊙ 1-11.30pm Mon-Thu, to 12.30am Fri

WORTH A TRIP

ROCK OF CASHEL

The **Rock of Cashel** (www.heritageireland.ie; adult/child €8/4; ⏲9am-7pm early Jun–mid-Sep, to 5.30pm mid-Mar–early Jun & mid-Sep–mid-Oct, to 4.30pm mid-Oct–mid-Mar) is one of Ireland's most spectacular historical sites: a prominent green hill, banded with limestone outcrops, rising from a grassy plain and bristling with ancient fortifications. Sturdy walls circle an enclosure containing a complete round tower, a 13th-century Gothic cathedral and the finest 12th-century Romanesque chapel in Ireland, home to some of the land's oldest frescoes.

Cashel Lodge & Camping Park (☎062-61003; www.cashel-lodge.com; Dundrum Rd; sites per person €10, s/d from €45/85; P wifi) is a good place to stay, with terrific views of the Rock and Hore Abbey. Bus Éireann runs eight buses daily between Cashel and Cork (€26.60, 1¾ hours).

& Sat, to 11pm Sun; wifi) The copper vats gleaming behind the bar give the game away: the Franciscan Well brews its own beer. The best place to enjoy it is in the enormous beer garden at the back. The pub holds regular beer festivals together with other small independent Irish breweries.

✩ Entertainment

Cork's cultural life is generally of a high calibre. To see what's happening, grab *WhazOn?* (www.whazon.com), a free monthly leaflet available from the tourist office, news agencies, shops, hostels and B&Bs.

★ **Cork Opera House** OPERA
(☎021-427 0022; www.corkoperahouse.ie; Emmet Pl; tickets €30-50; ⏲box office 10am-5.30pm Mon-Sat, pre-show to 7pm Mon-Sat & 6-7pm Sun) Given a modern makeover in the 1990s, this leading venue has been entertaining the city for more than 150 years with everything from opera and ballet to stand-up comedy, pop concerts and puppet shows. Around the back, the **Half Moon Theatre** (tickets €5-15) presents contemporary theatre, dance, art and occasional club nights.

★ **Triskel Arts Centre** ARTS CENTRE
(☎021-472 2022; www.triskelart.com; Tobin St; tickets €8-15; ⏲box office 10am-5pm Mon-Sat, 1-9pm Sun; wifi) A fantastic cultural centre housed partly in a renovated church building. Expect a varied program of live music, installation art, photography and theatre at this intimate venue. There's also a cinema (from 6.30pm) and a great cafe.

ℹ Information

Cork City Tourist Office (☎1850 230 330; www.discoverireland.ie/corkcity; Grand Pde; ⏲9am-5pm Mon-Sat year-round, plus 10am-5pm Sun Jul & Aug) Souvenir shop and information desk. Sells Ordnance Survey maps.

ℹ Getting There & Around

BICYCLE

Cycle Scene (☎021-430 1183; www.cyclescene.ie; 396 Blarney St; per day/week from €15/85) rents out bikes and accessories, including good-quality road-racing bikes (€45 a day).

BOAT

Brittany Ferries (☎021-427 7801; www.brittanyferries.ie; 42 Grand Pde) sails to Roscoff (France) weekly from the end of March to October. The ferry terminal is at Ringaskiddy, about 15 minutes by car southeast of the city centre along the N28.

BUS

Aircoach (☎01-844 7118; www.aircoach.ie) provides a direct service to Dublin city (€12.50) and Dublin Airport (€21.30) from St Patrick's Quay (3½ hours, hourly).

Cork bus station (cnr Merchant's Quay & Parnell Pl), east of the city centre, has services to the following:

Dublin €15.70, 3¾ hours, six daily
Kilkenny €15.70, 3½ hours, two daily
Killarney €18, 1½ hours, hourly

TRAIN

Cork's **Kent train station** (☎021-450 6766) is across the river. Destinations include the following:

Dublin €30, 2¼ hours, eight daily
Galway €20, four to six hours, seven daily, one or two changes
Killarney €12, 1½ to two hours, nine daily

Around Cork

If you need proof of the power of a good yarn, then join the queue to get into **Blarney Castle** (☎021-438 5252; www.blarneycastle.ie; Blarney; adult/child €18/8; ⏲9am-7pm Mon-Sat, to 6pm Sun Jun-Aug, shorter hours Sep-May; P), a 15th-century castle, one of Ireland's most popular tourist attractions. Everyone's here, of course, to plant their lips on the **Blarney Stone**, which supposedly gives one the gift of gab – a cliché that has entered every lexicon and tour route. Blarney is 8km northwest of Cork and buses run hourly from Cork bus station (€7.80 return, 20 minutes).

Killarney

POP 14,500

In the tourism game for more than 250 years, Killarney is a well-oiled machine set in the midst of sublime scenery that spans lakes, waterfalls and woodland beneath a skyline of 1000m-plus peaks. Competition keeps standards high and visitors on all budgets can expect to find good restaurants, great pubs and comfortable accommodation.

Mobbed in summer, Killarney is perhaps at its best in the late spring and early autumn when the crowds are manageable, but the weather is still good enough to enjoy its outdoor activities.

◉ Sights & Activities

Most of Killarney's attractions are just outside the town. The mountain backdrop is part of **Killarney National Park** (www.killarneynationalpark.ie), which takes in beautiful Lough Leane (the Lower Lake or 'Lake of Learning'), Muckross Lake and the Upper Lake, as well as the Mangerton, Torc, Shehy and Purple Mountains. In addition to Ross Castle and Muckross House, the park also has much to explore by foot, bike or boat.

The **Gap of Dunloe** is a wild and scenic mountain pass – studded with crags and bejewelled with lakes and waterfalls – that lies to the west of Killarney National Park, squeezed between Purple Mountain and the high summits of Macgillycuddy's Reeks (Ireland's highest mountain range).

⊨ Sleeping

★ Fleming's White Bridge

Caravan & Camping Park   CAMPGROUND €
(☑ 064-663 1590; www.killarneycamping.com; White Bridge, Ballycasheen Rd; unit plus 2 adults €28, hiker/cyclist €12; ⊘ mid-Mar–Oct; ☎) A lovely sheltered family-run campground 2.5km southeast of the town centre off the N22, Fleming's has a games room, bike hire, campers' kitchen, laundry and free trout fishing on the river that runs alongside. Your man Hillary at reception can arrange bus, bike and boat tours.

★ Crystal Springs   B&B €€
(☑ 064-663 3272; www.crystalspringsbandb.com; Ballycasheen Cross, Woodlawn Rd; s/d from €98/120; P☎) The timber deck of this wonderfully relaxing B&B overhangs the River Flesk, where trout anglers can fish for free. Rooms are richly furnished with patterned wallpapers and walnut timber; private bathrooms (most with spa baths) are huge. The glass-enclosed breakfast room also overlooks the rushing river. It's about a 15-minute stroll into town.

✖ Eating & Drinking

Jam   CAFE €
(☑ 064-663 7716; www.jam.ie; Old Market Lane; mains €4-11; ⊘ 8am-5pm Mon-Sat; ☎) Duck down the alley to this local hideout for deli sandwiches, coffee and cake, and a changing menu of hot lunch dishes such as shepherd's pie. It's all made with locally sourced produce. There are a few tables set up out the front in summer.

Treyvaud's   IRISH €€
(☑ 064-663 3062; www.treyvaudsrestaurant.com; 62 High St; mains €10-30; ⊘ 5-10pm Mon, noon-10pm Tue-Thu & Sun, noon-10.30pm Fri & Sat) Mustard-fronted Treyvaud's has a strong reputation for subtle dishes that merge trad Irish with European influences. The seafood chowder – a velvet stew of mussels, prawns and Irish salmon – makes a filling lunch; dinner mains incorporating local ingredients include cod with horseradish mash and tomato-and-caper salsa, and a hearty bacon and cabbage platter.

★ O'Connor's   PUB
(www.oconnorstraditionalpub.ie; 7 High St; ⊘ noon-11.30pm Sun-Thu, to 12.30am Fri & Sat; ☎) Live music plays every night at this tiny traditional pub with leaded-glass doors – one of Killarney's most popular haunts. In warmer weather, the crowds spill out onto the adjacent lane.

Courtney's   PUB
(www.courtneysbar.com; 24 Plunkett St; ⊘ 2-11.30pm Sun-Thu, to 12.30am Fri & Sat Jun-Sep, from 5pm Mon-Thu Oct-May) Inconspicuous on the outside, this cavernous 19th-century pub bursts at the seams with regular Irish music sessions (nightly in summer). Rock, blues, reggae and indie bands perform year-round on Fridays, with DJs taking over on Saturdays. This is where locals come to see their

SKELLIG MICHAEL

Portmagee (an 80km drive west of Killarney) is the jumping-off point for an unforgettable experience: the Skellig Islands, two tiny rocks 12km off the coast. The vertiginous climb up uninhabited **Skellig Michael** inspires an awe that monks could have clung to life in the meagre beehive-shaped stone huts that cluster on the tiny patch of level land on top. Skellig Michael famously featured as Luke Skywalker's Jedi temple in *Star Wars: The Force Awakens* (2015) and *Star Wars: The Last Jedi* (2017), attracting a whole new audience to the island's dramatic beauty. From spring to late summer, weather permitting, boat trips run from Portmagee to Skellig Michael; the standard rate is around €80 per person, with boats departing in the morning and returning at 3pm. Advance booking is essential; there are a dozen boat operators, including **Sea Quest** (☑ 087 236 2344; www.skelligsrock.com; per person €100; ☺ mid-May–Sep).

old mates perform and to kick off a night on the town.

❶ Information

Tourist Office (☑ 064-663 1633; www. killarney.ie; Beech Rd; ☺ 9am-5pm Mon-Sat; ☏) Killarney's tourist office can handle most queries and is especially good with transport intricacies.

❶ Getting There & Around

BUS

Bus Éireann operates from the bus station on Park Rd.

Cork €18, 2½ hours, hourly
Galway €24.70, 5½ hours, every two hours
Limerick €14.25, two hours, every two hours
Rosslare Harbour €26.60, six hours, six daily
Tralee €10.45, 40 minutes, six daily

TAXI

The town taxi rank is on College St. Taxi companies include **Killarney Taxi & Tours** (☑ 085 280 3333; www.killarneytaxi.com).

TRAIN

Killarney's **train station** (☑ 064-663 1067; Fair Hill) is behind the Malton Hotel, just east of the centre.

There are one or two direct services per day to Cork and Dublin; otherwise you'll have to change at Mallow.
Cork €12, 1½ hours
Dublin €31, 3¼ hours

Ring of Kerry

The Ring of Kerry, a 179km circuit around the dramatic coastal scenery of the Iveragh Peninsula (pronounced eev-raa), is one of Ireland's premier tourist attractions. Most travellers tackle the Ring by bus on guided day trips from Killarney, but you could spend days wandering here.

The Ring is dotted with picturesque villages (**Sneem** and **Portmagee** are worth a stop), **prehistoric sites** (ask for a guide at Killarney tourist office) and spectacular **viewpoints**, notably at Beenarourke just west of Caherdaniel, and Ladies' View (between Kenmare and Killarney). The **Ring of Skellig**, at the end of the peninsula, has fine views of the Skellig Rocks and is not as busy as the main route. You can forgo driving completely by walking part of the 200km **Kerry Way** (www.kerryway.com), which winds through the Macgillycuddy's Reeks mountains past Carrauntoohill (1040m), Ireland's highest mountain.

◎ Sights

Kerry Bog Village Museum   MUSEUM
(www.kerrybogvillage.ie; Ballincleave, Glenbeigh; adult/child €6.50/4.50; ☺ 9am-6pm; ℗) This museum recreates a 19th-century bog village, typical of the small communities that carved out a precarious living in the harsh environment of Ireland's ubiquitous peat bogs. You'll see the thatched homes of the turfcutter, blacksmith, thatcher and labourer, as well as a dairy, and meet Kerry bog ponies (a native breed) and Irish wolfhounds. It's on the N70, 8.3km southwest of Killorglin near Glenbeigh; buy a ticket at the neighbouring Red Fox Inn if no one's at the gate.

Old Barracks Heritage Centre   MUSEUM
(☑ 066-401 0430;   www.theoldbarrackscaher siveen.com; Bridge St; adult/child €4/2; ☺ 10am-5pm Mon-Sat, 11am-4pm Sun Mar-Nov; ℗) Established in response to the Fenian Rising of 1867, the Royal Irish Constabulary barracks at Cahersiveen were built in an eccentric Bavarian-Schloss style, complete with pointy turret and stepped gables. Burnt down in 1922 by anti-Treaty forces, the imposing

building has been restored and now houses fascinating exhibitions on the Fenian Rising and the life and works of local hero Daniel O'Connell.

★ **Derrynane National
Historic Park** HISTORIC SITE
(☑066-947 5113; http://derrynanehouse.ie; Derrynane; adult/child €5/3; ☺10.30am-6pm mid-Mar–Sep, 10am-5pm Oct, 10am-4pm Sat & Sun Nov–early-Dec; P🐕) Derrynane House was the home of Maurice 'Hunting Cap' O'Connell, a notorious local smuggler who grew rich on trade with France and Spain. He was the uncle of Daniel O'Connell, the 19th-century campaigner for Catholic emancipation, who grew up here in his uncle's care and inherited the property in 1825, when it became his private retreat. The house is furnished with O'Connell memorabilia, including the impressive triumphal chariot in which he lapped Dublin after his release from prison in 1844.

🛏 Sleeping & Eating

There are plenty of hostels and B&Bs along the Ring. It's wise to book ahead, as some places are closed out of season and others fill up quickly.

★ **Mannix Point Camping
& Caravan Park** CAMPGROUND €
(☑066-947 2806; www.campinginkerry.com; Mannix Point, Cahersiveen; hikers €8.50, vehicle plus 2 adults from €26; ☺late Apr–mid-Sep; 🐕) 🌿 Mortimer Moriarty's award-winning waterfront campground is one of Ireland's finest, with 42 pitches, an inviting kitchen, a campers' sitting room with peat fire (no TV, but regular music sessions and instruments if you haven't brought your own), laundry facilities, squeaky-clean showers (€1), a barbecue area and even a birdwatching platform. Sunsets here are stunning.

Moorings GUESTHOUSE €€
(☑066-947 7108; www.moorings.ie; s/d/tr from €90/120/165; 🐕) The Moorings is a friendly local hotel, **bar** (☺8am-11.30pm Mon-Sat, 8am-11pm Sun; 🍴) and **restaurant** (mains €24-35; ☺6-10pm Wed-Sun Apr-Oct; 🍴). It has 16 rooms, split between modern sea-view choices and simpler options, most refreshingly white in decor. Cots and pull-out sofas are available for kids.

★ **Smuggler's Inn** MODERN IRISH €€
(☑066-947 4330; www.smugglersinn.ie; Cliff Rd; 3-course lunch & early-bird menu €30, mains €20-27; ☺noon-2.45pm & 6-9.30pm; 🐕) At this diamond find near Waterville Golf Links, owner and chef Henry Hunt's gourmet creations incorporate fresh seafood and locally farmed poultry and meat, followed by artistic desserts (including homemade ice cream), served in a glass atrium dining room. Half-board deals are available at the inn's upstairs rooms (doubles from €85); cooked-to-order breakfasts include a catch of the day.

★ **Quinlan & Cooke** SEAFOOD €€
(☑066-947 2244; www.qc.ie; 3 Main St; mains €18-27; ☺food served 6-9pm, bar 3-10pm Thu-Mon Easter-Sep, shorter hrs Oct-Easter; 🐕🍴) 🌿 This is a modern take on a classic pub and as such is open pub hours for pints and craic. Some of the finest food on the Ring also pours forth, particularly locally sourced seafood from its own fishing fleet, such as Valentia crab and prawn bisque. Upstairs there are six boutique B&B bedrooms (doubles from €170).

ⓘ Getting Around

Bus Éireann runs a once-daily Ring of Kerry bus service (No 280; €23.50) from late June to late August. Buses leave Killarney at 11.30am, arriving back at Killarney at 4.45pm. En route, stops include (in order):

Killorglin €8, 30 minutes

Cahersiveen €17.50, 1½ hours

Waterville €20, 1¾ hours

Caherdaniel €21.80, 2¼ hours

The road is narrow and windy in places. Tour buses travel the Ring in an anticlockwise direction. Getting stuck behind one is tedious, so consider driving clockwise; just watch out on blind corners.

THE WEST COAST

Galway

POP 79,930

Arty and bohemian, Galway (Gaillimh) is legendary around the world for its entertainment scene. Students make up a quarter of the city's population and brightly painted pubs heave with live music on any given night. Here, street life is more important than sightseeing – cafes spill out onto cobblestone streets filled with a frenzy of fiddles, banjos, guitars and *bodhráns* (hand-held goatskin drums), while jugglers,

Galway City

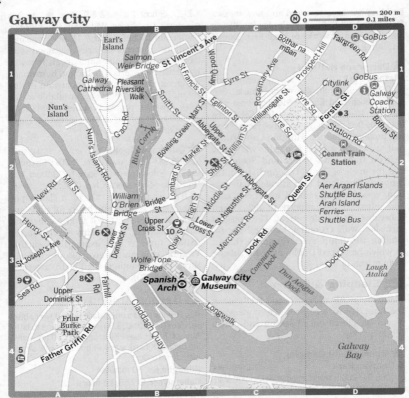

Galway City

◎ Top Sights
1 Galway City Museum	B3
2 Spanish Arch	B3

✪ Activities, Courses & Tours
3 Lally Tours	D1

🛏 Sleeping
4 Kinlay House	C2
5 Stop	A4

🍴 Eating
6 Aniar	A3
7 McCambridge's	C2
8 Oscar's	A3

🍸 Drinking & Nightlife
9 Crane Bar	A3
10 Tigh Neachtain	B3

painters, puppeteers and magicians in outlandish masks enchant passers-by.

◉ Sights

★ Galway City Museum
MUSEUM

(☏ 091-532 460; www.galwaycitymuseum.ie; Spanish Parade; ◷ 10am-5pm Tue-Sat, plus noon-5pm Sun Easter-Sep) FREE Exhibits at this modern, three-floor museum engagingly convey the city's archaeological, political, cultural and social history. Look out for an iconic Galway hooker fishing boat, a collection of *currachs* (boats made of a framework of laths covered with tarred canvas) and sections covering Galway's role in the revolutionary events that shaped the Republic of Ireland.

★ Spanish Arch
HISTORIC SITE

The Spanish Arch is thought to be an extension of Galway's medieval city walls, designed to protect ships moored at the nearby quay while they unloaded goods from Spain. It was partially destroyed by the tsunami that followed the 1755 Lisbon earthquake. Today it reverberates with buskers and drummers, and the lawns and riverside form a gathering place for locals and visitors on sunny days, as kayakers negotiate the tidal rapids of the River Corrib.

✯✯ Festivals

Galway International Arts Festival ART
(www.giaf.ie; ☉ mid-late Jul) Catch performances and exhibits by top drama groups, musicians and bands, comedians, artists and much more during this two-week fiesta of theatre, comedy, music and art.

Galway International
Oyster & Seafood Festival FOOD & DRINK
(www.galwayoysterfest.com; South Park; ☉ late Sep) Going strong since 1954, the world's oldest oyster festival draws thousands of visitors in late September. Events include the World Oyster Opening Championships, live music, a masquerade carnival and family activities.

🛏 Sleeping

★ Kinlay House HOSTEL €
(☏ 091-565 244; www.kinlaygalway.ie; Merchants Rd, Eyre Sq; dm/d €33/98; @ 🖧) The central location, cosy lounge, mellow vibe, pool table and smart kitchen and eating area make this large, brightly lit hostel a winner. Dorms vary in size but all the beds have individual curtains, lights and power and USB sockets. Tuesday night brings a pub crawl.

★ Stop B&B €€
(☏ 091-586 736; www.thestopbandb.com; 38 Father Griffin Rd; s/d/tr/f from €50/100/150/200; 🖧) Done up with contemporary artworks, stripped floorboards and bold colours, this 11-room house pulls out all the stops. The rooms are individually decorated and space – at a premium – is wisely used, so there are no wardrobes (just hangers), small work desks and no TV, but comfy beds. Breakfast includes freshly squeezed orange juice. There's a handy supermarket right across the street.

★ Glenlo Abbey Hotel HISTORIC HOTEL €€€
(☏ 091-519 600; www.glenloabbeyhotel.ie; Kentfield Bushy Park, N59; d/ste from €382/485; 🖧) Situated on the shores of Lough Corrib, 4km northwest of Galway, this 1740-built stone manor is the ancestral home of the Ffrench family, one of Galway's 14 tribes. Exceptionally preserved period architectural features are complemented by antique furnishings, sumptuous marble bathrooms, duck-down duvets and king-size pillows, along with lavish breakfasts. Its fine-dining **Pullman Restaurant** (2-/3-course menus €57/65; ☉ 6.30-10pm daily Mar-Oct, 6.30-9.30pm Fri & Sat Nov-Feb) occupies original *Orient Express* train carriages.

🍴 Eating & Drinking

McCambridge's CAFE, DELI €
(www.mccambridges.com; 38/39 Shop St; dishes €5-16; ☉ cafe 8.30am-5.30pm Mon-Thu, to 7pm Fri & Sat, 10am-4pm Sun, deli 8am-7pm Mon-Thu, to 8pm Fri & Sat, 10.30am-6pm Sun) Superb prepared salads are among the perfect picnic ingredients at this gourmet food emporium. All high ceilings, blond wood and busy staff, the upstairs cafe is lovely with a changing menu of modern Irish fare such as Galway Hooker beef stew, and more than 100 craft beers from Ireland's west. Brunch is served until 4.30pm on Sundays.

★ Oscar's SEAFOOD €€
(☏ 091-582 180; www.oscarsseafoodbistro.com; Upper Dominick St; mains €16-26; ☉ 6-9.30pm Mon-Fri, 5.30-9.30pm Sat) The menu changes daily at this outstanding seafood restaurant, but it might include monkfish poached in saffron and white wine and served with cockles; seaweed-steamed Galway Bay lobster with garlic-lemon butter; or lemon sole with samphire. From Monday to Thursday before 6.30pm, the two-course early-bird menu (€19.50) is a steal.

★ Aniar MODERN IRISH €€€
(☏ 091-535 947; www.aniarrestaurant.ie; 53 Lower Dominick St; 6/8/10 courses €72/89/99, with wine pairings €107-169; ☉ 6-9.30pm Tue-Thu, 5.30-9.30pm Fri & Sat) 🍴 Terroir specialist Aniar is passionate about the flavours and food producers of Galway and West Ireland. Owner and chef JP McMahon's multicourse tasting menus have earned him a Michelin star, yet the casual spring-green dining space remains refreshingly down to earth. The wine list favours small producers. Reserve at least a couple of weeks in advance.

★ Tigh Neachtain PUB
(www.tighneachtain.com; 17 Upper Cross St; ☉ 11.30am-midnight Mon-Thu, to 1am Fri, 10.30am-1am Sat, 12.30-11.30pm Sun) Painted a bright cornflower blue, this 19th-century corner pub – known simply as Neáchtain's (*nock-tans*) or Naughtons – has a wraparound terrace for watching Galway's passing parade,

CLIFFS OF MOHER

In good visibility, the Cliffs of Moher (Aillte an Mothair, or Ailltreacha Mothair) are staggeringly beautiful. The entirely vertical cliffs rise to a height of 214m, their edge abruptly falling away into a ceaselessly churning Atlantic.

A progression of vast heads, the dark limestone marches in a rigid formation. Views stretch to the Aran Islands and the hills of Connemara. Sunsets here see the sky turn a kaleidoscope of amber, amethyst, rose-pink and deep garnet-red.

One of Ireland's blockbuster sights, it includes a high-tech visitor centre, 19th-century lookout tower and wealth of walking trails.

The **Cliffs of Moher Visitor Centre** (🖉 065-708 6141; www.cliffsofmoher.ie; R478; adult/child incl parking €8/free; ⏰ 8am-9pm May-Aug, 8am-7pm Mar, Apr, Sep & Oct, 9am-5pm Nov-Feb; 🖥) has a spiralling exhibition covering the fauna, flora, geology and climate of the cliffs, and an interactive genealogy board with information on local family names. A number of bus tours leave Galway every morning for the Cliffs of Moher.

and a timber-lined interior with a roaring open fire, snugs and atmosphere to spare. Along with perfectly pulled pints of Guinness and 130-plus whiskeys, it has its own range of beers brewed by Galway Hooker.

★ **Crane Bar** PUB
(www.thecranebar.com; 2 Sea Rd; ⏰ 10.30am-11.30pm Mon-Thu, to 1am Fri, 12.30pm-1am Sat, to 11.30pm Sun) West of the Corrib, this atmospheric, always-crammed two-storey pub is the best spot in Galway to catch an informal *céilidh* (traditional music and dancing session). Music on both levels starts at 9.30pm.

ℹ Information

Galway Tourist Office (🖉 091-537 700; www.discoverireland.ie; Forster St; ⏰ 9am-5pm Mon-Sat) Galway's large, efficient tourist office can help arrange tours and has reams of information on the city and region.

ℹ Getting There & Around

BICYCLE

Galway's bike-share scheme (www.bikeshare.ie/galway.html) has 16 stations around town. For visitors, €3 (with €150 deposit) gets you a three-day pass. The first 30 minutes of each hire is free; up to two hours costs €1.50.

On Yer Bike (🖉 091-563 393; www.onyourbikecycles.com; 42 Prospect Hill; bike rental per day from €20; ⏰ 9.30am-7pm Mon-Fri, 11am-4pm Sat) offers bike rental.

BUS

Bus Éireann services depart from outside the train station. **Citylink** (www.citylink.ie; 17 Forster St; ⏰ office 9am-6pm Mon-Sat, 10am-6pm Sun; 🖥) and **GoBus** (www.gobus.ie; 🖥) use the coach station (New Coach Station; Fairgreen Rd) a block northeast. Citylink has buses to Clifden (€16, 1½ hours, six daily) and Dublin (€16, 2½ hours, hourly).

TRAIN

From the **train station** (www.irishrail.ie), just off Eyre Sq, there are up to 10 direct trains daily to/from Dublin's Heuston Station (from €17, 2½ hours), and five daily to Ennis (€7.50, 1¼ hours). Connections with other train routes can be made at Athlone (from €10.50, one hour).

Aran Islands

The windswept Aran Islands are one of western Ireland's major attractions. As well as their rugged beauty – they are an extension of The Burren's limestone plateau – the Irish-speaking islands have some of the country's oldest Christian and pre-Christian ruins.

There are three main islands in the group, all inhabited year-round. Most visitors head for the long and narrow (14.5km by a maximum 4km) **Inishmore** (Inis Mór). The land slopes up from the relatively sheltered northern shores and plummets on the southern side into the raging Atlantic. **Inishmaan** and **Inisheer** are much smaller and receive far fewer visitors.

The **tourist office** (🖉 099-61263; www.aranislands.ie; Kilronan; ⏰ 10am-5pm, to 6pm Jul & Aug) operates year-round at Kilronan, the arrival point and major village of Inishmore. You can leave your luggage here and change money. Around the corner is a Spar supermarket with an ATM (note, many places do not accept credit cards).

Inishmore

Three spectacular forts stand guard over Inishmore, each believed to be around 2000 years old. Chief among them is **Dún Aengus** (Dún Aonghasa; ☑099-61008; www.heritageireland.ie; adult/child €5/3; ☉9.30am-6pm Apr-Oct, to 4pm Nov-Mar), which has three massive drystone walls that run right up to sheer drops to the ocean below. It is protected by remarkable *chevaux de frise*, fearsome and densely packed defensive stone spikes. A small visitor centre has displays that put everything in context. A slightly strenuous 900m walkway wanders uphill to the fort itself.

Kilronan Hostel (☑099-61255; www.kilronanhostel.com; Kilronan; dm from €24; ☉late Feb-late Oct; @🛜), perched above Tí Joe Mac's pub, is a friendly hostel just a two-minute walk from the ferry. **Kilmurvey House** (☑099-61218; www.aranislands.ie/kilmurvey-house; Kilmurvey; s/d from €60/95; ☉Apr–mid-Oct; 🛜) offers B&B in a grand 18th-century stone mansion on the path leading to Dún Aengus.

❶ Getting There & Away

AIR

Aer Arann Islands (☑091-593 034; www.aerarannislands.ie; one way/return €25/49) Aer Arann Islands has flights to each of the islands up to six times a day; the flights take about 10 minutes. A connecting **shuttle bus** (☑091-593 034; www.aerarannislands.ie) links Galway city with **Connemara Regional Airport** (Aerfort Réigiúnach Chonamara; NNR; ☑091-593 034; Inverin).

BOAT

Aran Island Ferries (☑091-568 903; www.aranislandferries.com; one way/return €15/25) Aran Island Ferries has sailings to Inishmore (40 minutes, two to three daily), Inishmaan (45 minutes, two daily) and Inisheer (55 minutes, two daily). Crossings are subject to cancellation in high seas. Boats leave from **Rossaveal Ferry Terminal**, 37km west of Galway city and linked by **shuttle bus** (☑091-568 903; www.aranislandferries.com; Queen St). Contact the company in advance to arrange bike transport.

NORTHERN IRELAND
☑028

An exploding food scene, hip cities and the stunning Causeway Coast: there's plenty to pull visitors to the North. When you cross from the Republic into Northern Ireland you'll notice a couple of changes: the road signs are in miles and the prices are in pounds sterling – you're in the UK. At the time of research, there was no border checkpoint and not even a sign to mark the crossing point.

Belfast
POP 280,900

Belfast is in many ways a brand-new city. Once shunned by travellers unnerved by tales of the Troubles and sectarian violence, in recent years it has pulled off a remarkable transformation from bombs-and-bullets pariah to a hip-hotels-and-hedonism party town.

IRELAND BELFAST

WORTH A TRIP

CONNEMARA

With its shimmering black lakes, pale mountains, lonely valleys and more than the occasional rainbow, Connemara in the northwestern corner of County Galway is one of the most gorgeous pockets of Ireland. It's prime hill-walking country with plenty of wild terrain, none more so than the Twelve Bens, a ridge of rugged mountains that form part of **Connemara National Park** (☑076-100 2528; www.connemaranationalpark.ie; off N59; ☉24hr) FREE.

Connemara's 'capital', **Clifden** (An Clochán), is an appealing Victorian-era town with an oval of streets offering evocative strolls. Right in the centre of town is charmingly old-fashioned **Ben View House** (☑095-21256; www.benviewhouse.com; Bridge St; s €50-75 d €70-100; 🛜), and the gorgeous **Dolphin Beach B&B** (☑095-21204; www.dolphinbeachhouse.com; Lower Sky Rd; r from €110; 🅿🛜) 🚲 is 5km west of town.

From Galway, **Lally Tours** (☑091-562 905; www.lallytours.com; 4 Forster St; tours adult/child €30/20) runs day-long coach tours of Connemara.

Belfast

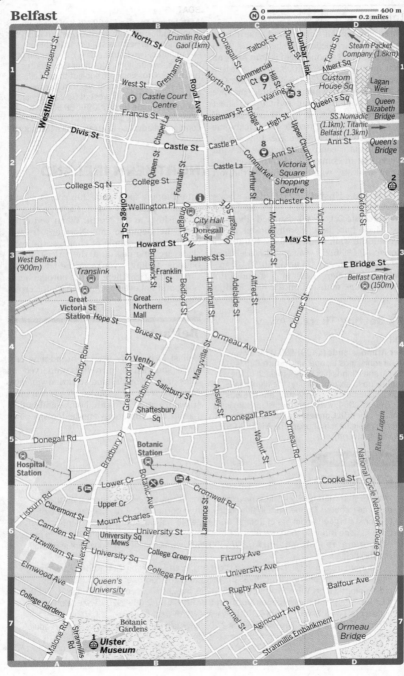

North St
Crumlin Road
Gaol (1km)
Donegall St
Talbot St
Dunbar St
Dunbar Link
Tomb St
Steam Packet
Company (1.8km)
Commercial
Ct
Hill St
Albert Sq
West St
Gresham St
North St
Waring St
Custom
House Sq
Lagan
Weir
Castle Court
Centre
Rosemary St
Bridge St
High St
Queen's Sq
Queen
Elizabeth
Bridge
Francis St
Chapel La
Royal Ave
Castle St
Castle Pl
Upper Church La
SS Nomadic
(1.1km); Titanic
Belfast (1.3km)
Queen's
Bridge
Queen St
Fountain St
Castle La
Cornmarket
Ann St
Ann St
College Sq N
College St
Arthur St
Victoria
Square
Shopping
Centre
Chichester St
Oxford St
Wellington Pl
Donegall Sq E
City Hall
Donegall
Sq
May St
Victoria St
Howard St
Donegall Sq W
James St S
Montgomery St
E Bridge St
Belfast Central
(150m)
West Belfast
(900m)
Translink
Brunswick St
Franklin
St
Bedford St
Linenhall St
Adelaide St
Alfred St
Cromac St
Great
Victoria St
Station
Hope St
Great
Northern
Mall
Bruce St
Ormeau Ave
Sandy Row
Great Victoria St
Ventry
St
Dublin Rd
Salisbury St
Maryville St
Aspley St
Donegall Pass
Ormeau Rd
Walnut St
Shaftesbury
Sq
Donegall Rd
Bradbury Pl
Botanic
Station
Cooke St
Hospital
Station
Lower Cr
Botanic Ave
Cromwell Rd
Lisburn Rd
Claremont St
Upper Cr
Mount Charles
Lawrence St
National Cycle Network Route 9
River Lagan
Camden St
University Rd
University St
Fitzwilliam St
University Sq
Mews
College Green
Fitzroy Ave
Elmwood Ave
University Sq
College Park
University Ave
Rugby Ave
Balfour Ave
College Gardens
Malone Rd
Stranmillis Rd
Queen's
University
Carmel St
Agincourt Ave
Ormeau
Bridge
Botanic
Gardens
Ulster
Museum
Stranmillis Embankment

0   400 m
0   0.2 miles

Belfast

◎ Sights

★ Titanic Belfast   MUSEUM
(www.titanicbelfast.com; Queen's Rd; adult/child
£18.50/8; ◷9am-7pm Jun & Jul, to 8pm Aug, to
6pm Apr, May & Sep, 10am-5pm Oct-Mar; ▣G2)
The head of the slipway where the RMS
Titanic was built is now occupied by the
gleaming, angular edifice of Titanic Belfast,
an unmissable multimedia extravaganza
that charts the history of Belfast and the
creation of the world's most famous ocean
liner. Cleverly designed exhibits enlivened
by historical images, animated projections
and soundtracks chart Belfast's rise to turn-
of-the-20th-century industrial superpower,
followed by a high-tech ride through a noisy,
smells-and-all recreation of the city's shipyards. Tickets also include entry to the SS
Nomadic.

SS Nomadic   HISTORIC SITE
(www.nomadicbelfast.com; Hamilton Dock, Queen's
Rd; adult/child £7/5; ◷10am-7pm Sun-Thu, to 8pm
Fri & Sat Jul & Aug, 10am-7pm Jun, 10am-6pm Apr,
May & Jun, 11am-5pm Oct-Mar; ▣G2) Built in
Belfast in 1911, the SS *Nomadic* is the last
remaining vessel of the White Star Line. The
little steamship ferried 1st- and 2nd-class
passengers between Cherbourg Harbour
and the ocean liners that were too big to
dock at the French port. On 10 April 1912 it
delivered 172 passengers to the ill-fated RMS
Titanic. Don't miss the luxurious 1st-class
toilets. Entry to the SS *Nomadic* (valid for
24 hours) is included in the ticket for Titanic
Belfast.

★ Ulster Museum   MUSEUM
(www.nmni.com; Botanic Gardens; ◷10am-5pm
Tue-Sun; ♿; ▣8A to 8D) 〔FREE〕 You could
spend hours browsing this state-of-the-art
museum, but if you're pressed for time don't
miss the Armada Room, with artefacts re-
trieved from the 1588 wreck of the Spanish
galleon Girona; the Egyptian Room, with
Takabuti, a 2500-year-old Egyptian mummy
unwrapped in Belfast in 1835; and the Early
Peoples Gallery, with the bronze Bann Disc,
a superb example of Celtic design from the
Iron Age.

★ Crumlin Road Gaol   HISTORIC BUILDING
(☎028-9074 1500; www.crumlinroadgaol.com;
53-55 Crumlin Rd; tour adult/child £12/7.50;
◷10am-5.30pm, last tour 4.30pm; ▣Agnes St)
Guided tours of Belfast's notorious Crumlin Road Gaol take you from the tunnel beneath Crumlin Rd, built in 1850 to convey
prisoners from the courthouse across the
street (and allegedly the origin of the judge's
phrase 'take him down'), through the echoing halls and cramped cells of C-Wing, to the
truly chilling execution chamber. Advance
tour bookings are recommended. The jail's
pedestrian entrance is on Crumlin Rd; the
car-park entrance is reached via Cliftonpark
Ave to the north.

⌂ Sleeping

Most budget and midrange accommodation
is south of the centre in the leafy university
district around Botanic Ave, University Rd
and Malone Rd, around a 20-minute walk
from City Hall. Business hotels and luxury
boutiques proliferate in the city centre.

★ Vagabonds   HOSTEL €
(☎028-9023 3017; www.vagabondsbelfast.com;
9 University Rd; dm £15-18, d & tw £50; @♾;
▣Shaftesbury Sq) Comfy bunks, lockable luggage baskets, private shower cubicles, a beer
garden, a pool table and a relaxed atmosphere are what you get at one of Belfast's
best hostels, run by a couple of experienced
travellers. It's conveniently located close to
both Queen's and the city centre.

Tara Lodge   GUESTHOUSE €€
(☎028-9059 0900; www.taralodge.com; 36 Cromwell Rd; s/d from £75/80; ℗@♾; ▣Upper Crescent Queens University) In a great location on
a quiet side street just a few paces from the
buzz of Botanic Ave, this guesthouse feels
more like a boutique hotel with its clean-cut,

IRELAND BELFAST

minimalist decor, friendly and efficient staff, and 34 bright and cheerful rooms. Delicious breakfasts include porridge with Bushmills whiskey.

★ **Merchant Hotel** HOTEL €€€
(☑ 028-9023 4888; www.themerchanthotel.com; 16 Skipper St; d/ste from £160/350; [P][@][🖫]; 🖫 Queen's Sq) Belfast's most flamboyant hotel occupies the palatial former Ulster Bank head office. Rooms are individually decorated with a fabulous fusion of contemporary styling and old-fashioned elegance; those in the original Victorian building have opulent floor-length silk curtains while newer rooms have an art deco–inspired theme. Facilities include a luxurious spa and an eight-person rooftop hot tub.

✕ Eating & Drinking

In recent years, Belfast's restaurant scene has been totally transformed by a wave of new restaurants whose standards compete with the best eateries in Europe.

Belfast's pub scene is lively and friendly, with the older traditional pubs complemented by a rising tide of stylish designer bars.

Maggie May's CAFE €
(☑ 028-9066 8515; www.maggiemaysbelfastcafe. co.uk; 50 Botanic Ave; mains £4.50-7.50; ☺ 8am-10pm Mon-Fri, 9am-11pm Sat & Sun; ☑🖫; 🖫7A to 7D) This is a classic little cafe with cosy wooden booths, murals of old Belfast and a host of hungover students wolfing down huge Ulster fry-ups. The all-day breakfast menu includes French toast and pancake stacks, while lunch can be soup and a sandwich or a burger.

★ **Holohan's at the Barge** MODERN IRISH €€
(☑ 028-9023 5973; www.holohansatthebarge. co.uk; Belfast Barge, Lanyon Quay; mains lunch £9-14, dinner £16-25; ☺ 1-4pm & 5-11pm Tue-Thu, 1-4pm & 5pm-midnight Fri & Sat, 1-7pm Sun; 🖫4, 6) Aboard the **Belfast Barge** (www.facebook.com/TheBelfastBarge; ☺ 10am-4pm Tue-Sat) [FREE], Holohan's is a sensational find for inspired twists on seafood and superb cooking of traditional Irish recipes such as *crabachain*, a mushroom, chestnut and tarragon fritter. Desserts are excellent too, and wines from around the world are served by the glass.

★ **Duke of York** PUB
(☑ 028-9024 1062; www.dukeofyorkbelfast.com; 11 Commercial Ct; ☺ 11.30am-11pm Mon, to 1am Tue & Wed, to 2am Thu & Fri, to midnight Sat, 3-9pm Sun; 🖫 Queen's Sq) In a cobbled alleyway off buzzing Hill St, the snug, traditional Duke feels like a living museum. There's regular live music; local band Snow Patrol played some of their earliest gigs here. Outside on Commercial Ct, a canopy of umbrellas leads to an outdoor area covered with murals depicting Belfast life; it takes on a street-party atmosphere in warm weather.

★ **Love & Death Inc** COCKTAIL BAR
(www.loveanddeathbelfast.com; 10A Ann St; ☺ 4pm-1am; 🖫 Victoria Sq) More like a cool inner-city house party, speakeasy-style Love & Death Inc is secreted up a flight of stairs above a pizza joint. Its living-room-style bar has outrageous decor, feisty Latin American–influenced food, feistier cocktails and a wild nightclub in the attic on weekends.

ℹ Information

Visit Belfast Welcome Centre (☑ 028-9024 6609; www.visitbelfast.com; 9 Donegall Sq N; ☺ 9am-7pm Mon-Sat, 11am-4pm Sun Jun-Sep, 9am-5.30pm Mon-Sat, 11am-4pm Sun Oct-May; 🖫; 🖫 Donegall Sq) Provides stacks of information about the whole of Northern Ireland, and books accommodation. Services include left luggage (not overnight), currency exchange and free wi-fi. There's also a gift shop selling local crafts and souvenirs.

ℹ Getting There & Away

AIR

Belfast International Airport (p644) is 30km northwest of the city, and has flights from the UK, Europe and the USA.

George Best Belfast City Airport (p644) is 6km northeast of the city centre, with flights from the UK and Europe.

BOAT

In addition to services with **Stena Line** (☑ 08447 707070; www.stenaline.co.uk; Victoria Terminal, 4 West Bank Rd; trips from £89; 🖫96) and **Steam Packet Company** (☑ 08722 992 992; www.steam-packet.com; Albert Quay; return fares from £98), car ferries to and from Scotland and England dock at Larne, 37km north of Belfast. Trains to the terminal at Larne Harbour depart from Great Victoria St station.

BUS

Europa Bus Centre, Belfast's main bus station, is behind the Europa Hotel and next door to Great Victoria St train station; it's reached via the Great Northern Mall beside the hotel. It's the main terminus for buses to Derry, Dublin and destinations in the west and south of Northern Ireland.

Ballycastle £12.50, 1¾ to 3¼ hours, hourly

Derry £12.50, 1¾ hours, half-hourly

Dublin £15.70, 2½ hours, hourly

Aircoach (www.aircoach.ie) operates a service from Glengall St, near Europa Bus Centre, to Dublin city centre and Dublin Airport.

TRAIN

For information on train fares and timetables, contact **Translink** (☑ 028-9066 6630; www.translink.co.uk; Europa Bus Centre).

Belfast Central Station (East Bridge St) East of the city centre. Trains run to Dublin and all destinations in Northern Ireland.

Great Victoria St Station (Great Victoria St, Great Northern Mall) Next to the Europa Bus Centre. Trains run to Portadown, Lisburn, Bangor, Larne Harbour and Derry.

Northern Ireland Railways (NIR; ☑ 028-9066 6630; www.translink.co.uk/Services/NI-Railways) Runs four routes from Belfast. One links with the system in the Republic via Newry to Dublin; the other three go east to Bangor, northeast to Larne and northwest to Derry via Coleraine.

❶ Getting Around

BICYCLE

Belfast Bikes (☑ 034-3357 1551; www.belfastbikes.co.uk; registration per 3 days £6, bikes per 30min/1hr/2hr/3hr free/£0.50/1.50/2.50; ☺ 6am-midnight) has 45 docking stations across the city centre. Register as a casual user for £6 through the website, app or on a terminal. The first 30 minutes of each trip are free.

BUS

Metro (☑ 028-9066 6630; www.translink.co.uk) operates the bus network in Belfast. Most city services depart from various stops on and around Donegall Sq, at City Hall and along Queen St. You can pick up a free bus map (and buy tickets) from the **Metro kiosk** (Donegall Sq; ☺ 8am-5.30pm Mon-Fri) at the northwest corner of the square.

You can also buy your ticket from the driver (change given); fares within the city zone are £2.

The Causeway & Antrim Coasts

Ireland isn't short of scenic coastlines, but the Causeway Coast between Portstewart (Port Stíobhaird) and Ballycastle (Baile an Chaibil) – climaxing in the spectacular rock formations of the Giant's Causeway – and

the Antrim Coast between Ballycastle and Belfast, are as magnificent as they come.

From April to September the **Ulsterbus** (☑ 028-9066 6630; www.translink.co.uk) Antrim Coaster (bus 252) links Larne with Coleraine via the Glens of Antrim, Ballycastle, the Giant's Causeway, Bushmills, Portrush and Portstewart.

From Easter to September the Causeway Rambler (bus 402) links Coleraine and Carrick-a-Rede (£9, 40 minutes, 12 daily) via Bushmills Distillery, the Giant's Causeway, White Park Bay and Ballintoy. The ticket allows unlimited travel in both directions for one day.

There are several hostels along the coast, including **Sheep Island View Hostel** (☑ 028-2076 9391; www.sheepislandview.com; 42A Main St; dm/s/tw from £18/25/45; [P][@][🖙]), **Ballycastle Backpackers** (☑ 077-7323 7890; www.ballycastlebackpackers.net; 4 North St; dm £17.50, d with/without bathroom £60/40; [P][@][🖙]) and **Bushmills Youth Hostel** (☑ 028-2073 1222; www.hini.org.uk; 49 Main St; dm £16-20, s £30-35, tw £50-60, tr £60-75; ☺ closed 11.30am-2.30pm Jul & Aug, 11.30am-3.30pm Mar-Jun, Sep & Oct; [@][🖙]).

◉ Sights

★ **Giant's Causeway**   LANDMARK

(www.nationaltrust.org.uk; ☺ dawn-dusk) **FREE** This spectacular rock formation – Northern Ireland's only Unesco World Heritage Site – is one of Ireland's most impressive and atmospheric landscape features, a vast expanse of regular, closely packed, hexagonal stone columns looking for all the world like the handiwork of giants. The phenomenon is explained in the **Giant's Causeway Visitor Experience** (☑ 028-2073 1855; 60 Causeway Rd; adult/child £12.50/6.25; ☺ 9am-7pm Jun-Sep, to 6pm Mar-May & Oct, to 5pm Nov-Feb; [🖙]) 🌿, housed in a new, ecofriendly building half-hidden in a hillside above the sea.

★ **Carrick-a-Rede Rope Bridge** BRIDGE
(☑ 028-2073 3335; www.nationaltrust.org.uk/car
rick-a-rede; 119 Whitepark Rd, Ballintoy; adult/child
£9/4.50; ⏰ 9.30am-6pm Apr-Oct, to 3.30pm Nov-
Mar) This 20m-long, 1m-wide bridge of wire
rope spans the chasm between the sea cliffs
and the little island of Carrick-a-Rede, swaying 30m above the rock-strewn water. Crossing the bridge is perfectly safe, but frightening
if you don't have a head for heights, especially if it's breezy (in high winds the bridge is
closed). From the island, views take in Rathlin
Island and Fair Head to the east.

There's a small National Trust information centre and cafe at the car park.

Derry (Londonderry)

POP 107,900

Northern Ireland's second-largest city continues to flourish as an artistic and cultural
hub. Derry's city centre was given a striking
makeover for its year as the UK City of Culture 2013, with the construction of the Peace
Bridge to Ebrington Sq, and the redevelopment of the waterfront and Guildhall area
making the most of the city's splendid riverside setting.

There's lots of history to absorb here,
from the Siege of Derry to the Battle of the
Bogside and Bloody Sunday. A stroll around
the 17th-century city walls that encircle the
city is a must, as is a tour of the Bogside
murals, along with taking in the burgeoning
live-music scene in the city's lively pubs.

⊙ Sights

★ **Derry's City Walls** WALLS
(⏰ dawn-dusk) FREE The best way to get a feel
for Derry's layout and history is to walk the
1.5km circumference of the city's walls. Completed in 1619, Derry's city walls are 8m high
and 9m thick, and are the only city walls in
Ireland to survive almost intact. The four
original gates (Shipquay, Ferryquay, Bishop's
and Butcher's) were rebuilt in the 18th and
19th centuries, when three new gates (New,
Magazine and Castle) were added.

★ **Tower Museum** MUSEUM
(www.derrystrabane.com/towermuseum; Union
Hall Pl; adult/child £3/1.50; ⏰ 10am-5.30pm, last
entry 4pm) Head straight to the 5th floor of
this award-winning museum inside a replica 16th-century tower house for a view
from the top. Then work your way down
through the excellent **Armada Shipwreck**

exhibition, and the **Story of Derry**, where
well-thought-out exhibits and audiovisuals
lead you through the city's history, from the
founding of the monastery of St Colmcille
(Columba) in the 6th century to the Battle of
the Bogside in the late 1960s. Allow at least
two hours.

People's Gallery Murals PUBLIC ART
(Rossville St) The 12 murals that decorate the
gable ends of houses along Rossville St, near
Free Derry Corner, are popularly referred to
as the People's Gallery. They are the work
of 'the Bogside Artists' (Kevin Hasson, Tom
Kelly, and Will Kelly, who passed away
in 2017). The three men lived through the
worst of the Troubles in Bogside. The murals
can be clearly seen from the northern part of
the City Walls.

🛏 Sleeping

★ **Merchant's House** B&B ££
(☑ 028-7126 9691; www.thesaddlershouse.com;
16 Queen St; d from £75; @ 🛜) This historical,
Georgian-style townhouse is a gem of a B&B.
It has an elegant lounge and dining room
with marble fireplaces and antique furniture, TV, coffee-making facilities, homemade
marmalade at breakfast and bathrobes in
the bedrooms (some rooms have shared
bathroom). Call at **Saddler's House** (36
Great James St; d from £75; 🛜) first to pick up
a key.

Abbey B&B B&B ££
(☑ 028-7127 9000; www.abbeyaccommodation.
com; 4 Abbey St; s/d/tr from £50/70/90; 🛜)
There's a warm welcome waiting at this
family-run B&B just a short walk from the
walled city, on the edge of the Bogside.
Rooms are spacious and modern.

🍴 Eating & Drinking

★ **Pyke 'n' Pommes** STREET FOOD £
(The POD; www.pykenpommes.ie; behind Foyle Marina, off Baronet St; mains £4-16; ⏰ noon-8.30pm
Fri & Sat, to 6pm Sun-Thu; 🚲) Derry's single-best
eatery is this quayside shipping container.
Chef Kevin Pyke's delectable, mostly organic burgers span his signature Notorious
PIG (pulled pork, crispy slaw, beetroot and
crème fraiche) and Veganderry (chickpeas,
lemon and coriander) to his Legenderry
Burger (Wagyu beef, pickled onions and
honey-mustard mayo). His Pykeos fish tacos
are another hit. Seasonal specials might include mackerel or oysters.

⭐ Peadar O'Donnell's   PUB

(www.facebook.com/Peadarsderry/; 59-63 Waterloo St; ⏱11.30am-1.30am Mon-Sat, 12.30pm-12.30am Sun) Done up as a typical Irish pub and grocery (with shelves of household items, shopkeeper's scales on the counter and a museum's-worth of old bric-a-brac), Peadar's has rowdy traditional-music sessions every night and often on weekend afternoons as well. Its adjacent **Gweedore Bar** (www.facebook.com/GweedoreRocks) hosts live rock bands every night, and a Saturday-night disco upstairs.

ℹ Information

Visit Derry Information Centre (📞028-7126 7284; www.visitderry.com; 44 Foyle St; ⏱9am-7pm Mon-Fri, 9am-6pm Sat, 10am-5pm Sun Jun-Aug, shorter hours Sep-May; 📶) A large tourist information centre with helpful staff and stacks of brochures for attractions in Derry and beyond. Also sells books and maps, and can book accommodation. **Claudy Cycles** (📞028-7133 8128; www.claudycycles.com; bike hire per half-/full day £8/12) can be rented here.

ℹ Getting There & Away

BUS

The **bus station** (📞028-7126 2261; Foyle St) is just northeast of the walled city. Services include the following:

Belfast £12, 1¾ hours, half-hourly

Dublin £20, four hours, every two hours daily

TRAIN

Derry's train station (always referred to as Londonderry in Northern Ireland timetables) is on the eastern side of the River Foyle; a free Rail Link bus connects with the bus station. Services run to Belfast (£12, 2½ hours) hourly Monday to Saturday, with six on Sunday.

SURVIVAL GUIDE

ℹ Directory A–Z

ACCOMMODATION

Hostels in Ireland can be booked solid in summer.

From June to September a dorm bed at most hostels costs €12 to €25 (£10 to £20), except for the more expensive hostels in Dublin, Belfast and a few other places.

Typical B&Bs cost around €40 to €60 (£35 to £50) per person per night (sharing a double room), though more luxurious B&Bs can cost upwards of €70 (£60) per person. Most B&Bs are small, so in summer they quickly fill up.

Commercial campgrounds typically charge €15 to €25 (£12 to £20) for a tent or campervan and two people. Unless otherwise indicated, prices quoted for 'sites' are for a tent, car and two people.

Useful resources:

An Óige (www.anoige.ie) Hostelling International (HI)–associated national organisation with 23 hostels scattered around the Republic.

HINI (www.hini.org.uk) HI-associated organisation with four hostels in Northern Ireland.

Independent Holiday Hostels of Ireland (www.hostels-ireland.com) Fifty-five tourist-board-approved hostels throughout all of Ireland.

Independent Hostel Owners of Ireland (www.independenthostelsireland.com) Independent hostelling association.

MONEY

The Republic of Ireland uses the euro (€). Northern Ireland uses the pound sterling (£), although the euro is also accepted in many places.

Tipping

Hotels €1/£1 per bag is standard; tip cleaning staff at your discretion.

Pubs Not expected unless table service is provided, then €1/£1 for a round of drinks.

Restaurants For decent service 10%; up to 15% in more expensive places.

Taxis Tip 10% or round up fare to the nearest euro/pound.

Toilet attendants Loose change; no more than €0.50/50p.

OPENING HOURS

Banks 10am–4pm Monday to Friday (to 5pm Thursday)

Pubs 10.30am–11.30pm Monday to Thursday, 10.30am–12.30am Friday and Saturday, noon–11pm Sunday (30 minutes 'drinking up' time allowed); closed Christmas Day and Good Friday

Restaurants noon–10.30pm; many close one day of the week

Shops 9.30am–6pm Monday to Saturday (to 8pm Thursday in cities), noon–6pm Sunday

PUBLIC HOLIDAYS

The main public holidays in the Republic of Ireland and Northern Ireland:

New Year's Day 1 January

St Patrick's Day 17 March

Easter (Good Friday to Easter Monday inclusive) March/April

May Holiday First Monday in May

Christmas Day 25 December

St Stephen's Day (Boxing Day) 26 December

Northern Ireland

Spring Bank Holiday Last Monday in May

Orangemen's Day 12 July
August Holiday Last Monday in August

Republic of Ireland
June Holiday 1st Monday in June
August Holiday 1st Monday in August
October Holiday Last Monday in October

TELEPHONE

The mobile-phone network in Ireland runs on the GSM 900/1800 system, which is compatible with the rest of Europe and Australia, but not the USA. Mobile numbers in the Republic begin with 085, 086 or 087; in Northern Ireland it's 07. A local pay-as-you-go SIM for your mobile will cost from around €10, but may work out free after the standard phone-credit refund (make sure your phone is compatible with the local provider).

To call Northern Ireland from the Republic, do not use 0044 as for the rest of the UK. Instead, dial 048 and then the local number. To dial the Republic from Northern Ireland, however, use the full international code, 00 353, then the local number.

VISAS

If you're a European Economic Area (EEA) national, you don't need a visa to visit (or work in) either the Republic or Northern Ireland. Citizens of Australia, Canada, New Zealand, South Africa and the USA can visit the Republic for up to three months, and Northern Ireland for up to six months. They are not allowed to work unless sponsored by an employer.

Full visa requirements for visiting the Republic are available online at www.dfa.ie; for Northern Ireland's visa requirements see www.gov.uk/government/organisations/uk-visas-and-immigration.

🚹 Getting There & Away

AIR

There are nonstop flights from Britain, Continental Europe and North America to Dublin, Shannon and Belfast International, and nonstop connections from Britain and Europe to Cork. International departure tax is included in the price of your ticket.

International airports in Ireland:

Belfast International Airport (Aldergrove; ☑ 028-9448 4848; www.belfastairport.com; Airport Rd) Located 30km northwest of the city. Flights serve the UK, Europe, and the USA (New York and Boston).

Dublin Airport (☑ 01-814 1111; www.dublinairport.com) Dublin Airport, 13km north of the centre, is Ireland's major international gateway airport. It has two terminals: most international flights (including most US flights) use the newer Terminal 2; Ryanair and select others use Terminal 1. Both terminals have the usual selection of pubs, restaurants, shops, ATMs and car-hire desks.

George Best Belfast City Airport (BHD; ☑ 028-9093 9093; www.belfastcityairport.com; Airport Rd) Located 6km northeast of Belfast city centre; flights serve the UK and Europe.

Shannon Airport (SNN; ☑ 061-712 000; www.shannonairport.ie) Ireland's third-busiest airport has ATMs, currency exchange, car-rental desks, taxis and a **tourist office** (☑ 061-712 000; www.shannonregiontourism.ie; Shannon Airport; ⊙7am-11pm) near the arrivals area. Numerous flights serve North America (with US pre-clearance facilities), the UK and Europe.

SEA

The main ferry routes between Ireland and the UK and mainland Europe:

➧ Belfast to Liverpool (England; eight hours)
➧ Belfast to Cairnryan (Scotland; 2½ hours)
➧ Cork to Roscoff (France; 14 hours; April to October only)
➧ Dublin to Liverpool (England; fast ferry – four hours, slow ferry – 8½ hours)
➧ Dublin to Holyhead (Wales; fast ferry – two hours, slow ferry – 3½ hours)
➧ Larne to Cairnryan (Scotland; two hours)
➧ Rosslare to Cherbourg/Roscoff (France; 18/20½ hours)
➧ Rosslare to Fishguard and Pembroke (Wales; 3½ hours)

Competition from budget airlines has forced ferry operators to discount heavily and offer flexible fares.

A useful website is www.aferry.co.uk, which covers all sea-ferry routes and operators to Ireland.

Main operators include the following:
Brittany Ferries (www.brittanyferries.com) Cork to Roscoff; March to October.
Irish Ferries (www.irishferries.com) Dublin to Holyhead ferries (up to five per day year-round); and France to Rosslare (twice per week).
P&O Ferries (www.poferries.com) Daily sailings year-round from Dublin to Liverpool, and Larne to Cairnryan.
Stena Line (www.stenaline.com) Daily sailings from Holyhead to Dublin Port, from Belfast to Liverpool and Cairnryan, and from Rosslare to Fishguard.

🚹 Getting Around

The big decision in getting around Ireland is whether to go by car or use public transport. Your own car will make the best use of your time and help you reach even the most remote of places. It's usually easy to get very cheap rentals –

BUS & RAIL PASSES

There are a few bus, rail and bus-and-rail passes worth considering:

Irish Explorer Offers customers five days of unlimited Irish Rail travel within 15 consecutive days (adult/child €160/80).

Open Road Pass Three days' travel within six consecutive days (€60) on Bus Éireann; extra days cost €16.50.

Sunday Day Tracker One day's unlimited travel (adult/child £7/3.75) on Translink buses and trains in Northern Ireland; Sunday only.

Trekker Four Day Four consecutive days of unlimited travel (€110) on Irish Rail.

Note that Eurail's one-country pass for Ireland is a bad deal in any of its permutations.

€10 per day or less is common – and if two or more are travelling together, the fee for rental and petrol can be cheaper than bus fares.

The bus network, made up of a mix of public and private operators, is extensive and generally quite competitive – although journey times can be slow and lots of the points of interest outside towns are not served. The rail network is quicker but more limited, serving only some major towns and cities. Both buses and trains get busy during peak times; you'll need to book in advance to be guaranteed a seat.

BICYCLE

Ireland's compact size and scenic landscapes make it a good cycling destination. However, dodgy weather, many very narrow roads and some very fast drivers are major concerns. Special tracks such as the 42km **Great Western Greenway** in County Mayo are a delight. A good tip for cyclists in the west is that the prevailing winds make it easier to cycle from south to north.

Buses will carry bikes, but only if there's room. For trains, bear the following in mind:
➡ Bikes are carried free on Intercity and off-peak commuter trains.
➡ Book in advance (www.irishrail.ie), as there's only room for two bikes per service.

BUS

Private buses compete – often very favourably – with Bus Éireann in the Republic and also run where the national buses are irregular or absent.

Distances are not especially long: few bus journeys will last longer than five hours. Bus Éireann bookings can be made online, but you can't reserve a seat for a particular service. Dynamic pricing is in effect on many routes: book early to get the lowest fares.

Note the following:

➡ Bus routes and frequencies are slowly contracting in the Republic.
➡ The National Journey Planner app by Transport for Ireland is very useful for planning bus and train journeys.

The main bus services in Ireland:

Bus Éireann (☑1850 836 6111; www.buseireann.ie) The Republic's main bus line.

Translink (☑028-9066 6630; www.translink.co.uk) Northern Ireland's main bus service; includes Ulsterbus and Goldline.

CAR & MOTORCYCLE

The majority of hire companies won't rent you a car if you're under 23 years of age and haven't had a valid driving licence for at least a year.

TRAIN

Given Ireland's relatively small size, train travel can be quick and advance-purchase fares are competitive with buses. Worth noting:

➡ Many of the Republic's most beautiful areas, such as whole swaths of the Wild Atlantic Way, are not served by rail.

➡ Most lines radiate out from Dublin, with limited ways of interconnecting between lines, which can complicate touring.

➡ There are four routes from Belfast in Northern Ireland; one links with the system in the Republic via Newry to Dublin.

➡ True 1st class only exists on the Dublin–Cork and Dublin–Belfast lines. On all other trains, seats are the same size as in standard class, despite any marketing come-ons such as 'Premier' class.

Irish Rail (Iarnród Éireann; ☑01-836 6222; www.irishrail.ie) Operates trains in the Republic.

Translink NI Railways (☑028-9066 6630; www.translink.co.uk) Operates trains in Northern Ireland.

1. Haute cuisine, France
Indulge in France's wealth of gastronomic pleasures.

2. Alfresco dining in Plaka, Athens, Greece
Athens' restaurant scene is marked by a delightful culture of casual, convivial alfresco dining.

3. Lokum
Eastern treat also known as Turkish delight.

4. Chefs at work, Milan, Italy
Milan is home to fine dining and regional specialities.

5. Rakija/raki
Fruit brandy found mainly in the Western Balkans.

Italy

POP 62.14 MILLION

Best Places to Eat

➡ Antiche Carampane (p691)

➡ Trattoria Mario (p701)

➡ Concettina Ai Tre Santi (p710)

➡ All'Osteria Bottega (p694)

Best Museums & Galleries

➡ Vatican Museums (p657)

➡ Galleria degli Uffizi (p696)

➡ Museo Archeologico Nazionale (p707)

➡ Museo del Novecento (p678)

➡ Museo e Galleria Borghese (p660)

Why Go?

A favourite destination since the days of the 18th-century Grand Tour, Italy may appear to hold few surprises. Its iconic monuments and masterpieces are known the world over, while cities like Rome, Florence and Venice need no introduction.

Yet Italy is far more than the sum of its sights. Its fiercely proud regions maintain centuries-old customs and culinary traditions, meaning enthralling festivals and delectable food appear at every turn. And then there are those timeless landscapes, from Tuscany's gentle hills to icy Alpine peaks, vertiginous coastlines and spitting volcanoes.

Drama is never far away in Italy and its streets and piazzas provide endless people-watching, ideally over a lazy lunch or *aperitivo* (evening drink). This is, after all, the land of *dolce far niente* (sweet idleness) where simply hanging out is a pleasure and time seems to matter just that little bit less.

When to Go
Rome

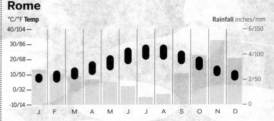

°C/°F **Temp** — Rainfall inches/mm

Apr–May Perfect spring weather; ideal for exploring vibrant cities and blooming countryside.

Jun–Jul Summer means beach weather and a packed festival calendar.

Sep–Oct Enjoy mild temperatures, autumn cuisine and the *vendemia* (grape harvest).

Entering the Country

Entering Italy from most other parts of the EU is generally uncomplicated, with no border checkpoints and no customs thanks to the Schengen Agreement. Document and customs checks remain standard if arriving from (or departing to) a non-Schengen country. A plethora of airlines link Italy with the rest of the world, and cut-rate carriers have significantly driven down the cost of flights from other European countries. Excellent rail and bus connections, especially with northern Italy, offer efficient overland transport, while car and passenger ferries run to ports throughout the Mediterranean.

ITINERARIES

One Week

A one-week whistle-stop tour of Italy is enough to take in the country's three most famous cities. After a couple of days exploring the unique canalscape of Venice (p686), head south to Florence (p696), Italy's great Renaissance city. Two days will whet your appetite for the artistic and architectural treasures that await in Rome (p651).

Two Weeks

After the first week, continue south for some sea and southern passion. Spend a day admiring art and lapping up the raw, high-octane energy of soul-stirring Naples (p707), a day investigating the ruins at Pompeii (p712), and a day or two enjoying the glitz and dramatic scapes of the Amalfi Coast (p714). Then backtrack to Naples for a ferry to Palermo (p718) and the gastronomic delights of Sicily.

Essential Food & Drink

Italian cuisine is highly regional in nature and wherever you go you'll find local specialities. That said, some staples are ubiquitous:

Pizza There are two varieties: Roman, with a thin crispy base; and Neapolitan, with a higher, more doughy base. The best are always prepared in a *forno a legna* (wood-fired oven).

Pasta Comes in hundreds of shapes and sizes and is served with everything from thick meat-based sauces to fresh seafood.

Gelato Classic flavours include *fragola* (strawberry), *pistacchio* (pistachio), *nocciola* (hazelnut) and *stracciatella* (milk with chocolate shavings).

Wine Ranges from big-name reds such as Piedmont's Barolo and Tuscany's Brunello di Montalcino to sweet Sicilian Malvasia and sparkling prosecco from the Veneto.

Caffè Italians take their coffee seriously, drinking cappuccino only in the morning, and espressos whenever, ideally standing at a bar.

Sleeping Price Ranges

The following price ranges refer to a double room with private bathroom (breakfast included) in high season.

€ less than €110

€€ €110–200

€€€ more than €200.

Eating Price Ranges

The following price ranges refer to a meal of two courses (antipasto/primo and secondo), a glass of house wine, and coperto (cover charge) for one person.

€ less than €25

€€ €25–45

€€€ more than €45

Resources

Lonely Planet (www.lonelyplanet.com/italy) Destination information.

ENIT (www.italia.it) Official tourism website.

The Local (www.thelocal.it) News from Italy.

ITALY

Italy Highlights

1 Rome (p651) Facing up to awe-inspiring art and iconic monuments.

2 Venice (p686) Taking to the water and cruising past Gothic palaces, domed churches and crumbling piazzas.

3 Florence (p696) Exploring this exquisite Renaissance time capsule.

4 Naples (p707) Working up an appetite for the world's best pizza in Naples' baroque backstreets.

5 Turin (p677) Visiting Turin's regal palaces and magnificent museums.

6 Siena (p705) Admiring glorious Gothic architecture and Renaissance art.

7 Amalfi Coast (p714) Basking in the Amalfi Coast's inspiring sea views.

8 Verona (p685) Enjoying an open-air opera in one of Italy's most romantic cities.

ROME

POP 2.87 MILLION

Ever since its glory days as an ancient superpower, Rome has been astonishing visitors. Its historical cityscape, piled high with haunting ruins and iconic monuments, is achingly beautiful, and its museums and basilicas showcase some of Europe's most celebrated masterpieces. But no list of sights and must-sees can capture the sheer elation of experiencing Rome's operatic streets and baroque piazzas, of turning a corner and stumbling across a world-famous fountain or a colourful neighbourhood market. Its street-side cafes are made for idling and elegant Renaissance *palazzi* (mansions) provide the perfect backdrop for romantic alfresco dining.

◉ Sights

◉ Ancient Rome

The neighbourhood's main sights are concentrated in a tightly packed area. Starting in the southeast, the Colosseum, Palatino and Roman Forum are all covered by a single ticket and are all within comfortable walking distance of each other.

★**Colosseum**   AMPHITHEATRE
(Colosseo; Map p652; ☑ 06 3996 7700; www.parcocolosseo.it; Piazza del Colosseo; adult/reduced incl Roman Forum & Palatino €16/7.50, Full Experience ticket €22/13.50; ⊗8.30am-1hr before sunset; ⓂColosseo) Rome's great gladiatorial arena is the most thrilling of the city's ancient sights. Inaugurated in 80 CE, the 50,000-seat Colosseum, also known as the Flavian Amphitheatre, was originally clad in travertine and covered by a huge canvas awning. Inside, tiered seating encircled the arena, itself built over an underground complex where animals were caged and stage sets prepared. Games involved gladiators fighting wild animals or each other.

Two thousand years on and it's Italy's top tourist attraction.

★**Palatino**   ARCHAEOLOGICAL SITE
(Palatine Hill; Map p652; ☑ 06 3996 7700; www.parcocolosseo.it; Via di San Gregorio 30, Piazza di Santa Maria Nova; adult/reduced incl Colosseum & Roman Forum €12/7.50, SUPER ticket €18/13.50; ⊗8.30am-1hr before sunset; some SUPER ticket sites Mon, Wed, Fri & morning Sun only; ⓂColosseo) Sandwiched between the Roman Forum and the Circo Massimo, the Palatino

(Palatine Hill) is one of Rome's most spectacular sights, a beautiful, atmospheric area of towering pine trees, majestic ruins and unforgettable views. This is where Romulus supposedly founded the city in 753 BCE and Rome's emperors lived in palatial luxury. Look out for the **stadio** (stadium), the ruins of the **Domus Flavia** (imperial palace), and grandstand views over the Roman Forum from the **Orti Farnesiani**.

★**Roman Forum**   ARCHAEOLOGICAL SITE
(Foro Romano; Map p652; ☑ 06 3996 7700; www.parcocolosseo.it; Largo della Salara Vecchia, Piazza di Santa Maria Nova; adult/reduced incl Colosseum & Palatino €12/7.50, SUPER ticket €18/13.50; ⊗8.30am-1hr before sunset; SUPER ticket sites Tue, Thu, Sat & afternoon Sun only; ☑Via dei Fori Imperiali) An impressive – if rather confusing – sprawl of ruins, the Roman Forum was ancient Rome's showpiece centre, a grandiose district of temples, basilicas and vibrant public spaces. The site, originally a marshy burial ground, was first developed in the 7th century BCE, growing over time to become the social, political and commercial hub of the Roman empire. Signature sights include the **Arco di Settimio Severo** (Arch of Septimius Severus), the **Curia**, the **Tempio di**

ITALY ROME

ⓘ COLOSSEUM & SUPER TICKETS

→ If queues are long, get your ticket at the Palatino, about 250m away at Via di San Gregorio 30.

→ Other queue-jumping tips: book your ticket online at www.coopculture.it (plus a €2 booking fee); get the Roma Pass; or join an official English-language tour (€5 on top of the regular ticket price).

→ You'll need to book a guided tour if you want to visit the underground area (hypogeum) and/or upper floors (Belvedere). These cost €9 (or €15 for both) plus the normal Colosseum ticket.

→ If you plan on visiting the Palatino and Roman Forum too, buy a SUPER ticket and plan carefully. The combo ticket, valid for all three sights for two consecutive days, is the only way to access internal sites at the Palatino and Roman Forum – all open a variety of different hours and days. Check schedules carefully to avoid missing out.

Ancient Rome

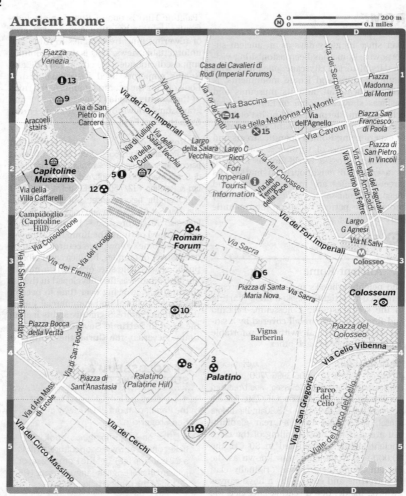

Saturno (Temple of Saturn) and the **Arco di Tito** (Arch of Titus).

★**Capitoline Museums**   MUSEUM
(Musei Capitolini; Map p652; ☎06 06 08; www.
museicapitolini.org; Piazza del Campidoglio 1;
adult/reduced €11.50/9.50; ☺9.30am-7.30pm,
last admission 6.30pm; ☐Piazza Venezia) Dating
from 1471, the Capitoline Museums are the
world's oldest public museums. Their collection of classical sculpture is one of Italy's
finest, boasting works such as the iconic
Lupa Capitolina (Capitoline Wolf), a life-
size bronze of a she-wolf suckling Romulus
and Remus, and the *Galata morente* (Dying

Gaul), a moving depiction of a dying warrior. There's also a formidable gallery with
masterpieces by the likes of Titian, Tintoretto, Rubens and Caravaggio.

Ticket prices increase when there's a temporary exhibition on.

Vittoriano   MONUMENT
(Victor Emanuel Monument; Map p652; Piazza Venezia; ☺9.30am-5.30pm summer, to 4.30pm winter;
☐Piazza Venezia) **FREE** Love it or loathe it, as
many Romans do, you can't ignore the Vittoriano (aka the Altare della Patria, Altar of the
Fatherland), the colossal mountain of white
marble that towers over Piazza Venezia. Built

Ancient Rome

at the turn of the 20th century to honour Italy's first king, Vittorio Emanuele II – who's immortalised in its vast equestrian statue – it provides the dramatic setting for the **Tomb of the Unknown Soldier** and, inside, the small **Museo Centrale del Risorgimento** (Map p652; ☎ 06 679 35 98; www.risorgimento.it; adult/reduced €5/2.50; ⊗ 9.30am-6.30pm), documenting Italian unification.

Bocca della Verità MONUMENT
(Mouth of Truth; Map p654; Piazza Bocca della Verità 18; voluntary donation; ⊗ 9.30am-5.50pm summer, to 4.50pm winter; 🚌 Piazza Bocca della Verità) A bearded face carved into a giant marble disc, the *Bocca della Verità* is one of Rome's most popular curiosities. Legend has it that if you put your hand in the mouth and tell a lie, the Bocca will slam shut and bite it off.

The mouth, which was originally part of a fountain, or possibly an ancient manhole cover, now lives in the portico of the **Chiesa di Santa Maria in Cosmedin**, a handsome medieval church.

⦾ Centro Storico

Bound by the River Tiber and Via del Corso, the *centro storico* is made for aimless wandering. Even without trying you'll come across some of Rome's great sights: the Pantheon, Piazza Navona and Campo de' Fiori, as well as a host of monuments, museums and churches. To the south, the lively Ghetto has been home to Rome's Jewish community since the 2nd century BCE.

★ Pantheon CHURCH
(Map p654; www.pantheonroma.com; Piazza della Rotonda; ⊗ 8.30am-7.30pm Mon-Sat, 9am-6pm Sun; 🚌 Largo di Torre Argentina) FREE A striking 2000-year-old temple, now a church, the Pantheon is the best preserved of Rome's ancient monuments and one of the most influential buildings in the Western world. Built by Hadrian over Marcus Agrippa's earlier 27 BCE temple, it has stood since around 125 CE, and while its greying, pockmarked exterior might look its age, it's still a unique and exhilarating experience to pass through its vast bronze doors and gaze up at the largest unreinforced concrete dome ever built.

Piazza Navona PIAZZA
(Map p654; 🚌 Corso del Rinascimento) With its showy fountains, baroque *palazzi* and colourful cast of street artists, hawkers and tourists, Piazza Navona is central Rome's elegant showcase square. Built over the 1st-century **Stadio di Domiziano** (Domitian's Stadium; Map p654; ☎ 06 6880 5311; www.stadiodomiziano.com; Via di Tor Sanguigna 3; adult/reduced €8/6; ⊗ 10am-6.30pm Sun-Fri, to 7.30pm Sat), it was paved over in the 15th century and for almost 300 years hosted the city's main market. Its grand centrepiece is Bernini's **Fontana dei Quattro Fiumi** (Fountain of the Four

ITALY ROME

Centro Storico & Trastevere

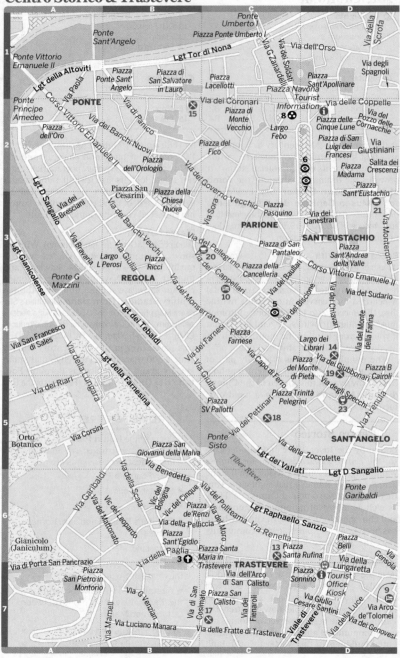

ITALY ROME

Rivers; Map p654; Piazza Navona), a flamboyant fountain featuring an Egyptian obelisk and muscular personifications of the rivers Nile, Ganges, Danube and Plate.

Campo de' Fiori PIAZZA

(Map p654; ☐ Corso Vittorio Emanuele II) Colourful and always busy, *Il Campo* is a major focus of Roman life: by day it hosts one of the city's best-known markets; by night it heaves with tourists and young drinkers who spill out of its many bars and restaurants. For centuries the square was the site of public executions. It was here that philosopher Giordano Bruno was burned for heresy in 1600, now marked by a sinister statue of the hooded monk, created by Ettore Ferrari in 1889.

★ Galleria Doria Pamphilj GALLERY

(Map p654; ☎ 06 679 73 23; www.doriapamphilj.it; Via del Corso 305; adult/reduced €12/8; ⊗ 9am–7pm, last entry 6pm; ☐ Via del Corso) Hidden behind the grimy grey exterior of Palazzo Doria Pamphilj, this wonderful gallery

VATICAN MUSEUMS ITINERARY

Follow this three-hour itinerary for the museums' greatest hits:

At the top of the escalator after the entrance, head out to the **Cortile della Pigna**, a courtyard named after the Augustan-era bronze pine cone in the monumental niche. Cross the courtyard into the long corridor that is the **Museo Chiaramonti** and head left up to the **Museo Pio-Clementino**, home of the Vatican's finest classical statuary. Follow through the **Cortile Ottagono** (Octagonal Courtyard) onto the **Sala Croce Greca** (Greek Cross Room) from where stairs lead up to the 1st floor. Continue through the **Galleria delle Carte Geografiche** (Map Gallery) to the **Sala di Costantino**, the first of the four **Stanze di Raffaello** (Raphael Rooms) – the others are the **Stanza d' Eliodoro**, the **Stanza della Segnatura**, home to Raphael's superlative *La scuola di Atene* (The School of Athens), and the **Stanza dell'Incendio di Borgo**. Anywhere else these frescoed chambers would be the star attraction, but here they're the warm-up act for the museums' grand finale, the **Sistine Chapel**. Originally built in 1484 for Pope Sixtus IV, this towering chapel boasts two of the world's most famous works of art: Michelangelo's ceiling frescoes (1508–12) and his *Giudizio universale* (Last Judgment; 1535–41).

boasts one of Rome's richest private art collections, with works by Raphael, Tintoretto, Titian, Caravaggio, Bernini and Velázquez, as well as several Flemish masters. Masterpieces abound, but the undisputed star is Velázquez' portrait of an implacable Pope Innocent X, who grumbled that the depiction was 'too real'. For a comparison, check out Gian Lorenzo Bernini's sculptural interpretation of the same subject.

⭐ **Trevi Fountain** FOUNTAIN
(Fontana di Trevi; Map p658; Piazza di Trevi; Ⓜ Barberini) The Fontana di Trevi, scene of movie star Anita Ekberg's late-night dip in *La Dolce Vita,* is a flamboyant baroque ensemble of mythical figures and wild horses taking up the entire side of 17th-century Palazzo Poli. Following a Fendi-sponsored restoration that finished in 2015, the fountain gleams brighter than it has for years. The tradition is to toss a coin into the water, thus ensuring that you'll return to Rome – on average about €3000 is thrown in every day.

Gallerie Nazionali:
Palazzo Barberini GALLERY
(Galleria Nazionale d'Arte Antica; Map p658; 🕿 06 481 45 91; www.barberinicorsini.org; Via delle Quattro Fontane 13; adult/reduced €12/6; ⏲ 8.30am-6pm Tue-Sun; Ⓜ Barberini) Commissioned to celebrate the Barberini family's rise to papal power, this sumptuous baroque palace impresses even before you view its breathtaking art collection. Many high-profile architects worked on it, including rivals Bernini and Borromini; the former contributed a square staircase, the latter a

helicoidal one. Amid the masterpieces on display, don't miss Filippo Lippi's *Annunciazione* (Annunciation; 1440–45) and Pietro da Cortona's ceiling fresco *Il Trionfo della Divina Provvidenza* (The Triumph of Divine Providence; 1632–39).

Piazza di Spagna &
the Spanish Steps PIAZZA
(Map p658; Ⓜ Spagna) A magnet for visitors since the 18th century, the Spanish Steps (Scalinata della Trinità dei Monti) provide a perfect people-watching perch. The 135 gleaming steps rise from Piazza di Spagna to the landmark **Chiesa della Trinità dei Monti** (Map p658; 🕿 06 679 41 79; http://trinitadeimonti.net/it/chiesa/; Piazza Trinità dei Monti 3; ⏲ 10.15am-8pm Tue-Thu, noon-9pm Fri, 9.15am-8pm Sat, 9am-8pm Sun).

Piazza di Spagna was named after the Spanish Embassy to the Holy See, although the staircase, designed by the Italian Francesco de Sanctis, was built in 1725 with money bequeathed by a French diplomat.

◉ Vatican City, Borgo & Prati

⭐ **St Peter's Basilica** BASILICA
(Basilica di San Pietro; Map p662; 🕿 06 6988 3731; www.vatican.va; St Peter's Sq; ⏲ 7am-7pm Apr-Sep, to 6pm Oct-Mar; 🚇 Piazza del Risorgimento, Ⓜ Ottaviano-San Pietro) FREE In this city of outstanding churches, none can hold a candle to St Peter's, Italy's largest, richest and most spectacular basilica. Built atop a 4th-century church, it was consecrated in 1626 after 120 years' construction. Its lavish interior contains many spectacular works of

art, including three of Italy's most celebrated masterpieces: Michelangelo's *Pietà,* his soaring dome, and Bernini's 29m-high baldachin over the papal altar.

Expect queues and note that strict dress codes are enforced (no shorts, miniskirts or bare shoulders).

★ **Vatican Museums** MUSEUM
(Musei Vaticani; Map p662; ☑ 06 6988 4676; www. museivaticani.va; Viale Vaticano; adult/reduced €17/8; ⊙ 9am-6pm Mon-Sat, to 2pm last Sun of month, last entry 2hr before close; ⬚ Piazza del Risorgimento, M Ottaviano-San Pietro) Founded by Pope Julius II in the early 16th century and enlarged by successive pontiffs, the Vatican Museums boast one of the world's greatest art collections. Exhibits, which are displayed along about 7km of halls and corridors, range from Egyptian mummies and Etruscan bronzes to ancient busts, old masters and modern paintings. Highlights include the spectacular collection of classical statuary in the **Museo Pio-Clementino**, a suite of rooms frescoed by Raphael, and the Michelangelo-painted **Sistine Chapel**.

Castel Sant'Angelo MUSEUM, CASTLE
(Map p662; ☑ 06 681 91 11; www.castelsantangelo. beniculturali.it; Lungotevere Castello 50; adult/reduced €14/7, free 1st Sunday of the month Oct-Mar; ⊙ 9am-7.30pm, ticket office to 6.30pm; ☎; ⬚ Piazza Pia) With its chunky round keep, this castle is an instantly recognisable landmark. Built as a mausoleum for the emperor Hadrian, it was converted into a papal fortress in the 6th century and named after an angelic vision that Pope Gregory the Great had in 590. Nowadays, it is a moody and dramatic keep that houses the **Museo Nazionale di Castel Sant'Angelo** and its grand collection of paintings, sculpture, military memorabilia and medieval firearms.

◉ Monti & Esquilino

Museo Nazionale Romano: Palazzo Massimo alle Terme MUSEUM
(Map p658; ☑ 06 3996 7700; www.coopculture.it; Largo di Villa Peretti 1; adult/reduced €10/5; ⊙ 9am-7.45pm Tue-Sun; M Termini) One of Rome's preeminent museums, this treasure trove of classical art is a must-see when you're in the city. The ground and 1st floors are devoted to sculpture, with some breathtaking pieces – don't miss *The Boxer*, a 2nd-century-BCE Greek bronze excavated on the Quirinale Hill in 1885, and the *Dying Niobid,* a 4th-

century-BCE Greek marble statue. But it's the magnificent and vibrantly coloured Villa Livia and Villa Farnesia frescoes on the 2nd floor that are the undisputed highlight.

Basilica di Santa Maria Maggiore BASILICA
(Map p658; ☑ 06 6988 6800; Piazza Santa Maria Maggiore; basilica free, adult/reduced museum €3/2, loggia €5; ⊙ 7am-6.45pm, loggia guided tours 9.30am-5.45pm; M Termini or Cavour) One of Rome's four patriarchal basilicas, this 5th-century church stands on Esquiline Hill's summit, on the spot where snow is said to have miraculously fallen in the summer of 358 CE. Every year on 5 August the event is recreated during a light show in Piazza Santa Maria Maggiore. Much altered over the centuries, the basilica is an architectural hybrid with 14th-century Romanesque campanile, Renaissance coffered ceiling, 18th-century baroque facade, largely baroque interior and a series of glorious 5th-century mosaics.

◉ Trastevere

Trastevere is one of central Rome's most vivacious neighbourhoods, an old-world warren of ochre *palazzi,* ivy-clad facades and cobbled lanes. Originally working class, it's now a trendy hang-out full of bars and restaurants – its very name, 'across the Tiber' *(tras tevere),* evokes both its geographical location and sense of difference.

Basilica di Santa Maria in Trastevere BASILICA
(Map p654; ☑ 06 581 48 02; Piazza Santa Maria in Trastevere; ⊙ 7.30am-9pm Sep-Jul, 8am-noon & 4-9pm Aug; ⬚ Viale di Trastevere, ⬚ Belli) Nestled in a quiet corner of Trastevere's focal square, this is said to be the oldest church dedicated to the Virgin Mary in Rome. In its original

---

ⓘ SKIP THE LINE AT THE VATICAN MUSEUMS
....

➜ Book tickets online at http:// biglietteriamusei.vatican.va/musei/ tickets/do (plus €4 booking fee).

➜ Minimise crowds: Tuesdays and Thursdays are quietest; Wednesday mornings are good as everyone is at the pope's weekly audience; afternoon is better than the morning; and avoid Mondays when many other museums are shut.

Termini, Esquiline and Quirinal

ITALY ROME

Termini, Esquiline and Quirinal

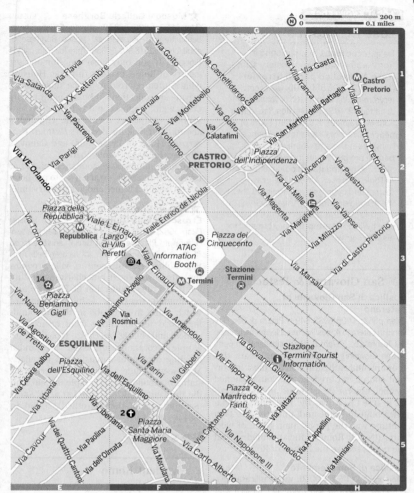

form, it dates from the early 3rd century, but a major 12th-century makeover saw the addition of a Romanesque bell tower and a glittering facade. The portico came later, added by Carlo Fontana in 1702. Inside, the 12th-century mosaics are the headline feature.

★ **Basilica di Santa Cecilia in Trastevere** BASILICA
(Map p662; ☎ 06 4549 2739; www.benedettinesan tacecilia.it; Piazza di Santa Cecilia 22; fresco & crypt each €2.50; ⊙ basilica & crypt 10am-12.30pm & 4-6pm Mon-Sat, 11.30am-12.30pm & 4.30-6.30pm Sun, fresco 10am-12.30pm Mon-Sat, 11.30am-12.30pm Sun; ☐ Viale de Trastevere, ☐ Belli) The last resting place of the patron saint of music features Pietro Cavallini's stunning 13th-century fresco, in the nuns' choir of the hushed convent adjoining the church. Inside the church itself, Stefano Maderno's mysterious sculpture depicts St Cecilia's miraculously preserved body, unearthed in the Catacombs of San Callisto in 1599. You can also visit the excavations of Roman houses, one of which was possibly Cecilia's. The church is fronted by a gentle fountain surrounded by roses.

LOSE THE CROWDS

Despite the roads that surround it, Rome's 'non-Catholic' cemetery, **Cimitero Acattolico per gli Stranieri** (Map p662; ☑ 06 574 19 00; www.cemeteryrome.it; Via Caio Cestio 6; voluntary donation €3; ◷ 9am-5pm Mon-Sat, to 1pm Sun; Ⓜ Piramide), is a verdant oasis of peace. An air of Grand Tour romance hangs over the site where up to 4000 people are buried, including poets Keats and Shelley, and Italian political thinker Antonio Gramsci. Among the gravestones and cypress trees, look out for the Angelo del Dolore (Angel of Grief), a much-replicated 1894 sculpture that US artist William Wetmore Story created for his wife's grave.

◉ San Giovanni & Testaccio

Basilica di San Giovanni in Laterano
BASILICA

(Map p662; ☑ 06 6988 6493; Piazza di San Giovanni in Laterano 4; basilica free, cloister incl Museo del Tesoro €5; ◷ 7am-6.30pm, cloister 9am-6pm; Ⓜ San Giovanni) For a thousand years this monumental cathedral was the most important church in Christendom. Commissioned by the emperor Constantine and consecrated in 324 CE, it was the first Christian basilica built in Rome and, until the late 14th century, was the pope's main place of worship. It's still Rome's official cathedral and the pope's seat as the bishop of Rome.

Basilica di San Clemente
BASILICA

(Map p662; ☑ 06 774 00 21; www.basilicasanclemente.com; Piazza di San Clemente; basilica free, excavations adult/reduced €10/5; ◷ 9am-12.30pm & 3-6pm Mon-Sat, 12.15-6pm Sun; Ⓠ Via Labicana) Nowhere better illustrates the various stages of Rome's turbulent past than this fascinating multilayered church. The ground-level 12th-century basilica sits atop a 4th-century church, which, in turn, stands over a 2nd-century pagan temple and a 1st-century Roman house. Beneath everything are foundations dating from the Roman Republic.

◉ Villa Borghese

Accessible from Piazzale Flaminio, Pincio Hill and the top of Via Vittorio Veneto, Villa Borghese is Rome's best-known park.

★ Museo e Galleria Borghese
MUSEUM

(Map p662; ☑ 06 3 28 10; http://galleriaborghese.beniculturali.it; Piazzale del Museo Borghese 5; adult/child €15/8.50; ◷ 9am-7pm Tue-Sun; Ⓠ Via Pinciana) If you only have time for one art gallery in Rome, make it this one. Housing what's often referred to as the 'queen of all private art collections', it boasts paintings by Caravaggio, Raphael and Titian, plus sensational sculptures by Bernini. Highlights abound, but look for Bernini's *Ratto di Proserpina* (Rape of Proserpina) and Canova's *Venere vincitrice* (Venus Victrix).

To limit numbers, visitors are admitted at two-hourly intervals – you'll need to pre-book tickets well in advance and get an entry time.

★ Museo Nazionale Etrusco di Villa Giulia
MUSEUM

(Map p662; ☑ 06 322 65 71; www.villagiulia.beniculturali.it; Piazzale di Villa Giulia; adult/reduced €8/4; ◷ 9am-8pm Tue-Sun; Ⓠ Via delle Belle Arti) Pope Julius III's 16th-century villa provides the often-overlooked but charming setting for Italy's finest collection of Etruscan and pre-Roman treasures. Exhibits, many of which came from tombs in the surrounding Lazio region, range from bronze figurines and black *bucchero* tableware to temple decorations, terracotta vases and a dazzling display of sophisticated jewellery. Must-sees include a polychrome terracotta statue of Apollo from a temple in Veio, and the 6th-century-BCE *Sarcofago degli Sposi* (Sarcophagus of the Betrothed), found in 1881 in Cerveteri.

🛏 Sleeping

🛏 Ancient Rome

★ Residenza Maritti
GUESTHOUSE €€

(Map p652; ☑ 06 678 82 33; www.residenzamaritti.com; Via Tor de' Conti 17; s €100, d €130-180, tr €150-200, q €170-210; ❄ 🎧; Ⓜ Cavour) Boasting stunning views over the nearby forums and Vittoriano, this hidden gem has 13 rooms spread over three floors. Some are bright and modern; others are more cosy with antiques, original tiled floors and family furniture. There's a fully equipped kitchen and a buffet breakfast is served in the bistro next door.

🛏 Centro Storico

Navona Essence
BOUTIQUE HOTEL €€

(Map p654; ☑ 06 8760 5186; www.navonaessencehotel.it; Via dei Cappellari 24; d €70-200; ❄ 🎧;

🚇 Corso Vittorio Emanuele II) Bed down in the heart of the action at this snug boutique hotel. Situated on a narrow backstreet near Campo de' Fiori, it's something of a squeeze but its location is handy for pretty much everywhere and its rooms are attractive, sporting a pared-down modern look and designer bathrooms.

Casa Fabbrini: Campo Marzio B&B €€
(Map p662; 🕿 06 324 37 06; https://campomarzio. casafabbrini.it; Vicolo delle Orsoline 13; r from €155; 🛜; 🚇 Spagna) There are only four B&B rooms on offer in this 16th-century townhouse secreted in a pedestrianised lane near the Spanish Steps, ensuring an intimate stay. Owner Simone Fabbrini has furnished these with a mix of antiques and contemporary pieces, and the result is quite delightful. Common areas include a mezzanine lounge and a kitchen where breakfast is served.

⭐ **Palazzo Scanderbeg** BOUTIQUE HOTEL €€€
(Map p658; 🕿 06 8952 90 01; www.palazzoscan derbeg.com; Piazza Scanderbeg 117; r/ste from €360/1000; 🌬🛜; 🚇 Barberini) Suite hotels are a dime a dozen in central Rome, but few are as attractive and comfortable as this boutique offering in a 15th-century *palazzo* near the Trevi Fountain. All of the guest rooms are spacious and elegantly appointed; suites have kitchens. Enjoy breakfast in the chic breakfast room or have the butler bring it to your room.

🛏 Vatican City, Borgo & Prati

Le Stanze di Orazio BOUTIQUE HOTEL €€
(Map p662; 🕿 06 3265 2474; www.lestanzediorazio. com; Via Orazio 3; r €80-200; 🌬🛜; 🚇 Via Cola di Rienzo, 🚇 Lepanto) This five-room boutique hotel makes for an attractive home away from home in the heart of the elegant Prati district, a single metro stop from the Vatican. The rooms have refined decor from a modern colour palette. There are top-end luxuries and well-appointed bathrooms. The breakfast area is small and stylish.

🛏 Monti & Esquilino

⭐ **RomeHello** HOSTEL €
(Map p658; 🕿 06 9686 00 70; https://theromehello. com/; Via Torino 45; dm/r from €15/45; 🌬@🛜; 🚇 Repubblica) 🌿 Funnelling all of its profits into worthy social enterprises, this street-art adorned hostel is the best in the city. It offers 200 beds, a communal kitchen, courtyard, lounge and laundry. Dorms max out at 10 beds (most have four) and have good mat-

tresses and en suite bathrooms; each bed has a locker, reading light, USB plug and power point.

⭐ **Beehive** HOSTEL €
(Map p658; 🕿 06 4470 4553; www.the-beehive. com; Via Marghera 8; dm from €25, s/d €70/100; without bathroom €50/80; ⏰ reception 7am-11pm; 🌬@🛜; 🚇 Termini) 🌿 More boutique chic than backpacker grungy, this small and stylish hostel has a glorious summer garden and a friendly traveller vibe. Dynamic American owners Linda and Steve exude energy and organise yoga sessions, storytelling evenings and tri-weekly vegetarian and organic dinners around a shared table (€10). Private rooms come with or without bathrooms and air-con; dorms are mixed or female-only.

🛏 Trastevere

⭐ **Arco del Lauro** GUESTHOUSE €€
(Map p654; 🕿 06 9784 0350; www.arcodellauro.it; Via Arco de' Tolomei 27; r €120-175; 🌬@🛜; 🚇 Viale di Trastevere, 🚇 Viale di Trastevere) Perfectly placed on a peaceful cobbled lane on the 'quiet side' of Trastevere, this ground-floor guesthouse sports six gleaming white rooms with parquet floors, a modern low-key look and well-equipped bathrooms. Guests share a fridge, a complimentary fruit bowl and cakes. Breakfast (€5) is served in a nearby cafe. Daniele and Lorenzo, who run the place, could not be friendlier or more helpful.

Relais Le Clarisse HOTEL €€
(Map p662; 🕿 06 5833 4437; www.leclarissetraste vere.com; Via Cardinale Merry del Val 20; r €120-200; 🌬🛜; 🚇 Viale di Trastevere, 🚇 Trastevere/Mastai) Set around a pretty internal courtyard with a gnarled old olive tree, orange trees and a scattering of tables, this is a peaceful 18-room oasis in Trastevere's bustling core. In

ITALY ROME

LOCAL KNOWLEDGE

THE SACROSANCT PASSEGGIATA

The *passeggiata* (traditional evening stroll) is a quintessential Roman experience. It's particularly colourful at weekends when families, friends and lovers take to the streets to strut up and down, slurp on gelato and window-shop. To join in, head to Via del Corso around 6pm. Alternatively, park yourself on the Spanish Steps and watch the theatrics unfold beneath you on Piazza di Spagna (p656).

Greater Rome

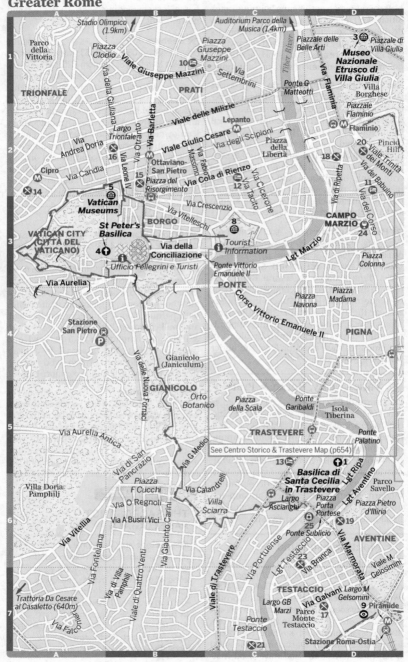

Parco della Vittoria

Stadio Olimpico (1.9km)

Auditorium Parco della Musica (1.4km)

Piazzale delle Belle Arti

Piazzale di Villa Giulia

3

Museo Nazionale Etrusco di Villa Giulia

Piazza Clodio

Viale Giuseppe Mazzini

Piazza Giuseppe Mazzini

Via Settembrini

10

Ponte G Matteotti

Villa Borghese

Via Flaminia

TRIONFALE

PRATI

Piazzale Flaminio

Via della Giuliana

Lepanto

Viale delle Milizie

Piazza della Libertà

Flaminio

Via Andrea Doria

Largo Trionfale

16

Via Oranto

Via Barletta

Viale Giulio Cesare

Via degli Scipioni

Pincio Hill

20

Viale Trinità dei Monti

Cipro

Via Leone IV

Via Candia

15

Ottaviano San Pietro

Via Fabio Massimo

Via Cola di Rienzo

Via Cicerone

Via Tacito

18

11

Via del Babuino

Via del Corso

14

5

Vatican Museums

Piazza del Risorgimento

Via Crescenzio

12

CAMPO MARZIO

Via di Ripetta

St Peter's Basilica

BORGO

Via Vitelleschi

8

24

VATICAN CITY (CITTÀ DEL VATICANO)

4

Via della Conciliazione

Tourist Information

Lgt Marzio

Piazza Colonna

Ufficio Pellegrini e Turisti

Ponte Vittorio Emanuele II

Via Aurelia

Ponte Vittorio Emanuele II

PONTE

Corso Vittorio Emanuele II

Piazza Navona

Piazza Madama

PIGNA

Stazione San Pietro

Gianicolo (Janiculum)

GIANICOLO

Orto Botanico

Piazza della Scala

Ponte Garibaldi

Isola Tiberina

Ponte Palatino

Via delle Nuova Fornaci

Via Aurelia Antica

TRASTEVERE

See Centro Storico & Trastevere Map (p654)

13

1

Via di San Pancrazio

Via G Medici

Basilica di Santa Cecilia in Trastevere

Lgt Ripa

Lgt Aventino

Parco Savello

Villa Doria Pamphilj

Piazza F Cucchi

Via Calandrelli

Villa Sciarra

Largo Ascianghi

Piazza Porta Portese

Piazza Pietro d'Illiria

Via Vitellia

Via O Regnoli

Via A Busiri Vici

Via Giacinto Carini

25

19

AVENTINE

Ponte Sublicio

Via Marmorata

Viale M Gelsomini

Via Fontelaiana

Via di Villa Pamphilj

Viale di Quattro Venti

Via di Trastevere

Via Portuense

Lgt Testaccio

23

Via Branca

Trattoria Da Cesare al Casaletto (640m)

Via Fati

TESTACCIO

Largo GB Marzi

Parco Monte Testaccio

Via Galvani

17

Largo M Gelsomini

9 Piramide

Ponte Testaccio

21

Stazione Roma-Ostia

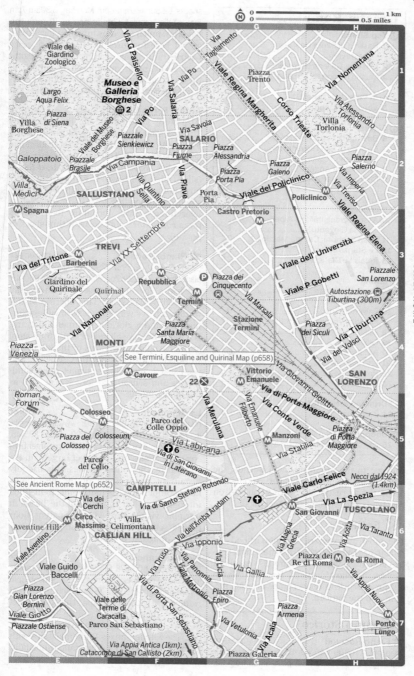

Greater Rome

◎ Top Sights

1 Basilica di Santa Cecilia in Trastevere	D5
2 Museo e Galleria Borghese	F1
3 Museo Nazionale Etrusco di Villa Giulia	D1
4 St Peter's Basilica	A3
5 Vatican Museums	B2

◎ Sights

6 Basilica di San Clemente	F5
7 Basilica di San Giovanni in Laterano	G6
8 Castel Sant'Angelo	C3
9 Cimitero Acattolico per gli Stranieri	D7

🛏 Sleeping

10 Associazione Italiana Alberghi per la Gioventù	B1
11 Casa Fabbrini: Campo Marzio	D2
12 Le Stanze di Orazio	C2
13 Relais Le Clarisse	C5

🍴 Eating

14 Bonci Pizzarium	A2
15 Fa-Bìo	B2
16 Fatamorgana	B2
17 Flavio al Velavevodetto	D7
18 Gelateria Dei Gracchi	D2
19 Giulietta	D6
20 Il Margutta	D2
21 La Tavernaccia	C7
22 Panella	F4
23 Trapizzino	C6

🍷 Drinking & Nightlife

24 Zuma Bar	D3

🛍 Shopping

25 Mercado de Porta Portese	D6

contrast to the urban mayhem outside, the hotel is all farmhouse charm. Rooms are decorated in rustic style with wrought-iron bedsteads and wood-beamed ceilings.

Eating

The most atmospheric neighbourhoods to dine in are the *centro storico* (historical centre) and Trastevere. There are also excellent choices in boho Monti and Testaccio. Watch out for overpriced tourist traps around Termini and the Vatican.

✕ Centro Storico

★ Forno Roscioli BAKERY €
(Map p654; ☑06 686 40 45; www.anticofornor oscioli.it; Via dei Chiavari 34; pizza slices from €2, snacks €2.50; ⊙7am-8pm Mon-Sat, 8.30am-7pm Sun; 🚌 Via Arenula) This is one of Rome's top bakeries, much loved by lunching locals who crowd here for luscious sliced pizza, prize pastries and hunger-sating *supplì* (risotto balls). The pizza margherita is superb, if messy to eat, and there's also a counter serving hot pastas and vegetable side dishes.

Antico Forno Urbani BAKERY €
(Map p654; ☑06 689 32 35; Piazza Costaguti 31; pizza slices from €1.50; ⊙7.40am-2.30pm & 5-7.45pm Mon-Fri, 8.30am-1.30pm Sat, 9.30am-1pm Sun; 🚌 Via Arenula) This Ghetto kosher bakery makes some of the best *pizza al taglio* (sliced pizza) in town. It can get extremely busy, but once you catch a whiff of the yeasty smell it's impossible to resist a quick stop. Everything's good, including its fabulous pizza *con patate* (topped with thin slices of potato).

★ Pianostrada RISTORANTE €€
(Map p654; ☑06 8957 2296; www.facebook.com/ pianostrada; Via delle Zoccolette 22; meals €40-45; ⊙1-4pm & 7pm-midnight Tue-Fri, 10am-midnight Sat & Sun; 🚌 Via Arenula) This uberhip bistro-restaurant, in a white space with vintage furnishings and a glorious summer courtyard, is a must. Reserve ahead, or settle for a stool at the bar and enjoy views of the kitchen at work. The cuisine is creative, seasonal and veg-packed, including gourmet open sandwiches and sensational focaccia, as well as full-blown mains.

La Ciambella ITALIAN €€
(Map p654; ☑06 683 29 30; www.la-ciambella. it; Via dell'Arco della Ciambella 20; meals €35-45; ⊙noon-11pm Tue-Sun; 🚌 Largo di Torre Argentina) Near the Pantheon but as yet largely undiscovered by the tourist hordes, this friendly restaurant beats much of the neighbourhood competition. Its handsome, light-filled interior is set over the ruins of the Terme di Agrippa, visible through transparent floor panels, setting an attractive stage for interesting, imaginative food.

Piccolo Arancio TRATTORIA €€
(Map p658; ☑06 678 61 39; www.piccoloarancio. it; Vicolo Scanderbeg 112; meals €38; ⊙noon-3pm & 7pm-midnight Tue-Sun; Ⓜ Barberini) In a 'hood riddled with tourist traps, this backstreet eatery – tucked inside a little house next to grandiose Palazzo Scanderberg – stands out. The kitchen mixes Roman classics with more contemporary options and, unusually, includes a hefty number of seafood choices –

the *linguini alla pescatora* (handmade pasta with shellfish and baby tomatoes) is sensational. Bookings essential.

Il Margutta
VEGETARIAN €€

(Map p662; ☑ 06 3265 0577; www.ilmargutta. bio; Via Margutta 118; lunch buffet weekdays/weekends €15/25, meals €35; ⊙ 8.30am-11.30pm; ☒; Ⓜ Spagna) This chic art-gallery-bar-restaurant is packed at lunchtime with Romans feasting on its good-value, eat-as-much-as-you-can buffet deal. Everything on its menu is organic, and the evening menu is particularly creative – vegetables and pulses combined and presented with care and flair. Among the various tasting menus is a vegan option.

★ Salumeria Roscioli
RISTORANTE €€€

(Map p654; ☑ 06 687 52 87; www.salumeriaroscioli.com; Via dei Giubbonari 21; meals €55; ⊙ 12.30-4pm & 7pm-midnight Mon-Sat; ☐ Via Arenula) The name Roscioli has long been a byword for foodie excellence in Rome, and this deli-restaurant is the place to experience it. Tables are set alongside the counter, laden with mouth-watering Italian and foreign delicacies, and in a small bottle-lined space behind. The food, including traditional Roman pastas, is top notch and there are some truly outstanding wines. Reservations essential.

✕ Vatican City, Borgo & Prati

Fa-Bìo
SANDWICHES €

(Map p662; ☑ 06 3974 6510; Via Germanico 71; meals €5-7; ⊙ 10.30am-5.30pm Mon-Fri, to 4pm Sat; ☐ Piazza del Risorgimento, Ⓜ Ottaviano-San Pietro) 🌿 Sandwiches, wraps, salads and fresh juices are all prepared with speed, skill and fresh organic ingredients at this busy takeaway. Locals, Vatican tour guides and in-the-know visitors come here to grab a quick lunchtime bite. If you can't find room in the small interior, there are stools along the pavement.

★ Bonci Pizzarium
PIZZA €

(Map p662; ☑ 06 3974 5416; www.bonci.it; Via della Meloria 43; pizza slices €5; ⊙ 11am-10pm Mon-Sat, from noon Sun; Ⓜ Cipro) Pizzarium, the takeaway of Gabriele Bonci, Rome's acclaimed pizza emperor, serves Rome's best sliced pizza, bar none. Scissor-cut squares of soft, springy base are topped with original combinations of seasonal ingredients and served for immediate consumption. Often jammed, there are only a couple of benches and stools for the tourist hordes; head across to the plaza at the metro station for a seat.

✕ Monti & Esquilino

★ Alle Carrette
PIZZA €

(Map p652; ☑ 06 679 27 70; www.facebook.com/allecarrette; Via della Madonna dei Monti 95; pizza €5.50-9; ⊙ 11.30am-4pm & 7pm-midnight; Ⓜ Cavour) Authentic pizza, super-thin and swiftly cooked in a wood-burning oven, is what this traditional Roman pizzeria on one of Monti's prettiest streets has done well for decades. Romans pile in here at weekends for good reason – it's cheap, friendly and delicious. All of the classic toppings are available, as well as gourmet choices such as anchovy and zucchini flower (yum!).

Panella
BAKERY €

(Map p662; ☑ 06 487 24 35; www.panellaroma. com; Via Merulana 54; meals €7-15; ⊙ 7am-11pm Mon-Thu & Sun, to midnight Fri & Sat; Ⓜ Vittorio Emanuele) Freshly baked pastries, fruit tartlets, *pizza al taglio* (pizza by the slice) and focaccia fill display cases in this famous bakery, and there's also a *tavola calda* ('hot table') where an array of hot dishes are on offer. Order at the counter and eat at bar

ITALY ROME

WORTH A TRIP

VIA APPIA ANTICA

Completed in 190 BCE, the Appian Way connected Rome with Brindisi on Italy's Adriatic coast. It's now a picturesque area of ancient ruins, grassy fields and towering pine trees. But it has a dark history – this is where Spartacus and 6000 of his slave rebels were crucified in 71 BCE, and where the ancients buried their dead. Well-to-do Romans built elaborate mausoleums while the early Christians went underground, creating a 300km network of subterranean burial chambers – the catacombs.

Highlights include the **Catacombe di San Sebastiano** (☑ 06 785 03 50; www.catacombe.org; Via Appia Antica 136; adult/reduced €8/5; ⊙ 10am-5pm Mon-Sat Jan-Nov; ☐ Via Appia Antica) and the nearby **Catacombe di San Callisto** (☑ 06 513 01 51; www.catacombe.roma. it; Via Appia Antica 110-126; adult/reduced €8/5; ⊙ 9am-noon & 2-5pm Thu-Tue Mar-Jan; ☐ Via Appia Antica).

To get to the Via, take bus 660 from Colli Albani metro station (line A) to the end of the line near Capo di Bove.

Roman Forum

A HISTORICAL TOUR

In ancient times, a forum was a market place, civic centre and religious complex all rolled into one, and the greatest of all was the Roman Forum (Foro Romano). Situated between the Palatino (Palatine Hill), ancient Rome's most exclusive neighbourhood, and the Campidoglio (Capitoline Hill), it was the city's busy, bustling centre. On any given day it teemed with activity. Senators debated affairs of state in the ❶ **Curia**, shoppers thronged the squares and traffic-free streets and crowds gathered under the ❷ **Colonna di Foca** to listen to politicians holding forth from the ❷ **Rostri**. Elsewhere, lawyers worked the courts in basilicas including the ❸ **Basilica di Massenzio**, while the Vestal Virgins quietly went about their business in the ❹ **Casa delle Vestali**.

Special occasions were also celebrated in the Forum: religious holidays were marked with ceremonies at temples such as ❺ **Tempio di Saturno** and ❻ **Tempio di Castore e Polluce**, and military victories were honoured with dramatic processions up Via Sacra and the building of monumental arches like ❼ **Arco di Settimio Severo** and ❽ **Arco di Tito**.

The ruins you see today are impressive but they can be confusing without a clear picture of what the Forum once looked like. This spread shows the Forum in its heyday, complete with temples, civic buildings and towering monuments to heroes of the Roman Empire.

TOP TIPS

➡ Get grandstand views of the Forum from the Palatino and Campidoglio.

➡ Visit first thing in the morning or late afternoon; crowds are worst between 11am and 2pm.

➡ In summer it gets hot in the Forum and there's little shade, so take a hat and plenty of water.

Colonna di Foca & Rostri
The free-standing, 13.5m-high Column of Phocus is the Forum's youngest monument, dating to AD 608. Behind it, the Rostri provided a suitably grandiose platform for pontificating public speakers.

Campidoglio (Capitoline Hill)

ADMISSION

Although valid for two days, admission tickets only allow for one entry into the Forum, Colosseum and Palatino.

Tempio di Saturno
Ancient Rome's Fort Knox, the Temple of Saturn was the city treasury. In Caesar's day it housed 13 tonnes of gold, 114 tonnes of silver and 30 million sestertii worth of silver coins.

IASDIC/SHUTTERSTOCK©

VIACHESLAV LOPATIN/SHUTTERSTOCK ©

Tempio di Castore e Polluce
Only three columns of the Temple of Castor and Pollux remain. The temple was dedicated to the Heavenly Twins after they supposedly led the Romans to victory over the Latin League in 496 BC.

Arco di Settimio Severo

One of the Forum's signature monuments, this imposing triumphal arch commemorates the military victories of Septimius Severus. Relief panels depict his campaigns against the Parthians.

Curia

This big barn-like building was the official seat of the Roman Senate. Most of what you see is a reconstruction, but the interior marble floor dates to the 3rd-century reign of Diocletian.

Basilica di Massenzio

Marvel at the scale of this vast 4th-century basilica. In its original form the central hall was divided into enormous naves; now only part of the northern nave survives.

Via Sacra

Tempio di Giulio Cesare

JULIUS CAESAR

Julius Caesar was cremated on the site where the Tempio di Giulio Cesare now stands.

Arco di Tito

Said to be the inspiration for the Arc de Triomphe in Paris, the well-preserved Arch of Titus was built by the emperor Domitian to honour his elder brother Titus.

Casa delle Vestali

White statues line the grassy atrium of what was once the luxurious 50-room home of the Vestal Virgins. The virgins played an important role in Roman religion, serving the goddess Vesta.

stools between shelves of gourmet groceries, or sit on the terrace for waiter service.

★ La Barrique ITALIAN €€
(Map p658; ☑ 06 4782 5953; www.facebook.com/la.barrique.94/; Via del Boschetto 41b; meals €40; ⓘ 1-2.30pm & 7.30-11pm Mon-Fri, 7.30-11.30pm Sat; Ⓜ Cavour) This traditional *enoteca* is a classy yet casual place to linger over a meal. There's a large wine list, mostly sourced from small producers, with lots of natural wines to choose from. A small menu of creative pastas and mains provide a great accompaniment – this is one of the best places to eat in Monti. Bookings recommended.

✖ Trastevere

★ Da Enzo TRATTORIA €€
(Map p654; ☑ 06 581 22 60; www.daenzoal29.com; Via dei Vascellari 29; meals €30-35; ⓘ 12.30-3pm & 7.30-11pm Mon-Sat; Ⓠ Lungotevere Ripa, Ⓠ Belli) Vintage ochre walls, yellow-checked tablecloths and a traditional menu featuring all the Roman classics are here, but what makes this tiny and staunchly traditional trattoria exceptional is its careful sourcing of local, quality products, many from nearby farms in Lazio. The seasonal, deep-fried Jewish artichokes and the *pasta cacio e pepe* (cheese-and-black-pepper pasta) are among the best in Rome.

★ La Tavernaccia TRATTORIA €€
(Map p662; ☑ 06 581 27 92; www.latavernacciaroma.com; Via Giovanni da Castel Bolognese 63; meals €30-45; ⓘ 12.45-3pm & 7.30-11pm Thu-Tue; Ⓠ Stazione Trastevere) This family-run trattoria bustles every minute it's open. Book in advance to get one of Rome's most sought-

---

ⓘ ROMA PASS

A cumulative sightseeing and transport card, available online or from tourist information points and participating museums, the **Roma Pass** (www.roma pass.it) comes in two forms:

72 hours (€38.50) Provides free admission to two museums or sites, as well as reduced entry to extra sites, unlimited city transport, and discounted entry to other exhibitions and events.

48 hours (€28) Gives free admission to one museum or site, and then as per the 72-hour pass.

---

after tables. Roman classics get stellar treatment here. First courses include various preserved meats and hams that melt away in your mouth. Besides pastas there are many roasts. Staff are cheery and helpful.

★ Trattoria Da Cesare al Casaletto TRATTORIA €€
(☑ 06 53 60 15; www.trattoriadacesare.it; Via del Casaletto 45; meals €25-50; ⓘ 12.45-3pm & 8-11pm Thu-Tue; Ⓠ Casaletto) Rome's best trattoria? Many think so and you will too after an amazing meal of Roman standards where virtually every dish is prepared just *so*. The restaurant is simplicity itself, with dozens of tables in a plain setting – in summer outside under a vine-covered arbour on a vast terrace. The food is rightfully the star. The service is efficient and relaxed.

✖ San Giovanni & Testaccio

Trapizzino FAST FOOD €
(Map p662; ☑ 06 4341 9624; www.trapizzino.it; Via Branca 88; trapizzini from €3.50; ⓘ noon-1am Tue-Sun; Ⓠ Via Marmorata) The original of what is now a growing countrywide chain, this is the birthplace of the *trapizzino,* a kind of hybrid sandwich made by stuffing a cone of doughy focaccia with fillers like *polpette al sugo* (meatballs in tomato sauce) or *pollo alla cacciatore* (stewed chicken). They're messy to eat but quite delicious.

Giulietta PIZZA €
(Map p662; ☑ 06 4522 9022; https://giuliettapizzeria.it; Piazza dell'Emporio 28; pizza €6.50-13; ⓘ 7.30pm-11.30pm; Ⓠ Via Marmorata) Occupying a former car showroom, this trendy pizzeria is part of a multi-space food hub part-owned by top Roman chef Cristina Bowerman. Its cavernous dining area, decorated in abstract contemporary style, sets the stage for sensational wood-fired pizzas topped with prime Italian ingredients.

★ Flavio al Velavevodetto ROMAN €€
(Map p662; ☑ 06 574 41 94; www.ristorantevelavevodetto.it; Via di Monte Testaccio 97-99; meals €30-35; ⓘ 12.30-3pm & 7.45-11pm; Ⓠ Via Galvani) The pick of Testaccio's trattorias, this casual spot is celebrated locally for its earthy, no-nonsense *cucina romana* (Roman cuisine). For a taste, start with *carciofo alla giudia* (deep-fried artichoke) before moving onto *rigatoni alla carbonara* (pasta tubes wrapped in a silky egg sauce spiked with morsels of cured pig's cheek) and finishing up with tiramisu.

ROME'S BEST GELATO

Fatamorgana (Map p662; ☑ 06 3751 9093; www.gelateriafatamorgana.it; Via Leone IV 52; gelato €2.50-5; ⊘ noon-11pm summer, to 9pm winter; Ⓜ Ottaviano-San Pietro) Rome's finest artisanal flavours, now in multiple central locations.

Gelateria del Teatro (Map p654; ☑ 06 4547 4880; www.gelateriadelteatro.it; Via dei Coronari 65; gelato from €3; ⊘ 11am-8pm winter, 10am-10.30pm summer; ☐ Via Zanardelli) Around 40 choices of delicious ice cream, all made on-site.

Otaleg (Map p654; ☑ 338 6515450; www.otaleg.com; Via di San Cosimato 14a; gelato from €2; ⊘ noon-midnight; ☑ ; ☐ Trastevere/Mastai) Classic and experimental flavours.

Gelateria Dei Gracchi (Map p662; ☑ 06 322 47 27; www.gelateriadeigracchi.it; Via di Ripetta 261; cones & tubs €2.50-5.50; ⊘ noon-10pm Tue-Sun; Ⓜ Flaminio) A taste of heaven in several locations across Rome.

Fior di Luna (Map p654; ☑ 06 6456 1314; http://fiordiluna.com; Via della Lungaretta 96; gelato from €2.50; ⊘ 1-8pm Sun & Mon, 1-11pm Tue-Sat; ☐ Belli, ☐ Viale di Trastevere) Great artisanal ice cream in Trastevere.

Drinking & Nightlife

Much of the drinking action is in the *centro storico*: Campo de' Fiori is popular with students, while the area around Piazza Navona hosts a more upmarket scene. Over the river, Trastevere is another favoured spot with dozens of bars and pubs. Rome's clubbing scene is centred on Testaccio and the Ostiense area, although you'll also find places in Trastevere and the *centro storico*. Admission to clubs is often free, but drinks are expensive.

Barnum Cafe
CAFE
(Map p654; ☑ 06 6476 0483; www.barnumcafe.com; Via del Pellegrino 87; ⊘ 9am-10pm Mon, 8.30am-2am Tue-Sat; ⊚ ; ☐ Corso Vittorio Emanuele II) A laid-back *Friends*-style cafe, evergreen Barnum is the sort of place you could quickly get used to. With its shabby-chic furniture and white bare-brick walls, it's a relaxed spot for a breakfast cappuccino, a light lunch or a late-afternoon drink. Come evening, a coolly dressed-down crowd sips expertly mixed craft cocktails.

★ Caffè Sant'Eustachio
COFFEE
(Map p654; ☑ 06 6880 2048; www.santeustachioilcaffe.it; Piazza Sant'Eustachio 82; ⊘ 7.30am-1am Sun-Thu, to 1.30am Fri, to 2am Sat; ☐ Corso del Rinascimento) Always busy, this workaday cafe near the Pantheon is reckoned by many to serve the best coffee in town. To make it, the bartenders sneakily beat the first drops of an espresso with several teaspoons of sugar to create a frothy paste to which they add the rest of the coffee. The result is superbly smooth.

★ Open Baladin
CRAFT BEER
(Map p654; ☑ 06 683 89 89; www.openbaladinroma.it; Via degli Specchi 6; ⊘ noon-2am; ⊚ ; ☐ Via Arenula) This modern pub near Campo de' Fiori has long been a leading light in Rome's craft-beer scene, and with more than 40 beers on tap and up to 100 bottled brews (many from Italian artisanal microbreweries) it's a top place for a pint. As well as great beer, expect a laid-back vibe and a young, international crowd.

Antico Caffè Greco
CAFE
(Map p658; ☑ 06 679 17 00; www.facebook.com/AnticoCaffeGreco; Via dei Condotti 86; ⊘ 9am-9pm; Ⓜ Spagna) Rome's oldest cafe, open since 1760, is still working the look with the utmost elegance: staff in black tails and bow tie or frilly white pinnies, scarlet flock walls and age-spotted gilt mirrors. Prices reflect this amazing heritage: pay €9 for a cappuccino sitting down or join locals for the same (€2.50) standing at the bar.

★ Zuma Bar
COCKTAIL BAR
(Map p662; ☑ 06 9926 6622; www.zumarestaurant.com; Via della Fontanella di Borghese 48, Palazzo Fendi; ⊘ 6pm-1am Sun-Thu, to 2am Fri & Sat; ⊚ ; Ⓜ Spagna) Dress up for a drink on the rooftop terrace of Palazzo Fendi of fashion-house fame – few cocktail bars in Rome are as sleek, hip or achingly sophisticated as this. City rooftop views are predictably fabulous; cocktails mix exciting flavours like shiso with juniper berries, elderflower and prosecco. DJs spin Zuma playlists at weekends.

NEIGHBOURHOOD SPECIALITIES

Most entrenched in culinary tradition is the Jewish Ghetto area, with its hearty Roman-Jewish cuisine. Deep-frying is a staple of *cucina ebraico-romanesca* (Roman-Jewish cooking), which developed between the 16th and 19th centuries when the Jews were confined to the city's ghetto. To add flavour to their limited ingredients – those spurned by the rich, such as courgette (zucchini) flowers – they began to fry everything from mozzarella to *baccalà* (salted cod). Particularly addictive are the locally grown artichokes, which are flattened out to form a kind of flower shape and then deep-fried to a golden crisp and salted to become *carciofo alla giudia* (Jewish-style artichokes). By contrast, *carciofo alla romana* (Roman-style artichokes) are stuffed with parsley, mint and garlic, then braised in an aromatic mix of broth and white wine until soft.

For the heart (and liver and brains) of the *cucina romana,* head to Testaccio, a traditional working-class district clustered around the city's former slaughterhouse. In the past, butchers who worked in the city abattoir were often paid in cheap cuts of meat as well as money. The Roman staple *coda alla vaccinara* translates as 'oxtail cooked butcher's style'. This is cooked for hours to create a rich sauce with tender slivers of meat. A famous Roman dish that's not for the faint-hearted is pasta with *pajata*, made with the entrails of young veal calves, considered a delicacy since they contain the mother's congealed milk. If you see the word *coratella* in a dish, it means you'll be eating *lights* (lungs), kidneys and hearts.

Ai Tre Scalini
WINE BAR

(Map p658; ☑ 06 4890 7495; www.facebook.com/aitrescalini; Via Panisperna 251; ⊙ 12.30pm-1am; Ⓜ Cavour) A firm favourite since 1895, the 'Three Steps' is always packed, with predominantly young patrons spilling out of its bar area and into the street. Its a perfect spot to enjoy an afternoon drink or a simple meal of cheese, salami and dishes such as *polpette al sugo* (meatballs with sauce), washed down with superb choices of wine or beer.

Blackmarket Hall
COCKTAIL BAR

(Map p658; ☑ 339 7351926; www.facebook.com/blackmarkethall/; Via de Ciancaleoni 31; ⊙ 6pm-3am; Ⓜ Cavour) One of Monti's best bars, this multi-roomed speakeasy in a former monastery has an eclectic vintage-style decor and plenty of cosy corners where you can enjoy a leisurely, convivial drink. It serves food up till midnight (burgers €12 to €15) and hosts live music – often jazz – on weekends. There's a second venue nearby on Via Panisperna 101.

Necci dal 1924
CAFE

(☑ 06 9760 1552; www.necci1924.com; Via Fanfulla da Lodi 68; ⊙ 8am-1am Sun-Thu, to 2am Fri & Sat; ☎⏍; ᰥ Prenestina/Officine Atac) An all-round hybrid in Pigneto, iconic Necci opened as a gelateria in 1924 and later became a favourite drinking destination of film director Pier Paolo Pasolini. These days it caters to a buoyant hipster crowd, offering a laid-back vibe, retro interior and all-day food. Huge kudos for the fabulous summertime terrace, which is very family friendly.

★ Niji Roma
COCKTAIL BAR

(Map p654; ☑ 06 581 95 20; www.facebook.com/niji.cafe.roma; Via dei Vascellari 35; ⊙ 7pm-3am; ᰥ Belli) A cosy, stylish, artistic bar that looks like a film set designed to portray just that. The range of cocktails continues the bar's themes. They are exquisitely poured and presented and are almost, *almost,* too good-looking to drink. The mood here is mellow but never slouchy.

Terra Satis
CAFE, WINE BAR

(Map p654; ☑ 06 9893 6909; Piazza dei Ponziani 1a; ⊙ 7am-1am Mon-Thu, to 2am Fri & Sat; ☎; ᰥ Viale di Trastevere, ᰥ Belli) This hip neighbourhood cafe and wine bar in Trastevere has it all: newspapers, great coffee and charming bar staff, not to mention vintage furniture, comfy banquette seating and really good snacks. On warm days the laid-back action spills out onto its bijou, vine-covered terrace on cobbled Piazza di Ponziani. Good wine and beer selection.

☆ Entertainment

Rome has a thriving cultural scene, with a year-round calendar of concerts, performances and festivals. Upcoming events are also listed on www.turismoroma.it and www.inromenow.com.

★ **Auditorium Parco della Musica**　CONCERT VENUE

(☎ 06 8024 1281; www.auditorium.com; Viale Pietro de Coubertin; ⬚ Viale Tiziano) The hub of Rome's thriving cultural scene, the Auditorium is the capital's premier concert venue. Its three concert halls offer superb acoustics, and together with a 3000-seat open-air arena stage everything from classical music concerts to jazz gigs, public lectures and film screenings.

The Auditorium is also home to Rome's world-class Orchestra dell'Accademia Nazionale di Santa Cecilia (www.santacecilia.it).

Teatro dell'Opera di Roma　OPERA

(Map p658; ☎ 06 48 16 01; www.operaroma.it; Piazza Beniamino Gigli 1; ⊗ box office 10am-6pm Mon-Sat, 9am-1.30pm Sun; Ⓜ Repubblica) Rome's premier opera house boasts a dramatic red-and-gold interior, a Fascist 1920s exterior and an impressive history: it premiered both Puccini's *Tosca* and Mascagni's *Cavalleria rusticana*. Opera and ballet performances are staged between November and June.

🛍 Shopping

Rome boasts the usual cast of flagship chain stores and glitzy designer outlets, but what makes shopping here fun is its legion of small, independent shops: family-run delis, small-label fashion boutiques, artisans' studios and neighbourhood markets.

Mercado de Porta Portese　MARKET

(Map p662; Piazza Porta Portese; ⊗ 6am-2pm Sun; ⬚ Viale di Trastevere, ⬚ Trastevere/Min P Istruzione) Head to this mammoth flea market to see Rome bargain-hunting. Thousands of stalls sell everything from rare books and fell-off-a-lorry bikes to Peruvian shawls and off-brand phones. It's crazily busy and a lot of fun. Keep your valuables safe and wear your haggling hat for the inevitable discovery of a treasure amid the dreck.

ℹ️ Information

SAFE TRAVEL

Rome is not a dangerous city, but petty theft can be a problem. Watch out for pickpockets around the big tourist sites, at Stazione Termini and on crowded public transport – the 64 Vatican bus is notorious.

MEDICAL SERVICES

Farmacia Gruppo Farmacrimi (☎ 06 474 54 21; https://farmacrimi.it; Via Marsala 29;

⊗ 7am-10pm) Pharmacy in Stazione Termini, next to Platform 1.

Policlinico Umberto I (☎ 06 4 99 71; www.policlinicoumberto1.it; Viale del Policlinico 155; Ⓜ Policlinico, Castro Pretorio) Rome's largest hospital is near Stazione Termini.

TOURIST INFORMATION

There are tourist information points at Fiumicino (p672) and Ciampino (p672) airports, as well as locations across the city. Each can provide city maps and sell the Roma Pass (p668). Online visit Rome's official tourist website, Turismo Roma (www.turismoroma.it).

Information points:

Pazza delle Cinque Lune (Map p654; ⊗ 9.30am-7pm; ⬚ Corso del Rinascimento) Near Piazza Navona.

Stazione Termini (Map p658; ☎ 06 06 08; www.turismoroma.it; Via Giovanni Giolitti 34; ⊗ 8am-6.45pm) In the hall adjacent to platform 24.

Imperial Forums (Map p652; Via dei Fori Imperiali; ⊗ 9.30am-7pm, to 8pm Jul & Aug; ⬚ Via dei Fori Imperiali)

Via Marco Minghetti (Map p654; ☎ 06 06 08; www.turismoroma.it; ⊗ 9.30am-7pm; ⬚ Via del Corso) Between Via del Corso and the Trevi Fountain.

Castel Sant'Angelo (Map p662; www.turismoroma.it; Piazza Pia; ⊗ 9.30am-7pm summer, 8.30am-6pm winter; ⬚ Piazza Pia)

Trastevere (Map p654; www.turismoroma.it; Piazza Sonnino; ⊗ 10.30am-8pm; ⬚ Viale di Trastevere, ⬚ Belli)

For information about the Vatican, contact the **Ufficio Pellegrini e Turisti** (Map p662; ☎ 06 6988 1662; www.vatican.va; St Peter's Sq; ⊗ 8.30am-6.30pm Mon-Sat; ⬚ Piazza del Risorgimento, Ⓜ Ottaviano-San Pietro).

ITALY ROME

A ROMAN PASSION

Football is a Roman passion, with support divided between the two local teams: Roma and Lazio. Both play their home games at the **Stadio Olimpico** (☎ 06 3685 7563; Viale dei Gladiatori 2, Foro Italico; ⬚ Lungotevere Maresciallo Cadorna), Rome's impressive Olympic stadium. If you go to a game, make sure you get it right – Roma play in red and yellow and its supporters stand in the *Curva Sud* (South Stand); Lazio plays in sky blue and its fans fill the *Curva Nord* (North Stand).

DAY TRIPS FROM ROME

Ostia Antica

An easy train ride from Rome, Ostia Antica is one of Italy's most under-appreciated archaeological sites. The ruins of ancient Rome's main seaport, the **Scavi Archeologici di Ostia Antica** (📞 06 5635 8099; www.ostiaantica.beniculturali.it; Viale dei Romagnoli 717; adult/reduced €10/5; ⊗ 8.30am-7.15pm Tue-Sun summer, last admission 6.15pm, shorter hours winter), are spread out and you'll need a few hours to do them justice.

From Rome, take the Roma–Lido train from Stazione Porta San Paolo (Piramide metro station) to Ostia Antica (every 15 minutes). The 25-minute trip is covered by a standard Rome public transport ticket (€1.50).

Tivoli

Tivoli, 30km east of Rome, is home to two Unesco–listed sites. Five kilometres from Tivoli proper, the ruins of the emperor Hadrian's sprawling **Villa Adriana** (📞 0774 38 27 33; www.villaadriana.beniculturali.it; Largo Marguerite Yourcenar 1; adult/reduced €10/5; ⊗ 8.30am-1hr before sunset) are quite magnificent. Up in Tivoli's hilltop centre, the Renaissance **Villa d'Este** (📞 0774 33 29 20; www.villadestetivoli.info; Piazza Trento 5; adult/reduced €10/5; ⊗ 8.30am-7.45pm Tue-Sun, from 2pm Mon, gardens close sunset, ticket office closes 6.45pm) is famous for its elaborate gardens and fountains.

Tivoli is accessible by Cotral bus (€1.30, 50 minutes, at least wtice-hourly) from Ponte Mammolo metro station.

The **Comune di Roma** (📞 06 06 08; www.060608.it; ⊗ 9am-7pm) runs a free multilingual tourist information phone line providing info on culture, shows, hotels, transport etc. Its website is also an excellent resource.

ℹ Getting There & Away

AIR

Rome's main international airport, **Leonardo da Vinci** (📞 06 6 59 51; www.adr.it/fiumicino), better known as Fiumicino, is on the coast 30km west of the city.

The much smaller **Ciampino Airport** (⊗ 8.30am-6pm), 15km southeast of the city centre, is the hub for European low-cost carrier Ryanair.

BOAT

The nearest port to Rome is at Civitavecchia, about 80km north.

Ferries sail here from Spain and Tunisia, as well as Sicily and Sardinia. Book tickets at travel agents or online at www.traghettiweb.it. You can also buy tickets directly at the port.

Half-hourly trains connect Civitavecchia with Roma Termini (€4.60 to €16, 45 minutes to 1½ hours).

BUS

Long-distance national and international buses use the **Autostazione Tibus** (Autostazione Tiburtina; 📞 06 44 25 95; www.tibusroma.it; Largo Guido Mazzoni; Ⓜ Tiburtina). Get tickets at the bus station or at travel agencies.

CAR & MOTORCYCLE

Rome is circled by the Grande Raccordo Anulare (GRA), to which all *autostrade* (motorways) connect, including the main A1 north–south artery, and the A12, which runs to Civitavecchia.

Car hire is available at the airport and Stazione Termini.

TRAIN

Rome's main station is **Stazione Termini** (www.romatermini.com; Piazza dei Cinquecento; Ⓜ Termini). It has regular connections to other European countries, all major Italian cities and many smaller towns.

Left luggage (1st 5hr €6, 6-12hr per hour €1, 13hr & over per hour €0.50; ⊗ 6am-11pm) is by platform 24 on the Via Giolitti side of the station.

ℹ Getting Around

TO/FROM THE AIRPORTS
Fiumicino

The easiest way to get to/from Fiumicino is by train, but there are also bus services. The set taxi fare to the city centre is €48 (valid for up to four people with luggage).

Leonardo Express Train (www.trenitalia.com; one way €14) Runs to/from Stazione Termini. Departures from Fiumicino airport every 30 minutes between 6.08am and 11.23pm; from Termini between 5.20am and 10.35pm. Journey time is approximately 30 minutes. Wheelchair accessible.

FL1 Train (www.trenitalia.com; one way €8) Connects to Trastevere, Ostiense and Tiburtina stations, but not Termini. Departures from Fiumicino airport every 15 minutes (half-hourly on Sundays and public holidays) between 5.57am and 10.42pm; from Tiburtina every 15 to 30 minutes between 5.01am and 10.01pm.

Ciampino

The best option from Ciampino is to take one of the regular bus services into the city centre. The set taxi fare to the city centre is €30.

SIT Bus – Ciampino (☑ 06 591 68 26; www.sitbusshuttle.com; to/from airport €6/5, return €9) Regular departures from the airport to Via Marsala outside Stazione Termini between 7.45am and 12.15am; from Termini between 4.30am and 9.30pm. Get tickets online, on the bus or at the desk at Ciampino. Journey time is 45 minutes.

Schiaffini Rome Airport Bus – Ciampino (☑ 06 713 05 31; www.romeairportbus.com; Via Giolitti; one way/return €5.90/9.90) Regular departures to/from Via Giolitti outside Stazione Termini. From the airport, services run between 4am and 11.45pm; from Via Giolitti, buses run from 4.20am to midnight. Buy tickets onboard, online, at the airport or at the bus stop. Journey time is approximately 40 minutes.

PUBLIC TRANSPORT

Rome's public transport system includes buses, trams, metro and a suburban train network.

Tickets are valid on all forms of public transport, except for routes to Fiumicino airport. They come in various forms:

BIT (€1.50) Valid for 100 minutes and one metro ride.

Roma 24h (€7) Valid for 24 hours.

Roma 48h (€12.50) Valid for 48 hours.

Roma 72h (€18) Valid for 72 hours.

Buy tickets at tabacchi (tobacconist shops), news-stands or from vending machines.

Bus

➡ Rome's buses and trams are run by **ATAC** (☑ 06 5 70 03; www.atac.roma.it).

➡ The main bus station is in front of Stazione Termini on Piazza dei Cinquecento, where there's an **information booth** (Map p658; ☺ 8am-8pm).

➡ Other important hubs are at Largo di Torre Argentina and Piazza Venezia.

➡ Buses generally run from about 5.30am until midnight, with limited services throughout the night.

Metro

➡ Rome has two main metro lines, A (orange) and B (blue), which cross at Termini.

➡ Trains run between 5.30am and 11.30pm (to 1.30am on Fridays and Saturdays).

TAXI

➡ Official licensed taxis are white with an ID number and Roma Capitale on the sides.

➡ Always go with the metered fare, never an arranged price (the set fares to and from the airports are exceptions).

➡ There are taxi ranks at the airports, Stazione Termini, Piazza della Repubblica, Piazza Barberini, Piazza di Spagna, Piazza Venezia, the Pantheon, the Colosseum, Largo di Torre Argentina, Piazza Belli, Piazza Pio XII and Piazza del Risorgimento.

NORTHERN ITALY

Italy's well-heeled north is a fascinating area of historical wealth and natural diversity. Bordered by the northern Alps and boasting some of the country's most spectacular coastline, it also encompasses Italy's largest lowland area, the fertile Po valley plain. Glacial lakes in the far north offer stunning scenery, while cities such as Venice, Milan and Turin harbour artistic treasures and lively cultural scenes.

Genoa

POP 583,600

Genoa (Genova) is an absorbing city of aristocratic palazzi, dark, malodorous alleyways, Gothic architecture and industrial sprawl. Formerly a powerful maritime republic known as La Superba (Christopher Columbus was born here in 1451), it's still an important transport hub, with ferry links to destinations across the Med and train links to the Cinque Terre.

◉ Sights

★ **Palazzo Reale**   PALACE
(☑ 010 271 02 36; www.palazzorealegenova.beni culturali.it; Via Balbi 10; adult/reduced €6/3; ☺ 9am-7pm Tue-Fri, 1.30-7pm Sat & Sun) If you only get the chance to visit one of the Palazzi dei Rolli (group of palaces belonging to the city's most eminent families), make it this one. A former residence of the Savoy dynasty, it has terraced gardens, exquisite furnishings, a fine collection of 17th-century art and a gilded Hall of Mirrors that is worth the entry fee alone.

★ **Musei di Strada Nuova**   MUSEUM
(Palazzi dei Rolli; ☑ 010 557 21 93; www.musei digenova.it; Via Garibaldi; combined ticket adult/

A BRIEF HISTORY OF ITALY

Ancient Times

The Etruscans were the first major force to emerge on the Italian peninsula. By the 7th century BCE they dominated central Italy, rivalled only by the Greeks from the southern colony of Magna Graecia. Both thrived until the emerging city of Rome began to flex its muscles.

Founded in the 8th century BCE (legend has it by Romulus), Rome flourished, becoming a republic in 509 BCE and growing to become the dominant force in the Western world. The end came for the Republic when internal rivalries led to the murder of Julius Caesar in 44 BCE and his great-nephew Octavian took power as Augustus, the first Roman emperor.

The empire's golden age came in the 2nd century CE, but a century later it was in decline. Diocletian split the empire into eastern and western halves, and when his successor, Constantine (the first Christian emperor), moved his court to Constantinople, Rome's days were numbered. In 476 the western empire fell to Germanic tribes.

City States & the Renaissance

The Middle Ages was a period of almost constant warfare as powerful city states fought across central and northern Italy. Eventually Florence, Milan and Venice emerged as regional powers. Against this fractious background, art and culture thrived, culminating in an explosion of intellectual and artistic activity in 15th-century Florence – the Renaissance.

Unification

By the end of the 16th century most of Italy was in foreign hands – the Austrian Habsburgs in the north and the Spanish Bourbons in the south. Three centuries later, Napoleon's brief Italian interlude inspired the unification movement, the Risorgimento. With Count Cavour providing the political vision and Guiseppe Garibaldi the military muscle, the movement brought about the 1861 unification of Italy. Ten years later Rome was wrested from the papacy to become Italy's capital.

Birth of a Republic

Italy's brief fascist interlude was a low point. Mussolini gained power in 1925 and in 1940 entered WWII on Germany's side. Defeat ensued and *Il Duce* was killed by partisans in April 1945. A year later, Italians voted in a national referendum to abolish the monarchy and create a constitutional republic.

The Modern Era

Italy's postwar era has been largely successful. A founding member of the European Economic Community, it survived a period of domestic terrorism in the 1970s and enjoyed sustained economic growth in the 1980s. But the 1990s heralded a period of crisis as corruption scandals rocked the nation, paving the way for billionaire media mogul Silvio Berlusconi to enter the political arena.

More recently, political debate has centred on the nation's sluggish economy and issues surrounding immigration. This culminated in the 2018 general election that gave rise to western Europe's first populist government, a coalition of the anti-establishment Five Star Movement and right-wing League party.

reduced €9/7; ⊘9am-7pm Tue-Fri, 10am-7.30pm Sat & Sun summer, to 6.30pm winter) Skirting the northern edge of the old city limits, pedestrianised Via Garibaldi (formerly Strada Nuova) was planned by Galeazzo Alessi in the 16th century. It quickly became the most sought-after quarter, lined with the palaces of Genoa's wealthiest citizens. Three of these *palazzi* – **Rosso**, **Bianco** and **Doria-Tursi** – today comprise the Musei di Strada Nuova. Between them, they hold the city's finest collection of old masters. Whether you visit the actual museums or not, the street is a must to wander.

Cattedrale di San Lorenzo   CATHEDRAL

(Piazza San Lorenzo; ⊙ 8am-noon & 3-7pm) Genoa's zebra-striped Gothic-Romanesque cathedral owes its continued existence to the poor quality of a British WWII bomb that failed to detonate here in 1941; it still sits on the right side of the nave like an innocuous museum piece.

The cathedral, fronted by three arched portals, twisting columns and crouching lions, was first consecrated in 1118. The two bell towers and cupola were added in the 16th century.

🛏 Sleeping & Eating

Hotel Cairoli   HOTEL €

(🖉 010 246 14 54; www.hotelcairoligenova.com; Via Cairoli 14/4; d €76-116, tr €104-149, q €122-172; ✳ @ 🛜) For five-star service at three-star prices, book at this artful hideaway. Rooms, on the 3rd floor of a towering *palazzo,* are themed on modern artists and feature works inspired by the likes of Mondrian, Dorazio and Alexander Calder. Add in a library, chillout area, small gym and terrace, and you have the ideal bolt-hole. Cheaper rates are available without breakfast.

★ Palazzo Grillo   DESIGN HOTEL €€

(🖉 010 247 73 56; www.hotelpalazzogrillo.it; Piazza delle Vigne 4; d €160-295; ✳ 🛜) Genovese locals Matteo and Laura have created the extraordinary place to stay that Genoa has been crying out for in a once-derelict *palazzo.* Stunning public spaces are dotted with spot-on contemporary design pieces, character-filled vintage finds and – look in any direction – original 15th-century frescoes. Rooms are simple but super-stylish with Vitra TVs and high ceilings.

★ Trattoria Rosmarino   TRATTORIA €€

(🖉 010 251 04 75; www.trattoriarosmarino.it; Salita del Fondaco 30; meals €30-35; ⊙ 12.30-2.30pm & 7.30-10.30pm Mon-Sat) Rosmarino cooks up the standard local specialities, yes, but the straightforwardly priced menu has an elegance and vibrancy that sets it apart. With two nightly sittings, there's always a nice buzz (though there are also enough nooks and crannies that a romantic night for two isn't out of the question). Call ahead for an evening table.

ℹ Information

Tourist Office (🖉 010 557 29 03; www.visit genoa.it; Via Garibaldi 12r; ⊙ 9am-6.20pm) Helpful office in the historical centre.

ℹ Getting There & Around

AIR

Genoa's **Cristoforo Colombo Airport** (🖉 010 6 01 51; www.airport.genova.it) is 6km west of the city.

To get to/from it, the **Volabus** (🖉 848 000 030; www.amt.genova.it; one-way €6) shuttle connects with Stazione Brignole and Stazione Principe. Buy tickets on board.

BOAT

Ferries sail to Spain, Sicily, Sardinia, Corsica, Morocco and Tunisia from the international passenger terminals, west of the city centre.

Grandi Navi Veloci (GNV; 🖉 010 209 45 91; www.gnv.it) Ferries to Sardinia (Porto Torres from €45) and Sicily (Palermo from €53). Also to Barcelona (Spain, from €51) and Tunis (Tunisia, from €77).

Moby Lines (🖉 199 30 30 40; www.moby.it) Ferries year-round to the Sardinian ports of Olbia (from €58) and Porto Torres (from €42).

BUS

Buses to international cities depart from **Piazza della Vittoria**, as does a daily bus to/from Milan's Malpensa airport (€25, three hours, 6am) and other interregional services. Tickets are sold at **Geotravels** (🖉 010 58 71 81; Piazza della Vittoria 57; ⊙ 9am-12.30pm & 3-7pm Mon-Fri, to noon Sat).

TRAIN

Genoa's Stazione Principe and Stazione Brignole are linked by very frequent trains to Milan (€13.45 to €21.50, 1½ to two hours), Pisa (€27, two hours), Rome (€63.50, five hours) and Turin (€12.40, two hours).

Stazione Principe tends to have more trains, particularly going west to San Remo (€12 to €18, two hours, eight daily) and Ventimiglia (€13.90 to €21, 2¼ hours, 10 daily).

Cinque Terre

Liguria's eastern Riviera boasts some of Italy's most dramatic coastline, the highlight of which is the Unesco–listed **Parco Nazionale delle Cinque Terre** (Cinque Terre National Park) just west of La Spezia. Running for 18km, this awesome stretch of plunging cliffs and vine-covered hills is named for its five tiny villages: Riomaggiore, Manarola, Corniglia, Vernazza and Monterosso.

🏃 Activities

The Cinque Terre offers excellent hiking with a 120km network of paths. The best known is the 12km **Sentiero Azzurro** (Blue

Trail), a one-time mule trail that links all five villages. To walk it (or any of the national park's trails) you'll need a **Cinque Terre Treking Card** (one/two days €7.50/14.50), or a **Cinque Terre Treno Card** (one/two days €16/29), which also provides unlimited train travel between La Spezia and the five villages. Both cards are available at park offices.

At the time of writing, two legs of the Sentiero Azzurro were closed for repair work – Riomaggiore to Manarola (the so-called Via dell'Amore) and Manarola to Corniglia. Check www.parconazionale5terre.it for the current situation.

If water sports are more your thing, you can hire snorkelling gear and kayaks at the **Diving Center 5 Terre** (☑ 0187 92 00 11; www.5terrediving.it; Via San Giacomo; ⊙ 10am-4pm Apr-Oct) in Riomaggiore.

ℹ Information

Parco Nazionale Offices (www.parconazionale5terre.it; ⊙ 8am-8pm summer, 8.30am-12.30pm & 1-5.30pm winter) Offices in the train stations of all five villages and La Spezia station; has comprehensive information about hiking trail closures.

ℹ Getting There & Away

BOAT

Golfo Paradiso SNC (☑ 0185 77 20 91; www.golfoparadiso.it) In summer, Golfo Paradiso runs boats to the Cinque Terre from Genoa (one way/return €21/36).

Consorzio Marittimo Turistico Cinque Terre Golfo dei Poeti (☑ 0187 73 29 87; www.navigazionegolfodeipoeti.it) From late March to October, this operator runs daily shuttle boats between all of the Cinque Terre villages (except Corniglia), costing €18 to €22 one way, €26 including all stops, or €35 for an all-day unlimited ticket.

TRAIN

From Genoa Brignole, direct trains run to Riomaggiore (€9.50, 1½ to two hours, at least 10 daily), stopping at each of the villages.

From La Spezia, one to three trains an hour run up the coast between 4.37am and 11.10pm. If you're using this route and want to stop at all the villages, get the Cinque Terre Treno Card.

Monterosso

The largest and most developed of the villages, Monterosso boasts the coast's only sandy beach, as well as a wealth of eating and accommodation options.

Ristorante Belvedere SEAFOOD €€
(☑ 0187 81 70 33; www.ristorante-belvedere.it; Piazza Garibaldi 38; meals €30; ⊙ noon-2.30pm & 6.30-10pm Wed-Mon) With tables overlooking the beach, this unpretentious seafood restaurant is a good place to try the local bounty. Start with *penne con scampi* (pasta tubes with scampi) before diving into *zuppa di pesce* (fish soup). Or partake of the speciality, the amphora Belvedere, where lobsters, mussels, clams, octopus and swordfish are stewed in a herb-scented broth in traditional earthenware.

Vernazza

Perhaps the most attractive of the five villages, Vernazza overlooks a small, picturesque harbour.

From near the harbour, a steep, narrow staircase leads up to **Castello Doria** (€1.50; ⊙ 10am-7pm summer, to 6pm winter), the oldest surviving fortification in the Cinque Terre. Dating from around 1000, it's now largely ruined except for the circular tower in the centre of the esplanade, but the castle is well worth a visit for the superb views it commands.

To overnight in Vernazza, try **La Mala** (☑ 334 2875718; www.lamala.it; Via San Giovanni Battista 29; d €160-250; ❄ 🛜), a contemporary boutique hotel in the cliffside heights of the village.

Corniglia

Corniglia, the only village with no direct sea access, sits atop a 100m-high rocky promontory surrounded by vineyards. To reach the village proper from the train station you must first tackle the **Lardarina**, a 377-step brick stairway, or jump on a shuttle bus (one way €2.50).

Once up in the village, you can enjoy dazzling 180-degree sea views from the **Belvedere di Santa Maria**, a heart-stopping lookout point at the end of Via Fieschi.

Manarola

One of the busiest of the villages, Manarola tumbles down to the sea in a helter-skelter of pastel-coloured buildings, cafes, trattorias and restaurants. Bequeathed with more grapevines than any other Cinque Terre village, it is famous for its sweet Sciacchetrà wine.

Riomaggiore

The Cinque Terre's largest and easternmost village, Riomaggiore acts as the unofficial HQ.

For a taste of classic seafood and local wine, search out **Dau Cila** (0187 76 00 32; www.ristorantedaucila.com; Via San Giacomo 65; meals €40-45; 12.30-3pm & 7-10.30pm), a smart restaurant–wine bar perched overlooking the twee harbour.

Turin

POP 886.800

With its regal *palazzi*, baroque piazzas, cafes and world-class museums, Turin (Torino) is a dynamic, cultured city. For centuries, it was the seat of the royal Savoy family, and between 1861 and 1864 it was Italy's first post-unification capital. Its now-booming contemporary art and architecture, live-music scene and innovative food and wine culture are definitely aspects you'll want to discover.

Sights

★ Museo Egizio   MUSEUM

(Egyptian Museum; 011 440 69 03; www.museo egizio.it; Via Accademia delle Scienze 6; adult/reduced €15/11; 9am-6.30pm Tue-Sun, 9am-2pm Mon) Opened in 1824 and housed in the austere Palazzo dell'Accademia delle Scienze, this Turin institution houses the most important collection of Egyptian treasure outside Cairo. Among its many highlights are a statue of Ramses II (one of the world's most important pieces of Egyptian art) and a vast papyrus collection.

There are also 500 funerary and domestic items from the tomb of royal architect Kha and his wife Merit, dating from 1400 BCE and found in 1906.

Mole Antonelliana   LANDMARK

(www.gtt.to.it/cms/turismo/ascensore-mole; Via Montebello 20; lift adult/reduced €8/6, incl Museo €15/12; lift 9am-8pm Sun, Mon & Wed-Fri, to 11pm Sat) The symbol of Turin, this 167m tower with its distinctive aluminium spire appears on the Italian two-cent coin. It was originally intended as a synagogue when construction began in 1862, but was never used as a place of worship, and nowadays houses the Museo Nazionale del Cinema (011 813 85 63; www.museocinema.it; adult/reduced €11/9, incl lift €15/12; 9am-8pm Sun, Mon & Wed-Fri, to 11pm Sat). For dazzling 360-degree

MUSEO NAZIONALE DELL'AUTOMOBILE

As the historical birthplace of one of the world's leading car manufacturers – the 'T' in Fiat stands for Torino – Turin is the obvious place for a car museum. **Museo Nazionale dell'Automobile** (011 67 76 66; www.museoauto.it; Corso Unità d'Italia 40; adult/reduced €12/10; 10am-2pm Mon, to 7pm Tue-Sun; Lingotto), a dashing modern museum, roughly 5km south of the city centre, doesn't disappoint with its precious collection of more than 200 automobiles – everything from an 1892 Peugeot to a 1980 Ferrari 308 (in red, of course).

views, take the **panoramic lift** up to the 85m-high outdoor viewing deck.

Cattedrale di San Giovanni Battista   CATHEDRAL

(011 436 15 40; www.duomoditorino.it; Via XX Settembre 87; 7am-12.30pm & 3-7pm) Turin's cathedral was built between 1491 and 1498 on the site of three 14th-century basilicas and, before that, a Roman theatre. Plain interior aside, as home to the **Shroud of Turin** (still alleged to be the burial cloth in which Jesus' body was wrapped, despite years of controversy), this is a highly trafficked church. The famous cloth is not on display, but you can see where it is kept and watch explanatory video presentations.

Piazza Castello   PIAZZA

Turin's central square is lined with museums, theatres and cafes. The city's Savoy heart, although laid out from the mid-1300s, was mostly constructed from the 16th to 18th centuries. Dominating it is the part-medieval, part-baroque **Palazzo Madama**, the original seat of the Italian parliament. To the north, is the exquisite facade of the **Palazzo Reale**, the royal palace built for Carlo Emanuele II in the mid-1600s.

Sleeping & Eating

★ Via Stampatori   B&B €

(339 2581330; www.viastampatori.com; Via Stampatori 4; s/d €90/110;) This utterly lovely B&B occupies the top floor of a frescoed Renaissance building, one of Turin's oldest. Its bright, stylish and individually furnished rooms overlook either a sunny

terrace or a leafy inner courtyard. The owner's personal collection of 20th-century design is used throughout, including in the two serene common areas. It's central but blissfully quiet.

DuParc Contemporary Suites DESIGN HOTEL €€
([☑] 011 012 00 00; www.duparcsuites.com; Corso Massimo D'Azeglio 21; r from €115; [P][❄][🛜]) A business-friendly location doesn't mean this isn't a great choice for all travellers. Staff are young, clued-up and friendly, and the building's iconic modern lines are matched with a fantastic contemporary art collection and comfortable furnishings, along with stunning Italian lighting. Best of all, even the cheapest rooms here are sumptuously large, with king beds, huge baths and floor-to-ceiling windows.

★**Banco vini e alimenti** PIEDMONTESE €€
([☑] 011 764 02 39; www.bancoviniealimenti.it; Via dei Mercanti 13f; meals €30-35; [🕐] 12.30pm-12.30am Tue-Sat, from 6.30pm Mon) A hybrid restaurant-bar-deli, this smartly designed, low-key place does clever small-dish dining for lunch and dinner. While it might vibe casual wine bar, with young staff in T-shirts, don't underestimate the food: this is serious Piedmontese cooking. Open all day, you can also grab a single-origin pour-over here in the morning, or a herbal house *spritz* in the late afternoon.

🍷 Drinking & Nightlife

Aperitivi and more substantial *apericenas* are a Turin institution. If you're on a tight budget, you can fill up on a generous buffet of bar snacks for the cost of a drink.

Nightlife concentrates in the riverside area around Piazza Vittoria Veneto, the Quadrilatero Romano district and the southern neighbourhoods of San Salvarino and Vanchiglia.

ℹ Information

Piazza Castello Tourist Office ([☑] 011 53 51 81; www.turismotorino.org; Piazza Castello; [🕐] 9am-6pm) Central and multilingual.

ℹ Getting There & Around

From **Turin Airport** ([☑] 011 567 63 61; www.aeroportoditorino.it; Strada Aeroporto 12), 16km northwest of the city centre in Caselle, airlines fly to Italian and European destinations.
Sadem ([☑] 800 801600; www.sadem.it; one way €7.50) runs an airport shuttle (€7.50, 50

minutes, half-hourly) to/from Piazza Carlo Felice near Porta Nuova train station.

Trains connect with Milan (€12.45 to €34, one to 1¾ hours, more than 30 daily), Florence (€71, three hours, 11 daily), Genoa (€12.40 to €27, 2¼ hours, up to 16 daily) and Rome (€98, 4½ hours, up to 21 daily).

Milan

POP 1.35 MILLION

Few Italian cities polarise opinion like Milan, Italy's financial and fashion capital. Some people love the cosmopolitan, can-do atmosphere, the vibrant cultural scene and sophisticated shopping; others grumble that it's dirty, ugly and expensive. Certainly, it lacks the picture-postcard beauty of many Italian towns, but in among the urban hustle are some truly great sights – Leonardo da Vinci's *Last Supper*, the immense Duomo and La Scala opera house.

◉ Sights

The **Civic Museum Card** (€12; www.turismo.milano.it) is a three-day ticket allowing a single admission to each of Milan's nine civic museums. Tickets can be purchased online or at any of the museums.

★**Duomo** CATHEDRAL
([☑] 02 7202 3375; www.duomomilano.it; Piazza del Duomo; adult/reduced Duomo €3/2, roof terraces via stairs €10/5, lift €14/7, archaeological area €7/3 (incl Duomo); [🕐] Duomo 8am-7pm, roof terraces 9am-7pm, archaeological area 9am-7pm; [Ⓜ] Duomo) A vision in pink Candoglia marble, Milan's extravagant Gothic cathedral, 600 years in the making, aptly reflects the city's creativity and ambition. Its pearly white facade, adorned with 135 spires and 3400 statues, rises like the filigree of a fairy-tale tiara, wowing the crowds with its extravagant detail. The interior is no less impressive, punctuated by three enormous stained-glassed apse windows, while in the crypt saintly Carlo Borromeo is interred in a rock-crystal casket.

★**Museo del Novecento** GALLERY
([☑] 02 8844 4061; www.museodelnovecento.org; Piazza del Duomo 8; adult/reduced €5/3; [🕐] 2.30-7.30pm Mon, from 9.30am Tue, Wed, Fri & Sun, to 10.30pm Thu & Sat; [🛜]; [Ⓜ] Duomo) Overlooking Piazza del Duomo, with fabulous views of the cathedral, is Mussolini's Arengario, from where he would harangue huge crowds in his heyday. Now it houses Milan's museum

of 20th-century art. Built around a futuristic spiral ramp (an ode to the Guggenheim), the museum's lower floors are cramped, but the heady collection, which includes the likes of Boccioni, Campigli, Giorgio de Chirico and Marinetti, more than distracts.

Pinacoteca di Brera
GALLERY
(☑ 02 7226 3264; www.pinacotecabrera.org; Via Brera 28; adult/reduced €12/8; ☺ 8.30am-7.15pm Tue-Sun; Ⓜ Lanza, Montenapoleone) Located upstairs from one of Italy's most prestigious art schools, this gallery houses Milan's collection of Old Masters, much of it 'lifted' from Venice by Napoleon. Rubens, Goya and Van Dyck all have a place, but you're here for the Italians: Titian, Tintoretto, Veronese and the Bellini brothers. Much of the work has tremendous emotional clout, most notably Mantegna's brutal *Lamentation over the Dead Christ*.

★ The Last Supper
ARTWORK
(Il Cenacolo; ☑ 02 9280 0360; www.cenacolovinciano.net; Piazza Santa Maria delle Grazie 2; adult/reduced €10/5, plus booking fee €2; ☺ 8.15am-7pm Tue-Sun; Ⓜ Cadorna) Milan's most famous mural, Leonardo da Vinci's *The Last Supper*, is hidden away on a wall of the refectory adjoining the **Basilica di Santa Maria delle Grazie** (☑ 02 467 61 11; www.legraziemilano.it; ☺ 7am-12.55pm & 3-7.30pm Mon-Sat, 7.30am-12.30pm, 3.30-9pm Sun) FREE. Depicting Christ and his disciples at the dramatic moment when Christ reveals he's aware of his betrayal, it's a masterful psychological study and one of the world's most iconic images. You may very well kick yourself if you miss it, so book in advance or sign up for a guided city tour.

Museo Nazionale Scienza e Tecnologia Leonardo da Vinci
MUSEUM
(☑ 02 48 55 51; www.museoscienza.org; Via San Vittore 21; adult/child €10/7.50, submarine tours €8; ☺ 9.30am-5pm Tue-Fri, to 6.30pm Sat & Sun; 🚻; Ⓜ Sant'Ambrogio) Kids and would-be inventors will go goggle-eyed at Milan's science museum, the largest of its kind in Italy. It is a fitting tribute in a city where arch-inventor Leonardo da Vinci did much of his finest work. The 16th-century monastery where it's housed features a collection of more than 15,000 items, including models based on da Vinci's sketches, with outdoor hangars housing steam trains, planes and Italy's first submarine, *Enrico Toti* (tours available in English and Italian).

QUADRILATERO D'ORO

A stroll around the **Quadrilatero d'Oro** (Golden Quadrilateral; Ⓜ Monte Napoleone), the world's most famous shopping district, is a must. This quaintly cobbled quadrangle of streets – bounded by Via Monte Napoleone, Via Sant'Andrea, Via della Spiga and Via Manzoni – has always been synonymous with elegance and money (Via Monte Napoleone was where Napoleon's government managed loans). Even if you don't have the slightest urge to sling a swag of glossy carriers, the window displays and people-watching are priceless.

🛏 Sleeping

Finding a room in Milan (let alone a cheap one) isn't easy, particularly during trade fairs and fashion weeks when rates skyrocket. The tourist office distributes *Milano Hotels*, a free annual listings guide to Milan's hotels.

★ Ostello Bello
HOSTEL €
(☑ 02 3658 2720; www.ostellobello.com; Via Medici 4; dm €45-50 d €145-175; ❄🛜; ☒ 2, 3, 14) A breath of fresh air in Milan's stiffly suited centre, this is the best hostel in town (and hands down the most social). Entrance is through its lively bar-cafe, where you're welcomed with a complimentary drink. Beds are in bright mixed dorms or private rooms, and there's a kitchen, sunny terrace, and basement lounge with board games and table football.

Babila Hostel
HOSTEL €
(☑ 02 3658 8490; www.babilahostel.it; Via Conservatorio 2a; dm €30-42, d €89-159, q 120-176; ❄🛜; Ⓜ San Babila) Set in a beautifully restored neo-Gothic *palazzo* with high, vaulted halls and steel-grey marble fireplaces, this is finally a design hostel worthy of Milan. Colourful Scandinavian furniture, Hugo Pratt prints, a music room and playroom (with table football) add comfort and character, and there's a gorgeous outdoor terrace, a good restaurant and a popular bar that serves cocktails and craft beer.

★ Atellani Apartments
APARTMENT €€
(☑ 375 528 99 22; www.atellaniapartments.com; Corso Magenta 65; 1-bed apt €170-230, 2-bed apt

Central Milan

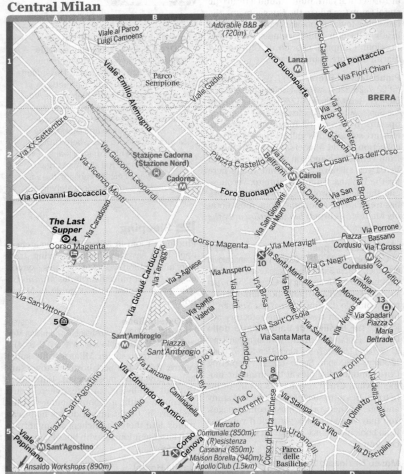

Adorabile B&B
(720m)

Corso Garibaldi

Via Pontaccio

Via Fiori Chiari

BRERA

Viale al Parco
Luigi Camoens

Foro Buonaparte

Lanza

Via Ponte Vetero

Via Arco

Viale Emilio Alemagna

Parco
Sempione

Viale Gadio

Via G Sacchi

Via Cusani   Via dell'Orso

Piazza Castello

Via Luca
Beltrami

Via XX Settembre

Via Giacomo Leopardi

Stazione Cadorna
(Stazione Nord)

Cadorna

Cairoli

Via San
Tomaso

Via Vicenza Monti

Via Giovanni Boccaccio

Foro Buonaparte

Via Dante

Via Broletto

Via San Giovanni
sul Muro

**The Last
Supper**
4

Via Caradosso

Corso Magenta
7

Corso Magenta

Via Meravigli
10

Via Santa Maria alla Porta

Via Porrone

Piazza
Cordusio   Bassano
Via T Grossi

Via G Negri

Cordusio

Via Orefici

Via Giosuè Carducci

Via Terraggio

Via S Agnese

Via Ansperto

Via Brisa

Via Borromei

Via Moneta

Via
Armorari

Via San Vittore

Via Santa
Valeria

Via Lupi

Via Sant'Orsola

Via Nerino

13

Via Spadari
Piazza S
Maria
Beltrade

Sant'Ambrogio

Piazza
Sant'Ambrogio

5

Via San Maurilio

Via San Pio V

Via Santa Marta

Via Cappuccio

Via Circo

Via Torino

Via della Palla

Via Lanzone

Via
Caminadella

Via C
Correnti

8

Via Stampa

Via Olmetto

Via Edmondo de Amicis

Piazza Sant'Agostino

Via Ariberto

Via Ausonio

Corso di Porta Ticinese

Via S Vito

Via Urbano III

Via Disciplini

**Viale
Papiniano**

Sant'Agostino

11

**Corso
Genova**

Mercato
Comunale (850m);
(R)esistenza
Caseria (850m);
Maison Borella (940m);
Apollo Club (1.5km)

Parco
delle
Basiliche

Ansaldo Workshops (890m)

€260-300; P ❋ ❧; M Conciliazione, ❷16) Now
you can bed down in the 15th-century *palazzo* where Leonardo himself lodged while
painting *The Last Supper*. Six boutique
apartments run by Portaluppi's grandchildren feature the architect's inspired modernist design, parquet floors, slick contemporary
decor by local artisans and views over the
Santa Maria delle Grazie. Guests can also
access the house museum and resplendent
garden with Leonardo's own vineyard.

★ **Adorabile B&B**   B&B €€
(❷391 114 2490; www.adorabile.it; Via Bramante
14; d €120; M Moscova) Step back in time in

this beautiful 1930s apartment with rosette
floor tiles, cast-iron radiators and Ariel
Soule artworks. Host Franz Iacono has impeccable taste (check out those Hästen beds)
and has created four characterful rooms. It's
a great place to plug into the city (don't miss
the 6pm *aperitivo*) in one of Milan's most
up-and-coming neighbourhoods.

★ **Maison Borella**   BOUTIQUE HOTEL €€€
(❷02 5810 9114; www.hotelmaisonborella.com;
Alzaia Naviglio Grande 8; d €195-260, ste €350-
600; P ❋ ❧; M Porta Genova) With balconies
overhanging the Naviglio Grande and striking vintage furniture selected by collector

ITALY MILAN

ITALY MILAN

★ **(R)esistenza Casearia**   CHEESE €
(☎ 02 3598 2848; Piazza XXIV Maggio; cheese boards €10-25; ⊙ 9am-10pm Tue-Thu, to midnight Fri-Sun; 🚋 9) Street-food guru Giuseppe Zen has done it again with this spectacular cheese bar in the **Mercato Comunale** (⊙ 8.30am-1pm & 4-7.30pm Tue-Sat, 8.30am-1pm Mon). Let them arrange a tasting plate of some of the finest raw-milk cheeses in Lombardy, all of which come from heritage producers with high-mountain pastures. Make a meal of it with a glass of biodynamic wine and the house-made tiramisu.

Luini   FAST FOOD €
(☎ 02 8646 1917; www.luini.it; Via Santa Radegonda 16; panzerotti €2.80; ⊙ 10am-3pm Mon, to 8pm Tue-Sat; ♦; Ⓜ Duomo) This historical joint is the go-to place for *panzerotti*, delicious pizza-dough parcels stuffed with a combination of mozzarella, spinach, tomato, ham or spicy salami, and then fried or baked in a wood-fired oven. Queues may be long but they move fast.

★ **Pasticceria Marchesi**   PASTRIES €
(☎ 02 86 27 70; www.pasticceriamarchesi.it; Via Santa Maria alla Porta 11/a; ⊙ 7.30am-8pm Tue-Sat, 8.30am-1pm Sun; Ⓜ Cairoli, Cordusio) Since 1824 the original Marchesi *pasticceria* (pastry

---

Raimondo Garau, this canalside hotel offers a touch of class in a dedicated bohemian neighbourhood. Converted from an old *casa di ringhiera,* its main rooms are arranged around an inner courtyard draped in ivy and offer charming features such as parquet floors and elegant *boiserie* (sculpted panelling).

✖ Eating & Drinking

Local specialities include *risotto alla milanese* (saffron-infused risotto cooked in bone marrow stock) and *cotoletta alla milanese* (breaded veal cutlet).

shop) has been charming customers with its refined 20th-century features and picture-perfect petit fours. Indulge your sweet tooth with any number of *bignes* (cream puffs), pralines, sugared almonds and fruit gels, and get your hands on some of the best *panettone* in Milan. The dining area out the back also makes for an elegant pit stop.

★ Trattoria del Pescatore SEAFOOD €€

(☑ 02 5832 0452; www.trattoriadelpescatore.it; Via Atto Vannucci 5; meals €40-45; ◷ 12.30-2.30pm & 8-11pm Mon-Sat; M Porta Romana) Milan's finest fish restaurant hides modestly behind a row of green awnings. At the helm are Sardinian couple Giuliano and Agnese and their son, who interned at three-Michelin-starred Arzak in San Sebastián. The pasta is handmade in their home town and the unmissable signature dish is the Catalan lobster drowned in Camone tomatoes and Tropea onions. Finish with green-apple sorbet and Sardinian cheeses.

Tipografia Alimentare ITALIAN €€

(☑ 02 8353 7868; www.tipografiaalimentare.it; Via Dolomiti 1; meals €20-35; ◷ 9am-10pm Wed-Mon; ☞ ✐; M Turro) ✐ Take a break from Milan at this laid-back food hub on the Martesana Canal. Run by fresh-food warriors Martina and Mattia, its vegetarian-focused menu showcases sustainable producers both on the plate and through wine tastings and food events. Matteo's grasp of texture and flavour is outstanding, resulting in layered dishes such as orzo topped with earthy beets and sprinkled with crunchy hazelnuts.

★ Tokuyoshi FUSION €€€

(☑ 02 8425 4626; www.ristorantetokuyoshi.com; Via San Calocero 3; meals €50-75; tasting menu €135; ◷ 7-10.30pm Tue-Sat, 12.30-2.30pm & 7-10.30pm Sun; ☐ 2, 14) Take a creative culinary voyage from Japan to Italy with Yoji Tokuyoshi at the helm. One-time sous-chef of world-renowned Osteria Francescana, this talented chef has already received a Michelin star for his efforts. Expect the unexpected, such as Parmesan tiramisu or cod-filled Sicilian *cannoli* (pastry shells).

☆ Nightlife & Entertainment

The tourist office stocks English-language entertainment guide *Hello Milano* (www.hello milano.it); while online Easy Milano (www.easymilano.it) serves the English-speaking community in Milan.

Apollo Club CLUB

(☑ 02 3826 0176; www.apollomilano.com; Via Giosuè Borsi 9; cocktails €8-10, meals €33-77; ◷ 7pm-3am Wed-Thu, to 4am Fri & Sat, noon-1am Sun; ☐ 3) Milan's creative crowd loves to hang at this multifunctional space incorporating a handsome vintage-style bar with club chairs and chesterfields, plus a 30-seat restaurant, a games room and a dance hall illuminated with a twinkling disco ball. Come for aperitif, dinner or brunch, but don't miss Friday's Rollover night, when a thousand people pack the dance floor thanks to international DJ talent.

Check out their Facebook posts for news and events (www.facebook.com/apolloclub milano).

LOCAL KNOWLEDGE

URBAN CHILLING

Conceived as a community hub by architect Luigi Secchi in 1939, **I Bagni Misteriosi** (☑ 02 8973 1800; www.bagnimisteriosi.com; Via Carlo Botta 18; adult €7-15, reduced €5-12 depending on time of day; ◷ 10am-6pm Sun-Mon & Wed, 10am-midnight Thu, 10am-10pm Fri & Sat; ☝; M Porta Romana) is a modernist *lido* with enormous heated pools, close-cropped lawns, shaded porticos, bistro and bar that has been painstakingly restored and is once again a favourite summer retreat. Besides the swimming, there's t'ai chi, art classes, evening *aperitivo*, and dance and music concerts hosted by the adjoining **Teatro Franco Parenti** (☑ 02 5999 5206; www.teatrofrancoparenti.it; Via Pier Lombardo 14; M Porta Romana).

One of the pools, featuring a fountain with flamingos, is dedicated to children, while the other, Olympic-sized pool is adults only. There are hammocks for snoozing, a hip background playlist, tip-top changing rooms and on-duty lifeguards. Both the bar and bistro are accessible from Via Sabina without having to pay the entry fee.

In winter the complex is made over into an ice-skating rink, while future renovations will return the tennis court to use. The best time to visit is between 6.30pm and 9pm for an unforgettable *aperitivo* around the pools.

Teatro alla Scala
OPERA

(La Scala; ☑ 02 7200 3744; www.teatroallascala. org; Piazza della Scala; tickets €30-300; Ⓜ Duomo) One of the most famous opera stages in the world, La Scala's season runs from early December to July. You can also see theatre, ballet and classical music concerts here year-round (except August). Buy tickets online or by phone up to two months before the performance, or from the **box office** (☑ 02 7200 3744; Largo Ghiringhelli; ⊙ 10.30am-6pm Mon-Sat, noon-6pm Sun; Ⓜ Duomo). Heavily discounted same-day tickets are also available from the box office.

San Siro Stadium
FOOTBALL

(Stadio Giuseppe Meazza; ☑ 02 4879 8201; www. sansiro.net; Piazzale Angelo Moratti; tickets from €35; Ⓜ San Siro Stadio, ☒16) San Siro Stadium wasn't designed to hold the entire population of Milan, but on a Sunday afternoon amid 80,000 football-mad citizens it can certainly feel like it. The city's two clubs, AC Milan and FC Internazionale Milano (aka Inter), play on alternate weeks from September to May.

Guided tours of the 1920s-built stadium take you behind the scenes to the players' locker rooms and include a visit to the **San Siro Museum** (☑ 02 404 24 32; Piazzale Angelo Moratti, Gate 8; museum & tour adult/reduced €15/11; ⊙ 9.30am-6pm Nov-Mar, to 7pm Apr-Oct), a shrine of memorabilia and film footage.

You can buy tickets for games on the clubs' websites (www.acmilan.com and www.inter.it).

🛍 Shopping

Beyond the hallowed streets of the Quadrilatero d'Oro, designer outlets and chains can be found along Corso Buenos Aires and Corso Vercelli; younger, hipper labels live along Via Brera and Corso Magenta; while Corso di Porta Ticinese and Navigli are home of the Milan street scene and subculture shops.

★ Peck
FOOD & DRINKS

(☑ 02 802 31 61; www.peck.it; Via Spadari 9; ⊙ 3-8pm Mon, from 9am Tue-Sat; 🛜; Ⓜ Duomo) Milan's historical deli is a bastion of the city's culinary heritage, with the huge ground floor turning out a colourful cornucopia of fabulous foods. It showcases a mind-boggling selection of cheeses, chocolates, pralines, pastries, freshly made gelato, pasta, seafood, meat, caviar, pâté, olive oils and balsamic vinegars; it also has a downstairs wine cellar.

ⓘ BACKSTAGE

Fashion alert: reserve ahead for fascinating behind-the-scenes **tours** (☑ 02 4335 3521; www.teatroallascala. org; Via Bergognone 34; per person €25; ⊙ 9am-noon & 2-4pm Tue & Thu; Ⓜ Porta Genova) of La Scala's costume and craft workshops.

ⓘ Information

Milan Tourist Office (☑ 02 8845 5555; www. turismo.milano.it; Galleria Vittorio Emanuele II 11-12; ⊙ 9am-7pm Mon-Fri, 10am-5.30pm Sat & Sun; Ⓜ Duomo) Centrally located in the Galleria with helpful English-speaking staff and lots of useful maps, brochures and information on new exhibitions and events. They also support the useful website www.yesmilano.it, which features the latest events in the city.

ⓘ Getting There & Away

AIR

Aeroporto Linate (LIN; ☑ 02 23 23 23; www. milanolinate-airport.com; Viale Forlanini) Located 7km east of Milan city centre; domestic and European flights only. Services at the airport include an exchange office, luggage storage and a VAT refund office.

Aeroporto Malpensa (MXP; ☑ 02 23 23 23; www.milanomalpensa-airport.com; ☒ Malpensa Express) Northern Italy's main international airport is about 50km northwest of Milan city. Services include car rental, banks, a VAT refund office and free wi-fi.

Orio al Serio (☑ 035 32 63 23; www.sacbo.it) Low-cost carriers link Bergamo airport with a wide range of European cities. There are direct transport links to Milan.

TRAIN

Regular fast trains depart Stazione Centrale for Venice (€45, 2½ hours), Bologna (€34.50 to €46, one to two hours), Florence (€56, 1¾ hours), Rome (€92, three hours) and other Italian and European cities.

Most regional trains also stop at Stazione Nord in Piazzale Cadorna.

ⓘ Getting Around

TO/FROM THE AIRPORT

Linate

Airport Bus Express (☑ 02 3008 9000; www. airportbusexpress.it; one way/return €5/9; Ⓜ Centrale) The Autostradale express airport bus departs from Milan's Stazione Centrale for Linate airport every half-hour between 5.30am and 10pm. Buses from the airport to Milan start at 7.45am and run until 10.45pm. Buses from Milan depart from Piazza Luigi di Savoia on the east side of the station. Tickets are sold on board.

Malpensa

Malpensa Shuttle (☑ 02 5858 3185; www.malpensashuttle.it; one way/return €10/16; Ⓜ Centrale) This Malpensa airport shuttle runs at least half-hourly between 5.15am and 10.45pm from Stazione Centrale, and roughly hourly throughout the rest of the night. The journey time is 50 minutes and buses depart from Piazza IV Novembre on the west side of the station. Terminal 2 stops need to be requested.

Malpensa Express (☑ 02 7249 4949; www.malpensaexpress.it; one way €13) Half-hourly trains run from Malpensa airport to Cadorna Stazione Nord (40 minutes) and Stazione Centrale (60 minutes). Services to Cadorna run between 5.40am and 12.20am; to Stazione Centrale from 5.37am to 10.37pm. The train also serves both airport terminals.

Orio al Serio

Orio Shuttle (☑ 035 31 93 66; www.orioshuttle.com; adult/reduced €7/5; Ⓜ Centrale) This shuttle bus service departs Piazza Luigi di Savoia at Stazione Centrale approximately every half-hour between 2.45am to 10.40pm, and from Orio al Serio airport between 7.45am and 12.15am. The journey takes 50 minutes.

PUBLIC TRANSPORT

Milan's metro, buses and trams are run by **ATM** (Azienda Trasporti Milano; ☑ 02 4860 7607; www.atm.it). Tickets (€1.50) are valid for one underground ride and up to 90 minutes' travel on city buses and trams. A day ticket costs €4.50.

The Lakes

Ringed by snowcapped mountains, gracious towns and landscaped gardens, the Italian lake district is an enchanting corner of the country.

Lago Maggiore

Snaking across the Swiss border, Lago Maggiore, the westernmost of the three main lakes, retains the belle époque glamour of its 19th-century heyday when it was a popular retreat for artists and writers.

Its headline sights are the Borromean islands, accessible from **Stresa** on the lake's western bank. **Isola Bella** is dominated by the 17th-century **Palazzo Borromeo**

(☑ 0323 93 34 78; www.isoleborromee.it; Isola Bella; adult/child €16/8.50, incl Palazzo Madre €21/10; ⊘ 9am-5.30pm mid-Mar–mid-Oct), a grand baroque palace with a wonderful art collection and beautiful tiered gardens. Over the water, **Palazzo Madre** (☑ 0323 93 34 78; www.isoleborromee.it; adult/child €13/6.50, incl Palazzo Borromeo €21/10; ⊘ 9am-5.30pm mid-Mar–mid-Oct) lords it over **Isola Madre**.

In Stresa's pedestrianised centre, **Ristorante Il Vicoletto** (☑ 0323 93 21 02; www.ristorantevicoletto.com; Vicolo del Pocivo 3; meals €30-45; ⊘ noon-2pm & 7-10pm Fri-Wed) is a refined restaurant serving excellent regional cooking. Nearby, the **Hotel Saini Meublè** (☑ 0323 93 45 19; www.hotelsaini.it; Via Garibaldi 10; s/d €75/102; 🛜) has warm, spacious rooms.

For further information, contact Stresa's **tourist office** (☑ 0323 3 13 08; www.stresaturismo.it; Piazza Marconi 16; ⊘ 10am-12.30pm & 3-6.30pm summer, closed Sat afternoon & Sun winter).

ⓘ Getting There & Around

The easiest way to get to Stresa is by train from Milan (€8.60 to €12.90, 1¼ hours, up to 20 daily).

Between April and September, **SAF** (☑ 0323 55 21 72; www.safduemila.com) operates an Alibus shuttle to/from Malpensa airport (€15, 1½ hours, six daily).

Navigazione Lago Maggiore (☑ 800 551801; www.navigazionelaghi.it) operates ferries across the lake. From Stresa, a return ticket to Isola Bella costs €6.80; to Isola Madre it's €10.

Lago di Como

Lago di Como, overshadowed by steep wooded hills and snowcapped peaks, is the most spectacular and least visited of the lakes. At its southwestern tip, **Como** is a prosperous town with an imposing **Duomo** (Cattedrale di Como; ☑ 031 331 22 75; Piazza del Duomo; ⊘ 9.30am-5.30pm Mon-Fri, 10.45am-4.30pm Sat, 1-4.30pm Sun) 🆓 and a charming medieval core.

For lunch head to the characterful **Osteria del Gallo** (☑ 031 27 25 91; www.osteriadelgallo-como.it; Via Vitani 16; meals €26-32; ⊘ 12.30-3pm Mon-Sat & 7-9pm Tue-Sat).

Also in the medieval centre, the modish **Avenue Hotel** (☑ 031 27 21 86; www.avenuehotel.it; Piazzolo Terragni 6; d €165-210, ste €250-290; 🅿❄🛜) offers slick four-star accommodation.

You can get more information at the **tourist office** (☑ 342 0076403; www.visitcomo.eu;

VERONA

Wander Verona's atmospheric streets and you'll understand why Shakespeare set *Romeo and Juliet* here – this is one of Italy's most beautiful and romantic cities. Known as *piccola Roma* (little Rome) for its importance in ancient times, its heyday came in the 13th and 14th centuries when it was ruled by the Della Scala (aka Scaligeri) family, who built *palazzi* and bridges, sponsored Giotto, Dante and Petrarch, oppressed their subjects, and feuded with everyone else.

Roman Arena (☑ 045 800 32 04; Piazza Brà; adult/reduced €10/7.50; ☺ 8.30am-7.30pm Tue-Sun, 1.30-7.30pm Mon) Built of pink-tinged marble in the 1st century CE, Verona's Roman amphitheatre survived a 12th-century earthquake to become the city's legendary open-air opera house, with seating for 30,000 people. You can visit the arena year-round, though it's at its best during the summer opera festival. In winter months, concerts are held at the **Teatro Filarmonico** (☑ 045 800 28 80; www.arena.it; Via dei Mutilati 4; opera/concerts from €23/25). From October to May, admission is €1 on the first Sunday of the month.

Giardino Giusti (☑ 045 803 40 29; Via Giardino Giusti 2; adult/reduced €8.50/5; ☺ 9am-7pm) Across the river from the historical centre, these sculpted gardens are considered a masterpiece of Renaissance landscaping, and are named after the noble family that has tended them since opening the gardens to the public in 1591. The vegetation is an Italianate mix of the manicured and natural, graced by soaring cypresses, one of which the German poet Goethe immortalised in his travel writings.

Casa di Giulietta (Juliet's House; ☑ 045 803 43 03; Via Cappello 23; adult/reduced €6/4.50, free with VeronaCard; ☺ 1.30-7.30pm Mon, 8.30am-7.30pm Tue-Sun) Juliet's house is a spectacle, but not for the reasons you might imagine – entering the courtyard off Via Cappello, you are greeted by a young multinational crowd, everyone milling around in the tiny space trying to take selfies with the well-rubbed bronze of Juliet. The walls are lined up to 2m high with love notes, many attached with chewing gum. Above you is the famous balcony, with tourists taking their turn to have pics taken against the 'romantic background'.

Verona Villafranca Airport (☑ 045 809 56 66; www.aeroportoverona.it) is 12km outside town and accessible by ATV Aerobus to/from the train station (€6, 15 minutes, every 20 minutes 5.15am to 11.30pm).

From the station, buses 11, 12 and 13 (90, 92, 96, 97 and 98 evenings and Sundays) run to Piazza Brà.

Trains connect with Milan (€12.75 to €25, 1¼ to two hours, up to three hourly), Venice (€9 to €27, 1¼ to 2¼ hours, at least twice hourly) and Bologna (€10 to €25, 50 minutes to 1½ hours, 20 daily).

ITALY THE LAKES

Como San Giovanni, Piazzale San Gottardo; ☺ 9am-5pm summer, 10am-4pm Wed-Mon winter) at San Giovanni train station.

ⓘ Getting There & Around

Regional trains run to Como San Giovanni from Milan's Stazione Centrale and Porta Garibaldi (€4.80, 40 minutes, 19 daily).

Navigazione Lago di Como (☑ 800 551801; www.navigazionelaghi.it; Lungo Lario Trento) operates year-round ferries from the jetty near Piazza Cavour.

Lago di Garda

The largest and most developed of the lakes, Lago di Garda straddles the border between Lombardy and the Veneto.

A good base is **Sirmione**, a picturesque village on its southern shores. Here you can investigate the **Grotte di Catullo** (☑ 030 91 61 57; www.polomuseale.lombardia.beniculturali.it/index.php/grotte-di-catullo; Piazzale Orti Manara 4; adult/reduced €8/4; ☺ 8.30am-7.30pm Mon & Wed-Sat & 9.30am-7pm Sun summer, 8.30am-5pm Mon & Wed-Sat & to 2pm Sun winter), a ruined Roman villa, and enjoy views over the lake's placid blue waters.

There is an inordinate number of eateries crammed into Sirmione's historical centre. One of the best is **La Fiasca** (☑ 030 990 61 11; www.trattorialafiasca.it; Via Santa Maria Maggiore 11; meals €30-35; ☺ noon-2.30pm & 6.45-10.15pm Thu-Tue), an authentic trattoria serving flavoursome lake fish.

Sirmione can be visited on a day trip from Verona, but if you want to overnight, **Meublé Grifone** (☑ 030 91 60 14; www.gardalakegrifonehotel.eu; Via Gaetano Bocchio 4; s €65-80, d €80-115; ❇ ⚡) boasts a superb lakeside location and relaxing views.

Get information from the **tourist office** (☑ 030 374 87 21; iat.sirmione@provincia.brescia.it; Viale Marconi 8; ⊙ 10am-12.30pm & 3-6pm Mon-Fri, 9.30am-12.30pm Sat) outside the medieval walls.

❶ Getting There & Around

Regular buses run to Sirmione from Verona (€3.60, one hour, hourly).

Navigazione Lago di Garda (☑ 800 551801; www.navigazionelaghi.it) operates the lake's ferries.

Venice

POP 261,905

Venice (Venezia) is a hauntingly beautiful city. At every turn you're assailed by unforgettable images – tiny bridges arching over limpid canals; chintzy gondolas sliding past working barges; and towers and distant domes silhouetted against the watery horizon. Its celebrated sights are legion, and its labyrinthine alleyways exude a unique, almost eerie atmosphere, redolent of cloaked passions and dark secrets.

◉ Sights

◉ San Marco

⭐**Basilica di San Marco**　　　　CATHEDRAL
(St Mark's Basilica; Map p690; ☑ 041 270 83 11; www.basilicasanmarco.it; Piazza San Marco; ⊙ 9.30am-5pm Mon-Sat, 2-5pm Sun summer, to 4.30pm Sun winter; ⛴ San Marco) **FREE** With a profusion of domes and over 8000 sq metres of luminous mosaics, Venice's cathedral is unforgettable. It was founded in the 9th century to house the corpse of St Mark after wily Venetian merchants smuggled it out of Egypt in a barrel of pork fat. When the original building burnt down in 932 Venice rebuilt the basilica in its own cosmopolitan image, with Byzantine domes, a Greek cross layout and walls clad in marble from Syria, Egypt and Palestine.

Campanile　　　　　　　　　TOWER
(Map p690; www.basilicasanmarco.it; Piazza San Marco; adult/reduced €8/4; ⊙ 8.30am-9pm summer, 9.30am-5.30pm winter, last entry 45min before closing; ⛴ San Marco) The basilica's 99m-tall bell tower has been rebuilt twice since its initial construction in 888 CE. Galileo Galilei tested his telescope here in 1609, but modern-day visitors head to the top for 360-degree lagoon views and close encounters with the **Marangona**, the booming bronze bell that originally signalled the start and end of the working day for the *marangoni* (artisans) at the Arsenale shipyards. Today it rings twice a day, at noon and midnight.

Palazzo Ducale　　　　　　　MUSEUM
(Ducal Palace; Map p690; ☑ 041 271 59 11; www.palazzoducale.visitmuve.it; Piazzetta San Marco 1; adult/reduced incl Museo Correr €20/13, with Museum Pass free; ⊙ 8.30am-7pm summer, to 5.30pm winter; ⛴ San Zaccaria) Holding pride of place on the waterfront, this pretty Gothic confection is an unlikely setting for the political and administrative seat of a great republic, but an exquisitely Venetian one. Beyond its dainty colonnades and geometrically patterned facade of white Istrian stone and pale pink Veronese marble lie grand rooms of state, the Doge's private apartments and a large complex of council chambers, courts and prisons.

Ponte dei Sospiri　　　　　　BRIDGE
(Bridge of Sighs; Map p690; ⛴ San Zaccaria) One of Venice's most photographed sights, the Bridge of Sighs connects the Palazzo Ducale to the 16th-century Priggione Nove (New Prisons). Its improbable popularity is due to British libertine Lord Byron (1788–1824), who mentioned it in one of his long narrative poems *Childe Harold's Pilgrimage*. Condemned prisoners were said to sigh as they passed through the enclosed bridge and glimpsed the beauty of the lagoon. Now the sighs are mainly from people trying to dodge the snapping masses.

◉ Dorsoduro

⭐**Gallerie dell'Accademia**　　　GALLERY
(Map p690; ☑ 041 522 22 47; www.gallerieaccademia.it; Campo de la Carità 1050; adult/reduced €12/2; ⊙ 8.15am-2pm Mon, to 7.15pm Tue-Sun; ⛴ Accademia) Venice's historical gallery traces the development of Venetian art from the 14th to 19th centuries, with works by all of the city's artistic superstars. The complex housing the collection maintained its serene composure for centuries until Napoleon installed his haul of art trophies here in 1807 –

Greater Venice

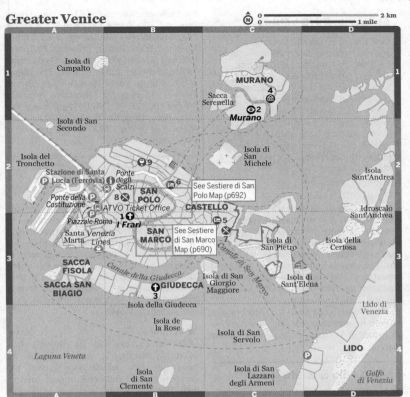

Greater Venice

looted from various religious institutions around town. Since then there's been non-stop visual drama on its walls. Note that the gallery is in the midst of a major refurbishment; some rooms may be closed.

★ Peggy Guggenheim Collection
MUSEUM

(Map p690; ☎041 240 54 11; www.guggenheim-venice.it; Calle San Cristoforo 701; adult/reduced €15/9; ☉10am-6pm Wed-Mon; ⚓Accademia) After losing her father on the *Titanic,* heiress Peggy Guggenheim became one of the great collectors of the 20th century. Her palatial canalside home, Palazzo Venier dei Leoni, showcases her stockpile of surrealist, futurist and abstract expressionist art with works by up to 200 artists, including her ex-husband Max Ernst, Jackson Pollock (among her many rumoured lovers), Pablo Picasso and Salvador Dalí.

Basilica di Santa Maria della Salute
BASILICA

(Our Lady of Health Basilica; Map p690; www.basilicasalutevenezia.it; Campo de la Salute 1; sacristy adult/reduced €4/2; ☉9.30am-noon & 3-5.30pm;

ⓘ NAVIGATING VENICE

Venice is not an easy place to navigate and even with a smartphone and satellite mapping you're bound to get lost. The main area of interest lies between Santa Lucia train station (signposted as the *ferrovia*) and Piazza San Marco (St Mark's Sq). The path between the two – Venice's main drag – is a good 40- to 50-minute walk. It also helps to know that the city is divided into six *sestieri* (districts): Cannaregio, Castello, San Marco, Dorsoduro, San Polo and Santa Croce.

▣ Salute) **FREE** Baldassare Longhena's magnificent basilica is prominently positioned near the entrance to the Grand Canal, its white stones, exuberant statuary and high domes gleaming spectacularly under the sun. The church makes good on an official appeal by the Venetian Senate directly to the Madonna in 1630, after 80,000 Venetians had been killed by plague.

The Senate promised the Madonna a church in exchange for her intervention on behalf of Venice – no expense or effort spared.

◉ San Polo & Santa Croce

★ **I Frari**   BASILICA

(Basilica di Santa Maria Gloriosa dei Frari; Map p687; ☑ 041 272 86 18; www.basilicadeifrari.it; Campo dei Frari 3072, San Polo; adult/reduced €3/1.50, with Chorus Pass free; ⊙ 9am-6pm Mon-Sat, 1-6pm Sun; ▣ San Tomà) A soaring Gothic church, the Friary's assets include marquetry choir stalls, Canova's pyramid mausoleum, Bellini's achingly sweet *Madonna with Child* triptych in the sacristy, and Longhena's creepy Doge Pesaro funereal monument.

Upstaging them all, however, is Titian's 1518 *Assunta* (Assumption) altarpiece, in which a radiant red-cloaked Madonna reaches heavenward, steps onto a cloud and escapes this mortal coil. Titian himself – lost to the plague in 1576 at the age 94 – has his memorial here.

◉ Giudecca

Chiesa del Santissimo Redentore   CHURCH

(Church of the Most Holy Redeemer; Map p687; www.chorusvenezia.org; Campo del SS Redentore

194, Giudecca; adult/reduced €3/1.50, with Chorus Pass free; ⊙ 10.30am-4.30pm Mon-Sat; ▣ Redentore) Built to celebrate the city's deliverance from the Black Death, Palladio's *Il Redentore* was completed under Antonio da Ponte (of Rialto Bridge fame) in 1592. The theme is taken up in Paolo Piazza's monochrome *Venice's Offering for Liberation from the Plague of 1575–77* (1619), high above the entry door. Look for Tintoretto's *The Flagellation of Christ* (1588) on the third altar to the right.

◉ The Islands

★ **Murano**   ISLAND

(Map p687; ▣ Faro) Murano has been the home of Venetian glass-making since the 13th century. Today artisans continue to ply their trade at workshops dotted around the island. To learn about local manufacturing traditions and view a collection of historical glass, visit the **Museo del Vetro** (Glass Museum; Map p687; ☑ 041 243 49 14; www.museovetro.visitmuve.it; Fondamenta Giustinian 8; adult/reduced €12/9.50, free with Museum Pass; ⊙ 10am-5pm; ▣ Museo).

★ **Burano**   ISLAND

(▣ Burano) Burano, with its cheery pastel-coloured houses, is renowned for its handmade lace, which once graced the décolletages and ruffs of European aristocracy. These days, with a couple of notable exceptions, much of the lace sold in local shops is imported. Still, tourists head here in droves to snap photos of the brightly painted houses reflecting in the canals – clogging up the bridges and driving the locals to distraction in the process. It's a much more peaceful place in the evening.

Torcello   ISLAND

(▣ Torcello) Torcello, the republic's original island settlement, was largely abandoned due to malaria and now counts only around 14 permanent residents. Its mosaic-clad Byzantine church, the **Basilica di Santa Maria Assunta** (☑ 041 73 01 19; Piazza Torcello; adult/reduced €5/4, incl museum & campanile €12/10; ⊙ 10.30am-5.30pm), is Venice's oldest.

🏃 Activities

The official rate for a gondola tour is €80 for 30 minutes (for up to six people). After 7pm it's €100 for 35 minutes.

✦ Festivals & Events

Carnevale CARNIVAL
(www.carnevale.venezia.it; ⊙ Jan/Feb) Masquerade madness stretches over two weeks in January or February before Lent. A Cannaregio Canal flotilla marks the outbreak of festivities, which feature masked balls, processions, public parties in every *campo* (square) and all manner of dressing up.

★ La Biennale di Venezia ART
(www.labiennale.org; Giardini della Biennale; ⊙ mid-May–Nov; 🚤 Giardini Biennale) Europe's premier arts showcase since 1907 is something of a misnomer: the Biennale is now actually held every year, but the spotlight alternates between art (odd-numbered years) and architecture (even-numbered years). Running alongside the two main events are annual showcases of dance, theatre, cinema and music.

Venice International Film Festival FILM
(Mostra Internazionale d'Arte Cinematografica; www.labiennale.org/en/cinema; Lungomare Marconi, Lido; ⊙ Aug-Sep) The only thing hotter than a Lido beach in August is the Film Festival's star-studded red carpet, usually rolled out from the last weekend in August through to the first week of September.

Regata Storica CULTURAL
(www.regatastoricavenezia.it; ⊙ Sep) Sixteenth-century costumes, eight-oared gondolas and ceremonial barques feature in this historical procession (usually held in early September) along the Grand Canal, which re-enacts the arrival of the Queen of Cyprus and precedes gondola races.

🛏 Sleeping

B&B San Marco B&B €
(Map p687; ☎ 041 522 75 89; www.realvenice. it; Fondamenta San Giorgio dei Schiavoni 3385I; r €135, without bathroom €105-135; ❄; 🚤 San Zaccaria) Alice and Marco welcome you warmly to their home overlooking Carpaccio's frescoed Scuola Dalmata. The 3rd-floor apartment (no lift), with its parquet floors and large windows, is furnished with family antiques and offers photogenic views over the terracotta rooftops and canals. The hosts live upstairs, so they're always on hand with great recommendations.

Oltre Il Giardino BOUTIQUE HOTEL €€
(Map p692; ☎ 041 275 00 15; www.oltreilgiardino-venezia.com; Fondamenta Contarini 2542; d/ste from €180/280; ❄ 🛜; 🚤 San Tomà) Live the dream in this garden villa, the 1920s home of Alma Mahler, the composer's widow. Hidden behind a lush walled garden, its six high-ceilinged guest rooms and suites marry historical charm with modern comfort: marquetry composer's desks, candelabras and 19th-century poker chairs sit alongside flat-screen TVs and designer bathrooms, while outside, pomegranate trees flower.

★ Locanda Ca' Le Vele B&B €€
(Map p687; ☎ 041 241 39 60; www.locandalevele. com; Calle de le Vele 3969; d €122-148, ste €165-183; ❄ 🛜; 🚤 Ca' d'Oro) The lane may be quiet and the house might look demure, but inside it's Venetian glam all the way. The six guestrooms are a surprisingly stylish riot of terrazzo floors, damask furnishings, Murano glass sconces and ornate gilded beds with busy covers. Pay a little extra for a canal view.

🍴 Eating

★ Osteria Trefanti VENETIAN €€
(Map p687; ☎ 041 520 17 89; www.osteriatrefanti.it; Fondamenta del Rio Marin o dei Garzoti 888; meals €40-45; ⊙ noon-2.30pm & 7-10.30pm Tue-Sun; 🛜; 🚤 Riva de Biasio) La Serenissima's spice trade lives on at simple, elegant Trefanti, where gnocchi might get an intriguing kick from cinnamon and turbot is flavoured with almond and coconut. Seafood is the focus; try the 'doge's fettucine', with mussels, scampi and clams. Furnished with recycled copper

---

ℹ VENICE DISCOUNT PASSES

Civic Museum Pass (www.visitmuve. it; adult/reduced €24/18) Valid for single entry to 11 civic museums, or just four sites around Piazza San Marco (€20/13). Buy online or at participating museums.

Chorus Pass (www.chorusvenezia.org; adult/reduced €12/8) Covers admission to 16 churches. Buy online or at participating sites.

VeneziaUnica (www.veneziaunica.it) A universal pass covering museum admission, transport, wi-fi and more. There's no standard pass; instead you tailor it to your needs and pay according to the services you include on it. See the website for details.

Sestiere di San Marco

200 m
0.1 miles

Basilica di San Marco
1

7
6
Ponte della Paglia
Ponte Capello

Piazzetta dei Leoni
C di Canonica
Ponte S Marco
C Larga San Marco

Piazzetta San Marco

5

Marzaria dell'Orologio

Procuratie Nuove

Bacino di San Marco

Procuratie Vecchie

San Marco Tourist Office
Giardini Ex Reali

San Marco Giardinetti

C Frubera
C dei Fabbri

Campo S Gallo

Rio del Palazzo

8
Fond del Fontego
San Marco Vallaresso

Canale della Giudecca

Rio Terà de le Colonne

Corte Zorzi
C Frezzaria
C d'Selvadego
Bocca di Piazza
C Vallaresso

San Marco

C dei Fuseri

C dei Fabbri

Frezzaria
C Venier

Ramo 1ª Cte Contarina
C Barozzi
C dei 13 Martiri

Fond Zattere ai Saloni

Piscina Frezzaria
C del Carro
C Bognolo

Campo di San Moisè

Corte Barozzi

Fond Dogana alla Salute

SAN MARCO

C de la Locande

Rio dei Bartaroli

Rio de la Veste

C Squero

C del Traghetto

Campo della Salute

Salute

4

Fond della Salute

Rio di S Luca

Campo S Anzolo

Campo S Fantin
C d la Chiesa

9

C de la Fenice
Cllo de la Fenice
C de Cristo

C Larga XXII Marzo

C Pedrocchi

C Veste

Salute

Rio Terà de la Mandola

C d Caffettier

C del Cristo

Fond Fenice

Campo di Santa Maria del Giglio

C de le Ostreghe

Santa Maria del Giglio

Campo Traghetto

Giglio

C Lanza

Rio delle Fornace

Rio di Ca' Garzoni

C del Avvocati

Campo S Anzolo

Campiello Drio la Chiesa

Rio di San Maurizio

Fond Corner Zaguri

C d Bastion

CS Cristoforo

C del Dose Da Ponte

Peggy Guggenheim Collection
3

Fond Ospedaleto

C del Pestrin

C de le Botteghe

Campo Santo Stefano

Campo di S Vidal

Campo San Vio

DORSODURO

C d Chiesa Bragadin

Fond di Ca' Bala

C Mocenigo Ca' Vecchia

Salizz Malipiero
C del Orbi
C d Muneghe

Ponte dell'Accademia

Grand Canal

Fond Venier dei

Piscina Forner

Ramo Lezze
Ramo Grassi

Salizz S Samuele
Campo S Samuele

C Vitturi

C Giustinian

Gallerie dell'Accademia
2

Accademia

Campo della Carità

Rio Terà Antonio Foscarini

Piscina Forner

Sestiere di San Marco

lamps, the space is small and deservedly popular – so book ahead.

★**CoVino** VENETIAN €€
(Map p687; ☑ 041 241 27 05; www.covinovenezia. com; Calle del Pestrin 3829; fixed-price menu lunch €27-36, dinner €40; ☺ 12.45-2.30pm & 7pm-midnight Thu-Mon; ☎; ☒ Arsenale) Tiny CoVino has only 14 seats but demonstrates bags of ambition with its inventive, seasonal menu inspired by the Venetian terroir. Speciality products are selected from Slow Food Foundation producers, and the charming waitstaff make enthusiastic recommendations from the wine list. Only a three-course set menu is available at dinner, but you can choose from two fixed-price options at lunch.

Osteria La Zucca ITALIAN €€
(Map p692; ☑ 041 524 15 70; www.lazucca.it; Calle del Tentor 1762; meals €32-38; ☺ noon-2.30pm & 7-10.30pm Mon-Sat; ☛; ☒ San Stae) With its menu of seasonal vegetarian creations and classic meat dishes, this cosy, woody restaurant consistently hits the mark. Herbs and spices are used to great effect in dishes such as nutmeg-tinged pumpkin and smoked ricotta flan. The small interior can get toasty, so reserve canalside seats in summer. Even in winter you're best to book ahead.

★**Antiche Carampane** VENETIAN €€€
(Map p692; ☑ 041 524 01 65; www.antichecaram pane.com; Rio Terà de le Carampane 1911; meals €55-63; ☺ 12.45-2.30pm & 7.30-10.30pm Tue-Sat; ☒ San Stae) Hidden in the once-dodgy lanes behind Ponte de le Tette, this culinary indulgence is hard to find but worth the effort.

Once you do, say hello to a market-driven menu of Venetian classics including *fegato alla veneziana* (veal liver with onions) and lots of seafood. Never short of a smart, convivial crowd, it's a good idea to book ahead.

🍷 Drinking & Nightlife

Al Prosecco WINE BAR
(Map p692; ☑ 041 524 02 22; www.alprosecco.com; Campo San Giacomo da l'Orio 1503; ☺ 10am-8pm Mon-Fri, to 5pm Sat; ☒ San Stae) Positioned on Venice's loveliest *campo* (square), this wine bar specialises in *vini naturali* (natural-process wines) – organic, biodynamic, wild-yeast fermented – from Italian winemakers. Order a glass of unfiltered 'cloudy' prosecco and toast the view over a plate of *cicheti*.

★**Al Timon** WINE BAR
(Map p687; ☑ 041 524 60 66; www.altimon.it; Fondamenta dei Ormesini 2754; ☺ 5pm-1am; ☒ San Marcuola) Find a spot in the wood-lined interior or, in summer, on the boat moored out the front along the canal and watch the motley parade of drinkers and dreamers arrive for steak platters and quality wines by the *ombra* (half-glass) or carafe.

Musicians play sets canalside when the weather obliges.

Harry's Bar BAR
(Map p690; ☑ 041 528 57 77; www.cipriani.com; Calle Vallaresso 1323; ☺ 10.30am-11pm; ☒ San Marco) Aspiring auteurs hold court at tables well scuffed by Ernest Hemingway, Charlie Chaplin, Truman Capote and Orson Welles, enjoying the signature €21 bellini (Giuseppe Cipriani's original 1948 recipe: white peach juice and *prosecco*) with a side of reflected glory.

☆ Entertainment

To find out what's on during your visit, check listings in free mags distributed citywide and online at Venezia da Vivere (www. veneziadavivere.com) and 2Venice (www. 2venice.it).

★**Teatro La Fenice** OPERA
(Map p690; ☑ 041 78 66 54; www.teatrolafenice. it; Campo San Fantin 1977; tickets €25-250; ☒ Giglio) One of Italy's top opera houses, La Fenice stages a rich roster of opera, ballet and classical music. The main opera season runs from January to July and September to October. The cheapest seats (€25) are in the boxes at the top. The view is extremely

Sestiere di San Polo

200 m
0.1 miles

CASTELLO

SAN MARCO

SANTA CROCE

SAN POLO

RIALTO

Strada Nova

Grand Canal

Grand Canal

Rio di San Salvador

Rio del Vin

Rio dei Meloni

Rio di San Polo

Rio di San Polo

Rio delle Due Torri

Rio di San Cassiano

Rio della Frescada

Rio Marin

Ca' d'Oro

Rialto

San Silvestro

C d Madonna
C Bondi
C d Widman
C Comello
Campo dei Miracoli
C Castelli
Ponte di Panada
Campo Santa Marina
C Pindemonte
C del Dose
C Scaletta
Saliz San Lio
C d Posta
Santa Maria Nova
Campo San Canzian
Saliz San Canzian
C del Forno
C de la Malvasia
C dei Carmini
C d Fava
C del Traghetto
Campiello della Cason
Rio dei Santi Apostoli
Corte del Tentor
Campo della Fava
Rio Tera d Franceschi
Campo dei SS Apostoli
C del Magazen
Zen
Corte Leoni
Campiello del Remer
C Modena
C dell'Aseo
Rio di S. Giovanni Crisostomo
Campo San Bartolomeo
Saliz Pio X
C dei Stagneri
SAN MARCO
Marzaria
Via 2 Aprile
C Larga Mazzini
Rio Tera d Pister
C Bembo
C del Oca
Campo Santa Sofia
Campo dei SS Apostoli
Corte Leoni Bianco
Campiello del Remer
Rialto-Mercato
Campo Cordaria
Campo San Giacomo di Rialto
Ruga dei Oreci
Rialto
C Bembo
C d Ca' d'Oro
Ca' d'Oro
Ca' d'Oro Traghetto
R dei Mori
Ruga Vecchia
C dei Cinque
C Sturion
C d Paradiso
Riva del Carbon
C del Forno
Fond de r'Oglio
C del'Angelo
C dei Botteri
C Raspi
C del Mori
Campo delle Beccarie
Ponte Raspi
Campiello Sansoni
Campo S Silvestro
C Oliera
San Silvestro
C Miani
Campo San Cassiano
C d Mori
C del Mutu
C dei Botteri
Riva
Campo Sant'Aponal
C dei Meloni
C Corner
C della Rosa
C d Regina
Rio di San Cassiano
RioTera delle Tette
RioTera delle Carampane
Ponte Storte
Campo Sant'Aponal
C della Madoneta
C del Traghetto della Madoneta
C Mocenigo
C del Tiozzi
C del Rajano
Fond Rimpetto
C d Chiesa
Ponte delle Tette
Antiche Carampane
C Albrizzi
Campiello Albrizzi
C dei Cavalli
SAN POLO
C dei Meloni
Saliz Carmini
Saliz di San Stae
C del Forno
C d Modena
Rio della Pietà
C Lunga
C Filosi
Campo Santa Maria Mater Domini
Campo Sant'Agostin
C dei Scaleter
Cristo
C del
Campo San Polo
C Pezzana
Osteria La Zucca
C del Megio
C Tentor
C Colombo
C Zambelli
C Larga
Rio Tera dell'Isola
C dell'Isola
Al Prosecco
C di Ruga Vecchia
SANTA CROCE
C del Tentor
Campo Sant'Agostin
Campiello Sant'Agostin
C d Albanesi
C della Vida
C Dona
Oltre Il Giardino
Campiello Rio Tera Zen
C Rio Tera
C Mora
Rio Tera S Polo
Saliz S Polo
C de Saoneri
Fond Contarini
Rio dei Frari
C Larga
Fond de le Grue
Ruga di San Stae

CICHETI

Venice's answer to tapas, *cicheti* are served at lunch and from around 6pm to 8pm with sensational Veneto wines by the glass. They range from basic bar snacks (spicy meatballs, fresh tomato and basil bruschetta) to highly inventive small plates: think white Bassano asparagus and plump lagoon shrimp wrapped in pancetta, pungent gorgonzola paired with spicy peperoncino (chilli) jam, wild boar salami, or fragrant, bite-sized bread rolls crammed with tuna, chicory and horseradish.

Prices start at €1 for meatballs and range from €3 to €6 for gourmet offerings, typically devoured standing up or perched atop stools at the bar.

restricted, but you will get to hear the music, watch the orchestra, soak up the atmosphere and people-watch.

ℹ️ Information

Marco Polo Airport Tourist Office (☑ 041 24 24; www.veneziaunica.it; Arrivals Hall, Marco Polo Airport; ⊙ 8.30am-7pm) Multilingual tourist information at the airport. It can help with information on transport to the city and offers a city map for €3.

Ospedale SS Giovanni e Paolo (☑ 041 529 43 11; www.aulss3.veneto.it; Campo Zanipolo 6777; 🚊 Ospedale) Venice's main hospital; for emergency care.

San Marco Tourist Office (Map p690; ☑ 041 24 24; www.veneziaunica.it; Piazza San Marco 71f; ⊙ 9am-7pm; 🚊 San Marco) Sells tickets for transport, concerts and sights, including the Museum Pass and Tourist City Pass.

Stazione Santa Lucia Tourist Office (Map p687; ☑ 041 24 24; www.veneziaunica.it; ⊙ 7am-9pm; 🚊 Ferrovia) Near platform 2, this office grudgingly dispenses information and sells maps, museum passes and tickets for public transport and concerts.

ℹ️ Getting There & Away

AIR

Most flights arrive at and depart from **Marco Polo Airport** (☑ flight information 041 260 92 60; www.veniceairport.it; Via Galileo Gallilei 30/1, Tessera), 12km outside Venice.

Ryanair flies to/from **Treviso Airport** (☑ 0422 31 51 11; www.trevisoairport.it; Via Noalese 63), about 30km away.

BOAT

Anek (☑ 041 528 65 22; www.anekitalia.com; Via Dell 'Elettronica, Fusina) runs regular ferries between Venice and Greece, and **Venezia Lines** (☑ 041 847 09 03; www.venezialines.com; ⊙ 9am-5pm daily May-Sep, Mon-Fri Oct-Apr; 🚊 San Basilio) runs high-speed boats to/from Croatia in summer.

BUS

ACTV (Azienda del Consorzio Trasporti Veneziano; ☑ 041 272 2111; http://actv.avmspa.it/en) buses service surrounding areas. Get tickets and information at the **bus station** (Piazzale Roma).

TRAIN

Regular trains serve Venice's **Stazione di Santa Lucia** from Padua (€4.25 to €18, 25 minutes) and Verona (€9 to €27, 50 minutes to 2¼ hours) as well as Bologna, Milan, Rome and Florence.

ℹ️ Getting Around

TO/FROM THE AIRPORT
Marco Polo Airport

Alilaguna (☑ 041 240 17 01; www.alilaguna.it; airport transfer one-way €15) operates four water shuttles that link the airport with various parts of Venice at a cost of €8 to Murano and €15 to all other landing stages. It takes approximately 1¼ hours to reach Piazza San Marco. Lines include the following:

Linea Blu (Blue Line) Stops at Lido, San Marco, Cruise Terminal and points in between.

Linea Rossa (Red Line) Serves Murano, Lido, San Marco and Giudecca.

Linea Arancia (Orange Line) Arrives at Santa Maria del Giglio via Rialto and the Grand Canal.

An **ATVO** (Map p687; ☑ 0421 59 46 71; www.atvo.it; Piazzale Roma 497g; ⊙ 6.40am-7.30pm; 🚊 Piazzale Roma) shuttle bus goes to/from Piazzale Roma (one way/return €8/15, 25 minutes, half-hourly), as does ACTV bus 5 (one way/return €8/15, 25 minutes, every 15 minutes).

Treviso Airport

ATVO buses run to/from Piazzale Roma (one way/return €12/22, 70 minutes, at least 13 daily).

BOAT

The city's main mode of public transport is the *vaporetto* (water bus).

Tickets, available from booths at major landing stations and on Piazzale Roma, cost €7.50 for a single trip. Passes are available for 24/48/72 hours at €20/30/40.

Useful routes:

1 Piazzale Roma to the train station and down the Grand Canal to San Marco and the Lido.

2 San Marco to Piazzale Roma and the train station, then along the Grand Canal to Rialto and the Lido.

4.1 Joins Murano to Fondamente Nove, then circles the perimeter of Venice.

Bologna

POP 388,400

Bologna is one of Italy's great unsung destinations. Its medieval centre is an eye-catching ensemble of red-brick *palazzi*, Renaissance towers and 40km of arcaded porticoes, and there are enough sights to excite without exhausting. A university town since 1088 (Europe's oldest), it's also a prime foodie destination, home to the eponymous bolognese sauce *(ragù)* as well as *tortellini*, lasagne and *mortadella* (Bologna sausage).

Sights

★ Basilica di San Petronio   CHURCH

(☑ 051 648 06 11; www.basilicadisanpetronio.org; Piazza Maggiore; photo pass €2; ☺ 7.45am-1.30pm & 3-6.30pm Mon-Fri, 7.45am-6.30pm Sat & Sun) Bologna's hulking Gothic basilica is Europe's sixth-largest church, measuring 132m by 66m by 47m. Work began on it in 1390, but it was never finished and still today its main facade remains incomplete. Inside, look for the huge sundial that stretches 67.7m down the eastern aisle. Designed in 1656 by Gian Cassini and Domenico Guglielmi, this was instrumental in discovering the anomalies of the Julian calendar and led to the creation of the leap year.

Le Due Torri   TOWER

(The Two Towers; Piazza di Porta Ravegnana) Standing sentinel over Piazza di Porta Ravegnana, Bologna's two leaning towers are the city's main symbol. The taller of the two, the 97.2m-high **Torre degli Asinelli** (www.duetorribologna.com; adult/reduced €5/3; ☺ 9.30am-7.30pm Mar-5 Nov, to 5.45pm 6 Nov-Feb) is open to the public, while the neighbouring 47m Torre Garisenda is sensibly out of bounds given its drunken 3.2m tilt.

★ Basilica di Santo Stefano   CHURCH

(www.abbaziassstefano.wixsite.com/abbaziassstefano; Via Santo Stefano 24; ☺ 9.15am-7.15pm Apr-Sep, to 6pm Oct-Mar) Bologna's most compelling religious site is this atmospheric labyrinth of interlocking ecclesiastical structures, whose architecture spans centuries of Bolognese history and incorporates Romanesque, Lombard and even ancient Roman elements. Originally there were seven churches – hence the basilica's nickname Sette Chiese – but only four remain intact today: Chiesa del Crocefisso, Chiesa della Trinità, Chiesa del Santo Sepolcro and Santi Vitale e Agricola.

Sleeping & Eating

★ Bologna nel Cuore   B&B €€

(☑ 329 2193354; www.bolognanelcuore.it; Via Cesare Battisti 29; s €90-120, d €125-145, apt €130-145; P ✳ ☎) This centrally located, immaculate and well-loved B&B features a pair of bright, high-ceilinged rooms with pretty tiled bathrooms and endless mod cons, plus two comfortable, spacious apartments with kitchen and laundry facilities. Owner and art historian Maria generously shares her knowledge of Bologna and serves breakfasts featuring jams made with fruit picked near her childhood home in the Dolomites.

Le Serre dei Giardini Margherita   BAR

(☑ 370 3336439; www.vetro.kilowatt.bo.it; Via Castiglione 134; ☺ 8am-1am Mon-Fri, 9am-1am Sat-Sun Mar-Dec, to 8pm Mon-Wed, to midnight Thu-Sat, 9am-8pm Sun Jan-Feb; ☎) ✿ Bologna's best time: parking yourself down with an Aperol spritz (€4) in hand among the cool kids and digital nomads at these formerly abandoned city greenhouses that have been transformed into an immensely cool and highly recommended co-working space, vegetarian/vegan restaurant (Vetro) and community gardens in the heart of Giardini Margherita, the city's largest green space.

★ All'Osteria Bottega   OSTERIA €€

(☑ 051 58 51 11; Via Santa Caterina 51; meals €36-41; ☺ 12.30-2.30pm & 8-10.30pm Tue-Sat) At Bologna's temple of culinary content, owners Daniele and Valeria lavish attention on every table between trips to the kitchen for astonishing plates of *culatello di Zibello* ham, tortellini in capon broth, Petroniana-style veal cutlets (breaded and fried, then topped with Parma ham and *parmigiano reggiano* and finished in broth), off-menu speciality pigeon and other Slow Food delights.

ℹ Information

Bologna Welcome (Tourist Office; ☑ 051 658 31 11; www.bolognawelcome.it; Piazza Maggiore

THE MOSAICS OF RAVENNA

A rewarding and worthwhile day trip from Bologna, Ravenna is famous for its Early Christian mosaics. These Unesco-listed treasures have been impressing visitors since the 13th century, when Dante described them in his *Divine Comedy* (much of which was written here). They are spread over five sites in the centre: the Basilica di San Vitale, the Mausoleo di Galla Placidia, the Basilica di Sant'Appollinare Nuovo, the Museo Arcivescovile and the Battistero Neoniano. These are covered by a single ticket (five-site combo ticket €9.50), available at any of the sites. The website www.ravennamosaici.it gives further information.

On the northern edge of the *centro storico*, the sombre exterior of the 6th-century **Basilica di San Vitale** (Via San Vitale; ⊘9am-7pm Mar-Oct, 10am-5pm Nov-May) hides a dazzling interior with mosaics depicting Old Testament scenes. In the same complex, the small **Mausoleo di Galla Placidia** (Via San Vitale; 5-site combo ticket €9.50 plus summer-only surcharge €2; ⊘9am-7pm Mar-Oct, 10am-5pm Nov-May) contains the city's oldest mosaics.

Adjoining Ravenna's unremarkable cathedral, the **Museo Arcivescovile** (Piazza Arcivescovado 1; ⊘9am-7pm Mar-Oct, 10am-5pm Nov-May) boasts an exquisite 6th-century ivory throne, while next door in the **Battistero Neoniano** (Piazza del Duomo 1; ⊘9am-7pm Mar-Oct, 10am-5pm Nov-May), the baptism of Christ is represented in the domed roof mosaic.

To the east, the **Basilica di Sant'Apollinare Nuovo** (Via di Roma 52; ⊘9am-7pm Mar-Oct, 10am-5pm Nov-May) boasts, among other things, a superb mosaic depicting a procession of martyrs headed towards Christ and his apostles.

Five kilometres southeast of the city, the apse mosaic of the **Basilica di Sant'-Apollinare in Classe** (Via Romea Sud 224; adult/reduced €5/2.50; ⊘8.30am-7.30pm Mon-Sat, 1-7.30pm Sun) is a must-see. Take bus 4 from the train station.

Regional trains run to/from Bologna (€7.35, 1½ hours, twice hourly) and destinations on the east coast.

1e; ⊘9am-7pm Mon-Sat, 10am-5pm Sun) Bologna's official tourist information hub offers daily, two-hour morning and afternoon walking tours (€15), among other excursions; can help with bookings; puts out a handy daily news and events brochure in English; and sells the **Bologna Welcome Card** (www.bolognawelcome.com/en/richiedicard; Easy/Plus card €25/40) and 24-hour bus passes (€5). Also has an office at the **airport** (Tourist Office; ☑051 647 22 01; www.bolognawelcome.com; Via Triumvirato 84, Guglielmo Marconi Airport; ⊘9am-7.30pm Mon-Sat, to 5pm Sun) and is an affiliate at **FICO Eataly World** (www.bolognawelcome.com; Via Paolo Canali 8, FICO Eataly World; ⊘10am-10pm).

ⓘ Getting There & Around

AIR
European and domestic flights serve **Guglielmo Marconi Airport** (☑051 647 96 15; www.bologna-airport.it; Via Triumvirato 84), 8km northwest of the city.

From the airport, an **Aerobus shuttle** (€6, 20 minutes, every 10 to 30 minutes) connects with the train station.

BUS
Bologna has an efficient bus system, run by **TPER** (☑051 29 02 90; www.tper.it).

Minibus A is the most direct of several buses that connect the bus station with the city centre.

TRAIN
Bologna is a major rail hub. From the station on Piazza delle Medaglie d'Oro, there are regular high-speed trains to Milan (€28.50 to €55, one to 2½ hours), Venice (€12.60 to €34, 1½ to 2½ hours), Florence (€28, 35 minutes) and Rome (€47.50 to €62, two to four hours).

TUSCANY & UMBRIA

Tuscany and its lesser-known neighbour, Umbria, are two of Italy's most beautiful regions. Tuscany's fabled landscape of rolling vine-covered hills dotted with cypress trees and stone villas has long been considered the embodiment of rural chic, while its historical cities and hilltop towns are home to a significant portfolio of the world's medieval and Renaissance art.

To the south, the predominantly rural region of Umbria, dubbed the 'green heart of Italy', harbours some of the country's best-preserved historical *borghi* (villages) and many important artistic, religious and architectural treasures.

Florence

POP 382,300

Visitors have been rhapsodising about Florence (Firenze) for centuries, and still it looms large on Europe's 'must-sees' list. Tourists flock here to feast on world-class art and explore its historical streets, laden with grand palaces, jewel-box churches, trattorias, wine bars and elegant boutiques. Cradle of the Renaissance and home of Machiavelli, Michelangelo and the Medici, it's a magnetic, romantic and brilliantly absorbing place.

⦿ Sights

⦿ Piazza del Duomo

★**Duomo** CATHEDRAL

(Cattedrale di Santa Maria del Fiore; ☑ 055 230 28 85; www.museumflorence.com; Piazza del Duomo; ⊙ 10am-5pm Mon-Wed & Fri, to 4.30pm Thu & Sat, 1.30-4.45pm Sun) FREE Florence's Duomo is the city's most iconic landmark. Capped by Filippo Brunelleschi's red-tiled cupola, it's a staggering construction whose breathtaking pink, white and green marble facade and graceful *campanile* (bell tower) dominate the Renaissance cityscape. Sienese architect Arnolfo di Cambio began work on it in 1296, but construction took almost 150 years and it wasn't consecrated until 1436. In the echoing interior, look out for frescoes by Vasari and Zuccari and up to 44 stained-glass windows.

★**Cupola del Brunelleschi** LANDMARK

(Brunelleschi's Dome; ☑ 055 230 28 85; www. museumflorence.com; Piazza del Duomo; adult/reduced incl baptistry, campanile, crypt & museum €18/3; ⊙ 8.30am-7pm Mon-Fri, to 5pm Sat, 1-4pm Sun) A Renaissance masterpiece, the Duomo's cupola – 91m high and 45.5m wide – was built between 1420 and 1436. Filippo Brunelleschi, taking inspiration from the Pantheon in Rome, designed a distinctive octagonal form of inner and outer concentric domes that rests on the drum of the cathedral rather than the roof itself. Four million bricks were used, laid in consecutive rings according to a vertical herringbone

pattern. Advance time-slot reservations, made online or at the cathedral's Piazza di San Giovanni ticket office, are obligatory.

★**Campanile** TOWER

(Bell Tower; ☑ 055 230 28 85; www.museum florence.com; Piazza del Duomo; adult/reduced incl baptistry, cupola, crypt & museum €18/3; ⊙ 8.15am-7pm) The 414-step climb up the cathedral's 84.7m-tall *campanile*, begun by Giotto in 1334, rewards with staggering city views. The first tier of bas-reliefs around the base of its elaborate Gothic facade are copies of those carved by Pisano depicting the Creation of Man and *attività umane* (arts and industries). The second tier depicts the planets, the cardinal virtues, the arts and the seven sacraments. The sculpted Prophets and Sibyls in the upper-storey niches are copies of works by Donatello and others.

Battistero di San Giovanni LANDMARK

(Baptistry; ☑ 055 230 28 85; www.museumflor ence.com; Piazza di San Giovanni; adult/reduced incl campanile, cupola, crypt & museum €18/3; ⊙ 8.15-10.15am & 11.15am-7.30pm Mon-Fri, 8.15am-6.30pm Sat, 8.15am-1.30pm Sun) This 11th-century baptistry – the oldest religious building on the vast cathedral square – is a Romanesque, octagonal-striped structure of white-and-green marble with three sets of doors conceived as panels illustrating the story of humanity and the Redemption. Most celebrated are Lorenzo Ghiberti's gilded bronze doors at the eastern entrance, the *Porta del Paradiso* (Gate of Paradise). What you see today are copies – the originals are in the Museo dell'Opera del Duomo. Buy tickets online or at the ticket office at Piazza di San Giovanni 7, opposite the main Baptistry entrance.

⦿ Piazza della Signoria & Around

★**Galleria degli Uffizi** GALLERY

(Uffizi Gallery; ☑ 055 29 48 83; www.uffizi.it; Piazzale degli Uffizi 6; adult/reduced Mar-Oct €20/10, Nov-Feb €12/6; ⊙ 8.15am-6.50pm Tue-Sun) Home to the world's greatest collection of Italian Renaissance art, Florence's premier gallery occupies the vast U-shaped Palazzo degli Uffizi (1560-80), built as government offices. The collection, bequeathed to the city by the Medici family in 1743 on condition that it never leave Florence, contains some of Italy's best-known paintings, including a room full of Botticelli masterpieces.

ITALIAN ART & ARCHITECTURE

Italy is littered with architectural and artistic reminders of its convoluted history. Etruscan tombs and Greek temples tell of glories long past, Roman amphitheatres testify to ancient blood lust and architectural brilliance, and Byzantine mosaics reveal influences sweeping in from the East.

The Renaissance left an indelible mark, giving rise to some of Italy's greatest masterpieces: Filippo Brunelleschi's dome atop Florence's Duomo, Botticelli's *The Birth of Venus*, and Michelangelo's Sistine Chapel frescoes. Contemporaries Leonardo da Vinci and Raphael further brightened the scene.

Caravaggio revolutionised the late-16th-century art world with his controversial and highly influential painting style. He worked in Rome and the south, where baroque art and architecture flourished in the 17th century.

In the late 18th and early 19th centuries neoclassicism saw a return to sober classical lines. Its main Italian exponent was sculptor Antonio Canova.

In sharp contrast to backward-looking neoclassicism, early 20th-century futurism sought new ways to express the dynamism of the machine age, while Italian rationalism saw the development of a linear, muscular style of architecture.

Continuing in this modernist tradition are Italy's two contemporary starchitects: Renzo Piano, the visionary behind Rome's Auditorium, and Rome-born Massimiliano Fuksas.

A combined ticket (valid three days) with Palazzo Pitti, Giardino di Boboli and Museo Archeologico is available for €38/21 (€18/11 November to February).

★ Palazzo Vecchio   MUSEUM
(🖉 055 276 85 58; www.musefirenze.it; Piazza della Signoria; adult/reduced museum €12.50/10, tower €12.50/10, museum & tower €17.50/15, museum & archaeological tour €16/13.50, archaeological tour €4, combination ticket €19.50/17.50; ⊙ museum 9am-11pm Fri-Wed, to 2pm Thu summer, 9am-7pm Fri-Wed, to 2pm Thu winter, tower 9am-9pm Fri-Wed, to 2pm Thu summer, 10am-5pm Fri-Wed, to 2pm Thu winter; 🕏) This fortress palace, with its crenellations and 94m-high tower, was designed by Arnolfo di Cambio between 1298 and 1314 for the *signoria* (city government). Today it is home to the mayor's office and the municipal council. From the top of the **Torre d'Arnolfo** (tower), you can revel in unforgettable views. Inside, Michelangelo's *Genio della Vittoria* (Genius of Victory) sculpture graces the Salone dei Cinquecento, a magnificent painted hall created for the city's 15th-century ruling Consiglio dei Cinquecento (Council of 500).

Piazza della Signoria   PIAZZA
(Piazza della Signoria) The hub of local life since the 13th century, Florentines flock here to meet friends and chat over early-evening *aperitivi* at historical cafes. Presiding over everything is Palazzo Vecchio, Florence's city hall, and the 14th-century **Loggia dei Lanzi**, an open-air gallery showcasing Renaissance sculptures, including Giambologna's *Rape of the Sabine Women* (c 1583), Benvenuto Cellini's bronze *Perseus* (1554) and Agnolo Gaddi's *Seven Virtues* (1384–89).

★ Museo del Bargello   MUSEUM
(🖉 055 238 86 06; www.bargellomusei.benicul turali.it; Via del Proconsolo 4; adult/reduced €8/4; ⊙ 8.15am-2pm, closed 2nd & 4th Sun, 1st, 3rd & 5th Mon of month) It was behind the stark walls of Palazzo del Bargello, Florence's earliest public building, that the *podestà* (governing magistrate) meted out justice from the 13th century until 1502. Today the building safeguards Italy's most comprehensive collection of Tuscan Renaissance sculpture, with some of Michelangelo's best early works and several by Donatello. Michelangelo was just 21 when a cardinal commissioned him to create the drunken grape-adorned *Bacchus* (1496–97). Unfortunately the cardinal didn't like the result and sold it.

◉ San Lorenzo

★ Museo delle Cappelle Medicee   MAUSOLEUM
(Medici Chapels; 🖉 055 238 86 02; www.bargel lomusei.beniculturali.it/musei/2/medicee; Piazza Madonna degli Aldobrandini 6; adult/reduced €8/4; ⊙ 8.15am-2pm, closed 2nd & 4th Sun, 1st, 3rd & 5th Mon of month) Nowhere is Medici conceit expressed so explicitly as in the Medici Chapels. Adorned with granite, marble, semi-precious stones and some of Michelangelo's most beautiful sculptures, it is the

Florence

Opera di Firenze (900m)

Via Luigi Alamanni

Via Guelfa

Via Nazionale

Via San Zanobi

Via XXVII Aprile

Via San Gallo

Via degli Alfani

Via B Cennini

Via Faenza

Via Panicale

Via Taddea

Piazza Adua

Via Valfonda

Via Fiume

Via dell'Ariento

Piazza del Mercato Centrale

Borgo la Noce

Via della Stufa

Via de' Ginori

Via Cavour

20

22

Teatro del Maggio Musicale Fiorentino (900m)

ATAF Ticketing Window

Stazione di Santa Maria Novella

Piazza della Stazione

Via Sant'Antonino

Via de' Pucci

Via Ricasoli

Bus Station

Via Santa Caterina da Siena

Piazza dell'Unità Italiana

Museo delle Cappelle Medicee
7

Piazza San Lorenzo

Via de' Martelli

Via degli Avelli

Piazza del Giglio

Piazza Madonna degli Aldobrandini

Borgo San Lorenzo

13

Via dell'Albero

Via della Scala

Via de' Panzani

Via de' Banchi

Via del'Alloro

Cupola del Brunelleschi
2

3

Duomo

Piazza di Santa Maria Novella

Piazza del Cavallari

Piazza di San Giovanni

9

1

Campanile

Piazza del Duomo

Via Palazzuolo

Via della Porcellana

Piazza degli Antinori

Via degli Agli

Via dei Pecori

Piazza del Adimari

18

Via dello Studio

Borgo d'Ognissanti

Via del Moro

Via del Campidoglio

Via Roma

Piazza del Giglio

Via del Corso

Piazza d'Ognissanti

Via de' Fossi

Via della Spada

Via de' Tornabuoni

Via de' Vecchietti

24

Piazza della Repubblica

Via Anselmi

Via Dante Alighieri

21

Piazza de' Cerchi

Piazza Carlo Goldoni

Via della Vigna Nuova

Via del Parione

16

Piazza Santa Trinita

Piazza de' Davanzati

Via Calimala

Piazza di Santa Cecilia

12

Piazza della Signoria

19

14

Via delle Terme

8

Ponte alla Carraia

Lungarno Corsini

Arno

Piazza Saltarelli

10

Palazzo Vecchio

28

26

17

Lungarno Guicciardini

Ponte Santa Trinita

Borgo SS Apostoli

Borgo San Frediano

Piazza N Sauro

Piazza de' Frescobaldi

Lungarno degli Acciaiuoli

Piazzale degli Uffizi

4

Piazza del Grano

Via dell'Ardiglione

Via di Santo Spirito

Via dello Sprone

Borgo San Jacopo

Galleria degli Uffizi

Via de' Serragli

Via Maffia

Via di Sant'Agostino

SANTO SPIRITO

Via dei Velluti

Via Sguazza

Via Guicciardini

27

Piazza dei Rossi

Piazza di Santa Maria Soprarno

Lungarno Generale Diaz

Lungarno Torrigiani

Via de' Bardi

Piazza Santo Spirito

Sdrucciolo de' Pitti

Piazza Santa Felicità

Costa di San Giorgio

Costa Scarpuccia

Via delle Caldaie

Via Mazzetta

15

Via Maggio

Piazza dei Pitti

Via Romana

Via della Meridiana

11

Florence

burial place of 49 dynastic members. Francesco I lies in the dark, imposing **Cappella dei Principi** (Chapel of Princes) alongside Ferdinando I and II and Cosimo I, II and III. Lorenzo il Magnifico is buried in the graceful **Sagrestia Nuova** (New Sacristy), which was Michelangelo's first architectural work.

◎ San Marco

★ Galleria dell'Accademia   GALLERY
(📞 055 238 86 09; www.galleriaaccademiafiren ze.beniculturali.it; Via Ricasoli 60; adult/reduced €12/6; ⊙ 8.15am-6.50pm Tue-Sun) A queue marks the door to this gallery, built to house one of the Renaissance's most iconic masterpieces, Michelangelo's *David*. But the world's most famous statue is worth the wait. The subtle detail – the veins in his sinewy arms, the leg muscles, the change in expression as you move around the statue –

BEST OF THE UFFIZI

Cut to the quick of the gallery's collection and start by getting to grips with pre-Renaissance Tuscan art in **Room 2**, home to several shimmering alterpieces by Giotto et al. Then work your way on to **Room 8** and Piero della Francesca's iconic profile portrait of the Duke and Duchess of Urbino. More familiar images await in the **Sala di Botticelli** (Rooms 10 to 14), including the master's great Renaissance masterpiece, *La nascita di Venere* (The Birth of Venus). Continue on to **Room 35** for Leonardo da Vinci's *Annunciazione* (Annunciation; 1472) and **Room 41** for Michelangelo's *Doni tondi* (The Holy Family).

is impressive. Carved from a single block of marble, Michelangelo's most famous work was his most challenging – he didn't choose the marble himself and it was veined.

◉ Oltrarno

Palazzo Pitti　　　　　　　　　MUSEUM
(☎ 055 29 48 83; www.uffizi.it/en/pitti-palace; Piazza dei Pitti; adult/reduced Mar-Oct €16/8, Nov-Feb €10/5, combined ticket with Uffizi Mar-Oct €38, Nov-Feb €18; ☺ 8.15am-6.50pm Tue-Sun) Commissioned by banker Luca Pitti in 1458, this Renaissance palace was later bought by the Medici family. Over the centuries, it was a residence of the city's rulers until the Savoys donated it to the state in 1919. Nowadays it houses an impressive collection of silver and jewellery, a couple of art museums and a series of rooms recreating life in the palace during House of Savoy times. Stop by at sunset when its entire facade is coloured a vibrant pink.

✦✦ Festivals & Events

Scoppio del Carro　　　　　　　FIREWORKS
(☺ Mar/Apr) A cart of fireworks is exploded in front of the cathedral on Piazza del Duomo at 11am on Easter Sunday.

Maggio Musicale Fiorentino PERFORMING ARTS
(www.maggiofiorentino.com; ☺ Apr-Jun) Italy's oldest arts festival features world-class performances of theatre, classical music, jazz, opera and dance. Events are staged at the **Teatro del Maggio Musicale Fiorentino** (☎ 055 200 12 78; Piazzale Vittorio Gui 1; ☺ box office 10am-6pm Mon-Sat).

Festa di San Giovanni　　　　　RELIGIOUS
(☺ 24 Jun) Florence celebrates its patron saint, John, with a *calcio storico* (historical football) match on Piazza di Santa Croce and fireworks over Piazzale Michelangelo.

🛏 Sleeping

★ Academy Hostel　　　　　　　HOSTEL €
(☎ 055 239 86 65; www.academyhostel.eu; Via Ricasoli 9; dm €30-45, d €70-90; ❄ @ 🛜) This classy hostel – definitely not a party hostel – sits on the 1st floor of Baron Ricasoli's 17th-century *palazzo*. The inviting lobby, with books to browse, was once a theatre and is a comfy spot to chill on the sofa over TV or a DVD. Dorms sport four, five or six beds, high moulded ceilings and brightly coloured lockers.

Hotel Scoti　　　　　　　　　　PENSION €
(☎ 055 29 21 28; www.hotelscoti.com; Via de' Tornabuoni 7; d/tr €140/165; 🛜) Wedged between designer boutiques on Florence's smartest shopping strip, this hidden *pensione* is a fabulous mix of old-fashioned charm and value for money. Its traditionally styled rooms are spread across the 2nd floor of a 16th-century *palazzo;* some have lovely rooftop views. Guests can borrow hairdryers, bottle openers etc, and the frescoed lounge (1780) is stunning.

★ Hotel Palazzo Guadagni　　HOTEL €€
(☎ 055 265 83 76; www.palazzoguadagni.com; Piazza Santo Spirito 9; d/tr/q €250/270/310; ❄ 🛜) This romantic midrange hotel overlooking Florence's liveliest summertime square is legendary – Zeffirelli shot scenes from *Tea with Mussolini* here. Housed in an artfully revamped Renaissance palace, it has 15 spacious rooms with old-world high ceilings and the occasional fresco or fireplace (decorative today). In summer bartenders serve cocktails on the impossibly romantic loggia terrace with wicker chairs and predictably dreamy views.

**Antica Torre di
Via de' Tornabuoni 1**　　BOUTIQUE HOTEL €€€
(☎ 055 265 81 61; www.tornabuoni1.com; Via de' Tornabuoni 1; d €355; 🛜) Footsteps from the Arno, inside beautiful 13th- to 19th-century Palazzo Gianfigliazzi, is this understated luxury hotel. Rooms are spacious and contemporary, but it's the stunning 6th-floor rooftop terrace that steals the show: lounge in the winter garden here, bask on the sun

terrace, drink at the bar and swoon over Florence graciously laid out at your feet.

✖ Eating

Mercato Centrale
FOOD HALL €

(☑ 055 239 97 98; www.mercatocentrale.it; Piazza del Mercato Centrale 4; dishes €5-15; ☺ market 7am-3pm Mon-Fri, to 5pm Sat, food hall 8am-midnight; ☎) Wander the maze of stalls rammed with fresh produce at Florence's oldest and largest food market, on the ground floor of an iron-and-glass structure designed by architect Giuseppe Mengoni in 1874. Head to the 1st floor's buzzing, thoroughly contemporary food hall with dedicated cookery school and artisan stalls cooking steaks, burgers, tripe *panini*, vegetarian dishes, pizza, gelato, pastries and pasta.

★ Trattoria Mario
TUSCAN €

(☑ 055 21 85 50; www.trattoria-mario.com; Via Rosina 2; meals €25; ☺ noon-3.30pm Mon-Sat, closed 3 weeks Aug) Arrive by noon to ensure a spot at this noisy, busy, brilliant trattoria – a legend that retains its soul (and allure with locals) despite being in every guidebook. Charming Fabio, whose grandfather opened the place in 1953, is front of house while big brother Romeo and nephew Francesco cook with speed in the kitchen. No advance reservations; cash only.

★ Osteria Il Buongustai
OSTERIA €

(☑ 055 29 13 04; www.facebook.com/ibuongustaifirenze; Via dei Cerchi 15r; meals €15-20; ☺ 9.30am-3.30pm Mon-Sat) Run with breathtaking speed and grace by Laura and Lucia, 'The Gourmand' is unmissable. Lunchtimes heave with locals and savvy students who flock here to fill up on tasty Tuscan home cooking at a snip of other restaurant prices. The place is brilliantly no-frills – watch women in hair caps at work in the kitchen, share a table and pay in cash.

Mariano
SANDWICHES €

(☑ 055 21 40 67; Via del Parione 19r; panini €3.50-6; ☺ 8am-3pm & 5-7.30pm Mon-Fri, 8am-3pm Sat) A local favourite for its simplicity and correct prices, it's been around since 1973. From sunrise to sunset, this brick-vaulted, 13th-century cellar gently buzzes with Florentines propped at the counter sipping coffee or wine or eating salads and *panini*. Come here for a coffee-and-pastry breakfast, light lunch, an *aperitivo* with cheese or salami tasting platter (€13 to €17), or a *panino* to eat on the move.

★ Il Teatro del Sale
TUSCAN €€

(☑ 055 200 14 92; www.teatrodelsale.com; Via dei Macci 111r; brunch/dinner €20/30; ☺ noon-2.30pm & 7-11pm Tue-Fri, noon-3pm & 7-11pm Sat, noon-3pm Sun, closed Aug) Florentine chef Fabio Picchi is one of Florence's living treasures who steals the Sant' Ambrogio show with this eccentric, good-value, members-only club (everyone welcome; membership €7) inside an old theatre. He cooks up brunch and dinner, culminating at 9.30pm in a live performance of drama, music or comedy arranged by his wife, artistic director and comic actress Maria Cassi.

Trattoria Cibrèo
TUSCAN €€

(www.cibreo.com; Via dei Macci 122r; meals €30-35; ☺ 12.50-2.30pm & 6.50-11pm, closed Aug) Dine at chez Fabio Picchi and you'll instantly understand why a queue gathers outside before it opens. Once inside, revel in top-notch Tuscan cuisine: perhaps *pappa al pomodoro* (a thick soupy mash of tomato, bread and basil) followed by *polpettine di pollo e ricotta* (chicken and ricotta meatballs). No reservations, no credit cards, no pasta and arrive early.

☕ Drinking & Nightlife

★ Le Volpi e l'Uva
WINE BAR

(☑ 055 239 81 32; www.levolpieluva.com; Piazza dei Rossi 1; ☺ 11am-9pm summer, 11am-9pm Mon-Sat winter) This humble wine bar remains as appealing as the day it opened over a decade ago. Its food and wine pairings are first class – taste and buy boutique wines by small Italian producers, matched perfectly with cheeses, cold meats and the finest crostini in town; the warm, melt-in-your-mouth *lardo di Cinta Sienese* (wafer-thin slices of aromatic of pork fat) is absolutely extraordinary.

ITALY FLORENCE

❶ CUT THE QUEUES

➡ Book tickets for the Uffizi and Galleria dell'Accademia, as well as several other museums, through **Firenze Musei** (Florence Museums; www.firenzemusei.it). Note that this entails a booking fee of €3 per museum (€4 for the Uffizi and Galleria dell'Accademia).

➡ Alternatively, the **Firenze Card** (€85, valid for 72 hours) allows you to bypass both advance booking and queues. Check details at www.firenzecard.it.

★ Mad Souls & Spirits
COCKTAIL BAR

(☑ 055 627 16 21; www.facebook.com/madsoul sandspirits; Borgo San Frediano 38r; ⊙ 6pm-2am; 🖥) At this uber-cool bar in San Frediano, cult alchemists Neri Fantechi and Julian Biondi woo a discerning crowd with their expertly crafted cocktails, served in a tiny aqua-green and red-brick space that couldn't be more spartan. A potted cactus decorates each scrubbed wood table and the humorous cocktail menu is the height of irreverence.

Check the 'Daily Madness' blackboard for specials.

★ Ditta Artigianale
CAFE

(☑ 055 274 15 41; www.dittaartigianale.it; Via de' Neri 32r; ⊙ 8am-10pm Mon-Thu, to midnight Fri, 9am-midnight Sat, to 11pm Sun; 🖥) With industrial decor and laid-back vibe, this ingenious coffee roastery is a perfect place to hang at any time of day. The creation of three-times Italian barista champion Francesco Sanapo, it's famed for its first-class coffee and outstanding gin cocktails. If you're yearning a flat white, cold brew tonic or cappuccino made with almond milk, come here.

La Cité
BAR

(www.facebook.com/lacitelibreriacafe; Borgo San Frediano 20r; ⊙ 10am-2am Mon-Sat, from 3pm Sun; 🖥) A hip cafe-bookshop with an eclectic choice of vintage seating, La Cité makes a wonderful, intimate venue for book readings, after-work drinks and fantastic live music – jazz, swing, world music. Check its Facebook page for the week's events.

FLORENCE'S BEST GELATO

Grom (☑ 055 21 61 58; www.grom.it; Via del Campanile 2; cones & tubs €2.60-5.50; ⊙ 10am-midnight Sun-Fri, to 1am Sat summer, 10.30am-10.30pm winter) Top-notch gelato, including outstanding chocolate, near the Duomo.

Vivoli (☑ 055 29 23 34; www.vivoli.it; Via dell'Isola delle Stinche 7; tubs €2-10; ⊙ 7.30am-midnight Tue-Sat, from 9am Sun, to 9pm winter) Vintage classic for coffee and cakes as well as gelato.

Gelateria La Carraia (☑ 055 28 06 95; www.lacarraiagroup.eu; Piazza Nazario Sauro 25r; cones & tubs €1.50-6; ⊙ 11am-midnight) Florentine favourite on the other side of the river.

Caffè Gilli
CAFE

(☑ 055 21 38 96; www.gilli.it; Piazza della Repubblica 39r; ⊙ 7.30am-1am) Popular with locals who sip coffee standing up at the long marble bar, this is the most famous of the historical cafes on the city's old Roman forum. Gilli has been serving delectable cakes, chocolates, fruit tartlets and *millefoglie* (lighter-than-light vanilla or custard slice) since 1733. It moved to this square in 1910 and has a beautifully preserved art nouveau interior.

ℹ Information

24-Hour Pharmacy (☑ 055 21 67 61; Stazione di Santa Maria Novella; ⊙ 24hr) All-hours pharmacy inside Florence's central train station; at least one member of staff usually speaks English.

Dr Stephen Kerr: Medical Service (☑ 335 8361682, 055 28 80 55; www.dr-kerr.com; Piazza Mercato Nuovo 1; ⊙ 3-5pm Mon-Fri, or by appointment 9am-3pm Mon-Fri) Resident British doctor.

Tourist Office (☑ 055 29 08 32; www.firenze turismo.it; Via Cavour 1r; ⊙ 9am-1pm Mon-Fri) Tourist office in the historical centre.

Tourist Office (☑ 055 21 22 45; www.firenze turismo.it; Piazza della Stazione 4; ⊙ 9am-7pm Mon-Sat, to 2pm Sun) Tourist office just across the street from Florence's central train station.

ℹ Getting There & Away

AIR

Florence airport (Aeroporto Amerigo Vespucci; ☑ 055 306 18 30, 055 3 06 15; www.aeroporto. firenze.it; Via del Termine 11) is 5km northwest of the city centre.

Pisa International Airport (p703) in Pisa, 80km west of Florence, serves flights to Italian destinations and major European cities.

BUS

Services from the **bus station** (Autostazione Busitalia-Sita Nord; ☑ 800 373760; www. fsbusitalia.it; Via Santa Caterina da Siena 17r; ⊙ 5.45am-8.40pm Mon-Sat, 6.25am-8.30pm Sun), just west of Piazza della Stazione, are limited; the train is better. Destinations served include Siena (€8.40, 1¼ hours, at least hourly) and Greve in Chianti (€4.50, one hour, hourly).

TRAIN

Florence's **Stazione di Santa Maria Novella** (www.firenzesantamarianovella.it; Piazza della Stazione) is on the main Rome–Milan line. There are regular direct services to/from Pisa (€8.60, 1¼ hours, every 15 minutes), Rome (€22 to €36, 1½ to 3¾ hours, at least twice hourly), Venice (€26 to €43, two hours, at least hourly) and

PISA

A handsome university city, Pisa is best known as the home of an architectural project gone terribly wrong. However, the Leaning Tower is just one of a number of noteworthy sights in its compact medieval centre.

Pisa's golden age came in the 12th and 13th centuries when it was a maritime power to rival Genoa and Venice.

Leaning Tower (Torre Pendente; ☎ 050 83 50 11; www.opapisa.it; Piazza dei Miracoli; €18; ⊗ 8.30am-10pm Jun-Aug, 9am-8pm Apr-May & Sep, to 7pm Oct & Mar, to 6pm Nov-Feb) One of Italy's signature sights, the Torre Pendente truly lives up to its name, leaning a startling 5.5 degrees off the vertical. The 58m-high tower, officially the Duomo's *campanile* (bell tower), took almost 200 years to build, but was already listing when it was unveiled in 1372. Over time, the tilt, caused by a layer of weak subsoil, steadily worsened until it was finally halted by a major stabilisation project in the 1990s.

Duomo (Duomo di Santa Maria Assunta; ☎ 050 83 50 11; www.opapisa.it; Piazza dei Miracoli; ⊗ 10am-8pm Apr-Sep, to 7pm Oct & Mar, to 6pm Nov-Feb) Pisa's magnificent Romanesque Duomo was begun in 1064 and consecrated in 1118. Its striking tiered exterior, with cladding of green-and-cream marble bands, conceals a vast columned interior capped by a gold wooden ceiling. The elliptical dome, the first of its kind in Europe at the time, was added in 1380.

Admission is free but you need a ticket from another Piazza dei Miracoli sight to get in or a fixed-timed free pass issued by **ticket offices** (⊗ 8am-7.30pm summer, to 5.30pm winter) behind the Leaning Tower or inside **Museo delle Sinopie** (€5, combination ticket with Battistero & Camposanto €8; ⊗ 8am-8pm Apr-Sep, 9am-7pm Oct & Mar, to 6pm Nov-Feb).

Battistero (Battistero di San Giovanni; ☎ 050 83 50 11; www.opapisa.it; Piazza dei Miracoli; €5, with Camposanto & Museo €8; ⊗ 8am-8pm Apr-Sep, 9am-7pm Oct & Mar, to 6pm Nov-Feb) Pisa's unusual round baptistery has one dome piled on top of another, each roofed half in lead, half in tiles, and topped by a gilt bronze John the Baptist (1395). Construction began in 1152, but it was remodelled and continued by Nicola and Giovanni Pisano more than a century later and finally completed in the 14th century. Inside, the hexagonal marble pulpit (1260) by Nicola Pisano is the highlight.

Ristorante Galileo (☎ 050 2 82 87; www.ristorantegalileo.com; Via San Martino 6-8; meals €25-35; ⊗ 12.30-3pm & 7.30-10.30pm) For good, honest, unpretentious Tuscan cooking, nothing beats this classical old-timer. From the cork-covered wine list to the complimentary plate of warm homemade focaccia and huge platters of tempting *cantuccini* (almond-studded biscuits), Galileo makes you feel welcome. Fresh pasta is strictly hand- and homemade, and most veggies are plucked fresh that morning from the restaurant's garden.

Pisa International Airport (Galileo Galilei Airport; ☎ 050 84 93 00; www.pisa-airport. com) is linked to the city centre by the **PisaMover** (www.pisa-mover.com) shuttle, which runs to Pisa Centrale train station (€2.70, five minutes, every seven to 15 minutes from 4.30am to 1.30am).

Frequent trains run to Lucca (€3.60, 30 minutes, half-hourly), Florence (€8.60, 1¼ hours, every 15 minutes) and La Spezia (€7.80 to €15.50, one to 1½ hours, half-hourly) for the Cinque Terre.

Milan (€37 to €46, 1¾ hours to four hours, at least hourly).

Getting Around

TO/FROM THE AIRPORT

Volainbus (☎ 800 373760; www.fsbusitalia.it) The Volainbus shuttle runs between Florence airport and the bus station on Via Santa Caterina da Siena, across from the train station. Going to the airport, departures are roughly half-hourly between 5am and 8.30pm and then hourly until 12.10am; from the airport between 5.30am and 8.30pm then hourly until 12.30am. Journey time is 20 to 30 minutes and a single/return ticket costs €6/10; drivers sell tickets.

PUBLIC TRANSPORT

City buses are operated by ATAF. Tickets are valid for 90 minutes (no return journeys), cost €1.50 (€2.50 on board) and are sold at the **ATAF ticketing window** (☑ 800 424500; www.ataf. net; Stazione di Santa Maria Novella, Piazza della Stazione; ☉ 6.45am-8pm) at Santa Maria Novella train station, at tobacconists and at kiosks.

Lucca

POP 88,400

Lucca is a love-at-first-sight type of place. Hidden behind monumental Renaissance walls, its historical centre is chock-full of handsome churches, alluring piazzas and excellent restaurants. Founded by the Etruscans, it became a city state in the 12th century and stayed that way for 600 years. Most of its streets and monuments date from this period.

◉ Sights

★ City Wall WALLS

Lucca's monumental *mura* (wall) was built around the old city in the 16th and 17th centuries and remains in almost perfect condition. It superseded two previous walls, the first built from travertine stone blocks in the 2nd century BCE. Twelve metres high and 4.2km long, today's ramparts are crowned with a tree-lined footpath looking down on the historical centre and – by the **Baluardo San Regolo** (San Regolo Bastion) – the city's vintage **Orto Botanico** (Botanical Garden; ☑ 0583 58 30 86; www.lemuradilucca.it/orto -botanico; Casermetta San Regolo; adult/reduced €4/3; ☉ 10am-7pm Jul-Sep, to 6pm May & Jun, to 5pm Mar, Apr & Oct) with its magnificent cedar trees.

★ Cattedrale di San Martino CATHEDRAL

(☑ 0583 49 05 30; www.museocattedralelucca.it; Piazza San Martino; €3, incl campanile, Museo della Cattedrale & Chiesa e Battistero dei SS Giovanni & Reparata adult/reduced €9/6; ☉ 9.30am-6pm Mon-Fri, to 6.45pm Sat, noon-6pm Sun summer, shorter hours winter) Lucca's predominantly Romanesque cathedral dates from the 11th century. Its stunning facade was constructed in the prevailing Lucca-Pisan style and designed to accommodate the pre-existing *campanile* (bell tower). The reliefs over the left doorway of the portico are believed to be by Nicola Pisano, while inside, treasures include the **Volto Santo** (literally, Holy Countenance) crucifix sculpture and a wonderful 15th-century tomb in the **sacristy**. The cathedral interior was rebuilt in the 14th and 15th centuries with a Gothic flourish.

🛏 Sleeping & Eating

Piccolo Hotel Puccini HOTEL €

(☑ 0583 5 54 21; www.hotelpuccini.com; Via di Poggio 9; s/d €75/100; 🕸 🗟) In a brilliant central location, this welcoming three-star hotel hides behind a discreet brick exterior. Its small guest rooms are attractive with wooden floors, vintage ceiling fans and colourful, contemporary design touches. Breakfast, optional at €3.50, is served at candlelit tables behind the small reception area. Rates are at least 30% lower in winter.

Da Felice PIZZA €

(☑ 0583 49 49 86; www.pizzeriadafelice.it; Via Buia 12; focaccia €1-4, pizza slices €1.40; ☉ 10am-8.30pm Mon-Sat) This buzzing spot behind Piazza San Michele is where the locals come for wood-fired pizza, *cecina* (salted chickpea pizza) and *castagnacci* (chestnut cakes). Eat in or take away, *castagnacci* come wrapped in crisp white paper, and, my, they're good married with a chilled bottle of Moretti beer.

★ Ristorante Giglio TUSCAN €€

(☑ 0583 49 40 58; www.ristorantegiglio.com; Piazza del Giglio 2; meals €40-50; ☉ 12.15-2.45pm & 7.30-10.30pm Thu-Mon, 7.30-10.30pm Wed) Splendidly at home in the frescoed 18th-century Palazzo Arnolfini, Giglio is stunning. Sip a complimentary *prosecco*, watch the fire crackle in the marble fireplace and savour traditional Tuscan with a modern twist: think fresh artichoke salad served in an edible parmesan-cheese wafer 'bowl', or risotto simmered in Chianti. End with Lucchese *buccellato* (sweet bread) filled with ice cream and berries.

ℹ Information

Tourist Office (☑ 0583 58 31 50; www.turismo. lucca.it; Piazzale Verdi; ☉ 9am-6.30pm) Offers free hotel reservations, left-luggage service (two bags €1.50/3 per hour/half-day) and two-hour guided city tours in English (€10 per person, under 15 years free) departing at 2pm daily, April to October, and on Saturdays and Sundays the rest of the year.

ℹ Getting There & Away

Regional trains run to/from Florence (€7.80 to €9.90, 1¾ hours) via Pisa (€3.60, 30 minutes, half-hourly).

Siena

POP 53,800

Siena is one of Italy's most enchanting medieval towns. Its walled centre is a beautifully preserved warren of dark lanes punctuated with Gothic *palazzi,* and at its heart is Piazza del Campo (Il Campo), the sloping square that is the venue for the city's famous annual horse race, Il Palio.

In the Middle Ages, the city was a political and artistic force to be reckoned with, a worthy rival for its larger neighbour Florence.

⊙ Sights

★ Piazza del Campo
PIAZZA

Popularly known as 'Il Campo', this sloping piazza has been Siena's social centre since being staked out by the ruling Consiglio dei Nove (Council of Nine) in the mid-12th century. Built on the site of a Roman marketplace, its paving is divided into nine sectors representing the number of members of the *consiglio* and these days acts as a carpet on which young locals meet and relax. The cafes around its perimeter are the most popular coffee and *aperitivi* spots in town.

Palazzo Pubblico
HISTORIC BUILDING

(Palazzo Comunale; Piazza del Campo) Built to demonstrate the enormous wealth, proud independence and secular nature of Siena, this 14th-century Gothic masterpiece is the visual focal point of the Campo, itself the true heart of the city. Architecturally clever (notice how its concave facade mirrors the opposing convex curve) it has always housed the city's administration and been used as a cultural venue. Its distinctive bell tower, the **Torre del Mangia** (✐ 0577 29 26 15; www.enjoysiena.it/it/attrattore/Torre-del-Mangia; €10; ⊙ 10am-6.15pm summer, to 3.15pm winter), provides magnificent views to those who brave the steep climb to the top.

★ Museo Civico
MUSEUM

(Civic Museum; ✐ 0577 29 26 15; www.enjoysiena.it/it/attrattore/Museo-Civico; Palazzo Pubblico, Piazza del Campo 1; adult/reduced €9/8; ⊙ 10am-6.15pm summer, to 5.15pm winter) Entered via the Palazzo Pubblico's **Cortile del Podestà** (Courtyard of the Podestà), this wonderful museum showcases rooms richly frescoed by artists of the Sienese school. Commissioned by the city's governing body rather than by the Church, some of the frescoes depict secular subjects – highly unusual at the time. The highlights are two huge frescoes: Ambrogio Lorenzetti's *Allegories of Good and Bad Government* (c 1338–40) and Simone Martini's celebrated *Maestà* (*Virgin Mary in Majesty;* 1315).

★ Duomo
CATHEDRAL

(Cattedrale di Santa Maria Assunta; ✐ 0577 28 63 00; www.operaduomo.siena.it; Piazza Duomo; summer/winter €5/free, when floor displayed €8; ⊙ 10.30am-7pm Mon-Sat, 1.30-6pm Sun summer, to 5.30pm winter) Consecrated on the former site of a Roman temple in 1179 and constructed over the 13th and 14th centuries, Siena's majestic *duomo* (cathedral) showcases the talents of many great medieval and Renaissance architects and artists: Giovanni Pisano designed the intricate white, green and red marble facade; Nicola Pisano carved the elaborate pulpit; Pinturicchio painted the frescoes in the extraordinary **Libreria Piccolomini** (Piccolomini Library; ✐ 0577 28 63 00; summer/winter free/€2; ⊙ 10.30am-7pm summer, to 5.30pm winter); and Michelangelo, Donatello and Gian Lorenzo Bernini all produced sculptures.

★ Museale Santa Maria della Scala
MUSEUM

(✐ 0577 28 63 00; www.santamariadellascala.com; Piazza Duomo 2; adult/reduced €9/7; ⊙ 10am-7pm Fri-Wed, to 10pm Thu summer, shorter hours winter) Built as a hospice for pilgrims travelling the Via Francigena, this huge complex opposite the Duomo dates from the 13th century. Its highlight is the upstairs **Pellegrinaio** (Pilgrim's Hall), featuring vivid 15th-century frescoes by Lorenzo di Pietro (aka Vecchietta), Priamo della Quercia and Domenico di Bartolo. All laud the good works of the hospital and its patrons; the most evocative is di Bartolo's *Il governo degli infermi* (Caring for the Sick; 1440–41), which depicts many activities that occurred here.

✯ Festivals & Events

Palio
PARADE

(Piazza del Campo; ⊙ 2 Jul & 16 Aug) Dating from the Middle Ages, this spectacular annual event includes a series of colourful pageants and a wild horse race in Piazza del Campo. Ten of Siena's 17 *contrade* (town districts) compete for the coveted *palio* (silk banner). Each *contrada* has its own traditions, symbol and colours, plus its own church and *palio* museum.

🛏 Sleeping & Eating

Hotel Alma Domus
HOTEL €

(📞0577 4 41 77; www.hotelalmadomus.it; Via Camporegio 37; s €46-55, d €83-140; ✳@🛜) Your chance to sleep in a convent: Alma Domus is owned by the church and is still home to several Dominican nuns. The economy rooms, although comfortable, are styled very simply and aren't as soundproofed as many would like. But the superior ones are lovely, with a stylish decor and modern fittings; many have mini-balconies with uninterrupted Duomo views.

★ Pensione Palazzo Ravizza
BOUTIQUE HOTEL €€€

(📞0577 28 04 62; www.palazzoravizza.it; Pian dei Mantellini 34; r €110-320; 🅿✳🛜) Occupying a Renaissance-era *palazzo* in a quiet but convenient corner of Siena, this gorgeous hotel offers rooms perfectly melding heritage features and modern amenities; the best face the large rear garden, which has a panoramic terrace. The breakfast buffet is generous, on-site parking is free and room rates are remarkably reasonable (especially in the low season).

Morbidi
DELI €

(📞0577 28 02 68; www.morbidi.com; Via Banchi di Sopra 75; lunch €12, aperitivo buffet from €8; ⏰8am-8pm Mon-Wed, to 9pm Thu & Fri, to 3pm Sat) A classy deli famed for its top-quality produce, Morbidi's excellent-value basement lunch buffet (€12; 12.15pm to 2.30pm Monday to Saturday) allows you to choose from freshly prepared antipasti, salads, risotto, pasta and dessert. Bottled water is supplied; wine and coffee cost extra. Buy your ticket upstairs before heading down. It also offers regular *aperitivo* buffets on Thursday and Friday evenings.

Enoteca I Terzi
TUSCAN €€

(📞0577 4 43 29; www.enotecaiterzi.it; Via dei Termini 7; meals €35-40; ⏰12.30-3pm & 7.30-11pm Mon-Sat) Close to the Campo but off the well-beaten tourist trail, this *enoteca* (wine bar) is located in a vaulted medieval building but has a contemporary feel. It's popular with sophisticated locals, who linger over working lunches, *aperitivi* sessions and slow-paced dinners featuring Tuscan *salumi* (cured meats), delicate handmade pasta, grilled meats and wonderful wines (many available by the glass).

ℹ Information

Tourist Office (📞0577 28 05 51; www.enjoysiena.it; Piazza Duomo 2, Santa Maria della Scala; ⏰9am-6pm summer, to 5pm winter) Siena's tourist information office is in the Museale Santa Maria della Scala, and can provide free maps of the city. The entrance is on the right (western) side of the museum building.

ℹ Getting There & Away

Buses run by **Tiemme** (📞800 922984; www.tiemmespa.it) link Siena with Florence (€8.40, 1¼ hours, at least hourly) and San Gimignano (€6.20, 1¼ hours, up to 17 daily), either direct or via Poggibonsi.

WORTH A TRIP

ORVIETO

Strategically located on the main train line between Rome and Florence, this spectacularly sited hilltop town has one major draw: its extraordinary Gothic **Duomo** (📞0763 34 24 77; www.opsm.it; Piazza Duomo 26; admission €4, incl Museo dell'Opera del Duomo di Orvieto €5; ⏰9.30am-7pm Mon-Sat, 1-5.30pm Sun summer, shorter hrs winter), built over 300 years from 1290. The facade is stunning, and the beautiful interior contains Luca Signorelli's awe-inspiring *Giudizio universale* (The Last Judgment) fresco cycle.

The **tourist office** (📞0763 34 17 72; Piazza Duomo 24; ⏰8.15am-1.50pm & 4-7pm Mon-Fri, 10am-6pm Sat & Sun) is opposite the cathedral; nearby sits **I Sette Consoli** (📞0763 34 39 11; www.isetteconsoli.it; Piazza Sant'Angelo 1a; meals €40-45, tasting menu €45; ⏰12.30-3pm & 7.30-10pm, closed Wed & Sun dinner), one of Umbria's best restaurants – its pasta and risotto are simply sublime. **Bottega Vera** (📞349 4300167; www.casaveraorvieto.it/it/bottega.html; Via del Duomo 36; ⏰8.30am-8.30pm Mon-Fri & Sun, to 10pm Sat; 🛜) is an excellent and non-touristy *enoteca* (wine bar).

Orvieto is a mere one-hour drive from both Montepulciano and Arezzo. Trains run to/from Florence (€16.70 to €25, 2½ hours, hourly) and Rome (€8.15 to €17.50, 1½ hours, hourly). From the train station you'll need to take the **funicular** (tickets €1.30; ⏰every 10min 7.15am-8.30pm Mon-Sat, every 15min 8am-8.30pm Sun) up to the town centre.

ASSISI

The birthplace of St Francis (1182–1226), the medieval town of Assisi is a major destination for millions of pilgrims. The main sight is the Basilica di San Francesco, one of Italy's most visited churches, but the hilltop historical centre is also well worth a look.

Basilica di San Francesco (www.sanfrancescoassisi.org; Piazza di San Francesco; ☻basilica superiore 8.30am-6.50pm, basilica inferiore 6am-6.50pm summer, shorter hours winter) Visible for miles around, the Basilica di San Francesco is the crowning glory of Assisi's Unesco-listed historical centre. The 13th-century complex comprises two churches: the Gothic Basilica Superiore (Upper Church), with its celebrated cycle of Giotto frescoes, and beneath, the older Basilica Inferiore (Lower Church) where you'll find works by Cimabue, Pietro Lorenzetti and Simone Martini. Also here, in the **Cripta di San Francesco**, is St Francis' much-venerated tomb.

Basilica di Santa Chiara (www.assisisantachiara.it; Piazza Santa Chiara; ☻6.30am-noon & 2-7pm summer, to 6pm winter) Built in a 13th-century Romanesque style, with muscular flying buttresses and a striking pink-and-white striped facade, this church is dedicated to St Clare, a spiritual contemporary of St Francis and founder of the *Sorelle Povere di Santa Chiara* (Order of the Poor Ladies), now known as the Poor Clares. She is buried in the church's crypt, alongside the original **Crocifisso di San Damiano**, a Byzantine cross before which St Francis was praying when he is said to have received his mission from God in 1205.

Tourist Office (☑075 813 86 80; www.visit-assisi.it; Piazza del Comune 10; ☻9am-7pm) Stop by here for maps, leaflets and accommodation lists.

Sena (☑0861 199 19 00; www.sena.it) operates services to/from Rome Tiburtina (€15 to €23, three to 3¾ hours, 10 daily), Milan (€24 to €31, 4½ to 8¾ hours, seven daily), Perugia (€11, 1½ hours, one daily) and Venice (€21 to €25, five to 5¾ hours, three daily).

Ticket offices are in the basement under the bus station on Piazza Gramsci.

SOUTHERN ITALY

A sun-bleached land of spectacular coastlines and rugged landscapes, southern Italy is a robust contrast to the more genteel north. Its stunning scenery, baroque towns and classical ruins exist alongside ugly urban sprawl and scruffy coastal development, sometimes in the space of just a few kilometres.

Yet for all its flaws, *il mezzogiorno* (the midday sun, as southern Italy is known) is an essential part of every Italian itinerary, offering charm, culinary good times and architectural treasures.

Naples

POP 966,145

A love-it-or-loathe-it sprawl of regal palaces, bombastic churches and chaotic streets, Na-

ples (Napoli) is totally exhilarating. Founded by Greek colonists, it became a thriving Roman city and was later the Bourbon capital of the Kingdom of the Two Sicilies. In the 18th century it was one of Europe's great cities, something you'll readily believe as you marvel at its art-crammed museums and great baroque buildings.

☻ Sights

★**Museo Archeologico Nazionale** MUSEUM (☑848 800 288; www.museoarcheologiconapoli.it; Piazza Museo Nazionale 19; adult/reduced €15/7.50; ☻9am-7.30pm Wed-Mon; Ⓜ Museo, Piazza Cavour) Naples' National Archaeological Museum serves up one of the world's finest collections of Graeco-Roman artefacts. Originally a cavalry barracks and later the seat of the city's university, the museum was established by the Bourbon king Charles VII in the late 18th century to house the antiquities he inherited from his mother, Elisabetta Farnese, as well as treasures looted from Pompeii and Herculaneum. Star exhibits include the celebrated *Toro Farnese* (Farnese Bull) sculpture and awe-inspiring mosaics from Pompeii's **Casa del Fauno** (House of the Faun).

★**Cappella Sansevero** CHAPEL (☑081 551 84 70; www.museosansevero.it; Via Francesco de Sanctis 19; adult/reduced €7/5;

Central Naples

Museo di Capodimonte (1.9km)

Museo Archeologico Nazionale

2

Via S Guiseppe dei Nudi

5

Via Tommasi

Via Francesco Saverio Correra

Piazza Cavour

Via M Maria Longo

Concettina Ai Tre Santi (650m)

Via Santissimi Apostoli

Museo

Piazza Museo Nazionale

Piazza Cavour

Via Santa Maria di Costantinopoli

Via Broggia

Via della Sapienza

Largo Regina Coeli

Via Pisanelli

Via Anticaglia

Vico Giganti

Via San Paolo

Via Atri

Via del Sole

3

Via Duomo

Via dei Tribunali

Via della Zite

Vico Zuroli

Via Enrico Pessina

Via Bellini

4

Piazza Bellini

Piazza Luigi Miraglia

Piazza San Gaetano

Via dei Tribunali

Vico Giuseppe Maffei

Via Vicaria Vecchia

Via G Brombeis

Vico S Domenico Soriano

Dante

Piazza Dante

Via Port'Alba

Via San Sebastiano

Via Nilo

Cappella Sansevero

1

Palazzo dei Di Sangrio

Piazzetta del Nilo

Via San Biagio dei Librai

Via S Severino

Piazza Museo Filangieri

Via d'Alagno

Via Montesanto

Via Tarsia

Via Pellegrini

Via Benedetto Croce

Via B Capasso

Duomo

Piazza Nicola Amore

Funicolare di Montesanto (170m); Certosa e Museo di San Martino (1.5km)

Piazza del Gesù Nuovo

7

Via Mezzocannone

Via G Paladino

Alibus (Stazione Central Stop) (850m); Metropark Napoli Centrale (1.1km); Circumvesuviana (1.2km); Stazione Centrale (1.2km)

Via Pasquale Scura

Via T Caravita

Via S Anna dei Lombardi

Via Santa Chiara

Largo Giusso

Largo Banchi Nuovi

Piazzetta Orefici

Via A Pignasecca

Via S Liborio

Via Formale

Piazza Carità

Via Donnalbina

Via Sedile di Porto

Corso Umberto I

Via Nuova Marina

Via G Simonelli

Vico P Galluppi

Via C Battisti

Via Monteoliveto

Via D. Cerriglio

Piazza Bovio

Università

Via Concezione a Montecalvario

Toledo

Via A Diaz

Via Bracco

Piazza Matteotti

Via dei Fiorentini

6

Via Graziella

Via A Depretis

Via S Nicola alla Dogana

Via Alside De Gasperi

Tirrenia

Via Potracarese a Montecalvario

Via S Tommaso d'Aquino

Via F Gioia

Via S Bartolomeo

Calata Porta di Massa

Varco Immacolatella

Via Speranzella

Via S Giacomo

Via Toledo

Via P E Imbriani

Piazza del Municipio

Via Medina

Piazza Francese

Via G Melisurgo

Via Cristoforo Colombo

Bacino del Piliero

Via G Verdi

Via Santa Brigida

Vico d'Aflitto

Municipio

Municipio

Molo Angioino

Funicolare Centrale

Via Vittorio Emanuele III

Piazza Trieste e Trento

San Carlo

9

Parco Castello

Via Chiaia

8

Pescheria Mattiucci (760m); L'Antiquario (820m); Pasticceria Mennella (1km)

SNAV

Alilauro

Caremar

Molo Beverello

Via A F Acton

Porto Immacolatella

Da Ettore (170m)

0 400 m
0 0.2 miles

Central Naples

⊙ 9am-7pm Wed-Mon; Ⓜ Dante) It's in this Masonic-inspired baroque chapel that you'll find Giuseppe Sanmartino's incredible sculpture, *Cristo velato* (Veiled Christ), its marble veil so realistic that it's tempting to try to lift it and view Christ underneath. It's one of several artistic wonders that include Francesco Queirolo's sculpture *Disinganno* (Disillusion), Antonio Corradini's *Pudicizia* (Modesty) and riotously colourful frescoes by Francesco Maria Russo, the latter untouched since their creation in 1749.

Duomo CATHEDRAL
(✆ 081 44 90 97; Via Duomo 149; cathedral/ baptistry free/€2; ⊙ cathedral 8.30am-1.30pm & 2.30-7.30pm Mon-Sat, 8.30am-1.30pm & 4.30-7.30pm Sun, baptistry 8.30am-12.30pm & 3.30-6.30pm Mon-Sat, 8.30am-1pm Sun, Cappella di San Gennaro 8.30am-1pm & 3-6.30pm Mon-Sat, 8.30am-1pm & 4.30-7pm Sun; 🚌 147, 182, 184 to Via Foria, Ⓜ Piazza Cavour) Whether you go for Giovanni Lanfranco's fresco in the Cappella di San Gennaro (Chapel of St Januarius), the 4th-century mosaics in the baptistry, or the thrice-annual 'miracle' of San Gennaro, do not miss Naples' cathedral. Kick-started by Charles I of Anjou in 1272 and consecrated in 1315, it was largely destroyed in a 1456 earthquake. It has had copious nips and tucks over the subsequent centuries.

Certosa e Museo
di San Martino MONASTERY, MUSEUM
(✆ 081 229 45 03; www.polomusealecampania. beniculturali.it/index.php/certosa-e-museo; Largo San Martino 5; adult/reduced €6/3; ⊙ 8.30am-7.30pm Tue & Thu-Sat, to 6.30pm Sun; Ⓜ Vanvitelli, 🚠 Montesanto to Morghen) The high point (quite literally) of the Neapolitan baroque, this charterhouse-turned-museum was built as a Carthusian monastery between 1325 and 1368. Centred on one of the most beautiful cloisters in Italy, it has been decorated, adorned and altered over the centuries by some of Italy's finest talent, most importantly architect Giovanni Antonio Dosio in the 16th century and baroque sculptor Cosimo Fanzago a century later. Nowadays, it's a superb repository of Neapolitan and Italian artistry.

⭐ **Museo di Capodimonte** MUSEUM
(✆ 081 749 91 11; www.museocapodimonte.be niculturali.it; Via Miano 2; adult/reduced €12/8; ⊙ 8.30am-7.30pm Thu-Tue; 🚋; 🚌 R4, 178 to Via Capodimonte, 🚌 Shuttle Capodimonte) Originally designed as a hunting lodge for Charles VII of Bourbon, the monumental Palazzo di Capodimonte was begun in 1738 and took more than a century to complete. It's now home to the **Museo di Capodimonte**, southern Italy's largest and richest art gallery. Its vast collection – much of which Charles inherited from his mother, Elisabetta Farnese – was moved here in 1759 and ranges from exquisite 12th-century altarpieces to works by Botticelli, Caravaggio, Titian and Warhol.

🛏 Sleeping

⭐ **Magma Home** B&B €
(✆ 320 4360272, 338 3188914; http://magmahome. it; Via San Giuseppe dei Nudi 18; d €70-150; 🌀🚋; Ⓜ Museo) ♪ Contemporary artworks, cultural soirées and impeccable hospitality plug you straight into Naples' cultural scene at Magma. Its eight rooms – each designed by a local artist – intrigue with their mix of Italian design classics, upcycled materials and specially commissioned artworks. There's a large, contemporary communal kitchen and living area, plus two inviting rooftop terraces with views of the city and Mt Vesuvius.

Neapolitan Trips HOSTEL €€
(✆ B&B 081 551 8977, hostel 081 1836 6402, hotel 081 1984 5933; www.neapolitantrips.com; Via dei Fiorentini 10; hostel dm €15-35, B&B d €45-90, hotel d €80-160; 🌀🚋; Ⓜ Toledo) Neapolitan Trips is a unique beast, with a clean, next-gen hostel on one floor, and both B&B and hotel rooms on another. The hostel is the standout, boasting a hip communal lounge-bar complete with electric guitars, amps and a piano for impromptu evening jams, a modern guest kitchen with complimentary pasta

ITALY NAPLES

ⓘ THE ARTECARD

The **Campania Artecard** (www.campaniartecard.it) offers discounted museum admission and transport. It comes in various forms, of which the most useful are the following:

Napoli (€21, valid for three days) Gives free entry to three sights in Naples, then discounts on others, as well as free city transport.

Tutta la regione (€34, valid for seven days) Provides free entry to five sights across the region and discounts on others.

Cards can be purchased online or at participating sites and museums.

to cook, and mixed-gender dorms with USB ports by each bed.

While the hostel floor has a buzzy outdoor terrace, hostel guests are also welcome to use the spectacular rooftop terrace, complete with sweeping city views and an upmarket restaurant. The work of emerging and established Neapolitan photographers grace the property, and the hostel also offers two triple rooms with communal bathroom. On-site laundry facilities are available, as well as a handy in-house 'shop' selling everything from phone chargers to batteries and portable tripods.

★ **Hotel Piazza Bellini**   BOUTIQUE HOTEL €€
(☑ 081 45 17 32; www.hotelpiazzabellini.com; Via Santa Maria di Costantinopoli 101; d €90-190; ❄ @ ⓢ; Ⓜ Dante) Only steps from the bars and nightlife of Piazza Bellini, this sharp, hip hotel occupies a 16th-century *palazzo*, its pure-white spaces spiked with original maiolica tiles, vaulted ceilings and *piperno*-stone paving. Rooms are modern and functional, with designer fittings, fluffy duvets and chic bathrooms with excellent showers. Four rooms on the 5th and 6th floors feature panoramic terraces.

✖ Eating

★ **Concettina Ai Tre Santi**   PIZZA €
(☑ 081 29 00 37; www.pizzeriaoliva.it; Via della Sanità 7; pizzas from €5; ⊙ noon-midnight Mon-Sat, to 5pm Sun; ⓢ; Ⓜ Piazza Cavour, Museo) Head in by noon (or 7.30pm at dinner) to avoid a long wait at this hot-spot pizzeria, made famous thanks to its young, driven *pizzaiolo* Ciro Oliva. The menu is an index of fastidiously sourced artisanal ingredients, used to top Ciro's flawless, wood-fired bases. Traditional Neapolitan pizza aside, you'll also find a string of creative seasonal options.

Pasticceria Mennella   PASTRIES €
(☑ 081 42 60 26; www.pasticceriamennella.it; Via Carducci 50-52; pastries from €1.50; ⊙ 6.30am-9.30pm Mon-Fri, to 10.30pm Sat, 7am-9.30pm Sun; Ⓜ Piazza Amedeo) If you eat only one sweet treat in Naples (good luck with that!), make it Mennella's spectacular *frolla al limone,* a shortbread pastry filled with heavenly lemon cream. Just leave room for the *mignon* (bite-size) version of its *sciù* (choux pastry) with *crema di nocciola* (hazelnut cream). Before you go feeling guilty, remember that everything is free of preservatives and artificial additives.

★ **Salumeria**   NEAPOLITAN €€
(☑ 081 1936 4649; www.salumeriaupnea.it; Via San Giovanni Maggiore Pignatelli 34/35; sandwiches from €5.50, charcuterie platters from €8.50, meals around €30; ⊙ 12.30-5pm & 7.15pm-midnight Thu-Tue; ⓢ; Ⓜ Dante) Small producers, local ingredients and contemporary takes on provincial Campanian recipes drive bistro-inspired Salumeria. Nibble on quality charcuterie and cheeses or fill up on artisanal *panini,* hamburgers or Salumeria's sublime *ragù napoletano* (pasta served in a rich tomato-and-meat sauce slow-cooked over two days). Even the ketchup here is made in-house, using DOP Piennolo tomatoes from Vesuvius.

★ **Da Ettore**   NEAPOLITAN €€
(☑ 081 764 35 78; Via Gennaro Serra 39; meals €25; ⊙ 1-3pm & 8-10pm Tue-Sat, 1-3pm Sun; ⓢ; ▯ R2 to Via San Carlo, Ⓜ Chiaia-Monte di Dio) This homey, eight-table trattoria has an epic reputation. Scan the walls for famous fans like comedy great Totò, and a framed passage from crime writer Massimo Siviero, who mentions Ettore in one of his tales. The draw is solid regional cooking, which includes one of the best *spaghetti alle vongole* (spaghetti with clams) in town. Book two days ahead for Sunday lunch.

Pescheria Mattiucci   SEAFOOD €€
(☑ 081 251 2215; www.pescheriamattiucci.com; Vico Belledonne a Chiaia 27; crudo €25, cooked dishes €12-15; ⊙ 12.30-3pm & 7-10.30pm Tue-Sat; ▯ E6 to Piazza dei Martiri, Ⓜ Piazza Amedeo) Run by brothers Francesco, Gennaro and Luigi, this local Chiaia fishmonger transforms daily

into a wonderfully intimate, sociable seafood eatery. Perch yourself on a bar stool, order a vino, and watch the team prepare your super-fresh, tapas-style *crudo* (raw seafood) to order. You'll also find a number of simple, beautifully cooked surf dishes.

Drinking & Nightlife

★ Caffè Gambrinus   CAFE

(☑ 081 41 75 82; www.grancaffegambrinus.com; Via Chiaia 1-2; ⊙ 7am-1am Sun-Fri, to 2am Sat; ⬚ R2 to Via San Carlo, Ⓜ Municipio) Gambrinus is Naples' oldest and most venerable cafe, serving superlative Neapolitan coffee under flouncy chandeliers. Oscar Wilde knocked back a few here and Mussolini had some rooms shut to keep out left-wing intellectuals. Sitdown prices are steep, but the *aperitivo* nibbles are decent and sipping a *spritz* or a luscious *cioccolata calda* (hot chocolate) in its belle époque rooms is something worth savouring.

★ L'Antiquario   COCKTAIL BAR

(☑ 081 764 53 90; www.facebook.com/Antiquario Napoli; Via Gaetani 2; ⊙ 7.30pm-2.30am; ⬚ 151, 154 to Piazza Vittoria) If you take your cocktails seriously, slip into this sultry, speakeasy-inspired den. Wrapped in art nouveau wallpaper, it's the domain of Neapolitan barkeep Alex Frezza, a finalist at the 2014 Bombay Sapphire World's Most Imaginative Bartender Awards. Straddling classic and contemporary, the drinks are impeccable, made with passion and meticulous attention to detail. Live jazz-centric tunes add to the magic on Wednesdays.

☆ Entertainment

★ Teatro San Carlo   OPERA, BALLET

(☑ box office 081 797 23 31; www.teatrosancarlo.it; Via San Carlo 98; ⊙ box office 10am-9pm Mon-Sat, to 6pm Sun; ⬚ R2 to Via San Carlo, Ⓜ Municipio) San Carlo's opera season runs from November or December to June, with occasional summer performances. Sample prices: a place in the 6th tier (from €35), the stalls (€75 to €130) or the side box (from €40). Ballet season runs from late October to April or early May; tickets range from €30 to €110.

ℹ Information

Naples is a relatively safe place, but be careful about walking alone late at night near Stazione Centrale and Piazza Dante. Also watch out for pickpockets (especially on public transport and at markets) and scooter thieves.

Loreto Mare Hospital (Ospedale San Maria di Loreto Nuovo; ☑ 081 254 21 11; www.aslnapo li1centro.it/818; Via Vespucci 26; ⬚ 154 to Via Vespucci) Central city hospital with an emergency department.

Police Station (Questura; ☑ 081 794 11 11, emergencies 112; Via Medina 75; Ⓜ Università) If your car has been clamped or removed, call 081 795 28 66.

Tourist Information Office (☑ 081 551 27 01; www.inaples.it; Piazza del Gesù Nuovo 7; ⊙ 9am-5pm Mon-Sat, to 1pm Sun; Ⓜ Dante) Tourist office in the *centro storico*.

Tourist Information Office (☑ 081 40 23 94; www.inaples.it; Via San Carlo 9; ⊙ 9am-5pm Mon-Sat, to 1pm Sun; ⬚ R2 to Via San Carlo, Ⓜ Municipio) Tourist office at Galleria Umberto I, directly opposite Teatro San Carlo.

ℹ Getting There & Away

AIR

Naples International Airport (Capodichino) (☑ 081 789 62 59; www.aeroportodinapoli.it; Viale F Ruffo di Calabria) Capodichino airport, 7km northeast of the city centre, is southern Italy's main airport. It's served by a number of major airlines and low-cost carriers, including easyJet, which operates flights to Naples from London, Paris, Amsterdam, Vienna, Berlin and several other European cities.

BOAT

Fast ferries and hydrofoils for Capri, Ischia, Procida and Sorrento depart from **Molo Beverello** (Ⓜ Municipio) in front of Castel Nuovo; hydrofoils for Capri, Ischia and Procida also sail from Mergellina.

Slow ferries for Sicily, the Aeolian Islands and Sardinia sail from **Molo Angioino** (Ⓜ Municipio) (right beside Molo Beverello) and neighbouring **Calata Porta di Massa** (Ⓜ Municipio).

As a rough guide, bank on about €22 for the 50-minute jet crossing to Capri, and €13 for the 35-minute sail to Sorrento.

Tickets for shorter journeys can be bought at the ticket booths on Molo Beverello, Calata Porta di Massa or at Mergellina. For longer journeys try the offices of the ferry companies or a travel agent.

Hydrofoil and ferry companies include the following:

Alilauro (☑ 081 497 22 38; www.alilauro.it; Molo Beverello)

Caremar (☑ 081 1896 6690; www.caremar.it; Molo Beverello)

Navigazione Libera del Golfo (NLG; ☑ 081 552 07 63; www.navlib.it; Marina Grande)

SNAV (☑ 081 428 55 55; www.snav.it; Molo Beverollo, Naples)

POMPEII & HERCULANEUM

On 24 August 79 CE, Mt Vesuvius erupted, submerging the thriving port of Pompeii in *lapilli* (burning fragments of pumice stone) and Herculaneum in mud. Both places were quite literally buried alive, leaving thousands of people dead. The Unesco-listed ruins of both provide remarkable models of working Roman cities, complete with streets, temples, houses, baths, forums, taverns, shops and even a brothel.

Pompeii

A stark reminder of the destructive forces that lie deep inside Vesuvius, the ruins of ancient **Pompeii** (081 857 53 47; www.pompeiisites.org; entrances at Porta Marina & Piazza Anfiteatro; adult/reduced €15/7.50, incl Oplontis & Boscoreale €18/9; 9am-7.30pm Mon-Fri, from 8.30am Sat & Sun, last entry 6pm Apr-Oct, shorter hours Nov-Mar; Circumvesuviana to Pompei Scavi–Villa dei Misteri) make for one of Europe's most compelling archaeological sites. The remains first came to light in 1594, when the architect Domenico Fontana stumbled across them while digging a canal, but systematic exploration didn't begin until 1748. Since then 44 of Pompeii's original 66 hectares have been excavated.

There's a huge amount to see at the site. Start with the **Terme Suburbane**, a public bathhouse decorated with erotic frescoes just outside **Porta Marina**, the most impressive of the city's original seven gates. Once inside the walls, continue down **Via Marina** to the grassy **foro** (forum). This was the ancient city's main piazza and is today flanked by limestone columns and what's left of the **basilica**, the 2nd-century-BCE seat of the city's law courts and exchange. Opposite the basilica, the **Tempio di Apollo** is the oldest and most important of Pompeii's religious buildings, while at the forum's northern end the **Granai del Foro** (forum granary) stores hundreds of amphorae and a number of body casts. These were made in the 19th century by pouring plaster into the hollows left by disintegrated bodies. A short walk away, the **Lupanare** (brothel) pulls in the crowds with its collection of red-light frescoes. To the south, the 2nd-century-BCE **Teatro Grande** is a 5000-seat theatre carved into the lava mass on which Pompeii was originally built. Other highlights include the **Anfiteatro**, the oldest known Roman amphitheatre in existence; the **Casa del Fauno**, Pompeii's largest private house, where many of the mosaics now in Naples' Museo Archeologico Nazionale (p707) originated; and the **Villa dei Misteri**, home to the Dionysiac frieze, the most important fresco still on-site. To get to Pompeii, take the Circumvesuviana train to Pompeii Scavi–Villa dei Misteri (€2.80, 36 minutes from Naples; €2.40, 30 minutes from Sorrento) near the main Porta Marina entrance.

Herculaneum (Ercolano)

Smaller and less daunting than Pompeii, **Herculaneum** (081 777 70 08; http://ercolano.beniculturali.it; Corso Resina 187, Ercolano; adult/reduced €11/5.50; 8.30am-7.30pm Apr-Oct, to 5pm Nov-Mar; ; Circumvesuviana to Ercolano–Scavi) can reasonably be visited in a morning or afternoon.

A modest fishing port and resort for wealthy Romans, Herculaneum, like Pompeii, was destroyed by the Vesuvius eruption. But because it was much closer to the volcano, it drowned in a 16m-deep sea of mud and debris rather than in the *lapilli* and ash that rained down on Pompeii. This essentially fossilised the town, ensuring that even delicate items like furniture and clothing were well preserved. Excavations began after the town was rediscovered in 1709 and continue to this day.

There are a number of fascinating houses to explore. Notable among them are the **Casa d'Argo**, a noble residence centred on a porticoed, palm-treed garden; the aristocratic **Casa di Nettuno e Anfitrite**, named after the extraordinary mosaic of Neptune in the *nymphaeum* (fountain and bath); and the **Casa dei Cervi** with its marble deer, murals and beautiful still-life paintings. Marking the sites' southernmost tip, the 1st-century-CE **Terme Suburbane** is a wonderfully preserved baths complex with deep pools, stucco friezes and bas-reliefs looking down on marble seats and floors. To reach Herculaneum, take the Circumvesuviana train to Ercolano–Scavi (€2.20, 20 minutes from Naples; €2.90, 45 minutes from Sorrento), from where it's a 500m walk from the station – follow signs downhill to the *scavi* (ruins).

Tirrenia (☎199 303040; www.tirrenia.it; Calata Porta di Massa) Runs ferries from Naples to Cagliari in Sardinia (from €46) twice weekly. Also runs once daily from Naples to Palermo in Sicily (from €40).

BUS

Most national and international buses leave from **Metropark Napoli Centrale** (☎800 650006; Corso Arnaldo Lucci; Ⓜ Garibaldi), on the southern side of Napoli Centrale train station. The bus station is home to **Biglietteria Vecchione** (☎331 88969217; ◷ 6.30am-9.15pm Mon-Fri, to 7pm Sat, 7am-7pm Sun), a ticket agency selling national and international bus tickets.

TRAIN

The city's main train station is **Napoli Centrale** (Stazione Centrale; ☎081 554 31 88; Piazza Garibaldi), just east of the *centro storico*. From here, the national rail company **Trenitalia** (☎892021; www.trenitalia.com) runs regular direct services to Rome (€13 to €48, 70 minutes to three hours, around 66 daily). High-speed private rail company **Italo** (☎892020; www. italotreno.it) also runs daily direct services to Rome (€15 to €40, 70 minutes, around 20 daily).

ⓘ Getting Around

TO/FROM THE AIRPORT

Airport shuttle **Alibus** (☎800 639525; www. anm.it; one way €5) connects the airport to Piazza Garibaldi (Napoli Centrale) and Molo Beverello.

PUBLIC TRANSPORT

You can travel around Naples by bus, metro and funicular.

Tickets come in various forms: a 90-minute ticket costs €1.60, a day ticket is €4.50.

Note that these tickets are only valid for Naples city; they don't cover travel on Circumvesuviana trains to Herculaneum, Pompeii and Sorrento.

Capri

POP 14,120

The most visited of the islands in the Bay of Naples, Capri deserves more than a quick day trip. Beyond the glamorous veneer of chichi cafes and designer boutiques is an island of rugged seascapes, desolate Roman ruins and a surprisingly unspoiled rural inland.

Ferries dock at Marina Grande, from where it's a short funicular ride up to Capri, the main town. A further bus ride takes you up to Anacapri.

◎ Sights

Grotta Azzurra   CAVE

(Blue Grotto; €14; ◷9am-5pm) Capri's most famous attraction is the Grotta Azzurra, an unusual sea cave illuminated by an otherworldly blue light. The easiest way to visit is to take a boat **tour** (☎081 837 56 46; www.mo toscafisticapri.com; Private Pier 0; Grotta Azzurra/ island trip €15/18) from Marina Grande; tickets include the return boat trip, but the rowing boat into the cave and admission are paid separately. Beautiful though it is, the Grotta is extremely popular in the summer, and the crowds coupled with long waiting times and tip-hungry guides can make the experience underwhelming for some.

Giardini di Augusto   GARDENS

(Gardens of Augustus; €1; ◷9am-7.30pm summer, reduced hours rest of year) As their name suggests, these gardens near the Certosa di San Giacomo were founded by Emperor Augustus. Rising in a series of flowered terraces, they lead to a lookout point offering breathtaking views over to the **Isole Faraglioni**, a group of three limestone stacks rising out of the sea.

★Villa Jovis   RUINS

(Jupiter's Villa; Via A Maiuri; adult/reduced €6/4; ◷10am-7pm Jun-Sep, to 6pm Apr, May & Oct, to 4pm Mar, Nov & Dec, closed Jan & Feb) Villa Jovis was the largest and most sumptuous of 12 Roman villas commissioned by Roman Emperor Tiberius (r 14–37 CE) on Capri, and his main island residence. A vast complex, now reduced to ruins, it famously pandered to the emperor's supposedly debauched tastes, and included imperial quarters and extensive bathing areas set in dense gardens and woodland. It's located a 45-minute walk east of Capri Town along Via Tiberio.

★Seggiovia del Monte Solaro   CABLE CAR

(☎081 837 14 38; www.capriseggiovia.it; Via Caposcuro; single/return €8/11; ◷9.30am-5pm May-Oct, 9am-4pm Mar & Apr, to 3.30pm Nov-Feb) Sitting in an old-fashioned chairlift above the white houses, terraced gardens and hazy hillsides of Anacapri as you rise to the top of Capri's highest mountain, the silence broken only by a distant dog barking or your own sighs of contentment, has to be one of the island's most sublime experiences. The ride takes an all-too-short 13 minutes, but when you get there, the views, framed by dismembered classical statues, are outstanding.

ITALY CAPRI

★ **Villa Lysis** HISTORIC BUILDING

(www.villalysiscapri.com; Via Lo Capo 12; €2; ⊙10am-7pm Thu-Tue Jun-Aug, to 6pm Apr, May, Sep & Oct, to 4pm Nov & Dec) This beautifully melancholic art nouveau villa is set on a clifftop on Capri's northeast tip and was the one-time retreat of French poet Jacques d'Adelsward-Fersen, who came to Capri in 1904 to escape a gay sex scandal in Paris. Unlike other stately homes, the interior has been left almost entirely empty; this is a place to let your imagination flesh out the details. It's a 40-minute walk from Piazza Umberto I and is rarely crowded.

🛏 Sleeping & Eating

★ **Casa Mariantonia** BOUTIQUE HOTEL €€

(☑081 837 29 23; www.casamariantonia.com; Via Orlandi 80, Anacapri; d €120-300; ⊙late Mar-Oct; P🅿❄🛜🏊) A family-run boutique hotel with a history (*limoncello di Capri* was supposedly invented here), it boasts nine fabulous rooms, a giant swimming pool, prestigious restaurant and a heavyweight list of former guests – philosopher Jean-Paul Sartre among them. If the tranquillity, lemon groves and personal *pensione* feel doesn't soothe your existential angst, nothing will.

★ **È Divino** ITALIAN €€

(☑081 837 83 64; www.edivinocapri.com/divino; Via Sella Orta 10a, Capri Town; meals €33-48; ⊙8pm-1am daily Jun-Aug, 12.30-2.30pm & 7.30pm-midnight Tue-Sun rest of year; 🕿) Proudly eccentric (what other restaurant has a bed in its dining room?), this diligent purveyor of Slow Food is a precious secret to those who know it. Whether dining among lemon trees

---

OTHER SOUTHERN SPOTS WORTH A VISIT

Lecce Known as the Florence of the south, it's a lively university town famous for its ornate baroque architecture.

Matera Europe's capital of culture 2019 is a prehistorical town set on two rocky ravines, known as *sassi*, studded with primitive cave dwellings.

Aeolian Islands An archipelago of seven tiny islands off Sicily's northeastern coast. Lipari is the largest and the main hub, while Stromboli is the most dramatic, with its permanently spitting volcano.

---

in the garden or among antiques, chandeliers, contemporary art (and that bed!) inside, expect a thoughtful, regularly changing menu dictated by what's fresh from the garden and market.

ⓘ Information

Tourist Office (☑081 837 06 34; www.capritourism.com; Banchina del Porto; ⊙8.30am-4.15pm, closed Sat & Sun Jan-Mar & Nov) Can provide a map of the island, plus accommodation listings, ferry timetables and other useful information.

ⓘ Getting There & Around

The two major ferry routes to Capri are from Naples and Sorrento, although there are also seasonal connections with Ischia and the Amalfi Coast (Amalfi, Positano and Salerno).

Caremar (☑081 837 07 00; www.caremar.it; Marina Grande) Operates hydrofoils and ferries to/from Naples (€12.50 to €18, 40 minutes to 1¼ hours, up to seven daily) and hydrofoils to/from Sorrento (€14.40, 25 minutes, four daily).

Navigazione Libera del Golfo (p711) Operates hydrofoils to/from Naples (from €19, 45 minutes, up to nine daily).

SNAV (☑081 428 55 55; www.snav.it; Marina Grande) Operates hydrofoils to/from Naples (from €22.50, 45 minutes, up to nine daily).

On the island, buses run from Capri Town to/from Marina Grande, Anacapri and Marina Piccola. Single tickets cost €2 (€2.50 if bought on board) on all routes, including the funicular.

Amalfi Coast

Stretching 50km along the southern side of the Sorrentine Peninsula, the Unesco-protected Amalfi Coast (Costiera Amalfitana) is a postcard-perfect vision of shimmering blue water fringed by vertiginous cliffs on which whitewashed villages and terraced lemon groves cling.

Sorrento

POP 16,400

Despite being a popular package-holiday destination, Sorrento manages to retain a laid-back southern Italian charm. There are very few sights to speak of, but there are wonderful views of Mt Vesuvius, and its small *centro storico* (historical centre) is an atmospheric place to explore. As the western gateway to the Amalfi, and close proximity to Pompeii and Capri, the town makes an excellent base for exploring the area.

☉ Sights & Activities

Museo Correale di Terranova   MUSEUM
(☎081 878 18 46; www.museocorreale.it; Via Correale 50; adult/reduced €8/5; ☉9.30am-6.30pm Mon-Sat, to 1.30pm Sat) East of the city centre, this wide-ranging museum is well worth a visit whether you're a clock collector, an archaeological egghead or into delicate ceramics. In addition to the rich assortment of 16th- to 19th-century Neapolitan art and crafts (including extraordinary examples of marquetry), you'll discover Japanese, Chinese and European ceramics, clocks, fans and, on the ground floor, ancient and medieval artefacts. Among these is a fragment of an ancient Egyptian carving uncovered in the vicinity of Sorrento's **Sedile Dominova** (Via San Cesareo).

**Chiesa & Chiostro
di San Francesco**   CHURCH
(☎081 878 12 69; Via San Francesco; ☉7am-7pm) Located next to the Villa Comunale Park, this church is best known for the peaceful 14th-century cloister abutting it, which is accessible via a small door from the church. The courtyard features an Arabic portico and interlaced arches supported by octagonal pillars. Replete with bougainvillea and birdsong, they're built on the ruins of a 7th-century monastery. Upstairs in the Sorrento International Photo School, the **Gallery Celentano** (☎344 0838503; www. raffaelecelentano.com; adult/reduced €3.50/free; ☉10am-9pm Mar-Dec) exhibits black-and-white photographs of Italian life and landscapes by contemporary local photographer Raffaele Celentano.

★ Nautica Sic Sic   BOATING
(☎081 807 22 83; www.nauticasicsic.com; Via Marina Piccola 43, Marina Piccola; ☉Apr-Oct) Seek out the best beaches by rented boat, with or without a skipper. This outfit rents out a variety of motor boats, starting at around €50 per hour or from €150 per day plus fuel. It also organises boat excursions and wedding shoots.

🛏 Sleeping & Eating

Ulisse   HOSTEL €
(☎081 877 47 53; www.ulissedeluxe.com; Via del Mare 22; dm/d from €35/139; P❀🛜🛌) Although it calls itself a hostel, the Ulisse is about as far from a backpackers' pad as a hiking boot is from a stiletto. Most rooms are plush, spacious affairs with swish if bland fabrics, gleaming floors and large en

---

PATH OF THE GODS

The **Sentiero degli Dei** (Path of the Gods) is by far the best-known walk on the Amalfi Coast for two reasons: first, it's spectacular from start to finish; and second, unlike most Amalfi treks, it doesn't involve inordinate amounts of stair-climbing.

The walk commences in the heart of Praiano, where a thigh-challenging 1000-step start takes you up to the path itself. You'll eventually emerge at **Nocelle**, from where a series of steps will take you through the olive groves and deposit you on the road just east of Positano.

---

suite bathrooms. There are two single-sex dorms, and quads for sharers. Breakfast is included in some rates but costs €10 with others.

Hotel Cristina   HOTEL €€
(☎081 878 35 62; www.hotelcristinasorrento.it; Via Privata Rubinacci 6, Sant'Agnello; d/tr/q from €150/220/240; ☉Mar-Oct; P❀🛜🛌) Located high above Sant'Agnello, this hotel has superb views, particularly from the swimming pool. The spacious rooms have sea-view balconies and combine inlaid wooden furniture with contemporary flourishes such as Philippe Starck chairs. There's an in-house restaurant and a free shuttle bus to/from Sorrento's Circumvesuviana train station.

★ Da Emilia   TRATTORIA €€
(☎081 807 27 20; www.daemilia.it; Via Marina Grande 62; meals €22-30; ☉noon-3pm & 6-10.30pm Mar-Nov; 🐾) Founded in 1947 and still run by the same family, this is a friendly, fast-moving place overlooking the fishing boats in Marina Grande. There's a large informal dining room, complete with youthful photos of former patron Sophia Loren, a romantic terrace by lapping waves, and a menu of straightforward dishes such as mussels with lemon, clam spaghetti and grilled calamari.

★ O'Puledrone   SEAFOOD €€
(☎081 012 41 34; www.opuledrone.com; Via Marina Grande 150; meals €25-30; ☉noon-3pm & 6.30pm-late Apr-Oct) The best fish you eat in Sorrento might be one you caught – a viable proposition at this congenial joint on the harbour at Marina Grande run by a cooperative of

local fishermen. Let them take you out on a three-hour fishing trip (€70) and the chef will cook your catch and serve it to you with a carafe of wine.

ℹ️ Information

Main Tourist Office (☎081 807 40 33; www. sorrentotourism.com; Via Luigi de Maio 35; ⊙9am-7pm Mon-Sat, to 1pm Sun Jun-Oct, 9am-4pm Mon-Fri, to 1pm Sat Nov-May; 🖥️) In the Circolo dei Forestieri (Foreigners' Club); lists ferry and train times. Ask for the useful publication *Surrentum,* published monthly from March to October.

ℹ️ Getting There & Away

Circumvesuviana (☎800 211388; www.eavsrl. it) trains run half-hourly between Sorrento and Naples (€3.90, 70 minutes) via Pompeii (€2.40, 30 minutes) and Ercolano (€2.90, 50 minutes).

Regular **SITA** (www.sitasudtrasporti.it) buses leave from the bus station across from the entrance to the Circumvesuviana train station for the Amalfi Coast, stopping at Positano (€2, one hour) and Amalfi (€2.90, 1¾ hours).

From the **Ferry & Hydrofoil Terminal** (Via Luigi de Maio), hydrofoils run to Capri (€20.50, 20 minutes, up to 13 daily) and Naples (€13, 20 minutes, up to six daily). There are also twice-daily summer sailings to Positano (€20, 30 minutes) and Amalfi (€21, 50 minutes).

Positano

POP 3915

Approaching Positano by boat, you're greeted by an unforgettable view of colourful, steeply stacked houses clinging to near-vertical green slopes. In town, the main activities are hanging out on the small beach, drinking and dining on flower-laden terraces, and browsing the expensive boutiques.

The **tourist office** (☎089 87 50 67; www. aziendaturismopositano.it; Via Regina Giovanna 13; ⊙8.30am-5pm Mon-Sat, to 3pm Sun) can provide information on walking in the densely wooded **Lattari Mountains.**

🛏️ Sleeping & Eating

Villa Nettuno   HOTEL €
(☎089 87 54 01; www.villanettunopositano.it; Viale Pasitea 208; d €80-150; ⊙Apr-Oct; 🅿️🖥️) Hidden behind a barrage of perfumed foliage, lofty Villa Nettuno is not short on charm. Go for one of the original rooms in the 300-year-old part of the building, decked out in robust rustic decor and graced with a communal terrace. Bathrooms are a little

old-fashioned, but this place is all about the view.

Albergo California   HOTEL €€
(☎089 87 53 82; www.hotelcaliforniapositano.it; Via Cristoforo Colombo 141; d €150-190; ⊙Mar-mid-Oct; 🅿️🖥️🖥️) If you were to choose the best place to take a quintessential Positano photo, it might be from the balcony of this hotel. But the view isn't all you get. The rooms in the older part of this grand 18th-century palace are magnificent, with original ceiling friezes and decorative doors. New rooms are simply decorated but tasteful, spacious and minimalist.

★**C'era Una Volta**   TRATTORIA, PIZZA €
(☎089 81 19 30; Via Marconi 127; meals €20-30; ⊙noon-3pm Wed-Mon, 6-11pm daily) Calling like a siren to any cash-poor budget traveller who thought Positano was for celebs only, this heroically authentic trattoria at the top of town specialises in honest, down-to-earth Italian grub. There's no need to look further than the *gnocchi alla sorrentina* (gnocchi in a tomato and basil sauce) and Caprese salad. Pizzas start at €4.50; beer is €2. In Positano, no less!

Amalfi

POP 5100

Amalfi, the main hub on the coast, makes a convenient base for exploring the surrounding coastline. It's a pretty place with a tangle of narrow alleyways, stacked whitewashed houses and sun-drenched piazzas, but it can get very busy in summer as day-trippers pour in to peruse its loud souvenir shops and busy eateries.

The **tourist office** (☎089 87 11 07; www. amalfitouristoffice.it; Corso delle Repubbliche Marinare 27; ⊙8.30am-1pm & 2-6pm Mon-Sat Apr-Oct, 8.30am-1pm Mon-Sat Nov-Mar; 🖥️) can provide information about sights, activities and transport.

👁️ Sights

★**Cattedrale di Sant'Andrea**   CATHEDRAL
(☎089 87 35 58; Piazza del Duomo; adult/reduced €3/1 between 10am-5pm; ⊙7.30am-8.30pm) A melange of architectural styles, Amalfi's cathedral is a bricks-and-mortar reflection of the town's past as an 11th-century maritime superpower. It makes a striking impression at the top of a sweeping 62-step staircase. Between 10am and 5pm, the cathedral is only accessible through the adjacent **Chi-**

ostro del Paradiso (⌨089 87 13 24; adult/reduced €3/1; ⊙9am-7.45pm Jul-Aug, reduced hours Sep-Jun), part of a four-section museum incorporating the cloisters, the 9th-century Basilica del Crocefisso, the crypt of St Andrew and the cathedral itself. Outside these times, you can enter the cathedral for free.

Grotta dello Smeraldo CAVE
(€5; ⊙9am-4pm) Four kilometres west of Amalfi, this grotto is named after the eerie emerald colour that emanates from the water. Stalactites hang down from the 24m-high ceiling, while stalagmites grow up to 10m tall. Buses regularly pass the car park above the cave entrance (from where you take a lift or stairs down to the rowing boats). Alternatively, **Coop Sant'Andrea** (⌨089 87 31 90; www.coopsantandrea.com; Lungomare dei Cavalieri 1) runs boats from Amalfi (€10 return, plus cave admission). Allow 1½ hours for the return trip.

🛏 Sleeping & Eating

Albergo Sant'Andrea HOTEL €
(⌨089 87 11 45; www.albergosantandrea.it; Salita Costanza d'Avalos 1; s/d €70/100; ⊙Mar-Dec; ❄🐾) Enjoy the atmosphere of busy Piazza del Duomo from the comfort of your own room. This modest two-star place has basic rooms with brightly coloured tiles and coordinating fabrics. Double glazing has helped cut down the piazza hubbub, which can reach fever pitch in high season – this is one place to ask for a room with a (cathedral) view.

★ DieciSedici B&B €€
(⌨089 87 22 52; www.diecisedici.it; Piazza Municipio 10-16; d from €145; ⊙Mar-Oct; ❄) DieciSedici (1016) dresses up an old medieval palace in the kind of style that only the Italians can muster. The half-dozen rooms dazzle with chandeliers, mezzanine floors, glass balconies and gorgeous linens. Two rooms (the Junior Suite and Family Classic) come with kitchenettes. All have satellite TV, aircon and Bose sound systems.

Trattoria Il Mulino TRATTORIA, PIZZA €
(⌨089 87 22 23; Via delle Cartiere 36; pizzas €6-11, meals €20-30; ⊙11.30am-4pm & 6.30pm-midnight Tue-Sun) A TV-in-the-corner, kids-running-between-the-tables sort of place, this is about as authentic an eatery as you'll find in Amalfi. There are few surprises on the menu, just hearty, honest pastas, grilled meats and fish. For a taste of local seafood,

---

WORTH A TRIP

RAVELLO

Elegant Ravello sits high in the clouds overlooking the coast. From Amalfi's Piazza Flavio Gioia, it's a nerve-tingling half-hour bus ride (€1.30, up to three an hour), but once you've made it up, you can unwind in the ravishing gardens of **Villa Rufolo** (⌨089 85 76 21; www.villarufolo.it; Piazza Duomo; adult/reduced €7/5; ⊙9am-9pm May-Sep, reduced hours Oct-Apr, tower museum 10am-6pm May-Sep, reduced hours Oct-Apr) and bask in awe-inspiring views at **Villa Cimbrone** (⌨089 85 74 59; www.hotelvillacimbrone.com/gardens; Via Santa Chiara 26; adult/reduced €7/4; ⊙9am-sunset).

---

try the octopus cake or pasta with swordfish. It's right at the top of the town under a simple plastic awning.

★ Ristorante La Caravella ITALIAN €€€
(⌨089 87 10 29; www.ristorantelacaravella.it; Via Matteo Camera 12; meals €50-90, tasting menus €50-135; ⊙noon-2.30pm & 7-11pm Wed-Mon) A restaurant of artists, art and artistry, Caravella once hosted Andy Warhol. It's no surprise that it doubles as a de-facto gallery with frescoes, creative canvases and a ceramics collection. And then there's the food on the seven-course tasting menu, prepared by some of the finest culinary Caravaggios in Italy.

Sicily

Everything about the Mediterranean's largest island is extreme, from the beauty of its rugged landscape to its hybrid cuisine and flamboyant architecture. Over the centuries Sicily has seen off a catalogue of foreign invaders, from the Phoenicians and ancient Greeks to the Spanish Bourbons and WWII Allies. All have contributed to the island's complex and fascinating cultural landscape.

ⓘ Getting There & Away

AIR

Flights from mainland Italian cities and European destinations serve Sicily's two main airports: Palermo's **Falcone-Borsellino** (⌨091 702 02 73, 800 541880; www.gesap.it) and Catania's **Fontanarossa** (⌨095 723 91 11; www.aeroporto.catania.it; 🐾).

BARI

Most travellers visit Puglia's regional capital to catch a ferry. And while there's not a lot to detain you, it's worth taking an hour or so to explore Bari Vecchia (Old Bari). Here, among the labyrinthine lanes, you'll find the **Basilica di San Nicola** (☑ 080 573 71 11; www.basilicasannicola.it; Piazza San Nicola; ⊙ 7am-8.30pm Mon-Sat, to 10pm Sun), the impressive home to the relics of St Nicholas (aka Santa Claus).

For lunch, **Terranima** (☑ 334 6608618, 080 521 97 25; www.terranima.com; Via Putignani 213; meals €30-35; ⊙ noon-3pm daily & 7-11pm Mon-Sat) serves delicious Puglian food.

Regular trains run to Bari from Rome (€50 to €69, four to 6½ hours, five daily).

Ferries sail to Greece, Croatia, Montenegro and Albania from the port, accessible by bus 50 from the main train station.

BOAT

Regular car and passenger ferries cross to Sicily (Messina) from Villa San Giovanni and Reggio di Calabria.

Ferries also sail from Genoa, Livorno, Civitavecchia, Naples, Salerno and Cagliari, as well as Malta and Tunisia.

Main operators:

Caronte & Tourist (☑ 090 5737; www.caronte tourist.it; Molo Norimberga) To Messina from Salerno.

Grandi Navi Veloci (☑ 010 209 45 91; www. gnv.it) To Palermo from Civitavecchia, Genoa, Naples and Tunis.

Grimaldi Lines (☑ 081 49 65 55, 091 611 36 91; www.grimaldi-lines.com; Molo Piave, Porto Stazione Marittima) To Palermo from Livorno, Salerno and Tunis.

Tirrenia (☑ 199 303040; www.tirrenia.it) To Palermo from Naples and Cagliari.

BUS

SAIS Trasporti (☑ 091 617 11 41; www. saistrasporti.it; Piazzetta Cairoli 2) operates long-distance buses between Sicily and Italian mainland destinations including Rome and Naples.

TRAIN

Trenitalia (☑ 892021; www.trenitalia.com) operates direct trains to Sicily from both Rome and Naples, along with direct night trains from Milan, Rome and Naples.

Palermo

POP 673,400

Still bearing the bruises of its WWII battering, Palermo is a compelling and chaotic city. It takes a little work, but once you've acclimatised to the congested and noisy streets you'll be rewarded with some of southern Italy's most imposing architecture, impressive art galleries and vibrant street markets, plus an array of tempting restaurants and cafes.

⊙ Sights

★ **Palazzo dei Normanni**   PALACE

(Palazzo Reale; ☑ 091 705 56 11; www.federicose condo.org; Piazza del Parlamento; adult/reduced incl exhibition Fri-Mon €12/10, Tue-Thu €10/8; ⊙ 8.15am-5.40pm Mon-Sat, to 1pm Sun) Home to Sicily's regional parliament, this venerable palace dates from the 9th century. However, it owes its current look (and name) to a major Norman makeover, during which spectacular mosaics were added to its royal apartments and magnificent chapel, the Cappella Palatina. Visits to the apartments, which are off-limits from Tuesday to Thursday, take in the mosaic-lined **Sala dei Venti**, and **Sala di Ruggero II**, King Roger's 12th-century bedroom.

★ **Cappella Palatina**   CHAPEL

(Palatine Chapel; ☑ 091 705 56 11; www.federico secondo.org; Piazza del Parlamento; adult/reduced incl exhibition Fri-Mon €12/10, Tue-Thu €10/8; ⊙ 8.15am-5.40pm Mon-Sat, to 1pm Sun) Designed by Roger II in 1130, this extraordinary chapel is Palermo's top tourist attraction. Located on the mid-level of Palazzo dei Normanni's three-tiered loggia, its glittering gold mosaics are complemented by inlaid marble floors and a wooden *muqarnas* ceiling, the latter a masterpiece of Arabic-style honeycomb carving reflecting Norman Sicily's cultural complexity.

Note that queues are likely, and you'll be refused entry if you're wearing shorts, a short skirt or a low-cut top.

Mercato di Ballarò   MARKET

(Via Ballaro 1; ⊙ 7.30am-8.30pm) Snaking for several city blocks southeast of Palazzo dei Normanni is Palermo's busiest street market, which throbs with activity well into the early evening. It's a fascinating mix of noises, smells and street life, and the cheapest place for everything from Chinese padded bras to fresh produce, fish, meat, olives and cheese – smile nicely for *un assaggio* (a taste).

Cattedrale di Palermo
CATHEDRAL

(☑ 329 3977513; www.cattedrale.palermo.it; Corso Vittorio Emanuele; cathedral free, royal tombs €1.50, treasury & crypt €3, roof €5, all-inclusive ticket adult/reduced €8/4; ⊙ 7am-7pm Mon-Sat, 8am-1pm & 4-7pm Sun; royal tombs, treasury, crypt & roof 9am-1.30pm Mon-Sat, royal tombs & roof also 9am-12.30pm Sun) A feast of geometric patterns, ziggurat crenellations, maiolica cupolas and blind arches, Palermo's cathedral has suffered aesthetically from multiple reworkings over the centuries, but remains a prime example of Sicily's unique Arab-Norman architectural style. The interior, while impressive in scale, is essentially a marble shell whose most interesting features are the **royal Norman tombs** (to the left as you enter), the **treasury** (home to Constance of Aragon's gem-encrusted 13th-century crown) and the panoramic views from the roof.

La Martorana
CHURCH

(Chiesa di Santa Maria dell'Ammiraglio; Piazza Bellini 3; adult/reduced €2/1; ⊙ 9.30am-1pm & 3.30-5.30pm Mon-Sat, 9-10.30am Sun) On the southern side of Piazza Bellini, this luminously beautiful 12th-century church was endowed by King Roger's Syrian emir, George of Antioch, and was originally planned as a mosque. Delicate Fatimid pillars support a domed cupola depicting Christ enthroned amid his archangels. The interior is best appreciated in the morning, when sunlight illuminates the magnificent Byzantine mosaics.

★ Teatro Massimo
THEATRE

(☑ box office 091 605 35 80; www.teatromassimo.it; Piazza Giuseppe Verdi; guided tours adult/reduced €8/5; ⊙ 9.30am-6pm) Taking over 20 years to complete, Palermo's neoclassical opera house is the largest in Italy and the second-largest in Europe. The closing scene of *The Godfather: Part III*, with its visually arresting juxtaposition of high culture, crime, drama and death, was filmed here and the building's richly decorated interiors are nothing short of spectacular. Guided 30-minute tours are offered throughout the day in English, Italian, French, Spanish and German.

🛏 Sleeping

★ Stanze al Genio Residenze
B&B €

(☑ 340 0971561; www.stanzealgeniobnb.it; Via Garibaldi 11; s €85-100, d €100-120; 🕸 🛜) Speckled

with Sicilian antiques, this B&B offers four gorgeous bedrooms, three with 19th-century ceiling frescoes. All four are spacious and thoughtfully appointed, with Murano lamps, old wooden wardrobes, the odd balcony railing turned bedhead, and top-quality, orthopaedic beds. That the property features beautiful maiolica tiles is no coincidence; the B&B is affiliated with the wonderful **Museo delle Maioliche** (☑ 380 3673773; www.stanzealgenio.it; adult/reduced €9/8; ⊙ guided tours in English 3pm Tue-Fri, 10am Sat, 11am Sun, in Italian 4pm Tue-Fri, 11am Sat & Sun) downstairs.

★ BB22 Palace
B&B €€

(☑ 091 32 62 14; www.bb22.it; cnr Via Roma & Via Bandiera; d €140-180, whole apt €700-1000) Occupying a flouncy *palazzo* in the heart of the city, BB22 Palace offers chic, contemporary rooms, each with its own style. Top billing goes to the Stromboli room, complete with spa bath and a bedroom skylight offering a glimpse of its 15th-century neighbour. Peppered with artworks, coffee-table tomes and an honour bar, the communal lounge makes for an airy retreat.

🍴 Eating & Drinking

★ Trattoria al Vecchio Club Rosanero
SICILIAN €

(☑ 349 4096880; Vicolo Caldomai 18; mains €3-12; ⊙ 1-3.30pm Mon-Sat & 8-11pm Thu-Sat; 🛜) A veritable shrine to the city's football team (*rosa nero* refers to the team's colours, pink and black), cavernous Vecchio Club scores goals with its bargain-priced, flavour-packed grub. Fish and seafood are the real fortes here; if it's on the menu, order the *caponata e pesce spada* (caponata with swordfish), a sweet-and-sour victory. Head in early to avoid a wait.

Osteria Ballarò
SICILIAN €€

(☑ 091 32 64 88; www.osteriaballaro.it; Via Calascibetta 25; meals €35-45; ⊙ noon-3pm & 7-11pm) Bare stone columns, exposed brick walls and vaulted ceilings set an atmospheric scene at this buzzing restaurant-wine bar. Approved by the Slow Food movement, its graze-friendly menu celebrates island produce and cooking, from artisanal cheeses and salumi (charcuterie) to arresting *crudite di pesce* (local sashimi), seafood *primi* and memorable Sicilian *dolci* (sweets). Quality local wines top it off. Reservations recommended.

Enoteca Buonivini
WINE BAR

(☑ 091 784 70 54; Via Dante 8; ⊘ 9.30am-1.30pm & 4pm-midnight Mon-Sat) Thirsty suits flock to this bustling, urbane *enoteca* (wine bar), complete with bar seating, courtyard and a generous selection of wines by the glass. There's no shortage of interesting local drops, not to mention artisanal cheese and charcuterie boards, beautiful pasta dishes and grilled meats.

When you're done, scan the shelves for harder-to-find craft spirits (Australian gin, anyone?) and Sicilian gourmet pantry essentials.

ℹ️ Information

Hospital (Ospedale Civico; ☑ 091 666 55 17; www.arnascivico.it; Via Tricomi; ⊘ 24hr) Has emergency facilities.

Municipal Tourist Office (☑ 091 740 80 21; http://turismo.comune.palermo.it; Piazza Bellini; ⊘ 8.45am-6.15pm Mon-Fri, from 9.45am Sat) The main branch of Palermo's city-run information booths. Other locations include Teatro Massimo, the Port of Palermo and Mondello, though these are only intermittently staffed, with unpredictable hours.

Police (Questura; ☑ 091 21 01 11; Piazza della Vittoria 8) Main police station.

ℹ️ Getting There & Away

AIR

Falcone-Borsellino Airport (p717) is at Punta Raisi, 35km northwest of Palermo on the A29 motorway. There are flights to mainland Italian airports and several European destinations.

BOAT

Numerous ferry companies operate from Palermo's port, just east of the city centre. These include the following:

Grandi Navi Veloci (☑ 010 209 45 91, 091 6072 6162; www.gnv.it; Molo Piave, Porto Stazione Marittima)

Grimaldi Lines (p718)

Tirrenia (☑ 091 611 65 18, 199 303040; www.tirrenia.it; Calata Marinai d'Italia)

BUS

The two main departure points are the **Piazzetta Cairoli bus terminal**, just south of the train station's eastern entrance, and the Intercity bus stop on Via Paolo Balsamo, two blocks due east of the train station.

Main bus companies:

Cuffaro (☑ 091 616 15 10; www.cuffaro.info; Via Paolo Balsamo 13) Services to Agrigento (€9, two hours, three to six daily).

Interbus (☑ 091 616 79 19; www.interbus.it; Piazzetta Cairoli Bus Terminal) To/from Syracuse (€13.50, 3½ hours, two to three daily).

SAIS Autolinee (☑ 091 616 60 28, 800 211020; www.saisautolinee.it; Piazzetta Cairoli Bus Terminal) To/from Catania (€13.50, 2¾ hours, nine to 14 daily) and Messina (€14, 2¾ hours, four to seven daily).

TRAIN

From Palermo Centrale station trains leave for Agrigento (€9, 2¼ hours, 10 daily) and Catania (€13.50 to €16.50, 3½ to five hours, five daily) via Messina (€12.80, three to 3¾ hours, 10 daily). There are also Intercity trains to Reggio di Calabria, Naples and Rome.

ℹ️ Getting Around

TO/FROM THE AIRPORT

Prestia e Comandè (☑ 091 58 63 51; www.prestiaecomande.it; one way/return €6.30/11) Runs an efficient half-hourly bus service between 5am and 12.30pm that transfers passengers from the airport to the centre of Palermo, dropping people off outside the Teatro Politeama Garibaldi (35 minutes) and Palermo Centrale train station (50 minutes). Get tickets from the office in the arrivals hall. Buses are parked to the right as you exit the hall.

BUS

Walking is the best way to get around Palermo's centre, but if you want to take a bus, most stop outside or near the train station. Tickets cost €1.40 (€1.80 on board) and are valid for 90 minutes.

Taormina

POP 10,900

Spectacularly perched on a clifftop terrace overlooking the Ionian Sea and Mt Etna, this sophisticated town has attracted socialites, artists and writers ever since Greek times. Its pristine medieval core, proximity to beaches, grandstand coastal views and chic social scene make it a hugely popular summer holiday destination.

◉ Sights & Activities

★ Teatro Greco
RUINS

(☑ 0942 2 32 20; Via Teatro Greco; adult/reduced €10/5; ⊘ 9am-1hr before sunset) Taormina's premier sight is this perfect horseshoe-shaped theatre, suspended between sea and sky, with Mt Etna looming on the southern horizon. Built in the 3rd century BCE, it's the most dramatically situated Greek theatre in the world and the second largest in Sicily (after Syracuse). In summer, it's used

MT ETNA

The dark silhouette of Mt Etna (3329m) broods ominously over Sicily's east coast, more or less halfway between Taormina and Catania. One of Europe's highest and most volatile volcanoes, it erupts frequently, most recently in 2021.

To get to Etna by public transport, take the AST bus from Catania. This departs from Piazza Papa Giovanni XXIII (opposite Catania's main train station) at 8.15am and drops you at the Rifugio Sapienza at 10.15am, where you can pick up the **Funivia dell'Etna** (☑ 095 91 41 41; www.funiviaetna.com; return €30, incl bus & guide €64; ☺ 9am-4.15pm Apr-Nov, to 3.45pm Dec-Mar) to 2500m. From there buses courier you up to the crater zone (2920m). If you want to walk, allow up to four hours for the round trip. The return journey leaves Rifugio Sapienza at 4.30pm, arriving in Catania at 6.30pm.

Gruppo Guide Alpine Etna Sud (☑ 095 791 47 55, 389 3496086; www.etnaguide.eu) is one of many outfits offering guided tours. Bank on around €85 for a full-day excursion.

Further Etna information is available from Catania's **tourist office** (☑ 095 742 55 73; www.comune.catania.it/la-citta/turismo; Via Vittorio Emanuele 172; ☺ 8am-7pm Mon-Sat, 8.30am-1.30pm Sun).

to stage concerts and festival events. To avoid the high-season crowds try to visit early in the morning.

Corso Umberto I STREET

Taormina's chief delight is wandering this pedestrian-friendly, boutique-lined thoroughfare. Start at the tourist office in **Palazzo Corvaja** (☺ varies), which dates back to the 10th century, before heading southwest for spectacular panoramic views from **Piazza IX Aprile**. Facing the square is the early-18th-century **Chiesa San Giuseppe** (Piazza IX Aprile; ☺ closed for restoration). Continue west through the **Torre dell'Orologio**, the 12th-century clock tower, into **Piazza del Duomo**, home to an ornate baroque fountain (1635) that sports Taormina's symbol, a two-legged centaur with the bust of an angel.

Villa Comunale PARK

(Parco Duchi di Cesarò; Via Bagnoli Croce; ☺ 8am-midnight summer, to 6pm winter) To escape the crowds, wander down to these stunningly sited public gardens. Created by Englishwoman Florence Trevelyan in the late 19th century, they're a lush paradise of tropical plants and delicate flowers, punctuated by whimsical follies. You'll also find a children's play area.

🛏 Sleeping & Eating

Le 4 Fontane B&B €

(☑ 333 6793876; www.le4fontane.com; Corso Umberto I 231; s €40-70, d €60-110; ✸ 🛜) An excellent budget B&B on the top floor of an old *palazzo*, Le 4 Fontane is run by a friendly

couple and has three homey rooms, two of which have views of Piazza del Duomo.

Isoco Guest House GUESTHOUSE €€

(☑ 0942 2 36 79; www.isoco.it; Via Salita Branco 2; r €78-220; ☺ Mar-Nov; ℗ ✸ @ 🛜) Each room at this welcoming, LGBT-friendly guesthouse is dedicated to an artist, from Botticelli to Keith Haring. While the older rooms are highly eclectic, the newer suites are chic and subdued, each with a modern kitchenette. Breakfast is served around a large table, while a pair of terraces offer stunning sea views and a hot tub. Multinight or prepaid stays earn the best rates.

Tischi Toschi SICILIAN €€

(☑ 339 3642088; www.tischitoschitaormina.com; Vico Paladini 3; meals €35-45; ☺ 12.30-2.30pm Wed-Sun & 7-10.30pm daily summer, 12.30-2.30pm & 7-10.30pm Wed-Sun winter) With only a handful of tables, this family-run, Slow Food–acclaimed trattoria offers a level of creativity and attention to detail that's generally lacking in touristy Taormina. The limited menu changes regularly based on what's in season, and is filled with less-common regional specialities, from succulent stewed rabbit with olives, carrots, pine nuts and celery, to heavenly wild-fennel 'meatballs'.

ℹ Information

Tourist Office (☑ 0942 2 32 43; Palazzo Corvaja, Piazza Santa Caterina; ☺ 8.30am-2.15pm & 3.30-6.45pm Mon-Fri year-round, also 9am-1pm & 4-6.30pm Sat summer) Has plenty of practical information, including transport timetables and a free map.

VALLEY OF THE TEMPLES

Sicily's most enthralling archaeological site, **Valley of the Temples** (Valle dei Templi; ☑ 0922 62 16 11; www.parcovalledeitempli.it; adult/reduced €10/5, incl Museo Archeologico €13.50/7; ☉ 8.30am-7pm year-round, plus 7.30-10pm Mon-Fri, 7.30-11pm Sat & Sun mid-Jul–mid-Sep) encompasses the ruined ancient city of Akragas, highlighted by the stunningly well-preserved **Tempio della Concordia** (Temple of Concordia), one of several ridge-top temples that once served as beacons for homecoming sailors. The 13-sq-km park, 3km south of Agrigento, is split into eastern and western zones. Ticket offices with car parks are at the park's southwestern corner (the main Porta V entrance) and at the northeastern corner near the Temple of Hera (Eastern Entrance).

For maps and information, ask at Agrigento's **tourist office** (☑ 0922 59 32 27; www.livingagrigento.it; Piazzale Aldo Moro 1; ☉ 8am-7pm Mon-Fri, to 1pm Sat) in the Provincia building.

❶ Getting There & Away

Bus is the easiest way to reach Taormina. The bus station is on Via Luigi Pirandello, 400m east of Porta Messina, the northeastern entrance to the old town. **Interbus** (☑ 0942 62 53 01; www.interbus.it; Via Luigi Pirandello) services leave daily for Messina (€4.30, 55 minutes to 1¾ hours, up to five daily), Catania (€5.10, 1¼ to two hours, twice hourly) and Catania airport (€8.20, 1½ hours, twice hourly). It also runs services to Castelmola (€1.90, 15 minutes, hourly).

Syracuse

POP 122,000

A tumultuous past has left Syracuse (Siracusa) a beautiful baroque centre and some of Sicily's finest ancient ruins. Founded in 734 BCE by Corinthian settlers, it became the dominant Greek city state on the Mediterranean and was known as the most beautiful city in the ancient world. A devastating earthquake in 1693 destroyed most of the city's buildings, paving the way for a city-wide baroque makeover.

◉ Sights

★ Piazza del Duomo   PIAZZA

Syracuse's showpiece square is a masterpiece of baroque town planning. A long, rectangular piazza flanked by flamboyant *palazzi*, it sits on what was once Syracuse's ancient acropolis (fortified citadel). Little remains of the original Greek building, but if you look along the side of the Duomo you'll see a number of thick Doric columns incorporated into the cathedral's structure.

★ Parco Archeologico
della Neapolis   ARCHAEOLOGICAL SITE

(☑ 0931 6 62 06; Viale Paradiso 14; adult/reduced €10/5, incl Museo Archeologico €13.50/7; ☉ 8.30am-1hr before sunset) For the classicist, Syracuse's real attraction is this archaeological park, home to the pearly white 5th century BCE **Teatro Greco**. Hewn out of the rocky hillside, this 16,000-capacity amphitheatre staged the last tragedies of Aeschylus (including *The Persians*), first performed here in his presence. In late spring it's brought to life with an annual season of classical theatre.

★ Museo Archeologico Paolo Orsi   MUSEUM

(☑ 0931 48 95 11; www.regione.sicilia.it/beniculturali/museopaoloorsi; Viale Teocrito 66; adult/reduced €8/4, incl Parco Archeologico €13.50/7; ☉ 9am-6pm Tue-Sat, to 1pm Sun) About 500m east of the archaeological park, this modern museum contains one of Sicily's largest and most interesting archaeological collections. Allow plenty of time to investigate the four sectors charting the area's prehistory, as well as Syracuse's development from foundation to the late Roman period.

🛏 Sleeping & Eating

★ Hotel Gutkowski   HOTEL €€

(☑ 0931 46 58 61; www.guthotel.it; Lungomare Vittorini 26; d €90-150, tr €150, q €160; ❈ 🛜) Book well in advance for one of the sea-view rooms at this stylish, eclectic hotel on the Ortygia waterfront, at the edge of the Giudecca neighbourhood. Divided between two buildings, its rooms are simple yet chic, with pretty tiled floors, walls in teals, greys, blues and browns, and a sharply curated mix of vintage and industrial details.

★ Sicily   PIZZA €

(☑ 392 9659949; www.sicilypizzeria.it; Via Cavour 67; pizzas €5.50-15; ☉ 7pm-midnight Tue-Sun; 🛜 🍴) Experimenting with pizzas is something you do at your peril in culinary-conservative Sicily. But that's what is done, and done well, at this funky retro-chic pizzeria. So if you're game for wood-fired pizzas topped with more-ish combos such as sausage, cheese, Swiss chard, pine nuts, sun-dried tomatoes and raisins, this is the place for you.

★ **Bistrot Bella Vita**   ITALIAN €€
(☑ 0931 46 49 38; Via Gargallo 60; meals €35-40; ⊙ cafe 8.30am-3pm & 5-10.30pm, restaurant 12.30-2.30pm & 7.30-10.30pm Tue-Sun) This casually elegant cafe-restaurant is one of Ortygia's stars. Stop by for good coffee (soy milk available) and *cornetti, biscotti* and pastries (try the sour orange-and-almond tart). Or book a table in the intimate back dining room, where local, organic produce drives beautifully textured, technically impressive dishes.

ⓘ Information

Tourist Office (☑ 800 055500; www.provincia.siracusa.it; Via Roma 31; ⊙ 7.30am-2pm Mon, Tue, Thu & Fri, to 4.30pm Wed) City maps and brochures.

ⓘ Getting There & Around

Buses are generally faster and more convenient than trains, with long-distance buses arriving and departing from the **bus terminal** (Corso Umberto I), just 180m southeast of the train station.

Interbus (☑ 0931 6 67 10; www.interbus.it) runs buses to Noto (€3.60, 55 minutes, three to six daily), Catania (€6.20, 1½ hours, 10 to 17 daily) and its airport, and Palermo (€13.50, 3½ hours, two to three daily). You can buy tickets at the kiosk by the bus stops.

SURVIVAL GUIDE

ⓘ Directory A–Z

ACCOMMODATION

➡ The bulk of Italy's accommodation is made up of *alberghi* (hotels) and *pensioni* (small, often family-run hotels). Other options are hostels, campgrounds, B&Bs, *agriturismi* (farm stays), mountain *rifugi* (Alpine refuges), monasteries and villa/apartment rentals.

➡ High-season rates apply at Easter, in summer (mid-June to August), and over the Christmas to New Year period.

➡ Many places in coastal resorts close between November and March.

ACTIVITIES

Cycling Tourist offices can provide details on trails and guided rides. The best time is spring. Favourite areas include Tuscany, the flatlands of Emilia-Romagna, and the peaks around Lago Maggiore and Lago del Garda.

Hiking Thousands of kilometres of *sentieri* (marked trails) criss-cross the country. The hiking season is from June to September. The Italian Parks organisation (www.parks.it) lists walking trails in Italy's national parks.

Skiing Italy's ski season runs from December through to March. Prices are generally high, particularly in the top Alpine resorts – the Apennines are cheaper. A popular option is to buy a *settimana bianca* (literally 'white week') package deal, covering accommodation, food and ski passes.

FOOD & DRINK
Eat Like an Italian

A full Italian meal consists of an *antipasto*, a *primo* (first course; pasta or rice dish), *secondo* (main course; usually meat or fish) with an *insalata* (salad) or *contorno* (vegetable side dish), *dolce* (dessert) and coffee. Most Italians only eat a meal this large at Sunday lunch or on a special occasion, and when eating out it's fine to mix and match and order, say, a *primo* followed by an *insalata* or *contorno*.

Italians are late diners, often not eating until after 8.30pm.

Where to Eat & Drink

Trattorias are traditional, often family-run places serving local food and wine; *ristoranti* (restaurants) are more formal, with a greater choice and smarter service; pizzerias, which usually open evenings only, often serve a full menu alongside pizzas.

At lunchtime bars and cafes sell *panini* (bread rolls), and many serve an evening *aperitivo* (aperitif) buffet. At an *enoteca* (wine bar) you can drink wine by the glass and snack on cheese and cured meats. Some also serve hot dishes. For a slice of pizza search out a *pizza al taglio* joint.

INTERNET ACCESS

➡ Numerous Italian cities and towns offer public wi-fi hotspots, including Rome, Bologna and Venice. To use them, you will need to register online using a credit card or an Italian mobile number. An easier option (no need for a local mobile number) is to head to a cafe or bar offering free wi-fi.

➡ Most hotels, B&Bs, hostels and *agriturismi* (farm stays) offer free wi-fi to guests, though signal quality can vary. There will sometimes be a computer for guest use.

ⓘ ROOM TAX

Most Italian hotels apply a room occupancy tax (tassa di soggiorno), which is charged on top of your regular hotel bill. The exact amount, which varies from city to city, depends on several factors, including the type of accommodation, a hotel's star rating and the number of people under your booking. As a rough guide reckon on €1 to €7 per person per night.

Prices quoted in this chapter do not include the tax.

LGBT+ TRAVELLERS

Homosexuality is legal (over the age of 16) and even widely accepted, but Italy is notably conservative in its attitudes, largely keeping in line with those of the Vatican. Overt displays of affection by LGBT couples can attract a negative response, especially in smaller towns.

There are gay venues in Rome, Milan and Bologna, and a handful in places such as Florence and Naples. Some coastal towns and resorts (such as the Tuscan town of Viareggio or Taormina in Sicily) are popular gay holiday spots in the summer.

Italy's main gay and lesbian organisation is **Arcigay** (🖉 051 095 7241; www.arcigay.it; Via Don Minzoni 18, Cassero LGBT Center, Bologna).

MONEY

ATMs Known as 'Bancomat', are widely available throughout Italy, and most will accept cards tied into the Visa, MasterCard, Cirrus and Maestro systems.

Credit cards Virtually all midrange and top-end hotels accept credit cards, as do most restaurants and large shops. Museums and some cheaper pensioni, trattorias and pizzerias often only accept cash. Major cards such as Visa, MasterCard, Eurocard, Cirrus and Eurocheques are widely accepted. Amex is also recognised, although it's less common.

Tipping If servizio is not included, leave up to 10% in restaurants and a euro or two in pizzerias. It's not necessary in bars or cafes, but many people leave small change (usually €0.10 per coffee) if drinking at the bar.

OPENING HOURS

Opening hours vary throughout the year. We've provided high-season opening hours, which will generally decrease in the shoulder and low seasons. 'Summer' times generally refer to the period from April to September or October, while 'winter' times generally run from October or November to March.

Banks 8.30am–1.30pm and 2.45pm–4.30pm Monday to Friday

Restaurants noon–3pm and 7.30pm–11pm or midnight

Cafes 7.30am–8pm, sometimes until 1am or 2am

Bars and clubs 10pm–4am or 5am

Shops 9am–1pm and 3.30pm–7.30pm (or 4pm–8pm) Monday to Saturday, some also open Sunday

PUBLIC HOLIDAYS

Most Italians take their annual holiday in August, with the busiest period occurring around 15 August, known locally as Ferragosto. As a result, many businesses and shops close for at least part of that month. Settimana Santa (Easter Holy Week) is another busy holiday period for Italians.

National public holidays include the following:

Capodanno (New Year's Day) 1 January

Epifania (Epiphany) 6 January

Pasquetta (Easter Monday) March/April

Giorno della Liberazione (Liberation Day) 25 April

Festa del Lavoro (Labour Day) 1 May

Festa della Repubblica (Republic Day) 2 June

Ferragosto (Feast of the Assumption) 15 August

Festa di Ognisanti (All Saints' Day) 1 November

Festa dell'Immacolata Concezione (Feast of the Immaculate Conception) 8 December

Natale (Christmas Day) 25 December

Festa di Santo Stefano (Boxing Day) 26 December

SAFE TRAVEL

Italy is generally a safe country, but watch out for pickpockets in popular tourist centres such as Rome, Florence, Venice and Naples.

TELEPHONE

➜ Area codes must be dialled even when calling locally.

➜ To call Italy from abroad, dial your international access number, then Italy's country code (39) followed by the relevant area code, including the leading 0, and the telephone number.

➜ To call abroad from Italy, dial 00, then the relevant country code followed by the telephone number.

➜ Italian mobile phone numbers begin with a three-digit prefix starting with a 3.

Mobile Phones

➡ The cheapest way of using your mobile is to buy a prepaid *(prepagato)* Italian SIM card. **TIM** (www.tim.it), **Wind** (www.wind.it), **Vodafone** (www.vodafone.it) and **Tre** (www.tre.it) all offer SIM cards and have retail outlets in most Italian cities and towns.

➡ All SIM cards must be registered in Italy, so make sure you have a passport or ID card with you when you buy one.

➡ You can easily top-up your Italian SIM with a recharge card *(ricarica)*, available from most tobacconists, some bars, supermarkets and banks.

ℹ Getting There & Away

AIR

Italy's main intercontinental gateway airports are Rome's Leonardo da Vinci (p672) and Milan's Aeroporto Malpensa (p683). Both are served by non-stop flights from around the world. Venice's Marco Polo Airport (p693) is also served by a handful of intercontinental flights.

Dozens of international airlines compete with the country's revamped national carrier, Alitalia, rated a three-star airline by UK aviation research company Skytrax. If you're flying from Africa or Oceania, you'll generally need to change planes at least once en route to Italy.

Intra-European flights serve plenty of other Italian cities; the leading mainstream carriers include Alitalia, Air France, British Airways, Lufthansa and KLM.

Cut-rate airlines, led by Ryanair and easyJet, fly from a growing number of European cities to more than two dozen Italian destinations, typically landing in smaller airports such as Rome's **Ciampino** (☎ 06 6 59 51; www.adr.it/ciampino).

LAND

Bus

Buses are the cheapest overland option to Italy, but services are less frequent, less comfortable and significantly slower than the train.

Eurolines (☎ 0861 199 19 00; www.eurolines. it) and **FlixBus** (www.flixbus.com) operate buses from European destinations to many Italian cities.

Train

Milan and Venice are Italy's main international rail hubs. International trains also run to/from Rome, Genoa, Verona, Padua, Bologna and Florence.

SEA

Multiple ferry companies connect Italy with countries throughout the Mediterranean. Many routes only operate in summer, when ticket prices also rise. Prices for vehicles vary according to their size.

The helpful website www.directferries.co.uk allows you to search routes and compare prices between the numerous international ferry companies servicing Italy. Another useful resource for ferries from Italy to Greece is www.ferries.gr.

International ferry companies that serve Italy include the following:

Adria Ferries (☎ 071 5021 1621; www.adria ferries.com)

Anek Lines (☎ 071 207 23 46; www.anekitalia. com)

GNV (Grandi Navi Veloci; ☎ 010 209 45 91; www.gnv.it)

Grimaldi Lines (☎ 081 49 64 44; www.grimaldi -lines.com)

Jadrolinija (☎ 071 228 41 00; www. jadrolinija.hr)

Minoan Lines (☎ 071 20 17 08; www.minoan.it)

Moby Lines (☎ 199 30 30 40; www.moby.it)

Montenegro Lines (☎ Bar 382 3030 3469; www.montenegrolines.net)

SNAV (☎ 081 428 55 55; www.snav.it)

Superfast (☎ Athens +30 210 891 97 00; www. superfast.com)

Venezia Lines (p693)

Ventouris (☎ 080 876 14 51; www.ventouris.gr; Nuova Stazione Marittima di Bari)

Virtu Ferries (☎ 095 703 12 11; www.virtu ferries.com)

ℹ Getting Around

BICYCLE

➡ Bikes can be taken on regional and certain international trains carrying the bike logo, but you'll need to purchase a separate bicycle ticket *(supplemento bici)*, valid for 24 hours (€3.50 on regional trains, €12 on international trains).

ITALY SURVIVAL GUIDE

ℹ ADMISSION PRICES

Admission to state-run museums, galleries and cultural sites is free to visitors under 18. EU citizens aged between 18 and 25 pay a token €2 to enter.

Between October and March admission to state-run museums and monuments is free to everyone on the first Sunday of each month. Watch out for other free days throughout the year, including six consecutive days during National Museum Week (first week in March).

→ Bikes can be carried free if dismantled and stored in a bike bag.

→ Check details at www.trenitalia.com/tcom-en/Services/Travelling-with-your-bike.

→ Most ferries also allow free bicycle passage.

BOAT

Craft *Navi* (large ferries) service Sicily and Sardinia, while *traghetti* (smaller ferries) and *aliscafi* (hydrofoils) service the smaller islands. Most ferries carry vehicles; hydrofoils do not.

Routes Main embarkation points for Sicily and Sardinia are Genoa, Livorno, Civitavecchia and Naples. Ferries for Sicily also leave from Villa

San Giovanni and Reggio di Calabria. Main arrival points in Sardinia are Cagliari, Arbatax, Olbia and Porto Torres; in Sicily they're Palermo, Catania, Trapani and Messina.

Timetables and tickets Comprehensive website **Direct Ferries** (www.directferries.co.uk) allows you to search routes, compare prices and book tickets for ferry routes in Italy.

Overnight ferries Travellers can book a two- to four-person cabin or a *poltrona,* which is an airline-type armchair. Deck class (which allows you to sit/sleep in lounge areas or on deck) is available only on some ferries.

MAIN INTERNATIONAL FERRY ROUTES

DESTINATION COUNTRY	DESTINATION PORT(S)	ITALIAN PORT(S)	COMPANY
Albania	Durrës	Bari	Ventouris, GNV
	Durrës	Bari, Ancona, Trieste	Adria Ferries
Croatia	Dubrovnik	Bari	Jadrolinija, Montenegro Lines
	Split, Stari Grad	Ancona	SNAV
	Split, Zadar, Stari Grad	Ancona	Jadrolinija
	Umag, Poreč, Rovinj, Pula	Venice	Venezia Lines
France (Corsica)	Bastia	Livorno, Genoa	Moby Lines
	Bonifacio	Santa Teresa di Gallura	Moby Lines
Greece	Corfu, Igoumenitsa, Patras	Bari	Superfast, Anek Lines
	Corfu, Igoumenitsa, Zakynthos, Cephalonia	Bari	Ventouris
	Igoumenitsa, Patras	Brindisi	Grimaldi Lines
	Igoumenitsa, Patras	Ancona	Superfast, Anek Lines, Grimaldi Lines, Minoan Lines
	Igoumenitsa, Patras	Venice	Superfast, Anek Lines, Grimaldi Lines, Minoan Lines
Malta	Valletta	Pozzallo	Virtu Ferries
Montenegro	Bar	Bari	Montenegro Lines, Jadrolinija
Morocco	Tangier	Genoa	GNV
	Tangier	Savona	Grimaldi Lines
Slovenia	Piran	Venice	Venezia Lines
Spain	Barcelona	Genoa	GNV
	Barcelona	Civitavecchia, Savona, Porto Torres	Grimaldi Lines
Tunisia	Tunis	Genoa, Civitavecccchia, Palermo	GNV
	Tunis	Civitavecchia, Palermo, Salerno	Grimaldi Lines

BUS

Routes Everything from meandering local routes to fast, reliable InterCity connections is provided by numerous bus companies.

Timetables and tickets These are available on bus-company websites and from local tourist offices. Tickets are generally competitively priced with the train and are often the only way to get to smaller towns. In larger cities most of the InterCity bus companies have ticket offices or sell tickets through agencies. In villages and even some good-sized towns, tickets are sold in bars or on the bus.

Advance booking Generally not required, but advisable for overnight or long-haul trips in high season.

CAR & MOTORCYCLE

Italy's extensive network of roads spans numerous categories. The main ones are as follows:

➡ Autostradas – An extensive, privatised network of motorways, represented on road signs by a white 'A' followed by a number on a green background. The main north–south link is the A1. Also known as the Autostrada del Sole (the 'Motorway of the Sun'), it extends from Milan to Naples. The main link from Naples south to Reggio di Calabria is the A3. There are tolls on most motorways, payable by cash or credit card as you exit.

➡ *Strade statali* (state highways) – Represented on maps by 'S' or 'SS'. Vary from toll-free, four-lane highways to two-lane main roads.

The latter can be extremely slow, especially in mountainous regions.

➡ *Strade regionali* (regional highways) – Coded 'SR' or 'R'.

➡ *Strade provinciali* (provincial highways) – Coded 'SP' or 'P'.

➡ *Strade locali* – Often not even paved or mapped.

For information in English about distances, driving times and fuel costs, see https://en.mappy.com. Additional information, including traffic conditions and toll costs, is available at www.autostrade.it.

TRAIN

Italy has an extensive rail network. Most services are run by **Trenitalia** (☑ 892021; www.trenitalia.com), but Italo (www.italotreno.it) also operates high-speed trains.

➡ Reservations are obligatory on AV and Intercity trains. On other services they're not, and outside peak holiday periods you should be fine without them.

➡ Both Trenitalia and Italo offer a variety of advance purchase discounts. Basically, the earlier you book, the greater the saving. Discounted tickets are limited, and refunds and changes are highly restricted. For all ticket options and prices, see the Trenitalia and Italo websites.

➡ *Regionale* train tickets must be validated in the green machines (usually found at the head of platforms) just before boarding. Failure to do so can result in a fine.

ITALY SURVIVAL GUIDE

Kosovo

POP 1.92 MILLION

Includes ➡

Best Places to Eat

Best Places to Stay

Why Go?

Europe's newest country, Kosovo is a fascinating land at the heart of the Balkans rewarding visitors with welcoming smiles, charming mountain towns, incredible hiking opportunities and 13th-century domed Serbian monasteries brushed in medieval art – and that's just for starters.

Kosovo declared independence from Serbia in 2008, and while it has been diplomatically recognised by 111 countries, there are still many nations that do not accept Kosovan independence, including Serbia. The country has been the recipient of massive aid from the international community, particularly the EU and NATO. Barbs of its past are impossible to miss, though: roads are dotted with memorials to those killed in 1999, while NATO forces still guard Serbian monasteries. No matter what many people who've never been to Kosovo might tell you, it's perfectly safe to travel here. Despite this, Kosovo remains one of the last truly off-the-beaten-path destinations in Europe.

When to Go
Pristina

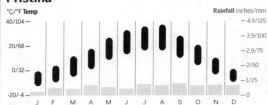

Dec–Mar Hit the powder on the still largely virgin ski slopes of Brezovica.

May–Sep Pleasant weather for hiking in the Rugova and Shar Mountains.

Aug The excellent Dokufest in Prizren is Kosovo's best arts event.

Entering the Country

Despite Kosovo's slightly ambiguous international status, it's well connected with other European countries by air and, with most neighbouring countries, by land. Whichever way you come, entering Kosovo is generally a breeze, with very welcoming and bureaucracy-free immigration and customs. One thing to be aware of, though, is that if you wish to travel between Serbia and Kosovo, you'll need to enter Kosovo from Serbia first.

ITINERARIES

Three Days

Spend a day in cool little Pristina (p730) and get to know Kosovo's charmingly chaotic capital. The next day, visit Visoki Dečani Monastery (p734), then head on to Prizren (p735) to see the old town's Ottoman sights and enjoy the view from the castle.

One Week

After a couple of days in the capital and visits to Gračanica Monastery (p735) and the Bear Sanctuary (p735), loop to lovely Prizren (p735) for a night before continuing to Peja (p734) for monasteries and markets. End with a few days of hiking and climbing in the beautiful Rugova Valley (p733).

Essential Food & Drink

Byrek Pastry with cheese or meat.

Gjuveç Baked meat and vegetables.

Fli Flaky pastry pie served with honey.

Kos Goat's-milk yoghurt.

Pershut Dried meat.

Qofta Flat or cylindrical minced-meat rissoles.

Tavë Meat baked with cheese and egg.

Vranac Red wine from the Rahovec (Orahovac) region of Kosovo.

AT A GLANCE

Area 10,887 sq km

Capital Pristina

Country Code ☑383

Currency euro (€)

Emergency Ambulance ☑94, Police ☑92

Language Albanian, Serbian

Time Central European Time (GMT/UTC plus one hour)

Visas Kosovo is visa-free for many travellers for a stay of up to 90 days.

Sleeping Price Ranges

The following price ranges are for a double room with bathroom.

€ less than €40

€€ €40–80

€€€ more than €80

Eating Price Ranges

The following price categories are for the average cost of a main course.

€ less than €5

€€ €5–10

€€€ more than €10

Resources

UN Mission in Kosovo Online (unmik.unmissions.org)

Balkan Insight (www.balkaninsight.com)

Kosovo Guide (www.kosovoguide.com)

KOSOVO

Kosovo Highlights

① **Prizren's old town**
(p735) Discovering the picturesque, mosque-studded streets of Prizren's charming old quarter and getting a breathtaking view from the fortress.

② **Visoki Dečani Monastery** (p734) Taking in gorgeous frescoes, then

buying monk-made wine and cheese at this serene 14th-century Serbian monastery.

③ **Pristina** (p730) Exploring Europe's youngest country through its plucky and idiosyncratic capital city and enjoying its excellent dining and nightlife.

④ **Patriarchate of Peć**

(p734) Travelling back in time as you listen to haunting chanting at this medieval church.

⑤ **Bear Sanctuary** (p735) Visiting the rescued bears living in excellent conditions at this wonderful lakeside sanctuary that's just a short trip from the capital.

PRISTINA

☏ 038 / POP 211,000

Pristina is a fast-changing city that feels full of optimism and potential, even if its traffic-clogged streets and mismatched architectural styles don't make it an obviously attractive place. While the city does have a couple of worthwhile museums and galleries and serves as a base for interesting near-

by sights, for most visitors Pristina is a place where the atmosphere is as much an attraction as any classic tourist sight.

☉ Sights

Central Pristina has been impressively redesigned and is focused on the Ibrahim Rugova Sq, the centrepiece of the city at the end of the attractive, pedestrianised Blvd Nënë

Tereza. On summer evenings the square comes alive with strolling families, street performers and little tots racing around on miniature cars.

★ Emin Gjiku Ethnographic Museum
HISTORIC BUILDING

(Rr Iliaz Agushi; ⊙10am-5pm Tue-Sat, to 3pm Sun) **FREE** This wonderful annex of the Museum of Kosovo is located in two beautifully preserved Ottoman houses enclosed in a large walled garden. The English-speaking staff will give you a fascinating tour of both properties and point out the various unique pieces of clothing, weaponry, jewellery and household items on display in each. There's no better introduction to Kosovar culture.

It's not the easiest place to find and it's not always open during stated hours. The best bet is to ask staff at the Museum of Kosovo.

Museum of Kosovo
MUSEUM

(Sheshi Adam Jashari; ⊙10am-6pm Tue-Sun) **FREE** Pristina's main museum has recently reopened after extensive renovations. Displays begin back in the misty times of the Bronze Age. There are some wonderful statues and monuments to Dardanian gods and goddesses, plus a large stone relief depicting a Dardanian funeral procession.

National Gallery of Kosovo
GALLERY

(✆038 225 627; Rr Agim Ramadani 60; ⊙10am-6pm Mon-Fri, to 5pm Sat & Sun) **FREE** This excellent space approaches Kosovan art from a contemporary perspective (don't expect to see paintings from the country's history here) and is worth a look around. Exhibitions change frequently and the gallery space is normally given over to a single artist at any one time. At the time of research, the 'art' included a stable of live cows.

🛏 Sleeping

★ White Tree Hostel
HOSTEL €

(✆049 166 777; www.whitetreehostel.com; Rr Mujo Ulqinaku 15; dm €10-12, d €34; ✶🛜) Pristina's best hostel is run by a group of well-travelled locals who took a derelict house into their care, painted the tree in the courtyard white and gradually began to attract travellers with a cool backpacker vibe. It feels more like an Albanian beach resort than a downtown Pristina bolthole.

Dorms have between four and eight beds plus there are a couple of decent double rooms with private bathrooms. There's also a fully equipped kitchen and it adjoins a very chilled, semi-open-air lounge bar (open to nonguests), which is a perfect place to meet other young travellers. With bicycles attached to the walls and giant metal sculptures, it's all very Instagramable. The crew also runs a cocktail bar/nightclub in the same building.

★ Hotel Prima
BOUTIQUE HOTEL €€

(✆044 111 298; LIdhja e Prizrenit 24; s/d incl breakfast from €30/50; ✶🛜) This small family-run hotel on a quiet side street gets pretty much everything right and is easily one of the best sleeps in Pristina. The understated rooms have work desks, wardrobes, and thoughtful extras such as hair-dryers. The beds are solid and comfortable and the showers are always hot. English-speaking staff are full of tips and ideas for Kosovo travel. Excellent value.

🍴 Eating & Drinking

★ Soma Book Station
MEDITERRANEAN €€

(✆038 748818; 4/a Fazli Grajqevci; mains €5-11; ⊙8am-1am Mon-Sat; 🛜) Soma is a local institution among the young, and nearly all visitors to Pristina end up here at some point. The shady garden hums with activity at lunchtime, while the red-brick industrial-chic interior is lined with bookshelves and has a relaxed vibe. Food combines various tastes of the Mediterranean, including tuna salad, beef carpaccio, grilled fish, steaks and burgers.

There's a terrific selection of books and vinyl on sale, the central bar area is one of the best places to drink in town, and the entire place is run with passion, politeness and an attention to detail you simply won't find anywhere else in the city.

Renaissance
BALKAN €€€

(Renesansa; ✆044 239 377; Rr Musine Kokollari 35; set meals €15; ⊙6pm-midnight Mon-Sat) This atmospheric place might be Pristina's best-kept secret. Wooden doors open to a traditional stone-walled dining room where tables are brimming with local wine, delicious mezze and meaty main courses prepared by the family's matriarch. There's no menu and you'll just be brought a whole array of different dishes. Come with friends and prepare for a long, leisurely meal.

Vegetarians can be catered for but should call ahead. The restaurant can be rather

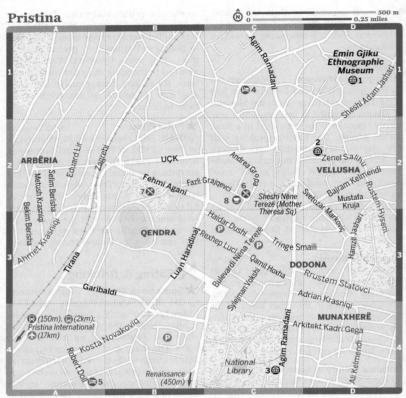

Pristina

N
0 _____ 500 m
0 _____ 0.25 miles

Pristina

Top Sights
1 Emin Gjiku Ethnographic
   Museum.................................D1

Sights
2 Museum of Kosovo D2
3 National Gallery of Kosovo C4

Sleeping
4 Hotel Prima C1

5 White Tree Hostel A4

Eating
6 Soma Book Station............................C2
7 Tiffany B2

Drinking & Nightlife
8 Dit' e Nat'..C2

tricky to find, as it's unsigned; taxi drivers usually know it.

Tiffany BALKAN €€€
(☏ 038 244 040; off Rr Fehmi Agani; meals €12; ◷ 9am-10.30pm Mon-Sat, from 6pm Sun; ☏) The organic menu here (delivered by efficient, if somewhat terse, English-speaking staff) is simply dazzling: sit on the sun-dappled terrace and enjoy the day's grilled special,

beautifully cooked seasonal vegetables drenched in olive oil, and freshly baked bread. Understandably much prized by the foreign community, this brilliant place is unsigned and somewhat hidden behind a well-tended bush on Fehmi Agani.

Dit' e Nat' CAFE
(☏ 038 742 037; www.ditenat.com/en; Rr Fazli Grajqevci 5; ◷ 8am-midnight Mon-Sat, from noon

Sun; ☎) 'Day and night', a bookshop-cafe-bar-performance space, is a home away from home for bookish expats and locals alike. There's a great selection of books in English, strong espresso, excellent cocktails, friendly English-speaking staff and occasional live music in the evenings, including jazz. Unusually for meat-loving Kosovo, Dit' e Nat' serves a few vegetarian light lunches and snacks.

ⓘ Getting There & Away

AIR
Pristina International Airport (☏ 038 501 502 1214; www.airportpristina.com) is 18km from the centre of town. There is currently no public transport to and from the airport, so you'll have to get a taxi into the city. Taxis charge €20 for the 20-minute trip to the city centre, though many will try to ask for more – always agree on a price before you get in. Going from the city to the airport, the cost is normally €13 to €15.

BUS
The **bus station** (Stacioni i Autobusëve; ☏ 038 550 011; Rr Lidja e Pejes) is 2km southwest of the centre off Blvd Bil Klinton. Taxis to the centre should cost €2, but drivers will often try to charge tourists €5 to €7.

International buses from Pristina include Belgrade (€15.50, seven hours, 11pm) and Novi Pazar (€7.50, three hours, three daily) in Serbia; Tirana, Albania (€10.50, five hours, every one to two hours); Skopje, North Macedonia (€5.50, two hours, hourly from 5.30am to 5pm); Podgorica, Montenegro (€15.50, seven hours, 7pm) and Ulcinj, Montenegro (€15.50, seven hours, 8am and 9pm).

Domestically there are buses to all corners of the country, including Prizren (€4, 75 minutes, every 20 minutes) and Peja (€4, 1½ hours, every 20 minutes).

TRAIN
Trains run from Pristina's small train station in the suburb of Fushë Kosovo to Peja (€3, two hours, twice daily at 8.01am and 4.41pm) and to Skopje in North Macedonia (€4, three hours, 7.22am daily).

ⓘ Getting Around
Pristina has a comprehensive bus network. Tickets cost 40c and can be bought on board. With the city centre being as small as it is, few travellers ever need to make use of these buses. Taxi meters start at €1.50, and most trips around the city can be done for under €3. Try **Radio Taxi Victory** (☏ 038 555 333).

OFF THE BEATEN TRACK

RUGOVA VALLEY

The **Rugova Valley** and the mountains that hem it in are Kosovo's adventure playground. The serpentine valley itself winds westward out of Peja and climbs steadily upwards towards the border of Montenegro. Narrow side-roads spin off this main route, giving access to high mountain pastures, glacial lakes and fairy-tale pine forests. Activities include caving, rafting, *via ferrata*, zip-lining, skiing and snowshoeing, but it's the hiking that really makes this a stand out tourist destination. This knot of mountains (which also extends into parts of Albania and Montenegro) is one of the most beautiful mountain ranges in eastern Europe and remains deliciously unspoiled. Slowly, though, facilities for trekkers are increasing.

The world-renowned **Peaks of the Balkans** long-distance hiking route crosses through the heart of these mountains, and throughout the area hiking trails are becoming better way-marked. If you don't have time to embark on the epic multi-day Peaks of the Balkans trail then there are lots of excellent day hikes. Two of our favourites are the half-day hike to the beautiful, forest-shrouded Kuqishta and Drelej lakes with a possible extension on to the summit of 2522m Mt Guni i Kuq (which would make for a full day hike) or the full day hike to the knife-ridge summit of Mt Hajila (2403m) with its extraordinary views down onto the plains of Montenegro. For any of these walks, it's advisable to hire an experienced guide through one of the Peja tour agencies such as Balkan Natural Adventure (p734).

WESTERN KOSOVO

Peja (Peć)

📞 039 / POP 97,000

Peja (Peć in Serbian) is Kosovo's third-largest city and one flanked by sites sacred to Orthodox Serbians. With a Turkish-style bazaar at its heart Peja would be a worthwhile stop on its own, but for most visitors the real reason to visit is to use the town as the launch pad to some wonderful mountain adventures in the spectacular nearby Rugova Valley and surrounding mountains. All of this means that Peja is fast becoming Kosovo's international tourism hub.

👁 Sights

★ Patriarchate of Peć   MONASTERY

(Pećka Patrijaršija; 📞 044 150 755; with audio guide €2; ⊙ 8am-6pm) This church and nunnery complex on the outskirts of Peja are a raw slice of Serbian Orthodoxy that has existed here since the late 13th century. Outside in the landscaped grounds all is bright and colourful, but once inside the church it feels more like you're within a dark cave with magnificent faded frescoes covering the walls and ceiling. The entire complex dates from between the 1230s and the 1330s.

👉 Tours

★ Balkan Natural Adventure   ADVENTURE

(📞 049 661 105; www.bnadventure.com; Mbretereesha Teute) Balkan Natural Adventure is easily the stand out local adventure tour operator. In fact, it was the friendly English-speaking team here who first established many of the trekking trails in the surrounding moun-

tains and put in the *via ferrata* and zipline. They can also organise caving, rock climbing or snowshoeing and they lead Peaks of the Balkans hiking tours.

🛏 Sleeping & Eating

Stone Bridge Guesthouse   HOTEL €

(📞 049 797 112; stonebridge.gh@gmail.com; Rr Lidhja e Pejës 6; d €25; ☎) This new, 10-room hotel in the heart of the town offers superb value for money. The modern, white-and-grey rooms have ubercomfortable mattresses and there are small, modern bathrooms. Try to nab a back room to cut out the worst of the street noise.

★ Dukagjini Hotel   HOTEL €€

(📞 038 771 177; www.hoteldukagjini.com; Sheshi i Dëshmorëve 2; d incl breakfast from €55; 🅿 ⊜ ❄ ☎ ✴) The regal stone-walled Dukagjini is the smartest address in town (and a popular wedding venue). Rooms can be rather small but are grandly appointed and have supremely comfortable beds; many on the 1st floor have huge terraces overlooking the central square. There's a pool and gym and a huge restaurant with views of the river. Free parking.

★ Art Design   BALKAN €

(📞 049 585 885, 044 222 254; Rr Enver Hadri 53; mains €3.50-6; ⊙ 8am-midnight) Despite sounding flash and modern, Art Design is actually an old house brimming with character and full of local arts and crafts. Choose between dining outside over a little stream or in one of the two rather chintzy dining rooms. Traditional dishes here include *sarma* (meat and rice rolled in grape leaves) and *speca dollma* (peppers filled with meat and rice).

WORTH A TRIP

VISOKI DEČANI MONASTERY

Built in the early 14th century by Serbian king Stefan Dečanski, the **Visoki Dečani Monastery** (📞 049 776 254; www.decani.org; ⊙ 10am-2.30pm & 3.30-5.30pm Mon-Sat, 10am-5.30pm Sun) FREE is in a beautiful spot beneath the mountains and surrounded by pine and chestnut trees. If you think the setting is attractive then you'll gasp in wonder as you push open the wooden doors of the church and first lay eyes on the treasures within. With its floor-to-ceiling, Biblical murals it's like stepping into an enormous medieval paintbox. There can be few more beautiful churches in Europe.

It's on the outskirts of Dečani, 15km south of Peja (Peć). Buses go to Dečani from Peja (€1, 30 minutes, frequent) on their way to Gjakova. It's a pleasant 1km walk to the monastery from the bus stop. From the roundabout in the middle of town, take the second exit if you're coming from Peja. You will need to leave your passport or ID card with the soldiers at the entrance gate if you wish to enter the complex.

GRAČANICA MONASTERY & BEAR SANCTUARY

Explore beyond Pristina by heading southeast to two of the country's best sights. Dusty fingers of sunlight pierce the darkness of **Gračanica Monastery** (€2; ⊗ 8am-6pm), completed in 1321 by Serbian King Milutin. It's an oasis in a town that is the cultural centre of Serbs in central Kosovo. Do dress respectably (that means no shorts or sleeveless tops for anyone, and head scarves for women) and you'll be very welcome to look around this historical complex and to view the gorgeous icons in the main church. The medieval-era paintings here are impressive enough but the real treat is saved for the smaller side chapel, which is an enchanted cavern of vivid, lifelike murals. Take a Gjilan-bound bus (€0.50, 15 minutes, every 30 minutes); the monastery's on your left.

Further along the road to Gjilan is the excellent **Bear Sanctuary** (☑ 045 826 072; www.facebook.com/PylliiArinjvePrishtina; Mramor; adult/child Apr-Oct €2/1, Nov-Mar €1/0.50c; ⊗ 10am-7pm Apr-Oct, to 4pm Nov-Mar), in the village of Mramor. Here you can visit a number of brown bears that were rescued from cruel captivity by the charity Four Paws. All the bears here were once kept in tiny cages as mascots for restaurants, but when the keeping of bears was outlawed in Kosovo in 2010, Four Paws stepped in to care for these wonderful animals. Sadly some of them still suffer from trauma and don't socialise well, but their excellent conditions are heartening indeed. Ask to be let off any Gjilan-bound bus by the Delfina gas station at the entrance to Mramor, then follow the road back past the lakeside, and then follow the track around to the right.

ⓘ Getting There & Away

BUS

The town's **bus station** (Rr Adem Jashar) is a 15-minute walk from the town centre. Frequent buses run to Pristina (€4, 1½ hours, every 20 minutes), Prizren (€3, 80 minutes to two hours, frequent) and Deçan (€1, 30 minutes, frequent). International buses link Peja with Ulclinj (€20, 10 hours, 10am and 8.30pm) and Podgorica in Montenegro (€15, seven hours, 10am).

TRAIN

Trains depart Peja for Pristina (€3, two hours, twice daily) from the town's small **train station** (Rr Emrush Miftari). To find the station, walk away from the Hotel Dukagjini down Rr Emrush Miftari for 1.4km.

SOUTHERN KOSOVO

Prizren

☑ 029 / POP 185,000

Picturesque Prizren, with its charming mosque- and church-filled old town, shines with an enthusiasm that's infectious. It's Kosovo's second city and most obvious tourist town, and is well worth a day or two's lingering exploration. Prizren is equally known for Dokufest, a documentary film festival held each August that attracts documentary makers and fans from all over the world.

◉ Sights

Prizren Fortress   CASTLE

(Kalaja; ⊗ dawn-dusk) FREE It's well worth making the steep 15-minute hike up from Prizren's old town (follow the road past the Orthodox Church on the hillside; it's well signed and pretty obvious) for the superb views over the city and on into the distance. The fortress itself is a little tumble-down but restoration work is currently underway. In the evening heaps of locals come up here and a slight carnival atmosphere prevails. In the white-heat of day, it can be quite lifeless.

⊨ Sleeping

Driza's House   HOSTEL €

(☑ 049 618 181; www.drizas-house.com; Remzi Ademaj 7; dm incl breakfast €9-15, tw/tr €25/42; ❄ ⊚) This former family home in a courtyard just off the river embankment retains a welcoming, homey vibe and is full of local charm. It's made up of two (10- and four-bed) dorms with custom-made bunk beds, all of which include curtains, reading lights, personal electricity plugs and lockable storage cupboards, and there's a comfortable private three-bed room.

★ Hotel Prizreni   HOTEL €

(☑ 029 225 200; www.hotelprizreni.com; Rr Shën Flori 2; s/d incl breakfast from €30/34; Ⓟ ❄ ⊚) With an unbeatable location just behind the Sinan Pasha Mosque (though some may be less pleased with the location during the dawn call to prayer), the Prizreni is a pleasant combination of traditional and modern, with 12 small but stylish and contemporary rooms, great views and enthusiastic staff. There's a good restaurant downstairs (open 8am to 11pm).

✕ Eating

★ Te Syla 'Al Hambra' KEBAB €

(☑ 049 157 400; www.tesyla.com; Shuaib Spahiu; kebabs €2-4; ☺ 8am-11pm) Unlike most riverside places in Prizren, there's nothing pretentious about this place. It was first established in the 1960s by a street vendor who just sizzled up kebabs on the corner. From such humble beginnings grew this local classic. The kebabs are as sensational as ever, with the meat literally melting in your mouth.

❶ Getting There & Away

Prizren is well connected by bus to Pristina (€4, two hours, every 20 minutes), Peja (€3, 80 minutes to two hours, frequent), Skopje in North Macedonia (€10, three hours, two daily) and Tirana in Albania (€12, three hours, seven daily).

The **bus station** is on the right bank of the river, a short walk from the old town: follow the right-hand side of the river embankment away from the castle until you come to the traffic circle, then turn left onto Rr De Rada. The bus station will be on your left after around 200m.

SURVIVAL GUIDE

❶ Directory A–Z

ACCOMMODATION

Accommodation is booming in Kosovo, with most large towns now offering a good range of options. There are now backpacker-style hostels in all major cities and plenty of midrange and even top-end accommodation in Pristina.

LGBTIQ+ TRAVELLERS

While legal, homosexuality remains taboo in Kosovo, and it's not a subject that many people will be comfortable broaching. That said, gay and lesbian travellers should generally have no problems, though public displays of affection are definitely inadvisable. There are no gay bars or clubs in the country, though there are a few gay-friendly bars in Pristina and Prizren. Most contact happens online.

MONEY

Kosovo's currency is the euro, despite not being part of the eurozone or the EU. ATMs are common, and established businesses accept credit cards.

OPENING HOURS

Opening hours vary, but these are the usual hours of business.

Banks 8am to 5pm Monday to Friday, until 2pm Saturday

Bars 8am to 11pm

Shops 8am to 6pm Monday to Friday, until 3pm Saturday

Restaurants 8am to midnight

PUBLIC HOLIDAYS

Note that traditional Islamic and Orthodox Christian holidays are also observed, including Ramadan.

New Year's Day 1 January

Independence Day 17 February

Kosovo Constitution Day 9 April

Labour Day 1 May

Europe Day 9 May

SAFE TRAVEL

Northern Kosovo Sporadic violence does occur in north Mitrovica and a few other flashpoints where Serbian and Kosovar communities live in close proximity.

Landmines Unexploded ordnance has been cleared from roads and paths, but you should seek KFOR advice (http://jfcnaples.nato.int/kfor) before venturing too remotely. That said, the situation is improving fast, with mine-clearance programmes all over the country.

Driving While it's perfectly legal, it's not a good idea to travel in Kosovo with Serbian plates on your car: you'll potentially leave yourself open to random attacks or vandalism from locals.

TELEPHONE

Mobile coverage is excellent throughout the country, and it's easy to obtain a SIM card with data for as little as €10; simply bring your passport to one of the offices of the three mobile phone providers. Kosovo uses the GSM phone system and American CDMA phones won't work here.

VISAS

Kosovo is visa-free for EU, Australian, Canadian, Japanese, New Zealand, South African and US passport holders for stays of up to 90 days.

❶ Getting There & Away

AIR

Pristina International Airport (p733) is 18km from the centre of Pristina. Airlines flying to Kosovo include Air Pristina, Adria, Austrian Airlines, easyJet, Norwegian, Pegasus and Turkish Airlines.

ⓘ BORDER CROSSINGS

Albania There are three border crossings between Kosovo and Albania. To get to Albania's Koman Ferry, use the Qafa Morina border crossing west of Gjakova. A short distance further south is the Qafë Prush crossing, though the road continuing into Albania is bad here. The busiest border is at Vërmicë, where a modern motorway connects to Tirana.

North Macedonia Cross into Blace from Pristina and Gllobocicë from Prizren.

Montenegro The main crossing is the Kulla/Rožaje crossing on the road between Rožaje and Peja.

Serbia There are six border crossings between Kosovo and Serbia. Be aware that Kosovo's independence is not recognised by Serbia, so if you plan to continue to Serbia but entered Kosovo via Albania, North Macedonia or Montenegro, officials at the Serbian border will deem that you entered Serbia illegally and you will not be let in. You'll need to exit Kosovo to a third country and then enter Serbia from there. If you entered Kosovo from Serbia, there's no problem returning to Serbia.

LAND

Kosovo has good bus connections between Albania, Montenegro and North Macedonia, with regular services from Pristina, Peja and Prizren to Tirana (Albania), Skopje (North Macedonia) and Podgorica (Montenegro). There's also a train line from Pristina to Skopje. You can take international bus trips to and from all neighbouring capital cities; note that buses to and from Belgrade in Serbia travel via Montenegro.

ⓘ Getting Around

BUS

Buses stop at distinct blue signs but can be flagged down anywhere. Bus journeys are generally cheap, but the going can be slow on Kosovo's single-lane roads.

CAR & MOTORCYCLE

Drivers should carry their licences with them whenever on the road, as police checks are not uncommon. Road conditions in Kosovo are generally good, though watch out for potholes on some poorly maintained stretches. Driving techniques in Kosovo are erratic at best. When driving, keep alert!

European Green Card vehicle insurance is not valid in Kosovo, so you'll need to purchase vehicle insurance at the border when you enter with a car; this is a hassle-free and inexpensive procedure.

It's perfectly easy to hire cars here and travel with them to neighbouring countries (with the exception of Serbia). Note that Serbian-plated cars have been attacked in Kosovo, and rental companies do not let cars hired in Kosovo travel to Serbia and vice versa.

TRAIN

The train system is something of a novelty, but services connect Pristina to Peja and to Skopje in neighbouring North Macedonia. Locals generally take buses.

KOSOVO SURVIVAL GUIDE

Latvia

POP 1.9 MILLION

Best Places to Eat

➜ Istaba (p746)
➜ 36.Line (p748)
➜ 3 Pavaru (p745)
➜ Fazenda Bazārs (p746)

Best Places to Stay

➜ Neiburgs (p745)
➜ Hotel Bergs (p745)
➜ Hotel MaMa (p748)
➜ Art Hotel Laine (p745)
➜ 2 Baloži (p750)

Why Go?

A tapestry of sea, lakes and woods, Latvia is best described as a vast, unspoilt parkland with just one real city – its cosmopolitan capital, Rīga. The country might be small, but the amount of personal space it provides is enormous. You can always secure a chunk of pristine nature all for yourself, be it for trekking, cycling or dreaming away on a white-sand beach amid pine-covered dunes.

Having been invaded by every regional power, Latvia has more cultural layers and a less homogenous population than its neighbours. People here fancy themselves to be the least pragmatic and the most artistic of the Baltic lot. They prove the point with myriad festivals and a merry, devil-may-care attitude – well, a subdued Nordic version of it.

When to Go
Rīga

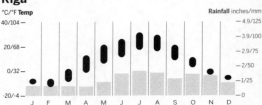

Jun–Aug Summer starts with an all-night solstice romp, then it's off to the beach.

Sep Refusing to let summer go, Rīgans sip lattes under heat lamps at alfresco cafes.

Dec Celebrate the festive season in the birthplace of the Christmas tree.

Entering the Country

Air travel to Latvia is primarily via Rīga International Airport (p747), about 13km southwest of the city centre. **Liepāja International Airport** (www.liepaja-airport.lv) serves more than 60 destinations with connections through Rīga.

Thanks to the Schengen Agreement, there are no border checks when traveling between Estonia and Lithuania by car. International bus service is operated by **Ecolines** (www.ecolines.net) and **Lux Express & Simple Express** (www.luxexpress.eu).

International trains head from Rīga to Moscow (16 hours), St Petersburg (15 hours) and Minsk (12 hours) daily. There are no direct trains to Estonia; you'll need to change at Valga.

Ferry services from Rīga, Liepāja and Ventspils connect Latvia to Swedish and German ports.

ITINERARIES

Three Days
Fill your first two days with a feast of architectural eye candy in Rīga (p741) and then take a day trip to opulent Rundāle Palace (p749).

One Week
After following the above itinerary, spend day four lazing on the beach and coveting the gracious wooden houses of Jūrmala (p748). The following morning head west to Kuldīga (p748) before continuing on to Ventspils (p750). Spend your last days exploring Sigulda (p751) and Cēsis (p752) within the leafy confines of Gauja National Park.

Essential Food & Drink

These are the pillars of Lavtian gastronomy:

Black Balzam The jet-black, 45%-proof concoction is a secret recipe of more than a dozen fairy-tale ingredients.

Mushrooms A national obsession; mushroom-picking takes the country by storm during the first showers of autumn.

Alus For such a tiny nation there's definitely no shortage of *alus* (beer) – each major town has its own brew. You can't go wrong with Užavas (Ventspils' contribution).

Kvass A beloved beverage made from fermented rye bread. It's surprisingly popular with kids!

Rye bread Apart from being tasty and arguably healthier than their wheat peers, these large brown loafs have aesthetic value too, matching nicely the dark wood of Latvia's Nordic interiors.

Berries Sold at markets all over the country, so you needn't go deep into the woods to collect a jar of them yourself.

AT A GLANCE

Area 64,589 sq km

Capital Rīga

Country Code 371

Currency euro (€)

Emergency 112

Language Latvian, Russian (unofficial)

Time Eastern European Time (GMT/UTC plus two hours)

Visas Not required for citizens of the EU, USA, Canada, Japan, New Zealand and Australia for stays of up to 90 days.

Sleeping Price Ranges

The following price ranges refer to the cost of a double room with private bathroom.

€ less than €40

€€ €40–80

€€€ more than €80

Eating Price Ranges

We've based the following Latvian price ranges on the average price of a main dish.

€ less than €7

€€ €7–14

€€€ more than €14

Resources

1188 (www.1188.lv)

Latvian Tourism Development Agency (www.latvia.travel)

Latvia Institute (www.li.lv)

Latvia Highlights

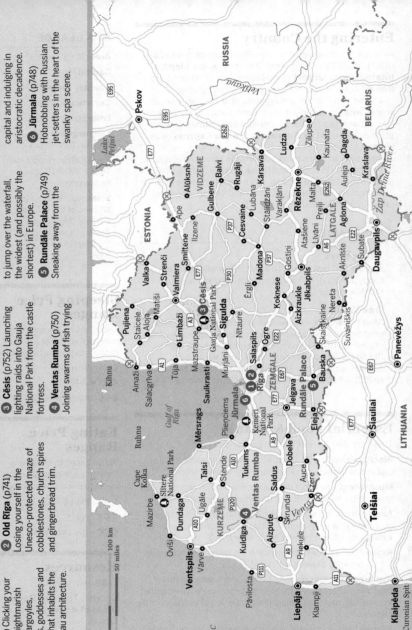

1 Riga (p741) Clicking your camera at the nightmarish menagerie of gargoyles, mythical beasts, goddesses and twisting vines that inhabits the city's art nouveau architecture.

2 Old Riga (p741) Losing yourself in the Unesco-protected maze of cobblestones, church spires and gingerbread trim.

3 Cēsis (p752) Launching lighting raids into Gauja National Park from the castle fortress.

4 Ventas Rumba (p750) Joining swarms of fish trying to jump over the waterfall, the widest (and possibly the shortest) in Europe.

5 Rundāle Palace (p749) Sneaking away from the capital and indulging in aristocratic decadence.

6 Jūrmala (p748) Hobnobbing with Russian jet-setters in the heart of the swanky spa scene.

RĪGA

POP 641,400

The Gothic spires that dominate Rīga's cityscape might suggest austerity, but it is the flamboyant art nouveau that forms the flesh and the spirit of this vibrant cosmopolitan city, the largest of all three Baltic capitals. Like all northerners, it is quiet and reserved on the outside, but there is some powerful chemistry going on inside its hip bars and modern art centres, and in the kitchens of its cool experimental restaurants. Standing next to a gulf named after itself, Rīga is a short drive from jet-setting sea resort, Jūrmala, which comes with a stunning white-sand beach. But if you are craving solitude and a pristine environment, gorgeous sea dunes and blueberry-filled forests begin right outside the city boundaries.

◎ Sights

Kalnciema Kvartāls   AREA

(☑ 6761 4322; www.kalnciemaiela.lv; Kalnciema iela 35) A lovingly restored courtyard was several wooden buildings is the location of a very popular weekend market, where Rīgans hawk their local produce – meats, cheeses, vegetables and even spirits. But there is more to it, with live concerts, performances and art exhibitions taking place outside the market days. Even if nothing is going on, sipping coffee in one of the on-site cafes and soaking in the atmosphere of an old Rīga suburb is worthwhile. Check the website for upcoming events.

◎ Old Rīga (Vecrīga)

The curving cobbled streets of Rīga's medieval core are best explored at random. Once you're sufficiently lost amid the tangle of gabled roofs, church spires and crooked alleyways, you will begin to uncover a stunning, World Heritage–listed realm of sky-scraping cathedrals, gaping city squares and crumbling castle walls.

★ Rīga Cathedral   CHURCH

(Rīgas Doms; ☑ 6722 7573; www.doms.lv; Doma laukums 1; €3; ⊙ 9am-6pm Mon-Tue & Sat, 9am-5pm Wed & Fri, 9am-5.30pm Thu, 2-5pm Sun May-Sep) Founded in 1211 as the seat of the Rīga diocese, this enormous (once Catholic, now Evangelical Lutheran) cathedral is the largest medieval church in the Baltic. The architecture is an amalgam of styles from the 13th to the 18th centuries: the eastern

end, the oldest portion, has Romanesque features; the tower is 18th-century baroque; and much of the rest dates from a 15th-century Gothic rebuilding.

St Peter's Church   CHURCH

(Sv Pētera baznīca; www.peterbaznica.riga.lv; Skārņu iela 19; adult/child €9/3; ⊙ 10am-7pm Tue-Sat, noon-7pm Sun) Forming the centrepiece of Rīga's skyline, this Gothic church is thought to be around 800 years old, making it one of the oldest medieval buildings in the Baltic. Its soaring red-brick interior is relatively unadorned, except for heraldic shields mounted on the columns. A colourful contrast is provided by the art exhibitions staged in the side aisles. At the rear of the church, a lift whisks visitors to a viewing platform 72m up the steeple.

★ Art Museum Rīga Bourse   MUSEUM

(Mākslas muzejs Rīgas Birža; ☑ 6732 4461; www.lnmm.lv; Doma laukums 6; adult/child €6/3; ⊙10am-6pm Tue-Thu, Sat & Sun, to 8pm Fri) Rīga's lavishly restored stock exchange building is a worthy showcase for the city's art treasures. The elaborate facade features a coterie of deities that dance between the windows, while inside, gilt chandeliers sparkle from ornately moulded ceilings. The Oriental section features beautiful Chinese and Japanese ceramics and an Egyptian mummy, but the main halls are devoted to Western art, including a Monet painting and a scaled-down cast of Rodin's *The Kiss*.

Rīga History & Navigation Museum   MUSEUM

(Rīgas vēstures un kuģniecības muzejs; ☑ 6735 6676; www.rigamuz.lv; Palasta iela 4; adult/child €5/1; ⊙10am-5pm) Founded in 1773, this is the oldest museum in the Baltic, situated in the old cathedral monastery. The permanent collection features artefacts from the Bronze Age all the way to WWII, ranging from lovely pre-Christian jewellery to preserved hands removed from medieval forgers. A highlight is the beautiful neoclassical Column Hall, built when Latvia was part of the Russian empire and filled with relics from that time.

★ Blackheads House   HISTORIC BUILDING

(Melngalvju nams; ☑ 6704 3678; www.melngalvju nams.lv; Rātslaukums 7; adult/child €6/3; ⊙11am-6pm Tue-Sun) Built in 1344 as a veritable fraternity house for the Blackheads guild of unmarried German merchants, the original house was bombed in 1941 and flattened by

Rīga

LATVIA RĪGA

Rīga Passenger Terminal (400m)

Auseklīa iela

Elizabetes iela

Pulkveža Brieža iela

Strēlnieku iela

Dzirnavu iela

26

1

Alberta Iela

QUIET CENTRE
(KLUSAIS CENTRS)

Emīla Melngaiļa iela

Hanzas iela

Zala iela

K Valdemāra iela

28

14

Skolas iela

23

25

22

Baznīcas iela

Antonijas iela

E. Melngaiļa iela

Elizabetes iela

Kronvalda parks

Kronvalda bulvāris

Kalpaka bulvāris

Alunāna iela

K Valdemāra iela

8

CENTRAL RĪGA
(CENTRS)

Mikela iela

Esplanāde

Citadeles iela

29

Kalpaka bulvāris

10

Raina bulvāris

Rīga
(12km)

K Valdemāra iela

Jēkaba iela

Basteja bulvāris

Bastejkalns

ZA Meierovica bulvāris

Brīvības bulvāris

Tērbatas iela

Elizabetes iela

Pils laukums

Torņa iela

2

Arsenāls Exhibition Hall

Trokšņu iela

21

Vērmanesdārzs

OLD RĪGA
(VECRĪGA)

Smilšu iela

Maza Pils iela

7

Vaļņu iela

Arhitektu

Alfrēda Kalniņa iela

Mazā Pils iela

Anglikāņu

Art Museum
Rīga Bourse

3

Zirgu iela

Merķela iela

Rīga Cathedral 5

Doma laukums

16

Kalēju iela

Vāgnera iela

Teātra iela

13

30

Audēju iela

15

Satekles iela

11 Novembra Krastmala

11

Pālasta iela

Jaunī iela

20

Skārņu iela

Kaļķu iela

9

17

Livu laukums

Vaļņu iela

Aspazijas bulvāris

Blackheads House

Rātslaukums

12

4

Grēcinieku iela

19

Audēju iela

Stacijas laukums

Tourist Information Centre

Kungu iela

Central Train Station

Latviešu Strēlnieku laukums

Peldu iela

Alberta laukums

Akmens Bridge

Marstaļu iela

Kungu iela

Kalēju iela

13 Janvāra iela

11 novembra krastmala iela

Tourist Information Centre - Bus Station

Gogoļa iela

Rīga International Bus Station

City Canal
(Pilsētas kanāls)

6

Rīga Central Market

Nēģu iela

Gogoļa iela

Pragas iela

Daugava River

0   400 m
0   0.2 miles

Rīga

◎ Top Sights
1 Alberta iela	C1
2 Arsenāls Exhibition Hall	A4
3 Art Museum Rīga Bourse	B5
4 Blackheads House	B5
5 Rīga Cathedral	A5
6 Rīga Central Market	C7

◎ Sights
7 Freedom Monument	C4
8 Latvian National Museum of Art	C2
9 Museum of Decorative Arts & Design	B5
10 Nativity of Christ Cathedral	C3
11 Rīga History & Navigation Museum	A5
12 St Peter's Church	B5

⊕ Activities, Courses & Tours
13 Rīga Bike Tours	C5

🛏 Sleeping
14 Art Hotel Laine	D2
15 Cinnamon Sally	D5
16 Dome Hotel	A5
17 Ekes Konvents	B5
18 Hotel Bergs	E4
19 Naughty Squirrel	C6
20 Neiburgs	B5

⊗ Eating
21 3 Pavaru	B4
22 Big Bad Bagels	D2
23 Fazenda Bazārs	D2
24 Istaba	F3
25 Miit	D2
26 Vincents	B1

◉ Drinking & Nightlife
27 Autentika (B2)	E1
28 Kaņepes Kultūras Centrs	D2
29 Leningrad	B3

✪ Entertainment
30 Latvian National Opera	C5

the Soviets seven years later. Somehow the original blueprints survived and an exact replica of this fantastically ornate structure was completed in 2001 for Rīga's 800th birthday.

Museum of Decorative Arts & Design
MUSEUM

(Dekoratīvi lietišķās mākslas muzejs; ☑ 6732 4461; www.lnmm.lv; Skārņu iela 10/20; adult/child €5/2.50; ⊙ 11am-5pm Tue & Thu-Sun, to 7pm Wed) The former St George's Church houses a museum devoted to applied art from the art

ART NOUVEAU IN RĪGA

If you ask any Rīgan where to find the city's world-famous art nouveau architecture, you will always get the same answer: 'Look up!'

Rīga has the greatest number of art nouveau buildings of any city in Europe. More than 750 buildings boast this flamboyant style of decor which is also known as *Jugendstil*, meaning 'youth style'. It was named after Munich-based magazine, *Die Jugend*, which popularised it around the turn of the 20th century.

Rīga's art nouveau district (known more formally as the 'Quiet Centre') is anchored around Alberta iela – check out 2a, 4 and 13 in particular – but you'll find fine examples throughout the city.

nouveau period to the present, including an impressive collection of furniture, woodcuts, tapestries and ceramics. The building's foundations date back to 1207 when the Livonian Brothers of the Sword erected their castle here. Since the rest of the original knights' castle was levelled by rioting citizens at the end of the same century, it is the only building that remains intact since the birth of Rīga.

★ **Arsenāls Exhibition Hall**　　GALLERY
(Izstāžu zāle Arsenāls; ☑ 6735 7527; www.lnmm. lv; Torņa iela 1; adult/child €3.50/2; ⊙ 11am-6pm Tue, Wed & Fri, to 8pm Thu, noon-5pm Sat & Sun) Behind a row of spooky granite heads depicting Latvia's most prominent artists, the imperial arsenal, constructed in 1832 to store weapons for the Russian tsar's army, is now a prime spot for international and local art exhibitions. Also check out the massive wooden stairs at the back of the building – their simple yet funky geometry predates modern architecture.

◉ Central Rīga (Centrs)

★ **Alberta iela**　　ARCHITECTURE
It's like a huge painting, which you can spend hours staring at, as your eye detects more and more intriguing details. But in fact, this must-see Rīga sight is a rather functional street with residential houses, restaurants and shops. Art nouveau, other-

wise known as *Jugendstil*, is the style, and the master responsible for most of these is Mikhail Eisenstein (father of filmmaker Sergei Eisenstein). Named after the founder of Rīga, Bishop Albert von Buxthoeven, the street was the architect's gift to Rīga on its 700th anniversary.

Freedom Monument　　MONUMENT
(Brīvības bulvāris) Affectionately known as 'Milda', Rīga's Freedom Monument towers above the city between Old and Central Rīga. Paid for by public donations, the monument was designed by Kārlis Zāle and erected in 1935 where a statue of Russian ruler Peter the Great once stood.

Latvian National Museum of Art　　GALLERY
(Latvijas Nacionālā mākslas muzejs; ☑ 6732 4461; www.lnmm.lv; K Valdemāra iela 10a; adult/child €6/3; ⊙ 10am-6pm Tue-Thu, to 8pm Fri, to 5pm Sat & Sun) Latvia's main gallery, sitting within the Esplanāde's leafy grounds, is an impressive building that was purpose-built in a baroque-classical style in 1905. Well-displayed paintings form a who's-who of Latvian art from the 18th to late 20th centuries. Temporary exhibitions supplement the interesting permanent collection.

Nativity of Christ Cathedral　　CHURCH
(Kristus Piedzimšanas katedrāle; ☑ 6721 1207; www.pravoslavie.lv; Brīvības bulvāris 23; ⊙ 7am-7pm) With gilded cupolas peeking through the trees, this Byzantine-styled Orthodox cathedral (1883) adds a dazzling dash of Russian bling to the skyline. During the Soviet period the church was converted into a planetarium, but it's since been restored to its former use. Mind the dress code – definitely no shorts; women are asked to cover their heads.

◉ Moscow Suburb (Maskavas forštate)

★ **Rīga Central Market**　　MARKET
(Rīgas Centrāltirgus; ☑ 6722 9985; www.rct.lv; Nēģu iela 7; ⊙ 7am-6pm) Haggle for your huckleberries at this vast market, housed in a series of WWI Zeppelin hangars and spilling outdoors as well. It's an essential Rīga experience, providing bountiful opportunities both for people-watching and to stock up for a picnic lunch. Although the number of traders is dwindling, the dairy and fish departments, each occupying a separate hangar, present a colourful picture of abundance

that activates ancient foraging instincts in the visitors.

☞ Tours

Rīga Bike Tours CYCLING
(📞 28225773; www.rigabiketours.com; Riharda Vagnera iela 14; ⊙ 10am-6pm) These folks run daily bicycle tours of Rīga that last for three hours and cost €20 (€15 with your own bike). Longer cycling tours of Latvia are also on offer. Its useful office operates under the Rīga Explorers Club brand.

E.A.T. Rīga WALKING, CYCLING
(📞 22469888; www.eatriga.lv; tours from €20) Foodies may be initially disappointed to discover that the name stands for 'Experience Alternative Tours' and the focus is on off-the-beaten-track themed walking tours (Old Rīga, Art Nouveau, Alternative Rīga, Retro Rīga). But don't fret – Rīga Food Tasting is an option. It also offers a cycling tour of Jūrmala.

🛏 Sleeping

🛏 Old Rīga (Vecrīga)

Cinnamon Sally HOSTEL €
(📞 22042280; www.cinnamonsally.com; Merķeļa iela 1; dm €11-17; @ 🛜) Convenient for the train and bus stations, Cinnamon Sally comes with perfectly clean rooms, very helpful staff and a common area cluttered with sociable characters. It might feel odd to be asked to take off your shoes at the reception, but it's all part of its relentless effort to create a homey atmosphere.

★ Naughty Squirrel HOSTEL €€
(📞 6722 0073; www.thenaughtysquirrel.com; Kaļķu iela 50; dm €12-16, r €45-80; ❋ @ 🛜) Slashes of bright paint and cartoon graffiti brighten up the city's capital of backpackerdom, which buzzes with travellers rattling the foosball table and chilling out in the TV room. Plush pillows and blankets in private rooms and homey wooden bunks in dorms make the place feel anything but institutional.

★ Ekes Konvents HOTEL €€
(📞 6735 8393; http://ekes-konvents.hotels-riga-lv; Skārņu iela 22; r €65; 🛜) Not to be confused with Konventa Sēta next door, the 600-year-old Ekes Konvents oozes wobbly medieval charm from every crooked nook and cranny. Curl up with a book in the adorable stone

alcoves on the landing of each storey. Breakfast is served down the block.

★ Dome Hotel HOTEL €€€
(📞 6750 9010; www.domehotel.lv; Miesnieku iela 4; r €261-432; 🛜) It's hard to imagine that this centuries-old structure was once part of a row of butcheries. Today a gorgeous wooden staircase leads guests up to a charming assortment of uniquely decorated rooms that sport eaved ceilings, wooden panelling, upholstered furniture and picture windows with city views.

★ Neiburgs HOTEL €€€
(📞 6711 5522; www.neiburgs.com; Jauņ iela 25/27; r €194-287; ❋ 🛜) Occupying one of Old Rīga's finest art nouveau buildings, Neiburgs blends preserved details with contemporary touches to achieve its signature boutique-chic style. Try for a room on one of the higher floors – you'll be treated to a view of a colourful clutter of gabled roofs and twisting medieval spires.

🛏 Central Rīga (Centrs)

★ Art Hotel Laine HOTEL €€
(📞 6728 8816; www.laine.lv; Skolas iela 11; s €55, d €65-77, superior d €126; P 🛜) Embedded in an apartment block with an antiquated lift taking guests to the reception on the 3rd floor, this place brings you closer to having your own home in Rīga than most hotels can or indeed wish to do. Dark green walls and armchair velvet, art on the walls, and bathtubs and furniture from yesteryear only complement the overall homey feeling.

Hotel Bergs HOTEL €€€
(📞 6777 0900; www.hotelbergs.lv; Elizabetes iela 83/85; ste from €203; P ❋ 🛜) A refurbished 19th-century building embellished with a Scandi-sleek extension, Hotel Bergs embodies the term 'luxury'. The spacious suites are lavished with high-quality monochromatic furnishings and some have kitchens. There's even a 'pillow menu', allowing guests to choose from an array of different bed pillows based on material and texture.

✕ Eating

✕ Old Rīga (Vecrīga)

★ 3 Pavaru MODERN EUROPEAN €€€
(📞 20370537; www.3pavari.lv; Torņa iela 4; mains €18-26; ⊙ noon-11pm) The stellar trio of chefs

who run this show have a jazzy approach to cooking, with improvisation at the heart of the compact and ever-changing menu. The emphasis is on experimentation (leg of lamb with anchovies, anyone?) and artful visual presentation that could have made Mark Rothko or Joan Miró gasp in admiration.

★ **Istaba** CAFE €€€

(☑ 6728 1141; www.facebook.com/galerijalSTABA; K Barona iela 31a; mains €17; ☺ noon-11pm) Owned by local chef and TV personality Mārtiņš Sirmais, 'The Room' sits in the rafters above a gallery and occasional performance space. There's no set menu – you're subject to the cook's fancy – but expect lots of free extras (bread, dips, salad, veggies), adding up to a massive serving.

✗ Central Rīga (Centrs)

Miit CAFE €

(www.miit.lv; Lāčplēša iela 10; mains €5; ☺ 7am-9pm Mon, to 11pm Tue-Thu, to 1am Fri, 9am-11pm Sat, 10am-6pm Sun) Rīga's hipster students head here to sip espresso and blog about Nietzsche amid comfy couches and discarded bicycle parts. The two-course lunch is a fantastic deal for penny-pinchers – expect a soup and a main course for under €5 (dishes change daily).

Big Bad Bagels BAGELS €

(☑ 24556585; www.bigbadbagels.lv; Baznīcas 8; bagels from €4.20; ☺ 8am-8pm Mon-Fri, 10am-7pm Sat, 10am-6pm Sun) US expats aching for lox or a bacon-egg-and-cheese bagel can get a fix at this real-deal joint. Fresh bagels come with cream cheese or as a sandwich with a destination theme (Chicken in Thailand, Prosciutto in Modena – you get the point). Fresh juice, smoothies and coffee are top notch, too.

★ **Fazenda Bazārs** MODERN EUROPEAN €€

(☑ 6724 0809; www.fazenda.lv; Baznīcas iela 14; mains €11-18; ☺ 9am-10pm Mon-Fri, from 10am Sat, from 11am Sun) Although right in the centre, this place feels like you've gone a long way and suddenly found a warm tavern in the middle of nowhere. Complete with a tiled stove, this wooden house oozes megatonnes of charm and the food on offer feels as homey as it gets, despite its international, fusion nature.

Vincents EUROPEAN €€€

(☑ 6733 2830; www.restorans.lv; Elizabetes iela 19; mains €29-39; ☺ 6-10pm Tue-Sat) 🍷 Rīga's ritz-iest restaurant has served royalty and rock stars (Emperor Akihito, Prince Charles, Elton John) amid its eye-catching van Gogh-inspired decor. The head chef, Martins Ritins, is a stalwart of the Slow Food movement and crafts his ever-changing menu mainly from produce sourced directly from small-scale Latvian farmers.

🍷 Drinking & Nightlife

★ **Kaņepes Kultūras Centrs** BAR

(☑ 6734 7050; www.kanepes.lv; Skolas iela 15; ☺ 3pm-2am or later) The crumbling building of a former musical school, which half of Rīgans over 40 seem to have attended, is now a bar with a large outdoor area filled with an artsy, studenty crowd. Wild dancing regularly erupts in the large room, where the parents of the patrons once suffered through their violin drills.

Autentika (B2) CLUB

(☑ 28348453; www.facebook.com/autentika.b2; Bruņinieku iela 2; ☺ 11am-11pm Mon-Tue, to midnight Wed, to 1am Thu, to 5am Sat, to 10pm Sun) Set in an old brewery, this multifunctional cultural space is a local hub for all things indie. Free-spirited locals mingle over cocktails, weekend brunch, art exhibitions, emerging live bands and more. Check the Facebook page for events.

Leningrad CAFE

(☑ 26161335; www.leningrad.lv; K Valdemāra iela 4; ☺ noon-3am Sun-Wed, to 7am Fri & Sat) Punk lives on at this Soviet-themed cafe – which indeed feels like the average cafe by day, but by night, shows a grittier side with a live music scene that can linger until morning. The beer selection is good and cheap, and the staff are friendly and relaxed.

Alus darbnīca Labietis BEER HALL

(☑ 25655958; www.labietis.lv; Aristida Briāna iela 9a-2; ☺ 1pm-1am) Its minimalist design making it feel a bit like a Gothic church, this place is on a mission to promote more obscure Latvian breweries and local craft beer. A great addition to the gradually gentrifying old factory area at the end of Miera iela.

☆ Entertainment

Latvian National Opera OPERA, BALLET

(Latvijas Nacionālajā operā; ☑ 6707 3777; www.opera.lv; Aspazijas bulvāris 3) With a hefty international reputation as one of the finest opera companies in all of Europe, the national opera is the pride of Latvia. It's also home to the Rīga Ballet; locally born lad Mikhail Baryshnikov got his start here. Performances happen most nights of the week – check the schedule on the website for details.

ℹ Information

Tourist Information Centre (🖉 6703 7900; www.liveriga.com; Rātslaukums 6; ⊗ 9am-7pm) Dispenses tourist maps and walking-tour brochures, helps with accommodation, books day trips and sells concert tickets. It also stocks the **Rīga Card** (www.liveriga.com), which offers discounts on sights and restaurants, and free rides on public transport. Satellite offices can be found in **Līvu laukums** (May to September only) and at the **bus station** (Prāgas iela 1).

ℹ Getting There & Away

AIR
Rīga International Airport (Starptautiskā Lidosta Rīga; 🖉 1817; www.riga-airport.com; Mārupe District; 🚌 22) is in the suburb of Skulte, 13km southwest of the city centre. It's the primary hub for air travel to the country – Latvia's national carrier, airBaltic (www.airbaltic.com), offers direct flights to 70 destinations within Europe.

BOAT
Rīga's **passenger ferry terminal** (🖉 6732 6200; www.portofriga.lv; Eksporta iela 3a), located about 1km downstream (north) of Akmens Bridge, offers services to Stockholm aboard Tallink (www.tallink.lv; 18 hours, three to four weekly).

It's possible to get to Jūrmala on the New Way (p748) river boat (daily, 2½ hours).

BUS
Buses depart from Rīga's **international bus station** (Rīgas starptautiskā autoosta; 🖉 9000 0009; www.autoosta.lv; Prāgas iela 1), located behind the railway embankment just beyond the southeastern edge of Old Rīga. International destinations include Tallinn, Vilnius, Warsaw, Pärnu, Kaunas, St Petersburg and Moscow. Try **Ecolines** (www.ecolines.net), **Eurolines Lux Express** (www.luxexpress.eu) or **Nordeka** (www.nordeka.lv).

TRAIN
Rīga's **central train station** (Centrālā stacija; 🖉 6723 2135; www.pv.lv; Stacijas laukums 2) is convenient to Old and Central Rīga, and is housed in a Soviet-era concrete box (now built into a glass-encased shopping mall), just outside Old Town.

Found in a large hall to the right from the main entrance, cash offices 1 to 6 sell tickets to international destinations, which now include Mos-

cow (from €153, 16 hours, daily), St Petersburg (from €92, 15 hours, daily) and Minsk (from €28, 12 hours, weekly). Domestic tickets are sold in cash offices 7 to 15. The information office (open 7am to 7pm) is located next to the latter.

ℹ Getting Around

BICYCLE
Zip around town with **Sixt Bicycle Rental** (Sixt velo noma; 🖉 6767 6780; www.sixtbicycle.lv; per 30min/day €1/10). A handful of stands are conveniently positioned around Rīga and Jūrmala; simply choose your bike, call the rental service and receive the code to unlock your wheels.

CAR
Rīga is divided into six parking zones. Municipal parking in the centre of Rīga costs between €2 and €3 per hour. If you need to drop a car in Rīga for longer, consult www.europark.lv – it runs parking lots all around the city and offers more flexibility time- and moneywise.

PUBLIC TRANSPORT
The centre of Rīga is too compact for most visitors even to consider public transport, but trams, buses or trolleybuses may come in handy if you are venturing further out. For routes and schedules, consult www.rigassatiksme.lv. Tickets cost €2; unlimited tickets are available for 24 hours (€5), three days (€10) and five days (€15). Tickets are available from Narvessen newspaper kiosks as well as vending machines on board new trams and in the underground pass by the train station.

OH CHRISTMAS TREE

Rīga's Blackheads House (p741) was known for its wild parties; it was, after all, a clubhouse for unmarried merchants. On a cold Christmas Eve in 1510, the squad of bachelors, full of holiday spirit (and other spirits, so to speak), hauled a great pine tree up to their clubhouse and smothered it with flowers. At the end of the evening they burned the tree to the ground in an impressive blaze. From then on, decorating the 'Christmas tree' became an annual tradition, which eventually spread across the globe (as you probably know, the burning part never really caught on).

An octagonal commemorative plaque, inlaid in cobbled Rātslaukums, marks the spot where the original tree once stood.

TAXI

Taxis charge €0.60 to €0.80 per kilometre. Insist on having the meter on before you set off. Meters usually start running at around €1.50. It shouldn't cost more than €5 for a short journey (like crossing the Daugava for dinner in Ķīpsala). There are taxi ranks outside the bus and train stations, at the airport and in front of a few major hotels in Central Rīga, such as Radisson Blu Hotel Latvija.

WESTERN LATVIA

Jūrmala

POP 48,600

Jūrmala (pronounced *yoor*-muh-lah) is a 32-km string of 14 townships with Prussian-style villas, each unique in shape and decor. Even during the height of communism, Jūrmala was always a place to '*sea*' and be seen. These days, on summer weekends vehicles clog the roads when jetsetters and day-tripping Rīgans flock to the resort town for some serious fun in the sun. Jomas iela is Jūrmala's main drag, with loads of tourist-centric venues. Unlike many European resort towns, most of Jūrmala's restaurants and hotels are several blocks away from the beach, which keeps the seashore (somewhat) pristine.

🛏 Sleeping & Eating

Hotel MaMa BOUTIQUE HOTEL €€€
(📞 6776 1271; www.hotelmama.lv; Tirgonu iela 22; r €175-360; 🖫) The bedroom doors have thick, mattress-like padding on the interior (psycho-chic?) and the suites themselves are a veritable blizzard of white drapery. A mix of silver paint and pixie dust accents the ultramodern furnishings and amenities. If heaven had a bordello, it would probably look something like this.

★ 36.Line LATVIAN €€€
(📞 22010696; www.36line.com; Līnija 36; mains €12-52; ⊙1-11pm; 🖉) Popular local chef Lauris Alekseyevs delivers modern twists on traditional Latvian dishes at this wonderful restaurant, occupying a slice of sand at the eastern end of Jūrmala. Enjoy the beach, then switch to casual attire for lunch or glam up for dinner. In the evening it's not uncommon to find DJs spinning beats.

ℹ Information

Tourist Office (📞 6714 7900; www.visitjurmala. lv; Lienes iela 5; ⊙9am-5pm Mon-Fri, 10am-5pm Sat, 10am-3pm Sun) Located across from Majori train station, this helpful office has scores of brochures outlining walks, bike routes and attractions. Staff can assist with accommodation bookings and bike rental. A giant map outside helps orient visitors when the centre is closed.

ℹ Getting There & Away

BOAT

The river boat **New Way** (📞 2923 7123; www.pie-kapteina.lv; return adult/child €30/15) departs from Rīga Riflemen Sq and docks in Majori, near the train station. The journey takes one hour, and only runs on weekends.

BUS

A common mode of transport between Rīga and Jūrmala; take minibuses (30 minutes) in the direction of Sloka, Jaunķemeri or Dubulti and ask the driver to let you off at Majori. These vans depart every five to 15 minutes between 6am and midnight and leave opposite Rīga's central train station. Catch the bus at Majori train station for a lift back. These regularly running minibuses can also be used to access other townships within Jūrmala's long sandy stretch. From 9am to midnight, minibuses also connect Jūrmala to Rīga International Airport.

CAR

Motorists driving into Jūrmala must pay a €2 toll per day from April to September before they cross the Lielupe river, even if you are just passing through. There is plenty of (mostly) free-of-charge parking space along Jūras iela.

TRAIN

Two to three trains per hour link the sandy shores of Jūrmala to Central Rīga. Take a suburban train bound for Sloka, Tukums or Dubulti and disembark at Majori station (€1.40 to €1.90, 20 to 50 minutes). The first train departs Rīga around 5.50am and the last train leaves Majori around 10.44pm. Jūrmala-bound trains usually depart from tracks 3 and 4, and stop six or seven times within the resort's 'city limits' if you wish to get off in another neighbourhood. Visit www.pv.lv or www.1188.lv for the most up-to-date information.

Kuldīga

POP 23,000

Home to what Latvians brand 'the widest waterfall in Europe', Kuldīga is also the place where your immersion into the epoch of chivalry won't be spoiled by day-tripping camera-clickers – the place is simply too far from Rīga. In its heyday, Kuldīga (or Goldingen, as its German founders called it) served as the capital of the Duchy of Courland (1596–1616), but it was badly damaged during the Great Northern War and was never quite able to regain its former lustre. Today, this blast from the past is a favourite spot to shoot Latvian period-piece films.

RUNDĀLE PALACE

Built as a grand residence for the Duke of Courland, this magnificent **palace** (Rundāles pils; ☑ 6396 2274; www.rundale.net; whole complex/house long route/short route & garden/garden €13/10/8/11/4; ☉10am-6pm) is a monument to 18th-century aristocratic ostentatiousness, and is rural Latvia's architectural highlight. It was designed by Italian baroque genius Bartolomeo Rastrelli, who is best known for the Winter Palace in St Petersburg. About 40 of the palace's 138 rooms are open to visitors, as are the wonderful formal gardens, inspired by those at Versailles.

Ernst Johann Biron started his career as a groom and lover of Anna Ioanovna, the Russian-born Duchess of Courland. She gave him the duchy when she became Russian empress, but he stayed with her in St Petersburg, turning into the most powerful political figure of the empire. In 1736 he commissoned the Italian architect Bartholomeo Rastrelli to construct his summer residence near Bauska.

Russian authors later blamed Biron for ushering in a era of terror, but many historians believe his role in the persecution of the nobility was exaggerated. On her death bed, the empress proclaimed Biron the Regent of Russia, but two months later his rivals arrested him and sentenced him to death by quartering. The sentence was commuted to exile. The unfinished palace stood as an empty shell for another 22 years when, pardoned by Catherine II, Ernst Johann returned home. Rastrelli resumed the construction and in 1768 the palace was finished. Ernst Johann died four years later at the age of 82. A succession of Russian nobles inhabited (and altered) the palace after the the Duchy of Courland was incorporated into Russian Empire in 1795.

The castle is divided into two halves; the **East Wing** was devoted to formal occasions, while the **West Wing** was the private royal residence. The **Royal Gardens**, inspired by the gardens at Versailles, were also used for public affairs. The rooms were heated by a network of 80 porcelain stoves (only six authentic stoves remain), as the castle was mostly used during the warmer months.

The palace was badly damaged in the Franco-Russian War in 1812 and again during the Latvian War of Independence in 1919 – what you see now is the result of a painstaking restoration started by experts from Leningrad in 1972 and officially finished in 2015. Definitely spend an extra €2 and opt for the 'long route' option when buying the ticket. Unlike the short route, it includes the duke's and duchess's private chambers, which is your chance to peek into the everyday life of 18th-century aristocrats as well as to admire the opulent interior design. Even the duke's chamber pot, adorned with a delightful painting of swimming salmon, is on display.

Like any good castle, Rundāle has loads of eerie ghost tales, but the most famous spectre that haunts the palace grounds is the 'White Lady'. In the 19th century the royal doctor had a young daughter who was courted by many men, but on her 18th birthday she suddenly grew ill and died. Obsessed with her untimely demise, the doctor kept her corpse in his laboratory to study her and tried to figure out why she was ravaged by illness (or was she poisoned by a lovelorn suitor?). Unable to rest eternally, the daughter's spirit began haunting the castle and cackling wildly in the middle of the night. During Rundāle's restorations, several art historians and masons heard her wicked laughter and brought in a priest to exorcise the grounds.

From Bauska (12km away) there are hourly buses to Rundāle Castle (€0.90 to 1.75) between 6am and 7.30pm. Make sure you get off at Pilsrundāle, the villlage before Rundāle.

◉ Sights

Ventas Rumba
WATERFALL

In a country that is acutely short of verticals but rich on horizontals, landscape features appear to be blatantly two-dimensional – even waterfalls. Spanning 240m, Ventas Rumba is branded Europe's widest, but as it is hardly taller than a basketball player, it would risk being dismissed by vile competitors a mere rapid, were it ever to attend an international waterfall congress. That said, it does look like a cute toy Niagara, when observed from the Kuldīga castle hill.

Kuldīga Historic Museum
MUSEUM

(Kuldīgas novada muzejs; ☑ 6335 0179; www.kuldi-gasmuzejs.lv; Pils iela; adult/child €1.50/1; ◷ noon-6pm Tue, 10am-6pm Wed-Sun) Founded by a local German school director, the museum is housed in what a local legend claims to be a Russian pavilion from the 1900 World Exhibition in Paris. Its 2nd floor has been redesigned as an apartment of a rich early-20th-century local family, which features an international playing-cards collection in the 'master's room'. A cluster of Duke Jakob's cannons sits on the front lawn.

⛏ Sleeping & Eating

★ 2 Baloži
GUESTHOUSE €€

(☑ 22000523; www.facebook.com/2balozi; Pasta iela 5; r from €50) Perched above the Alekšupīte stream, this old wooden house has rooms designed in the laconic Scandinavian style with lots of aged wood that creates a pleasant, nostalgic ambience. Goldingen Room restaurant, across the square, serves as the reception.

★ Pagrabiņš
INTERNATIONAL €€

(☑ 6632 0034; www.pagrabins.lv; Baznīcas iela 5; mains €5-15; ◷ 11am-11pm Mon-Thu, to 3am Fri & Sat, noon-11pm Sun; ☑) Pagrabiņš inhabits a cellar that was once used as the town's prison. Today a combination of Latvian and Asian dishes is served under low-slung alcoves lined with honey-coloured bricks. In warmer weather, enjoy your snacks on the small verandah, which sits atop the trickling Alekšupīte stream out the back.

ⓘ Information

Tourist Information Centre (☑ 6332 2259; www.visit.kuldiga.lv; Baznīcas iela 5; ◷ 9am-5pm)

ⓘ Getting There & Away

From the **bus station** (☑ 6332 2061; Adatu iela 9), buses run to/from Rīga (€6.40, 2½ to 3½ hours, every two hours), Liepāja (€3.85 to €4.70, 1¾ hours, seven daily), Ventspils (€3, 1¼ hours, six daily) and Alsunga (€1.60, 35 minutes, five daily).

Ventspils

POP 35,360

Fabulous amounts of oil and shipping money have turned Ventspils into one of Latvia's most beautiful and dynamic cities. The air is brisk and clean, and the well-kept buildings are done up in an assortment of cheery colours – even the towering industrial machinery is coated in bright paint. Latvia's biggest and busiest port wasn't always smiles and rainbows, though – Ventspils' strategic, ice-free location served as the naval and industrial workhorse for the original settlement of Cours in the 12th century, the Livonian Order in the 13th century, the Hanseatic League through the 16th century and finally the USSR in recent times.

Although locals coddle their Užavas beer and claim that there's not much to do, tourists will find a weekend's worth of fun in the form of brilliant beaches, interactive museums and winding Old Town streets dotted with the odd boutique and cafe.

◉ Sights

Ventspils Beach
BEACH

For Ventspils, the wide stretch of dazzlingly white sand south of the Venta River is what the Louvre is for Paris – its main treasure. During the warmer months, beach bums of every ilk – from nudists to kiteboarders – line the sands to absorb the sun's rays. Backed by a belt of dunes and a lush manicured park, the Blue Flag beach feels as pristine and well cared for as an urban beach can get.

⛏ Sleeping & Eating

Kupfernams
B&B €€

(☑ 27677107; www.hotelkupfernams.lv; Kārļa iela 5; s/d €44/65; ☜) This charming wooden house at the centre of Old Town has a set of cheery upstairs rooms with slanted ceilings, opening onto a communal lounge. Below, there's a cafe and a hair salon (which doubles as the reception).

Krogs Zītari　　EASTERN EUROPEAN €€

(📲 25708337; www.facebook.com/KrogsZitari; Tirgus iela 11; mains €7-15; ⊘ 11am-midnight) Tucked in the courtyard of a pretty timber-framed German house, this beer garden serves large portions of meat- and seafood-heavy fare. Whether it is beer-braised pork shank or fried rainbow trout with almond butter, all food is designed to make a perfect match for excellent Latvian brews.

❶ Information

Tourist Information Centre (📲 6362 2263; www.visitventspils.com; Dārzu iela 6; ⊘ 8am-6pm Mon-Fri, 10am-4pm Sat & Sun) In the ferry terminal.

❶ Getting There & Away

Ventspils' **bus terminal** (📲 6362 9904; Kuldīgas iela 5) is served by buses to/from Rīga (€7.55, 2¾ to four hours, hourly), Kuldīga (€3, 1¼ hours, six daily) and Liepāja (€5.20, 2¼ to three hours, six daily) via Jūrkalne (€2.50, one hour) and Pāvilosta (€3.25, 1¼ hours).

Stena Line (www.stenaline.lv) operates ferry service to Nynäshamn, Sweden, up to twice daily from the Ventspils **ferry terminal** (€49, 8½ hours).

NORTHERN LATVIA

Sigulda

POP 11,300

With a name that sounds like a mythical ogress, it comes as no surprise that the gateway to the Gauja Valley is an enchanting spot with delightful surprises tucked behind every dappled tree. Locals proudly call their town the 'Switzerland of Latvia', but if you're expecting the majesty of a mountainous snow-capped realm, you'll be rather disappointed. Instead, Sigulda mixes its own brew of scenic trails, extreme sports and 800-year-old castles steeped in legends.

◉ Sights & Activities

⭐ **Turaida Museum Reserve**　　CASTLE

(Turaidas muzejrezervāts; 📲 6797 1402; www.turaida-muzejs.lv; Turaidas iela 10; adult/child summer €6/1.15, winter €3.50/0.70; ⊘ 9am-8pm) Turaida means 'God's Garden' in ancient Livonian, and this green knoll capped with a fairy-tale castle is certainly a heavenly place. The red-brick castle with its tall cylindrical tower

was built in 1214 on the site of a Liv stronghold. A museum inside the castle's 15th-century granary offers an interesting account of the Livonian state from 1319 to 1561, and additional exhibitions can be viewed in the 42m-high Donjon Tower and the castle's western and southern towers.

Bobsled Track　　ADVENTURE SPORTS

(Bob trase; 📲 6797 3813; www.bobtrase.lv; Šveices iela 13; ⊘ noon-5pm Sat & Sun) Sigulda's 1200m bobsled track was built for the Soviet team. In winter you can fly down the 16-bend track at 80km/h in a five-person Vučko **soft bob** (per adult/child €10/7, from November to March). Summer speed fiends can ride a wheeled **summer bob** (per adult/child €10/7, from May to September).

✖ Eating

⭐ **Mr Biskvīts**　　CAFE, BAKERY €

(📲 6797 6611; www.mr.biskvits.lv; Ausekļa iela 9; mains €4-9; ⊘ 8am-9pm Mon-Fri, 9am-9pm Sat, 9am-7pm Sun) Mr Biskvīts' candy-striped lair is filled with delicious cakes and pastries, but it's also a good spot for a cooked breakfast, a lunchtime soup or sandwich, and an evening pasta or stir-fry. The coffee's great too.

❶ Information

Sigulda Tourism Information Centre (📲 6797 1335; www.tourism.sigulda.lv; Ausekļa iela 6; ⊘ 9am-6pm; 🛜) Located within the train station, this extremely helpful centre has stacks of information about activities and accommodation.

Gauja National Park Visitors Centre (📲 6130 3030; www.entergauja.com/en; Turaidas iela 2a; ⊘ 9am-7pm) Sells maps of the park, town and cycle routes nearby.

❶ Getting There & Away

Buses trundle the 50-odd kilometers between Sigulda's **bus station** and Rīga (€2.75, one hour, every 30 minutes between 8am and 10.30pm).

One train per hour (between 6am and 9pm) travels the Rīga–Sigulda–Cēsis–Valmiera line. Fares from Sigulda include Rīga (€1.90, one or 1¼ hours), Līgatne (€.70, 10 minutes) and Cēsis (€2, 40 minutes).

❶ Getting Around

Sigulda's attractions are quite spread out and after a long day of walking, bus 12 (€2.35) will become your new best friend. It plies the route to/from New Sigulda Castle, Turaida Castle and

Krimulda Manor hourly during business hours (more on weekends).

Cēsis

POP 18,600

With its stunning medieval castle, cobbled streets, green hills and landscaped gardens, Cēsis is simply the cutest little town in Latvia. There is a lot of history here, too: it started eight centuries ago as a Livonian Order's stronghold in the land of unruly pagans and saw horrific battles right under (or inside) the castle walls. Although it's an easy day trip from Rīga, Cēsis is definitely worth a longer stay, especially since there is the whole of Gauja National Park around it to explore.

◉ Sights

★ Cēsis Castle   CASTLE

(Cēsu pils; ☑ 6412 1815; www.cesupils.lv; adult/student €6/3.50, tours from €35; ◷ 10am-6pm) Cēsis Castle is actually two castles in one. The first is the sorrowful dark-stone towers of the old Wenden castle. Founded by Livonian knights in 1214, it was sacked by Russian tsar Ivan the Terrible in 1577, but only after its 300 defenders blew themselves up with gunpowder. The other is the more cheerful, castle-like, 18th-century manor house once inhabited by the dynasty of German counts von Sievers. It houses a museum that features original fin-de-siècle interiors.

🛏 Sleeping

Hotel Cēsis   HOTEL €€

(☑ 6412 0122; www.hotelcesis.com; Vienības laukums 1; s/d €45/60; @ 🛜) The exterior is vaguely neoclassical while the inside features rows of standard upmarket rooms. Its in-house restaurant serves top-notch Latvian and European cuisine in a formal setting or outdoors in the pristine garden.

① Information

Cēsis Tourism Information Centre

(☑ 28318318; www.tourism.cesis.lv; Baznīcas laukums 1; ◷ 10am-6pm) Just outside the walls of the Cēsis Castle.

① Getting There & Away

Cēsis' **bus station** and train station can be found in the same location, at the roundabout connecting Raunas iela to Raiņa iela. There are up to five trains per day between 6.35am and

9pm linking Cēsis and Rīga (€3.50, two hours). Bikes are allowed on board. Two or three buses per hour between 6.15am and 10.20pm ply the route from Cēsis to Rīga, stopping in Līgatne and Sigulda. Trains also run to Valmiera (€1.55, 30 minutes).

SURVIVAL GUIDE

① Directory A–Z

ACCOMMODATION

➡ We highly advise booking ahead during the high season (summer). Rates drop significantly in the colder months.

➡ Most rooms are en suite. Smoking in rooms is normally prohibited.

➡ Check out www.camping.lv for details on pitching a tent.

LGBTIQ+ TRAVELLERS

Rīga has a few gay venues and it was the first former-Soviet city to host EuroPride in 2015. The following organisations offer resources for LGBTIQ+ people in Latvia, as well as listings and events.

Mozaika (www.mozaika.lv) Latvia's only LGBTIQ+ alliance.

Latvian Gay Portal (www.gay.lv) Social networking and classifieds.

Latvia Pride (www.pride.lv) Resources, media and events

MONEY

Latvia abandoned its national currency, the lats, and switched to the euro in January 2014.

ATMs are easy to find and credit cards are widely accepted.

OPENING HOURS

Opening hours vary throughout the year. We list high-season opening hours, but remember these longer summer hours often decrease in shoulder and low seasons.

Shops 10am–7pm Monday to Friday, until 5pm on Saturdays. Some stay open on Sundays. Supermarkets are open up to 10pm, with some open 24 hours.

Restaurants Generally from 11am until 3pm for lunch and from 6pm to 11pm for dinner.

Banks 10am–2pm and 3pm-5pm Monday to Friday.

PUBLIC HOLIDAYS

The Latvia Institute website (www.li.lv) has a page devoted to special Latvian Remembrance Days under the 'About Latvia' link.

New Year's Day 1 January

Easter March/April

Labour Day 1 May

Restoration of Independence of the Republic of Latvia 4 May

Mothers' Day Second Sunday in May

Whitsunday A Sunday in May or June

Līgo Eve (Midsummer festival) 23 June

Jāņi (St John's Day and Summer Solstice) 24 June

National Day 18 November; Anniversary of the Proclamation of the Republic of Latvia, 1918

Christmas (Ziemsvētki) 25 December

Second Holiday 26 December

New Year's Eve 31 December

TELEPHONE

Latvian telephone numbers have eight digits; landlines start with '6' and mobile numbers start with '2'. To make any call within Latvia, simply dial the eight-digit number. To call a Latvian telephone number from abroad, dial the international access code, then the country code for Latvia (371) followed by the subscriber's eight-digit number.

ⓘ Getting Around

BICYCLE

Latvia's rural roads are forgivingly flat, to the delight of touring cyclists. Bikes and equipment can be hired from Rīga Bike Tours (p745), which also organises cycling holiday packages.

BUS

Buses are much more convenient than trains if you're travelling beyond the capital's clutch of suburban rail lines. Updated timetables are available at www.autoosta.lv and www.1188.lv.

TRAIN

Train travel is convenient for a limited number of destinations, most notably Jūrmala, Gauja National Park and Daugavpils. The city's network of commuter rails makes it easy for tourists to reach day-tripping destinations. Latvia's further attractions are best explored by bus.

Lithuania

POP 2.82 MILLION

Includes ➡

Best Places to Eat

➡ Saula (p760)

➡ Senoji Kibininė (p763)

➡ Balzac (p760)

➡ Tik Pas Joną (p767)

➡ Stora Antis (p766)

Best Places to Stay

➡ Hotel Pacai (p760)

➡ Bernardinu B&B (p760)

➡ Miško Namas (p767)

➡ Litinterp Guesthouse (p766)

➡ Domus Maria (p760)

➡ Narutis (p760)

Why Go?

Blame it on the Baltic sea breeze or the almost-endless mid-summer days: Lithuania has an otherworldly quality. In the southernmost of the Baltic states, beaches are spangled with amber and woodlands are alive with demonic statues.

Medieval-style mead and traditional wood-carving never went out of style but there's also a spirited counterculture, particularly in compact capital Vilnius. Less visited are second city Kaunas and spa resort Druskininkai, where 19th-century architecture nudges against brooding Soviet buildings.

As Europe's last country to be Christianised, pagan history still soaks the land. Curonian Spit, splintering from the Baltic coast, is awash in folklore. Cyclists, hikers and beach-goers eagerly board ferries to its voluptuous dunes. Cloaking the rest of Lithuania are lakes, forests of birch and pine, and pancake-flat farmland; in Lithuania, there's ample space to breathe.

When to Go
Vilnius

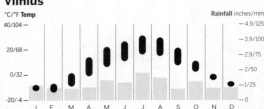

Jun–Aug Long days, short nights, numerous festivals and the Baltic Sea's swimmable.

Sep–Nov Autumn colours, plus classical music festivals and Vilnius' annual Mama Jazz.

Dec The winter deep freeze brings Vilnius' Christmas markets and snowy views.

Entering the Country

With budget flights into Vilnius and Kaunas, and rail routes from other destinations in Eastern Europe, it's easy and inexpensive to reach Lithuania from within Europe. Ryanair (www.ryanair.com) operates routes to Vilnius and Kaunas from several European cities. AirBaltic (www.airbaltic.com) flies to Vilnius from Rīga several times daily and from Tallinn on most days.

ITINERARIES

Three Days
Devote two days to exploring the baroque heart of Vilnius (p756). Then day-trip to Trakai (p762) to experience its island castle and the history and cuisine of the Karaite people, stopping off at Paneriai (p762) on the way.

One Week
Start by spending four nights in Vilnius (p756), including a day trip to Trakai (p762) and the memorial at Paneriai (p762). Travel cross-country to the Hill of Crosses (p766), near Šiauliai (p766), then explore some serious nature on Curonian Spit (p767) for a couple of days. Head back east via Klaipėda (p765) and Kaunas (p763).

Essential Food & Drink

Beer and mead Švyturys, Utenos and Kalnapilis are regional beers; *midus* (mead) is a honey-tinged nobleman's drink returning to popularity.

Beer snacks No drinking session is complete without smoked pigs' ears or *kepta duona* (deep-fried garlicky bread sticks).

Beetroot delight Cold *šaltibarščiai* (beetroot soup) is a summer speciality, served with potatoes; sour cream turns it neon pink. Hot beetroot soups, with or without cream, are common year-round.

Potato creations Pop a button for *cepelinai* (potato-dough 'zeppelins' stuffed with meat, mushrooms or curd cheese), *bulviniai blynai* (potato pancakes) or *žemaičių blynai* (heart-shaped mashed potato stuffed and fried), or *vedarai* (intestines stuffed with mashed potato).

Smoked fish Curonian Spit is famous for smoked fish, particularly the superb *rūkytas ungurys* (smoked eel).

Pastries Bite into Trakai specialities *kibinai*, pasties crammed with mutton, or sate your sweet tooth with *šakotis*, sweet, spit-roasted batter.

Hunter's table Sample local game, such as beaver stew or boar sausages.

AT A GLANCE

Area 65,300 sq km

Capital Vilnius

Country code ☑370

Currency euro (€)

Emergency General ☑112, fire ☑01, police ☑02, ambulance ☑03

Language Lithuanian

Time Eastern European Time (GMT/UTC plus two hours)

Visas Not required for citizens of the EU, USA, Canada, Japan, New Zealand and Australia for visits up to 90 days.

LITHUANIA

Sleeping Price Ranges

The following price ranges refer to the cost of a double room with private bathroom.

€ less than €50

€€ €50–100

€€€ more than €100

Eating Price Ranges

The following price ranges are based on the cost of a typical main course.

€ less than €7

€€ €7–14

€€€ more than €14

Resources

Lonely Planet (www.lonelyplanet.com/lithuania)

Visit Vilnius (www.vilnius-tourism.lt)

Lithuania Travel (https://www.lithuania.travel/en/)

Baltic Times (www.baltictimes.com/news_lithuania)

Lithuania Highlights

1 Vilnius (p756)
Wandering the backstreets of the beautiful baroque capital, looking for that perfect bar or bistro.

2 Curonian Spit (p767)
Cycling between beaches, birch forests and sand dunes on this peaceful sliver of land in the Baltic Sea.

3 Hill of Crosses (p766)
Being awestruck at this storied pilgrimage site, a hill entirely cloaked with crucifixes.

4 Trakai (p762) Exploring Lithuania's smallest national park and its postcard-perfect island castle.

5 Kaunas (p763) Drinking in Old Town's atmosphere and WWII history in Lithuania's spirited second city.

6 Grūtas Park (p764)
Feeling spooked by a Soviet sculpture gallery at forested 'Stalin World' near Druskininkai.

VILNIUS

♪ 5 / POP 574,147

There is a dreamy quality to Vilnius (vilnyus), especially in the golden glow of a midsummer evening. Lithuania's capital has an Old Town of rare authenticity: marvellously intact, its pebbly streets are lined with weather-worn period buildings that hide cafes, boutiques and dainty guesthouses.

Vilnius doesn't hide its battle scars. Reminders of loss are everywhere: museums dedicated to the Holocaust, former ghettos, preserved KGB torture chambers and cemeteries filled with the war dead.

Though carpeted with green spaces and studded with venerable Catholic and Orthodox church spires, this is no Eastern European antique. Artists, punks and even a self-declared micro-nation, the **Republic of Užupis**, keep Vilnius cutting-edge.

👁 Sights

👁 Cathedral Square & Gediminis Hill

⭐ Palace of the Grand Dukes of Lithuania   MUSEUM

(Valdovų Rumai; ☑ 5-262 0007; www.valdovuru mai.lt; Katedros aikštė 4; full admission €6, per exhibition €2-3, guided tour €20-30; ⏰ 10am-6pm Mon-Wed & Sun, to 8pm Thu-Sat) On a site that has been settled since at least the 4th century CE stands the latest in a procession of fortified palaces, repeatedly remodelled, destroyed and rebuilt. One of its grandest manifestations, the baroque palace built for the 17th-century grand dukes, has been faithfully rebuilt to house an atmospheric museum of art and history. Visitors with a couple of hours can opt for full admission, accessing four 'routes' through Lithuanian history; otherwise choose one or two.

Gediminas Castle & Museum   MUSEUM

(Gedimino Pilis ir Muziejus; ☑ 5-261 7453; www. lnm.lt; Gediminas Hill, Arsenalo gatvė 5; adult/child €5/2; ⏰ museum 10am-9pm, castle hill 7am-9pm) With its hilltop location above the junction of the Neris and Vilnia rivers, Gediminas Castle is the last of a series of settlements and fortified buildings occupying this site since Neolithic times. This brick version, built by Grand Duke Vytautas in the early

15th century, harbours a museum about the city with successive floors elaborating on past centuries of warfare, medieval weaponry and contemporary history. For most visitors, the highlight is the 360-degree panorama of Vilnius from the roof.

Vilnius Cathedral   CATHEDRAL

(Vilniaus Arkikatedra; ☑ 5-269 7800; www.katedra. lt; Katedros aikštė 4; cathedral admission free, crypt tours adult/child €4.50/2.50; ⏰ 7am-7pm, crypt tours 4pm Tue, Thu & Sat) Stately Vilnius Cathedral, divorced from its freestanding **belfry** (☑ 8-600 12080; www.bpmuziejus.lt; adult/student €4.50/2.50; ⏰ 10am-7pm Mon-Sat May-Sep), is a national symbol and the city's most instantly recognisable building. Known in full as the Cathedral of St Stanislav and St Vladislav, this columned neoclassical cathedral occupies a spot originally used for the worship of Perkūnas, the Lithuanian thunder god.

Register in advance to tour the crypts, the final resting place of many prominent Lithuanians including Vytautas the Great (1350–1430).

National Museum of Lithuania   MUSEUM

(Lietuvos Nacionalinis Muziejus; ☑ 5-262 7774; www.lnm.lt; Arsenalo gatvė 1; adult/child €3/1.50; ⏰ 10am-6pm Tue-Sun) This wide-ranging museum exhibits art and artefacts from Lithuanian life from Neolithic times to the present day. Early history is revealed in 2nd-millennium-BCE arrowheads and 7th-century grave hauls (signage isn't always good), while the lives of well-to-do Lithuanians of

LITHUANIA VILNIUS

JEWISH VILNIUS

Over the centuries, Vilnius developed into a leading centre of Jewish scholarship with more than 100 synagogues, earning itself the nickname 'Jerusalem of the north'. The Jewish community was largely destroyed in WWII. The former Jewish quarter lay in the streets west of Didžioji gatvė, including present-day Žydų gatvė (Jews St) and Gaono gatvė, named after Vilnius' most famous Jewish resident, Gaon Elijahu ben Shlomo Zalman (1720–97).

One of the three main branches of the Vilna Gaon Jewish State Museum, the **Tolerance Centre** (Tolerancijos Centras; ☑ 5-212 0112; www.jmuseum.lt; Naugarduko gatvė 10/2; adult/concession €4/2; ⏰ 10am-6pm Mon-Thu, to 4pm Fri & Sun) is simultaneously a museum of Jewish history and culture, and a performance space. The **Holocaust Museum** (Holokausto Ekspozicija; ☑ 5-262 0730; www.jmuseum.lt; Pamėnkalnio gatvė 12; adult/child €3/1.50; ⏰ 9am-5pm Mon-Thu, 9am-4pm Fri, 10am-4pm Sun), or 'Green House', exhibits the unvarnished truth behind the destruction of Lithuania's once-vibrant Jewish community, the Litvaks. This profoundly disturbing chapter of history is essential to understanding Vilnius. Many items on display were donated by survivors and victims' families.

The **Choral Synagogue** (Choralinė Sinagoga; ☑ 5-261 2523; Pylimo gatvė 39; €1; ⏰ 10am-4pm Mon-Fri, to 2pm Sun), built in 1903, is now Vilnius' sole surviving Jewish temple. The exterior is an intriguing blend of oriental and modern Romanesque styles; ring the buzzer to enter and view its vaulted interior and ornate Torah ark.

Central Vilnius

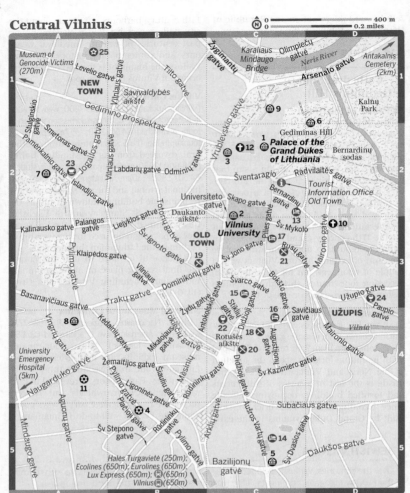

recent centuries are unveiled with velvet-lined sleds and elaborately painted furniture. The highlight is the colourful folk traditions room, replete with floral-decorated furnishings, linens and carved wooden crosses.

Old Town

★ Vilnius University   HISTORIC BUILDING
(Vilniaus Universitetas; ☎ 5-219 3029; www.muziejus.vu.lt; Universiteto gatvė 3; campus adult/child €1.50/0.50, bell tower adult/child €2.50/1.50; ☺ campus 9am-6pm Mon-Sat, bell tower 10am-7pm May-Sep) Founded in 1579 during the Catholic Counter Reformation, Vilnius University

was run by Jesuits for two centuries. During the 19th century it became one of Europe's greatest centres of learning, and the university survived shutdown by Tsar Nicholas I, rebranding under Soviet rule, and closure by the Nazis. Its spectacular architectural ensemble includes a 64m bell tower, baroque church, courtyard and fresco-laden hall, all of which are open to visitors.

Gates of Dawn   HISTORIC BUILDING
(Aušros Vartai; ☎ 5-212 3513; www.ausrosvartai.lt; Aušros Vartų gatvė 12; ☺ 6am-7pm) FREE The southern border of Old Town is marked by the last-standing of five 16th-century portals

Central Vilnius

that were once built into the city walls. A suitably grand way to enter the Old Town, the focal point of the Gates of Dawn is the Chapel of Mary the Mother of Mercy, housing the 'Vilnius Madonna'. Framed in silver, this 17th-century painting of the Virgin Mary attracts pilgrims from across Europe.

St Anne's Church
CHURCH
(Šv Onos Bažnyčia; www.onosbaznycia.lt; Maironio gatvė 8-1; ⊙10.30am-6.30pm Tue-Sat, 8am-7pm Sun) Flamboyant and Gothic St Anne's Church, a vision of undulating lines and red-brick arches, was built in 1500 on the site of a wooden church that burned to the ground. Today it's among Vilnius' most famous buildings; the turreted facade (marrying 33 different kinds of brick) inspires countless photo ops from the grassy plaza opposite. Within, rib vaults trace graceful lines of brick through a rosy interior. Napoleon was reportedly so charmed that he wanted to relocate the church to Paris.

MO Museum
GALLERY
(☑6-098 3764; https://mo.lt; Pylimo gatvė 17; adult/student/child under 7 €7/3.50/free; ⊙10am-8pm Sat-Mon, Wed & Thu, to 10pm Fri) Opened in October 2018, this assemblage of contemporary Lithuanian art and photography is the country's first private museum. An orderly union of sharp angles, polished glass and white plaster, the ultra-modern gallery was designed by visionary Daniel Libeskind, the architect behind Berlin's Jewish Museum. Around 5000 20th-century artworks are as-

sembled within, freshened by rotating exhibitions and occasional cultural events.

🔘 New Town & Beyond

★ Museum of Genocide Victims
MUSEUM
(Genocido Aukų Muziejus; ☑5-249 8156; www.genocid.lt/muziejus; Aukų gatvė 2a; adult/concession €4/1; ⊙10am-6pm Wed-Sat, to 5pm Sun) This former headquarters of the KGB (and before them the Gestapo, Polish occupiers and Tsarist judiciary) houses a museum dedicated to thousands of Lithuanians who were murdered, imprisoned or deported by the Soviet Union from WWII until the 1960s. Back-lit photographs, wooden annexes and a disorienting layout sharpen the impact of past horrors outlined in graphic detail. Most unsettling is the descent to the prison cells and execution yard.

Antakalnis Cemetery
CEMETERY
(Antakalnio Kapinės; off Karių kapų gatvė; ⊙9am-dusk) In this leafy suburb, little-visited by tourists, Antakalnis Cemetery is the final resting place of Lithuanian luminaries and locals lost to war. Brutalist, art-nouveau and modernist headstones give the cemetery, a half-hour walk east of the centre, the feel of an open-air sculpture gallery. Those killed by Soviet special forces on 13 January 1991 are memorialised by a sculpture of the Madonna.

A taxi or ride-share service from the train station costs around €6; hailing a ride back is near-impossible.

🛌 Sleeping

Jimmy Jumps House HOSTEL €
(☎5-231 3847; www.jimmyjumpshouse.com; Savičiaus gatvė 12-1; dm €9-15, d/tr with shared bathroom incl breakfast from €30/36; @🛜) Movie nights, pub crawls, free waffles...this clean, well-run, centrally located hostel is justifiably popular among backpackers. The pinewood bunks are in modest four- to 12-bed rooms, but hands-on service, lockers, a sociable lounge, games and a well-priced bar add up to money well spent.

Bernardinu B&B GUESTHOUSE €€
(☎5-261 5134; www.bernardinuhouse.com; Bernardinų gatvė 5; d €50-60, d/tr with shared bathroom from €45/69; P🛜) Baroque flourishes and original frescoes make every room unique at this friendly, family-owned B&B, stylishly restored within an 18th-century townhouse. Old timber flooring and ceilings have been carefully preserved, and stripped patches of brick allow you to see through the patina of the years. Breakfast (€6) is brought to your door on a tray.

Domus Maria GUESTHOUSE €€
(☎5-264 4880; www.domusmaria.lt; Aušros Vartų gatvė 12; s/d/tr/q incl breakfast from €60/83/100/113; P🛜) Austere and occasionally spooky, the guesthouse of the Vilnius archdiocese is housed in a former 17th-century monastery. Rooms are plain but ample, history almost echoes along the long corridors, and the location at the foot of Old-Town artery Aušros Vartų gatvė couldn't be better. Two rooms, 207 and 307, have views of the Gates of Dawn – book far in advance.

★Hotel Pacai DESIGN HOTEL €€€
(☎5-277 0000; https://hotelpacai.com; Didžioji gatvė 7; d from €180; P✳@🛜) Staying at luxurious Pacai, in a restored 17th-century palace,

---

SHOP LIKE A LOCAL

Traditional market stalls mingle effortlessly with on-trend cafes at **Halles Market** (Halės Turgavietė; ☎5-262 5536; www.halesturgaviete.lt; Pylimo gatvė 58; ⊙7am-6pm Tue-Sat, to 3pm Sun), one of the city's oldest food markets. The glossy metal and glass construction, completed in 1906, is a delightful place to browse fruit and veg, buckets of flowers and deli fare like honeys and jams.

---

you snooze beneath the same timber beams as past nobles...except nowadays there's modern art decking the walls, and individually styled chambers have discreet sundecks and lustrous marbled bathrooms. Murals and vaulted corridors preserve the history while a glamorous inner courtyard and top-end bar and restaurants bring Pacai bang up to date.

Narutis HISTORIC HOTEL €€€
(☎5-212 2894; www.narutis.com; Pilies gatvė 24; d/ste incl breakfast from €144/207; P✳@🛜🏊) In a townhouse built in 1581, rooms at this classy pad have satin drapes, huge comfy beds and, in some cases, original 19th-century frescoes. The opulence continues in the brick-lined spa (the pool and Jacuzzi are free in the mornings). Breakfast steals the show: served in a vaulted Gothic cellar, it's a banquet spread of bubbly, smoked fish and dainty desserts.

🍴 Eating

Senamiesčio Krautuvė DELI €
(☎5-231 2836; www.senamiesciokrautuve.lt; Literatų gatvė 5; ⊙10am-8pm Mon-Sat, 11am-5pm Sun) Look no further than this quiet hobbit-hole deli for the very best Lithuanian comestibles, many unique to the country. Wicker baskets brim with fruit and vegetables, cheeses and yoghurts fill the chiller cabinets, and jars of honey and jam line the shelves. Grab breads and cookies to eat on the hoof while admiring the arty tributes along Literatų gatvė.

★Saula LITHUANIAN, EUROPEAN €€
(☎5-250 7473; www.facebook.com/saularestoranas; Didžioji gatve 26; mains €9-16; ⊙11am-10pm Mon-Thu, to 11pm Fri & Sat, noon-10pm Sun) 🌿 Lithuanian staples find elegant expression at this contemporary cellar restaurant: herring with dill foam, duck drizzled with blackcurrant and buckthorn-garnished panna cotta. Birch tables and pale stone walls impart a light, airy feel, while pagan statuettes and modern-art knick-knacks mirror the old-meets-new menu. Best of all, the produce is locally sourced and informed by the seasons.

Balzac FRENCH €€
(☎8-614 89223; www.balzac.lt; Savičiaus gatvė 7; mains €11-17; ⊙11.30am-11pm Sun-Wed, to midnight Thu-Sat) This faithfully *français* bistro serves classic French dishes in an elegantly distressed setting: melt-in-mouth duck confit with lentils, *tournedos de boeuf* (beef tenderloin wrapped in bacon) and its signa-

ture *tarte tatin* (caramelised apple cake). The dining area is small, so book to avoid disappointment.

Meat Lovers' Pub
PUB FOOD €€

(📞 8-652 51233; www.meatloverspub.lt; Šv Ignoto gatvė14; mains €7-18; ⏰ 11.30am-midnight Mon-Fri, noon-midnight Sat, noon-8pm Sun; 📶) Order lager, wheat beer or dark ale. Nibble fried cheese and moreish smoked ribs. Find that you're thirsty again, and start the cycle anew. Meat Lovers' Pub delivers exactly what it promises: unapologetically carnivorous pub food, like German sausages, T-bone steaks and juicy burgers, in a convivial setting that somehow suits everyone from merry-making groups to solo travellers with books.

Drinking & Nightlife

Alinė Leičiai
PUB

(📞 5-260 9087; www.bambalyne.lt; Stiklių gatvė 4; ⏰ 11am-midnight; 📶) With draught mead, numerous local brews and a flower-filled beer garden, Leičiai is a cheerful place to clink glasses with locals. Mop up the damage with hearty Lithuanian fare: soup served in bread bowls, trout with hazelnuts and pork neck with cabbage.

Špunka
BAR

(📞 8-652 32361; www.spunka.lt; Užupio gatvė 9; ⏰ 3-10pm Tue-Sun, from 5pm Mon) This tiny, charismatic bar does a great line in craft ales from Lithuania and further afield. If you need sustenance to keep the drink and chat flowing, crunchy beer snacks, soups and garlic bread are close at hand.

Elska
COFFEE

(📞 8-608 21028; www.facebook.com/elska.coffee; Pamėnkalnio gatvė 1; ⏰ 7am-9pm Mon-Fri, 8am-8pm Sat & Sun; 📶) A front-runner of Vilnius' latest wave of smart coffee shops, Elska distinguishes itself with a pocket-sized library and adjoining gallery of modern art. This bookish cafe attracts a mix of grab-and-go commuters and students seeking to linger over avocado toast, chia-seed pudding and one of the best flat whites in the city.

☆ Entertainment

Lithuanian National Opera & Ballet Theatre
OPERA

(Lietuvos Nacionalinis Operos ir Baleto Teatras; 📞 5-262 0727; www.opera.lt; Vienuolio gatvė 1; ⏰ box of-fice 10am-7pm Mon-Fri, to 6.30pm Sat, to 3pm Sun) This stunning (or gaudy, depending on your taste) Soviet-era building, with huge, cascading chandeliers and grandiose dimensions, is home to Lithuania's national ballet and opera companies. You can see world-class performers for as little as €10.

ℹ️ Information

Tourist Information Office Old Town (📞 5-262 9660; www.vilnius-tourism.lt; cnr Pilies & Radvilaitės gatvė; ⏰ 9am-noon & 1-6pm) The head office of Vilnius' tourist information service has free maps, transport advice and can help book accommodation.

University Emergency Hospital (📞 5-236 5000; www.santa.lt; Santariškių gatvė 2; ⏰ 24hr) This teaching hospital takes serious and emergency cases.

ℹ️ Getting There & Away

BUS

Vilnius' **bus station** (Autobusų Stotis; 📞 1661; www.autobusustotis.lt; Sodų gatvė 22; ⏰ 5am-10.45pm) is just south of the Old Town. Inside its ticket hall, domestic tickets are sold from 6am to 7pm, and it has a *bagažinė* (left luggage service). Buses travel to/from Druskininkai (€11, two hours, 15 daily), Kaunas (€6 to €7, 1¾ hours, regular), Klaipėda (€17 to €21, four to 5¾ hours, 15 daily) and Šiauliai (€13.70 to €18, three to 4½ hours, 12 daily). Beyond Lithuania, direct services also reach Rīga in Latvia (€15 to €23, 4¼ to 6¼ hours, eight daily) and Tallinn in Estonia (€26 to €35, 9¼ hours, four daily).

Ecolines (📞 5-213 3300; www.ecolines.net; Geležinkelio gatvė 15; ⏰ 8.30am-9.30pm) Serves large cities across Europe.

Eurolines (📞 5-233 5277; www.eurolines.lt; Sodų gatvė 22; ⏰ 6.30am-9.30pm) A reliable long-distance carrier with services to Rīga, Tallinn, Warsaw (Poland) and Lviv (Ukraine).

Lux Express (📞 5-233 6666; www.luxexpress. eu; Sodų 20b-1; ⏰ 8am-7pm Mon-Fri, 9am-7pm Sat & Sun) Luxurious coaches connecting Vilnius with Rīga, Tallinn, St Petersburg, Warsaw and Helsinki.

TRAIN

There is no direct or convenient rail link between Vilnius' **train station** (Geležinkelio Stotis; 📞 5-269 3722; www.litrail.lt; Geležinkelio gatvė 16) and Rīga or Tallinn. Direct trains link Warsaw to Vilnius; browse schedules on www.intercity.pl. There are also regular services linking Minsk and Vilnius (see www.rw.by).

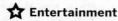

LITHUANIA VILNIUS

ⓘ Getting Around

TO/FROM THE AIRPORT

Buses 1 and 2 (€1) run between the **Vilnius International Airport** (Tarptautinis Vilniaus Oro Uostas; ☑ 6-124 4442; www.vno.lt; Rodūnios kelias 10a; ☎; ☐ 1, 2) and town, trains (€0.70) trundle to the main station.

BICYCLE

Vilnius is becoming increasingly bike-friendly, although bike lanes are rarer outside Old Town and along the banks of the Neris. The tourist office has free cycling maps, and orange **Cyclocity** (☑ 8-800 22008; www.cyclocity.lt; ☺ Apr-Oct) stations dot the city. A three-day ticket is €2.90 and the first half-hour is free, then charges are between €0.39 to €3.39 per 30 minutes.

PUBLIC TRANSPORT

The city is efficiently served by buses and trolley-buses from 5am to midnight; Sunday services are less frequent. Single-trip tickets cost €1 when bought from the driver. If you get a *Vilniečio kortelė* (electronic ticket) for €1.50, single journeys cost €0.65 or you can buy 24-/72-hour passes for €5/8 (www.vilniusticket.lt). Read more on www.vilniustransport.lt and www.stops.lt.

TAXI

Taxis are generally cheaper if ordered in advance by telephone (ask the hotel reception desk or restaurant to call). Reliable companies:
Ekipažas (☑ 1446; www.ekipazastaksi.lt)

EASTERN & SOUTHERN LITHUANIA

Paneriai

☑ 5 / POP 9000

A bleak chapter of Lithuania's wartime history is commemorated in this neighbourhood of Vilnius, 11km southwest of the centre. Paneriai is notorious as the site of 100,000 murders – the exact figure is unknown – by subunits of the Nazi secret police.

Around 70% of the people slaughtered in Paneriai were Jewish. Other victims were Lithuanian and Polish soldiers and partisan fighters, prisoners of war and priests.

A small **museum** (☑ tours 699 90 384; www.jmuseum.lt; Agrastų gatvė 15; ☺ 9am-5pm Tue-Sun May-Sep, by appointment Oct-Apr; ☐) **FREE** exhibits testimonies from the Burners Brigade, prisoners of war forced to dispose of bodies,

and eyewitness reports detailing how massacres unfolded to the glee of commanders. Nearby, a **walking path** connects Jewish, Soviet and Polish monuments and locations associated with the killings, such as prison bunkers and pits where victims were shot.

ⓘ Getting There & Away

Daily trains (some terminating in Trakai or Kaunas) travel between Vilnius and Paneriai station (€0.60, 10 minutes, at least hourly). To reach the museum, make a right down Agrastų gatvė upon leaving the train station and it's a 1km walk southwest.

Trakai

☑ 528 / POP 4500

Rising like an apparition from the waters of Lake Galvė, a rosy brick Gothic castle is the crowning attraction of Trakai. Spread along a 2km-long peninsula only 28km from Vilnius, this attractive town is a popular day trip.

With practically the entire town gazetted as an 82-sq-km **national park** (www.seniejitrakai.lt), it's fitting that Trakai's very name derives from the Lithuanian word for a forest glade. Its castle roosts on one of 21 islands in Lake Galvė, which opens out from the northern end of the peninsula.

★ **Trakai Castle**   CASTLE
(Trakų Pilis; ☑ 8-528 53946; www.trakaimuziejus.lt; adult/concession €8/4; ☺ 10am-7pm; ☐) Stepping across the wooden walkway to Trakai's Gothic castle is like tripping into a fairy tale. The castle is estimated to date from around 1400, when Grand Duke Vytautas needed stronger defences than the peninsula castle afforded. Arranged between its coral-coloured brick towers, the excellent **Trakai History Museum** conveys the flavour of past eras: chainmail, medieval weapons, 19th-century embroidery and glassware, plus talking knights, projected onto the stone walls.

North North East   KAYAKING
(☑ 8-677 93441; www.facebook.com/northnortheast kayaking; kayak rental €15, guided tour from €25; ☺ May-Oct) Trakai's castle is even lovelier when seen from the water, and on these beginner-friendly guided kayak tours – in Lithuanian, Russian or English – the epic views are amplified by local knowledge and the odd picnic. Our pick is the sunset tour, to see the lakes dappled with golden light.

DON'T MISS

KARAITE CULTURE

Trakai is well-known for Karaite culture and cuisine, belonging to a Judaic minority group who have lived here since medieval times. Grand Duke Vytautas brought 383 Karaite families from Crimea to Trakai, initially installing them as castle guards. The **Karaite Ethnographic Museum** (Karaimų etnografinė paroda; ☑ 528-55 286; www.trakaimuziejus. lt; Karaimų gatvė 22; adult/child €2/1; ⊙ 10am-6pm Wed-Sun) displays their traditional dress and arresting photographs of Karaite people, past and present.

Draped with antiques and wood-carved finery, **Senoji Kibininė** (☑ 528-55 865; www.kibi nas.lt; Karaimų gatvė 65; pasties from €1.50, mains €5.50-12; ⊙ 10am-10pm) is a popular place for the full Karaite culinary experience; it's worth braving the crowds for *kibinai* (pasties usually stuffed with lamb or mushrooms) served with a bowl of chicken broth. Alternatively, grab *ki- binai* from the takeaway counter at **Kybynlar** (☑ 8-698 06320; www.kybynlar.lt; Karaimų gatvė 29; pasties from €2, mains €7-12; ⊙ noon-9pm Mon, 11am-9pm Tue-Thu & Sun, 11am-10pm Fri & Sat).

❶ Getting There & Away

Eight or nine daily trains (€1.80, 30 minutes) travel between Trakai's **train station** (☑ 7005 5111; www.litrail.lt; Vilniaus gatvė 5) and Vilnius. Regular buses also link the two (€2, 30 minutes).

CENTRAL LITHUANIA

Kaunas

☑ 37 / POP 288,363

A scrappy little sister compared to debonair Vilnius, Kaunas (kow-nas) sprawls out from its dainty Old Town and 14th-century fort. Strategically wedged at the confluence of the Nemunas and Neris Rivers, Kaunas gained a taste for the limelight during a brief spell as Lithuania's capital in the interwar period; the town owes some of its most attractive ar- chitecture to this era. You'll find uninhibit- ed nightlife and arguably the country's best galleries, and plucky Kaunas is increasingly appealing as it prepares for a stint as Euro- pean Capital of Culture for 2022.

❍ Sights

◉ Old Town

The heart of Kaunas' lovely Old Town is the city's former **Town Hall** (Kauno rotušė; Rotušės aikštė 15), built in the mid-16th century and formerly a theatre, prison and palace.

House of Perkūnas　　　HISTORIC BUILDING
(Perkūno namas; ☑ 8-641 44614; www.perkunona mas.lt; Aleksoto gatvė 6; adult/child €2/1; ⊙ 10am- 4.30pm Mon-Fri) With ornate arches and turrets rippling from its brick facade, this late-15th-century mansion is a treasure of Kaunas' late-Gothic architecture. Built by merchants of the Hanseatic League, its inte- rior is laid out to evoke the noble lifestyles of yesteryear: chandeliers, dining tables and a library with a small exhibition dedicated to 19th-century Romantic poet Adam Mickiew- icz. The magnificent house is named for the thunder god Perkūnas, whose likeness was discovered during renovations in 1818.

**Maironis Lithuanian
Literary Museum**　　　MUSEUM
(Maironio Lietuvių Literatūros Muziejus; ☑ 37-206 842; http://maironiomuziejus.lt; Rotušės aikštė 13; adult/child €3/1; ⊙ 9am-5pm Tue-Sat) Even travel- lers unenthused by turn-of-the-20th-century literature will be enchanted by this museum dedicated to Lithuanian luminary Maironis (aka Jonas Mačiulis). The museum is inside a beautifully attired 18th-century mansion, bought and furnished by Maironis in 1909. Highlights include the rococo **Red Room** (actually baby blue) and the **Great Dining Room**, gloriously decorated with traditional heraldry rendered in bold graphic art.

**St Francis Xavier
Church & Monastery**　　　CHURCH
(☑ 37-432 098; www.kjb.lt; Rotušės aikštė 7-9; tower €1.50; ⊙ 4-6pm Mon-Fri, 7am-1pm & 4-6pm Sun) The southern side of Rotušės aikštė is dominated by rosy-pink late-Baroque facade of the St Francis Xavier Church, college and Jesuit monastery complex. Peek inside the twin-towered church, built between 1666 and 1720, and climb up to the viewing platform for a bird's-eye vantage point over Kaunas' Old Town.

◉ New Town

Laisvės alėja (Freedom Ave), a striking 1.7km pedestrian street, runs east from Old Town to New Town, ending at the blue-domed neo-Byzantine **St Michael the Archangel Church** (Šv Archangelo Mykolo Rektoratas; ☑37-226 676; Nepriklausomybės aikštė 14; ⏰9am-2.30pm).

★ MK Čiurlionis
National Museum of Art   GALLERY
(MK Čiurlionio Valstybinis Dailės Muziejus; ☑37-229 475; www.ciurlionis.lt; Putvinskio gatvė 55; adult/child €4/2, audio guide €4; ⏰11am-5pm Tue, Wed & Fri-Sun, to 7pm Thu) One Lithuania's oldest and grandest galleries, Kaunas' leading art museum (founded 1921) is the place to acquaint yourself with the dreamlike paintings of Mikalojus Konstantinas Čiurlionis (1875–1911), one of the country's greatest artists and composers. Elsewhere in the sizeable gallery are contemporary sculpture exhibitions flooded with natural light, Lithuanian folk and religious art, and 16th- to 20th-century European works.

Museum of the Ninth Fort   MUSEUM
(IX Forto Muziejus; ☑37-377 750; www.9fortomuziejus.lt; Žemaičių plentas 73; adult/child €3/1.50; ⏰10am-6pm Tue-Sun Apr-Oct) Lithuania's dark 20th-century history is powerfully and poignantly told at the Museum of the Ninth Fort, 7km north of Kaunas. Begin in the main **museum**, a modern gallery space with a churchlike interior, which details the country's WWII experience. With the same entrance ticket, continue uphill to the WWI-era **fort**, converted into a hard-labour prison in the early 20th century and a centre of torture, interrogation and mass killings in WWII.

Kaunas Picture Gallery   GALLERY
(Kauno Paveikslų Galerija; ☑37-221 789; www.ciurlionis.lt/kaunas-art-gallery; Donelaičio gatvė 16; adult/student €2/1; ⏰11am-5pm Tue, Wed & Fri-Sun, to 7pm Thu) This underrated gem, a branch of the many-tentacled Čiurlionis museum, exhibits works by 20th-century Lithuanian artists. Most explanation is in Lithuanian but the art does the talking: 1920s and '30s watercolours depict bucolic countryside and fishing villages (an enjoyable primer, if you're travelling into rural Lithuania) along with treasured artworks like a vivid triptych by 20th-century painter Adomas Galdikas.

🛏 Sleeping

Kauno Arkivyskupijos
Svečių Namai   GUESTHOUSE €
(Kaunas Archdiocese Guesthouse; ☑37-322 597; www.kaunas.lcn.lt/sveciunamai; Rotušės aikštė 21; s/d/tr without bathroom from €40/49; ⊞✱@🖤) The location of this Catholic archdiocesan guesthouse couldn't be better, snuggled between venerable churches and overlooking the Old Town square. Rooms are unadorned, but they have high ceilings and big windows. There's a communal kitchen to cook breakfast (which isn't offered) and parking spaces through the main archway – unless the local parishioners get there first.

Apple Economy Hotel   HOTEL €
(☑37-321 404; www.applehotel.lt; Valančiaus gatvė 19; s/d from €32/36; ⊞@🖤) Fourteen tiny but brightly decorated rooms are stacked into this simple but friendly hotel. There are no frills

---

WORTH A TRIP

FROM SPAS TO 'STALIN WORLD': DRUSKININKAI

Towering forests, toasty waters and a Soviet theme park...sound like your kind of trip? **Grūtas Park** (Grūto Parkas; ☑6-824 2320; www.grutoparkas.lt; Grūtas; adult/child €7.50/4; ⏰9am-10pm Jun-Aug; ⊞🍴) is a curious amusement park that educates with a gallery of socialist realist art and an information centre, packed with newspapers and USSR maps. Statues of Lenin that once dominated Lithuanian towns now sulk along tree-lined paths. Explore the surreal grounds, but it's better to skip the on-site zoo. It's 8km east of Druskininkai; take bus 2 via Viečiūnai (two to five daily).

The reputation of Druskininkai's healing mineral waters dates back centuries; test them at **Grand Spa Lietuva** (☑313-51 200; www.grandspa.lt; Kudirkos gatvė 43; ⏰9am-5pm Mon-Thu, to 6pm Fri & Sat, to 4pm Sun) then kick back in **Kolonada** (☑662 06062; www.sventejums.lt/kolonada; Kudirkos gatvė 22; mains €6-12; ⏰11am-11pm Sun-Thu, to 1am Fri & Sat) with a cocktail. Classic, slightly time-worn **Regina** (☑313-51 243; www.regina.lt; Kosciuškos gatvė 3; s/d/tr/q incl breakfast from €54/58/97/113; ⊞🖤), with its own little spa, is a good place to stay the night.

To reach Druskininkai, there are daily direct buses from Vilnius (€11, two hours, 10 daily) and Kaunas (€9 to €11, 2¼ to 3½ hours, 12 daily).

but it's a serviceable economy option in an excellent location, tucked into a quiet courtyard on the northwestern flank of Old Town.

Daugirdas BOUTIQUE HOTEL €€
(📞 37-301 561; www.daugirdas.lt; Daugirdo gatvė 4; s/d/ste incl breakfast €60/79/90; 🕸 🛜) This boutique hotel, wedged between central Old Town and the Nemunas, is one of the most charismatic in Kaunas. Parts of the building date to the 16th century, and the standard rooms are cosy and modern with good-quality beds and bathrooms with heated floors. For something extra special, luxuriate in a Jacuzzi in the timber-beamed Gothic Room (€175).

✖ Eating

Motiejaus Kepyklėlė BAKERY €
(📞 8-616 15599; Vilniaus gatvė 7; pastries from €1; ⏱ 7.30am-8pm Mon-Sat, 9am-7pm Sun) Perhaps the best bakery in Kaunas, Motiejaus prepares traditional Lithuanian cakes and cookies, alongside desserts and coffee with a Franco-Italian flavour. Cooked breakfasts can be hit and miss, but it's hard to go wrong with international dainties such as *canelés* (French vanilla cakes), muffins and croissants.

Senieji Rūsiai EUROPEAN €€€
(Old Cellars; 📞 37-202 806; www.seniejirusiai.lt; Vilniaus gatvė 34; mains €12-25; ⏱ 11am-midnight Mon-Thu, to 1am Fri, noon-1am Sat, noon-11pm Sun; 🛜) Named for its 17th-century subterranean vaults lined with frescoes, 'Old Cellars' is one of the most atmospheric places in Kaunas for a candlelit dinner. Choose flame-cooked beef or duck with wine-poached pears to match the medieval banquet ambience, or peruse pan-European options like steak with foie gras or salmon with cream of fennel.

☕ Drinking & Nightlife

Kultūra Kavinė PUB, CAFE
(www.facebook.com/kauno.kultura; Donelaičio gatvė 14-16; ⏱ noon-2am Tue-Fri, 3pm-2am Sat, noon-midnight Sun & Mon; 🛜) If revolution brews in Kaunas, they'll trace it back to Kultūra Kavinė. The town's dreamers and debaters spill out from this shabby-chic pub, smoking and sipping beers on the concrete terrace. Close to the New Town's galleries and beloved by students, this artful hangout has a raw, earnest feel and open-minded clientele. The best spot in town to mingle.

2½ Ubuolio PUB
(📞 8-650 66422; www.facebook.com/2supuseobuolio; Palangos gatvė 9; ⏱ 5pm-2am) A den for locals to glug a cold one over trivia nights and

VEGETARIAN KAUNAS

Discard those stereotypes about endless dumplings, Kaunas' dining scene is diverse. **Moksha** (📞 8-676 71649; www.facebook.com/cafemoksha; Vasario 16-osios gatvė 6; mains €6-12; ⏱ 11am-9pm Mon-Fri, noon-9pm Sat, noon-8pm Sun; 🌿) reels you in with ambient, plucked-string music, chilli-spiked aromas and personable service; try the vegan mango curry. Cosy **Radharanė** (📞 37-320 800; www.radharane.lt/kaunas; Daukšos gatvė 28; mains €4-6; ⏱ 11am-9pm; 🌿) also has a broad menu, from soy goulash to Thai vegetable curry and curried aubergine.

sports screenings, this cider pub in a vaulted cellar gets packed out even on weeknights. Bonus: there's free popcorn.

ℹ Information

Tourist Office (📞 8-616 50991; www.visit.kaunas.lt; Rotušės aikštė 15; ⏱ 9am-1pm & 2-6pm Mon-Fri, 10am-1pm & 2-4pm Sat, 10am-1pm & 2-3pm Sun) Inside Kaunas' Town Hall, this friendly and multilingual tourist office can book accommodation, sell maps and guides, and arrange bicycle rental and guided tours of the Old Town.

ℹ Getting There & Away

Kaunas' bus and train stations are not far from each other, about 2km south of the city centre. From the **bus station** (Autobusų Stotis; 📞 37-409 060; www.autobusubilietai.lt; Vytauto prospektas 24; ⏱ ticket office 6am-9.30pm), frequent services leave for Klaipėda (€14.50 to €16.80, 2¾ to four hours) and Vilnius (€6.40 to €7, 1¾ hours). From the **train station** (Geležinkelio Stotis; 📞 7005 5111; www.litrail.lt; MK Čiurlionio gatvė 16; ⏱ ticket office 4.10am-9.45pm) there are plenty of trains each day to Vilnius (€4.80 to €6.60, 1¼ to 1¾ hours).

There are also services to Tallinn in Estonia (two daily) and Rīga in Latvia (four daily).

WESTERN LITHUANIA

Klaipėda

📞 46 / POP 148,100
There's a distinctly German flavour to Klaipėda (klai-pey-da). Lithuania's third-largest city, formerly known as Memel, was part of

WORTH A TRIP

HILL OF CROSSES

Lithuania's fabled **Hill of Crosses** (Kryžių kalnas; ☑ 41-370 860; Jurgaičiai; ⊙ information centre 9am-6pm) is a symbol of defiance as much as a pilgrimage site. More than 100,000 crosses have been planted on this low hill, many of them strung with rosary beads that rattle softly in the breeze. The tradition began during the 1831 Uprising and reached its height in the 1960s, in defiance of anti-religious Soviet rule. At night locals crept here to lay crosses, infuriating their oppressors.

It's 12km north of Šiauliai (2km off Hwy A12) near Jurgaičiai. To reach the Hill of Crosses from Šiauliai, take a Joniškis-bound bus (€1.50, 10 minutes, up to seven daily) to the 'Domantai' stop and walk for 15 minutes, or grab a taxi (around €20).

the Prussian Kingdom until the region wrestled to autonomy in 1923. Most travellers barely glimpse Klaipėda as they rush headlong for the ferry to Curonian Spit, but it's rewarding to hang around. Buildings in compact, cobblestoned Old Town are constructed in the German *fachwerk* style (with distinctive half-timbered facades) and there's a bevy of bars in which to sip beers by the water.

⊙ Sights

Klaipėda Castle Museum MUSEUM
(Klaipėda Pilies Muziejus; ☑ 46-453 098; www. mlimuziejus.lt; Pilies gatvė 4; adult/child €1.74/0.87; ⊙ 10am-6pm Tue-Sat) Spread across four exhibition spaces around Klaipėda's castle, these warren-like galleries introduce different eras of regional history. The most atmospheric is the stone-lined medieval exhibition but the highlight is the **39/45 Museum**, a state-of-the-art space capturing the fear and disarray of wartime Klaipėda in evocative ways.

History Museum
of Lithuania Minor MUSEUM
(Mažosios Lietuvos Istorijos Muziejus; ☑ 46-410 524; www.mlimuziejus.lt; Didžioji Vandens gatvė 6; adult/child €1.45/0.72; ⊙ 10am-6pm Tue-Sat) This creaky-floored little museum traces the origins of 'Lithuania Minor' (Kleinlitauen) – as this coastal region was known during its several centuries as part of East Prussia. It exhibits Prussian maps, coins and artefacts

of the Teutonic order. Most attractive are the wooden furnishings, displays of folk art and traditional weaving machines.

🛏 Sleeping

Litinterp Guesthouse GUESTHOUSE €
(☑ 46-410 644; www.litinterp.com; Puodžių gatvė 17; s with/without bathroom €28/23, d €46/40; P ☜) For its price range, this guesthouse in an 18th-century building is a standout star. High ceilings with wooden beams and sizeable beds ensure charm and comfort in equal supply, and it's efficiently run, with English-speaking staff. The 19 rooms vary from standard doubles to kitchen-equipped suites; there's a shared kitchen and enclosed parking, too. Breakfast costs €3.

🍴 Eating

⭐ **Stora Antis** LITHUANIAN €€€
(☑ 6-862 5020; www.storaantis.lt; Tiltų gatvė 6; mains €15-18; ⊙ 5pm-midnight Tue & Thu-Sat) Taking full advantage of a stunning 19th-century cellar, brick-lined Stora Antis elevates classic Lithuanian fare (baked duck, bean soups, pan-fried plaice) to haute-cuisine heights. A restaurant was first established here in 1856 and it's retained its charms, laden with antiques and bric-a-brac. One of the best places to eat in Klaipėda's Old Town.

⭐ **Momo Grill** STEAK €€€
(☑ 8-693 12355; https://momogrill.lt; Liepų gatvė 20; mains €10-18; ⊙ 11am-10pm Tue-Fri, noon-10pm Sat; ☜) This tiny, modern, minimalist steakhouse is foodie heaven and the hardest table to book in town. The small menu consists of just three cuts of beef plus grilled fish and leg of duck, and allows the chef to focus on what he does best. The austere interior of white tiles is soothing and the wine list is marvellous.

🍷 Drinking & Nightlife

Timbered portside pub **Žvejų Baras** (☑ 6-866 0405; www.zvejubaras.lt; Kurpių gatvė 8; ⊙ 5pm-midnight Sun-Wed, to 2am Thu, to 4am Fri & Sat) lives up to its name (which means 'Fisherman's Bar'). Set aglow by lead-lined lamps, this is one of Klaipėda's nicest places to catch live music or sports screenings.

If you prefer your people-watching with a side-serve of meringues, macarons or little *sablés* (French shortbreads), head to cute corner cafe **Vanilės Namai** (☑ 8-612 02010; www.vanilesnamai.lt; cnr Manto & Vytauto gatvė; ⊙ 9am-8pm Sun-Thu, to 9pm Fri & Sat; ☜).

ℹ️ Information

Tourist Office (📱 46-412 186; www.klaipeda
info.lt; Turgaus gatvė 7; ⏰ 9am-6pm Mon-Fri)
Exceptionally efficient tourist office selling
maps and locally published guidebooks, and
arranging accommodation, tours and more.
Open weekends in summer.

ℹ️ Getting There & Away

BOAT

Smiltynės Perkėla (www.keltas.lt) runs car and
foot passenger ferries between Klaipėda and
Smiltynė on Curonian Spit.

BUS

Services to/from Klaipėda's **bus station** (Auto-
busų Stotis; 📱 46-411 547; www.klap.lt; Butkų
Juzės 9; ⏰ ticket office 3.30am-7.30pm) reach
Kaunas (€14 to €16, 2¾ to 4½ hours, 18 daily),
Šiauliai (€11, three to 3½ hours, seven daily) and
Vilnius (€18 to €21, four to 5½ hours, 16 daily).
Most buses to/from Juodkrantė and Nida depart
from Smiltynė ferry landing on Curonian Spit.

Buses also reach Kaliningrad in Russia
(€11.40, 4½ hours, two daily), Rīga in Latvia
(€19, five hours, one daily) and Tallinn in Estonia
(€47 to €56, 13 hours, one daily via Vilnius or
Kaunas). Ecolines (https://ecolines.net) sells
tickets for international destinations.

Curonian Spit

POP 3371

On this bewitching tendril of land, winds
caress the sand dunes, pine scents the
breeze and amber washes up on beaches.
Designated a **national park** (Kuršių Nerijos
Nacionalinis Parkas) in 1991, Curonian Spit
trails across the Baltic Sea from Lithuania to
Russian territory Kaliningrad. Pine forests
populated by deer, elk and wild boar cover
about 70% of the area and only a fraction
is urban. Until the first decades of the 20th
century, most of the spit was German territory. Today, locals joke that the spit's sand
dunes are 'Lithuania's Sahara'.

👁 Sights

⭐ Parnidis Dune
DUNES

(Parnidžio kopa) The 52m-high Parnidis Dune
is simultaneously mighty and fragile. Past
settlements around Nida have been engulfed
by the moving sand dune but this is a delicate landscape of mountain pines, meadows
and fine blonde sand speckled with purple
searocket flowers. A 1700m-long path picks
its way to a grand panorama at the height of

the dune, where you'll find a sundial with a
granite obelisk (constructed in 1995).

Don't stray from the footpath, and take all
rubbish with you.

Amber Gallery
GALLERY

(Gintaro Galerija; 📱 469-52 573; www.ambergal
lery.lt; Pamario gatvė 20; adult/child €2.50/1.20;
⏰ 10am-7pm Apr-Oct) In an old fisher's hut on
the north side of town is this museum and
shop devoted to amber. Staff introduce the
mythic and supposed health-boosting properties of this caramel-coloured fossilised
resin. Visitors can peer through magnifying
glasses at insects trapped in amber and explore the amber-ornamented garden. The
museum doubles as a boutique selling truly
unusual jewellery studded with amber. Enquire ahead for hour-long amber-processing
classes (€6).

🛏 Sleeping & Eating

⭐ Miško Namas
GUESTHOUSE €€

(📱 469-52 290; www.miskonamas.com; Pamario
gatvė 11; d €65-85, 2-/4-person apt from €85/95;
P 🛜) Overlooking a peaceful garden, this
immaculately maintained guesthouse is
picked out in Curonian blue-and-white and
filled with elegant furnishings, ornaments
and lace. Every room has a fridge and a kettle, and some have fully fledged kitchens and
balconies. Guests can browse books from the
small library or laze in the garden.

⭐ Tik Pas Joną
SEAFOOD €

(📱 8-620 82084; www.facebook.com/Rukytos
ZuvysTikPasJona; Naglių gatvė 6-1; mains €3;
⏰ 10am-10pm Apr-Nov, Sat & Sun only Dec-Mar)
Picture the scene: you select mackerel or eel
from a traditional smoking rack, lay it on a
paper plate with a slice of rye bread, and eat
with your hands while watching the lagoon
glow orange at sunset. This is the best spot
in Neringa to feast on the region's famous
smoked fish – accompany it with cold beer
and crunchy veggies.

Kepykla Gardumėlis
BAKERY €

(📱 469-52 021; www.kepykla-gardumelis.lt; Pamario
gatvė 3; snacks from €1.20; ⏰ 8am-6pm) Curonian Spit's best place for freshly baked goods,
Gardumėlis makes bread only with stone-
ground organic flour. Similar perfectionism is
applied to the ingredients destined for their
cookies, mille-feuille pastries and poppyseed
rolls. Their most unusual treat is *morkų sal-
dainiai*, bright-orange carrot candy: chewy,
zesty and with a slight vegetal note.

ℹ Information

Curonian Spit National Park Visitors Centre
(☑ 46-402 256; www.nerija.lt; Smiltynės gatvė 11; ⊘ 9am-noon & 1-6pm Tue-Sat Jun-Aug) The summer-only visitors centre in Smiltynė is packed with information about the park's ecology and attractions, and can arrange guided nature tours (€31 to €36, two to eight people).

Juodkrantė Tourist Information Centre
(☑ 469-53 490; www.visitneringa.com; L Rėzos gatvė 8; ⊘ 10am-8pm Mon-Sat, to 3pm Sun) Located opposite the bus stop inside the cultural centre.

Nida Tourist Information Centre (☑ 469-52 345; www.visitneringa.com; Taikos gatvė 4; ⊘ 9am-7pm Mon-Sat, 10am-5pm Sun; 🤳)

ℹ Getting There & Away

Curonian Spit is accessible only via boat or ferry (there are no bridges linking the spit to the mainland). From Klaipėda, two ferries run regularly: a passenger ferry goes to Smiltynė from the **Old Ferry Port** (Senoji perkėla; ☑ 46-311 117; www.keltas.lt; Danės gatvė 1; per passenger/bicycle €1/free) for cyclists and foot passengers (at least hourly between 7am and 9pm). There's a vehicle ferry from the **New Ferry Port** (Naujoji perkėla; ☑ 46-311 117; www.keltas.lt; Nemuno gatvė 8; per foot passenger/motorbike/car €1/4.90/12.30, bicycle free) 2km south of Klaipėda's Old Town that connects to a point on the spit around 2km south of Smiltynė (one to three ferries per hour between 5am and 9pm); pay as you drive on.

You can also reach the Russian Kaliningrad Region from here. The Russian border post is 3km south of Nida on the main road and daily buses depart from Nida (€7.80, two hours). Don't contemplate this without the necessary Russian visa and paperwork.

DON'T MISS

WITCHES' HILL

A coven of wooden sculptures is gathered on a forest-clad hill in Juodkrantė, carved by Lithuanian artists over the years since 1979. **Witches' Hill** (Raganų Kalnas; 🚶) is an open-air sculpture gallery where devils grimace beneath decorative arches, while warty-nosed witches and grinning peasants peep out from among the pine trees. The figures represent various characters from regional folklore, and some have an interactive quality: slide down a demon's tongue, sit on a throne, and try to resist taking a dozen photos.

ℹ Getting Around

Hire bikes in Klaipėda and take them across the lagoon via the passenger ferry for free. Alternatively, there are bike-rental places in Nida (usually around €3/10 per hour/day). There is a well-marked trail that runs the entire length of the spit from Smiltynė to Nida via Juodkrantė (about 50km).

Buses travel from the northerly ferry port Smiltynė to Juodkrantė (€1.90, 15 to 20 minutes) down to Nida (€4, one hour), between seven and 10 times daily.

SURVIVAL GUIDE

ℹ Directory A–Z

ACCOMMODATION

➡ Prices rise from June to August (book ahead) and drop outside the summer, when some places close.

➡ Most hostels are located in large cities like Vilnius and Kaunas; outside of these you're better off choosing guesthouses or farmstays.

LGBTIQ+ TRAVELLERS

Vilnius has a handful of LGBTIQ+-specific venues, and many more gay-friendly ones. The National LGBT Rights Organization (www.lgl.lt) has a map of gay venues on their website.

MONEY

➡ Cash is preferred for small purchases and at smaller-scale guesthouses.

➡ Tip 10% to reward good service in restaurants. Say *ačiū* (thank you) to show you aren't expecting change back.

OPENING HOURS

We have listed high-season opening hours, but remember these longer summer hours often decrease in shoulder and low seasons.

Banks 9am to 5pm Monday to Friday

Bars 11am to midnight Sunday to Thursday, 11am to 2am Friday and Saturday

Clubs 10pm to 3am Thursday or Friday to Saturday

Post offices 9am to 7pm Monday to Friday, 9am to 2pm Saturday

Restaurants noon to 11pm; later on weekends

Shops 9am or 10am to 6pm or 7pm Monday to Saturday; some open Sunday

TELEPHONE

➡ To call other cities from a landline within Lithuania, dial 8, wait for the tone, then dial the area code and telephone number.

➡ To make an international call from Lithuania, dial 00 followed by the country code.

➜ For travellers with unlocked phones, SIM cards are cheap (usually €1 or €2) and easy to pick up at convenience stores.

ℹ Getting There & Away

AIR

The airports at Vilnius (p762) and **Kaunas** (☑ 8-612 44442; www.kaunas-airport.lt; Vilniaus gatvė, Karmėlava; ⊘ 6am-midnight; ☐ 29, 29E) both have good connections within Europe. From the US and beyond, you're likely to change planes in a hub airport such as Amsterdam, Warsaw or Frankfurt.

➜ **AirBaltic** (www.airbaltic.com) flies to Vilnius from Rīga several times daily and from Tallinn on most days, and also offers scheduled if sporadic service from Rīga to Palanga. These flights are more frequent in summer (May to September).

➜ Many travellers arrive via low-cost carrier **Ryanair** (www.ryanair.com).

BOAT

From Klaipėda's **International Ferry Port** (☑ 46-499 799; www.portofklaipeda.lt; Perkėlos gatvė 10), **DFDS Seaways** (☑ 46-323 232; www.dfdsseaways.lt; Baltijos prospektas 40; ⊘ 10am-5.30pm) runs passenger and car ferries to/from Kiel, Germany (per pedestrian/car from €28/80, daily, 20 hours) and Karlshamn, Sweden (per pedestrian/car from €39/74, 14 hours, at least daily).

BUS

Long-distance bus routes link Vilnius to neighbouring countries Poland, **Belarus and the Baltics. Browse routes on Eurolines (www. eurolines.lt) and** Lux Express (https://lux express.eu), whose coaches link Vilnius with Rīga, Tallinn, St Petersburg, Warsaw and Helsinki.

CAR & MOTORCYCLE

➜ Poland and Latvia are part of the EU's common-border Schengen Agreement, so there are no border checks when driving between them and Lithuania.

➜ Inform your car-rental company ahead of time if you are planning to drive across borders.

➜ For neighbouring Belarus and Russian region Kaliningrad, where most visitors require a visa to enter, checks are stricter and cross-border car rental is unlikely to be possible.

TRAIN

➜ Direct trains link Warsaw to Kaunas and Vilnius; browse schedules on www.intercity.pl.

➜ There are regular services linking Minsk and Vilnius (see www.rw.by).

ℹ TICK WARNING

Travellers planning to spend time camping, hiking or walking in forests should strongly consider a tick-borne encephalitis (TBE) vaccination. Compared to other European countries, Lithuania has a relatively high incidence of TBE, a potentially very serious illness that attacks the brain. If you find a tick attached to your body, remove it as quickly as possible using a clean pair of tweezers and wash the affected area. TBE symptoms may not appear until one or two weeks after a tick bite; seek medical attention.

➜ To/from Rīga or Tallinn, buses are quicker and more direct.

ℹ Getting Around

BICYCLE

➜ Bike hire is offered in all major cities, and often in small villages along the coast.

➜ Curonian Spit, the Baltic coast and Šiauliai's surrounds are scenic, unchallenging destinations for cyclists. Ferries to Curonian Spit allow passengers to bring their bicycle for free.

➜ Some **Kautra** (www.kautra.lt) intercity buses have bike racks (no extra charge; look for the bicycle symbol next to routes when booking a ticket on www.autobusubilietai.lt).

BUS

➜ Most services are summarised on the extremely handy bus tickets website Autobusų Bilietai (www.autobusubilietai.lt).

CAR & MOTORCYCLE

➜ Car hire is offered in all the major cities and Lithuanian roads are generally very good.

➜ To cope with snowy conditions, winter tyres are compulsory from mid-November through March; rental vehicles should have them.

LOCAL TRANSPORT

➜ Lithuanian cities generally have good public transport, based on buses, trolleybuses and minibuses.

TRAIN

➜ The **Lithuanian Rail** website (www.litrail.lt) has routes, times and prices in English.

➜ For common train journeys like Vilnius to Kaunas or to Klaipėda, the train is often more comfortable and better value than the bus. For other routes, such as Klaipėda to Kaunas or Šiauliai to Kaunas, the opposite is true.

Moldova

POP 3.44 MILLION (INCLUDING TRANSDNIESTR)

Best Places to Eat

➜ Popasul Dacilor (p775)

➜ Gok-Oguz (p775)

➜ Kumanyok (p780)

➜ Vatra Neamului (p775)

➜ Stolovka SSSR (p780)

Best Places to Stay

➜ Art Rustic Hotel (p774)

➜ Butuceni Eco-Resort (p778)

➜ Château Purcari (p776)

➜ City Park Hotel (p774)

Why Go?

The world is finally waking up to the charms of this little nation wedged between Romania and Ukraine. Moldova was famously dubbed the world's least happy place in a bestselling book in 2008, but today it's better known for its unspoiled countryside and superb wine tours. As one of Europe's least visited countries, Moldova retains a measure of roads-less-travelled charm. But that's changing quickly as budget flights from Western Europe take off.

Moldova may be entering the consciousness of the global traveller, but those seeking the remote and obscure still have their Shangri-La in the form of the breakaway republic of Transdniestr, where the Soviet Union reigns supreme. As for the unhappy thing, well that's a thing of the past. According to the most recent UN survey, today's Moldova is the world's 65th *happiest* country.

When to Go
Chişinău

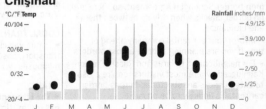

May–Jun Parks and restaurant terraces fill with students, and the weather is pleasant.

Jul High season hits its peak with hiking, wine tours and camping in full operation.

Oct Wine Festival takes place during the first weekend of October in Chişinău.

Entering the Country

Entering and leaving Moldova is usually a breeze, though you may experience queues and delays.

ITINERARIES

Three Days

Use the capital Chişinău (p772) as your base for a long-weekend getaway in Moldova. Spend day one strolling the pleasant parks of this fast-changing city, and checking out its museums and excellent restaurants. On the second day, take a day trip out to the stunning cave monastery at Orheiul Vechi (p777) and, if you don't mind a bit of driving, Tipova (p778) monastery with its incredible views of the Dniester River and Transdniestr beyond. On day three take a day trip to one of the many vineyards (p776) around Chişinău for a tour and wine tasting.

One Week

Spend a night or two in surreal Transdniestr (p779), a bastion of Russian-ness on the fringes of Moldova. Take an overnight trip to Soroca (p778) to see the impressive fortress on the lazy Dniestr. Lastly, reserve two or three days to explore more-remote bits of the country – kayaking on the Dniestr, birdwatching on the Lower Prut River near Cahul, exploring the Soviet sites of Gagauzia (p778) or staying a couple of nights in a boutique wine chalet.

Essential Food & Drink

Muşchi de vacă/porc/miel A cutlet of beef/pork/lamb.

Piept de pui The ubiquitous chicken breast.

Mămăligă Cornmeal mush with a consistency between porridge and bread that accompanies many dishes.

Brânză Moldova's most common cheese is a slightly salty-sour sheep's milk product that often comes grated. Put it on *mămăligă*.

Sarma Cabbage-wrapped minced meat or pilau rice packages, similar to Turkish dolma or Russian *goluptsy*.

Wine Look for bottles from quality local wineries like Cricova, Chateau Vartely and Purcari, among many others.

Fresh produce Moldova is essentially one big, very rewarding farmers market.

AT A GLANCE

Area 33,851 sq km

Capital Chişinău

Country Code ☑373

Currency Moldovan leu (plural lei)

Emergency Ambulance ☑903, fire ☑901, police ☑902

Language Moldovan

Time Eastern European Time (GMT/UTC plus three hours)

Visas None for EU, USA, Canada, Japan, Australia and New Zealand, but required for South Africa and many other countries

MOLDOVA

Sleeping Price Ranges

The following price ranges refer to the cost of a double room with private bathroom.

€ less than €35

€€ €35–85

€€€ more than €85

Eating Price Ranges

The following price ranges refer to the cost of an average main-course meal.

€ less than 90 lei

€€ 90–180 lei

€€€ more than 180 lei

Resources

Moldova Holiday (www.moldovaholiday.travel)

Moldova.org (www.moldova.org/en)

Fest (www.fest.md)

Moldova Highlights

1 Chişinău (p772)
Strolling the cafe-lined streets and leafy parks of Moldova's friendly capital.

2 Cricova (p776)
Designating a driver for tours to world-famous wine cellars and boutique wineries, like this one, outside Chişinău.

3 Orheiul Vechi (p777)
Exploring this fantastic historic cave monastery, burrowed by 13th-century monks.

4 Transdniestr (p779)
Leaving Europe behind in this self-styled 'republic', a surreal, living homage to the Soviet Union.

5 Soroca (p778) Ogling Gypsy-king mansions in Moldova's Roma capital, and visiting its medieval fortress.

6 Tipova (p778) Enjoying jaw-dropping views from this mystical monastery built into a cliff high above the Dniestr.

CHIŞINĂU

🎵 22 / POP 510,000

Pretty much all roads in Moldova lead to its wine-and-food-loving capital. Chişinău is a city of parks where retirees play chess in the shade of old-growth trees, of street festivals, and of sidewalk cafes where you can have a beverage and watch the world go by. A dozen superb wineries are within a 90-minute drive,

and the super-central location puts the entire country within a day trip. Throw in a hip and happening nightlife, and Chişinău ticks off all the boxes for an effective weekend break.

👁 Sights

Parcul Catedralei PARK
(Cathedral Park; B-dul Ştefan cel Mare; 🚶) Dab in the middle of Chişinău, this park is popu-

lar with families and canoodling teenagers on benches, and makes for great strolling. The highlight is the **Nativity of Christ Metropolitan Cathedral** (Catedrala Mitropolitană Naşterea Domnului; http://en.mitropolia.md) FREE, dating from the 1830s, and its lovely bell tower (1836). Along B-dul Ştefan cel Mare the main entrance to the park is marked by the Holy Gates (1841), also known as Chişinău's own **Arc de Triomphe**. On the northwestern side of the park is a colourful 24-hour **Flower Market** (Str Mitropolit G Bănulescu-Bodoni; ⊙10am-10pm).

Diagonally opposite Parcul Caedralei is **Grădina Publică Ştefan cel Mare şi Sfint** (Ştefan cel Mare Park; B-dul Ştefan cel Mare; 🚻), named after national hero Ştefan cel Mare, whose 1928 statue lords over the entrance.

National Archaeology & History Museum   MUSEUM
(Muzeul Naţional de Istorie a Moldovei; www.nationalmuseum.md/en; Str 31 August 1989, 121a; adult/student 10/5 lei, photos 15 lei, tour in English 100 lei; ⊙10am-6pm Sat-Thu Apr-Oct, to 5pm Nov-Mar) This impressive museum contains artefacts from the region of Orheiul Vechi, including Golden Horde coins and 14th-century ceramics; a rare, 2000-year-old Sarmatian fired-clay urn in the shape of a curly-coated ram; a beautiful amorpha (Greek jar) painted with anthropomorphic deities; and weapons dating from ancient times to the present. A huge late-Soviet-era diorama on the 1st floor depicts a battle near the village of Leuşeni on the Prut River during the pivotal WWII Iaşi-Chişinău Offensive.

Army Museum   MUSEUM
(Str Tighina 47; adult/child 10/3 lei, photos 10 lei; ⊙9am-5pm Tue-Sun) Occupying one end of the Centre of Culture and Military History, this once-musty museum now hosts a moving exhibit on Soviet-era repression. Stories of Red Terror, forced famines, mass deportations and gulag slave labour are told through photographs, videos, newspaper clippings and dioramas. While little is in English, the museum nevertheless gives you a good sense of the horrific scale of the crimes perpetrated by Lenin and Stalin.

National Art Museum   MUSEUM
(Muzeul Naţional de Artă al Moldovei; Str 31 August 1989, 115; adult/student 10/5 lei; ⊙10am-6pm Tue-Sun Apr-Oct, to 5pm Nov-Mar) The gorgeously restored main wing opened to visitors in 2018.

The focus is on contemporary Moldovan art, with a room or two of European works (mainly Dutch, Flemish and Italian) plus space for rotating exhibitions.

National Museum of Ethnography & Natural History   MUSEUM
(Muzeul Naţional de Etnografie şi Istorie Naturală; www.muzeu.md; Str M Kogălniceanu 82; adult/student 10/5 lei, photos 15 lei; ⊙10am-6pm Tue-Sun, closed last Wed of month; 🚻) The highlight of this massive and wonderful exhibition is a life-sized reconstruction of the skeleton of a dinothere – an 8-tonne elephant-like mammal that lived during the Pliocene epoch – 5.3 million to 1.8 million years ago – discovered in the Rezine region in 1966. Sweeping dioramas depict national customs and dress, while other exhibits cover geology, botany and zoology (including bizarre deformed animals in jars).

👉 Tours

Tour companies can arrange the standard wine, monastery and Transdniestr tours in addition to more specialised offerings, such as multiday excursions out of the capital. **Best Moldova** (☎022 874 027; www.bestmoldova.md; B-dul Ştefan cel Mare 71; ⊙9am-7pm Mon-Fri, to 4pm Sat) and **Tatra-Bis** (☎022 844 304; www.tatrabis.md; Str Alexandru Bernardazzi 59/3; ⊙9am-6pm Mon-Fri, 10am-3pm Sat) are two of the better ones.

🎊 Festivals & Events

⭐**Wine Festival**   WINE
(http://wineday.wineofmoldova.com; Piaţa Marii Adunări Naţionale; ⊙Oct) The nectar that makes Moldova tick is celebrated on the first weekend in October to coincide with the end of the grape harvest. A long block of B-dul Ştefan cel Mare is taken over by stalls selling wine, food and crafts as folk bands fill the air with traditional music. Tourists are encouraged to learn the national dances and don traditional clothing.

🛏 Sleeping

Ionika Hostel   HOSTEL €
(☎060 639 551; Str M Kogălniceanu 62; dm €7-9, d €19-20) The best all-around hostel in Chişinău, Ionika scores points with an excellent kitchen, flamboyant common areas, spacious dorms, individual bed lights and outlets, huge lockers, a musical massage shower and a pleasant outdoor patio.

Central Chişinău

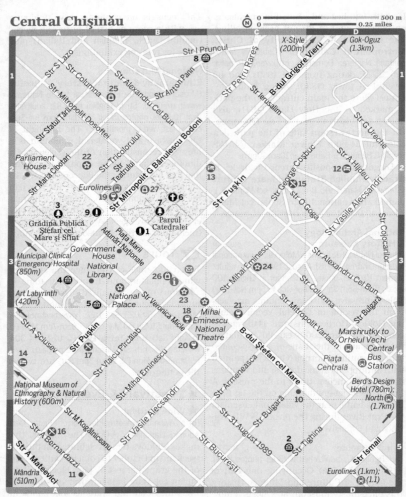

★ **City Park Hotel**   HOTEL €€

(☑ 022 249 249; www.citipark.md; Str E Doga 2; s/d incl breakfast €70/80; P 🛜) This fashionable hotel on the main walking street in town is popular, so book ahead to enjoy its bold, bright rooms, crisp English-speaking service and excellent breakfast in its street-side beer restaurant. Outstanding value, especially throwing in top-end perks like bathrobes and contemporary art.

★ **Art Rustic Hotel**   HOTEL €€

(☑ 022 232 593; www.art-rustic.md; Str Alexandru Hajdeu 79/1; s/d incl breakfast from €35/45; P ✳ 🛜) This small boutique hotel, a 15-minute walk from the centre, offers excellent value. The 13 rooms are individually and imaginatively furnished and come in two classes: '*standart*' and cheaper '*econom*', with the former being much bigger, and the latter boasting balconies.

Berd's Design Hotel   BOUTIQUE HOTEL €€€

(☑ 022 022 222; www.berdshotel.com; B-dul D Cantemir 12; s/d incl breakfast from €125/140, ste €290) Leviathan doors that must weigh several tonnes open to Chişinău's most design-conscious rooms, rendered in elegant silver tones. Quarters have plenty of space and giant beds, plus ultra-boutique bathrooms

Central Chişinău

◎ Sights

🎔 Activities, Courses & Tours

🛏 Sleeping

✪ Eating

◉ Drinking & Nightlife

✪ Entertainment

🛍 Shopping

with square sinks and wall-mounted toilets. Minimalism rules the day – no extra fabrics here.

✖ Eating

The neighbourhood along Str Bucureşti and Str 31 August 1989 is a good place to browse for restaurants. Northeast of the parks, pedestrianised Str E Doga is another cafe and restaurant row.

★ Coffee Molka
CAFE €

(Str Octavian Goga; dishes 25-50 lei; ⊙8am-10.30pm Mon-Fri, noon-10.30pm Sat & Sun; 🛜) The charismatic owner's love of coffee is on display everywhere, from Turkish coffee faithfully prepared according to an ancient style, to shelves of antique coffee grinders that make up part of the on-site coffee 'museum'. Vintage record and book collections and groovy lighting add to the ambience. Light bites are best taken on the rooftop terrace.

★ Popasul Dacilor
MOLDOVAN €€

(☑069 150 543; Str Valea Crucii St 13; mains 50-250 lei; ⊙11am-midnight; ❄🛜) Chişinău's most eccentric eatery is a bit like a *Game of Thrones* set, awash in furs, totem poles and gnarled wood. Out back open-air dining options take all shapes and sizes, and a two-tonne door leads to a secret stash of rare Moldovan wines. The traditional Bessarabian fare and service are superb. It's out towards the airport.

★ Gok-Oguz
MOLDOVAN €€

(☑022 468 852; Str Calea Orheiului 19a; mains 100-175 lei; ⊙10am-11pm) It's well worth the short taxi ride north of the centre to Chişinău's only Gagauzian restaurant. Gagauzian food has Turkic, Romanian and Russian influences, and the offerings here include *carne de miel po Gheorhievski* (baked mutton with rice and vegetables), lamb *cavurma* (a spicy stew) and *ghiozlemea* (gözleme – or Turkic pastries) with ewes' milk cheese.

Vatra Neamului
MOLDOVAN €€

(☑022 226 839; Str Puşkin 20b; mains 75-300 lei; ⊙11am-midnight; 🅿❄🛜) This superb place boasts charming old-world decor, unfailingly genial staff and – by night – a duet strumming traditional Moldovan instruments. A long menu of imaginatively dressed-up meats – think stewed pork with *mămăligă* (boiled cornmeal), baked rabbit and grilled trout, not to mention *varenyky* (Ukrainian dumplings) and *plăcintă* (stuffed pastries) – may prompt repeat visits.

Gastrobar
MEDITERRANEAN €€€

(☑068 906 545; Str A Bernardazzi 66; mains 100-250 lei; ⊙noon-11pm; ❄🛜✐) The food is both healthy and outstanding – what you might expect from a place with the motto 'bread, wine, life'. Warm up with a berry smoothie infused with flax seeds, then pick from light *meze* (tzatziki, hummus) or envelope-pushing mains like duck breast in orange and cranberry sauce or grilled octopus.

🍷 Drinking & Nightlife

★ Kira's Club
CLUB

(www.facebook.com/kirasclub; Str Veronica Micle 7; Fri & Sat cover 40 lei; ⊙ 11am-11pm Sun-Thu, to 5am Fri & Sat) More than a club, this intimate basement venue might better be described as a multifaceted counterculture haven. DJs are the norm, but on any given night you might encounter live music, hip-hop or poetry slams. In the warm months the party moves outside, taking over the sidewalk in front of the edgy Luceafărul theatre next door.

★ Invino enoteca
WINE BAR

(☑ 022 909 944; www.invino.md; Str Mitropolit G Bănulescu Bodini 41; ⊙ 11am-9pm; 🐕) Chişinău, as you might imagine, has its share of wine bars. Invino occupies a refined, minimalist space just off the central park. It has a big blonde-wood bar, an extensive wine list with virtually all of Moldova's wineries represented, plus cheeses and other hors d'oeuvres for pairing and palate cleansing. And this being Moldova, it ain't expensive.

Smokehouse
CRAFT BEER

(B-dul Ştefan cel Mare 128; ⊙ 11am-midnight Sun-Thu, to 2am Fri & Sat; 🐕) Twinned with the adjacent Taproom 27, the motto is 'hoppiness on tap' and they deliver with a small but carefully curated list of craft beers on tap. Grab a flight of four/eight beers for 65/130 lei. It's also known for ribs, corn succotash and other barbecuestaples of the American South.

☆ Entertainment

Posters listing what's on are displayed on boards outside the city's various theatres. Culture vultures should not miss a performance at the **Maria Bieşu National Opera & Ballet Theatre** (www.nationalopera.md; B-dul Ştefan cel Mare 152; tickets 50-200 lei; ⊙ box office 11am-6pm Tue-Mon, to 2pm Sat & Sun) or the architecturally splendid **Organ Hall** (Sala cu Orgă; www.organhall.md; B-dul Ştefan cel Mare 81; ⊙ box office 11am-6pm, performances 6pm).

🔒 Shopping

Wine is the most obvious gift. **Carpe Diem** (www.wineshop.md; Str Columna 136, 3a; ⊙ 11am-

---

TOURING MOLDOVA'S WINE COUNTRY

Moldova was the Rhone Valley of the Soviet Union, and two of the largest wineries in the world are within 20km of Chişinău: **Cricova** (☑ 069 077 734; www.cricovavin.md; Str Chişinăului 124, Cricova; ⊙ 10am-5pm Mon-Fri) and **Mileştii Mici** (☑ 069 500 262, 022 382 777; www.milestii-mici.md; Mileştii Mici town; tours 350-1500 lei; ⊙ 8am-5pm Mon-Fri). The latter has a collection of about 1.5 million bottles – which makes it the world's largest wine collection, according to the Guinness Book of World Records. Tours of these two giants are popular; email well in advance to book a spot.

To avoid crowds, you might consider booking a more intimate wine-tasting experience at one of the several boutique wineries around Chişinău. These have the added benefit of better wine. A few of the best:

Castel Mimi (☑ 062 001 893; www.castelmimi.md; Str Dacia 1, Bulboaca; tasting tours 300-780 lei; ⊙ 10am-6pm Wed-Sun, restaurant to 10pm) This legendary winery 40km southeast of Chişinău occupies a beautifully restored stone manor dating from 1893. It's a picture of modern luxury, with an interactive tasting table, an exquisite restaurant, and grove of *domiki* (small houses) and palatial rooms for rent.

Château Purcari (☑ 024 230 411; www.purcari.md; Purcari; tasting tours from 300 lei) Nestled in the extreme southeast corner of Moldova, about 115km from Chişinău, Purcari's wines are arguably Moldova's finest. Tours here can last from one to several days, with luxurious lakeside **accommodation** (☑ 060 121 221; https://purcari.md; Purcari; s/d from €65/75; ❄🐕) and an array of activities.

Château Vartely (☑ 022 829 891; www.vartely.md; Str Eliberării 170b, Orhei/New Orhei; basic tour without tasting 150 lei) Established in 2008, it offers not just very good whites and reds, but excellent food and cosy accommodation (rooms from €83) in one of 12 pretty wooden bungalows, just 50km north of Chişinău.

11pm) is the best wine shop in town, with highly knowledgeable, English-speaking owners. **Mândria** (www.mandria.md; Str Mitropolit G Bănulescu Bodini 5; ⊘9am-6pm Mon-Fri) is highly recommended for beautiful, hand-embroidered national outfits and blankets. For all-around souvenirs, drop into **Fantezie** (☑022 222 475; B-dul Ştefan cel Mare 83; ⊘9am-7pm Mon-Fri, 10am-5pm Sat, 10am-2pm Sun) in the marvellous city hall building.

❶ Information

Moldova Tourist Information Center (www.moldova.travel; B-dul Ştefan cel Mare 83; ⊘10am-7pm Mon-Fri, to 3pm Sat; 🕿) The enthusiastic staff can organise just about everything, from hotels to car rentals to guided excursions around Moldova.

Victoriabank (Str Puşkin 26; ⊘9am-5pm Mon-Fri, to 2pm Sat) Has ATM, Western Union and Moneygram.

❶ Getting There & Away

AIR

Moldova's only international airport is the modern **Chişinău International Airport** (KIV; ☑022 525 111; www.airport.md; Str Aeroportului 80/3), 13km southeast of the city centre, with regular flights to many major European capitals.

BUS

Buses heading south to Bucharest and east to Transdniestr and Odesa (Ukraine) use the **Central Bus Station** (Gara Centrala; ☑022 542 185; www.autogara.md; Str Mitropolit Varlaam 58). Most but not all buses to Odesa go via Palanca and avoid Transdniestr, and only a few go to the preferred Privoz Station in Odesa.

The **North Bus Station** (Autogara Nord; ☑022 411 338; Str Caleja Moşilor) serves Soroca and points north, and has international departures to Kyiv and Moscow. The **South Bus Station** (Autogara Sud; ☑022 713 983; Şoseaua Hînceşti 143) serves Comrat and most southern destinations, and also serves Iaşi, Romania.

With offices at the **train station** (☑022 549 813; www.eurolines.md; Aleea Garii 1; ⊘9am-6pm Mon-Fri) and in the **centre** (☑022 222 827; www.eurolines.md; Str Teatrului 4/1), Eurolines has nicer buses to major cities around Europe.

TRAIN

International trains depart from the eclectic **train station** (Gara Feroviară Chişinău; ☑022 833 333; Aleea Gării). Services run to Bucharest (from 600 lei, 14 hours, 4.56pm daily), Kyiv

(from 700 lei, 14 to 18 hours, two to three daily), Moscow (from 1500 lei, 29 to 32 hours, two to three daily) and Odesa (185 lei, 4 hours, 6.57am Thursday to Sunday). **Left luggage** (per day 11-15 lei; ⊘24hr) is available.

❶ Getting Around

TO/FROM THE AIRPORT

From the airport, trolleybus 30 (2 lei) services central Chişinău's main artery, B-dul Ştefan cel Mare (35 minutes).

Cabs ordered from taxi booths at the airport cost 100 lei to 120 lei to the centre.

CAR

Hiring a car is a good way to get around. Moldova's highways are in great shape, although rural roads still present some challenges.

The major rental agencies have booths at the airport. Several local companies prominently advertise cheaper rates around town, but be careful of these guys.

PUBLIC TRANSPORT

Buses, trolleybuses and *marshrutky* (fixed-route minivans; 2 lei to 3 lei) criss-cross the city in dizzying fashion from about 5.30am until 10.30pm. Trolleybus 30 wings its way down Str 31 August 1989 then veers onto B-dul Ştefan cel Mare and continues all the way to the airport. Trolleybuses 1, 5 and 8 connect the train station with the centre via B-dul Ştefan cel Mare, passing within a block of the Central Bus Station. See www.fest.md/en/map for route maps.

TAXI

Taxis ordered by phone or via a ride-hailing app (try Yandex taxi or iTaxi) cost just 30 lei to 50 lei for trips around the centre. Call 14 222, 14 428, 14 008 or 14 499.

AROUND CHIŞINĂU

Orheiul Vechi

The archaeological and ecclesiastical complex at **Orheiul Vechi** (Old Orhei; Butuceni), about 50km north of Chişinău, is the country's most important historical site and a place of stark natural beauty. Occupying a remote cliff high above the Răut River, the complex is known for its **Cave Monastery** (Mănăstire în Peşteră; Orheiul Vechi; voluntary donation; ⊘8am-6pm)

FREE, but also includes baths, fortifications and ruins dating back as much as 2000 years.

The complex is in the village of Butuceni, where a small bridge over the Răut takes you to the trailhead for a 15-minute hike up to the Cave Monastery, dug by Orthodox monks in the 13th century. Dress appropriately at the monastery: long skirts or pants for women, long shorts or trousers for men, and no tank tops.

The **Orheiul Vechi Exhibition Centre** (Butuceni; adult/student incl ethnographic museum 10/5 lei; ⊙ 9am-5pm Tue-Sun), located just before the bridge, contains objects recovered during archaeological digs, and also sells a handy English-language map and guide (40 lei) of the complex.

There are two fabulous sleeping options in Butuceni should you want to get a taste of village life. About 1km east of the bridge, **Eco-Resort Butuceni** (☑ 079 617 870; www. pensiuneabutuceni.md; Butuceni; s/d/tr/q incl breakfast €30/46/65/75; ❋ ❅ ☙) has 19 rooms done up in peasant style, a fabulous restaurant (mains 50–100 lei) and an indoor swimming pool. **Vila Etnica** (www.etnica.md; Butuceni; r €70-80; ❋ ❅) is a rambling complex with a pleasant restaurant on a babbling brook.

WORTH A TRIP

TIPOVA CAVE MONASTERY

This fantastic **monastery** (Tipova; 10 lei, photos 15 lei) FREE is built into cliffs that tower some 200m above the Dniestr River's right (west) bank, in the tiny village of Tipova some 95km northeast of Chişinău. The monastery consists of three religious chambers and monastic cells linked by precarious steps built into the rock face. The oldest of the three chambers, the **Elevation of the Holy Cross** cave church, is thought to date from the 11th century. Dress appropriately to enter any religious areas.

Arriving by private car is recommended. Otherwise, take the 10.30am *marshrutka* to Tipova (2½ hours) from Chişinău's North Bus Station. It returns to Chişinău in the late afternoon (around 3pm), so consider overnighting at lovely **Vila Serenada** (☑ 079 842 662; vent-dest@hotmail.fr; Horodişte; d incl breakfast €40; ❋) in nearby Horodişte.

ⓘ Getting There & Away

From Chişinău, *marshrutky* to Butuceni depart from a **bus stand** (Str Metropolit Varlaam) roughly opposite the Central Bus Station entrance (26 lei, 1¼ hours, five or six daily). Placards will say 'Butuceni', 'Trebujeni' or 'Orheiul Vechi'. The last trip back is at 4.15pm (6.20pm in the summer). A taxi round trip shouldn't cost more than €40.

Soroca

The northern city of Soroca (population 22,000) occupies a prominent position on the Dniestr River and is Moldova's unofficial 'Roma capital'. The incredibly gaudy, fantastical mansions of the Roma 'kings' that line the streets up on the hill above the centre are a sight to behold.

The gloriously solid **Soroca Fortress** (Cetatea Soroca; ☑ 069 323 734; Str Petru Rareş 1; adult/student 10/5 lei, tours in English 100 lei; ⊙ 9am-1pm & 2-6pm Wed-Sun) on the banks of the Dniestr dates to the late 15th century and the reign of Moldavian Prince Ştefan cel Mare. It was built on the remains of a wooden fortress in the shape of a circle, with five bastions. Today those bastions contain medieval-themed exhibits, with a few English placards posted about that shed light on the history of the fortress.

You can get fantastic views of the Dniestr and the perfectly partitioned fields of Ukraine beyond by climbing the 660 steps (not an exact count) up to the **Candle of Gratitude** (Str Independenţei) FREE on the town's southern outskirts.

There are a few passable places to stay in town but really only one restaurant of note, pizzeria **Salat** (Parcu Central; mains 40-100 lei; ⊙ 9am-11pm) on the town square.

From the **bus station** (Str Independenţei) south of town, *marshrutky* head to Chişinău's North Bus Station every hour or so until 6pm (75 lei, 2½ hours). There are daily buses to Bucharest and Kyiv.

Gagauzia

The autonomous region of Gagauzia (Gagauz Yeri) lies 100km due south of Chişinău but is a world apart from the cosmopolitan capital. This Turkic-influenced Christian ethnic minority forfeited full independence for autonomy in the early 1990s, thus making it subordinate to Moldova constitutionally and for defence. But politically the Gagauz

INTO THE WILD

Moldova has several playgrounds for lovers of the great outdoors. The bird-laden **Prutul de Jos (Lower Prut) Biosphere Reserve** in the country's extreme southwest corner was recognised as a Unesco site in 2018.

Other outdoorsy highlights around the country include multiday kayaking and camping expeditions on the **Dniestr River**; and the **Plaiul Fagului (Land of Beeches) Natural Scientific Reserve**, where you can bike through beech forests or climb Moldova's highest peak (430m). With a fleet of kayaks and mountain bikes, outdoor shop **X-Style** (📱 069 107 435, 069 692 265; www.xstyle.md; B-dul Grigore Vieru 27; ⊙ 9am-8pm) in Chişinău runs trips to these places, sometimes dipping into Romania. Ask for Natalie or Alexandru.

generally look towards Russia for patronage, while increasingly looking towards Turkey for both cultural inspiration and economic investment.

Comrat, the capital, has a nice church, the requisite Lenin statue and the eclectic **Comrat Regional History Museum** (vul Lenina 162; 10 lei; ⊙ 9am-4pm Tue-Sat), but its main appeal lies in being a cultural oddity. Tiraspol Hostel & Tours (p779) runs excellent tours to Gagauzia out of Chişinău or Tiraspol.

Comrat is easy to reach from Chişinău, with hourly *marshrutky* departures from the South Bus Station (45 lei, two hours).

TRANSDNIESTR

POP 469,000

The self-declared republic of Transdniestr, a narrow strip of land on the eastern bank of the Dniestr River, is a ministate that doesn't officially exist in anyone's eyes but its own.

From the Moldovan perspective, Transdniestr (also spelled Transnistria; in Russian: Prednestrove) is still officially part of its sovereign territory that was illegally grabbed in the early 1990s with Russian support. Officials in Transdniestr see it differently and proudly point to the territory having won its 'independence' in a bloody civil war in 1992. A bitter truce has ensued ever since.

These days, a trip to Transdniestr is easier than ever thanks to relaxed registration rules. Visitors will be stunned by this idiosyncratic region that still fully embraces the iconography of the Soviet period.

Tiraspol

📱 533 / POP 130,000

The 'capital' of Transdniestr is also, officially at least, the second-largest city in Moldova. With eerily quiet streets, flower beds tended

with military precision and old-school Soviet everything from street signs to parks named after communist grandees, Tiraspol will be one of the strangest places you'll ever visit.

◎ Sights & Activities

Noul Neamţ Monastery   MONASTERY
(Kitskany Monastery; Kitskany Village) A stunning 70m bell tower marks this serene monastery (1861), 7km south of Tiraspol. You can climb the bell tower for a bird's-eye view of the monastery's four churches and a sweeping panorama of the countryside. You'll need to ask around for the key to be let up. Frequent *marshrutky* serve Kitskany from Tiraspol (4 roubles, 10 minutes); the stop is just over the central bridge spanning the Dniestr.

**Tiraspol National
History Museum**   MUSEUM
(ul 25 Oktober 46; 26 roubles; ⊙ 9am-5pm Tue-Sun) No period of Transdniestran history is ignored at this relatively interesting museum, starting with photos of late-19th-century Tiraspol, moving to the Soviet period and the Great Patriotic War, to the civil war of 1992.

Kvint Factory   FACTORY
(📱 0533 96 577; www.kvint.md; ul Lenina 38; ⊙ store 9am-1pm & 2-10pm) Since 1897 Kvint has been making some of Moldova's finest brandies. Book private tasting tours in English two days in advance (US$10 to US$70 per person, five-person minimum). Wine tastings are also available (US$8 to US$17, three-person minimum), or join one-hour standard tours of the factory (in Russian), which take place Monday to Friday at 3pm (45 roubles per person, no tastings).

☞ Tours

Tiraspol Hostel & Tours   TOURS
(📱 068 571 472; www.moldovahostels.com) Run by Tim, an American, this operator runs

MOLDOVA TIRASPOL

truly creative tours to less explored corners of Transdniestr or multiday combo tours taking in Gagauzia and/or Odesa as well. The focus is on Soviet sights and experiences, often with a heavy local element (eg, a homestay and traditional meal in an isolated village).

Transnistria Tour TOURS
(☑ 069 427 502, 077 741 678; www.transnistria-tour. com) This highly recommended company offers a full range of tours and travel services to foreign visitors. Company head and guide Andrey Smolenskiy speaks German and Swedish in addition to English and Russian.

🛏 Sleeping

Like Home Hostel HOSTEL €
(☑ 0777 66 188; http://htno.ru; Sadovyi pereulok 9b; dm €10; ❄ 🌐) The best hostel in town, and not just because it's the only one with signage (making it viable for walk-ins). It's homey and friendly with a real common area, two spacious eight-bed dorm rooms with air-con, and some of the best food in town served in the Vkusnii Dom cafe at the back.

City Club HOTEL €€€
(☑ 0533 59 000; www.cityclub.md; ul Gorkogo 18; r without/with breakfast from €50/60; ℗ ❄ 🌐) One of the better deals in the region, City Club features lovely staff and well-appointed, spacious rooms. There are classy inside-and-out dining choices and a sauna, but the highlight is the truly impressive gym – even nongym-rats will be tempted to work out.

WORTH A TRIP

BENDERY FORTRESS

This impressive Ottoman **fortress** (Tighina Fortress; ☑ 077 908 728; www. bendery-fortress.com; ul Panina; 50 roubles, tours in English 150 roubles; ⊙ 9am-6pm Apr-Oct, 8am-5pm Nov-Mar), outside the centre near the Bendery–Tiraspol bridge, was built in the 16th century and saw keen fighting between Turkish and Russian forces before falling to Tsarist Russia permanently in the early 19th century. You can walk along the ramparts taking in the fine views of the Dniestr River, have a picnic on the grounds, and visit several museums on-site that document the fort's long and rich history.

To get to Bendery take trolleybus 19 (3 roubles, 20 minutes) from any stop along ul 25 Oktober in Tiraspol.

🍴 Eating & Drinking

⭐ Kumanyok UKRAINIAN €
(☑ 0533 72 034; ul Sverdlova 37; mains 50-125 roubles; ⊙ 9am-11pm; 🌐) This smart, super-friendly, traditional Ukrainian place is set in a kitsch faux-countryside home, where diners are attended to by a fleet of peasant-dressed waitresses. The menu is hearty Ukrainian fare; think *varenyky* (dumplings), *bliny* (pancakes), *golubtsi* (stuffed cabbage rolls) and, above all, authentic *borshch* (beetroot soup).

Stolovka SSSR CAFETERIA €
(Bus Station, ul Sovetskaya 1, 2nd fl, Bendery; dishes 8-18 roubles; ⊙ 9am-4pm; ❄ 🌐) In this retro-Soviet *stolovaya* (cafeteria) above the bus station, you can dine amid USSR-vintage paraphernalia on egalitarian fare like *solyanka* (pickled vegetables and potato soup), *olivye* (potato) salad and *kotleta* (minced meat cutlet). No English menu, just point and pick from the buffet.

Vintage CLUB
(www.clubvintage.ru; ul Klary Tsetkin 14/2; from 7pm Fri & Sat 100 roubles; ⊙ 24hr) The hottest club in Tiraspol, often pulling top DJs from Moscow and elsewhere. Serious fun.

ℹ Information

MONEY
The Transdniestran rouble is the only way to pay for stuff in the breakaway republic, as credit cards are not accepted. You can exchange dollars, euros, Russian roubles or Moldovan lei for roubles at exchange kiosks and banks.

TOURIST INFORMATION
Tourist Information Centre (☑ 0533 53 559; tourism@ngo.ardt.com; ul Sovetskaya 135; ⊙ 9.30am-6.30pm Mon-Sat) This helpful new office covers all of Transdniestr and is a good place to stop if you're planning to hit less-visited parts of the republic. They have the only decent map of Tiraspol, sell souvenirs and can help find guides.

ℹ Getting There & Away

From the bus station, *marshrutky* go to Chişinău (40 roubles, 1¾ hours, every 20 minutes) and Odesa in Ukraine (60 roubles, 2½ hours to three hours, six daily).

The Odesa–Chişinău train passes through Tiraspol, but it only runs from Friday to Sunday (plus Thursdays in summer). The departure to Odesa is at 8.06am (170 roubles, three hours), while to Chişinău the departure is at 9.21pm (110

ℹ CROSSING INTO TRANSDNIESTR

All visitors to Transdniestr are required to show a valid passport at the 'border' (if arriving by train this happens at the train station). The formalities are fairly straightforward and take about five minutes.

Your passport will be scanned and used to generate a slip of paper called a 'migration card'. You must keep the paper with your passport at all times and surrender it when leaving (so don't lose it!). Migration cards allow for stays of up to 45 days. If you plan to stay overnight you must provide the border officials with an address for each day of your stay.

Be sure to ask for a Moldovan entry stamp if you enter Transdniestr from Ukraine and plan on continuing to Moldova proper. If you fail to secure one, you must register your presence at the **Bureau for Migration and Asylum** (B-dul Ştefan cel Mare 124; ⊘9am-4pm Mon-Fri) in Chişinău within three business days of arriving in Moldova proper.

The above rules are subject to change, especially if tensions with Moldova increase.

roubles, one hour). There's an additional train to Chişinău on odd days (5.58pm).

The bus station and train station share a parking lot about 1.5km north of the centre. Trolley-bus 1 takes you into the centre via ul Lenina and ul 25 Oktober (3 roubles).

SURVIVAL GUIDE

ℹ Directory A–Z

MONEY
ATMs widely available, particularly in Chişinău and other cities. Credit cards usually accepted in urban centres, less so in rural areas. Transdniestr has its own currency.

OPENING HOURS
Banks 9am–3pm Monday to Friday
Businesses 8am–7pm Monday to Friday, to 4pm Saturday
Museums 9am–5pm Tuesday to Sunday
Restaurants 10am–11pm
Shops 9am or 10am–6pm or 7pm Monday to Saturday

PUBLIC HOLIDAYS
New Year's Day 1 January
Orthodox Christmas 7–8 January
International Women's Day 8 March
Orthodox Easter Sunday & Monday April/May
Labour Day 1 May
Victory (1945) Day 9 May
Independence Day 27 August
National Language Day 31 August
Western Christmas 25 December

TELEPHONE
It's straightforward to buy a local prepaid SIM card with one of the two main mobile-phone providers, Moldcell and Orange, and use it in any unlocked handset. To place a call or send a text from a local mobile phone, dial +373 or 0, plus the two-digit prefix and the six-digit number.

VISAS
None for European countries, USA, Canada, Japan, Australia and New Zealand, but required for South Africa and many other countries.

ℹ Getting There & Away

AIR
Moldova's only international airport is in Chişinău (p777). The national carrier, **Air Moldova** (✆022 830 830; www.airmoldova.md; B-dul Negruzzi 10, Chişinău; ⊘8am-8pm), and local budget carrier **Fly One** (✆022 100 003; www.flyone.aero) serve several European cities.

LAND
Motorists must purchase a highway sticker (vignette) to drive on Moldovan roads. Buy these online (http://vinieta.gov.md) or at border crossings. Rates per seven/15/30 days are €4/8/16.

ℹ Getting Around

Moldova has a comprehensive network of buses running to most towns and villages. *Marshrutky*, or fixed-route minivans (also known by their Romanian name, maxitaxis), follow the same routes as the buses and are quicker. Car hire makes sense as Moldova's roads are good these days and you can reach just about any part of the country on a day trip out of Chişinău.

Montenegro

382 / POP 676,900

Best Places to Eat

➡ Belveder (p790)

➡ Hotel Soa (p794)

➡ Restaurant Conte (p785)

➡ Antigona (p789)

➡ One (p787)

Best Places to Stay

➡ La Vecchia Casa (p791)

➡ Palazzo Drusko (p788)

➡ Palazzo Radomiri (p788)

➡ Old Town Hostel (p787)

➡ Hostel Pirate (p789)

Why Go?

Imagine a place with sapphire beaches as spectacular as Croatia's, rugged peaks as dramatic as Switzerland's, canyons nearly as deep as Colorado's, palazzi as elegant as Venice's and towns as old as Greece's. Now wrap it up in a Mediterranean climate and squish it into an area two-thirds the size of Wales, and you start to get a picture of Montenegro (Црна Гора).

More-adventurous travellers can easily sidestep the peak-season hordes on the coast by heading to the rugged mountains of the north. This is, after all, a country where wolves and bears still lurk in forgotten corners.

Montenegro, Crna Gora, Black Mountain: the name itself conjures up romance and drama. There are plenty of both on offer as you explore this perfumed land, bathed in the scent of wild herbs, conifers and Mediterranean blossoms. Yes, it really is as magical as it sounds.

When to Go
Podgorica

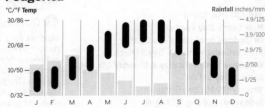

Jun Enjoy balmy weather without the peak-season prices and crowds.

Sep Warm water but fewer bods to share it with; shoulder-season prices.

Oct The leaves turn golden, making a rich backdrop for walks in the national parks.

Entering the Country

Whether you choose to fly, train, ferry, bus or drive, it's not difficult to get to Montenegro these days. New routes – including those served by low-cost carriers – are continually being added to the busy timetable at the country's two airports. It's also possible to make your way from neighbouring countries, especially Croatia. Dubrovnik's airport is very close to the border and the beautiful city makes an impressive starting point to a Montenegro holiday. Flights, cars and tours can be booked online at lonelyplanet.com/bookings.

ITINERARIES

Five Days

Basing yourself in the atmospheric walled town of Kotor (p785), spend an afternoon in palazzi-packed Perast (p785) and a whole day in buzzy Budva (p788). Allow another day to explore mountainous Lovćen National Park (p789) and the old royal capital, Cetinje (p789).

One Week

For your final two days, head north to the mountains of Durmitor National Park (p791), making sure to stop at the historic Ostrog Monastery (p791) on the way. Spend your time hiking, rafting (in season) and canyoning.

Essential Food & Drink

Loosen your belt; you're in for a treat. By default, most Montenegrin food is local, fresh and organic, and hence very seasonal. The food on the coast is virtually indistinguishable from Dalmatian cuisine: lots of grilled seafood, garlic, olive oil and Italian dishes. Inland it's much more meaty and Serbian-influenced. The village of Njeguši in the Montenegrin heartland is famous for its *pršut* (prosciutto, air-dried ham) and *sir* (cheese). Anything with Njeguški in its name is going to be a true Montenegrin dish and stuffed with these goodies.

Here are some local favourites:

Riblja čorba Fish soup, a staple of the coast.

Crni rižoto Black risotto, coloured and flavoured with squid ink.

Lignje na žaru Grilled squid, sometimes stuffed (*punjene*) with cheese and smoke-dried ham.

Jagnjetina ispod sača Lamb cooked (often with potatoes) under a metal lid covered with hot coals.

Rakija Domestic brandy, made from nearly anything. The local favourite is grape-based *loza*.

Vranac & Krstač The most famous indigenous red and white wine varietals (respectively).

MONTENEGRO

AT A GLANCE

Area 13,812 sq km

Capital Podgorica

Country Code ☑ 382

Currency euro (€)

Emergency Ambulance ☑ 124, Fire ☑ 123, Police ☑ 122

Language Montenegrin

Time Central European time (GMT/UTC plus one hour)

Visas None for citizens of EU, Canada, USA, Australia, New Zealand and many other countries.

Sleeping Price Ranges

The following price ranges are based on a standard double with bathroom in high season.

€ less than €45

€€ €45–100

€€€ more than €100

Eating Price Ranges

The following ranges refer to the average price of a main course.

€ less than €5

€€ €5–15

€€€ more than €15

Resources

Montenegrin National Tourist Organisation (www.montenegro.travel)

Montenegro Highlights

1 Kotor (p785) Randomly roaming the atmospheric streets until you're a little lost.

2 Lovćen National Park (p789) Driving the vertiginous route from Kotor to the Njegoš Mausoleum.

3 Perast (p785) Admiring the baroque palaces and churches.

4 Ostrog Monastery (p791) Seeking out the spiritual at this impressive cliff-clinging monastery.

5 Tara Canyon (p791) Floating through paradise, rafting between the plunging walls of this canyon.

6 Cetinje (p789) Diving into Montenegro's history, art and culture in the old royal capital.

7 Ulcinj (p788) Beaching by day and soaking up the Eastern-tinged vibe on the streets after dark.

8 Durmitor National Park (p791) Admiring the mountain vistas reflected in glacial lakes during walks.

COASTAL MONTENEGRO

There's less than 100km as the crow flies from the fjord-like Bay of Kotor in the north to the long sandy beaches abutting Albania, yet Montenegro's coast can still claim some of the most dramatic scenery on the entire Mediterranean.

Perast Пераст

☎ 032 / POP 270

Looking like a chunk of Venice that has floated down the Adriatic and anchored itself onto the Bay of Kotor, Perast hums with melancholy memories of the days when it was rich and powerful. Despite having only one main street, this tiny town boasts 16 churches and 17 formerly grand palazzi. While some are just enigmatic ruins sprouting bougainvillea and wild fig, others are caught up in the whirlwind of renovation that has hit the town.

The town slopes down from the highway to a narrow waterfront road (Obala Marka Martinovića) that runs along its length. At its heart is **St Nicholas' Church** (Crkva Sv Nikole; Obala Marka Martinovića bb; treasury €1; ⏲8am-6pm), set on a small square lined with date palms and the bronze busts of famous citizens.

Perast's most famous landmarks aren't on land at all: two peculiarly picturesque islands with equally peculiar histories.

Sights

★Gospa od Škrpjela ISLAND

(Our-Lady-of-the-Rock Island; ⏲church 9am-7pm Jul & Aug, to 5pm Apr-Jun & Sep-Nov, to 3pm Dec-Mar) This picturesque island was artificially created (on 22 July 1452, to be precise) around a rock where an image of the Madonna was found; every year on that same day, the locals row over with stones to continue the task. In summer, boats line up on the Perast waterfront to ferry people there and back (€5 return); off season, you may need to ask around.

The magnificent **church** at its centre was erected in 1630 and has sumptuous Venetian paintings, hundreds of silver votive tablets and a small museum (€1.50). The most unusual – and famous – exhibit is an embroidered icon of the Madonna and Child partly made with the hair of its maker.

Sleeping & Eating

GudCo Apartments APARTMENT €€

(☎032-373 589; gudco@t-com.me; Perast 152; apt from €75; ❄📶) There are only two spacious, stone-walled apartments available here, positioned directly above the extremely welcoming owners' house. Wake up to extraordinary bay views in your spacious Perast pad, then play with the kittens on the rear terrace while you catch up on your laundry (units have washing machines and dishwashers).

Konoba Školji MONTENEGRIN, SEAFOOD €€

(☎069-419 745; www.skolji.com; Obala Marka Martinovića bb; mains €8-24; ⏲10am-midnight; 📶) This appealing traditional restaurant is all about the thrill of the grill: fresh seafood and falling-off-the-bone meats are barbecued to perfection in full view of salivating diners. Thankfully they're not shy with the portion sizes; the delightful/maddening smell of the cooking and the sea air will have you ravenous by the time your meal arrives. The pasta is good too.

★Restaurant Conte SEAFOOD €€€

(☎032-373 722; www.hotelconte.me; Obala Marka Martinovića bb; mains €10-25; ⏲8am-midnight; 📶) If you don't fall in love here – with Perast, with your dining partner, with a random waiter – consider your heart stone; with its island views, table-top flowers and super-fresh oysters, this place is ridiculously romantic. You'll be presented with platters of whole fish to select from; the chosen one will return, cooked and silver-served, to your table.

Getting There & Away

- Paid parking is available on either approach to town (per day €2) but, in summer, it's in hot demand.
- Car access into the town itself is restricted.
- There's no bus station but buses to and from Kotor (€1.50, 25 minutes) stop at least every 30 minutes on the main road at the top of town.
- Water taxis zoom around the bay during summer and call into all ports, including Perast.
- Regular taxis from Kotor to Perast cost around €15.

Kotor Котор

☎ 032 / POP 13,000

Wedged between brooding mountains and a moody corner of the bay, achingly atmospheric Kotor is perfectly at one with its setting. Hemmed in by staunch walls snaking improbably up the surrounding slopes, the town is a medieval maze of museums, churches, cafe-strewn squares, and Venetian

Kotor

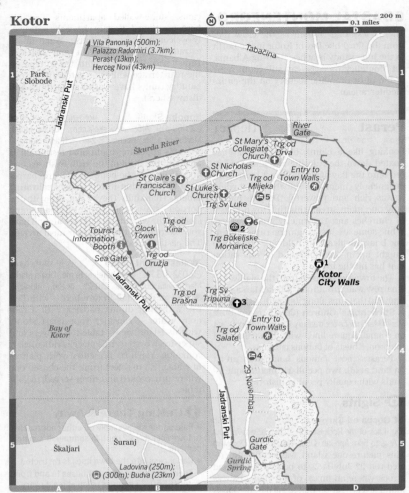

N ○ ━━━ 0 ━━━━━━━━━━━━━━━ 200 m
○ ━━━ 0 ━━━━━━━━━━━━━━━ 0.1 miles

MONTENEGRO KOTOR

Kotor

◎ Top Sights
1 Kotor City Walls D3

◎ Sights
2 Maritime Museum of
   Montenegro C3
3 St Tryphon's Cathedral C3

🛏 Sleeping
4 Old Town Hostel C4
5 Palazzo Drusko C2

🍷 Drinking & Nightlife
6 Letrika C3

palaces and pillories. It's a dramatic and delightful place where the past coexists with the present; its cobblestones ring with the sound of children racing to school in centuries-old buildings, lines of laundry flutter from wrought-iron balconies, and hundreds of cats – the descendants of seafaring felines – loll in marble laneways. Come nightfall, Kotor's spectacularly lit-up walls glow as serenely as a halo. Behind the bulwarks, the

WORTH A TRIP

TIVAT ТИВАТ

With its bobbing super yachts, a posh promenade and rows of swanky apartment blocks, visitors to Tivat could be forgiven for wondering if they're in Monaco or Montenegro. The erstwhile-mediocre seaside town has undergone a major makeover – courtesy of the multimillion-dollar redevelopment of its old naval base into a first-class marina – and while it bears no resemblance to anywhere else in the country, Tivat is now attracting the uberwealthy (and less-loaded rubberneckers) in droves.

Single-handedly responsible for Tivat's transformation is **Porto Montenegro** (www.portomontenegro.com), a surreal 24-hectare town-within-a-town occupying the former Arsenal shipyard and naval base. Primped, preening and planned right down to the last polished pebble, the almost impossibly glamorous marina complex includes upmarket apartment buildings; a 'lifestyle village' of fancy boutiques, bars, restaurants and leisure facilities; a **maritime museum** (Zbirka pomorskog nasljeđa; ☎067-637 781; Porto Montenegro; museum/submarine €3/2; ⏲9am-4pm Mon-Fri, 1-5pm Sat); a resort-style hotel; and berths for 450 yachts (with a total of 850 berths planned by completion). The best restaurant is brasserie-style **One** (☎067-486 045; www.facebook.com/jettyone; mains €10-22; ⏲8.30am-midnight), with views over the megayachts moored in the marina.

Tivat has a reputation as being one of the sunniest spots in the Bay of Kotor. While it will never rival Kotor for charm, it makes a pleasant stop on a trip around the bay.

streets buzz with bars, live music – from soul to serenades – and castle-top clubbing.

Budva's got the beaches, and nearby Dubrovnik's got the bling, but for romance, ambience and living history, this Old Town outflanks them all.

Sights

★Kotor City Walls FORTRESS

(Bedemi grada Kotora; €8; ⏲24hr, fees apply 8am-8pm May-Sep) Kotor's fortifications started to head up St John's Hill in the 9th century and by the 14th century a protective loop was completed, which was added to right up until the 19th century. The energetic can make a 1200m ascent up the fortifications via 1350 steps to a height of 260m above sea level; the views from St John's Fortress, at the top, are glorious. There are entry points near the River Gate and behind Trg od Salate.

St Tryphon's Cathedral CHURCH

(Katedrale Sv Tripuna; Trg Sv Tripuna; church & museum €2.50; ⏲9am-8pm Apr-Oct, to 5pm Nov, Dec & Mar, to 1pm Jan & Feb) Kotor's most impressive building, this Catholic cathedral was consecrated in 1166 but reconstructed after several earthquakes. When the entire frontage was destroyed in 1667, the baroque bell towers were added; the left one remains unfinished. The cathedral's gently hued interior is a masterpiece of Romanesque architecture with slender Corinthian columns alternating with pillars of pink stone, thrusting upwards to support a series of vaulted roofs. Look for the remains of Byzantine-style frescoes in the arches.

Maritime Museum of Montenegro MUSEUM

(Pomorski muzej Crne Gore; ☎032-304 720; www.museummaritimum.com; Trg Bokeljske Mornarice; adult/child €4/1; ⏲9am-8pm Mon-Sat, 10am-4pm Sun Jul & Aug, 8am-6pm Mon-Sat, 9am-1pm Sun May, Jun & Sep, 9am-5pm Mon-Fri, to noon Sat & Sun Oct-Apr) Kotor's proud history as a naval power is celebrated in three storeys of displays housed in a wonderful early-18th-century palace. An audio guide helps explain the collection of photographs, paintings, uniforms, exquisitely decorated weapons and models of ships.

Sleeping

Old Town Hostel HOSTEL €€

(☎032-325 317; www.hostel-kotor.me; 29 Novembar bb; dm from €14, r €75, without bathroom €60; ❄📶🏊) If the ghosts of the Bisanti family had any concerns when their 13th-century palazzo was converted into a hostel, they must be overjoyed now. Sympathetic renovations have brought the place to life, and the ancient stone walls echo with the cheerful chatter of happy travellers. A second building, directly across the road, has modern rooms and a small pool.

Vila Panonija HOTEL €€

(☎032-334 893; www.vilapanonija.com; Dobrota bb; r €80-110; 🅿❄📶) Set back from the waterfront in Dobrota, this old stone house has been converted into a small hotel – or is it a large guesthouse? The stained glass in the breakfast room is a little 'belle époque' but the bedrooms, with their midnight-blue feature walls, are much more modern. Some have balconies; all have en-suite bathrooms.

★ **Palazzo Drusko** BOUTIQUE HOTEL €€€
(📱067-333 172; www.palazzodrusko.me; near Trg od Mlijeka; s/d from €69/139; ✴️🛜) Loaded with character and filled with antiques, this venerable 600-year-old palazzo is a memorable place to stay, right in the heart of the Old Town. Thoughtful extras include water jugs loaded with lemon and mint, a guest kitchen, 3D TVs and old-fashioned radios rigged to play Montenegrin music.

Palazzo Radomiri HOTEL €€€
(📱032-333 176; www.palazzoradomiri.com; Dobrota 220; s/d/ste from €160/180/250; ⊙Apr-Oct; 🅿️✴️🛜♨️) This honey-coloured early-18th-century palazzo on the Dobrota waterfront, 4km north of Kotor's Old Town, has been transformed into a first-rate boutique hotel. Some rooms are bigger and grander than others, but all 10 have sea views and luxurious furnishings. Guests can avail themselves of a small workout area, sauna, pool, private jetty, bar and restaurant.

MONTENEGRO ULCINJ

WORTH A TRIP

BUDVA БУДВА

Budva is the poster child of Montenegrin tourism. Easily the country's most-visited destination, it attracts hordes of holidaymakers intent on exploring its atmospheric Stari Grad (Old Town), sunning themselves on the bonny beaches of the Budva Riviera and partying until dawn; with scores of buzzy bars and clanging clubs, it's not nicknamed 'the Montenegrin Miami' for nothing.

Though Budva has been settled since the 5th century BCE, you'll be hard-pressed finding much – outside of the Old Town – that isn't shiny and relatively new. Development has run rampant here, and not all of it appears to be particularly well thought out. In the height of the season, Budva's sands are blanketed with package holidaymakers from Russia and Ukraine, while the nouveau riche park their multimillion-dollar yachts in the town's guarded marina. That said, Budva has a hectic charm all of its own.

🍴 Eating & Drinking

Ladovina MONTENEGRIN, DALMATIAN €€
(📱063-422 472; www.ladovina.me; Njegoševa 209; mains €9-20; ⊙8am-1am) Tucked away in the Škaljari neighbourhood, south of the Old Town, this relaxed cafe-restaurant has tables beneath an open-sided pagoda under a canopy of trees. The menu includes veal, lamb and octopus claypots, and a mix of seafood and meat grills. There's a terrific selection of wine by the glass and craft beer. Save room for the Kotor cream pie.

★ **Letrika** COCKTAIL BAR
(www.facebook.com/artbarletrika; near Trg Bokeljske Mornarice; ⊙8am-1am) By day, Letrika is a quiet place for a sneaky drink, with a steampunk aesthetic and side-alley location. On summer nights DJs set up outside and the lane gets jammed with hip young things dancing and sipping cocktails.

ℹ️ Information

Kotor Health Centre (Dom zdravlja Kotor; 📱032-334 533; www.dzkotor.me; Jadranski Put bb) Kotor's main clinic.

Tourist Information Booth (📱032-325 951; www.tokotor.me; Jadranski Put; ⊙8am-8pm Apr-Oct, to 6pm Nov-Mar) Stocks free maps and brochures, and can help with contacts for private accommodation.

ℹ️ Getting There & Away

The **bus station** (📱032-325 809; www.autobus kastanicakotor.me; Škaljari bb; ⊙6am-8pm) is to the south of town, just off the road leading to the tunnel. Buses to Tivat (€1.50, 20 minutes), Budva (€4, 40 minutes) and Cetinje (€5, 1½ hours) are at least hourly.

A taxi to Tivat airport should cost around €10.

Ulcinj Улцињ

📱030 / POP 10,700

For a taste of Albania without actually crossing the border, head down to buzzy, beautiful Ulcinj. The population is 61% Albanian (68% Muslim), and in summertime it swells with Kosovar holidaymakers for the simple reason that it's a lot nicer than the Albanian seaside towns. The elegant minarets of numerous mosques give Ulcinj (Ulqin in Albanian) a distinctly Eastern feel, as does the lively music echoing out of the kebab stands around Mala Plaža (Small Beach). Ulcinj's ramshackle Old Town looms above the heaving beach and is a fantastic spot for people-watching without being surrounded by people.

★ Hostel Pirate
HOSTEL €

(☑ 068-212 552; www.hostel-pirate.com; Nikole Djakonovića bb; dm/r with shared bathroom from €12/30; ℗ ✳ 🛜) Just because it's Ulcinj's only hostel doesn't mean this jolly Pirate rests on its laurels. This is an immaculate, friendly, comfortable and flat-out-wonderful place that installs fierce love and loyalty in its guests. The hostel organises bike rentals, kayaking and boat trips. It also turns on free barbecue dinners fuelled by shots of equally gratis *rakija*.

★ Antigona
SEAFOOD €€€

(☑ 069-154 117; Stari Grad bb; mains €8-27; ⊙ 10am-midnight) Antigona's clifftop terrace offers perhaps the most romantic aspect of any eatery in Ulcinj, and handsome waiters in bow ties only add to the impression. The seafood is excellent too – but be sure to check the price and weight of the fish in advance if you wish to avoid any nasty surprises come bill time. It also rents rooms.

ℹ Information

Tourism Information Centre (☑ 030-412 333; www.ulcinj.travel; Gjergj Kastrioti Skënderbeu bb; ⊙ 7am-10pm Jun-Aug, 8am-3pm Mon-Fri Sep-May)

ℹ Getting There & Away

The **bus station** (☑ 030-413 225; www.bussta tionulcinj.com; Vëllazërit Frashëri bb; ⊙ 5am-10pm) is on the northeastern edge of town. Services head to Kotor (€9, 2½ hours, daily) and Budva (€7, two hours, nine daily).

INLAND MONTENEGRO

To truly get to know Montenegro, a visit to the country's mountainous core is a must. Its beating heart is Mt Lovćen, a symbol of national identity.

Lovćen National Park

Directly behind Kotor is **Mt Lovćen** (Ловћен; 1749m), the black mountain that gave Crna Gora (Montenegro) its name; *crna/negro* means 'black', and *gora/monte* means 'mountain' in Montenegrin and Italian respectively. This locale occupies a special place in the hearts of all Montenegrins. For most of its history it represented the entire nation – a rocky island of Slavic resistance in an Ottoman sea. A striking shrine to Montenegro's most famous son, Petar II Petrović Njegoš,

peers down from its heights, with views stretching as far as Albania and Croatia.

The park's main hub is **Ivanova Korita**, near its centre, where there are a few eateries and accommodation providers and, in winter, a beginners' ski slope. **Njeguši**, on the park's northern edge, is famous for being the home village of the Petrović dynasty and for making the country's best *pršut* (smoke-dried ham) and *sir* (cheese). Roadside stalls sell both, along with honey.

★ Njegoš Mausoleum
MAUSOLEUM

(Njegošev mauzolej; adult/child €3/1.50; ⊙ 9am-6pm) Lovćen's star attraction, this magnificent mausoleum (built 1970 to 1974) sits at the top of its second-highest peak, Jezerski Vrh (1657m). Take the 461 steps up to the entry where two granite giantesses guard the tomb of Montenegro's greatest hero. Inside, under a golden mosaic canopy, a 28-tonne Petar II Petrović Njegoš rests in the wings of an eagle, carved from a single block of black granite.

Konoba kod Radonjića
MONTENEGRIN €€

(☑ 041-239 820; Njeguši bb; mains €6-13; ⊙ 8am-7pm; 🛜) With stone walls and meat hanging from the ceiling, this atmospheric family-run tavern serves up delicious roast lamb as well as the local specialities, *pršut* and *sir*. Enjoy them along with olives on a Njeguški plate (€9.50) or in sandwiches (€2.50).

ℹ Information

National Park Visitor Centre (☑ 067-344 678; www.nparkovi.me; Ivanova Korita bb; ⊙ 9am-5pm) As well as providing information on the national park, this centre also rents bikes (per hour/day €2/10), offers accommodation in four-bed bungalows (€30) and takes camping bookings (from €3).

ℹ Getting There & Away

If you're driving, the park can be approached from either Kotor (20km) or Cetinje (7km); pay the entry fee (€2) at the booths on each approach. Tour buses are the only buses that head into the park. Be aware that this is a *very* twisty-turny and narrow road; the large tour buses that hog it in summer don't make the driving experience any easier. Don't be distracted by the beyond-spectacular views.

Cetinje
Цетиње

☑ 041 / POP 13,900

Rising from a green vale surrounded by rough grey mountains, Cetinje is an odd mix of erstwhile capital and overgrown village,

WORTH A TRIP

DELVE DEEP & DINE HIGH

Lipa Cave (Lipska pećina; ☑ 067-003 040; www.lipa-cave.me; adult/child €11/7; ☺ tours 10am, 11.30am, 1pm, 2.30pm and 4pm May-Oct) Cetinje may indeed be littered with old-time reminders of its days as Montenegro's capital city, but just 4km away lies an attraction that makes the town look positively modern. Millions of years old, Lipa Cave is one of the country's largest caves – and the only one open for organised visits – with 2.5km of illuminated passages and halls filled with stalactites, stalagmites and freaky natural pillars. Tours take 60 minutes, including a road-train ride and short walk to the entrance.

Belveder (☑ 067-567 217; mains €6-10; ☺ 10am-11pm; ☎) Occupying a scenic eyrie, well signposted on the way to Lipa Cave, this wonderful roadside restaurant serves traditional fare including freshwater fish, grilled squid, and lamb and veal slow-roasted *ispod sača* (under a domed metal lid topped with charcoal), accompanied by the smokiest paprika-laced potatoes you could hope for. The views from the wooden-roofed terrace gaze towards Lake Skadar.

where single-storey cottages and stately mansions share the same street. Several of those mansions – dating from the days when European ambassadors rubbed shoulders with Montenegrin princesses – have become museums or schools for art and music.

The city was founded in 1482 by Ivan Crnojević, the ruler of the Zeta state, after abandoning his previous capital near Lake Skadar, Žabljak Crnojevića, to the Ottomans. A large statue of him stands near the main square. Cetinje was the capital of Montenegro until the country was subsumed into the first Yugoslavia in 1918. After WWII, when Montenegro became a republic within federal Yugoslavia, it passed the baton – somewhat reluctantly – to Titograd (now Podgorica). Today it's billed as the 'royal capital', and is home to the country's most impressive collection of museums.

◉ Sights

Cetinje's collection of four museums (History, King Nikola, Njegoš Biljarda and Ethnographic) and two galleries (Montenegrin Art and its offshoot, Miodrag Dado Đurić) is known collectively as the **National Museum of Montenegro** (www.mnmuseum.org). A joint ticket (adult/child €10/5) will get you into all of them or you can buy individual tickets.

Some of the grandest buildings in town are former international embassies from Cetinje's days as Montenegro's capital.

History Museum   MUSEUM
(Istorijski muzej; ☑ 041-230 310; www.mnmuseum. org; Novice Cerovića 7; adult/child €3/1.50; ☺ 9am-5pm Apr-Oct, to 4pm Mon-Sat Nov-Mar) Housed in the imposing former parliament building (1910), this fascinating museum follows a timeline from the Stone Age onwards. His-

torical relics include the tunic that Prince Danilo was wearing when he was assassinated, and Prince Nikola's bullet-riddled standard from the battle of Vučji Do. It's also the most even-handed museum in the entire region in its coverage of the break-up of Yugoslavia, honestly examining Montenegrin involvement in the bombardment of Dubrovnik and war crimes in Bosnia.

Montenegrin Art Gallery   GALLERY
(Crnogorska galerija umjetnosti; www.mnmuseum. org; Novice Cerovića 7; adult/child €4/2; ☺ 9am-5pm Apr-Oct, to 4pm Mon-Sat Nov-Mar) All of Montenegro's great artists are represented here, with the most famous (Milunović, Lubarda, Đurić etc) having their own separate spaces. There's a small collection of icons, the most important being the precious 9th-century *Our Lady of Philermos,* traditionally believed to have been painted by St Luke himself. It's spectacularly presented in its own blue-lit 'chapel', but the Madonna's darkened face is only just visible behind its spectacular golden casing mounted with diamonds, rubies and sapphires.

Miodrag Dado Đurić Gallery   GALLERY
(Galerija; Balšića Pazar; ☺ 10am-2pm & 5-9pm Tue-Sun) FREE This edgy establishment is an offshoot of the Montenegrin Art Gallery, and is dedicated to one of Montenegro's most important artists, who died in 2010. Housed in a striking five-storey concrete and glass building, it promotes and displays 20th-century and contemporary Montenegrin art.

King Nikola Museum   PALACE
(Muzej kralja Nikole; www.mnmuseum.org; Dvorski Trg; adult/child €5/2.50; ☺ 9am-5pm Apr-Oct, to 4pm Mon-Sat Nov-Mar) Entry to this maroon-

and-white palace (1871), home to the last sovereign of Montenegro, is by guided tour (you may need to wait for a group to form). Although looted during WWII, more than enough plush furnishings, stern portraits and taxidermal animals remain to capture the spirit of the court.

🛏 Sleeping & Eating

⭐ La Vecchia Casa
GUESTHOUSE €

(📞 067-629 660; www.lavecchiacasa.com; Vojvode Batrica 6; s/d/apt €20/34/38; P ✳ 🔊) With its gorgeous rear garden and pervading sense of tranquillity, this period house captures the essence of old Cetinje. The clean, antique-strewn rooms retain a sense of the home's history, and there's a guest kitchen (stocked with do-it-yourself breakfast supplies) and a laundry.

Kole
MONTENEGRIN €€

(📞 069-606 660; www.restaurantkole.me; Bul Crnogorskih junaka 12; mains €4-16; ⊙ 7am-midnight) They serve omelettes and pasta at this popular restaurant, but it's worth delving into artery-clogging local specialities such as *Njeguški ražanj* (smoky spit-roasted meat stuffed with prosciutto and cheese) or *popeci na cetinjski način* ('Cetinje-style' veal schnitzel, similarly stuffed, rolled into logs, breaded and deep-fried). Serves are massive; try one between two, with a side salad.

ℹ Information

Accident & Emergency Clinic (Hitna pomoć; 📞 041-233 002; Vuka Mićunovića 2)

Tourist Information (📞 041-230 250; www. cetinje.travel; Novice Cerovića bb; ⊙ 8am-6pm Mar-Oct, to 4pm Nov-Feb) Helpful office which also rents bikes (per half-/full day €2/3). Short sightseeing tours start from here, taking to Cetinje's streets in golf buggies (30/45 minutes €2/3).

ℹ Getting There & Away

➡ Cetinje is just off the main Budva–Podgorica highway and can also be reached by a glorious back road from Kotor via Lovćen National Park.

➡ The **bus station** (📞 041-241 744; Trg Golootočkih Žrtava; ⊙ 6am-10pm) has regular services from Tivat (€5, 1¼ hours), Budva (€4, 40 minutes) and Kotor (€5, 1½ hours).

Durmitor National Park

The impossibly rugged and dramatic Durmitor (Дурмитор) is one of Montenegro's – and Mother Nature's – showpieces. Carved out by glaciers and underground streams, Durmitor stuns with dizzying canyons, glittering glacial lakes and nearly 50 limestone peaks soaring to over 2000m; the highest, **Bobotov Kuk**, hits 2523m. From December to March, Durmitor is a major ski resort, while in summer it's popular for hiking, rafting and other active pursuits.

The national park covers the Durmitor mountain range and a narrow branch heading east along the Tara River towards Mojkovac. West of the park, the mighty Tara marks the border with Bosnia and joins the Piva River near Šćepan Polje.

Durmitor is home to 163 bird species, about 50 types of mammals and purportedly the greatest variety of butterflies in Europe. It's very unlikely you'll spot bears and wolves, which is either a good or bad thing depending on your perspective.

⊙ Sights

⭐ Black Lake
LAKE

(Crno jezero) Eighteen glittering glacial lakes known as *gorske oči* (mountain eyes) dot the Durmitor range. The spectacular Black Lake, a pleasant 3km walk from Žabljak, is the largest of them and the most visited part of the national park. The rounded mass of **Međed** (the Bear; 2287m) rears up behind it, casting an inky shadow into the pine-walled waters. An easy 3.6km walking track circles the lake.

⭐ Tara Canyon
CANYON

Slicing through the mountains at the northern edge of the national park, the Tara River forms a canyon that is 1300m deep at its

MONTENEGRO DURMITOR NATIONAL PARK

DON'T MISS

OSTROG MONASTERY

Resting improbably – miraculously? – in a cliff face 900m above the Zeta valley, the gleaming white **Ostrog Monastery** (Manastir Ostrog; www.manastirostrog.com) is the most important site in Montenegro for Orthodox Christians, attracting up to a million visitors annually. Even with its numerous pilgrims, tourists and souvenir stands, it's a strangely affecting place. A **guesthouse** (📞 068-080 133; office@mostrog.me; dm €5) near the Lower Monastery offers tidy single-sex dorm rooms, while in summer sleeping mats are provided for free to pilgrims in front of the Upper Monastery.

peak (the Grand Canyon plummets a mere 200m deeper). The best views are from the water, and rafting along the river is one of the country's most popular tourist activities. If you'd rather admire the canyon from afar, head to the top of **Mt Ćurevac** (1625m) – although even this view is restricted by the canyon walls.

Tara Bridge — BRIDGE
(Đurđevića Tara) The elegant spans of the 150m-high Tara Bridge were completed just as WWII was starting. At the time it was the largest concrete arched vehicular bridge in Europe. Its 365m length is carried on five sweeping arches, the largest of which is 116m wide.

Dobrilovina Monastery — CHRISTIAN MONASTERY
Near the eastern boundary of the national park, 28km from Mojkovac, this monastery has an idyllic setting in lush fields hemmed in by the mountains and the Tara River. If you knock at the accommodation wing, a black-robed nun will unlock the church, but only if she's satisfied that you're appropriately attired. The frescoes that remain inside the church, dedicated to St George (Sv Đorđe), are faded but very beautiful.

Stećci Sites — CEMETERY
These mysterious carved stone tomb monuments – dating from between the 12th and 16th centuries – can be found across northern Montenegro and neighbouring Bosnia. There are two extremely significant *stećci* sites in Durmitor National Park (both were added to Unesco's World Heritage list in 2016): the Bare Žugića necropolis, with 300 *stećci*, and Grčko groblje (Greek graveyard) with 49. Many of the stones at both sites are intricately decorated.

🏃 Activities

Hiking
Durmitor is one of the best-marked mountain ranges in Europe, with 25 marked trails making up a total of 150km. Some suggest it's a little *too* well labelled, encouraging novices to wander around seriously high-altitude paths that are prone to fog and summer thunderstorms. Ask the staff at the National Park Visitors Centre (p794) about tracks that suit your level of experience and fitness.

One rewarding route is the hike to the two **Škrčka Lakes** (Škrčka jezera), in the centre of a tectonic valley, where you can enjoy magnificent scenery and stay overnight in a mountain hut (June to September only). Another popular hike is from the Black Lake to the **ice cave** *(ledina pećina)* – home in cooler months to stalactite- and stalagmite-like shapes made of ice – on Obla Glava. It's a six- to seven-hour return hike.

If you're considering an assault on **Bobotov Kuk** or a serious winter expedition, you're best to arrange a local guide.

In any case, check the weather forecast before you set out, stick to the tracks, and prepare for rain and sudden drops in temperature. A compass could be a lifesaver. *Durmitor and the Tara Canyon* by Branislav Cerović (€12 from the visitors centre) is a great resource for mountaineers and serious hikers. The **Mountaineering Association of Montenegro** (www.pscg.me) has contacts and info on the peaks and paths of Durmitor.

Via Dinarica Hiking Trail — HIKING
(www.viadinarica.com) The Montenegrin part of this 1930km 'megatrail' – which traverses Slovenia, Croatia, Bosnia, Montenegro and Albania – connects Durmitor with Bosnia's Sutjeska National Park. See the website for details, or contact **Black Mountain** (☑067-076 676; www.montenegroholiday.com) 🗲 to organise hiking tours.

Rafting
A rafting expedition along the Tara is the best way to revel in glorious river scenery that's impossible to catch from land. Trips are suitable for everyone from the white-water novice to experienced foam-hounds. Though it's not the world's most white-knuckled ride, there are a few rapids; if you're after speed, visit in April and May, when the last of the melting snow revs up the flow. Various operators run trips between April and October.

The 82km section that is raftable starts from Splavište, south of the Tara Bridge, and ends at Šćepan Polje on the Bosnian border. The classic two-day trip heads through the deepest part of the canyon on the first day, stopping overnight at Radovan Luka. **Summit Travel Agency** (☑068-535 535; www.summit.co.me; Njegoševa 12, Žabljak; half-/1-/2-day rafting trips €45/110/200) offers a range of rafting trips on this route, with transfers from Žabljak.

Most of the day tours from the coast traverse only the last 18km from Brstanovica – this is outside the national park and hence avoids hefty fees. You'll miss out on the canyon's depths, but it's still a beautiful stretch, including most of the rapids. The buses follow a spectacular road along the Piva River, giving you a double dose of canyon action.

It's important to use a reputable operator; in 2010 two people died in one day on a trip with inexperienced guides. At a minimum make sure you're given a helmet and life jacket – wear them and do them up. Some noteworthy operators are **Camp Grab** (☑ 069-101 002; www.tara-grab.com; half-day incl lunch €44, 3-day all-inclusive rafting trips from €200), **Tara Tour** (☑ 069-086 106; www.taratour.com; Šćepan Polje bb) and **Waterfall Rafting Centre** (☑ 069-310 848; www.raftingmontenegro.com). Many of the rafting groups also offer other activities, including horse riding, canyoning and jeep safaris. If you've got your own wheels you can save a few bucks and avoid a lengthy coach tour by heading directly to Šćepan Polje and hooking up with the rafting tours there.

Skiing

With 120 days of snow cover, Durmitor offers the most reliable – and cheapest – skiing in Montenegro.

Savin Kuk Ski Centar (☑ 052-363 036; www.tcdurmitor.me; ski passes day/week €12/60) and **Javorovača Ski Centar** (☑ 067-800 971; www.javorovaca.me; adult/child day passes €8/5, week passes €48/30) both rent out equipment and offer lessons. See www.skiresortmontenegro.com (in Montenegrin) for more information on all of Montenegro's ski centres.

Free-riding snowboarders and skiers should check out www.riders.me for off-piste adventure ideas.

Adventure Sports

Red Rock Zipline ADVENTURE SPORTS
(☑ 069-440 290; www.redrockzipline.com; Đurđevića Tara; adult €10; ⊙ 10am-8pm Apr-Oct)
Feel the wind in your hair (and the collywobbles in your stomach) with a 50km per hour flight across the Tara Canyon. The 350m-long zipline is strung alongside the magnificent Tara Bridge with a starting point 170m above the river. It's scary as hell, but fret not: it's run by an extremely professional outfit. Look for the red flags.

**Crno Jezero
Avanturistički Park** ADVENTURE SPORTS
(☑ 069-214 110; www.avanturistickipark.me; Black Lake; adult/child €9/8; ⊙ 10am-7pm Jul & Aug, 10am-6pm Sat & Sun Jun & Sep) Want to take flight? Two ziplines have been set up by the shores of Black Lake, offering criminal amounts of fun. The shorter one zips across the forest from a height of 14m, while the longer one will hurtle you for 350m clear across the lake. There are also obstacle courses and plenty of activities set up for kids, including a zipline with toboggan.

Nevidio Canyon CANYONING
Just south of the national park, near Šavnik, is the remarkable 2.7km-long Nevidio Canyon. Cut by the Komarnica River, at points it is only metres wide, hence the name (nevidio means 'invisible'). It's extremely beautiful but equally dangerous. Canyoning expeditions generally take about three to four hours and participants should be able to swim and have a high level of fitness.

July and August are the safest months to explore, and then only in the company of professional guides. **Montenegro Canyoning** (☑ 069-565 311; www.montenegro-canyoning.com; trips without/with lunch per person €90/100) is a highly recommended group that focuses solely on expeditions to Nevidio. Otherwise, **Anitra/Grab** (www.tara-grab.com) organises expeditions out of Nikšić (price on application), and Summit Travel Agency and **Durmitor Adventure** (☑ 069-629 516; www.durmitoradventure.com) do so out of Žabljak (€100 per person including lunch, minimum two people).

🛏 Sleeping & Eating

★**Hikers Den** HOSTEL €
(☑ 067-854 433; www.hostelzabljak.com; Božidara Žugića bb, Žabljak; dm/r from €13/35; ⊙ Apr-Oct; 🖫) Split between three neighbouring houses, this laid-back and sociable place is by far the best hostel in the north. If you're keen on rafting, canyoning or a jeep safari, the charming English-speaking hosts will happily make the arrangements. They also offer a four-hour 'Durmitor in a day' minivan tour (€20).

★**Eko-Oaza Tear of Europe** CAMPGROUND €
(Eko-Oaza suza Evrope; ☑ 069-444 590; www.eko-oaza.me; Gornja Dobrilovina; campsites per 1/2/3 people €7.50/11/15, campervans €13-15, cabins €50, without bathroom €20; ⊙ Apr-Oct; 🖫) Consisting of a handful of comfortable wooden cottages with bathrooms (each sleeping five people), small cabins without bathrooms, well-equipped apartments and a fine stretch of lawn above the river, this magical, family-run 'eco oasis' offers a genuine experience of Montenegrin hospitality. Home-cooked meals are provided on request, and rafting,

kayaking, canyoning and jeep safaris can be arranged. Truly memorable.

Hotel Soa
HOTEL €€€

(☑ 052-360 110; www.hotelsoa.com; Njegoševa bb, Žabljak; s/ste/apt from €67/105/124; P 🐾) The rooms at this snazzy, modern hotel are kitted out with monsoon shower heads, robes and slippers. There's also a playground, bikes for hire and one of the country's best restaurants (mains €5 to €17); try the lamb baked in cream, served with *ajvar* (roasted-red-capsicum dip).

O'ro
MONTENEGRIN €€

(Njegoševa bb, Žabljak; mains €8-11; ⊙ 7am-1am; 🐾) The focus is firmly on local specialities at this appealing wood-and-glass restaurant. In summer, grab a seat on the large terrace and tuck into a *Durmitorska večera* (Durmitor dinner) platter featuring air-dried beef, sausages, local cheese, *ajvar* and crispy roast potatoes. They also serve lamb, veal, trout and *kačamak* (polenta, cheese and potato porridge).

ⓘ Orientation

All roads (and ski runs and bumpy trails) lead to **Žabljak**, regional capital and – at 1450m – one of the highest towns in the Balkans. Quaintly ramshackle – though slowly smartening up – it's the gateway to Durmitor's mountain adventures. You'll find restaurants, hotels and a supermarket gathered around the car park that masquerades as Žabljak's main square.

ⓘ Information

The road to the Black Lake is blocked off just past the National Park Visitors Centre and an entry fee is charged (per person per one/three/seven days €3/6/12). Drivers will need to park outside the gates (€2) and walk the remaining 500m to the lake. Keep hold of your ticket, in case you bump into a ranger.

National Park Visitors Centre (☑ 052-360 228; www.nparkovi.me; Njegoševa bb, Žabljak; ⊙ 7am-5pm Mon-Fri, 10am-5pm Sat & Sun Jan & Jun–mid-Sep, 7am-3pm Mon-Fri mid-Sep–Dec & Feb-May) On the road to the Black Lake, this centre includes a wonderful micromuseum focusing on the park's flora and fauna. The knowledgeable staff answer queries and sell local craft, maps, hiking guides and fishing permits (€20). They also rent bikes (per hour/day €3/8), assist with accommodation and can organise local guides (€15 to €100, depending on the trail).

Žabljak Tourist Office (☑ 052-361 802; www.tozabljak.com; Trg Durmitorskih ratnika, Žabljak; ⊙ 7am-10pm mid-Jun–Sep, 8am-8pm Oct–mid-Jun) Operates in a wooden hut in Žabljak's main square/car park.

The website **www.durmitor.rs** has heaps of information on activities and accommodation in the region, plus the latest news and events listings.

ⓘ Getting There & Away

All of the approaches to Durmitor are spectacular. The most reliable road to Žabljak follows the Tara River west from Mojkovac. In summer this 70km drive takes about 90 minutes. If you're coming from Podgorica, the quickest way is through Nikšić and Šavnik. The main highway north from Nikšić follows the dramatic Piva Canyon to Šćepan Polje. There's a wonderful back road through the mountains leaving the highway near Plužine, but it's impassable as soon as the snows fall.

The bus station is at the southern edge of Žabljak, on the Šavnik road. Buses head to Podgorica (€8, 2½ hours, eight daily), Belgrade (€21, nine hours, daily) and, in summer, to the Bay of Kotor.

SURVIVAL GUIDE

ⓘ Directory A–Z

ACCOMMODATION

Montenegro offers a great variety of accommodation. Booking ahead in the summer – especially on the coast – is essential.

Hotels Range from slick seaside offerings to off-the-beaten-track Yugoslav-style digs. Prices range accordingly.

Hostels Popping up in popular destinations but thin on the ground elsewhere.

Campgrounds Usually offer million-dollar views for penny-pinching prices. Facilities vary wildly.

Private accommodation Almost every town and village has private rooms *(sobe)* and/or apartments *(apartmani)* for rent.

Eco villages Wooden cabins in the countryside.

MONEY

ATMs widely available. Credit cards are accepted in larger hotels but aren't widely accepted elsewhere.

OPENING HOURS

Montenegrins have a flexible approach to opening times. Even if hours are posted on the door of an establishment, don't be surprised if they're not heeded. Many tourist-orientated businesses close between November and March.

Banks 8am to 5pm Monday to Friday, 8am to noon Saturday.

Post offices 7am to 8pm Monday to Friday, sometimes Saturday. In smaller towns they may close midafternoon, or close at noon and reopen at 5pm.

Restaurants, cafes & bars 8am to midnight. If the joint is jumping, cafe-bars may stay open until 2am or 3am.

Shops 9am to 8pm. Sometimes they'll close for a few hours in the late afternoon.

PUBLIC HOLIDAYS

New Year's Day 1 and 2 January

Orthodox Christmas 6, 7 and 8 January

Orthodox Good Friday & Easter Monday date varies, usually April/May

Labour Day 1 and 2 May

Independence Day 21 and 22 May

Statehood Day 13 and 14 July

TELEPHONE

➔ The international access prefix is 00, or + from a mobile phone.

➔ The country code is 382.

➔ Press the *i* button on public phones for dialling commands in English.

➔ Mobile numbers start with 06.

➔ The prefix 80 indicates a toll-free number.

➔ You can make phone calls at most larger post offices. Phone boxes are otherwise few and far between.

ℹ Getting There & Away

ENTERING THE COUNTRY

Entering Montenegro doesn't pose any particular bureaucratic challenges. In fact, the country's dead keen to shuffle tourists in. Unfortunately, Croatia seems less happy to let them go, if the long waits at their side of the Adriatic highway checkpoint are any indication; if you need to be somewhere at a certain time, it pays to allow an hour. The main crossing from Serbia at Dobrakovo can also be slow at peak times.

AIR

➔ **Montenegro Airlines** (www.montenegroair lines.com) is the national carrier, running a small fleet of 116-seater planes.

➔ Montenegro's largest and most modern airport is immediately south of the capital, **Podgorica** (TGD; ✆ 020-444 244; www.monte negroairports.com).

➔ The second international airport, at **Tivat** (TIV; ✆ 032-670 930; www.montenegroair

ports.com; Jadranski Put bb), is well positioned for holidaymakers heading to the Bay of Kotor or Budva.

➔ Montenegro's de facto third airport is actually in neighbouring Croatia. Dubrovnik Airport (p277) is only 17km from the border and the closest airport to Herceg Novi.

LAND

Montenegro may be a wee slip of a thing but it borders five other states: Croatia, Bosnia and Hercegovina (BiH), Serbia, Kosovo and Albania. You can easily enter Montenegro by land from any of its neighbours.

Bus

There's a well-developed bus network linking Montenegro with the major cities of the former Yugoslavia and onward to Western Europe and Turkey. At the border, guards will often enter the bus and collect passports, checking the photos as they go. Once they're happy with them they return them to the bus conductor, who will return them as the driver speeds off.

Useful websites include www.busticket4.me, www.eurolines.com, www.getbybus.com and www.vollo.net.

Train

Montenegro's main train line starts at Bar and heads north through Podgorica and into Serbia. At least two trains head between Bar and Belgrade daily (€21, 11¾ hours). You'll find timetables on the website of **Montenegro Railways** (www.zcg-prevoz.me).

SEA

Montenegro Lines (www.montenegrolines. com) has boats from Bar to Bari (Italy), at least weekly from May to November (deck ticket €44 to €48, cabin €63 to €210, 11 hours); and from Bar to Ancona (Italy), at least weekly from July to August (deck €60, cabin €80 to €230, 16 hours). Cars cost €56 to €90.

ℹ Getting Around

Bus Buses link all major towns and are affordable, reliable and reasonably comfortable. Up-to-date timetable information and online booking can be found on www.busticket4.me.

Car While you can get to many places by bus, hiring a car will give you freedom to explore some of Montenegro's scenic back roads. Some of these are extremely narrow and cling to the sides of canyons, so they may not suit the inexperienced or faint-hearted.

The Netherlands

POP 17 MILLION

Best Places to Eat

- ➡ Vleminckx (p803)
- ➡ D'Vijff Vlieghen (p804)
- ➡ Fouquet (p811)
- ➡ AJÍ (p815)
- ➡ Heron (p818)
- ➡ In den Doofpot (p810)

Best Places to Stay

- ➡ Cocomama (p802)
- ➡ Sir Albert Hotel (p803)
- ➡ Hotel Indigo (p810)
- ➡ Citizen M (p815)
- ➡ King Kong Hostel (p815)
- ➡ Mother Goose Hotel (p817)

Why Go?

Tradition and innovation intertwine in the Netherlands. The legacies of great Dutch artists Rembrandt, Vermeer and Van Gogh, beautiful 17th-century canals, vintage windmills, tulip fields and quaint candlelit brown cafes coexist with visionary contemporary architecture, ecological fashion and homewares, cutting-edge design and food scenes, phenomenal nightlife and a progressive mindset.

Much of the Netherlands is below sea level and two-wheeling along pancake-flat landscape is one of Dutch life's greatest pleasures. Rental outlets are ubiquitous across the country, which is criss-crossed with dedicated cycling paths.

Allow ample time to revel in the magical, multifaceted capital Amsterdam, before ventureing further afield to charming canal-laced towns like Leiden and Delft. Explore exquisite Maastricht, with its city walls, ancient churches and grand squares, and the pulsing port city of Rotterdam, Dutch hub of urban renaissance.

When to Go
Amsterdam

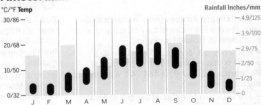

Jun–Aug High season: (the best odds for) balmy weather, alfresco cafe life and idyllic bike rides.

Mar–May See the world's largest flowering-bulb show in the Netherlands' fields.

Apr Europe's biggest street party celebrates the monarch's birthday on King's Day (Koningsdag).

Entering the Country

Schiphol International Airport (Amsterdam) Trains to Amsterdam Centraal Station cost €5.30 and take 15 minutes. Taxis to Amsterdam's centre (20 to 25 minutes) have a fixed rate of €39.

Duivendrecht and Sloterdijk bus stations Eurolines buses use Duivendrecht and FlixBus uses Sloterdijk; both have a fast metro or train link to Amsterdam Centraal.

Rotterdam The Hague Airport RET bus 33 (€3.50) makes the 20-minute run from the airport to Rotterdam Centraal Station every 15 minutes throughout the day; or hop off the bus at the Meijersplein metro station (line E) and continue by metro. Count on €25 for the 10-minute trip by taxi.

Eindhoven Airport Buses 400 and 401 travel up to six times hourly to/from Eindhoven train station (€3.50, 25 minutes).

ITINERARIES

One Week
Spend three days exploring canals, museum-hopping and cafe-crawling in Amsterdam (p799). Work your way through the ancient towns of the Randstad and edgy Rotterdam (p813); save a day for the grandeur of Maastricht (p818).

Two Weeks
Allow four days for Amsterdam's (p799) many delights, plus a day trip to the old towns of the north, and a day or two exploring some of the region's smaller towns. Then add a day each in beautiful Delft (p812), regal Den Haag (The Hague; p810), student-filled Utrecht (p816) and buzzing Rotterdam (p813). Finish off with two days in historic Maastricht (p818).

Essential Food & Drink

Vlaamse frites Iconic French fries smothered in mayonnaise or myriad other sauces.

Cheese Some Dutch say it makes them tall; others complain it causes nightmares. Nearly two-thirds of all Dutch *kaas* (cheese) sold is Gouda, classified by how long it's been aged. The tastiest hard, rich *oud* (old) varieties have strong, complex flavours.

Herring Street stalls sell raw, slightly salted *haring* (herring) cut into bite-sized pieces and served with onion and pickles.

Kroketten Croquettes are crumbed, deep-fried dough balls with various fillings, such as meat-filled *bitterballen*.

Jenever Dutch gin is made from juniper berries and drunk chilled from a tulip-shaped shot glass. *Jonge* (young) jenever is smooth; strongly flavoured *oude* (old) jenever can be an acquired taste.

AT A GLANCE

Area 41,543 sq km

Capital Amsterdam

Country code ☑ 31

Currency euro (€)

Emergency ☑ 112

Language Dutch, English widespread

Time Central European Time (GMT/UTC plus one hour)

Visas Schengen rules apply

Sleeping Price Ranges

The following price ranges refer to a double room with bathroom in high season. Unless otherwise stated, breakfast is not included in the price.

€ less than €100

€€ €100–180

€€€ more than €180

Eating Price Ranges

The following price ranges refer to a main course.

€ less than €12

€€ €12–25

€€€ more than €25

Resources

Netherlands Tourism Board (www.holland.com)

Holland Cycling Routes (www.hollandcyclingroutes.com)

Dutch Review (https://dutchreview.com)

Dutch News (www.dutchnews.nl)

THE NETHERLANDS

The Netherlands Highlights

1 Amsterdam (p799) Canal-cruising, brown-cafe lounging and admiring world-class art.

2 Rotterdam (p813) Marvelling at 20th-century and contemporary architecture.

3 Maastricht Underground (p818) Exploring centuries-old tunnels below Maastricht.

4 Vermeer Centrum Delft (p812) Learning about Vermeer's life and work in his evocative home town.

5 Den Haag (p810) Discovering the beautiful tree-lined boulevards, museums and palatial Binnenhof buildings.

6 Keukenhof Gardens (p809) Delving into Leiden's

dazzling tulip displays at its nearby gardens.

7 Zaanse Schans (p803) Watching windmills twirl at the delightful open-air museum.

8 Cycling (p811) Uncovering canals and tulip fields along the world's best cycling-route network.

AMSTERDAM

☑ 020 / POP 854,047

World Heritage–listed canals lined by tilted gabled houses, candlelit cafes, whirring bicycles, lush parks, treasure-packed museums, colourful markets, diverse dining, quirky shopping and legendary nightlife make the free-spirited Dutch capital an essential port of call.

Amsterdam has been a liberal place since the Netherlands' Golden Age, when it was at the forefront of European art and trade. Centuries later, in the 1960s, it again led the pack – this time in the principles of tolerance, with broad-minded views on drugs and same-sex relationships taking centre stage.

Explore its many worlds-within-worlds, where nothing ever seems the same twice. Better still, do it by boat or bike. Two-wheeling is a way of life here and abundant bike-rental shops make it easy to gear up and take a wind-in-your-hair spin through one of Europe's wildest cities.

◉ Sights

The I **Amsterdam City Card** (www.iamster dam.com; per 24/48/72/96 hours €59/74/87/98) provides admission to more than 30 museums, a canal cruise, and discounts at shops, entertainment venues and restaurants. It also includes a public-transport pass. Enquire at the tourist office.

◉ Medieval Centre

Crowned by the Royal Palace, the pigeon-, tourist- and busker-busy square that puts the 'Dam' in Amsterdam anchors the city's oldest quarter, which is also home to its infamous Red Light District.

★ Royal Palace   PALACE

(Koninklijk Paleis; Map p800; ☑ 020-522 61 61; www.paleisamsterdam.nl; Dam; adult/child €10/ free; ⊗ 10am-5pm; 🚊 4/14/24 Dam) Opened as a town hall in 1655, this resplendent building became a palace in the 19th century. The interiors gleam, especially the marble work – at its best in a floor inlaid with maps of the world in the great *burgerzaal* (citizens' hall) at the heart of the building. Pick up a free audioguide at the desk when you enter; it explains everything you see in vivid detail. King Willem-Alexander uses the palace only for ceremonies; check for periodic closures.

Begijnhof   COURTYARD

(Map p800; www.nicolaas-parochie.nl; ⊗ 9am-5pm; 🚊 2/11/12 Spui) **FREE** Dating from the early 14th century, this enclosed former convent is a surreal oasis of peace, with tiny houses and postage-stamp gardens around a well-kept courtyard off Gedempte Begijnensloot. The Beguines, a Catholic order of unmarried or widowed women who cared for the elderly, lived a religious life without taking monastic vows. The last Beguine died in 1971. Within the *hof* (courtyard) is the charming 1671 **Begijnhof Kapel** (Map p800; www.begijnhofkapelamsterdam.nl; Begijnhof 30; ⊗ 1-6.30pm Mon, 9am-6.30pm Tue-Fri, 9am-6pm Sat & Sun), and the **Engelse Kerk** (English Church; Map p800; www.ercadam.nl; Begijnhof 48; ⊗ 9am-5pm), built around 1392.

◉ Canal Ring

Amsterdam's Canal Ring was built during the 17th century after the seafaring port grew beyond its medieval walls, and authorities devised a ground-breaking expansion plan.

Wandering here amid architectural treasures and their reflections on the narrow waters of the Prinsengracht, Keizersgracht and Herengracht can cause days to vanish.

★ Anne Frank Huis   MUSEUM

(Map p800; ☑ 020-556 71 05; www.annefrank. org; Prinsengracht 263-267; adult/child €10.50/5; ⊗ 9am-10pm Apr-Oct, 9am-7pm Sun-Fri, to 9pm Sat Nov-Mar; 🚊 13/17 Westermarkt) The Anne Frank Huis draws more than one million

> **DON'T MISS**
>
> ### JORDAAN & THE WEST
>
> If Amsterdam's neighbourhoods held a 'best personality' contest, the Jordaan (once the workers' quarter) would win. Its intimacy is contagious, with modest 17th- and 18th- century merchants' houses and humble workers' homes, offbeat galleries and vintage shops peppering a grid of tiny lanes. This is the place for jovial bar sing-alongs and beery brown cafes (traditional Dutch pubs), the neighbourhood where you could spend a week wandering the narrow streets and still not discover all its hidden courtyards, tucked-away eateries and small-scale museums (cheese museum, tulip museum, houseboat museum). The 'hood abuts the West: industrial badlands that have transformed into an avant-garde cultural hub.

Central Amsterdam

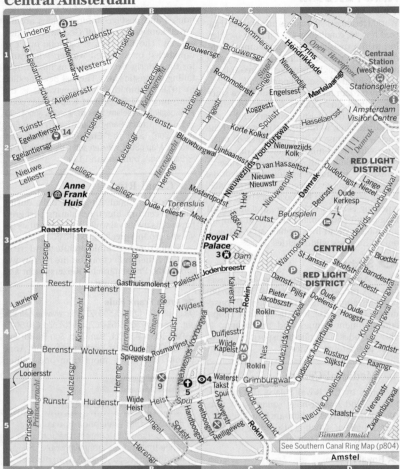

See Southern Canal Ring Map (p804)

See Southern Canal Ring Map (p804)

visitors annually. With Anne's melancholy bedroom and her actual diary – sitting alone in its glass case, filled with sunnily optimistic writing tempered by quiet despair – it's a powerful experience. It's compulsory to choose a timeslot and prepurchase tickets online. Renovations from 2018 include a new Westermarkt entrance and extensions to the museum.

👁 Museumplein

Amsterdam's most famous museums cluster around Museumplein, an urban playground of a city square with its skateboard ramp,

playground, ice-skating pond (in winter) and sky-high I Amsterdam sculpture (a favourite Instagram photo op).

⭐ **Rijksmuseum** MUSEUM
(National Museum; Map p804; 📞 020-674 70 00; www.rijksmuseum.nl; Museumstraat 1; adult/child €17.50/free; ⏰ 9am-5pm; 🚊 2/5/12 Rijksmuseum) The Rijksmuseum is among the world's finest art museums, packing works by local heroes Rembrandt, Vermeer and Van Gogh as well as 7500 other masterpieces over 1.5km of galleries. To avoid the biggest crowds, come before 10am or after 3pm. Prebooking tickets online provides fast-track entry.

THE NETHERLANDS AMSTERDAM

the world's largest collection of his work, both familiar paintings and wonderful little-known pieces. It's fascinating to see his work change from tentative beginnings to giddily bright sunflowers, and on to his frenzy of creative brilliance towards the end of his life. There are also paintings by contemporaries Gauguin, Toulouse-Lautrec, Monet and Bernard. You must choose a timeslot and prepurchase tickets online.

Stedelijk Museum   MUSEUM
(Map p804; ☑020-573 29 11; www.stedelijk.nl; Museumplein 10; adult/child €18.50/free; ⊙10am-6pm, to 10pm Fri; ☐2/3/5/12 Van Baerlestraat) This fabulous museum houses the collection amassed by postwar curator Willem Sandberg. Displays rotate but you'll see an amazing selection featuring works by Picasso, Matisse, Mondrian, Van Gogh, Rothko, De Kooning, Warhol and more, plus an exuberant Karel Appel mural and great temporary exhibitions. The building was originally a bank, built in 1895 to a neo-Renaissance design by AM Weissman, and the modern extension is nicknamed 'the bathtub' for reasons that will be obvious when you see it.

Start on the 2nd floor, with the astounding Golden Age works. Intimate paintings by Vermeer and De Hooch allow insight into everyday life in the 17th century, while Rembrandt's *The Night Watch* (1642) takes pride of place.

★ Van Gogh Museum   MUSEUM
(Map p804; ☑020-570 52 00; www.vangoghmuseum.nl; Museumplein 6; adult/child €18/free, audioguide €5/3; ⊙9am-7pm Sun-Thu, to 10pm Fri, to 9pm Sat late Jun-Aug, shorter hours rest of year; ☐2/3/5/12 Van Baerlestraat) It's a moving experience to visit this museum, which traces Van Gogh's life and development via

Vondelpark PARK
(Map p804; www.hetvondelpark.net; ☎2 Amstelveenseweg) A private park for the wealthy until 1953, Vondelpark now occupies a special place in Amsterdam's heart. It's a magical escape, but also supplies a busy social scene, encompassing cycle ways, pristine lawns, ponds with swans, quaint cafes, footbridges and winding footpaths. On a sunny day, an open-air party atmosphere ensues when tourists, lovers, cyclists, in-line skaters, pram-pushing parents, cartwheeling children, football-kicking teenagers, spliff-sharing friends and champagne-swilling picnickers all come out to play.

👁 Nieuwmarkt & Plantage

The streets around the Rembrandt House are prime wandering territory, offering a vibrant mix of old Amsterdam, canals and quirky shops and cafes.

★ Museum het Rembrandthuis MUSEUM
(Rembrandt House Museum; Map p800; ☎020-520 04 00; www.rembrandthuis.nl; Jodenbreestraat 4; adult/child €14/5; ⊙10am-6pm; Ⓜ Waterlooplein) This evocative museum is housed in Rembrandt's former home, where the master painter spent his most successful years, painting big commissions such as *The Night Watch* and running the Netherlands' largest painting studio. It wasn't to last, however: his work fell out of fashion, he had some expensive relationship problems and

DON'T MISS

DE PIJP

Immediately south of the Canal Ring, villagey De Pijp is Amsterdam's most spontaneous and creative quarter. Bohemian cafes, restaurants and bars spill out around its festive street market, **Albert Cuypmarkt** (Map p804; www.albertcuyp -markt.amsterdam; Albert Cuypstraat, btwn Ferdinand Bolstraat & Van Woustraat; ⊙9am-5pm Mon-Sat; Ⓜ De Pijp, ☎24 Albert Cuypstraat). Amsterdam's largest and busiest market, this is *the* hot spot in the city for buying gadgets, homewares, flowers, fruit and veg, herbs and spices, clothing and other goods. Snack vendors tempt passers-by with raw-herring sandwiches, fries, *poffertjes* (tiny Dutch pancakes dusted with icing sugar) and caramel syrup–filled *stroopwafels*.

bankruptcy came a-knocking. The inventory drawn up when he had to leave the house is the reason that curators have been able to refurnish the house so faithfully.

☞ Tours

Amsterdam has more canals than Venice and getting on the water is one of the best ways to feel the pulse of the city – the waterways are, after all, are a Unesco World Heritage Site.

★ Rederji Lampedusa BOATING
(http://rederjilampedusa.nl; Dijksgracht 6; 2hr canal tour €19; ⊙canal tours 11am & 1.30pm Sat May-Sep; ☎26 Muziekgebouw) Take a two-hour canal-boat tour around Amsterdam harbour in former refugee boats, brought from Lampedusa by Dutch founder Tuen. The tours are full of heart and offer a fascinating insight, not only into stories of contemporary migration, but also about how immigration shaped Amsterdam's history – especially the canal tour. Departs from next to Mediamatic.

Hungry Birds
Street Food Tours WALKING, FOOD
(☎06 1898 6268; www.hungrybirds.nl; day/night tour per person €79/89; ⊙by reservation) Guides take you 'off the eaten track' to chow on Dutch and ethnic specialities. Tours visit around 10 spots over four hours in De Pijp, Utrechtsestraat, Rembrandtplein and the Spui, from family-run eateries to street vendors. Prices include all food. The meet-up location is given after you make reservations.

✰ Festivals & Events

King's Day CULTURAL
(Koningsdag; ⊙27 Apr) King's Day is a celebration of the House of Orange, with hundreds of thousands of orange-clad locals and visitors filling Amsterdam's streets for drinking and dancing. The city also becomes one big flea market, as people sell off all their unwanted junk.

🛏 Sleeping

Amsterdam has loads of hotels in wild and wonderful spaces. But charm doesn't come cheap, and places fill fast – reserve as far ahead as possible, especially for summer bookings and weekends at any time.

★ Cocomama HOSTEL $
(Map p804; ☎020-627 24 54; www.cocomama hostel.com; Westeinde 18; dm/d from €42/120, minimum 2-night stay; 🛜; ☎4 Stadhouderskade) Once

WORTH A TRIP

ZAANSE SCHANS

The working, inhabited village Zaanse Schans functions as an open-air **windmill gallery** (☎075-681 00 00; www.dezaanseschans.nl; Kalverringdijk; per windmill adult/child €4.50/2; ⊙most windmills 9am-5pm Apr-Oct, hours vary Nov-Mar) on the Zaan river. Popular with tourists, its mills are completely authentic and operated with enthusiasm and love. You can explore the windmills at will, seeing the vast moving parts first-hand. The impressive **Zaans Museum** (☎075-681 00 00; www.zaansmuseum.nl; Schansend 7; adult/child €10/6; ⊙9am-5pm Apr-Sep, from 10am Oct-Mar) shows how wind and water were harnessed.

Trains (€3.20, 18 minutes, four per hour) run from Amsterdam Centraal Station (direction Alkmaar) to Koog Zaandijk, from where it's a well-signposted 1.5km walk.

a high-end brothel, this boutique hostel's doubles and dorms are light, bright and decorated with flair, with white walls and quirky designer Delftware or windmill themes. Amenities are way above typical hostel standard, with en suite bathrooms, in-room wifi, a relaxing back garden, a well-equipped kitchen, a book exchange and a super-comfy lounge open 24 hours. Breakfast is included.

St Christopher's at the Winston HOSTEL, HOTEL $
(Map p800; ☎020-623 13 80; www.st-christophers.co.uk; Warmoesstraat 129; dm/d from €47.80/153; @📶; 🚊4/14/24 Dam) This place hops 24/7 with rock-and-roll rooms, a busy nightclub with live bands nightly, a bar and restaurant, a beer garden and a smoking deck downstairs. En suite dorms sleep up to eight. Local artists were given free rein on the rooms, with super-edgy (entirely stainless steel) to questionably raunchy results. Rates include breakfast (and earplugs!).

★Sir Albert Hotel DESIGN HOTEL $$
(Map p804; ☎020-710 72 58; www.sirhotels.com/albert; Albert Cuypstraat 2-6; d/ste from €170/320; ❄@📶; Ⓜ De Pijp, 🚊3/12/24 De Pijp) A 19th-century diamond factory houses this glitzy design hotel. Its 90 creative rooms and suites have high ceilings and large windows, with custom-made linens and Illy espresso machines; iPads are available for use in the Persian-rug-floored study. Energetic staff are helpful and professional. Of the 10 balcony rooms, west-facing 336, 337 and 338 have sunset views over the canal.

W Amsterdam DESIGN HOTEL $$$
(Map p800; ☎020-811 25 00; www.wamsterdam.com; Spuistraat 175; d/ste from €380/567; ❄@📶🏊; 🚊2/11/12/13/17 Dam) Designer hotel chain W opened its Amsterdam premises in two landmark buildings, the Royal Dutch Post's former telephone exchange and a former bank – part of which now houses Dutch design mega-store **X Bank** (Map p800; www.xbank.amsterdam; Spuistraat 172; ⊙10am-8pm Mon-Sat, from noon Sun). Its 238 rooms (including connecting family rooms and 28 suites) combine design and vintage elements; there's also a state-of-the-art spa, a gym, an amazing rooftop lap pool, restaurants and bars.

✖ Eating

Amsterdam abounds with eateries. Superb streets for hunting include Utrechtsestraat, near Rembrandtplein; Amstelveenseweg, along the Vondelpark's western edge; and any of the little streets throughout the western canals.

★Vleminckx FAST FOOD $
(Map p800; www.vleminckxdesausmeester.nl; Voetboogstraat 33; fries €3-5, sauces €0.70; ⊙noon-7pm Sun & Mon, 11am-7pm Tue, Wed, Fri & Sat, to 8pm Thu; 🚊2/11/12 Koningsplein) Frying up *frites* (fries) since 1887, Amsterdam's best *friterie* has been based at this hole-in-the-wall takeaway shack near the Spui since 1957. The standard order of perfectly cooked crispy, fluffy *frites* is smothered in mayonnaise, though its 28 sauces also include apple, green pepper, ketchup, peanut, sambal and mustard. Queues almost always stretch down the block, but they move fast.

Braai BBQ Bar BARBECUE $
(☎020-221 13 76; www.braaiamsterdam.nl; Schinkelhavenkade 1; dishes €6.50-15.50; ⊙4-9.30pm; 🚊1/11/17 Surinameplein) Once a *haringhuis* (herring stand), this tiny place is now a street-food-style barbecue bar, with a great canal-side setting. Braai's speciality is marinated, barbecued ribs (half or full rack) and roasted sausages, but there are veggie options too. Cards are preferred, but it accepts

Southern Canal Ring

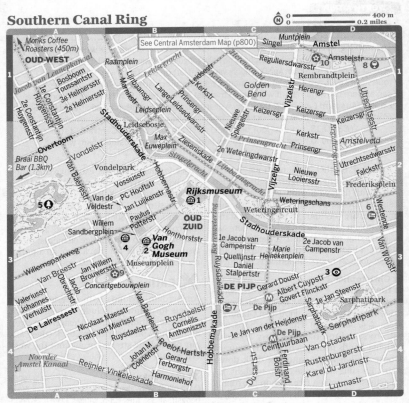

cash. Tables scatter under the trees alongside the water.

Tokoman   SURINAMESE $
(Map p800; www.tokoman.nl; Waterlooplein 327; sandwiches €3.75-5.50, dishes €6.50-12.50; ⊙11am-7pm, closed Sun; Ⓜ Waterlooplein) Queue with the folks getting their Surinamese spice on at Tokoman. It makes a sensational *broodje pom* (a sandwich filled with a tasty mash of chicken and a starchy Surinamese tuber). You'll want the *zuur* (pickled-cabbage relish) and *peper* (chilli) on it, plus a cold can of coconut water to wash it down.

★**D'Vijff Vlieghen**   DUTCH $$
(Map p800; ☎020-530 40 60; www.vijffvlieghen. nl; Spuistraat 294-302; mains €19-26; ⊙6-10pm; ☒2/11/12 Spui) Spread across five 17th-century canal houses, the 'Five Flies' is a jewel. Old-wood dining rooms overflow

with character, featuring Delft-blue tiles and original works by Rembrandt; chairs have copper plates inscribed with the names of famous guests (Walt Disney, Mick Jagger...). Exquisite dishes range from goose breast with apple, sauerkraut and smoked butter to candied haddock with liquorice sauce.

Greetje   DUTCH $$$

(Map p800; ☎020-779 74 50; www.restaurant greetje.nl; Peperstraat 23-25; mains €24-29; ☺6-10pm; ☒22/48 Prins Hendrikkade) 🍴 Greetje is Amsterdam's most creative Dutch restaurant, using the best seasonal produce to resurrect and re-create traditional Dutch recipes, like pickled beef, braised veal with apricots and leek *stamppot* (traditional mashed potatoes and vegetables), and pork belly with Dutch mustard sauce. Kick off with the Big Beginning (€17), a sampling of hot and cold starters.

🍷 Drinking & Nightlife

Amsterdam is one of the wildest nightlife cities in Europe and the world. Beyond the Red Light District and hotspots around Leidseplein and Rembrandtplein, the clubbing scene is also rapidly expanding thanks to 24-hour-licensed venues. Yet you can easily avoid a hardcore party scene: Amsterdam remains a *café* (pub) society where the pursuit of pleasure centres on cosiness and charm.

★'t Smalle   BROWN CAFE

(Map p800; www.t-smalle.nl; Egelantiersgracht 12; ☺10am-1am Sun-Thu, to 2am Fri & Sat; ☒13/17 Westermarkt) Dating back to 1786 as a *jenever* (Dutch gin) distillery and tasting house, and restored during the 1970s with antique porcelain beer pumps and lead-framed windows, locals' favourite 't Smalle is one of Amsterdam's most charming *bruin cafés*. Dock your boat right by the pretty stone terrace, which is wonderfully convivial by day and impossibly romantic at night.

Monks Coffee Roasters   COFFEE

(www.monkscoffee.nl; Bilderdijkstraat 46; ☺8am-5pm Tue-Sun; 🛜; ☒3/13/19 Bilderdijkstraat) Monks' phenomenal house blend, prepared with a variety of brewing methods, is hands down Amsterdam's best, but the cafe also serves superb coffee from small-scale specialists such as Amsterdam's Lot Sixty One and White Label Coffee, and Paris' Café Lomi. Its cavernous space is brilliant for brunch (try avocado toast with feta, chilli and lime, or banana bread with mascarpone and caramelised pineapple).

★Brouwerij 't IJ   BREWERY

(www.brouwerijhetij.nl; Funenkade 7; ☺brewery 2-8pm, English tour 3.30pm Fri-Sun; ☒7 Hoogte Kadijk) 🍴 Can you get more Dutch than drinking a craft beer beneath the creaking sails of the 1725-built De Gooyer Windmill? This is Amsterdam's leading microbrewery, with delicious standard, seasonal and limited-edition brews; try the smooth, fruity 'tripel' Zatte, their first creation back in 1985. Enjoy yours in the tiled tasting room, lined by an amazing bottle collection, or the plane-tree-shaded terrace.

Amsterdam Roest   BEER GARDEN

(www.amsterdamroest.nl; Jacob Bontiusplaats 1; ☺noon-midnight Sun-Wed, to 1am Thu, to 3am Fri & Sat; ☒22 Wittenburgergracht) This is one of those 'only in Amsterdam' places, and well worth the trip. Once-derelict shipyards now host an epically cool artist collective–bar-restaurant, Amsterdam Roest (Dutch for 'Rust'), with a canal-side terrace, mammoth playground of ropes and tyres, hammocks,

---

RED LIGHT DISTRICT

Just southeast of Centraal Station, on and around the parallel neon-lit canals Oudezijds Voorburgwal and Oudezijds Achterburgwal, the warren of medieval alleyways making up Amsterdam's Red Light District (locally known as De Wallen), is a carnival of vice, seething with skimpily clad prostitutes in brothel windows, raucous bars, haze-filled 'coffeeshops', strip shows, sex shows, mind-boggling museums and shops selling everything from cartoonish condoms to S&M gear and herbal highs.

The area is generally safe, but keep your wits about you and don't photograph or film prostitutes in the windows – out of respect, and to avoid having your camera flung in a canal by their enforcers. Seriously.

> ### ⓘ COFFEESHOP & SMART SHOP DOS & DON'T
>
> ....
>
> In the Netherlands, 'coffeeshops' are where one buys marijuana. 'Smart shops' sell mushroom truffles (psilocybin mushrooms, aka magic mushrooms, are now illegal in the Netherlands).
>
> ➡ Do ask coffeeshop staff for advice on what and how to consume, and heed it, even if nothing happens after an hour.
>
> ➡ Don't ask for hard (illegal) drugs.
>
> ➡ Don't drink alcohol – it's illegal in coffeeshops.
>
> ➡ Don't smoke tobacco, whether mixed with marijuana or on its own; it is forbidden inside all bars and restaurants, in accordance with the Netherlands' laws.

street art, a sandy beach in summer and bonfires in winter.

Pllek
BAR

(www.pllek.nl; TT Neveritaweg 59; ⊙9.30am-1am Sun-Thu, to 3am Fri & Sat; ⌷NDSM-werf) Uber-cool Pllek is a Noord magnet, with hip things of all ages streaming over to hang out in its interior made of old shipping containers and lie out on its artificial sandy beach when the weather allows. It's a terrific spot for a waterfront beer or glass of wine.

★ SkyLounge
COCKTAIL BAR

(Map p800; ☑020-530 08 75; www.skyloungeam sterdam.com; Oosterdoksstraat 4; ⊙11am-1am Sun-Tue, to 2am Wed & Thu, to 3am Fri & Sat; 🛜; ⌷2/4/11/12/13/14/17/24/26 Centraal Station) With wow-factor views whatever the weather, this bar offers a 360-degree panorama of Amsterdam from the 11th floor of the Double-Tree Amsterdam Centraal Station hotel – and it just gets better when you head out to its vast SkyTerrace, with an outdoor bar. Toast the view with a huge range of cocktails, craft beers and spirits. DJs regularly hit the decks from 9pm.

☆ Entertainment

Check what's on at I Amsterdam (www.iam sterdam.com).

Last Minute Ticket Shop sells same-day half-price tickets for concerts, performances and even club nights online. Events are handily marked 'LNP' (language no problem) if understanding Dutch isn't vital.

Pathé Tuschinskitheater
CINEMA

(Map p804; www.pathe.nl; Reguliersbreestraat 26-34; ⊙9.30am-12.30am; ⌷14/24 Rembrandt-plein) This fantastical cinema, with a facade that's a prime example of the Amsterdam School of architecture, is worth visiting for

its sumptuous art deco interior alone. The *grote zaal* (main auditorium) is the most stunning; it generally screens blockbusters, while the smaller theatres play arthouse and indie films. Visit the interior on an audio tour (€10) when films aren't playing.

Concertgebouw
CLASSICAL MUSIC

(Concert Hall; Map p804; ☑020-671 83 45; www.concertgebouw.nl; Concertgebouwplein 10; ⊙box office 1-7pm Mon-Fri, from 10am Sat & Sun; ⌷3/5/12 Museumplein) The Concert Hall was built in 1888 by AL van Gendt, who managed to engineer its near-perfect acoustics. Bernard Haitink, former conductor of the Royal Concertgebouw Orchestra, remarked that the world-famous hall was the orchestra's best instrument. Free half-hour concerts take place Wednesdays at 12.30pm from September to June; arrive early. Try the **Last Minute Ticket Shop** (www.lastminute ticketshop.nl; ⊙online ticket sales from 10am on day of performance) for half-price seats to all other performances.

🛍 Shopping

Stumbling across offbeat little boutiques is one of the great joys of shopping in Amsterdam. The best areas are the nexus of the Western Canal Ring and Jordaan, along Haarlemmerstraat and Haarlemmerdijk. To the south the Negen Straatjes (Nine Streets) offers a satisfying browse among its pint-sized, one-of-a-kind shops. Staalstraat in Nieuwmarkt is another bountiful vein.

★ Lindengracht Market
MARKET

(Map p800; www.jordaanmarkten.nl; Lindengracht; ⊙9am-4pm Sat; ⌷3 Nieuwe Willemsstraat) Dating from 1895, Saturday's Lindengracht Market is a wonderfully local affair, with 232 stalls selling bountiful fresh produce, including fish and a magnificent array of cheese, as well as gourmet goods, clothing and homewares. Arrive as early as possible for the best pickings and thinnest crowds.

ⓘ Information

I Amsterdam Visitor Centre (Map p800; ☑ 020-702 60 00; www.iamsterdam. com; Stationsplein 10; ⊙ 9am-5pm; 🚋 2/4/11/12/13/14/17/24/26 Centraal Station) Located outside Centraal Station.

I Amsterdam Visitor Centre Schiphol (www. iamsterdam.com; ⊙ 7am-10pm) Inside Schiphol International Airport in the Arrivals 2 hall.

ⓘ Getting There & Away

AIR

Most major airlines serve **Schiphol** (AMS; www. schiphol.nl), 18km southwest of the city centre.

BUS

Buses operated by Eurolines (www.eurolines. com) and FlixBus (www.flixbus.com) connect Amsterdam with all major European capitals and numerous smaller destinations. Book tickets online.

Eurolines buses use **Duivendrecht station** (Stationsplein 3, Duivendrecht; Ⓜ Duivendrecht), south of the centre, which has an easy metro link to Centraal Station (about a 20-minute trip via metros 50, 53 or 54).

FlixBus runs to/from **Sloterdijk train station**, west of the centre, which is linked to Centraal Station by metro number 50 (a six-minute trip).

TRAIN

Centraal Station (Map p800; Stationsplein; 🚋 2/4/11/12/13/14/17/24/26 Centraal Station) is in the city centre, with easy onward connections.

NS (www.ns.nl), aka Dutch Railways, runs the nation's rail service. Trains are frequent from Centraal Station and serve domestic destina-

tions such as Haarlem, Leiden and Delft several times per hour, making for easy day trips.

The main service centre to buy tickets for both national and international trains is on the station's west side.

ⓘ Getting Around

TO/FROM THE AIRPORT

Trains to Centraal Station depart every 10 minutes or so from 6am to 12.30am, and hourly at other times; the trip takes 15 minutes and costs €5.30. Taxis take 20 to 30 minutes and cost €39.

BICYCLE

The vast majority of Amsterdammers get around town on their *fietsen* (bikes). Rental companies are all over town; bikes cost about €12 per day.

BOAT

Free ferries to Amsterdam Noord depart from piers behind Centraal Station.

PUBLIC TRANSPORT

Most public transport within the city is by tram. Tickets are not sold on board. Buy a disposable **OV-chipkaart** (www.ov-chipkaart.nl; 1hr €3) or a day pass (one to seven days €7.50 to €34.50) from the **GVB information office** (www.gvb. nl; Stationsplein 10; ⊙ 7am-9pm Mon-Fri, from 8am Sat & Sun; 🚋 2/4/11/12/13/14/17/24/26 Centraal Station). When you enter *and* exit, wave your card at the machine to 'check in' and 'check out'.

THE RANDSTAD

One of the most densely populated places on the planet, the Randstad stretches from Amsterdam to Rotterdam and is crammed with classic Dutch towns and cities such as Den Haag, Utrecht, Leiden and Delft. A cycling network links the towns amid tulip fields.

Haarlem

☑ 023 / POP 159,556

This classic Dutch city of cobbled streets, historic buildings, grand churches, even grander museums, cosy bars, fine cafes and canals is just a 15-minute train ride from Amsterdam.

◉ Sights

Flanked by historic buildings, restaurants and cafes, the large Grote Markt is Haarlem's beating heart. Stalls crammed with

GAY AMSTERDAM

Amsterdam's gay scene is one of the largest in the world. Hubs include Warmoesstraat in the Red Light District and Reguliersdwarsstraat in the Southern Canal Ring. Gay Amsterdam (www. gayamsterdam.com) lists hotels, bars, clubs and more.

market produce fill the square Monday and Saturday.

★ **Frans Hals Museum – Hof**   MUSEUM
(www.franshalsmuseum.nl; Groot Heiligland 62; adult/child incl Frans Hals Museum – Hof €15/free; ☺ 11am-5pm Tue-Sat, from noon Sun) A must for anyone interested in the Dutch Masters, this superb museum is located in the poorhouse where Hals spent his final years. The collection focuses on the 17th-century Haarlem School; its pride and joy are eight group portraits of the Civic Guard that reveal Hals' exceptional attention to mood and psychological tone. Other greats represented here include Pieter Bruegel the Younger and Jacob van Ruisdael. Tickets include admission to the modern- and contemporary-art **Frans Hals Museum – Hal** (☎ 023-511 57 75; Grote Markt 16; ☺ 11am-5pm Tue-Sat, from noon Sun).

Grote Kerk van St Bavo   CHURCH
(www.bavo.nl; Oude Groenmarkt 22; adult/child €2.50/1.25; ☺ 10am-5pm Mon-Sat year-round, plus from noon Sun Jul & Aug) Topped by a towering 50m-high steeple, the Gothic Grote Kerk van St Bavo contains some fine Renaissance artworks, but the star attraction is its stunning Müller organ – one of the most magnificent in the world, standing 30m high and with about 5000 pipes, dating from 1738. It was played by Handel and a 10-year-old Mozart. Free hour-long **organ recitals** take place at 8.15pm Tuesday and 4pm Thursday from July to October, and on occasional Sundays at 2.30pm.

✖ Eating & Drinking

Cafes and restaurants abound along Zijlstraat, Spaarne and especially Lange Veerstraat, but you'll find gems scattered all over town.

★ **Restaurant Mr & Mrs**   BISTRO $$
(☎ 023-531 59 35; www.restaurantmrandmrs. nl; Lange Veerstraat 4; small plates €11-13, 4-/5-/6-course menu €40/48/56; ☺ 5-10pm Tue-Sat) Unexpectedly gastronomic cooking at this tiny restaurant is artfully conceived and presented. Small hot and cold plates designed for sharing might include steak tartare with black truffles, white asparagus with honey-poached egg, mackerel with Dutch shrimp and rose petals, chorizostuffed quail with *fregola* (bead-like pasta), and desserts like passionfruit tart with mint meringue and mango salsa. Definitely book ahead.

★ **Jopenkerk**   BREWERY
(www.jopenkerk.nl; Gedempte Voldersgracht 2; ☺ brewery & cafe 10am-1am, restaurant noon-3pm & 5.30-11pm; ⊕) Haarlem's most atmospheric place to drink is this independent brewery inside a stained-glass-windowed 1910 church. Enjoy brews such as citrusy Hopen, fruity Lente Bier and chocolatey Koyt along with Dutch bar snacks – *bitterballen* (meat-filled croquettes) and cheeses – beneath the gleaming copper vats. Or head to the mezzanine for dishes made from locally sourced, seasonal ingredients and Jopenkerk's beers (pairings available).

DeDakkas   ROOFTOP BAR
(www.dedakkas.nl; Parkeergarage de Kamp, 6th fl, De Witstraat; ☺ 9am-11pm Tue, Wed & Sun, to midnight Thu-Sat; ☎) From the ground, it looks like any other multistorey car park, but taking the lift to the 6th floor brings you out at this fabulous rooftop with a greenhouse-style glass cafe and timber-decked terrace with sweeping views over Haarlem (you can see Amsterdam on a clear day). Regular events include barbecues, cinema screenings, yoga, DJs and live music gigs.

ℹ Information

Tourist Office (VVV; ☎ 023-531 73 25; www.haarlemmarketing.nl; Grote Markt 2; ☺ 9.30am-5.30pm Mon-Fri, to 5pm Sat, noon-4pm Sun Apr-Sep, 1-5.30pm Mon, from 9.30am Tue-Fri, 10am-5pm Sat Oct-Mar)

ℹ Getting There & Away

Haarlem's 1908 art nouveau station is served by frequent trains to/from Amsterdam (€4.30, 15 minutes), Rotterdam (€12.40, one hour) and Den Haag (€8.50, 40 minutes).

Leiden

☑ 071 / POP 122,561
Vibrant Leiden is renowned for being Rembrandt's birthplace, the home of the Netherlands' oldest university (and 27,000 students) and the place America's pilgrims raised money to lease the *Mayflower* that took them to the New World in 1620. Beautiful 17th-century buildings line its canals.

◉ Sights

As you walk five minutes southeast from Centraal Station, the city's traditional character unfolds, especially around the Pieterskerk

KEUKENHOF GARDENS

One of the Netherlands' top attractions is 1km west of Lisse, between Haarlem and Leiden. **Keukenhof** (☑0252-465 555; www.keukenhof.nl; Stationsweg 166; ◷8am-7.30pm mid-Mar–mid-May; 🅿) is the world's largest bulb-flower garden, attracting around 1.4 million visitors during its eight-week season that coincides with the transient blooms in fields of multicoloured tulips, daffodils and hyacinths. Book ahead online to ensure a place.

In season, special buses link Keukenhof with Amsterdam's Schiphol Airport and Leiden's Centraal Station; combination tickets covering entry and transport are usually available.

and south. Leiden's district of historic waterways is worth at least a full day of wandering.

★**Museum Volkenkunde**　　MUSEUM
(National Museum of Ethnology; www.volkenkunde.nl; Steenstraat 1; adult/student/child 4-18yr €14/8/6; ◷10am-5pm Tue-Sun) Cultural achievements by civilisations worldwide are on show at this splendid museum, which has a collection of more than 300,000 artefacts from across the globe. Permanent galleries are dedicated to the cultures of Africa; the Arctic and North America; Asia; Central and South America; China; Indonesia; Japan and Korea; and Oceania. Highlights include the atmospherically lit Buddha Room next to the Japan and Korea section and the 'Mountain of the Immortals' carving in the China section. Temporary exhibitions are also impressive.

★**Rijksmuseum van Oudheden**　　MUSEUM
(National Museum of Antiquities; ☑071-516 31 63; www.rmo.nl; Rapenburg 28; adult/student/child 5-17yr €12.50/6/4; ◷10am-5pm Tue-Sun) Home to the Rijksmuseum's collection of Greek, Etruscan, Roman and Egyptian artefacts, this museum is best known for its Egyptian halls, which include the reconstructed **Temple of Taffeh**, a gift from Anwar Sadat to the Netherlands for helping to save ancient Egyptian monuments from flood. Other Egyptian exhibits include mastabas from Saqqara and a room of mummy cases. First-floor galleries are replete with Greek, Etruscan and Roman statuary and vases, as well as treasures from the ancient Near East.

Rijksmuseum Boerhaave　　MUSEUM
(☑071-751 99 99; www.rijksmuseumboerhaave.nl; Lange St Agnietenstraat 10; adult/student/child 4-17yr €12.50/7.50/5; ◷10am-5pm Tue-Sun) Named in honour of physician, botanist, chemist and University of Leiden teacher Herman Boerhaave (1668–1738), this impressive museum of science and medicine has exhibits profiling major discoveries in science in the Netherlands, and the doctors and scientists behind them. The museum is housed in a 15th-century convent that later became the first academic hospital in Northern Europe, and a multimedia introduction is presented in a recreated anatomical theatre. Teenagers will enjoy the opportunities for hands-on interaction in the Waterland exhibit.

Museum De Lakenhal　　MUSEUM
(www.lakenhal.nl; Oude Singel 28-32) Leiden's foremost museum, displaying works by native son Rembrandt among others, the Lakenhal reopened its doors in 2019 after undergoing a major renovation and expansion. Check online or with the tourist office for updates.

🍴 Sleeping & Eating

The city-centre canals and narrow old streets teem with choices. Market stalls line Botermarkt, Vismarkt, Aalmarkt and Nieuwe Rijn on Wednesday and Saturday.

★**Ex Libris**　　B&B $$
(☑071-240 86 36; www.hotelexlibris.com; Kloksteeg 4; r €120-200; ❄🅿) There are plenty of boutique B&Bs in the Netherlands, but few are as stylish, comfortable and welcoming as this one. Occupying a former bookshop and adjoining house near the Pieterskerk, it offers five quiet rooms accessed via steep stairs; these have coffee/tea and a smart TV. The chic downstairs breakfast room offers a €17 cafe-style repast (smoothies, granola, eggs, pancakes, toasties).

Borgman & Borman　　CAFE
(☑071-566 55 37; www.borgmanborgman.nl; Nieuwe Rijn 41; ◷9am-5pm Mon, 8am-6pm Tue-Sat,10.30am-5pm Sun; 🅿) The Giesen roaster in the window signals that this hip cafe is serious about its coffee, and once you've ordered you'll find that the baristas deliver on this promise. There's also a small menu of breakfast dishes, sandwiches (€5 to €7) and toasties. Service is friendly and the music on the sound system is excellent – not a '70s or '80s pop song to be heard. Cash only.

★ **In den Doopfot** EUROPEAN $$$
(☑ 071-512 24 34; www.indendoopfot.nl; Turfmarkt 9; mains €30, 3-/4-course lunch menu €39/45, 4-/5-/6-course dinner menu €55/65/75; ⊙ 12.30-3pm & 5.30-10pm Mon-Fri, 5.30-10pm Sat) Given the sky-high calibre of chef Patrick Brugman's food, In den Doopfot's prices are a veritable steal. This is extremely assured and creative cooking, as good to look at as it is to eat. Vegetarian menus are available on request, as are expert wine pairings by the glass (€8 per course). Highly recommended.

ℹ️ Information

Tourist Office (☑ 071-516 60 00; www.visit leiden.nl; Stationsweg 26; ⊙ 7am-7pm Mon-Fri, 10am-4pm Sat, 11am-3pm Sun; 🛜)

ℹ️ Getting There & Away

Leiden's train station is 400m northwest of the centre. There are frequent trains to/from Amsterdam (€9.10, 35 minutes), Den Haag (€3.50, 15 minutes) and Rotterdam (€7.40, 35 minutes).

Den Haag

☑ 070 / POP 519,988

Flanked by wide, leafy boulevards, Den Haag (The Hague) is the Dutch seat of government. The city enjoys an exciting cultural scene and top-notch dining. The party precinct of Grote Markt and the much-loved Paard live-music venue are essential stops for every visitor.

Den Haag's seaside suburb of Scheveningen (pronounced as s'CHay-fuh-ninger), 4km west, has a loud and lively kitsch, and a long stretch of beach.

👁️ Sights

★ **Mauritshuis** MUSEUM
(Royal Picture Gallery; ☑ 070-302 34 56; www.mau ritshuis.nl; Plein 29; adult/student/child under 19yr €15.50/12.50/free; ⊙ 1-6pm Mon, 10am-6pm Tue, Wed & Fri-Sun, 10am-8pm Thu; 🚊 Centrum) Offering a wonderful introduction to Dutch and Flemish art, this splendid museum is set in a 17th-century mansion built for wealthy sugar trader Johan Maurits. It became a museum housing the Royal Picture Collection in 1822, and acquired a swish modern wing in 2012-14. The 800-strong collection of paintings focuses on works created between the 15th and 18th centuries. It includes masterpieces such as Vermeer's *Girl with a Pearl Earring* (c1665) and Rembrandt's intriguing *The Anatomy Lesson of Dr Nicolaes Tulp* (1632).

Binnenhof PALACE
(🚊 Centrum) Home to both houses of the Dutch government, this complex of buildings next to the **Hofvijver** (Court Pond) is arranged around a central courtyard that was once used for executions. Its splendid ceremonial **Ridderzaal** (Knights Hall) dates back to the 13th century. The 17th-century North Wing is still home to the Upper House, but the Lower House meets in a chamber in the modern eastern part of the complex. Visitor organisation **ProDemos** (☑ 070-757 02 00; www.prodemos.nl; Hofweg 1; Ridderzaal tour €5.50, Ridderzaal, House of Representatives & Senate tour €11; ⊙ office 10am-5pm Mon-Sat, tours by reservation; 🚊 Kneuterdijk, Centrum) conducts guided tours.

★ **Escher in Het Paleis** MUSEUM
(☑ 070-427 77 30; www.escherinhetpaleis.nl; Lange Voorhout 74; adult/student/child 7-15yr/child under 7yr €10/8.50/6.50/free; ⊙ 11am-5pm Tue-Sun; 🚊 Korte Voorhout) Once home to members of the Dutch royal family, the 18th-century Lange Voorhout Palace now houses a collection of the work of Dutch graphic artist MC Escher (1898–1972). The permanent exhibition features notes, letters, photos and plenty of woodcuts and lithographs from various points of his career, including everything from the early realism to the later phantasmagoria. All are fascinating exercises in the blending of different perspectives, and the conjunction of mathematical rules and artistic subject matter.

🛏️ Sleeping

KingKool HOSTEL $
(☑ 070-215 83 39; www.kingkool.nl; Prinsegracht 51; dm €21-31, d with shared bathroom €55, d €69-76; 🅿️ 🛜; 🚊 Brouwersgracht) Close to **Paard** (☑ 070-750 34 34; www.paard.nl; Prinsegracht 12; ⊙ hours vary; 🚊 Grote Markt) and the Grote Markt party precinct, this is Den Haag's backpacker central. The ground-floor bar is a popular gathering spot and the mixed dorms (sleeping eight to 12, some on three-tier bunks) are made cheerful with street-art-style murals; those on the 1st floor are best. Shared bathrooms are barracks-like but clean, with plenty of hot water.

★ **Hotel Indigo** BOUTIQUE HOTEL $$$
(☑ 070-209 90 00; www.hotelindigo.com; Noordeinde 33; standard r €160-230, superior r €220-290; 🛜; 🚊 Kneuterdijk) A clever transformation of the former 1884 De Nederlandsche Bank headquarters, the Indigo is located on

DON'T MISS

THE NETHERLANDS BY BIKE

The Netherlands is the ultimate country to explore by *fiets* (bicycle). Cycling in the Netherlands (http://holland.cyclingaroundtheworld.nl) is a font of useful, inspiring information.

Cycling Routes & Maps

Bike routes web the country. Long-distance LF routes link one town to another and are well marked with distinctive, green-and-white signs. In 2017 work began on condensing the original 26 LP routes – comprising close to 4500km – into 12 longer themed routes.

Fietsersbond Routeplanner (https://en.routeplanner.fietsersbond.nl), powered by the Netherlands' national cycling federation, is a superb online route planner with an indispensable smartphone app.

The best overall maps are Falk/VVV *Fietskaart met Knooppuntennetwerk* maps (cycling network; www.falk.nl), with keys in English. Tourist offices often sell them.

Gearing Up

Rental shops are everywhere. Count on paying €12 per day. Many rent out e-bikes (electric bikes). Bikes always come with a lock. To brake on a traditional Dutch bicycle, back-pedal. Most Dutch cyclists don't wear a helmet, hence they're not standard with a rental.

Buy a day ticket for your bike (*dagkaart fiets;* €6.20) to take it on a train.

---

fashionable Noordeinde. Its 63 good-sized rooms are stylish, with smart furnishings and amenities – those in the attic have bags of character. Start the day with breakfast in the ground-floor cafe (included in the room rate) and finish with a cocktail in the basement speakeasy.

✖ Eating & Drinking

The cobbled streets and canals off Denneweg continually host adventurous new openings. For cheap eats, head to Chinatown. The main cafe strips are Denneweg and Noordeinde.

Lola Bikes & Coffee CAFE
(www.facebook.com/LolaBikesandCoffee; Noordeinde 91; ⊗8am-6pm Tue-Sun; 🚊Mauritskade) The owners and staff at this cafe are passionate cyclists, and operate a workshop at the rear where they repair racing bikes in between serving excellent coffee and cake to a host of regulars. Sit in the rear garden or relax in the shabby-chic front space. It's the home base of the Lola Cycling Club, which welcomes new members.

De Basiliek INTERNATIONAL $$
(☑070-360 61 44; www.debasiliek.nl; Korte Houtstraat 4a; mains €18-24, 3-course menu €37.50-42.50; ⊗noon-4pm & 6-10pm Mon-Fri, 6-10pm Sat; 🖀✎; 🚊Kalvermarkt-Stadhuis) Moody lighting, comfortable seating and unobtrusive service

set the scene for enjoyable meals at this classy choice. The menu is predominantly Italian and French, with a few Indian and Middle Eastern dishes thrown in as wildcards. The food is fresh and full of flavour, made with top-notch produce, and the stellar wine includes loads of by-the-glass options. Great coffee too.

★Fouquet DUTCH $$$
(☑070-360 62 73; www.fouquet.nl; Javastraat 31a; mains €25-28, 3-course menus €30-38; ⊗6-9.30pm Mon-Sat; ✎; 🚊Javastraat, Javabrug) The three-course 'market fresh' menu at this elegant restaurant is an excellent and bargain-priced introduction to Sebastiaan de Bruijn's seasonally inspired French-Mediterranean fare. The menu changes daily, responding to what is fresh in the local markets, and is prepared with love and great expertise. Presentation, service and the wine list are all equally impressive.

🛈 Information

Tourist Office (VVV; ☑070-361 88 60; www.denhaag.com; Spui 68; ⊗noon-6pm Mon, 10am-6pm Tue-Fri, 10am-5pm Sat, noon-5pm Sun; 🖀; 🚊Kalvermarkt-Stadhuis)

🛈 Getting There & Around

A one-hour/day pass for local trams costs €3.50/6.50.

THE NETHERLANDS DEN HAAG

Most trains use Den Haag **Centraal Station** (CS), but some through trains only stop at Den Haag **Hollands Spoor** (HS) station just south of the centre. Frequent trains serve Amsterdam (€11.70, 55 minutes) and Rotterdam (€4.70, 20 to 35 minutes). Den Haag's Centraal Station is also linked to Rotterdam by metro line E (€4.90, 30 minutes).

Delft

📞 015 / POP 101,034

An easy day trip by bicycle or train from Den Haag or Rotterdam, historic Delft has changed little since Golden Age artist Johannes Vermeer, a born-and-bred Delft lad, painted his famous *View of Delft* in 1660–61. The town is synonymous with its blue-and-white-painted porcelain and is usually heaving with visitors by noon; arrive early to beat the crowds.

⊙ Sights

Delft is best seen on foot: almost all the interesting sights lie within a 1km radius of the vast Markt. Much of the town dates from the 17th century and is remarkably well preserved.

★ Vermeer Centrum Delft   MUSEUM
(📞 015-213 85 88; www.vermee rdelft.nl/; Voldersgracht 21; adult/student/child 12-17yr €9/7/5; ⊙ 10am-5pm) Johannes Vermeer was born in Delft in 1632 and lived here until his death in 1675, aged only 43. Sadly, none of his works remain in Delft, making it hard for the town to make the most of its connection to the great painter. Hence this centre, where reproductions of his works are exhibited, a short film about his life is screened and displays about 17th-century painting techniques and materials give context.

Nieuwe Kerk   CHURCH
(New Church; 📞 015-212 30 25; https://oudeen nieuwekerkdelft.nl/; Markt 80; adult/child 6-11yr incl Oude Kerk €5/1, Nieuwe Kerk tower additional €4/2; ⊙ 9am-6pm Mon-Sat Apr-Oct, shorter hours rest of year) Construction of Delft's Nieuwe Kerk began in 1381; it was finally completed in 1655. The church has been the final resting place of almost every member of the House of Orange since 1584, including William of Orange (William the Silent), who lies in an over-the-top marble mausoleum designed by Hendrick de Keyser. Children under five are not permitted to climb the 109m-high tower, whose 376 narrow, spiralling steps lead to panoramic views.

Oude Kerk   CHURCH
(Old Church; 📞 015-212 30 15; https://oudeennieuwe kerkdelft.nl/; Heilige Geestkerkhof 25; adult/child 6-11yr incl Nieuwe Kerk €5/1; ⊙ 9am-6pm Mon-Sat Apr-Oct, shorter hours rest of year) Founded c 1246, the Oude Kerk is a surreal sight: its 75m-high tower, which was erected c 1350, leans nearly 2m from the vertical due to subsidence caused by its canal location, hence its nickname Scheve Jan ('Leaning John'). The older section features an austere barrel vault; the newer northern transept has a Gothic vaulted ceiling. One of the tombs inside the church is that of painter Johannes Vermeer.

Royal Delft   FACTORY
(Koninklijke Porceleyne Fles; 📞 015-760 08 00; www.royaldelft.com; Rotterdamseweg 196; adult/child 13-18yr/child under 13yr €13.50/8.50/free; ⊙ 9am-5pm Mar-Oct, 9am-5pm Mon-Sat, noon-5pm Sun Nov-Feb) Pottery fans will love visiting Royal Delft, the town's most famous earthenware factory. The admission ticket includes an audio tour that leads you through a painting demonstration, the company museum and the factory's production process; there's a €3 discount if you have a Museumkaart (p819). For many, of course, the tour highlight is the final stop in the gift shop.

✗ Eating & Drinking

There are plenty of cafes and restaurants on the Markt and surrounding streets. Drinking and partying unfolds in pubs on the Beestenmarkt and at renowned student hang-out **De Oude Jan** (📞 015-214 53 63; www.oudejan.nl; Heilige Geestkerkhof 4; ⊙ 10am-1am Mon, to 4am Tue-Thu & Sun, to 3am Fri & Sat Easter-Oct, from noon Nov-Easter; 🛜).

Kek   CAFE $
(📞 015-750 32 53; http://kekdelft.nl/; Voldersgracht 27; breakfast dishes €4-10, sandwiches €6-10; ⊙ 8.30am-6pm; 🛜🅿) 🍃 The baskets of organic fruit and vegetables at the front of this stylish cafe are a good indicator of what's on the menu – freshly squeezed juices, fruit smoothies and a tempting array of cakes, muffins, tarts and sandwiches made with local seasonal produce (sugar-free, vegan and gluten-free options available). Other draws include all-day breakfasts and coffee made using Giraffe beans.

ⓘ Information

Tourist Information Point (📞 015-215 40 51; www.delft.com; Kerkstraat 3; ⊙ 11am-3pm Sun & Mon, 10am-4pm Tue-Sat)

THE NETHERLANDS DELFT

ℹ Getting There & Around

There are bike trails from Den Haag (11km north-west) and Rotterdam (28km southeast).

Delft By Cycle (📞 06 2434 2610; https://delftbycycle.nl/en/; Phoenixstraat 112; per day €15; ⊙9am-5pm) rents out bikes.

Regular train services to/from Delft include Amsterdam (€13.20 to €15.60, one hour), Den Haag (€2.50, 15 minutes) and Rotterdam (€3.40, 15 minutes).

Rotterdam

📞 010 / POP 629,606

Futuristic architecture, a proliferation of art, and cutting-edge drinking, dining and nightlife scenes make Rotterdam one of Europe's most exhilarating cities right now. The Netherlands' second-largest metropolis has a diverse, multi-ethnic community, an absorbing maritime tradition centred on Europe's busiest port and a wealth of world-class museums.

The city was all but razed to the ground by WWII bombers, but rebuilding has continued unabated ever since with ingenuity and vision. Split by the vast Nieuwe Maas shipping channel, Rotterdam is crossed by a series of tunnels and bridges. On the north side of the water, the city centre is easily strolled – or pedalled around by bike.

◎ Sights

Rotterdam's not just an open-air gallery of extraordinary architecture – it's also home to streets filled with art. For a full list of sculptures and an interactive map, visit Sculpture International Rotterdam (www.sculptureinternationalrotterdam.nl).

★ Markthal   NOTABLE BUILDING

(Market Hall; https://markthal.klepierre.nl/; Nieuwstraat; ⊙10am-8pm Mon-Thu & Sat, to 9pm Fri, noon-6pm Sun; Ⓜ Blaak, ☒Blaak) One of the city's signature buildings, this extraordinary inverted-U-shaped market hall was designed by local architecture firm MVRDV and opened for business in 2014. It comprises highly sought-after glass-walled apartments arcing over a 40m-high market hall with a striking fruit-and-vegetable-muralled ceiling. Most of the stalls sell food to eat on the spot rather than produce to take home. There are also a number of sit-down eateries.

Huis Sonneveld   ARCHITECTURE

(Sonneveld House; www.huissonneveld.nl; Jongkindstraat 25; adult/student/child under 18yr €10/6.50/free; ⊙10am-5pm Tue-Sat; Ⓜ Eendrachtsplein,

ℹ ROTTERDAM WELCOME CARD

The **Rotterdam Welcome Card** (adult per 1/2/3 days €12/17/21) gives discounts of up to 25% on museum and attraction admission charges, as well as free public transport on RET metro, tram and bus services. Purchase it at Rotterdam's tourist offices.

☒Museumpark) When company director Albertus Sonneveld decided to commission an architect to design a contemporary home for his family, the obvious choice was Leendert van der Vlugt, who had designed the magnificent Van Nelle Factory. Working with Johannes Brinkman, Van der Vlugt designed a streamlined, state-of-the-art building that was hailed as an outstanding example of Dutch Functionalism as soon as its construction was completed in 1933. Replete with original fittings and furniture, it can now be visited with a fascinating audio tour.

Museum Rotterdam '40-'45 NU   MUSEUM

(War & Resistance Museum; www.40-45nu.nl; Coolhaven 375; adult/child 4-17yr €7.50/2.50; ⊙10am-5pm Sat, 11am-5pm Sun; Ⓜ Coolhaven) Good things often come in small packages, and so it is with this small but excellent museum sheltered under a bridge on the Coolhaven. An eight-minute immersive multimedia experience outlines the terror and destruction caused by the bombing of Rotterdam on 14 May 1940, when 54 German aircraft dropped 1300 bombs on the city over a 13-minute period. Artefact-driven displays focus on all aspects of the wartime experience, interspersing tales of optimism and bravery among many sad stories.

★ Van Nelle Fabriek   NOTABLE BUILDING

(Van Nelle Factory; www.vannellefabriek.com; Van Nelleweg 1, Spaanse Polder; ☒38 & B9 from Centraal Station) Designed and built between 1925 and 1931, this modernist World Heritage–listed factory northwest of the city centre is an icon of 20th-century industrial architecture. Often described as a 'glass palace' (it's largely constructed of steel and glass), it functioned as a state-of-the-art coffee, tea and tobacco factory until the 1990s and now houses creative industries. Though closed to the public, the factory sometimes offers guided tours on weekends at 1pm (adult/child under 13 years €8.50/5);

Rotterdam

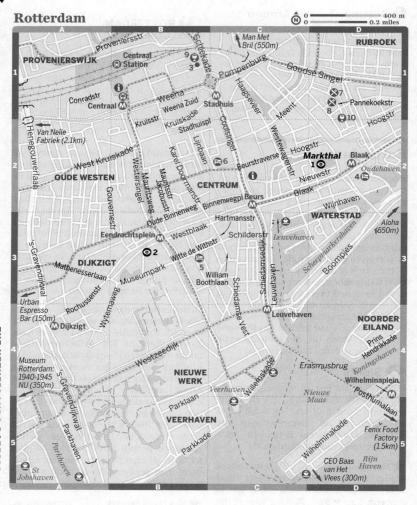

Rotterdam

check the factory website for details. **Urban Guides** (☏ 010-433 22 31; www.urbanguides.nl; Schiekade 205; boat tour adult/child under 12yr €17/free; ☉ office 10am-6pm Mon-Sat, noon-5pm Sun; Ⓜ Stadhuis, 🚋 Pompenburg, Weena, Stadhuis) also runs one-hour guided tours (€15 per person) at noon on most Saturdays and Sundays (book ahead).

🛏 Sleeping

★ King Kong Hostel   HOSTEL $
(☏ 010-818 87 78; www.kingkonghostel.com; Witte de Withstraat 74; dm €19-26, d €75-105; 🛜; Ⓜ Beurs, 🚋 Museumpark) There's plenty to like about this hip hostel in Rotterdam's major party precinct. Female and mixed-sex dorms sleep between four and 18, with bunks, under-bed lockers and plenty of power points. Shared bathrooms are modern and clean. Facilities include a laundry (€8 per load wash and dry), a luggage room, a communal kitchen, bike storage, a chill space and a ground-floor cafe.

★ Citizen M   BOUTIQUE HOTEL $$
(☏ 010-810 81 00; www.citizenm.com; Gelderse Plein 50; r from €66; 🅿@🛜; Ⓜ Blaak, 🚋 Blaak) A new-generation hostel for travellers who have progressed past dorms and shared bathrooms but want to recreate the casual conviviality of backpacker joints, Citizen M is as welcoming as it is well located. Capsule-like rooms are comfortable enough, with Smart TVs offering channels and free movies. The 1st floor bar, cafe and lounge are super-stylish spaces where you can relax or work.

Urban Residences   APARTMENT $$
(☏ 010-414 32 99; www.urbanresidences.com; Hennekijnstraat 104; studio €95-150, 2-bedroom apt €220-280; 🅿✳🛜; Ⓜ Beurs) You'll get a real taste of inner-city Rotterdam life when staying at these sleek apartments in the centre of town. Scattered over 15 floors of a recently constructed high-rise building, there are 76 generously sized apartments – many with impressive views. The Alessi interior fit-outs have a sternly minimalist decor but are very comfortable, offering couches, dining tables and well-equipped kitchens.

🍴 Eating

Rotterdam is replete with informal eateries and has two great food markets – the Markthal (p813) and **Fenix Food Factory** (www. fenixfoodfactory.nl; Veerlaan 19d, Katendrecht; ☉ 10am-7pm Tue-Thu, to 8pm Fri, to 6pm Sat, noon-6pm Sun, individual stall hours vary; 🅿🚻; Ⓜ Rijnhaven) 🌱 – with eateries alongside produce stalls.

★ Urban Espresso Bar   CAFE $
(UEB West; ☏ 010-477 01 88; www.urbanespresso bar.nl; Nieuwe Binnenweg 263; sandwiches €5-6, mains €7-9; ☉ 9am-6pm Mon-Sat, 10am-6pm Sun; 🛜🚻; 🚋 Claes de Vrieselaan) Could this be Rotterdam's best cafe? The coffee here is definitely a cut above most of its competitors (Giraffe beans, expert baristas), as is the food (artisanal breads and pastries, house-baked cakes, global flavours, organic ingredients). We can highly recommend the *tosties* (toasted sandwiches), soups and burgers, and we always enjoy chatting with fellow customers at the communal table. Cash only.

Tante Nel   FAST FOOD $
(www.tante-nel.com; Pannekoekstraat 53a; fries €2.50-8.75; ☉ noon-10pm Mon-Sat, to 9pm Sun; 🚋 Meent) Differing from traditional *patat* (fries) stands in a number of crucial ways, Tante Nel has pleasant street-side seating where its many and varied regulars settle in to enjoy treats such as hand-cut, expertly cooked fries with truffle mayonnaise or *patat stoofvlees* (fries topped with a rich meat stew), washed down with a gin and tonic, beer or milkshake.

★ AJÍ   INTERNATIONAL $$
(☏ 010-767 01 69; www.restaurantaji.nl; Pannekoekstraat 40a; snacks €5-24, small plates €16-24; ☉ noon-2pm & 5-10pm Tue-Thu, noon-11pm Fri & Sat; 🚋 Meent) Good-quality Asian food is hard to source in Rotterdam, so we were thrilled to discover this chic bistro serving dishes inspired by Asia and the Mediterranean. Build a meal with a few small plates, or just pop in for drinks and a platter of oysters or Spanish cured meats. There are good wines by the glass and bottle too.

★ CEO Baas van Het Vlees   STEAK $$$
(☏ 010-290 94 54; www.ceobaasvanhetvlees. nl; Sumatraweg 1-3, Katendrecht; mains €21-39;

DON'T MISS

WORLD-CLASS JAZZ FEST

North Sea Jazz Festival (www. northseajazz.nl; ☉ mid-Jul) One of the world's most respected jazz events sees hundreds of musicians perform. A free 'North Sea Round Town' festival in the weeks preceding the festival proper sees a variety of jazz acts performing in public spaces and concert halls around the city.

THE NETHERLANDS ROTTERDAM

⏱ 5-11pm Tue-Sat; Ⓜ Rijnhaven) Meat lovers should be sure to book a table at Rotterdam's best steakhouse. Working in their open kitchen, chefs cook spectacular cuts of beef to order. We love the fact that half portions of steak and delicious desserts are offered, and we have rarely been so impressed by a wine list (by both glass and bottle). Truly excellent.

🍷 Drinking & Nightlife

There's no lack of cafes, cocktail bars, microbreweries and pubs with alfresco summer seating. Witte de Withstraat is the main bar street.

★ Aloha
BAR

(📋 010-210 81 70; www.alohabar.nl; Maasboulevard 100; ⏱ noon-11pm Sun-Thu, to 1am Fri & Sat; Ⓜ Oostplein) 🌿 Sustainable, innovative and funky as anything, this bar-cafe in the former Tropicana baths has a large terrace boasting views across the Nieuwe Maas river. Operated by Blue City collective, a group of environmental entrepreneurs, it's a fabulous spot for summer lunches (sandwiches €6 to €9; snacks €5 to €13) or a drink accompanied by the house speciality, mushroom *bitterballen* (deep-fried croquette balls).

★ Biergarten
BEER GARDEN

(📋 010-233 05 56; www.biergartenrotterdam.nl; Schiestraat 18; ⏱ noon-midnight or later; Ⓜ Centraal Station) A sun-bleached labyrinth of wooden tables, brightly painted stairs, exotic foliage and low-slung festoon lighting, the Biergarten throngs with thirsty locals enjoying ice-cold pilsner, homemade lemonade and a tempting selection of barbecued

---

DON'T MISS

CRAFT COFFEE

Rotterdam's first artisanal coffee roastery (there are now 12), **Man Met Bril** (www.manmetbrilkoffie.nl; Vijverhofstraat 70; ⏱ 8am-5pm Mon-Fri, 9pm-6pm Sat & Sun; 🚊; 🚉 Schiekade, Walenburgerweg) sources direct-trade, 90% organic beans from across the globe and then roasts them in this hip space under a railway viaduct north of Centraal Station. The on-site cafe expertly prepared brews, cakes and sandwiches. Arrive before 10am to take advantage of the generous and dirt-cheap breakfast deal (€6.66).

---

meats. On Fridays, DJs preside over the always-inclusive action.

Bokaal
BAR

(📋 010-720 08 98; www.bokaalrotterdam.nl; Nieuwemarkt 11; ⏱ 11am-1am Sun-Thu, to 2am Fri & Sat; 🚉 Meent) In a *bokaal* (trophy) location at the heart of the enclave around pedestrian Nieuwemarkt and Pannekoekstraat, Bokaal has an indoor bar and a huge all-day sun terrace that heaves with people on summer nights. Beer (craft and Trappist) is its speciality, with nine on tap, and more than 80 in bottles. There's a food menu, but many take advantage of on-site food trucks.

ℹ Information

Tourist Office (📋 010-790 01 85; www.rotterdam.info; Coolsingel 114; ⏱ 9.30am-6pm; 🚊; Ⓜ Beurs) Main tourist office.

Tourist Office (www.rotterdam.info; Stationsplein 21, Centraal Station; ⏱ 9am-5.30pm Sun-Wed, 9am-8pm Thu-Sat mid-Aug–early Jul, 9am-7pm early Jul–mid-Aug) Centraal Station branch.

ℹ Getting There & Around

Rotterdam's main train station is **Rotterdam Centraal** (www.ns.nl/stationsinformatie/rtd/rotterdam-centraal; Stationsplein 1; Ⓜ Centraal Station, 🚉 Centraal) (CS). Major services include to/from Amsterdam (€15.40 to 17.80, 40 to 75 minutes), Schiphol airport (€12.40-14.80, 25-50 minutes) and Utrecht (€10.50, 40 minutes).

Rotterdam's tram, bus and metro services are provided by RET (www.ret.nl). Most converge near Rotterdam Centraal Station. A rechargeable two-hour ticket/day pass costs €3.50/13.50. **Zwann Bikes** (📋 010-412 62 20; www.czwaan.nl; Weena 703-707; per day standard/electric bike €12.50/17.50; ⏱ 7.30am-7.30pm Mon-Fri, 9am-7.30pm Sat & Sun) rents out bikes.

Utrecht

📋 030 / POP 345,100

It's hard not to fall in love with Utrecht, one of the Netherlands' oldest urban centres and a vibrant university city. Its compact medieval core radiates out from the iconic 15th-century Domtoren, ringed by a loop of very pretty tree-lined canals. Their central sections have distinctive double-level sides inset with what were once medieval warehouses – many now form fascinating venues to eat, drink, dance or sleep with terrace-walkways that extend right to the

DELFSHAVEN

Just 3km southwest of Rotterdam's centre, Delfshaven, once the official seaport for the city of Delft, survived the war and retains a village-like atmosphere. Take trams 4 or 8, or the metro to the Delfshaven station.

waterside. The brilliant cafe culture goes well beyond the canals – Utrecht's vibrant concert schedules are a big draw.

◉ Sights

There's plenty to see around **Domplein**, the heart of the city in a space where a cathedral should be. A tips-based three-hour 'free' walking tour starts outside Domtoren on Saturdays (noon) and Sundays (2pm).

Domtoren   HISTORIC BUILDING
(Cathedral Tower; www.domtoren.nl; Domplein 9; tower tour adult/student/child €9/7.50/5; ⊙11am-5pm Tue-Sat, noon-4pm Sun) Utrecht's most striking medieval landmark, this 112m tower is worth the 465-step climb for unbeatable city views: on a clear day you can see Amsterdam. Visits are by guided tour only, departing at least hourly on the hour. Buy tickets at the tourist office (p818) across the square or prebook online (advisable in summer). The tower was originally part of a splendid 14th or 15th-century **cathedral** (www.domkerk.nl; Achter de Dom 1; €2.50 donation; ⊙11am-3.30pm or longer Mon-Sat, 12.30-4pm Sun) complex whose nave was blown down by a freak hurricane in 1674.

★Dom Under   ARCHAEOLOGICAL SITE
(www.domunder.nl; Domplein 4; adult/child €12.50/10; ⊙tours hourly 11.30am-4.30pm Tue-Fri, from 10.30am Sat & Sun) Talented volunteer guides and fascinating educational films with CGI effects set the historical scene. Then it's your turn to become an amateur archaeologist as you're let loose in the subterranean half-dark beneath Domplein with your finger on the trigger of a smart-torch audio-gun. Finding clue-targets, you unravel the meaning of rubble-strata and the odd pottery piece, identifying relics of Utrecht's original Roman *castrum* and its early churches.

Museum Catharijneconvent   MUSEUM
(🖉030-231 38 35; www.catharijneconvent.nl; Lange Nieuwestraat 38; adult/senior/student &

child €14/12.50/7; ⊙10am-5pm Tue-Fri, from 11am Sat & Sun) Museum Catharijneconvent has the finest collection of medieval religious art in the Netherlands – virtually the history of Christianity, in fact – housed in a Gothic former convent and an 18th-century canal-side house. Marvel at the many beautiful illuminated manuscripts, look for the odd Rembrandt and enjoy the wide-ranging scope of the impressive special exhibitions.

★Rietveld-Schröderhuis   HISTORIC BUILDING
(🖉reservations 030-236 23 10; www.rietveldschroderhuis.nl; Prins Hendriklaan 50; €16.50; ⊙tours hourly 11am-4pm Tue-Sun, to 8pm some Fri; 🚍8) Years ahead of its time, this small but uniquely conceived house was built in 1924 by celebrated Utrecht designer Gerrit Rietveld. He'd be amazed to find that it's now a Unesco-recognised monument. Visiting feels like walking into a 3D Piet Mondrian abstract, and things get especially interesting when the walls start to move. To see a contextualising video, arrive 20 minutes before your assigned tour time (booking ahead is mandatory; an eight-language audio guide is included).

🛏 Sleeping

Strowis Hostel   HOSTEL $
(🖉030-238 02 80; www.strowis.nl; Boothstraat 8; dm €22-28, s/d €72.50/82.50, s/d/tr without bathroom €62.50/72.50/95; @🛜) Utrecht's most appealing hostel occupies a high-ceilinged 17th-century building; the dorms don't feel overly cramped even in the 16-bunk room. In the basement, luggage lockers (free with a €10 deposit) are good-sized and some incorporate a charger plug. The appealing cafe-lounge area opens on to a quirky rear garden. The small but well-equipped kitchen closes at 10.30pm.

★Mother Goose Hotel   HERITAGE HOTEL $$
(🖉030-303 63 00; www.mothergoosehotel.com; Ganzenmarkt 26; r €120-250; 🛜) Sensitively restored from what was originally a fortified 13th-century mansion, this 23-room boutique hotel incorporates many salvaged historic details and time-stressed artefacts into rooms full of contemporary comforts. The chatty local staff add a very personal touch, and the reception is wonderfully homey – you might even find a handwritten welcome postcard on your bed.

🍴 Eating & Drinking

Wharf-side restaurants on the Oudegracht and terrace places along narrow Dreiharingstraat

DUTCH DAYS OUT

Other Netherlands highlights worth considering for day trips or longer visits:

Alkmaar Its cheese ceremony (Fridays from the first Friday of April to the first Friday of September) dates from the 17th century.

Hoge Veluwe National Park Beautiful landscape of forests, dunes and marshes, with a bonus of a Van Gogh-rich art museum on-site.

Kinderdijk & Dordrecht A good day trip by fast ferry from Rotterdam is to visit Kinderdijk's Unesco-listed windmills then Dordrecht's medieval canals.

Gouda The perfect cheesy Dutch town.

Texel Largest of the Frisian Islands, with endless walks along dune-backed beaches and excellent local seafood.

are appealing but tourist-centred. Increasingly fashionable, student-oriented Voorstraat has bargain-value takeaway, oriental and snack foods. Cheap pizza places compete on Nobelstraat.

★**Heron** EUROPEAN $$
(☎030-230 22 29; www.heronrestaurant.nl; Schalkwijkstraat 26-28; 1-/2-/3-/4-/5-course meals €22/33/35/40/45; ☉5.30-9.30pm Tue-Sat) This adorable 'petit restaurant' presents expectant diners with a list of cryptic clues to a dinner that's brimming with imaginative flavours and is eminently seasonal. Expect 100% locally sourced fare including foraged plants collected by the forester owner. Six lucky guests get to sit right at the central cooking counter and watch every move of the expert chefs.

Olivier BROWN CAFE
(https://utrecht.cafe-olivier.be; Achter Clarenburg 6a; ☉11am-midnight Sun-Wed, 10am-2am Thu-Sat) Located unpromisingly beside the ugly Hoog Catharijne building is this blessed beer heaven, an astonishingly slick yet super-characterful reworking of a large former church, complete with organ.

ℹ Information

Tourist Office (VVV; ☎030-236 00 04; www.visit-utrecht.com; Domplein 9; ☉11.45am-5pm Mon, 10am-5pm Tue-Sat, noon-5pm Sun)

ℹ Getting There & Away

Regular direct services from Utrecht CS (Centraal Station) include Amsterdam (€7.60, 27 minutes), Den Haag (€11.20, 40 minutes), Maastricht (€23.90, two hours) and Rotterdam (€10.50, 37 minutes).

THE SOUTH

Actual hills rise on the Netherlands' southern edge, where Belgium and Germany are within range of a tossed wooden shoe. The star here is Maastricht.

Maastricht

☑043 / POP 122,500

Lively and energetic, Maastricht has Roman history, a maze of tunnel-caves and historical buildings aplenty, plus a Burgundian sophistication to its dining, a bacchanalian delight to its drinking culture, and a student-friendly street-life of all proportion to its size. *Everything* stops for the orgy of partying and carousing during Carnaval in February or March.

◉ Sights

Maastricht's greatest charm is exploring the compact area of narrow, cafe-filled streets on both sides of the pedestrianised Sint Servaasbrug, notably between the three main squares: Vrijthof, Markt and Onze Lieve Vrowplein.

★**St Servaasbasiliek** CHURCH
(www.sintservaas.nl; Keizer Karelplein 3; adult/child €4.50/3; ☉10am-5pm Mon-Sat, from 12.30pm Sun) Built above and around the shrine of St Servaas (Servatius), the first bishop of Maastricht, the basilica presents an architectural pastiche whose earliest sections date from 1000 CE. Its beautiful curved brick apse and towers dominate the Vrijthof. Tickets include access to the cloister garden and the four-room treasury whose star attractions are St Servaas' gilded bust and 11th-century sarcophagus.

Maastricht Underground CAVE
(☎043-325 21 21; www.maastrichtunderground.nl; Luikerweg 71; cave tour adult/child €6.25/5, combination tour €9.95/6.95) Maastricht Underground runs spooky, amusing and fascinating tours into sections of the vast tunnel network beneath St-Pietersberg massif. De-

partures run on a constantly shifting schedule, with up to five tours daily in summer, but very few in the off season – check the website.

Bonnefantenmuseum   GALLERY
(☑ 043-329 01 90; www.bonnefanten.nl; Ave Cèramique 250; adult/child €12.50/free; ☺ 11am-5pm Tue-Sun) Maastricht's star gallery has an excellent collection of early European painting and sculpture on the 1st floor, but is best known for contemporary art, with works by Limburg artists displayed upstairs; accessed via a dramatic sweep of stairs. There are regularly changing exhibitions.

🛏 Sleeping & Eating

Maastricht has many excellent dining addresses. Browse the eastern end of Tongersestraat and the little streets around the Vrijthof and Rechtstraat, just east of the river.

★ Kruisherenhotel   BOUTIQUE HOTEL $$$
(☑ 043-329 20 20; www.kruisherenhotel.nl; Kruisherengang 19-23; r weekday/weekend from €195/279; ❅ @ 🛜) This prize-winning design statement is housed inside the former Crutched Friar monastery complex, dating from 1483. Modern touches, such as moulded furniture and padded walls, accent the historical surroundings. Each of the 60 sumptuous rooms is unique. Some have murals and artwork; others are in the rafters of the old church. Breakfast is suitably heavenly.

★ Witloof   BELGIAN $$
(☑ 043-323 35 38; www.witloof.nl; Sint Bernardusstraat12; mains €17.50-21.50, 2-/3-course dinner €27/33; ☺ 5.30-9.30pm Wed-Sun) A decade after hitting the *New York Times'* list of world's trendiest restaurant concepts, Witloof still cuts the mustard with top-quality Belgian traditional food, an astounding beer cellar (do take a look!) and a tongue-in-cheek humour with decor worthy of a 21st-century Magritte.

ℹ Information

Tourist Office (VVV; ☑ 043-325 21 21; www.vvvmaastricht.nl; Kleine Straat 1; ☺ 10am-6pm Mon, 11am-5pm Sat & Sun)

ℹ Getting There & Away

There is an hourly international train service to Liège (€6.80, 33 minutes), from where fast trains depart for Brussels, Paris and Cologne. Domestic services include Amsterdam (€25.30,

2½ hours, two per hour) and Utrecht (€23.90, two hours, two per hour).

SURVIVAL GUIDE

ℹ Directory A–Z

ACCESSIBLE TRAVEL

The Netherlands ensures a certain level of accessibility for people with disabilities, particularly when it comes to public buildings, spaces and transport. However, older buildings may not be wheelchair-accessible and cobblestoned streets may be an issue for the mobility- or vision-impaired. The Dutch national organisation for people with a disability is **ANGO** (www.ango.nl).

ACCOMMODATION

Reserve ahead in high season (especially August) or during a big event.

B&Bs Very common in the countryside, and increasingly popular in towns and cities; some have automatic check-in.

Camping Campgrounds range from wild and remote to larger sites with luxury tents to rent and ample facilities.

Hostels Often design-driven, with dorms and private single and double rooms.

Hotels These embrace every budget. The bulk are standard and highly functional; a few are boutique.

DISCOUNT CARDS

Museumkaart (Museum Card; www.museumkaart.nl; adult/child €59.90/32.45, plus registration fee €4.95) offers free and discounted entry to some 400 museums all over the country, valid for one year, but strictly limited to five museum visits during the first 31 days. Purchase a temporary card at participating museums and validate online prior to initial one-month expiry.

INTERNET ACCESS

➡ Free wi-fi is widespread in hotels, restaurants, bars and coffeeshops, co-working cafes, tourist offices and other public places.

➡ In Amsterdam you can hire a pocket-sized mobile wi-fi device to carry around with you from **Pocket Wifi Amsterdam** (www.pocketwifi-amsterdam.com); order online and arrange delivery to your hotel or apartment or to Schiphol airport.

LEGAL MATTERS

➡ Technically, marijuana is illegal. However, possession of soft drugs (eg cannabis) up to 5g is tolerated. Larger amounts are subject to prosecution.

➡ In April 2018 Den Haag became the first Dutch city to officially ban smoking cannabis in its city centre, train station and major shopping areas.

➡ Smoking (anything) is banned in all public places. In a uniquely Dutch solution, you can still smoke tobacco-free pot in coffeeshops.

➡ Possession of hard drugs is treated as a serious crime.

MONEY

ATMs are widely available. Credit cards are accepted in most hotels, but not all restaurants, cafes and shops. Non-European credit cards are quite often rejected.

OPENING HOURS

Banks 9am–4pm Monday to Friday, some Saturday morning

Cafes and bars Open noon (exact hours vary); most close 1am Sunday to Thursday, 3am Friday and Saturday

Museums 10am–5pm daily, some close Monday

Restaurants Lunch 11am–2.30pm, dinner 6–10pm

Shops 10am or noon to 6pm Tuesday to Friday, 10am–5pm Saturday and Sunday, noon or 1pm to 5pm or 6pm Monday (if at all)

Supermarkets 8am–8pm

PUBLIC HOLIDAYS

Nieuwjaarsdag (New Year's Day) 1 January. Parties and fireworks galore.

Goede Vrijdag Good Friday

Eerste Paasdag Easter Sunday

Tweede Paasdag Easter Monday

Koningsdag (King's Day) 27 April (26 April if the 27th is a Sunday)

Bevrijdingsdag (Liberation Day) 5 May. Not a universal holiday: government workers have the day off, but almost everyone else has to work.

Hemelvaartsdag (Ascension Day) Fortieth day after Easter Sunday

Eerste Pinksterdag (Whit Sunday; Pentecost) Fiftieth day after Easter Sunday

Tweede Pinksterdag (Whit Monday) Fiftieth day after Easter Monday

ℹ HOLLAND OR THE NETHERLANDS?

'Holland' is a popular synonym for the Netherlands, yet it only refers to the combined provinces of Noord-Holland (North Holland) and Zuid-Holland (South Holland). The rest of the country is not Holland, even if the Dutch themselves often make the mistake.

Eerste Kerstdag (Christmas Day) 25 December

Tweede Kerstdag ('Second Christmas' aka Boxing Day) 26 December

SAFE TRAVEL

The Netherlands is a safe country, but be sensible all the same and always lock your bike. Never buy drugs on the street: it's illegal. And don't light up joints just anywhere – stick to coffeeshops.

TELEPHONE

The Dutch phone network, **KPN** (www.kpn.com), is efficient. Prices are reasonable by European standards.

ℹ Getting There & Away

AIR

Amsterdam's huge Schiphol International Airport (p807) is the country's main air-travel hub, with flights to/from cities all over the world. Within Europe, low-cost airlines land/take off in **Rotterdam** (RTM; ☎ 010-446 34 44; www.rotterdamthehagueairport.nl; ☎) and **Eindhoven** (EIN; www.vliegeindhovenairport.nl; Luchthavenweg 25; ⊘ 4.30am-midnight).

LAND
Bus

Eurolines (www.eurolines.com) Cheap international bus services to/from the Netherlands.

Busabout (www.busabout.com) From May to October, buses complete set circuits around Europe, stopping at major cities.

Flixbus (www.flixbus.com) Low-cost, intercity bus travel between 27 European countries aboard comfy buses.

IC Bus (www.dbicbus.com) Bus links between the Netherlands and Germany.

Car & Motorcycle

➡ Drivers need vehicle registration papers, third-party insurance and their domestic licence. Get a Green Card from your insurer to show you have coverage.

➡ **ANWB** (www.anwb.nl) provides information, maps, advice and services if you show a membership card from your own automobile association, like the AA or AAA.

➡ Hitching is uncommon.

Train

International train connections are good. All Eurail and Inter-Rail passes are valid on the Dutch national train service, **NS** (Nederlandse Spoorwegen; www.ns.nl). Many international services are operated by **NS International** (www.nsinternational.nl).

Thalys (www.thalys.com) fast trains serve Brussels (where you can connect to the Eurostar) and Paris. Twice-daily **Eurostar** (www.

ℹ FARES, TICKETS & OV-CHIPKAARTS

The easiest and cheapest way to travel with a ticket on trains and public transport (buses, trams and metros) is with a credit-loaded, plastic smart card known as an OV-chipkaart (www.ov-chipkaart.nl).

➡ Purchase an OV-chipkaart (€7.50), valid for five years, as soon as you arrive in the Netherlands at a train station, public-transport information office, supermarket or newsagent. Online, buy one in advance at www.public-transport-holland.com.

➡ Two types of OV-chipkaarts exist: 'anonymous' OV-chipkaarts are aimed at tourists and short-term visitors; 'personal' OV-chipkaarts require an address of residence in the Netherlands, Belgium, Germany or Luxembourg.

➡ To travel using your card, you must charge it with credit (minimum €10 on buses, or €20 to use it on NS trains) at any public-transport or station information counter or ticketing machine; the card must have sufficient credit to cover the cost of your journey.

➡ When you enter and exit a bus, tram or metro station, hold the card against a reader at the doors or station gates. The system then calculates your fare and deducts it from the card. If you don't check out, the system will deduct the highest fare possible. At train stations, card readers are strategically placed at platform entrances and exits.

➡ Upon departure from the county, you can retrieve any leftover credit from your card at any public-transport or station information counter; you'll pay a €1 fee to do this.

➡ For single journeys, if you don't have an OV-chipkaart, you can effectively purchase a more expensive, single-use, disposable OV-chipkaart each time you board a bus or tram, or buy a train ticket. On trains, this translates in reality as a €1 surcharge per transaction on top of the regular train fare.

➡ Some trams have conductors responsible for ticketing, while on others the drivers handle tickets. It is no longer possible to pay by cash on public transport in Amsterdam.

eurostar.com) services link London St Pancras with Rotterdam (three hours) and Amsterdam (3¾ hours).

German ICE high-speed trains run daily between Amsterdam and Cologne (from €35.90, three hours). Many continue to Frankfurt (from €45.90, four to 4¾ hours) via Frankfurt Airport.

Reserve seats in advance during peak periods. Buy tickets online at **SNCB Europe** (www.b-europe.com).

SEA

Several companies operate car/passenger ferries between the Netherlands and the UK:

Stena Line (www.stenaline.co.uk) sails between Harwich and Hoek van Holland, 31km northwest of Rotterdam, linked to central Rotterdam by train (30 minutes).

P&O Ferries (www.poferries.com) operates an overnight ferry every evening (11¾ hours) between Hull and Europoort, 39km west of central Rotterdam. Book bus tickets (40 minutes) to/from Rotterdam when you reserve your berth.

DFDS Seaways (www.dfdsseaways.co.uk) sails between Newcastle and IJmuiden, 30km northwest of Amsterdam, linked to Amsterdam by bus; the 15-hour sailings depart daily.

ℹ Getting Around

The Netherlands' compact size makes it a breeze to get around.

Bicycle Short- and long-distance bike routes lace the country and you are often pedalling through beautiful areas. All but the smallest train stations have bike-rental shops, as does every town and city.

Bus Cheaper and slower than trains but useful for remote villages not serviced by rail.

Car Good for visiting regions with minimal public transport. Drive on the right.

Train Service is fast, distances short, and trains frequent; buy an OV-chipkaart to get cheaper tickets and use on other forms of public transport too.

North Macedonia

📞 389 / POP 2.08 MILLION

Best Places to Eat

➡ Letna Bavča Kaneo (p836)

➡ Hotel Tutto Restaurant (p831)

➡ Vila Raskrsnica (p838)

➡ Nadžak (p828)

➡ Kebapčilnica Destan (p828)

Best Places to Stay

➡ Vila Raskrsnica (p838)

➡ Villa Dihovo (p838)

➡ Sunny Lake Hostel (p835)

➡ Villa Jovan (p835)

➡ Urban Hostel & Apartments (p827)

Why Go?

Part Balkan, part Mediterranean and rich in Greek, Roman and Ottoman heritage, North Macedonia has a fascinating past and a complex national identity.

Glittering Lake Ohrid and its historic town have etched out a place for North Macedonia on the tourist map, but there is a wealth of natural beauty in this small country.

Dramatic mountains have blissfully quiet walking trails, lakes and riding opportunities. The national parks of Mavrovo, Galičica and Pelister are cultivating some excellent cultural and culinary tourism initiatives; if you want to get off the beaten track in Europe – this is the place.

Skopje's centre has suffered from a building spree of grotesque faux-neoclassical monuments, buildings and fountains, funded by the previous government. Luckily, its Ottoman old town and buzzing modern areas are untouched, and remain charming and authentic.

When to Go
Skopje

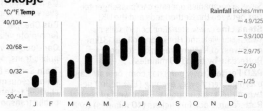

Jun–Aug Enjoy Ohrid's Summer Festival and dive into its 300m-deep lake.

Sep–Oct Partake in Skopje's jazz festival or merry-making at the Tikveš region's Wine Carnival.

Dec–Feb Ski Mavrovo, snuggle up beside fires in lodges and experience Ohrid out of season.

Entering the Country

Skopje and Ohrid are well connected to other Balkan tourist hubs as well as some international destinations further afield. Air connections have increased thanks to the growing number of budget airlines flying here. Buses are generally more frequent and cover a broader range of destinations than trains (they're also just as fast).

Some travellers have reported being denied entry to Serbia from North Macedonia if they have a stamp from Kosovo in their passport.

ITINERARIES

One Week

Spend a couple of days in Skopje (p824) amid the mind-boggling faux neoclassical architecture and in the Čaršija (p825) with its historic mosques, churches, museums and Ottoman castle. Visit the nearby Canyon Matka (p829) for kayaking and swimming in the cool waters.

Next head to North Macedonia's most charming and historic town, Ohrid (p833), for swimming in the spectacular lake. Stay in a village guesthouse on the edge of Pelister National Park (p837), with hiking and home cooking. Cross Lake Prespa for the pelican-inhabited, ruin-strewn island of Golem Grad (p833).

Two Weeks

Linger in Pelister National Park (p837) in order to stop in Bitola (p838), loved for its buzz, elegance and ancient Heraclea Lyncestis (p838) ruins.

Next visit Mavrovo National Park (p830) and stay in historic Janče (p831) and Galičnik (p831) villages for superb cuisine and horse riding. Visit the impressive Sveti Jovan Bigorski Monastery (p830).

Make a pit stop in the Tikveš Wine Region (p836) for tastings and a tour.

Essential Food & Drink

Ajvar Sweet red-capsicum dip; accompanies meats and cheeses.

Lukanci Homemade chorizo-like pork sausages, laced with paprika.

Pita A pie made of a coil of flaky pastry stuffed with local cheese and spinach or leek.

Rakija Grape-based fruit brandy.

Šopska salata Tomatoes, onions and cucumbers topped with grated *sirenje* (white cheese).

Tavče gravče Baked beans cooked with spices, onions and herbs, and served in earthenware.

Vranec & Temjanika North Macedonia's favourite red/white wine varietals.

AT A GLANCE

Area 25,713 sq km

Capital Skopje

Country Code ☑389

Currency North Macedonian denar (MKD)

Emergency Ambulance ☑194, Police ☑192

Language Macedonian, Albanian

Time Eastern European Time (GMT/UTC plus two hours)

Visas None for EU, US, Australian, Canadian or New Zealand citizens for stays of up to three months.

NORTH MACEDONIA

Sleeping Price Ranges

The following price ranges are based on a standard double with bathroom.

€ less than 3000MKD/€50

€€ 3000MKD/€50–5000MKD/€80

€€€ more than 5000MKD/€80

Eating Price Ranges

The following ranges refer to the average price of a main course.

€ less than 200MKD

€€ 200MKD–350MKD

€€€ more than 350MKD

Resources

Balkan Insight (www.balkaninsight.com)

Exploring Macedonia (www.exploringmacedonia.com)

North Macedonia Highlights

❶ Ohrid's Old Town
(p833) Exploring Ohrid's distinctive historic quarter, right to the end of the boardwalk and pebble beach, and up to the clifftop Church of Sveti Jovan at Kaneo.

❷ Skopje (p824) Diving into the historic Čaršija (Old Ottoman Bazaar) of North Macedonia's friendly capital, seeking out its modernist architecture and marvelling

at the supersized riverside monuments.

❸ Pelister National Park
(p837) Eating your fill on food-focused village tourism initiatives in this underrated national park, then walking it off the next day.

❹ Golem Grad (p833) Chasing ghosts, pelicans and tortoises around this eerie Lake Prespa island, fecund with overgrown ruins.

❺ Popova Kula (p836) Sipping your way through North Macedonia's premier wine region, Tikveš, using this wonderful winery hotel as your base.

❻ Sveti Jovan Bigorski Monastery (p830) Taking tea with monks at this majestic complex teetering in the hills of Mavrovo National Park.

SKOPJE СКОПЈЕ

♪ 02 / POP 506,930

Skopje has plenty of charm. Its Ottoman- and Byzantine-era sights are focused around the city's delightful Čaršija, bordered by the 15th-century Kameni Most (Stone Bridge)

and Tvrdina Kale Fortress – Skopje's guardian since the 5th century. Don't miss the excellent eating and drinking scene in Debar Maalo, a lovely tree-lined neighbourhood.

For most of its existence, Skopje has been a modest Balkan city known for its rich local life, but the last decade has seen its centre transformed into a bizarre set design for an ancient civilisation. Towering warrior statues, gleaming, enormous neoclassical buildings, marble-clad museums, hypnotic megafountains...and plenty of lions.

This is the result of a controversial, nationalistic project called 'Skopje 2014' implemented by ex–Prime Minister Nikola Gruevski. Some of the buildings along the riverbank are already suffering flooding and have unsteady foundations.

○ Sights

★ Čaršija
AREA

(Old Ottoman Bazaar) Čaršija is Skopje's hillside Ottoman old town, evoking the city's past with its winding lanes filled with teahouses, mosques, craftspeople's shops, and even good nightlife. It also boasts Skopje's best historic structures and a handful of museums, and is the first place any visitor should head. Čaršija runs from the Stone Bridge to the **Bit Pazar** (⊙8am-3pm), a big vegetable and household goods market. Expect to get pleasantly lost in its maze of narrow streets.

★ National Gallery of Macedonia
GALLERY

(Daut Paša Amam; www.nationalgallery.mk; Kruševska 1a; adult/student & child 50/20MKD; ⊙10am-6pm Tue-Sun Oct-Mar, to 9pm Apr-Sep) The Daut Paša Amam (1473) were once the largest Turkish baths outside of İstanbul and they make a magical setting for the permanent collection of Skopje's national art gallery, just by the entrance to the Čaršija. The seven restored rooms house mainly modern art and sculpture from North Macedonia, brought to life by the sun piercing through the small star-shaped holes in the domed ceilings. Two other National Gallery sites – **Čifte Amam** (Bitpazarska; adult/student & child 50/20MKD; ⊙10am-6pm Tue-Sun Oct-Mar, to 9pm Apr-Sep) and **Mala Stanica** (www.nationalgallery.mk; Jordan Mijalkov 18; adult/student & child 50/20MKD; ⊙8am-6pm Tue-Sun Oct-Mar, to 9pm Apr-Sep) – house rotating, temporary exhibitions.

★ Tvrdina Kale Fortress
FORTRESS

(Samoilova; ⊙7am-7pm) **FREE** Dominating the skyline of Skopje, this *Game of Thrones*-worthy, 6th-century CE Byzantine (and later, Ottoman) fortress is an easy walk up from the Čaršija and its ramparts offer great views over the city and river. Inside the ruins, two mini museums were being built at the time of writing to house various archaeological finds from Neolithic to Ottoman times. This will be a welcome addition to the site, as there are no information boards at the fortress at present.

Archaeological Museum of Macedonia
MUSEUM

(www.amm.org.mk; bul Goce Delčev; adult/student & child 300/150MKD; ⊙10am-6pm Tue-Sun) This supersized pile of Italianate-styled marble has been a giant receptacle for Skopje's recent splurge on government-led monuments to boost national pride. Inside, there are three floors displaying the cream of Macedonian archaeological excavations beneath the dazzle of hundreds of lights. Highlights include Byzantine treasures; sophisticated 3D reconstructions of early Macedonian faces from skulls; a pint-sized replica of an early Christian basilica showing the life phases of mosaic conservation; and a Phoenician royal necropolis.

Ploštad Makedonija
SQUARE

(Macedonia Sq) This gigantic square is the centrepiece of Skopje's audacious nation-building-through-architecture project and it has massive statues dedicated to national heroes, as well as an incongruous Triumphal Arch in the southeast corner. The towering, central warrior on a horse – Alexander the Great – is bedecked by fountains that are illuminated at night. Home to a number of cafes and hotels, it's a popular stomping ground for locals as well as tourists, particularly when the sun goes down.

Museum of Contemporary Art
MUSEUM

(NIMoCA; ☎02 311 7734; https://msu.mk; Samoilova 17; 300MKD, free 1st Fri of month; ⊙9am-5pm Tue-Sat, to 1pm Sun) Housed in a stunning modernist building with floor-to-ceiling windows and perched atop a hill with wonderful city views, this museum was built in the aftermath of Skopje's devastating 1963 earthquake. Artists and collections around the world donated works to form a collection that includes Picasso, Léger, Hockney, Meret Oppenheim and Bridget Riley. Unfortunately, its collection isn't always on display – you may come here and find its exhibitions extraordinary or mundane, depending on what's been put on display.

Sveti Spas Church
CHURCH

(Church of the Holy Saviour; Makarije Frčkoski 8; adult/student 120/50MKD; ⊙9am-5pm Tue-Fri, to 3pm Sat & Sun) Partially submerged 2m underground (the Ottomans banned churches from being taller than mosques), this church dates from the 14th century and is the most historically important in Skopje. Its sunken design means it doesn't look like a church, so you might not

Skopje

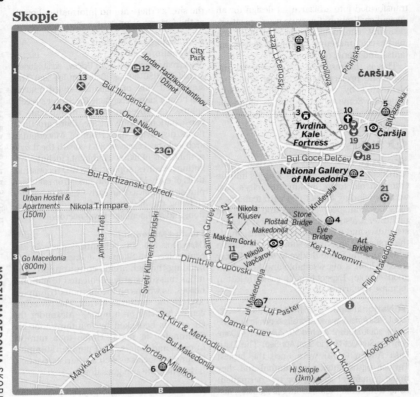

Skopje

◎ Top Sights

◎ Sights

✈ Activities, Courses & Tours

🛏 Sleeping

✖ Eating

◯ Drinking & Nightlife

✪ Entertainment

🛍 Shopping

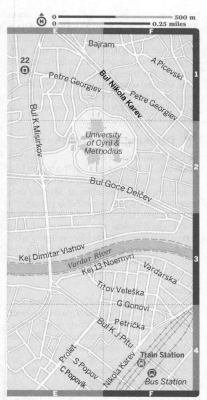

notice it at first: it's opposite the Old Town Brewery – look for the pretty bell tower that watches over it, built into its outer courtyard wall. Inside the church an elaborate carved iconostasis shines out of the dark.

Activities

Bicycle Tours & Guides Macedonia

CYCLING

(☏078 982 981; www.bicycle.mk; per day from 800MKD) Skopje's long riverside walkway is a magnet for cyclists, especially at dusk when joggers, strollers, kids playing football and anglers all come out too. Rent bikes by the day from this outfit; it'll even drop the bike (including helmet, lights and high-vis vest) at your hotel. Guided Skopje day tours and North Macedonia–wide adventures are also offered.

Tours

Skopje Walks

WALKING

(www.skopjewalks.com; ul Makedonija; donations welcome; ☉10am) **FREE** These excellent free tours run for three hours and cover every important corner of Skopje's inner city. Highly recommended for insights into the city, its history and residents from local guides who are passionate about Skopje. Tours meet outside the **Memorial House of Mother Teresa** (ul Makedonija 9) – look out for the blue ID badge – at 10am daily.

Festivals & Events

Skopje Jazz Festival

MUSIC

(☏02 313 1090; www.skopjejazzfest.com.mk; ☉Oct) The festival features artists from across the globe, always including a world-renowned player or group (Chick Corea, McCoy Tyner, Herbie Hancock and Tito Puente are some past headliners).

Sleeping

★Urban Hostel & Apartments

HOSTEL €

(☏02 614 2785; www.urbanhostel.com.mk; Adolf Ciborovski 22; dm/s/d €10/24/35, apt €35-70; ❋శ) In a converted residential house with a sociable front garden for summer lounging, Urban is an excellent budget option on the outskirts of the leafy Debar Maalo neighbourhood, a 15-minute walk west of central Skopje. Decor is eclectic, with a fireplace for cosy winter nights and even a piano. The hostel's modern apartments, on the same road, are great value.

Lounge Hostel

HOSTEL €

(☏076 547 165; www.loungehostel.mk; 1st fl, Naum Naumovski Borče 80; dm €9-10, s/d €25/30; ❋శ) A lovely large common area, orthopaedic mattresses and bright, breezy balconies attached to every room are some of the highlights of this sociable, retro-styled hostel with a view over City Park. Staff are a little less clued-up here than at some other hostels, but will bend over backwards to help make guests' lives easier.

Hi Skopje

HOSTEL €

(☏02 609 1242; www.hihostelskopje.com; Crniche 15; dm/d from €9/20) In a leafy, affluent suburb in the cool shade of Mt Vodno, this hostel's greatest assets are its garden and sprawling layout, which makes it feel more spacious than many others in town. It's a 15-minute walk to Ploštad Makedonija from here (and a 120MKD taxi ride from the bus and train stations), but the trade-off is a relaxing atmosphere.

★**Hotel Solun**   HOTEL €€€
(☑ 02 323 2512, 071 238 599; www.hotelsolun.com; Nikola Vapčarov 10; s/d from €83/103; ❋@🖥🌊) Accessed through an alley just off the main square, this is a stylish, beautifully designed place, with modern and elegantly decorated rooms, and an excellent art collection on the walls. A spa and an indoor pool beckon downstairs. Hotel Solun sits in a different stratosphere to most of North Macedonia's faded 'high-end' hotels.

✕ **Eating**

★**Nadžak**   MACEDONIAN €
(☑ 02 312 8113; Orce Nikolov 105; mains from 100MKD; ⏱8am-midnight; 🖥) It doesn't look like much, but the food at Nadžak is excellent, cheap and always fresh. All sorts of Macedonian specialities are on the menu, from *skara* (grilled meat) to liver to peppers and *tavče gravče* (oven-baked beans in tomato sauce). Everything tastes great – order several dishes and share. Seating is inside and on a covered terrace, in the heart of Debar Maalo.

★**Kebapčilnica Destan**   KEBAB €
(ul 104 6; mains 180MKD; ⏱8am-11pm) Skopje's best beef kebabs, accompanied by seasoned grilled bread, peppers and a little raw onion, are served at this classic Čaršija place. The terrace is often full. Ten stubby kebabs constitute a serious meat feast (180MKD), or you can ask for a half portion (120MKD). Pair the kebabs with *ajvar* (red-pepper dip) and a cabbage salad.

Barik   MACEDONIAN €
(☑070 360 601; Mihail Cokov 8; mains from 100MKD; ⏱8am-midnight) An excellent little taverna in Debar Maalo, with a great range of Macedonian specialities – try the veal liver with onion with some red wine or the baked cheese. Tables are scattered across the pavement and the whole place has a Mediterranean feel. It's very popular with the locals.

Sushico   ASIAN €€
(☑02 321 7874; www.sushico.com.mk; Aminta Treti 29; mains from 350MKD; ⏱11am-11.30pm; 🖥🍴) If you fancy a change of palate, this international chain serves a good range of pan-Asian specialities in an elegant setting (that includes the obligatory large Buddha statues). Try the avocado and quinoa rolls or the staple crispy duck, or choose from noodles, sushi or sashimi. There is a Sunday buffet brunch from noon to 4pm.

Kaj Pero   MACEDONIAN €€
(Orce Nikolov 109; mains 120-800MKD; ⏱9am-1am) This neighbourhood favourite in Debar Maalo has tables spilling out onto a leafy street, drawing a crowd of casual diners and drinkers. The menu is focused on *skara*, but there are also some inventive nongrill dishes and a good selection of local wines and *rakija* (fruit brandy). It's about a 10-minute walk west of central Skopje.

🍷 **Drinking & Nightlife**

★**Old Town Brewery**   CRAFT BEER
(Gradište 1; ⏱9am-midnight Sun-Thu, to 1am Fri & Sat; 🖥) The siren call of tasty craft beer sings to locals and tourists alike at Skopje's only microbrewery, which is justifiably popular for its Weiss beer, IPA, golden ale and dark beer – all brewed on-site and accompanied by a dependable menu of international pub grub. The sunny terrace, sandwiched between the walls of Tvrdina Kale Fortress (p825) and Sveti Spas Church, crowns its appeal.

Menada   BAR
(☑070 256 171; Kazandžiska 2; ⏱8am-1am) Popular with the local art and culture crowd, Menada often has live music – jazz, rock, folk – and a good atmosphere till the wee hours. The wood-panelled bar and terrace can get quite busy, so grab a table while you can. There are palatable snacks. It's right at the entry into the Čaršija.

Vinoteka Temov   WINE BAR
(Gradište 1a; ⏱9am-midnight) Skopje's best wine bar, in a restored wooden building near Sveti Spas Church, is refined and atmospheric. Knowledgeable staff offer a vast wine list starring the cream of North Macedonia's vineyards, though if you want to taste any of the better wines you'll need to buy a bottle as the glass selection is limited (as it is everywhere in North Macedonia, unfortunately).

☆ **Entertainment**

**Macedonian National
Opera and Ballet**   OPERA
(☑02 311 8451; http://mob.mk; Goce Delčev 4; tickets 400MKD) Set inside the most beautiful modernist building – designed by the Slovene architects Biro 71, completed in 1981 – this is where one can see classic opera and ballet pieces. Check the website for seasonal performances.

MT VODNO

Framing Skopje to the south, Vodno's towering mass – pinpointed by the 66m **Millennium Cross** – is an enduring symbol of the city. A popular (shaded) hiking trail cuts a swathe up its wooded slopes and there's also a gondola that climbs the mountainside from halfway up, where a couple of restaurants cater to day trippers. To get here, take the 'Millennium Cross' special bus (35MKD, 12 daily) from the bus station to the gondola. A taxi to the gondola costs about 200MKD, and the gondola round trip is 100MKD.

Up in the gods around the western side of Vodno, the village of Gorno Nerezi is home to **Sveti Pantelejmon Monastery** (1164), one of North Macedonia's most significant churches. Its Byzantine frescoes, such as the Lamentation of Christ, depict a pathos and realism predating the Renaissance by two centuries. It's 5km from Skopje city centre and it takes about 20 minutes to get here by taxi (350MKD, using the meter) because of the steep, windy road. The views from the monastery's terrace are sublime. Admission is 120MKD.

🛍 Shopping

⭐ **Monozero** ARTS & CRAFTS
(☑ 070 255 093; http://mono-zero.com; Kliment Ohridski 30; ⊙ 10.30am-6.30pm Mon-Fri, 10am-4pm Sat) A brilliant local carpentry enterprise, Monozero makes everything out of solid wood sourced from responsibly harvested forests. Each object is hand made using traditional craft techniques. You can pick up cheeseboards, chopping boards and candleholders, each smooth and beautiful and perfect for remembering North Macedonia, sustainably.

ℹ Information

Skopje's **tourist information centre** (Filip Makedonski; ⊙ 8.30am-4.30pm Mon-Fri) has maps and a range of countrywide promotional literature. Note that the advertised opening hours are not kept.

ℹ Getting There & Away

Skopje International Airport (☑ 02 314 8333; www.airports.com.mk; 1043, Petrovec) is located 21km east of the city centre.

Vardar Express (☑ 02 311 8263; www.vardar express.com) shuttle bus runs between the airport and the city; check the website for its timetable. Taxis to and from the airport cost 1200MKD.

Skopje's **bus station** (☑ 02 246 6313; www. sas.com.mk; bul Nikola Karev), with ATM, exchange office and English-language information office, adjoins the train station. Bus schedules are only available online in Macedonian (your hotel/hostel staff should be more than happy to translate for you, though).

ℹ Getting Around

➜ Buses congregate under the bus/train station; for Matka you need bus number 60 (70MKD) and for Vodno take the special 'Millennium Cross' bus (35MKD).

➜ Skopje's taxis aren't bad value, with the first kilometre costing just 40MKD, and 25MKD for subsequent kilometres.

➜ Drivers rarely speak English, but they do use their meters (if they don't, just ask/point).

AROUND SKOPJE

Canyon Matka

Ah, Matka. Early Christians, ascetics and revolutionaries picked a sublime spot when they retreated into the hills here from Ottoman advances: the setting is truly reverential. Matka means 'womb' in Macedonian and the site has a traditional link with the Virgin Mary.

Churches, chapels and monasteries have long been guarded by these forested mountains, though most have now been left to rack and ruin. Many of the modern-day villages in this area are majority Macedonian Albanian Muslim, though the population is sparse.

Canyon Matka is a popular day trip from Skopje and crowded at weekends; if you want peace and quiet, come early or stay overnight.

◉ Sights & Activities

⭐ **Sveta Bogorodica Monastery** MONASTERY
(Lake Matka; ⊙ 8am-8pm) **FREE** Framed by mountains and with a serene, peaceful atmosphere, Sveta Bogorodica is a really special spot. Still home to nuns, this working monastery has 18th-century wooden-balustraded living quarters. The beautiful 14th-century chapel has frescoes from the

1500s. A church has stood on this spot since the 6th century, evident from the crosses on the left-hand side of the entrance.

Bogorodica is clearly signposted from the road that leads to the Canyon Matka car park (buses drop passengers off here); walk up the short, steep hill directly above.

Church of Sveti Andrej CHURCH

(Lake Matka; ⊙ 10am-4pm) FREE The most easily accessible of Canyon Matka's 14th-century churches and also one of the finest, the petite Church of St Andrew (1389) is practically attached to the Canyon Matka Hotel and backed by the towering massif of the canyon walls. Inside, well-preserved painted frescoes depict apostles, holy warriors and archangels. Opening hours can be a bit erratic.

Cave Vrelo CAVE

(Matka boat kiosk; 400MKD; ⊙ 9am-7pm) A team of scuba divers from Italy and Belgium have explored Matka's underwater caverns to a depth of 212m and still not found the bottom, making these caves among the deepest in Europe. Cave Vrelo is open to the public – you can enter the inky depths of the bat-inhabited cave by boat or hired kayak.

Canyon Matka Kayaking KAYAKING

(single/double kayak per 30min 150/250MKD; ⊙ 9am-7pm) Kayaking through Matka's precipitous canyon is divine. This is a light paddle, where you can enjoy the rock formations and gorgeous sunlight – kayaks are the only watercraft allowed on the lake beside the licensed boat plying the route to Cave Vrelo. You can kayak to the cave and back; count on around two hours in total.

🛏 Sleeping & Eating

Canyon Matka Hotel LODGE €€

(☑ 02 205 2655; www.canyonmatka.mk; Lake Matka; d €39-60) The premium lakefront setting by the canyon walls makes this hotel a fine place for a night's rest, but it's more rough around the edges than might be expected and feels like an adjunct to its successful restaurant. The 2nd-floor rooms have charming wooden beams but are slightly smaller than those on the 1st floor.

Restaurant Canyon Matka MACEDONIAN €€

(☑ 02 205 2655; www.canyonmatka.mk/restaurant; Lake Matka; mains from 600MKD; ⊙ 8am-midnight) With a prime location just above the water, this is fine dining with a focus on the Macedonian and the Mediterranean. Order the grilled trout and salad with any of the good local wines and enjoy the beautiful views. Bring mosquito repellent for evenings.

ℹ Getting There & Away

From Skopje, catch bus 60 from Bul Partizanski Odredi or from the bus/train station (return 70MKD, 40 minutes, nine daily).

It is not possible to get to the main section of the lake, where the Canyon Matka Hotel and boat kiosk are, by car or bus. Taxis (450MKD) and the bus from Skopje will drop you about a 10- to 15-minute walk from there, at the public car park and a couple of riverside restaurants.

If you have your own wheels, the closest public car park to the lake is just before the pedestrian-only walkway, but it's a small car park up a steep hill and fills up quickly in summer and on weekends. Both car parks are free.

WESTERN NORTH MACEDONIA

Mavrovo National Park
Маврово Национален Парк

The gorges, pine forests, karst fields and waterfalls of Mavrovo National Park offer a breath of fresh, rarefied air for visitors travelling between Skopje and Ohrid. Beautiful vistas abound, and the park is home to North Macedonia's highest peak, Mt Korab (2764m). Locally the park is best known for its ski resort (the country's biggest) near Mavrovo town, but by international standards the skiing is fairly average. In summertime, the park is glorious.

Driving in the park is extremely scenic, but a word of caution: car GPS doesn't work well here and signposting is poor.

◉ Sights & Activities

★ Sveti Jovan
Bigorski Monastery MONASTERY

(⊙ services 5.30am, 4pm & 6pm) FREE This revered 1020 Byzantine monastery is located, fittingly, up in the gods along a track of switchbacks off the Debar road, close to Janče village. Legend attests an icon of Sveti Jovan Bigorski (St John the Baptist) miraculously appeared here, inspiring the monastery's foundation; since then the monastery has been rebuilt often – apparently, the icon has occasionally reappeared too. The complex went into demise during communist rule but has been painstakingly reconstructed and today is as impressive as ever, with some excellent views over Mavrovo's mountains.

Janče
VILLAGE

Just a blip on the map, the small village of Janče is one of the few places in Mavrovo (besides the ski resort) where it's possible to get decent accommodation. It's a picturesque spot that scales the hillside; the views from up here are awesome, even if the village itself feels like a forgotten corner of the country. Its cluster of stone houses includes some fascinating examples of decaying rural architecture with *bondruk* wooden frames, packed earthen walls and creaking wooden porches.

Galičnik
VILLAGE

Up a winding, tree-lined road ending in a rocky moonscape 17km southwest of Mavrovo, almost depopulated Galičnik features traditional houses along the mountainside. It's also famed for its traditional cheese-making. The village is placid except during the Galičnik Wedding Festival. A wonderful food and accommodation option is available with one of the few local families that live here year-round, and you can hike in the surrounding area, including to Janče.

Horse Club Bistra Galičnik
HORSE RIDING

(☑077 648 679; www.horseriding.com.mk) You can go on daily rides (2½ hours to 5½ hours) through Mavrovo's mountain valleys, departing from the village of Galičnik and dropping by traditional villages. The daily treks have cheese-tasting stops. Multiday excursions involve camping, cheese tasting and going up to the Medenica peak.

✵✰ Festivals & Events

★ Galičnik Wedding Festival
CULTURAL

(www.galichnik.mk; ⊙12–13 Jul) The small Mavrovo village of Galičnik is a placid rural outpost that bursts into life each July with a traditional wedding festival, when one or two lucky couples have their wedding here. It's a big two-day party that you can join, along with 3000 happy Macedonians. Everyone eats, drinks, and enjoys traditional folk dancing and music.

🛏 Sleeping & Eating

Baba i Dede
GUESTHOUSE €

(☑070 370 843, 077 854 256; Galičnik; r per person €20; ℙ🛜) Baba i Dede means Grandpa and Grandma – and indeed it's a pair of Galičnik ancients (more or less the only two people who live in the village year-round) who wel-

come you at this charming guesthouse with a restaurant. The four rooms are spacious and homely, and the traditional food is delicious, prepared by the ever-smiling Baba.

Sveti Jovan Bigorski Monastery
HOSTEL €

(☑Father Serges 070 304 316, Father Silvan 078 383 771; www.bigorski.org; Mavrovo National Park; dm €15-20; 🛎🛜) For a unique experience, you can bed down in one of North Macedonia's most famous monasteries for the night. Rooms are clustered in one wing of the religious complex and decorated, naturally, with traditional monastic furniture. Although the sleeping arrangements are effectively dorms, it's a far cry from the hard wooden bunks you might associate with the monks' pared-back lifestyle.

Hotel Tutto
HOTEL €€

(☑042 470 999; www.tutto.com.mk; Janče; s/d/tr €30/50/60, apt €40-50; ℙ🛎🛜) Welcome to one of North Macedonia's most enterprising community projects – an eco-hotel with a restaurant to die for. The setting in Janče is peaceful and lovely, and there are hiking trails at the hotel's front door. The 1st-floor rooms are exceedingly comfy: ask for one at the front to appreciate the view from your balcony.

★ Hotel Tutto Restaurant
MACEDONIAN €€

(☑042 470 999; www.tutto.com.mk; Janče; mains from 400MKD; ⊙8am-midnight) The owner of Tutto is a founding member of North Macedonia's Slow Food organisation, and his enthusiasm for local produce is infused in the restaurant kitchen. Macedonian specialities such as slow-roast lamb and *pita* (coiled filo pastry pies stuffed with spinach and cheese) are a must, and there are always fresh mushrooms on the menu, picked from the surrounding forest.

❶ Getting There & Away

➜ Without your own wheels, it's difficult to reach the various places of interest in the national park independently, or to do any hiking.

➜ For Sveti Jovan Bigorski Monastery, buses transiting Debar for Ohrid or Struga will be able to drop you off.

Lake Ohrid
☑046

Lake Ohrid, in its vastness and mystery, is a monumentally seductive attraction. Mirror-like and dazzling on sunny days, it's a truly beautiful place – especially in and around the ancient town of Ohrid.

At 300m deep, 34km long and three million years old, shared by North Macedonia (two-thirds) and Albania (one-third), Lake Ohrid is among Europe's deepest and oldest. The Macedonian portion is inscribed on the Unesco World Heritage list for its cultural heritage and unique nature – it's considered the most biodiverse lake of its size in the world.

◉ Sights

★ Sveti Naum Monastery   MONASTERY
(100MKD, parking 50MKD; ⊘ 7am-8pm Jun-Aug, closes at sunset rest of year) Sveti Naum, 29km south of Ohrid, is an imposing sight on a bluff near the Albanian border and a popular day trip from Ohrid. Naum was a contemporary of St Kliment, and their monastery an educational centre. The iconostasis inside the church dates to 1711 and the frescoes to the 19th century; it's well worth paying the fee to enter. Sandy beaches hem the monastery in on two sides and are some of the best places to swim around Lake Ohrid.

Vevčani   VILLAGE
Keeping one sleepy eye on Lake Ohrid from its mountain perch, Vevčani dates to the 9th century and is a quiet rural settlement beloved by locals for its traditional restaurants and natural springs (adult/child 20/10MKD; ⊘ 9am-5pm). The old brick streets flaunt distinctive 19th-century rural architecture and the village is watched over by the Church of St Nicholas. Vevčani lies 14km north of Struga, at the northerly edge of the lake. Buses from Struga run hourly (50MKD); a taxi should cost around 400MKD.

Museum on Water – Bay of Bones   MUSEUM
(☑ 078 909 806; adult/student & child 100/30MKD; ⊘ 9am-7pm Jul-Aug, to 4pm Sep-Jun, closed Mon Oct-Apr) In prehistoric times Lake Ohrid was home to a settlement of pile dwellers who lived literally on top of the water, on a platform supported by up to 10,000 wooden piles anchored to the lake bed. The remains of the settlement were discovered at this spot and were gradually excavated by an underwater team between 1997 and 2005; the museum is an elaborate reconstruction of the settlement as archaeologists think it would have looked between 1200 and 600 BCE.

🏃 Activities

Springs of St Naum   BOATING
(Sveti Naum Monastery; per boat 600MKD) Inside the Sveti Naum Monastery, colourful covered motorboats sit waiting to whisk visitors over the lake to see the Springs of St Naum. The water here is fed by Lake Prespa and is astoundingly clear – at some points it is 3.5m deep and still you can see the bottom.

🛏 Sleeping

Robinson Sunset House   HOSTEL €
(☑ 075 727 252; Lagadin; dm/d/apt €12/30/45; ❄ 🛜) Sweeping lake views, free surfboards (for paddling) and a sprawling garden with lots of relaxing nooks and crannies make this ramshackle hostel a winner if you don't fancy the bustle of Ohrid itself. It sits on a hill above the village of Lagadin, a short bus ride south of Ohrid town. Rooms are spacious and charming, if quite basic.

Hotel Sveti Naum   HOTEL €
(☑ 046 283 080; www.hotel-stnaum.com.mk; Sveti Naum; s/d/ste from 1890/2500/4990MKD; 🛜) Inside the grounds of the Sveti Naum Monastery, some of this hotel's rooms and suites have lovely lake views. Designed in line with traditional building principles, the rooms feature monastic-style furniture and are quite spacious, if a little dated. It's also right by one of Lake Ohrid's best beaches. For the price, it's a steal.

🍴 Eating & Drinking

Restaurant Ostrovo   MACEDONIAN €€
(Sveti Naum Monastery; mains 120-850MKD; ⊘ 8am-9pm) Of all the restaurants at Sveti Naum, this one has the prettiest setting by the water. Cross the little bridge and there's a seemingly endless garden for dining as well as a unique feature: moored pontoons that you can eat on. Staff speak very little English but are friendly and helpful. Fish features heavily on the menu and breakfast here is good.

Kutmičevica   MACEDONIAN €€
(☑ 046 798 399; www.kutmicevica.com.mk; Vevčani; mains 250-900MKD; ⊘ 9am-midnight) This restaurant, which reverberates with the chatter of locals, is a great find: the views from its dining room are immense, right out over the village. It spills onto a terrace on sunny days. The traditional wood-beamed setting matches the menu, where you'll see some Macedonian specialities you won't find in Ohrid, and some inventive takes on classic foods.

Orevche Beach Bar   BAR
(Orevche; ⊘ 10am-8pm; 🛜) A twisted cliffside path sloping steeply downwards into the unknown makes Orevche feel like a secret hideaway, and really it is because hardly any-

WORTH A TRIP

GALIČICA NATIONAL PARK

The rippling, rock-crested massif of Galičica separates Lakes Ohrid and Prespa, and is home to Magaro Peak (2254m), a handful of mountain villages and 1100 species of plant, 12 of which can be found only here. **Lake Prespa** is home to the island of **Golem Grad**. The whole area is protected as a 228-sq-km national park, stretching down to Sveti Naum.

Adrift on Lake Prespa, Golem Grad was once the king's summer playground but is now home to wild tortoises, cormorants and pelicans, and perhaps a few ghosts. A settlement endured here from the 4th century BCE to the 6th century CE and during medieval times there was a monastery complex. The ruins, birdlife and otherworldly beauty make it well worth exploring. Vila Raskrsnica (p838) or Dzani Dimovski ([✆]070 678 123), who owns the cafe at Dupeni Beach, organise trips.

Prespa is separated from its sister lake, Ohrid, by Galičica National Park and a road crosses the ridge of the park, linking the two. Prespa's mirrorlike surface stretches for 176.8 sq km and it is the highest tectonic lake in the Balkans (853m) – the borders of North Macedonia, Albania and Greece converge in its centre. **Dupeni Beach**, near the Greek border on its eastern side, is a (sandy!) spot for swimming.

body knows it's here. The Lake Ohrid water is clear and it would be easy to lose a few hours lounging on the rustic beach bar's day beds and swimming, particularly at sunset.

ⓘ Information

Once you leave Ohrid town, ATMs are surprisingly hard to find. There's a reliable one in the foyer of Hotel Bellevue, a giant waterfront high-rise just south of Ohrid town.

ⓘ Getting There & Away

The major regional bus hub is Ohrid town, and the northerly lake town of Struga also has some bus connections to other Macedonian towns.

ⓘ Getting Around

Bus Frequent buses ply the Ohrid–Sveti Naum route (€1) in summer, stopping off at various points along the lake road, including the village of Lagadin and the Bay of Bones (p832).

Boat Transfers from Ohrid to Sveti Naum (€10 return) run every day in summer.

Ohrid   Охрид

[✆]046 / POP 55,750

Sublime Ohrid is North Macedonia's most seductive destination. It sits on the edge of serene Lake Ohrid, with an atmospheric old quarter that cascades down steep streets, dotted with beautiful churches and topped by the bones of a medieval castle. Traditional restaurants and lakeside cafes liven up the cobblestone streets. Outside of July and August, the tourist circus subsides and the town becomes more lived in.

Ohrid is small enough to hop from historic monuments into a deck chair and dip your toes in the water – a lovely little town beach and boardwalk make the most of the town's natural charms. A holiday atmosphere prevails all summer, when it's a good idea to book accommodation in advance. Ohrid's busiest time is from mid-July to mid-August.

◉ Sights

⭐**Ohrid Boardwalk & City Beach**   BEACH
Skimming the surface of the water along Ohrid's shore, snaking towards Kaneo fishing village and the town's most famous church, this over-water boardwalk takes you to a beautiful outcrop of rocky beaches and a handful of restaurants and bars. On a hot day the area is thronged by bathers, drinkers and diners. The cool waters are translucent and inviting, the cliff-backed setting is sublime, and strolling this stretch of coast up to the Church of Sveti Jovan at Kaneo is an Ohrid must.

⭐**Church of Sveti Jovan at Kaneo**   CHURCH
(Kaneo; 100MKD; ⊙9am-6pm) This stunning 13th-century church is set on a cliff over the lake, about a 15-minute walk west of Ohrid's port area, and is possibly North Macedonia's most photographed structure. Peer down into the azure waters and you'll see why medieval monks found spiritual inspiration here. The small church has original frescoes behind the altar.

Plaošnik   CHURCH
(adult/student & child 100/30MKD; ⊙8am-7pm) Saluting the lake from Ohrid's hilltop, Plaošnik is home to the multidomed

Ohrid

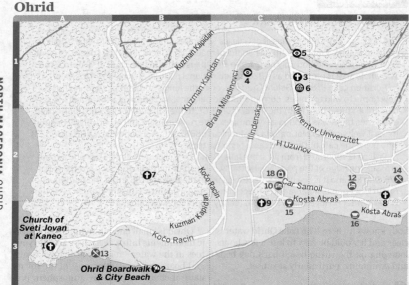

medieval Church of Sveti Kliment i Pantele-jmon, the foundations of a 5th-century basil-ica and a garden of intricate early Christian flora-and-fauna mosaics. The central church was restored in 2002; though it lacks the ancient wall frescoes of many other Macedonian churches, it is unusual in having glass floor segments revealing the original foundations and framed relics from the medieval church, which dated to the 9th century.

Sveta Bogorodica Bolnička & Sveti Nikola Bolnički
CHURCH

(off Car Samoil; admission to each church 50MKD; ⊙9am-1pm) *Bolnica* means 'hospital' in Macedonian; during plagues visitors faced 40-day quarantines inside the walled confines of these petite churches, which are thought to date to the 14th century. Sandwiched between Car Samoil and Kosta Abraš in the heart of the Old Town, the churches have somewhat irregular opening hours, but don't miss going in if they are open. Both are small and low-lying, but have intricate interiors heaving under elaborate icons.

Church of Sveta Bogorodica Perivlepta
CHURCH

(Klimentov Univerzitet; 100MKD; ⊙9am-4pm) Just inside the **Gorna Porta** (Upper Gate; Ilindenska), this 13th-century Byzantine church, whose name translates as 'Our Lady the Most Glorious', has vivid biblical frescoes painted by masters Michael and Eutychius, and superb lake and Old Town views from its terrace. There's also an **icon gallery** (⌨ 046 251 935; 100MKD; ⊙10am-2pm & 6-9pm Tue-Sun) highlighting the founders' artistic achievements.

Sveta Sofija Cathedral
CHURCH

(Car Samoil; adult/student & child 100/30MKD; ⊙9am-7pm) Ohrid's grandest church, 11th-century Sveta Sofija is supported by columns and decorated with elaborate, if very faded, Byzantine frescoes, though they are still well preserved and very vivid in the apse. Its superb acoustics mean it's often used for concerts. To one side of the church there's a peaceful, manicured garden providing a small oasis of green in the heart of the Old Town.

Tours

★ Free Pass Ohrid
TOURS

(⌨070 488 231; www.freepassohrid.mk; Kosta Abraš 74) Run by twin sisters and offering a whole array of tailored tours – from hiking in Galičica National Park, to wine touring around Tikveš, and boat trips and paragliding around Lake Ohrid, among others – this is local enterprise and alternative tourism at its best. They also have stacks of cultural and adventure tours from their Ohrid base.

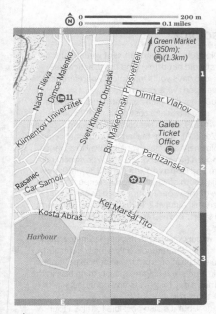

✷✷ Festivals & Events

★ **Ohrid Summer Festival**   PERFORMING ARTS
(📞 046 262 304; http://ohridskoleto.com.mk; Kej
Maršal Tito; ⊙ box office 9am-10pm Jul & Aug)
This is Ohrid's most celebrated festival and
one of the biggest cultural events in North
Macedonia. It hits town in late July and features classical and opera concerts, theatre
and dance staged at venues all over the city,
including the **Classical Amphitheatre** (Braka Miladinovci; ⊙ 24hr) FREE. Buy tickets from
the box office kiosk on Kej Maršal Tito, next
to the Jazz & Blues cafe-bar.

🛏 Sleeping

★ **Villa Jovan**   HISTORIC HOTEL €
(📞 076 236 606; vila.jovan@gmail.com; Car Samoil
44; s/d/ste €27/59/98; ✳🛜) By far the most
charming place to stay in Ohrid, this 1856
mansion offers nine rooms in the heart of
the Old Town. There are old-world furnishings, creaky floors and wooden beams, and
a cosy atmosphere. The two top-floor rooms
have quirky sunken baths sitting behind a
glass wall, looking out onto the tiny sun-trap
terraces.

Sunny Lake Hostel   HOSTEL €
(📞 075 629 571; www.sunnylakehostel.mk; 11 Oktombri 15; dm €10-12, d €24; ✳🛜) This excellent hostel is a bustling hub for backpackers.
Though it could be more spacious, nobody
cares because they have such a good time
here. The common areas are a highlight: a
snug upstairs terrace with lake views and a
garden down below for beer drinking. Facilities include a laundry, free breakfast, a
kitchen, lockers and bike hire (€5 per day).

★ **Jovanovic Guest House**   GUESTHOUSE €€
(📞 070 589 218; jovanovic.guesthouse@hotmail.com; Boro Šain 5; apt €40-65; ✳🛜) This
property has two studio apartments, both
of which sleep four, set in the heart of the
Old Town. Each is well equipped and comes
with a shady balcony. The apartment on the
1st floor is slightly bigger, but the top-floor
apartment's balcony is more private and has
one of the best views in town, right over the
lake and Sveta Sofija Cathedral.

TASTING TIKVEŠ WINES AT THE SOURCE

Five hundred years of Ottoman rule buried North Macedonia's ancient winemaking culture (the Ottomans, being Muslim, generally did not drink), and the practice was confined to monasteries for centuries. But these days you'll hear plenty of references to Tikveš – the country's most lauded (and developed) wine region.

None of the wineries accept walk-ins, so you'll need to plan appointments to taste and tour by calling ahead (if you're not driving, arrange a taxi at a cost of about €25 per car for five or so hours). **Tikveš Winery** (☑ 043 447 519; www.tikves.com.mk; 29 Noemvri 5; wine tasting per person from 300MKD; ☺10am-6pm Mon-Sat), one of the largest and most celebrated, can be virtually impossible to get an appointment at unless you plan way in advance.

Most vineyards – with the exceptions of **Bovin** (☑ 043 365 322; http://bovin.com.mk/; Industriska, 1440 Negotino; ☺8am-4pm Mon-Fri) and **Popova Kula** (☑ 043 367 400; www. popovakula.com.mk; bul Na Vinoto 1, Demir Kapija), both of which are well signposted – are extremely difficult to find on your own. Some of the winery 'tours', such as the one at **Stobi Winery** (☑ 078 221 427; www.stobiwinery.mk; Autopat 2, 1420 Gradsko; ☺9am-6pm) **FREE**, are really not worth bothering with. In short, Tikveš' reputation and Macedonian enthusiasm somewhat oversell the experience.

Happily, **Popova Kula** (☑ 043 367 400; www.popovakula.com.mk; bul Na Vinoto 1, Demir Kapija; s €35-45, d €50-110; 🅿✳🛜) in Demir Kapija, the region's only winery hotel and restaurant, is worth the effort. The owner took inspiration from the winery experiences of California and what he's achieved here is in a different league to everything else in the region. Tours of the property are held four times a day for guests and nonguests, with fascinating insight into the history of the site thrown in.

A stay at Popova Kula is highly recommended, but it's also possible to take a tour of the region from Ohrid (a long day) with Free Pass Ohrid (p834).

North Macedonia's key unique grape varietal is *vranac* (a full-bodied red), while Popova Kula in particular prizes a little-known grape called *stanushina*.

✖ Eating

Green Market
MARKET €

(off Goce Delčev; ☺7am-9pm Mon-Sat, to 2pm Sun, closes 7pm Mon-Sat in winter) Ohrid's main outdoor fruit and vegetable market is great for self-caterers and sells everything from local produce to electronics and kids' toys. Enter directly behind the fountain on Goce Delčev, near the Činar tree. Monday is the market's biggest day.

★ Letna Bavča Kaneo
SEAFOOD €€

(☑070 776 837; Kočo Racin 43; mains 220-500MKD; ☺8am-midnight; 🛜) Of the three terrace restaurants by the water at Kaneo, this one is the best – the atmosphere is right, the food is fantastic and the service professional. The traditional menu has had a facelift; truffle oil accompanies the potatoes, trout is both fresh and smoked, courgettes are stuffed with aromatic herbs and rice. There are good local wines.

Restaurant Antiko
MACEDONIAN €€

(Car Samoil 30; mains 200-800MKD; ☺11am-11pm) In an old Ohrid mansion in the middle of the Old Town, the famous Antiko has great traditional ambience and is a good place to try classic Macedonian dishes such as *tavče gravče* (beans and peppers baked in the oven with spices), and top-quality Macedonian wines.

🍷 Drinking & Nightlife

★ Jazz Inn
BAR

(Kosta Abraš 74; ☺9pm-1am) This unassuming little jazz-themed bar sways to a different rhythm than the strip of bars down on Ohrid's lakefront, with an alternative vibe, a distinct soundtrack and arty clientele. Tucked down a cobbled backstreet away from the touristy hubbub, the low-lit interior has a speakeasy feel, though revellers can be found spilling out onto the road by midnight on weekends and throughout summer.

Liquid
CAFE

(Kosta Abraš 17; ☺8am-1am; 🛜) Ohrid's most stylish lakefront bar is a relaxed chill-out place by day, serving coffee and drinks (no food). At night it morphs into the town's most lively bar with a beautiful crowd and pumping music. Its patio jutting into the lake has the best views and ambience on this strip. During the day this place is kid-friendly too.

🛍 Shopping

⭐Atelier Marta Pejoska   JEWELLERY

(☑070 691 251; whatisfiligree.tumblr.com/; Car Samoil 52; ⊘noon-6.30pm) Ohrid-born Marta trained as an architect and decided to dedicate herself to the traditional Macedonian craft of filigree – silver thread weaving that has the appearance of silver lace (pieces from €25). Marta is a charming host and works to order as well as displaying and selling her existing designs. She often has exhibitions in her small shop.

ℹ Information

Ohrid does not have an official tourist office (despite the fact that many city maps suggest it does); www.visitohrid.org is the municipal website.

ℹ Getting There & Away

Ohrid's **St Paul the Apostle Airport** (☑046 252 820; www.airports.com.mk) is 10km north of the town.

There is no public transport to and from the airport. Taxis cost 500MKD one way (don't bother haggling because it's a set fare) and are easy to pick up without prebooking.

Ohrid's **bus station** (cnr 7 Noemvri & Klanoec) is 1.5km northeast of the town centre. Tickets can either be bought at the station itself or from the **Galeb** (☑046 251 882; www.galeb.mk; Partizanska; ⊘9am-5pm) bus company ticket office just outside Ohrid Old Town. A taxi to Ohrid's bus station from the port area on the edge of the Old Town is a set fare of 150MKD.

CENTRAL NORTH MACEDONIA

Pelister National Park
Пелистер Национален Парк

North Macedonia's oldest national park, created in 1948, Pelister covers 171 sq km of the country's third-highest mountain range, the quartz-filled Baba massif. Eight peaks top 2000m, crowned by Mt Pelister (2601m). Two glacial lakes, known as 'Pelister's Eyes', sit at the top. Summiting both Mt Pelister and the lakes is one of the park's biggest hiking attractions.

Pelister has excellent village guesthouses nearby and is just 30 minutes away by car from historic Bitola. With its fresh alpine air and good day hikes, the park is an underrated Macedonian stopover.

👁 Sights

Dihovo   VILLAGE

Propping up the base of Pelister, just 5km from Bitola, the 830m-high mountainside hamlet of Dihovo is a charming spot, surrounded by thick pine forests and rushing mountain streams. The village's proximity to the main access road into the Pelister National Park makes it a popular base for walkers, and locals have shown impressive initiative in developing their traditional community into a pioneering village tourism destination.

Brajčino   VILLAGE

Cradled by the foothills on the western edge of Pelister, little Brajčino's lungs are fit to bursting with fresh mountain air, making it a thoroughly idyllic place to pitch up. Rushing water resounds around the village, cherry trees blossom in spring and migrating swallows stop by; traditional rural architecture adds further charm. There are five churches and a monastery hidden in the leafy environs circling this well-kept village and a two-to-three-hour, well-marked trail takes in all of them.

🏃 Activities

⭐Bee Garden BN   FOOD

(☑097 526 9535; www.pcelarnikbn.com; Dihovo; ⊘by appointment) A fantastic opportunity to learn about bee-keeping and taste local honey, pollen and royal jelly. The friendly apiarist will demonstrate the workings of the hives, and you can buy some of the delicious products – perfect for gifts back home. The bee-keeper's family also do excellent traditional home cooking, which can be booked by phoning in advance.

Mt Pelister & Lakes   WALKING

Pelister's signature hike is the full-day ascent to the national park's highest peak (2601m) and nearby mountain lakes – Big Lake and Small Lake – that puncture the mountain top like a pair of deep blue eyes, hence their nickname, 'Pelister's Eyes'. There are numerous starting points for the hike but none are reliably marked so it's advisable to take a guide.

🛏 Sleeping

★ Vila Raskrsnica
BOUTIQUE HOTEL €

(☑075 796 796; vila.raskrsnica@gmail.com; Brajčino; r per person €25; P ✳ 🤝) It's worth detouring from the tourist trail just to stay at this utterly lovely village hotel, which offers four rooms in a chalet-style house and lip-smacking country food. Rooms are comfortable and elegant, with exposed stone walls and wooden floors, but it's the expansive mountain-backed garden, rustic picnic tables and a peeping view of Lake Prespa that make Raskrsnica so special.

Villa Dihovo
GUESTHOUSE €€

(☑047 293 040, 070 544 744; www.villadihovo. com; Dihovo; room rates at your discretion; 🤝) A remarkable guesthouse, Villa Dihovo comprises three traditionally decorated rooms in a historic house that's home to former professional footballer Petar Cvetkovski and family. There's a big, private flowering lawn and cosy living room with an open fireplace for winter. The only fixed prices are for the homemade wine, beer and *rakija* (fruit brandy); all else, room price included, is your choice.

ℹ Information

Pelister National Park Information Centre
(☑047 237 010; www.park-pelister.com; Nizhepole; ⊙9am-3pm Tue-Sun) sells a detailed map of the park and its trails (120MKD). The centre is accessible from the Dihovo road shortly after you enter the park.

ℹ Getting There & Away

There is one main road into Pelister, which enters from the eastern side coming from Bitola and skirts very close to the village of Dihovo. If you enter the park in your own car, you'll be stopped at a checkpoint and charged 50MKD.

Public transport does not service the park. A taxi from Bitola or Dihovo costs 360MKD one way.

Bitola
Битола

☑047 / POP 95,390

Buttressing Pelister National Park, elevated Bitola (660m) has a sophistication inherited from its Ottoman days when it was known as the 'City of Consuls'. Macedonians wax lyrical about its elegant buildings, nationally important ruins and cafe culture – yet as far as tourists are concerned it's still a little off the beaten track.

Join the locals in sipping a coffee and people-watching along pedestrianised **Širok Sokak** (ul Maršal Tito), the main promenade and heart of the city, and explore the wonderful **Stara Čaršija** (Old Ottoman Bazaar).

★ Heraclea Lyncestis
ARCHAEOLOGICAL SITE

(adult/child 100MKD/20MKD; ⊙daylight-8pm) Located 1km south of central Bitola, Heraclea Lyncestis is among North Macedonia's best archaeological sites, though the neglected state of the on-site museum might make you think otherwise. See the Roman baths, portico and amphitheatre, and the striking early Christian basilica and episcopal palace ruins, with beautiful, well-preserved floor mosaics – they're unique in depicting endemic trees and animals. There's a small shady cafe in the grounds and the setting is bucolic.

★ Hotel Teatar
BOUTIQUE HOTEL €

(☑047 610 188; Stiv Naumov 35; s/d/t from €24/40/55; P ✳ 🤝) Sensitively designed in the image of a traditional Macedonian (Ottoman) house, Hotel Teatar is without doubt one of the loveliest hotels in the country. Rooms are spacious, simple and stylish, with large comfortable beds. The common areas display ethnographic costumes, and there's a secluded central courtyard with tables for drinks and breakfast.

Via Apartments
APARTMENT €

(☑075 552 343; www.via.mk; off ul Elpida Karamandi 4; s/d/tr/q €13/24/31/40; ✳ 🤝) Set back from the road, hidden away down a dingy alley, Via's lovely front garden/patio is a surprising oasis. Inside the well-designed, modern apartments share a kitchen, laundry and lounge. The location is excellent: just off Širok Sokak.

Vino Bar Bure
MEDITERRANEAN €

(☑047 227 744; Širok Sokak 37; mains from 90MKD; ⊙8am-midnight; 🤝) Positioned at the end of Širok Sokak, overlooking the street and the square, this restaurant specialises in Macedonian and Turkish cuisine, and good local wines. It has a modern terrace with a bustling atmosphere and a cosy interior. Order a *pide* – a flatbread with toppings of meat and/or cheese – or a *lahmacun* (Turkish pizza) and watch the world go by.

★ Porta Jazz
BAR

(Kiril i Metodij; ⊙8am-1am, to midnight Sep-May; 🤝) There's a notably bohemian vibe at this popular place that's packed every night in summer, and when live jazz and blues bands play during the rest of the year (September to May). It's located near the Church of Sveti Dimitrij, one block back from Širok Sokak.

Jagoda
BAR

(📞 047 203 030; Širok Sokak 154; ⏱ 7am-midnight; 📶) Right at the end of Širok Sokak, this is a great place for coffee, beer and DJ parties – the red-and-white chequered tablecloths, the good music and the airy terrace opposite the little park mean you can spend quite a few hours hanging out here. It's where the local art crowd goes. It serves meze, too.

ℹ️ Information

Bitola Tourist Office has no walk-in office. There is a decent website – http://bitola.info/ – with information about the town.

ℹ️ Getting There & Away

The **bus** and **train stations** (ul Nikola Tesla) are adjacent, 1km south of the centre.

SURVIVAL GUIDE

ℹ️ Directory A–Z

LGBTIQ+ TRAVELLERS

Macedonians are religious conservatives and the country's LGBTIQ+ scene is very small. The Rainbow Europe Index continues to rank the country's gay rights among the worst in the region.

MONEY

North Macedonia's national currency is the denar (MKD), but many tourist-related prices (such as transport and hotel costs) are quoted in euros – you may even find that the business owner doesn't immediately know the denar price if you ask for it. Hence Lonely Planet lists prices as they are quoted rather than in denars only.

Macedonian exchange offices *(menuvačnici)* work commission-free. ATMs are widespread. Credit cards can be used in larger cities (especially in restaurants), but don't rely on them outside Skopje.

OPENING HOURS

Banks 7am to 5pm Monday to Friday
Cafes 8am to midnight
Museums Many close on Mondays
Shops 9am to 6pm

PUBLIC HOLIDAYS

New Year's Day 1 January
Orthodox Christmas 7 January
Orthodox Easter Week March/April/May
Labour Day 1 May
Sts Cyril and Methodius Day 24 May
Ilinden Day 2 August
Independence Day 8 September
Revolution Day 11 October
St Clement of Ohrid Day 8 December

ℹ️ Getting There & Away

AIR

Budget airlines have improved Skopje's modest number of air connections, and it's now connected pretty well to major European cities. Wizz Air still flies Skopje–London, but has stopped its Ohrid–London flights.

See the Airports of Macedonia website (www. airports.com.mk) for information about flying in and out of North Macedonia, including timetables, carriers and weather conditions.

LAND
Bus

International routes generally arrive at and depart from Skopje or Ohrid. Pristina, Tirana, Sofia, Belgrade and Thessaloniki are the most common connections.

Car & Motorcycle

Bringing your own vehicle into North Macedonia is hassle free, though you do need a Green Card (proof of third-party insurance, issued by your insurer) endorsed for North Macedonia. You also need to bring the vehicle registration/ownership documents.

Train

→ The Macedonian Railway network is limited and trains are less frequent than buses.
→ Trains connect Skopje to Pristina, Belgrade and Thessaloniki (though the last is via a train-and-bus combo because of the fraught relationship with Greece).
→ Timetables and fares are viewable online (http://mktransport.mk/en).

ℹ️ Getting Around

BUS

→ Skopje serves most domestic destinations.
→ Larger buses are new and air-conditioned; kombis (minibuses) are usually not.
→ During summer, prebook for Ohrid.
→ Sunday is often the busiest day for intercity bus travel among locals, so book ahead.

CAR & MOTORCYCLE

There are occasional police checkpoints; make sure you have the correct documentation. Call 196 for roadside assistance.

TRAIN

Domestic trains are reliable but slow. From Skopje, one train line runs to Negotino and another to Bitola via Veles and Prilep. A smaller line runs Skopje–Kičevo. Ohrid does not have a train station.

Norway

POP 5.3 MILLION

Includes ➜

Best Places to Eat

➜ Sentralen (p848)

➜ Mathallen Oslo (p848)

➜ Pingvinen (p851)

➜ Baklandet Skydsstasjon (p857)

➜ Renaa Matbaren (p854)

Best Places to Stay

➜ The Thief (p845)

➜ Hotel Park (p851)

➜ Westerås Farm (p856)

➜ Darby's Inn (p854)

➜ Tromsø Bed & Books (p859)

Why Go?

Norway is a once-in-a-lifetime destination and the essence of its appeal is remarkably simple: this is one of the most beautiful countries on earth. Impossibly steep-sided fjords cut deep gashes into the interior; grand and glorious glaciers snake down from Europe's largest ice fields; and, with the chance to glimpse the soul-stirring Northern Lights, the appeal of the Arctic is primeval. The counterpoint to so much natural beauty is found in the country's vibrant cultural life. Norwegian cities are cosmopolitan, brimming with architecture that showcases the famous Scandinavian flair for design. Food, too, is a cultural passion through which Norwegians push the boundaries of innovation even as they draw deeply on a heartfelt love of tradition. Yes, Norway is one of the most expensive countries on the planet, but it'll pay you back with never-to-be-forgotten experiences many times over.

When to Go

Oslo

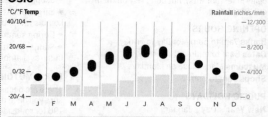

Feb Short days, but opportunities to enjoy winter sports and hunt for the Northern Lights.

Jun–Aug All attractions are open for high season and, beyond the Arctic Circle, the sun never sets.

Sep The stunning colours of autumn make this the prime time for hiking.

Entering the Country

Norway is well linked to other European countries by air. There are also regular bus and rail services to Norway from neighbouring Sweden and Finland (from where there are connections further afield to Europe), with less regular (and more complicated) services to/from Russia. Regular car and passenger ferries also connect southern Norwegian ports with Denmark, Sweden and Germany.

Flights, cars and tours can be booked online at lonelyplanet.com/bookings.

ITINERARIES

One Week

Begin in Oslo (p844) and soak up the Scandinavian sophistication of the city's museums, waterfront and culinary scene. Join the Norway in a Nutshell tour (p845), travelling by train across the stunning roof of Norway, down to Sognefjorden (p854) then on to Bergen (p849) via Gudvangen and Voss. Three days in Bergen will give you a taste of this beguiling city, then jump back on the train back to Oslo.

Two Weeks

With an extra week, allow for two days in Stavanger (p853), including the day excursion to Pulpit Rock (p853), a couple more days in Trondheim (p856), then three days exploring the length and breadth of the Lofoten Islands (p857) before flying back to Oslo (p844).

Essential Food & Drink

Reindeer Roast reindeer (reinsdyrstek) is something every nonvegetarian visitor should try at least once: ask for it cooked as you would enjoy a steak.

Elk Known elsewhere in the world as moose, elk (elg) comes in a variety of forms, including as a steak or burger.

Salmon An excellent salmon dish, gravat laks is made by marinating salmon in sugar, salt, brandy and dill, and serving it in a creamy sauce.

Wild berries The most popular edible wild berries include strawberries, blackcurrants, red currants, raspberries, blueberries (huckleberries) and the lovely amber-coloured moltebær (cloudberries).

Cheeses Norwegian cheeses have come to international attention as a result of the mild but tasty Jarlsberg. Try also the disconcertingly brown Gudbrandsdalsost (aka brunost) made from the whey of goat's and/or cow's milk, which has a slightly sweet flavour.

Aquavit Potent spirit distilled from grain and potatoes, typically flavoured with caraway and/or dill. Drink it neat and watch the hairs grow on your chest.

NORWAY

AT A GLANCE

Area 385,208 sq km

Capital Oslo

Country Code ☑ 47

Currency Norwegian krone (kr)

Emergency ☑ 112

Language Norwegian

Time GMT/UTC plus one hour

Visas Not required for stays of up to 90 days

Sleeping Price Ranges

The following price ranges refer to a double room with private bathroom in high season and, unless stated otherwise, include breakfast:

€ less than 750kr

€€ 750kr–1400kr

€€€ more than 1400kr

Eating Price Ranges

The following price ranges refer to a standard main course.

€ less than 125kr

€€ 125kr–200kr

€€€ more than 200kr

Resources

Visit Norway (www.visitnorway.com)

Fjord Norway (www.fjordnorway.com)

Lofoten (www.lofoten.info)

Lonely Planet (www.lonelyplanet.com/norway)

Norway Highlights

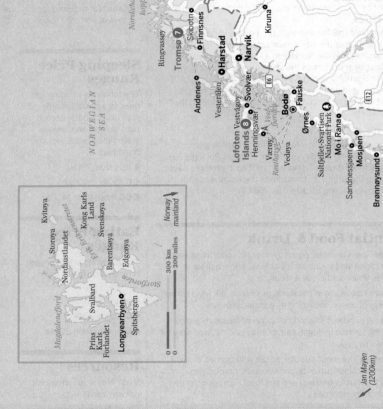

1 Oslo (p844)
Enjoying the capital's cosmopolitan charms and the stunning Opera House.

2 Geirangerfjord (p855) Exploring Norway's number-one fiord on the ferry from Hellesylt.

3 Bergen (p849)
Lingering amid enchanted Bryggen buildings along the waterfront.

4 Oslo to Bergen railway (p852)
Hopping aboard the train for Norway's most spectacular rail trip.

5 Pulpit Rock (p853) Hiking high above Lysefjord to Norway's most breathtaking lookout.

6 Hurtigruten coastal ferry (p852)
Journeying up Norway's peerless

coast from Bergen to
Kirkenes.

7 Tromsø (p858)
Experiencing one of
Norway's liveliest
towns and going dog-
sledding in winter.

8 Lofoten Islands
(p857) Heading
for the Arctic and
arguably Europe's
most beautiful
archipelago

OSLO

POP 988,873

Surrounded by mountains and sea, this compact, cultured and fun city has a palpable sense of reinvention. Come to Oslo to pay homage to Edvard Munch and Henrik Ibsen by all means, but don't leave without discovering something of its contemporary cultural life too. Explore one of its many museums, get to know its booming contemporary-art scene or just marvel at the work of its home-grown starchitects. Oslo has become a culinary destination in its own right, serving up everything from the Michelin-starred cuisine to down-home favourites such as peel-and-eat shrimp. And as night falls you'll discover a city that knows how to have fun, with its thriving cafe and bar culture. Meanwhile, the pull of the outdoors is ever-present: the city is blessed with a large number of bucolic parks, and the Oslofjord's waterways and islands are just minutes away from the centre.

◉ Sights

◉ Aker Brygge & Bygdøy

★Vikingskipshuset   MUSEUM
(Viking Ship Museum; ☑ 22 13 52 80; www.khm.uio. no; Huk Aveny 35; adult/child 100kr/free; ⊙ 9am-6pm May-Sep, 10am-4pm Oct-Apr; ☐ 30) Around 1100 years ago, Vikings dragged up two longships from the shoreline and used them as the centrepiece for grand ceremonial burials, most likely for important chieftains or nobility. Along with the ships, they buried many items for the afterlife: food, drink, jewellery, furniture, carriages, weapons, and even a few dogs for companionship. Discovered in Oslofjord in the late 19th and early 20th centuries, the ships and their wares are beautifully restored, offering an evocative, emotive insight into Viking life.

Astrup Fearnley Museet   GALLERY
(Astrup Fearnley Museum; ☑ 22 93 60 60; www. afmuseet.no; Strandpromenaden 2; adult/child 130kr/free; ⊙ noon-5pm Tue, Wed & Fri, to 7pm Thu, 11am-5pm Sat & Sun year-round, plus noon-5pm Mon Jul & Aug; ☐ 21, 54, ⛴ Aker Brygge) This private contemporary-art museum resides in an arresting, silvered-wood building designed by Renzo Piano, with a sail-like glass roof that feels both maritime and at one with the Oslofjord landscape. The collection is rich in American work from the '80s (artists such as Jeff Koons, Tom Sachs, Cindy Sherman and Richard Prince are well represented), but boundary-pushing pieces by other key artists such as Sigmar Polke and Anselm Kiefer reflect a now-broader collecting brief.

Polarship Fram Museum   MUSEUM
(Frammuseet; ☑ 23 28 29 50; www.frammuseum. no; Bygdøynesveien 39; adult/child 120/50kr, with Oslo Pass free; ⊙ 9am-6pm Jun-Aug, 10am-6pm May & Sep, to 5pm Oct-Apr; ☐ 30, ⛴ Bygdøynes) This museum is dedicated to one of the most enduring symbols of early polar exploration, the 39m schooner *Fram* (meaning 'Forward'). Wander the decks, peek inside the cramped bunk rooms and imagine life at sea and among the polar ice. Allow plenty of time, as there's an overwhelming volume of information to absorb, with detailed exhibits complete with maps, pictures and artefacts of various expeditions, from Nansen's attempt to ski across the North Pole to Amundsen's discovery of the Northwest Passage.

◉ Opera House & Bjørvika

★Oslo Opera House   ARCHITECTURE
(Den Norske Opera & Ballett; ☑ 21 42 21 21; www.op eraen.no; Kirsten Flagstads plass 1; foyer free; ⊙ foyer 10am-7pm Mon-Fri, 11am-6pm Sat, noon-6pm Sun; Ⓣ Sentralstasjonen) Centrepiece of Oslo's rapidly developing waterfront, the magnificent Opera House (2008), reminiscent of a glacier floating in the waters of the Oslofjord, is considered one of the most iconic buildings in Scandinavia. Conceived by Oslo-based architectural firm Snøhetta, its design is a thoughtful meditation on the notion of monumentality, the dignity of cultural production, Norway's unique place in the world

---

SEE THE SIGHTS FOR LESS

Oslo Pass (www.visitoslo.com/en/activ ities-and-attractions/oslo-pass; one/ two/three days adult 395/595/745kr, child 210/295/370kr), sold at the tourist office and available as an app for smartphones, is a good way of cutting transport and ticket costs around the city. The majority of the city's museums are free with the pass, as is all public transport within zones 1 and 2. Other perks include restaurant and tour discounts.

and the conversation between public life and personal experience. To fully appreciate the building's interior, join one of the **guided tours** (adult/child 120/70kr; ☺English tours 1pm Sun-Fri, noon Sat, additional tours Jul & Aug).

◉ City Centre

Akershus Festning   FORTRESS
(Akershus Fortress; www.akershusfestning.no; ☺6am-9pm; ☒Kontraskjæret) `FREE` When Oslo was named capital of Norway in 1299, King Håkon V ordered the construction of Akershus, strategically located on the eastern side of the harbour, to protect the city from external threats. Extended and modified over the centuries, it still dominates the Oslo harbourfront and the sprawling complex consists of **Akershus Slott** (Akershus Castle; ☒22 41 25 21; www.nasjonalefestningsverk.no; Kongens gate), which is currently closed for renovations, a fortress and assorted other buildings, including still-active military installations.

Nasjonalgalleriet   GALLERY
(National Gallery; ☒21 98 20 00; www.nasjonalmuseet.no; Universitetsgata 13; adult/child 120kr/free; ☺10am-6pm Tue, Wed & Fri, to 7pm Thu, 11am-5pm Sat & Sun; ☒Tullinløkka) The gallery houses the nation's largest collection of traditional and modern art, and many of Edvard Munch's best-known creations are on permanent display, including his most renowned piece, *The Scream.* But there's also a clutch of works by acclaimed European artists: Gauguin, Claudel, Picasso and El Greco, plus Manet, Degas, Renoir, Matisse, Cézanne and Monet are all in there. Nineteenth-century Norwegian artists have a strong showing too, including key figures such as JC Dahl and Christian Krohg.

◉ Frogner & Western Oslo

Vigelandsparken   PARK
(Vigeland Sculpture Park; www.vigeland.museum.no/no/vigelandsparken; Nobels gate 32; ☒Vigelandsparken) The centrepiece of **Frognerparken** (☒Vigelandsparken) is an extraordinary open-air showcase of work by Norway's best-loved sculptor, Gustav Vigeland, and is home to 212 granite and bronze pieces by the artist. His highly charged oeuvre includes entwined lovers, tranquil elderly couples, bawling babies and contempt-ridden beggars. Speaking of bawling babies, his most famous work here, *Sinnataggen* (Lit-

NORWAY IN A NUTSHELL

For maximum sights in minimal time, it's hard to beat the popular **Norway in a Nutshell** (Fjord Tours; ☒55 55 76 60; www.norwaynutshell.com). From Oslo, the classic route includes a train across Hardangervidda to Myrdal, a descent along the dramatic Flåm Railway, a cruise along Nærøyfjorden to Gudvangen, a bus to Voss, a connecting train to Bergen for a short visit, then an overnight return rail trip to Oslo (including a sleeper compartment); the return tour costs 3020kr.

tle Hot-Head), portrays a child in a mood of particular ill humour.

◉ Sofienberg, Grønland & Tøyen

Munchmuseet   GALLERY
(Munch Museum; ☒23 49 35 00; www.munchmuseet.no; Tøyengata 53; adult/child 120kr/free; ☺10am-4pm, to 5pm mid-May–early Sep; ☒20, ☒Tøyen) This monographic museum dedicated to Norway's greatest artist, Edvard Munch (1863–1944), houses the largest collection of his work in the world: some 28,000 items, including 1100 paintings and 4500 watercolours, many of which were gifted to the city by Munch himself. Don't come looking for *The Scream,* though – it's at the Nasjonalgalleriet, along with a number of his other masterworks.

🛏 Sleeping

🛏 Aker Brygge & Bygdøy

★**The Thief**   BOUTIQUE HOTEL €€€
(☒24 00 40 00; www.thethief.com; Landgangen 1; d 3390-4090kr; ☂☒; ☒Aker Brygge) Overlooking the Astrup Fearnley Museum, Oslo's best design hotel is more dark glamour than Scandinavian sparse, though is packed with playful touches from beautiful artisan objects to video art, and guests can max out on the luxe vibe at the hotel spa. Views from many of the rooms, and the rooftop bar, are stunning.

🛏 City Centre

★**Saga Poshtel Oslo**   HOSTEL €
(☒23 10 08 00; www.sagahoteloslo.com; Kongens gate 7; dm/d 425/1135kr; ☂; ☒Øvre Slottsgate) A

Oslo

500 m
0.25 miles

1
Majorstuen T-bane Station

Frognerparken (580m);
Vigelandsparken (800m)

Kirkeveien

Middelthuns gate

Gyldenløves gate

Marcus Thranes gate

Sannergata

Sannergata

Vøyensvingen

Toftes gate

15

Thorvald Meyers gate

Olaf Ryes plass

GRÜNERLØKKA

11

Maridalsveien

Waldemar Thranes gate

St Hanshaugen

Ullevålsveien

Thereses gate

Louises gate

Fagerborggata Pilestredet

Vibes gate

Bogstadveien

Josefines gate

Camilla Colletts vei

Oscars gate

Uranienborgveien

Holtegata

Niels Juels gate

Skovveien

Vestheimgata

Bygdøy allé

Drammensveien

Munkedamsveien

Finnmarkgata

Helgesens gata

Sofienberggata

Rathkes gate

Sars gate

Trondheimsveien

Botanisk Hage

5

Monrads gate

Jens Bjelkes gate

Tøyen T-bane Station

Åkebergveien

Tøyengata

Motzfeldts gate

Grønlandsleiret

Grønland T-bane Station

Tøyenbekken

Markveien

Nordre gate

Korsgata

Søndre gate

Torvbakgt

Torggata

Storgata

Hausmanns gate

Lakkegata

Nylandsveien

Vaterlands bro

Brugata

Galleri Oslo
Bus Terminal

Oslo Sentralstasjon

Grünerhagen Park

Østre Elvebakke

16

Brenneriveien

Møllerveien

Møllergata

(Hammersborggata)

Akersveien

Damstredet

Nordahl Bruns gate

Stensberggata

Var Frelsers Gravlund

TELTHUSBAKKEN

Ullevålsveien

14

Pilestredet

St Olavs gate

Holbergs plass

Holbergs gate

Pilestredet

Parkveien

Hegdehaugsveien

Wergelandsveien

Slottsparken

Inkognitogata

Riddervolds gate

Colbjørnsens gate

Henrik Ibsens gate

Parkveien

Hansteens gate

Huitfeldts gate

Ruseløkkveien

Cort Adelers gate

Råroussgata

6

Kristian IV's gate

Nationaltheatret T-bane Station

Haakon VII's gate

Tordenskiolds gate

Stortinget T-bane Station

Nedre Vollgate

Tollbugata

12

Prinsens gate

Karl Johans gate

Jernbanetorget (Oslo S) T-bane Station

Storgata

Biskop Gunnerus gate

Oslo Visitor Centre

Mariboes gate

Oslo

◎ **Top Sights**

◎ **Sights**

➕ **Activities, Courses & Tours**

🛏 **Sleeping**

🍴 **Eating**

🍷 **Drinking & Nightlife**

🎭 **Entertainment**

crossover hostel-hotel (posh-tel, if you didn't already get it), smartly designed and very central, with a big social lounge with decent wi-fi. Rooms are basic but spotless; there are lots of doubles, plus four- and six-bunk-bed dorms, some with en suites, some with shared facilities. Get yourself up in time for breakfast – it's top notch.

Citybox Oslo HOTEL €€
(☑ 21 42 04 80; www.citybox.no/oslo; Prinsens gate 6; s/d 780/980kr; 🛜; 🚆 Dronningens gate) This functional city chain champions its trademark brand: no-frills, essentials-only rooms at bargain prices (well, at least for Norway). Don't expect prison-block chic – it's surprisingly smart, with plain all-white rooms, Scandi-style furniture, free wi-fi and a great downtown location. Plush: no; practical: very.

✖ Eating

✖ Aker Brygge & Bygdøy

Freddy Fuego MEXICAN €
(www.freddyfuego.no; Lille Stranden 4; mains 115-130kr; ⊙11am-9pm Sun-Thu, to 10pm Fri & Sat;

Aker Brygge) The menu may be as simple as *un, dos, tres*, but this colourful burrito bar gets the basics right with melt-in-the-mouth meats which are marinated and slow-cooked for hours, and a range of salsas to match how fiery you're feeling. One taste of 'Freddy's Revenge' beside the Mexican wrestler mural and you might just be ready for some *lucha libre* yourself.

City Centre

Vippa
STREET FOOD €

(☑ 91 72 80 43; www.vippa.no; Akershusstranda 25; dishes 65-160kr; ☺ noon-9pm Wed-Sat, to 8pm Sun) It's a little out of the way, but if you find yourself in the vicinity of Vippetangen quay, duck into this popular hangar-turned-street-food-hall for international flavours galore. Grab a bowl of what tickles your fancy from Thai to Syrian, Chinese to Eritrean and pitch up at one of the communal benches for a chat with your table-mate.

★ Sentralen Restaurant
NEW NORDIC €€

(☑ 22 33 33 22; www.sentralen.no; Øvre Slottsgate 3; small plates 95-245kr; ☺ 11am-10pm Mon-Fri, from noon Sat; ☐ Øvre Slottsgate) One of Oslo's best dining experiences is also its most relaxed. A large dining room filled with old social-club chairs and painted in tones of deep, earthy green, draws city workers, visitors and natural-wine-obsessed locals in equal measure. Outstandingly prepared and presented, the small-plates concept makes it easy to sample across the appealing New Nordic menu.

Grünerløkka & Vulkan

Mathallen Oslo
FOOD HALL €€

(☑ 40 00 12 09; www.mathallenoslo.no; Maridalsveien 17, Vulkan; ☺ 10am-8pm Tue-Sat, 11am-6pm Sun; ☐ 54) Down by the river, this former industrial space is now a food hall dedicated to showcasing the very best Norwegian food, as well as some excellent international cuisines. Eating here is a casual affair – there are dozens of delis, cafes and miniature restaurants, and the place buzzes throughout the day and into the evening. Check the website for special culinary festivals held each month.

Drinking & Entertainment

★ Fuglen
COCKTAIL BAR, CAFE

(www.fuglen.com; Universitetsgaten 2, enter on Pilestredet; ☺ 7.30am-10pm Mon & Tue, to 1am Wed & Thu, to 3am Fri, 11am-3am Sat, 1... ☐ 33) Fuglen and its crew of m... preneurs are part of Oslo's dour-to... ...am-ily-cool reinvention. Since overhauling this cafe, they've launched a coffee and Norwegian design mini-empire in Japan, while in their home city they continue to roast and brew as well as mix some of the best cocktails around.

Grünerløkka Brygghus
PUB

(www.brygghus.no; Thorvald Meyers gate 30b; ☺ 4-11pm Mon-Wed, 4pm-1am Thu, 3pm-3.30am Fri, noon-3.30am Sat, noon-11pm Sun; ☐ Olaf Ryes plass) This atmospheric and amiable alehouse and microbrewery does a range of house brews from pilsners to *Weissbiers*, and also serves up some intriguing ales from guest breweries. Stomach liners – burgers, bangers and mash, and fish and chips – ca... be ordered at the bar. Street-side benches are at a premium but worth trying to snare.

★ Blå
LIVE MUSIC

(www.blaaoslo.no; Brenneriveien 9c; ☐ 54) Blå is all things to everyone, with DJs (it happens to be the city's best spot for hip-hop), live gigs and jazz. On Sundays there is a live big band that's been playing here every week for years, or just come early for a drink at one of the pretty riverside tables. Hours (much like the service) are vague; check listings for event timings.

ⓘ Information

Oslo Visitor Centre (☑ 23 10 62 00; www.visit oslo.com; Jernbanetorget 1; ☺ 9am-6pm; ☎; ☐ Jernbanetorget, ☐ Jernbanetorget, ☐ Oslo S) Oslo's excellent main tourist office is tucked in the Østbanehallen food hall inside the main train station. It can help you with accommodation, activities, cruises and cross-country trips, and also sells transport tickets and the Oslo Pass. Pick up one of the free city guides.

ⓘ Getting There & Away

AIR
Oslo Gardermoen International Airport (www.avinor.no/en/airport/oslo-airport), the city's main airport, is 50km north of the city. It's used by international and domestic carriers including Norwegian, SAS, Air France, British Airways and Widerøe. The airport has one terminal building.

A handful of budget carriers, including Ryanair, Wizz Air and Norwegian, operate flights to some destinations from Torp International Airport (www.torp.no), some 123km southwest of Oslo.

here but it's not all about railways: there are also fascinating photos of construction gangs and life in and around Flåm before cars and buses made it this far up the fjords.

★ **Flåmsbana Railway** RAIL
(www.visitflam.com/en/flamsbana; adult/child one way 390/195kr, return 550/274kr) This 20km-long engineering wonder hauls itself up 866m of altitude gain through 20 tunnels and, at a gradient of 1:18, is one of the world's steepest railway lines. It takes a full 45 minutes to climb to Myrdal, which sits on the bleak, treeless Hardangervidda plateau, with the vintage-styled train passing deep ravines and thundering waterfalls (there's a photo stop at awesome Kjosfossen). The railway runs year-round, with up to 10 departures daily in summer, dropping to four in winter.

🛏 Sleeping & Eating

★ **Flåm Camping & Hostel** HOSTEL, CAMPGROUND €
(☑940 32 681; www.flaam-camping.no; Nedre Brekkevegen 12; 1-/2-person tent 135/225kr, dm/s/tw 340/620/950kr, with shared bathroom 280/470/750kr; ⊗Apr-Oct; 🅿🛜) Everyone's favourite when looking for a budget place in Flåm, this immaculately kept and conveniently positioned hostel and campground has accommodation options to suit all wallets: bunk-bed dorms, singles, twins, triples and quads, in simple lodge buildings. There's also tonnes of green grassy space for caravans and campers and it's just a short walk to the marina.

Flåm Bakery BAKERY €
(cakes & pastries 30-45kr; ⊗8am-5pm) This very popular little bakery turns out muffins, Danish pastries, croissants and cakes, along with some delicious traditional Norwegian breads.

Ægir Bryggeri MICROBREWERY, PUB
(☑57 63 20 50; www.flamsbrygga.no/aegir-bryggeripub; Flåmsbrygga; ⊗noon-10pm May-Sep, from 6pm Oct-Dec, from 5pm Jan-Apr) Looking for all the world like a stave church, Ægir Brewery, all appealing woodwork and flagstones, offers six different kinds of draught beer, all brewed on the premises, plus a raft of choice in canned form. There's also a tasty line of Norwegian comfort food (185kr to 295kr). Spare Ribs Ragnarok, anyone?

ℹ Information

Tourist Office (☑57 63 14 00; www.visitflam.com; Stasjonsvegen; ⊗7am-7pm Jun-Aug,

to 4pm May & Sep) Located inside the Flåm Visitor Centre.

ℹ Getting There & Away

TRAIN
Flåm is the only Sognefjorden village with a rail link, via the magnificent Flåmsbana railway. There are train connections via Myrdal to Oslo (771kr, five hours, four daily) and Bergen (318kr, 2¾ hours, six daily).

Geirangerfjord

POP 200

This world-famous, Unesco-listed fjord is on the radar of nearly every visitor to Norway. A truly majestic combination of huge cliffs, plunging waterfalls and deep blue water, it's guaranteed to make a lasting imprint on your memory. But with scores of cruise ships docking at the port each day in summer, at certain times of day you're unlikely to enjoy much peace and quiet, especially around the main port of Geiranger. Thankfully, out on the fjord itself, peace and tranquillity remain and a ride on the Geiranger–Hellesylt ferry is an essential part of your Norwegian adventure.

◉ Sights

Flydalsjuvet VIEWPOINT
You'll have seen that classic photo somewhere, beloved of brochures, of the overhanging rock Flydalsjuvet, usually with a figure gazing down at a cruise ship in Geirangerfjord. The car park, signposted Flydalsjuvet, about 5km up a very steep and winding hill from Geiranger on the Stryn road, offers a great view of the fjord and the green river valley, but doesn't provide the postcard view down to the last detail.

☞ Tours

Geiranger Fjordservice BOATING
(☑70 26 30 07; www.geirangerfjord.no; Geirangervegen 2; 1½hr tours adult/child 405/202kr) This

long-running company runs sightseeing boat trips up and down the fjord from Geiranger. The standard 1½-hour trip runs up to five times daily in midsummer, just once daily in April and October, and not at all from November to March.

From May to October it also operates a smaller, 15-seater RIB boat (adult/child 695/395kr), and runs kayaking tours May to September (adult/child 680/580kr).

🛏 Sleeping & Eating

★ **Westerås Farm** CABIN €€
(☎932 64 497; Westerås; 2-bed cabin 870-1040kr, apt 1250kr; ⊙May-Sep) This idyllic old working farm, 4km along the Rv63 towards Grotli, sits at the end of a peaceful farm track, dizzyingly high above the bustle. Stay in one of the two farmhouse apartments, or five pine-clad cabins, each sleeping five to six. The barn, dating from 1603, houses a restaurant, where Arnfinn and Iris serve dishes made with their own produce.

Brasserie Posten BRASSERIE €€
(☎70 26 13 06; www.brasserieposten.no; Geirangervegen 4; mains 190-298kr; ⊙noon-11pm Apr-Sep, shorter hours rest of year) 🍴 A simple menu of sandwiches, burgers, steaks, fish and pizza is elevated above the norm by a passionate local chef who sources the best local produce and makes the most of fresh herbs and vegetables. The modern Scandi interior is bright and atmospheric, but the fjord-side terrace wins. It's not big, so expect a wait when the cruise rush hits.

ℹ Information

Tourist Office (☎70 26 30 99; www.geiranger. no; Geirangervegen 2; ⊙9am-7pm May–mid-Sep, 10am-6pm mid-Sep–Apr) This efficient, if occasionally overwhelmed, tourist office books boat and cruise tickets, hands out hiking leaflets, and generally aims to make your stay, however fleeting, as pleasurable as possible. It's located right beside the pier.

ℹ Getting There & Away

BOAT
The car ferry between Geiranger and Hellysylt is a stunner. There are three to eight sailings a day between April and October (adult/child one way 285/143kr, return 385/193kr, 1½ hours). With a car, the one-way fare is 580kr for one passenger or 1130kr with up to five people. Tickets can be booked online through the Visit Flåm (www. visitflam.com) website.

From June to August the Hurtigruten coastal ferry (p852) makes a detour from Ålesund (departs 9.30am) to Geiranger (departs 1.30pm) on its northbound run.

BUS
From mid-June to mid-August, sightseeing buses make the spectacular run from Geiranger to Åndalsnes (adult/child 478/239kr, three hours, twice daily), known as the 'Golden Route'.

Year-round there's a bus connection to Eidsdal (30 minutes, 69kr, up to four daily), from where it's a ferry and a further bus to Ålesund (two hours, 163kr).

NORTHERN NORWAY

With vibrant cities and some wondrous natural terrain, you'll be mighty pleased with yourself for undertaking an exploration of this huge territory that spans the Arctic Circle. An alternative to land travel is the Hurtigruten coastal ferry (p852), which pulls into every sizeable port, passing some of the best coastal scenery in Scandinavia.

Trondheim
POP 180,557

With its colourful warehouses, waterways and wooded hills, Norway's third-largest city is without doubt one of its most photogenic. Trondheim, the country's historic capital, is a pleasure to explore, with wide streets and a partly pedestrianised heart. Great cafes, restaurants and museums compete for attention, while Europe's northernmost Gothic cathedral doesn't need to try.

◉ Sights

★ **Nidaros Domkirke** CATHEDRAL
(☎73 89 08 00; www.nidarosdomen.no; Kongsgårdsgata; adult/child 100/40kr, tower 50kr, with Archbishop's Palace Museum & The Crown Regalia 180/80kr; ⊙9am-6pm Mon-Fri, to 2pm Sat, 1pm-5pm Sun Jun-Aug, shorter hours rest of year) Nidaros Cathedral is Scandinavia's largest medieval building, and the northernmost Gothic structure in Europe. Outside, the ornately embellished, altar-like west wall has top-to-bottom statues of biblical characters and Norwegian bishops and kings, sculpted in the early 20th century. Several are copies of medieval originals, nowadays housed in the adjacent museum. Note the glowing, vibrant colours of the modern stained glass in the rose window at the west end in striking

LOFOTEN ISLANDS

You'll never forget your first approach to Lofoten: the beauty of the islands' tall, craggy profiles is simply staggering.

The main islands, Austvågøy, Vestvågøy, Flakstadøy and Moskenesøy, are separated from the mainland by Vestfjorden, but all are connected by road bridges and tunnels. One of the best ways to appreciate the unparalleled views is to follow the E10 road, which runs along the islands from tip to toe.

The islands' appeal lies primarily in their astonishing landscapes, but don't miss the **Lofotr Viking Museum** (📞76 15 40 00; www.lofotr.no; adult/child incl guided tour mid-Jun–Aug 200/150kr, rest of year 170/130kr; ⏱10am-7pm Jun–mid-Aug, shorter hours rest of year; ♿), a 'living' museum borne of the ruins of an 83m-long dwelling of a powerful Viking chieftain, the largest building of its era ever discovered in Scandinavia.

Lofoten's principal town is Svolvær, and it's here you'll find the biggest range of accommodation, including the outstanding **Svinøya Rorbuer** (📞76 06 99 30; www.svinoya. no; Gunnar Bergs vei 2; cabins 1527-3310kr), the best-equipped **tourist office** (📞76 07 05 75; www.lofoten.info; Torget 18; ⏱9am-8.30pm Mon-Fri, to 6pm Sat & Sun mid-Jun–early Aug, shorter hours rest of year), and the primary (though tiny) airport. There are up to five flights daily from Bodø (25 minutes), and one flight direct to Oslo three times a week.

You'll find comprehensive information at www.lofoten.info.

contrast to the interior gloom. Photography not permitted.

Gamle Bybro
BRIDGE

(Old Town Bridge) There's been a bridge here since 1681, connecting the city with the **Kristiansten Fort** (Festningsgata; ⏱guided tours noon & 2pm daily Jun-Aug) FREE and guarded at each end by a watch-house (although only one now remains, currently occupied by a kindergarten). The present bridge dates from 1861, and it's a beauty – pedestrianised and clad in planks, it's the best place in town to get that essential shot of Trondheim's riverside warehouses. It's also the quickest way to get over to Bakklandet from the city centre.

Sverresborg Trøndelag Folkemuseum
MUSEUM, ARCHITECTURE

(📞73 89 01 00; www.sverresborg.no; Sverresborg Allé 13; adult/child incl guided tour mid-Jun–Aug 155kr/free, Sep–mid-Jun 115kr/free; ⏱10am-5pm Jun-Aug, 10am-3pm Tue-Fri, noon-4pm Sat & Sun Sep-May; 🚌8,18) Three kilometres west of the centre, this folk museum is one of the best of its kind in Norway. The indoor exhibition, Livsbilder (Images of Life), displays artefacts in use over the last 150 years – from clothing to school supplies to ornate sleds. The rest of the museum is open-air, comprising more than 60 period buildings, many of which you can enter, adjoining the ruins of King Sverre's castle and giving fine views of the city.

🛏 Sleeping

P-Hotel
HOTEL €

(📞73 60 40 05; www.p-hotels.no; Fosenkaia 7; s/d from 649/749kr; @🛜) Exit the train station and you're on the doorstep of the Trondheim branch of the P-Hotels chain. Staff are friendly and the 128 rooms are comfortable, if simply appointed. While the austere, box-like exterior and bland corridors lean more towards institutional than minimalist chic, its unique selling point is a rooftop terrace overlooking the Nidelven and the city beyond. Breakfast-in-a-bag is delivered to your door.

Scandic Nidelven Hotel
HOTEL €€

(📞73 56 80 00; www.scandichotels.com; Havnegata 1-3; r 1119-1643kr, ste from 2094kr; 🅿@🛜) A big business hotel with more than 340 rooms and the full suite of facilities including a gym. Beyond its vast atrium-like lobby, it's split into several box-shaped wings projecting over the water, so many rooms have river views. Standard rooms are smallish but Scandi-styled, and the breakfast is a corker – Twinings has awarded it 'Norway's best hotel breakfast' 11 times.

🍴 Eating

★ Baklandet Skydsstasjon
NORWEGIAN €€

(📞73 92 10 44; www.skydsstation.no; Øvre Bakklandet 33; mains 168-275kr; ⏱11am-1am Mon-Fri, from noon Sat & Sun) If you're still searching for that quintessentially Norwegian meal, you won't get much more traditional than this. Originally an 18th-century coaching inn, it's now everyone's favourite homely hang-out in Trondheim. The rambling rooms are crammed with old furniture and decorated with colourful wall hangings, while the menu is stuffed with comforting classics such as fish soup (unmissable), baked salmon and liver pâté.

Drinking & Nightlife

Jacobsen og Svart CAFE
(☏902 44 226; www.jacobsensvart.no; Ferjemannsveien 8; ☺7am-6pm Mon-Fri, from 9am Sat, from 11am Sun) Jacobsen og Svart manages to be unassuming yet achingly hip, and does what many claim to be the city's best coffee. Throw in a very cool soundtrack and near-perfect, freshly baked cinnamon rolls and you're somewhere close to cafe heaven.

Trondheim Microbryggeri MICROBREWERY
(☏73 51 75 15; www.tmb.no; Prinsens gate 39; ☺3pm-midnight Mon & Tue, 3pm-2am Wed & Thu, 2pm-2am Fri, noon-2am Sat) This splendid home-brew pub deserves a pilgrimage as reverential as anything accorded to St Olav from all committed *øl* (beer) quaffers. With up to eight of its own brews on tap and good light meals available, it's a place to linger, nibble and tipple. It's down a short lane, just off Prinsens gate.

ℹ Information

Tourist Office (☏73 80 76 60; www.visittrondheim.no; 1st fl, Nordre gate 11; ☺9am-6pm mid-Jun–mid-Aug, closed Sun rest of year) Up-to-the-minute tourist office in the heart of the city, with expert staff on hand offering stacks of information and accommodation bookings. Classy souvenirs and a bike-rental service (three hours/one day 175/295kr) are also available.

ℹ Getting There & Away

AIR
Værnes airport is 32km east of Trondheim, with flights operated by **SAS** (www.sas.no), **Norwegian** (www.norwegian.no) and **Widerøe** (www.wideroe.no).

BUS
The intercity bus terminal is the starting point for local and regional routes served by **AtB** (www.atb.no) and **FRAM Ekspress** (www.frammr.no) among others. Destinations include:
Alesund 655kr, 6½ hours, one daily

Bergen 823kr, 14 hours, one overnight bus daily

TRAIN
There are two to four trains daily to/from Oslo (992kr, 6½ hours). Two head north to Bodø (1118kr, 9¾ hours).

Tromsø

POP 72,681

Located 400km north of the Arctic Circle at 69°N, the small city of Tromsø bills itself as Norway's gateway to the Arctic, and there's definitely more than a hint of polar atmosphere around town. These days it's best known as one of the better places in Norway to spot the Northern Lights and, with a large university, animated nightlife and a happening cultural calendar, Tromsø is also a notoriously lively city.

◉ Sights

★**Arctic Cathedral** CHURCH
(Ishavskatedralen, Tromsdalen Church; ☏410 08 470; www.ishavskatedralen.no/en; Hans Nilsens vei 41; adult/child 50kr/free, organ concerts 80-180kr; ☺9am-7pm Mon-Sat, 1-7pm Sun Jun–mid-Aug, 2-6pm mid-Aug–Dec, from 1pm Jan-Mar, from 3pm Apr & May; ☒20,22) The 11 triangles of the Arctic Cathedral (1965) suggest glacial crevasses and auroral curtains. The glowing stained-glass window that occupies the east end depicts Christ descending to earth, while the west end is filled by a futuristic organ and icicle-like chandeliers of Czech crystal. Despite its position beside one of Tromsø's main thoroughfares, the serenity inside remains unspoiled. It's on the southern side of the Bruvegen bridge, a few minutes on the bus from Havnegata, or a 1km walk.

Fjellheisen CABLE CAR
(☏926 17 837; www.fjellheisen.no/en; Solliveien 12; return ticket adult/child 210/100kr; ☺10am-1am Jun–mid-Aug, to 11pm mid-Aug–May) For a fine view of the city and the midnight sun, take the cable car to the top of Mt Storsteinen (421m). There's a terrace and (pricey) restaurant at the top, from where a network of hiking routes radiates. Departures in both directions are on the hour and half hour. Take bus 26 from Havnegata.

Polar Museum MUSEUM
(Polarmuseet; ☏77 62 33 60; www.uit.no/tmu/polarmuseet; Søndre Tollbodgate 11; adult/child 60/30kr; ☺9am-6pm mid-Jun–mid-Aug, 11am-

5pm rest of year) Fittingly for a town that was the launch pad for many pioneering expeditions to the North Pole, Tromsø's Polar Museum is an old-fashioned romp through life in the Arctic, taking in everything from the history of trapping to the ground-breaking expeditions of Nansen and Amundsen. There are some fascinating artefacts and black-and-white archive photos; though the stuffed remains of various formerly fuzzy, once-blubbery polar creatures are rather less fun...and there are lots of them.

🏃 Activities

Active Tromsø   ADVENTURE
(🖉 481 37 133; www.activetromso.no) An excellent company offering the full range of summer and winter activities, including hiking, glacier walks and sea kayaking. Dog-sledding expeditions are a particular speciality, with overnight husky trips offering the chance to spot the aurora en route. Bookings can be made online or at the tourist office (p860).

👉 Tours

★ Mack Microbrewery   BREWERY
(Mack Ølbryggeri; 🖉 77 62 45 80; www.mack.no; Peder Hansens gate 4; 180kr; ⊙3.30pm Mon-Fri, 2.30pm Sat) Founded by Ludwig Markus Mack in 1877, this venerable institution – the most northerly brewery in the world – merits a pilgrimage. Having moved its main production to larger premises in 2012, Mack uses the original brewery to produce a variety of quaffable craft beers. Sample a couple on one of its daily tours, which leave from the brewery's own **Kjeller 5** (🖉94 78 46 35; https://mack.no/en/kjeller5; Storgata 4; ⊙11am-6pm Mon-Fri, to 3pm Sat).

🛏 Sleeping

Tromsø Bed & Books   GUESTHOUSE, HOSTEL €€
(🖉77 02 98 00; www.bedandbooks.no; Strandvegen 45; s/d 700/1000kr; 🛜) Run by a pair of seasoned globetrotters, this lovely establishment has a youthful, hostel-like vibe and has two 'homes', both stuffed with books, retro furniture, old maps and curios, and thoughtfully designed for budget travellers. Noise does carry in the vintage buildings, but that's part of the budget trade-off. There's no breakfast, but both houses have shared kitchens.

Scandic Ishavshotel   HOTEL €€€
(🖉77 66 64 00; www.scandichotels.no; Fredrik Langes gate 2; d/ste from 1269/2701kr; 🅿🛜)

This is the prime spot in Tromsø if you want a waterside view – the Scandic Ishavshotel's architecture evokes an ocean-going vessel, complete with a flag-topped mast and crow's nest. The rooms are sleek, smart and businesslike, in oranges and slate greys. Breakfast is included.

🍴 Eating

★ Risø   CAFE €
(🖉416 64 516; www.risoe-mk.no; Strandgata 32; mains 95-179kr; ⊙7.30am-5pm Mon-Fri, from 9am Sat) You'll find this popular coffee and lunch bar packed throughout most of the day: young trendies come in for their hand-brewed Chemex coffee, while local workers pop in for the daily specials, open-faced sandwiches and delicious cakes. It's small, and the tables are packed in tight, so you might have to queue.

Driv   CAFE €€
(🖉77 60 07 63; http://driv.no; Storgata 6; mains 99-180kr; ⊙noon-11.30am Mon-Thu, to 3am Fri & Sat, kitchen shuts 9pm) This student-run diner occupying part of the old Mack Brewery serves meaty burgers (try its renowned Driv burger), sandwiches and great salads.

Mathallen   BISTRO €€€
(🖉77 68 01 00; www.mathallentromso.no; Grønnegata 60; lunch mains 100-235kr, dinner mains from 315kr, 4-course tasting menu 735kr; ⊙bistro 11am-11pm Tue-Sat, deli 10am-6pm Mon-Fri, to 4pm Sat) With its industrial styling, exposed pipes and open-fronted kitchen, this elegant restaurant wouldn't look out of place in Oslo or Stockholm. It serves some of the best modern Norwegian food in town, majoring in fish and local meats; the lunchtime special is a steal at 100kr. There's a deli next door selling tapenades, cheeses, smoked salmon and *lutefisk* (stockfish).

🍺 Drinking & Nightlife

Ølhallen   PUB
(🖉77 62 45 80; www.olhallen.no; Storgata 4; ⊙11am-8.30pm Mon-Wed, to 12.30am Thu, to 1.30am Fri, 10am-1.30am Sat) Reputedly the oldest pub in town, and once the hang-out for salty fishermen and Arctic sailors, this is now the brewpub for the excellent Mack Brewery. There are 67 Norwegian ales on tap to try – including a selection from Mack's own brewery and microbrewery – so it might take you a while (and a few livers) to work your way through them all.

Bardus BAR

(☑ 92 67 48 88; www.bardus.no; Cora Sandelsgate 4; ⊙ 6pm-midnight Mon, 4pm-1.30am Tue-Thu, 3pm-3am Fri & Sat, 5pm-midnight Sun) Former cinema Bardus serves up Oscar-worthy cocktails and a selection of local beers to a mature crowd. It's smart without being pretentious, with weighty wooden tables, sofa seating and potted bamboo trees lending a relaxed vibe. Try its signature seaweed cocktail: a tongue-tingling sensation of gin, vermouth and distilled seaweed that tastes infinitely better than it sounds.

ⓘ Information

Tourist Office (☑ 77 61 00 00; www.vis-ittromso.no; Samuel Arnesens gate 5, Prostne-set; ⊙ 9am-6pm Mon-Fri, from 10am Sat & Sun Jan-Mar & Jun-Aug, shorter hours rest of year; 📶) Tromsø's busy, efficient tourist office is in smart premises on the 1st floor of the Prostne-set terminal building. Book activities through the available terminals, or ask for help from the knowledgeable staff. Also offers a selection of high-quality souvenirs and publishes the comprehensive *Tromsø Guide*.

ⓘ Getting There & Around

Tromsø Airport (☑ 67 03 46 00; www.avinor.no/flyplass/tromso) is about 5km from the town centre, on the western side of Tromsøya and is the main airport for the far north.

Flybussen (www.flybussen.no/tromso; one way/return 100/160kr) runs between the airport and Scandic Grand Storgata (15 minutes), but public buses 40 or 42 will take you to the city centre (15 minutes) for half the price – buy a discounted ticket (adult/child 31/19kr) from Point newsagent inside the airport, otherwise pay on board (adult/child 50/25kr).

The main bus terminal is in **Prostneset** (Samuel Arnesens gate 5, Prostneset). There are up to three daily express buses to/from Narvik (300kr, 4¼ hours) and one to Bodø (731kr, 12½ hours).

SURVIVAL GUIDE

ⓘ Directory A–Z

ACCOMMODATION

Norway offers a wide range of accommodation, from camping, hostels and pensions to world-class hotels. Booking ahead is always wise in high season and during festivals and major annual conferences.

MONEY

ATMs are widely available, and credit cards are accepted almost universally for transactions, including at hotels, shops and restaurants, and on taxis, ferries and buses.

Service charges and tips are generally included in restaurant bills and taxi fares.

OPENING HOURS

These standard opening hours are for high season (mid-June to mid-August) and tend to decrease outside that time. With the exception of restaurants and bars, pretty much everything is closed on Sundays.

Banks 8am to 4pm Monday to Friday

Post Offices 9am to 6pm Monday to Friday, 10am to 3pm Saturday

Restaurants Noon to 3pm and 6pm to 11pm; some don't close between lunch and dinner

Shops 10am to 5pm Monday to Saturday; some stay open to 7pm on Thursday

Supermarkets 9am to 11pm Monday to Friday, to 10pm Saturday

PUBLIC HOLIDAYS

New Year's Day (Nyttårsdag) 1 January

Maundy Thursday (Skjærtorsdag) March/April

Good Friday (Langfredag) March/April

Easter Monday (Annen Påskedag) March/April

Labour Day (Første Mai, Arbeidetsdag) 1 May

Constitution Day (Nasjonaldag) 17 May

Ascension Day (Kristi Himmelfartsdag) May/June, 40th day after Easter

Whit Monday (Annen Pinsedag) May/June, eighth Monday after Easter

Christmas Day (Første Juledag) 25 December

Boxing Day (Annen Juledag) 26 December

SMOKING

Smoking and vaping are forbidden in enclosed public spaces, including hotels, restaurants and bars.

TELEPHONE

Local SIM cards are widely available and can be used in most international mobile phones. There's mobile coverage in all but wilderness areas.

TOILETS

Public toilets at many shopping malls, train stations and bus terminals charge up to 10kr, and some are only accessible using a contactless credit or debit card.

❶ Getting There & Away

AIR

Norway is well connected with direct flights to/ from the rest of Europe and, to a lesser extent, North America.

The main international Norwegian airports are Oslo Gardermoen (p848), Bergen (p852), Stavanger (p854) and Tromsø (p860), and are well served by airlines including **Norwegian** (www.norwegian.com), **SAS** (www.sas.no) and **Widerøe** (www.wideroe.no).

LAND

Norway shares land borders with Sweden, Finland and Russia.

Train travel is possible between Oslo and Stockholm, Gothenburg, Malmö and Hamburg, with less-frequent services to selected Swedish cities from Trondheim.

Eurolines (www.eurolines.com), **Nor-Way Bussekspress** (www.nor-way.no) and **Swebus Express** (www.swebusexpress.se) offer international bus routes.

❶ Getting Around

AIR

The major Norwegian domestic routes are quite competitive, meaning that it is possible (if you're flexible about departure dates and book early) to travel for little more than the equivalent train fare.

BOAT

Norway's excellent system of ferries connects otherwise inaccessible, isolated communities with an extensive network of car ferries criss-crossing the fjords; express boats link offshore islands to the mainland. Most ferries accommodate motor vehicles, but queues and delays are possible at popular crossings in summer.

BUS

Buses on Norway's extensive local and long-distance bus network are comfortable and make a habit of running on time. You can check countrywide bus times (and some prices) at **EnTur** (www.en-tur.com).

CAR & MOTORCYCLE

There are no special requirements for bringing your car to Norway. Main highways, such as the E16 from Oslo to Bergen and the entire E6 from Oslo to Kirkenes, are open year-round; smaller, scenic mountain roads generally only open from June to September, snow conditions permitting.

Fuel and car rental is more expensive than in other parts of Europe, so factor this in to your budget when planning, as well as road tolls and fares for any ferry crossings.

Vegmeldingssentralen (☎ press 9 for English 22 07 30 00; www.vegvesen.no) provides 24-hour, up-to-date advice on road closures and conditions throughout the country.

TRAIN

NSB (Norwegian State Railways, Norges Statsbaner; ☎ press 9 for English 81 50 08 88; www.nsb.no), Norway's state railway company, operates an excellent, though limited, system of lines connecting Oslo with cities including Stavanger, Bergen, Trondheim, and Bodø; lines also connect Sweden with Oslo and Trondheim.

Look out for cheap *minipris* advance fares, which offer substantial discounts on standard ticket prices.

Poland

POP 38.5 MILLION

Best Places to Eat

➜ Warszawa Wschodnia (p868)

➜ Krako Slow Wines (p874)

➜ Kardamon (p877)

➜ Szeroka 9 (p889)

➜ Tawerna Mestwin (p887)

Best Places to Stay

➜ Dream Hostel (p867)

➜ Aparthotel Vanilla (p873)

➜ Mamas & Papas Hostel (p886)

➜ Puro Poznań Stare Miasto (p883)

➜ Hotel Spichrz (p888)

Why Go?

If they were handing out prizes for 'most eventful past', Poland would score a gold medal. The nation has spent centuries at the pointy end of history, grappling with war and invasion. Nothing, however, has succeeded in suppressing Poles' strong sense of nationhood and cultural identity. As a result, bustling centres like Warsaw and Kraków exude a sophisticated energy that's a heady mix of old and new.

Away from the cities, Poland is surprisingly diverse, from its northern beaches to the long chain of mountains on its southern border. In between, towns and cities are dotted with ruined castles, picturesque market squares and historic churches.

Although prices have steadily risen in the postcommunist era, Poland is still good value. As the Poles continue to reconcile their distinctive national identity with their location at the heart of Europe, it's a fascinating time to pay a visit.

When to Go
Warsaw

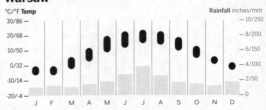

May–Jun Stately Kraków returns to life after a long winter.

Jul–Aug A brief but hot summer is good for swimming in the Baltic Sea or hiking in the mountains.

Sep–Oct Warm and sunny enough for an active city break to Warsaw.

Entering the Country

As a member of the EU, Poland has open borders (and plenty of rail and road crossings) on its western and southern frontiers with Germany, the Czech Republic and Slovakia. Crossings with EU-member Lithuania, on the northeastern end of the country, are also open.

It's a different story crossing into Ukraine, Belarus and Russia's Kaliningrad enclave, which form part of the EU's external border and may require visas and advance planning.

The following is a list of 24-hour border crossings into Poland's non-EU neighbours.

Belarusian border (south to north): Terespol, Kuźnica

Russian (Kaliningrad) border (east to west): Bezledy–Bagrationowsk, Gronowo

Ukrainian border (south to north): Medyka, Hrebenne–Rawa Ruska, Dorohusk

---

ITINERARIES

One Week

Spend a day exploring Warsaw (p864), with a stroll around the Old Town and a stop at the Museum of the History of Polish Jews. Next day, head to historic Kraków (p870) for three days, visiting the beautiful Old Town, Wawel Castle and former Jewish district of Kazimierz. Take a day trip to Auschwitz-Birkenau (p875), the former Nazi German extermination camp. Afterwards, head to Zakopane (p878) for a day in the mountains.

Two Weeks

Follow the above itinerary, then travel to Wrocław (p880) for two days, taking in its historic Cathedral Island. Head north to Gothic Toruń (p888) for a day, then onward to Gdańsk (p884) for two days, exploring the attractive Old Town, the superb Museum of WWII and the magnificent castle at Malbork (p886).

Essential Food & Drink

Barszcz Famous beetroot soup comes in two varieties: red (made from beetroot) and white (with wheat flour and sausage).

Bigos Thick stew with sauerkraut and meat.

Pierogi Flour dumplings, usually stuffed with cheese, mushrooms or meat.

Szarlotka Apple cake with cream; a Polish classic.

Wódka Vodka: try it plain, or ask for *myśliwska* (flavoured with juniper berries).

Żurek Hearty, sour rye soup includes sausage and hard-boiled egg.

AT A GLANCE

Area 312,696 sq km

Capital Warsaw

Country Code ☑ 48

Currency Polish złoty (zł)

Emergency Ambulance ☑ 999, fire ☑ 998, police ☑ 997; from mobile phones ☑ 112

Language Polish

Time GMT/UTC+1

Visas Generally not required for stays of up to 90 days

POLAND

Sleeping Price Ranges

Prices listed are for an average double room in high season, with private bathroom and including breakfast.

€ less than 150zł

€€ 150zł–400zł

€€€ more than 400zł

Eating Price Ranges

The following price ranges refer to the cost of an average main-course item.

€ less than 20zł

€€ 20zł–40zł

€€€ more than 40zł

Poland Highlights

1 Kraków (p870)
Experiencing the beauty and history of the Old Town.

2 Wrocław (p880)
Enjoying the city's student-fuelled party vibe.

3 Auschwitz-Birkenau (p875) Remembering the victims of the Holocaust.

4 Museum of WWII (p884) Discovering Poland's wartime history in Gdańsk's superb modern museum.

5 Zakopane (p878)
Skiing or hiking the Tatra Mountains from this alpine resort.

6 Warsaw Rising Museum (p865) Being dazzled by one of Warsaw's best museums.

WARSAW

POP 1.76 MILLION

Once you've travelled around Poland, you realise this: Warsaw is different. Rather than being centred on an old market square, the capital is spread across a broad area with diverse architecture: restored Gothic, communist concrete, modern glass and steel.

This jumble is a sign of the city's tumultuous past. Warsaw has suffered the worst history could throw at it, including near destruction at the end of WWII – and survived. As a result, it's a fascinating collection of neighbourhoods and landmarks. Excellent museums interpret its complex story, from the joys of Chopin's music to the tragedy of the Jewish ghetto.

It's not all about the past, however. Warsaw's restaurant and entertainment scene is the best in Poland. You can dine well and affordably here on cuisines from around the world, and take your choice of lively bars and clubs. This gritty city knows how to have fun.

⊙ Sights

★ Royal Castle   MUSEUM
(Zamek Królewski; ☎22 355 5170; www.zamek-krolewski.pl; Plac Zamkowy 4, Stare Miasto; adult/concession 30/20zł, free Wed; ☉10am-6pm Tue-Thu & Sat, to 8pm Fri, 11am-6pm Sun, closes 4pm Oct-Apr; 🚇Stare Miasto) This massive brick edifice, a copy of the original blown up by the Germans in WWII, began life as a wooden stronghold of the dukes of Mazovia in the 14th century. Its heyday came in the mid-17th century, when it became one of Europe's most splendid royal residences. It then served the Russian tsars and, in 1918, after Poland regained independence, became the residence of the president. Today it is filled with period furniture and works of art.

★ Old Town Square   SQUARE
(Rynek Starego Miasta, Stare Miasto; 🚇Stare Miasto) At the centre of the partially walled Old Town (Stare Miasto), the Old Town Square is, for those with an eye for historic buildings, the loveliest square in Warsaw. It's lined with tall houses exhibiting a fine blend of Renaissance, baroque, Gothic and neoclassical elements; aside from the facades at Nos 34 and 36, all were rebuilt after being reduced to rubble by the Germans at the close of WWII.

Church of the Holy Cross   CHURCH
(Kościół św Krzyża; ☎22 826 8910; www.swkrzyz.pl; ul Krakowskie Przedmieście 3, Śródmieście Północne; ☉10-11am & 1-4pm Mon-Sat, 2-4pm Sun; 🚇Nowy Świat-Uniwersytet) **FREE** Of Warsaw's many impressive churches, this is the one most visitors want to see. Not so much to admire the fine baroque altarpieces that miraculously survived the Warsaw Rising reprisals, but to glimpse a small urn by the second pillar on the left side of the nave. This urn, adorned with an epitaph to Frédéric Chopin, contains what remains of the composer's heart. It was brought here from Paris after the his death.

★ Palace of Culture & Science   HISTORIC BUILDING
(PKiN, Pałac Kultury i Nauki; ☎22 656 7600; www.pkin.pl; Plac Defilad 1, Śródmieście Północne; observation deck adult/concession 20/15zł; ☉observation deck 10am-8pm; 🚇Centrum) Love it or hate it, every visitor to Warsaw should visit the iconic, socialist-realist PKiN (as its full Polish name is abbreviated). This 'gift of friendship' from the Soviet Union was built in the early 1950s, and at 231m high remains the tallest building in Poland. It's home to a huge congress hall, theatres, a multiscreen cinema

and museums. Take the high-speed lift to the 30th-floor (115m) observation terrace *(taras widokowy)* to take it all in.

★ Warsaw Rising Museum   MUSEUM
(Muzeum Powstania Warszawskiego; www.1944.pl; ul Grzybowska 79, Czyste; adult/concession 25/20zł, Sun free; ☉8am-6pm Mon, Wed & Fri, to 8pm Thu, 10am-6pm Sat & Sun; 🚇Rondo Daszyńskiego, 🚇Muzeum Powstania Warszawskiego) One of Warsaw's best, this museum traces the history of the city's heroic but doomed uprising against the German occupation in 1944 via three levels of interactive displays, photographs, film archives and personal accounts. The volume of material is overwhelming, but the museum does an excellent job of instilling a sense of the desperation residents felt in deciding to oppose the occupation by force, and of illustrating the dark consequences, including the Germans' destruction of the city in the aftermath.

★ POLIN Museum of the History of Polish Jews   MUSEUM
(☎22 471 0301; www.polin.pl; ul Anielewicza 6, Muranów; main exhibition adult/concession 25/15zł, temporary exhibits adult/concession 12/8zł, Thu free; ☉10am-6pm Mon, Thu & Fri, to 8pm Wed, Sat & Sun; 🚇Ratusz Arsenał, 🚇Muranów, Anielewicza) This exceptional museum's permanent exhibition opened in late 2014. Impressive multimedia exhibits document 1000 years of Jewish history in Poland, from accounts of the earliest Jewish traders in the region through waves of mass migration, progress and pogroms, all the way to WWII and the destruction of Europe's largest Jewish community. It's worth booking online, and you can hire an audio guide (10zł) to get the most out of the many rooms of displays, interactive maps, photos and videos.

★ Fryderyk Chopin Museum   MUSEUM
(☎22 441 6251; www.chopin.museum; ul Okólnik 1, Śródmieście Północne; adult/concession 22/13zł, Wed free; ☉11am-8pm Tue-Sun; 🚇Nowy Świat-Uniwersytet) A high-tech, multimedia museum within the baroque Ostrogski Palace, showcasing the work of the country's most famous composer. You're encouraged to take your time through four floors of displays, including stopping by the listening booths in the basement where you can browse Chopin's oeuvre to your heart's content. Limited visitation is allowed each hour; your best bet is to book your visit in advance by phone or email. Entrance at ul Tamka 43.

Central Warsaw

N 0 ——————— 500 m
   0 ——————— 0.25 miles

POLIN Museum of the History of Polish Jews (300m)

Galeria Sztuki (1.6km)

Świętojerska

Polyester (250m)

Długa

Miodowa

2 ◎ **Old Town Square**

ℹ️ Tourist Office – Old Town

Jezuicka 6

Świętojańska

Bug[aj]

Podwale

Vistula

4 🏰 **Royal Castle**

POLAND WARSAW

Generała Andersa

Dłuuga

Al Solidarności

M 🅼 **Ratusz-Arsenał**

Senatorska

Kozia

7

Bednarska

Furmańska

Dobra

Senatorska

Wierzbowa

Trębacka

Mollera

Krakowskie Przedmieście

Browarna

Elektoralna

Saxon Gardens

Plac Piłsudskiego

Plac Małachowskiego

Traugutta

5 ✝

Oboźna

Seweryn[ów]

Dynasy

Warsaw Rising Museum (1.4km)

Grzybowska

Marszałkowska

Królewska

Kredytowa

Plac Dąbrowskiego

12 🏬

Czackiego

Nowy Świat - Uniwersytet 🅼

Fryderyk Chopin Museum

Jasna

Świętokrzyska

Mazowiecka

Tamka

Ordynacka

Okólnik

🏛 1

Plac Próżna Grzybowski

Zielna

9

Świętokrzyska 🅼

Moniuszki

13 🍴

Sienkiewicza

Warecka

Plac Powstańców Warszawy

Nowy Świat

Kopernika

Foksal

Twarda

Marszałkowska

Jasna

Złota

Zgoda

Górskiego

Szpitalna

Chmielna

10

Smolna

Palace of Culture & Science

3 🏛

Plac Defilad

Centrum 🅼

11 ✗

Bracka

Sienna

Emilii Plater

Złota

ℹ️ Tourist Office – PKiN

Widok

Al Jerozolimskie

Książęca

Warszawa Śródmieście Train Station

Nowogrodzka

Plac Trzech Krzyży

Wieska

Warszawa Centralna Train Station

🅿

Żurawia

Wspólna

Hoża

Wilcza

Al Jerozolimskie

Warszawa Zachodnia Terminal (2.2km)

Niepodległości

Emilii Plater

Wspólna

Poznańska

Marszałkowska

8

Hoża

Wilcza

Charlotte Chleb i Wino (500m); CMA (600m); Stodoła (2.2km)

Kluczka

Mokotowska

Al Ujazdowskie

Łazienki Park (1km)

Central Warsaw

Łazienki Park GARDENS
(Park Łazienkowski; ☎504 243 783; www.lazienki-krolewskie.pl; ul Agrykola 1, Ujazdów; ⊙24 hours; 🚊Plac Na Rozdrożu) **FREE** Pronounced wah-zhen-kee, this park is a beautiful place of man-icured greens, wooded glades and strutting peacocks. Once a hunting ground attached to **Ujazdów Castle** (ul Jazdów 2), Łazienki was ac-quired by King Stanisław August Poniatowski in 1764 and transformed into a splendid park complete with palace, amphitheatre, and var-ious follies and other buildings.

Neon Museum MUSEUM
(Muzeum Neonów; ☎665 711635; www.neon muzeum.org; ul Mińska 25, Kamionek; adult/con-cession 12/10zł; ⊙noon-5pm Mon, Tue, Thu & Fri, noon-6pm Sat, 11am-5pm Sun; 🚊Bliska) Situated within the cool Soho Factory complex of old industrial buildings housing designers and artists, this museum is devoted to the pres-ervation of the iconic neon signs of the com-munist era. The collection is arrayed within a historic factory, with many large pieces ful-ly lit. Other exhibits are dotted around the complex and are illuminated after dark. It's well worth the trek across the river. Get off the tram at the Bliska stop.

🛏 **Sleeping**

Warsaw has a huge range of accommoda-tion, from backpacker hostels to luxury bou-tique hotels, spread widely across the city centre. However, you'll get cheaper rates at places outside the centre in exchange for a short tram or metro ride. Many business ho-tels offer discounted rates at weekends.

★ **Dream Hostel** HOSTEL €
(☎22 419 4848; https://dream-hostels.com; Krakowskie Przedmieście 55, Śródmieście Północne; dm/d or tw from 50/193zł; 🛜; 🚊Plac Zamkowy) This large and lively hostel has everything go-ing for it – comfy beds, clean bathrooms, well-equipped kitchens, a choice of dorms (some women-only) and private rooms, a friendly on-site bar and helpful staff.

Oki Doki City Hostel HOSTEL €
(☎22 828 0122; www.okidoki.pl; Plac Dąbrowskie-go 3, Śródmieście Północne; dm/d from 38/168zł; 🛜; Ⓜ Świętokrzyska) Arguably Warsaw's most popular hostel and certainly one of the best, each of its bright, large rooms is individually named and decorated. Accommodation is in three- to eight-bed dorms, with a special three-bed dorm for women only. The own-ers are well travelled and know the needs of backpackers, providing a kitchen and a laundry service. Breakfast available (15zł).

Castle Inn HOTEL €€
(☎22 425 0100; http://castleinn.pl; ul Świętojańska 2, Stare Miasto; s/d from 356/376zł; ❄🛜; 🚊Stare Miasto) This 'art hotel' is housed in a 17th-century townhouse, one of the few that was not totally destroyed during WWII. All rooms overlook either Castle Sq or St John's Cathe-dral, and come in a range of quirky designs, such as 'Viktor', named for a reclusive street artist, complete with tasteful graffiti and a gorgeous castle view. Note: there are lots of steep stairs, and no lift.

Royal Route Residence APARTMENT €€
(☎22 887 9800; www.royalrouteresidencewarsaw. com; ul Nowy Świat 29/3, Śródmieście Północne; 2-person apt from 430zł; 🅿🛜📷; 🚊Foksal) Won-derfully central accommodation in an attrac-tive historic building, offering well-equipped apartments that sleep from two to seven people. Furnishings are bright and modern, and mod cons include microwave, espresso machine and washing machine. Go through the passageway into the courtyard; reception is tucked in the corner on the right.

★ **H15** BOUTIQUE HOTEL €€€
(☎22 553 8700; www.h15boutiqueapartments. com; ul Poznanska 15, Śródmieście Południowe; r/ apt from 540/1250zł; 🅿❄🛜; 🚊Hoża) Set in a gorgeous late-19th-century apartment block that once housed the Soviet Union's embassy,

this is one of Warsaw's most luxurious hotels. Modern art and designer furniture vie for your attention with elements of retained communist-era decor. Rooms are quirky and individual, and the location is bang in the middle of the city's trendiest district.

✗ Eating

The largest concentration of eateries is on and around Krakowskie Przedmieście and Nowy Świat, and south of al Jerozolimskie. The Old Town generally houses expensive tourist traps, but there are a few quality spots.

Mango
VEGAN €

(📞535 533 629; www.mangovegan.pl; ul Bracka 20, Śródmieście Północne; mains 19-45zł; ⊙11am-10pm; 🛜📶; Ⓜ Centrum) Mango is a stylish all-vegan eatery with a simple contemporary interior and pleasant outdoor terrace. Excellent menu items range from quinoa burgers to veggie kebabs. The 'Mango Plate' (*talerz mango*) of hummus, mango, falafel, eggplant, olives, sweet peppers and harissa paste served with pita bread is top value at 25zł.

Charlotte Chleb i Wino
FRENCH €

(📞662 204 555; www.bistrocharlotte.pl; Plac Zbawiciela, Śródmieście Południowe; mains 10-19zł; ⊙7am-midnight Mon-Thu, to 1am Fri, 8am-1am Sat, 8am-10pm Sun; 🛜; Ⓠ Plac Zbawiciela) This French-Polish bakery and bistro dishes up tantalising croissants and pastries at the break of dawn, then transitions to big salads and crusty sandwiches through the lunch and dinner hours, and finally to wine on the terrace in the evening. Great value for money.

★ĆMA
POLISH €€

(📞22 221 8176; www.mateuszgessler.com.pl; Unit 31, Hala Koszyki, ul Koszykowa 63, Śródmieście Południowe; mains 25-68zł; ⊙24hr; 🛜; Ⓠ Plac Konstytucji) 📝 Star chef Mateusz Gessler established this informal, brasserie-style eatery in the hipster heartland of the Hala Koszyki (a converted market hall filled with artisan shops and eateries). The menu brings a deft modern touch to the most traditional of Polish dishes, from head cheese (pig's-head brawn) to goose stomachs (stewed in gravy).

★Warszawa Wschodnia
MODERN EUROPEAN €€€

(📞22 870 2918; www.mateuszgessler.com.pl; Soho Factory, ul Mińska 25, Kamionek; mains 58-78zł, tasting menu 150zł; ⊙24hr; 🛜; Ⓠ Bliska) 📝 Fabulous restaurant in a huge industrial building, taking its name from the neon sign salvaged from the nearby train station of the same name. Serves a modern interpretation of Polish cuisine with French influences. The bar-kitchen area to the right of the entrance is open 24 hours.

🍷 Drinking & Nightlife

Bars are concentrated around the Old Town, ul Nowy Świat and south of Al Jerozolimskie. For clubbing check out ul Mazowiecka in the city centre, and ul Ząbkowska in Praga.

★Galeria Sztuki
CAFE

(📞22 619 8109; http://.caffee.stanowski.pl; ul Ząbkowska 13, Stara Praga; ⊙9am-11pm Mon-Thu, to midnight Fri, from 10am Sat, to 10pm Sun; 🛜; Ⓜ Dworzec Wileński) If you're staying on the east side of the river, this cosy spot – part cafe-bar, part antique shop – is a great place to escape to. It serves some of the best coffee in town, has a good choice of wines by the glass and does breakfasts (mostly egg-based) until noon.

Polyester
BAR

(📞733 464 600; ul Freta 49/51, Nove Miasto; ⊙noon-12.30am Sun-Thu, to 1.30am Fri-Sat; 🛜; Ⓠ Plac Krasińskich) Smooth establishment with retro furnishings and a laid-back vibe. Serves good cocktails, as well as a full range of coffee drinks and light food.

Enklawa
CLUB

(📞22 827 3151; www.enklawa.com; ul Mazowiecka 12, Śródmieście Północne; ⊙10pm-3am Tue, to 4am Wed-Sat; Ⓜ Świętokrzyska) Blue and purple light illuminates this space with comfy plush seating, mirrored ceilings, two bars and plenty of room to dance. Check out the extensive drinks menu, hit the dance floor or observe the action from a stool on the upper balcony. Wednesday night is 'old school' night, with music from the '70s to the '90s. Smart dress code.

☆ Entertainment

Filharmonia Narodowa
CLASSICAL MUSIC

(National Philharmonic; 📞22 551 7130; www.filharmonia.pl; ul Jasna 5, Śródmieście Północne; tickets from 60zł; ⊙box office 10am-2pm & 3-7pm Mon-Sat; Ⓜ Świętokrzyska) Home of the world-famous National Philharmonic Orchestra and Choir of Poland, founded in 1901, this venue has a concert hall (enter from ul Sienkiewicza 10) and a chamber-music hall (enter from ul Moniuszki 5), both of which stage regular concerts. There are box offices at both entrances.

Stodoła
LIVE MUSIC

(📞22 825 6031; www.stodola.pl; ul Batorego 10, Śródmieście Południowe; ⊙box office 9am-9pm Mon-Fri,

WORTH A TRIP

ŁÓDŹ

Łódź (pronounced *woodge*) is a red-brick city that grew fabulously wealthy in the 19th century on the back of its massive textile industry. Today it's famous for its architecture (both historic and modern), its colourful street art, its Jewish heritage and its many fine museums and art galleries. It is also the centre of Poland's film industry.

The city's abundant **street art** grew out of the Urban Forms Festival in 2009; today more than 100 murals and installations add colour and life to the city's rapidly rejuvenating centre. The **tourist office** (Centrum Informacji Turystycznej; ☑42 208 8181; www.lodz. travel; ul Piotrkowska 28; ☉9am-7pm Mon-Fri, 10am-6pm Sat, to-4pm Sun, shorter hours Oct-Apr; ☎; ☒Zachodnia-Więckowskiego) will point you to the best-known examples, and many are documented on the Urban Forms (www.urbanforms.org) website.

Łódź is an easy day trip from Warsaw, with a fast and frequent rail service (31zł, 90 minutes, at least hourly).

---

to 2pm Sat; Ⓜ Pole Mokotowskie) Opened in 1956, and originally a cafeteria and social club for builders working on the Palace of Culture & Science (p865), this venue is one of Warsaw's biggest and longest-running live-music stages. A great place to catch touring bands.

ⓘ Information

Tourist Office – PKiN (www.warsawtour.pl; Plac Defilad 1, Śródmieście Północne; ☉8am-7pm May-Sep, to 6pm Oct-Apr; ☎; Ⓜ Centrum, ☒Warszawa Śródmieście) The Palace of Culture & Science branch of Warsaw's official tourist information organisation is a central resource for maps and advice. The staff can also help with accommodation. There's no phone number, so visit in person. The entrance is on ul Emilii Plater.

Tourist Office – Old Town (www.warsawtour. pl; Rynek Starego Miasta 19/21, Stare Miasto; ☉9am-8pm May-Sep, to 6pm Oct-Apr; ☎; ☒Stare Miasto) Hands out free maps and booklets, and dispenses information on what to see and do during your stay. There's no phone, so visit in person or contact by email.

ⓘ Getting There & Away

AIR

Warsaw Chopin Airport (Lotnisko Chopina Warszawa; ☑22 650 4220; www.lotnisko-chopina.pl; ul Żwirki i Wigury 1, Włochy; ☒Warszawa Lotnisko Chopina) Warsaw's main airport lies in the suburb of Okęcie, 10km south of the city centre; it handles most domestic and international flights.

Warsaw Modlin Airport (Modlin Lotnisko; ☑22 315 1880; www.modlinairport.pl; ul Generała Wiktora Thommée 1a, Nowy Dwór Mazowiecki; ☒Modlin) Smaller airport 35km north of War-

saw used by budget carriers, including Ryanair for flights to and from the UK.

Buy tickets for public transport from the tourist office or from one of several newsagents.

BUS

Warszawa Zachodnia bus terminal (Dworzec Autobusowy Warszawa Zachodnia; ☑703 403 403; www.dawz.pl; al Jerozolimskie 144, Czyste; ☉information & tickets 5.30am-10pm), west of the city centre, handles the majority of international and domestic routes from the capital, run by various operators.

FlixBus (https://global.flixbus.com) operates buses to cities across Poland and beyond from **Młociny bus station** (Dworzec Autobusowy Młociny; ul Kasprowicza 145, Bielany; Ⓜ Młociny) north of the city centre, and **Wilanowska bus station** (Dworzec Autobusowy Wilanowska; ul Puławska 145, Wilanowska; Ⓜ Wilanowska) south of the centre, as well as from Warszawa Zachodnia. Each station is next to the Metro station of the same name. Book on its website for the lowest fares.

TRAIN

Warsaw has several train stations, but the one most travellers use is **Warszawa Centralna** (Warsaw Central; www.pkp.pl; al Jerozolimskie 54, Śródmieście Północne; ☉24hr; ☒Warszawa Centralna), with connections to every major Polish city and many other places in between; check the online timetable in English at http://rozklad-pkp.pl for times and fares.

You can buy tickets from ticket machines (instructions available in English), or one of the many ticket counters in both the main hall and the shopping concourse. It's best to write down your destination and travel dates/times to show the ticket seller, as not all ticket agents speak English.

POLAND WARSAW

ⓘ Getting Around

TO/FROM THE AIRPORT

Train is the easiest way of getting from **Warsaw Chopin Airport** to the city. Regular services run to Warszawa Centralna station every 30 minutes between 5am and 10.30pm (4.40zł, 20 minutes). Bus 175 (4.40zł, every 15 minutes, 5am to 11pm) runs to the city, passing along ul Jerozolimskie and ul Nowy Świat before terminating at Plac Piłsudskiego, within walking distance of the Old Town.

A shuttle bus transfers passengers from **Warsaw Modlin Airport** to nearby Modlin station, where you can catch a train to Warszawa Centralna (19zł, one hour, at least hourly). **Modlin Bus** (☑ 703 403 993; www.modlinbus.com) services run between Modlin airport and the Palace of Culture & Science in central Warsaw (35zł, one hour, hourly). Buy tickets from the driver; lower fares available online.

PUBLIC TRANSPORT

Warsaw's integrated public transport system is operated by **ZTM** (Zarząd Transportu Miejskiego, Urban Transport Authority; ☑ 19 115; www.ztm.waw.pl) and consists of tram, bus and metro lines, all using the same ticketing system.

Buy tickets at news stands – look for a sign saying 'Sprzedaży Biletów ZTM' – and ticket machines (*automat biletów*; instructions available in English) at metro stations and major tram and bus stops (coins, banknotes and credit cards). There are also machines on newer trams and buses (exact fare in coins only, or credit card).

For most trips, a *jednorazowy bilet* (single-journey ticket, 3.40zł) is sufficient. It is valid for 20 minutes, including transfers between bus, tram and metro. For longer journeys, consider a 40- or 90-minute ticket (4.40zł and 7zł respectively). These tickets also allow unlimited transfers.

KRAKÓW

POP 767,350

Many Polish cities are centred on an attractive Old Town, but none compare to Kraków (pronounced krak-oof) for effortless beauty. As it was the royal capital of Poland until 1596 and miraculously escaped destruction in WWII, Kraków is packed with appealing historic buildings and streetscapes. One of the most important sights is Wawel Castle, from where the ancient Polish kingdom was once ruled.

South of the castle lies the former Jewish quarter of Kazimierz. Its silent synagogues are a reminder of the tragedy of WWII. These days, the quarter has been injected with new life and is home to some of the city's best bars and clubs.

◉ Sights

◉ Wawel Hill

South of Old Town, this prominent hilltop is crowned with the former Royal Castle and cathedral – both enduring symbols of Poland.

★**Wawel Royal Castle** CASTLE
(Zamek Królewski na Wawelu; ☑ Wawel Visitor Centre 12 422 5155; www.wawel.krakow.pl; grounds free, attractions priced separately; ☉ grounds 6am-dusk; ⊕ 6, 8, 10, 13, 18) As the political and cultural heart of Poland through the 16th century, Wawel Castle is a potent symbol of national identity. It's now a museum containing five separate sections: Crown Treasury & Armoury, State Rooms, Royal Private Apartments, Lost Wawel and the Exhibition of Oriental Art. Each requires a separate ticket. Of the five, the State Rooms and Royal Private Apartments are the most impressive, but to be honest, the best part is just wandering around the castle grounds.

The Renaissance palace you see today dates from the 16th century. An original, smaller residence was built in the early 11th century by King Bolesław I Chrobry. Kazimierz III Wielki (Casimir III the Great) turned it into a formidable Gothic castle, but when it burned down in 1499, Zygmunt I Stary (Sigismund I the Old; 1506–48) commissioned a new residence. Within 30 years, the current Italian-inspired palace was in place. Despite further extensions and alterations, the three-storey structure, complete with a courtyard arcaded on three sides, has been preserved to this day.

Repeatedly sacked and vandalised by the Swedish and Prussian armies, the castle was occupied in the 19th century by the Austrians, who intended to make Wawel a barracks, while moving the royal tombs elsewhere. They never got that far, but they did turn the royal kitchen and coach house into a military hospital and raze two churches. They also built a new ring of massive brick walls, largely ruining the original Gothic fortifications.

After Kraków was incorporated into re-established Poland after WWI, restoration work began and continued until the outbreak of WWII. The work was resumed after the war and has been able to recover a good deal of the castle's earlier external form and interior decoration.

Wawel Cathedral
CHURCH

(📞 12 429 9515; www.katedra-wawelska.pl; cathedral free, combined entry for crypts, bell tower & museum adult/concession 12/7zł; ⊙ 9am-5pm Mon-Sat, from 12.30pm Sun Apr-Oct, to 4pm Nov-Mar; 🚌 6, 8, 10, 13, 18) Wawel Cathedral has witnessed many coronations, funerals and burials of Poland's monarchs and nobles over the centuries. The present-day cathedral is basically a Gothic structure, but chapels in different styles were built around it later. The showpiece chapel is the **Sigismund Chapel** (Kaplica Zygmuntowska) on the southern wall. It's often referred to as the most beautiful Renaissance chapel north of the Alps, recognisable from the outside by its gilded dome. An audio guide (7zł) helps to put it all in context.

👁 Old Town

The vast Rynek Główny (main square) is the focus of the Old Town, and is Europe's largest medieval town square (200m by 200m).

★ Rynek Underground
MUSEUM

(📞 12 426 5060; www.podziemiarynku.com; Rynek Główny 1; adult/concession 21/18zł, Tue free; ⊙ 10am-8pm Wed-Mon, to 4pm Tue, longer hours Apr-Oct; 🚌 1, 6, 8, 13, 18) This fascinating attraction beneath the market square consists of an underground route through medieval market stalls and other long-forgotten chambers. The

'Middle Ages meets 21st century' experience is enhanced by holograms and audiovisual wizardry. Buy tickets at an office on the western side of the Cloth Hall (Sukiennice 21), where an electronic board shows tour times and tickets available. The entrance to the tunnels is on the northeastern end of the Cloth Hall.

St Mary's Basilica
CHURCH

(Basilica of the Assumption of Our Lady; 📞 12 422 0521; www.mariacki.com; Plac Mariacki 5, Rynek Główny; adult/concession church 10/5zł, tower 15/10zł; ⊙ 11.30am-6pm Mon-Sat, from 2pm Sun; 🚌 1, 6, 8, 13, 18) This striking brick church, best known simply as St Mary's, is dominated by two towers of different heights. The first church here was built in the 1220s and following its destruction during a Tatar raid, construction of the basilica began. Tour the exquisite interior, with its remarkable carved wooden altarpiece, and in summer climb the tower for excellent views. Don't miss the hourly *hejnał* (bugle call) from the taller tower.

Cloth Hall
HISTORIC BUILDING

(Sukiennice; Rynek Główny 1/3; 🚌 1, 6, 8, 13, 18) **FREE** Dominating the middle of Rynek Główny, this building was once the centre of Kraków's medieval clothing trade. Created in the early 14th century when a roof was put over two rows of stalls, it was extended into a 108m-long Gothic structure, then rebuilt in Renaissance style after a 1555 fire; the arcades were a late-19th-century addition. The ground floor is now a busy trading centre for crafts and souvenirs; the upper

POLAND KRAKÓW

WORTH A TRIP

A UNESCO-PROTECTED SALT MINE

Some 14km southeast of Kraków, the **Wieliczka** (📞 12 278 7302; www.kopalnia.pl; ul Daniłowicza 10; adult/concession 94/74zł; ⊙ 7.30am-7.30pm Apr-Oct, 8am-5pm Nov-Mar; 📶 ♿) (vyeh-leech-kah) salt mine has been welcoming tourists since 1722 and today is one of Poland's most popular attractions. It's a subterranean labyrinth of tunnels and chambers – about 300km distributed over nine levels, the deepest being 327m underground – of which a small part is open to the public via two-hour guided tours.

The salt-hewn formations include chapels with altarpieces and figures, while others are adorned with statues and monuments – and there are even underground lakes. The climax of the tour is the vast chamber (54m by 18m, and 12m high) housing the ornamented **Chapel of St Kinga** (Kaplica Św Kingi). Every single element here, from chandeliers to altarpieces, is made of salt.

English-language tours depart every half-hour from 8.30am to 6pm. During the rest of the year there are between six and eight daily tours in English.

Minibuses to Wieliczka (3zł) depart Kraków frequently between 6am and 8pm from stands along ul Pawia, across from the Galeria Krakowska mall.

Kraków – Old Town & Wawel

0 ___ 200 m
0 ___ 0.1 miles

Kraków Główny Train Station

Bus Station

Kurniki

Plac Matejki

8

Plac Kolejowy

Fenn'a

Długa

Paderewskiego

Warszawska

Zacisze

Worcella

Pawia

Bosacka

Basztowa

Pijarska

Pijarska

Lubicz

Strzelecka

Reformacka

Św Tomasza

Sławkowska

Św Jana

Floriańska

Spitalna

Plac Św
Ducha

Św Marka

Zamenhofa

10

Szczepańska

**InfoKraków –
Old Town**

Św Tomasza

Św Krzyża

Skłodowskiej-Curie

Westerplatte

Radziwiłłowska

Blich

Jagiellońska

**Rynek
Główny**

Szewska

Rynek Underground

1

**InfoKraków –
Cloth Hall**

4

Plac
Mariacki

Mikołajska

Mikołajska

Kopernika

Kołłątaja

13

Wiślna

Bracka

Mały
Rynek

Sienna

Zyblikiewicza

Gen Sołtyka

**Kraków
Philharmonic
(100m)**

Gołębia

Grodzka

Stolarska

OLD TOWN

Planty

Wielopole

Bonerowska

WESOŁA

Franciszkańska

Plac
Dominikański

Dominikańska

Poselska

Plac
Wszystkich
Świętych

9

Senacka

Starowiślna

6

Metalowców

Siedleckiego

Straszewskiego

Plac
Św Marii
Magdaleny

Kanonicza

Grodzka

7

Sarego

Bogusławskiego

Św Gertrudy

Wrzesińska

Podzamcze

Św Idziego

Św Sebastiana

Dietla

Dietla

5

**Wawel
Royal
Castle**

2

Wawel
Hill

Droga do Zamku

Bernardyńska

Stradomska

Św Agnieszki

Krakowska

Joselewicza

Św Sebastiana

Starowiślna

Smocza

Koletek

Sukiennicza

Brzozowa

Podbrzezie

Miodowa

Warszauera

Jakuba

Szeroka

**Schindler's
Factory
(1.1km); Krako
Slow Wines
(1.2km)**

Dietla

Dietla

Bożego Ciała

Meiselsa

Nowa

Estery

Izaaka

12

Plac
Nowy

11

Izaaka

Józefa

Bartosza

Dajwór

**Marchewka z
Groszkiem (200m)**

**InfoKraków –
Kazimierz**

KAZIMIERZ

Józefa

Wąska

3

Św Wawrzyńca

14

A B C D

Kraków – Old Town & Wawel

⊙ Top Sights
1 Rynek Underground A3
2 Wawel Royal Castle A6

⊙ Sights
Cloth Hall .... (see 1)
3 Galicia Jewish Museum D7
Gallery of 19th-Century
Polish Painting .... (see 1)
4 St Mary's Basilica B3
5 Wawel Cathedral A6

⊜ Sleeping
6 Hotel Pugetów C4
7 Mundo Hostel B5

⊗ Eating
8 Glonojad C1
9 Miód Malina B4

⊙ Drinking & Nightlife
10 Bunkier Cafe A2
11 Cheder D7
12 Mleczarnia C7

⊛ Entertainment
13 Harris Piano Jazz Bar A3

⊙ Shopping
14 Galeria Krakowska C1

---

floor houses the **Gallery of 19th-Century Polish Painting** (☑ 12 433 5400; www.mnk.pl; adult/concession 20/15zł, Sun free; ☉ 9am-5pm Tue-Fri, 10am-6pm Sat, to 4pm Sun).

⊙ Kazimierz & Podgórze

Founded by King Kazimierz III Wielki in 1335, Kazimierz was originally an independent town that later became a Jewish district. During WWII, the Germans relocated Jews south across the Vistula River to a walled ghetto in Podgórze. They were exterminated in the nearby Płaszów Concentration Camp, as portrayed in the Steven Spielberg film *Schindler's List*. In addition to the attractions below, many synagogues are still standing and can be visited individually.

★ Schindler's Factory MUSEUM
(Fabryka Schindlera; ☑ 12 257 1017; www.muzeum krakowa.pl; ul Lipowa 4; adult/concession 24/18zł, Mon free; ☉ 10am-4pm Mon, 9am-8pm Tue-Sun; ☑ 3, 19, 24) This impressive interactive museum covers the German occupation of Kraków in WWII. It's housed in the former enamel factory of Oskar Schindler, the German industrialist who famously saved the lives of members of his Jewish labour force during the Holocaust. Well-organised, innovative exhibits tell the moving story of the city from 1939 to 1945. Take a tram to Plac Bohaterów Getta, then follow the signs east under the railway line to the museum.

Galicia Jewish Museum MUSEUM
(☑ 12 421 6842; www.galiciajewishmuseum.org; ul Dajwór 18; adult/concession 16/11zł; ☉ 10am-6pm; ☑ 3, 19, 24) This museum both commemorates Jewish victims of the Holocaust and celebrates the Jewish culture and history of the former Austro-Hungarian region of Galicia. It features an impressive photographic exhibition depicting modern-day remnants of southeastern Poland's once-thriving Jewish community, called 'Traces of Memory', along with video testimony of survivors and regular temporary exhibits. The museum also leads guided tours of the Jewish sites of Kazimierz; call or email for details.

⊨ Sleeping

As Poland's premier tourist destination, Kraków has plenty of accommodation options. However, advance booking is recommended for anywhere central.

★ Mundo Hostel HOSTEL €
(☑ 12 422 6113; www.mundohostel.eu; ul Sarego 10; dm 60-65zł, d 170-190zł; @ ☎; ☑ 1, 6, 8, 10, 13, 18) Attractive, well-maintained hostel in a quiet courtyard location neatly placed between the Old Town and Kazimierz. Each room is decorated for a different country; for example, the Tibet room is decked out with colourful prayer flags. Barbecues take place in summer. There's a bright, fully equipped kitchen for do-it-yourself meals.

★ Aparthotel Vanilla APARTMENT €€
(☑ 12 354 0150; www.aparthotelvanilla.pl; ul Bobrzyńskiego 33; apt from 250zł; P ❄ ☎; ☑ 11, 17, 18, 52) This place is a great choice for motorists, easily accessible from the A4 motorway, offering secure parking, and with a tram stop across the street (20 minutes to the centre). Standard rooms are superb value, effectively mini apartments with kitchenette and balcony; a buffet breakfast is served in the ground-floor restaurant.

Hamilton Suites APARTMENT €€
(☑ 12 346 4670; www.krakow-apartments.biz; apt 300-600zł; ☎) Provides high-quality

apartment rentals suited to longer stays (at least three days) and corporate rentals. The apartments are scattered around the Old Town as well as further afield in Podgórze. Most feature bright, modern design, and longer stays come with cleaning services. Check the website for an overview of the apartments.

★ Hotel Pugetów HISTORIC HOTEL €€€

(📞12 432 4950; www.donimirski.com/hotel-puge tow; ul Starowiślna 15a; s/d 500/700zł; P❋🛜; 🚌1, 3, 17, 19, 22, 24, 52) This charming historic hotel stands proudly next to the 19th-century neo-Renaissance palace of the same name. It offers just seven rooms with distinctive names (Conrad, Bonaparte) and identities. Think embroidered bathrobes, black-marble baths and a fabulous breakfast room in the basement.

✖ Eating

Glonojad VEGETARIAN €

(📞12 346 1677; www.glonojad.com; Plac Matejki 2; mains 15-22zł; ⊗8am-10pm Mon-Fri, from 9am Sat & Sun; 🛜🍴♿; 🚌2, 4, 14, 18, 20, 24, 44) This appealing and popular self-service cafeteria has a great view onto Plac Matejki, just north of the Barbican. The diverse menu has a variety of tempting vegetarian dishes including samosas, curries, potato pancakes, falafel, veggie lasagne and soups. The breakfast menu is served till noon, so there's no need to jump out of that hotel bed too early.

★ Krako Slow Wines INTERNATIONAL €€

(📞669 225 222; www.krakoslowwines.pl; ul Lipowa 6f; mains 22-40zł; ⊗10am-10pm Sun-Thu, to midnight Fri & Sat; 🛜🍴♿🍸; 🚌3, 19, 24) It's hard to accurately characterise this little wine bar and restaurant, which serves the best-value lunches within 100m of Schindler's Factory (p873). The emphasis is on the wine, but it also serves excellent beer, coffee, salads, snacks and hummus sandwiches, and its Caucasian barbecue (Tuesday to Saturday) turns out mouth-watering Georgian- and Armenian-style shashlik and kebab.

Marchewka z Groszkiem POLISH €€

(📞12 430 0795; www.marchewkazgroszkiem.pl; ul Mostowa 2; mains 15-35zł; ⊗9am-10pm; 🛜🍴♿; 🚌6, 8, 10, 13) Traditional Polish cooking, with hints of influence from neighbouring countries such as Ukraine, Hungary and Lithuania. Excellent potato pancakes and a delicious boiled beef with horseradish sauce are highlights of the menu. There are

a few sidewalk tables to admire the parade of people down one of Kazimierz's up-and-coming streets.

★ Miód Malina POLISH €€€

(📞12 430 0411; www.miodmalina.pl; ul Grodzka 40; mains 40-80zł; ⊗noon-11pm; 🛜🍴♿; 🚌1, 6, 8, 13, 18) The charmingly named 'Honey Raspberry' serves Polish dishes in colourful surrounds. Grab a window seat and order the wild mushrooms in cream, and any of the duck or veal dishes. There's a variety of beef steaks on the menu as well. The grilled sheep's-cheese appetiser, served with cranberry jelly, is a regional speciality. Reservations essential.

🍷 Drinking & Nightlife

The Rynek Główny is literally ringed on all sides by bars and cafes, where outdoor tables offer great people-watching spots. Kazimierz also has a lively bar scene, centred on Plac Nowy.

★ Bunkier Cafe CAFE

(📞12 431 0585; www.bunkiercafe.pl; Plac Szczepański 3a; ⊗9am-1am; 🛜; 🚌2, 4, 14, 18, 20, 24, 44) The 'Bunker' is a wonderful cafe with an enormous glassed-in terrace tacked on to the Bunkier Sztuki (Art Bunker), a cutting-edge gallery northwest of the Rynek. The garden space is heated in winter and always has a buzz. There is excellent coffee, nonfiltered beers and homemade lemonades, plus light bites such as burgers and salads. Enter from the Planty.

Cheder CAFE

(📞515 732 226; www.cheder.pl; ul Józefa 36; ⊗10am-10pm; 🚌3, 19, 24) Unlike most of the other Jewish-themed places in Kazimierz, this one aims to entertain *and* educate. Named after a traditional Hebrew school, the cafe offers access to a decent library in Polish and English, regular readings and films, real Israeli coffee, brewed in a traditional Turkish copper pot with cinnamon and cardamom, and snacks such as homemade hummus.

Mleczarnia CAFE

(📞12 421 8532; www.mle.pl; ul Meiselsa 20; ⊗10am-1am; 🛜; 🚌6, 8, 10, 13) Wins the prize for best beer garden – located across the street from the cafe. Shady trees and blooming roses make this place tops for a sunny-afternoon drink. If it's raining, the cafe itself is warm and cosy, with crowded bookshelves and portrait-covered walls. Interesting beverages available include mead and cocoa with cherry vodka. Self-service.

AUSCHWITZ-BIRKENAU MEMORIAL & MUSEUM

Many visitors combine a stay in Kraków with a trip to the **Auschwitz-Birkenau Memorial & Museum** (Auschwitz-Birkenau Miejsce Pamięci i Muzeum; guides 33 844 8100; www.auschwitz.org; ul Stanisławy Leszczyńskiej; 7.30am-7pm Jun-Aug, to 6pm Apr-May & Sep, to 5pm Mar & Oct, to 4pm Feb, to 3pm Jan & Nov, to 2pm Dec) **FREE**, a name synonymous with the horror of the Holocaust. More than a million Jews, and many thousands of Poles and Roma, were murdered here by German occupiers during WWII.

Both sections of the camp – **Auschwitz I** and the much larger outlying **Birkenau (Auschwitz II)** – have been preserved and are open to visitors free of charge. It's essential to visit both to appreciate the extent and the inhumanity of the place. From April to October it's compulsory to join a tour if you arrive between 10am and 3pm, otherwise you can explore at your own pace.

The tour begins at the main camp, Auschwitz I, which began life as a Polish military barracks but was co-opted by the Germans in 1940 as an extermination camp. Here is the infamous gate, displaying the grimly cynical message: 'Arbeit Macht Frei' (Work Makes You Free). Some 13 of 30 surviving prison blocks house museum exhibitions.

From here, the tour moves to Birkenau (Auschwitz II), 2km to the west, where most of the killing took place. Massive and purpose-built for efficiency, the camp had more than 300 prison barracks. Here you'll find the remnants of gas chambers and crematoria.

Auschwitz-Birkenau is a workable day trip from Kraków. There are hourly buses to Oświęcim (10zł, one hour), departing from the bus station in Kraków. There are also numerous minibuses to Oświęcim from the minibus stands off ul Pawia, next to Galeria Krakowska.

POLAND KRAKÓW

☆ Entertainment

★ Harris Piano Jazz Bar — JAZZ
(12 421 5741; www.harris.krakow.pl; Rynek Główny 28; tickets 20-80zł; 11am-2am; 1, 6, 8, 13, 18) This lively jazz haunt is housed in an atmospheric, intimate cellar space right on the Rynek Główny. Harris hosts jazz and blues bands most nights from around 9.30pm, but try to arrive an hour earlier to get a seat (or book in advance by phone). Wednesday nights see weekly jam sessions (admission free).

Kraków Philharmonic — CLASSICAL MUSIC
(Filharmonia im Karola Szymanowskiego w Krakowie; 12 619 8733; www.filharmonia.krakow.pl; ul Zwierzyniecka 1; box office 10am-2pm & 3-7pm Tue-Fri; 1, 2, 6) Home to one of Poland's best orchestras. Tickets cost 30zł to 40zł.

ⓘ Information

The official tourist information office, **Info-Kraków** (www.infokrakow.pl), maintains branches around town. Expect cheerful service, loads of free maps and promotional materials, help in sorting out accommodation and transport, and a computer on hand (in some branches) for free, short-term web-surfing.

ⓘ Getting There & Away

AIR
Kraków's **John Paul II International Airport** (KRK; 801 055 000, 12 295 5800; www.

krakowairport.pl; ul Kapitana Mieczysława Medweckiego 1, Balice;) is located in the town of Balice, about 15km west of the centre. The airport has car-hire desks, bank ATMs, a tourist information office and currency exchanges.

LOT (www.lot.com) flies to Warsaw, and Ryanair has direct flights to Gdańsk. There are also direct flights from Kraków to many cities in the UK and Europe.

BUS
Kraków's **bus station** (703 403 340; www.mda.malopolska.pl; ul Bosacka 18; information desk 9am-5pm; ; 2, 3, 4, 5, 10, 14, 17, 19, 20, 44, 50, 52) is next to the main train station northeast of the Old Town. Access the station through the train station and follow the signs. The station has ticket and information counters, storage lockers and vending machines.

Nearly all intercity coaches, both international and domestic, arrive at or depart from this station. Handy bus services include **FlixBus** (https://global.flixbus.com), **Leo Express** (www.leoexpress.com) and **Majer Bus** (www.majerbus.pl). Consult the websites for destinations, departure times and prices.

TRAIN
The modern **Kraków Main Station** (Kraków Główny; 22 391 9757; www.pkp.pl; ul Pawia 5a; information desk 7am-9pm; ; 2, 3, 4, 5, 10, 14, 17, 19, 20, 44, 50, 52) is on the northeastern edge of the Old Town, entered via the **Galeria Krakowska** (12 428 9902; www.galeriakrakowska.pl; ul Pawia 5; 9am-10pm

Mon-Sat, 10am-9pm Sun; 🚊 2, 3, 4, 10, 14, 20, 44, 52) shopping centre. Mostly underground, the station is beautifully laid out, with information booths and ticket offices on several levels. Find the left-luggage office (6zł/day) and storage lockers (per day big/small locker 12/8zł) below platform 5. There are plenty of bank ATMs, restaurants and shops.

❶ Getting Around

The city's extensive network of trams is operated by the **Kraków Public Transport Authority** (Miejskie Przedsiębiorstwo Komunikacyjne/ MPK; 📞 12 19150; www.mpk.krakow.pl) abbreviated as MPK. The system runs daily from about 5am to 11pm.

Rides require a valid ticket that can be bought from automated ticketing machines (automat biletów) onboard or at important stops. Some machines only take coins, while others also take bills and credit cards, though using coins remains the quickest way to buy a ticket. You can also buy tickets from some news kiosks.

Tickets are valid for various time periods, from 20 minutes (2.80zł) and 40 minutes (3.80zł) to 24/48/72 hours (15/24/36zł). Remember to validate your ticket in stamping machines when you first board; spot checks are frequent.

The network is logically laid out and tram numbers and routes are prominently displayed at stops. The only issue is that the routes and numbers change frequently as lines are upgraded and repaired. InfoKraków tourist offices can supply a transport map, though that may too be out of date.

MAŁOPOLSKA

Małopolska (literally 'Lesser Poland') covers southeastern Poland from the former royal capital of Kraków to the eastern Lublin Uplands. The name does not refer to size or relative importance, but rather that Lesser Poland was mentioned in atlases more recently than Wielkopolska ('Greater Poland'). It's a colourful region filled with remnants of traditional life and historic cities.

Lublin

POP 339,850

Lublin is the largest city in southeastern Poland, with a thriving cultural and academic scene. That said, it's not a looker. Lublin was ravaged during WWII and the forced industrialisation of the communist period added insult to injury. Nevertheless, the city's historic core, the Rynek, is slowly being gentrified, and trendy clubs and restaurants are giving new lustre to the Old Town's impressive stock of Renaissance and baroque town houses.

Lublin is of special interest to travellers seeking Poland's Jewish past. For centuries the city was a leading centre of Jewish scholarship, giving rise to Lublin's nickname the 'Jewish Oxford'. That heritage came to a brutal end in WWII, but here and there you can still find traces.

◉ Sights & Activities

Majdanek   HISTORIC SITE
(Państwowe Muzeum na Majdanku; 📞 81 710 2833; www.majdanek.eu; Droga Męczenników Majdanka 67; parking 5zł; ⊙ 9am-6pm Apr-Oct, to 4pm Nov-Mar, exhibition closed Mon; 🅿) **FREE** Majdanek extermination camp, where tens of thousands of people, mainly Jews, were murdered by the Germans during WWII, lies on the outskirts of Lublin – guard towers and barbed-wire fences interrupting the suburban sprawl are disquieting. Allow half a day for the 5km walk around the camp; if pushed for time, visit the historical exhibition in building 62, the photographic display in building 45, and the skin-crawlingly chilling gas chambers. Majdanek is 4km southeast of the Kraków Gate; take bus 23.

Lublin Castle   MUSEUM
(www.muzeumlubelskie.pl; ul Zamkowa 9; adult/ concession 30/23zł; ⊙ 10am-6pm Tue-Sun May-Sep, 9am-5pm Oct-Apr) Lublin's royal castle dates from the 12th and 13th centuries, though it's been rebuilt many times since; the oldest surviving part is the impressive Romanesque **round tower** that dominates the courtyard; it was here in 1569 that Poland's union with Lithuania was signed. The castle is home to **Lublin Museum** and the 14th-century Gothic **Chapel of the Holy Trinity**, which contains Poland's finest examples of medieval frescoes; the ticket gives access to both and also to the tower.

Kraków Gate   MUSEUM
(Brama Krakowska; www.muzeumlubelskie.pl; Plac Łokietka 3; adult/concession 5.50/4.50zł; ⊙ 10am-6pm Tue-Sun Jun-Aug, to 4pm Sep-May) The only significant remnant of the fortified walls that once surrounded the Old Town is the 14th-century Gothic Kraków Gate, built during the reign of Kazimierz III Wielki following the Mongol attack in 1341. It received its octagonal Renaissance superstructure in the

16th century, and its baroque crown in 1782. These days it's home to the **Historical Museum of Lublin** and its small collection of documents and photographs of the town's history.

Cathedral of St John the Baptist CHURCH
(www.archikatedra.kuria.lublin.pl; Plac Katedralny; church free, treasury & crypt adult/child 4/2zł; ☺treasury & crypt 10am-4pm Tue-Sat) This former Jesuit church dates from the 16th century and is the largest in Lublin; you can visit any time services are not taking place. The impressive interior is adorned with baroque trompe l'oeil frescoes by Moravian artist Józef Meyer. The **treasury** (*skarbiec*) houses precious gold and silverware, a 14th-century bronze baptismal font and more Meyer frescoes. The vaulted roof of the so-called **acoustic vestry** (*zakrystia akustyczna*) reflects whispers from one corner across to the other.

Underground Route WALKING
(☑ tour bookings 81 534 6570; www.teatrnn.pl/pod ziemia; Rynek 1; adult/concession 12/10zł; ☺10am-4pm Tue-Fri, noon-5pm Sat & Sun) This 280m trail winds its way through interconnected cellars beneath the Old Town, with historical exhibitions along the way. Entry is from the southwest side of the neoclassical Old Town Hall in the centre of Market Sq (Rynek) at approximately two-hourly intervals; check with the tourist office for exact times.

🛏 Sleeping

Folk Hostel HOSTEL €
(☑ 887 223 887; www.folkhostel.pl; ul Krakowskie Przedmieście 23; dm/tr 45/159zł; P ☎) This charming hostel ticks all the boxes, with friendly English-speaking staff, brightly decorated rooms and a superbly central location. Although it overlooks the main street, the entrance is around the back, via a gate on Zielona. Limited on-site parking.

Vanilla Hotel HOTEL €€
(☑ 81 536 6720; www.vanilla-hotel.pl; ul Krakowskie Przedmieście 12; s 265-335zł, d 315-405zł; P @ ☎) The name must be tongue-in-cheek – this sleekly gorgeous hotel on the main pedestrian plaza is anything but plain vanilla. The rooms are filled with inspired, even bold, styling: vibrant colours, big headboards, and retro lamps and furniture. There's lots of attention to detail here, which continues in the chic restaurant and coffee bar. Lower rates on weekends.

Rezydencja Waksman HOTEL €€
(☑ 81 532 5454; www.waksman.pl; ul Grodzka 19; s/d 210/230zł, apt from 290zł; P @ ☎) Hotel Waksman deserves a blue ribbon for many reasons, not least of which is the atmospheric Old Town location. Each standard room (named 'yellow', 'blue', 'green' or 'red' for its decor) has individual character. The two apartments on top are special; they offer ample space for lounging or working, and views over the Old Town and castle.

🍴 Eating & Drinking

Mandragora JEWISH €€
(☑ 81 536 2020; www.mandragora.lublin.pl; Rynek 9; mains 25-55zł; ☺8.30am-10pm Sun-Thu, to midnight Fri & Sat; ☎) There's good kitsch and there's bad kitsch, and at Mandragora, it's all good. Sure it's going for the *Fiddler on the Roof* effect with the lace tablecloths, knick-knacks and photos of old Lublin, but in the romantic Rynek setting it works wonderfully. The food is heartily Jewish, from roast duck with *tzimmes* (stewed carrots and dried fruit) to salt beef.

★ Kardamon INTERNATIONAL €€€
(☑ 81 448 0257; www.kardamon.eu; ul Krakowskie Przedmieście 41; mains 32-72zł; ☺noon-11pm Mon-Sat, to 10pm Sun; ☎) By many accounts, Lublin's best restaurant is this lush cellar on the main street. The menu is a mix of international staples such as grilled pork tenderloin, along with Polish favourites such as *żurek* (sour rye soup), roast duck served with beetroot and some regional specialities.

Czarna Owca PUB
(www.czarnaowcagastropub.pl; ul Narutowicza 9; ☺1-11pm Sun-Thu, to 2am Fri-Sat) The 'Black Sheep' is a legendary Lublin watering hole, going strong into the small hours at weekends. In addition to Żywiec and Paulaner on draught and a selection of bottled Polish craft beers, it has a menu of gourmet burgers, pub grub and snacks to munch on.

ℹ Information

Tourist Information Centre (LOITiK; ☑ 81 532 4412; www.lublintravel.pl; ul Jezuicka 1/3; ☺9am-7pm Apr-Oct, to 5pm Nov-Mar) Extremely helpful English-speaking staff. There are souvenirs for sale and lots of brochures, including handy maps of the most popular walking tours in Lublin. There's also a computer for internet access.

POLAND LUBLIN

WORTH A TRIP

ZAMOŚĆ: POLAND'S RENAISSANCE HEART

While most Polish cities' attractions centre on their medieval heart, Zamość (zah-moshch) is pure 16th-century Renaissance. It was founded in 1580 by nobleman Jan Zamoyski and designed by an Italian architect. The splendid architecture of Zamość's Old Town escaped serious destruction in WWII and was added to Unesco's World Heritage List in 1992.

The **Rynek Wielki** (Great Market Square) is the heart of Zamość's attractive Old Town. This impressive Italianate Renaissance square (exactly 100m by 100m) is dominated by a lofty, pink town hall and surrounded by colourful, arcaded burghers' houses. The **Museum of Zamość** (Muzeum Zamojskie; www.muzeum-zamojskie.pl; ul Ormiańska 30; adult/concession 12/6zł; ⊘9am-4pm Tue-Sun) is based in two of the loveliest buildings on the square and houses interesting exhibits, including paintings, folk costumes and a scale model of the 16th-century town.

The city's **synagogue** (www.zamosc.fodz.pl; ul Pereca 14; by donation; ⊘10am-6pm Tue-Sun Mar-Oct, to 2pm Nov-Feb) was built around 1620 and served as the Jewish community's main house of worship until WWII, when it was shuttered by the Germans. The highlight of the exhibition is a gripping computer presentation on the history of the town's Jewish community, including its roots in Sephardic Judaism.

Zamość is an easy day trip from Lublin by bus (15zł, two hours, every half-hour). The helpful **tourist office** (✆84 639 2292; www.travel.zamosc.pl; Rynek Wielki 13; ⊘8am-5pm Mon-Fri, from 9am Sat & Sun year-round, longer hours May-Sep; 🛜) in the town hall has maps, brochures and souvenirs.

ⓘ Getting There & Away

BUS
FlixBus (https://global.flixbus.com) services connect the **bus station** (ul Hutnicza 1, cross al Tysiąclecia) with major cities throughout Poland, including Warsaw (from 15zł, three hours, six daily) and Kraków (47zł, 5½ hours, four daily).

Private minibuses run from the **minibus station** (ul Nadstawna) north of the bus terminal to various destinations, including Zamość (15zł, two hours, hourly) and Kazimierz Dolny (8zł, one hour, every 30 minutes).

TRAIN
The train station is 2km south of the Old Town. There are direct trains to Warsaw (from 31zł, three hours, five daily); Kraków and Zamość are more easily reached by bus.

CARPATHIAN MOUNTAINS

The Carpathians (Karpaty) stretch from Poland's southern border with Slovakia into Ukraine, and their wooded hills and snowy mountains are a magnet for hikers, skiers and cyclists. The most popular destination here is the resort of Zakopane.

Zakopane
POP 27,270

Zakopane, 100km south of Kraków, is Poland's main alpine resort, situated at the foot of the Tatra Mountains. It's a popular jumping-off spot for trekking and mountain hikes, as well as skiing. The busy high street, ul Krupówki, is a jumble of souvenir shops, bars and restaurants, but away from the centre, the pace slows down. This was an artists' colony in the early 20th century, and the graceful timbered villas from those days – built in what's known as the 'Zakopane style' – are still scattered around town.

◎ Sights & Activities

Morskie Oko　LAKE
(national park per person 5zł) The most popular outing near Zakopane is to this emerald-green mountain lake, about 20km southeast of the town. Minibuses regularly depart from ul Kościuszki, across from the main bus station, for Polana Palenica (10zł, 45 minutes), from where a 9km-long road continues uphill to the lake. Cars, bikes and buses are not allowed, so you'll have to walk (about two hours each way) or take a horse-drawn carriage (50zł). Travel agencies organise day trips.

Kasprowy Wierch Cable Car
CABLE CAR

(☑18 201 5356; www.pkl.pl; Kuźnice; adult/
concession return 63/53zł; ⊙7.30am-4pm Jan-
Mar, to 6pm Apr-Jun & Sep-Oct, 7am-9pm Jul & Aug,
9am-4pm Nov-Dec) The cable-car trip from
Kuźnice (2km south of Zakopane) to the Mt
Kasprowy Wierch summit (1985m) is a classic tourist experience. At the end of the ascent (20 minutes, climbing 936m), you can
get off and stand with one foot in Poland
and the other in Slovakia. The view from the
top is spectacular (clouds permitting). The
cable car normally closes for two weeks in
May, and won't operate if the snow or wind
conditions are dangerous.

Old Church & Cemetery
CHURCH

(Stary Kościół i Cmentarz na Pęksowym Brzyzku;
ul Kościeliska 4; cemetery 2zł; ⊙8am-5pm) This
small wooden church and atmospheric cemetery date from the mid-19th century. The
Old Church has charming carved wooden
decorations and pews, and the Stations
of the Cross painted on glass on the windows. The adjoining cemetery is one of the
country's most beautiful, with a number of
amazing wood-carved headstones, some
resembling giant chess pieces. The noted
Polish painter and creator of the Zakopane
style, Stanisław Witkiewicz, is buried here
beneath a modest wooden grave marker.

🛌 Sleeping

Private rooms provide some of the best-
value accommodation in town (around 50zł
per person). Check at the tourist office for
details or look for signs reading 'pokoje', 'no-
clegi' or 'zimmer frei'.

Target Hostel
HOSTEL €

(☑18 207 4596, 730 955 730; www.targethostel.pl;
ul Sienkiewicza 3b; dm/tw from 39/150zł; @🛜)
This private, well-run hostel is within easy
walking distance of the bus station; the
entrance is downstairs from the street, beneath a clinic. Accommodation is in six- to
10-bed dorms, with classic pale-wood panelling and wooden floors. There's a common
room and communal kitchen, and the staff
are friendly and helpful.

Czarny Potok
HOTEL €€

(☑18 202 2760; www.czarnypotok.pl; ul Tetmajera
20; s/d from 219/259zł; P🛜🏊) The 'Black
Stream', set beside a pretty brook amid lovely gardens, is a 44-room pension-like hotel
on a quiet backstreet just south of the pedestrian mall. Bedrooms have alpine-style pine-

wood cladding, and there's a great fitness
centre with a pool and two saunas.

Hotel Sabała
HOTEL €€€

(☑18 201 5092; www.sabala.zakopane.pl; ul
Krupówki 11; s/d from 380/420zł; ⊜🛜🏊) Built in
1894 but thoroughly up to date, this striking
timber hotel has a superb location overlooking the picturesque pedestrian thoroughfare.
The hotel offers cosy, attic-style rooms, and
there's a sauna, solarium and swimming
pool. The restaurant here serves both local
specialities and international favourites.

🍴 Eating & Drinking

Karczma Zapiecek
POLISH €€

(☑18 201 5699; www.karczmazapiecek.pl; ul
Krupówki 43; mains 25-40zł; ⊙10am-11pm) One
of the better choices among a group of similar highlander-style restaurants along ul
Krupówki, with great food, an old stove and
a terrace. Traditional dishes on offer include
local oscypek grillowany (grilled smoked
cheese) served with bacon or cranberries,
Slovakian hałuski bryndzowe (potato
dumplings with sheep's cheese) and pstrąg
z pieca (baked trout).

Pstrąg Górski
SEAFOOD €€

(☑512 351 746; www.zakopane-restauracje.pl; ul
Krupówki 6a; mains 22-45zł; ⊙10am-10pm; 🛜)
This alpine-style restaurant (the 'Mountain
Trout') done up in timber-rich decor and
overlooking a narrow stream, serves some
of the freshest trout, salmon and sea fish in
town. Trout is priced at 6zł and up per 100g
(whole fish), bringing the price of a standard fish dinner to around 35zł, not including
sides.

La Mano
COFFEE

(www.facebook.com/lamanozakopane; ul Władysława Orkana 1f; ⊙9am-6pm Mon & Wed-Sat, 10am-
4pm Sun; 🛜) This cool and stylish cafe serves
the best coffee in town, a passion reflected
in the range of coffee-making equipment on
sale, alongside a neat line in locally produced
honey fruit juices and compotes. Sit out front
overlooking the street, or head through the
back for a view of the mountains.

ℹ️ Information

Tourist Office (Centrum Informacji Turystycznej; ☑18 201 2211; www.zakopane.pl; ul
Kościuszki 7; ⊙9am-5pm Mar-Aug, Mon-Fri
Sep-Feb) Small but helpful municipal tourist
office just south of the bus station on the walk
towards the centre. It has free city maps and
sells more-detailed hiking maps.

POLAND ZAKOPANE

Tatra National Park Information Point (Punkt Informacji Turystycznej; ☏18 20 23 300; www. tpn.pl; ul Chałubińskiego 42; ⊙7am-3pm) Located in a small building near the Rondo Jana Pawła II on the southern outskirts of the city. It's a good place for maps, guides and local weather and hiking information.

❶ Getting There & Around

Bus is far and away the best transport option for reaching Zakopane. The **bus station** (PKS; ☏300 300 143; ul Kościuszki 23) is about 400m northeast of the centre along ul Kościuszki. Most buses and minibuses depart from here or the small minibus station across the street.

Szwagropol (☏12 271 3550; www. szwagropol.pl) operates bus services to Kraków (20zł, two hours, twice hourly).

Dozens of privately owned minibuses depart regularly (when full) from the bus station to hiking trailheads, including Kuznice (5zł, 15 minutes, for the Kasprowy Wierch cable car) and Morskie Oko (8zł, 30 minutes).

SILESIA

Silesia (Śląsk in Polish; pronounced shlonsk), in the far southwest of the country, is a traditional industrial and mining region with a fascinating mix of landscapes.

Wrocław

POP 638,590

Everyone loves Wrocław (*vrots*-wahf) and it's easy to see why. Wrocław's location on the Odra River, with its 12 islands, 130 bridges and riverside parks, is idyllic, and the beautifully preserved Cathedral Island is a treat for lovers of Gothic architecture.

Though in some ways it's a more manageable version of Kraków, with all the cultural attributes and entertainment of that popular destination, the capital of Lower Silesia also has an appealing character all its own. Having absorbed Bohemian, Austrian and Prussian influences, the city has a unique architectural and cultural make-up, symbolised by its magnificent market square (Rynek).

But Wrocław is not just a pretty face. It is Poland's fourth-largest city and the major industrial, commercial and educational centre for the region. At the same time it's a lively cultural centre, with several theatres, major festivals, rampant nightlife and a large student community.

◉ Sights & Activities

The hub of city life is the magnificent Old Town square, the **Rynek**. Northeast of the Old Town lies historic Cathedral Island (Ostrów Tumski) – the birthplace of Wrocław.

★**Old Town Hall**   HISTORIC BUILDING
(Stary Ratusz; Rynek) This grand edifice took almost 200 years (1327–1504) to complete. The right-hand part of the eastern facade, with its austere early-Gothic features, is the oldest, while the delicate carving in the section to the left shows early-Renaissance style; the astronomical clock in the centre, made of larch wood, was built in 1580. The southern facade, dating from the early 16th century, is the most elaborate, with a pair of ornate bay windows and carved stone figures.

Wrocław Dwarves   PUBLIC ART
(Wrocławskie Krasnale; www.krasnale.pl) See if you can spot the tiny bronze statue of a dwarf resting on the ground, just to the west of the **Hansel & Gretel houses** (Jaś i Małgosia; ul Odrzańska 39/40). A few metres away you'll spot firefighter dwarves, rushing to put out a blaze. These figures are part of a collection of over 300 scattered through the city. Though whimsical, they're also a reference to the symbol of the Orange Alternative, a communist-era dissident group that used ridicule as a weapon.

★**Panorama of Racławice**   MUSEUM
(Panorama Racławicka; www.panoramaraclawicka.pl; ul Purkyniego 11; adult/concession 30/23zł; ⊙8am-7.30pm Apr-Oct, shorter hours & closed Mon Nov-Mar; ℗) Wrocław's pride and joy is this giant painting of the battle for Polish independence fought at Racławice on 4 April 1794, between the Polish army led by Tadeusz Kościuszko and Russian troops under General Alexander Tormasov. The Poles won but it was all for naught: months later the nationwide insurrection was crushed by the tsarist army. The canvas measures 15m by 114m, and is wrapped around the internal walls of a rotunda.

National Museum   MUSEUM
(Muzeum Narodowe; www.mnwr.pl; Plac Powstańców Warszawy 5; adult/concession 20/15zł, Sat free; ⊙10am-5pm Tue-Fri, 10.30am-6pm Sat & Sun, shorter hours Oct-Mar) A treasure trove of fine art. Medieval sculpture is displayed on the ground floor; exhibits include the Romanesque tympanum from the portal of the **Church of St Mary Magdalene** (ul Łaciarska; tower adult/concession 4/3zł; ⊙tower 10am-6pm Apr-Oct), depicting the Assumption of the

Virgin Mary, and 14th-century sarcophagi from the **Church of SS Vincent & James** (Kościół Św Wincentego i Św Jakuba; Plac Biskupa Nankiera 15a). There are also collections of Silesian paintings, ceramics, silverware and furnishings from the 16th to 19th centuries.

Cathedral of St John the Baptist   CHURCH
(Archikatedra Św Jana Chrzciciela; www.katedra.archi diecezja.wroc.pl; Plac Katedralny 18; tower & chapels adult/concession 10/8zł; ⊙ 10am-5pm Mon-Sat, from 2pm Sun) The centrepiece of Cathedral Island, this three-aisled Gothic basilica was built between 1244 and 1590. Seriously damaged during WWII, it was rebuilt in its original Gothic form. Entry to the church is free, but you need to buy a ticket to visit three beautiful baroque chapels, and to ascend to the viewpoint atop the 91m-high tower (there's a lift).

Gondola Bay   CANOEING
(Zatoka Gondol; www.visitwroclaw.eu/en/event/ gondola-bay; promenada Staromiejska; kayak per hour 15zł; ⊙ Apr-Sep) You can get a different perspective of the city by viewing it from the water. Rent a kayak, rowing boat (per hour 25zł) or motorboat (per hour 80zł) and take a tour around Ostrow Tumski.

🛏 Sleeping

Hostel Mleczarnia   HOSTEL €
(🗷 71 787 7570; www.mleczarniahostel.pl; ul Włodkowica 5; dm 40-50zł, tw 220zł; 🛜) Set in a quiet courtyard not far from the Rynek (go through the passage left of Restaurant Sarah), this hostel has bags of charm, having been decorated in a deliberately old-fashioned style with antique furniture. There's a women-only dorm available, along with a kitchen and free laundry facilities. In the courtyard is the excellent **Mleczarnia** (www.mle.pl; ⊙ 8am-4pm; 🛜) cafe-bar.

Hotel Patio   HOTEL €€
(🗷 71 375 0400; www.hotelpatio.pl; ul Kiełbaśnicza 24; s/d from 250/270zł; 🅿 ❄ 🛜) The Patio offers pleasant lodgings a short hop from the main square, within two buildings linked by a covered, sunlit courtyard. Rooms are clean and light, though the cheaper ones can be on the small side, and there's a spectacular breakfast spread.

Hotel Monopol   HOTEL €€€
(🗷 71 772 3777; www.monopolwroclaw.hotel.com. pl; ul Modrzejewskiego 2; r from 700zł; ❄ 🛜 🛝) In its heyday the elegant Monopol hosted such luminaries as Pablo Picasso and Marlene Dietrich (along with more notorious names such

as Adolf Hitler). Along with stylishly modernised bedrooms there's a choice of upmarket restaurants, bars, a cafe, a spa and boutiques, so you won't be short of pampering options.

🍴 Eating

★ Panczo   TEX-MEX €€
(🗷 884 009 737; www.facebook.com/panczobus; ul Świętego Antoniego 35/1a; mains 15-26zł; ⊙ noon-11pm Sun-Thu, to midnight Fri & Sat; 🛜) Part of a Polish trend that has seen street-food businesses opening up in permanent premises, Panczo serves up huge portions of lip-smacking tacos, enchiladas and – the house speciality – burritos. The food is fresh, zingy and authentic, as are the margaritas. Order food at the bar (ask for an English menu if there are none on the tables).

Vega Bar Wegański   VEGAN €€
(🗷 713 443 934; www.facebook.com/vega.bar.we ganski.wroclaw; Rynek 1/2; mains 15-30zł; ⊙ 8am-8pm Mon-Thu, to 9pm Fri & Sat, 9am-8pm Sun; 🛜) This buzzing vegan restaurant in the centre of the Rynek, with a cafe upstairs, serves everything from breakfasts of oatmeal and millet with vegan milk and seasonal fruits (till noon), to hot, filling lunch dishes such as tempeh burgers, Thai curries, pizzas and meat-free pierogi (Polish dumplings). There's a good choice of gluten-free options too, and even vegan ice cream.

★ Restauracja Jadka   POLISH €€€
(🗷 71 343 6461; www.jadka.pl; ul Rzeźnicza 24/25; mains 57-83zł; ⊙ 5-11pm Mon-Sat, to 10pm Sun) One of Wrocław's top fine-dining options, presenting impeccable modern versions of Polish classics such as ox tongue served with beetroot and chard, and halibut with tarragon and fried groats, with silver-service table settings (candles, crystal, linen) in delightful Gothic surroundings. Bookings are recommended, especially at weekends.

🍷 Drinking & Entertainment

Vinyl Cafe   BAR
(🗷 508 260 288; www.facebook.com/vinylcafe. wroclaw; ul Kotlarska 35/36; ⊙ 10am-midnight Mon-Thu, to 1am Fri-Sat, to 11pm Sun; 🛜) Hitting the retro button hard, this cool cafe-bar is a jumble of mismatched furniture, old framed photos and stacks of vinyl records. It's a great place to grab a drink, both day and night.

Bezsenność   CLUB
(www.facebook.com/klubbezsennosc; ul Ruska 51; ⊙ 7pm-3am Tue & Wed, to 5am Thu-Sat) With

its alternative/rock/dance line-up and distressed decor, 'Insomnia' attracts a high-end clientele and is one of the most popular clubs in town. It's located in the Pasaż Niepolda, home to a group of bars, clubs and restaurants, just off ul Ruska.

Filharmonia　　　　　　CLASSICAL MUSIC
(Philharmonic Hall; ☑ tickets 71 715 9700; www. nfm.wroclaw.pl; ul Piłsudskiego 19) The city's main concert hall stages performances of orchestral music, chamber music, jazz and popular artists.

ℹ Information

Tourist Office (☑ 71 344 3111; www.wroclaw-info.pl; Rynek 14; ⊙ 9am-7pm)

ℹ Getting There & Away

BUS
The **bus station** (Dworzec Centralny PKS; ☑ 703 400 444; ul Sucha 1/11) is 1.3km south of the Rynek, at the east end of the Wroclavia shopping mall, across the street from the main train station. Destination include Berlin (69zł, 4½ hours, four daily), Kraków (from 21zł, 3½ hours, hourly), Prague (69zł, 4½ hours, four daily) and Warsaw (29zł, 4½ to 5½ hours, hourly).

TRAIN
Trains depart from the impressive mock castle that is Wrocław Główny station, 1.2km south of the Rynek. Destination include Kraków (45zł, 3½ hours, hourly), Poznań (38zł, 2½ hours, hourly) and Warsaw (59zł, 3½ to six hours, 10 daily).

WIELKOPOLSKA

Wielkopolska (Greater Poland) is the region where Poland came to life in the Middle Ages. As a result of this ancient eminence, its cities and towns are full of historic and cultural attractions. The battles of WWII later caused widespread destruction in the area, though Poznań has resumed its prominent economic role.

Poznań

POP 554,700

Stroll into Poznań's Old Town square on any evening and you'll receive an instant introduction to the characteristic energy of Wielkopolska's capital. The city centre is buzzing at any time of the day, and positively jumping by night, full of people heading

to its many restaurants, pubs and clubs. The combination of international business travellers attending its numerous trade fairs and the city's huge student population has created a distinctive vibe quite independent of tourism.

In addition to its energetic personality, Poznań offers many historical attractions – this is, after all, the 1000-year-old birthplace of the Polish nation – and its plentiful transport links make it a great base from which to explore the quieter surrounding countryside.

◉ Sights

The main sights are split between the **Old Town** and the island of **Ostrów Tumski**, east of the main square and across the Warta River – the place where Poznań was founded, and with it the Polish state.

Town Hall　　　　　　HISTORIC BUILDING
(Ratusz; Stary Rynek 1; 🚌 Plac Wielkopolski, Wrocławska) Poznań's Renaissance town hall, topped with a 61m-high tower, instantly attracts attention. Its graceful form replaced a 13th-century Gothic structure, which burned down in the early 16th century. Every day at noon two metal goats appear through a pair of small doors above the clock and butt their horns together 12 times, in deference to an old legend. These days, the town hall is home to the city's Historical Museum.

Historical Museum of Poznań　　　MUSEUM
(Muzeum Historii Miasta Poznania; ☑ 61 856 8000 www.mnp.art.pl; Stary Rynek 1; adult/concession 7/5zł, Sat free; ⊙ 11am-5pm Tue-Thu, noon-9pm Fri, 11am-6pm Sat & Sun; 🚌 Plac Wielkopolski, Wrocławska) This museum (in the town hall) displays an interesting and well-presented exhibition on Poznań's history, though the building's original interiors are worth the entry price on their own. The richly ornamented Renaissance Hall on the 1st floor is a real gem, with its original stucco work and paintings from 1555. The 2nd floor contains artefacts from the Prussian/German period, documents illustrating city life in the 1920s and '30s, and a collection of interesting memorabilia from the past two centuries.

★**Porta Posnania**
Interactive Heritage Centre　　　MUSEUM
(Brama Poznania ICHOT; ☑ 61 647 7634 www. bramapoznania.pl; ul Gdańska 2; adult/concession

18/12zł incl audio guide; ⊘ 9am-6pm Tue-Fri, 10am-7pm Sat & Sun; ⓐ Katedra) This cutting-edge multimedia museum provides an easily digested introduction to the birth of the Polish nation, telling the tale of Ostrów Tumski's (Cathedral Island) eventful history via interactive displays, maps, movies and models. It's located opposite the island's eastern shore and is linked to the cathedral area by footbridge. The exhibitions are multilingual, but the audio guide helps bring everything together.

To reach the museum from the city centre, take tram 8 eastward to the Rondo Śródka stop.

★ **Poznań Cathedral**　　　CHURCH
(Katedra Poznańska; www.katedra.archpoznan.pl; ul Ostrów Tumski 17; church free, crypt adult/concession 3.50/2.50zł; ⊘ 9am-5pm Mon-Sat mid-Mar–mid-Nov, 9.30am-4pm mid-Nov–mid-Mar; ⓐ Katedra) Ostrów Tumski is dominated by this monumental double-towered cathedral. Basically Gothic with additions from later periods, notably the baroque upper towers, the cathedral was damaged in 1945 and took 11 years to rebuild. Early Polish kings were buried in the **crypt** – apart from fragments of their tombs, you can see the relics of the original church dating from 968, and of the Romanesque building from the second half of the 11th century.

🛏 Sleeping

Tey Hostel　　　HOSTEL €
(☑ 61 639 3497; www.tey-hostel.pl; ul Świętosławska 12; dm 25-40zł, s 58-150zł, d 70-200zł; ⓢ; ⓐ Wrocławska) Centrally located hostel offering comfortable accommodation with modern furniture and smart, contemporary decor in pastel shades. There's a spacious kitchen and lounge, and all beds have reading lamps and lockers. The cheaper private rooms have shared bathrooms.

Hotel Stare Miasto　　　HOTEL €€
(☑ 61 663 6242; www.hotelstaremiasto.pl; ul Rybaki 36; s/d from 275/340zł; P ❋ ⓢ; ⓐ Wrocławska) Stylish value-for-money hotel with a tastefully chandeliered foyer and spacious breakfast room. Rooms can be small but are clean and bright with lovely starched white sheets. Some upper rooms have skylights in place of windows.

★ **Puro Poznań**
Stare Miasto　　　BOUTIQUE HOTEL €€€
(☑ 61 333 1000; www.purohotel.pl/en/poznan; Stawna 12; r from 250zł; P ❋ ⓢ; ⓐ Plac Wielkopolski) The homegrown Puro hotel chain's Poznań outpost ticks all the boxes – central location, underground car park, designer decor, comfortable lobby with free coffee machine, fast reliable wi-fi, helpful staff, sharply styled bedrooms flooded with light and a buffet breakfast that has you coming back for more. What's not to like?

🍴 Eating

★ **Cybina 13**　　　POLISH €€
(☑ 61 663 6334; www.cybina13.pl; Cybińska 13/2; mains 29-49zł; ⊘ noon-10pm; ⓢ ⓘ; ⓐ Katedra, Rondo Śródka) ⏀ Set in the cute little enclave of Śródka, close to the Poznań Gate, this bright, modern restaurant is popular with locals, whether for a romantic dinner in the sharply styled dining room or a weekend lunch at the outdoor tables. The tempting menu puts a modern spin on traditional Polish dishes, and is accompanied by home-baked flavoured breads.

Wiejskie Jadło　　　POLISH €€
(☑ 61 853 6600; www.wiejskie-jadlo.pl; Stary Rynek 77; mains 22-55zł; ⊘ noon-11pm; ⓐ Marcinskowskiego) This compact Polish restaurant, hidden a short distance back from the Rynek, serves what it says on the sign – *wiejskie jadło* (countryside food). It offers a range of filling dishes including several kinds of pierogi (dumplings), *żurek* (sour rye soup) served in a hollow loaf, roast pork knuckle and beef with beetroot, all dished up in a rustic farmhouse setting.

🍷 Drinking & Nightlife

Stragan　　　CAFE
(☑ 789 233 965; www.facebook.com/stragankawiarnia; ul Ratajczaka 31; ⊘ 8am-9pm Mon-Fri, 9am-8pm Sat & Sun; ⓢ; ⓐ Gwarna) Cool, contemporary cafe in which even the most bearded hipster would feel at home. Coffee ranges from Chemex brews to flat whites, complemented by excellent cakes and light meals. Also serves breakfast (to noon) and bagels (all day); order at the counter.

Van Diesel Music Club　　　CLUB
(☑ 515 065 459; www.vandiesel.pl; Stary Rynek 88; ⊘ 9pm-5am Fri & Sat; ⓐ Plac Wielkopolski,

Wrocławska) Happening venue on the main square, with DJs varying their offerings between pop, house, R&B, soul and dance. Given the variety, you're sure to find a night that will get you on the dance floor.

☆ Entertainment

Centrum Kultury Zamek   CONCERT VENUE
(Castle Cultural Centre; ☑ 61 646 5260; www.ckzamek.pl; ul Św Marcin 80/82; ☏; ⊕ Gwarna, Zamek) Within the grand neo-Romanesque **Kaiserhaus** (ul Św Marcin 80/82), built from 1904 to 1910 for German emperor Wilhelm II, this active cultural hub hosts cinema, art and music events.

❶ Information

The Poznań City Card (one day, 49zł) is available at all city information centres. It provides free entry to major museums, sizeable discounts at restaurants and recreational activities, and unlimited public transport use.

Tourist Office (Informacja Turystyczna Stary Rynek; ☑ 61 852 6156; www.poznan.travel; Stary Rynek 59/60; ⊕ 9.30am-8pm Mon-Sat, 9.30am-5pm Sun; ⊕ Plac Wielkopolski, Wrocławska) Located conveniently on the main square.

Tourist Office – Train Station (Informacja Turystyczna Dworzec Główny PKP; ☑ 61 633 1016; www.poznan.travel; ul Dworcowa 2; ⊕ 9am-5pm; ⊕ Poznań Główny, Most Dworcowy) At Poznań Główny train station.

❶ Getting There & Away

BUS

The **bus station** (Dworzec autobusowy w Poznaniu; ☑ 703 303 330; www.pks.poznan.pl; ul Stanisława Matyi 2; ⊕ Poznań Główny, Most Dworcowy) is at the north end of the Avenida shopping mall, downstairs from the main train station. Destinations include:

Berlin from 49zł, three to four hours, six daily

Gdańsk 25zł, five hours, three daily

Prague 69zł, eight hours, twice daily

Warsaw 35zł, four to five hours, seven daily

Wrocław 15zł, 3½ hours, twice daily

TRAIN

Poznań Główny train station is 15km southwest of the old town square, entered via Level 1 of the Avenida shopping mall.

Gdańsk 56zł, 3½ hours, eight daily

Kraków 66zł, five to six hours, eight daily

Toruń 35zł, 1½ hours, 12 daily

Warsaw from 55zł, four hours, 12 daily

Wrocław 38zł, 2½ hours, hourly

POMERANIA

Pomerania (Pomorze in Polish) is an attractive region with diverse drawcards, from beautiful beaches to architecturally pleasing cities. The historic port city of Gdańsk is situated at the region's eastern extreme, while the attractive Gothic city of Toruń lies inland.

Gdańsk

POP 474,000

Like a ministate all to itself, Gdańsk has a unique feel that sets it apart from other cities in Poland. Centuries of maritime ebb and flow as a major Baltic port; streets of distinctively un-Polish architecture influenced by a united nations of wealthy merchants who shaped the city's past; the to-ing and fro-ing of Danzig/Gdańsk between Teutonic Prussia and Slavic Poland; and the destruction wrought by WWII have all bequeathed a special atmosphere that makes Gdańsk an increasingly popular destination.

Visitors throng in ever greater numbers to wander historical thoroughfares lined with grand, elegantly proportioned buildings, and to enjoy a treasure trove of characterful bars and cafes, seafood restaurants, amber shops and intriguing museums, not to mention pleasure-boat cruises along the river and a wealth of maritime history to soak up in between brews at dockside beer gardens.

◉ Sights

Most of Gdańsk's sights are situated in the Main Town (Główne Miasto), centred on the busy **Długi Targ** (Long Market), but two modern attractions – the Museum of WWII and the European Solidarity Centre – lie a short distance to the north of this compact central area.

★ Museum of WWII   MUSEUM
(Muzeum II Wojny Światowej; www.muzeum1939.pl; pl Władysława Bartoszewskiego 1; adult/concession 23/16zł; ⊕ 10am-7pm Tue-Fri, to 8pm Sat & Sun) Opened in 2016, this striking piece of modern architecture is a bold addition to the northern end of Gdańsk's waterfront. It has rapidly become one of the city's must-visit attractions, tracing the fate of Poland during the world's greatest conflict, from amazing footage of the German battleship *Schleswig-Holstein* firing on Westerplatte on 1 September 1939, to harrowing accounts of the

Gdańsk

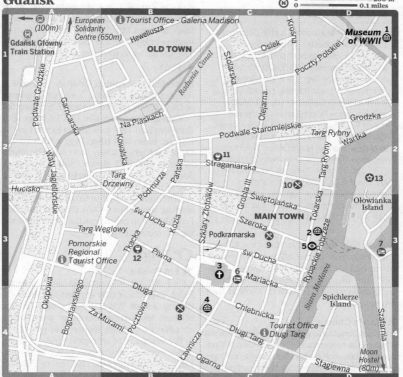

Gdańsk

◎ Top Sights
1 Museum of WWII	....D1

◎ Sights
Historical Museum of Gdańsk	...(see 4)
2 National Maritime Museum	...D3
3 St Mary's Church	...C3
4 Town Hall	...C4
5 Żuraw	...D3

🛏 Sleeping
6 Gotyk House	...C3
7 Hotel Podewils	...D3

🍽 Eating
8 Bar Neptun	...B4
9 Restauracja Pod Łososiem	...C3
10 Tawerna Mestwin	...C2

🍷 Drinking & Nightlife
11 Cafe Lamus	...C2
12 Józef K	...B3

★ Entertainment
13 Baltic Philharmonic Hall	...D2

horrors of Nazi extermination camps. An absolute minimum of three hours is needed to do it justice.

European Solidarity Centre MUSEUM
(Europejskie Centrum Solidarności; ☏ 58 772 4112; www.ecs.gda.pl; Plac Solidarności 1; building free, exhibition adult/concession 20/15zł; ⊙10am-6pm Mon-Fri, to 7pm Sat & Sun May-Sep, shorter hours Oct-Apr) Opened in 2014, and housed in a love-it-or-hate-it example of 21st-century architecture (its rusty steel plates designed to evoke ships under construction), this exhibition has quickly become one of Gdańsk's unmissables. Audio guides clamped to ears, visitors wander through seven halls examining Poland's

WORTH A TRIP

MALBORK

Magnificent **Malbork Castle** (Muzeum Zamkowe w Malborku; ☑ tickets 556 470 978; www.zamek.malbork.pl; ul Starościńska 1; adult/concession 29.50/20.50zł; ⊙ 9am-7pm May-Sep, 10am-3pm Oct-Apr; ℗) makes a great day trip from Gdańsk. It's the largest Gothic castle in Europe and was once headquarters of the medieval Teutonic Knights, its sinister form looming over the relatively small town and slow-moving Nogat River. Trains run regularly from Gdańsk Głowny station (13.60zł, 30 to 50 minutes, twice hourly). Once you get to Malbork station, turn right, cross the highway and follow ul Kościuszki to the castle. Visits are by self-guided tour with audio guide.

postwar fight for freedom, from the Gdańsk shipyard strikes of the 1970s to the round-table negotiations of the late 1980s and beyond, the displays blending state-of-the-art multimedia with real artefacts. Allow at least two hours.

St Mary's Church CHURCH

(www.bazylikamariacka.gdansk.pl; ul Podkramarska 5; tower adult/concession 10/5zł; ⊙ 8.30am-5.30pm Mon-Sat, 11am-noon & 1-5pm Sun year-round, longer hours May-Sep) Dominating the heart of the Old Town, St Mary's is often cited as the largest brick church in the world, its massive 78m-high tower dominating the Gdańsk cityscape. Begun in 1343, the building reached its present proportions in 1502. The high altar has a Gothic polyptych from the 1510s, with the Coronation of the Virgin depicted in its central panel. Don't miss the 15th-century astronomical clock in the northern transept, and the church tower (a climb of 405 steps).

National Maritime Museum MUSEUM

(Narodowe Muzeum Morskie w Gdańsku; ☑ Maritime Cultural Centre 58 329 8700, information 58 301 8611; www.nmm.pl; ul Ołowianka 9-13; combined ticket for all sites adult/concession 23/13zł; ⊙ 10am-4pm Tue-Fri, to 6pm Sat & Sun) This is a sprawling exhibition covering Gdańsk's role as a Baltic seaport through the centuries. The headquarters, the multimillion-euro Maritime Cultural Centre, has a permanent interactive exhibition 'People-Ships-Ports'. Other exhibitions (which can be visited individually with separate tickets) include the MS *Sołdek*, the first vessel to be built at

the Gdańsk shipyard in the postwar years, and the **Żuraw** (Crane; ul Szeroka 67/68; adult/concession 8/5zł; ⊙ 10am-6pm Jul & Aug, shorter hours & closed Mon Sep-Jun), a 15th-century loading crane that was the biggest in its day. The granaries across the river house more displays.

Historical Museum of Gdańsk MUSEUM

(Ratusza Głównego Miasta; www.muzeumgdansk. pl; Długa 46/47; adult/concession 12/6zł, tower 5zł; ⊙ 10am-1pm Tue, to 4pm Wed, Fri & Sat, to 6pm Thu, 11am-4pm Sun) This museum is located in the historic **town hall** (Długi Targ), which claims Gdańsk's highest tower at 81.5m. The showpiece is the Red Room (Sala Czerwona), done up in Dutch Mannerist style from the end of the 16th century. The 2nd floor houses exhibitions related to Gdańsk's history, including imitations of old Gdańsk interiors. From here you can access the tower for great views across the city.

☞ Tours

★ **Eat Polska** FOOD

(☑ 661 368 758; www.eatpolska.com; per person 290zł; ⊙ Food Tour daily at noon) Get beneath the surface of Polish food culture on one of these fascinating four-hour tours (bring an appetite!), which involve sampling food in the company of an expert guide at half a dozen venues, including a 1950s food market, a fish delicatessen and one of Poland's top restaurants. Vodka and beer tours are also available.

🛏 Sleeping

★ **Mamas & Papas Hostel** HOSTEL €

(☑ 792 578 933; www.facebook.com/hostelmamas papas; ul Nowiny 19; dm/tw from 50/130zł; ℗ @ 🖎) This family-run hostel set in a suburban home offers the best welcome in the Tri-City. It's a cosy affair with just 28 beds, a common room and kitchen, but it's the owners – experienced travellers who know what makes a good hostel experience – who make it special. The only drawback is the location, a 10-minute bus ride south of the centre.

Moon Hostel HOSTEL €

(☑ 58 691 6700; www.moonhostel.pl; ul Długie Ogrody 6a; s/d/q from 99/119/159zł; ℗ @ 🖎🖎) This colourfully decorated hostel has a superb location, a pleasant two-minute walk across the river from the Long Market. Accommodation is in bright, IKEA-furnished two- to six-bed rooms, with spotless shared or private bathrooms. Breakfast is available, but not really worth the price; there are several good breakfast cafes nearby.

Gotyk House
HOTEL €€

(Kamienica Gotyk; ☑58 301 8567; www.gotyk house.eu; ul Mariacka 1; r 339zł; ℗ 🕸) Wonderfully located near St Mary's Church, this neat, Gothic-themed guesthouse is squeezed into Gdańsk's oldest building. The seven compact rooms have Gothic touches such as pointy-arched doorways and hefty drapery, though most are thoroughly modern creations and bathrooms are definitely of the third millennium. Breakfast is served in your room. Four floors, no lift.

★ Hotel Podewils
HOTEL €€€

(☑58 300 9560; www.podewils.pl; ul Szafarnia 2; s/d from 355/455zł; ℗ 🕸 🕸) The view from the Podewils across the river to the Main Town can't be beaten, though the owners probably wish they could take its cheery baroque facade and move it away from the concrete riverside developments sprouting next door. Guestrooms are a vintage confection of elegant period furniture, classic prints and distinctive wallpaper.

✖ Eating

Bar Neptun
CAFETERIA €

(☑058 301 4988; www.barneptun.pl; ul Długa 33/34; mains 6-20zł; ⊙7.30am-7pm Mon-Fri, 10am-6pm Sat & Sun, 1hr later Jun-Sep; 🕸) It's surprising where some of Poland's communist-era milk bars have survived – this one is right on the main tourist drag. However, Neptun is a cut above your run-of-the-mill bar mleczny, with potted plants and decorative tiling. Popular with foreigners on a budget, it even has an English menu of Polish favourites such as naleśniki (crepes) and gołąbki (cabbage rolls).

★ Tawerna Mestwin
POLISH €€

(☑58 301 7882; www.tawernamestwin.com; ul Straganiarska 20/23; mains 22-38zł; ⊙11am-10pm Tue-Sun; 🕸🕸) ✔ The speciality here is Kashubian regional cooking from the northwest of Poland, and dishes such as potato pancakes, stuffed cabbage rolls, fish soup and fried herring are as close to home cooking as you'll get in a restaurant. The interior is done out like a traditional farm cottage and the exposed beams and dark-green walls make for a cosy atmosphere.

Restauracja Pod Łososiem
POLISH €€€

(☑58 301 7652; www.podlososiem.com.pl; ul Szeroka 52/54; mains 60-110zł; ⊙noon-11pm) Founded in 1598 and famous for its fish dishes, this is one of Gdańsk's most highly regarded restaurants. Red leather seats, brass chandeliers and a gathering of gas lamps fill out the rather sober interior, illuminated by the speciality drink – Goldwasser. This gooey, sweet liqueur with flakes of gold was produced in its cellars from the 16th century until WWII.

☕ Drinking & Nightlife

★ Józef K
BAR

(☑527 161 510; www.facebook.com/jozefk; ul Piwna 1/2; ⊙10am-2am Sun-Thu, to 4am Fri & Sat; 🕸) Is it a bar or a junk shop? You decide as you relax with a cocktail or a glass of excellent Polish perry on one of the battered sofas, illuminated by an old theatre spotlight. Downstairs is an open area where the party kicks off at weekends; upstairs is more intimate with lots of soft seating and well-stocked bookcases.

Cafe Lamus
BAR

(☑531 998 832; www.facebook.com/cafelamus; Lawendowa 8, enter from Straganiarska; ⊙noon-1am) This fun retro-style bar has a random scattering of 1970s sofas and armchairs (and deckchairs outside), big-print wallpaper from the same period, and a menu of Polish craft beers, cider and coffee. There's also a spillover bar for the Saturday-night crowd.

☆ Entertainment

Baltic Philharmonic Hall
CLASSICAL MUSIC

(☑58 320 6262; www.filharmonia.gda.pl; ul Ołowianka 1; ⊙box office 9.30am-4pm Tue, 10.30am-6pm Wed-Fri) The regular host of chamber-music concerts; also organises many of the major music festivals throughout the year.

❶ Information

Tourist Office – Długi Targ (☑58 301 4355; www.visitgdansk.com; Długi Targ 28/29; ⊙9am-7pm May-Aug, to 5pm Sep-Apr)

Tourist Office – Galeria Madison (www.visitgdansk.com; Galeria Madison, ul Rajska 10; ⊙9am-7pm Mon-Sat, from 10am Sun) Near the train station.

Tourist Office – Airport (☑58 348 1368; www.visitgdansk.com; ul Słowackiego 210, Gdańsk Lech Wałęsa Airport; ⊙24hr)

Pomorskie Regional Tourist Office (☑58 732 7041; www.pomorskie.travel; Brama Wyżynna, Wały Jagiellońskie 2a; ⊙9am-6pm year-round, to 8pm Mon-Fri Jun-Sep) Housed in the Upland Gate, this friendly regional tourist office has info on Gdańsk and the surrounding area.

Getting There & Away

AIR

Gdańsk Lech Wałęsa airport (☎801 066 808, 52 567 3531; www.airport.gdansk.pl; ul Słowackiego 210) is 14km west of the city centre. There are direct flights to Warsaw with LOT, and to Kraków and Wrocław with Ryanair.

International flights to many European and UK cities are operated by budget airlines Ryanair and Wizz Air.

BUS

Gdańsk's **bus terminal** (PKS Gdańsk; ul 3 Maja 12) is right behind the central train station, linked by an underground passageway.

There are plenty of connections from Gdańsk to Western European cities plus services east to Kaliningrad (40zł, 3½ hours, four daily).

TRAIN

The grand main train station, **Gdańsk Główny**, is on the western edge of the Old Town. Destinations include Malbork (13.50zł, 40 minutes, two or three an hour), Poznań (56zł, 3½ hours, eight daily), Toruń (47zł, 2½ hours, nine daily) and Warsaw (77zł, three to four hours, hourly).

Toruń

POP 202,560

Toruń escaped major damage in WWII and is famous for its well-preserved Gothic architecture, along with the quality of its famous gingerbread. The city is also renowned as the birthplace of Nicolaus Copernicus (Mikołaj Kopernik in Polish), who revolutionised the field of astronomy in 1543 by asserting the earth travelled around the sun. He's a figure you will not be able to escape – you can even buy gingerbread men in his likeness.

Sights

The usual starting point on Toruń's Gothic trail is the **Old Town Market Square** (Rynek Staromiejski), lined with finely restored houses. At the southeast corner, look for the picturesque **Statue of Copernicus**.

Old Town Hall MUSEUM
(Ratusz Staromiejski; www.muzeum.torun.pl; Rynek Staromiejski 1; adult/concession 15/10zł, tower 15/10zł, combined ticket 25/18zł; ⏲10am-6pm Tue-Sun May-Sep, to 4pm Oct-Apr) The Old Town Hall dates from the 14th century and hasn't changed much since, though some Renaissance additions lent an ornamental touch to the sober Gothic structure. Today it houses Gothic art (painting and stained glass), a display of local 17th- and 18th-century crafts and a gallery of Polish paintings from 1800 to the present, including a couple of Witkacys and Matejkos. Climb the tower for a fine panoramic view of Toruń's Gothic townscape.

Cathedral of SS John the Baptist & John the Evangelist CHURCH
(www.katedra.diecezja.torun.pl; ul Żeglarska 16; tower 9zł; ⏲9am-5.30pm Mon-Sat, from 2pm Sun, tower closed Nov-Mar) Toruń's mammoth Gothic cathedral was begun around 1260 but only completed at the end of the 15th century. Its massive tower houses Poland's second-largest historic bell, the Tuba Dei (God's Trumpet). On the southern side of the tower, facing the Vistula, is a large 15th-century clock; its original face and single hand are still in working order. Check out the dent above the VIII – it's from a cannonball that struck the clock during the Swedish siege of 1703.

Toruń Gingerbread Museum MUSEUM
(Muzeum Toruńskiego Piernika; www.muzeum.torun.pl; ul Strumykowa 4; adult/concession 12/9zł; ⏲10am-6pm Tue-Sun May-Sep, to 4pm Oct-Apr) Not to be confused with the commercial **Gingerbread Museum** (Muzeum Piernika; ☎56 663 6617; www.muzeumpiernika.pl; ul Rabiańska 9; adult/concession 17/12zł; ⏲10am-6pm, tours every hour, on the hour) across town, this branch of the Toruń Regional Museum is housed in a former gingerbread factory and looks at the 600-year-long history of the city's favourite sweet. You also get the chance to make your own gingerbread using dough prepared to the original recipe.

Sleeping

Toruń Główny Hostel HOSTEL €
(☎606 564 600; www.hosteltg.com; Toruń Główny train station; dm/d 39/70zł; 📶) This hostel is housed in the old post-office building right on the platform at Toruń's main train station, with attractive wall paintings of the Old Town. The six- and eight-bed dorms are spacious with suitcase-size lockers and reading lamps; free breakfast is served in the basement kitchen. Downsides include train noise (surprise!), and only one shower per floor.

★**Hotel Spichrz** HOTEL €€
(☎56 657 1140; www.spichrz.pl; ul Mostowa 1; s/d from 250/310zł; ❄📶) Wonderfully situated within a historic waterfront granary, this hotel's 19 rooms are laden with personality, featuring massive exposed beams above characterful timber furniture and contemporary

GREAT MASURIAN LAKES

The northeastern corner of Poland features a beautiful postglacial landscape dominated by thousands of lakes. About 200km of canals connect these bodies of water, making the area a prime destination for canoeists, as well as those who love to hike, fish and mountain bike.

The towns of **Giżycko** and **Mikołajki** make good bases. Both the **Giżycko tourist office** (☑ 87 428 5265; www.gizycko.turystyka.pl; ul Wyzwolenia 2; ⊙ 9am-6pm Mon-Fri, 10am-4pm Sat & Sun Jun-Aug, shorter hours Sep-May; ☎) and the **Mikołajki tourist office** (☑ 87 421 6850; www.mikolajki.eu; Plac Wolności 7; ⊙ 10am-6pm Mon-Sat, to 5pm Sun Jun-Aug, to 6pm Mon-Sat May & Sep) supply useful maps for sailing and hiking, provide excursion boat schedules and assist in finding accommodation.

Nature aside, there are some interesting fragments of history in this region. A grim reminder of the past is the **Wolf's Lair** (Wilczy Szaniec; ☑ 89 741 0031; www.wilczyszaniec. olsztyn.lasy.gov.pl; Gierłoż; adult/concession 15/10zł, parking 5zł; ⊙ 8am-8pm Apr-Sep, to 4pm Oct-Mar; ℗). Located at **Gierłoż**, 8km east of Kętrzyn, this ruined complex was Hitler's wartime headquarters for his invasion of the Soviet Union. In 1944 a group of high-ranking German officers tried to assassinate Hitler here. These dramatic events were reprised in the 2008 Tom Cruise movie *Valkyrie*.

bathrooms. The location by the river is within walking distance of the sights but away from the crowds. The hotel's Karczma Spichrz restaurant serves traditional Polish cuisine.

Hotel Petite Fleur
HOTEL €€

(☑ 56 621 5100; www.petitefleur.pl; ul Piekary 25; s/d from 210/270zł; ✴ ☎) One of the better midrange options in town, this place is full of historic character with an antique lobby, and understated rooms with timber beam ceilings and elegant prints, though the singles can be small and dark, and there's no lift. The French brick-cellar restaurant is one of Toruń's better dining options and the buffet breakfast is a delight.

✖ Eating & Drinking

Oberża
POLISH €

(☑ 56 622 0022; www.facebook.com/oberzatorun; ul Rabiańska 9; mains 8-17zł; ⊙ 11am-10pm Mon-Thu, to midnight Fri & Sat, to 9pm Sun; ☎) This self-service cafeteria stacks 'em high and sells 'em cheap for a hungry crowd of locals and tourists. Find your very own thatched minicottage or intimate hideout amid stained-glass windows, cartwheels, bridles and other rustic knick-knacks and enjoy 11 types of pierogi (dumplings), soups, salads and classic Polish mains from a menu tuned to low-cost belly-packing.

★ Szeroka 9
INTERNATIONAL €€€

(☑ 56 622 8424; www.szeroka9.pl; ul Szeroka 9; mains 35-50zł; ⊙ noon-11pm Mon-Fri, from 10am Sat & Sun) ✔ Arguably Toruń's top restaurant,

this place offers a changing menu of seasonal gourmet fare ranging from pickled trout with horseradish to pig cheeks with creamed potato and marinated beetroot; the dessert to plump for is local gingerbread in plum sauce. The decor is contemporary urban and the staff are friendly and knowledgeable. Reservations recommended for dinner.

Jan Olbracht
MICROBREWERY

(www.browar-olbracht.pl; ul Szczytna 15; ⊙ 10am-11pm Sun-Thu, to midnight Fri & Sat) Take a seat in a barrel-shaped indoor booth or at the street-side terrace to sample some of this microbrewery's unusual beers. These include pils, wheat beer, a special ale and, this being Toruń, gingerbread beer, all brewed in the gleaming copper vats at the street end of the bar.

☆ Entertainment

Dwór Artusa
CLASSICAL MUSIC

(☑ 56 655 4929; www.artus.torun.pl; Rynek Staromiejski 6; ⊙ box office noon-6pm Mon-Fri) The Artus Court, an impressive late-19th-century mansion overlooking the main square, houses a major cultural centre and has an auditorium hosting musical events, including concerts and recitals.

ℹ Information

Tourist Office (☑ 56 621 0930; www.it.torun. pl; Rynek Staromiejski 25; ⊙ 9am-6pm Mon-Fri, from 10am Sat & Sun; ☎) Free wi-fi access, heaps of info and professional staff who know their city.

890

Getting There & Away

BUS

Toruń bus station (Dworzec Autobusowy Toruń; ul Dąbrowskiego 8-24) is close to the northern edge of the Old Town and handles services to Gdańsk (from 20zł, 2½ hours, hourly) and Warsaw (from 28zł, three to four hours, at least hourly).

TRAIN

Toruń has two stations: **Toruń Główny** is about 2km south of the Old Town, on the opposite side of the Vistula, while the more convenient **Toruń Miasto** is on the Old Town's eastern edge. Not all services stop at both stations.

There are direct trains to Gdańsk (47zł, 2½ hours, four daily), Kraków (62zł, 5¼ hours, one daily) and Warsaw (from 50zł, 2¾ hours, hourly).

SURVIVAL GUIDE

Directory A–Z

ACCOMMODATION

Poland has a wide choice of accommodation to suit all budgets. Advanced booking is recommended for popular destinations such as Kraków, Zakopane and Gdańsk.

Hotels Hotels account for the majority of accommodation in Poland, encompassing a variety of old and new places, ranging from basic to ultraplush.

Pensions *Pensjonaty* (pensions) are small, privately run guesthouses that provide breakfast and occasionally half or full board. They are generally clean, comfortable and good value.

Hostels Polish hostels include both the newer breed of privately owned hostels and the older, publicly run or municipal hostels. There are also simple, rustic mountain lodges.

LGBTIQ+ TRAVELLERS

Homosexuality is legal in Poland but not openly tolerated. Polish society is conservative and for the most part remains hostile towards the LGBTIQ+ community.

The Polish gay and lesbian scene is fairly discreet; Warsaw and Kraków are the best places to find bars, clubs and gay-friendly accommodation, and Sopot is noted as gay-friendly compared to the rest of Poland. The best sources of information for Poland's scene are the Warsaw and Kraków city guides on www.queerinthe world.com, and www.queer.pl (in Polish only).

MONEY

➤ The Polish currency is the *złoty*, abbreviated to zł and pronounced *zwo*-ti. It is divided into 100 *groszy*, which are abbreviated to gr.

➤ Banknotes come in denominations of 10zł, 20zł, 50zł, 100zł and 200zł, and coins in 1gr, 2gr, 5gr, 10gr, 20gr and 50gr, and 1zł, 2zł and 5zł.

➤ Keep some small-denomination notes and coins for shops, cafes and restaurants – getting change for the 100zł and 200zł notes that ATMs often spit out can be a problem.

➤ ATMs are ubiquitous in cities and towns, and even the smallest hamlet is likely to have at least one. The majority accept Visa and MasterCard.

➤ Beware of the widespread Euronet ATMs, which give a much poorer rate of exchange than bank ATMs.

➤ The best exchange rates are obtained by changing money at banks, or by taking cash out of bank ATMs.

Tipping

When to tip Customary in restaurants and at service establishments such as hairdressers; optional everywhere else.

Restaurants At smaller establishments and for smaller tabs, round the bill to the nearest 5zł or 10zł increment. Otherwise, 10% is standard.

Taxis No need to tip, though you may want to round up the fare to reward good service.

OPENING HOURS

Most places adhere to the following hours. Shopping centres generally have longer hours and are open from 9am to 8pm at weekends. Museums are usually closed on Mondays, and have shorter hours outside high season.

Banks 9am–4pm Monday to Friday, to 1pm Saturday (varies)

Offices 9am–5pm Monday to Friday, to 1pm Saturday (varies)

Post Offices 8am–7pm Monday to Friday, to 1pm Saturday (cities)

Restaurants 11am–10pm daily

Shops 8am–6pm Monday to Friday, 10am–2pm Saturday

PUBLIC HOLIDAYS

New Year's Day 1 January
Epiphany 6 January
Easter Sunday March or April
Easter Monday March or April
State Holiday 1 May
Constitution Day 3 May
Pentecost Sunday Seventh Sunday after Easter
Corpus Christi Ninth Thursday after Easter
Assumption Day 15 August
All Saints' Day 1 November
Independence Day 11 November
Christmas 25 and 26 December

POLAND SURVIVAL GUIDE

TELEPHONE

➜ All telephone numbers, landline and mobile, have nine digits. Landlines are written 12 345 6789, with the first two numbers corresponding to the area code (there is no zero). Mobile-phone numbers are written 123 456 789.

➜ Poland uses the GSM 900/1800 system, the same as Europe, Australia and New Zealand. It's not compatible with most cell phones from North America or Japan (though many mobiles have multiband GSM 1900/900 phones that will work in Poland).

ⓘ Getting There & Away

Flights, cars and tours can be booked online at lonelyplanet.com/bookings.

AIR

➜ Most international flights to Poland arrive at Warsaw Chopin Airport (p869). Other international airports include Kraków, Gdańsk, Poznań and Wrocław.

➜ Poland's national airline is **LOT** (www.lot. com), offering regular flights to Poland from throughout Europe, and also to/from New York, Chicago, Toronto, Tel Aviv and Beijing, among others.

➜ Several budget carriers, including **Ryanair** (www.ryanair.com) and **Wizz Air** (www.wizzair. com), link European cities to Polish destinations.

LAND
Bus

➜ International buses head in all directions, including eastward to the Baltic States and Russia. From Zakopane, it's easy to hop into Slovakia via bus or minibus.

➜ Several companies operate long-haul coach services, including **Eurolines** (www.eurolines. pl), **Ecolines** (www.ecolines.net) and **FlixBus** (https://global.flixbus.com).

Car & Motorcycle

➜ The minimum legal driving age is 18.

➜ The maximum blood-alcohol limit is 0.02%.

➜ All drivers are required to carry their passport (with a valid visa if necessary), driving licence, vehicle registration document and proof of third-party insurance (called a Green Card).

Train

There are direct rail services from Warsaw to several surrounding capitals, including Berlin, Prague, Minsk and Moscow. Kraków also has useful international rail connections.

SEA

Ferry services operated by **Unity Line** (☑ 91 880 2909; www.unityline.pl) and **TT-Line** (www. ttline.com) connect Poland's Baltic coast ports of Gdańsk, Gdynia and Świnoujście to destinations in Scandinavia.

ⓘ Getting Around

AIR

LOT (www.lot.com) flies between Warsaw and Gdańsk, Katowice, Kraków, Poznań and Wrocław.

BUS

➜ Poland has a comprehensive bus network (far greater than the rail network) covering nearly every town and village accessible by road.

➜ Buy tickets at bus terminals or directly from the driver.

➜ **FlixBus** (https://global.flixbus.com) is the main nationwide coach operator between major cities and towns using modern coaches with free wi-fi.

CAR & MOTORCYCLE

➜ Major international car-rental companies are represented in larger cities and airports.

➜ Car-hire agencies require a passport, valid driving licence and credit card. You need to be at least 21 or 23 years of age (depending on the company).

TRAIN

➜ Poland's train network is extensive and reasonably priced.

➜ **PKP InterCity** (IC; ☑ from Poland 703 200 200, from abroad +48 22 391 97 57; www. intercity.pl) runs all of Poland's express trains, including ExpressInterCity Premium (EIP), ExpressInterCity (EIC), InterCity (IC), EuroCity (EC) and TLK trains.

➜ A second main operator, **PolRegio** (www. polregio.pl), takes care of most other trains, including relatively fast InterRegio trains and slower Regio trains.

➜ Buy tickets at ticket machines, station ticket windows or at special PKP passenger-service centres, located in major stations.

Portugal

POP 10.4 MILLION

Includes ➡

Best Places to Eat

➡ Alma (p900)

➡ Euskalduna Studio (p917)

➡ Taberna Típica Quarta Feira (p909)

➡ Antiga Confeitaria de Belém (p900)

➡ O Abocanhado (p922)

Best Places to Stay

➡ Casa do Príncipe (p899)

➡ Guest House Douro (p915)

➡ Albergaria do Calvario (p908)

➡ Dona Emilia (p919)

➡ Yeatman (p916)

➡ Moon Hill Hostel (p903)

Why Go?

With medieval castles, frozen-in-time villages, captivating cities and golden-sand bays, the Portuguese experience can mean many things. History, terrific food and wine, lyrical scenery and all-night partying are just the beginning. Portugal's cinematically beautiful capital, Lisbon, and its soulful northern rival, Porto, are two of Europe's most charismatic cities. Both are a joy to stroll, with gorgeous river views, rattling trams and tangled lanes hiding boutiques and vintage shops, new-wave bars, and a seductive mix of restaurants, fado (traditional Portuguese melancholic song) clubs and open-air cafes. Beyond the cities, Portugal's landscape unfolds in all its beauty. Here, you can stay overnight in converted hilltop fortresses fronting age-old vineyards, hike amid granite peaks or explore medieval villages in the little-visited hinterland. More than 800km of coast shelters some of Europe's best beaches.

When to Go
Lisbon

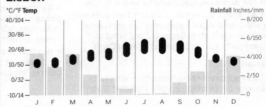

Apr & May Sunny days and wildflowers set the stage for hiking and outdoor activities.

Jun–Aug Lovely and lively, with a packed festival calendar and steamy beach days.

Late Sep & Oct Crisp mornings and sunny days; prices dip and crowds disperse.

Entering the Country

An increasingly popular destination, Portugal is well connected to North America and European countries by air. There are also handy overland links by bus and rail to and from Spain, from where you can continue on to other destinations on the continent – eg, the Sud Expresso train from Lisbon, which connects directly to Paris-bound TGV trains via the Spanish/French border at Irún/Hendaye.

ITINERARIES

One Week

Begin your journey in Porto (p914), gateway to the magical wine-growing region of the Douro valley (p915). Then head south to Coimbra (p912), Portugal's most venerable university town. Finish with three days to Lisbon (p895), including a night of fado in the Alfama, bar-hopping in Bairro Alto and pastry-eating in Belém.

Two Weeks

Explore Lisbon's environs, taking in the wooded wonderland of Sintra (p902), the crenellated charms of Óbidos (p910) and the Unesco-listed monastery at Tomar (p911). Next, head south, strolling the medieval lanes and Roman ruins of Évora (p908) before hitting the fabled beaches of the Algarve (p904). Follow the contours of Portugal's southern coast all the way to the dramatic end-of-the-continent cliffs at Sagres (p907) before flying home from Faro.

Essential Food & Drink

Cod for all seasons The Portuguese have dozens of ways to prepare *bacalhau* (dried salt cod). Try *bacalhau à brás* (grated cod fried with potatoes and eggs), *bacalhau espiritual* (cod soufflé) or *bacalhau com natas* (baked cod with cream and grated cheese).

Drink Port and red wines from the Douro valley, alvarinho and vinho verde (crisp, semi-sparkling wine) from the Minho and great, little-known reds from the Alentejo and the Beiras (particularly the Dão region).

Field and fowl *Porco preto* (sweet 'black' pork), *leitão* (roast suckling pig), *alheira* (bread and meat sausage – formerly Kosher), *cabrito assado* (roast kid) and *arroz de pato* (duck risotto).

Pastries The *pastel de nata* (custard tart) is legendary, especially in Belém. Other delicacies: *travesseiros* (almond and egg pastries) and *queijadas* (mini-cheese pastries).

Seafood Char-grilled *lulas* (squid), *polvo* (octopus) or *sardinhas* (sardines). Other treats: *cataplana* (seafood and sausage cooked in a copper pot), *caldeirada* (hearty fish stew) and *açorda de mariscos* (bread stew with shrimp).

AT A GLANCE

Area 88,323 sq km

Capital Lisbon

Country Code ☏ 351

Currency euro (€)

Emergency ambulance, fire and police ☏ 112

Language Portuguese

Time GMT/UTC in winter, GMT/UTC plus one hour in summer.

Visas Schengen rules apply.

Sleeping Price Ranges

The following price ranges refer to a double room with bathroom in high season. Unless otherwise stated breakfast is included in the price.

€ less than €60

€€ €60–120

€€€ more than €120

Eating Price Ranges

The following price ranges refer to a main course.

€ less than €10

€€ €10–20

€€€ more than €20

Resources

Lonely Planet (www.lonely planet.com/portugal)

Portugal Tourism (www. visitportugal.com)

Wines of Portugal (www. winesofportugal.info)

PORTUGAL

Portugal Highlights

1 **Alfama** (p895) Following the sound of fado spilling from the lamplit lanes of this enchanting old-world neighbourhood in the heart of Lisbon.

2 **Tavira** (p905) Taking in the town's laid-back charms, before hitting some of the Algarve's prettiest beaches.

3 **Coimbra** (p912) Catching live music in a backstreet bar in this festive university town with a stunning medieval centre.

4 **Sintra** (p902) Exploring the wooded hills, studded with fairy tale palaces, villas and gardens.

5 **Parque Nacional da Peneda-Gerês** (p921) Conquering the park's ruggedly scenic trails.

6 **Lagos** (p906) Enjoying heady beach days in this surf-loving town with a vibrant drinking and dining scene.

7 **Porto** (p914) Exploring the Unesco World Heritage–listed city centre and sampling velvety ports at riverside wine lodges.

LISBON

POP 547,733

Spread across steep hillsides that overlook the Rio Tejo, Lisbon has captivated visitors for centuries. Windswept vistas at breathtaking heights reveal the city in all its beauty: Roman and Moorish ruins, white-domed cathedrals and grand plazas lined with sun-drenched cafes. The real delight of discovery, though, is delving into the narrow cobblestone lanes.

As bright-yellow trams clatter through curvy tree-lined streets, *lisboêtas* (residents of Lisbon) stroll through lamplit old quarters and exchange gossip over glasses of wine while fado singers perform in the background. In other parts of town, Lisbon reveals its youthful alter ego at stylish dining rooms and lounges, late-night street parties, riverside nightspots, and boutiques selling all things classic and cutting-edge.

◎ Sights

★ Castelo de São Jorge   CASTLE

(www.castelodesaojorge.pt; adult/student/child €8.50/4/free; ⊙9am-9pm Mar-Oct, to 6pm Nov-Feb) Towering dramatically above Lisbon, the mid-11th-century hilltop fortifications of Castelo de São Jorge sneak into almost every snapshot. Roam its snaking ramparts and pine-shaded courtyards for superlative views over the city's red rooftops to the river. Three guided tours daily (in Portuguese, English and Spanish) at 10.30am, 1pm and 4pm are included in the admission price (additional tours available).

★ Mosteiro dos Jerónimos   MONASTERY

(www.mosteirojeronimos.pt; Praça do Império; adult/child €10/5, free Sun until 2pm for Portuguese citizens/residents only; ⊙10am-6.30pm Tue-Sun Jun-Sep, to 5.30pm Oct-May) Belém's undisputed heart-stealer is this Unesco-listed monastery. The *mosteiro* is the stuff of pure fantasy; a fusion of Diogo de Boitaca's creative vision and the spice and pepper dosh of Manuel I, who commissioned it to trumpet Vasco da Gama's discovery of a sea route to India in 1498.

★ Museu Calouste Gulbenkian – Coleção do Fundador   MUSEUM

(Founder's Collection; www.gulbenkian.pt; Av de Berna 45A; Coleção do Fundador/Coleção Moderna combo ticket adult/child €10/free, temporary exhibitions €3-6, free Sun from 2pm; ⊙10am-6pm Wed-Mon) Famous for its outstanding quality and breadth, the world-class Founder's Collection at Museu Calouste Gulbenkian showcases an epic collection of Western and Eastern art – from Egyptian treasures to Old Master and Impressionist paintings. Admission includes the separately housed **Coleção Moderna** (Modern Collection).

★ Tram 28E   TRAM

(Largo Martim Moniz) Don't leave the city without riding popular tram 28E from Largo Martim Moniz. This rickety, screechy, gloriously old-fashioned ride from Praça Martim Moniz to Campo de Ourique provides 45 minutes of mood-lifting views and absurdly steep climbs. With its polished wood panelling, bee-yellow paint job and chrome fittings, the century-old tram is like the full-scale model of a fastidious Hornby Railways collector.

Torre de Belém   TOWER

(www.torrebelem.pt; Av de Brasília; adult/child €6/3; ⊙10am-6.30pm Tue-Sun May-Sep, to 5.30pm Oct-Apr) Jutting out onto the Rio Tejo, this Unesco World Heritage–listed fortress epitomises the Age of Discoveries. You'll need to breathe in to climb the narrow spiral staircase to the tower, which affords sublime views over Belém and the river.

Praça do Comércio   PLAZA

(Terreiro do Paço; Praça do Comércio) With its grand 18th-century arcades, lemon-meringue facades and mosaic cobbles, the riverfront

---

HEAVENLY VIEWS

Lisbon's *miradouros* (lookouts) lift spirits with their heavenly views. Some have outdoor cafes for lingering.

Largo das Portas do Sol Moorish gateway with stunning views over Alfama's rooftops.

Miradouro da Graça (Largo da Graça) Pine-fringed square that's perfect for sundowners.

Miradouro da Senhora do Monte (Rua da Senhora do Monte) The highest lookout, with memorable castle views.

Miradouro de São Pedro de Alcântara (Rua São Pedro de Alcântara; ⊙viewpoint 24hr, kiosk 10am-midnight Sun-Wed, to 2am Thu-Sat) Drinks and sweeping views on the edge of Bairro Alto.

Miradouro de Santa Catarina (Rua de Santa Catarina; ⊙24hr) Youthful spot with guitar-playing rebels, artful graffiti and far-reaching views.

Central Lisbon

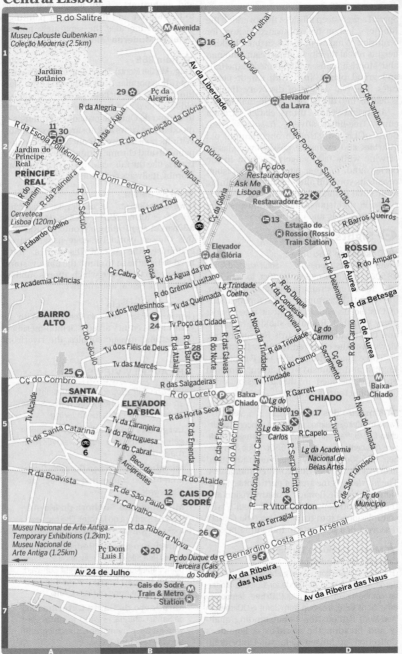

PORTUGAL LISBON

A · **B** · **C** · **D**

R do Salitre

Museu Calouste Gulbenkian –
Coleção Moderna (2.5km)

Jardim
Botânico

1

M Avenida
16

Av da Liberdade

R de São José

R do Telhal

Cç de Santano

29 ✪   Pç da
Alegria

R da Alegria

R das Portas de Santo Antão

Elevador
da Lavra

R da Mãe d'Água

R da Conceição da Glória

R da Glória

11 30

R da Escola Politécnica

Jardim do
Príncipe
Real

**PRÍNCIPE
REAL**

2

R do Jasmim

R da Palmeira

R Dom Pedro V

R das Taipas

R da Glória

Pç dos
Restauradores

Ask Me
Lisboa i
Restauradores M 22

13

R das Pretas

Estação do
Rossio (Rossio
Train Station)

14

R Barros Queirós

ROSSIO

R do Século

R Luísa Todi

Cerveteca
Lisboa (120m)

R Eduardo Coelho

7

Cç da Glória

Elevador
da Glória

R do Amparo

R de Aurea

R 1 de Dezembro

R da Betesga

3

R Academia Ciências

Cç Cabra

R da Rosa

Tv da Água da Flor

R do Grémio Lusitano

Lg Trindade
Coelho

R do Duque

R da Condessa

R da Oliveira

Lg do
Carmo

R do Carmo

R de Aurea

**BAIRRO
ALTO**

R do Século

Tv dos Inglesinhos

24

Tv da Queimada

Tv Poço da Cidade

R das Gáveas

R da Misericórdia

R Nova da Trindade

R da Trindade

Cç do
Sacramento

Baixa-
Chiado M

Tv do Carmo

Tv Trindade

4

Tv dos Fiéis de Deus

R da Atalaia

R da Barroca

28

R do Norte

Tv das Mercês

25

Cç do Combro

**SANTA
CATARINA**

R das Salgadeiras

R do Loreto P

Baixa-
Chiado

Lg do
Chiado M

19 ✕ 17

CHIADO

R Garrett

R Nova do Almada

R Serpa Pinto

R Ivens

Baixa-
Chiado M

5

Tv Alcaide

**ELEVADOR
DA BICA**

R de Santa Catarina

Tv da Laranjeira

Tv do Portuguesa

Tv do Cabral

6

Beco das
Arcipreste

R da Horta Seca

R da Emenda

R das Flores

10

R do Alecrim

R António Maria Cardoso

Lg de São
Carlos

R Capelo

Lg da Academia
Nacional de
Belas Artes

R da Boavista

R de São Paulo

Tv Carvalho

12

**CAIS DO
SODRÉ**

R do Ataíde

18

R Vitor Cordon

Cç de São Francisco

Pç do
Município

6

Museu Nacional de Arte Antiga –
Temporary Exhibitions (1.2km);
Museu Nacional de
Arte Antiga (1.25km)

R da Ribeira Nova

26

Pç Dom
Luís I

✕ 20

Tv Carvalho

Bernardino Costa

Pç do Duque da
Terceira (Cais
do Sodré)

9

R do Ferragial

R do Arsenal

Av da Ribeira
das Naus

7

Av 24 de Julho

Cais do Sodré
Train & Metro
Station M

Av da Ribeira das Naus

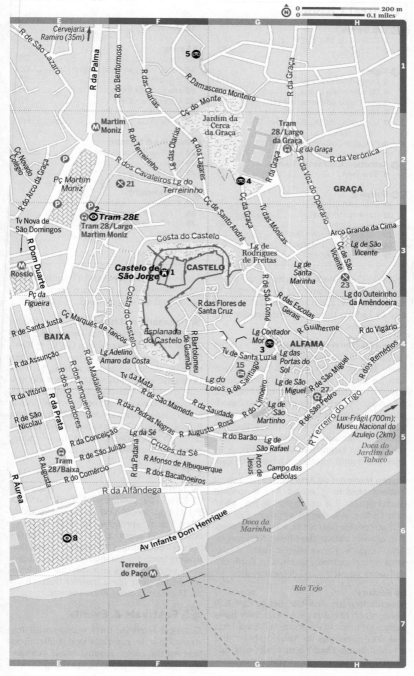

0 — 200 m
0 — 0.1 miles

Cervejaria
Ramiro (35m)

R de São Lázaro

R da Palma

R do Benformoso

R das Olarias

Cç do Monte

R Damasceno Monteiro

R da Graça

5

Jardim da
Cerca
da Graça

Tram
28/Largo
da Graça

Lg da Graça

R da Graça

R da Voz do Operário

R da Verónica

GRAÇA

Martim
Moniz

R do Terreirinho

R das Olarias

R dos Lagares

R dos Cavaleiros

Lg do
Terreirinho

Cç de Santo André

21

4

Cç da Graça

Tv das Mónicas

Cç Novidad
Colégio

Pç Martim
Moniz

Cç do Arco da Graça

R do Terreirinho

R Dom Duarte

2 Tram 28E
Tram 28/Largo
Martim Moniz

Costa do Castelo

Lg de
Rodrigues
de Freitas

CASTELO

Arco Grande da Cima

Cç de São Vicente

Lg de São
Vicente

Tv Nova de
São Domingos

Rossio

Pç da
Figueira

**Castelo de
São Jorge 1**

R de São Tomé

Lg de
Santa
Marinha

R das Escolas
Gerais

Lg do Outeirinho
da Amêndoeira

23

R de Santa Justa

Cç Marquês de Tancos

BAIXA

Lg Adelino
Amaro da Costa

R das Flores de
Santa Cruz

Lg Contador
Mor

R Guilherme

R do Vigário

3

ALFAMA

R da Assunção

R da Madalena

R dos Fanqueiros

R dos Douradores

Esplanada
do Castelo

R Bartolomeu
de Gusmão

Tv de Santa Luzia

15

Lg de
Santiago

Lg das
Portas do
Sol

R de São Miguel

27

R dos Remédios

R da Vitória

R de São
Nicolau

Tv da Mata

R de São Mamede

R das Pedras Negras

R da Saudade

Lg do
Loios

R de Santiago

R do Limoeiro

Lg de São
Miguel

Lg de
São
Martinho

R de São Pedro

R Terreiro do Trigo

Lux-Frágil (700m);
Museu Nacional do
Azulejo (2km)

R da Prata

R de São Julião

R da Conceição

Lg da
Sé

Cruzes da Sé

R Augusto
Rosa

R do Barão

Lg de
São Rafael

Doca do
Jardim do
Tabaco

R Áurea

R Augusta

Tram
28/Baixa

R do Comércio

R da Padaria

R Afonso de Albuquerque

R dos Bacalhoeiros

Arco
de
Jesus

Campo das
Cebolas

R da Alfândega

8

Av Infante Dom Henrique

Doca da
Marinha

Terreiro
do Paço

Rio Tejo

PORTUGAL LISBON

Central Lisbon

Praça do Comércio is a square to out-pomp them all. Everyone arriving by boat used to disembark here, and it still feels like the gateway to Lisbon, thronging with activity and rattling trams.

Museu Nacional do Azulejo MUSEUM
(📞 218 100 340; www.museudoazulejo.pt; Rua Madre de Deus 4; adult/child €5/free; ⊙10am-6pm Tue-Sun) Housed in a sublime 16th-century convent, Lisbon's Museu Nacional do Azulejo covers the entire *azulejo* (hand-painted tile) spectrum. Star exhibits feature a 36m-long panel depicting pre-earthquake Lisbon, a Manueline cloister with web-like vaulting and exquisite blue-and-white *azulejos,* and a gold-smothered baroque chapel.

Museu Nacional de Arte Antiga MUSEUM
(National Museum of Ancient Art; www.museudearteantiga.pt; Rua das Janelas Verdes; adult/child €6/free, with themed exhibitions €10/free; ⊙10am-6pm Tue-Sun) Set in a lemon-fronted, 17th-century palace, the Museu Nacional de Arte Antiga is Lapa's biggest draw. It presents a star-studded collection of European and Asian paintings and decorative arts.

LX Factory ARTS CENTRE
(www.lxfactory.com; Rua Rodrigues de Faria 103) Lisbon's hub of cutting-edge creativity hosts a dynamic menu of events from live concerts and film screenings to fashion shows and art exhibitions. There's a rustically cool cafe as well as a bookshop, several restaurants, design-minded shops and cultural spaces. On weekend nights there are parties with a dance- and art-loving crowd.

★**Oceanário de Lisboa** AQUARIUM
(www.oceanario.pt; Doca dos Olivais; adult/child €15/10, incl temporary exhibition €18/12; ⊙10am-8pm, to 7pm in winter) The closest you'll get to scuba diving without a wetsuit, Lisbon's Oceanário is mind-blowing. With 8000 marine creatures splashing in 7 million litres of seawater, no amount of hyperbole does it justice. Huge wrap-around tanks make you feel as if you're underwater, as you eyeball zebra sharks, honeycombed rays, gliding mantas and schools of neon fish.

☞ Tours

★**Taste of Lisboa** FOOD & DRINK
(📞 915 601 908; www.tasteoflisboa.com; tours €70-85) Lisbon foodie and radiant personality Filipa Valente specialises in neighbourhood-centric food tours in less touristy locales (Campo de Ourique, Mouraria) in addition to more traditional jaunts, but it's the off-the-beaten-path culinary crusades that will leave you feeling more like a traveller than a tourist. There are cooking classes as well.

⭐ Festivals & Events

Lisboêtas celebrate their seasons with fervour. Rio-style carnivals and indie flicks heat up the cooler months, while summer sees high-octane concerts, sparkly pride parading and saintly celebrations of feasting and matchmaking. *Fazer a festa* (partying) is considered a birthright in Portugal's live-wire capital. For up-to-date listings, pick up the tourist board's free magazine *Follow Me Lisboa* (www.visitlisboa.com/about-turismo -de-lisboa/publications).

🛏 Sleeping

★ Lisbon Calling
HOSTEL €

(📞 213 432 381; www.lisboncalling.net; Rua de São Paulo 126, 3rd fl; dm from €20, d with/without bathroom from €75/55; @ 🛜) This fashionable, unsigned backpacker favourite near Santa Catarina features original frescoes, *azulejos* and hardwood floors – all lovingly restored by friendly Portuguese owners. The bright, spacious dorms and a brick-vaulted kitchen are easy on the eye, but the private rooms – specifically room 1812 – will floor you: boutique-hotel-level dens of style and comfort that thunderously out-punch their price point.

Lisbon Destination Hostel
HOSTEL €

(📞 213 466 457; www.followyourdestination.com; Rossio train station, 2nd fl; dm €25, s/d without bathroom from €36/54, d from €107; @ 🛜) Housed in Lisbon's loveliest train station, this world-class hostel has a glass ceiling that lights the spacious plant-filled common area. Rooms are crisp and well kept, and there are loads of activities (bar crawls, beach day trips etc). Facilities include a shared kitchen, game consoles, movie room (with popcorn) and a 24-hour self-service bar. The breakfast with crêpes and fresh fruit is top-notch.

Lisbon Story Guesthouse
GUESTHOUSE €€

(📞 218 879 392; www.lisbonstoryguesthouse.com; Largo de São Domingos 18; d €80-100, without bathroom €50-70, apt €110-120; @ 🛜) 📁 Overlooking Largo de São Domingos, Lisbon Story is a small, extremely welcoming guesthouse with nicely maintained, light-drenched rooms, all of which sport Portuguese themes (the Tejo, tram 28E, fado etc), plus working antique radios, record players and the like. The lounge, with throw pillows and low tables, is a great place to chill.

★ Casa do Príncipe
B&B €€

(📞 218 264 183; www.casadoprincipe.com; Praça do Príncipe Real 23; d €108-209; ✳ 🛜) Perfectly located and exquisitely restored (and accordingly priced to shock!), this 14-room B&B is housed inside what was once the same 19th-century neo-Moorish palace as **Embaixada** (www.embaixadalx.pt; Praça do Príncipe Real 26; ⊘ noon-8pm Mon-Fri, 11am-7pm Sat & Sun, restaurants to 2am) next door. Original frescoes, *azulejos* and ornate moulded ceilings adorn the hardwood halls and spacious rooms, which are themed after the life of King Dom Pedro V. Indeed, you'll sleep like royalty here yourself.

Bairro Alto Hotel
BOUTIQUE HOTEL €€€

(📞 213 408 288; www.bairroaltohotel.com; Praça Luís de Camões 2; r from €380; P ✳ 🛜) On a pretty square is Lisbon's most storied luxury hotel, dating from 1921. It reopened in early 2019 after a massive €30 million re-design by Pritzker Prize–winning architect Eduardo Souto de Moura, who oversaw 32 new rooms, a redesigned reception and an entirely new 5th-floor restaurant (BAHR, by lauded chef Nuno Mendes) with a panoramic terrace for food and sundowners.

★ Santiago de Alfama
BOUTIQUE HOTEL €€€

(📞 213 941 616; www.santiagodealfama.com; Rua de Santiago 10; d/ste from €285/660; ✳ 🛜 🖥) In 2015 Dutch hospitality dreamer Heleen Uitenbroek turned a ruined 15th-century palace into luxury sleeps at this 19-room bastion of style. It's airy and awash in light pine-woods and contemporary art, and exquisite attention to detail is everywhere, from the Santiago-cross-inspired tile flooring and textured bathroom tiling to an encased glass hallway revealing uncovered Roman steps.

Valverde
BOUTIQUE HOTEL €€€

(📞 210 940 300; www.valverdehotel.com; Av da Liberdade 164; d €302-410, ste €446-646; P ✳ @ 🛜 🖥) Exquisite Valverde feels like a boutique town house (which it once was). Its facade is not showy, but once inside, an urban oasis of discerning design and personalised service is subtly unveiled. Reached by black-dominated, hushed hallways, the

---

CYCLING THE TEJO

A cycling/jogging path courses along the Tejo for 7km, between Cais do Sodré and Belém. Complete with artful touches – including the poetry of Pessoa printed along parts of it – the path takes in age-ing warehouses, weathered docks, and open-air restaurants and nightspots.

A handy place to rent bikes is a short stroll from Cais do Sodré: **Bike Iberia** (📞 969 630 369; www.bikeiberia.com; Largo Corpo Santo 5; bike hire per hour/day from €5/15, e-bike €20/35; ⊘ 9.30am-5.30pm).

25 rooms elicit style, form and function, and feature cultured European art and unique mid-century-modern pieces.

✗ Eating

Mercado da Ribeira
MARKET €

(www.timeoutmarket.com; Av 24 de Julho; ⊙ 10am-midnight Sun-Wed, to 2am Thu-Sat, traditional market 6am-2pm Mon-Sat; 🛜) Doing trade in fresh fruit and veg, fish and flowers since 1892, this domed market hall has been the word on everyone's lips since *Time Out* transformed half of it into a gourmet food court in 2014. Now it's Lisbon in chaotic culinary microcosm: Garrafeira Nacional wines, Café de São Bento steaks, Manteigaria Silva cold cuts and Michelin-star chef creations from Henrique Sá Pessoa.

Ti-Natércia
PORTUGUESE €

(🖉 218 862 133; Rua Escola Gerais 54; mains €5.50-12; ⊙ 7pm-midnight Tue-Fri, noon-3pm & 7pm-midnight Sat) 'Aunt' Natércia and her downright delicious Portuguese home cooking is a tough ticket: there are but a mere six tables and they fill up fast. She'll talk your ear off (and doesn't mince words – some have been rubbed the wrong way; vegetarians in particular should avoid) while you devour her excellent take on the classics. Reservations are essential (cash only).

Ao 26 – Vegan Food Project
VEGAN €

(🖉 967 989 184; www.facebook.com/ao26vegan foodproject; Rua Vítor Cordon 26; mains €5.50-7.50; ⊙ 12.30-6.30pm & 7.30-11pm Tue-Sat; 🛜🌱) So good it even lures in devout carnivores, this small, hip and bustling vegan place offers two elaborate, daily-changing chalkboard specials (eg Manchurian meatballs with tomato, coconut and masala). There's a fixed menu of loaded lentil burgers, beet burgers and veg sandwiches on *bolo do caco* (round bread cooked on a basalt stone slab), plus Lisbon craft beer.

★ Antiga Confeitaria de Belém
PASTRIES €

(Pastéis de Belém; www.pasteisdebelem.pt; Rua de Belém 84-92; pastries from €1.10; ⊙ 8am-11pm Oct-Jun, to midnight Jul-Sep) Since 1837 this patisserie has been transporting locals to sugar-coated nirvana with heavenly *pastéis de Belém*. The crisp pastry nests are filled with custard cream, baked at 200°C for that perfect golden crust, then lightly dusted with cinnamon. Admire *azulejos* in the vaulted rooms or devour a still-warm tart at the counter and try to guess the secret ingredient.

Pinóquio
PORTUGUESE €€

(🖉 213 465 106; www.restaurantepinoquio.pt; Praça dos Restauradores 79; mains €17-26; ⊙ noon-midnight; 🛜) Bustling Pinóquio is easy to miss as it's tucked into a *praça* corner partially obstructed by a souvenir kiosk. Dressed in white tablecloths against pea-green walls, it's distinctly old school, with indomitable waiters slinging a stunning slew of classic dishes: *arroz de pato* (duck rice), seafood *feijoada*, *arroz de bacalhau* (codfish rice), and pork chops with almonds and coriander.

★ O Zé da Mouraria
PORTUGUESE €€

(🖉 218 865 436; Rua João do Outeiro 24; mains for 2 €16.50-33.50; ⊙ noon-4pm Mon-Sat; 🛜) Don't be fooled by the saloon-like doors, there's a typical Portuguese *tasca* (tavern) inside. With homey local cuisine, blue-and-white-tiled walls and chequered tablecloths it's one of Lisbon's best. The house-baked cod loaded with chickpeas, onions, garlic and olive oil is rightfully popular, and daily specials (duck rice on Wednesday!) make return trips tempting.

★ Alma
MODERN PORTUGUESE €€€

(🖉 213 470 650; www.almalisboa.pt; Rua Anchieta 15; mains €32-36, tasting menus €110-120; ⊙ noon-3pm & 7-11pm Tue-Sun; 🛜) Two-Michelin-starred Henrique Sá Pessoa's flagship Alma is one of Portugal's destination restaurants and, in our humble opinion, Lisbon's best gourmet dining experience. The casual space exudes understated style amid the original stone flooring and gorgeous hardwood tables, but it's Pessoa's outrageously good nouveau Portuguese cuisine that draws the foodie flock from far and wide.

Cervejaria Ramiro
SEAFOOD €€€

(www.cervejariaramiro.pt; Av Almirante Reis 1; seafood per kg €12-91; ⊙ noon-12.30am Tue-Sun) Opened in 1956, Ramiro has legendary status among Lisbon's seafood lovers. Here you can feast on rich plates of giant tiger prawns, *percebes* (goose barnacles), lobster, crab and clams, and even juicy steak sandwiches.

Belcanto
PORTUGUESE €€€

(🖉 213 420 607; www.belcanto.pt; Largo de São Carlos 10; mains €49.50, tasting menu €165-185 with 5/9 wines €100/120; ⊙ 12.30-3pm & 7-11pm Tue-Sat; 🛜) José Avillez' two-Michelin-starred cathedral of cookery wows diners with painstaking creativity, polished service and a first-rate sommelier. Standouts among Lisbon's culinary adventure of a lifetime include suckling pig with orange purée; sea bass with seaweed and bivalves; and Avillez' masterstroke, the Garden of the Goose that Laid the Golden Eggs (egg, crunchy bread and mushrooms). Paired wines sometimes date from the '70s!

🍷 Drinking & Nightlife

⭐ Park
BAR

(www.facebook.com/parklisboaofficial; Calçada do Combro 58; ⏲1pm-2am Tue-Sat, to 8pm Sun; 🛜) If only all multistorey car parks were like this... Take the lift to the 5th floor, and head up and around to the top, which has been transformed into one of Lisbon's hippest rooftop bars, with sweeping views reaching right down to the Rio Tejo and over the bell towers of Igreja de Santa Catarina.

⭐ Cerveteca Lisboa
CRAFT BEER

(www.cervetecalisboa.com; Praça das Flores 62; ⏲3.30pm-1am Sun-Thu, to 2am Fri & Sat; 🛜) Lisbon's best craft-beer bar is a boozy godsend: 14 oft-changing taps (including two hand pumps) focusing on local and Northern European artisanal brews, including numerous local microbreweries. Not only will hopheads rejoice at IPAs from Lisbon including standouts such as Dois Corvos and 8ª Colina, but having choice alone inspires cartwheels. *Adeus,* tasteless lagers!

Pensão Amor
BAR

(www.pensaoamor.pt; Rua do Alecrím 19; ⏲2pm-3am Sun-Wed, to 4am Thu-Sat) Set inside a former brothel, this cheeky bar pays homage to its passion-filled past with colourful wall murals, a library of erotically tinged works, and a small stage where you can sometimes catch burlesque shows.

Lux-Frágil
CLUB

(www.luxfragil.com; Av Infante D Henrique, Armazém A, Cais de Pedra; ⏲11pm-6am Thu-Sat) Lisbon's ice-cool, must-see club, glammy Lux hosts big-name DJs spinning electro and house. It was started by late Lisbon nightlife impresario Marcel Reis and is part-owned by John Malkovich. Grab a spot on the terrace to see the sun rise over the Rio Tejo, or chill like a king or queen on the throne-like giant interior chairs.

BA Wine Bar do Bairro Alto
WINE BAR

(📞213 461 182; bawinebar@gmail.com; Rua da Rosa 107; ⏲6-11pm Tue-Sun; 🛜) Reserve ahead unless you want to get shut out of Bairro Alto's best wine bar, where the genuinely welcoming staff will offer you three fantastic tasting choices based on your wine proclivities (wines from €5; tasting boards for one/four €13/47). The cheeses (from small artisanal producers) and charcuterie (melt-in-your-mouth black-pork *presuntos*) are not to be missed, either. Reservations are essential.

☆ Entertainment

⭐ Hot Clube de Portugal
JAZZ

(📞213 460 305; www.hcp.pt; Praça da Alegria 48; ⏲10pm-2am Tue-Sat) As hot as its name suggests, this small, poster-plastered cellar (and newly added garden) has staged top-drawer jazz acts since the 1940s. It's considered one of Europe's best.

A Baiuca
LIVE MUSIC

(📞218 867 284; Rua de São Miguel 20; ⏲8pm-midnight Thu-Mon) On a good night, walking into A Baiuca is like gate-crashing a family party. It's a special place with *fado vadio* (street fado), where locals take a turn and spectators hiss if anyone dares to chat during the singing. There's a €25 minimum spend, which is as tough to swallow as the food, though the fado is spectacular. Reserve ahead.

A Tasca do Chico
LIVE MUSIC

(📞961 339 696; www.facebook.com/atasca.doch ico; Rua do Diário de Notícias 39; ⏲7pm-1.30am Sun-Thu, to 3am Fri & Sat) This crowded dive (reserve ahead), full of soccer banners and spilling over with people of all ilks, is a fado free-for-all. It's not uncommon for taxi drivers to roll up, hum a few bars, and hop right back into their cabs, speeding off into the night.

ℹ️ Information

British Hospital (📞217 104 600; www.british -hospital.pt; Rua Tomás da Fonseca) English-speaking doctors and staff.

Farmácia Estácio (Praça Dom Pedro IV 62; ⏲8.30am-8pm Mon-Fri, 10am-7pm Sat & Sun) A central, English-speaking pharmacy.

Ask Me Lisboa (📞213 463 314; www.askmelis boa.com; Praça dos Restauradores, Palácio Foz; ⏲9am-8pm) Lisbon's largest and most helpful tourist office has maps and information, and books accommodation and rental cars.

ℹ️ Getting There & Away

AIR

Around 6km north of the centre, **Aeroporto de Lisboa** (Lisbon Airport; 📞218 413 500; www. ana.pt/pt/lis/home; Alameda das Comunidades Portuguesas) operates direct flights to international hubs including London, New York, Paris and Frankfurt.

BUS

Lisbon's main long-distance bus terminal is **Sete Rios** (Praça General Humberto Delgado, Rua das

PORTUGAL LISBON

Laranjeiras), adjacent to both Jardim Zoológico metro station and Sete Rios train station. The big carriers, **Rede Expressos** (🌐 707 223 344; www.rede-expressos.pt; Praça General Humberto Delgado, Terminal Rodoviário de Sete Rios; ⏰ info booth 9am-1pm & 2-6pm Mon-Sat, 10am-2pm & 3-7pm Sun) and **Eva** (🌐 707 223 344; www.eva-bus.com; Praça General Humberto Delgado, Terminal Rodoviário de Sete Rios), run frequent services throughout Portugal.

The large bus terminal Gare do Oriente concentrates on services to the north and onto Spain and beyond. The biggest companies operating from here are **Renex/Rede Expressos/Citiexpress** (🌐 218 956 836; www.rede-expressos.pt; Via Recíproca 205, Gare do Oriente; ⏰7am-1pm) and Spanish operator **Avanza** (🌐 218 940 250; www.avanzabus.com; Av Dom João II, Gare do Oriente; ⏰ 8.30am-1pm & 2-8.15pm Mon-Fri, 8.30am-11am & 5-8.15pm Sat & Sun).

TRAIN

Gare do Oriente (Oriente Station; Av Dom João II) is Lisbon's biggest station. Trains to the Alentejo and the Algarve originate from here. **Santa Apolónia** is the terminal for trains from northern and central Portugal, **Cais do Sodré** serves Cascais and Estoril, and **Rossio** station offers frequent services to Sintra via Queluz. For fares and schedules, visit www.cp.pt.

ℹ Getting Around

TO/FROM THE AIRPORT

There's convenient metro access to the city centre from Aeroporto station; change at Alameda (green line) for Rossio and Baixa. A taxi for the 15-minute ride into central Lisbon costs around €16. Alternatively, buy a prepaid voucher to any address from Ask Me Lisboa in Arrivals. Uber and other app-based taxis pick up outside Departures (not Arrivals) and are considerably cheaper. You can also catch the Aerobus, which departs from outside Arrivals (adult/child €3.60/2, 25 to 35 minutes, every 20 minutes).

PUBLIC TRANSPORT

Public transport in Lisbon encompasses buses, trams, funiculars, lifts and a good metro system.

Metro Lisbon's subway is the quickest way around, running from 6.30am to 1am.

Tram The best way to get up into hilltop neighbourhoods (Alfama, Castelo, Graça) and western neighbourhoods (Estrela, Campo de Ourique). Runs from 5am/6am to about 10pm/11pm.

Bus An extensive network runs throughout the city. Buses operate from 5am/6am to about 10pm/11pm.

Elevadores and ascensors Lisbon's historic funiculars and lifts are the fastest way from lower neighbourhoods (Chiado, Baixa, Rossio) to hilltop neighbourhoods (Castelo, Glória, Graça).

Day passes (€6.40) allow unlimited travel over a 24-hour period on the entire bus, tram and metro network (€10.55 if you want to include Comboios de Portugal trains as well). If you're going to take more than five trips on the bus or metro on any given day, this is the best and easiest choice.

Lisboa Move-me (www.move-me.mobi; iOS/Android) and Lisboa Viagem by Transporlis (Android) are city-transportation apps for real-time routes and arrival/departure times.

AROUND LISBON

Sintra

POP 26,000

With its rippling mountains, dewy forests thick with ferns and lichen, exotic gardens and glittering palaces, Sintra is like a page torn from a fairy tale. Even Lord Byron waxed lyrical about Sintra's charms. Its Unesco World Heritage–listed centre, Sintra-Vila, is dotted with pastel-hued manors folded into luxuriant hills that roll down to the blue Atlantic. Sintra is *the* must-do side trip from Lisbon. Many do it in a day, but if time's not an issue, there's more than enough allure to keep you here for a few days.

◉ Sights

★**Palácio Nacional de Sintra** PALACE (www.parquesdesintra.pt; Largo Rainha Dona Amélia; adult/child €10/8.50; ⏰9.30am-7pm) The star of Sintra-Vila is this palace, with its iconic twin conical chimneys and lavish, whimsical interior, which is a mix of Moorish and Manueline styles, with arabesque courtyards, barley-twist columns and 15th- and 16th-century geometric *azulejos* (hand-painted tiles) that figure among Portugal's oldest.

Quinta da Regaleira NOTABLE BUILDING, GARDENS (www.regaleira.pt; Rua Barbosa du Bocage; adult/child €6/4, tours €12/8; ⏰9.30am-7pm Apr-Sep, to 5pm Oct-Mar) This magical villa and gardens is a neo-Manueline extravaganza, dreamed up by Italian opera-set designer Luigi Manini, under the orders of Brazilian coffee tycoon António Carvalho Monteiro, aka 'Monteiro dos Milhões' ('Moneybags Monteiro'). The villa is surprisingly homey inside, despite its ferociously carved fireplaces, frescos and

Venetian-glass mosaics. Keep an eye out for mythological and Knights Templar symbols.

Castelo dos Mouros CASTLE
(www.parquesdesintra.pt; adult/child €8/6.50; ☙9.30am-8pm) Soaring 412m above sea level, this mist-enshrouded ruined castle looms high above the surrounding forest. When the clouds peel away, the vistas over Sintra's palace-dotted hill and dale, across to the glittering Atlantic are – like the climb – breathtaking. The 10th-century Moorish castle's dizzying ramparts stretch across the mountain ridges and past moss-clad boulders the size of small buses. Tickets and info are available at the entrance (open 10am to 6pm).

Palácio Nacional da Pena PALACE
(www.parquesdesintra.pt; combined ticket with Parque da Pena adult/child €14/12.50; ☙9.45am-7pm) Rising from a thickly wooded peak and often enshrouded in swirling mist, Palácio Nacional da Pena is a wacky confection of onion domes, Moorish keyhole gates, writhing stone snakes and crenellated towers in pinks and lemons. It is considered the greatest expression of 19th-century romanticism in Portugal.

🛏 Sleeping & Eating

⭐ **Moon Hill Hostel** HOSTEL €
(☎219 243 755; www.moonhillhostel.com; Rua Guilherme Gomes Fernandes 17; dm €19-22, d with/without bathroom €75/55; ❄@☎) 🏊 This design-forward, minimalist newcomer easily outshines the competition. Book a bed in a four-bed mixed dorm (with lockers), or a boutique-hotel-level private room, with colourful reclaimed-wood headboards and wall-covering photos of enchanting Sintra forest scenes (go for 10 or 14 for Palácio Nacional da Pena views; 12 or 13 for Moorish castle views). Either way, you're sleeping in high style.

Sintra 1012 B&B €€
(☎918 632 997; www.sintra1012.com; Rua Gil Vicente 10 & 12; dm €25, d €65-120, villas €120-150; ❄@☎) You'll probably need to go to war to book one of the eight spacious and smart rooms in this highly recommended guesthouse run by a young Portuguese-American couple. Behind original medieval walls, it's a modern minimalist retreat that, in Roman times, was Sintra's first theatre. Today it's all comfort and class, right down to the basement studio – an astonishing deal (€65).

Nau Palatina PORTUGUESE €€
(☎219 240 962; www.facebook.com/barnaupalatina; Calçada São Pedro 18, São Pedro de Penaferrim;

tapas €1.50-11.90; ☙6pm-midnight Tue-Sat; ☎) Sintra's friendliest and most welcoming restaurant is a travel-highlight star in the making. Congenial owner Zé's creative tapas are as slightly off-centre as his location, a worthwhile 1km walk from Sintra centre in São Pedro de Penaferrim. Spice Route undertones are weaved throughout the small but tasty menu of tidbits, strongly forged from local and regional ingredients.

ⓘ Information

Ask Me Sintra (☎219 231 157; www.visitlisboa.com; Praça da República 23; ☙9.30am-6pm), near the centre of Sintra-Vila, is a helpful multilingual office with expert insight into Sintra and its surroundings. There's another small branch at **Sintra train station** (☎211 932 545; www.visitlisboa.com; Av Miguel Bombarda; ☙9am-7pm).

Parques da Sintra – Monte da Lua (☎219 237 300; www.parquesdesintra.pt; Largo Sousa Brandão; ☙9.30am-6pm Apr-Oct, 10am-5pm Nov-Mar), which manages most of Sintra's top sites, has a friendly information and ticket centre.

ⓘ Getting There & Around

Trains run half-hourly between Sintra and Lisbon's Rossio station (€2.25, 40 minutes).

Scotturb (www.scotturb.com) bus 434 (€6.90) is handy for accessing the Castelo dos Mouros; it runs frequently from the train station via Sintra-Vila to the castle (10 minutes), Palácio Nacional da Pena (15 minutes) and back. One ticket gives you hop-on, hop-off access (in one direction; no backtracking).

Cascais

POP 35,000

Cascais (kush-*kaish*) has rocketed from sleepy fishing village to much-loved summertime playground of wave-frolicking *lisboêtas*. It also boasts plenty of post-beach life, with winding lanes leading to small museums, cool gardens, a shiny marina and a pedestrianised old town dotted with designer boutiques, alfresco fish restaurants and lively bars.

⊙ Sights

Cascais' three sandy bays – **Praia da Conceição**, **Praia da Rainha** and **Praia da Ribeira** – are fine for a sunbake or a tingly Atlantic dip, but don't expect much towel space in summer. Atlantic waves pummel craggy **Boca do Inferno** (Mouth of Hell), 2km west of Cascais (about a 20-minute walk along the coast). The best beach is wild, windswept **Praia do**

Guincho, 9km northwest, a mecca to surfers and windsurfers with massive crashing rollers. The strong undertow can be dangerous for swimmers, but Guincho still lures nonsurfers with powder-soft sands, fresh seafood and magical sunsets.

Casa das Histórias Paula Rego
MUSEUM

(www.casadashistoriaspaularego.com; Avenida da República 300; adult/child €5/free; ⊙10am-6pm Tue-Sun, free 1st Sun of month) *✎* The Casa das Histórias Paula Rego showcases the disturbing, highly evocative paintings of Portugal's finest living artist. Biannually changing exhibits span Rego's career, from early work with collage in the 1950s to the twisted fairy tale–like tableaux of the 1980s, and up to the disturbing realism of more recent years.

Museu Condes de Castro Guimarães
MUSEUM

(www.cm-cascais.pt/equipamento/museu-condes-de-castro-guimaraes; adult/child €4/free, free 1st Sun of month; ⊙10am-6pm Tue-Sun) This whimsical early-19th-century mansion, complete with castle turrets and Arabic cloister, sits in the grounds of the **Parque Marechal Carmona** (www.cm-cascais.pt/equipamento/parque-marechal-carmona; Avenida Rei Humberto II; ⊙8.30am-8pm Apr-Sep, to 6pm Oct-Mar).

🛏️ Sleeping & Eating

Casa Vela
GUESTHOUSE **€€€**

(✆218 093 996; www.casavelahotel.com; Rua dos Bem Lembrados 17; d from €155; 🅿️❄️🛜🏊) The friendly Casa Vela has it all: 29 bright and attractive rooms with modern furnishings in decor schemes set to spice, colonial or garden themes in two upmarket residential homes; deceptively large and grand gardens with trickling fountains, hidden nooks and two tranquil pools; and a Portuguese-by-birth, Mozambican-by-upbringing manager, João Paulo, who is the epitome of jovial hospitality. Paradise found.

★ Bar do Guincho
PORTUGUESE **€€**

(✆214 871 683; www.bardoguincho.pt; Estrada do Abano, Praia do Guincho; mains €9-18; ⊙noon-7pm Sun & Tue-Thu, noon-11.45pm Fri & Sat, later hours Jul & Aug; 🛜) Sweeping the awards for most dramatic location in Cascais, this good-time bar-restaurant sits tucked behind a craggy ridge on the northern end of Guincho. From the sand, you would never know it's there, but it is – and it is packed! Revellers rake in the beach-friendly burgers, seafood and salads washed down with cold *cerveja* (beer). Settle in for the afternoon.

Café Galeria House of Wonders
CAFE **€€**

(www.facebook.com/houseofwonders; Largo da Misericórdia 53; meals €4.75-14.75; ⊙9am-10pm; 🛜🍴) *✎* This fantastically whimsical, Dutch-owned cafe is tucked away in the old quarter. Its astonishingly good Middle Eastern/Mediterranean vegetarian plates, refreshing juices (€4), fabulous cakes (always at least one vegan and gluten-free option), warm, welcoming ambience and artwork-filled interior are unmissable.

ℹ️ Information

Cascais Visitor Center (Turismo; ✆912 034 214; www.visitcascais.com; Praça 5 de Outubro 45A; ⊙9am-8pm May-Sep, to 6pm Oct-Apr) Has a handy map, events guide *(What's in Cascais)* and all sort of Cascais-branded merch.

ℹ️ Getting There & Away

Frequent trains run from Lisbon's Cais do Sodré station to Cascais (€2.25, 40 minutes) via Estoril.

THE ALGARVE

Soaring cliffs, sea caves, golden beaches, scalloped bays and sandy islands draw over four million visitors to the Algarve each year. In the south, tourist hotspots harbour holiday villas, brash resorts, splashy water parks, beach bars and sizzling nightclubs; elsewhere, the Algarve abounds in natural treasures, including the bird-filled lagoons and islands of the protected Parque Natural da Ria Formosa. Surrounded on two sides by the Atlantic, it's also a paradise for surfers, especially along the refreshingly undeveloped west coast.

Faro
POP 64,560

Exuding a more distinctly Portuguese feel than most resort towns, the Algarve's capital has an attractive marina, well-maintained parks and plazas, and a picturesque *cidade velha* (old town), ringed by medieval walls and home to museums, churches and al fresco cafes. On Faro's doorstep are the lagoons of the Parque Natural da Ria Formosa and the island beaches of Ilha de Faro and Ilha da Barreta.

★ **Parque Natural
da Ria Formosa**   NATURE RESERVE
(www.icnf.pt) Encompassing 18,000 hectares, this sizeable system of lagoons and islands stretches for 60km along the Algarve coastline from west of Faro to Cacela Velha. It encloses a vast area of *sapal* (marsh), *salinas* (salt pans), creeks and dune islands. The marshes are an important area for migrating and nesting birds. You can see a huge variety of wading birds, along with ducks, shorebirds, gulls and terns. It's the favoured nesting place of the little tern and the rare purple gallinule.

Formosamar   CRUISE, KAYAKING
(☑918 720 002; www.formosamar.com; Avenida da República, Stand 1, Faro Marina) ✐ This recommended outfit promotes environmentally responsible tourism. Among its excellent tours are two-hour birdwatching trips around the Parque Natural da Ria Formosa (€25), dolphin watching (€45), cycling (€37) and a two-hour kayak tour negotiating some of the narrower lagoon channels (€35). All trips have a minimum number of participants (usually two to four).

Casa d'Alagoa   HOSTEL €
(☑289 813 252; www.farohostel.com; Praça Alexandre Herculano 27; dm/d from €22/92; ☎) A renovated mansion on a pretty square houses this cool, laid-back hostel. Great facilities include a lounge with long, sociable tables and beanbags, an upstairs terrace, barbecue and communal kitchen, plus on-site bike hire. There's a range of clean, spacious dorms (larger dorms have balconies) and en suite doubles.

Vila Adentro   PORTUGUESE €€
(☑933 052 173; www.vilaadentro.pt; Praça Dom Afonso III 17; mains €9-17.50, cataplanas €39-49; ☺9am-midnight; ☛) With tables on the square in Faro's old town and a dining room decorated with floor-to-ceiling *azulejos* (hand-painted, blue-and-white tiles), this Moorish 15th-century building is a romantic spot for elevated Portuguese cuisine: pork, clam and lobster *cataplanas* (stew) for two, chargrilled octopus with fig and carob sauce, and tangerine-stuffed pork fillet. Wines hail from around the country.

O Castelo   BAR
(www.facebook.com/OCasteloBar.CidadeVelha. Faro; Rua do Castelo 11; ☺10.30am-4am Wed-Mon; ☎) O Castelo is all things to all people: bar, restaurant, club and performance space. Its

location atop the old town walls provides stunning Ria Formosa views, especially at sunset. Beer, wine and cocktails are accompanied by tapas such as flambéed chorizo and local cheeses.

ℹ Information

Turismo (www.visitalgarve.pt; Rua da Misericórdia 8; ☺9.30am-1pm & 2-5.30pm; ☎) Efficient office at the edge of the old town. There's another branch at the airport.

ℹ Getting There & Around

Faro Airport (FAO; ☑289 800 800; www.aeroportofaro.pt; ☎), 7km west of the centre, has both domestic and international flights.

One or two buses per hour depart from the bus station for Faro Airport (€2.20, 15 minutes) and Praia de Faro (€2.30, 20 minutes).

Buses to Lisbon (€20, 3¼ hours, six per day) and Algarve coastal destinations depart from the **bus station** (☑289 899 760; Avenida da República 5), on the northern side of the marina. Most services are run by **Eva** (☑289 899 760; www.eva-bus.com).

Faro's train station is 500m northwest of the centre. There are five direct trains from Lisbon daily (€22.90, four hours), plus service every hour or two to nearby coastal destinations.

Tavira

POP 26,167

Set on either side of the meandering Rio Gilão, Tavira is arguably the Algarve's most charming town, with the ruins of a hilltop castle, an old Roman bridge and a smattering of Gothic and Renaissance churches. It's also the launching point for the stunning, unspoilt beaches of Ilha de Tavira.

Tavira is ideal for wandering; the warren of cobblestone streets hides leafy gardens and shady squares. There's a small, active fishing port and a modern market.

Maria Nova   HOTEL €€€
(☑281 001 200; www.ap-hotelsresorts.com; Rua António Pinheiro 17; d/f from €122/180; ⓟ☀☷☒) Tavira's best hotel is set on a hill; it's worth paying extra for a south-facing room, with views from the balcony over the vast, free-form pool (and poolside bar), palm-planted gardens and the town. Contemporary, sand-toned rooms are up-to-the-minute; there's also an indoor pool spa, gym, gourmet restaurant and panoramic rooftop bar. Parking is first come, first served.

O Tonel   PORTUGUESE €€
(📞963 427 612; Rua Dr Augo Silva Carvalho 6;
tapas €3.50-7.50, mains €9-16; ⊘ 6.30-10pm Mon-
Sat) Contemporary Portuguese cuisine is
complemented by a striking dining room
of scarlet walls and *azulejos* (hand-painted
tiles). Begin with *petiscos* (tapas-style sharing dishes) like chorizo sautéed in Medron-
ho (local brandy) or clam-and-mackerel pâté
served in a tin with crusty bread, before
moving on to mains such as almond-crusted
pork or carob-marinated lamb. Wines come
from all over Portugal. Book ahead.

Fado Com História   TRADITIONAL MUSIC
(📞966 620 877; www.fadocomhistoria.com; Rua
Damião Augo de Brito Vasconcelos 4; adult/child
€8/free; ⊘ shows 12.15pm, 3.15pm & 5.15pm Mon-
Fri, 12.15pm & 5.15pm Sat, museum 10am-6pm
Mon-Sat) If you haven't experienced fado
(traditional song), this comprehensive introduction is even more worthwhile. Space is
limited, so buy your ticket a couple of hours
ahead. The 35-minute show begins with an
interesting film about fado's roots and history, followed by three live songs with explanations in English. On Saturdays the 3.15pm
performance takes place at the **Igreja da
Misericórdia** (www.diocese-algarve.pt; Largo da
Misericórdia; church incl museum €2, fado performances €8; ⊘ 10am-12.30pm & 3-6.30pm Tue-Sat
Jul & Aug, shorter hours Sep-Jun, fado performances
3.15pm Sat year-round).

ⓘ Information

Turismo (📞281 322 511; www.visitalgarve.pt;
Praça da República 5; ⊘ 9am-1pm & 2-5pm)
Provides local and some regional information.

ⓘ Getting There & Away

There are 12 trains daily to Faro (€3.20, 35
minutes).

Lagos
POP 22,000

As tourist towns go, Lagos *(lah-goosh)* has
got the lot. Its old town's pretty, cobbled
lanes and picturesque squares are enclosed
by 16th-century walls, while some truly fabulous beaches lie just beyond. With a huge
range of activities, excellent restaurants and
a pumping nightlife, Lagos attracts travellers of all ages.

Numerous operators offer boat excursions, with ticket stands at the marina or
along the promenade opposite. Lagos is also
a popular centre for surfing, diving, windsurfing, kite-surfing and stand-up paddle-
boarding (SUP) .

Ponta da Piedade   VIEWPOINT
(Point of Piety) Protruding 2.5km south of Lagos, Ponta da Piedade is a dramatic wedge
of headland with contorted, polychrome
sandstone cliffs and towers, complete with a
lighthouse and, in spring, hundreds of nesting egrets, with crystal-clear turquoise water below. The surrounding area blazes with
wild orchids in spring. On a clear day you
can see east to Carvoeiro and west to Sagres.
The only way to reach it is by car or on foot.

Lagos Atlantic Hotel   HOTEL €€
(📞282 761 527; www.facebook.com/lagos.atlantic.
hotel; Estrada do Monte Carapeto 9; d/f from
€115/125; 🅿✳🕸) Most of the spacious
rooms at this pristine, stylish hotel face
south and open to balconies overlooking the
pool. Family rooms have pull-out sofa beds;
kids under 12 stay free. Handy amenities
include shaded lock-up parking and a barbecue area.

O Camilo   SEAFOOD €€
(📞282 763 845; www.restaurantecamilo.pt; Praia
do Camilo; mains €11.50-23.50; ⊘ noon-4pm &
6-10pm Jun-Sep, to 9pm Oct-May; 🕸) Perched
above pretty Praia do Camilo, this sophisticated restaurant is renowned for its
high-quality seafood dishes. Specialities include razor clams, fried squid, lobster and
oysters in season, along with grilled fish.
The 40-seat dining room is light, bright and
airy, and the large 28-seat terrace overlooks
the ocean. Bookings are a good idea any
time and essential in high season.

Bon Vivant   BAR
(www.bonvivantbarinlagos.com; Rua 25 de Abril
105; ⊘ 4pm-3.30am Mon-Thu, to 4am Fri-Sun; 🕸)
Spread across five levels, including two underground rooms and a roof terrace, each
with its own bar, cherry-red-painted Bon
Vivant shakes up great house cocktails including the signature Mr Bonvivant (jenever, absinthe, strawberry-infused Aperol and
bitters). Happy hour runs from 5pm to 9pm;
DJs spin nightly downstairs.

ⓘ Information

Turismo (📞282 763 031; www.visitalgarve.pt;
Praça Gil Eanes 17; ⊘ 9.30am-1pm & 2-5.30pm)
Helpful office on Lagos' main square.

❶ Getting There & Away

Eva (www.eva-bus.com) and Rede Expressos (www.rede-expressos.pt) depart frequently from the **bus station** (Rua Mercado de Levante) for other Algarve towns. Lagos is at the western end of the Algarve train line, with services to points east including Faro (€7.40, 1¾ hours, nine daily). For Lisbon (€22.15, four hours, five daily), change at Tunes.

Silves

POP 10,867

Silves' winding backstreets of whitewashed buildings topped by terracotta roofs climb the hillside above the banks of the Rio Arade. Crowning the hill, hulking red-stone walls enclose one of the Algarve's best-preserved castles. The town makes a good base if you're after a less hectic, non-coastal Algarvian pace.

Castelo   CASTLE
(☑ 282 440 837; www.cm-silves.pt; Rua da Cruz de Portugal; adult/child €2.80/1.40, joint ticket with Museu Municipal de Arqueologia €3.90; ⊙ 9am-10pm Jul & Aug, to 8pm Sep–mid-Oct, to 7pm Jun, to 5.30pm mid-Oct–May) This russet-coloured, Lego-like castle – originally occupied in the Visigothic period – has great views over the town and surrounding countryside. What you see today dates mostly from the Moorish era, though the castle was heavily restored in the 20th century. Walking the parapets and admiring the vistas is the main attraction, but you can also gaze down on the excavated ruins of the Almohad-era palace. The whitewashed 12th-century water cisterns, 5m deep, now host temporary exhibitions.

Duas Quintas   GUESTHOUSE €€
(☑ 282 449 311; www.duasquintas.com; Santo Estevão; d/studio €110/135; **P ⊛ ⛲**) Set amid 6 hectares of orange groves, with views over the rolling hills from the terrace, this restored farmhouse has six partially antique-furnished rooms (including a spacious three-person studio with a kitchenette and washing machine), a communal lounge room, terraces and landscaped natural pool. Cots and high chairs are available for tots. It's 6km northeast of Silves along the N124.

Restaurante O Barradas   PORTUGUESE €€
(☑ 282 443 308; www.obarradas.com; Palmeirinha; mains €12.50-26.50, cataplanas €45-46; ⊙ 6-10pm Thu-Tue) 🌱 The star choice for foodies is this converted farmhouse 4.5km south of Silves, which utilises sustainably sourced fish and organic meat and vegetables in creations

like slow-cooked suckling pig, char-grilled octopus with sweet potato, and fava bean and chorizo stew. The owner is a winemaker, whose wares appear on the wine list alongside vintages from Portugal's finest wineries.

❶ Information

Centro de Interpretaçao do Património Islâmico (☑ 282 440 800; www.cm-silves.pt; Largo do Município; ⊙ 10am-1pm & 2-5pm Mon-Fri) Municipal tourist office within the Islamic history interpretative centre.

Turismo (☑ 282 098 927; www.visitalgarve.pt; Parque Ribeirinho de Silves; ⊙ 9.30am-1pm & 2-5.30pm Tue-Sat) Next to the main car park and bus stops.

❶ Getting There & Away

The train station is 2km south of town; take a local bus or a taxi, as it's along a major highway. Nine trains daily serve Lagos (€2.95, 30 minutes) and Faro €5.20, one hour).

Sagres

POP 1909

Overlooking some of the Algarve's most dramatic scenery, the small, elongated village of Sagres has an end-of-the-world feel, with its sea-carved cliffs and wind-whipped fortress high above the frothing ocean. It's the only place in the world where white storks are known to nest on cliff faces. Sagres has milder temperatures than other parts of the Algarve, with Atlantic winds keeping the summers cool. Outside town are some splendid beaches that are increasingly popular with surfers, and the striking cliffs of **Cabo de São Vicente** – the southwestern-most point of the European mainland, and a spectacular spot for sunset.

Fortaleza de Sagres   FORTRESS
(☑ 282 620 142; www.monumentosdoalgarve.pt; adult/child €3/1.50; ⊙ 9.30am-8pm May-Sep, to 5.30pm Oct-Apr) Blank, hulking and forbidding, Sagres' fortress offers breathtaking views over the sheer cliffs, and all along the coast to Cabo de São Vicente. Legend has it that this is where Prince Henry the Navigator established his navigation school and primed the early Portuguese explorers. It's quite a large site, so allow at least an hour to see everything.

Mar Ilimitado   WILDLIFE, CRUISE
(☑ 916 832 625; www.marilimitado.com; Porto da Baleira) 🌱 Mar Ilimitado's team of marine biologists lead a variety of highly recommended,

ecologically sound boat trips, from dolphin spotting (€35, 1½ hours) and seabird watching (€45, 2½ hours) to excursions up to Cabo de São Vicente (€25, one hour). Incredible marinelife you may spot includes loggerhead turtles, basking sharks, common and bottlenose dolphins, orcas, and minke and fin whales.

Pousada do Infante   BOUTIQUE HOTEL **€€€**
(☑ 282 620 240; www.pousadas.pt; Rua Patrão António Faustino; d/ste from €150/230; P❋@◌⊠)
On the promontory's clifftop, this modern *pousada* (upmarket inn) occupies a never-to-be-outbuilt position. All rooms and suites (with king-size beds and whirlpool baths) have balconies, but those at the front face the car park, so it's definitely worth paying extra for one overlooking the fortress and ocean to take in the dazzling sunsets and swimming pool (romantically floodlit at night).

A Eira do Mel   PORTUGUESE **€€**
(☑ 282 639 016; Estrada do Castelejo, Vila do Bispo; mains €11-22, cataplanas €27-35; ⊘ noon-2.30pm & 7.30-10pm Tue-Sat) A rustic former farmhouse 9km north of Sagres is the atmospheric setting for José Pinheiro's lauded slow-food cooking. Seafood is landed in Sagres, with meats, vegetables and fruit sourced from local farms. Dishes such as octopus *cataplana* (seafood stew) with sweet potatoes, spicy piri-piri Atlantic wild shrimp, rabbit in red wine and *javali* (wild boar) are accompanied by regional wines.

ℹ Information

Turismo (☑ 282 624 873; www.visitalgarve.pt; Rua Comandante Matoso 75; ⊘ 9.30am-1pm & 2-7pm daily Jul & Aug, 9.30am-1pm & 2-5.30pm Tue-Sat Sep-Jun) Situated on a patch of green lawn, 100m east of Praça da República.

ℹ Getting There & Away

From the **bus stop** (Rua Comandante Matoso) by the *turismo*, buses travel to/from Lagos (€4, one hour, hourly Monday to Friday, fewer on weekends) via Salema. There are twice-daily services to Cabo de São Vicente (€2.10, 10 minutes) Monday to Friday. Buy tickets on the bus.

CENTRAL PORTUGAL

The vast centre of Portugal is a rugged swath of rolling hillsides, whitewashed villages, olive groves and cork trees. Richly historical, it is scattered with prehistoric remains and medieval castles. It's also home to one of

Portugal's most architecturally rich towns, Évora, as well as several spectacular walled villages. There are fine local wines and, for the more energetic, plenty of outdoor exploring in the dramatic Beiras region.

Évora

POP 56.700

One of Portugal's most beautifully preserved medieval towns, Évora is an enchanting place to delve into the past. Inside the 14th-century walls, Évora's narrow, winding lanes lead to a striking Roman temple, a fortress-like medieval cathedral with rose granite towers, and a picturesque town square. Aside from its historical and aesthetic virtues, Évora is also a lively university town, surrounded by wineries and dramatic countryside.

★**Templo Romano**   RUINS
(Temple of Diana; Largo do Conde de Vila Flor) Once part of the Roman Forum, the remains of this temple, dating from the 2nd or early 3rd century CE, are a heady slice of drama right in town. It's among the best-preserved Roman monuments in Portugal, and probably on the Iberian Peninsula. Though it's commonly referred to as the Temple of Diana, there's no consensus about the deity to which it was dedicated, and some archaeologists believe it may have been dedicated to Julius Caesar.

Capela dos Ossos   CATACOMB
(Chapel of Bones; Praça 1 de Maio; adult/student €5/3.50; ⊘ 9am-6.30pm Jun-Sep, to 5pm Oct-May) One of Évora's most popular sights is also one of its most chilling. The walls and columns of this mesmerising *memento mori* (reminder of death) are lined with the bones and skulls of some 5000 people. This was the solution found by three 17th-century Franciscan monks for the overflowing graveyards of churches and monasteries.

Évora Inn   HOSTEL **€€**
(☑ 266 744 500; www.evorainn.com; Rua da República 11; s/d/tr/q €40/50/80/95; ◌) This friendly 10-room guesthouse in a 120-year-old building brings a serious dose of style to Évora. Pop art adorns the rooms and corridors, along with eye-catching wallpaper, modular chairs, a bold colour scheme and unusual features (including a telescope in the Mirante room up top).

★**Albergaria do Calvario**   BOUTIQUE HOTEL **€€€**
(☑ 266 745 930; www.albergariadocalvario.com; Travessa dos Lagares 3; r €118-155; P❋◌) Un-

pretentiously elegant, discreetly attentive and comfortable, this beautifully designed guesthouse has an ambience that travellers adore. The kind-hearted staff provide the best service in Évora, and breakfasts are outstanding, with locally sourced seasonal fruits, homemade cakes and egg dishes.

Salsa Verde VEGETARIAN €
(☑ 266 743 210; www.salsa-verde.org; Rua de Raimundo 93A; small plate €5; ☺ noon-3pm & 7-9.30pm Mon-Fri, noon-3pm Sat; ☜🖘🕮) Vegetarians (and Portuguese livestock) will be thankful for this veggie-popping paradise. Pedro, the owner, gives a wonderful twist to traditional Alentejan dishes such as the famous bread dish, *migas,* prepared with mushrooms. Low-playing bossa nova and a cheerful airy design make a fine complement to the dishes – all made from fresh, locally sourced products (organic when possible).

★Taberna Típica Quarta Feira PORTUGUESE €€€
(☑ 266 707 530; Rua do Inverno 16; dinner per person incl starters, house wine & dessert €30; ☺ 7.30-10pm Mon, 12.30-3pm & 7.30-10pm Tue-Sat) Don't bother asking for the menu since there's just one option on offer at this jovial eatery tucked away in the Moorish quarter. Luckily it's a stunner: slow-cooked black pork so tender it falls off the bone, plus freshly baked bread, grilled mushrooms (and other starters), dessert and ever-flowing glasses of wine – all served for one set price. Reserve ahead.

ℹ Information

Turismo (☑ 266 777 071; www.cm-evora. pt; Praça do Giraldo 73; ☺ 9am-7pm Apr-Oct, 9am-6pm Mon-Fri, 10am-2pm & 3-6pm Sat & Sun Nov-Mar) This central tourist office offers a great town map. Staff are more helpful if you have specific questions.

ℹ Getting There & Away

Évora station is outside the walls, 600m south of the Jardim Público. Two to five trains daily go to/from Lisbon (€13.70, two hours), Lagos (€25 to €28, 4¼ to five hours) and Faro (€26.20, 3½ to 4½ hours).

Peniche

POP 14,700

Popular for its nearby surf strands and also as a jumping-off point for the beautiful Ilhas Berlengas nature reserve, Peniche is spec-

tacularly set on a headland surrounded by sea. It remains a working port, giving it a slightly grittier, more 'lived in' feel than its resort neighbours.

Dominating the south of the peninsula, the seaside **Fortaleza de Peniche** (☑ 262 780 116; Campo da República; ☺ 9am-12.30pm & 2-5.30pm Tue-Fri, from 10am Sat & Sun) FREE, where Salazar's regime detained political prisoners in the 20th century, is a must-see for anyone interested in Portuguese history.

Peniche is a renowned surfing destination. Northeast of town, the scenic island-village of **Baleal** is a paradise of challenging but above all consistent waves that make it an ideal learners' beach. Surf hostels and surf schools abound here. Well-established operators include **Baleal Surfcamp** (☑ 262 769 277; www.balealsurfcamp.com; Rua Amigos do Baleal 2; 2-/3-/7-day course with lodging €180/255/528) and **Peniche Surfcamp** (☑ 962 336 295; www. penichesurfcamp.com; Avenida do Mar 162, Casais do Baleal; ☺ 1/2/10 surf classes €30/50/145).

About 10km offshore, **Berlenga Grande** is a spectacular, rocky and remote island, with twisting, shocked-rock formations and gaping caverns. There are good opportunities for diving here. **AcuaSubOeste** (☑ 918 393 444; www.acuasuboeste.com; Armazém 3, Avenida do Porto de Pesca; 2 dives €70; ☺ 9-10am & 5-7pm) and **Haliotis** (☑ 262 781 160; www. haliotis.pt; Casal da Ponte S/N, Atouguia da Baleia; 2-tank dive €75; ☺ 9am-1pm & 2-6pm) both offer a range of PADI certification courses.

Kitesurfing is big in Peniche. On the far side of high dunes about 500m east of the walled town, **Peniche Kite & Surf Center** (☑ 919 424 951; www.penichesurfcenter.com; Avenida Monsenhor Bastos, Praia de Peniche de Cima; ☺ 9.30am-8pm Mar-Oct) offers lessons and equipment.

Casa das Marés B&B €€
(☑ Casa 1 262 769 200, Casa 2 262 769 255, Casa 3 262 769 379; www.casadasmares1.com; Praia do Baleal; d/ste €70/120; ☜) At the picturesque, windswept tip of Baleal stands one of the area's most distinctive accommodation options. Three sisters originally inherited this dramatically perched house from their parents and divided it into three parts – each of which now serves as its own little B&B run by two surviving brothers-in-law and one of the sisters.

Nau dos Corvos PORTUGUESE €€€
(☑ 262 783 168; www.naudoscorvos.com; Marginal Norte, Cabo Carvoeiro; mains €17-23; ☺ noon-3pm & 7-10.30pm) It's just you and the sea out here

PORTUGAL PENICHE

at Cabo Carvoeiro, 2.5km from town at the tip of the peninsula. As you gaze out at the Atlantic from the windy rooftop viewing platform, it's nice to know that under your feet is an excellent, upmarket seafood restaurant (and Peniche's best).

It boasts some of the best sunset views in Portugal.

ⓘ Information

Posto de Turismo (☑ 262 789 571; www. cm-peniche.pt; Rua Alexandre Herculano 70; ◷ 9am-1pm & 2-5pm)

ⓘ Getting There & Away

Peniche's **bus station** (☑ 968 903 861; Rua Dr Ernesto Moreira) is served by served by Rodoviária do Oeste (www.rodoviariadooeste.pt), Rede Expressos (www.rede-expressos.pt) and Intercentro (www.internorte.pt). There are frequent services to Coimbra (€14.70, 2¾ hours), Lisbon (€9, 1½ hours) and Óbidos (€3.30, 40 minutes).

Óbidos

POP 3100

Surrounded by a classic crenellated wall, Óbidos' gorgeous historic centre is a labyrinth of cobblestone streets and flower-bedecked, whitewashed houses livened up by dashes of vivid yellow and blue paint. The 14th-century Porta da Vila gate leads directly into the main street, Rua Direita, which is lined with chocolate and sour cherry-liqueur shops. It's a delightful place to pass an afternoon, but overnight visitors will find its charms magnified after the tour buses leave, when you can explore Óbidos' nooks and crannies and wander along its imposing town walls in relative solitude.

Commanding centre-stage at the top of the village is **Castelo de Óbidos**, one of Dom Dinis' 13th-century creations. It's a stern edifice, with lots of towers, battlements and big gates. Converted into a palace in the 16th century (some Manueline touches add levity), it's now a deluxe **pousada** (☑ 210 407 630; www.pousadas.pt; Paço Real; d/ste from €200/320; ❄ ⑦).

The town's elegant main church, **Igreja de Santa Maria** (Praça de Santa Maria; ◷ 9.30am-12.30pm & 2.30-7pm summer, to 5pm winter), stands out for its interior, with a wonderful painted ceiling and walls done up in beautiful blue-and-white 17th-century *azulejos* (hand-painted tiles). Paintings by the renowned 17th-century painter Josefa de Óbidos are to the right of the altar.

★ **Muro de Óbidos**   HISTORIC SITE
Óbidos' dramatic, fully intact Moorish wall imposingly surrounds the historical centre of town and stretches in a completed loop of 1560m, all of which can be walked across the top, at a height of 13m in some spots (not including the towers). There are four staircases accessing the wall, but most folks climb up either at Porta da Vila or the castle. There are no guardrails, so take care, especially with children or anyone prone to vertigo or spontaneous face plants.

Casa d'Óbidos   HOTEL €€
(☑ 262 950 924; www.casadobidos.com; Quinta de São José; s/d €75/90, 2-/4-/6-person apt €90/140/175; P ⑦ ⛱) In a whitewashed, 1887 villa below town, this delightful option features spacious, breezy rooms with good modern bathrooms and period furnishings, plus a tennis court, swimming pool and lovely grounds with sweeping views of Óbidos' bristling walls and towers. Breakfast is served at a common dining table (fresh bread and breakfast fixings are delivered every morning to the apartments).

Ja!mon Ja!mon   PORTUGUESE €€
(☑ 916 208 162; Rua da Biquinha S/N; mains €10-14; ◷ noon-3pm & 7-10pm Tue-Sat, noon-3pm Sun) With the cheery Andre, his family and a young, enthusiastic staff, the hospitality is oh-so Portuguese (read: happy and generous) at this excellent *tasca* (tavern) featuring a wonderful terrace with lush hillside views.

ⓘ Information

Posto de Turismo (☑ 262 959 231; www. obidos.pt; Rua da Porta da Vila S/N; ◷ 9.30am-7.30pm May-Sep, to 6pm Oct-Apr) Just outside Porta da Vila, near the bus stop.

ⓘ Getting There & Away

Rodoviária do Oeste (www.rodoviariadooeste. pt) runs frequent buses to Peniche (€3.30, 40 minutes) and Lisbon (€7.85, 65 minutes) from the bus stop on the main road near Porta da Vila.

Nazaré

POP 10,500

With a warren of narrow, cobbled lanes running down to a wide, cliff-backed beach, Nazaré is Estremadura's most picturesque coastal resort. Its sands are packed wall-to-wall with multicoloured umbrellas in July and August. Nazaré is also one of Portugal's top draws for New Year's Eve and Carnaval celebrations, and is renowned for the monster surfing waves that roll in north of town at Praia do Norte each winter.

The **beaches** here are superb, although swimmers should be aware of dangerous currents. Climb or take the funicular to the clifftop promontory of **Sítio**, with its cluster of fishermen's cottages and outstanding views.

You'll likely be hit up by elderly local women offering rooms for rent. It never hurts to bargain and see what the going rate is. Rates drop 30% to 50% outside July and August.

Lab Hostel HOSTEL €

(☑ 262 382 339; www.labhostel.pt; Rua de Rio Maior 14; dm €17.50-18.50, d €55-100; ☞) One of Portugal's band of growing 'glostels' (glamorous hostels), stylish, minimal design, attention to detail and some of the whitest, brightest and cleanest rooms around make this worth a look. There's a female dorm, a family room and breakfast is included. It was a former laboratory (the owner's father-in-law was a pharmacist), and old chemist jars and bottles make for fun *objets d'art*.

A Tasquinha SEAFOOD €€

(☑ 262 551 945; Rua Adrião Batalha 54; mains €7.50-17.50; ☺ noon-3pm & 7-10.30pm Tue-Sun Carnival-New Year) This exceptionally friendly family affair has been running for 50-plus years, serving high-quality seafood in a pair of snug but prettily tiled dining rooms. Solo travellers delight: *Arroz de Marisco* (shellfish rice) for one person (€17.50)!

ⓘ Information

Posto de Turismo (☑ 262 561 194; www.cm-nazare.pt; Avenida Vieira Guimarães, Edifício do Mercado Municipal; ☺ 9.30am-1pm & 2.30-6pm Oct-Apr, to 7pm May, Jun & Sep, 9am-8pm Jul & Aug) In the front offices of the food market as well as next door to Igreja de Nossa Senhora da Nazaré in **Sítio** (☑ 930 424 860; www.cm-nazare.pt; Largo de Nossa Senhora da Nazaré; ☺ 9.30am-1pm & 2.30-6pm Oct-Apr, to 7pm May, Jun & Sep, 9am-8pm Jul & Aug). Helpful, multilingual staff.

ⓘ Getting There & Away

Rodoviária do Oeste (www.rodoviariadooeste.pt) and Rede Expressos (www.rede-expressos.pt) run frequent buses to Lisbon (€12, 1¾ hours) and Peniche (€10, 70 minutes) from Nazaré's bus station, a couple of blocks in from the ocean.

Tomar

POP 16,000

Tomar is one of central Portugal's most appealing small towns. With its pedestrian-friendly historical centre, its pretty riverside park frequented by swans, herons and families of ducks, and its charming natural setting adjacent to the lush Mata Nacional dos Sete Montes (Seven Hills National Forest), it wins lots of points for aesthetics. Its crowning glory is the medieval hilltop Convento de Cristo, whose crenellated walls form a beautiful backdrop from almost any vantage point.

Just northwest of Tomar, the double-decker Aqueduto de Pegões with its 180 arches was built between 1593 and 1613 to supply water to thirsty monks. It's best seen just off the Leiria road, 2.3km from town.

★ Convento de Cristo MONASTERY

(www.conventocristo.pt; Rua Castelo dos Templários; adult/under 12yr €6/free, with Alcobaça & Batalha €15; ☺ 9am-6.30pm Jun-Sep, to 5.30pm Oct-May) Wrapped in splendour and mystery, the Knights Templar held enormous power in Portugal from the 12th to 16th centuries and largely bankrolled the Age of Discoveries. Their headquarters sit on wooded slopes above the town and are enclosed within 12th-century walls. The Unesco World Heritage–listed Convento de Cristo is a stony expression of magnificence, founded in 1160 by Gualdim Pais. It has chapels, cloisters and choirs in diverging styles, added over the centuries by successive kings and Grand Masters.

Hostel 2300 Thomar HOSTEL €

(☑ 249 324 256; www.hostel2300thomar.com; Rua Serpa Pinto 43; dm/s/d/tr/q €18/30/45/60/80; ☞) One of Portugal's funkiest hostels, this cleverly renovated mansion right in the heart of town celebrates Portugal, with the rooms brightly decorated in an individual theme: from the Lisbon tram to sardines. Airy dorms (and doubles), lockers, modern bathrooms and a cool and fun living space are enough to convert those normally after luxe experiences into a backpacker.

Thomar Story BOUTIQUE HOTEL €€

(☑ 249 327 268; www.thomarstory.pt; Rua João Carlos Everard 53; s/d/tr €43/50/65; ☀ ☞) A major refurbishment of an old house has created 12 light and pleasant rooms along the lines of the current trend in Portugal: funky wall decorations and mirrors, bright accessories and modern bathrooms. The interior of each in some way reflects Tomar, from the town's convent to its synagogue. Breakfast costs €5. The best rooms have small patios and kitchenettes.

Restaurante Tabuleiro PORTUGUESE €€
(☑249 312 771; www.restaurantetabuleiro.word press.com; Rua Serpa Pinto 140; mains €15.80; ⊙noon-3pm & 7-10pm Mon-Sat; ➡) Located just off Tomar's main square, this family-friendly local hang-out features warm, attentive service, good traditional food and ridiculous (read: more-than-ample) portions. A great spot to experience local fare. The cod pie is a standout.

ℹ️ Information

Posto de Turismo (☑249 329 823; www. cm-tomar.pt; Avenida Dr Cândido Madureira; ⊙9.30am-6pm Apr-Sep, 10am-5pm Oct-Mar) Offers a good town map, an accommodation list and information about a historical trail.

ℹ️ Getting There & Away

Trains run to Lisbon (€9.80 to €11.10, 1¾ to two hours) every hour or two.

Coimbra

POP 143,396

Rising scenically from the Rio Mondego, Coimbra is an animated city steeped in history. It was Portugal's medieval capital for more than a century and it's home to the country's oldest and most prestigious university, the Unesco-listed Universidade de Coimbra. Coimbra's steeply stacked historic centre dates from Moorish times and is wonderfully atmospheric with its dark cobbled lanes and monumental cathedral. On summer evenings, the city's old stone walls reverberate with the haunting metallic notes of the *guitarra* (Portuguese guitar) and the full, deep voices of fado singers.

◉ Sights

⭐ **Biblioteca Joanina** LIBRARY
(Baroque Library; ☑239 242 744; www.uc.pt/ turismo; Pátio das Escolas, Universidade de Coimbra; adult/under 26yr/child incl Paço das Escolas, Capela de São Miguel & Museu da Ciência €12.50/10/free; ⊙9am-7.30pm Mar-Oct, 9am-1pm & 2pm-5pm Nov-Feb) The university's baroque library is Coimbra's headline sight. Named after King João V, who sponsored its construction between 1717 and 1728, it features a remarkable central hall decorated with elaborate ceiling frescoes and

huge rosewood, ebony and jacaranda tables. Towering gilt chinoiserie shelves hold some 40,000 books, mainly on law, philosophy and theology. Curiously, the library also houses a colony of bats to protect the books – they eat potentially harmful insects.

Sé Velha CATHEDRAL
(Old Cathedral; ☑239 825 273; www.sevelha-coim bra.org; Largo da Sé Velha, Rua do Norte 4; €2.50; ⊙10am-6pm Mon-Sat, 1-6pm Sun) Coimbra's 12th-century cathedral is one of Portugal's finest examples of Romanesque architecture. The main portal and facade are particularly striking, especially on warm summer evenings when the golden stone seems to glow in the soft light. Its construction was financed by Portugal's first king, Afonso Henriques, and completed in 1184 at a time when the nation was still threatened by the Moors, hence its crenellated exterior and narrow, slit-like lower windows. Interior highlights include an ornate late-Gothic retable and a lovely 13th-century cloister.

Museu Nacional de Machado de Castro MUSEUM
(☑239 853 070; www.museumachadocastro.pt; Largo Dr José Rodrigues; adult/child €6/3, cryptoportico only €3; ⊙2pm-6pm Tue, 10am-6pm Wed-Sun) This great museum is a highlight of central Portugal. Housed in a 12th-century bishop's palace, it stands over the city's ancient Roman forum, remains of which can be seen in the maze of spooky tunnels under the building – the *cryptoporticus*. Once you emerge from this, you can start on the fascinating art collection, which runs the gamut from Gothic religious sculpture to 16th-century Flemish painting and ornately crafted furniture.

🛏️ Sleeping & Eating

Serenata Hostel HOSTEL €
(☑239 853 130; www.serenatahostel.com; Largo da Sé Velha 21; dm €16, d €49-60, f €71; ❄️🛜) Occupying an elegant townhouse overlooking Coimbra's old cathedral, this fabulous hostel sits in the heart of the historical centre. Rooms, spread over three floors, come in an array of shapes and sizes, ranging from 10-bed dorms to spacious family rooms. White walls and artistic stencils create a modern feel, while high ceilings and creaking wood floors add a period touch.

Quinta das Lágrimas LUXURY HOTEL €€€
(☑239 802 380; www.quintadaslagrimas.pt; Rua António Augusto Gonçalves; r €160-450; 🅿️❄️🛜🏊)

Coimbra's sole five-star hotel is charmingly ensconced in the romantic **Jardim Quinta das Lágrimas** (Rua Vilarinho Raposo; adult/under 15yr/family €2.50/1/5; ☺10am-5pm Tue-Sun mid-Oct–mid-Mar, 10am-7pm mid-Mar–mid-Oct) on the west bank of the Mondego. Choose between classic richly furnished rooms in the original 18th-century palace, or go for something more minimalist in the modern annex. There's a formal fine-dining restaurant for gourmet dinners and a fully equipped spa.

Sete Restaurante   MODERN PORTUGUESE €€
(☎239 060 065; www.facebook.com/seterestaurante; Rua Dr. Martins de Carvalho 10; mains €11-19; ☺1-4pm & 7-midnight Wed-Mon) Squeezed into a corner behind the **Igreja de Santa Cruz** (Praça 8 de Maio; adult/child €3/free; ☺9.30am-4.30pm Mon-Sat, 1-5pm Sun), this intimate restaurant is one of the most popular in town. Its casual wine bar vibe, personable service and modern take on Portuguese cuisine ensure it's almost always buzzing. Book ahead to avoid disappointment.

Loggia   MODERN PORTUGUESE €€
(☎239 853 076; www.loggia.pt; Largo Dr José Rodrigues, Museu Nacional de Machado de Castro; mains €13-18; ☺10am-6pm Tue & Sun, to 10.30pm Wed-Sat) As much as its confident modern cuisine, the Loggia's big draw is its setting, on a panoramic terrace overlooking the old town. There's open-air seating for romantic sunset dinners or you can sit inside and admire the views from its glass-walled dining room. Its lunch buffet (€9.50) is great value.

🍷 Drinking & Entertainment

Galeria Santa Clara   BAR
(☎239 441 657; www.galeriasantaclara.com; Rua António Augusto Gonçalves 67; ☺2pm-2am Sun-Thu, to 3am Fri & Sat) An arty tea room by day and chilled-out bar by night, this is a terrific place to hang out. Inside it's all mismatched vintage furniture, books and chandeliers, while out the back the garden terrace boasts lovely views over the river to the historical centre. The atmosphere is laid-back and can feel like a house party when things get going.

Fado ao Centro   FADO
(☎239 837 060; www.fadoaocentro.com; Rua Quebra Costas 7; show incl drink €10; ☺show 6pm) At the bottom of the old town, this friendly cultural centre is a good place to acquaint yourself with fado. The evening 6pm show includes plenty of explanation, in Portuguese and English, about the history of the music and the meaning of each song. It's tourist-oriented, but the performers enjoy it and do it well.

ℹ️ Information

Turismo Largo da Portagem (☎239 488 120; www.turismodecoimbra.pt; Largo da Portagem; ☺9am-6pm Mon-Fri, 9.30am-1pm & 2-5.30pm Sat & Sun) Coimbra's main tourist office.

ℹ️ Getting There & Away

BUS
From the **bus station** (Av Fernão de Magalhães; ☺ticket office 8am-10pm), a 15-minute walk

PORTUGAL COIMBRA

WORTH A TRIP

LUSO & MATA NACIONAL DO BUÇACO

A retreat from the world for almost 2000 years, the **Mata Nacional do Buçaco** (☎231 937 000; www.fmb.pt; per car/cyclist/pedestrian €5/free/free; ☺8.30am-7pm Mon-Fri, to 8pm Sat & Sun) sits on the slopes of the Serra do Buçaco, some 30km north of Coimbra. This walled 105-hectare forest reserve harbours a network of paths and an astounding 700 plant species, from huge Mexican cedars to tree-sized ferns. Smack in the heart of the forest is the **Palace Hotel do Buçaco** (☎231 937 970; www.almeidahotels.pt/pt/hotel-coimbra-portugal; s €148-199, d €169-225; P), a fairy-tale royal palace now converted into a splurge-worthy overnight accommodation.

Generations of writers have enshrined Buçaco in the national imagination with breathless hymns to its natural and spiritual beauty. Access to the forest is through the quaint spa town of Luso at the foot of the Serra. Famed for its thermal waters, Luso is an easy day trip from Coimbra, but it also has some decent accommodation and the recommended **Pedra de Sal** (☎231 939 405; www.restaurantepedradesal.com; Rua Francisco A Dinis 33; mains €9-20; ☺noon-3pm & 7-10pm Wed-Mon) restaurant, specialising in succulent steak and Iberian pork.

Three weekday buses run from Coimbra's bus station to Luso (€3.75, 40 minutes) with two continuing on to Buçaco (€4, 50 minutes). Three daily trains run from Coimbra-B to Luso-Buçaco station (€2.55, 25 minutes). From here it's a 15-minute walk into town.

northwest of the centre, **Rede Expressos** (☑ 239 855 270; www.rede-expressos.pt) runs at least a dozen buses daily to Lisbon (€14.50, 2½ hours) and Porto (€12.50, 1½ hours), along with direct services to Braga (€14, 2¾ hours, six daily), and Faro (€28, six to 8½ hours, two daily).

TRAIN
Coimbra has two train stations: **Coimbra-B** and the more central **Coimbra A** (called just 'Coimbra' on timetables). Long-distance trains stop at Coimbra-B, 2km north of the city centre, from where local trains connect with Coimbra A – this connection is included in the price of tickets to/from Coimbra.

Coimbra has regular services to Lisbon (AP/IC €23.20/19.50, 1¾/two hours, hourly) and Porto (€17/13.40, one/1¼ hours, at least hourly).

THE NORTH

Beneath the edge of Spanish Galicia, northern Portugal is a land of lush river valleys, sparkling coastline, granite peaks and virgin forests. This region is also paradise for wine-lovers: it's home to Portugal's sprightly *vinho verde* (a young, slightly sparkling white or red wine) and ancient terraced Port vineyards along the dramatic Rio Douro. Gateway to the north is Porto, a beguiling riverside city blending both medieval and modern attractions. Smaller towns and villages also offer cultural allure, from majestic Braga, the country's religious heart, to seaside beauty Viana do Castelo.

Porto

☑ 22 / POP 237,600

Opening up like a pop-up book from the banks of the Rio Douro, edgy-yet-opulent Porto entices with its historical centre, sumptuous food and wine, and charismatic locals. A lively walkable city with chatter in the air and a tangible sense of history, Porto's old-world riverfront district is a Unesco World Heritage Site. Across the water twinkle the neon signs of Vila Nova de Gaia, headquarters of the major port wine manufacturers.

◉ Sights

★ **Palácio da Bolsa**   HISTORIC BUILDING
(Stock Exchange; www.palaciodabolsa.com; Rua Ferreira Borges; tours adult/child €10/6.50; ⊙ 9am-6.30pm Apr-Oct, 9am-12.30pm & 2-5.30pm Nov-Mar) This splendid neoclassical monument (built from 1842 to 1910) honours Porto's

past and present money merchants. Just past the entrance is the glass-domed **Pátio das Nações** (Hall of Nations), where the exchange once operated. But this pales in comparison with rooms deeper inside; to visit these, join one of the half-hour guided tours, which set off every 30 minutes.

★ **Igreja de São Francisco**   CHURCH
(Jardim do Infante Dom Henrique; adult/child €6/5; ⊙ 9am-8pm Jul-Sep, to 7pm Mar-Jun & Oct, to 5.30pm Nov-Feb) Igreja de São Francisco looks from the outside to be an austerely Gothic church, but inside it hides one of Portugal's most dazzling displays of baroque finery. Hardly a centimetre escapes unsmothered, as otherworldly cherubs and sober monks are drowned by nearly 100kg of gold leaf. If you see only one church in Porto, make it this one.

★ **Jardins do Palácio de Cristal**   GARDENS
(Rua Dom Manuel II; ⊙ 8am-9pm Apr-Sep, to 7pm Oct-Mar; ⊞) Sitting atop a bluff, this gorgeous botanical garden is one of Porto's best-loved escapes, with lawns interwoven with sun-dappled paths and dotted with fountains, sculptures, giant magnolias, camellias, cypress and olive trees. It's actually a mosaic of small gardens that open up little by little as you wander – as do the stunning views of the city and Rio Douro.

★ **Serralves**   MUSEUM
(www.serralves.pt; Rua Dom João de Castro 210; adult/child museums & park €10/free, park only €5/free, 10am-1pm 1st Sun of the month free; ⊙ 10am-7pm Mon-Fri, to 8pm Sat & Sun May-Sep, reduced hours Oct-Apr) This fabulous cultural institution combines a museum, a mansion and extensive gardens. Cutting-edge exhibitions, along with a fine permanent collection featuring works from the late 1960s to the present, are showcased in the **Museu de Arte Contemporânea**, an arrestingly minimalist, whitewashed space designed by the eminent Porto-based architect Álvaro Siza Vieira. The delightful, pink **Casa de Serralves** is a prime example of art deco, bearing the imprint of French architect Charles Siclis. One ticket gets you into both museums.

Museu Nacional Soares dos Reis   MUSEUM
(www.museusoaresdosreis.pt; Rua Dom Manuel II 44; adult/child €5/free; ⊙ 10am-6pm Tue-Sun) Porto's best art museum presents a stellar collection ranging from neolithic carvings to Portugal's take on modernism, all housed in the formidable Palácio das Carrancas.

Casa da Música
LANDMARK

(☑ 220 120 220; www.casadamusica.com; Avenida da Boavista 604-610; guided tour €10; ⊙ English guided tours 11am & 4pm) At once minimalist, iconic and daringly imaginative, the Casa da Música is the beating heart of Porto's cultural scene and the home of the Porto National Orchestra. Dutch architect Rem Koolhaas rocked the musical world with this crystalline creation – the jewel in the city's European Capital of Culture 2001 crown.

São Bento Train Station
HISTORIC BUILDING

(Praça Almeida Garrett; ⊙5am-1am) One of the world's most beautiful train stations, beaux arts São Bento wings you back to a more graceful age of rail travel. Completed in 1903, it seems to have been imported from 19th-century Paris with its mansard roof. But the dramatic *azulejo* panels of historical scenes in the front hall are the real attraction. Designed by Jorge Colaço in 1930, some 20,000 tiles depict historic battles (including Henry the Navigator's conquest of Ceuta), as well as the history of transport.

🖝 Tours

Taste Porto
FOOD & DRINK

(☑ 920 503 302; www.tasteporto.com; Downtown Food Tour adult/child €65/42, Vintage Food Tour €70/42; ⊙Downtown Food Tour 10.45am & 4pm Tue-Sat, Vintage Food Tour 10am & 4.15pm Mon-Sat, Photo Food Experience 9.45am daily) Loosen a belt notch for Taste Porto's superb Downtown Food Tours, where you'll sample everything from Porto's best slow-roast-pork sandwich to éclairs, fine wines, cheese and coffee. Friendly, knowledgeable guide André and his team lead these indulgent and insightful 3½-hour walking tours, which take in viewpoints and historical back lanes en route to restaurants, grocery stores and cafes.

🛏 Sleeping

Gallery Hostel
HOSTEL €

(☑ 224 964 313; www.gallery-hostel.com; Rua Miguel Bombarda 222; dm/d/tr/ste from €20/59/75/80; ❄🖥) A true travellers' hub, this hostel-gallery has clean and cosy dorms and doubles, a sunny, glass-enclosed back patio, a grassy terrace, a cinema room, a shared kitchen and a bar-music room. Throw in its free walking tours, homemade dinners on request, port-wine tastings and concerts, and you'll see why it's booked up so often – reserve ahead.

The Passenger
HOSTEL €

(☑ 963 802 000; www.thepassengerhostel.com; Estação de São Bento, Praça Almeida Garrett; dm €22-27, d €55-90, tr €95-110, q €115-190) A night spent at the station is no longer a miserable prospect since the opening of this cool hostel in São Bento train station. Decorated with vintage furniture and one-of-a-kind Portuguese artworks, it sure is a step up from most backpacker digs. Besides upbeat staff, there's a shared kitchen and a bar with a Mac and piano.

Canto de Luz
B&B €€

(☑ 225 492 142; www.cantodeluz.com; Rua do Almada 539; r €85-105; 🖥) *Ah oui*, this French-run guesthouse, just a five-minute walk from Trindade metro, is a delight. Rooms are light, spacious and make the leap between classic and contemporary, with vintage furnishings used to clever effect. Your kindly hosts André and Brigitte prepare delicious breakfasts, with fresh-squeezed juice, pastries and homemade preserves. There's also a pretty garden terrace.

★ Guest House Douro
BOUTIQUE HOTEL €€€

(☑ 222 015 135; www.guesthousedouro.com; Rua da Fonte Taurina 99-101; r €160-230; ❄@🖥) In

PORTUGAL PORTO

WORTH A TRIP

THROUGH THE GRAPEVINES OF THE DOURO

Portugal's best-known river flows through the country's rural heartland. In the upper reaches, port-wine grapes are grown on steep terraced hills, punctuated by remote stone villages and, in spring, splashes of dazzling white almond blossom. The Rio Douro is navigable right across Portugal. Highly recommended is the train journey from Porto to Pinhão (€11, 2½ hours, five daily), the last 70km clinging to the river's edge; from Pinhão, trains continue upstream as far as Pocinho (from Porto €13.30, 3¼ hours), or you can hop aboard a boat cruise for equally spellbinding perspectives on the river.

Cyclists and drivers can choose river-hugging roads along either bank – such as the N222 between Pinhão and Peso da Régua – and visit wineries along the way (check out www.dourovalley.eu for an extensive list of wineries open to visitors). You can also stay overnight in scenic wine lodges among the vineyards.

Porto

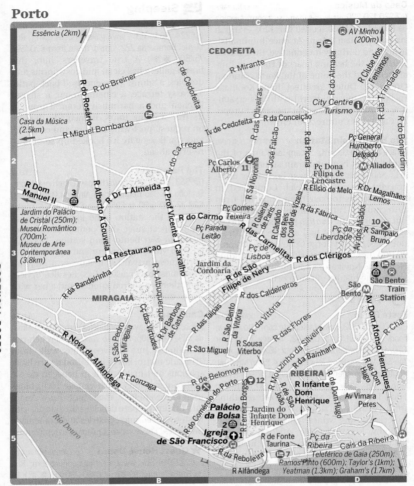

PORTUGAL PORTO

a restored relic overlooking the Rio Douro, these eight rooms have been blessed with gorgeous wooden floors, plush queen beds and marble baths; the best have dazzling river views. But it is the welcome that makes this place stand out from the crowd – your charming hosts Carmen and João bend over backwards to please.

★ **Yeatman** RESORT €€€
(☑ 220 133 185; www.the-yeatman-hotel.com; Rua do Choupelo 88; d €255-315, ste €485-2370; ✳ 🕏 ⌸) Named after one of port producer Taylor's original founders, the Yeatman is Porto's only true five-star resort, terraced

and tucked into the Gaia hillside with expansive Douro and Porto views. There's a two-Michelin-starred restaurant; huge, sumptuous guest rooms and suites with private terraces; a decanter-shaped pool; sunken Roman baths in the fantastic Caudalie spa; and it's close to everything else you could possibly wish for.

✗ Eating

Flor dos Congregados PORTUGUESE €€
(☑ 222 002 822; www.flordoscongregados.pt; Travessa dos Congregados 11; mains €8-16; ☺ 7-10pm Mon-Wed, noon-3pm & 7-11pm Thu-Sat) Tucked away down a narrow alley, this softly

frequently, but you'll always find superb steaks and to-die-for *empanadas* (savoury turnovers). Save an inch for the chocolate brownie with *dulce de leche*.

Essência VEGETARIAN €€
(☏ 228 301 813; www.essenciarestaurantevege tariano.com; Rua de Pedro Hispano 1190; mains €10.50-15; ⊙ 12.30-3pm & 8-10.30pm Mon-Thu, to midnight Fri & Sat; ✍) This bright, modern brasserie is famous Porto-wide for its generous vegetarian (and nonvegetarian!) dishes, stretching from wholesome soups and salads to curries, pasta dishes, risotto and *feijoada* (pork and bean casserole). There's a terrace for warm-weather dining.

O Paparico PORTUGUESE €€€
(☏ 225 400 548; www.opaparico.com; Rua de Costa Cabral 2343; menus €90-120; ⊙ 7.30-11pm Tue-Sat) It's worth the taxi hop north of town to O Paparico. Portuguese authenticity is the name of the game here, from the romantically rustic interior of stone walls, beams and white linen to the menu that sings of the seasons. Dishes such as veal with wild mushrooms and monkfish are cooked with passion, served with precision and expertly paired with wines.

★ Euskalduna Studio GASTRONOMY €€€
(☏ 935 335 301; www.euskaldunastudio.pt; Rua de Santo Ildefonso 404; 10-course tasting menu €95-110; ⊙ 7-10pm Wed-Sat) Everyone loves surprises, especially edible ones prepared with flawless execution, experimental finesse and a nod to the seasons. Just 16 lucky diners (eight at the

lit, family-run restaurant brims with stone-walled, wood-beamed, art-slung nooks. The frequently changing blackboard menu goes with the seasons.

Belos Aires ARGENTINE €€
(☏ 223 195 661; www.facebook.com/belosaires restaurante; Rua de Belomonte 104; mains €17-25; ⊙ 8-11.30am & 7pm-midnight Mon-Sat; ✍) At the heart of this intimate part-Argentine, part-Portuguese restaurant is Mauricio, a chef with a big personality and an insatiable passion for his homeland, revealed as you watch him dashing around in the open kitchen. The market-fresh menu changes

---

DON'T MISS

TASTING PORT WINE

Sitting just across the Rio Douro from Porto, **Vila Nova da Gaia** is woven into the city's fabric by stunning bridges and a shared history of port-wine making. Since the mid-18th century, port-wine bottlers and exporters have maintained their lodges here. Today some 30 of these lodges clamber up the riverbank and most open their doors to the public for cellar tours and tastings. Among the best are **Taylor's** (☑ 223 772 973; www.taylor.pt; Rua do Choupelo 250; tours incl tasting adult/child €15/6; ☉10am-6pm). **Graham's** (☑ 223 776 490, 223 776 492; www.grahams-port.com; Rua do Agro 141; tours incl tasting from €15; ☉ 9.30am-6.30pm Apr-Oct, to 6pm Nov-Mar) and **Ramos Pinto** (☑ 967 658 980, 936 809 283; www.ramospinto.pt; Av Ramos Pinto 400; tours incl tasting €10; ☉10am-6pm May-Oct, reduced hours Nov-Apr).

green marble counter peeking into the kitchen and eight at oak tables) get to sample Vasco Coelho Santos' stunning 10-course menus that allow flavours and textures to shine.

🍷 Drinking & Entertainment

★Prova
WINE BAR

(www.prova.com.pt; Rua Ferreira Borges 86; ☉5pm-1am Wed-Sun; 🛜) Diogo, the passionate owner, explains the finer nuances of Portuguese wine at this chic, stone-walled bar, where relaxed jazz plays. Stop by for a two-glass tasting (€5), or sample wines by the glass – including beefy Douros, full-bodied Dãos and crisp Alentejo whites. These marry well with sharing plates of local hams and cheeses (€14). Diogo's port tonics are legendary.

Aduela
BAR

(Rua das Oliveiras 36; ☉3pm-2am Mon, 10am-2am Tue-Thu, to 4am Fri & Sat, 3pm-midnight Sun) Retro and hip but not self-consciously so, chilled Aduela bathes in the nostalgic orange glow of its glass lights, which illuminate the green walls and mishmash of vintage furnishings. Once a sewing machine warehouse, today it's where friends gather to converse over wine and appetising *petiscos* (€3 to €8).

Terraplana
CAFE

(www.terraplanacafe.com; Avenida Rodrigues de Freitas 287; ☉6pm-midnight Sun-Thu, to 3am Fri & Sat) Totally relaxed and boho-cool without trying, Terraplana is the bar of the moment in this neck of Porto. Murals adorn the arty, stone-walled interior, and there's a pretty patio for summer imbibing. Besides inventive cocktails (around €10 a pop), they also have a solid selection of wines, gins and beers. These marry well with super-tasty pizzas (€8.50 to €9.50).

★Casa da Música
CONCERT VENUE

(House of Music; ☑220 120 220; www.casadamusica.com; Avenida da Boavista 604; ☉box office 9.30am-7pm Mon-Sat, to 6pm Sun) Grand and minimalist, sophisticated yet populist, Porto's cultural behemoth boasts a shoebox-style concert hall at its heart, meticulously engineered to accommodate everything from jazz duets to Beethoven's Ninth.

ℹ️ Information

City Centre Turismo (☑300 501 920; www.visitporto.travel; Rua Clube dos Fenianos 25; ☉9am-8pm May-Jul & Sep-Oct, to 9pm Aug, to 7pm Nov-Apr) The main city *turismo* has a detailed city map, a transport map and the *Agenda do Porto* cultural calendar, among other printed materials.

Santo António Hospital (☑222 077 500; www.chporto.pt; Largo Prof Abel Salazar) Has English-speaking staff.

ℹ️ Getting There & Away

AIR

Porto's gleaming, ultra-modern **Francisco de Sá Carneiro Airport** (☑229 432 400; www.aeroportoporto.pt; 4470-558 Maia), 16km northwest of the city centre, has excellent connections to international hubs including London, Brussels, Madrid, Frankfurt, New York and Toronto.

BUS

Bus services in Porto are regrettably dispersed, with no central bus terminal. On the plus side, there are frequent services to most places in northern Portugal, and express services to Coimbra, Lisbon and points south.

Renex-Rede Expressos (www.rede-expressos.pt; Campo 24 de Agosto) is the choice for Lisbon (€19, 3½ hours), with the most direct routes and eight to 12 departures daily, including one continuing on to the Algarve. Buses depart from Campo 24 de Agosto. **Transdev-Norte** (☑225 100 100; www.transdev.pt; Campo 24 de Agosto) runs to Braga (€6, one hour), and **AV Minho** (☑222 006 121; www.avminho.pt; Rua Régulo Maguanha 46) serves Viana do Castelo (€5.60, 2¼ hours).

TRAIN

Porto is northern Portugal's rail hub. Long-distance services start at **Campanhã** (Rua Monte da Estação) station, 3km east of the centre. Direct IC trains run hourly to Lisbon (€24.70 to €30.80, 2½ to three hours).

Most *urbano*, *regional* and *interregional* (IR) trains depart from **São Bento** (Praça Almeida Garrett) station, though they also pass through Campanhã.

❶ Getting Around

TO/FROM THE AIRPORT

The Metro do Porto violet line E links the airport with central Porto. A one-way ticket costs €2 and the journey takes around 45 minutes. Taxis charge €20 to €25 for the hour-long trip to the centre.

PUBLIC TRANSPORT

Public transport is inexpensive, clean and efficient in Porto. For maximum convenience, Porto's transport agency, **STCP** (Sociedade de Transportes Colectivos do Porto; ☑ 808 200 166; www.stcp.pt), offers the rechargeable **Andante Card** (€0.60; www.linhandante.com), allowing smooth movement between tram, metro, funicular and many bus lines. A 24-hour ticket for the entire public transport network, excluding trams, costs €7. For timetables, routes and fares, see www.stcp.pt and www.metrodoporto.pt.

Bus

STCP's extensive bus system has central hubs at Praça da Liberdade (the south end of Avenida dos Aliados), Praça Almeida Garrett (in front of São Bento train station) and Cordoaria. A one-way ticket bought on the bus costs €1.95, or €1.20 with an Andante Card.

Funicular

The panoramic **Funicular dos Guindais** (one way adult/child €2.50/1.25; ⊙ 8am-10pm Sun-Thu, to midnight Fri & Sat Apr-Oct, to 8pm Sun-Thu, to 10pm Fri & Sat Nov-Mar) shuttles up and down a steep incline from Avenida Gustavo Eiffel to Rua Augusto Rosa.

Metro

Running from around 6am to 1am daily, Porto's newish, easy-to-navigate **metro system** (http://en.metrodoporto.pt) comprises six metropolitan lines that all converge at the Trindade stop. Tickets cost €1.20/1.60/2 for zone 2/3/4 with an Andante Card.

Tram

Only three Porto tram lines remain, but they're very scenic. The Massarelos stop, on the riverfront near Palácio de Cristal, is the system's hub. From here, the most useful line (tram 1E) trundles along the Douro towards Foz do Douro. Trams run half-hourly from 8am to 9pm. One-way tickets cost €3; a two-day adult/child pass costs €10/5.

Viana do Castelo

POP 37,972

The jewel of the Costa Verde, Viana do Castelo is blessed with an appealing medieval centre, an attractive riverfront and lovely beaches just outside town. Viana's old quarter showcases leafy 19th-century boulevards and narrow lanes crowded with Manueline manors and rococo palaces, all dramatically presided over by the pearly-white, neo-Byzantine Santa Luzia church on the hilltop high above town. The stately heart of town is Praça da República, with its delicate Renaissance fountain and grandiose mansions and monuments.

Monte de Santa Luzia   HILL

There are two good reasons to visit Viana's 228m eucalyptus-clad hill. One is the wondrous view down the coast and up the Lima valley. The other is the fabulously over-the-top, 20th-century, neo-Byzantine **Templo do Sagrado Coração de Jesus** (Templo Monumento Santa Luzia, Temple of the Sacred Heart of Jesus; www.templosantaluzia.org; admission to dome €2; ⊙ 9am-6.45pm Apr-Oct, to 4.45pm Nov-Mar). You can get a little closer to heaven by climbing to the *zimbório* (lantern tower) atop its dome, via a lift, followed by an elbow-scraping stairway – take the museum entrance on the ground floor.

Praia do Cabedelo   BEACH

This is one of the Minho's best beaches: a 1km-long arc of blond, powdery sand that folds into grassy dunes backed by a grove of wind-blown pines. It's across the river from town, best reached on a five-minute **ferry trip** (one way/return adult €1.40/2.80, child under 12yr/under 6yr half price/free; ⊙ 9am-6pm May-Sep) from the pier south of Largo 5 de Outubro.

★ Dona Emília   GUESTHOUSE €€

(☑ 917 811 392; www.dona-emilia.com; Rua Manuel Espregueira 6; d with shared/private bathroom from €55/75; ❋) This phenomenal new B&B in a 19th-century town house commands front-row perspectives of Viana's historical centre from its luminous, high-ceilinged common areas and six guest rooms. Second-floor units have shared facilities, while suites under the eaves have beautifully tiled private bathrooms. All abound in period details; two have terraces with views over Viana's elegant main square or the leafy backyard.

O Marquês
PORTUGUESE €

(Rua do Marquês 72; meals from €6; ☺noon-3.30pm & 7-10pm Mon-Fri, noon-3.30pm Sat) A tremendous backstreet find, this place is absolutely jammed with locals for the *platos do dia* (daily specials; €6). Think baked cod with white beans or roasted turkey leg with potatoes and salad. It's a friendly, satisfying, family-run affair.

Confeitaria Natário
BAKERY €

(☑ 258 822 376; Rua Manuel Espregueira 37; pastries from €1; ☺9am-9pm Mon & Wed-Sat, 9am-1.30pm & 3.30-9pm Sun) This popular bakery is the place to try delicious *bolas de Berlim* (cream-filled doughnuts) – so good that you'll often have to wait in line. Get 'em warm from the oven at 11.30am and 4.30pm. Locals also convene here for *milfolhas* (flaky pastry filled with shrimp or meat), traditionally enjoyed with a glass of sparkling wine.

ⓘ Information

Viana Welcome Centre (☑ 258 098 415; www.vivexperiencia.pt; Praça do Eixo Atlântico; ☺10am-7pm Jul & Aug, 10am-1pm & 2-6pm Tue-Sun Sep-Oct & Mar-Jun, to 5pm Tue-Sun Nov-Feb) Centrally located down by the riverfront; offers tourist information, tours and activities.

ⓘ Getting There & Away

Viana is linked to Porto by direct trains (€6.85 to €7.95, 1¼ to two hours) and AV Minho buses (€6.50, two hours).

Braga

POP 136,885

Portugal's third-largest city boasts an elegant historical centre laced with ancient pedestrian lanes, grand plazas and a splendid array of baroque churches. Packed with cafes, boutiques, restaurants and bars, and enlivened by a large student population, Braga is also famous throughout Portugal for its religious festivals – particularly the elaborately staged **Semana Santa** (Holy Week) leading up to Easter Sunday. Just east of Braga stands the magnificent hillside sanctuary of **Bom Jesus do Monte**, one of Portugal's most iconic tourist attractions.

★ Sé
CATHEDRAL

(www.se-braga.pt; Rua Dom Paio Mendes; ☺9.30am-12.30pm & 2.30-6.30pm Apr-Oct, to 5.30pm Nov-Mar) Braga's extraordinary cathedral, the oldest in Portugal, was begun when the archdiocese was restored in 1070 and completed in the following century. It's a rambling complex made up of differing styles, and architecture buffs could spend half a day happily distinguishing the Romanesque bones from Manueline musculature and baroque frippery.

★ Escadaria do Bom Jesus do Monte
CHRISTIAN SITE

(Monte do Bom Jesus) Climbing dramatically to the hilltop pilgrimage site of Bom Jesus do Monte, 5km east of Braga, is this extraordinary staircase, with allegorical fountains, chapels and a superb view. City bus 2 runs frequently from Braga to the site, where you can climb the 580 steps (pilgrims sometimes do this on their knees) or ascend by funicular (one way/return €1.20/2).

Collector's Hostel
HOSTEL €

(☑ 253 048 124; www.collectorshostel.com; Rua Francisco Sanches 42; dm €17-20, d/tr €44/62, s/d with shared bath €27/40) This lovely hostel is lovingly run by two well-travelled women (one of whom was born in the hostel's living room) who met in Paris, restored the family house and all the furniture inside, and turned the three floors into a cosy hideaway where guests feel like they're in their grandparents' home, with a twist.

Vila Galé Collection Braga
LUXURY HOTEL €€€

(☑ 253 146 000; www.vilagale.com; Largo Carlos Amarante 150; r/ste from €144/195; ▣ ❊ @ ⓢ ⓢ) Braga's newest luxury hotel is this magnificent former hospital and convent dating from 1508, adopted by the Vila Galé hotel chain and reopened in 2018. Abounding in vaulted ceilings, interior courtyards, baroque fountains and other grandiose architectural touches, it houses 123 palatial rooms and suites with five-star amenities, complemented by a spa, two outdoor pools, two restaurants and a bar.

Livraria Centésima Página
CAFE €

(Avenida Central 118-120; snacks €3-5; ☺9am-7.30pm Mon-Sat) Tucked inside Centésima Página, an absolutely splendid bookshop with foreign-language titles, this charming cafe serves a rotating selection of tasty quiches along with salads and desserts, and has outdoor tables in the pleasantly rustic garden. Its lunch specials are a steal.

Casa de Pasto das Carvalheiras
FUSION €€

(☑ 253 046 244; www.facebook.com/casadepasto dascarvalheiras; Rua Dom Afonso Henriques 8;

small plates €5-15; ⊙ noon-3pm & 7pm-midnight Mon-Fri, noon-midnight Sat & Sun) This colourful eatery with a long bar serves up delectable, weekly changing *pratinhos* (small plates), from codfish confit with bok choy and noodles, to mushrooms with creamy polenta, to tasty cakes of *alheira* (a light garlicky sausage of poultry or game) and turnip greens. Weekday lunch menus go for €9 or €12, depending on the number of dishes you order.

ℹ Information

Turismo (🖉 253 262 550; www.visitbraga. travel; Avenida da Liberdade 1; ⊙ 9am-6.30pm Mon-Fri, 9.30am-1pm & 2-5.30pm Sat & Sun) Braga's helpful tourist office is in an art deco–style building facing busy Praça da República.

ℹ Getting There & Away

Hourly trains go to Porto (€3.25, about one hour). Direct trains also serve Coimbra (€21, 1¾ to 2¾ hours, four to seven daily) and Lisbon (€34, four hours, two to four daily).

Airport Bus (🖉 253 262 371; www.getbus.eu) travels to Porto's airport (one way/return €8/14, 50 minutes, 10 daily). **Transdev** (🖉 225 100 100; www.transdev.pt) runs buses to Viana do Castelo (€4.55, 1¾ hours).

Parque Nacional da Peneda-Gerês

Spread across four impressive granite massifs, this vast park encompasses boulder-strewn peaks, precipitous valleys, gorse-clad moorlands and forests of oak and pine. It also shelters more than 100 granite villages that, in many ways, have changed little since Portugal's founding in the 12th century.

For nature lovers, the stunning scenery here is unmatched in Portugal for outdoor adventures. There are trails and footpaths through the park, some between villages with accommodation. In Campo do Gerês (15km west of Vila do Gerês), **Equi Campo** (🖉 914 848 094, 253 357 022; www.equicampo. com; ⊙ 9am-7pm May-Sep, by arrangement Oct-Apr) organises hikes and horse-riding trips. Rio Caldo, 8km south of Vila do Gerês, is the base for water sports on the Caniçada Reservoir. English-run **Água Montanha Lazer** (🖉 925 402 000; www.aguamontanha.com; Rua da Raposeira 31; per hr kayak/SUP/pedalo €6/10/12, motorboat €35-45; 4-/10-person cottage per day €80/160, per week €525/980) rents a variety of boats and organises kayaking trips.

Convenient overnight bases for exploring the park include the old-fashioned hot springs resort of Vila do Gerês and the picturesque village of Soajo – at the park's southern and western edges respectively. Both boast a variety of sleeping and eating options. More remote villages offering simple accommodation include Campo do Gerês, Pitões das Júnias and Castro Laboreiro. Rental cottages throughout the park are available through **Adere Peneda-Gerês** (🖉 258 452 250; www.adere-pg.pt; Rua Dom

---

DON'T MISS

FIVE GREAT HIKES IN PARQUE NACIONAL PENEDA-GERÊS

Here are five of the national park's best walks, with starting point in parentheses. Park offices can provide further details.

Via Geira Roman Road (Portela do Homem, 12km north of Vila do Gerês) Trace the ancients' footsteps past dozens of intact mileposts as you follow this venerable Roman road downriver through the dense Albergaria da Mata forest to the Albufeira do Homem reservoir.

Caminhos do Pão & Caminhos da Fé (Soajo) Experience first-hand the interplay between Portuguese mountain people and their natural setting on this 8km loop through terraced fields and past ancient water mills.

Castro Laboreiro Loop (Castro Laboreiro) Climb 1km to the ruins of a medieval hilltop castle for spectacular views of the park's rugged northern mountains.

Mosteiro de Santa Maria das Júnias Loop (Pitões das Júnias) This 2.5km loop descends to a secluded valley where a 13th-century Cistercian monastery slumbers in solitude.

Trilho Pertinho do Céu (Gaviera; http://trilhos.arcosdevaldevez.pt/activities/trilho-pertinho-do-ceu) Loop through high pastures and picturesque stone villages on the 8km 'Close to Heaven Trail'.

Manuel I; ⊗9am-12.30pm & 2.30-6pm Mon-Fri) in Ponte da Barca.

★ Casa do Adro
INN €

(📞258 576 327; Largo do Eiró; r €50; 🅿🛜) This manor house (rather than a cottage), off Largo do Eiró by Soajo's parish church, dates from the 18th century. Rooms are huge, furnished with antiques and blessed with sweet vineyard and village vistas. There is a minimum two-night stay in August.

Parque Campismo Lamas de Mouro
CAMPGROUND €

(📝251 466 041; www.montesdelaboreiro.pt/parquecampismo.pdf; Lamas de Mouro; per adult/child/tent/car €4.20/2.80/3.70/3, 2-/4-/6-person bungalow €55/65/75) This tremendous private campground near boulder fields and flowering meadows has shady creekside tent sites plus four cosy pine-clad bungalows with kitchenettes. It rents out mountain bikes (€2.50/10 per hour/day) and offers treetop adventures, canyoning and hikes with shepherds. There are a couple of restaurants not too far away in the Lamas de Mouro village northwest of the park gate.

★ O Abocanhado
PORTUGUESE €€

(📝253 352 944; www.abocanhado.com; Brufe; mains €12-18; ⊗12.30-3.30pm & 7.30-9.30pm) With its stunning panoramic terrace high above the Rio Homem, this gorgeously situated restaurant is a temple to the finest ingredients that the surrounding countryside has to offer, including *javali* (wild boar), *veado* (venison) and *coelho* (rabbit), along with beef and goat raised in the adjacent fields. Finish with *requeijão* – a soft goat's cheese so fresh it's actually sweet.

ⓘ Information

Park Information Centre (Centro de Educação Ambiental do Vidoeiro; 📝253 390 110; www.icnf.pt; Lugar do Vidoeiro 99; ⊗9am-1pm & 2-5pm Mon-Fri) About 1km north of Vila do Gerês. Other park offices, from northwest to southeast, are located in the villages of Lamas de Mouro, Lindoso, Mezio, Campo do Gerês and Montalegre.

ⓘ Getting There & Away

Public transport within the park is extremely limited, so it's helpful to have your own wheels. You can rent cars from **Avic** (📝253 203 910; www.avic.pt; Rua Gabriel Pereira de Castro 28; ⊗9am-7pm Mon-Fri, 9am-12.30pm Sat) in Braga.

SURVIVAL GUIDE

ⓘ Directory A–Z

ACCOMMODATION

Although you can usually show up in any town and find a room on the spot, it's worthwhile booking ahead, especially for July and August.

LGBT+ TRAVELLERS

In 2010 Portugal legalised gay marriage, becoming the sixth European country to do so. Most Portuguese profess a laissez-faire attitude about same-sex couples, although how out you can be depends on where you are in Portugal. In Lisbon, Porto and the Algarve, acceptance has increased, whereas in most other areas, same-sex couples would be met with incomprehension. In this conservative Catholic country, homosexuality is still outside the norm. And while homophobic violence is extremely rare, discrimination has been reported in schools and workplaces.

Lisbon has the country's best gay and lesbian network and nightlife. Lisbon and Porto hold Gay Pride marches, but outside these events the gay community keeps a discreet profile.

MONEY

ATMs are widely available, except in the smallest villages. Credit cards are accepted in midrange and high-end establishments.

OPENING HOURS

Opening hours vary throughout the year. We provide high-season opening hours; hours will generally decrease in the shoulder and low seasons.

Banks 8.30am to 3pm Monday to Friday

Bars 7pm to 2am

Cafes 9am to 7pm

Clubs 11pm to 4am Thursday to Saturday

Restaurants noon to 3pm and 7 to 10pm

Shopping malls 10am to 10pm

Shops 9.30am to noon and 2 to 7pm Monday to Friday, 10am to 1pm Saturday

PUBLIC HOLIDAYS

Banks, offices, department stores and some shops close on the public holidays listed here. On New Year's Day, Easter Sunday, Labour Day and Christmas Day, even *turismos* close.

New Year's Day 1 January

Carnaval Tuesday February/March – the day before Ash Wednesday

Good Friday March/April

Liberty Day 25 April

Labour Day 1 May

Corpus Christi May/June – ninth Thursday after Easter

Portugal Day 10 June – also known as Camões and Communities Day

Feast of the Assumption 15 August
Republic Day 5 October
All Saints' Day 1 November
Independence Day 1 December
Feast of the Immaculate Conception
8 December
Christmas Day 25 December

TELEPHONE

To call Portugal from abroad, dial the international access code (00), then Portugal's country code (351), then the number. All domestic numbers have nine digits, and there are no area codes. The main domestic mobile operators are Vodafone, Optimus and TMN; all sell prepaid SIM cards that can be used in unlocked European, Australian and quad-band US mobiles.

Getting There & Away

AIR

Most international flights arrive in Lisbon, though Porto and Faro also receive some. For more information, including live arrival and departure schedules, see www.ana.pt.

LAND

Portugal shares a land border only with Spain, but there is both bus and train service linking the two countries, with onward connections to the rest of mainland Europe.

Bus

The major long-distance carriers that serve European destinations are **Busabout** (www.busabout.com) and **Eurolines** (www.eurolines.eu); though these carriers serve Portugal, the country is not currently included in the multicity travel passes of either company.

For some European routes, Eurolines is affiliated with the big Portuguese operators **Internorte** (☏ 707 200 512; www.internorte.pt) and **Eva Transportes** (☏ 289 589 055; www.eva-bus.com).

Train

There is nightly sleeper service between Madrid and Lisbon. Spanish trains also run from Vigo (Galicia) to Porto. Purchase tickets online through **Renfe** (www.renfe.com).

The train journey from Paris (Gare de Montparnasse) to Lisbon takes 21 hours and stops in a number of Spanish cities along the way. Buy tickets direct from **SNCF** (www.oui.sncf).

Getting Around

AIR

TAP (www.flytap.com) has multiple daily Lisbon–Porto and Lisbon–Faro flights (taking less than one hour) year-round.

BUS

A host of small private bus operators, most amalgamated into regional companies, run a dense network of services across the country. Among the largest are **Rede Expressos** (☏ 707 223 344; www.rede-expressos.pt), **Rodonorte** (☏ 259 340 710; www.rodonorte.pt) and the Algarve-based Eva Transportes.

Bus services are of four general types.

Alta Qualidade A fast deluxe category offered by some companies.

Carreiras Marked 'CR'; slow, seemingly stopping at every crossroads.

Expressos Comfortable, fast buses between major cities.

Rápidas Quick regional buses.

Even in summer you'll have little problem booking an *expresso* ticket for the same or next day. Fares and schedules are available online or at bus stations.

CAR & MOTORCYCLE
Automobile Associations

Automóvel Club de Portugal (ACP; ☏ 219 429 113, 24hr emergency assistance 808 222 222; www.acp.pt), Portugal's national auto club, has a reciprocal arrangement with several foreign automobile clubs, and can provide medical, legal and breakdown assistance.

Hire

To rent a car in Portugal you must be at least 25 years old and have held your driving licence for more than a year. The widest choice of car-hire companies is at Lisbon, Porto and Faro airports. Scooters/motorcycles (from €30/60 per day) are available in larger cities and all over coastal Algarve.

Road Rules

Speed limits for cars and motorcycles are generally 50km/h in towns and villages, 90km/h outside built-up areas and 120km/h on motorways. The legal blood-alcohol limit is 0.05%, and there are fines of up to €2500 for drink-driving. It's also illegal in Portugal to drive while talking on a mobile phone.

TRAIN

Train travel in Portugal is extremely affordable, with a decent network between major towns. Visit **Comboios de Portugal** (☏ 707 210 220; www.cp.pt) for schedules and prices.

There are four main types of long-distance service. Note that international services are marked IN on timetables.

Regional (R) Slow; stop everywhere.

Interregional (IR) Reasonably fast.

Intercidade (IC) *Rápido* or express trains.

Alfa Pendular Deluxe Marginally faster than express and much pricier.

Romania

POP 19.7 MILLION

Best Places to Eat

➡ Lacrimi şi Sfinţi (p930)

➡ Roata (p939)

➡ Homemade (p942)

➡ Caru' cu Bere (p930)

➡ Bistro de l'Arte (p934)

Best Places to Stay

➡ Casa Georgius Krauss (p935)

➡ Casa del Sole (p942)

➡ Little Bucharest Old Town Hostel (p929)

➡ Bella Muzica (p933)

➡ Lol & Lola (p939)

Why Go?

Beautiful and beguiling, Romania's rural landscape remains relatively untouched by the country's urban evolution. It's a land of aesthetically stirring hand-ploughed fields, sheep-instigated traffic jams and lots of homemade plum brandy. Most visitors focus their attention on Transylvania, with its legacy of fortified Saxon towns like Braşov and Sighişoara, plus tons of eye-catching natural beauty. Across the Carpathians, the Unesco-listed painted monasteries dot Bucovina. The Danube Delta has more than 300 species of birds, including many rare varieties, and is an ideal spot for bird-watching. Energetic cities like Timişoara, Sibiu, Cluj-Napoca and, especially, Bucharest offer culture – both high- and low-brow – and showcase Romania as a rapidly evolving European country.

When to Go
Bucharest

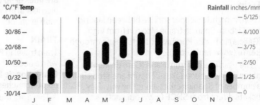

May Trees in full blossom; bird-watching in the Danube Delta at its best.

Jun Mountain hiking starts in mid-June; castles and museums are open and in high gear.

Sep The summer heat is gone, but sunny days are perfect for exploring big cities.

Entering the Country

Travel to Romania does not pose any unusual problems. Bucharest has air connections with many European capitals and large cities, and train and long-haul bus services are frequent. At the time of research, Romania was not a member of the EU's common customs and border area, the Schengen area, so even if you're entering from an EU member state (including Bulgaria or Hungary), you'll still have to show a passport or valid EU identity card. Border crossings can get crowded, particularly during weekends, so prepare for delays.

ITINERARIES

One Week
Spend a day ambling around the capital (p926), then take a train to Braşov (p932) – Transylvania's main event – for castles, activities and beer at street-side cafes. Spend a day in the medieval citadel of Sighişoara (p935), then catch a train back to Bucharest or on to Budapest.

Two Weeks
Arrive in Bucharest by plane or Timişoara by train, then head into Transylvania (p932), devoting a day or two each to Braşov (p932), Sighişoara (p935) and Sibiu (p936). Tour the southern painted monasteries in Bucovina (p940), then continue on to Bucharest (p926).

Essential Food & Drink

Romanian food borrows heavily from its neighbours, including Turkey, Hungary and the Balkans, and is centred on pork and other meats. Farm-fresh, organic fruits and vegetables are in abundance, lending flavour and colour to a long list of soups and salads. Condiments typically include sour cream, garlic sauce and grated sheep's cheese.

Ciorbă de burtă Garlicky tripe soup that's inexplicably a local favourite.

Ciorbă de perişoare A spicy soup with meatballs and vegetables.

Covrigi Oven-baked pretzels served warm from windows around town.

Mămăligă Cornmeal mush, sometimes topped with sour cream or cheese.

Papanaşi Arguably the county's most popular dessert and made of fried dough, stuffed with sweetened curd cheese and covered with jam and heavy cream.

Sarmale Spiced meat wrapped in cabbage or grape leaves.

Tochitură A hearty stew that's usually comprised of pan-fried pork, sometimes mixed with other meats, in a spicy tomato or wine sauce.

Ţuică Fiery plum brandy sold in water bottles at roadside rest stops.

AT A GLANCE

Area 238,391 sq km

Capital Bucharest

Country Code 40

Currency Romanian lei

Emergency 112

Language Romanian

Visas Not required for citizens of the EU, Australia, USA, Canada or New Zealand

Sleeping Price Ranges

The following price ranges refer to a double room with a bathroom, including breakfast (Bucharest prices tend to be higher).

€ less than 150 lei

€€ 150–300 lei

€€€ more than 300 lei

Eating Price Ranges

The following price ranges refer to an average main course.

€ less than 20 lei

€€ 20–40 lei

€€€ more than 40 lei

Resources

Autogari.ro (www.autogari.ro)

Lonely Planet (www.lonelyplanet.com/romania)

Romania Ministry of Tourism (www.romania.travel)

Romania Highlights

1 Braşov (p932) Basing yourself here to ascend castles and mountains (and castles on top of mountains).

2 Bucovina (p940) Following the Unesco World Heritage line of painted monasteries.

3 Sibiu (p936) Soaking in this beautifully restored Saxon town.

4 Sighişoara (p935) Exploring this medieval citadel and birthplace of Dracula.

5 Danube Delta (p937) Rowing through the tributaries and the riot of nature.

6 Bucharest (p926) Enjoying the museums and cacophonous nightlife of the capital.

BUCHAREST

🎵 021, 031 / POP 1.86 MILLION

Romania's capital sometimes gets a bad rap, but in fact it's dynamic, energetic and lots of fun. Many travellers give the city just a night or two before heading off to Transylvania, but that's not enough time. Allow at least a few days to take in the very good museums, stroll the parks and hang out at trendy cafes and drinking gardens. While much of the centre is modern and the buildings are in various stages of disrepair, you'll find splendid 17th- and 18th-century Orthodox churches and graceful belle époque villas tucked away in quiet corners. Communism changed the face of the city forever, and nowhere is this more evident than at the gargantuan Palace of Parliament, the grandest (and arguably crassest) tribute to dictatorial megalomania you'll ever see.

◉ Sights

◉ South of the Centre

★ Palace of Parliament   HISTORIC BUILDING
(Palatul Parlamentului, Casa Poporului; ⬚ tour bookings 0733-558 102; www.cic.cdep.ro; B-dul Naţiunile Unite; adult/student complete tours 45/23 lei, standard tours 40/20 lei; ⊙ 9am-5pm Mar-Oct, 10am-4pm Nov-Feb; Ⓜ Izvor) The Palace of Parliament is the world's second-largest administrative building (after the Pentagon) and former dictator Nicolae Ceauşescu's most infamous creation. Started in 1984 (and still unfinished), the 330,000-sq-metre building has more than 3000 rooms. Entry is by guided tour only (book ahead). Entry to the palace is from B-dul Naţiunile Unite on the building's northern side (to find it, face the front of the palace from B-dul Unirii and walk around the building to the right). Bring your passport.

Great Synagogue   SYNAGOGUE
(⬚ 0734-708 970; Str Adamache 11; ⊙ 10am-4pm Mon-Thu, to 1pm Fri & Sun; Ⓜ Piaţa Unirii) FREE This important synagogue dates from the mid-19th century and was established by migrating Polish Jews; entry is free, but a donation (10 lei) is expected. It's hard to find, hidden on three sides by public housing blocks, but worth the effort to see the meticulously restored interior and to take in the main exhibition on Jewish life and the Holocaust in Romania.

◉ Historic Centre & Piaţa Revoluţiei

Bucharest's Historic Centre (Centrul Istoric), sometimes referred to as the 'Old Town', lies south of Piaţa Revoluţiei. It was the seat of power in the 15th century but today is filled with clubs and bars. Piaţa Revoluţiei saw the heaviest fighting in the overthrow of communism in 1989. Those days are commemorated by the **Rebirth Memorial** (Memorialul Renaşterii; Calea Victoriei, Piaţa Revoluţiei; ⊙ 24hr; Ⓜ Universitate) in the centre of the square.

Stavropoleos Church   CHURCH
(⬚ 021-313 4747; www.stavropoleos.ro; Str Stavropoleos 4; ⊙ 8.30am-6pm; Ⓜ Piaţa Unirii) The tiny and lovely Stavropoleos Church, which dates from 1724, perches a bit oddly a block over from some of Bucharest's craziest Old Town carousing. It's one church, though, that will make a lasting impression, with its

courtyard filled with tombstones, an ornate wooden interior and carved wooden doors.

★ Romanian Athenaeum   HISTORIC BUILDING
(Ateneul Român; ⬚ box office 021-315 6875; www.fge.org.ro; Str Benjamin Franklin 1-3; tickets 20-70 lei; ⊙ box office noon-7pm Tue-Fri, from 4pm Sat, 10-11am Sun; Ⓜ Universitate, Piaţa Romană) The exquisite Athenaeum is the majestic heart of Romania's classical-music tradition. Scenes from Romanian history are featured on the interior fresco inside the Big Hall on the 1st floor; the dome is 41m high. A huge appeal dubbed 'Give a Penny for the Athenaeum' saved it from disaster after funds dried up in the late 19th century. Today it's home to the George Enescu Philharmonic Orchestra and normally only open during concerts, but you can often take a peek inside.

National Art Museum   MUSEUM
(Muzeul Naţional de Artă; ⬚ information 021-313 3030; www.mnar.arts.ro; Calea Victoriei 49-53; adult/child 25/10 lei; ⊙ 11am-7pm Wed-Sun; Ⓜ Universitate) Housed in the 19th-century Royal Palace, this massive, multipart museum – all signed in English – houses two permanent galleries: one for National Art and the other for European Masters. The national gallery is particularly strong on ancient and medieval art, while the European gallery includes some 12,000 pieces and is laid out by nationality.

◉ North of the Centre

Luxurious villas and parks line grand Şos Kiseleff, which begins at Piaţa Victoriei. The major landmark is the **Triumphal Arch** (Arcul de Triumf; Piaţa Arcul de Triumf; ⊙ closed to the public; Ⓜ Aviatorilor), which stands halfway up Şos Kiseleff.

★ Former Ceauşescu Residence   MUSEUM
(Primăverii Palace; ⬚ 021-318 0989; www.casaceausescu.ro; B-dul Primăverii 50; guided tours in English adult/child 50/40 lei; ⊙ 10am-5pm Tue-Sun; ⬚ 131, 282, 301, 331, 330, 335, Ⓜ Aviatorilor) This restored villa is the former main residence of Nicolae and Elena Ceauşescu, who lived here for around two decades up until the end in 1989. Everything has been returned to its former lustre, including the couple's bedroom and the private apartments of the three Ceauşescu children. Highlights include a cinema in the basement, Elena's opulent private chamber, and the back garden and swimming pool. Reserve a tour in advance by phone or on the website.

Central Bucharest

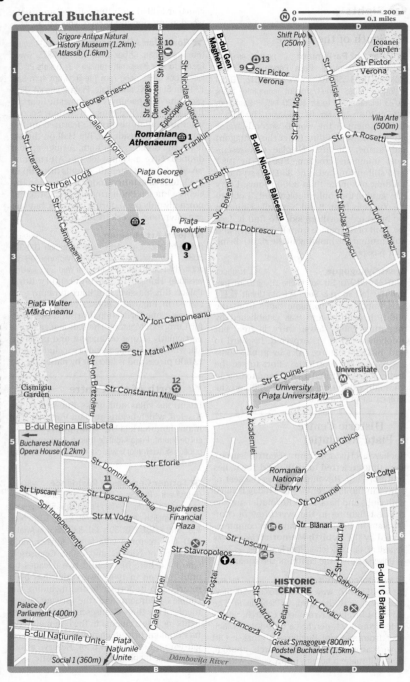

ROMANIA BUCHAREST

N 0 ————— 200 m
0 ————— 0.1 miles

Grigore Antipa Natural
History Museum (1.2km);
Atlassib (1.6km)

Shift Pub
(250m)

Icoanei
Garden

B-dul Gen Magheru

Str Mendeleev ⬤10

⬤13

9⬤ Str Pictor
Verona

Str Pictor
Verona

Str Georges
Clemenceau

Str Nicolae Golescu

Str
Episcopiei

Str George Enescu

Str Dionisie Lupu

Calea Victoriei

Romanian Athenaeum 🏛1

Str Franklin

B-dul Nicolae Bălcescu

Vila Arte
(500m)

Str Luterană

Piaţa George Enescu

Str C A Rosetti

Str Stirbei Vodă

Str C A Rosetti

Str Nicolae Filipescu

Str Tudor Arghezi

Str Ion Câmpineanu

🏛2

Piaţa
Revoluţiei

Str Boteanu

Str D I Dobrescu

❗3

Piaţa Walter
Mărăcineanu

Str Ion Câmpineanu

✉ Str Matei Millo

Str Ion Brezoianu

12 ✪

Str Constantin Mille

Str E Quinet

University
(Piaţa Universităţii)

Universitate
Ⓜ

ⓘ

Cişmigiu
Garden

Str Academiei

B-dul Regina Elisabeta

Bucharest National
Opera House (1.2km)

Str Domniţa Anastasia

Str Eforie

Str Ion Ghica

Romanian
National
Library

Str Colţei

Str Lipscani

11 ⬤
Str Lipscani

Str M Vodă

Bucharest
Financial
Plaza

Str Doamnei

Str Blănari

🖼6

🖼5

B-dul I C Brătianu

Spl Independenţei

Str Ilfov

✖7
Str Stavropoleos

🚹4

Str Lipscani

Str Hanul cu Tei

Str Gabroveni

HISTORIC
CENTRE

Str Covaci

8✖

Palace of
Parliament (400m)

Calea Victoriei

Str Poştei

Str Selari

Str Smârdan

Str Franceză

Great Synagogue (800m);
Podstel Bucharest (1.5km)

B-dul Naţiunile Unite

Piaţa
Naţiunile
Unite

Dâmboviţa River

Social 1 (360m)

Central Bucharest

Grigore Antipa Natural History Museum
MUSEUM

(Muzeul de Istorie Naturală Grigore Antipa; ☑ 021-312 8826; www.antipa.ro; Şos Kiseleff 1; adult/student 20/5 lei; ☉ 10am-8pm Tue-Sun Apr-Oct, to 6pm Tue-Fri, to 7pm Sat & Sun Nov-Mar; 🚌; Ⓜ Piaţa Victoriei) One of the few attractions in Bucharest aimed squarely at kids, this natural-history museum, showing off Romania's plant and animal life, has been thoroughly renovated. It features lots of modern bells and whistles, such as video displays, games and interactive exhibits. Much of it has English signage.

National Village Museum
MUSEUM

(Muzeul Naţional al Satului; ☑ 021-317 9103; www.muzeul-satului.ro; Şos Kiseleff 28-30; adult/child 15/4 lei; ☉ 9am-7pm Tue-Sun, to 5pm Mon; 🚌; Ⓜ Piaţa Victoriei) On the shores of Herăstrău Lake, this museum is a terrific open-air collection of several dozen homesteads, churches, mills and windmills relocated from rural Romania. Built in 1936 by royal decree, it is one of Europe's oldest open-air museums and a good choice for kids to boot.

🛏 Sleeping

Hotels in Bucharest are typically aimed at business people, and prices are higher than in the rest of the country; booking in

advance may help secure a discount. Room rates can drop by as much as half in midsummer (July and August), which is widely considered low season. The situation with hostels continues to improve and Bucharest now has some of the best cheap lodgings in the country.

★ Little Bucharest Old Town Hostel
HOSTEL €

(☑ 0786-055 287; www.littlebucharest.ro; Str Smârdan 15; dm 35-60 lei; r 145 lei; ❀@🤝; Ⓜ Piaţa Unirii) Bucharest's most central hostel, in the middle of the lively historic centre, is superclean, white-walled and well run. Accommodation is over two floors, with dorms ranging from six to 12 beds. Private doubles are also available. The staff are travel friendly and youth-oriented and can advise on sightseeing and fun. Book over the website or by email.

Podstel Bucharest
HOSTEL €

(☑ 021-336 2127; www.podstel.com; Str Olimpului 13a; dm 50-65 lei, d 150 lei; @🤝; Ⓜ Piaţa Unirii) Arguably the nicest and most chill of Bucharest's hostels is a 10-minute walk southwest of Piaţa Unirii. The location is quiet and mainly residential, and there's a beautiful garden set up like a Moroccan tearoom out back. Sleeping is in six-bed mixed dorms, with one good-value private double. Friendly and welcoming staff.

Vila Arte
BOUTIQUE HOTEL €€

(☑ 021-210 1035; www.vilaarte.ro; Str Vasile Lascăr 78; s/d 250/300 lei; ❀✱@🤝; Ⓜ Piaţa Romană, 🚌 5, 21) A renovated villa transformed into an excellent-value boutique hotel stuffed with original art that pushes the envelope on design and colour at this price point. The services are top drawer and the helpful reception makes every guest feel special. The 'Ottoman' room is done in an updated Turkish style, with deep-red spreads and fabrics, and oriental carpets.

Rembrandt Hotel
HOTEL €€€

(☑ 021-313 9315; www.rembrandt.ro; Str Smârdan 11; s/d tourist 300/400 lei, standard 500/600 lei, business from 700 lei; ❀✱@🤝; Ⓜ Universitate) Prices have gone through the roof here in the past couple of years, though the hotel's personal touch and stylish rooms, with big, comfy beds and parquet floors, still justify a short-stay splurge. The location, in the historic centre just opposite the landmark National Bank, is within easy reach of some of the best cafes and bars.

ROMANIA BUCHAREST

✕ Eating

Caru' cu Bere
ROMANIAN €€

(☎0726-282 373; www.carucubere.ro; Str Stavropoleos 3-5; mains 25-50 lei; ⊙8am-midnight Sun-Thu, to 2am Fri & Sat; 🐾; Ⓜ Piața Unirii) Despite a decidedly touristy-leaning atmosphere, with peasant-girl hostesses and sporadic traditional song-and-dance numbers, Bucharest's oldest beerhouse continues to draw in a strong local crowd. The colourful belle-époque interior and stained-glass windows dazzle, as does the classic Romanian food. Dinner reservations are essential.

Shift Pub
INTERNATIONAL €€

(☎021-211 2272; www.shiftpub.ro; Str General Eremia Grigorescu 17; mains 25-40 lei; ⊙noon-11pm Sun-Thu, to 1am Fri & Sat; 🐾; Ⓜ Piața Romană) Great choice for salads and burgers as well as numerous beef and pork dishes, often sporting novel Asian, Middle Eastern or Mexican taste touches. Try to arrive slightly before meal times to grab a coveted table in the tree-covered garden.

Social 1
INTERNATIONAL €€

(☎0733-222 200; www.social1.ro; B-dul Unirii 1; mains 27-50 lei; ⊙10am-midnight Tue-Sun, from noon Mon; 🐾🐾) Pair a visit to the Palace of Parliament with breakfast or lunch at this cheerful spot, conveniently situated just in front of Ceaușescu's behemoth. There's something for everyone on the menu: grills, burgers, ribs, fish and pasta. The quality is high, the prices are moderate and the service attentive. Sit outside in nice weather. Book in advance to be safe.

★ Lacrimi și Sfinți
ROMANIAN €€€

(☎0725-558 286; www.lacrimisisfinti.com; Str Șepcari 16; mains 30-60 lei; ⊙12.30pm-1am Tue-Sun, from 6.30pm Mon; 🐾; Ⓜ Piața Unirii) A true destination restaurant in the historic centre, Lacrimi și Sfinți takes modern trends such as farm-to-table freshness and organic sourcing and marries them to old-school Romanian recipes. The philosophy extends to the simple, peasant-inspired interior, where the woodworking and decorative elements come from old farmhouses. The result is food that feels authentic and satisfying. Book in advance.

🍸 Drinking & Nightlife

Bucharest excels at places to drink, whether you prefer coffee, wine, beer or cocktails. The city has an exploding artisanal coffee scene, and also some very good pubs and clubs – many of them to be found in the historic centre. In summer, look out for terraces and gardens, usually in a secluded spot under a canopy of trees.

★ Grădina Verona
CAFE

(☎0732-003 060; www.facebook.com/gradina verona; Str Pictor Verona 13-15; ⊙10am-midnight May-Sep; 🐾; Ⓜ Piața Romană) A garden oasis hidden behind the Cărturești bookshop, serving standard-issue but excellent espresso drinks and some of the most inspired iced-tea and lemonade infusions you're likely to find in Romania, such as peony flower, mango and lime (it's not bad).

M60
CAFE

(☎031-410 0010; www.facebook.com/m60cafeam zei; Str Mendeleev 2; ⊙8am-midnight Mon-Fri, from 10am Sat & Sun; 🐾; Ⓜ Piața Romană) M60 is a category-buster, transforming through the day from one of the city's preeminent morning coffee houses to a handy lunch spot (healthy salads and vegetarian options) and then morphing into a meet-up and drinks bar in the evening. It's been a hit since opening day, as city residents warmed to its clean, minimalist Scandinavian design and living-room feel.

Origo
CAFE

(☎0757-086 689; www.origocoffee.ro; Str Lipscani 9; ⊙7am-1am Sun, Tue & Wed, to 3am Thu-Sat; 🐾; Ⓜ Piața Unirii) Some of the best coffee in town and *the* best place to hang out in the morning, grab a table and gab with friends. Lots of special coffee roasts and an unlimited number of ways to imbibe. There are a dozen pavement tables for relaxing on a sunny day.

☆ Entertainment

Bucharest has a lively night scene of concerts, theatre, rock and jazz. Check the weekly guide *Șapte Seri* (www.sapteseri.ro) for entertainment listings. Another good source for what's on is the website www.iconcert.ro. To buy tickets online, visit the websites of the leading ticketing agencies: www.myticket. ro and www.eventim.ro.

Control
LIVE MUSIC

(☎0733-927 861; www.control-club.ro; Str Constantin Mille 4; ⊙1pm-late; 🐾; Ⓜ Universitate) This is a favourite among club-goers who like alternative, turbo-folk, indie and garage sounds. Hosts both live acts and DJs, depending on the night.

Bucharest National Opera House
OPERA

(Opera Națională București; ☎ box office 0743-278 335; www.operanb.ro; B-dul Mihail Kogălniceanu

70-72; tickets 20-80 lei; box office 10am-1pm & 2-7pm; M Eroilor) The city's premier venue for classical opera and ballet. Buy tickets online or at the venue box office.

 Shopping

Cărtureşti Verona   BOOKS
(📞 0728-828 916; www.carturesti.ro; Str Pictor Verona 13-15, cnr B-dul Nicolae Bălcescu; ⊘10am-10pm; M Piaţa Romană) This bookshop, music store, tearoom and funky backyard garden is a must-visit. Amazing collection of design, art and architecture books, as well as carefully selected CDs and DVDs, including many classic Romanian films with English subtitles. Also sells Lonely Planet guidebooks.

ℹ **Information**

You'll find hundreds of bank branches and ATMs in the centre. Banks usually have currency-exchange offices, but bring your passport as you'll have to show it to change money.

Bucharest Tourist Information Center
(📞 021-305 5500, ext 1003; http://seebucharest.ro; Piaţa Universităţii; ⊘10am-5pm Mon-Fri, to 2pm Sat & Sun; M Universitate) This small, poorly stocked tourist office in the underpass to the Universitate metro station is rarely open but seems to be the best the city can offer. While there's not much information on hand, the English-speaking staff can field basic questions.

Central Post Office (📞 021-315 9030; www.posta-romana.ro; Str Matei Millo 12; ⊘8am-7.30pm Mon-Fri, 9am-1pm Sat; M Universitate)

Emergency Clinic Hospital (Floreasca Hospital; 📞 021-599 2300; www.urgentafloreasca.ro; Calea Floreasca 8; ⊘24hr; M Ştefan cel Mare) The first port of call in any serious emergency. Arguably the city's, and country's, best emergency hospital.

ℹ **Getting There & Away**

AIR

All international and domestic flights use **Henri Coandă International Airport** (OTP; Otopeni; 📞 021-204 1000; www.bucharestairports.ro; Şos Bucureşti-Ploieşti, 📞 783), often referred to in conversation by its previous name, 'Otopeni'. Henri Coandă is 17km north of Bucharest on the main road to Braşov. Arrivals and departures use separate terminals (arrivals is to the north). The airport is a modern facility, with restaurants, newsagents, currency-exchange offices and ATMs. There are 24-hour information desks at both terminals.

The airport is the hub for the national carrier **Tarom** (📞 call centre 021-204 6464, office 021-316 0220; www.tarom.ro; Spl Independenţei 17,

city centre; ⊘9am-5pm Mon-Fri; M Piaţa Unirii). Tarom has a comprehensive network of internal flights to major Romanian cities as well as to capitals and big cities around Europe and the Middle East. At the time of writing, there were no direct flights from Bucharest to North America or Southeast Asia.

BUS

Several coach companies dominate the market for travel from Bucharest to cities around Romania.

The best bet for finding a connection is to consult the websites www.autogari.ro and www.cditransport.ro. Both keep up-to-date timetables and are fairly easy to manage, though www.cditransport.ro is only in Romanian. Be sure to follow up with a phone call just to make sure a particular bus is running on a particular day. Another option is to ask your hotel to help with arrangements or book through a travel agency.

Bucharest has several bus stations and they don't seem to follow any discernible logic for which station should serve which destination. Even residents have a hard time making sense of it. When purchasing a bus ticket, always ask where the bus leaves from.

CAR & MOTORCYCLE

Traffic in Bucharest is heavy and you won't want to drive around for very long. If you're travelling by car and just want to visit Bucharest for the day, it's more sensible to park at a metro station on the outskirts and take the metro into the city.

TRAIN

Gara de Nord (📞 reservations 021-9521; www.cfrcalatori.ro; Piaţa Gara de Nord 1; M Gara de Nord) is the central station for most national and all international trains. The station is accessible by metro from the centre of the city. Buy tickets at station ticket windows. A seat reservation is compulsory if you are travelling with an InterRail or Eurail pass. Check the latest train schedules on either www.cfr.ro or the German site www.bahn.de (when searching timetables, use German spellings for cities, ie 'Bukarest Nord' for Bucharest Gara de Nord).

Following are sample fares and destination times from Bucharest to major Romanian cities on faster IC (Inter-City) trains: Braşov (48 lei, three hours, 15 daily), Cluj-Napoca (90 lei, 7½ hours, five daily), Sibiu (70 lei, six hours, two daily), Sighişoara (70 lei, five hours, two daily) and Timişoara (112 lei, 9 to 10 hours, two daily).

ℹ **Getting Around**

TO/FROM THE AIRPORT
Bus

To get to Henri Coandă International Airport from the centre, take express bus 783, which leaves every 15 minutes between 6am and 11pm (every half-hour at weekends) from Piaţas Unirii and Victoriei and points in between. The Piaţa Unirii stop is on the south side.

Taxi

To hail a taxi at the airport, go to a series of touch screens located in the arrivals hall, where various taxi companies and their rates are listed. Choose any company offering rates from 1.69 to 1.89 lei per kilometre (there's little difference in quality). A reputable taxi to the centre should cost no more than 50 lei.

PUBLIC TRANSPORT

Bucharest's public transport system of the metro, buses, trams and trolleybuses is operated by the transport authority **RATB** (Regia Autonomă de Transport Bucureşti; 021-9391; www.ratb. ro). The system runs daily from about 4.30am to approximately 11.30pm.

To use buses, trams or trolleybuses, you must first purchase an 'Activ' or 'Multiplu' magnetic card (3.70 lei) from any STB street kiosk, which you then load with credit that is discharged as you enter the transport vehicles. Trips cost 1.30 lei each.

Metro stations are identified by a large letter 'M'. To use the metro, buy a magnetic-strip ticket available at ticketing machines or cashiers inside station entrances (have small bills handy). Tickets valid for two journeys cost 5 lei.

TRANSYLVANIA

After a century of being name-checked in literature and cinema, the word 'Transylvania' enjoys worldwide recognition. The mere mention conjures a vivid landscape of mountains, castles, spooky moonlight and at least one well-known count with a wicked overbite. Unexplained puncture wounds notwithstanding, Transylvania is all those things and more. A melange of architecture and chic sidewalk cafes punctuate the towns of Braşov, Sighişoara and Sibiu, while the vibrant student town Cluj-Napoca has some vigorous nightlife.

Braşov

0268 / POP 276,090

Gothic spires, medieval gateways, Soviet blocks and a huge Hollywood-style sign: Braşov's skyline is instantly compelling. A number of medieval watchtowers still glower over the town. Between them sparkle baroque buildings and churches, while easy-going cafes line main square Piaţa Sfat-

ului. Visible from here is forested Mt Tâmpa, sporting 'Braşov' in huge white letters.

◉ Sights

In addition to the sights below, explore the **Old Town Fortifications** that line the centre on the eastern and western flanks. Many have been restored.

Black Church CHURCH
(Biserica Neagră; 0268-511 824; www.honterus gemeinde.ro; Curtea Johannes Honterus 2; adult/student/child 10/6/3 lei; ⊙10am-7pm Tue-Sat, from noon Sun Apr-Oct, 10am-4pm Tue-Sat, from noon Sun Nov-Mar) Romania's largest Gothic church rises triumphantly over Braşov's old town. Built between 1385 and 1477, this German Lutheran church was named for its charred appearance after the town's Great Fire in 1689. Restoration of the church took a century. Today it stands 65m high at its bell tower's tallest point. Organ recitals are held in the church three times a week during July and August, usually at 6pm Tuesday, Thursday and Saturday.

St Nicholas' Cathedral CHURCH
(Biserica Sfântul Nicolae; Piaţa Unirii 1; ⊙7am-6pm) FREE With forested hills rising behind its prickly Gothic spires, St Nicholas' Cathedral is one of Braşov's most spectacular views. First built in wood in 1392, it was replaced by a Gothic stone church in 1495 and later embellished in Byzantine style. It was once enclosed by military walls; today the site has a small cemetery. Inside are murals of Romania's last king and queen, covered by plaster to protect them from communist leaders and uncovered in 2004.

Mt Tâmpa MOUNTAIN
(Muntele Tâmpa) Rising 940m high and visible around Braşov, Mt Tâmpa is adorned with its very own Hollywood-style sign. Hard as it is to imagine, it was the site of a mass-impaling of 40 noblemen by Vlad Ţepeş. Banish such ghoulish images from your head as you take the **cable car** (Telecabina; 0268-478 657; Aleea Tiberiu Brediceanu; one way/return adult 10/18 lei, child 6/10 lei; ⊙9.30am-5pm Tue-Sun, noon-6pm Mon), or hike (about an hour), to reach a small viewing platform offering stunning views over the city. There's a cafe at the top.

⌂ Sleeping

Rolling Stone Hostel HOSTEL €
(0268-513 965; www.rollingstone.ro; Str Piatra Mare 2a; dm/r from 46/170 lei; P @ 🕸) Powered

Braşov

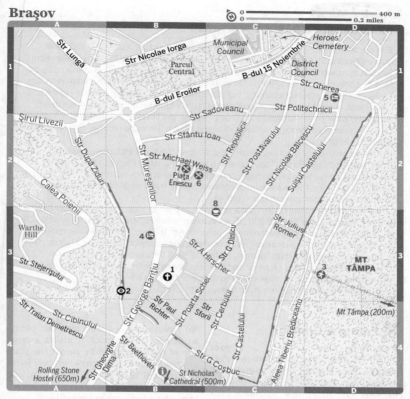

by enthusiastic staff, Rolling Stone has clean dorm rooms that sleep between six and 10. Most rooms have high ceilings and convenient touches like lockers and reading lamps for each bed. Private doubles are comfy, or sleep in the wood-beamed attic for a stowaway vibe. Maps and excellent local advice are supplied the moment you step through the door.

★ **Bella Muzica**　　　　　　　HOTEL €€
(☏ 0268-477 956; www.bellamuzica.ro; Piaţa Sfatului 19; s/d/apt from 250/290/560 lei; ❇ 🛜) A regal feel permeates Bella Muzica, housed within a 400-year-old building, thanks to its tastefully restored wooden beams, exposed brick, high ceilings and occasional antiques. The main square location of this refined hotel is hard to top.

Casa Reims　　　　　　　　B&B €€
(☏ 0368-467 325; www.casareims.ro; Str Castelului 85; s/d from 210/260 lei; 🅿 ❇ 🛜) Pastels and acid tones mingle beautifully with bare

Braşov

⊚ Sights
1 Black Church B3
2 Old Town Fortifications B3

⊕ Activities, Courses & Tours
3 Mt Tâmpa Cable Car D3

⊜ Sleeping
4 Bella Muzica B3
5 Casa Reims D1

⊗ Eating
6 Bistro de l'Arte B2
7 Pilvax B2

⊜ Drinking & Nightlife
8 Tipografia C3

brick and wooden beams at this boutique B&B. Personalised service from the friendly owners adds to the VIP feel, and most rooms have views of Mt Tâmpa.

WORTH A TRIP

BRAN CASTLE & RÂŞNOV FORTRESS

Rising above the town on a rocky promontory, **Bran Castle** (☎0268-237 700; www.bran-castle.com; Str General Traian Moşoiu 24; adult/student/child 40/25/10 lei; ⌚9am-6pm Tue-Sun, from noon Mon Apr-Sep, to 4pm Oct-Mar) holds visitors in thrall. Illuminated by the light of a pale moon, the vampire's lair glares down from its rocky bluff. An entire industry has sprouted around describing the pile as 'Dracula's Castle', and at first glance the claims look legit. Regrettably, though, Bran Castle's blood-drinking credentials don't withstand scrutiny. It's unlikely Vlad Ţepeş – either 'the Impaler' or 'protector of Wallachia' – ever passed through. Nor did the castle inspire Bram Stoker in writing his iconic Gothic novel *Dracula*.

These seem minor quibbles when you gaze up at the turreted fortress, guarded from the east by the Bucegi Mountains and from the west by Piatra Craiului massif. Meanwhile, the castle's museum pays greater homage to Romanian royals than immortal counts. Ignoring this, a gauntlet of souvenir sellers hawk fang-adorned mugs and Vlad-the-Impaler compact mirrors (really).

Commonly paired with Bran Castle on day trips from Braşov, nearby **Râşnov Fortress** (Cetatea Râşnov; ☎0268-230 115; www.rasnov-turism.ro; Strada Cetăţii; adult/child 12/6 lei; ⌚9am-6pm) might just be the more enchanting of the two. The medieval citadel, built by Teutonic Knights to guard against Tatar and Turkish invasion, roosts on a hilltop 19km southwest of Braşov by road. Visitors are free to stroll between sturdy watchtowers, browse medieval-themed souvenir and craft stalls, and admire views of rolling hills from the fortress' highest point. Walk from the village or take the lift.

Bran is a 45-minute bus ride from Braşov, with a stop in Râşnov, and makes an easy day trip.

Eating & Drinking

★Bistro de l'Arte BISTRO €€
(☎0720-535 566; www.bistrodelarte.ro; Piaţa Enescu 11; mains 32-40 lei; ⌚9am-midnight Mon-Sat, from noon Sun; 📶✍) Tucked down a charming side street, this bohemian joint can be spotted by the bike racks shaped like penny-farthings. There's an almost Parisian feel in Bistro de l'Arte's arty decor and Champagne breakfasts (59 lei), though its menu picks the best from France, Italy and beyond: bruschetta, fondue, German-style cream cake and a suitably hip cocktail list.

Pilvax HUNGARIAN €€
(☎0268-475 829; www.pilvax.ro; Str Michael Weiss 16; mains 25-60 lei; ⌚8am-10pm Tue-Sun, from 1pm Mon; 📶✍) Centrally located Pilvax offers an upscale fusion of Transylvanian and Hungarian food – think stuffed peppers or braised spare ribs with polenta – in a bright, modern setting. The wine list is among the best in the area and there's a big terrace out front for when it's too warm to sit inside. Reserve in advance for dinner or on weekends.

Tipografia TEAHOUSE
(☎0722-373 090; www.tipo-grafia.ro; Str Postăvarului 1; ⌚8am-1am Mon-Fri, from 9am Sat & Sun; 📶) Tipografia calls itself a teahouse, but it's an excellent all-rounder. It makes a mean cup of coffee too, and by sunset the place morphs into one of the city's best beer joints and cocktail bars. The crowd is local and chill, and weekend nights have been known to go on far longer than closing hour.

Information

You'll find numerous ATMs and banks on and around Str Republicii and B-dul Eroilor.

Tourist Information Centre (☎0268-327 298; www.brasovtourism.eu; Str Prundului 1; ⌚9am-5pm Mon-Thu, 10am-3pm Fri, 11am-2pm Sat & Sun) Cordial staff offer maps and local advice.

Getting There & Away

BUS

Maxitaxis and microbuses are the best way to reach places near Braşov, including Bran and Râşnov. The most accessible station is **Bus Station 1** (Autogara 1; ☎0268-427 267; www.autogari.ro; B-dul Gării 1), next to the train station. From 6am to 7.30pm maxitaxis leave every half-hour for Bucharest (from 40 lei, 2½ to 3½ hours). About 10 daily buses or maxitaxis leave for Sibiu (30 lei, 2½ hours). At least three go daily to Sighişoara (35 lei, two hours). Less frequent buses reach Cluj-Napoca (90 lei, four to five hours, four daily). For other destinations, check www.autogari.ro.

TRAIN

The **train station** (Gara Braşov; ☑ 0268-410 233; www.cfrcalatori.ro; B-dul Gării 5) is 2km northeast of the town centre. Left-luggage service is available at the station. Sample routes and fares: Bucharest (48 lei, three hours, 15 daily), Cluj-Napoca (75 lei, seven hours, six daily), Sibiu (45 lei, four hours, four daily) and Sighişoara (40 lei, three hours, six daily).

Sighişoara

☑ 0265 / POP 28,100

So resplendent are Sighişoara's pastel-coloured buildings, stony lanes and medieval towers, you'll rub your eyes in disbelief. Fortified walls encircle Sighişoara's lustrous merchant houses, now harbouring cafes, hotels and craft shops. Lurking behind the gingerbread roofs and turrets of the Unesco-protected old town is the history of Vlad Ţepeş, the bloodthirsty, 15th-century Wallachian prince. He was allegedly born here, in a house that is visitable to this day. Ţepeş is best remembered as Vlad the Impaler, or Dracula, fuelling a local industry of vampire-themed souvenirs. Allow time to lose yourself along Sighişoara's alleys, hike to its hilltop church and sip coffee at cafes half a millennium old.

◉ Sights

Citadel

FORTRESS

Sighişoara's delightful medieval buildings are enclosed within its citadel, a Unesco-listed complex of protective walls and watchtowers. Walking in the citadel is today a tranquil, fairy-tale-like experience, but these towers were once packed with weapons and emergency supplies, guarding Sighişoara from Turkish attacks (note the upper windows from which arrows could be fired).

Clock Tower

MUSEUM

(Turnul cu Ceas; Piaţa Muzeului 1; adult/child 15/4 lei; ⊙ 9am-6.30pm Tue-Fri, 10am-5.30pm Sat & Sun mid-May–mid-Sep, to 3.30pm mid-Sep–mid-May) The multicoloured-tiled roof of Sighişoara's Clock Tower glitters like the scales of a dragon. The tower was built in the 14th century and expanded 200 years later. It remains the prettiest sight in town, offering a magnificent panorama from the top. The views are as good a reason to visit as the museum

inside, a patchy collection of Roman vessels, scythes and tombstones, and a scale model of the fortified town (English-language explanation is variable).

Casa Vlad Dracul

HISTORIC BUILDING

(☑ 0744-518 108; www.facebook.com/restaurant-casa-vlad-dracul-229836943748789; Str Cositorarilor 5; 5 lei; ⊙ noon-8pm) Vlad Ţepeş (aka Dracula) was reputedly born in this house in 1431 and lived here until the age of four. It's now a decent restaurant, but for a small admission the staff will show you Vlad's old room (and give you a little scare). Bubble-burster: the building is indeed centuries old, but has been completely rebuilt since Vlad's days.

🛏 Sleeping

Burg Hostel

HOSTEL €

(☑ 0265-778 489; www.burghostel.ro; Str Bastionului 4-6; dm 45 lei, s/d 90/120 lei, without bathroom 85/110 lei; 🛜 🐝) A great budget choice without compromising on charm, Burg Hostel has spacious dorms (with handy touches like plug sockets close to beds). Common areas have chandeliers made from old cartwheels, plus ceramic lamps, vaulted ceilings and other rustic touches. Staff are friendly and there's a relaxing courtyard cafe. Breakfast isn't normally included, but you can buy meals from the cafe.

Pensiunea Legenda

GUESTHOUSE €€

(☑ 0748-694 368; www.legenda.ro; Str Bastionului 8; r 160 lei; 🛜) The owners of this historic guesthouse whisper that Vlad Ţepeş once wooed a beautiful young woman within these walls, a myth that will either charm or chill you. All five rooms at this well-run guesthouse have snug beds and occasional vampiric twists such as black chandeliers and dungeon-like doors. Breakfast not included.

★ Casa Georgius Krauss

BOUTIQUE HOTEL €€€

(☑ 0365-730 840; www.casakrauss.com; Str Bastionului 11; r 330-400 lei; 🅿 ❋ 🛜) This dazzling boutique hotel is hived out of an old burgher's house at the northern end of the citadel. The restoration left period details like wood-beamed ceilings, while adding tasteful modern bathrooms and plush-linened beds. The Krauss Room, number 2, has original paintings, including a medieval coat of arms, plus a four-poster bed.

ROMANIA SIGHIŞOARA

✕ Eating

Central Park INTERNATIONAL €€
(📋 0365-730 006; www.hotelcentralpark.ro; Central Park Hotel, Piața Hermann Oberth 25; mains 30-45 lei; ⊙ 11am-11pm; P 🛜) Even if you're not staying at the **hotel** (s/d 340/370 lei; P ✳ @ 🛜), plan a meal here. Sighișoara is short on good restaurants and this is one of the best. The food is a mix of Romanian and international dishes, including very good steaks, and the wine list offers the best domestic labels. Dress up for the lavish dining room or relax on the terrace.

Casa Vlad Dracul ROMANIAN €€
(📋 0265-771 596; www.facebook.com/restaurant-casa-vlad-dracul-229836943748789; Str Cositorarilor 5; mains 25-35 lei; ⊙ noon-8pm; 🔞) The link between Dracula and tomato soups, or medallions with potato and chicken roulade, we'll never quite understand. But the house where Vlad was born could have been dealt a worse blow than this atmospheric, wood-panelled restaurant. The menu of Romanian, Saxon and grilled specials is dotted with Dracula references. Embellish it a little and your kids will love it.

🛍 Shopping

★ Arts & Crafts ARTS & CRAFTS
(📋 0745-853 109; www.thespoonman.ro; Str Cositorarilor 5; ⊙ 10.30am-6.30pm) Inside Casa Vlad Dracul (p935), this wondrous handicraft shop is the brainchild of self-styled 'Spoonman' Mark Tudose, who employs traditional woodcarving methods to fashion Transylvanian spoons (each with a local legend behind it), as well as painted-glass icons, clay statues, painted eggs and much more. It's a beautiful place to browse, and your best bet for finding a culturally meaningful souvenir.

ℹ Information

There are numerous ATMs and banks lining Sighișoara's main street, Str 1 Decembrie 1918.
Tourist Information Centre (Centrul Național de Informare și Promovare Turistică; 📋 0365-882 937; www.sighisoara.org.ro; Str Turnului 1; ⊙ 9am-5pm; 🛜) Cordial, multilingual information service just behind the Clock Tower (p935) as you're approaching from town. Has free maps and transport information.

ℹ Getting There & Away

BUS

Close to the train station, the **main bus station** (Autogara Cambus; 📋 0265-771 260; www.autogari.ro; Str Libertății 53) sends buses of various sizes and colours to Brașov (from 26 lei, 2½ hours, five daily) and Sibiu (from 40 lei, 2½ hours, two daily). Note that some buses use stops other than the main bus station. Be sure to check with www.autogari.ro.

TRAIN

Direct trains connect Sighișoara's **train station** (📋 0265-771 886; www.cfrcalatori.ro; Str Libertății 51) with Brașov (40 lei, 2½ to 3½ hours, six daily), Bucharest (70 lei, five to 5½ hours, two daily, more via Brașov), Cluj-Napoca (40 to 60 lei, 4½ to six hours, four daily, more via Teius) and Sibiu (13 lei, 2½ to three hours, two daily, more via Medias).

Sibiu

📋 0269 / POP 147,250

Sibiu is awash in aristocratic elegance. Noble Saxon history emanates from every art nouveau facade and gold-embossed church, all parked elegantly around graceful squares. Renowned composers Strauss, Brahms and Liszt all played here during the 19th century, and Sibiu has stayed at the forefront of Romania's cultural scene. Houses with distinctive eyelid-shaped windows (imagine a benign Amityville Horror House) watch a cast of artists and buskers bustling below them. Cafes and bars inhabit brick-walled cellars and luminously decorated attics.

◉ Sights

★ St Mary's Evangelical Church CHURCH
(Catedrala Evanghelică Sfânta Maria; Piața Huet; adult/child 5/2 lei, with tower 8/3 lei; ⊙ 9am-8pm Mon-Sat, from 11.30am Sun) Sibiu's Gothic centrepiece rises more than 73m over the old town. Inside, marvel at ghoulish stone skeletons, 17th-century tombs and the largest organ in Romania, all framed by a magnificent arched ceiling. Built in stages from the mid-1300s to 1520, the church was planted atop the site of an older 12th-century sanctuary. At the time of research, the main chambers were closed for long-term renovation but it was still possible to visit the front room and tower.

DANUBE DELTA

After passing through several countries and absorbing countless lesser waterways, the Danube River empties into the Black Sea in eastern Romania, just south of the Ukrainian border.

The Danube Delta (Delta Dunării), included on Unesco's World Heritage list, is one of Romania's leading attractions. At the port of **Tulcea** (pronounced tool-cha), the river splits into three separate channels – the Chilia, Sulina and Sfântu Gheorghe arms – creating a constantly evolving 4187-sq-km wetland of marshes, floating reed islets and sandbars. The region provides sanctuary for 300 species of bird and 160 species of fish. Reed marshes cover 1563 sq km, constituting one of the largest single expanses of reed beds in the world.

The delta is a haven for wildlife lovers, birdwatchers, anglers and anyone wanting to get away from it all. There are beautiful, secluded beaches at both **Sulina** and **Sfântu Gheorghe**, and the fish and seafood, particularly the fish soup, are the best in Romania. Tulcea is the largest city in the delta and the main entry point for accessing the region. It's got good bus and minibus connections to the rest of the country, and is home to the main passenger ferries. There is no rail service in the delta and few paved roads, meaning the primary mode of transport is ferry boat. Regularly scheduled ferries, both traditional 'slow' ferries and faster (and more expensive) hydrofoils, leave from Tulcea's main port on select days throughout the week and access major points in the delta.

The helpful staff at the **Tourism Information Centre** (☑ 0240-519 130; www.cnipt tulcea.ro; Str Gării 26; ☺ 8am-4pm Mon-Fri) in Tulcea can help piece together a journey depending on your time and budget.

Brukenthal Palace GALLERY
(European Art Gallery; ☑ 0269-217 691; www. brukenthalmuseum.ro; Piața Mare 5; adult/student 20/5 lei; ☺ 9am-5pm Wed-Sun) Brukenthal Palace is worth visiting as much for its resplendent period furnishings as for the European art within. Duck beneath the Music Room's chandeliers to admire colourful friezes and 18th-century musical instruments, before sidling among chambers exhibiting 17th-century portraits amid satin chaise longues and cases packed with antique jewellery. Sumptuously curated.

History Museum MUSEUM
(Casa Altemberger; www.brukenthalmuseum.ro/istorie; Str Mitropoliei 2; adult/child 20/5 lei; ☺ 9am-5pm Wed-Sun) This impressive museum begins with re-enactments of cave dwellers squatting in the gloom and dioramas of Dacian life. Out of these shadowy corridors, the museum opens out to illuminating exhibitions about Saxon guilds and local handicrafts (most impressive is the 19th-century glassware from Porumbacu de Sus). There's plenty of homage to Saxon efficiency: you could expect a fine for improperly crafting a copper cake tin.

ASTRA National Museum Complex MUSEUM
(Muzeul Civilizației Populare Tradiționale ASTRA; ☑ 0269-202 447; www.muzeulastra.ro; Str Pă-durea Dumbrava 16-20; adult/child 17/3.50 lei; ☺ 8am-8pm May-Sep, 9am-5pm Oct-Apr) Five kilometres from central Sibiu, this is Europe's largest open-air ethnographic museum, where churches, mills and traditional homes number among 400 folk-architecture monuments on-site. In summer, ASTRA hosts numerous fairs, dance workshops and musical performances, so it's worthwhile checking the website for events. There's also a nice gift shop and restaurant with creekside bench seats.

🛏 Sleeping

B13 HOSTEL €
(☑ 0269-701 742; www.b13hostel.ro; Str Nicolea Bălcescu 13; dm 50-75 lei; ❄@🛜) Almost too chic to be dubbed a hostel, B13 offers comfy bunks in six- to 20-bed dorms (one is women-only). The best rooms face the street: they have more light and better views. There are lockers and a friendly chill-out room, and a handy American-style burger bar downstairs.

Council BOUTIQUE HOTEL €€
(☑ 0369-452 524; www.thecouncil.ro; Piața Mică 31; s/d/apt from €50/55/109; ❄🛜) Tapping into Sibiu's medieval lifeblood, this opulent hotel occupies a 14th-century hall in the heart of the old town. Individually designed rooms

are equipped with desks, security safes and plenty of contemporary polish, but there are aristocratic touches such as crimson throws, bare wooden rafters and Turkish-style rugs.

Am Ring
HOTEL €€

(☑ 0269-206 499; www.amringhotel.ro; Piața Mare 14; s/d/ste 250/290/390 lei; ❄ ☜) Centrally located and decorated in a smorgasbord of styles, this is arguably Sibiu's most lavish place to sleep. From the vaulted brick dining room to bedrooms styled with original wooden beams, throne-like chairs and baroque touches such as gold candelabra, Am Ring exudes old-world elegance.

✖ Eating & Drinking

★ Crama Sibiul Vechi
ROMANIAN €€

(☑ 0269-210 461; www.sibiulvechi.ro; Str Papiullarian 3; mains 25-35 lei; ☉ 11am-10pm) Hidden in an old wine cellar, this is the most evocative restaurant in Sibiu. Explore Romanian fare such as cheese croquettes, minced meatballs and peasant's stew with polenta. Show up early or reserve ahead; it's very popular.

Kulinarium
ROMANIAN, EUROPEAN €€

(☑ 0721-506 070; www.kulinarium.ro; Piața Mică 12; mains 30-40 lei; ☉ noon-midnight; ☜) Fresh, well-presented Italy- and France-leaning cuisine using seasonal ingredients graces plates at Kulinarium. The restaurant has an intimate, casual feel, with roughly painted stone walls and dangling modern lampshades. Choose from smoky Austrian sausages, spinach soup with quail eggs, rare-beef salad, trout with wild rice or well-executed pasta dishes.

Nod Pub
BAR

(☑ 0745-047 070; www.facebook.com/nod.pub; Piața Mică 27; ☉ 9am-midnight Mon-Fri, from 10am Sat & Sun; ☜) Superb coffee and authentic cocktails (try the mojito) make this a special spot, night or day. There's an organic feel to the wood-accented interior, but you're better off at an outdoor table, watching people mill around grand Piața Mică.

Music Pub
BAR

(☑ 0369-448 326; www.facebook.com/musicpub sibiu; Piața Mică 23; ☉ 8am-3am Mon-Fri, from 11am Sat & Sun; ☜) Skip down the graffitied corridor and rub your eyes in astonishment as a cellar bar and airy veranda open up. One of the merriest spots in town, Music Pub sparkles with straw lamps and little candles, while '90s dance and rock plays on. There's table service, it's friendly and there's occasional live music.

❶ Information

ATMs are located all over the centre.

Tourist Information Centre (☑ 0269-208 913; www.turism.sibiu.ro; Str Samuel Brukenthal 2, Piața Mare; ☉ 9am-8pm Mon-Fri, 10am-6pm Sat & Sun May-Sep, 9am-5pm Mon-Fri, to 1pm Sat & Sun Oct-Apr) Based at the town hall; staff can offer free maps and plenty of local transport advice.

❶ Getting There & Away

BUS

Sibiu has one useful bus station: the **Transmixt station** (Autogara Transmixt; ☑ 0269-217 757; www.autogari.ro; Piața 1 Decembrie 1918 no 6) is next to the train station. Ask locally or look on www.autogari.ro for destination information.

Services run to Brașov (30 lei, 2½ to three hours, 12 daily), Bucharest (60 lei, 4½ hours, 10 daily), Cluj-Napoca (35 lei, 3½ to 4½ hours, 15 daily), Timișoara (60 to 80 lei, six hours, seven daily) and Târgu Mureș (30 lei, 2½ to 3½ hours, six daily).

TRAIN

Sibiu's **train station** (Gara Sibiu; ☑ 0269-211 139; www.cfrcalatori.ro; Piața 1 Decembrie 1918, 6) has direct trains to Brașov (44 lei, three hours, four daily), Bucharest (70 lei, six to eight hours, two daily, more via Brașov), Sighișoara (13 lei, three hours, one daily, more via Copșa Mică or Mediaș) and Timișoara (61 lei, 6½ hours, one daily, more via Arad). Mostly indirect services reach Cluj-Napoca (66 lei, five hours, 12 daily); change at Copșa Mică or Vințu de Jos.

Cluj-Napoca

☑ 0264 / POP 324,500

Bohemian cafes, music festivals and vigorous nightlife are the soul of Cluj-Napoca, Romania's second-largest city. With increasing flight links to European cities, Cluj is welcoming more and more travellers, who usually shoot off to more-popular towns in southern Transylvania. But once arrived, first-time visitors inevitably lament their failure to allow enough time in Cluj. Don't make the same mistake. Start with the architecture, ranging from Romania's second-largest Gothic church to baroque buildings and medieval towers. Dip into galleries and gardens.

And allow at least one lazy morning to recover from Cluj's fiery nightlife.

◎ Sights

★ St Michael's Church
CHURCH
(Biserica Sfantul Mihail; ☏ 0264-592 089; Piaţa Unirii; ◷ 8am-6pm) FREE The showpiece of Piaţa Unirii is 14th- and 15th-century St Michael's, the second-biggest Gothic church in Romania, after Braşov's Black Church (p932). Its neo-Gothic clock tower (1859) stands 80m high, while original Gothic features – such as the 1444 front portal – can still be admired. Inside, soaring rib vaults lift the gaze towards fading frescoes.

At the time of research, the church was temporarily closed for renovation.

Parcul Etnografic Romulus Vuia
MUSEUM, PARK
(☏ 0264-586 776; www.muzeul-etnografic.ro; Aleea Muzeului Etnografic; adult/child 6/3 lei; ◷ 10am-6pm Wed-Sun Apr-Sep, 9am-4pm Oct-Mar) Traditional architecture from around Romania has been faithfully reassembled at this open-air museum, 5km northwest of central Cluj. Most impressive is the Cizer Church; get the attention of a caretaker to allow you inside to view frescoes covering its wooden interior.

Fabrica de Pensule
ARTS CENTRE
(Paintbrush Factory; ☏ 0727-169 569; www.fabricadepensule.ro; Str Henri Barbusse 59-61; ◷ tours 3-7pm Tue-Sat; ☐ 1, 6, 7, 24, 24B, 25, 30, 36B) FREE More of a living, breathing creative space than a gallery, Fabrica de Pensule teems with just-made artwork by local and foreign creators who use this former paintbrush factory as a studio. Visits are by free guided tour, and depending on how you like your art, you'll either adore visiting this artistic community in a postindustrial setting or be bemused by the work-in-progress art within boxy gallery spaces. It's 3km northeast of the centre. Walk or take the bus.

🛏 Sleeping

Youthink Hostel
HOSTEL €
(☏ 0743-014 630; www.youthinkhostel.com; Str Republicii 74; dm/d €15/35; P 🛜) 🌿 A labour-of-love restoration project has transformed a 1920 building into something between a hostel and an ecotourism retreat. Original wood beams, fireplace and hardwood floors retain the early-20th-century splendour, while the seven- and eight-bed dorms are clean and modern. Aptly for such a cheery

and eco-conscious hostel, you'll be greeted by friendly dogs and a cat.

★ Lol & Lola
BOUTIQUE HOTEL €€
(☏ 0264-450 498; www.loletlolahotel.ro; Str Neagră 9; s/d €67/79; P ❄ 🛜) This enjoyably zany hotel has a rainbow of individually styled rooms to choose from, with themes ranging from Hollywood, ballet, and a rock 'n' roll room with vinyl and guitars. It's ultramodern with friendly service. The hotel is a little tricky to find, situated on a small street just east of central Str Victor Babeş.

Hotel Confort
HOTEL €€
(☏ 0264-598 410; www.hotelconfort.ro; Calea Turzii 48; s/d/ste 220/240/270 lei; P ❄ 🛜) Huge rooms with wooden floors and fuzzy rugs are accented with flower arrangements and arty prints at this chic hotel. Four rooms have balconies, and most have big windows and billowy drapes. It's a car-friendly location, a 15-minute walk outside central Cluj. Parking is free but limited; ask ahead. Breakfast is an extra 30 lei.

🍴 Eating & Drinking

★ Roata
ROMANIAN €€
(☏ 0264-592 022; www.facebook.com/restaurantroatacluj; Str Alexandru Ciurea 6; mains 25-40 lei; ◷ noon-11pm; 🖋) Transylvanian cuisine just like Granny made it, in an untouristed part of Cluj. Settle in beneath the vine-covered trellis outdoors and agonise between roasted pork ribs and pike with capers. Or go all out with a 'Transylvanian platter' for two (52 lei), with homemade sausages, meatballs, sheep's cheese, aubergine stew and spare elastic for when your pants snap (we wish).

Bujole
ROMANIAN €€
(www.bujole.com; Piaţa Unirii 15; mains 35-70 lei; ◷ 8am-11pm Mon-Fri, from 9am Sat, from 10am Sun; 🛜) The excellent French-inspired Romanian cooking, with a few welcome atypical starters such as hummus, make this a must-visit. The convenient Piaţa Unirii location doesn't hurt. French influences include a very good foie gras and duck confit. If too many hotel breakfast buffets have you pining for something different, the breakfast menu includes the city's best eggs Benedict (25 lei).

Roots
CAFE
(B-dul Eroilor 4; ◷ 7.30am-11.30pm Mon-Fri, from 9am Sat, to 5pm Sun; 🛜) Competition for Cluj's

ROMANIA CLUJ-NAPOCA

WORTH A TRIP

PAINTED MONASTERIES OF BUCOVINA

Bucovina's painted monasteries are among the most distinctive in all Christendom. They're cherished not only for their beauty and quality of artisanship, but also for their endurance over the centuries and cultural significance. The half-dozen or so monasteries, scattered over a large swathe of Bucovina, date mainly from the 15th and 16th centuries, a time when Orthodox Moldavia was battling for its life with forces of the expanding Ottoman Empire.

The monasteries are hailed mainly for their colourful external frescoes, many of which have survived the region's cruel winters relatively intact. The external wall paintings served as both expressions of faith and as an effective method of conveying important biblical stories to a parish of mostly illiterate soldiers and peasants. But don't pass up the rich interiors, where every nook and cranny is filled with religious and cultural symbolism.

Arbore Monastery (Mănăstirea Arbore; ☑ 0740-154 213; Hwy DN2K 732, Arbore; adult/student 5/2 lei, photography 10 lei; ⊙ 8am-7pm May-Sep, to 4pm Oct-Apr), the smallest of the main monasteries, receives a fraction of the visitors the others receive. The smaller scale allows you to study the paintings up close, to appreciate the skills and techniques. The monastery dates from 1503.

Humor Monastery (Mănăstirea Humorului; ☑ 0230-572 837; Gura Humorului; adult/student 5/2 lei, photography 10 lei; ⊙ 8am-7pm May-Sep, to 4pm Oct-Apr), built in 1530 near the town of Gura Humorului, boasts arguably the most impressive interior frescoes.

Voroneţ Monastery (Mănăstirea Voroneţ; ☑ 0230-235 323; Str Voroneţ 166, Voroneţ; adult/child 5/2 lei, photography 10 lei; ⊙ dawn-dusk), also not far from Gura Humorului, is the only one to have a specific colour associated with it. 'Voroneţ Blue', a vibrant cerulean colour created from lapis lazuli, is prominent in its frescoes. The monastery was built in just three months and three weeks by Ştefan cel Mare following a 1488 victory over the Turks.

Built in 1532, **Moldoviţa Monastery** (Mânăstirea Moldoviţa; Vatra Moldoviţei; adult/student 5/2 lei, photography 10 lei; ⊙ 8am-7pm May-Sep, to 4pm Oct-Apr), 35km northwest of the Voroneţ Monastery, occupies a fortified quadrangular enclosure with tower, gates and flowery lawns. The central painted church has been partly restored, and features impressive frescoes from 1537.

The main gateway to the monasteries is **Suceava**, reachable by direct train from both Bucharest and Cluj-Napoca.

best brew is stiff, but Roots' silky coffee is the front runner. Staff are as friendly as the flat whites are smooth. Find it just next door to the Tourist Information Office.

Euphoria Biergarten   BEER GARDEN
(☑ 0745-393 333; www.euphoria.ro; Str Cardinal Iuliu Hossu 25; ⊙ 8am-2pm; 🐾) The perfect, quiet spot for evening beers (and good food too). Find a table out front by a small river or in the big garden out back and order from a wide range of national and craft beers. The food menu is fairly ambitious for a beer garden – mains (25 lei to 40 lei) include burgers, ribs and grilled meats.

Joben Bistro   CAFE
(www.jobenbistro.ro; Str Avram Iancu 29; ⊙ 8am-2am Mon-Thu, from noon Fri-Sun; 🐾) This steampunk cafe will lubricate the gears of any traveller with a penchant for Victoriana. Aside from the fantasy decor, with

skull designs, taxidermied deer heads and copper pipes on bare brick walls, it's a laid-back place to nurse a lavender-infused lemonade or perhaps the potent 'Drunky Hot Chocolate'.

ℹ Information

There are banks and ATMs scattered around the centre.

Tourist Information Office (☑ 0264-452 244; www.visitcluj.ro; B-dul Eroilor 6; ⊙ 8.30am-8pm Mon-Fri, 10am-6pm Sat & Sun; 🐾) Superfriendly office with free maps, thoughtful trekking advice and tons of info on transport links, accommodation, events and more.

ℹ Getting There & Away

BUS

Domestic and international bus services depart mostly from **Bus Station Beta** (Autogara Beta;

🚌 0264-455 249; www.autogarabeta-cluj.ro; Str Giordano Bruno 1-3; ⊙ 6am-10.45pm). The bus station is 350m northwest of the train station (take the overpass). Check www.autogari.ro for current routes and departure/arrival stations.

Popular routes and fares include: Braşov (65 lei, five hours, six daily), Bucharest (60 to 90 lei, nine hours, six daily) and Sibiu (30 to 40 lei, 3¼ to four hours, almost hourly).

TRAIN

Trains from Cluj-Napoca's **train station** (www. cfrcalatori.ro; Str Căii Ferate) reach the following destinations: Braşov (75 lei, seven hours, six daily), Bucharest (90 lei, 10 hours, five daily), Sighişoara (60 lei, 4½ hours, four daily) and Sibiu (50 lei, five hours, one daily).

The **Agenţia de Voiaj CFR** (🚆 0264-432 001; Piaţa Mihai Viteazu 20; ⊙ 8.30am-8pm Mon-Fri) sells domestic and international train tickets in advance.

BANAT

Western Romania, with its geographic and cultural ties to neighbouring Hungary and Serbia, and its historical links to the Austro-Hungarian Empire, enjoys an ethnic diversity that much of the rest of the country lacks. Timişoara, the regional hub, has a nationwide reputation as a beautiful and lively metropolis, and for a series of 'firsts'. It was the world's first city to adopt electric street lights (in 1884) and, more importantly, the first city to rise up against dictator Nicolae Ceauşescu in 1989.

Timişoara

🚆 0256 / POP 315,050

Romania's third-largest city (after Bucharest and Cluj-Napoca) is also one of the country's most attractive urban areas, built around a series of beautifully restored public squares and lavish parks and gardens. The city's charms have been recognised by the EU, which named Timişoara as the European Capital of Culture for 2023. Locally, Timişoara is known as 'Primul Oraş Liber' (The First Free City), for it was here that anti-Ceauşescu protests first exceeded the Securitate's capacity for violent suppression in 1989, eventually sending Ceauşescu and his wife to their deaths.

⊙ Sights

★ Museum of the
1989 Revolution   MUSEUM
(🚆 0256-294 936; www.memorialulrevolutiei.ro; Strada Popa Şapcă 3-5; adult/child 10/5 lei; ⊙ 8am-4pm Mon-Fri, 10am-2pm Sat) This is an ideal venue to brush up on the December 1989 anticommunist revolution that began here in Timişoara. Displays include documentation, posters and photography from those fateful days, capped by a graphic 20-minute video (not suitable for young children) with English subtitles. Enter from Str Oituz 2.

Synagogue in the Fortress   SYNAGOGUE
(Sinagoga din Cetate; Str Mărăşeşti 6) Built in 1865 by Viennese architect Ignatz Schuhmann, the synagogue acts as an important keynote in Jewish history – Jews in the Austro-Hungarian Empire were emancipated in 1864, when permission was given to build the synagogue. It was closed at the time of research for renovation, but the fine exterior is worth taking in.

Reformed Church   CHURCH
(Biserica Reformată; Str Timotei Cipariu 1) The 1989 revolution began at the Reformed Church, where Father László Tőkés spoke out against Ceauşescu. You can sometimes peek in at the church, and it is usually open during times of worship.

Timişoara Art Museum   MUSEUM
(Muzeul de Artă Timişoara; 🚆 0256-491 592; www. muzeuldeartatm.ro; Piaţa Unirii 1; adult 10 lei, child free; ⊙ 10am-6pm Tue-Sun) This museum displays a representative sample of paintings and visual arts over the centuries as well as regular, high-quality temporary exhibitions. It's housed in the baroque **Old Prefecture Palace** (built 1754), which is worth a look inside for the graceful interiors alone.

🛏 Sleeping

Hostel Costel   HOSTEL €
(🚆 0356-262 487; www.hostel-costel.ro; Str Petru Sfetca 1; dm 50-65 lei, d 135 lei; @ 🛜) This charming 1920s art-nouveau villa is the city's best-run hostel. The vibe is relaxed and congenial. There are three dorm rooms with six to 10 beds and one private double, plus ample chill rooms, a kitchen and a big garden with hammocks for relaxing.

⭐ Casa del Sole
BOUTIQUE HOTEL €€

(☑ 0356-457 771; www.casadelsole.ro; Str Romulus 12; s/d 260/370 lei; ⓟ ❋ 🛜 🏊) An unexpectedly attractive boutique hotel, located in a green residential district about 1km south of the centre. The hotel occupies an old villa, and the stylish, period-piece rooms are located in three buildings within the same complex. The back garden is lovely and has a restaurant and terrace for drinks. The pool is large and clean.

Vila La Residenza
HOTEL €€€

(☑ 0256-401 080; www.laresidenza.ro; Str Independenței 14; s/d/ste from 380/430/550 lei; ⓟ ❋ @ 🛜 🏊) This charming converted villa recalls an English manor, with a cosy reading room and library off the lobby and an enormous, well-tended garden in the back with swimming pool. Its 15 rooms are comfort-driven in a similarly understated way. A first choice for visiting celebrities and *the* place to stay if price is no object.

✕ Eating & Drinking

⭐ Homemade
INTERNATIONAL €€

(☑ 0730-832 299; www.facebook.com/pg/homemadetimisoara; Str Gheorghe Doja 40; mains 25-40 lei; ⊙ noon-11pm; 🛜) Push your way through the unmarked doorway into what looks like someone's living room, with dark-green walls and antique rugs on parquet floors. Homemade feels like a well-kept secret. The eclectic menu runs from very well-done burgers and fries to more intricate creations built around beef and pork. Plenty of vegetarian options on the menu as well. Reserve for evenings.

Casa Bunicii
ROMANIAN €€

(☑ 0356-100 870; www.casa-bunicii.ro; Str Virgil Onitiu 3; mains 25-60 lei; ⊙ noon-midnight) The name translates to 'Granny's House' and indeed this casual, family-friendly restaurant specialises in home cooking and regional specialities from Banat, with an emphasis on dishes based on *spätzle* (egg noodles). The duck soup with dumplings (12 lei) and grilled chicken breast served in sour cherry sauce (25 lei) both come recommended. Folksy surrounds.

La Căpițe
BEER GARDEN

(☑ 0371-397 706; www.facebook.com/lacapitetm; B-dul Pârvan Vasile 13; ⊙ 10am-1am Mar-Oct; 🛜) Shaggy riverside beer garden and alternative hang-out strategically located across the street from the university, ensuring lively crowds on warm summer evenings. Some nights have live music or DJs. The name translates as 'haystack', and bales of hay strewn everywhere make for comfy places to sit and chill.

Scârț Loc Lejer
CAFE

(☑ 0751-892 340; www.facebook.com/scartloclejer; Str Laszlo Szekely 1; ⊙ 10am-11pm Mon-Fri, from 11am Sat, from 2pm Sun; 🛜) An old villa that's been retro-fitted into a funky coffee house called something like the 'Creaky Door', with old prints on the walls and chill tunes on the turntable. There are several cosy rooms in which to read and relax, but our favourite is the garden out back, with shady nooks and even hammocks to stretch out on.

☆ Entertainment

National Theatre & Opera House
THEATRE, OPERA

(Teatrul Național și Opera Română; ☑ tickets 0256-201 117; www.tntimisoara.com; Str Mărășești 2) The National Theatre & Opera House features both dramatic works and classical opera, and is highly regarded. Buy tickets (from around 50 lei) at the **box office** (☑ 0256-201 117; www.ort.ro; Str Mărășești 2; ⊙ 11am-7pm Tue-Sun) or via email, but note that most of the dramatic works will be in Romanian.

ℹ Information

Timișoara Tourist Information Centre (Info Centru Turistic; ☑ 0256-437 973; www.timisoara-info.ro; Str Alba Iulia 2; ⊙ 9am-7pm Mon-Fri, 10am-4pm Sat May-Sep, 9am-6pm Mon-Fri, 10am-3pm Sat Oct-Apr) This tourist office can assist with accommodation and trains, and provide maps and Banat regional info.

ℹ Getting There & Away

BUS

Timișoara lacks a centralised bus station for its extensive domestic and international services. Buses and minibuses are privately operated and depart from different points around the city, depending on the company and destination. Many long-haul coach services use the **Normandia Bus Station** (Autogara Normandia; ☑ 0253-238 121; www.autogari.ro; Calea Stan Vidrighin 12), about 2km southeast of the centre. Another popular bus station, closer to the Northern Train station, is **Autotim** (Autogara Autotim; ☑ 0256-493 471; Splaiul Tudor Vladimirescu 30). Consult its website (www.autogari.ro) for departure points.

Sample fares include Bucharest (90 lei), Cluj-Napoca (60 lei) and Sibiu (75 lei). The main international operators include **Atlassib** (☎ 0757-112 370; www.atlassib.ro; Calea Stan Vidrighin 12; ⊙ 9am-6pm Mon-Fri, 10am-2pm Sat), **Eurolines** (☎ 0256-288 132; www.eurolines.ro; Calea Stan Vidrighin 12; ⊙ 9am-6pm Mon-Fri, 11am-3pm Sat) and **Flixbus** (www.flixbus.ro).

Belgrade-based **Gea Tours** (☎ 0316-300 257; www.geatours.rs) offers a daily minibus service between Timişoara and Belgrade (one way/return €15/30); book over the website.

TRAIN

Trains depart from the **Northern Train Station** (Gara Timişoara-Nord; ☎ 0256-493 806; www.cfrcalatori.ro; Str Gării 2; 🚋 1, 8), though it's actually 'west' of the centre. Daily express trains include services to Bucharest (112 lei, nine hours, two daily) and Cluj-Napoca (80 lei, six hours, one daily).

Agenţia de Voiaj CFR (☎ 0256-491 889, international trains 0256-294 131; www.cfr.ro; Piaţa Victoriei 7; ⊙ 10am-6pm Mon-Fri) sells domestic and international train tickets and seat reservations.

SURVIVAL GUIDE

ⓘ Directory A–Z

ACCESSIBLE TRAVEL

➡ Romania is not well equipped for people with disabilities, even though there has been some improvement over recent years. Wheelchair ramps are available only at some upmarket hotels and restaurants, and public transport is a challenge for anyone with mobility problems.

➡ **Romania Motivation Foundation** (www.motivation.ro) is a local organisation with offices around the country to assist people in wheelchairs and with mobility issues. It has a good website in English for people confined to wheelchairs.

➡ Download Lonely Planet's free Accessible Travel guide from http://lptravel.to/Accessible Travel.

ACCOMMODATION

Romania has a wide choice of accommodation options to suit most budgets, including hotels, pensions, hostels and camping grounds. Book summer accommodation in popular Transylvanian destinations such as Braşov and Sibiu well in advance.

Hostels Big cities like Bucharest and Cluj have modern-style hostels and are open to all age groups.

Hotels Hotels range from modest family-run affairs to boutiques and high-priced corporate chains – with a commensurate range of prices.

Pensions (pensiunes) Small, locally owned inns that offer excellent value and are occasionally borderline luxurious.

LEGAL MATTERS

Romanian police take a dim view towards illegal drug use of any kind, including cannabis, as well as obvious displays of public drunkenness.

LGBTIQ+ TRAVELLERS

Public attitudes towards homosexuality remain generally negative. In spite of this, Romania has made some legal progress towards decriminalising homosexual acts and adopting antidiscrimination laws.

➡ There is no legal provision for same-sex partnerships.

➡ Bucharest remains the most tolerant city in the country, though here, too, open displays of affection between same-sex couples are rare.

➡ The Bucharest-based **Accept Association** (www.acceptromania.ro) is an NGO that defends and promotes the rights of gays and lesbians at a national level. Each year in June the group helps to organise the six-day festival **Bucharest Pride** (www.bucharestpride.ro; ⊙ Jun), with films, parties, conferences and a parade.

MONEY

ATMs are widely available. Credit cards are widely accepted in hotels and restaurants.

Currency

The Romanian currency is the leu (plural: lei), listed in some banks and currency-exchange offices as RON. One leu is divided into 100 bani.

Money Changers

The best place to exchange money is at a bank. You'll pay a small commission, but get a decent rate. You can also change money at a private exchange booth (casa de schimb) but be wary of commission charges and always ask how many lei you will receive before handing over your bills.

You will need to show a passport to change money, so always have it handy. Never change money on the street with strangers; it's always a rip-off.

OPENING HOURS

Shopping centres and malls generally have longer hours and are open from 9am to 8pm Saturday to Sunday. Museums are usually closed on Monday, and have shorter hours outside high season.

Banks 9am to 5pm Monday to Friday, to 1pm Saturday (varies)

Museums 10am to 5pm Tuesday to Friday, to 4pm Saturday and Sunday

Offices 8am to 5pm Monday to Friday

Post Offices 8am to 7pm Monday to Friday, to 1pm Saturday (cities)

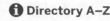

ℹ TIPPING

Restaurants 10% of the bill to reward good service.

Taxis Round the fare up to reward special service.

Hotels Tip cleaning staff 3 to 5 lei per night or 20 lei per week to reward good service.

Personal services Tip hairdressers 10%.

Restaurants 9am to 11pm Monday to Friday, 10am to 11pm Saturday and Sunday
Shops 9am to 6pm Monday to Friday, to 2pm Saturday

PUBLIC HOLIDAYS

If you'll be travelling during public holidays it's wise to book ahead, as some hotels in popular destinations may be full.

New Year 1 and 2 January

Orthodox Easter Monday April/May

Labour Day 1 May

Pentecost May/June, 50 days after Easter Sunday

Assumption of Mary 15 August

Feast of St Andrew 30 November

Romanian National Day 1 December

Christmas 25 and 26 December

SAFE TRAVEL

Watch out for jacked-up prices for tourists in Bucharest restaurants, taxis that charge extortionate fares (call for a taxi from companies recommended by your hotel) and a lifted wallet if you're not careful in public squares or jam-packed buses. Stray dogs are an occasional annoyance but rarely pose a danger. Avoid the temptation to pet them. The best strategy is to stay out of their way and they'll stay out of yours.

TELEPHONE
Domestic & International Calls

Romania has a modern telephone network of landlines and mobile (cell) phones. It's possible to receive and make direct international calls from anywhere in the country. Romania's country code is 40.

➡ All Romanian landline numbers have 10 digits, consisting of a zero, plus a city code and the number.

➡ The formula differs slightly depending on whether the number is in Bucharest or outside Bucharest. Bucharest numbers take the form:

0 + two-digit city code (21 or 31) + seven-digit number. Outside Bucharest, numbers take the form: 0 + three-digit city code + six-digit number.

➡ Mobile-phone numbers can be identified by a three-digit prefix starting with 7. All mobile numbers have 10 digits: 0 + three-digit prefix (7xx) + six-digit number.

Mobile Phones

Local SIM cards can be used in European, Australian and some American phones. Other phones must be set to roaming.

TOURIST INFORMATION

➡ The **Romanian Ministry of Tourism** (www.romania.travel) maintains a wonderful website with a trove of useful information. There's a large English-language section on festivals and events, accommodation and tips on what to see and do all around the country. Nearly all big cities have decent tourist offices. Tourist information can still be tough to track down in rural areas.

ℹ Getting There & Away

ENTERING THE COUNTRY
Passport

All international visitors to Romania are required to have a valid passport (EU members need only a valid EU ID card). The expiration date of the passport should exceed your travel dates by at least three months, though some airlines will not allow passengers to board unless the passport is valid for at least six months.

AIR

Romania has good air connections to Europe and the Middle East. At the time of research there were no direct flights to Romania from North America or Southeast Asia.

BUS

Long-haul bus services remain a popular way of travelling from Romania to Western Europe as well as to parts of southeastern Europe and Turkey. Bus travel is comparable in price to train travel, but can be faster and require fewer connections.

CAR & MOTORCYCLE

Romania has decent road and car-ferry connections to neighbouring countries, and entering the country by car or motorcycle will present no unexpected difficulties. At all border crossings, drivers should be prepared to show the vehicle's registration, proof of insurance (a green card) and a valid driver's licence. All visiting foreigners, including EU nationals, are required to show a valid passport (or EU identity card).

TRAIN

Romania is integrated into the European rail grid, and there are decent connections to Western Europe and neighbouring countries. Nearly all of these arrive at and depart from Bucharest's main station, Gara de Nord (p931). Budapest is the main rail gateway in and out of Romania from Western Europe. There are two daily direct trains between Budapest and Bucharest, with regular onward connections from Budapest to Prague, Munich and Vienna.

Getting Around

AIR

Given the distances and poor state of the roads, flying between cities is a feasible option if time is a primary concern. The Romanian national carrier **Tarom** (www.tarom.ro) operates a comprehensive network of domestic routes and has ticket offices around the country. The airline flies regularly between Bucharest and Cluj-Napoca, Sibiu and Timişoara. The budget carrier **Blue Air** (www.blueairweb.com) also has a comprehensive network of domestic destinations that overlap with Tarom.

BUS

A mix of buses, minibuses and 'maxitaxis' form the backbone of the Romanian national transport system. Unfortunately, bus routes change frequently; often these changes are communicated between people by word of mouth. Towns and cities will sometimes have a half-dozen different bus stations (autogara) and maxitaxi stops, depending on which company is oper-ating a particular route and the destination in question. The helpful website **Autogari.ro** (www. autogari.ro) is an up-to-date national timetable that is relatively easy to use and lists routes, times, fares and departure points.

CAR & MOTORCYCLE

Driving in Romania is not ideal, and if you have the chance to use alternatives like the train and bus, this can be a more relaxing option. Roads are generally crowded and in poor condition. The country has only a few stretches of motorway (autostrada), meaning most of your travel will be along two-lane highways. Western-style petrol stations are plentiful, but be sure to fill up before heading on long trips through the mountains or in remote areas. A litre of unleaded 95 octane cost about 5.50 lei at the time of research.

TRAIN

Romania's passenger rail network has been cut back considerably in recent years, though trains remain a reliable – if slow – way of moving between large cities.

➡ The national rail system is run by **Căile Ferate Române** (CFR, www.cfrcalatori.ro); the website has a handy online timetable (mersul trenurilor).

➡ Buy tickets at train-station windows, specialised Agenţia de Voiaj CFR ticket offices, private travel agencies or online at www.cfrcalatori.ro.

➡ Sosire means 'arrivals' and plecare, 'departures'. On posted timetables, the number of the platform from which the train departs is listed under linia.

1

2

1. Reine, Lofoten (p857), Norway
Astonishing and memorable Nordic landscapes.

2. Kirkjufell (p612), West Iceland
One of Iceland's most iconic mountains.

3. Plitvice Lakes National Park (p261), Croatia
Home to turquoise lakes and hundreds of waterfalls.

4. Dancers in Berat (p49), Albania
Learn about traditional culture in this mountain-set village.

5. Kamppi Chapel (p357), Helsinki, Finland
This contemporary Chapel of Silence is open to all.

5

3

4

Russia

POP 144.5 MILLION

Best Places to Eat

➜ Gran Cafe Dr Zhivago (p960)

➜ White Rabbit (p960)

➜ Lavka-Lavka (p960)

➜ Cococo (p972)

➜ Banshiki (p971)

➜ Russkaya Chaynaya (p965)

Best Places to Stay

➜ Brick Design Hotel (p959)

➜ Moss Boutique Hotel (p959)

➜ Godzillas Hostel (p959)

➜ Soul Kitchen Hostel (p971)

➜ Rossi Hotel (p971)

➜ Surikov Guest House (p964)

Why Go?

Europe's ultimate eastern frontier might be shrouded in ancient enigma and modern political intrigue, but it sizzles with creative energy and offers an entirely different perspective than its neighbours.

Could there be a more iconic image of Eastern Europe than the awe-inspiring architectural ensemble of Moscow's Red Square? Fresh from a thorough revamp, Russia's brash and wealthy capital is a must on any trip to the region. St Petersburg is another stunner. The former imperial capital is still Russia's most beautiful and alluring city, with its grand Italianate mansions, wending canals and opening bridges on the enormous Neva River. East of Moscow, there is entirely different scenery – that of millennia-old little towns packed with onion-domed churches and fortress-like monasteries.

When to Go
Moscow

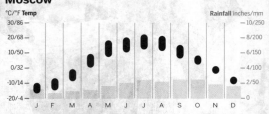

May Big military parades mark the end of WWII.

Jun–Jul Party during St Petersburg's White Nights, or chill out in gorgeous Suzdal.

Dec–Jan Snow makes even the bleakest places look magical as Russia enters the holiday season.

Entering the Country

There are many routes into and out of Russia. Most people fly into Moscow or St Petersburg. Using the main railway route via Belarus is now tricky due to visa squabbles between the two countries. Consider detouring via Finland, Latvia or Estonia.

ITINERARIES

One Week

Start your week in splendid St Petersburg (p966). Wander up Nevsky pr (p966), see Dvortsovaya pl and spend a half-day at the Hermitage (p967). Explore Peter & Paul Fortress (p970) and the wonderful Russian Museum (p966) the next day.

On day three, take an early-morning train to Moscow (p951). Touring the Kremlin (p951) and Red Square (p951) will take up one day, viewing the spectacular collections at the Tretyakov (p954) and Pushkin (p955) art museums another. On day five stretch your legs in the revamped Gorky Park (p955), taking in more art at New Tretyakov (p955) and Garage Museum (p955).

Take an afternoon train to Vladimir (p963) and continue to Suzdal (p964). Spend a day exploring this rural paradise before heading back to Vladimir in the morning on day seven. Check out its ancient monuments before visiting the Church of the Intercession on the Nerl (p963) just outside town. Catch a train back to Moscow in the evening.

Two Weeks

With two extra days in Moscow (p951), sweat it out in the luxurious Sanduny Baths (p960) or do a metro tour, then take a day trip to Sergiev Posad (p965). In St Petersburg (p966), spend more time in the Hermitage (p967) and other museums, and tack on an excursion to Peterhof (p972) or Tsarskoe Selo (p972).

Essential Food & Drink

Soups For example, the lemony, meat *solyanka* or the hearty fish *ukha*.

Bliny (pancakes) Served with *ikra* (caviar) or *tvorog* (cottage cheese).

Salads A wide variety usually slathered in mayonnaise, including the chopped potato Olivier.

Pelmeni (dumplings) Stuffed with meat and eaten with sour cream and vinegar.

Central Asian dishes Try *plov* (Uzbek pilaf), shashlyk (kebab) or *lagman* (noodles).

Vodka The quintessential Russian tipple.

Kvas A refreshing, beer-like nonalcoholic drink, or the red berry juice mix *mors*.

AT A GLANCE
....

Area 17,098,242 sq km

Capital Moscow

Country Code ☎ 7

Currency Rouble (R)

Emergency Stationary/mobile phone: Ambulance ☎ 03/103, Fire ☎ 01/101, Police ☎ 02/102

Language Russian

Time Moscow/St Petersburg (GMT/UTC plus three hours)

Visas Required by all – apply at least a month in advance of your trip

RUSSIA

Sleeping Price Ranges

The following price ranges refer to a double room with bathroom during high season.

€ less than R1500 (less than R3000 in Moscow and St Petersburg)

€€ R1500–4000 (R3000–15,000 in Moscow and St Petersburg)

€€€ more than R4000 (more than R15,000 in Moscow and St Petersburg)

Eating Price Ranges

The following price ranges refer to a main course.

€ less than R300 (less than R500 in Moscow and St Petersburg)

€€ R300–800 (R500–1000 in Moscow and St Petersburg)

€€€ more than R800 (more than R1000 in Moscow and St Petersburg)

Russia Highlights

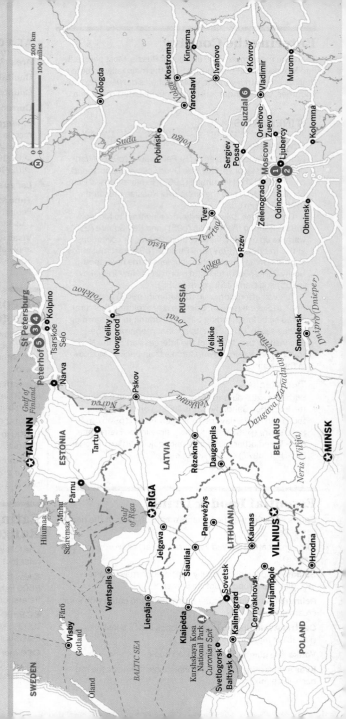

❶ **Moscow** (p951) Being amazed by the massive scale and riches of Russia's brash, energetic capital.

❷ **Kremlin** (p951) Sneaking inside Eastern Europe's most iconic fortress to marvel at imperial treasures.

❸ **St Petersburg** (p966) Taking a walking, bike or boat tour of a glorious Italianate slice of Old Europe incongruously placed in Russia.

❹ **State Hermitage Museum** (p967) Ogling the seemingly endless collection of masterpieces in St Petersburg's unrivalled museum.

❺ **Peterhof** (p972) Venturing into the open sea to marvel at a palace seemingly made of glittering gold.

❻ **Suzdal** (p964) Criss-crossing this beautiful town by bicycle or on foot, listening to the music of church bells and nightingales.

MOSCOW МОСКВА

☑ 495, 496, 498, 499 / POP 12.5 MILLION

Huge and prone to architectural gigantism, full of energy, both positive and dark, refined and tasteless at the same time, Moscow is overwhelming in every way. After the major spruce-up it has undergone in recent years, the mind-bogglingly eclectic Russian capital may look like hipster-ridden parts of Brooklyn at one point and a thoroughly glossed-over version of North Korea at another.

The sturdy stone walls of the Kremlin, the apex of Russian political power and once the centre of the Orthodox Church, occupy the city's founding site on the northern bank of the Moscow River. Remains of the Soviet state, such as Lenin's Tomb, are nearby in Red Square and elsewhere in the city, which radiates from the Kremlin in a series of ring roads.

⊙ Sights

⊚ Kremlin & Red Square

★**Moscow Kremlin** MUSEUM
(Кремль; ☑ 495-695 4146; www.kreml.ru; R700; ⊙ 9.30am-6pm 15 May-30 Sep, ticket office 9am-5pm Fri-Wed, ticket office 9.30am-4.30pm Fri-Wed 1 Oct-14 May, ticket office 9.30am-4.30pm Fri-Wed; Ⓜ Aleksandrovsky Sad) The apex of Russian political power and once the centre of the Orthodox Church, the Kremlin is the kernel of not only Moscow, but of the whole country. From here, autocratic tsars, communist dictators and modern-day presidents have done their best – and worst – for Russia.

Covering Borovitsky Hill on the Moscow River's north bank, it's enclosed by high walls 2.25km long (Red Square's outside the east wall). The best views of the complex are from Sofiyskaya nab across the river.

Much of what you see, both the red-brick walls and magnificent churches encircled by them, was designed by Italian architects invited to Moscow at the end of the 15th century by tsar Ivan III, or rather by his wife – Sophia Palaiologina. A niece of the last Byzantine emperor, she was raised as a fugitive in Rome and saw Moscow as heir to Constantinople and by extension – to Rome itself.

Before entering the Kremlin, deposit bags (free) at the **left-luggage office** (⊙ 9-11am, 11.30am-3.30pm & 4-6.30pm Fri-Wed), beneath the Kutafya Tower near the main **ticket office** (Кассы музеев Кремля; ⊙ 9am-5pm Fri-Wed May-Sep, 9.30am-4.30pm Fri-Wed Oct-Apr;

Ⓜ Aleksandrovsky Sad) in Alexander Garden. The entrance ticket covers admission to all five church-museums and the **Patriarch's Palace** (Патриарший дворец). It does not include the Armoury, the **Diamond Fund Exhibition** (Алмазный фонд России; ☑ 495-629 2036; www.gokhran.ru; R500; ⊙ 10am-1pm & 2-5pm Fri-Wed) or the **Ivan the Great Bell Tower** (Колокольня Ивана Великого; R250; ⊙ 10am-5pm Apr-Oct), which are priced separately.

During warm months (April to October), many people try to visit the Kremlin around noon in order to watch the change of guards at Sobornaya Sq in the centre of the fortress. The ceremony involves a few dozen horses and men in historical attire performing sophisticated square-bashing choreography.

Photography is not permitted inside the Armoury or any of the buildings on Sobornaya pl (Cathedral Sq).

★**Armoury** MUSEUM
(Оружейная палата; www.kreml.ru; adult/child R1000/free; ⊙ tours 10am, noon, 2.30pm & 4.30pm Fri-Wed; Ⓜ Aleksandrovsky Sad) The Armoury dates to 1511, when it was founded under Vasily III to manufacture and store weapons, imperial arms and regalia for the royal court. Later it also produced jewellery, icon frames and embroidery. To this day, the Armoury contains plenty of treasures for ogling, and remains a highlight of any visit to the Kremlin. If possible, buy your time-specific ticket to the Armoury when you buy your ticket to the Kremlin.

★**Red Square** HISTORIC SITE
(Красная площадь; Krasnaya pl; Ⓜ Ploshchad Revolyutsii) Immediately outside the Kremlin's northeastern wall is the celebrated Red Square, the 400m-by-150m area of cobblestones that is at the very heart of Moscow. Commanding the square from the southern end is St Basil's Cathedral (p954). This panorama never fails to send the heart aflutter, especially at night.

★**Lenin's Mausoleum** MEMORIAL
(Мавзолей Ленина; www.lenin.ru; Krasnaya pl; ⊙ 10am-1pm Tue-Thu & Sat; Ⓜ Ploshchad Revolyutsii) FREE Although Vladimir Ilych requested that he be buried beside his mum in St Petersburg, he still lies in state at the foot of the Kremlin wall, receiving visitors who come to pay their respects. Line up at the western corner of the square (near the entrance to Alexander Garden) to see the

The Kremlin

A DAY AT THE KREMLIN

Only at the Kremlin can you see 800 years of Russian history and artistry in one day. Enter the ancient fortress through the Trinity Gate Tower and walk past the impressive Arsenal, ringed with cannons. Past the Patriarch's Palace, you'll find yourself surrounded by white-washed walls and golden domes. Your first stop is ❶ **Assumption Cathedral** with the solemn fresco over the doorway. As the most important church in prerevolutionary Russia, this 15th-century beauty was the burial site of the patriarchs. The ❷ **Ivan the Great Bell Tower** now contains a nifty multimedia exhibit on the architectural history of the Kremlin. The view from the top is worth the price of admission. The tower is flanked by the massive ❸ **Tsar Cannon & Bell**.

In the southeast corner, ❹ **Archangel Cathedral** has an elaborate interior, where three centuries of tsars and tsarinas are laid to rest. Your final stop on Sobornaya pl is ❺ **Annunciation Cathedral**, rich with frescoes and iconography.

Walk along the Great Kremlin Palace and enter the ❻ **Armoury** at the time designated on your ticket. After gawking at the goods, exit the Kremlin through Borovitsky Gate and stroll through the Alexander Garden to the ❼ **Tomb of the Unknown Soldier**.

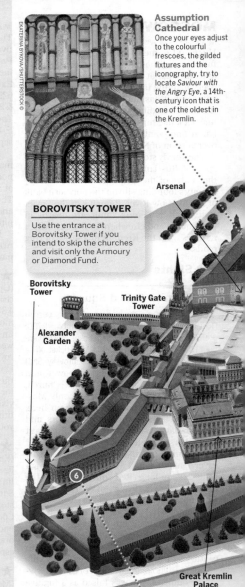

Assumption Cathedral
Once your eyes adjust to the colourful frescoes, the gilded fixtures and the iconography, try to locate *Saviour with the Angry Eye*, a 14th-century icon that is one of the oldest in the Kremlin.

Arsenal

BOROVITSKY TOWER
Use the entrance at Borovitsky Tower if you intend to skip the churches and visit only the Armoury or Diamond Fund.

Borovitsky Tower

Trinity Gate Tower

Alexander Garden

Great Kremlin Palace

Armoury
Take advantage of the free audio guide to direct you to the most intriguing treasures of the Armoury, which is chock-full of precious metalworks and jewellery, armour and weapons, gowns and crowns, carriages and sledges.

EKATERINA BYKOVA/SHUTTERSTOCK ©

DREAMER COMPANY/SHUTTERSTOCK ©

TOP TIPS

➡ **Online Purchase** Full-price tickets to the Kremlin churches and the Armoury can be purchased in advance on the Kremlin website.

➡ **Lunch** There are no eating options. Plan to eat before you arrive or stash a snack.

Tomb of the Unknown Soldier

Visit the Tomb of the Unknown Soldier honouring the heroes of the Great Patriotic War. Come at the top of the hour to see the solemn synchronicity of the changing of the guard.

TOWER TICKETS

Sessions at the Ivan the Great Bell Tower take place six or seven times a day, mid-May through September. Purchase tickets at the Kremlin ticket office 45 minutes before the session.

Patriarch's Palace

Ivan the Great Bell Tower

Check out the artistic electronic renderings of the Kremlin's history, then climb 137 steps to the belfry's upper gallery, where you will be rewarded with super, sweeping vistas of Sobornaya pl and beyond.

Moscow River

Sobornaya pl

Tsar Cannon & Bell

Peer down the barrel of the monstrous Tsar Cannon and pose for a picture beside the oversized Tsar Bell, both of which are too big to serve their intended purpose.

Annunciation Cathedral

Admire the artistic mastery of Russia's greatest icon painters – Theophanes the Greek and Andrei Rublyov – who are responsible for many of the icons in the deesis and festival rows of the iconostasis.

Archangel Cathedral

See the final resting place of princes and emperors who ruled Russia for more than 300 years, including the visionary Ivan the Great, the tortured Ivan the Terrible and the tragic Tsarevitch Dmitry.

embalmed leader, who has been here since 1924. Note that photography is not allowed and stern guards ensure that all visitors remain respectful and silent.

⭐ **St Basil's Cathedral** CHURCH
(Покровский собор, Храм Василия Блаженного; ☎ 495-698 3304; www.shm.ru; adult/concession R1000/150; ⏱ 11am-5pm Nov-Apr, to 6pm May-Oct, from 10am Jun-Aug; Ⓜ Ploshchad Revolyutsii) At the southern end of Red Square stands the icon of Russia: St Basil's Cathedral. This crazy confusion of colours, patterns and shapes is the culmination of a style that is unique to Russian architecture. In 1552 Ivan the Terrible captured the Tatar stronghold of Kazan on the Feast of Intercession. He commissioned this landmark church, officially the Intercession Cathedral, to commemorate the victory. Created from 1555 to 1561, this masterpiece would become the ultimate symbol of Russia.

State History Museum MUSEUM
(Государственный исторический музей; www.shm.ru; Krasnaya pl 1; adult/concession R700/100, audio guide R300; ⏱ ticket office 10am-5pm Mon, Wed, Thu & Sun, to 8pm Fri & Sat Sep-May, 10am-8pm daily Jun-Aug; Ⓜ Okhotny Ryad) At the northern end of Red Square, the State History Museum has an enormous collection covering Russian history from the time of the Stone Age. The building, dating from the late 19th century and designed in the Russian revivalist style, is itself an attraction – each room is in the style of a different period or region, some with highly decorated walls echoing old Russian churches.

South of the Moscow River

⭐ **State Tretyakov Gallery Main Branch** GALLERY
(Государственная Третьяковская Галерея; www.tretyakovgallery.ru; Lavrushinsky per 10; adult/concession R700/150; ⏱ 10am-6pm Tue, Wed & Sun, to 9pm Thu-Sat, last tickets 1hr before closing; Ⓜ Tretyakovskaya) The exotic boyar (high-ranking noble) castle on a little lane in Zamoskvorechie contains the main branch of the State Tretyakov Gallery, housing the world's best collection of Russian icons and an outstanding collection of other prerevolutionary Russian art. Show up early to beat the queues. The neighbouring **Engineer's Building** is reserved for special exhibits.

SOBORNAYA PLOSHCHAD

On the northern side of Sobornaya pl, with five golden helmet domes and four semicircular gables facing the square, is the **Assumption Cathedral** (Успенский собор), built between 1475 and 1479. As the focal church of prerevolutionary Russia, it's the burial place of most heads of the Russian Orthodox Church from the 1320s to 1700. The iconostasis dates from 1652, but its lowest level contains some older icons, including the Virgin of Vladimir (Vladimirskaya Bogomater), an early-15th-century Rublyov-school copy of Russia's most revered image, the Vladimir Icon of the Mother of God (Ikona Vladimirskoy Bogomateri).

The delicate little single-domed church beside the west door of the Assumption Cathedral is the **Church of the Deposition of the Robe** (Церковь Ризоположения), built between 1484 and 1486 by masons from Pskov.

With its two golden domes rising above the eastern side of Sobornaya pl, the 16th-century Ivan the Great Bell Tower (p951) is the Kremlin's tallest structure. Beside the bell tower stands the **Tsar Bell** (Царь-колокол), a 202-tonne monster that cracked before it ever rang. North of the bell tower is the mammoth **Tsar Cannon** (Царь-пушка), cast in 1586 but never shot.

The 1508 **Archangel Cathedral** (Архангельский собор), at the square's southeastern corner, was for centuries the coronation, wedding and burial church of tsars. The tombs of all of Russia's rulers from the 1320s to the 1690s are here bar one (Boris Godunov, who was buried at Sergiev Posad).

Finally, the **Annunciation Cathedral** (Благовещенский собор), at the southwest corner of Sobornaya pl and dating from 1489, contains the celebrated icons of master painter Theophanes the Greek. He probably painted the six icons at the right-hand end of the diesis row, the biggest of the six tiers of the iconostasis. Archangel Michael (the third icon from the left on the diesis row) and the adjacent St Peter are ascribed to Russian master Andrei Rublyov.

DON'T MISS

MOSCOW'S WHITE-HOT ART SCENE

Revamped old industrial buildings and other spaces in Moscow are where you'll find gems of Russia's super-creative contemporary art scene. Apart from the following recommended spots, also see www.artguide.ru.

Garage Museum of Contemporary Art (☑ 495-645 0520; www.garagemca.org; ul Krymsky val 9/32; adult/student R300/150; ⊙ 11am-10pm; Ⓜ Oktyabrskaya) Having moved into a permanent Gorky Park location, a Soviet-era building renovated by the visionary Dutch architect Rem Koolhaas, Garage hosts exciting exhibitions by top artists.

Vinzavod (Винзавод; www.winzavod.ru; 4-y Syromyatnichesky per 1; Ⓜ Chkalovskaya) **FREE** A former wine factory has morphed into this postindustrial complex of prestigious galleries, shops, a cinema and trendy cafe. Nearby, another converted industrial space, the **Artplay** (☑ 495-620 0882; www.artplay.ru; ul Nizhny Syromyatnichesky per 10; ⊙ noon-8pm Tue-Sun; Ⓜ Chkalovskaya) **FREE**, is home to firms specialising in urban planning and architectural design, as well as furniture showrooms and antique stores.

Red October (Завод Красный Октябрь; Bersenevskaya nab; Ⓜ Kropotkinskaya) **FREE** The red-brick buildings of this former chocolate factory now host the **Lumiere Brothers Photography Centre** (www.lumiere.ru; Bolotnaya nab 3, bldg 1; R250-400; ⊙ noon-9pm Tue-Fri, to 10pm Sat & Sun) plus other galleries, cool bars and restaurants. In an adjacent building the **Strelka Institute for Media, Architecture and Design** is worth checking out for its events, bookshop and bar. Also, look out for **GES-2**, a new large contemporary art space that was due to open in an old power station in 2021.

★ **Gorky Park** PARK
(Парк Горького; ⊙ 24hr; 🏄; Ⓜ Oktyabrskaya) **FREE** Moscow's main city escape isn't your conventional expanse of nature preserved inside an urban jungle. It's not a fun fair either, though it used to be one. Its official name says it all – Maxim Gorky's Central Park of Culture and Leisure. That's exactly what it provides: culture and leisure in all shapes and forms. Designed in the 1920s by avant-garde architect Konstantin Melnikov as a piece of communist utopia, these days it showcases the enlightened transformation Moscow has recently undergone.

Art Muzeon & Krymskaya Naberezhnaya PUBLIC ART
(Ⓜ Park Kultury) **FREE** Moscow's answer to London's South Bank, Krymskaya Nab (Crimea Embankment) features wave-shaped street architecture with Scandinavian-style wooden elements, beautiful flower beds and a moody fountain, which ejects water randomly from many holes in the ground to the excitement of children and adults alike. It has merged with the Art Muzeon park and its motley collection of Soviet stone idols (Stalin, Sverdlov and a selection of Lenins and Brezhnevs) that were ripped from their pedestals in the post-1991 wave of anti-Soviet feeling.

New Tretyakov Gallery GALLERY
(Новая Третьяковская галерея; www.tretya kovgallery.ru; ul Krymsky val 10; adult/child R500/250; ⊙ 10am-6pm Tue, Wed & Sun, to 9pm Thu-Sat, last tickets 1hr before closing; Ⓜ Park Kultury) Moscow's premier venue for 20th-century Russian art, this branch of the Tretyakov Gallery has much more than the typical socialist-realist images of muscle-bound men wielding scythes and busty women milking cows (although there's that, too). The exhibits showcase avant-garde artists such as Malevich, Kandinsky, Chagall, Goncharova and Popova, as well as nonconformist artists of the 1960s and 1970s who refused to accept the official style.

◎ **West of the Kremlin**

★ **Pushkin Museum of Fine Arts** MUSEUM
(Музей изобразительных искусств им Пушкина; ☑ 495-697 9578; www.arts-museum. ru; ul Volkhonka 12; single/combined galleries R400/600; ⊙ 11am-7pm Tue, Wed, Sat & Sun, to 9pm Thu & Fri; Ⓜ Kropotkinskaya) This is Moscow's premier foreign-art museum, split over three branches and showing off a broad selection of European works, including masterpieces from ancient civilisations, the Italian Renaissance and the Dutch Golden Age. To see the incredible collection of Impressionist

Central Moscow

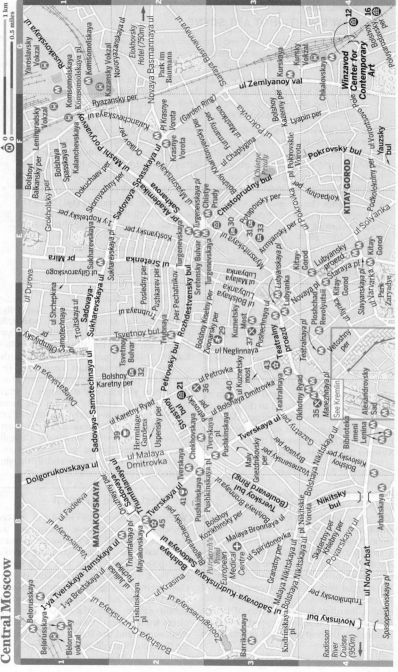

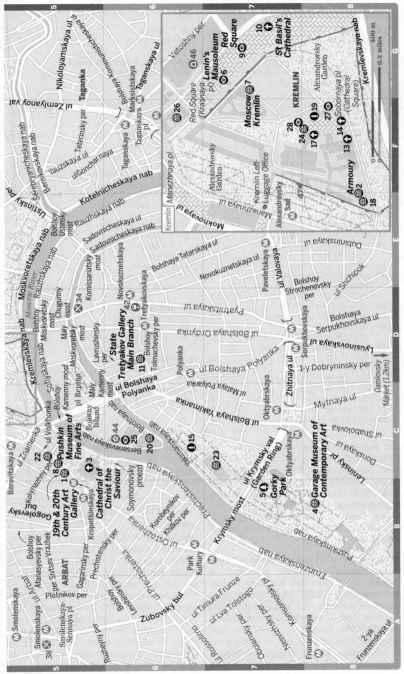

Central Moscow

and post-Impressionist paintings, visit the **19th & 20th Century Art Gallery** (ul Volkhonka 14; adult/student R300/150; ⊙11am-7pm Tue-Sun, to 9pm Thu). The **Museum of Private Collections** (Музей личных коллекций; www. artprivatecollections.ru; ul Volkhonka 10; entry prices vary; ⊙noon-8pm Wed-Sun, to 9pm Thu) shows off complete collections donated by private individuals.

★**Cathedral of Christ the Saviour** CHURCH (Храм Христа Спасителя; www.xxc.ru; ul Volkhonka 15; ⊙1-5pm Mon, from 10am Tue-Sun; ⓂKropotkinskaya) FREE This opulent and grandiose cathedral was completed in 1997 – just in time to celebrate Moscow's 850th birthday. The cathedral's sheer size and splendour guarantee its role as a love-it-or-hate-it landmark. Considering Stalin's plan for this site (a Palace of Soviets topped with a 100m statue of Lenin), Muscovites should at least be grateful they can admire the shiny domes of a church instead of the shiny dome of Ilyich's head.

◉ **Northern Moscow**

VDNKh PARK
(grounds free; ⓂVDNKh) Palaces for workers! There is no better place to see this Soviet slogan put into practice than at VDNKh, which stands for Exhibition of Achievements of the National Economy. The place feels like a Stalinesque theme park, with palatial pavilions, each designed in its own unique style to represent all the Soviet republics and various industries, from geology to space exploration. Fresh from a thorough, though not yet entirely completed reconstruction, the place looks more splendid than ever.

The top attraction is the reopened **Space Pavilion**, an opulent temple of retro-futurism filled with rockets and replicas of space stations, some of which you can walk through.

Tours

Radisson River Cruises BOATING
(www.radisson-cruise.ru; adult/child from R800/600; Ⓜ Kievskaya) The Radisson operates big riverboats that cart 140 people up and down the Moscow River on a 2½-hour cruise, departing from the dock in front of the hotel and from the dock in Gorky Park (p955). In summer, there are five or six daily departures from each location (check the website for times).

Sleeping

Godzillas Hostel HOSTEL €
(☎ 495-699 4223; www.godzillashostel.com; Bolshoy Karetny per 6; dm R700-950, s/d R2200/2800; ❄@📶; Ⓜ Tsvetnoy Bulvar) Tried and true, Godzillas is Moscow's best-known hostel, with dozens of beds spread out over four floors. The rooms come in various sizes, but they are all spacious and light-filled, and painted in different colours. To cater to the many guests, there are bathroom facilities on each floor, three kitchens and a big living room with satellite TV.

Fasol Hostel HOSTEL €
(☎ 495-240 9409; http://fasol.co; Arkhangelsky per 11/16 str 3; dm from R1000, d with shared bathroom R3500; Ⓜ Chistye Prudy) The entrance to this hostel, hidden in the courtyards amid 19th-century apartment blocks, looks unassuming. However, with over 80 beds, this popular and professionally run place is a major-league player. Dorms, sleeping six to eight, are decorated with psychedelic wall paintings; bunk beds come with body-friendly mattresses, curtains and individual lights, allowing guests to enjoy full autonomy.

Elokhovsky Hotel HOTEL €€
(Отель Елоховский; ☎ 495-632 2100; www.elohotel.ru; ul Spartakovskaya 24; s/d R4500/5300; ❄📶; Ⓜ Baumanskaya) Admittedly not very central and occupying the top floor of a shopping arcade, this hotel is nevertheless about the best value for money in Moscow. Rooms are painted in soothing colours, complemented by cityscapes of the world's major cities. The coffee machine in the lobby is available 24 hours. Baumanskaya metro and Yelokhovsky Cathedral are a stone's throw away.

★ **Brick Design Hotel** BOUTIQUE HOTEL €€
(☎ 499-110 2470; www.brickhotel.ru; Myasnitskaya ul 24/7 str 3/4; r from R8000; ❄📶; Ⓜ Chistye Prudy) Not only is this boutique hotel cosy, thoughtfully designed and very centrally located, it also doubles as an art gallery, with original works by Russian 20th-century conceptualist artists adorning the walls. That's in addition to a very tasteful combination of modern and antique furniture. Visitors also rave about the breakfast, which comes fresh from farms near Moscow.

Moss Boutique Hotel BOUTIQUE HOTEL €€€
(☎ 495-114 5572; www.mosshotel.ru; per Krivokoleyny 10 str 4; r from R13,000; ❄📶; Ⓜ Chistye Prudy) You get to see real moss growing in the elevator shaft of this elegant boutique hotel, with aged wood and black concrete surfaces dominating the interior. There's also a cool, relaxed ambience. Rooms – some really small, others bigger – are all equipped with superbly comfortable beds and formidable music centres that you can connect to your phone.

Eating

★ **Danilovsky Market** MARKET €€
(www.danrinok.ru; Mytnaya ul 74; mains R400-600; ⏲ 8am-8pm; Ⓜ Tulskaya) A showcase of the city's ongoing gentrification, this giant Soviet-era farmers market is now largely about deli food cooked and served in myriad little

METRO TOUR

For just R40 you can spend the day touring Moscow's magnificent metro stations. Many of the stations are marble-faced, frescoed, gilded works of art. Among our favourites are **Komsomolskaya**, a huge stuccoed hall, its ceiling covered with mosaics depicting military heroes; **Novokuznetskaya**, featuring military bas-reliefs done in sober khaki, and colourful ceiling mosaics depicting pictures of the happy life; and **Mayakovskaya**, Grand Prize winner at the 1939 World's Fair in New York. Another must-visit station is **Ploshchad Revolutsii**, filled with dozens of bronze statues of workers and soldiers.

eateries, including such gems as a Dagestani dumpling shop and a Vietnamese pho-soup kitchen. The market itself looks very orderly, if a tiny bit artificial, with uniformed vendors and thoughtfully designed premises.

★ **Lavka-Lavka** INTERNATIONAL €€

(Лавка-Лавка; ☑ 8-495-621 2036; www.restoran. lavkalavka.com; ul Petrovka 21 str 2; mains R500-1100; ⊘ noon-midnight Tue-Thu & Sun, to 1am Fri & Sat, 6pm-midnight Mon; 🛜 👪; Ⓜ Teatralnaya) 🔿 Welcome to the Russian Portlandia – all the food here is organic and hails from little farms where you can rest assured all the lambs and chickens lived a very happy life before being served to you on a plate. This is a great place to sample local food cooked in a funky improvisational style.

Moldova MOLDOVAN €€

(☑ 8-916-552 0353; www.restoran-moldova.ru; ul Rozhdestvenka 7; mains R450-600; ⊘ noon-midnight; Ⓜ Kuznetsky Most) When speakeasy meets post-Soviet political economy, it may result in something like this little gem tucked into the Moldovan embassy in Moscow's heart. Prepare for southern, Balkan-flavoured fare with *mititei* kebabs, *mamalyga* (polenta) with *brynza* soft cheese and paprika in all shapes and forms. The main highlight though is the excellent Moldovan wine.

THE BANYA

Taking a traditional Russian *banya* is a must. These wet saunas are a social hub and a fantastic experience for any visitor to Russia. Leave your inhibitions at home and be prepared for a beating with birch twigs (far more pleasant than it sounds). Ask at your accommodation for the nearest public *banya*. In Moscow, try the luxurious **Sanduny Baths** (☑ 495-782 1808; www.sanduny.ru; ul Neglinnaya 14; R1800-2800; ⊘ 8am-10pm Wed-Mon, 2nd male top class 10am-midnight Tue-Fri, 8am-10pm Sat & Sun; Ⓜ Kuznetsky Most), where they have several classes just like on trains, and in St Petersburg the traditional **Mytninskiye Bani** (Мытнинские бани; www.mybanya.spb.ru; ul Mytninskaya 17-19; per hour R200-350, lux banya per hour R1000-2000; ⊘ 8am-10pm Fri-Tue; Ⓜ Ploshchad Vosstaniya).

Gran Cafe Dr Zhivago RUSSIAN €€

(Гранд Кафе Dr Живаго; ☑ 499-922 0100; www. drzhivago.ru; Mokhovaya ul 15/1; mains R400-1200; ⊘ 24hr; Ⓜ Okhotny Ryad) An excellent breakfast choice before visiting the Kremlin, this round-the-clock place mixes Soviet nostalgia with a great deal of mischievous irony in both design and food. The chef has upgraded the menu of a standard pioneer camp's canteen to near-haute-cuisine level, with masterfully cooked porridge, pancakes, *vareniki* (boiled dumplings, like ravioli) and cottage-cheese pies.

★ **Björn** SCANDINAVIAN €€€

(☑ 495-953 9059; http://bjorn.rest; Pyatnitskaya ul 3; mains R700-1200; ⊘ noon-midnight; Ⓜ Novokuznetskaya) A neat cluster of fir trees on a busy street hides a Nordic gem that deserves a saga to glorify its many virtues. This is not an 'ethnic' restaurant, but a presentation of futuristic Scandinavian cuisine straight out of a science fiction movie. From salads to desserts, every dish looks deceptively simple, visually perfect and 23rd century.

White Rabbit INTERNATIONAL €€€

(☑ 495-510 5101; http://whiterabbitmoscow.ru; Smolenskaya pl 3; mains R800-1600; ⊘ noon-midnight, to 2am Thu-Sat; 🛜; Ⓜ Smolenskaya) Views from panoramic windows are breathtaking, but the real stunner here is the menu – playfully inventive, yet singularly Muscovite, marrying cutting-edge culinary thought with the lavishness of Tolstoy-era banquets. This results in such concoctions as baked-bean borscht with crucians or calf tongue in chokecherry dough. Definitely go for small snacks, especially pies. Booking is advisable.

🍷 Drinking & Nightlife

★ **Noor / Electro** BAR

(☑ 8-903-136 7686; www.noorbar.com; Tverskaya ul 23/12; ⊘ 8pm-3am Mon-Wed, to 6am Thu-Sun; Ⓜ Pushkinskaya) There is little to say about this misleadingly unassuming bar, apart from the fact that everything in it is close to perfection. It has it all – prime location, convivial atmosphere, eclectic DJ music, friendly bartenders and superb drinks. Though declared 'the best' by various magazines on several occasions, it doesn't feel like the owners care.

★ **Enthusiast** BAR

(Энтузиаст; Stoleshnikov per 7 str 5; ⊘ noon-11pm Sun-Thu, to 2am Fri & Sat; Ⓜ Teatralnaya) Scooter enthusiast, that is. But you don't have to be one in order to enjoy this superbly laid-back bar hidden at the far end of a fancifully shaped courtyard and disguised as a spare-parts shop. On a warm day, grab a beer or cider, settle into a beach chair and let harmony descend on you.

32.05
CAFE

(☑ 8-905-703 3205; www.veranda3205.ru; ul Karetny Ryad 3; ☉ 11am-3am; M Pushkinskaya) The biggest drinking and eating establishment in Hermitage Gardens, this veranda positioned at the back of the park's main building looks a bit like a greenhouse. In summer, tables (and patrons) spill out into the park, making it one of the city's best places for outdoor drinking. With its long bar and joyful atmosphere, the place also heaves in winter.

Cafe Mart
CAFE

(Кафе Март; www.cafemart.ru; ul Petrovka 25; ☉ 11am-midnight Sun-Wed, to 6am Thu-Sat, jazz concert 9pm Thu; 🖋; M Chekhovskaya) It looks like just another cellar bar, but if you walk all the way through the underground maze you'll find yourself in the huge overground 'orangerie' hall with mosaic-covered walls, warm lighting and possibly a jazz concert. When the weather is fine, Mart spills into the sculpture-filled courtyard of the adjacent **Moscow Museum of Modern Art** (Московский музей современного искусства; MMOMA; www.mmoma.ru; ul Petrovka 25; adult/student R450/250, joint ticket for 3 venues R500/300; ☉ noon-8pm Tue, Wed & Fri-Sun, 1-9pm Thu; M Chekhovskaya).

★ Bar Strelka
CAFE, CLUB

(www.barstrelka.com; Bersenevskaya nab 14/5, bldg 5a; ☉ 9am-midnight Mon-Thu, to 3am Fri, noon-3am Sat, noon-midnight Sun; 🛜; M Kropotkinskaya) Located just below the Patriarshy most, the bar-restaurant at the **Strelka Institute** (www.strelkainstitute.ru) is the ideal starting point for an evening in the Red October (p955) complex. The rooftop terrace has unbeatable Moscow River views, but the interior is equally cool in a shabby-chic sort of way. The bar menu is excellent and there is usually somebody tinkling the ivories.

Parka
CRAFT BEER

(☑ 8-926-160 6313; www.facebook.com/parka craft; Pyatnitskaya ul 22 str 1; ☉ 1pm-2am; M Novokuznetskaya) 'Parka' is a *banya* (bathhouse) term, hence the sauna-like decor, and just like a proper *banya*, this is a very relaxing place. The friendly bartenders let you try any beer before you commit to buying a pint; the brews, many with crazy Runglish names, are mostly local.

☆ Entertainment

★ Bolshoi Theatre
BALLET, OPERA

(Большой театр; ☑ 495-455 5555; www.bolshoi. ru; Teatralnaya pl 1; tickets R5500-12,000; ☉ closed late Jul-mid-Sep; M Teatralnaya) An evening at the Bolshoi is still one of Moscow's most romantic and entertaining options for a night on the town. The glittering six-tier auditorium has an electric atmosphere, evoking over 240 years of premier music and dance. Both the ballet and opera companies perform a range of Russian and foreign works here.

Tchaikovsky Concert Hall
CLASSICAL MUSIC

(Концертный зал имени Чайковского; ☑ 495-232 0400; www.meloman.ru; Triumfalnaya pl 4/31; tickets R800-3000; ☉ concerts 7pm, closed Aug; M Mayakovskaya) Established in 1921, the Tchaikovsky Concert Hall is the main venue for the country's best orchestras and stellar international acts. It's a huge auditorium, with seating for 1600 people. Expect to hear the Russian classics, such as Stravinsky, Rachmaninov and Shostakovich, as well as other European favourites. Look out for children's concerts, jazz ensembles and other special performances.

🛍 Shopping

GUM
MALL

(ГУМ; www.gum.ru; Krasnaya pl 3; ☉ 10am-10pm; M Ploshchad Revolyutsii) Behind its elaborate 240m-long facade on the northeastern side of Red Square, GUM is a bright, bustling shopping mall with hundreds of fancy stores and restaurants. With a skylight roof and three-level arcades, the spectacular interior was a revolutionary design when it was built in the 1890s, replacing the Upper Trading Rows that previously occupied this site.

Flakon
SHOPPING CENTRE

(www.flacon.ru; ul Bolshaya Novodmitrovskaya 36; M Dmitrovskaya) Flakon is arguably the most visually attractive of all the redeveloped industrial areas around town, looking a bit like the far end of London's Portobello Rd, especially on weekends. Once a glassware plant, it is now home to dozens of funky shops and other businesses. Shopping for designer clothes and unusual souvenirs is the main reason for coming here.

Izmaylovsky Market   MARKET
(www.kremlin-izmailovo.com; Izmaylovskoye sh 73; ⊘10am-8pm; Ⓜ Partizanskaya) Never mind the kitschy faux 'tsar's palace' it surrounds, this is the ultimate place to shop for *matryoshka* dolls, military uniforms, icons, Soviet badges and some real antiques. Huge and diverse, it is almost a theme park, including shops, cafes and a couple of not terribly exciting museums.

ℹ Information

Free wireless access is ubiquitous.

36.6 A chain of 24-hour pharmacies with many branches all around the city.

European Medical Centre (📞 495-933 6655; www.emcmos.ru; Spirodonevsky per 5; ⊘24hr; Ⓜ Mayakovskaya) Offers 24-hour emergency service, consultations and a full range of medical specialists.

ℹ BETWEEN CAPITALS

With excellent high-speed trains and numerous flights daily, travel between Moscow and St Petersburg couldn't be easier. The modern and comfortable Sapsan trains connect **Leningradsky train station** (Ленинградский вокзал; http://leningradsky.dzvr.ru; Komsomolskaya pl; 🛜; Ⓜ Komsomolskaya) in Moscow with **Moskovsky train station** (Moskovsky vokzal; Московский вокзал; www.moskovsky-vokzal.ru; Nevsky pr 85; Ⓜ Ploshchad Vosstaniya) in St Petersburg, in just four hours. To avoid queuing at the station, buy an e-ticket (from R3400), which you don't need to print out, using the RZD or Rail Russia app on your smartphone. Overnight trains range from scruffy cheapies to luxurious equivalents of the Orient Express.

Flights that connect St Petersburg's Pulkovo (p976) with all three main airports in Moscow are less convenient, given the time spent on getting to/from the airport, but tickets may cost as little as R2000. That said, consider how much you pay for airport trains or taxis.

Main Post Office (Myasnitskaya ul 26; ⊘24hr; Ⓜ Chistye Prudy)

Moscow Times (https://themoscowtimes.com) Country's main English-language publication.

ℹ Getting There & Around

ARRIVING IN MOSCOW

Airports The three main airports are accessible by the convenient **Aeroexpress Train** (📞 8-800 700 3377; www.aeroexpress.ru; one way R420; ⊘6am-midnight), which takes 35 to 45 minutes from the city centre. If you wish to take a taxi, book an official airport taxi through the dispatcher counter (R2000 to R2500). If you can order a taxi by phone or with a mobile-phone app it will be about 50% cheaper.

Train Stations Rail riders will arrive at one of the central train stations. All of the train stations are located in the city centre, with easy access to the metro. Alternatively, most taxi companies offer a fixed rate of R400 to R600 for a train-station transfer.

PUBLIC TRANSPORT

The rapidly expanding and super-efficient **Moscow metro** (www.mosmetro.ru; per ride R55) network is by far the most convenient way of getting around the city. But with the introduction of dedicated bus lanes and fleet upgrade, buses, trolleybuses and trams are becoming increasingly relevant.

Moscow has a unified ticketing system. Available from ticket booths and machines at metro stations and some bus stops, tickets are magnetic cards that you must tap on the reader at the turnstiles before entering a metro station or on the bus. Most convenient for short-term visitors is the red Ediny (Единый) ticket, which is good for all kinds of transport and available at metro stations. A single trip costs R55. A three-day unlimited pass goes for R438.

Metro stations are marked outside by 'M' signs. Many bus stops are now equipped with screens showing waiting time.

TAXI

Taxis are affordable, but you can't really flag them down in the street – not the metered ones anyway. These days, most people use mobile phone apps (such as Uber, Gett and Yandex Taxi) to order a cab. You can also order an official taxi by phone or book it online, or ask a Russian-speaker to do this for you. **Taxi Tsel** (📞 495-204 2244; www.taxicel.ru) is a reliable company, but operators don't speak English. **Lingo Taxi** (www.lingotaxi.com) promises English-speaking drivers and usually delivers.

GOLDEN RING
ЗОЛОТОЕ КОЛЬЦО

The Golden Ring is textbook Russia: onion-shaped domes, kremlins and gingerbread cottages with cherry orchards. It is a string of the country's oldest towns that formed the core of eastern Kyivan Rus. Too engrossed in fratricide, they failed to register the rise of Moscow, which elbowed them out of active politics. Largely untouched by Soviet industrialisation, places like Suzdal now attract flocks of Russian tourists in search of the lost idyll. The complete circular route, described in the Lonely Planet guide to Russia, requires about a week to be completed. But several gems can be seen on one- or two-day trips from Moscow.

Vladimir   Владимир

☑ 4922 / POP 347,000

Founded at the dawn of the 12th century on a bluff over the Klyazma River, Vladimir became the cradle of Russian history when Prince Andrei Bogolyubsky moved his capital there from Kyiv in 1169. Thus began Vladimir's Golden Age, when many of the beautifully carved white-stone buildings for which the area is renowned were built by Bogolyubsky and his brother, Prince Vsevolod the Big Nest. After a Mongol invasion devastated the town in 1238, power shifted some 200km west to a minor settlement called Moscow. Though Vladimir eventually rebounded from the ruins, it would never regain its former glory.

Today this bustling city is the administrative centre of Vladimir Oblast. Although not as charmingly bucolic as nearby Suzdal, Vladimir's easy access from Moscow, its cluster of centrally located Unesco-listed sights and its stunning river-valley panoramas make it an ideal starting point for a Golden Ring tour.

★ **Assumption Cathedral**   CHURCH
(Успенский собор; ☑ 4922-325 201; www.vlad museum.ru; Sobornaya pl; adult/student R150/75; ⊘ visitors 1-4.45pm Tue-Sun) Set dramatically high above the Klyazma River, this simple but majestic piece of pre-Mongol architecture is the legacy of Prince Andrei Bogolyubsky, the man who began shifting power from Kyiv to northeastern Rus (which eventually evolved into Muscovy). A white-stone version of Kyiv's brick Byzantine churches, the cathedral was constructed from 1158 to 1160,

WORTH A TRIP

CHURCH OF THE INTERCESSION ON THE NERL

Tourists and pilgrims all flock to Bogolyubovo, just 12km northeast of Vladimir, for this perfect little jewel of a 12th-century church standing amid a flower-covered floodplain. The **Church of the Intercession on the Nerl** (Церковь Покрова на Нерли; Bogolyubovo; ⊘ 10am-6pm Tue-Sun) FREE is the golden standard of Russian architecture. Apart from ideal proportions, its beauty lies in a brilliantly chosen waterside location (floods aside) and the sparing use of delicate carving.

To reach it, get bus 152 (R25) from the Golden Gate or Sobornaya pl in Vladimir and get off by the blue-domed Bogolyubsky Monastery. Walk past the monastery to Vokzalnaya ul, the first street on the right, and follow it down to the train station. Cross the pedestrian bridge over the railroad tracks and follow the stone path for 1km across the meadow.

though it was rebuilt and expanded after a fire in 1185. It was added to Unesco's World Heritage List in 1992.

Cathedral of St Dmitry   CHURCH
(Дмитриевский собор; www.vladmuseum.ru; Bolshaya Moskovskaya ul 60; adult/student R150/75; ⊘ 10am-6pm Mon-Thu, to 8pm Fri-Sun May-Sep, reduced hours Oct-Apr) Built between 1193 and 1197, this exquisite, Unesco-listed white-stone cathedral represents the epitome of Russian stone carving. The attraction here is the cathedral's exterior walls, which are covered in an amazing profusion of images. At their top centre, the north, south and west walls all show King David bewitching the birds and beasts with music.

Voznesenskaya Sloboda   HOTEL €€€
(Вознесенская слобода; ☑ 8-800 302 5494; www.vsloboda.ru; ul Voznesenskaya 14b; d from R4900; P ❈ 🛜) Perched on a bluff with tremendous views of the valley, this hotel has one of the most scenic locations in the area. Outside is a quiet neighbourhood of old wooden cottages and villas dominated by the elegant Ascension Church, whose bells chime idyllically throughout the day. The new building's interior is tastefully designed to resemble art nouveau style c 1900.

Ginger Cat
INTERNATIONAL €€

(Пшеничный кот; ☏4922-472 109; https://
pshenichniy-kot.ru; ul Bolshaya Moskovskaya 19;
mains R340-590; ☉11am-11pm, from 10am Sat
& Sun; 🛜) This cheerfully coloured modern
place is designed to keep children busy in
two playrooms while adults relax with a decent meal and a glass of wine. Children or
not, this is where you'll find competently
cooked international fare, such as steaks
and caesar *salat*. The extensive dessert
menu is a treat for any sweet tooth, young
or old.

★Four Brewers Pub
CRAFT BEER

(Паб Четыре Пивовара; www.4brewers.ru;
Bolshaya Moskovskaya ul 12; ☉2pm-midnight Sun-
Thu, to 2am Fri & Sat) This pocket-sized pub
offers 20 brews on tap and dozens more in
bottles – porter, IPA, stout, ale, you name
it – all from the brewers' own vats or other
Russian microbreweries, with such unforgettable names as 'Banana Kraken', 'Santa
Muerte', 'Roksana and the Endless Universe'
and (our personal favourite) 'Black Jesus,
White Pepper'. Bartenders happily offer recommendations and free tastes.

❶ Getting There & Away

Vladimir is on the main trans-Siberian line between Moscow and Nizhny Novgorod and on a
major highway leading to Kazan. There are nine
services a day from Moscow's Kursk Station
(Kursky vokzal), with modern Strizh and slightly
less comfortable Lastochka trains (R600 to
R1600, 1¾ hours).

Suzdal
Суздаль

☏49231 / POP 9750

The sparkling diamond in the Golden Ring
is undoubtedly Suzdal – if you have time
for only one of these towns, this is the one
to see. With rolling green fields carpeted
with dandelions, a gentle river curling lazi-
ly through a historic town centre, sunlight
bouncing off golden church domes and the
sound of horse clops and church bells carrying softly through the air, you may feel like
you've stumbled into a storybook Russia.

Suzdal served as a royal capital when
Moscow was still a cluster of cowsheds, and
was a major monastic centre and an important commercial hub for many years as
well. But in 1864, local merchants failed to
get the Trans-Siberian Railway built through
here (it went to Vladimir instead). Suzdal
was thus bypassed both by trains and 20th-

century progress, preserving its idyllic character for future visitors.

◉ Sights

★Kremlin
FORTRESS

(Кремль; ☏49231-21 624; www.vladmuseum.
ru; ul Kremlyovskaya; joint ticket adult/student
R350/200; ☉exhibitions 9am-6pm Sun-Thu, to
9pm Fri & Sat, grounds to 9pm) The grandfather
of the Moscow Kremlin, this citadel was the
12th-century base of Prince Yury Dolgoruky,
who ruled the vast northeastern part of Kyivan Rus (and, among other things, founded
a small outpost that would eventually become the Russian capital). The 1.4km-long
earthen ramparts of Suzdal's kremlin enclose a few streets of houses and a handful
of churches, as well as the main cathedral
group on ul Kremlyovskaya.

★Saviour Monastery of St Euthymius
MONASTERY

(Спасо-Евфимиев монастырь; ☏49231-20
746; www.vladmuseum.ru; ul Lenina; adult/student
R400/200; ☉10am-7pm Sun-Thu, to 9pm Fri &
Sat) Founded in the 14th century to protect
the town's northern entrance, Suzdal's biggest monastery grew mighty in the 16th and
17th centuries after Vasily III, Ivan the Terrible and the noble Pozharsky family funded
impressive new stone buildings and made
large land and property acquisitions. It was
girded with its great brick walls and towers
in the 17th century.

🛏 Sleeping

★Surikov Guest House
GUESTHOUSE €€

(Гостевой дом Суриковых; ☏8-915-752 4950,
8-961-257 9598; ul Krasnoarmeyskaya 53; d incl
breakfast R2500; ℗🛜) This 11-room boutique
guesthouse is positioned at a particularly
picturesque bend of the Kamenka River
across from the walls of the Saviour Monastery of St Euthymius. It has modestly sized
but comfortable rooms equipped with rustic-style furniture (some made by the owner himself) and a Russian restaurant (for
guests only) on the 1st floor. Visitors rave
about this place.

Pushkarskaya Sloboda
RESORT €€€

(Пушкарская слобода; ☏8-800 350 5303;
www.pushkarka.ru; ul Lenina 45; d from R4300;
℗❄🛜🛝) This attractive riverside holiday
village has everything you might want for a
Russian idyll, including accommodation options in traditionally styled log cabins (from

R7900). It has three restaurants (including a rustic country tavern and a formal dining room) and a spa centre with pool. The staff can also arrange all sorts of tours and classes around Suzdal.

✕ Eating & Drinking

★ Russkaya Chaynaya RUSSIAN €
(Русская чайная; www.tea-suzdal.ru; ul Kremlyovskaya 10g; mains R250-620; ⊙10am-9pm) It's hidden behind a kitsch crafts market, but this place is a gem. Russian standards – bliny, *shchi* (cabbage soup), mushroom dishes and pickles – are prominently represented, but it's all the unusual (and rather experimental) items on the menu that make Russkaya Chaynaya so special. Cabbage stewed in apple juice with raisins and thyme, anyone?

★ Gostiny Dvor RUSSIAN €€
(Гостиный дворъ; ☑ 49231-021190; www.suzdaldvor.ru; Trading Arcades, Torgovaya pl; mains R450-550; ⊙10am-10pm Mon-Thu, 9am-11pm Fri-Sun; 🛜📶) There are so many things to like about this place: eclectic decor of rustic antiques and warm wood; outside terrace tables offering river views; hearty Russian dishes (chicken, pike, *pelmeni* dumplings) prepared with modern flair; and friendly, attentive service, to start. Finish up with a tasting set of house-made *medovukha* (honey ale) while the kids amuse themselves in the playroom.

Graf Suvorov & Mead-Tasting Hall BEER HALL
(Граф Суворов и зал дегустаций; ☑ 49231-20 803, 8-905-734 5404; Trading Arcades, Torgovaya pl; tasting menu R300-500; ⊙10am-6pm Mon-Fri, to 8pm Sat & Sun) Sit beneath vaulted ceilings and contemplate kitsch murals of Russian military hero Count Suvorov's exploits in the Alps as you make your way through a tasting set (10 samples) of the few dozen varieties of locally produced *medovukha*. Flavours also include berry and herb infusions. Located on the back (river) side of the Trading Arcades.

ℹ Getting There & Away

There is no bus service to Suzdal from Moscow; you'll need to take a train to Vladimir and then switch to a Suzdal-bound bus there. Buses run very regularly throughout the day to and from Vladimir (R110, 45 minutes). The bus station is 2km east of the centre on Vasilievskaya ul. Some long-distance buses pass the central square on the way.

Sergiev Posad
Сергиев Посад
☑ 496 / POP 109,000

Blue-and-gold cupolas offset by snow-white walls – this colour scheme lies at the heart of the Russian perception of divinity and Sergiev Posad's monastery is a textbook example. It doesn't get any holier than this in Russia, for the place was founded in 1340 by the country's most revered saint, St Sergius of Radonezh. Since the 14th century, pilgrims have been journeying here to pay homage to him.

Although the Bolsheviks closed the monastery, it was reopened following WWII as a museum, residence of the patriarch and a working monastery. The patriarch and the church's administrative centre moved to the Danilovsky Monastery in Moscow in 1988, but the Trinity Monastery of St Sergius remains one of the most important spiritual sites in Russia.

★ Trinity Monastery of St Sergius MONASTERY
(Свято-Троицкая Сергиева Лавра; ☑ info 496-544 5334, tours 496-540 5721; www.stsl.ru; ⊙5am-9pm) FREE In 1340 St Sergius of Radonezh founded this *lavra* (senior monastery), which soon became the spiritual centre of Russian Orthodoxy. St Sergius was credited with providing mystic support to Prince Dmitry Donskoy in his improbable victory over the Tatars in the Battle of Kulikovo in 1380. Soon after his death at the age of 78, Sergius was named Russia's patron saint.

Old Hotel Lavra HOTEL €€
(Старая гостиница Лавры; ☑ 496-549 9000; www.lavrahotel.ru; pr Krasnoy Armii 133; s/d from R3000/3400; 🛜) Built in 1822 as pilgrim accommodation, this massive monastery hotel has been revived in its original capacity, with nothing to distract its supposedly puritan guests from prayer and contemplation – not even TV. But despite their blandness, rooms are modern and very clean. There's a vast restaurant on the premises. Unsurprisingly, alcohol is strictly banned throughout the complex. Breakfast is R200.

★ Gostevaya Izba RUSSIAN €€
(Гостевая Изба; ☑ 496-541 4343; www.sergiev-kanon.ru; Aptekarsky per 2; meals R350-850; ⊙10am-11pm; 🖉) Right by the monastery walls, this wonderful restaurant recreates classic dishes metropolitans of the past might

have eaten outside fasting periods, such as apple-roasted duck breast with lingonberry sauce. Portions are ample and the food delicious. Try some *kvas* (fermented rye bread water), fireweed tea or Siberian malt lemonade straight from the monastery's own brewery.

ℹ Getting There & Away

Considering the horrendous traffic jams on the road approaches to Moscow, train is a much better way of getting to Sergiev Posad from the capital. The fastest option is the express commuter train that departs from Moscow's Yaroslavsky vokzal (R230, one hour); there are four daily during the week, three on weekends. Cheaper but slower *elektrichki* (suburban trains; R176, 1½ hours) depart a few times per hour throughout the day.

ST PETERSBURG
САНКТ ПЕТЕРБУРГ

✆ 812 / POP 5,281,580

Affectionately known as Piter to locals, St Petersburg is a visual delight. The Neva River and surrounding canals reflect unbroken facades of handsome 18th- and 19th-century buildings that house a spellbinding collection of cultural storehouses, culminating in the incomparable Hermitage. Home to many of Russia's greatest creative talents (Pushkin, Dostoevsky, Tchaikovsky), Piter still inspires a contemporary generation of Russians, making it a liberal, hedonistic and exciting place to visit.

The city covers many islands, some real, some created through the construction of canals. The central street is Nevsky pr, which extends some 4km from the Alexander Nevsky Monastery to the Hermitage.

◉ Sights

◉ Historic Heart

Palace Square SQUARE

(Дворцовая площадь; Dvortsovaya pl; ℳ Admiralteyskaya) This vast expanse is simply one of the most striking squares in the world, still redolent of imperial grandeur almost a century after the end of the Romanov dynasty. For the most amazing first impression, walk from Nevsky pr, up Bolshaya Morskaya ul and under the **triumphal arch**.

★**Russian Museum** MUSEUM

(Русский музей; ✆ 812-595 4248; www.rusmuseum.ru; Inzhenernaya ul 4; adult/student R500/250; ⊙10am-8pm Mon, 10am-6pm Wed & Fri-Sun, 1-9pm Thu; ℳ Nevsky Prospekt) Focusing solely on Russian art, from ancient church icons to 20th-century paintings, the Russian Museum's collection is magnificent and can easily be viewed in half a day or less. The collection includes works by Karl Bryullov, Alexander Ivanov, Nicholas Ghe, Ilya Repin, Natalya Goncharova, Kazimir Malevich and

---

RUSSIA'S MOST FAMOUS STREET

Walking **Nevsky Prospekt** is an essential St Petersburg experience. Highlights along it include the Kazan Cathedral (p970), with its curved arms reaching out towards the avenue.

Opposite is the **Singer Building** (Nevsky pr 28; ℳ Nevsky Prospekt), a Style Moderne (art deco) beauty restored to all its splendour when it was the headquarters of the sewing-machine company; inside is the bookshop **Dom Knigi** (✆ 812-448 2355; www.spbdk.ru; Nevsky pr 28; ⊙9am-1am; 🛜; ℳ Nevsky Prospekt) and **Café Singer** (Кафе Зингеръ; ✆ 812-571 8223; www.singercafe.ru; Nevsky pr 28; mains R400-500; ⊙9am-11pm; 🛜; ℳ Nevsky Prospekt), serving good food and drinks with a great view over the street.

Further along are the covered arcades of Rastrelli's historic **Bolshoy Gostiny Dvor** (Большой Гостиный Двор; ✆ 812-630 5408; http://bgd.ru; Nevsky pr 35; ⊙10am-10pm; ℳ Gostiny Dvor) department store, while on the corner of Sadovaya ul is the Style Moderne classic **Kupetz Eliseevs** (✆ 812-456 6666; www.kupetzeliseevs.ru; Nevsky pr 56; ⊙10am-11pm; 🛜; ℳ Gostiny Dvor) reincarnated as a luxury grocery and cafe.

An enormous **statue of Catherine the Great** (pl Ostrovskogo) stands at the centre of **Ploshchad Ostrovskogo** (Площадь Островского; ℳ Gostiny Dvor), commonly referred to as the Catherine Gardens; at the southern end of the gardens is **Alexandrinsky Theatre** (✆ 812-710 4103; www.alexandrinsky.ru; pl Ostrovskogo 2; tickets R900-6000; ℳ Gostiny Dvor), where Chekhov's *The Seagull* premiered (to tepid reviews) in 1896.

DON'T MISS

STATE HERMITAGE MUSEUM

Mainly set in the magnificent Winter Palace and adjoining buildings, the **Hermitage** (Государственный Эрмитаж; www.hermitagemuseum.org; Dvortsovaya pl 2; combined ticket R700; ☉10.30am-6pm Tue, Thu, Sat & Sun, to 9pm Wed & Fri; M Admiralteyskaya) fully lives up to its sterling reputation. You can be absorbed by its treasures for days and still come out wanting more.

The enormous collection (over three million items, only a fraction of which are on display in around 360 rooms) almost amounts to a comprehensive history of Western European art. Viewing it demands a little planning, so choose the areas you'd like to concentrate on before you arrive. The museum consists of five connected buildings. From west to east:

Winter Palace Designed by Bartolomeo Rastrelli, its opulent state rooms, Great Church, Pavilion Hall and Treasure Rooms shouldn't be missed.

Small Hermitage and Old Hermitage Both were built for Catherine the Great, partly to house the art collection started by Peter the Great, which she significantly expanded. Here you'll find works by Rembrandt, Da Vinci and Caravaggio.

New Hermitage Built for Nicholas II, to hold the still-growing art collection. The Old and New Hermitages are sometimes grouped together and labelled the Large Hermitage.

General Staff Building Designed by Carlo Rossi in the 1820s, this building, located across the square from the Winter Palace, contains an amazing collection of Impressionist and post-Impressionist works.

State Hermitage Theatre Built in the 1780s by Giacomo Quarenghi. Concerts and ballets are still performed here.

Kuzma Petrov-Vodkin, among many others, and the masterpieces keep on coming as you tour the beautiful Carlo Rossi–designed Mikhailovsky Palace and its attached wings.

Entry is either from Arts Sq or via the connected **Benois Wing** (nab kanala Griboyedova; adult/student R450/200; ☉10am-8pm Mon, 10am-6pm Wed & Fri-Sun, 1-9pm Thu) on nab kanala Griboyedova. There's also an entrance from the lovely **Mikhailovsky Garden** (Михайловский сад; https://igardens.ru; ☉10am-10pm May-Sep, to 8pm Oct-Mar, closed Apr) FREE behind the palace. Permanent and temporary exhibitions by the Russian Museum are also held at the **Marble Palace** (Мраморный дворец; Millionnaya ul 5; adult/student R300/170; ☉10am-6pm Mon, Wed & Fri-Sun, 1-9pm Thu; M Nevsky Prospekt), the **Mikhailovsky Castle** (Михайловский замок; Sadovaya ul 2; adult/student R250/130; ☉10am-6pm Mon, Wed & Fri-Sun, 1-9pm Thu; M Gostiny Dvor) and the **Stroganov Palace** (Строгановский дворец; Nevsky pr 17; adult/student R250/130; ☉10am-6pm Wed & Fri-Mon, 1-9pm Thu; M Nevsky Prospekt). Combined tickets, available at each palace, cover entrance either to your choice of two the same day (adult/student R600/270) or to all four within a three-day period (R850/400).

★**Church of the Saviour on the Spilled Blood**   CHURCH
(Храм Спаса на Крови; ☏812-315 1636; http://eng.cathedral.ru/spasa_na_krovi; Konyushennaya pl; adult/student R350/200; ☉10.30am-6pm Thu-Tue; M Nevsky Prospekt) This five-domed dazzler is St Petersburg's most elaborate church, with a classic Russian Orthodox exterior and an interior decorated with some 7000 sq metres of mosaics. Officially called the Church of the Resurrection of Christ, its far more striking colloquial name references the assassination attempt on Tsar Alexander II here in 1881.

★**St Isaac's Cathedral**   MUSEUM
(Исаакиевский собор; ☏812-315 9732; www.cathedral.ru; Isaakievskaya pl; cathedral adult/student R250/150, colonnade R150; ☉cathedral 10.30am-10.30pm Thu-Tue May-Sep, to 6pm Oct-Apr, colonnade 10.30am-10.30pm May-Oct, to 6pm Nov-Apr; M Admiralteyskaya) The golden dome of St Isaac's Cathedral dominates the St Petersburg skyline. Its obscenely lavish interior is open as a museum, although services are held in the cathedral throughout the year. Many people bypass the museum to climb the 262 steps to the *kolonnada* (colonnade) around the drum of the dome, providing superb city views.

Central St Petersburg

Maly pr

Bolshoy pr

Sportivnaya

Sportivnaya

pr Dobrolyubova

Zverinskaya ul

ul Blokhina

ul Yablochkova

Kronverksky pr

Kronverksky Island

Alexandrovsky Park

Kronverkskaya nab

Zayachy Island

Proliv

Kronverksky

Peter & Paul Fortress

Troitskaya pl

Petrovskaya nab

Troitsky most

Tuchkov most

Petrogradsky Island

Malaya Neva

nab Makarova

Birzhevoy most

Suvorovskaya pl

27 Volkhovsky per

1-ya liniya / Kadetskaya liniya

ul Repina

VASILYEVSKY ISLAND

Birzhevaya pl 19

proezd 15

Birzhevoy Kunstkamera 2

Dvortsovy most

Dvortsovaya nab 10

Summer Garden

State Hermitage Museum 7

Millionnaya ul

Church of the Saviour on the Spilled Blood 1

Russian Museum 12

16 5

Vasileostrovets Gardens

Universitetskaya nab

Peterhof Express

ADMIRALTEYSKY

13

44

Dvortsovaya pl (Palace Square) 21

Zelyony most

Nevsky pr

Malaya Konyushennaya ul

43

17

38 Pl Iskusstv

Bolshaya Neva

Senatskaya pl (pl Dekabristov)

Admiralteysky

20

40

Nevsky Prospekt

Blagoveshchensky most

Angliyskaya nab

Galernaya ul

Alexander Garden

Isaakievskaya pl

Admiralteysky pr

Admiralteyskaya

Kazanskaya pl

9

39

28 Malaya Morskaya ul

6

St Isaac's Cathedral

Bolshaya Morskaya ul

nab reki Moyki

23

Gostiny Dvor

Konnogvardeysky bul

Pl Truda

Pochtamtskaya ul

29

New Holland 3

per Matveeva

Kryukov Canal

ul Truda

Bolshaya Morskaya ul

42

KAZANSKY

Grivtsova pr

25

30

Kazanskaya ul

Kazanskaya ul

nab kanala Griboyedova

Sadovaya ul

ul Lomonosova

SPASSKY

ul Dekabristov

36 37

Teatralnaya Pl

ul Glinki

Pr Rimskogo-Korsakova

Fonarny per

Stolyarny per

Voznesensky pr

Sadovaya

Sadovaya

Sennaya Pl

Sennaya pl

Spasskaya

Gorokhovaya ul

Moskovsky pr

SENNAYA

Semyonovsky most

ul Soyuza Pechatnikov

Griboyedov Canal

Nikolsky Gardens

Nikolsky per

Kryukov Canal

Yusupov Gardens

nab reki Fontanki

Obukhovsky most

Zvenigorodskaya

Pushkinskaya

Vitebskaya pl

Kanonerskaya ul

Sadovaya ul

nab reki Fontanki

Fontanka

Vitebsk Station (Vitebsky vokzal)

ul Labutina

POKROVSKY

Egypetsky most

Izmailovsky pr

Polsky Gardens

Tekhnologichesky Institut

Pulkovo (12km)

pr Moskvinoy

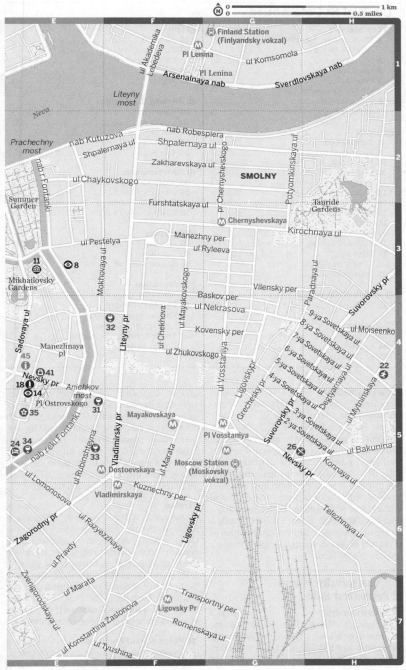

N 0 — 1 km
0 — 0.5 miles

ul Akademika Lebedeva

(R) Finland Station (Finlyandsky vokzal)

(M) Pl Lenina

Pl Lenina

ul Komsomola

Arsenalnaya nab

Sverdlovskaya nab

Liteyny most

Neva

Prachechny most

nab Kutuzova

nab Robespiera

Shpalernaya ul

Shpalernaya ul

Zakharevskaya ul

SMOLNY

nab r Fontanki

ul Chaykovskogo

pr Chernyshevskogo

Potyomkinskaya ul

Summer Garden

Furshtatskaya ul

Tauride Gardens

(M) Chernyshevskaya

ul Pestelya

Manezhny per

Kirochnaya ul

ul Ryleeva

11 🏛

⊚ 8

Mikhailovsky Gardens

Mokhovaya ul

Vilensky per

ParADnaya ul

Suvorovsky pr

Baskov per

ul Nekrasova

ul Mayakovskogo

ul Chekhova

9-ya Sovetskaya ul

ul Moiseenko

Sadovaya ul

🚇 32

Liteyny pr

Kovensky per

8-ya Sovetskaya ul

7-ya Sovetskaya ul

Manezhnaya pl

45

ⓘ

ul Zhukovskogo

Ligovsky pr

6-ya Sovetskaya ul

5-ya Sovetskaya ul

Degtyarnaya ul

22

🎭

Nevsky pr

🏠 41

ul Vosstaniya

Grechesky pr

4-ya Sovetskaya ul

ul Mytninskaya

18 ⓘ

⊚ 14

Anichkov most

3-ya Sovetskaya ul

Suvorovsky pr

Pl Ostrovskogo

🚇 31

Mayakovskaya

2-ya Sovetskaya ul

🎭 35

(M)

Pl Vosstaniya

ul Bakunina

24 34

🚇 33

(M)

26 🎭

Konnaya ul

📇

(M) Dostoevskaya

ul Marata

Moscow Station (Moskovsky vokzal) (R)

Nevsky pr

nab reki Fontanki

ul Rubinshteyna

Vladimirsky pr

Kuznechny per

Ligovsky pr

Telezhnaya ul

ul Lomonosova

Vladimirskaya

Zagorodny pr

ul Razyezzhaya

Zvenigorodskaya ul

ul Pravdy

ul Marata

Transportny per

Ligovsky Pr

Romenskaya ul

ul Konstantina Zaslonova

ul Tyushina

Central St Petersburg

Kazan Cathedral   CHURCH
(Казанский собор; ☎ 812-314 4663; http://
kazansky-spb.ru; Kazanskaya pl 2; ☉ 8.30am-
7.30pm; Ⓜ Nevsky Prospekt) FREE This neoclassical cathedral, partly modelled on St
Peter's in Rome, was commissioned by Tsar
Paul shortly before he was murdered in a
coup. Its 111m-long colonnaded arms reach
out towards Nevsky pr, encircling a garden
studded with statues. Inside, the cathedral
is dark and traditionally Orthodox, with a
daunting 80m-high dome. There is usually a
queue of believers waiting to kiss the icon of
Our Lady of Kazan, a copy of one of Russia's
most important icons.

◉ Vasilyevsky Island & Petrograd Side

★ **Kunstkamera**   MUSEUM
(Кунсткамера; ☎ 812-328 1412; www.kunstkamera.
ru; Universitetskaya nab 3, entrance on Tamozhenny
per; adult/child R300/100; ☉ 11am-7pm Tue-Sun;
Ⓜ Admiralteyskaya) Also known as the Museum
of Ethnology and Anthropology, this is the
city's first museum, founded in 1714 by Peter
himself. It is famous largely for its ghoulish
collection of monstrosities, preserved 'freaks',
two-headed mutant foetuses, deformed animals and odd body parts, all collected by
Peter. While most rush to see these sad specimens, there are also interesting exhibitions
on native peoples from around the world.

Strelka   LANDMARK
(Birzhevaya pl; Ⓜ Vasileostrovskaya) This eastern
tip of Vasilyevsky Island is where Peter the
Great wanted his new city's administrative
and intellectual centre to be. In fact, it became
the focus of the city's maritime trade, symbolised by the colonnaded Customs House (now
the Institute of Russian Literature) and the
Old Stock Exchange. The Strelka is flanked
by the pair of **Rostral Columns** (Ростральная
колонна), archetypal St Petersburg landmarks.

★ **Peter & Paul Fortress**   FORTRESS
(Петропавловская крепость; www.spbmuseum.
ru; grounds free, SS Peter & Paul Cathedral adult/

child R450/250, combined ticket for 5 exhibitions R600/350; ⏲grounds 9.30am-8pm, cathedral & bastion 10am-7pm Mon, Thu & Fri, 10am-5.45pm Sat, 11am-7pm Sun; Ⓜ Gorkovskaya) Housing a cathedral where the Romanovs are buried, a former prison and various exhibitions, this large defensive fortress on Zayachy Island is the kernel from which St Petersburg grew into the city it is today. History buffs will love it and everyone will swoon at the panoramic views from atop the fortress walls, at the foot of which lies a sandy riverside beach, a prime spot for sunbathing.

Beyond the Historic Heart

★New Holland ISLAND
(Новая Голландия; www.newhollandsp.ru; nab Admiralteyskogo kanala; ⏲9am-10pm Mon-Thu, to 11pm Fri-Sun; Ⓜ Sadovaya) This triangular island was closed for the most part of the last three centuries, and has opened to the public in dazzling fashion. There's plenty going on here, with hundreds of events happening throughout the year. There are summertime concerts, art exhibitions, yoga classes and film screenings, plus restaurants, cafes and shops. You can also come to enjoy a bit of quiet on the grass – or on one of the pontoons floating in the pond.

Golitsyn Loft CULTURAL CENTRE
(nab reky Fontanki 20; Ⓜ Gostiny Dvor) The new epicentre of creativity on the Fontanka River is this mazelike complex of shops, bars, cafes, beauty salons, tattoo parlours, galleries and even a hostel with capsule-style bunks. Enter via the archway into a large courtyard, which is spread with outdoor eating and drinking spots in the summer, then head up any of the stairwells into the five buildings for some urban exploration. On weekends the centre stages one-off events, such as craft markets, concerts and film screenings.

Sleeping

★Soul Kitchen Hostel HOSTEL €
(☎8-965-816 3470; www.soulkitchenhostel.com; nab reki Moyki 62/2, apt 9, Sennaya; dm R780-2200, d R3200-7500; @ 📶; Ⓜ Admiralteyskaya) Soul Kitchen blends boho hipness and boutique-hotel comfort, scoring perfect 10s in many key categories: private rooms (chic), dorm beds (double-width with privacy curtains), common areas and kitchen (all beautifully designed). The lounge is a fine place to hang out, with a record player, a big-screen projector (for movie nights) and an artful design.

★Rachmaninov Antique Hotel BOUTIQUE HOTEL €€
(☎812-571 9778; www.hotelrachmaninov.com; Kazanskaya ul 5; s/d from R6600/7500; @ 📶; Ⓜ Nevsky Prospekt) The long-established Rachmaninov still feels like a secret place for those in the know. Perfectly located and run by friendly staff, it's pleasantly old world, with hardwood floors and attractive Russian furnishings, particularly in the breakfast salon, which has a grand piano.

Rossi Hotel BOUTIQUE HOTEL €€€
(☎812-635 6333; www.rossihotels.com; nab reki Fontanki 55; s/d/ste from R8700/9600/18,000; ❄ @ 📶; Ⓜ Gostiny Dvor) Occupying a beautifully restored building on one of St Petersburg's prettiest squares, the Rossi's 65 rooms are all designed differently, but their brightness and moulded ceilings are uniform. Antique beds, super-sleek bathrooms, exposed brick walls and lots of cool designer touches create a great blend of old and new.

Eating

★Buter Brodsky EUROPEAN €€
(Бутер Бродский; ☎8-911-922 2606; https://vk.com/buterbrodskybar; nab Makarova 16; mains R260-780; ⏲noon-midnight; 📶; Ⓜ Sportivnaya) Shabby chic has never looked so good as it does at this cafe-bar dedicated to the poet Joseph Brodsky (the name is a pun on *buterbrod,* the Russian word for sandwich), a super-stylish part of Vasilyevsky Island's eating and drinking scene. The menu runs from excellent *smørrebrød* (open sandwiches; from R260) to fulsome Nordic- and Russian-themed mains.

Teplo MODERN EUROPEAN €€
(☎812-407 2702; www.v-teple.ru; Bolshaya Morskaya ul 45; mains R360-940; ⏲9am-midnight Mon-Fri, from 11am Sat & Sun; ❄ 📶 🌶 👪; Ⓜ Admiralteyskaya) This much-feted, eclectic and original restaurant has got it all just right. The venue itself is a lot of fun to nose around, with multiple small rooms, nooks and crannies. Service is friendly and fast (when it's not too busy) and the peppy, inventive Italian-leaning menu has something for everyone. Reservations are usually required, so call ahead.

Banshiki RUSSIAN €€
(Банщики; ☎8-921-941 1744; www.banshiki.spb.ru; Degtyarnaya ul 1; mains R500-1100; ⏲11am-

11pm; 🛜; Ⓜ Ploshchad Vosstaniya) Attached to a renovated *banya* (public baths) complex, this is currently the place to sample nostalgic Russian fare at affordable prices. Everything is made in-house, from its refreshing *kvas* (fermented rye bread water) to dried meats and eight types of smoked fish. Don't overlook cherry *vareniki* (dumplings) with sour cream, oxtail ragout or the rich borsch.

Cococo　　　　　　　　　　RUSSIAN €€€
(📞 812-418 2060; www.kokoko.spb.ru; Voznesensky pr 6; mains R650-1300; ⊙ 7-11am & 2pm-1am; 🛜; Ⓜ Admiralteyskaya) Cococo has charmed locals with its inventive approach to contemporary Russian cuisine. Your food is likely to arrive disguised as, say, a small bird's egg, a can of peas or a broken flowerpot – all rather gimmicky, theatrical and fun. The best way to sample what it does is with its tasting menu (R2900). Bookings are advised.

🍷 Drinking & Nightlife

★ **Top Hops**　　　　　　　　CRAFT BEER
(📞 8-966-757 0116; www.tophops.ru; nab reki Fontanki 55; ⊙ 4pm-1am Mon-Thu, 2pm-2am Fri-Sun; 🛜; Ⓜ Gostiny Dvor) One of the nicer craft-beer bars in town, this riverside space with friendly staff serves up a regularly changing menu of 20 beers on tap and scores more in bottles. The tasty Mexican snacks and food (go for nachos and chilli) go down exceptionally well while you sample your way through its range.

AROUND ST PETERSBURG

Several palace estates around St Petersburg, country retreats for the tsars, are now among the most spectacular sights in Russia.

Peterhof (Петергоф; also known as Petrodvorets), 29km west of the city and built for Peter the Great, is best visited for its **Grand Cascade** (⊙ 11am-5pm Mon-Fri, to 6pm Sat & Sun May-Oct) and Water Avenue, a symphony of over 140 fountains and canals located in the **Lower Park** (Нижний парк; www.peterhofmuseum.ru; adult/student May-Oct R750/400, Nov-Apr free; ⊙ 9am-7pm). There are several additional palaces, villas and parks here, each of which charges its own hefty admission price.

Tsarskoe Selo (Царское Село), 25km south of the city in the town of Pushkin, is home to the baroque **Catherine Palace** (Екатерининский дворец; www.tzar.ru; Sadovaya ul 7; adult/student R1000/350, audio guide R150; ⊙ 10am-4.45pm Wed-Sun), expertly restored following its near destruction in WWII. From May to September individual visits to Catherine's Palace are limited to noon to 2pm and 4pm to 5pm, other times being reserved for tour groups. The town itself is a pleasant place for a stroll, with a few nice places to eat along the route from the train station to the palace. **Borscht** (Борщ; Moskovskaya ul 20; ⊙ 11am-6pm) is a quirky place that serves nothing but the famed beetroot soup and vodka. For a more conventional dining experience try **Solenya Varenya** (Соленья-Варенья; 📞 8-812-465 2685; www.solenya-varenya.ru; Srednyaya ul 2; mains R420-880; ⊙ 10am-11pm; 🛜).

Pavlovsk (Павловск) A less visited destination a short bus ride away from Pushkin, this town is home to the stunning 18th-century **Pavlovsk Great Palace** (Большой Павловский дворец; www.pavlovskmuseum.ru; ul Sadovaya 20; adult/child R600/250; ⊙ 10am-6pm, closed Tue, Fri & 1st Mon of month) 🖉 and one of the finest green spaces in greater St Petersburg. To compare the tastes of its original owner to those of the current Russian leader, consider a lunch at Podvorye – reputedly one of Putin's favourite restaurants, located on the main road some 500m northeast from Pavlovsk train station.

By far the best (but also the priciest) way of reaching Peterhof is by **Peterhof Express** (www.peterhof-express.com; single/return adult R800/1500, student R600/1000; ⊙ 10am-6pm) hydrofoil, which leaves from jetties behind the Hermitage and the Admiralty from May to September. Buses and *marshrutky* (fixed-route minibuses) to Petrodvorets (R55, 30 minutes) run frequently from outside metro stations Avtovo and Leninsky Prospekt.

The easiest way to get to Tsarskoe Selo is by *marshrutka* (R35) from Moskovskaya metro station. For Pavlovsk; catch another *marshrutka* (R32) from Pavlovskoe sh near the southeast corner of Catherine Park. Infrequent suburban trains for Pushkin (R47, 30 minutes) and Pavlovsk, one stop away, leave from Vitebsk train station in St Petersburg.

Borodabar COCKTAIL BAR
([☑] 8-911-923 8940; www.facebook.com/Borod abar; Kazanskaya ul 11; ☺ 5pm-2am Sun-Thu, to 6am Fri & Sat; 🛜; M Nevsky Prospekt) *Boroda* means beard in Russian, and sure enough you'll see plenty of facial hair and tattoos in this hipster cocktail hang-out. Never mind, as the mixologists really know their stuff – we can particularly recommend their smoked Old Fashioned, which is infused with tobacco smoke, and their colourful (and potent) range of shots.

★ **Commode** BAR
(www.commode.club; 2nd fl, ul Rubinshteyna 1; per hour R180; ☺ 4pm-2am Sun-Thu, to 6am Fri & Sat) Stopping in for drinks at Commode feels more like hanging out in an upper-class friend's stylish apartment. After getting buzzed up, you can hang out in various high-ceilinged rooms, catch a small concert or po-etry slam, browse books in the quasi-library room, play a round of table football, or chat with the easy-going crowd that's fallen for the place.

Hat BAR
(ul Belinskogo 9; ☺ 7pm-5am; M Gostiny Dvor) The wonderfully retro-feeling Hat is a serious spot for jazz and whisky lovers, who come for the nightly live music and the cool-cat crowd that make this wonderfully designed bar feel like it's been transported out of 1950s Greenwich Village. A very welcome change of gear for St Petersburg's drinking options, but it can be extremely packed at weekends.

Kakhabar WINE BAR
([☑] 812-965 0524; https://kakhabar.ru; ul Rubin-shteyna 24; ☺ noon-11am, to 1am Fri & Sat) This is our ideal post-Soviet bar, specialising in Georgian wine accompanied by tapas-sized versions of succulent Georgian fare, includ-ing *khachapuri* (Georgian cheese bread) and *khinkali* (dumplings). Get a bottle of *saperavi* or *mukuzani* red if you need an introduction to Georgia's endemic wines and move on to the potent *chacha* (grappa equivalent) when things get lively.

☆ **Entertainment**

★ **Mariinsky Theatre** BALLET, OPERA
(Мариинский театр; [☑] 812-326 4141; www. mariinsky.ru; Teatralnaya pl 1; tickets R1200-6500; M Sadovaya) St Petersburg's most spectacular

venue for ballet and opera, the Mariinsky Theatre is an attraction in its own right. Tickets can be bought online or in per-son; book in advance during the summer months. The magnificent interior is the epit-ome of imperial grandeur, and any evening here will be an impressive experience.

Known as the Kirov Ballet during the So-viet era, the Mariinsky has an illustrious his-tory, with troupe members including such ballet greats as Nijinsky, Nureyev, Pavlova and Baryshnikov. In recent years the com-pany has been invigorated by the current artistic and general director, Valery Gergiev, who has worked hard to make the company solvent while overseeing the construction of the impressive and much-needed second theatre, the **Mariinsky II** (Мариинский II; ul Dekabristov 34; tickets R350-6000; ☺ ticket office 11am-7pm; M Sadovaya), across the Kryukov Canal from the company's green-and-white wedding cake of a building.

★ **Mikhailovsky Theatre** PERFORMING ARTS
(Михайловский театр; [☑] 812-595 4305; www. mikhailovsky.ru; pl Iskusstv 1; tickets R500-5000; M Nevsky Prospekt) This illustrious stage de-livers the Russian ballet or operatic expe-rience, complete with multitiered theatre, frescoed ceiling and elaborate productions. Pl Iskusstv (Arts Sq) is a lovely setting for this respected venue, which is home to the State Academic Opera & Ballet Company.

ℹ️ **Information**

Free wi-fi access is common across the city.
American Medical Clinic ([☑] 812-740 2090; www.amclinic.ru; nab reki Moyki 78; ☺ 24hr; M Admiralteyskaya) One of the city's largest private clinics.
Apteka Petrofarm ([☑] 812-571 3767; Nevsky pr 22-24; ☺ 24hr) An excellent, all-night pharmacy.
Main Post Office (Pochtamtskaya ul 9; M Ad-miralteyskaya) Worth visiting for its elegant Style Moderne interior.
St Petersburg Times Published every Tues-day and Friday, when it has an indispensable listings and arts review section.
Tourist Information Bureau ([☑] 812-242 3909, 812-303 0555; http://eng.ispb.info; Sadovaya ul 14/52; ☺ 10am-7pm Mon-Sat; M Gostiny Dvor) There are also branches outside the **Hermitage** ([☑] 8-931-326 5744; Dvortsovaya pl; ☺ 10am-7pm; M Admiralteyskaya) and **Pulkovo airport** (☺ 9am-8pm).

❶ Getting There & Around

ARRIVING IN ST PETERSBURG

Pulkovo Airport From St Petersburg's superb airport, an official taxi to the centre should cost between R800 and R1000; if you book one via an app it's likely to be R700. Alternatively, take bus 39 (35 minutes) or 39A (20 minutes) to Moskovskaya metro station for R35, then take the metro from Moskovskaya (Line 2) all over the city for R45.

Train Stations Main train stations are located in the city centre and connected to metro stations.

PUBLIC TRANSPORT

The metro is usually the quickest way around the city. *Zhetony* (tokens) and credit-loaded cards can be bought from booths in the stations (R45). Multiride cards are also available (R355 for 10 trips, R680 for 20 trips). Buses, trolleybuses and *marshrutky* fixed route minibuses (fare R40) often get you closer to the sights and are especially handy to cover long distances along main avenues like Nevsky pr.

TAXI

Taxi apps, such as Gett and Yandex Taxi, are all the rage in St Petersburg and they've brought down the prices of taxis in general, while improving the service a great deal. Aside from the apps, the best way to get a taxi is to order it by phone. **Taxi 6000000** (☑ 812-600 0000; http://6-000-000.ru) has English-speaking operators.

SURVIVAL GUIDE

❶ Directory A–Z

ACCESSIBLE TRAVEL

Travellers with disabilities are not well catered for in Russia. Many footpaths are in poor condition and potentially hazardous, and there is a lack of access ramps and lifts for wheelchairs. However, attitudes are enlightened and things are slowly changing.

ACCOMMODATION

For major cities and resorts it's a good idea to book a night or two in advance (especially during the busy summer season in St Petersburg). Elsewhere you can usually just turn up and find a room.

Hotels Range from contemporary and professionally run to moodily idiosyncratic DIY enterprises and an occasional Soviet-era dinosaur.

Hostels Moscow and St Petersburg have rich pickings but you'll now also find many good ones in other major cities and towns. At the time of research, laws were being passed that

outlaw hostels that occupy premises in apartment blocks. Many will likely close or relocate as a result of this.

B&Bs & homestays Not so common but worth searching out for a true experience of Russian hospitality.

INTERNET ACCESS

Installing a pay-as-you-go Russian SIM card with unlimited traffic on your smartphone is the easiest way to ensure constant access. These are available at airports and most shopping malls.

Wi-fi is common across Russia and usually access is free (or available for the cost of a cup of coffee). You may have to ask for a password (*parol*) to get online. Most of the time these days you also input your mobile phone number. Sometimes this will need to be a Russian number (ie one starting with +7); if you don't have one, ask a local if you can use their number.

If you don't have your own wi-fi-enabled device, it's probably easiest to get online in the business centres of hotels or at hostels that have a computer terminal.

LEGAL MATTERS

Avoid contact with the myriad types of police. It's not uncommon for them to bolster their incomes by extracting 'fines' from the unaware; you always have the right to insist to be taken to a police station (though we don't recommend this; if possible try to resolve the problem on the spot) or that the 'fine' be paid the legal way, through Sberbank. If you need police assistance (ie you've been the victim of a robbery or an assault), go to a station with a local for both language and moral support. Be persistent and patient.

If you are arrested, the police are obliged to inform your embassy or consulate immediately and allow you to communicate with it without delay. You can't count on the rules being followed, so be polite and respectful towards officials and hopefully things will go far more smoothly for you. In Russian, the phrase 'I'd like to call my embassy' is '*Pozhaluysta, ya khotel by pozvonit v posolstvo moyey strany*'.

LGBTIQ+ TRAVELLERS

➡ Russia is a conservative country and being gay is generally frowned upon. LGBTIQ+ people face stigma, harassment and violence in their everyday lives.

➡ Homosexuality isn't illegal, but promoting it (and other LGBTIQ+ lifestyles) is. What constitutes promotion is at the discretion of the authorities.

➡ There are active and relatively open gay and lesbian scenes in both Moscow and St Petersburg. Elsewhere, the gay scene tends to be underground.

➡ Visit http://english.gay.ru for information, good links and a resource for putting you in touch with personal guides for Moscow and St Petersburg.

→ Coming Out (www.comingoutspb.com) is the site of a St Petersburg–based support organisation.

MONEY

The Russian currency is the rouble, written as 'рубль' and abbreviated as 'руб' or 'р'. Roubles are divided into 100 almost worthless *kopeyki* (kopecks). Coins come in amounts of R1, R2, R5 and R10 roubles, with banknotes in values of R10, R50, R100, R200, R500, R1000, R2000 and R5000.

ATMs that accept all major credit and debit cards are everywhere, and most restaurants, shops and hotels in major cities gladly accept plastic. Visa and MasterCard are the most widespread card types, while American Express can be problematic in some hotels and shops. You can exchange dollars and euros (and some other currencies) at most banks; when they're closed, try the exchange counters at top-end hotels. You may need your passport. Note that crumpled or old banknotes are often refused.

OPENING HOURS

Banks 9am to 6pm Monday to Friday, some open 9am to 5pm Saturday

Bars and Clubs noon to midnight Sunday to Thursday, to 6am Friday and Saturday

Cafes 9am to 10pm

Post Offices 8am to 8pm or 9pm Monday to Friday, shorter hours Saturday and Sunday

Restaurants noon to midnight

Shops 10am to 8pm

Supermarkets and Food stores 9am to 11pm or 24 hours

PUBLIC HOLIDAYS

In addition to the following official days, many businesses (but not restaurants, shops and museums) close for a week of bank holidays between 1 January and at least 8 January. Bank holidays are typically declared to merge national holidays with the nearest weekend.

New Year's Day 1 January

Russian Orthodox Christmas Day 7 January

Defender of the Fatherland Day 23 February

International Women's Day 8 March

International Labour Day/Spring Festival 1 May

Victory Day 9 May

Russian Independence Day 12 June

Unity Day 4 November

SAFE TRAVEL

Despite the strain in relations with the West, Russia is generally a safe country in which to travel.

→ Don't leave any valuables or bags inside your car. Valuables lying around hotel rooms also tempt providence.

→ It's generally safe to leave your belongings unguarded when using the toilets on trains, but you'd be wise to get to know your fellow passengers first.

→ Pickpockets and purse-snatchers operate in big cities and major towns. Keep your valuables close.

→ Avoid drinking with dodgy strangers and discussing international politics when drunk.

TELEPHONE

Local calls from homes and most hotels are free. To make a long-distance call or to call a mobile from most phones, first dial 8, wait for a second dial tone, then dial the area code and phone number. To make an international call dial 8, wait for a second dial tone, then dial 10, then the country code etc. Some phones are for local calls only and won't give you that second dial tone.

To place an international call from a mobile phone, dial + and then the country code.

TIME

There are 11 time zones in Russia; the standard time is calculated from Moscow, which is GMT/UTC plus three hours year-round. In 2011, Russia abandoned the summer time switch, so the gap with European neighbours increases by an hour in winter.

TOILETS

→ Pay toilets are identified by the words платный туалет (*platny tualet*). In any toilet, Ж (*zhensky*) stands for women's and M (*muzhskoy*) stands for men's.

→ Public toilets are rare and can be dingy and uninviting. Toilets in major hotels, cafes or shopping centres are preferable.

→ In all public toilets, the babushka you pay your R20 to can also provide miserly rations of toilet paper; it's always a good idea to carry your own.

TOURIST INFORMATION

Official tourist offices are rare in Russia.

You're mainly dependent on hotel receptionists and administrators, service bureaus and travel firms for information. The latter two exist primarily to sell accommodation, excursions and transport – if you don't look like you want to book something, staff may or may not answer questions.

VISAS

Nationals of all Western countries require a visa, but most Latin American, as well as some East Asian countries, Israel and South Africa have visa-free arrangements with Russia. Arranging a visa is generally straightforward but is likely to be time-consuming, bureaucratic and – depending on how quickly you need the visa – costly. Start the application process at least a month before your trip.

ⓘ Getting There & Away

ENTERING THE COUNTRY

➡ Searches beyond the perfunctory are quite rare, but clearing customs when you leave Russia by a land border can be lengthy.

➡ Visitors are allowed to bring in and take out up to US$10,000 (or its equivalent) in currency, and goods up to the value of €10,000, weighing less than 50kg, without making a customs declaration.

➡ Fill in a customs declaration form if you're bringing into Russia major equipment, antiques, artworks or musical instruments (including a guitar) that you plan to take out with you – get it stamped in the red channel of customs to avoid any problems leaving with the same goods.

➡ If you plan to export anything vaguely 'arty' – instruments, coins, jewellery, antiques, antiquarian manuscripts and books (older than 50 years) or art (also older than 50 years) – it should first be assessed by the **Ministry of Culture** (Коллегия экспертизы; ☑ 499-391 4212; ul Akademika Korolyova 21, bldg 1, office 505, 5th fl; ⊙11am-5pm Mon-Fri; Ⓜ VDNKh); it is very difficult to export anything over 100 years old. Bring your item (or a photograph, if the item is large) and your receipt. If export is allowed, you'll be issued a receipt for tax paid, which you show to customs officers on your way out of the country.

AIR

Moscow's **Sheremetyevo** (Шереметьево; ☑ 495-578 6565; www.svo.aero), **Domodedovo** (Домодедово; ☑ 495-933 6666; www.domodedovo.ru) and **Vnukovo** (Внуково; ☑ 495-937 5555; www.vnukovo.ru) and St Petersburg's **Pulkovo International Airport** (LED; ☑ 812-337 3822; www.pulkovoairport.ru; Pulkovskoye sh) host the bulk of Russia's international flights.

Plenty of other cities have direct international connections, including Arkhangelsk, Irkutsk, Kaliningrad, Kazan, Khabarovsk, Krasnodar, Mineralnye Vody, Murmansk, Nalchik, Nizhny Novgorod, Novosibirsk, Perm, Yekaterinburg and Yuzhno-Sakhalinsk.

LAND

Russia borders 14 countries. Popular land approaches include trains and buses from Central European and Baltic countries or on either the trans-Manchurian or trans-Mongolian train routes from China and Mongolia.

Border Crossings

Russia shares borders with Azerbaijan, Belarus, China, Estonia, Finland, Georgia, Kazakhstan, Latvia, Lithuania, Mongolia, North Korea, Norway, Poland and Ukraine. Before planning a journey into or out of Russia from any of these countries, check the visa situation for your nationality.

On trains, border crossings are a straightforward but drawn-out affair, with a steady stream of customs and ticket personnel scrutinising your passport and visa. If you're arriving by car or motorcycle, you'll need to show your vehicle registration and insurance papers, and your driving licence, passport and visa. These formalities are usually minimal for Western European citizens. On the Russian side, most cars are subjected to cursory inspection, with only a small percentage getting a thorough check.

SEA

Ferry routes connect St Petersburg to Helsinki (Finland), Stockholm (Sweden) and Tallinn (Estonia).

ⓘ Getting Around

AIR

Major Russian airlines, including **Aeroflot** (☑ 495-223 5555, toll free in Russia 8-800 444 5555; www.aeroflot.com), **Rossiya** (☑ 8-495 139 7777, 8-800 444 5555; www.rossiya-airlines.com), **S7 Airlines** (☑ 495-783-0707, 8-800 700-0707; www.s7.ru), **Ural Airlines** (www.uralairlines.com), **UTAir** (www.utair.ru) and budget carrier **Pobeda** (www.pobeda.aero), have online booking, with the usual discounts for advance purchases. Otherwise, it's no problem buying a ticket at ubiquitous *aviakassa* (ticket offices), which may be able to tell you about flights that you can't easily find out about online overseas. Online agencies specialising in Russian air tickets with English interfaces include **Anywayanyday** (☑ 8-800 775 7753; www.anywayanyday.com), **Pososhok.ru** (☑ 8-800 333 8118; www.pososhok.ru), **One Two Trip!** (www.onetwotrip.ru) and **TicketsRU** (www.tickets.ru).

Whenever you book airline tickets in Russia you'll need to show your passport and visa. Tickets can also be purchased at the airport right up to the departure of the flight and sometimes even if the city centre office says that the plane is full. Return fares are usually double the one-way fares.

It's a good idea to check in online as early as possible and sign up for notifications about delays and cancellations. Most airlines have handy telephone apps, which you can use for both booking and online check-in.

Airlines may bump you if you don't check in at least an hour before departure and can be very strict about charging for checked bags that are overweight, which generally means anything over 20kg. Pobeda is notoriously strict (as well as unpredictable and arbitrary) about baggage allowances and carry-on luggage.

Have your passport and ticket handy throughout the various security and ticket checks that can occur, right up until you find a seat. Some flights have assigned seats, others don't. On the latter, seating is a free-for-all.

Many internal flights in Moscow use either Domodedovo or Vnukovo airports; if you're connecting to Moscow's Sheremetyevo international airport, allow a few hours to cross town (at least three hours if you need to go by taxi, rather than train and metro).

Big city airports are gradually being revamped and modernised, but in small towns airports offer facilities similar to the average bus shelter.

BUS & MARSHRUTKY

Long-distance buses tend to complement rather than compete with the rail network. They generally serve areas with no railway or routes on which trains are slow, infrequent or overloaded.

Most cities have an intercity bus station (автовокзал, avtovokzal). Tickets are sold at the station or on the bus. Fares are normally listed on the timetable and posted on a wall. As often as not you'll get a ticket with a seat assignment, either printed or scribbled on a till receipt. If you have luggage that needs to be stored in the bus baggage compartment, you may have to pay an extra fare, typically around 10% of the bus fare. Some bus stations may also apply a small fee for security measures.

Marshrutky (a Russian diminutive form of *marshrutnoye taksi,* meaning a fixed-route taxi) are minibuses that are often quicker than larger buses and rarely cost much more. Where roads are good and villages frequent, *marshrutky* can be twice as fast as buses and are well worth paying extra for.

CAR & MOTORCYCLE

Driving in Russia is not for the faint-hearted, but if you've a sense of humour, patience and a decent vehicle, it's an adventurous way to go. Both road quality and driving culture have improved a great deal in the last decade, so driving has become much more pleasant than before. There are also reliable car-hire companies.

The sheer number of vehicles and constant road improvements make traffic jams a largely unavoidable obstacle in the vicinities of Moscow, St Petersburg and other large cities. Russia's most popular navigation app, Yandex, monitors traffic jams in real time and sends you on the fastest route.

TRAIN

Russian Railways (РЖД, RZD; ☑ 8-800 775 0000; www.rzd.ru) trains are generally comfortable and, depending on the class of travel, relatively inexpensive for the distances covered. The network is highly centralised, with Moscow, which has nine large train stations, as the main transfer hub. Given large distances, a vast majority of carriages are equipped with sleeping berths, while only newer and shorter-distance trains have seats.

A handful of high-speed services aside, trains are rarely speedy, but have a remarkable record for punctuality – if you're a minute late for your train, the chances are you'll be left standing on the platform. The fact that RZD managers have a large portion of their pay determined by the timeliness of their trains not only inspires promptness, but also results in the creation of generous schedules. You'll notice this when you find your train stationary for hours in the middle of nowhere only to suddenly start up and roll into the next station right on time.

Serbia

POP 7.11 MILLION

Best Places to Eat

➜ Iris New Balkan Cuisine (p985)

➜ Šaran (p985)

➜ Bela Reka (p986)

➜ Ambar (p986)

➜ Stambolijski (p993)

Best Places to Stay

➜ Mama Shelter (p985)

➜ Savamala Bed & Breakfast (p984)

➜ Yugodom (p984)

➜ Varad Inn (p989)

➜ ArtLoft Hotel (p992)

Why Go?

Diverse, welcoming and a hell of a lot of fun – everything you never heard about Serbia is true. Best of all, this landlocked country in the heart of the Balkans is still delightfully off the tourist trail. While the feisty Serbian spirit is embodied in Belgrade's world-class nightlife and Novi Sad's epic EXIT festival, look beyond these historic metropolises and you'll discover a crucible of cultures and unsullied outdoors ripe for exploration.

The art nouveau town of Subotica revels in its Austro-Hungarian heritage, bohemian Niš echoes to the clip-clop of Roma horse carts, and minaret-studded Novi Pazar nudges the most sacred of Serbian Orthodox monasteries. Established wine regions and thermal spas cradled in rolling hills date back to Roman times. On the slopes of Kopaonik, Zlatibor and Stara Planina, ancient traditions coexist with après-ski bling, while super-scenic Tara and Đerdap national parks brim with hiking, biking, rafting and kayaking opportunities.

When to Go
Belgrade

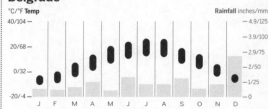

May & Sep Excellent time for hiking and mountain biking in the national parks.

Jul–Aug The festival season is in full swing; cool off by the lakes and on the rivers.

Dec–Mar Hit the ski resorts for alpine adventures or enjoy Belgrade's cultural calendar.

Entering the Country

Getting to Serbia is a cinch; it's connected to Europe by main roads, there are no seas to cross and its two airports welcome flights from across the continent and the world. All of Europe is accessible from Belgrade: Budapest, Zagreb, Sofia and Thessaloniki are a train ride away, and regular buses serve destinations including Vienna, Sarajevo and Podgorica.

ITINERARIES

Five Days

Revel in three days of cultural and culinary exploration in Belgrade (p981), allowing for at least one night of hitting the capital's legendary nightspots. Carry on north to laid-back Novi Sad (p988) on the Danube, and complete the Vojvodina tour with a day trip to Subotica (p989) to admire its art nouveau architecture.

Ten Days

Follow the above itinerary, then head to southern Serbia. Slice southwest for some hiking and a train ride in Tara National Park (p993) en route to Turkish-flavoured Novi Pazar (p989). Alternatively turn southeast for a boat trip and cycling through Đerdap National Park (p993), followed by the history and *kafana* cuisine of bohemian Niš (p992).

Essential Food & Drink

Kajmak Dairy delight akin to a salty clotted cream.

Ajvar Spread made from roasted peppers, aubergines and garlic.

Urnebes Creamy, spicy peppers-and-cheese spread.

Burek Flaky meat, cheese or vegetable pie eaten with yoghurt.

Pljeskavica Spicy hamburger, usually served with onions.

Ćevapi These skinless sausages are the national fast food.

Ražnjići Pork or veal shish kebabs.

Karađorđeva šnicla Similar to chicken Kiev, but with veal or pork and lashings of *kajmak* and tartar sauce.

Svadbarski kupus Sauerkraut and hunks of smoked pork slow-cooked in giant clay pots.

Riblja čorba Fish soup, most commonly from carp, spiced with paprika.

Gomboce Potato-dough dumplings, usually stuffed with plums.

Rakija Strong distilled spirit made from fruit – the most common variety is *šljivovica,* made from plums.

SERBIA

Sleeping Price Ranges

The following price categories are based on the cost of a high-season double room including breakfast.

€ less than 3000RSD

€€ 3000–8000RSD

€€€ more than 8000RSD

Eating Price Ranges

The following price categories are based on the cost of a main course.

€ less than 600RSD

€€ 600–1000RSD

€€€ more than 1000RSD

Serbia Highlights

1 Belgrade (p981) Revelling in the intriguing melange of faded Yugo-nostalgia, cutting-edge Balkan cool and fascinating history.

2 Tara National Park (p993) Hiking, rafting on the Drina or riding a narrow-gauge railway around the most scenic slice of Serbia.

3 EXIT Festival (p989) Joining thousands of revellers each July for eclectic beats at Novi Sad's formidable fortress.

4 Đerdap National Park (p993) Cycling or cruising through the Danube's astounding Iron Gates gorge and millennia of history.

5 Subotica (p989) Gawking at the marvellous art nouveau architecture of this leafy town in Vojvodina province.

6 Novi Pazar (p989) Exploring the melding cultural heritages of this Turkish-flavoured town and revered Serbian Orthodox sites nearby.

BELGRADE БЕОГРАД

📇 011 / POP 1.6 MILLION

Outspoken, adventurous, proud and audacious: Belgrade ('White City') is by no means a 'pretty' capital, but its gritty exuberance makes it one of Europe's most happening cities. While it hurtles towards a brighter future, its chaotic past unfolds before your eyes: socialist blocks are squeezed between art nouveau masterpieces, and remnants of the Habsburg legacy contrast with Ottoman relics and socialist modernist monoliths. This is where the Sava and Danube Rivers kiss, an old-world culture that at once evokes time-capsuled communist-era Yugoslavia and new-world, EU-contending cradle of cool.

Grandiose coffee houses and smoky dives pepper Knez Mihailova, a lively pedestrian boulevard flanked by historical buildings all the way to the ancient Belgrade Fortress. The riverside Savamala quarter has gone from ruin to resurrection, and is the city's creative headquarters (for now). Deeper in Belgrade's bowels are museums guarding the cultural, religious and military heritage of the country.

⊙ Sights

★ Belgrade Fortress   FORTRESS

(Beogradska tvrđava; www.beogradskatvrdjava.co.rs; ⊙ 24hr) FREE Some 115 battles have been fought over imposing, impressive Belgrade Fortress (aka Kalemegdan); the citadel was destroyed more than 40 times throughout the centuries. Fortifications began in Celtic times, and the Romans extended it onto the flood plains during the settlement of 'Singidunum', Belgrade's Roman name. Much of what stands today is the product of 18th-century Austro-Hungarian and Turkish reconstructions. The fort's bloody history, discernible despite today's jolly cafes and funfairs, only makes the fortress all the more fascinating.

Audio guides in six languages with a map (300RSD plus ID as deposit) are available from the souvenir shop within the Inner Stambol Gate, which is also where you must purchase tickets for the Clock Tower, Roman Well and Big Gunpowder Magazine.

★ Museum of Yugoslavia   MUSEUM

(www.muzej-jugoslavije.org; Botićeva 6; 400RSD, incl entry to Marshal Tito's Mausoleum, 4-6pm 1st Thu of month free; ⊙ 10am-6pm Tue-Sun) This must-visit museum houses an invaluable collection of more than 200,000 artefacts representing the fascinating, tumultuous history of Yugoslavia. Photographs, artworks, historical documents, films, weapons, priceless treasure: it's all here. It can be a lot to take in; English-speaking guides are available if booked in advance via email, or you can join a free tour on weekends (11am in English, Serbian at noon). **Marshal Tito's Mausoleum** (Kuća Cveća, House of Flowers) is also on the museum grounds; admission is included in the ticket price.

The museum's main building, known as the May 25 Museum, is the first purpose-designed and built museum in Belgrade. Take trolleybus 40 or 41 at the south end of Parliament on Kneza Miloša; ask the driver to let you out at Kuća Cveća.

★ Mt Avala   TOWER

(Mt Avala; tower 300RSD; ⊙ tower 9am-8pm Mar-Sept, to 5pm Oct-Feb) Looming over Belgrade and topped with the tallest tower in the Balkans (204.5m), Mt Avala is a city landmark that makes for a pleasant break from the capital's bustling streets. The **broadcasting tower**, originally completed in 1965 but levelled by NATO bombs in 1999, was rebuilt in 2010 and now offers picture-perfect panoramas over Belgrade and beyond from viewing platforms and a cafe. Nearby, the **Monument to the Unknown Hero** by Ivan Meštrović honours Serbian victims of WWI.

Mt Avala is 16km from the city centre; on weekends in summer, bus 400 runs to the top of Avala from the **Voždovac** (Joakima Rakovca) stop.

★ Museum of Contemporary Art   MUSEUM

(www.msub.org.rs; Ušće 10; 300RSD, free Wed; ⊙ 10am-6pm Mon, Wed & Fri-Sun, 10am-10pm Thu) One of Belgrade's top cultural sights, this recently renovated museum is a treasure trove of 20th-century art from the ex-Yugoslav cultural space. The 1960s concrete-and-glass modernist building, surrounded by a sculpture park, has great views towards the Belgrade Fortress across the Sava River.

Conceptual art features prominently, including a 1970s video called *Freeing the Memory* from the region's most famous artist (and Belgrade native), Marina Abramović. One section is dedicated to the 1920s Yugoslav avant-garde magazine *Zenit* and the Zenitism art movement associated with it.

National Museum   MUSEUM

(Narodni Muzej; www.narodnimuzej.rs; Trg Republike 1a; adult/child 300/150RSD, Sun free; ⊙ 10am-6pm Tue, Wed, Fri & Sun, Thu & Sat noon-8pm) Lack of funding for renovations kept Serbia's National Museum mostly shuttered for 15

Central Belgrade

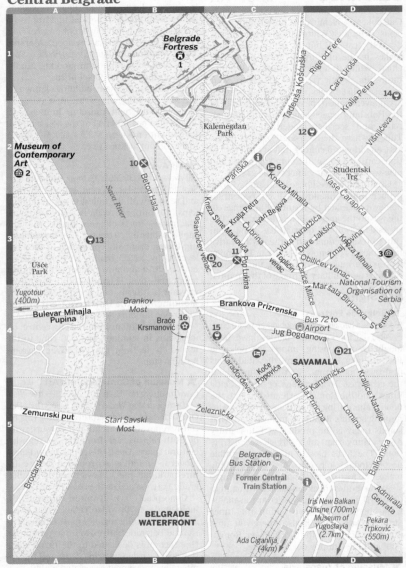

years, but its much ballyhooed 2018 reopening has been a great source of national pride – it awoke from the dead on Vidovdan (28 June), the country's national day – and for good reason. Built in 1903 and reconstructed multiple times over the years, the museum's latest €12 million makeover frames some 5000 sq metres of exhibition space over three floors.

Highlights include works by Croatian Ivan Meštrović, the most celebrated sculptor of the Kingdom of Yugoslavia; archaeological treasures from Roman-era Serbia; and extensive galleries dedicated to both 18th-

Central Belgrade

◎ Top Sights
1 Belgrade Fortress	B1
2 Museum of Contemporary Art	A2

◎ Sights
3 National Museum	D3

⊟ Sleeping
4 Hostel Bongo	E5
5 Hotel Moskva	E4
6 Mama Shelter	C2
7 Savamala Bed & Breakfast	C4
8 Smokvica Bed & Breakfast	E2
9 Yugodom	F3

⊗ Eating
10 Ambar	B2
11 Mayka	C3

◎ Drinking & Nightlife
12 Bar Central	D2
13 Klub 20/44	A3
14 Krafter	D1
15 Vinoteka	C4

✪ Entertainment
16 KC Grad	B4
17 National Theatre	E3

ⓐ Shopping
18 Bajloni Market	F3
19 Belgrade Design District	E4
20 Makadam	C3
21 Zeleni Venac Market	D4

Nikola Tesla Museum MUSEUM
(www.nikolateslamuseum.org; Krunska 51; admission incl guided tour in English 500RSD; ⊙10am-8pm Tue-Sun) Meet the man on the 100RSD note at one of Belgrade's best museums, where you can release your inner nerd with some wondrously sci-fi-ish interactive elements. Tesla's ashes are kept here in a glowing, golden orb: debate has been raging for years between the museum (and its secular supporters) and the Church as to whether the remains should be moved to Sveti Sava Temple.

Sveti Sava Temple CHURCH
(www.hramsvetogsave.com; Krušedolska 2a; ⊙7am-7pm) Sveti Sava is the Balkans' biggest (and the world's second biggest) Orthodox church, a fact made entirely obvious when looking at the city skyline from a distance or standing under its dome. The church is built on the site where the Turks apparently burnt relics of St Sava. Work on the church interior (frequently interrupted by wars) continues today as the cupola is being adorned with

and 19th-century Serbian art and 20th-century Yugoslavian art. Don't miss the museum's most haunting corner, where Stevan Aleksić's *The Burning of the Remains of St Sava* (1912) sits sidesaddle to Đorđe Krstić's *The Fall of Stalać* (1903), two hyper-realistic and menacing oils on canvas.

SERBIA BELGRADE

a 1248-sq-metre mosaic, one of the world's largest on a curved surface.

Visit the astonishing gold-ceilinged crypt and its ornate chandeliers, Murano glass mosaics and vibrant frescoes.

Ada Ciganlija BEACH
(www.adaciganlija.rs; parking 250RSD; ⊙24hr)
FREE In summertime, join the hordes of sea-starved locals (up to 250,000 a day) for sun and fun at this artificial island on the Sava. Cool down with a swim, kayak or windsurf after a leap from the 55m bungee tower. Take bus 52 or 53 from Zeleni Venac.

Gardoš Tower TOWER
(Tower of Sibinjanin Janko; www.kulanagardosu. com; Gardoš fortress; 200RSD; ⊙10am-7pm) This splendid brick tower (1896) has been renovated to house a free gallery, which hosts regular exhibitions. The views from the top, especially at sunset, are breathtaking. Somewhat confusingly, it's also known as the Millennium Tower.

From Zemun's buzzy Sinđelićeva, the tower is a five-minute walk up the cobbled street of Grobljanska.

☞ Tours

★ Yugotour DRIVING
(☑066 801 8614; www.yugotour.com; per person 2900-8900RSD; ⊙from 11am) Yugotour is a mini road trip through the history of Yugoslavia and the life of its president Tito. Belgrade's communist years are brought to life in the icon of Yugo-nostalgia: a Yugo car!

Tours are led by young locals happy to share their own perceptions of Yugoslavia; they take in the communist-era architecture of Novi Beograd, the Museum of Yugoslavia and Marshal Tito's Mausoleum, among other locations.

★ Taste Serbia FOOD & DRINK
(☑065 236 4866; www.tasteserbia.com; 4130-35400RSD) Take your taste buds on a holiday with these deliciously diverse tasting tours run by three local foodies. Explore Belgrade's gourmet scene, head north on a bacon-centric Vojvodinian voyage, stuff yourself in western Serbia and more; all tours are customisable, informative and fun. Pack your stretchy pants. Minimum two people and maximum of 16 people per group; advance bookings essential.

Belgrade Alternative Guide WALKING
(☑063 743 3055; www.belgradealtguide.com; tours per person 1700-9800RSD) Run by passionate

locals, these tours explore Savamala rooftop hang outs, central art galleries, street art, the history of Zemun, farmers markets, secret eateries and surrounding villages. Tours generally run between three and four hours.

🛏 Sleeping

Hostel Bongo HOSTEL €
(☑011 268 5515; www.hostelbongo.com; Terazije 36; dm/d with shared bathroom 1800/4800RSD; ❄@🤶) Guests at the modern, brightly painted and meticulously maintained Bongo can take their pick: plunge into the tons of attractions, bars and restaurants nearby, or hide from it all in the hostel's sweet garden terrace. Fantastic staff with oodles of hostelling experience.

★ Yugodom GUESTHOUSE €€
(☑065 984 6366; www.yugodom.com; Strahinjica Bana 80; d/ste 4200/8400RSD; ❄🤶) This evocative two-room guesthouse offers more than a comfortable bed; it's also a vessel for time travel. Billed as a 'stayover museum', Yugodom (*dom* means 'house' in Serbian) is decked out with gorgeous art and Yugoslavian mid-century modern furnishings from the Tito era (though you'll find all the mod cons and self-catering facilities you need disguised among the retro trappings).

The location is as impeccable as the surrounds; on a newly pedestrianised street smack in the middle of Dorćol and across the road from **Bajloni Market** (cnr Cetinjska & Džordža Vašingtona; ⊙6am-7pm).

★ Savamala Bed & Breakfast B&B €€
(☑011 406 0264; www.savamalahotel.rs; Kraljevića Marka 6, Savamala; s/d/tr from 6000/7200/9000RSD; ❄🤶) This brilliant B&B is all early-1900s charm out the front, and nouveau-Savamala graffiti-murals out the back. As hip as you'd expect from its location in Belgrade's coolest quarter, the digs here are furnished with a mix of period furniture and the work of up-and-coming Belgrade designers. It's close to the city's main sights, and there are tons of happening bars and restaurants within staggering distance.

Smokvica Bed & Breakfast B&B €€
(☑069 446 4002; www.smokvica.rs; Gospodar Jovanova 45, Dorćol; d 7700RSD; ❄🤶) Smokvica's shabby-chic cafe and accommodation empire has expanded to Dorćol, where the line-up's second B&B occupies a grand whitewashed 19th-century mansion. Spacious rooms with vaulted ceilings and hard-

wood floors are decked out in trademark sky blue, with supersonic showers. The designer cafe at this location is also a charming retreat just steps from the six rooms.

★**Mama Shelter** BOUTIQUE HOTEL €€€
(☑011 333 3000; www.mamashelter.com/en/belgrade; Kneza Mihaila 54a; d from 8300RSD; P❄@🛜) Belgrade is just the 7th city worldwide to receive one of Philippe Starck's whimsical designer Mama Shelter hotels – the city's hottest – this one sitting on prime real estate at the Belgrade Fortress end of Kneza Mihaila, on the top floor of the glitzy Rajićeva Shopping Centre.

Rooms are funky and fun, but the real coup here is the 1000-sq-metre rooftop restaurant, bar and hang-space, complete with arcade games, outdoor fire pit, stupendous views and oodles of beautiful people – one of the few places in Belgrade to get an aerial perspective with a cocktail in hand. Go at sunset!

Hotel Moskva HISTORIC HOTEL €€€
(Hotel Moscow; ☑011 364 2000; www.hotel moskva.rs; Terazije 20; s/d/ste from 10,500/12,800/24,700RSD; P❄@🛜) Art-nouveau icon and proud symbol of the best of Belgrade, the majestic 123-room Moskva has been wowing guests – including Albert Einstein, Indira Gandhi and Alfred Hitchcock – since 1906. Laden with ye olde glamour, this is the place to write your memoirs at a big old desk.

🍴 Eating

★**Pekara Trpković** BAKERY €
(www.facebook.com/pekaratrpkovic; Nemanjina 32; burek per 100g 32-55RSD; ⊙6am-8.30pm Mon-Sat, to 4pm Sun) The fact that this family business has existed for over a century in Belgrade's competitive bakery market is quite an achievement. The Serbian tradition of making pastries has reached its peak in this case. Trpković delicacies and sandwiches are extremely popular so you can often see queues, especially for breakfast and lunch break.

Sometimes there are two queues – one just for *burek* (heavenly filo pastries stuffed with veal, cheese, spinach etc).

★**Ribnjak** SERBIAN €€
(☑011 331 8894; Jojkićev Dunavac bb; mains 400-1000RSD, fish per kg 600-2900RSD; ⊙noon-10pm) An unremarkable houseboat moored far enough from the city centre that few people know about it (or ever see it!), this undeniably simple *restoran* (restaurant) does remarkable, extra effort-worthy things with river fish.

The speciality is rarely seen fish *mućkalica* (spicy stew) – order that as an appetiser (after the fish soup!) and follow with a perfectly griddle-seared whole zander (*grillovani smuđ*) and sides of Dalmatian-style potato and mangel (chard). No English menu. It's a 600RSD or so CarGo ride from Trg Republike.

Mayka VEGETARIAN €€
(☑011 328 8401; www.facebook.com/maykabeograd/; Kosančićev venac 2; mains 785-1050RSD; ⊙11am-midnight; 🛜🍴) Among Belgrade's slim offerings for vegetarians, here's a gem right in the city centre. Mayka serves up worldly vegetarian specialities in a Serbian way. Listen to the waiter's recommendations and don't miss dishes featuring their house-made seitan or stir-fried veggies with smoked sunflower cheese. Indian and Thai curries go down a treat as well, especially on the rustic front patio.

The interior evokes a bar atmosphere and, while enjoying world-class slow food, you can come across live jazz and piano acts too.

★**Iris New Balkan Cuisine** SERBIAN €€€
(☑064 129 6377; www.newbalkancuisine.com/iris; Sarajevska 54; tasting menus veg/non-veg 3000-3700RSD, with wine 5600/6300RSD; ⊙12.30-10pm Wed-Sat; 🛜🍴) 🌿 Belgrade's best foodie bang for the buck is this newcomer clandestinely occupying a 1st-floor apartment south of the old train station. Courses from the tasting menu are based around a single ingredient – whatever head chef Vanja Puškar has procured from organic farmers that week – and taken to new heights without leaving behind their Serbian origins.

Memorable examples when we dined: a stunning Buša beef carpaccio with yoghurt, olive oil and fried sourdough; a perfectly crisp pork schnitzel doused in green pea and mint cream with sage-perfumed zucchini foam; and a delightful fig-stuffed chicken roulade on triple-fried potato, with salty caramel and hop-orange foam. Natural wines often accompany the eight-course menus. Welcome to the New Balkans!

★**Šaran** SEAFOOD €€€
(☑011 261 8235; www.saran.co.rs; Kej Oslobođenja 53, Zemun; mains 1050-2090RSD; ⊙noon-11pm Sun & Mon, to 1am Tue-Sat; 🛜) Šaran (meaning 'carp') is rightfully renowned as Zemun's best quayside fish restaurant for its exceptional fish dishes, professional service and welcoming atmosphere. Freshwater river fish dishes like Smederevo-style pike

(grilled, then baked under an astonishingly flavourful smothering of tomatoes, garlic, onions and red peppers) and pricier whole saltwater options (6100RSD to 8400RSD) are absolute standouts.

Live Balkan music most nights.

Bela Reka
SERBIAN €€€

(📋 11 655 5098; www.restoranbelareka.rs; Tošin bunar 79, Novi Beograd; mains 630-1890RSD; 🕿) One of Belgrade's best new restaurants, Bela Reka is modern and sophisticated, but fiercely dedicated to the traditional craft of Serbian cuisine, and is well worth a trek to Novi Beograd, 5.5km west of Brankov Most. Gorgeously presented, meat-leaning dishes are some of Belgrade's best: perfectly spiced, Pirot-style *uštipci* (meatballs), walnut-and-hazelnut-crusted monastery chicken and *homolje* (sausage stuffed with cheese) are outstanding.

An award-winning baker fires up traditional *somun* flatbread in a clay oven and the goat's cheese comes direct from their own farm (you can pick some up in their artisan market). But wait, dessert! Go for *ledene kocke*, a dead-simple, dead-delicious sponge cake resurrected from Yugoslavian recipe books.

Ambar
BALKAN €€€

(📋 011 328 6637; www.ambarrestaurant.com; Karađorđeva 2-4, Beton Hala; small plates 310-1150RSD; 🕙 10am-2am; 🕿) Upmarket, innovative small-plate takes on Balkan cuisine are the go to at this chic spot – the best of a handful of trendy options overlooking the river. Everything from *ajvar* to mixed grills has been given a contemporary spin; even the *pljeskavica* (bunless hamburger) gets the five-star treatment.

Put your meal choices in the hands of the excellent and well-versed staff and you won't be disappointed, right down to the Serbian wines. You can try everything for 2990RSD.

🍷 Drinking & Nightlife

★ Restoran Tabor
TAVERNA

(📋 011 241 2464; www.restorantabor.com; Bulevar Kralja Aleksandra 348; 🕙 noon-2am Mon-Sat; 🕿) If you want an authentic Serbian Friday-night experience, this wildly popular (reserve several days ahead) *kafana* (tavern) in Zvezdara has it all: captivating folk music, great traditional food (don't skip the *mak pita* – baklava-like dessert made with poppy seeds), sexy lighting and a room full of good-time-seeking locals (and celebs) who will eventually be dancing on the tables!

It's 5.5km west of Knez Mihailova (a 300RSD or so CarGo ride from Savamala).

★ Klub 20/44
RIVER BARGE

(www.facebook.com/klub2044; Ušće bb; 🕙 5pm-2am Sun, Tue & Wed, to 4am Thu, to 5am Fri & Sat; 🕿) Retro, run-down and loads of fun, this alternative *splav* (river-barge nightclub) is named for Belgrade's map co-ordinates. Open year-round, it has become an electronica reference for top European DJs – despite its shabby appearance. Swimming up from the back might be your easiest way in!

★ Bar Central
COCKTAIL BAR

(www.facebook.com/BarCentral011; Kralja Petra 59; 🕙 9am-midnight Sun-Thu, to 1am Fri & Sat; 🕿) This is the HQ of Serbia's Association of Bartenders, a fact made evident after one sip of any of the sublime cocktails (515RSD to 1165RSD) on offer. With an interior as polished as a bottle flip-pour, this ain't the place for tacky tikis and those little umbrellas – this is serious mixology territory.

Krafter
CRAFT BEER

(www.facebook.com/kftbeerbar; Strahinjića Bana 44, Dorćol; 🕙 9am-midnight Mon-Thu, to 1pm Fri & Sat, 10am-midnight Sun; 🕿) Hopheads seeking local salvation should settle in at this intimate, industrial-chic craft beer bar featuring 14 rotating offerings on draught (pints 295RSD to 385RSD) – always Serbian – along with a small international selection in bottles. The menu is heavily weighted towards hoppy pale and India pale ales, and the lovely English-speaking staff are passionate about their suds devotion.

Vinoteka
WINE BAR

(www.facebook.com/vinotekasavamala; Karađorđeva 57, Savamala; 🕙 11am-midnight Sun-Thu, to 1am Fri & Sat; 🕿) If you want to take a deep dive into Serbian wine, this cosy Savamala wine bar boasts 40 domestic wines by the glass (290RSD to 450RSD) and nearly 300 ex-Yugoslavian regional wines by the bottle (it's a bottle shop by day). It's not a wild place but rather perfect for a bit of juice and a conversation in a more intimate setting.

☆ Entertainment

★ KC Grad
CULTURAL CENTRE

(www.gradbeograd.eu; Braće Krsmanović 4, Savamala; 🕙 noon-1am Mon-Thu, to 5.30am Fri & Sat, 2pm-midnight Sun; 🕿) A Savamala stalwart (it's been running since 2009), this wonderful warehouse space promotes local creativity with workshops, exhibitions, a restaurant and nightly music events.

Bitef Art Cafe LIVE MUSIC
(www.bitefartcafe.rs; Mitropolita Petra 8; ☺9am-4am; 🛜) There's something for everyone at this delightful hotchpotch of a cafe-club. Funk, soul and jazz get a good airing, as do rock, world and classical music. In summer, Bitef moves their stage to Belgrade Fortress.

National Theatre THEATRE
(☑011 262 0946; www.narodnopozoriste.rs; Francuska 3; ☺box office 11am-3pm & 5pm-performance time) This glorious old 1869 building hosts operas, dramas and ballets during autumn, winter and spring.

🔒 Shopping

★ Makadam ARTS & CRAFTS
(www.makadam.rs; Kosančićev venac 20; ☺noon-8pm Tue-Sun; 🛜) Make your way to Makadam across the original Turkish cobblestones of Kosančićev venac, a lovely slice of old Belgrade. The concept store only sells handmade products from across Serbia. Shoppers will find an impressive selection of carefully chosen items by local craftspeople and designers, with the accent on the use of natural and traditional materials.

The bistro (9am to midnight daily) serves local wines, beers and more. The sidewalk seating here – in fact along a large swath of Kosančićev venac – draws a lively, in-the-know happy hour crowd.

Belgrade Design District FASHION & ACCESSORIES
(Čumićevo Sokače; www.belgradedesigndistrict. blogspot.com; Čumićeva 2; ☺noon-8pm Mon-Fri, to 5pm Sat) Once Belgrade's first mall and later abandoned, this revitalised complex is now home to more than 30 boutiques showcasing up-and-coming local fashionistas, jewellers, artists and designers. It's a fabulous place to pick up original pieces you won't find anywhere else. It's in the middle of the city hidden behind buildings; follow the marked passage from Nušićeva by Trg Terazije.

ℹ️ Information

Tourist Organisation of Belgrade Hosts tourist information centres at **Nikola Tesla Airport** (Turistički informativni centri; ☑011 209 7828; www.tob.rs; Aerodrom Beograd 59, Belgrade Nikola Tesla Airport; ☺9am-9.30pm), **Knez Mihailova** (Turistički informativni centri; ☑011 263 5622; www.tob.rs; Knez Mihailova 56, Belgrade City Library; ☺9am-8pm) and the

now de-commissioned **Central Train Station** (Turistički informativni centri; ☑011 361 2732; www.tob.rs; Central Train Station; ☺9am-2pm Mon-Sat).

National Tourism Organisation of Serbia Operates the information centre at **Trg Republike** (Tourist information Centre; ☑011 328 2712; www.serbia.travel; Trg Republike 5; ☺10am-9pm Mon-Fri, to 6pm Sun) and **Mt Avala** (☑011 390 8517; www.serbia.travel; Mt Avala Tower; ☺9am-8pm Mar-Sep, to 5pm Oct-Feb). More info points are planned.

ℹ️ Getting There & Away

AIR
Belgrade Nikola Tesla Airport (☑011 209 4444; www.beg.aero; Aerodrom Beograd 59) is 18km from Belgrade. Air Serbia (www.airserbia. com) is Serbia's domestic carrier.

BUS
➡ Belgrade's **bus station** (Glavna Beogradska autobuska stanica; ☑011 263 6299; Železnička 4) is near the eastern banks of the Sava River; BAS (www.bas.rs) and Lasta (www.lasta.rs) are the two main carriers.

➡ Sample international routes include Sarajevo (2510RSD, eight hours, six daily), Ljubljana (4770RSD, 7½ hours, three daily) and Pristina (2020RSD, seven hours, five daily). For Vienna (2470RSD to 4570RSD, nine hours, three daily) and some other international destinations, tickets must be purchased at **Basturist** (☑011 263 8982; www.basturist.com; Železnička 4) at the eastern end of the station.

➡ Frequent domestic services include Subotica (1270RSD to 1440RSD, three hours, nine daily), Novi Sad (750RSD, one hour, every 15 minutes), Niš (1280RSD, three hours, every 30 minutes) and Novi Pazar (1470RSD, three hours, every 45 minutes).

TRAIN
➡ Most local and international trains depart from **Belgrade Centar** (Prokop Station; ☑011 397 5533; www.srbvoz.rs; Prokupačka), while trains for Bar (Montenegro), Sofia (Bulgaria) and Thessaloniki (Greece) leave from **Topčider Station** (☑011 360 2899; www.srbvoz.rs; Topčiderska, Topčider), south of the city centre. See www.serbianrailways.com for updates.

➡ Frequent trains go to Novi Sad (from 388RSD, 1½ hours, eight daily), Subotica (from 660RSD, three hours, six daily) and Niš (from 884RSD, four hours, six daily). International destinations include Bar (from 2833RSD, 11½ hours, 9.05pm), Budapest (from 1770RSD, eight hours, three daily), Sofia (from 2821RSD, 12 hours, 9.06am), Thessaloniki (from 4400RSD, 15 hours, 6.21pm) and Zagreb (from 2243RSD, seven hours, 10.20am and 9.19pm).

ⓘ Getting Around

TO/FROM THE AIRPORT

Local bus 72 (Jug Bogdanova, Zeleni Venac; 89RSD to 150RSD, half-hourly, 4.50am to midnight from airport, 4am to 11.40pm from town) connects the airport with Zeleni Venac (note the stop where passengers alight *from* the airport is different from the stop going *to* the airport); the cheapest tickets must be purchased from news stands. The **A1 minibus** (Kralja Milutina, Trg Slavija) also runs between the airport and central Trg Slavija (300RSD, 5am to 3.50am from airport, 4.20am to 3.20am from the square).

Don't get swallowed up by the airport taxi shark pit. Head to the taxi information desk (near the baggage claim area); they'll give you a taxi receipt with the name of your destination and the fare price (fixed according to six zones). A taxi from the airport to central Belgrade (Zone 2) is 1800RSD (a CarGo ride-share is about 500RSD less).

PUBLIC TRANSPORT

➡ **GSP Belgrade** (www.gsp.rs) runs the city's trams, trolleybuses and buses. Rechargeable **BusPlus** (www2.busplus.rs) smart cards can be bought (250RSD) and topped up (89RSD per ticket) at kiosks across the city; tickets are 150RSD if you buy from the driver. Fares are good for 90 minutes. Unlimited paper BusPlus passes relevant to tourists are available for one, three and five days for 250RSD, 700RSD and 1000RSD, respectively.

➡ Tram 2 connects Belgrade Fortress with Trg Slavija and the bus stations.

➡ Belgrade Centar (p987) train station is connected by **bus 36** (Prokupačka) with Trg Slavija and the bus stations, and by trolleybus 40 or 41 with the city centre.

➡ Zemun is a 45-minute walk from central Belgrade (across Brankov Most, along Nikole Tesle and the Kej Oslobođenja waterside walkway). Alternatively, take bus 15 or 84 from Zeleni Venac market.

TAXI

➡ Move away from obvious taxi traps and flag down a distinctly labelled cruising cab, or get a local to call you one. Flag fall is 170RSD; reputable cabs should charge about 65RSD per kilometre between 6am and 10pm Monday to Friday, 85RSD between 10pm and 6am, and weekends and holidays. Make absolutely sure the meter is turned on.

➡ Order a **Naxis Taxi** (ⓙ 011 19084; www. naxis.rs) by phone, text, Twitter or mobile app. Rates are fixed, drivers speak English and major credit cards are accepted. You can also rent a driver for a day trip out of the city. CarGo (www. appcargo.net) is a popular ride-share app.

VOJVODINA ВОЈВОДИНА

Novi Sad   Нови Сад

ⓙ 021 / POP 341,600

Novi Sad is a chipper town with all the spoils and none of the stress of the big smoke. Locals sprawl in pretty parks and outdoor cafes, and laneway bars pack out nightly. The looming Petrovaradin Fortress keeps a stern eye on proceedings, loosening its tie each July to host Serbia's largest music festival. You can walk to all of Novi Sad's attractions from the happening pedestrian thoroughfare, Zmaj Jovina, which stretches from the main square (Trg Slobode) to Dunavska.

Novi Sad isn't nicknamed the 'Athens of Serbia' for nothing: its history as a vibrant, creative city continues today in its established galleries, alternative music scene and a vibe that's generally more liberal than that of other Serbian cities. In 2022 Novi Sad will become the first non-EU city to spend a year with the prestigious title of European Capital of Culture.

⊙ Sights

★**Petrovaradin Fortress**   FORTRESS
(Petrovaradinska Tvrdjava; Beogradska; ⊙ 24hr) Towering over the river on a 40m-high volcanic slab, this mighty citadel, considered Europe's second-biggest fortress (and one of its best preserved), is aptly nicknamed 'Gibraltar on the Danube'. Constructed using slave labour between 1692 and 1780, its dungeons have held notable prisoners including Karađorđe (leader of the first Serbian uprising against the Turks and founder of a royal dynasty) and Yugoslav president Tito.

Have a good gawk at the iconic clock tower: the size of the minute and hour hands are reversed so far-flung fisherfolk can tell the time. Within the citadel walls, a **museum** (Muzej Grada Novog Sada; www.museumns.rs; 300RSD; ⊙ 9am-5pm Tue-Sun) offers insight into the site's history; it can also arrange tours (in English; 3500RSD) of Petrovaradin's 16km of creepy, but cool, unlit underground tunnels (*katakombe*). Petrovaradin hosts Novi Sad's wildly popular EXIT Festival each July.

★**Gallery of Matica Srpska**   MUSEUM
(www.galerijamaticesrpske.rs; Trg Galerija 1; 100RSD; ⊙ 10am-8pm Tue-Thu, to 10pm Fri, to 6pm Sat & Sun) First established in Pest (part of modern Budapest) in 1826 and moved to Novi Sad in 1864, this is one of Serbia's most

SUBOTICA & NOVI PAZAR

Sugar-spun art nouveau marvels, a laid-back populace and a sprinkling of Serbian and Hungarian flavours make Subotica (10km from the Hungarian border) a worthy day trip or stopover. Once an important hub of the Austro-Hungarian Empire, the town attracted some of the region's most influential architects and artists; their excellently preserved handiwork is today the town's biggest drawcard. The unmissable eye candy includes the 1904 **Raichle Palace**, which now houses a modern **art gallery** (Savremena galerija Subotica; www.sgsu.org.rs; Park Ferenca Rajhla 5; adult/child 100/50RSD; ☺8am-7pm Mon-Fri, 9am-1pm Sat); the 1910 **City Hall** (Gradska kuća; ☑024 555 128; Trg Slobode; tour with/without tower 300/150RSD; ☺tours noon Tue-Sat), with a soaring, 76m-high tower; and the 1902 **Synagogue** (Sinagoga; www.en.josu.rs; Trg Sinagoge 2; adult/child 250RSD/free; ☺10am-6pm Tue-Fri, to 2pm Sat & Sun) that was restored to its full glory in 2018.

Down south near the Montenegrin border, Novi Pazar is the cultural centre of the Raška (Sandžak) region, with a large Muslim population. Turkish coffee, cuisine and customs abound, yet some of the most sacred Orthodox sights are in the vicinity: this was the heartland of the Serbian medieval state. The 16th-century **Altun-Alem Mosque** (Altun-Alem džamija; 1.maja 79) is one of Serbia's oldest surviving Islamic buildings, while the small 9th-century **Church of St Peter** (Petrova crkva; ☑060 059 8401; foreigners €2; ☺8am-3pm), 3km from town, with a fascinating, photogenic cemetery, is the oldest intact church in the country. Around 14km west of town is the 13th-century, Unesco-listed **Sopoćani Monastery** (Manastir Sopoćani; foreigners €2; ☺8am-7pm); its frescoes are sublime examples of medieval art.

important and long-standing cultural institutions. It's not a mere gallery but rather a national treasure, with three floors covering priceless Serbian artworks from the 18th, 19th and 20th centuries in styles ranging from Byzantine to modernist, with countless icons, portraits, landscapes and graphic art (and more) in between.

Štrand
BEACH

(50RSD; ☺8am-7pm) One of Europe's best by-the-Danube beaches, this 700m-long stretch morphs into a city of its own come summertime, with bars, stalls and all manner of recreational diversions attracting thousands of sun- and fun-seekers from across the globe. It's also the ultimate Novi Sad party venue, hosting everything from local punk gigs to EXIT raves.

It's great for kids (watch them by the water: the currents here are strong), with playgrounds, trampolines and dozens of ice-cream and fast-food stalls.

Museum of Vojvodina
MUSEUM

(Muzej Vojvodine; www.muzejvojvodine.org.rs; Dunavska 35-7; 200RSD; ☺9am-7pm Tue-Fri, 10am-6pm Sat & Sun) This worthwhile museum houses historical, archaeological and ethnological exhibits. The main building covers Vojvodinian history from Palaeolithic times to the late 19th century. Nearby, at building 37, which also houses the **Museum of Contemporary**

Art Vojvodina (☑021 526 634; www.msuv.org; Dunavska 37; ☺10am-6pm Tue-Thu, Sat & Sun, to 8pm Fri) FREE, the story continues to 1945 with harrowing emphasis on WWI and WWII. The highlights include three gold-plated Roman helmets from the 4th century, excavated in Srem region not far from Novi Sad, and one of the city's first bicycles, dating from 1880.

☆ Festivals & Events

EXIT Festival
MUSIC

(www.exitfest.org; ☺Jul) The Petrovaradin Fortress is stormed by thousands of revellers each July during this epic festival. The first edition, in 2000, lasted 100 days and galvanised a generation of young Serbs against the Milošević regime. The festival has since been attended by the eclectic likes of Prodigy, Gogol Bordello and Motörhead...plus about 200,000 merrymakers from around the world each year.

🛌 Sleeping

★ Varad Inn
HOSTEL €

(☑021 431 400; www.varadinn.com; Štrosmajerova 16, Petrovaradin; dm/d/q from 1230/3960/4820RSD; ※🐾) Sitting in the shadow of Petrovaradin Fortress, this excellent budget option is housed in a gorgeous yellow baroque-style building constructed in 1714. Completely renovated but making beauti-

Novi Sad

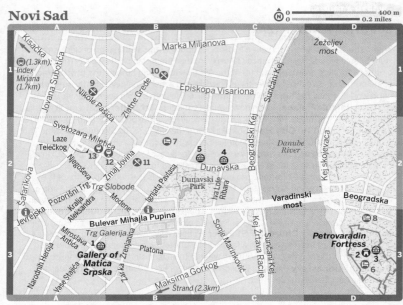

Novi Sad

◉ Top Sights
| 1 Gallery of Matica Srpska | A3 |
| 2 Petrovaradin Fortress | D3 |

◉ Sights
3 City Museum of Novi Sad	D3
4 Museum of Contemporary Art Vojvodina	C2
5 Museum of Vojvodina	B2

⊜ Sleeping
| 6 Leopold I | D3 |

| 7 Narator | B2 |
| 8 Varad Inn | D3 |

⊗ Eating
9 Fish i Zeleniš	A1
10 Project 72	B1
11 Toster Bar	B2

◯ Drinking & Nightlife
| 12 Beer Store | B2 |
| 13 PUBeraj | A2 |

ful use of salvaged historical bits and bobs, the Varad Inn (get it?) has beautiful feel-at-home rooms (all with their own bathrooms, lockers and towels), a lovely cafe and garden, and communal kitchen.

★ Narator
APARTMENT €€

(☏ 060 676 7886; www.en.narator.rs; Dunavska 17 / Trg Republike 16; s/d apt from 3600/4800RSD; ❄ 🛜) The super-central designer digs at Narator do indeed tell a story; four of them, in fact, one for every themed, individually decorated apartment. With names like 'Chambermaid from Eden', 'The Bookworm' and 'Captain Honeymoon', each room's tale unfolds via a series of exquisite, original

naive-style portraits scattered across the walls. All apartments are self-contained.

It's a bit tricky to find. Enter to the right of Laboratorija Medical Praxis from Dunavska and between Aldo and Jeodie's from Trg Republike.

Leopold I
LUXURY HOTEL €€€

(☏ 021 488 7878; www.leopoldns.com; Petrovaradin Fortress; 1st floor r/ste incl breakfast from 16,800/24,000RSD; 2nd floor r/ste incl breakfast from 10,800/16,800RSD; 🅿 ❄ 🛜) This rock-top, 59-room hotel in the Petrovaradin complex is split into two sections, with two different names: the 1st floor, **Leopold I**, is given over to indulgent baroque-style digs while the 2nd floor, **Garni Hotel Leopold I**, comprises modern, (slightly) economical rooms. The location is unbeatable, and breakfast at the terrace restaurant is a princely way to start the day.

Eating

★ Toster Bar
BURGERS €

(www.tosterbar.rs; Zmaj Jovina 24; burgers 320-860RSD; ⊙10am-11pm Mon-Thu, to 1am Fri & Sat, 11am-11pm Sun; 🛜) There are likely better Serbian-style *pljeskavica* (hamburgers) in Novi Sad, but there certainly aren't better American-style burgers, and the beauty of wildly popular Toster is that it does both! Tucked away in a jam-packed *pasaž* (passage), it's a Croatian-owned, cash-only joint doing fat, juicy and spicy (Carolina Reaper spicy!) burgers along with a wise devotion to craft beer.

Index Mirjana
FAST FOOD €

(Braće Popović 8; sandwiches 200-290RSD; ⊙7am-11pm Sun-Thu, to midnight Fri & Sat) The consensus among Novosadjani is that this hole-in-the-wall of a sandwich shop produces the best version of the locally famous Index sandwich – an indulgent, sauce-laden spin on a ham-and-cheese sandwich – in the friendliest of manners (many folks, both Serbian and foreigners, complain about nasty customer service at many of the Novi Sad sandwich shops).

★ Fish i Zeleniš
MEDITERRANEAN €€

(Fish and Greens; 🖉021 452 002; www.fishizelenis.com; Skerlićeva 2; mains 696-2900RSD; ⊙noon-11pm; 🛜🖉) This character-filled, snug little nook serves up the finest vegetarian and pescatarian meals in northern Serbia. Organic, locally sourced ingredients? Ambient? Ineffably delicious? Tick, tick, tick. Check the daily specials or spring for one of their excellently prepared Mediterranean staples, guided by the affable staff.

Project 72
SERBIAN €€

(🖉021 657 2720; www.wineanddeli.rs; Kosovska 15; small plates 242-898RSD, mains 725-1692RSD; ⊙9am-11pm Mon-Thu, to 1am Fri & Sat; 🛜) 🍷 This smart bistro with lovely sidewalk seating is brought to Novi Sad by the same owners as the excellent Fish i Zeleniš, but here the concentration is on creative tapas and heartier, Mediterranean/Serbian meat dishes, which pair wonderfully with the deep wine list featuring 21 Serbian wines by the glass.

Standout dishes include oxtail with celery purée and sweet *bermet* dessert wine; wild boar with orange and red fruits; and lamb with blanched broccoli. At least 80% of the produce used is organic.

🍷 Drinking & Nightlife

Beer Store
CRAFT BEER

(www.beerstore.rs; Svetozara Miletića 17; ⊙4pm-midnight Sun-Thu, to 1am Fri & Sat; 🛜) Don't let the name confuse you, Novi Sad's top craft beer destination features 20 mostly Serbian brews on draught, along with another 180 or so in bottles. Expect several pale ales and IPAs from Novi Sad's finest, 3Bir, which go down far too easily on the outdoor patio along this atmospheric pedestrianised street.

PUBeraj
BAR

(www.facebook.com/puberajcafee; Mite Ružića; ⊙8am-11pm Mon-Thu, to 1am Fri & Sat, noon-11pm Sun; 🛜) The hippest and certainly the most local of the smattering of bars around Laze Telečkog, PUBeraj is the brainchild of local Andrija Nikitović, who figured a stylish cocktail bar sandwiched between a barbershop and salon was just what Novi Sad needed. It features at least 30 whiskies, and hosts DJs and live music several times per week.

ⓘ Information

The Tourist Organisation of the City of Novi Sad operates two tourist information centres; one at **Jevrejska** (Turistički info centri; 🖉021 661 7343; www.novisad.travel; Jevrejska 10; ⊙7.30am-5pm Mon-Fri, 10am-3pm Sat) on the way to the main bus and railway stations; and on **Bulevar Mihajla Pupina** (Turistički info centri; 🖉021 421 811; www.novisad.travel; Bul Mihajla Pupina 9; ⊙7.30am-5pm Mon-Fri, 10am-5pm Sat) near Petrovaradin Fortress, Belgrade Quay and the Danube.

ⓘ Getting There & Away

The **bus station** (Međumesna autobuska stanica Novi Sad; 🖉021 444 022; Bul Jaše Tomića 6) has regular departures to Belgrade (700RSD, one hour, every 10 to 30 minutes) and Subotica (790RSD, 1¾ hours). There are a dozen or so buses to Niš (1780RSD, 5½ hours). Two buses go daily to Budapest (3130RSD, 5¾ hours, 9.15am and 10.15pm).

Frequent trains leave the **train station** (Železnička stanica Novi Sad; 🖉021 420 700; www.srbvoz.rs; Bul Jaše Tomića 4), next door to the bus station, for Belgrade (400RSD, 1¾ hours) and Subotica (490RSD, 2½ hours). At least three trains go daily to Budapest (1500RSD, 6½ hours, 9.26am, 1.17pm and 11.30pm).

ⓘ Getting Around

From the Novi Sad train station, city bus 4B (65RSD) will take you to the town centre.

Crveni i Red Taxi (www.crvenitaxi.co.rs/aplikacija) is the most reliable taxi app for Novi Sad.

SOUTH SERBIA
ЈУЖНА СРБИЈА

Niš   Ниш
📞 018 / POP 183,000

Serbia's third-largest metropolis is a lively city of curious contrasts, where Roma in horse-drawn carriages trot alongside new cars, and posh cocktails are sipped in antiquated alleyways. It's a buzzy kind of place, with a high number of university students, packed-out laneway bars, a happening live-music scene, and pop-up markets and funfairs come summertime.

Niš was settled in pre-Roman times, but hit its peak during the years of the Empire. Constantine the Great (280–337 CE) was born here, as were two other Roman emperors, Constantius III and Justin I. Turkish rule lasted from 1386 until 1877, despite several Serb revolts; Ćele Kula (Tower of Skulls) and Niš Fortress are reminders of Ottoman dominion. Niš also had it rough during WWII; the Nazis built one of Serbia's most notorious concentration camps here.

⊙ Sights

Mediana   RUINS
(Bul Cara Konstantina; 200RSD; ⊙ 9am-7pm Tue-Sun) Mediana is what remains of Constantine the Great's luxurious 4th-century Roman palace. The 1000 sq metres of gorgeous mosaics are the highlight here; they were hidden from public view until protective renovations were recently completed. Digging has revealed a palace, a forum, a church and an expansive grain-storage area. Mediana is on the eastern outskirts of Niš and a short walk from Ćele Kula.

Ćele Kula   MONUMENT
(Tower of Skulls; Bul Zoran Đinđić; 200RSD, with Red Cross Concentration Camp & Archaeological Hall 300RSD; ⊙ 9am-7pm Tue-Sun) With Serbian defeat imminent at the 1809 Battle of Čegar, the Duke of Resava kamikazed towards the Turkish defences, firing at their gunpowder stores, killing himself, 4000 of his men and 10,000 Turks. The Turks triumphed regardless, and to deter future acts of rebellion, they beheaded, scalped and embedded the skulls of the dead Serbs in this tower. Only 58 of the initial 952 skulls remain. Contra-

ry to Turkish intention, the tower serves as proud testament to Serbian resistance.

Catch bus 1 across the street from tourist information on Vožda Karađorđa (60RSD).

Red Cross Concentration Camp   MUSEUM
(Crveni Krst; Bul 12 Februar; 200RSD, with Archaeological Hall & Ćele Kula 300RSD; ⊙ 9am-7pm Tue-Sun) One of the best-preserved Nazi camps in Europe, the deceptively named Red Cross (named after the adjacent train station) held about 30,000 Serbs, Roma, Jews and Partisans during the German occupation of Serbia (1941–45). Harrowing displays tell their stories, and those of the prisoners who attempted to flee in the biggest-ever breakout from a concentration camp. This was a transit camp so few were killed on the premises – they were taken to **Bubanj** (Spomen park Bubanj; Vojvode Putnika; ⊙ 24hr), or on to Auschwitz, Dachau etc.

The English-speaking staff are happy to provide translations and explain the exhibits in depth: and the fact that you might have it all to yourself makes it all the more distressing. The camp is a short walk north of the Niš bus station.

⚑ Festivals & Events

Nišville International Jazz Festival   MUSIC
(www.nisville.com; Niš Fortress; from 3550RSD; ⊙ Aug) This jazz festival, held at Niš Fortress, attracts big-name musos from Serbia and around the world.

🛏 Sleeping

★ ArtLoft Hotel   BOUTIQUE HOTEL €€
(📞 018 305 800; www.artlofthotel.com; Oblačića Rada 8a/7; s/d/ste from 5612/6466/7320RSD; ❄ 🛜) Central and chic, this designer hotel takes its name literally, with original murals and paintings by local artists dominating every room. The modern feel extends to the professional staff, who take service to the next level by offering friendly assistance, advice and little touches including complimentary fruit and drinks. It's a short stroll from here to Trg Republike and Kopitareva.

★ Hotel Sole   HOTEL €€
(📞 018 524 555; www.hotelsole.rs; Kralja Stefana Prvovenčanog 11; s/d from 5782/6844RSD incl breakfast; 🅿 ❄ 🛜) Sitting pretty right in the heart of Niš, this refurbished hotel has modern, super-spacious rooms with boutique furnishings; ceiling murals are a very cool

GO WILD: TARA & ĐERDAP NATIONAL PARKS

If you need a breather from Serbia's urban destinations, two spectacular national parks provide fresh-air fun in droves. Contact **Wild Serbia** (☑ 063 273 852; www.wildserbia.com) for guided trips and outdoor adventures.

The sprawling **Đerdap National Park** (636 sq km) is home to the mighty Iron Gates gorge. Its formidable cliffs – some of which soar over 500m – dip and dive for 100km along the Danube on the border with Romania. The hulking **Golubac Fortress** (Tvrđava Golubački Grad; www.tvrdjavagolubackigrad.rs; Golubac; adult/child 600/120RSD; ⊙10am-7pm Tue-Sun Apr-Aug, to 6pm Sep, to 5pm Oct, to 4pm Nov-Mar) and the ancient settlement of **Lepenski Vir** (www.lepenski-vir.org; adult/child 400/250RSD; ⊙9am-8pm) are testimony to old-time tenacity. With marked paths and signposted viewpoints, Đerdap is an excellent hiking destination; the international EuroVelo 6 cycling path also runs through here. Boat tours through the gorge can be booked through **Serbian Adventures** (☑ 062 737 242; www.serbianadventures.com).

With forested slopes, dramatic ravines and jewel-like waterways, **Tara National Park** (220 sq km) is scenic Serbia at its best. Pressed up against Bosnia and Hercegovina, its main attraction is the Drina River canyon, the third-largest of its kind in the world. The emerald-green river offers ripper rafting; two lakes (Perućac and Zaovine) are ideal for calm-water kayaking. Nearby are the **Šargan Eight** (Šarganska osmica; ☑ Mon-Fri 031 510 288; www.sarganskaosmica.rs; Mokra Gora; adult/child 600/300RSD; ⊙3 daily Jul & Aug, 2 daily Apr-Jun, Sep & Oct, daily Dec-Feb) heritage railway, a 2½-hour journey with disorienting twists and tunnels, and the hilltop mini village of **Drvengrad** (Küstendorf; ☑ 064 883 0213; www.mecavnik.info; Mećavnik hill, Mokra Gora; adult/child 250/100RSD; ⊙7am-7pm) built by filmmaker Emir Kusturica for his movie *Life is a Miracle*.

touch. Hotel Sole also dishes up one of the best breakfasts you'll find anywhere and the staff were the best we met in Serbia's cities. They'll even throw in laundry at no extra charge.

✖ Eating

Pekara Anton Plus　　　BAKERY €
(www.pekara-brankovic.com; Trg Pavla Stojkovića 17; burek 45-120RSD; ⊙6am-8pm Mon-Fri, to 4pm Sat, to 2pm Sun) Prepare to hurry up and wait for the Serbian breakfast of champions: *burek* (hearty filo pastries stuffed with veal, cheese and other tasty fillings). This slick *pekara* (bakery) does the best in Niš. Four versions are available – veal, cheese, spinach and pizza (ham, cheese and mushroom) – and the Nišlije can't get enough of them.

Kafana Galija　　　SERBIAN €€
(www.kafanagalija.com; Nikole Pasica 35; mains 260-1700RSD; ⊙10am-midnight Mon-Thu, to 2am Fri & Sat, 11am-7pm Sun; 🕲) The chefs here grill to thrill, with exceptional takes on classics, including spicy meat platters and a good *pljeskavica* (bunless burger). Rouse yourself from your food coma by sticking around for the rollicking live music and associated crowd carousals – the patio spills out onto bustling Kopitareva. Save room for the wet and wonderful baklava.

★ Stambolijski　　　SERBIAN €€€
(☑ 018 300 440; www.restoranstambolijski.rs; Nikole Pašića 36; mains 390-1950RSD; ⊙noon-10.30pm; 🕲) This upscale, standout New Balkan restaurant elegantly occupies the oldest preserved home in Niš (dating to 1878) and is easily the city's top dining destination. The accolades were quickly showered on Chef Saša Mišić for his modern takes on classics like *jagnjetina ispod sača* (lamb cooked in a clay pot), coupled with creative dishes like pork neck with beer and honey.

🍷 Drinking & Nightlife

Vespa Bar　　　BAR
(www.vespabar.com; Trg Republike; ⊙8am-midnight Mon-Thu, to 2am Fri & Sat, 9am-midnight Sun; 🕲) There are literally Vespas coming out of the woodwork at this happy, happening bar in the centre of town. Chat with the friendly 'bikies' over beer (local and international) or something from the extensive cocktail list (195RSD to 420RSD). Ace people-watching.

Ministarstvo Beer Bar CRAFT BEER

(www.facebook.com/pg/ministarstvobeerbar; Vojvode Vuka 12; ⊙8.30am-midnight Mon-Thu, to 1.30am Fri, 10.30am-1.30am Sat, 5pm-midnight Sun; 🔊) Ministarstvo is one of Niš's go-to craft beer destinations, with 15 options on draught (mostly Serbian, a bit of mainstream German and Czech) and a gaggle more by the bottle. A fantastic soundtrack, lively patio and a fun, suds-swilling crowd make this a solid choice for hopheads who want to steer clear of more crowded areas such as Kopitareva.

ℹ Information

Tourist Organisation of Niš runs several tourist information centres, including one within the **Niš Fortress** (Turistički info centri; 🖉 018 250 222; www.visitnis.com; Tvrđava; ⊙9am-8pm Tue-Fri, 9.30am-2.30pm Sat & Sun). Other convenient branches in the city centre include **Vožda Karađorđa** (Turistički info centri; 🖉 018 523 118; www.visitnis.com; Vožda Karađorđa 7; ⊙9am-8pm Mon-Fri, to 2pm Sat), **Obreno-vićeva** (Turistički info centri; 🖉 018 520 207; www.visitnis.com; Obrenovićeva 38; ⊙9am-8pm Mon-Fri, to 2pm Sat) and **Dušanova** (Turis-tički info centri; 🖉 018 505 688; www.visitnis. com; Dušanova 30; ⊙8am-4pm Mon-Fri).

ℹ Getting There & Away

The **bus station** (Autobuska stanica Niš; 🖉 018 255 177; www.nis-ekspres.rs; Bul 12 Februar) has frequent services to Belgrade (1118RSD, three hours, hourly) and one daily bus to Novi Pazar (1280RSD, four hours, 3.15pm). **Niš Ekspres** (www.nis-ekspres.rs) heads to Sofia, Bulgaria (1225RSD, five hours, 4.30am) and Skopje, North Macedonia (1234RSD, four hours, six daily).

From the **train station** (Železnička stanica Niš; 🖉 018 264 625; www.srbvoz.rs; Dimitrija Tucovića bb), there are four daily trains to Belgrade (from 900RSD, 4½ hours), one to Sofia (from 1100RSD, six hours, 2.16pm) and one to Skopje (from 900RSD, five hours, 11.19pm).

The **Niš Constantine The Great Airport** (🖉 018 458 3336; www.nis-airport.com; Vazduhoplovaca 24) is 4km from downtown Niš; destinations include Germany, Italy, Slovakia and Switzerland. **Bus 34B** (60RSD, 10 minutes) heads from the bus station to the airport, leaving from a stop just outside the station on Bul 12 Februar. From the airport, it's 34A.

A taxi to/from the airport to town is around 400RSD – be weary of solo taxis waiting for passengers and changing the tariff period from 'one' to far more expensive 'three' (reserved for long-distance trips out of town).

SURVIVAL GUIDE

ℹ Directory A–Z

ACCOMMODATION

You'll find hotels and hostels in most Serbian towns. The **Serbian Youth Hostels Association** (Ferijalni Savez Beograd; 🖉 011 322 0762; www. hostels.rs; Makedonska 22/2, Belgrade) can help with hostel information and advice. Private rooms *(sobe)* and apartments *(apartmani)* offer good value and can be organised through tourist offices. 'Wild' camping is possible outside national parks; **Camping Association of Serbia** (www.camping.rs) lists official camping grounds. In rural areas, look out for *etno sela* (traditional village accommodation) or *salaši* (farmsteads). **Rural Tourism Serbia** (www.selo.co.rs) can organise village sleepovers.

Although accommodation prices are often quoted in euro, you must pay in dinar. City tax (130RSD to 155RSD per person per night) is levied on top of lodging bills.

LGBTIQ+ TRAVELLERS

As evidenced by the furore over Belgrade's early pride parades (chronicled in the 2011 film *Parada*), life is not all rainbows for homosexuals in this conservative country. Discretion is highly advised. Check out www.gay-serbia.com and www.gej.rs for the latest news in the Serbian LG-BTIQ+ community, or to make local connections.

MONEY

ATMs are widespread and cards are accepted by established businesses. There's an exchange office *(menjačnica)* on every street corner. Exchange machines accept euros, US dollars and British pounds.

OPENING HOURS

Banks 9am to 5pm Monday to Friday, 9am to 1pm Saturday

Bars 8am to midnight (later on weekends)

Restaurants 8am to midnight or 1am

Shops 8am to 6pm or 7pm Monday to Friday, 8am to 3pm Saturday

PUBLIC HOLIDAYS

New Year 1 and 2 January

Orthodox Christmas 7 January

Statehood Day 15 and 16 February

Orthodox Easter April/May

Labour Day 1 and 2 May

Armistice Day 11 November

SAFE TRAVEL

Travelling around Serbia is generally safe for visitors who exercise the usual caution. The exceptions can be border areas, particularly the southeast Kosovo border where Serb–Albanian tensions remain. Check the situation before attempting to cross overland, and think thrice about driving there in Serbian-plated cars.

TELEPHONE
The country code is 381. To call abroad from Serbia, dial 00 followed by the country code. Press the *i* button on public phones for dialling commands in English. Long-distance calls can also be made from booths in post offices. A variety of local and international phonecards can be bought in post offices and news stands.

❶ Getting There & Away

AIR
Belgrade's Nikola Tesla Airport (p987) handles most international flights. The airport website has a full list of airlines servicing Serbia. In the south, Niš Constantine the Great Airport links Niš with countries including Germany, Italy, Slovakia and Switzerland.

Serbia's national carrier is **Air Serbia** (www.airserbia.com). It code-shares with airlines including Etihad, Aeroflot, Alitalia and KLM.

LAND
Border Crossings
Because Serbia does not acknowledge crossing points into Kosovo as international border crossings, it may not be possible to enter Serbia from Kosovo unless you first entered Kosovo from Serbia. If you wish to enter Serbia from Kosovo, consider taking a route that transits another nearby country. Check with your embassy for updates.

Bus
Bus services to Western Europe and Turkey are well developed. When crossing borders, officers will usually board the bus, take everyone's passports then return them after processing them; passengers wait in their seats.

Car & Motorcycle
Drivers need International Driving Permits. If you're in your own car, you'll need your vehicle registration and ownership documents and locally valid insurance (such as European Green Card vehicle insurance). Otherwise, border insurance costs about €150 for a car, €95 for a motorbike; www.registracija-vozila.rs has updated price lists. Check your hire-car insurance cover to be sure it covers Serbia.

Driving Serbian-plated cars into Kosovo is not a good idea, and is usually not permitted by rental agencies or insurers anyway.

Train
International rail connections leaving Serbia originate in Belgrade. Heading north, most call in at Novi Sad and Subotica. Heading southeast, they go via Niš. The scenic route to Bar on the Montenegrin coast passes through Užice in the southwest.

At border stops, officials will board the train to stamp your passport and check for relevant visas. For more information, visit the website of **Serbian Railways** (www.serbianrailways.com).

❶ Getting Around

BICYCLE
Bicycle paths are improving in larger cities. Mountain biking in summer is popular in regions including Tara National Park. Picturesque winding roads come with the downside of narrow shoulders.

The international **Euro Velo 6** (www.eurovelo.com) route runs through parts of Serbia including Novi Sad, Belgrade and Đerdap National Park.

BUS
Bus services are extensive, though outside major hubs, sporadic connections may leave you in the lurch for a few hours. In southern Serbia particularly, you may have to double back to larger towns.

Reservations are only worthwhile for international buses and during festivals. Tickets can be purchased from the station before departure or on board.

CAR & MOTORCYCLE
The **Automobile & Motorcycle Association of Serbia** (Auto-Moto Savez Srbije; ☑ 011 333 1100, roadside assist 1987; www.amss.org.rs; Ruzveltova 18, Belgrade; ☺ 8am-4pm Mon-Fri) provides roadside assistance and extensive information on its website. A great resource for drivers is the **Planplus** (www.planplus.rs) interactive online road atlas; *Intersistem Kartografija* publishes a useful road map of Serbia (1:550,000).

Several car-hire companies have offices at Nikola Tesla Airport in Belgrade. Small-car hire typically costs €25 to €45 per day. Check where you are not able to take the car. In Belgrade and other large towns you may have to purchase parking tickets from machines, kiosks or via SMS (in Serbian only).

Traffic police are everywhere and accidents are workaday. The BAC limit is 0.02%. You must drive with your headlights on, even in the daytime. An International Driving Permit is required.

TRAIN
Serbian Railways (www.serbianrailways.com) links Belgrade, Novi Sad, Subotica, Niš and Užice in the west; check the website for smaller stations between the cities.

Trains usually aren't as regular and reliable as buses, and can be murderously slow, but they're a fun way to meet locals and other travellers.

Slovakia

POP 5.45 MILLION

Best Places to Eat

➜ Sky Bar & Restaurant (p1003)

➜ Vino & Tapas (p1007)

➜ Modrá Hviezda (p1003)

➜ Koliba Patria (p1010)

➜ Pán Ryba (p1013)

➜ Kupecká Bašta (p1010)

Best Places to Stay

➜ Marrol's Boutique Hotel (p1002)

➜ Penzión Sabato (p1006)

➜ Penzión Slovakia (p1013)

➜ Hostel Blues (p1002)

➜ Hotel Cafe Razy (p1006)

Why Go?

Right in the heart of Europe, Slovakia is a land of castles and mountains, occasionally punctuated by industrial sprawl. More than a quarter-century after Czechoslovakia's break-up, Slovakia has emerged as a self-assured, independent nation. Capital city Bratislava draws visitors to its resplendent old town but Slovakia shines brightest for lovers of the outdoors. Walking trails in the High Tatras wend through landscapes of unearthly beauty, with mirror-still glacier lakes backed by 2000m peaks.

Almost an alternate realm, Slovakia's less-visited east is speckled with quaint churches. Beyond eastern metropolis Košice, a boutique charmer of a city, the Tokaj wine region unfurls across thinly populated countryside.

Slovakia is small. For visitors, that can mean fortresses, hiking and beer-sloshing merriment – all in the space of a long weekend.

When to Go
Bratislava

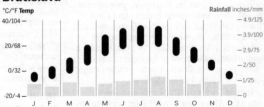

| **Jun–Aug** Festivals spark dancing and craft-making countrywide; all hiking trails are open. | **Sep & Oct** Fewer crowds but clement walking weather and music festivals galore. | **Late Dec–Feb** Bratislava's Christmas markets in late December, and ski season begins. |

Entering the Country

Bratislava and Košice are the country's main entry and exit points by air, road and rail. Poprad, with bus links to/from Zakopane in Poland and a few international flights, is in distant third place. Entering Slovakia from the EU, indeed from most of Europe, is a breeze. Lengthy customs checks make arriving from Ukraine more tedious.

Bratislava has the largest number of international flights. Well-connected Vienna International Airport is just 60km away from Bratislava, with frequent direct buses connecting the two.

Direct trains connect Bratislava to Austria, the Czech Republic, Poland, Hungary and Russia; from Košice, trains connect to the Czech Republic, Poland, Ukraine and Russia. Buses travel to Uzhhorod in Ukraine (three hours) from Košice.

ITINERARIES

Three Days

A long weekend in Bratislava (p999) is enough to experience the fine castle and old town, and take trips to forbidding Devín Castle (p1005) and uplifting Danubiana Meulensteen Art Museum (p1006). At nightfall, take your pick from avant-garde venues, merry beer halls and swish cocktail bars.

One Week

Spend three days experiencing Bratislava (p999), including one or two trips to castles or galleries outside the city. Press east to Poprad (p1006), a base for two glorious days of hiking or skiing. Storm Spiš Castle (p1010) and finish with a day or two in quirky Košice (p1012).

Essential Food & Drink

Bryndzové halušky National dish of potato dumplings with sheep's cheese and diced bacon.

Guláš Known elsewhere in Central Europe as goulash, a thick shepherd's stew often rich with venison.

Kapustnica Thick sauerkraut and sausage soup, commonly with ham or mushrooms.

Lokše Potato pancakes stuffed with cabbage, mince or other fillings.

Pirohy Pillowy dumplings with a crimped edge, crammed with cheese, meat or mushrooms.

Šulance Walnut- or poppyseed-topped dumplings.

Trdelník Barbecued cone of sweet pastry sprinkled with nuts and sugar.

Vývar Chicken or beef broth often with noodles, vegetables or dumplings.

Žemlovka Bread pudding with stewed fruit, frequently pears or apples.

AT A GLANCE

Area 49,034 sq km

Capital Bratislava

Country Code 421

Currency euro (€)

Emergency Ambulance 155, fire 150, general emergency 112, police 158

Language Slovak

Time Central European Time (GMT/UTC plus one hour)

Visas Not required for most visitors staying less than 90 days

SLOVAKIA

Sleeping Price Ranges

The following price ranges refer to a double room with bathroom.

€ less than €50

€€ €50–130

€€€ more than €130

Eating Price Ranges

The following price ranges refer to a main course.

€ less than €7

€€ €7–12

€€€ more than €12

Resources

Lonely Planet (www.lonelyplanet.com/slovakia)

Slovakia Tourist Board (http://slovakia.travel/en)

Englishman in Slovakia (www.englishmaninslovakia.co.uk)

Slovakia Highlights

1 High Tatras (p1007) Hiking between glacier lakes, snow-shrouded peaks and wildflower meadows.

2 Bratislava (p999) Strolling from hilltop castles to sci-fi monuments en route to your next coffee or beer.

3 Spiš Castle (p1010) Clambering around the ramparts of a 13th-century castle.

4 Košice (p1012) Exploring a postcard-perfect historic centre and bohemian nightlife in Slovakia's second city.

5 Slovenský Raj National Park (p1011) Clinging to ladders and being splashed by waterfalls.

6 Banská Štiavnica (p1004) Delighting in Gothic and Renaissance buildings and trendy cafes.

7 Vlkolínec (p1006) Gazing at folkloric woodcarvings and quaint houses.

8 Wine Country (p1013) Sipping sweet Tokaj wine in eastern Slovakia's countryside.

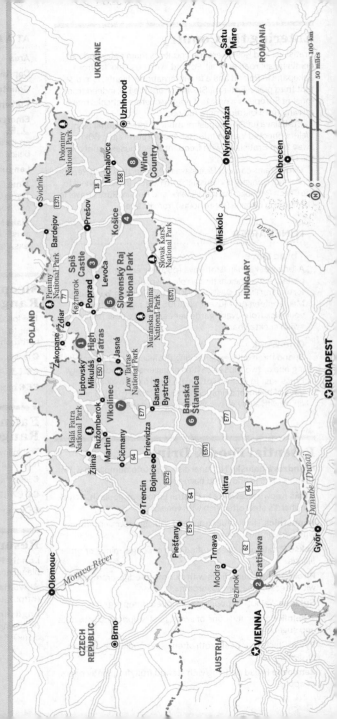

BRATISLAVA

📋 02 / POP 430,000

Slovakia's capital since the country's independence in 1993, Bratislava is a mosaic of illustrious history: a medieval and Gothic old town, baroque palaces commissioned by Hungarian nobles, and the crowning castle, rebuilt to Renaissance finery. Slicing through the city are stark-angled, communist-era blocks and a futurist bridge.

Recent years have added a cast of outlandish statues, boutiques and modish cafes, eagerly sought out by visiting stag party groups and day trippers from Vienna. Many arrive purely to enjoy the uproarious nightlife, from rowdy beer halls to hidden nightclubs.

Despite the march of modernism, Bratislava still has nature on its doorstep. The city banks the Danube River, only a few kilometres from the Austrian border. Rolling north are the Malé Karpaty (Small Carpathians), their lowlands draped with vineyards. Flitting between postcard-pretty, steely and gorgeously green, Bratislava never fails to intrigue.

History

First inhabited by Slavs during the 6th century, the earliest mention of Bratislava and its castle is found in 907 CE. By the 12th century, Bratislava (then called Poszony in Hungarian or Pressburg in German) was a large city in greater Hungary. Many of the imposing baroque palaces you see date to the 40-year reign of Austro-Hungarian empress Maria Theresa (1740–80). From the 16th-century Turkish occupation of Budapest to the mid-1800s, the Hungarian parliament met locally and monarchs were crowned in St Martin's Cathedral.

'Bratislava' was officially born as the second city of a Czechoslovakian state after WWI. When Europe was redivided, the city was coveted by various nations – not least Austria (the population was predominantly German-speaking). US President Woodrow Wilson supported Czechoslovakian requests to have a Danube port in their newly founded country and the city was almost called Wilsonovo Mesto (Wilson City). Post-WWII, the communists razed a large part of the old town, including the synagogue, to make space for a highway.

⊙ Sights

★ **Bratislava Castle**   CASTLE
(Bratislavský hrad; ☎ 02-2048 3110; www.bratislava-hrad.sk; grounds free, museum adult/student €8/4;

⊙ grounds 9am-1am, museum 10am-6pm Tue-Sun Apr-Oct, to 5pm Nov-Mar) Magnificently rebuilt in Renaissance style, Bratislava Castle looks as though it has been transplanted from a children's picture book. Inside is a **history museum**, though many chambers feel empty and underutilised. The castle's oldest original feature is the 13th-century **Crown Tower**; climb it for bird's-eye views. Another highlight is the late-baroque *Assumption of the Virgin Mary* (1762–3) painting by Anton Schmidt in the **Music Hall**. Without a ticket you can wander the manicured **baroque gardens** behind the castle.

Hlavné Námestie   SQUARE
The nucleus for Bratislava's history, festivals and chic cafe culture is Hlavné nám (Main Sq). There's architectural finery in almost every direction, notably the **Stará Radnica** (Old Town Hall), a complex of attractive 14th- and 15th-century Gothic buildings, and **Palugyayov Palác**, a neobaroque former palace.

★ **Museum of City History**   MUSEUM
(Aponiho Palace; ☎ 02-5910 0847; www.muzeum.bratislava.sk; Radničná 1; adult/child €5/2.50; ⊙ 10am-5pm Tue-Fri, 11am-6pm Sat & Sun) Rove through Bratislava's past in the former town hall. First, scale the tower for a lookout over Bratislava. Then tour the exhibition rooms; loveliest of all, despite the dreary name, is the **Hall of the Extended Municipal Council** and the **Court House**, with brightly coloured ceilings, Gothic flourishes and stained glass dating to the 17th century.

Spare some time at the end for the **Viticulture Museum** beneath, where you can sample regional wines with a lively explanation (from €5).

Blue Church   CHURCH
(Kostol sv Alžbety; https://modrykostol.fara.sk; Bezručova 2; ⊙ 7-7.30am & 5.30-7pm Mon-Sat, 7.30am-noon & 5.30-7pm Sun) Dedicated to St Elisabeth of Hungary in 1913, the early-20th-century 'Blue Church' is a vision in sapphire and powder-blue. From its undulating arches and ceramic roof tiles to the tip of its clock tower (36.8m), it's a marvel of art nouveau design.

St Martin's Cathedral   CHURCH
(Dóm sv Martina; ☎ 02-5443 1359; http://dom.fara.sk; Rudnayovo nám 1; ⊙ 9-11.30am & 1-6pm Mon-Sat, 1.30-4pm Sun May-Sep, to 4pm Mon-Sat Oct-Apr) The coronations of 19 royals have taken place within three-nave St Martin's

Central Bratislava

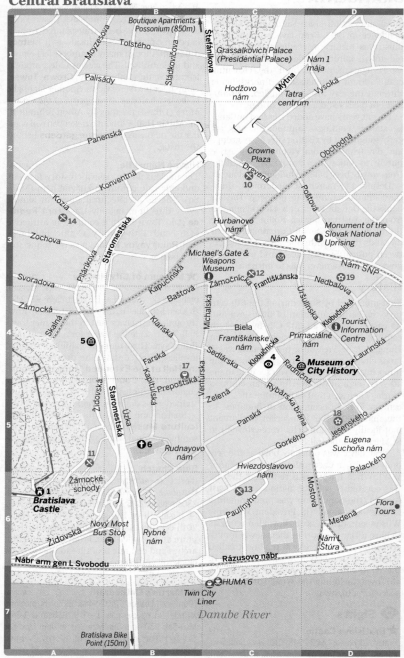

Boutique Apartments
Possonium (850m)

Grassalkovich Palace
(Presidential Palace)

Nám 1
mája

Štefánikova

Moyzesova

Tolstého

Sládkovičova

Palisády

Hodžovo
nám

Mýtna

Tatra
centrum

Vysoká

Panenská

Crowne
Plaza

Obchodná

Konventná

Drevená
10

Poštová

Kozia
14

Zochova

Staromestská

Pillárikova

Hurbanovo
nám

Nám SNP

Monument of the
Slovak National
Uprising

Nám SNP

Svoradova

Kapucínska

Michael's Gate &
Weapons Museum

Zámočnícka
12

Františkánska

Nedbalová
19

Zámocká

Baštová

Michalská

Ursulínska

Klobučnícka

Skalná

Klariská

Biela

Tourist
Information
Centre

5

Farská

Františkánske
nám

Sedlárska

Klobučnícka

Primaciálne
nám

Laurinská

Židovská

Kapitulská

17
Prepoštská

Venturska

4

2
Museum of
City History

Radničná

Zelená

Rybárska brána

Staromestská

Úzka

6

Rudnayovo
nám

Panská

Gorkého

18
Jesenského

Eugena
Suchoňa nám

Palackého

11

Hviezdoslavovo
nám

Mostová

Medená

Flora
Tours

1
Bratislava
Castle

Žámocké
schody

13

Paulínyho

Nový Most
Bus Stop

Rybné
nám

Nám Ľ
Štúra

Židovská

Nábr arm gen L Svobodu

Rázusovo nábr

HUMA 6
Twin City
Liner

Danube River

Bratislava Bike
Point (150m)

Cathedral, alluded to by the 300kg replica crown atop its spire. The interior of this 14th-century Gothic sanctuary has four chapels dedicated to saints and luminaries, a horseback statue of St Martin, and huge rib vaults and stained-glass windows that lift the gaze.

Museum of Jewish Culture MUSEUM
(Múzeum židovskej kultúry; ☎ 02-2049 0102; www.snm.sk; Židovská 17; adult/child €7/2; ☺ 11am-5pm Sun-Fri) This enriching museum unveils the stories of Bratislava's once-thriving Jewish community through photographs and objects from daily life, with a focus on the impressive Jewish architecture lost both during and after WWII.

🏃 Activities

Bratislava Bike Point CYCLING
(☎ 0907 683 112; www.bratislavabikepoint.com; Pri Suchom mlyne 84; bike rental 24hr €15, per day thereafter €13; ☺ bike rental by arrangement, tours Apr-Oct) Book at least a day in advance to

hire a bicycle from knowledgeable Bratislava Bike Point; for an extra €3, the bike can be brought to the central Bratislava address of your choice. Bike lock and helmet are included. The website is packed with cyclist-friendly info, too. Deposit €50 per bike.

⛳ Tours

★ Authentic Slovakia
CULTURAL

(☑0908 308 234; www.authenticslovakia.com; 2/4hr tour per person from €25/39) Always with ribald humour and an eye for the dark side, Authentic Slovakia leads you into Bratislava's seamy history and wacky architecture (usually aboard a retro Škoda car). Want to see 'Bratislava's Beverly Hills', brutalist cityscapes or drink your way around Devín Castle? You're in safe hands.

Bratislava Food Tours
FOOD & DRINK

(☑0910 902 315; http://bratislavafoodtours.com; per person €45-80) Guided by the well-honed taste buds of local foodies, learn about dining etiquette and Slovak staple foods in between bites of sheep's cheese, dumplings, cookies and optional swigs of beer and liqueur. Book ahead, and definitely don't dine before the tour.

✦ Festivals & Events

Coronation Festival
CULTURAL

(www.coronation.sk; ☺ late Jun; ♠) A historically accurate recreation of a coronation ceremony, plus markets, wine and folk music, unfolds annually in the old town over the last weekend of June. A different Hungarian monarch is 'crowned' each year, and there are historical tours of Bratislava, a concert in St Martin's Cathedral (p999) and lots of costume-clad tomfoolery – dress up and get your own royal portrait.

Cultural Summer & Castle Festival
CULTURAL

(www.visitbratislava.com; ☺ Jul-Sep; ♠) Bratislava's widest-ranging festival features classical music, folk, alternative theatre, jazz, brass bands and more, at venues across town throughout the summer. Historical buildings, town squares and even fountains transform into pop-up venues for DJs, dance parties, yoga classes and every genre of live music. Open-air theatre at Bratislava Castle (p999) is a highlight.

Bratislava Music Festival
MUSIC

(www.bhsfestival.sk; ☺ Oct/Nov) One of Slovakia's most important music festivals, with classical-music performances by international orchestras held in Slovak Philharmonic venues in late October or early November. They're presided over by visiting conductors, and include some premieres of Slovak compositions.

🛏 Sleeping

Midrange self-catering accommodation, like **Apartments Bratislava** (☑0918 397 924; www.apartmentsbratislava.com; studios/apt from €60/69; 🛜), is a great way to stay central without paying hotel prices.

★ Hostel Blues
HOSTEL €

(☑0905 204 020; www.hostelblues.sk; Špitálska 2; dm/d from €15/54; @🛜) A cracking hostel where social areas feel lovably grungy while facilities, like kitchens and bathrooms, are nicely up to date. Table football, guitars and cheap beer encourage mingling in the lounge, with its velvety sofas and blues posters. Choose from single-sex or mixed dorms, or private rooms with en-suite bathrooms (a steal for the price).

Patio Hostel
HOSTEL €

(☑02-5292 5797; www.patiohostel.com; Špitálska 2; dm €8-20, d/tr €70/85, tw/tr without bathroom from €59/74; 🅿🛜) A zesty colour scheme and on-the-ball staff make this modern backpackers a compelling choice. Accommodation options include four-bed, single-sex dorms, mixed 10-bed dorms and private rooms with or without bathrooms. A welcome drink sets the tone while lockers, free laundry service, complimentary coffee and a bar tick all the backpacker boxes.

Hotel Arcus
GUESTHOUSE €€

(☑02-5557 2522; www.hotelarcus.sk; Moskovská 5; s/d/tr incl breakfast €54/99/127; 🅿🛜) Family-run Arcus goes above and beyond: it's exceptionally clean with helpful reception staff and top-class breakfasts. Tucked away on a residential street, its room sizes vary but all have high ceilings and plenty of space, and there's a garden out back to relax in. Rates drop by 15% at weekends.

Marrol's Boutique Hotel
LUXURY HOTEL €€€

(☑02-5778 4600; www.hotelmarrols.sk; Tobrucká 4; d/ste incl breakfast from €138/254; 🅿❄🛜🏊) Even travellers with aristocratic tastes will raise an approving eyebrow at the neobaroque furnishings, sophisticated restaurant and exemplary service at Marrol's. Rooms are plush, in soft shades of ivory and gold, with king-sized beds. The breakfast buffet – sorry, banquet – is out of this world, and there's a lobby bar with fireplace.

✗ Eating

Štúr CAFE €
(☎ 0919 399 338; www.sturcafe.sk; Štúrova 8; cakes from €3, sandwiches from €4; ☺ 8.30am-10pm Mon-Fri, 9am-10pm Sat, 9am-9pm Sun; ☎ ✗) Wonderful coffee, gateaus in flavours ranging from carrot-almond to caramel cheesecake, and sandwiches are served in this bookish *kaviareň* (cafe) with flashes of art-nouveau style. It's named for Ľudovít Štúr, who codified the Slovak literary language.

Bratislavský Meštiansky Pivovar SLOVAK €€
(☎ 0944 512 265; www.mestianskypivovar.sk; Drevená 8; mains €7-22; ☺ 11am-midnight Mon-Thu & Sat, to 1am Fri, 11am-10pm Sun; ☎) Continuing Bratislava's 600-year-old beer-making tradition, this brewery and restaurant offers home-brewed and German beers to accompany its menu of Central European stomach liners (sometimes infusing the beer into the dishes). Settle in at the vaulted hall and choose from beer and onion goulash, confit duck, beer-roasted chicken and moreish snacks from cheese plates to crackling pork.

Prašná Bašta SLOVAK €€
(☎ 02-5443 4957; www.prasnabasta.sk; Zámočnicka 11; mains €8-21; ☺ 11am-11pm; ✗) Stained-glass windows cast a soft light inside Prašná Bašta, a cosy, low-ceilinged den. Similarly warm and reassuring are full-flavoured courses like chicken with camembert and walnuts, herbed trout, and veal drowned in mushroom sauce. A winning mix of atmosphere, friendly service and fine food.

★ Modrá Hviezda SLOVAK €€€
(☎ 0948 703 070; www.modrahviezda.sk; Beblavého 14; mains €12-24; ☺ 11am-11pm) The 'Blue Star' specialises in regally executed Slovak dishes: venison in cognac, tender lamb shank, and mangalica pork (from woolly pigs) on a silky pumpkin purée. The brick-lined cellar space, festooned with farm tools and a-twinkle with candles, feels equal parts romantic and rustic. A must-eat; reservations recommended.

★ Sky Bar & Restaurant THAI, EUROPEAN €€€
(☎ 0948 109 400; www.skybar.sk; Hviezdoslavovo nám 7; mains €10-20; ☺ noon-midnight Sun-Thu, to 1am Fri & Sat; ✗) Fusion cuisine is prepared with a nod and a wink by experimental chefs at this 7th-floor restaurant. You may not be able to read your menu amid the sultry, violet lighting but no matter: everything's delicious, from salmon with Thai basil to venison with veggies. Our highlight? The 'Wild Hunter' cocktail: part beverage, part primeval diorama.

● Drinking & Nightlife

Slovak Pub PUB
(☎ 02-5292 6367; www.slovakpub.sk; Obchodná 62; ☺ 11am-11pm Mon-Thu, to midnight Fri, noon-11pm Sat & Sun; ☎) The name suggests a by-the-numbers tourist trap, but this rustic tavern-restaurant is a guilty pleasure among locals, too. Grab a draught beer, or perhaps a wooden paddle of *slivovica* (plum brandy), and you'll likely stay longer than planned. Before you develop beer goggles, you might learn something from the knightly regalia and portraits of Slovak heroes on show.

Stupavar BEER HALL
(☎ 0948 343 252; www.facebook.com/stupavar beerpub; Prepoštská 4; ☺ 3pm-midnight) A local favourite for craft beer, this vaulted drinking haunt has an excellent selection of ales and microbrews for its small size.

☆ Entertainment

Keep an eye on **Kam do Mesta** (www.kam domesta.sk/bratislava) for entertainment listings.

KC Dunaj LIVE PERFORMANCE
(www.kcdunaj.sk; Nedbalova 3; ☺ 4pm-late Mon-Sat, to midnight Sun; ☎) An alternative cultural centre par excellence, hosting drama, live music, comedy, club nights, visual arts and more. A kicking international crowd can be found here almost nightly, particularly at the terrace bar with its rooftop view of the old town. It's generally open until early in the morning but exact hours vary depending on the event.

Historic SND THEATRE
(☎ box office 02-2049 4290; www.snd.sk; Gorkého; booking office cnr Jesenského & Komenského; tickets €18-40; ☺ box office 8am-7pm Mon-Fri, 9am-noon & 2-7pm Sat & Sun, plus 1hr before performances) The neo-Renaissance venue of the Slovak National Theatre, which dazzles with its silvery roof and statue-studded facade, hosts opera, ballet and modern drama within its 18th-century walls.

🛍 Shopping

Úľuv
ARTS & CRAFTS

(www.uluv.sk; Obchodná 64; ⏱noon-6pm Tue-Fri, to 2pm Sat) Woodcarving, pottery, weaving and other traditional Slovak art forms unfold expertly at this crafts cooperative. It's as much a gallery as a place to browse souvenirs, and everything is made with love.

ℹ Information

Bratislava's old town has banks and ATMs, especially along Poštova. The train and bus stations, and airport, have ATMs/exchange booths.

There is an expanding set of free wi-fi zones in the old town and beyond, including Hlavné nám, Hviezdoslavovo nám and Nám SNP.

Main Post Office (📞02-5443 0381; Nám SNP 35; ⏱7am-8pm Mon-Fri, to 6pm Sat) In a beautiful building.

Police station (📞0961 031 705, emergency 158, emergency 112; Štúrova 15)

Tourist Information Centre (📞02-5441 9410; www.visitbratislava.com; Klobučnícka 2; ⏱9am-7pm Apr-Oct, to 6pm Nov-Mar)

University Hospital (Univerzitná Nemocnica Bratislava; 📞02-5729 0111; www.unb.sk/nemocnica-stare-mesto; Mickiewiczova 13; 🚇Americké nám) The closest hospital to the old town.

Poliklinika Ruzinov (📞02-4827 9111; www.ruzinovskapoliklinika.sk; Ružinovská 10) Hospital with emergency services and 24-hour pharmacy.

ℹ Getting There & Away

AIR

Vienna's much busier international airport is only 60km west and connected by direct buses to both Bratislava's centre and its airport.

Bratislava Airport (BTS; 📞02-3303 3353; www.bts.aero; Ivanská cesta) is a 12km drive northeast of central Bratislava.

BOAT

LOD (📞02-5293 2226; www.lod.sk; Fajnorovo nábr 2, Passenger Port; adult one way/return €24/39, child one way/return €12/19.50; ⏱mid-Apr–mid-Oct) Daily hydrofoil departures between Bratislava and Vienna in July and August (and a few per week from April to June, and September to October), taking 1¾ hours there and slightly less coming back. Vessels depart from the **hydrofoil terminal** (Fajnorovo nábr 2).

Twin City Liner (📞in Austria +43 1 904 88 80; www.twincityliner.com; Rázusovo nábr) Boats to Vienna leave daily from the **HUMA 6 terminal** (Rázusovo nábr) from late March through October. You can book through **Flora Tours** (📞02-5443 5803; www.floratour.sk; Kúpeľná 6; ⏱9am-5pm Mon-Fri).

BUS

To reach Bratislava, trains are usually comparably priced and more convenient than the bus.
Bratislava Bus Station (Mlynské nivy; 🚌210) is 1km east of the old town; locals call it 'Mlynské Nivy' (the street name). For schedules, see https://cp.hnonline.sk.

WORTH A TRIP

TREASURES OF BANSKÁ ŠTIAVNICA

Gold, silver and around 140 different minerals brought enormous wealth to Banská Štiavnica, in rugged central Slovakia. A considerable swathe of the town is inscribed on Unesco's World Heritage list. Much of its architectural magnificence is in and around **Nám sv Trojice**, the old town's 'Holy Trinity Square'. Marching around the **Old Castle** (Starozámocká 1; guided/self-guided tour adult €4/3, child €2/1.50; ⏱9am-5pm daily May-Sep, 8am-4pm Wed-Sun Oct-Dec, 8am-4pm Tue-Sun Jan-Apr) is a riveting history lesson; don't miss navigating the creaking stairs of the Flamboyant Gothic clock tower. Many visitors arrive purely to see pilgrimage site **Kalvária** (Calvary; www.kalvaria.org; end of Pod Kalvlánou; ⏱9am-4pm Apr-Dec, Sat & Sun only Jan-Mar; 🅿) **FREE**, the apex of baroque art in Slovakia, on a volcanic hill 2km northeast of the old town.

Divná Pani (📞045-679 0945; www.divnapani.sk; A Kmeťa 8; snacks from €2; ⏱7.15am-10pm Mon-Thu, to midnight Fri, 8.30am-midnight Sat, 9am-10pm Sun) is a showy venue for cocktails and cake. Overnight, **Boutique Apartments** (📞0902 276 207; www.trotuarcafe.sk; A Kmeťa 14; apt from €39; 🐾) are comfy with a dash of steampunk chic.

Buses travel between Banská Štiavnica and Bratislava (€9.50, 3½ hours, two daily).

Slovak Lines (☑ 02-5542 2734; www.slovak lines.sk; Mlynské Nivy, Bratislava bus station; ⊙ ticket sales 6.30am-6.30pm) runs services throughout the country and to Vienna (€5.50, one hour, half-hourly).

Eurolines (☑ Bratislava office 02-5556 2195; www.eurolines.sk; Mlynské Nívy, Bratislava bus station) is the contact for most international buses, including to Budapest (from €5.50, 2½ to 4½ hours, hourly), Prague (from €9.50, 4¼ hours, eight daily), Paris (from €60, 19 hours, three weekly) and more, some of which also operate under the Slovak Lines banner.

TRAIN

InterCity (IC) and EuroCity (EC) trains are quickest. To and from Bratislava's **main station** (Hlavná Stanica; www.slovakrail.sk; Franza Liszta nám), *rychlík* (R; 'fast' trains) take slightly longer, but run more frequently and cost less. *Osobný* (Ob) trains connect smaller towns. For schedules, see https://cp.hnonline.sk.

Domestic trains run to Poprad (€15 to €19.50, 3½ to 4½ hours, 12 daily, some changing in Žilina) and Košice (€19, 4¾ to six hours, 12 daily, more with changes).

International trains run to Vienna (€10.50, one hour, hourly), Prague (from €12, 4¼ hours, two direct daily) and Budapest (from €15, 2¾ hours, eight daily).

❶ Getting Around

TO/FROM THE AIRPORT

➡ City bus 61 links Bratislava Airport (p1004) with the main train station, a 20-minute ride.

➡ Standing taxis (over)charge to town, some demanding as much as an eye-watering €25; ask the price before you get in or halve the cost by using a ride-share app like Taxify.

➡ Regular buses (€7, one hour, 14 daily) connect Vienna International Airport with Bratislava Airport (also stopping at Most SNP); find timetables on www.flixbus.com.

CAR

Abrix (☑ 0905 405 405; www.abrix.sk; Pestovateľská 1; ⊙ 8am-6pm Mon-Fri) Good-value operator offering pickup at the airport or any Bratislava address.

Buchbinder (☑ 02-4363 7821; www.buchbinder. sk; Stará Vajnorská 25; ⊙ 8am-6pm Mon-Fri, to noon Sat) Has an office at the airport.

PUBLIC TRANSPORT

The old town is small, so you won't always need to make use of Bratislava's extensive tram, bus and trolleybus network, run by Dopravný Podnik Bratislava (www.dpb.sk). Check https://imhd. sk/ba for city-wide schedules.

Tickets cost €0.70/0.90/1.20 for 15/30/60 minutes. Buy at machines next to stops and

WORTH A TRIP

ENCHANTING CASTLE TOUR

Blushing sandstone towers and crenellated turrets make **Bojnice Castle** (☑ 046-543 0624; www.bojnicecastle. sk; Zámok a okolie 1, Bojnice; adult/child €9/3.50; ⊙ 9am-5pm May-Sep, to 3pm Oct & Apr, 10am-3pm Nov-Mar) the most visited in Slovakia. An early-20th-century reconstruction by the Pálffy family took inspiration from the castles of France's Loire Valley, lifting Bojnice to the neobaroque splendour that stands today.

Prievidza, 4km east of the castle, has buses to Bratislava (€10.50, 3¼ to 4¼ hours, three daily). Local buses connect Prievidza and Bojnice (€0.60, 10 minutes).

news stands, and always validate on board (or risk a legally enforceable €50 to €70 fine). Passes start at €6.90/8 for 24/72 hours.

Bus 93 Main train station to Hodžovo nám then Petržalka train station

Trolleybus 207 Hodžovo nám to Bratislava Castle

Trolleybus 210 Bratislava bus station to main train station

TAXI

Taxi companies usually charge in the realm of €0.55 per kilometre in town (or €1.20 outside the city centre) but standing taxis compulsively overcharge foreigners. An around-town trip should never cost above €10. Ride-share apps like Uber and Taxify also operate in Bratislava.

AA Euro Taxi (☑ 0903 807 022, in Slovakia 02-16 022; www.aataxieuro.sk; minimum fare €3.89) Local taxi company.

Free Taxi (☑ 02-5596 9696; www.freetaxi.sk; minimum fare €3.90) Competitive fares...but no, it's not free.

Around Bratislava

Devín Castle

Perched between Slovakia and Austria, rugged **Devín Castle** (☑ 02-6573 0105; www. muzeum.bratislava.sk; Muránská 10, Devín; adult/ child €5/2.50; ⊙ 10am-6pm Mon-Fri, to 7pm Sat & Sun May-Sep, to 5pm daily Mar & Oct, to 4pm daily Nov-Feb) makes a popular day trip from Bratislava. From the ramparts there are admirable views of rivers and goat-speckled hills beyond. Inside, the museum hosts an archaeological exhibition with Neolithic grave finds and Bronze Age sculptures. In summer, kid-friendly medieval games and souvenir stalls consume the grounds. From November to March you can enter the grounds but exhibitions close. Bus 29 links Devin with Bratislava's Nový Most (stop 6); get a 30-minute ticket (€0.90).

Danubiana Meulensteen Art Museum

The windswept location of the world-class **Danubiana Meulensteen Art Museum** (☑ 02-6252 8501; www.danubiana.sk; Via Danubia, Čunovo; adult/child €10/5; ☺ 10am-6pm Tue-Sun) is as invigorating as the works on display. Inside, the gallery's floor-to-ceiling windows overlook the water, providing an organic backdrop to mostly contemporary art. It's 15km south of Bratislava with year-round bus links (bus 90, €1.20) and boat links at weekends from May to October (adult/child €16/10, including gallery entry).

TATRA MOUNTAINS

It's hard to overstate the majesty of the Tatras, whose 300-plus peaks form the central Carpathian Mountains' loftiest section. Together with the Polish national park of the same name, Slovakia's Tatra National Park is a Unesco-protected biosphere reserve.

DON'T MISS

THE VILLAGE TIME FORGOT

The squat, colourful houses of **Vlkolínec** (www.vlkolinec.sk; adult/child €2/1; ☺ 9am-6pm Mon-Fri, to 7pm Sat & Sun) evoke medieval Europe with just a hint of Hobbiton. This tiny Unesco-listed mountain hamlet, dating to the 14th century, has 45 traditional log buildings, including an 18th-century timber bell tower, baroque Catholic chapel and cottages painted peach and powder blue. Two weekday-only buses make the 30-minute (€0.50) journey to Vlkolínec from Ružomberok train station, which is reached by train from Bratislava (€11.70 to €14, 2¾ to 3½ hours), Poprad (€4.50 to €6, one hour) and Košice (€8.70 to €11, 2¼ to 3¾ hours).

Poprad

☑ 052 / POP 51.500 / ELEV 672M

Gateway to the High Tatras, Poprad is an excellent base for hiking or skiing day trips. By car or train, there are plenty of places to hike around lakes and through gorges or play in powder at winter-sports resorts. Rail links to Starý Smokovec and Štrbské Pleso are a cinch, and Slovenský Raj National Park is only a 15km drive south.

Poprad has its own attractions too, like the **Spišská Sobota** district, where well-preserved Renaissance buildings radiate charm, and the **Tatra Gallery** (Tatranská galéria; ☑ 052-772 1968; www.tatragaleria.sk; cnr Hviezdoslavova & Halatova; adult/child €3/1; ☺ 9am-6pm Mon-Fri, from 2pm Sun), housed in a former steam-power plant.

★ **Adventoura** ADVENTURE SPORTS
(☑ 0903 641 549; www.adventoura.eu) Dog sledding, trekking and adventure holidays, ski packages...this energetic outfit can arrange the works. Cultural and wildlife-spotting excursions are also expertly undertaken (with a high success rate on bear-watching trips). Day rates for private trips around the Tatras begin at around €30 per person. Book a week ahead (or a month, during peak season).

Aqua City SWIMMING, SPA
(☑ 052-785 1111; www.aquacity.sk; Športová 1397; day pass adult/student €22/19, 3hr pass adult/student €19/16; ☺ 8am-9pm; ⊞) ⊘ With indoor and outdoor pools, saunas and slides, this heavily hyped water park is a welcome destination after skiing or hiking. Mayan-themed water slides (summer only) suit the kids, the 'Sapphire' zone has pools bathed in sultry light, and there's a swim-up bar that prepares a passable piña colada (€6). The park is also an eco-pioneer in Central Europe.

Hotel Cafe Razy PENSION €
(☑ 0911 571 568; www.hotelcaferazy.sk; Sv Egídia nám 58; s/d from €25/40; ⓟ ☞) Hotel Cafe Razy's main-square location gives it reason to preen. The 16 rooms, some split-level, have individual flair: splashes of colour, tile floors and wooden beams. There's also zany clockwork on the outside of the building, which cranks into action after hours. Fortunately the 'c-razy' branding reflects the design rather than the service.

★ **Penzión Sabato** B&B €€
(☑ 052-776 9580; www.sabato.sk; Sobotské nám 6; d incl breakfast €70-110; ⓟ ☞) Within this

peach-coloured mansion, dating to 1730, find eight romantic rooms with billowy drapes, wood-beamed ceilings and handsome Renaissance-era furniture. Each one is different (they're priced by size) and five have fireplaces.

★ **Vino & Tapas** INTERNATIONAL **€€€**
(📞0918 969 101; www.facebook.com/vinotapaspoprad; Sobotské nám 38; 4-/8-course tasting menu €25/45; ☺5-11pm Tue-Sat) Truffled eggs, delicate ravioli, flower-strewn desserts... Vino & Tapas offers an exceptional dining experience in an atmospheric, brick-walled restaurant. Opt for a set menu with amuse-bouche to savour the best stuff. Phone ahead as it's rightly popular.

ℹ️ Information

Čistiareň Boja (Dlhé Hony 1, Max Shopping Mall; laundry per 3/6kg €12/15; ☺9am-8pm Mon-Sat) Overnight laundry service in the Max mall southwest of town.

City Information Centre (📞052-16 186; www.visitpoprad.sk; Svätého Egídia nám 86; ☺8am-6pm Mon-Fri, 9am-1pm Sat, 2-5pm Sun Jul & Aug, 9am-5pm Mon-Fri, to noon Sat Sep-Jun)

ℹ️ Getting There & Around

AIR
Poprad-Tatry International Airport (📞052-776 3875; www.airport-poprad.sk; Na Letisko 100), 4km west of town, has regular links to London Luton and seasonal ones to Rīga. There is no public transport to the airport. Metered **taxis** (📞0905 300 700, 052-776 8768; www.radiotaxi-poprad.sk) cost less than €4.

BUS
Buses serve Bratislava (€18, 5¾ hours, two daily), Košice (€4, 1¾ hours to 2½ hours, eight daily) and more. Between mid-June and mid-October there are buses to/from Zakopane in Poland (€5.50, two hours, two to four daily in season).

CAR
Good car-hire rates are offered by well-established **Car Rental Poprad** (📞0903 639 179; http://carrental-poprad.com; ☺by arrangement). Book ahead to pick up at Poprad's airport or train station.

TRAIN
Poprad-Tatry train station (Wolkera) is served by direct trains from Bratislava (€15 to €19.50, 3½ to 4½ hours, 12 daily, some changing in Žilina) and Košice (€5, 1¼ to two hours, almost hourly). From Poprad, direct trains travel to Starý Smokovec (€1.50, 25 minutes, hourly), from where electric trains zoom to other Tatras resorts.

High Tatras
📄052

The High Tatras (Vysoké Tatry), the tallest range in the Carpathian Mountains, occupy a near-mythic place in Slovak hearts. Instantly recognisable, the crooked summit of Mount Kriváň (2495m) has become a national symbol in literature and popular culture, with some Slovaks swearing it's their national duty to climb it. Twenty-five peaks reach higher than 2500m and the tallest mountains – like Gerlachovský štít (2654m) – attract the most hikers, revealing Slovakia as a nation of adventurers.

In winter, snow transforms hiking trails into small, family-friendly ski areas.

🏃 Activities

Hiking routes are colour-coded and easy to follow; unmarked routes cannot be undertaken without a mountain guide.

Pick up one of the numerous detailed maps and hiking guides available at bookshops and information offices, like VKU's 1:25,000 *Vysoké Tatry*. Distances are officially given in hours rather than kilometres (and we think these estimates assume a high level of fitness).

Many hiking routes criss-cross, or form part of, the Tatranská Magistrála. This mighty trail spans 45km, though you may see it described as longer, depending on the start or end village. Best trekked between mid-June and mid-October, the challenging trail runs beneath High Tatras peaks more than 2500m high, to the edge of the Western (Západné) Tatras. The route has some demanding, technical assisted sections as well as more level rambles.

ℹ️ Getting Around

Narrow-gauge electric trains trundle from Štrbské Pleso to Novy and Starý Smokovec, and on to Tatranská Lomnica. Tickets are priced by kilometre (€0.50 less than 2km, €1 up to 6km, etc). Maps at train stops show distances. Buy a multijourney ticket if touring resorts (one-/three-/seven-day pass €4/8/14, kids half-price).

Smokovec Resort Towns
📄052

The High Tatras are comfortably accessed from this string of resort towns. From west to east along Rte 537, they are Novy Smokovec, Starý Smokovec and Horný Smokovec. The region's history of holidaymaking is long: Starý Smokovec has been a mountain

ℹ MOUNTAIN SAFETY

Never set out into the mountains without the phone number for Slovakia's **Mountain Rescue Service** (Horská záchranná služba; ☏ 052-787 7711, emergency 18 300; www.hzs.sk), and always log your planned route and expected return time with your hostel or a friend who can raise the alarm. Download the **Mountain Rescue Service app**, which gives weather alerts and allows you to send an emergency SMS with your GPS coordinates; pre-fill the app with your information before hiking.

getaway since the late 18th century, and it retains a nostalgic air.

🏃 Activities

Hrebienok, reachable by **funicular** (Pozemná lanovka; http://hrebienok.lanovky.sk; Starý Smokovec; return adult/child Jul & Aug €11/8, Sep-Jun €9/6; ⊙ 7.30am-7pm Jul & Aug, 8.30am-6pm Sep-Jun) from Starý Smokovec, overlooks breathtaking views of the Veľká Studená Valley and has a few good hiking options, including short kid-friendly rambles. East and west from here, the red **Tatranská Magistrála Trail** transects the southern slopes of the High Tatras for 65km start to finish.

Bilíkova Chata (☏ 0949 579 777; www.bilik ovachata.sk; Hrebienok 14; s/tw without bathroom €29/46, ste from €80; 🐾), a log-lined overnight lodge and restaurant, is a short walk from the funicular railway terminus. An easy and well-signposted northbound walking trail (green) continues from Bilíkova Chata to **Studený potok waterfalls** (Vodopády Studeného potoka), taking about 20 minutes; 30 additional minutes brings you up to Zamkovského chata, a hiking lodge and restaurant. If you want to finish in Tatranská Lomnica, it's a further 3km to **Skalnaté pleso**, from where you can take a chairlift down.

Heading west from Hrebienok, you can hike along the base of Slavkovsky štít to lakeside **Sliezsky dom** hotel (red, two hours), then down a small connector trail to the yellow-marked trail back to Starý Smokovec (four hours total). Mountain climbers scale to the top of **Slavkovský štít** (2452m) via the blue trail from Starý Smokovec (eight to nine hours return).

To ascend peaks without marked trails, including the eight- or nine-hour odyssey to summit **Gerlachovský štít** (2654m), it's

mandatory to hire a certified guide; contact the **Mountain Guide Society** (☏ 0905 428 170; www.tatraguide.sk; Starý Smokovec 38; ⊙ noon-6pm daily, closed weekends Oct-May).

ℹ Information

Tatras Information Office (Tatranská informačná kancelária; ☏ 052-442 3440; www.tatry.sk; Starý Smokovec 23; ⊙ 8am-5.45pm Jan-Mar, to 4pm Apr-Dec) The area's largest info office, with helpful English-speaking staff and vast quantities of brochures.

ℹ Getting There & Away

Direct trains link Starý Smokovec and Poprad-Tatry (p1007) (€1.50, 25 minutes, hourly); Poprad is on the main west–east rail line between Bratislava and Košice.

Tatranská Lomnica

☏ 052 / POP 1300 / ELEV 903M

Overlooked by fearsome Lomnický štít, the country's second-highest peak, Tatranská Lomnica is home to a spine-chillingly precipitous cable car and the region's loftiest skiing – including its steepest piste. Summer also heaves with activity, as hikers embark on view-laden trails from Skalnaté pleso, a 1751m-altitude glacier lake.

Lomnický Štít Ascent CABLE CAR
(www.vt.sk; adult/child return Tatranská to Skalnaté pleso €22/18, return Skalnaté pleso to Lomnický štít €27/23; ⊙ 8.30am-5.30pm Jul & Aug, to 3.30pm Sep-Jun) From Lomnica, a gondola pauses midstation at **Štart**; change cars for the winter-sports area, restaurant and lake at Skalnaté pleso. From there, a cable car rises another 855m to the giddy summit of Lomnický štít (2634m), a hair-raising eight-minute journey. Prices are as steep as the ascent, and timeslots sell out quickly on sunny days; try queuing as early as 7.30am.

Ski Resort Tatranská Lomnica SKIING
(www.gopass.sk; adult one-/six-day pass €39/200; ⊙ late Nov–mid-Apr; ⛷) Nearly 12km of pistes – a mix of blue and red, with a couple of challenging black runs – make up the wondrously scenic skiing terrain above Tatranská Lomnica. Pistes top out at 2190m and there's a respectable 1300m vertical drop across the resort. Views of Slovakia's second-tallest peak, Lomnický štít, are remarkable throughout.

Zamkovského Chata HUT €
(☏ 0905 554 471; www.zamka.sk; dm €20; ⊙ year-round) Perched at 1475m above sea level, this

log chalet has been a guesthouse since the 1940s and is open year-round. Still catering to hikers, this no-frills refuge offers 23 dorm beds (crowded in summer) and a restaurant serving sausage and mustard, soups and dumplings. Breakfast (€6) and half-board (€16) are hearty and very reasonably priced.

Grandhotel Praha
HOTEL €€

(☑ 044-290 1338; www.ghpraha.sk; Tatranská Lomnica 8; d/ste incl breakfast from €114/184; P ☀ ☎ ☒) Stepping into this art nouveau hotel (1905), the indignities of ski-lift queues and mud-spattered hikes melt away. The marble staircase and sparkling chandeliers set the tone. Its ample rooms are similarly lavish, with gilt-edged mirrors and burnished wallpaper, and breakfast is exceptional. The spa, complete with sauna and steam room, is fragrant with mountain herbs, oils and soothing salt lamps.

Slnečný Dom
SLOVAK €€

(☑ 0903 406 470; www.slnecnydom.sk; Tatranská Lomnica 287; mains €8-12; ⊙ 9am-9pm Jul-Aug & Dec-Mar, reduced hours rest of year) Gaze at walls covered with antique skis while awaiting roasted trout, melt-in-your-mouth pork on lentils, or perhaps hot *encian* (soft, rinded cheese) at the 'Sunny House'. There's draft beer and central Slovak wines to wash it down.

★ Humno Tatry
BAR, CLUB

(☑ 0911 115 603; www.humnotatry.sk; Tatranská Lomnica; ⊙ 11am-11pm Thu, noon-4am Fri & Sat, noon-11pm Sun, closed Mon-Wed) Tumble straight from the cable-car base station into this big, wood-beamed club, diner and cocktail bar. There's an outdoor deck to bask in late-afternoon sun over beers, or perhaps an apple-sage or frozen-cherry refresher. Inside, the sound of thudding hiking boots is as loud as the music. On theme nights – DJs, house, old-school pop – it's packed to the rafters.

ℹ Information

TIK Tatranská Lomnica (☑ 052-446 8119; www.tatry.sk; Tatranská Lomnica 98; ⊙ 8am-4pm)

ℹ Getting There & Away

The **train station** is off Tatranská Lomnica's main road.

Reaching Poprad-Tatry (p1007) by train requires a change in Starý Smokovec or Studený Potok (€1.50, 45 minutes) but there are direct buses (€1.30, 30 minutes, hourly). Luggage storage is available at the bus station between 8.30am and 6.30pm.

Štrbské Pleso

☑ 052 / POP 3390 (REGION)

The tarn at Štrbské Pleso is one of the High Tatras' loveliest scenes – and don't visitors know it. This glacial lake (1346m) receives huge numbers of visitors around the year, thanks to lofty hiking trails and the country's longest ski season. Rent a **row boat** (☑ 0911 707 982; per 40min for 3/4 passengers €18/23; ⊙ 10am-6pm May-Sep) at the dock behind Grand Hotel Kempinski

✦ Activities

The easiest walk is the level 2.3km trail around the lake. For a longer hike, follow the red-marked, rocky **Magistrála Trail** uphill from Hotel Patria for about 1½ hours to **Popradské pleso**, an even more idyllic lake at 1494m. You can return to the train line by following the paved road down to the Popradské pleso stop (45 minutes). The Magistrála zigzags up the mountainside from Popradské pleso and then traverses east towards **Sliezsky dom** and the Hrebienok funicular above Starý Smokovec (5½ to six hours).

The year-round **Solisko Express chairlift** (return adult/child €13/9, 8am to 3.30pm) rises to **Chata pod Soliskom** (1840m), from where it's a one-hour walk north along a red trail to the 2093m summit of **Predné Solisko**.

Higher trails close from November to mid-June; check what's open at the **tourist office** (☑ 0911 333 466; www.strbskepleso.sk; Poštová; ⊙ 8am-4pm).

🛏 Sleeping & Eating

Chata Pod Soliskom
HOSTEL €

(☑ 0917 655 446; www.chatasolisko.sk; top of Solisko Express lift; dm/d €20/80) This modern hostel with a nine-bed dorm (no bunks) and one private room is located at the top of the Solisko Express (1840m). Lodgings are ornamented in modern chalet style with sheepskin rugs, rope sculptures, black-and-white landscape photography and pinewood everywhere you look. Breakfast is €6.

Grand Hotel Kempinski
HOTEL €€€

(☑ 052-326 2222; www.kempinski.com/hightatras; Kupelna 6; d/ste incl breakfast from €179/289; P ☀ @ ☎ ☒) Everything you'd expect from a sumptuous hotel chain, with the bonus of dreamy lake views, the Kempinski is Štrbské Pleso's best address. Elements of traditional Slovak design, like carved wooden headboards, are elegantly placed throughout the rooms, whose large windows offers views of lake or valley. Every luxury is here, from a heated pool with chandeliers to the suave restaurant.

★ **Koliba Patria** SLOVAK €€
(☑052-784 8870; http://hotelpatria.sk; eastern lakeshore, Štrbské Pleso; mains €8-18; ☉11.30am-10.30pm) On a lakeshore perch, Koliba Patria's earthy decor brings nature indoors: lamps are fashioned from cowbells, and a tree appears to burst from its wooden beams and slate walls. The refined Slovak menu offers familiar dishes done exceptionally well: perfectly spiced deer goulash, zesty sauerkraut and zander fillet on a silky bed of buttery potatoes. There's an outdoor terrace, too.

ⓘ Getting There & Away

Štrbské Pleso is connected by electric railway to the Smokovec Resort Towns (€1.50, 45 minutes) and Tatranská Lomnica (€2, 1½ hours). Direct buses also travel to/from Poprad (€1.70, one hour, five daily).

EASTERN SLOVAKIA

Welcome to Slovakia's untrammelled east, home to Andy Warhol history, medieval wine cellars, mysterious churches and the best wine region you've never heard of.

Levoča

☑053 / POP 14,700

The medieval wealth of Levoča, a former royal town, is writ large across its Unesco-listed centre. **Majstra Pavla nám**, the historic main square, is an architectural treasure chest: it's lined by burgher mansions with gabled roofs, and has a dazzlingly restored town hall.

The spindles-and-spires **Church of St Jacob** (Chrám sv Jakuba; www.chramsvjakuba.sk; Majstra Pavla nám; adult/child €3/2; ☉by tour 8.30am-4pm Tue-Sat, from 11.30am Sun & Mon), built in the 14th and 15th centuries, elevates the spirits with its soaring arches and precious art. The main attraction is the Gothic altar (1517), created by medieval woodcarver extraordinaire Master Paul of Levoča.

Beaming over the town is the **Church of Mariánska Hora** (Bazilika Panny Márie; ☑053-451 2826; http://rkc.levoca.sk; ☉hours vary, services 2.30pm Sun summer; ℗), a Catholic pilgrimage site glowing beatifically from a hill 2km north.

Hotel U Leva HOTEL €€
(☑053-450 2311; www.uleva.sk; Majstra Pavla nám 25; s/d/ste incl breakfast from €43/58/89; ℗♠)

Awash in the main square's golden colour scheme, Levoča's best hotel is spread across two pyramid-roofed buildings. Rooms are painted in warming sunset shades, with rustic accents like wooden beams but modern conveniences like fridges and good TVs. There's a welcome drink on arrival, too.

★ **Kupecká Bašta** SLOVAK, ITALIAN €€
(☑0908 989 626; www.kupeckabasta.sk; Kukučínová 2; mains €6-15; ☉10am-10pm Mon-Thu, 11am-11pm Fri & Sat) Dine within the very walls of Levoča's old town at this outstanding Slovak restaurant. A medley of Slovak and Hungarian influences grace the menu, like chicken stroganoff and schnitzels, along with unexpected combinations: pork encrusted with almonds, or served with mozzarella and cognac sauce, and Italian dishes like prawn and lime tagliatelle. It's all good, and the service is attentive.

ⓘ Information

Everything you're likely to need, ATMs, post office and the **tourist office** (☑053-451 3763; http://eng.levoca.sk; Majstra Pavla nám 58; ☉9am-4pm daily May-Sep, Mon-Fri only Oct-Apr) included, is on the main square.

ⓘ Getting There & Away

The **bus station** (Železničný riadok 31) is 1km by foot south of the main square. Direct services reach Košice (€5, two hours, four daily), Poprad (€1.70, 45 minutes, every one to two hours), Spišská Nová Ves (for Slovenský Raj, €0.90 to €2, 15 minutes to one hours, half-hourly) and Spišské Podhradie (for Spiš Castle, €0.90 to €2, 30 minutes, one or two hourly).

Spišské Podhradie

☑053 / POP 4040

Slovakia's most spectacular castle has propelled the otherwise dozy village of Spišské Podhradie to tourism stardom.

A former stomping ground of medieval watchmen and Renaissance nobles, **Spiš Castle** (Spišský hrad; ☑053-454 1336; www.facebook.com/spisskyhradsk; adult/student/child €8/6/4; ☉9am-6pm May-Sep, to 4pm Apr & Oct, 10am-4pm Nov, closed Dec-Mar) looms over the village from a limestone hill. This vast, Unesco-listed fortification is one of Central Europe's biggest castle complexes. Its bulwarks and thick defensive walls date to the 12th century (at the latest), and once guarded Hungarian royals and nobles from flying arrows. Highlights of the 4-hectare site include views from the

22m-high tower, and a **museum** of medieval history within the former palace.

Home-away-from-home **Penzión Podzámok** (☑ 053-454 1755; www.penzionpodzamok.eu; Podzámková 28; s/d/tr from €25/30/45, without bathroom s/d €12/20; P ☏ ☀) has nicely maintained rooms awash in candy colours. The view of Spiš Castle from the yard is spectacular.

By the highway, 6km west of the castle, **Spišsky Salaš** (☑ 053-454 1202; http://spisskysalas.sk; Levočská cesta 11; mains from €4; ☺ 10am-9pm; P ♿) pulls big crowds, with its lamb goulash and *pirohy* (dumplings).

❶ Getting There & Away

BUS

Buses connect with Levoča (€0.90 to €1.20, 30 minutes, one to two per hour), Poprad (from €2.20, one hour, six daily) and Košice (€4.30, 1½ hours, two direct daily, more via Prešov or Levoča).

TRAIN

Spišské Podhradie is connected by bus to Spišské Vlachy (€0.90, 20 minutes, 10 daily), which has direct rail links west to Spišská Nová Ves (for Slovenský Raj; €1.20, 25 minutes, every two hours) and east to Košice (€2.50, one hour, every two hours).

Slovenský Raj & Around

☑ 053

You don't simply visit **Slovenský Raj National Park** (www.slovenskyraj.eu; Jul & Aug adult/child €1.50/0.50, Sep-Jun free). It's more accurate to say that you clamber, scramble and get thoroughly drenched in the 328-sq-km park's dynamic landscape of caves, canyons and waterfalls. Hikers in 'Slovak Paradise' climb ladders over gushing cascades, trek to ruined monasteries and shiver within an ice cave – and that's just on day one.

Among several trailhead villages, three are the best served by accommodation and food options. Most popular is Podlesok, slightly west of Hrabušice. On the east side of the park is low-key Čingov, a convenient starting point for hikes and rock climbing.

◉ Sights & Activities

Before hiking, pick up VKÚ's 1:25,000 *Slovenský Raj* hiking map (No 4) or 1:50,000 regional map (No 124). Hikes involving via ferrata ladders are open from mid-June through October. In July and August, trails can get busy to the point of queues.

One of the best-loved ascents is from Podlesok through **Suchá Belá Gorge** to Kláštorisko Chata, the site of a medieval monastery. Begin early and allow between two and four hours for this often-steep (and often-crowded) trail, along which you'll be sprayed by waterfalls as you cling to metal ladders.

Dobšinská Ice Cave   CAVE
(Dobšinská ľadová jaskyňa; ☑ 058-788 1470; www.ssj.sk; Dobšiná; adult/child €8/4; ☺ 9am-4pm Tue-Sun by hourly tour late May-Sep, closed Oct–mid-May) More than 110,000 cubic metres of ice are packed into the gleaming walls of this Unesco-listed ice cave, near the southern edge of Slovenský Raj National Park. The atmosphere is otherworldly: icy stalagmites, resembling polished marble, bulge from the ground and chambers sparkle with dangling tendrils of frost. In places, the cave ice is 25m thick. The departure point is a half-hour walk from the car park, so arrive in good time ahead of guided tours (on the hour).

Ferrata HZS Kyseľ   CLIMBING
(per person €5; ☺ mid-Jun–mid-Oct) This one-way via-ferrata route is an exciting, hands-on way to experience Slovenský Raj's geological drama. Gear isn't included but you can hire it from operators in Podlesok or Čingov (€5 to €10); if you aren't confident, hire a guide (€50) from the national park office (p1012).

🛏 Sleeping & Eating

Autocamping Podlesok   CAMPGROUND €
(☑ 053-429 9165; www.podlesok.sk; Podlesok; per adult/child/campsite/motorhome €4.70/3.20/3.50/4, chalets €50-150; P ☏ ☀) Pitch a tent, hide out in a no-frills chalet or book a modern en-suite cottage at this well-located campground, right near Hrabušice's national park office and restaurants. Dogs are welcome (€2).

It's always a good idea to reserve in advance and it's essential to call ahead between November and March.

Reštaurácia Rumanka   SLOVAK €
(☑ 0907 289 262; www.podlesok.com; Podlesok; mains €4-8; ☺ 11am-9pm May-Sep, to 7pm Fri-Sun only Oct-Apr) Enormously popular Rumanka serves enough varieties of *halušky* (dumplings) to satisfy ravenous hikers, as well as crispy fried *pirohy* (stuffed with mushrooms or meat), pork chops, and sheep's cheese in handy takeaway portions (from €0.95). Excellent selection of homemade desserts, too, from strudels and mascarpone cupcakes to panna cotta.

ℹ Information

Outside July and August, stop off in Spišská Nová Ves for maps and advice.

Mountain Rescue Service (☑ 052-787 7711, emergency 18 300; www.hzs.sk) For emergencies in the park. Check the website for weather conditions.

National Park Information Centre (www.npslovenskyraj.sk; Hlavná, Podlesok; ◷ 7.30am-3pm Mon-Fri, 9.30am-4.30pm Sat & Sun Jul & Aug, closed Sep-Jun) Summer-only national park hub.

Tourist Information Centre (☑ 053-442 8292; www.spisskanovaves.eu/tic; Letná 49, Spišská Nová Ves; ◷ 8am-6pm Mon-Fri, 9am-1pm Sat, 2-6pm Sun May-Sep, to 7pm weekdays Jul & Aug, 9am-5pm Mon-Fri Oct-Mar) Year-round information and luggage storage in town.

ℹ Getting There & Away

Consider hiring a car from Poprad or Košice, particularly during low season when connections to the park can be a chore. By public transport, you'll have to transfer at least once.

BUS

Buses (https://cp.hnonline.sk) are most frequent in July and August, and services thin out on weekends.

There are up to five daily direct buses from Poprad to Hrabušice (€1.30, 45 minutes) and Dedinky (€2.10, 1¼ hours). Alternatively, change buses in Spišský Štvrtok.

More frequent buses from Poprad reach Slovenský Raj's transport hub Spišská Nová Ves (€1.70, 45 minutes, at least hourly Monday to Friday and every one to two hours Saturday and Sunday). From Spišská Nová Ves, it's easiest to hike, cycle or arrange a transfer through your accommodation but there are infrequent daily buses to Hrabušice (for Podlesok; €1.10, 30 minutes) and Čingov (€0.60, 15 minutes).

TRAIN

Trains run from Spišská Nová Ves to Poprad (€1.55, 20 minutes, at least hourly) and Košice (€4, one to 1½ hours, every one to two hours).

Košice

☑ 055 / POP 239,000

Equal parts pretty and gritty, Košice captures attention with its old town, a jewellery box of Gothic towers, medieval bastions and baroque sculpture. Since Košice's tenure as European Capital of Culture in 2013, the cultural scene has continued to bloom: offbeat bars, Soviet city tours and vegetarian dining share the limelight with cultural draws like the showstopping Gothic cathedral.

⊙ Sights

★ **Cathedral of St Elizabeth** CHURCH
(Dóm sv Alžbety; ☑ 055-622 1555; www.dom.rimkat.sk; Hlavné nám; tower adult/child €1.50/1, crypt €1; ◷ 1-5pm Mon, from 9am Tue-Fri, 9am-1pm Sat) This 14th-century cathedral dominates Košice's main square, its gables bristling above tall, stained-glass windows while colourful roof tiles evoke a resplendent scaled dragon. One of Europe's easternmost Gothic cathedrals, 60m-long St Elizabeth is the largest in the country. Ascend 160 stone steps up the narrow stairwell of 59.7m-tall **Sigismund Tower** to peep out across the city.

Hlavné Nám SQUARE
Much of Košice's finery is assembled along Hlavné nám, a long plaza with flower gardens, fountains and cafes on either side. Stroll past the central **musical fountain** (Hlavné nám) to experience its hourly chimes (and, at night, the multicoloured light show). Across from the fountain is the **State Theatre** (Štátne divadlo Košice; ☑ 055-245 2269; www.sdke.sk; Hlavné nám 58; ◷ box office 9am-12.30pm & 1-5.30pm Mon-Fri, 9am-1pm Sat), a baroque beauty from 1899. Walking south you'll see the 1779 **Shire Hall** (Župný dom; Hlavné nám 27), crowned with a coat of arms and home to the **East Slovak Gallery** (☑ 055-681 7511; www.vsg.sk; Hlavná 27; adult/child €3/2; ◷ 10am-6pm Tue-Sun).

Hrnčiarska HISTORIC SITE
(Ulička Remesiel; Hrnčiarska) FREE Art studios and traditional workshops line quaint Hrnčiarska, including herbalists, blacksmiths, potters and purveyors of precious stones. Some of their crafts haven't changed in 200 years; others use timeworn techniques to create contemporary designs. A few businesses along this cobbled lane have traditional crafts demonstrations, while others house arty coffee shops.

Rodošto & Mikluš Prison HISTORIC BUILDING, MUSEUM
(www.vsmuzeum.sk; Hrnčiarska; bastion adult/child €3/2, prison adult/child €2/1; ◷ 9am-5pm Tue-Sat, to 1pm Sun) This complex's motley attractions form a whirlwind tour of Košice's history. In the **bastion**, whose walls date to the 15th century, Košice is revealed as a powerhouse of medieval weapons production: you'll see cannonballs, coats of arms and well-dressed horse mannequins. Adjoining is a replica of the house in which Hungarian national hero Franz II Rákoczi was exiled in the 18th century. At the **prison**, you'll learn executioner

etiquette from a video presentation before seeing grisly restraints in the cells.

🛏 Sleeping

★ **Penzión Slovakia**　　GUESTHOUSE €€
(✆055-728 9820; www.penzionslovakia.sk; Orliá 6; s/d/apt incl breakfast from €64/74/95; P ✳ 🛜) Incongruous as it sounds, the patriotic Slovak guesthouse above this Argentine steakhouse is one of Košice's most compelling places to overnight. Framing an inner courtyard, rooms feel effortless (bare brick walls, brightly coloured trimmings) but they're exceptionally well designed and each is named after a Slovak city. Hot breakfasts are cooked to order. Our only gripe? The expensive parking (€10).

Hotel Zlatý Dukat　　BOUTIQUE HOTEL €€
(✆055-727 9333; www.zlatydukat.sk; Hlavná 16; s/d/ste incl breakfast from €65/85/145; P ✳ 🛜) Rooms at Zlatý Dukat have a classic, almost antique, style: high ceilings, areas of exposed brick and wooden beams, but modern fittings like flat-screen TVs and security boxes. There is a superb Slovak restaurant and wine cellar in the hotel's 13th-century basement.

🍴 Eating

★ **Republika Východu**　　INTERNATIONAL, CAFE €€
(✆0908 704 116; www.republikavychodu.sk; Hlavná 31; mains €5-12; ⊗8am-midnight Mon-Fri, from 10am Sat & Sun; 🛜🍴👶) With its tongue-in-cheek declaration of independence from Western Slovakia, Republika Východu (Republic of the East) sets a spirited tone. The menu, too, doesn't play by any rules: breakfast on avocado toast or quinoa porridge, studded with raspberries, then hang around to lunch on steak or goat's cheese salad. Bonus: it's lined with bookshelves and there's a children's play area.

Pán Ryba　　SEAFOOD €€
(✆0905 321 441; www.facebook.com/panrybakosice; Mlynská 13; mains €9-16; ⊗9am-10pm Mon-Fri, from 11am Sat) A revelation amid Košice's often doughy food scene, 'Mr Fish' brings inspiration from across Asia and the Mediterranean to its creative preparations of seafood. Tuna is seared beautifully, paella is generously laden with squid and mussels, and the open kitchen allows your hungry eyes a view of the proceedings.

12 Apoštolov　　SLOVAK, EUROPEAN €€
(✆0948 876 671; www.facebook.com/12apostolov Kosice; Kováčska 51; mains €6-8; ⊗11am-11pm Mon-Wed, to midnight Thu-Sat) High-backed

OFF THE BEATEN TRACK

WINE COUNTRY

South of Košice is Slovakia's best-known wine region, Tokaj (with a similarly named Hungarian wine region across the border). Villages in Košice's environs, like Čerhov, Malá Tŕňa and Viničky, produce great quantities of Tokaj's eponymous dessert wine. **Tokaj Macik** (✆0905 125 507; www.tokajmacik.sk; Medzipivničná 174, Malá Tŕňa; tasting per person €10-30; ⊗by arrangement), an hour southeast of Košice by road, is one of the best places to sip this golden nectar. Browse wineries on http://tokajregion.sk or ask at Košice's City Information Centre (p1014).

SLOVAKIA KOŠICE

pews and religious portraits seem to urge prayerful contemplation, but the chefs at 12 Apoštolov have something more decadent in mind. This venerable tavern (1910) specialises in Slovak soul food: gravy-soaked pork steak with bread dumplings, burgers, paprika-laced stews and fish with creamy risotto. There's also eight varieties of craft beer – not quite enough for each apostle.

Med Malina　　POLISH, SLOVAK €€
(✆055-622 0397; www.medmalina.sk; Hlavná 81; mains €6-14; ⊗11am-11pm Mon-Sat, to 10pm Sun) Sour soup *żurek*, roast duck with red cabbage, and *bigos* (cabbage and mushroom stew, flavoured with sausage meat): a medley of Polish and Slovak specialities are served with cheer in a simple but homely setting. Locals scramble for the few tables here, so it's worth reserving on weekends.

🍷 Drinking & Nightlife

Enoteca Centro　　WINE BAR
(✆0905 217 329; www.facebook.com/enotecacentro; Kováčska 10; ⊗10am-11pm Mon-Sat, 4-10pm Sun) A royal haul of Slovak wine is found in this cavernous bar, where old frescoes heighten the storied atmosphere. There's a sheltered terrace area for mild evenings – Italian-style, to suit Centro's excellent line in *aperitivi*.

Jazz Club　　CLUB, BAR
(www.jazzclub-ke.sk; Kováčska 39; ⊗bar 11.30am-midnight Mon-Thu, to 2am Fri & Sat, club 9pm-3am Tue-Sat) Part cafe-bar, part nightclub, Jazz Club has something to suit most revellers. An appealing mix of medieval-style arches, steampunk brass and wood decor and bright lights, the venue draws a messy young crowd to student nights and dance parties,

while a more chilled-out set lounge on its bar and terrace, or settle in for full-service meals.

ⓘ Information

City Information Centre (☑ 055-625 8888; www.visitkosice.org; Hlavná 59; ⊗9am-6pm Mon-Fri, to 3pm Sat & Sun)

Municipal Information Centre (Informačné centrum MiC; ☑ 0911 567 423; www.mickosice. sk; Hlavná 32; ⊗ 9.30am-6.30pm Mon-Fri, 10am-3pm Sat & Sun)

Nemocnica Košice-Šaca (☑ 055-723 4111; www.nemocnicasaca.sk; Lúčna 57, Šaca) Private hospital outside central Košice.

Police Station (☑158; Pribinova 6)

Post Office (☑ 055-674 1493; www.posta.sk; Poštová 20; ⊗7am-7pm Mon-Fri, 8am-noon Sat)

ⓘ Getting There & Away

AIR

Košice International Airport (KSC; www. airportkosice.sk; Košice-Barca) is 7km south-west of the city centre by road; bus 23 plies the route hourly.

Czech Airlines (www.csa.cz) flies to Bratislava and Prague; Austrian Airlines (www.austrian.com) to Vienna; Wizz Air (http://wizzair.com) to London Luton; LOT (www.lot.com) to Warsaw; and Turkish Airlines (www.turkishairlines.com) to Istanbul.

BUS

Direct buses reach Levoča (€5, two hours, seven daily), Poprad (€4, 1¾ to 2½ hours, eight daily) and Bratislava (€19.50 to €21, seven to 7¾ hours, two daily). There is a much bigger choice of west-bound routes if you change buses in Prešov.

Eurobus (☑ 055-680 7306; www.eurobus.sk; Staničné nám 9; ⊗ ticket office 6am-6pm Mon-Fri) has services to Uzhhorod in Ukraine (€7, four hours, six daily). Getting to Poland is easier from Poprad.

CAR

Several international car-hire companies, including Avis and Europcar, are represented at the airport. **Buchbinder** (☑ 0911 582 200, 055-683 2397; www.buchbinder.sk; Košice International Airport; ⊗ 8am-4.30pm Mon-Fri, or by arrangement) often has the most reasonable rates.

TRAIN

Direct trains from Košice **train station** (☑ general information 024-485 8188; Staničné nám, near Mestský park; ℝ) run to Bratislava (€19 to €22, 4¾ to seven hours, at least every 1½ hours), Poprad in the High Tatras (€5, 1¼ to two hours, almost hourly) and Spišská Nová Ves for Slovenský Raj (€4, one hour, hourly). There are also trains over the border to Budapest (€15, four hours, one or two daily) via Miskolc.

ⓘ Getting Around

The old town is small and walkable. Transport tickets (30-/60-minute ticket €0.60/0.70, 24-hour ticket €3.20) cover buses and trams; buy them at news stands and machines, and validate as soon as you board.

SURVIVAL GUIDE

ⓘ Directory A–Z

INTERNET ACCESS

➜ Wi-fi is widely available across the country. Slovak telecommunications companies are also aiming to bring high-speed internet to lesser-populated areas in Slovakia.

➜ Most hotels and cafes have wi-fi; in rural areas most guesthouses have a connection though it may not extend beyond the reception or dining area.

LGBTIQ+ TRAVELLERS

The Queer Slovakia (http://queerslovakia.sk) site lists events in Bratislava, Košice and beyond.

MONEY

➜ Visa and MasterCard are accepted at most hotels and restaurants in well-touristed places like Bratislava, Košice and High Tatras resorts.

➜ Guesthouses and apartments outside major cities often accept payment in cash only.

➜ Slovaks don't tip consistently, but rounding up bills to the nearest euro is common practice.

OPENING HOURS

Operating hours in villages and remote areas may be considerably shorter from October to April.

Banks 8am to 5pm Monday to Friday

Bars 11am to midnight Monday to Thursday, 11am to 2am Friday and Saturday, noon to midnight Sunday

Grocery Stores 6.30am to 6pm Monday to Friday, 7am to noon Saturday

Post Offices 8am to 6pm Monday to Friday, 8am to noon Saturday

Restaurants 11am to 10pm

PUBLIC HOLIDAYS

New Year's/Day of the Slovak Republic's Establishment 1 January

Epiphany/Three Kings Day 6 January

Good Friday and Easter Monday March/April

Labour Day 1 May

Victory over Fascism Day 8 May

Cyril and Methodius Day 5 July

SNP (National Uprising) Day 29 August

Constitution Day 1 September

Our Lady of Sorrows Day 15 September

All Saints' Day 1 November
Fight for Freedom and Democracy Day 17 November
Christmas 24 to 26 December

TELEPHONE

→ Slovakia has very good network coverage and you only need to bring a passport to buy a local SIM card. Major providers include Orange, T-Mobile and O2.

→ Landline numbers can have either seven or eight digits. Mobile phone numbers (10 digits) are often used for businesses; they start with 09.

→ When dialling from abroad, you need to drop the zero from both city area codes and mobile phone numbers.

TOURIST INFORMATION

Association of Information Centres of Slovakia (www.aices.sk) Runs a wide network of city information centres.

Slovak Tourist Board (http://slovakia.travel/en) The country's over-arching tourist resource online.

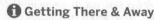 Getting There & Away

AIR

Vienna International Airport (VIE; ☎ 01-700 722 233; www.viennaairport.com; 🛜) in Austria, 60km away, has the nearest big international air hub.

There are other airports in Bratislava (p1004), Košice and Poprad (p1007).

The main airlines operating in Slovakia are:
Austrian Airlines (www.austrian.com) Connects Košice with Vienna.

Czech Airlines (www.csa.cz) Flies from Prague to Bratislava.

LOT (www.lot.com) Flies between Warsaw and Košice.

Ryanair (www.ryanair.com) Connects Bratislava with numerous destinations across the UK and Italy, coastal Spain, Dublin, Paris and Brussels.

Wizz Air (http://wizzair.com) Connects Košice to a few UK airports, Poprad to London Luton, and Bratislava to European cities including Kyiv, London Luton, Sofia and Warsaw.

LAND

→ Border posts between Slovakia and fellow EU Schengen member states – Czech Republic, Hungary, Poland and Austria – are almost nonexistent.

→ It's convenient to come in by road, but drivers must buy a vignette, a toll sticker granting access to Slovak highways, at the border (https://eznamka.sk).

→ Checks at the Ukrainian border are more strident, as you will be entering the EU (expect your vehicle to be searched). By bus or car, plan for one to two hours' wait.

→ Direct trains operate between Bratislava and Budapest (2¾ hours), Prague (from four hours) and Vienna (from one hour). From Košice, trains travel across the border with Hungary to Budapest (four hours) via Miskolc. Čierna nad Tisou has rail links to/from Ukraine.

→ Check www.slovakrail.sk for domestic train schedules and https://cp.hnonline.sk for domestic and international routes.

RIVER

Danube riverboats offer an alternative way to get between Bratislava and Vienna.

ⓘ Getting Around

AIR

Czech Airlines (www.csa.cz) offers the only domestic air service, between Bratislava and Košice (and you're probably better off catching the train).

BICYCLE

→ Roads can be narrow and potholed, and in towns cobblestones and tram tracks can prove dangerous for riders.

→ Bike rental isn't ubiquitous but it's common in mountain resorts and some national parks, and increasing in popularity in Bratislava and Košice.

→ Charges apply for bringing bikes aboard trains and cable cars (reservations may be necessary on long-distance trains).

BUS

Read timetables carefully; different schedules apply for weekends and holidays. Find up-to-date information at https://cp.hnonline.sk.

CAR & MOTORCYCLE

Highways are in great shape, distances are short and routes are scenic: Slovakia is a good country for a road trip.

LOCAL TRANSPORT

→ Bratislava and Košice have trams and trolleybuses, and High Tatras towns are linked by electric railway.

→ Public transport generally operates from 5am to 10.30pm (to 11pm in Bratislava). Reduced night-bus services run in Bratislava and Košice.

→ Buy tickets at ticket machines and news stands near the transport stop. Always validate your ticket in the machine on board or risk a fine.

TRAIN

The main Bratislava–Košice line slices west to east through the country, via Trenčín and Poprad. Search for up-to-date schedules and buy tickets through **Slovak Railways** (☎ 02-4485 8188; www.slovakrail.sk).

Slovenia

POP 2 MILLION

Includes ➡

Best Places to Eat

➡ Castle Restaurant (p1025)

➡ Monstera Bistro (p1022)

➡ Pri Mari (p1032)

➡ Štrud'l (p1027)

➡ Ek Bistro (p1021)

Best Places to Stay

➡ Jazz Hostel & Apartments (p1025)

➡ Adora Hotel (p1020)

➡ PachaMama (p1032)

➡ Youth Hostel Proteus Postojna (p1030)

➡ Vila Park (p1027)

Why Go?

It's a pint-sized place, with a surface area of just over 20,000 sq km, and two million people. But 'good things come in small packages', and never was that old chestnut more appropriate than in describing Slovenia. The country has everything – from beaches, snowcapped mountains, and hills awash in grape vines to Gothic churches, baroque palaces and art-nouveau buildings. Its incredible mixture of climates brings warm Mediterranean breezes up to the foothills of the Alps, where it can snow in summer. The capital, Ljubljana, is a culturally rich city that values sustainability over unfettered growth. This sensitivity towards the environment extends to rural and lesser-developed parts of the country.

When to Go

Ljubljana

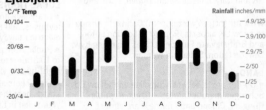

Apr–Jun Spring is a great time to be in the lowlands and the flower-carpeted valleys of the Julian Alps.

Sep This is the month made for everything – still warm enough to swim and tailor-made for hiking.

Dec–Mar Everyone dons their skis in this winter-sport-mad country.

Entering the Country

Entering Slovenia is usually a straightforward procedure. If you're arriving from an EU Schengen country, such as Austria, Italy or Hungary, you will not have to show a passport or go through customs, no matter which nationality you are. If you're coming from any non-Schengen country, ie outside of the EU but also including Croatia, full border procedures apply.

ITINERARIES

Three Days

Spend a couple of days in Ljubljana (p1018), then head north to unwind in romantic Bled (p1024) or Bohinj (p1026) beside idyllic mountain lakes. Alternatively, head south to visit the caves at Škocjan (p1030) or Postojna (p1029).

One Week

A full week will allow you to see the country's top highlights. After two days in the capital (p1018), head for Bled (p1024) and Bohinj (p1026). Depending on the season, take a bus or drive over the hair-raising Vršič Pass (p1028) into the valley of the vivid-blue Soča River and take part in some adventure sports in Bovec (p1028). Continue south to the caves at Škocjan (p1030) and Postojna (p1029), and then to the sparkling Venetian port of Piran (p1031) on the Adriatic.

Essential Food & Drink

Little Slovenia boasts an incredibly diverse cuisine, with as many as two dozen different regional styles of cooking. Here are some highlights:

Gibanica Layer cake stuffed with nuts, cheese and apple.

Jota Hearty bean-and-cabbage soup.

Postrv Trout, particularly from the Soča River, is a real treat.

Potica A nut roll eaten at teatime or as a dessert.

Prekmurska gibanica A rich concoction of pastry filled with poppy seeds, walnuts, apples and cheese, and topped with cream.

Pršut Air-dried, thinly sliced ham from the Karst region.

Štruklji Scrumptious dumplings made with curd cheese and served either savoury as a main course or sweet as a dessert.

Žganci The Slovenian stodge of choice – groats made from barley or corn but usually *ajda* (buckwheat).

Žlikrofi Ravioli-like parcels filled with cheese, bacon and chives.

AT A GLANCE

Area 20,273 sq km

Capital Ljubljana

Country Code ☑ 386

Currency euro (€)

Emergency Ambulance ☑ 112, Fire ☑ 112, Police ☑ 113

Language Slovene

Time Central European Time (GMT/UTC plus one hour)

Visas Not required for citizens of the EU, Australia, USA, Canada or New Zealand

Sleeping Price Ranges

The following price ranges refer to a double room with en suite toilet and bath or shower, and include tax and breakfast.

€ less than €50

€€ €50–100

€€€ more than €100

Eating Price Ranges

The following price ranges refer to a two-course, sit-down meal, including a drink, for one person. Many restaurants also offer an excellent-value set menu of two or even three courses at lunch.

€ less than €15

€€ €15–30

€€€ more than €30

SLOVENIA

0 — 50 km
0 — 25 miles

AUSTRIA

Graz

HUNGARY

Hodoš
Murska
Sobota
Beltinci Lendava

Klagenfurt

Krajnska
Gora

Jesenice

Ravne na   Dravograd Maribor
Koroškem

Slovenj   Slovenska   Ptuj Ormož
Gradec   Bistrica

Velenje   Zidani Most

Breg

Bovec   Mt Triglav   Bled   Celje   Rogaška
Kobarid   Ukanc   Lake   Kranj Kamnik Žalec   Slatina
              Bohinj Škofja   Rogaška   Rogatec
Cerkno   Loka   Domžale   Trbovlje   Slatina
Most   Hrastnik
na Soči   Ljubljana   Litija   Zagorje   Sevnica
Nova   Grosuplje ob Savi Krško   Brežice
Gorica   Idrija   ZAGREB
         Logatec   Vrhnika   Ivančna   Trebnje
Ajdovščina   Gorica
ITALY   Novo
         Postojna   Mesto
Divača   Cerknica   Ribnica
Škocjan Caves
Lipica   Kočevje   Metlika CROATIA
Trieste   Lokev   Pivka   Črnomelj
Piran   Ilirska   Karlovac
Izola Koper   Bistrica
                                                     Petrinja
Rijeka

Adriatic
Sea

CROATIA

BOSNIA &
HERCEGOVINA

Slovenia Highlights

❶ Ljubljana Castle
(p1019) Enjoying a 'flight'
on the funicular up to this
spectacular hilltop castle.

**❷ National & University
Library** (p1019) Considering
the genius of architect
Jože Plečnik at Ljubljana's
historic library.

❸ Lake Bled (p1024)
Gazing at the natural
perfection of this crystal-
clear green lake.

❹ Škocjan Caves (p1030)
Gawking in awe at the
100m-high walls of this
incredible cave system.

❺ Mt Triglav (p1027)
Climbing to the top of the
country's tallest mountain.

❻ Piran (p1031) Getting
lost wandering the narrow
Venetian alleyways of this
seaside town.

LJUBLJANA

☏ 01 / POP 279.750 / ELEV 297M

Slovenia's capital and largest city is one of
Europe's greenest and most liveable capitals.
Car traffic is restricted in the centre, leaving
the banks of the emerald-green Ljubljanica
River free for pedestrians and cyclists. Slovenia's master of early-modern, minimalist
design, Jože Plečnik, graced the capital with
beautiful bridges and buildings as well as

dozens of urban design elements, such as
pillars, pyramids and lamp posts. Some
50,000 students support an active clubbing
scene, and Ljubljana's museums and restaurants are among the best in the country.

◎ Sights

The easiest way to see Ljubljana is on foot.
The oldest part of town, with the most important historical buildings and sights (including

Ljubljana Castle) lies on the right (east) bank of the Ljubljanica River. Center, which has the lion's share of the city's museums and galleries, is on the left (west) side of the river.

★ Ljubljana Castle
CASTLE

(Ljubljanski Grad; ☑ 01-306 42 93; www.ljubljan skigrad.si; Grajska Planota 1; adult/child incl funicular & castle attractions €10/7, incl Time Machine tour €12/8.40, castle attractions only €7.50/5.20; ☉ castle 9am-11pm Jun-Sep, to 9pm Apr, May & Oct, 10am-8pm Jan-Mar & Nov, to 10pm Dec) Crowning a 375m-high hill east of the Old Town, this castle is an architectural mishmash, with most of it dating from the early 16th century when it was largely rebuilt after a devastating earthquake. It's free to ramble around the castle grounds, but you'll have to pay to enter the Watchtower and the Chapel of St George, and to see the worthwhile Slovenian History Exhibition, visit the Puppet Theatre and take the Time Machine tour.

National & University Library
ARCHITECTURE

(Narodna in Univerzitetna Knjižnica, NUK; ☑ 01-200 12 09; www.nuk.uni-lj.si; Turjaška ulica 1; ☉ 8am-8pm Mon-Fri, 9am-2pm Sat) **FREE** This library is architect Jože Plečnik's masterpiece, completed in 1941. To appreciate this great man's philosophy, enter through the main door (note the horse-head doorknobs) on Turjaška ulica – you'll find yourself in near darkness, entombed in black marble. As you ascend the steps, you'll emerge into a colonnade suffused with light – the light of knowledge, according to the architect's plans.

Triple Bridge
BRIDGE

(Tromostovje) Running south from **Prešernov trg** (Prešeren Sq) to the Old Town is the much celebrated Triple Bridge, originally called Špital (Hospital) Bridge. When it was built as a single span in 1842 it was nothing spectacular, but between 1929 and 1932 superstar architect Jože Plečnik added the two pedestrian side bridges, furnished all three with stone balustrades and lamps, and forced a name change. Stairways on each of the side bridges lead down to the poplar-lined terraces along the Ljubljanica River.

National Museum of Slovenia
MUSEUM

(Narodni Muzej Slovenije; ☑ 01-241 44 00; www. nms.si; Prešernova cesta 20; adult/student €6/4, with National Museum of Slovenia–Metelkova or Slovenian Museum of Natural History €8.50/6, lapidarium free; ☉ 10am-6pm, to 8pm Thu) Housed in a grand building from 1888 – the same building as the **Slovenian Museum of Natural**

History
(Prirodoslovni Muzej Slovenije; ☑ 01-241 09 40; www.pms-lj.si; adult/student €4/3, 1st Sun of month free; ☉ 10am-6pm Fri-Wed, to 8pm Thu) – highlights include the highly embossed *Vače situla* – a Celtic pail from the 6th century BCE that was unearthed in a town east of Ljubljana. There's also a Stone Age bone flute discovered near Cerkno in western Slovenia in 1995. You'll find examples of Roman jewellery found in 6th-century Slavic graves, as well as a glass-enclosed Roman lapidarium outside to the north.

City Museum of Ljubljana
MUSEUM

(Mestni Muzej Ljubljana; ☑ 01-241 25 00; www. mgml.si; Gosposka ulica 15; adult/child €6/4; ☉ 10am-6pm Tue, Wed & Fri-Sun, to 9pm Thu) The excellent city museum, established in 1935, focuses on Ljubljana's history, culture and politics via imaginative multimedia and interactive displays. The reconstructed street that once linked the eastern gates of the Roman colony of Emona (today's Ljubljana) to the Ljubljanica River and the collection of well-preserved classical artefacts in the basement treasury are worth a visit in themselves. So too are the models of buildings that the celebrated architect Jože Plečnik never got around to erecting.

🛏 Sleeping

★ Hostel Vrba
HOSTEL €

(☑ 064 133 555; www.hostelvrba.si; Gradaška ulica 10; dm €22-30, d €65-75; @ 🛜) Definitely one of our favourite budget digs in Ljubljana, this nine-room hostel on the Gradiščica Canal is just opposite the bars and restaurants of delightful Trnovo. There are three twin doubles, dorms with four to eight beds (including a popular all-female dorm), hardwood floors and an always warm welcome. Free bikes in summer.

Celica Hostel
HOSTEL €

(☑ 01-230 97 00; www.hostelcelica.com; Metelkova ulica 8; dm €18-26, s/d cell €58/62; @ 🛜) This stylishly revamped former prison (1882) in Metelkova (p1022) has 20 'cells', designed by different artists and architects, and complete with original bars. There are nine rooms and apartments with three to seven beds and a packed, popular 12-bed dorm. The ground floor is home to a cafe and restaurant (set lunch around €7). Bikes cost €3/6 for a half-/full day.

Hotel Galleria
BOUTIQUE HOTEL €€

(☑ 01-421 35 60; www.hotelgalleria.eu; Gornji trg 3; s €70-110, d €90-130; ❄ @ 🛜) This attractive

Ljubljana

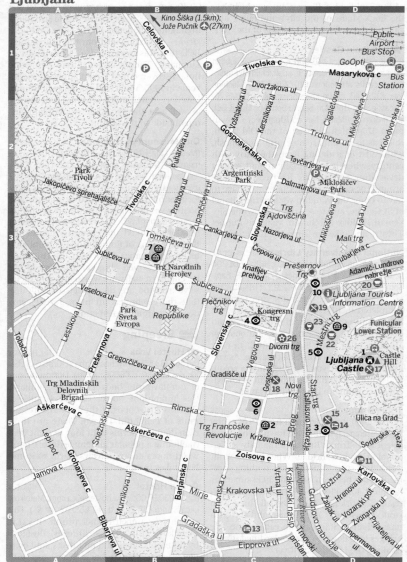

boutique hotel has been cobbled together from several Old Town town houses. There are 16 spacious rooms and a multitiered back garden. The decor is kitsch with a smirk and there are fabulous touches everywhere. Among our favourites are the enormous room 8, with views of the **Hercules**

Fountain (Levstikov trg), and room 13, with glimpses of Ljubljana Castle.

★ **Adora Hotel** HOTEL **€€€**
(📞082 057 240; www.adorahotel.si; Rožna ulica 7; s €115, d €125-155, apt €135-165; [P][✳][@][🛜]) This small hotel below Gornji trg is a wel-

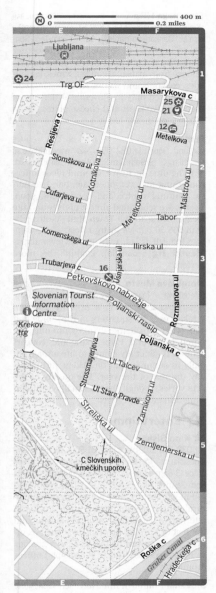

Ljubljana

🍴 Eating

★ Ek Bistro
INTERNATIONAL €

(☎041 937 534; www.facebook.com/eklubljana; Petkovškovo nabrežje 65; breakfasts €8-10; ⊗8am-8pm Mon-Thu, to 9pm Fri & Sat, to 3pm Sun; 📶🖋) Ljubljana's top spot for brunch, meaning in this case big slices of avocado toast on homemade bread, bowls of muesli and yoghurt, and eggs Benedict on fresh-baked English muffins. Wash it down with a glass of freshly squeezed something or a flat white. The fresh-cut flowers on the tables look great against the distressed brick walls.

Pop's Place
BURGERS €

(☎059 042 856; www.facebook.com/popsplace burgerbar; Cankarjevo nabrežje 3; burgers €8-10; ⊗noon-midnight; 📶) Centrally located craft-beer and burger bar that's evolved into a must-visit. The burgers, with locally sourced

come addition to accommodation in the Old Town. The 10 rooms are small but fully equipped, with lovely hardwood floors and tasteful furnishings. The breakfast room looks out onto a small garden, bikes are free for guests' use, and the staff are overwhelmingly friendly and helpful.

beef and brioche-style buns, are excellent, as are the beers and cocktails. The dining area feels festive, with an open kitchen behind the bar and communal tables out front for diners to rub elbows and compare burgers. Avoid traditional meal times: Pop's gets busy.

Druga Violina SLOVENIAN €
(☑ 082 052 506; www.facebook.com/drugaviolina; Stari trg 21; mains €6-10; ⊘ 8am-midnight; 🔊) Just opposite the Academy of Music, the 'Second Fiddle' is an extremely pleasant and affordable place for a meal in the Old Town. There are lots of Slovenian dishes, including *ajdova kaša z jurčki* (buckwheat groats with ceps) and *obara* (a thick stew of chicken and vegetables), on the menu. It's a social enterprise designed to help those with disabilities.

Gostilna na Gradu SLOVENIAN €€
(Inn at the Castle; ☑ 031 301 777; www.nagradu.si; Grajska planota 1; mains €12-18; ⊘ 10am-midnight Mon-Sat, noon-6pm Sun; 🔊) Right within the Ljubljana Castle (p1019) complex, Na Gradu is much too stylish to be just a *gostilna* (inn-like restaurant). The award-winning chefs use only Slovenian-sourced breads, cheeses and meats, and age-old recipes to prepare a meal to remember. If you really want to taste your way across the country, try the five-course gourmet tasting menu for €42.20.

★ Monstera Bistro SLOVENIAN €€€
(☑ 040 431 123; http://monsterabistro.si; Gosposka ulica 9; 3-course lunch €19, 7-course tasting menu €55; ⊘ 11.30am-5pm Mon-Wed, to 11pm Thu-Sat; 🔊🍽) 🍴 The concept bistro of star TV chef Bine Volčič delivers 'best-meal-of-the-trip' quality using locally sourced, seasonal ingredients and zero-waste food-prep concepts. Most diners opt for the three-course lunch (starter, main course, dessert), though the multicourse dinners are consistently good. The light-infused dining room, with white-brick walls and light woods, feels dressy without being overly formal. Book in advance.

🍷 Drinking & Nightlife

★ Magda CAFE
(☑ 01-620 26 10; https://barmagda.si; Pogačarjev trg 1; ⊘ 7am-1am Mon-Sat, from 10am Sun; 🔊) It's hard to put a finger on what makes Magda so special. Maybe it's the expertly prepared espresso (just €1 a cup purchased at the bar) or the unique 'tapas-style' breakfast menu, where you choose from local meats and cheeses, or the craft gins and local home-made brandies on offer. It's a great choice to start or end the day.

Slovenska Hiša COCKTAIL BAR
(Slovenian House; ☑ 083 899 811; www.slovenska hisa.si; Cankarjevo nabrežje 13; ⊘ 8am-1am Sun-Thu, to 3am Fri & Sat; 🔊) Our favourite boozer along the river is so cute it's almost twee. Choose from artisanal coffees, wines, lemonades, cocktails and spirits, featuring ingredients sourced only in Slovenia. Order one of the inventive meat and cheese plates (€4 to €7) to soak up the alcohol.

Pritličje CAFE
(Ground Floor; ☑ 082 058 742; www.pritlicje.si; Mestni trg 2; ⊘ 9am-1am Sun-Wed, to 3am Thu-Sat; 🔊) The ultra-inclusive 'Ground Floor' offers something for everyone: cafe, bar, live music, cultural centre and comic-book shop. Events are scheduled almost nightly and the location next to the **Town Hall** (Mestna Hiša; ☑ 01-306 30 00; Mestni trg 1; tours €5; ⊘ 8am-5pm Mon-Fri) FREE, with good views across **Mestni trg** (Town Sq), couldn't be more perfect.

Metelkova Mesto CLUB
(Metelkova Town; www.metelkovamesto.org; Masarykova cesta 24) This ex-army garrison – taken over by squatters in the 1990s and converted into a free-living commune – is home to several clubs, bars and concert venues. It generally comes to life after 11pm daily in summer, and on Friday and Saturday the rest of the year. The quality of the acts varies, though there's usually a little of something for everyone.

☆ Entertainment

★ Kino Šiška LIVE MUSIC
(☑ 030 310 110, box office 01-500 30 00; www.kinosiska.si; Trg Prekomorskih brigad 3; ⊘ box office 3-8pm Mon-Fri, pub 8am-midnight, events 8pm-2am; 🔊; 🚌 1, 3, 5, 8, 22, 25) This renovated old movie theatre now houses an urban cultural centre, hosting mainly indie, rock and alternative bands from around Slovenia and the rest of Europe. Buy tickets at the box office or at **Eventim** (☑ 090 55 77; www.eventim. si; Trg Osvobodilne Fronte 6; ⊘ 8am-4pm) offices around town.

Slovenia Philharmonic Hall CLASSICAL MUSIC
(Slovenska Filharmonija; ☑ 01-241 08 00; www.filharmonija.si; Kongresni trg 10; tickets €8-16; ⊘ box office 11am-1pm & 3-6pm Mon-Fri) Home to the Slovenian Philharmonic, founded in 1701, this small but atmospheric venue at the southeast corner of **Kongresni trg** (Congress Sq) also stages concerts and hosts performances of the Slovenian Chamber

Choir (Slovenski Komorni Zbor). Haydn, Beethoven and Brahms were honorary Philharmonic members, and Gustav Mahler was resident conductor for a season (1881–82).

Gala Hala LIVE MUSIC
(☑ 01-431 70 63; www.galahala.com; Metelkova Mesto, Masarykova cesta 24; tickets €3-10) Metelkova's biggest and best venue to catch live alternative, indie and rock music several nights a week. There's an open-air performance space from May to September.

ℹ Information

ATMs are everywhere, including several outside the Ljubljana TIC. Full-service banks are all around the centre; they're the best places to exchange cash.

Ljubljana Tourist Information Centre (TIC; ☑ 01-306 12 15; www.visitljubljana.com; Adamič-Lundrovo nabrežje 2; ⊙ 8am-9pm Jun-Sep, to 7pm Oct-May) Knowledgeable and enthusiastic staff dispense information, maps and useful literature, and help with accommodation. Offers a range of interesting city and regional tours, and maintains an excellent website.

Slovenian Tourist Information Centre (STIC; ☑ 01-306 45 76; www.slovenia.info; Krekov trg 10; ⊙ 8am-9pm daily Jun-Sep, 8am-7pm Mon-Fri, 9am-5pm Sat & Sun Oct-May; 🛜) Good source of information for travel to the rest of Slovenia, with internet and bicycle rental also available.

ℹ Getting There & Away

AIR

Jože Pučnik Airport (Aerodrom Ljubljana; ☑ 04-206 19 81; www.lju-airport.si; Zgornji Brnik 130a, Brnik), Slovenia's main international airport, is located 27km north of Ljubljana.

BUS

Buses to destinations both within Slovenia and abroad leave from the **bus station** (Avtobusna Postaja Ljubljana; ☑ 01-234 46 00; www.ap-ljubljana.si; Trg Osvobodilne Fronte 4; ⊙ 5am-10.30pm Mon-Fri, 5am-10pm Sat, 5.30am-10.30pm Sun) just next to the train station. The station website has an excellent timetable for checking departure times and prices. At the station, you'll find multilingual information phones and a touchscreen computer next to the ticket windows. You do not usually have to buy your ticket in advance; just pay as you board the bus.

Some sample one-way fares (return fares are usually double) from the capital: Bled (€7.80, 1½ hours, 57km, hourly), Bohinj (€9.80, two hours, 91km, hourly), Piran (€6, one hour, 53km, up to 24 daily).

TRAIN

Domestic and international trains arrive at and depart from central Ljubljana's **train station** (Železniška Postaja; ☑ 01-291 33 32; www.slo-zeleznice.si; Trg Osvobodilne Fronte 6; ⊙ 5am-10pm), where you'll find a separate information centre on the way to the platforms. The website has an excellent timetable with departure times and prices. Buy domestic tickets from windows No 1 to 8 and international ones from either window No 9 or the information centre.

Useful domestic destinations include Bled (€6.60, 55 minutes, 51km, up to 21 daily) and Koper (€9.60, 2½ hours, 153km, up to four services daily). Please note that these are one-way, 2nd-class domestic fares, travel times, distances and frequencies from Ljubljana. Return fares are double the price, and there's a surcharge of €1.80 on domestic InterCity (IC) and EuroCity (EC) train tickets.

ℹ Getting Around

TO/FROM THE AIRPORT

The cheapest way to Jože Pučnik Airport is by public bus (€4.10, 50 minutes, 27km) from **stop No 28** (€4.10 one way; ⊙ 5.20am-8.10pm) at the bus station. These run at 5.20am and hourly from 6.10am to 8.10pm Monday to Friday; at the weekend there's a bus at 6.10am and then one every two hours from 9.10am to 7.10pm. Buy tickets from the driver.

Two airport shuttle services that get consistently good reviews are **GoOpti** (☑ 01-320 45 30; www.goopti.com; Trg Osvobodilne Fronte 4; €9 one way) and **Markun Shuttle** (☑ reservations 041 792 865; www.prevozi-markun.com; €9 one way), which will transfer you from Brnik (where the airport is) to central Ljubljana in half an hour. Book by phone or online.

A taxi from the airport to Ljubljana will cost from €35 to €45.

BICYCLE

Ljubljana is a pleasure for cyclists, and there are bike lanes and special traffic lights everywhere. **Ljubljana Bike** (☑ 01-306 45 76; www.visitljubljana.si; Krekov trg 10; per 2hr/day €2/8; ⊙ 8am-7pm Mon-Fri, 9am-5pm Sat & Sun Apr, May & Oct, 8am-9pm Jun-Sep) rents two-wheelers in two-hour or full-day increments from April through October from the Slovenian Tourist Information Centre.

PUBLIC TRANSPORT

Ljubljana's city buses, many running on methane, operate every five to 15 minutes from 5am (6am on Sunday) to around 10.30pm. A flat fare of €1.20 (good for 90 minutes of unlimited travel, including transfers) is paid with a stored-value magnetic Urbana card, which can be purchased at newsstands, tourist offices and the public-transport authority's **Information Centre** (☑ 01-430 51 74; www.lpp.si/en; Slovenska cesta 56; ⊙ 6.30am-7pm Mon-Fri) for €2; credit can then be added (from €1 to €50).

THE JULIAN ALPS

This is the Slovenia of tourist posters: mountain peaks, postcard-perfect lakes and blue-green rivers. Prepare to be charmed by Lake Bled (with an island and a castle!) and surprised by Lake Bohinj (how does Bled score all that attention when down the road is Bohinj?). The lofty peak of Mt Triglav, at the centre of a national park of the same name, may dazzle you enough to prompt an ascent.

Lake Bled

☑ 04 / POP 5100 / ELEV 481M

Yes, it's every bit as lovely in real life. With its bluish-green lake, picture-postcard church on an islet, a medieval castle clinging to a rocky cliff and some of the highest peaks of the Julian Alps and the Karavanke as backdrops, Bled is Slovenia's most popular resort, drawing everyone from honeymooners lured by the over-the-top romantic setting to backpackers, who come for the hiking, biking, water-sports and canyoning possibilities.

That said, Bled can be overpriced and swarming with tourists in July and August. But as is the case with many popular destinations around the world, people come in droves – and will continue to do so – because the place is so special.

⊙ Sights

★**Lake Bled**   LAKE

(Blejsko jezero) Bled's greatest attraction is its exquisite blue-green lake, measuring just 2km by 1.4km. The lake is lovely to behold from almost any vantage point, and makes a beautiful backdrop for the 6km walk along the shore. Mild thermal springs warm the water to a swimmable 22°C (72°F) from June through August. The lake is naturally the focus of the entire town: you can rent rowing boats, splash around on stand-up paddleboards (SUPs) or simply snap countless photos.

Bled Island   ISLAND

(Blejski Otok; www.blejskiotok.si; ⊙ 9am-7pm) Tiny, tear-shaped Bled Island beckons from the shore. There's the **Church of the Assumption** (Cerkev Marijinega Vnebovzetja; ☑ 04-

576 79 79; adult/child €6/1; ⊙ 9am-7pm May-Sep, to 6pm Apr & Oct, to 4pm Nov-Mar) and a small museum, the **Provost's House** (☑ 04-576 79 78; adult/child €6/1, incl with admission to Church of the Assumption; ⊙ 9am-7pm May-Sep, to 6pm Apr & Oct, to 4pm Nov-Mar), but the real thrill is the ride out by *pletna* (gondola). The *pletna* will set you down on the south side at the monumental **South Staircase** (Južno Stopnišče), built in 1655. The staircase comprises 99 steps – a local tradition is for the husband to carry his new bride up them.

Bled Castle   CASTLE

(Blejski Grad; ☑ 04-572 97 82; www.blejski-grad.si; Grajska cesta 25; adult/child €11/5; ⊙ 8am-9pm Jun-Aug, to 8pm Apr-May & Sep-Oct, to 6pm Nov-Mar) Perched atop a steep cliff more than 100m above the lake, Bled Castle is how most people imagine a medieval fortress to be, with towers, ramparts, moats and a terrace offering magnificent views. The castle houses a **museum collection** that traces the lake's history from earliest times to the development of Bled as a resort in the 19th century.

🏃 Activities

Several local outfits organise outdoor activities in and around Bled, including trekking, mountaineering, rock climbing, ski touring, cross-country skiing, mountain biking, rafting, kayaking, canyoning, horse riding, paragliding and ballooning.

★**3glav Adventures**   ADVENTURE SPORTS

(☑ 041 683 184; www.3glav.com; Ljubljanska cesta 1; ⊙ 9am-noon & 4-7pm mid-Apr–Oct) Bled's number-one adventure-sport specialist. Its most popular trip is the Emerald River Adventure (from €80), an 11-hour hiking and swimming foray into Triglav National Park and along the Soča River that covers a sightseeing loop of the region (from Bled over the Vršič Pass and down the Soča Valley, with optional rafting trip). Book by phone or via the website.

Gondola Ride   BOATING

(Pletna; ☑ 041 427 155; www.bled.si; per person return €14; ⊙ 8am-9pm Mon-Sat, to 6pm Sun Jul & Aug, 8am-7pm Mon-Sat, 11am-5pm Sun Apr-Jun, Sep & Oct, 8am-6pm Mon-Sat, to 1pm Sun Nov-Mar) Riding a piloted gondola (known as a *pletna*) out to Bled Island is the archetypal tourist experience. There is a convenient jetty just below the TIC and another in Mlino on the south shore. You get about half an hour to explore the island. In all, the trip to the island and back takes about 1¼ hours.

SLOVENIA LAKE BLED

🛏 Sleeping & Eating

Bled has a wide range of accommodation, but book well in advance if you're travelling in July or August.

⭐ Jazz Hostel
& Apartments   HOSTEL, GUESTHOUSE €

(📱 040 634 555; www.jazzbled.com; Prešernova cesta 68; dm €35, d €80, without bathroom €60, apt d/q €90/100; 🅿 @ 🛜) If you don't mind being a little way (a short walk) from the action, this is a first-class budget choice. Guests rave about Jazz, mainly thanks to Jani, the superbly friendly owner who runs a sparkling, well-kitted-out complex. There are dorms (bunk-free, and with under-bed storage) and colourful en-suite rooms, plus family-sized apartments with a full kitchen. Book well in advance.

Camping Bled   CAMPGROUND €

(📱 04-575 20 00; www.sava-camping.com; Kidričeva cesta 10c; campsites from €23, glamping huts from €90; 🅿 @ 🛜) Bled's hugely popular, amenity-laden campground is in a rural valley at the western end of the lake, about 4km from the bus station. There's a rich array of family-friendly activities available, and a restaurant and a store on-site.

Old Parish House   GUESTHOUSE €€

(Stari Farovž; 📱 045 767 979; www.blejskiotok.si; Riklijeva cesta 22; s/d from €80/120; 🅿 🛜) In a privileged position, the Old Parish House belonging to the Parish Church of St Martin has been transformed into a simple, welcoming guesthouse, with timber beams, hardwood floors and neutral, minimalist style. Pros include car parking, lake views and waking to church bells.

Garden Village Bled   RESORT €€€

(📱 083 899 220; www.gardenvillagebled.com; Cesta Gorenjskega odreda 16; pier tent €130, tree house €320, glamping tent €370; ⊙ Apr-Oct; 🅿 @ 🛜 🏊) Garden Village embraces and executes the eco-resort concept with aplomb, taking glamping to a whole new level and delivering lashings of wow factor. Accommodation ranges from small two-person tents (with shared bathroom) on piers over a trout-filled stream, to family-sized tree houses and large safari-style tents. Plus there are beautiful grounds, a natural swimming pool and an organic restaurant.

Slaščičarna Zima   CAFE €

(📱 04-574 16 16; www.smon.si; Grajska cesta 3; kremna rezina €3; ⊙ 7.30am-9pm) Bled's culinary speciality is the delicious *kremna rezi-*

na, also known as the *kremšnita:* a layer of vanilla custard topped with whipped cream and sandwiched between two layers of flaky pastry. While this patisserie may not be its place of birth, it remains the best place in which to try it – retro decor and all.

Gostilna Murka   SLOVENIAN €€

(📱 04-574 33 40; www.gostilna-murka.com; Riklijeva cesta 9; mains €10-20; ⊙ 10am-10pm Mon-Fri, noon-11pm Sat & Sun; 🛜) This traditional restaurant set within a large, leafy garden may at first appear a bit theme-park-ish – but this is one of the first places locals recommend and the food is authentic (lots of old-school national dishes). Offers good-value lunch specials for around €6 (but you'll have to ask the server).

Castle Restaurant   SLOVENIAN €€€

(📱 advance booking 04-620 34 44; www.jezersek.si/en/bled-castle-restaurant; Grajska cesta 61; mains €20-40, tasting menu from €50; ⊙ 10.30am-10pm; 🛜) It's hard to fault the superb location of the castle's restaurant, with a terrace and views straight from a postcard. What a relief that the food is as good as it is: smoked trout, roast pork, poached fish. Note advance booking by phone is compulsory for dinner and only the multicourse tasting menu is available.

ℹ Information

Infocenter Triglavska Roža Bled (📱 04-578 02 05; www.tnp.si; Ljubljanska cesta 27; ⊙ 8am-6pm mid-Apr–mid-Oct, to 4pm mid-Oct–mid-Apr; 🛜)

Tourist Information Centre (📱 04-574 11 22; www.bled.si; Cesta Svobode 10; ⊙ 8am-9pm Mon-Sat, 9am-5pm Sun Jul & Aug, reduced hours Sep-Jun; 🛜) Open year-round: outside high season until at least 6pm Monday to Friday, to 3pm Sunday.

ℹ Getting There & Away

BUS

Bled is well connected by bus; the **bus station** (Cesta Svobode 4) is a hub of activity at the lake's northeast. **Alpetour** (📱 04-201 32 10; www.alpetour.si) runs most of the bus connections in the Julian Alps region, so check its website for schedules.

Popular services run to Lake Bohinj (€3.60, 37 minutes, 29km, up to 12 daily) and Ljubljana (€7.80, 70 to 80 minutes, 57km, up to 15 daily).

TRAIN

Bled has two train stations, though neither one is close to the town centre:

Lesce-Bled station Four kilometres east of Bled township on the road to Radovljica. It's on the rail line linking Ljubljana with Jesenice and Austria. Trains to/from Ljubljana (€5.20 to €7, 40 minutes to one hour, 51km, up to 20 daily) travel via Škofja Loka, Kranj and Radovljica. Buses connect the station with Bled.

Bled Jezero station On Kolodvorska cesta northwest of the lake. Trains to Bohinjska Bistrica (€1.85, 20 minutes, 18km, seven daily), from where you can catch a bus to Lake Bohinj, use this smaller station. You can travel on this line further south to Most na Soči and Nova Gorica.

Lake Bohinj

🖉 04 / POP 5100 / ELEV 542M

Many visitors to Slovenia say they've never seen a more beautiful lake than Bled...that is, until they've seen the blue-green waters of Lake Bohinj, 26km to the southwest. Admittedly, Bohinj lacks Bled's glamour, but it's less crowded and in many ways more authentic. It's an ideal summer-holiday destination. People come primarily to chill out or to swim in the crystal-clear water, with leisurely cycling and walking trails to occupy them as well as outdoor pursuits like kayaking, hiking and horse riding.

👁 Sights

⭐ **Church of St John the Baptist** CHURCH (Cerkev Sv Janeza Krstnika; 🖉 04-574 60 10; Ribčev Laz 56; church & bell tower €4, church only €2.50; ⊙ 10am-4pm Jun-Aug, group bookings only May & Sep) This postcard-worthy church and bell tower, at the head of the lake and beside the stone bridge, dates back at least 700 years and is what every medieval church should be: small, surrounded by natural beauty and full of exquisite frescoes. The nave is Romanesque, but the Gothic presbytery dates from about 1440. Many walls and ceilings are covered with 15th- and 16th-century frescoes.

Savica Waterfall WATERFALL (Slap Savica; 🖉 04-574 60 10; www.bohinj.si; Ukanc; adult/child €3/1.50; ⊙ 8am-8pm Jul & Aug, 9am-7pm Apr-Jun, to 5pm Sep-Nov) The magnificent Savica Waterfall, which cuts deep into a gorge 78m below, is 4km from Ukanc and can be reached by a walking path from there in 1½ hours. By car, you can continue past Ukanc via a sealed road to a car park beside the Savica restaurant, from where it's a 25-minute walk up more than 500 steps and over rapids and streams to the falls. Wear decent shoes for the slippery path.

Vogel MOUNTAIN (🖉 04-572 97 12; www.vogel.si; cable car return adult/child €20/10; ⊙ cable car 8am-7pm) The glorious setting and spectacular panoramas make it worth a trip up Vogel – during winter, when it's a popular **ski resort** (day pass adult/child €32/16; ⊙ mid-Dec–Mar), but also in its 'green season', when walks and photo ops abound. The cable car runs every 30 minutes or so from its base near Ukanc – the base station is at 569m, the top station at 1535m.

🏃 Activities

Lake Bohinj is filled with activities of all sorts, from active pursuits like canyoning and paragliding from Vogel to more-sedate pastimes like hiking, cycling and horse riding. The TIC in Ribčev Laz maintains a list of tour operators and equipment-rental outfits, and can help arrange trips and tours.

Alpinsport ADVENTURE SPORTS (🖉 04-572 34 86; www.alpinsport.si; Ribčev Laz 53; ⊙ 10am-6pm) Rents equipment: canoes, kayaks, SUPs and bikes in summer; skis and snowboards in winter. It also operates guided rafting and canyoning trips. Its base is opposite Hotel Jezero in Ribčev Laz.

PAC Sports ADVENTURE SPORTS (Perfect Adventure Choice; 🖉 04-572 34 61; www. pac.si; Hostel Pod Voglom, Ribčev Laz 60; ⊙ 8am-10pm Jun-Sep, to 8pm Oct-May) Popular sports and adventure company, based in Hostel Pod Voglom, 2km west of Ribčev Laz; also has a summertime lakeside kiosk at Camp Zlatorog. Rents bikes, canoes, SUPs and kayaks, and operates guided canyoning, rafting and caving trips. In winter, it rents sleds and offers ice climbing and snowshoeing.

🛏 Sleeping & Eating

Camp Zlatorog CAMPGROUND € (🖉 059 923 648; www.camp-bohinj.si; Ukanc 5; per person €11-15.50; ⊙ May-Sep; 🅿 🛜) This tree-filled campground can accommodate up to 750 guests and sits photogenically on the lake's southwestern corner, 5km from Ribčev Laz. Prices vary according to site location, with the most expensive (and desirable) sites right on the lake. Facilities are very good – including a restaurant, a laundry and water-sport rentals – and the tourist boat docks here. Tents can be hired.

Pension Stare PENSION €€ (🖉 040 558 669; www.bohinj-hotel.com; Ukanc 128; s/d €60/90; 🅿 🛜) This sweet 10-room

TRIGLAV NATIONAL PARK

Triglav National Park (Triglavski Narodni Park; commonly abbreviated as TNP), with an area of 840 sq km (over 4% of Slovenian territory), is one of the largest national reserves in Europe. It is a pristine, visually spectacular world of rocky mountains – the centrepiece of which is **Mt Triglav** (2864m), the country's highest peak – as well as river gorges, ravines, lakes, canyons, caves, rivers, waterfalls, forests and Alpine meadows.

The park has information centres in Bled (p1025), Stara Fužina in Bohinj, and **Trenta** (Dom Trenta; 05-388 93 30; www.tnp.si; Trenta; 9am-7pm Jul-Aug, 10am-6pm May, Jun, Sep & Oct, 10am-2pm Mon-Fri Jan-Apr, closed Nov-Dec) on the Vršič Pass. These centres have displays on park flora and fauna, and are well worth a stop.

Good online starting points for learning about the park are www.tnp.si and www.hiking-trail.net. Several hiking maps are available from TICs. Two decent options: the laminated 1:50,000-scale *Triglavski Narodni Park* (€9.10; buy online from shop.pzs.si) from the Alpine Association of Slovenia (PZS), and Kartografija's widely available 1:50,000-scale *Triglavski Narodni Park* (€8; www.kartografija.si).

pension is on the Savica River in Ukanc, surrounded by a large, peaceful garden. If you really want to get away from it all without having to climb mountains, this is your place. Rooms are no-frills; there's a half-board option too.

★ **Vila Park** BOUTIQUE HOTEL €€€
(04-572 3300; www.vila-park.si; Ukanc 129; d €100-120; P) Vila Park creates a great first impression, with sunloungers set in expansive riverside grounds, and balconies overflowing with flowers. The interior is equally impressive, with eight elegant rooms plus a handsome lounge and dining area. Note: it's a kid-free zone.

★ **Štrud'l** SLOVENIAN €
(041 541 877; www.facebook.com/gostilnica.trgovinica.strudl; Triglavska cesta 23, Bohinjska Bistrica; mains €6-12; 8am-10pm) This modern take on traditional farmhouse cooking is a must for foodies keen to sample local specialities. Overlook the incongruous location in the centre of Bohinjska Bistrica, and enjoy dishes like *ričet s klobaso* (barley porridge with sausage and beans).

Gostilna Pri Hrvatu SLOVENIAN €€
(031 234 300; Srednja Vas 76; mains €10-18; 10am-11pm Wed-Mon) Get an eyeful of mountain views from the sweet creek-side terrace of this relaxed inn in Srednja Vas. Flavourful homemade dishes include buckwheat dumplings, polenta with porcini, local chamois in piquant sauce, and grilled trout.

ⓘ Information

There are two main TICs in the Bohinj area: the office in **Ribčev Laz** (TIC; 04-574 60 10; www.

bohinj-info.com; Ribčev Laz 48; 8am-8pm Mon-Sat, to 6pm Sun Jul & Aug, 9am-5pm Mon-Sat, to 3pm Sun Nov & Dec, 8am-7pm Mon-Sat, 9am-3pm Sun Jan, Feb, May, Jun, Sep & Oct;) is closer to the lake and handier for most visitors than the office in **Bohinjska Bistrica** (LD TURIZEM; 04-574 76 00; www.ld-turizem.si; Mencingerjeva ulica 10; 8am-7pm Mon-Sat, to 1pm Sun Jul & Aug, 9am-noon & 2-6pm Mon-Fri, 9am-1pm Sat, to noon Sun Sep-Jun;). The **national park centre** (04-578 02 45; www.tnp.si; Stara Fužina 38; 8am-6pm Jul & Aug, 9am-5pm Apr-Jun, Sep & Oct) in Stara Fužina is worth a stop.

ⓘ Getting There & Away

BUS

The easiest way to get to Lake Bohinj is by **bus** (Ribčev Laz) – services run frequently from Ljubljana, via Bled and Bohinjska Bistrica. **Alpetour** (information 04-201 32 10; www.alpetour.si) is the major bus operator for the region.

Services from Lake Bohinj (departing from Ribčev Laz, near the TIC) run to Bled (€3.60, 40 minutes, 29km, up to 12 daily), Bohinjska Bistrica (€1.80, eight minutes, 7km, up to 20 daily) and Ljubljana (€9.80, two hours, 86km, up to nine daily)

TRAIN

Several trains daily make the run to Bohinjska Bistrica from Ljubljana (€7.30, two hours, six daily), though this route requires a change in Jesenice. There are also trains between Bled's small Bled Jezero station and Bohinjska Bistrica (€1.85, 20 minutes, 18km, seven daily).

From Bohinjska Bistrica, passenger trains to Nova Gorica (€5.80, 1¼ hours, 61km, up to eight daily) make use of a century-old, 6.3km tunnel under the mountains that provides the only direct option for reaching the Soča Valley.

CROSSING THE VRŠIČ PASS

A couple of kilometres from Kranjska Gora is one of the road-engineering marvels of the 20th century: a breakneck, Alpine road that connects Kranjska Gora with Bovec, 50km to the southwest. The trip involves no fewer than 50 pulse-quickening hairpin turns and dramatic vistas as you cross the **Vršič Pass** (Prelaz Vršič) at 1611m.

The road was commissioned during WWI by Germany and Austria-Hungary in their epic struggle with Italy. Much of the hard labour was done by Russian prisoners of war, and for that reason, the road from Kranjska Gora to the top of the pass is now called the Ruska cesta (Russian Road).

The road over the pass is usually open from May to October and is easiest to navigate by car, motorbike or bus (in summer, buses between Kranjska Gora and Bovec use this road). It is also possible – and increasingly popular – to cycle it.

SOČA VALLEY

The Soča Valley region (Posočje) stretches west of Triglav National Park and includes the outdoor activity centre of Bovec. Threading through it is the magically aquamarine Soča River. Most people come here for the rafting, hiking and skiing, though there are plenty of historical sights and locations, particularly relating to WWI, when millions of troops fought on the mountainous battlefront here.

Bovec

📍 05 / POP 3150 / ELEV 456M

Soča Valley's de facto capital, Bovec offers plenty for adventure-sports enthusiasts. With the Julian Alps above, the Soča River below and Triglav National Park (p1027) all around, you could spend a week here rafting, hiking, kayaking, mountain biking and, in winter, skiing, without ever doing the same thing twice. It's beautiful country and Bovec's a pleasant town in which to base yourself for these activities.

👁 Sights

⭐ **Boka Waterfall**   WATERFALL
(Slap Boka) With a sheer vertical drop of 106m (and a second drop of 30m), Boka is the highest waterfall in Slovenia – and it's especially stunning in the spring, when snowmelt gives it extra oomph. It's 5.5km southwest of Bovec – you can drive or cycle to the area and park by the bridge, then walk about 15 minutes to the viewpoint.

Kanin Cable Car   CABLE CAR
(📞 05-917 93 01; www.kanin.si; adult €10-34, child €8-28; ⏱ hours vary) This cable car whisks you up to the Bovec Kanin Ski Centre in a number of stages. It's most often used as an access for winter skiing or summer ac-

tivities, but it's equally rewarding for sightseers – the views from the top station and en route are sweepingly beautiful. In summer in particular, the last departure heading up the mountain can be as early as 2pm, so it's usually best to visit in the morning.

🏃 Activities

There are dozens of adrenaline-raising companies in Bovec; some specialise in one activity (often rafting), while others offer multiday packages so you can try various activities (rafting, canyoning, kayaking, paragliding, climbing, caving, ziplining).

Nature's Ways   ADVENTURE SPORTS
(📞 031 200 651; www.econaturesways.com; Čezsoča) Right by the river around 2km from Bovec, this company runs all the usual Bovec activities, including canyoning, rafting, kayaking, ziplining, caving and mountain biking. Reducing plastic pollution is part of its mantra.

Soca Rider   ADVENTURE SPORTS
(📞 041 596 104; www.socarider.com; Trg Golobarskih Žrtev 40) Does all of the usual trips, but distinguishes itself by making families and beginners a key part of its offering.

🛏 Sleeping & Eating

Bovec has some excellent accommodation, across a range of budgets. In addition to hotels and hostels, the TIC has dozens of private rooms and apartments (from €20 per person) on its lists. Don't discount the many scenic options along the road to Trenta towards the Vršič Pass, especially if you have a campervan.

Adrenaline Check Eco Place   CAMPGROUND €
(📞 041 383 662; www.adrenaline-check.com; Podklopca 4; campsite per person €15, s/d tent from €40/50, safari tent €120-150; ⏱ May-Sep; 🅿 🗑) About 3km southwest of town, this fun, fab-

ulous campground makes camping easy: hire a tent under a lean-to shelter that comes with mattresses and linen, or a big, furnished safari-style tent. Cars are left in a car park, and you walk through to a large, picturesque clearing (so it's not for campervans).

Hotel Sanje ob Soči
HOTEL €€

(☑ 05-389 60 00; www.sanjeobsoci.com; Mala Vas 105a; s/d €80/110; [P] [♠]) 'Dream on the Soča' is an architecturally striking hotel on the edge of town. Interiors are minimalist and colourful, and room sizes range from 'economy' on the ground floor to studios and family-sized apartments (named after the mountain you can see from the room's windows). There's friendly service, a sauna area, and a great breakfast spread (€12).

Dobra Vila
BOUTIQUE HOTEL €€€

(☑ 05-389 64 00; www.dobra-vila-bovec.si; Mala Vas 112; r €140-270; [P] [❄] [@] [♠]) This stunning 10-room boutique hotel is housed in an erstwhile telephone-exchange building dating from 1932. Peppered with art deco flourishes, interesting artefacts and objets d'art, it has its own library and a wine cellar, and a fabulous restaurant with a winter garden and an outdoor terrace.

Gostilna Sovdat
SLOVENIAN €€

(☑ 05-388 60 27; www.gostilna-sovdat.si; Trg Golobarskih Žrtev 24; mains €7-22; ☺10am-10pm) Sovdat isn't strong on aesthetics and its outdoor terrace isn't as pretty as others in town, but the crowd of locals attests to its popularity and value. Lots on the menu falls under €10, including plentiful pastas and bumper burgers. You can go upmarket, too, with the likes of gnocchi in a truffle sauce or roast beef with Gorgonzola.

Dobra Vila Restaurant
SLOVENIAN €€€

(☑ 05-389 64 00; www.dobra-vila-bovec.si; Mala Vas 112; 4-/6-course set menu €45/60) Easily the best place to eat in town is the polished restaurant at Dobra Vila – preferably in the pretty garden in summer. A carefully constructed menu of local, seasonal ingredients is served to an appreciative crowd. Setting, service and food are first-class; bookings are essential.

ℹ Information

Tourist Information Centre (TIC; ☑ 05-302 96 47; www.bovec.si; Trg Golobarskih Žrtev 22; ☺8am-8pm Jul & Aug, 9am-7pm Jun & Sep, 8.30am-12.30pm & 1.30-5pm Mon-Fri, 9am-5pm Sat & Sun May, shorter hours Oct-Apr) The TIC is open year-round. Winter hours will depend on the

reopening of the local ski centre – expect long hours when the ski season is fully operating.

ℹ Getting There & Away

Bus routes run to Ljubljana (€14, 3¾ hours, 151km, three daily). Busline **Alpetour** (☑ 04-532 04 45; www.alpetour.si) runs buses to Kranjska Gora (€7, 1¾ hours, 46km), via Trenta (€2.90, 30 minutes, 20km), for Vršič Pass.

SLOVENIAN KARST & COAST

The Karst region (*Kras* in Slovenian) of western Slovenia is a limestone plateau stretching inland from the Gulf of Trieste. Rivers, ponds and lakes can disappear and then resurface in the Karst's porous limestone through sinkholes and funnels, often resulting in underground caverns like the fabulous caves at Škocjan and Postojna. Slovenia has just 47km of coastline on the Adriatic Sea, but it certainly makes the most of it. Piran, the highlight, is full of Venetian architecture and has a lively seaside vibe.

Postojna

☑ 05 / POP 9420 / ELEV 546M

The karst cave at Postojna is one of the largest in the world, and its stalagmite and stalactite formations are unequalled anywhere. Among Slovenia's most popular attractions, it's a busy spot – the amazing thing is how the large crowds at the entrance seem to get swallowed whole by the size of the cave, and the tourist activity doesn't detract from the wonder. It's a big, slick complex, and it doesn't come cheap. But it's still worth every minute you can spend in this magical underground world. The adjacent town of Postojna serves as a gateway to the caves and is otherwise a fairly attractive provincial Slovenian town.

★Postojna Cave
CAVE

(Postojnska Jama; ☑05-700 01 00; www.postojnska-jama.eu; Jamska cesta 30; adult/child €25.80/15.50, with Predjama Castle €35.70/21.40; ☺tours hourly 9am-6pm Jul & Aug, to 5pm May, Jun & Sep, 10am, noon & 3pm Nov-Mar, 10am-noon & 2-4pm Apr & Oct) The jaw-dropping Postojna Cave system, a series of caverns, halls and passages some 24km long and two million years old, was hollowed out by the Pivka River, which enters a subterranean tunnel near the cave's entrance.

WORTH A TRIP

PREDJAMA CASTLE

Predjama Castle (Predjamski Grad; ☑05-700 01 00; www.postojnska-jama.eu; Predjama 1; adult/child €13.80/8.30, with Postojna Cave €35.70/21.40; ⊙9am-7pm Jul & Aug, to 6pm May, Jun & Sep, 10am-5pm Apr & Oct, to 4pm Nov-Mar), 9km from Postojna, is one of Europe's most dramatic castles. It teaches a clear lesson: if you want to build an impregnable fortification, put it in the gaping mouth of a cavern halfway up a 123m cliff. Its four storeys were built piecemeal over the years from 1202, but most of what you see today is from the 16th century. It looks simply unconquerable.

Visitors get to see 5km of the cave on 1½-hour tours; 3.2km of this is covered by a cool electric train. Postojna Cave has a constant temperature of 8°C to 10°C, with 95% humidity, so a warm jacket and decent shoes are advised.

Youth Hostel Proteus Postojna HOSTEL €
(☑05-850 10 20; www.proteus.sgls.si; Tržaška cesta 36; dm/s/d €15/23/34; P@☜) Don't be fooled by the institutional exterior – inside, this place is a riot of colour. It's surrounded by parkland and is a fun, chilled-out space, with three-bed rooms (shared bathrooms), kitchen and laundry access, and bike rental. The year-round hostel shares the building with student accommodation, so facilities are good. It's about 500m southwest of Titov trg.

★**Lipizzaner Lodge** GUESTHOUSE €€
(☑040 378 037; www.lipizzanerlodge.com; Landol 17; s/d/q from €55/80/100; P☜) In a relaxing rural setting 9km northwest of Postojna Cave, a Welsh-Finnish couple have established this very hospitable, affordable guesthouse. They offer seven well-equipped rooms (including family-sized, and a self-catering apartment); great-value, three-course evening meals on request (€20); brilliant local knowledge (check out their comprehensive website for an idea); forest walks (including to Predjama in 40 minutes); and bike rental.

Hotel Jama HOTEL €€€
(☑05-700 01 00; www.postojnska-jama.eu; Jamska cesta 30; r from €129) This huge, concrete, socialist-era hotel is part of the Postojna Cave complex and has undergone a stunning

renovation, reopening in 2016 with slick, contemporary rooms with striking colour schemes and lovely glass-walled bathrooms. It's worth paying extra (anywhere between €10 and €30) for a room with a view. There's also a restaurant and a bar, and the excellent buffet breakfast costs €12.

★**Restaurant Proteus** SLOVENIAN €€
(☑081 610 300; Titov trg 1; mains €12-22; ⊙8am-10pm) The fanciest place in town: inside is modern and white, with booths fringed by curtains, while the terrace overlooking the main square is a fine vantage point. Accomplished cooking showcases fine regional produce – house specialities include venison goulash and steak with *teran* (red wine) sauce. It's hard to go past the four-course Chef's Slovenian Menu (€38) for value and local flavour.

❶ Information

Tourist Information Centre Galerija (☑040 122 318; www.visit-postojna.si; Trg Padlih Borchev 5; ⊙9am-5pm Mon-Sat, to 3pm Sun) Well-stocked tourist office in the town centre.
Tourist Information Centre Postojna (TIC; ☑064 179 972; www.visit-postojna.si; Tržaška cesta 59; ⊙8am-4pm Mon-Fri, 10am-3pm Sat) A smart new pavilion has been built in the town's west, on the road into Postojna. It's handy for those driving into town and there's adequate parking.

❶ Getting There & Away

BUS

Postojna's **bus station** (Titova cesta 2) is 200m southwest of Titov trg. Note some intercity buses will stop at the cave complex too (on timetables this is Postojnska jama). Destinations from Postojna include Divača (for Škocjan; €3.90, 30 minutes, seven daily), Ljubljana (€6.80, one hour, hourly) and Piran (€9.60, 1¾ hours, four daily).

TRAIN

The train station is on Kolodvorska cesta about 800m east of the square.

Postojna is on the main train line linking Ljubljana (€5.80, one hour) with Sežana and Trieste via Divača, and is an easy day trip from the capital. As many as 20 trains a day make the run from Ljubljana to Postojna and back.

Škocjan Caves

★**Škocjan Caves** CAVE
(Škocjanske Jame; ☑05-708 21 00; www.park-skocjanske-jame.si; Škocjan 2; cave tour adult/child

Jul & Aug €20/10, Mar-Jun, Sep & Oct €18/9, Nov-Feb €16/7.50; ☉ tours hourly 10am-5pm Jun-Sep, 10am, noon, 1pm & 3.30pm Apr, May & Oct, 10am & 1pm Mon-Sat, 10am, 1pm & 3pm Sun Nov-Mar) Touring the huge, spectacular subterranean chambers of the 6km-long Škocjan Caves is a must. This remarkable cave system was carved out by the Reka River, which enters a gorge below the village of Škocjan and eventually flows into the Dead Lake, a sump at the end of the cave where it disappears. It surfaces again as the Timavo River at Duino in Italy, 34km northwest, before emptying into the Gulf of Trieste. Dress warmly and wear good walking shoes.

Etna ITALIAN €€

(☑ 031 727 568; www.etna.si; Kolodvorska ulica 3a, Divača; mains €8-19; ☉ 11am-11pm Tue-Sun) Etna takes the classic pizza-pasta-meat menu and gives it a creative twist, with surprisingly tasty (and beautifully presented) results. All the essentials are homemade (pasta, pizza dough from wholemeal flour); pizza choices are divided between classic or seasonal. The desserts are pretty as a picture.

❶ Getting There & Away

The Škocjan Caves are about 4.5km by road southeast of Divača. A bus connection runs from Divača's neighbouring train and bus stations to the caves a couple of times a day – the caves office recommends you call for times, as these change seasonally. Alternatively, there's a one-hour signed walking trail to the caves.

Buses between Ljubljana and the coast stop at Divača. Destinations include Ljubljana (€8.50, 1½ hours, seven daily) and Postojna (€3.90, 30 minutes, seven daily).

Train destinations from Divača include Ljubljana (€7.70, 1½ hours, up to 14 daily) and Postojna (€3.44, 35 minutes, up to 14 daily).

Piran

☑ 05 / POP 3800

One of the loveliest towns anywhere along the Adriatic coast, picturesque Piran (Pirano in Italian) sits prettily at the tip of a narrow peninsula. Its Old Town – one of the best-preserved historical towns anywhere in the Mediterranean – is a gem of Venetian Gothic architecture, but it can be a mob scene at the height of summer. In quieter times, it's hard not to fall instantly in love with the atmospheric winding alleyways, the sunsets and the seafood restaurants.

◉ Sights

★ **Tartinijev Trg** SQUARE

The pastel-toned Tartinijev trg is a marble-paved square (oval, really) that was the inner harbour until it was filled in 1894. The **statue** of a nattily dressed gentleman in the centre is of native son, composer and violinist Giuseppe Tartini (1692–1770). East is the 1818 **Church of St Peter** (Cerkev Sv Petra). Across from the church is **Tartini House** (Tartinijeva Hiša; ☑ 05-671 00 40; www.pomorskimuzej.si; Kajuhova ulica 12; adult/child €2/1; ☉ 9am-noon & 6-9pm Jul & Aug, shorter hours Sep-Jun), the composer's birthplace. The **Court House** (Sodniška Palača) and the porticoed 19th-century **Municipal Hall** (Občinska Palača), home to the tourist information centre, dominate the western edge of the square.

Cathedral of St George CATHEDRAL

(Župnijska Cerkev Sv Jurija; www.zupnija-piran.si; Adamičeva ulica 2) A cobbled street leads from behind the red Venetian House Tartinijev trg on to Piran's hilltop cathedral, baptistery and bell tower. The cathedral was built in baroque style in the early 17th century on the site of an earlier church from 1344.

The cathedral's doors are usually open and a metal grille allows you to see some of the richly ornate and newly restored interior, but full access is via the **Parish Museum of St George** (☑ 05-673 34 40; adult/child €2/1; ☉ 9am-1pm & 5-7.30pm Mon-Fri, 9am-2pm & 5-8pm Sat, from 11am Sun), which includes the church's treasury and catacombs.

Bell Tower TOWER

(Zvonik; Adamičeva ulica; €1; ☉ 10am-8pm summer, shorter hours rest of year) The Cathedral of St George's free-standing, 46.5m bell tower, built in 1609, was clearly modelled on the campanile of San Marco in Venice and provides a fabulous backdrop to many a town photo. Its 147 stairs can be climbed for fabulous views of the town and harbour. Next to it, the octagonal 17th-century baptistery contains altars and paintings. It is now sometimes used as an exhibition space. To the east is a 200m-long stretch of the 15th-century **town wall**.

🛏 Sleeping & Eating

Piran has a number of atmospheric choices and an unusually stable accommodation offering. Prices are higher here than elsewhere along the coast, and you'd be crazy to arrive without a booking in summer. If you're looking for a private room, start at **Maona Tourist Agency** (☑ 05-674 03 63; www.maona. si; Cankarjevo nabrežje 7; ☺ 9am-8pm Mon-Sat, 10am-1pm & 5-7pm Sun) or **Turist Biro** (☑ 05-673 25 09; www.turistbiro-ag.si; Tomažičeva ulica 3; ☺ 9am-1pm & 4-7pm Mon-Sat, 10am-1pm Sun).

Max Piran B&B €€
(☑ 041 692 928; www.maxpiran.com; Ulica IX Korpusa 26; d €70-88; ❄ 🛜) Piran's most romantic accommodation has just six handsome, compact rooms, each bearing a woman's name rather than a number, in a delightful, coral-coloured, 18th-century town house. It's just down from the Cathedral of St George, and is excellent value.

★ **PachaMama** GUESTHOUSE €€€
(PachaMama Pleasant Stay; ☑ 05-918 34 95; www. pachamama.si; Trubarjeva 8; r €80-175; ❄ 🛜) Built by travellers for travellers, this excellent guesthouse sits just off Tartinijev trg and offers 12 fresh rooms, decorated with timber and lots of travel photography. Cool private bathrooms and a 'secret garden' add appeal. There are also a handful of studios and family-sized apartments dotted around town, of an equally high standard.

Cantina Klet SEAFOOD €
(Trg 1 Maja 10; mains €5-10; ☺ 10am-11pm) This small wine bar sits pretty under a grapevine canopy on Trg 1 Maja. You order drinks from the bar (cheap local wine from the barrel or well-priced beers), but we especially love the self-service window (labelled 'Fritolin pri Cantini') where you order from a small blackboard menu of fishy dishes, like fish fillet with polenta, fried calamari or fish tortilla.

★ **Pri Mari** MEDITERRANEAN €€
(☑ 041 616 488, 05-673 47 35; www.primari-piran. com; Dantejeva ulica 17; mains €8-24; ☺ noon-4pm & 6-10pm Tue-Sun Apr-Oct, noon-4pm & 6-10pm Tue-Sat, noon-6pm Sun Nov-Mar) This stylishly rustic and welcoming restaurant run by an Italian-Slovenian couple serves the most inventive Mediterranean and Slovenian dishes in town – lots of fish – and a good selection of local wines. Space is limited, so it pays to book ahead.

❶ Information

Tourist Information Centre (TIC; ☑ 05-673 44 40; www.portoroz.si; Tartinijev trg 2; ☺ 9am-10pm Jul & Aug, to 7pm May, to 5pm Sep-Apr &

Jun) Your first stop for information on Piran and Portorož. It's in the impressive Municipal Hall.

❶ Getting There & Away

BUS

Arriva (☑ 090 74 11; www.arriva.si) buses serve the coast; see the website for schedules and prices. From the **bus station** (Dantejeva ulica) south of the centre, three buses daily make the journey to Ljubljana (€13, three hours), via Divača and Postojna.

SURVIVAL GUIDE

❶ Directory A–Z

ACCOMMODATION

Slovenia has all manner of places to bed down. You'll need to book well in advance if you're travelling during peak season (July and August on the coast and at Bled or Bohinj; spring and autumn in Ljubljana).

Hotels Runs the gamut between family-run operations and five-star boutiques.

Hostels Both indie hostels and HI-affiliated affairs are plentiful.

Pensions & Guesthouses Often family-owned and good value.

Private Rooms Single rooms or fully furnished flats. Locate via tourist information centres.

Mountain Huts Simple beds, with or without facilities, near hiking trails.

MONEY

ATMs are widely available or you can exchange money at banks. Credit and debit cards are accepted by most businesses throughout the country.

OPENING HOURS

Opening hours can vary throughout the year. We've provided high-season opening hours.

Banks 8.30am to 12.30pm and 2pm to 5pm Monday to Friday

Bars 11am to midnight Sunday to Thursday, to 1am or 2am Friday and Saturday

Restaurants 11am to 10pm

Shops 8am to 7pm Monday to Friday, to 1pm Saturday

PUBLIC HOLIDAYS

Slovenia celebrates 14 *prazniki* (holidays) each year. If any of them fall on a Sunday, the Monday becomes the holiday.

New Year's 1 and 2 January

Prešeren Day (Slovenian Culture Day) 8 February

Easter & Easter Monday March/April
Insurrection Day 27 April
Labour Day holidays 1 and 2 May
National Day 25 June
Assumption Day 15 August
Reformation Day 31 October
All Saints' Day 1 November
Christmas Day 25 December
Independence Day 26 December

TELEPHONE

Slovenia's country code is 386. Slovenia has six area codes (01 to 05 and 07). Ljubljana's area code is 01.

➡ To call a landline within Slovenia, include the area code if the number you are calling is outside the area code.

➡ To call abroad from Slovenia, dial 00 followed by the country and area codes, and then the number.

➡ To call Slovenia from abroad, dial the international access code, 386 (the country code for Slovenia), the area code (minus the initial zero) and the number.

ⓘ Getting There & Away

Most travellers arrive in Slovenia by air, or by rail and road connections from neighbouring countries. Flights, cars and tours can be booked online at lonelyplanet.com/bookings.

AIR

Ljubljana's Jože Pučnik Airport (p1023), 27km north of the capital, is the only air gateway for travelling to and from Slovenia. The arrivals hall has a branch of the **Slovenia Tourist Information Centre** (STIC; www.visitljubljana.si; Jože Pučnik Airport; ⊙ 8am-7pm Mon-Fri, 9am-5pm Sat & Sun Oct-May, 8am-9pm Jun-Sep) and a bank of ATMs (located just outside the terminal).

Budget carriers include **EasyJet** (www.easyjet.com) and **Wizz Air** (☑ Slovenia call centre 090 100 206; www.wizzair.com).

LAND
Bus

Several long-haul coach companies operate in Slovenia, connecting the country to destinations around Europe. This service is often cheaper and faster than trains. Buses are also useful for reaching areas where train connections from Slovenia are deficient, including to points in Italy and Bosnia & Hercegovina. Most international services arrive and depart from Ljubljana's main bus station (p1023).

Train

The **Slovenian Railways** (Slovenske Železnice, SŽ; ☑ info 1999; www.slo-zeleznice.si) network links up with the European railway network via Austria (Villach, Salzburg, Graz, Vienna), Italy (Trieste), Germany (Munich, Frankfurt), Czech Republic (Prague), Croatia (Zagreb, Rijeka), Hungary (Budapest), Switzerland (Zürich) and Serbia (Belgrade). The Slovenian Railways website has full information in English on current international connections.

SEA

During summer it's possible to travel by sea between Piran and the Italian ports of Venice and Trieste.

ⓘ Getting Around

BICYCLE

Cycling is a popular way to get around. Larger towns and cities have dedicated bicycle lanes and traffic lights. Bicycle-rental shops are generally concentrated in the more popular tourist areas. Expect to pay from €3/17 per hour/day.

BUS

The Slovenian bus network is extensive and you can reach every major city and town, and many smaller places, by bus. A range of companies serve the country, but prices tend to be uniform: around €4/6/10/17 for 25/50/100/200km of travel. Buy your ticket from ticket windows at the bus station (*avtobusna postaja*) or pay the driver as you board.

CAR & MOTORCYCLE

Roads in Slovenia are good. Tolls are not paid separately on motorways. Instead, cars must display a *vinjeta* (road-toll sticker) on the windscreen. The sticker costs €15/30/110 for a week/month/year for cars and €7.50/30/55 for motorbikes, and is available at petrol stations, post offices and tourist information centres. Failure to display a sticker risks a fine of up to €300. For emergency roadside assistance, call 1987 anywhere in Slovenia.

TRAIN

Domestic trains are operated by Slovenian Railways. The network is extensive and connects many major cities and towns. Trains tend to offer more space and are more comfortable than buses, and can occasionally be cheaper. Trains are useful mainly for covering long distances. The railways website has a timetable and extensive information in English.

SLOVENIA SURVIVAL GUIDE

Spain

POP 46.7 MILLION

Includes ➡

Best Places to Eat

➡ Casa Delfín (p1064)

➡ La Cuchara de San Telmo (p1073)

➡ El Poblet (p1080)

➡ Adolfo (p1055)

Best Places to Stay

➡ Un Patio en Santa Cruz (p1087)

➡ Balcón de Córdoba (p1090)

➡ Barceló Raval (p1062)

➡ Hotel Costa Vella (p1077)

Why Go?

Passionate, sophisticated and devoted to living the good life, Spain is at once a stereotype come to life and a country more diverse than you ever imagined.

Spanish landscapes stir the soul, from the jagged Pyrenees and wildly beautiful cliffs of the Atlantic northwest to charming Mediterranean coves, while astonishing architecture spans the ages at seemingly every turn. Spain's cities march to a beguiling beat with cutting-edge architecture and unrivalled nightlife, even as time-capsule villages serve as beautiful signposts to Old Spain. And then there's one of Europe's most celebrated (and varied) gastronomic scenes.

But, above all, Spain lives very much in the present. Perhaps you'll sense it along a crowded after-midnight street when all the world has come out to play. Or maybe that moment will come when a flamenco performer touches something deep in your soul. Whenever it happens, you'll find yourself nodding in recognition: *this* is Spain.

When to Go
Madrid

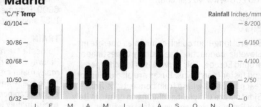

Mar & Apr Spring wildflowers, Semana Santa processions and mild southern temperatures.	May, Jun & Sep Balmy weather but without the crowds of high summer.	Jul & Aug Spaniards hit the coast in the summer heat, but quiet corners still abound.

Entering the Country

Immigration and customs checks usually involve a minimum of fuss, although there are exceptions. Your vehicle could be searched on arrival from Morocco; they're looking for controlled substances. Expect long delays at these borders, especially in summer. The tiny principality of Andorra is not in the EU, so border controls (and rigorous customs checks for contraband) remain in place.

ITINERARIES

One Week

Marvel at the art nouveau–influenced Modernista architecture and seaside style of Barcelona (p1055) before taking the train to San Sebastián (p1072). Head on to Bilbao (p1074) for the Guggenheim Museum and end the trip living it up in the legendary night-life scene of Madrid (p1038).

One Month

Fly into Seville (p1084) and embark on a route exploring this and Andalucía's other magical cities, Granada (p1091) and Córdoba (p1089). Take the train to Madrid (p1038), from where you can check out Toledo (p1054), Salamanca (p1049) and Segovia (p1051). Make east for the coast and Valencia (p1078). Head up to the Basque Country to see the epoch-making Guggenheim Museum in Bilbao (p1074) and feast on some of the world's best food in San Sebastián (p1072), then head east via the medieval villages of Aragón (p1070) and the dramatic Pyrenees (p1072) to Catalonia, spending time in Tarragona (p1068) before reaching Barcelona (p1055). Take a plane or boat for some R&R on the beautiful Balearic Islands (p1081) before catching a flight home.

Essential Food & Drink

Tapas or pintxos Possibly the world's most ingenious form of snacking. Madrid's La Latina *barrio* (district), Zaragoza's El Tubo and most Andalucían cities offer rich pickings, but a *pintxo* (Basque tapas) crawl in San Sebastián's Parte Vieja is one of life's most memorable gastronomic experiences.

Chocolate con churros These deep-fried doughnut strips dipped in thick hot chocolate are a Spanish favourite for breakfast, afternoon tea or at dawn on your way home from a night out. Madrid's Chocolatería de San Ginés (p1046) is the most famous purveyor.

Bocadillos Rolls filled with *jamón* (cured ham) or other cured meats, cheese or (in Madrid) deep-fried calamari.

Pa amb tomaquet Bread rubbed with tomato, olive oil and garlic – a staple in Catalonia and elsewhere.

AT A GLANCE

Area 505,370 sq km

Capital Madrid

Country Code ☏34

Currency euro (€)

Emergency ☏112

Languages Spanish (Castilian), Catalan, Basque, Galician (Gallego)

Time Central European Time (GMT/UTC plus one hour)

Visas Schengen rules apply

Sleeping Price Ranges

The following price ranges refer to a double room with private bathroom (Madrid and Barcelona/rest of Spain):

€ less than €75/65

€€ €75–200/€65–140

€€€ more than €200/140

Eating Price Ranges

The following price ranges refer to a standard main dish:

€ less than €12

€€ €12–20

€€€ more than €20

Resources

Fiestas.net (www.fiestas.net)

Tour Spain (www.tourspain.org)

Turespaña (www.spain.info)

Paradores (www.parador.es)

Spain Highlights

1 Alhambra
(p1091) Exploring the exquisite Islamic palace complex in Granada.

2 La Sagrada Família (p1059) Visiting Gaudí's singular work in progress in Barcelona, a cathedral that truly defies imagination.

3 Mezquita
(p1089) Wandering amid the horseshoe arches of Córdoba's great medieval mosque, close to perfection wrought in stone.

4 San Sebastián
(p1072) Eating your way through a food-lover's paradise with an idyllic setting.

5 Santiago de Compostela (p1076) Joining the pilgrims in Galicia's magnificent cathedral city.

6 Seville (p1084) Soaking up the scent of orange blossom, being carried away by the passion of flamenco and surrendering to the party atmosphere in this sunny southern city.

7 Madrid (p1038) Spending your days in some of Europe's best art galleries and nights amid its best nightlife.

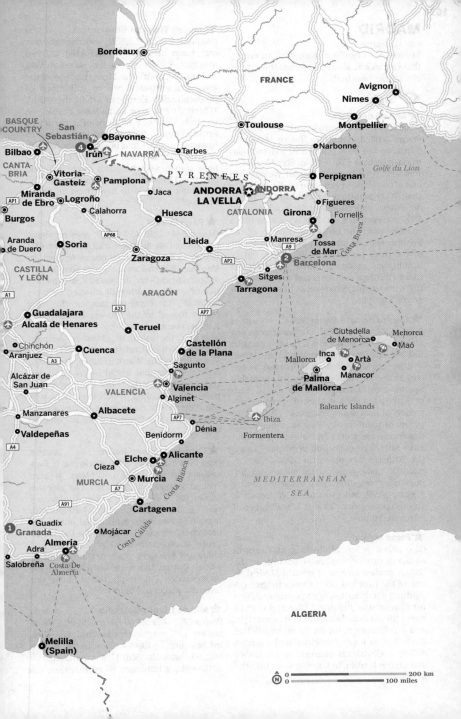

MADRID

POP 3.18 MILLION

Madrid is a beguiling place with an energy that carries one simple message: this city really knows how to live.

◉ Sights

★ Museo del Prado   MUSEUM

(Map p1044; www.museodelprado.es; Paseo del Prado; adult/child €15/free, 6-8pm Mon-Sat & 5-7pm Sun free, audio guide €3.50, admission plus official guidebook €24; ◐10am-8pm Mon-Sat, to 7pm Sun; ☏; Ⓜ Banco de España) Welcome to one of the world's premier art galleries. More than 7000 paintings are held in the Museo del Prado's collection (of which only around 1500 are currently on display), acting like a window onto the historical vagaries of the Spanish soul, at once grand and imperious in the royal paintings of Velázquez, darkly tumultuous in *Las pinturas negras* (The Black Paintings) of Goya, and outward looking with sophisticated works of art from all across Europe.

★ Centro de Arte Reina Sofía   MUSEUM

(Map p1044; ☏91 774 10 00; www.museoreinasofia.es; Calle de Santa Isabel 52; adult/concession €10/free, 1.30-7pm Sun, 7-9pm Mon & Wed-Sat free; ◐10am-9pm Mon & Wed-Sat, to 7pm Sun; Ⓜ Atocha) Home to Picasso's *Guernica*, arguably Spain's most famous artwork, the Centro de Arte Reina Sofía is Madrid's premier collection of contemporary art. In addition to plenty of paintings by Picasso, other major drawcards are works by Salvador Dalí and Joan Miró. The collection principally spans the 20th century up to the 1980s. The occasional non-Spanish artist makes an appearance (including Francis Bacon's *Lying Figure;* 1966), but most of the collection is strictly peninsular. Tickets are cheaper if purchased online.

★ Plaza Mayor   SQUARE

(Map p1044; Ⓜ Sol) Madrid's grand central square, a rare but expansive opening in the tightly packed streets of central Madrid, is one of the prettiest open spaces in Spain, a winning combination of imposing architecture, picaresque historical tales and vibrant street life. At once beautiful in its own right and a reference point for so many Madrid days, it also hosts the city's main tourist office, a Christmas market in December and arches leading to laneways out into the labyrinth.

★ Museo Thyssen-Bornemisza   MUSEUM

(Map p1044; ☏902 760511; www.museothyssen.org; Paseo del Prado 8; adult/child €12/free, Mon free; ◐10am-7pm Tue-Sun, noon-4pm Mon; Ⓜ Banco de España) The Thyssen is one of the most extraordinary private collections of predominantly European art in the world. Where the Prado or Reina Sofía enable you to study the body of work of a particular artist in depth, the Thyssen is the place to immerse yourself in a breathtaking breadth of artistic styles. Most of the big names are here, sometimes with just a single painting, but the Thyssen's gift to Madrid and the art-loving public is to have them all under one roof.

★ Palacio Real   PALACE

(Map p1044; ☏91 454 87 00; www.patrimonionacional.es; Calle de Bailén; adult/concession €11/6, guide/audio guide €3, EU citizens free last 2hr Mon-Thu; ◐10am-8pm Apr-Sep, to 6pm Oct-Mar; Ⓜ Ópera) Spain's lavish Palacio Real is a jewel box of a palace, although it's used only occasionally for royal ceremonies; the royal family moved to the modest Palacio de la Zarzuela years ago.

When the *alcázar* (Muslim fortress) burned down on Christmas Day 1734, Felipe V, the first of the Bourbon kings, decided to build a palace that would dwarf all its European counterparts. Felipe died before the palace was finished, which is perhaps why the Italianate baroque colossus has a mere 2800 rooms, just one-quarter of the original plan.

★ Parque del Buen Retiro   GARDENS

(Map p1040; Plaza de la Independencia; ◐6am-midnight Apr-Sep, to 10pm Oct-Mar; Ⓜ Retiro, Príncipe de Vergara, Ibiza, Atocha) The glorious gardens of El Retiro are as beautiful as any you'll find in a European city. Littered with marble monuments, landscaped lawns, the occasional elegant building (the Palacio de Cristal is especially worth seeking out) and abundant greenery, it's quiet and contemplative during the week but comes to life on weekends. Put simply, this is one of our favourite places in Madrid.

★ Museo Lázaro Galdiano   MUSEUM

(Map p1040; ☏91 561 60 84; www.flg.es; Calle de Serrano 122; adult/concession/child €6/3/free, last hour free; ◐10am-4.30pm Tue-Sat, to 3pm Sun; Ⓜ Gregorio Marañón) This imposing early-20th-century Italianate stone mansion, set

SPAIN MADRID

discreetly back from the street, belonged to Don José Lázaro Galdiano (1862–1947), a successful businessman and passionate patron of the arts. His astonishing private collection, which he bequeathed to the city upon his death, includes 13,000 works of art and objets d'art, a quarter of which are on show at any time.

✮✫ Festivals & Events

Fiestas de San Isidro Labrador CULTURAL
(www.esmadrid.com; ⊙May) Around 15 May Madrid's patron saint is honoured with a week of nonstop processions, parties and bullfights. Free concerts are held throughout the city, and this week marks the start of the city's bullfighting season.

🛏 Sleeping

🛏 Plaza Mayor & Royal Madrid

★ Central Palace Madrid HOTEL €€
(Map p1044; ☎91 548 20 18; www.centralpalace madrid.com; Plaza de Oriente 2; d without/with view €145/200; ❋🕿; MÓpera) Now here's something special. The views alone would be

reason enough to come to this hotel and definitely worth paying extra for – rooms with balconies look out over the Palacio Real and Plaza de Oriente. The rooms themselves are lovely and light filled, with tasteful, subtle faux-antique furnishings, comfortable beds, light wood floors and plenty of space.

🛏 La Latina

Posada del León de Oro BOUTIQUE HOTEL €€
(Map p1044; ☎91 119 14 94; www.posadadelle ondeoro.com; Calle de la Cava Baja 12; d/ste from €70/145; ❋🕿; MLa Latina) This rehabilitated inn has muted colour schemes and generally large rooms. There's a *corrala* (traditional internal or communal patio) at its core and thoroughly modern rooms along one of Madrid's best-loved streets. The downstairs bar is terrific.

🛏 Sol, Santa Ana & Huertas

Lapepa Chic B&B B&B €
(Map p1044; ☎648 474742; www.lapepa-bnb.com; 7th fl, Plaza de las Cortes 4; s/d from €55/60; ❋🕿; MBanco de España) A short step off Paseo del Prado and on a floor with an art nouveau

---

MUSEO DEL PRADO ITINERARY: ICONS OF SPANISH ART

The collection of the Museo del Prado (p1038) can be overwhelming in scope, and it's a good idea to come twice if you can – but if your time is limited, zero in on the museum's peerless collection of Spanish art.

Francisco José de Goya y Lucientes (Goya) is found on all three floors of the Prado, but we recommend starting at the southern end of the ground or lower level. In room 65, Goya's *El dos de mayo* and *El tres de mayo* rank among Madrid's most emblematic paintings; they bring to life the 1808 anti-French revolt and subsequent execution of insurgents in Madrid. Alongside, in rooms 67 and 68, are some of his darkest and most disturbing works, *Las pinturas negras;* they are so called in part because of the dark browns and black that dominate, but more for the distorted animalesque appearance of their characters.

There are more Goyas on the 1st floor in rooms 34 to 37. Among them are two more of Goya's best-known and most intriguing oils: *La maja vestida* and *La maja desnuda*. These portraits, in room 37, of an unknown woman, commonly believed to be the Duquesa de Alba (who may have been Goya's lover), are identical save for the lack of clothing in the latter. There are further Goyas on the top floor.

Having studied the works of Goya, turn your attention to Velázquez. Of all his works, *Las meninas* (room 12) is what most people come to see. Completed in 1656, it is more properly known as *La família de Felipe IV* (The Family of Felipe IV). The rooms surrounding *Las meninas* contain more fine works by Velázquez: watch out in particular for his paintings of various members of royalty who seem to spring off the canvas – Felipe II, Felipe IV, Margarita de Austria (a younger version of whom features in *Las meninas*), El Príncipe Baltasar Carlos and Isabel de Francia – on horseback.

Further, Bartolomé Esteban Murillo, José de Ribera, the stark figures of Francisco de Zurbarán and the vivid, almost surreal works of El Greco should all be on your itinerary.

Madrid

Canal **M**

C de Bravo Murillo

Av de Séneca

Parque del Oeste

C de Donoso Cortes

C de Hilario Eslava

C de Gaztambide

C de Andrés Mellado

C de Guzmán el Bueno

C de Blasco de Garay

C de Fernández de los Ríos

C de Fernando El Católico

Quevedo **M**

C de Fuencarral

M Moncloa

C Ruperto Chapi

Paseo de Moret

C de Meléndez Valdés

C de San Bernardo

Plaza del Conde del Valle de Suchil

Paseo del Pintor Rosales

C de Romero Robledo

C de Altamirano

C del Marqués de Urquijo

M Argüelles

C de Rodríguez San Pedro

C de Vallehermoso

ARGÜELLES

C de Alberto Aguilera

San Bernardo

C de Carranza

C de la Princesa

C del Acuerdo

C del Conde Duque

C de San Bernardo

MALASAÑA

C de Francisco Jacinto y Alcántara

C del Buen Suceso

C de Quintana

C de los Mártires de Alcalá

Plaza del Dos de Majo

C de la Palma

Glorieta de San Antonio de la Florida

C de la Rosaleda

La Rosaleda

C de Ferraz

Ventura Rodríguez **M**

C de San Bernardino

Noviciado **M**

C de San Bernardo

C de la Madera

Paseo de la Florida

Jardines de Ferraz

Plaza de España

M Noviciado

Parque de la Montaña

M Gran Vía

C de San Bernardo

Principe Pío

Santo Domingo

Paseo del Marqués de Monistrol

M Principe Pío

Cuesta de San Vicente

M Callao

Casa de Campo

CAMPO

Campo del Moro

M Ópera

C del Arenal

Sol **M**

Plaza de la Puerta del Sol

Plaza de la Armería

Puerta del Ángel **M**

Paseo de la Virgen del Puerto

Parque de Atenas

Parque del Emir Mohamed I

C Mayor

Plaza Mayor

LA LATINA

Tirso de Molina **M**

C de Segovia

C del Duque de Alba

C de Mesón de Paredes

Ronda de Segovia

C Juan Duque

C de Bailén

C de Toledo

C de la Ribera de los Curtidores

C de los Embajadores

Parque de Caramuel

Paseo de la Ermita del Santo

Av de Manzanares

Río Manzanares

Ronda de Segovia

Paseo Imperial

See Central Madrid Map (p1044)

M Puerta de Toledo

C de Toledo

Ronda de Toledo

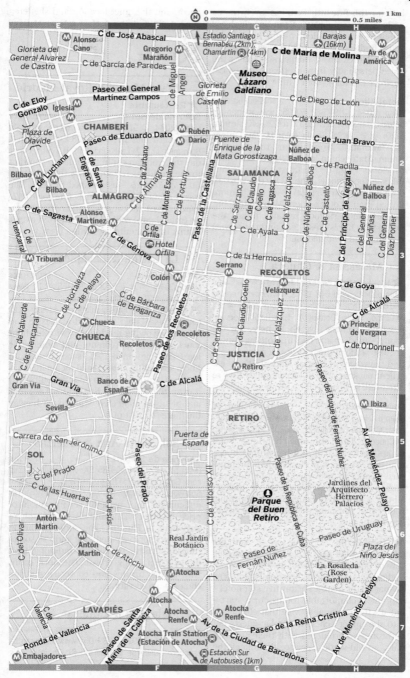

interior, this fine little B&B has lovely rooms with a contemporary, clean-line look so different from the dour *hostal* furnishings you'll find elsewhere. Modern art or even a bedhead lined with flamenco shoes gives the place personality in bucketloads. It's worth paying extra for a room with a view.

Hotel Alicia BOUTIQUE HOTEL €€
(Map p1044; ☑91 389 60 95; www.room-mate hoteles.com; Calle del Prado 2; d €120-140, ste from €170; ❋ ☎; Ⓜ Sol, Sevilla, Antón Martín) One of the landmark properties of the designer Room Mate chain of hotels, Hotel Alicia overlooks Plaza de Santa Ana with beautiful, spacious rooms. The style (the work of designer Pascua Ortega) is a touch more muted than in other Room Mate hotels, but the supermodern look remains intact, the downstairs bar is oh-so-cool, and the service is young and switched on.

🛏 Malasaña & Chueca

★ Hostal Main Street Madrid HOSTAL €
(Map p1044; ☑91 548 18 78; www.mainstreetma drid.com; 5th fl, Gran Vía 50; r from €140; ❋ ☎; Ⓜ Callao, Santo Domingo) Excellent service is what travellers rave about here, but the rooms – modern and cool in soothing greys – are also some of the best *hostal* rooms you'll find anywhere in central Madrid. It's an excellent package, and not surprisingly they're often full, so book well in advance.

Only You Hotel BOUTIQUE HOTEL €€
(Map p1044; ☑91 005 22 22; www.onlyyouhotels. com; Calle de Barquillo 21; d €205-285; ❋ @ ☎; Ⓜ Chueca) This stunning boutique hotel makes perfect use of a 19th-century Chueca mansion. The look is classy and contemporary thanks to respected interior designer Lázaro Rosa-Violán. Nice touches include all-day à la carte breakfasts and a portable router that you can carry out into the city to stay connected.

★ Hotel Orfila HOTEL €€€
(Map p1040; ☑91 702 77 70; www.hotelorfila.com; Calle de Orfila 6; r from €350; Ⓟ ❋ ☎; Ⓜ Alonso Martínez) One of Madrid's best hotels, Hotel Orfila has all the luxuries of any five-star hotel – supremely comfortable rooms, for a start – but it's the personal service that elevates it into the upper echelon; regular guests get bathrobes embroidered with their own initials. An old-world elegance dominates the

decor, and the quiet location and sheltered garden make it the perfect retreat at day's end.

 Eating

🍴 Plaza Mayor & Royal Madrid

★ Restaurante Sobrino de Botín CASTILIAN €€€
(Map p1044; ☑91 366 42 17; www.botin.es; Calle de los Cuchilleros 17; mains €18-27; ⊙1-4pm & 8pm-midnight; Ⓜ La Latina, Sol) It's not every day that you can eat in the oldest restaurant in the world (as recognised by the *Guinness Book of Records* – established in 1725). The secret of its staying power is fine *cochinillo asado* (roast suckling pig) and *cordero asado* (roast lamb) cooked in wood-fired ovens. Eating in the vaulted cellar is a treat.

🍴 La Latina & Lavapiés

★ Casa Lucio SPANISH €€€
(Map p1044; ☑91 365 32 52, 91 365 82 17; www. casalucio.es; Calle de la Cava Baja 35; mains €18-29; ⊙1-4pm & 8.30pm-midnight, closed Aug; Ⓜ La Latina) Casa Lucio is a Madrid classic and has been wowing *madrileños* with his light touch, quality ingredients and home-style local cooking since 1974, such as eggs (a Lucio speciality) and roasted meats in abundance. There's also *rabo de toro* (bull's tail) during the Fiestas de San Isidro Labrador and plenty of *rioja* (red wine) to wash away the mere thought of it.

🍴 Sol, Santa Ana & Huertas

La Finca de Susana SPANISH €
(Map p1044; ☑91 369 35 57; www.grupandilana. com; Calle del Príncipe 10; mains €8-14; ⊙1-11.30pm Sun-Wed, to midnight Thu-Sat; ☎; Ⓜ Sevilla) It's difficult to find a better combination of price, quality cooking and classy atmosphere anywhere in Huertas. The softly lit dining area has a sophisticated vibe and the sometimes-innovative, sometimes-traditional food draws a hip young crowd. The duck confit with plums, turnips and couscous is a fine choice. No reservations.

🍴 Malasaña & Chueca

Bazaar MODERN SPANISH €
(Map p1044; ☑91 523 39 05; www.restaurantba zaar.com; Calle de la Libertad 21; mains €8-13;

MADRID'S BEST SQUARES

Plaza de Oriente (Map p1044; Ⓜ Ópera) is a living, breathing monument to imperial Madrid. Here you'll find sophisticated cafes watched over by apartments that cost the equivalent of a royal salary; the **Teatro Real** (Map p1044; ☏ 902 244848; www.teatro-real. com), Madrid's opera house and one of Spain's temples to high culture; and Palacio Real (p1038), which once had aspirations to be the Spanish Versailles. Local legend has it that the marble statues surrounding the square get down off their pedestals at night to stretch their legs when no one's looking.

On the other hand, the intimate **Plaza de la Villa** (Map p1044; Ⓜ Ópera) is one of Madrid's prettiest. Enclosed on three sides by wonderfully preserved examples of 17th-century *barroco madrileño* (Madrid-style baroque architecture – a pleasing amalgam of brick, exposed stone and wrought iron), it was the permanent seat of Madrid's city government from the Middle Ages until recent years, when Madrid's city council relocated to the grand Palacio de Cibeles on **Plaza de la Cibeles** (Map p1044; Ⓜ Banco de España).

Plaza de Santa Ana (Map p1044; Ⓜ Sevilla, Sol, Antón Martín) is a delightful confluence of elegant architecture and irresistible energy. It presides over the upper reaches of the Barrio de las Letras and this literary personality makes its presence felt with statues of the 17th-century writer Calderón de la Barca and poet Federico García Lorca, and in the **Teatro Español** (Map p1044; ☏ 91 360 14 84; www.teatroespanol.es; Calle del Príncipe 25; Ⓜ Sevilla, Sol, Antón Martín), formerly the Teatro del Príncipe, at the plaza's eastern end. Apart from anything else, the plaza is the starting point for many a long Huertas night.

⊙ 1pm-11.30pm Sun-Wed, to midnight Thu-Sat; 🛜; Ⓜ Chueca) Bazaar's popularity among the well-heeled Chueca set shows no sign of abating. Its pristine white interior design, with theatre-style lighting and wall-length windows, may draw a crowd that looks like it's stepped out of the pages of *¡Hola!* magazine, but the food is extremely well priced and innovative, and the atmosphere is casual.

Yakitoro by Chicote JAPANESE, SPANISH €€
(Map p1044; ☏ 91 737 14 41; www.yakitoro.com; Calle de la Reina 41; tapas €3-9; ⊙ 1pm-midnight; Ⓜ Banco de España) Based around the idea of a Japanese tavern, driven by a spirit of innovation and a desire to combine the best in Spanish and Japanese flavours, Yakitoro is a hit. Apart from salads, it's all built around brochettes cooked over a wood fire, with wonderful combinations of vegetable, seafood and meat.

🍸 Drinking & Nightlife

Nights in the Spanish capital are the stuff of legend. They're invariably long and loud most nights of the week, rising to a deafening crescendo as the weekend nears. And what Ernest Hemingway wrote of the city in the 1930s remains true to this day: 'Nobody goes to bed in Madrid until they have killed the night.'

Delic BAR
(Map p1044; ☏ 91 364 54 50; www.delic.es; Costanilla de San Andrés 14; ⊙ 11am-2am Sun & Tue-Thu, to 2.30am Fri & Sat; Ⓜ La Latina) We could go on for hours about this long-standing cafe-bar, but we'll reduce it to its most basic elements: nursing an exceptionally good mojito or three on a warm summer's evening at Delic's outdoor tables on one of Madrid's prettiest plazas is one of life's great pleasures. Bliss.

★ **La Venencia** BAR
(Map p1044; ☏ 91 429 73 13; Calle de Echegaray 7; ⊙ 12.30-3.30pm & 7.30pm-1.30am; Ⓜ Sol, Sevilla) La Venencia is a *barrio* classic, with *manzanilla* (chamomile-coloured sherry) from Sanlúcar and sherry from Jeréz poured straight from the dusty wooden barrels, accompanied by a small selection of tapas with an Andalucian bent. There's no music, no flashy decorations; here it's all about you, your *fino* (sherry) and your friends.

★ **Museo Chicote** COCKTAIL BAR
(Map p1044; ☏ 91 532 67 37; www.museochicote. com; Gran Vía 12; ⊙ 7pm-3am Sun-Thu, to 3.30am Fri & Sat; Ⓜ Gran Vía) This place is a Madrid landmark, complete with its 1930s-era interior, and its founder is said to have invented more than 100 cocktails, which the likes of Ernest Hemingway, Ava Gardner, Grace Kel-

Central Madrid

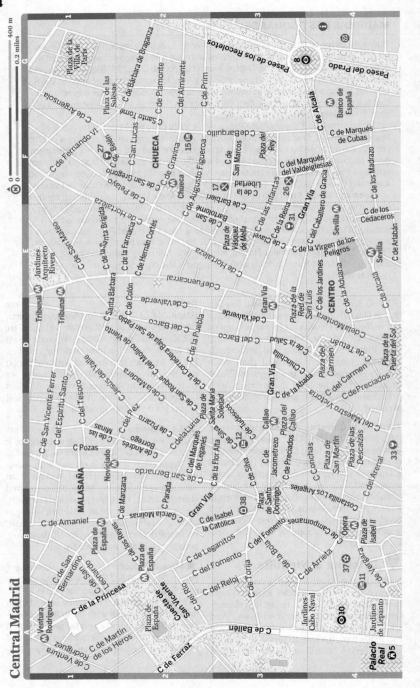

400 m
0.2 miles

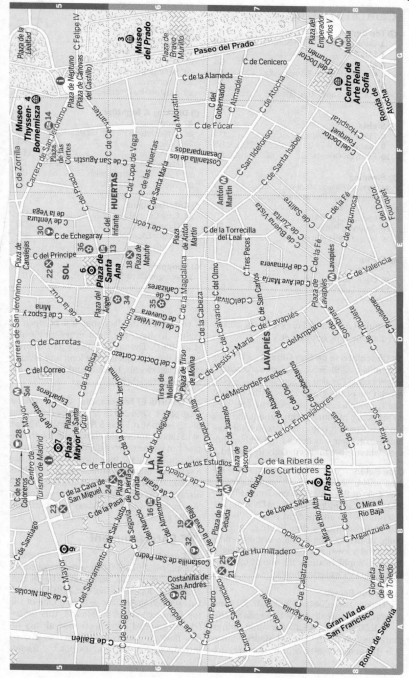

SPAIN MADRID

Central Madrid

ly, Sophia Loren and Frank Sinatra all enjoyed at one time or another.

★ **Chocolatería de San Ginés** CAFE
(Map p1044; ☎91 365 65 46; www.chocolateria
sangines.com; Pasadizo de San Ginés 5; ⊙24hr;
Ⓜ Sol) One of the grand icons of the Madrid night, this *chocolate con churros* cafe sees a sprinkling of tourists throughout the day, but locals pack it out in their search for sustenance on their way home from a nightclub somewhere close to dawn. Only in Madrid...

Café Belén BAR
(Map p1044; ☎91 308 27 47; www.elcafebelen.
com; Calle de Belén 5; ⊙3.30pm-3am Tue-Thu, to 3.30am Fri & Sat, 7-10pm Sun; 🛜; Ⓜ Chueca) Café Belén is cool in all the right places – lounge and chill-out music, dim lighting, a great range of drinks (the mojitos are especially good) and a low-key crowd that's the height of casual sophistication. It's one of our preferred Chueca watering holes.

Teatro Joy Eslava CLUB
(Joy Madrid; Map p1044; ☎91 366 37 33; www.
joy-eslava.com; Calle del Arenal 11; admission €10-18; ⊙11.30pm-6am; Ⓜ Sol) The only things guaranteed at this grand old Madrid dance club (housed in a 19th-century theatre) are

a crowd and the fact that it'll be open (it claims to have operated every single day since 1981). The music and the crowd are a mixed bag, but queues are long and invariably include locals, tourists and the occasional *famoso* (celebrity).

★ **Taberna El Tempranillo** WINE BAR
(Map p1044; ☎91 364 15 32; Calle de la Cava Baja 38; ⊙1-4pm Mon, 1-4pm & 8pm-midnight Tue-Sun; Ⓜ La Latina) You could come here for the tapas, but we recommend Taberna El Tempranillo primarily for its wines, of which it has a selection that puts numerous Spanish bars to shame. It's not a late-night place, but it's always packed in the early evening and on Sunday after El Rastro. Many wines are sold by the glass.

☆ Entertainment

★ **Casa Patas** FLAMENCO
(Map p1044; ☎91 369 04 96; www.casapatas.com;
Calle de Cañizares 10; admission incl drink €38;
⊙shows 10.30pm Mon-Thu, 8pm & 10.30pm Fri & Sat; Ⓜ Antón Martín, Tirso de Molina) One of the top flamenco stages in Madrid, this *tablao* (choreographed flamenco show) always offers flawless quality that serves as a good introduction to the art. It's not the friend-

liest place in town, especially if you're only here for the show, and you're likely to be crammed in a little, but no one complains about the standard of the performances.

★ **Café Central**   JAZZ
(Map p1044; ☑ 91 369 41 43; www.cafecentralmadrid.com; Plaza del Ángel 10; admission €12-18; ⊙ 11.30pm-2.30am Sun-Thu, to 3.30am Fri & Sat, performances 9pm; M Antón Martín, Sol) In 2011 the respected jazz magazine *Down Beat* included this art deco bar on the list of the world's best jazz clubs, the only place in Spain to earn the prestigious accolade (said by some to be the jazz equivalent of earning

a Michelin star). With well over 1000 gigs under its belt, it rarely misses a beat.

Estadio Santiago Bernabéu   STADIUM
(☑ tickets 90 232 43 24, tours 91 398 43 70; www.realmadrid.com; Avenida de Concha Espina 1; tours adult/child €25/18; ⊙ tours 10am-7pm Mon-Sat, 10.30am-6.30pm Sun, except match days; M Santiago Bernabéu) Football fans and budding Madridistas (Real Madrid supporters) will want to make a pilgrimage to the Estadio Santiago Bernabéu, a temple to all that's extravagant and successful in football. Self-guided tours take you up into the stands for a panoramic view of the stadium, then through

---

A TAPAS TOUR OF MADRID

Madrid's home of tapas is La Latina, especially along Calle de la Cava Baja and the surrounding streets.

Juana La Loca (Map p1044; ☑ 91 366 55 00; www.juanalalocamadrid.com; Plaza de la Puerta de Moros 4; tapas from €4, mains €10-30; ⊙ 1.30-5.30pm Tue-Sun, 7pm-midnight Sat-Wed, to 1am Thu-Fri; M La Latina) Juana La Loca does a range of creative tapas with tempting options lined up along the bar, and more on the menu that they prepare to order. But we love it above all for its brilliant *tortilla de patatas*, which is distinguished from others of its kind by the caramelised onions – simply wonderful.

Txirimiri (Map p1044; ☑ 91 364 11 96; www.txirimiri.es; Calle del Humilladero 6; tapas from €3; ⊙ noon-midnight; M La Latina) This *pintxos* (Basque tapas) bar is a great little discovery just down from the main La Latina tapas circuit. Wonderful wines, gorgeous *pinchos* (the *tortilla de patatas* – potato and onion omelette – is superb) and fine risottos add up to a pretty special combination.

Mercado de San Miguel (Map p1044; ☑ 91 542 49 36; www.mercadodesanmiguel.es; Plaza de San Miguel; tapas from €1.50; ⊙ 10am-midnight Sun-Thu, to 1am Fri & Sat; M Sol) This is one of Madrid's oldest and most beautiful markets, within early-20th-century glass walls and an inviting space strewn with tables. You can order tapas and sometimes more substantial plates at most of the counter bars, and everything here (from caviar to chocolate) is as tempting as the market is alive. Put simply, it's one of our favourite experiences in Madrid.

Casa Revuelta (Map p1044; ☑ 91 366 33 32; Calle de Latoneros 3; tapas from €3; ⊙ 10am-4pm & 7-11pm Tue-Sat, 10am-4pm Sun, closed Aug; M Sol, La Latina) Casa Revuelta puts out some of Madrid's finest tapas of *bacalao* (cod) bar none – unlike elsewhere, *tajadas de bacalao* don't have bones in them and slide down the throat with the greatest of ease. Early on a Sunday afternoon, as the Rastro crowd gathers here, it's filled to the rafters. Other specialities include *torreznos* (bacon bits), *callos* (tripe) and *albóndigas* (meatballs).

Casa Alberto (Map p1044; ☑ 91 429 93 56; www.casaalberto.es; Calle de las Huertas 18; tapas €3.25-10, raciones €7-16.50, mains €16-19; ⊙ restaurant 1.30-4pm & 8pm-midnight Tue-Sat, 1.30-4pm Sun, bar noon-1.30am Tue-Sat, 12.30-4pm Sun, closed Sun Jul & Aug; M Antón Martín) One of the most atmospheric old *tabernas* (taverns) of Madrid, Casa Alberto has been around since 1827 and occupies a building where Cervantes is said to have written one of his books. The secret to its staying power is vermouth on tap, excellent tapas at the bar and fine sit-down meals.

the presidential box, press room, dressing rooms, players' tunnel and even onto the pitch. The tour ends in the extraordinary Exposición de Trofeos (trophy exhibit). Better still, attend a game alongside 80,000 delirious fans.

🛍 Shopping

Our favourite aspect of shopping in Madrid is the city's small boutiques and quirky shops. Often run by the same families for generations, they counter the over commercialisation of mass-produced Spanish culture with everything from fashions to old-style ceramics to rope-soled espadrilles or gourmet Spanish food and wine.

★ El Rastro   MARKET
(Map p1044; Calle de la Ribera de los Curtidores; ⊙ 9am-3pm Sun; M La Latina) A Sunday morning at El Rastro flea market is a Madrid institution. You could easily spend an entire morning inching your way down the hill and the maze of streets. Cheap clothes, luggage, old flamenco records, even older photos of Madrid, faux-designer purses, grungy T-shirts, household goods and electronics are the main fare. For every 10 pieces of junk, there's a real gem (a lost masterpiece, an Underwood typewriter) waiting to be found.

Antigua Casa Talavera   CERAMICS
(Map p1044; ☎ 91 547 34 17; www.antiguacasatalavera.com; Calle de Isabel la Católica 2; ⊙ 10am-1.30pm & 5-8pm Mon-Fri, 10am-1.30pm Sat; M Santo Domingo) The extraordinary tiled facade of this wonderful old shop conceals an Aladdin's cave of ceramics from all over Spain. This is not the mass-produced stuff aimed at a tourist market, but instead comes from the small family potters of Andalucía and Toledo, ranging from the decorative (tiles) to the useful (plates, jugs and other kitchen items). The elderly couple who run the place are delightful.

ℹ Information

SAFE TRAVEL
Madrid is generally safe, but as in any large European city, keep an eye on your belongings and exercise common sense.

➔ El Rastro, around the Museo del Prado and the metro are favourite pickpocketing haunts, as are any areas where tourists congregate in large numbers.

➔ Avoid park areas (such as the Parque del Buen Retiro) after dark.

➔ Keep a close eye on your taxi's meter and try to keep track of the route to make sure you're not being taken for a ride.

TOURIST INFORMATION
The Madrid government's **Centro de Turismo** (Map p1044; ☎ 91 578 78 10; www.esmadrid.com; Plaza Mayor 27; ⊙ 9.30am-9.30pm; M Sol) is terrific. Housed in the Real Casa de la Panadería on the northern side of the Plaza Mayor, it allows access to its outstanding website and city database, and offers free downloads of the metro map to your phone. Staff are also helpful.

ℹ Getting There & Away

AIR
Madrid's **Adolfo Suárez Madrid-Barajas** (☎ 902 404704; www.aena.es; M Aeropuerto T1, T2 & T3, Aeropuerto T4) airport lies 15km northeast of the city, and it's Europe's sixth-busiest hub, with almost 50 million passengers passing through here every year. The airport has four terminals: terminal 4 (T4) deals mainly with flights of Iberia and its partners (eg British Airways, American Airlines and Vueling), while the remainder leave from the conjoined T1, T2 and (rarely) T3.

Direct flights connect the city with destinations across Europe, as well as the Americas, Asia and Africa.

BUS
Estación Sur de Autobuses (☎ 91 468 42 00; Calle de Méndez Álvaro 83; M Méndez Álvaro), just south of the M30 ring road, is the city's principal bus station. It serves most destinations to the south and many in other parts of the country. Most bus companies have a ticket office here, even if their buses depart from elsewhere. Avanzabus has services to Cáceres (€23, four to five hours, seven daily), Salamanca (€21, 2½ to 3½ hours, hourly) and Valencia (€28, 4¼ hours, nine daily). There are also international buses to Lisbon (€42 to €46, seven to 7½ hours, three daily).

TRAIN
All trains are run by **Renfe** (☎ 912 320 320; www.renfe.com). High-speed AVE (Tren de Alta Velocidad Española) services connect Madrid with Alicante, Barcelona, Córdoba, Huesca, León, Málaga, Seville, Valencia, Valladolid, Zaragoza and some towns en route.

North of the city centre, **Estación de Chamartín** (☎ 912 432 343; Paseo de la Castellana; M Chamartín) has numerous long-distance rail services, especially those to/from northern

Spain. This is also where long-haul international trains arrive from Paris and Lisbon.

Madrid's main train station **Puerta de Atocha** (www.renfe.es; Avenida de la Ciudad de Barcelona; Ⓜ Atocha Renfe) is at the southern end of the city centre. The bulk of trains for Spanish destinations depart from Atocha, especially those going south.

ⓘ Getting Around

TO/FROM THE AIRPORT
Bus

The **Exprés Aeropuerto** (Airport Express; www.emtmadrid.es; per person €5; ⊙ 24hr; 🛜) runs between Puerta de Atocha train station and the airport. From 11.55pm to 5.35am, departures are from the Plaza de Cibeles, not the train station. Services depart every 15 to 20 minutes from the station or every 35 minutes during the night from Plaza de Cibeles.

Metro

One of the easiest ways into town from the airport is line 8 of the metro to the Nuevos Ministerios transport interchange, which connects with lines 10 and 6 and the local overground *cercanías* (local trains serving suburbs and nearby towns). It operates from 6.05am to 1.30am. A single ticket costs €4.50 including the €3 airport supplement. If you're charging your public transport card with a 10-ride Metrobús ticket (€12.20), you'll need to top it up with the €3 supplement if you're travelling to/from the airport. The journey to Nuevos Ministerios takes around 15 minutes, around 25 minutes from T4.

Taxi

There is a fixed rate of €30 for taxis from the airport to the city centre (around 30 minutes, depending on traffic; 35 to 40 minutes from T4).

PUBLIC TRANSPORT

Madrid's modern metro (www.metromadrid.es), Europe's second largest, is a fast, efficient and safe way to navigate Madrid, and generally easier than getting to grips with bus routes. There are 11 colour-coded lines in central Madrid, in addition to the modern southern suburban MetroSur system, as well as lines heading east to the population centres of Pozuelo and Boadilla del Monte. Colour maps showing the metro system are available from any metro station or online. The metro operates from 6.05am to 1.30am.

TAXI

You can pick up a taxi at ranks throughout town or simply flag one down. From 7am to 9pm Monday to Friday, flag fall is €2.40 and you pay €1.05 per kilometre. The rest of the time flag fall is €2.90 and the per-kilometre charge is €1.20. Several supplementary charges, usually posted inside the taxi, apply; these include €3 from taxi ranks at train and bus stations.

CASTILLA Y LEÓN

Salamanca

POP 144,436

Whether floodlit by night or bathed in late-afternoon light, there's something magical about Salamanca. This is a city of rare beauty, awash with golden sandstone overlaid with ochre-tinted Latin inscriptions – an extraordinary virtuosity of plateresque and Renaissance styles. The monumental highlights are many and the exceptional Plaza Mayor is unforgettable. This is also Castilla's liveliest city, home to a massive Spanish and international student population that throngs the streets at night and provides the city with so much vitality.

⊙ Sights

★**Plaza Mayor**   SQUARE

Built between 1729 and 1755, Salamanca's grand square is widely considered to be Spain's most beautiful central plaza. The square is particularly memorable at night when illuminated (until midnight) to magical effect. Designed by Alberto Churriguera, it's a remarkably harmonious and controlled baroque display. The medallions placed around the square bear the busts of famous figures.

★**Universidad Civil**   HISTORIC BUILDING

(📞 923 29 44 00, ext 1150; www.salamanca.es; Calle de los Libreros; adult/concession €10/5, audio guide €2; ⊙ 10am-7pm Mon-Sat mid-Sep–Mar, 10am-8pm Mon-Sat, to 2pm Sun Apr–mid-Sep) Founded initially as the Estudio General in 1218, the university reached the peak of its renown in the 15th and 16th centuries. The visual feast of the entrance facade is a tapestry in sandstone, bursting with images of mythical heroes, religious scenes and coats of arms. It's dominated by busts of Fernando and Isabel. Behind the facade, the highlight of an otherwise-modest collection of rooms lies upstairs: the extraordinary **university library**, the oldest in Europe.

SPAIN SALAMANCA

Catedral Nueva
CATHEDRAL

(☑ 923 21 74 76; www.catedralsalamanca.org; Plaza de Anaya; adult/child incl audio guide & Catedral Vieja €5/3; ⊙ 10am-8pm Apr-Sep, 10am-6pm Oct-Mar) The tower of this late-Gothic cathedral lords over the city centre, its compelling Churrigueresque (an ornate style of baroque architecture) dome visible from almost every angle. The interior is similarly impressive, with elaborate choir stalls, main chapel and retrochoir, much of it courtesy of the prolific José Churriguera. The ceilings are also exceptional, along with the Renaissance doorways – particularly the **Puerta del Nacimiento** on the western face, which stands out as one of several miracles worked in the city's native sandstone.

Museo de Art Nouveau y Art Decó
MUSEUM

(Casa Lis; ☑ 923 12 14 25; www.museocasalis. org; Calle de Gibraltar; adult/under 12yr €4/free, 11am-2pm Thu free; ⊙ 11am-8pm Tue-Sun Apr-Oct, plus 11am-8pm Mon Aug, 11am-2pm & 4-8pm Tue-Fri, 11am-8pm Sat & Sun Nov–Mar; ♿) Utterly unlike any other Salamanca museum, this stunning collection of sculpture, paintings and art deco and art nouveau pieces inhabits a beautiful, light-filled Modernista (Catalan art nouveau) house. There's abundant stained glass and exhibits that include Lalique glass, toys by Steiff (inventor of the teddy bear), Limoges porcelain, Fabergé watches, fabulous bronze and marble figurines, and a vast collection of 19th-century children's dolls (some strangely macabre), which kids will love. There's also a cafe and an excellent gift shop.

🛏 Sleeping

Hostal Concejo
HOSTAL €

(☑ 92 087 521; https://hostalconcejo.com; Plaza de la Libertad 1; s €30, d €40-45; P ✱ 🕸) A cut above the average *hostal*, the stylish Concejo has polished-wood floors, tasteful furnishings, light-filled rooms and a superb central location. Try to snag one of the corner rooms, such as No 104, which has a traditional, glassed-in balcony, complete with a table, chairs and people-watching views.

Microtel Placentinos
BOUTIQUE HOTEL €€

(☑ 923 28 15 31; www.microtelplacentinos.com; Calle de Placentinos 9; s/d incl breakfast Sun-Thu €62/75, Fri & Sat €75/90; ✱ 🕸) One of Salamanca's most charming boutique hotels,

Microtel Placentinos is tucked away on a quiet street and has rooms with exposed stone walls and wooden beams. The service is faultless, and the overall atmosphere one of intimacy and discretion. All rooms have a hydromassage shower or tub and there's an outside whirlpool spa (summer only).

★ Don Gregorio
BOUTIQUE HOTEL €€€

(☑ 923 21 70 15; www.hoteldongregorio.com; Calle de San Pablo 80; r/ste incl breakfast from €200/310; P ✱ 🕸) A palatial hotel with part of the city's Roman wall flanking the garden. Rooms are decorated in soothing café-con-leche shades with crisp white linens and extravagant extras, including private saunas, espresso machines, complimentary minibar, king-size beds and vast hydromassage tubs. Sumptuous antiques and medieval tapestries adorn the public areas.

🍴 Eating & Drinking

La Cocina de Toño
TAPAS €€

(☑ 923 26 39 77; www.lacocinadetoño.es; Calle Gran Vía 20; tapas from €2, set menus €17-38, mains €18-23; ⊙ 11am-4.30pm & 8pm-midnight Tue-Sat, 11am-4.30pm Sun; 🕸) This place owes its loyal following to its creative *pinchos* (tapas-like snacks) and half-servings of dishes such as escalope of foie gras with roast apple and passionfruit gelatin. The restaurant serves more traditional fare as befits the decor, but the bar is one of Salamanca's gastronomic stars. Slightly removed from the old city, it draws a predominantly Spanish crowd.

★ Victor Gutierrez
CONTEMPORARY SPANISH €€€

(☑ 923 26 29 73; www.restaurantevictorgutierrez. com; Calle de Empedrada 4; set menus €65-95; ⊙ 1.30-4pm & 8.30pm-midnight Tue-Sat, 1.30-4pm Sun; 🕸) This is still the best table in town. Chef Victor Gutierrez has a Michelin star and his place has a justifiably exclusive vibe, with an emphasis on innovative dishes with plenty of colourful drizzle. The choice of what to order is largely made for you with some excellent set menus that change regularly. Reservations essential.

The Doctor Cocktail
COCKTAIL BAR

(☑ 923 26 31 51; www.facebook.com/thedoctor salamanca; Calle del Doctor Piñuela 5; ⊙ 4pm-late) Excellent cocktails, friendly bar staff and a cool crowd make for a fine mix just north of the Plaza Mayor. Apart from the creative list of cocktails, it has over 30 different kinds of

ÁVILA

Ávila's old city is one of Spain's best-preserved medieval bastions, surrounded by imposing city walls comprising eight monumental gates, 88 watchtowers and more than 2500 turrets. Ávila a deeply religious city that for centuries has drawn pilgrims to the cult of Santa Teresa de Ávila, with its many churches, convents and high-walled palaces. It's 1½ hours from Madrid by train or bus, and about halfway between Segovia and Salamanca.

Murallas (www.muralladeavila.com; adult/under 12yr €5/3.50; ⊙10am-8pm Apr-Jun & Sep-Oct, to 9pm Jul & Aug, to 6pm Tue-Sun Nov-Mar; 🖟) Ávila's splendid 12th-century walls stretch for 2.5km atop the remains of earlier Roman and Muslim battlements and rank among the world's best-preserved medieval defensive perimeters. Two sections of the walls can be climbed – a 300m stretch that can be accessed from just inside the Puerta del Alcázar, and a longer (1300m) stretch from Puerta de los Leales that runs the length of the old city's northern perimeter. The admission price includes a multilingual audio guide.

Catedral del Salvador (🖉920 21 16 41; Plaza de la Catedral; incl audio guide €6; ⊙10am-8pm Mon-Fri, to 9pm Sat, 11.45am-7.30pm Sun Apr-Jun, Sep & Oct, 10am-9pm Mon-Sat, 11.45am-9pm Sun Jul & Aug, 10am-6pm Mon-Fri, to 7pm Sat, to 5.30pm Sun Nov-Mar) Ávila's 12th-century cathedral is both a house of worship and an ingenious fortress: its stout granite apse forms the central bulwark in the historic city walls. The sombre, Gothic-style facade conceals a magnificent interior with an exquisite early-16th-century altar frieze showing the life of Jesus, plus Renaissance-era carved choir stalls. There is also a museum with an El Greco painting and a splendid silver monstrance by Juan de Arfe. (Push the buttons to illuminate the altar and the choir stalls.)

Hotel El Rastro (🖉920 35 22 25; www.elrastroavila.com; Calle Cepedas; s/d €45/90; ✺🛜) This atmospheric hotel occupies a former 16th-century palace with original stone, exposed brickwork and a natural, earth-toned colour scheme exuding a calm, understated elegance. Each room has a different form, but most have high ceilings and plenty of space. Note that the owners also run a marginally cheaper *hostal* (budget hotel) of the same name around the corner.

gin to choose from and above-average tonic to go with it.

❶ Information

Oficina de Turismo (🖉923 21 83 42; www.salamanca.es; Plaza Mayor 32; ⊙9am-7pm Mon-Fri, 10am-7pm Sat, to 2pm Sun) The municipal tourist office shares its space with the regional office on Plaza Mayor. An audio guide to city sights can be accessed on your smartphone via www.audioguiasalamanca.es.

❶ Getting There & Away

The bus and train stations are a 10- and 15-minute walk, respectively, from Plaza Mayor.

There are buses to Madrid (regular/express €15/24, 2½ to 3¼ hours, hourly) and Ávila (€7, 1½ hours, four daily).

Trains run to Madrid's Chamartín station (from €20, 1½ to 4½ hours, 13 daily), Ávila (€12.25, 1¼ hours, eight daily) and Valladolid (from €10.45, 1½ hours, eight daily).

Segovia

POP 51,756

Set amid the rolling hills of Castilla, Unesco World Heritage–listed Segovia is a city of warm terracotta and sandstone hues, with a stunning monument to Roman grandeur and a castle said to have inspired Walt Disney.

❍ Sights

★**Acueducto**   LANDMARK

Segovia's most recognisable symbol is El Acueducto (Roman Aqueduct), an 894m-long engineering wonder that looks like an enormous comb plunged into Segovia. First raised here by the Romans in the 1st century CE, the aqueduct was built with not a drop of mortar to hold together more than 20,000 uneven granite blocks. It's made up of 163 arches and, at its highest point in Plaza del Azoguejo, rises 28m high.

★ **Alcázar** CASTLE

(☑921 46 07 59; www.alcazardesegovia.com; Plaza de la Reina Victoria Eugenia; adult/concession/under 6yr €8/5.50/free, tower €2.50, audio guide €3; ⊙10am-6pm Nov-Mar, to 8pm Apr-Oct; ▣) Rapunzel towers, turrets topped with slate witches' hats and a deep moat at its base make the Alcázar a prototypical fairy-tale castle – so much so that its design inspired Walt Disney's vision of Snow White's castle. Fortified since Roman days, the site takes its name from the Arabic *al-qasr* (fortress). It was rebuilt in the 13th and 14th centuries, but the whole lot burned down in 1862. What you see today is an evocative, over-the-top reconstruction of the original.

Catedral CATHEDRAL

(☑921 46 22 05; www.turismodesegovia.com; Plaza Mayor; adult/concession €3/2.50, Sun morning free, tower tour €5; ⊙9am-9.30pm Apr-Oct, 9.30am-6.30pm Nov-Mar, tower tours 10.30pm, noon, 1.30pm & 4pm year-round) Started in 1525 on the site of a former chapel, Segovia's cathedral is a powerful expression of Gothic architecture that took almost 200 years to complete. The austere three-nave interior is anchored by an imposing choir stall and enlivened by 20-odd chapels, including the Capilla del Cristo del Consuelo, with its magnificent Romanesque doorway, and the Capilla de la Piedad, containing an important altarpiece by Juan de Juni. Join an hour-long guided tour to climb the tower for fabulous views.

🛏 Sleeping & Eating

Häb Urban Hostel HOSTAL €

(☑921 46 10 26; www.habhostel.com; Calle de Cervantes 16; r €60-90; ▣ ⚙) This bright and welcoming *hostal* has doubles with private bathrooms rather than dorms with bunk beds, despite the name. It's modern and has a fine location just where the pedestrian street begins the climb up into the old town. Some rooms are on the small side, but the look is light and contemporary.

★ **Hotel Palacio San Facundo** HISTORIC HOTEL €€

(☑921 46 30 61; www.hotelpalaciosanfacundo.com; Plaza San Facundo 4; s/d incl breakfast €95/145; ▣ @ ⚙) Segovia's hotels are proving adept at fusing stylishly appointed modern rooms with centuries-old architecture. This place is one of the best, with an attractive columned courtyard, a warm colour scheme, chic room decor and a central location. The breakfast buffet is more generous than most.

★ **Restaurante El Fogón Sefardí** JEWISH €€

(☑921 46 62 50; www.lacasamudejar.com; Calle de Isabel la Católica 8; tapas from €3.75, mains €12-26, set menus €20-35; ⊙1.30-4.30pm & 8.30-11.30pm) Located within the Hospedería La Gran Casa Mudéjar, this is one of the most original places in town. Sephardic Jewish cuisine is served either on the intimate patio or in the splendid dining hall with original 15th-century Mudéjar flourishes. The theme in the bar is equally diverse. Stop here for a taste of the award-winning tapas. Reservations recommended.

★ **Casa Duque** SPANISH €€€

(☑921 46 24 87; www.restauranteduque.es; Calle de Cervantes 12; mains €19.50-24, set menus €35-40; ⊙12.30-4.30pm & 8.30-11.30pm) *Cochinillo asado* (roast suckling pig) has been served at this atmospheric *mesón* (tavern) since the 1890s. For the uninitiated, try the *menú de degustación,* which includes *cochinillo*. Downstairs is the informal *cueva* (cave), where you can get tapas (snacks) and full-bodied *cazuelas* (stews). Reservations recommended.

ℹ Information

Centro de Recepción de Visitantes (☑921 46 67 21; www.turismodesegovia.com; Plaza del Azoguejo 1; ⊙10am-8pm Mon-Sat, to 7pm Sun Apr-Sep, 10am-6.30pm Mon-Sat, to 5pm Sun Oct-Mar) Segovia's main tourist office runs at least two guided tours of the city's monumental core daily (€10 to €17 per person), usually departing at 11am and 4pm (although check as this schedule can change). Reserve ahead.

Oficina de Turismo (☑921 46 03 34; www.segoviaturismo.es; Plaza Mayor 10; ⊙9.30am-2pm & 5-8pm Mon-Sat, 9.30am-5pm Sun Jul–mid-Sep, 9.30am-2pm & 4-7pm Mon-Sat, 9.30am-5pm Sun mid-Sep–Jun) On Plaza Mayor, with information on the wider region.

ℹ Getting There & Away

BUS

The bus station is just off Paseo de Ezequiel González. **La Sepulvedana** (☑902 11 96 99; www.lasepulvedana.es) buses run from Segovia to Madrid's Intercambiador de Moncloa (€4, one to 1½ hours, every 15 minutes). Buses also head to Ávila (€4.80, one hour, four daily) and Salamanca (€5.30, 3½ hours, two daily), among other destinations.

BURGOS & LEÓN: A TALE OF TWO CATHEDRALS

Burgos and León are cathedral towns par excellence, and both are well connected by train and bus to Madrid.

Burgos

Catedral (☏947 20 47 12; www.catedraldeburgos.es; Plaza del Rey Fernando; adult/under 14yr incl audio guide €7/2, from 4.30pm Tue free; ⊙9.30am-7.30pm mid-Mar–Oct, 10am-7pm Nov–mid-Mar) This Unesco World Heritage–listed cathedral, once a former modest Romanesque church, is a masterpiece. Work began on a grander scale in 1221; remarkably, within 40 years most of the French Gothic structure had been completed. You can enter from Plaza de Santa María for free for access to the Capilla del Santísimo Cristo, with its much-revered 13th-century crucifix, and the Capilla de Santa Tecla, with its extraordinary ceiling. However, we recommend that you visit the cathedral in its entirety.

Rimbombín (☏947 26 12 00; www.rimbombin.com; Calle Sombrería 6; d/tr/apt from €35/52/70; 🖳🛜) Opened in 2013, this 'urban *hostal*' has an upbeat, contemporary feel – its slick white furnishings and decor are matched with light-pine beams and modular furniture. Three of the rooms have balconies overlooking the pedestrian street. Conveniently, it's in the heart of Burgos' compact tapas district. The apartment is excellent value for longer stays, with the same chic modern look and two bedrooms.

Cervecería Morito (☏947 26 75 55; Calle de Diego Porcelos 1; tapas/raciones from €4/6; ⊙12.30-3.30pm & 7-11.30pm) Cervecería Morito is the undisputed king of Burgos tapas bars and as such it's always crowded. A typical order is *alpargata* (lashings of cured ham with bread, tomato and olive oil) or the *revueltos Capricho de Burgos* (scrambled eggs served with potatoes, blood sausage, red peppers, baby eels and mushrooms) – the latter is a meal in itself.

León

Catedral (☏987 87 57 70; www.catedraldeleon.org; Plaza Regia; adult/concession/under 12yr €6/5/free, combined ticket with Claustro & Museo Catedralicio-Diocesano €9/8/free; ⊙9.30am-1.30pm & 4-8pm Mon-Fri, 9.30am-noon & 2-6pm Sat, 9.30-11am & 2-8pm Sun May-Sep, 9.30am-1.30pm & 4-7pm Mon-Sat, 9.30am-2pm Sun Oct-Apr) León's 13th-century cathedral, with its soaring towers, flying buttresses and breathtaking interior, is the city's spiritual heart. Whether spotlit by night or bathed in glorious northern sunshine, the cathedral, arguably Spain's premier Gothic masterpiece, exudes a glorious, almost luminous quality. The show-stopping facade has a radiant rose window, three richly sculpted doorways and two muscular towers. The main entrance is lorded over by a scene of the Last Supper, while an extraordinary gallery of *vidrieras* (stained-glass windows) awaits you inside.

Panteón Real (www.turismoleon.org; Plaza de San Isidoro; adult/child €5/free; ⊙10am-2pm & 4-7pm Mon-Sat, 10am-2pm Sun) Attached to the **Real Basílica de San Isidoro** (☏987 87 61 61; ⊙7.30am-11pm), the stunning Panteón Real houses royal sarcophagi, which rest with quiet dignity beneath a canopy of some of the finest Romanesque frescos in Spain. Colourful motifs of biblical scenes drench the vaults and arches of this extraordinary hall, held aloft by marble columns with intricately carved capitals. The pantheon also houses a small **museum** where you can admire the shrine of San Isidoro, a mummified finger(!) of the saint and other treasures.

La Posada Regia (☏987 21 31 73; www.regialeon.com; Calle de Regidores 9-11; s €55-70, d €60-130; 🛜) This place has the feel of a *casa rural* (village or farmstead accommodation) despite being in the city centre. The secret is a 14th-century building, magnificently restored (with wooden beams, exposed brick and understated antique furniture), with individually styled rooms and supremely comfortable beds and bathrooms. As with anywhere in the Barrio Húmedo, weekend nights can be noisy.

TRAIN

There are a couple of services by train operated by **Renfe** (☎912 32 03 20; www.renfe.es): just three normal trains run daily from Madrid to Segovia (€8.25, two hours), leaving you at the main train station 2.5km from the aqueduct. The faster option is the high-speed Avant (€12.90, 28 minutes), which deposits you at the newer Segovia-Guiomar station, 5km from the aqueduct.

CASTILLA-LA MANCHA

Toledo

POP 83,741

Toledo is truly one of Spain's most magnificent cities. Dramatically sited atop a gorge overlooking the Río Tajo, it was known as the 'city of three cultures' in the Middle Ages, a place where – legend has it – Christian, Muslim and Jewish communities peacefully coexisted. Unsurprisingly, rediscovering the vestiges of this unique cultural synthesis remains modern Toledo's most compelling attraction. Horseshoe-arched mosques, Sephardic synagogues and one of Spain's finest Gothic cathedrals cram into its dense historical core. But the layers go much deeper. Further sleuthing will reveal Visigothic and Roman roots. Toledo's other forte is art, in particular the haunting canvases of El Greco, the influential, impossible-to-classify painter with whom the city is synonymous. Justifiably popular with day trippers, try to stay overnight to really appreciate the city in all its haunting glory.

⊙ Sights

★**Catedral de Toledo** CATHEDRAL
(☎925 22 22 41; www.catedralprimada.es; Plaza del Ayuntamiento; incl Museo de Textiles y Orfebrería adult/child €12.50/free; ⊙10am-6.30pm Mon-Sat, 2-6.30pm Sun) Toledo's illustrious main church ranks among the top 10 cathedrals in Spain. An impressive example of medieval Gothic architecture, its enormous interior is full of the classic characteristics of the style, rose windows, flying buttresses, ribbed vaults and pointed arches among them. The cathedral's sacristy is a veritable art gallery of old masters, with works by Velázquez, Goya and – of course – El Greco.

★**Alcázar** FORTRESS
(Museo del Ejército; ☎925 23 88 00; Calle Alféreces Provisionales; adult/child €5/free, Sun free;

⊙10am-5pm Thu-Tue) At the highest point in the city looms the foreboding Alcázar. Rebuilt under Franco, it has been reopened as a vast military museum. The usual displays of uniforms and medals are here, but the best part is the exhaustive historical section, with an in-depth examination of the nation's history in Spanish and English. The exhibition is epic in scale, but like a well-run marathon it's worth the physical (and mental) investment.

★**Sinagoga del Tránsito** SYNAGOGUE, MUSEUM
(☎925 22 36 65; www.culturaydeporte.gob.es; Calle Samuel Leví; adult/child €3/1.50, after 2pm Sat & all day Sun free; ⊙9.30am-7.30pm Tue-Sat Mar-Oct, to 6pm Tue-Sat Nov-Feb, 10am-3pm Sun year-round) This magnificent synagogue was built in 1355 by special permission from Pedro I. The synagogue now houses the **Museo Sefardí** (http://museosefardi.mcu.es; ⊙9.30am-6pm Mon-Sat, 10am-3pm Sun). The vast main prayer hall has been expertly restored and the Mudéjar decoration and intricately carved pine ceiling are striking. Exhibits provide an insight into the history of Jewish culture in Spain, and include archaeological finds, a memorial garden, costumes and ceremonial artefacts.

🛏 Sleeping & Eating

La Posada de Manolo BOUTIQUE HOTEL €€
(☎925 28 22 50; www.laposadademanolo.com; Calle de Sixto Ramón Parro 8; r €75-90; ❋🛜) This memorable hotel has themed each floor with furnishings and decor reflecting one of the three cultures of Toledo: Christian, Islamic and Jewish. Rooms vary in size and cost, depending on whether they are interior or exterior, and some have balconies. There are stunning views of the old town and cathedral from the terrace, where breakfast is served, weather permitting.

★**Hacienda del Cardenal** HISTORIC HOTEL €€
(☎925 22 49 00; www.haciendadelcardenal.com; Paseo de Recaredo 24; r incl breakfast €90-135; ❋🛜♿) This wonderful 18th-century former cardinal's mansion has pale ochre-coloured walls, Moorish-inspired arches and stately columns. Some rooms are grand and others are more simply furnished, but all come with dark furniture, plush fabrics and parquet floors.

Several overlook the glorious terraced gardens. Underground parking is available nearby (€15 per day).

★**Alfileritos 24**   MODERN SPANISH €€

(☑925 23 96 25; www.alfileritos24.com; Calle de los Alfileritos 24; mains €18-21, bar food €5-12; ☺1.30-4pm & 8-11.30pm) The 14th-century surroundings of columns, beams and barrel-vault ceilings are cleverly coupled with modern artwork and bright dining rooms in an atrium space spread over four floors. The menu demonstrates an innovative flourish in the kitchen, with dishes such as green rice with quail or loin of venison with baked-in-the-bag *reineta* (pippin) apple.

★**Adolfo**   MODERN EUROPEAN €€€

(☑925 22 73 21; www.adolforestaurante.com; Callejón Hombre de Palo 7; mains €25-28, set menu €76; ☺1-4pm & 8pm-midnight Mon-Sat) Toledo doffs its hat to fine dining at this temple of good food and market freshness. Run by notable La Mancha–born chef Adolfo Muñoz, the restaurant has been around for over 25 years, and in that time has morphed into one of Spain's best gourmet establishments. Partridge is the speciality.

❶ Information

Located virtually across from the cathedral, the **main tourist office** (☑925 25 40 30; www.toledo-turismo.com; Plaza Consistorio 1; ☺10am-6pm) could not be more central. There's an excellent free map and plenty of 'what's on' type of information.

❶ Getting There & Away

To get to most major destinations, you'll need to backtrack to Madrid.

Buses run from Madrid's Plaza Elíptica to Toledo's **bus station** (☑925 21 58 50; www.alsa.es; Bajada Castilla La Mancha), and back, roughly every half-hour (€5.40, 45 minutes to 1½ hours); some go direct, some via villages.

High-speed trains run from Madrid's Puerta de Atocha station (one way/return €13/21, 33 minutes, hourly) to Toledo's pretty **train station** (☑902 240202; www.renfe.es; Paseo de la Rosa).

CATALONIA

Barcelona

POP 1.62 MILLION

Barcelona is one of Europe's coolest cities. Despite two millennia of history, it's a forward-thinking place, always at the cutting edge of art, design and cuisine. Whether you explore its medieval palaces and plazas,

admire the Modernista masterpieces of Antoni Gaudí and others, shop for designer fashions along its bustling boulevards, sample its exciting nightlife or just soak up the sun on the beaches, you'll find it hard not to fall in love with this vibrant city.

As much as Barcelona is a visual feast, it will also lead you into culinary temptation. Anything from traditional Catalan cooking to the latest in avant-garde new Spanish cuisine will have your appetite in overdrive.

⊙ Sights & Activities

⊙ La Rambla & El Raval

★**La Rambla**   STREET

(Map p1060; Ⓜ Catalunya, Liceu, Drassanes) Barcelona's most famous street is both a tourist magnet and a window into Catalan culture, with cultural centres, theatres and intriguing architecture. Flanked by plane trees, the middle section of La Rambla is a broad pedestrian boulevard, crowded every day until the wee hours with a wide cross-section of society. Horrific terrorist attacks in 2017 did little to diminish its popularity either with the tourists or with the hawkers, pavement artists and handful of living statues.

★**Mercat de la Boqueria**   MARKET

(Map p1060; ☑93 318 20 17; www.boqueria.barcelona; La Rambla 91; ☺8am-8.30pm Mon-Sat; Ⓜ Liceu) Mercat de la Boqueria is possibly La Rambla's most interesting building, not so much for its Modernista-influenced design – it was actually built over a long period, from 1840 to 1914, on the site of the former St Joseph Monastery – but for the action of the food market within.

Gran Teatre del Liceu   ARCHITECTURE

(Map p1060; ☑93 485 99 14; www.liceubarcelona.cat; La Rambla 51-59; tours adult/concession/under 7yr 30min €6/5/free, 45min €9/7.50/free; ☺30min tours 1pm Mon-Sat, 45min tours hourly 2-5pm Mon-Fri, from 11am Sat; Ⓜ Liceu) If you can't catch a night at the opera, you can still have a look around one of Europe's greatest opera houses, known to locals as the Liceu. Smaller than Milan's La Scala but bigger than Venice's La Fenice, it can seat up to 2300 people in its grand auditorium.

⊙ Barri Gòtic

You could easily spend several days or even a week exploring the medieval streets of the

SPAIN BARCELONA

Barcelona

0 0.5 miles
0 1 km

1 Casa Batlló

3 La Pedrera

4 La Sagrada Família

G1 EL CLOT

Gran Via de les Corts Catalanes

SANT MARTÍ

CAMP DE L'ARPA

LA DRETA DE L'EIXAMPLE

SAGRADA FAMÍLIA

EL GUINARDÓ

L'EIXAMPLE

EL FORT PIENC

Estació del Nord

Arc de Triomf

Monumental

Av Meridiana

Plaça de les Glòries Catalanes

Plaça de les Arts

SANT GERVASI DE CASSOLES

GRÀCIA

EL CARMEL

Park Güell (200m)

Plaça de la Torre

Plaça de Lesseps

Av de l'Hospital Militar

Via Augusta

Av Diagonal

Hospital Clínic

Plaça de Joan Carles I

Plaça de Gràcia

Passeig de Gràcia

Plaça de Tetuan

Plaça de Raspall

Plaça de Joanic

Camp Nou (2km)

La Bonanova

Av Tibidabo

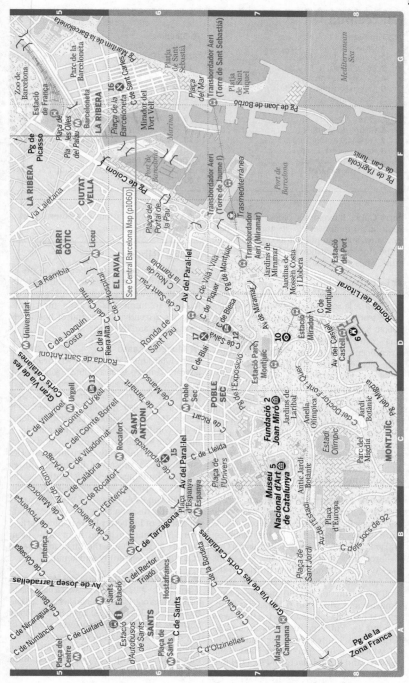

SPAIN BARCELONA

Barcelona

Barri Gòtic, Barcelona's oldest quarter. In addition to major sights, its tangle of narrow lanes and tranquil plazas conceals some of the city's most atmospheric shops, restaurants, cafes and bars.

★**La Catedral** CATHEDRAL
(Map p1060; ☑93 342 82 62; www.catedralbcn. org; Plaça de la Seu; donation €7 or choir €3, roof €3; ☺tourist visits 12.30-7.45pm Mon-Fri, 12.30-5.30pm Sat, 2-5.30pm Sun; Ⓜ Jaume I) Barcelona's central place of worship presents a magnificent image. The richly decorated main facade, dotted with gargoyles and the kinds of stone intricacies you would expect of northern European Gothic, sets it quite apart from other churches in Barcelona. The facade was actually added in 1870, although the rest of the building was built between 1298 and 1460. Its other facades are sparse in decoration, and the octagonal, flat-roofed towers are a clear reminder that, even here, Catalan Gothic architectural principles prevailed.

★**Museu d'Història de Barcelona** MUSEUM
(MUHBA; Map p1060; ☑93 256 21 00; www.museu historia.bcn.cat; Plaça del Rei; adult/concession/child €7/5/free, 3-8pm Sun & 1st Sun of month free; ☺10am-7pm Tue-Sat, to 8pm Sun; Ⓜ Jaume I) One of Barcelona's most fascinating museums takes you back through the centuries to the very foundations of Roman Barcino. You'll stroll over ruins of the old streets, sewers, laundries and wine- and fish-making factories that flourished here following the town's founding by Emperor Augustus around 10 BCE. Equally impressive is the building itself, which was once part of the Palau Reial Major (Grand Royal Palace) on Plaça del Rei,

among the key locations of medieval princely power in Barcelona.

◎ **La Ribera**

In medieval days, La Ribera was a stone's throw from the Mediterranean and the heart of Barcelona's foreign trade, with homes belonging to numerous wealthy merchants. Now it's a trendy district full of boutiques, restaurants and lively bars.

★**Museu Picasso** MUSEUM
(Map p1060; ☑93 256 30 00; www.museupicasso. bcn.cat; Carrer de Montcada 15-23; adult/concession/under 16yr permanent collection & temporary exhibit €14/7.50/free, 6-9.30pm Thu & 1st Sun of month free; ☺9am-7pm Tue, Wed & Fri-Sun, to 9.30pm Thu; 🛜; Ⓜ Jaume I) The setting alone, in five contiguous medieval stone mansions, makes the Museu Picasso unique (and worth the queues). The pretty courtyards, galleries and staircases preserved in the first three of these buildings are as delightful as the collection inside. While the collection concentrates on Pablo Picasso's formative years – potentially disappointing for those hoping for a feast of his better-known later works – there is enough material from subsequent periods to give you a thorough impression of the artist's versatility and genius.

★**Basílica de Santa Maria del Mar** CHURCH
(Map p1060; ☑93 310 23 90; www.santamariadel marbarcelona.org; Plaça de Santa Maria; guided tour €10; ☺9am-8.30pm Mon-Sat, 10am-8pm Sun, tours 1-5pm; Ⓜ Jaume I) At the southwestern end of Passeig del Born stands the apse of Barcelona's finest Catalan Gothic church, Santa Maria del Mar (Our Lady of the Sea). Built in the 14th century with record-breaking

alacrity for the time (it took just 54 years), the church is remarkable for its architectural harmony and simplicity.

⭐**Palau de la Música Catalana** ARCHITECTURE

(Map p1060; ☑ 93 295 72 00; www.palaumusica. cat; Carrer de Palau de la Música 4-6; adult/concession/under 10yr €20/11/free; ⊘ guided tours 10am-3.30pm Sep-Jun, to 6pm Easter & Jul, 9am-6pm Aug; Ⓜ Urquinaona) This concert hall is a high point of Barcelona's Modernista architecture, a symphony in tile, brick, sculpted stone and stained glass. Built by Domènech i Montaner between 1905 and 1908 for the Orfeo Català musical society, it was conceived as a temple for the Catalan Renaixença (Renaissance).

Parc de la Ciutadella PARK

(Map p1056; Passeig de Picasso; ⊘ 10am-10.30pm; ⛲; Ⓜ Arc de Triomf) Parc de la Ciutadella is perfect for winding down. Come for a stroll, a picnic, a boat ride on the lake or to inspect Catalonia's parliament in what is the most central green lung in the city.

◉ L'Eixample

Modernisme, the Catalan version of art nouveau, transformed Barcelona's cityscape in the early 20th century. Most Modernista works, including Antoni Gaudí's unfinished masterpiece, La Sagrada Família, were built in the elegant, if traffic-filled, L'Eixample (pronounced 'lay-sham-pluh'), a grid-plan district that was developed from the 1870s on.

⭐**La Sagrada Família** CHURCH

(Map p1056; ☑ 93 208 04 14; www.sagradafamilia. org; Carrer de la Marina; adult/child €15/free; ⊘ 9am-8pm Apr-Sep, to 7pm Mar & Oct, to 6pm Nov-Feb; Ⓜ Sagrada Família) If you have time for only one sightseeing outing, this should be it. La Sagrada Família inspires awe by its sheer verticality, and in the manner of the medieval cathedrals it emulates, it's still under construction. Work began in 1882 and is hoped (perhaps optimistically) to be completed in 2026, a century after the architect's death. Unfinished it may be, but it attracts more than 4.5 million visitors a year and is the most visited monument in Spain.

⭐**La Pedrera** ARCHITECTURE

(Casa Milà; Map p1056; ☑ 93 214 25 76; www. lapedrera.com; Passeig de Gràcia 92; adult/child €25/14; ⊘ 9am-8.30pm & 9-11pm Mar-Oct, 9am-6.30pm & 7-9pm Nov-Feb; Ⓜ Diagonal) This madcap Gaudí masterpiece was built in 1905–10 as a combined apartment and office block. Formally called Casa Milà, after the businessman who commissioned it, it is better known as La Pedrera (the Quarry) because of

SPAIN BARCELONA

DON'T MISS

LA SAGRADA FAMÍLIA HIGHLIGHTS

Roof The roof of La Sagrada Família is held up by a forest of extraordinary angled pillars. As the pillars soar towards the ceiling, they sprout a web of supporting branches, creating the effect of a forest canopy.

Nativity Facade The artistic pinnacle of the building. You can climb high up inside some of the four towers by a combination of lifts and narrow spiral staircases – a vertiginous experience.

Passion Facade The southwestern Passion Facade, on the theme of Christ's last days and death, was built between 1954 and 1978 based on surviving drawings by Gaudí, with four towers and a large, sculpture-bedecked portal by Josep Subirachs.

Glory Facade The Glory Facade is under construction and will, like the others, be crowned by four towers – the total of 12 representing the Twelve Apostles.

Museu Gaudí The Museu Gaudí, below ground level, includes interesting material on Gaudí's life and other works, as well as models and photos of La Sagrada Família.

Exploring La Sagrada Família Booking tickets online avoids what can be very lengthy queues. Although the church is essentially a building site, the completed sections and museum may be explored at leisure. Fifty-minute guided tours (€24) are offered. Alternatively, pick up an audio guide, for which you need ID. Enter from Carrer de Sardenya or Carrer de la Marina. Once inside, €14 (which includes the audio guide) will get you into lifts that rise up inside towers in the Nativity and Passion facades.

Central Barcelona

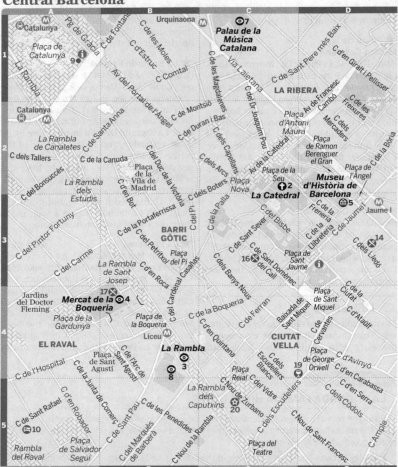

its uneven grey stone facade, which ripples around the corner of Carrer de Provença.

★ Casa Batlló ARCHITECTURE

(Map p1056; ☎93 216 03 06; www.casabatllo.es; Passeig de Gràcia 43; adult/child €28.50/25.50; ◎9am-9pm, last admission 8pm; ⊠Passeig de Gràcia) One of the strangest residential buildings in Europe, this is Gaudí at his hallucinatory best. The facade, sprinkled with bits of blue, mauve and green tiles and studded with wave-shaped window frames and balconies, rises to an uneven blue-tiled roof with a solitary tower.

Fundació Antoni Tàpies GALLERY

(Map p1056; ☎93 487 03 15; www.fundaciotapies. org; Carrer d'Aragó 255; adult/child €7/5.60; ◎10am-7pm Tue-Thu & Sat, to 9pm Fri, to 3pm Sun; ⊠Passeig de Gràcia) The Fundació Antoni Tàpies is both a pioneering Modernista building (completed in 1885) and the major collection of leading 20th-century Catalan artist Antoni Tàpies. Tàpies died in February 2012, aged 88; known for his esoteric work, he left behind a powerful range of paintings and a foundation intended to promote contemporary artists. Admission includes an audio guide.

mission fee). The rest of the park is free and can be visited without booking.

◎ Montjuïc

Southwest of the city centre, the hillside overlooking the port has some of the city's finest art collections, and also serves as a Central Park of sorts, and is a great place for a jog or stroll. The closest metro stops are Espanya, Poble Sec and Paral·lel. From Paral·lel a funicular railway runs up to Estació Parc Montjuïc, from where a cable car, the **Telefèric de Montjuïc** (Map p1056; ☑93 328 90 03; www.telefericdemontjuic. cat; Avinguda de Miramar 30; adult/child one way €8.40/6.60; ◎10am-9pm Jun-Sep, to 7pm Mar-May & Oct, to 6pm Nov-Feb; ☑55, 150), climbs to the Castell de Montjuïc. Bus 150 loops from Plaça d'Espanya to Castell de Montjuïc.

★**Park Güell** PARK
(☑93 409 18 31; www.parkguell.cat; Carrer d'Olot 7; adult/child €8.50/6; ◎8am-9.30pm May-Aug, to 8.30pm Apr, Sep & Oct, to 6.15pm Nov–mid-Feb, to 7pm mid-Feb–Mar; ☑24, 92, Ⓜ Lesseps, Vallcarca) North of Gràcia, Unesco-listed Park Güell is where architect Antoni Gaudí turned his hand to landscape gardening. It's a strange, enchanting place where his passion for natural forms really took flight and the artificial almost seems more natural than the natural.

The park is extremely popular, and access to the central area is limited to a certain number of people every half-hour – book ahead online (and you'll also save on the ad-

★ **Museu Nacional**
d'Art de Catalunya   MUSEUM
(MNAC; Map p1056; ☑ 936 22 03 76; www.museu
nacional.cat; Mirador del Palau Nacional; adult/child
€12/free, after 3pm Sat & 1st Sun of month free,
rooftop viewpoint only €2; ☉ 10am-8pm Tue-Sat,
to 3pm Sun May-Sep, to 6pm Tue-Sat, to 3pm Sun
Oct-Apr; ☜; ☐ 55, Ⓜ Espanya) From across the
city, the bombastic neobaroque silhouette
of the Palau Nacional can be seen on the
slopes of Montjuïc. Built for the 1929 World
Exhibition and restored in 2005, it houses a
vast collection of mostly Catalan art, spanning the early Middle Ages to the early 20th
century. The high point is the collection of
extraordinary Romanesque frescoes.

★ **Fundació Joan Miró**   MUSEUM
(Map p1056; ☑ 93 443 94 70; www.fmirobcn.org;
Parc de Montjuïc; adult/child €12/free; ☉ 10am-
8pm Tue, Wed, Fri & Sat, to 9pm Thu, to 3pm Sun
Apr-Oct, 10am-6pm Tue, Wed & Fri, to 9pm Thu,
to 8pm Sat, to 3pm Sun Nov-Mar; ☜; ☐ 55, 150,
☐ Paral·lel) Joan Miró, the city's best-known
20th-century artistic progeny, bequeathed
this art foundation to his home town in
1971. Its light-filled buildings, designed by
close friend and architect Josep Lluís Sert
(who also built Miró's Mallorca studios), are
crammed with seminal works, from Miró's
earliest timid sketches to paintings from his
last years.

Castell de Montjuïc   FORTRESS
(Map p1056; ☑ 93 256 44 40; http://ajuntament.
barcelona.cat/castelldemontjuic;   Carretera de
Montjuïc 66; adult/child €5/3, after 3pm Sun & all
day 1st Sun of month free; ☉ 10am-8pm Mar-Oct, to
6pm Nov-Feb; ☐ 150, ☐ Telefèric de Montjuïc, Castell de Montjuïc) This forbidding *castell* (castle
or fort) dominates the southeastern heights
of Montjuïc and enjoys commanding views
over the Mediterranean. It dates, in its present form, from the late 17th and 18th centuries. For most of its dark history, it has been
used to watch over the city and as a political
prison and killing ground.

◉ **La Barceloneta & the**
Waterfront

Since the late 20th century, Barcelona's formerly industrial waterfront has experienced
a dramatic transformation, and now boasts
sparkling beaches and seaside bars and restaurants, elegant sculptures, a 4.5km-long
boardwalk, ultramodern high-rises and
yacht-filled marinas. The gateway to the Med-

iterranean is the gridlike neighbourhood of
Barceloneta, an old-fashioned fishing quarter
full of traditional seafood restaurants, while
to the northeast, post-industrial El Poblenou
is worth a visit for its inviting roster of bars
and places to eat.

⚜ **Festivals & Events**

Festes de Santa Eulàlia   CULTURAL
(http://lameva.barcelona.cat/santaeulalia; ☉ Feb)
Around 12 February this big winter fest celebrates Barcelona's first patron saint with a
week of cultural events, including parades
of *gegants* (giants), theatre, *correfocs* (fire
runs) and *castells* (human castles). It's held
in conjunction with Llum BCN (which takes
place a few days later), during which light
installations are set up across the city.

Festes de la Mercè   CULTURAL
(www.bcn.cat/merce; ☉ Sep) The city's biggest
party involves four days of concerts, dancing and street theatre held in various locations across town. There are also *castells*
(human castles), a fireworks display synchronised with the Montjuïc fountains, a
parade of giants, and *correfocs* – a parade
of fireworks-spitting monsters and demons
who run with the crowd. Held around 24
September.

🛏 **Sleeping**

Accommodation in Barcelona is more expensive than anywhere else in Spain except
Madrid. La Rambla, the Barri Gòtic and El
Raval can be noisy but are close to the action with a big selection of boxy hotels, glorious boutique options, hostels and fleapits.
You'll find a few attractive boutique-style
guesthouses and hostels in Poble Sec and
up-and-coming Sant Antoni. L'Eixample has
the greatest range of hotels in most classes,
including some classic hotels and a long list
of decent midrange places, though some are
a bit far from the old city.

🛏 **El Raval**

★ **Barceló Raval**   DESIGN HOTEL €€
(Map p1060; ☑ 93 320 14 90; www.barceloraval.
com; Rambla del Raval 17-21; r from €185; ❋ ☜;
Ⓜ Liceu) Part of the city's plans to pull the
El Raval district up by the bootstraps, this
cylindrical designer hotel tower makes a
21st-century splash. The rooftop terrace
offers fabulous views and the B-Lounge
bar-restaurant is a lively joint for meals and

cocktails. Rooms have slick aesthetics (white with lime green or ruby red splashes of colour), coffee machines and iPod docks.

Barri Gòtic

Serras Hotel   BOUTIQUE HOTEL €€€
(Map p1060; ☎ 93 169 18 68; www.hoteltheserras barcelona.com; Passeig de Colom 9; r from €250; ❄ ☜ ⚞; M Barceloneta) This fresh five-star has every comfort – including a rooftop bar with a small dipping pool and a terrific view over the port – but never feels stuffy. Rooms at the front are brighter and have a better view (from the bathtub, in some cases), but rooms at the side are spared the traffic noise.

Poble Sec & Sant Antoni

Pars Tailor's Hostel   HOSTEL €
(Map p1056; ☎ 93 250 56 84; www.parshostels. com; Carrer de Sepúlveda 146; dm €25-30; ❄ ☜; M Urgell) Decorated like a mid-20th-century tailor's shop, with rooms themed around different fabrics, this popular hostel's common areas have old sewing machines, lovingly framed brassieres and vintage fixtures. You can shoot a round on the old billiard table, hang out in the comfy lounge, cook a meal in the well-equipped kitchen or join one of the activities on offer.

★Hotel Brummell   BOUTIQUE HOTEL €€
(Map p1056; ☎ 93 125 86 22; www.hotelbrummell. com; Carrer Nou de la Rambla 174; d from €140; ❄ ☜ ⚞; M Paral·lel) Stylish Brummell has been turning heads since its 2015 opening. It's a thoughtfully designed hotel with a creative soul and great atmosphere. The 20 bright rooms have a minimalist design, and the best of the bunch have sizeable terraces with views and even outdoor soaking tubs. The cheapest (the 'poolside classic' rooms) feel a little tight.

L'Eixample

Hostal Center Inn   HOSTAL €€
(Map p1056; ☎ 93 265 25 60; www.centerinnbarce lona.com; Gran Via de les Corts Catalanes 688; s/d/f from €65/75/115; ❄ @ ☜; M Tetuan) Set across two historic buildings 50m apart, Hostal Center Inn's simple rooms – some with balconies or terraces – have quirky touches such as wrought-iron bedsteads, Moroccan mosaic tables, gilded mirrors and, in one room, an antique escritoire.

La Barceloneta & the Waterfront

H10 Port Vell   BOUTIQUE HOTEL €€€
(Map p1060; ☎ 93 310 30 65; www.h10hotels.com; Pas de Sota Muralla 9; d from €150; ❄ @ ☜ ⚞; M Barceloneta) The location is excellent at this 58-room hotel within a short stroll of El Born and Barceloneta. Sleek, modern rooms have a trim, minimalist design with black-and-white bathrooms, and the best rooms (not all) have views over the marina. The rooftop terrace is the best feature, with sunloungers, a tiny plunge pool and evening cocktails.

✘ Eating

Barcelona has a celebrated food scene fuelled by a combination of world-class chefs, imaginative recipes and magnificent ingredients fresh from farms and the sea. Catalan culinary masterminds like brothers Ferran and Albert Adrià, and Carles Abellán have become international icons, reinventing the world of haute cuisine, while classic old-world Catalan recipes continue to earn accolades in dining rooms and tapas bars across the city.

✘ El Raval

Pinotxo Bar   TAPAS €€
(Map p1060; ☎ 93 317 17 31; www.pinotxobar.com; Mercat de la Boqueria, La Rambla 89; mains €9-17; ⊙ 6.30am-4pm Mon-Sat; M Liceu) Pinotxo is arguably La Boqueria's, and even Barcelona's, best tapas bar. The ever-charming owner, Juanito, might serve up chickpeas with pine nuts and raisins, a soft mix of potato and spinach sprinkled with salt, soft baby squid with cannellini beans, or a quivering cube of caramel-sweet pork belly.

✘ Barri Gòtic

La Vinateria del Call   SPANISH €€
(Map p1060; ☎ 93 302 60 92; www.lavinateria delcall.com; Carrer Salomó Ben Adret 9; raciones €7-12; ⊙ 7.30pm-1am; ☜; M Jaume I) In a magical setting in the former Jewish quarter, this tiny jewel-box of a wine bar serves up tasty Iberian dishes including Galician octopus, cider-cooked chorizo and the Catalan *escalivada* (roasted peppers, aubergine and onions) with anchovies. Portions are small and made for sharing, and there are over 160 varieties of wine to choose from.

Cafè de l'Acadèmia

CATALAN €€

(Map p1060; ☑ 93 319 82 53; Carrer dels Lledó 1; mains €8-20; ⊙ 1-3.30pm & 8-11.30pm Mon-Fri; ☜; Ⓜ Jaume I) Expect a mix of traditional Catalan dishes with the occasional creative twist. At lunchtime, local city hall workers pounce on the *menú del día* (€16). In the evening it is rather more romantic, as low lighting emphasises the intimacy of the beamed ceiling and stone walls. On warm days you can also dine in the pretty square at the front.

✗ Poble Sec & Sant Antoni

Quimet i Quimet

TAPAS €€

(Map p1056; ☑ 93 442 31 42; www.facebook.com/quimetyquimet; Carrer del Poeta Cabanyes 25; tapas €4-10, montaditos €3-4; ⊙ noon-4pm & 7-10.30pm Mon-Fri, noon-4pm Sat, closed Aug; Ⓜ Paral·lel) Quimet i Quimet is a family-run business that has been passed down from generation to generation. There's barely space to swing a *calamar* (squid) in this bottle-lined, standing-room-only place, but it is a treat for the palate, with *montaditos* (tapas on a slice of bread) made to order.

★ Enigma

GASTRONOMY €€€

(Map p1056; ☑ 616 696322; www.enigmaconcept. es; Carrer de Sepúlveda 38-40; tasting menu €220; ⊙ 7-9.30pm Tue-Fri, 1-2.30pm & 7-9.30pm Sat; Ⓜ Espanya) Resembling a 3D art installation, this conceptual offering from the famed Adrià brothers is a 40-course tour de force of cutting-edge gastronomy across six dining spaces. A meal takes 3½ hours and includes customised cocktail pairings (you can order additional drinks). There's a minimum of two diners; reserve months in advance. A €100 deposit per guest is required upon booking.

✗ La Ribera

Bormuth

TAPAS €

(Map p1060; ☑ 93 310 21 86; www.facebook.com/bormuthbarcelona; Carrer del Rec 31; tapas €4-10; ⊙ 12.30pm-1.30am Sun-Thu, to 2.30am Fri & Sat; ☜; Ⓜ Jaume I) Bormuth is a popular tapas bar with traditional decor, clad in bare brick and recycled wood. It serves typical favourites from around Spain, including *pimientos de Padrón* (fried green peppers), *buñelos de bacalao* (cod fritters) and *patatas mojo picón* (Canary Island baked potatoes, smothered in a spicy sauce). Bormuth also specialises in homemade vermouth, which it has on tap.

Casa Delfín

CATALAN €€

(Map p1060; ☑ 93 319 50 88; www.casadelfinrestaurant.com; Passeig del Born 36; mains €12-18; ⊙ noon-midnight Sun-Thu, to 1am Fri & Sat; ☜; Ⓜ Jaume I) One of Barcelona's culinary delights, Casa Delfín is everything you dream of when you think of Catalan (and Mediterranean) cooking. Start with salt-strewn *Padrón* peppers, moving on to plump anchovies from L'Escala in the Costa Brava, then tackle *suquet de los pescadores* (traditional Catalan fish stew; €14.50, minimum two people).

✗ L'Eixample

Tapas 24

TAPAS €

(Map p1056; ☑ 93 488 09 77; www.carlesabellan. com; Carrer de la Diputació 269; tapas €4-12; ⊙ 9am-midnight; ☜; Ⓜ Passeig de Gràcia) Hotshot chef Carles Abellán runs this basement tapas haven known for its gourmet versions of old faves. Highlights include the *bikini* (toasted ham and cheese sandwich – here the ham is cured and the truffle makes all the difference) and zesty *boquerones al limón* (lemon-marinated anchovies). You can't book, and service can be slow, but it's worth the wait.

★ Disfrutar

MODERN EUROPEAN €€€

(Map p1056; ☑ 93 348 68 96; www.disfrutarbarcelona.com; Carrer de Villarroel 163; tasting menus €150-190; ⊙ 1-2.30pm & 8-9.30pm Mon-Fri; Ⓜ Hospital Clínic) Disfrutar ('Enjoy' in Catalan) is among the city's finest restaurants, with two Michelin stars. Run by alumni of Ferran Adrià's game-changing (now closed) El Bulli restaurant, nothing is as it seems, such as black and green olives that are actually chocolate ganache with orange-blossom water.

✗ La Barceloneta & the Waterfront

La Cova Fumada

TAPAS €

(Map p1056; ☑ 93 221 40 61; Carrer del Baluard 56; tapas €4-12; ⊙ 9am-3.15pm Mon-Wed, 9am-3.15pm & 6-8.15pm Thu & Fri, 9am-1pm Sat; Ⓜ Barceloneta) There's no sign and the setting is decidedly downmarket, but this tiny, buzzing family-run tapas spot always packs in a crowd. The secret? Mouth-watering *pulpo* (octopus), calamari, sardines, *bombas* (meat and potato croquettes served with aioli) and grilled *carxofes* (artichokes) cooked in the open kitchen. Everything is amazingly fresh.

SEEING AN FC BARCELONA MATCH

Fútbol in Barcelona has the aura of religion, and for much of the city's population, support of FC Barcelona is an article of faith. FC Barcelona is traditionally associated with the Catalans and even Catalan nationalism.

Tickets to FC Barcelona matches are available at **Camp Nou** (☑902 189900; www. fcbarcelona.com; Carrer d'Arístides Maillol; Ⓜ Palau Reial), online via FC Barcelona's official website, and at various city locations. Tourist offices sell them (the branch at Plaça de Catalunya is a centrally located option) as do FC Botiga shops. Tickets can cost anything from €39 to upwards of €250, depending on the seat and match. On match day the ticket windows (at gates 9 and 15) are open from 9.15am until kick-off.

Fans who can't get to a game will still enjoy the self-guided **stadium tour and museum** (☑902 189900; www.fcbarcelona.com; Gate 9, Avinguda de Joan XXIII; adult/child self-guided tour €29.50/23.50, guided tour €50/35; ⊙9.30am-7.30pm mid-Apr–mid-Oct, 10am-6.30pm Mon-Sat, to 2.30pm Sun mid-Oct–mid-Apr; Ⓜ Palau Reial).

 Drinking & Nightlife

Barcelona is a town for nightlife lovers, with an enticing spread of candlelit wine bars, old-school taverns, stylish lounges and kaleidoscopic nightclubs where the party continues until daybreak. For something a little more sedate, the city's atmospheric cafes and teahouses make a fine retreat when the skies turn grey.

 Barri Gòtic

Marula Café BAR
(Map p1060; ☑93 318 76 90; www.marulacafe. com; Carrer dels Escudellers 49; cover up to €10; ⊙11pm-5am Wed, Thu & Sun, to 6am Fri & Sat; Ⓜ Liceu) A fantastic find in the heart of the Barri Gòtic, Marula will transport you to the 1970s and the best in funk and soul. James Brown fans will think they've died and gone to heaven. It's not, however, a mono-thematic place: DJs slip in other tunes, from breakbeat to house. Samba and other Brazilian dance sounds also penetrate here.

 La Ribera

El Born Bar BAR
(Map p1060; ☑93 319 53 33; www.elbornbar.com; Passeig del Born 26; ⊙10am-2.30am Mon-Thu, to 3am Fri, 11am-3am Sat, noon-2.30am Sun; 🤜; Ⓜ Jaume I) Moss-green paintwork, marble tables and a chequered black-and-white tiled floor create a timeless look for this popular little cafe-bar. A spiral wrought-iron staircase leads to a quieter room upstairs (the twisting steps mean that there is no table service and hot drinks can't be carried up-

stairs). El Born is ideal for either morning coffee, an afternoon vermouth or an evening cocktail.

 L'Eixample

Dry Martini BAR
(Map p1056; ☑93 217 50 72; www.drymartiniorg. com; Carrer d'Aribau 162-166; ⊙1pm-2.30am Mon-Thu, 1pm-3am Fri, 6.30pm-3am Sat, 6.30pm-2.30am Sun; 🄵FGC Provença) Waiters make expert cocktail suggestions, but the house drink, taken at the bar or on one of the plush green banquettes, is always a good bet. The gin and tonic comes in an enormous mug-sized glass – one will take you most of the night.

City Hall CLUB
(Map p1056; ☑93 238 07 22; www.cityhallbarcelona. com; Rambla de Catalunya 2-4; cover from €10; ⊙midnight-5am Mon-Thu, to 6am Sat; Ⓜ Catalunya) A long corridor leads to the dance floor of this venerable and popular club, located in a former theatre. Music styles, from house and techno to reggaeton, change nightly; check the agenda online. The cover charge includes a drink.

☆ **Entertainment**

★**Palau de la Música Catalana** CLASSICAL MUSIC
(Map p1060; ☑93 295 72 00; www.palaumusica.cat; Carrer de Palau de la Música 4-6; tickets from €18; ⊙box office 9.30am-9pm Mon-Sat, 10am-3pm Sun; Ⓜ Urquinaona) A feast for the eyes, this Modernista confection is also the city's most traditional venue for classical and choral music,

SPAIN BARCELONA

although it has a wide-ranging program, including flamenco, pop and – particularly – jazz. Just being here for a performance is an experience. In the foyer, its tiled pillars all a-glitter, you can sip a pre-concert tipple.

Shopping

Most mainstream fashion stores are along a shopping 'axis' that runs from Plaça de Catalunya along Passeig de Gràcia, then left (west) along Avinguda Diagonal.

In La Ribera, El Born and Carrer del Rec are the places for cool designer boutiques that sell high-end fashion. There are plenty of shops scattered throughout the Barri Gòtic (stroll Carrer d'Avinyò). El Raval is a haven for vintage fashion (especially Carrer de la Riera Baixa) and all kinds of original and arty independent shops.

Coquette FASHION & ACCESSORIES
(Map p1060; ☎ 93 310 35 35; www.coquettebcn. com; Carrer de Bonaire 5; ☺11am-3pm & 5-9pm Mon-Fri, 11.30am-9pm Sat; Ⓜ Barceloneta) With its spare, cut-back and designer look, this friendly fashion store is attractive in its own right. Women can browse through casual, feminine wear by such designers as Humanoid, Vanessa Bruno, UKE and Hoss Intropia.

Custo Barcelona FASHION & ACCESSORIES
(Map p1060; ☎ 93 268 78 93; www.custo.com; Plaça de les Olles 7; ☺10am-8pm Mon-Sat; Ⓜ Barceloneta) The psychedelic decor and casual atmosphere lend this avant-garde Barcelona fashion store a youthful edge. Custo presents daring new women's and men's collections each year on the New York catwalks. The dazzling colours and cut of everything from dinner jackets to hot pants are for the uninhibited. It has three other shops around town.

ℹ Information

Purse snatching and pickpocketing are major problems, especially around Plaça de Catalunya, La Rambla and Plaça Reial. Report thefts to the **Guàrdia Urbana** (Local Police; ☎ 092, 93 256 24 77; www.bcn.cat/guardiaurbana; La Rambla 43; ☺24hr; Ⓜ Liceu) on La Rambla. You're unlikely to recover your goods, but you will need to make this formal *denuncia* (police report) for insurance purposes. Avoid walking around El Raval and the southern end of La Rambla late at night.

Oficina d'Informació de Turisme de Barcelona (Map p1060; ☎ 93 285 38 34; www.bar celonaturisme.com; Plaça de Catalunya 17-S, underground; ☺8.30am-9pm; Ⓜ Catalunya) Barcelona's main tourist office is in Plaça de Catalunya. Helpful staff are clued up on the city. It also organises a great range of **walking tours** (Map p1060; ☎ 93 285 38 32; www. barcelonaturisme.com; Plaça de Catalunya 17; Ⓜ Catalunya).

Palau Robert Regional Tourist Office (Map p1056; ☎ 93 238 80 91; http://palaurobert. gencat.cat; Passeig de Gràcia 107; ☺9am-8pm Mon-Sat, to 2.30pm Sun; Ⓜ Diagonal) Inside the Palau Robert, Catalonia's regional tourist office has a host of info including audiovisual resources, a bookshop and a branch of Turisme Juvenil de Catalunya (for youth travel).

ℹ Getting There & Away

AIR

Barcelona's **El Prat airport** (☎ 91 321 10 00; www.aena.es; ☜) lies 17km southwest of Plaça de Catalunya at El Prat de Llobregat. The airport has two main terminal buildings: the newer T1 terminal and the T2, itself divided into three terminal areas (A, B and C). While the majority of international flights arrive at El Prat airport, there are two other airports in nearby cities, which are used by some budget airlines.

BOAT

Barcelona has ferry connections to the Balearic Islands and Italy. Boats depart from the port just south of the old city.

Passenger and vehicular ferries operated by **Trasmediterránea** (Map p1056; ☎ 902 454645; www.trasmediterranea.es; Moll de Sant Bertran; Ⓜ Drassanes) to/from the Balearic Islands dock around the Moll de Barcelona wharf in Port Vell. Information and tickets are available at the terminal buildings along Moll de Sant Bertran and on Moll de Barcelona or from travel agents. Fares vary enormously according to season, how far in advance you book and whether or not you want a cabin. Fares for a 'Butaca Turista' (seat) from Barcelona to any of the islands typically start around €60 on ferries in the summertime.

BUS

Long-distance buses leave from **Estació del Nord** (Map p1056; ☎ 93 706 53 66; www. barcelonanord.cat; Carrer d'Ali Bei 80; Ⓜ Arc de Triomf). A plethora of companies service different parts of Spain; many come under the umbrella of **ALSA** (☎ 902 422242; www.alsa. es). For other companies, ask at the bus station. There are frequent services (20 or more daily) to Madrid (seven to eight hours), Valencia (four to 4½ hours) and Zaragoza (3½ hours) and several daily departures to distant destinations such as Burgos, Santiago de Compostela and Seville.

GIRONA

A tight huddle of ancient arcaded houses, grand churches, cobbled streets and medieval baths, all enclosed by defensive walls and a lazy river, constitutes a powerful reason for visiting northern Catalonia's largest city, Girona (Castilian: Gerona). From Girona station there are trains to Figueres (€4.10 to €6.90, 30 to 40 minutes, at least 15 daily) and Barcelona (from €10, 40 minutes to 1¼ hours, 30 daily).

Catedral de Girona (www.catedraldegirona.cat; Plaça de la Catedral; adult/concession incl Basílica de Sant Feliu €7/5; ⊙10am-7.30pm Jul & Aug, to 6.30pm Apr-Jun, Sep & Oct, to 5.30pm Nov-Mar) Towering over a flight of 86 steps rising from Plaça de la Catedral, Girona's imposing cathedral is far more ancient than its billowing baroque facade suggests. Built over an old Roman forum, parts of its foundations date from the 5th century. Today, 14th-century Gothic styling – added over an 11th-century Romanesque church – dominates, though a beautiful, double-columned Romanesque **cloister** dates from the 12th century. With the world's second-widest Gothic nave, it's a formidable sight to explore, but audio guides are provided.

Museu d'Història dels Jueus (www.girona.cat/call; Carrer de la Força 8; adult/child €4/ free; ⊙10am-8pm Mon-Sat, to 2pm Sun Jul & Aug, 10am-2pm Mon & Sun, to 6pm Tue-Sat Sep-Jun) Until 1492, Girona was home to Catalonia's second-most important medieval Jewish community, after Barcelona, and one of the country's finest Jewish quarters. This excellent museum takes pride in Girona's Jewish heritage, without shying away from less salubrious aspects such as Inquisition persecution and forced conversions. You also see a rare 11th-century *miqvé* (ritual bath) and a 13th-century Jewish house.

Bells Oficis (☑972 22 81 70; www.bellsoficis.com; Carrer dels Germans Busquets 2; r incl breakfast €45-100; ✳🖥) A lovingly restored 19th-century apartment towards the southern end of the old town, Bells Oficis makes a stylish, ultra-welcoming base. It's the former home of Catalan artist Jaume Busquets i Mollera, and retains period details in the five very different rooms (one of which is a teeny two-bunk pad). Three rooms share a bathroom; one en suite room has no bathroom door.

El Celler de Can Roca (☑972 22 21 57; www.cellercanroca.com; Carrer Can Sunyer 48; degustation menus €180-215; ⊙bookings 12.30-2pm & 8-9.30pm Wed-Sat) Ever-changing avant-garde takes on Catalan dishes have catapulted El Celler de Can Roca to global fame. Holding three Michelin stars, it was named the best restaurant in the world in 2013, 2015 and 2018 by The World's 50 Best. Each year brings new innovations, from molecular gastronomy to multi-sensory food-art interplay to sci-fi dessert trolleys, all with mama's home cooking as the core inspiration.

Fares vary hugely depending on what time of day you travel and how far in advance you book.

Eurolines (www.eurolines.es), in conjunction with local carriers all over Europe, is the main international carrier. Its website provides links to national operators; it runs services across Europe and to Morocco from Estació del Nord, and from **Estació d'Autobusos de Sants** (Map p1056; Carrer de Viriat; Ⓜ Sants Estació), next to Estació Sants Barcelona.

TRAIN

The main station is **Estació Sants** (☑912 432343; www.adif.es; Plaça dels Països Catalans; Ⓜ Sants Estació), 2.5km west of La Rambla. Daily high-speed trains head for Madrid (€50 to more than €200, from 2½ hours, 30 daily) via Zaragoza; book well ahead for the lowest fares.

Other daily trains run to Valencia (€12 to €45, three to 4½ hours, up to 19 daily), Pamplona, San Sebastián, Bilbao, Santiago de Compostela, Seville and Málaga. Direct overnight trains from Paris, Geneva, Milan and Zürich also arrive at Estació Sants.

❶ Getting Around

TO/FROM THE AIRPORT

Frequent *aerobúses* (www.aerobusbcn.com) run between both airport terminals and Plaça de Catalunya (€5.90, 35 minutes, every five or 10 minutes), from 6am to 1am.

PUBLIC TRANSPORT

Barcelona's metro system spreads its tentacles around the city in such a way that most places of

WORTH A TRIP

ANDORRA

This mini-country wedged between France and Spain offers by far the best ski slopes and resort facilities in all the Pyrenees. Once the snows melt, there's an abundance of great walking, ranging from easy strolls to demanding day hikes in the principality's higher, more remote reaches. Strike out above the tight valleys and you can walk for hours, almost alone.

The only way to reach Andorra is by road from Spain or France. If driving, fill up in Andorra; fuel is substantially cheaper there. There are buses to/from Barcelona's Estació del Nord, Estació Sants and airport, Lleida, La Seu d'Urgell and Toulouse (France). All bus services arrive at and leave from Andorra la Vella.

interest are within a 10-minute walk of a station. It runs 5am to midnight Sunday to Thursday, till 2am on Friday and 24 hours on Saturday. Targeta T-10 (10-ride passes; €10.20) are the best value; otherwise, it's €2.20 per ride.

TAXI

Taxis charge €2.10 to €2.30 flagfall plus €1.10 to €1.30 per kilometre (the higher rates are for nights and weekends). You can flag a taxi down in the street, or call **Fonotaxi** (☏ 93 300 11 00; www.fonotaxi.net) or **Radio Taxi 033** (☏ 93 303 30 33; www.radiotaxi033.com). The call-out charge is €3.40 (€4.20 at night and on weekends).

Tarragona

POP 63,838

In this effervescent port city, Roman history collides with beaches, nightlife and a food scene that perfumes the air with freshly grilled seafood. The biggest lure is the wealth of remains from one of Spain's most important Roman cities, including mosaic-packed museums and a seaside amphitheatre. A roll-call of excellent places to eat gives you good reason to linger in the knot of lanes in the medieval centre, flanked by a broad cathedral with Gothic flourishes.

⊙ Sights

★ **Catedral de Tarragona**   CATHEDRAL
(www.catedraldetarragona.com; Plaça de la Seu; adult/child €5/3; ⊙10am-8pm Mon-Sat mid-Jun–mid-Sep, 10am-7pm Mon-Sat mid-Mar–mid-Jun & mid-Sep–Oct, 10am-5pm Mon-Fri, to 7pm Sat Nov–mid-Mar) Crowning the town, Tarragona's cathedral incorporates both Romanesque and Gothic features, as typified by the main facade. The flower-filled cloister has Gothic vaulting and Romanesque carved capitals, one of which shows rats conducting a cat's funeral...until the cat comes back to life! Chambers off the cloister display the remains of a Roman temple (unearthed in 2015) and the **Museu Diocesà**, its collection extending from Roman hairpins to 13th- and 14th-century polychrome Virgin woodcarvings. Don't miss the east nave's 14th-century frescos.

Passeig Arqueològic Muralles   WALLS
(Avinguda de Catalunya; adult/child €3.30/free; ⊙9am-9pm Tue-Sat, to 3pm Sun Easter-Sep, 9am-7pm Tue-Fri, to 3pm Sun Oct-Easter) A peaceful walk takes you around the inland part of the old town's perimeter between two lines of city walls. The inner walls are mainly Roman and date back to the 3rd century BCE, while the outer ones were put up by the British in 1709 during the War of the Spanish Succession. The earliest stretches are a mighty 4m thick. There's a helpful interpretation centre (Catalan, Spanish and English).

★ **Museu Nacional Arqueològic de Tarragona**   MUSEUM
(www.mnat.cat; Plaça del Rei 5; adult/child €4.50/free; ⊙8am-6pm Mon & Wed-Fri, 8am-3pm & 4-6.30 Tue Oct-May, 8am-3pm Mon-Fri Jun-Sep, 10am-2pm Sun year-round) This excellent museum does justice to the cultural and material wealth of Roman Tarraco. The mosaic collection traces changing trends from simple black-and-white designs to complex full-colour creations; highlights include the fine 2nd- or 3rd-century *Mosaic de la Medusa* and the large, almost complete 3rd-century *Mosaic dels Peixos de la Pineda*, showing fish and sea creatures. Explanations are mostly in Catalan and Spanish, but there are English-language booklets across the galleries.

🛏 Sleeping & Eating

Look for tapas bars and inexpensive cafes on the Plaça de la Font. The quintessential Tarragona seafood experience can be had in Serrallo, the town's fishing port, where a dozen bars and restaurants sell the day's catch.

Tarragona Hostel HOSTEL €

(📋877 05 58 96; www.tarragonahostel.com; Carrer de la Unió 26; dm/tr €12/40; 🗐) All the backpacker essentials are well executed at this friendly central hostel with chirpy staff, a leafy patio, a comfy common room, a shared kitchen and laundry facilities. Choose from two eight-bed dorms and a more modern four-bed dorm (all with air-con and personal lockers), or a private fan-cooled triple room.

Hotel Plaça de la Font HOTEL €€

(📋977 24 61 34; www.hotelpdelafont.com; Plaça de la Font 26; s/d/tr €60/80/100; ❄🗐) Comfortable modern rooms, individually decorated with photos of local monuments, make this cheerful, convenient hotel one of Tarragona's most attractive options. Rooms at the front have tiny balconies and are well soundproofed from the sociable murmur in bustling Plaça de la Font below. With tables right on the square, the cafe is perfect for light breakfasts (€6).

Barquet SEAFOOD €€

(📋977 24 00 23; www.restaurantbarquet.com; Carrer del Gasòmetre 16; mains €12-22; ⏰12.30-3.30pm Mon, 12.30-3.30pm & 8.30-10pm Tue-Fri, 1-3.30pm & 8.30-10.00pm Sat) This popular neighbourhood restaurant is a short downhill stroll south from Tarragona centre. It's deservedly famous for its expertly concocted rice dishes bursting with maritime flavour, and also does great seafood *raciones* (large plates). Don't be fooled by the nautical warehouse interior: fish dishes and desserts are executed with finesse.

AQ MEDITERRANEAN, FUSION €€

(📋977 21 59 54; www.aq-restaurant.com; Carrer de les Coques 7; mains €11-24; ⏰1.30-3.30pm & 8.30-11pm) The crisp interior design of this palm-patterned restaurant promises fine dining and AQ amply delivers, with its impeccably crafted, playfully executed fusion dishes taking inspiration from Catalan, Italian and Asian cuisines. Treat your taste buds to squid-ink croquettes, chunky strips of *patatas bravas*, grilled Wagyu steak, cod-and-aubergine teriyaki or wok-fried mussels.

DALÍ'S CATALONIA

The only name that could come into your head when you set eyes on the red castle-like building in central **Figueres**, topped with giant eggs and stylised Oscar-like statues and studded with plaster-covered croissants, is Salvador Dalí. With its entrance watched over by medieval suits of armour balancing baguettes on their heads, the **Teatre-Museu Dalí** (www.salvador-dali.org; Plaça de Gala i Salvador Dalí 5; adult/child under 9yr €14/free; ⏰9am-8pm Apr-Jul & Sep, 9am-8pm & 10pm-1am Aug, 9.30am-6pm Tue-Sun Oct & Mar, 10.30am-6pm Tue-Sun Nov-Feb) is an entirely appropriate final resting place for the master of surrealism. 'Theatre-museum' is an apt label for this trip through the incredibly fertile imagination of one of the great showmen of the 20th century. It's full of surprises, tricks and illusions, and contains a substantial portion of Dalí's life's work.

Port Lligat, 1km northeast of Cadaqués, is a tiny settlement around a lovely cove, with fishing boats pulled up on its beach. The **Casa Museu Dalí** (📋972 25 10 15; www.salvador-dali.org; adult/child under 8yr €12/free; ⏰9.30am-9pm mid-Jun–mid-Sep, 10.30am-6pm mid-Sep–Jan & mid-Feb–mid-Jun, closed mid-Jan–mid-Feb, plus Mon Nov–mid-Mar) started life as a fisherman's hut, but was steadily enlarged by Dalí and his wife Gala during their residence here from 1930 to 1982 (apart from a dozen or so years abroad around the Spanish Civil War). It provides a fascinating insight into the lives of the (excuse the pun) surreal couple. We probably don't need to tell you that it's the house with a lot of little white chimneypots and two egg-shaped towers, overlooking the western end of the beach. You must book ahead.

ℹ Information

The **tourist office** (☑ 977 25 07 95; www.tarragonaturisme.es; Carrer Major 39; ⊙10am-8pm late Jun-Sep, 10am-2pm & 3-5pm Mon-Fri, 10am-2pm & 3-7pm Sat, 10am-2pm Sun Oct-late Jun) is a good place for booking guided tours of the city. Opening hours are extended in high season.

ℹ Getting There & Away

BUS

The **bus station** (Plaça Imperial Tarraco) is 1.5km northwest of the old town along Rambla Nova. Destinations include Barcelona (€8.70, 1½ hours, seven daily) and Valencia (€22, three to 4½ hours, six daily).

TRAIN

Tarragona station is a 10-minute walk from the old town, while fast AVE trains stop at Camp de Tarragona station, 10km north. Departures from Tarragona station include trains to Barcelona (€10.50 to €17.30, one to 1½ hours, around every 30 minutes) and Valencia (€17 to €24, two to four hours, 15 to 17 daily).

ARAGÓN, BASQUE COUNTRY & NAVARRA

Zaragoza

POP 664,938

Zaragoza (Saragossa), on the banks of the mighty Río Ebro, is a vibrant, elegant and fascinating city. Its residents, who form over half of Aragón's population, enjoy a lifestyle that revolves around some superb tapas bars, great shopping and a vigorous nightlife. But Zaragoza is much more than just a good-time city: its host of historical sights spans all the great civilisations that have left their mark on the Spanish soul. This is also a good place to get acquainted with the artistic genius of Francisco de Goya, who was born a short horse-ride away in 1746.

◉ Sights

★ Basílica de Nuestra Señora del Pilar   CHURCH

(www.basilicadelpilar.es; Plaza del Pilar; ⊙6.45am-8.30pm Mon-Sat, to 9.30pm Sun) Brace yourself for this great baroque cavern of Catholicism. The faithful believe that here on 2 January 40 CE, the Virgin Mary appeared to Santiago

(St James the Apostle) atop a *pilar* (pillar) of jasper, and left the pillar behind as a testament to her visit. A chapel was built around the pillar, followed by a series of ever more grandiose churches, culminating in the enormous basilica.

★ Aljafería   PALACE

(☑ 976 28 96 83; www.cortesaragon.es; Calle de los Diputados; adult/concession/child €5/1/free, Sun free; ⊙10am-2pm & 4.30-8pm Apr-Oct, 10am-2pm & 4-6.30pm Nov-Mar) The Aljafería is Spain's finest Islamic-era edifice outside Andalucía. Built as a fortified palace for Zaragoza's Islamic rulers in the 11th century, it underwent various alterations after 1118 when Zaragoza passed into Christian hands. In the 1490s the Reyes Católicos (Catholic Monarchs), Fernando and Isabel, tacked on their own palace. From the 1590s the Aljafería was developed into more of a fortress than a palace. Twentieth-century restorations brought it back to life, and Aragón's regional parliament has been housed here since 1987.

La Seo   CATHEDRAL

(Catedral de San Salvador; ☑ 976 29 12 31; www.zaragozaturismo.es; Plaza de la Seo; adult/senior/child €4/3/free; ⊙10am-6.30pm & 7.30-9pm Mon-Thu, 10am-6.30pm Fri, 10am-noon, 3-8.30pm Sat, 10am-noon, 3-6.30pm & 7.30-9pm Sun mid-Jun–mid-Oct, 10am-2pm & 4-6.30pm Mon-Fri, 10am-noon & 4-6.30pm Sat & Sun mid-Oct–mid-Jun) Dominating the eastern end of Plaza del Pilar, La Seo is Zaragoza's finest work of Christian architecture, built between the 12th and 17th centuries and displaying a fabulous spread of styles from Romanesque to baroque. It stands on the site of Islamic Zaragoza's main mosque (which itself stood upon the temple of the Roman forum). The admission price includes La Seo's **Museo de Tapices** (⊙10am-6.30pm & 7.45-9pm Mon-Thu, 10am-6.30pm Fri, 10am-noon, 3-6.30pm & 7.45-9pm Sat & Sun mid-Jun–mid-Oct, 10am-2pm & 4-6.30pm mid-Oct–mid-Jun), a collection of Flemish and French tapestries considered the best of its kind in the world.

Museo Goya – Colección Ibercaja   MUSEUM

(☑ 976 39 73 87; http://museogoya.ibercaja.es; Calle de Espoz y Mina 23; adult/senior & child €4/free, audio guide or tablet €2; ⊙10am-8pm Mon-Sat, to 2pm Sun Apr-Oct, 10am-2pm & 4-8pm Mon-Sat, 10am-2pm Sun Nov-Mar) Apart from Madrid's Museo del Prado, this exceedingly well-laid-out museum contains arguably the best exposé of the work of one of Spain's most revered artists. Each of the three floors has a different focus, the 2nd floor being the one that exhibits Goya's own work. Four complete sets of his prints are included, most notably the groundbreaking, sometimes grotesque *Desastres de la Guerra* (Disasters of War), a bitter attack on the cruelty and folly of war.

Museo del Teatro de Caesaraugusta
MUSEUM

(☏ 976 72 60 75; www.zaragozaturismo.es; Calle de San Jorge 12; adult/student/senior & child €4/3/free; ☺ 10am-2pm & 5-9pm Tue-Sat, 10am-2.30pm Sun) The finest in Zaragoza's quartet of Roman museums was discovered during excavation of a building site in 1972. Great efforts, including an entertaining 15-minute audiovisual, have been made to help visitors visualise the splendour of this theatre that accommodated 6000 spectators on more than 30 rows of seating. The theatre is visible from the surrounding streets and is protected by a huge polycarbonate roof, 25m above ground, that is set at the height of the top of the original building.

🛏 Sleeping

★ Hotel Sauce
HOTEL €

(☏ 976 20 50 50; www.hotelsauce.com; Calle de Espoz y Mina 33; s €47-55, d €50-70; ❋ ☏) This stylish small hotel with a great central location is a superb option for its fresh, cheerful, contemporary rooms with tasteful watercolours, outstandingly friendly and helpful staff, and pleasant 24-hour cafe serving excellent breakfasts, cakes and cocktails. Its prices are very reasonable given everything that the hotel provides.

Catalonia El Pilar
HOTEL €€

(☏ 976 20 58 58; www.hoteles-catalonia.com; Calle de la Manifestación 16; s/d from €75/80; ❋ @ ☏) Ten out of 10 for the facade, a handsome Modernista construction that has been artfully renovated to house this eminently comfortable contemporary hotel. Inside, rooms are spacious and decorated in restful, muted earth tones with elegant marble-clad bathrooms. Some of the beds are king-size. Breakfast costs €14.

🍴 Eating & Drinking

Head to the tangle of lanes in El Tubo, north of Plaza de España, for one of Spain's richest gatherings of tapas bars.

After the tapas bars close around midnight, late-night and music bars come into their own. There's a good scattering of these in the historic centre.

Méli Melo
TAPAS €

(☏ 976 29 46 95; www.restaurantemelimelozaragoza.com; Calle Mayor 45; tapas €2.50-3; ☺ 1-5pm & 8pm-midnight Mon-Sat, 1-4pm Sun) The creative tapas at this tightly packed spot are arrayed very temptingly along the bar: you can just select those that appeal most; maybe prawnstuffed squid, or artichoke with ham, or a mini fish-and-shrimp burger. Or choose more substantial *raciones* from the board, such as *patatas a la gresca* (fried potato cubes) or *escalibada con bacalao* (baked veggies with cod).

Los Xarmientos
ARAGONESE €€

(☏ 976 29 90 48; www.facebook.com/xarmientos; Calle de Espoz y Mina 25; mains €12-16, set menus €26.50-35; ☺ 1.30-4pm & 8.30-11pm Wed-Sat, 1.30-4pm Tue & Sun) Aragonese meat dishes are a speciality at this artfully designed restaurant. It styles itself as a *parrilla*, meaning the dishes are cooked on a barbecue-style grill. It's a fine place to sample the local *ternasco* (lamb), Aragon's most emblematic dish, accompanied by a good Somontano wine and perhaps preceded by a spinach and goat's-cheese salad...or even some snails?

ℹ Information

Municipal Tourist Office (☏ 976 20 12 00; www.zaragozaturismo.es; Plaza del Pilar; ☺ 10am-8pm; ☏) Has branch offices around town, including at the train station.

Oficina de Turismo de Aragón (☏ 976 28 21 81; www.turismodearagon.com; Plaza de España 1; ☺ 9.30am-2.30pm & 4.30-7.30pm) Helpful place with plenty of brochures covering all of Aragón.

ℹ Getting There & Away

BUS

Dozens of bus lines fan out across Spain from the bus station attached to the Estación Intermodal Delicias train station, 3km west of the centre. **ALSA** (☏ 902 422242; www.alsa.es) runs to/from Madrid (from €16.80, three to four hours, 19 or more daily) and Barcelona (from €9.60, 3¾ hours, 16 or more daily). **Alosa** (☏ 974 21 07 00; www.avanzabus.com) runs buses to/from Huesca (€8, 1¼ hours, 14 or more daily) and Jaca (€16, 2½ hours, six or more daily).

SPAIN ZARAGOZA

TRAIN

Zaragoza's futuristic **Estación Intermodal Delicias** (Avenida de Navarra 80) is connected by around 20 daily high-speed AVE services to Madrid (€34 to €55, 1½ hours) and Barcelona (€37 to €60, 1¾ hours). Other destinations include Huesca (from €8, one hour, one or two daily), Jaca (€15, 3¼ hours, two daily) and Teruel (€20, 2½ hours, four daily).

Around Aragón

Aragón is a beautiful and fascinating region to explore if you have a few days to do so. In the south, little visited **Teruel** is home to some stunning Mudéjar architecture. Nearby, **Albarracín** is one of Spain's prettiest villages.

In the north, the **Parque Nacional de Ordesa y Monte Perdido** is the most spectacular stretch of the Spanish Pyrenees, with dramatic mountain scenery and superb hiking; the pretty village of **Torla** is the main gateway (though it gets overrun with visitors in July and August). En route to the mountains are several towns and villages with enchanting medieval quarters or fascinating medieval monuments, such as **Aínsa, Jaca** and **Huesca**.

In Aragón's northwest, **Sos del Rey Católico** is another gorgeous stone village draped along a ridge.

San Sebastián

POP 181,932

With Michelin stars apparently falling from the heavens onto its restaurants, not to mention a *pintxo* (tapas) culture almost unmatched anywhere else in Spain, stylish San Sebastián (Donostia in Basque) frequently tops lists of the world's best places to eat. Charming and well-mannered by day, cool and happening by night, the city has an idyllic location on the shell-shaped Bahía de la Concha, with crystalline waters, a flawless beach and green hills on all sides.

◉ Sights

★ Playa de la Concha   BEACH

(Paseo de la Concha) Fulfilling almost every idea of how a perfect city beach should be formed, Playa de la Concha (and its westerly extension, Playa de Ondarreta) is easily among the best city beaches in Europe. Throughout the long summer months a fiesta atmosphere prevails, with thousands of tanned and toned bodies spread across the sands. The swimming is almost always safe.

Monte Igueldo   VIEWPOINT

(www.monteigueldo.es; ⊙10am-9pm Mon-Fri, to 10pm Sat & Sun Jul, 10am-10pm daily Aug, 10am-8pm Mon-Fri, to 9pm Sat & Sun Jun & Sep, shorter hours rest of year) The views from the summit of Monte Igueldo, just west of town, will make you feel like a circling hawk staring down over the vast panorama of the Bahía de la Concha and the surrounding coastline and mountains. The best way to get there is via the old-world **funicular railway** (Plaza del Funicular; return adult/child €3.15/2.35; ⊙10am-9pm Jun-Aug, shorter hours rest of year) to the **Parque de Atracciones** (☑943 21 35 25; Paseo de Igeldo; ⊙10am-9pm Mon-Fri, to 10pm Sat & Sun Jul & Aug, 10am-7pm Mon-Fri, to 8pm Sat & Sun Jun & Sep, shorter hours rest of year), a small, old-fashioned theme park at the top of the hill. Opening hours vary throughout the year; check the website for details.

San Telmo Museoa   MUSEUM

(☑943 48 15 80; www.santelmomuseoa.com; Plaza Zuloaga 1; adult/concession/child €6/3/free, Tue free; ⊙10am-8pm Tue-Sun) One of the best museums in the Basque Country, the San Telmo Museoa has a thought-provoking collection that explores Basque history and culture in all its complexity. Exhibitions are spread between a restored convent dating back to the 16th century and a cutting-edge newer wing that blends into its plant-lined backdrop of Mount Urgull. The collection ranges from historical artefacts to bold fusions of contemporary art. San Telmo also stages some outstanding temporary exhibitions.

🛏 Sleeping

Pensión Altair   PENSIÓN €

(☑943 29 31 33; www.pension-altair.com; Calle Padre Larroca 3; s/d €60/110; ❋@🜚) This *pensión* is in a beautifully restored town house, with unusual church-worthy arched windows and modern, minimalist rooms that are a world away from the fusty decor of the old-town *pensiones*. Interior rooms lack the grandiose windows but are much larger.

Pensión Amaiur   BOUTIQUE HOTEL €€

(☑943 42 96 54; www.pensionamaiur.com; Calle 31 de Agosto 44; d with/without bathroom from €80/70; @🜚) A top-notch guesthouse in a prime old-town location, Amaiur has bright floral wallpapers and bathrooms tiled in Andalucian blue and white. The best rooms are those that overlook the main street, where you can sit on a little balcony and be completely enveloped in blushing red flowers. Some rooms share bathrooms. Guest kitchen and free snacks add to the value.

**Hotel de Londres
y de Inglaterra** HISTORIC HOTEL €€€
(☑ 943 44 07 70; www.hlondres.com; Calle de Zubieta 2; d €380; P ❄ ☎) Sitting pretty on the beachfront, Hotel de Londres y de Inglaterra (Hotel of London and England) is as proper as it sounds. Queen Isabel II set the tone for this hotel well over a century ago, and things have stayed pretty regal ever since. The place exudes elegance; some rooms have stunning views over Playa de la Concha.

✗ Eating & Drinking

With 18 Michelin stars, San Sebastián stands atop a pedestal as one of the culinary capitals of the planet. As if that alone weren't enough, the city is overflowing with bars – almost all of which have bar tops weighed down under a mountain of *pintxos* that almost every Spaniard will tell you are the best in country.

Most of the city's bars mutate through the day from calm morning-coffee hang-outs to pintxo-laden delights, before finally finishing up as noisy bars full of writhing, sweaty bodies. Nights in San Sebastián start late and go on until well into the wee hours.

★ La Fábrica BASQUE €€
(☑ 943 43 21 10; www.restaurantelafabrica.es; Calle del Puerto 17; mains €15-20, set menus from €30; ☉ 1-4pm & 7.30-11.30pm) The red-brick interior walls and white tablecloths lend an air of class to this restaurant, whose modern takes on Basque classics have been making waves with San Sebastián locals in recent years. La Fábrica only works with multicourse *menús,* which means you'll get to sample various delicacies like wild mushroom ravioli with foie gras cream or venison in red wine sauce. Advance reservations essential.

★ La Cuchara de San Telmo BASQUE €€
(☑ 943 44 16 55; www.lacucharadesantelmo. com; Calle de 31 de Agosto 28; pintxos from €2.50; ☉ 7.30-11pm Tue, 12.30-5.30pm & 7.30-11.30pm Wed-Sun) This bustling, always-packed bar offers miniature *nueva cocina vasca* (Basque nouvelle cuisine) from a supremely creative kitchen. Unlike many San Sebastián bars, this one doesn't have any *pintxos* laid out on

the bar top; instead you must order from the blackboard menu behind the counter.

Restaurante Kokotxa MODERN SPANISH €€€
(☑ 943 42 19 04; www.restaurantekokotxa.com; Calle del Campanario 11; mains €27-35, menús €85-115; ☉ 1.30-3.30pm & 8.30-10.30pm Tue-Sat) This Michelin-star restaurant is hidden away down an overlooked alley in the old town, but the food rewards those who search. Most people opt for the *menú de mercado* (€85) and enjoy the flavours of the traders from the busy city market. It's closed from mid-February through March and for two weeks in late October.

ℹ Information

The friendly **Oficina de Turismo** (☑ 943 48 11 66; www.sansebastianturismo.com; Alameda del Boulevard 8; ☉ 9am-8pm Mon-Sat, 10am-7pm Sun Jul-Sep, 9am-7pm Mon-Sat, 10am-2pm Sun Oct-May) offers comprehensive information on the city and the Basque Country in general.

ℹ Getting There & Away

AIR

Aeropuerto de San Sebastián (EAS; ☑ 902 404704; www.aena.es) is 22km northeast of the city. There are no international flights here, though there are several daily connections to Barcelona (1½ hours) and Madrid (1¼ hours).

BUS

San Sebastián's **bus station** (Estación Donostia Geltokia; www.estaciondonostia.com; Paseo Federico García Lorca 1) is on the eastern side of the river, just across from the Renfe train station. Services leave for Bilbao (from €7, 1¼ hours, frequent), Bilbao Airport (€17, 1¼ hours, hourly), Biarritz (France; from €7, 1¼ hours, six to eight daily) and Pamplona (from €8, 1¼ hours).

TRAIN

The main **Renfe train station** (Paseo de Francia) is just across Río Urumea, on a line linking Paris to Madrid. There are services to Madrid (from €29, 5½ hours, several daily) and to Barcelona (from €32, six hours, two daily).

For France you must first go to the Spanish/French border town of Irún (or sometimes trains go as far as Hendaye; from €2.25, 27 minutes), which is also served by Eusko Tren/Ferrocarril Vasco (www.euskotren.es), and change there. Trains depart every half-hour from **Amara train station** (Easo Plaza 9), about 1km south of the city centre, and also stop in Pasajes (from €1.70, 12 minutes) and Irún/Hendaye (€2.45, 25 minutes). Another ET/FV railway line heads west to Bilbao via Zarautz, Zumaia and Durango, but it's painfully slow, so the bus is usually a better plan.

Bilbao

POP 345,100

The commercial hub of the Basque Country, Bilbao (Bilbo in Basque) is best known for the magnificent Guggenheim Museum. An architectural masterpiece by Frank Gehry, the museum was the catalyst of a turnaround that saw Bilbao transformed from an industrial port city into a vibrant cultural centre (without losing its down-to-earth soul). After visiting this must-see temple to modern art, spend time exploring Bilbao's Casco Viejo (Old Quarter), a grid of elegant streets dotted with shops, cafes, *pintxo* bars and several small but worthy museums.

⊙ Sights

★ Museo Guggenheim Bilbao   GALLERY

(☑944 35 90 80; www.guggenheim-bilbao.es; Avenida Abandoibarra 2; adult/concession/child from €13/7.50/free; ⊙10am-8pm, closed Mon Sep-Jun) Shimmering titanium Museo Guggenheim Bilbao is one of modern architecture's most iconic buildings. It played a major role in helping to lift Bilbao out of its postindustrial depression and into the 21st century – and with sensation. It sparked the city's inspired regeneration, stimulated further development and placed Bilbao firmly in the international art and tourism spotlight.

★ Museo de Bellas Artes   GALLERY

(☑944 39 60 60; www.museobilbao.com; Plaza del Museo 2; adult/concession/child €10/8/free, free 6-8pm; ⊙10am-8pm Wed-Mon) The Museo de Bellas Artes houses a compelling collection that includes everything from Gothic sculptures to 20th-century pop art. There are

three main subcollections: classical art, with works by Murillo, Zurbarán, El Greco, Goya and van Dyck; contemporary art, featuring works by Gauguin, Francis Bacon and Anthony Caro; and Basque art, with works of the great sculptors Jorge Oteiza and Eduardo Chillida, and strong paintings by the likes of Ignacio Zuloaga and Juan de Echevarría.

Casco Viejo   OLD TOWN

The compact Casco Viejo, Bilbao's atmospheric old quarter, is full of charming streets, boisterous bars and plenty of quirky and independent shops. At the heart of the Casco are Bilbao's original seven streets, **Las Siete Calles**, which date from the 1400s.

🛏 Sleeping & Eating

The Bilbao tourism authority has a useful **reservations department** (☑946 94 12 12) for accommodation.

Pintxos (Basque tapas) are as good in Bilbao as they are in San Sebastián, and slightly cheaper (from around €2.50). Plaza Nueva, on the edge of the Casco Viejo, offers especially rich pickings, as do Calles de Perro and Jardines.

Casual Bilbao Gurea   PENSION €€

(☑944 16 32 99; www.casualhoteles.com; Calle de Bidebarrieta 14; s/d €75/85; 🖳) The family-run Gurea has arty, modern rooms with wooden floors, good natural light and exceptionally friendly staff. It's set on the 3rd and 4th floors of a building in the old town, with great dining options just steps from the entrance.

Miró Hotel   DESIGN HOTEL €€€

(☑946 61 18 80; www.mirohotelbilbao.com; Alameda Mazarredo 77; d from €210; ❋@🖳) This hip hotel facing the Museo Guggenheim Bilbao is the passion project of fashion designer Antonio Miró. It's filled with modern photography and art, quirky books, and minimalist decor – a perfect fit with art-minded Bilbao.

★ La Viña del Ensanche   PINTXOS €

(☑944 15 56 15; www.lavinadelensanche.com; Calle de la Diputación 10; small plates €5-15, set menu €30; ⊙8.30am-11pm Mon-Fri, noon-1am Sat) Set with old-fashioned wood-panelled walls and framed postcards written by adoring fans over the years, La Viña del Ensanche maintains a reputation as one of Bilbao's best eating spots – no small achievement for a place that has been in business since 1927. Mouth-watering morsels of ham, tender oc-

PAMPLONA & SAN FERMINES

Immortalised by Ernest Hemingway in *The Sun Also Rises*, the pre-Pyrenean city of Pamplona (Iruña in Basque) is home of the wild Sanfermines festival, but it is also an extremely walkable city that's managed to mix the charm of old plazas and buildings with modern shops and a lively nightlife.

The **Sanfermines festival** is held from 6 to 14 July, when Pamplona is overrun with thrill-seekers, curious onlookers and, yes, bulls. *El encierro* (running of the bulls) begins at 8am daily, when bulls are let loose from the Coralillos Santo Domingo. The 875m run through the streets to the bullring lasts just three minutes.

Since records began in 1924, 16 people have died during Pamplona's bullrun. Many of those who participate are full of bravado (and/or drink) and have little idea of what they're doing. For dedicated *encierro* news, check out www.sanfermin.com.

Animal rights groups oppose bullrunning as a cruel tradition, and the participating bulls will almost certainly all be killed in the afternoon bullfight. PETA (www.peta.org.uk) organises eye-catching protests in Pamplona at every Sanfermines.

topus and crispy asparagus tempura are just a few of the many temptations.

Agape Restaurante BASQUE €€
(944 16 05 06; www.restauranteagape.com; Calle de Hernani 13; menú del día €13.50, menús €24-37; 1-4pm Mon & Tue, 1-4pm & 9-11pm Wed-Sat;) With a solid reputation among locals for good-value meals that don't sacrifice quality, this is a highly recommended place for a slice of real Bilbao culinary life. Think sea bass served over shrimp and leek risotto, lamb confit with roasted aubergines and stir-fried vegetables with almond and sesame pesto – all served in a stylish but rustic setting.

ⓘ Information

The very helpful **main branch** (944 79 57 60; www.bilbaoturismo.net; Plaza Circular 1; 9am-8pm;) of the tourist office is near the Abando train station.

ⓘ Getting There & Away

BUS

Bilbao's main bus station, **Termibus** (944 39 50 77; www.termibus.es; Gurtubay 1, San Mamés), is west of the centre. Services operate to San Sebastián (from €7, 1¼ hours, frequent), Madrid (from €32, four to five hours, 15 daily), Barcelona (from €36, 8½ hours, four daily), Pamplona (€15, 2½ hours, six daily) and Santander (from €7, 1¼ hours, frequent).

TRAIN

Two Renfe trains run daily to Madrid (from €20, five to seven hours) and Barcelona (from €27, seven hours) from the Abando station. Slow **Renfe Feve** (www.renfe.com/viajeros/feve) trains from Concordia station next door head

west to Santander (from €9, three hours, three daily), where you can connect for places further west in Cantabria, Asturias and Galicia.

CANTABRIA, ASTURIAS & GALICIA

With a landscape reminiscent of parts of the British Isles, 'Green Spain' offers great walks and scenery in mountainous national and regional parks, seafood feasts in sophisticated towns or quaint fishing villages, and a spectacular coastline strung with oodles of beautiful beaches washed by the chilly waters of the north Atlantic.

Santillana del Mar

Thirty kilometres west of the Cantabrian capital, Santander, Santillana del Mar is a *bijou* medieval village and the obvious overnight base for visiting nearby Altamira. Buses run six times a day from Santander to Santillana del Mar.

Spain's finest prehistoric art, in the **Cueva de Altamira**, 2.5km southwest of Santillana, was discovered in 1879. It took more than 20 years, after further discoveries of cave art in France, before scientists accepted that these wonderful paintings of bison, horses and other animals really were the handiwork of primitive people many thousands of years ago. A replica cave here in the **Museo de Altamira** (942 81 80 05; http://museodealtamira.mcu.es; Avenida Marcelino Sanz de Sautuola, Santillana del Mar; adult/child €3/free, Sun & from 2pm Sat free; 9.30am-8pm Tue-Sat May-Oct, to 6pm Tue-Sat Nov-Apr, to 3pm Sun &

WORTH A TRIP

PICOS DE EUROPA

These jagged mountains straddling corners of Asturias, Cantabria and Castilla y León amount to some of the finest walking country in Spain. They comprise three limestone massifs (the highest peak rises to 2648m). The 674-sq-km **Parque Nacional de los Picos de Europa** covers all three massifs and is Spain's second-biggest national park.

There are numerous places to stay and eat all around the mountains, with Cangas de Onís (Asturias) and Potes (Cantabria) the main centres for accommodation and information. Getting here and around by public transport can be slow going, but the Picos are accessible by bus from Oviedo and Santander (the former is easier).

The official websites, www.mapama. gob.es and www.parquenacionalpico seuropa.es, are mostly in Spanish, but www.picosdeeuropa.com and www. liebanaypicosdeeuropa.com are useful for the Asturias and Cantabria sides respectively.

holidays year-round; P 🚻) now enables everyone to appreciate the inspired, 13,000- to 35,000-year-old paintings – advance bookings are advisable.

Santiago de Compostela

POP 80,326

The supposed burial place of St James (Santiago), this unique cathedral city and goal of pilgrims for nearly 1200 years is a bewitching place. The hundreds of thousands who walk here every year along the Camino de Santiago are often struck mute with wonder on entering the city's medieval centre. Fortunately, they usually regain their verbal capacities over a celebratory nocturnal foray into the city's lively bar scene.

👁 Sights & Activities

★ Catedral de Santiago de Compostela CATHEDRAL

(http://catedraldesantiago.es; Praza do Obradoiro; ⊗7am-8.30pm) The grand heart of Santiago, the cathedral soars above the city in a splendid jumble of spires and sculpture. Built piecemeal over several centuries, its beauty is a mix of the original Romanesque

structure (constructed between 1075 and 1211) and later Gothic and baroque flourishes. The tomb of Santiago beneath the main altar is a magnet for all who come here. The cathedral's artistic high point is the Pórtico de la Gloria inside the west entrance, featuring 200 masterly Romanesque sculptures.

★ Cathedral Rooftop Tour TOURS

(🖂881 55 79 45; www.catedraldesantiago.es; adult/concession/child €12/10/free, combined ticket with Museo da Catedral €15/12/free; ⊗tours hourly 10am-1pm & 4-7pm; 🚻) For unforgettable bird's-eye views of the cathedral interior from its upper storeys, and of the city from the cathedral roof, take the rooftop tour, which starts in the **visitor reception centre** (Praza do Obradoiro; ⊗9am-8pm Apr-Oct, 10am-8pm Nov-Mar). The tours are popular, so book beforehand, either at the visitor reception centre for same-day visits, or on the cathedral website up to several weeks ahead. Tours are given in Spanish, but some guides also speak some English.

Praza do Obradoiro PLAZA

The grand square in front of the cathedral's western facade earned its name (Workshop Sq) from the stonemasons' workshops set up here while the cathedral was being built. It's free of both traffic and cafes, and has a unique, magical atmosphere.

Museo da Catedral MUSEUM

(Colección Permanente; www.catedraldesantiago. es; Praza do Obradoiro; adult/concession/child €6/4/free; ⊗9am-8pm Apr-Oct, 10am-8pm Nov-Mar) The Cathedral Museum spreads over four floors and incorporates the cathedral's large 16th-century Gothic/plateresque cloister. You'll see a sizeable section of Maestro Mateo's original carved-stone choir (destroyed in 1604 but pieced back together in 1999), an impressive collection of religious art (including the *botafumeiros* in the 2nd-floor library), the lavishly decorated 18th-century *sala capitular* (chapter house), a room of tapestries woven from designs by Goya, and, off the cloister, the Panteón de Reyes, with tombs of kings of medieval León.

Museo das Peregrinacións e de Santiago MUSEUM

(http://museoperegrinacions.xunta.gal; Praza das Praterías; adult/pilgrim & student/senior & child €2.40/1.20/free; ⊗9.30am-8.30pm Tue-Fri, 11am-7.30pm Sat, 10.15am-2.45pm Sun) The brightly displayed Museum of Pilgrimages & Santiago gives fascinating insights into the phenomenon of Santiago (man, city and pilgrimage) down the centuries. Much of the explanatory material is in English as well as Spanish and Galician. There are also great close-up views of some of the cathedral's towers from the 3rd-floor windows.

🛌 Sleeping & Eating

Hostal Suso
HOSTAL €

(📞981 58 66 11; www.hostalsuso.com; Rúa do Vilar 65; r €42-80; ❄️@🛜) Stacked above a convenient cafe (with excellent-value breakfasts), the friendly, family-run 14-room Suso received a full makeover in 2016 and boasts immaculate, thoughtfully designed rooms in appealing greys and whites, with up-to-date bathrooms and firm beds. It's very good for the price. Everything is thoroughly soundproofed, too – the street outside is traffic-free but can get quite celebratory in summer.

Hotel Costa Vella
BOUTIQUE HOTEL €€

(📞981 56 95 30; www.costavella.com; Rúa da Porta da Pena 17; s €50-60, d €55-95; ❄️@🛜) Tranquil, well-designed rooms (some with typically Galician *galerías* – glassed-in balconies), a friendly welcome, super-helpful management and staff, and a lovely garden cafe make this family-run hotel a wonderful option. It's set in an old stone house just a 400m stroll from the cathedral; the €5 breakfast is substantial.

★Parador Hostal dos Reis Católicos
HISTORIC HOTEL €€€

(📞981 58 22 00; www.parador.es; Praza do Obradoiro 1; incl breakfast s €145-185, d €165-335; 🅿️❄️@🛜) Opened in 1509 as a pilgrims' hostel, and with a claim as the world's oldest hotel, this palatial *parador* occupies a wonderful building that is one of Santiago's major monuments in its own right. Even standard rooms are grand, if a little old-fashioned, with wooden floors, original art and good-sized bathrooms with big glass showers. Some have four-poster beds.

Café-Jardín Costa Vella
CAFE €

(www.costavella.com; Rúa da Porta da Pena 17; breakfast €2.70-4.50; ☺8am-11pm; 🛜) The garden cafe of Hotel Costa Vella is the most delightful spot for breakfast (or a drink later in the day), with its fountain, a scattering of statuary and beautiful flowering fruit trees. And if the weather takes a Santiago-esque rainy turn, you can still enjoy it from the glass pavilion or the *galería*.

★Abastos 2.0
GALICIAN €€

(📞654 015937; www.abastoscompostela.com; Rúa das Ameas; dishes €6-13, menú from €30; ☺noon-3.30pm & 8-11pm Mon-Sat) This highly original, incredibly popular marketside eatery offers new dishes concocted daily from the market's offerings, with an emphasis on seafood. Inside is one long 12-seat table where they serve a daily changing menu for €30-plus: reservations are highly advisable. Outside are a few tables (not reservable) where they serve small- to medium-size individual dishes. Almost everything in both sections is delicious.

★O Curro da Parra
GALICIAN, FUSION €€

(www.ocurrodaparra.com; Rúa do Curro da Parra 7; mains €17-23, starters & medias raciones €8-14; ☺1.30-3.30pm & 8.30-11.30pm Tue-Sun; 🛜) With a neat little stone-walled dining room upstairs and a narrow food-and-wine bar below, always-busy Curro da Parra serves thoughtfully created, market-fresh fare, changing weekly. Everything is delectable; typical offerings might include line-caught hake with cockles and green beans or beef tenderloin with shiitake mushrooms. The 2010 cheesecake has been a favourite ever since it opened.

ℹ️ Information

Turismo de Santiago (📞981 55 51 29; www.santiagoturismo.com; Rúa do Vilar 63; ☺9am-9pm May-Oct, 9am-7pm Mon-Fri, 9am-2pm & 4-7pm Sat & Sun Nov-Apr) is very efficient. Its website is a multilingual mine of information.

ℹ️ Getting There & Around

AIR
The busy **Santiago airport** (📞903 211 000; www.aena.es) has direct flights to/from some 20 European and Spanish cities, many of them operated by budget airlines easyJet, Ryanair and Vueling.

BUS
The **bus station** (📞981 54 24 16; Praza de Camilo Díaz Baliño; 🛜) is 1.5km northeast of the city centre. There are services to León (€31, six hours, one daily), Madrid (from €21, eight to 10 hours, four daily), Porto (Portugal; from €27, 4¼ hours, three daily), Santander (from €44, nine to 10 hours, two daily) and many places around Galicia.

TRAIN

From the **train station** (www.renfe.com; Rúa do Hórreo), plentiful trains run up and down the Galician coast as far as A Coruña and Vigo. There are regular services to Madrid (from €22, 5¼ hours).

Around Galicia

Galicia's dramatic coastline is one of Spain's best-kept secrets, with wild and precipitous cliffs, long inlets running far inland, splendid beaches and isolated fishing villages. The lively port city of **A Coruña** has a lovely city beach and fabulous seafood (a recurring Galician theme). It's also a gateway to the stirring landscapes of the **Costa da Morte** and **Rías Altas**; the latter's highlight among many is probably **Cabo Ortegal**. Inland Galicia is also worth exploring, especially the old town of **Lugo**, surrounded by what many consider the world's best preserved Roman walls.

VALENCIA

POP 787,808

Spain's third-largest city is a magnificent place, content for Madrid and Barcelona to grab the headlines while it gets on with being a wonderfully liveable city with thriving cultural, eating and nightlife scenes. The star attraction is the strikingly futuristic buildings of the Ciudad de las Artes y las Ciencias, designed by local boy Santiago Calatrava. Valencia also has an array of fabulous Modernista architecture, great museums and a large, characterful old quarter. Surrounded by fertile fruit-and-veg farmland, the city is famous as the home of rice dishes like paella, but its buzzy dining scene offers plenty more besides.

◉ Sights & Activities

★ Ciudad de las Artes y las Ciencias   ARCHITECTURE

(City of Arts & Sciences; ☑ 961 97 46 86; www. cac.es; Avenida del Professor López Piñero; ☒) This aesthetically stunning complex occupies a massive 350,000-sq-metre swath of the old Turia riverbed. It's occupied by a series of spectacular buildings that are mostly the work of world-famous, locally born architect Santiago Calatrava. The principal buildings are a majestic **opera house** (☑ tours 672 062523; www.lesarts.com;

guided visit adult/child €10.60/8.10; ⊘ guided visits 10.45am, noon & 1.30pm daily, plus 3.45pm & 5pm Mon-Sat), a **science museum** (☑ 961 97 47 86; adult/child €8/6.20, with Hemisfèric €12.60/9.60; ⊘ 10am-6pm or 7pm mid-Sep–Jun, 10am-9pm Jul–mid-Sep; ☒), a **3D cinema** (sessions adult/child €8.80/6.85, incl Museo de las Ciencias Príncipe Felipe €12.60/9.60; ⊘ from 10am) and an **aquarium** (☑ 960 47 06 47; www. oceanografic.org; Camino de las Moreras; adult/child €29.10/21.85, audio guide €3.70, combined ticket with Hemisfèric & Museo de las Ciencias Príncipe Felipe €37.40/28.40; ⊘ 10am-6pm Sun-Fri, to 8pm Sat mid-Sep–mid-Jun, 10am-8pm mid-Jun–mid-Jul & early Sep, 10am-midnight mid-Jul–Aug; ☒). Calatrava is a controversial figure for many Valencians, who complain about the expense and various design flaws. Nevertheless, if your taxes weren't involved, it's awe-inspiring and pleasingly family-oriented.

Catedral de Valencia   CATHEDRAL

(☑ 963 91 81 27; www.catedraldevalencia.es; Plaza de la Virgen; adult/child €7/5.50; ⊘ 10am-6.30pm Mon-Sat, 2-6.30pm Sun Apr-Oct, 10am-5.30pm Mon-Sat Nov-May; ☎) Valencia's cathedral was built over a mosque after the 1238 reconquest. Its low, wide, brick-vaulted triple nave is mostly Gothic, with neoclassical side chapels. Highlights are its **museum** (incl in cathedral entry; ⊘ 10am-6.30pm Mon-Sat, 2-6.30pm Sun Jun-Sep, 10am-5.30pm Mon-Sat, 10am-2pm Sun Oct-May, closed Sun Nov-Feb; ☎), rich Italianate frescos above the altarpiece, a pair of Goyas in the Capilla de San Francisco de Borja, and in the flamboyant Gothic Capilla del Santo Cáliz, what's claimed to be the Holy Grail from which Christ sipped during the Last Supper. It's a Roman-era agate cup, later modified, so at least the date is right. Admission includes an audio guide.

La Lonja   HISTORIC BUILDING

(☑ 962 08 41 53; www.valencia.es; Calle de la Lonja; adult/child €2/1, Sun free; ⊘ 10am-7pm Mon-Sat, to 2pm Sun) This splendid building, a Unesco World Heritage Site, was originally Valencia's silk and commodity exchange, built in the late 15th century when the city was booming. It's one of Spain's finest examples of a civil Gothic building. Two main structures flank a citrus-studded courtyard: the magnificent Sala de Contratación, a cathedral of commerce with soaring twisted pillars, and the Consulado del Mar, where a maritime tribunal sat. The top floor boasts a stunning coffered ceiling brought here from another building.

Mercado Central
MARKET

(☑963 82 91 00; www.mercadocentralvalencia.
es; Plaza del Mercado; ⊙7.30am-3pm Mon-Sat)
Valencia's vast Modernista covered market,
constructed in 1928, is a swirl of smells,
movement and colour. Spectacular seafood
counters display cephalopods galore and
numerous fish species, meat stalls groan
under the weight of sausages and giant
steaks, while the fruit and vegetables, many
produced locally in Valencia's *huerta* (area
of market gardens), are of special quality. A
tapas bar lets you sip a wine and enjoy the
atmosphere.

Museo de Bellas Artes
GALLERY

(San Pío V; ☑963 87 03 00; www.museobellasar
tesvalencia.gva.es; Calle de San Pío V 9; ⊙10am-
8pm Tue-Sun) **FREE** Bright and spacious, this
gallery ranks among Spain's best. Highlights
include a collection of magnificent late-
medieval altarpieces, and works by several
Spanish masters, including some great Goya
portraits, a haunting Velázquez self-portrait,
an El Greco *John the Baptist* and works by
Murillos, Riberas and the Ribaltas, father
and son.

Downstairs, an excellent series of rooms
focuses on the great, versatile Valencian
painter Joaquín Sorolla (1863–1923), who, at
his best, seemed to capture the spirit of an
age through sensitive portraiture.

Beaches

Valencia's town beaches are 3km from the
centre. Playa de las Arenas runs north into
Playa de la Malvarrosa and Playa de la Pataco-
na, forming a wide strip of sand some 4km
long. It's bordered by the Paseo Marítimo
promenade and a string of restaurants and
cafes. The marina and port area, refurbished
for the 2007 Americas Cup, is south of here
and backed by the intriguing and increasingly trendy fishing district of El Cabanyal,
which makes for excellent exploration.

🛏 Sleeping

Russafa Youth Hostel
HOSTEL €

(☑963 31 31 40; www.russafayouthhostel.com; Carrer del Padre Perera 5; dm €18-25, s with shared bathroom €30-50, d with shared bathroom €50-65; @ 🛜)
You'll feel instantly at home in this super-
welcoming, cute hostel set over various floors
of a venerable building in the heart of vibrant
Russafa. It's all beds, rather than bunks, and
with a maximum of three to a room, there's

WORTH A TRIP

LAS FALLAS

In mid-March, Valencia hosts one of
Europe's wildest street parties: **Las
Fallas de San José** (www.fallas.com).
From 15 to 19 March the city is engulfed
by an anarchic swirl of fireworks, music,
festive bonfires and all-night partying.
On the final night, hundreds of giant
effigies *(fallas)*, many of them representing political and social personages,
are torched. A popular vote spares the
most-cherished *ninot* (figure), which
gets housed for posterity in the **Museo
Fallero** (☑962 08 46 25; www.valencia.
es; Plaza Monteolivete 4; adult/child €2/
free, Sun free; ⊙10am-7pm Mon-Sat, to
2pm Sun).

no crowding. Sweet rooms and spotless bathrooms make for a mighty easy stay.

Hotel Sorolla Centro
HOTEL €€

(☑963 52 33 92; www.hotelsorollacentro.com;
Calle Convento Santa Clara 5; s/d from €55/70;
❇🛜) Neat and contemporary but without
any flashy design gimmicks, this hotel offers very solid value for comfortable, well-
thought-out modern rooms with powerful
showers and plenty of facilities. Staff are extremely helpful and the location, on a pedestrian street close to the main square, is fab.

★ Caro Hotel
HOTEL €€€

(☑963 05 90 00; www.carohotel.com; Calle
Almirante 14; r €165-325; P❇🛜) Housed in
a sumptuous 19th-century mansion, this
hotel sits atop two millennia of Valencian
history, with restoration revealing a hefty
hunk of the Arab wall, Roman column bases
and Gothic arches. Each room is furnished
in soothing dark shades, with a great king-
size bed and varnished concrete floors.
Bathrooms are tops. For special occasions,
reserve the 1st-floor grand suite, once the
ballroom.

🍴 Eating

The number of restaurants has to be seen
to be believed! In the centre there are numerous traditional options, as well as trendy
tapas choices. The main eating zones are
the Barrio del Carmen, L'Eixample and,
above all, the vibrant tapas-packed streets
of Russafa.

L'Ostrería del Carme
SEAFOOD €

(☎629 145026; www.laostreriadelcarmen.com; Plaza de Mossén Sorell; oysters €2-4; ⊙11am-3pm Mon-Sat, plus 5-8.30pm Thu & Fri) This little stall inside the **Mossén Sorell market** (⊙7.30am-3pm Mon-Sat, plus 5-8.30pm Thu & Fri except in Aug) is a cordial spot and a fabulous snack stop. It has oysters of excellent quality from Valencia and elsewhere; sit down with a glass of white wine and let them shuck you a few.

Navarro
VALENCIAN €€

(☎963 52 96 23; www.restaurantenavarro.com; Calle del Arzobispo Mayoral 5; rices €14-17, set menu €22; ⊙1-4pm Mon-Sat; 🐾) A byword in the city for decades for its quality rice dishes, Navarro is run by the grandkids of the original founders and it offers plenty of choice, outdoor seating and a set menu, including one of the rices as a main.

★ El Poblet
GASTRONOMY €€€

(☎961 11 11 06; www.elpobletrestaurante.com; Calle de Correos 8; degustation menus €85-125, mains €25-35; ⊙1.30-3.15pm & 8.30-10.15pm Mon & Wed-Sat; 🐾) This upstairs restaurant, overseen by famed Quique Dacosta and with Luis Valls as chef, offers elegance and fine gastronomic dining at prices that are very competitive for this quality. Modern French and Spanish influences combine to create sumptuous degustation menus. Some of the imaginative presentation has to be seen to be believed, and staff are genuinely welcoming and helpful.

🍷 Drinking & Nightlife

Russafa has the best bar scene, with a huge range of everything from family-friendly cultural cafes to quirky bars, as well as a couple of big clubs. The Barrio del Carmen is also famous nightlife territory. In summer the port area and Malvarrosa beach leap to life.

★ La Fábrica de Hielo
CAFE

(☎963 68 26 19; www.lafabricadehielo.net; Calle de Pavia 37; ⊙5pm-midnight Tue & Wed, to 1am Thu, to 1.30am Fri, 11am-1.30am Sat, to midnight Sun) It's difficult to know how to classify this former ice factory, converted with great charm into a sizeable multi-purpose space that does cultural events, drinks and tapas just back from the beach. Just drop by and see what's going down – Sundays are loads of fun, with paella and dancing, but there's always a great atmosphere.

★ Radio City
CLUB

(☎963 91 41 51; www.radiocityvalencia.es; Calle de Santa Teresa 19; ⊙10.30pm-4am Fri-Mon, from 10pm Tue, from 8pm Wed & Thu) Almost as much mini-cultural-centre as club, Radio City, which gets packed from around 1am, pulls in the punters with activities such as language exchange, and DJs or live music every night. There's everything from flamenco (Tuesday) to reggae and funk, and the crowd is eclectic and engaged.

L'Umbracle Terraza
BAR, CLUB

(☎671 668000; www.umbracleterraza.com; Avenida del Professor López Piñero 5; admission €12; ⊙midnight-7.30am Thu-Sat) At the southern end of the Umbracle walkway within the Ciudad de las Artes y las Ciencias, this is a touristy but atmospheric spot to spend a hot summer night. After the queue and laughable door attitude, catch the evening breeze under the stars on the terrace. The downstairs club **Mya** is a sweatier experience. Admission covers both venues.

ℹ Information

Tourist Info Valencia – Paz (☎963 98 64 22; www.visitvalencia.com; Calle de la Paz 48; ⊙9am-6.50pm Mon-Sat, 10am-1.50pm Sun; 🐾) has information about the city and region.

ℹ Getting There & Away

AIR

Valencia's **airport** (☎902 404 704; www.aena.es) is 10km west of the city centre along the A3, towards Madrid. Flights, including many budget routes, serve major European destinations, including London, Paris and Berlin.

BOAT

Trasmediterránea (☎902 454645; www.trasmediterranea.es) operates car and passenger ferries to Ibiza, Mallorca and Menorca. **Baleària** (☎902 160180, from overseas 912 66 02 14; www.balearia.com; Moll de la Pansa) goes to Mallorca and Ibiza.

BUS

Valencia's **bus station** (☎963 46 62 66; Avenida Menéndez Pidal) is located beside the riverbed. Bus 8 connects it to Plaza del Ayuntamiento. **Avanza** (www.avanzabus.com) operates regular bus services to/from Madrid (€28 to €36, 4½ to five hours). **ALSA** (www.alsa.es) has services to/from Barcelona (€29 to €38, four to six hours, up to 10 daily) and Alicante (€21 to €25, 2½ to 5½ hours, more than 10 daily), most via Benidorm.

TRAIN

All fast trains now use the **Valencia Joaquín Sorolla station** (www.adif.es; Calle San Vicente Mártir 171), 800m south of the old town. It's meant to be temporary, but looks like sticking around for a long time. It's linked with nearby **Estación del Norte** (Calle de Xàtiva; ☺5.30am-midnight; 🛜), 500m away, by free shuttle bus. Estación del Norte has slow trains to Gandia, Alicante and Madrid, as well as local *cercanía* lines.

Major destinations include Alicante (€17 to €20, 1½ to 2¼ hours, 12 daily), Barcelona (€22 to €28, 3¼ to 5½ hours, 14 daily) and Madrid (€21 to €51, 1¾ to 7¾ hours, 18 daily).

ℹ️ Getting Around

Valencia has an integrated bus, tram and metro network. Rides are €1.50; one-/two-/three-day travel cards cost €4/6.70/9.70. Metro lines 3 and 5 connect the airport, central Valencia and the port. The tram is a pleasant way to get to the beach and port. Pick it up at Pont de Fusta or where it intersects with the metro at Benimaclet.

BALEARIC ISLANDS

The Balearic Islands (Illes Balears in Catalan) adorn the glittering Mediterranean waters off Spain's eastern coastline. Beach tourism destinations par excellence, each of the islands has a quite distinct identity and they have managed to retain much of their individual character and beauty. All boast beaches second to none in the Med, but each offers reasons for exploring inland too.

Check out websites like www.illesbalears.es and www.platgesdebalears.com.

ℹ️ Getting There & Away

AIR

In summer, charter and regular flights converge on Palma de Mallorca and Ibiza from all over Europe.

BOAT

The major ferry companies are Trasmediterránea (p1066) and **Baleària** (☎902 16 01 80; www.balearia.com). Compare prices and look for deals at Direct Ferries (www.directferries.com).

The main ferry routes to the mainland, most operating only from Easter to late October, include the following:

Ibiza (Ibiza City) To/from Barcelona and Valencia (Trasmediterránea, Baleària) and Denia (Baleària)

Ibiza (Sant Antoni) To/from Valencia (Baleària)

Mallorca (Palma de Mallorca) To/from Barcelona and Valencia (Trasmediterránea, Baleària) and Denia (Baleària)

Mallorca (Port d'Alcúdia) To/from Barcelona (Baleària)

The main inter-island ferry routes include the following:

Ibiza (Ibiza City) To/from Palma de Mallorca (Trasmediterránea, Baleària)

Mallorca (Palma de Mallorca) To/from Ibiza City (Baleària) and Maó (Trasmediterránea)

Mallorca (Port d'Alcúdia) To/from Ciutadella (Trasmediterránea, Baleària)

Menorca (Ciutadella) To/from Port d'Alcúdia (Trasmediterránea, Baleària)

Menorca (Maó) To/from Palma de Mallorca (Trasmediterránea)

Mallorca

The ever-popular star of the Mediterranean, Mallorca has a sunny personality thanks to its ravishing beaches, azure views, remote mountains and soulful hill towns.

Palma de Mallorca

Palma de Mallorca is a graceful and historic Mediterranean city with some world-class attractions and equally impressive culinary, art and nightlife scenes.

POP 406,692

⦿ Sights

★**Catedral de Mallorca**   CATHEDRAL
(La Seu; www.catedraldemallorca.org; Carrer del Palau Reial 9; adult/child €7/free; ☺10am-6.15pm Mon-Fri Jun-Sep, to 5.15pm Apr, May & Oct, to 3.15pm Nov-Mar, 10am-2.15pm Sat year-round) Palma's vast cathedral ('La Seu' in Catalan) is the city's major architectural landmark. Aside from its sheer scale and undoubted beauty, its stunning interior features, designed by Antoni Gaudí and renowned contemporary artist Miquel Barceló, make this unlike any cathedral elsewhere in the world. The awesome structure is predominantly Gothic, apart from the main facade, which is startling, quite beautiful and completely mongrel.

Palau de l'Almudaina   PALACE
(https://entradas.patrimonionacional.es; Carrer del Palau Reial; adult/child €7/4, audio guide €3, guided tour €4; ☺10am-8pm Tue-Sun Apr-Sep, to 6pm Tue-Sun Oct-Mar) Originally an Islamic

fort, this mighty construction opposite the cathedral was converted into a residence for the Mallorcan monarchs at the end of the 13th century. The King of Spain resides here still, at least symbolically. The royal family is rarely in residence, except for the occasional ceremony, as they prefer to spend summer in the Palau Marivent (in Cala Major). At other times you can wander through a series of cavernous stone-walled rooms that have been lavishly decorated.

★**Palau March**   MUSEUM
(☑971 71 11 22; www.fundacionbmarch.es; Carrer del Palau Reial 18; adult/child €4.50/free; ⊙10am-6.30pm Mon-Fri Apr-Oct, to 5pm Nov-Mar, to 2pm Sat year-round) This house, palatial by any definition, was one of several residences of the phenomenally wealthy March family. Sculptures by 20th-century greats including Henry Moore, Auguste Rodin, Barbara Hepworth and Eduardo Chillida grace the outdoor terrace. Within lie many more artistic treasures from such luminaries of Spanish art as Salvador Dalí and Barcelona's Josep Maria Sert and Xavier Corberó. Not to be missed are the meticulously crafted figures of an 18th-century Neapolitan *belén* (nativity scene).

★**Es Baluard**   GALLERY
(Museu d'Art Modern i Contemporani; ☑971 90 82 00; www.esbaluard.org; Plaça de Porta de Santa Catalina 10; adult/child €6/free; ⊙10am-8pm Tue-Sat, to 3pm Sun; ☂) Built with flair and innovation into the shell of the Renaissance-era seaward walls, this contemporary art gallery is one of the finest on the island. Its temporary exhibitions are worth viewing, but the permanent collection – works by Miró, Barceló and Picasso – gives the gallery its cachet. Entry on Friday is by donation, and anyone turning up on a bike, on any day, is charged just €2.

🛏 **Sleeping & Eating**

Misión de San Miguel   BOUTIQUE HOTEL €€
(☑971 21 48 48; www.urhotels.com; Carrer de Can Maçanet 1A; d/ste from €110/175; 🅿❄@☂) This boutique hotel, with its 32 stylish designer rooms gathered discreetly around a quiet inner courtyard, is a real bargain. Good-quality mattresses and rain shower heads are typical of a place where the little things are always done well, although some rooms open onto public areas and can be a tad noisy. Service is friendly and professional.

★**Hotel Tres**   BOUTIQUE HOTEL €€€
(☑971 71 73 33; www.hoteltres.com; Carrer dels Apuntadors 3; s/d/ste €240/280/345; ❄@☂☒) Hotel Tres swings joyously between 16th-century town palace and fresh-faced Scandinavian design. Centred on a courtyard with a single palm, the rooms are cool and minimalist, with cowhide benches, anatomy-inspired prints, and nice details like rollaway desks and Durance aromatherapy cosmetics. Head up to the roof terrace at sunset for a steam and dip as the cathedral begins to twinkle.

★**Can Cera Gastro-Bar**   MEDITERRANEAN €€
(☑971 71 50 12; www.cancerahotel.com; Carrer del Convent de Sant Francesc 8; tapas €6-24; ⊙12.30-10.30pm) This restaurant spills onto a lovely inner patio at the Can Cera hotel, housed in a *palau* that dates originally from the 13th century. Dine by lantern light on tapas-sized dishes such as *frito mallorquín* (seafood fried with potato and herbs), Cantabrian anchovies, and pork ribs with honey and mustard. The vertical garden attracts plenty of attention from passers-by.

★**Marc Fosh**   MODERN EUROPEAN €€€
(☑971 72 01 14; www.marcfosh.com; Carrer de la Missió 7A; menús lunch €30-40, dinner €72-90; ⊙1-3pm & 7.30-10pm) The flagship of Michelin-starred Fosh's burgeoning flotilla of Palma restaurants, this stylish gastronomic destination introduces novel twists to time-honoured Mediterranean dishes and ingredients, all within the converted refectory of a 17th-century convent. The weekly lunch *menú* is a very reasonable way to enjoy dishes such as foie gras and duck terrine, or truffled pasta with burrata.

ℹ **Information**

Consell de Mallorca Tourist Office (☑971 17 39 90; www.infomallorca.net; Plaça de la Reina 2; ⊙8.30am-8pm Mon-Fri, to 3pm Sat; ☂)

Around Palma de Mallorca

Mallorca's northwestern coast is a world away from the high-rise tourism on the other side of the island. Dominated by the dramatic, razorback Serra de Tramuntana, it's a beautiful region of olive groves, pine forests and small villages with shuttered stone buildings. There are a couple of highlights for drivers: the hair-raising road down to the small port of **Sa Calobra**, and the amazing trip along the peninsula at the island's northern tip, **Cap Formentor**.

Sóller is a good place to base yourself for hiking and the nearby village of **Fornalutx** is one of the prettiest on Mallorca.

From Sóller, it's a 10km walk to the beautiful hilltop village of **Deià**, where Robert Graves, poet and author of *I Claudius,* lived for most of his life. From the village, you can scramble down to the small shingle beach of **Cala de Deià**. The pretty streets of **Valldemossa**, further southwest down the coast, are crowned by a fine monastery.

Further east, **Pollença** and **Artà** are attractive inland towns. Nice beaches include those at **Cala Sant Vicenç, Platja des Coll Baix** hidden on Cap des Pinar, **Cala Agulla** and others near Cala Ratjada, **Cala Mondragó** and **Cala Llombards**.

Buses and/or trains cover much of the island, but hiring a car (in any town or resort) is best for exploring the remoter beaches, hill towns and mountains.

Ibiza

Ibiza (Eivissa in Catalan) is an island of extremes. Its formidable party reputation is completely justified, with some of the world's greatest clubs attracting hedonists from the world over. The interior and northeast of the island, however, are another world. Peaceful country drives, hilly green territory, a sprinkling of mostly laid-back beaches and coves, and some wonderful inland accommodation and eateries are light years from the throbbing all-night dance parties that dominate the west.

Ibiza Town

⊙ Sights

Ibiza Town's port and nightlife area **Sa Penya** is crammed with funky and trashy clothing boutiques and arty-crafty market stalls. From here, you can wander up into Dalt Vila, the atmospheric old walled town.

★ **Dalt Vila**   OLD TOWN
Its formidable, floodlit, 16th-century bastions visible from across southern Ibiza, Dalt Vila is a fortified hilltop first settled by the Phoenicians and later occupied by a roster of subsequent civilisations. Tranquil and atmospheric, many of its cobbled lanes are accessible only on foot. It's mostly a residential area, but contains moody medieval

mansions and several key cultural sights. Enter via the Portal de Ses Taules gateway and wind your way uphill: all lanes lead to the cathedral-topped summit.

★ **Ramparts**   WALLS
Completely encircling Dalt Vila, Ibiza's colossal protective walls reach more than 25m in height and include seven bastions. Evocatively floodlit at night, these fortifications were constructed in the Renaissance era to protect Ibizans against the threat of attack by north African raiders and the Turkish navy. In under an hour, you can walk the entire 2km perimeter of the 16th-century ramparts, which were designed to withstand heavy artillery. Along the way, enjoy great views over the port and south across the water to Formentera.

🛏 Sleeping & Eating

Many of Ibiza City's hotels and *hostales* are closed in winter and heavily booked between April and October. Make sure you book ahead.

★ **Urban Spaces**   DESIGN HOTEL €€€
(📞 601 199302; info@urbanspacesibiza.com; Carrer de la Via Púnica 32; r €240-295; ⊙ Apr-early Jan; ❄ 🛜) Some of the world's most prolific street artists (N4T4, INKIE, JEROM) have pooled their creativity in this design hotel with an alternative edge. The roomy, muralsplashed suites sport clever backlighting, proper workstations and balconies with terrific views. Extras such as summer rooftop yoga and clubber-friendly breakfasts until 1pm are sure-fire people pleasers.

★ **S'Escalinata**   MEDITERRANEAN, CAFE €
(📞 971 30 61 93; www.sescalinata.es; Carrer des Portal Nou 10; dishes €7-13; ⊙ 10am-3am Apr-Oct; 🛜) With its low-slung tables and colourful cushions cascading down a steep stone staircase, this boho-chic cafe-bar-restaurant enjoys a magical location inside Dalt Vila. On the tempting menu are healthy breakfasts, tapas, *bocadillos* and delicious light dinners of hummus, tortilla or goat's-cheese salads. It's open late into the night, mixing up freshly squeezed juices, G&Ts and fruity cocktails.

Ca n'Alfredo   IBIZAN €€€
(📞 971 31 12 74; www.canalfredo.com; Passeig de Vara de Rey 16; mains €20-30; ⊙ 1-5pm & 8pm-1am Tue-Sat, 1-5pm Sun) Locals have been flocking to family-run Alfredo's on leafy Vara de Rey since 1934. It's a great place for the

CLUBBING IN IBIZA

Believe the hype. Despite being, essentially, a tiny island in the western Mediterranean, Ibiza can happily lay claim to being the world's queen of clubs. The globe's top DJs spin their magic here in summer, and the clubbing industry is very much the engine of the Ibizan economy. Sant Rafel, Ibiza Town, Platja d'en Bossa and Sant Antoni are the mega-club hubs. Expect to pay €15 to €20 for a *combinado* (spirit and mixer) and €10 to €12 for beer or water.

Pacha (www.pachaibiza.com; Avinguda 8 d'Agost; admission from €15; ⏱ midnight-7am May-Sep) Going strong since 1973, Pacha is Ibiza's original megaclub and the islanders' party venue of choice. It's built around the shell of a farmhouse, boasting a multilevel main dance floor, a Funky Room (for soul and disco beats), a huge VIP section and myriad other places to dance or lounge.

Amnesia (www.amnesia.es; Carretera Eivissa–Sant Antoni Km 5; admission €40-70; ⏱ midnight-6am late May-Oct) Amnesia is arguably Ibiza's most influential and legendary club, its decks welcoming such DJ royalty as Sven Väth, Paul Van Dyk, Paul Oakenfold, Tiësto and Avicii. There's a warehouse-like main room and a terrace topped by a graceful atrium. Big nights include techno-fests Cocoon and Music On, trance-mad Cream and foam-filled Espuma, which always draws a big local crowd.

Ushuaïa (☑ 971 92 81 93; www.ushuaiabeachhotel.com; Platja d'en Bossa 10; admission €45-75; ⏱ 3pm or 5pm-midnight May-Oct; ☎) Queen of daytime clubbing, ice-cool Ushuaïa is an open-air megaclub, packed with designer-clad hedonistas and waterside fun. The party starts early, with superstar DJs such as David Guetta, Martin Garrix, Luciano and Robin Schulz, and poolside lounging on Bali-style beds. Check out the Sky Lounge for sparkling sea views, or stay the night in the minimalist-chic **hotel** (r €390-840; ⏱ May-Oct; P❄☎≋).

freshest of seafood and other classic Ibiza dishes that are so good it's essential to book. Try John Dory fillets in almond sauce, or a traditional dish from the dedicated Ibizan cuisine menu, all accompanied by an impressive selection of Balearic wines.

🍷 Drinking & Nightlife

Sa Penya is the nightlife centre. Dozens of bars keep the port area jumping. Alternatively, various bars at Platja d'en Bossa combine sounds, sand, sea and sangria. Much cheaper than a taxi, the **Discobus** (www.discobus.es; per person €3-4; ⏱ midnight-6am Jun-Sep) does an all-night whirl of the major clubs, bars and hotels in Ibiza City, Platja d'en Bossa, Sant Rafel, Es Canar, Santa Eulària and Sant Antoni.

Bar 1805　　　　　　　　　　COCKTAIL BAR
(☑ 651 625972; www.bar1805ibiza.com; Carrer Baluard de Santa Llúcia 7; ⏱ 8pm-4am mid-Apr–Oct; ☎) Tucked away on a Sa Penya backstreet, this boho bar mixes some of the best cocktails in town, with lots of absinthe action on its beautifully illustrated menu. Try the signature Green Beast (served in a punch bowl) or a Gin-Basil Smash, which arrives in a teacup. Moules-frites, burgers, steaks, salads and other bites are served until 2am.

Bora Bora Beach Club　　　　　　　BAR
(www.boraboraibiza.net; Carrer d'es Fumarell 1; ⏱ 4pm-late May-Sep) A long beachside bar where sun and fun worshippers work off hangovers and prepare new ones. Entry is free and the ambience moves from chilled to party fever. It can get pretty messy in here with hundreds of swimwear-clad partygoers and jets screaming overhead (the airport is *very* close). There are also sun loungers to rent (€15).

ANDALUCÍA

So many of the most powerful images of Spain emanate from Andalucía that it can be difficult not to feel a sense of déjà vu. It's almost as if you've already been there in your dreams: the flashing fire of a flamenco dancer, the scent of orange blossom, a festive summer fair and magical nights in the shadow of the Alhambra. In the bright light of day, the picture is no less magical.

Seville

POP 689,434

It takes a stony heart not to be captivated by stylish but ancient, proud yet fun-loving Seville – home to two of Spain's most colourful festivals, fascinating and distinctive *barrios* (neighbourhoods) such as the flower-decked Santa Cruz, great historic monuments, and a population that lives life to the fullest. Being out among the celebratory, happy crowds in the tapas bars and streets on a warm spring night in Seville is an unforgettable experience. But try to avoid July and August, when it's so hot that most locals flee to the coast.

◎ Sights

★ Real Alcázar   PALACE
(☑ 954 50 23 24; www.alcazarsevilla.org; Plaza del Triunfo; adult/child €7/free; ⊙ 9.30am-7pm Apr-Sep, to 5pm Oct-Mar) A magnificent marriage of Christian and Mudéjar architecture, Seville's Unesco-listed palace complex is a breathtaking spectacle. The site, which was originally developed as a fort in 913, has been revamped many times over the 11 centuries of its existence, most spectacularly in the 14th century when King Pedro added the sumptuous Palacio de Don Pedro, still today the Alcázar's crown jewel. More recently, the Alcázar featured as a location for the *Game of Thrones* TV series.

★ Catedral de Sevilla & Giralda   CATHEDRAL
(☑ 902 09 96 92; www.catedraldesevilla.es; Plaza del Triunfo; adult/child €9/free, incl rooftop guided tour €15; ⊙ 11am-3.30pm Mon, to 5pm Tue-Sat, 2.30-6pm Sun) Seville's immense cathedral is awe-inspiring in its scale and majesty. The world's largest Gothic cathedral, it was built between 1434 and 1517 over the remains of what had previously been the city's main mosque. Highlights include the Giralda, the mighty bell tower, which incorporates the mosque's original minaret, the monumental tomb of Christopher Columbus, and the Capilla Mayor with an astonishing gold altarpiece. Note that children must be aged 11 years and over to access the rooftop tours. Audio guides cost €3.

Museo de Bellas Artes   MUSEUM
(Fine Arts Museum; ☑ 955 54 29 42; www.museodebellasartesdesevilla.es; Plaza del Museo 9; €1.50; ⊙ 9am-9pm Tue-Sat, to 3pm Sun) Housed in the beautiful former Convento de la Merced, Seville's Fine Arts Museum provides an elegant showcase for a comprehensive collection of Spanish and Sevillan paintings and sculptures. Works date from the 15th to 20th centuries, but the onus is very much on brooding religious paintings from the city's 17th-century *Siglo de Oro* (Golden Age).

★ Hospital de los Venerables Sacerdotes   MUSEUM
(☑ 954 56 26 96; www.focus.abengoa.es; Plaza de los Venerables 8; adult/child €8/4, 1st Thu of month free; ⊙ 10am-2pm Thu-Sun) This gem of a museum, housed in a former hospice for ageing priests, is one of Seville's most rewarding. The artistic highlight is the Focus-Abengoa Foundation's collection of 17th-century paintings in the Centro Velázquez. It's not a big collection, but each work is a masterpiece of its genre – highlights include Diego Velázquez' *Santa Rufina,* his *Inmaculada Concepción,* and a sharply vivid portrait of *Santa Catalina* by Bartolomé Murillo.

Plaza de España   SQUARE
(Avenida de Portugal, Parque de María Luisa) This bombastic plaza in the Parque de María Luisa was the most grandiose of the building projects completed for the 1929 Exposición Iberoamericana. A huge brick-and-tile confection, it's all very over the top, but it's undeniably impressive with its fountains, mini-canals and Venetian-style bridges. A series of gaudy tile pictures depict maps and historical scenes from each Spanish province.

⁂ Festivals & Events

Semana Santa   RELIGIOUS
(www.semana-santa.org; ⊙ Mar/Apr) Seville's Holy Week celebrations are legendary. Every day from Palm Sunday to Easter Sunday, large, life-size *pasos* (sculptural representations of events from Christ's Passion) are solemnly carried from the city's churches to the cathedral, accompanied by processions of marching *nazarenos* (penitents).

Feria de Abril   FERIA
(www.turismosevilla.org; El Real de la Feria; ⊙ Apr) The largest and most colourful of all Andalucía's *ferias* (fairs), Seville's weeklong spring fair is held in the second half of the month (sometimes edging into May) on El Real de la Feria, in the Los Remedios area west of the Río Guadalquivir. For six nights, *sevillanos* dress up in elaborate finery, parade around in horse-drawn carriages, eat, drink and dance till dawn.

⌂ Sleeping

Oasis Backpackers' Hostel   HOSTEL €
(☑ 955 26 26 96; www.oasissevilla.com; Calle Almirante Ulloa 1; dm €15-32, d €70-160; ✱ @ ☎ ☲) A veritable oasis in the busy city-centre

SPAIN SEVILLE

Seville

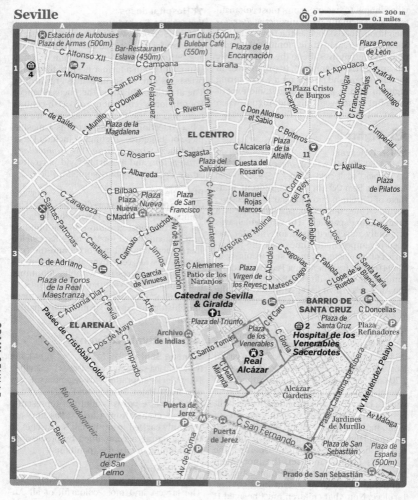

Seville

◎ Top Sights
1 Catedral de Sevilla & Giralda	C4
2 Hospital de los Venerables Sacerdotes	C4
3 Real Alcázar	C4

◎ Sights
4 Museo de Bellas Artes	A1

🛏 Sleeping
5 Hotel Adriano	A3
6 Hotel Casa 1800	C4
7 Oasis Backpackers' Hostel	A1
8 Un Patio en Santa Cruz	D3

✖ Eating
9 La Brunilda	A3
10 Restaurante Oriza	D5

◉ Drinking & Nightlife
11 El Garlochi	D2

district, this welcoming hostel is set in a palatial 19th-century mansion. There are various sleeping options ranging from mixed 14-person dorms to doubles with en suite bathrooms, and excellent facilities, including a cafe-bar, kitchen and rooftop deck with a small pool. Breakfast, not included in most rates, is available for €3.50.

Hotel Adriano
HOTEL €€

(☑954 29 38 00; www.adrianohotel.com; Calle de Adriano 12; s €65-70, d €75-140; P 🅿 ❄ 🛜) In the Arenal neighbourhood near the bullring, the three-star Adriano scores across the board with friendly staff, traditional, individually styled rooms and a lovely coffee shop, Pompeia, on the ground floor. Garage parking is available for €20 per day.

Un Patio en Santa Cruz
HOTEL €€€

(☑807 31 70 70; www.patiosantacruz.com; Calle Doncellas 15; s €65-140, d €75-200; ❄ 🛜) Feeling more like a gallery than a hotel, this place has stark white walls hung with bright works of art and lofty pot plants. The summery rooms, complete with parquet and dashes of purple, are good looking and comfortable, staff are friendly, and there's a cool rooftop terrace with Moroccan-mosaic tables.

★ Hotel Casa 1800
LUXURY HOTEL €€€

(☑954 56 18 00; www.hotelcasa1800sevilla.com; Calle Rodrigo Caro 6; d €125-525; ❄ @ 🛜) A short hop from the cathedral in the heart of Santa Cruz, this stately *casa* (house) is positively regal. Setting the tone is the elegant, old-school decor – wooden ceilings, chandeliers, parquet floors and plenty of gilt – but everything about the place charms, from the helpful staff to the rooftop terrace and complimentary afternoon tea.

✕ Eating

★ La Brunilda
TAPAS €

(☑954 22 04 81; www.labrunildatapas.com; Calle Galera 5; tapas €3.20-7.50; ⊙1-4pm & 8.30-11.30pm Tue-Sat, 1-4pm Sun) A regular fixture on lists of Seville's best tapas joints, this backstreet Arenal bar is at the forefront of the city's new wave of gourmet eateries. The look is modern casual with big blue doors, brick arches and plain wooden tables and the food is imaginative and good looking. The word is out, though, so arrive promptly or expect to queue.

CATEDRAL HIGHLIGHTS
....

The enormous Gothic cathedral was completed by 1507 after a century's work.

Puerta del Perdón A legacy of the great mosque.

Sala del Pabellón Art by 17th-century Golden Age masters.

Tomb of Christopher Columbus Inside the south entrance.

Capilla Mayor The fabulous Gothic retable is reckoned to be the world's biggest altarpiece.

Sacristía de los Cálices Art treasures including Goya's *Santas Justa y Rufina*.

Giralda Climb up inside the minaret of the great mosque, now the cathedral's bell tower.

★ Bar-Restaurante Eslava
FUSION, ANDALUCIAN €€

(☑954 90 65 68; www.espacioeslava.com; Calle Eslava 3; tapas €2.90-4.50, restaurant mains €16-24; ⊙bar 12.30-midnight Tue-Sat, 12.30-4pm Sun, restaurant 1-4pm & 8.30-midnight Tue-Sat, 1.30-4pm Sun) A hit with locals and savvy visitors, much-lauded Eslava shirks the traditional tilework and bullfighting posters of tapas-bar lore in favour of a simple blue space and a menu of creative contemporary dishes. Standouts include slow-cooked egg served on a mushroom cake, and memorable pork ribs in a honey and rosemary glaze. Expect crowds and a buzzing atmosphere.

Restaurante Oriza
BASQUE €€€

(☑954 22 72 54; www.restauranteoriza.com; Calle San Fernando 41; tapas €2.80-4.80, mains €23-35; ⊙1-5pm & 8pm-1am Mon-Thu, 1pm-1am Fri & Sat, 1pm-5pm Sun) The fabulous flavours of the Basque Country come to town at this upmarket eatery near the Parque de María Luisa. For the full-on à la carte experience, book at the restaurant; for a more casual meal, head to the in-house Bar España, which serves tapas and a €12 weekday lunch menu comprising starter, main course, dessert, coffee and drink.

🍺 Drinking & Nightlife

Drinking and partying really get going around midnight on Friday and Saturday

DON'T MISS

ALCÁZAR HIGHLIGHTS

Founded in 913 CE as a fort for Muslim Córdoba's local governors in Seville, the Alcázar (p1085) has been revamped many times since. Muslim rulers built at least two palaces inside it and after the Christians took Seville in 1248 they made further major modifications.

Patio del León (Lion Patio) The garrison yard of an 11th-century Islamic palace within the Alcázar. Off here is the Sala de la Justicia (Hall of Justice), with beautiful Mudéjar plasterwork and an *artesonado* (ceiling of interlaced beams with decorative insertions).

Patio de la Montería The rooms surrounding this patio are filled with interesting artefacts from Seville's history.

Cuarto Real Alto The Cuarto Real Alto (Upper Royal Quarters; used by the Spanish royal family on visits to Seville) are open for tours several times a day. The 14th-century Salón de Audiencias is still the monarch's reception room.

Palacio de Don Pedro Built by the Castilian king Pedro I ('the Cruel') in the 1360s, this is the single most stunning building in Seville. At its heart is the wonderful Patio de las Doncellas (Patio of the Maidens), surrounded by beautiful arches, plasterwork and tiling. The Alcoba Real (Royal Quarters), on the patio's northern side, has stunningly beautiful ceilings. The little Patio de las Muñecas (Patio of the Dolls), the heart of the palace's private quarters, features delicate Granada-style decoration. The Salón de Embajadores (Hall of Ambassadors), at the western end of the Patio de las Doncellas, was the throne room. Its fabulous wooden dome of multiple star patterns, symbolising the universe, was added in 1427.

Salones de Carlos V Reached via a staircase at the southeastern corner of the Patio de las Doncellas, these are the much-remodelled rooms of Alfonso X's 13th-century Gothic palace.

Gardens From the Salones de Carlos V you can go out and wander in the Alcázar's large and sleepy gardens, some with pools and fountains.

(daily when it's hot). Classic drinking areas include Plaza de la Alfalfa (cocktail and dive bars), the Barrio de Santa Cruz and the Alameda de Hércules. The latter is the hub for young *sevillanos* and the city's gay nightlife. In summer, dozens of open-air late-night bars *(terrazas de verano)* spring up along both banks of the river.

El Garlochi BAR
(Calle Boteros 26; ⊘9pm-3am Mon-Sat, to midnight Sun) There surely can't be many weirder places to drink than this dark temple of kitsch. Decked out in ultracamp religious decor, it's dedicated entirely to the iconography, smells and sounds of the Semana Santa (Holy Week). To get into the mood, try its signature cocktail, a Sangre de Cristo (Blood of Christ), made from grenadine, pink champagne and whisky.

Bulebar Café BAR
(☑955 29 42 12; www.facebook.com/bulebarcafe; Alameda de Hércules 83; ⊘12.30pm-2am) With its day-long opening hours and outdoor terrace overlooking the Alameda de Hércu-

les, this friendly spot is good for a leisurely people-watching break. Come for a late breakfast, a chilled early evening pick-me-up or a beer or two into the early hours.

☆ Entertainment

Seville is arguably Spain's flamenco capital and there are many opportunities to experience live performances.

Fun Club LIVE MUSIC
(☑636 669023; www.funclubsevilla.com; Alameda de Hércules 86; €5-12; ⊘9.30pm-7am Thu-Sat) Positively ancient by nightlife standards, the iconic Fun Club has been entertaining the nocturnal Alameda de Hércules crowd since the late 1980s. It still packs them in, hosting club nights and regular gigs – indie, rock and hip-hop.

❶ Getting There & Away

AIR

Seville's **airport** (Aeropuerto de Sevilla; ☑902 404704; www.aena.es; A4, Km 532) has a fair range of international and domestic flights.

BUS

Buses to Córdoba (€12, two hours, seven daily), Granada (€23 to €30, three hours, 10 daily), Málaga (€19 to €24, 2½ to four hours, 10 daily), Madrid (€23 to €33, 6½ hours, eight daily) and Lisbon (€45, seven to eight hours, five daily) go from the **Estación de Autobuses Plaza de Armas** (☑ 955 03 86 65; www.autobusesplaza dearmas.es; Avenida del Cristo de la Expiración).

TRAIN

Seville's principal train station, **Estación Santa Justa** (Avenida Kansas City), is 1.5km northeast of the centre.

High-speed AVE trains go to/from Madrid (from €35, 2½ to 3¼ hours, hourly) and Córdoba (from €21, 45 minutes to 1¼ hours, 25 daily). Slower trains head to Cádiz (€16, 1¾ hours, 15 daily), Huelva (€12, 1½ hours, three daily), Granada (€30, four hours, four daily) and Málaga (€24 to €44, two to 2½ hours, 11 daily).

Córdoba

POP 293,485

A little over a millennium ago Córdoba was the capital of Islamic Spain and Western Europe's biggest, most cultured city, where Muslims, Jews and Christians coexisted peaceably. Its past glories place it among Andalucía's top draws today. The centrepiece is the mesmerising, multiarched Mezquita. Surrounding it is an intricate web of winding streets, geranium-sprouting flower boxes and cool intimate patios that are at their most beguiling in late spring.

◉ Sights

★ **Mezquita**   MOSQUE, CATHEDRAL
(Mosque; ☑ 957 47 05 12; www.mezquita-catedral decordoba.es; Calle Cardenal Herrero; adult/child €10/5; ⊙ 10am-7pm Mon-Sat, 8.30-11.30am & 3-7pm Sun Mar-Oct, 8.30am-6pm Mon-Sat, 8.30-11.30am & 3-6pm Sun Nov-Feb, Mass 9.30am Mon-Sat, noon & 1.30pm Sun) It's impossible to overemphasise the beauty of Córdoba's great mosque, with its remarkably serene (despite tourist crowds) and spacious interior. One of the world's greatest works of Islamic architecture, the Mezquita hints, with all its lustrous decoration, at a refined age when Muslims, Jews and Christians lived side by side and enriched their city with a heady interaction of diverse, vibrant cultures.

★ **Palacio de Viana**   MUSEUM
(www.palaciodeviana.com; Plaza de Don Gome 2; whole house/patios €8/5; ⊙ 10am-7pm Tue-Sat, to 3pm Sun Sep-Jun, 9am-3pm Tue-Sun Jul & Aug) A stunning Renaissance palace with 12 beautiful, plant-filled patios, the Viana Palace is a particular delight to visit in spring. Occupied by the aristocratic Marqueses de Viana until 1980, the large building is packed with art and antiques. You can just walk round the lovely patios and garden with a self-guiding leaflet, or take a guided tour of the rooms as well. It's an 800m walk northeast from Plaza de las Tendillas.

★ **Alcázar de los Reyes Cristianos**   FORTRESS
(Fortress of the Christian Monarchs; ☑ 957 42 01 51; https://cultura.cordoba.es; Campo Santo de Los Mártires; adult/concession/child €4.50/2.25/free; ⊙ 8.30am-2.30pm Tue-Sat, from 9.30am Sun mid-Jun–mid-Sep, 8.30am-8.45pm Tue-Fri, to 4.30pm Sat, to 3pm Sun mid-Sep–mid-Jun; ⊞) Built under Castilian rule in the 13th and 14th centuries on the remains of a Moorish predecessor, this fort-cum-palace was where the Catholic Monarchs, Fernando and Isabel, made their first acquaintance with Columbus in 1486. One hall displays some remarkable Roman mosaics, dug up from Plaza de la Corredera in the 1950s. The Alcázar's terraced gardens – full of fish ponds, fountains, orange trees and flowers – are a delight to stroll around.

★ **Centro Flamenco Fosforito**   MUSEUM
(Posada del Potro; ☑ 957 47 68 29; https://cultura. cordoba.es; Plaza del Potro; ⊙ 8.30am-2.30pm Tue-Sat, from 9.30am Sun mid-Jun–mid-Sep, 8.30am-7.30pm Tue-Fri, to 2.30pm Sat & Sun mid-Sep–mid-Jun) **FREE** Possibly the best flamenco museum in Andalucía, the Fosforito centre has exhibits, film and information panels in English and Spanish telling you the history of the guitar and all the flamenco greats. Touch-screen videos demonstrate the important techniques of flamenco song, guitar, dance and percussion – you can test your skill at beating out the *compás* (rhythm) of different *palos* (song forms). Regular free live flamenco performances are held here, too, often at noon on Sunday (see the website).

⊨ Sleeping

★ **Patio del Posadero**   BOUTIQUE HOTEL €€
(☑ 957 94 17 33; www.patiodelposadero.com; Calle Mucho Trigo 21; r incl breakfast €95-155; ⊞ ⊛ ⊜ ⊠) A 15th-century building in a quiet lane 1km east of the Mezquita has been superbly converted into a welcoming boutique

hideaway combining comfort and unique contemporary design with that old-Córdoba Moorish style. At its centre is a charming cobble-floored, brick-arched patio, with steps leading up to a lovely upper deck with plunge pool, where the first-class home-made breakfasts are served.

Balcón de Córdoba BOUTIQUE HOTEL €€€
(📞957 49 84 78; www.balcondecordoba.com; Calle Encarnación 8; incl breakfast s €185-275, d €200-350; ❉🛜) Offering top-end boutique luxury a stone's throw from the Mezquita, the 10-room Balcón is a riveting place with a charming patio, slick rooms and ancient stone relics dotted around as if it were a wing of the nearby archaeological museum. Service doesn't miss a beat and the rooms have tasteful, soothing, contemporary decor with a little art but no clutter.

🍴 Eating

⭐**Mercado Victoria** FOOD HALL €
(www.mercadovictoria.com; Paseo de la Victoria; items €2-19; ⏰noon-1am Sun-Thu, noon-2am Fri & Sat mid-Jun–mid-Sep, 10am-midnight Sun-Thu, 10am-2am Fri & Sat mid-Sep–mid-Jun) The Mercado Victoria is, yes, a food court – but an unusually classy one, with almost everything, from Argentine empanadas and Mexican burritos to sushi and classic Spanish seafood and grilled meats, prepared fresh before your eyes. The setting is special too – a 19th-century wrought-iron-and-glass pavilion in the Victoria gardens just west of the old city.

La Boca FUSION €€
(📞957 47 61 40; www.facebook.com/restaurante.laboca; Calle de San Fernando 39; dishes €6-15; ⏰noon-midnight Wed-Mon; 🛜) If oxtail tacos, red-tuna *tataki,* or a salad of duck-prosciutto and mango in walnut vinaigrette sound appetising, you'll like La Boca. This inventive eatery serves up global variations in half a dozen appealingly arty, rustic-style *taberna* rooms or in its marginally more formal restaurant section. It's very well done, though portions are not large. Reservations advisable at weekends.

⭐**Bodegas Campos** ANDALUCIAN €€
(📞957 49 75 00; www.bodegascampos.com; Calle de Lineros 32; mains €12-24; ⏰1.30-4pm & 8.30-11pm) This atmospheric warren of rooms and patios is a Córdoba classic, and is popular with *cordobeses* and visitors alike. The restaurant and more informal *taberna* (tavern) serve up delicious dishes putting a slight creative twist on traditional Andalucian fare – the likes of cod-and-cuttlefish ravioli or pork tenderloin in grape sauce. Campos also produces its own house Montilla.

ℹ️ Information

Centro de Visitantes (Visitors Centre; 📞902 201774; www.turismodecordoba.org; Plaza del Triunfo; ⏰9am-7pm Mon-Fri, 9.30am-2.30pm Sat & Sun) The main tourist office has an

SPAIN CÓRDOBA

DON'T MISS

MEZQUITA HIGHLIGHTS

Emir Abd ar-Rahman I founded the Mezquita (p1089) in 785 CE. Three later extensions nearly quintupled its original size and brought it to the form you see today – except for one major alteration: a 16th-century cathedral plonked right in the middle.

Torre del Alminar You can climb inside the 54m-tall bell tower (originally the Mezquita's minaret) for fine panoramas.

Patio de los Naranjos This lovely courtyard, with its orange and palm trees and fountains, was the site of ritual ablutions before prayer in the mosque.

Prayer hall Divided into 19 'naves' by lines of two-tier arches striped in red brick and white stone. Their simplicity and number give a sense of endlessness to the Mezquita.

Mihrab and Maksura The arches of the *maksura* (the area where the caliphs and their retinues would have prayed) are the mosque's most intricate and sophisticated, forming a forest of interwoven horseshoe shapes. The portal of the mihrab itself is a sublime crescent arch in glittering gold mosaic.

The cathedral A 16th-century construction in the Mezquita's heart.

JEWISH CÓRDOBA

Jews were among the most dynamic and prominent citizens of Islamic Córdoba. The medieval *judería* (Jewish quarter), extending northwest from the Mezquita almost to Avenida del Gran Capitán, is today a maze of narrow streets and whitewashed buildings with flowery window boxes. The **Sinagoga** (☑ 957 74 90 15; www.turismodecordoba.org; Calle de los Judíos 20; €0.30; ☺ 9am-9pm Tue-Sat, to 3pm Sun), built in 1315, is one of the few surviving testaments to the Jewish presence in Andalucía. Across the street is the **Casa de Sefarad** (☑ 957 42 14 04; www.casadesefarad.es; cnr Calles de los Judíos & Averroes; €4; ☺ 11am-6pm Mon-Sat, to 2pm Sun), an interesting museum on the Sephardic (Iberian Peninsula Jewish) tradition.

exhibit on Córdoba's history, and some Roman and Visigothic remains downstairs.

🛈 Getting There & Away

BUS

The **bus station** (☑ 957 40 40 40; www.estacionautobusescordoba.es; Avenida Vía Augusta) is 2km northwest of the Mezquita, behind the train station. Destinations include Seville (€12, two hours, seven daily), Granada (€10, 2¾ hours, seven daily) and Málaga (€8 to €19, 2½ to 3½ hours, four daily).

TRAIN

Córdoba's **train station** (☑ 91 232 03 20; www.renfe.com; Plaza de las Tres Culturas) is on the high-speed AVE line between Madrid and Seville/Málaga. Rail destinations include Seville (€14 to €30, 45 minutes to 1¼ hours, more than 30 daily), Madrid (€33 to €66, 1¾ hours, 29 daily) and Málaga (€24 to €42, one hour, 18 daily). Trips to Granada (€24 to €36, two to 2¾ hours, four or more daily) include changing to a train or bus at Antequera.

Granada

ELEV 680M / POP 232,770

Granada's eight centuries as a Muslim city are symbolised in its keynote emblem, the remarkable Alhambra, one of the most graceful achievements of Islamic architecture. Granada is chock-full of history, the arts and life, with tapas bars filled to bursting and flamenco dives resounding to the heart-wrenching tones of the south. Today, Islam is more present than it has been for many centuries, in the shops, tearooms and mosque of a growing North African community around the maze of the Albayzín.

◉ Sights

★ Alhambra
ISLAMIC PALACE

(☑ 958 02 79 71, tickets 858 95 36 16; www.alhambra-patronato.es; adult/12-15yr/under 12yr €14/8/free, Generalife & Alcazaba adult/under 12yr €7/free; ☺ 8.30am-8pm Apr–mid-Oct, to 6pm mid-Oct–Mar, night visits 10-11.30pm Tue & Sat Apr–mid-Oct, 8-9.30pm Fri & Sat mid-Oct–Mar) The Alhambra is Granada's – and Europe's – love letter to Moorish culture. Set against a backdrop of brooding Sierra Nevada peaks, this fortified palace complex started life as a walled citadel before going on to become the opulent seat of Granada's Nasrid emirs. Their showpiece palaces, the 14th-century Palacios Nazaríes, are among the finest Islamic buildings in Europe and, together with the gorgeous Generalife gardens, form the Alhambra's great headline act.

★ Capilla Real
HISTORIC BUILDING

(Royal Chapel; ☑ 958 22 78 48; www.capillarealgranada.com; Calle Oficios; adult/concession/child €5/3.50/free; ☺ 10.15am-6.30pm Mon-Sat, 11am-6pm Sun) The Royal Chapel is the last resting place of Spain's Reyes Católicos (Catholic Monarchs), Isabel I de Castilla (1451–1504) and Fernando II de Aragón (1452–1516), who commissioned the elaborate Isabelline-Gothic-style mausoleum that was to house them. It wasn't completed until 1517, hence their interment in the Alhambra's **Convento de San Francisco** (www.parador.es; Calle Real de la Alhambra) until 1521.

Their monumental marble tombs (and those of their heirs) lie in the chancel behind a gilded wrought-iron screen created by Bartolomé de Jaén in 1520.

Granada

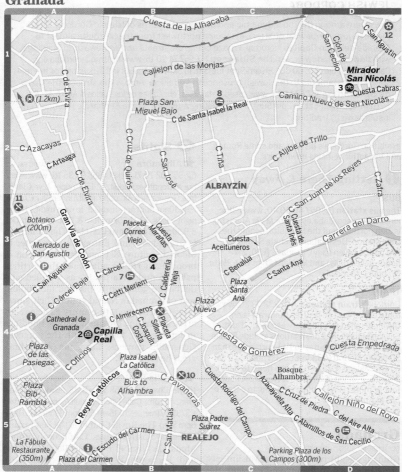

SPAIN GRANADA

👁 Albayzín

On the hill facing the Alhambra across the Darro valley, the Albayzín is an open-air museum in which you can lose yourself for most of a day. The cobbled streets are lined with gorgeous *cármenes* (large mansions with walled gardens). It survived as the Muslim quarter for several decades after the Christian conquest in 1492.

Calle Calderería Nueva STREET
Linking the upper and lower parts of the Albayzín, Calle Calderería Nueva is a narrow street famous for its *teterías* (tearooms). It's also a good place to shop for slippers, hookahs, jewellery and North African pottery from an eclectic cache of shops redolent of a Moroccan souk.

★ Mirador San Nicolás VIEWPOINT

(Plaza de San Nicolás) This is the place for those classic sunset shots of the Alhambra sprawled along a wooded hilltop with the dark Sierra Nevada mountains looming in the background. It's a well-known spot, accessible via Callejón de San Cecilio, so expect crowds of camera-toting tourists, students and buskers. It's also a haunt of pickpockets

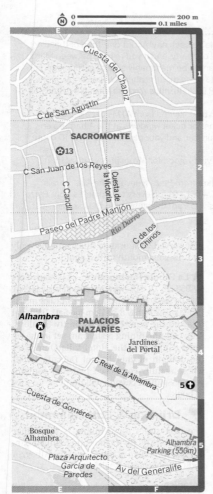

Granada

◎ **Top Sights**

◎ **Sights**

🛏 **Sleeping**

🍴 **Eating**

✪ **Entertainment**

SPAIN GRANADA

Carmen de la Alcubilla del Caracol
HISTORIC HOTEL €€

(☎ 958 21 55 51; www.alcubilladelcaracol.com; Calle del Aire Alta 12; r €165-185; ⊙ closed mid-Jul–Aug; ✳ ⚡) This much-sought-after small hotel inhabits a traditional whitewashed *carmen* on the slopes of the Alhambra (p1091). It feels more like a B&B than a hotel with its elegant homey interiors and seven quietly refined rooms washed in pale pastel colours. Outside, you can bask in fabulous views from the spectacular terraced garden.

★ Santa Isabel La Real
BOUTIQUE HOTEL €€€

(☎ 958 29 46 58; www.hotelsantaisabellareal. com; Calle de Santa Isabel La Real 19; r €115-210; ✳ @ ⚡) Up in hilltop Albayzín, this welcoming small hotel occupies a whitewashed 16th-century building. Many original architectural features endure, including marble columns and flagged stone floors, while a fireplace and sofa add a homey touch in the communal area. The guest rooms, which are set around a central patio, are individually decorated with embroidered pictures and hand-woven rugs.

🍴 Eating

Granada is a bastion of that fantastic practice of free tapas with every drink, and some have an international flavour. The labyrinthine Albayzín holds a wealth of eateries tucked away in the narrow streets. Calle

and bag-snatchers, so keep your wits about you as you enjoy the views.

🛏 Sleeping

Hotel Posada del Toro
HOTEL €

(☎ 958 22 73 33; www.posadadeltoro.com; Calle de Elvira 25; s/d/ste from €45/50/70; ✳ ⚡) A lovely little hotel in the lively Albayzín quarter. Bullfighting posters line a small passageway that leads to the main body of the hotel where tasteful rooms are decked out with parquet floors, Alhambra-style stucco and rustic furniture. Rates are a bargain considering its central location.

ℹ️ ALHAMBRA TICKETS

Up to 6600 tickets to the Alhambra are available each day. About one-third of these are sold at the entrance on the day, but they sell out early, and if you're here between March and October you need to start queuing by 7am to be reasonably sure of getting one. Fortunately, it's also possible to buy tickets up to three months ahead, online or by phone, from **Alhambra Advance Booking** (☑ 858 95 36 16; https://tickets.alhambra-patronato. es), for €0.85 extra per ticket.

Tickets purchased online or by phone can be collected from ATMs of La Caixa bank throughout Andalucía, or from ticket machines or ticket windows at the Alhambra entrance. You'll need your booking reference number and your payment card (or ID document if collecting at Alhambra ticket windows).

The Palacios Nazaríes are open for night visits, good for atmosphere rather than detail.

It's a pleasant (if uphill) walk of just over 1km from Plaza Nueva to the Alhambra's main entrance. Alternatively, buses C3 and C4 (€1.40) run every few minutes from Plaza Isabel La Católica. By car, follow 'Alhambra' signs from the highway to the car park, just uphill from the ticket office.

Calderería Nueva is a fascinating muddle of *teterías* (tearooms) and Arabic-influenced takeaways.

Bodegas Castañeda
TAPAS €

(☑ 958 21 54 64; Calle Almireceros 1; tapas €2-5; ⏲ 11.30am-4.30pm & 7.30pm-1am Mon-Thu, to 2am Fri-Sun) Eating becomes a contact sport at this traditional tapas bar where crowds of hungry punters jostle for food under hanging hams. Don't expect any experimental nonsense here, just classic tapas (and *raciones*) served lightning fast with booze poured from big wall-mounted casks.

Carmela Restaurante
SPANISH €€

(☑ 958 22 57 94; www.restaurantecarmela. com; Calle Colcha 13; tapas €7, mains €11-20; ⏲ 8am-midnight, kitchen noon-midnight) Traditional tapas updated for the 21st century are the star turn at this smart all-day cafe-restaurant at the jaws of the Realejo quarter. Bag a table in the cool brick-lined interior or on the outdoor terrace and bite into croquettes with black pudding and caramelised onion, or tuna *tataki* with soy reduction.

⭐ El Bar de Fede
INTERNATIONAL €€

(☑ 958 28 88 14; Calle Marqués de Falces 1; raciones €9-15; ⏲ 9am-2am Mon-Thu, to 3am Fri & Sat, 11am-2am Sun) The 'Fede' in the name refers to home-town poet Federico García Lorca, whose free spirit seems to hang over this hip, gay-friendly bar. It's a good-looking spot with patterned wallpaper and high tables set around a ceramic-tiled island, and the food is a joy. Standouts include chicken pâté served with orange sauce and heavenly melt-in-your mouth grilled squid.

⭐ La Fábula Restaurante
GASTRONOMY €€€

(☑ 958 25 01 50; www.restaurantelafabula.com; Calle de San Antón 28; mains €23-28, tasting menus €75-90; ⏲ 2-4pm & 8.30-11pm Tue-Sat) It's hard to avoid the pun: Fábula is pretty fabulous. A formal fine-dining restaurant set in the refined confines of the Hotel Villa Oniria, it's the domain of chef Ismael Delgado López whose artfully composed plates of contemporary Spanish cuisine will impress. Be sure to book.

🍷 Drinking & Entertainment

The best street for drinking is the rather scruffy Calle de Elvira, but other chilled bars line the Río Darro at the base of the Albayzín and Calle Navas in Realejo.

Botánico
BAR

(☑ 958 27 15 98; www.botanicocafe.es; Calle Málaga 3; ⏲ 1pm-1am Mon-Thu, to 2am Fri & Sat, to 6pm Sun) Dudes with designer beards, students finishing off their Lorca dissertations, and bohemians with arty inclinations hang out at Botánico, a casual eatery by day, a cafe at *merienda* (afternoon snack) time (5pm to 7pm), and a buzzing bar come the evening.

Peña La Platería
FLAMENCO

(☑ 958 21 06 50; www.laplateria.org.es; Placeta de Toqueros 7) Peña La Platería claims to be Spain's oldest flamenco club, founded in 1949. Unlike other more private clubs, it regularly opens its doors to nonmembers for performances on Thursday nights at 10pm. Tapas and drinks are available. Reservations recommended.

Jardines de Zoraya   FLAMENCO
(☑ 958 20 62 66; www.jardinesdezoraya.com; Calle Panaderos 32; ticket €20, dinner from €29; ⊙ shows 8pm & 10.30pm) Hosted in a restaurant in the Albayzín district, the Jardines de Zoraya appears, on first impression, to be a touristy *tablao* (choreographed flamenco show). But reasonable entry prices, talented performers and a highly atmospheric patio make it a worthwhile stop for any aficionado.

ⓘ Information

Municipal Tourist Office (☑ 958 24 82 80; www.granadatur.com; Plaza del Carmen 9; ⊙ 9am-7pm Mon-Sat, 10am-2pm Sun) Helpful English-speaking staff can provide maps and useful city information.

Provincial Tourist Office (☑ 958 24 71 28; www.turgranada.es; Calle Cárcel Baja 3; ⊙ 9am-8pm Mon-Fri, 10am-7pm Sat, 10am-3pm Sun) For information on Granada province.

ⓘ Getting There & Away

BUS

Granada's **bus station** (☑ 958 18 50 10; Avenida Juan Pablo II; ⊙ 6.30am-1.30am) is 3km northwest of the city centre. Destinations include Córdoba (€15 to €17, 2¾ hours, nine daily), Seville (€23 to €30, three hours, 10 daily), Málaga (€12 to €14, 1¾ hours, hourly) and Madrid (€19 to €45, five hours, 13 daily).

TRAIN

The **train station** (☑ 958 27 12 72; Avenida de Andaluces) is 1.5km west of the centre. Services run to Seville (€30, 3¾ hours, four daily), Almería (€20, three hours, four daily), Madrid (€30 to €47, four hours, six daily) and Barcelona (€40 to €85, eight hours, two daily).

WORTH A TRIP

ANDALUCÍA BEYOND THE CITIES
· ·
The Andalucian countryside, with its white villages, rugged mountains, winding country roads and appealing small towns, is every bit as magical as the region's famed cities – and packs in huge variety.

On the south flank of the Sierra Nevada (mainland Spain's highest mountain range), the jumble of valleys known as **Las Alpujarras** juxtaposes arid mountainsides and deep ravines with oasis-like, Berber-style villages set amid orchards and woodlands. There's great walking, a unique ambience derived from the area's Moorish past, and plenty of good accommodation in and around scenic villages like **Capileira**, **Ferreirola**, **Trevélez** and **Cádiar**, one to two hours' drive south from Granada.

Further afield, 200km northeast from Granada, the **Parque Natural Sierras de Cazorla, Segura y Las Villas** is 2099 sq km of craggy mountains, remote hilltop castles and deep green river valleys with some of the most abundant and visible wildlife in Spain – including three types of deer, ibex, wild boar, mouflon (a wild sheep), griffon vultures and golden eagles. The picturesque medieval town of **Cazorla** is a great base, and en route you shouldn't miss the gorgeous towns of **Úbeda** and **Baeza**, which are World Heritage–listed for their outstanding Renaissance architecture.

If you're starting from Seville, it's about an hour's drive west to the vast wetlands of the **Parque Nacional de Doñana**, Western Europe's biggest roadless region, where flocks of flamingos tinge the sky pink, huge herds of deer and boar roam the woodlands, and the iberian lynx fights for survival. Four-hour minibus safaris into the park go from **El Rocío**, **Sanlúcar de Barrameda** and **El Acebuche** visitors centre.

Along back roads between Seville and Málaga, hung from the skies between the spectacular clifftop towns of **Arcos de la Frontera** and **Ronda**, the gorgeously green limestone gorges and crags of the **Sierra de Grazalema** are criss-crossed by beautiful, marked trails between charming white villages such as **Grazalema**, **Benaoján** and **Zahara de la Sierra**.

All these areas have plenty of good accommodation, including many charming country guesthouses or small hotels. They can be reached by bus with a bit of effort: a car is the ideal way to get to and around them.

SPAIN GRANADA

Málaga

POP 569,002

Málaga is a world apart from the adjoining, overdeveloped Costa del Sol: an exuberant, historic port city that has rapidly emerged as a city of culture, its so-called 'mile of art' being compared to Madrid, and its dynamism and fine dining to Barcelona.

The tastefully restored historic centre is a delight, with a Gothic cathedral surrounded by narrow pedestrian streets flanked by traditional and modern bars, and shops that range from idiosyncratic and family owned to urban-chic and contemporary. The city's terrific bars and nightlife, the last word in Málaga *joie de vivre*, stay open very late.

◉ Sights

★Museo Picasso Málaga   MUSEUM
(📞952 12 76 00; www.museopicassomalaga.org; Calle San Agustín 8; €8, incl temporary exhibition €12; ⏰10am-8pm Jul & Aug, to 7pm Mar-Jun, Sep & Oct, to 6pm Nov-Feb; 🐾) This unmissable museum in the city of Picasso's birth provides a solid overview of the great master and his work, although, surprisingly, it only came to fruition in 2003 after more than 50 years of planning. The 200-plus works in the collection were donated and loaned to the museum by Christine Ruiz-Picasso (wife of Paul, Picasso's eldest son) and Bernard Ruiz-Picasso (Picasso's grandson) and catalogue the artist's sparkling career with a few notable gaps (the 'blue' and 'rose' periods are largely missing).

★Catedral de Málaga   CATHEDRAL
(📞952 22 03 45; www.malagacatedral.com; Calle Molina Lario; cathedral & Ars Málaga €6, incl roof €10; ⏰10am-8pm Mon-Fri, to 6.30pm Sat, 2-6.30pm Sun Apr, May & Oct, 10am-9pm Mon-Fri, to 6.30pm Sat, 2pm-6.30pm Sun Jun-Sep, closes 6.30pm daily Nov-Mar) Málaga's elaborate cathedral was started in the 16th century on the site of the former mosque. Of the mosque, only the **Patio de los Naranjos** survives, a small courtyard of fragrant orange trees. Inside, the fabulous domed ceiling soars 40m into the air, while the vast colonnaded nave houses an enormous cedar-wood choir. Aisles give access to 15 chapels with gorgeous 18th-century retables and religious art. It's worth taking the guided tour up to the *cubiertas* (roof) to enjoy panoramic city views.

★Alcazaba   CASTLE
(📞952 227 230; www.malagaturismo.com; Calle Alcazabilla; €3.50, incl Castillo de Gibralfaro €5.50; ⏰9am-8pm Apr-Oct, to 6pm Nov-Mar) No time to visit Granada's Alhambra? Then Málaga's Alcazaba can provide a taster. The entrance is next to the **Roman amphitheatre** (📞951 50 11 15; Calle Alcazabilla 8; ⏰10am-8pm) **FREE**, from where a meandering path climbs amid lush greenery: crimson bougainvillea, lofty palms, fragrant jasmine bushes and rows of orange trees. Extensively restored, this palace-fortress dates from the 11th-century Moorish period; the caliphal horseshoe arches, courtyards and bubbling fountains are evocative of this influential period in Málaga's history.

Centre Pompidou Málaga   MUSEUM
(📞951 92 62 00; www.centrepompidou.es; Pasaje Doctor Carrillo Casaux, Muelle Uno; €7, incl temporary exhibition €9; ⏰9.30am-8pm Wed-Mon; 🐾) Opened in 2015 in the port, this offshoot of Paris' Pompidou Centre is housed in a low-slung modern building crowned by a playful multicoloured cube. The permanent exhibition includes the extraordinary *Ghost,* by Kader Attia, depicting rows of Muslim women bowed in prayer and created from domestic aluminium foil, plus works by such modern masters as Frida Kahlo, Francis Bacon and Antoni Tàpies. There are also audiovisual installations, talking 'heads' and temporary exhibitions.

Castillo de Gibralfaro   CASTLE
(📞952 22 72 30; www.malagaturismo.com; Camino de Gibralfaro; €3.50, incl Alcazaba €5.50; ⏰9am-8pm Apr-Sep, to 6pm Oct-Mar) One remnant of Málaga's Islamic past is the craggy ramparts of the Castillo de Gibralfaro, spectacularly located high on the hill overlooking the city. Built by Abd ar-Rahman I, the 8th-century Córdoban emir, and later rebuilt in the 14th century when Málaga was the main port for the emirate of Granada, the castle originally acted as a lighthouse and military barracks. Nothing much is original in the castle's interior, but the protective walkway around the ramparts affords the best views over Málaga.

Museo Automovilístico Málaga   MUSEUM
(📞951 13 70 01; www.museoautomovilmalaga.com; Avenida Sor Teresa Prat 15; €8.50; ⏰10am-7pm; 🐾) Fashion and old cars might seem like weird bedfellows, but they're an inspired combo when viewed through the prism of

this slightly out-of-the-box museum in Málaga's erstwhile tobacco factory. The museum juxtaposes cars from the 1900s to the 1960s with haute couture from the same era. Imagine a 1936 Merc lined up next to a mannequin clothed in a Chanel jacket.

⊨ Sleeping

★ Dulces Dreams   HOSTEL €
(☑951 35 78 69; www.dulcesdreamshostel.com; Plaza de los Mártires 6; r incl breakfast €55-85; ✳ ☎) Managed by an enthusiastic young team, the rooms at Dulces (sweet) Dreams are, appropriately, named after desserts; 'Cupcake' is a good choice, with a terrace overlooking the imposing red-brick church across the way. This is an older building, so there's no lift and the rooms vary in size, but they're bright and whimsically decorated, using recycled materials as much as possible.

★ Molina Lario   HOTEL €€
(☑952 06 20 02; www.hotelmolinalario.com; Calle Molina Lario 20-22; r €170-210; ✳ ☎ ☒) Perfect for romantic couples, this hotel has a sophisticated, contemporary feel, with spacious rooms decorated in a cool palette of earthy colours. There are crisp white linens, marshmallow-soft pillows and tasteful paintings, plus a fabulous rooftop terrace and pool with views to the sea. Situated within confessional distance of the cathedral.

✗ Eating & Drinking

Málaga has a staggering number of tapas bars and restaurants, particularly around the historic centre (over 400 at last count). One of the city's biggest pleasures is a slow crawl round its numerous tapas bars and old bodegas (cellars). The best bar-hop areas are from Plaza de la Merced in the northeast to Calle Carretería in the northwest, plus Plaza Mitjana and Plaza de Uncibay.

★ El Mesón de Cervantes   TAPAS, ARGENTINE €€
(☑952 21 62 74; www.elmesondecervantes.com; Calle Álamos 11; medias raciones €4.50-8.50, raciones €7.50-14; ☺7pm-midnight Wed-Mon) Cervantes started as a humble tapas bar run by expat Argentine Gabriel Spatz, but has now expanded into four bar-restaurants (each with a slightly different bent), all within a block of each other. This one is the HQ, where pretty much everything on the menu is a show-stopper – lamb stew with cous-

cous, pumpkin and mushroom risotto, and, boy, the grilled octopus!

★ Óleo   FUSION €€
(☑952 21 90 62; www.oleorestaurante.es; Edificio CAC, Calle Alemania; mains €14-22; ☺1.15-4pm & 8.30pm-midnight Mon-Sat; ☎) Located at the city's **Centro de Arte Contemporáneo** (Contemporary Art Museum; www.cacmalaga.org; ☺9am-2pm & 5-9pm Tue-Sun) FREE with white-on-white minimalist decor, Óleo provides diners with the unusual choice of Mediterranean or Asian food, with some subtle combinations such as duck breast with a side of seaweed with hoisin, as well as more purist Asian dishes and gourmet palate-ticklers such as candied roasted piglet.

Los Patios de Beatas   WINE BAR
(☑952 21 03 50; www.lospatiosdebeatas.com; Calle Beatas 43; ☺1-5pm & 8pm-midnight Mon-Sat, 1-6pm Sun; ☎) Two 18th-century mansions have metamorphosed into this sumptuous space where you can sample fine wines from a selection reputed to be the most extensive in town. Stained-glass windows and beautiful resin tables inset with mosaics and shells add to the overall art-infused atmosphere.

ANDALUCÍA'S QUIETEST BEACHES

The coast east of Almería in eastern Andalucía is perhaps the last section of Spain's Mediterranean coast where you can (sometimes) have a beach to yourself. This is Spain's sunniest region – even in March it can be warm enough to strip off and take in the rays. The best thing about it is the wonderful coastline and semidesert scenery of the **Cabo de Gata** promontory. All along the 50km coast from El Cabo de Gata village to Agua Amarga, some of the most beautiful beaches on the Mediterranean, from long sandy strands to tiny rock-girt coves, alternate with precipitous cliffs and scattered villages. The main base is laid-back **San José**, with excellent beaches nearby, such as Playa de los Genoveses, Playa de Mónsul and the four isolated little beaches of the Calas de Barronal. The former gold-mining village of **Rodalquilar**, a few kilometres inland, is a bit of a boho-chic hideaway.

Innovative tapas and *raciones* (full-plate servings) are also on offer.

☆ Entertainment

★ Kelipe
FLAMENCO

(☑ 692 829885; Muro de Puerta Nueva 10; shows €25; ☺ shows 9.30pm Thu-Sat) There are many flamenco clubs springing up all over Andalucía, but few are as soul-stirring as Kelipe. Not only are the musicianship and dancing of the highest calibre, but the talented performers create an intimate feel and a genuine connection with the audience.

ℹ Information

The **municipal tourist office** (☑ 951 92 60 20; www.malagaturismo.com; Plaza de la Marina; ☺ 9am-8pm Apr-Oct, to 6pm Nov-Mar) offers a range of city maps and booklets. It also operates information kiosks at the Alcazaba entrance (Calle Alcazabilla), at the main train station (Explanada de la Estación), on Plaza de la Merced and on the eastern beaches (El Palo and La Malagueta).

ℹ Getting There & Around

AIR

Málaga's **airport** (AGP; ☑ 952 04 88 38; www.aena.es), 9km southwest of the city centre, is the main international gateway to Andalucía, served by top global carriers as well as budget airlines. Buses (€3, 15 minutes) and trains (€1.80, 12 minutes) run every 20 or 30 minutes between airport and city centre.

BUS

Málaga's **bus station** (☑ 952 35 00 61; www.estabus.emtsam.es; Paseo de los Tilos) is 1km southwest of the city centre. Destinations include Seville (€19, 2¾ hours, seven daily), Granada (€12, two hours, hourly) and Córdoba (€12, three to four hours, seven daily).

TRAIN

Málaga is the southern terminus of the Madrid–Málaga high-speed train line.

Málaga María Zambrano Train Station
(☑ 902 43 23 43; www.renfe.com; Explanada de la Estación; ☺ 6am-11pm) is near the bus station, a 15-minute walk from the city centre. Destinations include Córdoba (€27.50, one hour, 19 daily), Seville (€24, 2¾ hours, 11 daily) and Madrid (€80, 2¾ hours, 15 daily). Note that for Córdoba and Seville the daily schedule includes fast AVE trains at roughly double the cost.

EXTREMADURA

Cáceres
POP 95.917

Few visitors make it to the region of Extremadura, bordering Portugal, but those who do are rewarded with some true gems of old Spain, especially Roman Mérida and the 16th-century towns of Trujillo and Cáceres. The Ciudad Monumental, Cáceres' old centre, is truly extraordinary. Narrow cobbled streets twist and climb among ancient stone walls lined with palaces and mansions, while the skyline is decorated with turrets, spires, gargoyles and enormous storks' nests. Protected by defensive walls, it has survived almost intact from its 16th-century heyday.

◉ Sights

★ Palacio de los Golfines de Abajo
HISTORIC BUILDING

(☑ 927 21 80 51; www.palaciogolfinesdeabajo.com; Plaza de los Golfines; tours adult/child €2.50/free; ☺ tours hourly 10am-1pm & 5-7pm Tue-Sat, 10am-1pm Sun May-Sep, 10am-1pm & 4.30-6.30pm Tue-Sat, 10am-1pm Sun Oct-Apr) The sumptuous home of Cáceres' prominent Golfín family has been beautifully restored. Built piecemeal between the 14th and 20th centuries, it's crammed with historical treasures: original 17th-century tapestries and armoury murals, a 19th-century bust of Alfonso XII, and a signed 1485 troops request from the Reyes Católicos (Catholic Monarchs) to their Golfín stewards. But it's the detailed, theatrical tours (Spanish, English, French or Portuguese), through four richly decorated lounges, an extravagant chapel and a fascinating documents room, that make it a standout.

★ Museo de Cáceres
MUSEUM

(☑ 927 01 08 77; http://museodecaceres.juntaex.es; Plaza de las Veletas; €1.20; ☺ 9.30am-2.30pm & 4pm-8pm Tue-Fri, 10am-2.30pm & 4pm-8pm Sat, 10am-3pm Sun) The excellent Museo de Cáceres, spread across 12 buildings in a 16th-century mansion built over an evocative 12th-century *aljibe* (cistern), is the only surviving element of Cáceres' Moorish castle. The impressive archaeological section includes an elegant stone boar dated to the

4th to 2nd centuries BCE, while the equally appealing fine-arts display (behind the main museum; open only in the mornings) show-cases works by such greats as Picasso, Miró, Tàpies and El Greco. It's one of Spain's most underrated collections.

🛏 Sleeping & Eating

★Hotel Soho Boutique
Casa Don Fernando   BOUTIQUE HOTEL €€
(📞927 62 71 76; www.sohohoteles.com; Plaza Mayor 30; s/d from €55/70; 🅿❄🛜) Cáceres' smartest midrange choice sits on Plaza Mayor right opposite the Arco de la Estrel-la. Boutique-style rooms, spread over four floors, are tastefully modern, with gleaming bathrooms through glass doors. Pricier 'su-periors' enjoy the best plaza views (though weekend nights can be noisy), and attic-style top-floor rooms are good for families. Ser-vice hits that perfect professional-yet-friendly note.

★La Cacharrería   TAPAS €€
(📞927 10 16 79; lacacharreria@live.com; Calle de Orellana 1; tapas €4.50, raciones €10-18; ☺res-taurant 1-4pm & 8.30pm-midnight Thu-Mon, cafe 4pm-1.30am Thu-Sat, 4-11pm Sun; 🍴) Local fla-vours and ingredients combine in exquisite, international-inspired concoctions at this packed-out, minimalist-design tapas bar tucked into an old-town house. *Solomillo* (tenderloin) in Torta del Casar cheese arrives in martini glasses. Delicious guacamole, hummus, falafel and 'salsiki' are a godsend for vegetarians. No advance reservations: get here by 1.45pm or 8.30pm.

ⓘ Information

The **Oficina de Turismo** (📞927 25 55 97; www.turismocaceres.org; Palacio Carvajal, Calle Amargura 1; ☺8am-8.45pm Mon-Fri, 10am-1.45pm & 5-7.45pm Sat, 10am-1.45pm Sun) covers Cáceres city and province; it's inside the Palacio de Carvajal.

ⓘ Getting There & Away

BUS
The **bus station** (📞927 23 25 50; www.esta cionautobuses.es; Calle Túnez 1; ☺6.30am-10.30pm) has services to Madrid (from €23, four hours, seven daily) and Trujillo (€4, 45 minutes, six daily).

TRAIN
From the train station, 2.5km southwest of the old town, trains run to/from Madrid (€28 to €33, 3¾ hours to 4¼ hours, five daily), Mérida (€6 to €7, one hour, six daily) and Plasencia (€5 to €6, one hour, four daily).

SURVIVAL GUIDE

ⓘ Directory A–Z

ACTIVITIES

Hiking
➡ Top walking areas include the Pyrenees, Picos de Europa, Las Alpujarras (Andalucía) and the Galician coast.

➡ The best season is June to September in most areas, but April to June, September and October in most of Andalucía.

➡ Region-specific walking guides are published by Cicerone Press (www.cicerone.co.uk).

➡ GR (*Gran Recorrido;* long distance) trails are indicated with red-and-white markers; PR (*Pequeño Recorrido;* short distance) trails have yellow-and-white markers.

➡ Good hiking maps are published by Prames (www.prames.com), Editorial Alpina (www.ed itorialalpina.com) and the Institut Cartogràfic de Catalunya (www.icgc.cat).

➡ The Camino de Santiago pilgrim route to San-tiago de Compostela has many variations start-ing from all over Spain (and other countries). Most popular is the Camino Francés, running 783km from Roncesvalles, on Spain's border with France. Good websites: Caminolinks (www.santiago-compostela.net), Mundicamino (www.mundicamino.com) and Camino de Santiago (www.caminodesantiago.me).

Skiing
Skiing is cheaper but less varied than in much of the rest of Europe. The season runs from De-cember to mid-April. The best resorts are in the Pyrenees, especially in northwest Catalonia and in Aragón. The Sierra Nevada in Andalucía offers the most southerly skiing in Western Europe.

Surfing, Windsurfing & Kitesurfing
The Basque Country has good surf spots, includ-ing San Sebastián, Zarautz and the legendary left at Mundaka. Tarifa in Andalucía, with its long beaches and ceaseless wind, is generally considered to be the kitesurfing and windsurfing capital of Europe.

SPAIN SURVIVAL GUIDE

INTERNET ACCESS

Wi-fi is available at most hotels and in some cafes, restaurants and airports; generally (but not always) free.

LGBT+ TRAVELLERS

Homosexuality is legal in Spain. Same-sex marriage was legalised in 2005. Madrid, Barcelona, Sitges, Torremolinos and Ibiza have particularly active and lively gay scenes. Gay Iberia (www. gayiberia.com) has gay guides to the main destinations.

MONEY

➡ Many credit and debit cards can be used for withdrawing money from *cajeros automáticos* (ATMs) and for making purchases. The most widely accepted cards are Visa and Master-Card.

➡ Most banks will exchange major foreign currencies and offer the best rates. Ask about commissions and take your passport.

➡ Exchange offices, indicated by the word *cambio* (exchange), offer longer opening hours than banks, but have worse exchange rates and higher commissions.

➡ Value-added tax (VAT) is known as IVA *(impuesto sobre el valor añadido)*. Non-EU residents are entitled to a refund of the 21% IVA on purchases to be taken back to their country.

➡ Menu prices include a service charge. Most people leave some small change as a tip. Taxi drivers don't have to be tipped, but a little rounding up won't go amiss.

OPENING HOURS

Banks 8.30am–2pm Monday–Friday; some also open 4–7pm Thursday and 9am–1pm Saturday

Central post offices 8.30am–9.30pm Monday–Friday, 8.30am–2pm Saturday; most other branches 8.30am–2.30pm Monday–Friday, 9.30am–1pm Saturday

Nightclubs Midnight or 1am–5am or 6am

Restaurants Lunch 1–4pm; dinner 8.30–11pm or midnight

Shops 10am–2pm and 4.30–7.30pm or 5–8pm Monday–Friday or Saturday; big supermarkets and department stores generally open 10am–10pm Monday–Saturday

PUBLIC HOLIDAYS

The two main periods when Spaniards go on holiday are Semana Santa (the week leading up to Easter Sunday) and July or August. At these times accommodation can be scarce and transport heavily booked.

There are at least 14 official holidays a year – some observed nationwide, some locally. When a holiday falls close to a weekend, Spaniards like to make a *puente* (bridge), meaning they take the intervening day off too. Occasionally when some holidays fall close, they make an *acueducto* (aqueduct)! Here are the national holidays:

Año Nuevo (New Year's Day) 1 January

Viernes Santo (Good Friday) March/April

Fiesta del Trabajo (Labour Day) 1 May

La Asunción (Feast of the Assumption) 15 August

Fiesta Nacional de España (National Day) 12 October

La Inmaculada Concepción (Feast of the Immaculate Conception) 8 December

Navidad (Christmas) 25 December

Regional governments set five holidays and local councils two more. Common dates include the following:

Epifanía (Epiphany) or **Día de los Reyes Magos** (Three Kings' Day) 6 January

Jueves Santo (Good Thursday) March/April; not observed in Catalonia and Valencia

Corpus Christi June; the Thursday after the eighth Sunday after Easter Sunday

Día de Santiago Apóstol (Feast of St James the Apostle) 25 July

Día de Todos los Santos (All Saints' Day) 1 November

Día de la Constitución (Constitution Day) 6 December

SAFE TRAVEL

Most visitors to Spain never feel remotely threatened, but you should be aware of the possibility of petty theft (which may of course not seem so petty if your passport, cash, credit card and phone go missing). Stay alert and you can avoid most thievery techniques. Barcelona, Madrid and Seville are the worst offenders, as are popular beaches in summer (never leave belongings unattended).

TELEPHONE

The once widespread, but now fast disappearing, blue payphones accept coins, *tarjetas telefónicas* (phonecards) issued by the national phone company Telefónica and, in some cases, various credit cards. Calling from your smartphone, tablet or computer using an internet-based service such as WhatsApp, Skype or FaceTime is generally the cheapest and easiest option.

Mobile Phones

Local SIM cards are widely available and can be used in unlocked European and Australian mobile phones, but are not compatible with many North American or Japanese systems. The Spanish mobile-phone companies (Telefónica's MoviStar, Orange and Vodafone) offer *prepagado* (prepaid) accounts for mobiles. The SIM card costs from €10, to which you add some prepaid phone time.

Phone Codes

Spain has no area codes. All numbers are nine digits and you just dial that nine-digit number.

Numbers starting with 900 are national toll-free numbers, while those starting 901 to 905 come with varying costs; most can only be dialled from within Spain.

TOURIST INFORMATION

Most towns and large villages of any interest have a helpful *oficina de turismo* (tourist office) where you can get maps and brochures.

Turespaña (www.spain.info) is the country's national tourism body.

VISAS

Spain is one of 26 member countries of the Schengen Convention and Schengen visa rules apply.

Citizens or residents of EU and Schengen countries No visa required.

Citizens or residents of Australia, Canada, Israel, Japan, NZ and the USA No visa required for tourist visits of up to 90 days out of every 180 days.

Other countries Check with a Spanish embassy or consulate.

To work or study in Spain A special visa may be required – contact a Spanish embassy or consulate before travel.

❶ Getting There & Away

Flights, cars and tours can be booked online at lonelyplanet.com/bookings.

AIR

Flights from all over Europe (including numerous budget airlines), plus direct flights from North and South America, Africa, the Middle East and Asia, serve main Spanish airports. All of Spain's airports share the user-friendly website and flight information telephone number of **Aena** (☑ 91 321 10 00; www.aena.es), the national airports authority. Each airport's page on the website has details on practical information (such as parking and public transport) and a list of (and links to) airlines using that airport.

Madrid's airport (p1048) is Europe's sixth-busiest airport. Other major airports include Barcelona's Aeroport del Prat and the airports of Palma de Mallorca, Málaga, Alicante, Ibiza, Valencia, Seville, Bilbao, Menorca and Santiago de Compostela.

LAND

Spain shares land borders with France, Portugal and Andorra.

Bus

Aside from the main cross-border routes, numerous smaller services criss-cross Spain's borders with France and Portugal. Regular buses connect Andorra with Barcelona (including winter ski buses and direct services to the airport) and other destinations in Spain (including Madrid) and France.

Eurolines (www.eurolines.com) is the main operator of international bus services to Spain from most of Western Europe and Morocco. Services from France include Nice to Madrid, and Paris to Barcelona.

Avanza (www.avanzabus.com) runs daily buses between Lisbon and Madrid (€41 to €46, eight hours, two to three daily).

Train

Paris to Barcelona (from €49, 6½ hours, two to four daily) A high-speed service runs via Valence, Nîmes, Montpellier, Beziers, Narbonne, Perpignan, Figueres and Girona. Also high-speed services run from Lyon (from €39, five hours) and Toulouse (from €39, three to four hours).

Paris to Madrid (from €145 to €210, 9¾ hours to 11¼ hours, eight daily) The slow route runs via Les Aubrais, Blois, Poitiers, Irún, Vitoria, Burgos and Valladolid. The quicker route uses high-speed French TGV trains between Paris and Barcelona, where you change to a high-speed Spanish AVE to reach Madrid.

Lisbon to Madrid (chair/sleeper class from €61/95, 10½ hours, one daily)

Lisbon to Irún (chair/sleeper class €70/94, 13½ hours, one daily)

Porto to Vigo (€15, 2½ hours, two daily)

SEA

Trasmediterránea (www.trasmediterranea.es) This Spanish company runs many Mediterranean ferry services.

Brittany Ferries (www.brittany-ferries.co.uk) Services between Spain and the UK.

Grandi Navi Veloci (www.gnv.it) High-speed luxury ferries between Barcelona and Genoa.

Grimaldi Lines (www.grimaldi-lines.com) Barcelona to Civitavecchia (near Rome), Savona (near Genoa) and Porto Torres (northwest Sardinia).

❶ Getting Around

Students and seniors are eligible for discounts of 30% to 50% on most types of transport within Spain.

AIR

Air Europa (www.aireuropa.com) Madrid to A Coruña, Vigo, Bilbao and Barcelona, as well as other routes between Spanish cities.

Iberia (www.iberia.com) Spain's national airline has an extensive domestic network.

Ryanair (www.ryanair.com) Some domestic Spanish routes.

SPAIN SURVIVAL GUIDE

Volotea (www.volotea.com) Budget airline that flies domestically and internationally. Domestic routes take in Alicante, Bilbao, Málaga, Seville, Valencia, Zaragoza, Oviedo and the Balearics (but not Madrid or Barcelona).

Vueling (www.vueling.com) Spanish low-cost company with loads of domestic flights within Spain, especially from Barcelona.

BOAT

Regular ferries connect the Spanish mainland with the Balearic Islands.

BUS

Spain's bus network is operated by countless independent companies and reaches into the most remote towns and villages. Many towns and cities have one main bus station where most buses arrive and depart.

It is not necessary, and often not possible, to make advance reservations for local bus journeys. It is, however, a good idea to turn up at least 30 minutes before the bus leaves to guarantee a seat. For longer trips, you can and should buy your ticket in advance.

ALSA Countrywide bus network.

Avanza Buses from Madrid to Extremadura, western Castilla y León and Valencia.

Socibus Services between Madrid, western Andalucía and the Basque Country.

CAR & MOTORCYCLE

Spain's roads vary enormously but are generally good. Fastest are the *autopistas;* on some, you have to pay hefty tolls.

Every vehicle should display a nationality plate of its country of registration and you must always carry proof of ownership of a private vehicle. Third-party motor insurance is required throughout Europe. A warning triangle and a reflective jacket (to be used in case of breakdown) are compulsory.

Driving Licences

All EU member states' driving licences are recognised. Other foreign licences should be accompanied by an International Driving Permit (although in practice local licences are usually accepted). These are available from automobile clubs in your country and valid for 12 months.

Hire

To rent a car in Spain you have to have a licence, be aged 21 or over and have a credit or debit card. Rates vary widely: the best deals tend to be in major tourist areas, including airports. Prices are especially competitive in the Balearic Islands.

SPAIN SURVIVAL GUIDE

FERRIES TO SPAIN

A useful website for comparing routes and finding links to the relevant ferry companies is www.ferrylines.com.

From Italy

ROUTE	DURATION (HR)	FREQUENCY (WEEKLY)
Civitavecchia (near Rome) to Barcelona	20	6
Genoa to Barcelona	18	1–2
Porto Torres (Sardinia) to Barcelona	12	2–5
Savona (near Genoa) to Barcelona	20	1

From Morocco

ROUTE	DURATION	FREQUENCY
Nador to Almería	5–7hr	daily
Tangier to Barcelona	27–33hr	1–2 weekly
Tangier to Tarifa	35–40min	up to 15 daily
Tangier to Algeciras	1–2hr	up to 12 daily

From the UK

ROUTE	DURATION (HR)	FREQUENCY
Plymouth to Santander	20	weekly (mid-March to November)
Portsmouth to Bilbao	24	2 weekly
Portsmouth to Santander	24	3 weekly

Road Rules

➡ The blood-alcohol limit is 0.05%.

➡ The legal driving age for cars is 18. The legal driving age for motorcycles and scooters is 16 (80cc and over) or 14 (50cc and under). A licence is required.

➡ Motorcyclists must use headlights at all times and wear a helmet if riding a bike of 125cc or more.

➡ Drive on the right.

➡ In built-up areas, the speed limit is 50km/h (and in some cases, such as inner-city Barcelona, 30km/h), which increases to 100km/h on major roads and up to 120km/h on *autovías* and *autopistas* (toll-free and tolled dual-lane highways, respectively). Cars towing caravans are restricted to a maximum speed of 80km/h.

TRAIN

The national railway company is **Renfe** (☑ 91 232 03 20; www.renfe.com). Trains are mostly modern and comfortable, and late arrivals are the exception. The high-speed network is in constant expansion.

Passes are valid for all long-distance Renfe trains; Interrail users pay supplements on Talgo, InterCity and AVE trains. All pass-holders making reservations pay a small fee.

Types of Train

Among Spain's numerous types of train are the following:

Altaria, Alvia and Avant Long-distance intermediate-speed services.

AVE (Tren de Alta Velocidad Española) High-speed trains that link Madrid with Albacete, Alicante, Barcelona, Córdoba, Cuenca, Huesca, León, Lleida, Málaga, Palencia, Salamanca, Seville, Valencia, Valladolid and Zaragoza. There are also Barcelona–Seville, Barcelona–Málaga and Valencia–Seville services. In coming years,

Madrid–Bilbao should also come on line, and travel times to Galicia should fall. The same goes for Madrid–Granada and Madrid–Badajoz.

Cercanías (rodalies in Catalonia) For short hops and services to outlying suburbs and satellite towns in Madrid, Barcelona and 11 other cities.

Euromed Similar to AVE trains, they connect Barcelona with Valencia and Alicante.

Regionales Trains operating within one region, usually stopping at all stations.

Talgo & intercity Slower long-distance trains.

Trenhotel Overnight trains with sleeper berths.

Classes & Costs

➡ Fares vary enormously depending on the service (faster trains cost considerably more) and, for many long-distance trains, on the time and day of travel and how far ahead you book (the earlier the better).

➡ Long-distance trains have 2nd and 1st classes, known as *turista* and *preferente,* respectively. The latter is 20% to 40% more expensive.

➡ Children aged between four and 14 years are entitled to a 40% discount; those aged under four travel for free (but on long- and medium-distance trains only if they share a seat with a fare-paying passenger).

➡ Buying a return ticket gives a 20% discount on most long- and medium-distance trains.

➡ Students and people up to 25 years of age with a Euro<26 or GO 25 card are entitled to 20% off most ticket prices.

Reservations

Reservations are recommended for long-distance trips; you can make them in train stations, Renfe offices and travel agencies, as well as online. In a growing number of stations, you can pick up pre-booked tickets from machines scattered about the station concourse.

Sweden

POP 10.2 MILLION

Best Places to Eat

- ➡ Woodstockholm (p1109)
- ➡ Thörnströms Kök (p1118)
- ➡ Koksbaren (p1123)
- ➡ Bolaget (p1121)
- ➡ Camp Ripan Restaurang (p1124)

Best Places to Stay

- ➡ Icehotel (p1124)
- ➡ Rival Hotel (p1108)
- ➡ Dorsia Hotel (p1117)
- ➡ Stora Hotellet Umeå (p1122)
- ➡ Clarion Hotel Wisby (p1120)

Why Go?

Sweden is a Nordic dream date. Impeccable taste and attention to detail make much of the country look like a shoot for *Wallpaper* magazine. Almost everyone in Stockholm got the memo to 'look sharp', while Sweden's world-famous design imbues the everyday with beauty and whimsy. Across the country, walled medieval cities, seaside fortresses, turreted palaces and revealing museums attest to this land's complex and gripping backstory. Adding further depth are northern Sweden's Sami people. One of Europe's few indigenous people, their rich and ancient traditions offer a very different take on the Swedish experience. Then there are Sweden's natural assets. Whether you're sailing across an archipelago to a lonely island or trekking along a kingly trail flanked by snowcapped mountains, the sense of space, solitude and freedom is matched by few corners of Western Europe. If it's understated wonder you've been seeking, you may have found your match.

When to Go
Stockholm

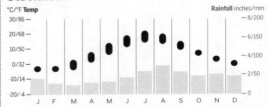

Mar There's still plenty of snow, but enough daylight to enjoy winter sports.

Jun–Aug Swedish summers are short but intense, and the Arctic Circle's White Nights are magical.

Sep The stunning colours of autumn make this prime hiking time up north.

Entering the Country

There is a good choice of flights to Sweden from most of the major cities in Europe. Trains also head here, many using Hamburg as a gateway to Scandinavia. Long-distance buses also make the trip with connections from the UK via the Channel Tunnel.

ITINERARIES

One Week

Spend four days exploring Stockholm (p1107), including a day in Uppsala (p1113) or, alternatively, a day exploring easily reached archipelago destinations like Waxholm (p1109) and Üto (p1109). Done, fly or ferry over to Gotland (p1120) and spend the rest of your time savouring the Unesco-lauded town of Visby (p1120) and cycling Gotland's pastoral landscapes.

Two Weeks

Start as above, but from Uppsala (p1113) go north to Östersund (p1121) for a day, then further up towards Kiruna (p1123) for two or three nights to check out the world-famous Icehotel, explore the Sweden's Arctic wilderness and learn about indigenous Sami culture. After three days on Gotland (p1120), head west to indie-cool Gothenburg (p1116) for a day or two before wrapping things up in continental Malmö (p1115).

Essential Food & Drink

Reindeer & Game Expect to see reindeer and other delicious game, especially up north in Sami cooking. Reindeer meat is known for its flavour, leanness and succulent quality.

Köttbullar Comforting Swedish meatballs are commonly served with potatoes and raw, stirred lingonberries.

Toast Skagen Butter-sautéed bread daintily topped with small prawns (shrimps), mayonnaise, sour cream, dijon mustard, whitefish roe and fresh dill.

Gravlax Ubiquitous and delicious, dill-cured salmon is a popular starter and *smörgåsbord* staple.

Herring The variety found off the west coast is locally known as *sill*, while that from the Baltic Sea is known as *strömming*. While the former is commonly pickled, the latter is popular breaded and fried.

Surströmming Stinky, fermented Baltic herring, traditionally eaten by the brave from late August to early September, particularly in Sweden's north.

Kanelbulle Sweden's most ubiquitous sweet treat, the spiced cinnamon bun is found in bakeries across the country.

Prinsesstårta Green 'Princess Cake' sees layers of sponge cake lined with jam and vanilla custard, thickly topped with whipped cream and encased in a marzipan shell.

AT A GLANCE

Area 450,295 sq km

Capital Stockholm

Currency Swedish Krona (kr)

Country Code ☑ 46

Emergency ☑ 112

Language Swedish (official), Finnish, Sami dialects, English

Time Central European Time (GMT/UTC plus one hour)

Visas Generally not required for stays of up to 90 days. Not required for members of EU or Schengen countries.

Sleeping Price Ranges

The following room prices are for a double room including breakfast in high season. Breakfast is normally included in hotel room prices, but usually costs extra in hostels.

€ less than 800kr

€€ 800–1600kr

€€€ more than 1600kr

Eating Price Ranges

The following price ranges refer to the average price of a main dish, not including drinks.

€ less than 100kr

€€ 100–200kr

€€€ more than 200kr

Resources

Visit Sweden (www.visitsweden.com)

The Local (www.thelocal.se)

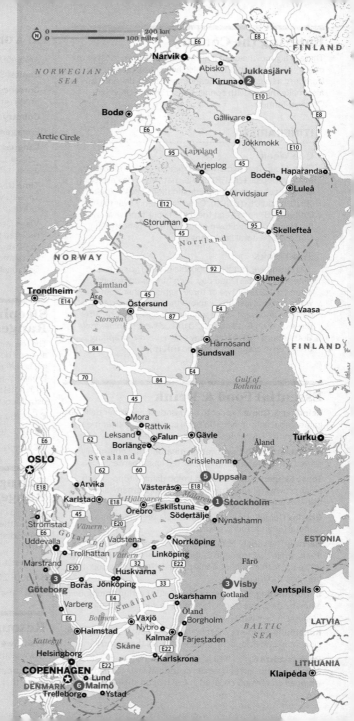

Sweden Highlights

1 Stockholm (p1107) Bouncing between world-class museums, restaurants and fairy-tale streetscapes in Sweden's confident, elegant capital.

2 Jukkasjärvi (p1124) Exploring indigenous Sami culture and slumbering in a hotel made of ice in a tiny Arctic hamlet.

3 Visby (p1120) Wandering time-stuck medieval streetscapes in Gotland's walled, World Heritage–listed capital.

4 Gothenburg (p1116) Shopping, grazing and museum hopping in Sweden's understatedly hip second city.

5 Uppsala (p1113) Roaming ancient ruins and taking in Scandinavia's largest church in one of Sweden's oldest cities.

6 Malmö (p1115) Hitting the streets of Sweden's most multicultural city, home to iconic architecture, arty bars and cafes, and spice-scented market stalls.

STOCKHOLM

📞 08 / POP 949,760

Beautiful capital cities are no rarity in Europe, but Stockholm is near the top of the list for sheer wow factor. Straddling 14 islands where the Baltic meets Lake Mälaren, this shiny Nordic star seems to have it all – edgy creativity, engrossing history, inner-city forests and waterways clean enough for a bracing dip. Saffron-and-cinnamon buildings rise starkly out of the surrounding ice-blue water, honeyed in sunlight and frostily elegant in cold weather. From its storybook Old Town (Gamla Stan) to its progressive design, fashion and culinary scenes, the city offers a crash course in style and taste. Across the city, world-class museums and galleries inform and provoke, serving up everything from glittering Viking treasures and an ill-fated warship, to ABBA props and subversive contemporary art. The result is a stimulating, inspiring hub, where the past, present and future constantly merge, converse and engage.

◉ Sights

◉ Djurgården & Skeppsholmen

★ Vasamuseet
MUSEUM

(📞08-51 95 48 80; www.vasamuseet.se; Galärvarvsvägen 14; adult/child 130kr/free; ⊙8.30am-6pm daily Jun-Aug, 10am-5pm Thu-Tue, to 8pm Wed Sep-May; 🅿; 🚊Djurgårdsfärjan, 🚌7) A good-humoured glorification of some dodgy calculations, Vasamuseet is the custom-built home of the massive warship *Vasa*; 69m long and 48.8m tall, it was the pride of the Swedish crown when it set off on its maiden voyage on 10 August 1628. Within minutes, the top-heavy vessel tipped and sank to the bottom of Saltsjön, along with many of the people on board.

★ Skansen
MUSEUM

(www.skansen.se; Djurgårdsvägen; adult/child 195/60kr; ⊙10am-8pm daily late Jun-Aug, reduced hours rest of year; 🅿🚻; 🚌69, 🚊Djurgårdsfärjan, 🚌7) The world's first open-air museum, Skansen was founded in 1891 by Artur Hazelius to provide an insight into how Swedes once lived. You could easily spend a day here and not see it all. Around 150 traditional houses and other exhibits dot the hilltop – it's meant to be 'Sweden in miniature', complete with villages, nature, commerce and industry. Note that prices and opening hours and days vary seasonally; check the website before you go.

★ Moderna Museet
MUSEUM

(📞08-52 02 35 00; www.modernamuseet.se; Exercisplan 4; ⊙10am-8pm Tue & Fri, to 6pm Wed & Thu, 11am-6pm Sat & Sun; 🅿; 🚌65, 🚊Djurgårdsfärjan) FREE Moderna Museet is Stockholm's modern-art maverick, its permanent collection ranging from paintings and sculptures to photography, video art and installations. Highlights include works by Pablo Picasso, Salvador Dalí, Andy Warhol, Damien Hirst and Robert Rauschenberg, plus several key figures in the Scandinavian and Russian art worlds and beyond. There are important pieces by Francis Bacon, Marcel Duchamp and Matisse, as well as their contemporaries, both household names and otherwise.

◉ Gamla Stan

★ Kungliga Slottet
PALACE

(Royal Palace; 📞08-402 61 00; www.theroyalpalace.se; Slottsbacken; adult/child 160/80kr; ⊙9am-5pm daily Jul & Aug, from 10am daily May-Jun & Sep, 10am-4pm Tue-Sun Oct-Apr; 🚇Gamla Stan) Kungliga Slottet was built on the ruins of Tre Kronor castle, which burned down in 1697. The north wing survived and was incorporated into the new building. Designed by court architect Nicodemus Tessin the Younger, it took 57 years to complete. Highlights include the decadent Karl XI Gallery, inspired by Versailles' Hall of Mirrors, and Queen Kristina's silver throne in the Hall of State.

Nobelmuseet
MUSEUM

(📞08-53 48 18 00; www.nobelcenter.se; Stortorget; adult/child 120kr/free; ⊙9am-8pm daily Jun-Aug, reduced hours rest of year; 🚇Gamla Stan) Nobelmuseet presents the history of the Nobel Prizes and their recipients, with a focus on the intellectual and cultural aspects of invention. It's a polished, contemporary space with fascinating displays, including short films on the theme of creativity, interviews with laureates like Ernest Hemingway and Martin Luther King, and cafe chairs signed by the visiting prize recipients (flip them over to see!).

◉ Östermalm & Ladugårdsgärdet

★ Historiska Museet
MUSEUM

(📞08-51 95 56 20; www.historiska.se; Narvavägen 13-17; ⊙10am-5pm daily Jun-Aug, 11am-5pm Tue-Sun, to 8pm Wed Sep-May; 🚌67, 69, 76, 🚌7,

🎟 Karlaplan, Östermalmstorg) FREE From Iron Age skates and a Viking boat to medieval textiles and Renaissance triptychs, Sweden's national historical collection spans over 10,000 years of Swedish culture and history. The exhibition about the Battle of Gotland (1361) is an undisputed highlight, as is the subterranean Gold Room, the latter gleaming with Viking plunder and other precious treasures.

👉 Tours

Strömma Kanalbolaget BOATING

(☑ 08-12 00 40 00; www.stromma.se; Nybrohamnen) This ubiquitous company offers tours large and small, from a 50-minute 'royal canal tour' around Djurgården (220kr) to a highly recommended 2¼-hour 'Under the Bridges of Stockholm' canal tour (280kr), the latter usually offered from mid-April to early November. There are also hop-on, hop-off tours by bus (from 320kr), boat (from 220kr) or both (from 450kr).

🛏 Sleeping

Major hotel chains are invariably cheaper booked online and in advance; rates are also much cheaper in summer and at weekends. Stockholm's Svenska Turistföreningen (STF) hostels are affiliated with Hostelling International (HI); a membership card yields a 50kr discount. Many have options for single, double and family rooms.

⭐ Vandrarhem af Chapman & Skeppsholmen HOSTEL €€

(☑ 08-463 22 66; www.stfchapman.com; Flaggmansvägen 8; dm/s/d from 240/695/1095kr; @ 🛜; 🚌 65 Skeppsholmen) The *af Chapman* is a storied vessel that has done plenty of travelling of its own. It's anchored in a superb location, swaying gently off Skeppsholmen. Bunks are in dorms below deck. Apart from showers and toilets, all facilities are on dry land in the Skeppsholmen hostel, including a good kitchen, a laid-back common room and a TV lounge.

Hotel C Stockholm HOTEL €€

(☑ 08-50 56 30 00; www.nordicchotel.com; Vasaplan 4; r from 1150kr; 🌀❄@🛜; 🚇 T-Centralen) A fantastic deal if you time it right and book ahead (especially in summer when prices drop), this sister hotel to the **Nordic Light** (☑ 08-50 56 30 00; www.nordiclighthotel.com; Vasaplan 7; r from 1400kr; 🌀❄@🛜; 🚇 T-Centralen) has small but well-designed rooms, great service and an enormous breakfast buffet. The cheapest rooms are windowless

and tiny but comfortable, with evocative Swedish-themed wallpaper. One of the two hotel bars is the famous **Icebar** (☑ 08-50 56 35 20; www.icebarstockholm.se; entry incl drink 175-215kr; ⏰ 3pm-midnight Sun-Thu, to 1am Fri & Sat, from 11.15am early May-late Sep).

Hotel Anno 1647 HISTORIC HOTEL €€

(☑ 08-442 16 80; www.anno1647.se; Mariagränd 3; s/d economy from 925/970kr, standard from 1600/1900kr; P🌀@🛜; 🚇 Slussen) Historic Hotel Anno 1647 lays on the charm with its snug wooden floors, spiral staircases and affable staff. The rooms, many of which overlook the colourful roofs of Gamla Stan across the water, come in numerous categories: economy rooms have shared showers and (tiny) bathrooms in the hall, while standard rooms and above offer superior (read: sublime) mattresses.

⭐ Rival Hotel HOTEL €€€

(☑ 08-54 57 89 00; www.rival.se; Mariatorget 3; s/d from 2395/2695kr; 🌀❄@🛜; 🚇 Mariatorget) Owned by ABBA's Benny Andersson and overlooking leafy Mariatorget, the Rival is one of the city's top design hotels. Deco accents and Swedish cinema photography nod to the Rival's picture-palace past, with rooms that are airy, stylish and complete with down duvets, pillow menu and speakers in smart, well-equipped bathrooms. In summer, consider booking a deluxe room with balcony for superlative views.

🍴 Eating

🍴 Gamla Stan

Under Kastanjen SWEDISH €€

(☑ 08-21 50 04; www.underkastanjen.se; Kindstugatan 1; sandwiches 110-125kr, daily lunch special 105kr, mains 182-289kr; ⏰ 8am-9pm Mon-Wed, to 11pm Thu & Fri, 9am-11pm Sat, 9am-9pm Sun; 🛜🚼; 🚇 Gamla Stan) The real reason to hit Under Kastanjen is for its picturesque setting, on a cobbled square, beside a chestnut tree, surrounded by ochre and yellow storybook houses. While the menu lacks wow factor, it does offer simple, comforting, generous home cooking, from soups and stews to classic Swedish meatballs. There's a good choice of gluten-free dishes, plus cakes for that mid-afternoon sugar hit.

Flying Elk PUB FOOD €€€

(☑ 08-20 85 83; www.theflyingelk.se; Mälartorget 15; mains 180-295kr; ⏰ 5pm-midnight daily; 🚇 Gamla Stan) Not your average pub – Michelin-starred chef Björn Frantzén has added contemporary vigour and polish to the traditional pub experience. The menu is all about quality produce and revamped comfort grub. Feel the love in dishes like a brioche burger laden with Gruyère, Parmesan and caramelised onion, or line-caught and seared ling served with saffron beurre blanc, deep-fried sage, walnuts and aged cheese.

Norrmalm

The Market SWEDISH €€€
(📞 08-51 73 42 00; www.scandichotels.com; Klarabergsgatan 41; weekday lunch special 145kr, mains 225-295kr; ⏰ 6.30am-11pm Mon-Fri, 7am-noon Sat & Sun; 🚇 T-Centralen) Located inside the Scandic Continental hotel, minimalist, light-filled The Market is notable for its expansive buffet breakfast and focus on sustainable, locally sourced ingredients. The à-la-carte menu offers sophisticated, seasonal dishes that might pair blackened perch with butternut gel, or grilled pigeon with leek purée, chestnuts and a chicken consommé. A set three-course vegan menu (395kr) is also available.

Södermalm

Blå Dörren SWEDISH €€
(📞 08-743 07 43; www.bla-dorren.se; Södermalmstorg 6; mains 145-260kr; ⏰ 10.30am-11pm Mon, to midnight Tue-Thu, to 1am Fri, 1pm-1am Sat, 1-11pm Sun; 🚇 Slussen) A stone's throw from Gamla Stan, Blå Dörren (The Blue Door) occupies the site of a 17th-century pub. Vaulted ceilings

and warm timber panelling set an appropriate scene for beautifully executed Swedish classics like fluffy, soul-coaxing elk meatballs, accompanied with juicy lingonberries. Libations include an extensive array of beers and *snaps* (the Swedes' favourite spirit).

★**Woodstockholm** SWEDISH €€€
(📞 08-36 93 99; www.woodstockholm.com; Mosebacketorg 9; mains 275-295kr; ⏰ 5-11pm Tue-Sat; 🚭📶; 🚇 Slussen) 🍴 Reservations are essential at this hip yet welcoming hotspot. The menu's theme changes every seven weeks or so, with a focus that ranges from specific geographic regions to more abstract concepts. What remains unchanging is a commitment to smaller, sustainable, local producers and honest, beautifully textured dishes cooked with flair.

Vasastan

★**Café Pascal** CAFE €€
(📞 08-31 61 10; www.cafepascal.se; Norrtullsgatan 4; breakfast 44-100kr, lunch dishes 69-149kr; ⏰ 7am-7pm Mon-Thu, to 6pm Fri, 9am-6pm Sat & Sun; 🚭📶; 🚇 Odenplan) Roughly hewn walls, lush foliage and rotating exhibitions of contemporary art and photography set the scene at this award-winning cafe. Food options are fresh, vibrant and not stock-standard, whether it be chia pudding with granola, yoghurt and fruit compote or salmon salad with lentils and seasonal vegetables. The Reuben sandwich is a local favourite, and the pastries suitably gorgeous and flaky.

STOCKHOLM ARCHIPELAGO

Buffering the city from the open Baltic Sea, the archipelago offers a beautiful sweep of rocky isles, graced with deep-green woods and little red cottages. And it's more accessible than many visitors imagine, with regular ferry services and tours.

Waxholmsbolaget (📞 08-600 10 00; www.waxholmsbolaget.se; Strömkajen; ⏰ 7am-2pm Mon, 8am-2pm Tue-Thu, 7.30am-4.30pm Fri, 8am-noon Sat, 8.30am-noon Sun; 🚇 Kungsträdgården), the main provider for island traffic, offers standard commuter routes and tours, as does Strömma Kanalbolaget (p1108).

Vaxholm is the gateway to the archipelago (just 35km northeast of Stockholm; take bus 670 from the Tekniska Högskolan tunnelbana station). On a sunny spring day, its crooked streets and storybook houses are irresistible. Explore the **Vaxholm Fortress Museum** (📞 08-54 17 18 90; www.vaxholmsfastning.se; Vaxholm Kastellet; adult/child 80kr/free; ⏰ noon-4pm daily early–mid-Jun, 11am-5pm daily late Jun-Aug, 11am-5pm Sat & Sun Sep), then tackle the dessert table at **Hembygdsgård** (📞 08-54 13 19 80; Trädgårdsgatan 19; ⏰ museum noon-4pm Fri-Mon Jun, to 4pm Fri-Sun Jul & Aug, cafe 11am-5pm Sat & Sun May, to 5pm daily Jun-early Sep) **FREE**

To the south, **Utö** has sandy beaches, fairy-tale forests, abundant bird life and an excellent **bakery** (📞 070-015 19 00; Gruvbryggan; pastries from 25kr, lunch from around 140kr, sandwiches 45-80kr; ⏰ 7am-5pm). Tiny Gruvbryggan is the main ferry stop. Ask at the guest harbour about cycle hire.

Stockholm

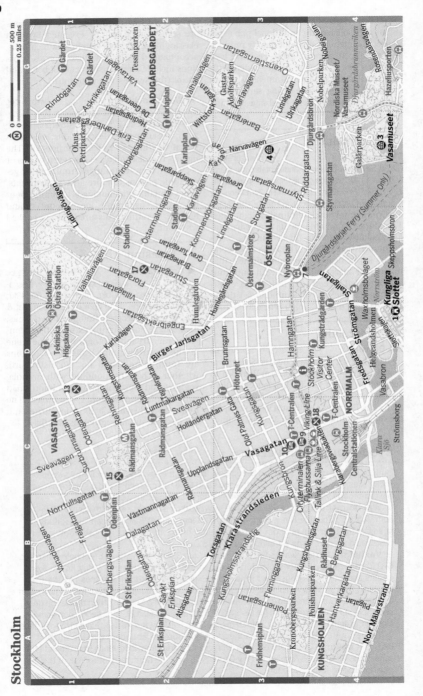

500 m
0.25 miles

LADUGÅRDSGÄRDET

VASASTAN

Birger Jarlsgatan

ÖSTERMALM

NORRMALM

Vasagatan

KUNGSHOLMEN

Torsgatan

Klarastrandsleden

Norr Mälarstrand

Kungliga Slottet

Vasamuseet

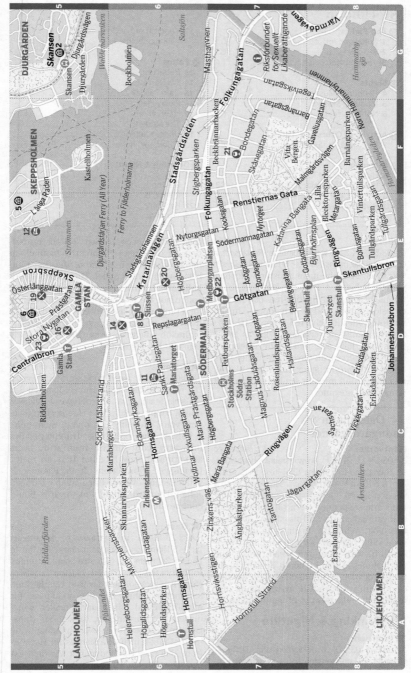

Stockholm

Babette ITALIAN €€

(⊉08-50 90 22 24; www.babette.se; Roslagsgatan 6; pizzas 165kr; mains 145kr; ☉5-10pm; ⊠Tekniska Högskolan) A white-neon rooster welcomes you to Babette, a friendly, compact, boisterous bistro with lipstick-red banquettes, curbside tables and a tiny open kitchen pumping out thin, charred Roman-style pizzas with satisfying crispiness. Pizzas aside, the short, daily changing menu celebrates other Mediterranean flavours, whether it be beans with *'nduja* (spicy Calabrian salami), feta cheese and mint, or sea-bass crudo with tomato and oregano.

✕ Östermalm & Ladugårdsgärdet

Hantverket SWEDISH €€

(⊉08-12 13 21 60; www.restauranghantverket. se; Sturegatan 15A; mains 125-195kr; ☉11.30am-2pm & 5-10pm Mon-Fri, 5-10pm Sat, closed lunch 3 weeks in Jul; ☏; ⊠Stadion) Green velvet curtains and suspended terracotta planters set a theatrical scene at this slinky, spacious bistro-bar. While the lunch menu includes a good-value *husmanskost* (traditional Swedish dish) with salad and bread (145kr), the place shines at night when it delivers beautiful, evocative creations like silky Swedish squid with white radish, oyster cream, rare oyster leaf and a powder of matured feta.

🍺 Drinking & Nightlife

★ Kvarnen BAR

(⊉08-643 03 80; www.kvarnen.com; Tjärhovsgatan 4; ☉11am-1am Mon & Tue, to 3am Wed-Fri, noon-3am Sat, noon-1am Sun; ⊠Medborgarplatsen) An old-school Hammarby football-fan hang-out, Kvarnen is one of the best (and best-loved) bars in Söder. The gorgeous beer hall dates from 1908 and seeps tradition; if you're not the clubbing type, get here early for a pint and a classic Swedish meal (mains from 225kr). As the night progresses, the nightclub vibe takes over. Queues are fairly constant but justifiable.

★ Tritonia CRAFT BEER

(⊉08-10 00 03; www.tritonia.se; Stora Nygatan 20; ☉6-11pm Tue-Thu, to 1am Fri, 1pm-1am Sat; ⊠Gamla Stan) If a microbrewery releases only a couple of kegs of a rare beer in Sweden, you'll probably find one of them here. A holy grail for beer buffs, Tritonia peddles intriguing craft brews, from fruit beers and tropical New England IPAs, to malty, barrel-aged concoctions from Estonia. If you're feeling overwhelmed, affable barkeep Johan Thor will guide you towards liquid enlightenment.

★ Gaston WINE BAR

(⊉08-20 85 83; www.gastonvin.se; Mälartorget 15; ☉5-11pm Mon & Sun, to midnight Tue-Thu, to 1am Fri, 3pm-1am Sat; ⊠Gamla Stan) Intimate, sophisticated yet relaxed, Gaston is where clued-in Stockholmers swill in Gamla Stan. Sommelier Janni Berndt's weakness for hand-harvested wines and smaller winemakers with fascinating backstories translates into an exciting, ever-changing wine list that might include a Suertes del Marqués from Tenerife or a biodynamic Vie on y Est from the Côtes du Rhône.

★**Folii** WINE BAR
(www.folii.se; Erstagatan 21; ⊘4pm-1am daily;
🐾; 🚇Medborgarpladsen) Dressed in on-point
shades of dusty pink and grey, intimate, laid-
back Folii is one of Stockholm's top wine
bars. You can sample any of its impeccably
chosen wines by the glass, with genial half-
glass serves (from 55kr) available for those
wanting to explore without a next-day hangover. And how can you not when options include adventurous winemakers and the odd
ancient varietal?

❶ Information

Stockholm Visitor Center (☑08-50 82 85
08; www.visitstockholm.com; Kulturhuset,
Sergels Torg 3; ⊘9am-7pm Mon-Fri, to 6pm
Sat, 10am-4pm Sun Jul–mid-Aug, reduced
hours rest of year; 🐾; 🚇T-Centralen) The main
visitors centre is inside Kulturhuset on Sergels
Torg. Free wi-fi.

❶ Getting There & Away

AIR

Stockholm Arlanda Airport (ARN; ☑010-109
10 00; www.swedavia.se/arlanda; 🐾) Stockholm's main airport, 43km north of the city
centre, is reached from central Stockholm by
bus, local train and express train.

BOAT

The main ferry lines with routes from Stockholm
are **Viking Line** (☑08-452 40 00; www.viking
line.se) and **Tallink & Sijla Line** (☑08-666 60
01; www.tallink.ee; Cityterminalen), both of which
operate regular ferry services to/from Helsinki
and Turku in Finland. Tallink & Sijlia Line also sails
to/from Tallinn (Estonia) and Rīga (Latvia).

BUS

Most long-distance buses arrive at and depart
from **Cityterminalen** (www.cityterminalen.com;
⊘3.15am-12.15am; 🚇T-Centralen), connected
to Centralstationen. The main counter sells
tickets for several bus companies, including
Flygbussarna (airport coaches). You can also
buy tickets from Pressbyrån shops and ticket
machines.

TRAIN

Stockholm is the hub for national train services
run by Sveriges Järnväg (p1125), with a network
of services that covers all the major towns and cities, as well as services to the rest of Scandinavia.

❶ Getting Around

TO/FROM THE AIRPORT

Arlanda Express (www.arlandaexpress.
com; Centralstationen; one-way adult/youth

280/150kr) trains link Arlanda airport to Centralstationen (adult/youth one way 280/150kr,
20 minutes, every six to 15 minutes). Trains run
less frequently after 11pm.

Cheaper **Flygbussarna** (www.flygbussarna.se;
Cityterminalen) buses run between Arlanda and
Cityterminalen (adult/child one way 99/89kr, 45
minutes, every 10 to 30 minutes).

PUBLIC TRANSPORT

Storstockholms Lokaltrafik (SL; ☑08-600
10 00; www.sl.se; Centralstationen; ⊘7am-
9pm) runs the tunnelbana (metro), local trains
and buses within Stockholm county. You can
buy tickets and passes at SL counters, ticket
machines at tunnelbana stations, Pressbyrån
kiosks and online at www.sl.se.

UPPSALA

☑018 / POP 219,920

The historical and spiritual heart of the
country, Uppsala has the upbeat party vibe
of a university town to balance the weight of
its university, castle, archaeological site and
cathedral (Scandinavia's largest). It's an easy
day trip from Stockholm, though it's worth
lingering overnight to properly soak up the
atmosphere.

◉ Sights

★**Domkyrka** CHURCH
(Cathedral; ☑018-430 35 00; www.svenskakyrkan.
se/uppsala/domkyrkan; Domkyrkoplan; ⊘8am-
6pm, tours in English 10am & 3pm Mon-Sat, 3pm
Sun late Jun–mid-Aug) FREE The Gothic Domkyrka dominates the city and is Scandinavia's
largest and tallest church, with towers soaring 119m. The interior is imposing, with the
French Gothic ambulatory flanked by small
chapels. Tombs here include those of St Erik,
Gustav Vasa and the scientist Carl von Linné.
Dating from 1710, the magnificent pulpit was
designed by baroque architect Nicodemus
Tessin the Younger, whose work includes
Stockholm's current Royal Palace.

★**Gamla Uppsala** ARCHAEOLOGICAL SITE
(☑018-23 93 00; www.arkeologigamlauppsala.
se; Disavägen; ⊘24hr; P; 🚌2) FREE One
of Sweden's largest and most important
burial sites, Gamla Uppsala (4km north of
Uppsala) contains 300 mounds from the 6th
to 12th centuries. The earliest are also the
three most impressive. Legend has it they
contain the pre-Viking kings Aun, Egil and
Adils, who appear in *Beowulf* and Icelandic
historian Snorre Sturlason's *Ynglingsaga*.

More recent evidence suggests the occupant of Östhögen (East Mound) was a woman, probably a female regent in her 20s or 30s.

Uppsala Slott
CASTLE

(☑ 018-727 24 82; www.uppsalaslott.com; Slottet; admission by guided tour only, ruins tour adult/child 120/60kr; ☺ hours vary) Built by Gustav Vasa in the 1550s, Uppsala Slott contains the state hall where kings were enthroned and Queen Kristina abdicated. The castle burned down in 1702 but was rebuilt and took on its present form in 1757. Guided tours of the original castle's ruins and the current state hall run from around mid-June to mid-August, while castle roof walks (595kr) are offered from May to September. Contact Destination Uppsala for more information.

Interestingly, the castle was also the scene of a brutal murder in 1567, when King Erik XIV and his guards killed Nils Sture and his two sons, Erik and Svante, after accusing them of high treason. At the castle entrance marked E, the **Uppsala Art Museum** (Uppsala konstmuseum; www.uppsalakonstmuseum.se; Drottning Christinas-vägen 1e; ☺ noon-4pm daily Jun–mid-Aug, to 4pm Tue, Wed & Fri-Sun, to 8pm Thu rest of year) **FREE** displays Swedish and international modern and contemporary art and ceramics as well as the art-study collection of Uppsala University.

🛏 Sleeping

⭐ **Sunnersta Herrgård**
HOSTEL €€

(☑ 018-32 42 20; www.sunnerstaherrgard.se; Sunnerstavägen 24; dm 290kr, s/d from 750/880kr; 🅿 @ 🛜; 🚃 8) In a historic manor house about 6km south of the city centre, this hostel has a parklike setting at the water's edge and a good restaurant on-site. Hotel-standard rooms include breakfast and share a bathroom with one other room; hostel guests can add breakfast for 105kr. Bike rental (per day/week 50/300kr) is also available.

Best Western Hotel Svava
HOTEL €€

(☑ 018-13 00 30; www.hotelsvava.se; Bangårdsgatan 24; s/d from 1350/1450kr; 🅿 ❄ 🛜) Named after one of Odin's Valkyrie maidens, Hotel Svava, right opposite the train station, is a comfortable top-end business-style hotel with renovated, carpeted rooms and great summer and weekend discounts.

🍴 Eating

⭐ **Kafferummet Storken**
CAFE €

(☑ 018-15 05 22; Stora Torget 3; cakes 39kr, lunch dishes 60-82kr; ☺ 9.30am-8pm Mon-Fri, to 7pm

Sat late Jun–mid-Aug, to 10pm daily rest of year; 📶) From a nondescript entrance on Stora Torget, stairs lead to this sprawling hideaway, its eclectically furnished rooms seemingly stuck in time. Order at the counter, where offerings include delicious quiches and especially popular 'filo cupcakes', savoury concoctions filled with the likes of Västerbotten cheese and chanterelle mushrooms. For a sugar high, opt for the *Fransk chokladkaka* (chocolate and hazelnut cake) or carrot cake.

Frenchi
FRENCH €€€

(☑ 018-15 01 55; www.frenchi.se; Stora Torget 10; mains 230-385kr; ☺ brasserie 10am-7pm Mon-Fri, to 5pm Sat, noon-5pm Sun, restaurant 5-9pm Mon-Thu, to 10pm Fri & Sat; 🛜) On Uppsala's main square, this sophisticated brasserie, restaurant and cocktail bar gives Gallic flavours East-Asian twists. This might translate into steak tartare with wasabi mayonnaise and pickled ginger, broccoli croquettes with roasted cauliflower, tofu crème and peanut dressing, or seafood dumplings in a decadent lobster broth. Daily lunch deals offer a main, salad, bread and coffee for 100/135kr on weekdays/weekends.

ℹ Information

Destination Uppsala (☑ 018-727 48 00; www.destinationuppsala.se) offers a helpful website and a number of staffed 'info-points' around town with maps, brochures, tips and information on sights, activities and events. See the website for locations and opening hours.

ℹ Getting There & Away

SJ Rail (Statens Järnvägar; ☑ 0771-75 75 75; www.sj.se) Operates regular services to/from Stockholm (from 95kr, 40 minutes) and Gävle (from 129kr, 1¼ hours), as well as less frequent services to/from Östersund (from 305kr, five hours) and Mora (from 255kr, 3¼ hours).

SOUTHERN SWEDEN

It's no wonder that so many artists call southern Sweden home – the light seems softer, the foliage brighter and the shoreline more dazzling. Skåne (Scania) was Danish property until 1658 and still openly flaunts its uniqueness – the heavy *Skånska* dialect, a wealth of half-timbered houses and the region's hybrid flag – a Swedish yellow cross on a red Danish background.

Malmö

📞 040 / POP 333,640

Malmö is the least Swedish of the country's major cities. Closer to cool-cat Copenhagen than Gothenburg and Stockholm, its multicultural market stalls, timber-beamed buildings and gritty, laid-back vibe exude a distinctly continental vibe. Take a couple of days to explore its beautiful parks, edgy contemporary architecture, engaging museums and impressive dining scene.

◎ Sights

★ Malmö Museer   MUSEUM

(📞 040-34 44 00; www.malmo.se/museer; Malmöhusvägen 6; adult/child 40kr/free; ⊙ 10am-5pm; ♿; 🚌 3, 7, 8) Located within the rambling **Malmöhus Slott** (📞 040 34 44 37; ⊙ tours 3pm Wed-Sun Jul-Sep), operating under the broad banner (and one low admission fee) of the Malmö Museer, are three main museums within a museum: the **Malmö Konstmuseum** (📞 040-34 44 37), **Stadsmuseum** (City Museum; 📞 040-34 44 37) and a large, unexpected **Aquarium** that's popular with younger visitors. Top billing goes to the Malmö Konstmuseum, which features a superb collection of Swedish furniture and handicrafts, plus a vast collection of 19th- and 20th-century Nordic art. There's a cafe and decent museum gift shop too.

★ Moderna Museet Malmö   MUSEUM

(📞 040-685 79 37; www.modernamuseet.se/malmo/en; Gasverksgatan 22; ⊙ 11am-6pm Tue-Fri, to 5pm Sat & Sun; 🚌 7, 8, 31, 32) FREE Architects Tham & Videgård chose to make the most of the distinct 1901 Rooseum, once a power-generating turbine hall, by adding a contemporary annexe, complete with a bright, perforated orange-red facade. Venue aside, the museum's galleries are well worth visiting, with regularly updated exhibitions that often include works from the museum's own collection, which includes works by Dalí and Picasso.

🛏 Sleeping

STF Vandrarhem Malmö City   HOSTEL €

(📞 040-611 62 20; www.svenskaturistforeningen.se; Rönngatan 1; dm/d from 280/730kr; ⊛ @ 🛜) Don't be put off by the exterior: this is a sparkling hostel right in the city centre with a bright and airy communal kitchen and an outdoor patio. Staff are enthusiastic and helpful.

THE BRIDGE

The **Öresund Bridge** (www.oresunds bron.com; motorcycle/car/minibus 280/ 515/1030kr) is the planet's longest cable-tied road and rail bridge, measuring 7.8km from Lernacken (on the Swedish side, near Malmö) to the artificial island of Peberholm (Pepper Island), south of Saltholm (Salt Island).

Local commuters pay via an electronic transmitter, while tolls for everyone else are payable by credit card, debit card or in euros, Danish or Swedish currency at the Lernacken toll booths or online. Tolls paid online (at least 30 minutes before crossing) are cheaper than paying at the toll booths; see the website for exact fares.

MJ's   HOTEL €€

(📞 040-664 64 00; www.mjs.life; Mäster Johansgatan 13; r from 1065kr; @ 🛜) After a nip and tuck, Mäster Johan is back as MJ's. Common areas revel in a kitsch-chic aesthetic, with everything from flamingo-pink ceilings to floral-print sofas and a hopping bar-restaurant. Rooms remain spacious, contrasting older wooden furnishings and the occasional antique with fashion-style photography and the odd leopard-print armchair. Breakfast is served in a garden-party-inspired atrium and the location is super central.

Best Western Hotel Royal   HOTEL €€

(📞 040-664 25 00; www.bwhotelroyal.se; Nora Vallgatan 94; s/d from 985/1145kr; @ 🛜) Run by two brothers, Hotel Royal has rooms spread over a historic 16th-century building and its modern counterpart. While the rooms are generally small, functional and uninspiring, they are comfortable, clean and can be very good value. The property includes a sauna and is within walking distance of Malmö's Centralstationen. On the downside, soundproofing isn't always great; light sleepers should bring earplugs.

✕ Eating

For sheer atmosphere, try the restaurant-bars on Lilla Torg. If you'd rather eat with the locals, head to Davishall, where some of the best restaurants are tucked away in the side streets. For fresh produce, hit **Möllevångstorget Produce Market** (Möllevångstorget; ⊙ 7am-3pm Mon-Sat).

WORTH A TRIP

LUND

The centrepiece of the appealing university town of Lund, just 15 minutes from Malmö by train, is the splendid Romanesque **Domkyrkan** (☑046-71 87 00; www.lundsdomkyrka.se; Kyrkogatan; ☺8am-6pm Mon-Fri, 9.30am-5pm Sat, to 6pm Sun), with some fantastic gargoyles over the side entrances, a giant turned to stone in the eerie crypt and an astronomical clock that sends the wooden figures whirring into action (at noon and 3pm Monday to Saturday, 1pm and 3pm on Sunday).

The town's most engaging museum, **Kulturen** (☑046-35 04 00; www.kulturen.com; Tegnerplatsen; adult May–mid-Sep 130kr, rest of year 90kr, child free; ☺10am-5pm daily May–mid-Sep, noon-4pm Tue-Fri, to 4pm Sat & Sun rest of year; ⁕), is a huge open-air space where you can wander among birch-bark hovels, perfectly preserved cottages, churches, farms and grand 17th-century houses.

Atmosfär   SWEDISH €€
(☑040-12 50 77; www.atmosfar.com; Fersensväg 4; mains 130-185kr; ☺11.30am-2.30pm & 5-10pm Mon-Fri, 5-10pm Sat; ☐1, 4, 41) A polished neighbourhood bistro with outdoor tables in the warmer months, Atmosfär serves good-value, flavourful combinations such as red cabbage with goat's cheese, chicken skin and browned butter, or beef tataki with carrot, macadamia and chive mayonnaise. The lunch menu is simpler and shorter, focussing on classic dishes like Swedish meatballs with lingonberries. Well-crafted cocktails too.

Mrs Saigon   VIETNAMESE €€
(☑040-788 35; www.mrs-saigon.se; Engelbrektsgatan 17; mains 90-215kr; ☺11.30am-3pm Mon, 11.30am-3pm & 5.30-11pm Tue-Thu, 11.30am-3pm & 5.30pm-midnight Fri & Sat; ☎; ☐1, 2, 4, 7, 8, 35, 54) Famed for her superb signature rice-noodle soup spiced with coriander, onion, basil and lime and served with chicken, beef or tofu, Mrs Saigon does her best to impress, and if the throngs of regular locals are any indication, she hits the mark. Other Vietnamese specialities include crispy shrimp rolls, homemade fish balls, sizzling crepes and rice-noodle salads.

❶ Information

Travel Shop (☑040-33 05 70; www.travelshop.se; Carlsgatan 4; ☺9am-5pm) sells tickets for bus and train companies, offers bike rental (per 24 hours 150kr) and can book a wide range of tours.

❶ Getting There & Away

BUS

FlixBus (p1125) operates regular direct services to Stockholm (from 279kr, 8½ hours, two to four daily), Jönköping (from 219kr, 4½ hours, four daily), Gothenburg (from 119kr, 3¼ hours, up to four daily) and Oslo (Norway; from 259kr, eight hours).

TRAIN

Pågatågen (local trains) operated by **Skånetrafiken** (☑0771-77 77 77; www.skanetrafiken.se) run regularly to Helsingborg (105kr, 40 to 65 minutes), Lund (50kr, 10 minutes) and other towns in Skåne. Bicycles require purchase of a child's fare.

SJ Rail (p1114) operates frequent trains per day to/from Gothenburg (from 295kr, 2½ to three hours) and Stockholm (from 395kr, 4½ to five hours).

GOTHENBURG

☑031 / POP 564,040

Gregarious Göteborg (yur-te-borry; Gothenburg in English) is the quintessential 'second city': understatedly hip and unexpectedly vibrant. Neoclassical architecture lines its tram-rattled streets, locals sun themselves beside canals, and there's always an interesting cultural or social event going on.

⊙ Sights

★**Konstmuseum**   GALLERY
(www.konstmuseum.goteborg.se; Götaplatsen; adult/child 60kr/free; ☺11am-6pm Tue & Thu, to 8pm Wed, to 5pm Fri-Sun; ⁕; ☐4, 5 Berzeliigatan) Home to Gothenburg's premier art collection, Konstmuseum traverses the Renaissance to the present day, with works by the French impressionists, Rubens, Van Gogh, Rembrandt and Picasso. Scandinavian masters such as Bruno Liljefors, Edvard Munch, Anders Zorn and Carl Larsson have pride of place in the **Fürstenburg Galleries**, with other highlights including a superb sculpture hall and the **Hasselblad Center**, the latter home to rotating photography exhibitions featuring both Nordic and global artists.

★**Universeum** MUSEUM
(☑031-335 64 00; www.universeum.se; Södra Vägen 50; adult/child 190/135kr; ☺10am-6pm; 🅿♿; ☒2, 4, 5, 6, 8, 10, 13 Korsvägen) In what is arguably the best museum for kids in Sweden, you find yourself in the midst of a humid rainforest, complete with trickling water, tropical birds and butterflies flitting through the greenery and tiny marmosets. On a level above, roaring dinosaurs maul each other, while next door, denizens of the deep float through the shark tunnel and venomous beauties lie coiled in the serpent tanks.

★**Röda Sten Konsthall** GALLERY
(www.rodastenkonsthall.se; Röda Sten 1; adult/child 40kr/free; ☺noon-5pm Tue, Thu & Fri, to 8pm Wed, to 6pm Sat & Sun; ☒3, 9 Vagnhallen Majorna) Occupying a defunct power station beside Älvsborgs bridge, Röda Sten Konsthall's four floors serve up edgy, contemporary exhibitions showcasing both Swedish and international artists working in mediums as varied as photography, sound art and installation art. It also hosts the Göteborg International Biennial for Contemporary Art (Gibca). The indie-style cafe serves delicious bites (sandwiches 79kr, dishes 139kr to 169kr), as well as hosting weekly live music. To get here, walk towards the Klippan precinct, continue under Älvsborgsbron and look for the brown-brick building.

Liseberg AMUSEMENT PARK
(www.liseberg.se; Södra Vägen; 1-day pass 475kr; ☺11am-11pm Jun–mid-Aug, hours vary rest of year; 🅿♿; ☒2, 4, 5, 6, 8, 10, 13) The attractions of Liseberg, Scandinavia's largest amusement park, are many and varied. Adrenalin blasts include the venerable wooden roller coaster Balder; AtmosFear, Europe's tallest (116m) free-fall tower; Loke, a fast-paced spinning 'wheel' that soars 42m into the air; and the Valkyria, Europe's longest-dive roller coaster, with a nerve-racking vertical drop of 50m. Softer options include carousels, fairy-tale castles, an outdoor dance floor, adventure playgrounds, and shows and concerts.

Haga District AREA
(www.hagashopping.se; ☒25 Pilgatan, ☒1, 3, 5, 6, 9, 10, 11 Hagakyrkan) The Haga district is Gothenburg's oldest suburb, dating back to 1648. A hardcore hippie hang-out in the 1960s and '70s, its cobbled streets and vintage buildings now host a blend of cafes and boutiques. During some summer weekends and at Christmas, store owners set up stalls along the neighbourhood's main strip, Haga Nygata, turning the street into one big market. The charming three-storey timber houses were built as housing for workers in the 19th century.

🛏 Sleeping

★**STF Göteborg City** HOSTEL €€
(☑031-756 98 00; www.svenskaturistforeningen.se; Drottninggatan 63-65; hostel r from 695kr, hotel s/d from 1300/1650kr; @🛜; ☒1, 2, 3, 4, 5, 6, 7, 9, 10, 11 Brunnsparken) A large, stylish, supercentral hostel with designer credentials. Industrial sleekness underscores the cafedining area and lounge, with plush comfort on each of the individually themed floors. All rooms are private, with en-suite bathroom, luxe carpeting, good soundproofing and comfortable bed-bunks. Best of all, bed linen and towels are provided. Breakfast is usually an optional 85kr.

★**Dorsia Hotel** BOUTIQUE HOTEL €€€
(☑031-790 10 00; www.dorsia.se; Trädgårdsgatan 6; r from 1990kr; 🅿❄@🛜; ☒1, 2, 3, 4, 5, 6, 7, 10, 11 Kungsportsplatsen) Richly textured and deliciously flamboyant, the Dorsia looks like the home of a moneyed 19th-century eccentric, complete with crinoline in the lobby, original artworks, and wallpapers and fabrics from the Swedish Designer Guild. Rooms are suitably furnished in hues of crimson and purple, with heavy velvet curtains, sublime Carpe Diem beds, espresso machines and mosaic-tile bathrooms. Breakfast is a notable buffet affair.

Hotel Flora BOUTIQUE HOTEL €€€
(☑031-13 86 16; www.hotelflora.se; Grönsakstorget 2; r from 1200kr; @🛜; ☒6, 11 Grönsakstorget) Fabulous Flora's slick, individually themed rooms flaunt black, white and spot colour interiors, designer chairs, flat-screen TVs and sparkling bathrooms, though lack of storage facilities may dismay those with extensive sartorial needs. Some of the top-floor rooms have air-con, several rooms offer river views, and rooms overlooking the chic split-level courtyard are for night owls rather than early birds.

🍴 Eating & Drinking

Da Matteo CAFE €
(☑031-13 05 15; www.damatteo.se; Magasinsgatan 17A; pastries from 27kr, sandwiches 72kr, pizzas 95-115kr; ☺7am-6pm Mon-Fri, from 8am Sat, 10am-5pm Sun; 🛜; ☒6, 9, 11 Domkyrkan)

Gothenburg

The perfect downtown lunch pit stop and a magnet for caffeine connoisseurs, this cafe and award-winning microroastery serves ethically sourced speciality coffee, as well as freshly made pastries, toasted sandwiches, salads and pizzas. Across the sun-soaked courtyard is another branch.

Saluhall Briggen MARKET €
(www.saluhallbriggen.se; Nordhemsgatan 28; ⊙9am-6pm Mon-Fri, to 3pm Sat; 📮1, 6 Prinsgatan) Originally built as a fire station in 1891, this handsome red-brick pile is now home to an appetite-piquing indoor market. Scan the counters for a plethora of treats, from freshly baked bread to glistening seafood, hearty cheeses and charcuterie, salads and global flavours. It's particularly handy for the hostel district.

★Thörnströms Kök SCANDINAVIAN €€€
(📋031-16 20 66; www.thornstromskok.com; Teknologgatan 3; mains 335-395kr, 4-/6-/8-course menu 675/895/1175kr; ⊙6pm-midnight Mon-Thu, to 1am Fri, 5pm-1am Sat; 🛜; 📮7, 10 Kapellplatsen) Classic technique, flawless presentation and a creative approach to local, seasonal ingredients helped chef Håkan earn his Michelin star. Hidden away in a quiet side street, his dining den is one of Gothenburg's culinary highlights, where impeccably cooked duck might conspire with Jerusalem artichokes and dried apricots, or where cherries reach new complexity in the company of pine nuts, sage and chocolate.

★Brewers Beer Bar CRAFT BEER
(📋031-388 77 66; www.magasinsgatan.brewers beerbar.se; Magasinsgatan 3; ⊙4pm-midnight Mon-Thu, 3pm-1am Fri, 1pm-1am Sat, 1-11pm Sun; 📮6, 9, 11 Domkyrkan) Should you sip an imperial stout brewed with almonds, coffee and vanilla or a guava-infused saison? This is the kind of predicament Brewers throws at you, its 14 taps showcasing some of the most thrilling microbreweries in Sweden and be-

to rustic Italian sausages with *farinata* (chickpea-flour pancake).

ℹ Information

Tourist Office (☏ 031-368 42 00; www.gote borg.com; Kungsportsplatsen 2; ◎ 9.30am-8pm late Jun–mid-Aug, shorter hours rest of year) Central and busy, with a good selection of free brochures and maps. There's a smaller **branch** (Nils Eriksongatan; ◎ 10am-8pm Mon-Fri, to 6pm Sat & Sun) inside the Nordstan shopping complex.

ℹ Getting There & Away

AIR

Göteborg Landvetter Airport (www.swedavia. se/landvetter; 🚌 Flygbuss) is located 25km east of the city, with frequent daily flights to/from Stockholm Arlanda and Stockholm Bromma airports. Nonstop flights to Visby (Gotland) depart once or twice daily (except Saturday) and once weekly to Umeå.

BOAT

Gothenburg is a major ferry terminal, with several services to Denmark and Germany with Stena Lines (www.stenaline.se).

BUS

FlixBus (☏ 08-50 51 37 50; www.flixbus.se) operates frequent buses to most major towns and cities; advance tickets usually work out considerably cheaper than on-the-spot purchases.

TRAIN

All trains depart from Centralstationen. The main lines in the west connect Gothenburg to

yond. A spacious, loftlike space with leafy outdoor tables to boot, it also offers bottled craft beers, beer-based cocktails and natural wines.

Top-notch edibles include snack-friendly olives with rosemary and pickled garlic, as well as Neapolitan-style sourdough pizzas heaped with fresh, quality ingredients. Card only; no cash.

★**Zamenhof** BAR
(☏ 031-797 87 50; www.zamenhof.se; Esperantoplatsen 5; ◎ 11am-1am Mon-Fri, from noon Sat, noon-9pm Sun; ☏; 🚋 1, 3, 5, 6, 9, 10, 11 Järntorget) Hip, loftlike Zamenhof incorporates three buzzing eateries and both front and back bars. The latter is packed with retro arcade games and pinball machines, while the front bar includes see-and-be-seen square-side tables. Polished barkeeps pour everything from craft beers to cleverly subversive cocktails (chocolate Negroni, anyone?), while food options range from poke bowls

Stockholm, Malmö and Oslo. Book tickets online via **Sveriges Järnväg** (SJ; www.sj.se) or purchase from ticket booths at the station.

ⓘ Getting Around

Buses, trams and ferries run by **Västtrafik** (☑ 0771-41 43 00; www.vasttrafik.se) make up the city's public-transport system; there is a Västtrafik information booth selling tickets and giving out timetables inside **Nils Ericson Terminalen**. The Västtrafik To Go app allows you to buy tickets on your phone.

GOTLAND

Gorgeous Gotland, adrift in the Baltic, has much to brag about: a Unesco-lauded medieval capital, truffle-sprinkled woods, A-list dining hot spots, talented artisans and more hours of sunshine than anywhere else in Sweden. It's also one of the country's richest historical regions, with around 100 medieval churches and countless prehistoric sites.

ⓘ Getting There & Away

Destination Gotland (☑ 0771-22 33 00; www.destinationgotland.se; Korsgatan 2, Visby) operates year-round car ferries between Visby and both Nynäshamn (3¼ hours, one to six times daily) and Oskarshamn (three hours, one or two daily). Fares vary wildly depending on a bunch of factors: date, time, occupancy, number of passengers, class of travel and whether you bring a vehicle. In the summer, ferries also depart from Västervik. Advance reservations are *strongly* recommended.

BRA (☑ 0771-44 00 10; www.flygbra.se) operates daily flights between Visby and Stockholm Bromma year-round.

ⓘ Getting Around

In Visby, hire bikes from **Gotlands Cykeluthyrning** (☑ 0498-21 41 33; www.gotlandscykeluthyrning.com; Skeppsbron 2; bikes per day adult/child from 120/80kr, per week from 600/400kr; ⊙ 9am-6pm daily late Jun–mid-Aug, reduced hours rest of year) at the harbour. It also rents camping equipment.

Kollektiv Trafiken (☑ 0498-21 41 12; www.gotland.se/kollektivtrafiken; 24hr ticket adult/child 160/130kr) runs buses to all corners of the island. A one-way ticket will not cost more than 80kr (to bring a bike on board add 40kr).

For car hire, try **Avis** (☑ 0498-21 98 10; www.avis.com; Donnersplats 2) or **Europcar** (☑ 0498-21 50 10; www.europcar.com/location/sweden; Visby Airport), both of which have desks at the airport.

Visby

☑ 0498 / POP 24,330

The port town of Visby is Scandinavia's best-preserved medieval town, not to mention one of Sweden's most photogenic destinations. Inside its thick city walls await twisting cobbled streets, fairy-tale wooden cottages and evocative ruins. And with more restaurants per capita than any other Swedish city, it's also a food-lovers' Valhalla.

⊙ Sights

★**Gotlands Museum**   MUSEUM
(☑ 0498-29 27 00; www.gotlandsmuseum.se; Strandgatan 14; adult/child 120kr/free; ⊙ 10am-6pm daily May-Sep, 11am-4pm Tue-Sun rest of year; ⊕) Gotlands Museum is one of the mightiest regional museums in Sweden. While highlights include amazing 8th-century, pre-Viking picture stones, human skeletons from chambered tombs and medieval wooden sculptures, the star turn is the legendary Spillings treasure horde. At 70kg it's the world's largest booty of preserved silver treasure.

🛏 Sleeping

Accommodation ranges from budget digs to luxe. Book in advance, particularly during the summer months.

Fängelse Vandrarhem   HOSTEL €
(☑ 0498-20 60 50; www.visbyfangelse.se; Skeppsbron 1; dm/s/d 400/600/1000kr; ⊛) This hostel offers beds year-round in the small converted cells of an old prison. It's in a handy location, between the ferry dock and the harbour restaurants, and there's an inviting terrace bar in summer. Reception is open from 8am to 3pm (from 9am to noon mid-August to late June), so call ahead if you are arriving outside these times.

Hotel Stenugnen   HOTEL €€
(☑ 0498-21 02 11; www.stenugnen.nu; Korsgatan 6; d from 945kr; 🅿🛜) With its chic white-on-white lounge and subtle nautical theme, the 15-room Hotel Stenugnen channels a Cape Cod vibe. Despite being a very short stroll from harbourside bars and central Visby's restaurant- and tourist-filled streets, the place feels like a tranquil, private home, its light-filled atrium the setting for decent, buffet-style breakfasts (complete with homemade bread).

★**Clarion Hotel Wisby**   HISTORIC HOTEL €€€
(☑ 0498-25 75 00; www.nordicchoicehotels.com; Strandgatan 6; r from 2065kr; 🅿⚜@🛜🏊)

Top of the heap in Visby is the luxurious, landmark Wisby. Medieval vaulted ceilings and sparkling candelabras contrast with eye-catching contemporary furnishings. The gorgeous pool (complete with medieval pillar) occupies a converted merchant warehouse. Don't miss the 11th-century chapel, just inside the entrance. The Kitchen & Table restaurant receives rave reviews from readers.

✖ Eating

Visby has plenty of eating options, with numerous options on Stora Torget, Södra Kyrkogatan and Hästgatan.

Jessens Saluhall & Bar   SWEDISH €€

(☑ 0498-21 42 14; www.saluhallochbar.se; Hästgatan 19; mains 129-295kr; ⊙ 11am-9pm Mon-Thu & Sun, to 10pm Fri & Sat late Jun–mid-Aug, to 6pm Mon-Thu, to 8pm Fri, to 4pm Sat rest of year) Strung with light bulbs and great for people watching, this fabulous deli-cum-eatery is run by three affable brothers. Daily specials generally include the perennially popular fish soup, given a Med-style makeover with the addition of gnocchi and chilli. Meat is sourced locally, and the seafood is fabulously fresh. You'll even find beers from the owners' sister's brewery.

Amarillo   INTERNATIONAL €€

(☑ 073-416 80 86; www.amarillovisby.se; Schweitzergränd 5b; dishes 120-175kr; ⊙ 5-11pm Wed-Sun Jul–mid-Aug, 5-11pm Tue-Thu, to midnight Fri & Sat rest of year; 🐾) Decked out in distressed wood panelling, cool, casual Amarillo serves small, tapas-style dishes with European, Pacific and Mexican influences. Expect tasty bites like homemade gnocchi with butter sauce, almonds and Västerbotten cheese, or tuna poke with puffed rice paper, teriyaki, ginger and grated kohlrabi. Libations include local craft beers and some interesting, organic wines.

★ Bolaget   FRENCH €€€

(☑ 0498-21 50 80; www.bolaget.fr; Stora Torget 16; mains 210-285kr; ⊙ 5-10pm Mon, Tue & Sat, 11.30am-2pm & 5-10pm Wed-Fri; 🐾) Take a defunct Systembolaget (state-owned alcohol shop), chip the 'System' off the signage, and reinvent the space as a buzzing, French bistro–inspired hot spot. Dishes are suitably Gallic, from duck-liver terrine with butter-fried sourdough bread and fig marmalade, to Toulouse sausage with sauerkraut, smoked pork belly and Dijon mustard.

Staffers are amiable and the summertime square-side bar seating is perfect for people watching.

ℹ️ Information

Gotlands Turistbyrå (☑ 0498-20 17 00; www.gotland.com; Donners Plats 1; ⊙ 9am-6pm daily Jun-Aug, reduced hours rest of year; 🐾) The large, helpful tourist office is conveniently located at Donners Plats and can help with accommodation and advise on what is going on during your stay. It also has free wi-fi.

NORRLAND

Norrland, the northern half of Sweden, is a paradise for nature lovers, its vast wilderness a veritable playground for hikers, skiers and others seeking natural, alfresco highs. In winter the landscape is transformed by snowmobiles, dog-sleds and the eerie natural phenomenon known as the aurora borealis (Northern Lights). The north is also home to the indigenous Sami people and their rich, proud traditions.

Östersund

☑ 063 / POP 50,960

This pleasant town by Storsjön lake, in whose chilly waters is said to lurk a rarely sighted monster, is a relaxed and scenic gateway town for further explorations of Norrland. Once a lucrative trading centre, it's now better known as a Unesco-designated 'city of gastronomy'.

⊙ Sights

★ Jamtli   MUSEUM

(☑ 063-15 01 00; www.jamtli.com; Museiplan; adult/child 80kr/free, late Jun-late Aug free; ⊙ 11am-5pm daily late Jun–mid Aug, Tue-Sun rest of year; 🅿️🐾) Jamtli, 1km north of the centre, consists of two parts: the open-air museum, comprising painstakingly reconstructed wooden buildings, complete with enthusiastic guides wearing 19th-century period costume; and the indoor museum, home to the **Överhogdal Tapestries**, the oldest of their kind in Europe – Christian Viking relics from 1100 CE that feature animals, people, ships and dwellings. Another fascinating display is devoted to Storsjöodjuret (the lake monster), including taped interviews with those who claim they have seen it, monster-catching gear and a pickled monster embryo.

🛏 Sleeping

Hotel Jämteborg   HOTEL €

(📞 063-51 01 01; www.jamteborg.se; Storgatan 54; hotel s/d from 1095/1250kr; 🅿 @ 🛜) Modest Hotel Jämteborg compensates for its dated, uninspiring interiors with friendly, helpful staff, a decent breakfast, and a central city location. Limited on-site facilities include a sauna and small fitness room, though the latter could use some TLC. Parking and wifi are free, the latter offering decent speeds.

★ Hotel Emma   HOTEL €€

(📞 063-51 78 40; www.hotelemma.com; Prästgatan 31; s/d from 850/990kr; 🅿 🛜) The individually styled rooms at super-central Emma nestle in crooked hallways on two floors, with homey touches like squishy armchairs and imposing ceramic stoves; some rooms have French doors facing the courtyard. The breakfast spread (98kr) is a delight and bike rental is available (per day 100kr). Reception hours are limited, so call ahead if arriving late or early.

🍴 Eating

Wedemarks Konditori & Bageri   CAFE €

(📞 063-51 03 83; http://wedemarks.se; Prästgatan 27; sandwiches from 63kr; ⊙ 8am-6pm Mon-Fri, 10am-5pm Sat, 11am-4pm Sun; 🛜) This glorious cafe has been sweet-toothing its customers since 1924. Sink your teeth into classic Swedish treats like Princess layer cake, topped with bright green marzipan or, in the warmer months, house-made Italian-style gelato. Savoury offerings include baguettes, panini and wraps, among them organic, house-made thin bread filled with hot-roasted salmon, cream cheese, mustard, salad and paprika. Bliss.

ⓘ Information

Tourist Office (📞 063-701 17 00; www.visit ostersund.se; Rådhusgatan 44; ⊙ 9am-5pm Mon-Fri, 10am-3pm Sat & Sun) Efficient office opposite the town hall.

ⓘ Getting There & Away

Åre Östersund Airport (📞 063-19 30 00; www. swedavia.se/ostersund; Frösön) lies 11km west of Östersund, with connections to Stockholm and Umeå. The airport bus (adult/child 90/45kr) leaves from the **bus station** (📞 0771-10 01 10; http://ltr.se; Gustav III Torg; ⊙ 6am-10.30pm Mon-Fri, 6.30am-7.30pm Sat, noon-10pm Sun).

SJ (p1125) runs one direct train daily to Stockholm (from 585kr, 4¾ hours) via Uppsala.

Umeå

📞 090 / POP 125,080

A vibrant college town, Umeå has claims to fame on several counts: it was the European Capital of Culture in 2014; it's home to Europe's greatest museum collection of vintage guitars; and it is the former residence of Stieg Larsson, author of *The Girl with the Dragon Tattoo*. Its location, a mere 400km below the Arctic Circle, means it is also popular with Northern Lights seekers.

◉ Sights

★ Västerbottens Museum   MUSEUM

(📞 090-16 39 00; www.vbm.se; Helena Elizabeths väg, Gammliavägen; ⊙ 10am-5pm, to 8pm Wed; 🅿) **FREE** The star of the Gammlia museum complex, the engrossing Västerbottens Museum traces the history of the province from prehistoric times to today. Exhibitions include an impressive ski-through-the ages collection starring the world's oldest ski (around 5400 years old), and an exploration of Sami rock art. The museum hosts excellent temporary exhibitions as well as regular workshops and activities for children. You'll also find a quality cafe specialising in organic fare. Catch bus 2 or 7 or walk 1km from the train station.

🛏 Sleeping

STF Vandrarhem Umeå   HOSTEL €

(📞 090-77 16 50; www.umeavandrarhem. com; Västra Esplanaden 10; dm/s/d from 240/385/520kr; 🛜) In a historic timber building, this efficient hostel has rooms of varying quality: try to nab a space in one of the newer rooms with beds, as opposed to the dorms with bunks. It's in a great location, at the edge of the town centre, and the facilities (two kitchens, laundry) are very handy for self-caterers. Bed linen, towels and the buffet breakfast cost extra.

★ Stora Hotellet Umeå   BOUTIQUE HOTEL €€

(📞 090-77 88 70; www.storahotelletumea.se; Storgatan 46; s/d/ste from 1000/1150/6000kr; 🅿 🛜) First opened as a hotel in 1895, the Stora Hotellet had major renovations to coincide with the city being named European Capital of Culture in 2014. The six categories of handsome rooms have names like Superstition, Adventure and Mystique, and if you're after a spot where historical ambience conspires with contemporary chic, this is a top place to stay.

Eating

★ Två Fiskare
SEAFOOD €€

(☑090-765 70 20; www.tvafiskare.se; Storgatan 44; dishes 139-169kr; ☺kitchen 11am-4pm Mon-Fri, to 3pm Sat, shop 10am-6pm Mon-Fri, to 4pm Sat) This white-tiled place takes Nordic fish very seriously indeed. Not only does it sell it fresh, it also prepares a handful of exquisite seafood and fish dishes daily for those in the know. From smoked shrimp to crab cakes and fish soup, dishes depend on what is flapping fresh that day. Undecided? Then opt for the classic fish and chips.

★ Koksbaren
SWEDISH €€€

(☑090-13 56 60; www.koksbaren.com; Rådhusesplanaden 17; mains 235-345kr; ☺5-11pm Mon-Thu, to midnight Fri & Sat late Jun-Aug, 11am-11pm Mon-Thu, 11am-midnight Fri, noon-midnight Sat rest of year; ☎) One of the best spots to dine in town, light-filled, contemporary Koksbaren puts sophisticated spins on quality produce, much of it regional. Expect anything from a Nordic take on the fish taco (toasted flatbread filled with smoked salmon and bean sprouts), to succulent dry-aged sirloin with mushrooms, French truffles and Parmesan cream. Great wines by the glass too.

ℹ Information

Tourist Office (☑090-16 16 16; www.visitumea.se; Rådhusesplanaden 6a; ☺10am-5pm Mon-Fri) Centrally located with helpful staff who can advise on places to stay and what's going on.

ℹ Getting There & Away

Umeå Airport (☑010-109 50 00; www.swedavia.com/umea; Flygplatsvägen) lies 5km south of the city centre, with daily flights to Stockholm's Arlanda and Bromma airports. Flights to Gothenburg and Kiruna depart several times weekly. An airport bus (route 80) runs to the city centre (70kr, 10 minutes).

Ybuss (p1125) runs buses south to Stockholm (473kr, 9¼ to 10¼ hours) twice daily, stopping at all the coastal towns.

Train services include four daily direct services to Stockholm (from 495kr, 6¼ to 11¼ hours). Frequent northbound trains to Luleå (from 314kr, 3¼ to five hours) stop in Boden, from where there are connections to Kiruna (from 515kr, 6½ to 11 hours).

Kiruna & Around

☑0980 / POP 23,120

Thousands of visitors flock to the workaday mining town of Kiruna every year to see the Icehotel in nearby Jukkasjärvi – northern Sweden's biggest attraction – and to take part in all manner of outdoor adventures: dog-sledding, snowmobiling and aurora borealis tours in the winter, and biking, hiking and canoeing during the luminous summer.

☞ Tours

Active Lapland
SNOW SPORTS

(☑076-104 55 08; www.activelapland.com; Solbacksvägen 22; tours from adult/child 1290/645kr) This experienced operator offers a number of excursions from mid-November to April. Options include a three-hour dog-sled ride and lunch package (adult/child 1590/795kr), highly recommended rides under the Northern Lights (adult/child 1390/695kr) and airport pickups by dog sleigh (5500kr for one to four passengers). They'll even let you drive your own dog-sled (adult/child 3290/1645kr).

Kiruna Guidetur
OUTDOORS

(☑0980-811 10; www.kirunaguidetur.com; Vänortsgatan 8; tours from adult/child 695/348kr) These popular all-rounders organise anything from overnighting in a self-made igloo, snowmobile safaris and cross-country skiing outings in winter, to overnight mountain-bike and canoeing tours, rafting and fishing trips in summer. They also offer mountain-bike rental (one day 295kr, each subsequent day 195kr). Book via the website, or visit the shop on the main square.

🛏 Sleeping

SPiS Hotel & Hostel
HOSTEL €

(☑0980-170 00; www.spiskiruna.se; Bergmästaregatan 7; dm/d from 315/535kr, hotel s/d from 895/995kr; ℗☎) This catch-all hotel-and-hostel combo features comfy, simple hotel rooms and dorms in central Kiruna; soundproofing isn't the best, so bring earplugs if you're an especially light sleeper. The complex includes a deli, a bakery and a top-quality restaurant, plus a handy communal guest kitchen and an even handier supermarket just a few minutes' stroll away. Look for the orange building.

Hotel Arctic Eden
BOUTIQUE HOTEL €€

(☑0980-611 86; www.hotelarcticeden.se; Föraregatan 18; s/d from 1295/1595kr; ℗☎☒) Kiruna's smartest digs offers functional rooms with Sami-inspired design touches, a spa and an indoor pool, and friendly staff happy to book all manner of outdoor adventures. The property also houses a notable restaurant and a

DON'T MISS

ICEHOTEL

The winter wonderland that is the **Icehotel** (☑0980-668 00; www.icehotel.com; Marknadsvägen 63; s/d/ste from 5000/5600/7000kr; ☺Dec-Apr; **P** 🛜) in Jukkasjärvi, 18km east of Kiruna, is an international phenomenon.

The enormous hotel is built using 30,000 tonnes of snow and 4000 tonnes of ice, with international artists and designers contributing innovative ice sculptures every year. The beds are covered with reindeer skins and army-grade sleeping bags, guaranteed to keep you warm despite the -5°C room temperature. There's even an Ice Ceremony Hall (popular for weddings) and a much-copied Absolut Icebar, serving drinks in glasses of ice.

Adjacent to the winter-only Icehotel is the year-round **Icehotel 365** (☑0980-668 00; www.icehotel.com; Jukkasjärvi; s/d/ste from 2400/2700/2700kr, cabins from 2000kr; **P** 🛜), which also includes spectacular ice sculptures and an ice bar. Day tours of the rooms are available; see the website.

quality handicraft store. The complex is also home to a popular East-Asian restaurant, Arctic Thai & Grill.

✖ Eating

FiKA by SPiS   CAFE €

(☑0980-170 00; www.spiskiruna.se/fika-by-spis; Meschplan 1; lunch dishes 69-125kr; ☺8am-6pm Mon-Fri, 10am-5pm Sat & Sun) You'll think you're in Stockholm at this sleek, modern cafe and providore. Lunch options include salads, grilled sandwiches and poke bowls, while the counter heaves with freshly made Swedish desserts and pastries. Speciality coffee and healthy, house-made smoothies are also in the mix, while its grocery shelves stock everything from jars of blackcurrant and liquorice curd to packs of Stockholm-roasted coffee beans.

★ Camp Ripan Restaurang   SWEDISH €€

(☑0980-630 00; www.ripan.se; Campingvägen 5; lunch dish 100-125kr, dinner mains 155-375kr; ☺noon-2pm & 5-9.30pm; **P** 🛜 🍴) It might be located at the local campground, but this popular restaurant is a smart, contemporary affair. Lunch options are limited and often *husmanskost* (Swedish home cooking) in nature, making dinner the real highlight (book ahead). Using no shortage of local, seasonal produce, dishes might include house-smoked reindeer fillet with a quiche-like pie of potato and robust Västerbotten cheese.

ℹ Information

Tourist Office (☑0980-188 80; www.kiruna lapland.se; Lars Janssonsgatan 17; ☺8.30am-6pm Mon-Fri, to 4pm Sat & Sun Jun-Aug, reduced hours rest of year) Inside the Folkets Hus visitor centre, the helpful tourist office offers free wi-fi and can book various tours.

ℹ Getting There & Away

AIR

Kiruna Airport (☑010-109 46 00; www. swedavia.com/kiruna), 7km east of the town, has nonstop flights to Stockholm (one to three daily), as well as several weekly nonstop flights to Umeå. The airport bus (one way adult/child 110/55kr) is timed to meet Stockholm flights and runs between the tourist office and central Kiruna.

BUS

Buses depart from the centrally located **bus station** (☑980-124 00; www.ltnbd.se/kiruna; Hjalmar Lundbohmsvägen 45; ☺7am-4pm Mon-Fri). Bus 501 runs to/from Jukkasjärvi (43kr, 30 minutes).

TRAIN

Destinations include Narvik (Norway; from 95kr, 2¾ to 3¼ hours), Luleå (from 295kr, 3½ to 5½ hours) and Gällivare (from 115kr, one to two hours). Travel to Stockholm (from 565kr, 15 to 16¾ hours) is overnight and requires at least one change.

SURVIVAL GUIDE

ℹ Directory A–Z

ACCOMMODATION

Sweden has a wide variety of accommodation that is generally of a very high standard. Book ahead in summer to secure the best prices.

CHILDREN

Most sights and activities are designed with kids in mind, with free or reduced admission for under-18s and plenty of hands-on exhibits. Dining, accommodation and transport providers are also well accustomed to handling families.

LGBT+ TRAVELLERS

Sweden is a famously liberal country. The national organisation for LGBT+ rights is **Riksförbundet för Sexuellt Likaberättigande** (RFSL; ☑ 08-50 16 29 00; www.rfsl.se; Alsnögatan 7, Danvikstull; ⊙10am-noon & 1-3pm Mon & Wed-Fri; ▣ 53, 71, 93, 402). For entertainment listings, club nights and other local information, visit www.qx.se (in Swedish).

MONEY

ATMs widely available. Credit cards accepted in most hotels and restaurants.

OPENING HOURS

Except where indicated, we list hours for high season (mid-June to August). Expect more limited hours the rest of the year.

Banks 9.30am to 3pm Monday to Friday; some city branches open to 5pm or 6pm

Bars and Pubs 11am or noon to 1am or 2am

Government Offices 9am to 5pm Monday to Friday

Restaurants 11am to 2pm and 5pm to 10pm, often closed on Sunday and/or Monday; high-end restaurants often closed for a week or two in July or August

Shops 9am to 6pm Monday to Friday, to 1pm Saturday

PUBLIC HOLIDAYS

Nyårsdag (New Year's Day) 1 January

Trettondedag Jul (Epiphany) 6 January

Långfredag, Påsk, Annandag Påsk (Good Friday, Easter Sunday and Monday) March/April

Första Maj (Labour Day) 1 May

Kristi Himmelsfärdsdag (Ascension Day) May/June

Pingst, Annandag Pingst (Whit Sunday and Monday) Late May or early June

Midsommardag (Midsummer's Day) Saturday between 19 and 25 June

Alla Helgons dag (All Saints Day) Saturday, late October or early November

Juldag (Christmas Day) 25 December

Annandag Jul (Boxing Day) 26 December

TELEPHONE

Swedish phone numbers have area codes followed by a varying number of digits. Local SIM cards are readily available from telco providers such as Telia, Comviq, Tre and Telenor. SIM cards can also be purchased from Pressbyrån locations (around 50kr to 100kr).

TIME

Sweden is one hour ahead of GMT/UTC and is in the same time zone as Norway and Denmark as well as most of Western Europe.

TOILETS

Public toilets in parks, shopping malls, libraries, and bus or train stations are rarely free in Sweden, though some churches and most museums and tourist offices have free toilets. Pay toilets cost 5kr to 10kr, usually payable by coin or text message.

ⓘ Getting There & Away

AIR

Sweden is well connected by air with numerous international airports. The main gateway is Stockholm Arlanda.

LAND

Direct access to Sweden by land is possible from Norway, Finland and Denmark (via the Öresund toll bridge). Bus companies **Nettbuss Express** (☑ 0771-15 15 15; www.nettbuss.se) and **FlixBus** (☑ 08-50 51 37 50; www.flixbus.se), and national rail company **Sveriges Järnväg** (SJ; ☑ 0771-75 75 75; www.sj.se), reach Norway and Denmark.

SEA

Ferry connections are frequent to various destinations in Sweden from Finland, Poland, Germany and Norway. Most lines offer substantial discounts for seniors, students and children.

ⓘ Getting Around

AIR

Domestic flights link various towns and cities in Sweden and can be a fast, if not particularly cheap, way of getting around.

BICYCLE

Sweden has a well-developed network of cycle paths in and around its towns and cities. There are also well-marked cycle routes around the country. Helmets are compulsory for all cyclists under age 15.

BUS

There is a comprehensive network of buses throughout Sweden and, in general, buses are cheaper than trains. The main long-distance companies are FlixBus, **Ybuss** (☑ 0771-33 44 44; www.ybuss.se), Nettbuss Express and **Svenska Buss** (☑ 0771-67 67 67; www.svenskabuss.se).

CAR & MOTORCYCLE

The blood-alcohol limit in Sweden is 0.02%. The minimum age to hire a car is 20 (sometimes 25).

TRAIN

Sweden has an extensive and reliable railway network, and trains are almost always faster than buses. Sveriges Järnväg covers most main lines.

Switzerland

POP 8.5 MILLION

Best Places to Eat

➜ Chez Vrony (p1136)

➜ Didi's Frieden (p1144)

➜ Volkshaus Basel (p1147)

➜ Cafe 3692 (p1141)

➜ Zur Werkstatt (p1139)

➜ Kraftwerk (p1144)

Best Places to Stay

➜ Hotel Widder (p1143)

➜ The Bed & Breakfast (p1139)

➜ Float Inn (p1130)

➜ Hotel Glacier (p1141)

Why Go?

What giddy romance Zermatt, St Moritz and other glitterati-encrusted names evoke. This is Sonderfall Schweiz ('special-case Switzerland'), a privileged neutral country set apart from others, proudly idiosyncratic, insular and unique. It's blessed with gargantuan cultural diversity: its four official languages alone speak volumes.

The Swiss don't do half measures: Zürich, their most gregarious urban centre, has cutting-edge art, legendary nightlife and one of the world's highest living standards. The national passion for sharing the great outdoors provides access (by public transport, no less!) to some of the world's most inspiring panoramic experiences.

So don't depend just on your postcard images of Bern's and Lucerne's chocolate-box architecture, the majestic Matterhorn or those pristine lakes – Switzerland is a place so outrageously beautiful it simply must be seen to be believed.

When to Go
Bern

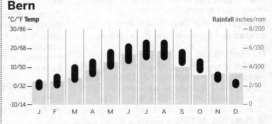

Dec–early Apr Carve through powder and eat fondue at an Alpine resort.

Jun–Sep Hike in the shadow of the mesmerising Matterhorn and be wowed by its perfection.

Aug Celebrate Swiss National Day on 1 August and witness Swiss national pride in full force.

Entering the Country

Formalities are minimal when arriving in Switzerland by air, rail or road thanks to the Schengen Agreement, which allows passengers coming from the EU to enter without showing a passport. When arriving from a non-EU country, you'll need your passport or EU identity card – and visa if required – to clear customs.

ITINERARIES

One Week

Starting in vibrant Zürich (p1142), shop famous Bahn-hofstrasse, then eat, drink and be merry. Next, head to the Jungfrau region (p1141) to explore some kick-arse Alpine scenery, whether it be by hiking or skiing. Take a pit stop in beautiful Lucerne (p1138) before finishing up in Switzerland's delightful capital, Bern (p1136).

Two Weeks

As above, then head west for a French flavour in Geneva (p1128) or lakeside Lausanne (p1133). Stop in Gruyères (p1134) to dip into a cheesy fondue and overdose on me-ringues drowned in thick double cream. Zip to Zermatt (p1135) or across to St Moritz (p1149) to frolic in snow or green meadows, then loop east to taste the Italian side of Switzerland at lakeside Lugano (p1148).

Essential Food & Drink

Fondue Switzerland's best-known dish, in which melted Em-mental and Gruyère cheese are combined with white wine in a large pot and eaten with small bread chunks.

Raclette Another popular artery-hardener of melted cheese served with potatoes.

Rösti German Switzerland's national dish of fried shredded potatoes is served with everything.

Veal Highly rated throughout the country; in Zürich, veal is thinly sliced and served in a cream sauce (*Zürcher Geschnetzeltes*).

Bündnerfleisch Dried beef, smoked and thinly sliced.

Chocolate Good at any time of day and available seemingly everywhere.

SWITZERLAND

Sleeping Price Ranges

The following price ranges refer to a double room with a private bathroom. Quoted rates are for high season and include breakfast, un-less otherwise noted.

$ less than Sfr170

$$ Sfr170–350

$$$ more than Sfr350

Eating Price Ranges

The following price ranges refer to a main course.

$ less than Sfr25

$$ Sfr25–50

$$$ more than Sfr50

Resources

My Switzerland (www.myswitzerland.com)

Swiss Info (www.swissinfo.ch)

SBB (www.sbb.ch)

Switzerland Highlights

1 Zürich (p1142)
Discovering this zesty city via a daytime stroll along the city's sublime lake followed by a rollicking night out.

2 Zermatt (p1135)
Marvelling at the iconic Matterhorn and wandering around this car-free Alpine village.

3 Bern (p1136) and **Lucerne** (p1138) Enjoying the charm of these famous beauties: think medieval Old Town appeal, folkloric fountains and art.

4 Jungfraujoch (p1141)
Being wowed by the Eiger's monstrous north face on a ride to the 'top of Europe', 3471m Jungfraujoch.

5 Geneva (p1128)
Boarding a boat in this sophisticated city for a serene Lake Geneva cruise to medieval Lausanne.

6 Bernina Express (p1149) Riding one of Switzerland's legendary scenic trains, such as the Bernina Express.

7 Lugano (p1148) Going Italian at Lugano, with its lovely, temperate lake setting.

GENEVA

POP 198,979 / ELEV 375M

Like the swans that frolic on its epony-mous Alpine lake (Europe's largest), Geneva (Genève) is a rare bird. Constantly perceived as the Swiss capital (it isn't), Switzerland's second-largest city is slick and cosmopolitan, and its people chatter in almost every language. The headquarters of the World Trade Organization, World Health Organization, International Committee of the Red Cross, and the second-largest branches of the United Nations and World Bank are here, along with an overload of luxury hotels, boutiques, jewellers, restaurants and chocolatiers.

◉ Sights

The city centre is so compact it's easy to see many of the main sights on foot. Begin your explorations on the southern side of Lake Geneva and visit the **Jardin Anglais** (English Garden; Quai du Général-Guisan) to see the **Horloge Fleurie** (Flower Clock). Crafted from 6500 flowers, the clock has ticked since 1955 and sports the world's longest second hand (2.5m).

⭐ **Jet d'Eau**   FOUNTAIN
(Quai Gustave-Ador) When landing by plane, this lakeside fountain is your first dramatic glimpse of Geneva. The 140m-tall structure shoots up water with incredible force – 200km/h, 1360 horsepower – to create the sky-high plume, kissed by a rainbow on sunny days. At any one time, 7 tonnes of water are in the air, much of which sprays spectators on the pier beneath. Two or three times a year it is illuminated pink, blue or another colour to mark a humanitarian occasion.

CERN   RESEARCH CENTRE
(☑ 022 767 84 84; www.cern.ch; Meyrin; ⊙ guid-ed tours in English 11am & 1pm Mon-Sat) FREE
Founded in 1954, the European Organiza-

tion for Nuclear Research (CERN), 8km west of Geneva, is a laboratory for research into particle physics. It accelerates protons down a 27km circular tube (the Large Hadron Collider, the world's biggest machine) and the resulting collisions create new matter. Come anytime to see the permanent exhibitions shedding light on its work, but for two-hour guided tours in English reserve online up to 15 days ahead and bring photo ID.

Musée International de la Croix-Rouge et du Croissant-Rouge   MUSEUM

(International Red Cross & Red Crescent Museum; ☑ 022 748 95 11; www.redcrossmuseum.ch; Av de la Paix 17; adult/child Sfr15/7; ⊙ 10am-6pm Tue-Sun Apr-Oct, to 5pm Nov-Mar) Compelling multimedia exhibits at Geneva's fascinating International Red Cross and Red Crescent Museum trawl through atrocities perpetuated by humanity. The litany of war and nastiness, documented in films, photos, sculptures and soundtracks, is set against the noble aims of the organisation founded by Geneva businessmen Henry Dunant in 1863. Excellent temporary exhibitions command an additional entrance fee. To get here take bus 8 from Gare CFF de Cornavin (p1132) to the Appia stop.

Cathédrale St-Pierre   CATHEDRAL

(www.cathedrale-geneve.ch; Cour de St-Pierre; towers adult/child Sfr5/2; ⊙ 9.30am-6.30pm Mon-Sat, noon-6.30pm Sun Jun-Sep, 10am-5.30pm Mon-Sat, noon-5.30pm Sun Oct-May) Geneva's cathedral is predominantly Gothic with an 18th-century neoclassical facade. Between 1536 and 1564 Protestant John Calvin preached here; see his seat in the north aisle. Inside the cathedral, 96 steps spiral up to the **northern tower**, offering a fascinating glimpse at the cathedral's architectural construction. From here, another 60 steps climb into the **south-**

ern tower, revealing close-up views of the bells and panoramic city vistas. From June to September, daily free carillon (5pm) and organ (6pm) concerts are a bonus.

Patek Philippe Museum   MUSEUM

(☑ 022 707 30 10; www.patekmuseum.com; Rue des Vieux-Grenadiers 7; adult/child Sfr10/free; ⊙ 2-6pm Tue-Fri, 10am-6pm Sat) An ode to Swiss timing, this elegant museum by one of Switzerland's leading luxury watchmakers displays exquisite timepieces and enamels from the 16th century to the present, with some 2000 exhibits on display.

🏃 Activities

Genève Plage   SWIMMING

(☑ 022 736 24 82; www.geneve-plage.ch; Quai de Cologny 5, Port Noir; adult/child Sfr7/3.50; ⊙ 10am-8pm mid-May–mid-Sep) This delightful swimming-pool complex, with its water slide and plenty of lawn to flop on, has been pleasing frolicking-in-the-sun Genevans since the 1930s. You can rent stand-up paddleboards for Sfr12 per hour, have fun surfing the artificial wave (Sfr10 per session) or get an Ayurvedic massage.

CGN Ferries & Cruises   BOATING

(Compagnie Générale de Navigation; ☑ 0900 929 929; www.cgn.ch; Quai du Mont-Blanc; 🖬) Lake Geneva's biggest ferry operator runs regular scheduled ferry services and a variety of themed lake cruises aboard beautiful belle époque steamers. Check the website for full details.

🎪 Festivals & Events

L'Escalade   CARNIVAL

(⊙ Dec) Smashing sweet marzipan-filled *marmites en chocolat* (chocolate cauldrons) and gorging on the broken pieces makes Geneva's biggest festival (second weekend of December) loads of fun. Torch-lit processions enliven the Vieille Ville and a bonfire is lit in the cathedral square to celebrate the defeat of Savoy troops in 1602.

🛏 Sleeping

When checking in, ask for your free Public Transport Card, covering public-transport travel for the duration of your hotel stay.

Le Jour et la Nuit   B&B $$

(☑ 079 214 73 87; www.lejouretlanuit-bnb.com; Av du Mervelet 8; ⊙ s/d Sfr210/230, ste Sfr250-270, apt Sfr135-250; 🅿 🖥) Alain and Sylvie are your affable hosts at this highly tasteful

SWITZERLAND GENEVA

GRAND TOUR OF SWITZERLAND
....

Imagine if you could see all of Switzerland's highlights in one unforgettable road trip. Well, the Swiss have done just that with this new 1600km route (www.grandtour.myswitzerland.com), linking 12 Unesco World Heritage Sites and taking in glaciers, mountain passes, cities, medieval villages, lakes, castles, abbeys – you name it. It's also doable by electric vehicle, with charging points en route.

Geneva

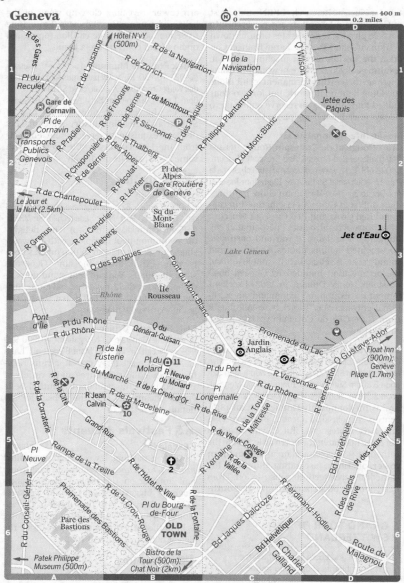

B&B, housed in a renovated 1920s villa. The three rooms and two apartments have been decorated with an eye for design, with Eames coat racks, Nespresso makers and Tivoli stereos. Generous breakfasts and a pretty garden are bonuses. Trams 14 and 18 to Bouchet stop close by.

Float Inn HOUSEBOAT **$$**
(☑ 078 797 51 97; www.floatinn.swiss; 55 Quai Gustave-Ador, Port des Eaux-Vives; d Sfr243; ☎) If you fancy spending the night adrift on Lake Geneva and waking up to eye-popping views of the Jet d'Eau, this catamaran turned luxe floating B&B makes that wish come true.

Geneva

Five portholed cabins with private bathrooms welcome guests, and there's also a bar, sun terrace and excellent home cooking.

Hôtel N'vY   HOTEL **$$**
(☑ 022 544 66 66; www.hotelnvygeneva.com; Rue de Richemont 18; d/f/ste from Sfr169/299/337; ✳ @ ☎) Contemporary flair abounds at this modish four-star place northeast of the train station, from the purple-lit bar downstairs to in-room amenities like international power outlets, Bluetooth connectivity and chromotherapy lighting. Among the five room categories, all but the standards come with big-screen TV, tea-making facilities and parquet wood floor. Upper-floor executive rooms have views of Lake Geneva and the Alps.

✕ Eating

Eateries crowd Place du Bourg-de-Four, Geneva's oldest square, in the lovely Old Town. Otherwise, head down the hill towards the river and Place du Molard, packed with tables and chairs for much of the year. In Pâquis, there's a tasty line-up of more affordable restaurants on Place de la Navigation.

Three Kids Bagel   BAGELS **$**
(☑ 022 311 24 24; www.threekids.ch; Rue du Vieux-Collège 10BIS; bagels Sfr9.50-16; ⊙ 11am-3.30pm Mon-Sat) How can you elevate the humble bagel to an art form? According to Three Kids, the devil is in the detail: they take local sourcing seriously, baking bagels daily to chewy perfection using unbleached, organic, stone-ground flour, then getting creative with fillings like raclette, Grisons ham, pickles, paprika chips, onions and honey-mustard.

Buvette des Bains   CAFETERIA **$**
(☑ 022 738 16 16; www.bains-des-paquis.ch; Quai du Mont-Blanc 30, Bains des Pâquis; mains Sfr14-23; ⊙ 7am-10.30pm; ☎) Meet Genevans at this earthy beach bar – rough and hip around the edges – at the Bains des Pâquis lakeside pool and sauna complex. Grab breakfast, a salad or the *plat du jour* (dish of the day), or dip into a *fondue au crémant* (sparkling-wine fondue). Dining is self-service on trays and alfresco in summer.

★ **La Finestra**   ITALIAN **$$**
(☑ 022 312 23 22; www.restaurant-lafinestra.ch/fr; Rue de la Cité 11; mains Sfr44-48, menus Sfr39-90; ⊙ noon-2.30pm & 7-10.30pm Mon-Fri, 7-10.30pm Sat) This handsome little restaurant nestled in the heart of the Old Town rustles up authentic haute-Italian cuisine in a casual yet refined setting. The low beams and tiny tables wedged into the basement level of this historic building make for an intimate setting. Freshness and a passion for herbs show in dishes as simple as risotto with rocket pesto and scallops.

Bistro de la Tour   BISTRO **$$**
(☑ 022 321 97 66; www.bistrodelatour.ch; Blvd de la Tour 2; mains Sfr29-38, 1-/2-/3-course lunch Sfr19/25/29; ⊙ noon-2pm & 7-10pm Mon-Fri) Just a handful of tables await lucky diners at this intimate bistro and wine place. And the menu? Succinct but *magnifique,* thanks to the combined passion of owners Philippe and Francis who source seasonal ingredients for homemade dishes as simple as bream with avocado, coriander and pomegranate, and succulent sirloin steak – all brilliantly cooked and matched with Swiss, Burgundy and Bordeaux wines.

☛ Drinking & Nightlife

Pâquis, the district in between the train station and lake, is particularly well endowed with bars. For a dose of Bohemia, head to Carouge on tram 12. This shady quarter of 17th-century houses and narrow streets has galleries, funky shops and hip nightlife.

★ **La Buvette du Bateau**　　　BAR
(☑ 022 508 56 89; www.bateaugeneve.ch; Quai Gustave-Ador 1; ☺ 4.30pm-midnight Tue-Thu, to 2am Fri & Sat) Few terraces are as dreamy as this. Moored permanently by the quay near Jet d'Eau, this fabulous belle époque paddle steamer, with flower boxes adorning its decks, sailed Lake Geneva's waters from 1896 until its retirement in 1974, and is now one of the busiest lounge bars in town in summer. Go for drinks, not food.

Chat Noir　　　BAR
(☑ 022 307 10 40; www.chatnoir.ch; Rue Vautier 13, Carouge; ☺ 5pm-2am Mon & Tue, to 4am Wed & Thu, to 5am Fri & Sat, 3pm-2am Sun) One of the busiest night spots in Carouge, the Black Cat is packed most nights thanks to its all-rounder vibe: arrive after work for an aperitif with a selection of tapas to nibble on, and stay until dawn for dancing, live music, jam sessions and DJ sets.

☆ Entertainment

★ **L'Usine**　　　PERFORMING ARTS
(www.usine.ch; Pl des Volontaires 4) At the gritty heart of Geneva's alternative culture scene, this nonprofit collection of 18 arts-related initiatives is housed beside the Rhône in a former gold-processing factory. On any given night, expect to see cutting-edge theatre at **TU** (www.theatredelusine.ch), live music at **Le Zoo** (www.lezoo.ch) or up-and-coming VJ artists at **Kalvingrad** (www.kalvingrad.com).

Alhambra　　　LIVE MUSIC
(☑ 078 966 07 97; www.alhambra-geneve.ch; Rue de la Rôtisserie 10) This gorgeous historic theatre with its cut-glass chandeliers, embossed silver ceilings and scarlet chairs makes a classy venue for live concerts ranging from Brazilian 'electrotropical' to African drumming, from disco to salsa, and from Afro-Caribbean to R&B.

🛍 Shopping

Designer shopping is wedged between Rue du Rhône and Rue de Rive; the latter has lots of chain stores. Grand-Rue in the Old Town and Carouge boast artsy boutiques. **Globus** (www.globus.ch/fr/store/116/globus-geneve; Rue du Rhône 48; ☺ 9am-7pm Mon-Wed, to 9pm Thu, to 7.30pm Fri, to 6pm Sat, food hall 7.30am-10pm Mon-Fri, 8.30am-10pm Sat) is Geneva's main department store, also home to a top-notch food hall.

❶ Getting There & Away

AIR

Geneva Airport (Aéroport International de Genève; www.gva.ch), 4km northwest of the town centre, is served by a wide variety of Swiss and international airlines.

BOAT

CGN (p1129) runs up to four steamers per day from Jardin Anglais and Pâquis to other Lake Geneva villages, including Nyon (adult return Sfr50, 1¼ hours) and Yvoire (Sfr50, 1¾ hours).

BUS

Gare Routière de Genève (☑ 022 732 02 30; www.gare-routiere.com; Pl Dorcière) operates buses across the border into neighbouring France.

TRAIN

More-or-less-hourly connections run from Geneva's central train station, **Gare CFF de Cornavin** (www.sbb.ch; Pl de Cornavin), to most Swiss towns and cities.
Bern (Sfr51, 1¾ hours)
Geneva Airport (Sfr4, seven minutes)
Lausanne (Sfr22.80, 36 to 50 minutes)
Zürich (Sfr88, 2¾ hours)

❶ Getting Around

TO/FROM THE AIRPORT

The quickest way to/from Geneva Airport is by train (Sfr4, seven minutes, several hourly); otherwise take bus 10 from the Rive stop (Sfr3, 30 minutes, four to nine hourly). When arriving at the airport, before leaving the luggage hall, grab a free public transport ticket from the machine next to the information desk.

A metered taxi into town costs Sfr35 to Sfr50 and takes about 15 minutes.

BICYCLE

Bike rental is available at **Genèveroule** (☑ 022 740 14 15; www.geneveroule.ch; Pl de Mont-brillant 17; city/mountain/e-bikes per half-day Sfr8/12/17, full day Sfr12/18/25; ☺ 8am-9pm May-Oct, to 6pm Nov-Apr), just outside the train station. A second office, known as **Terrassière**, is at Ruelle des Templiers 4 in the Eaux-Vives neighbourhood (left bank).

PUBLIC TRANSPORT

When you stay overnight in Geneva, you automatically receive a transport card, which enables you to use the entire public transport network (local trams, trains, buses, taxi-boats) for free. These are operated by **TPG** (TPG; www.tpg.ch; Rue de Montbrillant; ☺ 7am-7pm Mon-Fri, 9am-6pm Sat).

LAKE GENEVA & VAUD

Western Europe's largest lake – known by the francophones who people its shores as Lac Léman, but the rest of the world as Lake Geneva – is anchored by the city that claims it, wrapping around its southern shore.

Lausanne

POP 137,810 / ELEV 495M

In a fabulous location overlooking Lake Geneva, Lausanne is an enchanting beauty with several distinct personalities: the former fishing village of Ouchy, with its lakeside bustle; the Vieille Ville (Old Town), with charming cobblestone streets and covered staircases; and Flon, a warehouse district of bars and boutiques.

⊙ Sights

★ **AQUATIS Aquarium & Vivarium**   AQUARIUM
(www.aquatis.ch/en; Rte de Berne 144, Lausanne-Vennes; adult/child Sfr29/19; ⊙ 9am-7pm Apr-Oct, 10am-6pm Nov-Mar; 🚋) Not just another aquarium, AQUATIS has caused quite a stir since opening, giving Lausanne a striking landmark with a spherical facade that appears to be clad in shimmering fish scales. Using cutting-edge technology, it takes an immersive, eco-aware look at the world's freshwaters, whisking you around five continents, from Europe's glaciers to the Amazon.

★ **Musée Cantonal des Beaux Arts**   MUSEUM
(MCB-A; 📞 021 316 34 45; www.mcba.ch; Plateforme10, Av Benjamin-Constant) Housed in a contemporary new home at Plateforme10, the Fine Arts Museum showcases works by Swiss and foreign artists, ranging from Ancient Egyptian art to cubism, but the core collection comprises works by landscape painter Louis Ducros (1748–1810). Consult the website for the latest on opening times and prices.

★ **Olympic Museum**   MUSEUM
(Musée Olympique; 📞 021 621 65 11; www.olympic.org/museum; Quai d'Ouchy 1; adult/child Sfr18/10; ⊙ 9am-6pm daily May–mid-Oct, 10am-6pm Tue-Sun mid-Oct–Apr; 🅿🚋) Musée Olympique is easily Lausanne's most lavish museum and an essential stop for sports buffs (and kids). State-of-the-art installations recount the Olympic story from its inception to the present day through video, interactive displays, memorabilia and temporary themed exhibitions. Other attractions include tiered

landscaped gardens, site-specific sculptural works and a fabulous cafe with champion lake views from its terrace.

★ **Cathédrale de Notre Dame**   CATHEDRAL
(📞 021 316 71 60; www.patrimoine.vd.ch; Pl de la Cathédrale; ⊙ 9am-7pm Apr-Sep, to 5.30pm Oct-Mar) Lausanne's Gothic cathedral, Switzerland's finest, stands proudly at the heart of the Old Town. Raised in the 12th and 13th centuries on the site of earlier, humbler churches, it lacks the lightness of French Gothic buildings but is remarkable nonetheless. Pope Gregory X, in the presence of Rudolph of Habsburg (the Holy Roman Emperor) and an impressive following of European cardinals and bishops, consecrated the church in 1275.

🛏 Sleeping & Eating

BnB Lausanne   B&B $
(📞 021 616 77 22; www.bnblausanne.ch; Av Édouard Dapples 23; d/tr/q from Sfr100/120/130; 🛜) A warm *bienvenue* awaits at this early-20th-century apartment turned B&B, centrally located for exploring downtown Lausanne. Besides three well-looked-after rooms, with wood floors, warm colours, original paintings and antique furnishings, there is a guest lounge where you can grab a tea or coffee. Swiss produce features at breakfast. It's a couple of minutes' walk from the train station.

★ **Hôtel**
Beau-Rivage Palace   HISTORIC HOTEL $$$
(📞 021 613 33 33; www.brp.ch; Pl du Port 17-19; d from Sfr520; 🅿❄🛜🏊) Easily the most stunningly located hotel in Lausanne, this luxury lakeside address is sumptuous. A beautifully maintained early-19th-century mansion set in immaculate grounds, it tempts with magnificent lake and Alp views, a grand spa, and a number of bars and upmarket restaurants (including a superb gastronomic temple headed by Anne-Sophie Pic, the only French female chef with three Michelin stars).

Eat Me   TAPAS $
(📞 021 311 76 59; www.eat-me.ch; Rue Pépinet 3; small plates Sfr10-24; ⊙ noon-2pm & 6pm-midnight Tue-Sat; 🛜🍴) This fun, immensely popular and downright delicious resto-bar is all about global tapas, basically, with everything from baby burgers (sliders) to electric 'sashimiviche' (Sichuan sashimi à la ceviche!) and shrimp lollipops. Everything is well priced. Bring your friends!

DON'T MISS

MONTREUX

This tidy lakeside town boasts Switzerland's most extraordinary castle. Originally constructed on the shores of Lake Geneva in the 11th century, **Château de Chillon** (☑021 966 89 10; www.chillon.ch; Av de Chillon 21; adult/child Sfr12.50/6; ⊙9am-7pm Apr-Sep, 9.30am-6pm Mar & Oct, 10am-5pm Nov-Feb, last entry 1hr before close) was brought to the world's attention by Lord Byron and the world has been filing past ever since. Spend at least a couple of hours exploring its numerous courtyards, towers, dungeons and halls filled with arms, period furniture and artwork. The castle is a lovely 3km lakefront walk from Montreux. Alternatively, take bus 201 (10 minutes) or a CGN steamer (15 minutes). Crowds throng to the legendary (and not all-jazz) **Montreux Jazz Festival** (www.montreuxjazz.com; ⊙late Jun—mid-Jul). Free concerts take place every day (tickets for bigger-name artists cost anything from Sfr60 to Sfr450). There are frequent trains to Lausanne (Sfr13, 20 to 35 minutes) and other lakeside points. Montreux is also a stop on the scenic **GoldenPass** (☑021 989 81 90; www.golden pass.ch/en) route into the Bernese Oberland.

Le Pointu
CAFE $

(☑021 351 14 14; www.le-pointu.ch; Rue Neuve 2; snacks & light bites Sfr15-23, brunch items Sfr6-18; ⊙7am-midnight Mon-Wed, to 1am Thu, to 2am Fri, 9am-2am Sat, 10am-3pm Sun) Lodged in a turreted belle époque building on a street corner, this cafe-restaurant is a talking point, with its boho-flavoured vibe, green ceiling lit by bare bulbs, beautiful tilework and vintage-style furniture. Drop by for a coffee, cocktail, gourmet salad or open sandwich. Weekend brunches are worth raving about, with the likes of blueberry pancakes and açaí smoothie bowls.

ℹ Information

Lausanne Tourisme (Gare) (☑021 613 73 73; www.lausanne-tourisme.ch; Pl de la Gare 9; ⊙9am-7pm Jun-Aug, 9am-6pm Sep-May) At the train station.

Lausanne Tourisme (Ouchy) (☑021 613 73 73; www.lausanne-tourisme.ch; Av de Rhodanie 2; ⊙9am-7pm Apr-Sep, to 6pm Oct-Mar) By the lakeside.

ℹ Getting There & Around

Remember to collect your free Lausanne Transport Card for unlimited use of public transport during your stay. For timetables, visit www.t-l.ch.

BOAT

The **CGN** (www.cgn.ch; Quai Jean-Pascal Delamuraz; leisure cruises from Sfr25) runs passenger boats (no car ferries) from Ouchy to destinations around Lake Geneva.

Destinations include Montreux (Sfr27, 1½ hours, up to six daily), Vevey (Sfr21, one hour, up to seven daily), Nyon (Sfr35, 2¼ hours, up to four daily) and Geneva (Sfr45, 3½ to four hours, up to five daily).

TRAIN

You can travel by train to and from Geneva (Sfr22.80, 36 to 50 minutes, up to six hourly),

Geneva Airport (Sfr27, 45 to 56 minutes, up to four hourly) and Bern (Sfr34, 65 to 70 minutes, one or two hourly).

FRIBOURG, DREI-SEEN-LAND AND THE JURA

Gruyères

POP 2203 / ELEV 830M

Cheese and featherweight meringues drowned in thick cream are what this dreamy village is all about. Named after the emblematic *gru* (crane) brandished by the medieval Counts of Gruyères, it is a riot of 15th- to 17th-century houses tumbling down a hillock. Its heart is cobbled, a castle is its crowning glory and hard AOC Gruyère (the village is Gruyères, but the 's' is dropped for the cheese) has been made for centuries in its surrounding Alpine pastures. Fondue-serving cafes line the main square.

◎ Sights

★**Château de Gruyères**
CASTLE

(☑026 921 21 02; www.chateau-gruyeres.ch; Rue du Château 8; adult/child Sfr12/4; ⊙9am-6pm Apr-Oct, 10am-5pm Nov-Mar) This bewitching turreted castle, home to 19 different counts of Gruyères, who controlled the Sarine Valley from the 11th to 16th centuries, was rebuilt after a fire in 1493. Inside you can view period furniture, tapestries and modern 'fantasy art', plus watch a 20-minute multimedia film about Gruyères' history. Don't miss the short footpath that weaves its way around the castle. Combined tickets covering the château and other area attractions are available.

La Maison du Gruyère
FARM

(☑ 026 921 84 00; www.lamaisondugruyere.ch; Pl de la Gare 3, Pringy-Gruyères; adult/child Sfr7/6; ⊙ 9am-6.30pm Jun-Sep, to 6pm Oct-May) The secret behind Gruyère cheese is revealed in Pringy, directly opposite Gruyères train station (1.5km below town). Cheesemaking takes place three to four times daily between 9am and 11am, and 12.30pm and 2.30pm. A combined ticket for the dairy and Château de Gruyères (p1134) costs Sfr16 (no child combo).

✖ Eating

★ Chez Boudji
SWISS $$

(☑ 026 921 90 50; www.boudji.ch; Gite d'Avau 1, Broc; mains Sfr15-27; ⊙ 11.30am-2.30pm & 5.30-9pm May-Oct) Visitors love the authenticity of this Swiss mountain chalet with a panoramic terrace overlooking the Alps. Linger there in anticipation of the cheesy goodness you're about to consume. This is stodgy, hearty food: macaroni cheese, fondue, chalet soup and meringue with double cream for dessert! The rich flavour of the local cheese enlivening each simple dish is indescribably enjoyable.

ℹ Information

Pop in to see the friendly folks at **La Gruyère Tourisme** (☑ 084 842 44 24; www.la-gruyere.ch; Rue du Bourg 1; ⊙ 9.30am-5.30pm Jul & Aug, shorter hours rest of year) if you need clarification on the best way to use your time in this sprawling area.

ℹ Getting There & Away

Gruyères can be reached by hourly bus or train from Fribourg (Sfr6.80, 55 minutes, via Bulle) or Montreux (Sfr20.20, 1¼ hours, via Montbovon).

VALAIS

POP 335,700

This is Matterhorn country, an intoxicating land that seduces the toughest of critics with its endless panoramic vistas and breathtaking views. Switzerland's 10 highest mountains rise to the sky here, while snow fiends ski and board in one of Europe's top resorts, Zermatt.

Zermatt

POP 5643 / ELEV 1605M

Since the mid-19th century, Zermatt has starred among Switzerland's glitziest resorts. Today skiers cruise along well-kept pistes, spell-bound by the scenery, while style-conscious darlings flash designer threads in the town's swish lounge bars. But all are smitten with the Matterhorn (4478m), an unfathomable monolith you can't quite stop looking at.

◎ Sights & Activities

Zermatt is cruising heaven, with mostly long, scenic red runs, plus a smattering of blues for ski virgins and knuckle-whitening blacks for experts. The main skiing areas in winter are **Rothorn**, **Stockhorn** and **Klein Matterhorn** – 52 lifts and 360km of ski runs in all, with a link from Klein Matterhorn to the Italian resort of Cervinia and a **freestyle park** with a half-pipe for snowboarders. **Summer skiing** (20km of runs) and **boarding** (gravity park at Plateau Rosa on the Theodul glacier) is Europe's most extensive. One-/two-day summer ski passes cost Sfr84/125.

Zermatt is also excellent for **hiking**, with 400km of summer trails through some of the most incredible scenery in the Alps – the tourist office has trail maps. For Matterhorn close-ups, nothing beats the highly dramatic **Matterhorn Glacier Trail** (two hours, 6.5km) from Trockener Steg to Schwarzsee; 23 information panels en route tell you everything you could possibly need to know about glaciers and glacial life.

★ Matterhorn Glacier Paradise
CABLE CAR

(www.matterhornparadise.ch; Schluhmattstrasse; return adult/child Sfr100/50; ⊙ 8.30am-4.50pm) Views from Zermatt's cable cars are all remarkable, but the Matterhorn Glacier Paradise is the icing on the cake. Ride the world's highest-altitude 3S cable car to 3883m to gawp at 14 glaciers and 38 mountain peaks over 4000m from the **Panoramic Platform** (good weather only). Don't miss the **Glacier Palace**, an ice palace complete with glittering ice sculptures and an ice slide to swoosh down bum first. Finish with some exhilarating **snow tubing** outside in the snowy surrounds.

★ Gornergratbahn
RAIL

(www.gornergrat.ch; Bahnhofplatz 7; return adult/child Sfr98/49; ⊙ 7am-6.24pm) Europe's highest cogwheel railway has been climbing through staggeringly beautiful scenery to **Gornergrat** (3089m) – a 30-minute journey – since 1898. On the way up, sit on the right-hand side of the train to gaze at the Matterhorn. In summer an extra train runs once a week at sunrise and sunset – the most spectacular trips of all.

🛏 Sleeping & Eating

Most places close May to mid- (or late) June and again from October to mid-November.

Hotel Bahnhof   HOTEL $

(📞 027 967 24 06; www.hotelbahnhof.com; Bahnhofstrasse; dm Sfr35-50, s/d from Sfr80/120; ⊗ closed May–mid-Jun & mid-Oct–Nov; 🛜) Opposite the train station, these budget digs have comfy beds, spotless bathrooms and family-perfect rooms for four. Dorms are cosy and there's a stylish lounge with armchairs to flop in and books to read. There's no breakfast, but feel free to prepare your own in the snazzy, open-plan kitchen. Ski-storage room, lockers and laundry are available.

Snowboat   INTERNATIONAL $

(📞 027 967 43 33; www.zermattsnowboat.com; Vispastrasse 20; mains Sfr22-39; ⊗ 2pm-midnight Mon-Fri, from noon Sat & Sun; 🍴) This hybrid eating-drinking riverside address, with deckchairs sprawled across its rooftop sun terrace, is a blessing. When fondue tires, head here for barbecue-sizzled burgers (not just beef, but crab and veggie burgers, too), super-power creative salads (the Omega 3 buster is a favourite) and great cocktails. The vibe? Completely friendly, fun and funky.

★ Chez Vrony   SWISS $$

(📞 027 967 25 52; www.chezvrony.ch; Findeln; breakfast Sfr15-28, mains Sfr25-45; ⊗ 9.15am-5pm Dec-Apr & mid-Jun–mid-Oct) Ride the *Sunnegga Express* funicular to 2288m, then ski down or summer-hike 15 minutes to Zermatt's tastiest slope-side address in the Findeln hamlet. Delicious dried meats, homemade cheese and sausage come from Vrony's own cows, grazing away the summer on the high Alpine pastures (2100m) surrounding it, and the Vrony burger is legendary. Advance reservations essential in winter.

ℹ Information

The **tourist office** (📞 027 966 81 00; www. zermatt.ch; Bahnhofplatz 5; ⊗ 8.30am-8pm; 🛜) has a wealth of information, plus iPads to surf on and free wi-fi.

ℹ Getting There & Away

CAR

Zermatt is car-free. Motorists have to park in the **Matterhorn Terminal Täsch** (📞 027 967 12 14; www.matterhornterminal.ch; Täsch; per 24hr Sfr15.50) and ride the Zermatt Shuttle train (return adult/child Sfr16.40/8.20, 12 minutes, every 20 minutes from 6am to 9.40pm).

TRAIN

Direct trains to Zermatt depart hourly from Brig (Sfr38, 1½ hours), stopping at Visp en route. Zermatt is also the start/end point of the **Glacier Express** (www.glacierexpress.ch; adult/child one way St Moritz-Zermatt Sfr153/76.50, obligatory seat reservation summer/winter Sfr33/13; ⊗ 3 trains daily May-Oct, 1 daily mid-Dec–Feb) to/from St Moritz.

BERN

POP 142,479 / ELEV 540M

One of the planet's most underrated capitals, Bern is a fabulous find. With the genteel old soul of a Renaissance man and the heart of a high-flying 21st-century gal, the riverside city is both medieval and modern. The 15th-century Old Town is gorgeous enough to sweep you off your feet and make you forget the century (it's definitely worthy of its 1983 Unesco World Heritage Site status).

◉ Sights & Activities

Bern's flag-bedecked **medieval centre** is an attraction in its own right, with 6km of covered arcades and cellar shops and bars descending from the streets. After a devastating fire in 1405, the wooden city was rebuilt in today's sandstone. The city's 11 **decorative fountains** (1545) depict historical and folkloric characters. Most are along Marktgasse as it becomes Kramgasse and Gerechtigkeitsgasse, but the most famous lies in Kornhausplatz: the **Kindlifresserbrunnen** (Ogre Fountain) of a giant snacking...on children.

★ Zentrum Paul Klee   MUSEUM

(📞 031 359 01 01; www.zpk.org; Monument im Fruchtland 3; adult/child Sfr20/7; ⊗ 10am-5pm Tue-Sun) Bern's answer to the Guggenheim, Renzo Piano's architecturally bold, 150m-long wave-like edifice houses an exhibition space that showcases rotating works from Paul Klee's prodigious and often playful career. Interactive computer displays and audioguides help interpret the Swiss-born artist's work. Next door, the fun-packed **Kindermuseum Creaviva** (📞 031 359 01 61; www. creaviva-zpk.org) FREE lets kids experiment with hands-on art exhibits or create original artwork with the atelier's materials during the weekend program **Five Franc Studio** Sfr5; ⊗ 10am-4.30pm Sat & Sun; 🚼). Bus 12 runs from Bubenbergplatz direct to the museum.

SWITZERLAND'S SCENIC TRAINS

Swiss trains, buses and boats are more than a means of getting from A to B. Stunning views invariably make the journey itself the destination. Switzerland boasts the following routes among its classic sightseeing journeys. You're able to choose just one leg of the trip. Also, scheduled services often ply the same routes for standard fares; these are cheaper than the named trains, which often have cars with extra-large windows and require reservations.

Bernina Express (www.rhb.ch) This unforgettable four-hour train ride cuts 145km through the Engadine's glaciated realms, linking Chur, St Moritz and Tirano, Italy. Between May and October, continue for 2½ hours by bus from Tirano to Lugano along Italy's Lake Como and Ticino's palm-fringed Lake Lugano.

Centovalli Express (www.centovalli.ch) An underappreciated gem of a line (two hours) that snakes along fantastic river gorges in Switzerland and Italy, from Locarno to Domodossola. Trains run through the day and it is easy to connect to Brig and beyond from Domodossola in Italy.

Glacier Express (www.glacierexpress.ch) Hop aboard this red train with floor-to-ceiling windows for the famous eight-hour journey between St Moritz and Zermatt. Scenic highlights include the climb through Alpine meadows to Oberalp Pass (2033m) – the journey's high point between Disentis/Mustér and Andermatt – and the crossing of the iconic 65m-high Landwasser Viaduct between St Moritz and Chur.

GoldenPass Line (www.goldenpass.ch) Travels between Lucerne and Montreux. The journey is in three legs, and you must change trains twice. Regular trains, without panoramic windows, work the whole route hourly.

Jungfrau Region (www.jungfrau.ch) You can spend days ogling stunning Alpine scenery from the trains, cable cars and more here.

Zytglogge   TOWER
(Marktgasse) Bern's most famous Old Town sight, this ornate clock tower once formed part of the city's western gate (1191–1256). Crowds congregate to watch its revolving figures twirl at four minutes before the hour, after which the chimes begin. Tours enter the tower to see the clock mechanism from May to October; contact the tourist office for details. The clock tower supposedly helped Albert Einstein hone his special theory of relativity, developed while working as a patent clerk in Bern.

Münster   CATHEDRAL
(www.bernermuenster.ch; Münsterplatz 1; tower adult/child Sfr5/2; ⏰10am-5pm Mon-Sat, 11.30am-5pm Sun Apr–mid-Oct, noon-4pm Mon-Fri, 10am-5pm Sat, 11.30am-4pm Sun mid-Oct–Mar) Bern's 15th-century Gothic cathedral boasts Switzerland's loftiest spire (100m); climb the 344-step spiral staircase for vertiginous views. Coming down, stop by the **Upper Bells** (1356), rung at 11am, noon and 3pm daily, and the three 10-tonne **Lower Bells** (Switzerland's largest). Don't miss the main portal's **Last Judgement**, which portrays Bern's mayor going to heaven, while his Zürich counterpart is shown into hell. Afterwards wander through the adjacent **Münsterplattform**, a bijou clifftop park with a sunny pavilion cafe.

Aare Tubing   WATER SPORTS
(www.aaretubing.ch; ⏰Apr-Sep; 🛶) Urban swimming has become a big thing in Switzerland, and Bern is certainly in on the act. For even more action on the Aare River, this company will sort you out with tubes, inflatable rafts or stand-up paddleboards. Life jackets and safety instructions (phew!) are included. Visit the website for more details on locations, prices and bookings.

🛏 Sleeping & Eating

Am Pavillon   B&B $
(☎079 198 62 83; www.ampavillon.ch; Pavillonweg 1a; s Sfr100-110, d Sfr150-180; 🛜) An appealing conversion of a late-19th-century town house, this B&B is just a couple of minutes' stroll from the Hauptbahnhof. The rooms have plenty of original art nouveau charm (high ceilings, parquet floors and the like), and a palette of modern, neutral colours. Breakfast is served on the garden terrace when warm weather permits.

Hotel Landhaus   HOTEL $
(☎031 348 03 05; www.landhausbern.ch; Altenbergstrasse 4; dm/s/d from Sfr38/90/130; 🅿🛜) Fronted by the river and Old Town spires, this well-run boho hotel offers a mix of stylish six-bed dorms, family rooms and doubles.

Its buzzing ground-floor cafe and terrace attracts a cheery crowd. Breakfast (included with private rooms) costs Sfr12 extra for dorm-dwellers.

★ **Kornhauskeller** MEDITERRANEAN $$
(☑ 031 327 72 72; www.bindella.ch; Kornhausplatz 18; mains Sfr24-58; ◷ noon-2.30pm & 6pm-12.30am; 🖝) Fine dining takes place beneath vaulted frescoed arches at Bern's ornate former granary, now a stunning cellar restaurant serving Mediterranean cuisine. Beautiful people sip cocktails alongside historic stained-glass windows on the mezzanine, while in its neighbouring cafe, punters lunch in the sun on the busy pavement terrace. Children's menus are available.

❶ Information

The **Bern Tourismus** (☑ 031 328 12 12; www. bern.com; Bahnhofplatz 10a; ◷ 9am-7pm Mon-Sat, to 6pm Sun; 🖝) office at the train station is fully stocked with all you need to know about the capital. There's also a **branch** (☑ 031 328 12 12; www.bern.com; Grosser Muristalden 6, Bärengraben; ◷ 9am-6pm Jun-Sep, 10am-4pm Mar-May & Oct, 11am-4pm Nov-Feb) near the bear park.

❶ Getting There & Around

Frequent trains connect to most Swiss cities, including Geneva (Sfr51, 13/4 hours), Basel (Sfr41, 55 minutes) and Zürich (Sfr51, 55 minutes to 11/2 hours).

Buses and trams are operated by BernMobil (www.bernmobil.ch); many depart from stops near Bahnhofplatz.

CENTRAL SWITZERLAND

POP 718,400

To the Swiss, Central Switzerland – green, mountainous and soothingly beautiful – is the essence of 'Swissness'. It was here that the pact that kick-started a nation was signed in 1291, and here that hero William Tell gave a rebel yell against Habsburg rule. Geographically, politically and spiritually, this is the heartland. Nowhere does the flag fly higher.

Lucerne

POP 81,592 / ELEV 435M

Recipe for a gorgeous Swiss city: take a cobalt lake ringed by mountains of myth, add a medieval Old Town and sprinkle with covered bridges, sunny plazas, candy-coloured houses and waterfront promenades. Bright, beautiful Lucerne has been Little Miss Popular since the likes of Goethe, Queen Victoria and Wagner savoured her views in the 19th century.

◉ Sights & Activities

Your first port of call should be the medieval **Old Town**, with its ancient rampart walls and towers. Wander the cobblestone lanes and squares, pondering 15th-century buildings with painted facades and the two much-photographed covered bridges over the Reuss.

★ **Sammlung Rosengart** MUSEUM
(☑ 041 220 16 60; www.rosengart.ch; Pilatusstrasse 10; adult/child Sfr18/10; ◷ 10am-6pm) Lucerne's blockbuster cultural attraction is the Sammlung Rosengart, occupying a graceful neoclassical pile in the heart of town. It showcases the outstanding stash of Angela Rosengart, a Swiss art dealer and close friend of Picasso. Alongside works by the great Spanish master are paintings and sketches by Klee, Cézanne, Renoir, Chagall, Kandinsky, Miró, Matisse, Modigliani and Monet, among others. Complementing this collection are some 200 photographs by David Douglas Duncan documenting the last 17 years of Picasso's life.

★ **Kapellbrücke** BRIDGE
(Chapel Bridge) You haven't really been to Lucerne until you have strolled the creaky 14th-century Kapellbrücke, spanning the Reuss River in the Old Town. The octagonal water tower is original, but its gabled roof is a modern reconstruction, rebuilt after a disastrous fire in 1993. As you cross the bridge, note Heinrich Wägmann's 17th-century triangular roof panels, showing important events from Swiss history and mythology. The icon is at its most photogenic when bathed in soft golden light at dusk.

Lion Monument MONUMENT
(Löwendenkmal; Denkmalstrasse) By far the most touching of the 19th-century sights that lured so many British to Lucerne is the Lion Monument. Lukas Ahorn carved this 10m-long sculpture of a dying lion into the rock face in 1820 to commemorate Swiss soldiers who died defending King Louis XVI during the French Revolution. For *Narnia* fans, it often evokes Aslan at the stone table.

Verkehrshaus MUSEUM
(Swiss Museum of Transport; ☑ 0900 333 456; www.verkehrshaus.ch; Lidostrasse 5; adult/child

Sfr32/12; ⊙10am-6pm Apr-Oct, to 5pm Nov-Mar; ⊕) A great kid-pleaser, the fascinating interactive Verkehrshaus is deservedly Switzerland's most popular museum. Alongside rockets, steam locomotives, aeroplanes, vintage cars and dugout canoes are hands-on activities, such as pedalo boats, flight simulators, broadcasting studios and a walkable 1:20,000-scale map of Switzerland.

The museum also shelters a **planetarium** (www.verkehrshaus.ch/en/planetarium; adult/child Sfr16/7; ⊙hours vary), Switzerland's largest **3D cinema** (www.filmtheater.ch; evening film adult/child Sfr19/8) and the **Swiss Chocolate Adventure** (www.verkehrshaus.ch/en/swiss-chocolate-adventure; adult/child Sfr16/7), a 20-minute ride that whirls visitors through multimedia exhibits on the origins, history, production and distribution of chocolate, from Ghana to Switzerland and beyond.

🛌 Sleeping

⭐The Bed & Breakfast   B&B $
(☑041 310 15 14; www.thebandb.ch; Taubenhausstrasse 34; s Sfr85-130, d Sfr120-130, tr Sfr165-180, q Sfr200-220; P 🛜) This friendly B&B feels like home – with stylish, contemporary rooms, crisp white bedding and scatter cushions. Unwind in the garden or with a soak in the old-fashioned tub. Book ahead for the room under the eaves with private bathroom; all others share facilities. Take bus 1 to Eichhof or walk 15 minutes from the train station.

Backpackers Lucerne   HOSTEL $
(☑041 360 04 20; www.backpackerslucerne.ch; Alpenquai 42; dm Sfr30-35, d Sfr72-90, tr Sfr99-117; ⊙reception 7.30-10am & 4-11pm; 🛜) Just opposite the lake, a 15-minute walk southeast of Lucerne's train station, this is a soulful place to crash, with art-slung walls, bubbly staff and immaculate dorms with balconies. There's no breakfast, but guests have access to a well-equipped kitchen. Blades and mountain bikes for rent.

Hotel des Balances   HOTEL $$
(☑041 418 28 28; www.balances.ch; Weinmarkt 4; s/d/ste from Sfr150/220/305; P 🛜) Behind its elaborately frescoed facade, this perfectly positioned Old Town hotel flaunts a light and airy design ethos, with ice-white rooms, gilt mirrors and parquet floors. Suites have river-facing balconies. For the singles and doubles, expect to pay more for river-facing rooms. Breakfast is an additional Sfr35 per person.

✖ Eating & Drinking

⭐ Zur Werkstatt   INTERNATIONAL $$
(☑041 979 03 03; www.zurwerkstatt.ch; Waldstätterstrasse 18; lunch/dinner menus Sfr25/58; ⊙11.30am-1.30pm & 5pm-midnight Mon-Fri, 10am-2pm & 5pm-midnight Sat; ☑⊕) This funky, post-industrial, monochrome-toned restaurant revolves around a show kitchen and hip cocktail bar. Menus are kept simple (go meaty or veggie), but the food is anything but, singing of the seasons in dishes from mozzarella with wild asparagus and pomegranate to hand-cut steak tartare with crispy marrow and pumpkin chutney. It's popular – book ahead.

Wirtshaus Galliker   SWISS $$
(☑041 240 10 02; Schützenstrasse 1; mains Sfr27-49; ⊙9.30am-midnight Tue-Sat) Passionately run by the Galliker family for over four generations, this old-style, wood-panelled tavern attracts a lively bunch of regulars. Motherly waitresses dish up Lucerne soul food – rösti, *Chögalipaschtetli* (veal pastry pie) and the like – that is batten-the-hatches filling.

Rathaus Bräuerei   BREWERY
(☑041 410 61 11; www.rathausbrauerei.ch; Unter der Egg 2; ⊙9am-midnight Mon-Sat, to 11pm Sun) Sip home-brewed beer under the vaulted arches of this buzzy tavern near Kapellbrücke, or nab a pavement table and watch the river flow. You know this place is good as it's positively brimming with locals.

ℹ Information

Stamped by your hotel, the free **Lake Lucerne Region Visitors Card** entitles you to discounts on various museums, sporting facilities, cable cars and lake cruises.

Tourist Office (☑041 227 17 17; www.luzern.com; Zentralstrasse 5; ⊙8.30am-7pm Mon-Fri, 9am-7pm Sat, 9am-5pm Sun May-Oct, shorter hours Nov-Apr) Reached from Zentralstrasse or platform 3 of the Hauptbahnhof. Book day excursions around Lake Lucerne here.

ℹ Getting There & Around

Frequent trains connect Lucerne to Interlaken Ost (Sfr33, 1¾ hours), Bern (Sfr39, one to 1½ hours), Lugano (Sfr61, two hours) and Zürich (Sfr25, 45 minutes to one hour).

SNG (☑041 368 08 08; www.sng.ch; Alpenquai 11; pedalo/motorboat/pontoon boat per hour from Sfr30/60/90) operates extensive boat services on Lake Lucerne (including some paddle steamers). Rail passes are good for free or discounted travel.

BERNESE OBERLAND

POP 207,652

In the Bernese Oberland, nature works on an epic scale. Fittingly watched over by Mönch (Monk), Jungfrau (Virgin) and Eiger (Ogre), the Swiss Alps don't get more in-your-face beautiful than this.

Interlaken

POP 5673 / ELEV 570M

Once Interlaken made the Victorians swoon with mountain vistas from the chandelier-lit confines of grand hotels; today it makes daredevils scream with adrenaline-loaded activities. Straddling the glacier-fed Lakes Thun and Brienz and capped by the pearly white peaks of Eiger, Mönch and Jungfrau, the town is the gateway to Switzerland's fabled Jungfrau region and the country's hottest adventure destination bar none.

🏃 Activities

Switzerland is the world's second-biggest adventure-sports centre and Interlaken is its busiest hub. Some sample prices for these activities: around Sfr120 to Sfr170 for rafting or canyoning; Sfr140 for hydrospeeding; Sfr130 to Sfr180 for bungee or canyon jumping; Sfr170 for tandem paragliding; Sfr180 for ice climbing; Sfr220 for hang-gliding; and Sfr400 to Sfr450 for skydiving.

A good one-stop shop is **Outdoor Interlaken** (☎033 826 77 19; www.outdoor-interlaken.ch; Hauptstrasse 15; ⊗8am-7pm).

Harder Kulm   MOUNTAIN
(www.jungfrau.ch/harderkulm; adult/child Sfr32/16) For far-reaching views to the 4000m giants, take the eight-minute funicular ride to 1322m Harder Kulm. Many hiking paths begin here, and the vertigo-free can enjoy the panorama from the Zweiseensteg (Two Lake Bridge) jutting out above the valley. The wildlife park near the valley station is home to Alpine critters, including marmots and ibex.

🛏 Sleeping & Eating

Backpackers Villa Sonnenhof   HOSTEL $
(☎033 826 71 71; www.villa.ch; Alpenstrasse 16; dm Sfr43-49; 🅿🤶) Repeatedly voted one of Europe's best hostels, Sonnenhof is a slick, eco-friendly combination of ultramodern chalet and elegant art nouveau villa. Dorms are immaculate, and some have balconies with Jungfrau views. There's also a relaxed lounge, a well-equipped kitchen, a kids' play-room and a vast backyard for mountain gazing. Special family rates are available. Breakfast is included.

Hotel Alphorn   HOTEL $$
(☎033 822 30 51; www.hotel-alphorn.ch; Rothornstrasse 29a; s Sfr140-160, d Sfr160-180, tr Sfr225-240; 🅿🤶) Super-central yet peaceful, the Alphorn is a five-minute toddle from Interlaken West station. Decorated in cool blues and whites, the rooms are spotlessly clean, but you'll need to fork out an extra Sfr10 for a balcony.

The Barrel   CAFE $
(www.craft-cafe.ch; Postgasse 10; snacks & light meals Sfr7.50-19.50; ⊗noon-10pm Wed-Sat) Swiftly becoming one of Interlaken's preferred haunts, this easygoing cafe makes a fine pit stop for coffee with homemade cake, lunch or a craft beer (there are some great ones on tap). They whip up good salads, burgers, quiches and sandwiches using locally sourced ingredients.

ℹ Information

Tourist Office (☎033 826 53 00; www.interlakentourism.ch; Marktgasse 1; ⊗8am-7pm Mon-Fri, to 5pm Sat, 10am-5pm Sun Jul & Aug, shorter hours Sep-Jun) Right in the centre of things, Interlaken's tourist office has stacks of information on the town and surrounds. It also has a booking service.

ℹ Getting There & Away

There are two train stations: Interlaken West and Interlaken Ost.

Trains to Lucerne (Sfr33, 1¾ to two hours), Brig (Sfr46, 1¼ hours) and Montreux (Sfr74, 2¼ to 2¾ hours, via Spiez/Visp or Bern/Lausanne) depart frequently from Interlaken Ost train station.

Many trains up to mountain resorts begin in Lauterbrunnen (Sfr7.60, 20 minutes).

Grindelwald

POP 3818 / ELEV 1034M

Grindelwald's charms were discovered by skiers and hikers in the late 19th century, making it one of Switzerland's oldest resorts and the Jungfrau's largest. It has lost none of its appeal over the decades, with archetypal Alpine chalets and verdant pastures set against the chiselled features of the Eiger north face.

🏃 Activities

Stretching from Oberjoch at 2486m right down to the village, the region of First presents a fine mix of cruisey red and challenging black ski runs, plus 15.5km of well-groomed cross-country ski trails.

In summer, Grindelwald is outstanding hiking territory, with high-altitude trails commanding arresting views to massive mountain faces, crevassed glaciers and snowcapped peaks.

★ Kleine Scheidegg Walk
HIKING

One of the region's most stunning day hikes is the 15km trek from Grindelwald Grund to Wengen via Kleine Scheidegg, which heads up through wildflower-freckled meadows to skirt below the Eiger's north face and reach Kleine Scheidegg, granting arresting views of the 'Big Three': Eiger (3970m), Mönch (4107m) and Jungfrau (4158m). Allow around 5½ to six hours.

Grindelwald Sports
ADVENTURE SPORTS

(✆033 854 12 80; www.grindelwaldsports.ch; Dorfstrasse 103; ☺8.30am-7pm) Opposite the tourist office, this outfit arranges guided mountain climbing, glacier hikes, *vie ferrate* (protected climbing routes) and Alpine treks, plus ski and snowboard instruction in winter, and the heart-stopping canyon swing, a terrifying freefall at 120km/h between the canyon walls. It also houses a cosy cafe and sells walking guides.

🍴 Sleeping & Eating

Mountain Hostel
HOSTEL $

(✆033 854 38 38; www.mountainhostel.ch; Grundstrasse 58; dm Sfr42-47, d Sfr90-110, q Sfr168-208; P🛇) In a bright-blue building halfway between Grindelwald Grund train station and the Männlichen cable-car station, this is an ideal base for sports junkies, with well-kept dorms and a helpful crew. There's a beer garden, ski storage, TV lounge and mountain-bike and e-bike rental. Breakfast (included in rates) comes with locally sourced cheese, yoghurt, bread and honey.

Hotel Glacier
BOUTIQUE HOTEL $$

(✆033 853 10 04; www.hotel-glacier.ch; Endweg 55; d sfr280-450; P🛇) With astonishing views of the Eiger, this chic boutique hotel pays homage to its past as humble lodgings for the men who once harvested the ice from Grindelwald's glacier, with black-and-white photos, icicle lights and mountain murals. Retro-modern rooms in cool grey and blue tones come with hardwood floors, Marshall radios and Coco-Mat beds. The restaurant serves imaginative, region-driven food.

★ Cafe 3692
CAFE $$

(✆033 853 16 54; www.cafe3692.ch; Terrassenweg 61; snacks & light meals Sfr7-25, mains Sfr35-38; ☺8.30am-6pm Sun-Tue, to midnight Fri & Sat) Run by dream duo Myriam and Bruno, Cafe 3692 is a delight. Bruno is a talented carpenter and has let his imagination run riot – a gnarled apple tree is an eye-catching artwork, a mine-cart trolley cleverly transforms into a grill, and the ceiling is a wave of woodwork. Garden herbs and Grindelwald-sourced ingredients are knocked up into tasty specials.

❶ Getting There & Away

There are frequent train connections to Interlaken (Sfr11.20, 34 minutes) and Lauterbrunnen via Zweilütschinen (Sfr9, 36 minutes).

Wengen

POP 1292 / ELEV 1274M

Photogenically poised on a mountain ledge, Wengen has celestial views of the glacier-capped giant peaks' silent majesty as well as the shimmering waterfalls spilling into the Lauterbrunnen Valley below.

The village is car-free and can only be reached by train. It's a fabulous hub for **hiking** for much of the year as well as **skiing** in winter.

From Wengen's train station, loop back under the tracks and head three minutes downhill to **Hotel Bären** (✆033 855 14 19; www.baeren-wengen.ch; s Sfr190-230, d Sfr220-390, f Sfr390-490, all incl half-board; 🛇), a snug log chalet with bright, cosy rooms; the affable Brunner family serves a hearty breakfast and delicious seasonal cuisine in the attached restaurant. For superb regional fare in an even dreamier setting, check out the leafy mountain-facing terrace or the pine-clad, candlelit dining room at **Restaurant 1903** (✆033 855 34 22; www.hotel-schoenegg.ch; mains Sfr28-54; ☺6.30-10pm, closed May & mid-Oct–mid-Dec), a 250m walk uphill from the station.

The highlight of Wengen's calendar is the world-famous **Lauberhorn** (www.lauberhorn.ch; ☺mid-Jan) downhill ski race, where pros reach speeds of up to 160km/h.

Jungfraujoch

Jungfraujoch (3471m) is a once-in-a-lifetime trip and there's good reason why two million people a year visit Europe's highest train station. Clear good weather is essential; check www.jungfrau.ch for current conditions, and don't forget warm clothing, sunglasses and sunscreen.

From Interlaken Ost, the journey time is 2¼ to 2½ hours each way and the return fare is Sfr210.80. The last train back from Jungfraujoch leaves at 6.43pm in summer and 4.43pm in winter. From early May to late October you can qualify for a discounted Good Morning Ticket (Sfr145) by taking one of the first two trains from Interlaken Ost (6.35am or 7.05am) and boarding a return train from the summit no later than 1.13pm.

Gimmelwald

POP 101 / ELEV 1367M

Decades ago some anonymous backpacker scribbled these words in the guestbook at the Mountain Hostel: 'If heaven isn't what it's cracked up to be, send me back to Gimmelwald'. Enough said. When the sun is out in Gimmelwald, this pipsqueak of a village will simply take your breath away. Sit outside and listen to the distant roar of avalanches on the sheer mountain faces arrayed before you.

The charming **Esther's Guest House** (☑ 033 855 54 88; www.esthersguesthouse.ch; Kirchstatt; s Sfr60-90, d Sfr120-180, tr Sfr180, q Sfr200, apt Sfr240-250; ⬆) is run with love by Uri and his wife Dana, who extend a warm welcome and pay attention to guests' comfort.

Mürren

POP 418 / ELEV 1650M

Arrive on a clear evening when the sun hangs low on the horizon, and you'll think you've died and gone to heaven. Car-free Mürren is storybook Switzerland.

From the top station of Allmendhubel funicular, you can set out on many walks, including the spectacular **North Face Trail** (1½ hours), via Schiltalp, with big views to the glaciers and waterfalls of the Lauterbrunnen Valley and the monstrous Eiger north face. To up the challenge, try the head-spinning **Klettersteig** (☑ 033 856 86 86, tour bookings 033 854 12 80; www.kletter steig-muerren.ch; ⊘ mid-Jun–Oct) *via ferrata*.

Sleeping options near the train station include **Eiger Guesthouse** (☑ 033 856 54 60; www.eigerguesthouse.com; s Sfr60-170, d Sfr130-200, q Sfr180-210; ⬆), with its downstairs pub serving tasty food, and **Hotel Eiger** (☑ 033 856 54 54; www.hoteleiger.com; s Sfr183-270, d Sfr280-435, ste Sfr410-715; ⬆⬆), a huge wooden chalet with swimming pool and ravishing views.

Schilthorn

There's a tremendous 360-degree, 200-peak panorama from the 2970m Schilthorn, best appreciated from the Skyline view platform or Piz Gloria revolving restaurant. On a clear day, you can see from Titlis around to Mont Blanc, and across to the German Black Forest.

Note that this was the site of Blofeld's HQ in the 1969 James Bond film *On Her Majesty's Secret Service*, as explained at the interactive **Bond World 007** (www.schilthorn. ch; Schilthorn; free with cable-car ticket; ⊘ 8am-6pm). The Skyline Walk is a glass-and-steel platform dangling over a precipice, providing dizzying perspectives of the snow-dusted Jungfrau massif.

From Interlaken, the grand round-trip excursion to Schilthorn costs Sfr131.40 and goes via Lauterbrunnen, Grütschalp and Mürren, returning via Stechelberg to Interlaken. Ask about discounts for early-morning trips.

CANTON OF ZÜRICH

Naturally, the lakeside city of Zürich is the canton's centre of attention, but within half an hour of the city you can try out walking trails or mountain-bike routes in the heights of 871m Uetliberg, or explore castle-topped Rapperswil and the cutting-edge galleries of Winterthur, something of a cultural hot spot.

Zürich

POP 409.241

Culturally vibrant, efficiently run and attractively set at the meeting of river and lake, Zürich is regularly recognised as one of the world's most liveable cities. Long known as a savvy, hard-working financial centre, Switzerland's largest and wealthiest metropolis has also emerged in the 21st century as one of central Europe's hippest destinations, with an artsy, post-industrial edge that is epitomised in its exuberant summer **Street Parade**.

◉ Sights & Activities

The cobbled streets of the pedestrian Old Town line both sides of the river, while the bank vaults beneath Bahnhofstrasse, the city's most elegant shopping street, are said to be crammed with gold. On Sunday, seemingly all of Zürich strolls around the lake – on a clear day you'll glimpse the Alps in the distance.

★ **Fraumünster** CHURCH
(www.fraumuenster.ch/en; Stadthausquai 19; Sfr5 incl audioguide; ⊙10am-6pm Mar-Oct, to 5pm Nov-Feb; 🚊 6, 7, 10, 11, 14 to Paradeplatz) This 13th-century church is renowned for its stunning stained-glass windows, designed by the Russian-Jewish master Marc Chagall (1887–1985), who executed the series of five windows in the choir stalls in 1971 and the rose window in the southern transept in 1978. The rose window in the northern transept was created by Augusto Giacometti in 1945.

★ **Kunsthaus** MUSEUM
(📞044 253 84 84; www.kunsthaus.ch; Heimplatz 1; adult/child Sfr16/free, Wed free; ⊙10am-6pm Tue & Fri-Sun, to 8pm Wed & Thu; 🚊5, 8, 9, 10 to Kunsthaus) Zürich's impressive fine-arts gallery boasts a rich collection of largely European art. It stretches from the Middle Ages through a mix of Old Masters to Alberto Giacometti stick figures, Monet and van Gogh masterpieces, Rodin sculptures, and other 19th- and 20th-century art. It also hosts rotating exhibitions of the highest calibre.

Schweizerisches Landesmuseum MUSEUM
(Swiss National Museum; 📞058 466 65 11; www.nationalmuseum.ch/e/zuerich; Museumstrasse 2; adult/child Sfr10/free; ⊙10am-5pm Tue, Wed & Fri-Sun, to 7pm Thu; 🚊Zürich Hauptbahnhof, 🚉Zürich Hauptbahnhof) Inside a purpose-built cross between a mansion and a castle sprawls this eclectic and imaginatively presented museum. The permanent collection offers an extensive romp through Swiss history, with exhibits ranging from elaborately carved and painted sleds to domestic and religious artefacts, via a series of reconstructed historical rooms spanning six centuries. In 2016 the museum celebrated a major expansion with the opening of its archaeology section in a brand-new wing.

Lindenhof SQUARE
(🚊4, 6, 7, 10, 11, 13, 14, 15, 17 to Rennweg) Spectacular views across the Limmat to the Grossmünster can be enjoyed from a tree-shaded hilltop park, smack in the heart of the Old Town. Bring a picnic and watch the *boules* players while you eat.

Seebad Utoquai SWIMMING
(📞044 251 61 51; www.bad-utoquai.ch; Utoquai 49; adult/child Sfr8/4; ⊙7am-8pm mid-May–late Sep; 🚊2, 4, 10, 11, 14, 15 to Kreuzstrasse) Just north of leafy Zürichhorn park, 400m south of Bellevueplatz, this is the most popular bathing pavilion on the Zürichsee's eastern shore.

🛏 Sleeping

SYHA Hostel HOSTEL $
(📞043 399 78 00; www.youthhostel.ch; Mutschellenstrasse 114; dm Sfr40.50, s Sfr82-118, d Sfr92-139; @ 🛜; 🚊7 to Morgental, Ⓢ S8, S24 to Wollishofen) A pink 1960s landmark houses this busy, institutional hostel with 24-hour reception, dining hall, sparkling modern bathrooms and dependable wi-fi in the downstairs lounge. The included breakfast features miso soup and rice alongside all the Swiss standards. It's about 20 minutes south of the Hauptbahnhof.

LADYs FIRST HOTEL $$
(📞044 380 80 10; www.ladysfirst.ch; Mainaustrasse 24; d Sfr205-365, ste Sfr305-435; 📞; 🚊2, 4, 10, 11, 14, 15 to Feldeggstrasse) 🏊 Ladies come first here, as the name suggests, but gents are also welcome at this eco-aware, socially responsible hotel, housed in an art nouveau town house near the opera house and lake, though the spa and roof terrace are open to women only. The immaculate, generally spacious rooms abound in aesthetic touches such as traditional parquet flooring and designer furnishings.

Townhouse BOUTIQUE HOTEL $$
(📞044 200 95 95; www.townhouse.ch; Schützengasse 7; s Sfr195-365, d Sfr225-395, ste Sfr315-425; 📞; 🚊Zürich Hauptbahnhof, 🚉Zürich Hauptbahnhof) With a cracking location only steps from the train station and the shops of Bahnhofstrasse, this stylish five-storey hotel offers friendly service and a host of welcoming touches. The 26 rooms come in an assortment of sizes (from 15 to 35 sq metres), with luxurious wallpaper, wall hangings, parquet floors, retro furniture, DVD players and iPod docking stations.

★ **Hotel Widder** BOUTIQUE HOTEL $$$
(📞044 224 25 26; www.widderhotel.ch; Rennweg 7; d/ste from Sfr470/870; Ⓟ ❄ @ 🛜; 🚊4, 6, 7, 10, 11, 13, 14, 15, 17 to Rennweg) A supremely stylish boutique hotel in the equally grand district of Augustiner, the Widder is a pleasing fusion of five-star luxury and 12th-century charm. Rooms and public areas across the eight individually decorated town houses that make up this place are stuffed with designer furniture, art and original features – from oak beams to antique stoves and murals.

🍴 Eating

Traditional local cuisine is very rich, as epitomised by the city's signature dish, *Zürcher*

Zürich

Geschnetzeltes (sliced veal in a creamy mushroom and white wine sauce).

★ Kraftwerk
INTERNATIONAL $

(☎ 079 817 07 03; www.kraftwerk.coffee; Selnaustrasse 25; sharing plates Sfr29-65, lunch specials Sfr15-16.50; ☺ 8am-10pm Mon-Wed, to midnight Thu & Fri; ☒ 2, 9 to Sihlstrasse) This born-again *kraftwerk* (power station) now pumps out excellent locally roasted coffee, delicious meze and lunch specials in uberhip industrial surrounds. Vintage furniture is scattered around the high-ceilinged, crate-lined hall, where you can nibble on season-driven bites from aubergine caviar to spinach with smoked mozzarella, and fennel salad with hazelnuts and orange. The vibe is sociable and the service clued up.

Café Sprüngli
SWEETS $

(☎ 044 224 46 46; www.spruengli.ch; Bahnhofstrasse 21; sweets Sfr8-16; ☺ 7.30am-6.30pm Mon-Fri, 8am-6pm Sat, 9.30am-5.30pm Sun; ☒ 4, 6, 7, 10, 11, 13, 14, 15, 17 to Paradeplatz) Sit down for cakes,

chocolate, ice cream and exquisite coffee drinks at this epicentre of sweet Switzerland, in business since 1836. You can have a light lunch too, but whatever you do, don't fail to check out its heavenly chocolate shop, where you can buy delectable pralines and truffles, plus the house speciality – rainbow-bright Luxemburgerli macarons – to take home.

★ Didi's Frieden
SWISS $$

(☎ 044 253 18 10; www.didisfrieden.ch; Stampfenbachstrasse 32; 4-/5-course menu Sfr98/108, mains Sfr24-49; ☺ 11am-2.30pm & 5pm-midnight Mon-Fri, 6pm-midnight Sat; ☒ 7, 11, 14, 17 to Stampfenbachplatz) With its unique blend of familiarity and refinement, Didi's Frieden features among Zürich's top tables. The look is understated elegance, with wood floors, white tablecloths and wine-glass chandeliers. Service is discreet yet attentive, while menus sing of the seasons in dishes like venison steak with wild mushrooms and red wine-shallot jus – big on integral flavours and presented with panache.

Zürich

Alpenrose SWISS $$

(☑ 044 431 11 66; www.restaurantalpenrose.ch; Fabrikstrasse 12; mains Sfr24-38; ☺ 9am-11.30pm Tue-Fri, from 5pm Sat & Sun; ☒ 3, 4, 6, 10, 11, 13, 15, 17 to Quellenstrasse) With its tall, stencilled windows, warm wood panelling and stucco ceiling ornamentation, the Alpenrose exudes cosy Old World charm, and the cuisine here lives up to the promise. Hearty Swiss classics, such as herb-stuffed trout with homemade *Spätzli* (egg noodles) and buttered carrots, are exquisitely prepared and presented, and accompanied by a good wine list and a nice selection of desserts.

Zeughauskeller SWISS $$

(☑ 044 220 15 15; www.zeughauskeller.ch; Bahnhofstrasse 28a; lunch specials Sfr22.50, mains Sfr19-37; ☺ 11.30am-11pm; ☑; ☒ 4, 10, 11, 14, 15 to Paradeplatz) Tuck into the heartiest of Swiss grub under the heavy oak beams at this sprawling, atmospheric 15th-century beer hall with ample pavement seating. The menu (in eight languages) goes to town with a dozen varieties of sausage, along with other Swiss faves like pork roast with lashings of sauerkraut. Vegetarian options are also available.

🍺 Drinking & Entertainment

Options abound across town, but the bulk of the more animated drinking dens are in Züri-West, especially along Langstrasse in Kreis 4 and Hardstrasse in Kreis 5.

★ Frau Gerolds Garten BAR

(www.fraugerold.ch; Geroldstrasse 23/23a; ☺ bar-restaurant 11am-midnight Mon-Sat, noon-10pm Sun Apr-Sep, 6pm-midnight Mon-Sat Oct-Mar, market & shops 11am-7pm Mon-Fri, to 6pm Sat year-round; ☒ Hardbrücke) Hmm, where to start? The wine bar? The margarita bar? The gin bar? Whichever poison you choose, this wildly popular focal point of Zürich's summer drinking scene is pure unadulterated fun and one of the best grown-up playgrounds in Europe.

★ Rimini Bar BAR

(www.rimini.ch; Badweg 10; ☺ 5-11pm Mon-Wed, to midnight Thu-Sat, to 10pm Sun; ☒ 2, 8, 9, 13, 14, 17 to Sihlstrasse) Secluded behind a fence along the Sihl River, this bar at the **Männerbad** (☑ 044 211 95 94; ☺ 11am-7pm Mon-Thu & Sun, to 6.30pm Fri, to 5.30pm Sat Jun-Sep) public baths is one of Zürich's most inviting open-air drinking spots. Its vast wood deck is adorned with red-orange party lights, picnic tables and throw cushions for lounging, accompanied by the sound of water from the adjacent pools.

Open in good weather only.

Hive Club CLUB

(☑ 044 271 12 10; www.hiveclub.ch; Geroldstrasse 5; ☺ 11pm-4am Thu, to 7am Fri, to 9am Sat; ☒ Hardbrücke) Electronic music creates the buzz at this artsy, alternative club (cover Sfr35) adjacent to Frau Gerolds Garten in Kreis 5. Enter through an alley strung with multicoloured umbrellas, giant animal heads, mushrooms and watering cans. Big-name DJs keep things going into the wee hours three nights a week.

Rote Fabrik LIVE MUSIC

(☑ 044 485 58 58; www.rotefabrik.ch; Seestrasse 395; ☒ 161, 165 to Rote Fabrik) With a fabulous lakeside location, this multifaceted performing-arts centre stages rock, jazz and hip-hop concerts, original-language films, and theatre and dance performances. There's also a bar and a restaurant. Take bus 161 or 165 from Bürkliplatz.

ℹ Information

In the main train station, **Zürich Tourism** (☑ 044 215 40 00, hotel reservations 044 215 40 40; www.zuerich.com; Hauptbahnhof; ☺ 8am-8.30pm Mon-Sat, 8.30am to 6.30pm Sun May-Oct, 8.30am-7pm Mon-Sat, 9am-6pm Sun Nov-Apr) is an excellent first port of call.

ⓘ Getting There & Away

AIR

Zürich Airport (☑ 043 816 22 11; www.
zurich-airport.com) is 9km north of the city
centre, with flights to most capitals in Europe as
well as some in Africa, Asia and North America.

TRAIN

Direct trains run frequently to Stuttgart (Sfr70,
three hours), Munich (Sfr102, 4½ to 5½ hours),
Innsbruck (Sfr83, 3½ hours) and other international destinations. There are regular direct
departures to most major Swiss destinations,
such as Lucerne (Sfr25, 45 to 50 minutes), Bern
(Sfr51, one to 1½ hours) and Basel (Sfr34, 55
minutes to 1¼ hours).

ⓘ Getting Around

TO/FROM THE AIRPORT

Several trains an hour connect Zürich Airport
with the Hauptbahnhof (Sfr6.80, 12 minutes)
between around 5am and midnight. A taxi to the
centre costs around Sfr60.

BICYCLE

Züri Rollt (☑ 044 415 67 67; www.schweizrollt.
ch) is an innovative program that allows visitors
to borrow or rent bikes from a handful of locations, including Velostation Nord, across the
road from the north side of the Hauptbahnhof.
Bring ID and leave Sfr20 as a deposit. Rental is
free if you bring the bike back on the same day;
it costs Sfr10 per day if you keep it overnight.

PUBLIC TRANSPORT

The comprehensive, unified bus, tram and
S-Bahn public transit system **ZV** (☑ 0848 988
988; www.zvv.ch) includes boats plying the
Limmat River. Short trips under five stops are
Sfr2.70; typical trips are Sfr4.40. A 24-hour pass
for the city centre is Sfr8.80.

NORTHWESTERN SWITZERLAND

With businesslike Basel at its heart, this
region also prides itself on having the
country's finest Roman ruins (at Augusta
Raurica) and a gaggle of proud castles and
pretty medieval villages scattered across the
rolling countryside of Aargau Canton.

Basel

POP 175,940 / ELEV 273M

Tucked up against the French and German
borders in Switzerland's northwest corner,
Basel straddles the majestic Rhine. The
town is home to art galleries, 40-odd museums and galleries, avant-garde architecture
and an enchanting Old Town centre.

◉ Sights

★ Fondation Beyeler   MUSEUM

(☑ 061 645 97 00; www.fondationbeyeler.ch; Ba-
selstrasse 101, Riehen; adult/under 25yr Sfr25/
free; ⊙ 10am-6pm Thu-Tue, to 8pm Wed; ℗) This
astounding private-turned-public collection,
assembled by former art dealers Hildy and
Ernst Beyeler, is housed in a long, low, light-
filled, open-plan building designed by Italian
architect Renzo Piano. The varied exhibits
juxtapose 19th- and 20th-century works by
Picasso and Rothko against sculptures by
Miró and Max Ernst and tribal figures by
Oceania; there are also regular visiting exhibitions. Take tram 6 to Riehen from Barfüsserplatz or Marktplatz.

★ Museum Jean Tinguely   MUSEUM

(☑ 061 681 93 20; www.tinguely.ch; Paul Sacher-Anlage
2; adult/student/child Sfr18/12/free; ⊙ 11am-6pm Tue-
Sun; ℗) Designed by leading Ticino architect
Mario Botta, this museum showcases the
playful, mischievous and downright wacky
artistic concoctions of sculptor-turned-mad-
scientist Jean Tinguely. Buttons next to some
of Tinguely's 'kinetic' sculptures allow visitors
to set them in motion. It's great fun to watch
them rattle, shake and twirl, with springs,
feathers and wheels radiating at every angle, or to hear the haunting musical sounds
produced by the gigantic *Méta-Harmonies*
on the upper floor. Catch bus 31 or 36 from
Claraplatz.

🛏 Sleeping & Eating

Hotels are often full during Basel's trade
fairs and conventions; book ahead. Head to
the Marktplatz for a daily market and several stands selling excellent quick bites, such
as local sausages and sandwiches.

SYHA Youth Hostel Basel   HOSTEL $

(☑ 061 272 05 72; www.youthhostel.ch; St Alban-
Kirchrain 10; dm/s/tw with shared bathroom
from Sfr41/70/93, s/d from Sfr120/132; 🛜) Designed by Basel-based architects Buchner
& Bründler, this swanky, modern hostel in
a very pleasant neighbourhood is flanked by
tree-shaded squares and a rushing creek. It's
only a stone's throw from the Rhine, and 15
minutes on foot from the SBB Bahnhof (or
take tram 2 to Kunstmuseum and walk five
minutes downhill).

LIECHTENSTEIN

If Liechtenstein didn't exist, someone would have invented it. A tiny German-speaking mountain principality in the heart of 21st-century Europe, it certainly has novelty value. Only 25km long by 12km wide (at its broadest point) – just larger than Manhattan – Liechtenstein is mostly visited by people who want a glimpse of the turreted castle in capital **Vaduz**. Stay a little longer and you can escape into its pint-sized Alpine wilderness. The 75km **Liechtenstein Trail** (www.tourismus.li/en/activities/the-liechtenstein-trail), beginning in Vaduz, showcases the principality's greatest hits, from hilltop castles to serene villages. The **Liechtenstein Center** (☑ 239 63 63; www.tourismus.li; Städtle 39, Vaduz; ⊘ 9am-5pm Nov-Apr, 9am-6pm May-Oct; 🛜) offers brochures and souvenir passport stamps. From the Swiss border towns of Buchs (Sfr5.80, 27 minutes) and Sargans (Sfr7.20, 32 minutes), there are frequent buses to Vaduz.

Hotel Krafft   HOTEL $$
(☑ 061 690 91 30; www.krafftbasel.ch; Rheingasse 12; s Sfr144-225, d Sfr248-450, ste Sfr292-490; 🛜) Design-savvy urbanites gravitate to this renovated historic hotel for its smart, minimalist rooms that wonderfully fuse old and new; some have balconies. Free folding bikes, fresh fruit, tea and water stations impress, but the hotel's key feature is its prime riverside position, adjacent to Mittlere Brücke, peering out from Kleinbasel across the Rhine onto Grossbasel's gorgeous townscape. Ask for a room with a view.

★ Volkshaus Basel   BRASSERIE $$
(☑ 061 690 93 00; www.volkshaus-basel.ch/en; Rebgasse 12-14; mains Sfr32-46; ⊘ restaurant 11.30am-2pm & 6-10pm Mon-Fri & 6-10pm Sat, bar 10am-midnight Mon-Wed, to 1am Thu-Sat) This stylish Herzog & de Meuron–designed venue is part resto-bar, part gallery and part performance space. For relaxed dining, head for the atmospheric beer garden in a cobblestoned courtyard decorated with columns, vine-clad walls and light-draped rows of trees. The menu ranges from brasserie classics (*steak frites*) to more innovative offerings (salmon tartare with citrus fruits and gin cucumber).

ⓘ Information
Pop into **Basel Tourismus** (☑ 061 268 68 68; www.basel.com; Centralbahnstrasse 10; ⊘ 8-6pm Mon-Fri, 9am-5pm Sat, 9am-3pm Sun) or **Basel Tourismus** (☑ 061 268 68 68; www.basel.com; Barfüsserplatz; ⊘ 9am-6.30pm Mon-Fri, to 5pm Sat, 10am-3pm Sun) for information and maps on the city and its surrounds.

ⓘ Getting There & Around
Basel hotel guests automatically receive a 'mobility ticket' pass, providing free transport throughout the city, operated by **BVB** (☑ 061 685 14 14; www.bvb.ch/en).

AIR
The **EuroAirport** (☑ +33 3 89 90 31 11; www. euroairport.com), 5km northwest of town in France, is the main airport for Basel. It offers flights to numerous European cities on a variety of low-cost carriers. **Airport Bus 50** links the airport and Basel's main train station SBB Bahnhof (Sfr4.70, 22 minutes).

TRAIN
Basel is a major European rail hub. The main station has TGVs to Paris (three hours) and fast ICEs to major cities in Germany.

Frequent direct trains run from SBB Bahnhof to Zürich (Sfr34, 55 minutes to 1¼ hours) and Bern (Sfr41, 55 minutes). Services to Geneva (Sfr76, 2¾ hours) require a change of train in Bern, Biel/Bienne or Olten.

TICINO
POP 351,946

Switzerland meets Italy: in Ticino the summer air is rich and hot, and the peacock-proud posers propel their scooters in and out of traffic. Italian weather, Italian style. Not to mention the Italian ice cream, Italian pizza, Italian architecture and Italian language.

Locarno
POP 16,122 / ELEV 205M

Italianate architecture and the northern end of Lago Maggiore, plus more hours of sunshine than anywhere else in Switzerland (2300 hours, to be precise), give this laid-back town a summer resort atmosphere. Locarno is on the northeastern corner of Lago Maggiore, which mostly lies in Italy's Lombardy region. **Navigazione Lago Maggiore** (www.navigazionelaghi.it/lago-maggiore) operates boats across the entire lake.

◉ Sights

★ Santuario della Madonna del Sasso
CHURCH

(www.madonnadelsasso.org; Via Santuario 2; ◷7.30am-6.30pm) Overlooking the town, this sanctuary was built after the Virgin Mary supposedly appeared in a vision to a monk, Bartolomeo d'Ivrea, in 1480. There's a highly adorned church and several rather rough, near-life-size statue groups (including one of the Last Supper) in niches on the stairway. The best-known painting in the church is *La fuga in egitto* (Flight to Egypt), painted in 1522 by Bramantino.

Piazza Grande
AREA

Locarno's Italianate Città Vecchia (Old Town) fans out from Piazza Grande, a photogenic ensemble of arcades and Lombardstyle houses. A craft and fresh-produce market takes over the square every Thursday, and regular events are staged here during the warmer months.

ⓘ Information

Locarno's **tourist office** (☑084 809 10 91; www.ascona-locarno.com; Piazza Stazione; ◷9am-6pm Mon-Fri, 10am-6pm Sat, 10am-1.30pm & 2.30-5pm Sun) is housed in the train station. Ask about the free Ascona-Locarno Welcome Card.

ⓘ Getting There & Around

Locarno is well linked to Ticino and the rest of Switzerland via Bellinzona, or take the scenic Centovalli Express (www.centovalli.ch) to Brig via Domodossola in Italy.

A **funicular** (one way/return adult Sfr4.80/7.20, child Sfr2.20/3.60; ◷8am-10pm May, Jun & Sep, to midnight Jul & Aug, to 9pm Apr & Oct, to 7.30pm Nov-Mar) runs every 15 minutes from the Locarno town centre past the Santuario della Madonna del Sasso to Orselina.

Lugano

POP 63,932 / ELEV 270M

Ticino's lush, mountain-rimmed lake isn't its only liquid asset. Lugano is also the country's third-most-important banking centre. Suits aside, it's a vivacious city, with bars and pavement cafes huddling in the spaghetti maze of steep cobblestone streets that untangle at the edge of the lake and along the flowery promenade. The busy main square holds **markets** on Tuesday and Friday mornings.

◉ Sights & Activities

Take the stairs or the **funicular** (Piazzale della Stazione; Sfr1.30; ◷5am-midnight) from Lugano's train station down to the centre, a patchwork of interlocking *piazze*. Here, Lugano's early-16th-century cathedral **Cattedrale di San Lorenzo** (St Lawrence Cathedral; Via San Lorenzo; ◷6.30am-6pm) conceals some fine frescos and ornate baroque statues behind its Renaissance facade. **Società Navigazione del Lago di Lugano** (☑091 971 52 23; www.lakelugano.ch; Riva Vela; ◷Apr-Oct) runs hour-long cruises of the bay.

Museo d'Arte della Svizzera Italiana
GALLERY

(MASI; www.masilugano.ch; LAC Lugano Arte e Cultura, Piazza Bernardino Luini 6; adult/child Sfr20/free; ◷10am-6pm Tue, Wed, Fri-Sun, to 8pm Thu) The showpiece of Lugano's striking new **LAC cultural centre** (☑058 866 42 22; www.luganolac.ch), the MASI zooms in predominantly on 20th-century and contemporary art – from the abstract to the highly experimental, with exhibitions spread across three spaces. There is no permanent collection currently on display, but there is a high-calibre roster of rotating exhibitions. Recent focuses have included European pop art and the work of Belgian surrealist René Magritte.

🛏 Sleeping & Eating

Hotel & Hostel Montarina
HOTEL, HOSTEL $

(☑091 966 72 72; www.montarina.ch; Via Montarina 1; dm/s/d Sfr29/105/140; ⓟ⑤☒) Occupying a pastel-pink villa dating from 1860, this hotel-hostel duo extends a heartfelt welcome. Mosaic floors, high ceilings and wrought-iron balustrades are lingering traces of old-world grandeur. There's a shared kitchen-lounge, toys to amuse the kids, a swimming pool set in palm-dotted gardens and even a tiny vineyard.

★ Guesthouse Castagnola
GUESTHOUSE $$

(☑078 632 67 47; www.gh-castagnola.com; Salita degli Olivi 2; apt Sfr120-200; ⓟ⑤) Kristina and Maurizio bend over backwards to please at their B&B, lodged in a beautifully restored 16th-century town house. Exposed stone, natural fabrics and earthy colours dominate in four rooms kitted out with Nespresso coffee machines and flat-screen TVs. There's also a family-friendly apartment with a washing machine and full kitchen. Take bus 2 to Posta Castagnola, 2km east of the centre.

La Tinèra
SWISS $

(☑091 923 52 19; Via dei Gorini 2; mains Sfr19-24; ◷11.30am-3pm & 5.30-11pm Mon-Sat) Huddled down a backstreet near Piazza della Riforma, this convivial, rustic restaurant rolls out extremely tasty Ticinese home cooking. You might begin, say, with homemade *salumi* (cured meats), moving on to polenta with porcini mushrooms or meltingly tender osso buco. Simply pair with a good Merlot from the region.

ℹ Information

Lugano's main **tourist office** (☑ 058 220 65 00; www.lugano-tourism.ch; Piazza della Riforma, Palazzo Civico; ⊙ 9am-6pm Mon-Fri, 9am-5pm Sat, 10am-4pm Sun) is the starting point for guided tours of the city. There is also a **branch** (☑ 058 220 65 04; Piazzale della Stazione; ⊙ 9am-6pm Mon-Fri, 9am-1pm Sat) at the train station.

ℹ Getting There & Away

From Lugano's **train station** (Piazzale della Stazione) there are very frequent connections to Bellinzona (Sfr11, 30 minutes), with onward connections to destinations further north. Getting to Locarno (Sfr15.20, one hour) involves a change at Giubiasco.

GRAUBÜNDEN

POP 197,888

While you've probably heard about Davos' sensational downhill skiing, St Moritz' glamour and the tales of Heidi (fictionally born here), vast swaths of Graubünden remain little known and ripe for exploring. Strike into the Alps on foot or follow the lonely passes that corkscrew high into the mountains and the chances are you will be alone in exhilarating landscapes.

St Moritz

POP 5084 / ELEV 1856M

Switzerland's original winter wonderland and the cradle of Alpine tourism, St Moritz has been luring royals, celebrities and mon-eyed wannabes since 1864. With its shimmering aquamarine lake, emerald forests and aloof mountains, the town looks a million dollars.

🎿 Activities

Schweizer Skischule   SKIING

(☑ 081 830 01 01; www.skischool.ch; Via Stredas 14; ⊙ 8am-noon & 2-6pm Mon-Sat, 8-9am & 4-6pm Sun) The first Swiss ski school was founded in St Moritz in 1929. Today you can arrange skiing or snowboarding lessons here – check out the website for details.

🛏 Sleeping & Eating

Jugendherberge St Moritz   HOSTEL $

(☑ 081 836 61 11; www.youthhostel.ch/st.moritz; Via Surpunt 60; dm/s/d/q Sfr42.50/135.50/170/220; P 🐾 🛜) On the edge of the forest, this modern hostel has clean, quiet four-bed dorms and doubles. Considered a top family hostel, there's a children's toy room, bike hire and laundrette. Bus 3 offers door-to-door connections with the town centre (five minutes) and train station (10 minutes).

Chesa Spuondas   HOTEL $$

(☑ 081 833 65 88; www.chesaspuondas.ch; Via Somplaz 47; s/d/f incl half-board Sfr155/280/330; P 🛜) This family hotel nestles amid meadows at the foot of forest and mountains, 3km southwest of the town centre. Rooms have high ceilings, parquet floors and the odd antique. Kids are the centre of attention here, with dedicated meal times, activities and play areas, plus a children's ski school a 10-minute walk away.

Pizzeria Caruso   PIZZA $

(☑ 081 836 06 29; www.laudinella.ch; Via Tegiatscha 17; pizza Sfr13.50-22.50; ⊙ noon-1am; 🍴) Pizza lovers rave about the thin-crust Neapolitan numbers that fly out of the wood oven at Hotel Laudinella's pizzeria. These range from a simple Margherita to the gourmet Domenico with truffles and beef. Laudinella also offers a delivery service.

ℹ Information

The main **tourist office** (☑ 081 837 33 33; www.stmoritz.ch; Via Maistra 12; ⊙ 9am-6.30pm Mon-Fri, 10am-6pm Sat) is in St Moritz-Dorf, but if you're coming by train, visit the **sub-office** (⊙ 10am-2pm & 3-6.30pm) in the train station.

ℹ Getting There & Away

Trains run at least hourly from Zürich to St Moritz (Sfr76, three to 3½ hours), with one change (at Landquart or Chur).

Between mid-December and late October, one of Switzerland's most celebrated trains, the **Glacier Express** (www.glacierexpress.ch; one way adult/child Sfr153/76.50; ⊙ mid-May–late Oct & mid-Dec–early May), makes the scenic eight-hour journey from St Moritz to Zermatt (one to three times daily).

The **Bernina Express** (www.berninaexpress.ch; one way Chur-Tirano Sfr77; ⊙ mid-May–early Dec) provides seasonal links to Lugano from St Moritz, which include the stunning Unesco-recognised train line over the Bernina Pass to Tirano, Italy.

DON'T MISS

SWISS NATIONAL PARK

The Engadine's pride and joy is the **Swiss National Park** (www.nationalpark.ch) FREE, easily accessed from Scuol, Zernez and S-chanf. Spanning 172 sq km, Switzerland's only national park is a nature-gone-wild swath of dolomitic peaks, shimmering glaciers, larch woodlands, pastures, waterfalls and high moors strung with topaz-blue lakes. This was the first national park to be established in the Alps, on 1 August 1914, and more than 100 years later it remains true to its original conservation ethos, with the aims to protect, research and inform. Given that nature has been left to its own devices for a century, the park is a glimpse of the Alps before the dawn of tourism. There are some 80km of well-marked hiking trails, where, with a little luck and a decent pair of binoculars, ibex, chamois, marmots, deer, bearded vultures and golden eagles can be sighted. The **Swiss National Park Centre** (☑ 081 851 41 41; www.nationalpark.ch; exhibition adult/child Sfr7/3; ☉ 8.30am-6pm Jun-Oct, 9am-noon & 2-5pm Nov-May) should be your first port of call for information on activities and accommodation. It sells an excellent 1:50,000 park map (Sfr14, or Sfr20 with guidebook), which covers 21 walks through the park.

You can easily head off on your own, but you might get more out of one of the informative guided hikes (Sfr25) run by the centre from late June to mid-October. These include wildlife-spotting treks to the Val Trupchun and high-alpine hikes to the Offenpass and Lakes of Macun. Most are in German, but many guides speak a little English. Book ahead by phone or at the park office in Zernez. Entry to the park and its car parks is free. Conservation is paramount here, so stick to footpaths and respect regulations prohibiting camping, littering, lighting fires, cycling, picking flowers and disturbing the animals. For an overnight stay in the heart of the park, look no further than **Il Fuorn** (☑ 081 856 12 26; www.ilfuorn.ch; s Sfr85-120, d Sfr130-196, tr Sfr180-195, q Sfr200-220, half-board extra Sfr35; ☉ closed Nov, 2nd half Jan & Easter-late Apr; P ☏), an idyllically sited guesthouse that serves fresh trout and game at its excellent on-site restaurant.

SURVIVAL GUIDE

ⓘ Directory A–Z

INTERNET ACCESS

Free wi-fi hot spots can be found at airports, dozens of Swiss train stations and in many hotels and cafes. Public wi-fi, provided by **Swisscom** (www.swisscom.ch), costs from Sfr5 per day.

MONEY

➡ ATMs are at every airport, most train stations and on every second street corner in towns and cities; Visa, MasterCard and Amex are widely accepted.

➡ Swiss francs are divided into 100 centimes (Rappen in German-speaking Switzerland). Euros are accepted by many tourism businesses.

➡ Exchange money at large train stations.

➡ Tipping is not necessary, given that hotels, restaurants, bars and even some taxis are legally required to include service charge in bills. You can round up the bill after a meal for good service, as locals do.

OPENING HOURS

We list high-season opening hours for sights and attractions; hours tend to decrease during low season. Most businesses shut completely on Sunday.

Banks 8.30am to 4.30pm Monday to Friday

Museums 10am to 5pm, many close Monday and stay open late Thursday

Restaurants noon to 2.30pm and 6pm to 9.30pm; most close one or two days per week

Shops 10am to 6pm Monday to Friday, to 4pm Saturday

PUBLIC HOLIDAYS

New Year's Day 1 January

Good Friday March/April

Easter Sunday and Monday March/April

Ascension Day 40th day after Easter

Whit Sunday and Monday (Pentecost) 7th week after Easter

National Day 1 August

Christmas Day 25 December

St Stephen's Day 26 December

TELEPHONE

➡ Search for phone numbers online at http://tel.local.ch/en.

➡ National telecom provider Swisscom (www.swisscom.ch) provides public phone booths that accept coins and major credit cards.

➡ Prepaid local SIM cards are available from network operators Salt (www.salt.ch), Sunrise (www.sunrise.ch) and Swisscom Mobile (www.swisscom.ch/mobile) for as little as Sfr10.

TOURIST INFORMATION

My Switzerland (www.myswitzerland.com) is an in-depth, multilingual Switzerland Tourism website.

ⓘ Getting There & Away

AIR

The main international airports:

Geneva Airport (p1132) Geneva's airport is 4km northwest of the town centre.

Zürich Airport (p1146) The airport is 9km north of the centre, with flights to most European capitals as well as some in Africa, Asia and North America.

BUS

Eurolines (www.eurolines.com) has buses with connections across Western Europe.

TRAIN

Eco-friendly Switzerland makes rail travel a joy.
➸ Zürich is Switzerland's busiest international terminus, with trains to Munich and Vienna, from where there are extensive onward connections to cities in Eastern Europe.

➸ Most connections from Germany pass through Zürich or Basel.

➸ Nearly all connections from Italy pass through Milan before branching off to Zürich, Lucerne, Bern or Lausanne.

➸ Book tickets and get train information from Rail Europe (www.raileurope.com).

ⓘ Getting Around

Marketed as the Swiss Travel System, the network has a useful website (www.swisstravelsystem.co.uk). Excellent free maps covering the country are available at train stations and tourist offices.

BICYCLE

➸ For details on national, regional and local routes, rental, bike-friendly accommodation, guides and maps, visit www.schweizmobil.ch and click on 'Cycling in Switzerland'.

➸ **SBB Rent-a-Bike** (☑ 041 925 11 70; www.rentabike.ch; half-/full day from Sfr27/35), run by Swiss railways, offers bike hire at 100-odd train stations. For a Sfr10 surcharge they can be collected at one station and returned to another.

➸ Free bike hire is available from April to October through the eco-friendly initiative Schweiz Rollt, with outlets in Zürich and Geneva.

BOAT

All the larger lakes are serviced by steamers operated by Swiss Federal Railways (www.sbb.ch). These include Lakes Geneva, Constance, Lucerne, Lugano, Neuchâtel, Biel, Murten, Thun, Brienz and Zug, but not Lago Maggiore.

BUS

➸ Yellow post buses (www.postauto.ch) supplement the rail network, linking towns to difficult-to-access mountain regions.

➸ Services are regular, and departures (usually next to train stations) are linked to train schedules.

➸ Swiss national travel passes are valid.

➸ Purchase tickets on board; some scenic routes over the Alps (eg the Lugano–St Moritz run) require reservations.

CAR & MOTORCYCLE

➸ Major car-rental companies have offices at airports and in major cities and towns.

➸ Public transport is excellent in city centres – unlike parking cars, which is usually hard work.

➸ Headlights must be on at all times, and dipped (set to low-beam) in tunnels.

➸ The speed limit is 50km/h in towns, 80km/h on main roads outside towns, 100km/h on single-lane freeways and 120km/h on dual-lane freeways.

➸ Purchase a Sfr40 *vignette* (toll sticker) at the border or the nearest petrol station to use Swiss freeways and semi-freeways.

LOCAL TRANSPORT

The Swiss have many words to describe mountain transport: funicular (*Standseilbahn* in German, *funiculaire* in French, *funicolare* in Italian), cable car (*Luftseilbahn, téléphérique, funivia*), gondola (*Gondelbahn, télécabine, telecabina*) and chairlift (*Sesselbahn, télésiège, seggiovia*).

Always check what time the last cable car goes down the mountain – in winter it's as early as 4pm in mountain resorts.

TRAIN

The Swiss rail network combines state-run and private operations. The Swiss Federal Railway (www.sbb.ch) is abbreviated to SBB in German, CFF in French and FFS in Italian.

➸ Second-class compartments are perfectly acceptable but are often close to full; 1st-class carriages are more spacious and have fewer passengers.

➸ Train schedules are available online and at train stations. For information, see www.sbb.ch.

➸ Larger train stations have 24-hour left-luggage lockers (Sfr3 to Sfr6 per day), usually accessible 6am to midnight.

➸ Seat reservations (Sfr5) are advisable for longer journeys, particularly in high season.

➸ While European rail passes such as Eurail and Interrail passes are valid on Swiss national railways, a Swiss Travel Pass is a better option for exploring scenic Switzerland.

Turkey

POP 81.2 MILLION

Best Places to Eat

➡ Antiochia (p1159)
➡ Ayşa (p1166)
➡ Bi Lokma (p1171)
➡ Ocakbaşı Restoran (p1177)
➡ Vanilla (p1173)

Best Places to Stay

➡ Pera Palace Hotel (p1159)
➡ Hotel Empress Zoe (p1159)
➡ El Vino Hotel (p1168)
➡ Hotel Unique (p1170)
➡ Koza Cave Hotel (p1176)

Why Go?

Turkey walks the tightrope between Europe and Asia with ease. Its cities pack in towering minarets and spice-trading bazaars but also offer buzzing, modern street life. Out in the countryside, this country's reputation as a bridge between continents is laid bare. Its expansive steppes and craggy mountain slopes are scattered with the remnants of once-mighty empires. Lycian ruins peek from the undergrowth across the Mediterranean coast, the Roman era's pomp stretches out before you in Ephesus, while the swirling rock valleys of Cappadocia hide Byzantine monastery complexes whittled out by early Christian ascetics.

Of course, if you just want to sloth on a prime piece of beach, Turkey has you covered. But when you've brushed off the sand, this land where East meets West and the ancient merges seamlessly with the contemporary is a fascinating mosaic of culture, history and visceral natural splendour.

When to Go

İstanbul

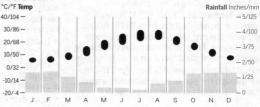

Apr & May İstanbul is a colourful kaleidoscope of tulips and it's prime hiking time on the coast.

Jun–Aug Summer temperatures sizzle and the Mediterranean resorts are in full swing.

Sep & Oct Plenty of crisp clear-sky days but the crowds have dispersed.

Entering the Country

Turkey is well connected to Europe and the rest of the world via land, air and sea.

Most visitors either don't need a tourist visa or can purchase one in advance from www.evisa.gov.tr.

ITINERARIES

One Week

Spend two days exploring İstanbul (p1156) then head south to laid-back Selçuk (p1166) and the grandiose ruins of Ephesus (p1167). After a two-night stop, catch a flight from nearby İzmir to the wacky fairy-chimney countryside of Cappadocia (p1175).

Two Weeks

Follow the one-week itinerary to Selçuk (p1166) then scoot to the Aegean coast for a day or two of chichi beach action in Bodrum (p1168). Next, trail south along the coast to Fethiye (p1169), for boat-trip fun and discovering the ghost village in nearby Kayaköy; or Kaş (p1171), to explore Kekova's submerged ruins. Move onto Antalya (p1172) to crane your neck at Aspendos' theatre and traipse through the old-district streets, before bussing it across the steppe to Cappadocia (p1175) for cave-hotel quirkiness and hot-air ballooning.

Essential Food & Drink

Balık ekmek Grilled fish fillets stuffed into bread with salad and a squeeze of lemon; sold at stands next to ferry docks around the country.

Simit Bread ring studded with sesame seeds; sold in bakeries and by street vendors.

Midye dolma Mussels stuffed with spiced rice and sold by street vendors.

Döner kebap Lamb cooked on a revolving upright skewer then thinly sliced and served in bread with salad and a sprinkling of sumac.

Gözleme Thin savoury pancakes filled with cheese, spinach, mushroom or potato; particularly popular in central Anatolia.

Ayvalık tost Toasted sandwich crammed with cheese, spicy sausage, pickles, tomatoes, ketchup, mayonnaise and anything else its creator can think of.

Pide Turkish-style pizza.

Kokoreç Seasoned lamb/mutton intestines stuffed with offal, grilled over coals and served in bread.

Türk kahvesi Turkish coffee is a thick and powerful brew and usually drunk in a couple of short sips.

TURKEY

Sleeping Price Ranges

Ranges are based on the cost of a double room in high season (İstanbul, İzmir & Bodrum Peninsula/elsewhere) and include breakfast, en-suite bathroom and taxes unless otherwise stated.

€ less than €80/ €25

€€ €80–180/ €26–60

€€€ more than €180/€60

Eating Price Ranges

Price ranges reflect the cost of a standard main-course dish.

€ less than ₺25

€€ ₺25–₺40

€€€ more than ₺40

BULGARIA

BLACK SEA
(KARADENİZ)

Burgas

Kapikule Edirne Kırklareli
GREECE İpsala Tekirdağ Çorlu İstanbul
Keşan
Gelibolu Darıca
Gallipoli Lapseki Yalova
Peninsula Çanakkale Bandırma Gemlik İznik
Troy (Truva) Bursa
Ayvacık Edremit Uludağ
Assos Balıkesir (2543m)
Lesvos Ayvalık
Bergama Pergamum Kütahya
Yeni Aliağa Manisa
Foça Uşak
Chios Sardis Afyon
Çeşme İzmir
Selçuk Odemiş Çivril
Kuşadası Aydın Nazilli Hierapolis
Ikaria Priene Denizli
Didyma Ephesus Afrodisias Isparta
Milas Yatağan Burdur
Güllük Muğla Çavdır
Bodrum Gökova
Kos (Akyaka) Ortaca Termessos
Marmaris Dalaman Antalya
Lycian Fethiye Side
Way Ölüdeniz Çıralı Kemer
Patara Çıralı Olympos Alanya
Beach Finike
Crete Kaş Anamurium
Anamur

Cide İnebolu Sinop
Amasra
Zonguldak Safranbolu Kastamonu
Karabük Tosya Osmancık
Kurşunlu Ilgaz
Bolu Gerede Çankırı Çorum
Adapazarı
Kocaelı Sungurlu
(İzmit) ANKARA Hattuşa
Eskişehir Gordion Kırıkkale
Polatlı Yozgat
Kırşehir
Cappadocia Göreme
Nevşehir Ürgüp
Aksaray Derinkuyu Yahyalı
Akşehir Niğde
Beyşehir Ereğli
Karaman
Akseki Adana
Kırobası Tarsus
Uzuncaburç Mersin (İçel)
Silifke Kızkalesi
Olukbaşı

NICOSIA
(LEFKOSIA)
CYPRUS

MEDITERRANEAN SEA
(AKDENİS)

The Bosphorus
Sea of Marmara
The Dardanelles
Sakarya River
Egirdir Gölü
Tuz Gölü (Salt Lake)
Beyşehir Gölü
Köprülü Kanyon
Suğla Gölü

Turkey Highlights

1 **İstanbul** (p1156) Ferry-hopping from Europe to Asia with your camera at the ready to capture the city's famous minaret-studded skyline.

2 **Cappadocia** (p1175) Bedding down in a cave-hotel to savour modern troglodyte style amid the bizarre lunarscape.

3 **Ephesus** (p1167) Fulfilling your toga-loaded daydreams

in one of the world's greatest surviving Graeco-Roman cities.

4 **Lycian Way** (p1169) Exploring the ruins of empires while relishing ridiculously

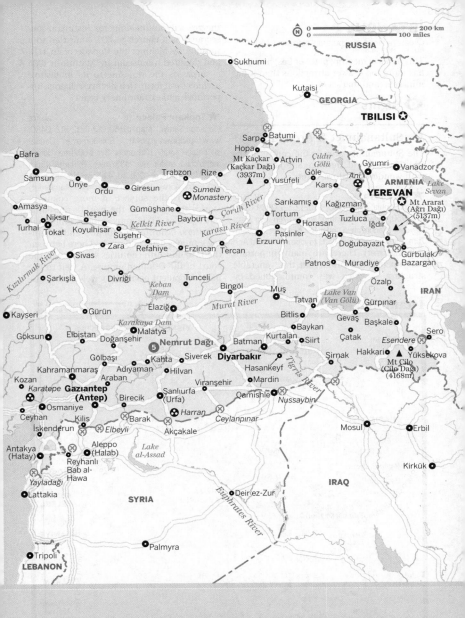

gorgeous coastal views along the long-distance trail.

⑤ Nemrut Dağı (Mt Nemrut; p1176) Marvelling at one king's egotism, amid the toppled statues on the summit.

⑥ Kaş (p1171) Paddling over Kekova's sunken city on a kayaking trip out of this fun-activity vortex.

⑦ Antalya (p1172) Strolling the narrow lanes between

Ottoman mansions and chunks of Roman wall in the old town quarter.

İSTANBUL

☑ 0212 (EUROPEAN İSTANBUL), 0216 (ASIAN İSTANBUL) / POP 14.8 MILLION

This magical meeting place of East and West has more top-drawer attractions than it has minarets (and that's a lot).

◉ Sights

◉ Sultanahmet & Around

The Sultanahmet area is the centre of the Old City, a World Heritage Site jam-packed with wonderful historic sights.

★ Aya Sofya   MUSEUM

(Hagia Sophia; Map p1160; ☑ 0212-522 0989, 0212-522 1750; www.ayasofyamuzesi.gov.tr/en; Aya Sofya Meydanı 1; adult/child under 8yr ₺60/free; ⊙ 9am-7pm Tue-Sun mid-Apr–Oct, to 5pm Nov–mid-Apr; ☐ Sultanahmet) There are many important monuments in İstanbul, but this venerable structure – which was commissioned by the great Byzantine emperor Justinian, consecrated as a church in 537, converted to a mosque by Mehmet the Conqueror in 1453 and declared a museum by Atatürk in 1935 – surpasses the rest due to its innovative architectural form, rich history, religious importance and extraordinary beauty.

★ Topkapı Palace   PALACE

(Topkapı Sarayı; Map p1160; ☑ 0212-512 0480; www.topkapisarayi.gov.tr; Babıhümayun Caddesi; palace adult/child under 8yr ₺60/free, Harem adult/child under 6yr ₺35/free; ⊙ 9am-6.45pm Wed-Mon mid-Apr–Oct, to 4.45pm Nov–mid-Apr, last entry 45min before closing; ☐ Sultanahmet) Topkapı is the subject of more colourful stories than most of the world's museums put together. Libidinous sultans, ambitious courtiers, beautiful concubines and scheming eunuchs lived and worked here between the 15th and 19th centuries when it was the court of the Ottoman empire. A visit to the palace's opulent pavilions, jewel-filled Treas-

İstanbul

ury and sprawling Harem gives a fascinating glimpse into their lives.

★ **Grand Bazaar** MARKET

(Kapalı Çarşı, Covered Market; Map p1160; www. kapalicarsi.org.tr; ⏰9am-7pm Mon-Sat, last entry 6pm; 🚇Beyazıt Kapalıçarşı) The colourful and chaotic Grand Bazaar is the heart of İstanbul's Old City and has been so for centuries. Starting as a small vaulted *bedesten* (warehouse) built by order of Mehmet the Conqueror in 1461, it grew to cover a vast area as lanes between the *bedesten,* neighbouring shops and *hans* (caravanserais) were roofed and the market assumed the sprawling, labyrinthine form that it retains today.

★ **Blue Mosque** MOSQUE

(Sultanahmet Camii; Map p1160; ☑0212-458 4468; Hippodrome; ⏰closed to non-worshippers during 6 daily prayer times; 🚇Sultanahmet) İstanbul's most photogenic building was the grand project of Sultan Ahmet I (r 1603–17), whose tomb is located on the north side of the site facing Sultanahmet Park. The mosque's wonderfully curvaceous exterior features a cascade of domes and six slender minarets. Blue İznik tiles adorn the interior and give the building its unofficial but commonly used name.

★ **Basilica Cistern** HISTORIC SITE

(Yerebatan Sarnıçı; Map p1160; ☑0212-512 1570; www.yerebatan.com; Yerebatan Caddesi; adult/child under 8yr ₺20/free; ⏰9am-5.30pm Nov–mid-Apr, to 6.30pm mid-Apr–Oct; 🚇Sultanahmet) This subterranean structure was commissioned by Emperor Justinian and built in 532. The largest surviving Byzantine cistern in İstanbul, it was constructed using 336 columns, many of which were salvaged from ruined temples and feature fine carved capitals. Its symmetry and sheer grandeur of conception are quite breathtaking, and its cavernous depths make a great retreat on summer days.

İstanbul Archaeology Museums MUSEUM

(İstanbul Arkeoloji Müzeleri; Map p1160; ☑0212-520 7740; www.istanbularkeoloji.gov.tr; Osman Hamdi Bey Yokuşu Sokak, Gülhane; adult/child under 8yr ₺30/free; ⏰9am-6pm Tue-Sun mid-Apr-Oct, 9am-4pm Tue-Sun Nov–mid-Apr; 🚇Gülhane) This superb museum showcases archaeological and artistic treasures from the Topkapı collections. Housed in three buildings, its exhibits include ancient artefacts, classical statuary and an exhibition tracing İstanbul's history. There are many highlights, but the sarcophagi from the Royal Necropolis of Si-

<table>
<tr><td>ⓘ MUSEUM PASS</td></tr>
</table>

The **Museum Pass İstanbul** (www. muze.gov.tr/en/museum-card) offers a possible ₺165 saving on entry to İstanbul's major sights, including Aya Sofya, and allows holders to skip admission queues.

You can also buy passes covering Cappadocia, the Aegean, the Mediterranean and the whole of Turkey.

don are particularly striking. Note that the ticket office closes one hour before the museum's official closing time.

Süleymaniye Mosque MOSQUE

(Map p1160; Professor Sıddık Sami Onar Caddesi; ⏰dawn-dusk; 🚇Vezneciler) The Süleymaniye crowns one of İstanbul's seven hills and dominates the Golden Horn, providing a landmark for the entire city. Though it's not the largest of the Ottoman mosques, it is certainly one of the grandest and most beautiful. It's also unusual in that many of its original *külliye* (mosque complex) buildings have been retained and sympathetically adapted for reuse.

◉ Beyoğlu

Beyoğlu is kilometre zero for galleries, boutiques, cafes, restaurants and nightlife. İstiklal Caddesi runs through the heart of the district right up to Taksim Meydanı (Taksim Square) and carries the life of the modern city up and down its lively promenade.

★ **Pera Museum** MUSEUM

(Pera Müzesi; Map p1158; ☑0212-334 9900; www. peramuseum.org; Meşrutiyet Caddesi 65, Tepebaşı; adult/student/child under 12yr ₺20/10/free; ⏰10am-7pm Tue-Thu & Sat, to 10pm Fri, noon-6pm Sun; 🚇Şişhane, 🚇Tünel) There's plenty to see at this impressive museum, but its major draw is undoubtedly the 2nd-floor exhibition of paintings featuring Turkish Orientalist themes. Drawn from Suna and İnan Kıraç's world-class private collection, the works provide fascinating glimpses into the Ottoman world from the 17th to 20th centuries and include the most beloved painting in the Turkish canon – Osman Hamdı Bey's *The Tortoise Trainer* (1906). Other floors host high-profile temporary exhibitions (past exhibitions have showcased Warhol, de Chirico, Picasso and Botero).

TURKEY İSTANBUL

Beyoğlu & Around

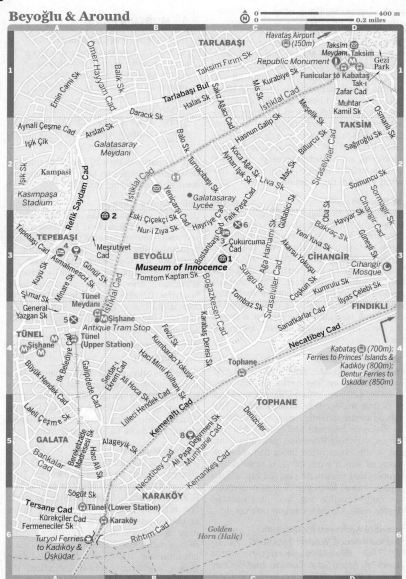

Museum of Innocence   MUSEUM
(Masumiyet Müzesi; Map p1158; ☎0212-252 9738; www.masumiyetmuzesi.org; Çukurcuma Caddesi, Dalgıç Çıkmazı 2; adult/student ₺40/30; ⊙10am–6pm Tue-Sun, to 9pm Thu; ☐Tophane) The painstaking attention to detail in this fascinating museum/piece of conceptual art will certainly provide every amateur psychologist with a theory or two about its creator, Nobel Prize–winning novelist Orhan Pamuk. Vitrines display a quirky collection of objects that evoke the minutiae of İstanbullu life in the mid- to late 20th century, when Pamuk's novel *The Museum of Innocence* is set.

Beyoğlu & Around

✗ Activities & Tours

İstanbul Walks (Map p1160; ☑0212-516 6300, 0554 335 6622; www.istanbulwalks.com; 1st fl, Şifa Hamamı Sokak 1; tours €60-130; ⬒Sultanahmet) and **Urban Adventures** (☑0532 641 2822; www.urbanadventures.com; tours adult €32-95, child €21-67) offer good guided walking tours. The latter also runs foodie walking tours and gastronomic evenings, while **Cooking Alaturka** (Map p1160; ☑0212-458 5919; www.cookingalaturka.com; Akbıyık Caddesi 72a, Cankurtaran; classes per person incl meal €65; ⊙10.30am & 4.30pm by reservation Mon-Sat; ⬒Sultanahmet) gives convivial two-hour cookery classes.

⬒ Sleeping

⬒ Sultanahmet & Around

★**Marmara Guesthouse** PENSION € (Map p1160; ☑0212-638 3638; Terbıyık Sokak 15, Cankurtaran; s €32-42, d €32-47, f €50-70; ⬒✱⬒; ⬒Sultanahmet) Few of Sultanahmet's family-run pensions can compete with the Marmara's cleanliness, comfort and thoughtful details. Owner Elif and team go out of their way to welcome guests, offering advice aplenty and serving a delicious breakfast on the vine-covered, sea-facing roof terrace. Rooms have comfortable beds, good bathrooms (small in some cases) and double-glazed windows.

★**Hotel Empress Zoe** BOUTIQUE HOTEL €€ (Map p1160; ☑0212-518 2504; www.emzoe.com; Akbıyık Caddesi 10, Cankurtaran; s €55-65, d €75-140, tr €120-155, ste €200-265; ⬒✱⬒; ⬒Sultanahmet) Named after the feisty Byzantine empress, this is one of İstanbul's most im-

pressive boutique hotels. The four buildings house 26 diverse rooms. The enticing garden suites overlook a 15th-century hamam and the gorgeous flower-filled courtyard where breakfast is served in warm weather. You can enjoy an early evening drink there, or while admiring the sea view from the terrace.

⬒ Beyoğlu & Around

★**Casa di Bava** BOUTIQUE HOTEL €€ (Map p1158; ☑0538 377 3877; www.casadibavaistanbul.com; Bostanbaşı Caddesi 28, Çukurcuma; economy ste from €90, 1-bedroom apt from €85, 2-bedroom penthouse €130; ⬒✱⬒; ⬒Taksim) The two-bedroom penthouse apartment at this suite hotel is an absolute knockout, and the 11 one-bedroom apartments in the 1880s building are impressive, too. All are stylishly decorated and well appointed, with original artworks, fully equipped kitchenettes and washing machines. The basement suites are smaller and less expensive; all have daily maid service. Breakfast is available on request.

★**Pera Palace Hotel** HISTORIC HOTEL €€€ (Map p1158; ☑0212-377 4000; www.perapalace.com; Meşrutiyet Caddesi 52, Tepebaşı; r €144-211, ste €230-513; ⬒⬒✱@⬒⬒; ⬒Şişhane) This famous hotel underwent a €23-million restoration in 2010 and the result is simply splendiferous. Rooms are luxurious and extremely comfortable, and facilities include an atmospheric bar and lounge (the latter often closed for private functions), spa, gym and restaurant. The most impressive feature of all is the service, which is both friendly and efficient. Breakfast costs €22.

✗ Eating

Sefa Restaurant TURKISH € (Map p1160; ☑0212-520 0670; www.sefarestaurant.com.tr; Nuruosmaniye Caddesi 11, Cağaloğlu; soups ₺6-12, portions ₺16-27; ⊙7am-5pm; ⬒⬒; ⬒Sultanahmet) Located between Sultanahmet and the Grand Bazaar, this clean and popular place offers *hazır yemek* (ready-made dishes) at reasonable prices. You can order from an English menu, but at busy times you may find it easier to just pick daily specials from the bain-marie. Try to arrive early-ish for lunch because many dishes run out by 1.30pm. No alcohol.

★**Antiochia** ANATOLIAN €€ (Map p1158; ☑0212-244 0820; www.antiochiaconcept.com; General Yazgan Sokak 3, Tünel; mezes & salads ₺15-20, pides ₺22, kebaps ₺33-62;

(sidebar) TURKEY İSTANBUL

Sultanahmet & Around

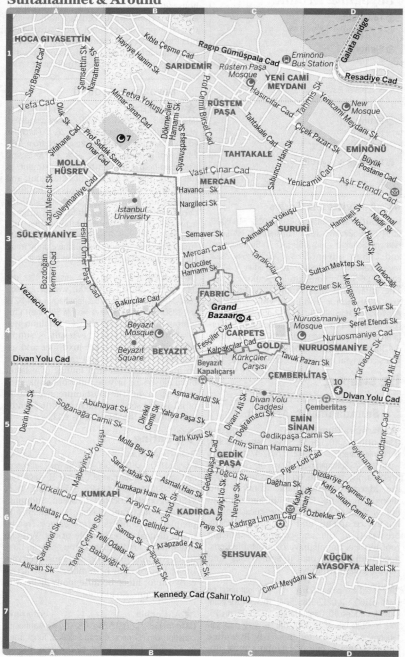

HOCA GIYASETTİN

Sarı Beyazıt Cad

Şemsettin Sk

Namahrem Sk

Hayriye Hanım Sk

Kıble Çeşme Cad

Ragıp Gümüşpala Cad

Eminönü
Bus Station

Galata Bridge

Reşadiye Cad

SARIDEMİR

Rüstem Paşa
Mosque

**YENİ CAMİ
MEYDANI**

New
Mosque

Vefa Cad

Oluk Sk

Fetva Yokuşu

Mimar Sinan Cad

Prof Cemil Birsel Cad

Hasırcılar Cad

Dökmeciler
Hamamı Sk

**RÜSTEM
PAŞA**

Tahtakale Cad

Çiçek Pazarı Sk

Yenicami Meydanı Sk

EMİNÖNÜ

7

Şifahane Cad

Prof Sıddık Sami
Onar Cad

Siyavuşpaşa Cad

TAHTAKALE

Sabuncu Hanı Sk

Tahmis Sk

Büyük
Postane Cad

**MOLLA
HÜSREV**

Kazlı Mescit Sk

Süleymaniye Cad

Vasıf Çınar Cad

MERCAN

Havancı
Sk

Nargileci Sk

Yenicamii Cad

Aşır Efendi Cad

Cemal
Nadir Sk

SÜLEYMANİYE

Bozdoğan
Kemeri Cad

Besim Ömer Paşa Cad

Istanbul
University

Semaver Sk

Mercan Cad

Örücüler
Hamamı Sk

Çakmakçılar Yokuşu

SURURİ

Tarakçılar Cad

Hanımeli Sk

Hoca Hanı Sk

Sultan Mektep Sk

Bezciler Sk

Mengene Sk

Türkocağı
Cad

Tasvir Sk

Şeref Efendi Sk

Vezneciler Cad

Bakırcılar Cad

FABRIC

**Grand
Bazaar** 4

Nuruosmaniye
Mosque

Nuruosmaniye Cad

NURUOSMANİYE

Beyazıt
Mosque

Fesçiler Cad

CARPETS

Kalpakçılar Cad

GOLD

Türbedar Sk

Babı-Ali Cad

Beyazıt
Square

BEYAZIT

Kürkçüler
Çarşısı

Tavuk Pazarı Cad

ÇEMBERLİTAŞ

Divan Yolu Cad

Beyazıt
Kapalıçarşı

10

Divan Yolu Cad

Derin Kuyu Sk

Abuhayat Sk

Soğanağa Camii Sk

Asma Kandil Sk

Direkli
Camii Sk

Yahya Paşa Sk

Divan Yolu
Caddesi

Divan-ı Ali Sk

Doğramacı Sk

Çemberlitaş

**EMİN
SİNAN**

Klodfarer Cad

Peykhane Cad

Mabeyinçi Yokuşu

Molla Bey Sk

Tatlı Kuyu Sk

Emin Sinan Hamamı Sk

Gedikpaşa Camii Sk

Türkeli Cad

Saraç İshak Sk

Asmalı Han Sk

**GEDİK
PAŞA**

Tüğcü Sk

Piyer Loti Cad

Dizdariye Çeşmesi Sk

Dağhan Sk

Katip Sinan Camii Sk

KUMKAPI

Kumkapı Hanı Sk

Arayıcı Sk

Gedikpaşa Cad

Saraylıçı Sk

Neviye Sk

Katip
Sinan Sk

Özbekler Sk

Mollataşı Cad

Üstad

KADIRGA

Paye Sk

Kadırga Limanı Cad

Çifte Gelinler Cad

Samsa Sk

Şarapnel Sk

Tavası Çeşme Sk

Telli Odalar Sk

Babayiğit Sk

Arapzade A Sk

Işık Sk

Capariz Sk

ŞEHSUVAR

**KÜÇÜK
AYASOFYA**

Kaleci Sk

Alişan Sk

Cinci Meydanı Sk

Kennedy Cad (Sahil Yolu)

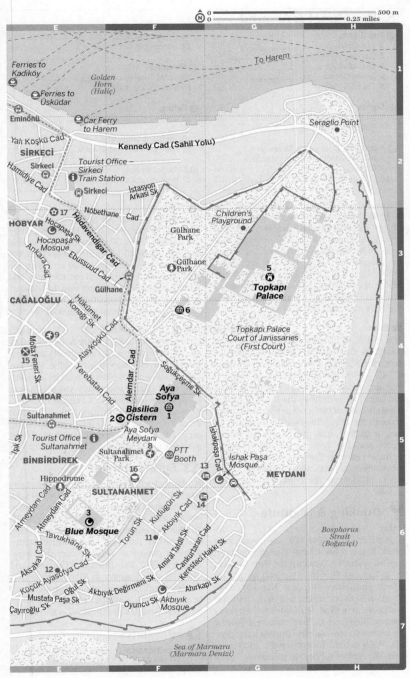

0 | 500 m
0 | 0.25 miles

Ferries to Kadıköy

Ferries to Üsküdar

Golden Horn (Haliç)

To Harem

Car Ferry to Harem

Seraglio Point

Eminönü

Yalı Köşkü Cad

Kennedy Cad (Sahil Yolu)

SİRKECİ

Sirkeci

Tourist Office – Sirkeci Train Station

Hamidiye Cad

Sirkeci

İstasyon Arkası Sk

Nöbethane Cad

HOBYAR

17

Hocapaşa Sk

Hocapaşa Mosque

Ankara Cad

Hüdavendigar Cad

Ebussuud Cad

Children's Playground

Gülhane Park

CAĞALOĞLU

Gülhane Park

Gülhane

Hükümet Konağı Sk

5

Topkapı Palace

9

Molla Fenari Sk

15

Alayköşkü Cad

Yerebatan Cad

Alemdar Cad

6

Soğukçeşme Sk

Topkapı Palace Court of Janissaries (First Court)

ALEMDAR

Aya Sofya

Sultanahmet

Basilica Cistern

2

1

Işık Sk

Tourist Office – Sultanahmet

Aya Sofya Meydanı

8

BİNBİRDİREK

Sultanahmet Park

PTT Booth

Ishak Paşa Mosque

16

13

MEYDANI

Hippodrome

SULTANAHMET

14

Atmeydanı Cad

Atmeydanı Cad

3

Kutlugün Sk

Bosphorus Strait (Boğaziçi)

Blue Mosque

Tavukhane Sk

11

Torun Sk

Akbıyık Cad

Amiral Tafdil Sk

Cankurtaran Cad

Keresteci Hakkı Sk

Aksakal Cad

12

Küçük Ayasofya Cad

Oğul Sk

Akbıyık Değirmeni Sk

Ahırkapı Sk

Mustafa Paşa Sk

Çayıroğlu Sk

Oyuncu Sk

Akbıyık Mosque

Sea of Marmara (Marmara Denizi)

Sultanahmet & Around

⏱ noon-midnight Mon-Fri, 3pm-midnight Sat; 🛜📶; 🚇 Tünel) Dishes from the southeastern city of Antakya (Hatay) are the speciality here. Cold and hot mezes are equally delicious, pides are flavoursome and the kebaps are exceptional – try the succulent *şiş et* (grilled lamb). The set menus of mezes and a choice of main dish (₺39 to ₺66) offer excellent value and there's a good range of Suvla wines by glass and bottle.

★ **Cuma** MODERN TURKISH €€€
(Map p1158; 🕿 0212-293 2062; www.cuma.cc; Çukurcuma Caddesi 53a, Çukurcuma; breakfast dishes ₺16-27, lunch dishes ₺25-40, dinner mains ₺27-45; ⏱ 9am-midnight Mon-Sat, to 8pm Sun; 🛜📶📶; 🚇 Taksim) Banu Tiryakioğulları's laid-back foodie oasis in the heart of Çukurcuma has one of the most devoted customer bases in the city. Tables are on the leafy terrace or in the atmospheric upstairs dining space, and the healthy, seasonally driven menu is heavy on flavour and light on fuss – breakfast is particularly delicious (regulars tend to share the *kahvaltı* – breakfast – plate).

🍷 **Drinking & Nightlife**

Unter BAR
(Map p1158; 🕿 0212-244 5151; www.unter.com.tr; Kara Ali Kaptan Sokak 4, Karaköy; ⏱ noon-midnight Tue-Thu, to 2am Fri, 9am-2am Sat, 9am-7pm Sun; 🛜; 🚇 Tophane) This cafe, bar and restaurant hybrid epitomises the new Karaköy style: it's glam without trying too hard, and has a vaguely arty vibe. Ground-floor windows open to the street in fine weather, allowing the action to spill outside during busy periods. Waiters tend to shift tables and chairs after the dinner service on weekends, opening the floor and laneway for dancing.

★ **Mikla** BAR
(Map p1158; 🕿 0212-293 5656; www.miklarestaurant.com; Marmara Pera Hotel, Meşrutiyet Caddesi 15, Tepebaşı; ⏱ 6-11.30pm Mon-Sat summer only; 🚇 Şişhane, 🚇 Tünel) It's worth overlooking the occasional bit of uppity service at this stylish rooftop bar to enjoy excellent cocktails and what could well be the best view in İstanbul. In winter the drinking action moves to the bar in the upmarket restaurant one floor down.

Derviş Cafe & Restaurant TEA GARDEN
(Map p1160; cnr Dalbastı Sokak & Kabasakal Caddesi; ⏱ 7am-midnight; 🚇 Sultanahmet) Superbly located directly opposite the Blue Mosque, the Derviş beckons patrons with its comfortable cane chairs and shady trees. Efficient service, reasonable prices and peerless people-watching opportunities make it a great place for a leisurely *çay* (₺4), *nargile* (water pipe; ₺35), *tost* (toasted sandwich; ₺10) and a game of backgammon.

☆ **Entertainment**

Hodjapasha Cultural Centre PERFORMING ARTS
(Map p1160; 🕿 0212-511 4626; www.hodjapasha.com; Hocapaşa Hamamı Sokak 3b, Sirkeci; performances adult ₺108-135, child under 12yr ₺80-92; 🚇 Sirkeci) Occupying a beautifully converted 550-year-old hamam, this cultural centre stages a one-hour whirling dervish performance at 7pm daily (Tuesday, Thursday and Saturday only January to March). Note that children under seven are not admitted, and be sure to switch off your phone, as readers have reported draconian crowd-control here.

ⓘ **Information**

American Hospital (Amerikan Hastenesi; 🕿 0212-444 3777, 0212-311 2000; www.americanhospitalistanbul.com; Güzelbahçe

Sokak 20, Nişantaşı; ⊘24hr; Ⓜ Osmanbey)
Private hospital with English-speaking staff and
a 24-hour emergency department.

Tourist Office – Sirkeci Train Station (Map
p1160; ☑ 0212-511 5888; Sirkeci Gar, Ankara
Caddesi, Sirkeci; ⊘ 9.30am-6pm mid-Apr–Sep,
9am-5pm Oct–mid-Apr; ⓟ Sirkeci) Maps and
brochures available.

ⓘ Getting There & Away

AIR

İstanbul Airport (IST, İstanbul Havalimanı;
☑ 444 1 442, WhatsApp 0 549 563 34 34; www.
igairport.com) is 42km northwest of Sultanahmet. İstanbul Airport opened in April 2019.

Sabiha Gökçen International Airport (SAW,
Sabiha Gökçen Havalimanı; ☑ 0216-588 8888;
www.sgairport.com) is 50km east, on the Asian
side of the city.

BOAT

Cruise ships currently arrive at a temporary
dock near the Fındıklı tram stop.

BUS

Büyük İstanbul Otogarı (Big İstanbul Bus Station; ☑ 0212-658 0505; www.otogaristanbul.
com), 10km northwest of Sultanahmet, is the
city's main otogar (bus station) and has buses
to towns and cities across the country, as well
as to European destinations.

Many bus companies offer a free *servis* (shuttle bus) to/from the otogar.

TRAIN

At the time of writing, the only international train
service to/from İstanbul was the nightly Sofia
Express. This was departing Halkali station at
10.40pm daily; ticket prices for seat only start
at ₺120. A transfer bus to Halkali departs from
Sirkeci Station at 9.30pm; the fare is included
in the İstanbul–Sofia (Bulgaria) ticket. You can
change in Sofia for Belgrade (Serbia) or in Dimitrovgrad and Gorna Oryahovitsa for Bucharest
(Romania).

A new fast train service to Ankara (from ₺70,
3½ hours) currently leaves, inconveniently, from
Pendik Station, 25km southeast of Kadıköy on
the Asian side of town.

Check **Turkish State Railways** (www.tcdd.
gov.tr) and **The Man in Seat Sixty-One** (www.
seat61.com/turkey2) for updates.

ⓘ Getting Around

Rechargeable **İstanbulkarts** (travel cards) can
be used on public transport citywide. Purchase
(₺10) and recharge them at kiosks and machines
at metro and tram stops, bus terminals and
ferry docks. If you're only using public transport
for a few city journeys, *jetons* (single-trip travel

HAMAMS: SQUEAKY-CLEAN THE TURKISH WAY

İstanbul's hamams may be pricey but
it's not often you get to soap-up amid
such historic finery. The following are
our top three Old City picks for sudsy relaxation after a long day of sightseeing:

Ayasofya Hürrem Sultan Hamamı
(Map p1160; ☑ 0212-517 3535; www.aya-
sofyahamami.com; Aya Sofya Meydanı 2;
bath treatments €80-160, massages €40-
75; ⊘ 8am-10pm; ⓟ Sultanahmet)

Çemberlitaş Hamamı (Map p1160;
☑ 0212-522 7974; www.cemberli-
tashamami.com; Vezir Han Caddesi 8, Çemberlitaş; self-service ₺140, bath, scrub &
soap massage ₺35; ⊘ men 6am-midnight,
women from 7.30am; ⓟ Çemberlitaş)

Cağaloğlu Hamamı (Map p1160;
☑ 0212-522 2424; www.cagalogluhamami.
com.tr; Prof Kazım İsmail Gürkan Caddesi
24; bath, scrub & massage packages
€40-120, self-service €30; ⊘ 9am-10pm;
ⓟ Sultanahmet)

---

tokens, ₺5) can be purchased from machines at
tram and metro stops.

BOAT

The most enjoyable way to get around town
is by ferry. Crossing between the Asian and
European shores, up and down the Golden
Horn and Bosphorus, and over to the Princes'
Islands, these vessels are as efficient as they
are popular with locals. Some are operated by
the government-owned İstanbul Şehir Hatları;
others by private companies, including **Dentur
Avrasya** (☑ 0216-444 6336; www.denturavra-
sya.com) and **Turyol** (☑ 0212-251 4421; www.
turyol.com). Timetables are posted at *iskelesi*
(ferry docks).

On the European side, the major ferry docks
are at the mouth of the Golden Horn (Eminönü
and Karaköy) and at Beşiktaş.

BUS

İstanbul's efficient bus system runs between
6am and midnight. You must have an İstan-
bulkart to use the buses. The major bus terminals are at Taksim Meydanı and at Beşiktaş,
Kabataş, Eminönü, Kadıköy and Üsküdar.

METRO

Metro services depart every five minutes between 6am and midnight. *Jetons* cost ₺5 and
İstanbulkarts can be used.

GETTING INTO İSTANBUL FROM THE AIRPORTS

İstanbul Airport (p1163) Havaist bus to Sultanahmet or Taksim (₺18); taxi ₺95 to Sultanahmet, ₺77 to Beyoğlu. At the time of writing, a new metro line to the airport was under construction.

Sabiha Gökçen International Airport (p1163) Havabüs bus to Taksim Meydanı (₺18, 3.30am to 1am), from where a funicular (₺5) and tram (₺5) travel to Sultanahmet; Havabüs bus to Kadıköy (₺14, 4am to 1am); taxi ₺175 to Sultanahmet and ₺165 to Beyoğlu.

TAXI

İstanbul is full of yellow taxis, all of them with meters – insist that drivers use them. It costs around ₺20 to travel between Beyoğlu and Sultanahmet.

TRAM & FUNICULAR

An excellent *tramvay* (tramway) service runs from Bağcılar, in the city's west, to Zeytinburnu and on to Sultanahmet and Eminönü. It then crosses the Galata Bridge to Karaköy (to connect with the Tünel funicular) and Kabataş (to connect with the funicular to Taksim Meydanı). A second service runs from Cevizlibağ, closer to Sultanahmet on the same line, through to Kabataş. Both services run every five minutes from 6am to midnight. The fare is ₺5; *jetons* are available from machines on every tram stop and İstanbulkarts can be used.

An antique tram rattles up and down İstiklal Caddesi between Tünel funicular station and Taksim Meydanı.

The one-stop Tünel funicular between Karaköy and the bottom of İstiklal Caddesi runs between 7am and 10.45pm. Another funicular runs from Kabataş (where it connects with the tram) up to the metro station at Taksim.

AEGEAN COAST

Gallipoli (Gelibolu) Peninsula

Antipodeans and many Brits won't need an introduction to Gallipoli; it's the backbone of the 'Anzac legend', in which an Allied campaign in 1915 to knock Turkey out of WWI and open a relief route to Russia turned into one of the war's greatest fiascos. Some 130,000 men died, roughly a third from Allied forces and the rest Turkish.

Today the battlefields are part of the **Gallipoli Historical National Park** and tens of thousands of Turks and foreigners alike come to pay their respects on pilgrimage every year. The Turkish officer responsible for the defence of Gallipoli was Mustafa Kemal (the future Atatürk); his victory is commemorated in Turkey on 18 March. On **Anzac Day** (25 April), a dawn service marks the anniversary of the Allied landings.

The easiest way to see the battlefields is with your own transport or on a tour from Çanakkale or Eceabat; try **Crowded House Tours** (☎0286-814 1565; www.crowdedhousegallipoli.com; Zubeyde Hanim Meydani 28, Eceabat).

If you want to sleep on the peninsula, options in Eceabat include hilltop **Hotel Casa Villa** (☎0286-814 1320; www.otelcasavilla.com; Çamburnu Sokak 75; r ₺160; ❄📶).

Çanakkale

☎0286 / POP 132,854

This sprawling harbour town has a fun and youthful vibe and would be worth visiting even if it didn't lie across the Dardanelles from the Gallipoli Peninsula and wasn't within easy day-tripping distance to Troy. After exploring these nearby sights, check out this university town's hip and alternative nightlife scene in the bars and cafes cramming the cobbled lanes around the five-storey Ottoman *saat kulesi* (clock tower), or go for a sunset stroll along the *kordon* (waterfront promenade).

Sleeping & Eating

Anzac Hotel HOTEL €€

(☎0286-217 7777; www.anzachotel.com; Saat Kulesi Meydanı 8; s/d/tr €30/35/40; P❄📶) An extremely professional management team ensures that this keenly priced hotel opposite the clock tower is well maintained and has high levels of service. Rooms are a good size, include tea- and coffee-making facilities and have double-glazed windows. The small bar on the mezzanine shows the movies *Gallipoli* and *Troy* nightly. Parking costs €3 per night.

★**Sardalya** SEAFOOD €

(Küçük Hamam Sokak 24b; fish sandwiches ₺7-10, fish & salad ₺11-19; ⏲11am-10pm Mon-Fri, 9am-10pm Sat, 9am-6pm Sun) On the corner of the Aynalı Çarşı, this no-frills place named in honour of a plentiful local fish (*sardalya* means sardine) serves everything from superfresh *balık ekmek* (fish sandwiches) to tasty plates of *midye tava* (fried mussels) or deep-fried fish. Sit at the counter on the street and chat with the locals between tasty mouthfuls, or order to go.

Cafe du Port INTERNATIONAL €€
(✆0286-217 2908; Yalı Caddesi 12; mains ₺22-28; ⊗8am-11pm) The restaurant at Hotel Limani is popular for good reason. The glass-fronted building on the *kordon* is stylish and inviting; the chefs are the most versatile in Çanakkale; and the service is brilliant. Specialities include steaks, salads, pastas and whatever else inspires the manager during his regular İstanbul sojourns. If nothing else, settle in for an end-of-day mojito.

ⓘ Getting There & Away

Regular buses go to İstanbul (₺60, six hours) and İzmir (₺59, 5¾ hours).

To Eceabat and the Gallipoli Peninsula there's an hourly ferry service (per person/car ₺3/35, 25 minutes) from the harbour dock.

Troy (Truva)

Not much remains of the great city of **Troy** (✆0286-283 0536; adult/child under 12yr ₺25/free; ⊗8.30am-7pm Apr-Oct, 8am-5pm Nov-Mar) and you'll have to use your imagination to envision the fateful day when the Greeks tricked the Trojans with their wooden horse. For history buffs and fans of Homer's *Iliad*, though, this is one of the most important stops on the Aegean.

The site is rather confusing for nonexpert eyes but the most conspicuous features, apart from the reconstruction of the **Trojan Horse**, include the **walls** from various periods; the Graeco-Roman **Temple of Athena**; the **Roman Odeon**; and the **Bouleuterion** (Council Chamber), built around Homer's time (c 800 BCE). The new state-of-the-art Troy archaeological museum is located nearby in the village of Tevfikiye.

Tour companies in Çanakkale and Eceabat offer half-day Troy tours (€35) and full-day Gallipoli battlefields and Troy excursions (around €75).

From Çanakkale, dolmuşes (minibuses) leave hourly to Troy (₺6, 35 minutes, between 9.30am and 5pm) from the Cuma Pazarı stop at the northern end of the bridge over the Çanakkale River.

Bergama (Pergamum)

✆0232 / POP 102.961

This workaday market town sits slap-bang below the remarkable ruins of Pergamum, site of ancient Rome's pre-eminent medical centre. During Pergamum's heyday (between Alexander the Great and the Roman domination of Asia Minor), it was one of the Middle East's richest and most powerful small kingdoms.

In town itself are the imposing remains of the **Red Hall** (Kızıl Avlu; Kınık Caddesi; ₺5; ⊗8am-6.30pm Apr-Sep, to 4.30pm Oct-Mar), a 2nd-century-CE temple dedicated to the Egyptian gods Serapis, Isis and Harpocrates. Upon the windswept hilltop, 5km from the Red Hall, and linked by a **cable car** (Bergama Akropolis Teleferik; ✆0232-631 0805; Akropol Caddesi; return ₺35; ⊗8am-7pm mid-Apr–Sep, 8.30am-5.30pm Oct–mid-Apr), is the **Acropolis** (Bergama Akropol; Akropol Caddesi 2; ₺35; ⊗8am-7pm mid-Apr–Sep, to 6.30pm Oct–mid-Apr), with its spectacular sloping theatre. The **Asklepion** (Prof Dr Frieldhelm Korte Caddesi 1; ₺30; ⊗8am-7pm Apr-Sep, to 6.30pm Oct-Mar), 2.5km uphill from town, was Pergamum's famed medical centre. The work Greek physician Galen did here in the 2nd century was the basis for Western medicine well into the 16th century. Back in town, **Bergama Archaeology Museum** (Bergama Müze Müdürlüğü; ✆0232-483 5117; Cumhuriyet Caddesi 6; ₺6; ⊗8am-7pm Apr-Oct, 8.30am-4.30pm Nov-Mar) has a small but impressive collection of artefacts.

Odyssey Guesthouse (✆0232-631 3501; www.odysseyguesthouse.com; Abacıhan Sokak 13; dm/s/d/tr €6/16/22/29, s/d without bathroom €10/17; ⊗closed Jan–mid-Feb; ❄🛜) has superb views of the archaeological sites, while **Aristonicus Boutique Hotel** (✆0232-632 4141; Taksim Caddesi 37; s/d/tw/tr & q €30/55/55/65; 🅿❄🛜) occupies two converted old stone houses.

Regular buses run to İzmir (₺10, two hours) and Çanakkale (₺30-35, 4½ hours), and there are nightly buses to Ankara (₺85, 8½ hours).

İzmir

✆0232 / POP 2.93 MILLION

Turkey's third-largest city is a sprawling harbourside hub with a proud history as one of the Mediterranean's cosmopolitan trading metropolises when it was known as Smyrna. Head to the ruins of the Roman **agora** (Agora

Caddesi; ₺10; ⊘ 8am-7pm mid-Apr–Sep, 8.30am-6.30pm Oct–mid-Apr; Ⓜ Çankaya) to see one of İzmir's few reminders of its grand past, and leave time for the rich repository of ancient artefacts at **İzmir Museum of History & Art** (İzmir Tarih ve Sanat Müzesi; ☑ 0232-445 6818; near Montrö Meydanı entrance, Kültürpark; ₺6; ⊘ 8am-7pm mid-Apr–Sep, 8.30am-6pm Oct–mid-Apr; ☐ 12, 253, Ⓜ Basmane). Afterwards sniff out a bargain (or five) within **Kemeraltı Market** (Kemeraltı Çarşısı; ⊘ 8am-7pm Mon-Sat; Ⓜ Çankaya, Konak), then soak up the city's energetic modern pulse along the *kordon* (waterfront promenade) and amid the student nightlife haunts of Alsancak district.

🛏 Sleeping & Eating

InHouse Hostel   HOSTEL €
(☑ 0232-404 0014; www.inhousehostel.com; 1460 Sokak 75, Alsancak; dm €9.50-12.75, d with shared bathroom €38; ✳ @ ᗰ; ☐ 12, 253, ᖴ Alsancak) Opened in 2015, this hostel offers 56 beds in private rooms and in cramped dorms sleeping between three and 10. Dorms have under-bed lockers, hard bunk beds and clean but limited shared bathrooms. There's 24-hour reception, a kitchen for common use, a small foyer lounge and an entertainment program predominantly consisting of nightly pub crawls. The Alsancak location is excellent.

★ **Swissôtel Büyük Efes**   HOTEL €€
(☑ 0232-414 0000; www.swissotel.com/hotels/izmir; Gazi Osmanpaşa Bulvarı 1; standard/executive r from €95/135; Ⓟ ✳ @ ᗰ ☲; Ⓜ Çankaya) Guests here have been known not to leave the premises at all during their city stay. Frankly, we're not at all surprised. Rooms are comfortable and well appointed, but it's the hotel's gorgeous garden and impressive facilities that are the real attraction. These include indoor and outdoor swimming pools, tennis court, spa, gym and rooftop bar with panoramic bay views.

★ **Ayşa**   TURKISH €
(☑ 0232-484 1525; Abacıoğlu Han, Anafartalar Caddesi 228, Kemeraltı Market; meze plates ₺9-10, portions from ₺10; ⊘ 8am-6pm Mon-Sat; Ⓜ; Ⓜ Konak, Çankaya) Serving Bosnian food that is remarkably similar to Turkish home cooking, this stylish *lokanta* (eatery with ready-made food) in the pretty Abacıoğlu Han offers both indoor and outdoor seating. Choose from the DIY meze display (yum!) and be sure to snaffle a piece of *börek* (filled pastry) if it's on offer. Main dishes are displayed in the bain-marie and include both meat and vegetable choices.

ℹ Getting There & Away

BUS

Bus company ticket offices mostly cluster on Dokuz Eylül Meydanı in Basmane. They usually provide a free *servis* to/from İzmir's mammoth otogar, 6.5km from the centre. Buses head to points across the country including frequent services to Bergama (₺15, two hours), Bodrum (₺40, three to 3½ hours) and Selçuk (₺10, one hour).

TRAIN

Most intercity services arrive at/depart from **Basmane station** (Basmane Gar). For northern or eastern Turkey, change at Ankara or Konya.

Six daily trains travel to Selçuk from Basmane station (₺6.50, 1½ hours) between 7.45am and 6.15pm.

There is one daily train to Ankara (₺44, 14 hours), leaving Basmane at 6.05pm and travelling via Eskişehir (₺40.50, 12 hours).

There is one daily train to Konya (₺43, 12½ hours), leaving Basmane at 8.15pm.

Selçuk

☑ 0232 / POP 35,991

This chilled-out provincial town is just the ticket if you want to take a break from your travels for a couple of days. The monumental ruins of Ephesus sit right on its doorstep, storks nest atop a preserved Roman-Byzantine aqueduct that runs right through the middle of town, and the quaint village vibe of the centre is complemented by a scattering of interesting sights hidden down the cobblestone lanes.

⊙ Sights

Ephesus Museum   MUSEUM
(☑ 0232-892 6010; Uğur Mumcu Sevgi Yolu Caddesi; ₺15; ⊘ 8am-9pm mid-Apr–Oct, 8.30am-6.30pm Nov–mid-Apr) An essential stop on every Ephesus itinerary, this small museum contains artefacts from the ancient city, including scales, jewellery and cosmetic boxes as well as coins, funerary goods and ancient statuary. Highlights include the famous phallic terracotta effigy of Bes in **room 2**, the huge statue of a resting warrior in **room 4** and the two extraordinary multibreasted marble statues of Artemis in **room 7**. The timelines on the walls are extremely useful for placing objects within their historical context.

Basilica of St John   CHURCH
(Aziz Yahya Kilisesi; St Jean Caddesi; incl Ayasuluk Fortress ₺10; ⊘ 8am-7pm Apr-Oct, to 5pm Nov-Mar) Despite a century of restoration, the once-great basilica built by Byzantine Emperor

EPHESUS (EFES)

Ephesus (Efes; www.ephesus.us; main site adult/child ₺60/free, Terraced Houses ₺30, parking ₺7.50; ☺8am-7pm Apr-Oct, to 5pm Nov-Mar) is a dazzlingly complete classical metropolis, once the capital of the Roman province of Asia Minor. A trip here is the closest you'll get to being able to conjure up daily life in the Roman age. There is a wealth of monuments to explore, but don't miss the following:

Curetes Way Named for the demigods who helped Lena give birth to Artemis and Apollo, the Curetes Way was Ephesus' main thoroughfare, 210m long and lined with statuary, religious and civic buildings, and rows of shops selling incense, silk and other goods, workshops and even restaurants.

Library of Celsus This magnificent library dating from the early 2nd century CE, the best-known monument in Ephesus, has been extensively restored. Originally built as part of a complex, the library looks bigger than it actually is: the convex facade base heightens the central elements, while the middle columns and capitals are larger than those at the ends. Facade niches hold replica statues of the Four Virtues. From left to right, they are Sophia (Wisdom), Arete (Goodness), Ennoia (Thought) and Episteme (Knowledge).

Temple of Hadrian One of Ephesus' star attractions and second only to the Library of Celsus, this ornate, Corinthian-style temple honours Trajan's successor and originally had a wooden roof when completed in 138 CE. Note its main arch; supported by a central keystone, this architectural marvel remains perfectly balanced, with no need for mortar. The temple's designers also covered it with intricate decorative details and patterns: Tyche, goddess of chance, adorns the first arch, while Medusa wards off evil spirits on the second.

Great Theatre Originally built under Hellenistic King Lysimachus, the Great Theatre was reconstructed by the Romans between 41 and 117 CE and it is thought St Paul preached here. However, they incorporated original design elements, including the ingenious shape of the *cavea* (seating area), part of which was under cover. Seating rows are pitched slightly steeper as they ascend, meaning that upper-row spectators still enjoyed good views and acoustics – useful, considering that the theatre could hold an estimated 25,000 people.

Dolmuşes (minibuses that stop anywhere along their prescribed route) serve the Lower Gate (₺3) every 10 minutes. A taxi to/from either gate costs about ₺20. Selçuk is roughly a 3.5km walk from both entrances.

Justinian (r 527–565) remains a skeleton of its former self. Nonetheless, it is an atmospheric site with excellent hilltop views, and the best place in the area for a sunset photo. The information panels and scale model highlight the building's original grandeur, as do the marble steps and monumental gate.

Ayasuluk Fortress   FORTRESS
(Ayasuluk Kalesi; St Jean Caddesi; incl Basilica of St John ₺10; ☺8am-5pm Apr-Oct, to 4pm Nov-Mar) Selçuk's crowning achievement is accessed on the same ticket as the Basilica of St John, once the citadel's principal structure. Earlier and extensive excavations here, concluded in 1998 after a quarter century, proved that there were castles on Ayasuluk Hill going back beyond the original Ephesian settlement to the Neolithic age. The fortress' partially restored remains, about 350m north of the church, date from Byzantine, Seljuk and Ottoman times and are well worth a visit.

🛏 Sleeping & Eating

Homeros Pension   PENSION €
(☑0507 715 7848, 0232-892 3995; www.homeros pension.com; 1048 Sokak 3; tw/d/tr €23/24/32; ❄️🛜) This long-time, family-run favourite offers 10 rooms in two buildings. The decor features colourful hanging textiles and handcrafted furniture made by owner Derviş, a carpenter, antiques collector and ultra-welcoming host. Enjoy some of the best views in town on the roof terraces (one at each house). The six rooms in the newer (main) building are the nicest.

★**Boomerang Guesthouse**   GUESTHOUSE €€
(☑0534 055 4761, 0232-892 4879; www.ephesus boomerangguesthouse.com; 1047 Sokak 10; dm/ s/d/f €10/40/55/80, s/d with shared bathroom €20/30; ❄️@🛜) People keep coming back to this welcoming Turkish/Australian-Chinese operation to spend chilled-out evenings

among the trees in the stone courtyard with its popular bar-restaurant. The best of the 10 rooms have balconies (ie Nos 13 and 14); all have kettles and fridges. The windowless basement dorm has 12 single beds, shares two bathrooms and has fans rather than air-con.

❶ Getting There & Away

At least six buses head to İstanbul (₺110, 10 hours) daily and there are frequent services to İzmir (₺10, one hour). For Pamukkale and destinations along the Mediterranean coast, you usually have to change buses at Denizli (₺35, three hours).

Eight trains head to İzmir (₺6.50, 1½ hours) daily via the city's Adnan Menderes Airport, and to Denizli (₺16.50, three hours). Note that the train's airport stop is a 20-minute walk from the departures terminal.

Pamukkale

📞 0258 / POP 2041

Inland from Selçuk is one of Turkey's premier natural wonders. Pamukkale's surreal hillside cascade of gleaming white calcite **travertines** (adult/child ₺35/free incl Hierapolis; ⊙8am-9pm mid-Apr–Sep, 8.30am-5pm Oct–mid-Apr), enclosing turquoise pools, has been a tourist attraction since the classical age. On the summit, the ruins of the ancient spa resort of **Hierapolis** (adult/child ₺35/free incl travertines; ⊙8am-9pm mid-Apr–Sep, 8.30am-5pm Oct–mid-Apr) lay testament to this area's enduring appeal.

The attendant farming turned tourist village is less impressive, so aim to pass straight through between Selçuk and the Mediterranean, or spend just one night if you'd like to experience the travertines at sunset. **Beyaz Kale Pension** (📞 0258-272 2064; www.beyaz kalepension.com; Oguzkaan Caddesi 4; s/d/tr/f €19/22/30/42; ❄️🛜🏊) has 10 spotless rooms on two floors, with some of the best local pension fare served on the relaxing rooftop terrace, and **Melrose House** (📞0258-272 2250; www.melrosehousehotel.com; Vali Vekfi Ertürk Caddesi 8; s/d €25/€28; ❄️🛜🏊) is the closest thing to a boutique hotel in Pamukkale.

Most services to/from Pamukkale involve changing in Denizli. Bus companies may provide a free *servis* from Denizli otogar to Pamukkale's main square. Otherwise, there are frequent dolmuşes (₺4, 30 minutes) between Pamukkale and Denizli otogar.

The convenient **Selçuk-Fethiye Bus** (📞0543-779 4732; www.selcukfethiyebus.com; ₺100) links Fethyie and Pamukkale. Trans-

port leaves Fethiye at 9.30am, arriving at Pamukkale at 1pm, before returning to Fethiye from Pamukkale at 4pm.

Bodrum

📞 0252 / POP 103,168

The beating heart of Turkey's holiday-resort peninsula, Bodrum hums with action during the summer months. Its natty whitewashed cottages all sporting blue trims are a post-card-maker's dream while the harbour is a hive for yachties and travellers alike.

Bodrum Castle   CASTLE
(Bodrum Kalesi; 📞0252-316 1095; www.bodrum-museum.com; İskele Meydanı) There are splendid views from the battlements of Bodrum's magnificent castle, built by the Knights Hospitaller in the early 15th century and dedicated to St Peter. In recent years it has housed the **Museum of Underwater Archaeology** (Sualtı Arkeoloji Müzesi), arguably the most important museum of its type in the world.

🛏 Sleeping

Kaya Apart & Pansiyon   PENSION €
(📞0535 737 7060; www.kayapansiyon.com.tr; Eski Hükümet Sokak 10; s/d ₺180/250; ⊙Apr-Oct; ❄️🛜) One of Bodrum's better pensions, the very central Kaya has 12 clean, simple rooms plus a studio apartment with hairdryer, safe and TV; six rooms count a balcony as well. There is a roof terrace with a castle view for breakfast, a flowering courtyard with a bar for lounging, and helpful owners Mustafa and Selda can arrange activities.

★**El Vino Hotel**   BOUTIQUE HOTEL €€
(📞0252-313 8770; www.elvinobodrum.com; Pamili Sokak; r/ste from €100/150; ❄️🛜🏊) This beautiful 'urban resort' with 31 rooms is contained in several stone buildings spread over an enormous garden in the backstreets of Bodrum that you'd never know was there. Try for a room with views of both the pool/garden and the sea (eg room 303). The rooftop restaurant is one of the best hotel ones in Bodrum. Great off-season rates.

🍴 Eating & Drinking

The loud bars and clubs of **Bar Street** (Dr Alim Bey Caddesi and Cumhuriyet Caddesi) get packed during summer nights. A more refined nightspot to rub shoulders with the

Turkish glitterati would be **White House** ([📱]0536 889 2066; www.facebook.com/WhiteHouse Bodrum; Cumhuriyet Caddesi 147; ⊘9am-5am).

Nazik Ana TURKISH €
([📱]0252-313 1891; www.nazikanarestaurant.com; Eski Hükümet Sokak 5; mezes ₺9-12, portion ₺14-18, pides ₺15-25; ⊘8.30am-11pm) This simple, back-alley place has a folksy, rustic decor. It offers hot and cold prepared dishes, viewable *lokanta*-style at the front counter, allowing you to sample different Turkish traditional dishes at shared tables. You can also order pides (Turkish-style pizzas) and *köfte* (meatballs). It gets busy with workers at lunchtime, offering one of Bodrum's most authentic and friendly eating experiences.

★ Kalamare SEAFOOD €€
([📱]0252-316 7076; www.facebook.com/kalamare 48; Sanat Okulu Sokak 9; mezes ₺10-15, mains ₺20-38; ⊘noon-1am) Though a bit cramped and inland, this distressed-looking place, with whitewashed tables and pastel-coloured walls, is one of our favourite seafood restaurants in Bodrum. Serving octopus, calamari, sea bass et al (as well as meat dishes for ichthyophobes), Kalamare attracts a cool young crowd, who hold court beneath the extravagant, Gaudí-style chimney.

❶ Getting There & Away

Bodrum otogar has numerous services including two buses daily to Antalya (₺70, six hours); four to İstanbul (₺120, 12 hours); and hourly buses to İzmir (₺40, 3½ hours).

Daily year-round ferries link Bodrum with Kos in Greece (one way/return from €17/19, 45 minutes). There are also Saturday and Sunday ferries to Rhodes (one way/return from €40/80, two hours) from August to mid-September. For information and tickets, contact the **Bodrum Ferryboat Association** (Bodrum Feribot İşletmeciliği; [📱]0252-316 0882; www.bodrumferryboat.com; Kale Caddesi 22; ⊘8am-7pm May-Sep, to 6pm Oct-Apr).

MEDITERRANEAN COAST

Fethiye

[📱]0252 / POP 98,799

The 1958 earthquake destroyed most of the ancient city of Telmessos, but the vibrant town of Fethiye – which rose in its place – is now the hub of the western Mediterranean. Its natural harbour, in a broad bay scattered with dinky

Acclaimed as one of the world's top-10 long-distance walks, the **Lycian Way** follows signposted paths around the Teke Peninsula to Antalya. The 500km route leads through pine and cedar forests beneath mountains rising almost 3000m, past villages, stunning coastal views and an embarrassment of ruins at Lycian cities. For those who don't have plenty of time to trek the entire trail, it can easily be walked in individual sections.

islands, is one of the finest in the region, and the town's lively vibe makes it an excellent base for forays both on and off the water.

◉ Sights & Activities

Tomb of Amyntas TOMB
(117 Sokak; ₺5; ⊘9am-7pm) Fethiye's most recognisable sight is the mammoth Tomb of Amyntas, an Ionic temple facade carved into a sheer rock face in 350 BCE, in honour of 'Amyntas son of Hermapias'. Located south of the centre, it is best visited at sunset. Other, smaller rock tombs lie about 500m to the east.

Fethiye Museum MUSEUM
([📱]0252-614 1150; www.lycianturkey.com/fethiye-museum.htm; 505 Sokak; ₺5; ⊘9am-7pm mid-Apr–mid-Oct, 8am-5pm mid-Oct–mid-Apr) Focusing on Lycian finds from Telmessos as well as the ancient settlements of Tlos and Kaunos, this small museum exhibits pottery, jewellery, small statuary and votive stones (including the important Grave Stelae and the Stelae of Promise). Its most prized significant possession, however, is the so-called **Trilingual Stele** from Letoön, dating from 338 BCE, which was used partly to decipher the Lycian language with the help of ancient Greek and Aramaic.

12-Island Tour Excursion Boats BOATING
(per person incl lunch ₺125-240; ⊘9.30am-6.30pm mid-Apr–Oct) Many visitors not joining the longer Blue Voyages opt for the 12-Island Tour, a day-long boat trip around Fethiye Körfezi (Fethiye Bay). The boats usually stop at five or six islands and cruise by the rest, but either way it's a great way to experience the coastline.

🛏 Sleeping & Eating

Most accommodation is up the hill behind the two Karagözler marinas.

TURKEY FETHIYE

BLUE VOYAGE

Fethiye is the hub of Turkey's cruising scene, and the most popular route is the 'Blue Voyage' *(Mavi Yolculuk)* to Olympos: a four-day, three-night journey on a *gület* (Turkish yacht). Boats usually call in at Ölüdeniz and Butterfly Valley and stop at Kaş, Kalkan and/or Kekova, with the final night at Gökkaya Bay opposite the eastern end of Kekova.

Prices vary by season; in summer they range from around €200 to €350 including food (but water, soft drinks and alcohol are extra). Thoroughly check out your operator before signing up – shoddy companies abound selling Blue Voyage trips with bad food, crews that speak no English and added extras that never materialise. Many people who end up disappointed have bought their trip from an agency in İstanbul; hold off on booking until you get to Fethiye. These owner-operated outfits run a tight ship:

Alaturka (☑0252-612 5423; www.alaturkacruises.com; Fevzi Çakmak Caddesi 29b; 3-night cruise per person from €225)

Before Lunch Cruises (☑0535 636 0076; www.beforelunch.com; Kordon Gezi Yolu; 3-night cruise per person €350)

V-GO Yachting & Travel (☑0252-612 2113; www.bluecruisesturkey.com; 3-night cruise €220; ⊙8.30am-11.30pm)

Duygu Pension   PENSION €€
(☑0252-614 3563, 0535 796 6701; www.duygu pension.com; 16 Sokak 54; s/d/tr €25/30/32; P✿❄@❋☼) Cute as a button, this warm and welcoming family-run pension near the Karagözler 2 marina has 11 homely rooms brightened by colourful wall stencils and frilly touches, while the rooftop terrace has blinding sea views. Birol is your man and a great source of information.

★**Hotel Unique**   BOUTIQUE HOTEL €€€
(☑0252-612 1145; www.hoteluniqueturkey.com; 30 Sokak 43a; r from €72; P✿❄☼☼) Opened in 2014, this stone building with colourful shutters seems considerably older, offering a contemporary seaside take on Ottoman-village chic. The service and attention to detail are impressive, with wooden beams, floors and hand-carved doors from Black Sea houses in the rooms, and pebbles from the beach in the bathroom floors.

★**Fish Market**   SEAFOOD €€
(Balık Pazarı, Balık Halı; Hal ve Pazar Yeri, btwn Hükümet & Belediye Caddesis; ⊙11am-10pm) This circle of fishmongers ringed by restaurants is Fethiye's most atmospheric eating experience: buy fresh fish (per kilo ₺10 to ₺35) and calamari (₺45), take it to a restaurant to have them cook it, and watch the fishmongers competing for attention with the waiter-touts, flower sellers and roaming *fasıl* (gypsy music) buskers.

Meğri Lokantası   TURKISH €€
(☑0252-614 4046; www.megrirestaurant.com; Çarşı Caddesi 26; dishes ₺12-60; ⊙9.30am-11:30pm; ☑) Looking for us at lunchtime in Fethiye? We're usually here. You can pick a meaty grill off the (more expensive) menu but do as the locals do: head inside and mix and match a plate (large mixed plate ₺20) from their glass counter display of hearty, homestyle vegetable and meat dishes. It's pretty much all delicious.

ℹ Information

The **tourist office** (☑0252-614 1527; İskele Meydanı; ⊙8am-noon & 1-5.30pm) is opposite the marina.

ℹ Getting There & Away

Fethiye's **otogar** (Fethiye Bus Station; İnönü Bulvarı) is 2.5km east of the centre. Buses head to Antalya (₺42, six hours) via Kaş (₺21, two hours) at least hourly.

Local dolmuşes for Ölüdeniz (₺5.50, 25 minutes), Kayaköy (₺4.50, 20 minutes) and surrounding villages leave from the dolmuş stop near the new mosque just off Atatürk Caddesi in the centre.

Catamarans sail daily to Rhodes in Greece (one way/return from €50/80, 1½ hours) from Fethiye pier, opposite the tourist office.

Patara

☑0242 / POP 776

There's always plenty of room to throw down your towel on Turkey's longest uninterrupted beach. Patara has 18km of sandy shore to stretch out on, and when you've finished with sun and sandcastles, the remnants of **Ancient Patara** (incl Patara Beach ₺20; ⊙8am-7pm mid-Apr–Sep, 8am-6pm Oct–mid-Apr) sprawl along the beach access road. If those ruins aren't enough, Patara is also within easy day-tripping distance to more ancient Lycian cities, including **Letoön** (admission ₺10; ⊙ 9am-7pm mid-Apr–Sep, 8am-5pm Oct–mid-Apr), which has three temples dedicated to Apollo, Artemis and Leto, and impressive **Xanthos** (☑ 0242-247 7660; admission ₺12; ⊙ 8.30am-6.30pm mid-Apr–Sep, 8.30am-5pm Oct–mid-Apr, ticket office shuts 30min before closure), with a Roman theatre and Lycian pillar tombs.

All the accommodation is in the postage-stamp-sized village of Gelemiş, 1.5km from the beachfront. **Akay Pension** (☑ 0532 410 2195, 0242-843 5055; www.pataraakaypension.com; s/d/tr/apt €25/36/45/65; P ⊜ ❄ 🛜 🛏) and **Flower Pension** (☑ 0242-843 5164; www.pataraflowerpension.com; s/d/tr/apt €24/33/40/75; P ⊜ ❄ @ 🛜 🛏) both have well-maintained rooms and balconies overlooking citrus groves.

Buses on the Fethiye–Kaş route drop you on the highway 3.5km from the village. From here dolmuşes run to the village (₺3) every 30 to 40 minutes between May and October.

Kaş

☑ 0242 / POP 7801

While other Mediterranean towns bank on their beaches for popularity, Kaş is all about adventure activities. This is Turkey's diving centre and a bundle of kayaking, hiking and boating trips are also easily organised here. It's a mellow kind of place with a squiggle of old town lanes wrapping around the small harbour, which is dominated by the craggy Greek island of Meis (Kastellorizo) just offshore.

⊙ Sights & Activities

Antiphellos Ruins RUINS

FREE Antiphellos was a small settlement and the port for Phellos, the much larger Lycian town further north in the hills. Its small Hellenistic **theatre** (Hastane Caddesi) FREE, 500m west of the main square, could seat 4000 spectators and is in very good condition. You can also walk to the **rock tombs** (Likya Caddesi) cut into the sheer cliffs above town, which are illuminated at night. The walk is strenuous so go at a cool time of day.

Dragoman OUTDOORS

(☑ 0242-836 3614; www.dragoman-turkey.com; Uzun Çarşı Sokak 15; 1-dive/6-dive pack €26/148, sea-kayaking tours €29-55; ⊙ 9am-9pm) This dynamic outdoor activities centre has built a reputation for its diving with professional and knowledgeable dive instructors. Its outdoor activities include sea kayaking day and multiday tours exploring the coast around Kekova and further afield, excellent hiking and mountain-biking trips, and SUP. For something more relaxing, there are also full-day boat trips tootling around the Kekova area (€50).

Bougainville Travel OUTDOORS

(☑ 0242-836 3737; www.bougainville-turkey.com; İbrahim Serin Caddesi 10) This reputable English-Turkish tour operator has much experience in organising any number of activities and tours, including Kekova island boat tours (€40), canyoning (€50), mountain biking (€40), tandem paragliding (€65 for flight lasting 20 to 30 minutes), scuba diving (€20 for one dive including equipment, €30 for a sample dive and €300 for a PADI course) and sea kayaking (€35).

🛏 Sleeping & Eating

⭐ **Hideaway Hotel** HOTEL €€

(☑ 0546 836 1887; www.hotelhideaway.com; Anfitiyatro Sokak 7; s/ste €46/76, d €57-66; P ⊜ ❄ @ 🛜 🛏) Run by the unstoppable Ahmet, a fount of local information, this lovely hotel has large, airy rooms (some with sea views) with a fresh white-on-white minimalist feel and gleaming modern bathrooms. There's a pool for cooling off and a chilled-out roof terrace that's the venue for morning yoga and sundowners at the bar with Meis views.

Ateş Pension PENSION €€

(☑ 0532 492 0680, 0242-836 1393; www.atespensionkas.com; Anfitiyatro Sokak 3; dm/s/d/tr/f €14/30/35/45/50; P ⊜ ❄ 🛜) Offering four-bed dorms and private rooms in two buildings, 'Hot Pension' is a cut above Kaş's other pensions, with snug duvets and modern bathrooms. Owners Recep and Ayşe are super-friendly hosts and serve Turkish feasts (₺30) and breakfasts of 55 items on the partly covered roof terrace, which is a relaxing lounge with a book exchange and partial sea views.

Bi Lokma ANATOLIAN €€

(☑ 0242-836 3942; www.bilokma.com.tr; Hükümet Caddesi 2; mains ₺22-40; ⊙ 8am-midnight; 🌱) Also known as 'Mama's Kitchen', this place has green tables in a terraced garden high above the harbour. The 'mama' in question is Sabo, whose daughters have taken the culinary baton, turning out traditional Turkish soul food, including excellent meze and their famous house *mantı* (Turkish ravioli) and *börek* (filled pastry).

ℹ Getting There & Away

The otogar is along Atatürk Bulvarı, 350m north of the centre. Dolmuşes leave half-hourly to Antalya (₺30, 3½ hours) via Olympos (₺15, 2½ hours). Buses to Fethiye (₺22, 2½ hours) leave every two hours.

Ferries to Meis (Kastellorizo; same-day return €25, 20 minutes) leave daily at 10am and return at 4pm. Buy tickets at the **Meis Express** (☑ 0242-836 1725; www.meisexpress.com; Cumhuriyet Meydanı; ◷ 8.30am-7pm) office near the harbour.

Olympos & Çıralı
☑ 0242

The tiny beach hamlets of Olympos and Çıralı are where you head if you're looking for days of beach action. Olympos is an old hippy hang-out with an all-night-party reputation in summer. The vine-covered ancient **Olympos ruins** (☑ 0242-247 7660; Olympos; incl Olympos Beach ₺20, parking ₺4; ◷ 8am-7pm mid-Apr–Sep, 8am-6pm Oct–mid-Apr) line the dirt track to the beach.

A couple of kilometres down the beach is more sedate Çıralı, where a clutch of pensions sit back from the sand and life is simplified to a choice between swinging in a hammock or sunning yourself on the beach.

In the evening, trips to the famed **Chimaera** (₺6; ◷ 24hr), a cluster of natural flames on the slopes of Mt Olympos, are the major activity. At night the 20-odd flames are visible at sea. Most Olympos accommodation runs nightly tours (it's around 7km from Olympos) or you can follow the signs 3.5km up the hill from Çıralı.

🛏 Sleeping & Eating

Olympos's 'tree house' camps, which line the track along the valley down to the ruins, have long been the stuff of travel legend. The 'tree houses' are actually rustic, platformed bungalows, and accommodation prices generally include breakfast and dinner. Most camps also offer bungalows with en suite.

Çıralı has better sleeping and eating options, from rustic pensions to beachfront lodges, and free access to Olympos Beach.

★ **Şaban Pension**　　　　BUNGALOW €
(☑ 0242-892 1265; www.sabanpansion.com; Yazırköyü, Olympos; incl half-board dm €9, bungalows s/d/tr €24/33/43, tree houses without bathroom s/d

€19/24; P ⊝ ❄ 🛜) Our personal favourite, this is the place to lounge in a hammock in the orchard or on a wooden platform by the stream enjoying sociable owner Meral's home cooking. Şaban isn't a party spot; it's a tranquil getaway where relaxed conversations strike up around the bonfire at night. Accommodation is in charming cabins and tree houses.

Orange Motel　　　　PENSION €€
(☑ 0242-825 7328; www.orangemotel.net; Yanartaş Yolu, Çıralı; s/d/tr €50/60/75, bungalows €70-90; P ⊝ ❄ 🛜) In the middle of an orange grove, the Orange feels like a farm despite its central location. Come here in spring and you'll never forget the overwhelming scent and buzz of bees. The garden is hung with hammocks, rooms are veritable wooden suites and there's a house travel agency. Breakfast features homemade orange and lemon marmalades and orange-blossom honey.

ℹ Getting There & Away

Buses and dolmuşes plying the Fethiye–Antalya coast road will stop at the Olympos and Çıralı junctions. From there, dolmuşes serve Olympos (10km) half-hourly from 8am to 8pm between May and October; and Çıralı (7km) roughly hourly in summer. Outside these months, ring your guesthouse beforehand to check dolmuş times or organise a pickup.

Antalya
☑ 0242 / POP 1.17 MILLION

The cultural capital of the Mediterranean, Antalya is a bustling modern city with a wonderfully preserved historic core. The old town of Kaleiçi is an atmospheric maze of Ottoman architecture, Roman ruins and Seljuk hamams, leading to an impressive harbour beneath a soaring cliff topped with cafes and bars – all overlooked by the snow-capped Beydağları (Bey Mountains). Just outside town, a clutch of dazzling ancient ruins sit on craggy slopes in easy reach for day trippers, providing another reason to dally here.

👁 Sights

★ **Antalya Museum**　　　　MUSEUM
(☑ 0242-247 7660; Konyaaltı Caddesi; ₺30; ◷ 8am-7pm mid-Apr–Oct, to 6pm Nov–mid-Apr) Do not miss this comprehensive museum with exhibitions covering everything from the Stone and Bronze Ages to Byzantium. The Hall of Regional Excavations exhibits finds from ancient cities in Lycia (such as

Patara and Xanthos) and Phrygia, while the Hall of Gods displays beautiful and evocative statues of 15 Olympian gods, many in excellent condition. Most of the statues were found at Perge, including the sublime Three Graces and the towering Dancing Woman dominating the first room.

Yivli Minare
HISTORIC SITE

(Fluted Minaret; Cumhuriyet Caddesi) This handsome and distinctive 'fluted' minaret, erected by Seljuk Sultan Aladdin Keykubad I in the early 13th century, is Antalya's symbol. The adjacent mosque (1373) is still in use.

🛏 Sleeping

★ White Garden Pansion
PENSION €€

(✆ 0242-241 9115; https://white-garden-pansion. antalyahotel.org; Hesapçı Geçidi 9; s/d ₺190/245; ❄ ❄ @ 🏠 🌐) A positively delightful place to stay, combining quirky Ottoman character, modern rooms with an old-world veneer, and excellent service from Metin and team. The building itself is a fine restoration and the courtyard is particularly charming with its large pool. The breakfast also gets top marks.

Tuvana Hotel
BOUTIQUE HOTEL €€€

(✆ 0242-247 6015; www.tuvanahotel.com; Karanlık Sokak 18; s/d from ₺489/611; P ❄ ❄ @ 🏠 🌐) This discreet compound of six Ottoman houses has been stylishly converted into a refined city hotel with 47 rooms and suites. The plush rooms have a historic feel, with varnished floorboards, rugs and wall hangings, plus mod-cons such as DVD players and safes. The swimming pool is a bonus and there are three on-site restaurants: Seraser (www.seraserrestaurant.com; mains ₺25-55; ⊙ noon-midnight), Il Vicino and Pio.

🍴 Eating & Drinking

For cheap eating, walk east to the Dönercil-er Çarşısı (Market of Döner Makers; İnönü Caddesi; mains ₺12-30; ⊙ 11am-11pm).

ÇaY-Tea's
CAFE €

(✆ 0542 233 4464; Hıdırlık Sokak 3; mains ₺20; ⊙ 10am-11pm Sun-Fri, to 11.30pm Sat; 🍴) Çay and coffee are served with ribbon-wrapped shortbread and a posy of fake flowers at this eclectic Dutch-Turkish cafe, where vintage furniture spills into the street and a wine cellar houses an inviting country-kitchen-style space. The menu is great light-lunch territory with sandwiches, omelettes, crepes,

vegan specialities and homemade cakes, including a lavender cheesecake.

★ Vanilla
INTERNATIONAL €€€

(✆ 0242-247 6013; www.vanillaantalya.com; Hesapçı Sokak 33; mains ₺25-66; ⊙ noon-10.15pm; 🍴) This outstanding, ultramodern restaurant, led by British chef Wayne, has a streamlined, unfussy atmosphere with its banquettes, glass surfaces and pleasant outside area dotted with cane-backed chairs. The menu is a beacon for vegetarians and anyone needing a kebap-break with Mediterranean-inspired dishes such as panko-crusted goat's-cheese salad and avocado risotto sitting alongside a Thai-style curry, pizzas and steak.

★ Castle Café
CAFE, BAR

(✆ 0242-248 6594; Hıdırlık Sokak 48/1; ⊙ 8.30am-midnight) This lively hang-out along the cliff edge is a local favourite, attracting a crowd of young Turks with its affordable drinks (300mL beer ₺11). Service can be slow, but the terrace's jaw-dropping views of the beaches and mountains west of town more than compensate, as does the well-priced menu (mains ₺14 to ₺24).

ℹ Information

Atatürk/Cumhuriyet Caddesi is lined with banks and ATMs. The **tourist office** (✆ 0242-247 7660 ext 133; Cumhuriyet Caddesi; ⊙ 8.30am-5.30pm) is just west of Cumhuriyet Meydanı.

ℹ Getting There & Away

The otogar is 4km north of the centre. A tram (₺2) runs from here to the city centre (İsmet Paşa stop). From the otogar, buses whizz to destinations across the country, including two overnight services to Göreme (₺85, nine hours); several daily to Konya (₺54, six hours); and frequent dolmuşes and buses to Fethiye, via either the inland route (₺30, 3½ hours) or the coastal towns (₺35, six hours).

CENTRAL ANATOLIA

This is the region where the whirling dervishes first swirled, Atatürk began his revolution, Alexander the Great cut the Gordion Knot and Julius Caesar uttered his famous line, '*Veni, vidi, vici*' ('I came, I saw, I conquered'). Turkey's central plains are both alive with mind-boggling history and the place where you'll best capture a sense of modern Anatolian life.

Ankara

📞 0312 / POP 4.9 MILLION

The Turkish capital established by Atatürk boasts two of the country's most important sights, plus a hilltop *hisar* (citadel) district that is full of old-fashioned charm and the cafe-crammed Kızılay neighbourhood that is one of Turkey's hippest urban quarters. İstanbullus may quip that the best view in Ankara is the train home, but the capital has plenty more substance than its reputation as a staid administrative centre suggests.

◉ Sights

★ Museum of Anatolian Civilisations   MUSEUM

(Anadolu Medeniyetleri Müzesi; 📞 0312-324 3160; www.anadolumedeniyetlerimuzesi.gov.tr; Gözcü Sokak 2; ₺30; ⏱ 8.30am-7pm mid-Apr–Sep, 8.30pm-5.15 Oct–mid-Apr; 🚌 Ulus) The superb Museum of Anatolian Civilisations is the perfect introduction to the complex weave of Turkey's ancient past, with beautifully curated exhibits housing artefacts cherry-picked from just about every significant archaeological site in Anatolia.

The central hall houses reliefs and statuary, while the surrounding halls take you on a journey of staggering history from Palaeolithic, Neolithic, Chalcolithic, Bronze Age, Assyrian, Hittite, Phrygian, Urartian and Lydian periods. Downstairs is a collection of Roman artefacts unearthed at excavations in and around Ankara.

Anıt Kabir   MONUMENT

(Atatürk Mausoleum & Museum; www.anitkabir. org; Gençlik Caddesi; audioguide ₺10; ⏱ 9am-noon & 1-5pm; 🚌 Anadolu) FREE The monumental mausoleum of Mustafa Kemal Atatürk (1881–1938), the founder of modern Turkey, sits high above the city with its abundance of marble and air of veneration. The tomb itself actually makes up only a small part of this complex, which consists of **museums** and a **ceremonial courtyard**. For many Turks a visit is virtually a pilgrimage, and it's not unusual to see people visibly moved. Allow at least two hours in order to visit the whole site.

🛌 Sleeping & Eating

Deeps Hostel   HOSTEL €

(📞 0312-213 6338; www.deepshostelankara. com; Ataç 2 Sokak 46; dm/s/d without breakfast €8.50/14/22; 🚻🖥; 🚌 Kızılay) At Ankara's best budget choice, friendly owner Şeyda has created a colourful, light-filled hostel with spacious dorms and small private rooms with squeaky-clean, modern shared bathrooms. It's all topped off by masses of advice and information, a fully equipped kitchen and a cute communal area downstairs where you can swap your Turkish travel tales.

★ Angora House Hotel   HISTORIC HOTEL €€

(📞 0312-309 8380; Kale Kapısı Sokak 16; s/d/tr €30/55/66; 🚻❄🖥; 🚌 Ulus) Be utterly charmed by this restored Ottoman house, which oozes subtle elegance at every turn. The six spacious rooms are infused with old-world atmosphere, featuring dark wood accents and colourful Turkish carpets, while the walled courtyard garden is the perfect retreat from the citadel streets. Delightfully helpful staff and a feast of a breakfast add to the appeal.

Leman Kültür   INTERNATIONAL €

(📞 0312-466 0620; www.lmk.com.tr; Bestekar Sokak 80; mains ₺10-18; ⏱ 9am-2am; 🖥) Named after a cult Turkish comic strip – and decorated accordingly – this is the pre-party pick for a substantial feed and for spotting beautiful young educated things. The food is generally of the meatballs, burgers, pizza and grilled meats variety. Drinks are reasonably priced and the speakers crank everything from indie-electro to Türk pop.

ⓘ Getting There & Away

BUS

From Ankara's huge **AŞTİ otogar** (Ankara Şehirlerarası Terminali İşletmesi; Mevlâna Bulvarı), buses depart to all corners of Turkey day and night. Services to İstanbul (₺50 to ₺75, six hours) leave numerous times daily. The AŞTİ is at the western end of Ankara's Ankaray metro line (fare ₺4), by far the easiest way to travel between the otogar and the centre.

TRAIN

Ankara's flash new **train station** (Ankara YHT Garı; www.tcdd.gov.tr; Celal Bayar Bulvarı), inaugurated in September 2016, has high-speed train services with Eskişehir (₺31, 1½ hours, 13 trains daily); İstanbul Pendik (a suburb 25km east of central İstanbul; ₺71, four hours, eight trains daily); and Konya (₺31, two hours, 10 trains daily). Trains are fast, comfortable and efficient. Ticket queues can be long so it's best to buy tickets the day before travel or buy online at www.tcdd.gov.tr.

Konya

📞 0332 / POP 1.3 MILLION

The home of the whirling dervish orders is both a modern economic boom town and a bastion of Seljuk culture. The centre is dotted with imposing historic monuments all topped off by the city's turquoise-domed **Mevlâna Museum** (📞 0332-351 1215; Asanlı Kışla Caddesi; audioguide ₺10; ⊙ 9am-7pm mid-Apr–Sep, 8am-5pm Oct–mid-Apr; 🚇 Mevlâna) **FREE**; the former dervish lodge is one of Turkey's finest sights and most important centres of pilgrimage.

Try to visit on a Saturday to see a whirling dervish *sema* ceremony at the **Mevlâna Culture Centre** (Whirling Dervish Performance; www.emav.org; Aslanlı Kışla Caddesi; ⊙ 7pm Sat; 🚇 Mevlâna Kültür Merkezi) **FREE**, and don't miss the **Tile Museum** (Karatay Medresesi Çini Müzesi; 📞 0332-351 1914; Ankara Caddesi, just off Alaaddin Meydanı; ₺6; ⊙ 9am-5pm), a former Seljuk theological school (1251) with finely preserved blue-and-white tilework and an outstanding ceramic collection.

For accommodation, **Ulusan Otel** (📞 0332-351 5004; ulusanhotel@hotmail.com; Çarşı PTT Arkasi 4; s/d €25/40; 🕸🛜) is the pick of the Konya cheapies and **Derviş Otel** (📞 0542 375 6261; www.dervishotel.com; Güngör Sokak 7; r €50-60, f €100; 🕸✳🛜) is a 200-year-old house converted into a rather wonderful boutique hotel. You can feast on Turkish classics at **Konak Konya Mutfağı** (📞 0332-352 8547; Piriesat Caddesi 5; mains ₺10-22; ⊙ 7.30am-11.45pm Tue-Sun, from 8am Mon; 🍴), run by well-known food writer Nevin Halıcı, while nearby **Somatçi** (📞 0332-352 4200; www.somatci.com; Mengüc Sokak 36; dishes ₺6.50-27; ⊙ 9am-10pm Tue-Sun; 🍴) rekindles old Seljuk and Ottoman recipes.

Konya otogar is 7km north of the centre and connected by tram. There are frequent buses to all major destinations, including Ankara (₺35, four hours); İstanbul (₺95, 10 hours); and Nevşehir, Cappadocia (₺50, three hours).

Seven express trains run to/from Ankara daily (economy/business class ₺30/43, two hours).

CAPPADOCIA

Cappadocia's cascading rock formations look like they've been plucked straight out of a fairy tale. Explore these rippling valleys, studded with cone-like rocks (called fairy chimneys), and you'll find the human history here just as fascinating as the geological wonderland. Rock-hewn churches covered in Byzantine frescoes are secreted into cliffs, the villages are honeycombed out of hillsides and vast subterranean complexes, where early Christians once hid, are tunnelled under the ground.

Göreme

📞 0384 / POP 2100

Surrounded by epic sweeps of moonscape valley, this remarkable honey-coloured village hollowed out of the hills may have long since grown beyond its farming-hamlet roots, but its charm has not diminished. Nearby, **Göreme Open-Air Museum** (Göreme Açık Hava Müzesi; 📞 0384-271 2167; Müze Caddesi; ₺30; ⊙ 8.30am-7pm Apr-Nov, to 5pm Dec-Mar) is a rock-cut Byzantine monastic settlement that housed some 20 monks, and if you wander out of town you'll find storybook landscapes and little-visited churches in the likes of Güllüdere (Rose) Valley. With its easy-going allure and stunning setting, it's no wonder Göreme continues to send travellers giddy.

👉 Tours

Heritage Travel TOURS

(📞 0384-271 2687; www.turkishheritagetravel.com; Uzundere Caddesi; day tours per person cash/credit card €45/55; ⊙ 9.30am-5.30pm) This highly recommended local agency offers day-tour itineraries that differ from most operators in Cappadocia, including an 'Undiscovered Cappadocia' trip that visits Soğanlı, Mustafapaşa and Derinkuyu Underground City. It also offers private day trips for those with particular interests, including jeep safaris, tours to Hacıbektaş and a fresco trip exploring Cappadocia's Byzantine heritage.

Yama Tours TOURS

(📞 0384-271 2508; www.yamatours.com; Müze Caddesi 7/6; group tours north/south €40/70; ⊙ 9.30am-6pm) This popular backpacker-friendly travel agency runs daily Cappadocia North (Göreme Open-Air Museum, Paşabağı and Avanos) and South (Ihlara Valley and Derinkuyu Underground City) tours. It can also organise a bag full of other Cappadocia adventures and activities for you, including private trips to Hacibektaş and Soğanlı, that take in plenty of sights along the way, and three-day trips to Mt Nemrut.

🛏 Sleeping & Eating

★ Kelebek Hotel
BOUTIQUE HOTEL €€€

(✆ 0384-271 2531; www.kelebekhotel.com; Yavuz Sokak 31; s/d €56/70, fairy chimney s €56-84, d €70-105, s/d without bathroom €44/55, s/d ste from €104/130; P🐾🌀🛜📶) Local guru Ali Yavuz leads a charming team at one of Göreme's original boutique hotels, which has seen a travel industry virtually spring from beneath its stunning terraces. Exuding Anatolian inspiration at every turn, the rooms are spread over a labyrinth of stairs and balconies interconnecting two gorgeous stone houses, each with a fairy chimney protruding skyward.

Koza Cave Hotel
BOUTIQUE HOTEL €€€

(✆ 0384-271 2466; Çakmaklı Sokak 49; d €165-200, ste €220-350; 🐾🌀🛜) 🥗 Bringing a new level of eco-inspired chic to Göreme, Koza Cave is a masterclass in stylish sustainable tourism. Passionate owner Derviş spent decades living in Holland and has incorporated Dutch eco-sensibility into every cave crevice of the 10 stunning rooms. Grey water is reused, and recycled materials and local handcrafted furniture are utilised in abundance to create sophisticated spaces. Highly recommended.

Seten Restaurant
MODERN TURKISH €€€

(✆ 0384-271 3025; www.setenrestaurant.com; Aydınlı Sokak; mains ₺25-65; ⊗ noon-11.30pm; 🍴) Brimming with an artful Anatolian aesthetic, Seten is a feast for the eye as well as for the stomach. Named after the old millstones used to grind bulgur wheat, this restaurant is an education for newcomers to Turkish cuisine and a treat for well-travelled palates. Attentive service complements classic main dishes and myriad luscious and unusual meze.

ℹ Getting There & Away

AIR

Kayseri Airport (Kayseri Erkilet Havalimanı; ✆ 0352-337 5494; www.kayseri.dhmi.gov.tr; Kayseri Caddesi) and **Nevşehir Airport** (Nevşehir Kapadokya Havalimanı; ✆ 0384-421 4455; Nevşehir Kapadokya Havaalanı Yolu, Gülşehir) serve central Cappadocia and have several daily flights to/from İstanbul.

Airport shuttle buses to Göreme from either airport must be prebooked. All hotels can do this for you or you can book directly through **Helios Transfer** (✆ 0384-271 2257; www.heliostransfer.com; Adnan Menderes Caddesi 25a; per passenger to/from Nevşehir/Kayseri airport €8/10; ⊗ 9am-6pm).

BUS

Most long-distance buses from western Turkey terminate in Nevşehir, where a free bus-company *servis* takes you on to Göreme. Make sure your ticket states your final destination, not Nevşehir. Beware of touts at Nevşehir otogar and only use the bus company's official *servis* shuttle.

The major bus companies all have offices in Göreme otogar and service destinations nationwide.

EASTERN TURKEY

Sadly, fighting between the PKK (Kurdistan Workers Party) and Turkish government forces, along with possible effects of the Syrian conflict in territory near the border, have rendered much of southeastern Anatolia risky for travellers. Check your government's travel advice before considering travelling here.

Nemrut Dağı Milli Parkı

Two thousand years ago, a megalomaniac Commagene king erected his own memorial sanctuary on **Nemrut Dağı** (Mt Nemrut; 2150m), the centrepiece of today's stunning national park (Nemrut Dağı National Park; ₺12). The fallen heads of the gigantic decorative statues of gods and kings, toppled by earthquakes, form one of the country's most enduring images.

Most people arrive on a sunrise or sunset tour arranged from **Malatya** or **Kahta**, or on a tour from Cappadocia. Note that the Cappadocia tours contain an extremely long drive here and back. In Kahta the pick of the accommodation is the **Kommagene Hotel** (✆ 0532 200 3856, 0416-725 9726; www.kommagenehotel.com; Mustafa Kemal Caddesi; s/d/tr €10/18/24, camping per car/tent €10/5; P🌀🛜), which organises decent Nemrut Dağı tours.

The closest base is the pretty village of **Karadut**, 12km from the summit. Accommodation here, including **Karadut Pension** (✆ 0416-737 2169, 0535 376 1102; karadutpansiyon@hotmail.com; per person incl breakfast ₺50, campsite ₺10; P🌀🛜) and **Nemrut Kervansaray Hotel** (✆ 0416-737 2190; osmanaydin.44@hotmail.com; d €43; P🛜📶), can arrange pick-ups from Kahta otogar as well as transport to the summit if you don't have your own car.

Kars

 0474 / POP 85,225

Kars' medieval fortress and stately, pastel-coloured Russian buildings are well worth a look, but most people come here to visit the dramatic ruins of **Ani** (₺8; ⊙8am-7pm Apr-Oct, to 5pm Nov-Mar; **P**), 45km east of the city.

Formerly a Silk Road entrepôt and capital of the Armenian kingdom, Ani was deserted after a Mongol invasion in 1236. The ghost city, with its lightning-cleaved **Church of the Redeemer**, now lies amid undulating grass overlooking the Armenian border. The site exudes an eerie ambience that is simply unforgettable.

In Kars, **Hotel Katerina Sarayı** (🖉0474-223 0636; www.katerinasarayi.com; Celalbaba Caddesi 52; s/d/tr €40/60/76; **P**📶) is all tsarist-style elegance and comfort, occupying a large 1879 Russian stone building, and the classy, 40-year-old, **Ocakbaşı Restoran** (🖉0474-212 0056; www.kaygisizocakbasi.com; Atatürk Caddesi; mains ₺13-22; ⊙8am-11.30pm; 📶🖉) serves tasty and unusual regional and Turkish dishes.

From the otogar, 4km northeast of central Kars and linked by *servis*, there are daily buses to destinations including Ankara (₺118, 18 hours) and İstanbul (₺130, 21 hours).

The easiest way to get to Ani is to take a taxi minibus (return trip ₺150 for one or two people and ₺50 per person for three or more). This includes three hours' waiting time and can be organised through English-speaking driver-guide **Celil Ersözoğlu** (🖉0532 226 3966; celilani@hotmail.com).

SURVIVAL GUIDE

❶ Directory A–Z

ACCOMMODATION

Budget travellers will find backpacker hostels with dorm beds in İstanbul, along the Aegean and Mediterranean coasts, and in Cappadocia. Camping grounds are also found along the coasts and in Cappadocia. There are plentiful hotels of all standards and family-run pensions in tourist areas. Pensions generally represent better value.

Outside tourist areas, solo travellers of both sexes should be cautious about the cheapest hotel options. Suss out the staff and atmosphere in reception; theft and even sexual assaults have occurred in budget establishments (albeit very rarely).

MONEY

➡ Turkish lira (₺) comes in notes of five, 10, 20, 50, 100 and 200; and coins of one, five, 10, 25 and 50 kuruş and one lira.

➡ Hotels and restaurants in more popular tourist destinations often quote their rates in euros.

➡ ATMs are widespread and dispense Turkish lira, and occasionally euros and US dollars, to Visa, MasterCard, Cirrus and Maestro cardholders.

➡ Credit cards (Visa and MasterCard) are widely accepted by hotels, shops and restaurants, although often not by establishments outside the main tourist areas. You can also get cash advances on these cards. Amex is less commonly accepted.

➡ US dollars and euros are the easiest currencies to change. You'll get better rates at exchange offices than at banks.

Tipping & Bargaining

➡ Tipping is customary in restaurants, hotels and for services such as guided tours.

➡ Round up metered taxi fares to the nearest 50 kuruş.

➡ Leave waiters around 10% to 15% of the bill.

➡ Check a *servis ücreti* (service charge) hasn't been automatically added to restaurant bills.

➡ Hotel prices are sometimes negotiable, especially outside of peak season.

➡ Bargaining for souvenirs is normal in bazaars.

OPENING HOURS

The working day shortens during the holy month of Ramazan (Ramadan). Friday is a normal working day in Turkey. Opening hours of tourist attractions and tourist information offices may shorten in the low season.

Tourist information 9am to 12.30pm and 1.30pm to 5pm Monday to Friday

Restaurants 11am to 10pm

Bars 4pm to late

Nightclubs 11pm to late

Shops 9am to 6pm Monday to Friday (longer in tourist areas and big cities – including weekend opening)

Government departments, offices and banks 8.30am to noon and 1.30pm to 5pm Monday to Friday

POST

Turkish *postanes* (post offices) are indicated by black-on-yellow 'PTT' signs. Postcards sent abroad cost about ₺2.80.

PUBLIC HOLIDAYS

New Year's Day (Yılbaşı) 1 January

National Sovereignty & Children's Day (Ulusal Egemenlik ve Çocuk Günü) 23 April

Labor & Solidarity Day (May Day) 1 May

Commemoration of Atatürk, Youth & Sports Day (Gençlik ve Spor Günü) 19 May

Şeker Bayramı (Sweets Holiday) Dates vary
Democracy and National Solidarity Day 15 July
Victory Day (Zafer Bayramı) 30 August
Kurban Bayramı (Festival of the Sacrifice) Dates vary
Republic Day (Cumhuriyet Bayramı) 29 October

SAFE TRAVEL

Turkey is not a dangerous country to visit, but it's always wise to be a little cautious, especially if you're travelling alone. To stay safe, you should watch out in particular for the following:

➡ A string of terrorist attacks by Islamic State (Isis) and Kurdish insurgents hit Ankara and İstanbul throughout 2016. The likelihood of being caught in such incidents remains statistically low, and the usual targets are government and military installations, but be vigilant and avoid political rallies and large gatherings of people.

➡ Marches and demonstrations are a regular sight in Turkish cities, especially İstanbul. These are best avoided as they can lead to clashes with the police.

➡ Do not visit areas in close proximity to the Syrian border, which are the most dangerous parts of Turkey. Here, there is the risk of being caught in the Turkish–Kurdish conflict and of being kidnapped or harmed by terrorists from Syria.

➡ For the same reasons, large areas of southeastern Anatolia were risky for travellers at the time of writing. Nemrut Dağı National Park was not among the areas considered risky, but check your government's travel advice before visiting the region.

➡ In İstanbul, single men are sometimes approached and lured to a bar by new 'friends'. The victim is then made to pay an outrageous bill, regardless of what he drank. Drugging is another occasional risk, especially for lone men. It pays to be a tad wary of who you befriend, especially when you're new to the country.

➡ Sexual assaults have occurred against travellers of both sexes in hotels in parts of Turkey. Make enquiries, check forums and do a little research in advance if you are travelling alone or heading off the beaten track.

TELEPHONE

➡ Payphones require cards that can be bought at telephone centres or, for a small mark-up, at some shops. Some accept credit cards.

➡ If you set up a roaming facility with your home phone provider, you should be able to connect your mobile to a network.

➡ SIM cards cost around ₺85 (including ₺30 in local call credit). An internet data pack with the SIM will cost around ₺25/30/40/60 for 1/2/4/8 GB.

➡ You can buy a local SIM and use it in your mobile from home, although the networks detect and bar foreign phones after 120 days.

VISAS

➡ At the time of research, nationals of countries including Denmark, Finland, France, Germany, Greece, Israel, Italy, Japan, New Zealand, Sweden and Switzerland don't need a visa to visit Turkey for up to 90 days.

➡ Nationals of countries including Australia, Austria, Belgium, Canada, India, Ireland, Mexico, the Netherlands, Norway, Portugal, Spain, Taiwan, the UK and USA need a visa, which should be purchased online at www.evisa.gov.tr before travelling.

➡ Most nationalities, including the above, are given a 60- or 90-day multiple-entry visa.

➡ In some cases, the 90-day visa stipulates 'per period 180 days'. This means you can spend three months in Turkey within a six-month period; when you leave after three months, you can't re-enter for three months.

➡ Visa fees cost US$15 to US$80, depending on nationality.

➡ Your passport must be valid for at least six months from the date you enter the country.

WOMEN TRAVELLERS

Travelling in Turkey is straightforward for women, provided you follow some simple guidelines.

➡ Tailor your behaviour and dress to your surroundings. Outside of İstanbul and heavily touristed destinations, you should dress modestly.

➡ Bring a shawl to cover your head when visiting mosques.

➡ In more conservative areas (particularly out east) your contact with men should be polite and formal, not chatty and friendly or they are likely to get the wrong idea about your intentions.

➡ Outside tourist areas, the cheapest hotels, as well as often being fleapits, are generally not suitable for lone women. Stick with family-oriented midrange hotels.

❶ Getting There & Away

AIR

The main international airports are in western Turkey. **Turkish Airlines** (☑1800-874 8875; www.turkishairlines.com), the national carrier, has an extensive international network.

Antalya International Airport (Antalya Havalimanı; ☑0242-444 7423; www.aytport.com; Serik Caddesi)

Milas-Bodrum International Airport (BJV; ☑0252-523 0215; www.milas-bodrumairport.com)

Dalaman International Airport (☑0252-792 5555; www.yda.aero)

İstanbul Airport (p1163)

İstanbul Sabiha Gökçen International Airport (p1163)

İzmir Adnan Menderes Airport (☑ 444 9828; www.adnanmenderesairport.com; ☎)

LAND

There are direct bus services to İstanbul from European destinations including Austria, Albania, Bulgaria, Georgia, Germany, Greece, Kosovo, Macedonia and Romania.

The major bus companies that operate these routes are **Metro Turizm** (☑ 0850-222 3455; www.metroturizm.com.tr) and Ulusoy (p1179).

Currently the only train route operating between Europe and İstanbul is the daily Sofia Express to/from Sofia (Bulgaria). You can change in Sofia for Belgrade (Serbia) or in Dimitrovgrad and Gorna Oryahovitsa for Bucharest (Romania). See Turkish State Railways and **The Man in Seat 61** (www.seat61.com/turkey) for details.

SEA

Departure times and routes change between seasons, with fewer ferries running in the winter. **Ferrylines** (www.ferrylines.com) is a good starting point for information. The following is a list of ferry routes from Turkey:

➡ Ayvalık–Lesvos (Midilli), Greece
➡ Bodrum–Kalymnos, Kos, Rhodes and Symi, Greece
➡ Çeşme–Chios, Greece
➡ İstanbul–Chornomorsk (Odessa), Ukraine
➡ Kaş–Meis (Kastellorizo), Greece
➡ Kuşadası–Samos, Greece
➡ Marmaris–Rhodes, Greece
➡ Turgetreis–Kalymnos and Kos, Greece

❶ Getting Around

AIR

Turkey is a vast country and domestic flights are an affordable way of reducing travel time, with more route choices if flying to/from İstanbul.

There are numerous regional airports, so it's well worth checking what's close to your Turkish destination. In addition to the international airports we've listed above, **Denizli Çardak Airport** is useful for visiting Pamukkale and **Kars Harakani Airport** for visiting Ani and northeastern Anatolia.

BUS

Turkey's intercity bus system is as good as any you'll find, with modern, comfortable coaches crossing the country at all hours and for very reasonable prices.

Major companies with extensive networks include **Kamil Koç** (☑ 0224-294 5562; www.

kamilkoc.com.tr), Metro Turizm (p1179) and **Ulusoy** (☑ 0850-811 1888; www.ulusoy.com.tr).

A town's otogar is often on the outskirts, but most bus companies provide a *servis* (free shuttle bus) to/from the centre.

Local routes are usually operated by dolmuşes (minibuses), which might run to a timetable or set off when full.

CAR & MOTORCYCLE

Turkey has the world's second-highest petrol prices. Petrol/diesel cost about ₺6.50 per litre.

An international driving permit (IDP) is not obligatory, but handy if your driving licence is from a country likely to seem obscure to a Turkish police officer.

You must be at least 21 years old to hire a car. Rental charges are similar to those in Europe. Try **Economy Car Rentals** (www.economycar rentals.com).

You must have international insurance, covering third-party damage, if you are bringing your own car into the country. Buying it at the border is a straightforward process (one month car/motorcycle €59/47).

Road accidents claim about 10,000 lives each year. To survive on Turkish roads:

➡ Drive defensively and cautiously.
➡ Don't expect fellow motorists to obey traffic signs or use indicators.
➡ Avoid driving at night, when you won't be able to see potholes, animals, and vehicles driving without lights or stopped in the middle of the road.

TRAIN

The **Turkish State Railways** (www.tcdd.gov.tr) network covers the country fairly well, with the notable exception of the coastlines. Most train journey times are notoriously long, but the entire system is currently being overhauled. Check out **The Man in Seat Sixty-One** (www.seat61.com/turkey2) for details on Turkish train travel.

High-Speed Routes

➡ Ankara–Konya
➡ İstanbul Pendik–Eskişehir–Ankara
➡ İstanbul Pendik–Eskişehir–Konya

Useful Long-Haul Routes (all departing from Ankara)

➡ Adana via Kayseri
➡ Diyarbakır via Kayseri, Sivas and Malatya
➡ İzmir via Eskişehir
➡ Kars via Kayseri, Sivas and Erzurum

InterRail Global and One Country passes and Balkan Flexipass cover the Turkish railway network, as do the Eurail Global and Select passes. ISIC cardholders get a 20% discount and Train Tour Cards are available at major stations.

Ukraine

POP 44.6 MILLION

Best Places to Eat

➡ Ostannya Barikada (p1185)

➡ Shoti (p1185)

➡ Baczewski (p1190)

➡ Trapezna Idey (p1190)

➡ Bernardazzi (p1192)

➡ Kotelok Mussels Bar (p1192)

Best Places to Stay

➡ Dream House Hostel (p1184)

➡ Hotel Bontiak (p1185)

➡ Villa Stanislavsky (p1190)

➡ Leopolis Hotel (p1190)

➡ Babushka Grand Hostel (p1192)

➡ Frederic Koklen (p1192)

Why Go?

Shaped like a broken heart, with the Dnipro River dividing it into two, this Slavic hinterland is a vast swathe of sage-flavoured steppe filled with sunflowers and wild poppies. Blessed with a near-ideal climate and the richest soil in Europe, it's one huge garden of a country where flowers are blossoming, fruit are ripening and farmers markets sing hymns of abundance.

If only its history were as idyllic. Just over two decades into a very troubled independence, Ukraine is dogged by a conflict with neighbouring Russia that has left Crimea and a small chunk of its eastern territory off limits to most travellers. But the country's main attractions, including eclectic and rebellious Kyiv, architecturally rich Lviv and flamboyant Odesa, are well away from the conflict zone. A long stretch of the Black Sea coast invites beach fun, while the Carpathians draw skiers in winter and cyclists in summer.

When to Go
Kyiv

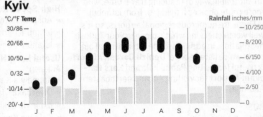

Jan Party on New Year's Eve then repent at an Orthodox Christmas service a week later.

May A great time to visit Kyiv when its countless horse chestnut trees are in blossom.

Aug Sip Ukraine's best coffee in one of Lviv's many outdoor cafes.

Entering the Country

The majority of visitors fly to Ukraine – generally to Kyiv. Some new direct train services to/from Poland have appeared and, as it has across Europe, international bus travel has made a big comeback.

ITINERARIES

Two Days

A couple of days are just enough to 'do' Kyiv (p1184), starting at its stellar attraction, the Kyevo-Pecherska Lavra (p1184; aka the Caves Monastery). Follow this with a hike up artsy Andriyivsky uzviz (p1184), before plunging into the beeswax-perfumed Byzantine interior of Unesco-listed St Sophia's Cathedral (p1184).

Five Days

Having seen the sights in Kyiv, hop aboard a slow night train to Lviv (p1189), Ukraine's most central European city complete with bean-scented coffee houses, Gothic and baroque churches, and quaintly rattling trams.

One Week

Take another overnight train or fly to Odesa (p1191), a flamboyant port city filled with elegant Parisian architecture and boasting an outstanding culinary culture that comes close to being regarded as 'Odesa cuisine'.

Essential Food & Drink

When it comes to food, Ukraine is the land of abundance, with distinct regional variations. Here are some of the Ukrainian staples you are certain to find on restaurant menus:

Borshch The national soup made with beetroot, pork fat and herbs.

Salo Cured pig fat, cut into slices and eaten with bread.

Varenyky Pasta pockets filled with everything from mashed potato to sour cherries.

Halushky Pasta cubes served with pieces of meat or liver.

Banosh A west Ukrainian version of polenta served with cottage cheese.

AT A GLANCE

Area 603,628 sq km

Capital Kyiv

Country Code ☑ 380

Currency Hryvnya (uah)

Emergency ☑ 112

Language Ukrainian, Russian

Time East European Time (GMT/UTC plus two hours)

Visas Not required for EU, UK, US and Canadian citizens for stays of up to 90 days

UKRAINE

Sleeping Price Ranges

The following price ranges refer to a double room in high season.

€ less than 500uah

€€ 500–1500uah

€€€ more than 1500uah

Eating Price Ranges

The following price ranges refer to a main course.

€ less than 100uah

€€ 100–200uah

€€€ more than 200uah

Ukraine Highlights

1 Kyevo-Pecherska Lavra (p1184) Inspecting Kyiv's collection of mummified monks by candlelight.

2 Andriyivsky Uzviz (p1184) Making an ascent of Kyiv's most atmospheric street.

3 Lviv (p1189) Doing a spot of cobble-surfing in the historical centre packed with churches, museums and eccentric restaurants.

4 Lychakivsky Cemetery (p1189) Exploring Lviv's final resting place of Ukraine's great and good.

KYIV КИЇВ

📌 044 / POP 2.9 MILLION

In the beginning there was Kyiv. Long before Ukraine and Russia existed, the city's inhabitants were already striding up and down the green hills, idling hot afternoons away on the Dnipro River and promenading along Khreshchatyk – then a stream, now the main avenue. From here, East Slavic civilisation spread all the way to Alaska.

Today, history continues to unfold. As revolution has come and gone, and as war in the east smoulders, Ukraine's capital has rebelled yet again, only this time culturally. A creative wave has swept over the city, embodied by urban art, vintage cafes and 24-hour parties. Seemingly overnight, Kyiv has become hip.

It's also cheap. You can eat at superb restaurants and drink at hidden cocktail bars for a fraction of what they would cost in the West. Kyiv's time is clearly now – or until the next revolution rolls around.

⊙ Sights

★ St Sophia's Cathedral CHURCH

(pl Sofiyska; grounds/cathedral/bell tower 20/80/40uah; ⏱ cathedral & museums 10am-6pm, grounds & bell tower 9am-7pm; Ⓜ Zoloti Vorota) The interior is the most astounding aspect of Kyiv's oldest standing church. Many of the mosaics and frescoes are original, dating back to 1017–31, when the cathedral was built to celebrate Prince Yaroslav's victory in protecting Kyiv from the Pechenegs (tribal raiders). While equally attractive, the building's gold domes and 76m-tall wedding-cake bell tower are 18th-century baroque additions. It's well worth climbing the bell tower for a bird's-eye view of the cathedral and 360-degree panoramas of Kyiv.

★ Kyevo-Pecherska Lavra MONASTERY

(Києво-Печерська лавра, Caves Monastery; 📌 044-406 6375; http://kplavra.kiev.ua; vul Lavrska 9; upper/lower Lavra 25uah/free; ⏱ 9am-7pm Apr-Sep, 9am-6pm Oct-Mar, caves 8.30am-4.30pm; Ⓜ Arsenalna) Tourists and Orthodox pilgrims alike flock to the Lavra, set on 28 hectares of grassy hills above the Dnipro River in Pechersk. It's easy to see why tourists come: the monastery's cluster of gold-domed churches is a feast for the eyes, the hoard of Scythian gold rivals that of the Hermitage, and the underground labyrinths lined with mummified monks are exotic and intriguing. For pilgrims, the rationale is much simpler:

to them, this is the holiest ground in the country.

★ Maidan Nezalezhnosti SQUARE

(майдан Незалежності, Independence Sq; Ⓜ Maidan Nezalezhnosti) Be it celebration or revolution, whenever Ukrainians want to get together – and they often do – 'Maidan' is the nation's meeting point. The square saw pro-independence protests in the 1990s and the Orange Revolution in 2004. But all of that was eclipsed by the Euromaidan Revolution in 2013–14, when it was transformed into an urban guerrilla camp besieged by government forces. In peaceful times, Maidan is more about festiveness than feistiness, with weekend concerts and a popular nightly fountain show.

Yet the echo of revolution is omnipresent. Makeshift memorials on vul Instytutska serve as a sombre reminder of those slain in Euromaidan. Images of burning tyres and army tents from that fateful winter will forever linger in the Ukrainian conscience.

Andriyivsky Uzviz STREET

(Андріївський узвіз, Andrew's Descent; Ⓜ Kontraktova Pl) According to legend, a man walked up the hill here, erected a cross and prophesied, 'A great city will stand on this spot.' That man was the Apostle Andrew, hence the name of Kyiv's quaintest thoroughfare, a steep cobbled street that winds its way up from Kontraktova pl to vul Volodymyrska, with a vaguely Montparnasse feel. Along the length of 'the *uzviz*' you'll find cafes, art galleries and vendors selling all manner of souvenirs and kitsch.

🛏 Sleeping

★ Dream House Hostel HOSTEL €

(📌 044-580 2169; https://dream-hostels.com; Andriyivsky uzviz 2D; dm/s/d without bathroom from 270/855/1100uah, d with bathroom 1350uah; ✳ @ 🛜; Ⓜ Kontraktova Pl) Kyiv's most happening hostel is this gleaming 100-bed affair superbly located at the bottom of Andriyivsky uzviz. An attached **cafe-bar** (⏱ 8am-midnight; 🛜), a basement kitchen, a laundry room, key cards, bike hire, and daily events and tours make this a comfortable and engaging base from which to explore the capital. A few doubles (some with bathroom) are available in addition to dorms.

★ Sunflower B&B Hotel B&B €€

(📌 044-279 3846; www.sunflowerhotel.kiev.ua; vul Kostyolna 9/41; s/d incl breakfast 1950/2300uah;

NUKES & CROOKS

Two of the country's most visited as well as most unusual attractions can be done as day trips from Kyiv. One is **Chornobyl**, the apocalyptic site of the world's worst nuclear catastrophe, which happened in April 1986. A trip into the vast 'exclusion zone' around the troubled nuclear plant, now covered by a massive sarcophagus, is a moving journey back to the days of the Soviet Union and the most thought-provoking nine hours you'll spend in Ukraine. Radiation is low enough for the place to be proclaimed safe to visit, so many travel companies in Kyiv, such as **SoloEast Travel** (☑044-279 3505; www.tourkiev.com; vul Prorizna 10, office 105; ⏥9am-6pm Mon-Fri, 10am-2pm Sat; Ⓜ Khreshchatyk), run Chornobyl tours, which typically involve bussing people from Maidan Nezalezhnosti to the site, located 110km north of Kyiv. Expect to pay US$80 to US$110 per person to join a group day tour.

Another product of Ukraine's turbulent recent history, Kyiv's newest tourist attraction is **Mezhyhirya** (☑050 664 0080; www.mnp.org.ua; vul Ivana Franka 19, Novi Petrivtsi; adult/child 120/50uah; ⏥8am-9.30pm May-Sep, 8am to dark Oct-Apr; ▣397), the estate that once 'belonged' to ex-president Viktor Yanukovych, who was ousted in the Euromaidan Revolution of 2014 and forced to escape to Russia. A wander through the opulent grounds – totalling 137 hectares and costing hundreds of millions of dollars to create – gives visitors an idea of just how corrupt the Yanukovych regime had become. Now a national park, the estate is centred around Yanukovych's personal dacha (country house), a 620 sq-metre pinewood behemoth. Mezhyhirya is about 15km north of Kyiv. Bus 397 goes right to the park, via Vyshhorod centre, from either Petrivka (50 minutes) or Heroyiv Dnipra (35 minutes) metro stations. Departures are every hour on the hour from Petrivka.

🌐@🛜; Ⓜ Maidan Nezalezhnosti) Just off maidan Nezalezhnosti but well hidden from noisy traffic and crowds, this B&B (and definitely not hotel) seems to have been designed by a super-tidy granny. The airy, light-coloured rooms have a retro feel and there are extras like umbrellas and a shoe-polishing machine that you wouldn't expect. Continental breakfast is served in your room.

Hotel Bontiak　　　　BOUTIQUE HOTEL €€€
(☑098 538 1538; www.bontiak.com; vul Irynynska 5; incl breakfast s 2500, d 2980-3390uah; 🌐@🛜; Ⓜ Zoloti Vorota) Tucked in a quiet courtyard a five-minute walk from maidan Nezalezhnosti, this cosy boutique hotel is built into Kyiv's hilly landscape, which is why the reception is on the top floor. The stylishly minimalist rooms are generously sized and well equipped, and breakfast is served in your room.

✖️ Eating

★**Kyivska Perepichka**　　　　PIES €
(Київська перепічка; vul Bohdana Khmelnytskoho 3; perepichka 15uah; ⏥8.30am-9pm Mon-Sat, 10am-9pm Sun; Ⓜ Teatralna) A perpetually long queue moves with lightning speed towards a window where two women hand out pieces of fried dough enclosing a mouth-watering sausage. The place became a local institution long before the first 'hot dog' hit town. An essential Kyiv experience.

★**Ostannya Barikada**　　　　UKRAINIAN €€
(Last Barricade; ☑068 907 1991; maidan Nezalezhnosti 1; mains 130-200uah; ⏥11am-midnight; 🌐🛜; Ⓜ Maidan Nezalezhnosti) Hidden in a 'secret bunker' under maidan Nezalezhnosti, this is both a nationalist shrine and one of Kyiv's best restaurants. Everything – from the cheeses and *horilka* (vodka) to the craft beer and steaks – is 100% homegrown. Ukraine's three modern revolutions are eulogised everywhere. Getting in is a quest, but as poet Taras Shevchenko said, 'Fight and you'll win.'

Tintin　　　　VIETNAMESE €€
(☑097 828 7878; www.facebook.com/TinTin.Velodrome; vul Lypynskoho 15; mains 120-200uah; ⏥noon-11pm; Ⓜ Zoloti Vorota) This gem enjoys a wonderfully surreal end-of-the-universe setting by the velodrome and doubles as a really cool bar. Owners seem to be positively obsessed with Vietnamese soups and curries, and super-friendly staff are trained to explain the ingredients and cooking methods. A frivolous chain of associations brings the Belgian cartoon character into the equation, but it's only for the better.

★**Shoti**　　　　GEORGIAN €€€
(Кафе Шоти; ☑044-339 9399; vul Mechnykova 9; mains 160-480uah; ⏥noon-11pm; 🌐🛜; Ⓜ Klovska) This is modern Georgian cuisine at its finest. Try the fork-whipped egg-and-butter

Central Kyiv

500 m
0.25 miles

PODIL

VERKHNIY GOROD

Dnipro River

Dniprovsky Park

Mezhyhirya (30km)

vul Naberezhno-Khreshchatytska

vul Poshtova

Naberezhne shose

Volodymyrsky uzviz

Park Askoldova Mohyla

Park Misky Sad

Petrivska aleya

pl Evropeyska

Maidan Nezalezhnosti

Maidan Nezalezhnosti

vul Ilyinska

vul Hryhoriya Skovorody

vul Voloska

Provulok Khoreviv

vul Khoreva

vul Spaska

Kontraktova pl

vul Bratska

vul Sahaydachnoho

Poshtova pl

Volodymyrska Hirka Park

Zhyvopysna aleya

vul Desyatynna

vul Mykhaylivska

vul Mala Zhytomyrska

7

11

1

vul Mykhaylivska

pl Mykhaylivska

pl Sofiyska

vul Sofiyska

prov Tarasa Shevchenka

vul Irynynska

vul Volodymyrska

6

St Sophia's Cathedral

2

vul Volodymyrska

Kontraktova pl

vul Pokrovska

vul Prytytsko Mykilska

5

vul Borychiv Tik

9

3

vul Striltelska

vul Reytarska

vul Yaroslaviv Val

15

vul Kostyantynivska

vul Kyrylivska

Andriyivsky Uzviz

vul Vozdvyzhenska

vul Kozhumyatska

vul Verkhniy Val

Peyzazhna aleya

pl Lvivska

vul Velyka Zhytomyrska

vul Lvivska

vul Vozdenesensky uzviz

vul Petrivska

vul Kudryavska

vul Obsevatorna

prov Chekhovsky

Bulvarno-Kudryavska

vul Oleksy Honchara

vul Lukyanivska

vul Hlybochytska

vul Sichovikh Striltsiv

16

vul Mykoly Pymonenka

vul Yuriya Kotsyubynskoho

vul Gogolivska

vul Turgenivska

Lukyanivska

vul Hlybochytska

vul Lukyanivska

pl Lukyanivska

vul Vyacheslava Chornovola

vul Pottava

vul Pavlivska

vul Dmytrivska

vul Zolotoustivska

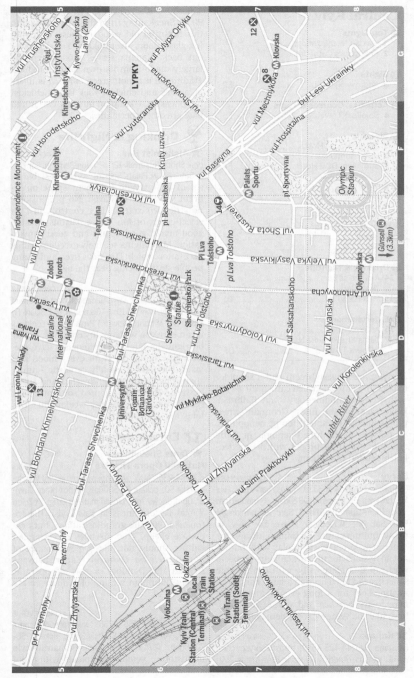

UKRAINE KYIV

Central Kyiv

khachapuri (cheese bread) and a shoulder of lamb or charcoal-grilled catfish, all served with fresh, complimentary *shoti* flatbread. Huge racks of the finest Georgian wines, professionally decanted, tempt oenophiles. Sit outside on the broad veranda, or settle into the restaurant proper with its meticulously scuffed wood floor.

Barvy   UKRAINIAN €€€
(Барви; ☏ 098 306 3333; http://barvy.rest; vul Mechnykova 3; mains 125-320uah; ☺ noon-11pm Mon, 10am-11pm Tue-Thu & Sun, 10am-midnight Fri & Sat; ☎; Ⓜ Klovska) There are only so many quintessential Ukrainian dishes for experiment-prone chefs to play with, but it's not an obstacle for the true culinary pioneers who run this place. Airy, with comfortable sofas instead of chairs and a large bar, it's an inviting spot for a long evening out. Come here to try *borshch* and *varenyky* dumplings like you've never seen them before.

★ **Kanapa**   UKRAINIAN €€€
(Канапа; ☏ 044-425 4548; https://borysov. ua/uk/kanapa; Andriyivsky uzviz 19A; mains 250-

400uah; ☺ 10am-midnight; ☎; Ⓜ Kontraktova Pl) ✎ Sneak away from the busy *uzviz* into this beautiful old wooden house with sliding-glass doors overlooking a lush ravine out back. Kanapa serves modern cuisine largely made from its own farm's produce. Traditional it is not: green *borshch* is made of nettles and chicken Kiev is not chicken but pheasant. Ukrainian mussels, caviar and pâté are other specialities.

🍷 Drinking & Nightlife

★ **Alchemist Bar**   COCKTAIL BAR
(vul Shota Rustaveli 12; ☺ noon-3am, to 5am Fri & Sat; ☎; Ⓜ Palats Sportu) Kyiv's best bar is set in an intimate basement space on vibrant vul Shota Rustaveli. No pretensions, no strict *feiskontrol* (face control), just an eclectic mix of fun-loving patrons chasing good music, good drinks and good conversation. Most nights see truly excellent bands play, after which DJs take over and many people start dancing near the bar.

★ **Pink Freud**   COCKTAIL BAR
(☏ 050 991 9818; www.facebook.com/pinkfreud kyiv; vul Nyzhniy Val 19; ☺ 6pm-1am, to 2.30am Fri & Sat; ☎; Ⓜ Kontraktova Pl) Pink Freud reckons it can cure you with quality cocktails. It may be right: its talented mixologists have created an original drink for every mood and taste. The food is equally cathartic – think spare ribs, boutique sandwiches and sinful desserts. There are talented solo musicians (guitar, sax, piano) most weeknights; DJs take over at weekends.

☆ Entertainment

★ **Taras Shevchenko National Opera Theatre**   OPERA
(☏ 044-235 2606; www.opera.com.ua; vul Volodymyrska 50; tickets 20-500uah; ☺ box office 11am-5.30pm, shows 7pm, closed mid-Jun–Aug; Ⓜ Zoloti Vorota) Performances at this lavish theatre (opened 1901) are grandiose affairs, but tickets are cheap. True disciples of Ukrainian culture should not miss a performance of *Zaporozhets za Dunaem* (Zaporizhzhyans Beyond the Danube), a sort of operatic, purely Ukrainian version of *Fiddler on the Roof*.

Atlas   CONCERT VENUE
(Атлас; ☏ 067 155 2255; www.facebook.com/ atlas37; vul Sichovykh Striltsiv 37-41; tickets 250-2000uah; ▣ Pl Lvivska) This industrial-style multistorey venue, complete with roof

terrace, caters to all musical tastes – from techno to heavy metal – with a sprinkling of theatre and poetry readings. The best of the best in Ukrainian and foreign music gravitate here these days.

ℹ️ Getting Around

TO/FROM THE AIRPORT
Boryspil airport is connected to Kyiv's main station by the round-the-clock **Skybus** service (90uah, 45 minutes to one hour). There is also a new train service between the two (80uah, 35 minutes), but it is not always reliable. Zhulyany airport is served by trolleybus 9 that departs from Bessarabska pl.

PUBLIC TRANSPORT
Kyiv's crowded, but efficient metro runs between around 6am and midnight. Plastic tokens are sold at windows and dispensers at stations. Buy tickets for buses, trolleybuses, trams and *marshrutky* (fixed-route minibuses) from the driver or conductor. One ride by metro or overground transport costs 8uah.

LVIV   ЛЬВІВ

📞 032 / POP 728,000

If you've spent time in other Ukrainian regions, Lviv will come as a shock. Mysterious and architecturally lovely, this Unesco-listed city is the country's least Soviet and exudes the same authentic Central European charm as pretourism Prague or Kraków once did. Its quaint cobbles, bean-perfumed coffeehouses and rattling trams are a continent away from the Soviet brutalism of the east. It's also a place where the candle of Ukrainian national identity burns brightest and where Russian is definitely a minority language.

But the secret is out, and those who foresaw that Lviv would become Ukraine's top tourist attraction are watching their prediction come true. No other city is more geared up for visitors and no other attracts so many of them. Lviv has the best range of hotels in the country, plus hostels, tour agencies, guides and English-language information abound, making this Ukraine's premier destination by a long way.

◉ Sights

★ Ploshcha Rynok   SQUARE
`FREE` Lviv was declared a Unesco World Heritage Site in 1998, and this old market square lies at its heart. The square was progressively rebuilt after a major fire in the early 16th century destroyed the original. Around 40 townhouses hem the square's perimeter. Most of these three- and four-storey buildings have uniform dimensions, with three windows per storey overlooking the square. This was the maximum number of windows allowed tax free and those buildings with four or more belonged to the extremely wealthy.

Pl Rynok is at its best on summer evenings when crowds of people emerge to enjoy the buskers, beer and generally good-natured atmosphere.

★ Lychakivsky Cemetery   CEMETERY
(Личаківський цвинтар; 📞 032-275 5415; www.lviv-lychakiv.com.ua; vul Pekarska; adult/student 25/15uah; ⊙ 9am-6pm Oct-Mar, to 8pm Apr-Sep; 🚋 7) Don't leave town until you've seen this amazing 42-hectare cemetery, only a short ride on tram 7 from the centre. This is the Père Lachaise of Eastern Europe, with the same sort of overgrown grounds and Gothic aura as the famous Parisian necropolis (but

UKRAINE LVIV

ℹ️ MOVING AROUND UKRAINE

Fast daytime trains are the preferable mode of transportation in Ukraine. These are modern, comfortable and usually have wi-fi. From Kyiv's **main train station** (Central Terminal; 📞 044-309 7005; pl Vokzalna 2; Ⓜ Vokzalna) there are three Intercity+ services daily for Lviv (360uah, five hours) and one to Odesa (370uah, 7¼ hours). There are also useful overnight services from Kyiv to Odesa (700uah, 7¾ hours) and from Odesa to Lviv (700uah, 10 hours).

Flights are also convenient, especially if you use Zhulyany airport (p1194) in Kyiv, which is closer to the city and more manageable than Boryspil airport (p1194). There are no direct flights between Odesa and Lviv.

Bus journeys can be arduous, so try and stick with well-established bus companies such as **Gunsel** (📞 044-525 4505; www.gunsel.com.ua; Central Bus Station), which runs useful services between Kyiv and Odesa (400uah, seven hours).

containing less-well-known people). Laid out in the late 18th century, it's packed full of western Ukraine's great and good. Pride of place goes to the grave of revered nationalist poet Ivan Franko.

Latin Cathedral CATHEDRAL
(www.lwowskabazylika.org.ua; pl Katedralna 1; ☺8.30am-5pm Mon-Sat, 2-5.30pm Sun) With various chunks dating from between 1370 and 1480, this working cathedral is one of Lviv's most impressive churches. The exterior is most definitely Gothic, while the heavily gilded interior, one of the city's highlights, has a more baroque feel, with colourfully wreathed pillars hoisting frescoed vaulting and mysterious side chapels glowing in candlelit half-light. Services are in four languages, including English.

If you walk around the outside of the cathedral, you'll eventually come to a relief of Pope John Paul II, erected to commemorate his visit to Lviv in 2001.

🛏 Sleeping

★ Old City Hostel HOSTEL €
(☎032-294 9644; www.oldcityhostel.lviv.ua; vul Beryndy 3; dm 160uah, d with/without bathroom 700/600uah; @☎) Occupying two floors of an elegantly fading tenement just steps from pl Rynok, this expertly run hostel, with period features and views of the Shevchenko statue from the wrap-around balcony, has long established itself as the city's best. Fluff-free dorms hold four to eight beds, shower queues are unheard of, sturdy lockers keep your stuff safe and there's a well-equipped kitchen.

★ Villa Stanislavsky BOUTIQUE HOTEL €€
(☎032-275 2505; www.villastanislavskyi.com. ua; vul Henerala Tarnavskoho 75; r from 850uah; P❄☎) This hilltop villa stands amid the splendid decay of what used to be a posh fin de siècle residential neighbourhood, 20 minutes on foot from the centre. The dark, polished wood of the stairs and furniture and the placid surroundings provide much-needed respite from the old town's hustle and bustle. A dedicated chess room is the cherry on the sundae.

★ Leopolis Hotel HOTEL €€€
(☎032-295 9500; www.leopolishotel.com; vul Teatralna 16; s/d 2700/3050uah; ❄@☎) One of the historical centre's finest places to catch some Zs. Every guest room in this 18th-century edifice is different, but all have a well-stocked minibar, elegant furniture and an Italian-marble bathroom with underfloor heating. Wheelchair-friendly facilities, a new spa/fitness area in the cellars and a pretty decent brasserie are extras you won't find anywhere else.

🍴 Eating

★ Trapezna Idey UKRAINIAN €
(Трапезна ідей; ☎032-254 6155; www.idem. org.ua; vul Valova 18A; mains 50-100uah; ☺11am-11pm) An unmarked door behind the paper-aeroplane monument leads into the bowels of a Bernardine monastery, where this lovely local-intelligentsia fave is hiding, together with a modern art gallery called the **Museum of Ideas**. People flock here for the hearty *bohrach* (a Ukrainian version of goulash) and *banosh* (Carpathian polenta with salty cottage cheese).

Tsukor Black BREAKFAST €
(Цукор Блэк; ☎098 679 8225; http://cukor.lviv. ua/; pr Kryva Lypa 3; mains 75-150uah; ☺8am-10pm) Come to Kryva Lypa for the best breakfasts in town. This two-storey place serves an array of wonderful toast- and waffle-based concoctions with eggs, avocado and other veggies. There is also a cool little souvenir shop in the premises, with most items featuring its trademark penguin.

★ Baczewski EASTERN EUROPEAN €€
(Ресторація Бачевських; ☎032-224 4444; vul Shevska 8; mains 100-330uah; ☺8am-midnight; ❄) Here's how you compress your Lviv cultural studies into one evening out. Start with Jewish *forschmak* (herring pate), eased down by Ukrainian *nalyvky* (digestifs) and followed by Hungarian fish soup. Proceed to Polish *pierogi* (dumplings) and finish with Viennese *Sachertorte* with Turkish coffee. An essential Lviv experience. Be sure to reserve a table for dinner at this mega-popular place.

🍺 Drinking & Nightlife

★ Pravda Beer Theatre BREWERY
(www.pravda.beer; pl Rynok 32; ☺10am-2am; ☎) The latest addition to Lviv's drinking scene is this dramatically industrial, multistorey beer temple right on pl Rynok. The master brewer here creates several types of beer, often given imaginative and sometimes political names such Obama Hope and Summer Lviv. Live music is provided by the brewery's very own orchestra, tours run throughout the day and there's a menu of good pub food.

★ **Pyana Vyshnya** BAR

(П'яна вишня; pl Rynok 11; ⊙ 10am-midnight) It's easy to find this one-drink bar – just look for the crowd of people on pl Rynok holding tiny glasses of something crimson, any time of the day. The tipple in question is the namesake, 18.5% volume, bitter-sweet cherry liqueur, sold by the crystal glass (36uah) or in bottles (200uah for 0.5L).

★ **Lvivska Kopalnya Kavy** CAFE

(Львівська копальня кави; pl Rynok 10; ⊙ 8am-midnight Mon-Thu, to 2am Fri-Sun; 🛜) Lviv is Ukraine's undisputed coffee capital, and the 'Lviv Coffee Mine' is where the stratum of arabica is excavated by local colliers from deep beneath pl Rynok. You can tour the mine or just sample the heart-pumping end product inside at tables as dark as the brews, or out on the covered courtyard.

ℹ️ Information

Tourist Information Centre (☑ 032-254 6079; www.lviv.travel; pl Rynok 1, Ratusha; ⊙ 9am-8pm May-Sep, 10am-6pm Oct-Apr) Ukraine's best tourist information centre. Branches at the **airport** (☑ 067 673 9194; www.lviv.travel; Lviv Airport; ⊙ open depending on flight schedule) and the **train station** (☑ 032-226 2005; www.lviv.travel; ticket hall, Lviv Train Station; ⊙ 9am-6pm).

ℹ️ Getting Around

TO/FROM THE AIRPORT

To reach the city centre from the airport, take trolleybus 9 to the university (vul Universytetska, 20 minutes) or bus 48 (28 minutes) to the corner of vul Doroshenka and pr Svobody.

PUBLIC TRANSPORT

The Tourist Information Centre has comprehensive maps of the entire tram and bus network, but you are unlikely to use it as central Lviv can be easily explored on foot.

ODESA ОДЕСА

☑ 048 / POP 1 MILLION

Odesa is a city straight from literature – an energetic, decadent boom town. Its famous Potemkin Steps sweep down to the Black Sea and Ukraine's biggest commercial port. Behind them, a cosmopolitan cast of characters makes merry among neoclassical pastel buildings lining a geometric grid of leafy streets.

Immigrants from all over Europe were invited to make their fortune here when Odesa was founded in the late 18th century by Russia's Catherine the Great. These new inhabitants, particularly Jews, gave Russia's southern window on the world a singular, subversive nature.

Having weathered recent political storms, Odesa is booming again – it now substitutes for Crimea as the main domestic holiday destination. It's a golden age for local businesses, but it puts a strain on the already crowded sandy beaches.

⊙ Sights

★ **Prymorsky Boulevard** STREET

(Приморський бульвар) Odesa's elegant facade, this tree-lined, clifftop promenade was designed to enchant the passengers of arriving boats with the neoclassical opulence of its architecture and civility, unexpected in these parts at the time of construction in the early 19th century. Imperial architects also transformed the cliff face into terraced gardens descending to the port, divided by the famous **Potemkin Steps** (Потьомкінські сходи) – the **Istanbul Park** lies east of the steps and the **Greek Park** west of them.

★ **Vul Derybasivska** STREET

(Дерибасівська вулиця) Odesa's main commercial street, pedestrian vul Derybasivska is jam-packed with restaurants, bars and, in the summer high season, tourists. At its quieter eastern end you'll discover the **statue of José de Ribas** (vul Derybasivska), the Spanish-Neapolitan general who built Odesa's harbour and who also has a central street named after him. At the western end of the thoroughfare is the pleasant and beautifully renovated **City Garden**, surrounded by several restaurants.

History of Odesa Jews Museum MUSEUM

(Музей історії євреїв Одеси; ☑ 048-728 9743; www.migdal.org.ua/migdal/museum/; vul Nizhynska 66; recommended donation 100uah, tour 200uah; ⊙ 1-7pm Mon-Thu, 10am-4pm Sun) Less than 2% of people call themselves Jewish in today's Odesa – against 44% in the early 1920s – but the resilient and humorous Jewish spirit still permeates every aspect of local life. Hidden inside a typical run-down courtyard with clothes drying on a rope and a rusty carcass of a prehistoric car, this modest but lovingly curated exhibition consists of items donated by Odessite families, many of whom have long emigrated to America or Israel.

🛌 Sleeping

Babushka Grand Hostel HOSTEL €

(☑ 063 070 5535; www.babushkagrand.com; vul Mala Arnautska 60; dm/d from 190/570uah; ✳ 🛜) While Odesa's other hostels are decidedly for the young, day-sleeping crowd, the wonderfully named Grand Babushka, occupying a palatial apartment near the train station, has a more laid-back, traveller vibe. The stuccoed interiors and crystal chandeliers are stunning, the staff fun and occasionally a real Ukrainian *babushka* arrives to cook up a feast.

Hotel Ayvazovsky HOTEL €€

(Готель Айвазовський; ☑ 067 997 9711; http://aivazovskiy-hotel.org.ua; vul Bunina 19; s/d incl breakfast from 1100/1500uah; ⊜ ✳ 🛜) From the Chesterfield sofas in the foyer to the spacious, European-standard bedrooms with high ceilings to the design-magazine-perfect bathrooms, this soothing, 27-room hotel in the heart of the city centre is worth every hryvnia. Continental breakfast is delivered to your room every morning, and staff can book tours and countless other services.

Frederic Koklen BOUTIQUE HOTEL €€€

(Фредерік Коклен; ☑ 048-737 5553; www.koklenhotel.com; prov Nekrasova 7; d incl breakfast from 1600uah; ✳ 🛜) Odesa's most sumptuous boutique hotel has guests gushing about the exceptional service, the luxurious period ambience and the great location. Rooms in this renovated mansion are studies in 18th- and 19th-century imperial-era style, and the attention to detail, quality of materials and standard of maintenance are exceptional for Ukraine.

🍴 Eating

Dva Karla MOLDOVAN €

(Bodega 2K; ☑ 096 524 1601; www.facebook.com/bodega2k; vul Hretska 22; mains 70-120uah; ⏱ 10am-11pm) This envoy from nearby Moldova occupies a super-quaint courtyard covered with a vine canopy in summer and pleasant cellar premises in winter. Come here to try *mamalyga* (a version of polenta with *brynza* goat's cheese or fried lard), paprika stuffed with rice and chopped meat, as well as juicy *mitityay* (kebabs).

Touting itself as a bodega, 2K also treats visitors to excellent Moldovan and (more experimental) Ukrainian wine. It's also a great breakfast option.

★ City Food Market FOOD HALL €€

(Міський продовольчий ринок; ☑ 048-702 1913; www.facebook.com/odessa.cityfood.market; Rishelyevska 9A; mains 100-200uah; ⏱ 11am-2am; 🛜 ✍) Once an itinerant tribe, congregating here and there for irregular jamborees, Odesa foodies now have a rather palatial indoors base. The two-storey building is divided between shops, each with its own kitchen dedicated to a particular product – from the Vietnamese *pho* soup and Greek pita gyros, to grilled ribs and oysters.

★ Bernardazzi EUROPEAN €€€

(Бернардацці; ☑ 067 000 2511; www.bernardazzi.com; Odessa Philharmonic Hall, vul Bunina 15; mains 200-420uah; ⏱ noon-midnight, to 2am Fri & Sat; ✳) Few Ukrainian restaurants have truly authentic settings, but the art nouveau dining room of this Italianesque palazzo (once a stock exchange, now the Philharmonic Hall) is the real deal. In addition to well-crafted Southern and Eastern European fare, there's an award-winning wine list, occasional live music and a secluded courtyard for summertime chilling.

Kotelok Mussels Bar SEAFOOD €€€

(☑ 048-736 6030; http://kotelok-musselsbar.com; vul Sadova 17; mains 180-400uah; ⏱ 9am-11pm, to midnight Fri & Sat) This may not be obvious, but mussels are as much a part of Odesa food culture as aubergine 'caviar' (cold vegetable stew). Furnished like a bar, with a row of seats facing an open kitchen, Kotelok is all about Black Sea mussels served with a variety of dips, including the quintessentially local mixture of paprika and *brynza* goat's cheese.

🍸 Drinking & Nightlife

★ Shkaf BAR

(Шкаф; ☑ 048-232 5017; www.shkaff.od.ua; vul Hretska 32; ⏱ 6pm-5am) It feels like entering a *shkaf* (wardrobe) from the outside, but what you find inside is a heaving basement bar–club, a surefire antidote to Odesa's trendy beach-club scene and pick-up bars. The inconspicuous, unmarked entrance is always surrounded by smoking/chilling-out patrons, so you won't miss it.

The Fitz BAR

(☑ 068 810 2070; www.facebook.com/TheFitzCocktailBar; vul Katerynynska 6; ⏱ 3pm-3am) Doubling as a barbershop by day, this little bar has an edgy, decadent feel enhanced by aged walls and a magnificent chandelier that bedazzles incoming customers. Some patrons occupy barbers' work stations, complete with sinks and mirrors, which adds to the overall surreality. Mostly rum-based cocktails include all-time favourites, as well as those you've likely never tried.

ⓘ Getting Around

To get to the city centre from the train station (about a 20-minute walk), go to the stop near the McDonald's and take any *marshrutka* (minibus) saying 'Грецька площа' (pl Hretska, vul Bunina side), such as bus 148. From the airport, trolleybus 14 goes to the train station, while the infrequent bus 117 trundles all the way into the centre, stopping at Pl Hretska Bus Stop.

SURVIVAL GUIDE

ⓘ Directory A–Z

ACCOMMODATION

Book well ahead during summer in Lviv and Odesa, and across the country in early January and early May. The Carpathians are busy in summer and to a lesser extent during ski season.

Hotels (готель) From standard Western chains to unreformed Soviet dinosaurs.

Mini-hotels (мини-готель) Typically occupy one floor in an apartment block; often good value.

Hostels (хостел) Some professionally run; many are semi-amateurish affairs in converted communal apartments.

Apartments (квартира) Vary in size and quality; a good alternative to city hotels.

Homestays (приватний сектор) Room or bed in seaside towns during high season; standards usually basic.

INTERNET ACCESS

Internet is more accessible for travellers in Ukraine than it is in most Western countries.

➡ SIM-cards with fast and unlimited internet access are ubiquitous and very cheap.

➡ Free wi-fi internet access is the norm in hotels, cafes and restaurants across the country, with or without a password.

➡ Bus stations, train stations and airports often have free wi-fi.

➡ Most cities have free wi-fi hotspots.

➡ Wi-fi is available on Intercity trains and on some long-distance coaches.

➡ Upmarket hotels often have a business centre with a couple of terminals hooked up to the internet.

➡ Internet cafes are uncommon these days; many of them have devolved into dodgy gaming centres.

LEGAL MATTERS

➡ Carry your passport with you at all times; if stopped by the police, you are obliged to show it.

➡ If you are stopped by the police, ask to see their ID immediately.

➡ The police must return your documents at once.

➡ Do not get involved with drugs; penalties can be severe and the process leading up to them labyrinthine.

➡ The US embassy in Kyiv maintains a list of English-speaking lawyers.

LGBTIQ+ TRAVELLERS

Homosexuality is legal in Ukraine, but few people are very out here and attitudes vary. Gay clubs do exist in large cities; elsewhere the gay scene is mostly underground. Ukraine lags behind most of Europe on gay rights, but pride marches do take place, heavily guarded by police and threatened by right-wing thugs.

MONEY

ATMs are widespread, even in small towns. Credit cards are accepted at most hotels and restaurants.

OPENING HOURS

Opening hours are consistent throughout the year with very few seasonal variations. Lunch breaks (1pm to 2pm or 2pm to 3pm) are an all-too-common throwback to Soviet days. Sunday closing is rare.

Banks 9am to 5pm Monday to Friday

Restaurants 11am to 11pm

Cafes 9am to 10pm

Bars and Clubs 10pm to 3am

Shops 9am to 9pm

Sights 9am to 5pm or 6pm, closed at least one day a week

PUBLIC HOLIDAYS

New Year's Day 1 January

Orthodox Christmas 7 January

International Women's Day 8 March

Orthodox Easter (Paskha) April/May

Labour Day 1–2 May

Victory Day (1945) 9 May

Constitution Day 28 June

Independence Day (1991) 24 August

Defender of Ukraine Day 14 October

SAFE TRAVEL

With Ukraine in the news for all the wrong reasons, safety is a major concern for travellers these days. But although crime is on the rise, Ukraine remains a rather safe European destination, unless you venture into the war zone, which accounts for a tiny part of the country's territory in the far east.

TELEPHONE

All numbers now start with 0, that zero being a part of the national code. If you see a number starting with 8, this is the old intercity and mobile prefix and should be left off.

VISAS

Generally, visas are not needed for stays of up to 90 days.

❶ Getting There & Away

AIR

Four international airports serve as gateways to Ukraine.

Kyiv Boryspil International Airport (☎ 044-364 4505; www.kbp.aero) Gets the bulk of international flights and serves as the hub for the national carrier, **Ukraine International Airlines** (☎ 044-581 5050; www.flyuia.com; vul Lysenka 4; ☺ 8am-7.30pm, to 5.30pm Sun; Ⓜ Maydan Nezalezhnosti).

Kyiv Zhulyany International Airport (☎ 044-585 0211; www.airport.kiev.ua; vul Medova 2; ☒ 9, marshrutka 302, 368, 805) Serves domestic flights and a growing number of international flights, including flights by budget carrier Wizz Air.

Lviv Danylo Halytsky International Airport (☎ 032 229 8112; www.lwo.aero; vul Lyubinska 168) Attracts a fair number of international flights, including Ryanair services to London.

Odesa International Airport (www.odessa. aero) Regular flights to Istanbul and several Central/Eastern European destinations.

LAND

Providing the most useful service by far, two trains daily connect Przemyśl in Poland to Lviv (two hours) and Kyiv (seven to nine hours). Considerably less convenient slow sleeper trains connect Kyiv and Lviv to Hungary and Slovakia.

Despite poor relations, trains were still running between Kyiv and Moscow (14 to 16 hours, seven daily) and destinations in Ukraine and Russia at the time of writing.

You'll find bus services to multiple European destinations at every major station in Ukraine. Check https://infobus.eu or https://busfor.ua for schedules.

❶ Getting Around

AIR

The network is very centralised, so more often than not you need to change flights in Kyiv when travelling between the southeast and the west. The number of domestic flights and carriers has fallen considerably in recent years.

BUS

Buses serve every city and small town, but they're best for short trips (three hours or less), as vehicles can often be small, old and overcrowded. However, luxury bus services run by big companies provide a good alternative to trains. Some bus stations have become quite orderly, others remain chaotic.

CAR & MOTORCYCLE

Travelling by car in Ukraine can be a rewarding if nerve-racking experience. However, road conditions are improving and drivers may even be becoming a little more disciplined.

LOCAL TRANSPORT

Ukrainian cities are navigable by trolleybus, tram, bus and (in Kyiv, Kharkiv and Dnipro) metro. Urban public-transport systems are usually overworked and overcrowded. There's no room for being shy or squeamish – learn to assert yourself quickly.

➡ A ticket (*kvytok* or *bilyet*) for one ride by bus/tram/trolleybus costs 2uah to 5uah.

➡ There are virtually no return, transfer, timed or day tickets available anywhere.

➡ It's always simplest to pay the driver or conductor.

➡ Tickets have to be punched on board (or ripped by the conductor).

➡ Unclipped or untorn tickets warrant an on-the-spot fine should you be caught.

➡ For the metros you need a plastic token (*zheton*), sold at the counters inside the stations. Top-up cards are now also available in Kyiv.

➡ Metros run from around 5.30am to midnight.

TRAIN

For long journeys, train is the preferred method of travel in Ukraine. The most useful and comfortable are the daytime Intercity+ trains. Many overnight trains have old, Soviet-era carriages. Services are mostly punctual.

Survival Guide

Directory A–Z

Accessible Travel

Cobbled medieval streets, 'classic' hotels, congested inner cities and underground subway systems make Europe a tricky destination for people with mobility issues. However, the train facilities are good and some destinations boast new tram services or lifts to platforms.

Download Lonely Planet's free Accessible Travel guide from http://lptravel.to/AccessibleTravel. The following websites can help with specific details.

Accessible Europe (www.accessibleurope.com) Specialist European tours with van transport.

DisabledGo.com (www.disabledgo.com) Detailed access information for thousands of venues across the UK and Ireland.

Mobility International Schweiz (www.mis-ch.ch) Good site (only partly in English) listing 'barrier-free' destinations in Switzerland and abroad, plus wheelchair-accessible hotels in Switzerland.

Mobility International USA (www.miusa.org) Publishes

guides and advises travellers with disabilities on mobility issues.

Society for Accessible Travel & Hospitality (SATH; www.sath.org) Reams of information for travellers with disabilities.

Accommodation

Price Ranges

Rates in our reviews are for high season and often drop outside high season by as much as 50%. High season in ski resorts is usually between Christmas and New Year and around the February to March winter holidays. Price categories are broken down differently for individual countries – see each country for full details.

Reservations

During peak holiday periods, particularly Easter, summer and Christmas – and any time of year in popular destinations such as London, Paris and Rome – it's wise to book ahead. Most places can be reserved online. Always try to book directly with the establishment; this means

you're paying just for your room, with no surcharge going to a hostel- or hotel-booking website.

B&Bs & Guesthouses

Guesthouses (pension, *Gasthaus, chambre d'hôte* etc) and B&Bs offer greater comfort than hostels for a marginally higher price. Most are simple affairs, normally with shared bathrooms.

In some destinations, particularly in Eastern Europe, locals wait in train stations touting rented rooms. Just be sure such accommodation isn't in a far-flung suburb that requires an expensive taxi ride to and from town. Confirm the price before agreeing to rent a room and remember that it's unwise to leave valuables in your room when you go out.

B&Bs in the UK and Ireland often aren't really budget accommodation – even the lowliest tend to have midrange prices and there is a new generation of 'designer' B&Bs, which are positively top end.

Camping

Camping is popular in Europe, although, on such a crowded continent, it's less of a wilderness experience than it is in North America or Africa. Glamping is also gaining in popularity. Most camping grounds are some distance from city centres.

National tourist offices provide lists of camping

BOOK YOUR STAY ONLINE

For more accommodation reviews by Lonely Planet authors, check out http://lonelyplanet.com/hotels/. You'll find independent reviews, as well as recommendations on the best places to stay. Best of all, you can book online.

grounds and camping organisations. Also see www.coolcamping.co.uk for details on prime campsites across Europe.

There will usually be a charge per tent or site, per person and per vehicle. In busy areas and in busy seasons, it's sometimes necessary to book in advance.

Camping other than at designated grounds is difficult in Western Europe, because it's hard to find a suitably private spot. Camping is also illegal without the permission of the local authorities (the police or local council office) or the landowner. Don't be shy about asking; you might be pleasantly surprised.

In some countries, such as Austria, the UK, France and Germany, free camping is illegal on all but private land, and in Greece it's illegal altogether but not enforced. This doesn't prevent hikers from occasionally pitching their tent, and you'll usually get away with it if you have a small tent, are discreet, stay just one or two nights, decamp during the day and don't light a fire or leave rubbish. At worst, you'll be woken by the police and asked to move on.

In Eastern Europe free camping is more widespread.

Homestays & Farmstays

You needn't volunteer on a farm to sleep on it. In Switzerland and Germany there's the opportunity to sleep in barns or 'hay hotels'. Farmers provide cotton undersheets (to avoid straw pricks) and woolly blankets for extra warmth, but guests need their own sleeping bag and torch. For further details visit Abenteuer im Stroh (www.schlaf-im-stroh.ch).

Italy in many ways invented the modern farmstay movement through its rich network of *agriturismi* that first grew up in the 1980s. Agriturismi are state-

regulated and participating farms must grow at least one of their own crops. Otherwise, accommodation runs the gamut from small rustic hideaways to grand country estates known as *massarías*. See www.agriturismo.it for more details.

Agritourism has since spread to the UK, France and other countries. See www.farmstayplanet.com.

Hostels

You can organise a lengthy excursion in Europe based purely in cheap hostels – as any nostalgic InterRailer will happy relate.

HI hostels (those affiliated to Hostelling International; www.hihostels.com) usually offer the cheapest (secure) roof over your head in Europe and you don't have to be particularly young to use them. That said, if you're over 26 you'll frequently pay a small surcharge (usually about €3) to stay in an official hostel.

Hostel rules vary per facility and country, but some ask that guests vacate the rooms for cleaning purposes or impose a curfew. Most offer a complimentary breakfast, although the quality varies. Hostels are also great places to meet other travellers and pick up all kinds of information on the region you are visiting. They often usurp tourist offices in this respect.

You need to be a YHA or HI member to use HI-affiliated

hostels, but nonmembers can stay by paying a few extra euros, which will be set against future membership. After sufficient nights (usually six), you automatically become a member. To join, ask at any hostel or contact your national hostelling office, which you'll find on the HI website – where you can also make online bookings.

Europe has many private hostelling organisations and hundreds of unaffiliated backpacker hostels. These have fewer rules, more self-catering kitchens and fewer large, noisy school groups. Dorms in many private hostels can be mixed sex. If you aren't happy to share mixed dorms, be sure to ask when you book.

Hotels

Hotels are usually the most expensive accommodation option, though at the lower end there is little to differentiate them from guesthouses or even hostels.

Cheap hotels around bus and train stations can be convenient for late-night or early-morning arrivals and departures, but some are also unofficial brothels or just downright sleazy. Check the room beforehand and make sure you're clear on the price and what it covers.

Discounts for longer stays are usually possible and hotel owners in southern Europe *might* be open to a little bargaining if times are slack. In many countries it's common for business hotels (usually more than two stars) to slash their rates by up to 40% on Friday and Saturday nights.

At the cutting edge of the market, boutique and design hotels continue to push the envelope. Look out for creative options set in old castles, monasteries or even former prisons.

University Accommodation

Some university towns rent out their student accommodation during the holiday periods. This is a popular practice in France, the UK and many Eastern European countries. University accommodation will sometimes be in single rooms (although it's more commonly in doubles or triples) and might have cooking facilities. For details ask at individual colleges or universities, at student information offices or local tourist offices.

Customs Regulations

The EU has a two-tier customs system: one for goods bought duty-free to import to or export from the EU, and one for goods bought in another EU country where taxes and duties have already been paid.

➡ When entering or leaving the EU, you are allowed to carry duty-free 200 cigarettes, 50 cigars or 250g of tobacco; 2L of still wine plus 1L of spirits over 22% alcohol or another 4L of wine (sparkling or otherwise); for other goods (eg, coffee, perfume, electronics) up to €430 (air/sea entry) or €300 (land entry).

➡ When travelling from one EU country to another, the duty-paid limits are 800 cigarettes, 200 cigars, 1kg of tobacco, 10L of spirits, 20L of fortified wine, 90L of wine

(of which not more than 60L is sparkling) and 110L of beer.

➡ Non-EU countries often have different regulations and many countries forbid the export of antiquities and cultural treasures.

Discount Cards

Camping Cards

The Camping Card International (CCI; www.camping cardinternational.com) is an ID that can be used instead of a passport when checking into a camping ground. Many camping grounds offer a small discount (up to 25%) if you sign in with one and it includes third-party insurance.

Rail Passes

If you plan to visit more than a few countries, or one or two countries in depth, you might save money with a rail pass.

European citizens or residents qualify for a one-month InterRail pass (p1213). There are special rates if you're under 27 years old. Children under 12 are free.

Non-European citizens can apply for a Eurail pass (p1213), valid in 28 countries for up to three months.

Student Cards

The **International Student Identity Card** (www.isic.org), available for full-time students at school, college or university, offers thousands of worldwide discounts on transport, museum entry, youth hostels and even some restaurants. Also available are the International Youth Travel Card (for under 30s) and the International Teacher Identity Card (for teachers and professors). Apply for the cards online or via issuing offices such as STA Travel (www.statravel.com).

For under-26s, there's also the **European Youth Card** (www.eyca.org). Many countries have raised the age limit for this card to under 31.

Electricity

Europe generally runs on 220V, 50Hz AC, but there are exceptions. The UK runs on 230/240V AC, and some old buildings in Italy and Spain have 125V (or even 110V in Spain). The continent is moving towards a 230V standard. If your home country has a vastly different voltage you will need a transformer for delicate and important appliances.

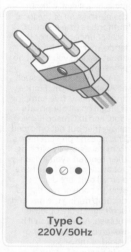

**Type C
220V/50Hz**

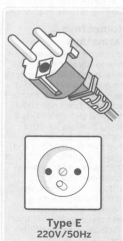

**Type E
220V/50Hz**

The UK and Ireland use three-pin square plugs. Most of Europe uses the 'europlug' with two round pins. Greece, Italy and Switzerland use a third round pin in a way that the two-pin plug usually – but not always in Italy and Switzerland – fits. Buy an adapter before leaving home; those on sale in Europe generally go the other way, but ones for visitors to Europe are also available – airports are always a good place to buy them.

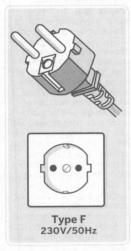

Type F
230V/50Hz

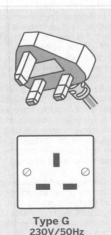

Type G
230V/50Hz

Embassies & Consulates

Generally speaking, your embassy won't be much help in emergencies if the trouble you're in is remotely your own fault. Remember, you're bound by the laws of the country you're in.

In genuine emergencies you might get some assistance, but only if other channels have been exhausted. For example, if you have all your money and documents stolen, it might assist with getting a new passport, but a loan for onward travel is out of the question.

LGBTIQ+ Travellers

Across Western Europe you'll find very liberal attitudes towards homosexuality. The Netherlands, Belgium and Spain were the first three countries in the world to legalise same-sex marriage, in 2001, 2003 and 2005 respectively.

London, Paris, Berlin, Munich, Amsterdam, Madrid and Lisbon have thriving gay communities and pride events. The Greek islands of Mykonos and Lesvos are popular gay beach destinations, while Gran Canaria and Ibiza in Spain are big centres for both gay clubbing and beach holidays.

Eastern Europe, and in particular Russia, tends to be far less progressive. Outside the big cities, attitudes become more conservative and discretion is advised, particularly in Turkey.

Health
Before You Go

No jabs are necessary to visit Europe. However, the World Health Organization (WHO) recommends that all travellers be covered for diphtheria, tetanus, measles, mumps, rubella and polio, regardless of their destination. Since most vaccines don't produce immunity until at least two weeks after they're given, visit a physician at least six weeks before departure.

Health Insurance

It is unwise to travel anywhere in the world without travel insurance. A good policy should include comprehensive health insurance including medical care and emergency evacuation. If you are engaging in hazardous sports, you may need to pay for extra cover.

If you're an EU citizen or a citizen of Iceland, Liechtenstein, Norway or Switzerland, the free EHIC (European Health Insurance Card) covers you for most medical care in 32 European countries, including maternity care and care for chronic illnesses such as diabetes (though not for emergency repatriation). However, you will normally have to pay for medicine bought from pharmacies, even if prescribed, and perhaps for some tests and procedures. The EHIC does not cover private medical consultations and treatment out of your home country; this includes nearly all dentists, and some of the better clinics and surgeries. In the UK, you can apply for an EHIC online, by telephone, or by filling out a form available at post offices.

Non-EU citizens should find out if there is a reciprocal arrangement for free medical care between their country and the EU country they are visiting.

Availability & Cost of Healthcare

Good healthcare is readily available in Western Europe, and for minor illnesses, pharmacists can give valuable advice and sell over-the-counter medication. They can also advise if you need specialised help and point you in the right direction. The

HEALTH RESOURCES

The World Health Organization (www.who.int) publishes the free online book *International Travel and Health*, which is revised annually. MD Travel Health (www.mdtravelhealth.com) provides up-to-date travel-health recommendations for every country.

It's usually a good idea to consult your government's website before departure, if one is available:

Australia (www.smartraveller.gov.au)

Canada (www.phac-aspc.gc.ca)

UK (www.gov.uk/foreign-travel-advice)

USA (www.cdc.gov/travel)

standard of dental care is usually good.

While the situation in Eastern Europe is improving since the EU accession of many countries, quality medical care is not always readily available outside major cities. Embassies, consulates and five-star hotels can usually recommend doctors or clinics.

Condoms are widely available in Europe, however emergency contraception may not be, so take the necessary precautions.

Following the implementation of Brexit (p1204) at the start of 2021, the EHIC health card (providing free state-provided healthcare in any EU country) will be valid for British citizens if you're travelling to an EU country (this doesn't apply in Switzerland, Norway, Iceland or Liechtenstein). Check www.nhs.uk for updates.

Tap Water

Tap water is generally safe to drink in Western Europe. However, bottled water is recommended in most of Eastern Europe and is a must in some countries, including Russia and Ukraine, where the giardia parasite can be a problem. Do not drink water from rivers or lakes as it may contain bacteria or viruses.

Insurance

It's foolhardy to travel without insurance to cover theft, loss and medical problems. There are a wide variety of policies, so check the small print. Some policies specifically exclude 'dangerous activities', which can include scuba diving, motorcycling, winter sports, adventure sports or even hiking. Check that the policy covers ambulances or an emergency flight home.

Internet Access

Internet access varies enormously across Europe. In most places you'll be able to find wi-fi (also called WLAN in some countries), although whether it's free varies greatly. Internet cafes are increasingly rare but not impossible to find.

Access is generally straightforward, although a few tips are in order. If you can't find the @ symbol on a keyboard, try AltGr + 2, or AltGr + Q. Watch out for German and some Balkans keyboards, which reverse the Z and the Y positions. Using a French keyboard is an art unto itself.

Where necessary in relevant countries, click on the language prompt in the bottom right-hand corner of the screen or hit Ctrl + Shift to switch between the Cyrillic and Latin alphabets.

Legal Matters

You can generally purchase alcohol (beer and wine) from between 16 and 18 (usually 18 for spirits), but if in doubt, ask. Although you can drive at 17 or 18, you might not be able to hire a car until you're 25.

Drugs are often quite openly available in Europe, but that doesn't mean they're legal. The Netherlands is most famed for its liberal attitudes, with coffee shops openly selling cannabis even though the drug is *not* technically legal. However, a blind eye is generally turned to the trade as the possession and purchase of small amounts (5g) of 'soft drugs' (ie marijuana and hashish) is allowed and users won't be prosecuted for smoking or carrying this amount. Don't take this relaxed attitude as an invitation to buy harder drugs; if you get caught, you'll be punished. Since 2008 magic mushrooms have been banned in the Netherlands.

Spain also has pretty liberal laws regarding marijuana, although its use is usually reserved for private places.

In Belgium the possession of up to 3g of cannabis is legal, but selling the drug isn't, so if you get caught at the point of sale, you could be in trouble. Switzerland, Italy, Moldova, Russia, Ukraine, Malta, Luxembourg, Estonia, Croatia, Austria, Slovenia and the Czech Republic have also decriminalised possession of marijuana, however, selling remains illegal. Portugal was the first country to decriminalise the use of all drugs in 2001.

Getting caught with drugs in some parts of Europe can lead to imprisonment. If in any doubt, err on the side of caution, and don't even think about taking drugs across international borders.

Money

ATMs

Across major European towns and cities international ATMs are common, but you should always have a back-up option, as there can be glitches. In some remote areas ATMs might be scarce.

Much of Western Europe now uses a chip-and-pin system for added security. You will have problems if you don't have a four-digit PIN and might have difficulties if your card doesn't have a metallic chip. Check with your bank.

Always cover the keypad when entering your PIN and make sure there are no unusual devices attached to the machine, which can copy your card's details or cause it to stick in the machine. If your card disappears and the screen goes blank before you've even entered your PIN, don't enter it – especially if a 'helpful' bystander tells you to do so. If you can't retrieve your card, call your bank's emergency number, if you can, before leaving the ATM.

Cash

It's a good idea to bring some local currency in cash, if only to cover yourself until you get to an exchange facility or find an ATM. The equivalent of €150 should be enough. Some extra cash in an easily exchanged currency is also a good idea, especially in Eastern Europe.

Credit Cards

Visa and MasterCard/Euro-card are more widely accepted in Europe than Amex and Diners Club; Visa (sometimes called Carte Bleue) is particularly strong in France and Spain.

There are, however, regional differences in the general acceptability of credit cards; in Germany, for example, it's less common for restaurants to take credit cards. Cards are not widely accepted off the beaten track.

To reduce the risk of fraud, always keep your card in view when making transactions; for example, in restaurants that do accept cards, pay as you leave, following your card to the till. Keep transaction records and either check your statements when you return home or check your account online while on the road.

Letting your credit-card company know roughly where you're going lessens the chance of fraud – or of your bank cutting off the card when it sees (your) unusual spending.

Debit Cards

It's always worthwhile having a Maestro-compatible debit or Visa-debit card, which differs from a credit card in deducting money straight from your bank account. Check with your bank or card provider for compatibility.

Exchanging Money

Euros, US dollars and UK pounds are the easiest currencies to exchange. You may have trouble exchanging some lesser-known ones at small banks.

Importing or exporting some currencies is restricted or banned, so try to get rid of any local currency before you leave. Get rid of Scottish pounds before leaving the UK; nobody outside Britain will touch them.

Most airports, central train stations, big hotels and many border posts have banking facilities outside regular business hours, at times on a 24-hour basis. Post offices in Europe often perform banking tasks, tend to open longer hours and outnumber banks in remote places. While they always exchange cash, they might baulk at handling travellers cheques not in the local currency.

The best exchange rates are usually at banks. *Bureaux de change* usually – but not always – offer worse rates or charge higher commissions. Hotels and airports are almost always the worst places to change money.

International Transfers

International bank transfers are good for secure one-off movements of large amounts of money, but they might take three to five days and there will be a fee (about £25 in the UK, for example). Be sure to specify the name of the bank, plus the sort code and address of the branch where you'd like to pick up your money. To avoid bank charges consider using an online transfer service such as TransferWise.

In an emergency it's quicker but more costly to have money wired via an Amex office or Western Union.

Taxes & Refunds

When non-EU residents spend more than a certain amount (around €175, but amounts vary from country to country) they can usually reclaim any sales tax when leaving the country.

Making a tax-back claim is straightforward. First make sure the shop offers duty-free sales (often a sign will be displayed reading 'Tax-Free Shopping'). When making your purchase, ask the shop attendant for a tax-refund voucher, filled in with the correct amount and the date. This can be used to claim a refund directly at international airports, or stamped at ferry ports or border crossings and mailed back for a refund.

Tipping & Bargaining

Service charges are increasingly added to bills. In theory this means you're not obliged to tip. In practice that money often doesn't go to the server. Don't pay twice. If the service charge is optional, remove it and pay a tip. If it's not optional, don't tip.

Tipping isn't such a big deal in Europe as it is, say,

in North America. Small change usually suffices in Italy or Spain. Between 10% to 12% is common in the UK. Unlike North America, credit-card machines generally don't have in-built tip requests meaning you'll have to leave your gratuity in cash.

Post

From major European centres, airmail typically takes about five days to North America and about a week to Australasian destinations. Mail from such countries as Albania or Russia is much slower.

Courier services such as DHL are best for essential deliveries.

Safe Travel

Travelling in Europe is usually very safe. With comprehensive healthcare, political stability and generally low crime rates, you'd be unlucky to encounter any serious problems

Discrimination

In some parts of Europe travellers of African, Arab or Asian descent might encounter unpleasant attitudes that are unrelated to them personally. In rural areas travellers whose skin colour marks them out as foreigners might experience unwanted attention.

Attitudes vary from country to country. People tend to be more accepting in cities than in the country. Race is also less of an issue in Western Europe than in parts of the former Eastern Bloc. For example, there has been a spate of racially motivated attacks in St Petersburg and other parts of Russia in recent years.

Druggings

Although rare, some drugging of travellers does occur in Europe. Travellers are especially vulnerable on trains and buses where a new 'friend' may offer you food or a drink that will knock you out, giving them time to steal your belongings.

Gassings have also been reported on a handful of overnight international trains. The best protection is to lock the door of your compartment (use your own lock if there isn't one) and to lock your bags to luggage racks, preferably with a sturdy combination cable.

If you can help it, never sleep alone in a train compartment.

Pickpockets & Thieves

Theft is definitely a problem in parts of Europe and you have to be aware of unscrupulous fellow travellers. The key is to be sensible with your possessions.

➡ Don't store valuables in train-station lockers or luggage-storage counters and be careful about people who offer to help you operate a locker. Also be vigilant if someone offers to carry your luggage: they might carry it away altogether.

➡ Don't leave valuables in your car, on train seats or in your room. When going out, don't flaunt cameras, laptops or other expensive electronic goods.

➡ Carry a small day pack, as shoulder bags are an open invitation for snatch-thieves. Consider using small zipper locks on your packs.

➡ Pickpockets are most active in dense crowds, especially in busy train stations and on public transport during peak hours. Be careful in these situations.

➡ Spread valuables, cash and cards around your body or in different bags.

➡ A money belt with your essentials (passport, cash, credit cards, airline tickets) is usually a good idea.

However, so you needn't delve into it in public, carry a wallet with a day's worth of cash.

➡ Having your passport stolen is less of a disaster if you've recorded the number and issue date or, even better, photocopied the relevant data pages. You can also scan them and email them to yourself. If you lose your passport, notify the police immediately to get a statement and contact your nearest consulate.

➡ Carry photocopies of your credit cards, airline tickets and other travel documents.

Scams

Most scams involve distracting you – either by kids running up to you, someone asking for directions or spilling something on you – while another person steals your wallet. Be alert in such situations.

In some countries, especially in Eastern Europe, you may encounter people claiming to be from the tourist police, the special police, the supersecret police, whatever. Unless they're wearing a uniform and have good reason for accosting you, treat their claims with suspicion.

Needless to say, never show your passport or cash to anyone on the street. Simply walk away. If someone flashes a badge, offer to accompany them to the nearest police station.

Unrest & Terrorism

Civil unrest and terrorist bombings are relatively rare in Europe, all things considered, but they do occur. A spike in attacks by extremists in the UK, France, Germany, Belgium and Spain occurred in the mid-2010s – seven of them between 2015 and 2017 – although things seemed to have quietened down somewhat since. Keep an eye on the news and avoid areas where any flare-up seems likely.

Telephone

Emergency Numbers

The number ☑112 can be dialled free for emergencies in all EU states. See individual countries for country-specific emergency numbers.

Mobile Phones

Even if you're not staying in Europe long, it's more cost-effective for travellers visiting from outside Europe to purchase a prepaid local SIM. In several countries you need your passport to buy a SIM card.

In order to use other SIM cards in your phone, you'll need to have your handset unlocked by your home provider. Even if your phone is locked, you can use apps such as Whatsapp to send free text messages internationally wherever you have wi-fi access or Skype to make free international calls whenever you're online.

Europe uses the GSM 900 network, which also covers Australia and New Zealand, but is not compatible with the North American GSM 1900 or the totally different system in Japan and South Korea. If you have a GSM phone, check with your service provider about using it in Europe. You'll need international roaming, but this is usually free to enable.

You can call abroad from almost any phone box in Europe. Public telephones accepting phonecards (available from post offices, telephone centres, news stands or retail outlets) are virtually the norm now; coin-operated phones are rare, if not impossible, to find.

Without a phonecard, you can ring from a telephone booth inside a post office or telephone centre and settle your bill at the counter. Reverse-charge (collect) calls are often possible. From many countries the Country Direct system lets you phone home by billing the long-distance carrier you use at home. These numbers can often be dialled from public phones without even inserting a phonecard.

Time

Nearly all of Europe, with several exceptions (Russia, Belarus, Iceland), observes daylight saving time on synchronised dates in late March (clocks go forward an hour) and late October (clocks go back an hour). The European parliament proposed to scrap daylight savings time from 2021, but Brexit and the Covid-19 pandemic delayed the implementation of this change.

Europe is divided into four time zones. From west to east:

UTC (Britain, Ireland, Portugal) GMT (GMT plus one hour in summer)

CET (the majority of European countries) GMT plus one hour (GMT plus two hours in summer)

EET (Greece, Turkey, Bulgaria, Romania, Moldova, Ukraine, Belarus, Lithuania, Latvia, Estonia, Kaliningrad, Finland) GMT plus two hours (GMT plus three in summer)

MSK (Russia) GMT plus three hours (GMT plus four hours in summer)

At 9am in Britain it's 1am (GMT/UTC minus eight hours) on the US west coast, 4am (GMT/UTC minus five hours) on the US east coast, 10am in Paris and Prague, 11am in Athens, noon in Moscow and 7pm (GMT/UTC plus 10 hours) in Sydney.

Toilets

Many public toilets require a small fee either deposited in a box or given to the attendant. Sit-down toilets are the rule in the vast majority of places, though squat toilets can very occasionally be found in rural areas.

Public-toilet provision is changeable from city to city. If you can't find one, simply drop into a hotel or restaurant and ask to use theirs, or make a nominal purchase at a cafe.

Tourist Information

Tourist offices are generally common and widespread, although their usefulness varies enormously.

Travel with Children

Hidden in the huge labyrinth that is Europe are tonnes of things that will appeal to kids, youths and teenagers, especially if you're willing to look beyond the obvious (Disneyland Paris, Costa del Sol) and seek out the obscure (cycling in Normandy or horse riding on the west coast of Ireland).

It is hard to generalise about kid friendliness in Europe. For more details, check the Lonely Planet website and search the specific countries you will be visiting. Lonely Planet (www.lonelyplanet.com/family-travel) also has regularly updated family-travel information, articles and advice, as well as numerous kids books.

Santorini Dave (www.santorinidave.com) has a comprehensive list of family-friendly hotels plus plenty of other advice.

Practicalities

➡ Europe, in particular Mediterranean Europe, is very family-oriented. Expect waitstaff to ruffle your kid's hair and bank on seeing young children sitting around at family meals in restaurants until late.

➡ Nappies (diapers) are widely available; baby-changing facilities vary from country to country but are generally pretty comprehensive.

➡ Baby formula and baby food are widely available

in all European countries. However, brands differ. You might want to bring your own stash as backup.

➡ For cheap rooms, check out Europe's hostels, many of which have at least one family room.

➡ Plan ahead and select a few preplanned big-ticket items aimed specifically at kids before you leave, such as Disneyland Paris or Legoland in Denmark.

➡ Don't write off the less obvious sights. Many of Europe's art galleries and iconic monuments give out kids activity books that lay out special interactive itineraries for children.

➡ Hit a festival. Many European festivals have a strong family bias and have been entertaining children for centuries, from Seville's Feria de Abril to France's Bastille Day.

➡ Most European countries have a pretty relaxed attitude to breastfeeding in public despite the fact that European women are less likely to breastfeed than women elsewhere.

➡ Cots are usually provided free of charge for young children in hotels on request. Reserve when booking.

➡ In the EU, some form of protective car seat must be used by all children under 1.35m (4ft 5 in). Check when booking a vehicle for seat availability.

Visas

➡ Citizens of the US, Canada, Australia, New Zealand and the UK currently need only a valid passport to enter nearly all countries in Europe, including the entire EU. However, in late 2022, the EU will introduce a new visa-waiver scheme called ETIAS (European Travel Information and Authorization System). Citizens of visa-exempt countries will subsequently have to fill in an online application and pay €7. The authorization will be valid for three years.

➡ Belarus offers 30 days of visa-free travel for citizens of 73 countries, including the EU, the US, Canada, Australia and New Zealand.

➡ Russia requires most visitors to have a prearranged visa before arrival and even an 'invitation' from (or booking with) a tour operator or hotel. It's simpler and safer to obtain these visas before leaving home. Citizens of South American countries, South Africa and many states of the former USSR can travel visa-free to Russia.

➡ Australians and New Zealanders need a visa for the Ukraine. Citizens of the EU, USA and Canada do not.

➡ Transit visas are usually cheaper than tourist or business visas but they allow only a very short stay (one to five days) and can be difficult to extend.

➡ All visas have a 'use-by' date and you'll be refused entry afterwards. In some cases it's easier to get visas as you go along rather than arranging them all beforehand. Carry spare passport photos (you may need from one to four every time you apply for a visa).

➡ Visas to neighbouring countries are usually issued immediately by consulates in Eastern Europe, although some may levy a hefty surcharge for 'express service'.

➡ Consulates are generally open weekday mornings (if there's both an embassy and a consulate, you want the consulate).

➡ Because regulations can change, double-check with the relevant embassy or consulate before travelling.

BREXIT

Following the now-famous 2016 referendum in which citizens of the UK narrowly voted in favour of leaving the EU, the status of UK travellers vis-à-vis EU entry requirements underwent some minor changes changes in January 2021.

➡ British citizens may stay in the Schengen area for 90 days within a 180-day period (and not indefinitely as before). From late 2022, they will also have to apply for an online ETIAS visa-waiver authorization which will cost €7 and be valid for three years.

➡ Citizens of the UK will need to check they have six months left on their passport when travelling to countries in the Schengen block.

➡ The EHIC health card (that formerly provided free state-provided healthcare in any EU country for British citizens) will be replaced by another scheme. In the meantime, the UK government recommends its citizens take out travel insurance.

➡ The guarantee of free-roaming for mobile phones has ended. UK citizens should check with their phone providers before travelling.

➡ UK citizens can no longer use EU passport holder lanes at European airports.

For the latest information on UK visas, visit www.gov.uk/browse/visas-immigration.

THE SCHENGEN AREA

Twenty-six European countries are signatories to the Schengen Agreement, which has effectively dismantled internal border controls between them. They are Austria, Belgium, the Czech Republic, Denmark, Estonia, Finland, France, Germany, Greece, Iceland, Italy, Hungary, Latvia, Liechtenstein, Lithuania, Luxembourg, Malta, the Netherlands, Norway, Poland, Portugal, Slovakia, Slovenia, Spain, Sweden and Switzerland.

Cyprus, Croatia, Bulgaria and Romania are prospective Schengen members, but have yet to officially join.

The UK and Ireland, as well as Russia and much of Eastern Europe, are not part of the Schengen Agreement. Visitors from non-EU countries will have to apply for visas to these countries separately.

Citizens of the US, Australia, New Zealand, Canada and the UK only need a valid passport to enter Schengen countries (as well as the UK and Ireland). However, from late 2022, citizens of these countries will need to fill out an online visa-waiver called ETIAS.

Other nationals, including South Africans, can apply for a single visa – a Schengen visa – when travelling throughout this region.

Non-EU visitors (with or without a Schengen visa) should expect to be questioned, however perfunctorily, when first entering the region. However, later travel within the zone is much like a domestic trip, with no border controls.

If you need a Schengen visa, you must apply at the consulate or embassy of the country that's your main destination, or your point of entry. You may then stay up to a maximum of 90 days in the entire Schengen area within a six-month period. Once your visa has expired, you must leave the zone and may only reenter after three months abroad. Shop around when choosing your point of entry, as visa prices may differ from country to country.

If you're a citizen of the US, Australia, New Zealand or Canada, you may stay visa-free a total of 90 days, during six months, within the entire Schengen region.

If you're planning a longer trip, you need to enquire personally as to whether you need a visa or visas. Your country might have bilateral agreements with individual Schengen countries allowing you to stay there longer than 90 days without a visa. However, you will need to talk directly to the relevant embassies or consulates.

Volunteering

If you want to spend more time living and working in Europe, a short-term volunteer project might seem a good idea, say, teaching English in Poland or building a school in Turkey. However, most voluntary organisations levy high charges for airfares, food, lodging and recruitment (from about €250 to €800 per week), making such work impractical for most shoestringers. One exception is WWOOF International (www.wwoof. org), which helps link volunteers with organic farms in Germany, Slovenia, the Czech Republic, Denmark, the UK, Austria and Switzerland. A small membership fee is required to join the national chapter but in exchange for your labour you'll receive free lodging and food.

For more information, see Lonely Planet's *Volunteer: A Traveller's Guide*.

Women Travellers

➡ Women might attract unwanted attention in Turkey, rural Spain and southern Italy, especially Sicily, where many men view whistling and catcalling as flattery. Conservative dress can help deter this.

➡ Hitchhiking alone is not recommended anywhere.

➡ Female readers have reported assaults at Turkish hotels with shared bathrooms, so women travelling to Turkey might want to consider a more expensive room with private bathroom.

➡ Journeywoman (www. journeywoman.com) maintains an online newsletter about solo female travels all over the world.

Work

EU citizens are allowed to work in any other EU country, but there can still be tiresome paperwork to complete. Other nationalities require special work permits that can be almost impossible to arrange, especially for temporary work. However, that doesn't prevent enterprising travellers from topping up their funds by working in the hotel or restaurant trades at beach

USEFUL WORK WEBSITES

EuroJobs (www.eurojobs.com) Links to hundreds of organisations looking to employ both non-Europeans (with the correct work permits) and Europeans.

Natives (www.natives.co.uk) Summer and winter resort jobs, plus various tips.

Picking Jobs (www.pickingjobs.com) Includes some tourism jobs.

Season Workers (www.seasonworkers.com) Best for ski-resort work and summer jobs, although it also has some childcare jobs.

Ski-jobs.co.uk (https://www.ski-jobs.co.uk) Mainly service jobs such as chalet hosts, bar staff and porters. Some linguistic skills required.

Teaching (www.teachaway.com) Details on jobs and training for teaching posts in Europe, from Andorra to Turkey.

or ski resorts, or teaching a little English – and they don't always have to do this illegally.

The UK, for example, issues special 'Youth Mobility Scheme' visas (www.gov. uk/tier-5-youth-mobility) to citizens from Australia, Canada, New Zealand, Japan, Hong Kong, South Korea, Taiwan and Monaco aged between 18 and 30, valid for two years of work. Similar versions of the Youth Mobility Scheme are offered by other European countries. Your national student-exchange organisation might also be able to arrange temporary work permits to several countries.

If you have a grandparent or parent who was born in an EU country, you may have certain rights of residency or citizenship. Ask that country's embassy about dual citizenship and work permits. With citizenship, also ask about any obligations, such as military service and residency. Beware that your home country may not recognise dual citizenship.

Seasonal Work

Typical tourist jobs (picking grapes in France, working at a bar in Greece) often come with board and lodging, and the pay is essentially pocket money, but you'll have a good time partying with other travellers.

Busking is fairly common in major European cities, but it's illegal in some parts of Switzerland and Austria. Crackdowns even occur in Belgium and Germany, where it has been tolerated in the past. Some other cities, including London, require permits and security checks. Talk to other buskers first.

Teaching English

Most schools prefer a bachelor's degree and a TEFL (Teaching English as a Foreign Language) certificate.

It is easier to find TEFL jobs in Eastern Europe than in Western Europe. The British Council (www.british council.org) can provide advice about training and job searches. Alternatively, try the big schools such as Berlitz (www.berlitz.com) and Wall Street English (www. wallstreetenglish.com).

Transport

GETTING THERE & AWAY

Flights, cars and tours can be booked online at www.lonely planet.com/bookings.

Entering Europe

Europe is one of the world's major destinations, sporting many of its busiest airports with routes fanning out to the far corners of the globe. More adventurous travellers can enter from Asia on some epic long-distance train routes. Numerous ferries jockey across the Mediterranean between Europe and Africa.

Air

To save money, it's best to travel off-season. This means, if possible, avoid mid-June to early September, Easter, Christmas and school holidays.

Regardless of your ultimate destination, it's sometimes better to pick a recognised transport 'hub' as your initial port of entry, where high traffic volumes help keep prices down. The busiest, and therefore most obvious, airports are London, Frankfurt, Paris and Rome. Sometimes tickets to Amsterdam, Athens, Barcelona, Berlin, İstanbul, Madrid and Vienna are worth checking out.

Long-haul airfares to Eastern Europe are rarely a bargain; you're usually better flying to a Western European hub and taking an onward budget-airline flight or train. The main hubs in Eastern Europe are Budapest, Moscow, Prague and Warsaw.

Most of the aforementioned gateway cities are also well serviced by low-cost carriers that fly to other parts of Europe.

Main European airports:

Schiphol Airport, Amsterdam (www.schiphol.nl)

Frankfurt Airport, Frankfurt (www.frankfurt-airport.com)

Heathrow Airport, London (www.heathrow.com)

Barajas Airport, Madrid (www. aeropuertomadrid-barajas.com)

Aéroport de Charles de Gaulle, Paris (www.easycdg.com)

Leonardo da Vinci Airport, Rome (www.adr.it)

Land

It's possible to reach Europe by various train routes from Asia. Most common is the Trans-Siberian Railway, connecting Moscow to Siberia, the Russian Far East, Mongolia and China.

It is also possible to reach Moscow from several Central Asian states and İstanbul from Iran and Jordan. See www.seat61.com for more information about these adventurous routes.

Sea

There are numerous ferry routes between Europe and

CLIMATE CHANGE & TRAVEL

Every form of transport that relies on carbon-based fuel generates CO_2, the main cause of human-induced climate change. Modern travel is dependent on aeroplanes, which might use less fuel per kilometre per person than most cars but travel much greater distances. The altitude at which aircraft emit gases (including CO_2) and particles also contributes to their climate change impact. Many websites offer 'carbon calculators' that allow people to estimate the carbon emissions generated by their journey and, for those who wish to do so, to offset the impact of the greenhouse gases emitted with contributions to portfolios of climate-friendly initiatives throughout the world. Lonely Planet offsets the carbon footprint of all staff and author travel.

Africa, including links from Spain to Morocco; Italy and Malta to Tunisia; and France to Morocco and Algeria. Check out www.traghettiweb. it for comprehensive information on all Mediterranean ferries. Ferries are often filled to capacity in summer, especially to and from Tunisia, so book well in advance if you're taking a vehicle across.

Passenger freighters (typically carrying up to 12 passengers) aren't nearly as competitively priced as airlines. Journeys also take a long time. However, if you have your heart set on a transatlantic journey, TravLtips Cruise & Freighter (www.travelofamerica.com) has information on freighter cruises.

GETTING AROUND

Air

Airlines

Low-cost carriers have revolutionised European transport. Over longer distances, airlines sometimes offer the cheapest transport connections, although flying is environmentally costly and often less comfortable than going by train and bus. Most budget airlines have a similar pricing system – namely that ticket prices rise with the number of seats sold on each flight, so book as early as possible to get a decent fare.

Some low-cost carriers – Ryanair being the prime example – have made a habit of flying to smaller, less convenient airports on the outskirts of their destination city, or even to the airports of nearby cities, so check the exact location of the departure and arrival airports before you book. Many flights also leave at the crack of dawn or arrive inconveniently late at night.

Departure and other taxes (including booking fees, checked-baggage fees and other surcharges) soon add up and are included in the final price by the end of the online booking process – usually a lot more than you were hoping to pay – but with careful choosing and advance booking you can get excellent deals.

In the face of competition from low-cost airlines, many national carriers have decided to drop their prices and/ or offer special deals. Some, such as British Airways, have even adopted the low-cost model of online booking, where the customer can opt to buy just a one-way flight, or can piece together their own return journey from two one-way legs.

For a comprehensive overview of which low-cost carriers fly to or from which European cities, check out www.flycheapo.com.

Air Passes

Various travel agencies and airlines offer air passes, including the three main airline alliances: Oneworld (www.oneworld.com), Star Alliance (www.staralliance. com) and SkyTeam (www. skyteam.com). Check with your travel agent for current promotions.

Bicycle

Much of Europe is ideally suited to cycling. Popular cycling areas include the whole of the Netherlands, the Belgian Ardennes, the west of Ireland, the upper reaches of the Danube in southern Germany and anywhere in northern Switzerland, Denmark or the south of France. Exploring the small villages of Turkey and Eastern Europe also provides up-close access to remote areas.

A primary consideration on a cycling trip is to travel light, but you should take a few tools and spare parts, including a puncture-repair kit and an extra inner tube. Panniers are essential to balance your possessions on either side of the bike frame. Wearing a helmet is not compulsory in most countries, but it is certainly sensible.

Seasoned cyclists can average 80km a day, but it depends on what you're carrying, the terrain and your level of fitness.

Rental & Purchase

It is easy to hire bikes throughout most of Europe. Many Western European train stations have bike-rental counters. It is sometimes possible to return the bike at a different outlet so you don't have to retrace your route. Hostels are another good place to find cheap bike hire.

There are plenty of places to buy bikes in Europe, but you'll need a specialist bicycle shop for a bike capable of withstanding a European trip. Cycling is very popular in the Netherlands and Germany, and those countries are good places to pick up a well-equipped touring bicycle.

Road bikes with drop handlebars are popular in Europe and, in many countries, still remain more common than off-road mountain bikes.

European prices are quite high (certainly higher than in North America); however, non-European residents should be able to claim back value-added tax (VAT) on the purchase.

A growing number of European cities have bike-sharing schemes where you can casually borrow a bike from a docking station for short hops around the city for a small cost. Most schemes have daily rates, although you usually need a credit card as deposit. Large bike-sharing schemes include Paris' Vélib (Europe's biggest), London's Santander Cycles and Barcelona's Bicing.

Transporting a Bicycle

For major cycling trips, it's best to have a bike you're familiar with, so consider bringing your own rather

CYCLING RESOURCES

Cyclists' Touring Club (CTC; www.ctc.org.uk) The national cycling association of the UK runs organised trips to Continental Europe.

European Cyclists' Federation (www.ecf.com) Has details of 'EuroVelo', the European cycle network of 12 pan-European cycle routes, plus tips for other tours.

SwitzerlandMobility (www.schweizmobil.ch/en/cycling-in-switzerland.html) Details of Swiss national routes and more.

than buying on arrival. If coming from outside Europe, ask about the airline's policy on transporting bikes before buying your ticket.

From the UK to the Continent, Eurostar (the train service through the Channel Tunnel) charges £30 to send a semidismantled bike as registered luggage with you. Book ahead. With a bit of tinkering and dismantling (eg removing wheels), you can put your bike into a bag or sack and take it on a Eurostar train as hand luggage if it measures less than 85cm.

Alternatively, the European Bike Express (www.bike-express.co.uk) is a UK-based coach service where cyclists can travel with their bicycles to various drop-off and pick-up points in France and northern Spain.

Once on the Continent, local and regional trains usually allow bikes to be transported as luggage, subject to space and a small supplementary fee (€5 to €15). Off-peak hours are best. Some cyclists have reported that Italian and French train attendants have refused bikes on slow trains, so be prepared for regulations to be interpreted differently in different countries.

Fast trains and international trains can rarely accommodate bikes; they might need to be sent as registered luggage and may end up on a different train from the one you take. This is often the case in France and Spain.

Boat

Several different ferry companies compete on the main ferry routes, resulting in a comprehensive but complicated service. The same ferry company can have a host of different prices for the same route, depending on the time of day or year, validity of the ticket and length of your vehicle. Vehicle tickets usually include the driver and often up to five passengers free of charge.

It's worth booking ahead where possible as there may be special reductions on off-peak crossings and advance-purchase tickets. On English Channel routes, apart from one-day or short-term excursion returns, there is little price advantage in buying a return ticket versus two singles.

Rail-pass holders are entitled to discounts or free travel on some lines. Food on ferries is often expensive (and lousy), so it is worth bringing your own. Also be aware that if you take your vehicle on board, you are usually denied access to it during the voyage.

Lake and river ferry services operate in many countries, Austria and Switzerland being just two. Some of these are very scenic.

Bus

International Buses

Often cheaper than trains, sometimes substantially so,

long-distance buses also tend to be slower and less comfortable. However in Portugal, Greece and Turkey, buses are often a better option than trains.

Europe's biggest organisation of international buses operates under the name Eurolines (www.eurolines.com), comprised of various national companies. A Eurolines Pass (www.eurolines.com/en/eurolines-pass) is offered for extensive travel, allowing passengers to visit a choice of 49 cities across Europe over 15 or 30 days. In the high season (mid-June to mid-September), the pass costs €315/405 for those aged under 26, or €375/490 for those 26 and over. It's cheaper in other periods.

Busabout (www.busabout.com) offers a 'hop-on, hop-off' service around Europe, stopping at major cities. Buses are often oversubscribed, so book each sector to avoid being stranded. It departs every two days from early May to early October.

National Buses

Domestic buses provide a viable alternative to trains in most countries. Again, they are usually slightly cheaper and somewhat slower. Buses are generally best for short hops, such as getting around cities and reaching remote villages, and they are often the only option in mountainous regions.

Reservations are rarely necessary. On many city buses you usually buy your ticket in advance from a kiosk or machine and validate it on entering the bus.

Car & Motorcycle

Travelling with your own vehicle gives flexibility and is the best way to reach remote places. However, the independence does sometimes isolate you from local life. Cars can also be a target for theft and are often impractical in city centres,

EUROPE'S BORDER CROSSINGS

Border formalities have been relaxed in most of the EU, but still exist in all their original bureaucratic glory in the more far-flung parts of Eastern Europe.

In line with the Schengen Agreement, there are officially no passport controls at the borders between 26 European states, namely: Austria, Belgium, the Czech Republic, Denmark, Estonia, Finland, France, Germany, Greece, Iceland, Italy, Hungary, Latvia, Liechtenstein, Lithuania, Luxembourg, Malta, the Netherlands, Norway, Poland, Portugal, Slovakia, Slovenia, Spain, Sweden and Switzerland. Sometimes, however, there are spot checks on trains crossing borders, so always have your passport. The UK was a nonsignatory to Schengen and thus maintains border controls over traffic from other EU countries (except Ireland, with which it shares an open border), although there is no customs control. The same goes for Ireland.

Bulgaria, Croatia, Cyprus and Romania are prospective Schengen area members – for up-to-date details see www.schengenvisainfo.com.

Most borders in Eastern Europe will be crossed via train, where border guards board the train and go through compartments checking passengers' papers. It is rare to get hit up for bribes, but occasionally in Belarus or Moldova you may face a difficulty that can only be overcome with a 'fine'. Travelling between Turkey and Bulgaria typically requires a change of trains and is subject to a lengthy border procedure.

where traffic jams, parking problems and getting thoroughly lost can make it well worth ditching your vehicle and using public transport. Some European cities, such as London, Milan and Stockholm, have implemented congestion charges.

Campervan

One popular way to tour Europe is for a group of three or four people to band together and buy or rent a campervan. London is the usual embarkation point. Look at the ads in London's free magazine *TNT* (www.tntmagazine.com) if you wish to form or join a group. *TNT* is also a good source for purchasing a van, as is Loot (www.loot.com).

Some secondhand dealers offer a 'buy back' scheme for when you return from the Continent, but check the small print before signing anything, and remember that if an offer is too good to be true, it probably is. Buying and reselling privately should be more advantageous if you have time. In the UK, DUInsure (www.duinsure.com) offers a campervan policy.

Fuel

➡ Fuel prices can vary enormously (though fuel is always more expensive than in North America or Australia).

➡ Only unleaded petrol is available throughout Europe. Diesel is usually cheaper, though the difference is marginal in Britain, Ireland and Switzerland.

➡ Ireland's Automobile Association maintains a webpage of European fuel prices at www.theaa.ie/aa/motoring-advice/petrol-prices.aspx.

Leasing

Leasing a vehicle involves fewer hassles than purchasing and can work out much cheaper than hiring for longer than 17 days. This program is limited to certain types of new cars, including Renault and Peugeot, but you save money because leasing is exempt from VAT and inclusive insurance plans are cheaper than daily insurance rates.

To lease a vehicle your permanent address must be outside the EU. In the US, contact Renault Eurodrive (www.renault-eurodrive.com) for more information.

Motorcycle Touring

Europe is made for motorcycle touring, with quality winding roads, stunning scenery and an active motorcycling scene. Just make sure your wet-weather gear is up to scratch.

➡ Rider and passenger crash helmets are compulsory everywhere in Europe.

➡ Austria, Belgium, France, Germany, Luxembourg, Portugal and Spain require that motorcyclists use headlights during the day; in other countries it is recommended.

➡ On ferries, motorcyclists rarely have to book ahead as they can generally be squeezed on board.

➡ Take note of the local custom about parking motorcycles on pavements (sidewalks). Though this is illegal in some countries, the police often turn a blind eye provided the vehicle doesn't obstruct pedestrians.

Insurance

➡ Third-party motor insurance is compulsory. Most UK policies automatically provide this for EU countries. Get your insurer to issue a Green Card (which may cost extra), an internationally recognised proof of insurance, and check that it lists every country you intend to visit. You'll need this in the event of an accident outside the country where the vehicle is insured.

➡ Ask your insurer for a European Accident Statement form, which can simplify things if worst comes to worst. Never sign statements that you can't read or understand – insist on a translation and sign that only if it's acceptable.

➡ For non-EU countries, check the requirements with your insurer. Travellers from the UK can obtain additional advice and information from the Association of British Insurers (www.abi.org.uk).

➡ Take out a European motoring assistance policy. Non-Europeans might find it cheaper to arrange international coverage with their national motoring organisation before leaving home. Ask your motoring organisation for details about the free services offered by affiliated organisations around Europe.

➡ Residents of the UK should contact the RAC (www.rac.co.uk) or the AA (www.theaa.co.uk) for more information. Residents of the US, contact AAA (www.aaa.com).

Purchase

Buying a car and then selling it at the end of your European travels may work out to be a better deal than renting one, although this isn't guaranteed and you'll need to do your sums carefully.

The purchase of vehicles in some European countries is illegal for nonnationals or non-EU residents. Britain is probably the best place to buy as secondhand prices are good there. Bear in mind that British cars have steering wheels on the right-hand side. If you wish to have left-hand drive and can afford to buy a new car, prices are generally reasonable in Greece, France, Germany,

Belgium, Luxembourg and the Netherlands.

Paperwork can be tricky wherever you buy, and many countries have compulsory roadworthiness checks on older vehicles.

Rental

➡ Renting a car is ideal for people who will need cars for 16 days or less. Anything longer, it's better to lease.

➡ Big international rental firms will give you reliable service and good vehicles. National or local firms can often undercut the big companies by up to 40%.

➡ Usually you will have the option of returning the car to a different outlet at the end of the rental period, but there's normally a charge for this and it can be very steep if it's a long way from your point of origin.

➡ Book early for the lowest rates and make sure you compare rates in different cities. Taxes range from 15% to 20% and surcharges apply if rented from an airport.

➡ If you rent a car in the EU you might not be able to take it outside the EU, and if you rent the car outside the EU, you will only be able to drive within the EU for eight days. Ask at the rental agencies for other such regulations.

➡ Make sure you understand what is included in the price (unlimited or paid kilometres, tax, injury insurance, collision damage waiver etc) and what your liabilities are. We recommend taking the collision damage waiver, though you can probably skip the injury insurance if you and your passengers have decent travel insurance.

➡ The minimum rental age is usually 21 years and sometimes 25. You'll need a credit card and to have held your licence for at least a year.

➡ Motorcycle and moped rental is common in some countries, such as Italy,

Spain, Greece and southern France.

Road Conditions & Road Rules

➡ Conditions and types of roads vary across Europe. The fastest routes are generally four- or six-lane highways known locally as motorways, autoroutes, autostrade, autobahns etc. These tend to skirt cities and plough through the countryside in straight lines, often avoiding the most scenic bits.

➡ Some highways incur tolls, which are often quite hefty (especially in Italy, France and Spain), but there will always be an alternative route. Motorways and other primary routes are generally in good condition.

➡ Road surfaces on minor routes are unreliable in some countries (eg Greece, Albania, Romania, Ireland, Russia and Ukraine), although normally they will be more than adequate.

➡ Except in Britain and Ireland, you should drive on the right. Vehicles brought to the Continent from any of these locales should have their headlights adjusted to avoid blinding oncoming traffic (a simple solution on older headlight lenses is to cover up a triangular section of the lens with tape). Priority is often given to traffic approaching from the right in countries that drive on the right-hand side.

➡ Speed limits vary from country to country. You may be surprised at the apparent disregard for traffic regulations in some places (particularly in Italy and Greece), but as a visitor it is always best to be cautious. Many driving infringements are subject to an on-the-spot fine. Always ask for a receipt.

➡ European drink-driving laws are particularly strict. The blood-alcohol concentration (BAC) limit when driving is usually between 0.05% and 0.08%, but in certain areas (such as Gibraltar, Romania and Belarus) it can be zero.

➡ Always carry proof of ownership of your vehicle (Vehicle Registration Document for British-registered cars). An EU driving licence is acceptable for those driving through Europe. If you have any other type of licence, you should obtain an International Driving Permit (IDP) from your motoring organisation. Check what type of licence is required in your destination prior to departure.

➡ Every vehicle that travels across an international border should display a sticker indicating its country of registration. A warning triangle, to be used in the event of breakdown, is compulsory almost everywhere.

➡ Some recommended accessories include a first-aid kit (compulsory in Austria, Slovenia, Croatia, Serbia, Montenegro and Greece), a spare bulb kit (compulsory in Spain), a reflective jacket for every person in the car (compulsory in France, Italy and Spain) and a fire extinguisher (compulsory in Greece and Turkey).

Hitching

Hitching is never entirely safe and we don't recommend it. Travellers who hitch should understand that they are taking a small but potentially

serious risk. It will be safer if they travel in pairs and let someone know where they plan to go.

➡ A man and woman travelling together is probably the best combination. A woman hitching on her own is taking a larger than normal risk.

➡ Don't try to hitch from city centres; take public transport to the suburban exit routes.

➡ Hitching is usually illegal on highways – stand on the slip roads or approach drivers at petrol stations and truck stops.

➡ Look presentable and cheerful, and make a cardboard sign indicating your intended destination in the local language.

➡ Never hitch where drivers can't stop in good time or without causing an obstruction.

➡ It is often possible to arrange a lift in advance: scan student noticeboards in colleges or check out services such as www.carpooling.co.uk or www.drive2day.de.

Local Transport

European towns and cities have excellent local-transport systems, often encompassing trams as well as buses and metro/subway/underground-rail networks.

Most travellers will find areas of interest in European cities can be easily traversed by foot or bicycle. In Greece

and Italy, travellers sometimes rent mopeds and motorcycles for scooting around a city or island.

Taxi

Taxis in Europe are metered and rates are usually high. There might also be surcharges for things such as luggage, time of day, pick-up location and extra passengers.

Good bus, rail and underground-railway networks often render taxis unnecessary, but if you need one in a hurry, they can be found idling near train stations or outside big hotels. Lower fares make taxis more viable in some countries such as Spain, Greece, Portugal and Turkey.

Uber operates in most of Europe's large cities, although you won't find it in Bulgaria, Denmark or Hungary where it is currently banned.

Train

Comfortable, frequent and reliable, trains are *the* way to get around Europe; whole trips can be organised purely around rail travel. France, Germany, the Low Countries and Switzerland score highly in quality and quantity of railways.

➡ Many state railways have interactive websites publishing their timetables and fares, including www.bahn.de (Germany) and www.sbb.ch (Switzerland), both of which have pages in English. Eurail (www.eurail.com) links to 28 European train companies.

➡ Man in Seat 61 (www.seat61.com) is very comprehensive, while the US-based Budget Europe Travel Service (www.budgeteuropetravel.com) can also help with tips.

➡ European trains sometimes split en route to

HITCHING FOR CASH

In parts of Eastern Europe including Russia, Ukraine and Turkey, traditional hitching is rarely practised. Instead, anyone with a car can be a taxi and it's quite usual to see locals stick their hands out (palm down) on the street, looking to hitch a lift. The difference with hitching here, however, is that you pay for the privilege. You will need to speak the local language (or at least know the numbers) to discuss your destination and negotiate a price.

service two destinations, so even if you're on the right train, make sure you're also in the correct carriage.

➡ A train journey to almost every station in Europe can be booked via www.voyages-sncf.com.

Express Trains

Eurostar (www.eurostar.com) links London's St Pancras International station with Paris' Gare du Nord (2¼ hours, up to 25 a day) via the Channel Tunnel; Brussels' international terminal (one hour 50 minutes, up to 12 a day); and Amsterdam Centraal Station (three hours 40 minutes; up to two daily) via Rotterdam. Some trains also stop at Lille and Calais in France. There are also several trains a week from London to Disneyland Paris; and seasonal service from London to Marseilles via Lyon and Avignon (May to September); and London to the French ski resorts (December to April).

The train stations at St Pancras International, Paris, Brussels and Amsterdam are much more central than the cities' airports. So, overall, the journey takes as little time as the equivalent flight, with less hassle.

Eurostar in London also sells onward tickets to some Continental destinations. Holders of Eurail and Inter-Rail passes are offered discounts on some Eurostar services; check when booking.

Within Europe, express trains are identified by the symbols 'EC' (EuroCity) or 'IC' (InterCity). The French TGV, Spanish AVE and German ICE trains are even faster, reaching up to 300km/h. Supplementary fares can apply on fast trains (which you often have to pay when travelling on a rail pass), and it is a good idea (sometimes obligatory) to reserve seats at peak times and on certain lines. The same applies for branded express trains, such as the Thalys (between Paris

and Brussels, Bruges, Amsterdam and Cologne), and the Freccia trains in Italy.

If you don't have a seat reservation, you can still obtain a seat that doesn't have a reservation ticket attached to it. Check which destination a seat is reserved for – you might be able to sit in it until the person boards the train.

International Rail Passes

If you're covering lots of ground, you should get a rail pass. But do some price comparisons of point-to-point ticket charges and rail passes beforehand to make absolutely sure you'll break even. Also shop around for rail-pass prices as they do vary between outlets. When weighing up options, look into cheap deals that include advance-purchase reductions, one-off promotions or special circular-route tickets, particularly over the internet.

Normal point-to-point tickets are valid for two months, and you can make as many stops as you like en route; make your intentions known when purchasing and inform train conductors how far you're going before they punch your ticket.

Supplementary charges (eg for some express and overnight trains) and seat reservation fees (mandatory on some trains, a good idea on others) are not covered by rail passes. Always ask. Note that European rail passes also give reductions on Eurostar, the Channel Tunnel and on certain ferries.

Pass-holders must always carry their passport with them for identification purposes. The railways' policy is that passes cannot be replaced or refunded if lost or stolen.

NON-EUROPEAN RESIDENTS

Eurail (www.eurail.com) passes can be bought only by residents of non-European countries and should be

purchased before arriving in Europe.

Similar to the InterRail pass, Eurail issues a 'Global Pass' covering 28 countries – the UK (except Northern Ireland) and North Macedonia are not included. While the pass is valid on some private train lines in the region, if you plan to travel extensively in Switzerland, be warned that the many private rail networks and cable cars, especially in the Jungfrau region around Interlaken, don't give Eurail discounts. A Swiss Pass or Half-Fare Card might be an alternative or necessary addition.

The pass is valid for a set number of consecutive days (up to three months) or a set number of days within a period of time (for up to two months). Those 27 or under can buy a Eurail Youth pass. For over 28s a full-fare Eurail pass is required. First- and 2nd-class options are available and up to two children aged between four and 11 can travel free on an adult pass.

Alternatively, there is the Select pass, which allows you to nominate two, three or four bordering countries in which you wish to travel, and then buy a pass allowing five, six, eight or 10 travel days in a two-month period. The five- and six-day passes offer an attractive price break, but for more expensive options, the continuous pass becomes better value.

There are also Eurail National Passes for just one country.

Two to five people travelling together can get a Saver version of all Eurail passes for a 15% discount.

EUROPEAN RESIDENTS

InterRail (www.interrail.eu) offers a 'Global Pass' to European residents for unlimited rail travel through 30 European countries (limited to two journeys in the pass-holder's country of residence). To qualify as a resident, you must have lived in a European country for six months.

SECURITY

Sensible security measures include always keeping your bags in sight (especially at stations), chaining them to the luggage rack, locking compartment doors overnight and sleeping in compartments with other people. However, horror stories are very rare.

Passes come in four types: youth (aged 27 and under), adult, senior (aged 60 and over) and family. They are valid for up to one month.

While an InterRail pass will get you further than a Eurail pass along the private rail networks of Switzerland's Jungfrau region (near Interlaken), its benefits are limited. A Swiss Pass or Half-Fare Card might be a necessary addition if you plan to travel extensively in that region.

InterRail also offers One Country passes valid in the country of your choice for up to one month.

National Rail Passes

National rail operators might also offer their own passes, or at least a discount card, offering substantial reductions on tickets purchased (eg the Bahn Card in Germany or the Half-Fare Card in Switzerland).

Such discount cards are usually only worth it if you're staying in the country a while and doing a lot of travelling.

Overnight Trains

There are usually two types of sleeping accommodation: dozing off upright in your seat or stretching out in a sleeper. Again, reservations are advisable, as sleeping options are allocated on a first-come, first-served basis. Couchette bunks are comfortable enough, if lacking in privacy. There are four per compartment in 1st class, six in 2nd class.

Sleepers are the most comfortable option, offering beds for one or two passengers in 1st class, or two or three passengers in 2nd class. Charges vary depending upon the journey, but they are significantly more costly than couchettes.

In the former Soviet Union, the most common options are either 2nd-class *kupeyny* compartments – which have four bunks – or the cheaper *platskartny*, which are open-plan compartments with reserved bunks (54 per coach). This 3rd-class equivalent is not great for those who value privacy.

Other options include the very basic bench seats in *obshchiy* (*zahalney* in Ukrainian) class, and 1st-class, two-person sleeping carriages (*myagki* in Russian). In Ukrainian, this last option is known as *spalney,* but is usually abbreviated to CB in Cyrillic (pronounced *es-ve*). First class is not available on every Russian or Ukrainian train.

Language

This chapter offers basic vocabulary to help you get around Europe. Read our coloured pronunciation guides as if they were English, and you'll be understood just fine. The stressed syllables are indicated with italics. Note the use of these abbreviations: (m) for masculine, (f) for feminine, (pol) for polite and (inf) for informal.

ALBANIAN

Note that uh is pronounced as the 'a' in 'ago'. Also, ll and rr in Albanian are pronounced stronger than when they are written as single letters. Albanian is also understood in Kosovo.

Hello.	Tungjatjeta.	toon·dya·tye·ta
Goodbye.	Mirupafshim.	mee·roo·paf·sheem
Please.	Ju lutem.	yoo loo·tem
Thank you.	Faleminderit.	fa·le·meen·de·reet
Excuse me.	Më falni.	muh fal·nee
Sorry.	Më vjen keq.	muh vyen kech
Yes./No.	Po./Jo.	po/yo
Help!	Ndihmë!	ndeeh·muh
Cheers!	Gëzuar!	guh·zoo·ar

I don't understand.
Unë nuk kuptoj.   oo·nuh nook koop·toy

Do you speak English?
A flisni anglisht?   a flees·nee ang·leesht

How much is it?
Sa kushton?   sa koosh·ton

Where's ...?
Ku është ...?   koo *uhsh*·tuh ...

Where are the toilets?
Ku janë banjat?   koo ya·nuh ba·nyat

BULGARIAN

Note that uh is pronounced as the 'a' in 'ago' and zh as the 's' in 'pleasure'.

Hello.	Здравейте.	zdra·vey·te
Goodbye.	Довиждане.	do·veezh·da·ne
Please.	Моля.	mol·ya
Thank you.	Благодаря.	bla·go·dar·ya
Excuse me.	Извинете.	iz·vee·ne·te
Sorry.	Съжалявам.	suh·zhal·ya·vam
Yes./No.	Да./Не.	da/ne
Help!	Помощ!	po·mosht
Cheers!	Наздраве!	na·zdra·ve

I don't understand.
Не разбирам.   ne raz·bee·ram

Do you speak English?
Говорите ли
английски?   go·vo·ree·te lee
ang·lees·kee

How much is it?
Колко струва?   kol·ko stroo·va

Where's ...?
Къде се намира ...?   kuh·de se na·mee·ra ...

Where are the toilets?
Къде има тоалетни?   kuh·de ee·ma to·a·let·nee

CROATIAN & SERBIAN

Croatian and Serbian are very similar and mutually intelligible (and using them you'll also be understood in Bosnia and Hercegovina, Montenegro and parts of Kosovo). In this section the significant differences between Croatian and Serbian are indicated with (C) and (S) respectively. Note that r is rolled and zh is pronounced as the 's' in 'pleasure'.

Hello.	Dobar dan.	daw·ber dan
Goodbye.	Zbogom.	zbo·gom
Please.	Molim.	mo·lim
Thank you.	Hvala.	hva·la
Excuse me.	Oprostite.	o·pro·sti·te
Sorry.	Žao mi je.	zha·o mi ye
Yes./No.	Da./Ne.	da/ne
Help!	Upomoć!	u·po·moch
Cheers!	Živjeli!	zhi·vye·li

I don't understand.
Ja ne razumijem. ya ne ra·zu·mi·yem

Do you speak English?
Govorite/Govoriš li go·vo·ri·te/go·vo·rish
engleski? (pol/inf) li en·gle·ski

How much is it?
Koliko stoji/ ko·li·ko sto·yi/
košta? (C/S) kosh·ta

Where's ...?
Gdje je ...? gdye ye ...

Where are the toilets?
Gdje se nalaze gdye se na·la·ze
zahodi/toaleti? (C/S) za·ho·di/to·a·le·ti

CZECH

An accent mark over a vowel in written Czech
indicates it's pronounced as a long sound.
Note that oh is pronounced as the 'o' in 'note',
uh as the 'a' in 'ago', and kh as the 'ch' in the
Scottish *loch*. Also, r is rolled in Czech and the
apostrophe (') indicates a slight y sound.

Hello.	Ahoj.	uh·hoy
Goodbye.	Na shledanou.	nuh·skhle·duh·noh
Please.	Prosím.	pro·seem
Thank you.	Děkuji.	dye·ku·yi
Excuse me.	Promiňte.	pro·min'·te
Sorry.	Promiňte.	pro·min'·te
Yes./No.	Ano./Ne.	uh·no/ne
Help!	Pomoc!	po·mots
Cheers!	Na zdraví!	nuh zdruh·vee

I don't understand.
Nerozumím. ne·ro·zu·meem

Do you speak English?
Mluvíte anglicky? mlu·vee·te uhn·glits·ki

How much is it?
Kolik to stojí? ko·lik to sto·yee

Where's ...?
Kde je ...? gde ye ...

Where are the toilets?
Kde jsou toalety? gde ysoh to·uh·le·ti

DANISH

All vowels in Danish can be long or short.
Note that aw is pronounced as in 'saw', and ew
as the 'ee' in 'see' with rounded lips.

Hello.	Goddag.	go·da
Goodbye.	Farvel.	faar·vel
Please.	Vær så venlig.	ver saw ven·lee
Thank you.	Tak.	taak
Excuse me.	Undskyld mig.	awn·skewl mai
Sorry.	Undskyld.	awn·skewl
Yes./No.	Ja./Nej.	ya/nai
Help!	Hjælp!	yelp
Cheers!	Skål!	skawl

I don't understand.
Jeg forstår ikke. yai for·stawr i·ke

Do you speak English?
Taler De/du ta·la dee/doo
engelsk? (pol/inf) eng·elsk

How much is it?
Hvor meget koster det? vor maa·yet kos·ta dey

Where's ...?
Hvor er ...? vor ir ...

Where's the toilet?
Hvor er toilettet? vor ir toy·le·tet

DUTCH

It's important to distinguish between the long
and short versions of each vowel sound. Note
that ew is pronounced as the 'ee' in 'see' with
rounded lips, oh as the 'o' in 'note', uh as the 'a'
in 'ago', and kh as the 'ch' in the Scottish *loch*
(harsh and throaty).

Hello.	Dag.	dakh
Goodbye.	Dag.	dakh
Please.	Alstublieft.	al·stew·bleeft
Thank you.	Dank u.	dangk ew
Excuse me.	Pardon.	par·don
Sorry.	Sorry.	so·ree
Yes./No.	Ja./Nee.	yaa/ney
Help!	Help!	help
Cheers!	Proost!	prohst

I don't understand.
Ik begrijp het niet. ik buh·khreyp huht neet

Do you speak English?
Spreekt u Engels? spreykt ew eng·uhls

How much is it?
Hoeveel kost het? hoo·veyl kost huht

Where's ...?
Waar is ...? waar is ...

Where are the toilets?
Waar zijn de toiletten? waar zeyn duh twa·le·tuhn

ESTONIAN

Double vowels in written Estonian indicate they are pronounced as long sounds. Note that air is pronounced as in 'hair'.

Hello.	Tere.	te·re
Goodbye.	Nägemist.	nair·ge·mist
Please.	Palun.	pa·lun
Thank you.	Tänan.	tair·nan
Excuse me.	Vabandage. (pol)	va·ban·da·ge
	Vabanda. (inf)	va·ban·da
Sorry.	Vabandust.	va·ban·dust
Yes./No.	Jaa./Ei.	yaa/ay
Help!	Appi!	ap·pi
Cheers!	Terviseks!	tair·vi·seks

I don't understand.
Ma ei saa aru. ma ay saa a·ru

Do you speak English?
Kas te räägite kas te rair·git·te
inglise keelt? ing·kli·se keylt

How much is it?
Kui palju see maksab? ku·i pal·yu sey mak·sab

Where's ...?
Kus on ...? kus on ...

Where are the toilets?
Kus on WC? kus on ve·se

FINNISH

In Finnish, double consonants are held longer than their single equivalents. Note that ew is pronounced as the 'ee' in 'see' with rounded lips, and uh as the 'u' in 'run'.

Hello.	Hei.	hay
Goodbye.	Näkemiin.	na·ke·meen
Please.	Ole hyvä.	o·le hew·va
Thank you.	Kiitos.	kee·tos
Excuse me.	Anteeksi.	uhn·tayk·si
Sorry.	Anteeksi.	uhn·tayk·si
Yes./No.	Kyllä./Ei.	kewl·la/ay
Help!	Apua!	uh·pu·uh
Cheers!	Kippis!	kip·pis

I don't understand.
En ymmärrä. en ewm·mar·ra

Do you speak English?
Puhutko englantia? pu·hut·ko en·gluhn·ti·uh

How much is it?
Mitä se maksaa? mi·ta se muhk·saa

Where's ...?
Missä on ...? mis·sa on ...

Where are the toilets?
Missä on vessa? mis·sa on ves·suh

FRENCH

The French r sound is throaty. French also has nasal vowels (pronounced as if you're trying to force the sound through the nose), indicated here with o or u followed by an almost inaudible nasal consonant sound m, n or ng. Syllables in French words are, for the most part, equally stressed.

Hello.	Bonjour.	bon·zhoor
Goodbye.	Au revoir.	o·rer·vwa
Please.	S'il vous plaît.	seel voo play
Thank you.	Merci.	mair·see
Excuse me.	Excusez-moi.	ek·skew·zay·mwa
Sorry.	Pardon.	par·don
Yes./No.	Oui./Non.	wee/non
Help!	Au secours!	o skoor
Cheers!	Santé!	son·tay

I don't understand.
Je ne comprends pas. zher ner kom·pron pa

Do you speak English?
Parlez-vous anglais? par·lay·voo ong·glay

How much is it?
C'est combien? say kom·byun

Where's ...?
Où est ...? oo ay ...

Where are the toilets?
Où sont les toilettes? oo son ley twa·let

GERMAN

Note that aw is pronounced as in 'saw', ew as the 'ee' in 'see' with rounded lips, while kh and r are both throaty sounds in German.

Hello.			
(in general)	Guten Tag.	goo·ten taak
(Austria)	Servus.	zer·vus
(Switzerland)	Grüezi.	grew·e·tsi
Goodbye.	Auf Wiedersehen.	owf vee·der·zey·en
Please.	Bitte.	bi·te
Thank you.	Danke.	dang·ke
Excuse me.	Entschuldigung.	ent·shul·di·gung
Sorry.	Entschuldigung.	ent·shul·di·gung
Yes./No.	Ja./Nein.	yaa/nain
Help!	Hilfe!	hil·fe
Cheers!	Prost!	prawst

I don't understand.
Ich verstehe nicht. ikh fer·shtey·e nikht

Do you speak English?
Sprechen Sie Englisch?   shpre·khen zee eng·lish

How much is it?
Wie viel kostet das?   vee feel kos·tet das

Where's ...?
Wo ist ...?   vaw ist ...

Where are the toilets?
Wo ist die Toilette?   vo ist dee to·a·le·te

GREEK

Note that dh is pronounced as the 'th' in 'that', and that gh and kh are both throaty sounds, similar to the 'ch' in the Scottish *loch*.

Hello.	Γεια σου.	yia su
Goodbye.	Αντίο.	a·di·o
Please.	Παρακαλώ.	pa·ra·ka·lo
Thank you.	Ευχαριστώ.	ef·kha·ri·sto
Excuse me.	Με συγχωρείτε.	me sing·kho·ri·te
Sorry.	Συγνώμη.	si·ghno·mi
Yes./No.	Ναι./Όχι.	ne/o·hi
Help!	Βοήθεια!	vo·i·thia
Cheers!	Στην υγειά μας!	stin i·yia mas

I don't understand.
Δεν καταλαβαίνω.   dhen ka·ta·la·ve·no

Do you speak English?
Μιλάς Αγγλικά;   mi·las ang·gli·ka

How much is it?
Πόσο κάνει;   po·so ka·ni

Where's ...?
Που είναι ...;   pu i·ne ...

Where are the toilets?
Που είναι η τουαλέτα;   pu i·ne i tu·a·le·ta

HUNGARIAN

A symbol over a vowel in written Hungarian indicates it's pronounced as a long sound. Double consonants should be drawn out a little longer than in English. Note that aw is pronounced as in 'law', eu as the 'u' in 'nurse', and ew as 'ee' with rounded lips. Also, r is rolled in Hungarian and the apostrophe (') indicates a slight y sound.

Hello. (to one person)
Szervusz.   ser·vus

Hello. (to more than one person)
Szervusztok.   ser·vus·tawk

Goodbye.	*Viszlát.*	vis·lat
Please.	*Kérem.* (pol)	key·rem
	Kérlek. (inf)	keyr·lek
Thank you.	*Köszönöm.*	keu·seu·neum

Excuse me.	*Elnézést kérek.*	el·ney·zeysht key·rek
Sorry.	*Sajnálom.*	shoy·na·lawm
Yes.	*Igen.*	i·gen
No.	*Nem.*	nem
Help!	*Segítség!*	she·geet·sheyg

Cheers! (to one person)
Egészségedre!   e·geys·shey·ged·re

Cheers! (to more than one person)
Egészségetekre!   e·geys·shey·ge·tek·re

I don't understand.
Nem értem.   nem eyr·tem

Do you speak English?
Beszél/Beszélsz angolul? (pol/inf)   be·seyl/be·seyls on·gaw·lul

How much is it?
Mennyibe kerül?   men'·nyi·be ke·rewl

Where's ...?
Hol van a ...?   hawl von o ...

Where are the toilets?
Hol a vécé?   hawl o vey·tsey

ITALIAN

The r sound in Italian is rolled and stronger than in English. Most other consonants can have a more emphatic pronunciation too (in which case they're written as double letters).

Hello.	*Buongiorno.*	bwon·jor·no
Goodbye.	*Arrivederci.*	a·ree·ve·der·chee
Please.	*Per favore.*	per fa·vo·re
Thank you.	*Grazie.*	gra·tsye
Excuse me.	*Mi scusi.* (pol)	mee skoo·zee
	Scusami. (inf)	skoo·za·mee
Sorry.	*Mi dispiace.*	mee dees·pya·che
Yes.	*Sì.*	see
No.	*No.*	no
Help!	*Aiuto!*	ai·yoo·to
Cheers!	*Salute!*	sa·loo·te

I don't understand.
Non capisco.   non ka·pee·sko

Do you speak English?
Parla inglese?   par·la een·gle·ze

How much is it?
Quant'è?   kwan·te

Where's ... ?
Dov'è ... ?   do·ve ...

Where are the toilets?
Dove sono i gabinetti?   do·ve so·no ee ga·bee·ne·tee

LATVIAN

A line over a vowel in written Latvian indicates it's pronounced as a long sound. Note that air is pronounced as in 'hair', ea as in 'ear', wa as in 'water', and dz as the 'ds' in 'adds'.

Hello.	Sveiks.	svayks
Goodbye.	Atā.	a·taa
Please.	Lūdzu.	loo·dzu
Thank you.	Paldies.	pal·deas
Excuse me.	Atvainojiet.	at·vai·nwa·yeat
Sorry.	Piedodiet.	pea·dwa·deat
Yes./No.	Jā./Nē.	yaa/nair
Help!	Palīgā!	pa·lee·gaa
Cheers!	Priekā!	prea·kaa

I don't understand.
Es nesaprotu.　　es ne·sa·prwa·tu

Do you speak English?
Vai Jūs runājat　　vai yoos ru·naa·yat
angliski?　　ang·li·ski

How much is it?
Cik maksā?　　tsik mak·saa

Where's ...?
Kur ir ...?　　kur ir ...

Where are the toilets?
Kur ir tualetes?　　kur ir tu·a·le·tes

LITHUANIAN

Symbols on vowels in written Lithuanian indicate that they're pronounced as long sounds. Note that ow is pronounced as in 'how'.

Hello.	Sveiki.	svay·ki
Goodbye.	Viso gero.	vi·so ge·ro
Please.	Prašau.	pra·show
Thank you.	Ačiū.	aa·choo
Excuse me.	Atleiskite.	at·lays·ki·te
Sorry.	Atsiprašau.	at·si·pra·show
Yes./No.	Taip./Ne.	taip/ne
Help!	Padėkit!	pa·dey·kit
Cheers!	Į sveikatą!	ee svay·kaa·taa

I don't understand.
Aš nesuprantu.　　ash ne·su·pran·tu

Do you speak English?
Ar kalbate angliškai?　　ar kal·ba·te aang·lish·kai

How much is it?
Kiek kainuoja?　　keak kain·wo·ya

Where's ...?
Kur yra ...?　　kur ee·ra ...

Where are the toilets?
Kur yra tualetai?　　kur ee·ra tu·a·le·tai

MACEDONIAN

Note that r is pronounced as a rolled sound in Macedonian.

Hello.	Здраво.	zdra·vo
Goodbye.	До гледање.	do gle·da·nye
Please.	Молам.	mo·lam
Thank you.	Благодарам.	bla·go·da·ram
Excuse me.	Извинете.	iz·vi·ne·te
Sorry.	Простете.	pros·te·te
Yes./No.	Да./Не.	da/ne
Help!	Помош!	po·mosh
Cheers!	На здравје!	na zdrav·ye

I don't understand.
Јас не разбирам.　　yas ne raz·bi·ram

Do you speak English?
Зборувате ли англиски? zbo·ru·va·te li an·glis·ki

How much is it?
Колку чини тоа?　　kol·ku chi·ni to·a

Where's ...?
Каде е ...?　　ka·de e ...

Where are the toilets?
Каде се тоалетите?　　ka·de se to·a·le·ti·te

NORWEGIAN

In Norwegian, each vowel can be either long or short. Generally, they're long when followed by one consonant and short when followed by two or more consonants. Note that aw is pronounced as in 'law', ew as 'ee' with pursed lips, and ow as in 'how'.

Hello.	God dag.	go·daag
Goodbye.	Ha det.	haa·de
Please.	Vær så snill.	veyr saw snil
Thank you.	Takk.	tak
Excuse me.	Unnskyld.	ewn·shewl
Sorry.	Beklager.	bey·klaa·geyr
Yes./No.	Ja./Nei.	yaa/ney
Help!	Hjelp!	yelp
Cheers!	Skål!	skawl

I don't understand.
Jeg forstår ikke.　　yai fawr·stawr i·key

Do you speak English?
Snakker du engelsk?　　sna·ker doo eyng·elsk

How much is it?
Hvor mye koster det?　　vor mew·e kaws·ter de

Where's ...?
Hvor er ...?　　vor ayr ...

Where are the toilets?
Hvor er toalettene?　　vor eyr to·aa·le·te·ne

POLISH

Polish vowels are generally pronounced short. Nasal vowels are pronounced as though you're trying to force the air through your nose, and are indicated with n or m following the vowel. Note also that r is rolled in Polish.

Hello.	Cześć.	cheshch
Goodbye.	Do widzenia.	do vee·dze·nya
Please.	Proszę.	pro·she
Thank you.	Dziękuję.	jyen·koo·ye
Excuse me.	Przepraszam.	pshe·pra·sham
Sorry.	Przepraszam.	pshe·pra·sham
Yes./No.	Tak./Nie.	tak/nye
Help!	Na pomoc!	na po·mots
Cheers!	Na zdrowie!	na zdro·vye

I don't understand.
Nie rozumiem.   nye ro·zoo·myem

Do you speak English?
Czy pan/pani mówi   chi pan/pa·nee moo·vee
po angielsku? (m/f)   po an·gyel·skoo

How much is it?
Ile to kosztuje?   ee·le to kosh·too·ye

Where's ...?
Gdzie jest ...?   gjye yest ...

Where are the toilets?
Gdzie są toalety?   gjye som to·a·le·ti

PORTUGUESE

Most vowel sounds in Portuguese have a nasal version (ie pronounced as if you're trying to force the sound through your nose), which is indicated in our pronunciation guides with ng after the vowel.

Hello.	Olá.	o·laa
Goodbye.	Adeus.	a·de·oosh
Please.	Por favor.	poor fa·vor
Thank you.	Obrigado. (m)	o·bree·gaa·doo
	Obrigada. (f)	o·bree·gaa·da
Excuse me.	Faz favor.	faash fa·vor
Sorry.	Desculpe.	desh·kool·pe
Yes./No.	Sim./Não.	seeng/nowng
Help!	Socorro!	soo·ko·rroo
Cheers!	Saúde!	sa·oo·de

I don't understand.
Não entendo.   nowng eng·teng·doo

Do you speak English?
Fala inglês?   faa·la eeng·glesh

How much is it?
Quanto custa?   kwang·too koosh·ta

Where's ...?
Onde é ...?   ong·de e ...

Where are the toilets?
Onde é a casa de   ong·de e a kaa·za de
banho?   ba·nyoo

ROMANIAN

Note that ew is pronounced as the 'ee' in 'see' with rounded lips, uh as the 'a' in 'ago', and zh as the 's' in 'pleasure'. The apostrophe (') indicates a very short, unstressed (almost silent) i. Moldovan is the official name of the variety of Romanian spoken in Moldova.

Hello.	Bună ziua.	boo·nuh zee·wa
Goodbye.	La revedere.	la re·ve·de·re
Please.	Vă rog.	vuh rog
Thank you.	Mulţumesc.	mool·tsoo·mesk
Excuse me.	Scuzaţi-mă.	skoo·za·tsee·muh
Sorry.	Îmi pare rău.	ewm' pa·re ruh·oo
Yes./No.	Da./Nu.	da/noo
Help!	Ajutor!	a·zhoo·tor
Cheers!	Noroc!	no·rok

I don't understand.
Eu nu înţeleg.   ye·oo noo ewn·tse·leg

Do you speak English?
Vorbiţi engleza?   vor·beets' en·gle·za

How much is it?
Cât costă?   kewt kos·tuh

Where's ...?
Unde este ...?   oon·de yes·te ...

Where are the toilets?
Unde este o toaletă?   oon·de yes·te o to·a·le·tuh

RUSSIAN

Note that zh is pronounced as the 's' in 'pleasure'. Also, r is rolled in Russian and the apostrophe (') indicates a slight y sound.

Hello.	Здравствуйте.	zdrast·vuyt·ye
Goodbye.	До свидания.	da svee·dan·ya
Please.	Пожалуйста.	pa·zhal·sta
Thank you.	Спасибо.	spa·see·ba
Excuse me./ Sorry.	Извините, пожалуйста.	eez·vee·neet·ye pa·zhal·sta
Yes./No.	Да./Нет.	da/nyet
Help!	Помогите!	pa·ma·gee·tye
Cheers!	Пей до дна!	pyey da dna

I don't understand.
Я не понимаю.   ya nye pa·nee·ma·yu

Do you speak English?
Вы говорите   vi ga·va·reet·ye
по-английски?   pa·an·glee·skee

How much is it?	Сколько стоит?	skol'·ka sto·eet
Where's ...?	Где (здесь) ...?	gdye (zdyes') ...
Where are the toilets?	Где здесь туалет?	gdye zdyes' tu·al·yet

How much is it?	Koliko stane?	ko·lee·ko sta·ne
Where's ...?	Kje je ...?	kye ye ...
Where are the toilets?	Kje je stranišče?	kye ye stra·neesh·che

SLOVAK

An accent mark over a vowel in written Slovak indicates it's pronounced as a long sound. Note also that uh is pronounced as the 'a' in 'ago', and kh as the 'ch' in the Scottish loch. The apostrophe (') indicates a slight y sound.

Hello.	Dobrý deň.	do·bree dyen'
Goodbye.	Do videnia.	do vi·dye·ni·yuh
Please.	Prosím.	pro·seem
Thank you.	Ďakujem	dyuh·ku·yem
Excuse me.	Prepáčte.	pre·pach·tye
Sorry.	Prepáčte.	pre·pach·tye
Yes./No.	Áno./Nie.	a·no/ni·ye
Help!	Pomoc!	po·mots
Cheers!	Nazdravie!	nuhz·druh·vi·ye

I don't understand.
Nerozumiem. — nye·ro·zu·myem

Do you speak English?
Hovoríte po anglicky? — ho·vo·ree·tye po uhng·lits·ki

How much is it?
Koľko to stojí? — kol'·ko to sto·yee

Where's ...?
Kde je ...? — kdye ye ...

Where are the toilets?
Kde sú tu záchody? — kdye soo tu za·kho·di

SLOVENE

Note that r is pronounced as a rolled sound in Slovene.

Hello.	Zdravo.	zdra·vo
Goodbye.	Na svidenje.	na svee·den·ye
Please.	Prosim.	pro·seem
Thank you.	Hvala.	hva·la
Excuse me.	Dovolite.	do·vo·lee·te
Sorry.	Oprostite.	op·ros·tee·te
Yes./No.	Da./Ne.	da/ne
Help!	Na pomoč!	na po·moch
Cheers!	Na zdravje!	na zdrav·ye

I don't understand.
Ne razumem. — ne ra·zoo·mem

Do you speak English?
Ali govorite angleško? — a·lee go·vo·ree·te ang·lesh·ko

SPANISH

Note that the Spanish r is strong and rolled, th is pronounced 'with a lisp', and v is soft, pronounced almost like a 'b'.

Hello.	Hola.	o·la
Goodbye.	Adiós.	a·dyos
Please.	Por favor.	por fa·vor
Thank you.	Gracias.	gra·thyas
Excuse me.	Perdón.	per·don
Sorry.	Lo siento.	lo syen·to
Yes./No.	Sí./No.	see/no
Help!	¡Socorro!	so·ko·ro
Cheers!	¡Salud!	sa·loo

I don't understand.
Yo no entiendo. — yo no en·tyen·do

Do you speak English?
¿Habla/Hablas inglés? (pol/inf) — a·bla/a·blas een·gles

How much is it?
¿Cuánto cuesta? — kwan·to kwes·ta

Where's ...?
¿Dónde está ...? — don·de es·ta ...

Where are the toilets?
¿Dónde están los servicios? — don·de es·tan los ser·vee·thyos

SWEDISH

Swedish vowels can be short or long – generally the stressed vowels are long, except when followed by double consonants. Note that aw is pronounced as in 'saw', air as in 'hair', eu as the 'u' in 'nurse', ew as the 'ee' in 'see' with rounded lips, and oh as the 'o' in 'note'.

Hello.	Hej.	hey
Goodbye.	Hej då.	hey daw
Please.	Tack.	tak
Thank you.	Tack.	tak
Excuse me.	Ursäkta mig.	oor·shek·ta mey
Sorry.	Förlåt.	feur·lawt
Yes./No.	Ja./Nej.	yaa/ney
Help!	Hjälp!	yelp
Cheers!	Skål!	skawl

I don't understand.
Jag förstår inte.   yaa feur-*shtawr* in-te

Do you speak English?
Talar du engelska?   taa-lar doo *eng*-el-ska

How much is it?
Hur mycket kostar det?   hoor *mew*-ke *kos*-tar de

Where's ...?
Var finns det ...?   var finns de ...

Where are the toilets?
Var är toaletten?   var air toh-aa-*le*-ten

TURKISH

Double vowels are pronounced twice in Turkish. Note also that eu is pronounced as the 'u' in 'nurse', ew as the 'ee' in 'see' with rounded lips, uh as the 'a' in 'ago', r is rolled and v is a little softer than in English.

Hello.	*Merhaba.*	*mer*-ha-ba
Goodbye.	*Hoşçakal.* (when leaving)	hosh-*cha*-kal
	Güle güle. (when staying)	gew-*le* gew-*le*
Please.	*Lütfen.*	*lewt*-fen
Thank you.	*Teşekkür ederim.*	te-shek-*kewr* e-*de*-reem
Excuse me.	*Bakar mısınız.*	ba-*kar* muh-suh-*nuhz*
Sorry.	*Özür dilerim.*	eu-*zewr* dee-*le*-reem
Yes./No.	*Evet./Hayır.*	e-*vet*/ha-*yuhr*
Help!	*İmdat!*	eem-*dat*
Cheers!	*Şerefe!*	she-re-*fe*

I don't understand.
Anlamıyorum.   an-*la*-muh-yo-room

Do you speak English?
İngilizce konuşuyor musunuz?   een-gee-*leez*-je ko-noo-*shoo*-yor moo-soo-*nooz*

How much is it?
Ne kadar?   ne ka-*dar*

Where's ...?
... nerede?   ... ne-re-de

Where are the toilets?
Tuvaletler nerede?   too-va-let-*ler* ne-re-de

UKRAINIAN

Ukrainian vowels in unstressed syllables are generally pronounced shorter and weaker than they are in stressed syllables. Note that ow is pronounced as in 'how' and zh as the 's' in 'pleasure'. The apostrophe (') indicates a slight y sound.

Hello.	Добрий день.	*do*-bry den'
Goodbye.	До побачення.	do po-*ba*-chen-nya
Please.	Прошу.	*pro*-shu
Thank you.	Дякую.	*dya*-ku-yu
Excuse me.	Вибачте.	*vy*-bach-te
Sorry.	Перепрошую.	pe-re-*pro*-shu-yu
Yes./No.	Так./Ні.	tak/ni
Help!	Допоможіть!	do-po-mo-*zhit*'
Cheers!	Будьмо!	*bud'*-mo

I don't understand.
Я не розумію.   ya ne ro-zu-*mi*-yu

Do you speak English?
Ви розмовляєте англійською мовою?   vy roz-mow-*lya*-ye-te an-*hliys'*-ko-yu *mo*-vo-yu

How much is it?
Скільки це він/вона коштує? (m/f)   *skil'*-ki tse vin/vo-*na* ko-shtu-ye

Where's ...?
Де ...?   de ...

Where are the toilets?
Де туалети?   de tu-a-*le*-ti

Behind the Scenes

SEND US YOUR FEEDBACK

We love to hear from travellers – your comments keep us on our toes and help make our books better. Our well-travelled team reads every word on what you loved or loathed about this book. Although we cannot reply individually to your submissions, we always guarantee that your feedback goes straight to the appropriate authors, in time for the next edition. Each person who sends us information is thanked in the next edition – the most useful submissions are rewarded with a selection of digital PDF chapters.

Visit **lonelyplanet.com/contact** to submit your updates and suggestions or to ask for help. Our award-winning website also features inspirational travel stories, news and discussions.

Note: We may edit, reproduce and incorporate your comments in Lonely Planet products such as guidebooks, websites and digital products, so let us know if you don't want your comments reproduced or your name acknowledged. For a copy of our privacy policy visit lonelyplanet.com/privacy.

ACKNOWLEDGEMENTS

Climate map data adapted from Peel MC, Finlayson BL & McMahon TA (2007) 'Updated World Map of the Köppen-Geiger Climate Classification', *Hydrology and Earth System Sciences*, 11, 1633–44.

Cover photograph: St Stephen's Cathedral, Vienna, Austria, Triff, Shutterstock©

Illustrations p386–7, p400–1, p666–7 and p952–3 by Javier Zarracina

THIS BOOK

This 4th edition of Lonely Planet's *Europe* guidebook was written by Isabel Albiston, Kate Armstrong, Alexis Averbuck, James Bainbridge, Mark Baker, Oliver Berry, Greg Bloom, Cristian Bonetto, Jade Bremner, Stuart Butler, Jean-Bernard Carillet, Kerry Christiani, Gregor Clark, Fionn Davenport, Marc Di Duca, Belinda Dixon, Peter Dragicevich, Mark Elliott, Steve Fallon, Duncan Garwood, Gemma Graham, Anthony Ham, Paula Hardy, Damian Harper, Anita

Isalska, Catherine Le Nevez, Jessica Lee, Ali Lemer, Vesna Maric, Virginia Maxwell, Hugh McNaughtan, Korina Miller, MaSovaida Morgan, Isabella Noble, John Noble, Stephanie Ong, Lorna Parkes, Christopher Pitts, Leonid Ragozin, Kevin Raub, Simon Richmond, Daniel Robinson, Brendan Sainsbury, Andrea Schulte-Peevers, Helena Smith, Regis St Louis, Andy Symington, Brana Vladisavljevic, Benedict Walker, Greg Ward, Nicola Williams and Neil Wilson.

This guidebook was produced by the following:

Senior Product Editor Daniel Bolger

Cartographers Julie Dodkins, Corey Hutchison

Product Editor Grace Dobell

Book Designer Clara Monitto

Assisting Editors Ronan Abayawickrema, Amy Lynch, Gabrelle Stefanos

Cover Researcher Fergal Condon

Thanks to Jennifer Carey, Clara Escriña, Amy Lysen, Aristea Parissi, Fiona Poot, Rachel Rawling, Alison Ridgway

Index

Map Legend

Sights

- Beach
- Bird Sanctuary
- Buddhist
- Castle/Palace
- Christian
- Confucian
- Hindu
- Islamic
- Jain
- Jewish
- Monument
- Museum/Gallery/Historic Building
- Ruin
- Shinto
- Sikh
- Taoist
- Winery/Vineyard
- Zoo/Wildlife Sanctuary
- Other Sight

Activities, Courses & Tours

- Bodysurfing
- Diving
- Canoeing/Kayaking
- Course/Tour
- Sento Hot Baths/Onsen
- Skiing
- Snorkelling
- Surfing
- Swimming/Pool
- Walking
- Windsurfing
- Other Activity

Sleeping

- Sleeping
- Camping
- Hut/Shelter

Eating

- Eating

Drinking & Nightlife

- Drinking & Nightlife
- Cafe

Entertainment

- Entertainment

Shopping

- Shopping

Information

- Bank
- Embassy/Consulate
- Hospital/Medical
- Internet
- Police
- Post Office
- Telephone
- Toilet
- Tourist Information
- Other Information

Geographic

- Beach
- Gate
- Hut/Shelter
- Lighthouse
- Lookout
- Mountain/Volcano
- Oasis
- Park
- Pass
- Picnic Area
- Waterfall

Population

- Capital (National)
- Capital (State/Province)
- City/Large Town
- Town/Village

Transport

- Airport
- Border crossing
- Bus
- Cable car/Funicular
- Cycling
- Ferry
- Metro station
- Monorail
- Parking
- Petrol station
- Subway station
- Taxi
- Train station/Railway
- Tram
- Underground station
- Other Transport

Routes

- Tollway
- Freeway
- Primary
- Secondary
- Tertiary
- Lane
- Unsealed road
- Road under construction
- Plaza/Mall
- Steps
- Tunnel
- Pedestrian overpass
- Walking Tour
- Walking Tour detour
- Path/Walking Trail

Boundaries

- International
- State/Province
- Disputed
- Regional/Suburb
- Marine Park
- Cliff
- Wall

Hydrography

- River, Creek
- Intermittent River
- Canal
- Water
- Dry/Salt/Intermittent Lake
- Reef

Areas

- Airport/Runway
- Beach/Desert
- Cemetery (Christian)
- Cemetery (Other)
- Glacier
- Mudflat
- Park/Forest
- Sight (Building)
- Sportsground
- Swamp/Mangrove

Note: Not all symbols displayed above appear on the maps in this book

Contributing Writers & Researchers

Isabel Albiston (Northern Ireland)

Kate Armstrong (Greece)

James Bainbridge (Turkey)

Oliver Berry (Britain & France)

Jean-Bernard Carillet (France)

Jade Bremner (Iceland)

Fionn Davenport (Britain & Ireland)

Marc Di Duca (Britain, Germany & Poland)

Belinda Dixon (Britain, Iceland & Ireland)

Duncan Garwood (Italy, Portugal & Spain)

Gemma Graham (Norway)

Paula Hardy (Italy)

Damian Harper (Britain & France)

Catherine Le Nevez (Britain, France, Germany, Luxembourg, the Netherlands & Portugal)

Jessica Lee (Croatia & Turkey)

Ali Lemer (Germany)

Virginia Maxwell (Italy, the Netherlands & Turkey)

Hugh McNaughtan (Britain, France, Germany & Poland)

Isabella Noble (Spain)

John Noble (Spain)

Stephanie Ong (Italy)

Lorna Parkes (Britain)

Christopher Pitts (France)

Kevin Raub (Portugal, Serbia)

Simon Richmond (Greece & Poland)

Daniel Robinson (France)

Andrea Schulte-Peevers (Germany)

Helena Smith (Belgium)

Regis St Louis (Belgium, France, Portugal & Spain)

Andy Symington (Britain, Greece & Spain)

Brana Vladisavljevic (Serbia)

Benedict Walker (Belgium & Germany)

Greg Ward (Britain & France)

Brendan Sainsbury

Italy, Spain Born and raised in the UK in a town that never merits a mention in any guidebook (Andover, Hampshire), Brendan spent the holidays of his youth caravanning in the English Lake District and didn't leave Blighty until he was 19. Making up for lost time, he's since squeezed 70 countries into a sometimes precarious existence as a writer and professional vagabond. His rocking chair memories will probably include staging a performance of 'A Comedy of Errors' at a school in war-torn Angola, running 150 miles across the Sahara Desert in the Marathon des Sables, and hitchhiking from Cape Town to Kilimanjaro with an early, dog-eared copy of LP's *Africa on a Shoestring*. In the last 11 years, he has written more than 40 books for Lonely Planet from Castro's Cuba to the canyons of Peru. When not scribbling research notes, Brendan likes partaking in ridiculous 'endurance' races, strumming old Clash songs on the guitar, and experiencing the pain and occasional pleasures of following Southampton Football Club. Brendan wrote the Plan and Survival Guide chapters.

Nicola Williams

France, Italy, the Netherlands Border-hopping is a way of life for British writer, runner, foodie, art aficionado and mum-of-three Nicola Williams, who has lived in a French village on the southern side of Lake Geneva for more than a decade. Nicola has authored more than 50 guidebooks on Paris, Provence, Rome, Tuscany, France, Italy and Switzerland for Lonely Planet and covers France as a destination expert for the Telegraph. She also writes for the *Independent*, *Guardian*, lonelyplanet.com, *Lonely Planet Magazine*, *French Magazine*, *Cool Camping France* and others. Catch her on the road on Twitter and Instagram at @tripalong.

Neil Wilson

Britain, Ireland, Poland Neil was born in Scotland and has lived there most of his life. Based in Perthshire, he has been a full-time writer since 1988, working on more than 80 guidebooks for various publishers, including the Lonely Planet guides to Scotland, England, Ireland and Prague. An outdoors enthusiast since childhood, Neil is an active hill-walker, mountain-biker, sailor, snowboarder, fly-fisher and rock-climber, and has climbed and tramped in four continents, including ascents of Jebel Toubkal in Morocco, Mount Kinabalu in Borneo, the Old Man of Hoy in Scotland's Orkney Islands and the Northwest Face of Half Dome in California's Yosemite Valley.

Steve Fallon
Hungary A native of Boston, Massachusetts, Steve graduated from Georgetown University with a Bachelor of Science in modern languages. After working for several years for a daily US newspaper and earning a master's degree in journalism, his fascination with the 'new' Asia led him to Hong Kong, where he lived for over a dozen years, working for a variety of media companies and running his own travel bookshop. Steve lived in Budapest for three years before moving to London in 1994. He has written or contributed to more than 100 Lonely Planet titles. Steve is a qualified London Blue Badge Tourist Guide. Visit his website on www.steveslondon.com.

Anthony Ham
Croatia, Finland, Germany, Slovenia, Spain Anthony is a freelance writer and photographer who specialises in Spain, East and Southern Africa, the Arctic and the Middle East. When he's not writing for Lonely Planet, Anthony writes about and photographs Spain, Africa and the Middle East for newspapers and magazines in Australia, the UK and the US.

Anita Isalska
France, Lithuania, Slovakia Anita Isalska is a travel journalist, editor and copywriter. After several merry years as a staff writer and editor – a few of them in Lonely Planet's London office – Anita now works freelance between San Francisco, the UK and any Baltic bolthole with good wi-fi. Anita specialises in Eastern and Central Europe, Southeast Asia, France and off-beat travel. Read her stuff on www.anitaisalska.com.

Vesna Maric
North Macedonia Vesna has been a Lonely Planet author for nearly two decades, covering places as far and wide as Bolivia, Algeria, Sicily, Cyprus, Barcelona, London and Croatia, among others. Her latest work has been updating Florida, Greece and North Macedonia.

Korina Miller
Greece Korina grew up on Vancouver Island and has been exploring the globe independently since she was 16, visiting or living in 36 countries and picking up a degree in Communications and Canadian Studies, an MA in Migration Studies and a diploma in Visual Arts en route. As a writer and editor, Korina has worked on nearly 60 titles for Lonely Planet and has also worked with lonelyplanet.com, BBC, The Independent, The Guardian, BBC5 and CBC, as well as many independent magazines, covering travel, art and culture. She has currently set up camp back in Victoria, soaking up the mountain views and the pounding surf.

MaSovaida Morgan
Estonia, Latvia MaSovaida is a travel writer and multimedia storyteller whose wanderlust has taken her to more than 40 countries and all seven continents. Previously, she was Lonely Planet's Destination Editor for South America and Antarctica for four years and worked as an editor for newspapers and NGOs in the Middle East and United Kingdom. Follow her on Instagram @MaSovaida.

Leonid Ragozin
Germany, Russia, Ukraine Leonid Ragozin studied beach dynamics at Moscow State University, but for want of decent beaches in Russia, he switched to journalism and spent 12 years voyaging through different parts of the BBC, with a break for a four-year stint as a foreign correspondent for Newsweek Russia. Leonid is currently a freelance journalist focusing largely on the conflict between Russia and Ukraine (both his Lonely Planet destinations), which prompted him to leave Moscow and find a new home in Rīga.

Cristian Bonetto

Denmark, Italy, Sweden Cristian has contributed to more than 30 Lonely Planet guides to date, including *New York City, Italy, Venice & the Veneto, Naples & the Amalfi Coast, Denmark, Copenhagen, Sweden* and *Singapore*. Lonely Planet work aside, his musings on travel, food, culture and design appear in numerous publications around the world, including *The Telegraph* (UK) and *Corriere del Mezzogiorno* (Italy). When not on the road, you'll find the reformed playwright and TV scriptwriter slurping espresso in his beloved hometown, Melbourne. Follow him on Instagram: @rexcat75.

Stuart Butler

Albania, Kosovo Stuart has been writing for Lonely Planet for a decade and during this time he's come eye to eye with gorillas in the Congolese jungles, met a man with horns on his head who could lie in fire, huffed and puffed over snow bound Himalayan mountain passes, interviewed a king who could turn into a tree, and had his fortune told by a parrot. Oh, and he's met more than his fair share of self-proclaimed gods. When not on the road for Lonely Planet he lives on the beautiful beaches of Southwest France with his wife and two young children. He also works as a photographer and was a finalist in both the 2015 and 2016 Travel Photographer of the Year Awards. In 2015 he walked for six weeks with a Maasai friend across part of Kenya's Maasai lands in order to gather material for a book he is writing (see www.walkingwiththemaasai.com). His website is www.stuartbutlerjournalist.com.

Kerry Christiani

Austria, France, Germany, Portugal, Switzerland Kerry is an award-winning travel writer, photographer and Lonely Planet author, specialising in Central and Southern Europe. Based in Wales, she has authored/co-authored more than a dozen Lonely Planet titles. An adventure addict, she loves mountains, cold places and true wilderness. She features her latest work at https://its-a-small-world.com and tweets @kerrychristiani.

Gregor Clark

France, Monaco, Portugal Gregor Clark is a US-based writer whose love of foreign languages and curiosity about what's around the next bend have taken him to dozens of countries on five continents. Chronic wanderlust has also led him to visit all 50 states and most Canadian provinces on countless road trips through his native North America. Since 2000, Gregor has regularly contributed to Lonely Planet guides, with a focus on Europe and the Americas. Titles include *Italy, France, Brazil, Costa Rica, Argentina, Portugal, Switzerland, Mexico, South America on a Shoestring, Montreal & Quebec City, France's Best Trips, New England's Best Trips,* cycling guides to Italy and California and coffee-table pictorials such as *Food Trails, The USA Book* and *The Lonely Planet Guide to the Middle of Nowhere*.

Peter Dragicevich

Bosnia & Hercegovina, Croatia, Italy, Montenegro After a successful career in niche newspaper and magazine publishing, both in his native New Zealand and in Australia, Peter finally gave in to Kiwi wanderlust, giving up staff jobs to chase his diverse roots around much of Europe. Over the last decade he's written literally dozens of guidebooks for Lonely Planet on an oddly disparate collection of countries, all of which he's come to love. He once again calls Auckland, New Zealand, his home – although his current nomadic existence means he's often elsewhere.

Mark Elliott

Belgium, the Netherlands Mark Elliott had already lived and worked on five continents when, in the pre-Internet dark ages, he started writing travel guides. He has since authored (or co-authored) around 60 books including dozens for Lonely Planet. He also acts as a travel consultant, occasional tour leader, video presenter, speaker, interviewer and blues harmonicist.

OUR STORY

A beat-up old car, a few dollars in the pocket and a sense of adventure. In 1972 that's all Tony and Maureen Wheeler needed for the trip of a lifetime – across Europe and Asia overland to Australia. It took several months, and at the end – broke but inspired – they sat at their kitchen table writing and stapling together their first travel guide, *Across Asia on the Cheap*. Within a week they'd sold 1500 copies. Lonely Planet was born.

Today, Lonely Planet has offices in the US, Ireland and China, with a network of over 2000 contributors in every corner of the globe. We share Tony's belief that 'a great guidebook should do three things: inform, educate and amuse'.

OUR WRITERS

Alexis Averbuck

Iceland, Italy (Rome), France Alexis has travelled and lived all over the world, from Sri Lanka to Ecuador, Zanzibar and Antarctica. In recent years she's been living on the Greek island of Hydra and exploring along her adopted homeland; sampling oysters in Brittany; and adventuring along Iceland's surreal lava fields, sparkling fjords and glacier tongues. A travel writer for more than two decades, Alexis has lived in Antarctica for a year, crossed the Pacific by sailboat and written books on her journeys through Asia, Europe and the Americas. She's also a painter – visit www.alexisaverbuck.com – and promotes travel and adventure on video and television. Alexis also wrote the Understand chapters.

Mark Baker

Bulgaria, Czech Republic, Poland, Romania, Slovenia Mark is a freelance travel writer with a penchant for offbeat stories and forgotten places. He's originally from the United States, but now makes his home in the Czech capital, Prague. He writes mainly on Eastern and Central Europe for Lonely Planet as well as other leading travel publishers, but finds real satisfaction in digging up stories in places that are too remote or quirky for the guides. Prior to becoming an author, he worked as a journalist for *The Economist*, *Bloomberg News* and *Radio Free Europe*, among other organisations. Follow him on Instagram and Twitter (@markbakerprague), and read his blog: www.markbakerprague.com.

Greg Bloom

Belarus, Moldova Greg is a freelance writer, editor, tour guide and travel planner based out of Manila and Anilao, Philippines. Greg began his writing career in the late '90s in Ukraine, working as a journalist and later editor-in-chief of the *Kyiv Post*, an English-language weekly. As a freelance travel writer, he has contributed to some 40 Lonely Planet titles, mostly in Eastern Europe and Asia. In addition to writing, he organises customised adventure tours in north Palawan and north Luzon (Philippines). Greg's travel articles have been published in the *Sydney Morning Herald*, the *South China Morning Post*, BBC.com and the Toronto *Globe and Mail*, among many other publications. Accounts of his Lonely Planet trips over the years are at www.mytripjournal.com/bloomblogs.

OVER MORE
PAGE WRITERS

Published by Lonely Planet Global Limited
CRN 554153
4th edition – January 2022
ISBN 978 1 7886 8390 6
© Lonely Planet 2022   Photographs © as indicated 2022
10 9 8 7 6 5 4 3 2 1
Printed in Singapore